DIRECTION OF TRADE STATISTICS YEARBOOK

Direction of Trade Statistics Yearbook

Prepared by the IMF Statistics Department
Adelheid Bürgi-Schmelz, Director

For information related to this publication, please:
fax the Statistics Department at (202) 623-6460,
or write Statistics Department
International Monetary Fund
Washington, D.C. 20431
or e-mail your query to **StatisticsQuery@imf.org**
For copyright inquiries, please fax the Editorial Division at (202) 623-6579.
For purchases only, please contact Publication Services (see information below).

Direction of Trade Statistics (DOTS): Quarterly issues of this publication provide, for about 158 countries, tables with current data (or estimates) on the value of imports from and exports to their most important trading partners. In addition, similar summary tables for the world, industrial countries, and developing countries are included. The yearbook provides, for the most recent seven years, detailed trade data by country for approximately 186 countries, the world, and major areas.

Last update of data: September 12, 2008

Address orders to:
International Monetary Fund
Attention: Publication Services
Washington, D.C. 20431
U.S.A.
Telephone: (202) 623-7430
Telefax: (202) 623-7201
E-mail: publications@imf.org
Internet: http://www.imf.org

ISSN 0252-306X
ISBN 978-1-58906-754-7

INTERNATIONAL MONETARY FUND

Direction of Trade Statistics

YEARBOOK

2008

SELECTION OF STATISTICAL PUBLICATIONS

International Financial Statistics (IFS)

Acknowledged as a standard source of statistics on all aspects of international and domestic finance, *IFS* publishes, for most countries of the world, current data on exchange rates, international liquidity, international banking, money and banking, interest rates, prices, production, international transactions (including balance of payments and international investment position), government finance, and national accounts. Information is presented in tables for specific countries and in tables for area and world aggregates. *IFS* is published monthly and annually. *Price:* Subscription price is US$695 a year (US$445 to university faculty and students) for twelve monthly issues and the yearbook. Single copy price is US$89 for a monthly issue and US$145 for a yearbook issue.

Balance of Payments Statistics Yearbook (BOPSY)

Issued in three parts, this annual publication contains balance of payments and international investment position data. Part 1 provides detailed tables on balance of payments statistics for approximately 171 countries and international investment position data for 111 countries. Part 2 presents tables of regional and world totals of major balance of payments components. Part 3 contains descriptions of methodologies, compilation practices, and data sources used by reporting countries. *Price:* US$129.

Direction of Trade Statistics (DOTS)

Quarterly issues of this publication provide, for 158 countries, tables with current data (or estimates) on the value of imports from and exports to their most important trading partners. In addition, similar summary tables for the world, industrial countries, and developing countries are included. The yearbook provides, for the most recent seven years, detailed trade data by country for approximately 182 countries, the world, and major areas. *Price:* Subscription price is US$209 a year (US$179 to university faculty and students) for the quarterly issues and the yearbook. Price for a quarterly issue only is US$34, the yearbook only is US$92, and a guide only is US$12.50.

Government Finance Statistics Yearbook (GFSY)

This annual publication provides detailed data on transactions in revenue, expense, net acquisition of assets and liabilities, other economic flows, and balances of assets and liabilities of general government and its subsectors. The data are compiled according to the framework of the 2001 *Government Finance Statistics Manual,* which provides for several summary measures of government fiscal performance. *Price:* US$94.

CD-ROM Subscriptions

International Financial Statistics (IFS), Balance of Payments Statistics (BOPS), Direction of Trade Statistics (DOTS), and *Government Finance Statistics (GFS)* are available on CD-ROM by annual subscription. The CD-ROMs incorporate a Windows-based browser facility, as well as a flat file of the database in scientific notation. *Price of each subscription:* US$520 a year for single-user PC license (US$295 for university faculty and students). Network and redistribution licenses are negotiated on a case-by-case basis. Please contact Publication Services for information.

Subscription Packages

Combined Subscription Package

The combined subscription package includes all issues of *IFS, DOTS, BOPSY, GFSY,* and *Staff Papers,* the Fund's economic journal. *Combined subscription price:* US$1,195 a year (US$889 for university faculty and students). Expedited delivery available at additional cost; please inquire.

Combined Statistical Yearbook Subscription

This subscription comprises *BOPSY, GFSY, IFSY,* and *DOTSY* at a combined rate of US$415. Because of different publication dates of the four yearbooks, it may take up to one year to service an order. Expedited delivery available at additional cost; please inquire.

IFS on the Internet

The Statistics Department of the Fund is pleased to make available to subscribers the *International Financial Statistics (IFS)* database through an easy-to-use online service. The *IFS* database contains time series data beginning in 1948. The browser software provides a familiar and easy-to-use Windows interface for browsing the database, selecting series of interest, displaying the selected series in a spreadsheet format, and saving the selected series for transfer to other software systems, such as Microsoft Excel®. Single user license price for the *IFS Online Service* is $575, and $345 for academic users. Dependent on certain criteria, a range of scaled discounts is available. For full details of qualification for these discounts and online payment, please visit http://www.imfstatistics.org or email us directly at publications@imf.org.

Address orders to

Publication Services, IMF, Washington, DC 20431, USA
Telephone: (202) 623-7430 Telefax: (202) 623-7201 E-mail: publications@imf.org
Internet: http://www.imf.org

Note: Prices include the cost of delivery by surface mail. Expedited delivery is available for an additional charge.

CONTENTS

"Country" in this publication does not always refer to a territorial entity that is a state as understood by international law and practice; the term also covers the euro area, the Eastern Caribbean Currency Union, and some nonsovereign territorial entities, for which statistical data are provided internationally on a separate basis.

COUNTRY AND AREA CODES

Code	Country	Page in latest yearbook	Page in current quarterly
001	**WORLD**	x	x
101	*Industrial Countries*	x	x
111	United States	x	x
156	Canada	x	x
193	Australia	x	x
158	Japan	x	x
196	New Zealand	x	x
122	Austria[1]	x	x
124	Belgium[1]	x	x
127	Belgium-Luxembourg not specified[1,6]		
128	Denmark[1]	x	x
172	Finland[1]	x	x
132	France[1,5]	x	x
134	Germany[1]	x	x
174	Greece[1]	x	x
176	Iceland	x	x
178	Ireland[1]	x	x
136	Italy[1]	x	x
137	Luxembourg[1]	x	x
138	Netherlands[1]	x	x
142	Norway	x	x
182	Portugal[1]	x	x
135	San Marino		
184	Spain[1]	x	x
144	Sweden[1]	x	x
146	Switzerland	x	x
112	United Kingdom[1]	x	x
202	*Developing Countries*	x	x
607	*Africa*	x	x
612	Algeria[2]	x	x
614	Angola	x	x
638	Benin	x	x
616	Botswana[3]		
748	Burkina Faso	x	x
618	Burundi	x	x
622	Cameroon	x	x
624	Cape Verde	x	
626	Central African Republic	x	x
628	Chad	x	x
632	Comoros	x	
636	Congo, Democratic Republic of	x	x
634	Congo, Republic of	x	x
662	Côte d'Ivoire	x	x
611	Djibouti	x	
642	Equatorial Guinea	x	
643	Eritrea		
644	Ethiopia	x	x
646	Gabon	x	x
648	Gambia, The	x	x
652	Ghana	x	x
656	Guinea	x	x
654	Guinea-Bissau	x	x
664	Kenya	x	x
666	Lesotho[3]		
668	Liberia	x	x
674	Madagascar	x	x
676	Malawi	x	x
678	Mali	x	x
682	Mauritania	x	x
684	Mauritius	x	x
686	Morocco	x	x
688	Mozambique	x	x
728	Namibia[3]		
692	Niger	x	x
694	Nigeria[2]	x	x
696	Réunion[5]		
714	Rwanda	x	x
856	St. Helena		
716	São Tomé & Príncipe	x	
722	Senegal	x	x
718	Seychelles	x	
724	Sierra Leone	x	x
726	Somalia	x	x
199	South Africa[3]	x	x
198	South African Common Customs Area[3]		
608	South African Com. Cust. Area excl. South Africa[3]	x	x
732	Sudan	x	x
734	Swaziland[3]		
738	Tanzania	x	x
742	Togo	x	x
744	Tunisia	x	x
746	Uganda	x	x
754	Zambia	x	x
698	Zimbabwe	x	x
799	Africa not specified		
507	*Asia*	x	x
512	Afghanistan, I.S. of	x	
859	American Samoa		
513	Bangladesh	x	x
514	Bhutan[4]		
516	Brunei Darussalam	x	x
522	Cambodia	x	x
924	China, People's Rep. of: Mainland	x	x
532	China, People's Rep. of: Hong Kong	x	x
546	China, People's Rep. of: Macao	x	x
819	Fiji	x	x
887	French Polynesia		
829	Guam		
534	India	x	x
536	Indonesia[2]	x	x
826	Kiribati		
542	Korea	x	x
544	Lao, P. D. Rep.	x	
548	Malaysia	x	x

[1]The data for the European Union (EU) for all periods cover Austria, Belgium, Cyprus, Czech Republic, Denmark, Estonia, Finland, France, Germany, Greece, Hungary, Ireland, Italy, Latvia, Lithuania, Luxembourg, Malta, Netherlands, Poland, Portugal, Slovak Republic, Slovenia, Spain, Sweden, and the United Kingdom.

[2]The Oil Exporting Countries comprise Algeria, Indonesia, the Islamic Republic of Iran, Iraq, Kuwait, Libya, Nigeria, Oman, Qatar, Saudi Arabia, the United Arab Emirates, and República Bolivariana de Venezuela.

[3]South African Common Customs Area includes Botswana, Lesotho, Namibia, South Africa, and Swaziland.

[4]Trade data for these countries and groups are incomplete. Because estimates are made from partner country data, the estimates do not cover trade in cases where no partner country data have been reported. For example, most trade among these countries is omitted, as is trade between these countries and "other countries not included elsewhere (n.i.e.)."

[5]Beginning in 1997, data for France include trade of French Guiana, Guadeloupe, Martinique, and Reunion.

[6]The data for Belgium-Luxembourg refer to the Belgium-Luxembourg Economic Union.

COUNTRY AND AREA CODES (continued)

Code	Country	Page in latest yearbook	Page in current quarterly
556	Maldives	x	
867	Marshall Islands		
868	Micronesia, Federated States of		
948	Mongolia	x	
518	Myanmar	x	x
836	Nauru		
558	Nepal	x	
839	New Caledonia	x	
564	Pakistan	x	x
565	Palau		
853	Papua New Guinea	x	x
566	Philippines	x	x
862	Samoa	x	x
576	Singapore	x	x
813	Solomon Islands	x	x
524	Sri Lanka	x	x
578	Thailand	x	x
866	Tonga	x	
869	Tuvalu		
846	Vanuatu	x	
582	Vietnam	x	x
598	Asia not specified		
170	*Europe*	x	x
914	Albania	x	x
911	Armenia	x	x
912	Azerbaijan	x	x
913	Belarus	x	x
963	Bosnia and Herzegovina[4]	x	x
918	Bulgaria[1]	x	x
960	Croatia	x	x
423	Cyprus[1]	x	x
935	Czech Republic[1]	x	x
934	Czechoslovakia		
937	Czechoslovakia not specified		
939	Estonia[1]	x	x
816	Faeroe Islands	x	
915	Georgia	x	x
823	Gibraltar		
944	Hungary[1]	x	x
916	Kazakhstan	x	x
917	Kyrgyz Republic	x	x
941	Latvia[1]	x	x
946	Lithuania[1]	x	x
962	Macedonia, Former Yug. Rep.	x	x
181	Malta[1]	x	x
921	Moldova	x	x
964	Poland[1]	x	x
968	Romania[1]	x	x
922	Russia	x	x
965	Serbia and Montenegro	x	x
936	Slovak Republic[1]	x	x
961	Slovenia[1]	x	x
923	Tajikistan	x	x
186	Turkey	x	x
925	Turkmenistan	x	x
930	U.S.S.R. (former) not specified		
926	Ukraine	x	x
927	Uzbekistan[4]	x	x
188	Yugoslavia, Socialist Fed. Rep. of		
966	Yugoslavia, not specified		
884	Europe not specified		
407	*Middle East*	x	x
419	Bahrain	x	x
469	Egypt	x	x
429	Iran, Islamic Republic of[2]	x	x
433	Iraq[2]	x	x
436	Israel	x	x
439	Jordan	x	x
443	Kuwait[2]	x	x
446	Lebanon	x	x
672	Libya[2]	x	x
449	Oman[2]	x	x
453	Qatar[2]	x	x
456	Saudi Arabia[2]	x	x
463	Syrian Arab Republic	x	x
466	United Arab Emirates[2]	x	x
487	West Bank/Gaza		
474	Yemen, Republic of	x	x
489	Middle East not specified		
207	*Western Hemisphere*	x	x
311	Antigua & Barbuda		
213	Argentina	x	x
314	Aruba	x	x
313	Bahamas, The	x	x
316	Barbados	x	x
339	Belize	x	
319	Bermuda	x	
218	Bolivia	x	x
223	Brazil	x	x
377	Cayman Islands		
228	Chile	x	x
233	Colombia	x	x
238	Costa Rica	x	x
321	Dominica	x	
243	Dominican Republic	x	x
248	Ecuador	x	x
253	El Salvador	x	x
323	Falkland Islands		
326	Greenland	x	
328	Grenada	x	
329	Guadeloupe[5]		
258	Guatemala	x	x
333	Guiana, French[5]		
336	Guyana	x	x

[1] The data for the European Union (EU) for all periods cover Austria, Belgium, Cyprus, Czech Republic, Denmark, Estonia, Finland, France, Germany, Greece, Hungary, Ireland, Italy, Latvia, Lithuania, Luxembourg, Malta, Netherlands, Poland, Portugal, Slovak Republic, Slovenia, Spain, Sweden, and the United Kingdom.

[2] The Oil Exporting Countries comprise Algeria, Indonesia, the Islamic Republic of Iran, Iraq, Kuwait, Libya, Nigeria, Oman, Qatar, Saudi Arabia, the United Arab Emirates, and República Bolivariana de Venezuela.

[3] South African Common Customs Area includes Botswana, Lesotho, Namibia, South Africa, and Swaziland.

[4] Trade data for these countries and groups are incomplete. Because estimates are made from partner country data, the estimates do not cover trade in cases where no partner country data have been reported. For example, most trade among these countries is omitted, as is trade between these countries and "other countries not included elsewhere (n.i.e.)."

[5] Beginning in 1997, data for France include trade of French Guiana, Guadeloupe, Martinique, and Reunion.

[6] The data for Belgium-Luxembourg refer to the Belgium-Luxembourg Economic Union.

COUNTRY AND AREA CODES (concluded)

Code	Country	Page in latest yearbook	Page in current quarterly
263	Haiti	x	x
268	Honduras	x	x
343	Jamaica	x	x
346	Leeward Islands		
349	Martinique[5]		
273	Mexico	x	x
351	Montserrat		
353	Netherlands Antilles	x	x
278	Nicaragua	x	x
283	Panama	x	x
288	Paraguay	x	x
293	Peru	x	x
361	St. Kitts and Nevis	x	
362	St. Lucia	x	
363	St. Pierre & Miquelon		
364	St. Vincent and the Grenadines	x	
366	Suriname	x	x
369	Trinidad and Tobago	x	x
298	Uruguay	x	x
299	Venezuela, República Bolivariana de[2]	x	x
376	Windward Islands		
399	Western Hemisphere not specified		
898	*Country or area not specified*		
899	*Special Categories*		
910	*Other countries not included elsewhere*	x	x
928	Cuba[4]	x	x
938	Eastern Germany		
954	North Korea[4]	x	
	Memorandum Items		
998	*European Union*[1]	x	
999	*Oil Exporting Countries*[2]	x	
201	*Non-Oil Developing Countries*[6]	x	

[1] The data for the European Union (EU) for all periods cover Austria, Belgium, Cyprus, Czech Republic, Denmark, Estonia, Finland, France, Germany, Greece, Hungary, Ireland, Italy, Latvia, Lithuania, Luxembourg, Malta, Netherlands, Poland, Portugal, Slovak Republic, Slovenia, Spain, Sweden, and the United Kingdom.

[2] The Oil Exporting Countries comprise Algeria, Indonesia, the Islamic Republic of Iran, Iraq, Kuwait, Libya, Nigeria, Oman, Qatar, Saudi Arabia, the United Arab Emirates, and República Bolivariana de Venezuela.

[3] South African Common Customs Area includes Botswana, Lesotho, Namibia, South Africa, and Swaziland.

[4] Trade data for these countries and groups are incomplete. Because estimates are made from partner country data, the estimates do not cover trade in cases where no partner country data have been reported. For example, most trade among these countries is omitted, as is trade between these countries and "other countries not included elsewhere (n.i.e.)."

[5] Beginning in 1997, data for France include trade of French Guiana, Guadeloupe, Martinique, and Reunion.

[6] The data for Belgium-Luxembourg refer to the Belgium-Luxembourg Economic Union.

INTRODUCTION

The quarterly issues, yearbook, and CD-ROM of the *Direction of Trade Statistics* (*DOTS*) present, for most member countries of the International Monetary Fund (the Fund), current figures on the value of merchandise exports and imports disaggregated according to their most important trading partners. The quarterly issues (*DOTSQ*) present current figures for about 158 countries. The yearbook (*DOTSY*) presents, for 182 countries, figures on the value of merchandise exports and imports by trade partners for the years 2001 through 2007. The CD-ROM presents the same information as *DOTSY* from 1980 onwards for annuals/quarters and months. Area and world aggregates showing trade flows between major areas of the world are presented in *DOTSQ*, *DOTSY* and the CD-ROM. Reported data are supplemented by estimates whenever such data are not current or are not available in monthly frequency.

World and area tables present (1) world aggregates comprising all countries, including about 26 small countries for which individual country tables are not presented in the quarterly issues, (2) industrial country aggregates derived from the figures for the 23 countries classified as industrial countries, (3) developing countries aggregates and subgroups, namely, Africa, Asia, Europe, Middle East, and Western Hemisphere, and (4) European Union aggregates. Aggregates for the World table are calculated as the sum of aggregates from the tables for the Industrial Countries and Developing Countries. It also includes trade of countries comprising the group "other countries n.i.e." and data for a country or area not specified and for "special categories."

The term "country," as used in this publication, does not in all cases refer to a territorial entity that is a state as understood by international law and practice; the term also covers some nonsovereign territorial entities, for which statistical data are maintained and provided internationally on a separate and independent basis.

The information on exports and imports by trading partners that countries report to the Fund varies in terms of frequency and currentness. Monthly data are made available on a regular and current basis (i.e., with a delay of four months or less from the current month) by approximately 46 countries which comprise virtually all of the industrial countries and about 23 developing countries. Together, these 46 countries have represented about four-fifths of the value of recorded world exports and imports in recent years.

Other countries may report monthly data that are less current, or the information may be compiled and made available in quarterly or annual frequency. For some countries, the data reported to the United Nations Statistical Division also have been used. Data for most of the European Union member countries are sourced from the COMEXT database maintained by EUROSTAT. However, the availability of partner data makes it possible to include in direction of trade statistics (DOTS) estimates for current months not only for countries less current or frequent in their reporting but also for countries for which data are not obtainable from other sources.

Estimation procedures

The estimation procedures are described in *A Guide to Direction of Trade Statistics* (1993), available on the CD-ROM and from the Fund's Publications Section (http://www.imf.org/external/pubs/cat/longres.cfm?sk=154.0). Reported data, including total imports and exports reported for publication in the Fund's *International Financial Statistics (IFS)*, are the basis of all estimates in DOTS. The entire DOTS database is continuously supplemented with estimates. *Briefly, the estimation procedures are as follows:*

Estimation occurs if a reporting country does not report trade with its partners for a specific period. Data are estimated for all partners and not for some of the partners. In the absence of some or all of the monthly DOTS, quarterly or annual reported DOTS are used. If quarterly data are available, then they are distributed over the relevant months using (1) the available monthly DOTS reported for other partner countries, (2) *IFS* monthly totals, or (3) an even distribution. If only annual data are available, then estimation procedures include, in addition to the techniques described above, DOTS reported from the most recent annual report or extrapolations of the most recent data or estimates. Where possible, estimates are computed first for months, and then annual totals are obtained by summation.

If data on total trade are reported for publication in *IFS* but DOTS data are not reported, then the sum of the direction of trade estimates is constrained to coincide with the *IFS* totals. In such cases, the data for total exports and total imports shown in the lines *IFS* World Total and *DOTS* World Total will be identical. If *IFS* data are not available, then extrapolation will determine the estimated value of trade, and *IFS* data will not appear on the country page.

When information is not reported and is inadequate to support the estimation techniques, the data are extrapolated using a matrix of trade among broad country groups. Projected trade growth by these country groups, consistent with trade growth estimates used in the Fund's *World Economic Outlook*, is combined with the available DOTS to derive extrapolation factors.

Estimates are not provided for trade flows between countries where data are unavailable for both trading partners during the latest ten years or more.

In summation, only a small portion of world trade is omitted from the DOTS; this portion comprises (1) a small amount of unreported trade among the developing countries; (2) a small amount of unreported trade between developing countries and the countries comprising the group "other countries n.i.e."; and (3) the trade among "other countries n.i.e.".

Table 1. DATA COVERAGE, 2003–2007

		DATA REPORTED FOR:						DATA NOT REPORTED	
		Complete Year			Part of the Year				
		Number of Countries[1]		Percent of World Trade	Number of Countries	Percent of World Trade		Number of Countries	Percent of World Trade
Exports	2007	72	(48)	90	3	0.29		107	10
	2006	87	(63)	91	2	0.11		93	9
	2005	104	(80)	93	0	0.00		78	7
	2004	111	(87)	94	0	0.00		71	6
	2003	119	(95)	95	0	0.00		63	5
Imports	2007	74	(50)	90	2	0.17		106	10
	2006	89	(65)	92	1	0.01		92	8
	2005	107	(83)	96	0	0.00		75	4
	2004	112	(88)	96	0	0.00		70	4
	2003	121	(97)	97	1	0.04		60	3

[1]The figures in parentheses indicate the number of developing countries that reported complete data for the respective year.

No estimates, however, are compiled for periods prior to 1981 or based on benchmark data referring to 1980 or earlier.

Moreover, data reported from countries' own records, even with longer delays, continually broaden the base of reported data, thereby replacing previously estimated figures. Area and world totals are compiled from reported data and these estimates. For a given year the percentage of world trade that is estimated declines over time, as data reported by countries replace the estimates (see Table 1, from *DOTSY*).

When partner data are used directly or indirectly to derive estimates, the data first are adjusted by a c.i.f./f.o.b. factor of 1.10 to allow for the cost of freight and insurance. Reported imports c.i.f. are divided by the c.i.f./f.o.b. factor to give partner country estimates of exports f.o.b. Similarly, reported exports f.o.b. are multiplied by the c.i.f./f.o.b. factor to give partner country imports c.i.f. For example, if country B has not reported data from its own records but country A has done so, then A's data for imports from B (reported c.i.f.) are divided by 1.10 to give the f.o.b. value of B's exports to A. Conversely, A's data for exports to B (reported f.o.b.) are multiplied by 1.10 to give the c.i.f. value of B's imports from A. Given the absence of timely data on cost, insurance, and freight, the 10 percent c.i.f./f.o.b. factor represents a simplified estimate of these costs, which vary widely across countries and transactions.

Symbols

To provide guidance regarding the sources of the figures for individual countries, figures in the country, world, and area pages are shown with symbols to the right of the figure. Figures shown without symbols are data reported from the respective country's own records; symbols indicate figures derived from partner records or by other methods of estimation, as follows:

Quarterly data

- G 2 months of reported data and 1 month of estimates
- L 1 month of reported data and 2 months of estimates
- V consolidated data derived solely from partner records
- Y consolidated data estimated by other methods, sometimes including the use of partner records; also used in world and area totals.

Annual data

- S 6–11 months of reported data and 1–6 months of estimates
- T 1–5 months of reported data and 7–11 months of estimates
- V consolidated data derived solely from partner records
- Y consolidated data estimated by other methods, sometimes including the use of partner records; also used in world and area totals.

The following symbols and abbreviations are used throughout DOTS as well:

A row of leaders (. . . .) indicates a lack of data.

A dash (–) indicates that a figure is zero or less than half a significant digit.

The letters **n.i.e.** mean not included elsewhere.

The letters **ns** mean not specified.

In the CD-ROM, estimates are indicated in blue and bold with text boxes attached to data observations.

Composition of country, world, and area pages

Country pages include lines for all partner countries that have been reported, estimated, or extrapolated. Where relevant, these pages also include lines for country or area data not specified and for "special categories." Trade included under "special categories" may cover military trade, transactions in free zones, or transactions in aircraft or ships. These data have not been designated to a partner country by the trade statistics compilers, nor have they been included by item in the reported data as an area not specified.

Country pages also include memorandum item lines for the European Union (EU), Oil Exporting Countries, and Non-Oil Developing Countries. Data in these memorandum lines show trade by all members of the group with the respective country. Similarly these memorandum lines appear on the area and world pages. The memorandum line represents trade by all individual members of the group. For example, the EU line on the world page represents trade by all EU members with the world, including trade among members. It does not present the EU data as if the EU was a single country. Users interested in such statistics would need to subtract intra-EU trade.

At the bottom of each country page in *DOTSY*, two sets of analytical lines appear, based on the data in the table. The first set shows the distribution (in percent) of the country's total exports and imports by area of the world. The other set of lines shows annual percentage changes for total imports and exports by area of the world.

Summary tables for the world and areas are calculated from the data shown on the country page. They show the trade by a group of countries to and from the individual countries listed in the table. This is analogous to stacking all the pages for the individual countries in an area and adding vertically to yield an aggregate table on the top of the stack.

While the country pages show the most important trading partners for each individual country, the world and area totals for each country's trade include trade not explicitly shown or not specified by partner countries. For comparison, total export and import data are also shown as given in terms of U.S. dollars in the world trade tables in *IFS* for countries that report trade statistics to the Fund.

When trade data are reported from a country's own records (both as world aggregates and by trading partner), the sums of exports to and of imports from all partner countries, including trade with unspecified partners, would, in principle, be identical with the aggregates reported independently for total exports and imports, respectively. In practice, however, discrepancies may arise—for example, when adjustments and/or revisions are applied to aggregates but are not carried through to individual partner data.

The CD ROM browser contains the cross country matrix view and economic concept view in addition to country tables and world and area tables view.

Currency

All data are expressed in terms of U.S. dollars. As most of the countries report in their national currency, U.S. dollar equivalents are obtained by converting data at period average exchange rates published in lines **rf** or **rh** on the country pages in *IFS*. Data are generally converted at their highest available frequency and are subsequently aggregated to longer periods: for example, monthly data are converted at monthly exchange rates and the resulting U.S. dollar equivalents are aggregated to quarterly and annual values.

Consistency between partner country data

It is sometimes assumed that corresponding export and import data between partner countries should be consistent. That is, the exports from Country A to B should be equal to the imports of Country B from A, after taking into account the insurance and freight costs under the generally observed case that Country B imports are valued on a c.i.f. basis. The DOTS estimation system uses this assumption in cases where one partner has not reported data.

However, notwithstanding the inclusion of insurance and freight in imports c.i.f., it should be noted that there are several complications that can cause inconsistency between exports to a partner and the partner's recorded imports f.o.b., or between imports f.o.b. from a partner and the partner's recorded exports. The principal reasons for inconsistent statistics on destination and origin for a given shipment are differences in 1) classification concepts and detail, 2) time of recording, 3) valuation, and 4) coverage, as well as 5) processing errors:

Classification concepts and detail

Destination/origin classification concepts in the presence of transshipment: Much trade is consigned via other countries, for example, a substantial volume of German trade passes through the Netherlands. An inconsistency in reported trade data can arise when the trade of the originating country is classified as going to either a first or proximate destination that is a transshipment point, whereas the ultimate destination country classifies the same trade according to its ultimate source.

Alternatively, the originating country may classify the shipment as going to the ultimate destination country, whereas the ultimate destination country classifies the same trade according to a proximate source that is a transshipment point. The lack of uniformity in the classification approach actually results from the application of different national customs instructions used in determining origin, transshipment, and destination countries.

Although there would be no classification inconsistency if all countries were to use a proximate destination/origin approach, this does not meet the analytical and operational needs of many data users whose interests align with the ultimate destination and/or origin of trade. That is, analytical information following the ultimate destination/origin principle requires countries to further distinguish, by trading partner, between the exports and imports involved in transshipment through their territory (re-imports and re-exports) from exports whose ultimate origin, and imports whose ultimate destination, is in their territory.

This, however, is often a difficult distinction to make in actual situations, and publication of such data is not uniform international practice. International recommendations note that no single way of attributing partner countries is ideal in view of the prevailing conditions under which trade is recorded.

Lack of destination/source country detail in published statistics: These conditions cause immediate problems in identifying trade counterparty information from published data. Destination/origin country for military and other confidential items and government goods may not be published or may be published only by regional aggregates. A destination can also be indeterminate and thus not be published, because the transshipment dispatcher may lack knowledge about the ultimate destination at the time of consignment. Regional aggregates without country detail may also be published when the trade of individual partners in a region is below a threshold level.

Time of recording

A lag occurs between shipment of an export and receipt of an import, especially for goods that are shipped over long distances. To avoid timing inconsistencies, international national accounts and balance of payments accounting standards recommend a change of ownership principle to assign a date to transactions. Under this principle, an exported good changes ownership at shipment from the exporting country, at which time the exporting country records an export and the destination country records an import (f.o.b.).

However, for practical reasons, the customs authorities of the importing country record the receipt of these goods later, when they arrive at the receiving country's frontier. This can cause a timing inconsistency. The result is that the same shipment can appear in an importing country's statistics for a month, quarter, and/or year that is later than the period that appears in the exporting country's statistics.

Valuation

Possible reasons for inconsistent valuation of a given shipment between source and destination include inconsistent currency version, evasion, anti-evasion procedures, values not known at the time of consignment, and differences in treatment of particular costs or procedures for assessment.

Coverage

Shipments to and from free-trade zones and bonded warehouses, exclusion of military and other confidential items and government goods, value thresholds for customs registration of shipments, returned goods, and other goods missed by customs (or surveys) are examples of coverage differences that can result in inconsistencies.

Processing errors

As a result of reporting and processing lags, trade data for a given period are often released before all customs documents for the period have been processed. These data are sometimes not revised, or, if data are revised, errors are nevertheless made in assigning the date on which goods are shipped or received and the late data are assigned to the wrong month, quarter, and/or year. Errors can also be made in assigning a destination to exports and an origin to imports during customs clearances, or in cases when the ultimate destination is changed after the initial consignment during transshipment, the change is not incorporated into published statistics via the release of revised data.

These issues should be considered in interpreting the data. International cooperation in harmonizing and reconciling customs procedures and definitions may assist in reducing differences, and, in a few cases, countries have reconciled data or have used partner data to make their own estimates.

A particular problem arises in DOTS for countries that have large inconsistencies with partners and sometimes fail to report data. In such cases, there will be anomalies in the time series between those periods based on reported data and those based on partner data.

INTRODUCTION

Les numéros trimestriels, l'annuaire et le disque optique compact (CD-ROM) de statistiques sur la répartition géographique des échanges (*Direction of Trade Statistics — DOTS*) présentent pour la plupart des pays membres du Fonds monétaire international (FMI) des données récentes sur la valeur des exportations et des importations de marchandises, ventilées par partenaires commerciaux importants. Les numéros trimestriels *(DOTSQ)* font état des données récentes provenant d'environ 158 pays. L'annuaire *(DOTSY)* présente, pour 182 pays, des données ventilées par partenaires commerciaux sur la valeur des marchandises qu'ils ont exportées et importées de 2001 à la fin de 2007. Le CD-ROM présente les mêmes informations que le *DOTSY*, mais à partir de 1980 et ventilées par année/trimestre et par mois. Le *DOTSQ*, le *DOTSY* et le CD-ROM contiennent en outre des agrégats mondiaux et régionaux des flux commerciaux entre les principales régions du monde. Lorsque les données ne sont pas communiquées sur une base régulière ou mensuelle, elles sont complétées par des estimations.

Les tableaux établis pour le monde et les régions présentent 1) les agrégats mondiaux couvrant l'ensemble des pays, y compris environ 26 petits pays dont les données ne figurent pas dans les pages des numéros trimestriels consacrées aux pays; 2) les agrégats des pays industrialisés dérivés des données transmises par les 23 pays faisant partie de cette catégorie; 3) les agrégats des pays en développement répartis en cinq régions — Afrique, Asie, Europe, Moyen-Orient et hémisphère occidental — et 4) les agrégats de l'Union européenne. Les agrégats du tableau mondial correspondent à la somme des agrégats des tableaux des pays industrialisés et des pays en développement. Le tableau présente également les données sur les échanges d'un ensemble de pays regroupés sous la rubrique « *Other countries n.i.e.* » (Autres pays n.i.a.), ainsi que les données de pays ou de régions non identifiées et celles appartenant aux « Catégories spéciales ».

Dans la présente publication, le terme « pays » ne recouvre pas toujours une entité territoriale constituant un État tel qu'il est défini selon la pratique et le droit internationaux. Ce terme recouvre également certaines entités territoriales qui ne sont pas des États souverains, mais sur lesquelles des données statistiques sont tenues à jour et fournies, séparément et indépendamment, au niveau international.

Les données que les pays communiquent au FMI sur leurs exportations et importations ventilées par partenaires commerciaux ne sont pas toutes communiquées avec la même fréquence et n'ont pas toutes le même degré d'actualité. Environ 46 pays, comprenant presque tous les pays industrialisés et environ 23 pays en développement, transmettent des données mensuelles sur une base régulière et pour la période en cours (c'est-à-dire, dans un délai de quatre mois ou moins). Ces dernières années, les échanges commerciaux de ces quelque 46 pays ont représenté ensemble environ 80 % de la valeur des exportations et importations mondiales enregistrées.

D'autres pays communiquent des données mensuelles moins récentes, ou n'établissent et ne transmettent des données que sur une base trimestrielle ou annuelle. Pour certains pays, les données communiquées à la Division de statistique des Nations Unies sont également utilisées. Pour la plupart des pays membres de l'Union européenne, les données sont tirées de la base de données COMEXT, qui est gérée par EUROSTAT. Par ailleurs, les renseignements communiqués par les partenaires commerciaux permettent d'établir dans *DOTS* des estimations mensuelles à jour non seulement pour les pays qui communiquent des données moins récentes, mais également pour ceux pour lesquels on ne dispose pas de statistiques d'autres sources.

Méthodes d'estimation

Les méthodes d'estimation sont décrites dans le Guide pour l'établissement des statistiques sur la répartition géographique des échanges (*A Guide to Direction of Trade Statistics*, 1993), disponible sur le CD-ROM et à la Section des publications du FMI (http:www.imf.org/external/pubs/cat/longres.cfm?sk=154.0). Les données communiquées, y compris les chiffres globaux d'importations et d'exportations transmis aux fins de publication dans *Statistiques financières internationales* (*SFI*), servent de base à toutes les estimations contenues dans *DOTS*. La base de données tout entière est régulièrement mise à jour avec de nouvelles estimations. *Les méthodes d'estimation utilisées sont décrites brièvement ci-dessous.*

On procède à une estimation lorsqu'un pays déclarant n'indique pas le montant de ses échanges avec un de ses partenaires commerciaux pour une période donnée. Les chiffres sont estimés pour tous les partenaires commerciaux et non pas simplement certains d'entre eux. Lorsque les statistiques mensuelles de *DOTS* font partiellement ou entièrement défaut, ce sont les statistiques trimestrielles ou annuelles communiquées pour *DOTS* qui sont utilisées. Si des données trimestrielles sont disponibles, elles sont alors ventilées entre les mois respectifs, en faisant appel : 1) aux données mensuelles de *DOTS* communiquées pour les autres partenaires commerciaux; 2) aux totaux mensuels de *SFI*; ou 3) à une répartition proportionnelle. Si on ne dispose que de données annuelles, les méthodes d'estimation couvrent, outre les techniques décrites susmentionnées, les statistiques de *DOTS* tirées du rapport annuel le plus récent ou les données ou estimations les plus récentes obtenues par extrapolation. Les estimations sont d'abord établies, dans la mesure du possible, sur une base mensuelle et les totaux annuels sont obtenus ensuite par addition.

Si des données sur les échanges sont communiquées aux fins de publication dans *SFI*, tandis que celles de *DOTS* ne le sont pas, la somme des estimations relatives à la répartition des échanges doit obligatoirement coïncider avec les totaux de *SFI*. En pareil cas, les données sur les exportations et importations totales présentées aux lignes « *IFS* World Total » et « *DOTS* World Total » seront identiques. Si l'on ne dispose pas de données pour *SFI*, la valeur estimée des échanges sera alors déterminée par extrapolation, et aucune donnée n'apparaîtra pour *SFI* à la page consacrée au pays.

Lorsque les renseignements font défaut ou lorsqu'ils sont inutilisables dans le cadre des méthodes d'estimation employées, les données sont calculées par extrapolation à l'aide d'une matrice des courants commerciaux entre grands groupes de pays. Des projections de croissance des échanges entre ces groupes, qui doivent concorder avec les estimations de croissance du commerce extérieur utilisées dans les *Perspectives de l'économie mondiale* du FMI, sont alors combinées aux statistiques disponibles de *DOTS* pour déterminer les coefficients d'extrapolation.

On n'établit pas d'estimations sur les échanges des partenaires commerciaux pour lesquels on ne dispose pas de données bilatérales pour les dix dernières années au moins.

Par conséquent, seule une faible part des échanges commerciaux n'est pas prise en compte dans *DOTS*; ce sont 1) un volume peu élevé d'échanges commerciaux entre pays en développement sur lesquels les données ne sont pas communiquées; 2) un faible volume d'échanges commerciaux entre les pays en développement et les pays du groupe « Autres pays n.i.a. » sur lesquels des données ne sont pas fournies; et 3) les échanges entre les pays appartenant à ce dernier groupe.

Toutefois, aucune estimation n'a été établie pour les périodes antérieures à 1981, et aucune n'est fondée sur des données de référence correspondant à 1980 où aux années antérieures. De plus, les données tirées des documents des pays, même si elles couvrent des périodes plus longues, enrichissent continuellement la base de données communiquées et viennent remplacer les estimations antérieures. Les totaux régionaux et mondiaux sont calculés à partir des données communiquées et à partir de ces estimations. Pour une année donnée, la proportion des statistiques du commerce mondial qui est estimative diminue à terme, à mesure que les données communiquées par les pays se substit6uent aux chiffres estimatifs (voir tableau 1 de *DOTSY*).

Lorsque les données des partenaires commerciaux servent directement ou indirectement à calculer les estimations, on commence par les ajuster en appliquant un coefficient c.a.f./f.à.b. égal à 1,10 pour tenir compte des coûts de fret et d'assurance. Les chiffres d'importations communiqués sur une base c.a.f sont divisés par le coefficient c.a.f./f.à.b. pour donner les chiffres estimatifs des exportations du pays partenaire sur une base f.à.b. Parallèlement, on multiplie les

Tableau 1. COUVERTURE DES DONNÉES, 2003–2007

		DONNÉES COMMUNIQUÉES POUR :						DONNÉES NON COMMUNIQUÉES	
		Année complète			Année partielle				
		Nombre de pays[1]		Pourcentage du commerce mondial	Nombre de pays	Pourcentage du commerce mondial		Nombre de pays	Pourcentage du commerce mondial
Exportations	2007	72	(48)	90	3	0,29		107	10
	2006	87	(63)	91	2	0,11		93	9
	2005	104	(80)	93	0	0,00		78	7
	2004	111	(87)	94	0	0,00		71	6
	2003	119	(95)	95	0	0,00		63	5
Importations	2007	74	(50)	90	2	0,17		106	10
	2006	89	(65)	92	1	0,01		92	8
	2005	107	(83)	96	0	0,00		75	4
	2004	112	(88)	96	0	0,00		70	4
	2003	121	(97)	97	1	0,04		60	3

[1]Les chiffres entre parenthèses indiquent le nombre de pays en développement qui ont fourni des données complètes pour l'année considérée.

chiffres d'exportations communiqués sur une base f.à.b. par le coefficient c.a.f./f.à.b. afin d'obtenir les estimations des importations du pays partenaire sur une base c.a.f. Par exemple, si le pays B n'a pas transmis de données tirées de ses propres documents, alors que le pays A l'a fait, les chiffres de A sur les importations en provenance de B (communiquées en valeur c.a.f.) sont divisés par 1,10 pour exprimer la valeur f.à.b. des exportations de B à destination de A. Inversement, les données de A sur les exportations à destination de B (transmises f.à.b.) sont multipliées par 1,10 pour déterminer la valeur c.a.f. des importations de B en provenance de A. En l'absence de données à jour sur les coûts d'assurance et de fret, le coefficient c.a.f./f.à.b. de 10 % ainsi appliqué est une estimation simplifiée de ces coûts, lesquels peuvent varier fortement d'un pays à l'autre et d'une opération à l'autre.

Symboles

Afin d'identifier les sources des données provenant de différents pays, un symbole apparaît à droite des chiffres présentés dans les pages consacrées aux pays, aux régions ou au monde entier. Les chiffres qui ne sont pas suivis d'un symbole sont ceux qui sont tirés des documents des pays en question; les symboles identifient les données calculées à partir de celles des partenaires commerciaux ou obtenues par une autre méthode d'estimation, comme suit :

Données trimestrielles

G données communiquées pour 2 mois; données esimées pour 1 mois

L données communiquées pour 1 mois; données estimées pour 2 mois

V données consolidées calculées uniquement à partir des relevés du partenaire

Y données consolidées estimées à l'aide d'autres méthodes, y compris, dans certains cas, par recours aux relevés du partenaire; utilisées aussi dans les totaux mondiaux et régionaux

Données annuelles

S données communiquées pour 6 à 11 mois; données estimées pour 1 à 6 mois

T données communiquées pour 1 à 5 mois; données estimées pour 7 à 11 mois

V données consolidées calculées uniquement à partir des relevés du partenaire

Y données consolidées estimées à l'aide d'autres méthodes, y compris, dans certains cas, par recours aux relevés du partenaire; utilisées aussi dans les totaux mondiaux et régionaux.

D'autres symboles et abréviations sont également utilisées dans *DOTS* :

Le symbole (. . . .) indique l'absence de données statistiques.

Le symbole (–) indique une valeur égale à zéro ou inférieure à la moitié d'un chiffre significatif.

Les lettres « **n.i.a.** » signifient « non inclus ailleurs ».

Les lettres « **ns** » signifient « non spécifié ».

Dans le CD-ROM, les estimations sont indiquées en caractères gras de couleur bleue. Des liens internes relient les observations sur les données à des zones textes.

Composition des pages consacrées aux pays, aux régions et au monde entier

Les pages consacrées aux pays comportent pour chacun des partenaires commerciaux du pays concerné des lignes de données communiquées directement ou obtenues par estimation ou par extrapolation. Le cas échéant, on ajoute une ligne se rapportant aux pays ou groupes de pays non spécifiés (*Country/area not specified*) ou pour des catégories spéciales (*Special categories*). Les échanges classés dans cette dernière catégorie peuvent recouvrir les opérations à caractère militaire, celles des zones franches ou celles qui concernent les aéronefs ou les navires. Ces données ne sont pas attribuées à un partenaire commercial déterminé par les statisticiens du commerce extérieur, et elles ne sont pas ventilées non plus sous un poste spécifique dans les données transmises pour la catégorie des groupes de pays non spécifiés.

Les pages consacrées aux pays comportent aussi des lignes de postes pour mémoire pour l'Union européenne (UE), les pays exportateurs de pétrole et les pays en développement non pétroliers. Les chiffres qui y figurent couvrent les échanges de l'ensemble des membres du groupe avec le pays concerné. Des postes pour mémoire similaires figurent aux pages des tableaux régionaux et mondiaux. Les chiffres inscrits à ces postes représentent la somme des échanges de tous les pays appartenant au groupe. Par exemple, le poste pour mémoire du tableau « *World* » qui se rapporte à l'UE recouvre les échanges de l'ensemble des pays membres de l'UE avec le reste du monde, y compris les échanges entre ces mêmes pays. Les données de l'UE n'y sont pas traitées comme s'il s'agissait d'un pays unique. Les utilisateurs intéressés par ces statistiques doivent donc soustraire du total les chiffres se rapportant aux échanges intra-UE.

Au bas des pages consacrées à chaque pays sont présentés deux groupes de lignes analytiques obtenues à partir des données du tableau. Le premier groupe de lignes indique la répartition (en pourcentage) des exportations et importations totales du pays par région du monde. L'autre présente les pourcentages de variation annuelle des importations et des exportations totales du pays par région du monde.

Des tableaux récapitulatifs sont établis pour le monde et les régions à partir des données figurant sur les pages consacrées aux pays. Ils indiquent la répartition des échanges globaux d'un groupe de pays à destination et en provenance de chacun des pays figurant dans le tableau. Le calcul s'apparente à empiler les pages de tous les pays d'une région et à ajouter verticalement tous les chiffres de façon à obtenir un tableau global au sommet de la pile.

Les pages consacrées aux pays identifient les principaux partenaires commerciaux de chaque pays en particulier, mais les totaux régionaux et mondiaux des échanges de chaque pays comprennent une portion des échanges qui ne sont pas identifiés explicitement ou qui ne sont pas ventilés par partenaire commercial. Aux fins de comparaison, les données sur le total des exportations et importations sont également exprimées en dollars EU, telles qu'elles figurent dans les tableaux établis pour le monde dans *SFI* pour les pays qui communiquent au FMI leurs statistiques sur les échanges commerciaux.

Lorsque les données sur les échanges sont tirées des propres documents du pays (agrégats pour le monde entier et données ventilées par partenaire commercial), les sommes des exportations à destination et des importations en provenance de l'ensemble des partenaires, y compris les échanges avec des partenaires non spécifiés, devraient en principe correspondre aux agrégats communiqués indépendamment pour les exportations et les importations totales respectivement. Toutefois, en pratique, certains écarts peuvent survenir sous l'effet, par exemple, d'ajustements ou de révisions des agrégats qui ne sont pas répercutés aux données correspondant aux partenaires individuels.

Outre une présentation par pages consacrées à chaque pays et par tableaux récapitulatifs établis pour le monde et les régions, le navigateur du CD-ROM offre une matrice des courants commerciaux entre pays et une présentation par tableaux synoptiques.

Monnaie

Toutes les données sont exprimées en dollars EU. Comme la plupart des pays communiquent leurs données en monnaie nationale, il convient d'obtenir leurs équivalents en dollars EU en utilisant les moyennes périodiques des taux de change des séries **rf** ou **rh** publiées aux pages consacrées aux pays dans *SFI*. Les données sont généralement converties à leur fréquence la plus élevée, et sont ensuite agrégées sur des périodes plus longues : ainsi, les données mensuelles sont converties à l'aide des valeurs mensuelles du taux de change, et les équivalents en dollars EU qui en découlent sont ensuite agrégés en valeurs trimestrielles et annuelles.

Cohérence des données entre pays partenaires

On présume parfois que les chiffres d'exportations et d'importations correspondants entre pays partenaires sont censés concorder. C'est-à-dire que le chiffre des exportations du pays A à destination du pays B devrait être égal à celui des importations du pays B en provenance du pays A, après ajustement pour coûts de fret et d'assurance, étant entendu que les importations du pays B sont généralement évaluées sur la base c.a.f. Le système d'estimation de *DOTS* se fonde sur cette hypothèse quand l'un des partenaires n'a pas communiqué de données.

Il convient toutefois de noter que, même après inclusion des coûts d'assurance et de fret dans les importations c.a.f., diverses autres difficultés peuvent provoquer une incohérence entre les chiffres des exportations à destination d'un pays partenaire et ceux des importations f.à.b. recensées par ledit partenaire, ou entre les chiffres des importations f.à.b. en provenance d'un pays partenaire et les exportations recensées par ledit partenaire. Le manque de concordance des statistiques entre le point d'origine et celui de destination d'une expédition donnée tient essentiellement à des différences dans 1) les critères et le niveau de détail de la classification; 2) les dates d'enregistrement; 3) les méthodes d'évaluation; 4) le champ couvert par les données; et 5) des erreurs de traitement.

Critères et niveaux de classification

Critères de classification en fonction de la destination ou de l'origine en cas de réexpédition : De nombreuses marchandises sont expédiées par l'intermédiaire d'autres pays (par exemple, un volume substantiel du commerce extérieur de l'Allemagne transite par les Pays-Bas). Une asymétrie peut se faire jour dans les chiffres recensés si l'opération commerciale du pays d'origine est classée en tant qu'expédition vers une première destination, ou destination la plus proche, qui constitue un point de réexpédition, alors que le pays de destination finale classe cette même opération sur la base de l'origine.

À l'inverse, le pays d'origine peut classer l'opération en tant qu'expédition vers le pays de destination finale, tandis que ce dernier l'enregistre sur la base de la provenance la plus proche qui constitue un point de réexpédition. Ce manque d'uniformité dans les méthodes de classement s'explique par les règles diverses qu'appliquent les administrations douanières nationales pour déterminer le pays d'origine, de réexpédition et de destination.

Il n'y aurait certes pas d'asymétrie de classement si tous les pays adoptaient le critère du lieu de destination ou de provenance le plus proche, mais ce critère ne répond pas aux besoins analytiques et opérationnels de nombreux utilisateurs de données dont les méthodes s'alignent sur le principe de la destination finale ou de l'origine. Cela signifie que l'analyse des informations basées sur le critère de la destination finale/l'origine exige des pays qu'ils établissent une distinction supplémentaire, par pays partenaire, entre les exportations et importations dont le transbordement a lieu sur leur territoire (réimportations et réexportations) et les exportations dont l'origine, et les importations dont la destination finale, se situent sur leur territoire.

Une telle distinction est toutefois difficile à établir dans la réalité, et la publication de ce type de données n'est pas uniformément pratiquée au niveau international. Les recommandations des instances internationales notent qu'il n'y a pas de moyen idéal de ventiler les opérations par pays partenaire dans les conditions actuelles de classification du commerce extérieur.

Absence de ventilation par pays de destination ou d'origine (ou de provenance) dans les statistiques publiées : Cette situation crée d'emblée des difficultés lorsqu'il s'agit d'identifier les informations sur les échanges entre pays partenaires à partir des données publiées. La ventilation, par pays de destination ou d'origine, des biens militaires et autres articles à caractère confidentiel et biens des administrations publiques peut ne pas être publiée, ou bien ne l'être qu'au niveau des agrégats régionaux. Il est possible aussi que la destination soit indéterminée, et donc non publiée, parce que le réexpéditeur ne connaît pas nécessairement la destination finale au moment de l'expédition. Enfin, les agrégats régionaux peuvent être pu-bliés sans ventilation par pays lorsque les transactions commerciales de certains partenaires n'atteignent pas une valeur minimale donnée.

Date d'enregistrement

Un délai s'écoule entre la date d'expédition d'une exportation et celle de la réception de l'importation, surtout lorsque les marchandises parcourent de grandes distances. Pour éviter les décalages entre les dates d'enregistrement des transactions, les normes internationales en matière de comptabilité nationale et de balance des paiements recommandent de dater les transactions sur la base du critère de changement de propriété. En vertu de ce principe, la marchandise exportée change de propriétaire au moment où elle est expédiée par le pays exportateur, date à laquelle celui-ci la comptabilise en tant qu'exportation et le pays destinataire, en tant qu'importation (f.à.b.).

Or, pour des raisons pratiques, les autorités douanières du pays importateur n'enregistrent la réception desdites marchandises qu'à une date ultérieure, lors de leur arrivée à la frontière du pays concerné, ce qui crée une asymétrie dans les dates d'enregistrement. La même expédition se trouve par conséquent enregistrée dans les statistiques du pays importateur au titre d'une période (mois, trimestre ou année) postérieure à celle où elle est recensée dans les statistiques du pays exportateur.

Évaluation

Les causes possibles du manque d'homogénéité entre l'évaluation d'une expédition donnée à son point d'origine et celui de destination sont notamment les suivantes : application de versions différentes du taux de change, fraude et manque de cohérence des dispositifs de lutte contre la fraude, valeur non encore connue au moment de la réexpédition et manières diverses de traiter certains coûts spécifiques ou de calculer la valeur.

Champ couvert par les données

Les expéditions à destination et en provenance de zones franches et d'entrepôts sous douane, l'exclusion des biens militaires et autres articles à caractère confidentiel et biens des administrations publiques, l'application de valeurs minimales pour l'immatriculation des expéditions en douane, les marchandises renvoyées et autres biens échappant à l'administration douanière (ou aux enquêtes) sont autant d'exemples de différences du champ couvert qui peuvent conduire à des anomalies.

Erreurs de traitement

En raison des décalages de communication et de traitement, les données du commerce extérieur d'une période donnée sont souvent diffusées avant que la documentation douanière de la période considérée n'ait été entièrement traitée. De telles données ne sont parfois pas révisées, ou, même si elles se sont, des erreurs se produisent néanmoins lorsqu'il s'agit de déterminer la date de l'expédition des biens ou celle de leur livraison, et les données tardives sont attribuées à un mois, trimestre ou année erronés. D'autres erreurs sont commises lorsqu'il convient d'attribuer une destination aux exportations ou une origine aux importations à l'occasion du dédouanement, ou encore lorsque la destination finale est modifiée postérieurement à la date d'expédition initiale, en cours de réexpédition, auquel cas le changement n'est pas diffusé sous forme de révision et n'est donc pas pris en considération dans les statistiques publiées.

Ces difficultés doivent donc être prises en compte pour l'interprétation des données. Un effort concerté d'harmonisation et d'alignement des réglementations et définitions douanières à l'échelon international peut aider à combler ces lacunes; dans quelques cas, les pays ont en outre procédé à un rapprochement des données ou se sont inspirés des statistiques des pays partenaires pour établir leurs propres estimations.

Un problème spécifique se pose dans *DOTS* à l'égard des pays dont les statistiques s'écartent notablement de celles de leurs partenaires et qui, parfois, s'abstiennent de communiquer des données. En pareils cas, des anomalies peuvent se faire jour dans les séries chronologiques entres les périodes basées sur les données communiquées et celles qui sont fondées sur les données des pays partenaires.

INTRODUCCIÓN

En los números trimestrales, el anuario y el CD-ROM de *Direction of Trade Statistics* (*DOTS*) se presentan, para la mayoría de los países miembros del Fondo Monetario Internacional (el Fondo), cifras actualizadas sobre el valor de las exportaciones e importaciones de mercancías, clasificadas según los principales países con que comercian. En los números trimestrales *(DOTSQ)* se presentan cifras actuali-zadas sobre unos 158 países. En el anuario *(DOTSY)* se presentan cifras sobre el valor de las exportaciones e importaciones de mercancías de 182 países, desglosadas por países con que comercian, referidas a los años 2001 a 2007 inclusive. En el CD-ROM se presenta la misma información que en el *DOTSY* de 1980 en adelante, clasificada por año, trimestre y mes. En el *DOTSQ*, el *DOTSY* y el CD-ROM se presentan agregados mundiales y regionales que muestran los flujos comerciales entre las principales regiones del mundo. Cuando los datos suministrados están desactualizados o no están disponibles mensualmente, se complementan con estimaciones.

En los cuadros mundiales y regionales se presentan: 1) agregados mundiales que abarcan todos los países, incluidos unos 26 países pequeños sobre los que no se presentan cuadros separados en los números trimestrales; 2) agregados sobre los países industriales, derivados de las cifras correspondientes a los 23 países clasificados como tales; 3) agregados de los países en desarrollo y de una serie de subgrupos, a saber: África, América, Asia, Europa y Oriente Próximo, y 4) agregados de la Unión Europea. Los agregados correspondientes al cuadro mundial se calculan como la suma de los agregados de los cuadros sobre los países industriales y los países en desarrollo. También se incluye el comercio de los países comprendidos en el grupo de "otros países no incluidos separadamente", así como datos sobre países o regiones no especificados y algunas "categorías especiales".

En esta publicación, el término "país" no siempre se refiere a una entidad territorial que sea un Estado, conforme al Derecho y a la práctica internacionales; dicho término abarca asimismo algunas entidades territoriales que no son Estados soberanos, sobre las cuales se declaran y mantienen estadísticas internacionales por separado y de forma independiente.

La información que los países suministran al Fondo en relación con sus exportaciones e importaciones, clasificada por países con que comercian, varía en cuanto a su frecuencia y grado de actualización. Alrededor de 46 países, incluidos prácticamente todos los países industriales y unos 23 países en desarrollo, facilitan datos mensuales de forma periódica y con carácter actualizado (es decir, en un plazo no superior a cuatro meses a partir del mes al que se refieren). En los últimos años estos 46 países, en conjunto, han representado, aproximadamente, un 80% del valor de las exportaciones e importaciones registradas mundiales.

Otros países declaran datos mensuales menos actualizados o compilan y suministran información de forma trimestral o anual. En algunos casos se han utilizado asimismo datos declarados por algunos países a la División de Estadística de las Naciones Unidas. Los datos correspondientes a la mayoría de los Estados miembros de la Unión Europea provienen de la base de datos COMEXT, gestionada por EUROSTAT. Con todo, la información disponible sobre los países con que se comercia permite incluir en *Direction of Trade Statistics* (*DOTS*) estimaciones relativas a cada mes, no sólo respecto de los países que transmiten sus datos con menor frecuencia y grado de actualización, sino también de aquellos cuyos datos no pueden obtenerse de otras fuentes.

Procedimientos de estimación

Los procedimientos de estimación se describen en la *Guía de las estadísticas sobre la distribución geográfica del comercio* (1993), disponible en el CD-ROM y que puede solicitarse a la Sección de Publicaciones del Fondo (http://www.imf.org/external/pubs/cat/longres.cfm?sk=154.0). Todas las estimaciones que aparecen en *DOTS* se basan en datos declarados, incluidos los correspondientes a las importaciones y exportaciones totales transmitidos para su publicación en *International Financial Statistics (IFS)* del Fondo. La base de datos de *DOTS* en su conjunto se complementa continuamente con estimaciones. *Los procedimientos de estimación pueden resumirse del modo siguiente:*

Cuando un país no declara cifras sobre el comercio con alguno de sus socios comerciales en determinado período, se realiza una estimación. Los datos estimados corresponden a la totalidad de los socios comerciales y no a unos cuantos. Si no se dispone de todos o de algunos datos mensuales de *DOTS*, se utilizan los datos trimestrales o anuales declarados de *DOTS*. Si se dispone de datos trimestrales, se distribuyen entre los meses pertinentes, utilizando: 1) los datos mensuales disponibles de *DOTS* declarados en relación con otros países con que se comercia; 2) los totales mensuales que se publican en *IFS* o 3) una distribución uniforme. Si sólo se dispone de datos anuales, los procedimientos de estimación incluyen, además de los métodos descritos anteriormente, los datos de *DOTS* que figuran en la declaración anual más reciente o extrapolaciones de los datos o de las estimaciones más recientes. En la medida de lo posible, se calculan primero las estimaciones correspondientes a los meses, y luego se suman los datos mensuales para obtener los totales anuales.

Si se declaran datos sobre el comercio exterior total para su publicación en *IFS*, pero no para *DOTS*, la suma de las estimaciones correspondientes al comercio con los distintos países deberá coincidir con los totales publicados en *IFS*. En estos casos, los datos correspondientes a las exportaciones e importaciones totales que aparecen en las líneas *IFS World Total* y *DOTS World Total* serán idénticos. Si no se dispone de datos de *IFS*, el valor estimado del comercio se determinará por extrapolación y no aparecerán datos de *IFS* en la página de país.

Si no se declaran datos, o si éstos no permiten aplicar adecuadamente los procedimientos de estimación, los datos se extrapolan utilizando una matriz del comercio entre grupos amplios de países. El crecimiento proyectado del comercio de estos grupos de países, que coincide con las estimaciones que al respecto se utilizan en la publicación del FMI *Perspectivas de la economía mundial*, se combina con los datos disponibles de *DOTS* para obtener los factores de extrapolación.

de un año determinado que se basa en estimaciones va reduciéndose con el tiempo a medida que se sustituyen las estimaciones por los datos declarados por los países (véase el cuadro 1 de *DOTSY*).

En los casos en que se utilizan, directa o indirectamente, datos de los países con los que se comercia para obtener estimaciones, dichos datos se ajustan primero en función del costo del flete y seguro mediante la aplicación de un factor c.i.f./f.o.b. de 1,10. Los datos declarados con respecto a las importaciones c.i.f. se dividen por el factor c.i.f./f.o.b. para obtener las estimaciones de las exportaciones f.o.b. del país con que se comercia. De forma análoga, los datos declarados con respecto a la exportación f.o.b. se multiplican por el factor c.i.f./f.o.b. para obtener las importaciones c.i.f. del país con que se comercia. Por ejemplo, si el país B no ha declarado datos basados en sus propios registros pero el país A sí lo ha hecho, los datos de A correspondientes a las importaciones (c.i.f.) procedentes de B se dividen por 1,10 para obtener el valor f.o.b. de las exportaciones de B a A y, viceversa, los datos de A con respecto a las exportaciones (f.o.b.) a B se multiplican por 1,10 para obtener el valor c.i.f. de las importaciones de B procedentes de A. Dado que no se dispone de datos puntuales con respecto al costo, seguro y flete, el factor c.i.f./f.o.b. del 10% constituye una estimación simplificada de estos costos, que varían mucho de un país a otro y según el tipo de transacción.

Cuadro 1. COBERTURA DE LOS DATOS, 2003–2007

		DATOS DECLARADOS CORRESPONDIENTES A:					DATOS NO DECLARADOS	
		Años completos			Años parciales			
		Número de países[1]		Porcentaje del comercio mundial	Número de países	Porcentaje del comercio mundial	Número de países	Porcentaje del comercio mundial
Exportaciones	2007	72	(48)	90	3	0,29	107	10
	2006	87	(63)	91	2	0,11	93	9
	2005	104	(80)	93	0	0,00	78	7
	2004	111	(87)	94	0	0,00	71	6
	2003	119	(95)	95	0	0,00	63	5
Importaciones	2007	74	(50)	90	2	0,17	106	10
	2006	89	(65)	92	1	0,01	92	8
	2005	107	(83)	96	0	0,00	75	4
	2004	112	(88)	96	0	0,00	70	4
	2003	121	(97)	97	1	0,04	60	3

[1]Las cifras entre paréntesis señalan la cantidad de países en desarrollo que declararon datos completos para el año correspondiente.

No se ofrecen estimaciones de las corrientes comerciales entre dos países si no se dispone de los datos respectivos de ninguno de ellos en relación con los últimos diez años, o más.

En suma, sólo una pequeña proporción del comercio mundial no queda incluida en *DOTS*; la misma comprende 1) un pequeño volumen de comercio no declarado entre los países en desarrollo, 2) un pequeño volumen de comercio no declarado entre los países en desarrollo y los países pertenecientes al grupo de "otros países no incluidos separadamente" y 3) el comercio entre los países que componen este último grupo.

No obstante, no se han elaborado estimaciones para los períodos anteriores a 1981 o basadas en datos de referencia correspondientes a 1980 o años anteriores. Por otra parte, los datos provenientes de los registros propios de los países, aun los declarados después de un plazo prolongado, amplían continuamente la base de los datos declarados, sustituyendo las cifras de las estimaciones previas. Los totales mundiales y regionales se compilan tomando como base los datos declarados y estas estimaciones. El porcentaje del comercio mundial

Símbolos

Para dar una indicación sobre las fuentes de los datos relativos a los distintos países, las cifras que aparecen en las páginas de países, del mundo y de regiones van seguidas de un símbolo. Las cifras que aparecen sin símbolos se refieren a datos provenientes de los registros propios de los países respectivos; los símbolos indican que las cifras se han obtenido a partir de registros de los países con que se comercia o mediante otros métodos de estimación, a saber:

Datos trimestrales

G 2 meses de datos declarados y 1 mes de estimaciones
L 1 mes de datos declarados y 2 meses de estimaciones
V datos consolidados obtenidos exclusivamente de registros de países con los que se comercia
Y datos consolidados estimados mediante otros métodos, que en algunos casos incluyen la utilización de registros de países con los que se comercia; se utilizan asimismo en los totales mundiales y regionales.

Datos anuales

S 6 a 11 meses de datos declarados y 1 a 6 meses de estimaciones
T 1 a 5 meses de datos declarados y 7 a 11 meses de estimaciones
V datos consolidados obtenidos exclusivamente de registros de países con los que se comercia
Y datos consolidados estimados mediante otros métdos, que en algunos casos incluyen la utilización de reistros de países con los que se comercia; se utilizan asimismo en los totales mundiales y regionales.

En *DOTS* se utilizan asimismo los siguientes símbolos y abreviaturas:

Los puntos suspensivos (. . . .) indican que no se dispone de datos.

Un guión (–) indica que la cifra es cero o inferior a la mitad de un dígito significativo.

Las letras **n.i.e.** significan "no incluido en otra parte".

Las letras **ns** significan "no especificado".

En el CD-ROM, las estimaciones se indican en azul y en negrita, con recuadros de texto adjuntos a observaciones sobre los datos.

Composición de las páginas de países, del mundo y de las regiones

En las páginas de países figuran líneas relativas a todos los países con los que se comercia que se hayan declarado, estimado o extrapolado. En los casos en que sea pertinente, se incluyen asimismo las líneas correspondientes a los datos de países o regiones no especificados y a "categorías especiales". El comercio incluido en estas últimas puede abarcar el comercio militar, las transacciones en las zonas francas o las transacciones de aeronaves o buques. Los compiladores de las estadísticas sobre el comercio no han asignado estos datos a ningún país con que se comercia, ni se han incluido por partidas en los datos declarados como región no especificada.

Las páginas de países también incluyen partidas informativas correspondientes a la Unión Europea (UE), los países exportadores de petróleo y los países en desarrollo no exportadores de petróleo. Los datos que figuran en esas partidas presentan el comercio exterior de todos los países miembros del grupo con el país respectivo. De igual forma, esas partidas aparecen en las páginas de las regiones y del mundo. La partida informativa representa el comercio exterior de cada uno de los países miembros del grupo. Por ejemplo, la línea UE de la página del mundo representa el comercio exterior de todos los países de la UE con el mundo, incluidos los intercambios entre los países miembros de la Unión. En esta línea no se presentan los datos de la UE como si ésta fuera un solo país. Los usuarios que deseen obtener estas estadísticas deberán restar el comercio interior entre los países de la UE.

Los dos conjuntos de renglones analíticos incluidos al final de cada página de país en *DOTSY* han sido calculados a partir de las cifras que figuran en el cuadro. El primer conjunto de renglones analíticos muestra la distribución, en porcentajes, de las exportaciones e importaciones totales del país por regiones del mundo. El otro conjunto de renglones muestra la variación porcentual anual de las exportaciones e importaciones totales de cada una de las regiones del mundo.

Los cuadros resumidos del mundo y las regiones se calculan a partir de los datos que figuran en las páginas de países. En esos cuadros se registra el comercio de un grupo de países con cada uno de los países enumerados en el cuadro. Esto equivale a colocar una sobre otra todas las páginas de los distintos países de una región y sumar todas las cifras verticalmente en una página superior que viene a ser un cuadro agregado.

En las páginas de países figuran los principales países con los que comercia cada país, mientras que en los totales mundiales y regionales del comercio de cada país se incluye el comercio que no se muestra explícitamente o no se especifica por país con que se comercia. A efectos comparativos, también se detallan los totales de exportación e importación, expresados en dólares de EE.UU., en los cuadros del comercio mundial de *IFS*, respecto de los países que declaran estadísticas comerciales al Fondo.

Cuando los datos declarados sobre el comercio provienen de los registros propios de un país (tanto como agregados mundiales como por países con los que se comercia), las sumas de las exportaciones hacia todos los países con los que comercia ese país y las importaciones procedentes de todos ellos, incluido el comercio con países no especificados, equivaldrían, en principio, a los agregados declarados de forma independiente para las exportaciones e importaciones totales, respectivamente. Sin embargo, en la práctica pueden surgir discrepancias; por ejemplo, cuando se aplican ajustes o revisiones a los agregados, que no se trasladan a los datos relativos a los distintos países con los que se comercia.

El buscador incluido en el CD-ROM permite visualizar la matriz de análisis multinacional y la presentación por concepto económico, además de los cuadros por países y los cuadros mundiales y regionales.

Moneda

Todos los datos se presentan en dólares de EE.UU. Puesto que la mayoría de los países declaran datos en su moneda nacional, los equivalentes en dólares de EE.UU. se obtienen convirtiendo los datos a los tipos de cambio medios del período publicados en las líneas **rf** o **rh** de las páginas de países de *IFS*. Por lo general, las conversiones se basan en los datos disponibles correspondientes al período más corto y luego son agregados para obtener datos con respecto a períodos más largos: por ejemplo, los datos mensuales se convierten usando los tipos de cambio mensuales y los equivalentes en dólares de EE.UU. se agregan para obtener los valores trimestrales y anuales.

Coherencia de los datos que proporcionan los países que comercian entre sí

Se da por supuesto a veces que los datos de exportación e importación correspondientes de los países que comercian entre sí deberán ser coherentes. Es decir, el monto de las exportaciones del país A al país B deberá ser igual al de las importaciones del país B provenientes del país A, tras los ajustes por concepto de los costos de flete y del seguro conforme al criterio de que las importaciones del país B se valo-ran generalmente sobre la base c.i.f.. El sistema de estimación de *DOTS* se basa en este supuesto en los casos en que uno de los dos países no ha declarado datos.

Sin embargo, cabe señalar que, aunque se incluyan los costos del flete y del seguro en las importaciones c.i.f., existen otras dificultades de diversa índole que pueden dar lugar a incoherencias entre las exportaciones con destino a un país con que se comercia y las importaciones f.o.b. registradas por ese país, o entre las importaciones f.o.b. provenientes del país con que se comercia y las exportaciones registradas por dicho país. La falta de coherencia de las estadísticas entre el punto de origen y el de destino de un envío determinado se debe principalmente a las diferencias en 1) los criterios y desglose de la clasificación, 2) el momento de registro, 3) la valoración y 4) la cobertura, así como 5) a los errores de procesamiento:

Criterios y desglose de la clasificación

Criterios de clasificación en función del origen o del destino en caso de reexpedición: Muchas mercancías se envían a través de otros países, por ejemplo, un gran volumen del comercio de Alemania se envía a través de los Países Bajos. Es posible que los datos declarados no sean coherentes si el comercio del país de origen se clasifica como comercio hacia un primer destino o a un destino más próximo que constituye el punto de reexpedición, mientras que el país de destino final clasifica el mismo comercio de acuerdo con el país de origen.

Por otra parte, el país de origen puede clasificar la operación como un envío hacia el país de destino final, mientras que este último clasifica dicha operación de acuerdo con el origen más próximo, que constituye un punto de reexpedición. La falta de uniformidad en lo que respecta a la clasificación se debe, de hecho, a las diferentes normas que aplican las administraciones aduaneras nacionales para determinar el país de origen, de reexpedición y de destino.

Si bien no existirían incoherencias en materia de clasificación si todos los países utilizaran el criterio del origen o del destino más próximo, este criterio no satisface las necesidades analíticas y operativas de muchos usuarios de datos que se basan en el criterio del destino final o del origen del comercio. Es decir, la información analítica basada en el criterio del origen o del destino final también exige a los países establecer una distinción, por país con que se comercia, entre las exportaciones y las importaciones cuya reexpedición se lleva a cabo a través de su territorio (reimportaciones y reexportaciones), y las exportaciones cuyo origen se encuentra en su territorio y las importaciones cuyo destino final se encuentra en dicho territorio.

Sin embargo, muchas veces es difícil establecer esta distinción y la publicación de estos datos no constituye una práctica establecida uniformemente a escala internacional. Las recomendaciones internacionales señalan que no existe un método ideal para desglosar las operaciones por países con que se comercia dadas las condiciones vigentes de registro del comercio exterior.

Falta de desglose por país de origen o de destino en las estadísticas publicadas. Esta situación crea inmediatamente problemas para identificar la información sobre el comercio entre los países a partir de los datos publicados. Es posible que no se publique información sobre el país de origen y de destino de los bienes militares y otros artículos de carácter confidencial y de los bienes públicos, o que esta información se publique en forma de agregados regionales. También es posible que no se determine el destino y que, por lo tanto, éste no se publique porque la persona encargada de la reexpedición no conoce el destino final en el momento del envío. Además, es posible que se publiquen agregados regionales sin un desglose por países si las transacciones comerciales de algunos países con que se comercia no alcanzan un nivel mínimo.

Momento de registro

Transcurre algún tiempo entre el envío de una exportación y el recibo de una importación, sobre todo si las mercancías se transportan lejos. Para evitar estas incoherencias en el momento de registro, las normas internacionales en materia de contabilidad nacional y de balanza de pagos recomiendan basarse en el criterio del traspaso de propiedad para asignar una fecha a las transacciones. Conforme a este criterio, un bien exportado cambia de propietario en el momento en que el país exportador envía dicho bien, fecha en que el país exportador registra dicha transacción como una exportación y el país de destino como una importación (f.o.b.).

Sin embargo, por razones prácticas, las autoridades aduaneras del país importador contabilizan el recibo de estos bienes en una fecha posterior, cuando llegan a la frontera del país receptor, lo que puede crear una incoherencia en cuanto al momento de registro. Por lo tanto, el mismo envío puede aparecer en las estadísticas del país importador correspondientes a un período (un mes, un trimestre o un año) posterior al período en que dicho envío aparece en las estadísticas del país exportador.

Valoración

Entre las causas posibles de la falta de coherencia entre la valoración de un envío determinado en el punto de origen y en el punto de destino cabe señalar la aplicación de versiones diferentes del tipo de cambio, el fraude, los procedi-mientos contra el fraude, los valores desconocidos en el momento del envío y los diferentes tratamientos de algunos costos específicos y los procedimientos de evaluación.

Cobertura

Los envíos destinados a las zonas francas y a los almacenes bajo control aduanero y provenientes de éstos, salvo los bienes militares u otros artículos de carácter confidencial y los bienes públicos, los valores mínimos para el registro aduanero de los envíos, y los bienes devueltos y otros bienes no registrados por la administración aduanera (ni incluidos en las encuestas) son algunos ejemplos de las diferencias en materia de cobertura que pueden dar lugar a incoherencias.

Errores de procesamiento

Debido a los desfases de declaración y de procesamiento, en muchos casos los datos sobre el comercio exterior correspondientes a un período determinado se divulgan antes de que se hayan procesado todos los documentos aduaneros correspondientes a dicho período. Estos datos a veces no se revisan o, si se revisan, se cometen errores al asignar la fecha en que se envían o se reciben los bienes y los datos desfasados se incluyen en el mes, el trimestre o el año equivocado. También pueden cometerse errores al asignar el destino de las exportaciones y el origen de las importaciones durante el despacho de aduana, o en los casos en que se modifica el destino final después del envío inicial durante la reexpedición, pero no se revisan los datos y, por lo tanto, el cambio no se incorpora en las estadísticas publicadas.

Deberán considerarse estas cuestiones al interpretar los datos. La cooperación internacional en materia de armonización y conciliación de los procedimientos aduaneros y las definiciones podría contribuir a reducir las diferencias; en algunos casos, los países han conciliado los datos o han utilizado los datos de los países con que comercian para preparar sus propias estimaciones.

En *DOTS* se plantea otro problema específico en el caso de los países cuyas estadísticas se diferencian en gran medida de las de los países con que comercian y que a veces no declaran datos. En estos casos, se producirán anomalías en las series cronológicas entre los períodos basados en los datos declarados y en los períodos basados en los datos de los países con que comercian.

WORLD *and* AREA TABLES

	Exports 2001	2002	2003	2004	2005	2006	2007	Imports 2001	2002	2003	2004	2005	2006	2007
	Billions of U.S. Dollars							*Billions of U.S. Dollars*						
IFS World Total	**6,139.9**	**6,434.3**	**7,483.8**	**9,150.0**	**10,468.6**	**12,150.7**	**13,851.9**	**6,351.4**	**6,587.7**	**7,673.5**	**9,382.3**	**10,665.1**	**12,257.3**	**14,124.9**
DOTS World Total 001	**6,139.5Y**	**6,433.0Y**	**7,519.5Y**	**9,131.9Y**	**10,359.3Y**	**11,960.8Y**	**13,820.6Y**	**6,381.2Y**	**6,628.8Y**	**7,750.3Y**	**9,486.6Y**	**10,753.4Y**	**12,362.6Y**	**14,312.8Y**
Industrial Countries 101	**4,084.4Y**	**4,216.5Y**	**4,873.1Y**	**5,792.4Y**	**6,437.2Y**	**7,250.9Y**	**8,147.0Y**	**3,932.2Y**	**4,025.3Y**	**4,630.7Y**	**5,478.7Y**	**5,941.0Y**	**6,621.9Y**	**7,624.0Y**
United States 111	1,098.69Y	1,124.35Y	1,215.98Y	1,423.01Y	1,611.35Y	1,790.31Y	1,895.74Y	783.30Y	750.35Y	782.14Y	883.82Y	962.34Y	1,056.68Y	1,188.84Y
Canada 156	217.48Y	218.57Y	235.25Y	265.61Y	304.13Y	338.65Y	370.45Y	269.19Y	261.29Y	278.68Y	322.44Y	364.41Y	387.08Y	416.22Y
Australia 193	60.17Y	68.19Y	81.61Y	100.08Y	112.74Y	126.49Y	147.42Y	68.40Y	68.11Y	72.68Y	93.43Y	113.45Y	131.55Y	152.08Y
Japan 158	316.18Y	305.45Y	345.22Y	409.41Y	464.79Y	525.65Y	563.99Y	447.23Y	457.85Y	514.86Y	619.25Y	657.82Y	699.79Y	766.30Y
New Zealand 196	12.50Y	13.57Y	16.88Y	21.00Y	23.65Y	24.04Y	27.37Y	15.52Y	15.68Y	17.91Y	21.28Y	22.79Y	23.47Y	27.41Y
Austria 122	66.56Y	70.83Y	88.01Y	107.51Y	116.40Y	134.93Y	155.82Y	60.55Y	66.72Y	82.34Y	101.75Y	107.45Y	129.73Y	157.94Y
Belgium 124	160.07Y	178.89Y	212.87Y	256.61Y	287.12Y	327.89Y	383.66Y	156.24Y	166.11Y	197.90Y	242.21Y	268.85Y	328.54Y	389.69Y
Belgium-Luxembourg n.s. 127	4.20Y	4.03Y	3.92Y	4.14Y	3.46Y	1.24Y	.82Y	2.73Y	2.86Y	3.32Y	2.91Y	2.05Y	.84Y	.65Y
Cyprus 423	6.38Y	7.28Y	10.32Y	13.25Y	13.08Y	15.46Y	16.85Y	1.45Y	1.33Y	1.61Y	1.81Y	1.93Y	3.84Y	3.96Y
Denmark 128	41.59Y	45.12Y	53.19Y	63.33Y	71.80Y	82.68Y	93.07Y	45.64Y	49.63Y	60.40Y	70.54Y	77.64Y	87.29Y	96.46Y
Finland 172	35.02Y	36.45Y	45.96Y	57.42Y	66.21Y	77.65Y	89.38Y	43.28Y	42.80Y	50.86Y	62.84Y	69.75Y	79.31Y	92.77Y
France 132	314.68Y	325.32Y	387.16Y	467.08Y	506.30Y	554.18Y	631.98Y	298.64Y	305.89Y	367.31Y	430.72Y	448.02Y	494.13Y	569.21Y
Germany 134	481.76Y	487.71Y	592.47Y	701.73Y	767.76Y	881.91Y	1,013.76Y	559.18Y	605.29Y	737.78Y	894.41Y	966.41Y	1,094.27Y	1,308.30Y
Greece 174	32.02Y	33.34Y	43.15Y	52.85Y	54.27Y	63.21Y	74.79Y	10.43Y	10.96Y	13.66Y	15.43Y	17.26Y	20.83Y	24.17Y
Iceland 176	2.33Y	2.01Y	2.60Y	3.37Y	4.57Y	5.13Y	6.05Y	2.29Y	2.53Y	2.73Y	3.19Y	3.26Y	3.75Y	4.24Y
Ireland 178	49.29Y	52.68Y	55.81Y	65.45Y	75.27Y	80.72Y	91.93Y	85.96Y	96.44Y	111.77Y	129.16Y	139.17Y	132.93Y	146.90Y
Italy 136	224.08Y	238.95Y	290.61Y	346.86Y	378.41Y	438.07Y	503.51Y	226.30Y	239.24Y	285.32Y	334.37Y	353.69Y	400.36Y	482.79Y
Luxembourg 137	12.32Y	12.77Y	16.10Y	20.64Y	22.31Y	24.99Y	25.68Y	8.66Y	8.87Y	13.33Y	17.04Y	17.22Y	21.11Y	23.98Y
Malta 181	4.33Y	4.57Y	4.88Y	5.61Y	5.29Y	7.10Y	8.31Y	2.32Y	2.60Y	3.04Y	3.32Y	3.36Y	3.87Y	4.98Y
Netherlands 138	218.00Y	229.27Y	271.65Y	329.86Y	376.91Y	444.34Y	520.55Y	199.87Y	204.00Y	246.06Y	302.54Y	338.78Y	424.42Y	505.71Y
Norway 142	31.14Y	32.90Y	39.12Y	46.71Y	52.46Y	61.75Y	75.96Y	55.21Y	57.76Y	73.21Y	88.62Y	107.69Y	123.07Y	133.17Y
Portugal 182	42.03Y	42.46Y	51.20Y	61.40Y	66.27Y	70.83Y	79.36Y	26.65Y	27.04Y	34.86Y	39.83Y	38.45Y	42.63Y	47.35Y
Slovenia 961	9.97Y	10.69Y	13.42Y	16.80Y	18.64Y	22.20Y	28.60Y	9.67Y	10.97Y	13.81Y	16.02Y	16.62Y	19.15Y	25.86Y
Spain 184	152.65Y	164.26Y	209.78Y	257.11Y	291.57Y	328.67Y	383.39Y	109.21Y	119.16Y	149.87Y	177.07Y	187.18Y	209.12Y	255.12Y
Sweden 144	64.44Y	67.76Y	82.40Y	99.31Y	109.34Y	116.32Y	146.86Y	79.06Y	81.91Y	101.94Y	124.31Y	134.03Y	150.05Y	173.31Y
Switzerland 146	91.88Y	95.08Y	111.89Y	132.08Y	145.07Y	165.47Y	191.52Y	96.70Y	103.80Y	116.83Y	138.27Y	151.53Y	158.10Y	183.51Y
United Kingdom 112	334.67Y	343.97Y	391.62Y	464.16Y	488.96Y	544.07Y	623.74Y	268.57Y	266.12Y	296.45Y	342.07Y	371.88Y	400.88Y	451.85Y
Developing Countries 202	**1,981.5Y**	**2,140.1Y**	**2,567.4Y**	**3,240.6Y**	**3,808.6Y**	**4,568.5Y**	**5,513.4Y**	**2,370.6Y**	**2,516.1Y**	**3,028.9Y**	**3,888.3Y**	**4,658.1Y**	**5,548.3Y**	**6,466.3Y**
Africa 607	**111.3Y**	**118.4Y**	**141.2Y**	**178.8Y**	**209.1Y**	**255.4Y**	**304.8Y**	**139.3Y**	**137.5Y**	**167.9Y**	**220.3Y**	**274.9Y**	**324.2Y**	**373.2Y**
Algeria 612	10.40Y	12.21Y	13.95Y	18.94Y	21.35Y	22.74Y	30.14Y	21.96Y	21.25Y	27.39Y	35.20Y	48.02Y	59.25Y	62.60Y
Angola 614	3.12Y	2.78Y	4.06Y	6.41Y	7.50Y	10.26Y	11.79Y	6.79Y	7.94Y	9.36Y	12.88Y	22.24Y	32.06Y	40.27Y
Benin 638	1.37Y	1.49Y	1.62Y	1.79Y	2.46Y	3.34Y	4.65Y	.41Y	.25Y	.29Y	.38Y	.37Y	.42Y	.51Y
Botswana 616	.29Y	.27Y	.35Y	.44Y	.44Y	.48Y	.75Y	1.74Y	1.78Y	2.17Y	2.69Y	2.91Y	3.21Y	2.31Y
Burkina Faso 748	.43Y	.56Y	.74Y	.87Y	.93Y	1.06Y	1.33Y	.16Y	.15Y	.23Y	.35Y	.34Y	.38Y	.42Y
Burundi 618	.13Y	.11Y	.14Y	.19Y	.22Y	.27Y	.29Y	.04Y	.03Y	.04Y	.04Y	.09Y	.06Y	.09Y
Cameroon 622	1.79Y	1.79Y	2.23Y	2.24Y	2.57Y	2.98Y	3.70Y	2.29Y	2.10Y	2.80Y	3.76Y	3.86Y	5.04Y	5.33Y
Cape Verde 624	.25Y	.29Y	.32Y	.39Y	.43Y	.56Y	.74Y	.02Y	.02Y	.03Y	.02Y	.03Y	.04Y	.03Y
Central African Rep. 626	.09Y	.10Y	.09Y	.13Y	.14Y	.20Y	.22Y	.18Y	.23Y	.13Y	.14Y	.13Y	.12Y	.14Y
Chad 628	.33Y	.42Y	.32Y	.38Y	.44Y	.48Y	.65Y	.08Y	.07Y	.10Y	1.18Y	2.02Y	2.51Y	2.50Y
Comoros 632	.07Y	.09Y	.11Y	.10Y	.10Y	.12Y	.14Y	.04Y	.03Y	.04Y	.04Y	.03Y	.03Y	.03Y
Congo, Dem. Rep. of 636	.62Y	.84Y	.95Y	1.26Y	1.48Y	2.05Y	2.76Y	1.25Y	1.46Y	1.08Y	1.24Y	1.57Y	1.74Y	2.12Y
Congo, Republic of 634	.86Y	.97Y	1.01Y	1.11Y	1.43Y	1.79Y	3.30Y	2.72Y	2.51Y	2.89Y	4.18Y	5.95Y	8.97Y	7.74Y
Côte d'Ivoire 662	2.47Y	2.40Y	2.66Y	3.35Y	3.87Y	4.30Y	5.43Y	4.09Y	4.83Y	5.62Y	6.50Y	6.99Y	7.60Y	8.88Y
Djibouti 611	.63Y	.58Y	.75Y	.78Y	1.05Y	1.36Y	1.68Y	.26Y	.22Y	.27Y	.28Y	.30Y	.37Y	.46Y
Equatorial Guinea 642	.29Y	.40Y	1.11Y	.67Y	1.02Y	1.47Y	1.21Y	1.71Y	1.91Y	2.90Y	4.35Y	6.82Y	8.21Y	9.02Y
Ethiopia 644	1.08Y	1.16Y	1.91Y	2.27Y	2.95Y	2.97Y	3.82Y	.47Y	.50Y	.61Y	.58Y	.88Y	1.02Y	1.14Y
Gabon 646	1.29Y	1.02Y	1.20Y	1.43Y	1.50Y	1.73Y	2.45Y	3.57Y	3.06Y	3.65Y	4.43Y	5.05Y	4.44Y	6.05Y
Gambia, The 648	.36Y	.37Y	.46Y	.52Y	.58Y	.64Y	.78Y	.03Y	.03Y	.02Y	.04Y	.03Y	.04Y	.05Y
Ghana 652	2.42Y	2.71Y	3.46Y	4.64Y	5.34Y	6.18Y	8.13Y	1.48Y	1.66Y	1.98Y	2.25Y	2.30Y	2.77Y	3.11Y
Guinea 656	.69Y	.80Y	.85Y	.96Y	1.21Y	1.32Y	1.66Y	.93Y	.91Y	.87Y	.98Y	1.26Y	1.26Y	1.54Y
Guinea-Bissau 654	.09Y	.08Y	.13Y	.11Y	.18Y	.16Y	.19Y	.14Y	.11Y	.08Y	.12Y	.12Y	.15Y	.41Y
Kenya 664	3.52Y	3.22Y	3.67Y	4.97Y	6.14Y	7.40Y	9.28Y	2.18Y	2.35Y	2.81Y	3.42Y	3.70Y	4.27Y	5.03Y
Lesotho 666	.12Y	.17Y	.22Y	.28Y	.23Y	.27Y	.28Y	.30Y	.36Y	.44Y	.54Y	.50Y	.52Y	.64Y
Liberia 668	4.01Y	4.58Y	3.90Y	4.47Y	5.23Y	6.89Y	8.00Y	1.07Y	1.18Y	1.02Y	1.05Y	1.09Y	1.72Y	1.13Y
Madagascar 674	1.04Y	.69Y	1.29Y	1.42Y	1.52Y	1.60Y	2.24Y	1.05Y	.87Y	1.17Y	1.36Y	1.08Y	1.15Y	1.31Y
Malawi 676	.39Y	.54Y	.53Y	.69Y	.67Y	.73Y	.85Y	.46Y	.46Y	.55Y	.55Y	.68Y	.68Y	.86Y
Mali 678	.83Y	.80Y	.87Y	1.14Y	1.26Y	1.44Y	1.78Y	.17Y	.17Y	.23Y	.34Y	.27Y	.42Y	.23Y
Mauritania 682	.59Y	.74Y	.83Y	.92Y	1.13Y	1.19Y	1.50Y	.60Y	.59Y	.64Y	.87Y	1.02Y	1.52Y	1.84Y
Mauritius 684	1.99Y	2.02Y	2.61Y	2.54Y	2.95Y	3.22Y	3.45Y	1.68Y	1.78Y	2.12Y	2.04Y	2.17Y	2.21Y	2.13Y
Morocco 686	10.48Y	11.73Y	13.58Y	17.16Y	22.54Y	22.56Y	29.35Y	8.35Y	8.83Y	10.03Y	11.82Y	15.65Y	14.22Y	17.05Y
Mozambique 688	1.14Y	1.47Y	1.58Y	1.87Y	2.29Y	2.22Y	2.87Y	.79Y	.98Y	.98Y	1.41Y	1.65Y	1.72Y	2.71Y
Namibia 728	.52Y	.33Y	.40Y	.50Y	.55Y	.67Y	.89Y	.92Y	.80Y	.89Y	1.48Y	1.58Y	2.13Y	2.12Y
Niger 692	.39Y	.47Y	.50Y	.65Y	.76Y	.92Y	1.00Y	.23Y	.11Y	.12Y	.34Y	.33Y	.47Y	.42Y
Nigeria 694	10.65Y	12.07Y	13.76Y	15.95Y	18.89Y	22.63Y	30.44Y	23.06Y	17.33Y	25.15Y	36.13Y	47.12Y	57.26Y	64.15Y
Rwanda 714	.18Y	.21Y	.26Y	.30Y	.35Y	.42Y	.52Y	.10Y	.12Y	.11Y	.35Y	.09Y	.11Y	.14Y
St. Helena 856	.03Y	.04Y	.03Y	.04Y	.06Y	.08Y	.11Y	.01Y	.02Y	.02Y	.02Y	.02Y	.02Y	.03Y
São Tomé & Príncipe 716	.05Y	.06Y	.06Y	.06Y	.06Y	.07Y	.07Y	.01Y	.01Y	.01Y	.01Y	.02Y	.01Y	.01Y
Senegal 722	1.78Y	1.96Y	2.35Y	2.85Y	3.62Y	3.45Y	4.50Y	.88Y	.91Y	1.04Y	1.10Y	1.61Y	1.25Y	1.59Y
Seychelles 718	.48Y	.35Y	.41Y	.45Y	.63Y	.69Y	.82Y	.26Y	.39Y	.40Y	.41Y	.45Y	.38Y	.36Y

World 001

		Exports							Imports						
		2001	2002	2003	2004	2005	2006	2007	2001	2002	2003	2004	2005	2006	2007
		Billions of U.S. Dollars							Billions of U.S. Dollars						
Sierra Leone	724	.37Y	.44Y	.53Y	.45Y	.53Y	.48Y	.54Y	.06Y	.11Y	.15Y	.20Y	.21Y	.22Y	.29Y
Somalia	726	.27Y	.31Y	.33Y	.43Y	.50Y	.63Y	.69Y	.08Y	.12Y	.17Y	.21Y	.28Y	.33Y	.42Y
South Africa	199	26.02Y	26.47Y	34.38Y	46.73Y	51.73Y	67.80Y	77.23Y	32.62Y	34.05Y	39.69Y	52.73Y	58.76Y	64.38Y	79.63Y
Sudan	732	1.71Y	1.98Y	2.84Y	4.42Y	6.64Y	15.35Y	7.11Y	1.87Y	2.13Y	2.74Y	4.20Y	5.48Y	6.31Y	8.63Y
Swaziland	734	.10Y	.11Y	.20Y	.18Y	.15Y	.17Y	.20Y	.37Y	.51Y	.56Y	.76Y	.89Y	.94Y	.98Y
Tanzania	738	1.63Y	1.77Y	2.16Y	2.66Y	3.15Y	3.92Y	4.73Y	.71Y	.77Y	.95Y	1.25Y	1.51Y	1.59Y	1.78Y
Togo	742	.80Y	1.34Y	1.28Y	1.61Y	1.92Y	2.62Y	4.06Y	.41Y	.36Y	.71Y	.53Y	.60Y	.67Y	.82Y
Tunisia	744	9.11Y	9.14Y	10.32Y	12.23Y	12.97Y	14.89Y	18.06Y	6.84Y	7.21Y	8.44Y	10.22Y	10.70Y	12.42Y	15.63Y
Uganda	746	.88Y	.96Y	1.10Y	1.34Y	1.53Y	1.92Y	2.55Y	.36Y	.40Y	.51Y	.58Y	.68Y	.69Y	.85Y
Zambia	754	.88Y	1.02Y	1.01Y	1.40Y	1.60Y	2.31Y	3.04Y	.74Y	.70Y	.96Y	1.71Y	2.64Y	3.70Y	3.89Y
Zimbabwe	698	1.22Y	1.46Y	1.40Y	1.65Y	1.95Y	1.86Y	2.24Y	1.73Y	1.71Y	1.85Y	1.91Y	1.89Y	2.17Y	2.55Y
Africa n.s.	799	1.02Y	.49Y	.38Y	.49Y	.38Y	.61Y	.60Y	1.03Y	1.08Y	.87Y	1.10Y	.83Y	.94Y	1.11Y
Asia	**507**	**1,031.8Y**	**1,142.6Y**	**1,398.4Y**	**1,755.8Y**	**2,031.3Y**	**2,395.9Y**	**2,810.2Y**	**1,267.0Y**	**1,390.0Y**	**1,660.2Y**	**2,110.9Y**	**2,468.6Y**	**2,908.1Y**	**3,389.7Y**
Afghanistan, I.S. of	512	.51Y	.94Y	1.46Y	1.78Y	2.73Y	3.48Y	4.40Y	.10Y	.10Y	.23Y	.20Y	.26Y	.30Y	.37Y
American Samoa	859	.08Y	.11Y	.06Y	.10Y	.23Y	.12Y	.18Y	.10Y	.03Y	.01Y	.01Y	.02Y	.02Y	.05Y
Bangladesh	513	7.76Y	7.48Y	8.91Y	11.03Y	12.92Y	15.17Y	16.78Y	6.53Y	6.41Y	7.63Y	9.34Y	9.87Y	12.31Y	13.27Y
Brunei Darussalam	516	1.19Y	1.48Y	1.68Y	1.49Y	1.51Y	1.81Y	3.57Y	3.66Y	3.77Y	4.37Y	4.97Y	6.18Y	7.58Y	7.62Y
Cambodia	522	2.07Y	2.34Y	2.67Y	3.26Y	3.90Y	5.06Y	5.86Y	1.71Y	1.95Y	2.31Y	2.85Y	3.16Y	3.89Y	4.47Y
China,P.R.: Mainland	924	221.02Y	270.69Y	375.99Y	491.45Y	585.55Y	714.83Y	858.42Y	412.65Y	482.23Y	609.17Y	803.42Y	999.61Y	1,212.32Y	1,487.84Y
China,P.R.:Hong Kong	532	173.69Y	195.44Y	229.43Y	277.42Y	310.63Y	364.62Y	410.34Y	56.95Y	60.02Y	63.33Y	73.89Y	75.98Y	80.63Y	76.37Y
China,P.R.:Macao	546	2.65Y	2.85Y	3.93Y	4.68Y	5.36Y	6.60Y	8.08Y	2.49Y	2.50Y	2.79Y	3.27Y	2.72Y	2.83Y	3.03Y
Fiji	819	.68Y	.76Y	.89Y	1.11Y	1.30Y	1.42Y	1.40Y	.61Y	.58Y	.68Y	.81Y	.77Y	.80Y	.83Y
French Polynesia	887	.90Y	1.22Y	1.53Y	1.29Y	1.72Y	1.46Y	1.61Y	.24Y	.26Y	.54Y	.42Y	.49Y	.33Y	.35Y
Guam	829	.53Y	.42Y	.50Y	.64Y	.88Y	1.08Y	.95Y	.06Y	.04Y	.07Y	.05Y	.05Y	.06Y	.09Y
India	534	41.89Y	45.84Y	58.23Y	76.47Y	99.87Y	124.99Y	171.60Y	48.27Y	54.75Y	67.22Y	91.92Y	112.02Y	133.80Y	166.98Y
Indonesia	536	31.80Y	33.78Y	54.87Y	69.15Y	79.74Y	84.15Y	103.18Y	62.62Y	64.31Y	80.37Y	95.06Y	106.94Y	125.06Y	142.41Y
Kiribati	826	.04Y	.08Y	.05Y	.06Y	.07Y	.06Y	.09Y	.04Y	.04Y	.03Y	.02Y	.01Y	.01Y	.01Y
Korea	542	129.92Y	140.44Y	163.91Y	203.90Y	235.42Y	280.96Y	328.89Y	159.90Y	171.77Y	205.26Y	271.89Y	306.67Y	358.64Y	399.26Y
Lao People's Dem.Rep.	544	.64Y	.64Y	.72Y	.94Y	1.13Y	1.48Y	1.88Y	.31Y	.32Y	.34Y	.41Y	.56Y	1.04Y	1.14Y
Malaysia	548	72.91Y	77.35Y	86.02Y	100.13Y	109.31Y	128.39Y	145.32Y	109.99Y	115.58Y	133.81Y	159.21Y	177.28Y	201.32Y	224.11Y
Maldives	556	.36Y	.32Y	.40Y	.61Y	.69Y	.81Y	1.56Y	1.09Y	1.25Y	1.07Y	1.17Y	.15Y	.19Y	.19Y
Mongolia	948	.60Y	.70Y	.81Y	1.04Y	1.20Y	1.46Y	2.10Y	.49Y	.50Y	.58Y	.86Y	.98Y	1.62Y	1.84Y
Myanmar	518	2.42Y	2.70Y	2.93Y	3.13Y	3.24Y	3.50Y	5.02Y	2.66Y	2.80Y	2.77Y	3.18Y	3.76Y	4.48Y	4.87Y
Nauru	836	.02Y	.03Y	.03Y	.02Y	.03Y	.03Y	.06Y	.02Y	.01Y	.02Y	.02Y	.01Y	—Y	.02Y
Nepal	558	1.15Y	.82Y	1.09Y	1.26Y	1.38Y	1.95Y	2.54Y	.79Y	.60Y	.62Y	.67Y	.67Y	.91Y	1.08Y
New Caledonia	839	.86Y	1.06Y	1.32Y	1.47Y	1.61Y	1.81Y	2.33Y	.52Y	.48Y	.74Y	1.00Y	1.08Y	1.50Y	2.59Y
Pakistan	564	9.87Y	11.64Y	14.27Y	20.18Y	25.27Y	30.08Y	34.68Y	9.41Y	9.63Y	10.99Y	13.72Y	15.35Y	17.84Y	20.20Y
Papua New Guinea	853	1.01Y	1.07Y	1.21Y	1.44Y	1.81Y	2.12Y	2.65Y	1.79Y	1.74Y	2.54Y	2.79Y	3.57Y	4.37Y	4.86Y
Philippines	566	39.96Y	39.42Y	44.24Y	50.14Y	52.54Y	58.43Y	66.05Y	42.81Y	46.66Y	51.52Y	57.75Y	63.82Y	70.12Y	77.18Y
Samoa	862	.25Y	.18Y	.23Y	.26Y	.27Y	.29Y	.31Y	.07Y	.08Y	.11Y	.10Y	.13Y	.14Y	.17Y
Singapore	576	109.67Y	112.06Y	120.97Y	148.20Y	174.08Y	203.13Y	228.77Y	91.97Y	95.34Y	108.46Y	134.61Y	159.20Y	183.73Y	201.68Y
Solomon Islands	813	.09Y	.07Y	.11Y	.12Y	.17Y	.21Y	.27Y	.08Y	.09Y	.12Y	.18Y	.21Y	.24Y	.33Y
Sri Lanka	524	5.20Y	5.66Y	6.47Y	7.84Y	9.11Y	10.32Y	10.92Y	4.81Y	4.56Y	5.10Y	6.17Y	6.65Y	7.19Y	7.90Y
Taiwan Province of China	528	100.91Y	107.29Y	121.33Y	157.27Y	168.64Y	186.58Y	200.73Y	151.26Y	162.68Y	182.76Y	226.51Y	247.80Y	283.11Y	310.70Y
Thailand	578	55.51Y	58.68Y	68.05Y	86.70Y	103.65Y	116.17Y	128.72Y	71.42Y	74.26Y	87.13Y	108.99Y	124.15Y	145.32Y	170.53Y
Tonga	866	.07Y	.08Y	.09Y	.11Y	.12Y	.13Y	.15Y	.03Y	.03Y	.03Y	.03Y	.02Y	.02Y	.02Y
Tuvalu	869	.01Y	.07Y	.02Y	.03Y	.04Y	.06Y	.06Y	—Y	—Y	—Y	—Y	—Y	—Y	—Y
Vanuatu	846	.16Y	.12Y	.19Y	.21Y	.24Y	.24Y	.28Y	.07Y	.06Y	.08Y	.21Y	.21Y	.27Y	.30Y
Vietnam	582	14.91Y	18.22Y	23.23Y	30.09Y	34.39Y	42.06Y	59.40Y	14.85Y	16.77Y	21.85Y	28.01Y	34.38Y	41.90Y	50.98Y
Asia n.s.	598	.52Y	.54Y	.47Y	.54Y	.38Y	.70Y	.87Y	6.59Y	7.75Y	5.49Y	7.10Y	3.66Y	5.15Y	7.15Y
Europe	**170**	**307.9Y**	**353.8Y**	**458.0Y**	**592.9Y**	**724.5Y**	**918.7Y**	**1,194.2Y**	**332.9Y**	**367.4Y**	**475.5Y**	**623.6Y**	**745.3Y**	**914.9Y**	**1,139.8Y**
Albania	914	1.22Y	1.37Y	1.67Y	2.07Y	2.29Y	2.69Y	3.53Y	.35Y	.35Y	.46Y	.61Y	.63Y	.73Y	1.05Y
Armenia	911	.53Y	.73Y	.92Y	1.12Y	1.32Y	1.81Y	2.52Y	.26Y	.37Y	.58Y	.57Y	.86Y	.77Y	.97Y
Azerbaijan	912	1.13Y	1.67Y	2.59Y	4.09Y	4.84Y	6.68Y	6.94Y	1.56Y	1.67Y	2.07Y	2.83Y	4.65Y	9.37Y	15.88Y
Belarus	913	2.35Y	8.38Y	10.80Y	4.26Y	13.54Y	10.93Y	26.74Y	2.38Y	6.61Y	8.54Y	5.47Y	11.95Y	11.58Y	20.16Y
Bosnia & Herzegovina	963	2.58Y	3.06Y	3.63Y	4.43Y	5.24Y	6.20Y	7.77Y	.81Y	.92Y	1.26Y	1.69Y	2.42Y	3.38Y	3.91Y
Bulgaria	918	6.00Y	6.68Y	9.06Y	12.67Y	16.04Y	21.88Y	27.13Y	5.44Y	5.81Y	7.53Y	10.01Y	11.58Y	14.67Y	17.08Y
Croatia	960	7.82Y	9.36Y	12.31Y	14.76Y	16.69Y	19.56Y	24.21Y	4.17Y	4.49Y	5.53Y	7.41Y	8.15Y	9.68Y	10.72Y
Czech Republic	935	34.24Y	38.34Y	48.37Y	60.41Y	71.59Y	89.18Y	113.38Y	32.91Y	37.97Y	49.47Y	60.08Y	69.52Y	87.01Y	115.07Y
Czechoslovakia n.s.	937	.16Y	.21Y	.20Y	.13Y	.01Y	.02Y	.04Y	.18Y	.19Y	.37Y	.55Y	.28Y	.32Y	.42Y
Estonia	939	5.25Y	6.31Y	7.50Y	9.09Y	11.29Y	15.33Y	16.30Y	4.38Y	4.34Y	5.32Y	7.13Y	8.16Y	10.07Y	10.46Y
Faroe Islands	816	.46Y	.42Y	.52Y	.58Y	.65Y	.68Y	.89Y	.46Y	.47Y	.57Y	.58Y	.59Y	.69Y	.80Y
Georgia	915	.90Y	.94Y	1.48Y	2.06Y	2.59Y	3.66Y	4.98Y	.62Y	.65Y	.92Y	1.20Y	1.37Y	2.08Y	1.84Y
Gibraltar	823	1.52Y	1.61Y	1.72Y	2.77Y	3.52Y	5.13Y	6.06Y	.15Y	.15Y	.29Y	.30Y	.34Y	.28Y	.38Y
Hungary	944	31.74Y	36.14Y	45.82Y	55.49Y	62.95Y	74.97Y	91.74Y	33.00Y	35.49Y	43.48Y	52.93Y	59.16Y	69.55Y	92.64Y
Kazakhstan	916	5.48Y	6.46Y	8.83Y	13.66Y	18.27Y	24.58Y	33.63Y	9.46Y	11.78Y	14.55Y	19.00Y	24.18Y	30.65Y	38.04Y
Kyrgyz Republic	917	.49Y	.65Y	.92Y	1.42Y	1.93Y	3.55Y	5.79Y	.37Y	.30Y	.40Y	.69Y	.71Y	.74Y	1.06Y
Latvia	941	5.54Y	5.75Y	7.19Y	8.42Y	9.60Y	12.84Y	17.89Y	3.16Y	3.27Y	4.03Y	5.68Y	6.48Y	7.63Y	9.56Y
Lithuania	946	6.91Y	8.18Y	10.54Y	12.29Y	14.40Y	18.27Y	23.12Y	4.10Y	4.79Y	6.36Y	8.16Y	9.83Y	11.44Y	14.10Y
Macedonia, FYR	962	1.65Y	1.65Y	1.85Y	2.29Y	2.46Y	3.26Y	4.16Y	.92Y	.83Y	1.06Y	1.40Y	1.70Y	2.33Y	3.45Y
Moldova	921	1.22Y	1.34Y	1.89Y	2.47Y	2.88Y	3.47Y	4.59Y	.85Y	.83Y	1.11Y	1.45Y	1.44Y	1.35Y	1.91Y
Poland	964	46.27Y	50.01Y	61.96Y	79.79Y	96.61Y	129.66Y	171.04Y	33.98Y	38.46Y	51.15Y	66.43Y	74.85Y	101.59Y	130.90Y
Romania	968	14.13Y	16.37Y	22.09Y	30.47Y	39.39Y	53.78Y	60.94Y	12.39Y	14.80Y	19.01Y	25.22Y	28.80Y	33.74Y	36.42Y
Russia	922	52.84Y	58.05Y	75.80Y	102.32Y	129.23Y	164.59Y	230.46Y	112.20Y	114.81Y	147.84Y	200.87Y	260.46Y	322.30Y	373.86Y
Serbia & Montenegro	965	3.78Y	4.66Y	5.82Y	7.37Y	7.89Y	2.94Y	3.19Y	1.41Y	1.77Y	2.11Y	2.72Y	3.37Y	.81Y	.94Y
Slovak Republic	936	13.71Y	15.54Y	20.99Y	26.45Y	32.02Y	42.59Y	57.88Y	12.59Y	15.07Y	22.40Y	27.34Y	29.29Y	37.49Y	53.35Y
Tajikistan	923	.52Y	.49Y	.68Y	.91Y	1.15Y	1.69Y	2.33Y	.48Y	.57Y	.66Y	.72Y	.90Y	1.03Y	1.19Y
Turkey	186	37.11Y	45.25Y	61.26Y	89.04Y	104.56Y	126.91Y	152.84Y	31.04Y	36.47Y	48.63Y	67.86Y	75.10Y	87.48Y	111.12Y

		Exports							Imports						
		2001	2002	2003	2004	2005	2006	2007	2001	2002	2003	2004	2005	2006	2007
		Billions of U.S. Dollars							Billions of U.S. Dollars						
Turkmenistan	925	1.32Y	1.25Y	1.68Y	2.48Y	2.46Y	2.53Y	3.31Y	2.43Y	2.75Y	3.47Y	4.38Y	6.10Y	6.66Y	7.88Y
Ukraine	926	15.56Y	17.74Y	23.43Y	31.28Y	40.02Y	53.19Y	68.74Y	16.28Y	17.83Y	22.25Y	34.57Y	36.77Y	42.84Y	56.54Y
U.S.S.R. n.s.	930	.11Y	.03Y	.01Y	.01Y	.07Y	.09Y	.06Y	.36Y	.45Y	.13Y	.11Y	.11Y	.10Y	.11Y
Uzbekistan	927	2.08Y	1.89Y	2.26Y	2.88Y	3.23Y	3.96Y	5.76Y	2.29Y	1.72Y	2.17Y	2.96Y	3.81Y	5.45Y	6.53Y
Yugoslavia n.s.	966	.55Y	.58Y	.78Y	.95Y	.90Y	.79Y	.42Y	.17Y	.18Y	.22Y	.27Y	.37Y	.26Y	.13Y
Europe n.s.	884	2.75Y	2.67Y	3.42Y	4.46Y	5.02Y	5.83Y	6.61Y	1.75Y	1.20Y	1.59Y	2.46Y	1.97Y	3.65Y	3.66Y
Middle East	**407**	**182.0Y**	**199.2Y**	**230.5Y**	**293.1Y**	**351.0Y**	**406.1Y**	**508.4Y**	**253.3Y**	**241.0Y**	**299.0Y**	**397.0Y**	**532.7Y**	**658.5Y**	**719.0Y**
Bahrain	419	3.87Y	4.25Y	5.07Y	6.22Y	7.67Y	9.42Y	11.31Y	3.26Y	2.99Y	3.40Y	4.45Y	5.55Y	6.91Y	7.84Y
Egypt	469	18.01Y	17.02Y	18.07Y	23.65Y	28.07Y	33.78Y	42.82Y	6.02Y	6.81Y	8.13Y	11.81Y	15.33Y	20.59Y	23.46Y
Iran, I.R. of	429	16.71Y	20.03Y	27.77Y	34.98Y	39.49Y	42.55Y	51.29Y	22.94Y	20.31Y	29.99Y	38.56Y	51.86Y	66.72Y	75.24Y
Iraq	433	5.11Y	5.52Y	4.05Y	9.31Y	11.74Y	12.33Y	14.24Y	12.18Y	10.05Y	8.95Y	17.64Y	19.42Y	26.30Y	32.32Y
Israel	436	29.16Y	29.05Y	30.60Y	38.10Y	41.03Y	44.35Y	51.97Y	29.38Y	29.28Y	30.68Y	37.01Y	42.04Y	45.94Y	53.11Y
Jordan	439	4.76Y	5.45Y	6.68Y	9.58Y	10.66Y	11.91Y	13.77Y	2.14Y	2.56Y	3.02Y	4.08Y	4.65Y	5.13Y	5.61Y
Kuwait	443	6.89Y	7.87Y	10.23Y	11.52Y	13.70Y	14.90Y	19.37Y	17.77Y	17.08Y	20.62Y	28.04Y	38.71Y	46.56Y	51.47Y
Lebanon	446	5.68Y	5.64Y	6.88Y	8.37Y	8.57Y	9.70Y	11.57Y	1.10Y	1.11Y	1.30Y	2.10Y	2.38Y	2.77Y	3.65Y
Libya	672	3.99Y	5.00Y	5.51Y	7.41Y	7.91Y	9.30Y	11.84Y	12.47Y	10.87Y	15.13Y	21.29Y	31.91Y	43.64Y	47.59Y
Oman	449	5.31Y	5.34Y	5.67Y	7.00Y	8.77Y	10.53Y	14.40Y	10.35Y	9.67Y	11.34Y	13.11Y	17.84Y	24.93Y	23.21Y
Qatar	453	3.64Y	3.89Y	5.28Y	7.82Y	9.48Y	14.98Y	20.68Y	12.38Y	11.53Y	14.58Y	19.14Y	26.67Y	35.85Y	42.52Y
Saudi Arabia	456	33.53Y	36.90Y	39.48Y	44.02Y	53.10Y	63.58Y	82.17Y	75.09Y	72.09Y	94.39Y	122.89Y	171.22Y	208.34Y	215.57Y
Syrian Arab Republic	463	4.79Y	5.38Y	6.39Y	11.75Y	14.32Y	17.17Y	21.36Y	6.67Y	7.30Y	6.44Y	9.63Y	11.25Y	13.31Y	15.91Y
United Arab Emirates	466	37.54Y	43.96Y	54.65Y	68.30Y	90.94Y	104.94Y	133.07Y	37.37Y	36.14Y	46.74Y	62.41Y	87.46Y	105.14Y	114.96Y
Yemen, Republic of	474	2.88Y	3.77Y	3.97Y	4.95Y	5.47Y	6.62Y	8.52Y	3.80Y	2.99Y	4.09Y	4.44Y	5.94Y	5.85Y	5.99Y
Middle East n.s.	489	.10Y	.11Y	.20Y	.14Y	.09Y	.08Y	.11Y	.36Y	.23Y	.25Y	.36Y	.43Y	.54Y	.65Y
Western Hemisphere	**207**	**348.4Y**	**326.2Y**	**339.3Y**	**420.0Y**	**492.6Y**	**592.5Y**	**695.7Y**	**378.2Y**	**380.3Y**	**426.1Y**	**536.5Y**	**636.6Y**	**742.7Y**	**844.6Y**
Antigua and Barbuda	311	.54Y	.63Y	.48Y	.64Y	.91Y	1.13Y	1.84Y	.34Y	.76Y	.40Y	.24Y	.19Y	.35Y	.23Y
Argentina	213	17.87Y	7.59Y	12.84Y	20.24Y	25.53Y	31.42Y	40.88Y	28.19Y	27.69Y	32.46Y	39.40Y	44.50Y	49.96Y	62.94Y
Aruba	314	.52Y	.72Y	.67Y	.96Y	2.83Y	2.87Y	2.67Y	1.28Y	.97Y	1.30Y	2.47Y	4.03Y	3.98Y	4.13Y
Bahamas, The	313	3.04Y	5.25Y	4.98Y	4.92Y	8.27Y	9.60Y	9.05Y	1.01Y	1.34Y	1.54Y	1.64Y	2.46Y	2.34Y	2.56Y
Barbados	316	.97Y	.83Y	.98Y	1.07Y	1.22Y	1.42Y	1.49Y	.31Y	.42Y	.44Y	.32Y	.61Y	.32Y	.43Y
Belize	339	.44Y	.44Y	.50Y	.51Y	.72Y	.70Y	.78Y	.30Y	.22Y	.31Y	.33Y	.33Y	.46Y	.40Y
Bermuda	319	4.49Y	4.77Y	4.71Y	3.84Y	3.14Y	4.30Y	4.13Y	1.42Y	.95Y	1.40Y	1.53Y	1.80Y	.68Y	.44Y
Bolivia	218	1.39Y	1.45Y	1.32Y	1.70Y	2.04Y	2.31Y	2.83Y	1.02Y	1.19Y	1.45Y	2.01Y	2.45Y	3.38Y	3.81Y
Brazil	223	56.51Y	49.20Y	48.65Y	64.85Y	75.42Y	94.74Y	122.89Y	64.10Y	65.42Y	82.13Y	110.09Y	132.93Y	152.69Y	180.59Y
Chile	228	15.49Y	14.70Y	16.76Y	21.40Y	28.66Y	34.19Y	40.99Y	19.48Y	19.21Y	22.96Y	34.59Y	42.55Y	60.20Y	70.44Y
Colombia	233	10.63Y	10.81Y	11.82Y	14.58Y	18.75Y	23.78Y	29.95Y	13.80Y	13.48Y	15.01Y	19.78Y	24.42Y	26.93Y	33.08Y
Costa Rica	238	5.38Y	6.49Y	6.89Y	7.40Y	8.26Y	9.93Y	11.13Y	7.01Y	8.31Y	10.60Y	12.03Y	13.08Y	14.77Y	16.47Y
Dominica	321	.23Y	.19Y	.18Y	.21Y	.24Y	.27Y	.34Y	.07Y	.07Y	.07Y	.07Y	.09Y	.10Y	.12Y
Dominican Republic	243	7.71Y	8.32Y	7.28Y	8.35Y	9.84Y	11.19Y	13.23Y	4.85Y	4.96Y	5.36Y	5.79Y	5.98Y	6.40Y	6.51Y
Ecuador	248	5.09Y	5.94Y	5.67Y	6.92Y	8.63Y	10.39Y	11.37Y	6.22Y	5.88Y	6.88Y	9.44Y	12.28Y	14.55Y	15.24Y
El Salvador	253	4.45Y	4.21Y	4.72Y	5.06Y	5.46Y	6.42Y	6.81Y	3.05Y	3.16Y	3.30Y	3.33Y	3.97Y	3.86Y	4.28Y
Falkland Islands	323	.06Y	.05Y	.07Y	.08Y	.06Y	.07Y	.09Y	.08Y	.09Y	.16Y	.14Y	.16Y	.15Y	.17Y
Greenland	326	.38Y	.40Y	.41Y	.54Y	.65Y	.64Y	.74Y	.40Y	.42Y	.49Y	.52Y	.55Y	.51Y	.63Y
Grenada	328	.17Y	.16Y	.20Y	.22Y	.28Y	.28Y	.32Y	.08Y	.05Y	.05Y	.04Y	.05Y	.04Y	.76Y
Guatemala	258	5.43Y	5.94Y	6.48Y	7.56Y	8.43Y	10.12Y	11.21Y	4.85Y	5.01Y	5.34Y	5.88Y	6.45Y	6.88Y	7.47Y
Guyana	336	.64Y	.51Y	.53Y	.55Y	.66Y	.86Y	.92Y	.63Y	.59Y	.63Y	.71Y	.70Y	.75Y	.88Y
Haiti	263	1.06Y	1.04Y	1.10Y	1.27Y	1.41Y	1.78Y	1.75Y	.32Y	.31Y	.41Y	.47Y	.57Y	.64Y	.68Y
Honduras	268	4.33Y	4.46Y	4.92Y	5.72Y	6.25Y	7.04Y	8.48Y	4.17Y	4.31Y	4.49Y	4.97Y	5.36Y	5.58Y	6.07Y
Jamaica	343	3.11Y	3.20Y	3.50Y	3.60Y	4.29Y	5.07Y	6.61Y	1.61Y	1.51Y	1.79Y	2.01Y	2.21Y	2.34Y	2.38Y
Mexico	273	136.22Y	134.98Y	136.94Y	161.01Y	178.48Y	210.44Y	225.77Y	160.47Y	162.37Y	168.56Y	192.98Y	215.92Y	253.17Y	278.54Y
Netherlands Antilles	353	7.44Y	5.87Y	4.66Y	8.89Y	10.69Y	9.61Y	11.58Y	2.04Y	1.64Y	1.77Y	2.18Y	3.21Y	4.12Y	4.05Y
Nicaragua	278	1.58Y	1.64Y	1.79Y	2.42Y	2.59Y	3.07Y	3.82Y	1.11Y	1.10Y	1.24Y	1.54Y	1.96Y	2.37Y	2.61Y
Panama	283	14.90Y	14.06Y	16.08Y	19.47Y	23.04Y	26.89Y	33.32Y	2.82Y	3.14Y	3.39Y	3.61Y	4.64Y	5.05Y	4.99Y
Paraguay	288	2.39Y	1.92Y	2.32Y	2.91Y	3.33Y	3.86Y	5.10Y	1.28Y	1.39Y	1.55Y	1.79Y	1.81Y	2.58Y	3.63Y
Peru	293	6.10Y	6.69Y	7.27Y	8.87Y	10.85Y	13.95Y	18.30Y	6.40Y	6.96Y	7.94Y	12.32Y	17.39Y	23.68Y	28.46Y
St. Kitts and Nevis	361	.15Y	.17Y	.22Y	.36Y	.27Y	.34Y	.42Y	.07Y	.07Y	.07Y	.07Y	.08Y	.09Y	.09Y
St. Lucia	362	.47Y	.51Y	.31Y	.34Y	.60Y	.64Y	1.62Y	.09Y	.07Y	.06Y	.09Y	.18Y	.32Y	.15Y
St. Pierre-Miquelon	363	.05Y	.04Y	.05Y	.06Y	.05Y	.04Y	.05Y	.01Y	.01Y	.01Y	.01Y	.01Y	.04Y	.02Y
St. Vincent & Grens.	364	.32Y	.35Y	.44Y	.51Y	.66Y	.53Y	.53Y	.20Y	.23Y	.21Y	.35Y	.37Y	.22Y	.17Y
Suriname	366	.61Y	.54Y	.59Y	.68Y	.84Y	.88Y	1.13Y	.55Y	.52Y	.64Y	.97Y	1.02Y	1.31Y	1.54Y
Trinidad and Tobago	369	3.18Y	2.74Y	3.31Y	4.60Y	4.82Y	5.31Y	6.29Y	4.48Y	4.78Y	7.15Y	9.22Y	12.02Y	14.36Y	16.10Y
Uruguay	298	3.60Y	2.37Y	2.76Y	3.67Y	4.38Y	5.58Y	6.70Y	2.48Y	2.38Y	2.81Y	3.59Y	4.14Y	4.63Y	5.49Y
Venezuela, Rep. Bol.	299	17.30Y	13.13Y	8.69Y	15.67Y	21.01Y	30.34Y	40.72Y	28.42Y	26.96Y	27.57Y	45.91Y	61.39Y	68.01Y	73.67Y
Western Hem. n.s.	399	4.13Y	3.86Y	8.23Y	8.34Y	9.06Y	10.48Y	9.90Y	3.17Y	2.33Y	4.19Y	4.13Y	4.71Y	5.11Y	4.49Y
Other Countries n.i.e.	**910**	**6.2Y**	**4.8Y**	**4.7Y**	**6.9Y**	**8.9Y**	**11.1Y**	**11.9Y**	**2.8Y**	**2.7Y**	**2.8Y**	**3.8Y**	**3.8Y**	**4.3Y**	**5.8Y**
Cuba	928	3.23Y	2.73Y	2.70Y	4.34Y	6.27Y	8.26Y	8.76Y	1.74Y	1.67Y	1.81Y	2.44Y	2.39Y	2.83Y	4.02Y
North Korea	954	2.99Y	2.07Y	2.04Y	2.54Y	2.63Y	2.85Y	3.13Y	1.05Y	1.06Y	1.00Y	1.36Y	1.37Y	1.47Y	1.77Y
Countries & Areas n.s.	**898**	**48.0Y**	**51.9Y**	**51.4Y**	**69.7Y**	**77.9Y**	**98.2Y**	**111.2Y**	**40.1Y**	**45.6Y**	**48.4Y**	**62.7Y**	**84.1Y**	**98.3Y**	**112.1Y**
Special Categories	**899**	**17.6Y**	**17.7Y**	**16.7Y**	**19.8Y**	**23.2Y**	**28.5Y**	**30.4Y**	**35.2Y**	**38.8Y**	**36.9Y**	**52.7Y**	**65.2Y**	**88.1Y**	**103.2Y**
Memorandum Items															
European Union	998	2,397.71Y	2,516.62Y	3,026.87Y	3,643.06Y	4,016.81Y	4,596.02Y	5,359.39Y	2,318.52Y	2,447.33Y	2,953.86Y	3,536.08Y	3,814.47Y	4,362.87Y	5,176.33Y
Oil Exporting Ctys.	999	182.87Y	199.69Y	243.92Y	310.06Y	376.13Y	432.93Y	551.48Y	336.60Y	317.58Y	402.21Y	535.42Y	708.54Y	867.00Y	945.68Y
Non-Oil Develop.Ctys.	201	1,798.59Y	1,940.40Y	2,323.53Y	2,930.57Y	3,432.45Y	4,135.60Y	4,961.88Y	2,034.03Y	2,198.50Y	2,626.66Y	3,352.91Y	3,949.54Y	4,681.30Y	5,520.63Y

	Exports 2001	2002	2003	2004	2005	2006	2007	Imports 2001	2002	2003	2004	2005	2006	2007
PERCENT DISTRIBUTION														
Industrial Countries................. 101	66.5	65.5	64.8	63.4	62.1	60.6	58.9	61.6	60.7	59.7	57.8	55.2	53.6	53.3
Developing Countries.............. 202	32.3	33.3	34.1	35.5	36.8	38.2	39.9	37.2	38.0	39.1	41.0	43.3	44.9	45.2
Africa..................................... 607	1.8	1.8	1.9	2.0	2.0	2.1	2.2	2.2	2.1	2.2	2.3	2.6	2.6	2.6
Asia.. 507	16.8	17.8	18.6	19.2	19.6	20.0	20.3	19.9	21.0	21.4	22.3	23.0	23.5	23.7
Europe.................................... 170	5.0	5.5	6.1	6.5	7.0	7.7	8.6	5.2	5.5	6.1	6.6	6.9	7.4	8.0
Middle East............................ 407	3.0	3.1	3.1	3.2	3.4	3.4	3.7	4.0	3.6	3.9	4.2	5.0	5.3	5.0
Western Hemisphere............. 207	5.7	5.1	4.5	4.6	4.8	5.0	5.0	5.9	5.7	5.5	5.7	5.9	6.0	5.9
Other Countries n.i.e................ 910	.1	.1	.1	.1	.1	.1	.1	—	—	—	—	—	—	—
ANNUAL PERCENT CHANGE														
World....................................... 001	–3.9	4.8	16.9	21.4	13.4	15.5	15.5	–3.2	3.9	16.9	22.4	13.4	15.0	15.8
Industrial Countries................. 101	–4.1	3.2	15.6	18.9	11.1	12.6	12.4	–3.9	2.4	15.0	18.3	8.4	11.5	15.1
Developing Countries.............. 202	–3.9	8.0	20.0	26.2	17.5	20.0	20.7	–2.7	6.1	20.4	28.4	19.8	19.1	16.5
Africa..................................... 607	4.2	6.3	19.3	26.6	17.0	22.1	19.3	.2	–1.3	22.2	31.2	24.8	17.9	15.1
Asia.. 507	–7.6	10.7	22.4	25.6	15.7	17.9	17.3	–4.2	9.7	19.4	27.1	16.9	17.8	16.6
Europe.................................... 170	1.8	14.9	29.5	29.5	22.2	26.8	30.0	4.2	10.4	29.4	31.1	19.5	22.7	24.6
Middle East............................ 407	5.8	9.5	15.7	27.2	19.8	15.7	25.2	–6.8	–4.8	24.1	32.8	34.2	23.6	9.2
Western Hemisphere............. 207	–4.1	–6.4	4.0	23.8	17.3	20.3	17.4	–1.2	.5	12.1	25.9	18.7	16.7	13.7
Other Countries n.i.e................ 910	15.8	–22.8	–1.4	45.4	29.4	24.8	7.0	–.1	–2.5	3.4	34.8	–1.0	14.3	34.8

		Exports							Imports						
		2001	2002	2003	2004	2005	2006	2007	2001	2002	2003	2004	2005	2006	2007
		Billions of U.S. Dollars							*Billions of U.S. Dollars*						
IFS World Total		**3,886.5**	**4,009.8**	**4,597.0**	**5,391.7**	**5,851.5**	**6,577.5**	**7,489.6**	**4,177.5**	**4,284.8**	**4,954.4**	**5,887.2**	**6,544.3**	**7,383.1**	**8,283.0**
DOTS World Total	**001**	**3,927.4Y**	**4,051.8**	**4,657.3**	**5,487.9Y**	**5,952.6**	**6,654.6**	**7,595.9**	**4,241.0Y**	**4,349.9**	**5,047.0**	**6,001.4Y**	**6,665.6**	**7,488.1**	**8,399.9**
Industrial Countries	**101**	**2,831.3Y**	**2,904.6**	**3,333.6**	**3,868.3Y**	**4,143.0**	**4,554.6**	**5,116.4**	**2,785.0Y**	**2,839.4**	**3,271.6**	**3,800.0Y**	**4,069.2**	**4,484.6**	**5,050.7**
United States	111	590.56Y	594.47	631.46	714.04Y	775.75	826.36	862.99	423.26Y	406.64	422.41	468.03Y	501.05	530.22	578.84
Canada	156	194.23Y	193.68	205.56	228.69Y	256.15	279.85	301.50	246.88Y	239.35	255.81	292.48Y	326.75	346.76	365.31
Australia	193	36.59Y	41.64	48.10	57.03Y	60.99	64.32	73.39	33.87Y	34.00	36.57	45.42Y	51.71	57.35	64.33
Japan	158	121.39Y	114.71	122.75	137.86Y	145.82	155.55	165.83	224.76Y	217.51	229.17	257.71Y	269.98	277.43	288.83
New Zealand	196	9.29Y	10.00	12.30	14.95Y	16.23	15.71	17.75	10.16Y	10.45	11.98	14.02Y	14.87	14.82	16.54
Austria	122	55.50Y	58.84	71.68	87.36Y	92.60	107.33	123.47	46.62Y	51.24	62.42	75.41Y	78.05	93.34	109.91
Belgium	124	136.58Y	153.36	182.97	218.36Y	239.20	268.41	310.58	132.26Y	139.93	168.28	204.50Y	224.40	274.04	321.72
Belgium-Luxembourg n.s.	127	.47	.52	.46	—	—	—	—	.48	.60	.85	—	—	—	—
Cyprus	423	3.36Y	3.57	4.03	4.82Y	5.12	7.18	7.67	1.02Y	.80	1.07	1.12Y	1.43	3.14	2.60
Denmark	128	34.83Y	37.79	44.11	51.00Y	56.82	65.39	73.07	37.36Y	40.57	49.85	57.88Y	63.55	71.03	76.37
Finland	172	26.19Y	27.37	33.22	38.88Y	42.79	50.54	58.47	30.53Y	30.80	36.18	42.44Y	45.63	51.35	59.19
France	132	262.84Y	270.94	319.68	377.64Y	402.40	437.17	493.58	232.28Y	238.95	282.18	325.24Y	335.08	364.76	414.91
Germany	134	364.60Y	366.20	435.88	507.18Y	537.16	609.84	693.03	416.76Y	447.71	543.85	649.91Y	688.80	759.75	890.25
Greece	174	22.73Y	23.83	30.94	37.90Y	35.82	39.71	48.10	6.77Y	7.13	9.07	9.79Y	10.65	12.80	14.25
Iceland	176	1.83Y	1.72	2.27	3.01Y	3.96	4.41	5.15	2.11Y	2.29	2.51	2.84Y	2.85	3.22	3.70
Ireland	178	42.82Y	46.66	47.92	56.26Y	64.33	67.98	78.13	77.19Y	87.50	101.84	116.79Y	125.25	117.16	128.45
Italy	136	159.90Y	171.83	208.97	237.66Y	246.84	270.93	311.72	163.25Y	170.29	204.43	236.62Y	246.33	272.41	317.34
Luxembourg	137	11.73Y	11.57	14.59	18.65Y	18.86	21.37	22.38	8.11Y	8.15	12.13	15.40Y	15.67	19.31	21.46
Malta	181	2.99	3.08	3.45	3.60Y	3.17	4.24	4.85	1.52	1.46	1.56	1.75Y	1.74	2.06	2.72
Netherlands	138	157.34Y	160.39	188.42	220.67Y	233.29	272.65	316.91	173.95Y	176.47	213.90	258.59Y	283.88	353.92	412.22
Norway	142	27.37Y	28.42	33.09	40.14Y	43.96	50.93	62.99	50.15Y	51.27	66.07	80.07Y	97.86	112.12	119.34
Portugal	182	36.54Y	36.58	44.66	52.25Y	53.08	56.10	61.35	23.98Y	23.97	30.65	34.56Y	32.46	35.75	38.16
Slovenia	961	7.96Y	8.59	10.71	13.26	13.85	16.27	20.32	6.53Y	7.18	9.13	10.15	10.22	11.91	15.00
Spain	184	121.49Y	130.48	167.52	200.68Y	217.39	234.79	272.61	86.96Y	94.81	120.16	139.91Y	147.06	161.13	187.68
Sweden	144	54.94Y	57.09	69.50	82.69Y	89.70	93.45	118.22	61.85Y	65.02	80.71	95.84Y	101.85	114.43	129.53
Switzerland	146	79.76Y	78.12	90.09	104.23Y	115.54	126.81	147.95	71.36Y	73.22	82.81	95.85Y	104.42	114.24	128.65
United Kingdom	112	267.45Y	273.11	309.23	359.52Y	372.20	407.31	464.42	215.01Y	212.13	236.01	267.67Y	287.65	310.21	343.44
Developing Countries	**202**	**1,070.4Y**	**1,120.7**	**1,297.9**	**1,583.7Y**	**1,771.1**	**2,051.3**	**2,430.9**	**1,423.4Y**	**1,479.3**	**1,754.9**	**2,174.8Y**	**2,567.9**	**2,972.7**	**3,320.7**
Africa	**607**	**68.4Y**	**71.2**	**83.5**	**100.6Y**	**115.6**	**133.4**	**153.4**	**98.3Y**	**96.4**	**119.5**	**148.2Y**	**190.4**	**219.9**	**244.8**
Algeria	612	8.28Y	9.31	10.04	13.50Y	14.87	14.27	18.37	18.20Y	17.62	23.58	29.84Y	40.72	51.92	53.14
Angola	614	1.61Y	1.80	2.77	2.98Y	3.77	5.82	7.28	5.14Y	5.79	5.86	6.02Y	12.44	16.17	20.28
Benin	638	.56Y	.59	.64	.61Y	.62	.77	1.20	.06Y	.06	.05	.04Y	.04	.09	.09
Botswana	616	.22Y	.18	.23	.29Y	.25	.18	.31	1.70Y	1.71	2.07	2.49Y	2.67	3.00	2.03
Burkina Faso	748	.22Y	.28	.40	.46Y	.42	.44	.54	.07Y	.06	.06	.06Y	.05	.05	.07
Burundi	618	.06Y	.05	.05	.10Y	.11	.12	.10	.03Y	.02	.03	.03Y	.07	.04	.05
Cameroon	622	1.26Y	1.23	1.43	1.27Y	1.25	1.34	1.66	1.72Y	1.68	2.17	2.62Y	2.82	3.72	3.74
Cape Verde	624	.22Y	.24	.27	.34Y	.35	.44	.59	.02Y	.02	.03	.02Y	.03	.04	.03
Central African Rep.	626	.07Y	.07	.06	.09Y	.09	.14	.14	.15Y	.17	.11	.11Y	.09	.08	.07
Chad	628	.29Y	.34	.22	.24Y	.28	.28	.36	.06Y	.05	.07	.91Y	1.67	2.08	2.37
Comoros	632	.04Y	.04	.06	.04Y	.04	.05	.04	.03Y	.03	.03	.03Y	.02	.03	.01
Congo, Dem. Rep. of	636	.28Y	.41	.49	.58Y	.71	.84	1.07	1.11Y	1.42	.99	1.05Y	1.18	.86	1.17
Congo, Republic of	634	.58Y	.57	.61	.67Y	.81	1.02	1.70	.91Y	.75	.84	1.26Y	2.09	3.69	3.67
Côte d'Ivoire	662	1.34Y	1.32	1.39	1.68Y	1.57	1.65	2.09	2.39Y	3.10	3.64	3.70Y	3.95	3.98	4.60
Djibouti	611	.22Y	.23	.22	.22Y	.23	.30	.36	.06Y	.01	.01	.01Y	.01	.01	.01
Equatorial Guinea	642	.25Y	.36	.94	.56Y	.84	1.07	.84	1.25Y	1.52	2.43	2.65Y	4.49	4.61	5.99
Ethiopia	644	.50Y	.58	1.00	1.09Y	1.37	1.04	1.28	.24Y	.33	.30	.38Y	.52	.57	.64
Gabon	646	1.15Y	.86	1.01	1.17Y	1.16	1.28	1.84	2.82Y	2.31	2.86	3.36Y	3.84	2.28	3.47
Gambia, The	648	.14Y	.13	.16	.15Y	.17	.16	.17	.02Y	.02	.01	.02Y	.01	.02	.02
Ghana	652	1.19Y	1.30	1.50	2.02Y	2.15	2.39	3.08	1.14Y	1.21	1.39	1.54Y	1.51	1.78	1.97
Guinea	656	.44Y	.52	.49	.52Y	.61	.68	.83	.64Y	.52	.49	.52Y	.63	.63	.83
Guinea-Bissau	654	.04Y	.04	.05	.05Y	.11	.09	.10	.01Y	.01	.01	.03Y	—	—	—
Kenya	664	1.69Y	1.39	1.34	1.84Y	2.19	2.48	3.07	1.01Y	1.07	1.25	1.54Y	1.61	1.74	1.89
Lesotho	666	.01Y	.01	.03	.03Y	.02	.03	.03	.25Y	.36	.43	.53Y	.50	.52	.64
Liberia	668	2.16Y	2.27	1.50	1.44Y	1.66	1.52	2.05	.76Y	.97	.77	.72Y	.83	1.12	.50
Madagascar	674	.44Y	.29	.52	.53Y	.51	.51	.72	.88Y	.79	1.04	1.23Y	.97	1.02	1.15
Malawi	676	.08Y	.13	.10	.15Y	.13	.19	.21	.30Y	.27	.33	.26Y	.37	.27	.36
Mali	678	.42Y	.38	.45	.53Y	.52	.61	.72	.05Y	.07	.07	.08Y	.07	.17	.06
Mauritania	682	.40Y	.45	.54	.59Y	.74	.69	.85	.40Y	.44	.47	.59Y	.76	.83	.91
Mauritius	684	.95Y	.90	1.35	1.08Y	1.25	1.32	1.35	1.52Y	1.63	1.94	1.74Y	1.66	1.62	1.67
Morocco	686	7.42Y	8.22	10.05	11.98Y	15.77	14.37	18.52	6.66Y	7.02	8.06	9.23Y	12.34	10.12	11.99
Mozambique	688	.33Y	.59	.48	.60Y	.71	.68	.84	.59Y	.64	.75	1.12Y	1.32	1.41	1.92
Namibia	728	.43Y	.24	.23	.34Y	.35	.35	.38	.88Y	.74	.80	1.36Y	1.32	1.65	1.69
Niger	692	.25Y	.26	.26	.32Y	.39	.44	.48	.13Y	.08	.10	.21Y	.23	.30	.27
Nigeria	694	6.17Y	6.44	7.38	8.72Y	9.66	11.85	15.47	15.71Y	12.17	19.47	25.66Y	37.22	45.10	48.14
Rwanda	714	.08Y	.09	.10	.13Y	.12	.16	.18	.06Y	.02	.02	.03Y	.05	.06	.06
St. Helena	856	.03Y	.03	.02	.03Y	.04	.06	.06	.01Y	.01	.01	.01Y	.01	.01	.01
São Tomé & Príncipe	716	.04Y	.05	.05	.05Y	.05	.06	.06	.01Y	.01	.01	.01Y	.02	.01	.01
Senegal	722	1.08Y	1.24	1.38	1.57Y	2.06	2.16	2.68	.52Y	.41	.41	.43Y	.67	.43	.56
Seychelles	718	.32Y	.18	.21	.23Y	.29	.29	.39	.23Y	.31	.33	.35Y	.40	.32	.28

		Exports							Imports						
		2001	2002	2003	2004	2005	2006	2007	2001	2002	2003	2004	2005	2006	2007
		Billions of U.S. Dollars							Billions of U.S. Dollars						
Sierra Leone	724	.27Y	.33	.36	.27Y	.29	.20	.23	.05Y	.10	.14	.17Y	.19	.20	.26
Somalia	726	.03Y	.04	.02	.03Y	.03	.04	.04	—Y	—	—	—Y	—	—	.01
South Africa	199	16.84Y	17.19	21.64	27.91Y	31.89	35.89	41.00	22.08Y	22.21	25.78	33.21Y	37.25	41.00	48.67
Sudan	732	.73Y	.72	1.00	1.47Y	2.22	10.39	2.04	.53Y	.49	.72	1.58Y	2.14	3.28	3.17
Swaziland	734	.03Y	.04	.03	.05Y	.06	.06	.08	.21Y	.29	.38	.47Y	.46	.39	.47
Tanzania	738	.59Y	.58	.66	.85Y	.92	1.12	1.47	.41Y	.45	.46	.59Y	.65	.63	.65
Togo	742	.36Y	.46	.56	.53Y	.75	1.05	1.28	.08Y	.09	.10	.12Y	.16	.16	.19
Tunisia	744	7.67Y	7.58	8.46	9.81Y	10.24	11.31	13.51	5.83Y	5.98	7.21	8.79Y	8.90	10.27	12.94
Uganda	746	.25Y	.25	.33	.41Y	.47	.54	.78	.26Y	.28	.33	.37Y	.41	.39	.50
Zambia	754	.15Y	.17	.18	.22Y	.28	.44	.57	.24Y	.19	.27	.37Y	.32	.54	.77
Zimbabwe	698	.26Y	.25	.28	.27Y	.24	.26	.34	.95Y	.84	.78	.77Y	.72	.70	.79
Africa n.s.	799	—Y	—	—	.03Y	—	—	—	—Y	.01	—	—Y	—	—	—
Asia	**507**	**456.1Y**	**486.5**	**571.1**	**699.5Y**	**758.5**	**851.9**	**987.2**	**697.6Y**	**739.9**	**871.9**	**1,076.8Y**	**1,233.4**	**1,403.1**	**1,562.1**
Afghanistan, I.S. of	512	.09Y	.29	.38	.55Y	.74	.98	1.09	.03Y	.03	.13	.07Y	.10	.10	.11
American Samoa	859	.04Y	.07	.06	.08Y	.19	.04	.06	.09Y	.01	.01	.01Y	.01	.01	.02
Bangladesh	513	1.84Y	1.67	1.72	2.20Y	2.35	2.59	3.07	5.90Y	5.72	6.86	8.45Y	8.75	10.84	11.47
Brunei Darussalam	516	.34Y	.56	.68	.43Y	.33	.53	2.07	2.43Y	2.32	2.89	3.15Y	3.59	4.08	4.19
Cambodia	522	.19Y	.22	.24	.29Y	.34	.36	.50	1.53Y	1.71	2.06	2.56Y	2.76	3.44	3.93
China,P.R.: Mainland	924	86.31Y	104.64	144.05	184.64Y	207.32	253.51	305.91	249.37Y	291.79	374.41	492.46Y	606.26	708.48	838.44
China,P.R.:Hong Kong	532	62.47Y	63.27	70.05	81.82Y	84.58	89.05	95.81	29.57Y	29.35	29.93	34.22Y	35.60	37.51	26.46
China,P.R.:Macao	546	.35Y	.52	.52	.43Y	.46	.63	.89	1.99Y	1.98	2.23	2.53Y	1.84	1.92	1.91
Fiji	819	.49Y	.49	.56	.65Y	.71	.72	.68	.49Y	.46	.53	.61Y	.57	.56	.54
French Polynesia	887	.84Y	1.13	1.46	1.10Y	1.35	1.07	1.23	.23Y	.25	.51	.34Y	.41	.24	.25
Guam	829	.14Y	.11	.14	.16Y	.18	.24	.29	.06Y	.04	.05	.04Y	.04	.05	.08
India	534	18.75Y	21.29	26.86	35.62Y	44.73	54.48	75.09	26.16Y	29.13	33.92	41.97Y	50.01	58.53	68.21
Indonesia	536	15.34Y	15.57	17.04	21.25Y	22.17	21.38	25.80	38.92Y	38.16	41.96	46.98Y	51.54	58.36	64.70
Kiribati	826	.03Y	.06	.03	.03Y	.04	.03	.04	.02Y	.02	.02	.02Y	—	.01	—
Korea	542	69.17Y	75.58	85.76	103.36Y	112.45	125.84	139.98	80.71Y	81.87	92.31	115.95Y	120.25	133.91	134.67
Lao People's Dem.Rep.	544	.05Y	.07	.07	.11Y	.10	.09	.15	.14Y	.14	.15	.19Y	.17	.18	.22
Malaysia	548	30.95Y	31.28	33.92	37.17Y	37.46	41.81	46.35	54.55Y	54.47	61.33	70.07Y	78.23	83.72	85.66
Maldives	556	.07Y	.07	.09	.13Y	.14	.16	.74	.14Y	.16	.14	.14Y	.06	.08	.08
Mongolia	948	.12Y	.17	.18	.23Y	.22	.26	.39	.20Y	.21	.24	.35Y	.36	.40	.42
Myanmar	518	.30Y	.23	.21	.24Y	.24	.24	.45	1.11Y	.94	.90	.76Y	.57	.63	.68
Nauru	836	.02Y	.02	.02	.02Y	.01	.02	.03	.01Y	.01	.02	.01Y	—	—	.01
Nepal	558	.13Y	.14	.14	.15Y	.17	.15	.23	.37Y	.28	.31	.31Y	.27	.25	.25
New Caledonia	839	.73Y	.92	1.11	1.20Y	1.20	1.35	1.72	.40Y	.34	.52	.61Y	.67	.98	1.59
Pakistan	564	3.29Y	3.91	4.90	7.57Y	8.26	9.58	9.62	5.69Y	5.85	6.77	7.84Y	7.94	8.79	9.22
Papua New Guinea	853	.66Y	.70	.75	.89Y	1.26	1.39	1.79	1.36Y	1.38	1.89	2.14Y	2.78	3.28	3.80
Philippines	566	21.24Y	20.01	22.07	22.60Y	21.94	22.83	24.54	26.23Y	26.20	26.26	27.40Y	27.20	27.35	27.53
Samoa	862	.18Y	.10	.13	.12Y	.14	.14	.14	.07Y	.07	.09	.08Y	.09	.07	.10
Singapore	576	50.15Y	48.68	51.75	62.01Y	66.00	73.78	83.23	38.37Y	37.53	42.32	50.35Y	54.95	60.88	63.27
Solomon Islands	813	.05Y	.04	.05	.06Y	.07	.11	.12	.03Y	.02	.03	.04Y	.04	.05	.06
Sri Lanka	524	1.64Y	1.57	1.84	2.22Y	2.28	2.53	2.57	3.91Y	3.67	3.86	4.46Y	4.65	5.09	5.47
Taiwan Province of China	528	58.90Y	60.98	65.77	85.27Y	88.89	91.16	97.65	77.40Y	73.69	78.03	89.31Y	91.14	98.13	100.58
Thailand	578	26.72Y	27.06	31.67	38.81Y	44.04	44.90	50.40	40.83Y	41.07	45.91	54.66Y	60.23	67.06	74.98
Tonga	866	.04Y	.05	.06	.07Y	.07	.07	.07	.02Y	.03	.03	.02Y	.02	.02	.02
Tuvalu	869	—Y	.01	.01	.01Y	.02	.02	.02	—Y	—	—	—Y	—	—	—
Vanuatu	846	.10Y	.07	.07	.09Y	.12	.14	.16	.02Y	.01	.02	.05Y	.04	.05	.04
Vietnam	582	4.34Y	4.92	6.72	7.81Y	7.92	9.71	14.30	9.28Y	10.97	15.24	18.66Y	22.29	28.01	33.18
Europe	**170**	**194.0Y**	**221.8**	**282.8**	**357.3Y**	**410.3**	**510.3**	**644.5**	**205.0Y**	**223.5**	**287.1**	**366.7Y**	**429.3**	**522.1**	**622.3**
Albania	914	1.01Y	1.07	1.27	1.53Y	1.62	1.79	2.34	.32Y	.33	.43	.53Y	.56	.64	.86
Armenia	911	.24Y	.35	.45	.48Y	.56	.65	.91	.10Y	.16	.32	.31Y	.53	.45	.50
Azerbaijan	912	.45Y	.63	1.09	1.84Y	2.02	2.83	2.39	1.04Y	1.10	1.24	1.24Y	2.43	6.37	11.35
Belarus	913	1.34Y	1.51	1.89	2.24Y	2.70	3.69	4.39	.76Y	.98	1.46	1.93Y	2.62	3.77	4.44
Bosnia & Herzegovina	963	1.56Y	1.80	2.04	2.55Y	2.84	2.88	3.58	.63Y	.69	.94	1.10Y	1.52	1.86	2.20
Bulgaria	918	3.84Y	4.31	5.74	7.33Y	8.44	10.36	12.36	3.66Y	3.83	4.92	6.20Y	7.00	8.56	8.94
Croatia	960	5.98Y	7.31	9.47	10.66Y	11.69	13.49	15.77	2.94Y	3.04	3.86	5.13Y	5.23	6.12	6.64
Czech Republic	935	26.73Y	29.83	37.03	45.46Y	51.89	62.41	79.08	24.88Y	28.86	36.85	42.09Y	48.35	60.24	79.04
Czechoslovakia n.s.	937	.09Y	.15	.11	—Y	.01	—	—	.01Y	.01	.02	—Y	.01	—	—
Estonia	939	2.94Y	3.61	4.44	5.33Y	6.27	8.69	9.58	3.57Y	3.59	4.32	5.42Y	5.88	6.35	6.26
Faroe Islands	816	.45Y	.41	.51	.53Y	.64	.66	.87	.45Y	.44	.52	.51Y	.52	.58	.66
Georgia	915	.37Y	.39	.53	.72Y	.78	1.12	1.49	.31Y	.28	.32	.45Y	.55	1.11	.85
Gibraltar	823	1.08Y	1.41	1.33	1.85Y	2.67	3.90	5.23	.13Y	.13	.25	.23Y	.29	.21	.28
Hungary	944	23.49Y	25.94	32.62	38.23Y	41.09	47.58	56.80	27.28Y	28.53	34.32	40.79Y	43.41	47.43	59.31
Kazakhstan	916	1.73Y	2.33	2.45	4.25Y	4.72	6.52	8.14	3.15Y	3.83	4.57	8.24Y	12.27	16.01	18.43
Kyrgyz Republic	917	.09Y	.12	.16	.13Y	.15	.26	.32	.12Y	.04	.06	.04Y	.04	.03	.03
Latvia	941	2.46Y	2.73	3.41	3.69Y	4.24	5.81	7.47	2.32Y	2.50	3.16	3.95Y	4.12	4.62	5.01
Lithuania	946	3.32Y	4.10	5.23	5.51Y	6.13	8.38	11.24	2.73Y	3.15	4.14	5.02Y	5.69	5.98	6.76
Macedonia, FYR	962	1.20Y	1.17	1.28	1.42Y	1.55	1.76	2.13	.74Y	.66	.84	1.06Y	1.24	1.49	2.22
Moldova	921	.40Y	.43	.63	.78Y	.80	.82	1.10	.29Y	.30	.43	.56Y	.45	.48	.58
Poland	964	34.51Y	37.90	46.52	58.20Y	67.62	89.51	118.52	26.11Y	29.49	38.80	48.37Y	52.34	69.00	87.95
Romania	968	10.05Y	11.43	15.41	20.14Y	23.98	29.83	35.23	9.39Y	11.05	14.16	17.64Y	19.27	20.97	21.18
Russia	922	29.91Y	33.75	43.84	58.43Y	72.30	93.72	126.48	57.01Y	57.08	74.94	102.06Y	135.43	168.48	186.21
Serbia & Montenegro	965	2.48Y	3.32	3.98	5.36Y	5.16	.19	—	1.04Y	1.34	1.58	2.06Y	2.46	.11	—
Slovak Republic	936	7.51Y	8.76	12.11	14.27Y	15.99	20.76	27.93	8.15Y	10.12	15.71	18.54Y	18.56	22.73	32.48
Tajikistan	923	.06Y	.07	.10	.12Y	.11	.14	.15	.07Y	.13	.16	.22Y	.48	.43	.49
Turkey	186	23.32Y	28.81	38.41	52.68Y	58.41	66.17	75.78	22.59Y	26.16	33.27	44.61Y	48.39	53.93	62.69
Turkmenistan	925	.52Y	.37	.44	.85Y	.66	.61	.73	.19Y	.24	.37	.43Y	.55	.54	.59

		Exports							Imports						
		2001	2002	2003	2004	2005	2006	2007	2001	2002	2003	2004	2005	2006	2007
		Billions of U.S. Dollars							Billions of U.S. Dollars						
Ukraine	926	5.02Y	5.90	7.93	10.20Y	12.73	17.12	22.87	4.33Y	4.82	4.60	7.22Y	8.32	9.47	10.96
Uzbekistan	927	.67Y	.60	.77	.80Y	.73	.70	1.01	.62Y	.52	.50	.60Y	.71	.72	.99
Yugoslavia n.s.	966	.08Y	.10	.15	—Y	—	—	—	.02Y	.01	.01	—Y	—	—	—
Europe n.s.	884	1.08Y	1.18	1.45	1.76Y	1.75	1.73	1.78	.05Y	.06	.08	.10Y	.15	.15	.14
Middle East	**407**	**110.3Y**	**115.9**	**131.4**	**157.9Y**	**183.6**	**202.2**	**246.3**	**142.8Y**	**133.9**	**164.3**	**208.3Y**	**279.0**	**331.2**	**352.9**
Bahrain	419	1.57Y	1.77	2.11	2.40Y	2.46	3.06	3.56	1.21Y	1.03	1.08	1.31Y	1.59	2.15	2.36
Egypt	469	11.51Y	10.31	10.96	13.85Y	14.84	16.96	21.12	4.03Y	4.68	5.17	6.99Y	8.95	12.77	13.06
Iran, I.R. of	429	7.73Y	9.29	13.23	16.72Y	18.30	16.44	16.20	11.34Y	10.42	15.62	18.91Y	24.81	28.99	31.48
Iraq	433	2.47Y	2.44	1.64	3.05Y	3.58	3.35	3.64	10.14Y	7.33	7.65	14.45Y	15.62	21.35	23.95
Israel	436	22.60Y	21.46	21.67	26.98Y	28.37	29.95	34.91	23.03Y	23.06	23.75	27.88Y	31.71	33.97	38.82
Jordan	439	2.30Y	2.61	3.02	3.36Y	3.92	4.43	4.92	.45Y	.72	1.00	1.52Y	1.74	1.89	1.82
Kuwait	443	4.45Y	5.15	6.68	7.41Y	8.59	8.59	10.90	9.02Y	8.17	9.43	12.15Y	16.63	18.95	20.23
Lebanon	446	3.47Y	3.52	4.46	4.87Y	4.59	5.15	5.76	.49Y	.37	.50	.55Y	.57	.56	.86
Libya	672	2.87Y	3.56	3.92	4.85Y	4.84	5.43	6.78	10.68Y	9.36	12.92	18.03Y	27.21	36.74	42.39
Oman	449	2.60Y	2.69	3.03	3.88Y	4.41	5.07	7.43	3.21Y	3.10	3.71	2.65Y	4.00	4.38	5.14
Qatar	453	2.55Y	2.65	3.60	5.64Y	6.18	9.67	13.73	7.49Y	6.41	8.06	9.81Y	13.25	18.30	20.58
Saudi Arabia	456	23.67Y	25.29	26.12	27.33Y	32.73	37.37	47.77	39.90Y	38.68	50.57	63.17Y	88.49	103.19	101.19
Syrian Arab Republic	463	2.43Y	2.61	2.95	3.46Y	3.93	4.28	5.19	4.07Y	4.21	3.71	3.45Y	4.00	4.59	4.74
United Arab Emirates	466	19.12Y	21.24	26.85	32.49Y	45.31	50.93	61.95	17.39Y	15.89	20.86	27.09Y	39.34	42.34	45.14
Yemen, Republic of	474	1.00Y	1.28	1.18	1.61Y	1.51	1.56	2.48	.37Y	.44	.29	.34Y	1.07	1.01	1.16
Middle East n.s.	489	.01	—	—	—Y	—	—	—	—	—	—	—Y	—	—	—
Western Hemisphere	**207**	**241.5Y**	**225.4**	**229.1**	**268.3Y**	**303.1**	**353.5**	**399.5**	**279.6Y**	**285.7**	**312.2**	**374.8Y**	**435.7**	**496.4**	**538.6**
Antigua and Barbuda	311	.32Y	.40	.27	.24Y	.47	.65	.85	.32Y	.74	.38	.09Y	.15	.29	.20
Argentina	213	9.28Y	3.99	6.00	8.64Y	10.07	12.04	15.37	9.25Y	10.35	11.56	12.68Y	13.96	14.25	17.48
Aruba	314	.43Y	.63	.55	.59Y	.75	.83	.92	1.20Y	.89	1.14	2.19Y	3.59	3.39	3.47
Bahamas, The	313	1.92Y	3.27	2.94	2.50Y	3.63	4.97	5.54	.81Y	.98	1.07	1.16Y	1.97	1.69	1.43
Barbados	316	.51Y	.51	.62	.64Y	.72	.81	.84	.13Y	.10	.11	.11Y	.15	.10	.10
Belize	339	.26Y	.22	.29	.23Y	.35	.32	.34	.22Y	.16	.22	.23Y	.24	.37	.26
Bermuda	319	2.83Y	2.26	2.20	2.93Y	2.18	2.75	2.20	1.38Y	.89	1.33	1.44Y	1.77	.57	.35
Bolivia	218	.41Y	.38	.36	.41Y	.49	.50	.64	.31Y	.32	.33	.52Y	.58	.80	1.04
Brazil	223	36.62Y	30.51	28.86	35.85Y	40.47	47.42	61.34	37.12Y	38.89	45.83	56.60Y	65.36	70.89	82.68
Chile	228	7.35Y	6.45	7.04	8.79Y	11.65	14.04	17.41	11.72Y	11.52	13.32	19.75Y	24.68	34.14	36.29
Colombia	233	6.50Y	6.29	6.99	8.11Y	9.79	11.75	14.87	8.94Y	8.92	10.10	12.43Y	14.78	15.60	16.94
Costa Rica	238	3.56Y	4.38	4.82	4.78Y	5.19	6.11	6.66	5.39Y	5.97	6.93	7.94Y	8.27	8.61	9.14
Dominica	321	.08Y	.08	.08	.08Y	.10	.11	.16	.03Y	.03	.03	.03Y	.04	.03	.02
Dominican Republic	243	5.85Y	5.69	5.23	5.48Y	6.15	6.91	8.15	4.70Y	4.78	5.12	5.41Y	5.51	5.72	5.65
Ecuador	248	2.70Y	2.95	2.80	3.03Y	3.58	4.48	4.97	3.62Y	3.86	4.76	6.57Y	8.52	9.89	9.41
El Salvador	253	2.55Y	2.25	2.53	2.53Y	2.53	3.25	3.27	2.08Y	2.20	2.30	2.37Y	2.37	2.22	2.44
Falkland Islands	323	.06Y	.04	.07	.08Y	.06	.07	.09	.08Y	.08	.15	.13Y	.15	.14	.16
Greenland	326	.38Y	.39	.41	.54Y	.65	.64	.74	.36Y	.39	.43	.47Y	.50	.46	.57
Grenada	328	.09Y	.09	.12	.12Y	.15	.13	.15	.06Y	.03	.03	.02Y	.02	.01	.02
Guatemala	258	2.65Y	2.95	3.17	3.65Y	3.97	4.99	5.56	3.26Y	3.42	3.65	3.93Y	4.07	4.12	4.08
Guyana	336	.23Y	.25	.28	.24Y	.29	.34	.35	.50Y	.47	.50	.55Y	.49	.51	.60
Haiti	263	.69Y	.74	.79	.81Y	.88	1.07	.91	.30Y	.29	.37	.42Y	.51	.56	.57
Honduras	268	2.74Y	2.89	3.30	3.69Y	3.83	4.21	5.17	3.71Y	3.83	3.92	4.41Y	4.59	4.61	4.87
Jamaica	343	2.08Y	2.23	2.37	2.26Y	2.51	2.85	3.17	1.41Y	1.30	1.49	1.57Y	1.78	1.74	1.98
Mexico	273	121.93Y	118.11	119.85	137.65Y	152.06	172.67	181.54	150.41Y	153.18	158.63	180.21Y	199.60	231.72	251.05
Netherlands Antilles	353	1.48Y	1.31	1.29	1.45Y	2.00	2.92	3.30	.72Y	.51	.81	.64Y	1.15	1.69	1.22
Nicaragua	278	.58Y	.62	.70	.81Y	.86	.99	1.21	.79Y	.83	.92	1.19Y	1.41	1.82	1.98
Panama	283	7.48Y	7.66	9.25	10.26Y	11.13	13.41	16.09	.89Y	.99	1.05	1.10Y	1.36	1.73	1.44
Paraguay	288	.68Y	.64	.69	.87Y	1.17	1.20	1.64	.29Y	.23	.44	.50Y	.43	.49	.71
Peru	293	2.95Y	2.93	3.10	3.71Y	4.25	5.30	7.30	3.84Y	4.20	4.89	7.31Y	10.47	13.98	15.79
St. Kitts and Nevis	361	.10Y	.13	.17	.14Y	.19	.25	.30	.06Y	.07	.07	.07Y	.08	.08	.07
St. Lucia	362	.15Y	.17	.19	.21Y	.36	.45	.35	.08Y	.06	.04	.05Y	.12	.28	.10
St. Pierre-Miquelon	363	.05Y	.04	.05	.06Y	.04	.04	.05	.01Y	.01	—	.01Y	.01	.03	.01
St. Vincent & Grens.	364	.16Y	.24	.31	.29Y	.42	.28	.25	.16Y	.19	.17	.26Y	.34	.16	.13
Suriname	366	.31Y	.34	.43	.44Y	.54	.55	.71	.48Y	.44	.51	.82Y	.84	1.05	1.22
Trinidad and Tobago	369	1.87Y	1.67	1.99	3.05Y	2.57	2.68	3.07	3.18Y	3.27	5.43	7.01Y	9.20	10.99	11.47
Uruguay	298	1.21Y	.74	.90	1.00Y	1.07	1.68	1.79	.83Y	.84	1.12	1.62Y	1.83	1.67	1.90
Venezuela, Rep. Bol.	299	10.52Y	8.45	5.35	8.66Y	11.47	15.52	18.04	19.96Y	19.41	21.02	30.30Y	41.95	47.46	50.54
Western Hem. n.s.	399	2.00Y	2.47	2.73	3.49Y	4.56	4.27	4.22	1.00Y	1.05	1.97	2.70Y	2.89	2.54	1.28
Other Countries n.i.e.	**910**	**2.9Y**	**1.9**	**2.1**	**2.4Y**	**2.8**	**3.3**	**3.4**	**1.2Y**	**1.2**	**1.2**	**1.7Y**	**1.7**	**1.8**	**2.1**
Cuba	928	1.62Y	1.46	1.75	1.99Y	2.54	3.07	3.23	.87Y	.88	1.00	1.45Y	1.47	1.57	1.97
North Korea	954	1.33Y	.49	.39	.43Y	.28	.21	.14	.31Y	.33	.24	.25Y	.21	.27	.09
Countries & Areas n.s.	**898**	**15.1Y**	**15.9**	**14.6**	**22.0Y**	**23.7**	**30.3**	**26.0**	**16.0Y**	**16.5**	**13.2**	**18.5Y**	**22.1**	**23.6**	**20.8**
Special Categories	**899**	**7.1Y**	**7.9**	**8.3**	**10.4Y**	**10.7**	**14.1**	**17.5**	**15.3Y**	**13.3**	**5.8**	**6.1Y**	**3.7**	**3.9**	**4.5**
Memorandum Items															
European Union	998	1,871.22Y	1,954.65	2,329.31	2,739.05Y	2,917.87	3,273.79	3,789.52	1,817.47Y	1,910.95	2,301.56	2,707.77Y	2,878.04	3,244.83	3,761.99
Oil Exporting Ctys	999	105.76Y	112.09	124.90	153.49Y	182.11	199.87	246.08	201.95Y	186.73	234.84	299.04Y	400.78	477.07	506.62
Non-Oil Develop.Ctys	201	964.63Y	1,008.63	1,173.05	1,430.26Y	1,588.97	1,851.42	2,184.87	1,221.44Y	1,292.54	1,520.11	1,875.80Y	2,167.11	2,495.63	2,814.11
PERCENT DISTRIBUTION															
Industrial Countries	**101**	**72.1**	**71.7**	**71.6**	**70.5**	**69.6**	**68.4**	**67.4**	**65.7**	**65.3**	**64.8**	**63.3**	**61.0**	**59.9**	**60.1**
Developing Countries	**202**	**27.3**	**27.7**	**27.9**	**28.9**	**29.8**	**30.8**	**32.0**	**33.6**	**34.0**	**34.8**	**36.2**	**38.5**	**39.7**	**39.5**
Africa	**607**	**1.7**	**1.8**	**1.8**	**1.8**	**1.9**	**2.0**	**2.0**	**2.3**	**2.2**	**2.4**	**2.5**	**2.9**	**2.9**	**2.9**
Asia	**507**	**11.6**	**12.0**	**12.3**	**12.7**	**12.7**	**12.8**	**13.0**	**16.4**	**17.0**	**17.3**	**17.9**	**18.5**	**18.7**	**18.6**
Europe	**170**	**4.9**	**5.5**	**6.1**	**6.5**	**6.9**	**7.7**	**8.5**	**4.8**	**5.1**	**5.7**	**6.1**	**6.4**	**7.0**	**7.4**

	Exports 2001	2002	2003	2004	2005	2006	2007	Imports 2001	2002	2003	2004	2005	2006	2007
Middle East............................ 407	2.8	2.9	2.8	2.9	3.1	3.0	3.2	3.4	3.1	3.3	3.5	4.2	4.4	4.2
Western Hemisphere.............. 207	6.2	5.6	4.9	4.9	5.1	5.3	5.3	6.6	6.6	6.2	6.2	6.5	6.6	6.4
Other Countries n.i.e................ 910	.1	—	—	—	—	—	—	—	—	—	—	—	—	—
ANNUAL PERCENT CHANGE														
World....................................... 001	–2.8	3.2	14.9	17.8	8.5	11.8	14.1	–3.5	2.6	16.0	18.9	11.1	12.3	12.2
Industrial Countries................. 101	–2.9	2.6	14.8	16.0	7.1	9.9	12.3	–3.9	2.0	15.2	16.2	7.1	10.2	12.6
Developing Countries.............. 202	–3.4	4.7	15.8	22.0	11.8	15.8	18.5	–3.7	3.9	18.6	23.9	18.1	15.8	11.7
Africa...................................... 607	5.1	4.0	17.4	20.5	14.9	15.4	15.0	.6	–2.0	24.0	24.1	28.4	15.5	11.3
Asia.. 507	–9.0	6.7	17.4	22.5	8.4	12.3	15.9	–6.0	6.1	17.8	23.5	14.5	13.8	11.3
Europe.................................... 170	4.5	14.3	27.5	26.4	14.8	24.4	26.3	6.3	9.0	28.5	27.7	17.1	21.6	19.2
Middle East............................ 407	4.2	5.0	13.4	20.1	16.2	10.2	21.8	–9.7	–6.3	22.7	26.8	33.9	18.7	6.6
Western Hemisphere.............. 207	–3.4	–6.7	1.7	17.1	13.0	16.6	13.0	–2.6	2.2	9.3	20.1	16.2	13.9	8.5
Other Countries n.i.e................ 910	51.8	–33.8	9.4	13.6	16.5	16.4	2.8	–14.8	3.2	2.5	36.9	–.8	9.8	11.6

		Exports							Imports						
		2001	2002	2003	2004	2005	2006	2007	2001	2002	2003	2004	2005	2006	2007
		Billions of U.S. Dollars							*Billions of U.S. Dollars*						
IFS World Total		**2,253.6**	**2,424.3**	**2,886.7**	**3,758.1**	**4,613.9**	**5,566.4**	**6,362.0**	**2,173.9**	**2,302.9**	**2,719.0**	**3,496.1**	**4,121.9**	**4,876.2**	**5,845.9**
DOTS World Total	**001**	**2,209.6Y**	**2,378.8Y**	**2,859.6Y**	**3,640.6Y**	**4,403.3Y**	**5,302.3Y**	**6,219.4Y**	**2,133.4Y**	**2,273.6Y**	**2,698.1Y**	**3,477.7Y**	**4,078.0Y**	**4,862.3Y**	**5,899.8Y**
Industrial Countries	**101**	**1,252.1Y**	**1,310.8Y**	**1,538.3Y**	**1,922.6Y**	**2,292.7Y**	**2,694.7Y**	**3,028.7Y**	**1,144.0Y**	**1,183.7Y**	**1,356.8Y**	**1,676.0Y**	**1,868.7Y**	**2,133.7Y**	**2,569.6Y**
United States	111	508.14Y	529.88Y	584.52Y	708.97Y	835.60Y	963.95Y	1,032.75Y	360.04Y	343.52Y	359.44Y	415.33Y	460.89Y	526.07Y	609.51Y
Canada	156	23.00Y	24.68Y	29.42Y	36.47Y	47.53Y	58.24Y	67.96Y	22.04Y	21.75Y	22.66Y	29.68Y	37.23Y	39.80Y	50.31Y
Australia	193	23.58Y	26.54Y	33.51Y	43.04Y	51.74Y	62.15Y	74.02Y	34.51Y	34.09Y	36.11Y	48.00Y	61.73Y	74.20Y	87.73Y
Japan	158	194.55Y	190.51Y	222.28Y	271.37Y	318.82Y	370.01Y	398.15Y	221.27Y	240.16Y	285.52Y	361.33Y	387.57Y	422.17Y	477.26Y
New Zealand	196	3.21Y	3.58Y	4.58Y	6.05Y	7.42Y	8.33Y	9.62Y	5.31Y	5.19Y	5.88Y	7.20Y	7.86Y	8.60Y	10.77Y
Austria	122	11.06Y	11.99Y	16.33Y	20.15Y	23.79Y	27.59Y	32.35Y	13.91Y	15.46Y	19.92Y	26.33Y	29.40Y	36.38Y	48.01Y
Belgium	124	23.46Y	25.52Y	29.89Y	38.24Y	47.92Y	59.47Y	73.08Y	23.94Y	26.15Y	29.58Y	37.65Y	44.38Y	54.43Y	67.92Y
Belgium-Luxembourg n.s.	127	3.73Y	3.52Y	3.46Y	4.14Y	3.46Y	1.24Y	.82Y	2.26Y	2.26Y	2.47Y	2.91Y	2.05Y	.84Y	.65Y
Cyprus	423	3.01Y	3.71Y	6.28Y	8.42Y	7.96Y	8.28Y	9.17Y	.43Y	.53Y	.54Y	.69Y	.50Y	.70Y	1.36Y
Denmark	128	6.75Y	7.33Y	9.07Y	12.33Y	14.98Y	17.29Y	19.99Y	8.25Y	9.04Y	10.52Y	12.62Y	14.06Y	16.21Y	20.06Y
Finland	172	8.82Y	9.08Y	12.73Y	18.53Y	23.42Y	27.11Y	30.91Y	12.74Y	12.00Y	14.68Y	20.39Y	24.11Y	27.95Y	33.57Y
France	132	51.80Y	54.35Y	67.45Y	89.42Y	103.87Y	116.98Y	138.36Y	66.11Y	66.71Y	84.96Y	105.36Y	112.78Y	129.23Y	154.16Y
Germany	134	117.11Y	121.45Y	156.54Y	194.49Y	230.52Y	272.04Y	320.70Y	142.23Y	157.35Y	193.73Y	244.26Y	277.19Y	333.89Y	417.69Y
Greece	174	9.29Y	9.51Y	12.20Y	14.95Y	18.45Y	23.41Y	26.68Y	3.66Y	3.82Y	4.59Y	5.64Y	6.60Y	8.02Y	9.92Y
Iceland	176	.49Y	.28Y	.33Y	.37Y	.61Y	.72Y	.90Y	.18Y	.24Y	.23Y	.35Y	.41Y	.53Y	.54Y
Ireland	178	6.47Y	6.02Y	7.89Y	9.18Y	10.94Y	12.74Y	13.80Y	8.75Y	8.94Y	9.94Y	12.37Y	13.91Y	15.77Y	18.46Y
Italy	136	64.16Y	67.08Y	81.62Y	109.19Y	131.56Y	167.12Y	191.77Y	62.76Y	68.67Y	80.58Y	97.49Y	107.08Y	127.55Y	165.10Y
Luxembourg	137	.59Y	1.20Y	1.51Y	1.99Y	3.44Y	3.62Y	3.30Y	.55Y	.71Y	1.19Y	1.63Y	1.55Y	1.81Y	2.52Y
Malta	181	1.34Y	1.50Y	1.44Y	2.01Y	2.12Y	2.87Y	3.45Y	.80Y	1.14Y	1.49Y	1.56Y	1.62Y	1.80Y	2.27Y
Netherlands	138	60.41Y	68.60Y	82.89Y	108.68Y	143.05Y	171.09Y	203.18Y	25.83Y	27.42Y	31.99Y	43.75Y	54.71Y	70.35Y	93.30Y
Norway	142	3.77Y	4.48Y	6.03Y	6.58Y	8.50Y	10.82Y	12.96Y	5.05Y	6.48Y	7.14Y	8.55Y	9.82Y	10.95Y	13.80Y
Portugal	182	5.48Y	5.87Y	6.52Y	9.11Y	13.17Y	14.72Y	17.98Y	2.66Y	3.06Y	4.21Y	5.27Y	5.99Y	6.87Y	9.19Y
Slovenia	961	2.00Y	2.10Y	2.70Y	3.53Y	4.79Y	5.94Y	8.28Y	3.14Y	3.78Y	4.68Y	5.87Y	6.40Y	7.25Y	10.86Y
Spain	184	31.05Y	33.64Y	42.12Y	56.29Y	74.03Y	93.72Y	110.61Y	21.60Y	23.84Y	29.13Y	36.56Y	39.45Y	47.11Y	66.44Y
Sweden	144	9.50Y	10.66Y	12.90Y	16.62Y	19.64Y	22.86Y	28.64Y	17.18Y	16.87Y	21.20Y	28.42Y	32.12Y	35.56Y	43.73Y
Switzerland	146	12.11Y	16.93Y	21.77Y	27.83Y	29.50Y	38.64Y	43.55Y	25.32Y	30.56Y	34.00Y	42.40Y	47.09Y	43.84Y	54.84Y
United Kingdom	112	67.21Y	70.85Y	82.38Y	104.62Y	116.74Y	136.72Y	159.29Y	53.49Y	53.95Y	60.39Y	74.37Y	84.20Y	90.63Y	108.37Y
Developing Countries	**202**	**909.6Y**	**1,018.0Y**	**1,268.1Y**	**1,655.0Y**	**2,035.6Y**	**2,515.0Y**	**3,079.0Y**	**943.6Y**	**1,033.7Y**	**1,271.1Y**	**1,708.6Y**	**2,083.5Y**	**2,567.0Y**	**3,136.2Y**
Africa	**607**	**42.8Y**	**47.1Y**	**57.6Y**	**78.1Y**	**93.4Y**	**121.9Y**	**151.2Y**	**40.6Y**	**40.6Y**	**48.1Y**	**71.7Y**	**84.1Y**	**103.7Y**	**127.7Y**
Algeria	612	2.11Y	2.87Y	3.89Y	5.41Y	6.44Y	8.42Y	11.72Y	3.66Y	3.51Y	3.66Y	5.16Y	7.02Y	6.98Y	9.04Y
Angola	614	1.51Y	.98Y	1.29Y	3.43Y	3.73Y	4.44Y	4.51Y	1.65Y	2.15Y	3.50Y	6.86Y	9.79Y	15.89Y	19.98Y
Benin	638	.81Y	.90Y	.98Y	1.18Y	1.84Y	2.57Y	3.44Y	.35Y	.19Y	.24Y	.33Y	.33Y	.33Y	.42Y
Botswana	616	.07Y	.09Y	.12Y	.15Y	.19Y	.30Y	.44Y	.04Y	.06Y	.11Y	.19Y	.24Y	.22Y	.28Y
Burkina Faso	748	.21Y	.27Y	.34Y	.41Y	.51Y	.62Y	.78Y	.08Y	.09Y	.16Y	.28Y	.29Y	.33Y	.36Y
Burundi	618	.07Y	.07Y	.09Y	.09Y	.10Y	.16Y	.19Y	.01Y	.01Y	.01Y	.02Y	.02Y	.02Y	.03Y
Cameroon	622	.53Y	.56Y	.81Y	.97Y	1.33Y	1.64Y	2.04Y	.58Y	.42Y	.64Y	1.14Y	1.05Y	1.33Y	1.58Y
Cape Verde	624	.03Y	.05Y	.05Y	.05Y	.08Y	.12Y	.15Y	—Y	—Y	—Y	—Y	—Y	—Y	.01Y
Central African Rep.	626	.03Y	.03Y	.03Y	.04Y	.05Y	.06Y	.08Y	.03Y	.06Y	.03Y	.03Y	.04Y	.04Y	.06Y
Chad	628	.04Y	.09Y	.10Y	.13Y	.16Y	.20Y	.29Y	.02Y	.02Y	.03Y	.27Y	.35Y	.43Y	.13Y
Comoros	632	.03Y	.04Y	.05Y	.05Y	.06Y	.07Y	.10Y	.01Y	—Y	—Y	.01Y	.01Y	.01Y	.02Y
Congo, Dem. Rep. of	636	.34Y	.43Y	.46Y	.68Y	.78Y	1.21Y	1.69Y	.13Y	.05Y	.09Y	.19Y	.39Y	.88Y	.95Y
Congo, Republic of	634	.28Y	.40Y	.40Y	.45Y	.62Y	.77Y	1.60Y	1.58Y	1.46Y	1.92Y	2.84Y	3.77Y	5.17Y	3.93Y
Côte d'Ivoire	662	1.14Y	1.08Y	1.27Y	1.66Y	2.30Y	2.66Y	3.34Y	1.71Y	1.72Y	1.98Y	2.81Y	3.05Y	3.62Y	4.29Y
Djibouti	611	.41Y	.36Y	.54Y	.55Y	.82Y	1.06Y	1.32Y	.20Y	.21Y	.26Y	.27Y	.29Y	.36Y	.45Y
Equatorial Guinea	642	.04Y	.04Y	.17Y	.11Y	.18Y	.40Y	.37Y	.47Y	.39Y	.47Y	1.69Y	2.33Y	3.60Y	3.03Y
Ethiopia	644	.58Y	.58Y	.91Y	1.18Y	1.58Y	1.93Y	2.53Y	.22Y	.17Y	.31Y	.20Y	.37Y	.45Y	.50Y
Gabon	646	.14Y	.15Y	.20Y	.26Y	.35Y	.45Y	.60Y	.75Y	.74Y	.79Y	1.07Y	1.21Y	2.15Y	2.57Y
Gambia, The	648	.22Y	.24Y	.30Y	.37Y	.41Y	.48Y	.60Y	.01Y	.01Y	.01Y	.02Y	.02Y	.02Y	.04Y
Ghana	652	1.20Y	1.38Y	1.93Y	2.57Y	3.15Y	3.72Y	4.98Y	.33Y	.43Y	.57Y	.68Y	.76Y	.95Y	1.09Y
Guinea	656	.25Y	.28Y	.36Y	.44Y	.59Y	.64Y	.83Y	.29Y	.38Y	.38Y	.46Y	.63Y	.63Y	.71Y
Guinea-Bissau	654	.05Y	.04Y	.08Y	.05Y	.06Y	.06Y	.09Y	.13Y	.09Y	.07Y	.09Y	.12Y	.14Y	.41Y
Kenya	664	1.83Y	1.83Y	2.33Y	3.12Y	3.94Y	4.92Y	6.21Y	1.17Y	1.28Y	1.55Y	1.88Y	2.09Y	2.53Y	3.14Y
Lesotho	666	.10Y	.16Y	.19Y	.25Y	.21Y	.24Y	.25Y	.05Y	—Y	—Y	—Y	—Y	.01Y	—Y
Liberia	668	1.85Y	2.31Y	2.40Y	3.02Y	3.57Y	5.38Y	5.95Y	.31Y	.21Y	.25Y	.33Y	.26Y	.61Y	.63Y
Madagascar	674	.60Y	.40Y	.76Y	.88Y	.99Y	1.06Y	1.48Y	.17Y	.09Y	.12Y	.12Y	.11Y	.13Y	.15Y
Malawi	676	.31Y	.41Y	.43Y	.54Y	.55Y	.54Y	.64Y	.16Y	.19Y	.22Y	.28Y	.31Y	.40Y	.51Y
Mali	678	.42Y	.42Y	.43Y	.61Y	.74Y	.84Y	1.07Y	.11Y	.10Y	.16Y	.27Y	.20Y	.25Y	.17Y
Mauritania	682	.19Y	.29Y	.29Y	.32Y	.39Y	.50Y	.66Y	.20Y	.15Y	.18Y	.27Y	.27Y	.69Y	.93Y
Mauritius	684	1.04Y	1.12Y	1.25Y	1.46Y	1.70Y	1.90Y	2.10Y	.16Y	.15Y	.18Y	.30Y	.50Y	.59Y	.46Y
Morocco	686	3.06Y	3.51Y	3.53Y	5.18Y	6.76Y	8.19Y	10.83Y	1.68Y	1.81Y	1.97Y	2.59Y	3.30Y	4.11Y	5.06Y
Mozambique	688	.81Y	.88Y	1.11Y	1.27Y	1.58Y	1.53Y	2.03Y	.20Y	.35Y	.23Y	.29Y	.32Y	.31Y	.80Y
Namibia	728	.10Y	.10Y	.16Y	.17Y	.20Y	.32Y	.51Y	.05Y	.06Y	.08Y	.12Y	.26Y	.48Y	.44Y
Niger	692	.14Y	.21Y	.24Y	.33Y	.38Y	.48Y	.52Y	.10Y	.03Y	.02Y	.14Y	.10Y	.17Y	.16Y
Nigeria	694	4.48Y	5.63Y	6.38Y	7.23Y	9.24Y	10.78Y	14.96Y	7.35Y	5.17Y	5.68Y	10.47Y	9.90Y	12.16Y	16.01Y
Rwanda	714	.10Y	.12Y	.16Y	.17Y	.23Y	.26Y	.33Y	.05Y	.09Y	.09Y	.32Y	.04Y	.05Y	.08Y
St. Helena	856	.01Y	.01Y	.01Y	.01Y	.02Y	.02Y	.04Y	—Y	.01Y	.01Y	.01Y	.01Y	.01Y	.02Y
São Tomé & Príncipe	716	.01Y	.01Y	.01Y	.01Y	.01Y	.01Y	.01Y	—Y	—Y	—Y	—Y	—Y	—Y	—Y
Senegal	722	.70Y	.72Y	.97Y	1.28Y	1.56Y	1.29Y	1.82Y	.36Y	.50Y	.63Y	.67Y	.93Y	.82Y	1.03Y
Seychelles	718	.16Y	.17Y	.19Y	.22Y	.34Y	.41Y	.43Y	.03Y	.07Y	.07Y	.05Y	.05Y	.06Y	.08Y

		Exports							Imports						
		2001	2002	2003	2004	2005	2006	2007	2001	2002	2003	2004	2005	2006	2007
		Billions of U.S. Dollars							*Billions of U.S. Dollars*						
Sierra Leone	724	.10Y	.11Y	.17Y	.19Y	.24Y	.28Y	.32Y	.01Y	.01Y	.01Y	.02Y	.02Y	.02Y	.03Y
Somalia	726	.24Y	.28Y	.31Y	.40Y	.47Y	.59Y	.65Y	.08Y	.12Y	.16Y	.21Y	.27Y	.33Y	.41Y
South Africa	199	9.18Y	9.28Y	12.74Y	18.82Y	19.83Y	31.90Y	36.23Y	10.54Y	11.83Y	13.90Y	19.52Y	21.50Y	23.30Y	30.81Y
Sudan	732	.97Y	1.27Y	1.84Y	2.95Y	4.43Y	4.96Y	5.07Y	1.34Y	1.64Y	2.02Y	2.63Y	3.34Y	3.03Y	5.46Y
Swaziland	734	.06Y	.08Y	.16Y	.12Y	.10Y	.11Y	.11Y	.16Y	.22Y	.18Y	.29Y	.43Y	.55Y	.51Y
Tanzania	738	1.04Y	1.19Y	1.49Y	1.81Y	2.23Y	2.79Y	3.26Y	.30Y	.32Y	.49Y	.65Y	.86Y	.96Y	1.12Y
Togo	742	.44Y	.88Y	.72Y	1.08Y	1.17Y	1.57Y	2.78Y	.33Y	.26Y	.61Y	.42Y	.43Y	.51Y	.63Y
Tunisia	744	1.43Y	1.55Y	1.85Y	2.41Y	2.73Y	3.57Y	4.55Y	1.00Y	1.22Y	1.23Y	1.43Y	1.80Y	2.15Y	2.69Y
Uganda	746	.64Y	.71Y	.78Y	.93Y	1.06Y	1.38Y	1.77Y	.10Y	.11Y	.18Y	.21Y	.27Y	.29Y	.35Y
Zambia	754	.73Y	.85Y	.83Y	1.17Y	1.32Y	1.87Y	2.47Y	.50Y	.51Y	.70Y	1.35Y	2.32Y	3.16Y	3.11Y
Zimbabwe	698	.96Y	1.20Y	1.12Y	1.38Y	1.72Y	1.60Y	1.89Y	.77Y	.87Y	1.07Y	1.14Y	1.17Y	1.47Y	1.75Y
Africa n.s.	799	1.02Y	.49Y	.38Y	.46Y	.38Y	.61Y	.60Y	1.03Y	1.07Y	.87Y	1.10Y	.83Y	.94Y	1.11Y
Asia	**507**	**575.3Y**	**655.6Y**	**826.7Y**	**1,055.4Y**	**1,271.8Y**	**1,542.8Y**	**1,821.2Y**	**567.7Y**	**648.6Y**	**786.7Y**	**1,032.1Y**	**1,232.5Y**	**1,501.3Y**	**1,823.9Y**
Afghanistan, I.S. of	512	.42Y	.65Y	1.08Y	1.24Y	1.99Y	2.50Y	3.31Y	.07Y	.07Y	.10Y	.14Y	.16Y	.20Y	.27Y
American Samoa	859	.03Y	.04Y	.01Y	.01Y	.04Y	.08Y	.12Y	.01Y	.03Y	—Y	.01Y	.01Y	.01Y	.03Y
Bangladesh	513	5.88Y	5.78Y	7.18Y	8.82Y	10.55Y	12.56Y	13.70Y	.62Y	.68Y	.76Y	.88Y	1.11Y	1.44Y	1.78Y
Brunei Darussalam	516	.85Y	.92Y	1.00Y	1.06Y	1.18Y	1.28Y	1.50Y	1.23Y	1.44Y	1.48Y	1.82Y	2.59Y	3.50Y	3.43Y
Cambodia	522	1.88Y	2.11Y	2.44Y	2.97Y	3.56Y	4.70Y	5.35Y	.18Y	.24Y	.25Y	.29Y	.40Y	.45Y	.54Y
China,P.R.: Mainland	924	134.46Y	165.70Y	231.46Y	306.14Y	377.57Y	460.42Y	550.98Y	162.29Y	189.58Y	233.81Y	309.73Y	391.46Y	501.10Y	646.58Y
China,P.R.:Hong Kong	532	111.18Y	132.15Y	159.37Y	195.58Y	226.04Y	275.56Y	314.51Y	27.32Y	30.63Y	33.39Y	39.66Y	40.37Y	43.09Y	49.89Y
China,P.R.:Macao	546	2.30Y	2.33Y	3.41Y	4.24Y	4.89Y	5.97Y	7.19Y	.50Y	.52Y	.57Y	.75Y	.88Y	.91Y	1.12Y
Fiji	819	.19Y	.27Y	.33Y	.46Y	.60Y	.70Y	.72Y	.12Y	.12Y	.15Y	.19Y	.20Y	.23Y	.29Y
French Polynesia	887	.05Y	.09Y	.07Y	.18Y	.36Y	.39Y	.39Y	.01Y	.01Y	.03Y	.08Y	.08Y	.09Y	.11Y
Guam	829	.38Y	.31Y	.36Y	.48Y	.70Y	.83Y	.66Y	.01Y	.01Y	.02Y	.01Y	.01Y	.01Y	.01Y
India	534	23.12Y	24.54Y	31.37Y	40.85Y	55.09Y	70.46Y	96.45Y	21.93Y	25.41Y	33.11Y	49.79Y	61.91Y	75.16Y	98.62Y
Indonesia	536	16.46Y	18.20Y	37.83Y	47.90Y	57.56Y	62.77Y	77.37Y	23.70Y	26.15Y	38.41Y	48.07Y	55.39Y	66.68Y	77.71Y
Kiribati	826	.02Y	.02Y	.02Y	.02Y	.03Y	.03Y	.05Y	.02Y	.01Y	—Y	—Y	—Y	—Y	.01Y
Korea	542	60.73Y	64.84Y	78.15Y	100.54Y	122.96Y	155.12Y	188.91Y	79.20Y	89.90Y	112.94Y	155.93Y	186.42Y	224.50Y	264.36Y
Lao People's Dem.Rep	544	.59Y	.57Y	.65Y	.83Y	1.04Y	1.39Y	1.73Y	.17Y	.18Y	.19Y	.22Y	.39Y	.86Y	.92Y
Malaysia	548	41.96Y	46.07Y	52.09Y	62.96Y	71.85Y	86.58Y	98.97Y	55.44Y	61.10Y	72.47Y	89.11Y	99.02Y	117.59Y	138.44Y
Maldives	556	.29Y	.26Y	.31Y	.49Y	.56Y	.64Y	.82Y	.95Y	1.09Y	.93Y	1.03Y	.09Y	.11Y	.10Y
Mongolia	948	.48Y	.53Y	.63Y	.80Y	.97Y	1.17Y	1.68Y	.29Y	.29Y	.34Y	.51Y	.63Y	1.22Y	1.43Y
Myanmar	518	2.10Y	2.44Y	2.70Y	2.87Y	2.97Y	3.22Y	4.53Y	1.54Y	1.84Y	1.85Y	2.39Y	3.16Y	3.82Y	4.14Y
Nauru	836	—Y	—Y	—Y	—Y	.01Y	.01Y	.03Y	.01Y	.01Y	.01Y	.01Y	—Y	—Y	.01Y
Nepal	558	1.02Y	.68Y	.95Y	1.12Y	1.22Y	1.80Y	2.31Y	.42Y	.32Y	.31Y	.36Y	.40Y	.66Y	.83Y
New Caledonia	839	.13Y	.14Y	.21Y	.27Y	.40Y	.46Y	.61Y	.13Y	.13Y	.22Y	.39Y	.41Y	.52Y	1.01Y
Pakistan	564	6.59Y	7.73Y	9.37Y	12.60Y	16.99Y	20.48Y	25.04Y	3.72Y	3.78Y	4.22Y	5.87Y	7.41Y	9.05Y	10.98Y
Papua New Guinea	853	.34Y	.37Y	.46Y	.54Y	.55Y	.72Y	.86Y	.42Y	.36Y	.65Y	.65Y	.79Y	1.09Y	1.06Y
Philippines	566	18.73Y	19.41Y	22.17Y	27.54Y	30.61Y	35.60Y	41.51Y	16.58Y	20.46Y	25.26Y	30.35Y	36.62Y	42.77Y	49.64Y
Samoa	862	.07Y	.08Y	.10Y	.14Y	.13Y	.15Y	.17Y	.01Y	.01Y	.02Y	.02Y	.04Y	.06Y	.07Y
Singapore	576	59.51Y	63.37Y	69.22Y	86.18Y	108.07Y	129.34Y	145.53Y	53.47Y	57.71Y	66.06Y	84.20Y	104.16Y	122.77Y	138.34Y
Solomon Islands	813	.04Y	.03Y	.06Y	.06Y	.09Y	.10Y	.16Y	.05Y	.07Y	.10Y	.14Y	.17Y	.19Y	.27Y
Sri Lanka	524	3.55Y	4.09Y	4.62Y	5.62Y	6.82Y	7.79Y	8.35Y	.90Y	.90Y	1.24Y	1.71Y	2.00Y	2.10Y	2.43Y
Taiwan Province of China	528	42.00Y	46.31Y	55.55Y	72.00Y	79.74Y	95.41Y	103.08Y	73.82Y	88.95Y	104.69Y	137.17Y	156.63Y	184.94Y	210.09Y
Thailand	578	28.76Y	31.58Y	36.33Y	47.81Y	59.50Y	71.20Y	78.29Y	30.46Y	33.00Y	40.99Y	54.06Y	63.68Y	78.00Y	95.35Y
Tonga	866	.02Y	.03Y	.03Y	.04Y	.05Y	.05Y	.07Y	—Y	—Y	—Y	.01Y	—Y	.01Y	—Y
Tuvalu	869	.01Y	.06Y	.01Y	.02Y	.02Y	.03Y	.03Y	—Y	—Y	—Y	—Y	—Y	—Y	—Y
Vanuatu	846	.05Y	.05Y	.12Y	.11Y	.12Y	.10Y	.13Y	.04Y	.05Y	.06Y	.16Y	.17Y	.23Y	.25Y
Vietnam	582	10.58Y	13.30Y	16.50Y	22.27Y	26.47Y	32.35Y	45.10Y	5.51Y	5.74Y	6.54Y	9.24Y	11.86Y	13.72Y	17.80Y
Asia n.s.	598	.52Y	.54Y	.47Y	.54Y	.38Y	.70Y	.87Y	6.59Y	7.75Y	5.49Y	7.10Y	3.66Y	5.15Y	7.15Y
Europe	**170**	**113.5Y**	**131.6Y**	**175.0Y**	**235.3Y**	**314.1Y**	**408.3Y**	**549.5Y**	**127.7Y**	**143.8Y**	**188.2Y**	**256.6Y**	**315.5Y**	**392.2Y**	**517.0Y**
Albania	914	.22Y	.29Y	.40Y	.54Y	.67Y	.90Y	1.19Y	.03Y	.02Y	.03Y	.08Y	.07Y	.09Y	.19Y
Armenia	911	.29Y	.38Y	.47Y	.64Y	.76Y	1.16Y	1.61Y	.16Y	.21Y	.26Y	.27Y	.33Y	.32Y	.47Y
Azerbaijan	912	.68Y	1.04Y	1.50Y	2.25Y	2.81Y	3.85Y	4.55Y	.52Y	.57Y	.83Y	1.59Y	2.22Y	3.00Y	4.53Y
Belarus	913	1.00Y	6.85Y	8.89Y	1.99Y	10.84Y	7.23Y	22.34Y	1.60Y	5.62Y	7.07Y	3.53Y	9.31Y	7.79Y	15.70Y
Bosnia & Herzegovina	963	1.03Y	1.27Y	1.59Y	1.88Y	2.39Y	3.33Y	4.19Y	.18Y	.23Y	.32Y	.58Y	.91Y	1.52Y	1.71Y
Bulgaria	918	2.16Y	2.36Y	3.31Y	5.34Y	7.60Y	11.51Y	14.76Y	1.78Y	1.98Y	2.61Y	3.80Y	4.58Y	6.10Y	8.14Y
Croatia	960	1.84Y	2.05Y	2.84Y	4.10Y	4.99Y	6.06Y	8.44Y	1.23Y	1.45Y	1.67Y	2.28Y	2.91Y	3.56Y	4.08Y
Czech Republic	935	7.50Y	8.51Y	11.34Y	14.95Y	19.68Y	26.77Y	34.30Y	8.02Y	9.10Y	12.62Y	17.97Y	21.16Y	26.74Y	36.01Y
Czechoslovakia n.s.	937	.07Y	.06Y	.10Y	.13Y	—Y	.02Y	.04Y	.17Y	.18Y	.35Y	.55Y	.27Y	.32Y	.42Y
Estonia	939	2.31Y	2.70Y	3.06Y	3.76Y	5.03Y	6.64Y	6.71Y	.80Y	.75Y	1.00Y	1.70Y	2.28Y	3.71Y	4.20Y
Faroe Islands	816	.01Y	.01Y	.01Y	.05Y	.01Y	.01Y	.02Y	.01Y	.03Y	.04Y	.08Y	.08Y	.11Y	.14Y
Georgia	915	.54Y	.55Y	.95Y	1.34Y	1.82Y	2.55Y	3.50Y	.31Y	.37Y	.60Y	.75Y	.82Y	.97Y	.99Y
Gibraltar	823	.44Y	.19Y	.40Y	.92Y	.85Y	1.23Y	.83Y	.02Y	.02Y	.04Y	.06Y	.06Y	.07Y	.11Y
Hungary	944	8.25Y	10.20Y	13.19Y	17.26Y	21.86Y	27.39Y	34.94Y	5.72Y	6.96Y	9.16Y	12.14Y	15.75Y	22.11Y	33.33Y
Kazakhstan	916	3.75Y	4.11Y	6.37Y	9.39Y	13.52Y	18.03Y	25.45Y	6.32Y	7.94Y	9.97Y	10.74Y	11.90Y	14.63Y	19.59Y
Kyrgyz Republic	917	.40Y	.52Y	.76Y	1.28Y	1.78Y	3.29Y	5.47Y	.25Y	.26Y	.34Y	.65Y	.67Y	.71Y	1.04Y
Latvia	941	3.08Y	3.02Y	3.78Y	4.73Y	5.36Y	7.03Y	10.41Y	.84Y	.78Y	.87Y	1.73Y	2.36Y	3.01Y	4.55Y
Lithuania	946	3.59Y	4.08Y	5.31Y	6.78Y	8.27Y	9.89Y	11.88Y	1.37Y	1.64Y	2.22Y	3.14Y	4.14Y	5.46Y	7.33Y
Macedonia, FYR	962	.46Y	.48Y	.58Y	.87Y	.91Y	1.49Y	2.03Y	.17Y	.17Y	.23Y	.34Y	.46Y	.84Y	1.23Y
Moldova	921	.82Y	.91Y	1.26Y	1.69Y	2.09Y	2.65Y	3.50Y	.56Y	.52Y	.68Y	.89Y	.99Y	.87Y	1.34Y
Poland	964	11.75Y	12.10Y	15.43Y	21.58Y	28.97Y	40.14Y	52.52Y	7.87Y	8.96Y	12.33Y	18.04Y	22.49Y	32.58Y	42.93Y
Romania	968	4.06Y	4.93Y	6.67Y	10.32Y	15.41Y	23.95Y	25.71Y	3.00Y	3.74Y	4.84Y	7.58Y	9.53Y	12.77Y	15.24Y
Russia	922	22.52Y	24.03Y	31.79Y	43.71Y	56.87Y	70.81Y	103.88Y	55.06Y	57.64Y	72.74Y	98.53Y	124.64Y	153.41Y	187.27Y
Serbia & Montenegro	965	1.30Y	1.33Y	1.83Y	2.01Y	2.73Y	2.75Y	3.18Y	.38Y	.43Y	.52Y	.65Y	.91Y	.71Y	.93Y
Slovak Republic	936	6.20Y	6.78Y	8.88Y	12.17Y	16.02Y	21.83Y	29.95Y	4.44Y	4.95Y	6.69Y	8.80Y	10.71Y	14.75Y	20.84Y
Tajikistan	923	.46Y	.42Y	.58Y	.79Y	1.05Y	1.55Y	2.18Y	.40Y	.44Y	.51Y	.50Y	.42Y	.60Y	.70Y
Turkey	186	13.79Y	16.44Y	22.85Y	36.35Y	46.14Y	60.74Y	77.07Y	8.44Y	10.30Y	15.36Y	23.24Y	26.70Y	33.54Y	48.39Y

		Exports							Imports						
		2001	2002	2003	2004	2005	2006	2007	2001	2002	2003	2004	2005	2006	2007
		Billions of U.S. Dollars							*Billions of U.S. Dollars*						
Turkmenistan	925	.80Y	.88Y	1.24Y	1.62Y	1.80Y	1.91Y	2.57Y	2.23Y	2.51Y	3.11Y	3.96Y	5.55Y	6.11Y	7.29Y
Ukraine	926	10.52Y	11.83Y	15.48Y	21.07Y	27.29Y	36.07Y	45.87Y	11.94Y	13.00Y	17.64Y	27.33Y	28.43Y	33.34Y	45.55Y
U.S.S.R. n.s.	930	.11Y	.03Y	.01Y	.01Y	.07Y	.09Y	.06Y	.36Y	.45Y	.13Y	.11Y	.11Y	.10Y	.11Y
Uzbekistan	927	1.41Y	1.29Y	1.49Y	2.08Y	2.50Y	3.26Y	4.74Y	1.66Y	1.20Y	1.67Y	2.36Y	3.10Y	4.73Y	5.54Y
Yugoslavia n.s.	966	.47Y	.48Y	.63Y	.95Y	.90Y	.78Y	.42Y	.16Y	.16Y	.20Y	.27Y	.37Y	.26Y	.13Y
Europe n.s.	884	1.67Y	1.49Y	1.97Y	2.70Y	3.27Y	4.10Y	4.83Y	1.71Y	1.14Y	1.51Y	2.36Y	1.82Y	3.49Y	3.53Y
Middle East	**407**	**71.6Y**	**83.2Y**	**99.0Y**	**135.0Y**	**167.3Y**	**203.6Y**	**261.8Y**	**110.4Y**	**107.1Y**	**134.7Y**	**188.6Y**	**253.6Y**	**327.2Y**	**366.0Y**
Bahrain	419	2.30Y	2.48Y	2.96Y	3.81Y	5.20Y	6.35Y	7.75Y	2.05Y	1.96Y	2.32Y	3.14Y	3.95Y	4.76Y	5.48Y
Egypt	469	6.49Y	6.71Y	7.11Y	9.79Y	13.23Y	16.82Y	21.70Y	1.98Y	2.13Y	2.97Y	4.82Y	6.38Y	7.83Y	10.40Y
Iran, I.R. of	429	8.97Y	10.71Y	14.50Y	18.20Y	21.12Y	26.02Y	34.98Y	11.61Y	9.89Y	14.37Y	19.64Y	27.05Y	37.73Y	43.76Y
Iraq	433	2.64Y	3.08Y	2.41Y	6.26Y	8.16Y	8.97Y	10.59Y	2.04Y	2.71Y	1.30Y	3.18Y	3.80Y	4.95Y	8.38Y
Israel	436	6.56Y	7.58Y	8.93Y	11.12Y	12.66Y	14.40Y	17.06Y	6.34Y	6.23Y	6.93Y	9.13Y	10.34Y	11.97Y	14.28Y
Jordan	439	2.46Y	2.83Y	3.66Y	6.22Y	6.75Y	7.48Y	8.85Y	1.69Y	1.85Y	2.01Y	2.56Y	2.91Y	3.23Y	3.79Y
Kuwait	443	2.44Y	2.72Y	3.55Y	4.11Y	5.12Y	6.31Y	8.46Y	8.75Y	8.91Y	11.19Y	15.89Y	22.08Y	27.60Y	31.24Y
Lebanon	446	2.19Y	2.10Y	2.38Y	3.45Y	3.93Y	4.49Y	5.73Y	.60Y	.73Y	.80Y	1.54Y	1.80Y	2.20Y	2.77Y
Libya	672	1.12Y	1.44Y	1.58Y	2.56Y	3.08Y	3.87Y	5.06Y	1.77Y	1.49Y	2.19Y	3.24Y	4.66Y	6.86Y	5.14Y
Oman	449	2.71Y	2.64Y	2.64Y	3.12Y	4.36Y	5.45Y	6.97Y	7.13Y	6.56Y	7.63Y	10.47Y	13.84Y	20.56Y	18.08Y
Qatar	453	1.09Y	1.25Y	1.68Y	2.14Y	3.30Y	5.31Y	6.95Y	4.89Y	5.11Y	6.52Y	9.33Y	13.42Y	17.55Y	21.94Y
Saudi Arabia	456	9.84Y	11.55Y	13.36Y	16.69Y	20.34Y	26.17Y	34.34Y	35.17Y	33.39Y	43.80Y	59.69Y	82.69Y	105.10Y	114.31Y
Syrian Arab Republic	463	2.35Y	2.76Y	3.43Y	8.29Y	10.40Y	12.89Y	16.18Y	2.60Y	3.10Y	2.73Y	6.18Y	7.25Y	8.72Y	11.18Y
United Arab Emirates	466	18.42Y	22.72Y	27.80Y	35.81Y	45.63Y	54.02Y	71.12Y	19.98Y	20.25Y	25.88Y	35.32Y	48.12Y	62.80Y	69.82Y
Yemen, Republic of	474	1.88Y	2.49Y	2.79Y	3.34Y	3.96Y	5.06Y	6.04Y	3.43Y	2.55Y	3.79Y	4.10Y	4.87Y	4.84Y	4.83Y
Middle East n.s.	489	.09Y	.10Y	.20Y	.13Y	.08Y	.08Y	.11Y	.36Y	.23Y	.25Y	.36Y	.43Y	.54Y	.65Y
Western Hemisphere	**207**	**106.4Y**	**100.6Y**	**109.8Y**	**151.3Y**	**189.0Y**	**238.5Y**	**295.3Y**	**97.2Y**	**93.6Y**	**113.4Y**	**159.6Y**	**197.9Y**	**242.7Y**	**301.7Y**
Antigua and Barbuda	311	.23Y	.23Y	.21Y	.41Y	.44Y	.47Y	.99Y	.01Y	.02Y	.02Y	.14Y	.05Y	.05Y	.04Y
Argentina	213	8.59Y	3.60Y	6.84Y	11.59Y	15.46Y	19.37Y	25.50Y	18.89Y	17.32Y	20.88Y	26.62Y	30.43Y	35.61Y	45.34Y
Aruba	314	.09Y	.08Y	.12Y	.36Y	2.08Y	2.04Y	1.75Y	.08Y	.08Y	.16Y	.27Y	.44Y	.58Y	.65Y
Bahamas, The	313	1.12Y	1.98Y	2.04Y	2.42Y	4.64Y	4.63Y	3.50Y	.19Y	.36Y	.48Y	.49Y	.50Y	.65Y	1.13Y
Barbados	316	.46Y	.31Y	.35Y	.43Y	.51Y	.61Y	.65Y	.19Y	.32Y	.33Y	.20Y	.46Y	.21Y	.33Y
Belize	339	.16Y	.20Y	.19Y	.24Y	.34Y	.33Y	.38Y	.08Y	.06Y	.09Y	.10Y	.09Y	.09Y	.14Y
Bermuda	319	1.66Y	2.51Y	2.50Y	.91Y	.96Y	1.55Y	1.93Y	.04Y	.06Y	.07Y	.09Y	.03Y	.10Y	.08Y
Bolivia	218	.99Y	1.07Y	.96Y	1.29Y	1.54Y	1.81Y	2.19Y	.70Y	.87Y	1.13Y	1.49Y	1.87Y	2.57Y	2.77Y
Brazil	223	19.82Y	18.59Y	19.71Y	28.88Y	34.84Y	47.19Y	61.35Y	26.62Y	26.34Y	36.15Y	53.16Y	67.23Y	81.36Y	97.41Y
Chile	228	8.12Y	8.24Y	9.72Y	12.62Y	17.01Y	20.15Y	23.58Y	7.73Y	7.64Y	9.59Y	14.77Y	17.76Y	25.99Y	34.03Y
Colombia	233	4.11Y	4.52Y	4.81Y	6.46Y	8.96Y	12.02Y	15.06Y	4.84Y	4.49Y	4.84Y	7.31Y	9.57Y	11.27Y	16.08Y
Costa Rica	238	1.70Y	2.11Y	2.07Y	2.61Y	3.06Y	3.81Y	4.46Y	1.61Y	2.33Y	3.66Y	4.08Y	4.80Y	6.14Y	7.31Y
Dominica	321	.15Y	.11Y	.11Y	.13Y	.14Y	.16Y	.19Y	.04Y	.03Y	.04Y	.04Y	.06Y	.07Y	.10Y
Dominican Republic	243	1.84Y	2.59Y	2.00Y	2.82Y	3.63Y	4.20Y	4.98Y	.14Y	.16Y	.23Y	.36Y	.45Y	.65Y	.82Y
Ecuador	248	2.39Y	2.99Y	2.87Y	3.89Y	5.06Y	5.91Y	6.39Y	2.59Y	2.02Y	2.12Y	2.82Y	3.75Y	4.66Y	5.83Y
El Salvador	253	1.90Y	1.97Y	2.19Y	2.53Y	2.93Y	3.17Y	3.53Y	.97Y	.96Y	1.00Y	.96Y	1.59Y	1.62Y	1.83Y
Falkland Islands	323	—Y	—Y	—Y	—Y	—Y	—Y	—Y	—Y	.01Y	.01Y	.01Y	.01Y	.01Y	.01Y
Greenland	326	—Y	.01Y	—Y	—Y	—Y	—Y	—Y	.04Y	.04Y	.06Y	.04Y	.05Y	.05Y	.06Y
Grenada	328	.08Y	.07Y	.08Y	.10Y	.13Y	.15Y	.17Y	.02Y	.03Y	.02Y	.02Y	.02Y	.03Y	.74Y
Guatemala	258	2.77Y	2.98Y	3.30Y	3.90Y	4.45Y	5.12Y	5.64Y	1.59Y	1.58Y	1.68Y	1.93Y	2.34Y	2.72Y	3.34Y
Guyana	336	.38Y	.23Y	.21Y	.27Y	.31Y	.45Y	.49Y	.12Y	.11Y	.12Y	.15Y	.20Y	.22Y	.25Y
Haiti	263	.35Y	.30Y	.30Y	.45Y	.52Y	.70Y	.82Y	.02Y	.03Y	.03Y	.05Y	.06Y	.08Y	.12Y
Honduras	268	1.58Y	1.57Y	1.61Y	2.02Y	2.42Y	2.82Y	3.30Y	.46Y	.48Y	.57Y	.56Y	.75Y	.96Y	1.18Y
Jamaica	343	1.03Y	.97Y	1.12Y	1.34Y	1.77Y	2.22Y	3.42Y	.20Y	.20Y	.30Y	.44Y	.43Y	.60Y	.40Y
Mexico	273	14.26Y	16.85Y	17.06Y	23.34Y	26.40Y	37.72Y	44.21Y	9.86Y	9.03Y	9.75Y	12.58Y	16.08Y	21.24Y	27.29Y
Netherlands Antilles	353	5.96Y	4.56Y	3.37Y	7.44Y	8.69Y	6.68Y	8.28Y	1.19Y	1.06Y	.93Y	1.49Y	2.01Y	2.36Y	2.75Y
Nicaragua	278	1.00Y	1.02Y	1.10Y	1.62Y	1.74Y	2.08Y	2.60Y	.32Y	.28Y	.32Y	.34Y	.55Y	.55Y	.63Y
Panama	283	7.42Y	6.40Y	6.82Y	9.21Y	11.89Y	13.46Y	17.20Y	1.92Y	2.14Y	2.33Y	2.51Y	3.28Y	3.32Y	3.54Y
Paraguay	288	1.70Y	1.27Y	1.62Y	2.03Y	2.13Y	2.64Y	3.44Y	.99Y	1.16Y	1.11Y	1.29Y	1.38Y	2.09Y	2.92Y
Peru	293	3.14Y	3.76Y	4.16Y	5.16Y	6.60Y	8.64Y	11.00Y	2.55Y	2.76Y	3.05Y	5.00Y	6.92Y	9.67Y	12.64Y
St. Kitts and Nevis	361	.05Y	.04Y	.05Y	.22Y	.07Y	.09Y	.12Y	.01Y	—Y	—Y	.01Y	.01Y	.01Y	.01Y
St. Lucia	362	.33Y	.35Y	.12Y	.13Y	.24Y	.19Y	1.27Y	.02Y	.02Y	.02Y	.04Y	.06Y	.04Y	.05Y
St. Vincent & Grens.	364	.15Y	.12Y	.13Y	.22Y	.24Y	.25Y	.29Y	.03Y	.04Y	.04Y	.09Y	.03Y	.05Y	.05Y
Suriname	366	.30Y	.20Y	.16Y	.23Y	.29Y	.32Y	.41Y	.07Y	.08Y	.13Y	.15Y	.17Y	.25Y	.32Y
Trinidad and Tobago	369	1.31Y	1.07Y	1.32Y	1.55Y	2.25Y	2.63Y	3.21Y	1.29Y	1.50Y	1.70Y	2.19Y	2.79Y	3.34Y	4.59Y
Uruguay	298	2.39Y	1.63Y	1.86Y	2.67Y	3.31Y	3.90Y	4.91Y	1.65Y	1.54Y	1.69Y	1.96Y	2.28Y	2.92Y	3.53Y
Venezuela, Rep. Bol	299	6.77Y	4.68Y	3.24Y	6.90Y	9.44Y	14.79Y	22.39Y	7.93Y	7.20Y	6.54Y	14.43Y	17.55Y	18.18Y	20.28Y
Western Hem. n.s.	399	2.13Y	1.39Y	5.50Y	4.85Y	4.51Y	6.21Y	5.67Y	2.18Y	1.27Y	2.21Y	1.43Y	1.82Y	2.57Y	3.20Y
Other Countries n.i.e.	**910**	**3.3Y**	**2.9Y**	**2.6Y**	**4.5Y**	**6.1Y**	**7.8Y**	**8.5Y**	**1.6Y**	**1.5Y**	**1.6Y**	**2.1Y**	**2.1Y**	**2.4Y**	**3.7Y**
Cuba	928	1.61Y	1.27Y	.95Y	2.35Y	3.73Y	5.19Y	5.52Y	.87Y	.79Y	.81Y	.99Y	.91Y	1.25Y	2.05Y
North Korea	954	1.67Y	1.58Y	1.65Y	2.11Y	2.35Y	2.63Y	2.99Y	.75Y	.73Y	.76Y	1.11Y	1.16Y	1.19Y	1.68Y
Countries & Areas n.s.	**898**	**32.9Y**	**35.9Y**	**36.9Y**	**47.7Y**	**54.2Y**	**67.8Y**	**85.2Y**	**24.1Y**	**29.1Y**	**35.2Y**	**44.2Y**	**62.0Y**	**74.7Y**	**91.3Y**
Special Categories	**899**	**10.5Y**	**9.8Y**	**8.4Y**	**9.4Y**	**12.5Y**	**14.4Y**	**12.9Y**	**20.0Y**	**25.5Y**	**31.1Y**	**46.6Y**	**61.5Y**	**84.2Y**	**98.6Y**
Memorandum Items															
European Union	998	525.91Y	561.33Y	696.89Y	903.11Y	1,098.03Y	1,321.23Y	1,569.05Y	499.35Y	534.85Y	650.65Y	826.67Y	934.43Y	1,115.53Y	1,412.01Y
Oil Exporting Ctys.	999	77.05Y	87.48Y	118.85Y	156.34Y	193.77Y	232.85Y	304.87Y	133.98Y	130.32Y	167.16Y	234.88Y	305.51Y	387.10Y	435.65Y
Non-Oil Develop.Ctys.	201	832.55Y	930.52Y	1,149.22Y	1,498.68Y	1,841.83Y	2,282.17Y	2,774.15Y	809.65Y	903.34Y	1,103.90Y	1,473.73Y	1,778.00Y	2,179.91Y	2,700.56Y
PERCENT DISTRIBUTION															
Industrial Countries	**101**	**56.7**	**55.1**	**53.8**	**52.8**	**52.1**	**50.8**	**48.7**	**53.6**	**52.1**	**50.3**	**48.2**	**45.8**	**43.9**	**43.6**
Developing Countries	**202**	**41.2**	**42.8**	**44.3**	**45.5**	**46.2**	**47.4**	**49.5**	**44.2**	**45.5**	**47.1**	**49.1**	**51.1**	**52.8**	**53.2**
Africa	**607**	**1.9**	**2.0**	**2.0**	**2.1**	**2.1**	**2.3**	**2.4**	**1.9**	**1.8**	**1.8**	**2.1**	**2.1**	**2.1**	**2.2**
Asia	**507**	**26.0**	**27.6**	**28.9**	**29.0**	**28.9**	**29.1**	**29.3**	**26.6**	**28.5**	**29.2**	**29.7**	**30.2**	**30.9**	**30.9**

	Exports 2001	2002	2003	2004	2005	2006	2007	Imports 2001	2002	2003	2004	2005	2006	2007
Europe....170	5.1	5.5	6.1	6.5	7.1	7.7	8.8	6.0	6.3	7.0	7.4	7.7	8.1	8.8
Middle East....407	3.2	3.5	3.5	3.7	3.8	3.8	4.2	5.2	4.7	5.0	5.4	6.2	6.7	6.2
Western Hemisphere....207	4.8	4.2	3.8	4.2	4.3	4.5	4.7	4.6	4.1	4.2	4.6	4.9	5.0	5.1
Other Countries n.i.e....910	.1	.1	.1	.1	.1	.1	.1	.1	.1	.1	.1	.1	.1	.1
ANNUAL PERCENT CHANGE														
World....001	–5.6	7.7	20.2	27.3	21.0	20.4	17.3	–2.7	6.6	18.7	28.9	17.3	19.2	21.3
Industrial Countries....101	–6.7	4.7	17.4	25.0	19.3	17.5	12.4	–4.2	3.5	14.6	23.5	11.5	14.2	20.4
Developing Countries....202	–4.5	11.9	24.6	30.5	23.0	23.6	22.4	–1.1	9.5	23.0	34.4	21.9	23.2	22.2
Africa....607	2.7	10.0	22.3	35.6	19.7	30.4	24.1	–.9	.2	18.4	49.0	17.3	23.3	23.1
Asia....507	–6.5	14.0	26.1	27.7	20.5	21.3	18.0	–2.0	14.2	21.3	31.2	19.4	21.8	21.5
Europe....170	–2.5	16.0	32.9	34.5	33.5	30.0	34.6	1.1	12.6	30.9	36.4	22.9	24.3	31.8
Middle East....407	8.5	16.2	19.0	36.4	23.9	21.7	28.6	–2.8	–3.0	25.8	40.0	34.5	29.0	11.9
Western Hemisphere....207	–5.8	–5.5	9.2	37.7	25.0	26.2	23.8	3.2	–3.7	21.1	40.8	24.0	22.6	24.3
Other Countries n.i.e....910	–4.6	–12.9	–8.9	71.4	36.4	28.7	8.8	14.2	–6.6	4.1	33.1	–1.1	17.9	52.4

		Exports							Imports						
		2001	2002	2003	2004	2005	2006	2007	2001	2002	2003	2004	2005	2006	2007
		Billions of U.S. Dollars							Billions of U.S. Dollars						
IFS World Total		**117.5**	**121.2**	**148.9**	**196.4**	**264.2**	**303.2**	**348.6**	**111.1**	**112.4**	**140.9**	**180.3**	**216.5**	**248.9**	**314.6**
DOTS World Total	**001**	**119.2Y**	**124.4Y**	**151.2Y**	**190.5Y**	**241.9Y**	**287.5Y**	**332.0Y**	**112.0Y**	**118.4Y**	**148.8Y**	**194.7Y**	**230.0Y**	**279.6Y**	**355.1Y**
Industrial Countries	**101**	**76.1Y**	**78.8Y**	**99.3Y**	**124.6Y**	**162.3Y**	**192.4Y**	**212.9Y**	**67.1Y**	**70.6Y**	**87.0Y**	**105.3Y**	**120.7Y**	**134.9Y**	**173.6Y**
United States	111	19.40Y	18.15Y	26.91Y	39.17Y	56.40Y	69.57Y	79.33Y	8.70Y	8.88Y	10.24Y	11.67Y	13.70Y	16.67Y	20.18Y
Canada	156	1.41Y	1.65Y	3.16Y	3.28Y	5.40Y	6.73Y	7.93Y	1.07Y	1.14Y	1.12Y	1.25Y	4.84Y	1.83Y	2.81Y
Australia	193	.53Y	.64Y	.90Y	1.13Y	1.65Y	1.77Y	1.64Y	1.39Y	1.41Y	1.52Y	1.87Y	2.00Y	2.31Y	2.68Y
Japan	158	2.51Y	3.78Y	5.31Y	6.67Y	7.59Y	9.42Y	10.86Y	4.69Y	5.60Y	5.96Y	8.06Y	8.85Y	9.81Y	11.92Y
New Zealand	196	.11Y	.15Y	.18Y	.25Y	.30Y	.25Y	.33Y	.16Y	.18Y	.21Y	.29Y	.38Y	.55Y	.71Y
Austria	122	.14Y	.14Y	.28Y	.54Y	.80Y	.96Y	.72Y	.58Y	.61Y	.72Y	1.04Y	1.18Y	1.38Y	1.90Y
Belgium	124	3.54Y	4.32Y	4.38Y	4.42Y	6.05Y	6.45Y	7.19Y	2.34Y	2.50Y	3.06Y	3.58Y	4.07Y	5.92Y	8.18Y
Belgium-Luxembourg n.s.	127	.32Y	.34Y	.41Y	.48Y	.48Y	.24Y	—Y	.39Y	.47Y	.54Y	.56Y	.57Y	.22Y	—Y
Cyprus	423	.01Y	.01Y	.02Y	.02Y	.02Y	.03Y	.03Y	.02Y	.03Y	.03Y	.04Y	.03Y	.04Y	.04Y
Denmark	128	.15Y	.18Y	.19Y	.47Y	.24Y	.26Y	.36Y	.46Y	.57Y	.65Y	.71Y	.79Y	.90Y	.90Y
Finland	172	.16Y	.14Y	.12Y	.30Y	.19Y	.33Y	.36Y	.63Y	.53Y	.66Y	1.07Y	1.23Y	1.67Y	2.07Y
France	132	12.47Y	12.57Y	15.13Y	16.88Y	19.27Y	20.56Y	21.48Y	15.07Y	14.30Y	19.49Y	24.15Y	25.45Y	26.60Y	31.20Y
Germany	134	4.88Y	5.65Y	6.56Y	6.92Y	8.54Y	10.39Y	11.94Y	8.94Y	9.90Y	11.50Y	14.07Y	15.32Y	17.58Y	21.18Y
Greece	174	.43Y	.35Y	.40Y	.42Y	.38Y	.51Y	.63Y	.26Y	.26Y	.29Y	.36Y	.55Y	.59Y	.58Y
Iceland	176	.01Y	.07Y	.06Y	.02Y	.02Y	.04Y	.05Y	.02Y	.02Y	.02Y	.06Y	.07Y	.07Y	.07Y
Ireland	178	.28Y	.28Y	.26Y	.28Y	.39Y	.37Y	.40Y	.65Y	.71Y	.84Y	1.35Y	1.41Y	1.44Y	1.76Y
Italy	136	9.02Y	8.64Y	10.19Y	11.80Y	13.79Y	16.88Y	17.32Y	6.09Y	6.55Y	8.11Y	9.35Y	10.96Y	12.63Y	16.52Y
Luxembourg	137	.01Y	.02Y	.02Y	.02Y	.03Y	.02Y	.02Y	.06Y	.06Y	.07Y	.10Y	.10Y	.10Y	.11Y
Malta	181	.03Y	.04Y	.02Y	.03Y	.03Y	.05Y	.02Y	.02Y	.03Y	.05Y	.05Y	.06Y	.09Y	.09Y
Netherlands	138	4.62Y	5.46Y	5.42Y	6.60Y	9.31Y	10.39Y	11.93Y	2.48Y	2.52Y	3.77Y	4.56Y	5.56Y	7.29Y	10.46Y
Norway	142	.20Y	.20Y	.13Y	.17Y	.22Y	.30Y	.52Y	.32Y	.35Y	.47Y	.34Y	.67Y	.71Y	1.00Y
Portugal	182	1.31Y	1.38Y	1.39Y	2.01Y	3.32Y	3.05Y	3.71Y	1.01Y	1.20Y	1.57Y	1.90Y	2.05Y	2.80Y	3.98Y
Slovenia	961	.01Y	.01Y	.06Y	.09Y	.12Y	.14Y	.18Y	.01Y	.02Y	.03Y	.04Y	.10Y	.17Y	.20Y
Spain	184	6.80Y	7.39Y	9.10Y	11.17Y	15.10Y	18.20Y	20.27Y	3.16Y	3.70Y	5.14Y	6.17Y	7.26Y	8.82Y	17.44Y
Sweden	144	.20Y	.15Y	.19Y	.31Y	.43Y	.56Y	.62Y	1.01Y	1.24Y	1.37Y	2.02Y	2.67Y	2.65Y	3.73Y
Switzerland	146	.56Y	.81Y	1.65Y	2.53Y	2.81Y	4.77Y	4.06Y	1.13Y	1.16Y	1.38Y	1.59Y	1.75Y	1.96Y	2.25Y
United Kingdom	112	7.04Y	6.36Y	6.88Y	8.62Y	9.43Y	10.18Y	10.95Y	6.43Y	6.71Y	8.19Y	9.04Y	9.10Y	10.12Y	11.60Y
Developing Countries	**202**	**32.7Y**	**36.4Y**	**44.5Y**	**57.6Y**	**71.5Y**	**91.2Y**	**114.4Y**	**43.7Y**	**46.2Y**	**58.1Y**	**84.2Y**	**103.3Y**	**137.5Y**	**172.3Y**
Africa	**607**	**11.1Y**	**12.7Y**	**14.9Y**	**18.1Y**	**21.7Y**	**25.4Y**	**32.3Y**	**11.7Y**	**12.3Y**	**14.5Y**	**19.8Y**	**23.2Y**	**28.3Y**	**35.5Y**
Algeria	612	.15Y	.19Y	.22Y	.26Y	.37Y	.52Y	.58Y	.31Y	.30Y	.34Y	.37Y	.58Y	.72Y	.86Y
Angola	614	.42Y	.43Y	.52Y	.58Y	.64Y	.80Y	.92Y	.01Y	.04Y	.01Y	.30Y	.34Y	.42Y	1.85Y
Benin	638	.13Y	.25Y	.25Y	.28Y	.34Y	.35Y	.43Y	.22Y	.08Y	.07Y	.10Y	.08Y	.11Y	.13Y
Botswana	616	.02Y	.04Y	.07Y	.05Y	.07Y	.15Y	.20Y	.04Y	.06Y	.02Y	.10Y	.12Y	.11Y	.14Y
Burkina Faso	748	.17Y	.21Y	.25Y	.31Y	.37Y	.48Y	.59Y	.03Y	.03Y	.05Y	.07Y	.06Y	.08Y	.10Y
Burundi	618	.04Y	.05Y	.07Y	.07Y	.06Y	.06Y	.08Y	—Y	—Y	—Y	.01Y	.01Y	.01Y	.02Y
Cameroon	622	.33Y	.28Y	.51Y	.57Y	.71Y	.90Y	1.09Y	.16Y	.21Y	.26Y	.33Y	.35Y	.40Y	.50Y
Cape Verde	624	.01Y	.02Y	.02Y	.02Y	.04Y	.06Y	.07Y	—Y	—Y	—Y	—Y	—Y	—Y	—Y
Central African Rep.	626	.01Y	.02Y	.02Y	.03Y	.03Y	.04Y	.06Y	.01Y	.05Y	.01Y	.01Y	.01Y	.01Y	.01Y
Chad	628	.02Y	.05Y	.06Y	.09Y	.10Y	.12Y	.15Y	.01Y	.01Y	.01Y	.01Y	.01Y	.01Y	.01Y
Comoros	632	.02Y	.02Y	.03Y	.02Y	.02Y	.03Y	.03Y	—Y	—Y	—Y	—Y	—Y	—Y	—Y
Congo, Dem. Rep. of	636	.28Y	.35Y	.37Y	.55Y	.64Y	1.02Y	1.50Y	.12Y	.03Y	.04Y	.06Y	.14Y	.12Y	.23Y
Congo, Republic of	634	.12Y	.15Y	.15Y	.11Y	.17Y	.16Y	.19Y	.06Y	.07Y	.06Y	.08Y	.11Y	.09Y	.12Y
Côte d'Ivoire	662	.47Y	.46Y	.61Y	1.09Y	1.56Y	1.74Y	2.12Y	1.18Y	1.05Y	1.14Y	1.96Y	2.18Y	2.64Y	3.32Y
Djibouti	611	.15Y	.07Y	.13Y	.04Y	.07Y	.09Y	.11Y	.15Y	.17Y	.20Y	.24Y	.26Y	.33Y	.41Y
Equatorial Guinea	642	.03Y	.03Y	.15Y	.07Y	.12Y	.15Y	.18Y	.04Y	—Y	—Y	—Y	.01Y	.03Y	.04Y
Ethiopia	644	.09Y	.11Y	.10Y	.13Y	.17Y	.21Y	.21Y	.14Y	.07Y	.14Y	.04Y	.07Y	.10Y	.12Y
Gabon	646	.07Y	.09Y	.11Y	.16Y	.19Y	.23Y	.27Y	.14Y	.15Y	.10Y	.13Y	.24Y	.37Y	.25Y
Gambia, The	648	.05Y	.06Y	.07Y	.10Y	.14Y	.15Y	.18Y	—Y	—Y	—Y	—Y	—Y	—Y	—Y
Ghana	652	.62Y	.71Y	.88Y	1.12Y	1.40Y	1.68Y	2.04Y	.10Y	.15Y	.18Y	.22Y	.23Y	.29Y	.36Y
Guinea	656	.09Y	.09Y	.13Y	.15Y	.20Y	.19Y	.23Y	.07Y	.03Y	.07Y	.02Y	.03Y	.03Y	.04Y
Guinea-Bissau	654	.02Y	.02Y	.06Y	.04Y	.05Y	.04Y	.05Y	—Y	—Y	.02Y	.02Y	.02Y	.03Y	.04Y
Kenya	664	.39Y	.40Y	.47Y	.57Y	.60Y	.66Y	.87Y	.65Y	.79Y	.99Y	1.26Y	1.42Y	1.73Y	2.16Y
Lesotho	666	—Y	—Y	—Y	.01Y	—Y	.01Y	—Y	—Y	—Y	—Y	—Y	—Y	—Y	—Y
Liberia	668	.06Y	.05Y	.06Y	.08Y	.13Y	.17Y	.20Y	.01Y	.01Y	.02Y	.02Y	.02Y	.23Y	.03Y
Madagascar	674	.16Y	.12Y	.24Y	.21Y	.23Y	.21Y	.33Y	.05Y	.03Y	.06Y	.04Y	.03Y	.03Y	.04Y
Malawi	676	.27Y	.35Y	.35Y	.44Y	.45Y	.41Y	.47Y	.07Y	.08Y	.12Y	.14Y	.15Y	.21Y	.24Y
Mali	678	.32Y	.31Y	.29Y	.46Y	.55Y	.63Y	.80Y	.02Y	.02Y	.02Y	.02Y	.02Y	.02Y	.03Y
Mauritania	682	.07Y	.08Y	.09Y	.09Y	.11Y	.14Y	.17Y	.13Y	.08Y	.11Y	.15Y	.19Y	.21Y	.26Y
Mauritius	684	.30Y	.30Y	.35Y	.34Y	.40Y	.37Y	.38Y	.11Y	.09Y	.11Y	.19Y	.21Y	.21Y	.26Y
Morocco	686	.38Y	.37Y	.36Y	.44Y	.71Y	.82Y	1.05Y	.19Y	.24Y	.26Y	.34Y	.43Y	.54Y	.67Y
Mozambique	688	.68Y	.65Y	.81Y	.85Y	1.08Y	.97Y	1.34Y	.14Y	.24Y	.13Y	.16Y	.12Y	.11Y	.48Y
Namibia	728	.01Y	.02Y	.04Y	.03Y	.04Y	.04Y	.07Y	.02Y	.02Y	.02Y	.04Y	.05Y	.05Y	.06Y
Niger	692	.09Y	.10Y	.12Y	.15Y	.18Y	.22Y	.26Y	.01Y	.02Y	.02Y	.07Y	.09Y	.11Y	.14Y
Nigeria	694	.46Y	.95Y	.70Y	1.18Y	1.39Y	1.54Y	1.90Y	1.57Y	1.65Y	2.02Y	3.21Y	3.88Y	4.89Y	6.11Y
Rwanda	714	.07Y	.09Y	.13Y	.14Y	.16Y	.19Y	.24Y	.01Y	.01Y	—Y	.01Y	.01Y	.01Y	.01Y
St. Helena	856	.01	.01	.01Y	.01Y	.01Y	.02Y	.04Y	—Y	—Y	.01Y	.01Y	.01Y	.01Y	.02Y
São Tomé & Príncipe	716	—Y	—Y	—Y	.01Y	—Y	—Y	.01Y	—Y	—Y	—Y	—Y	—Y	—Y	—Y
Senegal	722	.32Y	.27Y	.46Y	.55Y	.67Y	.44Y	.54Y	.23Y	.32Y	.44Y	.47Y	.62Y	.66Y	.82Y
Seychelles	718	.04Y	.05Y	.05Y	.05Y	.12Y	.09Y	.08Y	.01Y	.04Y	.01Y	.03Y	.02Y	.04Y	.05Y

		Exports							Imports						
		2001	2002	2003	2004	2005	2006	2007	2001	2002	2003	2004	2005	2006	2007
		Billions of U.S. Dollars							*Billions of U.S. Dollars*						
Sierra Leone	724	.03Y	.04Y	.06Y	.08Y	.11Y	.09Y	.11Y	.01Y	—Y	—Y	—Y	.01Y	.01Y	.01Y
Somalia	726	.12Y	.16Y	.17Y	.20Y	.23Y	.29Y	.35Y	.01Y	.01Y	.01Y	.01Y	.01Y	.01Y	.02Y
South Africa	199	.86Y	1.30Y	1.95Y	2.47Y	2.54Y	3.72Y	5.55Y	4.01Y	4.20Y	4.62Y	6.68Y	7.05Y	8.52Y	10.57Y
Sudan	732	.06Y	.08Y	.13Y	.16Y	.21Y	.17Y	.21Y	.02Y	.01Y	.02Y	.03Y	.06Y	.07Y	.04Y
Swaziland	734	—Y	—Y	.02Y	—Y	.01Y	.01Y	.02Y	.06Y	.11Y	.08Y	.13Y	.15Y	.22Y	.29Y
Tanzania	738	.39Y	.46Y	.61Y	.75Y	.82Y	1.01Y	.95Y	.07Y	.11Y	.17Y	.22Y	.29Y	.31Y	.35Y
Togo	742	.13Y	.50Y	.21Y	.19Y	.16Y	.20Y	.26Y	.24Y	.19Y	.50Y	.27Y	.28Y	.35Y	.43Y
Tunisia	744	.18Y	.18Y	.21Y	.25Y	.22Y	.30Y	.37Y	.16Y	.22Y	.26Y	.29Y	.46Y	.52Y	.66Y
Uganda	746	.46Y	.51Y	.49Y	.59Y	.66Y	.81Y	1.03Y	.05Y	.05Y	.10Y	.12Y	.13Y	.17Y	.20Y
Zambia	754	.61Y	.71Y	.66Y	.88Y	1.06Y	1.34Y	1.81Y	.14Y	.16Y	.33Y	.57Y	1.31Y	1.42Y	.91Y
Zimbabwe	698	.82Y	.90Y	.99Y	1.08Y	1.40Y	1.31Y	1.51Y	.37Y	.48Y	.68Y	.70Y	.76Y	1.12Y	1.33Y
Africa n.s.	799	.51Y	.02Y	.01Y	.01Y	.01Y	.02Y	.02Y	.56Y	.54Y	.62Y	.47Y	.50Y	.54Y	.57Y
Asia	**507**	**12.7Y**	**14.4Y**	**18.8Y**	**24.1Y**	**30.5Y**	**41.9Y**	**52.6Y**	**15.3Y**	**17.5Y**	**22.5Y**	**33.4Y**	**43.7Y**	**59.3Y**	**76.7Y**
Afghanistan, I.S. of	512	.04Y	.05Y	.07Y	.04Y	.05Y	.05Y	.07Y	—Y	—Y	—Y	.01Y	.01Y	.01Y	.01Y
American Samoa	859	—Y	.01Y	—Y	—Y	—Y	—Y	—Y	—Y	—Y	—Y	—Y	—Y	—Y	—Y
Bangladesh	513	.04Y	.04Y	.08Y	.10Y	.11Y	.08Y	.09Y	.03Y	.04Y	.07Y	.05Y	.06Y	.08Y	.11Y
Brunei Darussalam	516	—Y	—Y	—Y	—Y	.01Y	—Y	—Y	—Y	—Y	.01Y	.01Y	.02Y	.02Y	.03Y
Cambodia	522	—Y	—Y	—Y	—Y	—Y	—Y	—Y	—Y	—Y	—Y	—Y	—Y	—Y	.01Y
China,P.R.: Mainland	924	3.14Y	3.69Y	7.14Y	11.06Y	16.86Y	25.15Y	32.74Y	4.03Y	5.04Y	7.84Y	11.83Y	17.43Y	26.12Y	36.72Y
China,P.R.:Hong Kong	532	.44Y	.44Y	.56Y	.66Y	.83Y	1.06Y	1.13Y	.68Y	.69Y	.88Y	1.09Y	1.08Y	1.27Y	1.52Y
China,P.R.:Macao	546	—Y	.01Y	.01Y	—Y	—Y	—Y	.02Y	—Y	—Y	—Y	—Y	—Y	—Y	—Y
Fiji	819	—Y	—Y	—Y	—Y	—Y	.02Y	—Y	—Y	—Y	—Y	—Y	—Y	—Y	—Y
French Polynesia	887	—Y	—Y	—Y	—Y	.01Y	—Y	—Y	—Y	—Y	—Y	.06Y	.06Y	.08Y	.10Y
India	534	3.38Y	3.63Y	3.81Y	1.90Y	2.74Y	2.48Y	3.47Y	1.86Y	2.33Y	3.10Y	4.08Y	6.02Y	8.03Y	9.90Y
Indonesia	536	1.18Y	1.43Y	1.48Y	2.09Y	1.38Y	.57Y	1.19Y	.90Y	1.05Y	1.11Y	1.25Y	1.41Y	1.69Y	2.14Y
Korea	542	1.01Y	1.20Y	1.57Y	2.07Y	2.36Y	3.72Y	3.66Y	3.40Y	3.16Y	3.62Y	6.92Y	7.78Y	9.48Y	10.69Y
Malaysia	548	.20Y	.22Y	.34Y	.46Y	.48Y	.76Y	1.50Y	.68Y	.77Y	1.07Y	1.35Y	1.78Y	2.18Y	2.96Y
Maldives	556	—Y	—Y	—Y	.01Y	—Y	—Y	—Y	.01Y	.01Y	.01Y	.02Y	.01Y	.02Y	.02Y
Myanmar	518	—Y	—Y	—Y	—Y	—Y	—Y	—Y	.02Y	.03Y	.02Y	.01Y	.01Y	.02Y	.03Y
Nauru	836	—Y	—Y	—Y	—Y	—Y	—Y	—Y	—Y	—Y	—Y	.01Y	—Y	—Y	—Y
New Caledonia	839	—Y	—Y	—Y	—Y	—Y	—Y	—Y	—Y	—Y	.02Y	.05Y	.05Y	.05Y	.18Y
Pakistan	564	.27Y	.28Y	.32Y	.45Y	.57Y	.61Y	.86Y	.29Y	.25Y	.34Y	.71Y	.66Y	.85Y	1.02Y
Papua New Guinea	853	.01Y	.01Y	—Y	—Y	.01Y	.01Y	.01Y	—Y	—Y	—Y	—Y	—Y	—Y	—Y
Philippines	566	.07Y	.05Y	.05Y	.07Y	.08Y	.06Y	.05Y	.07Y	.08Y	.12Y	.14Y	.15Y	.21Y	.21Y
Singapore	576	.44Y	.53Y	.40Y	.61Y	.64Y	1.07Y	.97Y	.99Y	1.63Y	1.31Y	1.72Y	2.41Y	3.35Y	3.95Y
Sri Lanka	524	.03Y	.03Y	.03Y	.04Y	.04Y	.03Y	.04Y	.03Y	.03Y	.04Y	.04Y	.05Y	.06Y	.06Y
Taiwan Province of China	528	1.88Y	1.99Y	2.25Y	3.51Y	3.08Y	4.64Y	4.87Y	1.00Y	1.12Y	1.33Y	1.46Y	1.62Y	1.94Y	2.02Y
Thailand	578	.45Y	.63Y	.54Y	.84Y	1.02Y	1.24Y	1.60Y	.99Y	1.12Y	1.38Y	2.25Y	2.51Y	3.12Y	4.61Y
Vietnam	582	.04Y	.06Y	.11Y	.13Y	.18Y	.12Y	.06Y	.18Y	.13Y	.22Y	.33Y	.47Y	.45Y	.16Y
Asia n.s.	598	.06Y	.04Y	.04Y	.05Y	.05Y	.20Y	.22Y	.15Y	.03Y	.04Y	.04Y	.09Y	.24Y	.27Y
Europe	**170**	**2.3Y**	**2.5Y**	**2.7Y**	**3.6Y**	**4.6Y**	**5.9Y**	**7.5Y**	**4.5Y**	**4.8Y**	**6.1Y**	**8.7Y**	**11.0Y**	**12.7Y**	**17.6Y**
Albania	914	—Y	.01Y	—Y	—Y	.01Y	.01Y	.01Y	—Y	—Y	—Y	—Y	—Y	—Y	—Y
Azerbaijan	912	—Y	—Y	—Y	—Y	.04Y	.04Y	.01Y	—Y	—Y	—Y	—Y	—Y	—Y	—Y
Belarus	913	.01Y	.01Y	.01Y	.01Y	.02Y	.03Y	.03Y	.02Y	.04Y	.05Y	.02Y	.03Y	.06Y	.07Y
Bosnia & Herzegovina	963	—	—	—Y	—Y	—Y	—Y	—Y	—Y	—Y	—Y	—Y	—Y	.01Y	.01Y
Bulgaria	918	.04Y	.02Y	.02Y	.04Y	.05Y	.12Y	.15Y	.08Y	.09Y	.08Y	.12Y	.16Y	.15Y	.28Y
Croatia	960	.03Y	.07Y	.03Y	.03Y	.04Y	.05Y	.07Y	.15Y	.23Y	.13Y	.30Y	.37Y	.22Y	.09Y
Czech Republic	935	.03Y	.04Y	.06Y	.18Y	.19Y	.15Y	.31Y	.14Y	.17Y	.28Y	.38Y	.56Y	.66Y	.84Y
Czechoslovakia n.s.	937	—Y	—Y	—Y	—Y	—Y	—Y	—Y	.01Y	—Y	—Y	.01Y	.01Y	—Y	—Y
Estonia	939	.01Y	.02Y	.02Y	.01Y	.01Y	.01Y	.01Y	.02Y	.02Y	.02Y	.02Y	.05Y	.19Y	.43Y
Faroe Islands	816	—Y	—Y	—Y	—Y	—Y	—Y	—Y	.01Y	.02Y	.03Y	.04Y	.05Y	.07Y	.09Y
Georgia	915	—Y	—Y	—Y	.01Y	—Y	.01Y	.01Y	—Y	.01Y	.01Y	—Y	—Y	.01Y	.01Y
Gibraltar	823	.02Y	.03Y	.03Y	.03Y	.04Y	.03Y	.04Y	—Y	—Y	—Y	—Y	—Y	.01Y	.01Y
Hungary	944	.02Y	.02Y	.03Y	.03Y	.04Y	.03Y	.06Y	.15Y	.19Y	.31Y	.45Y	.75Y	1.08Y	1.28Y
Kazakhstan	916	.01Y	.01Y	.01Y	.02Y	.02Y	.03Y	.05Y	—Y	.04Y	.02Y	.02Y	.02Y	.04Y	.04Y
Latvia	941	—Y	—Y	—Y	.01Y	.01Y	.01Y	.01Y	—Y	.01Y	.01Y	.02Y	.03Y	.06Y	.15Y
Lithuania	946	.02Y	.03Y	.02Y	.03Y	.03Y	.06Y	.05Y	.02Y	.01Y	.02Y	.03Y	.05Y	.05Y	.13Y
Macedonia, FYR	962	—Y	—Y	—Y	.01Y	—Y	.01Y	.01Y	—Y	—Y	—Y	—Y	—Y	—Y	—Y
Moldova	921	—Y	—Y	—Y	—Y	—Y	—Y	—Y	.01Y	.01Y	—Y	.02Y	.01Y	.01Y	.02Y
Poland	964	.23Y	.26Y	.31Y	.37Y	.34Y	.61Y	.79Y	.47Y	.39Y	.42Y	.59Y	.75Y	.83Y	1.25Y
Romania	968	.05Y	.07Y	.05Y	.06Y	.09Y	.09Y	.14Y	.18Y	.18Y	.21Y	.28Y	.42Y	.43Y	.49Y
Russia	922	.15Y	.39Y	.36Y	.45Y	.71Y	.73Y	1.16Y	1.05Y	1.32Y	1.69Y	2.03Y	2.63Y	2.49Y	3.93Y
Serbia & Montenegro	965	.04	.04Y	.04Y	.06Y	.08Y	.10Y	.12Y	.01Y	.02Y	.02Y	.03Y	.04Y	.05Y	.06Y
Slovak Republic	936	.01Y	.01Y	.01Y	.01Y	.01Y	.04Y	.04Y	.02Y	.03Y	.04Y	.09Y	.15Y	.19Y	.25Y
Tajikistan	923	.01Y	.01Y	—Y	—Y	—Y	.02Y	—Y	.01Y	.02Y	.02Y	.03Y	.03Y	.04Y	.05Y
Turkey	186	1.24Y	1.32Y	1.50Y	1.90Y	2.44Y	2.98Y	3.49Y	.94Y	1.07Y	1.54Y	2.36Y	2.72Y	3.46Y	4.89Y
Ukraine	926	.06Y	.10Y	.11Y	.17Y	.30Y	.35Y	.46Y	.51Y	.72Y	.89Y	1.56Y	1.76Y	2.17Y	2.75Y
U.S.S.R. n.s.	930	.08Y	—Y	—Y	—Y	—Y	—Y	—Y	.12Y	.13Y	.12Y	.07Y	.05Y	.03Y	.04Y
Uzbekistan	927	—	—	—	—	—	—Y	—Y	.01Y	—Y	—Y	—Y	—Y	—Y	—Y
Yugoslavia n.s.	966	—Y	.01Y	.01Y	.01Y	.01Y	.01Y	.01Y	—Y	.01Y	—Y	—Y	—Y	—Y	—Y
Europe n.s.	884	.18Y	.05Y	.07Y	.10Y	.12Y	.33Y	.40Y	.60Y	.12Y	.16Y	.24Y	.30Y	.40Y	.49Y
Middle East	**407**	**2.6Y**	**2.8Y**	**3.5Y**	**3.7Y**	**4.5Y**	**5.7Y**	**7.1Y**	**8.7Y**	**8.2Y**	**10.5Y**	**15.0Y**	**16.1Y**	**25.3Y**	**26.9Y**
Bahrain	419	.02Y	.03Y	.06Y	.03Y	.04Y	.04Y	.06Y	.33Y	.29Y	.45Y	.62Y	.89Y	.77Y	.85Y
Egypt	469	.40Y	.41Y	.46Y	.60Y	.71Y	.86Y	1.25Y	.30Y	.36Y	.59Y	.74Y	1.11Y	1.33Y	1.52Y
Iran, I.R. of	429	.14Y	.11Y	.14Y	.14Y	.22Y	.33Y	.37Y	1.46Y	1.33Y	1.57Y	3.08Y	3.32Y	4.01Y	4.49Y
Iraq	433	.16Y	.15Y	.08Y	.11Y	.10Y	.14Y	.17Y	.49Y	.37Y	.01Y	.07Y	.06Y	.25Y	.38Y
Israel	436	.56Y	.61Y	.55Y	.68Y	.82Y	.73Y	.92Y	.24Y	.24Y	.32Y	.45Y	.57Y	.64Y	.93Y

	Exports 2001	Exports 2002	Exports 2003	Exports 2004	Exports 2005	Exports 2006	Exports 2007	Imports 2001	Imports 2002	Imports 2003	Imports 2004	Imports 2005	Imports 2006	Imports 2007
	Billions of U.S. Dollars							*Billions of U.S. Dollars*						
Jordan........ 439	.07Y	.06Y	.07Y	.06Y	.08Y	.06Y	.09Y	.08Y	.11Y	.12Y	.15Y	.17Y	.19Y	.23Y
Kuwait........ 443	.03Y	.03Y	.05Y	.05Y	.07Y	.08Y	.11Y	.15Y	.27Y	.20Y	.19Y	.24Y	.25Y	.25Y
Lebanon........ 446	.05Y	.06Y	.07Y	.09Y	.12Y	.11Y	.15Y	.08Y	.14Y	.10Y	.13Y	.17Y	.20Y	.26Y
Libya........ 672	.31Y	.41Y	.42Y	.40Y	.52Y	.67Y	.86Y	.42Y	.42Y	.45Y	.50Y	.63Y	.87Y	1.07Y
Oman........ 449	.01Y	.02Y	.03Y	.04Y	.05Y	.08Y	.08Y	.07Y	.06Y	.09Y	.11Y	.28Y	2.20Y	.67Y
Qatar........ 453	.01Y	.01Y	.01Y	.01Y	.02Y	.04Y	.06Y	.07Y	.08Y	.09Y	.19Y	.29Y	.36Y	.31Y
Saudi Arabia........ 456	.27Y	.41Y	.75Y	.56Y	.37Y	.69Y	1.00Y	3.48Y	3.05Y	4.48Y	5.83Y	4.12Y	8.97Y	9.79Y
Syrian Arab Republic........ 463	.05Y	.05Y	.07Y	.11Y	.14Y	.17Y	.20Y	.07Y	.18Y	.18Y	.26Y	.37Y	.42Y	.53Y
United Arab Emirates........ 466	.41Y	.29Y	.65Y	.71Y	1.04Y	1.47Y	1.63Y	1.12Y	.97Y	1.55Y	2.21Y	3.29Y	4.23Y	4.82Y
Yemen, Republic of........ 474	.12Y	.10Y	.12Y	.11Y	.15Y	.21Y	.20Y	.18Y	.10Y	.08Y	.16Y	.15Y	.07Y	.25Y
Middle East n.s........ 489	—Y	—Y	.01Y	—Y	—Y	—Y	—Y	.16Y	.18Y	.22Y	.33Y	.41Y	.51Y	.61Y
Western Hemisphere........ 207	**4.0Y**	**4.0Y**	**4.6Y**	**8.1Y**	**10.1Y**	**12.3Y**	**14.9Y**	**3.4Y**	**3.4Y**	**4.5Y**	**7.2Y**	**9.3Y**	**11.9Y**	**15.5Y**
Antigua and Barbuda........ 311	.01Y	—Y	—Y	—Y	.01Y	.01Y	.01Y	—Y	—Y	—Y	—Y	—Y	—Y	.01Y
Argentina........ 213	.16Y	.12Y	.11Y	.12Y	.13Y	.19Y	.18Y	.86Y	.87Y	1.10Y	2.01Y	2.02Y	2.75Y	4.48Y
Aruba........ 314	.01Y	.01Y	.01Y	.01Y	.02Y	.02Y	.02Y	.01Y	.01Y	.01Y	.01Y	.01Y	.02Y	.02Y
Bahamas, The........ 313	—Y	.03Y	—Y	—Y	.01Y	.01Y	.01Y	—Y	—Y	—Y	—Y	.01Y	—Y	.02Y
Barbados........ 316	—Y	—Y	—Y	—Y	—Y	—Y	.01Y	—Y	—Y	—Y	.01Y	—Y	—Y	—Y
Belize........ 339	—Y	—Y	—Y	—Y	—Y	—Y	—Y	—Y	—Y	.01Y	.02Y	.02Y	.03Y	.04Y
Bermuda........ 319	—Y	—Y	—Y	—Y	—Y	—Y	.09Y	.01Y	—Y	—Y	.01Y	—Y	.01Y	.01Y
Bolivia........ 218	—Y	—Y	—Y	—Y	—Y	—Y	—Y	—Y	—Y	—Y	—Y	—Y	—Y	.02Y
Brazil........ 223	2.73Y	2.92Y	3.27Y	6.06Y	6.50Y	7.82Y	10.27Y	1.73Y	1.76Y	2.24Y	3.83Y	5.26Y	6.50Y	7.51Y
Chile........ 228	.18Y	.22Y	.21Y	.88Y	1.44Y	1.86Y	1.20Y	.04Y	.05Y	.10Y	.10Y	.13Y	.18Y	.22Y
Colombia........ 233	.03Y	.04Y	.06Y	.04Y	.05Y	.06Y	.10Y	.03Y	.03Y	.06Y	.09Y	.06Y	.09Y	.31Y
Costa Rica........ 238	—Y	—Y	.01Y	.01Y	—Y	.01Y	.01Y	.01Y	.02Y	.02Y	.05Y	.06Y	.05Y	.05Y
Dominican Republic........ 243	—Y	—Y	.03Y	.04Y	.05Y	.06Y	.07Y	—Y	.01Y	.01Y	.01Y	.01Y	.01Y	.02Y
Ecuador........ 248	.02Y	.02Y	.01Y	.01Y	.09Y	.10Y	.12Y	.02Y	.07Y	.04Y	.07Y	.11Y	.11Y	.13Y
El Salvador........ 253	—Y	—Y	—Y	—Y	.01Y	.01Y	.01Y	—Y	—Y	—Y	—Y	—Y	—Y	—Y
Guatemala........ 258	—Y	—Y	—Y	—Y	—Y	.01Y	—Y	.01Y	.01Y	.02Y	.01Y	.01Y	.01Y	.02Y
Honduras........ 268	—Y	—Y	—Y	.01Y	.01Y	.01Y	.01Y	—Y	—Y	—Y	—Y	—Y	—Y	—Y
Jamaica........ 343	—Y	—Y	—Y	.01Y	.03Y	.01Y	.07Y	.03Y	.03Y	.02Y	.01Y	.02Y	.01Y	—Y
Mexico........ 273	.29Y	.23Y	.21Y	.26Y	.29Y	.62Y	.84Y	.27Y	.22Y	.26Y	.23Y	.41Y	.53Y	.54Y
Netherlands Antilles........ 353	—Y	.01Y	.01Y	.01Y	.01Y	.01Y	.01Y	.02Y	.01Y	.04Y	.04Y	.08Y	.08Y	.10Y
Nicaragua........ 278	—Y	—Y	.01Y	—Y	.01Y	.05Y	.03Y	—Y	—Y	—Y	—Y	—Y	—Y	—Y
Panama........ 283	.13Y	.01Y	.02Y	.03Y	.34Y	.23Y	.02Y	.02Y	.01Y	.24Y	.02Y	.07Y	.02Y	.01Y
Paraguay........ 288	—Y	—Y	—Y	—Y	—Y	—Y	—Y	.01Y	.01Y	.03Y	.08Y	.05Y	.04Y	.05Y
Peru........ 293	.04Y	.05Y	.15Y	.02Y	.39Y	.34Y	.61Y	.02Y	.02Y	.04Y	.05Y	.06Y	.12Y	.24Y
St. Vincent & Grens........ 364	—Y	—Y	—Y	—Y	—Y	—Y	—Y	.01Y	—Y	—Y	—Y	—Y	—Y	—Y
Suriname........ 366	—Y	—Y	—Y	—Y	—Y	—Y	—Y	.01Y	.02Y	.01Y	.02Y	.02Y	.02Y	.03Y
Trinidad and Tobago........ 369	.07Y	.15Y	.22Y	.29Y	.35Y	.41Y	.50Y	.01Y	.01Y	.01Y	.01Y	.02Y	.03Y	.04Y
Uruguay........ 298	.08Y	.05Y	.07Y	.15Y	.31Y	.38Y	.63Y	.02Y	.05Y	.07Y	.08Y	.12Y	.18Y	.20Y
Venezuela, Rep. Bol........ 299	.14Y	.03Y	.02Y	.03Y	.03Y	.03Y	.05Y	.05Y	.06Y	.06Y	.11Y	.15Y	.25Y	.33Y
Western Hem. n.s........ 399	.10Y	.06Y	.12Y	.12Y	.04Y	.02Y	.03Y	.20Y	.07Y	.05Y	.34Y	.60Y	.87Y	1.14Y
Other Countries n.i.e........ 910	**.3Y**	**.4Y**	**.3Y**	**.3Y**	**.4Y**	**.5Y**	**.7Y**	**.1Y**	**.1Y**	**.1Y**	**.1Y**	**.2Y**	**.2Y**	**.2Y**
Cuba........ 928	.03Y	.02Y	.02Y	.02Y	.03Y	.04Y	.04Y	.04Y	.05Y	.05Y	.06Y	.07Y	.08Y	.10Y
North Korea........ 954	.30Y	.40Y	.28Y	.26Y	.34Y	.50Y	.65Y	.03Y	.04Y	.06Y	.08Y	.09Y	.11Y	.14Y
Countries & Areas n.s........ 898	**8.0Y**	**8.0Y**	**6.2Y**	**7.3Y**	**6.8Y**	**2.6Y**	**3.2Y**	**1.0Y**	**1.3Y**	**3.4Y**	**4.6Y**	**5.3Y**	**6.4Y**	**8.3Y**
Special Categories........ 899	**1.9Y**	**.7Y**	**.9Y**	**.7Y**	**.9Y**	**.7Y**	**.8Y**	**.1Y**	**.2Y**	**.2Y**	**.5Y**	**.4Y**	**.5Y**	**.6Y**
Memorandum Items														
European Union........ 998	51.74Y	53.79Y	61.47Y	71.99Y	88.56Y	100.47Y	109.41Y	50.44Y	52.72Y	67.17Y	81.75Y	90.81Y	104.05Y	136.28Y
Oil Exporting Ctys........ 999	3.27Y	4.04Y	4.54Y	5.59Y	5.58Y	6.16Y	8.00Y	10.10Y	9.63Y	11.95Y	17.13Y	18.27Y	28.69Y	31.21Y
Non-Oil Develop.Ctys........ 201	29.48Y	32.33Y	39.93Y	52.03Y	65.88Y	85.03Y	106.37Y	33.60Y	36.57Y	46.10Y	67.03Y	85.05Y	108.80Y	141.13Y
PERCENT DISTRIBUTION														
Industrial Countries........ 101	**63.9**	**63.4**	**65.7**	**65.4**	**67.1**	**66.9**	**64.1**	**59.9**	**59.7**	**58.4**	**54.1**	**52.5**	**48.3**	**48.9**
Developing Countries........ 202	**27.5**	**29.2**	**29.4**	**30.2**	**29.5**	**31.7**	**34.5**	**39.0**	**39.0**	**39.0**	**43.2**	**44.9**	**49.2**	**48.5**
Africa........ 607	**9.3**	**10.2**	**9.8**	**9.5**	**9.0**	**8.8**	**9.7**	**10.5**	**10.4**	**9.7**	**10.1**	**10.1**	**10.1**	**10.0**
Asia........ 507	**10.7**	**11.5**	**12.4**	**12.7**	**12.6**	**14.6**	**15.8**	**13.7**	**14.8**	**15.1**	**17.2**	**19.0**	**21.2**	**21.6**
Europe........ 170	**1.9**	**2.0**	**1.8**	**1.9**	**1.9**	**2.0**	**2.2**	**4.1**	**4.1**	**4.1**	**4.5**	**4.8**	**4.5**	**5.0**
Middle East........ 407	**2.2**	**2.2**	**2.3**	**1.9**	**1.8**	**2.0**	**2.1**	**7.8**	**6.9**	**7.0**	**7.7**	**7.0**	**9.0**	**7.6**
Western Hemisphere........ 207	**3.4**	**3.2**	**3.0**	**4.3**	**4.2**	**4.3**	**4.5**	**3.0**	**2.8**	**3.0**	**3.7**	**4.1**	**4.3**	**4.4**
Other Countries n.i.e........ 910	**.3**	**.3**	**.2**	**.1**	**.2**	**.2**	**.2**	**.1**	**.1**	**.1**	**.1**	**.1**	**.1**	**.1**
ANNUAL PERCENT CHANGE														
World........ 001	**−11.2**	**4.4**	**21.5**	**26.0**	**27.0**	**18.8**	**15.5**	**4.3**	**5.7**	**25.7**	**30.8**	**18.1**	**21.6**	**27.0**
Industrial Countries........ 101	**−11.3**	**3.5**	**26.0**	**25.4**	**30.3**	**18.5**	**10.6**	**2.2**	**5.3**	**23.1**	**21.0**	**14.7**	**11.8**	**28.7**
Developing Countries........ 202	**−12.8**	**11.1**	**22.3**	**29.6**	**24.0**	**27.6**	**25.4**	**7.7**	**5.7**	**25.7**	**45.0**	**22.8**	**33.1**	**25.3**
Africa........ 607	**−1.9**	**14.3**	**16.8**	**21.9**	**19.9**	**16.9**	**27.0**	**6.9**	**4.5**	**18.1**	**36.4**	**17.6**	**21.9**	**25.3**
Asia........ 507	**−22.8**	**13.0**	**31.1**	**28.1**	**26.6**	**37.3**	**25.4**	**11.0**	**14.4**	**28.5**	**48.4**	**30.7**	**35.7**	**29.5**
Europe........ 170	**−13.4**	**12.4**	**6.1**	**32.1**	**28.9**	**27.5**	**27.3**	**23.3**	**6.7**	**26.0**	**42.9**	**25.9**	**15.8**	**38.8**
Middle East........ 407	**8.5**	**5.9**	**28.1**	**4.8**	**20.6**	**27.1**	**25.5**	**−10.0**	**−6.0**	**28.1**	**43.4**	**7.0**	**57.1**	**6.6**
Western Hemisphere........ 207	**−14.7**	**−1.3**	**14.1**	**78.4**	**24.8**	**21.4**	**21.3**	**38.0**	**−.8**	**32.1**	**61.9**	**29.3**	**27.7**	**30.4**
Other Countries n.i.e........ 910	**9.8**	**26.3**	**−27.1**	**−6.2**	**31.6**	**44.0**	**29.0**	**20.1**	**22.4**	**28.4**	**27.6**	**12.5**	**23.4**	**25.8**

	Exports							Imports						
	2001	2002	2003	2004	2005	2006	2007	2001	2002	2003	2004	2005	2006	2007
	Billions of U.S. Dollars							Billions of U.S. Dollars						
IFS World Total	**1,183.6**	**1,300.8**	**1,540.6**	**1,958.1**	**2,323.9**	**2,768.5**	**3,237.9**	**1,125.1**	**1,223.0**	**1,465.1**	**1,880.0**	**2,212.4**	**2,578.4**	**2,977.4**
DOTS World Total 001	**1,189.6Y**	**1,302.0Y**	**1,570.6Y**	**1,963.9Y**	**2,320.3Y**	**2,772.8Y**	**3,246.7Y**	**1,126.0Y**	**1,218.0Y**	**1,468.7Y**	**1,881.0Y**	**2,189.4Y**	**2,574.3Y**	**3,010.1Y**
Industrial Countries 101	**610.6Y**	**639.6Y**	**739.9Y**	**907.5Y**	**1,051.0Y**	**1,220.3Y**	**1,363.0Y**	**510.0Y**	**530.0Y**	**617.6Y**	**768.7Y**	**835.1Y**	**933.8Y**	**1,082.5Y**
United States 111	242.18Y	262.22Y	289.24Y	347.17Y	400.08Y	466.22Y	497.96Y	134.43Y	132.45Y	144.57Y	174.78Y	187.79Y	215.02Y	248.84Y
Canada 156	13.59Y	14.93Y	16.83Y	21.21Y	25.34Y	31.54Y	36.78Y	10.39Y	10.27Y	11.38Y	15.59Y	16.99Y	19.03Y	24.84Y
Australia 193	20.80Y	23.52Y	29.65Y	38.01Y	45.89Y	55.04Y	65.49Y	27.19Y	27.26Y	29.51Y	39.53Y	52.22Y	62.68Y	74.15Y
Japan 158	141.98Y	139.81Y	160.05Y	192.47Y	214.14Y	238.03Y	253.84Y	180.34Y	196.65Y	238.97Y	299.05Y	316.31Y	338.79Y	373.34Y
New Zealand 196	2.43Y	2.80Y	3.60Y	4.84Y	5.88Y	6.65Y	7.88Y	4.09Y	3.98Y	4.45Y	5.51Y	5.83Y	6.23Y	7.61Y
Austria 122	1.98Y	2.17Y	2.59Y	3.23Y	3.74Y	4.18Y	4.69Y	2.42Y	2.78Y	3.21Y	4.27Y	4.81Y	6.14Y	7.52Y
Belgium 124	11.10Y	11.66Y	13.59Y	17.00Y	20.40Y	25.45Y	30.56Y	9.29Y	10.20Y	11.82Y	13.99Y	15.07Y	17.76Y	21.09Y
Belgium-Luxembourg n.s. 127	.12Y	.26Y	.17	.30Y	.32Y	.36Y	.40Y	.16Y	.17Y	.20	.21Y	.24Y	.24Y	.22Y
Cyprus 423	.90Y	1.12Y	.89Y	1.69Y	1.41Y	2.08Y	2.32Y	.04Y	.05Y	.06Y	.12Y	.07Y	.06Y	.46Y
Denmark 128	2.99Y	3.00Y	4.02Y	5.33Y	6.61Y	7.82Y	8.55Y	2.50Y	2.51Y	3.03Y	3.66Y	3.95Y	4.38Y	5.14Y
Finland 172	3.06Y	3.58Y	4.95Y	7.36Y	9.58Y	10.84Y	11.94Y	4.96Y	3.71Y	4.34Y	6.22Y	6.32Y	6.80Y	8.40Y
France 132	16.43Y	16.66Y	22.17Y	27.83Y	32.35Y	35.89Y	45.25Y	19.18Y	17.85Y	21.33Y	25.96Y	30.10Y	36.44Y	43.79Y
Germany 134	40.36Y	40.67Y	51.52Y	65.21Y	78.32Y	90.43Y	104.46Y	41.60Y	45.82Y	59.54Y	72.02Y	77.29Y	91.91Y	109.69Y
Greece 174	2.96Y	3.38Y	4.11Y	4.64Y	5.53Y	6.94Y	7.37Y	.29Y	.28Y	.37Y	.41Y	.41Y	.54Y	.71Y
Iceland 176	.11Y	.06Y	.10Y	.11Y	.16Y	.17Y	.20Y	.05Y	.06Y	.06Y	.08Y	.08Y	.08Y	.08Y
Ireland 178	4.28Y	4.08Y	5.11Y	6.13Y	7.48Y	8.73Y	9.17Y	4.29Y	4.20Y	4.65Y	5.72Y	6.38Y	6.91Y	8.02Y
Italy 136	14.01Y	15.09Y	19.03Y	24.62Y	29.12Y	36.36Y	44.01Y	14.45Y	15.23Y	16.99Y	20.70Y	22.82Y	27.42Y	32.96Y
Luxembourg 137	.38Y	.90Y	1.16Y	1.52Y	2.63Y	2.66Y	2.38Y	.13Y	.12Y	.23Y	.28Y	.33Y	.37Y	.53Y
Malta 181	.91Y	1.01Y	.93Y	1.34Y	1.25Y	1.73Y	1.67Y	.54Y	.87Y	1.07Y	1.08Y	.84Y	1.08Y	1.46Y
Netherlands 138	33.83Y	35.18Y	40.98Y	50.99Y	62.18Y	69.87Y	84.15Y	9.40Y	9.46Y	10.17Y	13.77Y	15.44Y	17.96Y	22.74Y
Norway 142	1.64Y	1.79Y	2.56Y	2.38Y	3.00Y	4.03Y	4.41Y	1.84Y	2.45Y	2.47Y	3.18Y	3.50Y	3.91Y	6.02Y
Portugal 182	1.28Y	1.28Y	1.47Y	1.88Y	2.58Y	3.10Y	4.16Y	.34Y	.43Y	.67Y	.97Y	1.05Y	1.04Y	1.57Y
Slovenia 961	.25Y	.27Y	.37Y	.49Y	.63Y	.92Y	1.50Y	.09Y	.16Y	.20Y	.17Y	.19Y	.28Y	.34Y
Spain 184	9.36Y	9.76Y	12.79Y	16.41Y	20.76Y	26.56Y	33.76Y	3.19Y	3.35Y	4.03Y	4.97Y	5.81Y	7.39Y	9.82Y
Sweden 144	3.43Y	3.34Y	4.22Y	5.17Y	6.35Y	7.64Y	9.42Y	6.16Y	5.67Y	7.05Y	9.10Y	9.51Y	10.68Y	12.23Y
Switzerland 146	4.46Y	4.06Y	4.92Y	5.94Y	6.59Y	8.72Y	10.49Y	11.06Y	13.54Y	16.02Y	21.03Y	23.72Y	19.21Y	23.99Y
United Kingdom 112	35.82Y	36.96Y	42.86Y	54.24Y	58.70Y	68.32Y	80.16Y	21.57Y	20.41Y	21.20Y	26.30Y	28.01Y	31.40Y	36.95Y
Developing Countries 202	**571.9Y**	**655.7Y**	**820.2Y**	**1,048.8Y**	**1,258.8Y**	**1,542.2Y**	**1,869.1Y**	**589.2Y**	**651.0Y**	**799.1Y**	**1,040.3Y**	**1,251.1Y**	**1,509.0Y**	**1,769.6Y**
Africa 607	**17.4Y**	**19.4Y**	**24.5Y**	**33.6Y**	**41.3Y**	**53.4Y**	**68.4Y**	**17.0Y**	**17.3Y**	**21.2Y**	**32.9Y**	**37.9Y**	**47.6Y**	**58.3Y**
Algeria 612	.58Y	.88Y	1.24Y	1.87Y	2.39Y	3.07Y	4.45Y	.68Y	.46Y	.54Y	.80Y	.82Y	1.30Y	2.40Y
Angola 614	.88Y	.23Y	.41Y	2.32Y	2.29Y	2.43Y	2.01Y	1.44Y	2.06Y	3.33Y	6.05Y	7.82Y	13.33Y	15.50Y
Benin 638	.65Y	.59Y	.69Y	.83Y	1.42Y	2.12Y	2.87Y	.10Y	.10Y	.17Y	.23Y	.24Y	.21Y	.27Y
Botswana 616	.03Y	.03Y	.04Y	.08Y	.09Y	.12Y	.19Y	—Y	—Y	.08Y	.09Y	.12Y	.11Y	.14Y
Burkina Faso 748	.02Y	.03Y	.05Y	.05Y	.05Y	.06Y	.10Y	.03Y	.04Y	.10Y	.20Y	.23Y	.25Y	.24Y
Burundi 618	.01Y	.01Y	.01Y	.02Y	.03Y	.04Y	.05Y	—Y	—Y	—Y	—Y	—Y	.01Y	.01Y
Cameroon 622	.11Y	.18Y	.19Y	.28Y	.41Y	.47Y	.63Y	.39Y	.18Y	.27Y	.66Y	.52Y	.74Y	.77Y
Cape Verde 624	—Y	.01Y	.01Y	.01Y	.01Y	.01Y	.02Y	—Y	—Y	—Y	—Y	—Y	—Y	—Y
Central African Rep. 626	.01Y	—Y	.01Y	.01Y	.01Y	.01Y	.02Y	.02Y	.01Y	.01Y	.02Y	.02Y	.02Y	.03Y
Chad 628	—Y	.01Y	.01Y	.01Y	.02Y	.02Y	.08Y	—Y	.01Y	.01Y	.26Y	.34Y	.41Y	.11Y
Comoros 632	.01Y	.02Y	.01Y	.02Y	.02Y	.03Y	.04Y	.01Y	—Y	—Y	.01Y	.01Y	—Y	—Y
Congo, Dem. Rep. of 636	.04Y	.06Y	.07Y	.08Y	.09Y	.11Y	.14Y	.01Y	.01Y	.03Y	.12Y	.19Y	.38Y	.48Y
Congo, Republic of 634	.13Y	.16Y	.19Y	.26Y	.34Y	.48Y	1.19Y	1.40Y	1.16Y	1.75Y	2.73Y	3.54Y	4.67Y	3.59Y
Côte d'Ivoire 662	.48Y	.45Y	.47Y	.38Y	.46Y	.64Y	.93Y	.20Y	.19Y	.24Y	.39Y	.40Y	.49Y	.34Y
Djibouti 611	.12Y	.13Y	.21Y	.26Y	.43Y	.56Y	.67Y	—Y	.01Y	.01Y	.01Y	.01Y	.01Y	.01Y
Equatorial Guinea 642	—Y	.01Y	.01Y	.02Y	.03Y	.20Y	.11Y	.39Y	.37Y	.47Y	1.67Y	1.98Y	3.41Y	2.90Y
Ethiopia 644	.21Y	.23Y	.30Y	.34Y	.48Y	.69Y	1.06Y	.03Y	.04Y	.03Y	.04Y	.13Y	.16Y	.14Y
Gabon 646	.05Y	.05Y	.06Y	.06Y	.10Y	.15Y	.23Y	.46Y	.40Y	.49Y	.59Y	.64Y	1.33Y	1.82Y
Gambia, The 648	.12Y	.13Y	.17Y	.18Y	.20Y	.23Y	.29Y	—Y	.01Y	.01Y	.01Y	.02Y	.02Y	.03Y
Ghana 652	.43Y	.49Y	.81Y	1.12Y	1.30Y	1.59Y	2.26Y	.09Y	.09Y	.12Y	.19Y	.25Y	.36Y	.39Y
Guinea 656	.12Y	.14Y	.18Y	.23Y	.29Y	.34Y	.47Y	.05Y	.19Y	.15Y	.16Y	.20Y	.18Y	.28Y
Guinea-Bissau 654	.03Y	.01Y	.02Y	.01Y	.02Y	.02Y	.03Y	.11Y	.06Y	.05Y	.07Y	.09Y	.11Y	.14Y
Kenya 664	.52Y	.68Y	.80Y	1.13Y	1.45Y	1.93Y	2.46Y	.31Y	.29Y	.34Y	.37Y	.39Y	.47Y	.55Y
Lesotho 666	.10Y	.16Y	.19Y	.24Y	.20Y	.24Y	.25Y	.05Y	—Y	—Y	—Y	—Y	—Y	—Y
Liberia 668	1.47Y	1.85Y	2.06Y	2.47Y	2.93Y	4.77Y	5.18Y	.18Y	.08Y	.10Y	.11Y	.15Y	.16Y	.37Y
Madagascar 674	.29Y	.17Y	.37Y	.44Y	.49Y	.53Y	.76Y	.12Y	.05Y	.06Y	.07Y	.07Y	.08Y	.10Y
Malawi 676	.04Y	.05Y	.07Y	.10Y	.09Y	.12Y	.15Y	.01Y	.02Y	.01Y	.02Y	.02Y	.03Y	.05Y
Mali 678	.08Y	.08Y	.10Y	.11Y	.11Y	.13Y	.19Y	.07Y	.07Y	.13Y	.23Y	.17Y	.22Y	.11Y
Mauritania 682	.08Y	.10Y	.11Y	.13Y	.15Y	.21Y	.29Y	.02Y	.03Y	.02Y	.06Y	.01Y	.41Y	.57Y
Mauritius 684	.60Y	.61Y	.68Y	.77Y	.80Y	1.08Y	1.52Y	.04Y	.05Y	.05Y	.05Y	.08Y	.08Y	.07Y
Morocco 686	.63Y	.85Y	1.23Y	1.61Y	1.93Y	2.50Y	3.38Y	.76Y	.75Y	.80Y	1.07Y	1.46Y	1.84Y	2.10Y
Mozambique 688	.09Y	.17Y	.21Y	.30Y	.37Y	.37Y	.50Y	.04Y	.09Y	.08Y	.11Y	.14Y	.14Y	.23Y
Namibia 728	.05Y	.05Y	.07Y	.09Y	.09Y	.18Y	.29Y	.02Y	.04Y	.05Y	.07Y	.19Y	.41Y	.36Y
Niger 692	.04Y	.09Y	.09Y	.15Y	.15Y	.22Y	.20Y	.06Y	.01Y	—Y	.06Y	—Y	.01Y	.01Y
Nigeria 694	2.92Y	3.48Y	4.15Y	4.34Y	5.16Y	5.79Y	8.90Y	3.39Y	1.79Y	1.50Y	2.58Y	2.08Y	1.21Y	2.19Y
Rwanda 714	.01Y	.01Y	.01Y	.01Y	.03Y	.03Y	.05Y	.03Y	.08Y	.08Y	.31Y	.03Y	.04Y	.06Y
São Tomé & Príncipe 716	—Y	—Y	—Y	—Y	.01Y	—Y	—Y	—Y	—Y	—Y	—Y	—Y	—Y	—Y
Senegal 722	.29Y	.31Y	.32Y	.44Y	.51Y	.47Y	.76Y	.12Y	.18Y	.18Y	.20Y	.30Y	.12Y	.16Y
Seychelles 718	.05Y	.05Y	.05Y	.06Y	.08Y	.11Y	.11Y	.02Y	.02Y	.06Y	.01Y	.02Y	.01Y	.02Y
Sierra Leone 724	.05Y	.05Y	.05Y	.07Y	.10Y	.12Y	.16Y	—Y	.01Y	.01Y	.01Y	.01Y	.01Y	.01Y

		Exports							Imports						
		2001	2002	2003	2004	2005	2006	2007	2001	2002	2003	2004	2005	2006	2007
		Billions of U.S. Dollars							Billions of U.S. Dollars						
Somalia	726	.05Y	.05Y	.06Y	.08Y	.09Y	.11Y	.13Y	.01Y	.03Y	.02Y	.03Y	.03Y	.03Y	.03Y
South Africa	199	3.81Y	4.16Y	5.63Y	8.36Y	10.68Y	14.44Y	16.68Y	4.19Y	5.80Y	7.09Y	9.36Y	10.25Y	9.66Y	13.67Y
Sudan	732	.55Y	.76Y	.85Y	1.38Y	2.12Y	2.55Y	2.58Y	1.15Y	1.32Y	1.64Y	2.04Y	2.85Y	2.33Y	4.92Y
Swaziland	734	.06Y	.08Y	.14Y	.12Y	.09Y	.10Y	.10Y	.09Y	.11Y	.10Y	.15Y	.24Y	.28Y	.17Y
Tanzania	738	.33Y	.42Y	.59Y	.63Y	.79Y	1.01Y	1.39Y	.18Y	.15Y	.22Y	.30Y	.40Y	.44Y	.53Y
Togo	742	.28Y	.34Y	.46Y	.81Y	.93Y	1.15Y	1.98Y	.06Y	.06Y	.09Y	.13Y	.14Y	.14Y	.18Y
Tunisia	744	.34Y	.36Y	.43Y	.54Y	.63Y	.76Y	.95Y	.14Y	.18Y	.14Y	.24Y	.25Y	.30Y	.30Y
Uganda	746	.11Y	.12Y	.17Y	.19Y	.20Y	.29Y	.39Y	.03Y	.03Y	.03Y	.05Y	.06Y	.05Y	.07Y
Zambia	754	.07Y	.08Y	.10Y	.13Y	.14Y	.21Y	.39Y	.22Y	.20Y	.22Y	.61Y	.75Y	1.37Y	1.57Y
Zimbabwe	698	.10Y	.10Y	.10Y	.18Y	.20Y	.20Y	.27Y	.25Y	.26Y	.26Y	.29Y	.29Y	.26Y	.28Y
Africa n.s.	799	.31Y	.31Y	.24Y	.29Y	.31Y	.33Y	.49Y	—Y	.17Y	—Y	—Y	—Y	—Y	.06Y
Asia	**507**	**466.7Y**	**538.1Y**	**674.8Y**	**853.8Y**	**1,010.7Y**	**1,210.2Y**	**1,418.2Y**	**458.5Y**	**519.1Y**	**628.5Y**	**802.9Y**	**945.3Y**	**1,124.9Y**	**1,314.2Y**
Afghanistan, I.S. of	512	.31Y	.45Y	.72Y	.79Y	1.40Y	1.76Y	2.31Y	.06Y	.05Y	.07Y	.10Y	.12Y	.14Y	.18Y
American Samoa	859	.03Y	.03Y	.01Y	.01Y	.04Y	.08Y	.12Y	.01Y	.03Y	—Y	—Y	.01Y	.01Y	.03Y
Bangladesh	513	5.18Y	5.12Y	6.11Y	7.14Y	7.84Y	9.32Y	10.24Y	.39Y	.40Y	.47Y	.53Y	.64Y	.78Y	.87Y
Brunei Darussalam	516	.85Y	.91Y	1.00Y	1.05Y	1.16Y	1.26Y	1.48Y	1.22Y	1.44Y	1.47Y	1.80Y	2.56Y	3.46Y	3.40Y
Cambodia	522	1.87Y	2.10Y	2.42Y	2.95Y	3.53Y	4.66Y	5.31Y	.18Y	.23Y	.23Y	.27Y	.35Y	.40Y	.45Y
China,P.R.: Mainland	924	112.20Y	136.98Y	186.85Y	245.13Y	293.96Y	349.36Y	407.85Y	131.47Y	150.10Y	175.58Y	223.52Y	271.94Y	330.71Y	397.63Y
China,P.R.:Hong Kong	532	107.21Y	127.28Y	153.52Y	188.45Y	217.76Y	266.35Y	303.95Y	23.21Y	25.85Y	28.45Y	32.03Y	32.63Y	33.72Y	39.01Y
China,P.R.:Macao	546	2.27Y	2.29Y	2.77Y	3.24Y	3.57Y	4.40Y	5.39Y	.33Y	.41Y	.47Y	.57Y	.67Y	.66Y	.78Y
Fiji	819	.19Y	.26Y	.32Y	.45Y	.59Y	.67Y	.70Y	.12Y	.12Y	.15Y	.19Y	.19Y	.22Y	.28Y
French Polynesia	887	.05Y	.05Y	.07Y	.18Y	.35Y	.38Y	.38Y	—Y	.01Y	.02Y	.02Y	.02Y	.01Y	.01Y
Guam	829	.38Y	.30Y	.36Y	.48Y	.70Y	.83Y	.66Y	—Y	.01Y	.02Y	.01Y	.01Y	.01Y	.01Y
India	534	11.91Y	13.39Y	18.24Y	24.67Y	34.52Y	45.20Y	64.24Y	11.95Y	13.48Y	17.75Y	26.48Y	31.87Y	37.67Y	50.14Y
Indonesia	536	12.40Y	13.92Y	32.71Y	40.70Y	49.98Y	54.92Y	67.48Y	18.95Y	20.77Y	32.79Y	40.99Y	47.22Y	56.42Y	64.67Y
Kiribati	826	.01Y	.02Y	.02Y	.02Y	.03Y	.03Y	.05Y	.02Y	.01Y	—Y	—Y	—Y	—Y	—Y
Korea	542	35.19Y	40.43Y	47.72Y	61.08Y	73.98Y	90.61Y	107.60Y	57.87Y	67.04Y	86.37Y	115.64Y	136.70Y	161.53Y	181.92Y
Lao People's Dem.Rep	544	.58Y	.57Y	.65Y	.81Y	1.02Y	1.38Y	1.72Y	.17Y	.17Y	.18Y	.21Y	.37Y	.85Y	.90Y
Malaysia	548	38.47Y	42.93Y	48.22Y	58.46Y	66.29Y	78.28Y	89.77Y	48.53Y	53.49Y	61.93Y	75.56Y	84.13Y	99.53Y	115.22Y
Maldives	556	.26Y	.22Y	.27Y	.39Y	.42Y	.48Y	.62Y	.05Y	.06Y	.06Y	.06Y	.08Y	.10Y	.08Y
Mongolia	948	.23Y	.26Y	.30Y	.36Y	.44Y	.59Y	.92Y	.24Y	.23Y	.29Y	.47Y	.55Y	1.15Y	1.35Y
Myanmar	518	2.08Y	2.31Y	2.64Y	2.81Y	2.93Y	3.16Y	4.45Y	1.51Y	1.78Y	1.81Y	2.34Y	3.09Y	3.72Y	4.01Y
Nauru	836	—Y	—Y	—Y	—Y	.01Y	.01Y	.03Y	.01Y	.01Y	.01Y	—Y	—Y	—Y	.01Y
Nepal	558	.90Y	.59Y	.88Y	1.05Y	1.15Y	1.73Y	2.22Y	.41Y	.32Y	.31Y	.35Y	.39Y	.64Y	.81Y
New Caledonia	839	.12Y	.14Y	.20Y	.26Y	.39Y	.44Y	.60Y	.12Y	.13Y	.19Y	.32Y	.34Y	.45Y	.80Y
Pakistan	564	2.77Y	3.66Y	4.79Y	6.25Y	8.11Y	9.57Y	12.04Y	2.29Y	2.16Y	2.31Y	2.64Y	3.71Y	4.42Y	5.14Y
Papua New Guinea	853	.33Y	.35Y	.45Y	.53Y	.54Y	.69Y	.85Y	.42Y	.36Y	.65Y	.64Y	.78Y	1.08Y	1.05Y
Philippines	566	15.28Y	16.51Y	18.67Y	23.98Y	25.84Y	29.42Y	34.69Y	14.80Y	18.02Y	22.92Y	27.87Y	33.51Y	39.43Y	46.11Y
Samoa	862	.06Y	.07Y	.10Y	.13Y	.13Y	.14Y	.17Y	—Y	.01Y	.02Y	.01Y	.04Y	.06Y	.07Y
Singapore	576	48.13Y	51.74Y	56.94Y	70.27Y	85.57Y	100.61Y	115.58Y	47.59Y	50.43Y	59.10Y	73.55Y	89.55Y	106.89Y	120.12Y
Solomon Islands	813	.04Y	.03Y	.06Y	.06Y	.09Y	.10Y	.15Y	.05Y	.07Y	.10Y	.14Y	.17Y	.19Y	.27Y
Sri Lanka	524	2.93Y	3.14Y	3.93Y	4.53Y	5.56Y	6.34Y	6.70Y	.37Y	.38Y	.52Y	.70Y	.90Y	.99Y	1.06Y
Taiwan Province of China	528	32.57Y	35.39Y	40.97Y	51.65Y	55.67Y	64.96Y	69.21Y	64.18Y	77.37Y	92.88Y	121.66Y	138.87Y	162.79Y	183.98Y
Thailand	578	21.74Y	24.16Y	27.32Y	35.13Y	42.45Y	51.20Y	56.98Y	25.36Y	27.18Y	33.60Y	43.65Y	51.01Y	61.64Y	73.18Y
Tonga	866	.02Y	.03Y	.03Y	.04Y	.05Y	.05Y	.07Y	—Y	—Y	—Y	.01Y	—Y	.01Y	—Y
Tuvalu	869	.01Y	.01Y	.01Y	.02Y	.02Y	.03Y	.03Y	—Y	—Y	—Y	—Y	—Y	—Y	—Y
Vanuatu	846	.05Y	.05Y	.12Y	.11Y	.09Y	.10Y	.12Y	.04Y	.05Y	.06Y	.16Y	.17Y	.22Y	.25Y
Vietnam	582	9.91Y	12.10Y	15.07Y	20.33Y	24.24Y	30.65Y	42.99Y	4.29Y	4.57Y	5.48Y	7.81Y	9.82Y	11.05Y	14.80Y
Asia n.s.	598	.22Y	.21Y	.23Y	.18Y	.23Y	.30Y	.41Y	2.30Y	2.41Y	2.16Y	2.50Y	2.82Y	3.77Y	5.35Y
Europe	**170**	**19.6Y**	**24.5Y**	**36.5Y**	**51.1Y**	**69.0Y**	**98.9Y**	**142.8Y**	**20.7Y**	**24.3Y**	**29.5Y**	**39.6Y**	**46.8Y**	**53.3Y**	**68.8Y**
Albania	914	.03Y	.03Y	.05Y	.08Y	.10Y	.10Y	.12Y	—Y	—Y	—Y	.01Y	.02Y	.02Y	.08Y
Armenia	911	.01Y	.01Y	.02Y	.03Y	.04Y	.07Y	.10Y	—Y	.01Y	.01Y	—Y	.01Y	.02Y	.05Y
Azerbaijan	912	.03Y	.11Y	.31Y	.30Y	.31Y	.47Y	.69Y	.01Y	—Y	.04Y	.23Y	.04Y	.18Y	.76Y
Belarus	913	.04Y	.04Y	.06Y	.11Y	.13Y	.35Y	.42Y	.17Y	.19Y	.19Y	.24Y	.67Y	.78Y	.97Y
Bosnia & Herzegovina	963	.01Y	.01	.02	.07	.03	.05Y	.09Y	—Y	.01	.01	—	.11Y	.12Y	.03Y
Bulgaria	918	.32Y	.31Y	.49Y	.84Y	.87Y	2.24Y	1.39Y	.11Y	.11Y	.20Y	.30Y	.39Y	.62Y	.70Y
Croatia	960	.25Y	.25Y	.33Y	.55Y	.80Y	1.19Y	1.98Y	.04Y	.02Y	.02Y	.05Y	.09Y	.11Y	.13Y
Czech Republic	935	1.18Y	1.64Y	2.41Y	2.75Y	3.31Y	4.95Y	7.59Y	.60Y	.62Y	.95Y	1.11Y	1.39Y	1.94Y	2.70Y
Czechoslovakia n.s.	937	.06Y	.05Y	.08Y	.09Y	—Y	.02Y	.03Y	.05Y	.08Y	.11Y	.15Y	—Y	—Y	—Y
Estonia	939	.39Y	.26Y	.30Y	.46Y	.63Y	.95Y	1.12Y	.19Y	.07Y	.06Y	.09Y	.12Y	.37Y	.28Y
Faroe Islands	816	—Y	—Y	—Y	—Y	—Y	—Y	—Y	—Y	—Y	—Y	—Y	—Y	.01Y	.01Y
Georgia	915	.02Y	.04Y	.16Y	.11Y	.10Y	.14Y	.28Y	.01Y	.01Y	.03Y	.08Y	.04Y	.10Y	.04Y
Gibraltar	823	.01Y	—Y	.02Y	.01Y	.02Y	—Y	—Y	—Y	.01Y	—Y	—Y	—Y	—Y	—Y
Hungary	944	2.50Y	3.62Y	4.63Y	6.10Y	6.53Y	7.76Y	10.90Y	.65Y	.99Y	.90Y	1.18Y	1.20Y	1.82Y	2.39Y
Kazakhstan	916	.51Y	.81Y	1.92Y	2.67Y	4.38Y	5.30Y	8.29Y	1.10Y	1.55Y	2.14Y	2.84Y	3.44Y	4.15Y	7.02Y
Kyrgyz Republic	917	.10Y	.19Y	.31Y	.60Y	.97Y	2.21Y	3.82Y	.05Y	.07Y	.08Y	.13Y	.13Y	.21Y	.30Y
Latvia	941	.10Y	.13Y	.23Y	.33Y	.50Y	.76Y	1.03Y	.03Y	.05Y	.03Y	.10Y	.07Y	.16Y	.21Y
Lithuania	946	.14Y	.21Y	.34Y	.53Y	.69Y	.87Y	1.24Y	.03Y	.08Y	.15Y	.09Y	.11Y	.13Y	.20Y
Macedonia, FYR	962	.02Y	.03Y	.04Y	.04Y	.03Y	.06Y	.12Y	—Y	—Y	.02Y	—Y	.02Y	—Y	.01Y
Moldova	921	.01Y	.01Y	.02Y	.03Y	.07Y	.06Y	.08Y	.01Y	.03Y	.01Y	.01Y	.01Y	—Y	.01Y
Poland	964	2.25Y	2.46Y	3.14Y	4.03Y	5.48Y	8.94Y	13.44Y	.63Y	.59Y	.82Y	1.15Y	1.33Y	1.82Y	2.33Y
Romania	968	.53Y	.69Y	.91Y	1.66Y	2.16Y	7.33Y	3.91Y	.33Y	.70Y	.82Y	.83Y	.89Y	.82Y	1.12Y
Russia	922	5.40Y	6.73Y	10.26Y	14.61Y	20.77Y	25.47Y	42.43Y	13.18Y	14.58Y	17.37Y	23.81Y	29.34Y	32.21Y	38.38Y
Serbia & Montenegro	965	.12Y	.11	.22	.25	.27Y	.38Y	.44Y	.02Y	.01	.03	.02	.04Y	.01Y	.01Y
Slovak Republic	936	.15Y	.18Y	.34Y	.72Y	1.37Y	2.53Y	5.22Y	.11Y	.08Y	.19Y	.24Y	.36Y	.59Y	1.14Y
Tajikistan	923	.04Y	.02Y	.03Y	.07Y	.17Y	.34Y	.58Y	.02Y	.02Y	.04Y	.05Y	.05Y	.05Y	.07Y
Turkey	186	3.08Y	3.94Y	6.24Y	9.02Y	12.27Y	16.82Y	23.09Y	1.01Y	1.30Y	1.49Y	1.84Y	1.99Y	2.38Y	4.11Y
Turkmenistan	925	.06Y	.12Y	.14Y	.12Y	.12Y	.20Y	.35Y	.04Y	.05Y	.10Y	.15Y	.18Y	.21Y	.33Y

		Exports							Imports						
		2001	2002	2003	2004	2005	2006	2007	2001	2002	2003	2004	2005	2006	2007
		Billions of U.S. Dollars							Billions of U.S. Dollars						
Ukraine	926	.75Y	1.12Y	1.75Y	2.60Y	4.14Y	5.89Y	9.25Y	1.83Y	2.55Y	3.23Y	4.17Y	3.76Y	3.21Y	4.06Y
U.S.S.R. n.s.	930	.01Y	.01Y	—Y	—Y	—Y	—Y	—Y	.23Y	.31Y	—Y	.03Y	—Y	—Y	—Y
Uzbekistan	927	.42Y	.32Y	.42Y	.58Y	.78Y	1.12Y	1.61Y	.22Y	.23Y	.43Y	.65Y	.73Y	.93Y	.85Y
Yugoslavia n.s.	966	.04Y	.02	—	—	—Y	—Y	—Y	.03Y	—	—	—	—Y	—Y	—Y
Europe n.s.	884	.97Y	1.01Y	1.29Y	1.76Y	1.92Y	2.39Y	3.13Y	.04Y	.03Y	.03Y	.04Y	.27Y	.32Y	.53Y
Middle East	**407**	**35.2Y**	**41.2Y**	**50.9Y**	**63.9Y**	**78.6Y**	**97.4Y**	**130.8Y**	**74.8Y**	**69.8Y**	**90.3Y**	**122.7Y**	**171.3Y**	**219.0Y**	**241.4Y**
Bahrain	419	.41Y	.44Y	.47Y	.59Y	.89Y	.98Y	1.28Y	1.06Y	.84Y	.91Y	1.15Y	1.38Y	1.76Y	1.72Y
Egypt	469	2.69Y	2.66Y	3.02Y	3.72Y	4.96Y	6.82Y	9.14Y	.66Y	.66Y	.86Y	1.19Y	1.38Y	1.52Y	2.18Y
Iran, I.R. of	429	3.27Y	4.38Y	6.62Y	7.98Y	8.91Y	11.32Y	16.09Y	8.14Y	6.52Y	9.67Y	12.47Y	17.30Y	24.33Y	27.77Y
Iraq	433	1.17Y	1.43Y	.50Y	.87Y	1.01Y	1.24Y	1.44Y	.47Y	1.06Y	.46Y	1.61Y	2.09Y	2.81Y	6.00Y
Israel	436	3.38Y	3.63Y	4.30Y	5.43Y	6.48Y	7.47Y	9.44Y	3.49Y	3.53Y	4.01Y	5.28Y	6.00Y	6.94Y	7.97Y
Jordan	439	.87Y	1.11Y	1.54Y	2.45Y	2.31Y	2.47Y	2.66Y	.43Y	.41Y	.47Y	.60Y	.70Y	.71Y	.89Y
Kuwait	443	1.02Y	1.18Y	1.85Y	1.89Y	2.33Y	3.02Y	4.43Y	7.86Y	7.99Y	10.17Y	14.56Y	20.31Y	25.44Y	28.59Y
Lebanon	446	.71Y	.65Y	.75Y	.93Y	.92Y	.99Y	1.36Y	.03Y	.07Y	.06Y	.06Y	.06Y	.09Y	.13Y
Libya	672	.35Y	.54Y	.49Y	1.03Y	1.06Y	1.55Y	1.93Y	.09Y	.05Y	.14Y	.46Y	1.04Y	2.14Y	2.28Y
Oman	449	.76Y	.60Y	.72Y	.87Y	1.32Y	1.74Y	2.50Y	6.67Y	6.08Y	6.61Y	9.29Y	12.10Y	16.57Y	15.27Y
Qatar	453	.53Y	.49Y	.78Y	.78Y	1.47Y	2.42Y	3.41Y	4.41Y	4.31Y	5.87Y	7.84Y	11.61Y	15.18Y	19.23Y
Saudi Arabia	456	5.86Y	6.55Y	7.45Y	8.81Y	11.34Y	14.84Y	20.36Y	24.96Y	23.33Y	30.37Y	40.51Y	60.67Y	74.33Y	79.22Y
Syrian Arab Republic	463	1.02Y	1.23Y	1.47Y	1.83Y	2.19Y	2.78Y	3.57Y	.15Y	.21Y	.21Y	.15Y	.07Y	.14Y	.05Y
United Arab Emirates	466	12.51Y	15.52Y	19.94Y	25.56Y	32.03Y	37.82Y	50.75Y	13.19Y	12.57Y	17.18Y	23.97Y	32.50Y	42.97Y	46.53Y
Yemen, Republic of	474	.67Y	.83Y	.98Y	1.15Y	1.35Y	1.88Y	2.36Y	3.01Y	2.18Y	3.30Y	3.56Y	4.10Y	4.03Y	3.58Y
Middle East n.s.	489	.01Y	.01Y	.01Y	.04Y	.03Y	.03Y	.06Y	.14Y	.02Y	—Y	—Y	—Y	—Y	—Y
Western Hemisphere	**207**	**33.0Y**	**32.5Y**	**33.6Y**	**46.3Y**	**59.2Y**	**82.4Y**	**108.9Y**	**18.1Y**	**20.4Y**	**29.7Y**	**42.3Y**	**49.8Y**	**64.1Y**	**86.8Y**
Antigua and Barbuda	311	.08Y	.10Y	.06Y	.23Y	.27Y	.30Y	.60Y	—Y	—Y	—Y	—Y	.01Y	—Y	—Y
Argentina	213	1.76Y	.46Y	1.10Y	2.03Y	2.89Y	3.92Y	6.02Y	3.31Y	3.36Y	5.26Y	6.25Y	7.36Y	7.50Y	11.05Y
Aruba	314	.01Y	.01Y	.02Y	.02Y	.02Y	.03Y	.03Y	—Y	—	—	—	—	—Y	—Y
Bahamas, The	313	.77Y	1.24Y	1.25Y	1.27Y	2.10Y	1.80Y	1.98Y	.02Y	.05Y	.05Y	.04Y	.07Y	.09Y	.44Y
Barbados	316	.02Y	.03Y	.06Y	.05Y	.05Y	.12Y	.08Y	—Y	—Y	—Y	—Y	—Y	—Y	—Y
Belize	339	.04Y	.03Y	.03Y	.05Y	.05Y	.04Y	.05Y	.04Y	.01Y	.01Y	.02Y	.01Y	.01Y	.03Y
Bermuda	319	.07Y	.40Y	.21Y	.80Y	.82Y	1.36Y	1.72Y	.03Y	.01Y	.01Y	.01Y	—Y	—Y	.02Y
Bolivia	218	.03Y	.03Y	.03Y	.05Y	.08Y	.09Y	.14Y	.03Y	.03Y	.04Y	.09Y	.08Y	.22Y	.25Y
Brazil	223	5.57Y	5.26Y	5.67Y	9.04Y	12.45Y	17.62Y	23.93Y	5.96Y	7.28Y	11.17Y	16.46Y	19.00Y	22.37Y	29.39Y
Chile	228	2.38Y	2.32Y	2.66Y	3.42Y	4.48Y	6.18Y	9.14Y	2.95Y	3.43Y	4.61Y	7.80Y	9.61Y	13.87Y	19.77Y
Colombia	233	.84Y	.98Y	1.15Y	1.83Y	2.53Y	3.49Y	4.76Y	.13Y	.17Y	.25Y	.44Y	.54Y	.82Y	1.47Y
Costa Rica	238	.35Y	.35Y	.33Y	.46Y	.64Y	1.00Y	1.19Y	.25Y	.46Y	1.42Y	1.46Y	1.85Y	3.04Y	3.85Y
Dominica	321	.10Y	.07Y	.05Y	.06Y	.07Y	.09Y	.09Y	—Y	—Y	—Y	—Y	.01Y	.01Y	.03Y
Dominican Republic	243	.41Y	.51Y	.37Y	.48Y	.62Y	.77Y	.92Y	.04Y	.03Y	.09Y	.17Y	.16Y	.27Y	.35Y
Ecuador	248	.48Y	.54Y	.58Y	.82Y	1.20Y	1.53Y	1.89Y	.40Y	.35Y	.32Y	.59Y	.13Y	.22Y	.29Y
El Salvador	253	.36Y	.38Y	.44Y	.48Y	.47Y	.64Y	.67Y	.01Y	.03Y	.03Y	.03Y	.06Y	.10Y	.09Y
Greenland	326	—Y	—Y	—Y	—Y	—Y	—Y	—Y	.04Y	.03Y	.05Y	.04Y	.05Y	.05Y	.05Y
Grenada	328	—Y	—Y	—Y	—Y	.01Y	.01Y	.01Y	—Y	.01Y	—Y	—Y	—Y	—Y	—Y
Guatemala	258	.84Y	.98Y	1.10Y	1.28Y	1.33Y	1.59Y	1.56Y	.20Y	.15Y	.10Y	.14Y	.23Y	.23Y	.24Y
Guyana	336	.03Y	.03Y	.03Y	.04Y	.06Y	.13Y	.11Y	.01Y	.01Y	.01Y	.02Y	.04Y	.06Y	.06Y
Haiti	263	.06Y	.08Y	.10Y	.12Y	.12Y	.16Y	.23Y	—Y	—Y	—Y	—Y	.01Y	.01Y	.03Y
Honduras	268	.36Y	.41Y	.37Y	.47Y	.44Y	.57Y	.65Y	.02Y	.01Y	.02Y	.03Y	.06Y	.07Y	.10Y
Jamaica	343	.16Y	.15Y	.18Y	.22Y	.27Y	.34Y	.44Y	.04Y	.06Y	.11Y	.28Y	.23Y	.38Y	.07Y
Mexico	273	8.86Y	10.49Y	9.99Y	12.83Y	14.64Y	22.33Y	27.44Y	2.63Y	2.73Y	3.26Y	4.03Y	4.24Y	5.97Y	7.55Y
Netherlands Antilles	353	.14Y	.17Y	.08Y	.11Y	.24Y	.20Y	.16Y	.14Y	.10Y	.20Y	.09Y	.08Y	.22Y	.31Y
Nicaragua	278	.17Y	.23Y	.24Y	.33Y	.37Y	.45Y	.53Y	.03Y	—Y	—Y	.01Y	.03Y	.01Y	.02Y
Panama	283	5.40Y	4.66Y	4.81Y	5.90Y	7.85Y	9.83Y	13.67Y	.24Y	.31Y	.35Y	.50Y	.63Y	.45Y	.45Y
Paraguay	288	.27Y	.23Y	.31Y	.49Y	.52Y	.60Y	.76Y	.07Y	.05Y	.05Y	.12Y	.10Y	.10Y	.07Y
Peru	293	.63Y	.74Y	.86Y	1.05Y	1.36Y	1.92Y	2.91Y	.97Y	1.20Y	1.26Y	2.25Y	3.04Y	4.35Y	6.10Y
St. Kitts and Nevis	361	—Y	—Y	—Y	—Y	—Y	—Y	.01Y	—Y	—	—	—	—	—Y	—Y
St. Lucia	362	—Y	.01Y	—Y	.01Y	.01Y	.01Y	.01Y	—Y	—Y	—Y	—Y	.03Y	—Y	—Y
St. Vincent & Grens	364	.08Y	.05Y	.05Y	.09Y	.10Y	.11Y	.11Y	—Y	.01Y	—Y	—Y	—Y	—Y	—Y
Suriname	366	.17Y	.08Y	.04Y	.07Y	.10Y	.09Y	.13Y	.01Y	.01Y	.02Y	.01Y	.02Y	.01Y	.02Y
Trinidad and Tobago	369	.13Y	.14Y	.17Y	.24Y	.33Y	.50Y	.64Y	.01Y	.02Y	.03Y	.05Y	.04Y	.12Y	.30Y
Uruguay	298	.49Y	.23Y	.29Y	.38Y	.48Y	.65Y	.90Y	.18Y	.18Y	.20Y	.27Y	.37Y	.46Y	.56Y
Venezuela, Rep. Bol.	299	1.53Y	.91Y	.48Y	1.22Y	1.92Y	3.40Y	4.94Y	.34Y	.26Y	.71Y	1.02Y	1.63Y	3.09Y	3.69Y
Western Hem. n.s.	399	.41Y	.24Y	.44Y	.41Y	.28Y	.54Y	.44Y	.02Y	.03Y	.01Y	.02Y	.03Y	.06Y	.16Y
Other Countries n.i.e.	**910**	**1.5Y**	**1.4Y**	**1.5Y**	**1.8Y**	**2.4Y**	**3.4Y**	**3.3Y**	**.5Y**	**.6Y**	**.6Y**	**1.0Y**	**1.0Y**	**1.3Y**	**2.0Y**
Cuba	928	.42Y	.40Y	.34Y	.49Y	.89Y	1.71Y	1.44Y	.13Y	.14Y	.14Y	.22Y	.26Y	.57Y	1.15Y
North Korea	954	1.04Y	.97Y	1.12Y	1.32Y	1.53Y	1.70Y	1.86Y	.33Y	.41Y	.50Y	.75Y	.76Y	.72Y	.83Y
Countries & Areas n.s.	**898**	**3.3Y**	**3.2Y**	**2.7Y**	**3.2Y**	**4.4Y**	**2.7Y**	**5.3Y**	**15.8Y**	**19.5Y**	**22.9Y**	**31.2Y**	**45.5Y**	**54.6Y**	**67.5Y**
Special Categories	**899**	**1.2Y**	**.9Y**	**1.3Y**	**1.4Y**	**1.7Y**	**1.9Y**	**2.2Y**	**10.6Y**	**16.9Y**	**26.2Y**	**39.8Y**	**56.5Y**	**75.5Y**	**88.4Y**
Memorandum Items															
European Union	998	190.16Y	198.87Y	244.30Y	310.30Y	368.43Y	436.66Y	526.48Y	142.86Y	145.76Y	173.25Y	213.87Y	233.24Y	275.65Y	332.88Y
Oil Exporting Ctys	999	42.90Y	49.87Y	76.94Y	95.91Y	118.92Y	141.14Y	186.68Y	89.15Y	85.19Y	116.03Y	156.11Y	209.38Y	265.77Y	297.84Y
Non-Oil Develop.Ctys	201	529.00Y	605.82Y	743.23Y	952.88Y	1,139.88Y	1,401.10Y	1,682.39Y	500.01Y	565.78Y	683.08Y	884.22Y	1,041.77Y	1,243.18Y	1,471.75Y

	Exports 2001	2002	2003	2004	2005	2006	2007	Imports 2001	2002	2003	2004	2005	2006	2007
PERCENT DISTRIBUTION														
Industrial Countries................. 101	51.3	49.1	47.1	46.2	45.3	44.0	42.0	45.3	43.5	42.1	40.9	38.1	36.3	36.0
Developing Countries.............. 202	48.1	50.4	52.2	53.4	54.3	55.6	57.6	52.3	53.4	54.4	55.3	57.1	58.6	58.8
Africa...................................... 607	1.5	1.5	1.6	1.7	1.8	1.9	2.1	1.5	1.4	1.4	1.7	1.7	1.8	1.9
Asia.. 507	39.2	41.3	43.0	43.5	43.6	43.6	43.7	40.7	42.6	42.8	42.7	43.2	43.7	43.7
Europe.................................... 170	1.6	1.9	2.3	2.6	3.0	3.6	4.4	1.8	2.0	2.0	2.1	2.1	2.1	2.3
Middle East............................ 407	3.0	3.2	3.2	3.3	3.4	3.5	4.0	6.6	5.7	6.1	6.5	7.8	8.5	8.0
Western Hemisphere.............. 207	2.8	2.5	2.1	2.4	2.5	3.0	3.4	1.6	1.7	2.0	2.2	2.3	2.5	2.9
Other Countries n.i.e................ 910	.1	.1	.1	.1	.1	.1	.1	—	—	—	.1	—	.1	.1
ANNUAL PERCENT CHANGE														
World....................................... 001	–6.3	9.4	20.6	25.0	18.1	19.5	17.1	–5.8	8.2	20.6	28.1	16.4	17.6	16.9
Industrial Countries................. 101	–8.0	4.7	15.7	22.7	15.8	16.1	11.7	–8.1	3.9	16.5	24.5	8.6	11.8	15.9
Developing Countries.............. 202	–4.6	14.7	25.1	27.9	20.0	22.5	21.2	–4.3	10.5	22.8	30.2	20.3	20.6	17.3
Africa...................................... 607	7.4	11.6	26.2	37.3	23.0	29.1	28.1	–8.3	1.6	22.6	55.1	15.5	25.5	22.5
Asia.. 507	–6.0	15.3	25.4	26.5	18.4	19.7	17.2	–4.7	13.2	21.1	27.8	17.7	19.0	16.8
Europe.................................... 170	2.6	25.1	48.9	40.2	34.9	43.4	44.4	7.1	17.3	21.2	34.4	18.0	14.0	29.1
Middle East............................ 407	.5	17.1	23.4	25.6	22.9	23.9	34.3	–6.3	–6.6	29.3	35.9	39.6	27.8	10.3
Western Hemisphere.............. 207	.8	–1.5	3.3	38.0	27.7	39.2	32.2	10.4	12.6	45.5	42.3	17.8	28.9	35.4
Other Countries n.i.e................ 910	16.2	–6.4	7.0	23.5	33.7	40.7	–3.1	36.7	21.0	15.0	51.7	5.9	25.4	53.6

Developing Countries: Europe 170

	Exports 2001	2002	2003	2004	2005	2006	2007	Imports 2001	2002	2003	2004	2005	2006	2007
	Billions of U.S. Dollars							Billions of U.S. Dollars						
IFS World Total	**349.0**	**385.7**	**497.3**	**671.2**	**823.2**	**1,012.3**	**1,254.5**	**359.4**	**406.2**	**521.5**	**689.1**	**798.5**	**1,016.2**	**1,317.5**
DOTS World Total 001	**303.7Y**	**356.4Y**	**454.3Y**	**598.0Y**	**746.3Y**	**907.9Y**	**1,133.3Y**	**316.4Y**	**361.9Y**	**466.6Y**	**599.0Y**	**718.1Y**	**906.9Y**	**1,192.3Y**
Industrial Countries 101	**184.8Y**	**213.3Y**	**273.4Y**	**363.7Y**	**436.4Y**	**526.1Y**	**627.7Y**	**189.2Y**	**214.8Y**	**270.9Y**	**346.4Y**	**392.0Y**	**482.8Y**	**623.0Y**
United States 111	14.76Y	15.96Y	17.37Y	23.86Y	24.75Y	28.25Y	27.06Y	14.80Y	14.39Y	15.44Y	18.17Y	19.90Y	23.12Y	30.55Y
Canada 156	.70Y	.89Y	1.22Y	2.04Y	2.21Y	2.50Y	2.30Y	.98Y	1.17Y	1.47Y	1.76Y	2.28Y	3.05Y	3.59Y
Australia 193	.20Y	.33Y	.35Y	.67Y	.76Y	.93Y	1.14Y	.70Y	.66Y	.70Y	.88Y	.97Y	1.25Y	1.81Y
Japan 158	3.21Y	2.76Y	3.59Y	4.89Y	5.70Y	7.02Y	10.20Y	7.03Y	7.71Y	10.52Y	15.00Y	17.18Y	19.92Y	27.35Y
New Zealand 196	.03Y	.04Y	.06Y	.11Y	.12Y	.11Y	.16Y	.10Y	.13Y	.16Y	.14Y	.16Y	.20Y	.22Y
Austria 122	8.05Y	8.83Y	12.60Y	15.35Y	18.11Y	20.69Y	24.13Y	9.12Y	10.24Y	13.55Y	17.94Y	19.62Y	24.37Y	32.84Y
Belgium 124	5.23Y	5.68Y	7.05Y	10.17Y	12.61Y	14.66Y	17.73Y	6.02Y	6.70Y	8.14Y	10.69Y	13.51Y	17.35Y	23.09Y
Belgium-Luxembourg n.s. 127	.30	.33	.50	.66	.06Y	.06Y	.08Y	.25	.27	.34	.42	.21Y	.23Y	.30Y
Cyprus 423	1.71Y	2.15Y	4.93Y	6.05Y	5.65Y	5.15Y	5.46Y	.14Y	.25Y	.20Y	.23Y	.24Y	.32Y	.66Y
Denmark 128	2.68Y	3.32Y	3.79Y	5.16Y	6.20Y	7.40Y	9.08Y	3.22Y	3.65Y	4.31Y	5.26Y	6.12Y	7.78Y	9.94Y
Finland 172	5.16Y	4.89Y	7.07Y	9.99Y	12.62Y	14.33Y	16.80Y	4.90Y	5.40Y	6.80Y	8.78Y	10.47Y	13.29Y	15.91Y
France 132	11.29Y	13.91Y	18.15Y	24.63Y	31.20Y	37.51Y	47.33Y	14.68Y	17.38Y	22.81Y	28.94Y	31.33Y	38.87Y	47.06Y
Germany 134	59.38Y	63.61Y	83.96Y	105.61Y	122.02Y	143.95Y	173.71Y	60.69Y	68.50Y	87.82Y	114.37Y	132.40Y	167.20Y	217.73Y
Greece 174	3.03Y	3.53Y	4.45Y	5.58Y	7.15Y	9.43Y	11.75Y	2.40Y	2.54Y	3.18Y	3.71Y	4.09Y	5.14Y	7.07Y
Iceland 176	.32Y	.08Y	.12Y	.17Y	.34Y	.39Y	.52Y	.08Y	.13Y	.12Y	.18Y	.23Y	.30Y	.25Y
Ireland 178	1.10Y	1.11Y	1.87Y	2.01Y	2.26Y	2.70Y	3.19Y	1.59Y	1.86Y	2.05Y	2.59Y	2.78Y	3.65Y	4.55Y
Italy 136	25.14Y	27.49Y	33.43Y	43.84Y	55.79Y	72.03Y	81.23Y	23.42Y	27.75Y	34.37Y	41.25Y	44.56Y	54.86Y	69.04Y
Luxembourg 137	.18Y	.26Y	.31Y	.41Y	.42Y	.50Y	.80Y	.24Y	.41Y	.75Y	1.09Y	.82Y	.95Y	1.42Y
Malta 181	.27Y	.39Y	.44Y	.48Y	.76Y	.99Y	1.62Y	.10Y	.10Y	.19Y	.25Y	.29Y	.28Y	.36Y
Netherlands 138	10.79Y	15.50Y	19.31Y	30.19Y	42.84Y	57.56Y	69.57Y	7.23Y	8.49Y	10.60Y	15.51Y	21.34Y	29.23Y	40.07Y
Norway 142	1.25Y	1.90Y	2.52Y	3.11Y	4.17Y	5.07Y	6.26Y	1.88Y	2.37Y	3.25Y	3.46Y	3.97Y	4.24Y	4.32Y
Portugal 182	1.22Y	1.30Y	1.50Y	2.45Y	4.12Y	4.30Y	4.82Y	.59Y	.78Y	1.00Y	1.15Y	1.34Y	1.64Y	1.96Y
Slovenia 961	1.61Y	1.69Y	2.11Y	2.74Y	3.78Y	4.59Y	6.13Y	2.77Y	3.39Y	4.18Y	5.26Y	5.71Y	6.33Y	9.58Y
Spain 184	4.72Y	5.87Y	7.75Y	11.56Y	15.66Y	19.62Y	24.83Y	5.87Y	7.12Y	9.28Y	11.89Y	13.12Y	15.71Y	20.64Y
Sweden 144	4.57Y	5.85Y	6.95Y	9.39Y	10.82Y	12.84Y	16.21Y	5.24Y	6.15Y	7.73Y	10.52Y	12.03Y	14.37Y	18.43Y
Switzerland 146	4.19Y	8.72Y	11.49Y	15.76Y	14.89Y	17.68Y	21.04Y	4.62Y	5.80Y	7.39Y	9.19Y	9.77Y	10.43Y	13.52Y
United Kingdom 112	13.73Y	16.91Y	20.46Y	26.79Y	32.25Y	38.86Y	48.12Y	10.56Y	11.41Y	14.60Y	17.78Y	19.50Y	23.61Y	29.47Y
Developing Countries 202	**115.5Y**	**138.4Y**	**177.2Y**	**230.3Y**	**304.7Y**	**375.9Y**	**498.3Y**	**124.5Y**	**143.8Y**	**192.8Y**	**250.1Y**	**323.6Y**	**420.5Y**	**564.4Y**
Africa 607	**3.3Y**	**4.1Y**	**4.7Y**	**6.6Y**	**8.3Y**	**10.7Y**	**14.6Y**	**3.7Y**	**3.9Y**	**4.3Y**	**5.5Y**	**6.6Y**	**7.9Y**	**9.8Y**
Algeria 612	.99Y	1.19Y	1.52Y	1.87Y	2.05Y	2.91Y	4.29Y	1.18Y	1.25Y	1.14Y	1.39Y	1.86Y	1.99Y	2.41Y
Angola 614	.05Y	.08Y	.05Y	.07Y	.08Y	.17Y	.13Y	—Y	—Y	—Y	—Y	.01Y	.03Y	—Y
Benin 638	.01Y	.02Y	.01Y	.02Y	.02Y	.02Y	.06Y	.01Y	.01Y	—Y	—Y	—Y	—Y	—Y
Botswana 616	—Y	—Y	—Y	—Y	—Y	.01Y	.01Y	—Y	—Y	—Y	—Y	—Y	—Y	—Y
Burkina Faso 748	.01Y	.01Y	.02Y	.02Y	.03Y	.03Y	.04Y	—Y	—Y	—Y	—Y	—Y	—Y	.01Y
Cameroon 622	.03Y	.04Y	.05Y	.05Y	.06Y	.07Y	.09Y	.02Y	.03Y	.03Y	.05Y	.05Y	.04Y	.07Y
Cape Verde 624	—Y	.01Y	.01Y	.01Y	—Y	.01Y	.01Y	—Y	—Y	—Y	—Y	—Y	—Y	—Y
Central African Rep. 626	—Y	—Y	—Y	—Y	—Y	—Y	—Y	—Y	—Y	—Y	.01Y	.01Y	.01Y	.01Y
Chad 628	.01Y	.02Y	.01Y	.01Y	.01Y	.02Y	.01Y	.01Y	.01Y	.01Y	.01Y	—Y	—Y	—Y
Comoros 632	—Y	—Y	—Y	—Y	—Y	—Y	.01Y	—Y	—Y	—Y	—Y	—Y	—Y	.01Y
Congo, Dem. Rep. of 636	—Y	—Y	.01Y	.01Y	.01Y	.01Y	.01Y	—Y	—Y	—Y	—Y	—Y	.03Y	.05Y
Congo, Republic of 634	.01Y	.01Y	.02Y	.02Y	.03Y	.03Y	.04Y	—Y	.01Y	.01Y	.02Y	.02Y	.04Y	.04Y
Côte d'Ivoire 662	.05Y	.07Y	.07Y	.07Y	.08Y	.09Y	.12Y	.29Y	.43Y	.53Y	.40Y	.37Y	.39Y	.48Y
Djibouti 611	.01Y	.01Y	.01Y	.02Y	.02Y	.03Y	.10Y	—Y	—Y	—Y	—Y	—Y	—Y	—Y
Equatorial Guinea 642	—Y	—Y	—Y	.01Y	.01Y	.03Y	.03Y	—Y	—Y	—Y	—Y	.01Y	.03Y	.05Y
Ethiopia 644	.06Y	.08Y	.16Y	.21Y	.20Y	.19Y	.27Y	.01Y	.01Y	.03Y	.03Y	.04Y	.04Y	.06Y
Gabon 646	—Y	.01Y	.01Y	.01Y	.01Y	.01Y	.03Y	.01Y	.01Y	.02Y	.08Y	.10Y	.12Y	.15Y
Gambia, The 648	.01Y	.01Y	.01Y	.03Y	.02Y	.02Y	.03Y	—Y	—Y	—Y	—Y	—Y	—Y	—Y
Ghana 652	.06Y	.06Y	.08Y	.11Y	.13Y	.14Y	.23Y	.12Y	.14Y	.25Y	.21Y	.21Y	.24Y	.27Y
Guinea 656	.02Y	.02Y	.02Y	.04Y	.05Y	.04Y	.05Y	.17Y	.15Y	.16Y	.27Y	.41Y	.41Y	.39Y
Kenya 664	.03Y	.03Y	.06Y	.09Y	.16Y	.25Y	.29Y	.02Y	.03Y	.04Y	.05Y	.06Y	.08Y	.10Y
Liberia 668	.30Y	.39Y	.23Y	.39Y	.45Y	.37Y	.48Y	.11Y	.12Y	.12Y	.19Y	.09Y	.22Y	.23Y
Madagascar 674	—Y	.01Y	.01Y	.01Y	.01Y	.01Y	.02Y	—Y	—Y	—Y	—Y	—Y	—Y	—Y
Malawi 676	—Y	—Y	—Y	—Y	—Y	—Y	.01Y	.05Y	.06Y	.05Y	.07Y	.07Y	.08Y	.12Y
Mali 678	.01Y	.01Y	.03Y	.03Y	.05Y	.06Y	.07Y	.01Y	.01Y	.01Y	.01Y	.01Y	—Y	—Y
Mauritania 682	.03Y	.07Y	.06Y	.03Y	.04Y	.04Y	.05Y	.04Y	.03Y	.04Y	.05Y	.06Y	.06Y	.08Y
Mauritius 684	.01Y	.01Y	.01Y	.02Y	.07Y	.09Y	.04Y	—Y	—Y	.01Y	.02Y	.02Y	.02Y	.03Y
Morocco 686	.48Y	.59Y	.51Y	1.05Y	1.21Y	1.34Y	2.08Y	.22Y	.31Y	.34Y	.39Y	.52Y	.67Y	.86Y
Mozambique 688	—Y	.01Y	.01Y	.01Y	.03Y	.05Y	.05Y	.01Y	.01Y	.01Y	.02Y	.05Y	.05Y	.07Y
Namibia 728	—Y	—Y	.02Y	.01Y	—Y	—Y	.03Y	—Y	.01Y	.01Y	.01Y	.02Y	.01Y	.02Y
Niger 692	.01Y	.01Y	.01Y	.01Y	.01Y	.01Y	.02Y	—Y	—Y	—Y	—Y	—Y	.05Y	.01Y
Nigeria 694	.43Y	.37Y	.49Y	.53Y	.83Y	.95Y	1.08Y	.26Y	.21Y	.26Y	.20Y	.24Y	.39Y	.52Y
Rwanda 714	—Y	.01Y	—Y	—Y	.01Y	—Y	.01Y	.01Y	.01Y	—Y	—Y	.01Y	.01Y	—Y
Senegal 722	.04Y	.04Y	.06Y	.09Y	.10Y	.13Y	.18Y	—Y	—Y	—Y	—Y	—Y	—Y	—Y
Seychelles 718	.01Y	.01Y	.02Y	.01Y	.02Y	.06Y	.06Y	—Y	—Y	—Y	.01Y	.01Y	.01Y	—Y
Sierra Leone 724	.01Y	.01Y	.04Y	.01Y	.01Y	.02Y	.03Y	—Y	—Y	—Y	.01Y	—Y	—Y	.01Y
Somalia 726	—Y	—Y	—Y	—Y	.01Y	.01Y	.01Y	—Y	—Y	—Y	—Y	—Y	—Y	—Y
South Africa 199	.17Y	.30Y	.36Y	.59Y	1.05Y	1.48Y	1.84Y	.71Y	.59Y	.80Y	1.54Y	1.85Y	2.43Y	3.12Y
Sudan 732	.10Y	.14Y	.18Y	.31Y	.36Y	.47Y	.41Y	.01Y	.02Y	.02Y	.02Y	.01Y	.02Y	.02Y
Swaziland 734	—Y	—Y	—Y	—Y	—Y	—Y	—Y	.01Y	—Y	—Y	—Y	—Y	—Y	—Y

		Exports							Imports						
		2001	2002	2003	2004	2005	2006	2007	2001	2002	2003	2004	2005	2006	2007
		Billions of U.S. Dollars							Billions of U.S. Dollars						
Tanzania	738	.02Y	.02Y	.01Y	.02Y	.10Y	.11Y	.13Y	.03Y	.03Y	.05Y	.07Y	.09Y	.11Y	.13Y
Togo	742	.02Y	.02Y	.02Y	.04Y	.03Y	.15Y	.46Y	.01Y	.01Y	.01Y	.01Y	.01Y	.01Y	.01Y
Tunisia	744	.33Y	.41Y	.51Y	.73Y	.90Y	1.20Y	1.65Y	.17Y	.21Y	.23Y	.23Y	.24Y	.25Y	.36Y
Uganda	746	.01Y	.01Y	.02Y	.02Y	.02Y	.05Y	.08Y	.02Y	.02Y	.03Y	.03Y	.05Y	.03Y	.04Y
Zambia	754	—Y	—Y	—Y	—Y	—Y	.01Y	.01Y	—Y	—Y	—Y	—Y	.01Y	.01Y	.08Y
Zimbabwe	698	—Y	—Y	—Y	—Y	—Y	.01Y	.01Y	.11Y	.10Y	.08Y	.09Y	.05Y	.04Y	.08Y
Asia	**507**	**13.8Y**	**20.8Y**	**25.9Y**	**32.9Y**	**39.4Y**	**44.8Y**	**57.9Y**	**22.6Y**	**30.2Y**	**41.8Y**	**54.6Y**	**73.7Y**	**99.2Y**	**145.9Y**
Afghanistan, I.S. of	512	.07Y	.15Y	.27Y	.39Y	.51Y	.65Y	.88Y	.01Y	.01Y	.01Y	.02Y	.02Y	.03Y	.05Y
Bangladesh	513	.10Y	.12Y	.21Y	.28Y	.56Y	.74Y	.67Y	.07Y	.08Y	.11Y	.18Y	.20Y	.32Y	.46Y
Brunei Darussalam	516	—Y	—Y	—Y	—Y	—Y	.01Y	—Y	—Y	—Y	—Y	—Y	.01Y	—Y	—Y
Cambodia	522	.01Y	.01Y	.01Y	.01Y	.02Y	.02Y	.02Y	—Y	.01Y	.01Y	.02Y	.03Y	.02Y	.04Y
China,P.R.: Mainland	924	6.11Y	9.88Y	12.94Y	15.62Y	19.86Y	24.02Y	28.05Y	8.71Y	12.75Y	19.13Y	25.38Y	38.38Y	54.89Y	86.01Y
China,P.R.:Hong Kong	532	.51Y	.86Y	.89Y	.99Y	.97Y	1.14Y	1.37Y	.45Y	.61Y	.77Y	1.28Y	.66Y	.90Y	1.12Y
China,P.R.:Macao	546	—Y	.01Y	—Y	—Y	—Y	—Y	.01Y	.01Y	.01Y	.02Y	.03Y	.02Y	.02Y	.02Y
Fiji	819	—Y	—Y	—Y	—Y	—Y	—Y	.01Y	—Y	—Y	—Y	—Y	—Y	—Y	—Y
French Polynesia	887	—Y	.03Y	—Y	—Y	—Y	—Y	—Y	—Y	—Y	—Y	—Y	—Y	—Y	—Y
India	534	1.30Y	2.25Y	3.41Y	3.74Y	4.43Y	5.33Y	7.32Y	1.60Y	1.93Y	2.39Y	3.09Y	3.69Y	4.53Y	6.49Y
Indonesia	536	.24Y	.29Y	.59Y	.79Y	.70Y	.76Y	1.59Y	.98Y	1.31Y	1.57Y	1.91Y	2.05Y	2.59Y	3.44Y
Korea	542	1.42Y	1.87Y	1.99Y	3.09Y	3.47Y	3.39Y	8.06Y	3.70Y	4.39Y	6.25Y	9.44Y	13.93Y	19.22Y	26.80Y
Lao People's Dem.Rep.	544	.01Y	.01Y	—Y	.01Y	.01Y	—Y	.01Y	—Y	—Y	.01Y	.01Y	.01Y	.01Y	.01Y
Malaysia	548	.48Y	.79Y	.85Y	.41Y	.47Y	.66Y	1.02Y	1.79Y	2.21Y	2.92Y	3.26Y	3.28Y	3.71Y	4.65Y
Mongolia	948	.25Y	.27Y	.33Y	.44Y	.53Y	.58Y	.76Y	.04Y	.06Y	.05Y	.03Y	.06Y	.05Y	.07Y
Myanmar	518	.02Y	.12Y	.05Y	.04Y	.02Y	.04Y	.06Y	.01Y	.02Y	.01Y	.01Y	.01Y	.02Y	.02Y
Nepal	558	.01Y	.01Y	.01Y	.02Y	.01Y	.02Y	.02Y	—Y	—Y	.01Y	.01Y	.01Y	.01Y	.01Y
New Caledonia	839	—Y	—Y	—Y	.01Y	.01Y	.01Y	.01Y	—Y	—Y	—Y	.02Y	.02Y	.02Y	.02Y
Pakistan	564	.19Y	.26Y	.33Y	.66Y	1.09Y	1.27Y	1.31Y	.23Y	.27Y	.37Y	.46Y	.55Y	.71Y	.91Y
Papua New Guinea	853	—Y	—Y	—Y	.01Y	—Y	—Y	—Y	—Y	—Y	—Y	—Y	—Y	.01Y	.01Y
Philippines	566	.29Y	.36Y	.49Y	.46Y	.47Y	.31Y	.35Y	.40Y	.89Y	.80Y	.74Y	.66Y	.76Y	.85Y
Singapore	576	1.27Y	1.06Y	.74Y	.97Y	1.90Y	2.75Y	2.97Y	1.18Y	1.31Y	1.35Y	1.68Y	1.89Y	1.71Y	1.87Y
Sri Lanka	524	.06Y	.05Y	.06Y	.09Y	.15Y	.16Y	.17Y	.17Y	.19Y	.22Y	.27Y	.28Y	.35Y	.45Y
Taiwan Province of China	528	.61Y	1.13Y	1.35Y	2.72Y	1.99Y	1.53Y	1.58Y	1.82Y	2.46Y	3.63Y	4.37Y	5.00Y	6.60Y	8.13Y
Thailand	578	.45Y	.56Y	.55Y	1.01Y	1.06Y	.82Y	.79Y	1.00Y	1.23Y	1.69Y	1.86Y	2.29Y	2.87Y	4.21Y
Tuvalu	869	—Y	.05Y	—Y	—Y	—Y	—Y	—Y	—Y	—Y	—Y	—Y	—Y	—Y	—Y
Vanuatu	846	—Y	—Y	—Y	—Y	.02Y	—Y	—Y	....	....	....	....	....	....	....
Vietnam	582	.37Y	.68Y	.79Y	1.11Y	1.09Y	.66Y	.95Y	.40Y	.43Y	.47Y	.55Y	.61Y	1.03Y	1.62Y
Europe	**170**	**83.0Y**	**95.5Y**	**123.4Y**	**161.6Y**	**218.7Y**	**275.4Y**	**367.8Y**	**86.9Y**	**97.7Y**	**129.6Y**	**170.6Y**	**218.3Y**	**281.3Y**	**371.9Y**
Albania	914	.18Y	.24Y	.31Y	.42Y	.51Y	.73Y	.97Y	.02Y	.02Y	.03Y	.06Y	.04Y	.07Y	.10Y
Armenia	911	.13Y	.18Y	.25Y	.43Y	.50Y	.86Y	1.30Y	.10Y	.08Y	.13Y	.13Y	.17Y	.21Y	.36Y
Azerbaijan	912	.56Y	.84Y	1.10Y	1.86Y	2.34Y	3.17Y	3.57Y	.48Y	.53Y	.72Y	1.18Y	1.91Y	2.36Y	2.51Y
Belarus	913	.94Y	6.79Y	8.80Y	1.84Y	10.66Y	6.80Y	21.81Y	1.26Y	5.24Y	6.65Y	2.72Y	8.23Y	6.51Y	14.39Y
Bosnia & Herzegovina	963	1.01Y	1.25Y	1.56Y	1.80Y	2.34Y	3.25Y	4.08Y	.16Y	.21Y	.29Y	.55Y	.77Y	1.36Y	1.63Y
Bulgaria	918	1.65Y	1.82Y	2.48Y	3.92Y	5.98Y	8.14Y	12.17Y	1.38Y	1.53Y	2.07Y	2.91Y	3.49Y	4.67Y	6.32Y
Croatia	960	1.23Y	1.47Y	2.02Y	3.04Y	3.90Y	4.60Y	6.03Y	.95Y	1.14Y	1.45Y	1.78Y	2.16Y	2.84Y	3.57Y
Czech Republic	935	6.07Y	6.54Y	8.41Y	11.68Y	15.79Y	21.28Y	26.00Y	6.75Y	7.73Y	10.83Y	15.29Y	17.36Y	22.17Y	30.12Y
Estonia	939	1.90Y	2.39Y	2.70Y	3.21Y	4.31Y	5.59Y	5.50Y	.56Y	.61Y	.86Y	1.52Y	2.02Y	2.94Y	3.33Y
Faroe Islands	816	—Y	—Y	—Y	.02Y	—Y	.01Y	.01Y	.01Y	.01Y	.01Y	.03Y	.02Y	.04Y	.04Y
Georgia	915	.48Y	.47Y	.70Y	1.07Y	1.52Y	2.17Y	2.83Y	.27Y	.33Y	.53Y	.64Y	.76Y	.80Y	.87Y
Gibraltar	823	.39Y	.15Y	.32Y	.85Y	.75Y	1.08Y	.75Y	—Y	.01Y	.03Y	.05Y	.04Y	.06Y	.09Y
Hungary	944	5.51Y	6.37Y	8.32Y	10.89Y	14.96Y	19.30Y	23.48Y	4.33Y	5.16Y	7.01Y	8.73Y	11.59Y	16.75Y	26.94Y
Kazakhstan	916	3.15Y	3.19Y	4.34Y	6.60Y	8.98Y	12.50Y	16.87Y	3.50Y	3.74Y	4.88Y	6.84Y	7.19Y	8.88Y	10.58Y
Kyrgyz Republic	917	.28Y	.32Y	.43Y	.67Y	.79Y	1.06Y	1.63Y	.19Y	.18Y	.24Y	.32Y	.35Y	.48Y	.71Y
Latvia	941	2.94Y	2.85Y	3.51Y	4.35Y	4.77Y	6.13Y	9.31Y	.49Y	.58Y	.75Y	1.52Y	2.16Y	2.70Y	3.85Y
Lithuania	946	3.38Y	3.79Y	4.89Y	6.12Y	7.43Y	8.83Y	10.41Y	1.30Y	1.52Y	2.03Y	2.98Y	3.91Y	5.15Y	6.72Y
Macedonia, FYR	962	.42Y	.43Y	.52Y	.80Y	.84Y	1.37Y	1.83Y	.16Y	.16Y	.20Y	.33Y	.43Y	.82Y	1.20Y
Moldova	921	.80Y	.89Y	1.23Y	1.64Y	1.98Y	2.52Y	3.36Y	.53Y	.48Y	.65Y	.84Y	.95Y	.83Y	1.28Y
Poland	964	8.78Y	8.95Y	11.39Y	15.98Y	21.98Y	28.92Y	36.48Y	5.97Y	7.22Y	10.21Y	15.09Y	18.69Y	27.85Y	36.72Y
Romania	968	3.02Y	3.78Y	5.25Y	7.99Y	12.31Y	15.36Y	20.02Y	1.81Y	2.04Y	3.00Y	4.97Y	6.78Y	9.66Y	11.62Y
Russia	922	15.04Y	14.69Y	18.56Y	25.50Y	30.18Y	38.01Y	52.92Y	36.94Y	37.64Y	48.46Y	63.80Y	83.12Y	108.93Y	130.58Y
Serbia & Montenegro	965	1.01Y	1.04Y	1.40Y	1.45Y	2.07Y	1.87Y	2.19Y	.32Y	.37Y	.44Y	.53Y	.74Y	.54Y	.73Y
Slovak Republic	936	6.02Y	6.57Y	8.48Y	11.36Y	14.58Y	19.20Y	24.65Y	4.22Y	4.76Y	6.35Y	8.26Y	9.86Y	13.56Y	18.95Y
Tajikistan	923	.39Y	.37Y	.51Y	.68Y	.82Y	1.12Y	1.48Y	.36Y	.39Y	.39Y	.38Y	.29Y	.42Y	.49Y
Turkey	186	5.90Y	7.34Y	9.47Y	15.25Y	21.21Y	27.81Y	36.40Y	3.28Y	4.52Y	6.37Y	8.27Y	10.58Y	14.72Y	21.56Y
Turkmenistan	925	.49Y	.52Y	.81Y	1.11Y	1.16Y	1.06Y	1.45Y	2.15Y	2.42Y	2.39Y	2.87Y	4.27Y	4.54Y	5.10Y
Ukraine	926	9.56Y	10.43Y	13.38Y	17.88Y	22.34Y	29.21Y	35.43Y	7.84Y	7.93Y	11.19Y	16.01Y	18.24Y	22.29Y	31.73Y
U.S.S.R. n.s.	930	.01	.02	.01Y	.01Y	—	—Y	—Y	.01Y	.02Y	.01Y	.01Y	—Y	—Y	—Y
Uzbekistan	927	.97Y	.93Y	1.05Y	1.48Y	1.69Y	2.12Y	3.10Y	1.38Y	.90Y	1.17Y	1.62Y	2.26Y	3.66Y	4.51Y
Yugoslavia n.s.	966	.42	.45	.62Y	.94Y	.88Y	.76Y	.38Y	.11	.15	.19Y	.25Y	.34Y	.23Y	.08Y
Europe n.s.	884	.36Y	.41Y	.58Y	.76Y	1.21Y	1.35Y	1.06Y	.04Y	.10Y	.07Y	.09Y	.17Y	1.38Y	1.73Y
Middle East	**407**	**10.8Y**	**13.3Y**	**16.7Y**	**23.9Y**	**29.6Y**	**33.3Y**	**43.3Y**	**6.2Y**	**6.3Y**	**8.3Y**	**10.1Y**	**13.6Y**	**17.8Y**	**19.8Y**
Bahrain	419	.02Y	.03Y	.05Y	.09Y	.08Y	.12Y	.16Y	.02Y	.02Y	.02Y	.02Y	.02Y	.05Y	.15Y
Egypt	469	1.49Y	1.53Y	1.42Y	2.18Y	3.32Y	3.96Y	5.24Y	.20Y	.23Y	.35Y	.47Y	.58Y	.88Y	1.24Y
Iran, I.R. of	429	2.30Y	2.28Y	3.56Y	5.06Y	5.96Y	6.71Y	9.22Y	1.22Y	1.29Y	2.28Y	2.45Y	4.20Y	6.65Y	8.18Y
Iraq	433	.53Y	.58Y	1.05Y	2.21Y	3.23Y	3.07Y	3.37Y	.13Y	—Y	.13Y	.48Y	.46Y	.49Y	.80Y
Israel	436	1.90Y	2.79Y	3.44Y	4.23Y	4.35Y	5.19Y	5.46Y	1.40Y	1.37Y	1.43Y	1.86Y	2.10Y	2.50Y	3.16Y
Jordan	439	.25Y	.29Y	.38Y	.73Y	.84Y	.87Y	1.42Y	.03Y	.04Y	.06Y	.08Y	.09Y	.05Y	.06Y
Kuwait	443	.16Y	.29Y	.26Y	.38Y	.39Y	.43Y	.50Y	.12Y	.03Y	.02Y	.03Y	.04Y	.18Y	.10Y
Lebanon	446	.65Y	.53Y	.54Y	.75Y	.89Y	.89Y	1.13Y	.05Y	.06Y	.09Y	.17Y	.17Y	.16Y	.16Y

	Exports 2001	2002	2003	2004	2005	2006	2007	Imports 2001	2002	2003	2004	2005	2006	2007
	Billions of U.S. Dollars							Billions of U.S. Dollars						
Libya........ 672	.23Y	.27Y	.41Y	.58Y	.77Y	.80Y	1.18Y	1.15Y	.92Y	1.35Y	1.83Y	2.44Y	2.77Y	1.04Y
Oman........ 449	.04Y	.05Y	.05Y	.08Y	.18Y	.24Y	.38Y	.01Y	.01Y	.01Y	.01Y	.01Y	.01Y	.04Y
Qatar........ 453	.01Y	.03Y	.05Y	.09Y	.16Y	.44Y	.58Y	.01Y	.01Y	.01Y	.02Y	.05Y	.07Y	.05Y
Saudi Arabia........ 456	.91Y	1.20Y	1.52Y	1.62Y	2.25Y	2.61Y	3.74Y	.76Y	.84Y	1.05Y	1.36Y	2.02Y	2.37Y	2.68Y
Syrian Arab Republic........ 463	.75Y	.86Y	1.15Y	1.66Y	1.99Y	2.40Y	3.38Y	.69Y	.98Y	.96Y	.64Y	.46Y	.33Y	.64Y
United Arab Emirates........ 466	1.41Y	2.12Y	2.55Y	3.74Y	4.78Y	5.19Y	7.08Y	.37Y	.49Y	.56Y	.73Y	.93Y	1.33Y	1.57Y
Yemen, Republic of........ 474	.16Y	.40Y	.30Y	.48Y	.46Y	.44Y	.59Y	—Y	—Y	.02Y	—Y	—Y	—Y	—Y
Western Hemisphere........ 207	**4.6Y**	**4.8Y**	**6.4Y**	**5.4Y**	**8.7Y**	**11.7Y**	**14.7Y**	**5.2Y**	**5.7Y**	**8.8Y**	**9.3Y**	**11.4Y**	**14.3Y**	**16.9Y**
Antigua and Barbuda........ 311	.06Y	.05Y	.07Y	.07Y	.05Y	.02Y	.21Y	—Y	—Y	.01Y	.12Y	.01Y	.01Y	—Y
Argentina........ 213	.13Y	.06Y	.09Y	.18Y	.30Y	.40Y	.67Y	.38Y	.56Y	.85Y	1.14Y	1.57Y	2.10Y	2.53Y
Aruba........ 314	—Y	—Y	.01Y	.06Y	.03Y	—Y	—Y	—Y	—Y	.01Y	—Y	—Y	—Y	.02Y
Bahamas, The........ 313	.07Y	.10Y	.11Y	.29Y	.55Y	.67Y	.40Y	.06Y	.03Y	.08Y	.23Y	.23Y	.36Y	.38Y
Barbados........ 316	—Y	.02Y	—Y	—Y	.02Y	.01Y	.01Y	—Y	.05Y	.01Y	—Y	.01Y	—Y	.01Y
Belize........ 339	—Y	.01Y	.01Y	.04Y	.10Y	.07Y	.08Y	—Y	—Y	—Y	.01Y	.01Y	—Y	.01Y
Bermuda........ 319	1.38Y	2.08Y	2.25Y	.07Y	.13Y	.13Y	.10Y	—Y	.01Y	.01Y	.03Y	—Y	—Y	—Y
Bolivia........ 218	—Y	—Y	—Y	—Y	—Y	.01Y	.02Y	.01Y	.01Y	.04Y	—Y	.01Y	—Y	.01Y
Brazil........ 223	.62Y	.66Y	.87Y	1.17Y	1.51Y	1.81Y	3.02Y	2.56Y	2.59Y	3.76Y	4.33Y	5.53Y	6.69Y	7.83Y
Chile........ 228	.09Y	.12Y	.08Y	.12Y	.17Y	.21Y	.32Y	.17Y	.18Y	.33Y	.51Y	.70Y	1.34Y	1.66Y
Colombia........ 233	.07Y	.11Y	.10Y	.19Y	.22Y	.29Y	.46Y	.13Y	.13Y	.22Y	.29Y	.40Y	.40Y	.51Y
Costa Rica........ 238	.03Y	.03Y	.02Y	.06Y	.06Y	.05Y	.06Y	.10Y	.34Y	.33Y	.28Y	.23Y	.13Y	.13Y
Dominica........ 321	—Y	—Y	.01Y	.01Y	—Y	—Y	—Y	—Y	—Y	—Y	—Y	—Y	—Y	—Y
Dominican Republic........ 243	.07Y	.09Y	.04Y	.10Y	.09Y	.11Y	.09Y	.01Y	.01Y	.01Y	.02Y	.01Y	.02Y	.03Y
Ecuador........ 248	.09Y	.06Y	.05Y	.12Y	.09Y	.18Y	.15Y	.38Y	.41Y	.52Y	.63Y	.85Y	.83Y	1.12Y
El Salvador........ 253	.07Y	.05Y	.05Y	.05Y	.05Y	.08Y	.08Y	.12Y	.03Y	.06Y	.07Y	.08Y	.06Y	.06Y
Falkland Islands........ 323	—Y	—Y	—Y	—Y	—Y	—Y	—Y	—Y	.01Y	.01Y	.01Y	.01Y	.01Y	.01Y
Greenland........ 326	—Y	.01Y	—Y	—Y	—Y	—Y	—Y	—Y	—Y	—Y	—Y	—Y	—Y	.01Y
Guatemala........ 258	.06Y	.05Y	.06Y	.07Y	.07Y	.11Y	.10Y	.08Y	.05Y	.09Y	.02Y	.02Y	.03Y	.04Y
Guyana........ 336	—Y	—Y	—Y	—Y	—Y	—Y	.01Y	.02Y	—Y	—Y	—Y	—Y	—Y	—Y
Haiti........ 263	.01Y	.01Y	.01Y	.01Y	.01Y	.01Y	.01Y	—Y	—Y	—Y	—Y	—Y	—Y	—Y
Honduras........ 268	.03Y	.04Y	.04Y	.07Y	.03Y	.05Y	.06Y	.04Y	.06Y	.08Y	.02Y	.03Y	.02Y	.01Y
Jamaica........ 343	.02Y	.02Y	.02Y	.03Y	.02Y	.04Y	.03Y	.03Y	.02Y	.07Y	.03Y	.04Y	.07Y	.18Y
Mexico........ 273	.48Y	.49Y	.42Y	.88Y	.97Y	1.44Y	1.40Y	.39Y	.44Y	.57Y	.57Y	.72Y	.97Y	1.35Y
Netherlands Antilles........ 353	.06Y	—Y	.14Y	.03Y	.02Y	.10Y	.05Y	—Y	—Y	—Y	.03Y	.01Y	—Y	—Y
Nicaragua........ 278	.01Y	.02Y	.01Y	.03Y	.02Y	.02Y	.01Y	.06Y	.02Y	.02Y	—Y	.02Y	.02Y	.01Y
Panama........ 283	.28Y	.26Y	.23Y	.30Y	.45Y	.32Y	.50Y	.10Y	.20Y	.13Y	.24Y	.11Y	.12Y	.07Y
Paraguay........ 288	—Y	—Y	—Y	—Y	—Y	.01Y	.01Y	.02Y	.05Y	.01Y	.05Y	.10Y	.24Y	.18Y
Peru........ 293	.09Y	.13Y	.12Y	.15Y	.18Y	.20Y	.32Y	.17Y	.14Y	.15Y	.22Y	.24Y	.37Y	.36Y
St. Kitts and Nevis........ 361	—Y	—Y	—Y	.17Y	.01Y	.01Y	.02Y	—Y	—Y	—Y	—Y	—Y	.01Y	.01Y
St. Vincent & Grens........ 364	.01Y	.02Y	.01Y	.06Y	.04Y	.04Y	.05Y	—Y	.01Y	.01Y	.06Y	—Y	.02Y	.01Y
Suriname........ 366	—Y	—Y	—Y	—Y	.01Y	—Y	.01Y	—Y	—Y	—Y	.01Y	—Y	.01Y	.03Y
Trinidad and Tobago........ 369	.02Y	.03Y	.02Y	.04Y	.03Y	.05Y	.06Y	—Y	—Y	—Y	—Y	.01Y	.01Y	—Y
Uruguay........ 298	.03Y	.07Y	.21Y	.09Y	.16Y	.05Y	.11Y	.05Y	.08Y	.11Y	.08Y	.09Y	.27Y	.18Y
Venezuela, Rep. Bol........ 299	.14Y	.08Y	.07Y	.13Y	.19Y	.63Y	1.40Y	.10Y	.08Y	.09Y	.14Y	.19Y	.26Y	.19Y
Western Hem. n.s........ 399	.62Y	.11Y	1.28Y	.79Y	3.13Y	4.57Y	4.87Y	.19Y	.23Y	1.17Y	.09Y	.15Y	.12Y	.10Y
Other Countries n.i.e........ 910	**.2Y**	**.1Y**	**.2Y**	**.3Y**	**.5Y**	**.5Y**	**.5Y**	**.6Y**	**.4Y**	**.3Y**	**.3Y**	**.2Y**	**.2Y**	**.2Y**
Cuba........ 928	.10Y	.07Y	.09Y	.09Y	.21Y	.30Y	.38Y	.50Y	.38Y	.25Y	.27Y	.12Y	.11Y	.14Y
North Korea........ 954	.07Y	.06Y	.13Y	.23Y	.26Y	.22Y	.15Y	.06Y	.04Y	.04Y	.05Y	.06Y	.05Y	.06Y
Countries & Areas n.s........ 898	**2.1Y**	**2.9Y**	**1.3Y**	**1.0Y**	**1.5Y**	**2.1Y**	**2.6Y**	**1.7Y**	**1.9Y**	**1.5Y**	**1.1Y**	**1.5Y**	**2.4Y**	**3.3Y**
Special Categories........ 899	**1.0**	**1.6**	**2.2Y**	**2.6Y**	**3.1Y**	**3.1Y**	**3.1Y**	**.4**	**1.0**	**.9Y**	**1.0Y**	**.8Y**	**1.0Y**	**1.2Y**
Memorandum Items														
European Union........ 998	194.76Y	220.10Y	284.34Y	376.63Y	467.11Y	573.15Y	694.37Y	182.68Y	209.98Y	269.93Y	351.02Y	402.52Y	511.12Y	666.02Y
Oil Exporting Ctys........ 999	7.39Y	8.75Y	12.12Y	17.09Y	21.48Y	24.70Y	34.37Y	6.29Y	6.42Y	8.46Y	10.54Y	14.48Y	19.07Y	20.96Y
Non-Oil Develop.Ctys........ 201	108.14Y	129.65Y	165.08Y	213.23Y	283.21Y	351.20Y	463.97Y	118.17Y	137.36Y	184.36Y	239.58Y	309.10Y	401.37Y	543.43Y
PERCENT DISTRIBUTION														
Industrial Countries........ 101	**60.9**	**59.9**	**60.2**	**60.8**	**58.5**	**57.9**	**55.4**	**59.8**	**59.3**	**58.1**	**57.8**	**54.6**	**53.2**	**52.3**
Developing Countries........ 202	**38.0**	**38.8**	**39.0**	**38.5**	**40.8**	**41.4**	**44.0**	**39.3**	**39.7**	**41.3**	**41.8**	**45.1**	**46.4**	**47.3**
Africa........ 607	**1.1**	**1.1**	**1.0**	**1.1**	**1.1**	**1.2**	**1.3**	**1.2**	**1.1**	**.9**	**.9**	**.9**	**.9**	**.8**
Asia........ 507	**4.5**	**5.8**	**5.7**	**5.5**	**5.3**	**4.9**	**5.1**	**7.1**	**8.3**	**9.0**	**9.1**	**10.3**	**10.9**	**12.2**
Europe........ 170	**27.3**	**26.8**	**27.2**	**27.0**	**29.3**	**30.3**	**32.5**	**27.5**	**27.0**	**27.8**	**28.5**	**30.4**	**31.0**	**31.2**
Middle East........ 407	**3.6**	**3.7**	**3.7**	**4.0**	**4.0**	**3.7**	**3.8**	**1.9**	**1.7**	**1.8**	**1.7**	**1.9**	**2.0**	**1.7**
Western Hemisphere........ 207	**1.5**	**1.3**	**1.4**	**.9**	**1.2**	**1.3**	**1.3**	**1.6**	**1.6**	**1.9**	**1.5**	**1.6**	**1.6**	**1.4**
Other Countries n.i.e........ 910	**.1**	**—**	**—**	**.1**	**.1**	**.1**	**—**	**.2**	**.1**	**.1**	**.1**	**—**	**—**	**—**
ANNUAL PERCENT CHANGE														
World........ 001	**-.2**	**17.4**	**27.5**	**31.6**	**24.8**	**21.7**	**24.8**	**2.9**	**14.4**	**28.9**	**28.4**	**19.9**	**26.3**	**31.5**
Industrial Countries........ 101	**1.7**	**15.4**	**28.2**	**33.0**	**20.0**	**20.6**	**19.3**	**4.1**	**13.5**	**26.2**	**27.9**	**13.2**	**23.2**	**29.0**
Developing Countries........ 202	**-3.5**	**19.8**	**28.0**	**30.0**	**32.3**	**23.4**	**32.6**	**1.8**	**15.5**	**34.1**	**29.7**	**29.4**	**29.9**	**34.2**
Africa........ 607	**5.5**	**22.9**	**16.1**	**39.2**	**25.7**	**28.4**	**36.9**	**6.6**	**5.4**	**11.9**	**28.1**	**19.0**	**19.8**	**24.9**
Asia........ 507	**-11.8**	**51.1**	**24.4**	**27.0**	**19.7**	**13.9**	**29.2**	**13.6**	**33.7**	**38.5**	**30.8**	**34.9**	**34.6**	**47.1**
Europe........ 170	**-4.1**	**15.0**	**29.3**	**30.9**	**35.3**	**26.0**	**33.5**	**-2.0**	**12.5**	**32.6**	**31.6**	**28.0**	**28.8**	**32.2**
Middle East........ 407	**18.0**	**22.4**	**26.2**	**42.7**	**24.2**	**12.3**	**30.2**	**-1.7**	**1.9**	**32.6**	**21.9**	**33.8**	**31.1**	**11.2**
Western Hemisphere........ 207	**-10.9**	**4.3**	**34.6**	**-16.4**	**62.5**	**34.1**	**25.3**	**27.2**	**10.3**	**53.2**	**5.1**	**23.2**	**25.4**	**18.5**
Other Countries n.i.e........ 910	**-9.2**	**-23.7**	**73.5**	**47.4**	**44.8**	**8.4**	**3.3**	**20.7**	**-24.7**	**-31.0**	**9.5**	**-43.6**	**-7.8**	**17.7**

	Exports 2001	2002	2003	2004	2005	2006	2007	Imports 2001	2002	2003	2004	2005	2006	2007
	Billions of U.S. Dollars							Billions of U.S. Dollars						
IFS World Total........................	**271.6**	**283.3**	**341.7**	**495.6**	**676.6**	**860.3**	**816.9**	**207.0**	**217.5**	**241.4**	**323.4**	**394.0**	**438.0**	**542.0**
DOTS World Total.................... 001	**247.5Y**	**243.0Y**	**297.0Y**	**410.2Y**	**519.2Y**	**643.2Y**	**716.9Y**	**175.6Y**	**193.8Y**	**226.7Y**	**325.8Y**	**384.4Y**	**442.4Y**	**559.5Y**
Industrial Countries................. 101	**127.1Y**	**121.7Y**	**148.7Y**	**200.4Y**	**253.9Y**	**302.3Y**	**322.6Y**	**105.3Y**	**115.2Y**	**127.2Y**	**168.0Y**	**196.2Y**	**213.4Y**	**264.5Y**
United States.............................. 111	35.28Y	33.90Y	40.85Y	51.94Y	62.86Y	72.67Y	78.18Y	20.09Y	20.70Y	21.30Y	27.38Y	35.22Y	41.91Y	50.62Y
Canada....................................... 156	1.48Y	1.63Y	2.05Y	2.44Y	3.27Y	4.06Y	4.21Y	1.49Y	1.51Y	1.42Y	1.86Y	2.41Y	3.01Y	4.04Y
Australia.................................... 193	1.53Y	1.39Y	1.80Y	2.27Y	2.26Y	3.03Y	3.81Y	4.23Y	3.77Y	3.22Y	4.44Y	4.44Y	5.54Y	6.63Y
Japan.. 158	40.49Y	37.52Y	46.10Y	57.82Y	79.93Y	100.58Y	105.01Y	10.99Y	12.11Y	14.28Y	17.33Y	19.87Y	22.93Y	30.34Y
New Zealand............................... 196	.55Y	.49Y	.63Y	.73Y	.97Y	1.16Y	1.03Y	.32Y	.36Y	.50Y	.65Y	.76Y	.89Y	1.22Y
Austria.. 122	.76Y	.70Y	.75Y	.86Y	.91Y	1.50Y	2.38Y	.92Y	1.11Y	1.53Y	1.99Y	2.41Y	2.76Y	3.39Y
Belgium...................................... 124	2.40Y	2.79Y	3.70Y	5.16Y	6.52Y	6.50Y	8.81Y	5.21Y	5.94Y	5.80Y	8.51Y	9.70Y	10.18Y	11.83Y
Cyprus.. 423	.36Y	.38Y	.40Y	.58Y	.76Y	.74Y	.90Y	.22Y	.19Y	.24Y	.29Y	.15Y	.19Y	.19Y
Denmark..................................... 128	.24Y	.15Y	.17Y	.42Y	.86Y	.57Y	.40Y	1.00Y	1.09Y	1.32Y	1.60Y	1.68Y	1.37Y	1.93Y
Finland....................................... 172	.11Y	.10Y	.10Y	.15Y	.14Y	.16Y	.20Y	1.12Y	1.29Y	1.57Y	2.91Y	4.17Y	3.99Y	4.59Y
France.. 132	6.66Y	6.34Y	7.02Y	13.70Y	13.76Y	14.27Y	15.25Y	8.85Y	9.84Y	12.52Y	17.27Y	16.87Y	17.22Y	20.35Y
Germany..................................... 134	5.68Y	5.06Y	6.38Y	7.42Y	10.10Y	12.44Y	12.10Y	14.00Y	16.64Y	19.16Y	24.80Y	29.23Y	32.42Y	38.12Y
Greece.. 174	2.56Y	1.88Y	2.83Y	3.82Y	4.91Y	5.86Y	5.77Y	.59Y	.62Y	.65Y	1.03Y	1.43Y	1.55Y	1.30Y
Iceland.. 176	—Y	—Y	.01Y	.01Y	.01Y	.04Y	.02Y	.01Y	.01Y	.01Y	.01Y	.02Y	.06Y	.10Y
Ireland.. 178	.20Y	.12Y	.15Y	.24Y	.23Y	.21Y	.31Y	1.04Y	1.02Y	1.00Y	1.28Y	1.39Y	1.50Y	1.89Y
Italy.. 136	11.24Y	10.94Y	13.27Y	21.99Y	24.87Y	31.23Y	36.48Y	9.99Y	11.48Y	13.34Y	17.21Y	18.76Y	20.46Y	29.95Y
Luxembourg................................ 137	.01Y	.02Y	.02Y	.05Y	.36Y	.40Y	.06Y	.09Y	.09Y	.09Y	.13Y	.17Y	.23Y	.25Y
Malta.. 181	.11Y	.05Y	.02Y	.10Y	.05Y	.08Y	.12Y	.10Y	.12Y	.14Y	.16Y	.17Y	.14Y	.16Y
Netherlands................................ 138	5.19Y	5.54Y	6.90Y	9.46Y	15.14Y	16.06Y	15.56Y	4.17Y	4.31Y	4.67Y	7.05Y	8.42Y	10.37Y	12.82Y
Norway....................................... 142	.08Y	.09Y	.09Y	.11Y	.16Y	.18Y	.34Y	.26Y	.26Y	.30Y	.62Y	.45Y	.71Y	.71Y
Portugal..................................... 182	.68Y	.74Y	.96Y	1.23Y	1.44Y	2.05Y	2.48Y	.23Y	.23Y	.29Y	.34Y	.44Y	.37Y	.49Y
Slovenia...................................... 961	.05Y	.04Y	.05Y	.04Y	.08Y	.08Y	.16Y	.18Y	.17Y	.22Y	.31Y	.31Y	.36Y	.60Y
Spain.. 184	4.98Y	4.98Y	6.07Y	9.25Y	11.26Y	14.80Y	15.16Y	2.69Y	2.86Y	3.49Y	4.50Y	4.27Y	4.81Y	6.64Y
Sweden....................................... 144	.81Y	.48Y	.75Y	.67Y	.72Y	.45Y	.47Y	2.14Y	1.98Y	2.70Y	3.74Y	4.15Y	4.09Y	4.80Y
Switzerland................................ 146	1.14Y	1.51Y	1.93Y	2.25Y	3.15Y	3.32Y	3.39Y	5.54Y	7.08Y	5.86Y	6.93Y	7.73Y	7.80Y	9.37Y
United Kingdom.......................... 112	4.51Y	4.90Y	5.70Y	7.67Y	9.22Y	9.82Y	9.97Y	9.83Y	10.44Y	11.61Y	15.64Y	21.56Y	18.50Y	22.17Y
Developing Countries............. 202	**102.8Y**	**102.0Y**	**124.8Y**	**179.3Y**	**228.7Y**	**295.9Y**	**338.7Y**	**64.4Y**	**72.6Y**	**91.7Y**	**150.1Y**	**178.3Y**	**217.6Y**	**281.7Y**
Africa....................................... 607	**8.2Y**	**7.7Y**	**9.5Y**	**13.7Y**	**14.4Y**	**22.8Y**	**24.2Y**	**2.7Y**	**2.9Y**	**3.3Y**	**4.4Y**	**5.3Y**	**6.5Y**	**7.6Y**
Algeria....................................... 612	.17Y	.34Y	.38Y	.49Y	.63Y	.73Y	.93Y	.07Y	.27Y	.32Y	.41Y	.58Y	.69Y	.83Y
Angola.. 614	.01Y	—Y	.01Y	.01Y	.01Y	.01Y	.02Y	—Y	—Y	—Y	—Y	—Y	—Y	—Y
Benin.. 638	.01Y	.02Y	.02Y	.02Y	.02Y	.03Y	.03Y	—Y	—Y	—Y	—Y	—Y	—Y	.01Y
Botswana.................................... 616	.02Y	.01Y	—Y	.01Y	.01Y	.02Y	.04Y	—Y	—Y	—Y	—Y	—Y	—Y	—Y
Burkina Faso............................... 748	.02Y	.02Y	.02Y	.03Y	.04Y	.05Y	.06Y	—Y	—Y	—Y	—Y	—Y	—Y	—Y
Burundi...................................... 618	.02Y	—Y	—Y	—Y	.01Y	.05Y	.06Y	—Y	—Y	—Y	—Y	—Y	—Y	.01Y
Cameroon................................... 622	.03Y	.04Y	.03Y	.03Y	.04Y	.06Y	.07Y	—Y	.01Y	.01Y	.01Y	.01Y	.01Y	.02Y
Chad... 628	.01Y	.01Y	.02Y	.02Y	.03Y	.04Y	.05Y	—Y	—Y	—Y	—Y	—Y	—Y	—Y
Comoros..................................... 632	—Y	—Y	.01Y	.01Y	.01Y	.01Y	.02Y	—Y	—Y	—Y	—Y	—Y	—Y	—Y
Congo, Dem. Rep. of.................. 636	—Y	—Y	—Y	—Y	—Y	.01Y	.01Y	—Y	—Y	—Y	—Y	—Y	—Y	—Y
Congo, Republic of..................... 634	.01Y	.05Y	.01Y	—Y	.01Y	.01Y	.02Y	—Y	—Y	—Y	.01Y	.01Y	.01Y	.01Y
Côte d'Ivoire............................... 662	.05Y	.06Y	.05Y	.07Y	.10Y	.07Y	.07Y	.01Y	.01Y	.01Y	.03Y	.04Y	.04Y	.05Y
Djibouti....................................... 611	.13Y	.14Y	.17Y	.22Y	.29Y	.37Y	.45Y	.05Y	.04Y	.05Y	.02Y	.02Y	.02Y	.03Y
Equatorial Guinea....................... 642	—Y	—Y	—Y	.01Y	.01Y	.01Y	.01Y	—Y	—Y	—Y	—Y	—Y	—Y	—Y
Ethiopia...................................... 644	.21Y	.15Y	.33Y	.48Y	.69Y	.78Y	.95Y	.05Y	.05Y	.11Y	.09Y	.12Y	.15Y	.18Y
Gabon... 646	—Y	—Y	.01Y	.01Y	.01Y	.01Y	.01Y	—Y	—Y	—Y	—Y	—Y	—Y	—Y
Gambia, The............................... 648	.01Y	.01Y	.01Y	.02Y	.02Y	.03Y	.04Y	—Y	—Y	—Y	—Y	—Y	—Y	—Y
Ghana.. 652	.02Y	.02Y	.03Y	.03Y	.05Y	.05Y	.07Y	.01Y	.01Y	.02Y	.03Y	.04Y	.05Y	.07Y
Guinea.. 656	.01Y	.01Y	.01Y	.02Y	.02Y	.03Y	.04Y	—Y	—Y	—Y	—Y	—Y	—Y	—Y
Kenya.. 664	.83Y	.68Y	.97Y	1.24Y	1.62Y	2.01Y	2.47Y	.18Y	.17Y	.17Y	.18Y	.21Y	.25Y	.31Y
Liberia.. 668	—Y	—Y	—Y	.01Y	.01Y	.01Y	.01Y	—Y	—Y	—Y	—Y	—Y	—Y	—Y
Madagascar................................. 674	.13Y	.09Y	.13Y	.17Y	.23Y	.29Y	.35Y	—Y	—Y	—Y	—Y	—Y	.01Y	.01Y
Malawi.. 676	—Y	—Y	—Y	—Y	—Y	—Y	—Y	.03Y	.03Y	.04Y	.05Y	.05Y	.07Y	.08Y
Mali.. 678	—Y	—Y	—Y	—Y	.01Y	.01Y	.01Y	—Y	—Y	—Y	—Y	—Y	—Y	—Y
Mauritania.................................. 682	.01Y	.01Y	.01Y	.02Y	.03Y	.03Y	.04Y	.01Y	.01Y	.01Y	.01Y	.01Y	.01Y	.02Y
Mauritius.................................... 684	.12Y	.16Y	.18Y	.28Y	.40Y	.29Y	.12Y	—Y	—Y	—Y	.03Y	.19Y	.28Y	.09Y
Morocco...................................... 686	1.25Y	1.33Y	.99Y	1.47Y	2.23Y	2.81Y	3.40Y	.27Y	.23Y	.25Y	.34Y	.33Y	.41Y	.53Y
Mozambique............................... 688	.01Y	.01Y	.05Y	.04Y	.04Y	.06Y	.07Y	—Y	—Y	—Y	.01Y	—Y	—Y	.01Y
Namibia...................................... 728	.02Y	.02Y	.02Y	.03Y	.05Y	.08Y	.11Y	—Y	—Y	—Y	—Y	—Y	—Y	—Y
Niger... 692	.01Y	.02Y	.01Y	.02Y	.03Y	.03Y	.03Y	—Y	—Y	—Y	—Y	—Y	—Y	—Y
Nigeria.. 694	.14Y	.18Y	.42Y	.49Y	.65Y	.80Y	1.06Y	.01Y	—Y	.02Y	.06Y	.08Y	.10Y	.12Y
Rwanda....................................... 714	.02Y	.01Y	.01Y	.01Y	.04Y	.03Y	.03Y	—Y	—Y	—Y	—Y	—Y	—Y	—Y
Senegal....................................... 722	.02Y	.04Y	.05Y	.08Y	.09Y	.06Y	.07Y	—Y	—Y	—Y	—Y	.01Y	.02Y	.03Y
Seychelles................................... 718	.06Y	.06Y	.07Y	.09Y	.12Y	.15Y	.18Y	—Y	—Y	—Y	—Y	—Y	—Y	—Y
Sierra Leone............................... 724	.01Y	—Y	.01Y	.01Y	.01Y	.01Y	.01Y	—Y	—Y	—Y	—Y	—Y	—Y	—Y
Somalia....................................... 726	.04Y	.05Y	.05Y	.07Y	.10Y	.13Y	.15Y	.06Y	.08Y	.13Y	.17Y	.23Y	.28Y	.36Y
South Africa................................ 199	3.52Y	2.69Y	3.64Y	5.64Y	3.36Y	9.48Y	8.66Y	1.03Y	.79Y	.94Y	1.33Y	1.47Y	1.57Y	1.92Y
Sudan.. 732	.25Y	.27Y	.67Y	1.04Y	1.64Y	1.68Y	1.78Y	.15Y	.29Y	.35Y	.53Y	.40Y	.60Y	.46Y
Swaziland.................................... 734	—Y	—Y	—Y	—Y	—Y	—Y	—Y	—Y	—Y	—Y	.01Y	.03Y	.04Y	.04Y
Tanzania..................................... 738	.30Y	.28Y	.28Y	.37Y	.47Y	.62Y	.74Y	.02Y	.02Y	.05Y	.06Y	.07Y	.09Y	.12Y
Togo... 742	.01Y	.02Y	.02Y	.03Y	.02Y	.02Y	.03Y	.01Y	—Y	—Y	—Y	—Y	—Y	—Y

		Exports							Imports						
		2001	2002	2003	2004	2005	2006	2007	2001	2002	2003	2004	2005	2006	2007
		Billions of U.S. Dollars							*Billions of U.S. Dollars*						
Tunisia	744	.44Y	.42Y	.54Y	.65Y	.75Y	1.01Y	1.22Y	.47Y	.55Y	.52Y	.56Y	.75Y	.92Y	1.19Y
Uganda	746	.06Y	.07Y	.09Y	.12Y	.17Y	.21Y	.26Y	—Y	—Y	.02Y	.02Y	.03Y	.03Y	.04Y
Zambia	754	.05Y	.05Y	.07Y	.14Y	.10Y	.30Y	.25Y	.14Y	.14Y	.14Y	.15Y	.25Y	.35Y	.55Y
Zimbabwe	698	.02Y	.20Y	.02Y	.10Y	.11Y	.08Y	.10Y	.02Y	.02Y	.05Y	.05Y	.04Y	.04Y	.04Y
Africa n.s.	799	.11Y	.10Y	.06Y	.07Y	.06Y	.25Y	.08Y	.06Y	.12Y	.02Y	.25Y	.32Y	.40Y	.46Y
Asia	**507**	**68.2Y**	**65.2Y**	**82.5Y**	**112.9Y**	**151.4Y**	**194.6Y**	**222.0Y**	**29.8Y**	**34.4Y**	**44.3Y**	**70.5Y**	**83.8Y**	**104.8Y**	**142.5Y**
Afghanistan, I.S. of	512	—Y	.01Y	.02Y	.02Y	.03Y	.04Y	.05Y	—Y	—Y	.01Y	.01Y	.01Y	.02Y	.02Y
Bangladesh	513	.38Y	.36Y	.55Y	.95Y	1.71Y	1.97Y	2.15Y	.11Y	.14Y	.11Y	.10Y	.14Y	.16Y	.19Y
Brunei Darussalam	516	—Y	—Y	—Y	.01Y	.01Y	.01Y	.01Y	.01Y	—Y	—Y	—Y	—Y	—Y	—Y
Cambodia	522	—Y	—Y	—Y	—Y	—Y	—Y	.01Y	—Y	—Y	—Y	—Y	—Y	—Y	—Y
China,P.R.: Mainland	924	8.01Y	8.76Y	13.39Y	19.81Y	28.17Y	38.09Y	44.65Y	7.60Y	9.34Y	13.78Y	20.97Y	26.37Y	35.83Y	53.79Y
China,P.R.:Hong Kong	532	2.20Y	2.68Y	3.16Y	4.06Y	4.56Y	4.97Y	5.38Y	1.57Y	2.02Y	1.87Y	3.77Y	4.05Y	4.78Y	5.67Y
China,P.R.:Macao	546	.01Y	.01Y	.01Y	.01Y	.01Y	.02Y	.03Y	—Y	—Y	—Y	—Y	—Y	—Y	.01Y
India	534	5.45Y	3.61Y	4.00Y	8.29Y	10.25Y	13.09Y	15.91Y	4.94Y	6.03Y	8.11Y	13.72Y	16.68Y	20.42Y	26.26Y
Indonesia	536	2.27Y	2.09Y	2.52Y	3.44Y	4.28Y	5.39Y	5.61Y	1.69Y	1.77Y	1.77Y	2.34Y	2.84Y	3.61Y	4.64Y
Korea	542	20.57Y	18.60Y	23.34Y	29.81Y	37.86Y	49.93Y	60.43Y	5.87Y	5.99Y	7.26Y	11.33Y	11.61Y	14.01Y	19.92Y
Malaysia	548	2.19Y	1.48Y	1.84Y	2.68Y	3.50Y	5.04Y	4.77Y	1.44Y	1.78Y	2.67Y	4.11Y	4.35Y	5.22Y	6.76Y
Maldives	556	.03Y	.03Y	.03Y	.09Y	.12Y	.16Y	.19Y	—Y	—Y	—Y	—Y	—Y	—Y	—Y
Myanmar	518	—Y	.01Y	.01Y	.01Y	.01Y	.01Y	.01Y	.01Y	.01Y	.02Y	.03Y	.03Y	.04Y	.06Y
Nepal	558	.11Y	.08Y	.04Y	.04Y	.06Y	.06Y	.07Y	—Y	—Y	—Y	—Y	—Y	—Y	—Y
Pakistan	564	3.25Y	3.42Y	3.80Y	5.07Y	6.87Y	8.72Y	10.55Y	.72Y	.90Y	1.02Y	1.81Y	2.16Y	2.66Y	3.43Y
Philippines	566	2.79Y	2.12Y	2.48Y	2.43Y	3.58Y	4.94Y	5.10Y	.18Y	.18Y	.23Y	.31Y	.39Y	.48Y	.61Y
Singapore	576	9.01Y	9.12Y	10.20Y	12.70Y	18.10Y	22.17Y	22.87Y	1.61Y	1.93Y	1.94Y	3.71Y	6.11Y	6.23Y	7.25Y
Sri Lanka	524	.48Y	.81Y	.55Y	.84Y	.95Y	1.14Y	1.40Y	.25Y	.21Y	.37Y	.60Y	.53Y	.56Y	.68Y
Taiwan Province of China	528	5.91Y	6.35Y	9.34Y	12.57Y	17.30Y	22.14Y	25.39Y	1.49Y	1.50Y	2.24Y	3.46Y	3.47Y	4.16Y	4.99Y
Thailand	578	5.37Y	5.39Y	6.84Y	9.56Y	13.40Y	16.21Y	16.92Y	1.76Y	1.97Y	2.55Y	3.78Y	4.50Y	6.05Y	7.83Y
Vietnam	582	.16Y	.26Y	.34Y	.45Y	.59Y	.41Y	.39Y	.50Y	.56Y	.30Y	.46Y	.49Y	.52Y	.41Y
Asia n.s.	598	.04Y	.04Y	.03Y	.03Y	.01Y	.06Y	.07Y	.02Y	.01Y	.01Y	.01Y	.01Y	.01Y	.01Y
Europe	**170**	**5.4Y**	**5.7Y**	**7.7Y**	**12.4Y**	**12.7Y**	**16.5Y**	**18.5Y**	**9.6Y**	**10.6Y**	**15.8Y**	**29.8Y**	**31.5Y**	**35.2Y**	**46.7Y**
Albania	914	—Y	.01Y	.02Y	.01Y	.02Y	.02Y	.03Y	.01Y	—Y	—Y	—Y	—Y	—Y	—Y
Armenia	911	.15Y	.18Y	.19Y	.17Y	.20Y	.22Y	.20Y	.06Y	.12Y	.13Y	.14Y	.15Y	.10Y	.07Y
Azerbaijan	912	.08Y	.08Y	.08Y	.08Y	.11Y	.15Y	.23Y	.03Y	.03Y	.07Y	.18Y	.26Y	.37Y	.55Y
Belarus	913	.01Y	.01Y	.01Y	.01Y	.02Y	.03Y	.05Y	.09Y	.08Y	.06Y	.29Y	.15Y	.16Y	.23Y
Bosnia & Herzegovina	963	—Y	—Y	—Y	.01Y	—Y	—Y	.01Y	.01Y	.01Y	.02Y	.02Y	.03Y	.04Y	.05Y
Bulgaria	918	.03Y	.06Y	.09Y	.12Y	.09Y	.10Y	.14Y	.15Y	.15Y	.17Y	.34Y	.35Y	.45Y	.53Y
Croatia	960	.28Y	.23Y	.39Y	.37Y	.14Y	.06Y	.12Y	.07Y	.05Y	.05Y	.14Y	.28Y	.33Y	.27Y
Czech Republic	935	.17Y	.22Y	.35Y	.21Y	.25Y	.22Y	.20Y	.40Y	.44Y	.42Y	.96Y	1.20Y	1.18Y	1.47Y
Czechoslovakia n.s.	937	—Y	—Y	—Y	—Y	—Y	—Y	—Y	—Y	—Y	.10Y	.13Y	.18Y	.22Y	.29Y
Estonia	939	—Y	.01Y	.01Y	.01Y	.01Y	.02Y	.02Y	.02Y	.03Y	.02Y	.02Y	.02Y	.10Y	.14Y
Georgia	915	.02Y	.02Y	.03Y	.06Y	.10Y	.16Y	.26Y	.02Y	.02Y	.01Y	.01Y	.01Y	.04Y	.05Y
Gibraltar	823	.02Y	.01Y	.02Y	.03Y	.04Y	.09Y	.03Y	—Y	—Y	—Y	—Y	—Y	—Y	—Y
Hungary	944	.09Y	.07Y	.09Y	.10Y	.11Y	.14Y	.29Y	.31Y	.33Y	.66Y	1.36Y	1.70Y	1.88Y	2.11Y
Kazakhstan	916	.07Y	.09Y	.08Y	.08Y	.10Y	.13Y	.18Y	.36Y	.32Y	.49Y	.99Y	1.18Y	1.43Y	1.85Y
Kyrgyz Republic	917	.01Y	.01Y	.01Y	.01Y	.01Y	.02Y	.02Y	.01Y	.01Y	.01Y	.21Y	.20Y	.02Y	.03Y
Latvia	941	.02Y	.02Y	.02Y	.02Y	.03Y	.04Y	.04Y	.02Y	.03Y	.03Y	.03Y	.02Y	.04Y	.31Y
Lithuania	946	.01Y	.01Y	.01Y	.02Y	.03Y	.04Y	.06Y	.02Y	.01Y	.01Y	.01Y	.04Y	.06Y	.16Y
Macedonia, FYR	962	.01Y	.01Y	.01Y	.01Y	.01Y	.02Y	.02Y	.01Y	.01Y	.01Y	—Y	.01Y	.01Y	.02Y
Moldova	921	—Y	—Y	—Y	.01Y	.01Y	.01Y	.02Y	—Y	.01Y	.01Y	.02Y	.02Y	.02Y	.03Y
Poland	964	.17Y	.17Y	.23Y	.29Y	.24Y	.39Y	.43Y	.31Y	.37Y	.44Y	.62Y	.92Y	1.11Y	1.31Y
Romania	968	.25Y	.21Y	.17Y	.23Y	.40Y	.68Y	1.06Y	.56Y	.71Y	.74Y	1.39Y	1.27Y	1.64Y	1.71Y
Russia	922	.24Y	.31Y	.35Y	.53Y	.74Y	1.08Y	1.21Y	2.51Y	2.96Y	3.75Y	6.44Y	6.79Y	6.67Y	10.39Y
Serbia & Montenegro	965	.12Y	.13Y	.16Y	.22Y	.29Y	.36Y	.43Y	.03Y	.03Y	.04Y	.07Y	.09Y	.10Y	.12Y
Slovak Republic	936	.02Y	.02Y	.02Y	.02Y	.03Y	.02Y	.03Y	.05Y	.06Y	.08Y	.15Y	.26Y	.31Y	.33Y
Tajikistan	923	.01Y	.02Y	.04Y	.04Y	.05Y	.06Y	.12Y	.01Y	.01Y	.06Y	.03Y	.04Y	.09Y	.09Y
Turkey	186	3.24Y	3.39Y	4.87Y	9.15Y	8.93Y	11.56Y	12.13Y	2.83Y	3.03Y	5.60Y	10.24Y	10.73Y	12.03Y	16.05Y
Turkmenistan	925	.24Y	.24Y	.29Y	.38Y	.51Y	.64Y	.77Y	.02Y	.02Y	.56Y	.86Y	1.10Y	1.36Y	1.76Y
Ukraine	926	.08Y	.09Y	.12Y	.19Y	.21Y	.25Y	.31Y	1.41Y	1.47Y	1.87Y	4.62Y	3.91Y	4.76Y	5.94Y
Uzbekistan	927	.02Y	.04Y	.01Y	.01Y	.01Y	.02Y	.03Y	.05Y	.07Y	.07Y	.09Y	.11Y	.13Y	.17Y
Yugoslavia n.s.	966	—Y	—Y	—Y	—Y	—Y	—Y	—Y	.01Y	.01Y	.01Y	.01Y	.01Y	.02Y	.02Y
Europe n.s.	884	.03Y	.01Y	.01Y	.01Y	.02Y	.02Y	.03Y	.26Y	.25Y	.31Y	.38Y	.45Y	.55Y	.69Y
Middle East	**407**	**18.3Y**	**20.8Y**	**22.3Y**	**36.5Y**	**46.0Y**	**56.7Y**	**68.3Y**	**17.7Y**	**20.1Y**	**22.7Y**	**36.6Y**	**48.0Y**	**59.1Y**	**71.3Y**
Bahrain	419	1.78Y	1.89Y	2.29Y	2.98Y	4.04Y	5.07Y	6.14Y	.65Y	.80Y	.94Y	1.34Y	1.65Y	2.11Y	2.76Y
Egypt	469	1.13Y	1.28Y	1.26Y	2.00Y	2.69Y	3.35Y	4.07Y	.69Y	.81Y	1.09Y	2.32Y	3.10Y	3.92Y	4.94Y
Iran, I.R. of	429	2.27Y	2.97Y	3.15Y	3.70Y	4.79Y	5.76Y	6.78Y	.77Y	.73Y	.83Y	1.52Y	2.19Y	2.64Y	3.14Y
Iraq	433	.68Y	.80Y	.71Y	2.97Y	3.74Y	4.34Y	5.50Y	.71Y	.77Y	.40Y	.49Y	.61Y	.74Y	.90Y
Israel	436	.30Y	.16Y	.13Y	.14Y	.16Y	.20Y	.24Y	.13Y	.15Y	.16Y	.20Y	.26Y	.28Y	.32Y
Jordan	439	1.11Y	1.23Y	1.56Y	2.83Y	3.33Y	3.89Y	4.35Y	1.14Y	1.28Y	1.36Y	1.72Y	1.93Y	2.27Y	2.59Y
Kuwait	443	1.12Y	1.14Y	1.27Y	1.61Y	2.07Y	2.51Y	3.00Y	.53Y	.58Y	.72Y	1.08Y	1.41Y	1.73Y	2.16Y
Lebanon	446	.70Y	.77Y	.93Y	1.54Y	1.84Y	2.27Y	2.80Y	.45Y	.45Y	.53Y	1.15Y	1.39Y	1.73Y	2.20Y
Libya	672	.16Y	.16Y	.19Y	.37Y	.44Y	.52Y	.66Y	.09Y	.09Y	.20Y	.37Y	.50Y	.63Y	.75Y
Oman	449	1.83Y	1.90Y	1.76Y	2.05Y	2.70Y	3.23Y	3.84Y	.38Y	.42Y	.92Y	1.06Y	1.45Y	1.77Y	2.09Y
Qatar	453	.50Y	.68Y	.77Y	1.18Y	1.48Y	2.26Y	2.70Y	.39Y	.70Y	.53Y	1.28Y	1.45Y	1.86Y	2.19Y
Saudi Arabia	456	2.02Y	2.58Y	2.65Y	4.52Y	4.68Y	5.78Y	7.05Y	4.77Y	5.18Y	6.69Y	10.27Y	13.90Y	17.16Y	19.86Y
Syrian Arab Republic	463	.35Y	.40Y	.53Y	4.39Y	5.71Y	7.16Y	8.65Y	1.66Y	1.72Y	1.35Y	5.12Y	6.29Y	7.73Y	9.93Y
United Arab Emirates	466	3.49Y	3.80Y	3.81Y	4.76Y	6.60Y	8.09Y	9.83Y	5.14Y	6.09Y	6.56Y	8.33Y	11.27Y	13.82Y	16.42Y
Yemen, Republic of	474	.79Y	1.02Y	1.24Y	1.43Y	1.74Y	2.18Y	2.63Y	.20Y	.26Y	.38Y	.38Y	.60Y	.74Y	1.00Y
Middle East n.s.	489	.03Y	.03Y	.10Y	.06Y	.04Y	.04Y	.05Y	.02Y	.02Y	.01Y	.02Y	.02Y	.03Y	.04Y

	Exports 2001	2002	2003	2004	2005	2006	2007	Imports 2001	2002	2003	2004	2005	2006	2007
	Billions of U.S. Dollars							Billions of U.S. Dollars						
Western Hemisphere................ 207	**2.7Y**	**2.7Y**	**2.8Y**	**3.8Y**	**4.2Y**	**5.3Y**	**5.8Y**	**4.6Y**	**4.7Y**	**5.6Y**	**8.7Y**	**9.8Y**	**12.0Y**	**13.6Y**
Argentina................................ 213	.12Y	.03Y	.05Y	.09Y	.08Y	.12Y	.25Y	1.18Y	1.14Y	1.28Y	2.08Y	1.85Y	1.67Y	2.40Y
Aruba...................................... 314	—Y	—Y	—Y	—Y	—Y	—Y	—Y	.01Y	—Y	—Y	—Y	.02Y	.01Y	.01Y
Bahamas, The........................... 313	.02Y	.02Y	.04Y	.04Y	.05Y	.06Y	.07Y	—Y	—Y	—Y	—Y	—Y	—Y	—Y
Bermuda.................................. 319	—Y	—Y	—Y	—Y	—Y	—Y	—Y	—Y	—Y	—Y	—Y	—Y	—Y	.01Y
Bolivia.................................... 218	—Y	—Y	—Y	.01Y	—Y	.01Y	.01Y	—Y	—Y	—Y	.01Y	.01Y	.01Y	.01Y
Brazil...................................... 223	1.45Y	1.49Y	1.70Y	2.39Y	2.57Y	3.59Y	3.25Y	2.60Y	2.73Y	3.27Y	5.15Y	5.68Y	7.99Y	8.35Y
Chile....................................... 228	.06Y	.04Y	.05Y	.05Y	.09Y	.10Y	.13Y	.13Y	.12Y	.25Y	.31Y	.41Y	.42Y	.52Y
Colombia................................. 233	.06Y	.07Y	.08Y	.10Y	.10Y	.14Y	.17Y	.10Y	.16Y	.14Y	.18Y	.58Y	.51Y	.62Y
Costa Rica............................... 238	.16Y	.25Y	.20Y	.15Y	.17Y	.08Y	.04Y	—Y	—Y	.01Y	.02Y	.03Y	.03Y	.04Y
Dominican Republic.................. 243	.01Y	.02Y	.01Y	.01Y	.02Y	.02Y	.03Y	—Y	—Y	—Y	—Y	—Y	—Y	—Y
Ecuador................................... 248	.06Y	.01Y	.03Y	.04Y	.08Y	.10Y	.10Y	.04Y	.03Y	.03Y	.13Y	.06Y	.03Y	.03Y
El Salvador.............................. 253	—Y	—Y	.02Y	.01Y	.01Y	.01Y	.02Y	.01Y	—Y	—Y	—Y	—Y	—Y	—Y
Guatemala............................... 258	.01Y	.02Y	.01Y	.02Y	.04Y	.03Y	.03Y	.07Y	.09Y	.08Y	.10Y	.07Y	.09Y	.12Y
Guyana.................................... 336	—Y	—Y	—Y	—Y	—Y	—Y	—Y	—Y	—Y	—Y	—Y	.01Y	.01Y	.01Y
Haiti.. 263	—Y	—Y	—Y	—Y	.01Y	.01Y	.01Y	—Y	—Y	—Y	—Y	—Y	.01Y	.01Y
Honduras................................. 268	—Y	.01Y	.01Y	.01Y	.01Y	.01Y	.02Y	—Y	—Y	—Y	—Y	—Y	—Y	—Y
Jamaica................................... 343	—Y	.01Y	.01Y	.01Y	.01Y	.02Y	.01Y	—Y	—Y	—Y	.01Y	.03Y	—Y	—Y
Mexico..................................... 273	.38Y	.39Y	.42Y	.62Y	.73Y	.73Y	1.35Y	.26Y	.24Y	.32Y	.34Y	.56Y	.62Y	.74Y
Netherlands Antilles................. 353	.19Y	.14Y	—Y	—Y	—Y	—Y	—Y	—Y	.01Y	—Y	—Y	—Y	—Y	—Y
Nicaragua................................ 278	—Y	.01Y	—Y	.01Y	—Y	.01Y	—Y	—Y	—Y	—Y	—Y	—Y	—Y	—Y
Panama.................................... 283	.02Y	.02Y	.01Y	.01Y	.01Y	.01Y	.02Y	—Y	—Y	.01Y	.02Y	.01Y	.02Y	.01Y
Paraguay.................................. 288	—Y	—Y	—Y	—Y	—Y	.01Y	.01Y	.02Y	—Y	.01Y	.04Y	.05Y	.03Y	.04Y
Peru.. 293	.03Y	.02Y	.02Y	.03Y	.06Y	.04Y	.10Y	.06Y	.05Y	.04Y	.03Y	.03Y	.06Y	.07Y
Suriname................................. 366	—Y	—Y	—Y	—Y	—Y	—Y	—Y	—Y	—Y	.05Y	.06Y	.08Y	.09Y	.12Y
Trinidad and Tobago................ 369	.01Y	.02Y	.01Y	.02Y	.03Y	.03Y	.03Y	—Y	—Y	.01Y	.03Y	—Y	—Y	—Y
Uruguay.................................. 298	.03Y	.02Y	.01Y	.12Y	.02Y	.01Y	.02Y	.08Y	.12Y	.08Y	.14Y	.20Y	.27Y	.32Y
Venezuela, Rep. Bol.................. 299	.06Y	.03Y	.03Y	.06Y	.07Y	.13Y	.12Y	.06Y	.02Y	.03Y	.05Y	.06Y	.10Y	.11Y
Western Hem. n.s...................... 399	.03Y	.03Y	.02Y	.02Y	.02Y	.03Y	.03Y	.01Y	—Y	—Y	.02Y	.03Y	.01Y	.02Y
Other Countries n.i.e............... 910	**—Y**	**—Y**	**—Y**	**.1Y**	**.1Y**	**.1Y**	**.1Y**	**.1Y**	**.1Y**	**.1Y**	**.2Y**	**.2Y**	**.2Y**	**.3Y**
Cuba.. 928	.02Y	.02Y	.02Y	.03Y	.04Y	.05Y	.06Y	.02Y	.05Y	.06Y	.07Y	.08Y	.11Y	.14Y
North Korea.............................. 954	.02Y	.03Y	.03Y	.07Y	.05Y	.06Y	.07Y	.05Y	.10Y	.04Y	.10Y	.10Y	.12Y	.15Y
Countries & Areas n.s.............. 898	**16.5Y**	**18.1Y**	**22.2Y**	**28.7Y**	**34.5Y**	**42.5Y**	**52.4Y**	**4.8Y**	**4.8Y**	**6.4Y**	**5.9Y**	**7.8Y**	**9.0Y**	**10.1Y**
Special Categories.................. 899	**1.1Y**	**1.1Y**	**1.3Y**	**1.6Y**	**2.0Y**	**2.5Y**	**3.1Y**	**1.1Y**	**1.0Y**	**1.2Y**	**1.6Y**	**1.9Y**	**2.3Y**	**2.8Y**
Memorandum Items														
European Union......................... 998	47.02Y	45.72Y	55.96Y	83.50Y	102.02Y	118.10Y	127.65Y	63.47Y	70.68Y	82.01Y	111.93Y	129.45Y	135.19Y	167.30Y
Oil Exporting Ctys...................... 999	14.72Y	16.66Y	17.67Y	25.64Y	32.12Y	39.54Y	47.08Y	14.61Y	16.63Y	18.99Y	27.24Y	36.34Y	44.84Y	53.21Y
Non-Oil Develop.Ctys................. 201	88.06Y	85.37Y	107.09Y	153.71Y	196.53Y	256.33Y	291.61Y	49.83Y	56.01Y	72.68Y	122.82Y	142.01Y	172.71Y	228.49Y
PERCENT DISTRIBUTION														
Industrial Countries................ 101	**51.4**	**50.1**	**50.1**	**48.9**	**48.9**	**47.0**	**45.0**	**60.0**	**59.5**	**56.1**	**51.6**	**51.0**	**48.2**	**47.3**
Developing Countries............. 202	**41.5**	**42.0**	**42.0**	**43.7**	**44.0**	**46.0**	**47.2**	**36.7**	**37.5**	**40.4**	**46.1**	**46.4**	**49.2**	**50.4**
Africa...................................... 607	**3.3**	**3.2**	**3.2**	**3.3**	**2.8**	**3.5**	**3.4**	**1.5**	**1.5**	**1.4**	**1.4**	**1.4**	**1.5**	**1.4**
Asia....................................... 507	**27.6**	**26.8**	**27.8**	**27.5**	**29.2**	**30.2**	**31.0**	**17.0**	**17.7**	**19.5**	**21.7**	**21.8**	**23.7**	**25.5**
Europe.................................... 170	**2.2**	**2.3**	**2.6**	**3.0**	**2.4**	**2.6**	**2.6**	**5.5**	**5.5**	**7.0**	**9.1**	**8.2**	**8.0**	**8.4**
Middle East............................ 407	**7.4**	**8.6**	**7.5**	**8.9**	**8.9**	**8.8**	**9.5**	**10.1**	**10.4**	**10.0**	**11.2**	**12.5**	**13.4**	**12.7**
Western Hemisphere............. 207	**1.1**	**1.1**	**.9**	**.9**	**.8**	**.8**	**.8**	**2.6**	**2.4**	**2.5**	**2.7**	**2.5**	**2.7**	**2.4**
Other Countries n.i.e............... 910	**—**	**—**	**—**	**—**	**—**	**—**	**—**	**—**	**.1**	**—**	**.1**	**—**	**.1**	**.1**
ANNUAL PERCENT CHANGE														
World....................................... 001	**–7.7**	**–1.8**	**22.2**	**38.1**	**26.6**	**23.9**	**11.5**	**.7**	**10.3**	**17.0**	**43.7**	**18.0**	**15.1**	**26.5**
Industrial Countries................ 101	**–11.3**	**–4.2**	**22.1**	**34.8**	**26.7**	**19.0**	**6.7**	**–1.4**	**9.4**	**10.4**	**32.0**	**16.8**	**8.8**	**24.0**
Developing Countries............. 202	**–3.9**	**–.7**	**22.3**	**43.8**	**27.5**	**29.4**	**14.5**	**7.4**	**12.7**	**26.2**	**63.7**	**18.8**	**22.0**	**29.5**
Africa...................................... 607	**–8.4**	**–5.8**	**23.5**	**44.5**	**4.7**	**58.7**	**6.1**	**3.0**	**7.3**	**13.6**	**35.8**	**20.2**	**21.5**	**17.6**
Asia....................................... 507	**–8.2**	**–4.4**	**26.5**	**36.8**	**34.1**	**28.5**	**14.1**	**2.0**	**15.4**	**28.9**	**59.3**	**18.8**	**25.1**	**36.1**
Europe.................................... 170	**–2.3**	**5.0**	**35.7**	**61.5**	**2.3**	**30.3**	**11.6**	**10.8**	**10.3**	**49.0**	**88.0**	**5.8**	**11.9**	**32.7**
Middle East............................ 407	**17.8**	**13.9**	**7.4**	**63.5**	**26.0**	**23.1**	**20.5**	**19.1**	**13.2**	**13.1**	**61.5**	**31.0**	**23.2**	**20.5**
Western Hemisphere............. 207	**–.2**	**–2.3**	**3.6**	**39.0**	**9.2**	**26.9**	**9.7**	**–.7**	**1.6**	**18.9**	**55.1**	**12.3**	**22.5**	**13.2**
Other Countries n.i.e............... 910	**–64.0**	**22.5**	**6.2**	**107.8**	**–15.3**	**25.3**	**21.2**	**–35.7**	**104.5**	**–30.6**	**60.3**	**11.2**	**23.8**	**27.4**

	Exports							Imports						
	2001	2002	2003	2004	2005	2006	2007	2001	2002	2003	2004	2005	2006	2007
	Billions of U.S. Dollars							*Billions of U.S. Dollars*						
IFS World Total	**340.8**	**344.2**	**374.7**	**460.7**	**558.2**	**667.9**	**757.9**	**383.2**	**358.0**	**370.4**	**450.8**	**531.6**	**633.3**	**757.8**
DOTS World Total............ 001	**349.7Y**	**353.0Y**	**386.4Y**	**478.0Y**	**575.6Y**	**690.9Y**	**790.4Y**	**403.3Y**	**381.5Y**	**387.3Y**	**477.2Y**	**556.2Y**	**659.2Y**	**783.0Y**
Industrial Countries............ 101	**253.4Y**	**257.4Y**	**277.1Y**	**326.4Y**	**389.0Y**	**453.6Y**	**502.6Y**	**272.3Y**	**253.1Y**	**254.0Y**	**287.6Y**	**324.8Y**	**368.8Y**	**426.0Y**
United States............ 111	196.51Y	199.66Y	210.14Y	246.83Y	291.50Y	327.24Y	350.22Y	182.03Y	167.09Y	167.89Y	183.32Y	204.28Y	229.35Y	259.32Y
Canada............ 156	5.83Y	5.59Y	6.16Y	7.49Y	11.31Y	13.41Y	16.74Y	8.10Y	7.66Y	7.27Y	9.23Y	10.71Y	12.88Y	15.03Y
Australia............ 193	.51Y	.65Y	.81Y	.96Y	1.18Y	1.38Y	1.93Y	1.00Y	.98Y	1.15Y	1.28Y	2.09Y	2.42Y	2.47Y
Japan............ 158	6.37Y	6.65Y	7.23Y	9.52Y	11.46Y	14.97Y	18.24Y	18.22Y	18.08Y	15.80Y	21.88Y	25.36Y	30.71Y	34.30Y
New Zealand............ 196	.08Y	.10Y	.10Y	.13Y	.15Y	.16Y	.22Y	.63Y	.54Y	.57Y	.60Y	.74Y	.73Y	1.01Y
Austria............ 122	.13Y	.15Y	.11Y	.17Y	.24Y	.26Y	.44Y	.86Y	.73Y	.90Y	1.10Y	1.37Y	1.75Y	2.35Y
Belgium............ 124	1.19Y	1.07Y	1.17Y	1.49Y	2.33Y	6.41Y	8.80Y	1.08Y	.81Y	.77Y	.89Y	2.02Y	3.22Y	3.72Y
Belgium-Luxembourg n.s............ 127	2.99Y	2.59Y	2.38Y	2.71Y	2.60Y	.58Y	.34Y	1.46Y	1.35Y	1.39Y	1.71Y	1.02Y	.16Y	.13Y
Cyprus............ 423	.04Y	.04Y	.04Y	.08Y	.13Y	.27Y	.46Y	—Y	.02Y	—Y	.02Y	.01Y	.10Y	—Y
Denmark............ 128	.70Y	.69Y	.90Y	.95Y	1.06Y	1.25Y	1.60Y	1.07Y	1.22Y	1.20Y	1.37Y	1.51Y	1.77Y	2.15Y
Finland............ 172	.33Y	.37Y	.49Y	.73Y	.89Y	1.43Y	1.59Y	1.13Y	1.07Y	1.31Y	1.42Y	1.92Y	2.20Y	2.60Y
France............ 132	4.94Y	4.87Y	4.96Y	6.38Y	7.29Y	8.75Y	9.04Y	8.33Y	7.34Y	8.81Y	9.04Y	9.04Y	10.10Y	11.77Y
Germany............ 134	6.81Y	6.46Y	8.11Y	9.32Y	11.55Y	14.82Y	18.49Y	17.00Y	16.47Y	15.72Y	19.00Y	22.95Y	24.78Y	30.97Y
Greece............ 174	.32Y	.37Y	.42Y	.49Y	.47Y	.66Y	1.16Y	.12Y	.11Y	.11Y	.12Y	.13Y	.21Y	.26Y
Iceland............ 176	.06Y	.07Y	.05Y	.06Y	.06Y	.09Y	.11Y	.02Y	.02Y	.01Y	.02Y	.02Y	.02Y	.04Y
Ireland............ 178	.60Y	.43Y	.51Y	.52Y	.58Y	.72Y	.74Y	1.18Y	1.15Y	1.39Y	1.42Y	1.95Y	2.27Y	2.24Y
Italy............ 136	4.75Y	4.92Y	5.71Y	6.94Y	7.99Y	10.62Y	12.72Y	8.81Y	7.66Y	7.77Y	8.99Y	9.98Y	12.18Y	16.63Y
Luxembourg............ 137	.01Y	—Y	—Y	—Y	.01Y	.05Y	.04Y	.02Y	.02Y	.05Y	.03Y	.13Y	.16Y	.21Y
Malta............ 181	.01Y	.01Y	.02Y	.06Y	.03Y	.02Y	.02Y	.03Y	.03Y	.03Y	.03Y	.26Y	.22Y	.20Y
Netherlands............ 138	5.98Y	6.92Y	10.28Y	11.44Y	13.59Y	17.20Y	21.98Y	2.55Y	2.64Y	2.78Y	2.86Y	3.95Y	5.50Y	7.21Y
Norway............ 142	.60Y	.49Y	.73Y	.81Y	.95Y	1.24Y	1.42Y	.75Y	1.06Y	.65Y	.95Y	1.23Y	1.37Y	1.75Y
Portugal............ 182	.99Y	1.17Y	1.19Y	1.54Y	1.72Y	2.22Y	2.80Y	.49Y	.42Y	.69Y	.90Y	1.10Y	1.02Y	1.18Y
Slovenia............ 961	.09Y	.09Y	.12Y	.18Y	.18Y	.21Y	.32Y	.09Y	.05Y	.06Y	.08Y	.09Y	.11Y	.15Y
Spain............ 184	5.18Y	5.63Y	6.40Y	7.91Y	11.24Y	14.54Y	16.60Y	6.68Y	6.81Y	7.20Y	9.03Y	8.99Y	10.38Y	11.90Y
Sweden............ 144	.49Y	.84Y	.79Y	1.08Y	1.32Y	1.39Y	1.92Y	2.62Y	1.83Y	2.35Y	3.03Y	3.75Y	3.77Y	4.54Y
Switzerland............ 146	1.77Y	1.84Y	1.78Y	1.36Y	2.07Y	4.16Y	4.56Y	2.97Y	2.98Y	3.34Y	3.67Y	4.14Y	4.44Y	5.71Y
United Kingdom............ 112	6.10Y	5.71Y	6.48Y	7.30Y	7.15Y	9.54Y	10.09Y	5.10Y	4.98Y	4.79Y	5.62Y	6.04Y	6.99Y	8.18Y
Developing Countries............ 202	**86.6Y**	**85.5Y**	**101.5Y**	**138.9Y**	**172.0Y**	**209.8Y**	**258.5Y**	**121.9Y**	**120.1Y**	**129.4Y**	**183.9Y**	**227.1Y**	**282.6Y**	**348.2Y**
Africa............ 607	**2.8Y**	**3.2Y**	**4.0Y**	**6.0Y**	**7.7Y**	**9.6Y**	**11.8Y**	**5.5Y**	**4.4Y**	**4.9Y**	**9.1Y**	**11.0Y**	**13.4Y**	**16.4Y**
Algeria............ 612	.23Y	.28Y	.52Y	.91Y	1.01Y	1.18Y	1.48Y	1.42Y	1.23Y	1.31Y	2.18Y	3.19Y	2.28Y	2.54Y
Angola............ 614	.16Y	.24Y	.31Y	.45Y	.70Y	1.02Y	1.43Y	.19Y	.06Y	.16Y	.51Y	1.63Y	2.11Y	2.63Y
Benin............ 638	.01Y	.01Y	.02Y	.02Y	.04Y	.05Y	.05Y	.02Y	—Y	—Y	—Y	—Y	.01Y	.01Y
Burkina Faso............ 748	—Y	—Y	.01Y	.01Y	.02Y	.01Y	—Y	.02Y	.02Y	.02Y	—Y	—Y	—Y	.01Y
Cameroon............ 622	.02Y	.02Y	.03Y	.04Y	.11Y	.14Y	.16Y	.01Y	—Y	.07Y	.09Y	.11Y	.14Y	.22Y
Cape Verde............ 624	.01Y	.01Y	.01Y	.02Y	.03Y	.03Y	.04Y	—Y	—Y	—Y	—Y	—Y	—Y	—Y
Central African Rep............ 626	—Y	—Y	—Y	—Y	—Y	.01Y	—Y	—Y	—Y	—Y	—Y	—Y	—Y	—Y
Congo, Dem. Rep. of............ 636	.01Y	—Y	.01Y	.03Y	.03Y	.06Y	.03Y	—Y	—Y	.02Y	.01Y	.07Y	.35Y	.19Y
Congo, Republic of............ 634	.01Y	.02Y	.04Y	.06Y	.08Y	.08Y	.16Y	.11Y	.22Y	.09Y	.01Y	.10Y	.36Y	.17Y
Côte d'Ivoire............ 662	.09Y	.05Y	.06Y	.06Y	.08Y	.11Y	.10Y	.03Y	.03Y	.05Y	.03Y	.06Y	.06Y	.10Y
Djibouti............ 611	—Y	—Y	.01Y	.01Y	.01Y	.01Y	—Y	—Y	—Y	—Y	—Y	—Y	—Y	—Y
Equatorial Guinea............ 642	—Y	—Y	—Y	—Y	.01Y	.01Y	.04Y	.03Y	.02Y	—Y	.02Y	.34Y	.13Y	.04Y
Ethiopia............ 644	.01Y	.01Y	.01Y	.02Y	.04Y	.06Y	.04Y	—Y	—Y	—Y	—Y	—Y	—Y	—Y
Gabon............ 646	.01Y	.01Y	.01Y	.02Y	.04Y	.04Y	.06Y	.14Y	.18Y	.17Y	.26Y	.23Y	.34Y	.35Y
Gambia, The............ 648	.03Y	.02Y	.03Y	.03Y	.04Y	.05Y	.07Y	—Y	—Y	—Y	—Y	—Y	—Y	—Y
Ghana............ 652	.07Y	.10Y	.13Y	.19Y	.26Y	.26Y	.38Y	—Y	.03Y	—Y	.03Y	.03Y	.01Y	.01Y
Guinea............ 656	—Y	.01Y	.02Y	.02Y	.03Y	.03Y	.04Y	—Y	—Y	—Y	—Y	—Y	—Y	—Y
Guinea-Bissau............ 654	—Y	—Y	—Y	—Y	—Y	—Y	—Y	.02Y	.03Y	—Y	—Y	—Y	—Y	.23Y
Kenya............ 664	.06Y	.03Y	.03Y	.10Y	.11Y	.07Y	.12Y	.01Y	.01Y	.01Y	.02Y	.01Y	.01Y	.02Y
Liberia............ 668	.02Y	.01Y	.04Y	.07Y	.05Y	.06Y	.07Y	—Y	—Y	.01Y	.01Y	—Y	—Y	—Y
Madagascar............ 674	.01Y	.01Y	.01Y	.04Y	.03Y	.02Y	.03Y	—Y	—Y	—Y	—Y	—Y	—Y	—Y
Malawi............ 676	—Y	—Y	—Y	.01Y	—Y	.01Y	.01Y	—Y	—Y	—Y	.01Y	.01Y	.01Y	.01Y
Mali............ 678	—Y	.01Y	.01Y	.01Y	.02Y	.02Y	—Y	.01Y	—Y	—Y	—Y	—Y	.01Y	.02Y
Mauritania............ 682	.01Y	.03Y	.03Y	.05Y	.05Y	.08Y	.11Y	—Y	—Y	—Y	—Y	—Y	—Y	—Y
Mauritius............ 684	.03Y	.04Y	.03Y	.05Y	.04Y	.06Y	.03Y	—Y	.01Y	.01Y	—Y	.01Y	.01Y	.01Y
Morocco............ 686	.33Y	.37Y	.44Y	.61Y	.69Y	.72Y	.93Y	.25Y	.28Y	.32Y	.44Y	.55Y	.64Y	.90Y
Mozambique............ 688	.02Y	.04Y	.03Y	.07Y	.07Y	.09Y	.06Y	—Y	—Y	—Y	—Y	—Y	—Y	.01Y
Namibia............ 728	.02Y	.01Y	.01Y	.01Y	.01Y	.02Y	—Y	—Y	—Y	—Y	—Y	—Y	—Y	—Y
Niger............ 692	—Y	—Y	—Y	.01Y	.01Y	.02Y	.01Y	.04Y	—Y	—Y	—Y	—Y	—Y	—Y
Nigeria............ 694	.53Y	.65Y	.61Y	.70Y	1.20Y	1.72Y	2.02Y	2.12Y	1.51Y	1.88Y	4.40Y	3.61Y	5.57Y	7.08Y
Senegal............ 722	.04Y	.05Y	.08Y	.11Y	.19Y	.19Y	.27Y	—Y	—Y	—Y	—Y	.01Y	.01Y	.01Y
Seychelles............ 718	—Y	—Y	—Y	—Y	—Y	—Y	—Y	—Y	—Y	—Y	—Y	—Y	—Y	.01Y
Sierra Leone............ 724	.01Y	—Y	.01Y	.01Y	.01Y	.04Y	.01Y	—Y	—Y	—Y	—Y	—Y	—Y	—Y
Somalia............ 726	.03Y	.03Y	.02Y	.04Y	.04Y	.06Y	—Y	—Y	—Y	—Y	—Y	—Y	—Y	—Y
South Africa............ 199	.82Y	.84Y	1.17Y	1.75Y	2.22Y	2.79Y	3.49Y	.61Y	.44Y	.45Y	.61Y	.89Y	1.12Y	1.53Y
Sudan............ 732	.02Y	.02Y	.01Y	.06Y	.09Y	.09Y	.09Y	.01Y	—Y	—Y	—Y	.01Y	.02Y	.02Y
Tanzania............ 738	.01Y	.01Y	.01Y	.04Y	.05Y	.05Y	.06Y	—Y	—Y	—Y	—Y	—Y	—Y	—Y
Togo............ 742	—Y	—Y	.01Y	.02Y	.03Y	.04Y	.05Y	.01Y	—Y	.01Y	.01Y	.01Y	.01Y	.01Y
Tunisia............ 744	.14Y	.17Y	.16Y	.23Y	.23Y	.31Y	.36Y	.05Y	.06Y	.07Y	.11Y	.10Y	.16Y	.19Y
Uganda............ 746	—Y	—Y	—Y	.01Y	.01Y	.01Y	.01Y	—Y	—Y	—Y	—Y	—Y	—Y	—Y

	Exports 2001	Exports 2002	Exports 2003	Exports 2004	Exports 2005	Exports 2006	Exports 2007	Imports 2001	Imports 2002	Imports 2003	Imports 2004	Imports 2005	Imports 2006	Imports 2007
	Billions of U.S. Dollars							*Billions of U.S. Dollars*						
Zambia.......... 754	—Y	—Y	.01Y	.01Y	.01Y	.01Y	—Y	—Y	—Y	.01Y	.01Y	—Y	—Y	.01Y
Zimbabwe.......... 698	.01Y	—Y	.01Y	.01Y	—Y	—Y	—Y	.01Y	.01Y	.01Y	.01Y	.03Y	.02Y	.01Y
Africa n.s.......... 799	.08Y	.06Y	.06Y	.09Y	.01Y	.01Y	—Y	.40Y	.25Y	.23Y	.38Y	.01Y	.01Y	.01Y
Asia.......... 507	**13.9Y**	**17.2Y**	**24.8Y**	**31.8Y**	**39.8Y**	**51.2Y**	**70.5Y**	**41.5Y**	**47.4Y**	**49.7Y**	**70.6Y**	**86.0Y**	**113.1Y**	**144.5Y**
Afghanistan, I.S. of.......... 512	—Y	—Y	—Y	—Y	—Y	—Y	—Y	—Y	—Y	—Y	—Y	.01Y	.01Y	.01Y
Bangladesh.......... 513	.18Y	.14Y	.23Y	.35Y	.33Y	.44Y	.55Y	.02Y	.02Y	.02Y	.02Y	.07Y	.10Y	.15Y
Brunei Darussalam.......... 516	—Y	—Y	—Y	—Y	—Y	—Y	—Y	—Y	—Y	—Y	—Y	—Y	.02Y	—Y
Cambodia.......... 522	—Y	—Y	—Y	—Y	.01Y	—Y	.01Y	—Y	—Y	—Y	—Y	.01Y	.02Y	.04Y
China,P.R.: Mainland.......... 924	5.00Y	6.39Y	11.15Y	14.52Y	18.72Y	23.80Y	37.68Y	10.48Y	12.36Y	17.48Y	28.03Y	37.34Y	53.55Y	72.42Y
China,P.R.:Hong Kong.......... 532	.83Y	.89Y	1.24Y	1.43Y	1.92Y	2.03Y	2.68Y	1.41Y	1.46Y	1.42Y	1.48Y	1.95Y	2.43Y	2.56Y
China,P.R.:Macao.......... 546	.01Y	.01Y	.62Y	.99Y	1.29Y	1.54Y	1.75Y	.16Y	.10Y	.07Y	.14Y	.20Y	.22Y	.31Y
Fiji.......... 819	—Y	—Y	—Y	—Y	—Y	—Y	—Y	—Y	—Y	—Y	—Y	—Y	.01Y	.01Y
French Polynesia.......... 887	—Y	.01Y	—Y	—Y	.01Y	.01Y	.01Y	—Y	—Y	—Y	—Y	—Y	—Y	—Y
India.......... 534	1.07Y	1.66Y	1.90Y	2.25Y	3.14Y	4.35Y	5.50Y	1.58Y	1.64Y	1.76Y	2.41Y	3.66Y	4.51Y	5.83Y
Indonesia.......... 536	.36Y	.47Y	.54Y	.88Y	1.21Y	1.13Y	1.50Y	1.18Y	1.25Y	1.17Y	1.59Y	1.87Y	2.37Y	2.83Y
Korea.......... 542	2.54Y	2.75Y	3.53Y	4.49Y	5.29Y	7.47Y	9.16Y	8.36Y	9.32Y	9.44Y	12.60Y	16.40Y	20.27Y	25.04Y
Malaysia.......... 548	.62Y	.66Y	.84Y	.96Y	1.11Y	1.85Y	1.92Y	2.99Y	2.85Y	3.88Y	4.83Y	5.48Y	6.96Y	8.85Y
Maldives.......... 556	—Y	—Y	—Y	—Y	—Y	—Y	—Y	.90Y	1.02Y	.86Y	.95Y	—Y	—Y	—Y
Mongolia.......... 948	—	—Y	—Y	—Y	—Y	—Y	—Y	—Y	—Y	—Y	—Y	.02Y	.01Y	.01Y
Myanmar.......... 518	—Y	—Y	.01Y	—Y	—Y	—Y	—Y	—Y	—Y	—Y	—Y	.01Y	.02Y	.02Y
New Caledonia.......... 839	—Y	—Y	—Y	.01Y	.01Y	.01Y	—Y	—Y	—Y	—Y	—Y	—Y	—Y	—Y
Pakistan.......... 564	.10Y	.11Y	.12Y	.16Y	.36Y	.31Y	.28Y	.19Y	.19Y	.17Y	.26Y	.32Y	.40Y	.47Y
Papua New Guinea.......... 853	.01Y	—Y	—Y	—Y	—Y	.02Y	.01Y	—Y	—Y	—Y	—Y	—Y	—Y	—Y
Philippines.......... 566	.30Y	.36Y	.49Y	.60Y	.64Y	.87Y	1.32Y	1.13Y	1.28Y	1.19Y	1.27Y	1.91Y	1.89Y	1.86Y
Samoa.......... 862	.01Y	—Y	—Y	.01Y	.01Y	—Y	—Y	—Y	—Y	—Y	—Y	—Y	—Y	—Y
Singapore.......... 576	.67Y	.93Y	.95Y	1.63Y	1.86Y	2.73Y	3.15Y	2.10Y	2.42Y	2.36Y	3.55Y	4.20Y	4.60Y	5.15Y
Solomon Islands.......... 813	—Y	—Y	—Y	—Y	—Y	—Y	.01Y	—Y	—Y	—Y	—Y	—Y	—Y	—Y
Sri Lanka.......... 524	.06Y	.06Y	.04Y	.12Y	.12Y	.12Y	.04Y	.08Y	.09Y	.09Y	.10Y	.23Y	.14Y	.17Y
Taiwan Province of China.......... 528	1.03Y	1.45Y	1.65Y	1.54Y	1.71Y	2.13Y	2.03Y	5.32Y	6.50Y	4.62Y	6.21Y	7.67Y	9.45Y	10.98Y
Thailand.......... 578	.76Y	.84Y	1.08Y	1.27Y	1.57Y	1.73Y	2.00Y	1.36Y	1.51Y	1.77Y	2.52Y	3.38Y	4.32Y	5.51Y
Vanuatu.......... 846	—Y	—Y	—Y	—Y	—Y	—Y	—Y	—Y	—Y	—Y	—Y	—Y	.01Y	—Y
Vietnam.......... 582	.10Y	.18Y	.20Y	.25Y	.38Y	.51Y	.72Y	.15Y	.06Y	.06Y	.09Y	.47Y	.67Y	.81Y
Asia n.s.......... 598	.20Y	.26Y	.17Y	.28Y	.08Y	.15Y	.15Y	4.12Y	5.30Y	3.28Y	4.56Y	.74Y	1.13Y	1.52Y
Europe.......... 170	**3.2Y**	**3.4Y**	**4.7Y**	**6.6Y**	**9.2Y**	**11.5Y**	**13.0Y**	**5.9Y**	**6.2Y**	**7.2Y**	**7.9Y**	**7.9Y**	**9.7Y**	**11.9Y**
Albania.......... 914	—Y	.01Y	.02Y	.03Y	.04Y	.03Y	.06Y	—Y	—Y	—Y	.01Y	—Y	—Y	—Y
Armenia.......... 911	—	—	.01Y	.01Y	.01Y	.02Y	.02Y	—	—Y	—Y	—Y	—Y	—Y	—Y
Azerbaijan.......... 912	—Y	—Y	.01Y	.01Y	.02Y	.03Y	.05Y	—Y	—Y	—Y	—Y	—Y	.09Y	.71Y
Belarus.......... 913	—Y	—Y	.01Y	.01Y	.01Y	.02Y	.03Y	.06Y	.08Y	.12Y	.27Y	.24Y	.27Y	.04Y
Bosnia & Herzegovina.......... 963	—	—Y	.01	.01	.02	.02Y	.01Y	—Y	—Y	—Y	—Y	—Y	—Y	—Y
Bulgaria.......... 918	.12Y	.15Y	.23Y	.42Y	.60Y	.91Y	.91Y	.06Y	.10Y	.09Y	.13Y	.19Y	.21Y	.31Y
Croatia.......... 960	.05Y	.04Y	.07Y	.10Y	.12Y	.17Y	.23Y	.01Y	—Y	.02Y	—Y	.02Y	.07Y	.02Y
Czech Republic.......... 935	.05Y	.06Y	.12Y	.13Y	.15Y	.17Y	.20Y	.13Y	.14Y	.14Y	.23Y	.64Y	.79Y	.87Y
Czechoslovakia n.s.......... 937	.02Y	.01Y	.01Y	.03Y	—Y	—Y	.01Y	.11Y	.10Y	.14Y	.25Y	.08Y	.10Y	.13Y
Estonia.......... 939	.01Y	.01Y	.02Y	.07Y	.07Y	.07Y	.06Y	.02Y	.02Y	.03Y	.05Y	.06Y	.10Y	.03Y
Faroe Islands.......... 816	—Y	—Y	—Y	.02Y	—Y	.01Y	.01Y	—Y	—Y	—Y	—Y	—Y	—Y	—Y
Georgia.......... 915	.01Y	.03Y	.06Y	.09Y	.09Y	.07Y	.12Y	.01Y	—Y	.01Y	.02Y	.01Y	.03Y	.02Y
Gibraltar.......... 823	—Y	—Y	—Y	—Y	—Y	.01Y	—Y	.01Y	—Y	—Y	.01Y	—Y	—Y	—Y
Hungary.......... 944	.13Y	.12Y	.12Y	.14Y	.21Y	.16Y	.20Y	.28Y	.29Y	.28Y	.42Y	.50Y	.57Y	.61Y
Kazakhstan.......... 916	.01Y	.01Y	.01Y	.02Y	.04Y	.06Y	.06Y	1.36Y	2.30Y	2.44Y	.06Y	.08Y	.11Y	.10Y
Latvia.......... 941	.01Y	.01Y	.02Y	.02Y	.06Y	.09Y	.02Y	.31Y	.12Y	.04Y	.07Y	.08Y	.04Y	.04Y
Lithuania.......... 946	.04Y	.04Y	.04Y	.08Y	.10Y	.10Y	.12Y	.01Y	.02Y	.01Y	.04Y	.04Y	.07Y	.11Y
Macedonia, FYR.......... 962	.01Y	.01Y	.01Y	.02Y	.01Y	.04Y	.06Y	—Y	—Y	—Y	—Y	—Y	.01Y	—Y
Moldova.......... 921	—Y	—Y	—Y	.01Y	.03Y	.05Y	.04Y	—Y	—Y	—Y	—Y	—Y	—Y	—Y
Poland.......... 964	.32Y	.26Y	.36Y	.90Y	.93Y	1.28Y	1.38Y	.50Y	.39Y	.44Y	.60Y	.81Y	.96Y	1.33Y
Romania.......... 968	.21Y	.17Y	.29Y	.37Y	.45Y	.48Y	.57Y	.12Y	.12Y	.07Y	.10Y	.17Y	.22Y	.30Y
Russia.......... 922	1.68Y	1.90Y	2.26Y	2.62Y	4.46Y	5.53Y	6.16Y	1.37Y	1.14Y	1.47Y	2.45Y	2.76Y	3.10Y	3.99Y
Serbia & Montenegro.......... 965	.01Y	.01Y	.02Y	.03Y	.03Y	.03Y	—Y	—Y	—Y	—Y	—Y	—Y	—Y	.01Y
Slovak Republic.......... 936	.01Y	.01Y	.03Y	.06Y	.04Y	.03Y	.01Y	.04Y	.02Y	.03Y	.05Y	.08Y	.10Y	.16Y
Turkey.......... 186	.33Y	.44Y	.78Y	1.04Y	1.29Y	1.58Y	1.95Y	.39Y	.38Y	.35Y	.54Y	.69Y	.96Y	1.79Y
Turkmenistan.......... 925	—Y	—Y	.01Y	.01Y	—Y	.01Y	—Y	.02Y	.02Y	.06Y	.07Y	.01Y	—Y	.11Y
Ukraine.......... 926	.06Y	.08Y	.12Y	.22Y	.30Y	.36Y	.41Y	.36Y	.33Y	.46Y	.97Y	.75Y	.92Y	1.05Y
U.S.S.R. n.s.......... 930	—Y	—Y	—Y	—Y	.07Y	.09Y	.06Y	—Y	—Y	—Y	—Y	.05Y	.07Y	.06Y
Uzbekistan.......... 927	—Y	—Y	—Y	.01Y	.01Y	.01Y	.01Y	—Y	—Y	.01Y	—Y	—Y	—Y	—Y
Yugoslavia n.s.......... 966	—Y	.01Y	—Y	—Y	.01Y	.01Y	.02Y	—Y	—Y	—Y	—Y	.01Y	.01Y	.02Y
Europe n.s.......... 884	.13Y	.02Y	.03Y	.07Y	.01Y	.01Y	.19Y	.77Y	.65Y	.94Y	1.61Y	.63Y	.84Y	.09Y
Middle East.......... 407	**4.6Y**	**5.1Y**	**5.5Y**	**7.0Y**	**8.5Y**	**10.6Y**	**12.3Y**	**3.0Y**	**2.7Y**	**2.9Y**	**4.1Y**	**4.6Y**	**6.0Y**	**6.5Y**
Bahrain.......... 419	.07Y	.08Y	.08Y	.12Y	.15Y	.15Y	.12Y	.01Y	—Y	—Y	—Y	.01Y	.06Y	.01Y
Egypt.......... 469	.80Y	.83Y	.95Y	1.30Y	1.55Y	1.83Y	2.00Y	.12Y	.08Y	.08Y	.09Y	.21Y	.18Y	.51Y
Iran, I.R. of.......... 429	.98Y	.96Y	1.03Y	1.32Y	1.24Y	1.90Y	2.51Y	.02Y	.02Y	.02Y	.13Y	.03Y	.09Y	.17Y
Iraq.......... 433	.10Y	.12Y	.06Y	.10Y	.07Y	.19Y	.11Y	.24Y	.51Y	.31Y	.52Y	.58Y	.66Y	.30Y
Israel.......... 436	.41Y	.40Y	.51Y	.63Y	.85Y	.81Y	1.00Y	1.08Y	.93Y	1.01Y	1.35Y	1.40Y	1.61Y	1.91Y
Jordan.......... 439	.17Y	.14Y	.12Y	.16Y	.19Y	.18Y	.34Y	.01Y	—Y	—Y	—Y	.01Y	.02Y	.02Y
Kuwait.......... 443	.11Y	.08Y	.12Y	.18Y	.25Y	.27Y	.42Y	.08Y	.04Y	.09Y	.03Y	.06Y	.01Y	.15Y
Lebanon.......... 446	.07Y	.09Y	.10Y	.14Y	.17Y	.22Y	.29Y	—Y	.01Y	.01Y	.01Y	.01Y	.01Y	.02Y
Libya.......... 672	.06Y	.05Y	.08Y	.18Y	.28Y	.32Y	.43Y	.02Y	.01Y	.05Y	.08Y	.04Y	.45Y	.01Y
Oman.......... 449	.07Y	.07Y	.09Y	.08Y	.11Y	.17Y	.17Y	—Y	—Y	—Y	—Y	—Y	—Y	.01Y
Qatar.......... 453	.05Y	.04Y	.07Y	.07Y	.17Y	.15Y	.20Y	.01Y	—Y	.01Y	—Y	.01Y	.09Y	.16Y

	Exports							Imports						
	2001	2002	2003	2004	2005	2006	2007	2001	2002	2003	2004	2005	2006	2007
	Billions of U.S. Dollars							*Billions of U.S. Dollars*						
Saudi Arabia.......456	.78Y	.81Y	1.00Y	1.20Y	1.69Y	2.25Y	2.19Y	1.19Y	1.00Y	1.21Y	1.72Y	1.99Y	2.26Y	2.75Y
Syrian Arab Republic.......463	.18Y	.22Y	.22Y	.31Y	.37Y	.37Y	.38Y	.02Y	.01Y	.02Y	.01Y	.07Y	.09Y	.03Y
United Arab Emirates.......466	.61Y	.99Y	.85Y	1.03Y	1.19Y	1.44Y	1.83Y	.16Y	.11Y	.04Y	.10Y	.12Y	.46Y	.49Y
Yemen, Republic of.......474	.14Y	.14Y	.15Y	.16Y	.26Y	.36Y	.27Y	.04Y	—Y	.01Y	—Y	.02Y	—Y	—Y
Middle East n.s.......489	.05Y	.07Y	.09Y	.03Y	—Y	—Y	—Y	.03Y	.02Y	.02Y	.01Y	—Y	—Y	—Y
Western Hemisphere.......207	**62.1Y**	**56.6Y**	**62.5Y**	**87.6Y**	**106.8Y**	**126.8Y**	**151.0Y**	**65.8Y**	**59.4Y**	**64.8Y**	**92.2Y**	**117.6Y**	**140.4Y**	**168.8Y**
Antigua and Barbuda.......311	.08Y	.08Y	.08Y	.11Y	.12Y	.14Y	.18Y	.01Y	.01Y	.01Y	.02Y	.02Y	.04Y	.02Y
Argentina.......213	6.41Y	2.93Y	5.49Y	9.18Y	12.06Y	14.74Y	18.39Y	13.16Y	11.39Y	12.39Y	15.14Y	17.63Y	21.59Y	24.89Y
Aruba.......314	.06Y	.06Y	.09Y	.27Y	2.00Y	1.99Y	1.69Y	.07Y	.07Y	.13Y	.26Y	.40Y	.56Y	.60Y
Bahamas, The.......313	.25Y	.59Y	.65Y	.82Y	1.93Y	2.09Y	1.05Y	.11Y	.27Y	.34Y	.21Y	.19Y	.21Y	.29Y
Barbados.......316	.43Y	.26Y	.29Y	.37Y	.43Y	.48Y	.55Y	.18Y	.26Y	.31Y	.19Y	.45Y	.21Y	.31Y
Belize.......339	.12Y	.15Y	.15Y	.15Y	.19Y	.22Y	.25Y	.03Y	.04Y	.06Y	.06Y	.05Y	.05Y	.06Y
Bermuda.......319	.21Y	.03Y	.04Y	.04Y	.02Y	.06Y	.01Y	.01Y	.05Y	.05Y	.04Y	.02Y	.10Y	.04Y
Bolivia.......218	.95Y	1.04Y	.93Y	1.24Y	1.46Y	1.70Y	2.03Y	.66Y	.83Y	1.04Y	1.39Y	1.78Y	2.34Y	2.49Y
Brazil.......223	9.46Y	8.27Y	8.20Y	10.22Y	11.80Y	16.34Y	20.88Y	13.77Y	11.97Y	15.71Y	23.38Y	31.75Y	37.81Y	44.33Y
Chile.......228	5.41Y	5.54Y	6.71Y	8.14Y	10.84Y	11.80Y	12.79Y	4.44Y	3.86Y	4.31Y	6.05Y	6.90Y	10.19Y	11.87Y
Colombia.......233	3.11Y	3.32Y	3.42Y	4.30Y	6.06Y	8.03Y	9.57Y	4.45Y	4.01Y	4.17Y	6.31Y	7.99Y	9.46Y	13.17Y
Costa Rica.......238	1.16Y	1.49Y	1.51Y	1.93Y	2.19Y	2.66Y	3.17Y	1.24Y	1.51Y	1.87Y	2.27Y	2.63Y	2.89Y	3.25Y
Dominica.......321	.04Y	.04Y	.05Y	.06Y	.06Y	.07Y	.09Y	.03Y	.03Y	.03Y	.04Y	.04Y	.06Y	.06Y
Dominican Republic.......243	1.34Y	1.97Y	1.55Y	2.19Y	2.85Y	3.25Y	3.87Y	.08Y	.11Y	.12Y	.17Y	.26Y	.34Y	.42Y
Ecuador.......248	1.74Y	2.35Y	2.19Y	2.91Y	3.60Y	4.00Y	4.13Y	1.75Y	1.16Y	1.20Y	1.40Y	2.60Y	3.48Y	4.26Y
El Salvador.......253	1.47Y	1.52Y	1.68Y	1.99Y	2.39Y	2.43Y	2.75Y	.83Y	.90Y	.91Y	.86Y	1.45Y	1.46Y	1.66Y
Grenada.......328	.07Y	.07Y	.08Y	.10Y	.12Y	.14Y	.16Y	.01Y	.02Y	.02Y	.02Y	.02Y	.02Y	.74Y
Guatemala.......258	1.85Y	1.93Y	2.13Y	2.52Y	3.01Y	3.38Y	3.94Y	1.23Y	1.29Y	1.39Y	1.66Y	2.00Y	2.36Y	2.93Y
Guyana.......336	.35Y	.20Y	.17Y	.22Y	.25Y	.32Y	.37Y	.09Y	.09Y	.10Y	.12Y	.14Y	.15Y	.18Y
Haiti.......263	.28Y	.19Y	.18Y	.32Y	.38Y	.51Y	.57Y	.02Y	.02Y	.03Y	.04Y	.05Y	.06Y	.08Y
Honduras.......268	1.17Y	1.11Y	1.19Y	1.47Y	1.93Y	2.17Y	2.56Y	.39Y	.40Y	.47Y	.50Y	.66Y	.86Y	1.06Y
Jamaica.......343	.84Y	.79Y	.90Y	1.08Y	1.44Y	1.83Y	2.87Y	.10Y	.09Y	.10Y	.11Y	.11Y	.14Y	.14Y
Mexico.......273	4.25Y	5.25Y	6.02Y	8.75Y	9.76Y	12.60Y	13.18Y	6.30Y	5.41Y	5.34Y	7.40Y	10.14Y	13.15Y	17.11Y
Netherlands Antilles.......353	5.58Y	4.24Y	3.15Y	7.29Y	8.41Y	6.37Y	8.07Y	1.03Y	.94Y	.69Y	1.33Y	1.85Y	2.06Y	2.34Y
Nicaragua.......278	.82Y	.77Y	.83Y	1.25Y	1.33Y	1.55Y	2.03Y	.24Y	.25Y	.29Y	.33Y	.49Y	.52Y	.59Y
Panama.......283	1.59Y	1.46Y	1.76Y	2.97Y	3.24Y	3.06Y	2.99Y	1.56Y	1.62Y	1.60Y	1.73Y	2.46Y	2.72Y	3.00Y
Paraguay.......288	1.42Y	1.03Y	1.30Y	1.53Y	1.60Y	2.03Y	2.66Y	.87Y	1.06Y	1.00Y	1.01Y	1.08Y	1.68Y	2.57Y
Peru.......293	2.35Y	2.83Y	3.02Y	3.92Y	4.60Y	6.14Y	7.05Y	1.33Y	1.34Y	1.56Y	2.46Y	3.55Y	4.77Y	5.87Y
St. Kitts and Nevis.......361	.04Y	.04Y	.04Y	.06Y	.06Y	.08Y	.10Y	—Y	—Y	—Y	—Y	—Y	—Y	.01Y
St. Lucia.......362	.32Y	.34Y	.12Y	.13Y	.23Y	.18Y	1.25Y	.02Y	.02Y	.02Y	.04Y	.03Y	.03Y	.04Y
St. Vincent & Grens.......364	.06Y	.05Y	.06Y	.07Y	.11Y	.10Y	.12Y	.02Y	.02Y	.02Y	.03Y	.03Y	.03Y	.04Y
Suriname.......366	.13Y	.11Y	.12Y	.16Y	.19Y	.22Y	.27Y	.05Y	.05Y	.05Y	.06Y	.06Y	.11Y	.12Y
Trinidad and Tobago.......369	1.08Y	.72Y	.90Y	.97Y	1.51Y	1.65Y	1.98Y	1.28Y	1.46Y	1.65Y	2.10Y	2.73Y	3.18Y	4.25Y
Uruguay.......298	1.77Y	1.27Y	1.28Y	1.93Y	2.35Y	2.81Y	3.24Y	1.32Y	1.11Y	1.22Y	1.38Y	1.51Y	1.75Y	2.27Y
Venezuela, Rep. Bol.......299	4.89Y	3.63Y	2.63Y	5.46Y	7.24Y	10.59Y	15.88Y	7.38Y	6.78Y	5.64Y	13.11Y	15.53Y	14.48Y	15.95Y
Western Hem. n.s.......399	.97Y	.95Y	3.64Y	3.50Y	1.03Y	1.05Y	.32Y	1.76Y	.94Y	.98Y	.96Y	1.01Y	1.50Y	1.78Y
Other Countries n.i.e.......910	**1.3Y**	**.9Y**	**.6Y**	**1.9Y**	**2.7Y**	**3.3Y**	**3.9Y**	**.5Y**	**.3Y**	**.4Y**	**.5Y**	**.5Y**	**.6Y**	**1.0Y**
Cuba.......928	1.05Y	.77Y	.47Y	1.71Y	2.57Y	3.10Y	3.61Y	.18Y	.16Y	.31Y	.37Y	.38Y	.39Y	.53Y
North Korea.......954	.23Y	.13Y	.09Y	.22Y	.16Y	.16Y	.25Y	.28Y	.14Y	.13Y	.14Y	.15Y	.19Y	.50Y
Countries & Areas n.s.......898	**3.0Y**	**3.7Y**	**4.6Y**	**7.6Y**	**7.0Y**	**18.0Y**	**21.8Y**	**.8Y**	**1.6Y**	**1.0Y**	**1.5Y**	**1.8Y**	**2.2Y**	**2.1Y**
Special Categories.......899	**5.4Y**	**5.5Y**	**2.7Y**	**3.1Y**	**4.8Y**	**6.2Y**	**3.6Y**	**7.8Y**	**6.4Y**	**2.5Y**	**3.7Y**	**1.9Y**	**5.0Y**	**5.6Y**
Memorandum Items														
European Union.......998	42.22Y	42.85Y	50.81Y	60.68Y	71.91Y	92.85Y	111.14Y	59.90Y	55.72Y	58.29Y	68.10Y	78.42Y	89.52Y	109.54Y
Oil Exporting Ctys.......999	8.77Y	8.16Y	7.59Y	12.10Y	15.67Y	21.30Y	28.74Y	13.83Y	12.45Y	11.72Y	23.86Y	27.04Y	28.72Y	32.44Y
Non-Oil Develop.Ctys.......201	77.87Y	77.34Y	93.89Y	126.83Y	156.33Y	188.51Y	229.80Y	108.04Y	107.63Y	117.68Y	160.07Y	200.07Y	253.84Y	315.76Y
PERCENT DISTRIBUTION														
Industrial Countries.......101	**72.5**	**72.9**	**71.7**	**68.3**	**67.6**	**65.7**	**63.6**	**67.5**	**66.3**	**65.6**	**60.3**	**58.4**	**55.9**	**54.4**
Developing Countries.......202	**24.8**	**24.2**	**26.3**	**29.1**	**29.9**	**30.4**	**32.7**	**30.2**	**31.5**	**33.4**	**38.5**	**40.8**	**42.9**	**44.5**
Africa.......607	**.8**	**.9**	**1.0**	**1.3**	**1.3**	**1.4**	**1.5**	**1.4**	**1.1**	**1.3**	**1.9**	**2.0**	**2.0**	**2.1**
Asia.......507	**4.0**	**4.9**	**6.4**	**6.6**	**6.9**	**7.4**	**8.9**	**10.3**	**12.4**	**12.8**	**14.8**	**15.5**	**17.2**	**18.5**
Europe.......170	**.9**	**1.0**	**1.2**	**1.4**	**1.6**	**1.7**	**1.6**	**1.5**	**1.6**	**1.8**	**1.7**	**1.4**	**1.5**	**1.5**
Middle East.......407	**1.3**	**1.4**	**1.4**	**1.5**	**1.5**	**1.5**	**1.6**	**.8**	**.7**	**.7**	**.9**	**.8**	**.9**	**.8**
Western Hemisphere.......207	**17.8**	**16.0**	**16.2**	**18.3**	**18.6**	**18.4**	**19.1**	**16.3**	**15.6**	**16.7**	**19.3**	**21.2**	**21.3**	**21.6**
Other Countries n.i.e.......910	**.4**	**.3**	**.1**	**.4**	**.5**	**.5**	**.5**	**.1**	**.1**	**.1**	**.1**	**.1**	**.1**	**.1**
ANNUAL PERCENT CHANGE														
World.......001	**–4.3**	**.9**	**9.5**	**23.7**	**20.4**	**20.0**	**14.4**	**–1.2**	**–5.4**	**1.5**	**23.2**	**16.6**	**18.5**	**18.8**
Industrial Countries.......101	**–5.2**	**1.6**	**7.7**	**17.8**	**19.2**	**16.6**	**10.8**	**–4.3**	**–7.1**	**.3**	**13.2**	**12.9**	**13.6**	**15.5**
Developing Countries.......202	**–2.2**	**–1.3**	**18.7**	**36.9**	**23.8**	**22.0**	**23.2**	**5.2**	**–1.5**	**7.8**	**42.1**	**23.5**	**24.4**	**23.2**
Africa.......607	**35.9**	**12.8**	**24.9**	**50.3**	**27.8**	**25.4**	**22.6**	**2.2**	**–20.5**	**11.8**	**87.0**	**20.8**	**21.7**	**22.2**
Asia.......507	**10.9**	**23.8**	**44.4**	**28.2**	**25.3**	**28.8**	**37.6**	**18.9**	**14.1**	**4.8**	**42.2**	**21.7**	**31.6**	**27.8**
Europe.......170	**23.0**	**6.7**	**36.3**	**40.2**	**40.0**	**25.5**	**12.5**	**–.2**	**4.9**	**15.1**	**10.8**	**–.3**	**22.2**	**23.0**
Middle East.......407	**22.0**	**9.9**	**7.7**	**27.5**	**22.1**	**24.1**	**15.6**	**–.7**	**–10.3**	**5.3**	**41.2**	**12.4**	**31.1**	**9.4**
Western Hemisphere.......207	**–8.1**	**–8.8**	**10.4**	**40.1**	**21.9**	**18.7**	**19.1**	**–1.0**	**–9.8**	**9.2**	**42.2**	**27.6**	**19.3**	**20.3**
Other Countries n.i.e.......910	**–19.3**	**–30.0**	**–37.2**	**244.3**	**40.9**	**19.5**	**18.4**	**2.5**	**–34.1**	**43.3**	**16.6**	**4.5**	**8.3**	**78.0**

Other Countries n.i.e. 910

	Exports							Imports						
	2001	2002	2003	2004	2005	2006	2007	2001	2002	2003	2004	2005	2006	2007
	Billions of U.S. Dollars							Billions of U.S. Dollars						
DOTS World Total.................... 001	**2.5Y**	**2.5Y**	**2.6Y**	**3.4Y**	**3.4Y**	**3.9Y**	**5.3Y**	**6.8Y**	**5.3Y**	**5.2Y**	**7.6Y**	**9.8Y**	**12.2Y**	**13.1Y**
Industrial Countries................ 101	**1.1Y**	**1.1Y**	**1.1Y**	**1.5Y**	**1.5Y**	**1.7Y**	**1.9Y**	**3.2Y**	**2.1Y**	**2.3Y**	**2.7Y**	**3.1Y**	**3.6Y**	**3.7Y**
United States............................ 111	—Y	—Y	—Y	—Y	—Y	—Y	—Y	.01Y	.19Y	.30Y	.47Y	.40Y	.38Y	.49Y
Canada..................................... 156	.24Y	.21Y	.27Y	.45Y	.46Y	.56Y	.99Y	.27Y	.19Y	.21Y	.28Y	.43Y	.51Y	.60Y
Australia................................... 193	.01Y	.01Y	.01Y	.02Y	.02Y	.02Y	.01Y	.02Y	.02Y	.01Y	.01Y	.01Y	.01Y	.01Y
Japan.. 158	.23Y	.23Y	.18Y	.17Y	.15Y	.08Y	.02Y	1.20Y	.17Y	.17Y	.21Y	.26Y	.19Y	.21Y
New Zealand............................. 196	—Y	—Y	—Y	—Y	—Y	—Y	—Y	.05Y	.03Y	.04Y	.06Y	.05Y	.05Y	.09Y
Austria...................................... 122	—Y	—Y	—Y	—Y	—Y	—Y	—Y	.02Y	.02Y	.01Y	.01Y	.01Y	.01Y	.01Y
Belgium.................................... 124	.02Y	.01Y	.01Y	.01Y	.01Y	—Y	—Y	.03Y	.03Y	.04Y	.05Y	.07Y	.07Y	.05Y
Cyprus...................................... 423	.01Y	.01Y	.01Y	.01Y	—Y	—Y	—Y	—Y	—Y	—Y	—Y	—Y	—Y	—Y
Denmark................................... 128	—Y	—Y	—Y	—Y	—Y	—Y	.01Y	.03Y	.03Y	.03Y	.04Y	.04Y	.05Y	.04Y
Finland..................................... 172	—Y	—Y	—Y	.01Y	—Y	—Y	.01Y	—Y	—Y	—Y	.01Y	.01Y	.01Y	.01Y
France...................................... 132	.04Y	.04Y	.03Y	.02Y	.03Y	.03Y	.05Y	.25Y	.23Y	.17Y	.12Y	.15Y	.14Y	.13Y
Germany................................... 134	.05Y	.05Y	.05Y	.06Y	.07Y	.03Y	.04Y	.19Y	.23Y	.20Y	.23Y	.42Y	.63Y	.36Y
Greece...................................... 174	—Y	—Y	—Y	—Y	—Y	.08Y	.01Y	—Y	.01Y	—Y	—Y	—Y	—Y	—Y
Ireland...................................... 178	.01Y	—Y	—Y	.01Y	—Y	—Y	—Y	.02Y	—Y	—Y	—Y	—Y	—Y	—Y
Italy.. 136	.02Y	.04Y	.02Y	.02Y	.01Y	.02Y	.02Y	.29Y	.28Y	.32Y	.26Y	.28Y	.40Y	.35Y
Netherlands.............................. 138	.26Y	.28Y	.34Y	.51Y	.56Y	.60Y	.45Y	.09Y	.11Y	.17Y	.20Y	.18Y	.15Y	.18Y
Norway..................................... 142	—Y	—Y	—Y	—Y	—Y	—Y	.02Y	—Y	—Y	—Y	—Y	—Y	—Y	.03Y
Portugal.................................... 182	.02Y	.02Y	.02Y	.04Y	.01Y	.02Y	.03Y	.01Y	—Y	—Y	—Y	.01Y	.01Y	.01Y
Spain.. 184	.12Y	.14Y	.14Y	.15Y	.16Y	.16Y	.18Y	.65Y	.51Y	.58Y	.60Y	.67Y	.88Y	1.00Y
Sweden..................................... 144	—Y	—Y	—Y	—Y	—Y	—Y	—Y	.03Y	.02Y	.03Y	.06Y	.06Y	.05Y	.05Y
Switzerland............................... 146	.02Y	.02Y	.02Y	.02Y	.02Y	.02Y	.02Y	.02Y	.02Y	.01Y	.02Y	.02Y	.02Y	.03Y
United Kingdom......................... 112	.02Y	.01Y	.01Y	.02Y	.02Y	.03Y	.02Y	.07Y	.05Y	.05Y	.03Y	.03Y	.04Y	.04Y
Developing Countries............. 202	**1.5Y**	**1.4Y**	**1.4Y**	**1.9Y**	**1.9Y**	**2.2Y**	**3.4Y**	**3.6Y**	**3.1Y**	**2.9Y**	**4.9Y**	**6.7Y**	**8.6Y**	**9.4Y**
Africa...................................... 607	**.1Y**	**.1Y**	**.1Y**	**.1Y**	**.1Y**	**.2Y**	**.2Y**	**.4Y**	**.5Y**	**.3Y**	**.3Y**	**.4Y**	**.6Y**	**.8Y**
Algeria..................................... 612	.01Y	.02Y	.02Y	.03Y	.04Y	.04Y	.06Y	.10Y	.13Y	.15Y	.20Y	.28Y	.35Y	.42Y
Congo, Republic of..................... 634	—Y	—Y	—Y	—Y	—Y	—Y	—Y	.23Y	.30Y	.14Y	.08Y	.09Y	.11Y	.14Y
Ethiopia.................................... 644	—Y	—Y	—Y	—Y	.01Y	.01Y	.01Y	—Y	—Y	—Y	—Y	—Y	—Y	—Y
Ghana....................................... 652	.02Y	.03Y	.03Y	.04Y	.05Y	.06Y	.07Y	.01Y	.02Y	.02Y	.03Y	.03Y	.04Y	.05Y
Guinea-Bissau........................... 654	—Y	—Y	—Y	—Y	.01Y	.01Y	.01Y	—Y	—Y	—Y	—Y	—Y	—Y	—Y
Kenya.. 664	—Y	—Y	—Y	—Y	—Y	—Y	.01Y	—Y	—Y	—Y	—Y	—Y	—Y	—Y
Madagascar............................... 674	—Y	—Y	.01Y	.02Y	.02Y	.02Y	.03Y	—Y	—Y	—Y	—Y	—Y	—Y	—Y
South Africa............................... 199	—Y	—Y	—Y	—Y	—Y	—Y	.01Y	—Y	.01Y	.01Y	—Y	.01Y	.09Y	.15Y
Tunisia...................................... 744	.01Y	.01Y	.01Y	.01Y	—Y	—Y	.01Y	.02Y	—Y	—Y	—Y	—Y	—Y	—Y
Asia... 507	**.4Y**	**.5Y**	**.6Y**	**.8Y**	**.9Y**	**1.2Y**	**1.8Y**	**1.6Y**	**1.5Y**	**1.6Y**	**2.0Y**	**2.7Y**	**3.7Y**	**3.6Y**
Bangladesh................................ 513	.04Y	.03Y	.01Y	.01Y	.02Y	.02Y	.01Y	.01Y	.01Y	.01Y	.01Y	.01Y	.02Y	.03Y
China,P.R.: Mainland.................. 924	.26Y	.35Y	.47Y	.67Y	.67Y	.91Y	1.53Y	.99Y	.86Y	.95Y	1.23Y	1.89Y	2.74Y	2.82Y
China,P.R.:Hong Kong................ 532	.04Y	.02Y	.01Y	.02Y	.01Y	.02Y	.02Y	.06Y	.04Y	.02Y	.02Y	.02Y	.03Y	.02Y
China,P.R.:Macao....................... 546	—Y	—Y	—Y	—Y	—Y	—Y	.01Y	—Y	—Y	—Y	—Y	—Y	—Y	—Y
India... 534	.02Y	.01Y	—Y	—Y	.04Y	.05Y	.07Y	.18Y	.20Y	.19Y	.15Y	.09Y	.11Y	.14Y
Indonesia.................................. 536	—Y	—Y	—Y	.01Y	.01Y	—Y	—Y	.01Y	—Y	—Y	.01Y	.01Y	.02Y	.01Y
Korea.. 542	.01Y	.02Y	—Y	—Y	—Y	—Y	—Y	—Y	—Y	—Y	.01Y	—Y	.22Y	.24Y
Malaysia.................................... 548	—Y	—Y	—Y	—Y	—Y	—Y	—Y	.01Y	.01Y	.01Y	.02Y	.02Y	.01Y	.01Y
Mongolia................................... 948	—Y	—Y	—Y	—Y	—Y	.03Y	.03Y	—Y	—Y	—Y	—Y	—Y	—Y	—Y
Myanmar................................... 518	.02Y	.02Y	.02Y	.03Y	.03Y	.04Y	.05Y	.02Y	.02Y	.02Y	.03Y	.03Y	.04Y	.05Y
Pakistan.................................... 564	—Y	—Y	—Y	.01Y	.01Y	.02Y	.02Y	—Y	—Y	—Y	.01Y	.01Y	.01Y	.01Y
Singapore.................................. 576	—Y	.01Y	—Y	—Y	.01Y	.01Y	—Y	.13Y	.09Y	.07Y	.06Y	.08Y	.08Y	.07Y
Taiwan Province of China............ 528	—Y	.01Y	.01Y	.01Y	.01Y	.01Y	.01Y	.04Y	.03Y	.04Y	.03Y	.03Y	.04Y	.03Y
Thailand.................................... 578	.02Y	.04Y	.05Y	.08Y	.11Y	.06Y	.03Y	.12Y	.19Y	.23Y	.28Y	.24Y	.26Y	.20Y
Vietnam..................................... 582	—Y	—Y	—Y	—Y	—Y	—Y	—Y	.05Y	.06Y	.07Y	.12Y	.23Y	.17Y	—Y
Europe..................................... 170	**.5Y**	**.4Y**	**.3Y**	**.3Y**	**.2Y**	**.2Y**	**.2Y**	**.2Y**	**.1Y**	**.2Y**	**.4Y**	**.5Y**	**.6Y**	**.6Y**
Belarus..................................... 913	.01Y	.02Y	.02Y	.03Y	.01Y	.01Y	.01Y	.01Y	.01Y	.01Y	.01Y	.02Y	.01Y	.02Y
Bulgaria.................................... 918	.01Y	.01Y	.01Y	.01Y	—Y	.01Y	.01Y	—Y	—Y	—Y	.01Y	—Y	.01Y	.01Y
Czech Republic........................... 935	—Y	—Y	—Y	.01Y	.01Y	—Y	—Y	.01Y	—Y	.01Y	.02Y	.02Y	.04Y	.02Y
Kazakhstan................................ 916	.01Y	.02Y	.01Y	.02Y	.03Y	.03Y	.04Y	—Y	—Y	.01Y	.01Y	.02Y	.02Y	.02Y
Moldova.................................... 921	—Y	.01Y	—Y	—Y	—Y	—Y	—Y	—Y	—Y	—Y	—Y	—Y	—Y	—Y
Poland...................................... 964	.01Y	.01Y	.01Y	.01Y	.02Y	.01Y	—Y	.01Y	.01Y	.02Y	.01Y	.02Y	.02Y	.02Y
Romania.................................... 968	.02Y	.02Y	.02Y	.01Y	.01Y	—Y	—Y	—Y	—Y	.01Y	—Y	—Y	—Y	—Y
Russia....................................... 922	.41Y	.27Y	.17Y	.17Y	.06Y	.06Y	.09Y	.13Y	.09Y	.16Y	.28Y	.39Y	.41Y	.38Y
Slovak Republic.......................... 936	—Y	—Y	—Y	—Y	—Y	—Y	—Y	—Y	—Y	—Y	—Y	.02Y	.01Y	.03Y
Tajikistan.................................. 923	.01Y	—Y	—Y	—Y	—Y	—Y	—Y	—Y	—Y	—Y	—Y	—Y	—Y	—Y
Turkey...................................... 186	.01Y	—Y	—Y	—Y	.01Y	—Y	—Y	.01Y	—Y	.01Y	—Y	—Y	.01Y	.04Y
Turkmenistan............................. 925	—Y	—Y	—Y	.01Y	.01Y	.01Y	.01Y	—Y	—Y	—Y	—Y	—Y	—Y	—Y
Ukraine..................................... 926	.02Y	.01Y	.02Y	.01Y	—Y	—Y	—Y	.01Y	.01Y	.01Y	.01Y	.02Y	.03Y	.04Y
Middle East............................. 407	**.1Y**	**.1Y**	**.1Y**	**.2Y**	**.2Y**	**.2Y**	**.3Y**	**—Y**	**—Y**	**.1Y**	**.1Y**	**.1Y**	**.1Y**	**.1Y**
Iran, I.R. of................................ 429	.01Y	.04Y	.04Y	.06Y	.07Y	.09Y	.12Y	—Y	—Y	—Y	—Y	—Y	—Y	—Y
Lebanon.................................... 446	.03Y	.03Y	.04Y	.05Y	.05Y	.07Y	.08Y	—Y	—Y	.01Y	.01Y	.01Y	.01Y	.01Y
Libya... 672	—Y	—Y	—Y	—Y	—Y	—Y	—Y	.02Y	.02Y	.02Y	.03Y	.04Y	.05Y	.06Y
Qatar.. 453	—Y	—Y	—Y	.03Y	—Y	—Y	—Y	....	....	....	....	....	....	....
Saudi Arabia.............................. 456	.02Y	.06Y	—Y	—Y	.03Y	.04Y	.05Y	.02Y	.02Y	.03Y	.03Y	.05Y	.06Y	.07Y
Syrian Arab Republic.................. 463	.01Y	.01Y	.01Y	—Y	—Y	—Y	—Y	—Y	—Y	—Y	—Y	—Y	—Y	—Y
Yemen, Republic of..................... 474	—Y	—Y	—Y	.01Y	—Y	—Y	—Y	—Y	—Y	—Y	—Y	—Y	—Y	—Y

Other Countries n.i.e. 910

	Exports							Imports						
	2001	2002	2003	2004	2005	2006	2007	2001	2002	2003	2004	2005	2006	2007
	Billions of U.S. Dollars							Billions of U.S. Dollars						
Western Hemisphere................ 207	**.4Y**	**.3Y**	**.4Y**	**.5Y**	**.5Y**	**.5Y**	**.9Y**	**1.4Y**	**1.0Y**	**.6Y**	**2.1Y**	**3.0Y**	**3.6Y**	**4.2Y**
Argentina.................................. 213	—Y	—Y	—Y	—Y	—Y	—Y	—Y	.05Y	.02Y	.03Y	.10Y	.11Y	.11Y	.11Y
Belize....................................... 339	.02Y	.02Y	.03Y	.04Y	.04Y	.05Y	.06Y	—Y	—Y	—Y	—Y	—Y	—Y	—Y
Brazil.. 223	.07Y	.09Y	.09Y	.12Y	.11Y	.12Y	.20Y	.35Y	.19Y	.16Y	.33Y	.34Y	.45Y	.49Y
Chile... 228	.03Y	.01Y	—Y	—Y	—Y	—Y	—Y	.04Y	.05Y	.05Y	.07Y	.11Y	.07Y	.11Y
Colombia.................................. 233	.02Y	.01Y	.02Y	.01Y	.01Y	.01Y	.02Y	.03Y	.07Y	.07Y	.04Y	.07Y	.06Y	.06Y
Costa Rica................................ 238	.12Y	—Y	—Y	.01Y	.01Y	.01Y	.01Y	.01Y	.01Y	.01Y	.01Y	.01Y	.01Y	.02Y
Dominican Republic.................... 243	.03Y	.03Y	.04Y	.05Y	.06Y	.08Y	.09Y	.01Y	.01Y	.02Y	.02Y	.03Y	.03Y	.04Y
Ecuador.................................... 248	—Y	—Y	—Y	—Y	—Y	—Y	—Y	.01Y	.01Y	.01Y	.04Y	.01Y	.01Y	.01Y
El Salvador............................... 253	—Y	—Y	—Y	—Y	—Y	—Y	—Y	—Y	—Y	—Y	—Y	.01Y	.01Y	.01Y
Guatemala................................ 258	.02Y	.01Y	.01Y	.01Y	.01Y	.01Y	.01Y	.01Y	.01Y	.01Y	.01Y	.04Y	.05Y	.06Y
Guyana..................................... 336	.03Y	.03Y	.04Y	.05Y	.05Y	.07Y	.08Y	.01Y	.01Y	.01Y	.01Y	.02Y	.02Y	.03Y
Haiti.. 263	.01Y	.01Y	.01Y	.01Y	.01Y	.01Y	.01Y	—Y	—Y	—Y	—Y	—Y	—Y	—Y
Honduras.................................. 268	.01Y	—Y	.01Y	.01Y	.01Y	.01Y	.01Y	—Y	.01Y	.01Y	.01Y	.01Y	.01Y	.02Y
Jamaica.................................... 343	.01Y	—Y	.01Y	—Y	.01Y	—Y	.02Y	—Y	—Y	—Y	—Y	—Y	.01Y	.01Y
Mexico...................................... 273	.03Y	.02Y	.02Y	.02Y	.02Y	.04Y	.02Y	.19Y	.16Y	.18Y	.19Y	.24Y	.21Y	.21Y
Netherlands Antilles.................... 353	—Y	—Y	—Y	—Y	—Y	—Y	—Y	.13Y	.07Y	.04Y	.05Y	.05Y	.07Y	.08Y
Nicaragua................................. 278	—Y	—Y	—Y	—Y	—Y	—Y	.01Y	—Y	—Y	—Y	—Y	—Y	—Y	—Y
Panama..................................... 283	—Y	—Y	—Y	—Y	.01Y	.02Y	.02Y	—Y	—Y	—Y	—Y	—Y	—Y	—Y
Paraguay................................... 288	—Y	—Y	—Y	.01Y	.02Y	.02Y	.03Y	—Y	—Y	—Y	—Y	—Y	—Y	—Y
Peru.. 293	—Y	.01Y	—Y	—Y	—Y	—Y	—Y	.01Y	—Y	—Y	.01Y	—Y	.03Y	.04Y
Suriname................................... 366	—Y	—Y	—Y	.01Y	.01Y	.01Y	.01Y	—Y	—Y	—Y	—Y	—Y	—Y	—Y
Trinidad and Tobago.................... 369	—Y	—Y	—Y	—Y	—Y	.01Y	.01Y	.01Y	.01Y	.02Y	.02Y	.03Y	.03Y	.04Y
Uruguay..................................... 298	—Y	—Y	—Y	—Y	—Y	—Y	—Y	—Y	—Y	—Y	.01Y	.04Y	.05Y	.06Y
Venezuela, Rep. Bol..................... 299	.02Y	.01Y	.10Y	.11Y	.09Y	.03Y	.30Y	.53Y	.35Y	.01Y	1.19Y	1.88Y	2.37Y	2.85Y
Memorandum Items														
European Union.......................... 998	.58Y	.64Y	.67Y	.90Y	.91Y	1.01Y	.83Y	1.69Y	1.54Y	1.65Y	1.64Y	1.99Y	2.51Y	2.33Y
Oil Exporting Ctys....................... 999	.06Y	.12Y	.17Y	.23Y	.24Y	.21Y	.53Y	.66Y	.53Y	.21Y	1.50Y	2.25Y	2.83Y	3.41Y
Non-Oil Develop.Ctys.................. 201	1.42Y	1.25Y	1.26Y	1.64Y	1.65Y	2.01Y	2.86Y	2.94Y	2.61Y	2.65Y	3.39Y	4.43Y	5.77Y	5.95Y
PERCENT DISTRIBUTION														
Industrial Countries................ 101	**41.9**	**44.4**	**44.0**	**45.1**	**44.7**	**43.0**	**35.6**	**47.3**	**40.6**	**45.0**	**35.3**	**31.7**	**29.6**	**28.4**
Developing Countries.............. 202	**58.1**	**55.6**	**56.0**	**54.9**	**55.3**	**57.0**	**64.4**	**52.7**	**59.4**	**55.0**	**64.7**	**68.3**	**70.4**	**71.6**
Africa..................................... 607	**2.4**	**3.0**	**3.8**	**3.6**	**4.1**	**4.4**	**4.1**	**5.3**	**8.6**	**6.4**	**4.1**	**4.2**	**4.8**	**5.8**
Asia.. 507	**16.5**	**20.4**	**22.7**	**24.8**	**27.3**	**30.0**	**34.2**	**23.5**	**28.5**	**31.0**	**26.2**	**27.2**	**30.6**	**27.7**
Europe.................................... 170	**20.0**	**15.5**	**10.3**	**8.5**	**4.8**	**3.8**	**3.4**	**2.7**	**2.7**	**4.7**	**4.8**	**5.3**	**4.6**	**4.5**
Middle East............................ 407	**2.6**	**5.5**	**3.7**	**4.4**	**4.9**	**5.3**	**5.0**	**.6**	**.9**	**1.0**	**1.5**	**.9**	**1.0**	**1.1**
Western Hemisphere.............. 207	**16.6**	**11.2**	**15.5**	**13.6**	**14.2**	**13.4**	**17.7**	**20.6**	**18.7**	**11.9**	**28.2**	**30.6**	**29.4**	**32.5**
ANNUAL PERCENT CHANGE														
World....................................... 001	**–.1**	**–2.5**	**3.4**	**33.4**	**.1**	**14.3**	**34.8**	**15.8**	**–22.8**	**–1.4**	**45.1**	**29.6**	**24.8**	**7.0**
Industrial Countries................ 101	**–14.8**	**3.2**	**2.5**	**36.9**	**–.8**	**9.8**	**11.6**	**51.8**	**–33.8**	**9.4**	**13.6**	**16.5**	**16.4**	**2.8**
Developing Countries.............. 202	**14.2**	**–6.7**	**4.2**	**30.7**	**.8**	**17.9**	**52.4**	**–4.6**	**–12.9**	**–8.9**	**70.9**	**36.7**	**28.7**	**8.8**
Africa..................................... 607	**19.8**	**21.3**	**29.1**	**27.6**	**12.5**	**23.4**	**25.8**	**9.7**	**26.3**	**–27.0**	**–6.3**	**31.6**	**44.0**	**29.0**
Asia.. 507	**36.7**	**21.0**	**15.1**	**45.3**	**10.5**	**25.4**	**53.6**	**16.1**	**–6.4**	**7.0**	**22.6**	**34.5**	**40.7**	**–3.1**
Europe.................................... 170	**20.6**	**–24.7**	**–31.0**	**10.1**	**–43.9**	**–7.8**	**17.6**	**–9.2**	**–23.7**	**73.4**	**47.4**	**44.8**	**8.5**	**3.2**
Middle East............................ 407	**–35.7**	**104.5**	**–30.6**	**60.3**	**11.2**	**23.8**	**27.4**	**–64.4**	**22.8**	**6.0**	**109.0**	**–15.9**	**25.3**	**21.2**
Western Hemisphere.............. 207	**2.6**	**–34.0**	**43.3**	**16.6**	**4.5**	**8.3**	**78.0**	**–19.3**	**–30.0**	**–37.3**	**244.4**	**40.9**	**19.5**	**18.4**

MEMORANDUM TABLES

European Union 998

	Exports 2001	2002	2003	2004	2005	2006	2007	Imports 2001	2002	2003	2004	2005	2006	2007
	Billions of U.S. Dollars							*Billions of U.S. Dollars*						
IFS World Total	**2,399.9**	**2,558.4**	**3,050.1**	**3,636.5**	**3,917.6**	**4,438.3**	**5,180.9**	**2,384.1**	**2,482.1**	**2,992.4**	**3,609.9**	**3,948.3**	**4,545.6**	**5,310.7**
DOTS World Total 001	**2,435.8Y**	**2,595.1**	**3,108.0Y**	**3,714.9Y**	**4,015.0**	**4,518.2**	**5,270.3**	**2,424.0Y**	**2,523.1**	**3,058.7Y**	**3,690.0Y**	**4,041.1**	**4,609.8**	**5,386.5**
Industrial Countries 101	**1,905.2Y**	**2,018.3**	**2,411.1Y**	**2,845.3Y**	**3,023.4**	**3,349.8**	**3,835.8**	**1,802.5Y**	**1,869.0**	**2,251.9Y**	**2,667.8Y**	**2,830.5**	**3,188.3**	**3,711.5**
United States 111	220.15Y	232.08	257.54Y	293.22Y	313.65	337.21	357.38	187.23Y	175.99	183.47Y	205.50Y	213.89	217.93	247.31
Canada 156	19.84Y	21.46	24.25Y	27.30Y	29.49	33.35	35.35	17.01Y	16.39	18.32Y	21.24Y	22.48	25.01	31.71
Australia 193	14.06Y	16.03	19.77Y	24.68Y	25.78	26.75	31.15	8.51Y	8.59	9.39Y	11.43Y	12.52	14.11	15.92
Japan 158	40.95Y	40.65	46.09Y	53.75Y	54.42	56.01	59.77	75.23Y	72.19	84.80Y	98.95Y	99.06	95.27	106.46
New Zealand 196	2.10Y	2.27	3.03Y	3.77Y	3.88	3.54	3.99	2.61Y	2.72	3.27Y	3.65Y	3.88	3.78	4.15
Austria 122	55.07Y	58.61	74.26Y	91.07Y	96.14	110.93	129.06	43.44Y	47.92	59.24Y	72.56Y	74.57	89.94	106.54
Belgium 124	117.09Y	134.04	160.89Y	193.78Y	212.61	239.26	276.66	120.00Y	127.87	155.67Y	188.69Y	208.46	258.05	306.32
Cyprus 423	2.72Y	2.97	3.50Y	4.21Y	4.76	6.58	6.94	1.02Y	.94	1.13Y	1.22Y	1.45	3.18	2.92
Denmark 128	31.07Y	34.57	40.73Y	46.99Y	53.04	61.27	69.39	29.39Y	32.20	40.35Y	47.68Y	51.93	59.80	64.90
Finland 172	23.61Y	24.48	30.21Y	36.28Y	40.14	45.69	53.50	26.18Y	26.41	31.76Y	37.66Y	40.81	46.25	53.61
France 132	225.89Y	234.93	286.77Y	337.93Y	362.93	396.99	451.91	187.03Y	195.10	236.15Y	275.06Y	281.76	308.95	355.29
Germany 134	331.62Y	340.08	415.29Y	491.53Y	521.50	592.94	679.44	343.88Y	372.42	465.41Y	566.42Y	602.60	681.66	820.41
Greece 174	20.04Y	21.63	27.92Y	33.98Y	33.43	36.88	45.01	6.17Y	6.31	8.33Y	8.88Y	9.47	11.54	12.98
Iceland 176	1.62Y	1.35	1.84Y	2.34Y	3.17	3.66	4.35	1.59Y	1.79	1.97Y	2.32Y	2.34	2.66	3.14
Ireland 178	33.44Y	37.40	37.30Y	45.10Y	51.01	55.83	65.39	50.31Y	56.74	66.44Y	79.01Y	84.76	77.61	85.48
Italy 136	141.59Y	152.56	187.57Y	217.13Y	226.46	250.69	293.07	129.22Y	135.52	166.91Y	193.97Y	199.40	224.46	267.78
Luxembourg 137	10.85Y	10.93	14.04Y	17.51Y	17.56	20.40	21.11	7.70Y	7.79	11.85Y	15.14Y	15.40	18.79	21.19
Malta 181	2.30	2.59	2.90Y	3.27Y	2.79	3.69	4.39	1.17	1.14	1.20Y	1.41Y	1.52	1.62	2.29
Netherlands 138	120.52Y	126.52	150.63Y	177.55Y	186.70	216.50	254.61	158.37Y	160.92	197.05Y	242.61Y	269.02	340.75	400.99
Norway 142	24.51Y	26.53	31.45Y	38.14Y	41.86	47.91	58.86	41.82Y	42.23	57.40Y	70.03Y	85.56	99.16	105.47
Portugal 182	34.04Y	34.69	42.67Y	49.77Y	50.88	53.48	57.76	21.83Y	21.75	28.10Y	31.65Y	29.38	32.09	34.67
Slovenia 961	8.38Y	9.01	11.22Y	14.05Y	14.94	17.51	22.07	6.81Y	7.57	9.58Y	10.84Y	11.04	13.03	16.97
Spain 184	110.42Y	120.08	155.05Y	185.50Y	202.60	220.57	257.64	80.21Y	87.76	111.37Y	129.63Y	134.58	147.42	174.44
Sweden 144	46.68Y	51.14	63.26Y	76.93Y	82.35	93.15	111.75	45.42Y	48.03	60.74Y	73.77Y	78.54	90.20	106.26
Switzerland 146	68.67Y	69.54	81.35Y	94.47Y	103.97	111.67	128.59	57.96Y	60.08	68.10Y	79.27Y	84.91	92.64	106.41
United Kingdom 112	198.00Y	212.20	241.60Y	285.09Y	287.33	307.31	356.70	152.37Y	152.65	173.88Y	199.23Y	211.15	232.40	257.91
Developing Countries 202	**508.4Y**	**552.7**	**673.7Y**	**837.0Y**	**956.5**	**1,123.1**	**1,390.2**	**594.8Y**	**627.6**	**790.1Y**	**999.5Y**	**1,186.6**	**1,395.4**	**1,651.0**
Africa 607	**53.5Y**	**56.4**	**67.8Y**	**79.9Y**	**91.8**	**98.4**	**119.9**	**65.4Y**	**65.5**	**75.3Y**	**86.5Y**	**107.0**	**116.0**	**128.9**
Algeria 612	6.92Y	7.86	9.02Y	11.70Y	12.98	12.41	15.19	14.40Y	13.67	16.42Y	19.09Y	25.94	30.42	29.09
Angola 614	1.23Y	1.32	2.15Y	2.02Y	2.50	3.82	5.51	1.81Y	2.12	1.27Y	1.22Y	3.26	2.70	5.68
Benin 638	.49Y	.53	.58Y	.53Y	.52	.61	.87	.06Y	.06	.05Y	.04Y	.04	.09	.08
Botswana 616	.17Y	.14	.17Y	.16Y	.18	.11	.22	1.60Y	1.61	1.87Y	2.20Y	2.13	2.33	1.16
Burkina Faso 748	.20Y	.25	.38Y	.43Y	.38	.41	.48	.06Y	.05	.05Y	.05Y	.04	.04	.05
Burundi 618	.05Y	.04	.04Y	.07Y	.09	.10	.09	.02Y	.02	.03Y	.02Y	.06	.03	.05
Cameroon 622	1.03Y	1.04	1.30Y	1.14Y	1.09	1.18	1.47	1.59Y	1.49	1.93Y	2.27Y	2.64	3.39	3.42
Cape Verde 624	.21Y	.23	.26Y	.29Y	.34	.42	.58	.01Y	.02	.03Y	.02Y	.02	.04	.03
Central African Rep. 626	.06Y	.06	.05Y	.06Y	.07	.11	.12	.15Y	.17	.10Y	.10Y	.08	.08	.07
Chad 628	.15Y	.20	.15Y	.20Y	.22	.20	.27	.06Y	.05	.05Y	.09Y	.09	.04	.04
Comoros 632	.03Y	.04	.04Y	.04Y	.04	.05	.04	.02Y	.02	.03Y	.01Y	.01	.03	.01
Congo, Dem. Rep. of 636	.25Y	.35	.44Y	.49Y	.60	.71	.86	.93Y	1.17	.79Y	.91Y	.90	.80	1.00
Congo, Republic of 634	.47Y	.50	.51Y	.57Y	.68	.84	1.42	.37Y	.46	.37Y	.32Y	.37	.47	.41
Côte d'Ivoire 662	1.19Y	1.19	1.24Y	1.45Y	1.40	1.44	1.84	2.13Y	2.83	3.28Y	2.96Y	2.63	3.11	3.74
Djibouti 611	.19Y	.16	.16Y	.15Y	.13	.20	.25	.06Y	—	.01Y	.01Y	.01	.01	.01
Equatorial Guinea 642	.16Y	.21	.54Y	.33Y	.57	.50	.59	.68Y	.71	1.10Y	1.04Y	2.06	2.18	3.20
Ethiopia 644	.37Y	.36	.51Y	.51Y	.74	.77	.98	.16Y	.25	.22Y	.25Y	.36	.37	.44
Gabon 646	1.04Y	.76	.91Y	1.03Y	.99	1.08	1.29	1.06Y	.56	.61Y	.69Y	.72	.76	1.04
Gambia, The 648	.13Y	.12	.13Y	.13Y	.13	.13	.15	.02Y	.02	.01Y	.02Y	.01	.01	.01
Ghana 652	.86Y	.99	1.13Y	1.49Y	1.55	1.83	2.30	.86Y	.98	1.14Y	1.23Y	1.19	1.41	1.57
Guinea 656	.32Y	.42	.41Y	.42Y	.46	.54	.71	.51Y	.41	.38Y	.42Y	.52	.49	.65
Guinea-Bissau 654	.04Y	.04	.05Y	.05Y	.10	.08	.09	—Y	.01	.01Y	.01Y	—	—	—
Kenya 664	.88Y	.87	.91Y	1.12Y	1.21	1.48	1.81	.83Y	.81	.92Y	1.09Y	1.16	1.29	1.45
Lesotho 666	.01Y	.01	.02Y	.02Y	.02	.02	.02	.02Y	.01	.01Y	.03Y	.07	.08	.17
Liberia 668	1.58Y	1.35	.78Y	.48Y	.48	.73	.80	.77Y	.99	.81Y	.76Y	.78	1.12	.51
Madagascar 674	.39Y	.26	.44Y	.46Y	.45	.44	.62	.55Y	.52	.59Y	.68Y	.58	.67	.75
Malawi 676	.05Y	.07	.06Y	.11Y	.09	.13	.14	.19Y	.18	.21Y	.20Y	.21	.19	.28
Mali 678	.37Y	.36	.40Y	.47Y	.48	.56	.67	.05Y	.07	.07Y	.08Y	.06	.14	.05
Mauritania 682	.35Y	.39	.47Y	.47Y	.60	.57	.71	.36Y	.40	.38Y	.47Y	.61	.69	.79
Mauritius 684	.76Y	.71	1.16Y	.84Y	1.07	1.15	1.07	1.17Y	1.28	1.58Y	1.41Y	1.40	1.35	1.42
Morocco 686	6.77Y	7.33	9.23Y	11.04Y	14.56	13.04	16.76	5.75Y	6.14	7.29Y	8.31Y	11.40	9.01	10.66
Mozambique 688	.18Y	.30	.24Y	.24Y	.28	.32	.35	.56Y	.61	.73Y	1.10Y	1.32	1.38	1.91
Namibia 728	.16Y	.16	.20Y	.24Y	.23	.20	.24	.83Y	.66	.64Y	1.06Y	1.11	1.39	1.31
Niger 692	.18Y	.20	.21Y	.27Y	.28	.26	.36	.12Y	.08	.09Y	.15Y	.16	.17	.25
Nigeria 694	4.60Y	4.94	5.76Y	6.52Y	7.31	8.81	11.65	5.82Y	4.78	6.97Y	6.55Y	10.39	13.64	13.10
Rwanda 714	.06Y	.07	.08Y	.11Y	.10	.13	.15	.05Y	.02	.02Y	.03Y	.04	.05	.05
St. Helena 856	.02Y	.03	.02Y	.02Y	.04	.06	.04	—Y	.01	.01Y	—Y	—	—	—
São Tomé & Príncipe 716	.03Y	.05	.05Y	.04Y	.04	.06	.05	.01Y	.01	.01Y	.01Y	.02	.01	.01
Senegal 722	.93Y	1.12	1.23Y	1.42Y	1.84	1.99	2.45	.41Y	.39	.39Y	.40Y	.65	.38	.51
Seychelles 718	.13Y	.16	.20Y	.22Y	.27	.26	.37	.18Y	.26	.29Y	.31Y	.35	.27	.23
Sierra Leone 724	.24Y	.29	.33Y	.22Y	.24	.15	.16	.04Y	.10	.13Y	.17Y	.18	.15	.18

European Union 998

		Exports							Imports						
		2001	2002	2003	2004	2005	2006	2007	2001	2002	2003	2004	2005	2006	2007
		Billions of U.S. Dollars							*Billions of U.S. Dollars*						
Somalia	726	.02Y	.03	.02Y	.02Y	.01	.02	.02	—Y	—	—Y	—Y	—	—	.01
South Africa	199	11.28Y	11.96	15.39Y	20.12Y	22.84	24.99	28.10	13.61Y	13.86	15.56Y	20.12Y	22.85	23.55	28.58
Sudan	732	.57Y	.53	.76Y	1.06Y	1.66	1.93	1.50	.23Y	.20	.20Y	.27Y	.23	.14	.20
Swaziland	734	.02Y	.02	.02Y	.03Y	.04	.03	.04	.13Y	.12	.13Y	.17Y	.14	.15	.22
Tanzania	738	.37Y	.36	.46Y	.56Y	.66	.79	1.03	.31Y	.31	.33Y	.47Y	.40	.41	.52
Togo	742	.30Y	.41	.51Y	.47Y	.70	1.01	1.31	.06Y	.07	.07Y	.09Y	.15	.15	.19
Tunisia	744	7.16Y	7.19	8.15Y	9.41Y	9.87	10.86	12.97	5.70Y	5.91	7.12Y	8.53Y	8.57	9.58	12.27
Uganda	746	.18Y	.19	.24Y	.28Y	.34	.39	.58	.23Y	.25	.28Y	.32Y	.38	.36	.46
Zambia	754	.11Y	.11	.13Y	.16Y	.20	.32	.40	.16Y	.12	.18Y	.23Y	.23	.46	.62
Zimbabwe	698	.20Y	.17	.19Y	.19Y	.16	.18	.20	.71Y	.61	.57Y	.55Y	.48	.45	.48
Asia	**507**	**128.9Y**	**138.0**	**165.9Y**	**205.3Y**	**223.9**	**254.8**	**305.0**	**216.7Y**	**230.2**	**292.7Y**	**372.3Y**	**423.8**	**484.0**	**580.8**
Afghanistan, I.S. of	512	.04Y	.13	.21Y	.32Y	.40	.52	.57	.02Y	.02	.07Y	.04Y	.03	.05	.03
Bangladesh	513	.78Y	.72	.79Y	1.11Y	1.18	1.33	1.41	3.07Y	3.14	4.16Y	5.33Y	5.16	6.54	6.98
Brunei Darussalam	516	.15Y	.16	.51Y	.23Y	.15	.26	1.76	.06Y	.07	.10Y	.13Y	.07	.14	.09
Cambodia	522	.10Y	.11	.11Y	.14Y	.16	.17	.21	.42Y	.47	.56Y	.73Y	.63	.82	.94
China,P.R.: Mainland	924	27.77Y	33.20	46.33Y	59.83Y	64.20	79.99	98.30	68.89Y	80.73	115.31Y	156.90Y	197.52	234.56	314.85
China,P.R.:Hong Kong	532	19.54Y	19.37	20.66Y	23.84Y	25.63	27.23	28.59	16.05Y	16.17	17.39Y	20.95Y	21.75	24.63	14.82
China,P.R.:Macao	546	.16Y	.32	.33Y	.17Y	.18	.21	.29	.62Y	.58	.70Y	.84Y	.44	.56	.68
Fiji	819	.04Y	.02	.03Y	.05Y	.06	.06	.05	.09Y	.09	.12Y	.13Y	.13	.15	.14
French Polynesia	887	.55Y	.79	1.05Y	.74Y	1.03	.76	.83	.10Y	.11	.37Y	.17Y	.24	.03	.03
India	534	11.17Y	13.28	16.32Y	21.09Y	26.20	30.43	40.02	12.23Y	13.00	16.09Y	20.59Y	24.09	28.28	35.52
Indonesia	536	4.09Y	4.38	4.75Y	6.18Y	5.94	6.26	7.45	10.38Y	10.53	11.90Y	13.06Y	13.75	15.14	17.42
Kiribati	826	.01Y	.02	—Y	—Y	—	—	—	—Y	—	—Y	.01Y	—	—	—
Korea	542	14.06Y	15.96	18.57Y	22.15Y	25.36	28.71	33.92	21.33Y	23.94	29.63Y	38.65Y	42.97	50.45	53.35
Lao People's Dem.Rep.	544	.03Y	.04	.04Y	.08Y	.05	.04	.08	.12Y	.13	.14Y	.17Y	.15	.13	.18
Malaysia	548	8.52Y	7.95	9.47Y	10.85Y	11.47	12.89	15.57	15.75Y	15.70	18.77Y	21.01Y	21.55	21.97	24.57
Maldives	556	.04Y	.04	.06Y	.08Y	.09	.09	.11	.02Y	.02	.02Y	.03Y	.04	.06	.07
Mongolia	948	.08Y	.07	.11Y	.13Y	.12	.13	.22	.04Y	.02	.03Y	.03Y	.06	.07	.11
Myanmar	518	.08Y	.09	.06Y	.10Y	.10	.10	.22	.45Y	.40	.42Y	.55Y	.34	.36	.36
Nauru	836	—Y	—	—Y	—Y	—	—	—	—Y	—	—Y	.01Y	—	—	—
Nepal	558	.07Y	.09	.09Y	.08Y	.10	.08	.10	.12Y	.09	.10Y	.13Y	.12	.11	.12
New Caledonia	839	.53Y	.68	.84Y	.89Y	.81	.96	1.18	.23Y	.20	.31Y	.31Y	.37	.59	.88
Pakistan	564	1.85Y	2.12	2.55Y	3.68Y	4.80	5.23	5.19	2.67Y	2.90	3.57Y	4.26Y	3.93	4.18	4.72
Papua New Guinea	853	.03Y	.04	.04Y	.04Y	.04	.06	.09	.26Y	.25	.40Y	.47Y	.50	.51	.63
Philippines	566	4.16Y	3.14	3.80Y	4.45Y	4.50	4.67	5.42	7.23Y	7.65	7.88Y	8.50Y	8.53	8.01	7.70
Samoa	862	.01Y	—	.01Y	—Y	—	.01	.01	—Y	—	—Y	—Y	—	—	—
Singapore	576	13.63Y	14.06	16.10Y	20.05Y	21.48	24.47	28.01	14.99Y	14.55	17.64Y	22.81Y	24.11	24.70	25.09
Solomon Islands	813	—Y	—	—Y	—Y	.01	.01	.01	—Y	—	—Y	.01Y	.02	.01	.03
Sri Lanka	524	.89Y	.86	1.06Y	1.37Y	1.34	1.34	1.39	1.47Y	1.44	1.59Y	2.00Y	2.05	2.38	2.85
Taiwan Province of China	528	12.06Y	11.87	12.36Y	15.97Y	16.23	16.60	18.22	23.66Y	21.88	26.29Y	30.87Y	30.91	32.69	35.38
Thailand	578	6.78Y	6.59	7.22Y	8.75Y	9.84	9.13	10.81	12.15Y	11.67	13.77Y	16.83Y	17.18	18.33	22.62
Tonga	866	—Y	—	.01Y	—Y	.01	.02	—	—Y	—	—Y	—Y	—	—	—
Tuvalu	869	—Y	.05	—Y	—Y	.01	.01	—	—Y	—	—Y	—Y	—	—	—
Vanuatu	846	.03Y	.01	.01Y	.01Y	.03	.01	.01	.01Y	—	.01Y	.03Y	.03	.01	.01
Vietnam	582	1.64Y	1.80	2.33Y	2.77Y	2.34	2.98	4.92	4.23Y	4.43	5.40Y	6.70Y	7.08	8.57	10.68
Europe	**170**	**199.6Y**	**229.9**	**295.1Y**	**377.8Y**	**441.0**	**554.3**	**705.5**	**207.1Y**	**228.5**	**297.2Y**	**379.0Y**	**450.8**	**560.1**	**676.6**
Albania	914	.99Y	1.06	1.26Y	1.52Y	1.64	1.81	2.36	.32Y	.32	.41Y	.49Y	.52	.62	.85
Armenia	911	.20Y	.24	.35Y	.41Y	.50	.58	.80	.06Y	.13	.28Y	.26Y	.49	.41	.46
Azerbaijan	912	.35Y	.53	.89Y	1.55Y	1.86	2.46	2.16	1.14Y	1.26	1.48Y	1.48Y	2.97	6.57	10.10
Belarus	913	1.86Y	2.01	2.54Y	3.26Y	3.99	5.51	6.61	1.25Y	1.48	2.23Y	3.16Y	4.18	5.50	5.86
Bosnia & Herzegovina	963	1.83Y	2.15	2.49Y	2.99Y	3.37	3.32	4.19	.62Y	.69	.95Y	1.17Y	1.62	2.07	2.43
Bulgaria	918	3.93Y	4.42	5.87Y	7.60Y	8.90	11.16	13.74	3.36Y	3.52	4.56Y	5.86Y	6.68	8.32	8.78
Croatia	960	6.29Y	7.79	10.04Y	11.70Y	12.98	15.15	17.84	2.88Y	2.97	3.75Y	4.96Y	5.01	6.03	6.64
Czech Republic	935	29.09Y	32.37	40.26Y	50.31Y	58.20	71.62	91.34	27.91Y	31.99	42.04Y	50.04Y	56.84	71.15	94.29
Czechoslovakia n.s.	937	.09Y	.15	.11	—Y	—	—	—	.01Y	.01	.02	—Y	—	—	—
Estonia	939	3.18Y	3.89	4.88Y	6.15Y	7.57	10.60	12.29	3.43Y	3.51	4.40Y	5.73Y	6.32	7.02	7.68
Faroe Islands	816	.31Y	.30	.36Y	.41Y	.47	.48	.64	.40Y	.37	.46Y	.45Y	.47	.48	.52
Georgia	915	.27Y	.30	.39Y	.50Y	.62	.87	1.13	.26Y	.26	.26Y	.36Y	.31	.94	.59
Gibraltar	823	1.02Y	1.33	1.20Y	1.61Y	2.54	3.93	4.46	.11Y	.09	.22Y	.20Y	.25	.17	.22
Hungary	944	23.70Y	26.60	33.17Y	39.89Y	44.11	52.71	63.39	25.25Y	27.09	33.58Y	40.93Y	44.33	51.15	65.44
Kazakhstan	916	1.60Y	1.75	2.34Y	3.99Y	4.40	6.27	8.14	2.93Y	3.64	4.28Y	8.07Y	11.34	15.04	16.97
Kyrgyz Republic	917	.06Y	.10	.12Y	.12Y	.14	.21	.31	.11Y	.03	.02Y	.03Y	.02	.03	.03
Latvia	941	3.42Y	3.72	4.67Y	5.36Y	6.50	8.73	11.81	2.34Y	2.50	3.00Y	4.39Y	5.05	5.98	7.13
Lithuania	946	4.35Y	5.38	6.97Y	7.20Y	8.04	11.04	15.05	3.13Y	3.46	4.62Y	5.93Y	6.75	7.72	9.86
Macedonia, FYR	962	1.20Y	1.20	1.31Y	1.51Y	1.67	1.92	2.39	.62Y	.57	.77Y	.98Y	1.19	1.45	2.14
Moldova	921	.46Y	.49	.73Y	.91Y	.99	1.04	1.37	.23Y	.27	.40Y	.57Y	.45	.50	.73
Poland	964	35.57Y	39.18	48.30Y	61.56Y	72.37	95.89	126.40	27.54Y	31.21	41.52Y	52.69Y	57.68	77.55	100.08
Romania	968	10.76Y	12.42	16.72Y	22.37Y	27.18	34.33	42.52	9.16Y	10.66	13.96Y	17.81Y	19.39	22.22	22.55
Russia	922	28.52Y	32.90	42.58Y	56.81Y	70.13	90.52	121.57	56.69Y	58.25	75.80Y	98.20Y	137.04	172.88	189.68
Serbia & Montenegro	965	2.68Y	3.58	4.41Y	5.29Y	5.70	.01	—	1.11Y	1.41	1.67Y	2.00Y	2.58	.01	—
Slovak Republic	936	10.84Y	12.45	17.29	21.82Y	25.58	32.74	43.96	11.04Y	13.30	19.17	23.23Y	24.57	30.85	43.53
Tajikistan	923	.04Y	.04	.07Y	.08Y	.11	.15	.15	.14Y	.22	.24Y	.22Y	.13	.26	.33
Turkey	186	18.81Y	24.10	33.36Y	47.20Y	52.44	58.58	67.32	19.38Y	22.67	29.66Y	39.56Y	43.01	48.40	58.43
Turkmenistan	925	.24Y	.31	.39Y	.51Y	.41	.44	.48	.16Y	.19	.33Y	.51Y	.99	.69	.35
Ukraine	926	6.38Y	7.43	10.09Y	12.84Y	16.24	22.47	29.80	4.80Y	5.80	6.65Y	9.09Y	9.75	10.98	14.09
Uzbekistan	927	.56Y	.49	.51Y	.58Y	.71	.73	.98	.65Y	.47	.40Y	.51Y	.66	1.22	1.75
Yugoslavia n.s.	966	.09Y	.13	.13Y	.21Y	.09	—	—	.02Y	.03	.04Y	.01Y	.03	—	—
Europe n.s.	884	.94Y	1.05	1.31Y	1.51Y	1.57	1.56	1.65	.05Y	.11	.08Y	.10Y	.14	.15	.13

European Union 998

		Exports							Imports						
		2001	2002	2003	2004	2005	2006	2007	2001	2002	2003	2004	2005	2006	2007
		Billions of U.S. Dollars							Billions of U.S. Dollars						
Middle East	**407**	**68.5Y**	**74.1**	**87.7Y**	**106.8Y**	**122.6**	**127.7**	**153.4**	**54.0Y**	**50.8**	**61.7Y**	**82.1Y**	**112.6**	**129.3**	**138.5**
Bahrain	419	.85Y	.90	1.09Y	1.48Y	1.47	1.80	1.96	.47Y	.37	.41Y	.44Y	.68	.69	1.05
Egypt	469	6.49Y	6.27	7.04Y	9.18Y	10.31	11.17	13.95	2.99Y	3.15	3.80Y	5.30Y	6.47	9.59	9.47
Iran, I.R. of	429	6.06Y	7.81	11.36Y	14.81Y	16.12	14.06	13.71	6.04Y	5.36	7.85Y	10.26Y	14.25	17.76	18.46
Iraq	433	1.75Y	1.69	1.07Y	1.72Y	1.99	1.55	1.92	3.12Y	2.64	1.72Y	3.14Y	4.44	6.34	9.43
Israel	436	13.21Y	12.96	13.29Y	15.92Y	16.77	17.33	19.36	9.29Y	8.77	9.16Y	11.17Y	12.41	12.34	15.24
Jordan	439	1.68Y	1.91	2.13Y	2.42Y	2.88	3.31	3.61	.14Y	.20	.23Y	.29Y	.32	.28	.29
Kuwait	443	2.51Y	2.79	3.54Y	4.37Y	4.79	4.55	5.96	2.19Y	1.74	2.15Y	2.78Y	4.02	5.02	5.27
Lebanon	446	2.85Y	2.90	3.84Y	4.03Y	3.74	3.81	4.33	.28Y	.19	.23Y	.31Y	.27	.28	.42
Libya	672	2.71Y	3.08	3.63Y	4.41Y	4.42	4.61	5.68	10.33Y	8.96	12.40Y	17.03Y	24.43	32.78	37.53
Oman	449	1.30Y	1.30	1.47Y	2.04Y	2.18	2.18	3.32	.26Y	.43	.28Y	.44Y	.57	.52	.46
Qatar	453	1.74Y	1.83	2.52Y	4.22Y	3.88	6.41	8.62	.61Y	.45	.96Y	1.13Y	1.65	2.27	2.55
Saudi Arabia	456	11.91Y	14.42	15.32Y	15.58Y	19.27	21.98	27.34	11.78Y	11.58	14.86Y	20.27Y	27.80	29.78	25.00
Syrian Arab Republic	463	2.02Y	2.10	2.51Y	2.98Y	3.44	3.66	4.19	3.86Y	4.10	3.45Y	3.19Y	3.63	4.34	4.62
United Arab Emirates	466	12.73Y	13.41	18.13Y	22.49Y	30.45	30.34	38.04	2.56Y	2.75	4.14Y	6.20Y	11.44	7.16	8.42
Yemen, Republic of	474	.68Y	.76	.76Y	1.12Y	.93	.94	1.46	.08Y	.11	.08Y	.10Y	.23	.17	.30
Western Hemisphere	**207**	**57.9Y**	**54.4**	**57.2Y**	**67.2Y**	**77.1**	**87.9**	**106.3**	**51.6Y**	**52.6**	**63.1Y**	**79.6Y**	**92.5**	**105.9**	**126.2**
Antigua and Barbuda	311	.27Y	.34	.14Y	.16Y	.28	.38	.60	.32Y	.74	.37Y	.21Y	.15	.29	.18
Argentina	213	4.54Y	2.05	3.04Y	4.51Y	5.02	6.12	8.16	5.32Y	6.22	7.45Y	8.08Y	8.35	9.12	11.63
Aruba	314	.15Y	.16	.18Y	.20Y	.18	.30	.29	.10Y	.08	.12Y	.29Y	.51	.30	.31
Bahamas, The	313	.63Y	1.26	1.45Y	.78Y	1.52	1.30	1.72	.46Y	.47	.53Y	.62Y	1.36	1.37	1.07
Barbados	316	.17Y	.19	.22Y	.18Y	.19	.24	.24	.08Y	.11	.07Y	.07Y	.11	.05	.06
Belize	339	.06Y	.06	.07Y	.05Y	.12	.07	.10	.08Y	.07	.10Y	.10Y	.13	.20	.14
Bermuda	319	2.23Y	1.78	1.72Y	1.43Y	1.58	1.88	1.44	1.23Y	.86	1.11Y	1.41Y	1.66	.54	.27
Bolivia	218	.15Y	.15	.13Y	.17Y	.21	.22	.27	.10Y	.10	.12Y	.14Y	.17	.18	.25
Brazil	223	16.64Y	14.85	13.96Y	17.55Y	19.92	22.26	29.16	17.98Y	17.82	22.02Y	27.84Y	30.89	33.14	44.09
Chile	228	3.33Y	2.99	3.33Y	3.88Y	4.86	5.38	6.39	4.50Y	4.46	5.54Y	8.95Y	10.55	15.31	16.70
Colombia	233	1.92Y	1.78	2.28Y	2.40Y	3.03	3.40	4.15	2.31Y	2.30	2.77Y	3.98Y	4.34	4.45	5.60
Costa Rica	238	.73Y	.78	.90Y	.93Y	1.01	1.37	1.32	2.00Y	2.54	3.06Y	4.08Y	4.11	3.74	4.11
Dominica	321	.04Y	.02	.03Y	.03Y	.02	.03	.03	.02Y	.03	.02Y	.02Y	.03	.03	.02
Dominican Republic	243	1.01Y	1.00	.80Y	.88Y	.99	1.11	1.40	.32Y	.38	.41Y	.59Y	.61	.89	1.09
Ecuador	248	.74Y	.90	.95Y	.89Y	1.09	1.13	1.23	1.07Y	1.22	1.52Y	1.65Y	2.11	1.93	2.34
El Salvador	253	.64Y	.44	.56Y	.51Y	.49	.89	.76	.15Y	.12	.18Y	.23Y	.28	.22	.27
Falkland Islands	323	.06Y	.05	.07Y	.08Y	.05	.06	.09	.07Y	.08	.15Y	.12Y	.14	.13	.15
Greenland	326	.31Y	.35	.36Y	.51Y	.61	.58	.68	.25Y	.29	.34Y	.38Y	.39	.37	.44
Grenada	328	.02Y	.02	.03Y	.03Y	.05	.04	.05	.04Y	.02	.02Y	.01Y	.02	—	.01
Guatemala	258	.51Y	.61	.53Y	.66Y	.67	.86	.91	.31Y	.26	.31Y	.33Y	.40	.44	.45
Guyana	336	.07Y	.10	.14Y	.07Y	.07	.11	.10	.18Y	.18	.21Y	.24Y	.22	.22	.28
Haiti	263	.10Y	.11	.11Y	.09Y	.14	.20	.13	.02Y	.01	.01Y	.02Y	.02	.02	.04
Honduras	268	.20Y	.21	.32Y	.49Y	.44	.36	.48	.33Y	.33	.40Y	.44Y	.50	.55	.59
Jamaica	343	.44Y	.51	.61Y	.47Y	.51	.44	.41	.52Y	.49	.60Y	.80Y	.83	.58	.69
Mexico	273	13.82Y	14.36	16.12Y	18.21Y	20.89	23.94	28.64	6.80Y	6.14	7.24Y	8.30Y	10.61	12.03	16.32
Netherlands Antilles	353	.52Y	.48	.45Y	.51Y	.76	1.36	1.06	.18Y	.13	.13Y	.17Y	.16	.45	.33
Nicaragua	278	.09Y	.11	.13Y	.14Y	.14	.13	.18	.11Y	.08	.07Y	.10Y	.12	.15	.20
Panama	283	1.07Y	1.47	1.83Y	2.08Y	1.82	2.48	3.48	.55Y	.70	.68Y	.74Y	.91	1.26	.89
Paraguay	288	.23Y	.17	.16Y	.19Y	.21	.22	.31	.23Y	.15	.34Y	.39Y	.33	.38	.58
Peru	293	.89Y	.91	.98Y	1.14Y	1.32	1.60	2.17	1.25Y	1.41	1.59Y	2.23Y	2.99	4.31	5.57
St. Kitts and Nevis	361	.02Y	.03	.07Y	.05Y	.05	.06	.07	.01Y	.01	.02Y	.02Y	.02	.01	.01
St. Lucia	362	.04Y	.05	.05Y	.08Y	.20	.25	.14	.04Y	.04	.03Y	.04Y	.08	.25	.06
St. Pierre-Miquelon	363	.03Y	.02	.03Y	.04Y	.03	.03	.03	—Y	—	—Y	.01Y	.01	.03	.01
St. Vincent & Grens.	364	.11Y	.19	.25Y	.25Y	.35	.19	.15	.14Y	.17	.18Y	.31Y	.33	.16	.13
Suriname	366	.12Y	.18	.19Y	.21Y	.24	.24	.33	.15Y	.11	.20Y	.22Y	.23	.29	.32
Trinidad and Tobago	369	.55Y	.41	.66Y	1.51Y	.67	.64	.80	.44Y	.48	.52Y	.60Y	.63	1.67	1.43
Uruguay	298	.68Y	.43	.45Y	.52Y	.56	1.03	.95	.45Y	.56	.70Y	.81Y	.79	.89	1.08
Venezuela, Rep. Bol.	299	3.37Y	3.02	1.96Y	2.84Y	3.53	4.41	5.40	2.61Y	2.58	2.16Y	2.63Y	4.67	7.60	7.41
Other Countries n.i.e.	**910**	**1.5Y**	**1.4**	**1.5Y**	**1.5Y**	**1.8**	**2.3**	**2.1**	**.6Y**	**.7**	**.7Y**	**1.0Y**	**1.0**	**1.1**	**.9**
Cuba	928	1.29Y	1.10	1.24Y	1.20Y	1.61	2.12	2.03	.55Y	.60	.66Y	.90Y	.92	.92	.82
North Korea	954	.25Y	.30	.26Y	.29Y	.20	.16	.09	.09Y	.10	.07Y	.09Y	.09	.19	.09
Countries & Areas n.s.	**898**	**13.8Y**	**14.9**	**13.8Y**	**21.3Y**	**23.2**	**29.8**	**25.0**	**16.1Y**	**16.4**	**13.4Y**	**18.7Y**	**22.0**	**24.2**	**22.6**
Special Categories	**899**	**6.6Y**	**7.3**	**7.7Y**	**9.4Y**	**9.6**	**13.0**	**16.3**	**9.9Y**	**9.3**	**2.4Y**	**2.9Y**	**.1**	**—**	**—**
Memorandum Items															
European Union	998	1,623.48Y	1,732.01	2,101.35Y	2,499.93Y	2,669.56	3,013.00	3,520.66	1,511.11Y	1,602.09	1,973.47Y	2,358.37Y	2,507.39	2,889.15	3,418.97
Oil Exporting Ctys.	999	59.69Y	66.51	78.53Y	96.89Y	112.84	117.58	144.29	70.10Y	65.49	81.81Y	102.59Y	143.35	168.42	174.13
Non-Oil Develop.Ctys.	201	448.70Y	486.24	595.13Y	740.07Y	843.63	1,005.56	1,245.89	524.69Y	562.10	708.30Y	896.90Y	1,043.28	1,226.94	1,476.82
PERCENT DISTRIBUTION															
Industrial Countries	**101**	**78.2**	**77.8**	**77.6**	**76.6**	**75.3**	**74.1**	**72.8**	**74.4**	**74.1**	**73.6**	**72.3**	**70.0**	**69.2**	**68.9**
Developing Countries	**202**	**20.9**	**21.3**	**21.7**	**22.5**	**23.8**	**24.9**	**26.4**	**24.5**	**24.9**	**25.8**	**27.1**	**29.4**	**30.3**	**30.6**
Africa	**607**	**2.2**	**2.2**	**2.2**	**2.2**	**2.3**	**2.2**	**2.3**	**2.7**	**2.6**	**2.5**	**2.3**	**2.6**	**2.5**	**2.4**
Asia	**507**	**5.3**	**5.3**	**5.3**	**5.5**	**5.6**	**5.6**	**5.8**	**8.9**	**9.1**	**9.6**	**10.1**	**10.5**	**10.5**	**10.8**
Europe	**170**	**8.2**	**8.9**	**9.5**	**10.2**	**11.0**	**12.3**	**13.4**	**8.5**	**9.1**	**9.7**	**10.3**	**11.2**	**12.1**	**12.6**
Middle East	**407**	**2.8**	**2.9**	**2.8**	**2.9**	**3.1**	**2.8**	**2.9**	**2.2**	**2.0**	**2.0**	**2.2**	**2.8**	**2.8**	**2.6**
Western Hemisphere	**207**	**2.4**	**2.1**	**1.8**	**1.8**	**1.9**	**1.9**	**2.0**	**2.1**	**2.1**	**2.1**	**2.2**	**2.3**	**2.3**	**2.3**
Other Countries n.i.e.	**910**	**.1**	**.1**	**—**	**—**	**—**	**.1**	**—**	**—**	**—**	**—**	**—**	**—**	**—**	**—**
ANNUAL PERCENT CHANGE															
World	**001**	**1.1**	**6.5**	**19.8**	**19.5**	**8.1**	**12.5**	**16.6**	**–1.2**	**4.1**	**21.2**	**20.6**	**9.5**	**14.1**	**16.8**
Industrial Countries	**101**	**—**	**5.9**	**19.5**	**18.0**	**6.3**	**10.8**	**14.5**	**–2.4**	**3.7**	**20.5**	**18.5**	**6.1**	**12.6**	**16.4**

European Union 998

	Exports							Imports						
	2001	2002	2003	2004	2005	2006	2007	2001	2002	2003	2004	2005	2006	2007
Developing Countries.............. 202	4.3	8.7	21.9	24.2	14.3	17.4	23.8	.5	5.5	25.9	26.5	18.7	17.6	18.3
Africa.......................................607	5.5	5.5	20.2	17.8	14.9	7.2	21.8	4.3	.1	15.0	14.9	23.7	8.4	11.1
Asia.. 507	1.2	7.0	20.2	23.8	9.1	13.8	19.7	−3.2	6.2	27.2	27.2	13.8	14.2	20.0
Europe.......................................170	6.5	15.2	28.4	28.0	16.7	25.7	27.3	8.2	10.3	30.1	27.5	18.9	24.2	20.8
Middle East............................. 407	4.8	8.2	18.3	21.7	14.8	4.2	20.1	−14.5	−5.9	21.5	32.9	37.2	14.9	7.1
Western Hemisphere..............207	2.0	−6.1	5.2	17.6	14.7	14.1	20.9	1.0	2.0	19.9	26.2	16.2	14.5	19.1
Other Countries n.i.e................910	4.1	−9.0	7.1	−.5	21.7	26.0	−7.2	−18.3	10.2	4.1	35.2	1.7	10.0	−17.9

	Exports 2001	2002	2003	2004	2005	2006	2007	Imports 2001	2002	2003	2004	2005	2006	2007
			Billions of U.S. Dollars							Billions of U.S. Dollars				
IFS World Total	**323.2**	**327.5**	**396.7**	**567.8**	**801.8**	**998.8**	**982.8**	**197.1**	**199.7**	**226.2**	**307.6**	**389.2**	**446.7**	**555.6**
DOTS World Total 001	**312.8Y**	**304.8Y**	**370.0Y**	**489.2Y**	**651.1Y**	**802.8Y**	**902.7Y**	**176.1Y**	**182.2Y**	**211.8Y**	**307.6Y**	**388.3Y**	**446.9Y**	**576.0Y**
Industrial Countries 101	**172.4Y**	**161.3Y**	**199.9Y**	**257.3Y**	**352.2Y**	**417.4Y**	**454.6Y**	**101.0Y**	**104.1Y**	**115.7Y**	**158.5Y**	**195.2Y**	**212.8Y**	**266.1Y**
United States 111	53.36Y	47.59Y	59.18Y	82.69Y	112.76Y	127.58Y	150.98Y	21.16Y	19.01Y	19.89Y	26.50Y	38.34Y	46.84Y	55.52Y
Canada 156	3.10Y	3.06Y	4.70Y	5.17Y	7.68Y	9.14Y	10.21Y	2.08Y	2.01Y	1.77Y	2.48Y	3.03Y	3.65Y	5.27Y
Australia 193	3.13Y	3.02Y	3.23Y	3.61Y	3.92Y	5.53Y	6.66Y	5.23Y	4.80Y	4.40Y	5.83Y	6.50Y	7.88Y	8.96Y
Japan 158	52.78Y	49.26Y	59.87Y	74.10Y	97.57Y	121.58Y	127.57Y	14.90Y	15.66Y	16.65Y	21.19Y	25.30Y	26.40Y	34.33Y
New Zealand 196	.66Y	.64Y	.79Y	.81Y	1.23Y	1.40Y	1.38Y	.55Y	.50Y	.64Y	.87Y	1.03Y	1.28Y	1.86Y
Austria 122	.53Y	.48Y	.64Y	1.00Y	1.28Y	1.89Y	2.44Y	.90Y	.96Y	1.37Y	1.82Y	2.31Y	2.57Y	3.28Y
Belgium 124	2.13Y	2.57Y	3.46Y	4.58Y	5.69Y	6.78Y	7.88Y	2.94Y	3.13Y	3.01Y	4.65Y	5.42Y	6.81Y	8.50Y
Cyprus 423	.05Y	.04Y	.06Y	.07Y	.13Y	.15Y	.18Y	.08Y	.08Y	.05Y	.12Y	.09Y	.16Y	.07Y
Denmark 128	.23Y	.16Y	.19Y	.44Y	.88Y	.60Y	.41Y	.74Y	.88Y	1.01Y	1.38Y	1.44Y	1.26Y	1.66Y
Finland 172	.14Y	.15Y	.14Y	.16Y	.19Y	.25Y	.14Y	.84Y	.94Y	1.28Y	2.47Y	3.78Y	3.73Y	4.09Y
France 132	9.69Y	9.20Y	11.05Y	13.46Y	18.10Y	19.93Y	18.96Y	9.14Y	9.70Y	13.78Y	20.38Y	20.64Y	20.53Y	24.60Y
Germany 134	5.07Y	4.80Y	6.38Y	8.42Y	11.69Y	13.44Y	13.44Y	12.24Y	14.24Y	15.95Y	21.67Y	26.20Y	28.61Y	34.12Y
Greece 174	2.48Y	1.71Y	2.63Y	3.40Y	4.71Y	5.63Y	5.52Y	.31Y	.40Y	.35Y	.61Y	.89Y	1.08Y	.85Y
Iceland 176	.01Y	—Y	—Y	—Y	.02Y	.01Y	—Y	.01Y	.02Y	.01Y	.06Y	.06Y	.11Y	.15Y
Ireland 178	.10Y	.12Y	.10Y	.15Y	.13Y	.19Y	.21Y	.70Y	.73Y	.74Y	1.05Y	1.19Y	1.42Y	1.81Y
Italy 136	14.72Y	13.50Y	17.02Y	21.35Y	30.36Y	38.38Y	42.39Y	8.39Y	9.41Y	11.27Y	14.51Y	16.23Y	18.19Y	26.68Y
Luxembourg 137	.02Y	.02Y	.03Y	.05Y	.38Y	.40Y	.08Y	.08Y	.07Y	.06Y	.14Y	.15Y	.18Y	.21Y
Malta 181	.07Y	.04Y	.01Y	.03Y	.03Y	.02Y	.04Y	.08Y	.11Y	.11Y	.14Y	.16Y	.14Y	.14Y
Netherlands 138	7.46Y	8.08Y	10.31Y	11.20Y	19.71Y	20.60Y	20.94Y	3.24Y	3.22Y	3.56Y	6.36Y	7.63Y	9.79Y	12.96Y
Norway 142	.11Y	.11Y	.09Y	.10Y	.12Y	.13Y	.27Y	.23Y	.22Y	.34Y	.65Y	.50Y	.74Y	.70Y
Portugal 182	1.39Y	1.56Y	1.67Y	2.45Y	3.72Y	3.83Y	4.37Y	.18Y	.16Y	.24Y	.28Y	.43Y	.35Y	.44Y
Slovenia 961	.04Y	.03Y	.08Y	.11Y	.16Y	.23Y	.23Y	.08Y	.11Y	.15Y	.20Y	.26Y	.34Y	.53Y
Spain 184	8.84Y	8.86Y	10.65Y	13.92Y	19.09Y	24.95Y	25.80Y	2.77Y	2.65Y	3.47Y	4.42Y	5.37Y	5.54Y	8.00Y
Sweden 144	.86Y	.68Y	.77Y	.68Y	.74Y	.45Y	.78Y	1.75Y	1.73Y	2.33Y	3.62Y	4.33Y	4.03Y	4.85Y
Switzerland 146	.78Y	1.02Y	1.31Y	1.93Y	2.52Y	3.20Y	2.61Y	3.58Y	4.48Y	3.49Y	3.70Y	4.59Y	4.95Y	6.44Y
United Kingdom 112	4.70Y	4.59Y	5.57Y	7.44Y	9.38Y	11.08Y	11.10Y	8.75Y	8.92Y	9.81Y	13.37Y	19.34Y	16.28Y	20.08Y
Developing Countries 202	**127.1Y**	**128.5Y**	**152.4Y**	**206.5Y**	**267.7Y**	**337.1Y**	**389.9Y**	**71.7Y**	**75.2Y**	**92.4Y**	**144.5Y**	**187.5Y**	**227.1Y**	**301.3Y**
Africa 607	**9.4Y**	**9.3Y**	**11.1Y**	**15.7Y**	**17.0Y**	**26.2Y**	**28.6Y**	**4.0Y**	**4.1Y**	**4.5Y**	**6.8Y**	**7.0Y**	**7.5Y**	**9.6Y**
Algeria 612	.12Y	.14Y	.14Y	.18Y	.29Y	.27Y	.34Y	.49Y	.24Y	.27Y	.25Y	.20Y	.31Y	.39Y
Angola 614	.02Y	.03Y	.02Y	.02Y	.04Y	.05Y	.05Y	—Y	.01Y	.10Y	.34Y	.01Y	.01Y	.01Y
Benin 638	.02Y	.11Y	.03Y	.06Y	.09Y	.11Y	.13Y	.19Y	.05Y	.03Y	.04Y	.03Y	.03Y	.04Y
Botswana 616	.01Y	—Y	—Y	—Y	—Y	—Y	—Y	—Y	—Y	—Y	—Y	—Y	—Y	—Y
Burkina Faso 748	.02Y	.02Y	.02Y	.03Y	.04Y	.05Y	.05Y	—Y	.01Y	.01Y	.01Y	.01Y	.02Y	.02Y
Burundi 618	.02Y	.01Y	—Y	—Y	.01Y	.05Y	.06Y	—Y	—Y	—Y	—Y	—Y	—Y	—Y
Cameroon 622	.15Y	.14Y	.34Y	.45Y	.60Y	.75Y	.90Y	.01Y	.04Y	.01Y	.03Y	.02Y	.03Y	.03Y
Cape Verde 624	—Y	.01Y	.01Y	.01Y	.02Y	.02Y	.03Y	—Y	—Y	—Y	—Y	—Y	—Y	—Y
Central African Rep. 626	—Y	—Y	—Y	—Y	—Y	—Y	—Y	—Y	—Y	.01Y	.01Y	.01Y	.01Y	.03Y
Chad 628	.01Y	.01Y	.02Y	.03Y	.04Y	.05Y	.06Y	—Y	—Y	—Y	—Y	—Y	—Y	.01Y
Comoros 632	.01Y	.01Y	.01Y	.01Y	.01Y	.01Y	.02Y	—Y	—Y	—Y	—Y	—Y	—Y	—Y
Congo, Dem. Rep. of 636	—Y	.01Y	—Y	—Y	—Y	—Y	—Y	—Y	—Y	—Y	—Y	—Y	—Y	—Y
Congo, Republic of 634	.02Y	.03Y	.02Y	.01Y	.01Y	.02Y	.02Y	—Y	.03Y	—Y	—Y	.01Y	.01Y	.01Y
Côte d'Ivoire 662	.39Y	.33Y	.41Y	.91Y	1.34Y	1.52Y	1.83Y	.15Y	.10Y	.10Y	.66Y	.74Y	.77Y	.99Y
Djibouti 611	.13Y	.14Y	.17Y	.23Y	.33Y	.40Y	.48Y	—Y	—Y	.01Y	.01Y	.01Y	.01Y	.01Y
Ethiopia 644	.19Y	.12Y	.31Y	.39Y	.60Y	.73Y	.86Y	.03Y	.03Y	.07Y	.05Y	.07Y	.09Y	.11Y
Gabon 646	—Y	.01Y	.01Y	.02Y	.03Y	.03Y	.06Y	.01Y	.01Y	.01Y	.02Y	.02Y	.02Y	.03Y
Gambia, The 648	.01Y	.01Y	.01Y	.01Y	.02Y	.02Y	.02Y	—Y	—Y	—Y	—Y	—Y	—Y	—Y
Ghana 652	.31Y	.42Y	.49Y	.66Y	.88Y	1.13Y	1.38Y	.02Y	.03Y	.04Y	.05Y	.07Y	.09Y	.11Y
Guinea 656	.02Y	.04Y	.03Y	.03Y	.04Y	.04Y	.05Y	.01Y	.01Y	.03Y	—Y	—Y	—Y	—Y
Guinea-Bissau 654	—Y	—Y	—Y	—Y	—Y	—Y	—Y	—	—	.01Y	.02Y	.02Y	.03Y	.03Y
Kenya 664	.74Y	.60Y	.75Y	.96Y	1.33Y	1.63Y	1.98Y	.07Y	.06Y	.06Y	.07Y	.09Y	.10Y	.13Y
Liberia 668	—Y	—Y	—Y	—Y	.01Y	.01Y	.01Y	.13Y	.01Y	.01Y	.01Y	—Y	.01Y	.03Y
Madagascar 674	.10Y	.05Y	.12Y	.15Y	.21Y	.26Y	.32Y	.01Y	—Y	—Y	—Y	.01Y	.01Y	.01Y
Malawi 676	—Y	—Y	—Y	—Y	—Y	—Y	.01Y	—Y	—Y	—Y	.01Y	.01Y	.01Y	.02Y
Mali 678	.03Y	.01Y	.01Y	.01Y	.01Y	.01Y	.02Y	.01Y	—Y	.01Y	.01Y	.01Y	.01Y	.01Y
Mauritania 682	.03Y	.03Y	.03Y	.04Y	.05Y	.05Y	.06Y	.06Y	.03Y	.02Y	.02Y	.03Y	.04Y	.05Y
Mauritius 684	.11Y	.14Y	.10Y	.16Y	.26Y	.28Y	.15Y	.03Y	.01Y	.02Y	.03Y	.19Y	.28Y	.09Y
Morocco 686	1.39Y	1.42Y	1.04Y	1.53Y	2.37Y	3.02Y	3.62Y	.24Y	.20Y	.20Y	.26Y	.33Y	.44Y	.52Y
Mozambique 688	.02Y	.02Y	.07Y	.07Y	.06Y	.09Y	.10Y	—Y	.01Y	.01Y	.01Y	.01Y	.01Y	.02Y
Namibia 728	.02Y	.02Y	.02Y	.03Y	.03Y	.04Y	.04Y	.01Y	—Y	.01Y	.01Y	.01Y	.03Y	.02Y
Niger 692	.01Y	.01Y	.02Y	.07Y	.08Y	.10Y	.12Y	—Y	.01Y	—Y	.06Y	.07Y	.09Y	.11Y
Nigeria 694	.39Y	.39Y	.62Y	.62Y	.76Y	.85Y	1.01Y	.66Y	1.14Y	.88Y	1.09Y	.98Y	.03Y	.64Y
Rwanda 714	.01Y	.01Y	.01Y	.01Y	.02Y	.02Y	.03Y	—Y	.06Y	.07Y	.27Y	—Y	—Y	—Y
Senegal 722	.21Y	.15Y	.30Y	.36Y	.40Y	.15Y	.18Y	—Y	—Y	.03Y	.01Y	.01Y	.03Y	.04Y
Seychelles 718	.06Y	.06Y	.07Y	.09Y	.12Y	.15Y	.18Y	—Y	—Y	—Y	—Y	—Y	—Y	—Y
Sierra Leone 724	.01Y	—Y	.01Y	.01Y	.01Y	.01Y	.02Y	—Y	—Y	—Y	—Y	—Y	—Y	—Y
Somalia 726	.04Y	.04Y	.04Y	.05Y	.08Y	.10Y	.12Y	.06Y	.07Y	.11Y	.14Y	.17Y	.21Y	.28Y
South Africa 199	3.54Y	2.99Y	4.21Y	6.31Y	4.09Y	10.73Y	10.48Y	.89Y	.84Y	1.06Y	1.70Y	2.10Y	2.40Y	2.73Y
Sudan 732	.24Y	.27Y	.56Y	.75Y	1.12Y	1.19Y	1.24Y	.06Y	.17Y	.19Y	.36Y	.25Y	.47Y	.64Y
Swaziland 734	—Y	—Y	—Y	—Y	—Y	—Y	—Y	.01Y	.01Y	.01Y	.01Y	.03Y	.03Y	.04Y

	Exports							Imports						
	2001	2002	2003	2004	2005	2006	2007	2001	2002	2003	2004	2005	2006	2007
	Billions of U.S. Dollars							Billions of U.S. Dollars						
Tanzania 738	.27Y	.27Y	.26Y	.32Y	.42Y	.51Y	.59Y	.03Y	.02Y	.06Y	.07Y	.09Y	.11Y	.14Y
Togo 742	.03Y	.41Y	.03Y	.06Y	.05Y	.06Y	.08Y	.11Y	.03Y	.25Y	.02Y	.03Y	.02Y	.03Y
Tunisia 744	.48Y	.45Y	.60Y	.69Y	.77Y	1.05Y	1.29Y	.50Y	.60Y	.60Y	.62Y	.88Y	1.05Y	1.36Y
Uganda 746	.06Y	.07Y	.09Y	.12Y	.16Y	.21Y	.25Y	—Y	—Y	.02Y	.02Y	.03Y	.03Y	.04Y
Zambia 754	.05Y	.05Y	.07Y	.14Y	.09Y	.29Y	.24Y	.09Y	.14Y	.14Y	.15Y	.17Y	.19Y	.30Y
Zimbabwe 698	.02Y	.20Y	.02Y	.10Y	.12Y	.08Y	.10Y	.02Y	.02Y	.03Y	.03Y	.03Y	.03Y	.03Y
Africa n.s. 799	.01Y	.01Y	.01Y	.01Y	.01Y	.01Y	.01Y	.06Y	.11Y	.01Y	.25Y	.32Y	.38Y	.45Y
Asia 507	**83.4Y**	**82.9Y**	**102.3Y**	**134.1Y**	**179.0Y**	**226.2Y**	**263.0Y**	**35.9Y**	**40.3Y**	**50.1Y**	**79.2Y**	**103.1Y**	**124.7Y**	**169.8Y**
Afghanistan, I.S. of 512	.01Y	.02Y	.04Y	.04Y	.04Y	.05Y	.06Y	—Y	—Y	.01Y	.01Y	.01Y	.01Y	.02Y
Bangladesh 513	.57Y	.60Y	.81Y	1.23Y	2.05Y	2.35Y	2.76Y	.09Y	.10Y	.08Y	.10Y	.14Y	.15Y	.18Y
Brunei Darussalam 516	.02Y	.03Y	.04Y	.04Y	.05Y	.05Y	.06Y	.04Y	.04Y	.13Y	.31Y	1.22Y	1.63Y	1.90Y
Cambodia 522	.07Y	.07Y	.08Y	.07Y	.10Y	.11Y	.13Y	—Y	—Y	.01Y	—Y	—Y	—Y	.01Y
China,P.R.: Mainland 924	9.56Y	10.78Y	15.31Y	22.83Y	32.90Y	43.62Y	55.54Y	8.36Y	10.07Y	14.78Y	21.89Y	30.20Y	39.23Y	58.62Y
China,P.R.:Hong Kong 532	2.20Y	2.51Y	2.80Y	3.46Y	3.52Y	3.89Y	3.95Y	1.07Y	.96Y	1.11Y	2.79Y	2.99Y	3.68Y	4.60Y
China,P.R.:Macao 546	.01Y	.02Y	.05Y	.05Y	.02Y	.03Y	.03Y	.14Y	.08Y	.06Y	.12Y	.17Y	.19Y	.27Y
Fiji 819	.01Y	.01Y	.01Y	.02Y	.02Y	.02Y	.02Y	—Y	—Y	—Y	—Y	.01Y	—Y	—Y
French Polynesia 887	.01Y	.01Y	.01Y	.01Y	.01Y	.01Y	.01Y	—Y	—Y	—Y	—Y	—Y	—Y	—Y
India 534	6.79Y	5.45Y	6.98Y	8.46Y	10.38Y	13.38Y	16.99Y	4.67Y	5.60Y	7.35Y	13.09Y	16.23Y	20.15Y	25.89Y
Indonesia 536	2.97Y	2.99Y	3.28Y	4.35Y	5.01Y	5.39Y	6.22Y	1.46Y	1.51Y	1.52Y	1.95Y	2.60Y	3.01Y	3.80Y
Korea 542	23.48Y	21.76Y	27.31Y	34.16Y	44.13Y	56.84Y	67.21Y	6.97Y	6.65Y	7.77Y	11.35Y	13.03Y	15.19Y	22.74Y
Malaysia 548	3.05Y	2.96Y	3.66Y	5.15Y	6.63Y	8.84Y	9.57Y	2.14Y	2.31Y	2.96Y	4.75Y	5.80Y	7.53Y	12.19Y
Maldives 556	.04Y	.04Y	.04Y	.08Y	.13Y	.16Y	.19Y	—Y	.01Y	.01Y	.01Y	.01Y	.01Y	.02Y
Mongolia 948	—Y	—Y	—Y	—Y	—Y	—Y	.01Y	—Y	—Y	—Y	—Y	—Y	—Y	—Y
Myanmar 518	.07Y	.06Y	.05Y	.06Y	.08Y	.15Y	.27Y	.02Y	.04Y	.03Y	.04Y	.04Y	.05Y	.07Y
Nepal 558	.12Y	.08Y	.04Y	.04Y	.07Y	.06Y	.08Y	—Y	—Y	—Y	—Y	—Y	—Y	—Y
New Caledonia 839	.01Y	.01Y	.01Y	.01Y	.01Y	.01Y	—Y	—Y	—Y	—Y	—Y	—Y	—Y	—Y
Pakistan 564	3.34Y	3.57Y	3.94Y	5.22Y	7.31Y	9.24Y	11.20Y	.81Y	.83Y	.88Y	1.95Y	2.12Y	2.59Y	3.37Y
Papua New Guinea 853	.03Y	.03Y	.03Y	.04Y	.05Y	.07Y	.07Y	.01Y	.07Y	.12Y	.09Y	.05Y	.18Y	.01Y
Philippines 566	3.31Y	2.74Y	3.18Y	3.49Y	4.83Y	6.19Y	6.73Y	.24Y	.26Y	.37Y	.49Y	.66Y	.68Y	.85Y
Samoa 862	.01Y	.01Y	.01Y	.01Y	.01Y	.01Y	.02Y	—Y	—Y	.02Y	.01Y	—Y	—Y	—Y
Singapore 576	13.46Y	14.02Y	15.06Y	18.41Y	25.57Y	31.22Y	32.96Y	4.51Y	6.09Y	5.77Y	9.51Y	14.95Y	15.60Y	16.30Y
Solomon Islands 813	—Y	—Y	—Y	—Y	—Y	—Y	.01Y	—	—	—Y	—Y	—Y	—Y	—Y
Sri Lanka 524	.56Y	.82Y	.68Y	.99Y	1.25Y	1.51Y	1.73Y	.13Y	.09Y	.23Y	.29Y	.41Y	.43Y	.54Y
Taiwan Province of China 528	7.81Y	8.05Y	11.30Y	14.94Y	18.96Y	24.05Y	27.03Y	1.85Y	1.89Y	2.49Y	3.58Y	3.83Y	4.18Y	5.10Y
Thailand 578	5.44Y	5.63Y	6.79Y	9.88Y	14.61Y	17.52Y	18.43Y	2.25Y	2.65Y	3.57Y	5.89Y	7.35Y	8.18Y	10.98Y
Vanuatu 846	—Y	—Y	—Y	—Y	—Y	—Y	—Y	—	.01	.01Y	—Y	—Y	—Y	—Y
Vietnam 582	.45Y	.64Y	.76Y	1.01Y	1.23Y	1.40Y	1.66Y	.66Y	.78Y	.70Y	.81Y	.90Y	1.33Y	1.33Y
Asia n.s. 598	.01Y	.02Y	.01Y	.05Y	.07Y	.04Y	.03Y	.43Y	.25Y	.09Y	.19Y	.41Y	.71Y	1.01Y
Europe 170	**5.0Y**	**5.0Y**	**6.9Y**	**8.7Y**	**12.6Y**	**16.5Y**	**18.3Y**	**6.6Y**	**6.7Y**	**11.7Y**	**19.1Y**	**24.3Y**	**27.3Y**	**37.8Y**
Albania 914	—Y	.01Y	.01Y	—Y	—Y	.01Y	.01Y	—Y	—Y	—Y	—Y	—Y	—Y	—Y
Armenia 911	.11Y	.10Y	.06Y	.07Y	.10Y	.12Y	.15Y	.04Y	.05Y	.03Y	.04Y	.04Y	.04Y	.05Y
Azerbaijan 912	.07Y	.07Y	.08Y	.07Y	.10Y	.12Y	.15Y	.02Y	.03Y	.06Y	.35Y	.21Y	.42Y	.62Y
Belarus 913	—Y	—Y	—Y	.01Y	.01Y	.02Y	.02Y	.06Y	.05Y	.05Y	.09Y	.08Y	.11Y	.14Y
Bulgaria 918	.08Y	.08Y	.13Y	.08Y	.08Y	.04Y	.10Y	.09Y	.10Y	.09Y	.11Y	.19Y	.24Y	.30Y
Croatia 960	.14Y	.04Y	.08Y	.08Y	.07Y	.04Y	.11Y	.03Y	.03Y	.03Y	.14Y	.27Y	.25Y	.21Y
Czech Republic 935	.13Y	.09Y	.15Y	.19Y	.22Y	.15Y	.26Y	.28Y	.26Y	.30Y	.73Y	1.01Y	.99Y	1.19Y
Czechoslovakia n.s. 937	.01	—	—	.01Y	—Y	.02Y	.03Y	—Y	—Y	.10Y	.13Y	.18Y	.22Y	.29Y
Estonia 939	—Y	.01Y	.01Y	.01Y	.01Y	.01Y	.02Y	.15Y	.02Y	.01Y	.02Y	.04Y	.07Y	.13Y
Faroe Islands 816	—Y	—Y	—Y	—Y	—Y	—Y	—Y	.01Y	.02Y	.03Y	.04Y	.05Y	.07Y	.09Y
Georgia 915	.02Y	.02Y	.03Y	.06Y	.10Y	.15Y	.21Y	.02Y	.02Y	.01Y	.01Y	.01Y	.03Y	.04Y
Gibraltar 823	—Y	—Y	—Y	—Y	—Y	—Y	—Y	—	—	—	—Y	—Y	—Y	.01Y
Hungary 944	.05Y	.08Y	.11Y	.11Y	.08Y	.09Y	.10Y	.19Y	.21Y	.45Y	.97Y	1.35Y	1.31Y	1.55Y
Kazakhstan 916	.05Y	.06Y	.05Y	.04Y	.05Y	.06Y	.07Y	.35Y	.30Y	.55Y	.97Y	1.14Y	1.38Y	1.80Y
Kyrgyz Republic 917	.01Y	.01Y	.01Y	.01Y	.01Y	.02Y	.02Y	.01Y	.01Y	.02Y	.21Y	.20Y	.02Y	.03Y
Latvia 941	—Y	—Y	.01Y	.01Y	.02Y	.01Y	.01Y	—Y	.01Y	.02Y	.02Y	.03Y	.05Y	.06Y
Lithuania 946	.01Y	.01Y	.01Y	.01Y	.01Y	.02Y	.05Y	.03Y	.02Y	.01Y	.01Y	.02Y	.06Y	.19Y
Macedonia, FYR 962	—Y	.01Y	—Y	.01Y	—Y	.01Y	.02Y	—Y	—Y	—Y	—Y	.01Y	—Y	.01Y
Moldova 921	—Y	—Y	—Y	—Y	—Y	—Y	—Y	.01Y	.01Y	—Y	—Y	.01Y	.01Y	.01Y
Poland 964	.13Y	.18Y	.22Y	.24Y	.21Y	.32Y	.34Y	.33Y	.31Y	.41Y	.53Y	.88Y	.99Y	1.39Y
Romania 968	.07Y	.05Y	.04Y	.07Y	.18Y	.35Y	.75Y	.28Y	.35Y	.36Y	.57Y	.87Y	1.11Y	1.13Y
Russia 922	.12Y	.15Y	.20Y	.31Y	.51Y	.69Y	.74Y	1.82Y	2.13Y	2.76Y	3.80Y	4.51Y	4.48Y	7.57Y
Serbia & Montenegro 965	.15Y	.16Y	.19Y	.25Y	.34Y	.43Y	.52Y	.03Y	.04Y	.04Y	.06Y	.07Y	.09Y	.12Y
Slovak Republic 936	.01Y	.01Y	.01Y	.04Y	.06Y	.05Y	.05Y	.04Y	.02Y	.02Y	.06Y	.21Y	.28Y	.27Y
Tajikistan 923	.02Y	.02Y	.04Y	.04Y	.05Y	.06Y	.12Y	.02Y	.03Y	.08Y	.06Y	.07Y	.12Y	.14Y
Turkey 186	3.49Y	3.55Y	5.03Y	6.56Y	9.68Y	12.76Y	13.27Y	1.64Y	1.60Y	4.04Y	6.51Y	8.58Y	9.81Y	13.65Y
Turkmenistan 925	.24Y	.24Y	.28Y	.37Y	.51Y	.64Y	.77Y	.02Y	.02Y	.56Y	.86Y	1.10Y	1.36Y	1.76Y
Ukraine 926	.04Y	.06Y	.10Y	.10Y	.20Y	.25Y	.41Y	1.01Y	.96Y	1.54Y	2.68Y	3.02Y	3.63Y	4.82Y
U.S.S.R. n.s. 930	—Y	—Y	—Y	—Y	—Y	—Y	—Y	—Y	—Y	—Y	.03Y	—Y	—Y	—Y
Uzbekistan 927	—Y	—Y	—Y	—Y	—Y	—Y	.01Y	.05Y	.07Y	.07Y	.09Y	.12Y	.14Y	.20Y
Yugoslavia n.s. 966	—Y	—Y	—Y	—Y	—Y	—Y	—Y	.01Y	—Y	.01Y	.01Y	.01Y	.01Y	.01Y
Europe n.s. 884	.04Y	—Y	—Y	—Y	—Y	—Y	.01Y	.05Y	.01Y	.01Y	.01Y	.02Y	.03Y	.02Y
Middle East 407	**16.0Y**	**17.9Y**	**19.2Y**	**26.4Y**	**35.3Y**	**43.4Y**	**51.5Y**	**14.7Y**	**16.1Y**	**18.3Y**	**26.0Y**	**34.2Y**	**42.2Y**	**50.3Y**
Bahrain 419	1.74Y	1.86Y	2.24Y	2.95Y	4.00Y	5.03Y	6.07Y	.59Y	.75Y	.86Y	1.34Y	1.67Y	1.98Y	2.54Y
Egypt 469	1.27Y	1.47Y	1.44Y	1.88Y	2.59Y	3.33Y	4.05Y	.53Y	.63Y	.83Y	1.07Y	1.67Y	2.09Y	2.69Y
Iran, I.R. of 429	2.30Y	2.96Y	3.17Y	3.68Y	4.84Y	5.77Y	6.91Y	.80Y	.69Y	.79Y	1.01Y	1.50Y	1.80Y	2.09Y
Iraq 433	.19Y	.18Y	.10Y	.14Y	.21Y	.21Y	.18Y	.02Y	.12Y	.02Y	.09Y	.03Y	.04Y	.04Y
Israel 436	—Y	—Y	—Y	—Y	—Y	—Y	—Y	.05	.03	.03Y	.05Y	.10Y	.11Y	.28Y

Oil Exporting Ctys 999

		Exports							Imports						
		2001	2002	2003	2004	2005	2006	2007	2001	2002	2003	2004	2005	2006	2007
		Billions of U.S. Dollars							Billions of U.S. Dollars						
Jordan	439	1.00Y	1.06Y	1.25Y	2.04Y	2.77Y	3.15Y	3.14Y	1.02Y	1.11Y	1.17Y	1.28Y	1.59Y	1.82Y	2.10Y
Kuwait	443	.93Y	.92Y	1.02Y	1.20Y	1.50Y	1.79Y	2.00Y	1.00Y	.98Y	1.07Y	1.57Y	1.90Y	2.28Y	2.62Y
Lebanon	446	.32Y	.34Y	.39Y	.52Y	.67Y	.83Y	1.02Y	.36Y	.42Y	.46Y	.55Y	.70Y	.89Y	1.16Y
Libya	672	.05Y	.06Y	.09Y	.12Y	.15Y	.18Y	.21Y	.02Y	.01Y	.16Y	.13Y	.23Y	.62Y	.88Y
Oman	449	1.77Y	1.77Y	1.60Y	1.85Y	2.43Y	2.92Y	3.49Y	.26Y	.29Y	.80Y	.92Y	1.27Y	1.56Y	1.83Y
Qatar	453	.44Y	.60Y	.67Y	.98Y	1.34Y	2.01Y	2.40Y	.33Y	.36Y	.43Y	1.11Y	1.34Y	1.77Y	2.10Y
Saudi Arabia	456	1.62Y	1.79Y	1.92Y	2.28Y	3.01Y	3.66Y	4.46Y	3.61Y	3.59Y	4.45Y	5.60Y	7.36Y	9.10Y	10.11Y
Syrian Arab Republic	463	.29Y	.30Y	.36Y	3.10Y	4.19Y	5.27Y	6.37Y	1.26Y	1.37Y	.83Y	3.68Y	4.68Y	5.79Y	7.45Y
United Arab Emirates	466	3.23Y	3.61Y	3.77Y	4.41Y	6.00Y	7.22Y	8.59Y	4.68Y	5.45Y	6.00Y	7.21Y	9.59Y	11.64Y	13.52Y
Yemen, Republic of	474	.82Y	1.01Y	1.17Y	1.29Y	1.65Y	2.06Y	2.62Y	.18Y	.29Y	.37Y	.35Y	.56Y	.69Y	.90Y
Middle East n.s.	489	—Y	—Y	.04Y	—Y	—Y	—Y	—Y	.01Y	—Y	—Y	—Y	—Y	—Y	—Y
Western Hemisphere	**207**	**13.3Y**	**13.4Y**	**12.9Y**	**21.5Y**	**23.6Y**	**24.9Y**	**28.5Y**	**10.5Y**	**8.0Y**	**7.9Y**	**13.5Y**	**18.8Y**	**25.4Y**	**33.8Y**
Antigua and Barbuda	311	.01Y	.01Y	—Y	—Y	—Y	—Y	—Y	—	—	—Y	—Y	—Y	.03Y	—Y
Argentina	213	.22Y	.10Y	.11Y	.32Y	.19Y	.56Y	.30Y	1.10Y	.81Y	.94Y	1.94Y	2.28Y	2.92Y	4.27Y
Aruba	314	—Y	—Y	—Y	—Y	—Y	—Y	.02Y	.01Y	—Y	—Y	—Y	.02Y	.01Y	.01Y
Bahamas, The	313	.03Y	.24Y	.09Y	.09Y	.18Y	.41Y	.49Y	—Y	.01Y	—Y	.05Y	.01Y	.02Y	—Y
Barbados	316	.01Y	—Y	—Y	—Y	—Y	.01Y	.01Y	—Y	—Y	—Y	—Y	—Y	—Y	.01Y
Belize	339	—Y	—Y	—Y	—Y	—Y	—Y	—Y	—Y	—Y	.01Y	.01Y	.01Y	.01Y	.02Y
Bermuda	319	—Y	—Y	—Y	—Y	—Y	—Y	.01Y	.01Y	—Y	—Y	—Y	—Y	—Y	—Y
Bolivia	218	—Y	—Y	.01Y	.01Y	.01Y	.01Y	.01Y	.11Y	.10Y	.07Y	.07Y	.02Y	.03Y	.04Y
Brazil	223	3.63Y	4.43Y	4.56Y	7.78Y	8.14Y	10.08Y	11.13Y	3.39Y	3.23Y	3.57Y	5.97Y	7.97Y	11.24Y	13.13Y
Chile	228	.33Y	.33Y	.23Y	.54Y	.48Y	.71Y	.64Y	.49Y	.39Y	.46Y	.69Y	.91Y	1.21Y	1.67Y
Colombia	233	.75Y	.78Y	.71Y	1.12Y	1.20Y	1.27Y	1.40Y	1.61Y	1.08Y	.82Y	1.90Y	2.69Y	3.46Y	6.27Y
Costa Rica	238	.10Y	.29Y	.23Y	.31Y	.41Y	.54Y	.66Y	.03Y	.03Y	.03Y	.04Y	.06Y	.09Y	.06Y
Dominican Republic	243	.21Y	.77Y	.20Y	.54Y	.78Y	.90Y	1.09Y	.01Y	.02Y	.01Y	.01Y	.01Y	.02Y	.03Y
Ecuador	248	.23Y	.37Y	.21Y	.42Y	.41Y	.41Y	.47Y	.22Y	.14Y	.10Y	.17Y	.21Y	.31Y	.51Y
El Salvador	253	.01Y	.06Y	.10Y	.17Y	.13Y	.12Y	.13Y	.02Y	—Y	.01Y	—Y	.01Y	.02Y	—Y
Guatemala	258	.20Y	.21Y	.08Y	.10Y	.08Y	.04Y	.05Y	.07Y	.08Y	.08Y	.12Y	.10Y	.11Y	.16Y
Guyana	336	.01Y	.01Y	.01Y	.01Y	.01Y	.03Y	.03Y	—Y	—Y	—Y	—Y	—Y	—Y	—Y
Haiti	263	.02Y	.02Y	.01Y	.01Y	.01Y	.02Y	.03Y	—Y	—Y	—Y	—Y	—Y	.01Y	.01Y
Honduras	268	.02Y	.08Y	.05Y	.07Y	.03Y	.04Y	.04Y	—Y	—Y	—Y	—Y	—Y	—Y	.01Y
Jamaica	343	.13Y	.11Y	.07Y	.09Y	.28Y	.52Y	.59Y	.01Y	.01Y	.01Y	.03Y	.05Y	.05Y	.05Y
Mexico	273	.86Y	.88Y	.88Y	1.22Y	1.17Y	1.56Y	2.39Y	1.22Y	.91Y	.85Y	1.15Y	2.31Y	2.68Y	3.17Y
Netherlands Antilles	353	4.58Y	3.56Y	2.54Y	7.00Y	8.11Y	5.77Y	6.96Y	.23Y	.22Y	.05Y	.11Y	.19Y	.18Y	.14Y
Nicaragua	278	.19Y	.14Y	.13Y	.39Y	.11Y	.12Y	.22Y	.03Y	—Y	—Y	—Y	—Y	—Y	.01Y
Panama	283	.35Y	.24Y	.16Y	.09Y	.31Y	.12Y	.11Y	.52Y	.29Y	.43Y	.50Y	.98Y	1.64Y	2.28Y
Paraguay	288	.01Y	.01Y	.01Y	—Y	.01Y	.01Y	.01Y	.03Y	.02Y	.02Y	.03Y	.02Y	.02Y	.01Y
Peru	293	.33Y	.26Y	.38Y	.60Y	.34Y	.78Y	.70Y	.25Y	.20Y	.18Y	.26Y	.40Y	.64Y	1.02Y
St. Lucia	362	.05Y	.02Y	.02Y	—Y	.04Y	—Y	—Y	—	—	—Y	—Y	—Y	—Y	—Y
St. Vincent & Grens.	364	—Y	—Y	—Y	—Y	.03Y	—Y	—Y	—Y	.01Y	—Y	—Y	—Y	—Y	—Y
Suriname	366	—Y	—Y	—Y	.01Y	—Y	—Y	—Y	—	—	.05Y	.06Y	.08Y	.10Y	.12Y
Trinidad and Tobago	369	.60Y	.36Y	.39Y	.14Y	.29Y	.44Y	.53Y	.05Y	.17Y	.05Y	.07Y	.04Y	.06Y	.07Y
Uruguay	298	.06Y	.08Y	.03Y	.25Y	.21Y	.27Y	.33Y	.14Y	.14Y	.10Y	.21Y	.28Y	.35Y	.44Y
Venezuela, Rep. Bol.	299	.15Y	.03Y	.03Y	.06Y	.09Y	.12Y	.14Y	.06Y	.01Y	.03Y	.03Y	.09Y	.05Y	.06Y
Western Hem. n.s.	399	.17Y	.03Y	1.67Y	.15Y	.57Y	—Y	—Y	.86Y	.14Y	.03Y	.05Y	.07Y	.12Y	.24Y
Other Countries n.i.e.	**910**	**.6Y**	**.5Y**	**.2Y**	**1.4Y**	**2.0Y**	**2.6Y**	**3.1Y**	**.1Y**	**.1Y**	**.2Y**	**.3Y**	**.3Y**	**.2Y**	**.6Y**
Cuba	928	.49Y	.32Y	.03Y	1.11Y	1.75Y	2.19Y	2.65Y	.04Y	.06Y	.18Y	.20Y	.20Y	.16Y	.22Y
North Korea	954	.11Y	.16Y	.16Y	.26Y	.30Y	.39Y	.45Y	.03Y	.08Y	.01Y	.06Y	.07Y	.07Y	.37Y
Countries & Areas n.s.	**898**	**12.6Y**	**14.4Y**	**17.4Y**	**24.0Y**	**29.2Y**	**45.7Y**	**55.1Y**	**.2Y**	**.3Y**	**3.1Y**	**4.1Y**	**4.9Y**	**6.2Y**	**7.9Y**
Special Categories	**899**	**.1Y**	**—Y**	**—Y**	**—Y**	**—Y**	**—Y**	**—Y**	**3.2Y**	**2.4Y**	**.3Y**	**.2Y**	**.3Y**	**.5Y**	**.1Y**
Memorandum Items															
European Union	998	58.84Y	56.98Y	71.28Y	89.48Y	126.96Y	149.44Y	155.75Y	54.23Y	58.29Y	69.76Y	99.56Y	119.42Y	124.73Y	157.64Y
Oil Exporting Ctys	999	14.16Y	15.44Y	16.42Y	19.86Y	25.63Y	30.40Y	35.96Y	13.39Y	14.39Y	16.42Y	20.97Y	27.09Y	32.21Y	38.08Y
Non-Oil Develop.Ctys	201	112.92Y	113.11Y	136.00Y	186.69Y	242.06Y	306.75Y	353.94Y	58.27Y	60.85Y	75.99Y	123.57Y	160.42Y	194.88Y	263.24Y
PERCENT DISTRIBUTION															
Industrial Countries	**101**	55.1	52.9	54.0	52.6	54.1	52.0	50.4	57.3	57.1	54.6	51.5	50.3	47.6	46.2
Developing Countries	**202**	40.6	42.2	41.2	42.2	41.1	42.0	43.2	40.7	41.3	43.6	47.0	48.3	50.8	52.3
Africa	**607**	3.0	3.0	3.0	3.2	2.6	3.3	3.2	2.3	2.3	2.1	2.2	1.8	1.7	1.7
Asia	**507**	26.7	27.2	27.6	27.4	27.5	28.2	29.1	20.4	22.1	23.6	25.7	26.6	27.9	29.5
Europe	**170**	1.6	1.7	1.9	1.8	1.9	2.0	2.0	3.7	3.7	5.5	6.2	6.3	6.1	6.6
Middle East	**407**	5.1	5.9	5.2	5.4	5.4	5.4	5.7	8.4	8.8	8.6	8.4	8.8	9.4	8.7
Western Hemisphere	**207**	4.2	4.4	3.5	4.4	3.6	3.1	3.2	5.9	4.4	3.7	4.4	4.9	5.7	5.9
Other Countries n.i.e.	**910**	.2	.2	.1	.3	.3	.3	.3	—	.1	.1	.1	.1	.1	.1
ANNUAL PERCENT CHANGE															
World	**001**	−12.0	−2.6	21.4	32.2	33.1	23.3	12.4	9.5	3.5	16.2	45.2	26.2	15.1	28.9
Industrial Countries	**101**	−14.6	−6.5	23.9	28.7	36.9	18.5	8.9	7.9	3.2	11.1	37.0	23.2	9.0	25.0
Developing Countries	**202**	−9.7	1.1	18.6	35.5	29.6	26.0	15.6	11.6	5.0	22.8	56.4	29.7	21.1	32.7
Africa	**607**	−13.0	−.9	20.1	41.4	8.1	53.8	9.3	33.7	2.6	9.3	50.2	4.3	5.8	28.3
Asia	**507**	−10.6	−.6	23.4	31.1	33.5	26.3	16.2	4.1	12.4	24.2	58.2	30.2	20.9	36.1
Europe	**170**	−8.8	.3	36.8	27.2	44.4	30.3	11.3	23.6	1.3	74.7	64.1	26.9	12.4	38.3
Middle East	**407**	9.7	12.1	7.3	37.5	33.7	22.9	18.6	19.0	9.4	13.6	42.1	31.6	23.4	19.2
Western Hemisphere	**207**	−19.9	1.0	−3.9	66.8	9.9	5.1	14.6	15.5	−23.2	−1.8	70.5	39.9	34.8	33.3
Other Countries n.i.e.	**910**	−48.4	−20.7	−59.1	595.4	50.2	25.9	20.2	−31.0	118.8	37.0	36.7	3.9	−12.8	151.2

		Exports							Imports						
		2001	2002	2003	2004	2005	2006	2007	2001	2002	2003	2004	2005	2006	2007
		Billions of U.S. Dollars							Billions of U.S. Dollars						
IFS World Total		**1,943.7**	**2,112.1**	**2,508.2**	**3,211.8**	**3,837.2**	**4,598.9**	**5,423.8**	**1,995.1**	**2,122.6**	**2,516.7**	**3,218.1**	**3,764.9**	**4,466.9**	**5,336.4**
DOTS World Total	**001**	**1,896.8Y**	**2,074.0Y**	**2,489.7Y**	**3,151.4Y**	**3,752.2Y**	**4,499.5Y**	**5,316.7Y**	**1,957.2Y**	**2,091.3Y**	**2,486.3Y**	**3,170.1Y**	**3,689.7Y**	**4,415.5Y**	**5,323.8Y**
Industrial Countries	**101**	**1,079.6Y**	**1,149.5Y**	**1,338.4Y**	**1,665.3Y**	**1,940.5Y**	**2,277.3Y**	**2,574.1Y**	**1,043.1Y**	**1,079.6Y**	**1,241.0Y**	**1,517.5Y**	**1,673.5Y**	**1,920.9Y**	**2,303.5Y**
United States	111	454.77Y	482.29Y	525.34Y	626.28Y	722.83Y	836.37Y	881.77Y	338.88Y	324.51Y	339.55Y	388.83Y	422.54Y	479.23Y	553.98Y
Canada	156	19.90Y	21.62Y	24.72Y	31.30Y	39.85Y	49.10Y	57.75Y	19.95Y	19.74Y	20.90Y	27.21Y	34.20Y	36.16Y	45.04Y
Australia	193	20.45Y	23.51Y	30.28Y	39.42Y	47.82Y	56.61Y	67.36Y	29.29Y	29.29Y	31.71Y	42.17Y	55.23Y	66.31Y	78.77Y
Japan	158	141.78Y	141.25Y	162.41Y	197.27Y	221.25Y	248.43Y	270.58Y	206.37Y	224.50Y	268.88Y	340.14Y	362.27Y	395.77Y	442.93Y
New Zealand	196	2.54Y	2.94Y	3.79Y	5.25Y	6.19Y	6.93Y	8.23Y	4.76Y	4.69Y	5.24Y	6.33Y	6.83Y	7.32Y	8.91Y
Austria	122	10.53Y	11.51Y	15.68Y	19.15Y	22.51Y	25.70Y	29.91Y	13.01Y	14.50Y	18.54Y	24.51Y	27.09Y	33.82Y	44.73Y
Belgium	124	21.33Y	22.94Y	26.43Y	33.67Y	42.23Y	52.69Y	65.20Y	21.00Y	23.02Y	26.58Y	33.00Y	38.96Y	47.62Y	59.42Y
Belgium-Luxembourg n.s.	127	3.73Y	3.52Y	3.46Y	4.14Y	3.46Y	1.24Y	.82Y	2.26Y	2.26Y	2.47Y	2.91Y	2.05Y	.84Y	.65Y
Cyprus	423	2.96Y	3.67Y	6.22Y	8.35Y	7.82Y	8.13Y	9.00Y	.35Y	.45Y	.49Y	.57Y	.41Y	.54Y	1.28Y
Denmark	128	6.52Y	7.17Y	8.88Y	11.89Y	14.10Y	16.69Y	19.58Y	7.51Y	8.16Y	9.51Y	11.24Y	12.62Y	14.95Y	18.40Y
Finland	172	8.69Y	8.92Y	12.59Y	18.37Y	23.22Y	26.85Y	30.76Y	11.90Y	11.07Y	13.40Y	17.92Y	20.33Y	24.22Y	29.49Y
France	132	42.11Y	45.14Y	56.39Y	75.96Y	85.77Y	97.05Y	119.40Y	56.96Y	57.01Y	71.18Y	84.98Y	92.14Y	108.70Y	129.56Y
Germany	134	112.05Y	116.65Y	150.15Y	186.07Y	218.83Y	258.61Y	307.26Y	129.99Y	143.10Y	177.78Y	222.60Y	250.99Y	305.29Y	383.57Y
Greece	174	6.81Y	7.79Y	9.58Y	11.55Y	13.74Y	17.78Y	21.17Y	3.35Y	3.42Y	4.24Y	5.02Y	5.72Y	6.94Y	9.08Y
Iceland	176	.49Y	.28Y	.32Y	.37Y	.59Y	.71Y	.89Y	.17Y	.23Y	.21Y	.30Y	.35Y	.43Y	.39Y
Ireland	178	6.37Y	5.90Y	7.79Y	9.03Y	10.80Y	12.54Y	13.59Y	8.04Y	8.21Y	9.20Y	11.32Y	12.72Y	14.35Y	16.65Y
Italy	136	49.44Y	53.58Y	64.61Y	87.84Y	101.20Y	128.74Y	149.38Y	54.37Y	59.26Y	69.31Y	82.99Y	90.85Y	109.37Y	138.42Y
Luxembourg	137	.57Y	1.17Y	1.48Y	1.94Y	3.07Y	3.22Y	3.22Y	.47Y	.65Y	1.13Y	1.49Y	1.40Y	1.63Y	2.32Y
Malta	181	1.27Y	1.46Y	1.42Y	1.98Y	2.09Y	2.85Y	3.41Y	.72Y	1.03Y	1.38Y	1.42Y	1.45Y	1.67Y	2.12Y
Netherlands	138	52.95Y	60.52Y	72.59Y	97.48Y	123.35Y	150.49Y	182.25Y	22.59Y	24.20Y	28.43Y	37.39Y	47.08Y	60.56Y	80.34Y
Norway	142	3.66Y	4.37Y	5.94Y	6.48Y	8.38Y	10.69Y	12.69Y	4.82Y	6.26Y	6.80Y	7.90Y	9.32Y	10.21Y	13.10Y
Portugal	182	4.09Y	4.31Y	4.85Y	6.67Y	9.45Y	10.89Y	13.61Y	2.48Y	2.89Y	3.97Y	4.99Y	5.56Y	6.52Y	8.75Y
Slovenia	961	1.96Y	2.07Y	2.62Y	3.43Y	4.63Y	5.71Y	8.05Y	3.06Y	3.68Y	4.52Y	5.67Y	6.14Y	6.91Y	10.34Y
Spain	184	22.20Y	24.78Y	31.46Y	42.37Y	54.94Y	68.77Y	84.81Y	18.83Y	21.19Y	25.66Y	32.14Y	34.08Y	41.57Y	58.44Y
Sweden	144	8.64Y	9.98Y	12.12Y	15.94Y	18.90Y	22.42Y	27.87Y	15.43Y	15.14Y	18.87Y	24.79Y	27.78Y	31.54Y	38.88Y
Switzerland	146	11.33Y	15.91Y	20.46Y	25.90Y	26.98Y	35.44Y	40.94Y	21.73Y	26.08Y	30.51Y	38.70Y	42.50Y	38.89Y	48.40Y
United Kingdom	112	62.51Y	66.25Y	76.80Y	97.18Y	107.36Y	125.65Y	148.19Y	44.75Y	45.04Y	50.58Y	61.00Y	64.85Y	74.35Y	88.30Y
Developing Countries	**202**	**782.5Y**	**889.5Y**	**1,115.7Y**	**1,448.5Y**	**1,767.9Y**	**2,177.9Y**	**2,689.1Y**	**872.0Y**	**958.4Y**	**1,178.7Y**	**1,564.1Y**	**1,896.0Y**	**2,339.9Y**	**2,834.9Y**
Africa	**607**	**33.5Y**	**37.8Y**	**46.4Y**	**62.3Y**	**76.4Y**	**95.7Y**	**122.6Y**	**36.6Y**	**36.5Y**	**43.6Y**	**65.0Y**	**77.1Y**	**96.3Y**	**118.1Y**
Algeria	612	1.99Y	2.73Y	3.74Y	5.23Y	6.15Y	8.15Y	11.38Y	3.17Y	3.27Y	3.39Y	4.90Y	6.82Y	6.67Y	8.65Y
Angola	614	1.49Y	.95Y	1.28Y	3.40Y	3.69Y	4.39Y	4.46Y	1.65Y	2.15Y	3.40Y	6.52Y	9.79Y	15.89Y	19.97Y
Benin	638	.78Y	.78Y	.94Y	1.12Y	1.75Y	2.46Y	3.31Y	.16Y	.14Y	.22Y	.30Y	.30Y	.30Y	.38Y
Botswana	616	.07Y	.09Y	.12Y	.14Y	.19Y	.30Y	.44Y	.04Y	.06Y	.11Y	.19Y	.24Y	.22Y	.28Y
Burkina Faso	748	.20Y	.26Y	.32Y	.39Y	.47Y	.57Y	.73Y	.08Y	.09Y	.16Y	.27Y	.28Y	.31Y	.33Y
Burundi	618	.05Y	.05Y	.09Y	.09Y	.10Y	.11Y	.13Y	.01Y	.01Y	.01Y	.02Y	.02Y	.02Y	.03Y
Cameroon	622	.38Y	.42Y	.46Y	.53Y	.73Y	.89Y	1.13Y	.56Y	.38Y	.62Y	1.11Y	1.02Y	1.30Y	1.55Y
Cape Verde	624	.03Y	.04Y	.04Y	.04Y	.06Y	.09Y	.13Y	—Y	—Y	—Y	—Y	—Y	—Y	.01Y
Central African Rep.	626	.02Y	.03Y	.03Y	.04Y	.05Y	.06Y	.08Y	.03Y	.06Y	.02Y	.02Y	.03Y	.03Y	.03Y
Chad	628	.03Y	.07Y	.08Y	.10Y	.12Y	.15Y	.23Y	.02Y	.02Y	.03Y	.27Y	.35Y	.42Y	.12Y
Comoros	632	.03Y	.04Y	.04Y	.05Y	.05Y	.06Y	.08Y	.01Y	—Y	—Y	.01Y	.01Y	.01Y	.02Y
Congo, Dem. Rep. of	636	.34Y	.42Y	.46Y	.67Y	.77Y	1.21Y	1.69Y	.13Y	.05Y	.09Y	.19Y	.39Y	.88Y	.95Y
Congo, Republic of	634	.25Y	.37Y	.39Y	.43Y	.61Y	.75Y	1.58Y	1.58Y	1.43Y	1.91Y	2.84Y	3.77Y	5.16Y	3.92Y
Côte d'Ivoire	662	.75Y	.76Y	.86Y	.75Y	.95Y	1.14Y	1.51Y	1.55Y	1.62Y	1.87Y	2.14Y	2.31Y	2.85Y	3.30Y
Djibouti	611	.28Y	.21Y	.36Y	.32Y	.50Y	.66Y	.85Y	.20Y	.21Y	.26Y	.26Y	.28Y	.35Y	.43Y
Equatorial Guinea	642	.04Y	.04Y	.16Y	.10Y	.18Y	.40Y	.37Y	.47Y	.39Y	.47Y	1.69Y	2.33Y	3.60Y	3.03Y
Ethiopia	644	.38Y	.45Y	.60Y	.79Y	.98Y	1.19Y	1.67Y	.19Y	.14Y	.24Y	.15Y	.30Y	.36Y	.40Y
Gabon	646	.14Y	.14Y	.18Y	.24Y	.32Y	.41Y	.55Y	.74Y	.73Y	.78Y	1.05Y	1.19Y	2.13Y	2.54Y
Gambia, The	648	.21Y	.23Y	.28Y	.35Y	.39Y	.46Y	.58Y	.01Y	.01Y	.01Y	.02Y	.02Y	.02Y	.04Y
Ghana	652	.90Y	.96Y	1.43Y	1.92Y	2.26Y	2.59Y	3.60Y	.30Y	.39Y	.52Y	.62Y	.69Y	.85Y	.98Y
Guinea	656	.23Y	.24Y	.33Y	.41Y	.56Y	.60Y	.79Y	.28Y	.38Y	.36Y	.46Y	.63Y	.63Y	.71Y
Guinea-Bissau	654	.05Y	.04Y	.08Y	.05Y	.06Y	.06Y	.08Y	.13Y	.09Y	.05Y	.07Y	.09Y	.12Y	.37Y
Kenya	664	1.09Y	1.22Y	1.58Y	2.16Y	2.62Y	3.29Y	4.23Y	1.10Y	1.22Y	1.50Y	1.81Y	2.00Y	2.43Y	3.01Y
Lesotho	666	.10Y	.16Y	.19Y	.25Y	.21Y	.24Y	.25Y	.05Y	—Y	—Y	—Y	—Y	—Y	—Y
Liberia	668	1.84Y	2.31Y	2.39Y	3.02Y	3.56Y	5.37Y	5.94Y	.18Y	.21Y	.24Y	.32Y	.26Y	.59Y	.60Y
Madagascar	674	.50Y	.35Y	.64Y	.73Y	.78Y	.80Y	1.16Y	.16Y	.08Y	.12Y	.12Y	.10Y	.12Y	.14Y
Malawi	676	.31Y	.41Y	.43Y	.54Y	.54Y	.54Y	.64Y	.16Y	.19Y	.22Y	.28Y	.31Y	.39Y	.49Y
Mali	678	.38Y	.41Y	.42Y	.60Y	.73Y	.83Y	1.05Y	.10Y	.09Y	.15Y	.26Y	.20Y	.24Y	.15Y
Mauritania	682	.16Y	.26Y	.27Y	.29Y	.34Y	.45Y	.59Y	.14Y	.12Y	.16Y	.25Y	.24Y	.65Y	.88Y
Mauritius	684	.93Y	.98Y	1.15Y	1.31Y	1.44Y	1.62Y	1.95Y	.13Y	.14Y	.15Y	.27Y	.32Y	.31Y	.37Y
Morocco	686	1.67Y	2.09Y	2.50Y	3.65Y	4.39Y	5.17Y	7.20Y	1.44Y	1.61Y	1.78Y	2.33Y	2.97Y	3.67Y	4.54Y
Mozambique	688	.78Y	.86Y	1.04Y	1.20Y	1.52Y	1.45Y	1.93Y	.20Y	.34Y	.23Y	.28Y	.31Y	.30Y	.78Y
Namibia	728	.08Y	.08Y	.14Y	.14Y	.17Y	.29Y	.47Y	.04Y	.06Y	.08Y	.11Y	.25Y	.45Y	.42Y
Niger	692	.13Y	.20Y	.22Y	.27Y	.29Y	.38Y	.40Y	.10Y	.02Y	.02Y	.08Y	.03Y	.08Y	.04Y
Nigeria	694	4.09Y	5.24Y	5.76Y	6.62Y	8.47Y	9.93Y	13.96Y	6.69Y	4.02Y	4.80Y	9.37Y	8.92Y	12.13Y	15.38Y
Rwanda	714	.09Y	.12Y	.15Y	.16Y	.21Y	.24Y	.31Y	.05Y	.03Y	.02Y	.04Y	.04Y	.05Y	.08Y
St. Helena	856	.01Y	.01Y	.01Y	.01Y	.02Y	.02Y	.04Y	—Y	.01Y	.01Y	.01Y	.01Y	.01Y	.02Y
São Tomé & Príncipe	716	—Y	.01Y	.01Y	.01Y	.01Y	.01Y	.01Y	—Y	—Y	—Y	—Y	—Y	—Y	—Y
Senegal	722	.49Y	.57Y	.67Y	.92Y	1.16Y	1.14Y	1.64Y	.36Y	.50Y	.60Y	.67Y	.92Y	.79Y	.99Y
Seychelles	718	.10Y	.11Y	.12Y	.13Y	.22Y	.26Y	.25Y	.03Y	.07Y	.07Y	.05Y	.05Y	.06Y	.08Y

		Exports							Imports						
		2001	2002	2003	2004	2005	2006	2007	2001	2002	2003	2004	2005	2006	2007
		Billions of U.S. Dollars							Billions of U.S. Dollars						
Sierra Leone	724	.09Y	.10Y	.16Y	.18Y	.23Y	.27Y	.30Y	.01Y	.01Y	.01Y	.02Y	.02Y	.02Y	.03Y
Somalia	726	.20Y	.24Y	.27Y	.34Y	.39Y	.49Y	.53Y	.02Y	.05Y	.06Y	.07Y	.10Y	.11Y	.13Y
South Africa	199	5.63Y	6.29Y	8.54Y	12.51Y	15.75Y	21.17Y	25.75Y	9.65Y	10.99Y	12.84Y	17.82Y	19.40Y	20.90Y	28.08Y
Sudan	732	.73Y	.99Y	1.28Y	2.20Y	3.31Y	3.76Y	3.82Y	1.28Y	1.47Y	1.84Y	2.27Y	3.09Y	2.56Y	4.82Y
Swaziland	734	.06Y	.08Y	.16Y	.12Y	.09Y	.11Y	.11Y	.15Y	.22Y	.18Y	.28Y	.40Y	.52Y	.47Y
Tanzania	738	.77Y	.92Y	1.24Y	1.49Y	1.82Y	2.28Y	2.67Y	.27Y	.30Y	.43Y	.58Y	.77Y	.85Y	.98Y
Togo	742	.41Y	.47Y	.68Y	1.03Y	1.12Y	1.51Y	2.70Y	.22Y	.24Y	.36Y	.39Y	.41Y	.49Y	.60Y
Tunisia	744	.95Y	1.10Y	1.25Y	1.72Y	1.96Y	2.52Y	3.26Y	.49Y	.62Y	.63Y	.81Y	.92Y	1.10Y	1.33Y
Uganda	746	.58Y	.64Y	.68Y	.81Y	.90Y	1.17Y	1.52Y	.10Y	.11Y	.16Y	.19Y	.24Y	.26Y	.31Y
Zambia	754	.69Y	.80Y	.76Y	1.03Y	1.23Y	1.58Y	2.23Y	.41Y	.37Y	.55Y	1.20Y	2.16Y	2.97Y	2.82Y
Zimbabwe	698	.94Y	1.01Y	1.10Y	1.28Y	1.60Y	1.52Y	1.79Y	.75Y	.85Y	1.04Y	1.11Y	1.14Y	1.44Y	1.72Y
Africa n.s.	799	1.00Y	.48Y	.37Y	.45Y	.37Y	.60Y	.59Y	.97Y	.96Y	.85Y	.84Y	.51Y	.56Y	.65Y
Asia	**507**	**491.9Y**	**572.7Y**	**724.5Y**	**921.3Y**	**1,092.7Y**	**1,316.6Y**	**1,558.2Y**	**531.9Y**	**608.3Y**	**736.7Y**	**952.9Y**	**1,129.3Y**	**1,376.5Y**	**1,654.1Y**
Afghanistan, I.S. of	512	.41Y	.63Y	1.04Y	1.20Y	1.95Y	2.45Y	3.25Y	.07Y	.06Y	.09Y	.13Y	.15Y	.19Y	.25Y
American Samoa	859	.03Y	.04Y	.01Y	.01Y	.04Y	.08Y	.12Y	.01Y	.03Y	—Y	.01Y	.01Y	.01Y	.03Y
Bangladesh	513	5.30Y	5.18Y	6.38Y	7.59Y	8.50Y	10.21Y	10.94Y	.54Y	.58Y	.68Y	.78Y	.97Y	1.29Y	1.60Y
Brunei Darussalam	516	.83Y	.88Y	.97Y	1.02Y	1.14Y	1.23Y	1.44Y	1.18Y	1.41Y	1.35Y	1.51Y	1.38Y	1.87Y	1.53Y
Cambodia	522	1.81Y	2.04Y	2.36Y	2.90Y	3.46Y	4.59Y	5.23Y	.18Y	.23Y	.24Y	.28Y	.40Y	.44Y	.53Y
China,P.R.: Mainland	924	124.91Y	154.92Y	216.16Y	283.31Y	344.67Y	416.79Y	495.43Y	153.93Y	179.51Y	219.02Y	287.84Y	361.25Y	461.87Y	587.96Y
China,P.R.:Hong Kong	532	108.98Y	129.64Y	156.57Y	192.13Y	222.51Y	271.67Y	310.56Y	26.25Y	29.67Y	32.28Y	36.86Y	37.38Y	39.41Y	45.28Y
China,P.R.:Macao	546	2.29Y	2.31Y	3.36Y	4.19Y	4.87Y	5.94Y	7.16Y	.36Y	.44Y	.51Y	.63Y	.71Y	.72Y	.84Y
Fiji	819	.18Y	.25Y	.31Y	.44Y	.58Y	.68Y	.70Y	.12Y	.11Y	.15Y	.19Y	.19Y	.23Y	.29Y
French Polynesia	887	.04Y	.08Y	.07Y	.18Y	.36Y	.38Y	.38Y	.01Y	.01Y	.03Y	.08Y	.08Y	.09Y	.11Y
Guam	829	.38Y	.30Y	.36Y	.48Y	.70Y	.83Y	.66Y	.01Y	.01Y	.02Y	.01Y	.01Y	.01Y	.01Y
India	534	16.32Y	19.10Y	24.38Y	32.39Y	44.71Y	57.08Y	79.45Y	17.26Y	19.81Y	25.76Y	36.71Y	45.68Y	55.01Y	72.74Y
Indonesia	536	13.49Y	15.20Y	34.55Y	43.56Y	52.55Y	57.37Y	71.16Y	22.23Y	24.64Y	36.89Y	46.12Y	52.79Y	63.67Y	73.91Y
Kiribati	826	.02Y	.02Y	.02Y	.02Y	.03Y	.03Y	.05Y	.02Y	.01Y	—Y	—Y	—Y	—Y	.01Y
Korea	542	37.25Y	43.08Y	50.85Y	66.37Y	78.83Y	98.28Y	121.70Y	72.22Y	83.25Y	105.17Y	144.58Y	173.40Y	209.31Y	241.62Y
Lao People's Dem.Rep	544	.59Y	.57Y	.65Y	.83Y	1.03Y	1.39Y	1.73Y	.17Y	.18Y	.19Y	.22Y	.38Y	.86Y	.92Y
Malaysia	548	38.91Y	43.12Y	48.43Y	57.81Y	65.22Y	77.74Y	89.40Y	53.30Y	58.80Y	69.51Y	84.36Y	93.22Y	110.06Y	126.24Y
Maldives	556	.25Y	.22Y	.27Y	.41Y	.43Y	.49Y	.63Y	.95Y	1.08Y	.93Y	1.02Y	.08Y	.10Y	.09Y
Mongolia	948	.48Y	.53Y	.63Y	.80Y	.97Y	1.17Y	1.67Y	.29Y	.29Y	.34Y	.51Y	.63Y	1.22Y	1.42Y
Myanmar	518	2.03Y	2.39Y	2.65Y	2.80Y	2.89Y	3.07Y	4.25Y	1.51Y	1.81Y	1.82Y	2.35Y	3.12Y	3.76Y	4.06Y
Nauru	836	—Y	—Y	—Y	—Y	.01Y	.01Y	.03Y	.01Y	.01Y	.01Y	.01Y	—Y	—Y	.01Y
Nepal	558	.91Y	.60Y	.90Y	1.07Y	1.15Y	1.74Y	2.23Y	.42Y	.32Y	.31Y	.36Y	.40Y	.66Y	.82Y
New Caledonia	839	.12Y	.14Y	.20Y	.27Y	.39Y	.45Y	.61Y	.13Y	.13Y	.22Y	.39Y	.41Y	.52Y	1.01Y
Pakistan	564	3.25Y	4.16Y	5.44Y	7.38Y	9.68Y	11.24Y	13.84Y	2.91Y	2.95Y	3.34Y	3.93Y	5.29Y	6.46Y	7.61Y
Papua New Guinea	853	.31Y	.34Y	.42Y	.51Y	.50Y	.65Y	.79Y	.41Y	.29Y	.53Y	.56Y	.74Y	.90Y	1.04Y
Philippines	566	15.41Y	16.67Y	18.99Y	24.05Y	25.77Y	29.42Y	34.78Y	16.33Y	20.19Y	24.89Y	29.86Y	35.97Y	42.09Y	48.79Y
Samoa	862	.06Y	.07Y	.10Y	.13Y	.12Y	.14Y	.15Y	.01Y	.01Y	.01Y	.01Y	.04Y	.06Y	.07Y
Singapore	576	46.05Y	49.35Y	54.17Y	67.77Y	82.50Y	98.12Y	112.58Y	48.96Y	51.62Y	60.29Y	74.69Y	89.21Y	107.17Y	122.04Y
Solomon Islands	813	.04Y	.03Y	.05Y	.06Y	.09Y	.10Y	.15Y	.05Y	.07Y	.10Y	.14Y	.17Y	.19Y	.27Y
Sri Lanka	524	2.99Y	3.26Y	3.94Y	4.62Y	5.58Y	6.28Y	6.61Y	.77Y	.81Y	1.00Y	1.43Y	1.60Y	1.67Y	1.89Y
Taiwan Province of China	528	34.20Y	38.26Y	44.25Y	57.05Y	60.79Y	71.36Y	76.05Y	71.97Y	87.06Y	102.20Y	133.60Y	152.80Y	180.77Y	204.99Y
Thailand	578	23.32Y	25.95Y	29.54Y	37.92Y	44.89Y	53.68Y	59.86Y	28.21Y	30.35Y	37.42Y	48.17Y	56.34Y	69.82Y	84.37Y
Tonga	866	.02Y	.03Y	.03Y	.04Y	.04Y	.05Y	.07Y	—Y	—Y	—Y	.01Y	—Y	.01Y	—Y
Tuvalu	869	.01Y	.06Y	.01Y	.02Y	.02Y	.03Y	.03Y	—Y	—Y	—Y	—Y	—Y	—Y	—Y
Vanuatu	846	.05Y	.05Y	.12Y	.11Y	.12Y	.10Y	.12Y	.04Y	.04Y	.05Y	.16Y	.17Y	.23Y	.25Y
Vietnam	582	10.13Y	12.66Y	15.74Y	21.26Y	25.24Y	30.94Y	43.45Y	4.85Y	4.96Y	5.83Y	8.43Y	10.96Y	12.39Y	16.48Y
Asia n.s.	598	.51Y	.52Y	.46Y	.50Y	.31Y	.67Y	.83Y	6.16Y	7.50Y	5.40Y	6.92Y	3.24Y	4.44Y	6.13Y
Europe	**170**	**108.5Y**	**126.6Y**	**168.1Y**	**226.5Y**	**301.5Y**	**391.8Y**	**531.2Y**	**121.1Y**	**137.1Y**	**176.5Y**	**237.5Y**	**291.2Y**	**364.8Y**	**479.2Y**
Albania	914	.22Y	.29Y	.40Y	.54Y	.67Y	.89Y	1.18Y	.03Y	.02Y	.03Y	.08Y	.06Y	.09Y	.19Y
Armenia	911	.17Y	.28Y	.41Y	.57Y	.66Y	1.04Y	1.46Y	.11Y	.16Y	.23Y	.22Y	.28Y	.28Y	.42Y
Azerbaijan	912	.61Y	.96Y	1.42Y	2.18Y	2.71Y	3.73Y	4.40Y	.50Y	.54Y	.77Y	1.24Y	2.01Y	2.58Y	3.91Y
Belarus	913	1.00Y	6.84Y	8.89Y	1.98Y	10.83Y	7.21Y	22.32Y	1.54Y	5.58Y	7.02Y	3.44Y	9.23Y	7.68Y	15.56Y
Bosnia & Herzegovina	963	1.03Y	1.27Y	1.59Y	1.88Y	2.39Y	3.32Y	4.19Y	.18Y	.23Y	.32Y	.58Y	.91Y	1.52Y	1.71Y
Bulgaria	918	2.08Y	2.28Y	3.18Y	5.26Y	7.51Y	11.47Y	14.66Y	1.69Y	1.89Y	2.52Y	3.68Y	4.39Y	5.86Y	7.84Y
Croatia	960	1.70Y	2.01Y	2.76Y	4.02Y	4.92Y	6.02Y	8.32Y	1.20Y	1.41Y	1.64Y	2.14Y	2.65Y	3.31Y	3.88Y
Czech Republic	935	7.37Y	8.43Y	11.18Y	14.76Y	19.46Y	26.62Y	34.03Y	7.74Y	8.84Y	12.31Y	17.24Y	20.15Y	25.74Y	34.81Y
Czechoslovakia n.s.	937	.06Y	.06Y	.09Y	.12Y	—Y	—Y	.01Y	.17Y	.18Y	.25Y	.42Y	.09Y	.10Y	.13Y
Estonia	939	2.31Y	2.69Y	3.05Y	3.75Y	5.02Y	6.63Y	6.69Y	.65Y	.74Y	.99Y	1.68Y	2.24Y	3.64Y	4.07Y
Faroe Islands	816	.01Y	.01Y	.01Y	.04Y	.01Y	.01Y	.02Y	.01Y	.01Y	.01Y	.03Y	.03Y	.05Y	.05Y
Georgia	915	.52Y	.53Y	.91Y	1.28Y	1.72Y	2.39Y	3.28Y	.29Y	.35Y	.59Y	.74Y	.81Y	.94Y	.95Y
Gibraltar	823	.44Y	.19Y	.40Y	.92Y	.85Y	1.23Y	.83Y	.02Y	.02Y	.04Y	.06Y	.05Y	.07Y	.10Y
Hungary	944	8.20Y	10.12Y	13.08Y	17.15Y	21.78Y	27.30Y	34.83Y	5.53Y	6.75Y	8.70Y	11.17Y	14.40Y	20.80Y	31.78Y
Kazakhstan	916	3.70Y	4.05Y	6.31Y	9.36Y	13.47Y	17.97Y	25.38Y	5.97Y	7.65Y	9.42Y	9.77Y	10.75Y	13.24Y	17.79Y
Kyrgyz Republic	917	.38Y	.51Y	.75Y	1.27Y	1.77Y	3.27Y	5.45Y	.23Y	.25Y	.32Y	.44Y	.47Y	.69Y	1.01Y
Latvia	941	3.07Y	3.02Y	3.77Y	4.72Y	5.35Y	7.02Y	10.40Y	.84Y	.77Y	.85Y	1.71Y	2.33Y	2.96Y	4.49Y
Lithuania	946	3.58Y	4.07Y	5.30Y	6.77Y	8.26Y	9.87Y	11.83Y	1.34Y	1.62Y	2.20Y	3.13Y	4.12Y	5.40Y	7.14Y
Macedonia, FYR	962	.45Y	.48Y	.57Y	.87Y	.90Y	1.49Y	2.01Y	.17Y	.17Y	.22Y	.34Y	.46Y	.84Y	1.22Y
Moldova	921	.82Y	.91Y	1.26Y	1.69Y	2.08Y	2.65Y	3.50Y	.55Y	.51Y	.68Y	.89Y	.99Y	.86Y	1.33Y
Poland	964	11.62Y	11.92Y	15.21Y	21.34Y	28.76Y	39.82Y	52.18Y	7.54Y	8.65Y	11.92Y	17.51Y	21.61Y	31.59Y	41.54Y
Romania	968	3.99Y	4.88Y	6.63Y	10.25Y	15.23Y	23.59Y	24.96Y	2.72Y	3.39Y	4.49Y	7.01Y	8.66Y	11.66Y	14.11Y
Russia	922	22.40Y	23.87Y	31.59Y	43.41Y	56.35Y	70.12Y	103.14Y	53.25Y	55.52Y	69.97Y	94.72Y	120.13Y	148.93Y	179.70Y
Serbia & Montenegro	965	1.15Y	1.18Y	1.64Y	1.76Y	2.38Y	2.32Y	2.66Y	.35Y	.39Y	.48Y	.59Y	.84Y	.62Y	.82Y
Slovak Republic	936	6.20Y	6.77Y	8.87Y	12.14Y	15.96Y	21.79Y	29.90Y	4.40Y	4.93Y	6.67Y	8.74Y	10.49Y	14.46Y	20.56Y
Tajikistan	923	.44Y	.40Y	.54Y	.75Y	1.00Y	1.49Y	2.06Y	.38Y	.41Y	.43Y	.44Y	.34Y	.47Y	.56Y
Turkey	186	10.30Y	12.88Y	17.83Y	29.79Y	36.46Y	47.97Y	63.80Y	6.80Y	8.70Y	11.32Y	16.73Y	18.12Y	23.73Y	34.74Y

	Exports							Imports						
	2001	2002	2003	2004	2005	2006	2007	2001	2002	2003	2004	2005	2006	2007
	Billions of U.S. Dollars							*Billions of U.S. Dollars*						
Turkmenistan.......... 925	.56Y	.64Y	.96Y	1.25Y	1.29Y	1.27Y	1.80Y	2.21Y	2.49Y	2.55Y	3.09Y	4.45Y	4.76Y	5.53Y
Ukraine.......... 926	10.48Y	11.76Y	15.38Y	20.97Y	27.08Y	35.81Y	45.46Y	10.93Y	12.04Y	16.10Y	24.65Y	25.42Y	29.71Y	40.72Y
U.S.S.R. n.s.......... 930	.11Y	.03Y	.01Y	.01Y	.07Y	.09Y	.06Y	.35Y	.45Y	.13Y	.07Y	.11Y	.10Y	.11Y
Uzbekistan.......... 927	1.41Y	1.29Y	1.49Y	2.08Y	2.49Y	3.25Y	4.74Y	1.62Y	1.14Y	1.61Y	2.28Y	2.98Y	4.59Y	5.35Y
Yugoslavia n.s.......... 966	.47Y	.48Y	.63Y	.95Y	.89Y	.78Y	.41Y	.15Y	.16Y	.20Y	.26Y	.36Y	.25Y	.11Y
Europe n.s.......... 884	1.62Y	1.48Y	1.97Y	2.70Y	3.27Y	4.10Y	4.82Y	1.66Y	1.13Y	1.51Y	2.34Y	1.81Y	3.47Y	3.50Y
Middle East.......... 407	**55.6Y**	**65.2Y**	**79.7Y**	**108.6Y**	**131.9Y**	**160.2Y**	**210.3Y**	**95.7Y**	**91.0Y**	**116.4Y**	**162.6Y**	**219.4Y**	**285.0Y**	**315.7Y**
Bahrain.......... 419	.55Y	.62Y	.71Y	.86Y	1.20Y	1.32Y	1.68Y	1.46Y	1.21Y	1.46Y	1.80Y	2.28Y	2.78Y	2.94Y
Egypt.......... 469	5.22Y	5.24Y	5.67Y	7.91Y	10.64Y	13.48Y	17.65Y	1.46Y	1.50Y	2.13Y	3.74Y	4.72Y	5.74Y	7.71Y
Iran, I.R. of.......... 429	6.67Y	7.74Y	11.33Y	14.53Y	16.28Y	20.25Y	28.06Y	10.81Y	9.20Y	13.58Y	18.64Y	25.55Y	35.93Y	41.67Y
Iraq.......... 433	2.45Y	2.90Y	2.31Y	6.12Y	7.95Y	8.76Y	10.41Y	2.01Y	2.59Y	1.28Y	3.09Y	3.77Y	4.91Y	8.34Y
Israel.......... 436	6.56Y	7.58Y	8.93Y	11.11Y	12.65Y	14.40Y	17.05Y	6.30Y	6.20Y	6.90Y	9.08Y	10.24Y	11.86Y	14.01Y
Jordan.......... 439	1.46Y	1.77Y	2.41Y	4.18Y	3.97Y	4.33Y	5.70Y	.67Y	.74Y	.84Y	1.28Y	1.32Y	1.41Y	1.69Y
Kuwait.......... 443	1.50Y	1.81Y	2.52Y	2.91Y	3.62Y	4.52Y	6.46Y	7.76Y	7.93Y	10.12Y	14.33Y	20.18Y	25.32Y	28.62Y
Lebanon.......... 446	1.86Y	1.76Y	2.00Y	2.93Y	3.26Y	3.65Y	4.71Y	.24Y	.31Y	.33Y	.99Y	1.10Y	1.31Y	1.62Y
Libya.......... 672	1.07Y	1.37Y	1.49Y	2.43Y	2.93Y	3.69Y	4.85Y	1.75Y	1.48Y	2.04Y	3.10Y	4.43Y	6.24Y	4.26Y
Oman.......... 449	.94Y	.87Y	1.05Y	1.27Y	1.92Y	2.53Y	3.47Y	6.88Y	6.27Y	6.83Y	9.55Y	12.58Y	19.00Y	16.25Y
Qatar.......... 453	.65Y	.65Y	1.01Y	1.16Y	1.96Y	3.29Y	4.55Y	4.55Y	4.75Y	6.08Y	8.22Y	12.08Y	15.78Y	19.84Y
Saudi Arabia.......... 456	8.22Y	9.76Y	11.43Y	14.42Y	17.32Y	22.52Y	29.88Y	31.57Y	29.80Y	39.34Y	54.09Y	75.33Y	95.99Y	104.20Y
Syrian Arab Republic.......... 463	2.06Y	2.46Y	3.08Y	5.20Y	6.20Y	7.62Y	9.81Y	1.34Y	1.73Y	1.90Y	2.51Y	2.57Y	2.93Y	3.72Y
United Arab Emirates.......... 466	15.19Y	19.11Y	24.02Y	31.40Y	39.63Y	46.79Y	62.54Y	15.30Y	14.80Y	19.88Y	28.11Y	38.52Y	51.16Y	56.30Y
Yemen, Republic of.......... 474	1.06Y	1.48Y	1.63Y	2.05Y	2.31Y	3.00Y	3.41Y	3.25Y	2.26Y	3.42Y	3.75Y	4.31Y	4.15Y	3.93Y
Middle East n.s.......... 489	.09Y	.10Y	.15Y	.13Y	.08Y	.08Y	.11Y	.35Y	.23Y	.25Y	.36Y	.43Y	.54Y	.65Y
Western Hemisphere.......... 207	**93.2Y**	**87.1Y**	**96.9Y**	**129.7Y**	**165.3Y**	**213.6Y**	**266.8Y**	**86.7Y**	**85.6Y**	**105.5Y**	**146.1Y**	**179.1Y**	**217.3Y**	**267.8Y**
Antigua and Barbuda.......... 311	.22Y	.22Y	.20Y	.40Y	.44Y	.47Y	.99Y	.01Y	.01Y	.02Y	.14Y	.04Y	.03Y	.03Y
Argentina.......... 213	8.36Y	3.50Y	6.73Y	11.27Y	15.26Y	18.81Y	25.20Y	17.79Y	16.51Y	19.94Y	24.68Y	28.16Y	32.69Y	41.07Y
Aruba.......... 314	.09Y	.08Y	.12Y	.36Y	2.07Y	2.04Y	1.72Y	.08Y	.08Y	.16Y	.27Y	.42Y	.58Y	.64Y
Bahamas, The.......... 313	1.09Y	1.74Y	1.95Y	2.33Y	4.46Y	4.22Y	3.01Y	.19Y	.35Y	.47Y	.44Y	.49Y	.64Y	1.13Y
Barbados.......... 316	.45Y	.31Y	.35Y	.43Y	.50Y	.60Y	.65Y	.18Y	.32Y	.33Y	.20Y	.46Y	.21Y	.32Y
Belize.......... 339	.16Y	.20Y	.19Y	.24Y	.33Y	.33Y	.38Y	.08Y	.06Y	.08Y	.10Y	.08Y	.08Y	.12Y
Bermuda.......... 319	1.66Y	2.51Y	2.50Y	.91Y	.96Y	1.55Y	1.92Y	.04Y	.06Y	.07Y	.08Y	.03Y	.10Y	.08Y
Bolivia.......... 218	.98Y	1.07Y	.96Y	1.28Y	1.54Y	1.80Y	2.18Y	.59Y	.77Y	1.05Y	1.43Y	1.85Y	2.54Y	2.74Y
Brazil.......... 223	16.20Y	14.16Y	15.15Y	21.10Y	26.70Y	37.11Y	50.22Y	23.23Y	23.11Y	32.58Y	47.19Y	59.26Y	70.12Y	84.28Y
Chile.......... 228	7.79Y	7.91Y	9.49Y	12.07Y	16.53Y	19.44Y	22.94Y	7.24Y	7.25Y	9.13Y	14.08Y	16.85Y	24.78Y	32.36Y
Colombia.......... 233	3.35Y	3.74Y	4.10Y	5.34Y	7.75Y	10.74Y	13.66Y	3.22Y	3.41Y	4.02Y	5.41Y	6.88Y	7.81Y	9.82Y
Costa Rica.......... 238	1.60Y	1.83Y	1.84Y	2.30Y	2.65Y	3.26Y	3.80Y	1.58Y	2.30Y	3.63Y	4.03Y	4.74Y	6.05Y	7.25Y
Dominica.......... 321	.15Y	.10Y	.10Y	.12Y	.13Y	.16Y	.18Y	.04Y	.03Y	.04Y	.04Y	.06Y	.07Y	.10Y
Dominican Republic.......... 243	1.63Y	1.81Y	1.80Y	2.28Y	2.85Y	3.30Y	3.90Y	.13Y	.15Y	.22Y	.35Y	.44Y	.64Y	.79Y
Ecuador.......... 248	2.16Y	2.62Y	2.66Y	3.47Y	4.65Y	5.50Y	5.92Y	2.37Y	1.87Y	2.01Y	2.65Y	3.54Y	4.35Y	5.31Y
El Salvador.......... 253	1.89Y	1.91Y	2.09Y	2.35Y	2.81Y	3.06Y	3.41Y	.95Y	.96Y	.99Y	.95Y	1.58Y	1.61Y	1.82Y
Falkland Islands.......... 323	—Y	—Y	—Y	—Y	—Y	—Y	—Y	—Y	.01Y	.01Y	.01Y	.01Y	.01Y	.01Y
Greenland.......... 326	—Y	.01Y	—Y	—Y	—Y	—Y	—Y	.04Y	.04Y	.06Y	.04Y	.05Y	.05Y	.06Y
Grenada.......... 328	.07Y	.07Y	.08Y	.10Y	.13Y	.15Y	.17Y	.02Y	.03Y	.02Y	.02Y	.02Y	.03Y	.74Y
Guatemala.......... 258	2.57Y	2.78Y	3.22Y	3.80Y	4.37Y	5.08Y	5.59Y	1.52Y	1.50Y	1.60Y	1.81Y	2.24Y	2.61Y	3.18Y
Guyana.......... 336	.37Y	.23Y	.20Y	.26Y	.30Y	.42Y	.46Y	.12Y	.11Y	.11Y	.14Y	.19Y	.22Y	.25Y
Haiti.......... 263	.34Y	.27Y	.28Y	.44Y	.51Y	.67Y	.79Y	.02Y	.02Y	.03Y	.04Y	.06Y	.07Y	.11Y
Honduras.......... 268	1.56Y	1.49Y	1.57Y	1.95Y	2.38Y	2.78Y	3.25Y	.45Y	.48Y	.56Y	.56Y	.75Y	.95Y	1.18Y
Jamaica.......... 343	.90Y	.86Y	1.04Y	1.25Y	1.50Y	1.71Y	2.83Y	.19Y	.19Y	.29Y	.40Y	.38Y	.55Y	.35Y
Mexico.......... 273	13.41Y	15.96Y	16.19Y	22.12Y	25.22Y	36.17Y	41.83Y	8.65Y	8.12Y	8.90Y	11.43Y	13.77Y	18.56Y	24.11Y
Netherlands Antilles.......... 353	1.38Y	1.01Y	.84Y	.45Y	.58Y	.91Y	1.32Y	.96Y	.85Y	.88Y	1.38Y	1.83Y	2.18Y	2.61Y
Nicaragua.......... 278	.81Y	.88Y	.97Y	1.23Y	1.62Y	1.95Y	2.38Y	.30Y	.27Y	.32Y	.34Y	.55Y	.55Y	.62Y
Panama.......... 283	7.08Y	6.16Y	6.67Y	9.12Y	11.58Y	13.34Y	17.09Y	1.40Y	1.85Y	1.91Y	2.01Y	2.31Y	1.67Y	1.26Y
Paraguay.......... 288	1.69Y	1.27Y	1.62Y	2.03Y	2.12Y	2.64Y	3.43Y	.96Y	1.14Y	1.09Y	1.26Y	1.36Y	2.07Y	2.90Y
Peru.......... 293	2.81Y	3.50Y	3.79Y	4.57Y	6.26Y	7.86Y	10.30Y	2.30Y	2.56Y	2.87Y	4.75Y	6.52Y	9.02Y	11.62Y
St. Kitts and Nevis.......... 361	.05Y	.04Y	.05Y	.22Y	.07Y	.09Y	.12Y	.01Y	—Y	—Y	.01Y	.01Y	.01Y	.01Y
St. Lucia.......... 362	.27Y	.33Y	.10Y	.13Y	.20Y	.19Y	1.27Y	.02Y	.02Y	.02Y	.04Y	.06Y	.04Y	.05Y
St. Vincent & Grens.......... 364	.15Y	.12Y	.13Y	.22Y	.21Y	.25Y	.29Y	.03Y	.03Y	.03Y	.09Y	.03Y	.05Y	.05Y
Suriname.......... 366	.29Y	.19Y	.16Y	.23Y	.29Y	.31Y	.41Y	.07Y	.08Y	.08Y	.09Y	.09Y	.16Y	.20Y
Trinidad and Tobago.......... 369	.70Y	.70Y	.93Y	1.41Y	1.95Y	2.19Y	2.69Y	1.24Y	1.33Y	1.66Y	2.12Y	2.75Y	3.28Y	4.52Y
Uruguay.......... 298	2.33Y	1.55Y	1.82Y	2.42Y	3.10Y	3.63Y	4.58Y	1.51Y	1.40Y	1.59Y	1.75Y	1.99Y	2.57Y	3.10Y
Venezuela, Rep. Bol.......... 299	6.62Y	4.65Y	3.21Y	6.84Y	9.36Y	14.67Y	22.25Y	7.88Y	7.19Y	6.51Y	14.40Y	17.46Y	18.13Y	20.21Y
Western Hem. n.s.......... 399	1.96Y	1.36Y	3.83Y	4.70Y	3.94Y	6.20Y	5.67Y	1.32Y	1.13Y	2.18Y	1.38Y	1.75Y	2.45Y	2.96Y
Other Countries n.i.e.......... 910	**2.7Y**	**2.4Y**	**2.4Y**	**3.1Y**	**4.0Y**	**5.2Y**	**5.4Y**	**1.6Y**	**1.4Y**	**1.4Y**	**1.8Y**	**1.8Y**	**2.2Y**	**3.1Y**
Cuba.......... 928	1.12Y	.95Y	.92Y	1.24Y	1.98Y	3.00Y	2.87Y	.84Y	.73Y	.64Y	.79Y	.72Y	1.09Y	1.84Y
North Korea.......... 954	1.55Y	1.43Y	1.49Y	1.85Y	2.05Y	2.25Y	2.54Y	.72Y	.65Y	.75Y	1.05Y	1.09Y	1.12Y	1.31Y
Countries & Areas n.s.......... 898	**20.4Y**	**21.6Y**	**19.5Y**	**23.8Y**	**25.0Y**	**22.2Y**	**30.2Y**	**23.9Y**	**28.7Y**	**32.1Y**	**40.2Y**	**57.1Y**	**68.5Y**	**83.4Y**
Special Categories.......... 899	**10.4Y**	**9.8Y**	**8.4Y**	**9.4Y**	**12.5Y**	**14.4Y**	**12.9Y**	**16.7Y**	**23.1Y**	**30.8Y**	**46.4Y**	**61.2Y**	**83.8Y**	**98.6Y**
Memorandum Items														
European Union.......... 998	467.07Y	504.34Y	625.61Y	813.63Y	971.06Y	1,171.78Y	1,413.30Y	445.12Y	476.56Y	580.89Y	727.11Y	815.01Y	990.80Y	1,254.37Y
Oil Exporting Ctys.......... 999	62.89Y	72.05Y	102.44Y	136.48Y	168.14Y	202.44Y	268.91Y	120.59Y	115.93Y	150.74Y	213.91Y	278.41Y	354.88Y	397.57Y
Non-Oil Develop.Ctys.......... 201	719.63Y	817.41Y	1,013.22Y	1,311.99Y	1,599.78Y	1,975.42Y	2,420.20Y	751.39Y	842.49Y	1,027.92Y	1,350.16Y	1,617.58Y	1,985.03Y	2,437.32Y
PERCENT DISTRIBUTION														
Industrial Countries.......... 101	**56.9**	**55.4**	**53.8**	**52.8**	**51.7**	**50.6**	**48.4**	**53.3**	**51.6**	**49.9**	**47.9**	**45.4**	**43.5**	**43.3**
Developing Countries.......... 202	**41.3**	**42.9**	**44.8**	**46.0**	**47.1**	**48.4**	**50.6**	**44.6**	**45.8**	**47.4**	**49.3**	**51.4**	**53.0**	**53.2**
Africa.......... 607	**1.8**	**1.8**	**1.9**	**2.0**	**2.0**	**2.1**	**2.3**	**1.9**	**1.7**	**1.8**	**2.0**	**2.1**	**2.2**	**2.2**
Asia.......... 507	**25.9**	**27.6**	**29.1**	**29.2**	**29.1**	**29.3**	**29.3**	**27.2**	**29.1**	**29.6**	**30.1**	**30.6**	**31.2**	**31.1**

	Exports							Imports						
	2001	2002	2003	2004	2005	2006	2007	2001	2002	2003	2004	2005	2006	2007
Europe.......170	5.7	6.1	6.8	7.2	8.0	8.7	10.0	6.2	6.6	7.1	7.5	7.9	8.3	9.0
Middle East.......407	2.9	3.1	3.2	3.4	3.5	3.6	4.0	4.9	4.4	4.7	5.1	5.9	6.5	5.9
Western Hemisphere.......207	4.9	4.2	3.9	4.1	4.4	4.7	5.0	4.4	4.1	4.2	4.6	4.9	4.9	5.0
Other Countries n.i.e.......910	.1	.1	.1	.1	.1	.1	.1	.1	.1	.1	.1	—	.1	.1
ANNUAL PERCENT CHANGE														
World.......001	–4.5	9.3	20.0	26.6	19.1	19.9	18.2	–3.7	6.9	18.9	27.5	16.4	19.7	20.6
Industrial Countries.......101	–5.3	6.5	16.4	24.4	16.5	17.4	13.0	–5.2	3.5	15.0	22.3	10.3	14.8	19.9
Developing Countries.......202	–3.6	13.7	25.4	29.8	22.1	23.2	23.5	–2.0	9.9	23.0	32.7	21.2	23.4	21.2
Africa.......607	8.2	13.0	22.8	34.2	22.6	25.2	28.2	–3.6	–.1	19.5	48.9	18.6	24.9	22.7
Asia.......507	–5.8	16.4	26.5	27.2	18.6	20.5	18.4	–2.4	14.4	21.1	29.4	18.5	21.9	20.2
Europe.......170	–2.2	16.7	32.8	34.8	33.1	30.0	35.6	.1	13.2	28.8	34.5	22.6	25.3	31.3
Middle East.......407	8.2	17.4	22.2	36.2	21.5	21.4	31.3	–5.5	–4.9	27.9	39.7	34.9	29.9	10.8
Western Hemisphere.......207	–3.3	–6.5	11.2	33.8	27.4	29.2	24.9	1.9	–1.3	23.3	38.5	22.5	21.4	23.2
Other Countries n.i.e.......910	18.1	–11.2	1.3	28.6	30.3	30.1	3.2	17.3	–11.7	.9	32.7	–1.8	22.4	42.0

COUNTRY TABLES

Afghanistan, Islamic Republic of 512

		Exports							Imports						
		2001	2002	2003	2004	2005	2006	2007	2001	2002	2003	2004	2005	2006	2007
		Millions of U.S. Dollars							*Millions of U.S. Dollars*						
DOTS World Total	**001**	**90.5Y**	**87.2Y**	**209.8Y**	**185.1Y**	**239.5Y**	**276.9Y**	**340.1Y**	**565.6Y**	**1,034.1Y**	**1,607.9Y**	**1,973.0Y**	**3,007.4Y**	**3,824.4Y**	**4,879.9Y**
Industrial Countries	**101**	**23.7Y**	**25.1Y**	**119.0Y**	**60.8Y**	**95.3Y**	**91.0Y**	**96.6Y**	**100.2Y**	**321.4Y**	**419.4Y**	**602.6Y**	**815.2Y**	**1,075.0Y**	**1,202.9Y**
United States	111	.64V	4.27V	57.18V	22.91V	61.55V	41.64V	69.82V	6.60V	87.89V	66.66V	173.36V	287.54V	459.25V	537.57V
Canada	156	.27V	.23V	.45V	.28V	.38V	.70V	.71V	.11V	1.31V	6.52V	7.95V	17.23V	6.95V	14.13V
Australia	193	.02V	.10V	.09V	.15V	.16V	.37V	.09V	.41V	1.84V	2.43V	5.92V	4.56V	16.45V	11.32V
Japan	158	.16V	1.54V	1.78V	.98V	2.56V	.55V	.24V	49.42V	92.15V	114.10V	72.89V	84.33V	75.07V	98.39V
New Zealand	196	.27V	.15V	.12V	.09V	1.00V	.44V	.18V	.09V	.43V	.71V	.55V	.32V	.33V	.36V
Austria	122	.07V	.03V	.01V	.01V	.03V	.15V	.03V	.16V	6.09V	3.95V	29.33V	21.61V	17.34V	16.80V
Belgium	124	4.42V	4.50V	6.28V	6.36V	5.58V	3.78V	3.78V	7.93V	6.85V	7.14V	9.15V	19.30V	15.71V	19.64V
Cyprus	423	.04V	.02V	.05V	—V	.05Y	.02V	.03V	—V	.04V	.01V	.07V	.05V	.19V	.54V
Denmark	128	2.06V	.99V	1.74V	2.63V	3.01V	5.74V	.48V	.95V	10.74V	8.15V	22.34V	9.19V	8.94V	14.38V
Finland	172	6.31V	5.99V	6.26V	5.02V	9.66V	12.21V	9.66V	.01V	.39V	.61V	.30V	1.48V	2.80V	4.23V
France	132	.38V	.97V	37.51V	4.13V	.39V	.90V	2.15V	5.23V	15.64V	36.99V	58.44V	33.81V	51.87V	72.05V
Germany	134	6.56V	4.97V	4.50V	10.27V	3.67V	2.80V	5.71V	15.94V	57.32V	103.23V	130.03V	166.89V	275.42V	204.06V
Greece	174	.01V	.03V	.55V	.01V	.44V	1.56V	.01V	.33V	.41V	.23V	.48V	.76V	.74V	.30V
Iceland	176	.01V	—V	—V	—V	.01V	—V	—V	—V	—V	—V	—V	—V	—V	—V
Ireland	178	.01V	.02V	.05V	.09V	2.37V	.04V	.16V	.60V	1.88V	3.18V	3.11V	3.27V	7.52V	10.57V
Italy	136	.70V	.38V	.63V	3.45V	1.82V	1.12V	.61V	1.47V	8.36V	21.53V	27.01V	29.22V	17.91V	34.18V
Luxembourg	137	—V	—V	—V	.01V	.01V	.14V	.07V	.01V	.15V	.02V	.08V	.55V	.15V	.62V
Malta	181	—Y	—V	—V	—V	.01V	—V	—V	—Y	—V	—V	.01V	.55V	.02V	—V
Netherlands	138	.03V	.05V	.04V	.18V	.10V	.18V	.16V	3.89V	19.78V	17.65V	16.05V	87.70V	33.32V	35.83V
Norway	142	.32V	.20V	.13V	.11V	.13V	.39V	1.15V	.70V	.07V	3.03V	4.78V	2.31V	13.24V	6.62V
Portugal	182	.01V	.03V	.05V	.01V	—V	.01V	—V	.12V	.02V	.35V	.08V	.22V	.18V	—V
Slovenia	961	.01V	.01V	.12V	.15Y	—V	—V	—V	—V	.47V	.56V	.73Y	.67V	6.61V	.47V
Spain	184	.05V	.01V	.01V	.06V	1.03V	.07V	.26V	.15V	2.80V	2.82V	4.24V	9.87V	10.62V	9.16V
Sweden	144	.14V	.09V	.07V	.05V	.01V	.02V	.03V	.02V	.51V	.96V	5.00V	2.30V	7.79V	19.84V
Switzerland	146	.48V	.19V	.70V	.16V	.17V	.37V	.30V	.08V	1.38V	.89V	2.01V	2.85V	.95V	1.04V
United Kingdom	112	.76V	.35V	.69V	3.69V	1.19V	17.77V	.96V	6.04V	4.90V	17.72V	28.66V	28.67V	45.66V	90.78V
Developing Countries	**202**	**66.8Y**	**62.1Y**	**90.8Y**	**124.3Y**	**144.2Y**	**185.9Y**	**243.5Y**	**465.4Y**	**712.6Y**	**1,188.5Y**	**1,370.5Y**	**2,192.2Y**	**2,749.4Y**	**3,677.0Y**
Africa	**607**	**1.9Y**	**3.4Y**	**3.9Y**	**4.9Y**	**5.4Y**	**6.3Y**	**8.1Y**	**40.7Y**	**51.4Y**	**77.9Y**	**43.1Y**	**56.2Y**	**58.9Y**	**73.2Y**
Algeria	612	.05V	2.09V	2.32Y	3.02Y	3.84Y	4.74Y	6.14Y	—V	—V	—Y	—Y	—Y	—Y	—Y
Benin	638	—V	.22V	.08V	—V	—V	—Y	—Y	—V	—V	—V	—V	—V	—Y	—Y
Cameroon	622	—V	—V	.02V	.02Y	.03Y	.03Y	.04Y	—V	—V	—V	—Y	—Y	—Y	—Y
Côte d'Ivoire	662	—V	—V	—V	—V	—V	.07V	.09Y	—V	.04V	—V	—V	—V	.01V	.02Y
Kenya	664	.20V	.03V	—V	.08V	.10Y	.12Y	.15Y	39.80V	50.79V	70.92V	40.43V	46.19Y	57.09Y	70.85Y
Madagascar	674	—V	—V	—V	—Y	—Y	—Y	—Y	—V	—V	.08V	.11Y	.12Y	.15Y	.19Y
Mauritius	684	—V	—V	.02V	.02V	.01V	.03V	.04V	—V	—V	—V	.04V	—V	—V	.02V
Morocco	686	.07V	—V	—V	.01V	—V	—Y	—Y	—V	.01V	.07V	.05V	.14V	.18Y	.22Y
Niger	692	—V	—V	—V	—V	—Y	—Y	.01Y	—V	—V	—V	—V	—Y	—Y	—Y
Senegal	722	.12V	—V	.01V	.10V	.08V	—V	—Y	—V	—V	—V	.06V	.05V	.02V	.02Y
Somalia	726	—Y	—Y	—Y	—Y	—Y	—Y	—Y	.01Y	.01Y	.01Y	.01Y	.01Y	.02Y	.02Y
South Africa	199	—V	—V	.06V	.90V	.22V	—V	—V	.81V	.14V	6.44V	1.03V	8.81V	—V	—V
Tanzania	738	.02V	.02V	.02Y	.03Y	.03Y	.04Y	.05Y	—V	.31V	.39Y	.52Y	.59Y	.73Y	.91Y
Tunisia	744	1.40V	1.03V	1.37V	.71V	1.10V	1.28V	1.59Y	.10V	.06V	.03V	.77V	.30V	.74V	.92Y
Zimbabwe	698	—V	—V	—V	—V	—V	—V	—Y	—V	—V	—V	.05V	—V	—V	—Y
Asia	**507**	**52.1Y**	**45.6Y**	**66.5Y**	**89.9Y**	**106.6Y**	**130.8Y**	**165.3Y**	**338.4Y**	**491.4Y**	**793.5Y**	**865.8Y**	**1,537.9Y**	**1,931.7Y**	**2,537.8Y**
Bangladesh	513	—V	—V	3.72V	3.32V	3.05V	2.83V	4.11V	6.13V	5.12V	3.57V	2.18V	.92V	.81Y	1.64Y
Brunei Darussalam	516	.04Y	.04Y	.05V	.07Y	.08Y	.10Y	.12Y	—Y	—Y	.01V	.01Y	.02Y	.02Y	.03Y
Cambodia	522	.02V	—V	—V	—V	—V	—V	—Y	—V	—V	—V	—V	.05V	.03V	.03Y
China,P.R.: Mainland	924	.15V	.07V	.56V	.75V	1.42V	.17V	2.16V	18.99V	21.91V	29.13V	64.22V	56.32V	110.71V	186.36V
China,P.R.:Hong Kong	532	—V	.02V	—V	—V	.01V	.12V	.07V	3.63V	3.54V	1.82V	1.92V	1.96V	1.88V	2.51V
China,P.R.:Macao	546	—V	—V	—V	.07V	—V	—V	—V	—V	—V	—V	—V	—V	—V	—V
India	534	25.32Y	16.57V	31.82V	39.42V	50.63V	62.57Y	77.65Y	33.67Y	56.84V	136.72V	169.84V	158.31V	195.66Y	242.81Y
Indonesia	536	1.30V	.57V	1.07V	.18V	.04V	.22V	.24V	7.18V	10.15V	18.78V	15.32V	6.82V	6.66V	8.07V
Korea	542	.07V	.23V	.15V	.08V	.07V	.06V	.12V	104.51V	140.70V	137.06V	84.89V	65.59V	86.40V	119.94V
Malaysia	548	1.24V	.01V	.02V	.32V	.04V	.01V	.01V	2.59V	2.54V	2.02V	3.77V	5.97V	4.63V	4.45V
Mongolia	948	—V	.03V	—V	—V	.04V	—Y	—Y	—V	.06V	—V	.01V	.02V	—Y	—Y
New Caledonia	839	—V	—V	—V	—V	.01Y	.01Y	.01Y	....	....	....	....	....	....	....
Pakistan	564	23.66V	27.78V	28.33V	44.57V	48.36V	59.77Y	74.17Y	157.04V	245.49V	449.41V	511.36V	1,171.57V	1,447.97Y	1,796.92Y
Philippines	566	.03V	—V	.08V	—V	—V	.02V	.01V	.03V	.10V	.38V	.11V	.04V	.28V	.17V
Singapore	576	—V	.19V	.25V	.45V	2.37V	4.34V	5.79V	2.81V	1.46V	2.13V	1.45V	4.13V	6.61V	8.95V
Sri Lanka	524	.02V	.08V	.25V	.11V	.11V	.28V	—V	.06V	.44V	.53V	1.41V	2.24V	.75V	—V
Taiwan Province of China	528	—V	—V	.03V	.02V	—V	—V	.02V	.02V	.06V	.07V	.38V	.50V	.35V	.48V
Thailand	578	.21V	.04V	.16V	.49V	.35V	.24V	.78V	1.74V	3.06V	11.87V	8.95V	63.47V	68.92V	165.44V
Vietnam	582	.05V	—V	—V	—V	—V	—V	—V	—V	—V	—V	—V	—V	—V	—V
Europe	**170**	**5.7Y**	**6.6Y**	**11.5Y**	**16.3Y**	**15.6Y**	**28.5Y**	**46.9Y**	**79.3Y**	**160.4Y**	**294.2Y**	**432.4Y**	**558.6Y**	**709.0Y**	**1,009.8Y**
Albania	914	—V	—V	—V	—V	—V	—V	—V	—V	.11V	—V	—V	—V	—V	2.26V
Azerbaijan	912	—V	—V	—V	—V	—V	—V	—V	.21V	.76V	.68V	2.41V	12.85V	35.43V	52.34V
Belarus	913	.27V	.35V	.57V	.41V	.12V	1.33V	1.19V	2.03V	9.90V	17.67V	15.06V	12.90V	8.52V	6.89V
Bulgaria	918	.01V	—V	.04V	.04V	—V	.02V	.01V	2.38V	3.01V	6.23V	5.42V	.57V	2.71V	37.90V
Croatia	960	.18V	—V	—V	—V	—V	—V	—V	—V	—V	—V	—V	—V	—V	—V
Czech Republic	935	.13V	.03V	.07V	1.20V	.42V	.69V	.02V	.17V	.87V	1.57V	5.69V	5.23V	4.90V	16.59V

Afghanistan, Islamic Republic of 512

	Exports 2001	2002	2003	2004	2005	2006	2007	Imports 2001	2002	2003	2004	2005	2006	2007
	Millions of U.S. Dollars							*Millions of U.S. Dollars*						
Estonia.......... 939	.01V	—V	.01V	.01V	—V	—V	.01V	—V	—V	.10V	.01V	.02V	1.10V	2.35V
Georgia.......... 915	—V	—V	—V	—V	—V	.05V	.04Y	.02V	.14V	.03V	—V	.97V	.83V	.85Y
Hungary.......... 944	.01V	.10V	.11V	.02V	.01V	.02V	.02V	.01V	.03V	3.30V	3.68V	3.02V	7.03V	7.69V
Kazakhstan.......... 916	.03V	.01V	—V	.24V	.27Y	.33Y	.41Y	20.00V	34.24V	54.39V	95.03V	108.57Y	134.19Y	166.53Y
Kyrgyz Republic.......... 917	—V	—V	.06V	.21V	.16V	—V	.21V	1.73V	4.85V	6.74V	8.83V	13.63V	82.23V	170.12V
Latvia.......... 941	—V	—V	.01V	—V	—V	—V	—V	.21V	.43V	.42V	.30V	.33V	.46V	1.19V
Lithuania.......... 946	—V	—V	.08V	.03V	.01V	—V	—V	—V	.19V	.09V	.28V	11.42V	3.87V	8.36V
Macedonia, FYR.......... 962	—V	—V	.01V	—V	—V	.01V	.01Y	—V	.08V	—V	.03V	.03V	.02V	.03Y
Poland.......... 964	1.00V	.42V	.36V	.21V	.04V	.40V	.22V	3.46V	1.97V	3.70V	2.84V	5.79V	22.24V	3.74V
Romania.......... 968	—V	—V	—V	.01V	.02V	.07V	.01V	—V	.47V	2.08V	3.15V	.13V	.23V	12.80V
Russia.......... 922	2.51V	4.41V	5.87V	3.75V	3.55V	10.46V	8.14V	8.49V	35.52V	59.86V	83.55V	114.92V	90.64V	137.61V
Slovak Republic.......... 936	—V	—V	—Y	—Y	—V	—V	.01V	.71V	.99V	1.25Y	1.64Y	.48V	33.59V	50.38V
Tajikistan.......... 923	.09V	.27V	1.45V	3.64V	3.09V	5.91V	24.64V	3.41V	6.93V	6.38V	8.47V	13.31V	20.51V	13.31V
Turkey.......... 186	.38V	.96V	2.44V	6.16V	7.55V	8.72V	11.38V	7.68V	22.25V	40.14V	77.75V	124.74V	100.22V	119.91V
Turkmenistan.......... 925	1.09V	.01V	.22V	.29Y	.34Y	.41Y	.51Y	24.09V	31.42V	81.14V	106.56Y	121.75Y	150.47Y	186.74Y
Ukraine.......... 926	.02V	.07V	.14V	.10V	.06V	.07Y	.09Y	4.66V	6.27V	8.47V	11.70V	7.95V	9.83Y	12.20Y
Middle East.......... 407	**3.5Y**	**3.7Y**	**7.3Y**	**9.8Y**	**11.7Y**	**14.1Y**	**17.4Y**	**5.2Y**	**9.2Y**	**21.9Y**	**27.6Y**	**36.8Y**	**45.9Y**	**55.9Y**
Bahrain.......... 419	.05Y	.06Y	.07Y	.10Y	.11Y	.14Y	.17Y	.17Y	.18Y	.23Y	.31Y	.35Y	.43Y	.54Y
Egypt.......... 469	1.13V	1.22Y	1.55Y	2.03Y	2.32Y	2.87Y	3.56Y	—V	—Y	—Y	—Y	—Y	—Y	—Y
Iran, I.R. of.......... 429	.65V	.12V	.13Y	.17Y	.21Y	.26Y	.34Y	—Y	—Y	—Y	—Y	—Y	—Y	—Y
Jordan.......... 439	.27V	.57V	.84V	1.15V	.72V	1.20V	.93V	—V	.03V	.24V	.81V	.57V	.30V	.87V
Kuwait.......... 443	.14Y	.15Y	.17Y	.22Y	.28Y	.34Y	.44Y	—Y	—Y	—Y	—Y	—Y	—Y	—Y
Lebanon.......... 446	.99Y	1.08Y	1.36Y	1.79Y	2.05Y	2.53Y	3.14Y	—Y	—Y	—Y	—Y	—Y	—Y	—Y
Oman.......... 449	—V	—V	—V	—Y	—Y	—Y	—Y	1.33V	5.20V	15.63V	20.68Y	28.14Y	35.37Y	42.67Y
Qatar.......... 453	—V	.02V	—V	.02V	.59V	.07V	.10Y	.33V	.18V	1.52V	.08V	—V	—V	—Y
Saudi Arabia.......... 456	.28V	.46V	.20V	.34V	.48V	.59Y	.76Y	.37Y	.40Y	.48Y	.64Y	.87Y	1.09Y	1.31Y
United Arab Emirates.......... 466	—V	—V	3.00V	3.90Y	4.97Y	6.13Y	7.94Y	2.97Y	3.16Y	3.83Y	5.07Y	6.90Y	8.67Y	10.47Y
Yemen, Republic of.......... 474	.01V	—V	—Y	.08V	—V	—Y	—Y	—V	—V	—Y	—V	—V	—Y	—Y
Western Hemisphere.......... 207	**3.5Y**	**2.7Y**	**1.6Y**	**3.5Y**	**4.9Y**	**6.2Y**	**5.8Y**	**1.8Y**	**.2Y**	**.9Y**	**1.6Y**	**2.6Y**	**3.9Y**	**.4Y**
Argentina.......... 213	—V	—V	.12V	—V	.02V	.06V	.24V	—V	.09V	.18V	.50V	.54V	.27V	.16V
Barbados.......... 316	—V	—V	—V	—V	—V	—V	—Y	—V	—V	.02V	—V	—V	—V	—Y
Bermuda.......... 319	—Y	—Y	—Y	—Y	—V	—V	.01Y	—Y	—Y	—Y	—Y	—Y	—Y	—Y
Brazil.......... 223	1.49V	.93V	.22V	.31V	.32V	.39V	—V	.02V	—V	.37V	.21V	1.58V	3.24V	—V
Chile.......... 228	.02V	—V	.03V	—V	—V	—V	—V	1.46V	—V	—V	.05V	.01V	—V	—V
Colombia.......... 233	.28V	.94V	.17V	.45V	.02V	.40V	.08V	—V	—V	.05V	.09V	.01V	.11V	.02V
Costa Rica.......... 238	.05V	.36V	.12V	.08V	.04V	.05Y	.06Y	....	....	....	....	....	....	....
Ecuador.......... 248	1.27V	.15V	—V	—V	—V	—V	—Y	.30V	.12V	—V	.23V	.17V	.09V	.12Y
El Salvador.......... 253	.14V	—V	—V	—V	.07V	.30V	.01V	—V	—V	—V	—V	—V	—V	—V
Guatemala.......... 258	.06V	.08V	.52V	.10V	.17V	.21Y	.26Y	—V	.02V	.23V	.43Y	.04V	.04Y	.04Y
Honduras.......... 268	.06V	.13V	.31V	2.34V	2.68Y	3.31Y	4.10Y	—V	—V	.02V	—V	—Y	—Y	—Y
Mexico.......... 273	—V	—V	—V	—V	.38V	.94V	.55V	—V	—V	—V	—V	.18V	.13V	.03V
Peru.......... 293	.06V	.01V	—V	.01V	.07V	.06V	.05Y	—V	—V	—V	.09V	.02V	—V	—Y
St. Kitts and Nevis.......... 361	.02Y	.02Y	.02Y	.03Y	.04Y	.05Y	.06Y	....	....	....	....	....	....	....
St. Vincent & Grens.......... 364	.04V	—V	—V	.01V	—V	—Y	—Y	—V	—V	—V	—V	—V	—Y	—Y
Trinidad and Tobago.......... 369	.02V	.05V	.06Y	.08Y	.09Y	.11Y	.14Y	—V	—V	—Y	—Y	—Y	—Y	—Y
Uruguay.......... 298	.02V	.03Y	—V	.01V	—V	—Y	—Y	—V	—Y	.03V	—V	.03V	.03Y	.04Y
Venezuela, Rep. Bol.......... 299	.01V	.04V	.02V	.02V	.95V	.29V	.26V	—V	—V	—V	—V	—V	—V	—Y
Memorandum Items														
European Union.......... 998	22.72Y	19.00Y	59.19Y	37.58Y	29.85Y	47.61Y	24.37Y	47.41Y	140.86Y	235.51Y	349.56Y	442.39Y	575.99Y	623.74Y
Oil Exporting Ctys.......... 999	2.43Y	3.45Y	6.90Y	7.86Y	11.35Y	12.65Y	16.23Y	12.19Y	19.09Y	40.24Y	41.79Y	42.73Y	51.80Y	62.52Y
Non-Oil Develop.Ctys.......... 201	64.35Y	58.64Y	83.88Y	116.45Y	132.85Y	173.25Y	227.31Y	453.18Y	693.54Y	1,148.24Y	1,328.67Y	2,149.46Y	2,697.59Y	3,614.50Y
PERCENT DISTRIBUTION														
Industrial Countries.......... 101	**26.2**	**28.8**	**56.7**	**32.8**	**39.8**	**32.9**	**28.4**	**17.7**	**31.1**	**26.1**	**30.5**	**27.1**	**28.1**	**24.6**
Developing Countries.......... 202	**73.8**	**71.2**	**43.3**	**67.2**	**60.2**	**67.1**	**71.6**	**82.3**	**68.9**	**73.9**	**69.5**	**72.9**	**71.9**	**75.4**
Africa.......... 607	**2.1**	**3.9**	**1.9**	**2.6**	**2.3**	**2.3**	**2.4**	**7.2**	**5.0**	**4.8**	**2.2**	**1.9**	**1.5**	**1.5**
Asia.......... 507	**57.6**	**52.3**	**31.7**	**48.5**	**44.5**	**47.2**	**48.6**	**59.8**	**47.5**	**49.3**	**43.9**	**51.1**	**50.5**	**52.0**
Europe.......... 170	**6.3**	**7.6**	**5.5**	**8.8**	**6.5**	**10.3**	**13.8**	**14.0**	**15.5**	**18.3**	**21.9**	**18.6**	**18.5**	**20.7**
Middle East.......... 407	**3.9**	**4.2**	**3.5**	**5.3**	**4.9**	**5.1**	**5.1**	**.9**	**.9**	**1.4**	**1.4**	**1.2**	**1.2**	**1.1**
Western Hemisphere.......... 207	**3.9**	**3.1**	**.8**	**1.9**	**2.0**	**2.2**	**1.7**	**.3**	**—**	**.1**	**.1**	**.1**	**.1**	**—**
ANNUAL PERCENT CHANGE														
World.......... 001	**–36.3**	**–3.6**	**140.5**	**–11.8**	**29.4**	**15.6**	**22.8**	**–8.9**	**82.8**	**55.5**	**22.7**	**52.4**	**27.2**	**27.6**
Industrial Countries.......... 101	**–55.0**	**5.9**	**373.7**	**–48.9**	**56.8**	**–4.6**	**6.2**	**–15.1**	**220.6**	**30.5**	**43.7**	**35.3**	**31.9**	**11.9**
Developing Countries.......... 202	**–25.3**	**–7.0**	**46.2**	**36.9**	**16.0**	**28.9**	**31.0**	**–7.4**	**53.1**	**66.8**	**15.3**	**60.0**	**25.4**	**33.7**
Africa.......... 607	**427.5**	**82.1**	**15.0**	**25.7**	**10.6**	**16.8**	**28.1**	**17.1**	**26.1**	**51.8**	**–44.8**	**30.6**	**4.8**	**24.1**
Asia.......... 507	**–24.6**	**–12.4**	**45.7**	**35.2**	**18.6**	**22.7**	**26.4**	**9.9**	**45.2**	**61.5**	**9.1**	**77.6**	**25.6**	**31.4**
Europe.......... 170	**–43.0**	**15.8**	**72.4**	**42.3**	**–4.2**	**82.4**	**64.7**	**–49.0**	**102.4**	**83.4**	**47.0**	**29.2**	**26.9**	**42.4**
Middle East.......... 407	**9.3**	**4.4**	**98.6**	**33.6**	**19.8**	**20.7**	**23.0**	**24.2**	**76.6**	**139.6**	**25.8**	**33.4**	**24.6**	**21.8**
Western Hemisphere.......... 207	**–47.4**	**–22.5**	**–41.2**	**114.1**	**40.5**	**27.2**	**–5.6**	**478.4**	**–87.3**	**293.0**	**79.2**	**61.4**	**51.5**	**–89.7**

	Exports							Imports						
	2001	2002	2003	2004	2005	2006	2007	2001	2002	2003	2004	2005	2006	2007
	Millions of U.S. Dollars							*Millions of U.S. Dollars*						
IFS World Total	**307.2**	**339.6**	**447.9**	**605.4**	**658.2**	**797.7**	**1,072.6**	**1,326.9**	**1,503.2**	**1,864.1**	**2,308.8**	**2,618.1**	**3,058.5**	**4,196.2**
DOTS World Total 001	**307.3**	**338.8**	**447.0**	**604.4**	**631.6**	**759.1**	**1,011.7**	**1,323.1**	**1,499.6**	**1,842.3**	**2,287.4**	**2,606.1**	**3,029.0**	**4,090.9**
Industrial Countries 101	**285.8**	**320.2**	**421.7**	**548.9**	**590.0**	**697.9**	**885.0**	**1,044.3**	**1,134.8**	**1,334.7**	**1,626.9**	**1,690.0**	**1,868.0**	**2,577.3**
United States 111	2.01	5.42	2.27	3.09	6.59	3.29	6.88	14.31	25.62	18.53	34.73	37.57	31.35	48.35
Canada 156	—	.02	.06	—	.05	—	.01	2.28	1.97	4.19	3.98	5.08	5.41	5.02
Australia 193	—	—	—	.03	—	—	.05	.33	.76	.50	.49	.90	1.21	2.04
Japan 158	.08	.04	.08	.02	.09	.05	.02	6.09	8.57	8.21	11.24	11.57	13.04	19.93
New Zealand 196	—	—	—	.05	—	.01	—	.15	.32	.31	.21	.48	.74	.93
Austria 122	.73	.75	5.54	2.03	1.52	2.23	2.40	10.78	19.09	29.92	25.77	45.67	36.61	56.34
Belgium 124	.44	.03	.12	.36	.32	.57	.45	.05	.02	.78	17.99	20.40	26.00	14.37
Cyprus 423	—	.05	.16	—	—	.07	.73	3.74	3.19	4.80	3.00	4.18	5.10	4.17
Denmark 128	.77	.20	.19	.18	.26	.44	.24	2.41	3.52	7.01	7.15	6.39	4.89	5.25
Finland 172	—	—	—	.02	—	.01	.18	27.24	5.00	3.02	4.86	14.06	7.80	14.99
France 132	2.03	2.08	2.09	3.09	4.57	5.53	6.72	12.61	16.66	20.21	37.57	32.44	29.16	45.06
Germany 134	16.83	18.27	15.24	18.76	21.91	25.03	26.15	77.71	84.22	104.85	141.88	143.31	172.69	227.84
Greece 174	39.81	42.71	57.28	72.46	68.95	74.60	88.99	341.12	325.92	371.62	424.63	431.25	479.42	606.65
Iceland 176	.07	.01	.12	—	—	—	—	.01	.18	.29	.48	.07	.06	.21
Ireland 178	—	—	—	.02	—	.13	—	3.82	4.50	2.25	7.44	11.22	9.46	11.67
Italy 136	217.06	245.17	334.90	441.24	477.37	574.32	728.06	423.63	518.14	620.75	746.37	768.94	856.22	1,130.57
Luxembourg 137	—	—	—	—	—	.02	.31	.12	.35	.22	.74	1.08	.95	3.17
Malta 181	—	.77	—	1.72	—	—	—	.26	.29	.25	.08	.01	.01	.05
Netherlands 138	.39	.40	.46	1.06	.89	1.82	.60	9.87	8.57	12.71	18.66	23.88	16.17	23.20
Norway 142	—	—	—	.01	.03	.01	.03	4.97	.29	.30	.64	.89	2.24	2.46
Portugal 182	—	—	—	—	.01	.01	.01	.12	1.62	.34	1.57	2.58	2.23	3.60
Slovenia 961	.12	.44	.43	.45	2.56	1.02	.87	14.65	18.27	26.53	17.75	18.88	23.80	29.02
Spain 184	.27	.90	.33	.65	.60	.83	2.05	16.19	20.69	31.76	34.23	44.38	51.75	55.39
Sweden 144	.55	.95	.63	2.93	3.01	6.65	16.98	12.38	8.04	6.29	13.43	15.26	15.18	11.43
Switzerland 146	4.48	.54	1.32	.57	.40	.66	.83	12.41	12.90	14.30	57.21	25.19	33.32	203.55
United Kingdom 112	.19	1.43	.46	.20	.90	.61	2.45	47.00	46.07	44.81	14.77	24.31	43.16	52.05
Developing Countries 202	**21.5**	**18.4**	**25.3**	**55.2**	**41.6**	**61.2**	**126.7**	**278.9**	**364.3**	**507.5**	**660.0**	**915.1**	**1,160.7**	**1,509.8**
Africa 607	**—**	**—**	**—**	**.1**	**.5**	**.2**	**.2**	**2.1**	**6.1**	**5.3**	**2.9**	**4.7**	**12.3**	**7.5**
Algeria 612	—	—	—	.06	—	.03	.01	.14	.24	.18	—	.14	3.27	4.19
Benin 638	—	—	—	—	—	—	.01	—	—	—	—	—	—	—
Cameroon 622	—	—	—	—	—	—	.11	—	—	—	—	.03	.02	.06
Central African Rep. 626	—	—	—	—	—	—	—	—	—	.02	—	—	—	—
Congo, Republic of 634	—	—	—	—	.01	—	—	—	—	—	—	—	—	.01
Ethiopia 644	—	—	—	—	—	—	—	—	—	—	—	.01	.06	.08
Gabon 646	—	—	—	—	.52	—	—	—	—	—	—	—	—	—
Ghana 652	—	—	—	—	—	—	—	—	.02	—	.01	.05	.03	.04
Madagascar 674	—	—	—	—	—	.13	.02	—	—	—	—	.02	.01	—
Mali 678	—	—	—	—	—	—	—	—	.36	—	.06	.13	.03	.02
Morocco 686	—	—	—	—	—	—	—	—	.05	—	.01	.67	.68	.80
Niger 692	—	—	—	—	—	—	—	.02	—	.02	.21	.01	—	—
Nigeria 694	—	—	—	—	—	—	—	—	—	—	—	—	—	.03
Senegal 722	—	—	—	—	.01	—	—	—	—	—	—	.05	—	—
Sierra Leone 724	—	—	—	—	—	—	—	—	.02	.06	.04	.03	.02	.01
South Africa 199	—	—	—	—	—	—	—	—	.56	.35	.19	.02	.14	.55
Sudan 732	—	—	—	—	—	—	—	—	2.02	2.02	.10	.01	—	.01
Tunisia 744	—	—	—	—	—	—	.02	1.92	2.81	2.64	2.26	3.54	7.97	1.71
Zambia 754	—	—	—	—	—	—	.01	—	—	—	—	—	—	—
Zimbabwe 698	—	—	—	—	—	—	—	.01	—	—	.01	—	.06	.02
Asia 507	**—**	**.1**	**1.6**	**.7**	**3.4**	**9.9**	**37.7**	**37.7**	**48.2**	**79.9**	**125.7**	**207.5**	**239.4**	**342.8**
Afghanistan, I.S. of 512	—	.10	—	—	—	—	2.05	—	—	—	—	—	—	—
Bangladesh 513	—	—	—	—	—	—	—	.01	.01	—	—	—	.13	1.00
Cambodia 522	—	—	—	—	.02	.02	—	—	.02	—	—	—	—	.01
China,P.R.: Mainland 924	—	.01	1.59	.61	3.24	9.01	26.95	26.91	37.50	65.15	101.70	173.19	181.89	277.36
China,P.R.:Hong Kong 532	—	—	—	—	—	.81	.01	.53	.46	.81	.51	1.23	3.51	2.59
China,P.R.:Macao 546	—	—	—	—	—	.01	—	.01	.01	—	.04	—	.12	.02
India 534	—	—	—	—	.01	.01	8.42	3.94	2.60	4.49	6.13	10.09	7.03	15.50
Indonesia 536	—	—	—	.01	—	—	—	.09	.11	.29	1.62	1.45	2.07	4.30
Korea 542	—	—	—	—	—	—	.11	3.10	4.26	5.29	7.91	12.65	33.27	23.13
Malaysia 548	—	—	—	—	—	—	.09	2.32	.27	.32	1.52	1.88	1.62	2.49
Mongolia 948	—	—	—	—	—	—	—	—	—	.10	—	—	—	—
Pakistan 564	—	—	—	—	—	—	—	—	.03	.03	.01	.04	.21	.59
Philippines 566	—	—	—	—	—	—	—	—	.48	.05	.25	.30	.30	.35
Samoa 862	—	—	—	—	—	—	—	—	—	—	—	—	.02	—
Singapore 576	—	—	.02	.03	.09	.05	.01	.40	.84	1.35	2.15	2.65	3.63	1.32
Sri Lanka 524	—	—	—	—	.01	—	—	—	—	—	.01	.04	.07	.15
Taiwan Province of China 528	—	—	—	—	—	—	—	.27	.79	1.55	1.87	—	—	—
Thailand 578	—	—	—	—	—	—	—	.05	.79	.45	1.86	2.77	4.35	12.43
Vietnam 582	—	—	—	—	.02	—	—	.05	.02	—	.11	1.16	1.17	1.60
Europe 170	**20.6**	**16.9**	**21.8**	**53.7**	**35.6**	**49.2**	**87.6**	**221.4**	**283.7**	**372.3**	**464.2**	**640.5**	**837.2**	**1,033.6**
Azerbaijan 912	—	—	—	.04	—	—	—	.79	.02	—	—	2.30	.81	1.80
Belarus 913	—	—	—	—	—	—	—	9.50	6.62	8.35	.58	6.76	4.12	.28
Bosnia & Herzegovina 963	.01	.07	.04	.38	1.09	4.31	4.33	.07	.68	1.27	1.20	3.34	8.25	12.49

	Exports 2001	Exports 2002	Exports 2003	Exports 2004	Exports 2005	Exports 2006	Exports 2007	Imports 2001	Imports 2002	Imports 2003	Imports 2004	Imports 2005	Imports 2006	Imports 2007
	Millions of U.S. Dollars							*Millions of U.S. Dollars*						
Bulgaria....918	.09	.10	.19	1.59	3.61	3.31	7.41	26.28	28.52	40.72	46.03	73.54	83.08	74.08
Croatia....960	.05	.16	.32	.40	.18	2.23	.98	16.92	32.30	28.38	29.85	31.11	43.49	40.35
Czech Republic....935	.49	.42	.27	1.22	.41	.60	.23	6.26	5.43	13.30	20.64	25.72	32.51	32.13
Estonia....939	—	—	—	—	—	—	—	—	—	—	—	.20	—	.07
Georgia....915	—	—	—	—	.04	3.06	—	.02	.77	.95	4.24	8.99	7.73	18.47
Hungary....944	.05	.07	1.11	.06	.79	.49	.37	14.25	12.54	12.51	16.57	19.49	24.45	40.00
Kazakhstan....916	—	—	—	—	—	—	—	—	—	.25	.03	1.16	1.86	2.16
Kyrgyz Republic....917	—	—	—	—	—	—	—	—	—	.03	.37	.33	.25	.36
Latvia....941	—	—	—	—	—	—	.07	—	—	.53	—	.01	.05	.05
Lithuania....946	—	—	—	—	.01	—	—	.02	.02	.04	.01	.10	.05	.10
Macedonia, FYR....962	7.12	4.96	3.05	7.66	10.34	12.59	24.31	15.28	16.54	15.60	23.94	32.09	48.69	80.56
Moldova....921	—	—	—	—	—	.01	—	.54	1.11	.58	3.26	5.72	5.49	3.63
Poland....964	—	.06	.03	.16	.07	.05	.31	.93	1.76	4.64	6.64	11.86	16.32	33.20
Romania....968	.03	.06	.08	.23	1.59	.65	3.22	12.00	15.78	15.17	9.93	19.03	52.57	17.63
Russia....922	.04	.04	2.43	.44	.46	.44	2.77	16.98	38.91	52.41	64.12	105.77	124.24	169.99
Serbia & Montenegro....965	9.55	7.48	10.54	30.06	5.53	10.73	19.28	5.99	12.95	8.48	13.17	16.36	27.13	87.48
Slovak Republic....936	.05	.02	.01	.03	.05	.26	.06	.55	.32	.99	3.21	5.02	6.78	5.69
Tajikistan....923	—	—	—	—	—	.08	—	—	—	—	—	—	—	—
Turkey....186	3.09	3.40	3.70	11.46	11.35	10.34	24.21	80.78	91.30	121.69	163.10	196.50	232.33	303.69
Ukraine....926	.02	.04	—	—	.05	.01	.01	14.21	18.15	46.42	57.01	75.05	116.90	109.23
Europe n.s....884	—	—	—	—	—	—	—	—	—	.01	.24	.08	.05	.20
Middle East....407	**.4**	**.2**	**.9**	**.6**	**1.1**	**1.4**	**.4**	**6.6**	**14.2**	**26.2**	**18.2**	**24.3**	**25.6**	**44.9**
Bahrain....419	—	—	—	—	.01	.08	—	.01	—	.04	—	.02	—	—
Egypt....469	—	—	—	—	.03	.03	.09	3.56	3.88	10.59	8.85	11.26	18.64	23.69
Iran, I.R. of....429	—	.02	.03	.17	.76	.34	.10	.42	1.25	2.33	1.62	1.86	1.35	1.22
Iraq....433	—	—	—	—	.24	—	.07	—	—	.53	—	—	—	—
Israel....436	.10	—	—	.39	—	.87	—	.14	.34	.29	4.67	5.29	1.61	11.36
Jordan....439	.09	—	—	—	.03	.02	—	.03	.01	.08	.17	.28	.38	.52
Kuwait....443	.10	—	—	.06	—	—	—	—	—	.02	.02	—	.02	—
Lebanon....446	.10	—	.89	—	—	.02	—	.05	5.06	9.58	.03	1.53	.13	3.23
Libya....672	—	.01	.02	.01	—	—	—	—	.67	—	—	.53	—	1.16
Saudi Arabia....456	—	.18	—	—	—	—	.01	.90	.97	1.78	.54	.81	1.36	.45
Syrian Arab Republic....463	—	—	—	—	—	—	—	1.05	.22	.33	.86	1.47	1.09	1.34
United Arab Emirates....466	—	—	—	—	—	.02	—	.48	1.75	.60	1.41	1.29	1.00	1.74
Yemen, Republic of....474	—	—	—	—	—	—	.10	—	—	—	—	—	—	.16
Western Hemisphere....207	**.5**	**1.2**	**1.0**	**.1**	**1.0**	**.5**	**.9**	**11.1**	**12.2**	**23.9**	**49.1**	**38.1**	**46.3**	**80.9**
Argentina....213	—	—	—	—	—	—	.72	1.92	1.32	.81	4.74	2.17	.62	3.75
Bahamas, The....313	—	—	—	—	—	—	—	—	—	—	—	—	—	.12
Barbados....316	—	—	—	—	—	—	—	.01	.02	.02	—	.01	—	.01
Brazil....223	—	—	.04	.08	.90	.49	.06	3.57	6.02	13.48	32.05	23.46	30.36	55.32
Chile....228	—	—	—	—	—	—	—	—	—	.05	—	.13	.15	.32
Colombia....233	—	—	—	—	—	—	—	.81	.47	.01	.44	2.08	.39	.58
Costa Rica....238	—	—	—	—	—	—	.01	.08	—	.78	.02	.51	.65	.05
Ecuador....248	—	—	—	—	—	—	—	4.63	3.93	7.17	6.79	7.91	9.65	16.24
El Salvador....253	—	—	—	—	—	—	—	—	—	—	.02	.03	—	—
Guatemala....258	—	—	—	—	.02	.04	—	—	—	—	.08	.19	.12	.01
Honduras....268	—	—	—	—	—	—	—	.01	.09	.25	—	.02	—	—
Jamaica....343	—	—	—	—	—	—	.02	—	—	—	—	—	.01	—
Mexico....273	—	—	—	—	—	.01	—	.03	.01	.08	.47	.62	1.28	1.97
Nicaragua....278	—	—	—	—	—	—	—	—	—	—	.04	—	—	—
Panama....283	.49	1.24	.96	—	.05	.01	.02	—	—	—	—	—	—	—
Paraguay....288	—	—	—	—	—	—	—	—	—	.86	1.84	.78	2.13	2.01
Peru....293	—	—	—	—	—	—	—	—	—	—	—	—	—	.11
Suriname....366	—	—	—	—	—	—	—	—	.22	.04	—	.02	.02	.05
Trinidad and Tobago....369	—	—	—	—	—	—	—	—	—	—	.02	.03	.02	—
Uruguay....298	—	—	—	—	.01	—	.06	.01	.11	.09	2.46	.17	.86	.35
Venezuela, Rep. Bol....299	—	—	—	—	.03	—	—	.01	—	.22	.13	—	.01	.07
Western Hem. n.s....399	—	—	—	—	.01	—	—	—	—	—	—	—	—	—
Other Countries n.i.e....910	**—**	**—**	**—**	**—**	**—**	**—**	**—**	**—**	**—**	**—**	**—**	**—**	**—**	**.1**
Cuba....928	—	—	—	—	—	—	—	—	—	.02	.02	.01	.02	.08
Countries & Areas n.s....898	**—**	**.2**	**—**	**.3**	**—**	**—**	**—**	**—**	**.5**	**—**	**.5**	**.9**	**.4**	**3.7**
Memorandum Items														
European Union....998	279.78	314.71	419.27	546.64	584.19	695.28	878.21	1,025.72	1,104.26	1,320.13	1,564.98	1,670.62	1,860.75	2,406.06
Oil Exporting Ctys....999	.10	.21	.05	.31	1.03	.40	.18	2.05	5.00	5.95	5.34	6.08	9.08	13.16
Non-Oil Develop.Ctys....201	21.37	18.23	25.28	54.86	40.57	60.76	126.47	276.80	359.34	501.55	654.65	909.06	1,151.60	1,496.68
PERCENT DISTRIBUTION														
Industrial Countries....101	**93.0**	**94.5**	**94.3**	**90.8**	**93.4**	**91.9**	**87.5**	**78.9**	**75.7**	**72.5**	**71.1**	**64.8**	**61.7**	**63.0**
Developing Countries....202	**7.0**	**5.4**	**5.7**	**9.1**	**6.6**	**8.1**	**12.5**	**21.1**	**24.3**	**27.5**	**28.9**	**35.1**	**38.3**	**36.9**
Africa....607	**—**	**—**	**—**	**—**	**.1**	**—**	**—**	**.2**	**.4**	**.3**	**.1**	**.2**	**.4**	**.2**
Asia....507	**—**	**—**	**.4**	**.1**	**.5**	**1.3**	**3.7**	**2.8**	**3.2**	**4.3**	**5.5**	**8.0**	**7.9**	**8.4**
Europe....170	**6.7**	**5.0**	**4.9**	**8.9**	**5.6**	**6.5**	**8.7**	**16.7**	**18.9**	**20.2**	**20.3**	**24.6**	**27.6**	**25.3**
Middle East....407	**.1**	**.1**	**.2**	**.1**	**.2**	**.2**	**—**	**.5**	**.9**	**1.4**	**.8**	**.9**	**.8**	**1.1**
Western Hemisphere....207	**.2**	**.4**	**.2**	**—**	**.2**	**.1**	**.1**	**.8**	**.8**	**1.3**	**2.1**	**1.5**	**1.5**	**2.0**

Albania 914

	Exports							Imports						
	2001	2002	2003	2004	2005	2006	2007	2001	2002	2003	2004	2005	2006	2007
ANNUAL PERCENT CHANGE														
World.. 001	19.9	10.3	31.9	35.2	4.5	20.2	33.3	21.1	13.3	22.8	24.2	13.9	16.2	35.1
Industrial Countries.................. 101	17.1	12.0	31.7	30.2	7.5	18.3	26.8	19.7	8.7	17.6	21.9	3.9	10.5	38.0
Developing Countries.............. 202	81.1	−14.1	37.3	117.8	−24.6	47.0	107.1	26.9	30.7	39.3	30.0	38.7	26.8	30.1
Africa...................................... 607	....	....	....	—	771.8	−69.9	12.5	357.8	190.5	−13.1	−45.4	63.3	160.9	−38.6
Asia... 507	−92.8	—	—	−59.3	419.6	192.7	279.7	79.0	27.9	65.8	57.4	65.1	15.4	43.2
Europe..................................... 170	74.5	−18.0	28.9	146.9	−33.8	38.2	78.1	19.8	28.2	31.2	24.7	38.0	30.7	23.5
Middle East............................. 407	—	−46.1	348.2	−34.1	73.8	27.0	−73.4	−16.4	113.1	84.9	−30.6	34.0	5.0	75.5
Western Hemisphere............. 207	—	154.1	−18.7	−91.9	—	−46.6	64.8	96.5	10.1	95.8	105.7	−22.4	21.4	75.0
Other Countries n.i.e................ 910	—	—	—	....	....	....	....	12.9	30.7	—	−9.5	−35.3	8.9	435.4

Algeria 612

	Exports 2001	Exports 2002	Exports 2003	Exports 2004	Exports 2005	Exports 2006	Exports 2007	Imports 2001	Imports 2002	Imports 2003	Imports 2004	Imports 2005	Imports 2006	Imports 2007
	Millions of U.S. Dollars							*Millions of U.S. Dollars*						
IFS World Total	**19,092**	**18,700**	**24,470**	**32,210**	**46,372**	**54,755**	**59,518**	**9,482**	**12,010**	**13,322**	**17,954**	**19,857**	**21,010**	**27,439**
DOTS World Total 001	**18,319**	**18,528**	**24,905Y**	**31,903Y**	**43,657Y**	**53,866Y**	**56,916Y**	**9,750**	**11,809**	**15,375Y**	**20,849Y**	**23,535Y**	**25,056Y**	**33,213Y**
Industrial Countries 101	**15,190**	**15,494**	**21,437Y**	**27,130Y**	**37,018Y**	**47,202Y**	**48,311Y**	**7,472**	**8,712**	**11,048Y**	**14,853Y**	**16,360Y**	**15,702Y**	**20,206Y**
United States 111	2,616	2,633	4,660V	7,206V	9,850V	14,626V	16,756V	1,025	1,161	536V	1,069V	1,277V	1,212V	1,818V
Canada 156	663	929	1,717V	2,380V	3,451V	4,366V	4,772V	259	335	278V	224V	207V	246V	527V
Australia 193	23	28	—V	—V	—V	357V	119V	41	64	38V	56V	73V	85V	61V
Japan 158	75	37	54V	107V	39V	115V	355V	201	440	303V	575V	588V	478V	938V
New Zealand 196	—	—	—V	—V	—V	—V	—V	51	63	58V	81V	106V	153V	201V
Austria 122	—	—	70V	74V	9V	136V	255V	114	108	99V	150V	189V	183V	289V
Belgium 124	526	456	1,272V	1,481V	1,895V	2,307V	1,725V	264	287	563V	773V	755V	768V	1,172V
Cyprus 423	—	—	1V	—V	—Y	4V	13V	4	6	3V	3V	4V	4V	3V
Denmark 128	3	—	3V	1V	—V	—V	—V	40	56	43V	82V	61V	82V	97V
Finland 172	—	2	2V	—V	—V	56V	—V	89	97	102V	133V	99V	144V	226V
France 132	2,786	2,517	3,433V	3,624V	4,359V	4,707V	4,215V	2,398	2,682	4,731V	6,271V	6,585V	5,543V	6,208V
Germany 134	176	432	887V	934V	1,836V	1,286V	1,250V	790	851	844V	1,337V	1,478V	1,480V	1,772V
Greece 174	69	64	90V	77V	104V	171V	191V	67	59	43V	51V	54V	241V	122V
Iceland 176	—	—	—V	—V	—V	—V	—V	5	3	—V	—V	—V	—V	—V
Ireland 178	—	16	—V	—V	—V	36V	1V	24	47	25V	46V	71V	65V	46V
Italy 136	4,144	3,720	4,800V	5,475V	6,950V	9,126V	7,879V	1,040	1,136	1,463V	1,699V	1,822V	2,151V	2,812V
Luxembourg 137	—	—	—V	—V	1V	2V	—V	7	7	9V	29V	28V	13V	19V
Malta 181	12	14	2V	—V	—V	2V	—V	6	5	1V	2V	1V	2V	8V
Netherlands 138	1,311	1,671	813V	1,173V	1,661V	1,834V	2,858V	148	215	284V	345V	320V	379V	561V
Norway 142	40	7	1V	9V	1V	1V	—V	9	19	4V	3V	5V	15V	17V
Portugal 182	285	335	227V	556V	1,238V	1,014V	728V	49	44	52V	57V	75V	100V	121V
Slovenia 961	4	3	50V	66Y	95V	105V	105V	3	6	10V	13Y	68V	118V	138V
Spain 184	2,157	2,234	2,863V	3,213V	4,595V	5,239V	5,491V	522	620	940V	1,127V	1,681V	1,476V	1,994V
Sweden 144	11	14	14V	4V	29V	18V	44V	67	98	161V	218V	391V	205V	327V
Switzerland 146	—	—	89V	124V	148V	94V	5V	—	—	116V	170V	131V	218V	361V
United Kingdom 112	289	383	388V	624V	755V	1,601V	1,548V	251	304	341V	338V	290V	341V	369V
Developing Countries 202	**3,040**	**2,919**	**3,328Y**	**4,588Y**	**6,388Y**	**6,347Y**	**8,224Y**	**2,269**	**3,075**	**4,303Y**	**5,966Y**	**7,136Y**	**9,306Y**	**12,944Y**
Africa 607	**281**	**285**	**312Y**	**338Y**	**531Y**	**655Y**	**786Y**	**154**	**212**	**248Y**	**284Y**	**411Y**	**577Y**	**641Y**
Angola 614	—	—	—Y	—Y	—Y	—Y	—Y	—	—	—Y	—Y	—Y	—Y	1Y
Benin 638	—	25	—V	—V	1V	1Y	2Y	—	—	—V	—V	—V	—Y	—Y
Botswana 616	7	—	—Y	—Y	—Y	—Y	—Y	—	—	—Y	—Y	—Y	—Y	—Y
Burkina Faso 748	—	—	—Y	—Y	—Y	—Y	—Y	—	1	1Y	1Y	1Y	1Y	2Y
Burundi 618	—	7	—V	—V	—V	—V	—Y	—	—	—V	—V	—V	—V	—Y
Cameroon 622	—	—	1V	1Y	1Y	2Y	2Y	4	2	6V	8Y	10Y	13Y	17Y
Cape Verde 624	2	8	9Y	12Y	17Y	21Y	25Y	1	—	—Y	—Y	—Y	—Y	—Y
Congo, Republic of 634	—	—	—V	—V	—Y	—Y	—Y	—	1	—V	—V	—Y	—Y	—Y
Côte d'Ivoire 662	—	—	—V	—V	—V	—V	—Y	58	55	45V	57V	47V	69V	89Y
Ethiopia 644	—	—	—V	—V	—V	—Y	—Y	1	2	—V	—V	—V	—Y	—Y
Gabon 646	—	5	6Y	7Y	10Y	13Y	15Y	4	1	1Y	1Y	1Y	1Y	2Y
Kenya 664	—	—	—V	1V	1Y	1Y	1Y	2	2	—V	—V	—Y	—Y	1Y
Liberia 668	—	—	—Y	—Y	—Y	—Y	—Y	1	—	—Y	—Y	1Y	1Y	1Y
Malawi 676	—	—	—Y	—Y	—Y	—Y	—Y	1	3	3Y	5Y	6Y	7Y	9Y
Mauritania 682	11	10	12Y	16Y	22Y	28Y	33Y	3	5	6Y	8Y	10Y	12Y	16Y
Morocco 686	175	141	159V	147V	315V	396Y	478Y	6	17	26V	45V	55V	68Y	89Y
Niger 692	—	—	4V	4V	6Y	7Y	9Y	—	—	—V	—V	—Y	—Y	1Y
Nigeria 694	2	3	1V	1Y	1Y	1Y	1Y	1	2	1V	1Y	1Y	1Y	1Y
Senegal 722	1	2	1V	6V	2V	1V	1Y	—	1	—V	1V	—V	—V	—Y
South Africa 199	—	—	—V	1V	23V	3V	1V	10	10	39V	32V	70V	187V	136V
Sudan 732	—	—	—Y	—V	9V	4V	3V	1	1	—V	1V	1V	1V	—V
Tanzania 738	—	—	—Y	—Y	—Y	—Y	—Y	1	3	3Y	4Y	5Y	6Y	8Y
Tunisia 744	81	84	119V	142V	123V	177V	213Y	59	102	114V	120V	201V	207V	268Y
Uganda 746	—	—	—V	—Y	—Y	—Y	—Y	—	1	—V	—Y	—Y	—Y	—Y
Zimbabwe 698	—	—	—V	—V	—V	—V	—Y	—	1	1V	—V	—V	—V	—Y
Asia 507	**285**	**336**	**492Y**	**631Y**	**744Y**	**1,181Y**	**2,183Y**	**541**	**882**	**1,375Y**	**2,055Y**	**2,636Y**	**3,380Y**	**4,895Y**
Afghanistan, I.S. of 512	—	—	—Y	—Y	—Y	—Y	—Y	—	2	3Y	3Y	4Y	5Y	7Y
Bangladesh 513	—	—	—V	—V	—V	1V	—V	—	1	1V	1V	1V	1Y	3Y
China,P.R.: Mainland 924	—	77	90V	135V	329V	127V	1,022V	191	340	711V	1,066V	1,545V	2,147V	2,980V
China,P.R.:Hong Kong 532	—	—	—V	—V	—V	2V	1V	8	19	14V	9V	14V	24V	28V
India 534	18	67	3V	5V	11V	14Y	17Y	39	83	119V	218V	285V	352Y	456Y
Indonesia 536	256	126	160V	131V	54V	125V	169V	71	94	60V	79V	140V	116V	161V
Korea 542	—	9	174V	219V	151V	525V	588V	159	207	247V	390V	374V	430V	845V
Malaysia 548	1	2	2V	—V	1V	6V	5V	36	66	83V	100V	56V	74V	125V
Maldives 556	—	—	—V	—V	—V	—Y	—Y	1	5	6Y	7Y	9Y	11Y	15Y
Pakistan 564	—	—	—V	—V	1V	1Y	1Y	2	2	9V	9V	14V	17Y	22Y
Philippines 566	—	—	1V	—V	4V	7V	1V	2	5	3V	2V	1V	1V	2V
Singapore 576	9	47	—V	26V	—V	—V	20V	10	19	5V	18V	14V	29V	48V
Sri Lanka 524	—	—	—Y	—Y	—Y	—Y	—Y	1	—	—Y	—Y	1Y	1Y	1Y
Taiwan Province of China 528	—	—	—V	—V	—V	91V	51V	—	—	30V	41V	40V	40V	52V
Thailand 578	—	7	61V	115V	193V	281V	308V	12	32	65V	96V	102V	95V	150V
Vietnam 582	—	—	—V	—V	—V	—V	—V	8	6	20V	15V	34V	38V	—V

	Exports 2001	2002	2003	2004	2005	2006	2007	Imports 2001	2002	2003	2004	2005	2006	2007
	Millions of U.S. Dollars							Millions of U.S. Dollars						
Europe 170	**990**	**1,041**	**1,040Y**	**1,263Y**	**1,687Y**	**1,809Y**	**2,193Y**	**1,005**	**1,140**	**1,688Y**	**2,084Y**	**2,286Y**	**3,241Y**	**4,759Y**
Albania 914	—	—	—V	—V	—V	3V	4V	—	—	—V	—V	—V	—V	—V
Belarus 913	—	—	—V	—V	—V	—V	—V	3	—	13V	7V	5V	4V	1V
Bosnia & Herzegovina 963	....	....	....	....	....	....	....	—	—	—Y	—Y	1Y	1Y	1Y
Bulgaria 918	—	1	—V	—V	9V	—V	—V	17	38	18V	14V	31V	13V	106V
Croatia 960	3	24	3V	1V	—V	—V	—V	2	6	8V	5V	8V	15V	7V
Czech Republic 935	—	1	—V	52V	56V	9V	138V	37	34	74V	71V	88V	70V	70V
Estonia 939	—	—	—V	—V	—V	—V	—V	3	2	1V	2V	4V	3V	1V
Georgia 915	—	—	—V	—V	—V	—V	—Y	2	5	—V	—V	—V	4V	5Y
Hungary 944	1	—	—V	—V	—V	—V	—V	15	28	27V	24V	54V	80V	68V
Kazakhstan 916	—	—	—V	—V	—Y	—Y	—Y	—	—	4V	—V	—Y	—Y	—Y
Latvia 941	—	—	—V	—V	—V	—V	—V	—	—	10V	2V	9V	35V	29V
Lithuania 946	—	—	2V	—V	—V	—V	—V	14	5	2V	1V	1V	—V	16V
Macedonia, FYR 962	—	—	—V	4V	—V	—V	—Y	—	—	—V	—V	—V	—V	—Y
Moldova 921	—	—	—V	—V	—V	—Y	—Y	9	9	—V	—V	—V	—Y	—Y
Poland 964	—	1	5V	2V	—V	—V	1V	123	85	95V	93V	130V	130V	225V
Romania 968	—	27	—V	1V	—V	—V	1V	21	40	57V	67V	77V	93V	116V
Russia 922	—	4	1V	1V	2V	—V	10V	239	268	321V	202V	227V	708V	1,541V
Serbia & Montenegro 965	39	35	42Y	56Y	76Y	95Y	115Y	9	19	21Y	27Y	35Y	43Y	56Y
Slovak Republic 936	—	—	—Y	—Y	—V	—V	—V	—	1	1Y	1Y	17V	40V	22V
Tajikistan 923	6	—	—Y	—Y	—Y	—Y	—Y	11	17	19Y	25Y	32Y	39Y	51Y
Turkey 186	941	948	983V	1,142V	1,539V	1,695V	1,917V	379	391	630V	887V	888V	1,123V	1,355V
Ukraine 926	1	—	4V	4V	4V	6Y	7Y	110	191	386V	653V	679V	838Y	1,086Y
Europe n.s. 884	—	—	—Y	—Y	—Y	—Y	—Y	9	1	1Y	2Y	2Y	3Y	4Y
Middle East 407	**316**	**266**	**296Y**	**374Y**	**526Y**	**630Y**	**755Y**	**181**	**366**	**419Y**	**544Y**	**689Y**	**808Y**	**1,022Y**
Bahrain 419	—	—	—Y	—Y	—Y	—Y	—Y	12	22	24Y	31Y	40Y	49Y	64Y
Egypt 469	105	156	189Y	250Y	339Y	427Y	515Y	29	58	64Y	84Y	107Y	132Y	171Y
Iran, I.R. of 429	—	1	1Y	2Y	2Y	3Y	3Y	—	—	—Y	—Y	—Y	—Y	—Y
Iraq 433	40	50	56Y	64Y	85Y	102Y	120Y	1	—	—Y	—Y	—Y	—Y	—Y
Jordan 439	22	16	1V	1V	21V	—V	—V	31	46	63V	76V	94V	77V	96V
Kuwait 443	2	15	17Y	20Y	26Y	31Y	37Y	2	1	1Y	2Y	2Y	3Y	3Y
Lebanon 446	8	10	12Y	17Y	22Y	28Y	34Y	17	26	29Y	38Y	48Y	60Y	77Y
Libya 672	1	9	10Y	12Y	16Y	19Y	22Y	3	2	2Y	2Y	3Y	4Y	4Y
Oman 449	—	—	—V	—Y	—Y	—Y	—Y	1	2	1V	1Y	2Y	2Y	2Y
Qatar 453	—	—	—V	—V	—V	3V	3Y	—	1	2V	9V	6V	8V	10Y
Saudi Arabia 456	16	—	—V	1V	2V	3Y	3Y	37	30	33Y	38Y	51Y	61Y	72Y
Syrian Arab Republic 463	9	7	9Y	8V	11Y	14Y	17Y	25	126	140Y	196V	250Y	308Y	399Y
United Arab Emirates 466	113	2	1V	1Y	1Y	1Y	2Y	24	51	57Y	66Y	87Y	105Y	123Y
Yemen, Republic of 474	—	—	—Y	—V	—V	—Y	—Y	—	1	1Y	—V	—V	—Y	1Y
Western Hemisphere 207	**1,170**	**991**	**1,188Y**	**1,982Y**	**2,900Y**	**2,072Y**	**2,307Y**	**388**	**475**	**572Y**	**999Y**	**1,114Y**	**1,300Y**	**1,626Y**
Argentina 213	17	25	—V	—V	1V	14V	17V	181	161	229V	497V	498V	592V	842V
Bahamas, The 313	—	—	—Y	—Y	—Y	—Y	—Y	1	—	—Y	—Y	—Y	—Y	—Y
Barbados 316	3	—	—V	—V	—V	—V	—Y	—	—	—V	—V	—V	—V	—Y
Brazil 223	987	881	1,114V	1,935V	2,838V	1,976V	2,234V	51	107	169V	383V	423V	518V	551V
Chile 228	—	—	—V	—V	—V	—V	—V	—	—	1V	1V	2V	2V	3V
Colombia 233	—	—	—V	—V	—V	—V	—V	9	8	5V	4V	1V	1V	1V
Costa Rica 238	—	—	—V	—V	—V	—Y	—Y	1	1	—V	—V	—V	—Y	—Y
Ecuador 248	12	13	—V	—V	20V	—V	—Y	11	60	24V	10V	4V	—V	—Y
Guatemala 258	—	3	—V	—V	—V	—Y	—Y	—	—	5V	—V	4V	5Y	6Y
Honduras 268	—	—	—V	—V	—Y	—Y	—Y	—	3	—V	—V	—Y	—Y	—Y
Mexico 273	148	70	73V	46V	41V	81V	55V	125	101	96V	71V	107V	95V	104V
Panama 283	—	—	—V	—V	—V	—V	—V	1	2	—V	—V	—V	—V	—V
Paraguay 288	—	—	—V	—V	—V	—V	—Y	—	2	—V	—V	—V	—V	—Y
Peru 293	—	—	—V	—V	—V	—V	—Y	5	3	16V	20V	32V	65V	89Y
St. Kitts and Nevis 361	—	—	—Y	—Y	—Y	—Y	—Y	—	—	—Y	—Y	—Y	1Y	1Y
St. Vincent & Grens. 364	—	—	—Y	—Y	—Y	—Y	—Y	1	—	—Y	—Y	—Y	—Y	—Y
Uruguay 298	—	—	—V	—V	—V	—Y	—Y	—	20	27V	11V	17V	20Y	26Y
Venezuela, Rep. Bol. 299	1	—	—V	—V	—V	—V	—V	—	7	—V	—V	26V	1V	1Y
Other Countries n.i.e. 910	**89**	**115**	**140Y**	**185Y**	**252Y**	**316Y**	**382Y**	**9**	**21**	**24Y**	**31Y**	**39Y**	**49Y**	**63Y**
Cuba 928	—	—	—Y	—Y	—Y	—Y	—Y	3	11	12Y	16Y	20Y	24Y	32Y
North Korea 954	89	115	140Y	185Y	252Y	316Y	381Y	5	11	12Y	15Y	19Y	24Y	31Y
Memorandum Items														
European Union 998	11,774	11,860	14,923Y	17,358Y	23,585Y	27,654Y	26,443Y	6,073	6,783	9,924Y	12,869Y	14,275Y	13,653Y	16,714Y
Oil Exporting Ctys 999	430	207	246Y	231Y	186Y	286Y	359Y	140	190	158Y	198Y	317Y	300Y	378Y
Non-Oil Develop.Ctys 201	2,611	2,712	3,082Y	4,358Y	6,201Y	6,061Y	7,865Y	2,129	2,885	4,145Y	5,768Y	6,819Y	9,006Y	12,567Y
PERCENT DISTRIBUTION														
Industrial Countries 101	**82.9**	**83.6**	**86.1**	**85.0**	**84.8**	**87.6**	**84.9**	**76.6**	**73.8**	**71.9**	**71.2**	**69.5**	**62.7**	**60.8**
Developing Countries 202	**16.6**	**15.8**	**13.4**	**14.4**	**14.6**	**11.8**	**14.4**	**23.3**	**26.0**	**28.0**	**28.6**	**30.3**	**37.1**	**39.0**
Africa 607	**1.5**	**1.5**	**1.3**	**1.1**	**1.2**	**1.2**	**1.4**	**1.6**	**1.8**	**1.6**	**1.4**	**1.7**	**2.3**	**1.9**
Asia 507	**1.6**	**1.8**	**2.0**	**2.0**	**1.7**	**2.2**	**3.8**	**5.5**	**7.5**	**8.9**	**9.9**	**11.2**	**13.5**	**14.7**
Europe 170	**5.4**	**5.6**	**4.2**	**4.0**	**3.9**	**3.4**	**3.9**	**10.3**	**9.7**	**11.0**	**10.0**	**9.7**	**12.9**	**14.3**
Middle East 407	**1.7**	**1.4**	**1.2**	**1.2**	**1.2**	**1.2**	**1.3**	**1.9**	**3.1**	**2.7**	**2.6**	**2.9**	**3.2**	**3.1**
Western Hemisphere 207	**6.4**	**5.3**	**4.8**	**6.2**	**6.6**	**3.8**	**4.1**	**4.0**	**4.0**	**3.7**	**4.8**	**4.7**	**5.2**	**4.9**
Other Countries n.i.e. 910	**.5**	**.6**	**.6**	**.6**	**.6**	**.6**	**.7**	**.1**	**.2**	**.2**	**.1**	**.2**	**.2**	**.2**

Algeria 612

	Exports 2001	2002	2003	2004	2005	2006	2007	Imports 2001	2002	2003	2004	2005	2006	2007
ANNUAL PERCENT CHANGE														
World.. 001	−16.2	1.1	34.4	28.1	36.8	23.4	5.7	8.0	21.1	30.2	35.6	12.9	6.5	32.6
Industrial Countries.................. 101	−16.4	2.0	38.4	26.6	36.4	27.5	2.3	6.5	16.6	26.8	34.4	10.1	−4.0	28.7
Developing Countries.............. 202	−16.0	−4.0	14.0	37.8	39.2	−.6	29.6	13.0	35.5	39.9	38.6	19.6	30.4	39.1
Africa...................................... 607	−5.6	1.4	9.6	8.5	56.9	23.4	19.9	−4.1	37.7	17.2	14.5	44.6	40.4	11.0
Asia.. 507	232.9	18.0	46.5	28.3	17.9	58.8	84.8	−4.3	63.1	55.9	49.4	28.3	28.2	44.8
Europe.................................... 170	−28.6	5.2	—	21.4	33.6	7.2	21.2	13.6	13.5	48.1	23.4	9.7	41.8	46.9
Middle East............................ 407	452.2	−15.6	11.1	26.4	40.6	19.7	19.9	27.6	101.8	14.4	29.8	26.7	17.2	26.6
Western Hemisphere.............. 207	−34.9	−15.3	19.9	66.8	46.3	−28.5	11.3	51.3	22.3	20.6	74.5	11.5	16.7	25.1
Other Countries n.i.e................ 910	7.8	29.6	21.2	32.3	36.0	25.7	20.6	86.8	146.3	11.2	30.1	27.3	23.5	29.5

		Exports 2001	Exports 2002	Exports 2003	Exports 2004	Exports 2005	Exports 2006	Exports 2007	Imports 2001	Imports 2002	Imports 2003	Imports 2004	Imports 2005	Imports 2006	Imports 2007
		Millions of U.S. Dollars							*Millions of U.S. Dollars*						
IFS World Total		**6,379.9**	**7,515.8**	**9,508.0**	**13,475.0**	**24,109.0**	**31,083.6**	....	....	....	....	....	....	....	....
DOTS World Total	**001**	**6,170.2Y**	**7,220.1Y**	**8,506.0Y**	**11,541.3Y**	**20,216.2Y**	**29,149.7Y**	**36,604.3Y**	**3,436.3Y**	**3,063.0Y**	**4,465.4Y**	**7,033.5Y**	**8,250.0Y**	**11,282.5Y**	**12,964.2Y**
Industrial Countries	**101**	**4,672.0Y**	**5,262.9Y**	**5,325.2Y**	**5,475.9Y**	**11,312.8Y**	**14,702.5Y**	**18,438.6Y**	**1,775.8Y**	**1,983.1Y**	**3,043.6Y**	**3,282.5Y**	**4,151.5Y**	**6,403.7Y**	**8,008.4Y**
United States	111	2,979.36V	2,977.55V	4,096.64V	4,360.82V	8,042.18V	1,067.64V	1,750.82V	303.71V	409.75V	541.09V	653.73V	1,020.80V	1,705.33V	1,408.22V
Canada	156	29.95V	.03V	.03V	.04V	283.24V	528.82V	1,158.57V	3.23V	4.68V	18.96V	18.42V	68.01V	59.00V	85.58V
Australia	193	.01V	.05V	.29V	—V	.04V	49.77V	.05V	2.12V	2.14V	3.72V	2.19V	2.00V	4.50V	6.39V
Japan	158	20.19V	356.14V	74.54V	7.87V	17.22V	543.31V	175.18V	33.67V	38.46V	58.08V	341.52V	130.38V	205.58V	204.68V
New Zealand	196	—V	.01V	.01V	.01V	—V	—V	—V	1.27V	1.53V	1.96V	4.79V	9.56V	15.75V	12.79V
Austria	122	—V	2.01V	—V	.02V	.04V	.02V	.03V	1.76V	2.26V	8.24V	5.77V	4.52V	13.26V	21.74V
Belgium	124	507.41V	451.76V	222.22V	108.56V	472.24V	323.53V	258.45V	124.00V	155.95V	150.62V	159.90V	182.34V	265.85V	386.95V
Cyprus	423	—V	—V	—V	—V	—Y	—V	—V	.09V	.69V	1.01V	.29V	.08V	.23V	.08V
Denmark	128	.19V	.96V	.47V	1.17V	.01V	.29V	1.42V	22.71V	10.52V	12.42V	9.80V	7.03V	10.12V	10.31V
Finland	172	.01V	.01V	—V	—V	.02V	.01V	.01V	1.41V	1.17V	1.14V	3.18V	1.48V	3.03V	13.19V
France	132	603.74V	577.37V	631.04V	746.72V	1,584.51V	1,412.22V	2,158.41V	162.93V	197.79V	291.09V	307.39V	411.37V	694.95V	819.03V
Germany	134	49.34V	190.35V	54.24V	3.69V	69.67V	68.71V	178.13V	42.57V	58.51V	104.32V	106.51V	157.53V	276.04V	559.96V
Greece	174	—V	—V	—V	—V	—V	—V	—V	.18V	.86V	.92V	1.65V	2.55V	2.15V	1.66V
Ireland	178	.01V	.05V	.02V	.01V	.02V	.02V	.02V	3.78V	7.63V	8.82V	9.54V	8.82V	16.65V	14.39V
Italy	136	50.40V	262.88V	178.62V	32.50V	74.20V	46.63V	180.14V	116.53V	115.60V	114.67V	136.62V	181.32V	207.12V	301.63V
Luxembourg	137	—V	.01V	.02V	—V	—V	—V	—V	.53V	1.39V	1.14V	2.70V	.55V	.39V	.67V
Malta	181	—Y	—V	—V	—V	—V	—V	—V	.04Y	1.05V	3.05V	4.88V	3.91V	4.41V	3.70V
Netherlands	138	91.04V	39.20V	19.19V	3.99V	96.06V	83.85V	1,101.64V	120.85V	117.16V	524.25V	181.93V	205.26V	270.76V	391.79V
Norway	142	.04V	.05V	.18V	.41V	4.22V	6.10V	2.26V	74.46V	66.52V	52.19V	38.73V	178.39V	211.71V	227.78V
Portugal	182	105.58V	55.90V	2.52V	2.08V	29.64V	62.66V	462.02V	492.96V	594.58V	810.03V	920.12V	1,093.29V	1,677.50V	2,548.95V
Slovenia	961	—V	—V	.02V	.03Y	.03V	.29V	.16V	.12V	.03V	.05V	.07Y	.21V	.34V	.94V
Spain	184	139.44V	311.76V	30.34V	191.15V	610.09V	426.48V	538.56V	85.46V	62.90V	116.37V	91.73V	122.02V	271.83V	265.89V
Sweden	144	.93V	.07V	—V	.10V	4.71V	.11V	.02V	18.73V	12.72V	27.76V	31.04V	32.88V	44.73V	82.52V
Switzerland	146	.14V	.07V	.18V	.04V	.04V	54.92V	185.90V	16.15V	9.08V	6.26V	10.64V	13.10V	24.52V	37.30V
United Kingdom	112	94.22V	36.64V	14.58V	16.66V	24.67V	27.12V	286.80V	146.51V	110.18V	185.50V	239.40V	314.10V	417.91V	602.25V
Developing Countries	**202**	**1,498.2Y**	**1,957.2Y**	**3,180.9Y**	**6,065.5Y**	**8,903.4Y**	**14,447.2Y**	**18,165.7Y**	**1,660.5Y**	**1,079.9Y**	**1,421.7Y**	**3,750.9Y**	**4,098.5Y**	**4,878.8Y**	**4,955.8Y**
Africa	**607**	**11.0Y**	**32.5Y**	**9.6Y**	**270.3Y**	**307.9Y**	**379.8Y**	**1,677.1Y**	**460.2Y**	**467.7Y**	**573.1Y**	**637.6Y**	**705.8Y**	**881.7Y**	**1,015.9Y**
Algeria	612	.01V	.20V	.22Y	.28Y	.36Y	.44Y	.57Y	—V	.03V	.04Y	.05Y	.07Y	.09Y	.11Y
Benin	638	.30V	—V	.15V	—V	—V	—Y	—Y	—V	.02V	.02V	4.17V	.35V	.43Y	.54Y
Burkina Faso	748	—Y	—Y	—Y	—Y	—Y	—Y	—Y	.01Y	.01Y	.01Y	.01Y	.01Y	.02Y	.02Y
Cameroon	622	1.41V	.26V	.99V	1.30Y	1.48Y	1.84Y	2.28Y	16.11V	.91V	2.17V	2.85Y	3.26Y	4.03Y	5.00Y
Cape Verde	624	.40V	.43Y	.54Y	.71Y	.81Y	1.01Y	1.25Y	.02V	.02Y	.02Y	.03Y	.04Y	.05Y	.06Y
Congo, Republic of	634	4.61V	2.46V	.43V	.24V	.28Y	.34Y	.42Y	5.72V	10.74V	5.30V	8.58V	9.81Y	12.12Y	15.04Y
Côte d'Ivoire	662	.06V	.55V	.05V	.36V	.48V	.14V	.18Y	67.22V	33.24V	24.77V	16.29V	9.60V	11.69V	14.50Y
Gabon	646	.48Y	.53Y	.67Y	.87Y	1.00Y	1.23Y	1.53Y	1.41Y	1.53Y	1.93Y	2.54Y	2.90Y	3.58Y	4.44Y
Ghana	652	1.45Y	1.58Y	2.00Y	2.62Y	2.99Y	3.70Y	4.59Y	18.47Y	20.05Y	25.37Y	33.32Y	38.07Y	47.05Y	58.39Y
Guinea	656	.01V	.01Y	—V	—V	—Y	—Y	—Y	—V	—Y	.01V	—V	—Y	—Y	—Y
Guinea-Bissau	654	—Y	—Y	—Y	—Y	—Y	—Y	—Y	.01Y	.01Y	.01Y	.01Y	.01Y	.01Y	.02Y
Kenya	664	.06V	.28V	.01V	—V	—Y	—Y	—Y	.43V	.90V	3.76V	1.67V	1.90Y	2.35Y	2.92Y
Madagascar	674	.01V	—V	—V	—Y	—Y	—Y	—Y	—V	—V	—V	—Y	—Y	—Y	—Y
Mauritius	684	—V	—V	—V	—V	—V	—V	—V	.01V	.06V	—V	1.10V	.06V	3.15V	2.53V
Morocco	686	—V	.07V	.02V	.09V	.29V	.36Y	.44Y	7.32V	8.27V	7.98V	16.29V	15.17V	18.74Y	23.26Y
Mozambique	688	.06V	—V	.11V	.09V	—V	—V	—Y	.55V	.15V	.94V	.71V	.90V	1.69V	2.10Y
Nigeria	694	.76V	5.43V	2.21V	2.87Y	3.65Y	4.51Y	5.84Y	.98V	22.40V	.47V	.62Y	.84Y	1.05Y	1.27Y
Senegal	722	—V	9.29V	.03V	.02V	—V	—V	—Y	.20V	.35V	1.32V	2.51V	1.68V	2.67V	3.31Y
South Africa	199	1.31V	11.37V	2.04V	260.67V	296.30V	366.18V	1,659.81V	335.45V	352.99V	488.97V	524.91V	599.85V	746.91V	850.01V
Sacca exc. South Afr.	608	—Y	—Y	—Y	—Y	—Y	—Y	—Y	4.54V	9.87V	3.63V	13.77V	15.74Y	19.45Y	24.14Y
Sudan	732	—Y	—Y	—Y	—V	.18V	—V	.09V	—Y	—Y	—V	—V	—V	—V	—V
Tanzania	738	—V	—V	—Y	—Y	—Y	—Y	—Y	.56V	1.54V	1.95Y	2.56Y	2.92Y	3.61Y	4.48Y
Togo	742	—V	.01V	—V	—V	—V	—Y	—Y	....	....	....	....	....	....	....
Tunisia	744	—V	—V	—V	—V	—V	.02V	.02Y	.11V	.34V	.54V	1.15V	1.14V	2.48V	3.08Y
Zambia	754	—V	.01V	—V	.10V	.01V	.02V	.07V	.04V	.35V	1.23V	.44V	.66V	.44V	.63V
Zimbabwe	698	.01V	—V	.13V	.03V	.04V	—V	—Y	1.05V	3.94V	2.69V	4.06V	.85V	.06V	.08Y
Asia	**507**	**1,310.7Y**	**1,873.1Y**	**3,025.6Y**	**5,333.9Y**	**7,105.2Y**	**12,121.3Y**	**14,091.2Y**	**963.2Y**	**257.5Y**	**447.3Y**	**2,527.8Y**	**2,524.5Y**	**2,676.1Y**	**2,207.2Y**
Bangladesh	513	—Y	—Y	—Y	—Y	—V	—V	—V	—V	—V	.77V	.97V	.24V	.29Y	.36Y
Cambodia	522	—V	—V	—V	—V	.18V	—V	—Y	—V	—V	—V	—V	.03V	.03V	.04Y
China,P.R.: Mainland	924	656.21V	988.23V	2,004.50V	4,120.74V	5,982.44V	9,937.16V	1,713.36V	50.48V	67.43V	160.34V	193.61V	410.15V	983.81V	1,364.69V
China,P.R.:Hong Kong	532	.32V	.14V	.47V	.41V	80.09V	136.60V	45.24V	18.41V	21.08V	24.10V	20.36V	31.52V	35.26V	47.65V
China,P.R.:Macao	546	—V	—V	—V	—V	—V	—V	—V	—V	—V	—V	.64V	—V	—V	—V
India	534	—Y	4.91V	1.64V	.52V	2.34V	2.90Y	3.60Y	15.51Y	37.66V	68.47V	74.78V	143.99V	177.97Y	220.85Y
Indonesia	536	.04V	—V	86.18V	302.48V	1.04V	.37V	.97V	17.45V	13.12V	15.08V	23.62V	34.97V	48.17V	47.05V
Korea	542	199.74V	161.56V	243.30V	124.91V	.62V	198.79V	311.44V	765.11V	20.40V	27.23V	1,995.52V	1,669.13V	1,140.80V	191.03V
Malaysia	548	—V	—V	.01V	—V	—V	.01V	.11V	3.96V	6.93V	15.45V	23.90V	25.82V	45.93V	61.01V
Pakistan	564	—V	—V	—V	—V	.52V	.64Y	.79Y	—V	4.26V	8.76V	10.35V	11.18V	13.82Y	17.15Y
Philippines	566	—V	—V	.33V	.23V	—V	.09V	—V	.66V	.38V	.44V	.38V	.58V	.24V	1.10V
Singapore	576	.28V	58.91V	1.18V	.29V	41.94V	18.67V	7.50V	40.90V	38.53V	55.67V	62.50V	70.18V	102.98V	111.77V
Taiwan Province of China	528	416.28V	544.11V	686.20V	780.97V	894.08V	1,697.20V	1,926.15V	1.47V	2.07V	12.58V	2.44V	3.07V	5.25V	8.42V
Thailand	578	37.87V	115.24V	1.73V	3.38V	101.93V	128.87V	82.02V	18.38V	23.01V	27.71V	80.48V	39.79V	55.25V	136.07V
Vietnam	582	—V	.03V	.03V	—V	—V	—V	—V	30.85V	22.62V	30.76V	38.28V	83.82V	66.33V	—V

	Exports 2001	Exports 2002	Exports 2003	Exports 2004	Exports 2005	Exports 2006	Exports 2007	Imports 2001	Imports 2002	Imports 2003	Imports 2004	Imports 2005	Imports 2006	Imports 2007
	Millions of U.S. Dollars							Millions of U.S. Dollars						
Europe 170	**1.3Y**	**.4Y**	**—Y**	**.4Y**	**8.6Y**	**25.5Y**	**3.1Y**	**53.5Y**	**85.5Y**	**55.7Y**	**77.4Y**	**85.7Y**	**180.4Y**	**139.8Y**
Azerbaijan 912	—V	.06V	—V	—V	—V	.02V	.03V	.09V	.04V	—V	.38V	—V	.11V	.01V
Belarus 913	—V	.12V	—V	—V	—V	—V	—V	1.80V	8.12V	1.64V	.15V	2.63V	5.66V	.04V
Bulgaria 918	.01V	.01V	—V	—V	—V	—V	—V	.29V	.10V	.16V	.50V	.60V	1.07V	1.77V
Czech Republic 935	1.31V	—V	—V	.15V	—V	.02V	.35V	1.45V	.24V	.28V	2.56V	3.95V	8.66V	8.67V
Estonia 939	—V	—V	—V	—V	—V	—V	—V	.13V	1.17V	.32V	.17V	.08V	.30V	4.06V
Hungary 944	—V	.09V	.01V	—V	—V	—V	—V	.35V	.36V	1.42V	1.12V	4.08V	5.51V	4.98V
Kazakhstan 916	—V	.01V	—V	—V	—Y	—Y	—Y	....	....	....	....	....	....	....
Lithuania 946	—V	—V	—V	—V	—V	—V	—V	.13V	.21V	.99V	.86V	.39V	.40V	.42V
Macedonia, FYR 962	.02V	—V	—V	—V	—V	—V	—Y	—V	—V	.01V	—V	—V	—V	—Y
Moldova 921	—V	—V	—V	—V	—V	—Y	—Y	.22V	.11V	.63V	—V	.54V	.66Y	.82Y
Poland 964	—V	.03V	.01V	.04V	.43V	1.24V	1.09V	3.11V	1.39V	2.09V	1.30V	1.57V	3.39V	6.36V
Romania 968	—V	—V	—V	—V	.01V	—V	—V	.91V	.98V	2.37V	4.33V	1.45V	1.47V	1.75V
Russia 922	—V	.03V	.01V	.01V	—V	.04V	.72V	22.50V	55.77V	26.17V	37.95V	29.50V	88.70V	40.01V
Slovak Republic 936	—V	—V	—Y	—Y	—V	—V	—V	4.47V	.71V	.90Y	1.18Y	5.75V	8.27V	9.65V
Turkey 186	—V	.07V	.01V	.24V	8.17V	24.18V	.89V	9.20V	12.13V	15.28V	24.43V	29.53V	49.12V	52.53V
Ukraine 926	—V	—V	.01V	—V	.01V	.01Y	.02Y	8.81V	4.15V	3.49V	2.49V	5.68V	7.02Y	8.71Y
Middle East 407	**—Y**	**—Y**	**.1Y**	**.1Y**	**—Y**	**—Y**	**—Y**	**6.4Y**	**5.5Y**	**6.3Y**	**8.4Y**	**10.0Y**	**14.1Y**	**17.0Y**
Bahrain 419	—Y	—Y	—Y	—Y	—Y	—Y	—Y	.16Y	.17Y	.22Y	.28Y	.32Y	.40Y	.50Y
Egypt 469	—V	—Y	—Y	.01Y	.01Y	.01Y	.01Y	.63V	.69Y	.87Y	1.14Y	1.30Y	1.61Y	2.00Y
Jordan 439	—V	—V	—V	—V	—V	—V	—V	.04V	.12V	.09V	.18V	.14V	1.89V	1.99V
Lebanon 446	.01Y	.01Y	.01Y	.02Y	.02Y	.03Y	.03Y	2.77Y	3.00Y	3.80Y	4.99Y	5.71Y	7.05Y	8.75Y
Oman 449	—V	.01V	—V	—Y	—Y	—Y	—Y	2.57V	1.24V	1.04V	1.37Y	1.87Y	2.35Y	2.83Y
Qatar 453	—V	—V	.10V	.08V	.01V	—V	—Y	....	....	....	....	....	....	....
Saudi Arabia 456	—V	—V	—V	—V	—V	—Y	—Y	.23Y	.24Y	.30Y	.39Y	.53Y	.67Y	.81Y
Yemen, Republic of 474	—V	—V	—Y	—V	—V	—Y	—Y	—V	—V	—Y	.02V	.08V	.10Y	.12Y
Western Hemisphere 207	**175.2Y**	**51.2Y**	**145.5Y**	**460.7Y**	**1,481.7Y**	**1,920.5Y**	**2,394.3Y**	**177.3Y**	**263.7Y**	**339.2Y**	**499.7Y**	**772.5Y**	**1,126.5Y**	**1,575.9Y**
Argentina 213	—V	—V	—V	—V	—V	.01V	—V	20.06V	32.01V	70.27V	89.03V	153.19V	152.19V	182.48V
Barbados 316	—V	—V	—V	—V	—V	—V	—Y	—V	.83V	—V	—V	.02V	—V	—Y
Bolivia 218	—V	—V	—V	—V	.01V	.02Y	.02Y	—V	.01V	—V	—V	—Y	—Y	—Y
Brazil 223	175.07V	11.63V	7.54V	3.58V	.12V	464.42V	944.79V	156.15V	219.40V	258.52V	392.33V	572.44V	919.68V	1,340.06V
Chile 228	—V	—V	58.63V	391.67V	1,088.31V	1,197.46V	875.00V	.09V	—V	1.74V	3.81V	1.19V	2.91V	5.05V
Colombia 233	—V	.01V	.02V	.05V	—V	30.48V	.01V	.30V	.04V	.06V	.36V	1.22V	.62V	.86V
Costa Rica 238	.01V	—V	—V	—V	.05V	.06Y	.07Y	—V	—Y	—Y	—Y	—Y	—Y	—Y
Ecuador 248	—V	.06V	—V	—V	20.57V	32.40V	40.20Y	.01V	.66V	2.21V	.03V	.47V	.65V	.81Y
El Salvador 253	.06V	—V	—V	.02V	—V	—V	—V	.01V	—V	—V	—V	—V	—V	—V
Guatemala 258	—V	—V	—V	.01Y	—V	—Y	—Y	—V	—V	.03V	—V	—V	—Y	—Y
Mexico 273	—V	—V	—V	—V	.14V	.15V	53.32V	—V	—V	—V	—V	34.22V	24.74V	14.95V
Netherlands Antilles 353	—V	—V	—Y	—Y	—Y	—Y	—Y	—V	—V	.03V	.04Y	.05Y	.06Y	.07Y
Panama 283	—V	—V	—V	—V	—V	—V	—V	—V	—V	.13V	.02V	.02V	.05V	.05V
Paraguay 288	—V	—V	—V	—V	—V	—V	—Y	.16V	.45V	4.46V	7.46V	7.21V	22.71V	28.18Y
Peru 293	—V	—V	—V	—V	259.02V	55.33V	306.87Y	.03V	9.41V	.80V	5.37V	.26V	.81V	.72Y
Trinidad and Tobago 369	—V	39.33V	49.78Y	65.37Y	74.70Y	92.32Y	114.57Y	—V	.43V	.55Y	.72Y	.82Y	1.02Y	1.27Y
Uruguay 298	—V	—Y	29.51V	—V	38.72V	47.86Y	59.39Y	.42V	.45Y	.37V	.48V	.88V	1.09Y	1.35Y
Venezuela, Rep. Bol 299	.03V	.13V	.04V	—V	.02V	—V	—V	.05V	.03V	.04V	—V	.50V	.01V	.02Y
Memorandum Items														
European Union 998	1,643.62Y	1,929.08Y	1,153.31Y	1,106.88Y	2,966.33Y	2,453.20Y	5,167.23Y	1,350.81Y	1,455.06Y	2,367.40Y	2,219.72Y	2,745.09Y	4,203.81Y	6,059.81Y
Oil Exporting Ctys 999	.85Y	5.77Y	88.74Y	305.72Y	5.08Y	5.33Y	7.39Y	21.29Y	37.06Y	16.96Y	26.06Y	38.79Y	52.35Y	52.10Y
Non-Oil Develop.Ctys 201	1,497.39Y	1,951.44Y	3,092.12Y	5,759.73Y	8,898.29Y	4,441.84Y	8,158.30Y	1,639.24Y	1,042.81Y	1,404.78Y	3,724.87Y	4,059.71Y	4,826.43Y	4,903.69Y
PERCENT DISTRIBUTION														
Industrial Countries 101	**75.7**	**72.9**	**62.6**	**47.4**	**56.0**	**50.4**	**50.4**	**51.7**	**64.7**	**68.2**	**46.7**	**50.3**	**56.8**	**61.8**
Developing Countries 202	**24.3**	**27.1**	**37.4**	**52.6**	**44.0**	**49.6**	**49.6**	**48.3**	**35.3**	**31.8**	**53.3**	**49.7**	**43.2**	**38.2**
Africa 607	**.2**	**.4**	**.1**	**2.3**	**1.5**	**1.3**	**4.6**	**13.4**	**15.3**	**12.8**	**9.1**	**8.6**	**7.8**	**7.8**
Asia 507	**21.2**	**25.9**	**35.6**	**46.2**	**35.1**	**41.6**	**38.5**	**28.0**	**8.4**	**10.0**	**35.9**	**30.6**	**23.7**	**17.0**
Europe 170	**—**	**—**	**—**	**—**	**—**	**.1**	**—**	**1.6**	**2.8**	**1.2**	**1.1**	**1.0**	**1.6**	**1.1**
Middle East 407	**—**	**—**	**—**	**—**	**—**	**—**	**—**	**.2**	**.2**	**.1**	**.1**	**.1**	**.1**	**.1**
Western Hemisphere 207	**2.8**	**.7**	**1.7**	**4.0**	**7.3**	**6.6**	**6.5**	**5.2**	**8.6**	**7.6**	**7.1**	**9.4**	**10.0**	**12.2**
ANNUAL PERCENT CHANGE														
World 001	**−15.6**	**17.0**	**17.8**	**35.7**	**75.2**	**44.2**	**25.6**	**56.0**	**−10.9**	**45.8**	**57.5**	**17.3**	**36.8**	**14.9**
Industrial Countries 101	**1.7**	**12.6**	**1.2**	**2.8**	**106.6**	**30.0**	**25.4**	**29.1**	**11.7**	**53.5**	**7.8**	**26.5**	**54.2**	**25.1**
Developing Countries 202	**−45.0**	**30.6**	**62.5**	**90.7**	**46.8**	**62.3**	**25.7**	**100.8**	**−35.0**	**31.7**	**163.8**	**9.3**	**19.0**	**1.6**
Africa 607	**−31.7**	**196.4**	**−70.4**	**—**	**13.9**	**23.4**	**341.6**	**2.9**	**1.6**	**22.5**	**11.3**	**10.7**	**24.9**	**15.2**
Asia 507	**−49.1**	**42.9**	**61.5**	**76.3**	**33.2**	**70.6**	**16.3**	**427.7**	**−73.3**	**73.7**	**465.1**	**−.1**	**6.0**	**−17.5**
Europe 170	**—**	**−68.5**	**−90.4**	**995.6**	**—**	**195.9**	**−87.9**	**−11.7**	**59.9**	**−34.8**	**38.9**	**10.7**	**110.3**	**−22.5**
Middle East 407	**−64.5**	**66.6**	**324.8**	**−4.3**	**−64.6**	**−15.2**	**24.1**	**19.0**	**−14.7**	**15.7**	**32.8**	**18.7**	**41.3**	**20.9**
Western Hemisphere 207	**32.8**	**−70.8**	**184.4**	**216.6**	**221.6**	**29.6**	**24.7**	**35.0**	**48.8**	**28.6**	**47.3**	**54.6**	**45.8**	**39.9**

	Exports 2001	Exports 2002	Exports 2003	Exports 2004	Exports 2005	Exports 2006	Exports 2007	Imports 2001	Imports 2002	Imports 2003	Imports 2004	Imports 2005	Imports 2006	Imports 2007
	Millions of U.S. Dollars							*Millions of U.S. Dollars*						
IFS World Total	**26,543**	**25,650**	**29,566**	**34,576**	**40,351**	**46,569**	**55,779**	**20,320**	**8,990**	**13,834**	**22,445**	**28,688**	**34,158**	**44,707**
DOTS World Total 001	**26,543**	**25,709**	**29,566**	**34,575**	**40,384**	**46,455**	**54,814**	**20,320**	**8,990**	**13,833**	**22,424**	**28,695**	**34,151**	**42,348**
Industrial Countries 101	**8,214**	**8,903**	**9,739**	**10,537**	**11,952**	**13,249**	**15,401**	**9,661**	**4,404**	**5,736**	**8,629**	**10,090**	**11,430**	**14,322**
United States 111	2,884	2,957	3,134	3,818	4,572	4,116	4,345	3,781	1,804	2,264	3,432	4,046	4,294	5,352
Canada 156	225	190	216	177	303	437	347	202	65	88	130	160	185	293
Australia 193	66	95	116	124	145	135	210	59	49	63	73	136	138	162
Japan 158	351	408	344	363	304	398	666	767	314	396	612	789	933	1,200
New Zealand 196	6	10	11	11	15	14	31	19	7	7	12	14	12	15
Austria 122	4	7	8	12	11	10	17	81	36	57	88	103	119	151
Belgium 124	290	250	232	249	262	298	409	168	82	107	140	168	228	246
Cyprus 423	20	21	25	20	15	24	26	—	—	—	—	—	—	—
Denmark 128	228	208	260	289	291	292	350	79	44	68	102	110	115	165
Finland 172	49	62	84	77	59	112	142	81	32	59	74	111	129	140
France 132	273	325	346	316	400	568	605	736	262	320	586	584	909	1,061
Germany 134	455	632	721	727	871	1,126	1,221	1,052	554	769	1,093	1,303	1,545	2,131
Greece 174	66	72	117	115	70	77	122	9	4	7	12	11	7	8
Iceland 176	—	—	—	—	1	1	2	—	1	—	—	—	—	—
Ireland 178	24	31	69	46	61	93	116	79	31	42	48	72	76	93
Italy 136	853	847	931	948	984	1,095	1,387	839	312	444	623	748	908	1,072
Luxembourg 137	4	1	—	1	1	1	1	6	4	4	8	9	11	7
Malta 181	2	3	3	5	2	4	2	1	—	1	1	1	2	3
Netherlands 138	813	1,046	1,094	1,243	1,352	1,443	1,797	152	75	106	172	182	207	237
Norway 142	17	16	14	23	30	29	24	22	11	13	24	20	23	27
Portugal 182	135	131	136	131	121	80	193	42	30	35	50	53	65	86
Slovenia 961	12	3	14	12	16	28	46	6	2	4	4	5	6	11
Spain 184	1,093	1,146	1,388	1,355	1,567	1,824	2,061	712	311	392	517	571	614	813
Sweden 144	21	42	70	49	27	35	55	174	58	93	267	316	256	315
Switzerland 146	30	19	22	21	97	519	535	187	120	182	249	257	261	288
United Kingdom 112	291	382	385	407	376	491	693	407	195	215	312	319	386	445
Developing Countries 202	**17,907**	**16,529**	**19,478**	**23,533**	**27,687**	**32,378**	**39,311**	**10,574**	**4,508**	**8,004**	**13,393**	**18,273**	**22,033**	**28,023**
Africa 607	**887**	**840**	**1,084**	**1,905**	**1,821**	**2,524**	**3,265**	**258**	**86**	**115**	**163**	**164**	**215**	**227**
Algeria 612	158	114	208	452	452	538	765	3	—	—	—	1	16	19
Angola 614	18	29	64	81	139	138	166	—	—	—	—	—	—	—
Benin 638	—	1	2	3	2	5	5	—	—	—	—	—	—	—
Botswana 616	—	—	—	—	2	—	—	—	—	—	—	—	—	—
Burkina Faso 748	—	—	—	—	—	2	1	—	—	—	—	—	—	—
Cameroon 622	1	3	2	4	7	11	11	—	—	—	—	—	—	—
Cape Verde 624	—	—	—	—	2	2	1	—	—	—	—	—	—	—
Chad 628	—	—	1	—	—	—	1	—	—	—	—	—	—	—
Congo, Dem. Rep. of 636	2	2	—	17	13	35	27	—	—	—	—	—	—	—
Congo, Republic of 634	5	11	22	36	43	45	55	—	5	4	2	—	—	—
Côte d'Ivoire 662	6	7	4	5	14	12	17	1	1	—	—	1	2	1
Equatorial Guinea 642	1	1	1	1	2	1	3	—	—	—	—	—	—	—
Eritrea 643	—	—	—	—	2	—	—	—	—	—	—	—	—	—
Ethiopia 644	—	—	—	—	—	—	1	—	—	—	—	—	—	—
Gabon 646	5	2	5	6	8	12	10	—	—	—	—	—	1	—
Gambia, The 648	—	1	1	2	1	2	4	—	—	—	—	—	—	—
Ghana 652	2	7	10	13	26	21	32	—	—	1	31	16	1	—
Guinea 656	—	1	—	1	2	2	3	—	—	—	—	—	—	—
Kenya 664	43	17	7	79	26	15	50	—	—	—	—	—	—	—
Liberia 668	—	—	6	4	3	3	14	—	—	—	—	—	—	—
Madagascar 674	4	4	4	23	14	14	31	—	—	—	—	—	—	1
Malawi 676	—	—	—	2	3	5	9	1	1	1	1	2	2	2
Mali 678	—	3	—	1	1	5	2	—	—	—	—	—	—	—
Mauritania 682	1	1	—	4	4	2	10	—	—	—	—	—	—	—
Mauritius 684	21	28	21	25	26	45	26	—	—	—	—	—	—	—
Morocco 686	117	98	175	210	200	233	353	7	11	3	5	20	63	56
Mozambique 688	15	12	19	49	31	36	60	—	2	—	—	—	—	1
Namibia 728	5	5	—	3	1	2	3	—	—	—	—	—	—	—
Niger 692	—	2	2	6	8	11	7	—	—	—	—	—	—	—
Nigeria 694	60	74	70	99	108	158	303	114	21	38	15	—	1	1
Rwanda 714	—	—	—	—	—	1	—	—	—	—	—	—	—	—
Senegal 722	14	23	15	21	30	73	56	—	—	—	—	2	—	—
Sierra Leone 724	—	1	1	4	3	8	6	—	—	—	—	—	—	—
South Africa 199	312	292	333	600	491	917	999	123	33	54	91	109	119	131
Sudan 732	5	4	1	5	13	4	5	—	—	—	—	—	—	—
Tanzania 738	1	3	2	26	24	20	45	—	—	—	—	—	—	—
Togo 742	1	—	1	2	4	9	8	—	—	—	—	—	—	—
Tunisia 744	83	93	101	114	111	132	167	5	10	13	16	6	10	13
Uganda 746	—	—	—	2	1	2	6	1	—	—	—	—	—	—
Zambia 754	1	—	—	1	1	—	—	—	—	—	—	—	—	—
Zimbabwe 698	3	1	2	5	—	—	—	1	1	1	—	4	—	—

	Exports 2001	Exports 2002	Exports 2003	Exports 2004	Exports 2005	Exports 2006	Exports 2007	Imports 2001	Imports 2002	Imports 2003	Imports 2004	Imports 2005	Imports 2006	Imports 2007
	Millions of U.S. Dollars							Millions of U.S. Dollars						
Asia.......... 507	**3,038**	**3,056**	**5,005**	**5,153**	**6,409**	**6,943**	**9,498**	**2,474**	**711**	**1,515**	**2,596**	**4,018**	**5,276**	**7,658**
Bangladesh.......... 513	101	83	140	143	163	140	310	3	1	—	1	2	3	4
Cambodia.......... 522	1	—	—	1	2	2	3	—	—	—	—	—	2	3
China,P.R.: Mainland.......... 924	1,124	1,092	2,478	2,628	3,193	3,473	5,167	1,066	330	721	1,402	2,237	3,122	5,093
China,P.R.:Hong Kong.......... 532	100	83	98	108	143	170	193	43	12	22	28	33	31	34
China,P.R.:Macao.......... 546	—	—	—	—	—	—	—	3	—	—	—	—	—	1
Fiji.......... 819	—	1	2	—	—	—	—	—	—	—	—	—	—	—
India.......... 534	435	443	558	567	739	910	859	151	88	136	161	262	303	384
Indonesia.......... 536	43	72	74	248	370	317	409	105	34	68	107	144	185	214
Korea.......... 542	390	355	434	319	369	432	675	410	70	212	308	412	439	526
Malaysia.......... 548	292	218	216	276	420	532	568	143	43	85	131	173	224	325
Mongolia.......... 948	—	—	—	—	1	1	1	—	—	—	—	1	—	—
Myanmar.......... 518	—	—	—	—	—	—	—	2	1	1	5	8	10	10
Nepal.......... 558	—	—	2	1	—	—	—	—	—	—	—	—	—	—
Pakistan.......... 564	20	59	55	43	39	58	80	31	5	17	27	31	40	45
Philippines.......... 566	104	155	236	235	302	287	422	27	8	14	21	34	41	47
Singapore.......... 576	28	16	10	15	17	44	26	85	28	39	65	105	143	126
Sri Lanka.......... 524	3	9	1	51	33	3	2	4	2	3	5	6	6	7
Taiwan Province of China.......... 528	31	84	126	83	108	84	86	230	60	131	187	226	279	330
Thailand.......... 578	304	312	435	288	312	285	367	128	27	55	130	321	403	456
Vietnam.......... 582	60	72	137	146	197	205	331	10	3	6	12	22	45	52
Asia n.s.......... 598	—	—	1	—	—	—	—	34	—	4	6	2	1	—
Europe.......... 170	**289**	**374**	**614**	**939**	**1,503**	**1,804**	**1,820**	**560**	**324**	**463**	**798**	**1,056**	**1,409**	**997**
Albania.......... 914	—	2	4	3	2	1	2	—	—	—	—	—	—	—
Armenia.......... 911	—	1	—	2	2	3	5	—	—	—	—	—	—	—
Azerbaijan.......... 912	1	—	—	—	1	1	3	—	—	—	—	—	—	—
Belarus.......... 913	—	1	1	3	4	5	9	—	—	4	2	4	8	20
Bosnia & Herzegovina.......... 963	—	—	1	5	13	3	6	—	—	—	1	—	—	—
Bulgaria.......... 918	6	21	22	22	123	75	14	3	1	4	4	8	11	29
Croatia.......... 960	3	5	8	22	19	37	41	2	1	1	—	3	1	1
Czech Republic.......... 935	3	17	19	20	21	23	34	17	13	22	39	43	61	64
Estonia.......... 939	1	4	4	3	4	5	6	—	—	—	1	2	1	2
Georgia.......... 915	—	—	1	1	1	4	3	4	—	12	—	11	21	—
Hungary.......... 944	9	10	10	11	9	10	12	22	9	19	22	23	37	54
Kazakhstan.......... 916	3	4	—	1	3	17	16	2	2	2	14	21	18	11
Latvia.......... 941	3	3	4	8	30	28	—	7	27	1	27	27	23	—
Lithuania.......... 946	4	5	11	14	16	14	19	—	7	—	—	4	3	15
Macedonia, FYR.......... 962	1	—	1	2	2	3	3	—	1	—	—	2	3	—
Moldova.......... 921	—	—	—	—	1	1	—	—	—	—	—	—	—	—
Poland.......... 964	33	53	128	183	301	334	417	28	12	28	43	54	86	107
Romania.......... 968	13	9	16	14	19	36	82	15	6	9	24	28	26	42
Russia.......... 922	151	149	199	359	671	901	784	109	78	111	136	195	244	430
Serbia & Montenegro.......... 965	3	1	2	2	3	8	—	1	—	—	—	—	1	—
Slovak Republic.......... 936	—	—	1	—	—	3	4	21	3	8	12	12	18	26
Tajikistan.......... 923	—	1	1	—	1	—	—	—	—	—	—	—	—	—
Turkey.......... 186	55	78	168	235	211	243	272	31	8	11	26	43	59	76
Turkmenistan.......... 925	—	—	—	—	—	—	2	—	—	—	—	—	—	—
Ukraine.......... 926	3	7	12	25	47	49	80	11	7	7	18	28	29	119
Uzbekistan.......... 927	—	2	2	2	—	—	5	—	—	5	—	—	—	—
Europe n.s.......... 884	—	—	—	—	—	—	—	286	148	219	430	548	759	—
Middle East.......... 407	**1,450**	**1,432**	**1,306**	**1,572**	**1,732**	**1,494**	**2,213**	**148**	**46**	**58**	**98**	**91**	**140**	**260**
Bahrain.......... 419	19	2	9	10	5	6	4	2	—	—	—	4	8	1
Egypt.......... 469	347	405	447	597	559	324	577	8	2	7	18	4	16	39
Iran, I.R. of.......... 429	417	339	47	1	—	6	319	2	—	1	1	1	1	2
Iraq.......... 433	54	50	15	34	19	31	17	—	—	—	—	—	—	—
Israel.......... 436	87	62	100	175	208	135	213	76	26	39	58	80	95	125
Jordan.......... 439	121	108	72	76	68	47	25	—	—	—	—	—	—	—
Kuwait.......... 443	26	17	26	25	30	63	40	2	4	4	6	—	10	20
Lebanon.......... 446	17	33	31	33	28	28	46	—	—	—	—	—	—	—
Libya.......... 672	24	18	22	54	60	84	123	6	—	—	—	—	8	5
Oman.......... 449	35	38	35	26	44	49	25	—	—	—	—	—	—	—
Qatar.......... 453	7	8	12	8	29	20	15	6	—	—	—	—	—	25
Saudi Arabia.......... 456	57	87	137	175	233	344	372	14	12	5	11	1	—	24
Syrian Arab Republic.......... 463	101	113	133	128	163	130	144	—	—	—	1	—	—	1
United Arab Emirates.......... 466	100	112	182	190	217	159	191	32	2	2	3	1	1	18
West Bank/Gaza Strip.......... 487	—	—	—	—	1	1	—	—	—	—	—	—	—	—
Yemen, Republic of.......... 474	37	39	38	40	68	69	102	—	—	—	—	—	—	—
Western Hemisphere.......... 207	**12,243**	**10,827**	**11,470**	**13,965**	**16,222**	**19,613**	**22,514**	**7,134**	**3,341**	**5,853**	**9,739**	**12,943**	**14,994**	**18,882**
Antigua and Barbuda.......... 311	—	1	—	—	1	—	—	—	—	—	—	—	—	—
Aruba.......... 314	—	—	—	4	7	7	4	—	—	—	22	47	10	5
Bahamas, The.......... 313	8	7	1	25	20	5	2	1	—	1	1	2	2	35
Barbados.......... 316	1	11	1	3	2	2	2	—	—	—	—	—	—	—
Belize.......... 339	1	1	2	1	1	2	2	—	—	—	—	—	—	—
Bolivia.......... 218	269	300	242	299	380	380	463	21	16	23	139	269	323	221
Brazil.......... 223	6,188	4,828	4,663	5,605	6,335	8,132	10,486	5,278	2,518	4,708	7,603	10,293	11,871	14,660
Chile.......... 228	2,850	2,961	3,537	3,835	4,500	4,404	4,176	506	177	290	404	549	599	708
Colombia.......... 233	187	189	227	274	361	551	576	50	16	20	47	53	56	91

	Exports 2001	Exports 2002	Exports 2003	Exports 2004	Exports 2005	Exports 2006	Exports 2007	Imports 2001	Imports 2002	Imports 2003	Imports 2004	Imports 2005	Imports 2006	Imports 2007
	Millions of U.S. Dollars							*Millions of U.S. Dollars*						
Costa Rica........ 238	34	27	35	59	56	99	103	6	2	6	17	22	21	21
Dominica........ 321	—	—	—	—	1	—	—	—	—	—	—	—	—	—
Dominican Republic........ 243	62	70	70	108	123	149	197	1	—	1	1	1	2	4
Ecuador........ 248	103	162	136	196	265	302	345	117	23	40	55	60	72	110
El Salvador........ 253	51	10	19	57	60	95	93	—	—	—	—	—	—	—
Grenada........ 328	—	—	—	1	1	1	1	1	—	1	1	1	—	—
Guatemala........ 258	44	47	75	88	126	172	154	1	—	—	—	—	1	3
Guyana........ 336	—	1	1	1	2	2	2	—	—	—	—	—	—	—
Haiti........ 263	20	11	12	13	12	22	15	—	—	—	—	—	—	—
Honduras........ 268	7	9	10	32	48	86	61	—	—	—	—	—	—	—
Jamaica........ 343	10	4	5	10	10	17	13	1	—	—	—	—	—	—
Mexico........ 273	485	670	796	1,036	1,159	1,519	1,434	437	158	238	758	793	1,111	1,337
Netherlands Antilles........ 353	—	—	—	47	80	118	44	—	—	—	6	2	7	5
Nicaragua........ 278	2	3	7	13	47	56	55	—	—	—	—	—	—	—
Panama........ 283	36	31	60	85	70	107	133	1	1	—	—	—	—	1
Paraguay........ 288	500	341	445	522	509	621	779	303	255	295	380	453	505	1,056
Peru........ 293	394	444	414	500	600	729	958	21	14	17	33	45	52	116
St. Kitts and Nevis........ 361	—	—	—	—	—	—	—	—	—	—	—	—	—	1
St. Lucia........ 362	—	—	1	1	40	1	1	—	—	—	—	—	—	—
Suriname........ 366	1	1	2	3	4	4	5	5	—	—	—	—	—	—
Trinidad and Tobago........ 369	6	7	16	24	27	29	27	—	3	—	4	—	—	16
Uruguay........ 298	746	542	543	684	864	1,196	1,205	329	122	164	227	274	309	468
Venezuela, Rep. Bol........ 299	235	148	140	438	513	806	1,176	25	7	9	34	32	25	24
Western Hem. n.s........ 399	—	—	8	—	—	—	—	30	25	41	7	43	26	—
Other Countries n.i.e........ 910	**49**	**22**	**23**	**91**	**97**	**96**	**101**	**3**	**1**	**1**	**2**	**2**	**3**	**3**
Cuba........ 928	49	22	23	91	97	96	101	3	1	1	2	2	3	3
Countries & Areas n.s........ 898	**53**	—	**325**	**413**	—	—	—	**31**	**15**	**92**	**400**	**80**	**440**	—
Special Categories........ 899	**320**	**256**	—	**2**	**648**	**732**	—	**50**	**61**	—	—	**250**	**245**	—
Memorandum Items														
European Union........ 998	4,686	5,300	6,059	6,241	6,867	8,019	9,732	4,719	2,103	2,801	4,238	4,832	5,813	7,252
Oil Exporting Ctys........ 999	1,218	1,079	968	1,750	2,077	2,575	3,756	309	81	127	178	180	247	350
Non-Oil Develop.Ctys........ 201	16,690	15,450	18,510	21,782	25,611	29,803	35,555	10,265	4,427	7,877	13,216	18,092	21,786	27,673
PERCENT DISTRIBUTION														
Industrial Countries........ 101	**30.9**	**34.6**	**32.9**	**30.5**	**29.6**	**28.5**	**28.1**	**47.5**	**49.0**	**41.5**	**38.5**	**35.2**	**33.5**	**33.8**
Developing Countries........ 202	**67.5**	**64.3**	**65.9**	**68.1**	**68.6**	**69.7**	**71.7**	**52.0**	**50.1**	**57.9**	**59.7**	**63.7**	**64.5**	**66.2**
Africa........ 607	**3.3**	**3.3**	**3.7**	**5.5**	**4.5**	**5.4**	**6.0**	**1.3**	**1.0**	**.8**	**.7**	**.6**	**.6**	**.5**
Asia........ 507	**11.4**	**11.9**	**16.9**	**14.9**	**15.9**	**14.9**	**17.3**	**12.2**	**7.9**	**11.0**	**11.6**	**14.0**	**15.5**	**18.1**
Europe........ 170	**1.1**	**1.5**	**2.1**	**2.7**	**3.7**	**3.9**	**3.3**	**2.8**	**3.6**	**3.3**	**3.6**	**3.7**	**4.1**	**2.4**
Middle East........ 407	**5.5**	**5.6**	**4.4**	**4.5**	**4.3**	**3.2**	**4.0**	**.7**	**.5**	**.4**	**.4**	**.3**	**.4**	**.6**
Western Hemisphere........ 207	**46.1**	**42.1**	**38.8**	**40.4**	**40.2**	**42.2**	**41.1**	**35.1**	**37.2**	**42.3**	**43.4**	**45.1**	**43.9**	**44.6**
Other Countries n.i.e........ 910	**.2**	**.1**	**.1**	**.3**	**.2**	**.2**	**.2**	—	—	—	—	—	—	—
ANNUAL PERCENT CHANGE														
World........ 001	**.8**	**–3.1**	**15.0**	**16.9**	**16.8**	**15.0**	**18.0**	**–19.6**	**–55.8**	**53.9**	**62.1**	**28.0**	**19.0**	**24.0**
Industrial Countries........ 101	**–5.9**	**8.4**	**9.4**	**8.2**	**13.4**	**10.9**	**16.2**	**–21.5**	**–54.4**	**30.3**	**50.4**	**16.9**	**13.3**	**25.3**
Developing Countries........ 202	**4.7**	**–7.7**	**17.8**	**20.8**	**17.7**	**16.9**	**21.4**	**–17.5**	**–57.4**	**77.6**	**67.3**	**36.4**	**20.6**	**27.2**
Africa........ 607	**34.9**	**–5.3**	**29.0**	**75.7**	**–4.4**	**38.6**	**29.4**	**–40.1**	**–66.7**	**34.2**	**41.3**	**.8**	**30.8**	**5.7**
Asia........ 507	**32.1**	**.6**	**63.8**	**3.0**	**24.4**	**8.3**	**36.8**	**–12.7**	**–71.2**	**112.9**	**71.3**	**54.8**	**31.3**	**45.1**
Europe........ 170	**14.1**	**29.2**	**64.2**	**52.9**	**60.1**	**20.0**	**.9**	**–17.7**	**–42.2**	**43.0**	**72.4**	**32.4**	**33.4**	**–29.3**
Middle East........ 407	**14.6**	**–1.3**	**–8.8**	**20.4**	**10.2**	**–13.8**	**48.2**	**–11.9**	**–68.7**	**26.1**	**67.5**	**–6.6**	**52.8**	**86.2**
Western Hemisphere........ 207	**–3.0**	**–11.6**	**5.9**	**21.8**	**16.2**	**20.9**	**14.8**	**–18.0**	**–53.2**	**75.2**	**66.4**	**32.9**	**15.8**	**25.9**
Other Countries n.i.e........ 910	**–8.0**	**–54.7**	**5.3**	**292.9**	**6.0**	**–1.1**	**5.1**	**–6.8**	**–65.6**	**1.6**	**29.7**	**16.3**	**49.3**	**15.1**

Armenia, Republic of 911

	Exports 2001	2002	2003	2004	2005	2006	2007	Imports 2001	2002	2003	2004	2005	2006	2007
	Millions of U.S. Dollars							*Millions of U.S. Dollars*						
IFS World Total	**342.8**	**505.2**	**685.6**	**715.0**	**950.4**	**1,004.0**	**1,219.1**	**874.3**	**987.2**	**1,279.5**	**1,351.0**	**1,767.9**	**2,194.4**	**3,281.8**
DOTS World Total 001	**341.6**	**504.5**	**685.6**	**722.9**	**973.9**	**985.1**	**1,152.2**	**876.8**	**986.8**	**1,279.5**	**1,350.7**	**1,801.7**	**2,191.6**	**3,267.7**
Industrial Countries 101	**167.9**	**257.0**	**356.1**	**406.9**	**605.6**	**611.2**	**640.2**	**385.9**	**328.4**	**489.1**	**494.3**	**677.7**	**768.2**	**1,203.0**
United States 111	52.27	46.89	57.19	97.10	109.51	65.82	75.89	84.20	54.15	90.97	89.12	111.49	106.30	145.75
Canada 156	.91	1.46	3.04	8.23	11.48	11.13	5.94	6.93	2.28	5.36	8.30	18.65	10.85	11.29
Australia 193	.57	.35	.10	.75	.08	.26	1.26	2.86	1.55	1.31	1.79	1.73	1.84	7.45
Japan 158	.08	.80	.11	.22	1.12	.31	4.70	2.89	.46	16.42	12.67	23.72	39.95	104.86
New Zealand 196	.04	.09	—	.01	—	.07	.07	—	.06	.94	1.72	.29	.84	.82
Austria 122	.01	.07	.10	1.64	3.04	3.84	5.50	4.08	3.24	3.74	5.83	5.16	44.85	123.43
Belgium 124	46.49	92.27	123.83	107.93	124.60	108.85	100.22	41.78	91.11	125.99	102.34	144.25	119.98	116.44
Cyprus 423	2.67	1.29	.37	.06	1.15	.09	.39	8.20	2.46	1.15	1.66	.83	.81	4.56
Denmark 128	—	.02	.01	.02	.02	.03	.10	1.10	1.09	1.80	1.63	2.74	2.92	4.15
Finland 172	.62	.07	.09	.37	1.44	3.84	8.82	1.67	2.50	2.63	3.05	4.50	4.95	11.31
France 132	.75	1.12	1.93	1.83	2.02	4.13	9.42	12.05	12.20	17.18	18.82	47.42	71.07	150.23
Germany 134	11.12	28.16	44.42	83.18	152.11	148.03	169.68	33.96	42.86	58.83	79.17	141.36	145.33	221.14
Greece 174	2.03	1.17	5.22	.83	.81	.65	2.74	13.58	12.19	24.54	28.89	25.40	51.39	40.72
Iceland 176	—	.53	.61	1.97	—	—	—	.10	.02	.42	.34	.12	.47	.01
Ireland 178	.01	.01	.01	.02	—	—	—	.38	.40	1.24	1.52	1.99	2.83	4.23
Italy 136	6.07	11.70	19.32	28.43	25.59	28.93	30.04	29.64	36.63	44.51	44.91	60.03	86.77	113.95
Luxembourg 137	—	.33	1.15	.70	1.20	1.49	1.59	6.63	10.69	.01	.06	1.59	1.49	.52
Malta 181	—	—	—	—	—	.01	—	—	—	—	—	—	—	—
Netherlands 138	1.26	11.22	21.91	26.27	133.11	126.95	156.01	6.96	10.08	9.07	7.33	9.01	11.57	21.18
Norway 142	—	.02	—	—	—	—	—	.04	.50	.97	.71	.46	.55	1.11
Portugal 182	.01	—	.02	—	—	—	—	.46	.80	.91	1.33	.56	.70	2.24
Slovenia 961	—	—	—	—	—	.01	.03	.67	.83	1.51	1.85	4.44	4.73	6.33
Spain 184	.11	.31	1.22	.81	3.03	26.78	15.51	3.11	3.07	8.09	6.72	10.20	10.49	20.54
Sweden 144	—	.14	.20	.02	.18	.23	.24	5.37	.63	5.49	5.73	4.63	5.71	26.17
Switzerland 146	23.04	7.83	32.70	45.35	34.67	72.10	49.26	28.32	10.48	39.14	57.64	45.84	19.68	22.30
United Kingdom 112	19.85	51.09	42.57	1.19	.42	7.62	2.79	90.94	28.12	26.90	11.18	11.28	22.12	42.25
Developing Countries 202	**172.3**	**247.4**	**329.0**	**313.0**	**365.8**	**370.8**	**510.2**	**488.9**	**657.2**	**781.1**	**853.1**	**1,120.9**	**1,422.3**	**2,061.2**
Africa 607	**—**	**.2**	**.6**	**.3**	**.2**	**.2**	**.6**	**.3**	**.9**	**3.5**	**4.3**	**2.8**	**8.3**	**13.2**
Algeria 612	....	....	....	....	....	....	....	—	—	—	—	—	—	.20
Burundi 618	....	....	....	....	....	....	....	—	—	—	—	—	—	.01
Cameroon 622	—	—	.02	.02	—	—	—	—	—	—	—	—	.06	.23
Central African Rep. 626	....	....	....	....	....	....	....	—	—	—	—	—	.02	—
Chad 628	....	....	....	....	....	....	....	—	—	—	—	—	—	.01
Congo, Dem. Rep. of 636	—	—	—	—	—	.03	—	....	....	....	....	....	....	....
Congo, Republic of 634	—	—	.01	.05	.04	—	—	—	—	—	—	—	—	.02
Côte d'Ivoire 662	.01	—	—	—	.01	—	—	—	—	.94	.88	.44	1.64	3.01
Ethiopia 644	....	....	....	....	....	....	....	—	—	—	—	—	.23	.35
Ghana 652	—	—	—	—	—	—	—	—	—	.17	—	—	1.57	2.40
Guinea 656	—	—	—	—	—	—	.01	—	—	—	—	—	.08	.04
Kenya 664	—	—	—	—	—	.06	—	—	—	—	—	—	—	—
Liberia 668	—	—	—	—	—	—	—	.07	—	—	—	—	—	—
Madagascar 674	....	....	....	....	....	....	....	—	—	—	—	—	—	.05
Malawi 676	....	....	....	....	....	....	....	—	—	—	—	—	.16	.21
Mauritania 682	—	—	—	—	—	—	—	—	—	—	—	—	—	.03
Mauritius 684	—	—	—	—	—	—	.55	—	—	—	—	—	—	.01
Morocco 686	—	—	—	—	—	.01	—	—	—	.02	—	—	.06	.07
Namibia 728	—	—	.29	.07	.02	.04	—	—	—	—	—	—	—	—
Seychelles 718	—	—	—	—	—	—	—	—	—	—	—	.02	.08	—
Sierra Leone 724	—	—	.09	—	—	—	—	—	—	.27	—	—	.24	.17
Somalia 726	—	—	—	—	—	—	.03	—	—	—	—	—	—	.02
South Africa 199	—	.24	.13	—	.12	.01	.03	.16	.92	2.11	3.39	2.35	3.98	6.03
Sudan 732	—	—	.03	.19	.01	.04	—	—	—	—	—	—	—	—
Tanzania 738	—	—	—	—	—	—	—	.07	—	—	—	—	.03	.12
Tunisia 744	—	—	—	—	—	—	—	—	—	—	—	—	.08	.15
Uganda 746	—	—	—	—	—	—	—	—	—	—	—	—	—	.04
Zimbabwe 698	—	—	—	—	—	—	—	—	—	.02	—	—	—	—
Asia 507	**2.8**	**10.2**	**9.8**	**29.6**	**12.5**	**6.2**	**16.4**	**18.8**	**28.7**	**82.8**	**99.2**	**134.3**	**203.8**	**343.9**
Afghanistan, I.S. of 512	—	—	.02	—	—	.05	.02	—	—	—	—	—	—	—
Bangladesh 513	—	—	—	.03	—	—	—	—	—	—	—	—	.09	.11
Cambodia 522	—	—	—	—	—	—	.02	—	—	—	—	—	.07	.12
China,P.R.: Mainland 924	.07	4.05	4.60	21.75	9.25	.46	7.87	7.81	10.13	31.45	38.50	65.58	111.07	194.76
China,P.R.:Hong Kong 532	2.42	4.52	2.06	4.43	.24	2.15	1.30	2.23	.81	1.26	.39	.81	1.57	1.94
India 534	.07	.33	.04	.29	.37	.58	3.22	5.25	4.28	13.11	17.06	16.16	22.79	21.52
Indonesia 536	—	—	.01	—	—	—	—	.12	4.64	7.56	9.08	12.19	15.15	17.44
Korea 542	—	.95	.11	.57	.23	.76	.48	.88	2.08	9.95	9.32	13.36	22.32	58.42
Malaysia 548	—	.06	—	.01	.11	.17	.44	.46	.63	7.86	9.13	9.72	9.03	9.75
Mongolia 948	—	—	—	—	—	—	.02	—	—	—	—	—	—	.01
Nepal 558	....	....	....	....	....	....	....	—	—	—	—	—	.02	.01
Pakistan 564	.11	—	.17	.02	—	—	—	.75	.12	1.47	1.68	2.95	3.47	5.62

	Exports							Imports						
	2001	2002	2003	2004	2005	2006	2007	2001	2002	2003	2004	2005	2006	2007
	Millions of U.S. Dollars							*Millions of U.S. Dollars*						
Papua New Guinea.......853	....	....	....	....	....	....	....	—	—	—	—	—	.01	—
Philippines.......566	—	—	.02	—	—	.34	.18	—	—	.11	.12	.13	.51	1.08
Singapore.......576	—	—	—	.01	.08	—	.01	.47	1.11	1.30	1.31	1.50	2.04	4.41
Sri Lanka.......524	—	—	—	.04	.17	.01	.10	.10	.44	.66	.60	.83	.75	3.14
Taiwan Province of China.......528	—	.28	.39	2.14	.50	.08	.10	.35	.61	3.18	3.86	2.93	4.17	4.26
Thailand.......578	.01	—	2.37	.32	.80	1.44	2.53	.42	.91	2.70	3.51	3.71	6.44	11.36
Vietnam.......582	.09	.02	—	—	.74	.19	.10	—	2.92	2.15	4.63	4.37	4.32	9.93
Europe.......170	**94.0**	**101.1**	**133.0**	**131.8**	**195.0**	**225.4**	**418.5**	**268.3**	**414.6**	**480.5**	**540.5**	**723.6**	**951.0**	**1,437.7**
Azerbaijan.......912	—	—	—	—	—	—	—	—	—	.01	—	—	—	—
Belarus.......913	1.20	1.49	2.10	2.04	2.53	3.80	2.49	1.09	2.04	5.71	6.99	12.99	17.54	23.60
Bosnia & Herzegovina.......963	—	—	—	—	—	.01	—	—	—	.17	.03	.01	—	.01
Bulgaria.......918	.33	1.60	1.52	4.72	.84	1.29	46.93	6.42	49.50	49.27	53.06	27.35	41.61	87.49
Croatia.......960	—	—	—	—	.05	.01	.25	.33	.02	1.56	—	—	.29	1.01
Czech Republic.......935	—	.19	.07	.05	.22	.31	2.30	2.53	2.86	3.03	1.89	7.48	8.65	15.96
Estonia.......939	—	.26	.04	.07	.01	1.03	.48	.16	.30	.14	.36	.34	1.06	.73
Georgia.......915	12.41	16.61	18.67	29.06	46.83	54.65	87.87	18.50	31.47	10.58	13.13	19.21	35.46	46.33
Gibraltar.......823	3.69	—	.07	—	—	—	—	.06	.23	.02	.13	.35	.06	.24
Hungary.......944	.73	.18	.06	.65	1.48	.02	.67	1.69	2.26	4.30	5.68	6.57	7.00	23.75
Kazakhstan.......916	1.13	.81	1.05	1.75	2.64	3.99	7.25	.50	1.73	8.19	12.01	1.05	159.42	240.60
Kyrgyz Republic.......917	.13	.09	.11	.02	.02	.16	.15	.06	.01	.01	—	.76	.01	.02
Latvia.......941	.36	.66	.69	.84	1.83	.09	1.27	.74	.64	.43	.32	.54	.75	1.22
Lithuania.......946	.07	.07	.14	.14	.15	1.38	.20	.41	4.44	.99	.35	.44	.48	1.35
Macedonia, FYR.......962	—	.12	—	—	—	—	—	.13	.18	.16	.34	.21	.23	.22
Moldova.......921	.19	.08	.30	.18	.76	.84	2.47	.44	1.34	1.74	1.96	3.09	2.72	1.69
Montenegro, Rep. of.......943	—	—	—	—	—	—	.24	—	—	—	—	—	.42	.91
Poland.......964	.03	.11	.14	.07	.72	7.87	7.08	2.65	3.34	3.89	9.20	11.62	9.94	17.62
Romania.......968	—	.09	.02	.25	.30	.04	.71	.20	7.23	16.46	34.01	75.24	83.78	68.38
Russia.......922	60.50	64.63	94.42	77.90	119.00	121.16	201.54	173.65	192.90	174.91	159.69	242.63	304.17	494.46
Serbia, Rep. of.......942	—	—	—	—	—	.66	—	....	....	....	....	....	....	....
Serbia & Montenegro.......965	—	—	.01	.05	—	—	—	—	.21	.28	.61	.48	—	—
Slovak Republic.......936	—	—	.02	.03	—	.01	.02	.89	3.22	4.03	3.55	4.08	5.03	9.44
Tajikistan.......923	.24	.15	—	—	—	.24	.06	—	—	—	—	—	—	.24
Turkey.......186	1.13	1.44	1.15	2.02	2.47	2.37	3.03	33.76	38.23	40.89	44.80	66.93	95.42	130.63
Turkmenistan.......925	.82	2.78	3.64	.61	1.03	1.80	2.52	.80	24.98	96.78	103.07	113.53	11.86	9.54
Ukraine.......926	10.98	8.09	6.99	10.48	13.70	22.55	46.26	22.10	45.74	55.27	80.72	125.39	163.19	251.79
Uzbekistan.......927	.06	.26	.51	.85	.44	1.17	1.52	1.21	1.19	1.54	8.54	3.11	1.86	10.43
Europe n.s.......884	—	1.39	1.29	.01	—	—	3.22	—	.55	.09	.10	.15	—	.03
Middle East.......407	**72.9**	**134.1**	**182.6**	**139.7**	**152.1**	**123.9**	**72.3**	**164.9**	**191.1**	**192.1**	**177.1**	**219.0**	**234.7**	**212.9**
Bahrain.......419	.01	—	—	—	.02	—	.03	—	—	—	—	—	—	.46
Egypt.......469	.01	—	.09	.03	.02	.02	.07	—	.13	.32	.34	.70	2.23	4.59
Iran, I.R. of.......429	31.87	31.47	22.48	30.56	28.51	29.64	38.50	78.12	62.62	51.28	62.28	89.17	—	—
Iraq.......433	—	—	—	.22	.03	.42	.02	.06	—	—	—	—	114.40	141.66
Israel.......436	33.39	87.71	142.35	98.36	112.24	87.45	26.43	27.59	82.70	122.98	98.42	103.80	87.78	34.76
Jordan.......439	.05	—	.02	—	—	.09	.08	—	.01	—	—	.04	.09	.09
Kuwait.......443	.01	.01	—	.01	.22	.04	—	—	—	.01	.05	.05	.04	.20
Lebanon.......446	.20	.42	.21	.49	.15	.37	.28	5.98	1.52	.76	.96	1.76	5.83	8.28
Oman.......449	—	—	—	—	—	—	—	.08	—	.25	.49	.05	.08	.05
Qatar.......453	—	—	—	—	—	—	—	—	—	—	—	—	.06	.04
Saudi Arabia.......456	—	.05	.37	.40	.10	—	—	—	—	—	—	—	.74	1.66
Syrian Arab Republic.......463	.07	.20	.49	.73	.47	.23	.15	5.60	1.20	1.20	1.00	2.09	4.34	1.96
United Arab Emirates.......466	7.28	14.20	16.61	8.92	10.38	5.60	6.77	47.42	42.95	15.33	13.54	21.33	19.14	19.12
Western Hemisphere.......207	**2.6**	**1.8**	**3.0**	**11.5**	**6.0**	**15.0**	**2.3**	**36.6**	**21.9**	**22.2**	**32.0**	**41.2**	**24.5**	**53.6**
Argentina.......213	.01	—	.02	—	—	—	.01	.04	.89	.74	2.06	2.77	3.55	6.68
Bahamas, The.......313	.20	1.58	1.09	.32	.42	2.77	—	.73	—	—	.01	.01	.01	.02
Barbados.......316	—	—	—	—	—	—	—	—	—	—	—	—	—	4.62
Belize.......339	.01	.07	1.30	10.96	5.45	12.14	2.08	—	—	—	—	—	.01	.26
Brazil.......223	—	—	—	.02	—	—	.01	.23	15.58	20.29	23.30	29.14	14.67	26.20
Chile.......228	—	—	—	—	—	—	—	—	—	.02	.04	3.54	.55	.36
Colombia.......233	—	—	—	—	—	.05	.15	—	—	—	—	—	.10	1.15
Costa Rica.......238	—	—	—	—	—	—	—	—	1.02	.08	.02	.04	.84	.61
Dominica.......321	—	—	—	—	—	.04	.01	.14	.05	—	.10	—	.08	.05
Dominican Republic.......243	....	....	....	....	....	....	....	.30	.19	—	.67	.02	.03	.03
Ecuador.......248	—	.01	—	—	—	—	—	.01	.71	—	2.18	4.03	3.70	10.11
El Salvador.......253	....	....	....	....	....	....	....	—	—	—	—	—	.03	.15
Guatemala.......258	....	....	....	....	....	....	....	—	—	—	—	—	.03	.06
Honduras.......268	....	....	....	....	....	....	....	—	—	—	—	—	.01	.04
Mexico.......273	—	.01	—	.02	.01	.02	.02	—	—	.21	.75	.73	.71	1.24
Nicaragua.......278	.39	—	—	—	—	—	—	—	—	—	—	—	.01	.07
Panama.......283	—	.16	.29	.20	.12	—	.05	19.33	3.29	—	2.38	—	.08	1.65
Paraguay.......288	....	....	....	....	....	....	....	—	—	—	—	—	—	.13
Peru.......293	—	—	—	—	—	—	—	—	—	.46	.18	.75	.03	.15
St. Kitts and Nevis.......361	.27	—	.32	—	—	—	.01	.29	.11	.16	.01	—	.01	.01
Suriname.......366	—	—	—	—	—	—	—	—	—	—	—	—	—	.01
Uruguay.......298	—	—	—	—	—	—	.01	.02	.04	—	.06	.22	.07	.01
Venezuela, Rep. Bol.......299	—	—	—	—	—	—	—	—	—	.26	.29	—	—	—
Western Hem. n.s.......399	1.70	—	—	—	—	—	—	15.55	—	—	—	—	—	—

	Exports							Imports						
	2001	2002	2003	2004	2005	2006	2007	2001	2002	2003	2004	2005	2006	2007
	Millions of U.S. Dollars							Millions of U.S. Dollars						
Other Countries n.i.e................910	—	—	—	—	—	—	—	1.8	—	.1	.1	.1	.2	.1
Cuba..928	—	—	—	—	—	.02	—	1.78	—	—	.13	.06	.23	.07
North Korea...............................954	—	—	—	—	—	—	—	—	—	.15	—	.02	—	.05
Countries & Areas n.s..............898	1.4	.1	.5	3.0	2.5	3.2	1.8	.2	1.2	9.1	3.1	3.1	.9	3.4
Memorandum Items														
European Union.........................998	92.21	200.44	263.52	255.17	453.11	472.16	515.11	269.63	275.96	350.38	343.35	506.46	620.63	979.47
Oil Exporting Ctys......................999	39.16	45.73	39.48	40.12	39.24	35.70	45.29	125.80	110.20	74.69	85.74	122.80	149.62	180.38
Non-Oil Develop.Ctys..................201	133.14	201.67	289.54	272.86	326.59	335.05	464.92	363.14	546.98	706.43	767.38	998.07	1,272.69	1,880.84
PERCENT DISTRIBUTION														
Industrial Countries................ 101	49.2	50.9	51.9	56.3	62.2	62.0	55.6	44.0	33.3	38.2	36.6	37.6	35.1	36.8
Developing Countries............. 202	50.4	49.0	48.0	43.3	37.6	37.6	44.3	55.8	66.6	61.0	63.2	62.2	64.9	63.1
Africa.....................................607	—	—	.1	—	—	—	.1	—	.1	.3	.3	.2	.4	.4
Asia....................................... 507	.8	2.0	1.4	4.1	1.3	.6	1.4	2.1	2.9	6.5	7.3	7.5	9.3	10.5
Europe...................................170	27.5	20.0	19.4	18.2	20.0	22.9	36.3	30.6	42.0	37.6	40.0	40.2	43.4	44.0
Middle East........................... 407	21.3	26.6	26.6	19.3	15.6	12.6	6.3	18.8	19.4	15.0	13.1	12.2	10.7	6.5
Western Hemisphere.............207	.8	.4	.4	1.6	.6	1.5	.2	4.2	2.2	1.7	2.4	2.3	1.1	1.6
Other Countries n.i.e................910	—	—	—	—	—	—	—	.2	—	—	—	—	—	—
ANNUAL PERCENT CHANGE														
World...................................... 001	13.7	47.7	35.9	5.4	34.7	1.1	17.0	–.9	12.5	29.7	5.6	33.4	21.6	49.1
Industrial Countries................ 101	7.2	53.0	38.6	14.3	48.8	.9	4.8	–13.2	–14.9	48.9	1.1	37.1	13.4	56.6
Developing Countries............. 202	50.7	43.6	33.0	–4.9	16.9	1.3	37.6	24.4	34.4	18.9	9.2	31.4	26.9	44.9
Africa.....................................607	70.7	—	141.8	–41.0	–43.4	.4	234.1	426.2	208.0	286.1	20.5	–34.4	193.9	59.5
Asia....................................... 507	196.2	267.8	–4.0	202.4	–57.9	–49.9	162.3	58.1	52.3	188.6	19.8	35.4	51.8	68.7
Europe...................................170	21.6	7.5	31.6	–.9	48.0	15.6	85.7	16.7	54.5	15.9	12.5	33.9	31.4	51.2
Middle East........................... 407	102.2	83.9	36.2	–23.5	8.9	–18.6	–41.6	26.4	15.9	.5	–7.8	23.7	7.2	–9.3
Western Hemisphere.............207	....	–29.8	66.0	281.7	–48.0	150.7	–84.5	74.9	–40.3	1.5	44.3	28.7	–40.5	118.7
Other Countries n.i.e................910	—	—	—	31.3	14.3	....	....	....	8.5	26.6	–8.8	–41.5	191.1	–49.2

		Exports							Imports						
		2001	2002	2003	2004	2005	2006	2007	2001	2002	2003	2004	2005	2006	2007
		Millions of U.S. Dollars							*Millions of U.S. Dollars*						
IFS World Total		**148.9**	**128.4**	**83.4**	**79.6**	**106.6**	**109.0**	**98.1**	**841.4**	**841.4**	**847.8**	**875.2**	**1,031.1**	**1,041.3**	**1,114.4**
DOTS World Total	**001**	**148.9**	**128.4**	**82.2**	**79.6**	**106.2**	**109.0**	**98.1**	**836.4**	**841.5**	**846.6**	**874.9**	**1,030.0**	**1,041.3**	**1,114.4**
Industrial Countries	**101**	**47.0**	**54.3**	**39.7**	**33.3**	**52.3**	**48.6**	**21.0**	**674.5**	**682.2**	**681.9**	**693.9**	**820.6**	**815.4**	**879.1**
United States	111	8.02	15.63	7.55	8.30	11.96	11.64	11.04	459.79	460.25	467.76	485.82	576.05	563.78	608.71
Canada	156	.03	.06	.07	.12	.05	.03	.07	5.43	5.33	4.45	4.90	4.61	6.03	7.18
Australia	193	.19	.50	—	.08	—	—	—	.55	.34	.40	.73	.81	.42	.90
Japan	158	—	.01	—	—	—	.01	—	18.77	19.85	21.38	20.59	20.10	24.16	19.09
New Zealand	196	—	—	—	—	—	—	—	1.04	.10	.19	.05	.24	.28	.32
Austria	122	—	—	—	.02	—	—	—	.18	.21	.05	.08	.75	.58	.20
Belgium	124	—	—	.52	.63	3.87	1.50	—	1.27	2.99	.28	.33	1.83	1.04	.77
Cyprus	423	—	—	—	—	.03	—	—	.16	.14	.17	.16	.07	.44	.18
Denmark	128	—	.34	—	—	—	—	—	1.48	2.47	1.09	1.77	2.33	1.31	2.21
Finland	172	—	—	—	—	—	—	.03	.19	.01	.01	.01	.29	13.53	1.02
France	132	.02	.02	.55	.01	—	.04	—	4.79	6.14	9.44	7.85	12.06	6.73	7.63
Germany	134	.08	.18	.22	.06	.02	.11	.09	9.18	6.53	19.39	3.65	5.33	5.28	4.08
Greece	174	.02	—	.05	.07	.04	—	—	.04	.06	.07	.22	.22	.07	.05
Ireland	178	.05	.06	.18	—	—	—	—	.39	.02	.02	—	.03	.39	2.95
Italy	136	.06	.04	—	—	—	—	.01	5.29	5.90	5.36	4.78	4.68	5.31	6.35
Luxembourg	137	—	—	—	.01	—	—	—	.05	.01	—	—	.01	—	—
Malta	181	—	—	—	—	—	—	—	—	—	.07	—	.07	—	—
Netherlands	138	37.64	36.68	28.35	22.70	35.60	34.19	9.04	97.21	106.63	109.83	123.76	132.65	135.28	133.58
Norway	142	—	—	—	—	—	—	—	.38	.19	.22	.07	.04	.04	.01
Portugal	182	—	—	.01	—	.01	—	—	.21	.10	.13	.06	.05	.11	.04
Spain	184	.18	.01	1.11	.17	.07	.01	.04	6.21	4.95	4.84	4.50	8.16	6.80	18.22
Sweden	144	—	.01	—	.02	—	—	.05	1.87	4.48	4.32	2.63	1.58	1.57	.87
Switzerland	146	.01	.02	.03	—	—	.01	.01	2.04	7.28	8.79	9.72	9.16	3.82	12.39
United Kingdom	112	.66	.76	1.03	1.10	.63	1.08	.66	58.04	48.24	23.67	22.24	39.47	38.45	52.39
Developing Countries	**202**	**100.9**	**72.3**	**41.7**	**45.5**	**53.7**	**60.2**	**76.5**	**160.8**	**158.3**	**163.9**	**179.6**	**208.5**	**223.8**	**233.0**
Africa	**607**	**.3**	**.1**	**.1**	**.1**	**—**	**—**	**.2**	**4.7**	**4.7**	**.8**	**.2**	**.3**	**.6**	**.3**
Central African Rep.	626	.23	.05	—	—	—	—	—	....	....	....	....	....	....	....
Liberia	668	—	—	.02	.09	—	—	.15	—	—	.63	.11	—	.44	.02
South Africa	199	.04	—	.04	—	—	—	.02	.03	4.67	.13	.09	.11	.11	.20
Sudan	732	....	....	....	....	....	....	....	4.69	.04	.02	.05	.17	.05	.04
Asia	**507**	**.4**	**.4**	**—**	**1.4**	**.3**	**—**	**2.1**	**19.5**	**16.4**	**19.3**	**25.6**	**32.8**	**39.1**	**43.2**
China,P.R.: Mainland	924	.06	.10	.02	.04	.05	.02	.13	5.83	3.47	2.38	5.22	7.93	10.91	14.95
China,P.R.:Hong Kong	532	.03	—	—	—	—	.01	.21	3.23	2.36	4.69	3.38	3.46	5.79	8.87
India	534	—	—	—	.05	.01	—	—	.80	1.33	1.04	1.96	1.39	.85	1.70
Indonesia	536	—	—	—	—	—	—	—	.44	.42	.52	.68	.85	.92	1.45
Korea	542	.17	.18	—	—	—	—	.48	6.63	6.45	7.87	12.10	16.39	16.73	12.56
Malaysia	548	—	—	—	—	—	—	—	.89	.84	1.09	.93	.89	—	—
Pakistan	564	....	....	....	....	....	....	....	.04	—	.04	.04	.02	.04	.04
Philippines	566	.03	—	—	—	—	—	.01	.19	.27	.24	.21	.31	.28	.41
Singapore	576	.07	—	—	—	—	—	—	.64	.16	.13	.17	.26	.14	.21
Taiwan Province of China	528	—	—	—	1.33	.20	—	1.25	.42	.22	.43	.42	.21	1.00	.63
Thailand	578	—	.06	.01	—	.02	—	—	.39	.92	.93	.52	1.12	2.46	2.40
Europe	**170**	**.5**	**—**	**.3**	**.1**	**—**	**.3**	**.9**	**.8**	**.7**	**.4**	**.7**	**.9**	**.6**	**1.1**
Bulgaria	918	—	—	—	—	—	.01	—	—	.02	.02	.06	.13	.01	.13
Hungary	944	—	—	—	—	—	—	—	.26	.23	.11	.27	.34	.16	.39
Poland	964	.15	—	—	—	—	.27	.89	—	—	.01	—	.02	—	.09
Romania	968	—	—	—	—	—	—	—	—	—	—	—	.03	—	.14
Turkey	186	—	—	—	.01	—	—	—	.40	.30	.26	.32	.27	.38	.32
Ukraine	926	—	—	.03	.04	.01	—	—	.03	.05	—	.06	.02	.02	—
U.S.S.R. n.s.	930	.34	—	.29	—	—	.02	.03	.15	.12	.05	.02	.07	.02	.03
Middle East	**407**	**—**	**.1**	**.2**	**.1**	**.1**	**—**	**—**	**.5**	**.7**	**3.0**	**.8**	**.5**	**1.5**	**1.1**
Bahrain	419	—	.06	—	.02	.06	.04	—	.02	.10	.05	—	—	.02	.10
Iran, I.R. of	429	—	—	—	—	—	—	—	—	.11	.01	.41	.06	—	—
Israel	436	—	—	.08	.04	—	—	—	.37	.36	2.67	.28	.22	1.22	.91
Lebanon	446	—	—	—	—	—	—	.03	.08	.03	.04	.02	.05	.03	.03
Qatar	453	....	....	....	....	....	....	....	—	—	.02	.01	—	.13	—
Saudi Arabia	456	—	—	—	—	—	—	—	.04	.01	.06	.04	.04	.11	—
United Arab Emirates	466	—	—	.08	—	—	—	—	—	.05	.16	.03	.10	—	.09
Western Hemisphere	**207**	**99.8**	**71.8**	**41.1**	**43.9**	**53.3**	**59.8**	**73.3**	**135.2**	**135.7**	**140.3**	**152.2**	**174.0**	**181.9**	**187.2**
Antigua and Barbuda	311	.14	.81	.01	.20	.40	.06	.27	.48	.93	—	.86	.07	.01	.14
Argentina	213	—	.04	.08	—	—	—	—	4.18	3.19	5.06	5.04	8.12	8.33	5.26
Bahamas, The	313	.08	.05	.03	.06	.03	.20	—	.02	1.42	1.33	2.16	3.70	5.47	4.44
Barbados	316	.18	.18	.04	.04	.02	.01	—	.74	.60	.93	.86	1.23	.99	1.24
Belize	339	—	—	—	—	—	—	—	—	—	—	—	—	.06	—
Bermuda	319	.04	.05	.02	.01	.02	.01	.01	.20	.23	.61	.52	.50	.37	.07
Bolivia	218	.02	—	—	.11	—	.02	—	.01	.29	.15	.16	.05	.02	—
Brazil	223	.04	.01	.12	.01	.05	—	.09	7.31	8.11	10.02	14.75	18.63	20.23	20.27
Chile	228	.30	.03	—	.01	.02	—	—	1.85	1.78	1.86	1.10	2.10	1.96	2.14

	Exports							Imports						
	2001	2002	2003	2004	2005	2006	2007	2001	2002	2003	2004	2005	2006	2007
	Millions of U.S. Dollars							Millions of U.S. Dollars						
Colombia.......233	42.82	27.87	9.96	8.52	12.68	12.74	16.71	15.71	16.22	20.09	21.76	24.91	25.23	33.51
Costa Rica.......238	—	—	—	—	.02	.02	.57	2.92	2.54	2.44	2.21	2.53	1.65	3.71
Dominica.......321	—	—	—	.01	.01	—	—	—	—	—	.17	.04	.67	.10
Dominican Republic.......243	.12	.02	.13	.05	.10	.11	.09	1.85	1.20	2.03	1.60	2.41	5.22	5.29
Ecuador.......248	—	—	—	—	.01	—	—	.28	.33	.24	.21	.30	.19	.17
El Salvador.......253	—	—	—	—	—	—	—	.34	.47	.33	.15	.43	.28	.33
Grenada.......328	.06	.05	.05	.01	.02	.03	—	—	—	—	—	—	—	—
Guatemala.......258	.01	—	.02	.01	—	—	—	.28	1.54	.31	.44	.27	.05	.11
Guyana.......336	—	—	—	—	—	—	—	4.22	2.67	1.96	1.38	.82	.97	1.20
Haiti.......263	.01	.01	—	.01	.03	.08	.08	.08	.09	.10	.03	.01	.01	.06
Honduras.......268	.02	—	—	—	.05	.09	—	.46	.86	.66	1.03	1.78	2.05	2.20
Jamaica.......343	.01	.03	1.13	.02	.10	.08	.62	.80	.57	.84	.70	1.50	1.35	1.39
Mexico.......273	.05	.28	.01	—	.09	.01	.01	15.28	14.60	11.28	8.88	16.87	10.50	9.05
Netherlands Antilles.......353	12.12	10.62	9.78	8.90	9.51	9.01	12.94	27.57	26.09	26.37	24.94	27.89	33.41	31.35
Nicaragua.......278	—	—	—	—	—	—	—	.01	—	—	—	—	—	.01
Panama.......283	30.34	21.62	10.50	13.85	17.77	24.09	29.15	16.40	16.16	18.74	23.27	23.81	25.83	30.52
Paraguay.......288	—	—	—	—	.10	—	.07	—	—	.20	2.15	.26	1.58	2.26
Peru.......293	—	.04	.01	.02	.03	—	.01	3.76	2.66	1.06	1.76	1.98	2.20	2.37
St. Kitts and Nevis.......361	.01	—	—	.01	—	.02	—	.04	—	—	.10	—	—	.04
St. Lucia.......362	.10	.08	.05	.04	.03	—	—	—	—	—	—	—	.09	—
St. Vincent & Grens.......364	—	—	.01	—	—	—	—	....	....	....	....	....	....	....
Suriname.......366	.03	.09	.05	.20	.82	.98	1.66	3.03	3.17	.64	.68	.32	.51	1.27
Trinidad and Tobago.......369	.25	.08	.14	.03	.54	.67	.20	3.50	5.46	5.78	5.12	5.81	5.15	3.72
Uruguay.......298	—	—	—	.01	.07	—	—	.16	.09	1.00	1.39	.50	1.10	.65
Venezuela, Rep. Bol.......299	13.00	9.82	8.92	11.73	10.74	11.50	10.73	23.74	24.44	26.21	28.78	27.15	26.48	24.36
Western Hem. n.s.......399	.08	.07	.08	.04	.07	.06	.05	.03	—	—	—	—	—	.01
Other Countries n.i.e.......910	**.6**	**.2**	**.1**	**.2**	**—**	**—**	**.1**	**.8**	**.4**	**.3**	**1.0**	**.3**	**1.0**	**1.2**
Cuba.......928	.60	.22	.06	.17	.02	.02	.06	.79	.40	.30	1.02	.28	1.01	1.17
Countries & Areas n.s.......898	**.4**	**1.5**	**.8**	**.6**	**.2**	**.2**	**.5**	**.2**	**.7**	**.5**	**.4**	**.7**	**1.1**	**1.2**
Memorandum Items														
European Union.......998	38.86	38.11	32.02	24.78	40.28	37.19	10.81	186.81	189.11	178.85	172.32	209.94	217.05	231.02
Oil Exporting Ctys.......999	13.00	9.82	9.00	11.73	10.74	11.50	10.73	24.22	25.04	26.99	29.96	28.20	27.63	25.90
Non-Oil Develop.Ctys.......201	87.93	62.50	32.70	33.79	42.96	48.67	65.75	136.58	133.23	136.88	149.65	180.28	196.13	207.05
PERCENT DISTRIBUTION														
Industrial Countries.......101	**31.5**	**42.3**	**48.3**	**41.8**	**49.2**	**44.6**	**21.5**	**80.7**	**81.1**	**80.5**	**79.3**	**79.7**	**78.3**	**78.9**
Developing Countries.......202	**67.8**	**56.3**	**50.7**	**57.2**	**50.6**	**55.2**	**78.0**	**19.2**	**18.8**	**19.4**	**20.5**	**20.2**	**21.5**	**20.9**
Africa.......607	**.2**	**—**	**.1**	**.1**	**—**	**—**	**.2**	**.6**	**.6**	**.1**	**—**	**—**	**.1**	**—**
Asia.......507	**.2**	**.3**	**—**	**1.8**	**.3**	**—**	**2.1**	**2.3**	**2.0**	**2.3**	**2.9**	**3.2**	**3.8**	**3.9**
Europe.......170	**.3**	**—**	**.4**	**.1**	**—**	**.3**	**.9**	**.1**	**.1**	**.1**	**.1**	**.1**	**.1**	**.1**
Middle East.......407	**—**	**—**	**.2**	**.1**	**.1**	**—**	**—**	**.1**	**.1**	**.4**	**.1**	**—**	**.1**	**.1**
Western Hemisphere.......207	**67.1**	**56.0**	**50.0**	**55.2**	**50.2**	**54.9**	**74.7**	**16.2**	**16.1**	**16.6**	**17.4**	**16.9**	**17.5**	**16.8**
Other Countries n.i.e.......910	**.4**	**.2**	**.1**	**.2**	**—**	**—**	**.1**	**.1**	**—**	**—**	**.1**	**—**	**.1**	**.1**
ANNUAL PERCENT CHANGE														
World.......001	**–14.0**	**–13.8**	**–36.0**	**–3.2**	**33.5**	**2.6**	**–10.0**	**5.4**	**.6**	**.6**	**3.3**	**17.7**	**1.1**	**7.0**
Industrial Countries.......101	**–28.8**	**15.7**	**–27.0**	**–16.1**	**57.1**	**–7.0**	**–56.7**	**10.1**	**1.1**	**—**	**1.8**	**18.3**	**–.6**	**7.8**
Developing Countries.......202	**–4.6**	**–28.3**	**–42.3**	**9.2**	**18.0**	**12.1**	**27.1**	**–10.3**	**–1.6**	**3.5**	**9.6**	**16.1**	**7.3**	**4.1**
Africa.......607	**137.7**	**–80.1**	**9.7**	**52.0**	**–98.2**	**....**	**....**	**–59.0**	**–.3**	**–83.4**	**–69.0**	**13.7**	**121.0**	**–56.9**
Asia.......507	**639.9**	**–1.8**	**–89.4**	**—**	**–79.9**	**–87.3**	**—**	**27.0**	**–15.5**	**17.6**	**32.5**	**28.1**	**19.1**	**10.5**
Europe.......170	**—**	**–99.5**	**—**	**–83.6**	**–76.9**	**—**	**210.3**	**–63.7**	**–14.2**	**–39.3**	**65.0**	**22.3**	**–34.5**	**89.6**
Middle East.......407	**–66.5**	**—**	**151.0**	**–60.2**	**–6.3**	**–24.2**	**–30.4**	**–57.4**	**27.3**	**354.9**	**–73.6**	**–41.8**	**223.9**	**–25.1**
Western Hemisphere.......207	**–5.5**	**–28.0**	**–42.8**	**6.7**	**21.5**	**12.1**	**22.5**	**–9.2**	**.4**	**3.4**	**8.5**	**14.3**	**4.6**	**2.9**
Other Countries n.i.e.......910	**135.6**	**–63.4**	**–74.3**	**194.0**	**–86.1**	**–2.8**	**159.4**	**72.5**	**–49.3**	**–24.5**	**236.5**	**–72.4**	**258.1**	**16.5**

	Exports 2001	2002	2003	2004	2005	2006	2007	Imports, f.o.b 2001	2002	2003	2004	2005	2006	2007
	Millions of U.S. Dollars							*Millions of U.S. Dollars*						
IFS World Total	**63,387**	**65,033**	**71,546**	**86,420**	**105,832**	**123,293**	**141,099**	**60,690**	**68,897**	**84,716**	**103,653**	**118,783**	**132,496**	**157,651**
DOTS World Total 001	**63,399**	**65,221**	**70,900**	**86,162**	**105,055**	**121,827**	**141,450**	**60,779**	**69,558**	**84,735**	**103,724**	**119,045**	**132,842**	**157,767**
Industrial Countries 101	**30,626**	**31,846**	**35,444**	**40,575**	**47,956**	**54,693**	**62,075**	**36,901**	**41,797**	**49,596**	**58,076**	**63,532**	**65,991**	**77,973**
United States 111	6,126	6,248	6,141	6,995	7,053	7,547	8,514	11,154	12,749	13,551	15,310	16,550	18,789	20,239
Canada 156	915	999	1,099	1,419	1,369	1,212	1,520	904	961	1,169	1,355	1,425	1,680	1,713
Japan 158	12,212	12,051	12,840	16,095	21,305	23,865	26,677	7,878	8,580	10,606	12,262	13,069	12,752	15,184
New Zealand 196	3,645	4,239	5,220	6,361	6,822	6,708	7,944	2,452	2,660	3,272	3,826	4,134	4,213	5,255
Austria 122	34	20	36	49	50	57	53	261	362	501	614	742	763	844
Belgium 124	—	—	—	527	729	793	1,225	—	—	—	888	1,034	1,171	1,357
Belgium-Luxembourg n.s. 127	469	516	457	—	—	—	—	434	544	773	—	—	—	—
Cyprus 423	7	7	7	8	8	10	12	2	2	3	2	3	5	6
Denmark 128	54	63	100	120	140	153	142	290	410	513	724	723	789	822
Finland 172	223	207	304	404	469	884	1,006	390	364	421	539	637	608	751
France 132	624	794	746	737	843	923	1,206	1,338	1,768	2,502	3,077	3,805	3,191	3,950
Germany 134	756	880	832	985	1,056	1,066	1,186	3,450	3,998	5,191	6,044	6,657	6,782	8,193
Greece 174	51	26	33	41	77	33	98	55	231	92	102	110	111	131
Iceland 176	1	1	1	2	5	12	6	3	3	3	9	7	18	22
Ireland 178	96	101	111	142	117	118	191	659	844	1,059	1,335	1,501	1,409	1,762
Italy 136	1,130	1,092	1,031	1,021	1,152	1,415	1,318	1,778	2,064	2,690	3,254	3,329	3,354	4,055
Luxembourg 137	—	—	—	—	1	1	1	—	—	—	2	2	9	20
Malta 181	8	7	8	9	4	34	4	3	3	7	7	9	11	13
Netherlands 138	848	768	871	1,117	1,637	2,153	2,316	527	652	786	924	975	1,054	1,220
Norway 142	69	96	64	58	93	98	104	117	133	136	112	211	163	322
Portugal 182	30	37	40	24	35	47	34	89	120	130	135	124	103	148
Slovenia 961	8	8	8	8	9	10	14	22	27	37	39	46	46	46
Spain 184	422	376	448	486	762	892	837	388	497	682	941	982	1,029	1,534
Sweden 144	106	109	146	170	288	268	296	795	948	1,173	1,327	1,583	1,895	1,965
Switzerland 146	137	163	177	153	200	289	1,372	663	692	747	1,008	1,145	1,358	1,666
United Kingdom 112	2,655	3,037	4,723	3,642	3,732	6,107	6,000	3,249	3,182	3,551	4,241	4,727	4,688	6,756
Developing Countries 202	**31,052**	**31,953**	**34,141**	**43,920**	**55,503**	**65,322**	**77,380**	**23,619**	**27,454**	**34,827**	**45,104**	**54,948**	**65,818**	**78,515**
Africa 607	**1,188**	**1,278**	**1,390**	**1,975**	**2,352**	**2,667**	**3,035**	**533**	**695**	**892**	**1,049**	**1,444**	**1,774**	**1,510**
Algeria 612	33	42	35	51	66	77	55	1	30	—	—	—	357	119
Angola 614	2	2	3	2	2	4	6	—	—	—	—	—	50	—
Benin 638	—	1	1	—	—	1	1	—	—	—	—	—	—	—
Botswana 616	2	2	1	4	2	4	6	—	—	—	—	—	—	—
Burkina Faso 748	—	—	—	1	1	1	6	—	—	—	—	—	—	—
Burundi 618	—	—	—	1	1	—	—	—	—	—	—	—	—	—
Cameroon 622	2	1	2	1	9	2	3	—	—	—	—	1	1	1
Central African Rep. 626	—	1	—	—	—	—	—	—	—	—	—	—	—	—
Chad 628	—	4	—	1	1	3	—	—	—	—	—	—	—	—
Congo, Dem. Rep. of 636	—	3	—	—	2	1	6	—	—	1	1	—	—	—
Congo, Republic of 634	—	1	1	2	1	2	5	—	—	—	—	3	—	61
Côte d'Ivoire 662	1	2	1	3	2	2	12	8	11	15	14	11	8	10
Djibouti 611	—	1	—	1	2	1	2	—	—	—	—	—	—	—
Equatorial Guinea 642	—	—	—	—	—	1	—	—	—	—	—	—	—	—
Eritrea 643	—	—	4	1	—	1	1	....	....	....	....	....	....	....
Ethiopia 644	3	4	5	5	3	3	2	1	1	1	1	2	3	4
Gabon 646	1	—	—	1	1	1	1	—	31	—	—	101	—	—
Gambia, The 648	—	—	—	—	5	—	—	—	—	—	—	—	—	—
Ghana 652	34	31	44	69	75	70	88	2	3	3	3	5	8	7
Guinea 656	6	4	8	7	6	13	27	—	—	1	—	—	—	—
Guinea-Bissau 654	—	—	—	—	—	1	—	—	—	—	—	—	—	—
Kenya 664	49	44	19	29	32	43	44	11	12	13	11	11	12	13
Lesotho 666	—	—	—	—	—	—	—	—	—	—	—	—	1	—
Liberia 668	—	—	—	4	4	1	2	—	—	—	—	—	1	—
Madagascar 674	3	3	7	4	3	5	9	1	1	1	—	1	—	—
Malawi 676	1	11	1	—	1	—	1	6	4	6	1	8	11	7
Mali 678	1	2	8	9	9	10	22	—	1	1	—	7	15	8
Mauritania 682	3	2	1	1	9	4	6	—	—	—	—	3	—	—
Mauritius 684	69	76	66	94	77	90	72	3	3	4	4	2	3	3
Morocco 686	24	41	4	23	43	26	16	19	15	19	15	46	37	39
Mozambique 688	99	97	148	240	308	237	292	—	—	1	—	—	—	1
Namibia 728	1	2	1	2	3	3	7	4	5	5	7	6	8	8
Niger 692	2	—	1	2	2	4	3	—	—	—	—	1	7	7
Nigeria 694	21	22	20	21	22	34	28	—	—	—	—	—	—	—
Rwanda 714	1	—	—	—	—	—	—	—	—	—	—	—	—	—
St. Helena 856	—	—	—	2	1	—	—	—	—	—	—	—	—	—
São Tomé & Príncipe 716	—	—	—	—	—	1	—	—	—	—	—	—	—	—
Senegal 722	4	9	3	3	10	10	14	—	—	—	—	—	1	2
Seychelles 718	3	3	4	3	3	5	11	1	1	1	1	2	3	3
Sierra Leone 724	1	—	1	1	2	3	4	—	—	—	—	—	3	2
Somalia 726	—	1	—	—	—	—	—	—	—	—	—	—	—	—

	Exports							Imports, f.o.b						
	2001	2002	2003	2004	2005	2006	2007	2001	2002	2003	2004	2005	2006	2007
	Millions of U.S. Dollars							*Millions of U.S. Dollars*						
South Africa 199	672	709	863	1,178	1,435	1,744	2,108	446	527	746	920	1,169	1,185	1,136
Sudan 732	68	79	95	142	164	214	119	—	—	10	—	—	—	—
Swaziland 734	1	—	—	1	—	—	—	2	18	30	40	47	33	46
Tanzania 738	65	61	35	55	31	25	23	5	4	3	2	4	8	4
Togo 742	—	1	—	—	1	3	2	3	10	9	12	2	2	—
Tunisia 744	3	7	4	3	3	3	12	2	3	3	4	5	6	9
Uganda 746	7	1	1	3	2	4	4	6	8	8	5	4	4	7
Zambia 754	1	3	1	4	6	7	12	—	—	—	1	—	1	1
Zimbabwe 698	3	3	4	3	3	2	1	11	7	9	5	3	5	9
Asia 507	**24,722**	**25,623**	**27,437**	**35,794**	**46,607**	**54,552**	**64,908**	**20,499**	**24,130**	**30,516**	**39,814**	**48,468**	**58,058**	**69,235**
Afghanistan, I.S. of 512	—	2	2	5	4	15	10	—	—	—	—	—	—	—
American Samoa 859	20	41	24	9	152	8	9	79	2	1	2	2	5	7
Bangladesh 513	183	172	147	196	179	140	169	24	25	28	32	34	29	32
Brunei Darussalam 516	23	28	28	29	23	21	26	219	314	366	505	524	775	927
Cambodia 522	6	8	12	19	36	32	35	2	2	3	3	6	5	17
China,P.R.: Mainland 924	3,904	4,528	5,929	7,946	12,075	14,987	20,067	5,333	7,006	9,340	13,183	16,291	19,146	24,461
China,P.R.:Hong Kong 532	2,142	1,912	1,854	1,987	2,048	2,337	2,365	736	722	755	938	1,014	1,215	1,182
China,P.R.:Macao 546	19	21	28	31	28	36	62	4	4	4	6	8	7	8
Fiji 819	303	284	316	290	313	337	308	124	120	139	164	147	130	101
French Polynesia 887	109	145	182	109	51	55	68	1	4	2	2	2	3	6
Guam 829	9	9	11	10	12	11	11	—	—	—	—	—	—	30
India 534	1,243	1,354	2,194	3,995	5,266	6,739	7,774	409	511	639	824	928	961	1,225
Indonesia 536	1,664	1,696	1,863	2,377	2,757	3,328	3,275	1,942	2,362	2,604	2,671	2,816	3,233	4,003
Kiribati 826	17	21	19	19	23	20	26	—	—	2	—	—	1	1
Korea 542	4,929	5,425	5,253	6,665	8,252	9,187	11,359	2,393	2,596	3,105	3,611	3,959	5,176	4,989
Lao People's Dem.Rep. 544	8	11	7	17	18	19	22	1	—	—	—	7	27	5
Malaysia 548	1,336	1,244	1,355	1,766	1,915	2,079	2,643	2,012	2,117	2,820	4,069	4,666	5,148	6,182
Maldives 556	9	13	10	15	15	17	20	—	—	—	—	—	1	1
Mongolia 948	1	10	16	11	10	12	14	—	—	—	—	—	11	1
Myanmar 518	20	9	8	20	31	26	30	11	10	10	12	11	16	18
Nauru 836	12	17	17	12	10	14	19	2	2	2	—	—	—	4
Nepal 558	6	6	6	9	6	6	27	1	1	1	2	2	2	3
New Caledonia 839	118	136	136	147	214	207	285	29	26	41	41	37	64	92
Pakistan 564	222	230	237	380	360	234	360	96	111	113	114	107	116	127
Palau 565	1	1	1	1	2	1	1	....	....	....	....	....	....	....
Papua New Guinea 853	522	536	547	677	1,003	1,116	1,385	646	645	980	1,198	1,507	1,895	2,022
Philippines 566	673	624	619	712	635	774	920	262	421	517	542	565	539	671
Samoa 862	32	26	36	23	28	25	25	48	47	67	63	65	58	78
Singapore 576	2,768	2,641	2,233	2,369	3,044	3,460	3,413	2,052	2,339	2,887	4,538	6,698	7,956	8,837
Solomon Islands 813	30	29	34	36	49	59	77	1	1	3	4	3	3	6
Sri Lanka 524	177	162	105	156	137	127	117	43	48	57	58	66	70	79
Taiwan Province of China 528	2,751	2,597	2,428	2,988	4,202	4,677	5,010	1,566	1,821	2,180	2,639	2,739	3,049	3,634
Thailand 578	1,177	1,371	1,462	2,234	3,144	3,239	3,700	1,374	1,699	2,369	2,791	3,665	4,684	6,621
Tonga 866	8	10	10	10	12	10	11	—	—	—	—	—	—	—
Tuvalu 869	2	2	3	3	3	3	3	—	—	—	—	—	1	—
Vanuatu 846	25	27	30	35	45	51	60	2	3	4	2	3	2	2
Vietnam 582	255	278	275	486	509	1,144	1,202	1,084	1,172	1,476	1,798	2,593	3,728	3,862
Wallis-Futuna 857	—	—	—	2	5	5	6	....	....	....	....	....	....	....
Europe 170	**426**	**421**	**521**	**592**	**816**	**1,153**	**1,467**	**246**	**377**	**490**	**765**	**1,037**	**1,010**	**1,427**
Albania 914	3	—	7	1	1	—	2	—	3	14	—	—	—	—
Armenia 911	1	—	1	1	9	1	6	—	—	—	—	—	—	1
Azerbaijan 912	2	4	6	5	2	5	7	—	—	—	—	—	—	—
Belarus 913	1	—	—	—	—	—	1	1	1	1	1	3	30	9
Bosnia & Herzegovina 963	—	2	—	3	1	2	1	2	1	1	1	9	2	2
Bulgaria 918	11	25	44	49	57	29	45	4	7	11	14	18	18	22
Croatia 960	3	8	9	5	3	11	5	4	7	8	14	16	14	15
Czech Republic 935	50	41	45	58	50	73	78	36	58	79	112	132	148	192
Estonia 939	—	—	1	1	2	7	14	1	1	3	10	13	10	8
Georgia 915	2	3	1	2	5	5	3	—	—	1	2	1	5	5
Gibraltar 823	1	2	3	2	4	2	2	—	—	—	—	—	—	—
Hungary 944	13	14	16	12	16	18	10	49	93	89	114	153	174	279
Kazakhstan 916	6	2	2	4	8	5	12	1	1	2	3	6	8	7
Kyrgyz Republic 917	—	—	—	—	—	—	2	—	—	—	—	—	—	—
Latvia 941	3	4	4	8	7	8	11	2	1	1	1	2	3	4
Lithuania 946	2	1	5	8	6	3	5	1	3	6	9	12	25	27
Macedonia, FYR 962	1	1	1	—	1	1	2	2	2	2	1	1	1	3
Poland 964	12	8	12	20	37	21	23	24	47	64	156	260	145	245
Romania 968	29	17	39	26	36	79	120	7	8	14	23	26	21	32
Russia 922	95	89	99	121	258	506	558	12	24	25	35	77	53	104
Serbia & Montenegro 965	—	2	1	2	1	—	3	—	1	2	2	3	3	4
Slovak Republic 936	5	6	6	2	4	2	3	7	7	12	16	18	34	114
Tajikistan 923	—	1	—	—	1	—	3	—	—	—	—	—	—	—
Turkey 186	154	161	175	219	259	309	484	89	110	153	241	268	294	330
Turkmenistan 925	—	—	—	—	—	1	1	—	—	—	—	—	1	—
Ukraine 926	28	28	41	38	45	61	67	2	3	3	9	17	21	22
Uzbekistan 927	2	1	1	1	1	1	1	—	—	—	—	—	—	—
Yugoslavia n.s. 966	2	—	—	—	—	1	—	1	—	—	—	1	1	—

	Exports 2001	Exports 2002	Exports 2003	Exports 2004	Exports 2005	Exports 2006	Exports 2007	Imports, f.o.b 2001	Imports, f.o.b 2002	Imports, f.o.b 2003	Imports, f.o.b 2004	Imports, f.o.b 2005	Imports, f.o.b 2006	Imports, f.o.b 2007
	Millions of U.S. Dollars							*Millions of U.S. Dollars*						
Middle East.......... 407	**3,992**	**3,854**	**3,853**	**4,428**	**3,981**	**5,046**	**6,051**	**1,555**	**1,476**	**1,894**	**2,239**	**2,391**	**3,101**	**3,820**
Bahrain.......... 419	52	53	69	82	88	97	112	26	34	70	97	86	92	123
Egypt.......... 469	373	359	158	477	263	315	305	7	15	10	26	10	13	15
Iran, I.R. of.......... 429	388	332	169	112	132	311	163	14	21	34	21	26	29	30
Iraq.......... 433	439	363	163	346	218	92	8	—	21	28	4	—	116	—
Israel.......... 436	143	135	128	94	120	133	152	232	298	301	383	447	480	524
Jordan.......... 439	48	64	85	89	69	80	61	4	1	2	2	3	2	3
Kuwait.......... 443	251	286	364	384	360	406	447	63	87	89	83	181	165	247
Lebanon.......... 446	23	15	13	27	20	19	17	3	4	7	6	8	8	12
Libya.......... 672	21	49	6	10	12	8	15	—	—	—	—	33	—	—
Oman.......... 449	107	95	132	181	176	206	306	1	1	7	1	2	2	3
Qatar.......... 453	61	45	83	90	99	149	164	189	111	109	149	236	224	199
Saudi Arabia.......... 456	1,352	1,284	1,183	1,516	1,324	1,676	1,642	579	674	585	763	1,023	946	841
Syrian Arab Republic.......... 463	11	12	12	9	11	4	5	1	1	1	1	1	2	2
United Arab Emirates.......... 466	658	691	1,227	945	945	1,439	2,565	438	208	633	691	296	947	1,821
Yemen, Republic of.......... 474	63	68	59	67	144	112	88	—	—	20	11	39	76	—
Middle East n.s.......... 489	4	2	3	—	—	—	—	—	—	—	—	—	—	—
Western Hemisphere.......... 207	**724**	**776**	**941**	**1,131**	**1,746**	**1,904**	**1,919**	**785**	**775**	**1,035**	**1,237**	**1,608**	**1,876**	**2,523**
Antigua and Barbuda.......... 311	—	1	1	1	—	1	1	—	—	—	—	—	—	—
Argentina.......... 213	43	34	56	59	113	129	96	82	95	123	124	159	128	221
Aruba.......... 314	—	—	—	—	—	—	—	—	—	—	—	—	20	—
Bahamas, The.......... 313	5	3	8	12	5	3	3	1	1	2	2	3	3	2
Barbados.......... 316	2	2	4	2	2	2	6	—	—	—	—	1	1	1
Belize.......... 339	—	1	—	—	1	—	1	—	—	—	—	—	2	2
Bermuda.......... 319	1	1	—	6	1	2	2	—	—	—	2	3	—	—
Bolivia.......... 218	—	—	—	—	1	1	2	1	1	3	2	4	5	4
Brazil.......... 223	245	219	302	408	643	696	762	271	254	316	403	550	620	765
Chile.......... 228	69	80	80	111	138	183	169	43	49	96	75	104	112	291
Colombia.......... 233	14	17	50	27	15	26	24	10	15	16	21	21	18	19
Costa Rica.......... 238	4	2	2	4	5	12	35	7	8	13	22	22	35	50
Dominica.......... 321	—	—	—	—	1	1	—	—	—	—	—	—	—	—
Dominican Republic.......... 243	5	10	4	3	5	6	7	3	3	3	4	9	14	19
Ecuador.......... 248	8	6	9	18	4	6	7	2	2	3	4	5	10	14
El Salvador.......... 253	7	5	6	7	8	13	33	—	1	1	1	1	3	2
Falkland Islands.......... 323	—	—	—	—	1	—	1	—	—	—	—	—	—	—
Grenada.......... 328	1	1	2	1	—	—	—	—	—	—	—	—	—	—
Guatemala.......... 258	5	7	6	7	12	17	27	1	2	2	2	3	4	5
Guyana.......... 336	1	1	4	1	1	1	5	1	—	—	1	1	1	1
Haiti.......... 263	4	—	—	1	—	—	1	—	—	1	1	1	1	2
Honduras.......... 268	4	6	6	3	4	5	11	2	2	3	5	8	8	9
Jamaica.......... 343	16	16	18	18	17	24	27	1	3	1	1	1	1	1
Mexico.......... 273	210	240	295	317	633	632	554	318	280	384	506	647	792	953
Netherlands Antilles.......... 353	3	2	4	2	8	6	4	1	3	4	3	6	8	8
Nicaragua.......... 278	3	1	1	1	—	2	1	1	1	2	3	3	4	7
Panama.......... 283	2	2	4	8	12	6	10	2	—	—	—	—	3	2
Paraguay.......... 288	—	—	—	—	1	5	1	—	—	—	—	—	—	—
Peru.......... 293	32	32	35	52	52	69	71	33	42	53	41	44	59	112
St. Lucia.......... 362	1	2	2	2	1	2	1	—	—	—	—	—	—	—
St. Vincent & Grens.......... 364	2	1	2	1	1	—	1	—	—	—	—	—	—	—
Suriname.......... 366	1	1	1	1	1	2	2	—	—	—	—	—	—	—
Trinidad and Tobago.......... 369	19	16	24	18	10	17	17	1	1	3	2	3	4	5
Uruguay.......... 298	9	13	8	9	9	14	17	3	5	4	8	9	12	22
Venezuela, Rep. Bol.......... 299	7	51	4	9	15	18	15	1	4	2	1	2	2	2
Western Hem. n.s.......... 399	1	3	5	24	27	2	5	1	3	2	1	1	6	5
Other Countries n.i.e.......... 910	**14**	**15**	**5**	**11**	**7**	**6**	**13**	**6**	**15**	**9**	**18**	**17**	**21**	**15**
Cuba.......... 928	11	12	3	2	6	6	13	4	5	3	3	3	7	7
North Korea.......... 954	3	3	2	8	—	—	—	2	10	6	15	14	14	7
Countries & Areas n.s.......... 898	**1,169**	**852**	**577**	**700**	**491**	**606**	**664**	**13**	**12**	**22**	**73**	**149**	**17**	**12**
Special Categories.......... 899	**496**	**492**	**626**	**792**	**932**	**1,092**	**1,172**	**234**	**274**	**276**	**370**	**377**	**563**	**653**
Memorandum Items														
European Union.......... 998	7,607	8,124	9,991	9,600	11,232	15,096	16,081	13,851	16,227	20,366	24,613	27,581	27,555	34,442
Oil Exporting Ctys.......... 999	5,001	4,956	5,248	6,040	6,126	7,743	8,684	3,227	3,520	4,089	4,385	4,614	6,021	7,266
Non-Oil Develop.Ctys.......... 201	26,051	26,997	28,893	37,879	49,377	57,579	68,696	20,392	23,934	30,739	40,719	50,334	59,797	71,249
PERCENT DISTRIBUTION														
Industrial Countries.......... 101	**48.3**	**48.8**	**50.0**	**47.1**	**45.6**	**44.9**	**43.9**	**60.7**	**60.1**	**58.5**	**56.0**	**53.4**	**49.7**	**49.4**
Developing Countries.......... 202	**49.0**	**49.0**	**48.2**	**51.0**	**52.8**	**53.6**	**54.7**	**38.9**	**39.5**	**41.1**	**43.5**	**46.2**	**49.5**	**49.8**
Africa.......... 607	**1.9**	**2.0**	**2.0**	**2.3**	**2.2**	**2.2**	**2.1**	**.9**	**1.0**	**1.1**	**1.0**	**1.2**	**1.3**	**1.0**
Asia.......... 507	**39.0**	**39.3**	**38.7**	**41.5**	**44.4**	**44.8**	**45.9**	**33.7**	**34.7**	**36.0**	**38.4**	**40.7**	**43.7**	**43.9**
Europe.......... 170	**.7**	**.6**	**.7**	**.7**	**.8**	**.9**	**1.0**	**.4**	**.5**	**.6**	**.7**	**.9**	**.8**	**.9**
Middle East.......... 407	**6.3**	**5.9**	**5.4**	**5.1**	**3.8**	**4.1**	**4.3**	**2.6**	**2.1**	**2.2**	**2.2**	**2.0**	**2.3**	**2.4**
Western Hemisphere.......... 207	**1.1**	**1.2**	**1.3**	**1.3**	**1.7**	**1.6**	**1.4**	**1.3**	**1.1**	**1.2**	**1.2**	**1.4**	**1.4**	**1.6**
ANNUAL PERCENT CHANGE														
World.......... 001	**–.2**	**2.9**	**8.7**	**21.5**	**21.9**	**16.0**	**16.1**	**–10.0**	**14.4**	**21.8**	**22.4**	**14.8**	**11.6**	**18.8**
Industrial Countries.......... 101	**–.7**	**4.0**	**11.3**	**14.5**	**18.2**	**14.0**	**13.5**	**–11.5**	**13.3**	**18.7**	**17.1**	**9.4**	**3.9**	**18.2**
Developing Countries.......... 202	**–.5**	**2.9**	**6.9**	**28.6**	**26.4**	**17.7**	**18.5**	**–7.4**	**16.2**	**26.9**	**29.5**	**21.8**	**19.8**	**19.3**
Africa.......... 607	**.4**	**7.6**	**8.7**	**42.1**	**19.1**	**13.4**	**13.8**	**–9.8**	**30.3**	**28.3**	**17.6**	**37.6**	**22.9**	**–14.9**

	Exports							Imports, f.o.b						
	2001	2002	2003	2004	2005	2006	2007	2001	2002	2003	2004	2005	2006	2007
Asia.. 507	−3.1	3.6	7.1	30.5	30.2	17.0	19.0	−6.4	17.7	26.5	30.5	21.7	19.8	19.3
Europe.................................... 170	−6.8	−1.2	23.6	13.6	38.0	41.3	27.2	−11.4	53.1	30.1	56.1	35.6	−2.7	41.3
Middle East............................ 407	23.1	−3.5	—	14.9	−10.1	26.7	19.9	−18.8	−5.1	28.3	18.2	6.8	29.7	23.2
Western Hemisphere.............. 207	−11.0	7.2	21.3	20.2	54.4	9.1	.8	−5.0	−1.3	33.6	19.5	30.0	16.6	34.5
Other Countries n.i.e................ 910	263.1	2.5	−62.7	94.6	−37.7	−6.3	107.0	—	132.3	−40.9	104.1	−6.6	25.3	−29.9

	Exports 2001	Exports 2002	Exports 2003	Exports 2004	Exports 2005	Exports 2006	Exports 2007	Imports 2001	Imports 2002	Imports 2003	Imports 2004	Imports 2005	Imports 2006	Imports 2007
	Millions of U.S. Dollars							Millions of U.S. Dollars						
IFS World Total	**66,481**	**73,081**	**89,240**	**111,686**	**117,711**	**130,370**	**156,650**	**70,479**	**72,765**	**91,578**	**113,307**	**119,939**	**130,939**	**156,134**
DOTS World Total 001	**70,743**	**78,515**	**97,179**	**118,317**	**124,997**	**136,832**	**163,759**	**74,648**	**78,076**	**99,540**	**119,924**	**127,149**	**137,318**	**163,243**
Industrial Countries 101	**54,190**	**59,992**	**73,975**	**89,092**	**91,461**	**98,802**	**114,450**	**59,617**	**61,351**	**77,364**	**95,156**	**99,631**	**107,223**	**128,118**
United States 111	3,635	3,885	4,750	7,060	7,279	7,923	8,018	2,867	2,719	2,223	2,311	2,831	3,079	3,625
Canada 156	519	511	688	996	1,082	1,208	1,237	308	257	303	298	431	370	526
Australia 193	250	373	521	655	737	788	922	41	38	46	59	76	96	103
Japan 158	848	925	1,042	1,423	1,446	1,528	1,553	944	870	1,097	1,487	1,320	1,414	1,398
New Zealand 196	52	66	77	105	110	111	125	11	10	13	22	22	25	36
Belgium 124	1,225	1,226	1,562	1,690	2,051	2,164	2,339	1,849	1,983	2,379	2,646	2,798	3,212	3,551
Cyprus 423	34	100	55	51	58	66	88	4	4	3	52	49	98	99
Denmark 128	509	563	698	802	821	986	1,115	412	402	529	652	699	685	780
Finland 172	397	472	618	606	620	716	784	635	577	753	768	801	834	896
France 132	3,497	3,654	4,586	5,019	5,180	5,144	5,877	2,842	2,871	3,766	4,619	4,778	4,338	5,099
Germany 134	22,872	24,712	30,622	37,816	38,834	41,170	48,816	32,418	33,249	43,157	55,558	58,286	62,400	74,296
Greece 174	385	449	673	673	587	765	1,043	94	104	123	148	150	149	202
Iceland 176	14	14	18	26	38	64	51	3	3	5	8	6	7	10
Ireland 178	220	240	289	828	288	452	452	385	389	455	825	598	661	700
Italy 136	6,150	7,307	9,425	10,498	10,813	12,317	14,478	5,010	5,166	6,693	8,174	8,446	9,588	11,574
Luxembourg 137	152	136	153	368	229	245	236	152	161	209	376	345	349	352
Malta 181	24	20	23	28	39	267	64	3	3	3	5	8	9	16
Netherlands 138	1,732	1,928	2,213	2,276	2,238	2,472	2,941	3,404	3,467	4,220	4,647	4,766	5,610	7,056
Norway 142	270	278	304	393	417	522	795	45	42	57	73	61	309	530
Portugal 182	369	367	506	470	443	559	655	176	189	232	262	241	248	300
Slovenia 961	1,176	1,330	1,770	2,494	2,150	2,529	3,502	1,012	1,113	1,557	1,843	1,328	1,574	1,872
Spain 184	1,825	2,417	2,596	2,907	3,368	3,804	4,622	802	1,159	1,227	1,398	1,452	1,540	1,781
Sweden 144	809	909	1,153	1,223	1,256	1,390	1,803	892	973	1,211	1,581	1,577	1,731	2,087
Switzerland 146	3,838	4,233	5,031	5,672	6,421	6,414	7,093	3,508	3,739	5,016	5,142	5,742	6,156	8,151
United Kingdom 112	3,387	3,878	4,602	5,012	4,953	5,198	5,840	1,801	1,865	2,088	2,204	2,818	2,739	3,075
Developing Countries 202	**16,502**	**18,301**	**22,943**	**29,075**	**33,228**	**37,774**	**49,046**	**15,023**	**16,582**	**22,015**	**24,692**	**27,422**	**30,000**	**35,044**
Africa 607	**704**	**656**	**810**	**1,088**	**1,217**	**1,498**	**1,899**	**624**	**600**	**789**	**687**	**944**	**1,200**	**894**
Algeria 612	92	70	90	137	171	166	263	111	45	77	82	10	150	281
Angola 614	2	2	7	5	4	12	20	—	2	—	—	—	—	—
Benin 638	6	4	4	4	3	3	4	—	—	—	—	—	—	—
Botswana 616	4	1	1	1	4	2	1	—	—	—	—	—	—	—
Burkina Faso 748	1	1	—	1	1	1	1	—	—	—	—	—	—	—
Burundi 618	5	1	1	—	1	—	—	—	—	—	—	—	1	—
Cameroon 622	3	4	4	2	2	2	6	1	3	—	1	1	2	2
Cape Verde 624	1	1	1	—	—	—	—	—	—	—	—	—	—	—
Central African Rep. 626	—	—	—	—	—	—	1	—	—	—	—	—	—	—
Chad 628	—	—	3	1	7	6	2	—	—	—	—	—	—	—
Congo, Dem. Rep. of 636	1	1	1	1	1	3	4	—	—	—	—	—	—	—
Congo, Republic of 634	1	1	2	4	9	12	13	—	—	—	1	1	—	—
Côte d'Ivoire 662	7	7	5	7	5	7	9	1	1	1	1	1	1	—
Djibouti 611	3	1	—	1	1	5	1	—	—	—	—	—	—	—
Equatorial Guinea 642	—	—	—	—	1	1	2	—	—	—	—	—	—	—
Eritrea 643	—	—	1	1	—	—	—	—	—	—	—	—	—	—
Ethiopia 644	8	7	6	7	7	7	21	1	1	—	—	1	—	—
Gabon 646	7	14	16	18	21	16	40	—	—	—	—	—	—	—
Gambia, The 648	1	2	1	1	—	1	1	—	—	—	—	—	—	—
Ghana 652	18	12	9	53	9	11	16	8	1	1	1	1	1	1
Guinea 656	17	14	—	1	9	17	13	—	—	1	—	—	—	—
Kenya 664	6	5	6	5	9	23	17	2	2	2	1	1	1	1
Liberia 668	1	—	—	2	2	2	3	1	—	—	—	—	—	—
Madagascar 674	1	1	4	1	1	1	2	2	1	1	1	1	—	1
Malawi 676	1	1	1	1	—	1	—	4	2	8	3	4	3	4
Mali 678	4	4	7	6	7	11	16	—	—	—	—	—	—	—
Mauritania 682	1	2	3	2	3	3	5	—	—	—	—	—	—	—
Mauritius 684	3	3	5	4	7	6	7	4	5	6	6	8	6	7
Morocco 686	35	33	48	62	64	100	94	29	34	54	54	39	40	49
Mozambique 688	1	1	1	3	1	2	5	—	—	—	—	—	—	9
Namibia 728	3	1	4	1	1	4	9	—	—	—	1	—	—	1
Niger 692	—	—	—	1	—	1	1	—	—	—	—	—	—	—
Nigeria 694	74	82	98	124	130	122	225	264	286	270	207	536	646	163
Rwanda 714	1	—	—	—	—	1	—	—	1	—	—	3	5	8
Senegal 722	12	7	8	6	7	7	11	—	—	—	—	—	—	—
Seychelles 718	1	1	1	2	1	1	1	1	1	—	—	—	—	—
Sierra Leone 724	2	7	6	1	—	—	1	—	—	—	—	—	—	—
Somalia 726	3	1	—	—	1	—	—	—	—	—	—	—	—	—
South Africa 199	312	298	388	519	628	732	878	174	183	226	255	254	243	232
Sudan 732	7	10	18	23	33	116	71	—	—	—	—	1	—	—
Tanzania 738	8	4	4	6	4	11	8	1	11	22	35	7	1	5
Togo 742	2	2	2	2	2	5	3	—	—	—	—	—	—	—

	Exports 2001	2002	2003	2004	2005	2006	2007	Imports 2001	2002	2003	2004	2005	2006	2007
	Millions of U.S. Dollars							*Millions of U.S. Dollars*						
Tunisia 744	38	44	49	68	52	67	106	7	9	101	29	71	93	127
Uganda 746	2	2	1	1	1	4	9	—	—	1	1	1	1	—
Zambia 754	2	1	2	1	2	4	8	1	—	—	1	—	4	1
Zimbabwe 698	9	4	3	3	2	2	1	9	10	14	5	2	1	1
Asia 507	**2,500**	**3,080**	**3,330**	**4,451**	**5,441**	**5,343**	**6,711**	**2,596**	**2,733**	**3,422**	**4,011**	**5,073**	**5,842**	**7,421**
Afghanistan, I.S. of 512	—	6	4	27	20	16	15	—	—	—	—	—	—	—
Bangladesh 513	11	15	16	20	20	22	16	23	25	28	35	34	61	66
Bhutan 514	1	1	4	10	—	1	1	—	—	—	—	—	—	—
Brunei Darussalam 516	1	1	—	2	1	4	2	—	—	—	—	—	—	—
Cambodia 522	1	1	1	1	1	1	3	3	3	3	5	3	7	16
China,P.R.: Mainland 924	785	1,130	1,026	1,430	1,979	1,619	2,295	936	1,110	1,782	1,885	2,640	3,138	4,025
China,P.R.:Hong Kong 532	373	548	500	510	551	578	654	299	66	75	96	94	114	116
China,P.R.:Macao 546	1	2	3	5	11	13	14	7	8	6	7	2	4	5
Fiji 819	—	—	—	—	—	1	—	—	—	—	—	—	—	—
French Polynesia 887	1	—	1	1	5	1	1	—	—	—	—	—	—	—
India 534	138	191	239	375	415	513	738	113	107	135	172	198	222	275
Indonesia 536	117	100	103	141	173	157	269	67	63	76	84	85	98	97
Korea 542	283	330	395	504	608	721	854	265	367	404	613	671	673	888
Lao People's Dem.Rep 544	—	—	—	1	—	—	1	—	—	—	—	1	1	1
Malaysia 548	96	91	102	229	278	312	372	102	221	77	158	211	348	329
Maldives 556	1	—	3	2	1	2	4	—	—	—	—	—	—	—
Mongolia 948	1	2	4	6	3	5	8	—	—	—	—	—	—	1
Myanmar 518	3	3	6	7	6	7	9	4	5	6	9	9	8	9
Nepal 558	2	3	1	2	2	1	1	2	2	1	2	2	2	2
New Caledonia 839	4	1	4	3	2	3	6	—	—	—	—	—	—	—
Pakistan 564	29	51	63	73	115	156	138	35	34	35	39	36	39	48
Papua New Guinea 853	—	—	—	—	—	—	6	—	—	—	1	1	1	—
Philippines 566	84	65	186	200	286	94	100	58	50	146	151	271	128	137
Singapore 576	208	196	183	327	324	371	452	62	121	52	86	72	90	212
Sri Lanka 524	12	18	16	35	35	27	34	10	8	9	10	10	14	17
Taiwan Province of China 528	216	183	263	309	390	444	369	426	373	372	332	389	485	642
Thailand 578	94	88	166	176	170	202	257	136	129	160	245	253	296	397
Vietnam 582	39	51	39	55	44	71	94	46	41	54	79	93	112	138
Europe 170	**11,262**	**12,729**	**16,620**	**20,696**	**23,126**	**26,855**	**35,259**	**10,675**	**12,169**	**16,660**	**18,590**	**19,766**	**20,623**	**23,273**
Albania 914	8	16	20	31	53	42	69	1	2	3	3	2	2	3
Armenia 911	4	4	5	9	7	48	125	1	—	2	1	1	1	6
Azerbaijan 912	26	17	18	37	34	37	63	42	38	37	44	134	89	18
Belarus 913	38	41	66	77	119	165	200	17	28	45	52	58	63	73
Bosnia & Herzegovina 963	168	226	248	293	365	324	477	84	92	116	121	160	264	333
Bulgaria 918	226	265	345	505	601	742	1,057	107	127	202	293	337	410	316
Croatia 960	810	957	1,192	1,554	1,558	1,689	2,082	337	419	582	852	725	864	960
Czech Republic 935	1,957	2,140	2,785	3,476	3,672	4,337	5,848	1,939	2,176	3,065	3,663	3,916	4,192	5,018
Estonia 939	48	66	83	106	290	127	193	16	20	42	37	30	29	49
Faroe Islands 816	—	—	1	—	—	3	3	—	—	—	—	—	—	—
Georgia 915	13	11	15	24	20	35	59	1	1	1	1	2	2	4
Gibraltar 823	—	1	4	5	1	2	2	—	—	—	—	—	—	—
Hungary 944	3,217	3,394	3,865	4,322	4,167	4,663	5,972	3,859	3,996	5,358	4,632	3,704	3,441	4,006
Kazakhstan 916	36	49	113	138	173	218	317	182	337	244	566	632	819	1,087
Kosovo 967	—	—	—	—	14	33	44	—	—	—	—	1	2	3
Kyrgyz Republic 917	1	1	4	3	2	3	4	—	—	—	—	1	—	1
Latvia 941	59	82	95	112	137	204	247	14	15	18	22	20	24	49
Lithuania 946	58	69	144	140	188	187	230	17	19	37	35	34	39	53
Macedonia, FYR 962	54	70	68	77	84	91	117	8	7	8	8	15	19	20
Moldova 921	14	19	24	31	36	37	66	11	5	10	9	13	17	30
Montenegro, Rep. of 943	—	—	—	—	—	58	70	—	—	—	—	—	3	2
Poland 964	1,110	1,245	1,609	2,094	2,403	3,134	4,421	813	853	1,050	1,221	1,568	1,735	2,173
Romania 968	648	828	1,279	1,747	2,333	2,559	2,967	430	580	927	1,298	1,655	1,529	857
Russia 922	911	1,001	1,465	1,997	2,558	3,133	3,997	943	879	1,411	1,626	2,645	2,772	2,281
Serbia, Rep. of 942	—	—	—	—	—	615	804	—	—	—	—	—	236	369
Serbia & Montenegro 965	249	349	460	578	561	—	—	49	92	118	172	186	—	—
Slovak Republic 936	886	1,049	1,404	1,756	2,074	2,329	3,258	1,023	1,626	2,172	2,261	1,956	2,213	3,206
Tajikistan 923	—	—	3	3	1	4	4	2	6	1	5	5	6	9
Turkey 186	390	541	829	1,050	978	1,109	1,374	514	603	892	1,207	1,417	1,450	1,788
Turkmenistan 925	9	7	30	17	41	8	48	18	8	—	14	—	—	39
Ukraine 926	306	271	430	476	633	903	1,109	231	231	293	382	425	397	522
Uzbekistan 927	12	9	18	31	29	42	69	17	8	25	65	126	4	2
Europe n.s. 884	1	3	3	8	9	6	7	—	—	—	—	—	—	—
Middle East 407	**1,219**	**1,183**	**1,437**	**1,804**	**2,183**	**2,537**	**3,131**	**816**	**767**	**810**	**928**	**1,001**	**1,647**	**2,623**
Bahrain 419	16	12	24	45	27	30	44	2	2	3	3	2	1	4
Egypt 469	101	121	120	137	167	213	269	11	10	11	12	14	14	16
Iran, I.R. of 429	230	219	371	449	549	462	478	12	14	11	73	230	178	304
Iraq 433	77	82	23	52	49	37	55	170	188	39	46	—	57	509
Israel 436	146	146	148	199	193	212	288	68	82	72	82	81	87	137
Jordan 439	27	32	28	39	44	47	70	1	1	1	1	1	3	4
Kuwait 443	29	41	76	74	82	110	141	—	—	1	—	—	—	—
Lebanon 446	27	26	31	34	37	42	52	1	—	1	1	1	3	2
Libya 672	46	57	49	89	77	76	99	247	137	196	285	138	592	966

		Exports							Imports						
		2001	2002	2003	2004	2005	2006	2007	2001	2002	2003	2004	2005	2006	2007
		Millions of U.S. Dollars							*Millions of U.S. Dollars*						
Oman	449	29	17	30	54	55	62	106	—	—	2	1	1	—	—
Qatar	453	8	25	15	34	53	82	139	—	—	—	—	3	—	1
Saudi Arabia	456	156	186	257	264	386	568	598	113	151	333	373	404	371	294
Syrian Arab Republic	463	30	33	37	40	87	57	64	186	177	131	44	63	280	330
United Arab Emirates	466	290	179	221	278	362	524	701	5	5	10	9	62	58	55
West Bank/Gaza Strip	487	—	—	—	2	1	1	1	—	—	—	—	—	—	—
Yemen, Republic of	474	6	8	8	15	16	16	28	—	—	—	—	—	1	—
Western Hemisphere	**207**	**818**	**653**	**745**	**1,037**	**1,262**	**1,543**	**2,045**	**312**	**313**	**334**	**476**	**638**	**688**	**833**
Antigua and Barbuda	311	4	—	—	1	2	1	1	—	—	—	—	—	—	—
Argentina	213	87	32	54	89	98	123	142	8	43	80	71	95	126	168
Aruba	314	—	—	—	1	1	—	1	—	—	—	—	9	—	—
Bahamas, The	313	1	1	1	2	2	5	28	—	—	2	—	—	—	—
Barbados	316	2	1	1	1	2	3	2	—	—	—	—	—	—	—
Belize	339	1	1	2	4	5	3	5	—	—	—	—	—	—	—
Bermuda	319	—	—	—	—	—	—	1	—	—	—	—	—	—	—
Bolivia	218	2	2	2	2	3	3	6	1	1	3	2	4	7	8
Brazil	223	333	239	226	303	403	452	698	115	108	118	216	168	161	229
Chile	228	35	42	47	69	102	110	146	43	32	39	76	173	169	185
Colombia	233	25	30	34	45	55	96	110	4	4	3	3	4	7	5
Costa Rica	238	10	9	9	49	10	12	13	3	2	4	3	6	18	3
Dominica	321	—	—	1	—	—	2	—	—	—	—	—	—	—	—
Dominican Republic	243	5	6	4	7	8	11	18	1	—	2	1	3	11	11
Ecuador	248	6	9	8	9	15	17	26	4	2	3	3	3	3	6
El Salvador	253	8	6	5	6	7	5	7	1	1	1	1	2	1	1
Guatemala	258	12	7	10	8	10	17	17	4	3	2	3	3	2	2
Guyana	336	—	—	—	—	—	—	1	—	—	—	—	—	—	—
Haiti	263	2	4	2	1	1	1	2	—	—	—	—	—	—	—
Honduras	268	5	3	4	5	5	4	4	1	2	3	3	4	2	1
Jamaica	343	2	3	1	2	3	16	13	—	—	—	—	—	—	—
Mexico	273	161	151	213	307	335	404	534	119	107	67	88	121	132	108
Netherlands Antilles	353	5	6	6	5	6	6	8	—	—	—	—	1	—	—
Nicaragua	278	1	1	8	1	3	2	1	2	2	2	2	2	2	1
Panama	283	19	6	7	9	39	14	28	4	—	—	—	—	—	—
Paraguay	288	4	3	3	2	7	5	6	—	—	—	—	—	—	—
Peru	293	15	21	23	25	28	39	54	2	3	3	3	2	10	8
St. Kitts and Nevis	361	—	—	—	—	—	1	1	—	—	—	—	—	—	—
St. Lucia	362	1	—	—	—	—	1	2	—	—	—	—	—	—	—
St. Vincent & Grens	364	1	—	—	—	1	—	—	—	—	—	—	—	—	—
Suriname	366	—	—	1	1	1	1	6	—	—	—	—	—	—	3
Trinidad and Tobago	369	8	20	9	7	12	9	15	—	1	—	—	—	—	—
Uruguay	298	7	6	4	9	13	75	26	—	2	—	1	—	1	2
Venezuela, Rep. Bol	299	53	43	56	62	75	98	114	—	1	2	2	2	3	89
Western Hem. n.s	399	2	2	5	5	10	8	9	—	—	—	—	36	33	1
Other Countries n.i.e	**910**	**21**	**15**	**5**	**9**	**6**	**8**	**13**	**3**	**2**	**4**	**3**	**3**	**3**	**3**
Cuba	928	3	2	3	4	4	5	11	2	1	2	2	2	2	2
North Korea	954	18	13	2	5	2	2	2	1	1	1	1	1	1	1
Countries & Areas n.s	**898**	**—**	**165**	**202**	**103**	**206**	**186**	**162**	**—**	**130**	**152**	**72**	**88**	**85**	**78**
Special Categories	**899**	**29**	**42**	**54**	**38**	**96**	**61**	**86**	**5**	**10**	**5**	**1**	**5**	**7**	**—**
Memorandum Items															
European Union	998	52,100	57,752	71,528	84,767	86,861	95,225	114,825	59,572	62,379	80,348	97,631	100,368	107,439	128,293
Oil Exporting Ctys	999	1,201	1,101	1,388	1,758	2,163	2,463	3,188	990	891	1,017	1,162	1,471	2,154	2,759
Non-Oil Develop.Ctys	201	15,302	17,200	21,555	27,317	31,066	35,311	45,858	14,033	15,691	20,997	23,530	25,951	27,846	32,285
PERCENT DISTRIBUTION															
Industrial Countries	**101**	**76.6**	**76.4**	**76.1**	**75.3**	**73.2**	**72.2**	**69.9**	**79.9**	**78.6**	**77.7**	**79.3**	**78.4**	**78.1**	**78.5**
Developing Countries	**202**	**23.3**	**23.3**	**23.6**	**24.6**	**26.6**	**27.6**	**29.9**	**20.1**	**21.2**	**22.1**	**20.6**	**21.6**	**21.8**	**21.5**
Africa	**607**	**1.0**	**.8**	**.8**	**.9**	**1.0**	**1.1**	**1.2**	**.8**	**.8**	**.8**	**.6**	**.7**	**.9**	**.5**
Asia	**507**	**3.5**	**3.9**	**3.4**	**3.8**	**4.4**	**3.9**	**4.1**	**3.5**	**3.5**	**3.4**	**3.3**	**4.0**	**4.3**	**4.5**
Europe	**170**	**15.9**	**16.2**	**17.1**	**17.5**	**18.5**	**19.6**	**21.5**	**14.3**	**15.6**	**16.7**	**15.5**	**15.5**	**15.0**	**14.3**
Middle East	**407**	**1.7**	**1.5**	**1.5**	**1.5**	**1.7**	**1.9**	**1.9**	**1.1**	**1.0**	**.8**	**.8**	**.8**	**1.2**	**1.6**
Western Hemisphere	**207**	**1.2**	**.8**	**.8**	**.9**	**1.0**	**1.1**	**1.2**	**.4**	**.4**	**.3**	**.4**	**.5**	**.5**	**.5**
ANNUAL PERCENT CHANGE															
World	**001**	**4.9**	**11.0**	**23.8**	**21.8**	**5.6**	**9.5**	**19.7**	**3.5**	**4.6**	**27.5**	**20.5**	**6.0**	**8.0**	**18.9**
Industrial Countries	**101**	**3.2**	**10.7**	**23.3**	**20.4**	**2.7**	**8.0**	**15.8**	**1.7**	**2.9**	**26.1**	**23.0**	**4.7**	**7.6**	**19.5**
Developing Countries	**202**	**10.7**	**10.9**	**25.4**	**26.7**	**14.3**	**13.7**	**29.8**	**11.1**	**10.4**	**32.8**	**12.2**	**11.1**	**9.4**	**16.8**
Africa	**607**	**17.0**	**–6.8**	**23.5**	**34.2**	**11.9**	**23.1**	**26.8**	**–4.0**	**–3.8**	**31.4**	**–12.9**	**37.4**	**27.2**	**–25.5**
Asia	**507**	**6.1**	**23.2**	**8.1**	**33.7**	**22.2**	**–1.8**	**25.6**	**24.2**	**5.3**	**25.2**	**17.2**	**26.5**	**15.2**	**27.0**
Europe	**170**	**9.1**	**13.0**	**30.6**	**24.5**	**11.7**	**16.1**	**31.3**	**9.5**	**14.0**	**36.9**	**11.6**	**6.3**	**4.3**	**12.8**
Middle East	**407**	**35.0**	**–3.0**	**21.5**	**25.5**	**21.0**	**16.2**	**23.4**	**11.5**	**–6.1**	**5.6**	**14.6**	**7.9**	**64.5**	**59.3**
Western Hemisphere	**207**	**12.8**	**–20.1**	**14.0**	**39.2**	**21.6**	**22.3**	**32.6**	**4.1**	**.3**	**6.8**	**42.6**	**34.0**	**7.7**	**21.1**
Other Countries n.i.e	**910**	**–15.4**	**–29.4**	**–65.7**	**82.8**	**–40.5**	**40.1**	**62.0**	**32.9**	**–18.0**	**58.5**	**–27.8**	**4.0**	**–4.4**	**15.9**

Azerbaijan, Republic of 912

		Exports							Imports						
		2001	2002	2003	2004	2005	2006	2007	2001	2002	2003	2004	2005	2006	2007
		Millions of U.S. Dollars							*Millions of U.S. Dollars*						
IFS World Total		**2,314.9**	**2,166.7**	**2,590.1**	**3,615.4**	**4,347.2**	**6,372.2**	**6,058.3**	**1,430.9**	**1,665.5**	**2,625.7**	**3,515.9**	**4,211.3**	**5,266.7**	**5,712.2**
DOTS World Total	**001**	**2,314.9**	**2,166.7**	**2,590.1**	**3,615.4**	**4,347.2**	**6,372.2**	**6,058.3**	**1,430.9**	**1,665.5**	**2,625.7**	**3,515.9**	**4,211.3**	**5,266.7**	**5,712.2**
Industrial Countries	**101**	**1,728.1**	**1,572.5**	**1,811.5**	**1,850.1**	**2,055.1**	**3,645.5**	**1,869.0**	**605.9**	**596.7**	**1,162.9**	**1,547.3**	**1,498.5**	**1,993.6**	**2,226.5**
United States	111	13.66	51.97	63.86	25.99	43.20	98.19	289.17	230.93	98.70	132.62	131.89	141.41	197.99	268.91
Canada	156	.55	.30	.32	.24	.31	.72	2.26	1.58	2.52	22.13	15.39	13.87	25.68	21.45
Australia	193	.01	—	.09	.09	.01	.02	.12	1.18	2.55	5.71	10.89	8.14	8.42	7.06
Japan	158	.19	.26	19.80	.35	.02	.04	—	66.66	48.44	101.49	127.12	70.61	188.29	295.09
New Zealand	196	—	—	—	.01	—	—	2.52	8.52	9.02	7.94	5.91	2.85	4.10	6.68
Austria	122	.06	.01	.43	1.12	1.57	2.13	2.54	20.26	15.18	8.17	17.18	24.40	40.43	46.62
Belgium	124	.62	1.22	1.43	.69	6.31	9.54	14.82	19.99	10.91	25.66	30.85	17.23	29.90	42.47
Cyprus	423	—	.22	3.82	7.73	3.82	27.00	34.39	.16	.22	.41	.15	.41	.19	.85
Denmark	128	.07	.06	.03	.11	.07	.05	.22	6.34	4.81	6.76	5.66	6.38	13.14	15.19
Finland	172	.06	—	.06	.03	.14	—	.08	5.43	8.11	6.81	6.89	26.53	167.73	151.49
France	132	66.47	166.28	209.73	66.89	406.72	347.58	258.84	26.14	118.11	155.95	120.13	121.81	55.84	103.80
Germany	134	12.86	28.77	7.31	37.60	34.80	9.00	19.73	72.84	83.45	169.90	198.48	256.34	403.82	471.20
Greece	174	50.83	54.12	71.43	20.23	95.67	181.98	115.06	8.42	5.42	7.77	4.53	5.03	5.37	30.78
Iceland	176	85.85	—	—	—	—	—	—	.01	.06	.04	—	.23	7.34	.02
Ireland	178	.02	—	—	.08	—	.01	.01	2.36	1.64	3.96	8.34	7.76	8.58	9.19
Italy	136	1,324.07	1,082.72	1,345.95	1,614.86	1,315.74	2,845.41	940.93	24.67	26.36	73.98	106.75	94.61	124.68	140.94
Luxembourg	137	—	4.54	7.73	13.54	5.83	—	—	.18	.55	1.43	2.39	1.27	1.58	1.58
Malta	181	8.67	30.17	12.51	15.98	41.69	22.44	119.64	.20	—	—	—	.11	.13	.48
Netherlands	138	15.61	9.58	6.37	14.32	2.80	14.64	7.35	13.38	15.90	43.96	152.66	160.44	90.94	100.74
Norway	142	1.80	1.03	2.26	1.17	1.61	.69	.07	3.65	20.24	33.63	73.22	29.94	14.70	14.06
Portugal	182	—	2.98	.03	2.93	8.55	19.22	—	2.50	1.93	.27	1.90	6.23	3.15	5.09
Slovenia	961	1.69	4.81	7.08	11.45	3.76	3.46	—	.90	.33	.90	.65	.88	1.75	5.50
Spain	184	101.82	103.99	43.33	5.61	75.98	52.84	52.83	3.35	10.27	9.27	11.01	17.62	16.18	18.52
Sweden	144	.06	—	.01	.01	.28	.08	.08	13.91	5.63	40.89	66.57	72.40	84.37	13.65
Switzerland	146	7.72	20.37	.30	2.49	1.71	4.83	5.25	18.35	21.11	17.08	26.93	27.01	45.55	43.82
United Kingdom	112	35.44	9.09	7.66	6.60	4.50	5.60	3.08	53.96	85.24	286.12	421.81	384.95	453.77	411.33
Developing Countries	**202**	**584.8**	**593.5**	**777.3**	**1,764.6**	**2,291.7**	**2,726.2**	**4,189.1**	**824.9**	**1,068.3**	**1,462.2**	**1,968.4**	**2,712.1**	**3,272.9**	**3,485.6**
Africa	**607**	**27.1**	**5.0**	**.5**	**8.4**	**1.8**	**15.6**	**1.4**	**3.8**	**4.9**	**1.3**	**25.1**	**52.2**	**46.2**	**15.1**
Algeria	612	.06	—	.18	—	—	—	—	—	.06	—	—	.01	.01	.03
Angola	614	.09	.03	—	.34	—	.10	.01	—	.07	—	—	.01	.02	.03
Botswana	616	—	—	—	—	—	—	—	.02	—	—	—	—	—	—
Cameroon	622	.06	.04	—	—	—	—	—	—	—	.01	—	—	.01	—
Central African Rep.	626	—	—	—	—	—	—	—	—	.04	—	.05	.02	—	—
Congo, Dem. Rep. of	636	—	—	—	—	—	—	.08	—	—	—	—	—	—	.05
Congo, Republic of	634	—	.06	—	.03	—	—	—	—	—	—	—	.01	—	—
Côte d'Ivoire	662	—	—	—	—	—	—	—	.01	—	—	—	.01	—	—
Djibouti	611	—	.18	—	—	—	—	—	—	—	—	—	—	—	—
Equatorial Guinea	642	—	.26	.10	—	—	—	—	.01	—	—	—	—	.02	—
Eritrea	643	....	....	....	....	....	....	....	.16	.01	.01	.15	—	—	—
Ethiopia	644	—	—	—	—	—	—	—	.01	—	—	—	—	—	—
Gabon	646	—	—	—	—	—	—	—	—	—	—	—	—	.01	—
Ghana	652	—	3.78	—	—	—	—	—	—	—	—	—	—	—	—
Guinea	656	—	—	.16	—	.68	—	—	.18	—	—	24.12	32.47	40.43	11.67
Kenya	664	—	—	—	—	—	—	—	—	—	—	.13	.09	.19	.26
Malawi	676	—	—	—	—	—	—	—	—	.08	.01	—	—	.02	.07
Mauritania	682	—	—	—	—	—	.03	—	—	—	—	—	—	—	—
Morocco	686	24.28	—	—	—	.02	—	—	.02	.01	.01	.02	.24	.83	.56
Mozambique	688	....	....	....	....	....	....	....	—	—	—	—	—	—	.06
Niger	692	—	.28	—	—	—	—	—	—	—	—	—	—	—	—
Nigeria	694	.60	.39	—	—	.99	.06	—	.01	—	.01	.02	—	—	—
Senegal	722	—	—	—	7.73	—	—	—	—	—	—	—	—	—	—
Seychelles	718	—	—	—	.03	—	—	—	—	—	.03	.02	1.26	—	.05
Sierra Leone	724	—	.02	—	—	—	—	—	—	—	—	—	—	—	.04
South Africa	199	.05	—	.09	.01	—	—	—	.02	1.62	.40	.45	17.81	4.27	1.94
Sudan	732	—	—	—	—	.11	.02	1.16	—	—	—	—	—	—	—
Tanzania	738	—	—	—	—	—	—	—	—	.55	.01	—	—	—	—
Tunisia	744	1.93	—	—	.23	—	15.42	.16	—	—	.01	.01	.02	.01	—
Zimbabwe	698	—	—	—	—	—	—	—	3.50	2.50	.83	.26	.22	.35	.36
Asia	**507**	**9.0**	**8.3**	**29.8**	**193.7**	**249.8**	**228.6**	**791.2**	**92.9**	**134.2**	**282.6**	**368.4**	**700.3**	**362.0**	**499.7**
Afghanistan, I.S. of	512	.19	.69	.61	2.19	11.68	32.21	47.58	—	—	—	—	—	—	—
American Samoa	859	—	—	—	—	—	—	—	—	—	—	—	—	.04	—
Bangladesh	513	—	—	—	—	—	—	—	.02	.01	—	.06	.03	.02	—
Brunei Darussalam	516	.01	—	—	—	—	—	—	—	—	—	—	—	—	—
Cambodia	522	—	.01	—	—	—	—	—	—	—	—	—	—	—	—
China,P.R.: Mainland	924	2.44	1.31	19.29	31.72	99.24	6.39	10.10	41.99	51.02	92.39	145.50	173.81	222.49	278.79
China,P.R.:Hong Kong	532	.07	.04	7.21	18.07	12.65	50.63	45.76	—	.04	—	.06	1.68	1.15	.29
French Polynesia	887	—	—	—	—	—	—	—	—	.05	—	—	—	—	—
India	534	.80	2.25	1.31	5.39	1.63	1.01	144.95	15.10	19.42	35.40	47.02	55.89	57.45	71.98
Indonesia	536	.01	—	.03	129.36	—	.01	390.29	.27	.34	15.96	1.66	2.04	2.24	6.01

		Exports							Imports						
		2001	2002	2003	2004	2005	2006	2007	2001	2002	2003	2004	2005	2006	2007
		Millions of U.S. Dollars							Millions of U.S. Dollars						
Korea	542	1.19	—	.97	3.79	.49	68.35	124.77	5.54	7.29	15.96	24.13	41.63	46.93	91.56
Lao People's Dem.Rep.	544	—	.11	—	.23	—	—	—	—	—	—	—	—	—	—
Malaysia	548	—	—	—	.02	.25	—	.04	2.40	4.21	100.28	125.40	22.45	4.07	16.53
Mongolia	948	.32	—	—	—	.06	.01	.02	—	—	—	—	.05	.10	—
Nauru	836	—	—	—	—	—	—	—	—	—	—	.01	—	—	—
Nepal	558	—	—	—	—	—	—	.10	—	—	—	—	—	—	—
New Caledonia	839	—	—	—	—	—	—	—	—	—	—	—	—	.02	—
Pakistan	564	3.58	2.53	.02	—	.68	.93	1.24	.76	1.05	1.11	1.59	2.27	1.46	2.49
Philippines	566	—	—	—	—	—	—	.02	—	.06	.05	.09	.13	.32	.40
Singapore	576	.03	.82	.10	2.77	123.09	33.97	9.23	3.06	34.64	10.37	8.91	384.88	6.17	8.68
Sri Lanka	524	.01	—	.07	.01	—	.01	—	18.31	10.72	6.01	9.07	8.65	9.08	10.23
Taiwan Province of China	528	.01	—	—	.02	—	.01	.03	3.50	2.32	1.43	1.15	2.08	2.67	3.75
Thailand	578	—	.30	—	.06	.01	34.79	.01	1.90	3.04	3.09	3.22	3.70	7.72	8.59
Tuvalu	869	—	—	—	—	—	—	—	—	—	.10	—	—	—	—
Vietnam	582	.32	.24	.18	.05	.07	.25	17.08	.02	.01	.48	.52	.98	.06	.34
Europe	**170**	**336.0**	**376.5**	**537.2**	**1,064.2**	**1,605.0**	**1,452.2**	**2,343.1**	**631.5**	**831.1**	**1,082.7**	**1,475.3**	**1,817.2**	**2,609.1**	**2,633.8**
Albania	914	—	—	—	1.65	—	.64	11.19	—	—	.04	—	—	—	—
Belarus	913	1.03	.91	.95	.79	1.17	1.47	2.32	4.62	3.17	6.21	10.95	18.12	20.69	76.97
Bosnia & Herzegovina	963	.30	—	—	—	—	—	—	.08	—	—	—	—	.08	.04
Bulgaria	918	1.79	2.59	13.93	49.31	100.86	6.31	5.69	12.15	6.68	4.80	5.58	4.55	15.47	10.18
Croatia	960	24.35	7.28	61.08	109.17	176.91	3.56	39.86	2.31	.13	.14	.87	.44	1.55	1.01
Czech Republic	935	.06	.15	.68	.24	.79	.04	.37	2.05	1.91	9.83	5.27	17.63	25.49	19.50
Estonia	939	.26	.02	.18	.10	1.46	.53	.50	.23	.24	.38	1.27	1.08	1.65	14.56
Georgia	915	103.24	80.83	110.06	188.78	208.44	285.28	343.82	4.93	12.74	10.23	14.49	45.50	49.20	62.93
Gibraltar	823	3.04	.09	—	.65	5.90	27.77	28.74	.07	.14	.04	.11	.18	.37	.22
Hungary	944	—	—	—	—	—	.01	—	3.77	2.01	3.12	2.49	4.82	10.41	12.16
Kazakhstan	916	6.62	11.57	10.13	9.42	17.17	105.66	127.59	99.54	149.79	138.71	236.74	95.35	127.25	222.29
Kyrgyz Republic	917	.26	1.10	.18	.34	1.84	7.03	2.70	1.36	.68	.79	1.39	1.53	.47	.92
Latvia	941	2.68	2.54	11.12	11.52	5.37	8.38	3.61	.56	.57	.88	2.86	1.51	1.88	1.71
Lithuania	946	1.24	3.12	4.87	6.05	4.94	2.77	5.11	1.18	.74	1.52	2.26	2.03	3.97	11.83
Macedonia, FYR	962	—	—	—	—	—	—	—	—	—	.08	.22	.24	.26	.46
Moldova	921	.07	.16	.14	.14	.20	.34	.11	.34	1.64	1.13	3.08	2.71	4.67	9.80
Poland	964	1.51	1.64	2.83	2.64	7.37	4.07	3.79	11.77	7.13	8.94	19.24	15.36	22.48	27.80
Romania	968	9.04	28.35	1.64	82.30	119.12	80.12	85.40	3.74	3.93	6.18	8.03	5.55	39.26	3.02
Russia	922	77.56	95.69	147.88	209.76	285.42	344.26	527.12	152.99	280.94	383.90	569.46	717.22	1,181.58	1,003.89
Serbia & Montenegro	965	—	—	—	—	—	—	—	—	—	—	—	—	.75	.22
Slovak Republic	936	.27	.99	.98	.71	.96	.16	.04	.22	.57	.25	1.48	1.30	2.24	4.03
Tajikistan	923	12.11	27.98	34.44	46.49	78.94	130.90	51.56	.86	.42	.98	.01	.11	.29	.51
Turkey	186	67.38	83.40	107.04	182.59	275.96	388.14	1,056.32	148.17	156.22	195.25	225.00	313.00	385.04	624.69
Turkmenistan	925	12.05	8.67	5.83	143.42	273.58	9.52	13.60	135.17	119.78	188.36	114.44	242.95	369.01	40.29
Ukraine	926	6.84	12.98	21.20	12.26	35.79	38.40	29.19	39.33	79.98	118.83	170.36	226.25	317.51	465.56
Uzbekistan	927	3.11	3.83	1.48	2.81	2.84	6.86	4.45	6.09	1.41	2.06	79.66	99.80	27.49	19.13
Yugoslavia n.s.	966	1.20	2.61	.58	3.04	—	—	—	—	.26	.07	.05	.04	—	—
Middle East	**407**	**197.4**	**194.5**	**208.7**	**498.3**	**434.8**	**1,022.3**	**867.4**	**83.5**	**87.9**	**83.3**	**84.1**	**126.3**	**155.1**	**193.5**
Bahrain	419	—	—	—	—	.01	—	.01	—	—	—	—	.10	.01	.01
Egypt	469	5.26	.17	.03	.57	38.89	.03	.04	.38	.14	.18	.57	.63	1.31	2.30
Iran, I.R. of	429	9.14	29.88	49.13	153.56	166.47	295.90	434.73	55.42	57.93	50.61	45.32	76.32	85.92	105.24
Iraq	433	—	—	1.48	3.56	10.37	11.99	33.80	—	.11	.04	.02	.98	.27	—
Israel	436	164.13	154.06	138.11	323.74	195.06	684.83	369.85	6.00	6.74	2.91	4.10	10.76	26.18	30.84
Jordan	439	.03	.41	.21	—	—	—	.14	.02	—	.35	1.25	2.05	1.03	1.75
Kuwait	443	—	—	—	—	—	—	—	.11	.05	.03	.03	.20	.01	.03
Lebanon	446	8.57	2.57	6.71	.02	4.45	15.18	6.00	.05	.01	.28	.12	.03	.09	.20
Libya	672	—	—	1.35	—	.40	.03	.06	—	—	—	—	—	—	.15
Oman	449	—	.01	—	—	—	.37	.01	.12	.98	.21	.09	.15	.48	.18
Qatar	453	—	.21	.01	.01	—	.12	.01	—	—	—	.01	.06	.08	.14
Saudi Arabia	456	.04	—	.08	—	.06	—	—	1.88	1.90	1.63	.93	1.27	1.15	1.38
Syrian Arab Republic	463	—	.05	.92	6.62	.29	.01	18.06	.82	.85	.52	.51	.59	.79	1.27
United Arab Emirates	466	10.21	7.16	6.03	8.05	15.43	11.62	4.72	18.74	19.17	26.51	31.16	33.15	37.78	50.06
Yemen, Republic of	474	—	.01	4.68	2.22	3.39	2.24	—	—	.04	.04	—	.01	.01	—
Middle East n.s.	489	....	....	....	....	....	....	....	—	—	.01	—	—	—	—
Western Hemisphere	**207**	**15.4**	**9.1**	**1.0**	**—**	**.2**	**7.5**	**185.9**	**13.2**	**10.2**	**12.2**	**15.5**	**16.1**	**100.6**	**143.5**
Argentina	213	15.02	2.08	—	.01	.12	.09	.07	.40	.69	.44	.32	1.87	5.30	8.59
Barbados	316	—	—	—	—	—	—	—	—	—	—	—	—	—	.08
Belize	339	....	....	....	....	....	....	....	—	—	—	—	.01	.04	.02
Bolivia	218	.02	—	—	—	—	—	—	—	—	—	—	—	—	—
Brazil	223	.25	6.89	—	.01	.01	.03	69.17	6.63	7.53	9.09	11.12	9.09	85.29	117.56
Chile	228	—	.03	—	—	—	—	114.63	.03	.01	.05	.06	.18	.05	.08
Colombia	233	—	—	—	—	—	.04	.37	.01	—	.02	.18	.12	.02	.07
Costa Rica	238	—	—	—	—	—	—	—	—	—	—	.01	.01	.32	.52
Dominican Republic	243	—	—	—	—	—	—	—	—	—	—	—	.19	—	—
Ecuador	248	—	—	—	—	—	—	—	.83	.14	.47	1.28	2.34	3.14	3.79
El Salvador	253	....	....	....	....	....	....	....	—	—	.02	.14	.24	.35	.71
Guatemala	258	—	—	—	—	—	—	—	—	.16	.06	—	—	.06	—
Guyana	336	....	....	....	....	....	....	....	—	—	.02	—	—	—	—
Honduras	268	—	—	—	—	—	—	—	.11	—	—	—	—	—	—
Jamaica	343	—	—	—	—	—	—	—	.08	.01	.02	.01	—	—	.01
Mexico	273	—	—	.99	—	—	—	.02	2.31	.68	1.47	1.91	.72	.55	.94

Azerbaijan, Republic of 912

	Exports 2001	Exports 2002	Exports 2003	Exports 2004	Exports 2005	Exports 2006	Exports 2007	Imports 2001	Imports 2002	Imports 2003	Imports 2004	Imports 2005	Imports 2006	Imports 2007
	Millions of U.S. Dollars							*Millions of U.S. Dollars*						
Netherlands Antilles......353	—	—	—	—	—	—	—	—	.03	—	—	.01	—	—
Panama......283	—	—	—	—	.03	—	.03	—	—	.07	.02	—	1.10	6.31
Paraguay......288	—	—	—	—	—	—	.02	—	—	—	—	.14	.29	.10
Peru......293	—	—	—	—	—	.10	—	—	—	.03	—	—	.02	.01
St. Kitts and Nevis......361	—	—	.01	—	—	.52	—	.91	.11	.22	.40	.81	3.61	2.90
Suriname......366	—	.04	—	—	—	—	—	.01	—	—	—	—	—	—
Trinidad and Tobago......369	.03	—	—	—	—	.01	.01	—	—	.04	.05	.01	—	.04
Uruguay......298	—	—	—	—	—	—	—	—	.65	.10	—	.02	.02	.10
Venezuela, Rep. Bol......299	—	.01	—	.01	—	.42	.10	.07	.02	—	—	.15	.02	.03
Western Hem. n.s......399	.05	—	.01	—	—	6.28	1.51	1.80	.12	.11	—	.21	.39	1.67
Other Countries n.i.e......910	**1.1**	**.7**	**1.3**	**.7**	**.4**	**.5**	**.3**	**.2**	**.3**	**.6**	**.2**	**.8**	**.1**	**—**
Cuba......928	1.12	.70	1.27	.71	.41	.47	.26	—	.31	—	.05	.07	—	—
North Korea......954	—	—	—	.01	—	—	—	.16	.01	.59	.15	.70	.15	—
Countries & Areas n.s......898	**—**	**—**	**—**	**—**	**—**	**—**	**—**	**—**	**.1**	**—**	**—**	**—**	**—**	**—**
Memorandum Items														
European Union......998	1,624.38	1,507.04	1,745.57	1,841.03	2,029.11	3,556.93	1,583.03	294.78	407.24	867.16	1,190.81	1,248.12	1,569.65	1,661.02
Oil Exporting Ctys......999	20.08	37.66	58.28	294.54	193.72	320.53	863.72	76.61	80.56	95.00	79.23	114.34	127.96	163.24
Non-Oil Develop.Ctys......201	564.73	555.80	719.01	1,470.04	2,097.93	2,405.70	3,325.36	748.27	987.74	1,367.24	1,889.15	2,597.79	3,144.98	3,322.39
PERCENT DISTRIBUTION														
Industrial Countries......101	**74.7**	**72.6**	**69.9**	**51.2**	**47.3**	**57.2**	**30.8**	**42.3**	**35.8**	**44.3**	**44.0**	**35.6**	**37.9**	**39.0**
Developing Countries......202	**25.3**	**27.4**	**30.0**	**48.8**	**52.7**	**42.8**	**69.1**	**57.6**	**64.1**	**55.7**	**56.0**	**64.4**	**62.1**	**61.0**
Africa......607	**1.2**	**.2**	**—**	**.2**	**—**	**.2**	**—**	**.3**	**.3**	**.1**	**.7**	**1.2**	**.9**	**.3**
Asia......507	**.4**	**.4**	**1.1**	**5.4**	**5.7**	**3.6**	**13.1**	**6.5**	**8.1**	**10.8**	**10.5**	**16.6**	**6.9**	**8.7**
Europe......170	**14.5**	**17.4**	**20.7**	**29.4**	**36.9**	**22.8**	**38.7**	**44.1**	**49.9**	**41.2**	**42.0**	**43.2**	**49.5**	**46.1**
Middle East......407	**8.5**	**9.0**	**8.1**	**13.8**	**10.0**	**16.0**	**14.3**	**5.8**	**5.3**	**3.2**	**2.4**	**3.0**	**2.9**	**3.4**
Western Hemisphere......207	**.7**	**.4**	**—**	**—**	**—**	**.1**	**3.1**	**.9**	**.6**	**.5**	**.4**	**.4**	**1.9**	**2.5**
ANNUAL PERCENT CHANGE														
World......001	**32.6**	**-6.4**	**19.5**	**39.6**	**20.2**	**46.6**	**-4.9**	**22.1**	**16.4**	**57.7**	**33.9**	**19.8**	**25.1**	**8.5**
Industrial Countries......101	**47.9**	**-9.0**	**15.2**	**2.1**	**11.1**	**77.4**	**-48.7**	**38.4**	**-1.5**	**94.9**	**33.1**	**-3.2**	**33.0**	**11.7**
Developing Countries......202	**1.4**	**1.5**	**31.0**	**127.0**	**29.9**	**19.0**	**53.7**	**12.4**	**29.5**	**36.9**	**34.6**	**37.8**	**20.7**	**6.5**
Africa......607	**162.6**	**-81.4**	**-89.4**	**—**	**-78.4**	**764.6**	**-91.0**	**-84.5**	**31.6**	**-73.1**	**—**	**108.0**	**-11.5**	**-67.2**
Asia......507	**-45.0**	**-7.6**	**258.0**	**550.2**	**29.0**	**-8.5**	**246.1**	**45.8**	**44.5**	**110.6**	**30.3**	**90.1**	**-48.3**	**38.0**
Europe......170	**-14.1**	**12.1**	**42.7**	**98.1**	**50.8**	**-9.5**	**61.3**	**14.4**	**31.6**	**30.3**	**36.3**	**23.2**	**43.6**	**.9**
Middle East......407	**31.6**	**-1.4**	**7.3**	**138.8**	**-12.7**	**135.1**	**-15.2**	**-2.1**	**5.2**	**-5.2**	**1.0**	**50.2**	**22.8**	**24.8**
Western Hemisphere......207	**70.7**	**-41.1**	**-88.7**	**-97.2**	**446.5**	**—**	**—**	**51.4**	**-23.0**	**20.5**	**26.7**	**4.1**	**523.6**	**42.7**
Other Countries n.i.e......910	**—**	**-36.9**	**80.6**	**-43.0**	**-44.0**	**15.9**	**-44.8**	**27.7**	**105.3**	**82.2**	**-65.2**	**272.0**	**-80.5**	**-99.4**

		Exports							Imports						
		2001	2002	2003	2004	2005	2006	2007	2001	2002	2003	2004	2005	2006	2007
		Millions of U.S. Dollars							*Millions of U.S. Dollars*						
IFS World Total		**423.1**	**446.2**	**424.7**	**477.0**	**562.0**	**674.4**	**484.8**	**1,912.4**	**1,728.1**	**1,761.6**	**1,905.0**	**2,230.0**	**2,400.6**	**2,449.4**
DOTS World Total	**001**	**916.1Y**	**1,220.6Y**	**1,406.8Y**	**1,495.8Y**	**2,243.4Y**	**2,136.6Y**	**2,332.5Y**	**3,416.9Y**	**5,852.7Y**	**5,578.8Y**	**5,554.6Y**	**9,238.3Y**	**10,738.5Y**	**10,172.6Y**
Industrial Countries	**101**	**738.3Y**	**891.4Y**	**972.1Y**	**1,050.4Y**	**1,788.2Y**	**1,537.0Y**	**1,295.8Y**	**2,116.5Y**	**3,602.9Y**	**3,236.3Y**	**2,749.6Y**	**3,988.4Y**	**5,468.9Y**	**6,094.7Y**
United States	111	298.45V	434.36V	454.55V	606.73V	660.27V	432.18V	475.64V	1,124.09V	1,072.61V	1,192.73V	1,300.31V	1,945.79V	2,516.91V	2,720.41V
Canada	156	8.91V	10.49V	34.73V	43.15V	46.54V	20.38V	58.94V	20.49V	25.84V	23.83V	29.18V	60.97V	55.76V	100.18V
Australia	193	1.39V	1.50V	1.67V	1.85V	3.00V	3.05V	2.18V	5.18V	3.83V	9.13V	12.70V	5.53V	3.35V	3.10V
Japan	158	2.38V	1.84V	.42V	.70V	.92V	77.68V	2.74V	169.17V	528.17V	323.65V	459.93V	243.02V	1,337.57V	1,376.12V
New Zealand	196	.04V	—V	.18V	.07V	.18V	.09V	.04V	.87V	1.17V	.61V	1.69V	.93V	16.03V	1.30V
Austria	122	—V	.34V	1.60V	—V	.01V	.01V	.03V	1.18V	1.34V	.92V	2.15V	1.75V	5.00V	30.34V
Belgium	124	.86V	.05V	.11V	.05V	.28V	1.28V	5.50V	2.60V	6.55V	3.37V	3.00V	8.94V	3.23V	3.93V
Cyprus	423	.29V	.28V	.31V	—V	—V	.01V	—V	.16V	.13V	.32V	.19V	.17V	.13V	.10V
Denmark	128	.03V	.02V	10.03V	.17V	.45V	.78V	.08V	23.20V	113.95V	3.86V	16.60V	7.76V	45.97V	11.63V
Finland	172	—V	—V	4.21V	.55V	.02V	.02V	—V	.16V	2.32V	18.34V	3.88V	1.92V	6.17V	8.16V
France	132	129.45V	82.13V	99.07V	64.78V	48.50V	41.62V	36.01V	68.14V	28.77V	521.05V	58.75V	30.51V	147.61V	32.79V
Germany	134	118.55V	136.36V	100.93V	88.38V	118.44V	238.15V	154.99V	82.44V	610.82V	62.15V	11.97V	462.32V	20.40V	56.18V
Greece	174	8.78V	24.86V	20.83V	1.33V	28.99V	1.03V	77.75V	20.82V	16.89V	5.61V	6.02V	9.68V	13.82V	8.31V
Iceland	176	1.66V	1.18V	1.94V	.31V	1.65V	1.23V	.94V	—V	.10V	—V	—V	—V	.78V	.76V
Ireland	178	.11V	—V	—V	—V	.03V	—V	.01V	3.45V	3.43V	2.96V	3.46V	3.16V	3.05V	4.45V
Italy	136	3.91V	7.72V	30.23V	3.62V	6.51V	39.64V	5.36V	253.75V	382.43V	653.62V	452.56V	68.26V	68.62V	759.94V
Luxembourg	137	—V	—V	—V	—V	—V	—V	—V	.04V	.17V	.17V	—V	—V	3.82V	—V
Malta	181	.30Y	.14V	.20V	.15V	.35V	.65V	.02V	—Y	—V	—V	—V	.17V	.12V	.13V
Netherlands	138	.51V	1.40V	2.62V	.76V	4.58V	.31V	.34V	72.52V	8.39V	15.03V	22.85V	51.51V	110.82V	120.14V
Norway	142	6.84V	.05V	.94V	8.41V	2.07V	2.97V	6.02V	87.13V	538.17V	45.20V	83.32V	272.47V	260.77V	202.99V
Portugal	182	.03V	.08V	.05V	.10V	7.82V	.41V	.15V	.57V	.42V	.44V	.86V	.50V	6.19V	.43V
Slovenia	961	.01V	.06V	.07V	.09Y	—V	.02V	—V	.31V	—V	—V	—Y	.01V	—V	.04V
Spain	184	99.99V	120.35V	137.32V	184.41V	698.63V	486.90V	338.53V	103.09V	119.27V	166.81V	144.77V	675.13V	630.58V	437.16V
Sweden	144	.04V	.26V	.01V	.57V	46.38V	.78V	.07V	2.43V	6.46V	31.27V	2.20V	3.39V	3.08V	49.78V
Switzerland	146	46.53V	39.88V	62.46V	36.28V	39.78V	62.93V	121.60V	50.78V	72.10V	105.96V	55.09V	60.78V	87.89V	125.50V
United Kingdom	112	9.23V	27.99V	7.67V	7.97V	72.78V	124.83V	8.90V	23.99V	59.63V	49.26V	78.16V	73.78V	121.20V	40.82V
Developing Countries	**202**	**176.1Y**	**327.3Y**	**432.3Y**	**442.3Y**	**451.7Y**	**595.2Y**	**1,031.1Y**	**1,229.8Y**	**2,173.1Y**	**2,245.5Y**	**2,677.6Y**	**5,104.3Y**	**5,089.8Y**	**3,854.8Y**
Africa	**607**	**3.0Y**	**3.2Y**	**3.0Y**	**1.0Y**	**5.1Y**	**4.3Y**	**14.5Y**	**2.8Y**	**36.2Y**	**3.1Y**	**3.6Y**	**7.3Y**	**13.1Y**	**8.2Y**
Algeria	612	.70V	—V	—Y	—Y	—Y	—Y	—Y	.07V	.01V	.02Y	.02Y	.03Y	.04Y	.04Y
Benin	638	.03V	.01V	—V	—V	—V	—Y	—Y	—V	—V	—V	—V	—V	—Y	—Y
Cameroon	622	—V	—V	—V	—Y	—Y	—Y	—Y	—V	—V	.29V	.38Y	.44Y	.54Y	.67Y
Congo, Republic of	634	—V	—V	—V	—V	—Y	—Y	—Y	—V	—V	.05V	—V	—Y	—Y	—Y
Côte d'Ivoire	662	—V	1.38V	1.95V	—V	—V	.01V	.02Y	.63V	.49V	.88V	1.31V	4.10V	1.63V	2.03Y
Gabon	646	—Y	—Y	—Y	—Y	—Y	—Y	—Y	—Y	—Y	—Y	—Y	.01Y	.01Y	.01Y
Kenya	664	.65V	.12V	.01V	.02V	.02Y	.03Y	.03Y	—V	.06V	.04V	.17V	.20Y	.24Y	.30Y
Liberia	668	—Y	—Y	—Y	—Y	—Y	—Y	—Y	.02Y	.02Y	.02Y	.03Y	.03Y	.04Y	.05Y
Madagascar	674	.18V	—V	.03V	.04Y	.05Y	.06Y	.07Y	—V	—V	—V	—Y	—Y	—Y	.01Y
Mauritius	684	.01V	.01V	.04V	.02V	.02V	.16V	.12V	.01V	—V	—V	—V	.01V	.02V	—V
Morocco	686	.20V	.11V	.19V	.13V	.13V	.16Y	.20Y	—V	—V	.01V	.02V	—V	.01Y	.01Y
Nigeria	694	.43V	.57V	.46V	.60Y	.77Y	.95Y	1.23Y	—V	—V	—V	—Y	—Y	—Y	—Y
Senegal	722	—V	—V	—V	.01V	.01V	.01V	.01Y	—V	—V	—V	—V	—V	—V	—Y
South Africa	199	.57V	.86V	.31V	.06V	4.05V	2.93V	12.79V	2.01V	35.57V	1.76V	1.55V	2.47V	10.54V	5.06V
Togo	742	.28V	.09V	.03V	.01V	—V	—Y	—Y	—Y	—Y	—Y	—V	—V	—Y	—Y
Tunisia	744	—V	.02V	.01V	.01V	—V	.02V	.02Y	.03V	.05V	.02V	.04V	—V	.02V	.02Y
Zambia	754	—V	.01V	—V	—V	—V	—V	—V	—V	—V	—V	.05V	—V	—V	—V
Zimbabwe	698	—V	—V	—V	.12V	—V	—V	—Y	—V	—V	—V	.01V	—V	—V	—Y
Asia	**507**	**20.1Y**	**46.8Y**	**45.8Y**	**37.3Y**	**66.4Y**	**79.7Y**	**398.2Y**	**852.4Y**	**1,360.5Y**	**1,372.2Y**	**1,417.0Y**	**2,314.0Y**	**1,976.3Y**	**2,173.7Y**
Bangladesh	513	1.57V	—V	1.10V	—V	—V	10.28V	—V	—V	—V	—V	—V	—V	—Y	—Y
China,P.R.: Mainland	924	.02V	.05V	.71V	.63V	.17V	.06V	16.47V	38.24V	69.15V	133.90V	124.80V	170.99V	181.06V	178.93V
China,P.R.:Hong Kong	532	.06V	.01V	.01V	.01V	.03V	.17V	.01V	3.32V	3.16V	2.05V	1.98V	2.50V	6.09V	4.77V
India	534	.08Y	.24V	.13V	.02V	10.46V	12.93Y	16.05Y	2.52Y	2.80V	3.54V	5.50V	9.08V	11.22Y	13.93Y
Indonesia	536	—V	12.86V	—V	.19V	5.21V	—V	.19V	.60V	.92V	.58V	.58V	.88V	1.13V	1.28V
Korea	542	9.74V	.01V	.17V	11.58V	26.49V	.17V	.23V	555.11V	1,064.00V	999.88V	1,097.32V	1,741.79V	1,235.32V	1,438.50V
Malaysia	548	.19V	.33V	.41V	.37V	.24V	.60V	.45V	.77V	.26V	.45V	.71V	1.38V	2.15V	2.93V
Maldives	556	.14V	.20V	.02V	.02V	.04V	.05Y	.06Y	....	....	....	....	....	....	....
New Caledonia	839	.03V	—V	—V	—V	—Y	—Y	—Y	....	....	....	....	....	....	....
Pakistan	564	.23V	.14V	—V	.07V	.23V	.28Y	.35Y	2.13V	2.53V	2.09V	2.36V	1.51V	1.86Y	2.31Y
Philippines	566	—V	—V	.01V	.04V	—V	—V	—V	.85V	2.74V	1.00V	1.62V	.84V	1.06V	1.80V
Samoa	862	—Y	—Y	—Y	—Y	.55V	.68Y	.84Y	.01Y	.01Y	.01Y	.01Y	.02Y	.02Y	.02Y
Singapore	576	.31V	32.74V	41.01V	24.00V	22.64V	53.66V	361.93V	180.15V	159.42V	169.61V	178.01V	274.61V	325.71V	525.04V
Taiwan Province of China	528	.09V	.06V	.04V	.02V	.03V	.70V	.81V	67.21V	54.40V	57.84V	2.53V	107.25V	206.90V	.82V
Thailand	578	.05V	.01V	1.42V	.34V	.26V	.12V	.86V	1.10V	.94V	.94V	1.57V	3.18V	3.75V	3.39V
Vietnam	582	7.58V	.09V	.80V	—V	—V	—V	—V	.40V	.21V	.30V	—V	—V	—V	—V
Europe	**170**	**51.8Y**	**31.6Y**	**75.8Y**	**209.8Y**	**207.3Y**	**323.5Y**	**349.1Y**	**75.9Y**	**108.1Y**	**115.8Y**	**316.6Y**	**609.8Y**	**738.7Y**	**436.6Y**
Albania	914	—V	—V	—V	—V	—V	—V	.11V	—V	—V	—V	—V	—V	—V	—V
Belarus	913	.23V	.23V	.67V	.03V	.04V	.07V	.10V	—V	—V	—V	16.82V	—V	—V	—V
Bulgaria	918	—V	.03V	—V	.19V	.16V	.38V	.52V	.15V	.26V	.30V	.39V	.82V	1.80V	13.36V
Croatia	960	.40V	.38V	.36V	.37V	.28V	6.39V	.49V	.19V	.51V	.36V	.08V	.13V	.49V	.63V
Czech Republic	935	.32V	.37V	.47V	1.04V	.87V	.35V	—V	.69V	2.52V	1.02V	3.05V	5.55V	7.49V	1.64V

		Exports							Imports						
		2001	2002	2003	2004	2005	2006	2007	2001	2002	2003	2004	2005	2006	2007
		Millions of U.S. Dollars							Millions of U.S. Dollars						
Estonia	939	.10V	.06V	.24V	—V	—V	—V	—V	2.44V	4.31V	5.14V	.11V	.20V	.28V	.09V
Georgia	915	.28V	2.88V	.01V	—V	—V	.06V	.04Y	.59V	—V	.22V	—V	.18V	—V	—Y
Hungary	944	.10V	.17V	.48V	2.96V	.18V	—V	.02V	.61V	.70V	.36V	.28V	.01V	.10V	.31V
Kazakhstan	916	.74V	1.40V	.55V	.32V	.37Y	.46Y	.57Y	—V	32.28V	10.86V	32.48V	37.12Y	45.87Y	56.93Y
Latvia	941	—V	—V	—V	—V	—V	—V	—V	.06V	.27V	1.39V	.29V	1.25V	1.34V	1.95V
Lithuania	946	.14V	1.87V	.07V	2.93V	2.71V	17.89V	10.93V	.18V	.02V	.01V	3.85V	4.30V	.49V	.05V
Macedonia, FYR	962	.10V	—V	.02V	.01V	.01V	.01V	.01Y	—V	—V	—V	—V	—V	—V	—Y
Moldova	921	—V	—V	—V	.01V	.01V	.01Y	.01Y	—V	—V	—V	—V	—V	—Y	—Y
Poland	964	46.77V	21.59V	68.99V	200.36V	197.23V	294.48V	334.45V	26.83V	12.38V	49.90V	46.53V	262.79V	234.76V	321.69V
Romania	968	.44V	.25V	.24V	.26V	.22V	.31V	.05V	.03V	13.81V	11.68V	.10V	.08V	.51V	2.15V
Russia	922	.21V	.47V	.32V	.50V	.64V	.94V	.47V	15.85V	13.17V	.84V	148.75V	256.89V	390.99V	—V
Serbia & Montenegro	965	....	....	....	....	....	....	....	.01Y	.01Y	.01Y	.01Y	.01Y	.02Y	.02Y
Slovak Republic	936	.07V	.09V	.11Y	.15Y	—V	—V	—V	.39V	—V	.01Y	.01Y	.15V	.14V	.01V
Tajikistan	923	—V	—V	—V	—V	.36V	.09V	—V	—Y	—Y	—Y	—Y	—Y	—Y	—Y
Turkey	186	.20V	.35V	3.23V	.53V	3.68V	1.30V	.47V	19.90V	25.85V	32.04V	61.63V	36.78V	50.00V	32.41V
Turkmenistan	925	.09V	.14V	.01V	.01Y	.01Y	.02Y	.02Y	—V	—V	1.66V	2.18Y	2.49Y	3.08Y	3.82Y
Ukraine	926	1.59V	1.36V	—V	.10V	.56V	.69Y	.86Y	8.02V	2.02V	—V	.08V	1.04V	1.28Y	1.59Y
Middle East	**407**	**.2Y**	**.8Y**	**1.4Y**	**.9Y**	**.5Y**	**.7Y**	**.9Y**	**24.4Y**	**24.3Y**	**39.0Y**	**40.4Y**	**52.8Y**	**66.7Y**	**78.9Y**
Bahrain	419	.04Y	.04Y	.05Y	.07Y	.08Y	.10Y	.12Y	—Y	—Y	—Y	—Y	—Y	—Y	—Y
Israel	436	—V	.73V	1.09V	.36V	—V	.09V	.18V	2.20V	.66V	10.34V	2.42V	1.10V	1.76V	.55V
Lebanon	446	.04Y	.04Y	.06Y	.07Y	.08Y	.10Y	.13Y	—Y	—Y	—Y	—Y	—Y	—Y	—Y
Oman	449	.04V	—V	—V	—Y	—Y	—Y	—Y	....	....	....	....	....	....	....
Saudi Arabia	456	.08V	.01V	—V	—V	.02V	.02Y	.03Y	22.24Y	23.65Y	28.67Y	37.94Y	51.61Y	64.88Y	78.27Y
United Arab Emirates	466	—V	—V	.18V	.24Y	.30Y	.37Y	.48Y	—Y	—Y	—Y	—Y	—Y	—Y	—Y
Yemen, Republic of	474	—V	—V	—Y	.19V	—V	—Y	—Y	—V	—V	—Y	—V	.07V	.08Y	.10Y
Western Hemisphere	**207**	**101.0Y**	**245.0Y**	**306.2Y**	**193.2Y**	**172.5Y**	**187.0Y**	**268.3Y**	**274.2Y**	**644.0Y**	**715.4Y**	**900.0Y**	**2,120.4Y**	**2,295.1Y**	**1,157.3Y**
Antigua and Barbuda	311	.11Y	.12Y	.15Y	.20Y	.22Y	.28Y	.34Y	.05Y	.05Y	.07Y	.09Y	.10Y	.12Y	.15Y
Argentina	213	.79V	.43V	.51V	1.04V	2.06V	2.25V	32.16V	9.19V	8.14V	1.64V	27.37V	21.97V	5.67V	2.41V
Aruba	314	.02V	1.29V	1.21V	1.96V	3.37V	4.97V	4.03V	.09V	.05V	.03V	.06V	.03V	.22V	—V
Barbados	316	.22V	.16V	.12V	.17V	1.07V	.16V	.20Y	3.31V	2.27V	2.15V	3.02V	3.36V	3.50V	4.34Y
Belize	339	.24Y	.26Y	.33Y	.44Y	.50Y	.62Y	.77Y	.02Y	.02Y	.02Y	.03Y	.04Y	.04Y	.06Y
Bermuda	319	.62Y	.68Y	.86Y	1.13Y	.10V	.01V	.01Y	.31Y	.34Y	.43Y	.56Y	.64Y	.80Y	.99Y
Bolivia	218	—V	—V	.03V	.01V	.03V	.04Y	.05Y	.06V	.10V	.06V	.04V	.05Y	.06Y	.08Y
Brazil	223	2.70V	4.33V	.42V	2.35V	5.70V	2.05V	—V	12.46V	111.96V	430.63V	536.53V	1,637.14V	1,601.72V	330.12V
Chile	228	.04V	—V	.10V	.09V	.11V	.12V	.05V	1.51V	1.10V	1.80V	1.60V	1.93V	2.30V	3.63V
Colombia	233	.11V	.09V	.30V	—V	.03V	—V	.50V	9.90V	51.84V	42.82V	48.65V	77.52V	17.35V	3.05V
Costa Rica	238	.01V	15.04V	7.65V	6.87V	.14V	.18Y	.22Y	2.40V	2.46V	4.15V	23.53V	6.10V	7.54Y	9.36Y
Dominica	321	.05V	.06Y	.07Y	.09Y	.10Y	.13Y	.16Y	.05V	.06Y	.07Y	.10Y	.11Y	.14Y	.17Y
Dominican Republic	243	.71V	.77Y	.97Y	1.28Y	1.46Y	1.81Y	2.24Y	.76V	.83Y	1.05Y	1.38Y	1.57Y	1.95Y	2.41Y
Ecuador	248	9.32V	.06V	34.21V	—V	.90V	.30V	.37Y	2.82V	9.71V	3.01V	1.55V	1.94V	1.70V	2.11Y
El Salvador	253	8.63V	12.52V	2.62V	4.00V	—V	—V	3.22V	.95V	.74V	1.07V	1.43V	1.04V	.70V	.94V
Greenland	326	.02Y	.03Y	.03Y	.04Y	.05Y	.06Y	.08Y	—Y	—Y	—Y	—Y	—Y	—Y	—Y
Grenada	328	.10Y	.11Y	.13Y	.18Y	.20Y	.25Y	.31Y	—Y	—Y	—Y	—Y	—Y	—Y	—Y
Guatemala	258	2.99V	26.65V	60.60V	.02V	86.63V	107.07Y	132.87Y	.23V	.67V	.08V	1.90V	1.35V	1.66Y	2.07Y
Guyana	336	.01Y	.01Y	.01Y	.01Y	.02Y	.02Y	.02Y	—Y	—Y	—Y	—Y	—Y	—Y	—Y
Haiti	263	.05V	.63V	.14V	.04V	.05Y	.06Y	.08Y	.13Y	.14Y	.17Y	.23Y	.26Y	.32Y	.40Y
Honduras	268	.04V	2.74V	.35V	.59V	.68Y	.83Y	1.04Y	.43V	.59V	.30V	.25V	.29Y	.35Y	.44Y
Jamaica	343	.80V	.81V	5.30V	.79V	1.10V	1.76V	1.39V	3.35V	2.64V	2.22V	2.05V	1.76V	1.99V	2.37V
Mexico	273	9.54V	47.91V	51.22V	36.16V	24.33V	.29V	24.75V	48.13V	10.31V	15.07V	9.70V	15.11V	13.62V	20.60V
Netherlands Antilles	353	.01V	—V	24.14V	31.71Y	36.23Y	44.78Y	55.57Y	141.48V	142.90V	97.97V	128.67Y	147.01Y	181.70Y	225.49Y
Panama	283	.01V	—V	.15V	—V	—V	—V	—V	.33V	13.99V	.26V	.32V	.50V	1.23V	.55V
Paraguay	288	42.78V	28.48V	54.37V	8.86V	2.26V	—V	—Y	—V	—V	—V	—V	—V	—V	—Y
Peru	293	.17V	99.00V	55.14V	50.75V	.03V	—V	—Y	5.10V	16.05V	6.36V	3.56V	2.90V	3.41V	4.14Y
St. Kitts and Nevis	361	.01Y	.01Y	.01Y	.02Y	.02Y	.02Y	.03Y	—Y	—Y	—Y	—Y	—Y	—Y	—Y
St. Lucia	362	.05Y	.05Y	.06Y	.08Y	.10Y	.12Y	.15Y	—Y	—Y	—Y	—Y	—Y	.01Y	.01Y
St. Vincent & Grens.	364	.13V	.14V	.13V	.02V	.04V	.04Y	.05Y	—V	.01V	—V	—V	.01V	.01Y	.01Y
Suriname	366	.07Y	.08Y	.10Y	.13Y	.15Y	.19Y	.23Y	—Y	—Y	—Y	—Y	—Y	—Y	—Y
Trinidad and Tobago	369	20.06V	2.08V	2.63Y	3.46Y	3.95Y	4.88Y	6.06Y	21.50V	26.17V	33.12Y	43.50Y	49.70Y	61.43Y	76.24Y
Uruguay	298	—V	—Y	.01V	.04V	.02V	.03Y	.04Y	.65V	.71Y	.34V	.71V	1.74V	2.15Y	2.67Y
Venezuela, Rep. Bol.	299	.14V	—V	1.70V	40.24V	.38V	13.24V	.90V	8.80V	239.91V	70.26V	62.80V	145.88V	383.02V	462.07Y
Western Hem. n.s.	399	.45Y	.45Y	.45Y	.45Y	.45Y	.45Y	.45Y	.20Y	.24Y	.28Y	.31Y	.35Y	.39Y	.43Y
Other Countries n.i.e.	**910**	**—Y**	**—Y**	**—Y**	**—Y**	**—Y**	**—Y**	**—Y**	**.4Y**	**.4Y**	**.5Y**	**.7Y**	**.8Y**	**.9Y**	**1.2Y**
Cuba	928	—Y	—Y	—Y	—Y	—Y	—Y	—Y	.23Y	.25Y	.31Y	.41Y	.47Y	.58Y	.72Y
North Korea	954	—Y	—Y	—Y	—Y	—Y	—Y	—Y	.14Y	.15Y	.20Y	.26Y	.29Y	.36Y	.45Y
Countries & Areas n.s.	**898**	**1.7Y**	**1.9Y**	**2.4Y**	**3.1Y**	**3.6Y**	**4.4Y**	**5.5Y**	**70.2Y**	**76.2Y**	**96.5Y**	**126.7Y**	**144.7Y**	**178.9Y**	**222.0Y**
Memorandum Items															
European Union	998	419.59Y	426.21Y	485.61Y	560.37Y	1,234.77Y	1,249.17Y	973.16Y	690.04Y	1,381.17Y	1,592.99Y	861.52Y	1,673.21Y	1,434.40Y	1,890.07Y
Oil Exporting Ctys	999	1.37Y	13.44Y	2.35Y	41.27Y	6.67Y	14.58Y	2.82Y	31.72Y	264.49Y	99.53Y	101.34Y	198.39Y	449.07Y	541.67Y
Non-Oil Develop.Ctys	201	174.69Y	313.91Y	429.93Y	400.99Y	445.01Y	580.62Y	1,028.33Y	1,198.07Y	1,908.65Y	2,146.00Y	2,576.23Y	4,905.92Y	4,640.77Y	3,313.11Y
PERCENT DISTRIBUTION															
Industrial Countries	**101**	**80.6**	**73.0**	**69.1**	**70.2**	**79.7**	**71.9**	**55.6**	**61.9**	**61.6**	**58.0**	**49.5**	**43.2**	**50.9**	**59.9**
Developing Countries	**202**	**19.2**	**26.8**	**30.7**	**29.6**	**20.1**	**27.9**	**44.2**	**36.0**	**37.1**	**40.3**	**48.2**	**55.3**	**47.4**	**37.9**
Africa	**607**	**.3**	**.3**	**.2**	**.1**	**.2**	**.2**	**.6**	**.1**	**.6**	**.1**	**.1**	**.1**	**.1**	**.1**
Asia	**507**	**2.2**	**3.8**	**3.3**	**2.5**	**3.0**	**3.7**	**17.1**	**24.9**	**23.2**	**24.6**	**25.5**	**25.0**	**18.4**	**21.4**
Europe	**170**	**5.6**	**2.6**	**5.4**	**14.0**	**9.2**	**15.1**	**15.0**	**2.2**	**1.8**	**2.1**	**5.7**	**6.6**	**6.9**	**4.3**
Middle East	**407**	**—**	**.1**	**.1**	**.1**	**—**	**—**	**—**	**.7**	**.4**	**.7**	**.7**	**.6**	**.6**	**.8**
Western Hemisphere	**207**	**11.0**	**20.1**	**21.8**	**12.9**	**7.7**	**8.8**	**11.5**	**8.0**	**11.0**	**12.8**	**16.2**	**23.0**	**21.4**	**11.4**

	Exports							Imports						
	2001	2002	2003	2004	2005	2006	2007	2001	2002	2003	2004	2005	2006	2007
ANNUAL PERCENT CHANGE														
World.......................................001	4.4	33.2	15.3	6.3	50.0	–4.8	9.2	–13.2	71.3	–4.7	–.4	66.3	16.2	–5.3
Industrial Countries.................101	–7.0	20.7	9.1	8.1	70.2	–14.0	–15.7	–19.2	70.2	–10.2	–15.0	45.1	37.1	11.4
Developing Countries..............202	114.9	85.9	32.1	2.3	2.1	31.8	73.2	–1.6	76.7	3.3	19.2	90.6	–.3	–24.3
Africa.....................................607	135.8	3.8	–3.7	–66.1	389.1	–14.4	235.2	–94.6	—	–91.4	15.9	102.9	79.5	–37.4
Asia..507	467.4	132.8	–2.0	–18.6	77.9	20.1	399.6	16.7	59.6	.9	3.3	63.3	–14.6	10.0
Europe....................................170	775.0	–38.9	139.5	176.8	–1.2	56.0	7.9	–33.4	42.4	7.1	173.4	92.6	21.1	–40.9
Middle East............................407	–93.5	330.3	68.4	–32.4	–48.9	42.5	37.4	16.7	–.5	60.5	3.5	30.8	26.4	18.3
Western Hemisphere.............207	48.0	142.6	25.0	–36.9	–10.7	8.4	43.5	–17.7	134.8	11.1	25.8	135.6	8.2	–49.6
Other Countries n.i.e................910	—	—	....	....	....	....	....	10.4	8.5	26.6	31.3	14.3	23.6	24.1

		Exports							Imports						
		2001	2002	2003	2004	2005	2006	2007	2001	2002	2003	2004	2005	2006	2007
		Millions of U.S. Dollars							Millions of U.S. Dollars						
IFS World Total		**5,578.5**	**5,785.9**	**6,623.7**	**7,555.9**	**10,160.4**	**11,562.8**	**13,394.1**	**4,306.1**	**4,987.8**	**5,657.2**	**7,384.8**	**8,790.2**	**8,944.4**	**11,293.1**
DOTS World Total	**001**	**8,254.8Y**	**8,455.2Y**	**10,354.4Y**	**13,592.5Y**	**15,943.7Y**	**19,755.3Y**	**23,846.2Y**	**3,685.6Y**	**4,062.5Y**	**4,839.4Y**	**5,861.5Y**	**7,098.1Y**	**8,682.9Y**	**10,423.1Y**
Industrial Countries	**101**	**1,102.0Y**	**937.3Y**	**979.8Y**	**1,192.7Y**	**1,449.4Y**	**1,958.2Y**	**2,145.1Y**	**1,730.3Y**	**1,943.8Y**	**2,322.9Y**	**2,644.3Y**	**2,709.8Y**	**3,367.6Y**	**3,911.9Y**
United States	111	410.36V	381.27V	364.82V	392.36V	413.45V	594.36V	595.27V	476.30V	461.12V	559.68V	330.55V	385.77V	539.77V	650.54V
Canada	156	7.63V	8.15V	7.65V	4.87V	6.28V	90.68V	7.33V	9.40V	9.98V	12.97V	18.13V	25.64V	30.15V	42.41V
Australia	193	26.38V	34.14V	69.96V	96.89V	85.56V	91.50V	122.69V	56.66V	58.73V	75.97V	90.35V	96.38V	106.29V	123.74V
Japan	158	202.29V	145.73V	128.78V	250.48V	286.50V	461.74V	390.82V	181.48V	281.53V	380.40V	430.20V	471.08V	594.06V	745.97V
New Zealand	196	3.66V	3.11V	5.84V	7.45V	6.24V	8.35V	8.31V	8.61V	8.19V	9.04V	12.93V	12.79V	11.46V	17.49V
Austria	122	1.68V	1.38V	2.49V	2.57V	1.87V	1.32V	3.24V	17.50V	13.63V	25.87V	49.55V	29.58V	32.60V	47.96V
Belgium	124	23.45V	21.80V	24.96V	27.91V	33.79V	34.72V	35.11V	48.59V	48.17V	70.15V	102.64V	72.76V	90.34V	95.54V
Cyprus	423	.19V	.24V	.45V	.64V	.46V	4.01V	2.31V	2.12V	1.98V	1.90V	1.66V	2.85V	3.09V	3.47V
Denmark	128	34.88V	16.71V	.57V	.85V	1.37V	1.51V	.67V	19.35V	19.30V	25.18V	23.35V	22.40V	29.21V	30.16V
Finland	172	8.43V	.07V	.56V	3.11V	4.56V	6.74V	9.42V	11.35V	18.16V	28.89V	72.76V	53.73V	62.54V	131.60V
France	132	98.18V	65.33V	32.83V	121.02V	59.31V	34.11V	78.25V	106.23V	104.31V	159.88V	280.64V	126.75V	144.17V	187.19V
Germany	134	20.76V	12.52V	92.32V	30.81V	40.56V	50.04V	104.33V	194.07V	258.82V	265.36V	360.69V	455.03V	440.14V	489.04V
Greece	174	7.76V	12.56V	2.18V	2.24V	1.62V	5.35V	23.11V	5.16V	3.30V	3.72V	4.68V	5.60V	5.25V	14.75V
Iceland	176	.09V	—V	—V	—V	5.32V	29.76V	5.92V	.13V	.01V	—V	.04V	—V	—V	—V
Ireland	178	3.48V	.69V	.45V	.95V	1.69V	7.49V	9.65V	22.55V	22.55V	14.24V	13.38V	14.09V	18.78V	35.45V
Italy	136	53.01V	42.99V	57.63V	42.03V	59.33V	43.72V	94.83V	110.17V	121.25V	143.00V	169.37V	191.21V	265.48V	277.04V
Luxembourg	137	.05V	.43V	.01V	—V	—V	—V	.08V	.80V	.29V	1.60V	4.56V	21.58V	4.35V	3.78V
Malta	181	7.43Y	—V	.12V	.19V	.14V	.11V	.10V	.84Y	.78V	.86V	.60V	1.55V	1.60V	1.48V
Netherlands	138	14.18V	15.45V	10.62V	24.83V	66.53V	109.72V	210.75V	74.67V	75.26V	86.99V	112.64V	129.93V	158.91V	178.14V
Norway	142	12.42V	5.06V	5.85V	6.99V	8.61V	19.80V	17.94V	3.12V	4.99V	5.26V	6.86V	6.80V	7.80V	9.80V
Portugal	182	2.47V	10.09V	10.74V	6.37V	16.82V	8.33V	3.94V	1.78V	6.67V	5.15V	5.98V	2.82V	4.49V	7.33V
Slovenia	961	.74V	.01V	—V	—Y	.30V	1.35V	8.34V	.27V	.41V	.35V	.46Y	16.39V	18.09V	7.33V
Spain	184	19.11V	28.49V	16.37V	14.17V	61.52V	38.00V	114.99V	31.74V	37.30V	38.11V	46.04V	56.37V	70.84V	83.11V
Sweden	144	.11V	.94V	1.07V	1.30V	.75V	2.74V	.38V	35.38V	28.41V	34.94V	32.63V	28.59V	35.16V	35.02V
Switzerland	146	9.88V	24.07V	25.38V	36.57V	19.77V	36.10V	55.08V	64.42V	138.07V	95.14V	155.72V	122.05V	154.46V	224.34V
United Kingdom	112	133.38V	106.07V	118.16V	118.05V	267.01V	276.62V	242.26V	247.62V	220.52V	278.20V	317.92V	358.01V	538.51V	469.25V
Developing Countries	**202**	**1,865.1Y**	**1,779.4Y**	**2,111.5Y**	**2,860.9Y**	**3,595.4Y**	**4,326.9Y**	**4,984.5Y**	**1,937.4Y**	**2,099.3Y**	**2,492.0Y**	**3,184.9Y**	**4,351.5Y**	**5,269.8Y**	**6,454.6Y**
Africa	**607**	**297.3Y**	**266.3Y**	**411.0Y**	**569.9Y**	**813.0Y**	**700.7Y**	**773.5Y**	**27.6Y**	**36.1Y**	**67.7Y**	**34.0Y**	**41.5Y**	**43.1Y**	**61.9Y**
Algeria	612	11.26V	19.73V	21.92Y	28.51Y	36.31Y	44.82Y	58.06Y	—V	—V	—Y	—Y	—Y	—Y	—Y
Angola	614	.14Y	.16Y	.20Y	.26Y	.29Y	.36Y	.45Y	—Y	—Y	—Y	—Y	—Y	—Y	—Y
Benin	638	2.42V	9.85V	10.71V	8.17V	4.27V	5.27Y	6.54Y	—V	—V	.13V	.55V	—V	—Y	—Y
Burkina Faso	748	—Y	.01Y	.01Y	.01Y	.01Y	.01Y	.01Y	1.10Y	1.19Y	1.51Y	1.98Y	2.26Y	2.80Y	3.47Y
Cameroon	622	—V	1.87V	—V	—Y	—Y	—Y	—Y	—V	—V	—V	—Y	—Y	—Y	—Y
Central African Rep.	626	—Y	—Y	—Y	—Y	—Y	—Y	—Y	.28Y	.30Y	.38Y	.50Y	.57Y	.70Y	.87Y
Congo, Republic of	634	—V	1.78V	.51V	.03V	.03Y	.04Y	.05Y	—V	—V	—V	—V	—Y	—Y	—Y
Côte d'Ivoire	662	13.83V	8.77V	.04V	—V	.13V	.25V	.31Y	3.38V	.56V	.02V	—V	.46V	.12V	.15Y
Djibouti	611	—Y	—Y	—Y	—Y	—Y	—Y	—Y	.01Y	.01Y	.01Y	.01Y	.01Y	.01Y	.02Y
Ethiopia	644	—V	—V	—V	—V	—V	—Y	—Y	.02Y	.02Y	.02Y	.03Y	.03Y	.04Y	.05Y
Gabon	646	1.33Y	1.44Y	1.83Y	2.40Y	2.74Y	3.39Y	4.20Y	—Y	—Y	—Y	—Y	—Y	—Y	—Y
Ghana	652	.51Y	.55Y	.70Y	.92Y	1.05Y	1.30Y	1.61Y	.01Y	.01Y	.01Y	.01Y	.01Y	.02Y	.02Y
Kenya	664	71.57V	32.67V	145.91V	182.66V	208.70Y	257.94Y	320.10Y	.48V	7.60V	.62V	2.53V	2.89Y	3.57Y	4.44Y
Madagascar	674	47.14V	51.51V	16.83V	22.10Y	25.25Y	31.21Y	38.73Y	—V	.41V	.04V	.05Y	.06Y	.07Y	.09Y
Mauritania	682	—Y	—Y	—Y	—Y	—Y	—Y	—Y	.02Y	.02Y	.03Y	.03Y	.04Y	.05Y	.06Y
Mauritius	684	30.10V	33.55V	83.76V	132.93V	156.74V	38.66V	.17V	1.22V	—V	—V	.34V	.01V	.08V	—V
Morocco	686	3.92V	4.83V	9.09V	14.34V	28.10V	34.73Y	43.10Y	.52V	.65V	.61V	.81V	.85V	1.05Y	1.30Y
Niger	692	2.67V	10.04V	7.33V	3.87V	4.43Y	5.47Y	6.79Y	—V	—V	—V	—V	—Y	—Y	—Y
Nigeria	694	.53V	.56V	.89V	1.15Y	1.47Y	1.81Y	2.35Y	—V	—V	—V	—Y	—Y	.01Y	.01Y
Senegal	722	.87V	5.01V	5.54V	.65V	.03V	.25V	.31Y	—V	—V	—V	.01V	.41V	.23V	.29Y
Seychelles	718	6.92V	.05V	.07V	.09Y	.10Y	.12Y	.15Y	—V	.18V	—V	—Y	—Y	—Y	—Y
Somalia	726	.01Y	.01Y	.01Y	.01Y	.01Y	.01Y	.02Y	2.31Y	2.50Y	3.17Y	4.16Y	4.75Y	5.88Y	7.29Y
South Africa	199	44.33V	10.62V	2.35V	23.75V	47.18V	33.93V	35.50V	6.86V	10.43V	12.46V	13.11V	16.65V	13.13V	24.85V
Sudan	732	—Y	—Y	12.56Y	33.38V	166.49V	77.95V	54.39V	2.32Y	2.51Y	41.72V	—V	—V	—V	—V
Swaziland	734	—Y	—Y	—Y	—Y	—Y	—Y	—Y	.21Y	.23Y	.28Y	.37Y	.43Y	.53Y	.66Y
Tanzania	738	51.61V	63.97V	80.97Y	106.34Y	121.50Y	150.16Y	186.35Y	.05V	—V	—Y	—Y	—Y	—Y	—Y
Togo	742	.68V	3.42V	2.19V	2.55V	.67V	.83Y	1.03Y	.01V	.03V	—V	—V	—V	—Y	—Y
Tunisia	744	7.37V	5.82V	7.38V	5.58V	7.03V	10.42V	12.93Y	8.73V	9.40V	6.63V	9.36V	11.93V	14.69V	18.23Y
Uganda	746	.04V	.01V	.16V	.21Y	.24Y	.30Y	.37Y	.02V	—V	—V	—Y	—Y	—Y	—Y
Zambia	754	.08V	.06V	.02V	.01V	.27V	1.43V	.01V	—V	—V	—V	—V	—V	—Y	—Y
Zimbabwe	698	—V	—V	—V	—V	—V	—V	—Y	—V	.01V	—V	—V	—V	.01V	.01Y
Africa n.s.	799	—Y	—Y	—Y	—Y	—Y	—Y	—Y	.05Y	.06Y	.07Y	.08Y	.10Y	.11Y	.12Y
Asia	**507**	**960.7Y**	**762.6Y**	**827.3Y**	**1,053.0Y**	**1,254.9Y**	**1,603.5Y**	**1,559.8Y**	**446.0Y**	**488.2Y**	**521.6Y**	**653.4Y**	**980.9Y**	**1,076.7Y**	**1,410.8Y**
Afghanistan, I.S. of	512	.15Y	.17Y	.21Y	.28Y	.32Y	.39Y	.49Y	.06Y	.07Y	.08Y	.11Y	.12Y	.15Y	.19Y
Bangladesh	513	4.05V	—V	—V	—V	—V	17.21V	1.79V	1.60V	.99V	1.56V	1.86V	2.32V	1.56Y	2.28Y
Bhutan	514	—Y	—Y	—Y	—Y	—Y	—Y	—Y	.02Y	.03Y	.03Y	.04Y	.05Y	.06Y	.08Y
Brunei Darussalam	516	.03Y	.03Y	.01V	.01Y	.01Y	.01Y	.01Y	3.80Y	4.13Y	.01V	.01Y	.01Y	.02Y	.02Y
Cambodia	522	—V	—V	—V	—V	.06V	.07V	.09Y	—V	—V	—V	—V	.06V	.01V	.02Y
China,P.R.: Mainland	924	70.61V	47.31V	47.39V	89.48V	62.67V	58.92V	92.97V	57.41V	63.70V	91.45V	133.02V	205.65V	313.08V	423.10V
China,P.R.:Hong Kong	532	12.14V	8.94V	12.78V	24.74V	41.55V	19.96V	5.45V	58.69V	52.24V	44.64V	45.16V	40.97V	47.08V	62.21V
China,P.R.:Macao	546	.01V	—V	—V	—V	—V	—V	—V	.01V	—V	—V	.01V	—V	—V	—V

	Exports							Imports						
	2001	2002	2003	2004	2005	2006	2007	2001	2002	2003	2004	2005	2006	2007
	Millions of U.S. Dollars							*Millions of U.S. Dollars*						
India.......534	246.69Y	113.05V	78.34V	93.62V	155.14V	191.74Y	237.95Y	89.96Y	102.91V	119.47V	147.50V	199.63V	246.72Y	306.18Y
Indonesia.......536	21.65V	38.66V	42.55V	97.95V	125.66V	36.37V	27.58V	19.70V	18.34V	19.15V	21.74V	19.63V	28.80V	38.51V
Korea.......542	116.83V	140.83V	228.45V	261.46V	279.61V	310.03V	291.11V	51.26V	67.55V	57.97V	90.15V	130.19V	137.75V	222.43V
Malaysia.......548	50.70V	35.10V	40.24V	71.14V	98.33V	127.85V	111.71V	29.83V	35.34V	36.46V	38.10V	45.86V	60.02V	67.54V
Maldives.......556	.42V	2.38V	.73V	31.57V	13.64V	16.86Y	20.92Y	—V	—V	—V	—V	—V	—Y	—Y
Mongolia.......948	—V	—Y	—Y	—Y	—Y	—Y	—Y	.03Y	.04Y	.04Y	.06Y	.07Y	.08Y	.10Y
Myanmar.......518	—Y	—Y	—Y	—Y	—Y	—Y	—Y	.45Y	.49Y	.62Y	.82Y	.94Y	1.16Y	1.44Y
Nepal.......558	1.18V	.64V	.18V	—V	.09V	.79V	.97Y	—V	—V	—V	—V	—V	.03V	.04Y
New Caledonia.......839	—V	—V	.01V	—V	—Y	—Y	—Y	—V	—V	—V	—V	—Y	—Y	—Y
Pakistan.......564	38.81V	40.56V	71.74V	57.71V	40.07V	49.52Y	61.46Y	49.56V	47.42V	43.34V	48.50V	45.84V	56.66Y	70.32Y
Papua New Guinea.......853	.02Y	.02Y	.02Y	.03Y	.03Y	.04Y	.05Y	.01Y	.01Y	.01Y	.02Y	.02Y	.02Y	.03Y
Philippines.......566	12.22V	3.92V	6.45V	1.53V	5.62V	6.29V	4.89V	3.63V	3.03V	2.77V	3.09V	3.47V	6.03V	18.09V
Singapore.......576	180.90V	67.18V	55.76V	67.90V	132.99V	321.06V	228.57V	23.00V	33.04V	34.65V	42.21V	187.44V	61.18V	59.04V
Solomon Islands.......813	—Y	—Y	—Y	—Y	—Y	—Y	—Y	.02Y	.02Y	.02Y	.03Y	.03Y	.04Y	.05Y
Sri Lanka.......524	17.57V	95.13V	3.67V	33.00V	3.32V	5.76V	4.94V	1.99V	2.91V	3.63V	5.56V	5.33V	4.52V	4.37V
Taiwan Province of China.......528	125.57V	111.09V	147.92V	135.70V	181.57V	233.86V	350.23V	18.23V	17.41V	20.62V	18.82V	20.78V	24.54V	28.82V
Thailand.......578	51.88V	52.03V	85.35V	79.01V	106.95V	194.70V	118.57V	36.32V	38.41V	44.75V	56.56V	72.45V	87.17V	105.95V
Vietnam.......582	9.30V	5.53V	5.55V	7.91V	7.27V	12.00V	—V	.40V	.19V	.28V	—V	—V	—V	—V
Europe.......170	**14.4Y**	**18.9Y**	**14.7Y**	**17.2Y**	**19.5Y**	**46.5Y**	**133.0Y**	**21.9Y**	**33.2Y**	**57.1Y**	**94.1Y**	**90.1Y**	**130.6Y**	**170.5Y**
Albania.......914	—V	—V	.03V	—V	.02V	—V	—V	—V	—V	—V	—V	.01V	.09V	—V
Armenia.......911	—Y	—Y	—Y	—Y	—Y	—V	.42V	.01V	—V	—V	—V	.02V	—V	.03V
Azerbaijan.......912	—V	—V	—V	—V	.09V	.01V	.01V	—V	—V	—V	—V	.01V	—V	.01V
Belarus.......913	—V	—V	—V	—V	—V	—V	—V	—V	—V	.01V	.20V	.50V	.01V	.03V
Bosnia & Herzegovina.......963	—Y	—Y	—Y	—Y	—Y	—Y	—Y	.14Y	.15Y	.19Y	.26Y	.29Y	.36Y	.45Y
Bulgaria.......918	—V	1.01V	—V	—V	—V	—V	.06V	.15V	.55V	.53V	.46V	.41V	2.24V	1.28V
Czech Republic.......935	.05V	—V	.04V	.07V	.23V	.07V	.12V	2.37V	1.81V	2.36V	5.15V	6.33V	6.20V	9.69V
Estonia.......939	—V	—V	—V	—V	.10V	.05V	.53V	.29V	.01V	.06V	.04V	.05V	3.12V	.10V
Gibraltar.......823	—Y	—Y	—Y	—Y	—Y	—Y	—Y	.01Y	.01Y	.02Y	.02Y	.03Y	.04Y	.04Y
Hungary.......944	.23V	—V	.05V	.09V	.05V	4.60V	12.44V	1.39V	3.19V	7.24V	12.43V	15.67V	34.31V	28.54V
Kazakhstan.......916	—V	—V	—V	.25V	.29Y	.35Y	.44Y	—V	—V	—V	—V	—Y	—Y	—Y
Kyrgyz Republic.......917	—V	—V	—V	—V	—V	—V	.02V	—V	—V	—V	—V	—V	—V	—V
Latvia.......941	—V	.01V	.06V	—V	—V	—V	—V	.04V	.03V	.06V	.03V	.09V	.07V	.16V
Lithuania.......946	—V	.03V	—V	—V	.02V	—V	.11V	.05V	.09V	.05V	.11V	.18V	.29V	.40V
Macedonia, FYR.......962	—V	.08V	—V	—V	—V	.06V	.08Y	—V	.04V	.03V	—V	.01V	.09V	.12Y
Poland.......964	.05V	.14V	.01V	.20V	.06V	.04V	.18V	1.42V	1.74V	2.03V	8.36V	3.40V	8.35V	16.95V
Romania.......968	.74V	.29V	.22V	.05V	.24V	.21V	.44V	2.50V	4.99V	9.08V	4.82V	6.99V	10.39V	7.04V
Russia.......922	.01V	—V	.40V	.04V	1.18V	.39V	9.57V	.74V	.02V	1.37V	.80V	.38V	11.50V	5.01V
Serbia & Montenegro.......965	....	....	....	....	....	....	....	.03Y	.03Y	.04Y	.06Y	.07Y	.08Y	.10Y
Slovak Republic.......936	—V	—V	—Y	—Y	—V	—V	.04V	.11V	.37V	.47Y	.61Y	2.66V	5.74V	5.24V
Turkey.......186	13.29V	17.26V	13.79V	16.46V	17.21V	40.73V	108.57V	12.28V	18.63V	31.74V	59.86V	45.83V	38.83V	84.31V
Turkmenistan.......925	—Y	—Y	—Y	—Y	—Y	—Y	—Y	—V	—V	.01V	.01Y	.01Y	.01Y	.01Y
Ukraine.......926	—V	.10V	.04V	—V	—V	—Y	—Y	.01V	1.15V	1.35V	.25V	6.44V	7.96Y	9.88Y
Uzbekistan.......927	....	....	....	....	....	....	....	.36Y	.39Y	.50Y	.65Y	.74Y	.92Y	1.14Y
Middle East.......407	**587.3Y**	**728.0Y**	**857.2Y**	**1,219.1Y**	**1,503.1Y**	**1,921.9Y**	**2,508.3Y**	**1,362.7Y**	**1,455.8Y**	**1,754.8Y**	**2,275.3Y**	**3,076.6Y**	**3,857.7Y**	**4,674.3Y**
Egypt.......469	13.38V	14.52Y	18.38Y	24.14Y	27.58Y	34.08Y	42.30Y	2.55V	2.76Y	3.50Y	4.59Y	5.25Y	6.48Y	8.05Y
Iran, I.R. of.......429	65.69V	51.28V	57.00Y	74.13Y	94.38Y	116.52Y	150.94Y	—Y	—Y	—Y	—Y	—Y	—Y	—Y
Iraq.......433	.06Y	.07Y	.07Y	.10Y	.12Y	.15Y	.20Y	.01Y	.01Y	.01Y	.01Y	.01Y	.02Y	.02Y
Jordan.......439	7.16V	9.48V	17.04V	5.15V	5.50V	30.99V	68.31V	20.53V	21.18V	20.08V	21.10V	22.69V	25.36V	49.45V
Kuwait.......443	56.06Y	57.98Y	64.45Y	83.82Y	106.73Y	131.76Y	170.68Y	16.43Y	17.47Y	21.18Y	28.02Y	38.12Y	47.92Y	57.81Y
Lebanon.......446	49.28Y	53.48Y	67.69Y	88.90Y	101.57Y	125.54Y	155.79Y	6.86Y	7.45Y	9.42Y	12.38Y	14.14Y	17.48Y	21.69Y
Libya.......672	2.70Y	2.79Y	3.10Y	4.03Y	5.14Y	6.34Y	8.21Y	.01Y	.01Y	.02Y	.02Y	.03Y	.04Y	.04Y
Oman.......449	39.26V	78.62V	120.82V	157.13Y	200.07Y	246.99Y	319.95Y	16.89V	24.68V	23.43V	31.00Y	42.17Y	53.01Y	63.95Y
Qatar.......453	20.00V	30.59V	58.69V	72.22V	55.95V	110.98V	143.76Y	32.54V	32.18V	38.92V	40.55V	50.21V	57.10V	68.88Y
Saudi Arabia.......456	180.85V	250.20V	185.29V	409.50V	520.72V	642.82Y	832.73Y	1,116.98Y	1,187.71Y	1,439.87Y	1,905.29Y	2,591.75Y	3,258.30Y	3,930.76Y
Syrian Arab Republic.......463	3.95Y	4.29Y	5.43Y	6.85V	7.83Y	9.68Y	12.01Y	12.49Y	13.55Y	17.15Y	17.07V	19.51Y	24.11Y	29.92Y
United Arab Emirates.......466	138.27V	147.00V	224.27V	291.67Y	371.39Y	458.48Y	593.93Y	125.61Y	133.56Y	161.92Y	214.25Y	291.44Y	366.40Y	442.02Y
Yemen, Republic of.......474	10.59V	27.66V	35.01Y	1.49V	6.17V	7.62Y	9.46Y	11.43V	14.83V	18.77Y	.39V	.59V	.72Y	.90Y
Middle East n.s.......489	—Y	—Y	—Y	—Y	—Y	—Y	—Y	.34Y	.43Y	.51Y	.60Y	.69Y	.77Y	.86Y
Western Hemisphere.......207	**5.4Y**	**3.6Y**	**1.3Y**	**1.7Y**	**4.8Y**	**54.3Y**	**9.9Y**	**79.2Y**	**85.9Y**	**90.8Y**	**128.2Y**	**162.5Y**	**161.6Y**	**137.0Y**
Antigua and Barbuda.......311	....	....	....	....	....	....	....	—Y	—Y	—Y	.01Y	.01Y	.01Y	.01Y
Argentina.......213	2.22V	—V	—V	—V	4.05V	7.33V	1.30V	20.75V	2.51V	9.60V	10.87V	5.82V	6.58V	4.04V
Aruba.......314	.02V	.09V	.04V	—V	—V	.01V	.09V	.01V	.07V	—V	.02V	.06V	.05V	—V
Bahamas, The.......313	—Y	—Y	—Y	—Y	—Y	—Y	—Y	.04Y	.05Y	.06Y	.07Y	.09Y	.11Y	.13Y
Barbados.......316	.04V	.10V	.01V	.03V	—V	.03V	.03Y	—V	.06V	.08V	.02V	—V	—V	—Y
Bermuda.......319	—Y	—Y	—Y	—Y	.04V	.01V	.01Y	—Y	—Y	—Y	—Y	—Y	—Y	—Y
Bolivia.......218	—V	.03V	—V	—V	—V	—Y	—Y	—V	—V	—V	—V	—Y	—Y	—Y
Brazil.......223	—V	.03V	—V	—V	—V	32.62V	—V	56.43V	75.02V	77.92V	113.48V	151.47V	150.31V	125.22V
Chile.......228	—V	—V	.35V	.28V	—V	—V	—V	1.24V	1.54V	1.73V	2.33V	2.56V	1.71V	2.92V
Colombia.......233	2.18V	2.37V	.80V	1.35V	.17V	2.77V	1.98V	.03V	.60V	.50V	.23V	.73V	.40V	.59V
Costa Rica.......238	.01V	.01V	—V	.01V	.01V	.02Y	.02Y	.09V	.04V	—V	—V	—V	.01Y	.01Y
Ecuador.......248	.01V	—V	—V	—V	—V	—V	—Y	.01V	.01V	.03V	.02V	.08V	.11V	.14Y
Falkland Islands.......323	—Y	—Y	—Y	—Y	—Y	—Y	—Y	.05Y	.06Y	.07Y	.10Y	.11Y	.14Y	.17Y
Guatemala.......258	—V	—V	—V	—V	—V	—Y	—Y	.54V	.51V	.33V	.50V	.45V	.56Y	.69Y
Honduras.......268	—Y	—Y	—Y	—Y	—Y	—Y	—Y	.03Y	.03Y	.04Y	.06Y	.07Y	.08Y	.10Y
Mexico.......273	—V	—V	—V	—V	.39V	11.17V	6.33V	—V	—V	—V	—V	.48V	1.04V	2.22V
Netherlands Antilles.......353	—V	—V	—Y	—Y	—Y	—Y	—Y	—V	5.35V	—V	—Y	—Y	—Y	—Y
Paraguay.......288	—V	—V	—V	—V	—V	—V	—Y	—V	—V	—V	.26V	.43V	.45V	.56Y

Exports

	2001	2002	2003	2004	2005	2006	2007
	Millions of U.S. Dollars						
Peru 293	.01V	—V	.07V	—V	.17V	.30V	.16Y
Uruguay 298	.90V	.98Y	—V	—V	—V	—Y	—Y
Venezuela, Rep. Bol 299	.03V	—V	—V	—V	—V	—V	—V
Other Countries n.i.e 910	**—Y**	**—Y**	**—Y**	**—Y**	**—Y**	**—Y**	**—Y**
Cuba 928	—Y	—Y	—Y	—Y	—Y	—Y	—Y
North Korea 954	—Y	—Y	—Y	—Y	—Y	—Y	—Y
Countries & Areas n.s 898	**5,287.7Y**	**5,738.5Y**	**7,263.1Y**	**9,538.9Y**	**10,899.0Y**	**13,470.3Y**	**16,716.6Y**
Memorandum Items							
European Union 998	429.63Y	335.93Y	371.68Y	397.43Y	618.07Y	630.63Y	955.19Y
Oil Exporting Ctys 999	536.37Y	677.49Y	779.06Y	1,220.21Y	1,517.93Y	1,797.04Y	2,308.39Y
Non-Oil Develop.Ctys 201	1,328.77Y	1,101.88Y	1,332.42Y	1,640.71Y	2,077.48Y	2,529.82Y	2,676.12Y
PERCENT DISTRIBUTION							
Industrial Countries 101	13.3	11.1	9.5	8.8	9.1	9.9	9.0
Developing Countries 202	22.6	21.0	20.4	21.0	22.6	21.9	20.9
Africa 607	3.6	3.1	4.0	4.2	5.1	3.5	3.2
Asia 507	11.6	9.0	8.0	7.7	7.9	8.1	6.5
Europe 170	.2	.2	.1	.1	.1	.2	.6
Middle East 407	7.1	8.6	8.3	9.0	9.4	9.7	10.5
Western Hemisphere 207	.1	—	—	—	—	.3	—
ANNUAL PERCENT CHANGE							
World 001	6.9	2.4	22.5	31.3	17.3	23.9	20.7
Industrial Countries 101	13.9	−14.9	4.5	21.7	21.5	35.1	9.5
Developing Countries 202	−4.9	−4.6	18.7	35.5	25.7	20.3	15.2
Africa 607	−5.0	−10.4	54.3	38.7	42.7	−13.8	10.4
Asia 507	−13.7	−20.6	8.5	27.3	19.2	27.8	−2.7
Europe 170	−50.5	31.7	−22.6	17.2	13.5	138.8	185.8
Middle East 407	17.7	24.0	17.8	42.2	23.3	27.9	30.5
Western Hemisphere 207	−25.6	−33.6	−64.6	29.9	192.7	—	−81.7
Other Countries n.i.e 910	—	—	....	....	....	....	....

Imports

	2001	2002	2003	2004	2005	2006	2007
	Millions of U.S. Dollars						
Peru 293	.01V	.05V	.17V	.16V	.09V	.08V	.19Y
Uruguay 298	—V	—Y	—V	—V	—V	—Y	—Y
Venezuela, Rep. Bol 299	—V	—V	.29V	.03V	—V	—V	—Y
Other Countries n.i.e 910	**1.2Y**	**1.3Y**	**1.7Y**	**2.2Y**	**2.5Y**	**3.1Y**	**3.9Y**
Cuba 928	.91Y	.99Y	1.25Y	1.64Y	1.88Y	2.32Y	2.88Y
North Korea 954	.32Y	.35Y	.44Y	.58Y	.66Y	.82Y	1.01Y
Countries & Areas n.s 898	**16.7Y**	**18.1Y**	**22.9Y**	**30.1Y**	**34.4Y**	**42.5Y**	**52.7Y**
Memorandum Items							
European Union 998	935.85Y	988.38Y	1,196.64Y	1,626.28Y	1,617.60Y	1,981.66Y	2,158.73Y
Oil Exporting Ctys 999	1,328.15Y	1,413.95Y	1,704.77Y	2,240.92Y	3,033.36Y	3,811.59Y	4,601.99Y
Non-Oil Develop.Ctys 201	609.20Y	685.34Y	787.23Y	943.98Y	1,318.13Y	1,458.17Y	1,852.62Y
PERCENT DISTRIBUTION							
Industrial Countries 101	46.9	47.8	48.0	45.1	38.2	38.8	37.5
Developing Countries 202	52.6	51.7	51.5	54.3	61.3	60.7	61.9
Africa 607	.7	.9	1.4	.6	.6	.5	.6
Asia 507	12.1	12.0	10.8	11.1	13.8	12.4	13.5
Europe 170	.6	.8	1.2	1.6	1.3	1.5	1.6
Middle East 407	37.0	35.8	36.3	38.8	43.3	44.4	44.8
Western Hemisphere 207	2.1	2.1	1.9	2.2	2.3	1.9	1.3
ANNUAL PERCENT CHANGE							
World 001	4.1	10.2	19.1	21.1	21.1	22.3	20.0
Industrial Countries 101	5.5	12.3	19.5	13.8	2.5	24.3	16.2
Developing Countries 202	2.8	8.4	18.7	27.8	36.6	21.1	22.5
Africa 607	39.3	31.0	87.5	−49.8	22.1	3.9	43.7
Asia 507	−10.1	9.5	6.8	25.3	50.1	9.8	31.0
Europe 170	−40.6	51.7	71.9	64.7	−4.2	44.9	30.6
Middle East 407	10.2	6.8	20.5	29.7	35.2	25.4	21.2
Western Hemisphere 207	−17.2	8.4	5.7	41.1	26.8	−.5	−15.2
Other Countries n.i.e 910	10.4	8.5	26.6	31.3	14.3	23.6	24.1

		Exports							Imports						
		2001	2002	2003	2004	2005	2006	2007	2001	2002	2003	2004	2005	2006	2007
		Millions of U.S. Dollars							*Millions of U.S. Dollars*						
IFS World Total		**4,826.0**	**4,565.7**	**5,262.7**	**6,614.7**	**7,232.7**	**9,102.5**	**10,233.1**	**8,349.8**	**7,913.7**	**9,516.2**	**12,599.4**	**12,881.0**	**14,963.5**	**17,263.0**
DOTS World Total	**001**	**5,735.6**	**5,443.3**	**6,229.4**	**7,585.6**	**8,494.4**	**11,650.2Y**	**12,717.1Y**	**9,011.5**	**7,847.8**	**9,834.9**	**11,590.0**	**13,850.9**	**16,095.6**	**18,476.3**
Industrial Countries	**101**	**4,273.7**	**4,033.9**	**4,688.5**	**5,921.8**	**6,355.0**	**8,874.2Y**	**9,437.7Y**	**2,289.5**	**1,996.5**	**2,060.7**	**2,413.5**	**2,649.6**	**3,168.6**	**3,581.4**
United States	111	1,696.62	1,504.41	1,488.64	1,697.52	2,003.48	2,869.93S	2,930.68S	264.91	234.19	231.09	268.19	326.54	376.71	470.41
Canada	156	95.62	82.56	165.52	247.44	275.36	407.70S	416.06S	78.40	51.70	93.32	65.72	62.53	106.52	250.48
Australia	193	13.60	13.16	12.23	13.57	29.55	27.09S	29.56S	214.61	172.11	204.90	266.38	268.01	269.33	335.30
Japan	158	62.00	55.84	51.49	61.60	64.36	103.93S	114.45S	720.71	594.86	566.70	613.95	570.99	749.82	653.84
New Zealand	196	2.72	2.59	2.07	2.04	1.81	4.01S	3.21S	10.42	14.03	14.12	20.14	17.98	22.32	28.28
Austria	122	10.47	10.88	12.08	19.18	23.51	45.19S	49.80S	19.61	11.03	25.31	21.59	25.47	33.52	30.63
Belgium	124	179.81	187.91	225.86	252.76	268.82	421.81S	509.10S	26.47	27.72	25.46	27.60	24.11	77.56	65.94
Cyprus	423	.88	.48	.51	.73	1.21	1.49S	1.48S	.28	—	—	—	—	—	1.30
Denmark	128	58.59	58.83	69.23	82.54	73.79	111.50S	115.81S	26.59	53.32	71.80	27.12	29.62	41.46	45.20
Finland	172	16.98	17.71	16.37	19.72	18.09	19.56S	24.43S	14.22	11.73	7.21	14.89	16.29	39.05	61.64
France	132	308.35	311.49	367.54	526.42	544.53	624.04S	702.47S	78.63	80.53	83.14	67.04	55.80	112.88	96.55
Germany	134	588.17	566.16	849.63	1,101.52	1,143.72	1,567.19S	1,648.10S	192.80	158.21	174.31	223.26	316.32	301.63	413.68
Greece	174	3.70	4.74	7.65	11.13	14.43	22.00S	25.96S	5.07	1.47	—	—	—	8.06	2.67
Iceland	176	.77	.49	.57	.47	.72	2.07S	1.67S	—	—	—	—	—	—	—
Ireland	178	22.16	23.48	33.67	47.58	52.17	60.38S	62.17S	.94	1.26	2.08	1.56	8.14	2.51	2.13
Italy	136	263.03	216.01	240.76	305.14	326.23	460.19S	460.50S	77.86	78.96	95.46	135.03	156.77	175.25	222.15
Luxembourg	137	.34	.74	.07	.29	.22	.18S	.07S	.22	—	—	—	—	6.64	1.57
Malta	181	—	—	—	.36	.83	1.51S	.98S	.78	.89	—	—	—	—	3.90
Netherlands	138	251.47	207.89	227.44	254.00	241.40	378.95S	425.75S	87.66	63.37	76.38	61.11	62.87	93.66	127.48
Norway	142	16.77	18.06	15.02	12.83	11.59	40.77S	45.19S	39.29	15.19	49.05	12.56	7.91	12.21	23.83
Portugal	182	7.68	7.22	4.93	7.62	12.05	14.91S	16.56S	1.39	6.19	2.74	5.92	2.02	2.59	3.20
Slovenia	961	.04	—	.07	.34	2.38	7.12S	3.64S	—	.22	—	—	—	—	—
Spain	184	88.38	103.53	158.88	239.78	298.77	409.83S	442.58S	20.78	20.17	31.97	46.79	38.22	61.17	54.39
Sweden	144	83.42	85.54	109.62	147.84	130.60	168.37S	188.17S	67.23	60.86	47.81	113.61	128.22	222.11	205.37
Switzerland	146	15.64	22.49	24.55	20.14	20.56	49.34S	57.92S	102.94	115.03	107.11	137.97	209.07	160.73	220.68
United Kingdom	112	486.50	531.66	604.11	849.25	794.78	1,055.16S	1,161.36S	237.70	223.42	150.75	283.03	322.73	292.85	260.79
Developing Countries	**202**	**542.7**	**528.8**	**557.1**	**652.7**	**850.4**	**1,214.3Y**	**1,484.1Y**	**5,370.7**	**4,955.3**	**6,556.5**	**8,050.4**	**9,902.9**	**11,603.6**	**13,518.5**
Africa	**607**	**24.9**	**40.8**	**49.6**	**50.4**	**45.4**	**71.2Y**	**98.2Y**	**73.5**	**38.2**	**66.2**	**77.8**	**53.4**	**63.9**	**109.9**
Algeria	612	.53	.36	.76	.82	1.22	1.04S	2.50S	—	—	—	—	—	1.35	—
Angola	614	—	—	.70	.88	.21	.27S	.33S	—	—	—	—	—	—	—
Benin	638	—	.36	.15	.25	.36	.44S	2.87S	3.45	2.13	7.32	6.82	.58	1.05	6.61
Burkina Faso	748	—	—	—	—	—	—S	—S	—	.79	7.73	17.57	2.72	—	2.56
Burundi	618	—	—	—	.26	—	.02S	.03S	.19	—	—	—	—	—	—
Cameroon	622	.98	.93	1.37	1.41	1.31	1.20S	1.23S	1.70	3.23	7.41	7.64	2.11	.81	—
Chad	628	—	—	—	—	—	—S	—S	—	—	—	—	—	1.89	3.04
Congo, Dem. Rep. of	636	.02	—	—	.02	.63	.78S	.96S	....	....	....	....	....	....	....
Congo, Republic of	634	—	—	.16	.20	—	—S	—S	—	—	—	—	—	—	—
Côte d'Ivoire	662	4.73	6.04	3.05	1.93	4.58	16.94S	20.84S	2.06	.97	.86	—	—	4.38	6.08
Djibouti	611	1.36	.93	3.38	.98	.64	.77S	1.06S	—	—	—	—	—	—	—
Equatorial Guinea	642	—	.05	—	—	—	—S	—S	—	—	—	—	—	—	—
Ethiopia	644	.41	.10	—	1.16	1.73	.80S	.96S	—	—	—	—	—	—	10.63
Gabon	646	—	—	—	—	.30	.37S	.46S	—	—	—	—	—	—	—
Gambia, The	648	—	.06	—	—	—	—S	—S	—	—	—	—	—	—	—
Ghana	652	.86	1.99	.63	4.32	1.71	2.17S	6.93S	—	—	—	—	—	—	1.33
Guinea	656	—	.04	.16	.44	.51	.79S	1.25S	—	—	—	—	—	—	—
Guinea-Bissau	654	—	—	—	—	.37	.46S	.82S	—	—	—	—	—	—	—
Kenya	664	2.55	3.96	2.31	4.45	2.93	3.52S	4.20S	—	—	—	—	—	—	—
Liberia	668	—	.12	.05	.15	.03	.04S	.04S	4.62	—	—	—	—	—	—
Madagascar	674	.12	.18	.11	.14	.90	1.26S	1.34S	—	—	—	—	—	—	—
Malawi	676	.07	—	.08	—	—	—S	—S	—	—	—	—	—	—	—
Mali	678	—	—	—	—	—	—S	—S	—	2.01	14.44	15.88	12.19	6.32	7.81
Mauritius	684	.02	.04	.14	—	—	.12S	.22S	—	—	—	—	—	1.54	6.61
Morocco	686	.63	.59	.73	.93	2.07	2.71S	3.94S	—	—	—	—	—	—	7.28
Mozambique	688	.27	.18	.46	.91	.66	.35S	1.79S	—	—	—	—	—	—	—
Namibia	728	—	.02	—	—	—	—S	—S	—	—	—	—	—	—	—
Niger	692	—	—	—	—	.03	.04S	.05S	—	—	—	—	—	.43	—
Nigeria	694	.84	.92	1.17	2.13	4.87	3.75S	3.26S	5.53	2.12	6.26	6.11	12.18	7.76	11.28
Senegal	722	.11	.33	.84	1.23	.33	.16S	.20S	—	—	—	—	—	—	—
Sierra Leone	724	.22	.16	.08	1.03	.11	.13S	.16S	—	—	—	—	—	—	—
Somalia	726	—	.08	—	—	—	—S	—S	—	—	—	—	—	—	—
South Africa	199	2.02	3.09	3.95	4.89	5.59	10.93S	20.45S	13.38	6.87	8.72	12.26	9.03	9.63	16.84
Sudan	732	2.47	16.68	23.51	19.47	9.11	15.40S	13.96S	5.55	4.44	10.76	11.52	14.56	15.30	11.18
Swaziland	734	.45	.41	.67	.52	.46	.94S	.84S	23.70	4.52	1.31	—	—	—	—
Tanzania	738	1.05	.13	2.45	.37	.34	.24S	.42S	.96	—	—	—	—	1.33	1.27
Togo	742	.10	—	—	.22	1.88	2.32S	2.88S	—	.81	—	—	—	—	—
Tunisia	744	1.32	.28	1.95	.87	1.04	1.69S	2.27S	10.83	9.79	1.42	—	—	2.80	—
Uganda	746	.96	1.12	.70	.47	1.43	1.54S	1.92S	.42	—	—	—	—	—	—
Zambia	754	.44	.13	—	—	—	.01S	—S	—	—	—	—	—	5.21	10.97
Zimbabwe	698	2.34	1.49	.08	—	—	—S	—S	1.15	.49	—	—	—	4.13	6.39

		Exports							Imports						
		2001	2002	2003	2004	2005	2006	2007	2001	2002	2003	2004	2005	2006	2007
		Millions of U.S. Dollars							*Millions of U.S. Dollars*						
Asia	**507**	**309.5**	**270.1**	**325.4**	**378.0**	**510.9**	**655.7Y**	**769.3Y**	**4,669.3**	**4,324.2**	**5,551.5**	**6,428.6**	**7,251.7**	**8,363.1**	**9,832.2**
Afghanistan, I.S. of	512	5.57	4.66	3.25	1.98	.84	.74S	1.49S	—	—	4.10	3.66	3.35	3.12	4.52
American Samoa	859	—	—	—	—	—	—S	—S	.26	—	—	—	—	—	—
Bhutan	514	1.48	1.41	2.38	3.64	3.30	3.65S	4.85S	5.07	3.30	3.84	6.05	10.44	10.69	10.42
Brunei Darussalam	516	.64	.93	.51	.16	.53	.61S	.70S	.47	—	—	—	—	—	—
Cambodia	522	—	.05	.15	.75	.64	1.01S	.61S	—	—	—	—	—	—	—
China,P.R.: Mainland	924	5.54	12.19	13.17	30.67	46.33	78.43S	87.84S	772.40	910.30	1,090.84	1,445.68	1,870.35	2,332.22	2,771.64
China,P.R.:Hong Kong	532	101.00	101.19	87.07	94.38	105.50	112.74S	113.33S	461.75	421.79	437.83	518.14	566.71	702.81	769.05
China,P.R.:Macao	546	—	.02	—	—	—	.06S	.05S	—	—	—	—	—	.30	9.89
Fiji	819	.03	.05	—	—	—	—S	—S	1.68	—	—	—	—	—	—
India	534	60.80	39.33	55.34	66.15	118.88	152.85S	209.71S	1,195.49	1,145.83	1,494.22	1,745.06	1,951.24	2,061.71	2,646.58
Indonesia	536	4.86	7.08	8.23	9.00	23.10	16.28S	19.48S	179.52	171.50	209.24	261.05	269.53	312.76	378.68
Kiribati	826	—	—	—	—	—	—S	—S	2.32	—	—	—	—	—	—
Korea	542	13.41	12.56	15.64	25.36	22.86	51.86S	122.38S	403.74	340.84	366.98	418.57	446.16	514.57	550.61
Lao People's Dem.Rep	544	.05	—	—	—	—	—S	—S	.46	.24	—	—	—	—	—
Malaysia	548	4.76	5.55	3.88	7.74	10.36	15.82S	21.84S	146.48	147.84	215.21	274.78	299.67	347.82	327.06
Maldives	556	.24	—	—	—	—	—S	—S	.90	—	.40	—	—	—	—
Mongolia	948	—	—	—	—	—	—S	—S	.49	.26	—	—	—	—	—
Myanmar	518	.68	.97	2.44	1.89	1.51	3.29S	5.77S	19.72	23.77	33.23	27.30	32.28	26.90	29.66
Nepal	558	1.95	3.91	2.98	4.59	3.48	2.35S	4.48S	4.15	5.38	4.86	2.14	2.94	3.73	15.67
New Caledonia	839	—	—	—	—	—	—S	—S	.31	—	—	—	—	—	—
Pakistan	564	25.60	27.18	42.70	40.46	52.00	56.95S	73.52S	85.63	59.78	95.49	121.19	143.88	170.33	196.90
Papua New Guinea	853	.53	1.13	1.32	.91	1.40	1.06S	1.91S	.58	—	—	—	—	—	—
Philippines	566	.51	.33	7.82	2.65	4.82	6.44S	4.22S	9.18	14.41	18.01	12.39	24.12	20.92	35.52
Samoa	862	.13	—	—	—	—	—S	—S	—	—	—	—	—	—	—
Singapore	576	35.65	26.56	37.54	33.17	53.14	74.15S	50.07S	827.07	905.55	1,040.73	873.07	852.31	965.17	1,137.49
Solomon Islands	813	.04	.04	—	—	—	—S	—S	1.45	—	—	—	—	—	—
Sri Lanka	524	2.02	1.94	5.80	9.68	8.81	7.20S	10.15S	7.87	6.79	9.24	9.32	10.05	16.40	13.45
Taiwan Province of China	528	14.43	3.94	15.86	15.75	18.27	16.40S	18.11S	359.24	—	348.27	413.54	438.51	481.54	477.89
Thailand	578	16.73	11.12	9.45	12.52	14.50	33.26S	12.70S	179.69	163.28	176.56	291.20	316.29	381.05	442.02
Vanuatu	846	—	—	—	—	—	—S	—S	.75	—	—	—	—	—	—
Vietnam	582	12.84	8.01	9.91	16.54	20.69	20.49S	6.08S	2.59	3.36	2.49	5.50	13.85	11.06	15.13
Europe	**170**	**48.1**	**48.8**	**53.8**	**92.8**	**124.8**	**267.1Y**	**335.6Y**	**113.7**	**111.9**	**213.4**	**283.4**	**506.8**	**795.5**	**821.7**
Albania	914	.06	.13	.06	.07	.35	.19S	.62S	.34	—	—	—	—	—	—
Armenia	911	—	—	—	—	—	.03S	.03S	—	—	—	—	—	—	—
Azerbaijan	912	—	—	—	—	—	.01S	—S	.22	—	.60	—	—	.35	—
Belarus	913	—	—	.07	—	—	.59S	2.43S	—	—	—	—	—	—	20.51
Bulgaria	918	.72	.62	.86	.13	.81	2.35S	1.11S	3.90	.36	—	—	—	2.26	7.31
Croatia	960	—	—	.07	.29	.80	.18S	.26S	—	—	—	—	—	5.23	4.44
Czech Republic	935	4.22	2.60	1.58	2.04	4.52	16.38S	13.26S	7.01	6.41	2.39	7.48	10.24	13.86	15.17
Czechoslovakia n.s.	937	—	—	—	.10	—	—S	—S	—	—	—	—	—	—	—
Estonia	939	—	.15	—	—	.24	.39S	.24S	—	—	—	—	—	—	—
Georgia	915	—	—	—	—	—	.01S	1.31S	—	—	—	—	—	—	—
Gibraltar	823	.06	—	—	.12	.10	.12S	.15S	.23	—	—	—	—	—	—
Hungary	944	3.83	3.33	3.18	5.72	8.84	11.12S	6.35S	2.07	2.90	4.86	5.70	13.65	17.07	44.26
Kazakhstan	916	.63	1.86	1.70	1.40	1.41	1.27S	1.43S	3.62	3.48	11.21	17.64	19.43	17.55	17.06
Kyrgyz Republic	917	—	—	—	—	—	.07S	.15S	—	—	—	—	—	—	—
Latvia	941	.02	.02	.18	.50	.10	.12S	.08S	—	—	—	—	—	2.12	.13
Lithuania	946	—	—	—	.08	.03	.36S	.15S	—	—	—	—	—	1.05	—
Macedonia, FYR	962	—	—	—	—	—	.29S	.35S	—	—	—	—	—	—	—
Moldova	921	—	—	—	—	.73	.89S	.87S	—	—	—	—	—	—	—
Poland	964	6.64	5.94	6.13	10.24	14.60	29.28S	33.48S	1.65	2.02	2.17	5.75	11.42	9.71	3.21
Romania	968	1.19	.94	.51	1.70	1.33	5.54S	3.74S	1.88	.33	—	—	—	36.74	23.83
Russia	922	8.65	3.56	4.63	6.06	9.32	22.51S	56.32S	47.57	30.37	35.39	74.69	147.51	249.00	249.91
Slovak Republic	936	—	.24	.44	.94	1.71	9.60S	26.97S	—	—	—	—	—	—	—
Tajikistan	923	—	—	—	—	—	—S	.04S	.81	.98	2.48	10.99	8.68	6.95	6.00
Turkey	186	21.81	29.05	33.30	60.17	75.41	159.28S	179.35S	12.39	10.38	31.41	21.77	62.51	88.63	65.44
Turkmenistan	925	—	—	—	—	—	—S	—S	4.82	6.10	7.23	12.10	11.67	14.73	51.26
Ukraine	926	.18	.20	.89	2.26	3.23	3.81S	5.46S	2.68	2.44	14.21	15.71	42.22	76.00	29.48
Uzbekistan	927	.12	.12	.25	1.04	1.31	2.72S	1.45S	24.53	46.07	101.47	111.56	179.45	254.29	283.72
Middle East	**407**	**140.1**	**126.4**	**104.1**	**106.5**	**132.3**	**151.9Y**	**179.1Y**	**421.4**	**397.0**	**599.0**	**1,063.7**	**1,887.5**	**2,164.7**	**2,376.9**
Bahrain	419	1.45	.90	1.42	1.70	2.11	1.42S	2.07S	4.45	—	—	—	—	18.93	1.97
Egypt	469	7.02	11.76	5.99	8.70	11.67	12.24S	13.18S	2.25	7.23	10.28	6.80	21.04	25.08	18.24
Iran, I.R. of	429	36.84	38.24	36.55	34.85	46.05	53.90S	65.07S	10.27	9.99	19.91	16.91	23.42	43.47	38.08
Iraq	433	2.45	—	—	—	—	—S	—S	.24	—	—	—	—	—	—
Israel	436	—	—	—	—	—	—S	.09S	—	—	—	—	—	—	—
Jordan	439	1.30	1.31	1.23	1.79	1.75	1.79S	3.82S	1.75	2.56	.86	9.42	3.45	10.58	18.67
Kuwait	443	2.76	3.68	2.93	3.67	5.52	6.19S	7.91S	28.06	117.40	173.45	638.59	1,178.76	1,238.54	1,536.71
Lebanon	446	.57	.75	.47	.63	.39	.27S	.33S	—	—	—	—	—	6.85	5.83
Libya	672	.11	.04	.65	.65	.36	.44S	.57S	—	—	—	—	—	—	—
Oman	449	.95	1.12	.85	.79	.67	.64S	.73S	.28	.29	—	—	—	.58	13.19
Qatar	453	1.82	2.31	1.65	2.64	3.19	3.35S	4.36S	4.15	1.72	5.58	10.67	15.09	22.25	51.81
Saudi Arabia	456	11.78	12.00	11.29	17.91	26.06	31.61S	35.22S	237.32	103.84	199.99	163.56	292.50	400.57	343.33
Syrian Arab Republic	463	21.54	30.66	16.97	11.03	9.14	13.77S	11.79S	19.67	1.83	—	—	—	6.51	5.10
United Arab Emirates	466	50.56	21.88	22.26	20.43	21.12	21.29S	27.75S	112.52	152.18	188.94	217.70	353.24	391.31	343.99
Yemen, Republic of	474	.99	1.77	1.80	1.69	4.26	4.96S	6.25S	.43	—	—	—	—	—	—
Western Hemisphere	**207**	**20.0**	**42.7**	**24.1**	**24.9**	**37.0**	**68.5Y**	**101.8Y**	**92.9**	**84.1**	**126.3**	**196.9**	**203.5**	**216.4**	**377.7**
Antigua and Barbuda	311	.07	—	—	.42	—	—S	—S	.28	—	—	—	—	—	—
Argentina	213	1.34	.59	.22	.32	.86	1.90S	2.62S	39.64	44.99	72.84	63.40	95.67	81.23	156.92
Bahamas, The	313	—	—	—	—	—	—S	—S	1.73	—	1.21	—	—	11.31	—

	Exports							Imports						
	2001	2002	2003	2004	2005	2006	2007	2001	2002	2003	2004	2005	2006	2007
	Millions of U.S. Dollars							Millions of U.S. Dollars						
Barbados.......316	—	—	—	—	—	.04S	.05S	—	—	—	—	—	—	—
Belize.......339	—	—	—	—	—	—S	—S	.74	—	—	—	—	—	—
Bermuda.......319	—	—	—	—	—	.01S	.02S	.56	—	—	—	—	—	—
Bolivia.......218	.05	—	.76	—	—	—S	—S	—	—	—	3.94	—	—	—
Brazil.......223	7.07	7.20	6.53	5.82	3.05	8.50S	14.62S	36.93	24.43	43.29	120.35	94.15	106.05	211.72
Chile.......228	.18	.97	.22	.18	1.00	1.87S	2.40S	2.76	2.50	2.58	6.06	9.35	3.49	1.17
Colombia.......233	.06	.12	.16	.04	.14	.42S	1.76S	—	—	—	—	—	—	—
Costa Rica.......238	.17	.31	.22	.33	.18	.22S	.28S	—	—	—	—	—	—	—
Dominican Republic.......243	.17	—	.10	—	—	—S	—S	—	—	—	—	—	1.88	3.08
Ecuador.......248	—	—	—	—	—	.05S	.06S	—	—	—	—	—	—	—
El Salvador.......253	.12	.06	.12	—	.39	.46S	.40S	—	—	—	—	—	—	—
Greenland.......326	—	—	—	—	—	—S	—S	.19	—	—	—	—	—	—
Grenada.......328	—	—	—	—	—	—S	—S	2.36	5.19	—	—	—	—	—
Guatemala.......258	.11	.25	.22	.44	.08	.10S	.12S	.21	.24	3.26	2.27	4.36	2.48	1.56
Guyana.......336	—	—	—	—	—	—S	—S	—	—	—	—	—	1.48	—
Haiti.......263	1.45	.37	—	—	—	—S	—S	—	—	—	—	—	—	—
Honduras.......268	.24	.10	—	—	.07	.08S	.10S	—	—	—	—	—	—	—
Jamaica.......343	.04	—	—	—	—	.52S	.29S	—	—	—	—	—	—	—
Mexico.......273	6.58	10.43	15.43	15.80	21.11	48.68S	71.43S	5.34	—	—	—	—	1.49	1.55
Netherlands Antilles.......353	.03	21.34	—	.35	1.98	1.05S	1.43S	—	—	—	—	—	—	—
Nicaragua.......278	.05	.04	—	.10	.06	—S	—S	—	—	—	—	—	—	—
Panama.......283	.27	.29	.03	.22	.76	1.18S	1.54S	.77	—	1.28	—	—	1.40	—
Paraguay.......288	—	.14	—	—	—	—S	—S	.76	—	—	—	—	—	—
Peru.......293	.21	.26	.09	.30	7.32	3.31S	4.51S	.63	—	1.88	.89	—	3.24	—
Trinidad and Tobago.......369	—	—	—	—	—	—S	—S	—	—	—	—	—	1.96	—
Uruguay.......298	1.26	.15	—	—	—	—S	—S	—	—	—	—	—	.36	1.76
Venezuela, Rep. Bol.......299	.55	.12	.05	.23	—	.09S	.21S	—	2.16	—	—	—	—	—
Western Hem. n.s.......399	—	—	—	.37	—	—S	—S	—	4.56	—	—	—	—	—
Other Countries n.i.e.......910	**4.6**	**5.5**	**6.6**	**12.0**	**11.2**	**20.8Y**	**27.7Y**	**41.9**	**28.9**	**14.3**	**11.4**	**23.0**	**18.9**	**12.0**
Cuba.......928	—	.99	—	1.63	.36	1.08S	.33S	....	....	....	....	....	....	....
North Korea.......954	4.61	4.48	6.64	10.33	10.81	19.73S	27.34S	41.92	28.88	14.35	11.43	23.02	18.92	12.00
Countries & Areas n.s.......898	**3.4**	**6.9**	**7.8**	**10.2**	**13.8**	**19.6S**	**32.1S**	**76.5**	**37.0**	**270.6**	**211.2**	**320.3**	**229.6**	**158.7**
Special Categories.......899	**911.2**	**868.2**	**969.3**	**988.9**	**1,264.0**	**1,521.2S**	**1,735.5S**	**1,232.0**	**830.1**	**770.1**	**903.5**	**955.1**	**1,074.9**	**1,205.7**
Memorandum Items														
European Union.......998	2,384.69	2,346.53	2,939.94	3,885.71	3,977.58	5,436.62Y	5,919.46Y	868.94	810.69	803.83	1,047.48	1,221.88	1,514.76	1,661.37
Oil Exporting Ctys.......999	114.05	87.74	86.39	93.12	132.15	138.59Y	167.05Y	577.88	561.18	803.37	1,314.59	2,144.73	2,418.59	2,717.07
Non-Oil Develop.Ctys.......201	428.62	441.08	470.74	559.56	718.22	1,075.71Y	1,317.04Y	4,792.86	4,394.15	5,753.15	6,735.79	7,758.13	9,185.00	10,801.43
PERCENT DISTRIBUTION														
Industrial Countries.......101	**74.5**	**74.1**	**75.3**	**78.1**	**74.8**	**76.2**	**74.2**	**25.4**	**25.4**	**21.0**	**20.8**	**19.1**	**19.7**	**19.4**
Developing Countries.......202	**9.5**	**9.7**	**8.9**	**8.6**	**10.0**	**10.4**	**11.7**	**59.6**	**63.1**	**66.7**	**69.5**	**71.5**	**72.1**	**73.2**
Africa.......607	**.4**	**.7**	**.8**	**.7**	**.5**	**.6**	**.8**	**.8**	**.5**	**.7**	**.7**	**.4**	**.4**	**.6**
Asia.......507	**5.4**	**5.0**	**5.2**	**5.0**	**6.0**	**5.6**	**6.0**	**51.8**	**55.1**	**56.4**	**55.5**	**52.4**	**52.0**	**53.2**
Europe.......170	**.8**	**.9**	**.9**	**1.2**	**1.5**	**2.3**	**2.6**	**1.3**	**1.4**	**2.2**	**2.4**	**3.7**	**4.9**	**4.4**
Middle East.......407	**2.4**	**2.3**	**1.7**	**1.4**	**1.6**	**1.3**	**1.4**	**4.7**	**5.1**	**6.1**	**9.2**	**13.6**	**13.4**	**12.9**
Western Hemisphere.......207	**.3**	**.8**	**.4**	**.3**	**.4**	**.6**	**.8**	**1.0**	**1.1**	**1.3**	**1.7**	**1.5**	**1.3**	**2.0**
Other Countries n.i.e.......910	**.1**	**.1**	**.1**	**.2**	**.1**	**.2**	**.2**	**.5**	**.4**	**.1**	**.1**	**.2**	**.1**	**.1**
ANNUAL PERCENT CHANGE														
World.......001	**2.6**	**–5.1**	**14.4**	**21.8**	**12.0**	**37.2**	**9.2**	**.1**	**–12.9**	**25.3**	**17.8**	**19.5**	**16.2**	**14.8**
Industrial Countries.......101	**1.1**	**–5.6**	**16.2**	**26.3**	**7.3**	**39.6**	**6.3**	**–2.5**	**–12.8**	**3.2**	**17.1**	**9.8**	**19.6**	**13.0**
Developing Countries.......202	**–.2**	**–2.6**	**5.4**	**17.1**	**30.3**	**42.8**	**22.2**	**5.9**	**–7.7**	**32.3**	**22.8**	**23.0**	**17.2**	**16.5**
Africa.......607	**–23.8**	**63.8**	**21.8**	**1.6**	**–10.1**	**57.0**	**37.9**	**–12.3**	**–48.1**	**73.5**	**17.5**	**–31.4**	**19.8**	**71.9**
Asia.......507	**4.9**	**–12.7**	**20.5**	**16.2**	**35.2**	**28.3**	**17.3**	**9.3**	**–7.4**	**28.4**	**15.8**	**12.8**	**15.3**	**17.6**
Europe.......170	**–15.4**	**1.3**	**10.4**	**72.4**	**34.4**	**114.0**	**25.7**	**–7.5**	**–1.6**	**90.8**	**32.8**	**78.8**	**57.0**	**3.3**
Middle East.......407	**2.9**	**–9.8**	**–17.7**	**2.3**	**24.2**	**14.8**	**18.0**	**–8.4**	**–5.8**	**50.9**	**77.6**	**77.5**	**14.7**	**9.8**
Western Hemisphere.......207	**–12.1**	**113.6**	**–43.5**	**3.2**	**48.4**	**85.2**	**48.7**	**–29.5**	**–9.5**	**50.3**	**55.9**	**3.4**	**6.3**	**74.6**
Other Countries n.i.e.......910	**–11.9**	**18.7**	**21.4**	**80.0**	**–6.7**	**86.4**	**32.9**	**–36.0**	**–31.1**	**–50.3**	**–20.3**	**101.4**	**–17.8**	**–36.6**

Exports

Millions of U.S. Dollars

		2001	2002	2003	2004	2005	2006	2007
IFS World Total		**259.4**	**241.5**	**249.8**	**278.3**	**359.5**	**385.0**	**418.7**
DOTS World Total	**001**	**259.3**	**241.5**	**193.0**	**208.9**	**260.0**	**323.9**	**391.1Y**
Industrial Countries	**101**	**89.7**	**80.0**	**78.0**	**87.9**	**98.7**	**146.4**	**92.9Y**
United States	111	38.81	35.58	36.11	43.05	48.38	89.37	36.27V
Canada	156	7.15	4.51	3.92	5.25	6.49	7.80	7.57V
Australia	193	.43	.36	.22	.03	.08	.07	.73V
Japan	158	.21	.13	.12	.05	.07	.25	.47V
New Zealand	196	.92	.48	.44	.03	.02	.13	.74V
Austria	122	.13	.09	.07	.01	—	.11	—V
Belgium	124	.86	.40	.19	.07	.19	.95	.08V
Cyprus	423	.04	.04	.01	.02	.02	.01	—V
Denmark	128	.34	.28	.04	.34	.22	.60	.32V
Finland	172	.17	.02	.01	.03	.01	.02	.01V
France	132	2.47	3.27	1.59	2.53	3.71	1.52	2.73V
Germany	134	.58	1.17	1.15	1.01	1.43	4.17	3.47V
Greece	174	.02	.09	.14	.36	.07	.82	.89V
Iceland	176	—	—	—	.02	—	—	.28V
Ireland	178	.35	.03	.05	.13	.10	.15	—V
Italy	136	2.03	1.70	.88	.25	.83	1.27	.65V
Luxembourg	137	.01	.03	—	—	—	—	—V
Malta	181	.01	.01	—	—	—	.02	—V
Netherlands	138	2.45	.97	.90	2.46	1.54	1.22	1.67V
Norway	142	.09	.08	.02	.02	—	.02	.04V
Portugal	182	.16	.59	.46	.01	.14	.07	.01V
Slovenia	961	.04	—	—	—	—	.03	—V
Spain	184	.28	2.89	.87	1.23	3.04	.65	.01V
Sweden	144	.63	.40	2.43	.23	.04	.15	.03V
Switzerland	146	1.22	1.19	.87	.53	.94	3.99	.20V
United Kingdom	112	30.32	25.69	27.49	30.22	31.38	33.02	36.77V
Developing Countries	**202**	**126.0**	**120.5**	**115.0**	**121.1**	**161.3**	**177.5**	**298.2Y**
Africa	**607**	**.9**	**1.2**	**.6**	**.6**	**.3**	**.5**	**.6Y**
Algeria	612	.01	—	—	.03	—	—	—Y
Angola	614	—	.75	—	—	.02	—	—Y
Cameroon	622	—	.01	—	.31	—	—	—Y
Cape Verde	624	—	—	—	—	.02	—	—Y
Central African Rep.	626	.01	—	—	—	—	.01	.01Y
Comoros	632	—	—	.01	—	—	—	—Y
Côte d'Ivoire	662	—	.01	—	—	—	.01	—Y
Eritrea	643	....	....	....	....	....	....	....
Ethiopia	644	—	—	—	—	—	—	—Y
Gabon	646	.01	—	—	—	.01	—	—Y
Gambia, The	648	.01	.01	—	—	.01	—	—Y
Ghana	652	—	—	—	.04	—	.01	.01Y
Guinea	656	—	.01	—	—	—	—	—Y
Kenya	664	.01	—	—	—	—	.01	.01Y
Liberia	668	.04	—	—	—	—	.03	.03Y
Madagascar	674	—	—	—	—	—	—	—Y
Malawi	676	—	—	—	—	—	—	—Y
Mali	678	.01	—	—	—	—	—	—Y
Mauritania	682	.01	—	—	—	—	—	—Y
Mauritius	684	—	—	—	—	—	—	—V
Morocco	686	—	.03	.01	—	—	.01	.01Y
Mozambique	688	—	—	—	—	—	—	—Y
Namibia	728	.05	—	.05	—	.02	.05	.08Y
Niger	692	.02	—	—	—	—	—	—Y
Nigeria	694	.02	.11	—	.01	—	.01	.01Y
Rwanda	714	.01	—	—	—	—	—	—Y
St. Helena	856	.38	.10	—	—	—	.04	.05Y
São Tomé & Príncipe	716	.08	—	.11	—	—	—	—Y
Senegal	722	—	.05	.05	—	—	—	—Y
Seychelles	718	—	—	—	—	.04	—	—Y
Sierra Leone	724	—	—	.01	.01	.05	.13	.16Y
Somalia	726	—	—	—	—	—	—	—Y
South Africa	199	—	.04	.08	.22	.06	.08	.07V
Sudan	732	.01	.01	—	—	—	—	—V
Swaziland	734	.20	—	.19	—	—	.05	.06Y
Tanzania	738	—	—	—	—	.03	—	—Y
Tunisia	744	.03	.02	.03	—	.02	.04	.05Y
Uganda	746	—	—	—	—	—	—	—Y
Zambia	754	—	—	—	—	—	—	—V
Zimbabwe	698	.01	—	—	—	—	—	—Y
Asia	**507**	**1.3**	**1.3**	**1.3**	**2.1**	**3.2**	**5.4**	**4.1Y**
Afghanistan, I.S. of	512	—	—	.01	—	—	—	—Y
Bangladesh	513	—	.02	.02	—	—	—	—V
Cambodia	522	—	—	—	—	—	—	—Y

Imports

Millions of U.S. Dollars

		2001	2002	2003	2004	2005	2006	2007
IFS World Total		**1,068.7**	**1,070.8**	**1,195.3**	**1,413.0**	**1,604.5**	**1,586.1**	**1,709.5**
DOTS World Total	**001**	**1,068.6**	**1,070.8**	**1,202.1**	**1,476.2**	**1,599.6**	**1,620.8**	**1,648.6Y**
Industrial Countries	**101**	**737.2**	**720.8**	**778.3**	**924.2**	**982.6**	**990.7**	**923.9Y**
United States	111	449.38	440.12	453.03	519.80	595.28	611.77	502.26V
Canada	156	40.17	37.40	42.39	53.90	57.26	60.08	64.00V
Australia	193	3.58	2.75	4.88	3.85	3.65	4.90	6.23V
Japan	158	44.55	45.04	53.45	64.04	82.76	59.86	53.57V
New Zealand	196	10.78	11.52	12.66	16.41	13.46	12.51	17.10V
Austria	122	1.17	1.26	1.13	1.46	1.41	2.97	2.40V
Belgium	124	3.63	4.54	4.96	4.93	9.03	6.05	6.11V
Cyprus	423	.24	.29	.34	.48	.41	.44	.09V
Denmark	128	6.19	9.96	9.04	53.90	7.49	6.68	5.87V
Finland	172	1.13	.42	1.22	1.18	1.34	1.97	.31V
France	132	14.79	19.06	26.59	24.02	28.77	28.37	21.96V
Germany	134	18.23	17.81	19.73	20.92	26.12	22.35	33.03V
Greece	174	.26	.14	.17	.10	.19	.19	.34V
Iceland	176	.03	.06	.05	.03	.08	.06	—V
Ireland	178	2.76	1.86	2.83	5.98	3.93	4.14	2.26V
Italy	136	12.81	10.39	12.00	12.53	14.94	13.84	17.43V
Luxembourg	137	.03	.03	.05	—	—	.30	.16V
Malta	181	.03	.03	.03	.05	—	.01	—V
Netherlands	138	9.71	18.61	12.71	16.32	.49	12.14	40.25V
Norway	142	2.52	2.96	3.13	4.98	1.14	1.27	1.44V
Portugal	182	1.56	.44	.74	1.25	.40	.13	.83V
Slovenia	961	.01	.01	.02	.02	.04	.07	.03V
Spain	184	6.82	4.29	6.16	10.58	8.52	6.16	8.45V
Sweden	144	13.05	5.78	27.17	7.60	8.46	19.91	17.40V
Switzerland	146	7.79	7.30	9.34	16.59	28.86	19.62	14.98V
United Kingdom	112	85.96	78.70	74.46	83.24	88.52	94.94	107.38V
Developing Countries	**202**	**331.1**	**349.6**	**423.4**	**551.6**	**615.4**	**628.2**	**722.4Y**
Africa	**607**	**1.6**	**2.1**	**1.8**	**2.8**	**.8**	**2.7**	**15.9Y**
Algeria	612	.02	.02	.04	.05	—	—	—Y
Angola	614	—	—	—	—	—	—	—Y
Cameroon	622	.02	.01	.01	.03	—	.84	1.04Y
Cape Verde	624	—	—	—	—	—	—	—Y
Central African Rep.	626	.01	.01	.01	—	—	—	—Y
Comoros	632	—	—	—	—	—	—	—Y
Côte d'Ivoire	662	—	—	—	—	.02	—	—Y
Eritrea	643	—	—	—	.04	—	.02	.02Y
Ethiopia	644	—	—	—	.03	—	—	—Y
Gabon	646	—	—	—	.07	.01	—	—Y
Gambia, The	648	—	—	—	—	.01	.01	.01Y
Ghana	652	.01	.08	.01	—	—	.03	.03Y
Guinea	656	—	—	—	—	.02	—	—Y
Kenya	664	—	—	.05	.11	.02	.02	.02Y
Liberia	668	—	—	.01	—	—	—	—Y
Madagascar	674	.01	.02	.02	—	—	—	—Y
Malawi	676	.02	.02	.02	.02	.04	.03	.04Y
Mali	678	.01	.03	.09	.04	.06	.05	.06Y
Mauritania	682	—	—	—	—	—	—	—Y
Mauritius	684	.01	.02	.01	.03	.12	.03	.41V
Morocco	686	.04	.03	.02	—	.05	.03	.04Y
Mozambique	688	.04	.01	—	.01	.02	—	—Y
Namibia	728	—	—	—	—	.05	.03	.02Y
Niger	692	.13	.01	—	.01	—	—	—Y
Nigeria	694	—	—	—	—	—	.04	.05Y
Rwanda	714	—	—	—	—	—	—	—Y
St. Helena	856	.39	.16	.34	.75	.15	—	—Y
São Tomé & Príncipe	716	—	.02	.02	—	.01	—	—Y
Senegal	722	.02	.01	.01	.02	—	—	—Y
Seychelles	718	—	—	—	—	—	—	—Y
Sierra Leone	724	.07	.12	.11	—	.06	.01	.01Y
Somalia	726	—	.01	.01	.01	—	—	—Y
South Africa	199	.71	1.50	.95	1.49	—	1.25	13.83V
Sudan	732	—	—	.01	.01	.03	.03	—V
Swaziland	734	.02	.02	.05	.04	.11	.17	.21Y
Tanzania	738	—	—	.01	—	—	—	—Y
Tunisia	744	.05	.01	.02	—	—	.01	.01Y
Uganda	746	—	—	—	—	.01	—	—Y
Zambia	754	—	—	.01	—	—	—	—V
Zimbabwe	698	—	.02	—	.03	.02	.07	.09Y
Asia	**507**	**50.4**	**54.6**	**60.4**	**103.9**	**94.6**	**101.5**	**83.6Y**
Afghanistan, I.S. of	512	—	—	—	—	—	—	—Y
Bangladesh	513	.05	.04	.04	.07	.10	.10	.06Y
Cambodia	522	.02	—	—	—	—	.03	.03Y

	Exports							Imports						
	2001	2002	2003	2004	2005	2006	2007	2001	2002	2003	2004	2005	2006	2007
	Millions of U.S. Dollars							*Millions of U.S. Dollars*						
China,P.R.: Mainland.................. 924	.22	.39	.48	.64	.85	1.79	1.03V	21.74	26.63	31.24	39.15	46.62	48.08	38.41V
China,P.R.:Hong Kong................ 532	.13	.14	.03	.34	.88	.55	.13V	2.99	3.78	3.00	2.89	5.45	7.28	2.84V
China,P.R.:Macao....................... 546	—	—	—	—	—	—	—V	—	.01	—	—	—	.02	—V
Fiji... 819	—	—	—	—	—	—	—Y	—	.01	—	—	—	.16	.19Y
French Polynesia......................... 887	.01	—	—	—	.01	.01	.01Y	—	—	—	—	—	—	—Y
Guam... 829	—	—	—	—	—	.01	.01Y	—	—	—	—	—	—	—Y
India.. 534	.01	.01	.02	.05	.05	.10	.12Y	1.84	1.93	3.07	2.69	3.24	5.32	6.60Y
Indonesia.................................... 536	.03	.01	—	.02	—	—	—V	1.86	2.00	1.70	2.27	2.22	2.52	5.87V
Kiribati....................................... 826	—	—	—	—	—	—	—Y	.27	.02	—	—	—	—	—Y
Korea.. 542	.06	.06	.04	.01	.04	.02	.02V	6.05	5.73	6.37	35.98	13.31	12.07	11.65V
Lao People's Dem.Rep................. 544	—	—	—	—	—	—	—Y	.02	.01	.01	.01	.01	—	—Y
Malaysia..................................... 548	—	.01	—	.04	.03	.15	.10V	2.22	2.76	2.42	5.09	4.24	3.30	1.62V
Nauru... 836	—	—	—	—	—	—	—Y	—	—	—	.01	—	—	—Y
Nepal.. 558	—	—	—	—	—	—	—Y	.02	—	.01	—	—	—	—Y
Pakistan...................................... 564	—	.01	—	—	—	.01	.02Y	.27	.26	.25	.32	.20	.31	.39Y
Philippines.................................. 566	.17	.01	.01	—	—	.04	—V	.81	.89	1.50	.70	1.12	1.08	.27V
Singapore.................................... 576	.16	.04	.02	.02	.55	1.11	—V	.82	.87	1.01	1.54	1.20	.97	—V
Sri Lanka..................................... 524	—	—	—	—	.03	.02	—V	.93	.09	.28	.15	.22	.28	.05V
Taiwan Province of China............ 528	.20	.57	.65	.93	.71	1.54	2.17V	6.93	6.34	6.10	8.40	7.52	7.49	4.46V
Thailand...................................... 578	.33	.02	.05	—	—	.03	.48V	3.32	2.97	3.14	4.41	8.80	12.08	11.17V
Vietnam...................................... 582	—	—	—	—	—	.07	—V	.24	.21	.28	.21	.36	.42	—V
Europe.................................... 170	**1.3**	**.3**	**.2**	**.2**	**.7**	**2.2**	**9.0Y**	**3.4**	**3.5**	**4.0**	**4.4**	**4.2**	**6.3**	**6.7Y**
Albania....................................... 914	—	—	—	—	—	—	.01V	—	—	—	—	—	.01	—V
Armenia...................................... 911	—	—	—	—	—	—	4.20V	—	—	—	—	—	.02	.02Y
Azerbaijan.................................. 912	—	—	—	—	—	—	.07V	—	—	—	—	—	—	—V
Belarus....................................... 913	—	—	—	—	—	—	.02V	—	—	—	—	—	—	.08V
Bosnia & Herzegovina................. 963	—	—	—	—	—	.01	.01Y	—	—	—	.02	—	—	—Y
Bulgaria...................................... 918	—	—	—	—	—	—	—V	.09	.05	.02	.18	.02	.06	.57V
Czech Republic........................... 935	.11	.06	.08	.02	.19	.67	1.14V	1.18	1.09	1.31	1.42	.67	.77	.24V
Estonia....................................... 939	—	—	—	—	—	—	—V	—	—	.01	—	—	—	—V
Georgia...................................... 915	.02	—	—	—	—	—	—Y	—	.06	.10	—	—	.03	.04Y
Hungary...................................... 944	.15	.01	.03	.06	—	.01	.03V	.14	.10	.15	.39	.71	.58	.96V
Kazakhstan................................. 916	1.00	—	—	—	—	—	—Y	—	—	—	—	—	—	—Y
Latvia... 941	—	—	—	—	—	—	—V	—	—	—	—	—	.02	.25V
Lithuania.................................... 946	—	—	—	—	—	—	—V	—	—	.03	—	—	—	.01V
Macedonia, FYR.......................... 962	—	—	—	—	—	—	.01Y	—	—	—	—	—	—	—Y
Moldova...................................... 921	.01	—	.01	—	—	.02	.02Y	—	—	—	—	—	—	—Y
Poland.. 964	—	—	—	—	.02	.02	2.39V	.17	.07	.15	.23	.13	.48	.15V
Romania..................................... 968	—	—	—	—	.01	—	.02V	.03	.05	.02	.03	.04	.12	.11V
Russia.. 922	.01	—	—	—	—	.01	.05V	.01	.07	.08	.05	.07	.12	—V
Slovak Republic.......................... 936	—	—	—	—	—	.15	.09V	—	.02	—	.01	.05	.04	.19V
Turkey.. 186	.02	.25	.06	.06	.44	1.33	.94V	1.39	1.89	1.63	1.89	1.82	3.61	3.54V
Turkmenistan.............................. 925	—	—	—	—	—	—	—Y	.03	—	—	—	—	—	—Y
Ukraine...................................... 926	.01	—	—	.03	.03	—	—Y	.34	.05	.45	.16	.59	.37	.46Y
Uzbekistan.................................. 927	—	—	—	—	—	.01	.02Y	—	—	—	.01	—	—	—Y
Yugoslavia n.s............................ 966	—	—	—	—	—	—	—Y	—	.01	—	.01	.06	.04	.05Y
Europe n.s.................................. 884	—	—	—	—	—	—	—Y	—	—	—	—	—	.03	.03Y
Middle East............................ 407	**.2**	**.1**	**1.5**	**.1**	**.1**	**.5**	**.6Y**	**6.5**	**1.2**	**4.0**	**2.9**	**2.4**	**3.2**	**4.5Y**
Bahrain....................................... 419	—	.06	.07	.02	—	—	—Y	.04	.11	.01	.03	—	.03	.04Y
Egypt.. 469	—	—	—	—	—	—	—Y	.02	.02	.17	.10	.12	.08	.10Y
Iran, I.R. of................................ 429	.10	—	—	—	—	—	—Y	.06	.04	.06	.15	.01	.03	.04Y
Israel.. 436	—	.01	.04	.06	.04	.04	—V	6.07	.93	3.36	.96	1.84	2.56	3.96V
Jordan.. 439	—	—	—	—	—	—	—Y	.01	—	.01	.01	.06	.13	—V
Kuwait.. 443	—	—	—	—	—	—	—Y	—	—	—	.02	—	—	—Y
Lebanon...................................... 446	—	—	—	—	.01	—	—Y	.06	.03	.06	1.61	.03	.01	.01Y
Oman.. 449	—	—	—	—	—	.01	.01Y	—	—	—	.01	.23	.06	.07Y
Saudi Arabia............................... 456	.04	—	1.39	.01	.01	.03	.04Y	—	.02	.13	.05	.11	.08	.09Y
Syrian Arab Republic.................. 463	—	—	—	—	—	—	—Y	.01	.01	.01	—	—	—	—Y
United Arab Emirates................. 466	—	—	—	—	—	.40	.52Y	.18	.07	.13	—	—	.19	.23Y
Western Hemisphere............... 207	**122.3**	**117.7**	**111.4**	**118.1**	**157.1**	**168.9**	**283.9Y**	**269.2**	**288.3**	**353.2**	**437.6**	**513.4**	**514.5**	**611.6Y**
Antigua and Barbuda.................. 311	6.11	7.21	6.32	6.08	9.17	11.49	14.26Y	.09	.08	.08	.33	.07	.48	.60Y
Argentina.................................... 213	.07	.16	.10	.06	.06	.09	—V	.84	.98	1.48	2.33	3.81	2.48	2.40V
Aruba.. 314	.24	.42	.44	.44	.88	.90	1.12V	.01	.01	.01	—	1.12	.03	—V
Bahamas, The............................. 313	3.01	2.06	1.95	2.74	3.05	3.18	3.95Y	.24	.18	.14	.19	1.17	.18	.22Y
Belize.. 339	2.71	2.49	1.33	1.39	1.69	1.91	2.36Y	1.04	2.05	1.46	1.44	1.60	1.57	1.95Y
Bermuda...................................... 319	.90	.58	.58	1.04	.82	.87	1.08Y	.01	.06	.04	.10	.14	.01	.01Y
Bolivia.. 218	—	.03	.17	—	—	—	—Y	.10	.13	.01	.17	.14	.66	.82Y
Brazil.. 223	.07	—	.09	.08	.04	.35	32.40V	12.29	16.70	17.50	20.60	32.18	30.89	—V
Chile... 228	.03	.03	.04	.02	.05	.08	.06V	1.31	2.31	1.72	2.22	2.62	2.33	4.32V
Colombia.................................... 233	.01	.09	.06	.11	.03	.11	.06V	4.53	3.50	4.68	4.32	5.36	6.31	36.18V
Costa Rica.................................. 238	.34	.18	.06	.06	.09	.10	.13Y	2.33	2.40	3.99	4.21	6.55	—	—Y
Dominica.................................... 321	3.62	4.09	5.25	4.20	5.30	5.16	6.40Y	2.00	1.65	2.32	1.94	2.27	2.60	3.23Y
Dominican Republic.................... 243	1.13	1.48	.94	.72	1.27	1.50	1.86Y	2.74	3.00	3.11	3.16	4.00	5.99	7.43Y
Ecuador...................................... 248	—	—	.06	—	.02	.05	.07Y	.60	.53	.44	.77	.76	1.17	1.45Y

	Exports 2001	2002	2003	2004	2005	2006	2007	Imports 2001	2002	2003	2004	2005	2006	2007
	Millions of U.S. Dollars							*Millions of U.S. Dollars*						
El Salvador 253	—	—	.04	.05	.06	.03	.18V	.24	2.14	1.19	.61	.38	.54	.25V
Grenada 328	7.38	6.66	7.38	8.05	12.08	8.79	10.91Y	1.50	1.37	1.31	1.34	1.69	1.52	1.88Y
Guatemala 258	.08	.03	.01	.02	.01	.02	.02Y	4.53	2.04	1.62	1.81	2.96	1.08	1.34Y
Guyana 336	6.35	8.52	6.19	7.13	6.19	6.47	8.03Y	10.23	10.58	12.28	15.60	14.93	17.41	21.61Y
Haiti 263	.51	.40	.44	.67	.89	1.25	1.55Y	.20	—	.10	.11	—	.09	.11Y
Honduras 268	.08	.01	—	—	—	.03	.04Y	2.10	3.10	5.26	4.16	7.53	6.38	7.91Y
Jamaica 343	20.14	15.04	15.39	13.70	20.64	21.09	52.92V	9.94	9.33	10.10	10.78	11.60	12.12	10.78V
Mexico 273	.38	.04	.53	.12	.08	.30	2.39V	11.38	10.43	11.36	17.86	14.17	13.22	9.07V
Netherlands Antilles 353	2.54	2.31	1.86	3.48	2.00	3.80	4.71Y	1.13	1.50	13.37	16.89	13.05	1.13	1.40Y
Nicaragua 278	—	—	—	.02	.11	.23	—V	—	—	—	—	.01	.01	—V
Panama 283	.18	1.15	1.02	.67	.78	.66	7.30V	1.88	2.78	3.29	3.19	5.26	4.31	.15V
Paraguay 288	—	—	.05	—	—	.04	.05Y	—	.01	—	—	—	—	—Y
Peru 293	—	—	.01	.03	—	.02	.05Y	.31	.21	.32	.55	.73	.89	.95Y
St. Kitts and Nevis 361	5.67	6.52	6.70	7.81	10.26	10.80	13.41Y	.41	.19	.11	.18	.08	.14	.17Y
St. Lucia 362	13.80	11.42	11.71	14.34	21.84	22.66	28.12Y	6.63	5.55	.53	5.21	5.80	5.19	6.44Y
St. Vincent & Grens. 364	9.14	9.07	9.23	10.69	11.85	14.03	17.42Y	3.75	4.42	3.56	4.05	4.58	4.91	6.09Y
Suriname 366	4.67	5.31	3.24	3.69	3.34	2.31	2.87Y	8.17	14.08	12.25	12.83	7.21	16.83	20.89Y
Trinidad and Tobago 369	28.63	28.88	28.36	29.14	38.87	48.70	60.44Y	174.24	182.27	236.44	295.59	353.04	366.10	454.32Y
Uruguay 298	—	—	—	—	—	—	—Y	.06	.10	.07	.85	2.77	3.53	4.38Y
Venezuela, Rep. Bol. 299	1.21	.83	.02	.04	.19	.05	8.17V	4.38	4.48	3.07	4.12	5.55	4.19	5.05Y
Western Hem. n.s. 399	3.27	2.64	1.85	1.55	5.45	1.80	1.60Y	.03	.10	.05	.05	.31	.22	.14Y
Other Countries n.i.e. 910	**.2**	**—**	**—**	**—**	**—**	**—**	**—Y**	**.3**	**.3**	**.4**	**.4**	**1.6**	**1.9**	**2.3Y**
Cuba 928	.15	.05	.04	—	—	.01	.01Y	.25	.29	.38	.41	.43	.26	.32Y
North Korea 954	—	—	—	—	—	—	—Y	—	—	.05	.01	1.15	1.61	2.00Y
Countries & Areas n.s. 898	**—**	**—**	**—**	**—**	**—**	**—**	**—Y**	**.1**	**.1**	**—**	**—**	**—**	**—**	**—Y**
Special Categories 899	**43.5**	**40.9**	**—**	**—**	**—**	**—**	**—Y**	**—**	**—**	**—**	**—**	**—**	**—**	**—Y**
Memorandum Items														
European Union 998	41.14	37.76	36.38	38.97	42.93	45.64	50.28Y	179.91	174.92	200.99	246.61	201.63	222.55	266.09Y
Oil Exporting Ctys 999	1.42	.95	1.41	.09	.20	.50	8.75Y	6.50	6.63	5.14	6.68	8.12	7.10	11.40Y
Non-Oil Develop.Ctys 201	124.57	119.56	113.60	120.98	161.06	177.01	289.43Y	324.61	343.01	418.28	544.90	607.32	621.05	710.97Y
PERCENT DISTRIBUTION														
Industrial Countries 101	**34.6**	**33.1**	**40.4**	**42.1**	**38.0**	**45.2**	**23.8**	**69.0**	**67.3**	**64.7**	**62.6**	**61.4**	**61.1**	**56.0**
Developing Countries 202	**48.6**	**49.9**	**59.6**	**57.9**	**62.0**	**54.8**	**76.2**	**31.0**	**32.7**	**35.2**	**37.4**	**38.5**	**38.8**	**43.8**
Africa 607	**.3**	**.5**	**.3**	**.3**	**.1**	**.1**	**.1**	**.1**	**.2**	**.2**	**.2**	**.1**	**.2**	**1.0**
Asia 507	**.5**	**.5**	**.7**	**1.0**	**1.2**	**1.7**	**1.0**	**4.7**	**5.1**	**5.0**	**7.0**	**5.9**	**6.3**	**5.1**
Europe 170	**.5**	**.1**	**.1**	**.1**	**.3**	**.7**	**2.3**	**.3**	**.3**	**.3**	**.3**	**.3**	**.4**	**.4**
Middle East 407	**.1**	**—**	**.8**	**—**	**—**	**.2**	**.1**	**.6**	**.1**	**.3**	**.2**	**.2**	**.2**	**.3**
Western Hemisphere 207	**47.2**	**48.7**	**57.7**	**56.5**	**60.4**	**52.1**	**72.6**	**25.2**	**26.9**	**29.4**	**29.6**	**32.1**	**31.7**	**37.1**
Other Countries n.i.e. 910	**.1**	**—**	**—**	**—**	**—**	**—**	**—**	**—**	**—**	**—**	**—**	**.1**	**.1**	**.1**
ANNUAL PERCENT CHANGE														
World 001	**−5.0**	**−6.9**	**−20.1**	**8.3**	**24.4**	**24.6**	**20.7**	**−7.6**	**.2**	**12.3**	**22.8**	**8.4**	**1.3**	**1.7**
Industrial Countries 101	**43.5**	**−10.8**	**−2.6**	**12.7**	**12.3**	**48.4**	**−36.5**	**−7.3**	**−2.2**	**8.0**	**18.7**	**6.3**	**.8**	**−6.8**
Developing Countries 202	**−24.0**	**−4.3**	**−4.6**	**5.3**	**33.2**	**10.1**	**68.0**	**−8.1**	**5.6**	**21.1**	**30.3**	**11.6**	**2.1**	**15.0**
Africa 607	**154.1**	**27.8**	**−52.1**	**13.5**	**−58.2**	**79.7**	**18.9**	**−.7**	**33.5**	**−14.3**	**51.3**	**−70.5**	**227.6**	**495.4**
Asia 507	**−57.0**	**−2.2**	**4.1**	**52.5**	**53.6**	**72.1**	**−24.7**	**−4.7**	**8.2**	**10.8**	**71.9**	**−8.9**	**7.3**	**−17.6**
Europe 170	**−98.3**	**−74.5**	**−42.3**	**−12.2**	**302.2**	**225.0**	**302.9**	**−71.2**	**1.7**	**14.5**	**10.9**	**−5.4**	**51.4**	**6.6**
Middle East 407	**−96.6**	**−55.3**	**—**	**−94.3**	**−31.7**	**731.2**	**18.2**	**131.7**	**−81.0**	**221.8**	**−25.5**	**−18.5**	**32.0**	**43.4**
Western Hemisphere 207	**52.6**	**−3.8**	**−5.3**	**6.0**	**33.0**	**7.5**	**68.1**	**−7.6**	**7.1**	**22.5**	**23.9**	**17.3**	**.2**	**18.9**
Other Countries n.i.e. 910	**—**	**−68.0**	**−16.9**	**−96.3**	**216.7**	**69.7**	**24.1**	**−5.6**	**13.9**	**48.7**	**−1.2**	**273.6**	**18.7**	**24.1**

	Exports 2001	Exports 2002	Exports 2003	Exports 2004	Exports 2005	Exports 2006	Exports 2007	Imports 2001	Imports 2002	Imports 2003	Imports 2004	Imports 2005	Imports 2006	Imports 2007
	Millions of U.S. Dollars							*Millions of U.S. Dollars*						
IFS World Total	**7,450.6**	**8,020.9**	**9,945.6**	**13,773.7**	**15,979.3**	**19,733.7**	**24,275.3**	**8,286.4**	**9,092.3**	**11,558.0**	**16,490.8**	**16,708.1**	**22,351.2**	**28,693.1**
DOTS World Total 001	**7,457.2**	**8,020.8**	**9,943.3**	**13,751.7**	**15,976.2**	**19,732.7**	**24,331.1**	**8,292.9**	**9,092.3**	**11,558.0**	**16,345.5**	**16,708.1**	**22,351.1**	**28,674.4**
Industrial Countries 101	**940.3**	**1,580.9**	**2,429.1**	**3,581.9**	**5,493.7**	**7,283.9**	**7,721.5**	**1,527.9**	**1,720.9**	**2,100.5**	**2,647.7**	**3,079.7**	**4,349.8**	**5,507.3**
United States 111	77.43	91.32	102.47	209.28	251.17	446.96	348.54	131.63	103.33	150.20	195.79	232.26	284.09	387.68
Canada 156	3.13	4.92	7.21	7.55	9.67	9.03	10.47	6.50	10.66	11.59	10.70	46.52	29.73	49.33
Australia 193	2.32	2.97	2.36	1.42	5.75	24.74	6.30	2.38	.78	1.22	1.24	3.59	2.75	3.55
Japan 158	1.90	1.48	2.39	2.64	4.46	7.03	38.43	22.85	27.21	39.27	44.43	58.21	140.73	208.28
New Zealand 196	.14	—	.02	.03	.12	.31	6.34	.11	.17	.34	1.49	2.48	2.34	4.35
Austria 122	10.98	10.06	16.16	18.12	16.78	21.97	29.69	46.28	45.38	64.76	72.01	81.05	103.16	175.87
Belgium 124	16.56	39.86	63.72	96.00	78.71	95.86	101.35	62.01	69.15	77.38	91.91	118.37	165.03	206.98
Cyprus 423	2.83	4.06	.18	2.04	16.81	30.03	46.54	3.60	4.24	15.96	3.08	5.44	13.85	13.28
Denmark 128	24.26	26.24	105.78	131.06	66.58	56.02	34.20	31.04	32.26	40.45	54.38	53.86	86.89	90.34
Finland 172	15.99	13.91	19.69	41.86	30.66	28.33	37.57	33.47	30.02	34.82	47.02	51.24	75.92	102.84
France 132	40.77	44.80	55.31	104.63	274.73	202.96	76.96	87.21	94.89	116.43	165.07	176.14	270.77	349.85
Germany 134	241.04	347.94	421.18	516.27	708.46	752.84	730.64	604.08	693.08	820.67	1,081.04	1,121.05	1,672.04	2,171.31
Greece 174	3.49	2.93	6.04	2.97	4.42	3.59	2.54	4.14	5.65	4.93	7.79	9.56	10.23	14.74
Iceland 176	1.78	1.52	2.87	6.16	3.54	10.98	12.60	2.02	5.86	12.21	26.74	39.52	53.72	49.99
Ireland 178	.46	4.06	3.34	7.84	3.49	.86	1.80	5.43	7.17	7.76	16.17	19.55	23.52	23.02
Italy 136	85.41	130.06	135.25	142.96	159.78	173.13	181.44	164.14	215.22	283.98	300.46	393.56	498.30	638.12
Luxembourg 137	3.35	3.25	4.97	4.88	4.97	3.95	3.65	1.37	.85	.78	1.20	2.69	2.27	8.53
Malta 181	—	—	—	.04	.05	.01	.03	—	—	.09	.45	.34	.08	.47
Netherlands 138	125.78	279.01	413.81	924.38	2,408.30	3,494.50	4,331.82	81.95	84.12	93.40	118.70	161.28	220.00	250.28
Norway 142	20.35	27.34	24.28	29.09	38.76	51.74	76.35	24.80	19.90	25.44	27.21	43.68	74.93	85.54
Portugal 182	.11	2.15	2.55	4.33	5.46	3.50	2.70	1.54	1.69	2.39	2.85	3.90	4.75	7.23
Slovenia 961	2.57	2.21	5.22	5.05	4.93	7.49	3.16	22.47	22.31	28.44	34.42	35.81	48.34	65.11
Spain 184	9.98	15.08	27.60	31.78	8.32	11.20	24.33	26.61	36.14	52.35	56.72	63.50	89.45	136.22
Sweden 144	20.33	27.23	65.38	137.27	262.61	365.71	77.09	60.37	99.60	98.48	98.42	89.02	114.82	134.96
Switzerland 146	6.36	4.79	3.08	6.73	4.76	6.21	9.19	40.47	43.49	37.85	60.10	123.04	177.28	140.13
United Kingdom 112	222.93	493.73	938.27	1,147.56	1,120.40	1,474.92	1,527.79	61.41	67.73	79.31	128.35	144.05	184.81	189.36
Developing Countries 202	**6,458.7**	**6,390.4**	**7,463.5**	**10,108.8**	**10,386.2**	**12,357.1**	**16,537.8**	**6,600.8**	**7,114.7**	**9,153.8**	**13,372.8**	**13,110.2**	**17,452.5**	**22,525.5**
Africa 607	**55.4**	**64.0**	**75.3**	**34.7**	**42.7**	**68.2**	**86.0**	**22.7**	**26.2**	**39.2**	**33.5**	**35.2**	**36.2**	**42.5**
Algeria 612	23.52	16.47	11.41	6.24	4.90	3.77	1.36	—	—	.05	—	—	—	.28
Angola 614	1.64	7.38	1.49	.13	2.39	5.15	.04	—	.14	—	—	—	—	—
Benin 638	.50	—	.04	—	—	—	.56	—	—	—	—	—	.02	—
Botswana 616	—	.02	—	.03	—	2.79	.94	—	—	—	—	—	—	—
Burkina Faso 748	—	.34	1.40	—	1.69	1.73	.22	—	—	—	—	—	—	—
Burundi 618	—	—	—	.02	.03	—	—	—	—	—	—	—	—	—
Cameroon 622	1.93	1.84	2.10	.69	.95	2.16	5.52	—	.21	.01	.50	.01	.14	.01
Cape Verde 624	—	—	—	—	—	—	—	—	—	—	—	—	—	.01
Central African Rep. 626	.02	—	.01	—	—	—	—	—	.04	—	2.89	—	—	—
Chad 628	.01	.05	.36	.06	—	—	—	—	—	—	—	—	—	—
Comoros 632	—	—	—	—	—	—	—	—	—	—	—	.01	—	—
Congo, Dem. Rep. of 636	—	—	—	—	.27	—	—	—	—	—	.05	—	.01	—
Congo, Republic of 634	.09	.12	.25	.23	.74	1.27	3.10	—	.01	—	.01	—	.01	.09
Côte d'Ivoire 662	2.38	9.95	11.64	5.58	6.20	9.34	12.72	2.00	1.55	5.44	3.05	4.25	1.52	.33
Eritrea 643	—	—	—	—	—	—	8.28	—	—	—	—	—	—	—
Ethiopia 644	.45	.29	.57	1.59	6.79	7.97	1.59	—	—	—	.01	.19	.24	.28
Gabon 646	—	—	—	—	—	—	.03	.01	.05	—	—	.20	—	—
Gambia, The 648	—	—	.02	—	—	—	—	—	.02	—	—	.03	.01	—
Ghana 652	.29	.34	.68	.29	.36	.14	9.12	4.58	8.65	6.30	11.73	10.78	11.60	15.93
Guinea 656	.71	.30	.69	.66	5.06	2.81	1.97	—	.06	.05	1.37	.35	.03	—
Guinea-Bissau 654	—	—	.15	—	—	—	—	—	—	—	—	—	—	—
Kenya 664	.15	.07	.03	.05	.40	.01	1.10	—	.03	.02	.09	.02	.21	.39
Lesotho 666	—	—	—	—	—	—	—	.04	.07	—	—	.01	—	—
Liberia 668	.03	—	—	—	—	.07	—	—	—	—	.50	.63	.08	—
Madagascar 674	.08	—	.07	—	.13	.32	.36	—	—	—	.10	—	—	.03
Malawi 676	—	—	.37	—	—	.07	—	.26	.02	—	—	.09	.20	.71
Mali 678	.12	.11	.07	—	—	—	—	—	—	—	—	—	—	—
Mauritania 682	—	—	.12	—	—	—	.38	2.62	2.82	2.19	1.79	1.21	3.58	.67
Mauritius 684	—	—	—	.01	—	.01	—	.01	.01	.01	.02	.05	.06	.20
Morocco 686	4.88	6.99	16.61	.74	.12	3.76	5.78	8.33	9.62	10.51	10.65	12.42	11.68	11.90
Mozambique 688	—	—	.01	.07	.03	.08	.17	—	—	—	—	—	—	.16
Namibia 728	—	—	—	—	—	—	—	—	—	—	.04	.05	.05	.07
Niger 692	—	—	—	.07	.06	.02	—	—	—	—	—	—	—	—
Nigeria 694	4.24	2.41	4.68	4.34	3.75	18.46	4.28	.01	.28	.02	.18	.01	.08	.01
Rwanda 714	.03	—	—	.48	—	—	.03	—	.04	—	—	—	—	—
Senegal 722	3.06	2.31	2.92	3.48	.26	.02	.37	—	—	—	—	—	—	.01
Seychelles 718	—	—	—	—	.02	.02	.94	—	.24	—	—	.05	—	—
Sierra Leone 724	—	.04	.01	.02	.58	.05	.14	—	—	—	—	.49	.04	.11
South Africa 199	5.86	4.87	3.32	3.01	2.66	1.18	18.94	4.11	1.84	13.95	—	3.40	5.61	9.15
Sudan 732	4.26	9.24	12.02	6.35	3.57	2.53	10.35	—	.01	—	.02	—	—	—
Swaziland 734	—	—	—	—	—	—	—	—	.02	—	—	.10	—	.07

	Exports							Imports						
	2001	2002	2003	2004	2005	2006	2007	2001	2002	2003	2004	2005	2006	2007
	Millions of U.S. Dollars							Millions of U.S. Dollars						
Tanzania 738	—	.19	.15	.12	.83	.12	.41	.12	.10	.05	—	.04	.07	.22
Togo 742	.28	.37	—	.01	—	—	—	—	—	—	—	—	—	—
Tunisia 744	.01	.27	3.54	.32	.72	4.29	5.43	.01	.02	.05	.11	.23	.24	.93
Uganda 746	—	.03	.09	.02	—	—	.01	.34	—	—	—	.01	.01	.01
Zambia 754	.36	.03	—	.01	.05	.03	.13	—	—	—	—	.01	—	.05
Zimbabwe 698	.50	—	.48	.04	.11	.04	.07	.21	.29	.52	.35	.52	.72	.91
Asia 507	**304.6**	**375.5**	**331.2**	**583.6**	**857.9**	**830.0**	**941.8**	**126.2**	**128.6**	**176.0**	**335.6**	**523.1**	**912.5**	**1,322.3**
Afghanistan, I.S. of 512	1.84	9.00	16.06	13.69	11.73	7.74	6.26	.30	.39	.63	.45	.13	1.46	1.31
Bangladesh 513	5.19	7.80	10.83	17.22	9.60	22.01	31.12	.11	.05	.08	.66	.82	1.19	2.49
Cambodia 522	—	.02	—	—	—	—	—	.07	—	—	.17	.13	.09	.20
China,P.R.: Mainland 924	143.05	217.43	162.25	282.87	430.87	398.67	484.65	41.29	46.47	71.78	157.08	284.11	553.64	815.82
China,P.R.:Hong Kong 532	—	—	—	18.62	8.54	7.66	9.02	—	—	—	.94	1.28	.73	1.21
China,P.R.:Macao 546	—	—	—	—	—	—	—	—	—	—	.02	—	.08	.13
French Polynesia 887	—	—	—	—	—	—	—	.02	—	—	—	—	—	—
India 534	64.97	50.35	33.28	82.61	197.46	112.93	101.98	13.76	20.74	28.62	35.63	45.99	58.61	81.06
Indonesia 536	10.19	6.27	12.79	15.79	24.22	37.54	27.47	4.18	4.61	7.09	10.55	17.33	23.13	36.59
Korea 542	12.31	9.55	9.80	9.98	9.48	8.70	18.03	21.48	17.99	23.68	50.50	47.67	77.83	125.63
Lao People's Dem.Rep 544	—	—	—	—	—	—	—	—	—	—	—	—	—	.01
Malaysia 548	17.23	25.16	21.97	26.43	16.46	34.73	41.32	6.58	5.78	5.74	19.04	53.56	97.93	90.10
Mongolia 948	3.40	5.11	3.74	5.11	7.66	4.71	3.82	—	—	—	—	.01	.05	—
Myanmar 518	—	—	—	—	—	—	.35	—	.11	—	—	—	.06	.01
Nauru 836	—	—	—	—	—	—	—	.01	—	—	—	—	—	—
Nepal 558	.50	—	2.08	—	.14	—	.37	.02	.01	.02	.02	.03	.03	.05
Pakistan 564	2.06	4.79	5.19	17.80	58.89	73.95	84.28	.14	1.15	1.74	3.09	4.68	7.76	10.78
Papua New Guinea 853	—	—	—	—	—	.02	—	—	—	—	—	—	—	.01
Philippines 566	.62	.04	2.37	.56	4.94	6.30	11.40	.93	.84	1.26	2.08	2.26	3.44	5.15
Singapore 576	1.00	2.15	1.48	1.93	5.20	31.90	15.51	.79	1.56	1.70	3.22	5.91	7.67	21.63
Sri Lanka 524	4.47	3.45	3.15	8.23	5.01	15.46	18.43	1.53	2.09	2.13	3.04	5.07	7.43	8.48
Taiwan Province of China 528	6.82	15.85	19.90	46.65	25.76	24.97	38.47	18.59	16.32	17.58	34.90	36.17	44.57	67.14
Thailand 578	1.83	1.38	3.98	9.54	2.00	1.90	1.20	4.40	5.84	4.44	10.40	15.43	18.25	38.94
Tuvalu 869	—	—	—	—	—	—	—	—	—	—	—	—	—	.01
Vietnam 582	29.08	17.20	22.29	26.57	39.97	40.77	48.10	11.94	4.64	9.51	3.84	2.48	8.52	15.53
Europe 170	**5,858.0**	**5,723.5**	**6,832.3**	**9,133.1**	**9,125.6**	**11,056.2**	**14,825.2**	**6,297.0**	**6,820.2**	**8,802.9**	**12,854.7**	**12,318.9**	**16,126.6**	**20,849.1**
Albania 914	.03	.02	.02	.06	5.11	1.96	—	—	—	—	—	—	.04	.07
Armenia 911	1.23	2.93	7.35	8.76	12.85	19.51	20.27	1.69	2.11	2.28	2.06	2.13	4.12	3.47
Azerbaijan 912	4.99	4.48	8.73	14.92	28.04	34.46	86.43	3.50	2.22	1.72	1.21	1.95	2.72	3.26
Bosnia & Herzegovina 963	.63	4.02	.08	4.21	11.79	5.41	6.78	—	.01	—	.08	.04	.10	.09
Bulgaria 918	7.81	7.95	11.56	24.98	23.55	35.29	32.49	11.44	12.07	12.70	18.44	21.80	30.93	34.81
Croatia 960	13.47	10.46	14.58	18.15	20.74	23.26	32.42	4.61	3.19	12.48	9.80	8.90	16.08	12.19
Czech Republic 935	35.43	36.28	49.29	53.23	55.77	69.10	79.99	57.19	54.23	74.48	111.09	99.37	139.49	197.31
Estonia 939	129.21	63.35	62.02	89.98	106.42	94.50	227.46	4.09	3.58	5.54	14.19	17.75	37.68	43.26
Faroe Islands 816	—	—	—	—	—	—	—	—	1.43	2.83	2.07	5.86	5.84	7.42
Georgia 915	2.24	.74	.88	2.61	6.64	18.09	29.30	2.24	3.04	3.72	3.56	2.46	3.41	4.59
Gibraltar 823	1.80	.01	.04	.02	.43	.08	.02	1.09	1.65	.23	—	.03	—	—
Hungary 944	75.40	70.82	105.47	136.63	134.58	97.77	140.02	28.26	28.10	37.80	55.91	80.05	111.83	130.43
Kazakhstan 916	28.51	39.11	68.05	121.29	183.51	259.41	361.27	8.36	14.90	13.00	23.52	31.07	74.37	151.74
Kyrgyz Republic 917	7.12	2.68	4.79	4.10	8.80	20.03	23.07	6.41	2.82	3.38	3.27	2.04	1.46	2.72
Latvia 941	492.27	520.11	344.35	310.71	322.57	462.00	995.83	36.14	36.07	44.31	85.04	90.58	111.89	127.52
Lithuania 946	275.80	256.74	264.98	284.86	351.78	432.70	564.59	107.35	109.36	154.24	175.59	134.58	170.30	180.12
Macedonia, FYR 962	1.04	1.05	4.66	5.25	.12	.44	.30	.34	.32	.72	.82	1.14	1.62	3.36
Moldova 921	43.77	43.20	55.88	73.51	102.21	95.68	144.55	38.56	43.36	48.14	68.49	72.34	81.07	81.93
Poland 964	248.00	273.28	434.17	728.77	847.35	1,032.81	1,224.08	201.97	221.80	348.49	474.97	578.95	765.88	819.70
Romania 968	26.58	35.12	43.94	79.74	61.49	66.24	119.10	3.67	4.33	4.25	9.12	9.91	18.11	23.14
Russia 922	3,962.72	3,977.11	4,879.86	6,462.98	5,715.79	6,845.34	8,886.59	5,437.89	5,922.30	7,601.92	11,142.57	10,118.15	13,099.06	17,186.68
Serbia, Rep. of 942	—	—	—	—	—	—	32.74	—	—	—	—	—	—	21.22
Serbia & Montenegro 965	15.61	16.37	17.21	27.40	35.15	16.59	—	6.41	7.65	4.80	7.71	12.31	20.95	—
Slovak Republic 936	25.36	18.24	22.33	46.90	50.85	70.58	70.27	14.44	16.10	25.46	42.45	42.84	69.62	111.91
Tajikistan 923	2.55	2.99	4.08	11.76	8.63	13.56	27.72	1.72	1.55	1.91	4.77	3.46	4.44	6.26
Turkey 186	15.86	25.25	22.96	26.41	37.65	38.65	67.78	23.15	24.95	25.62	41.36	72.28	114.47	139.01
Turkmenistan 925	2.17	20.62	39.73	16.95	43.86	14.53	86.94	1.43	.43	.04	.44	1.09	1.09	.91
Ukraine 926	421.82	271.58	343.52	539.81	907.85	1,234.00	1,472.13	277.43	290.66	362.07	544.94	893.91	1,223.75	1,534.35
Uzbekistan 927	16.62	18.96	21.73	39.14	42.09	54.24	93.07	17.58	11.96	10.67	11.26	13.87	16.24	21.63
Europe n.s. 884	—	—	—	—	—	—	—	.08	.10	.07	—	—	—	.04
Middle East 407	**136.1**	**118.8**	**96.2**	**147.2**	**144.8**	**158.9**	**216.8**	**17.5**	**12.9**	**15.1**	**24.7**	**33.3**	**54.5**	**72.4**
Bahrain 419	—	—	.01	.18	.46	.01	.03	—	—	—	—	—	—	—
Egypt 469	19.98	12.00	8.45	22.73	32.49	37.02	57.08	.72	.30	.71	2.72	5.38	9.06	14.11
Iran, I.R. of 429	37.89	16.64	20.50	33.30	35.80	31.67	66.50	.82	.73	.93	3.44	2.79	3.91	9.44
Iraq 433	26.09	32.62	8.06	1.03	.08	.48	.05	—	—	—	—	—	—	—
Israel 436	1.20	1.15	1.08	1.46	1.74	7.47	5.78	14.63	10.63	11.28	15.73	21.67	32.53	37.97
Jordan 439	.03	1.09	2.68	4.18	9.12	5.14	11.53	.12	—	.11	.08	.08	.08	.11
Kuwait 443	1.90	—	.20	.06	.09	.05	.33	—	—	—	—	—	—	—
Lebanon 446	10.90	1.25	.06	4.25	10.02	3.33	3.25	.12	.26	.07	.07	.10	.59	1.16
Libya 672	—	4.16	.71	14.72	15.78	1.61	4.00	.04	.03	.50	—	—	.88	—
Oman 449	—	—	—	.01	—	—	—	.11	—	—	—	—	—	.01
Qatar 453	—	—	—	—	—	—	.10	—	—	—	—	.04	.07	.30
Saudi Arabia 456	.13	—	1.56	6.36	3.47	3.62	7.07	.02	.13	.43	.39	.84	4.34	1.77
Syrian Arab Republic 463	15.38	14.64	15.43	37.57	31.19	44.10	42.83	.03	.12	.15	.53	.34	1.24	3.95

	Exports							Imports						
	2001	2002	2003	2004	2005	2006	2007	2001	2002	2003	2004	2005	2006	2007
	Millions of U.S. Dollars							Millions of U.S. Dollars						
United Arab Emirates.................. 466	22.56	34.83	37.30	20.60	4.21	24.35	16.63	.86	.72	.88	1.67	2.07	1.79	3.59
Yemen, Republic of..................... 474	.02	.40	.21	.78	.39	.01	1.58	—	—	—	—	—	.04	—
Western Hemisphere............... 207	**104.6**	**108.5**	**128.6**	**210.1**	**215.2**	**243.9**	**468.0**	**137.5**	**126.8**	**120.7**	**124.3**	**199.8**	**322.7**	**239.1**
Argentina.................................... 213	.11	—	.65	1.64	3.41	3.56	6.04	6.54	2.14	3.98	6.33	23.22	71.31	67.85
Bahamas, The.............................. 313	—	—	—	15.29	—	—	—	.25	.25	.74	.04	.04	.08	.11
Barbados..................................... 316	—	—	—	—	—	—	.07	—	—	—	—	—	—	.02
Belize.. 339	—	.68	—	.05	—	.30	.47	—	—	.07	—	—	—	—
Bermuda...................................... 319	—	—	—	—	—	—	—	.01	.02	.02	.01	.01	.02	.02
Bolivia... 218	—	.01	.01	—	—	—	.06	.01	.02	.02	.01	.02	.02	.07
Brazil... 223	76.71	89.42	113.37	155.53	167.45	207.38	372.75	60.76	104.48	89.19	96.98	142.25	209.96	105.86
Chile.. 228	.07	.99	.98	.14	3.25	2.09	3.81	.45	.88	.77	1.83	4.56	6.43	12.31
Colombia...................................... 233	2.35	1.87	3.71	1.26	.80	1.91	23.25	6.71	.21	8.78	3.14	2.51	5.70	6.10
Costa Rica.................................... 238	—	—	.01	—	1.34	2.75	1.30	3.22	.15	.33	2.96	2.89	2.80	3.42
Dominica...................................... 321	—	—	—	—	—	—	.62	—	—	—	.01	—	—	1.39
Dominican Republic..................... 243	2.65	.01	—	—	.10	.30	.38	—	.01	.01	.10	.10	.37	.34
Ecuador....................................... 248	2.41	.81	2.50	2.03	—	6.55	8.29	4.58	5.19	6.36	2.97	7.20	12.76	15.91
El Salvador.................................. 253	.27	.13	—	—	2.34	1.45	.05	22.10	—	1.91	.27	1.16	—	.03
Falkland Islands........................... 323	—	—	—	—	—	—	—	—	—	—	.01	—	.02	—
Greenland.................................... 326	—	—	—	—	—	—	—	—	—	—	—	—	—	.01
Grenada....................................... 328	—	—	—	—	—	—	—	.02	—	—	.06	—	—	—
Guatemala.................................... 258	.56	—	—	.04	1.36	1.64	.01	2.96	1.64	—	3.12	.09	.10	.05
Haiti... 263	—	—	—	—	—	—	.20	—	—	—	—	—	—	—
Honduras..................................... 268	—	.88	.05	—	—	—	—	4.28	.02	.77	.03	4.89	.28	.08
Jamaica.. 343	—	—	—	—	—	—	—	.02	—	.01	.01	.03	.05	.03
Mexico... 273	4.31	3.42	3.72	8.99	7.63	6.01	4.40	1.09	3.16	3.37	4.42	5.95	10.17	16.88
Netherlands Antilles..................... 353	—	—	—	—	—	—	—	.35	.23	—	—	—	—	—
Nicaragua..................................... 278	.65	.75	.43	3.15	1.48	.98	1.15	12.50	.20	—	.01	2.33	.04	4.39
Panama.. 283	.04	.63	.01	1.44	5.15	.50	—	.14	.47	.25	.26	.07	.62	.34
Paraguay...................................... 288	—	—	—	.01	—	—	—	—	—	—	—	.01	—	.07
Peru... 293	1.45	.04	.01	2.20	3.19	1.99	2.35	4.87	1.40	1.36	.46	1.34	.98	1.76
St. Kitts and Nevis....................... 361	—	—	—	—	—	.41	—	—	—	—	—	—	—	—
St. Vincent & Grens...................... 364	—	—	—	—	—	—	.14	—	—	—	—	—	—	—
Trinidad and Tobago.................... 369	—	—	—	—	—	—	—	.01	.01	.01	—	—	—	—
Uruguay....................................... 298	1.25	—	.61	3.13	2.07	.03	—	.12	.08	.50	1.09	1.12	.92	1.22
Venezuela, Rep. Bol..................... 299	4.78	2.22	1.18	15.20	15.59	5.98	42.65	—	—	—	.20	.02	.05	.87
Western Hem. n.s........................ 399	7.01	6.66	1.34	—	—	—	—	6.48	6.26	2.26	—	—	—	—
Other Countries n.i.e................ 910	**10.0**	**7.2**	**8.3**	**9.0**	**18.9**	**11.8**	**16.5**	**13.8**	**26.9**	**18.0**	**30.1**	**7.8**	**13.7**	**8.8**
Cuba... 928	7.15	5.28	5.91	6.89	13.18	10.34	14.81	13.55	26.76	17.92	28.26	5.71	11.64	6.40
North Korea................................. 954	2.89	1.94	2.38	2.09	5.69	1.43	1.65	.28	.10	.08	1.87	2.13	2.04	2.36
Countries & Areas n.s.............. 898	**48.2**	**42.3**	**42.3**	**52.0**	**77.5**	**76.6**	**55.3**	**150.4**	**229.8**	**285.7**	**294.8**	**510.3**	**535.2**	**632.8**
Memorandum Items														
European Union.......................... 998	2,108.32	2,685.38	3,567.06	4,970.12	7,044.79	8,986.31	10,515.53	1,746.57	1,978.74	2,512.73	3,239.27	3,574.53	4,990.91	6,188.75
Oil Exporting Ctys........................ 999	131.31	115.62	98.38	117.67	107.89	127.52	170.45	6.03	6.51	9.90	16.44	23.11	34.23	52.87
Non-Oil Develop.Ctys................... 201	6,327.40	6,274.75	7,365.11	9,991.10	10,278.33	12,229.57	16,367.35	6,594.78	7,108.23	9,143.93	13,356.36	13,087.10	17,418.22	22,472.64
PERCENT DISTRIBUTION														
Industrial Countries................. 101	12.6	19.7	24.4	26.0	34.4	36.9	31.7	18.4	18.9	18.2	16.2	18.4	19.5	19.2
Developing Countries.............. 202	86.6	79.7	75.1	73.5	65.0	62.6	68.0	79.6	78.2	79.2	81.8	78.5	78.1	78.6
Africa..................................... 607	.7	.8	.8	.3	.3	.3	.4	.3	.3	.3	.2	.2	.2	.1
Asia.. 507	4.1	4.7	3.3	4.2	5.4	4.2	3.9	1.5	1.4	1.5	2.1	3.1	4.1	4.6
Europe.................................... 170	78.6	71.4	68.7	66.4	57.1	56.0	60.9	75.9	75.0	76.2	78.6	73.7	72.2	72.7
Middle East............................ 407	1.8	1.5	1.0	1.1	.9	.8	.9	.2	.1	.1	.2	.2	.2	.3
Western Hemisphere............. 207	1.4	1.4	1.3	1.5	1.3	1.2	1.9	1.7	1.4	1.0	.8	1.2	1.4	.8
Other Countries n.i.e............... 910	.1	.1	.1	.1	.1	.1	.1	.2	.3	.2	.2	—	.1	—
ANNUAL PERCENT CHANGE														
World...................................... 001	1.7	7.6	24.0	38.3	16.2	23.5	23.3	–4.1	9.6	27.1	41.4	2.2	33.8	28.3
Industrial Countries................. 101	12.9	68.1	53.7	47.5	53.4	32.6	6.0	–2.5	12.6	22.1	26.1	16.3	41.2	26.6
Developing Countries.............. 202	–.2	–1.1	16.8	35.4	2.7	19.0	33.8	–4.9	7.8	28.7	46.1	–2.0	33.1	29.1
Africa..................................... 607	–55.0	15.6	17.5	–53.9	23.0	59.9	26.1	–12.7	15.4	49.8	–14.5	5.0	3.0	17.5
Asia.. 507	–5.8	23.3	–11.8	76.2	47.0	–3.3	13.5	–26.6	1.9	36.9	90.7	55.9	74.4	44.9
Europe.................................... 170	.3	–2.3	19.4	33.7	–.1	21.2	34.1	–5.1	8.3	29.1	46.0	–4.2	30.9	29.3
Middle East............................ 407	73.6	–12.7	–19.0	53.0	–1.6	9.7	36.5	13.7	–26.0	16.5	63.7	35.1	63.7	32.8
Western Hemisphere............. 207	–2.6	3.7	18.5	63.4	2.4	13.3	91.9	52.7	–7.8	–4.8	3.0	60.8	61.5	–25.9
Other Countries n.i.e............... 910	12.6	–28.1	15.0	8.2	110.2	–37.6	39.9	–69.4	94.3	–33.0	67.4	–74.0	74.6	–36.0

	Exports							Imports						
	2001	2002	2003	2004	2005	2006	2007	2001	2002	2003	2004	2005	2006	2007
	Millions of U.S. Dollars							*Millions of U.S. Dollars*						
IFS World Total	**190,327**	**215,779**	**255,549**	**306,721**	**335,837**	**366,923**	**432,315**	**178,683**	**198,036**	**234,902**	**285,506**	**318,738**	**351,893**	**413,975**
DOTS World Total 001	**188,066**	**213,497**	**250,244**	**307,903**	**334,270**	**366,926**	**432,309**	**178,453**	**197,512**	**224,951**	**285,951**	**318,589**	**351,919**	**413,962**
Industrial Countries 101	**160,615**	**180,475**	**212,931**	**261,531**	**280,786**	**306,125**	**356,236**	**147,446**	**164,114**	**187,079**	**235,653**	**258,209**	**282,910**	**327,460**
United States 111	10,583	16,804	16,859	19,961	21,384	22,616	24,732	12,430	12,606	13,311	15,678	17,070	18,849	22,424
Canada 156	797	1,430	1,631	1,812	2,322	2,701	2,946	1,322	1,020	1,149	1,295	1,340	1,628	2,479
Australia 193	792	1,116	1,208	1,375	1,504	1,436	1,719	501	586	547	784	1,090	1,574	1,784
Japan 158	1,970	2,085	2,423	3,306	3,405	3,182	3,355	5,098	6,133	7,117	8,238	8,544	9,200	10,382
New Zealand 196	137	168	192	206	203	185	211	291	329	413	502	518	501	499
Austria 122	2,053	2,224	2,642	3,362	3,202	3,740	4,398	1,221	1,101	1,362	1,524	1,953	2,250	2,345
Cyprus 423	91	89	92	146	134	221	257	24	28	40	77	86	82	151
Denmark 128	1,539	1,597	2,006	2,414	2,667	2,905	3,669	805	874	1,098	1,303	1,288	1,344	1,636
Finland 172	1,043	1,089	1,342	1,768	1,899	2,362	2,833	1,126	1,128	1,531	1,784	1,757	2,002	2,369
France 132	32,891	34,751	43,457	52,964	57,797	61,928	72,020	23,965	25,230	29,734	35,624	36,295	39,346	46,285
Germany 134	34,304	39,700	48,747	61,399	64,725	72,334	84,406	28,888	33,913	39,741	52,712	54,888	61,043	73,395
Greece 174	1,240	1,314	1,610	2,016	2,060	2,344	3,018	273	243	222	218	244	303	394
Iceland 176	44	37	55	60	82	103	150	35	40	49	75	90	94	108
Ireland 178	1,510	1,658	1,635	2,325	3,636	2,978	3,036	5,804	13,911	12,881	17,970	20,848	20,184	20,128
Italy 136	10,932	11,498	13,507	16,142	17,658	18,973	22,447	7,602	7,815	7,461	9,162	10,119	11,873	15,534
Luxembourg 137	3,719	3,829	4,671	6,161	6,671	6,885	7,450	1,043	1,202	1,473	2,143	2,125	2,180	3,100
Malta 181	61	64	75	95	95	96	122	70	79	67	34	66	22	32
Netherlands 138	22,897	24,829	29,217	36,443	39,086	43,937	51,576	30,267	30,819	37,088	48,587	56,587	64,395	73,028
Norway 142	657	756	856	1,148	1,318	1,567	1,827	1,944	1,508	2,081	2,482	5,062	5,095	4,169
Portugal 182	1,431	1,404	1,599	1,961	2,195	2,193	2,694	1,764	1,593	1,527	1,725	1,774	1,333	1,481
Slovenia 961	180	205	280	372	448	519	687	96	85	99	154	146	178	206
Spain 184	7,289	7,726	9,850	12,034	12,548	13,486	15,726	3,441	3,634	4,520	5,645	5,792	6,488	7,597
Sweden 144	2,625	2,906	3,501	4,214	4,661	5,358	6,476	4,135	4,271	4,876	6,297	6,315	7,302	8,890
Switzerland 146	2,775	2,696	2,837	3,240	3,781	5,156	7,556	1,559	1,538	1,709	2,108	2,552	2,456	3,349
United Kingdom 112	19,055	20,500	22,637	26,606	27,304	28,921	32,925	13,743	14,430	16,982	19,531	21,659	23,187	25,695
Developing Countries 202	**27,419**	**31,753**	**35,924**	**45,341**	**51,496**	**57,972**	**72,419**	**30,985**	**33,369**	**37,846**	**50,259**	**59,862**	**68,939**	**86,498**
Africa 607	**3,077**	**3,295**	**3,724**	**4,736**	**5,172**	**6,508**	**8,099**	**4,917**	**5,892**	**5,743**	**6,726**	**8,221**	**8,506**	**9,020**
Algeria 612	377	405	512	703	686	698	1,066	445	1,074	1,399	1,629	2,084	2,538	1,897
Angola 614	113	142	137	145	166	242	352	558	497	244	119	519	356	284
Benin 638	37	48	62	57	68	85	140	6	4	4	1	5	14	21
Botswana 616	2	2	6	3	8	20	57	8	15	11	17	25	47	53
Burkina Faso 748	18	20	39	34	29	38	45	2	1	2	3	3	7	6
Burundi 618	15	15	14	17	25	27	31	3	4	5	4	12	4	6
Cameroon 622	102	112	142	156	146	161	192	65	55	88	102	194	214	179
Cape Verde 624	9	9	13	14	21	16	24	—	—	—	—	—	—	—
Central African Rep. 626	4	4	4	9	7	7	8	108	133	56	56	44	38	31
Chad 628	9	12	10	17	30	24	22	2	1	1	—	—	—	—
Comoros 632	4	3	3	3	5	4	3	—	—	—	—	—	—	—
Congo, Dem. Rep. of 636	111	120	142	174	230	224	283	777	1,002	655	578	575	513	502
Congo, Republic of 634	56	61	54	62	65	97	127	8	8	41	30	3	7	16
Côte d'Ivoire 662	79	91	101	118	111	132	198	156	231	270	312	188	267	283
Djibouti 611	7	9	10	14	6	30	20	—	1	—	2	—	—	1
Equatorial Guinea 642	3	9	13	17	16	28	42	—	—	1	2	1	1	4
Eritrea 643	6	8	7	4	8	5	4	—	—	—	—	—	—	—
Ethiopia 644	26	18	24	26	48	65	124	21	8	13	18	29	36	43
Gabon 646	34	31	41	46	61	77	135	14	13	13	14	16	20	23
Gambia, The 648	25	17	12	14	13	18	21	3	2	1	1	1	1	2
Ghana 652	46	61	83	108	123	293	306	50	81	79	118	150	161	156
Guinea 656	55	58	56	56	70	90	91	132	88	55	54	66	48	54
Guinea-Bissau 654	3	3	2	4	6	4	2	—	—	—	—	—	—	—
Kenya 664	62	67	76	91	95	107	158	38	32	32	32	35	50	80
Lesotho 666	—	—	—	1	—	—	1	9	6	5	27	64	78	166
Liberia 668	9	4	11	12	10	10	12	3	1	2	—	443	25	31
Madagascar 674	32	27	49	56	43	40	50	27	12	15	14	16	26	19
Malawi 676	3	8	6	13	9	16	12	4	9	10	16	7	6	17
Mali 678	32	29	29	45	54	83	93	3	6	5	6	4	3	6
Mauritania 682	50	58	46	43	53	91	97	46	59	50	64	88	104	93
Mauritius 684	30	36	34	50	56	62	54	54	92	63	72	75	86	104
Morocco 686	222	291	329	396	470	679	727	275	282	320	339	470	454	515
Mozambique 688	6	7	9	8	15	12	10	314	342	302	470	510	566	555
Namibia 728	15	3	11	7	14	28	24	15	13	15	18	22	14	14
Niger 692	23	20	18	23	35	36	85	10	10	—	—	—	—	2
Nigeria 694	246	251	237	216	269	541	841	39	68	89	64	93	126	112
Rwanda 714	21	23	21	29	28	29	41	3	5	2	4	8	8	5
São Tomé & Príncipe 716	2	3	3	2	3	4	3	—	1	1	1	2	2	2
Senegal 722	70	123	113	135	119	127	201	29	32	23	22	15	34	54
Seychelles 718	5	5	4	4	4	4	6	1	3	—	7	—	1	1
Sierra Leone 724	15	12	15	15	10	16	15	23	46	90	125	142	120	145
Somalia 726	1	—	—	—	—	1	1	—	—	—	—	—	—	—

	Exports 2001	2002	2003	2004	2005	2006	2007	Imports 2001	2002	2003	2004	2005	2006	2007
	Millions of U.S. Dollars							Millions of U.S. Dollars						
South Africa......199	590	593	700	1,134	1,178	1,353	1,527	1,018	1,035	1,178	1,680	1,681	1,842	2,715
Sudan......732	25	20	31	62	121	144	59	4	4	7	9	4	8	12
Swaziland......734	1	—	—	—	1	1	1	4	4	4	2	—	2	2
Tanzania......738	22	26	29	38	44	70	74	77	55	41	39	29	36	35
Togo......742	29	32	47	46	42	137	79	4	10	7	19	9	38	29
Tunisia......744	397	365	391	453	485	478	554	455	449	452	457	418	449	534
Uganda......746	18	22	20	43	52	36	48	58	61	44	68	85	75	92
Zambia......754	7	9	5	6	16	18	22	24	21	33	86	67	61	101
Zimbabwe......698	10	9	9	10	7	8	13	23	17	13	23	18	17	16
Asia......507	**8,821**	**10,854**	**12,275**	**14,710**	**16,864**	**17,048**	**20,674**	**12,385**	**13,245**	**15,046**	**19,266**	**23,400**	**27,887**	**36,028**
Afghanistan, I.S. of......512	7	6	6	8	18	14	18	5	5	7	7	6	4	4
Bangladesh......513	43	50	47	52	55	56	60	270	275	351	427	433	555	611
Bhutan......514	1	1	—	—	—	—	—	—	—	—	—	—	—	—
Brunei Darussalam......516	—	—	3	5	3	4	13	—	—	—	—	—	—	—
Cambodia......522	10	17	19	20	23	26	37	12	10	9	22	16	26	47
China,P.R.: Mainland......924	1,510	1,885	2,472	2,840	3,359	3,668	4,583	3,840	4,471	5,934	8,208	10,628	12,841	17,171
China,P.R.:Hong Kong......532	1,363	1,653	1,715	2,036	2,204	2,461	2,832	694	981	542	719	860	947	912
China,P.R.:Macao......546	2	1	1	1	1	1	20	15	15	17	20	9	11	15
Fiji......819	—	2	1	1	1	1	3	—	—	—	—	3	1	4
French Polynesia......887	—	—	21	25	22	26	29	—	—	1	1	2	2	1
Guam......829	1	1	1	1	—	—	1	—	—	—	—	—	—	—
India......534	2,696	3,842	4,378	5,278	6,428	5,811	7,395	1,509	1,666	1,911	2,791	3,046	3,797	4,533
Indonesia......536	202	221	220	511	343	350	372	863	970	1,037	1,084	1,110	1,171	1,482
Kiribati......826	—	—	—	—	—	—	—	—	—	—	—	1	—	—
Korea......542	616	708	778	957	1,134	1,081	1,390	760	771	1,110	1,394	1,826	2,256	3,254
Lao People's Dem.Rep......544	3	3	3	10	11	7	9	11	15	20	15	17	18	12
Malaysia......548	255	263	289	326	328	347	483	620	551	598	576	607	705	809
Maldives......556	1	1	1	1	1	2	2	—	—	—	—	—	—	—
Mongolia......948	3	3	7	4	7	3	7	2	1	1	1	1	1	10
Myanmar......518	8	10	4	2	5	9	6	20	23	23	25	18	11	10
Nepal......558	7	8	17	12	14	13	8	5	4	5	4	6	4	5
New Caledonia......839	9	30	18	20	27	59	40	11	2	4	15	49	110	270
Pakistan......564	118	157	193	205	327	289	302	169	194	216	267	287	310	362
Papua New Guinea......853	1	1	1	2	1	1	3	8	15	15	20	29	20	43
Philippines......566	143	153	176	174	204	239	257	192	235	221	249	346	485	411
Samoa......862	—	—	1	1	—	—	—	—	—	—	—	—	—	—
Singapore......576	431	463	470	521	613	656	751	572	574	423	436	744	1,042	1,484
Solomon Islands......813	—	—	—	—	—	—	—	—	—	1	3	4	2	1
Sri Lanka......524	158	180	200	239	274	293	326	205	230	238	325	345	392	442
Taiwan Province of China......528	555	496	408	562	573	611	584	774	572	646	893	934	944	1,225
Thailand......578	584	601	716	783	730	843	893	1,378	1,201	1,199	1,102	1,322	1,356	1,829
Tonga......866	—	—	1	—	—	—	—	—	—	—	—	—	—	—
Vanuatu......846	—	—	—	—	—	—	—	—	1	1	12	7	6	2
Vietnam......582	92	99	108	110	157	175	247	453	466	516	649	746	869	1,079
Europe......170	**7,443**	**8,926**	**11,144**	**14,815**	**17,066**	**21,274**	**27,456**	**7,198**	**7,456**	**9,345**	**14,066**	**16,041**	**18,501**	**22,435**
Albania......914	7	9	12	16	13	17	17	1	3	11	1	2	1	4
Armenia......911	47	90	125	121	136	137	131	34	83	112	106	110	105	96
Azerbaijan......912	14	11	30	57	36	31	48	3	2	2	1	5	4	12
Belarus......913	64	55	62	80	115	139	186	20	39	58	93	79	106	117
Bosnia & Herzegovina......963	26	27	36	45	52	54	78	9	7	9	11	13	14	33
Bulgaria......918	145	137	187	228	266	338	569	287	307	465	630	706	1,004	1,154
Croatia......960	170	209	235	259	283	321	323	58	52	50	75	44	42	55
Czech Republic......935	960	1,271	1,390	1,843	2,129	2,678	3,652	750	695	894	1,530	1,909	2,513	3,038
Estonia......939	75	95	122	165	202	260	327	81	65	137	177	194	102	153
Faroe Islands......816	1	1	1	1	2	2	4	—	—	—	1	—	—	—
Georgia......915	9	9	17	23	26	34	45	3	3	4	8	12	30	26
Gibraltar......823	23	7	6	20	3	54	112	6	5	1	2	—	—	7
Hungary......944	856	991	1,218	1,361	1,603	1,745	1,997	1,411	1,350	1,146	1,141	1,246	1,487	1,667
Kazakhstan......916	54	44	66	133	99	148	161	27	31	40	37	34	55	173
Kosovo......967	—	—	—	—	2	6	4	—	—	—	—	—	—	3
Kyrgyz Republic......917	3	3	3	4	7	9	16	—	3	3	2	1	1	—
Latvia......941	85	96	100	124	161	208	315	55	42	43	69	33	53	65
Lithuania......946	148	171	200	248	306	436	674	100	105	154	299	174	175	283
Macedonia, FYR......962	13	18	20	19	24	39	35	17	29	40	34	54	87	200
Moldova......921	16	18	24	30	39	44	45	5	6	7	10	14	13	10
Montenegro, Rep. of......943	—	—	—	—	—	6	8	—	—	—	—	—	—	—
Poland......964	1,591	1,831	2,243	3,165	3,746	4,654	6,190	1,051	1,186	1,501	2,371	2,461	2,841	3,610
Romania......968	326	360	454	600	752	994	1,393	279	305	406	631	639	575	472
Russia......922	1,080	1,186	1,450	1,970	2,485	3,518	4,494	1,698	1,749	2,452	3,865	5,218	5,935	6,685
Serbia, Rep. of......942	—	—	—	—	—	189	244	—	—	—	—	—	84	116
Serbia & Montenegro......965	62	89	123	162	167	—	—	20	24	30	49	62	—	—
Slovak Republic......936	265	326	440	656	674	836	1,143	216	220	289	387	420	497	889
Tajikistan......923	3	3	2	2	1	2	3	7	6	10	9	6	24	4
Turkey......186	1,137	1,553	2,203	3,003	3,247	3,724	4,403	890	952	1,303	2,189	2,328	2,478	3,305
Turkmenistan......925	8	5	8	19	15	12	17	3	1	—	7	3	5	1
Ukraine......926	239	290	350	441	458	621	786	115	150	138	290	246	236	230
Uzbekistan......927	11	13	13	13	14	18	34	49	37	39	42	27	33	30
Europe n.s......884	6	5	5	5	4	7	8	—	—	1	—	1	1	2

	Exports 2001	2002	2003	2004	2005	2006	2007	Imports 2001	2002	2003	2004	2005	2006	2007
	Millions of U.S. Dollars							Millions of U.S. Dollars						
Middle East 407	**5,548**	**6,150**	**6,291**	**7,982**	**8,747**	**9,062**	**10,810**	**2,872**	**3,100**	**3,335**	**4,961**	**6,194**	**6,497**	**8,878**
Bahrain 419	44	44	64	93	66	82	87	26	24	27	31	37	38	39
Egypt 469	327	306	341	450	583	613	779	93	67	117	205	306	499	483
Iran, I.R. of 429	256	320	488	624	580	553	550	35	22	28	106	125	168	273
Iraq 433	88	109	59	91	67	73	65	—	1	—	1	1	1	1
Israel 436	2,745	2,889	2,722	3,610	3,779	3,254	4,036	1,934	2,083	1,838	2,468	2,980	2,635	3,671
Jordan 439	105	113	124	121	154	164	156	4	3	3	7	13	17	14
Kuwait 443	84	98	135	145	163	194	249	40	34	21	19	112	32	50
Lebanon 446	222	258	245	268	250	240	289	31	33	33	28	34	34	49
Libya 672	111	130	100	154	150	215	168	27	60	58	83	58	121	187
Oman 449	65	60	70	87	75	125	127	3	18	7	12	22	6	5
Qatar 453	32	54	49	61	139	244	363	5	18	13	40	119	151	727
Saudi Arabia 456	507	650	737	813	949	1,184	1,310	205	244	293	401	761	1,179	1,374
Syrian Arab Republic 463	159	175	207	257	243	265	209	30	64	32	50	26	25	70
United Arab Emirates 466	780	924	927	1,174	1,494	1,805	2,329	439	425	862	1,507	1,596	1,587	1,928
West Bank/Gaza Strip 487	—	2	1	1	—	1	1	—	—	—	—	1	1	4
Yemen, Republic of 474	22	21	23	34	56	52	95	2	3	4	5	4	4	8
Western Hemisphere 207	**2,531**	**2,528**	**2,490**	**3,099**	**3,647**	**4,080**	**5,380**	**3,613**	**3,676**	**4,377**	**5,240**	**6,006**	**7,547**	**10,137**
Antigua and Barbuda 311	1	—	—	—	1	1	3	—	—	—	—	—	1	1
Argentina 213	224	105	153	188	228	364	546	318	319	322	355	378	404	540
Aruba 314	2	3	2	2	3	1	2	5	8	10	14	39	—	7
Bahamas, The 313	2	6	3	3	8	3	4	1	—	—	—	—	1	6
Barbados 316	3	4	4	4	4	5	6	1	—	—	—	—	—	—
Belize 339	—	1	—	—	1	2	2	—	2	—	1	1	1	—
Bermuda 319	2	2	2	3	2	2	1	—	—	—	—	—	—	—
Bolivia 218	6	8	6	8	12	11	11	3	5	1	20	23	8	41
Brazil 223	869	809	888	1,211	1,397	1,610	2,077	1,416	1,557	1,817	1,820	2,060	2,889	4,047
Chile 228	120	117	126	163	237	269	373	140	134	167	238	289	322	420
Colombia 233	97	110	100	108	145	157	218	218	227	351	540	557	599	577
Costa Rica 238	22	28	29	28	28	36	105	193	203	285	392	375	364	579
Dominica 321	1	—	2	1	1	1	1	—	—	—	—	—	—	—
Dominican Republic 243	42	39	65	34	42	46	62	27	46	49	84	106	155	242
Ecuador 248	39	35	32	35	43	56	58	112	107	151	231	253	305	438
El Salvador 253	13	13	15	14	23	17	19	4	6	7	6	13	10	12
Greenland 326	6	3	1	2	2	3	1	—	—	—	—	—	—	—
Grenada 328	—	1	1	—	1	1	1	—	1	2	2	1	1	—
Guatemala 258	25	37	39	38	47	51	46	30	11	15	16	24	22	20
Guyana 336	2	3	2	2	2	3	4	37	25	41	46	26	32	29
Haiti 263	5	12	4	3	6	5	6	6	2	3	3	6	9	14
Honduras 268	9	15	13	14	11	11	13	35	57	62	82	104	129	108
Jamaica 343	23	33	17	16	25	33	40	1	1	1	—	2	3	2
Mexico 273	641	785	668	777	853	888	1,028	645	541	550	698	877	1,024	1,441
Netherlands Antilles 353	18	17	12	14	20	25	23	19	21	16	22	15	31	28
Nicaragua 278	4	9	11	15	9	12	35	5	4	4	6	12	12	13
Panama 283	52	91	70	65	113	72	91	53	39	108	77	57	62	103
Paraguay 288	6	2	3	4	7	7	10	1	3	2	4	4	4	11
Peru 293	58	52	50	60	78	87	123	82	71	87	151	179	394	573
St. Kitts and Nevis 361	1	—	—	1	3	4	—	—	—	—	—	1	—	—
St. Lucia 362	1	1	2	1	13	2	3	—	—	—	—	—	—	—
St. Pierre-Miquelon 363	—	—	—	—	2	—	—	—	—	—	3	3	4	4
St. Vincent & Grens. 364	2	1	1	2	3	—	6	12	—	2	—	—	—	—
Suriname 366	10	10	13	16	21	13	17	4	21	79	99	100	138	142
Trinidad and Tobago 369	14	11	21	28	19	18	28	25	16	22	15	64	42	25
Uruguay 298	26	12	28	23	20	21	57	20	20	22	26	16	26	59
Venezuela, Rep. Bol. 299	183	151	105	212	212	242	318	200	229	201	284	411	557	652
Western Hem. n.s. 399	1	1	1	3	6	2	39	—	2	—	5	7	1	1
Other Countries n.i.e. 910	**31**	**31**	**40**	**48**	**63**	**65**	**48**	**21**	**15**	**12**	**12**	**6**	**5**	**3**
Cuba 928	24	21	28	33	53	52	45	15	11	8	7	6	4	2
North Korea 954	7	10	12	15	11	13	3	7	5	4	5	—	—	1
Countries & Areas n.s. 898	—	—	—	—	—	—	—	—	—	**15**	**4**	—	—	—
Special Categories 899	—	**1,238**	**1,346**	**981**	**1,923**	**2,764**	**3,604**	—	**15**	—	**23**	—	—	—
Memorandum Items														
European Union 998	146,841	160,166	192,582	237,985	255,608	279,996	328,039	127,932	144,017	164,866	210,465	228,381	251,180	291,971
Oil Exporting Ctys 999	2,932	3,371	3,639	4,791	5,127	6,223	7,757	2,301	3,165	4,007	5,230	6,491	7,637	8,687
Non-Oil Develop.Ctys 201	24,487	28,382	32,285	40,550	46,369	51,749	64,662	28,685	30,204	33,838	45,030	53,371	61,302	77,811
PERCENT DISTRIBUTION														
Industrial Countries 101	**85.4**	**84.5**	**85.1**	**84.9**	**84.0**	**83.4**	**82.4**	**82.6**	**83.1**	**83.2**	**82.4**	**81.0**	**80.4**	**79.1**
Developing Countries 202	**14.6**	**14.9**	**14.4**	**14.7**	**15.4**	**15.8**	**16.8**	**17.4**	**16.9**	**16.8**	**17.6**	**18.8**	**19.6**	**20.9**
Africa 607	**1.6**	**1.5**	**1.5**	**1.5**	**1.5**	**1.8**	**1.9**	**2.8**	**3.0**	**2.6**	**2.4**	**2.6**	**2.4**	**2.2**
Asia 507	**4.7**	**5.1**	**4.9**	**4.8**	**5.0**	**4.6**	**4.8**	**6.9**	**6.7**	**6.7**	**6.7**	**7.3**	**7.9**	**8.7**
Europe 170	**4.0**	**4.2**	**4.5**	**4.8**	**5.1**	**5.8**	**6.4**	**4.0**	**3.8**	**4.2**	**4.9**	**5.0**	**5.3**	**5.4**
Middle East 407	**3.0**	**2.9**	**2.5**	**2.6**	**2.6**	**2.5**	**2.5**	**1.6**	**1.6**	**1.5**	**1.7**	**1.9**	**1.8**	**2.1**
Western Hemisphere 207	**1.3**	**1.2**	**1.0**	**1.0**	**1.1**	**1.1**	**1.2**	**2.0**	**1.9**	**1.9**	**1.8**	**1.9**	**2.1**	**2.4**
ANNUAL PERCENT CHANGE														
World 001	**.8**	**13.5**	**17.2**	**23.0**	**8.6**	**9.8**	**17.8**	**1.9**	**10.7**	**13.9**	**27.1**	**11.4**	**10.5**	**17.6**
Industrial Countries 101	**1.3**	**12.4**	**18.0**	**22.8**	**7.4**	**9.0**	**16.4**	**2.1**	**11.3**	**14.0**	**26.0**	**9.6**	**9.6**	**15.7**

	Exports							Imports						
	2001	2002	2003	2004	2005	2006	2007	2001	2002	2003	2004	2005	2006	2007
Developing Countries.............. 202	−1.8	15.8	13.1	26.2	13.6	12.6	24.9	1.0	7.7	13.4	32.8	19.1	15.2	25.5
Africa...................................... 607	—	7.1	13.0	27.2	9.2	25.8	24.4	−8.6	19.8	−2.5	17.1	22.2	3.5	6.0
Asia... 507	−4.7	23.0	13.1	19.8	14.6	1.1	21.3	.9	6.9	13.6	28.1	21.5	19.2	29.2
Europe.................................... 170	1.5	19.9	24.9	32.9	15.2	24.7	29.1	12.3	3.6	25.3	50.5	14.0	15.3	21.3
Middle East............................ 407	−6.3	10.8	2.3	26.9	9.6	3.6	19.3	−6.8	7.9	7.6	48.8	24.8	4.9	36.6
Western Hemisphere.............. 207	7.9	−.1	−1.5	24.5	17.7	11.9	31.9	2.3	1.7	19.1	19.7	14.6	25.7	34.3
Other Countries n.i.e................ 910	−12.8	−1.9	31.2	20.0	31.1	2.4	−26.4	−8.5	−28.0	−23.9	3.8	−51.5	−20.4	−36.6

	Exports 2001	Exports 2002	Exports 2003	Exports 2004	Exports 2005	Exports 2006	Exports 2007	Imports 2001	Imports 2002	Imports 2003	Imports 2004	Imports 2005	Imports 2006	Imports 2007
	Millions of U.S. Dollars							Millions of U.S. Dollars						
IFS World Total	**169.0**	**169.0**	**205.0**	**213.0**	**208.0**	**266.2**	**253.9**	**516.8**	**524.5**	**551.7**	**519.7**	**592.9**	**676.0**	**684.4**
DOTS World Total 001	**249.4Y**	**196.7Y**	**278.9Y**	**298.2Y**	**303.1Y**	**419.8Y**	**359.2Y**	**484.0Y**	**478.5Y**	**550.3Y**	**551.1Y**	**768.1Y**	**734.7Y**	**826.2Y**
Industrial Countries 101	**196.7Y**	**145.1Y**	**200.9Y**	**206.6Y**	**218.9Y**	**337.3Y**	**239.4Y**	**281.9Y**	**240.0Y**	**314.6Y**	**258.0Y**	**381.5Y**	**352.1Y**	**376.4Y**
United States 111	93.36V	76.09V	96.55V	103.00V	94.64V	141.82V	103.09V	190.08V	151.03V	219.45V	166.76V	238.48V	262.68V	257.62V
Canada 156	2.41V	4.26V	3.24V	6.39V	7.95V	8.44V	10.07V	2.51V	3.44V	4.15V	5.22V	6.59V	9.81V	7.34V
Australia 193	.02V	.08V	.07V	.06V	.21V	1.96V	2.01V	.32V	.84V	.22V	.05V	.69V	.11V	.88V
Japan 158	31.84V	7.12V	8.63V	8.68V	7.38V	4.96V	6.24V	27.54V	25.08V	16.95V	22.60V	11.41V	7.76V	4.70V
New Zealand 196	—V	—V	.01V	.06V	.01V	.02V	.02V	.22V	.20V	.14V	.16V	.16V	.43V	.49V
Austria 122	—V	.02V	.06V	—V	.15V	.19V	—V	.97V	1.29V	2.11V	4.54V	5.13V	2.98V	5.08V
Belgium 124	—V	1.36V	.12V	1.00V	1.10V	.60V	.45V	.30V	.99V	.54V	.50V	.62V	2.58V	2.14V
Cyprus 423	.02V	—V	—V	.15V	.02Y	—V	—V	—V	—V	.01V	—V	—V	—V	—V
Denmark 128	.01V	.10V	.15V	.24V	.20V	.09V	.01V	2.39V	4.57V	5.26V	2.20V	3.27V	1.86V	2.72V
Finland 172	—V	—V	—V	—V	—V	8.25V	14.92V	.04V	—V	.03V	.02V	.78V	10.30V	.30V
France 132	.03V	.04V	9.50V	.05V	14.92V	1.18V	1.47V	2.39V	1.23V	15.99V	1.40V	20.40V	2.65V	8.40V
Germany 134	2.84V	1.87V	1.63V	.77V	1.08V	.12V	.22V	21.24V	7.70V	5.81V	5.39V	10.45V	7.73V	12.65V
Greece 174	2.21V	1.10V	.61V	—V	.04V	.04V	.22V	.39V	.33V	.20V	.01V	1.50V	.45V	.31V
Iceland 176	—V	—V	—V	—V	.02V	—V	—V	.04V	.02V	—V	.01V	—V	—V	.02V
Ireland 178	2.20V	3.93V	5.54V	.15V	4.05V	1.76V	4.49V	.32V	.28V	.23V	.74V	4.43V	.26V	.69V
Italy 136	2.82V	.07V	3.39V	.21V	.37V	.14V	.04V	2.07V	.79V	1.80V	4.48V	11.99V	3.00V	20.92V
Luxembourg 137	—V	—V	—V	—V	—V	—V	—V	—V	—V	—V	—V	.73V	.20V	—V
Malta 181	—Y	—V	—V	1.35V	—V	—V	—V	—Y	—V	—V	—V	—V	—V	—V
Netherlands 138	9.24V	5.32V	8.17V	5.50V	6.58V	12.31V	14.01V	5.59V	9.47V	5.67V	6.95V	8.54V	5.76V	7.25V
Norway 142	—V	—V	—V	—V	—V	.02V	—V	.13V	.12V	.12V	12.49V	.10V	2.21V	.88V
Portugal 182	1.93V	.01V	—V	3.61V	.13V	8.46V	8.62V	.22V	.55V	.08V	.18V	—V	.03V	.12V
Slovenia 961	—V	—V	.01V	.02Y	—V	—V	—V	—V	—V	—V	—Y	.29V	.97V	2.11V
Spain 184	2.21V	.04V	.85V	.33V	2.73V	6.40V	14.50V	2.00V	6.21V	3.43V	4.12V	34.59V	11.42V	9.90V
Sweden 144	.04V	.22V	.52V	.72V	.06V	.01V	.03V	1.13V	2.16V	.73V	1.01V	.75V	.26V	.96V
Switzerland 146	—V	.04V	.01V	—V	.06V	.14V	.47V	.16V	.93V	.51V	.99V	2.02V	1.85V	5.09V
United Kingdom 112	45.52V	43.46V	61.87V	74.33V	77.17V	140.41V	58.58V	21.84V	22.75V	31.14V	18.17V	18.60V	16.83V	25.83V
Developing Countries 202	**52.6Y**	**51.5Y**	**77.8Y**	**91.4Y**	**84.1Y**	**82.3Y**	**119.5Y**	**179.8Y**	**214.3Y**	**205.1Y**	**252.9Y**	**340.7Y**	**325.9Y**	**379.4Y**
Africa 607	**2.3Y**	**2.7Y**	**7.8Y**	**14.2Y**	**20.0Y**	**26.2Y**	**33.3Y**	**1.7Y**	**4.9Y**	**2.4Y**	**1.6Y**	**3.5Y**	**3.6Y**	**2.1Y**
Algeria 612	—V	—V	—Y	—Y	—Y	—Y	—Y	.01V	—V	—Y	—Y	—Y	—Y	—Y
Benin 638	—V	—V	.01V	—V	—V	—Y	—Y	....	....	....	....	....	....	....
Congo, Republic of 634	—V	—V	—V	—V	—Y	—Y	—Y	—V	3.85V	—V	—V	—Y	—Y	—Y
Côte d'Ivoire 662	1.37V	1.20V	.73V	4.49V	7.87V	15.54V	19.29Y	1.58V	.73V	.92V	.83V	2.02V	1.08V	1.34Y
Kenya 664	.01V	.04V	.01V	.05V	.05Y	.07Y	.08Y	—V	.01V	—V	—V	—Y	—Y	—Y
Madagascar 674	—V	—V	—V	—Y	—Y	—Y	—Y	—V	—V	.01V	.01Y	.01Y	.01Y	.01Y
Mauritius 684	.14V	—V	.15V	.05V	—V	.12V	.41V	.01V	—V	.83V	.31V	—V	—V	—V
Morocco 686	.02V	—V	—V	—V	—V	—Y	—Y	—V	—V	.02V	—V	—V	—Y	—Y
Nigeria 694	.50V	.46V	5.00V	6.51Y	8.29Y	10.23Y	13.25Y	—V	—V	—V	—Y	—Y	—Y	—Y
South Africa 199	.05V	.76V	1.81V	3.02V	3.60V	—V	—V	.14V	.31V	.63V	.47V	.60V	2.47V	.76V
Tanzania 738	.17V	.04V	.05Y	.07Y	.08Y	.10Y	.12Y	—V	—V	—Y	—Y	—Y	—Y	—Y
Togo 742	—V	.01V	—V	—V	—V	—Y	—Y	—V	—Y	—Y	—Y	—Y	—Y	—Y
Tunisia 744	—V	—V	.01V	—V	.03V	.01V	.01Y	—V	—V	—V	—V	.85V	—V	—Y
Uganda 746	—V	—V	.04V	.06Y	.07Y	.08Y	.10Y	—V	—V	.01V	.02Y	.02Y	.02Y	.03Y
Zambia 754	.04V	.18V	—V	—V	—V	.07V	—V	—V	—V	—V	—V	—V	—V	—V
Zimbabwe 698	—V	—V	—V	—V	.02V	—V	—Y	—V	—V	—V	—V	—V	—V	—Y
Asia 507	**16.9Y**	**11.4Y**	**10.3Y**	**16.9Y**	**10.2Y**	**6.2Y**	**28.1Y**	**39.3Y**	**36.2Y**	**33.1Y**	**52.5Y**	**55.8Y**	**48.1Y**	**50.2Y**
Bangladesh 513	.67V	—V	—V	—V	—V	—V	—V	—V	—V	—V	—V	—V	—Y	—Y
Brunei Darussalam 516	—Y	—Y	.05V	.06Y	.07Y	.09Y	.11Y	—Y	—Y	—V	—Y	—Y	—Y	—Y
Cambodia 522	—V	—Y	—Y	—Y	—Y	—Y	—Y	—V	—V	—V	—V	—V	.12V	.15Y
China,P.R.: Mainland 924	—V	.14V	.90V	—V	.19V	.02V	—Y	6.90V	9.84V	11.18V	23.02V	35.28V	31.64V	28.44V
China,P.R.:Hong Kong 532	.10V	.11V	.04V	.12V	.11V	.45V	.03V	1.44V	2.09V	1.56V	1.40V	.81V	.64V	.83V
China,P.R.:Macao 546	—V	—V	—V	.01V	—V	—V	—V	—V	—V	—V	—V	—V	—V	—V
India 534	.19Y	.33V	.11V	.01V	.02V	.03Y	.04Y	.25Y	.61V	2.45V	1.53V	2.47V	3.05Y	3.78Y
Indonesia 536	.14V	.62V	.37V	—V	.05V	.14V	.04V	3.23V	.87V	.43V	.63V	.54V	.65V	.52V
Korea 542	8.96V	2.78V	1.20V	4.61V	4.71V	.48V	4.74V	13.09V	5.25V	4.15V	15.94V	3.96V	4.03V	5.60V
Malaysia 548	.02V	.16V	5.10V	.96V	.28V	.11V	.28V	.39V	.44V	.96V	1.33V	.45V	.89V	.61V
Pakistan 564	—V	.08V	.06V	.11V	.18V	.22Y	.27Y	.04V	.15V	.16V	.48V	.04V	.05Y	.07Y
Philippines 566	.75V	.09V	.44V	.01V	—V	—V	—V	3.72V	1.12V	2.47V	.08V	.08V	.09V	.02V
Taiwan Province of China 528	.34V	6.02V	.31V	1.56V	2.22V	2.47V	1.67V	5.73V	11.27V	6.61V	6.86V	8.87V	4.51V	6.66V
Thailand 578	5.73V	1.03V	1.68V	9.40V	2.33V	2.23V	20.90V	4.55V	4.58V	3.11V	1.20V	3.32V	2.41V	3.57V
Europe 170	**3.3Y**	**1.2Y**	**4.0Y**	**5.8Y**	**8.0Y**	**1.8Y**	**2.9Y**	**4.4Y**	**6.2Y**	**7.1Y**	**28.7Y**	**77.8Y**	**36.1Y**	**49.4Y**
Belarus 913	—V	—V	.06V	—V	—V	—V	—V	—V	.74V	—V	.06V	—V	.33V	.51V
Bulgaria 918	.03V	.01V	.08V	—V	—V	.03V	.36V	.12V	.35V	.13V	1.14V	.40V	3.38V	.56V
Czech Republic 935	—V	.09V	—V	.04V	—V	.01V	.02V	1.62V	1.11V	1.88V	.13V	.32V	1.52V	1.65V
Estonia 939	.01V	—V	—V	.01V	—V	—V	—V	.37V	1.86V	1.35V	2.51V	.07V	.39V	1.11V
Hungary 944	.12V	.10V	.51V	1.51V	.12V	—V	—V	.09V	.34V	.17V	.57V	—V	.40V	.54V
Latvia 941	—V	.94V	1.16V	.11V	1.59V	.11V	—V	.34V	.02V	.04V	.19V	.76V	.81V	.98V
Poland 964	.08V	.10V	.83V	2.82V	4.54V	—V	—V	.39V	1.33V	1.40V	1.35V	7.20V	1.89V	3.66V
Romania 968	—V	—V	.01V	.01V	—V	.01V	—V	.14V	.13V	.15V	.25V	.03V	.02V	.10V
Russia 922	2.55V	—V	.12V	—V	.61V	.87V	.87V	1.23V	.20V	1.76V	21.87V	67.91V	26.46V	38.24V
Turkey 186	.48V	—V	1.18V	1.35V	1.13V	.74V	1.67V	.04V	.07V	.17V	.65V	1.04V	.93V	2.10V

	Exports							Imports						
	2001	2002	2003	2004	2005	2006	2007	2001	2002	2003	2004	2005	2006	2007
	Millions of U.S. Dollars							*Millions of U.S. Dollars*						
Middle East............................ 407	**—Y**	**—Y**	**—Y**	**—Y**	**—Y**	**—Y**	**—Y**	**—Y**	**—Y**	**—Y**	**—Y**	**—Y**	**—Y**	**—Y**
Yemen, Republic of..................... 474	—V	—V	—Y	.01V	—V	—Y	—Y	—V	—V	—Y	—V	—V	—Y	—Y
Western Hemisphere............... 207	**30.2Y**	**36.2Y**	**55.8Y**	**54.5Y**	**45.9Y**	**48.0Y**	**55.2Y**	**134.4Y**	**167.0Y**	**162.6Y**	**170.1Y**	**203.6Y**	**238.1Y**	**277.5Y**
Antigua and Barbuda.................. 311	.29Y	.32Y	.40Y	.53Y	.61Y	.75Y	.93Y	.07Y	.08Y	.10Y	.13Y	.15Y	.19Y	.23Y
Argentina.................................. 213	—V	—V	—V	—V	—V	—V	—V	1.56V	1.05V	2.32V	1.11V	1.42V	2.08V	2.52V
Aruba.. 314	—V	—V	—V	—V	—V	.05V	—V	—V	—V	—V	—V	—V	—V	—V
Bahamas, The............................ 313	.02Y	.02Y	.02Y	.03Y	.03Y	.04Y	.05Y	.27Y	.29Y	.37Y	.48Y	.55Y	.68Y	.85Y
Barbados.................................. 316	.94V	1.86V	1.32V	1.31V	1.45V	1.43V	1.77Y	2.98V	2.74V	1.46V	1.53V	1.85V	2.10V	2.60Y
Bolivia...................................... 218	—V	—V	—V	—V	—V	—Y	—Y	—V	—V	.01V	—V	—Y	.01Y	.01Y
Brazil.. 223	.16V	.53V	.27V	.32V	.16V	.01V	—V	3.45V	3.61V	3.02V	1.93V	3.58V	4.20V	—V
Chile... 228	—V	—V	.03V	—V	.01V	—V	—V	.22V	—V	6.45V	.39V	.78V	2.08V	.87V
Colombia.................................. 233	—V	—V	.10V	—V	—V	—V	5.97V	.39V	1.34V	1.39V	1.12V	.59V	1.06V	.90V
Costa Rica................................ 238	1.94V	.75V	.49V	.56V	.62V	.77Y	.95Y	2.27V	2.27V	4.97V	5.35V	6.14V	7.59Y	9.42Y
Dominica................................... 321	.02V	.02Y	.03Y	.03Y	.04Y	.05Y	.06Y	—V	—Y	—Y	—Y	—Y	—Y	—Y
Dominican Republic................... 243	3.25V	3.53Y	4.47Y	5.87Y	6.70Y	8.28Y	10.28Y	.06V	.06Y	.08Y	.10Y	.12Y	.15Y	.18Y
Ecuador..................................... 248	.01V	.04V	—V	—V	.01V	—V	—Y	.05V	.08V	.01V	.43V	.09V	.06V	.08Y
El Salvador................................ 253	.37V	1.00V	.37V	.61V	.67V	2.49V	2.59V	7.89V	8.29V	9.48V	9.63V	10.50V	13.12V	14.01V
Grenada.................................... 328	—Y	—Y	—Y	—Y	—Y	—Y	—Y	—Y	—Y	—Y	—Y	.01Y	.01Y	.01Y
Guatemala................................. 258	1.49V	1.77V	27.37V	1.59V	2.27V	2.81Y	3.49Y	15.14V	23.53V	34.84V	41.13V	42.95V	53.08Y	65.88Y
Guyana...................................... 336	.47Y	.51Y	.65Y	.85Y	.97Y	1.20Y	1.49Y	.38Y	.42Y	.53Y	.69Y	.79Y	.98Y	1.21Y
Haiti.. 263	—V	—V	—V	.01V	.02Y	.02Y	.02Y	—Y	—Y	—Y	—Y	—Y	—Y	—Y
Honduras................................... 268	.06V	.66V	.16V	.51V	.58Y	.71Y	.89Y	2.61V	3.27V	6.44V	6.66V	7.61Y	9.40Y	11.67Y
Jamaica..................................... 343	3.86V	5.57V	9.62V	29.25V	12.22V	12.00V	5.59V	3.54V	4.22V	3.91V	3.84V	3.65V	4.16V	3.32V
Mexico....................................... 273	1.55V	1.59V	2.83V	5.13V	8.39V	7.56V	7.76V	39.55V	73.67V	64.88V	66.48V	89.18V	95.61V	112.72V
Netherlands Antilles.................... 353	.01V	.03V	.92V	1.21Y	1.38Y	1.70Y	2.11Y	43.63V	28.69V	6.81V	8.94Y	10.21Y	12.62Y	15.66Y
Panama...................................... 283	.66V	.04V	—V	.09V	.08V	—V	.10V	.22V	.40V	.16V	.15V	.63V	.55V	.41V
Paraguay.................................... 288	—V	—V	.01V	—V	—V	—V	—Y	.96V	.74V	.04V	.11V	—V	—V	—Y
Peru... 293	—V	13.81V	2.36V	.71V	—V	—V	—Y	.04V	—V	.31V	.80V	.60V	1.06V	1.17Y
St. Lucia.................................... 362	—Y	—Y	—Y	—Y	—Y	—Y	—Y	.16Y	.18Y	.22Y	.29Y	.34Y	.42Y	.52Y
St. Vincent & Grens..................... 364	.07V	.10V	.04V	.05V	.09V	.11Y	.13Y	—V	—V	—V	—V	—V	—Y	—Y
Suriname.................................... 366	.01Y	.01Y	.01Y	.01Y	.01Y	.01Y	.02Y	—Y	—Y	—Y	—Y	—Y	—Y	—Y
Trinidad and Tobago.................... 369	14.53V	3.19V	4.04Y	5.30Y	6.06Y	7.49Y	9.30Y	8.54V	10.83V	13.70Y	18.00Y	20.56Y	25.41Y	31.54Y
Uruguay..................................... 298	.02V	.02Y	.04V	.02V	.02V	.02Y	.03Y	.18V	.19Y	.04V	.03V	.22V	.28Y	.34Y
Venezuela, Rep. Bol.................... 299	.32V	.62V	.01V	.15V	3.16V	.06V	1.18V	.18V	1.06V	.98V	.71V	1.00V	1.11V	1.34Y
Western Hem. n.s........................ 399	.13Y	.19Y	.26Y	.32Y	.39Y	.45Y	.52Y	.02Y	.03Y	.04Y	.04Y	.05Y	.06Y	.07Y
Other Countries n.i.e............... 910	**.1Y**	**.1Y**	**.1Y**	**.1Y**	**.2Y**	**.2Y**	**.2Y**	**22.3Y**	**24.2Y**	**30.6Y**	**40.2Y**	**45.9Y**	**56.7Y**	**70.4Y**
Cuba.. 928	.07Y	.08Y	.10Y	.13Y	.15Y	.19Y	.23Y	22.26Y	24.16Y	30.58Y	40.16Y	45.88Y	56.71Y	70.38Y
Memorandum Items														
European Union.......................... 998	69.29Y	58.78Y	94.93Y	92.93Y	114.84Y	180.06Y	117.57Y	63.72Y	62.99Y	77.86Y	54.46Y	130.44Y	72.28Y	107.33Y
Oil Exporting Ctys........................ 999	.96Y	1.70Y	5.39Y	6.66Y	11.49Y	10.43Y	14.47Y	3.41Y	1.93Y	1.41Y	1.34Y	1.54Y	1.76Y	1.86Y
Non-Oil Develop.Ctys................... 201	51.69Y	49.78Y	72.45Y	84.77Y	72.61Y	71.83Y	105.04Y	176.41Y	212.39Y	203.72Y	251.56Y	339.13Y	324.12Y	377.51Y
PERCENT DISTRIBUTION														
Industrial Countries................. 101	**78.9**	**73.8**	**72.1**	**69.3**	**72.2**	**80.4**	**66.7**	**58.2**	**50.2**	**57.2**	**46.8**	**49.7**	**47.9**	**45.6**
Developing Countries............. 202	**21.1**	**26.2**	**27.9**	**30.7**	**27.7**	**19.6**	**33.3**	**37.2**	**44.8**	**37.3**	**45.9**	**44.4**	**44.4**	**45.9**
Africa...................................... 607	**.9**	**1.4**	**2.8**	**4.8**	**6.6**	**6.2**	**9.3**	**.4**	**1.0**	**.4**	**.3**	**.5**	**.5**	**.3**
Asia.. 507	**6.8**	**5.8**	**3.7**	**5.7**	**3.4**	**1.5**	**7.8**	**8.1**	**7.6**	**6.0**	**9.5**	**7.3**	**6.5**	**6.1**
Europe................................... 170	**1.3**	**.6**	**1.4**	**2.0**	**2.6**	**.4**	**.8**	**.9**	**1.3**	**1.3**	**5.2**	**10.1**	**4.9**	**6.0**
Western Hemisphere............. 207	**12.1**	**18.4**	**20.0**	**18.3**	**15.2**	**11.4**	**15.4**	**27.8**	**34.9**	**29.5**	**30.9**	**26.5**	**32.4**	**33.6**
Other Countries n.i.e............... 910	**—**	**—**	**—**	**—**	**—**	**—**	**.1**	**4.6**	**5.0**	**5.6**	**7.3**	**6.0**	**7.7**	**8.5**
ANNUAL PERCENT CHANGE														
World...................................... 001	**35.5**	**−21.1**	**41.8**	**6.9**	**1.7**	**38.5**	**−14.4**	**9.4**	**−1.1**	**15.0**	**.1**	**39.4**	**−4.3**	**12.5**
Industrial Countries................. 101	**13.9**	**−26.2**	**38.4**	**2.8**	**5.9**	**54.1**	**−29.0**	**−4.4**	**−14.9**	**31.1**	**−18.0**	**47.9**	**−7.7**	**6.9**
Developing Countries............. 202	**365.9**	**−2.2**	**51.2**	**17.4**	**−8.0**	**−2.2**	**45.3**	**41.0**	**19.2**	**−4.3**	**23.3**	**34.7**	**−4.3**	**16.4**
Africa...................................... 607	**....**	**17.7**	**189.6**	**82.2**	**40.5**	**31.0**	**26.9**	**....**	**181.5**	**−50.6**	**−32.5**	**114.4**	**2.5**	**−40.3**
Asia.. 507	**—**	**−32.8**	**−9.6**	**64.1**	**−39.7**	**−38.7**	**350.6**	**363.3**	**−7.9**	**−8.6**	**58.5**	**6.4**	**−13.9**	**4.5**
Europe................................... 170	**....**	**−62.1**	**218.4**	**47.5**	**36.9**	**−77.9**	**66.1**	**510.0**	**41.4**	**14.5**	**307.1**	**170.7**	**−53.5**	**36.8**
Middle East........................... 407	**—**	**—**	**....**	**....**	**−98.0**	**23.6**	**24.1**	**35.5**	**—**	**....**	**....**	**....**	**....**	**....**
Western Hemisphere............. 207	**171.9**	**19.9**	**54.2**	**−2.4**	**−15.7**	**4.6**	**15.0**	**13.7**	**24.3**	**−2.7**	**4.6**	**19.7**	**16.9**	**16.6**
Other Countries n.i.e............... 910	**10.4**	**8.5**	**26.6**	**31.3**	**14.3**	**23.6**	**24.1**	**10.4**	**8.5**	**26.6**	**31.3**	**14.3**	**23.6**	**24.1**

		Exports							Imports						
		2001	2002	2003	2004	2005	2006	2007	2001	2002	2003	2004	2005	2006	2007
		Millions of U.S. Dollars							Millions of U.S. Dollars						
IFS World Total		**371.6**	**450.1**	**555.2**	**563.8**	**564.5**	**570.0**	**590.0**	**623.0**	**724.8**	**891.8**	**893.8**	**894.0**	**990.0**	**1,110.0**
DOTS World Total	**001**	**591.0**	**241.5**	**271.4**	**290.1**	**300.4**	**343.6Y**	**415.5Y**	**622.2**	**720.9**	**886.0**	**897.2**	**892.9**	**3,476.2Y**	**4,871.4Y**
Industrial Countries	**101**	**40.4**	**38.9**	**40.0**	**34.1**	**26.3**	**81.3Y**	**79.4Y**	**333.0**	**364.8**	**456.9**	**414.8**	**448.3**	**844.0Y**	**1,324.5Y**
United States	111	.60	.36	.74	.13	.29	.55V	4.55V	29.69	20.90	24.88	9.75	18.23	127.16V	318.23V
Canada	156	.38	.05	.69	—	—	.02V	.23V	3.28	2.86	3.12	1.62	3.25	15.66V	10.97V
Australia	193	.06	.06	—	—	—	.01V	—V	.13	.19	.01	.25	.16	1.42V	1.20V
Japan	158	.28	.31	.31	.06	—	.03V	.03V	20.37	20.31	30.11	20.34	13.81	18.03V	22.02V
New Zealand	196	—	—	—	.12	.01	—V	—V	—	.08	.36	1.00	.91	1.56V	.82V
Austria	122	—	—	—	—	—	—V	—V	2.91	.47	.11	.17	.13	2.84V	4.95V
Belgium	124	5.31	2.97	3.47	1.56	.56	13.10V	18.94V	17.70	13.65	37.89	40.10	43.49	93.61V	153.74V
Cyprus	423	—	.02	—	—	—	—V	—V	.29	.01	.05	.03	—	.23V	—V
Denmark	128	1.18	.38	7.53	.25	3.23	10.14V	9.16V	5.16	5.12	5.47	4.16	7.88	2.05V	2.62V
Finland	172	—	—	—	—	—	—V	—V	.34	.79	.46	.20	.05	.96V	1.16V
France	132	5.25	6.85	4.43	8.49	3.63	9.00V	5.59V	144.37	172.91	214.70	165.20	194.54	257.32V	397.63V
Germany	134	3.73	2.99	1.98	2.29	1.51	8.24V	6.78V	17.90	20.84	22.59	18.14	15.44	61.64V	75.83V
Greece	174	.17	—	.01	—	.01	—V	—V	1.31	.09	.11	.01	.01	3.36V	7.43V
Iceland	176	.05	.02	—	—	—	—V	—V	.09	—	.07	—	.07	—V	—V
Ireland	178	.90	.66	.02	—	—	—V	—V	1.75	2.10	2.94	7.53	6.22	2.51V	3.45V
Italy	136	9.26	9.86	6.59	4.27	3.67	3.59V	5.30V	23.29	23.27	19.21	10.76	14.38	38.78V	46.62V
Luxembourg	137	—	.01	—	—	.02	—V	—V	.21	.18	.37	.15	.06	.08V	1.07V
Malta	181	.14	—	—	—	—	—V	—V	.02	—	.07	—	—	.16V	.14V
Netherlands	138	1.35	3.26	1.51	.35	.39	24.17V	15.23V	24.73	28.81	27.14	27.48	26.13	77.60V	92.01V
Norway	142	.05	—	.39	—	—	.01V	—V	.21	.98	1.49	13.86	7.96	1.12V	.40V
Portugal	182	1.86	2.82	1.96	3.19	3.83	6.65V	11.72V	.90	.80	1.13	.45	.78	.72V	1.29V
Slovenia	961	—	.05	.04	.45	.84	.54V	—V	—	—	.12	.08	—	.34V	.07V
Spain	184	5.34	4.47	4.29	4.32	2.06	4.70V	1.55V	13.18	13.17	18.43	15.54	23.50	31.84V	47.45V
Sweden	144	.73	.03	.80	3.07	1.95	.01V	—V	1.27	.47	2.44	3.26	4.11	14.35V	19.00V
Switzerland	146	1.45	2.35	3.28	4.92	1.99	.09V	.04V	2.57	1.09	2.32	23.37	20.53	14.13V	22.18V
United Kingdom	112	2.29	1.36	1.93	.66	2.34	.46V	.32V	21.35	35.70	41.27	51.35	46.66	76.50V	94.21V
Developing Countries	**202**	**550.1**	**201.1**	**231.4**	**255.9**	**273.8**	**262.0Y**	**335.7Y**	**283.0**	**349.4**	**428.6**	**479.1**	**444.2**	**2,631.7Y**	**3,546.2Y**
Africa	**607**	**433.3**	**77.2**	**57.5**	**81.1**	**81.0**	**108.7Y**	**138.2Y**	**167.2**	**192.4**	**247.9**	**248.0**	**266.4**	**367.6Y**	**449.8Y**
Algeria	612	—	.01	—	.01	—	—Y	—Y	—	—	—	—	1.20	1.50Y	1.81Y
Angola	614	—	.02	.02	3.79	.32	.40Y	.49Y	.33	—	.17	—	—	—Y	—Y
Burkina Faso	748	1.08	1.11	2.16	2.19	4.38	5.41Y	6.72Y	.05	.04	.38	.26	.09	.12Y	.14Y
Cameroon	622	.33	2.96	1.03	.62	.46	.57Y	.71Y	.79	.83	4.61	10.02	9.63	11.91Y	14.78Y
Central African Rep.	626	.01	.03	.04	—	.01	.02Y	.02Y	.03	—	—	—	—	—Y	—Y
Chad	628	.27	.22	.92	4.17	2.06	2.55Y	3.16Y	.01	.02	.03	—	—	—Y	—Y
Comoros	632	—	.01	—	—	—	—Y	—Y	—	—	—	—	—	—Y	—Y
Congo, Dem. Rep. of	636	—	—	.04	.26	.01	.01Y	.02Y	.08	.01	—	.01	.01	.01Y	.02Y
Congo, Republic of	634	.22	.22	.25	.20	.32	.40Y	.49Y	.83	1.42	1.23	2.81	1.81	2.24Y	2.77Y
Côte d'Ivoire	662	1.02	1.15	1.37	4.49	1.12	8.03V	9.97Y	33.90	40.47	47.50	62.32	62.38	121.44V	150.71Y
Djibouti	611	—	—	—	.03	—	—Y	—Y	—	—	—	—	.01	.01Y	.01Y
Equatorial Guinea	642	.11	—	.02	1.27	.75	.93Y	1.16Y	—	—	—	—	—	—Y	—Y
Ethiopia	644	—	—	—	—	—	—Y	—Y	—	.15	—	.06	.01	.01Y	.01Y
Gabon	646	.17	.31	.27	1.65	.42	.52Y	.64Y	.07	.31	1.97	.08	.89	1.10Y	1.37Y
Gambia, The	648	—	—	.05	.01	.02	.03Y	.03Y	.14	.14	.07	—	.10	.13Y	.16Y
Ghana	652	15.15	13.46	4.84	5.48	3.44	4.26Y	5.28Y	29.38	40.09	54.43	64.24	63.84	78.90Y	97.92Y
Guinea	656	.04	.01	.01	.13	.07	.09Y	.11Y	.02	.01	.09	.05	.13	.16Y	.20Y
Guinea-Bissau	654	—	—	—	.01	—	—Y	—Y	—	—	—	—	.01	.01Y	.01Y
Kenya	664	.01	.01	.12	—	.01	.01Y	.01Y	.02	.04	.03	.10	.02	.03Y	.04Y
Liberia	668	—	—	.01	.02	—	—Y	—Y	.11	.03	.02	2.64	—	—Y	.01Y
Madagascar	674	—	—	.41	.39	.13	.16Y	.20Y	.01	.03	—	.01	.02	.02Y	.03Y
Malawi	676	—	—	—	—	—	—Y	—Y	.17	—	—	.02	—	—Y	—Y
Mali	678	.12	.06	.40	7.67	7.36	9.09Y	11.28Y	.10	—	.14	.01	.11	.14Y	.17Y
Mauritania	682	.01	—	1.45	.17	.04	.05Y	.07Y	3.99	2.81	4.79	7.45	4.68	5.78Y	7.18Y
Mauritius	684	—	.25	.58	1.12	1.13	.31V	.74V	.04	.01	1.17	.72	.51	.49V	.59V
Morocco	686	4.78	8.95	3.19	2.14	3.17	3.91Y	4.86Y	.72	.95	1.97	2.64	2.81	3.47Y	4.31Y
Mozambique	688	—	—	—	—	—	—Y	—Y	.08	—	—	.09	—	—Y	—Y
Namibia	728	—	—	—	—	3.30	6.60Y	9.90Y	—	—	.12	—	.05	.09Y	.14Y
Niger	692	4.97	5.12	7.75	15.23	17.91	22.13Y	27.47Y	.11	—	.13	.37	.22	.27Y	.34Y
Nigeria	694	13.38	35.78	12.77	16.68	13.71	16.92Y	21.92Y	29.87	27.55	37.73	26.73	35.89	45.11Y	54.43Y
St. Helena	856	....	....	....	....	....	....	....	—	—	—	—	—	.01Y	.01Y
São Tomé & Príncipe	716	—	—	—	—	—	—Y	—Y	—	.03	—	—	—	—Y	—Y
Senegal	722	1.51	.78	2.90	.42	2.66	3.44V	4.27Y	11.83	21.49	11.04	7.61	18.10	14.59V	18.11Y
Seychelles	718	....	....	....	....	....	....	....	—	—	.01	—	—	—Y	—Y
Sierra Leone	724	.07	—	.03	.02	—	—Y	—Y	.04	.33	.33	—	1.19	1.47Y	1.82Y
Somalia	726	—	—	—	—	—	—Y	—Y	—	—	.03	—	—	—Y	—Y
South Africa	199	1.91	2.56	4.30	2.64	3.69	3.78V	4.99V	11.77	17.95	42.39	6.31	19.72	25.57V	26.82V
Swaziland	734	—	—	—	—	—	—Y	—Y	—	.02	.06	.92	.31	.38Y	.48Y
Tanzania	738	—	—	—	.01	—	—Y	—Y	.29	—	—	—	.32	.39Y	.48Y
Togo	742	2.76	4.13	12.40	10.00	14.53	17.95Y	22.28Y	40.53	35.74	35.49	50.72	39.83	49.22Y	61.09Y
Tunisia	744	1.01	—	.16	.23	.01	.99V	1.23Y	1.47	1.91	1.91	1.81	2.14	2.55V	3.16Y

		Exports							Imports						
		2001	2002	2003	2004	2005	2006	2007	2001	2002	2003	2004	2005	2006	2007
		Millions of U.S. Dollars							*Millions of U.S. Dollars*						
Uganda	746	—	—	—	—	—	—Y	—Y	—	.01	.05	—	.29	.36Y	.45Y
Zambia	754	—	—	—	—	—	—V	—V	.42	.01	—	—	—	—V	—V
Zimbabwe	698	—	—	—	—	—	.13V	.16Y	—	—	.01	—	—	—V	—Y
Africa n.s.	799	384.37	—	—	—	—	—Y	—Y	—	—	—	—	.07	.13Y	.20Y
Asia	**507**	**96.7**	**115.7**	**161.7**	**170.5**	**183.9**	**133.8Y**	**176.8Y**	**95.5**	**105.8**	**140.4**	**188.2**	**138.6**	**2,168.9Y**	**2,952.1Y**
Afghanistan, I.S. of	512	—	—	—	—	—	—Y	—Y	—	.24	.09	—	—	—Y	—Y
Bangladesh	513	2.61	2.95	10.82	1.20	7.55	.95V	6.01V	.11	.01	.01	.32	.35	.43Y	3.09Y
Brunei Darussalam	516	....	....	....	....	....	....	....	—	—	—	—	.03	.03Y	.04Y
Cambodia	522	—	—	—	—	—	—Y	—Y	—	—	—	—	.01	—V	—Y
China,P.R.: Mainland	924	.80	16.26	62.34	104.87	93.89	81.28V	102.83V	46.50	46.30	62.69	78.92	59.49	1,597.61V	2,168.82V
China,P.R.:Hong Kong	532	1.32	.42	.05	1.30	.01	.26V	2.24V	2.25	2.62	1.63	4.63	.92	45.04V	48.32V
French Polynesia	887	.07	—	—	—	—	—Y	—Y	.13	.05	—	.04	—	—Y	—Y
India	534	61.30	42.22	27.45	20.04	22.13	27.35Y	33.94Y	8.31	13.97	14.68	14.11	9.21	11.39Y	14.13Y
Indonesia	536	11.33	23.94	25.31	10.55	24.47	2.84V	8.20V	5.65	5.16	5.26	6.91	8.48	58.66V	64.29V
Korea	542	.01	.01	1.08	—	—	.26V	2.11V	6.17	6.75	3.92	5.89	4.51	22.90V	38.45V
Lao People's Dem.Rep.	544	—	—	—	—	—	—Y	—Y	.04	—	—	—	—	—Y	—Y
Malaysia	548	1.76	.67	1.29	8.00	—	.05V	1.83V	.89	2.92	12.39	5.43	8.81	108.34V	231.85V
Mongolia	948	....	....	....	....	....	....	....	—	—	—	—	.01	.01Y	.01Y
Myanmar	518	—	—	—	—	—	—Y	—Y	.08	.06	—	—	—	—Y	—Y
Nauru	836	—	—	—	—	—	—Y	—Y	.01	—	—	—	—	—Y	—Y
Nepal	558	—	—	—	—	—	—Y	—Y	—	.02	—	—	.03	.04Y	.05Y
Pakistan	564	1.33	12.70	4.41	1.59	6.02	7.45Y	9.24Y	1.89	.77	.10	.89	.22	.27Y	.34Y
Philippines	566	.57	.66	1.63	—	.36	—V	—V	—	—	—	—	—	.62V	1.31V
Samoa	862	....	....	....	....	....	....	....	—	—	.02	—	—	—Y	—Y
Singapore	576	.60	1.32	1.19	4.23	3.65	.18V	.39V	1.43	4.98	6.96	5.49	7.35	102.11V	61.30V
Sri Lanka	524	—	.01	—	—	—	—Y	—Y	—	—	.01	—	.09	.12Y	.14Y
Taiwan Province of China	528	3.19	.85	6.36	3.71	1.43	2.26V	2.47V	3.15	1.60	1.26	3.29	.97	15.97V	10.47V
Thailand	578	8.58	12.51	15.72	10.58	14.33	10.90V	7.51V	18.88	20.27	31.13	59.68	37.43	205.04V	309.07V
Vietnam	582	3.25	1.21	4.07	4.48	10.08	—V	—V	.07	.06	.27	2.55	.68	—V	—V
Asia n.s.	598	—	—	—	—	—	—Y	—Y	—	—	—	—	—	.34Y	.37Y
Europe	**170**	**6.2**	**5.4**	**.8**	**1.7**	**.5**	**3.9Y**	**2.3Y**	**7.8**	**13.0**	**10.2**	**3.8**	**3.8**	**14.4Y**	**55.1Y**
Albania	914	—	—	—	—	—	—V	—V	—	.02	—	—	—	—V	.01V
Belarus	913	—	—	—	—	—	.02V	—V	.14	.43	.27	—	—	—V	.61V
Bulgaria	918	—	.02	.01	—	.10	.01V	—V	.02	.24	.02	—	.01	.34V	.50V
Croatia	960	—	—	—	—	—	—V	—V	—	—	—	.37	.28	—V	—V
Czech Republic	935	.31	—	.04	.25	.08	.53V	.03V	1.07	.48	.08	.07	.19	1.56V	2.22V
Estonia	939	—	—	—	—	—	—V	—V	—	—	—	.02	.07	.03V	.30V
Faroe Islands	816	....	....	....	....	....	....	....	.02	—	—	—	—	—Y	—Y
Gibraltar	823	—	—	—	—	—	—Y	—Y	—	—	—	.41	—	.01Y	.01Y
Hungary	944	—	—	—	—	—	—V	.02V	.08	.18	.01	.04	.02	2.43V	6.11V
Kazakhstan	916	—	—	—	—	.17	.21Y	.26Y	—	—	—	—	—	—Y	—Y
Kyrgyz Republic	917	—	—	—	—	—	—V	—V	—	—	—	—	—	—V	.03V
Latvia	941	—	—	.44	.03	—	—V	—V	—	—	—	—	.07	.24V	.21V
Lithuania	946	—	—	.04	.04	.10	.18V	—V	—	—	—	.19	.18	.51V	1.05V
Poland	964	—	.08	—	—	—	.02V	.02V	.26	.74	.91	.40	.79	1.34V	2.31V
Romania	968	—	—	—	—	—	.05V	—V	.07	.05	.93	—	.10	.02V	.06V
Russia	922	—	—	—	—	—	—V	—V	—	—	—	.12	.06	.46V	.08V
Slovak Republic	936	—	—	—	—	.01	.01V	—V	—	—	—	.01	.07	.76V	.47V
Tajikistan	923	—	—	—	—	—	—V	—V	—	—	—	—	—	—V	.11V
Turkey	186	3.57	3.72	.06	1.42	.01	2.86V	2.00V	3.61	5.12	4.49	1.91	1.87	6.60V	40.86V
Ukraine	926	2.29	1.36	—	—	—	—Y	—Y	2.14	5.35	3.28	—	.11	.13Y	.16Y
Yugoslavia n.s.	966	—	.21	.18	—	—	—Y	—Y	.35	.39	—	—	—	—Y	—Y
Europe n.s.	884	—	—	—	—	—	—Y	—Y	—	—	.23	.24	—	—Y	—Y
Middle East	**407**	**2.0**	**.8**	**7.0**	**1.3**	**7.2**	**8.8Y**	**11.4Y**	**10.7**	**27.7**	**19.8**	**24.4**	**25.7**	**29.4Y**	**35.9Y**
Bahrain	419	—	—	.12	.50	—	—Y	—Y	2.66	10.84	11.78	8.99	4.69	5.80Y	7.20Y
Egypt	469	.03	—	—	.01	.01	.01Y	.01Y	.49	4.28	1.51	.57	4.19	5.17Y	6.42Y
Iran, I.R. of	429	.13	—	—	—	—	—Y	—Y	.16	.43	.37	1.29	.10	.13Y	.16Y
Iraq	433	.13	—	—	—	—	—Y	—Y	—	—	—	—	—	—Y	—Y
Israel	436	—	.04	—	—	.01	—V	—V	1.30	.89	2.08	.20	.52	—V	—V
Jordan	439	—	—	.03	—	.03	—V	—V	—	—	—	—	—	—V	.01V
Kuwait	443	—	—	—	—	—	—Y	—Y	.01	5.48	.07	1.31	1.61	2.02Y	2.44Y
Lebanon	446	.02	.04	.03	.02	.03	.04Y	.05Y	.24	.22	.40	2.36	1.13	1.39Y	1.73Y
Libya	672	—	.01	—	—	—	—Y	—Y	.03	—	—	.01	.01	.01Y	.01Y
Qatar	453	—	—	—	—	—	—V	—Y	—	—	—	—	1.57	—V	—Y
Saudi Arabia	456	1.59	.65	1.09	.29	4.20	5.19Y	6.72Y	5.48	4.64	1.80	1.45	9.86	12.40Y	14.96Y
Syrian Arab Republic	463	—	—	—	—	—	—Y	—Y	.18	.30	.19	.09	.04	.05Y	.07Y
United Arab Emirates	466	.09	.01	5.71	.50	2.90	3.58Y	4.64Y	.19	.56	1.53	8.13	1.95	2.45Y	2.95Y
Yemen, Republic of	474	—	—	—	—	—	—Y	—Y	.01	.05	—	—	—	—Y	—Y
Middle East n.s.	489	—	—	—	—	—	—Y	—Y	—	—	.03	—	—	—Y	—Y
Western Hemisphere	**207**	**11.9**	**2.0**	**4.5**	**1.3**	**1.2**	**6.8Y**	**7.0Y**	**1.8**	**10.5**	**10.3**	**14.7**	**9.7**	**51.3Y**	**53.3Y**
Antigua and Barbuda	311	—	—	—	—	—	—Y	—Y	—	—	.01	—	—	—Y	—Y
Argentina	213	—	.15	—	—	—	—V	—V	.12	1.81	.17	.47	.05	5.42V	5.29V
Bahamas, The	313	—	—	—	—	—	—Y	—Y	.03	.01	—	—	—	—Y	—Y
Belize	339	—	—	—	—	—	—Y	—Y	—	—	.01	—	—	—Y	—Y
Bolivia	218	—	—	—	—	—	—Y	—Y	—	—	.01	—	—	—Y	—Y
Brazil	223	9.01	.91	.88	—	.63	5.63V	5.20V	.87	6.96	8.59	9.82	8.98	42.92V	44.93V
Chile	228	—	.02	—	—	—	—V	—V	.23	.16	.11	.05	.09	.11V	.26V

	Exports 2001	2002	2003	2004	2005	2006	2007	Imports 2001	2002	2003	2004	2005	2006	2007
	Millions of U.S. Dollars							*Millions of U.S. Dollars*						
Colombia.......233	.31	.15	3.33	.56	.50	.59V	.29V	.03	.08	.35	.43	.36	.47V	—V
Costa Rica.......238	—	—	—	—	—	—Y	—Y	.01	—	—	—	—	—Y	—Y
Ecuador.......248	—	.23	.11	.19	—	—V	—Y	—	—	.01	—	.01	—V	—Y
El Salvador.......253	.24	—	—	—	—	—Y	—Y	.05	—	—	—	—	—Y	—Y
Falkland Islands.......323	—	—	—	—	—	—Y	—Y	—	—	—	.01	—	—Y	—Y
Greenland.......326	—	—	—	—	—	—Y	—Y	—	—	—	—	.05	.07Y	.08Y
Grenada.......328	—	.03	—	—	—	—Y	—Y	—	—	—	—	—	—Y	—Y
Guatemala.......258	—	.01	—	—	—	—Y	—Y	.07	—	—	—	—	—Y	—Y
Guyana.......336	—	—	—	.20	—	—Y	—Y	.09	—	.02	—	—	—Y	—Y
Honduras.......268	—	.34	—	—	.03	.03Y	.04Y	.02	—	—	.17	—	—Y	—Y
Jamaica.......343	—	—	—	—	—	—V	—V	.02	—	—	—	—	—V	—V
Mexico.......273	—	—	—	—	—	.08V	.07V	.05	.03	.25	—	.02	.18V	.03V
Netherlands Antilles.......353	—	—	—	—	—	—Y	—Y	.04	—	.09	—	.05	.06Y	.08Y
Panama.......283	.03	—	—	.16	—	—V	—V	.02	—	.03	3.66	.01	.01Y	.02Y
Paraguay.......288	—	—	—	—	—	—V	—Y	.01	—	—	—	—	—V	—Y
Peru.......293	1.42	—	—	.15	—	.42V	1.34Y	—	—	.02	—	—	.48V	.78Y
St. Kitts and Nevis.......361	....	....	....	....	....	....	....	.01	—	—	—	—	—Y	—Y
Suriname.......366	—	—	—	—	—	—Y	—Y	.01	—	—	—	—	—Y	—Y
Trinidad and Tobago.......369	—	—	—	—	—	—Y	—Y	—	.09	.01	—	—	.01Y	.01Y
Uruguay.......298	—	—	—	—	—	—Y	—Y	.04	.01	.05	.05	.05	.06Y	.08Y
Venezuela, Rep. Bol.......299	.88	.19	.12	—	—	—V	—V	.02	1.40	.52	.01	—	1.45V	1.75Y
Western Hem. n.s.......399	—	—	.02	—	—	—Y	—Y	—	—	.02	.05	.01	.01Y	.01Y
Other Countries n.i.e.......910	**—**	**1.4**	**—**	**—**	**.3**	**.4Y**	**.4Y**	**1.3**	**.7**	**.5**	**3.3**	**.5**	**.6Y**	**.7Y**
Cuba.......928	—	—	—	—	—	—Y	—Y	—	.02	—	.03	—	—Y	—Y
North Korea.......954	—	1.35	.02	—	.29	.35Y	.44Y	1.33	.69	.54	3.24	.46	.57Y	.71Y
Countries & Areas n.s.......898	**.5**	**.2**	**—**	**—**	**—**	**—Y**	**—Y**	**4.6**	**5.9**	**—**	**—**	**—**	**—Y**	**—Y**
Memorandum Items														
European Union.......998	37.83	35.80	35.08	29.22	24.22	81.36Y	74.66Y	278.08	319.79	395.50	345.35	384.76	671.76Y	961.35Y
Oil Exporting Ctys.......999	27.54	60.60	44.99	28.03	45.28	28.54Y	41.49Y	41.41	45.22	47.29	45.83	60.66	123.73Y	142.80Y
Non-Oil Develop.Ctys.......201	522.56	140.47	186.39	227.90	228.49	233.41Y	294.18Y	241.60	304.22	381.29	433.23	383.51	2,507.96Y	3,403.38Y
PERCENT DISTRIBUTION														
Industrial Countries.......101	**6.8**	**16.1**	**14.7**	**11.8**	**8.8**	**23.7**	**19.1**	**53.5**	**50.6**	**51.6**	**46.2**	**50.2**	**24.3**	**27.2**
Developing Countries.......202	**93.1**	**83.3**	**85.3**	**88.2**	**91.1**	**76.2**	**80.8**	**45.5**	**48.5**	**48.4**	**53.4**	**49.7**	**75.7**	**72.8**
Africa.......607	**73.3**	**31.9**	**21.2**	**27.9**	**27.0**	**31.6**	**33.3**	**26.9**	**26.7**	**28.0**	**27.6**	**29.8**	**10.6**	**9.2**
Asia.......507	**16.4**	**47.9**	**59.6**	**58.8**	**61.2**	**38.9**	**42.5**	**15.4**	**14.7**	**15.8**	**21.0**	**15.5**	**62.4**	**60.6**
Europe.......170	**1.0**	**2.2**	**.3**	**.6**	**.2**	**1.1**	**.6**	**1.2**	**1.8**	**1.2**	**.4**	**.4**	**.4**	**1.1**
Middle East.......407	**.3**	**.3**	**2.6**	**.5**	**2.4**	**2.6**	**2.7**	**1.7**	**3.8**	**2.2**	**2.7**	**2.9**	**.8**	**.7**
Western Hemisphere.......207	**2.0**	**.8**	**1.6**	**.4**	**.4**	**2.0**	**1.7**	**.3**	**1.5**	**1.2**	**1.6**	**1.1**	**1.5**	**1.1**
Other Countries n.i.e.......910	**—**	**.6**	**—**	**—**	**.1**	**.1**	**.1**	**.2**	**.1**	**.1**	**.4**	**.1**	**—**	**—**
ANNUAL PERCENT CHANGE														
World.......001	**202.2**	**–59.1**	**12.4**	**6.9**	**3.6**	**14.4**	**20.9**	**10.6**	**15.8**	**22.9**	**1.3**	**–.5**	**289.3**	**40.1**
Industrial Countries.......101	**2.5**	**–3.8**	**2.9**	**–14.6**	**–22.9**	**208.9**	**–2.3**	**3.1**	**9.5**	**25.2**	**–9.2**	**8.1**	**88.3**	**56.9**
Developing Countries.......202	**252.3**	**–63.4**	**15.1**	**10.6**	**7.0**	**–4.3**	**28.1**	**20.0**	**23.5**	**22.6**	**11.8**	**–7.3**	**492.5**	**34.7**
Africa.......607	**—**	**–82.2**	**–25.5**	**41.0**	**—**	**34.1**	**27.1**	**31.8**	**15.1**	**28.8**	**—**	**7.4**	**38.0**	**22.3**
Asia.......507	**2.8**	**19.7**	**39.7**	**5.5**	**7.8**	**–27.3**	**32.1**	**22.9**	**10.7**	**32.8**	**34.0**	**–26.3**	**—**	**36.1**
Europe.......170	**–39.6**	**–12.6**	**–85.9**	**129.2**	**–73.0**	**727.3**	**–40.0**	**–6.4**	**67.7**	**–21.5**	**–63.0**	**.8**	**278.0**	**281.8**
Middle East.......407	**–19.1**	**–62.1**	**819.7**	**–81.1**	**445.6**	**22.8**	**29.5**	**–47.2**	**158.0**	**–28.6**	**23.3**	**5.3**	**14.6**	**22.1**
Western Hemisphere.......207	**–43.2**	**–83.0**	**120.1**	**–71.7**	**–7.6**	**480.3**	**3.0**	**–34.8**	**498.8**	**–2.7**	**43.4**	**–34.2**	**428.9**	**4.0**
Other Countries n.i.e.......910	**—**	**—**	**–98.7**	**31.3**	**14.3**	**23.6**	**24.1**	**33.4**	**–46.8**	**–23.6**	**503.6**	**–85.9**	**23.6**	**24.1**

		Exports							Imports, f.o.b						
		2001	2002	2003	2004	2005	2006	2007	2001	2002	2003	2004	2005	2006	2007
		Millions of U.S. Dollars							*Millions of U.S. Dollars*						
DOTS World Total	**001**	**1,347.4Y**	**919.2Y**	**1,352.1Y**	**1,486.2Y**	**1,752.6Y**	**756.9Y**	**569.5Y**	**4,491.6Y**	**4,765.9Y**	**4,705.7Y**	**3,837.7Y**	**884.7**	**1,056.1**	**4,217.2Y**
Industrial Countries	**101**	**1,253.5Y**	**807.1Y**	**1,212.3Y**	**1,307.5Y**	**1,610.7Y**	**522.0Y**	**319.2Y**	**2,826.4Y**	**2,256.3V**	**2,202.0V**	**2,932.0Y**	**816.5**	**947.8**	**2,199.3V**
United States	111	60.73V	21.27V	14.18V	22.91V	80.09V	15.09V	22.09V	371.30V	415.10V	401.30V	471.90V	693.03	758.50	660.00V
Canada	156	1.51V	2.43V	2.05V	9.53V	14.37V	14.79V	2.82V	23.42V	71.11V	32.90V	51.69V	36.09	69.62	62.36V
Australia	193	—V	.10V	—V	1.92V	3.06V	.07V	.01V	.53V	.55V	.45V	5.66V	1.15	3.04	2.01V
Japan	158	2.15V	3.61V	3.97V	3.42V	4.44V	.02V	.02V	220.80V	21.56V	18.57V	961.44V	15.42	17.35	16.38V
New Zealand	196	.02V	—V	.01V	—V	—V	.01V	.11V	1.58V	1.99V	1.95V	2.72V	.89	1.78	2.89V
Austria	122	.01V	—V	.01V	—V	—V	—V	.01V	.03V	.05V	.06V	.04V	.24	1.52	.54V
Belgium	124	—V	.01V	.01V	—V	—V	—V	.19V	1.70V	2.00V	1.86V	2.77V	.52	.80	.90V
Cyprus	423	—V	—V	—V	—V	.02Y	—V	—V	.01V	—V	—V	.02V	—	—	—V
Denmark	128	.14V	—V	.08V	.05V	1.24V	.04V	37.48V	2.10V	1.32V	2.00V	6.06V	2.08	1.66	38.58V
Finland	172	.01V	—V	.04V	.19V	.02V	—V	.27V	.17V	9.57V	.56V	.69V	.09	.03	.16V
France	132	986.70V	682.13V	832.22V	1,076.35V	1,164.95V	19.65V	21.39V	1,220.00V	1,058.72V	1,529.06V	1,192.41V	10.98	15.40	150.41V
Germany	134	.08V	.14V	.09V	.10V	5.76V	20.48V	66.68V	410.82V	99.91V	6.88V	17.42V	4.80	11.73	557.10V
Greece	174	.77V	.63V	3.48V	.43V	.77V	1.18V	1.23V	.53V	.44V	.02V	.02V	.01	.03	.38V
Iceland	176	—V	—V	—V	—V	—V	—V	—V	—V	—V	—V	—V	.14	.04	.02V
Ireland	178	.10V	.07V	.03V	.09V	.02V	.03V	.09V	.83V	1.02V	1.69V	1.23V	.39	.38	1.17V
Italy	136	8.92V	4.49V	.02V	18.62V	27.74V	.02V	2.98V	479.17V	450.95V	10.07V	46.54V	8.94	13.26	499.69V
Luxembourg	137	—V	—V	—V	—V	—V	.17V	.01V	.01V	.02V	.01V	.06V	—	.01	—V
Malta	181	.11Y	.16V	—V	—V	—V	—V	—V	.01Y	—V	—V	—V	—	—	—V
Netherlands	138	15.19V	17.35V	9.98V	9.23V	3.78V	.48V	.66V	4.31V	41.80V	56.07V	32.32V	5.03	7.52	94.77V
Norway	142	54.77V	.23V	184.78V	.02V	.04V	.12V	.05V	.34V	.51V	.10V	.41V	.30	.12	5.92V
Portugal	182	—V	.01V	.07V	.08V	.23V	.26V	.21V	.91V	.55V	.52V	.55V	.71	1.41	1.19V
Slovenia	961	.01V	.01V	.03V	.03Y	—V	—V	—V	—V	.01V	.02V	.02Y	—	—	.05V
Spain	184	42.71V	13.31V	20.53V	34.87V	208.41V	269.65V	78.82V	28.11V	19.35V	15.22V	54.36V	1.19	1.31	2.26V
Sweden	144	—V	36.16V	34.74V	22.29V	68.48V	56.91V	.03V	.41V	2.77V	12.46V	2.15V	1.37	.88	.86V
Switzerland	146	20.47V	.01V	6.41V	16.30V	.07V	2.96V	49.92V	10.22V	10.69V	41.58V	21.59V	3.93	5.13	11.93V
United Kingdom	112	59.11V	24.95V	99.60V	91.13V	27.19V	120.05V	34.15V	49.06V	46.27V	68.68V	59.97V	29.20	36.33	89.75V
Developing Countries	**202**	**38.9Y**	**52.5Y**	**64.2Y**	**79.4Y**	**28.5Y**	**94.8Y**	**76.4Y**	**1,664.5Y**	**2,508.9Y**	**2,502.7Y**	**904.3Y**	**67.4**	**107.8**	**2,017.4Y**
Africa	**607**	**5.7Y**	**1.2Y**	**2.1Y**	**5.3Y**	**4.0Y**	**5.5Y**	**10.8Y**	**.9Y**	**1.7Y**	**1.2Y**	**.7Y**	**1.9**	**1.9**	**91.7Y**
Algeria	612	—V	—V	—Y	—Y	—Y	—Y	—Y	—V	—V	—Y	—Y	.01	—	—Y
Cameroon	622	—V	—V	—V	—Y	—Y	—Y	—Y	—V	—V	—V	—Y	—	.02	.02Y
Cape Verde	624	—V	—Y	—Y	—Y	—Y	—Y	—Y	—V	—Y	—Y	—Y	—	.84	1.04Y
Congo, Republic of	634	—V	—V	—V	—V	—Y	—Y	—Y	.12V	.40V	.26V	.08V	—	—	—Y
Côte d'Ivoire	662	—V	—V	—V	—V	—V	—V	—Y	.03V	.01V	—V	—V	—	—	—Y
Gabon	646	....	....	....	....	....	....	....	—Y	—Y	—Y	—Y	—	.03	.03Y
Gambia, The	648	....	....	....	....	....	....	....	—Y	—Y	—Y	—Y	.34	.24	.30Y
Kenya	664	1.09V	—V	—V	—V	—Y	—Y	—Y	—V	.01V	—V	—V	—	.01	.01Y
Madagascar	674	—V	—V	—V	—Y	—Y	—Y	—Y	—V	—V	—V	.01Y	—	—	—Y
Mauritania	682	—Y	—Y	—Y	—Y	—Y	—Y	—Y	.01Y	.01Y	.01Y	.01Y	—	—	—Y
Mauritius	684	—V	—V	—V	—V	—V	—V	—V	.01V	—V	—V	—V	—	.01	—V
Morocco	686	.10V	—V	—V	—V	—V	—Y	—Y	—V	—V	—V	—V	.07	.13	.17Y
Namibia	728	—Y	—Y	—Y	—Y	—Y	—Y	—Y	.06Y	.07Y	.07Y	.08Y	—	—	—Y
Niger	692	—V	—V	—V	—V	—Y	—Y	—Y	—V	—V	—V	—V	1.17	—	—Y
Nigeria	694	3.53V	.68V	1.65V	2.15Y	2.74Y	3.38Y	4.38Y	—V	—V	—V	—Y	—	—	—Y
St. Helena	856	....	....	....	....	....	....	....	.01Y	.01Y	.01Y	.01Y	—	—	—Y
Senegal	722	—V	—V	—V	1.49V	.12V	.12V	.15Y	—V	—V	—V	—V	—	—	—Y
Somalia	726	—Y	—Y	—Y	—Y	—Y	—Y	—Y	.03Y	.04Y	.05Y	.06Y	—	—	—Y
South Africa	199	.87V	.14V	—V	.04V	—V	—V	3.73V	.20V	.25V	.36V	.29V	.33	.56	90.06V
Swaziland	734	....	....	....	....	....	....	....	.06Y	.06Y	.08Y	.10Y	.01	.02	.03Y
Tanzania	738	—V	.35V	.44Y	.58Y	.67Y	.82Y	1.02Y	—V	—V	—Y	—Y	—	—	—Y
Togo	742	....	....	....	....	....	....	....	.35V	.50V	.28V	.03V	—	—	—Y
Tunisia	744	.14V	—V	.03V	.04V	.02V	—V	—Y	.02V	.35V	.05V	—V	—	.04	.05Y
Zambia	754	—V	.01V	—V	—V	—V	—V	—V	—V	—V	—V	—V	—	—	—V
Zimbabwe	698	—V	—V	—V	.99V	.42V	1.20V	1.49Y	—V	.01V	—V	—V	—	—	—Y
Asia	**507**	**24.0Y**	**5.1Y**	**5.9Y**	**6.5Y**	**.6Y**	**.7Y**	**18.5Y**	**72.5Y**	**397.2Y**	**214.4Y**	**793.6Y**	**7.7**	**15.7**	**1,723.7Y**
Afghanistan, I.S. of	512	—Y	—Y	—Y	—Y	—Y	—Y	—Y	—Y	—Y	—Y	—Y	—	—	.01Y
American Samoa	859	....	....	....	....	....	....	....	.01Y	.01Y	.01Y	.02Y	—	.01	.01Y
Bangladesh	513	.51V	—V	—V	—V	—V	—V	—V	—V	—V	—V	—V	.01	.03	.02Y
Cambodia	522	....	....	....	....	....	....	....	—V	—V	—V	—V	.01	.01	.01Y
China,P.R.: Mainland	924	—V	—V	—V	—V	—V	—V	.02V	11.09V	14.23V	31.63V	123.24V	1.73	4.75	81.99V
China,P.R.:Hong Kong	532	—V	—V	—V	—V	—V	—V	—V	—V	—V	—V	—V	1.28	1.51	—V
China,P.R.:Macao	546	—V	—V	—V	.01V	—V	—V	—V	.20V	.11V	.11V	.04V	—	—	—V
Fiji	819	—Y	—Y	—Y	—Y	—Y	—Y	—Y	—Y	—Y	—Y	—Y	—	.08	.10Y
India	534	—Y	.06V	—V	.89V	.32V	.40Y	.49Y	.61Y	.30V	.47V	.55V	.37	1.26	1.56Y
Indonesia	536	.04V	.38V	.35V	.31V	.02V	—V	.01V	.47V	.48V	.42V	1.07V	.54	.64	6.61V
Korea	542	—V	—V	4.16V	4.99V	—V	.02V	—V	36.39V	361.41V	163.41V	646.43V	1.79	3.77	1,534.96V
Lao People's Dem.Rep	544	—Y	—Y	—Y	—Y	—Y	—Y	—Y	—Y	—Y	—Y	—Y	.02	—	—Y
Malaysia	548	.03V	.01V	.02V	.02V	—V	—V	.01V	.22V	.13V	.24V	.09V	.05	.72	.31V
New Caledonia	839	—V	.02V	.01V	—V	—Y	—Y	—Y	—V	—V	—Y	—Y	.01	.01	.01Y
Pakistan	564	.58V	.37V	.50V	.23V	.23V	.29Y	.36Y	.13V	.01V	.01V	.02V	.02	.08	.11Y

		Exports							Imports, f.o.b						
		2001	2002	2003	2004	2005	2006	2007	2001	2002	2003	2004	2005	2006	2007
		Millions of U.S. Dollars							*Millions of U.S. Dollars*						
Philippines	566	.49V	.03V	.12V	.06V	—V	—V	17.38V	1.59V	.38V	.72V	.20V	.07	.18	.11V
Singapore	576	22.36V	4.20V	.71V	—V	.01V	—V	.24V	21.31V	19.56V	16.81V	21.22V	.20	.66	96.25V
Sri Lanka	524	—V	—V	—Y	—Y	—Y	—Y	—Y	—V	—V	—Y	—Y	.08	.15	.19Y
Taiwan Province of China	528	—V	—V	—Y	—V	—V	—V	—V	—V	—V	—Y	—V	.88	.85	—V
Thailand	578	—V	.03V	.05V	.03V	—V	—V	—V	.48V	.57V	.53V	.73V	.62	.94	1.45V
Vietnam	582	—V	—Y	—V	—V	—V	—V	—V	—V	—Y	.04V	—V	.05	.07	—V
Europe	**170**	**.2Y**	**4.9Y**	**10.6Y**	**29.0Y**	**4.3Y**	**.8Y**	**.5Y**	**1,382.2Y**	**2,077.7Y**	**2,248.5Y**	**67.3Y**	**.9**	**1.2**	**99.7Y**
Belarus	913	.01V	.02V	.02V	.01V	.01V	.01V	.02V	—V	—V	—V	—V	—	—	—V
Bulgaria	918	—V	—V	—V	—V	—V	—V	.01V	—V	.01V	.02V	.01V	—	.01	.01V
Czech Republic	935	—V	—V	—V	—V	—V	—V	—V	.05V	.34V	—V	.80V	.01	.03	.08V
Czechoslovakia n.s.	937	....	....	....	....	....	....	....	.03Y	.04Y	.05Y	.06Y	—	—	—Y
Estonia	939	.02V	—V	3.96V	28.89V	—V	—V	—V	.15V	.23V	.03V	2.61V	—	—	—V
Hungary	944	.04V	—V	.11V	—V	—V	—V	—V	.63V	.74V	4.57V	5.73V	.35	.08	.30V
Kazakhstan	916	....	....	....	....	....	....	....	1,221.21V	2,011.30V	2,192.63V	—V	—	—	—Y
Latvia	941	—V	—V	—V	—V	—V	—V	—V	.02V	.02V	—V	—V	—	—	.04V
Poland	964	—V	4.82V	6.36V	—V	4.11V	—V	—V	26.95V	47.32V	7.43V	.29V	.02	.23	.65V
Romania	968	—V	—V	—V	—V	—V	—V	—V	—V	—V	—V	.01V	.02	.09	.90V
Russia	922	.12V	.03V	.07V	.08V	.22V	.80V	.50V	117.59V	—V	.50V	2.09V	—	—	.07V
Slovak Republic	936	—V	—V	—Y	—Y	—V	—V	—V	—V	—V	—Y	—Y	—	—	.03V
Turkey	186	—V	—V	.11V	.05V	—V	—V	—V	.07V	.19V	.17V	.12V	.19	.41	.23V
Turkmenistan	925	—V	—V	—V	—Y	—Y	—Y	—Y	15.30V	17.36V	42.11V	55.30Y	—	—	96.92Y
Ukraine	926	—V	—V	—V	—V	—V	—Y	—Y	—V	—V	.81V	—V	.35	.36	.45Y
U.S.S.R. n.s.	930	....	....	....	....	....	....	....	.05Y	.05Y	.07Y	.09Y	—	.01	.01Y
Yugoslavia n.s.	966	....	....	....	....	....	....	....	.11Y	.12Y	.15Y	.20Y	.01	—	.01Y
Middle East	**407**	**.7Y**	**.1Y**	**.1Y**	**—Y**	**—Y**	**.1Y**	**5.7Y**	**.3Y**	**.8Y**	**1.0Y**	**.6Y**	**.3**	**.4**	**.5Y**
Bahrain	419	—Y	—Y	—Y	—Y	—Y	—Y	—Y	.04Y	.04Y	.06Y	.07Y	.04	.01	.01Y
Egypt	469	—V	—Y	—Y	—Y	—Y	—Y	—Y	—V	—Y	—Y	—Y	.05	.16	.20Y
Iran, I.R. of	429	—V	—V	—Y	—Y	—Y	—Y	—Y	—Y	—Y	—Y	—Y	.03	.01	.01Y
Israel	436	—V	—V	—V	—V	—V	.09V	5.64V	—V	.50V	.60V	.10V	.08	.12	.20V
Jordan	439	—V	—V	—V	—V	—V	—V	—V	—V	—V	—V	—V	—	.06	—V
Kuwait	443	....	....	....	....	....	....	....	.16Y	.17Y	.20Y	.27Y	—	—	—Y
Lebanon	446	—Y	—Y	—Y	—Y	—Y	—Y	—Y	.07Y	.07Y	.09Y	.12Y	—	—	—Y
Saudi Arabia	456	.69V	.08V	.14V	.03V	.02V	.03Y	.04Y	—Y	—Y	—Y	—Y	.01	.03	.03Y
Syrian Arab Republic	463	—Y	—Y	—Y	—Y	—Y	—Y	—Y	—Y	—Y	—Y	—V	.01	—	—Y
United Arab Emirates	466	....	....	....	....	....	....	....	—Y	—Y	—Y	—Y	.04	.01	.02Y
Western Hemisphere	**207**	**8.3Y**	**41.2Y**	**45.4Y**	**38.5Y**	**19.6Y**	**87.6Y**	**40.9Y**	**208.7Y**	**31.5Y**	**37.6Y**	**42.2Y**	**56.5**	**88.5**	**101.8Y**
Antigua and Barbuda	311	—Y	—Y	—Y	—Y	—Y	—Y	—Y	2.91Y	3.16Y	4.00Y	5.25Y	.01	.01	.02Y
Argentina	213	—V	—V	—V	—V	—V	—V	—V	—V	—V	—V	—V	.14	.19	—V
Aruba	314	.18V	.21V	.55V	.47V	.46V	.34V	.07V	.04V	.05V	.02V	.01V	.02	.01	.01V
Bahamas, The	313	.28Y	.31Y	.39Y	.51Y	.58Y	.72Y	.90Y	.62Y	.68Y	.86Y	1.13Y	.10	.01	.01Y
Barbados	316	.01V	.06V	.04V	.09V	.13V	.01V	.01Y	.90V	.58V	.58V	1.04V	.59	.84	1.05Y
Bolivia	218	—V	—V	.03V	.03V	—V	—Y	—Y	—V	—V	—V	—V	—	—	—Y
Brazil	223	—V	1.25V	—V	.02V	3.53V	69.50V	18.83V	.65V	.59V	.71V	2.52V	.60	1.09	—V
Chile	228	—V	—V	—V	—Y	—Y	—Y	—Y	—V	—V	—Y	—Y	.51	.66	.82Y
Colombia	233	.02V	.05V	1.10V	.44V	—V	—V	—V	.37V	.12V	.16V	.23V	.22	.17	.21V
Costa Rica	238	.63V	1.41V	3.84V	1.27V	1.13V	1.39Y	1.73Y	.53V	.95V	2.04V	3.26V	.54	.87	1.08Y
Dominica	321	—V	—Y	—Y	—Y	—Y	—Y	—Y	.03V	.03Y	.04Y	.05Y	—	—	—Y
Dominican Republic	243	.52V	.57Y	.72Y	.95Y	1.08Y	1.34Y	1.66Y	.05V	.06Y	.07Y	.10Y	.04	.13	.16Y
Ecuador	248	.19V	.17V	.07V	—V	—V	—V	—Y	—V	.03V	—V	—V	—	—	—Y
El Salvador	253	.05V	—V	—V	—V	—V	—V	—V	.11V	.11V	.12V	.27V	.01	.03	.03V
Guatemala	258	2.81V	6.96V	7.78V	.62V	9.27V	11.46Y	14.23Y	—V	.05V	.03V	.12V	.15	.06	.07Y
Guyana	336	—Y	—Y	—Y	—Y	—Y	—Y	—Y	.01Y	.01Y	.01Y	.01Y	.01	.02	.02Y
Haiti	263	1.20V	—V	—V	—V	—Y	—Y	—Y	—Y	—Y	—Y	—Y	—	.01	.01Y
Honduras	268	—V	—V	—V	—V	—Y	—Y	—Y	—Y	—Y	—Y	—Y	.04	.19	.23Y
Jamaica	343	.13V	.36V	.46V	.73V	.73V	.59V	.29V	.97V	.95V	3.82V	.68V	.53	1.13	1.38V
Mexico	273	.98V	1.99V	.17V	.02V	.02V	.01V	.01V	170.05V	3.18V	6.97V	4.94V	1.50	3.58	2.79V
Netherlands Antilles	353	.52V	.65V	1.10V	1.45Y	1.66Y	2.05Y	2.54Y	10.56V	7.33V	—V	—Y	.43	.33	.41Y
Nicaragua	278	....	....	....	....	....	....	....	—V	—V	—V	—V	—	.01	—V
Panama	283	.03V	—V	—V	—V	—V	—V	—V	—V	.07V	.07V	.10V	1.03	1.63	.02V
Paraguay	288	—V	—V	.11V	—V	—V	—V	—Y	—V	—V	—V	—V	—	—	—Y
Peru	293	.20V	27.04V	28.08V	30.58V	—V	.16V	.60Y	.77V	—V	.04V	.04V	.01	.08	.07Y
St. Kitts and Nevis	361	—Y	—Y	—Y	—Y	—Y	—Y	.01Y	—Y	—Y	—Y	—Y	—	—	—Y
St. Vincent & Grens.	364	—V	—V	.02V	.06V	—V	—Y	—Y	—V	—V	—V	—V	—	—	—Y
Trinidad and Tobago	369	.01V	.01V	.01Y	.01Y	.01Y	.01Y	.01Y	19.10V	13.38V	16.94Y	22.25Y	1.50	2.79	3.46Y
Uruguay	298	.10V	.11Y	.11V	—V	—V	—Y	—Y	—V	—Y	—V	.02V	—	.01	.01Y
Venezuela, Rep. Bol.	299	.38V	.10V	.79V	1.26V	1.00V	.04V	—V	.86V	—V	1.01V	—V	47.03	73.00	88.07Y
Western Hem. n.s.	399	—Y	—Y	—Y	—Y	—Y	—Y	—Y	.12Y	.14Y	.16Y	.17Y	1.46	1.66	1.85Y
Other Countries n.i.e	**910**	**—Y**	**—Y**	**—Y**	**—Y**	**—Y**	**—Y**	**—Y**	**.7Y**	**.8Y**	**1.0Y**	**1.3Y**	**.9**	**.4**	**.5Y**
Cuba	928	—Y	—Y	—Y	—Y	—Y	—Y	—Y	.43Y	.46Y	.59Y	.77Y	.88	.42	.52Y
North Korea	954	—Y	—Y	—Y	—Y	—Y	—Y	—Y	.29Y	.32Y	.40Y	.53Y	—	—	—Y
Countries & Areas n.s.	**898**	**55.0Y**	**59.7Y**	**75.6Y**	**99.2Y**	**113.4Y**	**140.1Y**	**173.9Y**	**—Y**	**—Y**	**—Y**	**—Y**	**—**	**—**	**—Y**
Memorandum Items															
European Union	998	1,113.93Y	784.22Y	1,011.37Y	1,282.34Y	1,512.75Y	488.91Y	244.21Y	2,225.98Y	1,783.39V	1,717.21Y	1,426.06Y	65.93	92.60	1,438.90V
Oil Exporting Ctys.	999	4.65Y	1.24Y	2.93Y	3.76Y	3.78Y	3.45Y	4.43Y	1.49Y	.65Y	1.64Y	1.34Y	47.66	73.69	94.74Y
Non-Oil Develop.Ctys.	201	34.25Y	51.24Y	61.27Y	75.67Y	24.74Y	91.36Y	71.93Y	1,663.03Y	2,508.24Y	2,501.07Y	902.98Y	19.71	34.11	1,922.67Y
PERCENT DISTRIBUTION															
Industrial Countries	**101**	**93.0**	**87.8**	**89.7**	**88.0**	**91.9**	**69.0**	**56.1**	**62.9**	**47.3**	**46.8**	**76.4**	**92.3**	**89.8**	**52.2**
Developing Countries	**202**	**2.9**	**5.7**	**4.7**	**5.3**	**1.6**	**12.5**	**13.4**	**37.1**	**52.6**	**53.2**	**23.6**	**7.6**	**10.2**	**47.8**
Africa	**607**	**.4**	**.1**	**.2**	**.4**	**.2**	**.7**	**1.9**	**—**	**—**	**—**	**—**	**.2**	**.2**	**2.2**

	Exports							Imports, f.o.b						
	2001	2002	2003	2004	2005	2006	2007	2001	2002	2003	2004	2005	2006	2007
Asia.......................... 507	1.8	.6	.4.	.4	—	.1	3.2	1.6	8.3	4.6	20.7	.9	1.5	40.9
Europe.......................... 170	—	.5	.8	2.0	.2	.1	.1	30.8	43.6	47.8	1.8	.1	.1	2.4
Middle East.......................... 407	.1	—	—	—	—	—	1.0	—	—	—	—	—	—	—
Western Hemisphere.......................... 207	.6	4.5	3.4	2.6	1.1	11.6	7.2	4.6	.7	.8	1.1	6.4	8.4	2.4
Other Countries n.i.e.......................... 910	—	—	—	—	—	—	—	—	—	—	—	.1	—	—
ANNUAL PERCENT CHANGE														
World.......................... 001	68.2	−31.8	47.1	9.9	17.9	−56.8	−24.8	18.9	6.1	−1.3	−18.4	−76.9	19.4	299.3
Industrial Countries.......................... 101	72.7	−35.6	50.2	7.9	23.2	−67.6	−38.8	24.9	−20.2	−2.4	33.2	−72.2	16.1	132.0
Developing Countries.......................... 202	53.8	34.9	22.3	23.7	−64.1	232.4	−19.5	9.9	50.7	−.2	−63.9	−92.5	60.0	—
Africa.......................... 607	22.3	−79.4	80.4	148.1	−25.0	39.4	94.8	8.0	90.8	−30.6	−43.4	190.1	−1.2	—
Asia.......................... 507	362.7	−78.7	16.1	10.4	−91.1	22.0	—	66.4	447.8	−46.0	270.1	−99.0	103.7	—
Europe.......................... 170	−93.0	—	118.0	173.2	−85.0	−81.0	−35.6	4.1	50.3	8.2	−97.0	−98.6	29.2	—
Middle East.......................... 407	−85.4	−88.7	75.1	−76.1	−27.4	404.7	—	−22.8	195.4	21.2	−40.8	−53.0	49.8	17.7
Western Hemisphere.......................... 207	4.7	399.6	10.0	−15.1	−49.1	347.0	−53.4	45.9	−84.9	19.5	12.1	34.0	56.7	15.0
Other Countries n.i.e.......................... 910	—	—	....	....	....	....	....	10.4	8.5	26.6	31.3	−32.5	−52.1	24.1

		Exports							Imports						
		2001	2002	2003	2004	2005	2006	2007	2001	2002	2003	2004	2005	2006	2007
		Millions of U.S. Dollars							*Millions of U.S. Dollars*						
IFS World Total		**1,284.8**	**1,298.7**	**1,597.8**	**2,146.0**	**2,791.1**	**3,874.5**	**4,458.3**	**1,707.7**	**1,770.1**	**1,615.9**	**1,844.2**	**2,341.3**	**2,814.3**	**3,457.0**
DOTS World Total	**001**	**1,352.9**	**1,374.9**	**1,676.6**	**2,254.4**	**2,239.6Y**	**3,080.7Y**	**3,479.3Y**	**1,709.4**	**1,832.0**	**1,692.1**	**1,887.8**	**2,343.3**	**2,554.3Y**	**3,133.0Y**
Industrial Countries	**101**	**528.5**	**519.6**	**542.9**	**657.8**	**529.6Y**	**728.4Y**	**941.9Y**	**571.4**	**584.7**	**555.2**	**549.6**	**714.2**	**552.5Y**	**703.9Y**
United States	111	187.89	192.15	236.66	359.19	279.64V	343.27V	342.64V	314.35	310.03	309.87	261.34	324.03	236.94V	305.47V
Canada	156	20.21	7.75	6.04	13.25	20.47V	43.36V	101.17V	19.76	12.55	7.90	13.15	17.08	25.24V	15.83V
Australia	193	.91	1.11	2.76	1.91	3.54V	4.81V	4.21V	.89	.29	.31	.43	1.31	.58V	1.66V
Japan	158	2.81	5.86	18.58	68.40	73.33V	174.12V	263.57V	58.39	101.31	83.61	105.26	142.88	43.53V	70.17V
New Zealand	196	.43	1.38	.33	.19	.33V	.75V	.71V	2.71	2.11	1.53	2.54	.86	1.74V	2.57V
Austria	122	.46	1.09	2.39	2.06	3.67V	6.15V	7.62V	1.94	1.67	2.28	3.26	3.64	2.90V	6.65V
Belgium	124	14.04	8.71	15.88	32.73	21.15V	7.18V	37.25V	6.97	7.48	7.72	6.97	9.47	12.07V	12.26V
Cyprus	423	—	—	—	—	—Y	.01V	.02V	.01	—	.02	.01	—	—V	.05V
Denmark	128	.14	.14	.44	.30	.49V	1.62V	1.10V	2.25	2.15	1.98	2.62	2.60	6.35V	6.39V
Finland	172	4.09	10.31	6.73	4.18	1.19V	.07V	.10V	3.87	5.27	1.84	2.06	4.25	7.21V	9.31V
France	132	3.35	4.05	4.87	5.77	9.72V	12.51V	13.90V	17.03	19.85	19.63	21.68	31.16	25.79V	24.49V
Germany	134	8.44	6.64	6.78	10.27	24.72V	24.24V	24.30V	37.49	31.55	36.67	36.82	44.75	71.00V	76.07V
Greece	174	.07	.03	4.12	7.34	.06V	.01V	.21V	.07	.05	.09	.32	.08	.19V	.08V
Iceland	176	—	—	—	—	.50V	.02V	.02V	—	—	.02	.01	—	—V	—V
Ireland	178	.06	.11	.11	.01	.06V	.06V	.06V	.93	1.04	.37	.74	.79	.80V	.78V
Italy	136	13.28	13.78	16.44	15.40	20.49V	30.94V	39.07V	29.51	24.33	21.29	18.67	23.02	26.27V	33.74V
Luxembourg	137	—	—	—	—	.10V	—V	—V	—	—	—	—	—	.42V	.03V
Malta	181	—	—	—	—	—V	—V	—V	—	.02	—	—	.07	—V	—V
Netherlands	138	16.03	13.37	13.69	18.98	22.70V	37.74V	45.77V	7.44	7.70	5.13	7.04	6.09	13.68V	18.35V
Norway	142	.08	.09	.01	.13	1.02V	.96V	1.41V	1.51	.55	1.02	.39	.73	4.92V	7.37V
Portugal	182	.47	.52	.32	.40	.48V	.71V	.92V	.55	.50	.28	.47	.59	1.12V	2.90V
Slovenia	961	—	—	—	—	—V	—V	—V	.10	.09	.19	.07	.13	.12V	.88V
Spain	184	6.39	5.17	6.19	10.58	20.22V	20.44V	24.64V	26.78	24.34	23.56	27.25	35.91	28.06V	42.30V
Sweden	144	1.27	.38	.35	.72	.80V	.40V	.73V	11.53	15.19	9.70	21.12	37.93	24.16V	36.11V
Switzerland	146	176.55	214.97	165.91	52.45	1.21V	2.18V	1.07V	13.07	5.10	6.65	6.17	6.70	7.17V	14.20V
United Kingdom	112	71.51	31.99	34.29	53.57	23.73V	16.90V	31.45V	14.24	11.55	13.56	11.18	20.12	12.30V	16.23V
Developing Countries	**202**	**810.8**	**844.2**	**1,122.2**	**1,587.7**	**1,699.9Y**	**2,339.8Y**	**2,521.8Y**	**1,133.8**	**1,244.8**	**1,131.3**	**1,333.3**	**1,624.1**	**1,995.6Y**	**2,421.4Y**
Africa	**607**	**.2**	**.8**	**.9**	**1.1**	**1.4Y**	**3.1Y**	**19.1Y**	**1.0**	**2.2**	**1.4**	**1.3**	**5.0**	**2.9Y**	**3.8Y**
Algeria	612	.02	.02	—	—	—Y	—Y	—Y	—	.01	—	.01	—	—Y	—Y
Angola	614	—	—	—	—	—Y	—Y	—Y	—	—	—	—	.01	.02Y	.02Y
Benin	638	—	—	.01	—	—V	—Y	—Y	—	—	—	—	—	—Y	—Y
Burundi	618	—	—	—	—	—V	—V	—Y	.02	—	—	—	—	—V	—Y
Cameroon	622	.01	—	—	—	—Y	—Y	—Y	—	.04	—	—	—	—Y	—Y
Central African Rep.	626	—	—	—	—	—Y	—Y	—Y	.01	—	.01	.02	—	—Y	—Y
Congo, Republic of	634	—	—	—	.07	.07Y	.09Y	.11Y	—	—	—	—	—	—Y	—Y
Côte d'Ivoire	662	—	—	—	—	—V	.02V	.03Y	—	—	—	—	—	—V	—Y
Djibouti	611	....	....	....	....	....	....	....	.02	—	—	—	—	—Y	—Y
Equatorial Guinea	642	—	—	—	—	—Y	—Y	—Y	—	—	—	.03	—	—Y	—Y
Ethiopia	644	—	—	.09	.02	.02Y	.03Y	.03Y	—	—	—	—	—	—Y	—Y
Gabon	646	—	—	—	.01	.01Y	.01Y	.01Y	—	—	—	—	—	—Y	—Y
Ghana	652	—	—	.10	.39	.44Y	.55Y	.68Y	.04	.01	—	—	—	—Y	—Y
Guinea	656	—	—	.01	—	—Y	—Y	—Y	—	—	—	—	—	—Y	—Y
Kenya	664	.02	—	—	—	—Y	—Y	—Y	.01	—	—	—	—	.01Y	.01Y
Madagascar	674	—	.04	—	—	—Y	—Y	—Y	—	.01	—	—	—	—Y	—Y
Mali	678	....	....	....	....	....	....	....	.01	.10	.01	—	—	—Y	—Y
Mauritius	684	—	—	—	—	—V	—V	.09V	—	—	—	—	—	—V	—V
Morocco	686	—	—	—	.03	—V	—Y	—Y	—	.03	.08	.05	1.16	1.43Y	1.78Y
Mozambique	688	—	—	—	—	—Y	—Y	—Y	—	—	—	.01	—	.01Y	.01Y
Namibia	728	—	—	—	—	—Y	—Y	—Y	—	.01	—	—	—	—Y	—Y
Nigeria	694	.02	.13	—	—	—Y	—Y	—Y	.02	.12	—	.01	—	—Y	—Y
São Tomé & Príncipe	716	....	....	....	....	....	....	....	—	—	—	.01	.05	.06Y	.08Y
Senegal	722	—	—	.01	—	—V	—V	—Y	—	.01	—	—	.05	—V	—Y
South Africa	199	.13	.22	.32	.13	.36V	1.73V	17.41V	.87	1.32	1.28	1.04	3.63	1.28V	1.80V
Sudan	732	—	—	—	.09	—V	—V	—V	—	—	—	—	—	—V	—V
Swaziland	734	—	—	—	—	—Y	—Y	—Y	—	.34	.01	.08	.06	.07Y	.09Y
Tunisia	744	—	—	—	—	—V	.02V	.03Y	—	.19	—	—	—	.02V	.03Y
Zambia	754	—	—	—	—	—V	—V	—V	—	—	—	—	.01	—V	—V
Zimbabwe	698	—	—	—	—	—V	—V	—Y	.01	—	—	—	.03	—V	—Y
Africa n.s.	799	.03	.38	.31	.41	.51Y	.62Y	.72Y	—	—	—	—	—	—Y	—Y
Asia	**507**	**15.6**	**20.7**	**45.6**	**109.0**	**69.1Y**	**197.0Y**	**224.0Y**	**143.9**	**145.3**	**130.0**	**152.3**	**193.1**	**105.9Y**	**162.1Y**
Bangladesh	513	—	—	—	—	—V	—V	—V	.01	.01	.43	.11	.34	—Y	—Y
Bhutan	514	....	....	....	....	....	....	....	—	—	—	—	.02	.03Y	.04Y
Brunei Darussalam	516	—	—	—	—	—Y	—Y	—Y	—	—	—	.01	—	—Y	—Y
Cambodia	522	....	....	....	....	....	....	....	.02	.01	—	—	—	—Y	—Y
China,P.R.: Mainland	924	5.07	7.72	11.55	23.50	28.49V	42.76V	51.39V	86.34	95.89	87.11	107.54	136.02	64.27V	106.48V
China,P.R.:Hong Kong	532	.67	1.89	3.00	4.83	3.12V	2.88V	2.54V	1.42	1.09	1.19	2.20	2.16	5.72V	8.86V
China,P.R.:Macao	546	—	—	—	—	.01V	—V	.01V	—	—	—	.01	—	—V	.01V
French Polynesia	887	—	—	—	—	—Y	—Y	—Y	—	—	—	.11	—	—Y	—Y
India	534	3.04	1.03	1.56	.32	.69V	.85Y	1.06Y	4.20	5.37	6.97	10.83	11.71	14.47Y	17.96Y

		Exports							Imports						
		2001	2002	2003	2004	2005	2006	2007	2001	2002	2003	2004	2005	2006	2007
		Millions of U.S. Dollars							*Millions of U.S. Dollars*						
Indonesia	536	.65	.35	.19	1.58	.23V	.04V	.09V	3.81	4.11	2.46	1.75	4.40	1.55V	1.61V
Korea	542	1.85	3.41	16.95	56.68	31.05V	146.95V	165.47V	20.84	17.16	17.48	13.96	18.06	8.44V	11.21V
Malaysia	548	1.89	4.93	11.04	20.90	3.04V	.74V	1.11V	2.08	1.48	1.58	1.61	2.82	.91V	1.97V
Nepal	558	—	—	—	—	—Y	—Y	—Y	—	.01	—	—	—	—Y	—Y
New Caledonia	839	—	—	—	—	—Y	—Y	—Y	—	—	—	—	.01	.01Y	.01Y
Pakistan	564	—	.15	—	.07	.08V	.10Y	.13Y	.55	.34	.20	.23	.21	.25Y	.32Y
Philippines	566	—	.01	—	—	—V	—V	—V	.58	.44	.44	.45	.90	.05V	.86V
Singapore	576	.76	.03	.27	.13	—V	—V	—V	.34	.75	.56	.77	1.22	—V	—V
Sri Lanka	524	—	—	—	—	.01V	.01V	—V	.87	.80	.46	.52	.56	1.82V	1.78V
Taiwan Province of China	528	.03	.14	.02	.15	.63V	1.07V	1.04V	20.79	15.21	7.23	8.04	9.39	4.11V	3.76V
Thailand	578	1.67	.73	.72	.78	1.72V	1.59V	1.16V	1.76	2.52	3.73	4.06	4.49	4.25V	7.24V
Vietnam	582	—	.32	.33	.03	—V	—V	—V	.16	.08	.12	.10	.83	—V	—V
Asia n.s.	598	—	—	—	—	—Y	—Y	—Y	.08	—	—	—	—	—Y	—Y
Europe	**170**	**.4**	**1.0**	**.8**	**2.1**	**5.0Y**	**3.6Y**	**8.2Y**	**3.4**	**4.1**	**9.3**	**3.4**	**8.8**	**11.5Y**	**20.1Y**
Albania	914	—	—	—	—	—V	—V	—V	—	—	.03	.02	.04	—V	—V
Azerbaijan	912	—	—	—	—	—V	—V	—V	.02	—	—	—	—	—V	—V
Belarus	913	—	—	—	—	.01V	.02V	.06V	—	.01	.01	.01	—	—V	.07V
Bosnia & Herzegovina	963	....	....	....	....	....	....	....	—	.01	—	—	—	—Y	—Y
Bulgaria	918	.01	—	—	—	—V	.04V	—V	.02	.01	.28	.02	.06	.03V	.10V
Croatia	960	—	—	—	—	—V	—V	—V	.06	—	.03	.04	.18	—V	—V
Czech Republic	935	.05	.03	.08	.05	.30V	.20V	.15V	.92	1.00	.59	.67	1.06	1.88V	2.50V
Estonia	939	—	—	—	—	.07V	.13V	.08V	.01	.04	.03	.05	.18	.30V	.43V
Georgia	915	....	....	....	....	....	....	....	—	.03	—	—	.01	—V	—Y
Gibraltar	823	....	....	....	....	....	....	....	—	—	—	.01	.01	.01Y	.01Y
Hungary	944	—	—	—	.03	—V	—V	.08V	.38	.21	.14	.30	.57	4.63V	8.79V
Kazakhstan	916	.02	—	—	—	—Y	—Y	—Y	—	—	—	—	—	—Y	—Y
Latvia	941	—	—	—	—	.05V	.06V	.35V	—	—	—	—	—	.02V	.07V
Lithuania	946	.03	—	.07	—	.17V	.26V	.30V	.03	.01	.01	.01	.01	.03V	.06V
Macedonia, FYR	962	—	—	—	—	.01V	—V	—Y	—	—	—	—	—	—V	—Y
Moldova	921	—	—	—	—	—V	—Y	—Y	—	.01	—	—	—	—Y	—Y
Poland	964	.05	.08	—	.14	.18V	.50V	1.25V	.56	.56	.30	.47	.58	.09V	1.30V
Romania	968	.10	.01	.02	.17	.08V	.07V	.07V	.02	.05	.06	.12	.15	.18V	.02V
Russia	922	.08	.78	.62	1.58	3.83V	2.22V	3.86V	.52	.85	.29	.50	2.12	.07V	.67V
Serbia & Montenegro	965	—	—	—	—	—Y	—Y	—Y	—	—	.01	—	.01	.01Y	.01Y
Slovak Republic	936	—	—	—	—	—V	—V	.17V	.02	.07	.14	.25	.48	.20V	.14V
Tajikistan	923	....	....	....	....	....	....	....	—	—	.04	—	—	—Y	—Y
Turkey	186	.02	—	.03	.15	.23V	.10V	1.74V	.40	.52	.40	.86	.71	.79V	1.91V
Ukraine	926	—	—	—	—	.02V	.03Y	.04Y	.48	.66	6.95	.07	2.60	3.21Y	3.99Y
Europe n.s.	884	—	.10	—	.01	.01Y	.01Y	.02Y	—	—	—	—	.02	.02Y	.03Y
Middle East	**407**	**1.2**	**1.7**	**2.7**	**5.3**	**6.6Y**	**8.7Y**	**10.7Y**	**3.9**	**3.4**	**2.4**	**6.9**	**3.2**	**5.7Y**	**5.9Y**
Bahrain	419	—	—	—	—	—Y	—Y	—Y	—	.03	—	—	—	—Y	—Y
Egypt	469	.53	1.10	.56	2.71	3.10Y	3.83Y	4.76Y	.03	.03	.01	.04	.08	.09Y	.12Y
Iran, I.R. of	429	—	—	—	—	—Y	—Y	—Y	.01	.04	.03	.01	.02	.02Y	.03Y
Iraq	433	—	—	—	—	—Y	—Y	—Y	.01	.01	—	—	—	—Y	—Y
Israel	436	.35	.27	.22	.43	.64V	1.36V	1.45V	3.51	3.02	2.15	6.34	2.91	5.39V	5.39V
Jordan	439	—	—	—	.04	.05V	—V	—V	—	—	—	.01	—	—V	.07V
Kuwait	443	.01	—	—	—	—Y	—Y	—Y	—	—	—	—	—	—Y	—Y
Lebanon	446	.11	—	.04	.07	.09Y	.11Y	.13Y	—	—	—	—	—	—Y	—Y
Oman	449	—	—	.01	—	—Y	—Y	—Y	—	—	—	—	—	—Y	—Y
Qatar	453	—	—	—	—	—Y	—Y	.01Y	.01	—	—	—	—	—V	—Y
Saudi Arabia	456	—	.01	—	—	.12V	.15Y	.20Y	.01	.02	.04	.05	—	—Y	.01Y
Syrian Arab Republic	463	—	.04	—	—	—Y	—Y	—Y	.13	.17	.14	.09	.16	.19Y	.24Y
United Arab Emirates	466	.18	.25	1.90	2.06	2.62Y	3.23Y	4.19Y	.13	.07	.01	.31	.02	.02Y	.02Y
Western Hemisphere	**207**	**793.4**	**820.1**	**1,072.1**	**1,470.1**	**1,617.8Y**	**2,127.4Y**	**2,259.8Y**	**981.7**	**1,089.9**	**988.3**	**1,169.5**	**1,414.0**	**1,869.6Y**	**2,229.5Y**
Antigua and Barbuda	311	—	—	.02	—	—Y	—Y	—Y	—	—	—	—	—	—Y	—Y
Argentina	213	67.46	27.65	57.18	131.48	244.77V	293.28V	200.83V	307.95	308.50	284.39	295.28	391.16	417.88V	508.95V
Aruba	314	—	—	—	.05	.05V	.02V	—V	—	—	—	.02	—	.02V	—V
Bahamas, The	313	.06	.09	.05	.04	.05Y	.06Y	.07Y	—	—	.04	.02	.04	.04Y	.05Y
Barbados	316	—	—	—	.01	.13V	.60V	.75Y	—	—	—	—	—	—V	—Y
Belize	339	—	—	.01	—	—Y	.01Y	.01Y	—	—	—	—	—	—Y	—Y
Bermuda	319	—	—	—	—	—V	—V	—Y	—	—	.03	.03	—	—Y	—Y
Brazil	223	299.55	336.57	503.97	713.56	989.77V	1,448.38V	1,601.15V	276.44	392.45	347.79	486.59	513.71	763.34V	935.78V
Chile	228	30.31	32.80	44.00	51.15	34.42V	53.32V	51.80V	144.80	126.12	125.41	111.42	162.40	314.83V	329.68V
Colombia	233	191.93	139.47	157.77	119.72	174.28V	106.54V	130.07V	47.88	42.56	48.11	61.24	57.27	64.35V	72.11V
Costa Rica	238	.17	5.12	.09	.19	.24V	.30Y	.37Y	.64	.48	.31	.54	.59	.74Y	.91Y
Dominica	321	—	—	.02	—	—Y	—Y	—Y	—	.02	—	.05	.01	.01Y	.01Y
Dominican Republic	243	.96	1.10	1.18	1.66	1.89Y	2.34Y	2.90Y	.01	.03	.25	.70	.31	.38Y	.47Y
Ecuador	248	10.21	3.14	13.79	5.32	2.16V	4.49V	5.57Y	6.05	6.57	7.45	9.68	12.24	10.22V	12.68Y
El Salvador	253	.01	.02	.16	7.75	.25V	.25V	.10V	.07	43.05	.10	.32	.13	.03V	.11V
Guatemala	258	.21	.34	.38	1.50	.24V	.30Y	.37Y	.21	.09	.09	.23	.30	.38Y	.47Y
Guyana	336	—	—	.07	.09	.11Y	.13Y	.17Y	.02	—	—	—	—	—Y	—Y
Haiti	263	.02	.02	.13	.10	.12Y	.15Y	.18Y	.01	—	—	—	—	—Y	—Y
Honduras	268	.14	.18	.20	.17	.19Y	.23Y	.29Y	.07	.03	.32	.09	.02	.03Y	.04Y
Jamaica	343	.02	—	.02	.96	.08V	—V	—V	.01	—	—	—	.01	—V	—V
Mexico	273	8.32	19.85	21.10	26.99	29.94V	38.95V	58.67V	37.79	32.92	34.68	36.25	50.94	39.02V	53.16V
Netherlands Antilles	353	.03	—	—	—	—Y	—Y	—Y	.60	.58	.60	.12	.01	.01Y	.01Y
Nicaragua	278	—	—	.03	.04	—V	—V	—V	.08	.05	.02	.04	.11	—V	—V

		Exports							Imports						
		2001	2002	2003	2004	2005	2006	2007	2001	2002	2003	2004	2005	2006	2007
		Millions of U.S. Dollars							*Millions of U.S. Dollars*						
Panama	283	3.86	.44	.35	7.95	.06V	.08V	.08V	6.88	5.30	4.41	6.40	5.51	.36V	.67V
Paraguay	288	4.68	2.66	4.28	17.59	12.71V	25.80V	32.02Y	22.98	18.13	16.73	19.15	22.76	32.43V	40.25Y
Peru	293	67.52	73.75	89.92	137.82	112.44V	122.97V	142.55Y	107.87	94.98	104.71	127.30	152.25	210.08V	255.24Y
St. Kitts and Nevis	361	.04	—	—	—	—Y	—Y	—Y	—	—	—	—	—	—Y	—Y
St. Vincent & Grens	364	—	—	—	—	—V	—Y	—Y	.05	—	—	—	—	.01Y	.01Y
Suriname	366	.10	—	—	—	—Y	—Y	—Y	.01	—	—	—	—	—Y	—Y
Trinidad and Tobago	369	.11	.34	.36	.05	.06Y	.07Y	.09Y	.18	.17	.21	.12	.05	.06Y	.08Y
Uruguay	298	9.45	1.12	.85	1.43	1.09V	1.34Y	1.67Y	3.91	3.87	3.92	3.83	5.20	6.43Y	7.98Y
Venezuela, Rep. Bol	299	98.24	175.42	176.20	244.46	12.70V	27.75V	30.06V	17.14	13.98	8.69	10.04	38.93	8.97V	10.82Y
Western Hem. n.s	399	—	—	—	.01	.02Y	.02Y	.03Y	.01	—	—	—	—	—Y	—Y
Other Countries n.i.e	**910**	**.3**	**—**	**.4**	**.4**	**.4Y**	**.5Y**	**.6Y**	**1.9**	**2.2**	**1.1**	**1.1**	**1.7**	**2.1Y**	**2.6Y**
Cuba	928	.21	—	.07	.03	.03Y	.04Y	.05Y	.75	.68	.43	.36	1.36	1.69Y	2.09Y
North Korea	954	.08	.02	.35	.34	.39Y	.48Y	.59Y	1.12	1.49	.69	.70	.32	.40Y	.49Y
Countries & Areas n.s	**898**	**10.3**	**8.4**	**8.5**	**6.0**	**6.8Y**	**8.4Y**	**10.5Y**	**2.3**	**.2**	**4.4**	**3.8**	**3.3**	**4.1Y**	**5.1Y**
Special Categories	**899**	**3.0**	**2.7**	**2.6**	**2.5**	**2.9Y**	**3.6Y**	**4.4Y**	**—**	**—**	**—**	**—**	**—**	**—Y**	**—Y**
Memorandum Items															
European Union	998	139.73	96.40	112.76	162.54	150.36Y	160.11Y	229.52Y	162.62	154.68	145.51	162.03	223.48	239.57Y	299.90Y
Oil Exporting Ctys	999	99.12	176.18	178.31	248.10	15.67Y	31.18Y	34.54Y	21.15	18.35	11.23	12.18	43.37	10.57Y	12.49Y
Non-Oil Develop.Ctys	201	711.66	668.06	943.88	1,339.57	1,684.21Y	2,308.58Y	2,487.28Y	1,112.65	1,226.48	1,120.08	1,321.12	1,580.72	1,985.02Y	2,408.90Y
PERCENT DISTRIBUTION															
Industrial Countries	**101**	**39.1**	**37.8**	**32.4**	**29.2**	**23.6**	**23.6**	**27.1**	**33.4**	**31.9**	**32.8**	**29.1**	**30.5**	**21.6**	**22.5**
Developing Countries	**202**	**59.9**	**61.4**	**66.9**	**70.4**	**75.9**	**75.9**	**72.5**	**66.3**	**68.0**	**66.9**	**70.6**	**69.3**	**78.1**	**77.3**
Africa	**607**	**—**	**.1**	**.1**	**.1**	**.1**	**.1**	**.5**	**.1**	**.1**	**.1**	**.1**	**.2**	**.1**	**.1**
Asia	**507**	**1.2**	**1.5**	**2.7**	**4.8**	**3.1**	**6.4**	**6.4**	**8.4**	**7.9**	**7.7**	**8.1**	**8.2**	**4.1**	**5.2**
Europe	**170**	**—**	**.1**	**—**	**.1**	**.2**	**.1**	**.2**	**.2**	**.2**	**.5**	**.2**	**.4**	**.4**	**.6**
Middle East	**407**	**.1**	**.1**	**.2**	**.2**	**.3**	**.3**	**.3**	**.2**	**.2**	**.1**	**.4**	**.1**	**.2**	**.2**
Western Hemisphere	**207**	**58.6**	**59.6**	**63.9**	**65.2**	**72.2**	**69.1**	**65.0**	**57.4**	**59.5**	**58.4**	**61.9**	**60.3**	**73.2**	**71.2**
Other Countries n.i.e	**910**	**—**	**—**	**—**	**—**	**—**	**—**	**—**	**.1**	**.1**	**.1**	**.1**	**.1**	**.1**	**.1**
ANNUAL PERCENT CHANGE															
World	**001**	**–8.3**	**1.6**	**21.9**	**34.5**	**–.7**	**37.6**	**12.9**	**–15.5**	**7.2**	**–7.6**	**11.6**	**24.1**	**9.0**	**22.7**
Industrial Countries	**101**	**–32.4**	**–1.7**	**4.5**	**21.2**	**–19.5**	**37.5**	**29.3**	**–30.2**	**2.3**	**–5.0**	**–1.0**	**30.0**	**–22.6**	**27.4**
Developing Countries	**202**	**20.1**	**4.1**	**32.9**	**41.5**	**7.1**	**37.6**	**7.8**	**–5.4**	**9.8**	**–9.1**	**17.9**	**21.8**	**22.9**	**21.3**
Africa	**607**	**181.8**	**255.3**	**9.0**	**34.2**	**25.1**	**114.9**	**522.7**	**–29.7**	**119.4**	**–36.5**	**–10.2**	**297.7**	**–42.0**	**31.2**
Asia	**507**	**2.3**	**32.5**	**120.4**	**138.9**	**–36.6**	**185.2**	**13.7**	**–3.8**	**1.0**	**–10.5**	**17.2**	**26.8**	**–45.2**	**53.1**
Europe	**170**	**–24.8**	**182.3**	**–16.3**	**155.9**	**133.4**	**–27.3**	**125.3**	**–36.9**	**18.7**	**128.9**	**–63.3**	**157.9**	**30.5**	**75.3**
Middle East	**407**	**–66.4**	**41.0**	**64.5**	**93.9**	**24.5**	**31.2**	**23.5**	**–18.2**	**–12.0**	**–29.7**	**187.8**	**–53.6**	**79.7**	**2.5**
Western Hemisphere	**207**	**21.0**	**3.4**	**30.7**	**37.1**	**10.0**	**31.5**	**6.2**	**–5.4**	**11.0**	**–9.3**	**18.3**	**20.9**	**32.2**	**19.2**
Other Countries n.i.e	**910**	**483.4**	**–93.5**	**—**	**–12.8**	**14.3**	**23.6**	**24.1**	**–44.3**	**16.3**	**–48.6**	**–4.0**	**57.7**	**23.6**	**24.1**

		Exports							Imports						
		2001	2002	2003	2004	2005	2006	2007	2001	2002	2003	2004	2005	2006	2007
		Millions of U.S. Dollars							*Millions of U.S. Dollars*						
DOTS World Total	**001**	**736.3Y**	**837.8Y**	**1,144.4Y**	**1,506.0Y**	**2,189.8Y**	**2,763.1Y**	**3,144.8Y**	**2,842.0Y**	**3,370.3Y**	**3,997.8Y**	**4,875.6Y**	**5,758.4Y**	**6,000.6Y**	**7,521.8Y**
Industrial Countries	**101**	**569.7Y**	**626.0Y**	**852.6Y**	**1,004.3Y**	**1,377.5Y**	**1,689.2Y**	**2,000.4Y**	**1,713.7Y**	**1,975.7Y**	**2,249.4Y**	**2,808.2Y**	**3,125.0Y**	**3,167.0Y**	**3,937.5Y**
United States	111	11.45V	15.36V	11.45V	11.18V	66.09V	24.55V	24.09V	47.30V	35.09V	23.21V	30.36V	19.36V	56.54V	22.22V
Canada	156	.92V	1.71V	3.02V	3.01V	2.26V	3.37V	5.00V	.90V	.48V	2.17V	1.47V	2.18V	5.20V	5.52V
Australia	193	1.94V	.56V	.74V	.71V	8.58V	1.79V	2.45V	.17V	1.71V	.47V	2.96V	1.32V	2.13V	1.13V
Japan	158	.21V	.34V	.52V	1.24V	1.42V	2.74V	3.42V	1.46V	1.79V	.88V	1.15V	4.05V	1.70V	5.47V
New Zealand	196	.05V	.05V	.08V	.04V	.10V	.12V	.14V	.14V	.04V	.12V	.01V	—V	.02V	—V
Austria	122	76.44V	83.47V	105.29V	110.11V	145.52V	239.62V	302.74V	184.78V	248.44V	272.52V	322.43V	401.03V	356.37V	524.55V
Belgium	124	8.17V	6.07V	7.90V	10.28V	11.38V	12.58V	30.04V	29.05V	29.69V	39.94V	49.43V	57.44V	58.98V	85.76V
Cyprus	423	.02V	.12V	.60V	.11V	.05Y	.05V	.07V	.24V	.34V	.16V	.15V	.08V	1.00V	.37V
Denmark	128	3.04V	5.34V	1.28V	1.96V	1.52V	2.27V	6.44V	20.50V	17.37V	14.29V	18.43V	23.79V	15.31V	25.61V
Finland	172	8.49V	.21V	.54V	.17V	.18V	.30V	1.56V	1.60V	2.05V	5.53V	3.50V	6.04V	12.78V	7.02V
France	132	22.89V	19.99V	41.44V	42.85V	51.96V	77.40V	64.33V	52.36V	54.04V	70.32V	63.63V	113.00V	91.48V	98.09V
Germany	134	113.83V	108.02V	194.76V	311.40V	286.25V	338.98V	419.55V	400.40V	459.53V	544.51V	721.71V	790.89V	867.07V	982.40V
Greece	174	14.62V	35.27V	24.72V	7.23V	8.68V	9.61V	7.46V	10.39V	13.73V	20.72V	27.22V	28.96V	25.44V	39.83V
Iceland	176	.03V	.03V	.05V	.06V	.11V	.17V	.22V	.09V	.04V	—V	—V	—V	.05V	.02V
Ireland	178	.08V	.05V	.18V	.21V	.37V	1.36V	1.09V	5.59V	5.49V	4.85V	11.32V	9.68V	21.82V	17.39V
Italy	136	219.93V	261.11V	326.93V	332.76V	382.02V	423.25V	507.35V	382.27V	425.19V	483.08V	552.88V	635.72V	599.01V	779.00V
Luxembourg	137	.04V	.08V	.09V	.12V	.09V	.08V	.20V	1.08V	1.37V	1.27V	1.38V	1.70V	1.73V	1.49V
Netherlands	138	10.68V	12.55V	12.43V	9.27V	23.23V	15.74V	27.29V	47.08V	58.50V	62.15V	85.22V	109.32V	98.71V	128.93V
Norway	142	.69V	.83V	1.49V	2.85V	3.17V	5.29V	6.98V	2.56V	2.29V	1.15V	3.81V	4.15V	3.67V	3.06V
Portugal	182	4.30V	.23V	2.67V	2.73V	2.82V	3.92V	1.31V	.60V	1.10V	3.21V	.44V	3.47V	8.81V	16.41V
Slovenia	961	56.68V	59.46V	80.75V	106.05Y	327.95V	462.25V	518.54V	436.78V	512.68V	586.45V	770.20Y	756.81V	792.50V	1,001.36V
Spain	184	6.71V	3.33V	19.66V	27.45V	26.95V	20.39V	13.08V	32.53V	39.16V	39.93V	43.09V	36.72V	38.78V	47.60V
Sweden	144	3.13V	3.52V	5.81V	6.94V	11.93V	17.48V	25.64V	13.80V	14.14V	19.99V	31.93V	31.42V	24.86V	34.47V
Switzerland	146	2.03V	3.06V	4.22V	9.43V	6.03V	12.55V	15.51V	18.69V	25.10V	29.92V	34.70V	39.81V	44.64V	69.47V
United Kingdom	112	3.41V	5.21V	5.97V	6.17V	8.81V	13.33V	15.87V	23.29V	26.38V	22.59V	30.76V	48.08V	38.39V	40.35V
Developing Countries	**202**	**166.5Y**	**211.9Y**	**291.8Y**	**501.6Y**	**812.3Y**	**1,074.0Y**	**1,144.4Y**	**1,128.4Y**	**1,394.6Y**	**1,748.4Y**	**2,067.4Y**	**2,633.4Y**	**2,833.7Y**	**3,584.2Y**
Africa	**607**	**3.4Y**	**2.8Y**	**3.0Y**	**3.8Y**	**3.7Y**	**4.9Y**	**4.8Y**	**.7Y**	**.6Y**	**.3Y**	**1.5Y**	**1.6Y**	**1.9Y**	**3.9Y**
Algeria	612	—V	.29V	.32Y	.42Y	.53Y	.66Y	.85Y	....	....	....	....	....	....	....
Gabon	646	.01Y	.01Y	.01Y	.01Y	.01Y	.01Y	.02Y	....	....	....	....	....	....	....
Kenya	664	....	....	....	....	....	....	....	.01V	.01V	.01V	.11V	.13Y	.16Y	.19Y
Morocco	686	1.72V	.97V	.85V	1.27V	1.14V	1.41Y	1.76Y	—V	.18V	.07V	.08V	.41V	.50Y	.62Y
South Africa	199	.44V	.75V	.65V	.91V	1.45V	1.91V	1.05V	.64V	.42V	.21V	1.18V	.67V	1.10V	2.82V
Tanzania	738	—V	—V	—Y	—Y	—Y	—Y	—Y	.02V	—V	—Y	—Y	.01Y	.01Y	.01Y
Tunisia	744	1.19V	.81V	1.13V	1.16V	.53V	.94V	1.16Y	—V	—V	.03V	.09V	.40V	.17V	.21Y
Asia	**507**	**2.0Y**	**5.3Y**	**5.1Y**	**3.9Y**	**95.8Y**	**113.1Y**	**28.6Y**	**11.2Y**	**13.5Y**	**20.9Y**	**70.3Y**	**36.5Y**	**50.0Y**	**94.0Y**
China,P.R.: Mainland	924	.61V	.35V	.58V	.70V	94.01V	109.18V	24.81V	1.70V	3.39V	6.28V	14.36V	21.53V	26.48V	59.32V
China,P.R.:Hong Kong	532	.09V	.01V	.25V	—V	.11V	.01V	—V	1.30V	.91V	.92V	1.36V	1.55V	1.77V	1.16V
China,P.R.:Macao	546	.02V	.03V	.03V	.04V	.08V	.08V	.04V	.01V	—V	—V	.03V	—V	—V	—V
India	534	—Y	2.27V	2.14V	.55V	.29V	.36Y	.45Y	—Y	2.29V	3.38V	3.17V	1.85V	2.28Y	2.83Y
Indonesia	536	.24V	.62V	.01V	1.74V	.01V	.02V	.04V	.27V	.23V	.62V	1.13V	.42V	.50Y	1.18V
Korea	542	.02V	.07V	.02V	.10V	.20V	1.13V	.42V	5.31V	3.11V	6.05V	47.54V	8.07V	15.63V	23.16V
Malaysia	548	.01V	1.63V	.68V	.37V	.55V	1.76V	2.30V	.23V	.95V	.72V	.08V	.09V	.18V	1.23V
New Caledonia	839	—V	—V	—V	.02V	.02Y	.03Y	.04Y	....	....	....	....	....	....	....
Pakistan	564	.05V	.01V	.35V	—V	.01V	.01Y	.02Y	.76V	.14V	.17V	.80V	1.05V	1.29Y	1.60Y
Philippines	566	.02V	.11V	.61V	.19V	—V	—V	—V	.77V	1.32V	1.50V	.35V	.16V	.18V	.65V
Taiwan Province of China	528	.08V	.22V	.34V	.21V	.52V	.54V	.53V	.64V	1.01V	1.15V	1.43V	1.83V	1.67V	2.82V
Vietnam	582	.87V	—V	.07V	—V	—V	—V	—V	.17V	.17V	.09V	—V	—V	—V	—V
Europe	**170**	**147.6Y**	**189.8Y**	**266.8Y**	**470.3Y**	**686.0Y**	**922.2Y**	**1,068.8Y**	**1,110.5Y**	**1,375.0Y**	**1,715.4Y**	**1,976.8Y**	**2,569.4Y**	**2,754.1Y**	**3,469.6Y**
Albania	914	.07V	.62V	1.15V	1.09V	3.03V	7.50V	11.36V	.01V	.08V	.05V	.42V	1.20V	4.74V	4.76V
Azerbaijan	912	.08V	—V	—V	—V	—V	.07V	.04V	.33V	.01V	—V	—V	—V	—V	—V
Belarus	913	—V	.01V	—V	.07V	.04V	.09V	.09V	.70V	4.42V	.08V	4.63V	12.97V	5.95V	7.46V
Bulgaria	918	.43V	.80V	.65V	1.65V	6.09V	20.45V	29.17V	11.11V	11.67V	10.61V	12.93V	72.59V	139.62V	41.26V
Croatia	960	112.55V	148.45V	208.05V	316.42V	410.98V	541.45V	660.47V	610.21V	767.84V	974.93V	1,156.57V	1,385.47V	1,440.02V	1,859.94V
Czech Republic	935	3.42V	4.73V	6.97V	7.00V	24.65V	27.99V	35.74V	76.87V	85.88V	95.41V	116.81V	146.09V	160.04V	178.62V
Estonia	939	.11V	.10V	.10V	—V	—V	.04V	.32V	—V	.09V	.10V	.01V	.42V	1.88V	1.67V
Georgia	915	—V	.06V	.15V	—V	1.32V	.48V	.34Y	—V	—V	—V	—V	—V	—V	—Y
Hungary	944	4.59V	8.32V	20.90V	71.50V	117.26V	145.01V	178.74V	231.36V	253.55V	311.16V	296.59V	317.38V	312.29V	408.63V
Kyrgyz Republic	917	....	....	....	....	....	....	....	—V	—V	—V	—V	—V	.19V	.04V
Latvia	941	—V	.01V	—V	.06V	.06V	.89V	—V	.08V	.11V	.16V	.13V	.32V	.07V	.78V
Lithuania	946	.15V	.21V	.14V	.15V	.16V	.21V	.21V	.34V	.68V	1.74V	1.10V	1.31V	.95V	1.15V
Macedonia, FYR	962	3.77V	13.00V	10.68V	14.82V	21.43V	24.12V	29.94V	17.86V	20.14V	26.17V	36.55V	55.50V	71.17V	88.32Y
Moldova	921	—V	.05V	.11V	.17V	.65V	.81Y	1.00Y	.14V	.61V	.45V	.13V	—V	—Y	—Y
Poland	964	4.02V	4.30V	4.24V	7.77V	34.90V	62.12V	39.30V	45.62V	80.72V	96.66V	92.73V	132.41V	73.99V	99.83V
Romania	968	7.95V	.53V	.61V	17.65V	41.38V	68.56V	44.39V	13.48V	16.06V	18.94V	44.09V	139.95V	197.77V	79.81V
Russia	922	4.73V	.47V	1.94V	17.06V	2.56V	3.61V	5.98V	43.97V	31.12V	58.16V	47.44V	88.78V	104.36V	98.67V
Slovak Republic	936	1.21V	2.04V	2.59Y	3.40Y	4.54V	6.63V	7.72V	16.46V	29.73V	37.63Y	49.42Y	57.43V	54.72V	83.59V
Turkey	186	4.48V	5.74V	7.58V	10.43V	14.00V	8.53V	19.52V	30.34V	47.59V	69.55V	109.81V	141.04V	165.92V	489.69V
Ukraine	926	.02V	.36V	.89V	1.02V	2.95V	3.65Y	4.53Y	11.58V	24.67V	13.64V	7.43V	16.55V	20.46Y	25.39Y
Middle East	**407**	**12.8Y**	**13.6Y**	**16.6Y**	**22.5Y**	**25.8Y**	**33.1Y**	**41.7Y**	**3.1Y**	**3.0Y**	**3.5Y**	**7.2Y**	**4.2Y**	**4.8Y**	**5.9Y**
Bahrain	419	.13Y	.14Y	.18Y	.23Y	.27Y	.33Y	.41Y	....	....	....	....	....	....	....
Egypt	469	11.64V	12.63Y	15.98Y	20.99Y	23.98Y	29.64Y	36.78Y	.47V	.51Y	.65Y	.85Y	.97Y	1.20Y	1.49Y
Israel	436	.82V	.55V	.09V	.73V	.18V	1.27V	1.91V	2.31V	1.76V	1.21V	2.97V	1.76V	1.43V	1.76V

	Exports 2001	Exports 2002	Exports 2003	Exports 2004	Exports 2005	Exports 2006	Exports 2007	Imports 2001	Imports 2002	Imports 2003	Imports 2004	Imports 2005	Imports 2006	Imports 2007
	Millions of U.S. Dollars							*Millions of U.S. Dollars*						
Jordan.......... 439	.01V	—V	—V	.04V	.06V	.04V	.25V	.18V	.55V	1.42V	3.17V	1.16V	1.83V	2.21V
Kuwait.......... 443	.02Y	.02Y	.02Y	.03Y	.03Y	.04Y	.05Y	....	....	....	....	....	....	....
Lebanon.......... 446	.04Y	.04Y	.06Y	.07Y	.08Y	.10Y	.13Y	.13Y	.14Y	.18Y	.24Y	.28Y	.34Y	.42Y
Qatar.......... 453	—V	.06V	.05V	.04V	.19V	.37V	.49Y	....	....	....	....	....	....	....
Saudi Arabia.......... 456	.14V	.14V	.18V	.35V	.54V	.67Y	.87Y	—Y	—Y	—Y	—Y	—Y	—Y	—Y
Yemen, Republic of.......... 474	—V	—V	—Y	.06V	.51V	.63Y	.78Y	.04V	—V	—Y	—V	—V	—Y	—Y
Western Hemisphere.......... 207	**.8Y**	**.3Y**	**.4Y**	**1.1Y**	**1.0Y**	**.6Y**	**.4Y**	**3.0Y**	**2.5Y**	**8.2Y**	**11.7Y**	**21.7Y**	**22.8Y**	**10.9Y**
Argentina.......... 213	.23V	.15V	.28V	.56V	.35V	.22V	.15V	.23V	.44V	.92V	5.14V	13.82V	3.55V	6.51V
Bolivia.......... 218	—V	.01V	—V	—V	—V	—Y	—Y	....	....	....	....	....	....	....
Brazil.......... 223	.03V	.01V	—V	.02V	.03V	.04V	—V	2.73V	1.99V	7.28V	6.45V	6.19V	15.68V	—V
Chile.......... 228	—V	—V	.03V	.02V	.06V	.19V	.11V	—V	—V	.02V	—V	—V	—V	—V
Colombia.......... 233	.51V	.11V	.11V	.51V	.48V	.08V	.03V	—V	.10V	.02V	.01V	—V	.01V	.01V
Ecuador.......... 248	—V	.05V	—V	—V	—V	—V	—Y	....	....	....	....	....	....	....
Peru.......... 293	.02V	.01V	.01V	.03V	.02V	.03V	.10Y	—V	—V	—V	.03V	.46V	2.08V	2.58Y
Uruguay.......... 298	—V	—Y	—V	—V	.01V	.01Y	.01Y	—V	—Y	—V	.06V	1.20V	1.49Y	1.85Y
Memorandum Items														
European Union.......... 998	565.94Y	623.74Y	865.96Y	1,065.69Y	1,471.29Y	1,881.50Y	2,204.59Y	2,013.08Y	2,359.96Y	2,734.35Y	3,290.49Y	3,709.51Y	3,656.97Y	4,604.91Y
Oil Exporting Ctys.......... 999	.40Y	1.12Y	.59Y	2.58Y	1.31Y	1.76Y	2.29Y	.27Y	.23Y	.62Y	1.13Y	.42Y	.50Y	1.18Y
Non-Oil Develop.Ctys.......... 201	166.13Y	210.73Y	291.18Y	499.05Y	811.01Y	1,072.19Y	1,142.11Y	1,128.12Y	1,394.36Y	1,747.74Y	2,066.27Y	2,632.98Y	2,833.17Y	3,583.07Y
PERCENT DISTRIBUTION														
Industrial Countries.......... 101	**77.4**	**74.7**	**74.5**	**66.7**	**62.9**	**61.1**	**63.6**	**60.3**	**58.6**	**56.3**	**57.6**	**54.3**	**52.8**	**52.3**
Developing Countries.......... 202	**22.6**	**25.3**	**25.5**	**33.3**	**37.1**	**38.9**	**36.4**	**39.7**	**41.4**	**43.7**	**42.4**	**45.7**	**47.2**	**47.7**
Africa.......... 607	**.5**	**.3**	**.3**	**.3**	**.2**	**.2**	**.2**	**—**	**—**	**—**	**—**	**—**	**—**	**.1**
Asia.......... 507	**.3**	**.6**	**.4**	**.3**	**4.4**	**4.1**	**.9**	**.4**	**.4**	**.5**	**1.4**	**.6**	**.8**	**1.2**
Europe.......... 170	**20.0**	**22.7**	**23.3**	**31.2**	**31.3**	**33.4**	**34.0**	**39.1**	**40.8**	**42.9**	**40.5**	**44.6**	**45.9**	**46.1**
Middle East.......... 407	**1.7**	**1.6**	**1.4**	**1.5**	**1.2**	**1.2**	**1.3**	**.1**	**.1**	**.1**	**.1**	**.1**	**.1**	**.1**
Western Hemisphere.......... 207	**.1**	**—**	**—**	**.1**	**—**	**—**	**—**	**.1**	**.1**	**.2**	**.2**	**.4**	**.4**	**.1**
ANNUAL PERCENT CHANGE														
World.......... 001	**10.0**	**13.8**	**36.6**	**31.6**	**45.4**	**26.2**	**13.8**	**7.5**	**18.6**	**18.6**	**22.0**	**18.1**	**4.2**	**25.3**
Industrial Countries.......... 101	**9.1**	**9.9**	**36.2**	**17.8**	**37.2**	**22.6**	**18.4**	**2.7**	**15.3**	**13.9**	**24.8**	**11.3**	**1.3**	**24.3**
Developing Countries.......... 202	**13.1**	**27.2**	**37.7**	**71.9**	**61.9**	**32.2**	**6.6**	**15.7**	**23.6**	**25.4**	**18.2**	**27.4**	**7.6**	**26.5**
Africa.......... 607	**48.9**	**–15.7**	**4.5**	**27.5**	**–2.6**	**34.3**	**–1.9**	**198.7**	**–9.7**	**–47.4**	**361.6**	**10.5**	**20.0**	**99.7**
Asia.......... 507	**–50.5**	**164.2**	**–4.7**	**–22.8**	**—**	**18.1**	**–74.7**	**59.9**	**21.3**	**54.4**	**236.3**	**–48.0**	**36.8**	**87.9**
Europe.......... 170	**18.6**	**28.6**	**40.6**	**76.3**	**45.9**	**34.4**	**15.9**	**15.2**	**23.8**	**24.8**	**15.2**	**30.0**	**7.2**	**26.0**
Middle East.......... 407	**–19.7**	**6.1**	**22.0**	**36.1**	**14.7**	**28.0**	**25.9**	**21.9**	**–5.4**	**16.8**	**108.7**	**–42.4**	**15.3**	**22.6**
Western Hemisphere.......... 207	**52.3**	**–56.2**	**25.6**	**164.7**	**–15.6**	**–39.5**	**–29.0**	**54.3**	**–14.7**	**226.7**	**41.7**	**85.4**	**5.2**	**–52.0**

	Exports 2001	2002	2003	2004	2005	2006	2007	Imports, f.o.b 2001	2002	2003	2004	2005	2006	2007
	Millions of U.S. Dollars							*Millions of U.S. Dollars*						
IFS World Total	**58,287**	**60,439**	**73,203**	**96,678**	**118,529**	**137,807**	**160,649**	**55,602**	**47,243**	**48,326**	**62,836**	**73,600**	**91,351**	**120,622**
DOTS World Total 001	**59,003**	**60,354**	**73,667**	**97,672**	**118,469**	**138,365**	**157,094**	**55,852**	**47,232**	**48,456**	**62,867**	**73,571**	**91,976**	**120,608**
Industrial Countries 101	**33,399**	**34,518**	**39,402**	**49,085**	**55,602**	**62,725**	**73,806**	**33,668**	**27,993**	**27,249**	**32,566**	**37,078**	**41,854**	**54,642**
United States 111	14,379	15,535	16,901	20,342	22,742	24,680	25,343	13,038	10,438	9,727	11,519	12,852	14,856	18,901
Canada 156	555	782	978	1,199	1,944	2,275	2,362	927	740	749	866	1,020	1,193	1,708
Australia 193	247	254	305	368	462	509	614	265	213	293	374	628	738	776
Japan 158	1,986	2,098	2,311	2,768	3,476	3,884	4,321	3,064	2,347	2,521	2,868	3,407	3,839	4,610
New Zealand 196	23	30	36	51	54	57	72	35	34	23	28	30	28	29
Austria 122	84	57	61	107	148	143	220	325	265	271	330	386	467	794
Belgium 124	—	—	—	—	—	2,994	3,886	210	—	—	—	—	957	1,142
Belgium-Luxembourg n.s. 127	2,434	1,892	1,795	1,931	2,196	—	—	585	535	515	640	760	—	—
Cyprus 423	12	11	12	57	106	172	222	1	1	1	8	4	44	—
Denmark 128	122	76	107	128	151	219	279	188	157	185	188	237	268	357
Finland 172	118	114	157	237	362	458	525	378	376	268	400	322	482	843
France 132	1,665	1,525	1,752	2,235	2,561	2,741	3,472	2,083	1,747	1,768	2,288	2,703	2,843	3,531
Germany 134	2,502	2,537	3,136	4,036	5,023	5,675	7,211	4,812	4,398	4,205	5,072	6,144	6,503	8,675
Greece 174	155	147	137	193	173	247	370	19	27	24	49	26	60	41
Iceland 176	3	1	9	9	4	2	—	2	4	3	4	2	4	5
Ireland 178	323	114	165	188	232	353	347	245	204	224	267	288	322	424
Italy 136	1,809	1,817	2,208	2,904	3,224	3,829	4,464	2,185	1,762	1,757	2,053	2,280	2,572	3,347
Luxembourg 137	—	—	—	—	—	21	—	—	—	—	—	—	43	48
Malta 181	6	5	18	48	26	14	—	25	22	26	16	18	30	34
Netherlands 138	2,863	3,182	4,246	5,917	5,283	5,744	8,841	533	537	509	618	586	786	1,116
Norway 142	213	171	280	321	444	584	651	227	214	265	341	294	349	528
Portugal 182	506	582	628	962	1,015	1,461	1,805	196	169	144	191	228	313	341
Slovenia 961	58	68	87	132	129	174	232	48	12	14	19	21	28	38
Spain 184	1,042	1,120	1,552	1,984	2,173	2,324	3,476	1,226	975	974	1,175	1,332	1,431	1,843
Sweden 144	175	183	297	503	547	495	634	812	575	641	819	912	951	1,349
Switzerland 146	413	447	327	348	534	846	1,156	1,004	898	941	1,078	1,219	1,331	2,205
United Kingdom 112	1,705	1,772	1,899	2,117	2,591	2,822	3,301	1,235	1,341	1,202	1,355	1,376	1,417	1,955
Developing Countries 202	**24,230**	**24,724**	**32,998**	**46,987**	**60,495**	**72,750**	**82,841**	**21,961**	**19,097**	**21,000**	**30,065**	**36,299**	**49,920**	**65,657**
Africa 607	**1,528**	**1,944**	**2,342**	**3,501**	**4,885**	**5,934**	**6,866**	**3,271**	**2,660**	**3,193**	**6,083**	**6,601**	**7,889**	**10,279**
Algeria 612	45	87	154	349	384	471	501	1,096	1,014	1,114	1,935	2,838	1,976	2,234
Angola 614	142	199	235	357	520	836	1,218	175	12	8	4	—	464	945
Benin 638	9	9	14	19	32	39	41	12	1	—	1	—	6	5
Botswana 616	1	2	1	2	2	4	—	—	—	—	—	—	—	—
Burkina Faso 748	1	2	5	7	19	5	—	3	—	1	—	—	—	5
Cameroon 622	13	13	20	29	88	104	121	—	1	1	2	1	2	11
Cape Verde 624	5	5	9	17	24	28	36	—	—	—	—	—	—	—
Central African Rep. 626	—	—	1	—	2	4	—	—	—	—	—	—	—	—
Chad 628	—	—	—	—	1	1	—	—	—	—	—	—	—	—
Comoros 632	—	—	2	1	2	2	—	—	—	—	—	—	—	—
Congo, Dem. Rep. of 636	4	2	9	13	17	20	—	—	—	—	1	—	195	175
Congo, Republic of 634	4	6	13	22	36	34	84	73	51	64	1	66	291	136
Côte d'Ivoire 662	33	36	26	41	44	72	60	19	25	41	15	18	35	63
Djibouti 611	2	4	8	10	4	8	—	—	—	—	—	—	—	—
Equatorial Guinea 642	—	3	3	4	7	11	34	10	4	—	14	285	93	—
Eritrea 643	—	—	—	—	9	7	—	—	—	—	—	—	—	—
Ethiopia 644	14	13	8	23	35	55	37	—	—	—	—	—	—	—
Gabon 646	6	3	8	15	27	27	41	62	54	—	—	—	—	—
Gambia, The 648	27	22	27	31	32	42	63	—	—	—	—	—	—	—
Ghana 652	24	57	105	169	219	223	321	1	27	2	—	1	2	3
Guinea 656	3	14	13	15	20	30	32	3	—	—	—	—	—	—
Guinea-Bissau 654	—	—	—	—	1	4	—	—	—	—	—	—	—	209
Kenya 664	10	14	15	20	76	48	59	1	—	—	—	—	1	3
Lesotho 666	—	—	—	—	1	—	—	—	—	—	—	—	—	—
Liberia 668	2	1	2	28	9	11	—	—	—	—	—	—	—	—
Madagascar 674	7	3	7	13	13	7	—	—	—	—	—	—	—	—
Malawi 676	—	1	3	4	1	1	—	2	—	3	3	4	2	5
Mali 678	2	9	7	5	14	13	—	9	1	—	—	—	5	11
Mauritania 682	5	24	19	40	44	73	97	—	—	—	—	—	—	—
Mauritius 684	4	5	4	15	8	6	—	—	3	4	2	—	4	—
Morocco 686	189	235	226	349	414	391	438	97	146	202	241	311	331	532
Mozambique 688	3	28	11	23	28	35	—	1	1	4	—	—	—	—
Namibia 728	2	4	10	11	13	13	—	—	—	—	—	—	—	—
Niger 692	—	—	1	3	1	2	—	1	—	—	—	—	—	—
Nigeria 694	417	508	470	505	953	1,373	1,512	1,372	1,091	1,493	3,499	2,652	3,943	5,273
Rwanda 714	—	—	1	—	—	1	—	—	—	—	—	—	—	—
São Tomé & Príncipe 716	—	—	—	—	1	1	—	—	—	—	—	—	—	—
Senegal 722	19	29	56	74	129	74	159	2	1	—	1	—	—	—
Seychelles 718	1	—	—	—	—	—	—	—	—	—	—	—	—	—
Sierra Leone 724	3	3	5	7	9	35	—	—	—	—	—	—	—	—

		Exports							Imports, f.o.b						
		2001	2002	2003	2004	2005	2006	2007	2001	2002	2003	2004	2005	2006	2007
		Millions of U.S. Dollars							*Millions of U.S. Dollars*						
Somalia	726	31	28	22	44	45	62	—	—	—	—	—	—	—	—
South Africa	199	424	478	733	1,036	1,369	1,459	1,758	286	182	202	268	342	435	522
Sudan	732	8	15	8	49	69	80	47	—	—	—	—	—	—	—
Swaziland	734	—	—	—	—	—	—	—	—	—	—	—	—	1	—
Tanzania	738	6	3	5	8	14	19	—	—	—	—	—	—	—	—
Togo	742	1	3	7	15	27	31	38	3	1	4	7	9	5	11
Tunisia	744	54	67	56	113	109	158	169	34	38	42	74	58	83	121
Uganda	746	1	2	2	4	4	2	—	—	—	—	—	—	1	—
Zambia	754	1	1	6	8	8	7	—	—	—	1	8	2	3	8
Zimbabwe	698	3	2	4	3	2	3	—	6	7	5	5	12	8	6
Africa n.s.	799	—	—	—	—	6	7	—	—	—	—	—	—	—	—
Asia	**507**	**4,759**	**6,605**	**9,300**	**11,640**	**15,022**	**16,895**	**20,615**	**5,799**	**5,576**	**6,337**	**9,341**	**13,395**	**18,956**	**26,989**
Afghanistan, I.S. of	512	—	—	—	—	1	3	—	1	1	—	—	—	—	—
American Samoa	859	—	—	—	—	—	1	—	—	—	—	—	—	—	—
Bangladesh	513	67	45	85	202	150	275	231	17	11	12	11	7	12	25
Brunei Darussalam	516	—	—	—	—	1	1	—	—	—	—	—	—	16	—
Cambodia	522	—	1	1	1	1	2	—	—	—	—	1	1	1	4
China,P.R.: Mainland	924	1,902	2,520	4,533	5,440	6,834	8,400	10,749	1,328	1,554	2,148	3,710	5,353	7,989	12,618
China,P.R.:Hong Kong	532	469	527	694	768	888	1,030	1,336	348	295	250	337	386	664	599
China,P.R.:Macao	546	—	—	—	—	—	1	—	2	3	7	9	9	6	9
Fiji	819	—	1	1	2	1	1	—	—	—	—	—	—	—	—
French Polynesia	887	—	4	1	2	2	2	—	—	—	—	—	—	—	—
Guam	829	—	—	1	1	1	1	—	—	—	—	—	—	—	—
India	534	285	654	553	652	1,137	937	958	543	573	486	556	1,203	1,474	2,165
Indonesia	536	210	257	323	383	498	496	693	231	318	319	370	456	650	894
Korea	542	736	852	1,223	1,429	1,896	1,962	2,047	1,574	1,067	1,079	1,730	2,327	3,106	3,391
Malaysia	548	167	282	225	283	406	647	680	347	357	444	515	637	901	2,275
Maldives	556	1	1	1	2	2	3	—	—	—	—	—	—	—	—
Mongolia	948	—	—	—	1	2	2	—	—	—	—	—	—	—	—
Myanmar	518	1	1	5	3	2	3	—	—	—	—	—	—	1	—
Nepal	558	—	—	—	—	1	1	—	—	—	—	—	—	—	—
New Caledonia	839	—	1	3	6	6	5	—	—	—	—	—	—	—	—
Pakistan	564	67	27	46	98	290	194	148	7	6	4	7	11	30	50
Papua New Guinea	853	1	1	1	2	2	18	—	—	—	—	—	—	—	—
Philippines	566	83	127	117	243	244	272	394	121	186	241	209	283	343	336
Samoa	862	2	1	1	1	1	1	—	—	—	—	—	3	—	—
Singapore	576	213	469	338	571	844	943	1,379	310	312	415	425	815	1,188	1,209
Solomon Islands	813	—	—	—	—	—	1	—	—	—	—	—	—	—	—
Sri Lanka	524	19	25	18	32	38	76	—	4	2	3	6	11	12	17
Taiwan Province of China	528	312	430	689	832	826	759	816	735	687	646	981	1,323	1,749	2,285
Thailand	578	208	350	416	648	887	731	968	212	187	261	440	522	737	1,005
Vietnam	582	11	28	25	38	62	129	216	18	15	22	32	48	76	107
Europe	**170**	**1,918**	**2,008**	**2,690**	**3,656**	**5,162**	**5,964**	**6,147**	**1,209**	**984**	**1,238**	**1,841**	**1,808**	**2,333**	**3,843**
Albania	914	2	5	8	20	32	26	45	—	—	—	1	2	2	—
Armenia	911	2	2	8	10	9	16	—	—	—	—	—	—	—	—
Azerbaijan	912	3	3	6	13	16	23	36	1	—	—	—	—	78	643
Belarus	913	—	2	7	9	5	13	—	52	67	91	225	203	221	—
Bosnia & Herzegovina	963	2	2	7	6	6	14	—	—	—	—	—	—	—	—
Bulgaria	918	65	57	86	160	201	269	199	10	18	24	61	74	44	47
Croatia	960	41	29	57	70	88	97	138	5	1	14	1	3	11	7
Czech Republic	935	40	35	66	80	57	48	60	52	55	65	110	216	237	275
Estonia	939	3	6	11	33	51	51	39	4	—	8	15	21	17	13
Faroe Islands	816	—	—	—	16	—	—	—	1	—	—	—	—	—	—
Georgia	915	13	24	54	80	85	46	71	1	—	—	7	1	6	17
Gibraltar	823	—	—	—	1	1	10	—	2	1	1	1	—	—	—
Hungary	944	75	48	49	61	153	78	82	99	83	101	133	114	115	133
Kazakhstan	916	2	5	7	13	32	42	41	3	39	3	5	9	37	11
Kyrgyz Republic	917	—	—	—	1	2	1	—	—	—	—	—	—	—	—
Latvia	941	2	2	4	5	12	44	—	239	58	3	16	—	—	—
Lithuania	946	9	11	12	24	45	41	70	1	3	2	1	5	2	—
Macedonia, FYR	962	5	8	5	16	12	25	33	—	—	—	—	1	2	—
Moldova	921	2	1	1	8	28	52	35	—	—	—	—	—	1	3
Montenegro, Rep. of	943	—	—	—	—	—	3	—	....	....	....	....	....	....	....
Poland	964	168	100	77	285	272	299	272	105	99	120	139	134	212	268
Romania	968	172	134	246	314	301	341	317	11	7	7	10	16	31	49
Russia	922	1,103	1,252	1,500	1,658	2,917	3,443	3,741	464	428	555	808	722	943	1,709
Serbia, Rep. of	942	—	—	—	—	—	62	—	....	....	....	....	....	....	....
Serbia & Montenegro	965	3	9	12	27	23	22	—	—	—	—	1	1	1	5
Slovak Republic	936	4	6	23	38	21	20	—	8	11	13	22	32	38	75
Tajikistan	923	—	—	—	—	1	3	—	—	—	—	—	—	—	—
Turkey	186	166	205	337	453	559	639	693	88	63	58	76	108	160	210
Turkmenistan	925	—	—	7	8	4	9	—	1	1	8	2	3	—	—
Ukraine	926	34	62	93	183	220	220	274	59	49	163	206	143	151	378
Uzbekistan	927	—	—	3	10	8	5	—	4	—	—	—	1	1	—
Europe n.s.	884	—	—	—	52	1	—	—	—	—	—	—	—	—	—
Middle East	**407**	**2,489**	**2,747**	**3,320**	**4,427**	**5,367**	**7,312**	**7,876**	**1,526**	**1,505**	**1,679**	**2,394**	**2,575**	**3,600**	**3,256**
Bahrain	419	51	68	71	103	138	137	114	—	—	—	—	—	33	—
Egypt	469	425	386	462	623	868	1,349	1,238	47	25	35	33	31	38	53
Iran, I.R. of	429	442	492	869	1,133	968	1,568	1,838	3	9	14	3	3	31	11

	Exports							Imports, f.o.b						
	2001	2002	2003	2004	2005	2006	2007	2001	2002	2003	2004	2005	2006	2007
	Millions of U.S. Dollars							*Millions of U.S. Dollars*						
Iraq.......... 433	6	71	42	62	50	158	90	26	329	280	473	523	597	272
Israel.......... 436	138	110	187	213	262	272	356	414	335	318	494	468	474	676
Jordan.......... 439	40	27	37	63	105	113	284	4	1	1	—	2	6	8
Kuwait.......... 443	65	59	74	128	192	167	231	55	28	74	22	33	1	114
Lebanon.......... 446	46	46	55	90	124	178	226	1	5	7	10	6	7	15
Libya.......... 672	35	30	53	116	213	204	239	8	2	26	57	34	401	—
Oman.......... 449	28	31	44	42	54	60	93	—	—	—	—	—	1	5
Qatar.......... 453	32	27	31	42	116	87	135	—	—	7	—	3	8	64
Saudi Arabia.......... 456	570	558	673	826	1,203	1,485	1,478	816	677	888	1,232	1,340	1,617	1,709
Syrian Arab Republic.......... 463	65	88	67	161	166	204	196	12	4	11	5	55	41	10
United Arab Emirates.......... 466	440	653	551	707	728	1,045	1,197	104	91	19	64	77	347	320
Yemen, Republic of.......... 474	105	103	105	118	180	284	162	36	—	—	—	—	—	—
Western Hemisphere.......... 207	**13,536**	**11,421**	**15,346**	**23,764**	**30,059**	**36,644**	**41,337**	**10,157**	**8,371**	**8,552**	**10,407**	**11,918**	**17,141**	**21,290**
Antigua and Barbuda.......... 311	1	1	1	2	4	6	—	—	—	1	—	—	—	—
Argentina.......... 213	5,002	2,342	4,561	7,373	9,915	11,714	14,417	6,207	4,747	4,673	5,572	6,239	8,057	10,410
Aruba.......... 314	4	5	34	179	356	232	75	27	30	35	101	117	183	273
Bahamas, The.......... 313	11	102	391	488	1,488	1,456	300	3	4	—	2	6	2	—
Barbados.......... 316	8	9	12	14	13	24	—	6	7	3	38	7	19	32
Belize.......... 339	3	3	3	2	3	4	—	—	1	—	—	—	—	—
Bermuda.......... 319	1	1	1	3	1	48	—	—	1	—	—	4	70	19
Bolivia.......... 218	333	421	360	535	580	694	851	256	396	520	714	990	1,448	1,601
Chile.......... 228	1,352	1,461	1,880	2,546	3,612	3,896	4,264	862	654	798	1,390	1,700	2,908	3,483
Colombia.......... 233	606	637	749	1,038	1,406	2,143	2,339	188	108	99	147	138	248	427
Costa Rica.......... 238	100	161	211	356	413	428	482	37	33	49	77	92	118	155
Dominica.......... 321	1	1	1	3	2	2	—	—	—	—	1	—	—	—
Dominican Republic.......... 243	132	209	226	268	332	364	459	2	2	2	2	3	4	13
Ecuador.......... 248	211	388	355	493	646	873	662	18	15	19	83	92	30	30
El Salvador.......... 253	52	75	87	137	237	214	176	—	—	—	—	1	3	4
Grenada.......... 328	2	2	2	3	5	5	—	—	—	—	—	—	—	—
Guatemala.......... 258	83	113	164	253	333	319	256	1	—	—	1	2	6	12
Guyana.......... 336	6	9	10	14	17	20	—	—	—	—	—	—	1	—
Haiti.......... 263	23	24	32	25	46	66	77	—	—	—	—	—	—	—
Honduras.......... 268	35	48	72	90	139	141	131	—	—	—	1	2	2	5
Jamaica.......... 343	60	68	84	116	156	181	247	—	—	—	—	8	2	4
Mexico.......... 273	1,868	2,342	2,741	3,948	4,064	4,440	4,260	695	580	533	704	844	1,310	1,979
Netherlands Antilles.......... 353	221	34	40	77	81	297	830	24	8	9	8	7	3	8
Nicaragua.......... 278	13	20	25	45	49	60	55	—	—	—	—	—	—	—
Panama.......... 283	105	126	183	214	277	310	386	24	12	7	24	14	13	17
Paraguay.......... 288	720	558	707	872	961	1,231	1,648	300	383	475	298	319	296	434
Peru.......... 293	286	436	488	631	933	1,501	1,649	231	217	234	349	458	815	996
St. Kitts and Nevis.......... 361	—	—	—	1	1	2	—	—	—	—	—	—	—	—
St. Lucia.......... 362	176	244	2	2	3	4	1,035	—	—	—	10	—	—	—
St. Vincent & Grens.......... 364	1	1	1	2	2	3	—	—	—	—	6	—	—	—
Suriname.......... 366	9	11	16	28	36	31	37	—	—	—	1	—	30	19
Trinidad and Tobago.......... 369	97	145	223	538	691	634	690	13	25	45	49	95	108	113
Uruguay.......... 298	641	410	404	667	850	1,006	1,288	503	485	538	523	494	618	786
Venezuela, Rep. Bol.......... 299	1,092	797	606	1,465	2,216	3,555	4,724	748	627	276	200	256	592	346
Western Hem. n.s.......... 399	278	218	673	1,337	192	743	—	10	35	237	106	31	255	125
Other Countries n.i.e.......... 910	**320**	**173**	**143**	**302**	**312**	**408**	**447**	**73**	**87**	**88**	**115**	**110**	**124**	**198**
Cuba.......... 928	112	74	70	132	246	343	324	11	14	22	45	39	32	89
North Korea.......... 954	208	99	74	170	66	64	123	62	73	66	70	72	92	109
Countries & Areas n.s.......... 898	—	—	—	—	—	—	—	**37**	**55**	**119**	**121**	**84**	**77**	**111**
Special Categories.......... 899	**1,030**	**925**	**1,123**	**1,297**	**2,059**	**2,482**	—	**90**	—	—	—	—	—	—
Memorandum Items														
European Union.......... 998	15,881	15,408	18,498	24,205	26,551	30,468	39,810	15,613	13,414	13,041	15,924	18,146	20,139	26,643
Oil Exporting Ctys.......... 999	3,382	3,567	3,888	5,756	7,577	10,670	12,732	4,459	4,185	4,509	7,855	8,215	10,163	11,241
Non-Oil Develop.Ctys.......... 201	20,848	21,157	29,110	41,231	52,918	62,080	70,110	17,502	14,911	16,490	22,210	28,083	39,757	54,416
PERCENT DISTRIBUTION														
Industrial Countries.......... 101	**56.6**	**57.2**	**53.5**	**50.3**	**46.9**	**45.3**	**47.0**	**60.3**	**59.3**	**56.2**	**51.8**	**50.4**	**45.5**	**45.3**
Developing Countries.......... 202	**41.1**	**41.0**	**44.8**	**48.1**	**51.1**	**52.6**	**52.7**	**39.3**	**40.4**	**43.3**	**47.8**	**49.3**	**54.3**	**54.4**
Africa.......... 607	**2.6**	**3.2**	**3.2**	**3.6**	**4.1**	**4.3**	**4.4**	**5.9**	**5.6**	**6.6**	**9.7**	**9.0**	**8.6**	**8.5**
Asia.......... 507	**8.1**	**10.9**	**12.6**	**11.9**	**12.7**	**12.2**	**13.1**	**10.4**	**11.8**	**13.1**	**14.9**	**18.2**	**20.6**	**22.4**
Europe.......... 170	**3.3**	**3.3**	**3.7**	**3.7**	**4.4**	**4.3**	**3.9**	**2.2**	**2.1**	**2.6**	**2.9**	**2.5**	**2.5**	**3.2**
Middle East.......... 407	**4.2**	**4.6**	**4.5**	**4.5**	**4.5**	**5.3**	**5.0**	**2.7**	**3.2**	**3.5**	**3.8**	**3.5**	**3.9**	**2.7**
Western Hemisphere.......... 207	**22.9**	**18.9**	**20.8**	**24.3**	**25.4**	**26.5**	**26.3**	**18.2**	**17.7**	**17.6**	**16.6**	**16.2**	**18.6**	**17.7**
Other Countries n.i.e.......... 910	**.5**	**.3**	**.2**	**.3**	**.3**	**.3**	**.3**	**.1**	**.2**	**.2**	**.2**	**.2**	**.1**	**.2**
ANNUAL PERCENT CHANGE														
World.......... 001	**–1.1**	**2.3**	**22.1**	**32.6**	**21.3**	**16.8**	**13.5**	**–.7**	**–15.4**	**2.6**	**29.7**	**17.0**	**25.0**	**31.1**
Industrial Countries.......... 101	**1.7**	**3.4**	**14.1**	**24.6**	**13.3**	**12.8**	**17.7**	**2.6**	**–16.9**	**–2.7**	**19.5**	**13.9**	**12.9**	**30.6**
Developing Countries.......... 202	**–5.5**	**2.0**	**33.5**	**42.4**	**28.7**	**20.3**	**13.9**	**–5.1**	**–13.0**	**10.0**	**43.2**	**20.7**	**37.5**	**31.5**
Africa.......... 607	**43.9**	**27.2**	**20.5**	**49.5**	**39.5**	**21.5**	**15.7**	**14.1**	**–18.7**	**20.0**	**90.5**	**8.5**	**19.5**	**30.3**
Asia.......... 507	**22.5**	**38.8**	**40.8**	**25.2**	**29.1**	**12.5**	**22.0**	**2.3**	**–3.8**	**13.7**	**47.4**	**43.4**	**41.5**	**42.4**
Europe.......... 170	**49.5**	**4.7**	**34.0**	**35.9**	**41.2**	**15.5**	**3.1**	**–.1**	**–18.6**	**25.8**	**48.7**	**–1.7**	**29.0**	**64.7**
Middle East.......... 407	**44.1**	**10.3**	**20.9**	**33.3**	**21.2**	**36.2**	**7.7**	**–4.8**	**–1.4**	**11.6**	**42.5**	**7.6**	**39.8**	**–9.6**
Western Hemisphere.......... 207	**–23.5**	**–15.6**	**34.4**	**54.9**	**26.5**	**21.9**	**12.8**	**–14.0**	**–17.6**	**2.2**	**21.7**	**14.5**	**43.8**	**24.2**
Other Countries n.i.e.......... 910	**57.1**	**–45.9**	**–17.4**	**111.0**	**3.2**	**30.8**	**9.6**	**–52.4**	**19.7**	**.6**	**30.8**	**–4.1**	**11.9**	**60.3**

		Exports							Imports						
		2001	2002	2003	2004	2005	2006	2007	2001	2002	2003	2004	2005	2006	2007
		Millions of U.S. Dollars							Millions of U.S. Dollars						
DOTS World Total	**001**	**3,336.4Y**	**3,439.8Y**	**4,422.2**	**4,510.2Y**	**5,633.3Y**	**6,906.6Y**	**6,944.0Y**	**1,314.9Y**	**1,630.1Y**	**1,340.9**	**1,639.7Y**	**1,669.5Y**	**1,989.8Y**	**3,933.4Y**
Industrial Countries	**101**	**2,209.6Y**	**2,113.1Y**	**2,644.9**	**2,868.0Y**	**3,261.7Y**	**3,707.5Y**	**3,813.5Y**	**373.0Y**	**617.0Y**	**494.6**	**470.1Y**	**364.9Y**	**579.9Y**	**2,277.1Y**
United States	111	385.45V	278.36V	342.73	389.91V	536.00V	522.73V	382.91V	114.29V	51.15V	152.70	54.23V	54.67V	52.91V	153.67V
Canada	156	2.24V	3.94V	2.68	2.72V	2.76V	1.67V	1.97V	.77V	1.22V	3.19	3.84V	2.88V	16.93V	3.19V
Australia	193	218.75V	313.79V	369.59	504.68V	523.98V	775.35V	927.28V	25.83V	30.92V	56.74	32.29V	24.92V	22.83V	28.51V
Japan	158	1,541.51V	1,377.17V	1,811.45	1,720.18V	2,074.49V	2,066.72V	2,275.82V	61.06V	351.21V	132.71	118.65V	115.23V	111.30V	135.76V
New Zealand	196	11.27V	72.26V	103.23	133.15V	67.49V	199.37V	128.85V	1.45V	1.69V	2.07	2.62V	2.52V	73.65V	2.43V
Austria	122	.02V	.01V	.03	.01V	.02V	—V	.04V	.83V	1.64V	.42	2.55V	.76V	4.87V	1.71V
Belgium	124	—V	—V	.06	.12V	.10V	.26V	.05V	—V	—V	5.00	5.39V	3.25V	3.95V	14.81V
Cyprus	423	.08V	—V	—	.05V	.06Y	—V	—V	—V	—V	—	.05V	.08V	.06V	.15V
Denmark	128	.04V	—V	.05	—V	—V	.08V	.14V	.48V	.84V	.62	.57V	.76V	.71V	1.42V
Finland	172	.01V	.01V	—	—V	.04V	—V	—V	.41V	.29V	.54	.46V	.23V	.31V	.40V
France	132	.22V	.24V	.35	1.00V	.76V	.67V	2.25V	8.36V	12.27V	22.17	11.25V	6.98V	20.78V	9.86V
Germany	134	3.55V	1.43V	4.22	1.49V	1.71V	.36V	2.93V	24.30V	37.78V	42.81	62.86V	30.08V	37.50V	40.72V
Greece	174	—V	—V	—	—V	.03V	—V	—V	.01V	—V	.01	.02V	.06V	.03V	.13V
Iceland	176	....	....	....	....	....	....	....	—V	—V	.02	—V	—V	.07V	—V
Ireland	178	—V	—V	—	—V	.09V	—V	.01V	7.69V	1.03V	1.60	1.06V	.72V	.25V	3.09V
Italy	136	.51V	.16V	.08	.58V	.16V	.18V	.07V	15.12V	8.30V	9.23	12.82V	11.68V	35.46V	11.01V
Luxembourg	137	.10V	.04V	—	—V	.07V	.07V	.01V	.06V	.96V	—	—V	.12V	.19V	.54V
Netherlands	138	.49V	.31V	.89	2.12V	.65V	.10V	.13V	10.63V	8.46V	6.28	13.51V	10.73V	10.74V	15.62V
Norway	142	—V	—V	.16	—V	.08V	.01V	.03V	.10V	1.19V	1.37	.83V	2.00V	2.21V	3.68V
Portugal	182	—V	—V	—	—V	—V	—V	—V	.05V	.05V	.01	.03V	.18V	—V	3.11V
Slovenia	961	—V	—V	—	.03Y	—V	—V	.01V	—V	—V	—	—Y	—V	.05V	.05V
Spain	184	.04V	12.59V	.05	.01V	1.26V	.03V	.01V	1.01V	2.30V	3.62	6.60V	5.97V	3.27V	.93V
Sweden	144	.14V	.04V	.05	.06V	.04V	.07V	—V	2.32V	2.42V	1.80	1.37V	1.46V	5.90V	2.19V
Switzerland	146	.04V	3.77V	.32	.01V	5.36V	12.40V	10.56V	3.16V	3.07V	2.93	2.87V	1.66V	14.54V	17.63V
United Kingdom	112	45.12V	48.98V	8.97	111.88V	46.53V	127.46V	80.48V	95.08V	100.26V	48.76	136.21V	87.96V	161.39V	1,826.53V
Developing Countries	**202**	**1,126.8Y**	**1,326.7Y**	**1,777.2**	**1,642.1Y**	**2,371.5Y**	**3,198.9Y**	**3,130.3Y**	**939.3Y**	**1,010.2Y**	**844.1**	**1,166.7Y**	**1,301.3Y**	**1,405.8Y**	**1,651.2Y**
Africa	**607**	**15.0Y**	**17.1Y**	**.8**	**25.7Y**	**30.3Y**	**34.5Y**	**39.1Y**	**1.3Y**	**.6Y**	**.7**	**3.2Y**	**5.5Y**	**2.5Y**	**2.5Y**
Algeria	612	—V	—V	—	—Y	—Y	—Y	—Y	—V	—V	.02	.02Y	.03Y	.04Y	.04Y
Benin	638	—V	—V	—	—V	.02V	.03Y	.04Y	....	....	....	....	....	....	....
Botswana	616	....	....	....	....	....	....	....	.02Y	.02Y	—	—Y	—Y	—Y	—Y
Congo, Dem. Rep. of	636	—Y	—Y	—	—Y	—Y	—Y	—Y	—Y	—Y	.08	.11Y	.12Y	.15Y	.19Y
Congo, Republic of	634	—V	—V	—	—V	—Y	—Y	—Y	—V	—V	.09	—V	—Y	—Y	—Y
Ghana	652	—Y	—Y	.04	.05Y	.05Y	.07Y	.08Y	—Y	—Y	—	—Y	—Y	—Y	—Y
Kenya	664	—V	—V	—	—V	—Y	—Y	—Y	—V	—V	—	.01V	.01Y	.01Y	.01Y
Malawi	676	....	....	....	....	....	....	....	.02Y	.02Y	—	—Y	—Y	.01Y	.01Y
Mauritius	684	.12V	—V	.09	.01V	.14V	—V	.02V	.05V	.05V	—	—V	.04V	.13V	.05V
Morocco	686	—V	.07V	—	—V	.02V	.02Y	.03Y	.01V	.03V	.03	.01V	—V	—Y	—Y
Nigeria	694	2.29V	.52V	.66	.86Y	1.09Y	1.35Y	1.75Y	—V	—V	—	—Y	—Y	—Y	—Y
Senegal	722	—V	.01V	—	—V	—V	—V	—Y	—V	—V	—	1.01V	.08V	.01V	.01Y
South Africa	199	—V	—V	—	—V	—V	—V	—V	1.10V	.42V	.43	1.96V	5.11V	2.04V	2.03V
Swaziland	734	....	....	....	....	....	....	....	.05Y	.06Y	—	.01Y	.01Y	.01Y	.01Y
Tanzania	738	.12V	—V	—	—Y	—Y	—Y	—Y	—V	—V	.07	.10Y	.11Y	.14Y	.17Y
Tunisia	744	.07V	—V	—	.02V	—V	—V	—Y	.04V	—V	—	—V	—V	—V	—Y
Uganda	746	....	....	....	....	....	....	....	—V	.02V	—	—Y	—Y	—Y	—Y
Africa n.s.	799	12.41Y	16.54Y	—	24.80Y	28.93Y	33.06Y	37.19Y	—Y	—Y	—	—Y	—Y	—Y	—Y
Asia	**507**	**1,105.2Y**	**1,305.1Y**	**1,774.4**	**1,614.5Y**	**2,328.5Y**	**3,144.0Y**	**3,086.7Y**	**934.5Y**	**1,005.6Y**	**836.7**	**1,154.9Y**	**1,281.7Y**	**1,382.1Y**	**1,628.8Y**
Afghanistan, I.S. of	512	—Y	—Y	.01	.01Y	.01Y	.02Y	.02Y	.04Y	.05Y	.06	.08Y	.09Y	.11Y	.13Y
Bangladesh	513	.43V	—V	.01	—V	—V	—V	—V	.70V	1.02V	.08	.18V	.58V	.67Y	.77Y
Cambodia	522	.01V	—V	.12	—V	.29V	.02V	.03Y	.11V	—V	.15	—V	.09V	.11V	.13Y
China,P.R.: Mainland	924	134.76V	219.83V	294.78	203.12V	188.84V	195.74V	219.58V	18.94V	23.16V	64.58	50.16V	58.51V	109.60V	123.99V
China,P.R.:Hong Kong	532	.70V	.38V	2.42	2.36V	.49V	1.08V	1.10V	56.46V	63.74V	87.13	62.02V	35.15V	31.88V	32.64V
China,P.R.:Macao	546	—V	—V	—	.02V	.14V	—V	—V	—V	.02V	—	—V	—V	—V	—V
Fiji	819	.04Y	.04Y	—	—Y	—Y	—Y	—Y	—Y	—Y	—	—Y	—Y	—Y	—Y
India	534	.21Y	.30V	89.56	.44V	.72V	.89Y	1.11Y	4.17Y	4.46V	7.32	5.28V	36.78V	45.46Y	56.41Y
Indonesia	536	33.76V	31.55V	112.90	268.40V	1,088.63V	1,460.85V	1,695.20V	23.78V	35.31V	35.42	34.94V	43.27V	41.31V	47.70V
Korea	542	411.30V	420.11V	494.82	630.24V	715.35V	1,096.03V	849.96V	18.10V	29.43V	31.25	34.75V	67.53V	24.68V	29.27V
Malaysia	548	4.59V	3.35V	163.01	12.90V	11.78V	68.66V	87.05V	300.25V	282.53V	265.40	348.19V	388.59V	380.12V	442.66V
Myanmar	518	—Y	—Y	.02	.03Y	.03Y	.04Y	.05Y	.29Y	.32Y	.13	.17Y	.20Y	.24Y	.30Y
Nauru	836	.05Y	.06Y	—	—Y	—Y	—Y	—Y	—Y	—Y	—	—Y	—Y	—Y	—Y
Nepal	558	.36V	.27V	.31	1.00V	.36V	.07V	.09Y	—V	—V	—	—V	—V	.11V	.14Y
Pakistan	564	1.40V	.33V	.12	.19V	1.19V	1.47Y	1.82Y	.87V	2.76V	.40	.74V	2.00V	2.47Y	3.06Y
Papua New Guinea	853	.06Y	.06Y	—	—Y	—Y	—Y	—Y	.01Y	.01Y	—	—Y	—Y	—Y	—Y
Philippines	566	.20V	21.44V	.98	.28V	.84V	.07V	.17V	4.28V	3.15V	2.78	4.43V	10.34V	6.80V	6.44V
Singapore	576	164.89V	194.18V	197.67	140.72V	135.26V	199.66V	127.38V	451.19V	501.23V	267.05	537.01V	545.33V	631.67V	766.21V
Sri Lanka	524	—V	—V	.03	.04Y	.05Y	.06Y	.08Y	—V	—V	.21	.28Y	.32Y	.39Y	.49Y
Taiwan Province of China	528	.14V	.06V	.06	.18V	.03V	1.99V	.87V	12.63V	12.98V	19.92	14.58V	18.12V	15.11V	18.28V
Thailand	578	352.27V	413.09V	416.86	354.53V	184.48V	117.38V	102.14V	41.09V	43.88V	53.88	62.06V	74.75V	91.43V	100.16V
Vietnam	582	.01V	.06V	.75	—V	—V	—V	—V	1.63V	1.52V	.91	—V	—V	—V	—V
Europe	**170**	**.2Y**	**.1Y**	**.3**	**—Y**	**10.1Y**	**1.5Y**	**.2Y**	**.2Y**	**.2Y**	**.2**	**1.2Y**	**2.5Y**	**7.1Y**	**4.9Y**
Azerbaijan	912	—V	—V	—	—V	—V	—V	—V	.01V	—V	—	—V	—V	—V	—V
Czech Republic	935	.03V	.03V	—	—V	.64V	.47V	—V	.03V	.03V	.02	—V	—V	3.20V	.27V
Hungary	944	.12V	—V	—	.02V	4.10V	.67V	—V	—V	—V	.02	.01V	.11V	.12V	.46V

	Exports 2001	2002	2003	2004	2005	2006	2007	Imports 2001	2002	2003	2004	2005	2006	2007
	Millions of U.S. Dollars							Millions of U.S. Dollars						
Latvia.......... 941	—V	—V	—	—V	.06V	—V	—V	....	....	....	....	....	....	....
Poland.......... 964	.01V	.01V	—	.01V	—V	—V	.01V	.03V	.11V	.01	.02V	—V	.57V	.83V
Romania.......... 968	—V	—V	—	—V	—V	.02V	—V	.01V	—V	—	—V	—V	1.22V	—V
Russia.......... 922	—V	.02V	.25	—V	—V	.01V	—V	—V	—V	—	—V	—V	.02V	—V
Slovak Republic.......... 936	—V	—V	—	—Y	5.18V	.20V	—V	.06V	.01V	—	.01Y	1.74V	1.20V	2.34V
Turkey.......... 186	—V	—V	—	—V	.02V	.01V	.01V	.03V	.07V	.10	1.16V	.65V	.76V	1.05V
Ukraine.......... 926	—V	—V	—	—V	.10V	.13Y	.16Y	—V	—V	.01	—V	—V	—Y	—Y
Europe n.s.......... 884	—Y	.01Y	—	—Y	—Y	—Y	—Y	—Y	—Y	—	—Y	—Y	—Y	—Y
Middle East.......... 407	**6.0Y**	**4.0Y**	**1.6**	**1.8Y**	**2.5Y**	**3.1Y**	**3.9Y**	**3.1Y**	**3.4Y**	**5.2**	**6.8Y**	**9.3Y**	**11.8Y**	**14.0Y**
Bahrain.......... 419	3.46Y	3.75Y	.01	.01Y	.01Y	.02Y	.02Y	.04Y	.04Y	.01	.01Y	.01Y	.01Y	.02Y
Egypt.......... 469	.10V	.10Y	.03	.04Y	.04Y	.05Y	.07Y	.01V	.01Y	.11	.14Y	.16Y	.20Y	.25Y
Iran, I.R. of.......... 429	—V	—V	—	—Y	—Y	—Y	—Y	.68Y	.73Y	.56	.74Y	1.01Y	1.27Y	1.53Y
Iraq.......... 433	—Y	—Y	—	—Y	—Y	—Y	—Y	.01Y	.01Y	—	—Y	—Y	—Y	—Y
Israel.......... 436	—V	—V	—	—V	—V	—V	—V	—V	—V	.02	—V	—V	—V	—V
Jordan.......... 439	.01V	—V	—	—V	—V	.01V	—V	.02V	.01V	.01	.01V	.03V	.22V	.01V
Kuwait.......... 443	—Y	—Y	.02	.02Y	.02Y	.03Y	.04Y	—Y	—Y	—	—Y	—Y	—Y	—Y
Lebanon.......... 446	—Y	—Y	—	—Y	—Y	—Y	—Y	—Y	—Y	.01	.01Y	.01Y	.02Y	.02Y
Libya.......... 672	—Y	—Y	.01	.01Y	.01Y	.01Y	.02Y	—Y	—Y	—	—Y	—Y	—Y	—Y
Oman.......... 449	1.95V	.03V	.25	.32Y	.41Y	.51Y	.66Y	.11V	.15V	.10	.14Y	.18Y	.23Y	.28Y
Qatar.......... 453	—V	.02V	.11	—V	—V	—V	—Y	—Y	—Y	.01	.01Y	.01Y	.01Y	.01Y
Saudi Arabia.......... 456	.45V	.02V	.03	.12V	.28V	.34Y	.45Y	.09Y	.09Y	1.39	1.83Y	2.49Y	3.14Y	3.78Y
Syrian Arab Republic.......... 463	.04Y	.04Y	.09	—V	—Y	—Y	—Y	.16Y	.17Y	.03	—V	—Y	—Y	—Y
United Arab Emirates.......... 466	—V	—V	1.02	1.32Y	1.68Y	2.08Y	2.69Y	2.03Y	2.15Y	2.96	3.91Y	5.32Y	6.69Y	8.07Y
Yemen, Republic of.......... 474	....	....	....	....	....	....	....	—V	—V	—	—V	.02V	.02Y	.02Y
Western Hemisphere.......... 207	**.5Y**	**.4Y**	**.2**	**—Y**	**.2Y**	**15.8Y**	**.4Y**	**.2Y**	**.5Y**	**1.3**	**.6Y**	**2.3Y**	**2.2Y**	**.9Y**
Argentina.......... 213	—V	—V	—	—V	—V	—V	—V	.12V	.05V	.66	.17V	.39V	.50V	.21V
Belize.......... 339	—Y	—Y	—	—Y	—Y	—Y	—Y	—Y	—Y	.05	.07Y	.08Y	.10Y	.12Y
Bolivia.......... 218	—V	—V	—	.01V	—V	—Y	—Y	—V	—V	—	—V	—Y	—Y	—Y
Brazil.......... 223	.01V	—V	—	.01V	.03V	15.71V	—V	.06V	.42V	.21	.27V	.69V	1.14V	—V
Chile.......... 228	—V	—V	—	—V	—V	—V	—V	—V	—V	.11	—V	—V	—V	—V
Colombia.......... 233	.07V	—V	—	—V	.03V	.01V	—V	—V	—V	—	—V	—V	—V	—V
Dominican Republic.......... 243	.30V	.33Y	—	—Y	—Y	—Y	—Y	—V	—Y	—	—Y	.01Y	.01Y	.01Y
Ecuador.......... 248	.08V	—V	—	—V	.01V	—V	—Y	—V	—V	.06	—V	—V	—V	—Y
Honduras.......... 268	....	....	....	....	....	....	....	—Y	—Y	.02	.02Y	.02Y	.03Y	.04Y
Mexico.......... 273	—V	—V	.19	—V	.10V	.06V	.40V	—V	—V	.14	—V	1.13V	.39V	.53V
Netherlands Antilles.......... 353	—V	—V	—	—Y	—Y	—Y	.01Y	—V	—V	—	—Y	—Y	—Y	—Y
Panama.......... 283	—V	—V	—	—V	—V	—V	—V	—V	—V	.05	—V	—V	—V	—V
Paraguay.......... 288	—V	.03V	—	—V	—V	—V	—Y	—V	—V	—	—V	—V	—V	—Y
Peru.......... 293	.02V	—V	—	.02V	—V	—V	—Y	—V	—V	.03	.01V	—V	—V	—Y
Uruguay.......... 298	—V	—Y	—	—V	—V	—Y	—Y	—V	—Y	.01	—V	—V	—Y	—Y
Venezuela, Rep. Bol.......... 299	—V	.01V	.01	—V	—V	—V	—V	—V	—V	—	.04V	—V	—V	—Y
Western Hem. n.s.......... 399	.01Y	.02Y	—	—Y	—Y	—Y	—Y	—Y	—Y	—	—Y	—Y	—Y	—Y
Other Countries n.i.e.......... 910	**—Y**	**—Y**	**—**	**.1Y**	**.1Y**	**.1Y**	**.1Y**	**.2Y**	**.3Y**	**.1**	**.1Y**	**.1Y**	**.2Y**	**.2Y**
North Korea.......... 954	.01Y	.01Y	.04	.06Y	.06Y	.08Y	.10Y	.24Y	.26Y	.08	.11Y	.12Y	.15Y	.19Y
Countries & Areas n.s.......... 898	**—Y**	**—Y**	**—**	**—Y**	**—Y**	**—Y**	**.1Y**	**1.9Y**	**2.0Y**	**2.1**	**2.8Y**	**3.2Y**	**4.0Y**	**4.9Y**
Special Categories.......... 899	....	....	....	....	....	....	....	**.5Y**	**.5Y**	**—**	**—Y**	**—Y**	**—Y**	**—Y**
Memorandum Items														
European Union.......... 998	50.46Y	63.87Y	14.76	117.38Y	61.50Y	130.62Y	86.13Y	166.46Y	176.74Y	142.93	254.80Y	162.88Y	290.56Y	1,936.17Y
Oil Exporting Ctys.......... 999	38.45Y	32.15Y	115.00	271.05Y	1,092.14Y	1,465.17Y	1,700.80Y	26.69Y	38.46Y	40.45	41.63Y	52.31Y	52.69Y	61.43Y
Non-Oil Develop.Ctys.......... 201	1,088.40Y	1,294.53Y	1,662.24	1,371.07Y	1,279.39Y	1,733.74Y	1,429.51Y	912.63Y	971.79Y	803.63	1,125.05Y	1,248.96Y	1,353.06Y	1,589.76Y
PERCENT DISTRIBUTION														
Industrial Countries.......... 101	**66.2**	**61.4**	**59.8**	**63.6**	**57.9**	**53.7**	**54.9**	**28.4**	**37.9**	**36.9**	**28.7**	**21.9**	**29.1**	**57.9**
Developing Countries.......... 202	**33.8**	**38.6**	**40.2**	**36.4**	**42.1**	**46.3**	**45.1**	**71.4**	**62.0**	**62.9**	**71.2**	**77.9**	**70.6**	**42.0**
Africa.......... 607	**.5**	**.5**	**—**	**.6**	**.5**	**.5**	**.6**	**.1**	**—**	**.1**	**.2**	**.3**	**.1**	**.1**
Asia.......... 507	**33.1**	**37.9**	**40.1**	**35.8**	**41.3**	**45.5**	**44.5**	**71.1**	**61.7**	**62.4**	**70.4**	**76.8**	**69.5**	**41.4**
Europe.......... 170	**—**	**—**	**—**	**—**	**.2**	**—**	**—**	**—**	**—**	**—**	**.1**	**.2**	**.4**	**.1**
Middle East.......... 407	**.2**	**.1**	**—**	**—**	**—**	**—**	**.1**	**.2**	**.2**	**.4**	**.4**	**.6**	**.6**	**.4**
Western Hemisphere.......... 207	**—**	**—**	**—**	**—**	**—**	**.2**	**—**	**—**	**—**	**.1**	**—**	**.1**	**.1**	**—**
ANNUAL PERCENT CHANGE														
World.......... 001	**5.5**	**3.1**	**28.6**	**2.0**	**24.9**	**22.6**	**.5**	**−7.9**	**24.0**	**−17.7**	**22.3**	**1.8**	**19.2**	**97.7**
Industrial Countries.......... 101	**13.5**	**−4.4**	**25.2**	**8.4**	**13.7**	**13.7**	**2.9**	**−22.4**	**65.4**	**−19.8**	**−5.0**	**−22.4**	**58.9**	**292.7**
Developing Countries.......... 202	**−7.3**	**17.7**	**34.0**	**−7.6**	**44.4**	**34.9**	**−2.1**	**−.5**	**7.6**	**−16.4**	**38.2**	**11.5**	**8.0**	**17.5**
Africa.......... 607	**44.7**	**14.2**	**−95.4**	**—**	**17.6**	**14.1**	**13.2**	**−14.1**	**−52.1**	**18.6**	**339.0**	**71.5**	**−54.0**	**−.2**
Asia.......... 507	**−7.9**	**18.1**	**36.0**	**−9.0**	**44.2**	**35.0**	**−1.8**	**−.4**	**7.6**	**−16.8**	**38.0**	**11.0**	**7.8**	**17.8**
Europe.......... 170	**−58.0**	**−56.9**	**266.4**	**−86.9**	**—**	**−85.0**	**−88.2**	**−12.5**	**34.0**	**−24.1**	**608.8**	**109.3**	**182.8**	**−30.3**
Middle East.......... 407	**41.8**	**−33.7**	**−60.8**	**18.3**	**33.9**	**23.7**	**29.2**	**6.4**	**7.1**	**54.2**	**31.0**	**36.1**	**27.6**	**18.5**
Western Hemisphere.......... 207	**23.2**	**−23.7**	**−47.1**	**−80.9**	**346.3**	**—**	**−97.4**	**−88.0**	**155.2**	**181.2**	**−55.0**	**292.1**	**−7.0**	**−58.1**
Other Countries n.i.e.......... 910	**10.4**	**8.5**	**350.8**	**31.3**	**14.3**	**23.6**	**24.1**	**10.4**	**8.5**	**−68.2**	**31.3**	**14.3**	**23.6**	**24.1**

	Exports							Imports						
	2001	2002	2003	2004	2005	2006	2007	2001	2002	2003	2004	2005	2006	2007
	Millions of U.S. Dollars							Millions of U.S. Dollars						
IFS World Total	**5,115.2**	**5,748.9**	**7,540.2**	**9,931.3**	**11,739.4**	**15,101.5**	**18,575.1**	**7,263.0**	**7,987.0**	**10,901.5**	**14,467.4**	**18,162.5**	**23,269.6**	**30,086.4**
DOTS World Total 001	**5,062.1**	**5,630.9**	**7,376.2**	**9,859.8**	**11,734.5**	**15,142.9**	**18,476.5**	**7,182.3**	**7,830.5**	**10,681.3**	**14,392.9**	**18,194.6**	**19,559.6**	**30,102.1**
Industrial Countries 101	**3,233.7**	**3,633.3**	**4,710.8**	**6,054.8**	**6,828.8**	**8,456.3**	**10,158.4**	**4,005.0**	**4,424.4**	**6,023.3**	**7,873.1**	**9,142.2**	**10,923.2**	**14,731.3**
United States 111	282.56	268.41	331.39	442.98	353.62	428.40	428.19	190.61	171.34	272.83	325.65	465.81	467.71	325.03
Canada 156	19.08	24.13	25.81	36.76	55.83	54.43	75.71	22.22	25.14	18.60	37.74	62.99	76.35	32.46
Australia 193	3.62	5.01	7.23	11.47	12.36	11.57	13.57	6.74	27.51	70.06	72.19	72.78	55.23	37.06
Japan 158	12.86	10.83	14.30	13.86	17.08	26.51	36.14	76.57	88.07	135.89	188.85	218.97	311.18	118.61
New Zealand 196	.09	.12	.18	.59	.70	.46	1.17	.27	1.06	.52	.91	2.47	6.21	3.15
Austria 122	85.04	95.40	150.84	218.81	221.47	293.76	340.00	144.34	164.51	235.27	342.02	393.96	499.29	1,283.19
Belgium 124	—	—	—	—	697.95	991.04	1,141.32	—	—	—	—	225.16	263.23	535.30
Belgium-Luxembourg n.s. 127	254.93	277.88	455.16	595.39	—	—	—	110.60	113.87	150.38	213.83	—	—	—
Cyprus 423	26.52	28.28	25.70	38.81	112.38	111.14	68.62	7.90	2.97	3.01	4.41	29.11	20.21	72.09
Denmark 128	25.85	25.86	28.47	33.37	36.76	46.67	44.93	57.06	62.51	71.10	84.08	94.00	100.00	144.00
Finland 172	7.09	8.95	11.01	11.64	13.52	65.47	51.94	50.72	35.88	37.82	49.50	57.15	110.98	119.59
France 132	286.32	299.83	378.06	447.95	539.21	632.83	736.87	437.66	443.52	606.12	768.08	855.13	953.56	1,043.83
Germany 134	487.20	542.24	802.40	1,015.55	1,154.04	1,459.25	1,899.58	1,105.58	1,125.15	1,533.64	2,109.60	2,474.99	2,897.98	3,713.51
Greece 174	448.15	520.41	772.83	979.73	1,110.84	1,204.00	1,675.88	411.09	475.14	712.63	830.31	913.12	1,218.69	1,861.56
Iceland 176	.33	.09	.16	.30	.07	.21	1.47	.34	.44	.28	1.86	.84	1.44	2.60
Ireland 178	7.97	10.86	13.79	17.04	10.12	13.82	18.37	19.40	19.69	23.04	46.97	63.84	80.36	103.30
Italy 136	766.43	874.50	1,041.68	1,298.38	1,413.17	1,526.76	1,882.96	695.28	892.40	1,099.70	1,420.53	1,634.15	2,049.55	2,621.43
Luxembourg 137	—	—	—	—	2.87	8.51	5.70	—	—	—	—	6.54	9.30	32.31
Malta 181	11.21	8.64	6.93	21.60	67.69	101.29	50.11	.19	.25	3.42	.20	11.13	2.75	11.10
Netherlands 138	79.37	101.91	114.12	126.47	144.07	208.82	220.40	132.35	159.26	191.06	239.65	260.86	297.39	768.64
Norway 142	5.99	7.45	7.74	10.49	11.34	12.87	24.75	4.46	6.89	10.84	11.37	10.32	21.80	13.81
Portugal 182	18.94	15.17	14.29	15.33	25.56	64.01	28.06	21.41	23.11	29.97	38.96	37.85	36.22	24.97
Slovenia 961	19.41	24.43	28.74	29.52	52.49	113.08	289.69	36.89	44.36	65.98	92.45	99.98	121.23	248.53
Spain 184	165.37	191.85	203.09	334.44	380.66	489.23	438.39	120.07	153.17	239.73	303.56	336.61	406.24	436.16
Sweden 144	26.66	30.41	36.95	44.09	51.96	70.01	110.23	90.14	83.10	123.37	167.06	216.37	225.66	283.86
Switzerland 146	58.02	95.34	51.34	64.42	84.15	132.78	112.41	84.45	99.44	120.69	172.60	181.81	247.55	399.09
United Kingdom 112	134.72	165.28	188.61	245.77	258.92	389.43	461.92	178.70	205.64	267.36	350.75	416.29	443.06	496.05
Developing Countries 202	**1,786.8**	**1,982.4**	**2,633.5**	**3,762.2**	**4,730.5**	**6,485.2**	**8,248.2**	**3,160.3**	**3,140.9**	**4,558.7**	**6,510.7**	**8,980.8**	**8,482.6**	**15,362.0**
Africa 607	**66.8**	**73.6**	**72.3**	**97.9**	**155.3**	**109.0**	**269.1**	**40.8**	**33.3**	**30.1**	**42.7**	**70.4**	**111.1**	**124.3**
Algeria 612	8.07	29.71	16.62	12.53	28.00	12.01	96.64	.07	.54	.09	.04	9.86	.09	.02
Angola 614	.27	.09	.15	.45	.54	.98	1.61	.01	.01	—	—	—	—	—
Benin 638	.08	.09	.09	1.38	.15	.31	.45	—	.02	.03	.27	—	.02	—
Botswana 616	.42	.69	—	—	—	.01	.12	—	—	—	—	—	.01	.01
Burkina Faso 748	.39	.04	.27	—	—	.03	.04	—	—	—	.07	.10	—	—
Burundi 618	.01	.02	—	—	.03	.03	.01	—	—	—	.03	—	—	—
Cameroon 622	.53	.87	.81	.62	.68	1.43	.17	.11	.05	.14	.41	.12	.09	.32
Cape Verde 624	.53	.01	—	—	—	—	.01	—	—	—	—	—	—	—
Central African Rep. 626	—	—	—	.01	—	.01	.01	—	—	—	—	—	—	—
Chad 628	.01	.01	—	—	.94	.87	.09	—	—	—	—	.02	—	—
Comoros 632	—	.09	.85	1.05	.82	2.07	1.03	.01	—	—	.01	—	.01	.03
Congo, Dem. Rep. of 636	.01	.13	.05	—	.02	.03	.95	—	.07	—	—	—	.01	.12
Congo, Republic of 634	.53	.03	.93	.30	.35	2.15	.07	—	—	—	—	1.78	21.91	20.73
Côte d'Ivoire 662	.49	2.23	1.53	1.90	1.19	.93	.48	2.20	1.09	.74	.65	1.96	3.51	2.56
Djibouti 611	.05	.17	.06	.02	.01	.02	.04	—	—	—	—	—	—	—
Equatorial Guinea 642	.17	.03	—	.19	—	—	.45	—	—	—	.11	—	—	—
Eritrea 643	.01	.01	.02	.02	.03	.01	.02	—	—	—	—	—	—	—
Ethiopia 644	.47	1.05	.55	.88	—	1.36	3.22	.12	.25	.01	.01	—	.09	.17
Gabon 646	—	.04	—	.03	.13	.01	.10	.08	.05	.03	—	—	—	2.33
Gambia, The 648	1.94	.29	.78	1.47	2.16	.13	—	.65	.20	.23	.24	.01	.21	.03
Ghana 652	2.14	1.31	.75	1.82	2.55	4.15	4.54	.35	.17	.43	.80	.43	.39	.29
Guinea 656	.10	.07	.21	.25	.37	.40	.35	.01	—	.23	.04	.07	.03	—
Guinea-Bissau 654	—	—	.02	—	—	—	—	—	—	—	.01	—	—	—
Kenya 664	.13	.07	.57	.28	15.80	5.32	2.01	.01	.02	.08	.12	.17	.25	.27
Lesotho 666	—	—	—	—	—	—	.01	—	.01	—	—	—	—	—
Liberia 668	.18	.27	.52	1.81	8.58	1.99	1.34	.01	.03	.74	3.00	7.11	.02	.04
Madagascar 674	—	.01	—	.06	.05	1.17	.25	.08	.04	.12	.17	1.40	.37	.05
Malawi 676	.06	.04	—	—	.04	.11	.16	.23	.15	.07	.07	—	.01	—
Mali 678	.02	.02	.02	.01	.14	1.70	1.30	—	—	—	—	.01	—	—
Mauritania 682	1.27	2.33	3.21	2.09	3.85	.05	.18	.22	.22	.09	.01	.01	.03	—
Mauritius 684	.05	.05	.08	.08	.17	.33	.22	.01	.04	.14	.05	.15	.20	.28
Morocco 686	6.26	5.74	8.31	17.94	8.14	9.09	18.68	17.44	10.24	9.58	12.93	25.64	41.32	62.76
Mozambique 688	.01	.03	.03	.06	.16	.21	.36	—	.02	.61	.01	.01	.01	—
Namibia 728	.29	.01	.30	—	—	—	23.32	—	—	.01	.06	.04	.05	.04
Niger 692	2.19	3.01	1.90	2.30	.76	.74	.10	—	—	—	—	.03	.02	—
Nigeria 694	11.09	6.69	14.95	10.83	7.09	2.85	9.03	.05	.11	.04	.02	.31	3.36	8.56
Rwanda 714	.01	.02	.02	—	—	.01	.03	—	—	—	—	—	—	—
São Tomé & Príncipe 716	.31	.05	—	—	.01	—	—	—	—	—	—	—	—	—
Senegal 722	.72	.44	.12	.09	1.33	1.25	1.09	—	—	.01	—	.02	.05	—
Seychelles 718	.31	.13	.02	.09	—	.05	10.49	.01	—	—	.01	.01	—	.13

		Exports							Imports						
		2001	2002	2003	2004	2005	2006	2007	2001	2002	2003	2004	2005	2006	2007
		Millions of U.S. Dollars							*Millions of U.S. Dollars*						
Sierra Leone	724	.04	.02	.05	—	—	.45	.30	.01	.01	—	—	—	.01	.06
Somalia	726	—	—	—	—	—	—	—	—	.01	.01	—	—	—	—
South Africa	199	1.88	1.47	2.33	3.90	21.23	16.93	8.01	9.95	9.23	5.63	6.11	10.68	28.84	13.91
Sudan	732	3.31	2.88	4.68	3.96	15.82	4.71	4.67	.90	.63	.60	1.12	.24	.26	.08
Swaziland	734	—	—	—	—	—	—	.21	—	.02	—	.01	.01	.05	—
Tanzania	738	.10	.10	.09	.43	.26	.53	.12	.02	.02	.11	.15	.22	.10	.15
Togo	742	.03	.03	.20	2.96	3.64	3.62	7.95	.01	—	.01	.05	.02	—	—
Tunisia	744	22.11	13.15	10.84	28.07	29.93	28.45	67.23	.50	.73	2.60	7.46	3.86	3.16	5.37
Uganda	746	.11	.04	.10	—	.21	2.05	.36	.19	.18	.20	.15	.49	.52	.93
Zambia	754	.10	.09	.13	.04	.02	.42	1.08	.11	—	—	—	.13	—	1.23
Zimbabwe	698	—	—	.17	—	.13	.05	.18	7.48	9.12	7.49	8.51	5.47	6.13	3.86
Africa n.s.	799	—	—	—	—	—	—	—	—	.01	—	—	—	—	—
Asia	**507**	**58.7**	**78.3**	**194.0**	**249.6**	**372.7**	**622.5**	**645.9**	**341.5**	**401.5**	**645.5**	**886.1**	**1,220.6**	**1,575.1**	**1,367.8**
Afghanistan, I.S. of	512	2.17	2.73	5.67	4.93	.52	2.46	34.46	.01	—	.04	.05	—	.02	.01
Bangladesh	513	1.80	.44	.44	4.66	.74	1.52	1.08	.63	1.72	1.91	1.38	2.90	3.88	1.00
Bhutan	514	—	.01	.01	.01	—	—	—	—	—	—	—	—	—	—
Cambodia	522	.82	1.50	2.42	.60	.32	3.22	1.27	—	.01	.05	.10	10.30	.20	.02
China,P.R.: Mainland	924	9.58	12.41	60.32	36.25	71.54	79.18	95.54	87.13	136.76	279.03	471.16	703.05	971.13	836.71
China,P.R.:Hong Kong	532	1.05	2.96	2.92	5.82	5.43	13.94	18.99	11.11	16.08	21.72	21.85	21.82	32.44	91.56
China,P.R.:Macao	546	—	—	—	.06	.04	1.02	.44	.02	.01	.06	.23	.26	.69	1.63
Fiji	819	—	.02	.08	.03	.02	.95	.06	—	—	—	—	—	—	—
French Polynesia	887	—	—	—	—	—	.03	—	.01	—	—	—	—	—	—
India	534	11.00	6.97	8.43	21.96	17.41	32.71	78.42	19.06	16.72	23.21	33.98	36.88	47.53	84.88
Indonesia	536	1.60	3.14	8.40	14.84	13.64	16.56	12.87	105.11	74.72	101.75	50.60	60.46	33.71	19.57
Kiribati	826	—	—	—	—	—	—	—	—	—	—	—	—	.02	—
Korea	542	6.24	10.47	14.10	12.82	19.95	37.50	38.04	30.35	46.58	73.68	110.75	143.40	197.44	104.15
Lao People's Dem.Rep.	544	—	—	—	—	—	.01	.02	.01	.18	.01	.03	.07	.09	.11
Malaysia	548	1.71	3.83	3.10	4.20	4.98	8.12	18.32	12.24	18.41	20.82	32.02	42.22	50.43	40.11
Maldives	556	—	—	—	—	.02	—	.05	—	—	—	—	.02	—	—
Mongolia	948	1.42	.83	1.24	1.62	1.77	3.67	2.03	—	.04	—	.01	.02	.06	.01
Myanmar	518	—	—	.02	—	.07	—	.19	—	1.30	.04	.11	.16	.16	.15
Nauru	836	—	.10	—	—	—	—	—	—	.02	—	—	—	—	—
Nepal	558	.06	.37	.08	.15	.23	.85	.06	—	—	.02	.01	.03	.04	.04
New Caledonia	839	—	.02	.07	.04	.04	.05	.06	—	—	—	—	—	—	—
Pakistan	564	3.66	3.23	7.82	4.85	6.11	44.71	10.59	.48	.44	1.03	2.44	2.89	3.06	6.11
Papua New Guinea	853	—	—	—	.02	—	—	—	.33	.01	—	.04	.03	.02	—
Philippines	566	1.48	1.66	4.71	7.01	11.04	19.35	12.59	1.54	3.77	6.16	5.63	13.92	15.44	15.45
Singapore	576	2.43	3.20	44.54	95.45	181.09	297.31	282.91	7.33	7.72	13.30	16.12	18.84	21.96	9.39
Sri Lanka	524	4.13	2.30	4.41	4.83	4.60	4.14	5.12	.44	.38	.46	.95	1.03	1.16	1.44
Taiwan Province of China	528	5.56	10.77	15.23	15.94	18.30	14.59	15.05	32.74	48.08	72.21	103.40	117.34	125.67	85.28
Thailand	578	2.08	8.75	4.78	10.54	10.24	33.27	10.42	12.06	14.16	17.93	21.69	27.43	46.06	22.52
Tonga	866	.07	.34	.35	.05	.02	—	—	—	—	—	—	—	—	—
Tuvalu	869	—	—	—	—	—	.50	.01	—	—	—	—	—	.01	—
Vanuatu	846	.01	—	—	—	—	—	—	—	—	—	.02	—	.08	—
Vietnam	582	1.89	2.24	4.90	2.87	4.56	6.72	7.32	20.93	14.43	12.11	13.50	17.42	23.74	47.65
Asia n.s.	598	—	—	—	—	.01	.05	—	—	—	—	—	.06	.05	—
Europe	**170**	**1,471.3**	**1,614.5**	**2,123.0**	**3,035.4**	**3,752.8**	**5,155.6**	**6,580.9**	**2,575.6**	**2,459.6**	**3,497.0**	**4,925.1**	**6,855.9**	**5,496.6**	**12,705.6**
Albania	914	27.28	38.20	29.94	38.95	62.39	103.09	72.07	.09	.14	.25	1.40	3.68	3.88	11.57
Armenia	911	5.62	6.09	10.76	13.20	14.21	15.82	23.11	.13	.66	12.19	10.20	.19	16.72	24.55
Azerbaijan	912	3.87	3.38	6.98	8.87	10.39	10.51	19.97	.70	.62	.03	.30	.80	2.73	.53
Belarus	913	6.61	7.58	7.46	12.15	14.30	24.36	27.44	5.93	7.24	11.60	26.64	23.87	32.74	34.77
Bosnia & Herzegovina	963	10.10	10.61	9.64	11.76	65.99	126.92	37.51	.47	.88	.71	1.82	6.70	22.50	32.09
Croatia	960	5.74	15.85	42.64	40.90	164.13	254.59	175.38	2.31	14.09	30.27	32.90	42.67	52.65	109.94
Czech Republic	935	21.87	27.41	41.64	58.46	60.28	102.42	131.56	116.16	122.24	174.67	244.98	264.19	343.24	618.46
Estonia	939	3.50	2.46	4.90	4.49	5.76	8.23	6.16	.46	.33	1.16	2.78	3.73	5.21	9.38
Faroe Islands	816	—	.01	—	—	—	—	—	—	.01	—	—	—	—	—
Georgia	915	53.55	48.86	43.91	64.68	65.14	98.34	227.43	7.81	.20	28.64	28.45	55.30	29.55	79.76
Gibraltar	823	3.74	5.45	7.60	54.90	37.40	51.41	84.19	.01	—	.02	.26	—	—	.09
Hungary	944	33.26	38.20	61.80	86.36	91.86	136.20	193.93	80.50	99.87	133.44	175.63	212.11	299.05	919.15
Kazakhstan	916	7.26	5.98	8.88	11.72	10.91	23.91	62.95	4.57	25.41	128.00	147.11	194.73	18.29	4.01
Kosovo	967	—	—	—	—	—	.05	47.04	—	—	—	—	—	—	3.30
Kyrgyz Republic	917	.10	.10	.14	.70	.64	1.05	.91	.14	.14	.22	.96	.22	.52	3.73
Latvia	941	5.76	6.70	8.63	9.53	9.07	14.16	25.51	.58	1.03	1.52	2.54	2.33	2.42	8.83
Lithuania	946	7.56	8.21	10.59	14.42	16.48	21.53	30.07	2.75	5.52	13.02	12.15	13.31	15.57	28.60
Macedonia, FYR	962	112.33	125.98	152.32	207.26	233.27	289.29	396.56	19.54	17.87	23.62	51.25	83.18	176.18	389.47
Moldova	921	19.20	17.11	20.41	19.45	20.23	23.96	55.10	2.55	3.72	6.46	7.47	6.37	11.38	23.16
Montenegro, Rep. of	943	—	—	—	—	—	—	6.86	—	—	—	—	—	—	.52
Poland	964	34.74	40.94	61.15	100.11	128.44	224.14	301.41	106.71	99.24	151.25	215.97	295.36	457.02	595.04
Romania	968	128.84	158.48	226.89	400.99	443.46	585.29	909.54	172.19	162.63	260.14	426.60	677.93	876.85	1,364.48
Russia	922	119.06	91.33	103.83	125.56	151.50	230.54	451.97	1,441.72	1,146.45	1,348.82	1,829.72	2,830.74	506.24	3,716.39
Serbia, Rep. of	942	—	—	—	—	—	489.77	830.86	—	—	—	—	—	211.28	241.90
Serbia & Montenegro	965	212.58	173.13	248.63	346.17	349.49	—	—	20.50	23.88	33.86	52.70	86.48	—	—
Slovak Republic	936	8.86	17.82	17.69	38.13	41.59	81.19	143.31	37.85	45.02	70.66	106.00	114.53	150.28	262.12
Tajikistan	923	.18	.30	.28	.61	.58	1.38	.76	7.15	19.82	29.63	37.25	16.53	19.33	6.16
Turkey	186	413.13	529.20	679.51	995.84	1,229.47	1,751.22	2,131.88	272.64	389.28	657.63	872.55	1,101.87	1,389.36	2,062.69
Turkmenistan	925	1.22	1.71	.97	1.01	.76	2.98	1.06	1.47	.64	.03	1.43	.04	.08	—
Ukraine	926	61.76	52.87	58.54	74.92	80.67	112.39	227.98	231.70	244.56	342.39	585.65	696.97	729.34	2,156.25
Uzbekistan	927	3.00	2.84	1.96	2.69	2.54	4.10	5.35	6.56	2.02	.52	1.03	2.22	9.69	1.87
Europe n.s.	884	160.57	177.69	255.31	291.52	441.87	366.82	.07	32.41	26.13	36.27	49.36	119.82	114.52	.08

		Exports							**Imports**						
		2001	2002	2003	2004	2005	2006	2007	2001	2002	2003	2004	2005	2006	2007
		Millions of U.S. Dollars							*Millions of U.S. Dollars*						
Middle East	**407**	**151.9**	**146.5**	**165.4**	**284.6**	**335.6**	**452.0**	**521.8**	**36.7**	**62.8**	**95.3**	**101.0**	**100.3**	**105.4**	**152.8**
Bahrain	419	.14	.50	.49	.42	.37	2.04	1.17	—	1.11	—	—	.01	—	.07
Egypt	469	22.44	27.92	43.46	52.14	66.50	46.40	64.63	5.49	4.03	4.83	8.05	10.61	16.43	28.68
Iran, I.R. of	429	16.61	5.76	19.11	12.12	15.08	44.18	38.90	.64	1.39	1.88	2.36	6.62	9.65	12.39
Iraq	433	5.35	1.34	.68	8.04	20.19	7.99	16.56	—	—	1.16	—	—	.32	—
Israel	436	32.18	43.30	38.69	75.17	67.68	74.55	95.67	18.80	18.50	19.41	24.60	34.85	44.25	57.82
Jordan	439	7.62	5.55	7.20	7.28	9.86	18.69	6.95	5.07	2.88	14.14	21.66	17.76	2.62	2.89
Kuwait	443	.47	1.05	2.20	2.38	15.88	3.57	3.98	.14	.09	.31	.34	.16	.23	1.14
Lebanon	446	18.03	12.00	11.50	68.22	44.47	62.19	91.47	.29	.58	.57	.74	.40	.36	1.38
Libya	672	2.39	1.36	3.07	6.66	22.00	3.93	2.91	.33	1.00	.06	.11	.14	.92	3.16
Oman	449	1.37	.09	.21	.51	.66	1.38	3.01	—	—	—	.03	.01	—	.01
Qatar	453	.14	.08	.28	.26	.29	.31	1.39	—	—	—	—	.05	.13	.46
Saudi Arabia	456	17.39	17.76	10.97	16.73	30.43	39.68	65.20	.36	.62	.52	.79	2.61	3.87	1.32
Syrian Arab Republic	463	20.02	17.83	12.32	22.78	20.64	35.50	103.57	4.24	29.10	26.32	10.64	16.75	18.58	19.97
United Arab Emirates	466	7.61	9.46	13.87	10.14	21.52	78.42	18.08	1.28	3.49	26.11	31.71	10.30	8.03	23.50
Yemen, Republic of	474	.16	2.53	1.31	1.76	—	33.19	8.32	.10	.05	—	—	—	—	.02
Western Hemisphere	**207**	**38.1**	**69.4**	**78.8**	**94.7**	**114.1**	**146.1**	**230.5**	**165.7**	**183.6**	**290.7**	**555.8**	**733.7**	**1,194.3**	**1,011.5**
Antigua and Barbuda	311	.13	10.45	5.64	.38	.55	3.71	60.18	—	—	—	—	—	.01	—
Argentina	213	1.02	.52	1.83	3.27	3.62	6.70	21.23	9.90	21.62	22.33	19.35	78.15	104.03	16.56
Aruba	314	.01	—	—	—	—	.03	—	—	—	—	—	—	.07	—
Bahamas, The	313	.13	.23	.27	.36	.75	1.64	12.15	—	.04	—	.21	.18	.42	.57
Barbados	316	.05	.02	.06	.12	.05	.54	.52	—	—	—	—	—	—	—
Belize	339	.11	.32	.12	1.04	.36	3.08	.51	.04	.01	.09	—	—	.03	.40
Bermuda	319	—	.01	.02	.01	—	—	.01	—	—	—	—	—	—	.01
Bolivia	218	.07	.04	.04	.11	.02	.03	.09	.01	.02	—	—	—	.04	—
Brazil	223	6.96	15.02	19.74	36.08	39.57	26.86	32.12	81.48	71.63	117.05	237.85	320.83	461.90	256.03
Chile	228	.37	.40	.60	.58	.86	.90	6.99	42.36	22.25	58.84	181.61	171.54	409.48	495.94
Colombia	233	1.06	2.84	4.80	5.52	4.54	2.14	2.63	.40	.69	1.05	1.96	2.46	2.19	6.80
Costa Rica	238	.12	.16	.04	.56	.70	.08	.25	.61	.75	1.99	2.87	1.55	2.52	.01
Dominica	321	—	—	—	.08	.07	.42	.05	—	—	—	—	—	.01	.02
Dominican Republic	243	1.77	1.73	1.64	.51	1.29	1.13	.29	.01	.02	.06	.14	.26	.44	.25
Ecuador	248	.23	.09	.20	.17	.26	.98	.50	3.94	5.21	9.50	9.53	13.11	12.14	14.49
El Salvador	253	.04	1.11	.98	1.17	.01	1.11	.08	.01	.01	.01	6.54	.05	.04	—
Falkland Islands	323	—	—	—	—	—	—	—	.02	.07	—	—	—	—	—
Greenland	326	—	.01	—	—	—	.01	—	—	—	.02	.02	.05	.06	—
Grenada	328	—	—	—	—	—	—	—	—	—	—	—	.01	—	—
Guatemala	258	2.13	1.11	.94	.31	.63	1.02	.40	—	2.29	5.38	.01	.01	.14	.96
Guyana	336	—	—	—	—	—	—	.01	—	—	—	—	.01	—	.01
Haiti	263	.01	.01	.02	—	.02	.64	.20	—	—	—	—	—	—	—
Honduras	268	.44	.44	1.01	.71	.54	.42	.46	.39	1.02	1.41	.09	.22	.09	.17
Jamaica	343	.04	.08	.04	—	.39	.22	.01	.01	.02	.01	.03	.02	.01	.03
Mexico	273	12.36	20.49	11.20	14.52	25.62	29.11	16.95	7.89	3.73	13.68	8.12	9.78	18.10	11.82
Netherlands Antilles	353	.01	.19	—	.02	.14	.55	.26	—	—	—	—	—	—	.01
Nicaragua	278	.02	.04	—	.01	.01	.97	.06	—	.01	—	.01	.02	.04	.01
Panama	283	1.77	1.58	12.36	14.30	6.94	3.22	4.07	.74	.58	.75	.71	5.35	.76	.58
Paraguay	288	.02	.03	.87	.53	.38	1.77	.25	1.26	—	.15	.30	.24	.33	.27
Peru	293	7.11	7.26	6.05	6.78	22.28	30.32	25.81	9.88	35.84	39.07	76.16	106.53	165.11	183.61
St. Kitts and Nevis	361	—	—	—	—	—	1.06	11.27	—	.01	—	—	—	—	—
St. Lucia	362	—	.02	—	—	—	—	—	—	.01	—	—	.01	—	—
St. Pierre-Miquelon	363	—	—	—	—	—	—	—	—	—	—	—	.07	—	—
St. Vincent & Grens	364	.91	.73	4.34	2.34	2.07	3.90	3.61	—	—	—	—	.01	.02	.01
Suriname	366	.01	—	—	—	.01	.01	.12	.09	—	.01	—	—	—	.02
Trinidad and Tobago	369	.07	—	.03	.03	.08	17.95	22.93	—	—	—	—	.02	—	—
Uruguay	298	.35	1.54	2.10	.20	.36	1.38	.11	.22	1.53	2.58	1.31	1.59	3.30	7.26
Venezuela, Rep. Bol	299	.70	.94	1.76	2.50	.72	1.13	4.01	6.34	16.09	16.01	8.02	18.69	11.26	15.51
Western Hem. n.s.	399	.11	2.01	2.10	2.49	1.28	3.07	2.36	.10	.18	.71	.95	2.95	1.80	.14
Other Countries n.i.e.	**910**	**2.5**	**1.2**	**1.5**	**4.7**	**4.2**	**8.8**	**6.2**	**11.7**	**11.6**	**9.5**	**9.1**	**5.1**	**14.5**	**7.4**
Cuba	928	2.08	1.03	.23	.52	1.19	7.71	5.97	9.20	8.99	6.94	6.06	.60	11.23	7.28
North Korea	954	.37	.12	1.27	4.15	3.00	1.07	.18	2.49	2.63	2.55	3.04	4.53	3.24	.16
Countries & Areas n.s.	**898**	**39.2**	**14.0**	**30.3**	**38.1**	**152.2**	**149.6**	**40.0**	**5.3**	**253.6**	**89.8**	—	**48.2**	**119.5**	**1.4**
Special Categories	**899**	—	—	—	—	—	**41.9**	—	—	—	—	—	—	**19.8**	—
Memorandum Items															
European Union	998	2,966.71	3,363.63	4,479.10	5,785.41	6,647.16	8,376.97	10,296.93	3,964.37	4,377.76	5,939.31	7,822.01	9,031.80	11,008.49	16,241.02
Oil Exporting Ctys	999	72.77	77.37	92.12	97.55	175.51	212.02	272.59	114.30	98.05	147.94	94.04	109.20	71.58	85.65
Non-Oil Develop.Ctys	201	1,713.98	1,904.99	2,541.38	3,664.60	4,555.03	6,273.19	7,975.61	3,046.02	3,042.83	4,410.74	6,416.65	8,871.57	8,410.99	15,276.36
PERCENT DISTRIBUTION															
Industrial Countries	**101**	**63.9**	**64.5**	**63.9**	**61.4**	**58.2**	**55.8**	**55.0**	**55.8**	**56.5**	**56.4**	**54.7**	**50.2**	**55.8**	**48.9**
Developing Countries	**202**	**35.3**	**35.2**	**35.7**	**38.2**	**40.3**	**42.8**	**44.6**	**44.0**	**40.1**	**42.7**	**45.2**	**49.4**	**43.4**	**51.0**
Africa	**607**	**1.3**	**1.3**	**1.0**	**1.0**	**1.3**	**.7**	**1.5**	**.6**	**.4**	**.3**	**.3**	**.4**	**.6**	**.4**
Asia	**507**	**1.2**	**1.4**	**2.6**	**2.5**	**3.2**	**4.1**	**3.5**	**4.8**	**5.1**	**6.0**	**6.2**	**6.7**	**8.1**	**4.5**
Europe	**170**	**29.1**	**28.7**	**28.8**	**30.8**	**32.0**	**34.0**	**35.6**	**35.9**	**31.4**	**32.7**	**34.2**	**37.7**	**28.1**	**42.2**
Middle East	**407**	**3.0**	**2.6**	**2.2**	**2.9**	**2.9**	**3.0**	**2.8**	**.5**	**.8**	**.9**	**.7**	**.6**	**.5**	**.5**
Western Hemisphere	**207**	**.8**	**1.2**	**1.1**	**1.0**	**1.0**	**1.0**	**1.2**	**2.3**	**2.3**	**2.7**	**3.9**	**4.0**	**6.1**	**3.4**
Other Countries n.i.e.	**910**	—	—	—	—	—	**.1**	—	**.2**	**.1**	**.1**	**.1**	—	**.1**	—

Bulgaria 918

	Exports							Imports						
	2001	2002	2003	2004	2005	2006	2007	2001	2002	2003	2004	2005	2006	2007
ANNUAL PERCENT CHANGE														
World.. 001	6.3	11.2	31.0	33.7	19.0	29.0	22.0	12.9	9.0	36.4	34.7	26.4	7.5	53.9
Industrial Countries................. 101	14.7	12.4	29.7	28.5	12.8	23.8	20.1	23.1	10.5	36.1	30.7	16.1	19.5	34.9
Developing Countries.............. 202	−6.5	10.9	32.8	42.9	25.7	37.1	27.2	1.9	−.6	45.1	42.8	37.9	−5.5	81.1
Africa..................................... 607	46.6	10.3	−1.8	35.4	58.6	−29.8	146.8	−4.7	−18.4	−9.6	41.8	64.9	57.9	11.9
Asia....................................... 507	−33.1	33.3	147.8	28.6	49.3	67.0	3.8	68.2	17.6	60.8	37.3	37.8	29.0	−13.2
Europe.................................... 170	−7.7	9.7	31.5	43.0	23.6	37.4	27.6	−2.3	−4.5	42.2	40.8	39.2	−19.8	131.2
Middle East............................ 407	−.4	−3.5	12.9	72.1	17.9	34.7	15.4	14.0	71.1	51.7	6.0	−.8	5.1	45.0
Western Hemisphere............. 207	24.0	82.2	13.5	20.2	20.5	28.0	57.8	−11.4	10.8	58.3	91.2	32.0	62.8	−15.3
Other Countries n.i.e................ 910	−82.4	−53.0	29.8	211.5	−10.4	110.0	−30.0	388.6	−.6	−18.3	−4.0	−43.7	182.2	−48.5

		Exports							Imports						
		2001	2002	2003	2004	2005	2006	2007	2001	2002	2003	2004	2005	2006	2007
		Millions of U.S. Dollars							Millions of U.S. Dollars						
IFS World Total		**226.3**	**248.4**	**320.5**	**479.3**	**468.0**	**588.0**	**660.0**	**655.4**	**746.2**	**925.0**	**1,270.0**	**1,380.0**	**1,500.0**	**1,700.0**
DOTS World Total	**001**	**173.6Y**	**173.0Y**	**247.9Y**	**375.5Y**	**373.3Y**	**419.2Y**	**477.2Y**	**508.4Y**	**649.7Y**	**863.0Y**	**1,024.5Y**	**1,096.0Y**	**1,257.9Y**	**1,572.2Y**
Industrial Countries	**101**	**67.0Y**	**56.6Y**	**57.5Y**	**58.8Y**	**46.0Y**	**44.4Y**	**62.5Y**	**238.6Y**	**313.2Y**	**437.9Y**	**504.9Y**	**459.3Y**	**486.6Y**	**598.0Y**
United States	111	4.55V	2.64V	.82V	.36V	2.09V	.73V	1.36V	4.84V	20.46V	11.99V	24.20V	27.61V	19.69V	36.30V
Canada	156	.63V	.02V	.08V	.14V	.18V	.07V	.28V	3.58V	1.32V	2.34V	7.92V	13.47V	3.84V	13.98V
Australia	193	—V	—V	.02V	.02V	—V	.02V	.03V	.16V	.42V	.30V	.92V	1.23V	1.52V	6.45V
Japan	158	4.61V	7.67V	8.39V	9.92V	8.13V	8.58V	14.75V	7.88V	9.45V	8.02V	4.63V	4.90V	8.03V	6.87V
New Zealand	196	—V	—V	—V	—V	—V	—V	—V	—V	—V	.01V	.01V	.01V	.36V	.07V
Austria	122	.02V	.04V	.03V	.06V	.05V	.03V	.03V	.73V	1.04V	.53V	.78V	.91V	.86V	.84V
Belgium	124	1.63V	1.15V	1.46V	3.11V	3.14V	5.98V	5.64V	20.31V	22.01V	42.38V	37.49V	32.40V	42.26V	49.82V
Cyprus	423	—V	—V	—V	.01V	.03Y	.02V	—V	—V	—V	—V	—V	—V	.02V	.02V
Denmark	128	3.07V	.90V	3.91V	.71V	.54V	.46V	9.51V	6.41V	4.72V	4.44V	8.06V	2.15V	2.98V	2.93V
Finland	172	—V	—V	—V	—V	.02V	—V	—V	.31V	2.49V	.65V	9.25V	1.45V	2.92V	1.92V
France	132	11.50V	13.43V	12.45V	7.49V	8.05V	6.60V	6.03V	128.25V	176.55V	263.64V	298.04V	260.18V	287.18V	323.61V
Germany	134	1.91V	2.02V	2.59V	4.91V	2.64V	2.37V	2.98V	11.00V	10.92V	25.28V	21.71V	18.79V	24.90V	24.73V
Greece	174	.14V	.16V	.61V	.01V	.23V	—V	—V	.37V	.23V	.16V	.11V	.02V	.11V	.10V
Iceland	176	—V	—V	.01V	—V	—V	.01V	.01V	—V	1.00V	—V	—V	—V	—V	—V
Ireland	178	—V	—V	—V	.40V	—V	—V	.03V	1.78V	1.37V	.94V	1.17V	1.48V	1.68V	2.84V
Italy	136	21.80V	19.84V	15.76V	14.42V	8.10V	9.53V	12.02V	17.84V	22.13V	26.92V	37.87V	30.66V	31.58V	39.13V
Luxembourg	137	—V	.01V	—V	—V	.03V	.01V	.05V	.21V	.18V	.12V	.31V	.27V	.19V	.57V
Malta	181	—Y	—V	—V	—V	—V	—V	—V	—Y	—V	—V	—V	.06V	.08V	—V
Netherlands	138	1.01V	.79V	1.23V	2.88V	2.78V	1.41V	3.01V	8.66V	10.31V	17.33V	15.42V	18.44V	19.08V	18.90V
Norway	142	—V	.01V	—V	.01V	—V	—V	.01V	.05V	.17V	.14V	.38V	.38V	.61V	.39V
Portugal	182	6.54V	3.09V	5.87V	6.49V	6.09V	4.22V	1.84V	.95V	1.20V	1.74V	2.07V	1.87V	1.34V	2.39V
Slovenia	961	.23V	.37V	.47V	.62Y	.06V	.95V	.80V	—V	—V	—V	—Y	—V	.09V	—V
Spain	184	4.33V	3.15V	2.59V	5.93V	2.44V	.86V	1.23V	12.19V	21.70V	21.77V	24.66V	23.70V	20.33V	40.46V
Sweden	144	.32V	.19V	.22V	.32V	.18V	1.33V	.02V	.26V	.33V	1.12V	1.80V	9.40V	9.14V	14.88V
Switzerland	146	.54V	.78V	.72V	.59V	.25V	.27V	.41V	.74V	1.01V	1.33V	1.56V	1.46V	2.29V	2.44V
United Kingdom	112	4.16V	.31V	.23V	.41V	.92V	.92V	2.47V	12.09V	4.18V	6.79V	6.54V	8.49V	5.48V	8.41V
Developing Countries	**202**	**103.2Y**	**112.6Y**	**185.6Y**	**310.4Y**	**320.2Y**	**365.9Y**	**403.6Y**	**248.9Y**	**313.9Y**	**396.4Y**	**482.0Y**	**593.7Y**	**718.2Y**	**908.2Y**
Africa	**607**	**29.9Y**	**28.9Y**	**44.9Y**	**65.1Y**	**55.9Y**	**69.9Y**	**87.0Y**	**187.7Y**	**232.6Y**	**274.7Y**	**339.4Y**	**412.7Y**	**522.5Y**	**650.4Y**
Algeria	612	—V	.56V	.62Y	.81Y	1.03Y	1.28Y	1.65Y	—V	—V	—Y	—Y	—Y	.01Y	.01Y
Angola	614	.01Y	.01Y	.01Y	.01Y	.01Y	.02Y	.02Y	—Y	—Y	—Y	—Y	—Y	—Y	—Y
Benin	638	.05V	.04V	.34V	.24V	.08V	.11Y	.13Y	1.19V	1.22V	2.37V	2.40V	4.82V	5.96Y	7.39Y
Botswana	616	....	....	....	....	....	....	....	—Y	—Y	—Y	—Y	—Y	—Y	.01Y
Cameroon	622	—V	—V	—V	—Y	—Y	—Y	—Y	—V	.03V	.06V	.08Y	.10Y	.12Y	.15Y
Central African Rep.	626	.01Y	.02Y	.02Y	.03Y	.03Y	.04Y	.05Y	—Y	—Y	—Y	—Y	—Y	—Y	—Y
Chad	628	.02Y	.03Y	.03Y	.04Y	.05Y	.06Y	.08Y	.01Y	.01Y	.02Y	.02Y	.03Y	.03Y	.04Y
Congo, Republic of	634	—V	—V	.28V	—V	—Y	—Y	—Y	—V	—V	—V	—V	—Y	—Y	—Y
Côte d'Ivoire	662	.68V	1.05V	1.22V	.30V	.80V	.80V	.99Y	134.80V	159.38V	124.45V	210.27V	255.11V	326.40V	405.07Y
Djibouti	611	—Y	—Y	—Y	—Y	—Y	—Y	—Y	.01Y	.01Y	.02Y	.02Y	.03Y	.03Y	.04Y
Gabon	646	.01Y	.01Y	.01Y	.02Y	.02Y	.03Y	.03Y	.01Y	.01Y	.02Y	.02Y	.03Y	.03Y	.04Y
Ghana	652	9.72Y	10.55Y	13.35Y	17.53Y	20.03Y	24.76Y	30.73Y	7.74Y	8.40Y	10.63Y	13.97Y	15.96Y	19.72Y	24.48Y
Guinea-Bissau	654	.03Y	.03Y	.04Y	.05Y	.05Y	.07Y	.08Y	.01Y	.01Y	.01Y	.01Y	.01Y	.02Y	.02Y
Kenya	664	.03V	—V	.05V	—V	—Y	.01Y	.01Y	.21V	2.26V	2.26V	1.18V	1.35Y	1.67Y	2.07Y
Liberia	668	—Y	—Y	—Y	—Y	—Y	—Y	—Y	—Y	—Y	—Y	.01Y	.01Y	.01Y	.01Y
Madagascar	674	—V	.02V	.19V	.25Y	.28Y	.35Y	.43Y	.03V	.03V	—V	—Y	—Y	—Y	—Y
Malawi	676	—Y	—Y	—Y	—Y	—Y	—Y	—Y	.01Y	.01Y	.01Y	.02Y	.02Y	.02Y	.03Y
Mali	678	3.38Y	3.67Y	4.64Y	6.09Y	6.96Y	8.61Y	10.68Y	2.33Y	2.53Y	3.20Y	4.21Y	4.81Y	5.94Y	7.37Y
Mauritania	682	.01Y	.01Y	.01Y	.02Y	.02Y	.03Y	.03Y	.43Y	.47Y	.60Y	.78Y	.89Y	1.11Y	1.37Y
Mauritius	684	3.78V	.77V	3.76V	2.03V	.35V	.76V	1.00V	.17V	.58V	.05V	.08V	.01V	.62V	.26V
Morocco	686	3.96V	2.79V	2.86V	5.39V	5.17V	6.39Y	7.92Y	4.60V	4.97V	7.16V	9.11V	15.02V	18.57Y	23.04Y
Niger	692	7.03V	4.38V	9.73V	13.06V	14.93Y	18.45Y	22.89Y	1.38V	1.13V	2.25V	1.24V	1.42Y	1.76Y	2.18Y
Nigeria	694	.07V	1.01V	1.42V	1.84Y	2.35Y	2.90Y	3.75Y	—V	.03V	.11V	.15Y	.20Y	.25Y	.30Y
Senegal	722	.06V	.09V	.04V	.05V	.09V	.06V	.08Y	3.29V	7.02V	32.34V	24.71V	16.49V	18.95V	23.52Y
South Africa	199	.03V	.10V	.40V	.68V	—V	—V	—V	3.33V	2.25V	4.93V	8.51V	10.29V	16.94V	23.56V
Swaziland	734	—Y	—Y	—Y	—Y	—Y	—Y	—Y	—Y	—Y	.01Y	.01Y	.01Y	.01Y	.01Y
Tanzania	738	.01V	—V	—Y	—Y	—Y	—Y	—Y	—V	—V	—Y	—Y	—Y	—Y	—Y
Togo	742	.77V	3.10V	4.91V	16.41V	2.53V	3.13Y	3.89Y	25.15V	35.60V	75.97V	55.89V	73.01V	90.23Y	111.98Y
Tunisia	744	.28V	.62V	.90V	.28V	1.05V	2.08V	2.58Y	2.89V	6.53V	8.21V	6.67V	13.08V	14.05V	17.44Y
Uganda	746	—V	—V	—V	—Y	—Y	—Y	—Y	—V	—V	.01V	.01Y	.01Y	.02Y	.02Y
Zambia	754	—V	—V	—V	—V	—V	—V	—V	—V	—V	—V	—V	—V	—V	.01V
Zimbabwe	698	—V	—V	—V	—V	—V	—V	—Y	.05V	.11V	—V	.03V	—V	—V	—Y
Asia	**507**	**50.2Y**	**60.4Y**	**119.8Y**	**232.2Y**	**256.1Y**	**283.5Y**	**292.1Y**	**22.6Y**	**37.5Y**	**55.8Y**	**55.4Y**	**58.9Y**	**70.4Y**	**116.7Y**
Bangladesh	513	—V	.72V	7.03V	15.97V	2.47V	—V	2.33V	—V	—V	—V	—V	—V	—Y	—Y
China,P.R.: Mainland	924	—V	.64V	29.40V	118.81V	148.45V	175.65V	141.23V	4.47V	6.40V	12.88V	14.42V	17.75V	21.28V	48.15V
China,P.R.:Hong Kong	532	.01V	—V	—V	—V	—V	—V	.13V	3.91V	8.13V	8.74V	6.95V	6.06V	6.50V	11.01V
India	534	11.09Y	9.43V	9.31V	8.13V	3.75V	4.64Y	5.76Y	7.44Y	16.02V	24.02V	22.64V	21.50V	26.57Y	32.98Y
Indonesia	536	3.18V	3.94V	3.47V	9.87V	7.65V	10.96V	14.39V	.79V	1.34V	2.55V	1.94V	4.62V	2.49V	2.29V
Korea	542	2.19V	4.58V	4.07V	6.47V	2.68V	.04V	—V	.56V	.46V	1.23V	1.04V	1.12V	3.17V	8.00V
Malaysia	548	2.48V	.90V	—V	—V	.05V	.02V	.56V	—V	1.53V	.35V	.05V	.05V	—V	.69V
Maldives	556	—V	—V	—V	—V	.34V	.42Y	.52Y	—Y	—Y	—Y	—Y	—Y	—Y	—Y

	Exports							Imports						
	2001	2002	2003	2004	2005	2006	2007	2001	2002	2003	2004	2005	2006	2007
	Millions of U.S. Dollars							*Millions of U.S. Dollars*						
Pakistan.......... 564	—V	.01V	.63V	4.40V	2.62V	3.24Y	4.02Y	.16V	—V	.13V	.11V	.03V	.04Y	.04Y
Papua New Guinea.......... 853	....	....	....	....	....	....	....	.01Y	.01Y	.01Y	.01Y	.01Y	.01Y	.02Y
Philippines.......... 566	—V	.25V	.19V	—V	—V	—V	—V	.16V	.02V	.16V	—V	.04V	—V	—V
Singapore.......... 576	23.65Y	25.67Y	32.49Y	42.67Y	48.75Y	60.25Y	74.77Y	1.94Y	2.11Y	2.67Y	3.50Y	4.00Y	4.95Y	6.14Y
Taiwan Province of China.......... 528	2.31V	5.07V	9.34V	12.12V	17.13V	7.89V	14.10V	.76V	.26V	.18V	.76V	.60V	.24V	1.35V
Thailand.......... 578	4.13V	7.46V	19.70V	13.72V	22.18V	20.36V	34.33V	1.28V	1.14V	2.66V	3.97V	3.15V	5.15V	5.97V
Vietnam.......... 582	1.20V	1.76V	4.14V	—V	—V	—V	—V	1.13V	.11V	.18V	—V	—V	—V	—V
Asia n.s.......... 598	—Y	—Y	—Y	—Y	—Y	—Y	—Y	—Y	.01Y	.01Y	.01Y	.01Y	.01Y	.01Y
Europe.......... 170	**2.1Y**	**2.0Y**	**1.3Y**	**3.5Y**	**.5Y**	**2.8Y**	**6.2Y**	**19.9Y**	**20.3Y**	**36.4Y**	**46.8Y**	**59.9Y**	**67.7Y**	**79.3Y**
Belarus.......... 913	—V	—V	—V	—V	—V	—V	—V	—V	.37V	1.54V	—V	1.86V	1.91V	.24V
Bulgaria.......... 918	—V	—V	—V	.06V	.09V	—V	—V	.43V	.04V	.30V	—V	—V	.03V	.04V
Czech Republic.......... 935	.32V	.34V	.07V	1.04V	.12V	—V	.02V	.26V	.10V	.28V	1.47V	2.68V	1.22V	.68V
Czechoslovakia n.s.......... 937	—Y	—Y	—Y	—Y	—Y	—Y	—Y	.74Y	.80Y	1.01Y	1.33Y	1.52Y	1.87Y	2.33Y
Estonia.......... 939	—V	—V	—V	—V	—V	—V	—V	—V	—V	—V	—V	—V	.02V	.05V
Hungary.......... 944	.03V	—V	.04V	—V	—V	.01V	—V	.12V	.07V	.08V	.02V	.22V	.67V	.48V
Kazakhstan.......... 916	—V	—V	—V	.06V	.06Y	.08Y	.10Y	—V	—V	—V	.49V	.56Y	.70Y	.86Y
Lithuania.......... 946	.26V	—V	—V	—V	—V	—V	—V	.01V	.04V	.07V	.47V	.48V	.52V	.08V
Poland.......... 964	.15V	.20V	.12V	.64V	—V	.36V	.09V	1.28V	.70V	.63V	.56V	.67V	1.62V	.42V
Romania.......... 968	—V	.27V	—V	—V	.01V	.02V	—V	.08V	.04V	.13V	3.39V	.30V	.13V	.12V
Russia.......... 922	.53V	—V	—V	—V	—V	—V	—V	2.62V	1.15V	3.63V	3.91V	8.62V	7.05V	9.11V
Serbia & Montenegro.......... 965	....	....	....	....	....	....	....	.01Y	.01Y	.01Y	.01Y	.02Y	.02Y	.03Y
Slovak Republic.......... 936	—V	—V	—Y	.01Y	—V	—V	—V	.11V	.25V	.31Y	.41Y	.08V	.12V	.07V
Turkey.......... 186	.76V	1.20V	1.02V	1.67V	.23V	2.34V	5.98V	.80V	1.76V	3.40V	2.87V	4.31V	4.11V	5.55V
Ukraine.......... 926	—V	—V	—V	—V	—V	.01Y	.01Y	1.10V	1.60V	8.05V	9.60V	13.15V	16.25Y	20.17Y
U.S.S.R. n.s.......... 930	—Y	—Y	—Y	—Y	—Y	—Y	—Y	12.36Y	13.41Y	16.97Y	22.29Y	25.47Y	31.48Y	39.06Y
Middle East.......... 407	**1.6Y**	**1.1Y**	**1.4Y**	**1.9Y**	**2.1Y**	**2.6Y**	**3.3Y**	**16.7Y**	**20.6Y**	**23.2Y**	**31.1Y**	**39.7Y**	**49.0Y**	**59.5Y**
Bahrain.......... 419	1.00Y	1.08Y	1.37Y	1.80Y	2.06Y	2.54Y	3.16Y	.01Y	.01Y	.01Y	.01Y	.01Y	.01Y	.02Y
Egypt.......... 469	—V	—Y	—Y	—Y	—Y	—Y	—Y	.17V	.19Y	.24Y	.31Y	.35Y	.44Y	.54Y
Israel.......... 436	—V	—V	—V	—V	—V	—V	.09V	—V	2.86V	1.54V	2.42V	1.10V	.44V	.88V
Jordan.......... 439	—V	—V	—V	.03V	—V	—V	—V	—V	—V	—V	—V	—V	—V	—V
Kuwait.......... 443	—Y	—Y	—Y	—Y	—Y	—Y	—Y	.03Y	.04Y	.04Y	.06Y	.08Y	.10Y	.12Y
Lebanon.......... 446	.02Y	.02Y	.03Y	.04Y	.04Y	.05Y	.06Y	.44Y	.47Y	.60Y	.79Y	.90Y	1.11Y	1.38Y
Libya.......... 672	—Y	—Y	—Y	—Y	—Y	—Y	—Y	15.88Y	16.89Y	20.47Y	27.09Y	36.85Y	46.32Y	55.89Y
Qatar.......... 453	—Y	—Y	—Y	—Y	—V	—V	—Y	—V	—V	.05V	.09V	—V	—V	—Y
Saudi Arabia.......... 456	.57V	—V	—V	—V	—V	—Y	—Y	—Y	—Y	—Y	—Y	—Y	—Y	—Y
United Arab Emirates.......... 466	—V	—V	—Y	—Y	—Y	—Y	—Y	.18Y	.19Y	.23Y	.31Y	.42Y	.53Y	.64Y
Western Hemisphere.......... 207	**19.3Y**	**20.2Y**	**18.4Y**	**7.7Y**	**5.6Y**	**7.1Y**	**14.9Y**	**2.0Y**	**2.8Y**	**6.3Y**	**9.2Y**	**22.4Y**	**8.6Y**	**2.4Y**
Argentina.......... 213	.01V	—V	—V	.01V	.01V	—V	—V	.01V	.08V	.07V	.53V	.51V	2.53V	1.00V
Brazil.......... 223	2.63V	—V	1.30V	.15V	.03V	.03V	5.13V	1.14V	2.07V	5.58V	7.59V	21.26V	5.00V	—V
Chile.......... 228	—V	—V	—V	—V	—V	—V	—V	.11V	—V	—V	.21V	.03V	—V	—V
Colombia.......... 233	13.94V	16.94V	13.29V	3.41V	—V	.18V	—V	—V	—V	—V	.08V	—V	.20V	1.04V
Costa Rica.......... 238	—V	—V	.15V	—V	—V	—Y	—Y	—V	—Y	—Y	—Y	—Y	—Y	—Y
Falkland Islands.......... 323	....	....	....	....	....	....	....	—Y	—Y	—Y	—Y	—Y	.01Y	.01Y
Mexico.......... 273	—V	—V	—V	—V	—V	.01V	.09V	—V	—V	—V	—V	—V	—V	.03V
Peru.......... 293	.10V	.14V	—V	—V	.90V	1.70V	3.99Y	.49V	.34V	.36V	.51V	.28V	.52V	—Y
Trinidad and Tobago.......... 369	.06V	—V	—Y	—Y	—Y	—Y	—Y	—V	.01V	.02Y	.02Y	.03Y	.03Y	.04Y
Uruguay.......... 298	—V	—Y	—V	—V	—V	—V	—Y	—V	—Y	—V	—V	.01V	.01Y	.01Y
Western Hem. n.s.......... 399	2.60Y	3.12Y	3.64Y	4.16Y	4.68Y	5.20Y	5.72Y	.28Y	.28Y	.28Y	.28Y	.28Y	.28Y	.28Y
Other Countries n.i.e.......... 910	**—Y**	**—Y**	**—Y**	**—Y**	**—Y**	**—Y**	**—Y**	**.3Y**	**.3Y**	**.4Y**	**.5Y**	**.5Y**	**.7Y**	**.8Y**
North Korea.......... 954	—Y	—Y	—Y	—Y	—Y	—Y	—Y	.26Y	.28Y	.36Y	.47Y	.54Y	.66Y	.82Y
Countries & Areas n.s.......... 898	**—Y**	**—Y**	**—Y**	**—Y**	**—Y**	**—Y**	**—Y**	**1.0Y**	**1.0Y**	**1.3Y**	**1.7Y**	**2.0Y**	**2.5Y**	**3.1Y**
Special Categories.......... 899	**3.5Y**	**3.8Y**	**4.8Y**	**6.3Y**	**7.2Y**	**8.9Y**	**11.1Y**	**19.6Y**	**21.3Y**	**27.0Y**	**35.4Y**	**40.5Y**	**50.0Y**	**62.1Y**
Memorandum Items														
European Union.......... 998	57.41Y	45.97Y	47.66Y	49.45Y	35.41Y	35.07Y	45.76Y	223.14Y	280.49Y	415.16Y	468.18Y	414.40Y	454.40Y	533.33Y
Oil Exporting Ctys.......... 999	3.83Y	5.52Y	5.51Y	12.53Y	11.04Y	15.14Y	19.79Y	16.88Y	18.48Y	23.46Y	29.64Y	42.16Y	49.70Y	59.24Y
Non-Oil Develop.Ctys.......... 201	99.33Y	107.09Y	180.13Y	297.85Y	309.13Y	350.76Y	383.83Y	232.06Y	295.42Y	372.93Y	452.32Y	551.53Y	668.46Y	848.98Y
PERCENT DISTRIBUTION														
Industrial Countries.......... 101	**38.6**	**32.7**	**23.2**	**15.7**	**12.3**	**10.6**	**13.1**	**46.9**	**48.2**	**50.7**	**49.3**	**41.9**	**38.7**	**38.0**
Developing Countries.......... 202	**59.4**	**65.1**	**74.9**	**82.7**	**85.8**	**87.3**	**84.6**	**49.0**	**48.3**	**45.9**	**47.0**	**54.2**	**57.1**	**57.8**
Africa.......... 607	**17.2**	**16.7**	**18.1**	**17.3**	**15.0**	**16.7**	**18.2**	**36.9**	**35.8**	**31.8**	**33.1**	**37.7**	**41.5**	**41.4**
Asia.......... 507	**28.9**	**34.9**	**48.3**	**61.8**	**68.6**	**67.6**	**61.2**	**4.4**	**5.8**	**6.5**	**5.4**	**5.4**	**5.6**	**7.4**
Europe.......... 170	**1.2**	**1.2**	**.5**	**.9**	**.1**	**.7**	**1.3**	**3.9**	**3.1**	**4.2**	**4.6**	**5.5**	**5.4**	**5.0**
Middle East.......... 407	**.9**	**.6**	**.6**	**.5**	**.6**	**.6**	**.7**	**3.3**	**3.2**	**2.7**	**3.0**	**3.6**	**3.9**	**3.8**
Western Hemisphere.......... 207	**11.1**	**11.7**	**7.4**	**2.1**	**1.5**	**1.7**	**3.1**	**.4**	**.4**	**.7**	**.9**	**2.0**	**.7**	**.2**
Other Countries n.i.e.......... 910	**—**	**—**	**—**	**—**	**—**	**—**	**—**	**.1**	**—**	**—**	**—**	**—**	**.1**	**.1**
ANNUAL PERCENT CHANGE														
World.......... 001	**1.7**	**–.4**	**43.3**	**51.5**	**–.6**	**12.3**	**13.8**	**2.1**	**27.8**	**32.8**	**18.7**	**7.0**	**14.8**	**25.0**
Industrial Countries.......... 101	**.7**	**–15.6**	**1.6**	**2.3**	**–21.9**	**–3.4**	**40.8**	**–6.4**	**31.3**	**39.8**	**15.3**	**–9.0**	**5.9**	**22.9**
Developing Countries.......... 202	**2.1**	**9.2**	**64.8**	**67.2**	**3.2**	**14.3**	**10.3**	**10.9**	**26.1**	**26.3**	**21.6**	**23.2**	**21.0**	**26.5**
Africa.......... 607	**13.5**	**–3.6**	**55.4**	**45.2**	**–14.3**	**25.2**	**24.5**	**10.1**	**23.9**	**18.1**	**23.6**	**21.6**	**26.6**	**24.5**
Asia.......... 507	**–1.9**	**20.3**	**98.1**	**93.9**	**10.3**	**10.7**	**3.1**	**18.9**	**65.9**	**48.7**	**–.7**	**6.4**	**19.5**	**65.7**
Europe.......... 170	**–44.7**	**–2.2**	**–37.8**	**177.7**	**–85.4**	**452.0**	**120.9**	**15.9**	**2.1**	**79.0**	**28.6**	**28.0**	**13.0**	**17.1**
Middle East.......... 407	**56.3**	**–30.5**	**26.6**	**33.8**	**12.2**	**23.6**	**27.6**	**5.4**	**23.5**	**12.3**	**34.1**	**27.8**	**23.3**	**21.5**
Western Hemisphere.......... 207	**3.3**	**4.5**	**–9.0**	**–58.0**	**–27.2**	**26.6**	**109.7**	**5.8**	**37.1**	**126.2**	**46.3**	**142.5**	**–61.6**	**–71.9**
Other Countries n.i.e.......... 910	**—**	**—**	**....**	**....**	**....**	**....**	**....**	**10.4**	**8.5**	**26.6**	**31.3**	**14.3**	**23.6**	**24.1**

		Exports							Imports						
		2001	2002	2003	2004	2005	2006	2007	2001	2002	2003	2004	2005	2006	2007
		Millions of U.S. Dollars							*Millions of U.S. Dollars*						
IFS World Total		**38.5**	**30.2**	**37.7**	**46.9**	**94.8**	**58.4**	**62.4**	**139.3**	**129.4**	**156.6**	**176.2**	**267.2**	**430.6**	**319.1**
DOTS World Total	**001**	**38.5**	**31.0**	**37.5**	**47.9**	**56.9**	**58.7**	**90.4Y**	**138.8**	**130.1**	**156.8**	**175.9**	**267.3**	**430.2**	**386.2Y**
Industrial Countries	**101**	**31.5**	**17.6**	**23.4**	**23.6**	**33.0**	**32.5**	**49.2Y**	**61.4**	**56.1**	**61.4**	**73.4**	**121.9**	**176.7**	**111.4Y**
United States	111	.04	.06	.61	.25	.32	.32	.91V	4.28	1.99	3.32	1.90	6.89	9.97	7.70V
Canada	156	—	.02	—	—	.23	.22	.06V	.37	.82	.82	1.59	2.00	2.59	2.00V
Australia	193	—	—	.02	—	—	—	—V	.17	.03	—	.09	.27	.37	.01V
Japan	158	—	—	.02	.22	.30	.30	.13V	6.97	7.46	6.81	10.54	18.31	33.38	2.35V
New Zealand	196	—	—	—	—	—	—	—V	—	—	—	—	—	—	.04V
Austria	122	—	—	—	—	—	—	.17V	—	—	—	—	—	—	.23V
Belgium	124	—	—	—	—	—	—	5.20V	—	—	—	—	—	—	33.65V
Belgium-Luxembourg n.s.	127	4.05	2.63	2.14	1.77	2.19	2.47	—Y	21.51	21.36	23.27	23.94	32.78	50.38	—Y
Cyprus	423	—	—	—	—	—	—	—V	—	—	—	—	—	—	.08V
Denmark	128	—	—	—	—	—	—	.65V	2.74	3.25	3.97	4.14	4.95	9.61	.76V
Finland	172	—	—	—	—	—	—	1.13V	—	—	—	—	—	—	.01V
France	132	.44	.47	.30	.38	.50	.49	3.83V	10.76	9.14	7.59	11.29	13.98	19.05	23.42V
Germany	134	3.01	.78	.41	1.07	1.39	1.43	28.31V	3.53	3.43	5.40	7.04	14.34	10.13	20.89V
Greece	174	—	—	—	—	—	—	—V	.26	.13	.18	.14	.62	.12	.13V
Ireland	178	—	—	—	—	—	—	.04V	.10	.11	.46	.01	.12	.01	.17V
Italy	136	.22	.03	.07	—	—	.04	.92V	2.98	3.26	3.34	6.09	14.42	13.69	6.77V
Luxembourg	137	—	—	—	—	—	—	—V	—	—	—	—	—	—	.08V
Malta	181	—	—	—	—	—	—	—V	—	—	—	—	—	—	2.21V
Netherlands	138	2.79	1.61	1.67	.34	.20	.31	2.81V	2.84	2.32	2.75	3.39	4.52	5.57	4.62V
Norway	142	—	—	—	—	—	—	—V	—	—	—	—	—	—	.03V
Portugal	182	—	—	—	—	—	—	—V	.07	.02	1.04	—	—	—	.16V
Slovenia	961	—	—	—	—	—	—	.03V	—	—	—	—	—	—	.05V
Spain	184	.09	—	—	—	.01	—	.24V	.72	.23	.36	.34	.77	1.11	2.87V
Sweden	144	.01	.01	.01	.01	—	.02	3.91V	—	—	—	—	—	—	.16V
Switzerland	146	10.35	6.06	12.00	13.83	20.73	19.77	.68V	.69	.90	.82	1.32	1.63	.98	.65V
United Kingdom	112	10.54	5.88	6.14	5.77	7.12	7.19	.19V	3.40	1.61	1.21	1.62	6.28	19.80	2.36V
Developing Countries	**202**	**6.3**	**10.6**	**4.9**	**14.7**	**23.6**	**25.9**	**40.9Y**	**76.0**	**72.5**	**94.7**	**100.8**	**144.9**	**252.9**	**274.2Y**
Africa	**607**	**6.0**	**9.9**	**3.4**	**6.0**	**5.0**	**6.4**	**14.7Y**	**33.5**	**43.9**	**69.0**	**71.8**	**88.2**	**93.5**	**101.7Y**
Congo, Dem. Rep. of	636	.16	.52	.31	.29	.60	.84	1.04Y	.73	.60	1.38	2.21	1.02	.80	1.00Y
Congo, Republic of	634	.10	.06	.03	.03	.04	—	—Y	—	—	—	—	—	—	—Y
Djibouti	611	—	—	—	—	—	—	—Y	.08	—	—	—	—	.02	.03Y
Kenya	664	2.64	5.80	.03	.36	.37	1.19	1.47Y	9.34	15.70	22.51	27.50	34.05	35.45	43.99Y
Mauritius	684	—	—	—	—	—	—	—V	—	—	—	—	—	—	.25V
Morocco	686	—	—	—	—	—	—	.28Y	—	—	—	—	—	—	—Y
Rwanda	714	2.20	3.12	2.14	4.20	2.70	3.12	3.87Y	.48	.83	.73	.73	.90	1.03	1.28Y
South Africa	199	—	.01	.12	.27	.34	.03	2.84V	4.04	4.72	5.04	4.52	14.98	9.50	7.34V
Sudan	732	—	—	—	—	—	—	3.65V	—	—	—	—	—	—	—V
Tanzania	738	.05	.04	.03	.16	—	—	.01Y	11.23	13.44	18.38	14.90	12.88	7.59	9.41Y
Uganda	746	.81	.29	.75	.69	.92	1.17	1.46Y	.80	1.27	9.25	11.04	11.37	16.92	21.00Y
Zambia	754	.01	.01	—	—	.01	—	.04V	3.66	4.64	8.11	6.68	9.93	12.92	2.00V
Zimbabwe	698	—	—	—	—	—	—	—Y	.51	.87	.17	.25	.16	.25	.31Y
Africa n.s.	799	—	—	—	—	—	—	—Y	2.61	1.80	3.41	3.91	2.91	9.01	15.11Y
Asia	**507**	**—**	**—**	**.2**	**5.6**	**5.2**	**5.7**	**7.2Y**	**22.8**	**23.0**	**21.7**	**25.9**	**38.4**	**75.6**	**93.1Y**
Bangladesh	513	—	—	—	—	—	—	—V	—	—	.36	.38	.32	.05	.03Y
China,P.R.: Mainland	924	—	—	—	—	—	—	.61Y	5.98	6.44	6.53	6.35	11.83	18.77	14.34V
China,P.R.:Hong Kong	532	—	—	—	—	—	—	.04V	1.35	.62	.40	.08	.44	.37	.32V
India	534	—	—	—	—	—	—	—Y	5.41	5.48	6.86	9.15	10.46	14.82	18.39Y
Indonesia	536	....	....	....	....	....	....	....	—	—	—	—	—	—	.13V
Korea	542	—	—	—	—	—	—	—V	.87	1.40	.54	.96	.28	.66	.63V
Malaysia	548	—	—	—	—	—	—	.01V	—	—	—	—	—	—	.03V
Pakistan	564	—	—	—	5.11	4.43	4.98	6.18Y	.10	.02	.04	.11	—	13.04	16.18Y
Philippines	566	—	—	—	—	—	—	.09V	—	—	—	—	—	—	.34V
Singapore	576	—	—	.18	.52	.78	.70	—V	—	—	—	—	—	—	—V
Taiwan Province of China	528	—	—	—	—	—	—	.04V	.09	.07	.13	.05	.40	—	.03V
Thailand	578	—	—	—	—	—	—	.16V	—	—	—	—	—	—	1.46V
Asia n.s.	598	—	—	—	—	—	—	—Y	9.04	8.97	6.82	8.77	14.63	27.92	41.21Y
Europe	**170**	**.2**	**.7**	**1.3**	**.5**	**10.3**	**10.1**	**14.3Y**	**3.2**	**1.9**	**2.0**	**1.5**	**6.8**	**28.0**	**12.1Y**
Bulgaria	918	—	—	—	—	—	—	—V	—	—	—	—	—	—	.01V
Czech Republic	935	—	—	—	—	—	—	—V	.05	.04	.08	.52	.07	—	.25V
Hungary	944	—	—	—	—	—	—	.07V	—	—	—	—	—	—	—V
Poland	964	—	—	—	—	—	—	.40V	—	—	—	—	—	—	.01V
Romania	968	—	—	—	—	—	—	.45V	.63	.04	.02	.01	.13	.04	—V
Russia	922	—	—	—	.50	.68	.67	1.61V	1.75	.91	.77	.05	.49	20.21	.06V
Slovak Republic	936	....	....	....	....	....	....	....	—	—	—	—	—	—	1.35V
Turkey	186	—	—	—	—	—	—	.05V	—	—	—	—	—	—	.84V
Europe n.s.	884	.24	.72	1.26	—	9.62	9.48	11.76Y	.73	.87	1.11	.94	6.09	7.74	9.61Y
Middle East	**407**	**.1**	**—**	**—**	**2.6**	**3.1**	**3.7**	**4.6Y**	**16.0**	**3.7**	**1.4**	**.9**	**10.3**	**54.6**	**65.8Y**
Egypt	469	—	—	—	2.55	2.21	2.49	3.09Y	—	—	—	—	—	—	—Y
Iran, I.R. of	429	—	—	—	—	—	—	—Y	.89	.04	—	.52	.36	.27	.32Y
Oman	449	—	.01	.02	.01	.89	1.01	1.31Y	—	—	—	—	—	—	—Y
Saudi Arabia	456	.07	—	—	—	—	—	—Y	15.14	3.62	1.45	.42	9.92	54.30	65.51Y
United Arab Emirates	466	—	—	—	.04	—	.20	.26Y	—	—	—	—	—	—	—Y

	Exports							Imports						
	2001	2002	2003	2004	2005	2006	2007	2001	2002	2003	2004	2005	2006	2007
	Millions of U.S. Dollars							*Millions of U.S. Dollars*						
Western Hemisphere................ 207	—	—	—	—	—	—	—Y	.5	.2	.6	.7	1.3	1.3	1.4Y
Colombia.................................... 233	—	—	—	—	—	—	.02V	—	—	—	—	—	—	—V
Mexico.. 273	—	—	—	—	—	—	.02V	—	—	—	—	—	—	.16V
Western Hem. n.s........................ 399	—	—	—	—	—	—	—Y	.47	.18	.60	.70	1.26	1.26	1.27Y
Other Countries n.i.e................ 910	—	—	—	—	—	—	—Y	.3	—	—	.1	.2	.1	.1Y
North Korea.................................. 954	—	—	—	—	—	—	—Y	.29	—	—	.06	.22	.08	.10Y
Countries & Areas n.s.............. 898	.7	2.9	9.2	9.5	.3	.2	.3Y	1.1	1.5	.7	1.6	.2	—	—Y
Memorandum Items														
European Union........................... 998	21.14	11.41	10.75	9.34	11.41	11.94	47.90Y	48.96	44.90	49.67	58.51	92.84	129.47	100.24Y
Oil Exporting Ctys........................ 999	.07	.01	.02	.05	.89	1.21	1.56Y	16.03	3.66	1.45	.94	10.27	54.57	65.97Y
Non-Oil Develop.Ctys................... 201	6.21	10.57	4.86	14.70	22.71	24.68	39.30Y	59.94	68.89	93.23	99.83	134.62	198.38	208.25Y
PERCENT DISTRIBUTION														
Industrial Countries................. 101	81.9	56.6	62.4	49.4	58.0	55.5	54.4	44.2	43.1	39.1	41.8	45.6	41.1	28.8
Developing Countries............. 202	16.3	34.1	13.0	30.8	41.5	44.1	45.2	54.7	55.8	60.4	57.3	54.2	58.8	71.0
Africa..................................... 607	15.5	31.8	9.1	12.6	8.8	10.8	16.2	24.1	33.7	44.0	40.8	33.0	21.7	26.3
Asia....................................... 507	—	—	.5	11.8	9.2	9.7	7.9	16.4	17.7	13.8	14.7	14.4	17.6	24.1
Europe................................... 170	.6	2.3	3.4	1.0	18.1	17.3	15.9	2.3	1.4	1.3	.9	2.5	6.5	3.1
Middle East........................... 407	.2	—	.1	5.4	5.4	6.3	5.1	11.5	2.8	.9	.5	3.8	12.7	17.0
Western Hemisphere............. 207	—	—	—	—	—	—	—	.3	.1	.4	.4	.5	.3	.4
Other Countries n.i.e............... 910	—	—	—	—	—	—	—	.2	—	—	—	.1	—	—
ANNUAL PERCENT CHANGE														
World....................................... 001	−21.2	−19.5	21.0	27.5	18.8	3.2	54.0	−5.7	−6.3	20.6	12.2	52.0	60.9	−10.2
Industrial Countries................. 101	−3.1	−44.3	33.3	1.0	39.6	−1.3	51.2	−9.1	−8.7	9.5	19.7	66.0	45.0	−37.0
Developing Countries............. 202	−61.4	68.5	−53.8	201.7	60.0	9.7	57.8	−2.8	−4.5	30.5	6.4	43.8	74.6	8.4
Africa..................................... 607	−28.0	64.9	−65.3	76.2	−17.0	27.4	130.7	−12.3	31.0	57.3	4.0	22.9	6.0	8.8
Asia....................................... 507	2.0	....	—	—	−7.4	9.0	25.9	18.1	.7	−5.8	19.3	48.4	97.1	23.1
Europe................................... 170	−97.0	200.1	75.3	−60.5	—	−1.5	41.4	45.2	−41.4	7.2	−23.4	345.8	313.0	−56.6
Middle East........................... 407	−32.3	−87.2	189.9	—	18.9	19.3	25.9	−10.9	−77.2	−60.5	−34.7	988.9	431.3	20.6
Western Hemisphere............. 207	—	—	—	....	15.5	23.1	....	−4.3	−61.5	229.3	17.0	80.3	.2	13.2
Other Countries n.i.e............... 910	—	—	....	....	....	....	....	....	—	....	—	266.7	−63.4	24.1

	Exports 2001	2002	2003	2004	2005	2006	2007	Imports 2001	2002	2003	2004	2005	2006	2007
	Millions of U.S. Dollars							*Millions of U.S. Dollars*						
IFS World Total	**1,499.6**	**1,923.0**	**2,118.0**	**2,798.0**	**3,200.0**	**3,800.0**	**4,400.0**	**2,094.0**	**2,318.0**	**2,559.9**	**3,193.3**	**3,927.0**	**4,749.2**	**5,300.0**
DOTS World Total 001	**1,295.8**	**1,488.7**	**1,770.7**	**2,187.6**	**3,014.0**	**3,561.6**	**4,066.4Y**	**1,455.6**	**1,674.7**	**1,732.3**	**2,074.6**	**2,548.1**	**2,985.2**	**6,456.7Y**
Industrial Countries 101	**1,185.1**	**1,268.5**	**1,494.7**	**2,038.5**	**2,289.5**	**2,713.7**	**3,572.4Y**	**68.5**	**155.6**	**140.8**	**227.1**	**392.4**	**298.7**	**553.5Y**
United States 111	832.20	960.37	1,126.39	1,312.03	1,595.33	1,898.92	2,363.09V	16.56	15.60	16.30	23.16	36.19	25.51	152.68V
Canada 156	10.40	—	—	94.49	107.00	115.16	189.03V	.74	—	—	1.41	1.75	2.59	6.12V
Australia 193	1.30	—	—	3.23	5.24	6.54	17.02V	1.66	—	—	10.32	15.55	13.19	38.69V
Japan 158	13.30	18.88	21.66	25.08	62.82	34.07	126.22V	19.65	63.90	74.82	83.70	100.21	129.60	122.64V
New Zealand 196	.40	—	—	—	.35	.39	.82V	.15	—	—	—	2.63	.32	1.44V
Austria 122	.70	—	—	2.69	2.85	11.10	14.68V	.25	—	—	.31	.42	.27	2.98V
Belgium 124	3.00	—	—	9.97	10.13	22.94	42.99V	.45	—	—	4.32	5.78	6.20	40.97V
Cyprus 423	.10	—	—	—	.25	.08	.20V	.03	—	—	—	.37	.31	.72V
Denmark 128	2.40	—	—	2.16	.99	7.64	10.62V	2.11	—	—	3.23	4.69	2.98	1.77V
Finland 172	.40	—	—	1.10	.51	.13	.48V	.11	—	—	12.69	.21	23.77	.36V
France 132	35.00	38.39	48.84	62.49	52.17	55.14	50.14V	12.63	52.00	38.17	47.69	176.78	47.39	83.01V
Germany 134	98.70	118.20	154.35	237.67	225.06	233.49	298.27V	4.18	9.04	5.74	12.42	8.65	8.64	30.76V
Greece 174	.20	—	—	—	1.78	2.82	4.06V	—	—	—	—	.29	.01	1.11V
Iceland 176	—	—	—	—	—	.04	.67V	—	—	—	—	—	.11	—V
Ireland 178	11.00	—	—	13.90	10.00	15.32	17.22V	2.07	—	—	2.05	7.05	3.80	2.88V
Italy 136	2.80	—	—	9.36	6.55	11.03	23.41V	2.44	—	—	4.59	3.27	5.45	23.25V
Luxembourg 137	1.60	—	—	4.20	5.92	6.76	7.03V	—	—	—	5.88	6.22	5.88	6.76V
Malta 181	—	—	—	—	—	—	.09V	—	—	—	—	—	—	—V
Netherlands 138	25.70	—	—	32.86	21.41	27.59	31.95V	.21	—	—	—	2.37	3.04	7.07V
Norway 142	2.80	—	—	4.89	5.17	4.99	9.44V	.11	—	—	.19	.84	.65	.09V
Portugal 182	.50	—	—	—	.05	.22	.21V	.08	—	—	—	.04	.06	.18V
Slovenia 961	.10	—	—	—	.03	1.09	1.08V	—	—	—	—	—	—	3.64V
Spain 184	6.70	—	—	30.64	33.89	85.34	115.08V	.28	—	—	.87	1.71	1.62	2.79V
Sweden 144	6.70	—	—	7.72	9.45	11.93	17.54V	.10	—	—	1.63	1.38	1.63	9.42V
Switzerland 146	2.80	—	—	8.78	8.54	7.96	19.33V	2.94	—	—	5.67	8.38	5.45	8.50V
United Kingdom 112	126.30	132.67	143.49	175.30	124.05	153.03	211.72V	1.75	15.05	5.73	6.96	7.63	10.21	5.66V
Developing Countries 202	**110.4**	**110.1**	**115.5**	**139.8**	**723.5**	**844.1**	**489.3Y**	**1,386.2**	**1,448.8**	**1,515.6**	**1,804.9**	**2,149.5**	**2,676.5**	**5,890.8Y**
Africa 607	**4.2**	**—**	**—**	**—**	**.9**	**1.9**	**5.9Y**	**.5**	**—**	**—**	**—**	**1.3**	**2.0**	**1.5Y**
Algeria 612	—	—	—	—	—	—	—Y	.08	—	—	—	—	—	—Y
Angola 614	—	—	—	—	.03	.03	.04Y	—	—	—	—	.20	—	—Y
Burundi 618	—	—	—	—	—	.01	.01Y	....	....	....	....	....	....	....
Cameroon 622	—	—	—	—	.02	—	—Y	—	—	—	—	—	.02	.03Y
Congo, Dem. Rep. of 636	—	—	—	—	—	—	—Y	—	—	—	—	.01	—	—Y
Congo, Republic of 634	—	—	—	—	.03	—	—Y	....	....	....	....	....	....	....
Ethiopia 644	—	—	—	—	—	.13	.16Y	—	—	—	—	—	—	—Y
Kenya 664	—	—	—	—	.01	—	—Y	—	—	—	—	—	—	—Y
Madagascar 674	—	—	—	—	—	.01	.01Y	—	—	—	—	—	.01	.01Y
Mali 678	—	—	—	—	—	.05	.06Y	....	....	....	....	....	....	....
Mauritius 684	—	—	—	—	—	—	.02V	—	—	—	—	—	.03	.01V
Morocco 686	—	—	—	—	—	.01	.01Y	—	—	—	—	.03	.43	.54Y
Senegal 722	—	—	—	—	—	—	—Y	—	—	—	—	—	.02	.03Y
Sierra Leone 724	—	—	—	—	.02	—	—Y	—	—	—	—	—	—	—Y
South Africa 199	.10	—	—	—	.67	1.39	5.21V	.37	—	—	—	.16	1.32	.50V
Sudan 732	—	—	—	—	—	.07	.09Y	....	....	....	....	....	....	....
Swaziland 734	—	—	—	—	.12	.19	.24Y	—	—	—	—	.85	.18	.22Y
Tanzania 738	—	—	—	—	.04	—	—Y	....	....	....	....	....	....	....
Tunisia 744	—	—	—	—	—	.01	.01Y	—	—	—	—	—	—	—Y
Uganda 746	4.10	—	—	—	—	—	—Y	—	—	—	—	—	—	.12Y
Asia 507	**103.5**	**110.1**	**115.5**	**130.7**	**705.8**	**807.9**	**408.2Y**	**1,380.1**	**1,448.8**	**1,515.6**	**1,802.8**	**2,135.3**	**2,660.4**	**5,848.6Y**
Afghanistan, I.S. of 512	—	—	—	—	.04	.02	.03Y	.02	—	—	—	—	—	—Y
American Samoa 859	....	....	....	....	....	....	....	—	—	—	—	.13	.10	.12Y
Bangladesh 513	—	—	—	—	.01	.08	—V	.42	—	—	—	.37	.57	.67Y
Brunei Darussalam 516	.10	—	—	—	.08	.10	.12Y	.01	—	—	—	.32	.03	.03Y
China,P.R.: Mainland 924	16.70	8.34	6.49	12.63	14.24	15.50	46.44V	86.93	197.79	223.39	341.82	423.51	523.85	969.38V
China,P.R.:Hong Kong 532	4.50	6.00	4.88	5.17	540.87	542.56	17.09V	116.92	371.66	408.90	413.11	449.73	539.22	673.29V
China,P.R.:Macao 546	—	—	—	—	.03	—	.04V	—	—	—	—	1.29	1.28	15.40V
India 534	.10	—	—	—	.21	.55	.68Y	2.85	—	—	—	16.74	27.54	34.18Y
Indonesia 536	.60	.95	1.74	1.53	1.19	1.62	1.14V	9.91	77.56	81.96	78.62	82.63	85.34	134.04V
Korea 542	1.00	1.45	1.46	25.09	2.01	3.20	8.07V	49.62	94.76	80.73	99.58	150.68	146.09	309.57V
Lao People's Dem.Rep 544	.80	—	—	—	.21	.28	.34Y	.02	—	—	—	.20	.96	1.19Y
Malaysia 548	10.30	22.82	16.43	9.06	8.55	7.25	19.41V	19.25	58.47	77.79	77.65	92.48	89.37	147.54V
Mongolia 948	....	....	....	....	....	....	....	.02	—	—	—	—	.21	.26Y
Myanmar 518	—	—	—	—	.07	.03	.04Y	.07	—	—	—	.42	.13	.16Y
Nepal 558	—	—	—	—	—	—	—Y	—	—	—	—	.01	.08	.10Y
New Caledonia 839	—	—	—	—	.03	.01	.01Y	—	—	—	—	—	—	—Y
Pakistan 564	—	—	—	—	.77	.06	.07Y	.42	—	—	—	10.94	13.17	16.34Y
Papua New Guinea 853	—	—	—	—	.01	.02	.03Y	—	—	—	—	.01	.05	.07Y
Philippines 566	4.20	—	—	2.08	1.77	1.97	.46V	2.51	—	—	4.41	6.03	7.25	9.38V
Singapore 576	28.00	26.59	29.12	10.47	69.53	138.83	76.67V	399.49	122.49	119.65	144.53	136.15	156.84	482.24V

	Exports							Imports						
	2001	2002	2003	2004	2005	2006	2007	2001	2002	2003	2004	2005	2006	2007
	Millions of U.S. Dollars							Millions of U.S. Dollars						
Sri Lanka 524	.40	—	—	1.18	.10	.45	.56Y	.02	—	—	.28	.32	1.60	1.98Y
Taiwan Province of China 528	4.70	3.59	4.34	3.90	4.85	5.20	8.38V	78.18	189.26	188.01	242.71	291.14	381.84	471.61V
Thailand 578	7.60	7.94	11.78	17.14	15.22	15.14	44.75V	503.93	238.38	215.96	231.35	290.56	415.03	1,491.11V
Vietnam 582	24.50	32.41	39.22	42.42	46.05	75.04	183.91V	109.51	98.44	119.16	168.69	181.61	269.91	1,089.88V
Europe 170	**1.1**	**—**	**—**	**5.2**	**6.3**	**14.2**	**34.8Y**	**5.0**	**—**	**—**	**1.6**	**4.7**	**6.3**	**25.1Y**
Albania 914	—	—	—	—	—	.04	.01V	—	—	—	—	.02	.03	—V
Belarus 913	—	—	—	—	—	—	.18V	—	—	—	—	1.06	1.23	—V
Bulgaria 918	—	—	—	—	.01	—	.01V	1.91	—	—	—	—	.03	1.39V
Croatia 960	—	—	—	—	.02	.01	—V	—	—	—	—	—	—	—V
Czech Republic 935	.10	—	—	—	.19	.96	1.54V	—	—	—	—	.01	.41	.20V
Estonia 939	—	—	—	—	—	—	.61V	—	—	—	—	—	—	.02V
Georgia 915	....	....	....	....	....	....	....	.02	—	—	—	—	—	—Y
Hungary 944	.10	—	—	—	.10	.59	.18V	.09	—	—	—	.04	.04	.12V
Kazakhstan 916	—	—	—	—	—	—	.02Y	—	—	—	—	—	—	—Y
Kyrgyz Republic 917	—	—	—	—	—	—	.30V	—	—	—	—	—	—	—V
Latvia 941	—	—	—	—	—	—	.08V	—	—	—	—	—	—	.38V
Lithuania 946	—	—	—	—	—	—	.21V	—	—	—	—	—	—	.01V
Poland 964	.30	—	—	1.12	.41	1.66	.56V	—	—	—	.02	.04	.10	4.00V
Romania 968	—	—	—	—	.03	.06	.56V	—	—	—	—	—	—	.24V
Russia 922	.40	—	—	2.71	3.41	5.50	16.07V	2.83	—	—	1.02	3.23	2.72	12.32V
Slovak Republic 936	—	—	—	—	.07	.34	1.39V	—	—	—	—	.04	.02	.49V
Turkey 186	.20	—	—	1.40	1.71	3.32	10.95V	.12	—	—	.56	.20	1.63	5.83V
Ukraine 926	—	—	—	—	.34	1.74	2.16Y	—	—	—	—	.07	.11	.14Y
Middle East 407	**.3**	**—**	**—**	**1.6**	**2.0**	**3.0**	**3.6Y**	**.1**	**—**	**—**	**.2**	**3.8**	**5.2**	**8.7Y**
Bahrain 419	—	—	—	—	.06	.01	.02Y	—	—	—	—	.06	.08	.10Y
Egypt 469	—	—	—	—	.05	.09	.11Y	—	—	—	—	1.66	—	—Y
Iran, I.R. of 429	—	—	—	—	—	—	—Y	—	—	—	—	.04	1.50	1.81Y
Israel 436	.10	—	—	—	.11	.26	.09V	.02	—	—	—	.02	.05	.22V
Jordan 439	—	—	—	—	.04	.03	—V	.01	—	—	—	.03	.44	2.86V
Kuwait 443	—	—	—	—	—	.01	.02Y	—	—	—	—	—	—	—Y
Lebanon 446	—	—	—	—	.03	.09	.11Y	—	—	—	—	—	—	—Y
Libya 672	—	—	—	—	—	—	—Y	—	—	—	—	—	.01	.01Y
Oman 449	....	....	....	....	....	....	....	—	—	—	—	.05	.06	.08Y
Qatar 453	—	—	—	—	.02	.01	.02Y	—	—	—	—	—	—	—Y
Saudi Arabia 456	—	—	—	—	.06	.14	.18Y	.01	—	—	—	.48	1.69	2.04Y
Syrian Arab Republic 463	—	—	—	—	—	.11	.13Y	—	—	—	—	.01	—	—Y
United Arab Emirates 466	.20	—	—	1.59	1.63	2.22	2.87Y	.03	—	—	.24	1.41	1.34	1.62Y
Western Hemisphere 207	**1.3**	**—**	**—**	**2.3**	**8.4**	**17.1**	**36.9Y**	**.6**	**—**	**—**	**.4**	**4.4**	**2.6**	**6.9Y**
Argentina 213	.10	—	—	—	.65	1.41	2.32V	.36	—	—	—	.71	.58	3.28V
Aruba 314	....	....	....	....	....	....	....	.01	—	—	—	.06	.15	.18Y
Belize 339	—	—	—	—	—	.11	.13Y	—	—	—	—	—	—	—Y
Brazil 223	—	—	—	—	.52	.82	3.78V	—	—	—	—	.96	1.13	—V
Chile 228	.10	—	—	—	1.12	3.00	6.60V	.10	—	—	—	—	.12	.08V
Colombia 233	—	—	—	—	.12	.12	.34V	—	—	—	—	—	—	—V
Costa Rica 238	—	—	—	—	—	.01	.01Y	....	....	....	....	....	....	....
Dominican Republic 243	—	—	—	—	—	—	—Y	—	—	—	—	.11	—	—Y
Ecuador 248	—	—	—	—	.08	.16	.20Y	....	....	....	....	....	....	....
El Salvador 253	—	—	—	—	.08	—	.12V	—	—	—	—	1.72	.25	.76V
Falkland Islands 323	....	....	....	....	....	....	....	.04	—	—	—	—	.17	.21Y
Guatemala 258	—	—	—	—	.01	—	—Y	—	—	—	—	—	—	—Y
Haiti 263	—	—	—	—	.15	—	—Y	—	—	—	—	—	—	—Y
Jamaica 343	—	—	—	—	—	.04	—V	—	—	—	—	.01	—	—V
Mexico 273	1.00	—	—	2.29	3.80	8.28	22.61V	—	—	—	.35	.10	.03	.99V
Nicaragua 278	—	—	—	—	.10	.03	—V	—	—	—	—	.71	.14	—V
Panama 283	.10	—	—	—	1.05	2.75	—V	—	—	—	—	—	—	—Y
Paraguay 288	—	—	—	—	—	.01	.01Y	.08	—	—	—	—	—	—Y
Peru 293	—	—	—	—	.51	.14	.29Y	—	—	—	—	.07	.01	—Y
St. Pierre-Miquelon 363	—	—	—	—	.17	.02	.02Y	....	....	....	....	....	....	....
Trinidad and Tobago 369	—	—	—	—	—	—	.26Y	—	—	—	—	—	—	—Y
Uruguay 298	—	—	—	—	.04	.11	.14Y	—	—	—	—	—	—	1.38Y
Venezuela, Rep. Bol. 299	—	—	—	—	.02	.05	.03V	—	—	—	—	—	—	—Y
Other Countries n.i.e. 910	**—**	**—**	**—**	**—**	**—**	**.1**	**.1Y**	**.7**	**—**	**—**	**—**	**3.3**	**4.2**	**5.2Y**
North Korea 954	—	—	—	—	.01	.10	.12Y	.74	—	—	—	3.28	4.18	5.18Y
Countries & Areas n.s. 898	**.3**	**110.1**	**160.5**	**9.3**	**1.0**	**3.6**	**4.5Y**	**.2**	**70.3**	**76.0**	**42.6**	**2.9**	**5.8**	**7.2Y**
Memorandum Items														
European Union 998	322.40	289.26	346.68	591.16	505.84	649.22	851.34Y	26.78	76.09	49.64	102.66	226.99	121.82	228.56Y
Oil Exporting Ctys 999	.80	.95	1.74	3.12	2.92	4.06	4.26Y	10.03	77.56	81.96	78.86	84.62	89.95	139.59Y
Non-Oil Develop.Ctys 201	109.60	109.14	113.72	136.66	720.55	840.02	485.09Y	1,376.15	1,371.25	1,433.59	1,726.08	2,064.85	2,586.59	5,751.19Y
PERCENT DISTRIBUTION														
Industrial Countries 101	**91.5**	**85.2**	**84.4**	**93.2**	**76.0**	**76.2**	**87.9**	**4.7**	**9.3**	**8.1**	**10.9**	**15.4**	**10.0**	**8.6**
Developing Countries 202	**8.5**	**7.4**	**6.5**	**6.4**	**24.0**	**23.7**	**12.0**	**95.2**	**86.5**	**87.5**	**87.0**	**84.4**	**89.7**	**91.2**
Africa 607	**.3**	**—**	**—**	**—**	**—**	**.1**	**.1**	**—**	**—**	**—**	**—**	**—**	**.1**	**—**
Asia 507	**8.0**	**7.4**	**6.5**	**6.0**	**23.4**	**22.7**	**10.0**	**94.8**	**86.5**	**87.5**	**86.9**	**83.8**	**89.1**	**90.6**
Europe 170	**.1**	**—**	**—**	**.2**	**.2**	**.4**	**.9**	**.3**	**—**	**—**	**.1**	**.2**	**.2**	**.4**
Middle East 407	**—**	**—**	**—**	**.1**	**.1**	**.1**	**.1**	**—**	**—**	**—**	**—**	**.1**	**.2**	**.1**
Western Hemisphere 207	**.1**	**—**	**—**	**.1**	**.3**	**.5**	**.9**	**—**	**—**	**—**	**—**	**.2**	**.1**	**.1**

	Exports							Imports						
	2001	2002	2003	2004	2005	2006	2007	2001	2002	2003	2004	2005	2006	2007
Other Countries n.i.e................ 910	—	—	—	—	—	—	—	.1	—	—	—	.1	.1	.1
ANNUAL PERCENT CHANGE														
World.. 001	15.4	14.9	18.9	23.5	37.8	18.2	14.2	2.2	15.1	3.4	19.8	22.8	17.2	116.3
Industrial Countries.................. 101	19.4	7.0	17.8	36.4	12.3	18.5	31.6	–68.9	127.1	–9.5	61.3	72.8	–23.9	85.3
Developing Countries.............. 202	–8.2	–.3	4.9	21.1	417.5	16.7	–42.0	16.6	4.5	4.6	19.1	19.1	24.5	120.1
Africa...................................... 607	—	–89.6	.3	144.3	–18.1	101.8	208.2	164.7	–44.8	575.1	–56.0	40.7	59.6	–27.8
Asia... 507	–12.3	6.4	4.9	13.2	440.1	14.5	–49.5	16.5	5.0	4.6	19.0	18.4	24.6	119.8
Europe..................................... 170	–4.3	422.5	27.3	80.3	20.3	126.4	144.7	233.6	51.7	42.8	73.5	195.1	33.7	298.1
Middle East............................. 407	400.0	11.1	–49.0	305.7	24.8	49.7	19.7	–90.9	911.2	–41.4	–8.1	—	37.4	68.8
Western Hemisphere.............. 207	49.4	–73.9	99.9	123.3	268.2	102.8	116.0	–55.6	265.6	–46.0	45.7	—	–41.8	166.9
Other Countries n.i.e................ 910	–105.4	—	....	....	....	—	24.1	–78.3	8.5	26.6	31.3	14.3	27.3	24.1

Cameroon 622

		Exports							Imports						
		2001	2002	2003	2004	2005	2006	2007	2001	2002	2003	2004	2005	2006	2007
		Millions of U.S. Dollars							*Millions of U.S. Dollars*						
IFS World Total		**1,749.0**	**1,802.0**	**2,282.6**	**2,476.8**	**2,797.7**	**3,576.4**	**3,750.0**	**1,852.0**	**1,866.0**	**2,163.4**	**2,406.3**	**2,735.0**	**3,150.5**	**3,760.0**
DOTS World Total	**001**	**1,748.8**	**1,800.5**	**2,240.0**	**3,464.8Y**	**3,624.6Y**	**4,725.6Y**	**5,017.5Y**	**1,850.9**	**1,805.1**	**1,788.5**	**2,248.4Y**	**2,535.1Y**	**2,906.1Y**	**3,612.7Y**
Industrial Countries	**101**	**1,256.2**	**1,401.8**	**1,601.8**	**2,377.4Y**	**2,561.6Y**	**3,377.8Y**	**3,403.9Y**	**1,142.7**	**1,138.0**	**1,074.5**	**1,396.5Y**	**1,370.9Y**	**1,479.3Y**	**1,825.4Y**
United States	111	35.95	121.93	168.69	304.91V	155.55V	265.55V	286.09V	145.85	155.75	102.23	109.56V	128.92V	132.00V	146.30V
Canada	156	7.52	.18	.87	10.79V	8.23V	5.32V	6.72V	19.76	20.51	16.20	8.29V	14.15V	9.40V	20.39V
Australia	193	.03	.05	.24	.47V	.85V	.59V	1.06V	2.24	2.00	2.02	.85V	10.03V	2.58V	3.28V
Japan	158	1.62	1.16	1.79	6.52V	5.63V	18.98V	2.38V	84.21	84.21	121.96	21.75V	19.75V	20.25V	26.03V
New Zealand	196	.08	.12	.10	.15V	.30V	.18V	.30V	.09	.23	.21	.24V	2.53V	2.81V	4.95V
Austria	122	—	.03	.10	.57V	1.27V	1.75V	2.21V	2.12	4.40	6.44	2.61V	1.72V	2.35V	6.16V
Belgium	124	—	—	—	92.54V	175.96V	194.99V	162.87V	—	—	—	171.31V	160.90V	177.25V	210.98V
Belgium-Luxembourg n.s.	127	39.73	38.20	56.22	—Y	—Y	—Y	—Y	85.08	74.41	84.59	—Y	—Y	—Y	—Y
Cyprus	423	.04	.08	.12	.22V	.15Y	.15V	.24V	.02	.10	.47	.03V	—V	.01V	.06V
Denmark	128	1.69	.63	.40	1.82V	3.03V	2.06V	2.53V	2.43	3.50	3.32	5.56V	2.68V	3.09V	3.37V
Finland	172	.21	.13	.01	.17V	.33V	4.20V	.80V	11.17	8.94	10.75	11.43V	5.48V	5.40V	8.50V
France	132	189.46	233.27	243.18	315.75V	344.28V	543.94V	587.94V	445.88	451.63	391.86	636.15V	611.40V	686.87V	844.96V
Germany	134	24.85	25.81	25.54	63.30V	81.35V	54.18V	71.79V	138.21	86.82	77.19	103.59V	107.40V	103.79V	140.34V
Greece	174	3.69	2.82	4.85	7.50V	9.27V	6.54V	7.92V	2.59	2.53	11.57	4.53V	8.42V	3.24V	11.85V
Iceland	176	.01	—	—	.03V	.20V	—V	.02V	.26	.01	—	—V	—V	—V	—V
Ireland	178	10.67	7.10	12.68	30.28V	33.82V	14.32V	22.74V	10.24	11.15	10.48	14.25V	9.36V	10.05V	11.51V
Italy	136	473.26	341.55	301.30	425.73V	499.31V	723.23V	788.85V	56.44	62.09	67.94	91.57V	90.21V	88.79V	137.71V
Luxembourg	137	—	—	—	.24V	—V	.01V	—V	—	—	—	1.05V	.69V	.63V	1.18V
Malta	181	.04	.03	.05	.02V	.07V	.04V	.21V	.01	.09	.49	.72V	1.17V	1.49V	.94V
Netherlands	138	157.27	230.22	237.67	149.72V	286.27V	336.11V	308.18V	33.86	51.99	64.20	80.87V	67.00V	77.05V	84.35V
Norway	142	.03	.01	.03	.05V	.07V	.11V	.27V	3.08	3.44	4.84	2.39V	3.81V	7.84V	8.04V
Portugal	182	17.35	14.28	15.37	63.34V	24.14V	66.31V	35.47V	2.17	4.29	6.79	3.02V	3.20V	10.85V	5.95V
Slovenia	961	—	—	—	6.10Y	7.02V	12.41V	3.49V	—	.70	.99	1.31Y	.10V	.03V	.31V
Spain	184	263.59	358.15	489.73	524.19V	628.58V	1,000.15V	995.51V	28.58	27.56	26.95	45.57V	44.71V	36.79V	53.31V
Sweden	144	.18	.18	.11	17.70V	.07V	.25V	.14V	16.99	14.67	17.08	11.90V	13.28V	30.38V	29.48V
Switzerland	146	.11	.21	.24	3.82V	2.95V	8.30V	3.00V	7.38	7.21	6.17	13.67V	11.75V	20.02V	12.85V
United Kingdom	112	28.81	25.67	42.48	351.48V	292.92V	118.17V	113.16V	44.08	59.73	39.74	54.31V	52.29V	46.37V	52.64V
Developing Countries	**202**	**477.6**	**375.9**	**595.2**	**1,030.8Y**	**998.4Y**	**1,267.9Y**	**1,514.5Y**	**677.7**	**655.0**	**705.3**	**840.4Y**	**1,151.1Y**	**1,410.6Y**	**1,767.2Y**
Africa	**607**	**160.3**	**183.4**	**286.6**	**330.9Y**	**359.6Y**	**408.5Y**	**513.9Y**	**435.8**	**355.3**	**354.5**	**398.1Y**	**468.0Y**	**601.9Y**	**728.8Y**
Algeria	612	—	1.43	5.70	7.41Y	9.44Y	11.65Y	15.10Y	—	—	.78	1.03Y	1.40Y	1.76Y	2.12Y
Angola	614	14.65	.83	1.98	2.59Y	2.96Y	3.66Y	4.55Y	1.55	.29	1.09	1.43Y	1.63Y	2.02Y	2.51Y
Benin	638	1.34	1.39	3.07	9.11V	8.76V	10.82Y	13.43Y	.47	4.83	5.85	.68V	.51V	.63Y	.78Y
Burkina Faso	748	—	.03	.06	.08Y	.09Y	.11Y	.13Y	—	—	—	—Y	—Y	—Y	—Y
Cape Verde	624	—	—	1.89	2.48Y	2.83Y	3.50Y	4.34Y	—	—	—	—Y	—Y	—Y	—Y
Central African Rep.	626	5.20	14.21	13.04	17.13Y	19.57Y	24.19Y	30.02Y	.02	—	—	—Y	—Y	—Y	.01Y
Chad	628	11.60	38.74	45.61	59.90Y	68.44Y	84.59Y	104.98Y	.11	.32	.09	.11Y	.13Y	.16Y	.20Y
Comoros	632	.03	.02	—	—Y	—Y	—Y	—Y	—	—	—	—Y	—Y	—Y	—Y
Congo, Dem. Rep. of	636	27.10	11.42	—	—Y	—Y	—Y	—Y	.01	—	.13	.17Y	.20Y	.24Y	.30Y
Congo, Republic of	634	18.85	21.20	20.33	10.17V	11.62Y	14.36Y	17.83Y	4.94	10.13	14.89	1.15V	1.31Y	1.62Y	2.01Y
Côte d'Ivoire	662	2.89	11.90	2.47	16.64V	22.74V	1.92V	2.39Y	19.98	28.38	34.66	61.36V	44.46V	75.19V	93.31Y
Equatorial Guinea	642	10.00	—	—	—Y	—Y	—Y	—Y	39.94	—	—	—Y	—Y	—Y	—Y
Gabon	646	15.66	18.64	42.78	56.19Y	64.20Y	79.35Y	98.47Y	3.44	3.13	2.27	2.98Y	3.40Y	4.20Y	5.21Y
Gambia, The	648	—	.06	1.49	1.95Y	2.23Y	2.76Y	3.42Y	—	.01	.04	.06Y	.06Y	.08Y	.10Y
Ghana	652	.22	10.87	32.66	42.89Y	49.01Y	60.57Y	75.17Y	.62	18.07	10.00	13.14Y	15.01Y	18.55Y	23.03Y
Guinea	656	.03	.75	2.08	1.02V	1.17Y	1.45Y	1.80Y	33.86	13.65	25.72	.01V	.01Y	.01Y	.01Y
Guinea-Bissau	654	—	—	—	—Y	—Y	—Y	—Y	1.07	.21	—	—Y	—Y	—Y	—Y
Kenya	664	—	—	—	.08V	.09Y	.12Y	.14Y	.29	.11	.20	1.96V	2.23Y	2.76Y	3.43Y
Liberia	668	—	—	2.79	3.66Y	4.18Y	5.17Y	6.42Y	—	—	—	—Y	—Y	—Y	—Y
Madagascar	674	—	—	.10	.13Y	.15Y	.18Y	.22Y	—	—	.01	.01Y	.01Y	.02Y	.02Y
Malawi	676	—	—	—	—Y	—Y	—Y	—Y	.03	.05	—	—Y	—Y	—Y	—Y
Mali	678	.02	.12	.19	.24Y	.28Y	.34Y	.43Y	—	—	.02	.02Y	.03Y	.03Y	.04Y
Mauritania	682	—	—	.05	.06Y	.07Y	.09Y	.11Y	15.61	14.25	18.87	24.78Y	28.32Y	35.00Y	43.43Y
Mauritius	684	—	2.17	1.65	2.91V	1.41V	1.02V	4.93V	—	.11	.92	.09V	.07V	1.57V	.95V
Morocco	686	8.48	10.37	10.94	15.02V	11.55V	14.27Y	17.71Y	2.56	4.27	4.16	6.58V	6.18V	7.63Y	9.47Y
Mozambique	688	—	—	.05	.06Y	.07Y	.08Y	.10Y	—	—	—	—Y	—Y	—Y	—Y
Namibia	728	—	.65	4.63	8.61Y	12.58Y	16.56Y	20.54Y	2.84	2.78	4.02	5.26Y	6.51Y	7.75Y	8.99Y
Niger	692	11.16	—	.01	.43V	.49Y	.61Y	.76Y	—	—	—	—V	—Y	—Y	—Y
Nigeria	694	13.43	15.07	16.64	21.64Y	27.55Y	34.01Y	44.06Y	258.59	199.55	169.26	223.97Y	304.66Y	383.01Y	462.06Y
Rwanda	714	—	.05	.44	.58Y	.66Y	.82Y	1.02Y	—	—	—	—Y	—Y	—Y	—Y
São Tomé & Príncipe	716	—	.96	.43	.56Y	.64Y	.79Y	.98Y	—	.05	.05	.07Y	.08Y	.10Y	.13Y
Senegal	722	6.69	6.42	9.50	11.53V	12.03V	10.67V	13.24Y	10.37	8.32	11.32	11.33V	9.19V	11.01V	13.67Y
Seychelles	718	—	—	—	—Y	—Y	—Y	—Y	—	—	—	—Y	—Y	.01Y	.01Y
Sierra Leone	724	.02	.03	1.46	1.92Y	2.19Y	2.71Y	3.36Y	—	.01	—	—Y	.01Y	.01Y	.01Y
South Africa	199	1.02	4.02	53.10	29.31V	2.75V	1.40V	2.63V	32.31	38.01	44.03	36.28V	39.01V	43.74V	51.15V
Sudan	732	—	—	.12	—V	—V	—V	—V	—	—	—	—V	—V	—V	—V
Swaziland	734	—	—	—	—Y	—Y	—Y	—Y	.02	.01	.02	.02Y	.03Y	.03Y	.04Y
Tanzania	738	.06	.02	.07	.09Y	.10Y	.13Y	.16Y	.25	—	.07	.09Y	.10Y	.13Y	.16Y
Togo	742	3.31	3.37	5.12	.95V	10.50V	12.98Y	16.11Y	1.72	3.58	1.53	.18V	.09V	.11Y	.13Y
Tunisia	744	8.55	8.63	6.14	5.54V	9.23V	7.55V	9.36Y	3.66	3.68	4.21	4.87V	3.22V	4.49V	5.57Y

		Exports							Imports						
		2001	2002	2003	2004	2005	2006	2007	2001	2002	2003	2004	2005	2006	2007
		Millions of U.S. Dollars							Millions of U.S. Dollars						
Uganda	746	—	—	—	—Y	—Y	—Y	—Y	—	.19	—	—Y	—Y	—Y	—Y
Zambia	754	—	—	—	—V	—V	.01V	.02V	—	—	—	—V	—V	—V	.01V
Zimbabwe	698	—	—	—	—V	.02V	—V	—Y	1.51	1.31	.33	.41V	.14V	—V	—Y
Asia	**507**	**297.8**	**161.4**	**218.9**	**555.7Y**	**470.1Y**	**668.9Y**	**704.1Y**	**122.1**	**164.6**	**205.0**	**302.5Y**	**449.8Y**	**512.6Y**	**698.0Y**
Afghanistan, I.S. of	512	—	—	—	—Y	—Y	—Y	—Y	—	—	.02	.02Y	.03Y	.03Y	.04Y
Bangladesh	513	4.74	5.42	9.62	6.95V	1.92V	.74V	—V	1.11	.76	1.33	1.55V	1.44V	1.32Y	1.35Y
Brunei Darussalam	516	—	—	—	—Y	—Y	—Y	—Y	—	—	.01	.02Y	.02Y	.03Y	.03Y
Cambodia	522	—	—	—	—V	—V	.02V	.03Y	—	—	.01	—V	.02V	—V	.01Y
China,P.R.: Mainland	924	103.16	77.76	97.96	91.62V	60.71V	181.63V	145.30V	49.97	66.47	86.60	108.75V	142.87V	210.27V	326.46V
China,P.R.:Hong Kong	532	1.24	7.07	8.63	15.57V	4.22V	12.06V	7.60V	4.46	5.42	10.32	32.96V	37.49V	42.08V	49.71V
China,P.R.:Macao	546	—	—	—	.01V	.01V	—V	—V	—	—	—	—V	—V	—V	—V
India	534	15.68	27.00	7.62	10.16V	10.92V	13.49Y	16.74Y	10.46	25.10	31.22	27.62V	37.98V	46.94Y	58.25Y
Indonesia	536	3.83	1.07	2.68	8.57V	6.13V	10.09V	5.80V	16.48	11.46	19.13	17.43V	15.33V	17.66V	18.86V
Korea	542	.45	.59	.61	244.99V	294.45V	387.11V	472.90V	6.23	12.63	11.86	16.77V	14.69V	12.56V	27.45V
Malaysia	548	1.25	1.42	8.14	40.48V	26.87V	38.16V	18.81V	3.54	3.80	8.53	7.27V	10.15V	25.40V	39.07V
Myanmar	518	—	—	—	—Y	—Y	—Y	—Y	—	5.06	1.29	1.69Y	1.94Y	2.39Y	2.97Y
New Caledonia	839	—	—	—	—V	—Y	—Y	.01Y	—	—	—	—Y	—Y	—Y	—Y
Pakistan	564	3.59	7.89	12.66	13.44V	9.59V	11.85Y	14.71Y	11.43	1.81	1.74	9.01V	51.43V	63.57Y	78.89Y
Philippines	566	—	.32	.02	.03V	—V	—V	—V	.10	.09	.24	—V	—V	.13V	.16V
Singapore	576	4.67	.05	.25	29.08V	.50V	.65V	2.59V	1.56	1.81	3.10	23.63V	16.59V	20.98V	21.93V
Sri Lanka	524	—	.11	—	—Y	—Y	—Y	—Y	.32	.11	.20	.27Y	.30Y	.38Y	.47Y
Taiwan Province of China	528	141.64	20.01	58.94	84.64V	44.51V	1.63V	1.25V	2.55	4.36	3.22	14.29V	4.75V	8.48V	16.56V
Thailand	578	15.14	12.19	11.68	10.13V	10.24V	11.50V	18.33V	12.72	25.44	21.44	41.20V	114.73V	60.41V	55.83V
Vietnam	582	2.41	.47	.12	—V	—V	—V	—V	1.15	.26	4.78	—V	—V	—V	—V
Europe	**170**	**8.1**	**19.6**	**17.5**	**51.6Y**	**53.3Y**	**44.4Y**	**76.1Y**	**73.1**	**58.7**	**73.0**	**56.0Y**	**64.9Y**	**77.3Y**	**96.4Y**
Albania	914	—	—	—	—V	.03V	.02V	.06V	—	—	.03	—V	—V	—V	.12V
Azerbaijan	912	—	—	—	—V	—V	.01V	—V	—	—	—	.01V	—V	—V	—V
Belarus	913	—	—	—	.46V	.01V	.13V	.01V	—	—	—	.76V	1.04V	2.37V	6.07V
Bulgaria	918	—	—	—	.37V	.11V	.08V	.29V	1.52	1.69	2.17	.68V	.75V	1.57V	.19V
Czech Republic	935	—	—	—	4.19V	4.51V	.62V	.27V	—	3.38	2.97	.43V	1.76V	1.64V	1.86V
Czechoslovakia n.s.	937	—	—	—	—Y	—Y	—Y	—Y	3.90	—	—	—Y	—Y	—Y	—Y
Estonia	939	—	—	—	—V	—V	—V	—V	—	—	—	.62V	1.03V	.14V	.17V
Georgia	915	—	—	—	.09V	.11V	—V	—Y	—	—	—	—Y	—Y	—Y	—Y
Gibraltar	823	—	—	.28	.37Y	.42Y	.52Y	.64Y	—	—	—	—Y	—Y	—Y	—Y
Hungary	944	—	—	—	.72V	.62V	.78V	.06V	.45	2.38	3.16	1.25V	2.74V	2.11V	1.99V
Kazakhstan	916	—	—	—	—V	—Y	—Y	—Y	—	—	—	.01V	.01Y	.01Y	.01Y
Lithuania	946	—	.01	—	.06V	.39V	.52V	.38V	—	.26	7.48	.68V	.29V	9.24V	4.75V
Macedonia, FYR	962	—	—	—	.02V	.02V	.08V	.10Y	—	—	—	—V	—V	—Y	—Y
Poland	964	2.47	.64	.78	3.18V	2.53V	5.05V	6.25V	2.98	5.24	6.31	4.66V	8.06V	4.44V	9.22V
Romania	968	.24	.39	.08	.85V	1.04V	.34V	3.18V	5.85	6.53	7.61	8.12V	11.19V	15.84V	11.32V
Russia	922	1.11	—	.06	2.22V	2.16V	1.83V	3.65V	9.83	13.18	7.70	1.55V	.70V	1.09V	5.61V
Serbia & Montenegro	965	2.35	3.02	—	—Y	—Y	—Y	—Y	.16	.18	.05	.06Y	.07Y	.09Y	.11Y
Slovak Republic	936	—	—	—	.59Y	.33V	.04V	.08V	—	.63	.92	1.21Y	.50V	.06V	.30V
Turkey	186	1.95	12.00	11.04	31.42V	32.27V	23.48V	47.67V	9.75	14.30	20.48	23.12V	18.59V	16.30V	26.82V
Ukraine	926	—	—	—	.20V	.93V	1.15Y	1.43Y	10.25	10.83	14.06	12.79V	18.12V	22.40Y	27.80Y
U.S.S.R. n.s.	930	—	.50	1.72	2.26Y	2.59Y	3.20Y	3.97Y	—	—	—	—Y	—Y	—Y	—Y
Yugoslavia n.s.	966	—	3.02	3.51	4.61Y	5.27Y	6.51Y	8.08Y	—	—	—	—Y	—Y	—Y	—Y
Europe n.s.	884	—	—	—	—Y	—Y	—Y	—Y	28.39	.07	.02	.02Y	.02Y	.03Y	.04Y
Middle East	**407**	**6.3**	**6.7**	**11.9**	**11.8Y**	**11.8Y**	**14.6Y**	**19.0Y**	**28.1**	**37.7**	**27.0**	**36.6Y**	**46.3Y**	**64.8Y**	**70.8Y**
Bahrain	419	—	—	—	—Y	—Y	—Y	—Y	—	2.06	—	—Y	—Y	—Y	—Y
Egypt	469	.11	.43	1.10	1.44Y	1.65Y	2.03Y	2.53Y	3.42	10.10	11.67	15.33Y	17.52Y	21.65Y	26.87Y
Iran, I.R. of	429	—	—	—	—Y	—Y	—Y	—Y	1.65	1.27	2.08	2.75Y	3.74Y	4.70Y	5.67Y
Israel	436	.77	.11	.07	—V	—V	—V	.18V	1.33	3.03	2.73	4.40V	6.27V	14.85V	9.68V
Jordan	439	—	.07	.28	.17V	.15V	.10V	.36V	—	—	.02	.01V	—V	—V	.04V
Kuwait	443	.09	.31	.22	.28Y	.36Y	.44Y	.57Y	—	.06	.03	.04Y	.05Y	.07Y	.08Y
Lebanon	446	.59	.50	3.03	3.98Y	4.54Y	5.62Y	6.97Y	4.65	1.51	.95	1.25Y	1.43Y	1.76Y	2.19Y
Libya	672	—	—	—	—Y	—Y	—Y	—Y	—	.03	—	—Y	—Y	—Y	—Y
Oman	449	—	—	.28	.36Y	.46Y	.57Y	.74Y	—	.01	.37	.49Y	.67Y	.84Y	1.02Y
Qatar	453	—	—	—	.55V	.04V	.20V	.26Y	—	.11	.18	.66V	.69V	.86V	1.04Y
Saudi Arabia	456	2.51	3.94	4.60	2.94V	1.97V	2.44Y	3.16Y	17.02	12.06	2.95	3.90Y	5.31Y	6.67Y	8.05Y
Syrian Arab Republic	463	1.03	.32	.79	—V	—Y	—Y	—Y	.01	.03	.10	—V	—Y	—Y	—Y
United Arab Emirates	466	1.25	.97	1.57	2.05Y	2.61Y	3.22Y	4.17Y	—	7.42	5.91	7.81Y	10.63Y	13.36Y	16.12Y
Yemen, Republic of	474	—	—	—	—V	.02V	.03Y	.03Y	—	—	—	—V	—V	—Y	—Y
Western Hemisphere	**207**	**5.1**	**5.0**	**60.3**	**80.9Y**	**103.6Y**	**131.4Y**	**201.4Y**	**18.7**	**38.7**	**45.7**	**47.2Y**	**122.2Y**	**154.0Y**	**173.2Y**
Argentina	213	—	—	—	.04V	—V	—V	—V	1.04	1.75	1.86	3.87V	7.94V	11.62V	12.35V
Bahamas, The	313	—	—	.27	.35Y	.40Y	.49Y	.61Y	—	—	—	—Y	—Y	—Y	—Y
Barbados	316	—	—	—	.03V	—V	.76V	.94Y	—	—	—	.34V	—V	—V	—Y
Bermuda	319	—	—	—	—Y	—V	.02V	.02Y	—	—	—	—Y	—Y	—Y	—Y
Brazil	223	.43	.72	.90	2.07V	.74V	2.08V	11.14V	8.29	16.90	28.19	31.69V	96.46V	114.89V	133.23V
Chile	228	—	—	—	—V	—V	—V	—V	1.11	1.19	1.52	1.44V	1.26V	6.61V	2.58V
Colombia	233	—	.11	—	.01V	—V	.06V	.01V	.53	1.38	2.17	.81V	.74V	1.26V	1.63V
Costa Rica	238	—	—	—	—V	—V	—Y	—Y	1.50	2.65	2.13	6.51V	6.66V	8.23Y	10.22Y
Dominican Republic	243	—	.06	28.49	37.41Y	42.75Y	52.83Y	65.56Y	—	—	—	—Y	—Y	—Y	—Y
Ecuador	248	—	—	—	—V	—V	.02V	.03Y	—	.19	.37	—V	.02V	.04V	.04Y
El Salvador	253	—	—	—	—V	—V	.01V	—V	—	—	—	—V	—V	—V	—V
Guatemala	258	—	—	—	.01V	—V	—Y	—Y	—	—	—	—V	.18V	.22Y	.28Y
Honduras	268	—	—	—	.27V	.31Y	.38Y	.47Y	—	—	—	—V	—Y	—Y	—Y

	Exports 2001	2002	2003	2004	2005	2006	2007	Imports 2001	2002	2003	2004	2005	2006	2007
	Millions of U.S. Dollars							*Millions of U.S. Dollars*						
Jamaica.......343	—	—	—	—V	.07V	—V	.04V	—	—	—	—V	—V	—V	—V
Mexico.......273	4.53	3.75	—	—V	.27V	.56V	32.48V	.07	.19	.13	—V	.92V	.24V	.37V
Netherlands Antilles.......353	—	—	—	—Y	—Y	—Y	—Y	—	—	.01	.01Y	.01Y	.01Y	.01Y
Panama.......283	—	—	—	—V	—V	—V	—V	1.51	.20	.14	—V	—V	—V	—V
Paraguay.......288	—	—	—	—V	—V	—V	—Y	—	.01	—	—V	—V	.05V	.06Y
Peru.......293	—	—	—	.02V	.21V	.12V	.05Y	1.73	1.43	1.64	1.12V	2.29V	3.77V	3.69Y
Suriname.......366	—	—	—	—Y	—Y	—Y	—Y	2.86	—	—	—Y	—Y	—Y	—Y
Trinidad and Tobago.......369	—	—	30.10	39.53Y	45.17Y	55.83Y	69.28Y	—	.16	—	—Y	—Y	—Y	—Y
Uruguay.......298	—	—	—	—V	13.55V	16.74Y	20.78Y	—	—	1.06	1.42V	5.67V	7.00Y	8.69Y
Venezuela, Rep. Bol.......299	.11	.30	.50	1.13V	.13V	1.53V	—V	.04	12.68	6.52	—V	—V	—V	—Y
Other Countries n.i.e.......910	**—**	**—**	**—**	**—Y**	**—Y**	**—Y**	**—Y**	**—**	**—**	**.2**	**.2Y**	**.2Y**	**.3Y**	**.4Y**
North Korea.......954	—	—	—	—Y	—Y	—Y	—Y	—	.01	.15	.20Y	.23Y	.29Y	.36Y
Countries & Areas n.s.......898	**14.9**	**22.8**	**43.1**	**56.6Y**	**64.6Y**	**79.9Y**	**99.1Y**	**30.5**	**12.1**	**8.6**	**11.2Y**	**12.8Y**	**15.9Y**	**19.7Y**
Memorandum Items														
European Union.......998	1,213.31	1,278.78	1,430.59	2,059.41Y	2,396.21Y	3,085.82Y	3,111.10Y	883.30	876.51	841.72	1,248.65Y	1,194.39Y	1,302.07Y	1,621.92Y
Oil Exporting Ctys.......999	21.23	23.09	32.19	44.93Y	48.69Y	64.15Y	73.85Y	293.77	244.66	207.19	258.08Y	342.47Y	428.93Y	515.02Y
Non-Oil Develop.Ctys.......201	456.41	352.82	562.97	985.88Y	949.68Y	1,203.73Y	1,440.63Y	383.93	410.37	498.09	582.30Y	808.64Y	981.63Y	1,252.17Y
PERCENT DISTRIBUTION														
Industrial Countries.......101	**71.8**	**77.9**	**71.5**	**68.6**	**70.7**	**71.5**	**67.8**	**61.7**	**63.0**	**60.1**	**62.1**	**54.1**	**50.9**	**50.5**
Developing Countries.......202	**27.3**	**20.9**	**26.6**	**29.8**	**27.5**	**26.8**	**30.2**	**36.6**	**36.3**	**39.4**	**37.4**	**45.4**	**48.5**	**48.9**
Africa.......607	**9.2**	**10.2**	**12.8**	**9.6**	**9.9**	**8.6**	**10.2**	**23.5**	**19.7**	**19.8**	**17.7**	**18.5**	**20.7**	**20.2**
Asia.......507	**17.0**	**9.0**	**9.8**	**16.0**	**13.0**	**14.2**	**14.0**	**6.6**	**9.1**	**11.5**	**13.5**	**17.7**	**17.6**	**19.3**
Europe.......170	**.5**	**1.1**	**.8**	**1.5**	**1.5**	**.9**	**1.5**	**3.9**	**3.3**	**4.1**	**2.5**	**2.6**	**2.7**	**2.7**
Middle East.......407	**.4**	**.4**	**.5**	**.3**	**.3**	**.3**	**.4**	**1.5**	**2.1**	**1.5**	**1.6**	**1.8**	**2.2**	**2.0**
Western Hemisphere.......207	**.3**	**.3**	**2.7**	**2.3**	**2.9**	**2.8**	**4.0**	**1.0**	**2.1**	**2.6**	**2.1**	**4.8**	**5.3**	**4.8**
ANNUAL PERCENT CHANGE														
World.......001	**–4.6**	**3.0**	**24.4**	**54.7**	**4.6**	**30.4**	**6.2**	**24.2**	**–2.5**	**–.9**	**25.7**	**12.8**	**14.6**	**24.3**
Industrial Countries.......101	**2.3**	**11.6**	**14.3**	**48.4**	**7.7**	**31.9**	**.8**	**35.7**	**–.4**	**–5.6**	**30.0**	**–1.8**	**7.9**	**23.4**
Developing Countries.......202	**–11.5**	**–21.3**	**58.3**	**73.2**	**–3.1**	**27.0**	**19.5**	**11.6**	**–3.3**	**7.7**	**19.2**	**37.0**	**22.5**	**25.3**
Africa.......607	**8.2**	**14.4**	**56.3**	**15.5**	**8.7**	**13.6**	**25.8**	**.3**	**–18.5**	**–.2**	**12.3**	**17.6**	**28.6**	**21.1**
Asia.......507	**–15.8**	**–45.8**	**35.7**	**153.8**	**–15.4**	**42.3**	**5.2**	**37.8**	**34.8**	**24.6**	**47.5**	**48.7**	**14.0**	**36.2**
Europe.......170	**–70.1**	**141.2**	**–10.7**	**195.4**	**3.3**	**–16.7**	**71.5**	**30.2**	**–19.7**	**24.3**	**–23.3**	**16.0**	**19.2**	**24.6**
Middle East.......407	**–.8**	**5.0**	**79.3**	**–1.5**	**.4**	**24.0**	**29.5**	**83.3**	**34.3**	**–28.4**	**35.7**	**26.4**	**39.9**	**9.2**
Western Hemisphere.......207	**21.3**	**–2.3**	**—**	**34.2**	**28.1**	**26.9**	**53.2**	**47.0**	**107.2**	**18.1**	**3.2**	**158.8**	**26.0**	**12.5**
Other Countries n.i.e.......910	**—**	**—**	**....**	**....**	**....**	**....**	**....**	**639.5**	**....**	**—**	**31.3**	**14.3**	**23.6**	**24.1**

		Exports							Imports, f.o.b						
		2001	2002	2003	2004	2005	2006	2007	2001	2002	2003	2004	2005	2006	2007
		Millions of U.S. Dollars							*Millions of U.S. Dollars*						
IFS World Total		**259,850**	**252,393**	**272,819**	**304,528**	**359,431**	**389,531**	**416,669**	**221,748**	**221,951**	**239,051**	**273,104**	**323,466**	**348,928**	**379,800**
DOTS World Total	**001**	**261,300**	**252,382**	**271,593**	**315,950**	**360,573**	**388,210**	**420,838**	**221,495**	**221,989**	**239,402**	**271,880**	**314,547**	**349,442**	**380,029**
Industrial Countries	**101**	**247,304**	**238,817**	**255,898**	**294,408**	**333,785**	**354,588**	**378,967**	**179,966**	**178,592**	**188,275**	**207,859**	**234,760**	**254,747**	**273,733**
United States	111	228,991	221,292	235,241	269,028	302,358	316,746	332,065	141,095	139,063	145,118	160,234	177,634	191,950	205,734
Australia	193	682	709	943	1,183	1,354	1,618	1,636	1,027	1,087	1,148	1,361	1,439	1,255	1,663
Japan	158	5,203	5,152	5,610	6,526	7,579	8,309	8,559	9,534	9,817	9,801	10,255	12,220	13,519	14,427
New Zealand	196	137	131	256	339	296	339	380	338	354	385	412	462	435	478
Austria	122	195	152	173	225	373	403	383	576	618	741	987	1,065	1,255	1,338
Belgium	124	1,075	996	1,117	1,254	1,889	2,121	2,777	655	888	831	1,039	1,481	1,732	2,202
Cyprus	423	10	13	6	21	9	13	17	9	2	2	1	14	3	3
Denmark	128	345	252	176	215	240	276	361	524	655	771	769	1,300	1,256	1,242
Finland	172	165	169	243	238	358	418	678	443	448	663	749	1,008	985	789
France	132	1,357	1,239	1,525	1,811	2,096	2,541	2,922	3,591	3,734	3,545	4,036	4,116	4,577	4,762
Germany	134	1,853	1,794	1,930	2,012	2,676	3,488	3,631	5,149	5,278	6,185	7,231	8,477	9,810	10,781
Greece	174	165	91	125	225	115	136	147	67	68	81	100	120	180	125
Iceland	176	16	34	33	73	75	138	90	38	34	24	24	46	27	28
Ireland	178	204	221	344	349	346	336	326	927	1,095	1,357	1,339	1,698	2,256	2,277
Italy	136	1,032	912	1,195	1,330	1,591	1,663	2,400	2,612	2,739	3,226	3,506	3,783	4,029	4,737
Luxembourg	137	55	54	162	85	60	143	214	49	53	43	59	73	84	100
Malta	181	8	18	10	11	8	7	11	7	8	19	20	23	21	23
Netherlands	138	1,001	1,086	1,099	1,481	1,810	2,704	3,751	905	935	1,207	1,177	1,262	1,404	1,649
Norway	142	581	583	650	955	1,277	1,667	3,430	2,208	2,504	3,073	2,979	4,991	4,808	4,972
Portugal	182	69	91	77	139	136	133	166	174	160	200	230	261	314	325
Slovenia	961	23	20	29	36	56	41	86	27	36	36	42	51	61	76
Spain	184	523	583	598	935	986	1,048	1,142	565	652	848	967	991	1,240	1,188
Sweden	144	192	175	200	286	398	403	509	1,103	1,184	1,455	1,662	1,894	2,078	1,966
Switzerland	146	214	323	342	490	878	956	1,355	917	978	1,015	1,283	1,752	1,874	2,115
United Kingdom	112	3,206	2,724	3,812	5,163	6,821	8,940	11,928	7,424	6,202	6,503	7,396	8,600	9,589	10,734
Developing Countries	**202**	**13,751**	**13,389**	**15,500**	**21,279**	**26,386**	**33,149**	**41,311**	**36,671**	**39,699**	**47,841**	**60,834**	**76,388**	**91,167**	**101,825**
Africa	**607**	**837**	**885**	**947**	**1,037**	**1,384**	**1,818**	**2,668**	**1,446**	**1,963**	**3,043**	**3,606**	**5,560**	**7,237**	**8,385**
Algeria	612	187	265	253	204	189	223	479	715	1,099	1,717	2,380	3,451	4,366	4,772
Angola	614	3	4	17	17	62	54	78	30	—	—	—	283	529	1,159
Benin	638	5	3	4	4	3	14	10	—	—	—	—	—	—	—
Botswana	616	1	2	3	13	5	12	11	—	1	2	17	1	—	106
Burkina Faso	748	3	1	2	7	12	3	13	1	—	—	—	—	—	—
Burundi	618	—	—	2	—	2	1	2	—	—	—	—	—	—	—
Cameroon	622	19	9	14	8	13	9	19	13	7	6	11	8	5	7
Cape Verde	624	—	—	—	—	1	—	—	—	—	—	—	—	—	—
Central African Rep.	626	—	—	—	1	—	—	—	—	—	—	—	—	—	—
Chad	628	2	1	2	3	5	10	14	—	—	—	—	—	—	—
Comoros	632	—	—	—	—	1	1	—	—	—	1	—	—	—	—
Congo, Dem. Rep. of	636	3	7	7	7	13	18	37	—	—	—	—	—	—	—
Congo, Republic of	634	5	3	4	9	10	15	24	1	1	1	4	1	2	4
Côte d'Ivoire	662	10	13	4	7	11	17	17	33	45	71	86	112	171	258
Djibouti	611	—	1	—	2	2	2	1	—	—	—	—	—	—	—
Equatorial Guinea	642	2	1	2	1	2	1	2	70	188	335	266	454	206	225
Eritrea	643	—	—	2	—	1	1	1	....	....	....	....	....	....	....
Ethiopia	644	6	4	16	11	22	14	15	4	4	4	5	7	6	8
Gabon	646	3	4	2	9	9	15	19	1	2	2	1	1	1	2
Gambia, The	648	—	—	—	—	—	1	1	2	—	—	—	—	—	—
Ghana	652	43	44	42	50	78	97	149	14	26	35	24	24	48	20
Guinea	656	4	4	3	4	7	7	10	18	26	27	18	24	30	42
Kenya	664	17	13	10	17	34	49	64	7	8	10	12	13	13	16
Lesotho	666	—	—	—	—	—	—	—	6	3	6	11	12	9	7
Liberia	668	1	1	1	2	4	4	8	1	1	3	7	11	17	18
Madagascar	674	1	1	1	1	1	2	10	4	3	14	21	12	14	17
Malawi	676	4	4	2	2	3	5	5	1	1	1	1	1	1	2
Mali	678	3	2	3	7	6	10	7	4	2	1	—	—	—	—
Mauritania	682	1	2	1	4	3	4	8	—	—	1	—	—	—	1
Mauritius	684	2	2	1	3	2	2	5	11	9	8	8	5	6	11
Morocco	686	164	112	103	122	175	149	234	57	55	67	73	126	150	205
Mozambique	688	12	8	11	14	19	26	17	—	—	—	—	1	1	—
Namibia	728	1	1	1	1	1	12	5	—	13	13	31	46	113	128
Niger	692	1	1	6	1	5	6	6	1	1	1	2	2	2	1
Nigeria	694	69	51	51	61	92	199	172	138	130	320	74	148	648	260
Rwanda	714	1	1	1	1	2	1	2	—	1	—	—	—	—	—
St. Helena	856	—	—	—	—	—	—	1	—	—	—	—	—	—	—
São Tomé & Príncipe	716	—	—	—	—	—	—	—	1	1	2	—	—	—	—
Senegal	722	28	7	9	20	20	22	33	1	1	1	1	1	1	1
Seychelles	718	1	1	—	—	1	1	1	—	1	1	3	3	4	4
Sierra Leone	724	1	3	2	2	4	4	11	2	2	2	3	2	2	11
Somalia	726	2	—	—	—	1	2	2	—	—	—	—	—	—	—

		Exports							Imports, f.o.b						
		2001	2002	2003	2004	2005	2006	2007	2001	2002	2003	2004	2005	2006	2007
		Millions of U.S. Dollars							Millions of U.S. Dollars						
South Africa	199	122	158	215	282	375	579	734	292	312	362	498	576	720	980
Sudan	732	37	33	42	58	92	80	197	—	—	—	12	66	63	61
Swaziland	734	—	—	1	2	3	3	6	1	1	2	2	3	2	2
Tanzania	738	8	11	19	23	27	33	44	1	2	2	11	132	38	2
Togo	742	15	9	7	4	9	7	14	—	—	1	1	—	2	2
Tunisia	744	40	87	60	28	33	57	102	8	10	14	18	27	60	47
Uganda	746	2	3	4	4	8	7	12	1	—	3	4	3	3	2
Zambia	754	3	5	8	13	14	35	63	—	1	—	—	—	—	—
Zimbabwe	698	2	3	6	7	5	5	6	3	6	6	3	2	5	3
Asia	**507**	**7,082**	**7,198**	**8,633**	**11,990**	**14,267**	**17,415**	**21,323**	**20,553**	**22,504**	**27,349**	**34,904**	**41,652**	**50,031**	**56,828**
Afghanistan, I.S. of	512	—	1	6	7	16	6	13	—	—	—	—	—	1	1
American Samoa	859	1	1	1	2	1	2	1	—	—	2	—	1	1	2
Bangladesh	513	74	36	72	85	85	145	340	124	105	252	377	405	480	506
Brunei Darussalam	516	1	1	1	3	3	15	3	2	4	3	3	3	2	2
Cambodia	522	1	1	1	1	2	3	6	15	13	61	108	109	131	189
China,P.R.: Mainland	924	2,650	2,549	3,215	5,040	5,867	6,755	8,701	8,207	10,182	13,326	18,576	24,427	30,438	35,890
China,P.R.:Hong Kong	532	753	736	799	1,056	1,184	1,406	1,442	794	636	611	555	462	452	495
China,P.R.:Macao	546	1	1	2	23	25	27	41	51	58	62	66	35	33	31
Fiji	819	2	4	4	3	8	3	5	2	4	3	4	6	8	7
French Polynesia	887	6	5	8	10	13	13	15	1	2	2	2	2	2	2
Guam	829	1	1	3	5	4	4	3	1	1	1	—	—	—	—
India	534	371	359	504	662	900	1,478	1,673	745	846	1,017	1,212	1,476	1,691	1,852
Indonesia	536	295	309	321	513	571	703	935	621	614	663	717	790	836	929
Korea	542	1,246	1,251	1,312	1,712	2,331	2,881	2,814	2,981	3,097	3,665	4,483	4,440	5,088	5,035
Lao People's Dem.Rep	544	—	—	—	1	1	1	1	2	2	4	7	6	5	6
Malaysia	548	213	290	342	336	340	458	557	1,225	1,286	1,637	2,026	2,159	2,594	2,729
Maldives	556	5	2	2	3	6	6	557	9	2	5	2	—	—	1
Mongolia	948	—	2	2	6	12	8	9	1	6	12	45	131	171	179
Myanmar	518	—	—	—	1	—	—	1	41	30	30	19	9	7	7
Nauru	836	—	—	—	—	—	—	—	—	—	—	—	1	—	—
Nepal	558	1	2	2	9	5	9	11	10	6	7	11	10	12	13
New Caledonia	839	1	1	1	2	10	6	22	—	—	—	—	1	—	—
Pakistan	564	44	53	215	270	262	351	412	178	185	196	189	205	248	227
Papua New Guinea	853	2	1	2	3	6	6	3	5	1	2	1	2	3	3
Philippines	566	219	192	263	320	303	355	428	634	709	696	734	762	873	714
Singapore	576	241	324	304	467	528	652	860	734	629	748	754	804	870	1,396
Sri Lanka	524	19	13	33	41	101	225	230	77	71	73	88	90	100	104
Taiwan Province of China	528	621	685	847	931	1,120	1,231	1,415	2,850	2,703	2,691	3,022	3,214	3,422	3,642
Thailand	578	277	330	312	391	397	478	552	1,088	1,133	1,340	1,556	1,637	1,986	2,153
Tonga	866	—	1	—	—	—	—	1	—	—	—	—	—	—	—
Vanuatu	846	—	—	—	—	1	—	—	—	—	—	1	4	—	—
Vietnam	582	37	44	58	84	167	186	270	153	181	239	346	462	576	710
Europe	**170**	**622**	**632**	**928**	**1,269**	**1,844**	**2,581**	**3,233**	**1,174**	**1,256**	**1,927**	**2,901**	**4,125**	**4,490**	**4,284**
Albania	914	2	2	2	2	5	11	12	—	—	1	23	1	1	2
Armenia	911	1	2	2	2	4	5	9	1	2	2	2	1	2	2
Azerbaijan	912	3	2	20	10	15	19	30	—	1	1	1	—	1	122
Belarus	913	2	3	6	4	7	11	6	3	7	7	9	17	25	49
Bosnia & Herzegovina	963	1	—	2	1	2	5	5	1	2	3	3	2	3	5
Bulgaria	918	13	10	11	39	40	47	30	39	44	48	63	74	99	113
Croatia	960	9	9	9	15	17	22	26	10	11	15	19	21	23	35
Czech Republic	935	33	52	66	87	116	192	225	107	113	127	181	251	301	296
Estonia	939	3	3	6	8	24	25	31	59	35	33	19	43	46	56
Faroe Islands	816	—	—	—	2	2	2	2	—	11	6	2	7	8	3
Georgia	915	5	1	2	7	9	13	14	5	—	3	8	39	49	66
Gibraltar	823	—	—	7	15	34	31	41	—	—	—	—	—	—	—
Hungary	944	26	47	71	42	58	116	192	106	106	137	161	182	240	298
Kazakhstan	916	23	24	25	55	95	107	172	19	7	13	37	30	33	27
Kyrgyz Republic	917	1	1	2	3	4	7	8	—	—	13	—	18	1	—
Latvia	941	7	9	16	22	30	47	37	12	8	9	10	12	13	13
Lithuania	946	3	6	12	18	26	28	40	22	16	45	117	427	413	146
Macedonia, FYR	962	1	1	1	5	8	31	15	2	3	2	2	3	4	8
Moldova	921	1	—	1	2	1	1	1	1	2	3	2	16	21	2
Poland	964	143	80	121	181	221	274	285	191	199	266	298	441	864	623
Romania	968	19	23	82	68	132	189	134	60	81	102	131	173	183	151
Russia	922	184	149	216	311	466	772	1,072	234	243	586	1,093	1,439	1,224	1,348
Serbia & Montenegro	965	—	5	6	7	9	13	—	—	5	5	7	11	12	—
Slovak Republic	936	6	7	11	23	17	19	94	26	35	100	88	100	156	158
Tajikistan	923	1	—	1	1	1	2	2	—	—	—	—	—	—	—
Turkey	186	111	169	192	278	398	476	614	204	256	332	468	524	589	618
Turkmenistan	925	2	7	1	13	27	17	7	1	8	5	3	3	5	1
Ukraine	926	12	17	35	43	68	94	121	41	54	56	126	241	172	110
Uzbekistan	927	9	2	1	3	7	4	7	27	5	8	28	46	—	33
Yugoslavia n.s.	966	3	—	2	3	—	1	—	3	—	—	—	—	1	—
Europe n.s.	884	—	—	—	—	—	—	—	—	—	—	—	—	1	—
Middle East	**407**	**1,155**	**1,052**	**1,230**	**1,792**	**2,272**	**2,818**	**3,680**	**1,610**	**1,729**	**2,184**	**2,593**	**3,502**	**4,298**	**4,394**
Bahrain	419	9	9	12	16	23	27	39	8	8	8	5	6	91	7
Egypt	469	121	112	164	149	260	374	327	27	37	83	153	118	123	153
Iran, I.R. of	429	313	94	163	143	229	272	255	29	35	45	62	37	39	41

	Exports							Imports, f.o.b						
	2001	2002	2003	2004	2005	2006	2007	2001	2002	2003	2004	2005	2006	2007
	Millions of U.S. Dollars							*Millions of U.S. Dollars*						
Iraq....... 433	4	9	3	25	63	129	247	524	695	798	843	995	1,473	1,396
Israel....... 436	220	246	154	293	356	392	398	403	401	441	534	672	769	895
Jordan....... 439	22	19	20	32	101	50	57	3	3	4	5	7	13	15
Kuwait....... 443	37	47	54	58	98	79	106	12	16	33	—	51	56	1
Lebanon....... 446	21	24	21	35	41	53	65	5	5	7	8	9	10	15
Libya....... 672	12	29	26	76	70	59	191	—	—	6	70	77	58	—
Oman....... 449	12	14	34	47	19	49	109	2	2	5	6	4	5	3
Qatar....... 453	16	18	26	101	70	93	84	9	—	15	28	38	47	—
Saudi Arabia....... 456	206	219	278	444	365	478	648	502	477	650	790	1,415	1,505	1,761
Syrian Arab Republic....... 463	10	11	14	30	55	43	60	40	32	68	18	18	22	77
United Arab Emirates....... 466	130	171	237	315	486	696	1,071	47	19	21	71	54	84	28
Yemen, Republic of....... 474	22	30	24	28	38	24	25	—	—	—	—	—	—	—
Western Hemisphere....... 207	**4,055**	**3,622**	**3,761**	**5,191**	**6,620**	**8,516**	**10,407**	**11,887**	**12,246**	**13,337**	**16,831**	**21,550**	**25,111**	**27,934**
Antigua and Barbuda....... 311	7	6	13	12	15	63	18	—	—	1	—	—	—	1
Argentina....... 213	85	28	53	97	144	169	239	227	206	270	222	395	505	445
Aruba....... 314	—	3	4	6	10	9	12	—	3	6	36	47	129	87
Bahamas, The....... 313	19	23	22	27	55	51	91	9	10	35	43	47	20	59
Barbados....... 316	20	23	30	36	51	58	58	6	5	4	6	6	12	8
Belize....... 339	2	3	4	5	6	9	7	2	4	3	6	8	8	10
Bermuda....... 319	23	71	33	52	65	68	62	2	2	2	10	14	15	3
Bolivia....... 218	10	4	5	9	13	23	14	7	9	11	16	20	43	101
Brazil....... 223	585	470	611	697	911	1,171	1,418	987	1,215	1,432	1,804	2,606	3,008	3,138
Chile....... 228	225	174	225	270	345	417	714	415	424	628	1,012	1,374	1,646	1,575
Colombia....... 233	225	217	215	302	371	452	618	268	250	268	320	481	559	441
Costa Rica....... 238	39	48	47	57	70	61	77	122	157	210	242	291	343	342
Dominica....... 321	2	2	6	4	4	5	5	—	1	—	—	1	—	—
Dominican Republic....... 243	68	80	60	75	121	144	187	61	75	81	98	99	101	106
Ecuador....... 248	86	83	104	126	130	139	229	86	102	100	96	94	115	206
El Salvador....... 253	14	21	32	39	46	44	44	29	35	32	41	46	60	41
Greenland....... 326	5	3	3	10	17	22	19	4	1	1	1	—	—	43
Grenada....... 328	2	3	4	5	7	7	7	1	1	1	1	1	1	1
Guatemala....... 258	70	71	87	109	144	161	121	95	91	104	139	170	206	204
Guyana....... 336	5	7	6	9	14	22	25	135	144	145	151	121	125	151
Haiti....... 263	17	22	14	15	28	27	30	7	7	13	17	21	17	21
Honduras....... 268	10	10	18	18	36	33	48	81	81	70	102	107	105	116
Jamaica....... 343	64	100	86	127	126	135	186	209	166	190	264	324	368	341
Mexico....... 273	1,547	1,509	1,546	2,261	2,786	3,859	4,627	7,773	8,067	8,693	10,359	12,066	14,122	16,073
Netherlands Antilles....... 353	9	11	15	19	17	23	54	15	1	17	27	1	57	18
Nicaragua....... 278	6	7	9	13	16	16	20	28	29	29	46	45	61	83
Panama....... 283	73	24	44	49	50	74	81	7	8	6	35	36	32	28
Paraguay....... 288	4	6	2	5	8	6	8	2	7	9	14	13	12	15
Peru....... 293	123	104	93	136	218	254	310	162	186	188	364	1,126	1,850	2,009
St. Kitts and Nevis....... 361	13	16	10	4	6	8	10	4	5	6	6	7	8	4
St. Lucia....... 362	6	6	6	7	8	12	16	—	—	—	—	—	—	—
St. Pierre-Miquelon....... 363	12	13	14	16	15	13	15	—	—	1	—	—	—	1
St. Vincent & Grens....... 364	3	2	4	4	6	9	10	—	—	—	—	—	—	1
Suriname....... 366	4	3	5	11	9	9	9	35	30	1	110	152	191	375
Trinidad and Tobago....... 369	100	92	90	120	132	177	211	126	106	166	115	198	271	393
Uruguay....... 298	13	6	9	31	20	21	24	89	31	97	101	108	48	87
Venezuela, Rep. Bol....... 299	513	343	216	390	567	695	714	861	782	508	1,014	1,514	1,060	1,400
Western Hem. n.s....... 399	46	10	17	19	31	50	71	29	4	9	8	9	10	7
Other Countries n.i.e....... 910	**243**	**174**	**189**	**258**	**389**	**468**	**547**	**244**	**207**	**267**	**453**	**456**	**555**	**986**
Cuba....... 928	231	160	167	234	371	452	528	234	207	267	453	456	555	985
North Korea....... 954	12	13	22	24	18	15	19	9	—	—	—	—	—	—
Countries & Areas n.s....... 898	**1**	**2**	**3**	**—**	**2**	**—**	**1**	**—**	**—**	**—**	**—**	**1**	**—**	**—**
Special Categories....... 899	**—**	**—**	**—**	**1**	**—**	**—**	**—**	**4,603**	**3,482**	**3,011**	**2,723**	**2,930**	**2,964**	**3,476**
Memorandum Items														
European Union....... 998	11,701	10,795	13,126	16,195	20,461	25,517	32,355	25,331	25,268	28,426	32,183	37,672	42,910	45,908
Oil Exporting Ctys....... 999	1,794	1,569	1,662	2,377	2,817	3,676	5,011	3,460	3,869	4,781	6,053	8,574	10,178	10,593
Non-Oil Develop.Ctys....... 201	11,957	11,820	13,838	18,902	23,570	29,473	36,300	33,211	35,830	43,060	54,781	67,815	80,988	91,232
PERCENT DISTRIBUTION														
Industrial Countries....... 101	**94.6**	**94.6**	**94.2**	**93.2**	**92.6**	**91.3**	**90.1**	**81.3**	**80.5**	**78.6**	**76.5**	**74.6**	**72.9**	**72.0**
Developing Countries....... 202	**5.3**	**5.3**	**5.7**	**6.7**	**7.3**	**8.5**	**9.8**	**16.6**	**17.9**	**20.0**	**22.4**	**24.3**	**26.1**	**26.8**
Africa....... 607	**.3**	**.4**	**.3**	**.3**	**.4**	**.5**	**.6**	**.7**	**.9**	**1.3**	**1.3**	**1.8**	**2.1**	**2.2**
Asia....... 507	**2.7**	**2.9**	**3.2**	**3.8**	**4.0**	**4.5**	**5.1**	**9.3**	**10.1**	**11.4**	**12.8**	**13.2**	**14.3**	**15.0**
Europe....... 170	**.2**	**.3**	**.3**	**.4**	**.5**	**.7**	**.8**	**.5**	**.6**	**.8**	**1.1**	**1.3**	**1.3**	**1.1**
Middle East....... 407	**.4**	**.4**	**.5**	**.6**	**.6**	**.7**	**.9**	**.7**	**.8**	**.9**	**1.0**	**1.1**	**1.2**	**1.2**
Western Hemisphere....... 207	**1.6**	**1.4**	**1.4**	**1.6**	**1.8**	**2.2**	**2.5**	**5.4**	**5.5**	**5.6**	**6.2**	**6.9**	**7.2**	**7.4**
Other Countries n.i.e....... 910	**.1**	**.1**	**.1**	**.1**	**.1**	**.1**	**.1**	**.1**	**.1**	**.1**	**.2**	**.1**	**.2**	**.3**
ANNUAL PERCENT CHANGE														
World....... 001	**–5.0**	**–3.4**	**7.6**	**16.3**	**14.1**	**7.7**	**8.4**	**–7.3**	**.2**	**7.8**	**13.6**	**15.7**	**11.1**	**8.8**
Industrial Countries....... 101	**–5.1**	**–3.4**	**7.2**	**15.0**	**13.4**	**6.2**	**6.9**	**–7.8**	**–.8**	**5.4**	**10.4**	**12.9**	**8.5**	**7.5**
Developing Countries....... 202	**–3.8**	**–2.6**	**15.8**	**37.3**	**24.0**	**25.6**	**24.6**	**–5.7**	**8.3**	**20.5**	**27.2**	**25.6**	**19.3**	**11.7**
Africa....... 607	**–8.2**	**5.8**	**7.0**	**9.4**	**33.5**	**31.3**	**46.8**	**–20.9**	**35.8**	**55.0**	**18.5**	**54.2**	**30.2**	**15.9**
Asia....... 507	**–5.8**	**1.6**	**19.9**	**38.9**	**19.0**	**22.1**	**22.4**	**–7.3**	**9.5**	**21.5**	**27.6**	**19.3**	**20.1**	**13.6**

	Exports							Imports, f.o.b						
	2001	2002	2003	2004	2005	2006	2007	2001	2002	2003	2004	2005	2006	2007
Europe....170	–.8	1.6	46.8	36.8	45.3	40.0	25.3	–18.3	6.9	53.4	50.5	42.2	8.8	–4.6
Middle East....407	–11.6	–8.9	17.0	45.6	26.8	24.1	30.6	–7.1	7.4	26.3	18.7	35.1	22.7	2.2
Western Hemisphere....207	3.2	–10.7	3.8	38.0	27.5	28.6	22.2	1.3	3.0	8.9	26.2	28.0	16.5	11.2
Other Countries n.i.e....910	8.9	–28.3	8.4	36.7	50.6	20.4	16.8	–11.4	–14.9	28.5	69.9	.8	21.7	77.5

Cape Verde 624

		Exports							Imports						
		2001	2002	2003	2004	2005	2006	2007	2001	2002	2003	2004	2005	2006	2007
		Millions of U.S. Dollars							*Millions of U.S. Dollars*						
IFS World Total		**10.0**	**10.5**	**12.7**	**15.1**	**17.5**	**20.6**	**19.2**	**234.0**	**276.0**	**351.0**	**431.3**	**437.5**	**543.0**	**749.9**
DOTS World Total	**001**	**9.8**	**22.1Y**	**29.0Y**	**20.7Y**	**25.7Y**	**37.4Y**	**30.3Y**	**247.7**	**333.1Y**	**361.1Y**	**453.1Y**	**497.6Y**	**637.9Y**	**846.5Y**
Industrial Countries	**101**	**9.6**	**20.9Y**	**28.3Y**	**19.6Y**	**23.6Y**	**33.4Y**	**25.2Y**	**210.2**	**265.3Y**	**294.2Y**	**374.3Y**	**385.7Y**	**481.9Y**	**646.8Y**
United States	111	1.73	1.73V	5.36V	3.55V	2.36V	.82V	2.00V	7.99	10.56V	10.12V	55.99V	10.67V	14.85V	6.27V
Canada	156	—	.02V	.01V	.01V	.02V	.15V	.02V	3.11	.10V	.05V	.03V	.75V	.27V	.16V
Australia	193	—	—V	—V	—V	—V	.11V	.01V	.04	.03V	—V	.34V	—V	.02V	.01V
Japan	158	—	—V	.05V	.06V	—V	—V	—V	14.53	—V	3.38V	.69V	—V	—V	1.10V
New Zealand	196	—	—V	—V	—V	—V	—V	—V	—	—V	—V	.02V	.01V	.03V	—V
Austria	122	—	.02V	.01V	—V	—V	—V	—V	1.33	1.01V	1.25V	.32V	.53V	.22V	.38V
Belgium	124	—	.01V	.01V	—V	.12V	—V	.32V	9.39	9.88V	14.09V	15.32V	22.74V	17.81V	26.75V
Cyprus	423	—	—V	—V	—V	—Y	—V	—V	—	—V	—V	.01V	—V	—V	—V
Denmark	128	—	.02V	.37V	.53V	—V	.08V	—V	.67	1.50V	1.25V	1.08V	1.04V	1.08V	.75V
Finland	172	—	—V	—V	—V	—V	—V	.01V	—	.14V	.15V	.15V	.11V	.32V	.54V
France	132	—	4.83V	7.52V	.23V	.31V	.05V	.09V	8.29	11.19V	15.19V	11.33V	23.36V	14.37V	55.26V
Germany	134	.06	.18V	.55V	.35V	.70V	.07V	.05V	7.81	18.33V	7.91V	8.07V	7.98V	9.69V	18.20V
Greece	174	—	—V	—V	—V	—V	.63V	.07V	.02	.04V	—V	.04V	.01V	.05V	—V
Ireland	178	—	—V	.10V	—V	—V	—V	—V	.01	.08V	.15V	.68V	1.60V	2.24V	1.11V
Italy	136	—	.07V	.07V	.03V	.34V	.24V	.68V	7.58	11.48V	11.70V	19.18V	38.99V	34.73V	39.41V
Luxembourg	137	—	.03V	—V	.02V	—V	—V	—V	1.20	1.61V	1.70V	.24V	.33V	.08V	.12V
Malta	181	—	—V	—V	—V	—V	—V	—V	.09	.22V	.10V	.83V	2.07V	2.48V	2.02V
Netherlands	138	.02	.02V	.16V	.04V	.38V	4.72V	.22V	18.11	22.59V	32.75V	38.15V	35.65V	67.37V	92.07V
Norway	142	—	—V	—V	—V	—V	—V	—V	.45	.02V	—V	.07V	.07V	.32V	.51V
Portugal	182	7.72	7.98V	9.13V	12.25V	8.56V	8.12V	9.06V	113.40	153.91V	170.30V	190.57V	203.06V	262.46V	344.22V
Slovenia	961	—	—V	—V	—Y	—V	—V	—V	—	—V	—V	—Y	—V	.20V	.05V
Spain	184	.02	.03V	.06V	.15V	9.83V	16.55V	11.28V	10.35	12.15V	13.01V	23.80V	27.11V	41.19V	47.44V
Sweden	144	—	—V	—V	.01V	—V	—V	—V	1.54	.15V	.20V	.51V	.40V	3.09V	3.00V
Switzerland	146	—	.42V	.01V	.01V	.06V	.84V	.20V	.09	.63V	.39V	.40V	.57V	.65V	1.08V
United Kingdom	112	.01	5.50V	4.92V	2.34V	.92V	1.06V	1.19V	4.21	9.71V	10.54V	6.51V	8.69V	8.37V	6.39V
Developing Countries	**202**	**.2**	**1.2Y**	**.6Y**	**1.1Y**	**2.1Y**	**3.9Y**	**5.0Y**	**32.9**	**62.8Y**	**60.6Y**	**70.5Y**	**102.4Y**	**144.4Y**	**185.2Y**
Africa	**607**	**.2**	**.7Y**	**.2Y**	**.3Y**	**1.7Y**	**2.1Y**	**2.6Y**	**5.5**	**27.3Y**	**23.5Y**	**24.8Y**	**42.9Y**	**68.4Y**	**82.4Y**
Algeria	612	—	—V	—Y	—Y	—Y	—Y	—Y	.04	8.45V	10.25Y	13.56Y	18.45Y	23.19Y	27.98Y
Angola	614	.02	.02Y	.02Y	.03Y	.03Y	.04Y	.05Y	.43	.47Y	.60Y	.78Y	.90Y	1.11Y	1.37Y
Cameroon	622	—	—V	—V	—Y	—Y	—Y	—Y	—	—V	2.07V	2.73Y	3.11Y	3.85Y	4.78Y
Congo, Republic of	634	—	—V	—V	—V	—Y	—Y	—Y	—	.27V	.30V	—V	—Y	—Y	—Y
Côte d'Ivoire	662	—	—V	—V	—V	.01V	—V	—Y	2.01	9.67V	4.72V	2.00V	11.51V	33.33V	41.37Y
Guinea	656	—	—Y	.06V	.02V	.02Y	.02Y	.03Y	.02	.02Y	—V	—V	—Y	—Y	—Y
Guinea-Bissau	654	—	—Y	—Y	—Y	—Y	—Y	—Y	.05	.06Y	.07Y	.10Y	.11Y	.14Y	.17Y
Kenya	664	—	—V	—V	—V	—Y	—Y	—Y	—	—V	—V	.68V	.78Y	.96Y	1.19Y
Mauritania	682	.06	.06Y	.08Y	.10Y	.12Y	.14Y	.18Y	—	—Y	—Y	—Y	—Y	—Y	—Y
Morocco	686	—	—V	—V	.01V	1.39V	1.72Y	2.13Y	.23	.43V	.77V	1.45V	.91V	1.13Y	1.40Y
Nigeria	694	—	.60V	.03V	.04Y	.05Y	.06Y	.08Y	.02	—V	.02V	.02Y	.03Y	.04Y	.05Y
São Tomé & Príncipe	716	.01	.01Y	.01Y	.01Y	.02Y	.02Y	.02Y	—	—Y	—Y	—Y	—Y	—Y	—Y
Senegal	722	.08	.05V	.01V	.06V	.07V	—V	.01Y	.93	6.38V	1.77V	1.79V	4.43V	2.39V	2.96Y
South Africa	199	—	—V	—V	—V	—V	.05V	.10V	1.73	1.41V	2.89V	1.59V	2.62V	2.29V	1.11V
Togo	742	—	—V	—V	—V	—V	—Y	—Y	—	.14V	—V	—V	—V	—Y	—Y
Tunisia	744	—	—V	—V	—V	—V	—V	—Y	—	—V	—V	.06V	.04V	—V	—Y
Zimbabwe	698	—	—V	—V	—V	—V	—V	—Y	—	—V	—V	—V	.03V	—V	—Y
Asia	**507**	**—**	**.2Y**	**.4Y**	**.1Y**	**—Y**	**—Y**	**.7Y**	**11.0**	**13.2Y**	**8.0Y**	**6.7Y**	**9.4Y**	**14.3Y**	**25.1Y**
China,P.R.: Mainland	924	—	—V	—V	—V	—V	—V	—Y	2.34	2.02V	2.85V	3.07V	5.71V	11.12V	16.17V
China,P.R.:Hong Kong	532	—	—V	—V	.03V	—V	—V	—V	.12	—V	.59V	.39V	.71V	.15V	.10V
French Polynesia	887	—	—Y	—Y	—Y	—Y	—Y	—Y	—	—Y	—Y	—Y	.01Y	.01Y	.01Y
India	534	—	—V	—V	—V	—V	—Y	—Y	.14	.12V	.07V	.49V	.29V	.36Y	.44Y
Indonesia	536	—	.05V	.27V	.02V	—V	—V	—V	1.41	.50V	.46V	.25V	.42V	.38V	.25V
Korea	542	—	.05V	—V	—V	—V	—V	.21V	.36	.05V	.08V	.44V	.37V	.70V	1.28V
Malaysia	548	—	.08V	—V	.02V	—V	—V	—V	.11	.05V	.30V	.07V	.07V	.19V	1.41V
Nauru	836	—	—Y	—Y	—Y	—Y	—Y	—Y	.01	.01Y	.01Y	.02Y	.02Y	.02Y	.03Y
Philippines	566	—	.01V	.04V	—V	—V	—V	—V	—	.01V	.04V	.14V	—V	.11V	—V
Singapore	576	—	—V	.02V	.05V	—V	—V	.22V	.04	.28V	1.85V	1.28V	1.08V	.14V	.30V
Sri Lanka	524	—	—V	—Y	—Y	—Y	—Y	—Y	.01	—V	—Y	—Y	—Y	—Y	—Y
Taiwan Province of China	528	—	—V	—V	—V	—V	.02V	.26V	.02	.16V	.73V	.12V	.17V	.08V	.31V
Thailand	578	—	.04V	.04V	—V	—V	.02V	—V	.09	3.16V	1.04V	.39V	.55V	1.00V	4.76V
Vietnam	582	—	—Y	—V	—V	—V	—V	—V	6.34	6.88Y	.01V	—V	—V	—V	—V
Europe	**170**	**—**	**—Y**	**—Y**	**.3Y**	**.1Y**	**.6Y**	**.1Y**	**6.8**	**8.6Y**	**8.2Y**	**6.0Y**	**4.5Y**	**7.8Y**	**11.6Y**
Bulgaria	918	—	—V	—V	—V	—V	—V	—V	.68	.01V	—V	—V	—V	—V	.01V
Czech Republic	935	—	—V	—V	—V	—V	.62V	.01V	—	—V	.38V	—V	—V	1.29V	.82V
Czechoslovakia n.s.	937	....	....	....	....	....	....	....	.06	.06Y	.08Y	.11Y	.12Y	.15Y	.18Y
Gibraltar	823	—	—Y	—Y	—Y	—Y	—Y	—Y	.01	.01Y	.02Y	.02Y	.03Y	.03Y	.04Y
Hungary	944	—	—V	—V	—V	—V	—V	—V	.16	—V	.01V	.02V	—V	.04V	.17V
Latvia	941	—	—V	—Y	—V	—V	—V	.01V	....	....	....	....	....	....	....
Poland	964	—	.01V	.01V	.01V	—V	—V	—V	—	.44V	.06V	.01V	.01V	.03V	.21V
Romania	968	—	—V	—V	—V	—V	—V	—V	.77	.37V	.68V	.21V	—V	—V	—V
Russia	922	—	—V	—V	.32V	—V	.01V	—V	.35	.06V	.74V	.04V	.08V	.04V	.10V

Cape Verde 624

	Exports 2001	2002	2003	2004	2005	2006	2007	Imports 2001	2002	2003	2004	2005	2006	2007
	Millions of U.S. Dollars							*Millions of U.S. Dollars*						
Serbia & Montenegro.................. 965	....	....	....	....	....	....	....	.01	.01Y	.01Y	.01Y	.02Y	.02Y	.02Y
Slovak Republic.......................... 936	—	—V	—Y	—Y	.13V	—V	.10V	—	.08V	.11Y	.14Y	.01V	.03V	.25V
Turkey.. 186	—	—V	—V	—V	—V	—V	.01V	4.57	7.43V	6.15V	5.49V	3.43V	5.12V	8.58V
Ukraine...................................... 926	—	—V	—V	—V	—V	—Y	—Y	.20	.13V	—V	—V	.82V	1.01Y	1.26Y
Middle East............................. 407	**—**	**—Y**	**—Y**	**—Y**	**—Y**	**—Y**	**—Y**	**3.5**	**5.6Y**	**8.1Y**	**10.7Y**	**13.4Y**	**16.0Y**	**18.6Y**
Israel... 436	—	—V	—V	—V	—V	—V	—V	.53	—V	—V	—V	—V	—V	—V
Oman... 449	....	....	....	....	....	....	....	.02	.02Y	.02Y	.03Y	.04Y	.05Y	.06Y
Saudi Arabia............................... 456	—	—Y	—Y	—Y	—Y	—Y	—Y	.04	.04Y	.05Y	.07Y	.09Y	.11Y	.14Y
United Arab Emirates.................. 466	....	....	....	....	....	....	....	.06	.07Y	.08Y	.11Y	.14Y	.18Y	.22Y
Middle East n.s........................... 489	—	—Y	—Y	—Y	—Y	—Y	—Y	2.86	5.42Y	7.98Y	10.54Y	13.10Y	15.66Y	18.22Y
Western Hemisphere............... 207	**—**	**.3Y**	**—Y**	**.4Y**	**.2Y**	**1.2Y**	**1.6Y**	**6.1**	**8.1Y**	**12.7Y**	**22.3Y**	**32.2Y**	**37.9Y**	**47.4Y**
Argentina.................................. 213	—	—V	—V	—V	—V	—V	—V	.01	.05V	.26V	.55V	2.17V	2.24V	1.34V
Barbados.................................... 316	....	....	....	....	....	....	....	—	—V	—V	—V	.02V	—V	—Y
Bermuda..................................... 319	—	—Y	—Y	—Y	—V	.84V	1.04Y	—	—Y	—Y	—Y	—Y	—Y	—Y
Bolivia.. 218	—	—V	—V	—V	—V	—Y	—Y	.05	—V	—Y	—Y	—Y	—Y	—Y
Brazil.. 223	—	.15V	.02V	.02V	.02V	.02V	—V	5.61	5.99V	9.84V	18.36V	26.24V	30.82V	39.65V
Chile... 228	—	—V	.02V	.19V	—V	.03V	.01V	.04	—V	—V	—V	—V	—V	.07V
Colombia.................................... 233	—	—V	—V	—V	—V	—V	.09V	.08	—V	—V	.07V	—V	—V	—V
Ecuador...................................... 248	—	—V	—V	—V	—V	.03V	.03Y	—	.05V	—V	—V	—V	—V	—Y
Guatemala.................................. 258	—	.05V	—V	—Y	—V	—Y	—Y	—	—V	—V	—Y	—Y	—Y	—Y
Guyana....................................... 336	....	....	....	....	....	....	....	.02	.02Y	.02Y	.03Y	.03Y	.04Y	.05Y
Honduras.................................... 268	—	.05V	—V	.17V	.19Y	.24Y	.29Y	.01	—V	—V	—V	—Y	—Y	—Y
Mexico.. 273	—	—V	—V	—V	—V	.02V	.08V	.17	—V	—V	—V	—V	.02V	.06V
Peru.. 293	—	—V	—V	—V	—V	—V	—Y	.02	—V	.05V	.07V	—V	.19V	.55Y
St. Vincent & Grens..................... 364	—	—Y	—Y	—Y	—Y	—Y	—Y	.06	—V	—V	—V	—V	—Y	—Y
Trinidad and Tobago................... 369	—	—V	—Y	—Y	—Y	—Y	—Y	.02	1.93V	2.44Y	3.21Y	3.66Y	4.53Y	5.62Y
Uruguay..................................... 298	—	—Y	—V	—V	—V	—Y	—Y	.01	—Y	.03V	.01V	—V	—Y	—Y
Venezuela, Rep. Bol.................... 299	—	—V	—V	—V	.02V	—V	—V	—	—V	—V	—V	—V	—V	—Y
Western Hem. n.s........................ 399	—	—Y	—Y	—Y	—Y	—Y	—Y	.01	.02Y	.03Y	.04Y	.05Y	.06Y	.06Y
Other Countries n.i.e............... 910	**—**	**—Y**	**—Y**	**—Y**	**—Y**	**—Y**	**—Y**	**.2**	**.2Y**	**.3Y**	**.4Y**	**.4Y**	**.5Y**	**.7Y**
Cuba... 928	—	—Y	—Y	—Y	—Y	—Y	—Y	.02	.03Y	.03Y	.04Y	.05Y	.06Y	.08Y
North Korea................................ 954	—	—Y	—Y	—Y	—Y	—Y	—Y	.19	.21Y	.26Y	.34Y	.39Y	.48Y	.60Y
Countries & Areas n.s.............. 898	**—**	**—Y**	**—Y**	**.1Y**	**.1Y**	**.1Y**	**.1Y**	**4.0**	**4.3Y**	**5.5Y**	**7.2Y**	**8.2Y**	**10.2Y**	**12.6Y**
Special Categories.................. 899	**—**	**—Y**	**—Y**	**—Y**	**—Y**	**—Y**	**—Y**	**—**	**—Y**	**—Y**	**.1Y**	**.1Y**	**.1Y**	**.1Y**
Memorandum Items														
European Union.......................... 998	7.83	18.70Y	22.91Y	15.96Y	21.30Y	32.13Y	23.11Y	184.16	254.52Y	280.83Y	316.97Y	373.71Y	467.15Y	639.15Y
Oil Exporting Ctys....................... 999	—	.65Y	.30Y	.06Y	.07Y	.06Y	.08Y	1.58	9.08Y	10.88Y	14.04Y	19.17Y	23.96Y	28.70Y
Non-Oil Develop.Ctys.................. 201	.16	.58Y	.34Y	1.05Y	2.02Y	3.87Y	4.91Y	31.32	53.70Y	49.69Y	56.51Y	83.20Y	120.40Y	156.48Y
PERCENT DISTRIBUTION														
Industrial Countries................ 101	**98.0**	**94.3**	**97.7**	**94.4**	**91.7**	**89.3**	**83.2**	**84.9**	**79.7**	**81.5**	**82.6**	**77.5**	**75.5**	**76.4**
Developing Countries............. 202	**1.7**	**5.5**	**2.2**	**5.3**	**8.1**	**10.5**	**16.5**	**13.3**	**18.8**	**16.8**	**15.6**	**20.6**	**22.6**	**21.9**
Africa...................................... 607	**1.7**	**3.3**	**.8**	**1.3**	**6.6**	**5.5**	**8.6**	**2.2**	**8.2**	**6.5**	**5.5**	**8.6**	**10.7**	**9.7**
Asia.. 507	**—**	**1.0**	**1.3**	**.6**	**.1**	**.1**	**2.3**	**4.4**	**4.0**	**2.2**	**1.5**	**1.9**	**2.2**	**3.0**
Europe.................................... 170	**—**	**—**	**—**	**1.6**	**.5**	**1.7**	**.5**	**2.8**	**2.6**	**2.3**	**1.3**	**.9**	**1.2**	**1.4**
Middle East............................ 407	**—**	**—**	**—**	**—**	**—**	**—**	**—**	**1.4**	**1.7**	**2.3**	**2.4**	**2.7**	**2.5**	**2.2**
Western Hemisphere............. 207	**—**	**1.1**	**.2**	**1.8**	**.9**	**3.2**	**5.1**	**2.5**	**2.4**	**3.5**	**4.9**	**6.5**	**5.9**	**5.6**
Other Countries n.i.e............... 910	**—**	**—**	**—**	**—**	**—**	**—**	**—**	**.1**	**.1**	**.1**	**.1**	**.1**	**.1**	**.1**
ANNUAL PERCENT CHANGE														
World....................................... 001	**–10.4**	**126.8**	**31.1**	**–28.5**	**24.2**	**45.4**	**–19.1**	**4.3**	**34.5**	**8.4**	**25.5**	**9.8**	**28.2**	**32.7**
Industrial Countries................ 101	**–9.9**	**118.2**	**35.8**	**–30.9**	**20.6**	**41.7**	**–24.6**	**4.1**	**26.2**	**10.9**	**27.2**	**3.0**	**24.9**	**34.2**
Developing Countries............. 202	**–22.4**	**648.8**	**–47.9**	**72.9**	**88.5**	**88.7**	**26.9**	**2.4**	**90.8**	**–3.5**	**16.5**	**45.1**	**41.0**	**28.3**
Africa...................................... 607	**–14.7**	**349.7**	**–70.4**	**26.5**	**517.5**	**21.2**	**25.9**	**15.1**	**398.4**	**–14.0**	**5.5**	**73.3**	**59.4**	**20.4**
Asia.. 507	**—**	**....**	**57.3**	**–67.3**	**–88.7**	**251.2**	**—**	**–8.6**	**20.5**	**–39.3**	**–17.2**	**41.1**	**51.9**	**75.8**
Europe.................................... 170	**—**	**....**	**5.4**	**—**	**–59.3**	**376.2**	**–78.1**	**–10.6**	**26.6**	**–4.4**	**–26.6**	**–25.3**	**71.8**	**50.1**
Middle East............................ 407	**9.1**	**—**	**....**	**....**	**....**	**....**	**....**	**316.1**	**57.9**	**46.6**	**32.1**	**24.5**	**19.7**	**16.4**
Western Hemisphere............. 207	**—**	**....**	**–81.0**	**702.9**	**–39.5**	**410.6**	**31.4**	**–11.5**	**32.0**	**57.4**	**76.2**	**44.1**	**17.8**	**25.1**
Other Countries n.i.e............... 910	**—**	**—**	**....**	**....**	**....**	**....**	**....**	**81.2**	**8.5**	**26.6**	**31.3**	**14.3**	**23.6**	**24.1**

	Exports 2001	2002	2003	2004	2005	2006	2007	Imports 2001	2002	2003	2004	2005	2006	2007
	Millions of U.S. Dollars							*Millions of U.S. Dollars*						
IFS World Total	**142.3**	**147.0**	**127.5**	**126.2**	**129.0**	**158.0**	**195.0**	**107.7**	**120.0**	**118.6**	**151.6**	**172.8**	**203.0**	**230.0**
DOTS World Total 001	**166.0Y**	**212.4Y**	**122.5Y**	**126.9Y**	**115.1Y**	**111.8Y**	**123.2Y**	**134.7Y**	**140.8Y**	**147.5Y**	**201.3Y**	**222.9Y**	**299.0Y**	**341.4Y**
Industrial Countries 101	**136.5Y**	**154.2Y**	**97.7Y**	**97.9Y**	**82.3Y**	**75.7Y**	**68.0Y**	**74.4Y**	**73.9Y**	**66.7Y**	**97.1Y**	**96.6Y**	**149.1Y**	**150.9Y**
United States 111	2.18V	1.91V	1.82V	8.09V	5.18V	4.00V	2.91V	4.07V	7.15V	8.14V	33.00V	16.28V	27.50V	21.67V
Canada 156	.03V	.23V	.04V	.06V	.17V	.09V	.24V	.19V	.29V	.11V	.64V	.29V	.25V	.47V
Australia 193	—V	.01V	—V	—V	.06V	.06V	.07V	.02V	.63V	.07V	.14V	.20V	.09V	.25V
Japan 158	1.70V	.97V	1.82V	2.03V	1.94V	1.46V	2.07V	3.46V	2.71V	2.31V	2.25V	1.29V	.92V	1.56V
New Zealand 196	—V	—V	.03V	.04V	.02V	—V	.11V	—V	—V	—V	—V	—V	—V	.03V
Austria 122	.09V	.07V	—V	—V	.04V	.02V	—V	.12V	.10V	.10V	.06V	.10V	.10V	1.02V
Belgium 124	98.08V	120.99V	51.05V	51.27V	40.23V	34.68V	27.97V	4.30V	4.28V	4.70V	10.21V	7.92V	7.62V	9.30V
Cyprus 423	.16V	.54V	.05V	.06V	.03Y	—V	—V	.16V	.02V	.12V	.26V	—V	—V	.02V
Denmark 128	.04V	—V	.01V	.03V	—V	—V	.03V	.50V	.35V	.75V	.92V	.87V	.74V	1.96V
Finland 172	—V	.04V	—V	—V	—V	—V	—V	.03V	.05V	.15V	.19V	.04V	.02V	.09V
France 132	4.95V	4.75V	9.31V	7.96V	11.11V	8.77V	8.74V	40.67V	41.70V	41.02V	35.66V	36.99V	45.95V	56.71V
Germany 134	2.32V	1.50V	2.46V	3.02V	.70V	4.18V	2.41V	5.36V	4.25V	2.36V	2.83V	4.13V	6.40V	5.54V
Greece 174	—V	.02V	—V	—V	—V	—V	—V	.02V	.02V	—V	.10V	.07V	.02V	.10V
Iceland 176	—V	—V	—V	—V	—V	.01V	—V	—V	—V	—V	—V	—V	.01V	.01V
Ireland 178	—V	—V	—V	—V	.02V	.01V	.07V	.13V	.11V	.21V	.66V	.09V	.30V	.08V
Italy 136	6.63V	6.88V	12.70V	11.31V	9.31V	5.32V	9.46V	2.55V	2.13V	2.08V	2.59V	1.68V	3.91V	2.72V
Luxembourg 137	—V	—V	—V	—V	—V	—V	—V	.03V	.10V	.01V	.04V	.06V	.04V	.01V
Malta 181	—Y	—V	—V	—V	—V	—V	—V	—Y	—V	—V	—V	.04V	.03V	.05V
Netherlands 138	.05V	.01V	.18V	.06V	.10V	1.12V	.40V	1.82V	1.98V	1.92V	3.86V	22.99V	45.00V	44.40V
Norway 142	—V	.03V	—V	.01V	—V	—V	.08V	.06V	.06V	.05V	.07V	.05V	.05V	.17V
Portugal 182	4.25V	4.40V	4.41V	2.61V	2.99V	3.63V	4.25V	.15V	.20V	.12V	.27V	.04V	.39V	.10V
Slovenia 961	.03V	.01V	.03V	.04Y	—V	—V	.60V	—V	—V	.05V	.07Y	.01V	.08V	.05V
Spain 184	15.64V	11.54V	11.91V	10.64V	10.03V	12.11V	8.47V	6.99V	4.35V	.73V	1.79V	.96V	5.20V	1.42V
Sweden 144	—V	—V	—V	.03V	.02V	.10V	.03V	.11V	.05V	.05V	.22V	.76V	1.81V	1.63V
Switzerland 146	.03V	.07V	.03V	.09V	.05V	—V	.07V	.38V	.19V	.08V	.19V	.65V	1.41V	.23V
United Kingdom 112	.30V	.27V	1.81V	.51V	.27V	.16V	.04V	3.31V	3.17V	1.62V	1.09V	1.02V	1.28V	1.29V
Developing Countries 202	**29.5Y**	**58.1Y**	**24.8Y**	**29.0Y**	**32.8Y**	**36.1Y**	**55.2Y**	**29.3Y**	**33.2Y**	**38.1Y**	**48.3Y**	**62.5Y**	**71.0Y**	**92.5Y**
Africa 607	**4.8Y**	**45.3Y**	**6.4Y**	**7.3Y**	**7.8Y**	**9.5Y**	**12.6Y**	**14.3Y**	**23.9Y**	**25.7Y**	**31.7Y**	**36.8Y**	**49.2Y**	**62.9Y**
Algeria 612	.40V	.15V	.16Y	.21Y	.27Y	.33Y	.43Y	—V	—V	—Y	—Y	—Y	—Y	—Y
Benin 638	.03V	—V	—V	—V	—V	—Y	—Y	.01V	.03V	.04V	—V	.02V	.02Y	.02Y
Burkina Faso 748	.02Y	.02Y	.03Y	.04Y	.04Y	.05Y	.07Y	.02Y	.02Y	.02Y	.03Y	.03Y	.04Y	.05Y
Cameroon 622	.02V	—V	—V	—Y	—Y	—Y	.01Y	5.72V	15.63V	14.35V	18.84Y	21.53Y	26.61Y	33.02Y
Chad 628	.24Y	.26Y	.33Y	.43Y	.49Y	.60Y	.75Y	2.41Y	2.62Y	3.31Y	4.35Y	4.97Y	6.15Y	7.63Y
Congo, Dem. Rep. of 636	2.64Y	2.87Y	3.63Y	4.77Y	5.45Y	6.73Y	8.35Y	1.72Y	1.86Y	2.36Y	3.09Y	3.54Y	4.37Y	5.42Y
Congo, Republic of 634	.12V	.12V	.19V	.15V	.17V	.21Y	.27Y	1.05V	.73V	1.02V	.21V	.24Y	.30Y	.37Y
Côte d'Ivoire 662	.01V	—V	—V	—V	—V	—V	—Y	1.49V	1.02V	1.64V	.84V	.88V	1.55V	1.93Y
Gabon 646	.02Y	.02Y	.03Y	.03Y	.04Y	.05Y	.06Y	.05Y	.05Y	.06Y	.08Y	.09Y	.12Y	.14Y
Guinea 656	—V	—Y	.01V	—V	—Y	—Y	—Y	—V	—Y	—V	—V	—Y	—Y	—Y
Kenya 664	—V	.05V	.14V	.03V	.04Y	.05Y	.06Y	—V	—V	—V	.02V	.02Y	.02Y	.03Y
Lesotho 666	....	....	....	....	....	....	....	.05Y	.06Y	.07Y	.09Y	.11Y	.13Y	.16Y
Madagascar 674	.01V	—V	—V	—Y	—Y	—Y	—Y	.05V	—V	.04V	.05Y	.06Y	.08Y	.10Y
Mali 678	—Y	—Y	—Y	—Y	—Y	—Y	—Y	.02Y	.02Y	.02Y	.03Y	.04Y	.04Y	.05Y
Mauritius 684	.05V	.31V	—V	—V	—V	—V	—V	.01V	—V	—V	—V	—V	—V	—V
Morocco 686	.36V	.10V	.34V	.79V	.96V	1.19Y	1.48Y	.20V	.31V	.45V	.78V	1.28V	1.58Y	1.96Y
Namibia 728	—Y	—Y	—Y	—Y	—Y	—Y	—Y	.21Y	.21Y	.21Y	.21Y	.21Y	.21Y	.21Y
Niger 692	—V	—V	.10V	—V	—Y	—Y	—Y	—V	—V	—V	—V	—Y	—Y	—Y
Nigeria 694	.18V	.27V	.11V	.14Y	.18Y	.23Y	.29Y	—V	—V	.46V	.61Y	.82Y	1.03Y	1.25Y
Senegal 722	.03V	—V	.07V	.07V	.08V	.01V	.02Y	.65V	.73V	.94V	1.11V	.94V	.65V	.80Y
South Africa 199	—V	.11V	.59V	.13V	—V	—V	.80V	.58V	.57V	.34V	.86V	1.45V	5.32V	8.48V
Sudan 732	.40Y	.43Y	.27Y	—V	—V	—V	—V	.01Y	.01Y	—V	—V	—V	—V	—V
Togo 742	—V	.02V	—V	—V	—V	—Y	—Y	.05V	.06V	.02V	.08V	.03V	.04Y	.05Y
Tunisia 744	.28V	.52V	.40V	.44V	.11V	.02V	.03Y	—V	—V	—V	—V	.09V	.40V	.50Y
Uganda 746	—V	40.02V	—V	—Y	—Y	—Y	—Y	—V	—V	.30V	.39Y	.45Y	.55Y	.68Y
Zimbabwe 698	—V	—V	—V	—V	—V	—V	—Y	—V	—V	.06V	—V	—V	.01V	.01Y
Asia 507	**22.3Y**	**11.0Y**	**12.6Y**	**15.3Y**	**16.4Y**	**16.7Y**	**31.2Y**	**10.8Y**	**4.9Y**	**6.4Y**	**10.7Y**	**14.3Y**	**5.9Y**	**19.7Y**
China,P.R.: Mainland 924	1.26V	1.14V	2.10V	6.40V	8.17V	7.83V	6.01V	.63V	.76V	2.34V	3.61V	7.80V	1.86V	9.75V
China,P.R.:Hong Kong 532	1.02V	2.96V	.32V	—V	.05V	.01V	—V	.43V	.09V	.08V	.05V	.12V	.15V	2.74V
India 534	.08Y	1.03V	.08V	.20V	.31V	.38Y	.47Y	.85Y	2.63V	1.38V	1.48V	1.36V	1.68Y	2.09Y
Indonesia 536	3.26V	3.86V	8.23V	7.65V	7.29V	7.69V	23.77V	1.04V	.43V	.95V	.98V	.78V	.36V	.51V
Korea 542	.22V	.03V	.01V	.12V	.09V	.20V	.26V	.15V	.23V	.70V	.49V	.68V	.33V	.16V
Malaysia 548	.10V	.01V	.12V	.43V	.04V	.01V	.03V	.03V	.07V	.04V	2.98V	.41V	.09V	1.45V
Myanmar 518	....	....	....	....	....	....	....	.34Y	.37Y	.47Y	.62Y	.71Y	.87Y	1.09Y
New Caledonia 839	—V	—V	.01V	—V	—Y	—Y	—Y	—V	—V	—V	—V	—Y	—Y	—Y
Pakistan 564	13.83V	—V	—V	.08V	.31V	.38Y	.47Y	6.88V	.01V	.06V	.08V	.42V	.52Y	.64Y
Philippines 566	—V	.01V	.01V	—V	—V	—V	—V	—V	.10V	—V	.04V	.07V	.01V	—V
Taiwan Province of China 528	2.33V	1.00V	.44V	.17V	.05V	.20V	.16V	.03V	.04V	.25V	.03V	1.84V	.01V	.18V
Thailand 578	.16V	.96V	.99V	.22V	.14V	.03V	.06V	.20V	.10V	.02V	.36V	.12V	.05V	1.11V
Vietnam 582	.05V	.01V	.25V	—V	—V	—V	—V	.22V	.05V	.10V	—V	—V	—V	—V
Europe 170	**1.9Y**	**1.1Y**	**3.0Y**	**4.8Y**	**5.6Y**	**6.0Y**	**6.2Y**	**.9Y**	**1.2Y**	**1.3Y**	**.9Y**	**3.4Y**	**2.0Y**	**2.2Y**
Albania 914	—V	—V	.02V	—V	—V	—V	—V	—V	—V	—V	—V	—V	—V	—V
Belarus 913	—V	.04V	—V	—V	—V	—V	—V	.02V	—V	.01V	—V	—V	—V	—V
Bulgaria 918	—V	—V	—V	—V	—V	—V	—V	—V	—V	—V	.01V	—V	.01V	.01V

	Exports							Imports						
	2001	2002	2003	2004	2005	2006	2007	2001	2002	2003	2004	2005	2006	2007
	Millions of U.S. Dollars							*Millions of U.S. Dollars*						
Czech Republic........ 935	.55V	.21V	.58V	.61V	.41V	.06V	—V	.12V	.10V	.42V	.21V	.33V	.07V	.11V
Estonia........ 939	—V	—V	—V	—V	—V	—V	—V	—V	—V	—V	.01V	—V	—V	—V
Georgia........ 915	.01V	—V	—V	—V	—V	—V	—Y	—V	—V	—V	—V	—V	—V	—Y
Hungary........ 944	.08V	—V	.03V	.11V	—V	—V	—V	—V	—V	.04V	.05V	.17V	.01V	—V
Kazakhstan........ 916	.01V	—V	—V	—V	—Y	—Y	—Y	—V	—V	—V	—V	—Y	—Y	—Y
Kyrgyz Republic........ 917	....	....	....	....	....	....	....	—V	.01V	.02V	—V	—V	—V	.02V
Latvia........ 941	—V	—V	—Y	—V	—V	.29V	.12V	—V	—V	—Y	—V	—V	—V	.05V
Lithuania........ 946	—V	—V	—V	—V	—V	—V	—V	—V	—V	—V	.02V	.03V	—V	.04V
Macedonia, FYR........ 962	—V	.01V	—V	—V	—V	—V	—Y	—V	—V	—V	—V	—V	—V	—Y
Poland........ 964	.38V	.09V	.10V	.06V	—V	—V	.18V	.02V	.04V	.14V	.02V	.07V	.14V	.04V
Romania........ 968	—V	.02V	.01V	.02V	.02V	.02V	.14V	—V	—V	—V	.03V	.10V	—V	.17V
Russia........ 922	.11V	—V	.02V	.04V	—V	.02V	.02V	.03V	—V	.11V	—V	—V	.08V	—V
Slovak Republic........ 936	.39V	.11V	.14Y	.18Y	—V	—V	—V	—V	—V	—Y	—Y	1.71V	.74V	.60V
Turkey........ 186	.35V	.54V	2.14V	3.77V	5.16V	5.60V	5.77V	.61V	.63V	.36V	.23V	.67V	.55V	.72V
Ukraine........ 926	—V	.08V	—V	—V	—V	—Y	—Y	—V	.27V	—V	.07V	.05V	.07Y	.08Y
U.S.S.R. n.s........ 930	—Y	—Y	—Y	—Y	—Y	—Y	—Y	.13Y	.14Y	.18Y	.24Y	.27Y	.33Y	.41Y
Yugoslavia n.s........ 966	....	....	....	....	....	....	....	—Y	—Y	—Y	—Y	—Y	—Y	.01Y
Middle East........ 407	**.4Y**	**.6Y**	**2.6Y**	**1.1Y**	**2.1Y**	**2.6Y**	**3.3Y**	**1.2Y**	**1.4Y**	**2.0Y**	**2.7Y**	**3.1Y**	**4.1Y**	**5.1Y**
Bahrain........ 419	.25Y	.27Y	.35Y	.45Y	.52Y	.64Y	.80Y	....	....	....	....	....	....	....
Egypt........ 469	.02V	.02Y	.03Y	.04Y	.05Y	.06Y	.07Y	.03V	.03Y	.04Y	.05Y	.06Y	.07Y	.09Y
Israel........ 436	—V	—V	1.82V	—V	—V	—V	—V	—V	—V	—V	—V	—V	.22V	.33V
Lebanon........ 446	.09Y	.10Y	.12Y	.16Y	.19Y	.23Y	.29Y	1.21Y	1.32Y	1.67Y	2.19Y	2.50Y	3.09Y	3.84Y
Oman........ 449	—V	—V	—V	—Y	—Y	—Y	—Y	—V	—V	.31V	.41Y	.56Y	.71Y	.85Y
Saudi Arabia........ 456	.05V	.17V	.32V	.43V	1.34V	1.66Y	2.15Y	—Y	—Y	—Y	—Y	—Y	—Y	—Y
Yemen, Republic of........ 474	—V	—V	—Y	.02V	—V	—Y	—Y	—V	.01V	.02Y	—V	—V	—Y	—Y
Western Hemisphere........ 207	**.1Y**	**.2Y**	**.2Y**	**.6Y**	**.8Y**	**1.2Y**	**1.8Y**	**2.0Y**	**1.9Y**	**2.7Y**	**2.3Y**	**4.9Y**	**9.7Y**	**2.6Y**
Argentina........ 213	—V	—V	—V	—V	—V	—V	—V	.02V	—V	—V	.05V	.08V	.02V	.17V
Aruba........ 314	....	....	....	....	....	....	....	.25V	.06V	—V	—V	—V	—V	—V
Barbados........ 316	.01V	.01V	.01V	—V	—V	—V	—Y	.01V	—V	—V	—V	—V	.01V	.01Y
Bolivia........ 218	.01V	—V	.01V	.01V	—V	—Y	—Y	—V	—V	—V	—V	—Y	—Y	—Y
Brazil........ 223	.01V	.07V	.04V	.24V	.11V	.34V	—V	.39V	.32V	.86V	.45V	2.25V	4.70V	—V
Chile........ 228	—V	—V	—V	—V	—V	—V	—V	—V	—V	—V	—V	.02V	—V	—V
Colombia........ 233	.01V	.02V	—V	.01V	—V	.06V	.17V	.01V	.02V	—V	.03V	.21V	1.87V	.02V
Costa Rica........ 238	.01V	.01V	.02V	.02V	—V	—Y	—Y	—V	—V	—V	.02V	.02V	.02Y	.03Y
Ecuador........ 248	—V	—V	—V	—V	—V	—V	—Y	.08V	—V	—V	.01V	.02V	.02V	.03Y
El Salvador........ 253	—V	—V	—V	—V	.02V	—V	—V	—V	—V	—V	—V	—V	—V	—V
Honduras........ 268	—V	.04V	.07V	.27V	.31Y	.38Y	.47Y	....	....	....	....	....	....	....
Mexico........ 273	—V	—V	—V	—V	.28V	.23V	.90V	—V	—V	—V	—V	.23V	.01V	.01V
Netherlands Antilles........ 353	.04V	—V	.03V	.04Y	.05Y	.06Y	.07Y	—V	—V	—Y	—Y	—Y	—Y	—Y
Paraguay........ 288	—V	—V	—V	—V	—V	—V	—Y	—V	.06V	.25V	—V	—V	—V	—Y
Peru........ 293	—V	—V	—V	—V	—V	—V	—Y	—V	—V	—V	—V	.09V	.95V	—Y
Trinidad and Tobago........ 369	—V	.01V	.02Y	.02Y	.02Y	.03Y	.03Y	—V	—V	—Y	—Y	—Y	—Y	—Y
Venezuela, Rep. Bol........ 299	—V	—V	—V	—V	.06V	.13V	.17V	—V	—V	—V	—V	—V	—V	—Y
Western Hem. n.s........ 399	—Y	—Y	—Y	—Y	—Y	—Y	—Y	1.25Y	1.42Y	1.60Y	1.77Y	1.95Y	2.13Y	2.30Y
Other Countries n.i.e........ 910	**—Y**	**—Y**	**—Y**	**—Y**	**—Y**	**—Y**	**—Y**	**.7Y**	**.7Y**	**.9Y**	**1.2Y**	**1.4Y**	**1.7Y**	**2.1Y**
North Korea........ 954	....	....	....	....	....	....	....	.68Y	.74Y	.93Y	1.23Y	1.40Y	1.73Y	2.15Y
Countries & Areas n.s........ 898	**—Y**	**—Y**	**—Y**	**—Y**	**—Y**	**—Y**	**—Y**	**30.3Y**	**32.9Y**	**41.6Y**	**54.7Y**	**62.5Y**	**77.2Y**	**95.9Y**
Memorandum Items														
European Union........ 998	133.96Y	151.42Y	94.78Y	88.50Y	75.26Y	70.46Y	62.77Y	66.40Y	63.01Y	56.60Y	61.13Y	80.11Y	119.86Y	127.30Y
Oil Exporting Ctys........ 999	3.90Y	4.46Y	8.83Y	8.44Y	9.14Y	10.04Y	26.82Y	1.04Y	.43Y	1.72Y	2.00Y	2.16Y	2.10Y	2.61Y
Non-Oil Develop.Ctys........ 201	25.61Y	53.67Y	16.02Y	20.60Y	23.67Y	26.02Y	28.39Y	28.24Y	32.80Y	36.42Y	46.30Y	60.33Y	68.85Y	89.90Y
PERCENT DISTRIBUTION														
Industrial Countries........ 101	**82.2**	**72.6**	**79.7**	**77.1**	**71.5**	**67.7**	**55.2**	**55.3**	**52.5**	**45.3**	**48.2**	**43.3**	**49.9**	**44.2**
Developing Countries........ 202	**17.8**	**27.4**	**20.3**	**22.9**	**28.5**	**32.3**	**44.8**	**21.7**	**23.6**	**25.9**	**24.0**	**28.0**	**23.7**	**27.1**
Africa........ 607	**2.9**	**21.3**	**5.2**	**5.7**	**6.8**	**8.5**	**10.2**	**10.6**	**17.0**	**17.4**	**15.7**	**16.5**	**16.5**	**18.4**
Asia........ 507	**13.4**	**5.2**	**10.3**	**12.0**	**14.3**	**15.0**	**25.4**	**8.0**	**3.5**	**4.3**	**5.3**	**6.4**	**2.0**	**5.8**
Europe........ 170	**1.1**	**.5**	**2.5**	**3.8**	**4.9**	**5.4**	**5.1**	**.7**	**.8**	**.9**	**.4**	**1.5**	**.7**	**.7**
Middle East........ 407	**.2**	**.3**	**2.2**	**.9**	**1.8**	**2.3**	**2.7**	**.9**	**1.0**	**1.4**	**1.3**	**1.4**	**1.4**	**1.5**
Western Hemisphere........ 207	**.1**	**.1**	**.2**	**.5**	**.7**	**1.1**	**1.5**	**1.5**	**1.3**	**1.8**	**1.2**	**2.2**	**3.3**	**.8**
Other Countries n.i.e........ 910	—	—	—	—	—	—	—	**.5**	**.5**	**.6**	**.6**	**.6**	**.6**	**.6**
ANNUAL PERCENT CHANGE														
World........ 001	**–26.5**	**27.9**	**–42.3**	**3.6**	**–9.3**	**–2.9**	**10.2**	**11.7**	**4.5**	**4.8**	**36.5**	**10.7**	**34.1**	**14.2**
Industrial Countries........ 101	**–31.2**	**13.0**	**–36.7**	**.2**	**–15.9**	**–8.0**	**–10.2**	**10.8**	**–.7**	**–9.7**	**45.4**	**–.5**	**54.4**	**1.2**
Developing Countries........ 202	**6.5**	**96.9**	**–57.3**	**16.9**	**13.0**	**9.9**	**53.1**	**15.7**	**13.5**	**14.7**	**26.7**	**29.4**	**13.5**	**30.4**
Africa........ 607	**23.8**	**843.2**	**–85.9**	**13.4**	**8.1**	**21.1**	**32.9**	**–3.1**	**67.5**	**7.5**	**23.1**	**16.1**	**33.7**	**27.7**
Asia........ 507	**19.6**	**–50.7**	**14.2**	**21.5**	**7.6**	**1.8**	**86.6**	**166.7**	**–54.9**	**30.7**	**68.3**	**33.4**	**–58.6**	**233.1**
Europe........ 170	**–51.8**	**–42.1**	**178.2**	**58.1**	**16.7**	**7.2**	**3.7**	**–71.0**	**26.8**	**8.3**	**–30.3**	**280.5**	**–41.3**	**12.2**
Middle East........ 407	**13.0**	**37.4**	**364.0**	**–58.1**	**89.2**	**23.5**	**27.6**	**–37.4**	**9.5**	**49.5**	**30.5**	**17.7**	**31.0**	**24.9**
Western Hemisphere........ 207	**–89.6**	**73.8**	**20.8**	**209.9**	**37.2**	**47.4**	**48.1**	**53.8**	**–6.3**	**44.0**	**–13.7**	**107.7**	**100.0**	**–73.6**
Other Countries n.i.e........ 910	—	—	....	....	....	....	....	**10.4**	**8.5**	**26.6**	**31.3**	**14.3**	**23.6**	**24.1**

		Exports							Imports						
		2001	2002	2003	2004	2005	2006	2007	2001	2002	2003	2004	2005	2006	2007
		Millions of U.S. Dollars							*Millions of U.S. Dollars*						
IFS World Total		**189.0**	**185.0**	**601.0**	**2,191.0**	**3,149.0**	**3,408.0**	**3,450.0**	**679.0**	**1,646.0**	**790.0**	**953.0**	**950.0**	**1,308.0**	**1,500.0**
DOTS World Total	**001**	**74.8Y**	**62.5Y**	**91.4Y**	**1,110.8Y**	**1,840.0Y**	**2,281.3Y**	**2,274.8Y**	**365.6Y**	**462.5Y**	**351.4Y**	**411.6Y**	**488.2Y**	**529.2Y**	**717.2Y**
Industrial Countries	**101**	**55.2Y**	**45.4Y**	**64.9Y**	**826.5Y**	**1,517.5Y**	**1,893.3Y**	**2,159.1Y**	**318.4Y**	**368.5Y**	**243.3Y**	**269.3Y**	**312.0Y**	**310.6Y**	**401.5Y**
United States	111	5.82V	5.55V	22.18V	752.55V	1,436.36V	1,837.55V	2,036.36V	150.81V	140.14V	70.84V	44.22V	59.07V	66.33V	78.21V
Canada	156	.12V	.03V	.03V	.08V	.01V	.03V	.02V	2.35V	.79V	2.67V	3.14V	5.41V	11.53V	14.88V
Australia	193	—V	—V	.05V	.01V	.03V	.03V	—V	.48V	4.07V	.05V	.78V	1.55V	3.13V	.26V
Japan	158	.68V	.07V	.02V	.11V	.27V	10.97V	85.23V	2.23V	.84V	1.59V	.56V	.59V	1.17V	5.62V
New Zealand	196	—V	—V	—V	.01V	—V	—V	—V	—V	—V	.12V	—V	—V	—V	—V
Austria	122	.36V	—V	—V	.01V	—V	.01V	.06V	.33V	.16V	3.06V	1.63V	7.49V	6.43V	2.67V
Belgium	124	1.70V	.84V	1.29V	.02V	.03V	.05V	.24V	10.38V	12.94V	10.68V	18.87V	32.92V	25.90V	24.41V
Cyprus	423	.01V	—V	—V	.02V	.03Y	—V	—V	—V	—V	—V	—V	—V	.04V	.01V
Denmark	128	.02V	—V	—V	—V	—V	—V	—V	3.20V	3.54V	1.95V	1.43V	1.23V	1.86V	2.79V
Finland	172	—V	—V	—V	—V	—V	—V	—V	.10V	.11V	.68V	.19V	10.24V	.50V	.90V
France	132	5.25V	4.08V	5.74V	7.90V	14.25V	12.96V	7.50V	104.12V	140.57V	98.64V	89.50V	103.36V	98.58V	145.96V
Germany	134	12.07V	10.03V	14.66V	11.34V	11.15V	9.87V	11.15V	9.88V	24.53V	13.39V	26.21V	15.25V	38.79V	54.12V
Greece	174	—V	—V	—V	—V	.02V	—V	—V	.12V	.14V	.10V	.05V	.01V	.09V	—V
Ireland	178	—V	—V	—V	.01V	—V	—V	—V	.19V	.15V	.95V	.22V	.22V	.08V	.55V
Italy	136	.86V	.42V	.90V	.48V	.36V	.18V	.08V	7.65V	8.87V	8.52V	7.19V	7.20V	6.72V	13.36V
Luxembourg	137	—V	—V	—V	—V	—V	—V	—V	.06V	.22V	.15V	—V	.01V	.01V	.25V
Malta	181	—Y	—V	—V	—V	—V	—V	—V	—Y	—V	—V	—V	—V	.27V	.55V
Netherlands	138	—V	—V	.08V	.05V	.03V	.16V	.04V	15.91V	9.47V	15.56V	14.27V	19.82V	14.73V	21.65V
Norway	142	—V	—V	—V	—V	—V	—V	.14V	—V	.11V	.11V	1.11V	.18V	.78V	.24V
Portugal	182	22.35V	19.98V	13.77V	48.08V	48.99V	13.52V	14.91V	1.20V	12.05V	4.79V	42.72V	22.26V	.47V	1.21V
Slovenia	961	1.82V	.47V	.95V	1.24Y	.30V	—V	—V	.24V	.20V	—V	—Y	—V	—V	—V
Spain	184	4.09V	3.73V	3.35V	1.47V	.32V	—V	.69V	.86V	1.30V	1.29V	1.77V	1.40V	5.11V	5.60V
Sweden	144	—V	—V	—V	2.65V	4.75V	2.86V	1.25V	.94V	.38V	1.51V	4.48V	12.09V	8.73V	12.01V
Switzerland	146	—V	—V	.23V	.18V	—V	4.73V	—V	1.56V	.51V	.55V	1.51V	1.91V	13.07V	3.13V
United Kingdom	112	.05V	.16V	1.69V	.27V	.59V	.41V	1.40V	5.82V	7.41V	6.11V	9.46V	9.79V	6.25V	13.09V
Developing Countries	**202**	**19.6Y**	**17.2Y**	**26.5Y**	**284.3Y**	**322.5Y**	**387.9Y**	**115.7Y**	**47.2Y**	**94.0Y**	**108.1Y**	**142.3Y**	**176.2Y**	**218.6Y**	**315.8Y**
Africa	**607**	**7.4Y**	**5.2Y**	**8.9Y**	**7.1Y**	**8.4Y**	**11.9Y**	**13.5Y**	**25.2Y**	**52.0Y**	**71.2Y**	**96.4Y**	**110.1Y**	**134.4Y**	**164.2Y**
Algeria	612	—V	.02V	.02Y	.03Y	.04Y	.05Y	.06Y	—V	—V	—Y	—Y	—Y	—Y	—Y
Benin	638	.01V	.02V	.03V	—V	—V	—Y	—Y	.30V	.25V	1.02V	4.59V	2.27V	2.80Y	3.48Y
Burkina Faso	748	.01Y	.01Y	.02Y	.02Y	.02Y	.03Y	.04Y	.03Y	.03Y	.04Y	.05Y	.06Y	.07Y	.08Y
Cameroon	622	.10V	.29V	.08V	.10Y	.12Y	.15Y	.18Y	12.76V	42.61V	50.17V	65.89Y	75.29Y	93.05Y	115.47Y
Central African Rep.	626	2.19Y	2.38Y	3.01Y	3.96Y	4.52Y	5.59Y	6.93Y	.26Y	.28Y	.36Y	.47Y	.54Y	.66Y	.82Y
Congo, Republic of	634	.03V	.06V	.01V	.03V	.03Y	.04Y	.05Y	.02V	.12V	.09V	—V	—Y	—Y	—Y
Côte d'Ivoire	662	.02V	.01V	—V	.01V	.03V	.02V	.02Y	2.10V	3.55V	4.10V	4.17V	4.36V	5.03V	6.25Y
Gabon	646	.01Y	.01Y	.01Y	.01Y	.02Y	.02Y	.02Y	—Y	—Y	—Y	—Y	—Y	—Y	—Y
Ghana	652	.04Y	.04Y	.06Y	.07Y	.08Y	.10Y	.13Y	....	....	....	....	....	....	....
Guinea	656	—V	—Y	.01V	.01V	.01Y	.01Y	.01Y	.01V	.01Y	—V	—V	—Y	—Y	.01Y
Kenya	664	—V	—V	—V	—V	—Y	—Y	—Y	—V	.03V	.05V	.16V	.18Y	.23Y	.28Y
Madagascar	674	.01V	—V	.05V	.07Y	.08Y	.09Y	.12Y	—V	.01V	.04V	.05Y	.06Y	.07Y	.09Y
Mauritania	682	....	....	....	....	....	....	....	.01Y	.01Y	.02Y	.02Y	.02Y	.03Y	.04Y
Mauritius	684	.01V	.02V	.13V	—V	1.07V	2.87V	2.32V	—V	—V	—V	—V	—V	—V	—V
Morocco	686	2.92V	1.74V	4.71V	2.25V	1.66V	2.05Y	2.55Y	.17V	.90V	1.13V	1.57V	2.04V	2.53Y	3.13Y
Niger	692	—V	.01V	—V	.01V	.01Y	.01Y	.01Y	.70V	.15V	.11V	.42V	.48Y	.59Y	.74Y
Nigeria	694	.21V	.14V	.41V	.53Y	.67Y	.83Y	1.07Y	2.27V	.37V	7.43V	9.83Y	13.37Y	16.81Y	20.28Y
Senegal	722	—V	—V	—V	—V	—V	—V	—Y	2.36V	.55V	1.25V	3.97V	1.47V	.93V	1.16Y
Somalia	726	—Y	—Y	—Y	—Y	—Y	—Y	—Y	.01Y	.01Y	.01Y	.02Y	.02Y	.02Y	.03Y
South Africa	199	—V	—V	.04V	—V	—V	—V	—V	2.32V	1.00V	3.75V	3.19V	5.76V	5.99V	5.37V
Sudan	732	.42Y	.46Y	.28Y	—V	—V	—V	—V	—Y	—Y	—V	—V	—V	—V	—V
Togo	742	—V	—V	—V	—V	—V	—Y	—Y	1.48V	1.43V	1.22V	1.37V	2.38V	2.94Y	3.65Y
Tunisia	744	1.46V	—V	.01V	.02V	—V	—V	—Y	.42V	.65V	.42V	.67V	1.81V	2.65V	3.29Y
Zambia	754	—V	—V	—V	—V	—V	—V	—V	—V	—V	—V	—V	—V	—V	.01V
Asia	**507**	**2.7Y**	**4.8Y**	**10.8Y**	**272.1Y**	**311.3Y**	**375.0Y**	**101.3Y**	**5.1Y**	**6.2Y**	**6.3Y**	**12.3Y**	**23.6Y**	**25.3Y**	**88.0Y**
Bangladesh	513	—V	—V	—V	—V	—V	1.71V	2.77V	—V	—V	—V	—V	—V	—Y	—Y
China,P.R.: Mainland	924	.01V	1.39V	2.58V	238.39V	181.56V	236.62V	76.43V	.31V	1.88V	1.85V	4.94V	16.42V	15.56V	72.03V
China,P.R.:Hong Kong	532	—V	.40V	.22V	—V	.59V	—V	—V	.14V	.02V	.10V	—V	.02V	.74V	6.42V
India	534	—Y	1.28V	2.77V	1.85V	.40V	.50Y	.62Y	3.58Y	2.09V	2.48V	3.71V	4.37V	5.40Y	6.70Y
Indonesia	536	.39V	—V	.63V	.08V	1.04V	1.37V	6.35V	—V	.11V	.25V	.10V	.42V	.03V	.23V
Korea	542	—V	.01V	1.19V	27.53V	48.49V	52.94V	.76V	.36V	1.38V	.68V	.15V	.51V	1.38V	.44V
Malaysia	548	—V	—V	—V	.16V	.12V	—V	.40V	—V	.02V	.06V	.06V	.05V	—V	.49V
Pakistan	564	.28V	.58V	.08V	.40V	.78V	.97Y	1.20Y	.48V	.34V	.36V	2.99V	.58V	.72Y	.89Y
Taiwan Province of China	528	1.50V	.61V	2.67V	.71V	74.90V	51.92V	.46V	.02V	.01V	.06V	.04V	.33V	.21V	.05V
Thailand	578	.51V	.47V	.65V	2.94V	3.37V	29.00V	12.33V	.23V	.36V	.41V	.29V	.87V	1.27V	.70V
Vietnam	582	.02V	.04V	.03V	—V	—V	—V	—V	—V	—V	.07V	—V	—V	—V	—V
Europe	**170**	**9.1Y**	**6.4Y**	**6.5Y**	**4.8Y**	**2.3Y**	**.1Y**	**.2Y**	**6.7Y**	**22.5Y**	**12.2Y**	**9.2Y**	**9.3Y**	**16.5Y**	**13.1Y**
Belarus	913	—V	—V	—V	—V	—V	—V	—V	.01V	.06V	.40V	.07V	—V	—V	—V
Bulgaria	918	—V	—V	—V	—V	.02V	—V	—V	.01V	.01V	—V	—V	1.03V	.95V	.10V
Czech Republic	935	4.21V	2.44V	2.94V	2.10V	1.85V	—V	—V	.06V	.17V	.42V	.04V	.10V	.61V	.14V
Estonia	939	—V	—V	—V	—V	—V	—V	—V	.06V	—V	—V	—V	—V	—V	—V
Hungary	944	.31V	.01V	.03V	—V	—V	—V	—V	.03V	1.91V	.28V	—V	.21V	.01V	.01V

	Exports							Imports						
	2001	2002	2003	2004	2005	2006	2007	2001	2002	2003	2004	2005	2006	2007
	Millions of U.S. Dollars							Millions of U.S. Dollars						
Macedonia, FYR.......... 962	.01V	—V	.01V	.02V	.13V	.06V	.08Y	—V	—V	—V	—V	—V	—V	—Y
Poland.......... 964	3.62V	2.72V	2.73V	2.29V	.11V	—V	.05V	.81V	.27V	.67V	.61V	.41V	.64V	.69V
Romania.......... 968	—V	—V	.04V	—V	—V	—V	—V	—V	.01V	—V	.64V	.13V	.01V	—V
Russia.......... 922	—V	—V	.12V	.04V	.03V	.04V	.02V	—V	9.52V	.79V	.08V	1.39V	6.50V	1.02V
Slovak Republic.......... 936	—V	.22V	.28Y	.37Y	—V	—V	—V	.32V	—V	—Y	—Y	—V	.03V	.06V
Turkey.......... 186	.44V	.98V	.32V	—V	.13V	—V	—V	.81V	3.69V	1.97V	1.17V	1.10V	1.65V	3.55V
Ukraine.......... 926	.55V	—V	—V	—V	.01V	.01Y	.01Y	4.56V	6.88V	7.70V	6.55V	4.93V	6.09Y	7.56Y
Middle East.......... 407	**.2Y**	**.4Y**	**.2Y**	**.3Y**	**.3Y**	**.4Y**	**.5Y**	**9.6Y**	**13.0Y**	**17.4Y**	**23.3Y**	**32.2Y**	**40.5Y**	**49.9Y**
Egypt.......... 469	.16V	.18Y	.22Y	.29Y	.34Y	.42Y	.52Y	.11V	.12Y	.16Y	.21Y	.23Y	.29Y	.36Y
Israel.......... 436	—V	.09V	—V	—V	—V	—V	—V	—V	—V	—V	.22V	.88V	1.10V	1.65V
Jordan.......... 439	—V	—V	—V	—V	—V	—V	—V	.04V	.01V	—V	.07V	.04V	.07V	.77V
Lebanon.......... 446	—Y	—Y	—Y	—Y	—Y	—Y	—Y	.04Y	.04Y	.05Y	.07Y	.08Y	.09Y	.12Y
Oman.......... 449	—V	.05V	—V	—Y	—Y	—Y	—Y	.37V	3.27V	5.61V	7.42Y	10.10Y	12.69Y	15.31Y
Saudi Arabia.......... 456	.04V	.03V	.02V	.02V	—V	.01Y	.01Y	9.00Y	9.57Y	11.60Y	15.36Y	20.89Y	26.26Y	31.68Y
Western Hemisphere.......... 207	**.1Y**	**.4Y**	**.1Y**	**—Y**	**.3Y**	**.5Y**	**.2Y**	**.6Y**	**.3Y**	**.9Y**	**1.1Y**	**1.1Y**	**1.9Y**	**.6Y**
Argentina.......... 213	—V	—V	—V	—V	—V	.01V	—V	.36V	—V	.56V	.50V	.43V	.23V	.61V
Brazil.......... 223	—V	—V	.02V	—V	.01V	.01V	—V	.17V	.29V	.38V	.30V	.57V	1.58V	—V
Colombia.......... 233	—V	.43V	.06V	—V	.02V	—V	.03V	—V	—V	—V	.26V	—V	.09V	—V
Costa Rica.......... 238	—V	—V	—V	.01V	—V	—Y	—Y	....	....	....	....	....	....	....
Ecuador.......... 248	.05V	.01V	—V	—V	—V	—V	—Y	.08V	—V	—V	—V	—V	—V	—Y
Mexico.......... 273	—V	—V	—V	—V	.25V	.49V	.18V	—V	—V	—V	—V	.06V	—V	—V
Memorandum Items														
European Union.......... 998	56.73Y	45.11Y	48.41Y	78.31Y	82.78Y	40.02Y	37.37Y	162.27Y	224.41Y	168.73Y	218.64Y	244.01Y	215.84Y	300.04Y
Oil Exporting Ctys.......... 999	.64Y	.24Y	1.08Y	.66Y	1.76Y	2.26Y	7.50Y	11.64Y	13.32Y	24.89Y	32.71Y	44.77Y	55.79Y	67.50Y
Non-Oil Develop.Ctys.......... 201	18.92Y	16.94Y	25.41Y	283.66Y	320.77Y	385.68Y	108.23Y	35.53Y	80.64Y	83.20Y	109.57Y	131.47Y	162.81Y	248.25Y
PERCENT DISTRIBUTION														
Industrial Countries.......... 101	**73.8**	**72.5**	**71.0**	**74.4**	**82.5**	**83.0**	**94.9**	**87.1**	**79.7**	**69.2**	**65.4**	**63.9**	**58.7**	**56.0**
Developing Countries.......... 202	**26.2**	**27.5**	**29.0**	**25.6**	**17.5**	**17.0**	**5.1**	**12.9**	**20.3**	**30.8**	**34.6**	**36.1**	**41.3**	**44.0**
Africa.......... 607	**10.0**	**8.3**	**9.7**	**.6**	**.5**	**.5**	**.6**	**6.9**	**11.2**	**20.3**	**23.4**	**22.6**	**25.4**	**22.9**
Asia.......... 507	**3.6**	**7.7**	**11.8**	**24.5**	**16.9**	**16.4**	**4.5**	**1.4**	**1.3**	**1.8**	**3.0**	**4.8**	**4.8**	**12.3**
Europe.......... 170	**12.2**	**10.2**	**7.1**	**.4**	**.1**	**—**	**—**	**1.8**	**4.9**	**3.5**	**2.2**	**1.9**	**3.1**	**1.8**
Middle East.......... 407	**.3**	**.6**	**.3**	**—**	**—**	**—**	**—**	**2.6**	**2.8**	**5.0**	**5.7**	**6.6**	**7.7**	**7.0**
Western Hemisphere.......... 207	**.1**	**.7**	**.1**	**—**	**—**	**—**	**—**	**.2**	**.1**	**.3**	**.3**	**.2**	**.4**	**.1**
ANNUAL PERCENT CHANGE														
World.......... 001	**–12.8**	**–16.4**	**46.2**	**—**	**65.6**	**24.0**	**–.3**	**162.2**	**26.5**	**–24.0**	**17.1**	**18.6**	**8.4**	**35.5**
Industrial Countries.......... 101	**–5.4**	**–17.8**	**43.2**	**—**	**83.6**	**24.8**	**14.0**	**213.4**	**15.7**	**–34.0**	**10.7**	**15.9**	**–.5**	**29.3**
Developing Countries.......... 202	**–28.6**	**–12.1**	**54.2**	**973.4**	**13.4**	**20.3**	**–70.2**	**24.7**	**99.2**	**15.0**	**31.6**	**23.9**	**24.0**	**44.4**
Africa.......... 607	**–24.2**	**–29.9**	**70.1**	**–19.7**	**17.4**	**41.9**	**14.0**	**29.9**	**106.0**	**37.1**	**35.4**	**14.2**	**22.1**	**22.1**
Asia.......... 507	**–42.5**	**76.3**	**125.9**	**—**	**14.4**	**20.5**	**–73.0**	**–23.1**	**21.0**	**1.8**	**94.6**	**91.9**	**7.3**	**247.6**
Europe.......... 170	**4.4**	**–30.2**	**1.3**	**–25.5**	**–52.7**	**–95.4**	**45.4**	**152.4**	**237.7**	**–45.7**	**–25.1**	**1.4**	**77.6**	**–20.3**
Middle East.......... 407	**—**	**69.7**	**–30.8**	**30.0**	**8.6**	**23.6**	**24.2**	**5.7**	**36.1**	**33.9**	**34.0**	**38.0**	**25.7**	**23.2**
Western Hemisphere.......... 207	**–98.7**	**715.1**	**–80.1**	**–84.9**	**—**	**82.1**	**–58.8**	**779.7**	**–53.0**	**226.7**	**12.6**	**.6**	**78.3**	**–67.9**

	Exports							Imports						
	2001	2002	2003	2004	2005	2006	2007	2001	2002	2003	2004	2005	2006	2007
	Millions of U.S. Dollars							*Millions of U.S. Dollars*						
IFS World Total....................	**18,272**	**18,180**	**21,664**	**32,520**	**41,267**	**58,485**	**67,644**	**17,429**	**17,091**	**19,322**	**24,793**	**32,735**	**38,405**	**47,125**
DOTS World Total.................... 001	**18,555**	**18,285**	**21,464**	**32,548**	**39,544**	**57,299**	**67,498**	**17,830**	**17,014**	**19,413**	**24,788**	**30,893**	**35,891**	**43,797**
Industrial Countries................ 101	**10,629**	**10,118**	**11,223**	**17,007**	**21,083**	**31,292**	**32,670**	**7,185**	**6,642**	**6,981**	**8,426**	**11,508**	**12,791**	**16,314**
United States.................... 111	3,428	3,484	3,468	4,568	6,248	8,940	8,420	2,867	2,528	2,525	3,402	4,722	5,593	7,294
Canada.................... 156	259	263	414	779	1,069	1,289	1,201	426	320	332	348	406	483	979
Australia.................... 193	41	60	98	88	95	134	279	86	98	87	141	165	203	216
Japan.................... 158	2,134	1,928	2,247	3,696	4,536	6,039	7,091	556	540	635	803	1,021	1,150	1,614
New Zealand.................... 196	9	9	21	23	26	22	26	28	18	19	25	41	43	44
Austria.................... 122	13	10	10	8	6	6	17	40	38	53	67	102	121	142
Belgium.................... 124	232	228	272	329	377	732	755	110	126	111	104	178	166	218
Cyprus.................... 423	1	—	—	—	—	—	—	—	—	—	—	—	—	—
Denmark.................... 128	57	59	75	82	117	115	128	66	67	77	68	108	118	157
Finland.................... 172	36	51	71	116	149	276	220	84	103	252	197	514	263	251
France.................... 132	603	631	733	1,286	1,387	2,412	2,391	574	622	595	511	683	712	793
Germany.................... 134	518	426	592	901	930	1,758	1,661	689	736	711	832	1,198	1,259	1,574
Greece.................... 174	42	65	91	122	147	221	365	5	10	3	5	8	29	9
Iceland.................... 176	14	30	1	2	2	3	3	4	3	2	3	3	3	5
Ireland.................... 178	25	30	35	42	44	52	59	43	39	44	44	47	62	52
Italy.................... 136	801	857	905	1,338	1,658	2,812	3,455	436	354	387	446	524	630	737
Luxembourg.................... 137	1	—	—	1	—	—	—	7	13	13	14	15	12	8
Malta.................... 181	—	—	2	1	1	1	1	—	—	—	—	1	1	1
Netherlands.................... 138	535	534	771	1,653	2,301	3,815	3,909	108	102	113	186	171	301	255
Norway.................... 142	42	28	26	28	36	28	49	51	24	30	63	61	62	109
Portugal.................... 182	21	16	25	29	29	28	31	54	47	54	57	60	73	74
Slovenia.................... 961	—	—	1	1	—	1	1	3	4	3	4	5	4	5
Spain.................... 184	345	389	477	730	963	1,380	1,338	465	417	451	516	618	710	847
Sweden.................... 144	80	146	113	169	282	426	411	181	150	199	265	451	354	392
Switzerland.................... 146	158	78	86	158	62	137	181	110	99	103	106	139	137	170
United Kingdom.................... 112	1,232	797	690	857	616	665	679	194	184	181	220	267	301	368
Developing Countries............. 202	**6,851**	**7,027**	**8,902**	**13,408**	**16,803**	**23,579**	**31,996**	**8,746**	**8,744**	**10,286**	**13,754**	**18,456**	**19,954**	**23,059**
Africa.................... 607	**116**	**65**	**97**	**98**	**116**	**144**	**195**	**238**	**250**	**255**	**964**	**1,597**	**2,055**	**1,327**
Algeria.................... 612	—	—	1	1	2	1	3	14	—	—	—	—	—	—
Angola.................... 614	—	—	2	3	1	3	5	—	—	64	431	1,197	1,317	962
Benin.................... 638	1	1	—	—	—	—	—	—	—	—	—	—	—	—
Cameroon.................... 622	2	1	1	1	1	6	2	—	—	—	—	—	—	—
Congo, Dem. Rep. of.................... 636	—	—	—	1	1	1	2	—	—	—	—	64	136	—
Congo, Republic of.................... 634	—	—	—	—	—	—	—	22	5	—	—	2	15	2
Côte d'Ivoire.................... 662	2	1	—	—	—	—	—	—	—	—	—	—	—	—
Equatorial Guinea.................... 642	—	—	—	—	—	1	1	6	—	—	—	—	—	—
Gabon.................... 646	—	—	—	1	—	—	—	—	—	22	67	—	58	—
Ghana.................... 652	2	1	3	3	5	7	11	—	—	—	—	—	—	—
Guinea.................... 656	—	—	—	—	1	—	1	—	—	—	—	—	—	—
Kenya.................... 664	1	—	—	1	2	2	3	—	—	1	1	1	2	1
Liberia.................... 668	1	2	2	1	—	—	—	—	—	—	—	—	—	—
Mauritius.................... 684	1	1	1	1	2	2	2	1	—	—	—	—	—	—
Morocco.................... 686	7	6	9	10	14	13	3	1	1	1	2	2	3	1
Mozambique.................... 688	—	—	1	—	1	—	1	—	—	—	—	—	—	—
Namibia.................... 728	9	—	—	—	—	—	—	—	—	—	—	—	—	—
Nigeria.................... 694	9	14	14	22	27	47	54	123	188	107	376	260	454	278
Seychelles.................... 718	—	—	—	—	—	—	—	—	—	—	—	—	—	6
South Africa.................... 199	33	37	58	48	58	58	104	70	53	58	86	70	66	73
Sudan.................... 732	—	—	—	—	1	—	—	—	—	—	—	—	—	—
Tanzania.................... 738	—	—	—	—	1	—	1	—	—	—	—	—	—	—
Tunisia.................... 744	—	—	1	1	—	—	—	—	3	—	—	—	2	1
Zambia.................... 754	—	—	—	—	—	—	1	—	—	—	—	—	—	—
Zimbabwe.................... 698	2	—	—	—	—	—	—	—	—	—	—	—	—	—
Africa n.s.................... 799	44	—	2	2	1	1	—	—	—	—	—	—	—	—
Asia.................... 507	**2,298**	**2,964**	**4,474**	**7,128**	**9,050**	**12,487**	**19,038**	**2,241**	**2,190**	**2,514**	**3,399**	**5,140**	**4,866**	**6,416**
Afghanistan, I.S. of.................... 512	1	—	—	—	—	—	—	—	—	—	—	—	—	—
Bangladesh.................... 513	4	—	2	1	—	—	—	—	1	1	1	2	2	2
Cambodia.................... 522	—	—	—	—	—	—	—	—	—	—	—	—	2	7
China,P.R.: Mainland.................... 924	1,015	1,233	1,847	3,212	4,390	4,933	9,980	1,014	1,102	1,289	1,847	2,535	3,491	4,886
China,P.R.:Hong Kong.................... 532	34	—	73	132	91	100	101	28	41	69	73	89	112	53
China,P.R.:Macao.................... 546	—	—	582	957	1,282	1,533	1,746	—	—	—	—	—	—	—
Fiji.................... 819	—	—	1	1	1	2	2	—	—	—	—	—	—	—
French Polynesia.................... 887	3	2	2	2	1	2	1	—	—	—	—	—	—	—
India.................... 534	111	180	222	426	493	1,489	2,211	75	82	70	101	135	165	208
Indonesia.................... 536	42	64	77	152	189	183	237	86	86	78	130	144	175	188
Kiribati.................... 826	—	—	—	—	1	—	—	—	—	—	—	—	—	—
Korea.................... 542	553	714	1,014	1,804	2,192	3,405	3,849	540	439	540	700	1,560	9	3
Malaysia.................... 548	32	22	50	124	94	114	73	104	71	80	109	135	188	170
Mongolia.................... 948	—	—	—	—	—	—	—	—	1	—	—	—	—	—

	Exports							Imports						
	2001	2002	2003	2004	2005	2006	2007	2001	2002	2003	2004	2005	2006	2007
	Millions of U.S. Dollars							Millions of U.S. Dollars						
Myanmar.......518	2	—	—	—	—	—	—	—	1	—	—	—	—	—
Pakistan.......564	—	—	1	1	2	2	2	37	37	35	39	45	57	63
Papua New Guinea.......853	—	—	—	1	—	—	—	—	—	—	—	—	—	—
Philippines.......566	55	38	53	60	13	131	315	24	8	12	15	13	16	30
Samoa.......862	1	—	4	3	4	3	2	—	—	—	—	—	—	—
Singapore.......576	25	36	41	59	73	55	113	25	24	19	28	31	28	114
Sri Lanka.......524	13	17	17	15	23	22	29	15	12	10	13	18	20	21
Taiwan Province of China.......528	352	530	414	—	—	—	—	174	169	196	204	236	272	241
Thailand.......578	45	51	56	138	131	406	266	92	94	103	117	158	273	374
Tonga.......866	—	—	—	1	1	—	1	—	—	—	—	—	—	—
Tuvalu.......869	—	—	—	1	—	—	—	—	—	—	—	—	—	—
Vanuatu.......846	—	—	—	—	—	—	—	—	—	—	1	—	—	—
Vietnam.......582	9	77	17	38	69	107	108	27	22	11	22	39	54	55
Europe.......170	**152**	**224**	**247**	**476**	**675**	**1,214**	**1,396**	**138**	**173**	**143**	**175**	**257**	**307**	**1,043**
Armenia.......911	—	—	—	—	—	—	1	—	—	—	—	—	—	—
Belarus.......913	—	—	—	—	—	1	2	1	—	—	—	—	4	—
Bulgaria.......918	35	31	65	158	169	416	474	—	6	1	1	4	2	20
Croatia.......960	—	—	1	1	1	3	3	1	1	1	2	2	46	1
Czech Republic.......935	1	1	2	4	4	5	9	7	10	7	13	20	28	24
Estonia.......939	2	4	2	4	8	7	6	3	—	11	2	6	8	2
Georgia.......915	—	—	—	—	—	1	—	—	—	—	—	—	—	—
Hungary.......944	—	—	1	1	2	2	3	9	6	12	11	12	13	18
Kazakhstan.......916	—	—	—	—	—	—	—	1	1	1	2	3	1	—
Latvia.......941	9	6	6	7	10	15	14	11	16	—	—	12	2	1
Lithuania.......946	2	3	7	9	15	9	10	—	—	—	—	1	2	3
Poland.......964	11	6	7	21	20	176	185	10	13	24	22	37	43	36
Romania.......968	1	—	1	9	29	12	3	16	12	5	5	19	13	6
Russia.......922	17	89	41	91	147	158	228	33	36	25	24	22	28	44
Slovak Republic.......936	—	—	—	—	—	—	—	1	1	3	4	5	8	14
Tajikistan.......923	—	—	—	2	—	—	—	—	—	—	—	—	—	—
Turkey.......186	72	83	112	163	261	394	440	20	22	19	29	32	37	844
Ukraine.......926	—	1	2	3	7	15	19	24	49	33	59	83	72	31
Yugoslavia n.s.......966	—	—	1	—	—	—	—	—	—	—	—	—	—	—
Middle East.......407	**166**	**255**	**210**	**255**	**361**	**379**	**477**	**73**	**52**	**51**	**56**	**70**	**79**	**133**
Bahrain.......419	1	1	2	2	2	2	3	—	—	—	—	—	—	—
Egypt.......469	5	—	3	5	9	5	13	1	1	1	1	—	—	—
Iran, I.R. of.......429	57	25	56	84	148	178	182	2	1	1	1	1	2	1
Iraq.......433	—	—	—	—	1	—	—	—	—	—	—	—	—	—
Israel.......436	6	10	12	15	19	21	21	59	44	45	50	58	57	73
Jordan.......439	—	—	1	—	1	1	2	—	—	—	—	1	—	—
Kuwait.......443	2	—	8	10	9	9	13	—	—	—	—	—	—	—
Lebanon.......446	1	1	1	1	1	1	2	—	—	—	—	—	—	—
Libya.......672	1	—	—	—	—	—	—	—	—	—	—	—	—	—
Oman.......449	2	3	9	9	14	25	17	—	—	—	—	—	—	—
Qatar.......453	1	2	2	—	4	2	3	3	1	1	—	1	2	22
Saudi Arabia.......456	56	76	66	72	71	74	100	5	4	—	2	6	2	34
Syrian Arab Republic.......463	1	—	—	—	—	—	5	—	—	—	—	1	1	1
United Arab Emirates.......466	33	136	51	56	80	61	116	1	1	1	1	2	15	2
Yemen, Republic of.......474	—	—	2	1	2	—	—	—	—	—	—	—	—	—
Western Hemisphere.......207	**4,119**	**3,519**	**3,873**	**5,450**	**6,601**	**9,355**	**10,892**	**6,057**	**6,079**	**7,323**	**9,160**	**11,393**	**12,647**	**14,141**
Antigua and Barbuda.......311	—	—	—	6	—	—	—	—	—	—	—	—	—	—
Argentina.......213	555	233	324	448	626	769	877	3,057	3,059	3,768	4,152	4,791	4,509	4,347
Bahamas, The.......313	1	1	2	1	2	2	3	—	—	—	—	—	—	—
Barbados.......316	86	1	1	1	1	2	4	2	9	—	—	—	—	—
Belize.......339	—	—	6	—	1	2	1	—	—	—	—	—	—	—
Bolivia.......218	144	139	140	139	211	286	300	25	23	41	53	38	59	57
Brazil.......223	835	694	839	1,403	1,728	2,758	3,356	1,492	1,615	2,022	2,780	3,782	4,243	4,501
Colombia.......233	243	275	284	309	347	492	617	189	207	203	294	344	364	883
Costa Rica.......238	52	65	73	97	116	188	171	3	4	9	9	9	8	19
Dominican Republic.......243	29	35	27	29	36	35	41	—	1	2	3	4	5	8
Ecuador.......248	231	253	293	323	341	422	461	123	93	78	139	246	607	758
El Salvador.......253	17	21	31	56	85	98	93	3	—	1	3	2	1	3
Guatemala.......258	58	71	137	166	129	152	249	4	9	10	12	14	7	45
Guyana.......336	96	—	—	—	1	1	1	3	9	—	—	1	2	1
Haiti.......263	5	5	4	5	6	5	4	—	—	—	—	—	—	—
Honduras.......268	18	20	24	57	52	48	41	1	—	—	1	1	1	1
Jamaica.......343	7	7	11	18	8	11	10	1	—	—	—	—	—	2
Mexico.......273	827	909	921	1,307	1,582	2,288	2,368	532	475	480	621	765	1,003	1,350
Netherlands Antilles.......353	3	3	3	4	3	3	3	—	6	32	24	19	14	12
Nicaragua.......278	5	5	6	8	9	25	28	—	—	—	—	—	1	4
Panama.......283	24	37	101	168	111	178	178	5	3	5	22	11	11	13
Paraguay.......288	46	24	24	34	40	62	69	90	79	41	97	118	182	221
Peru.......293	478	464	425	523	724	932	1,034	285	256	421	695	1,106	1,427	1,687
St. Lucia.......362	—	—	—	—	—	1	1	—	—	—	—	—	—	—
Suriname.......366	—	—	—	1	1	1	1	—	—	—	—	—	—	—
Trinidad and Tobago.......369	3	4	6	5	6	11	15	—	—	—	7	7	—	19
Uruguay.......298	63	41	39	67	73	91	99	56	64	85	74	—	—	—

	Exports							Imports						
	2001	2002	2003	2004	2005	2006	2007	2001	2002	2003	2004	2005	2006	2007
	Millions of U.S. Dollars							*Millions of U.S. Dollars*						
Venezuela, Rep. Bol..................... 299	286	207	148	273	358	492	866	185	158	124	173	135	202	213
Western Hem. n.s........................ 399	7	6	3	2	2	—	—	—	8	—	—	—	—	—
Other Countries n.i.e................ 910	**38**	**43**	**42**	**61**	**96**	**62**	**103**	**30**	**13**	**4**	**1**	**2**	**2**	**4**
Cuba... 928	37	42	38	47	43	44	64	1	1	1	1	2	1	3
North Korea................................. 954	1	1	4	14	54	17	39	29	12	3	1	—	—	1
Countries & Areas n.s.............. 898	**—**	**—**	**—**	**716**	**—**	**77**	**—**	**—**	**—**	**—**	**—**	**—**	**—**	**—**
Special Categories................... 899	**1,036**	**1,098**	**1,297**	**1,356**	**1,562**	**2,289**	**2,728**	**1,869**	**1,614**	**2,141**	**2,607**	**927**	**3,145**	**4,419**
Memorandum Items														
European Union........................... 998	4,568	4,258	4,886	7,712	9,068	14,915	15,647	3,100	3,058	3,306	3,587	5,041	5,220	5,981
Oil Exporting Ctys........................ 999	489	527	431	678	902	1,073	1,591	420	438	313	683	549	852	738
Non-Oil Develop.Ctys.................. 201	6,363	6,499	8,471	12,730	15,901	22,506	30,406	8,326	8,306	9,973	13,071	17,907	19,102	22,321
PERCENT DISTRIBUTION														
Industrial Countries................. 101	**57.3**	**55.3**	**52.3**	**52.3**	**53.3**	**54.6**	**48.4**	**40.3**	**39.0**	**36.0**	**34.0**	**37.3**	**35.6**	**37.3**
Developing Countries.............. 202	**36.9**	**38.4**	**41.5**	**41.2**	**42.5**	**41.2**	**47.4**	**49.1**	**51.4**	**53.0**	**55.5**	**59.7**	**55.6**	**52.7**
Africa...................................... 607	**.6**	**.4**	**.4**	**.3**	**.3**	**.3**	**.3**	**1.3**	**1.5**	**1.3**	**3.9**	**5.2**	**5.7**	**3.0**
Asia.. 507	**12.4**	**16.2**	**20.8**	**21.9**	**22.9**	**21.8**	**28.2**	**12.6**	**12.9**	**12.9**	**13.7**	**16.6**	**13.6**	**14.7**
Europe.................................... 170	**.8**	**1.2**	**1.2**	**1.5**	**1.7**	**2.1**	**2.1**	**.8**	**1.0**	**.7**	**.7**	**.8**	**.9**	**2.4**
Middle East............................ 407	**.9**	**1.4**	**1.0**	**.8**	**.9**	**.7**	**.7**	**.4**	**.3**	**.3**	**.2**	**.2**	**.2**	**.3**
Western Hemisphere............. 207	**22.2**	**19.2**	**18.0**	**16.7**	**16.7**	**16.3**	**16.1**	**34.0**	**35.7**	**37.7**	**37.0**	**36.9**	**35.2**	**32.3**
Other Countries n.i.e................ 910	**.2**	**.2**	**.2**	**.2**	**.2**	**.1**	**.2**	**.2**	**.1**	**—**	**—**	**—**	**—**	**—**
ANNUAL PERCENT CHANGE														
World....................................... 001	**–3.8**	**–1.5**	**17.4**	**51.6**	**21.5**	**44.9**	**17.8**	**–3.8**	**–4.6**	**14.1**	**27.7**	**24.6**	**16.2**	**22.0**
Industrial Countries................. 101	**–1.4**	**–4.8**	**10.9**	**51.5**	**24.0**	**48.4**	**4.4**	**–6.5**	**–7.6**	**5.1**	**20.7**	**36.6**	**11.1**	**27.6**
Developing Countries.............. 202	**–8.9**	**2.6**	**26.7**	**50.6**	**25.3**	**40.3**	**35.7**	**–1.6**	**—**	**17.6**	**33.7**	**34.2**	**8.1**	**15.6**
Africa...................................... 607	**65.0**	**–43.8**	**48.8**	**1.3**	**18.8**	**23.6**	**35.5**	**–53.6**	**5.4**	**1.8**	**278.1**	**65.8**	**28.7**	**–35.4**
Asia.. 507	**–18.8**	**29.0**	**50.9**	**59.3**	**27.0**	**38.0**	**52.5**	**3.5**	**–2.3**	**14.8**	**35.2**	**51.2**	**–5.3**	**31.9**
Europe.................................... 170	**–14.8**	**47.5**	**10.4**	**92.7**	**41.6**	**80.0**	**14.9**	**–14.5**	**25.3**	**–17.0**	**22.1**	**46.8**	**19.5**	**239.4**
Middle East............................ 407	**–42.4**	**53.1**	**–17.4**	**21.2**	**41.3**	**5.2**	**25.7**	**–16.9**	**–27.9**	**–3.5**	**11.2**	**24.7**	**13.1**	**67.4**
Western Hemisphere............. 207	**–.8**	**–14.6**	**10.1**	**40.7**	**21.1**	**41.7**	**16.4**	**1.6**	**.4**	**20.5**	**25.1**	**24.4**	**11.0**	**11.8**
Other Countries n.i.e................ 910	**–5.2**	**13.4**	**–.9**	**44.8**	**57.3**	**–35.8**	**67.1**	**—**	**–56.4**	**–65.1**	**–69.9**	**47.4**	**–10.5**	**124.3**

	Exports							Imports						
	2001	2002	2003	2004	2005	2006	2007	2001	2002	2003	2004	2005	2006	2007
	Millions of U.S. Dollars							*Millions of U.S. Dollars*						
IFS World Total (Billions).........	**266**	**326**	**438**	**593**	**762**	**969**	**1,218**	**244**	**295**	**413**	**561**	**660**	**792**	**956**
DOTS World Total (Billions)...... 001	**267**	**326**	**438**	**593**	**762**	**969**	**1,218**	**244**	**295**	**413**	**561**	**660**	**792**	**956**
Industrial Countries................. 101	**149,222**	**177,892**	**239,267**	**319,939**	**410,701**	**501,114**	**603,984**	**117,409**	**132,809**	**177,700**	**233,078**	**251,540**	**296,696**	**356,290**
United States.............................. 111	54,395	70,064	92,633	125,155	163,348	203,898	233,181	26,221	27,251	33,939	44,773	48,994	59,326	69,998
Canada.. 156	3,350	4,305	5,633	8,162	11,658	15,520	19,363	4,030	3,627	4,375	7,354	7,516	7,667	10,975
Australia...................................... 193	3,574	4,589	6,263	8,838	11,065	13,626	17,998	5,430	5,852	7,301	11,553	16,147	19,195	25,758
Japan.. 158	45,078	48,483	59,423	73,514	84,097	91,772	102,116	42,810	53,489	74,151	94,372	100,468	115,811	133,903
New Zealand................................ 196	435	596	803	1,077	1,354	1,620	2,161	737	803	1,024	1,413	1,327	1,314	1,537
Austria... 122	354	481	674	781	883	1,048	1,552	662	893	1,105	1,511	1,611	2,054	2,465
Belgium....................................... 124	2,548	2,877	3,934	5,860	7,740	9,909	12,681	1,721	2,022	2,768	3,520	4,006	4,304	4,971
Cyprus... 423	116	225	218	185	287	351	698	1	1	1	2	3	3	8
Denmark...................................... 128	899	917	1,494	1,946	2,790	3,648	4,594	626	637	964	1,206	1,195	1,308	1,824
Finland.. 172	912	1,154	1,674	2,495	3,627	4,958	6,566	2,376	1,513	1,788	3,021	2,628	3,124	3,798
France... 132	3,706	4,088	7,330	9,967	11,701	13,967	20,460	4,243	4,299	6,102	7,670	9,027	11,298	13,365
Germany...................................... 134	9,759	11,382	17,536	23,756	32,537	40,302	48,729	13,695	16,434	24,341	30,368	30,668	37,888	45,422
Greece... 174	694	732	1,114	1,380	1,936	2,180	3,254	58	55	75	86	87	104	168
Iceland... 176	34	18	46	46	75	78	92	19	14	23	27	47	40	36
Ireland... 178	530	770	1,392	2,140	3,184	3,917	4,437	613	689	951	1,188	1,423	1,545	1,925
Italy... 136	4,005	4,828	6,654	9,226	11,697	15,981	21,179	3,784	4,320	5,080	6,451	6,934	8,606	10,217
Luxembourg................................ 137	39	51	311	918	2,040	2,016	2,053	58	50	116	129	151	169	252
Malta... 181	80	116	124	273	301	475	328	71	180	228	252	238	351	376
Netherlands................................ 138	7,294	9,070	13,505	18,519	25,876	30,843	41,411	1,456	1,573	1,934	2,969	2,925	3,648	4,935
Norway.. 142	412	527	899	1,029	1,322	1,700	2,200	570	924	865	1,398	1,145	1,249	1,614
Portugal...................................... 182	261	301	406	588	914	1,360	1,825	72	83	195	281	324	354	394
Slovenia...................................... 961	77	95	151	207	266	447	696	13	30	36	42	57	95	111
Spain... 184	2,299	2,612	3,932	5,534	8,486	11,547	16,600	714	901	1,361	1,746	2,083	3,014	4,430
Sweden....................................... 144	932	910	1,453	1,860	2,577	3,273	4,548	2,173	1,792	2,716	3,339	3,130	3,451	4,153
Switzerland................................. 146	653	638	842	1,512	1,956	2,519	3,609	1,730	2,041	2,693	3,645	3,894	4,269	5,872
United Kingdom........................... 112	6,786	8,059	10,824	14,968	18,983	24,158	31,654	3,525	3,337	3,570	4,761	5,511	6,510	7,784
Developing Countries............. 202	**116,570**	**147,035**	**198,118**	**272,161**	**349,614**	**465,197**	**611,039**	**117,108**	**147,260**	**209,514**	**288,861**	**352,741**	**420,690**	**512,525**
Africa.. 607	**5,058**	**6,007**	**9,012**	**12,083**	**16,308**	**22,888**	**31,843**	**4,522**	**5,429**	**8,168**	**15,041**	**19,961**	**26,856**	**34,442**
Algeria... 612	223	352	646	981	1,405	1,952	2,709	70	82	99	259	362	140	1,124
Angola... 614	46	61	146	194	373	894	1,241	722	1,087	2,206	4,717	6,581	10,931	12,885
Benin... 638	521	421	471	577	953	1,452	1,972	—	17	68	111	140	89	113
Botswana.................................... 616	14	19	23	50	59	62	118	—	—	2	3	4	8	26
Burkina Faso............................... 748	4	6	12	13	16	19	44	—	1	32	124	163	193	155
Burundi.. 618	1	2	3	5	12	10	13	—	—	2	—	—	2	1
Cameroon.................................... 622	29	44	65	100	130	191	297	184	115	115	149	67	200	160
Cape Verde.................................. 624	2	2	3	3	5	10	15	—	—	—	—	—	—	—
Central African Rep...................... 626	1	1	2	3	7	2	9	1	1	2	6	9	9	7
Chad.. 628	—	2	2	6	15	14	65	—	2	3	223	200	260	84
Comoros...................................... 632	—	1	1	1	2	6	8	—	—	—	—	—	—	—
Congo, Dem. Rep. of.................. 636	13	19	25	37	50	69	93	7	12	26	100	176	368	460
Congo, Republic of...................... 634	38	40	60	93	145	242	420	182	232	815	1,569	2,278	2,785	2,828
Côte d'Ivoire............................... 662	258	220	228	123	137	227	413	8	14	37	108	85	126	41
Djibouti....................................... 611	48	50	66	72	111	155	164	—	—	—	1	1	—	2
Equatorial Guinea........................ 642	3	3	5	10	19	41	93	372	341	412	997	1,486	2,538	1,697
Eritrea... 643	3	6	5	8	8	38	27	—	—	—	1	—	1	3
Ethiopia....................................... 644	79	96	153	194	285	432	775	2	4	5	14	86	132	87
Gabon.. 646	6	5	9	14	41	64	103	259	232	301	400	348	817	1,092
Gambia, The................................ 648	73	82	116	124	125	163	185	—	—	2	—	—	—	9
Ghana.. 652	146	182	322	510	673	803	1,224	37	30	34	80	96	80	53
Guinea... 656	44	43	73	93	144	176	263	—	12	10	15	3	12	92
Guinea-Bissau.............................. 654	6	4	12	6	6	6	7	—	—	—	—	—	—	—
Kenya.. 664	139	183	242	349	457	622	932	6	6	9	17	18	24	28
Lesotho.. 666	17	25	25	47	56	64	59	1	—	—	—	—	1	1
Liberia... 668	113	30	26	182	150	530	806	29	56	42	17	14	2	3
Madagascar.................................. 674	73	40	112	152	183	223	333	9	11	7	14	14	24	30
Malawi... 676	4	7	11	19	16	31	42	—	1	—	—	2	1	1
Mali... 678	23	22	35	59	66	75	125	1	2	28	107	80	114	36
Mauritania................................... 682	30	52	56	64	74	109	137	4	10	8	50	4	402	567
Mauritius..................................... 684	87	90	107	151	177	198	284	9	5	3	7	8	7	5
Morocco....................................... 686	300	451	696	943	1,206	1,570	2,162	84	122	161	214	277	359	423
Mozambique................................. 688	22	26	45	75	91	128	160	11	23	27	44	74	80	124
Namibia....................................... 728	21	20	38	53	60	133	246	11	29	37	47	76	122	158
Niger... 692	7	15	19	25	34	72	31	—	—	—	—	—	1	—
Nigeria.. 694	919	1,047	1,787	1,720	2,305	2,856	3,800	227	134	72	463	527	278	537
Rwanda.. 714	3	4	4	5	12	12	35	6	5	7	16	12	22	24
São Tomé & Príncipe.................... 716	1	—	—	—	1	1	2	—	—	—	1	—	—	—
Senegal....................................... 722	53	58	73	108	133	187	333	—	1	6	4	8	9	23
Seychelles................................... 718	1	1	2	2	3	5	7	—	—	—	—	—	1	4
Sierra Leone................................ 724	12	14	17	28	31	39	58	—	—	—	2	1	1	6

	Exports 2001	Exports 2002	Exports 2003	Exports 2004	Exports 2005	Exports 2006	Exports 2007	Imports 2001	Imports 2002	Imports 2003	Imports 2004	Imports 2005	Imports 2006	Imports 2007
	Millions of U.S. Dollars							*Millions of U.S. Dollars*						
Somalia........ 726	1	2	4	10	17	28	27	1	2	7	8	3	3	2
South Africa........ 199	1,051	1,312	2,030	2,952	3,826	5,769	7,429	1,173	1,269	1,841	2,960	3,444	4,095	6,608
Sudan........ 732	227	392	478	816	1,294	1,417	1,536	938	1,157	1,442	1,706	2,615	1,941	4,114
Swaziland........ 734	3	5	7	11	11	7	13	7	11	15	15	23	25	19
Tanzania........ 738	90	121	191	216	304	383	596	3	7	28	68	171	152	199
Togo........ 742	109	138	263	399	538	704	1,374	—	5	22	46	32	22	26
Tunisia........ 744	106	144	184	245	295	358	482	3	38	17	34	44	51	30
Uganda........ 746	17	28	51	76	79	138	202	1	6	4	12	20	18	20
Zambia........ 754	39	35	35	51	49	103	198	36	46	48	171	252	269	394
Zimbabwe........ 698	33	32	30	113	125	136	198	115	160	167	141	158	139	142
Africa n.s........ 799	2	58	2	2	2	2	6	—	143	—	—	1	1	—
Asia........ 507	**87,691**	**110,696**	**145,053**	**198,339**	**249,711**	**318,356**	**397,024**	**86,190**	**112,071**	**156,574**	**211,212**	**250,808**	**291,007**	**344,818**
Afghanistan, I.S. of........ 512	17	20	26	57	51	101	169	—	—	1	1	2	—	2
Bangladesh........ 513	958	1,068	1,335	1,906	2,404	3,084	3,345	17	32	33	57	79	99	114
Bhutan........ 514	2	1	2	—	—	—	5	—	—	—	—	—	—	—
Brunei Darussalam........ 516	17	21	34	48	53	100	113	148	242	312	251	208	215	242
Cambodia........ 522	206	252	295	452	536	698	881	35	25	26	30	27	35	51
China,P.R.:Hong Kong........ 532	46,503	58,483	76,289	100,878	124,505	155,435	184,289	9,424	10,788	11,119	11,800	12,232	10,795	12,824
China,P.R.:Macao........ 546	743	876	1,281	1,612	1,602	2,181	2,643	119	142	186	216	264	257	282
Fiji........ 819	26	31	26	33	43	68	64	—	1	5	6	2	1	3
French Polynesia........ 887	1	3	3	8	16	19	27	—	—	—	1	1	2	1
India........ 534	1,903	2,673	3,344	5,927	8,937	14,588	24,036	1,700	2,274	4,251	7,677	9,780	10,469	14,659
Indonesia........ 536	2,847	3,427	4,481	6,257	8,369	9,457	12,618	3,888	4,501	5,748	7,224	8,430	9,621	12,380
Kiribati........ 826	—	—	1	1	1	1	17	—	—	—	—	—	—	—
Korea........ 542	12,544	15,508	20,096	27,818	35,117	44,558	56,129	23,396	28,581	43,135	62,250	76,874	89,818	104,045
Lao People's Dem.Rep........ 544	54	54	98	101	105	169	177	7	10	11	13	26	50	85
Malaysia........ 548	3,223	4,975	6,141	8,087	10,618	13,540	17,702	6,206	9,295	13,987	18,174	20,108	23,577	28,737
Maldives........ 556	2	3	3	8	17	15	25	—	—	—	—	—	1	—
Mongolia........ 948	123	140	156	233	319	434	684	239	223	284	460	540	1,144	1,323
Myanmar........ 518	498	725	908	939	935	1,207	1,692	134	137	170	207	274	253	371
Nepal........ 558	149	105	122	163	188	260	386	5	5	5	8	8	8	15
New Caledonia........ 839	3	4	8	8	15	19	31	1	—	6	58	78	164	378
Pakistan........ 564	718	1,243	1,855	2,466	3,423	4,241	5,785	582	557	575	595	833	1,007	1,105
Palau........ 565	2	—	—	—	1	1	1	—	—	—	—	—	—	—
Papua New Guinea........ 853	19	27	61	53	66	126	213	122	160	231	244	309	392	468
Philippines........ 566	1,622	2,042	3,094	4,269	4,689	5,738	7,505	1,945	3,217	6,306	9,059	12,870	17,676	23,129
Samoa........ 862	2	3	3	6	6	13	12	—	—	—	1	—	—	—
Singapore........ 576	5,795	6,969	8,869	12,687	16,716	23,188	29,680	5,143	7,054	10,484	13,997	16,531	17,675	17,520
Solomon Islands........ 813	1	1	2	3	5	5	10	6	18	33	58	96	125	182
Sri Lanka........ 524	395	338	504	695	941	1,107	1,386	6	11	20	23	37	35	48
Taiwan Province of China........ 528	5,006	6,590	9,005	13,545	16,559	20,740	23,480	27,344	38,082	49,362	64,779	74,655	87,141	100,986
Thailand........ 578	2,504	2,959	3,828	5,802	7,819	9,763	11,979	4,713	5,599	8,827	11,542	13,994	17,962	22,652
Timor-Leste........ 537	—	—	1	2	1	2	—	—	—	—	—	—	—	—
Tonga........ 866	1	5	2	6	3	4	7	—	—	—	—	—	—	—
Tuvalu........ 869	—	—	—	2	6	11	7	—	—	—	—	—	—	—
Vanuatu........ 846	1	1	3	7	8	18	21	—	—	—	—	—	1	—
Vietnam........ 582	1,805	2,150	3,179	4,261	5,639	7,468	11,906	1,010	1,115	1,456	2,482	2,549	2,486	3,214
Wallis-Futuna........ 857	—	—	—	—	—	—	1	—	—	—	—	—	—	—
Asia n.s........ 598	1	1	—	—	—	—	—	—	—	—	—	—	—	—
Europe........ 170	**7,770**	**10,708**	**18,160**	**25,322**	**36,356**	**56,147**	**82,816**	**10,504**	**11,978**	**15,378**	**18,848**	**23,438**	**26,580**	**33,861**
Albania........ 914	16	19	32	63	84	66	89	—	—	—	6	7	13	67
Armenia........ 911	2	2	5	12	23	33	51	1	7	2	2	—	8	38
Azerbaijan........ 912	11	94	204	144	234	347	475	4	1	35	40	24	22	1
Belarus........ 913	9	16	32	65	81	216	227	35	64	97	154	490	429	613
Bosnia & Herzegovina........ 963	2	3	6	14	20	24	54	1	—	1	1	103	120	27
Bulgaria........ 918	89	98	166	338	442	1,783	813	28	21	59	67	90	82	157
Croatia........ 960	143	113	169	345	574	878	1,515	5	6	7	22	44	55	68
Czech Republic........ 935	524	808	1,282	1,351	1,668	2,364	4,143	92	155	297	442	372	517	831
Estonia........ 939	268	137	140	202	312	456	585	11	36	30	21	58	285	90
Faroe Islands........ 816	—	—	—	—	—	—	1	—	—	—	—	—	3	7
Georgia........ 915	4	8	20	23	41	78	176	3	4	8	34	3	7	16
Gibraltar........ 823	1	1	21	1	1	1	1	—	—	—	—	—	—	—
Hungary........ 944	1,031	1,449	2,286	2,652	2,495	3,288	5,016	130	169	301	476	366	699	1,209
Kazakhstan........ 916	328	601	1,566	2,212	3,899	4,752	7,447	961	1,355	1,721	2,286	2,902	3,607	6,419
Kyrgyz Republic........ 917	77	146	245	493	866	2,113	3,666	42	56	69	110	105	113	113
Latvia........ 941	47	68	111	179	282	439	685	5	5	19	20	9	14	22
Lithuania........ 946	59	98	170	274	361	555	802	4	12	17	14	11	16	20
Macedonia, FYR........ 962	10	17	24	26	22	28	75	—	1	15	1	10	3	10
Moldova........ 921	2	2	7	24	51	32	50	13	4	8	—	—	1	1
Montenegro, Rep. of........ 943	—	—	—	—	—	—	48	—	—	—	—	—	—	1
Poland........ 964	1,017	1,165	1,620	1,844	2,598	3,998	6,562	226	219	359	487	558	668	1,111
Romania........ 968	255	362	506	1,057	1,371	6,085	2,085	104	390	470	327	292	233	282
Russia........ 922	2,715	3,522	6,035	9,102	13,211	15,829	28,484	7,959	8,405	9,726	12,129	15,886	17,539	19,630
Serbia, Rep. of........ 942	—	—	—	—	—	—	36	—	—	—	—	—	—	6
Serbia & Montenegro........ 965	88	73	136	163	201	300	323	10	3	14	13	21	7	7
Slovak Republic........ 936	61	92	137	160	309	577	1,473	13	38	122	129	183	336	735
Tajikistan........ 923	5	7	21	54	144	306	514	5	6	18	15	14	18	10
Turkey........ 186	676	1,089	2,065	2,822	4,252	7,307	10,483	231	289	533	591	633	765	1,293

	Exports							Imports						
	2001	2002	2003	2004	2005	2006	2007	2001	2002	2003	2004	2005	2006	2007
	Millions of U.S. Dollars							Millions of U.S. Dollars						
Turkmenistan.......925	31	87	79	85	90	162	302	1	1	4	14	19	16	49
Ukraine.......926	248	528	929	1,444	2,492	3,723	5,867	610	706	1,246	1,044	785	437	666
Uzbekistan.......927	51	104	147	172	230	406	766	8	27	200	403	451	566	363
Europe n.s.......884	—	—	1	2	3	1	1	—	—	—	—	—	1	—
Middle East.......407	**8,028**	**10,485**	**14,382**	**18,593**	**24,488**	**33,280**	**49,352**	**9,307**	**9,570**	**14,642**	**22,244**	**32,294**	**42,733**	**49,634**
Bahrain.......419	52	58	83	121	187	285	385	78	52	52	92	69	65	102
Egypt.......469	875	853	937	1,389	1,935	2,976	4,432	80	92	153	188	211	217	237
Iran, I.R. of.......429	900	1,396	2,316	2,555	3,298	4,479	7,288	2,424	2,347	3,308	4,492	6,796	9,946	13,330
Iraq.......433	398	421	56	150	408	491	687	73	96	—	320	416	653	762
Israel.......436	833	901	1,141	1,541	1,955	2,573	3,658	483	516	690	943	1,074	1,316	1,650
Jordan.......439	227	305	464	623	832	978	1,104	48	53	61	88	79	53	82
Kuwait.......443	192	263	675	484	628	862	1,338	453	464	513	765	1,021	1,924	2,288
Lebanon.......446	236	276	365	484	472	500	705	3	4	5	10	4	9	19
Libya.......672	41	112	175	255	360	704	864	54	1	41	417	942	1,694	1,548
Oman.......449	67	60	82	111	191	339	548	1,610	1,447	1,986	4,278	4,142	6,130	6,719
Qatar.......453	32	50	62	104	203	437	622	379	175	293	334	473	562	588
Saudi Arabia.......456	1,356	1,673	2,147	2,776	3,825	5,054	7,815	2,723	3,436	5,195	7,524	12,286	15,086	17,546
Syrian Arab Republic.......463	223	357	481	693	888	1,357	1,869	—	14	26	28	18	51	8
United Arab Emirates.......466	2,381	3,452	5,037	6,842	8,733	11,411	17,036	448	445	773	1,304	2,045	2,796	3,007
Yemen, Republic of.......474	210	305	354	458	547	806	964	451	426	1,546	1,459	2,718	2,231	1,748
Middle East n.s.......489	5	4	7	10	24	28	38	—	—	—	—	—	—	—
Western Hemisphere.......207	**8,022**	**9,139**	**11,511**	**17,824**	**22,751**	**34,527**	**50,005**	**6,586**	**8,211**	**14,751**	**21,516**	**26,241**	**33,514**	**49,770**
Antigua and Barbuda.......311	1	3	3	119	147	161	395	—	—	—	—	—	—	—
Argentina.......213	574	185	447	852	1,325	2,003	3,566	1,281	1,240	2,729	3,255	3,800	3,696	6,313
Aruba.......314	4	3	2	4	6	10	10	—	—	—	—	—	—	—
Bahamas, The.......313	35	63	122	99	155	165	163	—	—	1	1	—	—	18
Barbados.......316	5	10	9	10	19	76	35	—	—	—	—	—	—	1
Belize.......339	6	9	10	23	32	29	26	—	—	1	—	—	—	—
Bermuda.......319	11	14	32	127	122	148	82	—	—	—	—	—	—	—
Bolivia.......218	8	10	12	24	50	58	97	10	12	7	30	31	47	57
Brazil.......223	1,363	1,466	2,145	3,675	4,829	7,380	11,377	2,347	3,003	5,844	8,684	9,982	12,907	18,342
Chile.......228	816	998	1,283	1,689	2,151	3,110	4,416	1,303	1,565	2,245	3,676	4,943	5,689	10,239
Colombia.......233	205	287	398	630	930	1,497	2,263	26	29	60	176	205	264	1,095
Costa Rica.......238	63	82	99	154	229	409	568	27	184	561	641	919	1,747	2,307
Dominica.......321	88	45	34	46	49	61	73	1	1	1	2	1	8	31
Dominican Republic.......243	38	106	148	233	264	402	513	—	2	4	16	29	94	100
Ecuador.......248	134	195	239	344	467	715	942	28	14	40	92	43	87	141
El Salvador.......253	100	133	158	197	176	315	352	—	2	2	4	10	4	5
Greenland.......326	—	—	1	—	2	—	1	10	12	22	21	29	30	38
Grenada.......328	—	—	—	1	3	4	3	—	—	—	—	—	—	—
Guatemala.......258	163	245	306	393	473	687	797	—	1	2	43	95	44	47
Guyana.......336	12	14	18	21	27	82	65	2	4	—	1	7	18	18
Haiti.......263	14	23	26	22	30	60	82	—	—	—	—	—	1	6
Honduras.......268	65	59	78	123	134	224	273	—	1	3	12	14	19	16
Jamaica.......343	85	66	102	126	104	180	246	34	49	105	270	221	359	38
Mexico.......273	1,819	2,864	3,267	4,973	5,537	8,824	11,707	763	1,115	1,677	2,140	2,227	2,606	3,260
Netherlands Antilles.......353	47	41	46	68	86	121	69	—	—	1	1	1	—	—
Nicaragua.......278	34	49	69	102	114	163	212	—	—	—	3	14	1	3
Panama.......283	1,240	1,274	1,480	2,187	3,151	3,868	5,581	2	4	29	15	22	14	8
Paraguay.......288	72	79	126	235	252	327	465	3	8	13	58	59	54	20
Peru.......293	177	247	354	418	609	1,012	1,678	498	732	760	1,524	2,265	2,875	4,297
St. Kitts and Nevis.......361	—	—	—	—	1	1	3	—	—	—	—	—	—	—
St. Lucia.......362	3	3	2	2	2	4	7	—	—	—	—	33	—	—
St. Vincent & Grens.......364	13	8	8	13	14	15	27	—	—	—	—	—	—	—
Suriname.......366	152	67	20	30	54	43	67	8	6	16	1	7	4	3
Trinidad and Tobago.......369	35	42	59	76	95	165	263	—	5	10	4	18	10	21
Uruguay.......298	189	95	128	210	255	407	615	96	78	76	110	158	270	342
Venezuela, Rep. Bol.......299	444	333	199	596	837	1,699	2,835	146	145	542	738	1,106	2,651	3,004
Western Hem. n.s.......399	4	21	82	5	17	103	133	—	1	1	—	1	13	—
Other Countries n.i.e.......910	**904**	**778**	**864**	**1,130**	**1,720**	**2,494**	**2,562**	**281**	**387**	**516**	**781**	**734**	**996**	**1,687**
Cuba.......928	333	310	236	331	635	1,262	1,169	114	116	121	195	237	528	1,105
North Korea.......954	571	467	628	800	1,085	1,232	1,392	167	271	395	586	497	468	582
Countries & Areas n.s.......898	**2**	**7**	—	—	—	—	—	—	**1**	**12**	**38**	**19**	**44**	**59**
Special Categories.......899	—	—	—	—	—	—	—	**8,769**	**14,984**	**25,094**	**38,665**	**55,178**	**73,366**	**85,696**
Memorandum Items														
European Union.......998	44,300	52,487	78,473	107,265	143,851	182,058	242,531	36,344	39,440	54,477	70,131	73,559	90,362	110,614
Oil Exporting Ctys.......999	9,800	12,584	17,662	22,828	30,563	39,741	58,160	12,495	13,275	18,571	28,119	38,547	51,482	62,833
Non-Oil Develop.Ctys.......201	106,770	134,450	180,455	249,333	319,050	425,456	552,879	104,613	133,985	190,943	260,742	314,195	369,208	449,692
PERCENT DISTRIBUTION														
Industrial Countries.......101	**55.9**	**54.6**	**54.6**	**53.9**	**53.9**	**51.7**	**49.6**	**48.2**	**45.0**	**43.0**	**41.5**	**38.1**	**37.5**	**37.3**
Developing Countries.......202	**43.7**	**45.1**	**45.2**	**45.9**	**45.9**	**48.0**	**50.2**	**48.1**	**49.8**	**50.7**	**51.5**	**53.4**	**53.1**	**53.6**
Africa.......607	**1.9**	**1.8**	**2.1**	**2.0**	**2.1**	**2.4**	**2.6**	**1.9**	**1.8**	**2.0**	**2.7**	**3.0**	**3.4**	**3.6**
Asia.......507	**32.9**	**34.0**	**33.1**	**33.4**	**32.8**	**32.8**	**32.6**	**35.4**	**37.9**	**37.9**	**37.6**	**38.0**	**36.8**	**36.1**
Europe.......170	**2.9**	**3.3**	**4.1**	**4.3**	**4.8**	**5.8**	**6.8**	**4.3**	**4.1**	**3.7**	**3.4**	**3.6**	**3.4**	**3.5**
Middle East.......407	**3.0**	**3.2**	**3.3**	**3.1**	**3.2**	**3.4**	**4.1**	**3.8**	**3.2**	**3.5**	**4.0**	**4.9**	**5.4**	**5.2**
Western Hemisphere.......207	**3.0**	**2.8**	**2.6**	**3.0**	**3.0**	**3.6**	**4.1**	**2.7**	**2.8**	**3.6**	**3.8**	**4.0**	**4.2**	**5.2**

	Exports 2001	2002	2003	2004	2005	2006	2007	Imports 2001	2002	2003	2004	2005	2006	2007
Other Countries n.i.e................910	.3	.2	.2	.2	.2	.3	.2	.1	.1	.1	.1	.1	.1	.2
ANNUAL PERCENT CHANGE														
World....................................... 001	7.0	22.1	34.6	35.4	28.5	27.1	25.7	8.2	21.3	39.7	36.0	17.6	19.9	20.8
Industrial Countries................. 101	6.1	19.2	34.5	33.7	28.4	22.0	20.5	11.0	13.1	33.8	31.2	7.9	18.0	20.1
Developing Countries.............. 202	8.0	26.1	34.7	37.4	28.5	33.1	31.4	4.5	25.7	42.3	37.9	22.1	19.3	21.8
Africa.....................................607	21.9	18.8	50.0	34.1	35.0	40.3	39.1	−16.5	20.1	50.4	84.2	32.7	34.5	28.2
Asia.. 507	5.8	26.2	31.0	36.7	25.9	27.5	24.7	4.2	30.0	39.7	34.9	18.7	16.0	18.5
Europe....................................170	11.3	37.8	69.6	39.4	43.6	54.4	47.5	23.5	14.0	28.4	22.6	24.4	13.4	27.4
Middle East............................ 407	14.3	30.6	37.2	29.3	31.7	35.9	48.3	−7.9	2.8	53.0	51.9	45.2	32.3	16.1
Western Hemisphere.............207	16.1	13.9	26.0	54.8	27.6	51.8	44.8	23.8	24.7	79.6	45.9	22.0	27.7	48.5
Other Countries n.i.e...............910	32.2	−14.0	11.1	30.8	52.2	45.0	2.7	128.8	37.6	33.5	51.3	−6.0	35.7	69.4

		Exports							Imports						
		2001	2002	2003	2004	2005	2006	2007	2001	2002	2003	2004	2005	2006	2007
		Millions of U.S. Dollars							*Millions of U.S. Dollars*						
IFS World Total		**189,894**	**200,092**	**223,762**	**259,260**	**289,337**	**316,816**	**344,509**	**201,076**	**207,644**	**231,896**	**271,074**	**299,533**	**334,681**	**367,647**
DOTS World Total	001	**190,081**	**200,320**	**224,040**	**259,423**	**289,509**	**316,819**	**344,738**	**201,474**	**208,024**	**232,580**	**271,458**	**299,967**	**334,691**	**368,223**
Industrial Countries	101	**87,920**	**87,259**	**91,045**	**100,847**	**110,949**	**114,930**	**116,974**	**61,626**	**59,252**	**65,933**	**75,905**	**78,067**	**82,391**	**89,487**
United States	111	42,413	42,878	41,780	43,964	46,505	47,874	47,316	13,486	11,822	12,784	14,500	15,444	16,047	17,953
Canada	156	2,933	3,018	2,927	3,137	3,354	3,492	3,401	1,184	1,055	1,076	1,204	1,223	1,425	1,487
Australia	193	2,246	2,410	2,732	3,195	3,455	3,704	4,446	1,625	1,614	1,613	1,736	1,747	2,116	2,093
Japan	158	11,250	10,745	12,088	13,813	15,258	15,495	15,343	22,705	23,477	27,561	32,957	33,028	34,549	36,893
New Zealand	196	276	284	355	415	467	468	522	357	293	283	319	289	344	381
Austria	122	438	358	446	583	578	597	707	340	564	478	505	588	599	613
Belgium	124	1,257	1,298	1,452	1,683	1,936	2,132	1,959	1,375	1,467	1,607	1,825	1,915	2,393	2,595
Cyprus	423	34	53	31	31	37	36	44	5	6	6	7	7	12	10
Denmark	128	599	590	680	808	1,106	920	862	397	424	474	566	578	694	607
Finland	172	365	363	528	908	1,243	1,258	1,214	389	459	444	395	381	399	380
France	132	2,981	2,631	2,834	3,415	4,077	4,294	4,563	3,096	1,959	2,097	2,305	2,532	2,661	2,962
Germany	134	6,624	6,270	7,225	8,082	9,358	9,751	10,408	4,278	4,237	5,291	5,143	5,285	5,709	6,165
Greece	174	202	184	233	262	285	269	300	45	44	32	47	41	33	28
Iceland	176	6	4	5	6	8	8	15	—	1	2	3	3	7	3
Ireland	178	369	324	360	419	395	406	396	615	464	816	984	858	876	1,121
Italy	136	2,053	2,081	2,479	3,005	3,409	3,879	4,213	2,836	2,696	2,805	3,344	3,417	3,684	4,120
Luxembourg	137	—	—	—	—	—	—	53	—	—	—	—	—	—	42
Malta	181	24	34	31	21	22	24	28	53	69	75	82	64	125	212
Netherlands	138	3,253	3,368	3,594	4,257	5,473	5,286	5,697	1,396	1,378	1,362	1,555	1,702	1,654	1,821
Norway	142	293	298	320	339	367	362	365	123	114	139	178	215	248	272
Portugal	182	125	116	121	151	183	181	249	66	64	52	64	103	95	61
Slovenia	961	20	24	31	39	44	51	63	8	7	10	13	22	31	31
Spain	184	1,423	1,386	1,685	1,883	2,249	2,400	2,398	429	422	417	471	502	551	654
Sweden	144	660	618	680	769	872	940	988	478	361	427	508	450	465	531
Switzerland	146	969	962	1,051	1,200	1,351	1,620	1,820	2,623	2,912	2,967	3,484	3,681	3,625	4,573
United Kingdom	112	7,106	6,960	7,377	8,460	8,914	9,481	9,604	3,717	3,344	3,115	3,709	3,991	4,047	3,880
Developing Countries	202	**101,833**	**112,885**	**132,789**	**158,397**	**178,406**	**201,736**	**227,655**	**139,796**	**148,715**	**166,593**	**195,487**	**221,824**	**252,235**	**278,662**
Africa	607	**1,298**	**1,163**	**1,345**	**1,580**	**1,444**	**1,706**	**1,901**	**660**	**656**	**825**	**983**	**1,057**	**1,067**	**1,016**
Algeria	612	11	10	13	8	13	22	26	—	—	—	—	—	2	1
Angola	614	17	19	22	19	29	32	43	—	—	1	—	88	150	50
Benin	638	18	15	8	6	13	41	44	—	—	—	—	—	—	2
Botswana	616	3	3	4	3	2	14	26	—	—	—	—	—	—	—
Burkina Faso	748	4	7	8	6	6	6	10	—	—	—	—	—	—	—
Burundi	618	1	1	1	—	—	—	—	—	—	—	—	—	—	—
Cameroon	622	18	25	25	30	34	38	45	5	6	11	17	5	13	8
Cape Verde	624	—	—	1	—	1	—	—	—	—	—	—	—	—	—
Central African Rep.	626	—	—	—	—	—	—	2	1	3	—	—	—	—	—
Chad	628	—	—	—	—	—	1	6	—	—	—	—	1	—	—
Comoros	632	—	1	—	—	—	—	2	—	—	—	—	—	—	—
Congo, Dem. Rep. of	636	11	15	28	31	23	21	16	—	—	1	1	—	—	—
Congo, Republic of	634	22	19	13	13	12	13	14	5	2	4	3	7	4	5
Côte d'Ivoire	662	17	8	5	4	4	9	12	1	1	—	—	—	2	—
Djibouti	611	1	1	1	2	6	3	2	1	1	2	1	1	1	2
Equatorial Guinea	642	—	1	1	3	2	2	2	—	—	—	—	—	—	—
Ethiopia	644	1	1	1	3	4	4	5	1	1	1	2	2	2	3
Gabon	646	8	6	5	4	5	5	8	26	10	9	1	1	2	3
Gambia, The	648	15	13	14	12	9	6	6	—	—	—	—	—	—	—
Ghana	652	22	21	26	24	17	19	27	1	1	1	1	2	2	4
Guinea	656	18	18	19	18	14	13	11	3	2	3	4	3	4	4
Guinea-Bissau	654	—	—	—	—	—	—	4	—	—	—	—	—	—	1
Kenya	664	34	39	47	67	65	68	83	44	32	40	49	38	43	41
Lesotho	666	22	51	76	87	69	69	58	—	—	—	—	—	—	—
Liberia	668	6	5	6	9	8	6	7	—	2	—	—	—	—	1
Madagascar	674	87	31	86	104	86	88	124	13	9	8	8	12	8	9
Malawi	676	3	1	3	2	1	2	1	—	—	—	—	—	—	—
Mali	678	16	15	10	13	12	12	13	—	—	—	1	—	2	—
Mauritania	682	5	3	2	2	3	2	1	1	1	1	2	2	1	2
Mauritius	684	102	100	87	64	42	45	50	11	6	11	9	6	10	12
Morocco	686	30	28	32	31	30	66	96	2	9	46	111	152	199	221
Mozambique	688	3	4	9	5	4	4	2	18	27	16	12	3	2	8
Namibia	728	1	2	4	8	5	11	3	—	3	5	1	11	4	2
Niger	692	2	2	2	1	2	2	1	—	—	—	1	—	—	—
Nigeria	694	180	151	149	122	87	124	195	5	7	6	19	25	53	49
Rwanda	714	—	—	1	—	1	1	—	14	10	4	4	5	1	13
Senegal	722	22	22	23	25	26	20	20	9	8	10	11	13	11	13
Seychelles	718	1	1	1	1	1	2	2	1	1	1	1	2	3	2
Sierra Leone	724	11	10	10	9	8	9	11	—	—	—	1	1	—	—
Somalia	726	—	—	—	—	—	—	—	—	—	—	1	1	—	—
South Africa	199	463	401	512	747	699	802	783	435	452	586	661	620	494	493

	Exports 2001	2002	2003	2004	2005	2006	2007	Imports 2001	2002	2003	2004	2005	2006	2007
	Millions of U.S. Dollars							*Millions of U.S. Dollars*						
Sudan........ 732	3	4	5	7	9	10	12	5	5	6	8	7	8	4
Swaziland........ 734	15	17	17	19	12	18	20	10	12	4	—	—	1	1
Tanzania........ 738	13	12	12	17	21	29	33	17	14	19	21	19	19	27
Togo........ 742	57	46	34	30	30	27	20	3	2	3	3	3	5	5
Tunisia........ 744	13	13	12	15	16	25	33	2	2	3	5	6	6	11
Uganda........ 746	7	6	4	4	6	9	11	19	12	14	12	12	12	14
Zambia........ 754	1	2	2	2	4	3	5	1	5	1	2	2	3	1
Zimbabwe........ 698	9	6	4	3	2	1	1	3	8	4	8	3	—	5
Africa n.s........ 799	3	6	1	1	—	2	2	1	—	—	—	1	—	—
Asia........ 507	**92,250**	**103,200**	**123,181**	**146,667**	**165,574**	**186,888**	**210,495**	**135,379**	**143,210**	**160,099**	**188,063**	**213,880**	**243,685**	**269,288**
Afghanistan, I.S. of........ 512	3	3	2	2	2	2	2	—	—	—	—	—	—	—
Bangladesh........ 513	435	442	457	508	572	703	645	85	90	85	88	106	113	110
Bhutan........ 514	—	—	—	—	—	—	—	—	—	—	—	19	63	67
Brunei Darussalam........ 516	51	58	54	56	32	29	30	1	—	2	3	1	1	1
Cambodia........ 522	256	339	374	452	498	556	612	12	9	7	8	9	8	19
China,P.R.: Mainland........ 924	70,095	78,744	95,477	114,180	130,283	148,853	167,786	87,522	92,032	101,260	118,051	135,084	153,651	170,575
China,P.R.:Macao........ 546	1,158	1,060	1,120	1,248	1,597	1,860	2,244	149	210	237	289	330	322	381
Fiji........ 819	20	18	23	19	9	11	8	13	7	7	8	5	6	9
Guam........ 829	—	33	57	57	41	39	40	—	1	2	1	2	2	4
India........ 534	1,202	1,444	1,906	2,097	2,805	2,958	4,467	2,296	2,499	3,182	3,778	4,593	4,743	6,132
Indonesia........ 536	843	865	1,001	1,108	1,265	1,430	1,816	1,491	1,495	1,562	1,753	1,929	1,927	2,076
Kiribati........ 826	—	—	—	—	—	—	1	—	—	—	—	—	—	—
Korea........ 542	3,329	3,905	4,570	5,661	6,205	6,672	6,790	9,130	9,771	11,238	12,927	13,272	15,424	15,338
Lao People's Dem.Rep........ 544	9	6	7	7	8	14	13	—	—	—	—	—	—	—
Malaysia........ 548	1,614	1,983	1,981	2,294	2,391	2,807	3,240	5,044	5,098	5,741	6,684	7,353	7,775	8,060
Maldives........ 556	4	2	2	2	2	4	5	2	1	2	1	1	1	1
Mongolia........ 948	14	16	21	27	13	10	9	—	1	2	7	1	1	3
Myanmar........ 518	64	64	44	44	36	40	49	28	25	29	40	48	54	80
Nepal........ 558	53	37	24	31	18	19	27	1	1	1	1	1	2	1
Pakistan........ 564	79	96	109	127	140	157	171	541	498	500	603	585	654	634
Palau........ 565	4	3	—	—	—	—	—	—	—	—	—	—	—	—
Papua New Guinea........ 853	9	9	7	7	7	5	10	6	6	7	8	9	8	16
Philippines........ 566	1,926	2,308	2,227	2,521	2,607	2,637	2,812	1,977	2,711	3,754	4,367	4,924	5,189	6,132
Samoa........ 862	1	1	1	1	1	1	2	—	9	1	—	—	—	—
Singapore........ 576	3,793	4,053	4,589	5,596	5,986	6,226	6,471	9,364	9,717	11,647	14,263	17,412	21,226	25,005
Solomon Islands........ 813	3	1	2	1	2	2	2	4	3	2	1	1	1	2
Sri Lanka........ 524	358	349	404	436	430	442	439	47	48	81	54	43	62	61
Taiwan Province of China........ 528	4,538	4,438	5,436	6,307	6,492	6,705	6,794	13,885	14,922	16,134	19,806	21,671	25,002	26,324
Thailand........ 578	1,852	2,155	2,304	2,652	2,843	3,190	3,696	3,516	3,797	4,270	4,871	5,984	6,824	7,510
Tonga........ 866	—	—	—	—	—	—	—	—	—	—	—	—	1	—
Vanuatu........ 846	1	1	2	2	2	2	2	1	1	1	1	1	1	1
Vietnam........ 582	539	769	979	1,223	1,286	1,510	2,310	262	259	347	450	498	623	745
Europe........ 170	**1,347**	**1,668**	**1,840**	**2,691**	**3,244**	**3,906**	**4,802**	**633**	**1,088**	**1,081**	**992**	**946**	**925**	**1,005**
Albania........ 914	—	—	—	1	1	1	2	—	—	—	—	—	—	—
Armenia........ 911	2	2	4	2	1	1	2	—	1	2	1	1	1	1
Azerbaijan........ 912	—	1	1	2	2	8	6	—	—	—	—	—	—	—
Belarus........ 913	2	1	4	4	4	6	12	18	50	22	14	7	5	6
Bosnia & Herzegovina........ 963	1	1	1	1	1	2	1	—	—	—	—	—	—	—
Bulgaria........ 918	15	19	44	46	37	48	57	4	8	4	6	4	11	17
Croatia........ 960	20	23	32	35	35	44	52	3	1	1	2	5	3	2
Czech Republic........ 935	121	133	182	274	345	603	582	86	109	128	139	177	172	184
Estonia........ 939	51	47	60	73	95	145	125	3	2	4	5	9	11	9
Georgia........ 915	2	5	4	2	3	5	14	1	1	2	—	—	1	2
Gibraltar........ 823	1	1	1	1	1	1	2	—	7	1	1	1	2	1
Hungary........ 944	348	587	433	776	995	984	1,153	23	367	186	101	87	70	117
Kazakhstan........ 916	13	8	4	10	8	11	20	3	1	1	—	1	3	2
Kyrgyz Republic........ 917	—	—	—	1	1	2	5	—	—	—	—	—	—	1
Latvia........ 941	12	11	19	28	31	43	55	4	—	3	—	2	2	4
Lithuania........ 946	9	12	15	26	30	32	39	2	7	2	3	6	7	13
Macedonia, FYR........ 962	1	1	2	3	2	7	4	—	—	—	—	—	—	—
Moldova........ 921	—	—	1	1	1	11	4	—	—	—	—	—	—	—
Poland........ 964	208	222	240	291	355	464	612	19	24	23	39	36	47	72
Romania........ 968	23	20	31	44	47	85	163	16	32	24	11	8	10	8
Russia........ 922	212	216	282	428	504	581	900	281	323	498	483	451	431	375
Serbia & Montenegro........ 965	5	6	8	13	12	14	17	3	1	1	—	—	—	—
Slovak Republic........ 936	20	19	24	45	44	63	133	1	4	9	11	13	12	10
Tajikistan........ 923	—	—	—	—	—	1	7	—	—	—	—	—	—	—
Turkey........ 186	227	286	390	515	598	605	625	162	132	133	155	126	127	165
Turkmenistan........ 925	—	—	—	1	1	1	—	—	—	—	—	—	—	—
Ukraine........ 926	49	45	54	62	83	134	203	2	17	37	17	9	9	15
Uzbekistan........ 927	2	1	3	6	3	4	5	—	—	1	2	1	—	1
Europe n.s........ 884	—	—	1	1	2	1	1	—	—	—	—	—	—	—
Middle East........ 407	**2,625**	**2,742**	**3,275**	**3,712**	**3,928**	**4,468**	**5,227**	**1,779**	**2,326**	**2,782**	**3,528**	**3,943**	**4,236**	**4,328**
Bahrain........ 419	53	47	41	41	37	43	57	13	10	14	27	46	22	6
Egypt........ 469	173	132	129	131	132	152	175	23	32	40	64	136	88	126
Iran, I.R. of........ 429	31	27	38	50	61	85	84	57	104	161	127	190	168	190
Iraq........ 433	1	2	—	2	2	3	5	—	—	—	—	—	—	—

	Exports 2001	Exports 2002	Exports 2003	Exports 2004	Exports 2005	Exports 2006	Exports 2007	Imports 2001	Imports 2002	Imports 2003	Imports 2004	Imports 2005	Imports 2006	Imports 2007
	Millions of U.S. Dollars							*Millions of U.S. Dollars*						
Israel........ 436	646	657	801	871	1,096	1,323	1,488	712	878	966	1,128	1,511	1,755	1,840
Jordan........ 439	70	120	158	202	199	227	216	4	9	2	5	3	5	5
Kuwait........ 443	50	51	50	52	53	56	58	48	73	84	413	224	208	71
Lebanon........ 446	67	57	44	46	40	57	44	7	8	7	8	6	4	5
Libya........ 672	2	2	2	1	2	2	3	—	—	—	—	—	—	—
Oman........ 449	23	20	20	17	16	23	31	26	30	28	36	30	53	77
Qatar........ 453	25	18	26	27	23	41	35	10	11	22	26	22	28	20
Saudi Arabia........ 456	330	268	266	296	301	367	408	184	222	261	373	436	483	471
Syrian Arab Republic........ 463	24	22	22	42	41	18	25	4	2	—	1	—	2	2
United Arab Emirates........ 466	1,124	1,314	1,672	1,926	1,921	2,066	2,591	682	940	1,193	1,304	1,325	1,406	1,502
Yemen, Republic of........ 474	5	4	4	6	3	6	8	9	6	6	16	14	14	13
Western Hemisphere........ 207	**4,312**	**4,113**	**3,148**	**3,747**	**4,217**	**4,768**	**5,229**	**1,344**	**1,436**	**1,805**	**1,921**	**1,999**	**2,321**	**3,025**
Argentina........ 213	269	29	91	174	246	258	351	175	176	181	221	224	223	263
Aruba........ 314	2	2	2	2	2	2	3	—	—	—	1	—	—	—
Bahamas, The........ 313	3	3	2	2	2	6	4	—	—	—	—	—	—	—
Barbados........ 316	2	3	3	2	2	2	3	—	—	—	1	—	—	—
Belize........ 339	1	2	1	1	1	1	1	—	—	—	—	—	—	—
Bolivia........ 218	3	2	2	3	3	5	8	—	1	3	3	3	3	3
Brazil........ 223	629	614	572	835	1,006	1,176	1,332	557	633	757	881	921	1,084	1,430
Chile........ 228	413	310	277	313	327	395	400	135	150	171	191	165	170	166
Colombia........ 233	92	93	85	92	105	140	188	12	15	15	17	14	16	21
Costa Rica........ 238	36	32	33	27	30	33	35	46	91	344	272	264	351	499
Dominican Republic........ 243	37	43	27	29	38	34	38	1	2	4	7	10	18	12
Ecuador........ 248	38	38	33	36	32	52	54	8	7	8	11	13	25	22
El Salvador........ 253	64	74	77	103	96	78	53	2	2	4	8	19	39	45
Greenland........ 326	—	—	—	—	—	—	1	—	—	—	—	—	—	—
Guatemala........ 258	57	73	91	116	105	79	73	2	2	3	3	5	4	6
Guyana........ 336	2	2	2	1	2	2	1	2	4	3	6	6	5	7
Haiti........ 263	4	4	7	11	3	2	3	—	1	—	1	—	1	1
Honduras........ 268	33	44	58	81	54	51	42	2	1	2	2	2	2	2
Jamaica........ 343	15	15	14	11	9	7	6	2	1	3	—	2	—	1
Mexico........ 273	1,159	1,655	921	939	1,176	1,456	1,601	290	225	178	168	211	259	299
Netherlands Antilles........ 353	49	46	—	—	—	—	—	1	—	—	—	—	—	—
Nicaragua........ 278	14	21	31	38	47	76	65	1	—	1	—	1	1	1
Panama........ 283	930	701	530	583	549	476	495	19	14	18	16	18	22	29
Paraguay........ 288	117	84	109	132	109	89	102	18	22	21	22	15	8	8
Peru........ 293	54	55	56	62	66	84	117	22	28	38	38	48	38	53
Suriname........ 366	2	3	2	2	2	2	5	1	1	2	2	4	3	3
Trinidad and Tobago........ 369	11	9	9	9	8	8	7	—	—	—	—	—	—	—
Uruguay........ 298	64	26	21	25	37	34	37	35	34	32	30	32	28	36
Venezuela, Rep. Bol........ 299	207	112	40	76	121	168	153	11	12	15	15	18	15	110
Western Hem. n.s........ 399	4	19	51	43	42	53	53	3	14	3	8	5	5	5
Other Countries n.i.e........ 910	**53**	**36**	**16**	**18**	**17**	**26**	**20**	**39**	**21**	**15**	**18**	**16**	**18**	**21**
Cuba........ 928	10	6	4	7	7	18	5	7	7	8	12	11	15	19
North Korea........ 954	43	30	12	11	10	8	16	33	14	7	6	5	3	2
Countries & Areas n.s........ 898	**10**	—	—	—	—	—	—	**1**	—	—	—	—	—	—
Special Categories........ 899	**25**	**30**	**23**	**23**	**18**	**17**	**23**	**5**	**5**	**5**	**6**	**10**	**6**	**8**
Memorandum Items														
European Union........ 998	28,303	27,687	30,761	36,289	42,079	44,239	46,447	19,661	18,476	19,862	21,823	22,767	24,351	26,240
Oil Exporting Ctys........ 999	2,828	2,839	3,277	3,686	3,865	4,389	5,405	2,513	2,895	3,332	4,066	4,200	4,343	4,566
Non-Oil Develop.Ctys........ 201	99,005	110,046	129,512	154,710	174,541	197,347	222,250	137,282	145,820	163,261	191,421	217,624	247,892	274,095
PERCENT DISTRIBUTION														
Industrial Countries........ 101	**46.3**	**43.6**	**40.6**	**38.9**	**38.3**	**36.3**	**33.9**	**30.6**	**28.5**	**28.3**	**28.0**	**26.0**	**24.6**	**24.3**
Developing Countries........ 202	**53.6**	**56.4**	**59.3**	**61.1**	**61.6**	**63.7**	**66.0**	**69.4**	**71.5**	**71.6**	**72.0**	**73.9**	**75.4**	**75.7**
Africa........ 607	**.7**	**.6**	**.6**	**.6**	**.5**	**.5**	**.6**	**.3**	**.3**	**.4**	**.4**	**.4**	**.3**	**.3**
Asia........ 507	**48.5**	**51.5**	**55.0**	**56.5**	**57.2**	**59.0**	**61.1**	**67.2**	**68.8**	**68.8**	**69.3**	**71.3**	**72.8**	**73.1**
Europe........ 170	**.7**	**.8**	**.8**	**1.0**	**1.1**	**1.2**	**1.4**	**.3**	**.5**	**.5**	**.4**	**.3**	**.3**	**.3**
Middle East........ 407	**1.4**	**1.4**	**1.5**	**1.4**	**1.4**	**1.4**	**1.5**	**.9**	**1.1**	**1.2**	**1.3**	**1.3**	**1.3**	**1.2**
Western Hemisphere........ 207	**2.3**	**2.1**	**1.4**	**1.4**	**1.5**	**1.5**	**1.5**	**.7**	**.7**	**.8**	**.7**	**.7**	**.7**	**.8**
ANNUAL PERCENT CHANGE														
World........ 001	**−6.0**	**5.4**	**11.8**	**15.8**	**11.6**	**9.4**	**8.8**	**−5.6**	**3.3**	**11.8**	**16.7**	**10.5**	**11.6**	**10.0**
Industrial Countries........ 101	**−9.1**	**−.8**	**4.3**	**10.8**	**10.0**	**3.6**	**1.8**	**−4.9**	**−3.9**	**11.3**	**15.1**	**2.8**	**5.5**	**8.6**
Developing Countries........ 202	**−3.1**	**10.9**	**17.6**	**19.3**	**12.6**	**13.1**	**12.8**	**−5.8**	**6.4**	**12.0**	**17.3**	**13.5**	**13.7**	**10.5**
Africa........ 607	**−13.1**	**−10.4**	**15.7**	**17.4**	**−8.6**	**18.2**	**11.4**	**−3.6**	**−.7**	**25.7**	**19.1**	**7.6**	**1.0**	**−4.8**
Asia........ 507	**−2.5**	**11.9**	**19.4**	**19.1**	**12.9**	**12.9**	**12.6**	**−6.0**	**5.8**	**11.8**	**17.5**	**13.7**	**13.9**	**10.5**
Europe........ 170	**−3.4**	**23.8**	**10.4**	**46.2**	**20.6**	**20.4**	**22.9**	**−10.4**	**71.7**	**−.6**	**−8.3**	**−4.7**	**−2.1**	**8.6**
Middle East........ 407	**−7.8**	**4.5**	**19.4**	**13.4**	**5.8**	**13.8**	**17.0**	**−.8**	**30.7**	**19.6**	**26.8**	**11.8**	**7.4**	**2.2**
Western Hemisphere........ 207	**−10.6**	**−4.6**	**−23.4**	**19.0**	**12.5**	**13.1**	**9.7**	**5.0**	**6.8**	**25.7**	**6.4**	**4.0**	**16.1**	**30.3**
Other Countries n.i.e........ 910	**−34.3**	**−32.1**	**−54.4**	**9.3**	**−6.2**	**55.3**	**−22.3**	**−20.6**	**−46.6**	**−29.2**	**20.1**	**−8.8**	**9.0**	**20.4**

Exports

Millions of U.S. Dollars

		2001	2002	2003	2004	2005	2006	2007
IFS World Total		**2,299.5**	**2,355.8**	**2,580.8**	**2,811.8**	**2,475.9**	**2,557.3**	**2,542.7**
DOTS World Total	**001**	**2,297.9**	**2,359.0**	**2,533.2**	**2,811.8**	**2,475.9**	**2,557.3**	**2,542.6**
Industrial Countries	**101**	**1,788.3**	**1,757.2**	**1,901.6**	**2,050.1**	**1,680.2**	**1,669.5**	**1,554.6**
United States	111	1,106.98	1,145.34	1,252.06	1,369.60	1,204.98	1,127.66	1,031.93
Canada	156	43.53	42.83	40.92	41.50	22.07	17.80	19.38
Australia	193	4.03	2.37	2.78	3.45	4.75	4.59	7.05
Japan	158	14.56	14.39	17.96	22.99	21.31	19.86	28.96
New Zealand	196	.76	.57	1.29	.69	1.02	1.05	3.16
Austria	122	5.01	4.87	3.96	3.63	3.04	4.55	3.81
Belgium	124	8.19	6.20	7.46	4.69	4.49	2.82	6.59
Cyprus	423	.06	.04	.03	.17	.46	.17	.11
Denmark	128	20.91	20.82	20.68	21.66	16.57	17.77	15.85
Finland	172	3.06	2.78	2.57	2.98	1.73	2.28	2.98
France	132	97.80	78.22	85.70	86.98	66.68	84.69	77.03
Germany	134	176.52	175.27	206.14	232.58	146.62	186.82	161.54
Greece	174	1.73	1.05	1.66	3.03	.64	.83	1.08
Iceland	176	.20	.05	.03	—	.01	—	—
Ireland	178	7.06	6.10	6.25	8.21	4.84	6.93	5.00
Italy	136	23.39	18.33	30.31	39.24	26.54	28.32	29.86
Luxembourg	137	—	—	.03	.01	.08	.07	.04
Malta	181	.01	.01	.03	.01	.05	.09	.01
Netherlands	138	74.25	65.12	53.77	48.95	33.39	32.34	27.21
Norway	142	3.17	3.27	2.54	2.01	.86	.88	1.10
Portugal	182	5.20	3.14	4.31	2.70	2.02	.90	.34
Slovenia	961	.03	.16	.08	.46	.26	.10	.15
Spain	184	21.83	19.06	29.17	13.61	9.29	11.91	15.19
Sweden	144	18.17	17.69	15.66	14.79	13.51	10.97	11.40
Switzerland	146	4.96	2.35	3.03	2.54	2.29	1.42	2.67
United Kingdom	112	146.83	127.20	113.18	123.60	92.67	104.64	102.17
Developing Countries	**202**	**495.8**	**573.8**	**598.8**	**692.4**	**694.9**	**752.1**	**837.4**
Africa	**607**	**1.7**	**.3**	**.3**	**1.5**	**.6**	**.6**	**3.3**
Algeria	612	—	—	—	—	—	—	—
Angola	614	—	—	—	.58	—	—	—
Cameroon	622	—	—	—	—	—	—	—
Congo, Republic of	634	—	—	—	—	—	—	—
Djibouti	611	—	—	—	—	—	—	—
Ethiopia	644	—	—	—	—	—	—	—
Gabon	646	.03	—	—	—	—	—	—
Guinea	656	—	—	—	—	—	—	—
Kenya	664	—	—	—	—	—	—	—
Madagascar	674	—	—	—	—	—	—	—
Malawi	676	—	—	—	—	—	—	—
Mauritius	684	1.02	.08	.01	.05	.29	.03	.26
Morocco	686	—	.01	—	.05	.02	.03	.06
Mozambique	688	—	—	—	—	—	—	—
Namibia	728	—	—	—	—	—	—	—
Niger	692	—	—	—	—	—	—	—
Nigeria	694	—	.03	—	.02	—	.12	.01
Senegal	722	.08	—	—	—	—	—	—
Sierra Leone	724	—	—	—	—	—	—	.03
South Africa	199	.53	.17	.31	.82	.33	.43	2.95
Sudan	732	—	—	—	—	—	—	—
Tanzania	738	—	—	—	—	—	—	—
Tunisia	744	—	—	—	—	—	—	—
Uganda	746	—	—	—	.01	—	—	—
Zimbabwe	698	—	—	—	.01	—	—	—
Asia	**507**	**473.0**	**555.5**	**584.3**	**673.4**	**679.3**	**723.0**	**802.4**
Afghanistan, I.S. of	512	—	—	—	—	—	—	—
Bangladesh	513	.44	.80	.70	.88	.75	.74	1.45
Brunei Darussalam	516	—	.02	.07	—	—	—	—
Cambodia	522	1.31	1.37	2.11	2.63	1.42	1.40	14.00
China,P.R.: Mainland	924	268.47	365.87	357.33	391.38	367.79	377.41	377.42
China,P.R.:Hong Kong	532	147.16	136.86	168.77	212.33	242.65	288.55	332.91
Fiji	819	—	—	—	.03	.01	.09	.02
Guam	829	.03	.01	.03	.02	.03	.04	.04
India	534	.24	.04	—	.07	.14	.02	.67
Indonesia	536	.41	.08	.43	.12	.07	.37	1.28
Korea	542	2.32	3.56	2.43	4.42	3.66	3.11	3.08
Lao People's Dem.Rep	544	.05	—	—	—	—	—	—
Malaysia	548	3.82	4.31	5.21	6.82	6.67	2.98	4.87
Maldives	556	—	—	—	—	—	.01	.01
Myanmar	518	.38	.11	.01	—	—	.01	.02

Imports

Millions of U.S. Dollars

		2001	2002	2003	2004	2005	2006	2007
IFS World Total		**2,386.3**	**2,529.8**	**2,755.2**	**3,477.9**	**3,913.4**	**4,564.8**	**5,365.6**
DOTS World Total	**001**	**2,386.7**	**2,529.7**	**2,746.7**	**3,477.9**	**3,913.4**	**4,558.6**	**5,365.0**
Industrial Countries	**101**	**572.7**	**620.9**	**736.0**	**984.0**	**1,186.1**	**1,390.2**	**1,839.1**
United States	111	99.08	104.87	107.44	140.92	159.34	249.39	302.26
Canada	156	3.72	2.63	4.92	5.02	6.37	12.30	11.30
Australia	193	28.20	30.87	37.98	48.60	44.21	73.19	78.22
Japan	158	129.63	170.53	240.00	334.60	426.04	381.02	482.28
New Zealand	196	5.66	4.98	5.61	5.49	5.33	6.80	5.73
Austria	122	.72	1.60	1.39	4.99	8.61	6.22	21.69
Belgium	124	3.90	2.66	3.06	4.45	4.73	3.62	7.08
Cyprus	423	.13	.11	.10	.14	.13	.13	.09
Denmark	128	4.03	3.96	15.79	8.83	12.41	7.57	12.54
Finland	172	7.43	19.81	20.67	23.02	40.54	36.57	51.02
France	132	100.29	108.22	92.24	110.80	129.45	184.02	223.87
Germany	134	55.83	46.85	71.91	127.81	146.71	146.68	238.12
Greece	174	.25	.28	.51	.50	.81	1.28	.54
Iceland	176	—	—	—	.05	—	—	.01
Ireland	178	1.86	3.57	2.14	2.07	3.80	7.94	11.67
Italy	136	24.98	28.87	35.19	44.50	48.46	59.45	84.94
Luxembourg	137	—	—	—	.03	.01	.01	.09
Malta	181	—	—	.01	—	—	—	—
Netherlands	138	10.27	11.74	11.98	15.95	16.20	14.44	19.00
Norway	142	.78	1.07	1.12	1.39	2.31	2.21	2.21
Portugal	182	12.28	11.86	11.26	14.40	13.11	16.52	18.82
Slovenia	961	.21	.43	.62	.97	.61	.50	2.85
Spain	184	4.07	4.43	3.32	8.37	7.24	9.66	15.29
Sweden	144	9.17	6.28	7.35	10.13	11.64	17.28	29.27
Switzerland	146	6.42	6.78	9.91	14.92	30.44	74.50	123.38
United Kingdom	112	63.77	48.52	51.51	56.10	67.65	78.85	96.80
Developing Countries	**202**	**1,812.6**	**1,908.0**	**2,009.2**	**2,492.0**	**2,724.2**	**3,164.4**	**3,520.3**
Africa	**607**	**5.9**	**8.9**	**7.8**	**10.8**	**18.5**	**15.3**	**18.4**
Algeria	612	—	—	—	—	—	.12	—
Angola	614	—	—	—	—	—	—	—
Cameroon	622	.02	.01	.01	.01	.01	—	—
Congo, Republic of	634	.01	—	—	—	—	—	—
Djibouti	611	.02	.01	—	—	—	—	—
Ethiopia	644	—	.01	—	—	.06	.07	.11
Gabon	646	—	—	—	—	—	—	—
Guinea	656	.01	—	—	—	—	—	—
Kenya	664	.03	.10	.04	.24	.34	.35	.29
Madagascar	674	—	—	—	.01	.01	.04	.03
Malawi	676	—	—	—	.02	—	—	—
Mauritius	684	.02	—	.02	1.30	.01	.02	.03
Morocco	686	.02	.07	.09	.10	.08	.13	.18
Mozambique	688	—	—	—	—	—	—	.31
Namibia	728	—	—	—	—	—	—	.03
Niger	692	—	—	—	—	.01	.10	.01
Nigeria	694	—	—	—	—	—	—	—
Senegal	722	—	—	—	—	.03	.03	.01
Sierra Leone	724	—	—	—	—	—	—	—
South Africa	199	5.62	8.54	7.54	8.73	17.50	13.82	16.73
Sudan	732	—	—	—	—	.01	—	—
Tanzania	738	.02	.02	.01	.01	.01	—	—
Tunisia	744	.03	.07	.13	.38	.32	.58	.66
Uganda	746	.01	—	—	—	—	.01	—
Zimbabwe	698	.04	.04	—	—	.10	—	.06
Asia	**507**	**1,783.7**	**1,872.2**	**1,962.4**	**2,431.8**	**2,661.2**	**3,100.0**	**3,436.3**
Afghanistan, I.S. of	512	—	—	—	.08	—	—	—
Bangladesh	513	.03	.05	.01	.13	.06	.11	.16
Brunei Darussalam	516	—	—	.01	.02	.15	—	—
Cambodia	522	.01	.10	.05	.12	.20	.03	.04
China,P.R.: Mainland	924	1,018.24	1,055.15	1,180.52	1,544.67	1,687.84	2,062.50	2,287.66
China,P.R.:Hong Kong	532	331.42	367.99	350.32	367.71	390.39	465.23	542.00
Fiji	819	—	—	—	—	—	—	.03
Guam	829	—	—	—	—	—	—	—
India	534	2.85	1.73	1.61	3.77	7.44	5.83	4.76
Indonesia	536	10.75	13.79	12.47	14.51	17.24	19.10	25.29
Korea	542	141.70	125.60	94.21	101.92	83.21	89.49	82.04
Lao People's Dem.Rep	544	—	—	—	—	—	.01	—
Malaysia	548	22.69	27.14	30.74	30.34	41.09	51.33	64.22
Maldives	556	—	—	—	—	—	—	—
Myanmar	518	.15	.20	.10	.07	.03	.14	.20

	Exports 2001	2002	2003	2004	2005	2006	2007	Imports 2001	2002	2003	2004	2005	2006	2007
	Millions of U.S. Dollars							Millions of U.S. Dollars						
Nepal........ 558	—	—	—	—	—	—	—	.01	—	—	—	—	.02	—
Pakistan........ 564	.01	.14	.14	.11	—	.01	.04	2.36	1.29	1.54	1.38	1.13	.74	.85
Papua New Guinea........ 853	—	—	.01	—	—	—	—	—	—	—	.01	—	—	—
Philippines........ 566	5.14	3.79	9.29	12.07	16.20	11.13	12.24	4.54	3.26	5.09	7.46	8.41	7.94	6.75
Samoa........ 862	—	—	.02	—	—	—	—	—	—	—	—	—	—	—
Singapore........ 576	13.05	8.69	9.20	3.43	2.60	2.82	4.31	63.22	74.53	97.83	144.02	202.40	186.19	167.66
Sri Lanka........ 524	.15	.25	.05	.04	.07	.11	.09	.65	.54	1.06	.90	.65	1.88	.83
Taiwan Province of China........ 528	18.34	16.12	17.29	25.22	22.76	16.91	31.73	159.06	168.97	155.44	168.81	157.41	146.66	186.60
Thailand........ 578	2.47	2.49	1.37	4.75	6.98	1.75	1.49	25.31	30.37	29.52	40.08	55.62	54.05	55.99
Vietnam........ 582	9.19	11.01	9.81	9.04	7.51	15.49	16.69	.75	1.51	1.87	5.78	7.89	8.78	11.20
Europe........ 170	**1.7**	**1.6**	**2.4**	**4.7**	**1.9**	**4.8**	**5.4**	**3.6**	**10.5**	**15.6**	**13.6**	**15.8**	**10.3**	**13.3**
Albania........ 914	—	—	—	—	—	—	—	—	—	—	—	.01	.02	—
Armenia........ 911	....	....	....	....	....	....	....	.01	.05	.05	—	—	.10	—
Belarus........ 913	....	....	....	....	....	....	....	—	—	—	.01	—	.08	—
Bosnia & Herzegovina........ 963	.01	—	—	.03	—	—	—	.02	.03	.03	.04	.09	.09	.05
Bulgaria........ 918	—	—	.01	—	.01	—	—	.03	.06	.07	.23	.15	.30	.22
Croatia........ 960	.02	.02	.02	.06	.02	.01	.04	.03	.10	.12	.21	.29	.20	.12
Czech Republic........ 935	.10	.04	.12	.72	.05	1.01	.74	.12	5.52	.06	.18	.41	.29	.64
Estonia........ 939	.03	.03	.01	.10	.08	.05	.04	—	—	—	—	—	.01	2.57
Hungary........ 944	.52	.13	.10	.40	.21	.04	.10	.11	.23	.10	.23	.59	.37	1.94
Latvia........ 941	.01	—	—	.10	.12	.07	.08	—	.01	.03	.03	—	.02	.06
Lithuania........ 946	—	—	—	—	—	.03	—	—	—	—	.05	.05	.01	.02
Macedonia, FYR........ 962	—	.02	—	—	—	—	—	—	—	—	—	—	—	—
Moldova........ 921	—	—	—	—	—	—	—	—	—	—	.02	.02	.01	.04
Poland........ 964	.19	.14	.50	.97	.44	1.17	1.78	.13	.36	.58	.54	.62	.50	.51
Romania........ 968	.01	—	—	—	—	.08	—	.19	.42	.53	.78	.87	1.64	1.29
Russia........ 922	.09	.13	.01	.25	.63	.21	.17	.05	.02	6.26	3.10	6.37	.82	.04
Serbia, Rep. of........ 942	—	—	—	—	—	—	—	—	—	—	—	—	.01	.06
Serbia & Montenegro........ 965	.02	—	—	.05	.04	—	—	—	—	—	—	.02	—	—
Slovak Republic........ 936	.02	.02	.01	.11	.01	.71	.31	—	.03	.05	.04	.18	.54	.56
Turkey........ 186	.53	.82	1.56	1.93	.31	1.26	2.09	2.79	3.56	4.64	3.92	4.03	4.68	4.53
Ukraine........ 926	.13	.21	.01	.01	—	.12	.02	.09	.12	3.06	4.17	2.05	.61	.62
Middle East........ 407	**6.4**	**5.0**	**2.6**	**2.5**	**1.8**	**1.4**	**2.6**	**14.2**	**10.3**	**14.1**	**16.1**	**15.0**	**24.5**	**29.3**
Bahrain........ 419	.01	—	—	.01	—	—	—	.01	—	—	—	—	—	—
Egypt........ 469	.08	.01	.01	.01	—	—	.01	.02	.15	.03	—	.12	.24	.15
Iran, I.R. of........ 429	—	.01	.02	—	—	—	—	—	.02	.04	.23	.03	.07	.04
Israel........ 436	1.63	1.93	1.10	.38	.36	.09	.15	3.85	.79	3.75	3.68	1.48	4.07	1.37
Jordan........ 439	4.28	2.19	.97	.19	.44	—	.03	—	—	—	—	—	—	.02
Kuwait........ 443	.02	.02	.03	.04	.03	.01	—	—	—	.01	.03	—	.06	—
Lebanon........ 446	—	.02	.06	.08	.05	.05	.07	—	—	—	—	—	—	—
Oman........ 449	—	—	—	—	—	—	—	—	—	—	.01	—	.01	.01
Qatar........ 453	.07	.08	.07	.12	.38	—	—	—	—	—	—	.02	—	—
Saudi Arabia........ 456	.08	.12	.06	.28	.26	.44	.38	10.12	9.16	10.03	12.11	13.25	19.91	27.59
United Arab Emirates........ 466	.24	.55	.24	1.36	.30	.78	1.97	.17	.15	.21	.02	.09	.11	.08
Yemen, Republic of........ 474	—	.03	.05	—	—	—	—	—	—	.01	—	—	—	—
Western Hemisphere........ 207	**13.1**	**11.5**	**9.3**	**10.3**	**11.2**	**22.4**	**23.7**	**5.3**	**6.1**	**9.3**	**19.7**	**13.8**	**14.3**	**23.0**
Argentina........ 213	2.94	.35	.16	.03	.09	.20	.33	.24	.55	1.02	.64	.72	.69	1.04
Belize........ 339	—	—	—	—	—	—	—	—	—	—	.02	—	—	—
Bermuda........ 319	.20	.11	.11	.04	.03	—	—	—	—	—	.01	—	—	—
Bolivia........ 218	—	—	—	—	—	—	.01	—	—	—	—	.01	.01	.01
Brazil........ 223	.13	.04	.10	.07	.32	2.83	.86	2.89	3.72	4.50	11.54	6.87	7.69	12.80
Chile........ 228	.43	.45	.25	.23	.14	1.50	.41	.22	.22	.38	.68	.78	.72	1.44
Colombia........ 233	.18	.01	.03	—	—	.07	.17	.07	.09	.12	.13	.32	.29	.64
Costa Rica........ 238	.03	—	—	.01	—	—	.06	.02	.04	.14	.06	.01	.01	.03
Dominica........ 321	—	—	—	—	—	—	—	.02	.04	.37	.11	.10	.03	.05
Dominican Republic........ 243	—	—	—	—	—	.03	—	.37	.44	.69	.86	1.12	1.60	2.39
Ecuador........ 248	.18	.01	.02	.04	.01	.01	—	—	—	—	.01	.01	.01	.03
Greenland........ 326	—	.05	.01	—	—	—	—	—	—	—	.01	—	—	.01
Guatemala........ 258	—	—	.03	—	—	—	—	—	.01	.03	.01	—	.01	.01
Guyana........ 336	—	—	—	—	—	—	—	—	.01	—	—	—	—	—
Honduras........ 268	.83	.61	.10	—	—	—	—	.01	.04	.06	.05	.13	.04	.06
Jamaica........ 343	—	—	.01	—	—	—	.01	.01	.02	.03	.02	.02	.02	.02
Mexico........ 273	6.80	8.62	7.27	9.10	9.44	14.58	17.53	.98	.57	1.26	2.93	2.72	2.49	3.38
Netherlands Antilles........ 353	.03	—	—	—	—	—	—	—	—	—	—	—	—	—
Nicaragua........ 278	—	—	.09	.06	—	—	—	—	—	.04	.02	.07	.10	.10
Panama........ 283	1.26	.95	.94	.63	.84	1.53	4.18	—	—	—	—	—	.02	.04
Paraguay........ 288	—	—	—	—	—	—	—	.04	.01	.03	.05	.01	—	—
Peru........ 293	.05	.11	.15	.03	.32	.04	.08	.05	.06	.31	.14	.04	.06	.59
St. Pierre-Miquelon........ 363	....	....	....	....	....	....	....	—	—	—	.01	—	—	—
St. Vincent & Grens........ 364	....	....	....	....	....	....	....	—	—	.02	—	—	—	—
Trinidad and Tobago........ 369	—	—	—	—	—	—	—	—	—	—	.06	.01	.02	—
Uruguay........ 298	.02	.04	.03	—	—	.05	.02	.35	.26	.29	2.36	.80	.51	.35
Venezuela, Rep. Bol........ 299	.02	.11	—	.02	.02	1.56	.01	—	—	—	—	—	—	.01
Western Hem. n.s........ 399	—	—	—	.02	—	—	—	—	—	—	.01	—	—	—
Other Countries n.i.e........ 910	**—**	**.3**	**—**	**.2**	**—**	**—**	**—**	**1.4**	**.8**	**1.4**	**1.9**	**3.1**	**4.0**	**5.7**
Cuba........ 928	....	....	....	....	....	....	....	.75	.78	1.42	1.85	2.96	4.04	5.65
North Korea........ 954	.02	.25	.03	.20	.03	—	—	.64	.01	—	.01	.11	—	—

	Exports 2001	2002	2003	2004	2005	2006	2007	Imports 2001	2002	2003	2004	2005	2006	2007
	Millions of U.S. Dollars							Millions of U.S. Dollars						
Countries & Areas n.s.............898	13.4	27.7	32.8	69.1	100.8	135.8	150.6	—	—	—	—	—	—	—
Memorandum Items														
European Union............998	610.93	546.42	581.73	609.70	423.80	499.28	463.42	299.56	305.35	329.87	434.13	513.97	592.51	839.98
Oil Exporting Ctys............999	.84	.99	.84	1.97	1.07	3.27	3.64	21.05	23.13	22.77	26.90	30.64	39.37	53.03
Non-Oil Develop.Ctys............201	495.00	572.80	597.99	690.42	693.84	748.83	833.71	1,791.58	1,884.83	1,986.44	2,465.05	2,693.54	3,125.03	3,467.24
PERCENT DISTRIBUTION														
Industrial Countries............101	77.8	74.5	75.1	72.9	67.9	65.3	61.1	24.0	24.5	26.8	28.3	30.3	30.5	34.3
Developing Countries............202	21.6	24.3	23.6	24.6	28.1	29.4	32.9	75.9	75.4	73.2	71.7	69.6	69.4	65.6
Africa............607	.1	—	—	.1	—	—	.1	.2	.4	.3	.3	.5	.3	.3
Asia............507	20.6	23.5	23.1	23.9	27.4	28.3	31.6	74.7	74.0	71.4	69.9	68.0	68.0	64.1
Europe............170	.1	.1	.1	.2	.1	.2	.2	.2	.4	.6	.4	.4	.2	.2
Middle East............407	.3	.2	.1	.1	.1	.1	.1	.6	.4	.5	.5	.4	.5	.5
Western Hemisphere............207	.6	.5	.4	.4	.5	.9	.9	.2	.2	.3	.6	.4	.3	.4
Other Countries n.i.e.............910	—	—	—	—	—	—	—	.1	—	.1	.1	.1	.1	.1
ANNUAL PERCENT CHANGE														
World............001	-9.5	2.7	7.4	11.0	-11.9	3.3	-.6	5.8	6.0	8.6	26.6	12.5	16.5	17.7
Industrial Countries............101	-11.3	-1.7	8.2	7.8	-18.0	-.6	-6.9	9.3	8.4	18.5	33.7	20.5	17.2	32.3
Developing Countries............202	-1.8	15.7	4.4	15.6	.4	8.2	11.3	5.1	5.3	5.3	24.0	9.3	16.2	11.2
Africa............607	71.2	-82.6	9.3	387.8	-58.6	-5.5	450.5	15.9	51.4	-11.5	37.8	70.9	-17.4	20.8
Asia............507	-2.8	17.4	5.2	15.2	.9	6.4	11.0	4.9	5.0	4.8	23.9	9.4	16.5	10.8
Europe............170	-25.6	-6.4	51.2	100.3	-59.4	148.6	13.0	47.0	192.9	48.3	-12.9	16.1	-34.5	28.5
Middle East............407	78.7	-22.8	-47.6	-4.8	-26.3	-24.8	90.6	16.3	-27.5	37.1	14.2	-6.8	63.2	19.6
Western Hemisphere............207	12.6	-12.5	-19.0	10.7	9.1	99.7	5.7	-3.0	15.4	52.9	112.0	-30.2	4.1	60.4
Other Countries n.i.e.............910	25.5	—	-88.1	551.1	-83.7	-35.6	....	-76.4	-43.2	79.8	30.8	65.1	31.8	39.8

	Exports 2001	Exports 2002	Exports 2003	Exports 2004	Exports 2005	Exports 2006	Exports 2007	Imports 2001	Imports 2002	Imports 2003	Imports 2004	Imports 2005	Imports 2006	Imports 2007
	Millions of U.S. Dollars							*Millions of U.S. Dollars*						
IFS World Total	**12,290**	**11,911**	**13,080**	**16,223**	**21,146**	**24,388**	**29,786**	**12,834**	**12,711**	**13,888**	**16,746**	**21,204**	**26,046**	**33,164**
DOTS World Total 001	**12,307**	**12,099**	**13,128**	**16,788**	**21,190**	**24,391**	**29,991**	**12,820**	**12,695**	**14,155**	**17,033**	**21,202**	**26,162**	**32,897**
Industrial Countries 101	**7,465**	**7,541**	**8,577**	**10,021**	**12,463**	**14,621**	**16,713**	**7,778**	**6,935**	**8,053**	**8,987**	**10,206**	**12,105**	**14,878**
United States 111	5,345	5,343	6,142	7,056	8,852	9,948	10,609	4,443	4,032	4,261	5,113	6,033	6,961	8,631
Canada 156	143	164	177	156	298	275	266	344	274	357	386	389	501	649
Australia 193	14	14	13	22	17	16	17	20	21	48	30	22	24	27
Japan 158	165	194	202	263	330	324	395	559	614	645	649	705	945	1,231
New Zealand 196	2	2	3	3	4	4	5	12	9	3	11	3	5	7
Austria 122	3	3	3	3	4	5	4	29	34	43	47	59	105	108
Belgium 124	210	241	228	290	368	369	389	75	81	89	94	94	124	132
Cyprus 423	1	1	—	—	—	65	206	—	—	—	—	—	—	—
Denmark 128	18	37	76	60	57	79	143	33	31	29	21	30	46	45
Finland 172	65	50	57	65	24	37	64	57	51	117	96	274	220	161
France 132	140	144	156	213	184	378	484	350	236	395	306	386	430	541
Germany 134	417	332	265	265	339	360	553	560	511	624	677	774	933	1,205
Greece 174	7	3	3	5	5	8	11	2	1	2	1	6	1	4
Iceland 176	—	—	—	—	2	1	1	—	—	—	—	—	1	2
Ireland 178	26	20	15	43	59	56	26	41	39	45	51	58	55	64
Italy 136	196	225	287	364	439	479	556	401	275	293	321	332	395	520
Luxembourg 137	—	—	—	—	—	—	—	1	1	1	2	3	2	3
Malta 181	—	—	—	—	—	1	1	—	—	—	—	1	—	—
Netherlands 138	114	129	302	386	440	513	836	85	79	132	127	168	291	301
Norway 142	9	10	11	16	19	19	28	34	12	13	17	18	20	24
Portugal 182	71	57	88	113	148	158	185	6	8	262	266	340	36	13
Slovenia 961	9	8	10	26	22	3	7	5	5	4	4	4	5	9
Spain 184	141	206	197	214	349	516	581	247	260	255	259	—	387	456
Sweden 144	33	30	27	30	42	49	50	134	63	79	89	108	137	137
Switzerland 146	51	166	129	152	140	561	885	159	147	191	218	209	249	341
United Kingdom 112	287	160	185	275	320	395	410	180	150	165	199	190	234	269
Developing Countries 202	**4,673**	**4,245**	**4,295**	**6,430**	**8,288**	**9,256**	**12,616**	**4,748**	**5,111**	**5,773**	**7,566**	**10,223**	**13,242**	**16,829**
Africa 607	**20**	**24**	**61**	**75**	**49**	**88**	**170**	**61**	**64**	**106**	**88**	**79**	**90**	**113**
Algeria 612	1	—	5	3	1	1	1	—	—	—	—	—	—	—
Angola 614	—	—	—	—	1	1	1	—	—	—	—	—	34	—
Benin 638	—	—	1	1	—	—	—	—	—	1	1	1	1	—
Burkina Faso 748	—	—	—	—	—	—	1	15	19	15	4	—	—	—
Cameroon 622	1	2	1	1	1	1	1	—	—	—	—	—	—	—
Central African Rep. 626	—	—	—	—	—	2	—	—	—	—	—	—	—	—
Congo, Dem. Rep. of 636	—	—	—	—	—	—	—	—	—	18	10	3	—	—
Congo, Republic of 634	—	—	1	1	—	1	1	—	—	15	—	—	—	1
Côte d'Ivoire 662	1	—	4	4	1	1	1	—	1	1	1	—	1	1
Djibouti 611	—	—	—	—	1	—	—	—	—	—	—	1	—	—
Eritrea 643	—	1	—	—	—	—	—	—	—	—	—	—	—	—
Gambia, The 648	—	—	1	—	—	—	—	—	—	—	—	—	—	—
Ghana 652	—	—	2	1	2	2	2	—	—	—	—	—	—	—
Guinea 656	—	—	4	—	—	—	—	—	—	—	—	—	—	—
Kenya 664	3	—	—	—	—	—	1	—	—	2	10	—	—	—
Liberia 668	1	—	4	1	1	—	1	—	—	—	—	—	—	1
Mali 678	—	1	—	—	—	—	—	—	—	—	—	—	—	—
Mauritania 682	—	3	5	—	—	—	—	—	—	—	—	—	—	—
Morocco 686	1	2	4	23	9	8	35	1	3	2	5	9	8	13
Nigeria 694	1	4	9	2	2	4	1	8	—	—	—	21	—	41
Rwanda 714	—	—	—	—	—	—	—	—	—	—	—	—	—	1
Senegal 722	1	1	2	1	1	1	—	—	—	—	2	—	3	9
South Africa 199	7	4	15	34	27	63	118	27	40	50	53	42	37	39
Togo 742	—	—	—	1	—	—	—	6	—	—	—	—	—	—
Tunisia 744	—	6	3	2	1	1	—	—	—	—	—	—	—	—
Zambia 754	—	—	—	—	—	1	1	—	—	—	—	—	—	—
Zimbabwe 698	—	—	—	—	—	—	—	—	—	1	—	—	5	4
Asia 507	**134**	**171**	**267**	**400**	**554**	**883**	**1,167**	**1,235**	**1,343**	**1,570**	**2,233**	**3,102**	**4,190**	**5,752**
Afghanistan, I.S. of 512	—	—	—	—	—	—	—	—	1	—	—	—	—	—
Bangladesh 513	—	1	—	1	5	1	1	—	—	—	—	—	1	2
China,P.R.: Mainland 924	20	30	83	138	237	452	785	475	532	686	1,055	1,617	2,219	3,327
China,P.R.:Hong Kong 532	16	16	16	18	13	13	23	42	45	39	43	48	58	85
India 534	3	4	6	8	5	63	77	73	88	113	180	248	346	476
Indonesia 536	2	2	2	3	4	2	4	63	60	59	80	104	118	134
Korea 542	44	47	76	93	136	201	111	266	310	337	452	594	761	897
Malaysia 548	1	1	1	1	2	3	3	33	35	62	64	75	140	161
Pakistan 564	—	—	1	2	3	8	3	13	10	7	12	21	34	44
Philippines 566	6	8	6	5	7	5	7	5	7	7	15	10	13	13
Samoa 862	—	—	—	—	—	—	1	—	—	—	—	—	—	—
Singapore 576	9	7	11	27	23	15	71	35	31	34	40	53	62	55
Sri Lanka 524	1	3	2	12	16	10	1	3	3	3	4	4	6	7

	Exports 2001	Exports 2002	Exports 2003	Exports 2004	Exports 2005	Exports 2006	Exports 2007	Imports 2001	Imports 2002	Imports 2003	Imports 2004	Imports 2005	Imports 2006	Imports 2007
	Millions of U.S. Dollars							*Millions of U.S. Dollars*						
Taiwan Province of China............528	24	44	54	81	90	94	65	166	162	165	197	227	277	305
Thailand............578	7	7	8	11	12	14	15	53	53	54	82	90	129	204
Vietnam............582	—	—	—	—	—	—	—	5	5	5	10	12	26	42
Europe............170	**78**	**68**	**127**	**150**	**245**	**249**	**289**	**130**	**167**	**168**	**242**	**332**	**289**	**334**
Albania............914	—	—	1	—	—	—	—	—	—	—	—	—	1	1
Belarus............913	—	—	—	—	—	1	—	—	1	14	—	—	5	—
Bosnia & Herzegovina............963	—	—	—	—	—	—	—	1	—	—	1	1	—	—
Bulgaria............918	—	—	—	—	2	2	16	3	6	8	7	9	7	8
Croatia............960	2	—	5	5	4	21	8	—	—	—	—	4	1	3
Czech Republic............935	1	1	14	8	12	4	5	9	11	11	15	16	16	22
Estonia............939	1	—	—	—	1	4	8	—	2	—	1	7	3	2
Georgia............915	—	—	—	3	4	—	—	—	—	—	—	—	—	1
Gibraltar............823	2	—	1	—	1	—	—	—	—	—	—	—	—	—
Hungary............944	—	—	—	1	2	2	2	9	5	3	19	41	13	14
Kazakhstan............916	—	—	—	—	—	—	—	—	5	4	1	1	1	8
Latvia............941	—	—	—	—	1	—	2	—	2	15	9	9	2	11
Lithuania............946	—	—	—	1	1	1	—	2	5	5	1	1	4	26
Macedonia, FYR............962	—	—	—	—	—	7	11	—	—	—	—	—	—	—
Moldova............921	—	—	—	—	—	—	—	—	—	—	4	—	—	—
Poland............964	6	4	7	3	7	15	17	12	12	15	24	21	30	31
Romania............968	8	6	2	3	5	4	4	6	6	6	6	3	9	4
Russia............922	52	41	36	55	74	55	74	49	82	43	82	139	118	108
Serbia & Montenegro............965	—	—	—	—	—	—	—	—	—	—	—	—	1	1
Slovak Republic............936	—	—	—	—	3	1	2	4	3	4	3	4	4	4
Turkey............186	—	6	56	65	115	127	132	12	11	12	14	20	24	36
Ukraine............926	2	2	2	3	5	6	5	21	15	26	55	57	50	55
Yugoslavia n.s............966	3	6	2	—	9	—	—	—	—	1	—	—	—	—
Europe n.s............884	—	—	—	—	—	—	2	—	—	—	—	—	—	—
Middle East............407	**89**	**115**	**119**	**130**	**234**	**221**	**201**	**64**	**85**	**91**	**118**	**116**	**157**	**187**
Bahrain............419	—	1	—	—	1	—	1	2	3	1	1	—	3	2
Egypt............469	1	1	12	1	1	2	1	1	1	2	3	3	4	5
Iran, I.R. of............429	—	6	3	3	4	3	—	—	—	1	1	—	1	3
Iraq............433	—	—	—	1	1	—	1	—	—	—	—	—	—	—
Israel............436	77	89	89	104	198	188	168	55	77	73	100	99	137	165
Jordan............439	1	1	1	1	1	1	3	—	—	—	—	—	—	1
Kuwait............443	1	—	1	2	1	1	2	—	—	—	—	—	—	—
Lebanon............446	1	4	1	1	2	1	3	—	—	—	—	—	—	—
Libya............672	—	—	—	—	—	—	—	—	—	9	10	5	4	—
Qatar............453	—	—	—	—	—	—	—	—	—	—	—	1	1	6
Saudi Arabia............456	4	5	3	2	4	4	5	1	1	3	1	5	3	2
Syrian Arab Republic............463	2	6	7	6	2	13	10	3	2	1	1	2	1	1
United Arab Emirates............466	2	2	1	5	14	5	8	—	—	1	1	1	1	2
West Bank/Gaza Strip............487	—	—	—	—	—	—	—	—	—	—	—	2	—	—
Yemen, Republic of............474	—	—	—	3	5	1	—	—	—	—	—	—	—	—
Western Hemisphere............207	**4,352**	**3,867**	**3,720**	**5,675**	**7,207**	**7,815**	**10,790**	**3,258**	**3,452**	**3,838**	**4,885**	**6,593**	**8,516**	**10,443**
Antigua and Barbuda............311	—	1	4	3	1	2	11	—	—	—	—	1	—	—
Argentina............213	37	14	19	38	47	51	74	202	211	257	322	412	586	712
Aruba............314	11	8	13	43	136	229	15	12	1	4	2	17	72	107
Bahamas, The............313	9	47	39	44	70	16	3	—	—	—	—	—	—	1
Barbados............316	3	2	2	2	3	37	33	—	—	—	—	15	—	—
Belize............339	—	1	1	1	1	1	1	—	—	—	—	—	—	7
Bermuda............319	—	—	—	—	—	3	—	—	—	1	—	—	—	—
Bolivia............218	42	39	36	60	50	59	66	131	137	198	170	192	117	143
Brazil............223	167	110	93	141	141	191	471	582	641	768	973	1,383	1,885	2,394
Chile............228	168	177	189	255	296	259	376	262	281	300	359	377	512	661
Costa Rica............238	150	155	199	240	219	242	283	15	16	19	23	25	36	38
Dominica............321	1	1	1	1	1	2	3	—	—	—	—	—	—	—
Dominican Republic............243	103	170	343	437	583	583	622	2	3	3	3	3	8	10
Ecuador............248	700	825	780	1,015	1,324	1,237	1,276	318	366	410	412	529	697	733
El Salvador............253	29	33	38	46	51	50	50	1	1	1	1	1	3	6
Grenada............328	1	—	—	—	—	1	—	—	—	—	—	—	—	—
Guatemala............258	77	84	92	128	142	157	161	11	9	12	14	15	21	25
Guyana............336	3	3	3	4	5	6	8	1	—	—	2	1	1	1
Haiti............263	29	38	34	39	44	68	55	—	—	—	—	—	—	7
Honduras............268	25	30	36	37	46	44	58	2	6	12	4	6	3	4
Jamaica............343	28	23	30	69	93	59	46	3	1	1	2	2	1	2
Mexico............273	261	311	360	526	611	582	495	596	677	748	1,044	1,757	2,291	3,073
Netherlands Antilles............353	27	23	22	61	33	38	28	3	4	3	8	3	7	12
Nicaragua............278	6	5	6	6	11	10	10	1	—	—	1	1	25	3
Panama............283	265	216	172	216	264	257	246	59	34	48	64	63	92	139
Paraguay............288	5	1	1	2	2	2	4	45	71	66	67	11	15	20
Peru............293	277	353	396	548	710	692	806	159	160	193	261	350	517	608
St. Kitts and Nevis............361	1	—	—	—	—	—	1	—	—	—	—	—	1	—
St. Lucia............362	2	1	1	2	3	4	5	—	—	—	—	—	—	—
St. Vincent & Grens............364	—	—	1	1	1	2	2	—	—	—	—	—	—	—
Suriname............366	3	4	5	6	9	9	16	—	—	—	—	—	1	—
Trinidad and Tobago............369	171	58	99	71	198	207	342	34	25	33	39	177	93	310

	Exports							Imports						
	2001	2002	2003	2004	2005	2006	2007	2001	2002	2003	2004	2005	2006	2007
	Millions of U.S. Dollars							*Millions of U.S. Dollars*						
Uruguay.......... 298	10	5	4	6	7	6	9	22	23	23	28	28	31	40
Venezuela, Rep. Bol.......... 299	1,737	1,127	696	1,627	2,098	2,702	5,210	793	785	728	1,082	1,219	1,498	1,366
Western Hem. n.s.......... 399	4	2	1	1	2	9	4	2	—	9	2	6	2	24
Other Countries n.i.e.......... 910	**24**	**63**	**61**	**33**	**66**	**52**	**52**	**19**	**9**	**23**	**16**	**6**	**13**	**17**
Cuba.......... 928	24	63	61	33	64	49	51	13	4	5	7	6	4	9
North Korea.......... 954	—	—	—	—	2	4	1	6	5	18	10	—	9	8
Countries & Areas n.s.......... 898	**—**	**126**	**1**	**17**	**—**	**1**	**—**	**2**	**641**	**—**	**—**	**224**	**—**	**—**
Special Categories.......... 899	**144**	**125**	**194**	**287**	**373**	**461**	**610**	**274**	**—**	**305**	**463**	**543**	**802**	**1,172**
Memorandum Items														
European Union.......... 998	1,747	1,654	1,922	2,367	2,828	3,499	4,542	2,243	1,866	2,589	2,634	2,924	3,474	4,075
Oil Exporting Ctys.......... 999	1,749	1,147	720	1,648	2,129	2,724	5,233	866	847	801	1,174	1,356	1,626	1,554
Non-Oil Develop.Ctys.......... 201	2,924	3,098	3,575	4,782	6,159	6,532	7,383	3,882	4,263	4,972	6,392	8,867	11,615	15,275
PERCENT DISTRIBUTION														
Industrial Countries.......... 101	**60.7**	**62.3**	**65.3**	**59.7**	**58.8**	**59.9**	**55.7**	**60.7**	**54.6**	**56.9**	**52.8**	**48.1**	**46.3**	**45.2**
Developing Countries.......... 202	**38.0**	**35.1**	**32.7**	**38.3**	**39.1**	**37.9**	**42.1**	**37.0**	**40.3**	**40.8**	**44.4**	**48.2**	**50.6**	**51.2**
Africa.......... 607	**.2**	**.2**	**.5**	**.4**	**.2**	**.4**	**.6**	**.5**	**.5**	**.8**	**.5**	**.4**	**.3**	**.3**
Asia.......... 507	**1.1**	**1.4**	**2.0**	**2.4**	**2.6**	**3.6**	**3.9**	**9.6**	**10.6**	**11.1**	**13.1**	**14.6**	**16.0**	**17.5**
Europe.......... 170	**.6**	**.6**	**1.0**	**.9**	**1.2**	**1.0**	**1.0**	**1.0**	**1.3**	**1.2**	**1.4**	**1.6**	**1.1**	**1.0**
Middle East.......... 407	**.7**	**.9**	**.9**	**.8**	**1.1**	**.9**	**.7**	**.5**	**.7**	**.6**	**.7**	**.5**	**.6**	**.6**
Western Hemisphere.......... 207	**35.4**	**32.0**	**28.3**	**33.8**	**34.0**	**32.0**	**36.0**	**25.4**	**27.2**	**27.1**	**28.7**	**31.1**	**32.6**	**31.7**
Other Countries n.i.e.......... 910	**.2**	**.5**	**.5**	**.2**	**.3**	**.2**	**.2**	**.2**	**.1**	**.2**	**.1**	**—**	**—**	**.1**
ANNUAL PERCENT CHANGE														
World.......... 001	**–6.5**	**–1.7**	**8.5**	**27.9**	**26.2**	**15.1**	**23.0**	**13.2**	**–1.0**	**11.5**	**20.3**	**24.5**	**23.4**	**25.7**
Industrial Countries.......... 101	**–15.8**	**1.0**	**13.7**	**16.8**	**24.4**	**17.3**	**14.3**	**12.2**	**–10.8**	**16.1**	**11.6**	**13.6**	**18.6**	**22.9**
Developing Countries.......... 202	**12.5**	**–9.2**	**1.2**	**49.7**	**28.9**	**11.7**	**36.3**	**10.2**	**7.6**	**13.0**	**31.0**	**35.1**	**29.5**	**27.1**
Africa.......... 607	**–33.5**	**24.0**	**149.6**	**23.4**	**–34.9**	**79.6**	**93.4**	**17.6**	**5.3**	**65.8**	**–16.9**	**–10.6**	**13.8**	**25.8**
Asia.......... 507	**–13.3**	**27.1**	**56.5**	**49.7**	**38.3**	**59.4**	**32.1**	**55.8**	**8.7**	**16.9**	**42.2**	**38.9**	**35.1**	**37.3**
Europe.......... 170	**–7.8**	**–13.1**	**86.9**	**17.4**	**63.8**	**1.6**	**16.0**	**56.4**	**28.4**	**.7**	**44.1**	**37.4**	**–12.9**	**15.6**
Middle East.......... 407	**95.4**	**29.1**	**3.7**	**9.0**	**80.4**	**–5.6**	**–8.9**	**.9**	**33.0**	**7.8**	**29.3**	**–1.7**	**34.8**	**19.5**
Western Hemisphere.......... 207	**13.4**	**–11.1**	**–3.8**	**52.6**	**27.0**	**8.4**	**38.1**	**–1.8**	**6.0**	**11.2**	**27.3**	**35.0**	**29.2**	**22.6**
Other Countries n.i.e.......... 910	**–24.1**	**161.9**	**–3.4**	**–45.5**	**98.2**	**–20.2**	**–1.2**	**79.5**	**–54.7**	**161.3**	**–28.4**	**–66.2**	**135.7**	**31.2**

		Exports							Imports						
		2001	2002	2003	2004	2005	2006	2007	2001	2002	2003	2004	2005	2006	2007
		Millions of U.S. Dollars							Millions of U.S. Dollars						
IFS World Total		**17.0**	**19.0**	**26.7**	**18.7**	**12.0**	**9.9**	**8.5**	**51.0**	**53.0**	**70.0**	**86.0**	**98.7**	**115.2**	**120.0**
DOTS World Total	**001**	**37.5Y**	**28.5Y**	**33.0Y**	**34.5Y**	**24.1Y**	**32.0Y**	**30.4Y**	**82.6Y**	**95.8Y**	**123.5Y**	**111.3Y**	**114.0Y**	**141.7Y**	**156.3Y**
Industrial Countries	**101**	**29.3Y**	**23.9Y**	**28.9Y**	**25.5Y**	**16.7Y**	**24.2Y**	**12.1Y**	**43.6Y**	**47.1Y**	**66.0Y**	**49.2Y**	**46.8Y**	**56.5Y**	**44.1Y**
United States	111	9.73V	4.91V	3.73V	15.09V	1.36V	1.45V	.45V	1.54V	.11V	.66V	.66V	.33V	—V	.22V
Canada	156	.38V	.14V	.76V	.07V	.08V	.10V	.04V	.15V	.02V	.18V	.23V	.80V	.78V	.49V
Australia	193	—V	.01V	—V	—V	—V	.01V	—V	.10V	.15V	.29V	.02V	—V	.02V	.06V
Japan	158	1.60V	.88V	1.34V	.51V	3.53V	.06V	.01V	6.22V	5.37V	16.02V	.48V	.40V	1.93V	.84V
New Zealand	196	—V	—V	—V	.02V	—V	—V	—V	—V	—V	—V	—V	—V	.02V	.43V
Austria	122	—V	—V	—V	—V	.15V	—V	—V	—V	—V	—V	.01V	—V	.05V	—V
Belgium	124	.07V	.07V	.06V	.09V	.06V	.14V	.04V	4.05V	3.31V	3.71V	3.46V	5.29V	4.24V	3.79V
Denmark	128	—V	.08V	—V	.03V	—V	—V	—V	.03V	.08V	.15V	.24V	.13V	.06V	.03V
Finland	172	—V	—V	—V	—V	—V	—V	—V	—V	—V	.03V	.02V	—V	—V	.01V
France	132	7.44V	9.05V	15.13V	6.43V	6.50V	5.84V	8.38V	22.61V	30.41V	37.14V	27.19V	25.29V	35.39V	28.43V
Germany	134	3.42V	5.34V	6.49V	1.57V	3.20V	.83V	.71V	2.02V	.65V	1.30V	1.63V	1.05V	1.58V	.98V
Greece	174	.10V	.87V	.59V	.48V	.09V	.11V	.51V	1.01V	.55V	.14V	.46V	1.25V	1.93V	1.00V
Ireland	178	—V	—V	—V	—V	—V	—V	.01V	.70V	—V	.25V	.76V	1.01V	.72V	2.52V
Italy	136	.07V	.36V	—V	.34V	.12V	4.07V	1.09V	.94V	1.25V	1.40V	5.63V	4.80V	5.97V	1.53V
Luxembourg	137	—V	—V	—V	—V	—V	—V	—V	.07V	.23V	.34V	.33V	—V	—V	.07V
Netherlands	138	1.62V	1.84V	.71V	.68V	1.20V	11.44V	.53V	1.92V	2.63V	1.72V	2.29V	2.04V	2.47V	1.82V
Norway	142	—V	—V	.01V	.01V	.05V	.04V	.01V	—V	.23V	.01V	—V	.11V	.02V	.01V
Portugal	182	—V	.02V	—V	—V	—V	—V	—V	.23V	.05V	.03V	.47V	.07V	.06V	.01V
Spain	184	—V	—V	—V	—V	.06V	.02V	.03V	.38V	.61V	1.78V	2.72V	3.62V	.49V	.56V
Sweden	144	—V	—V	—V	—V	.03V	—V	—V	—V	.16V	.03V	—V	—V	.47V	.47V
Switzerland	146	.10V	.09V	.09V	.14V	.02V	.03V	—V	.01V	.09V	.08V	.09V	.03V	.16V	.15V
United Kingdom	112	4.75V	.29V	.05V	.09V	.21V	.11V	.23V	1.60V	1.23V	.74V	2.54V	.61V	.18V	.69V
Developing Countries	**202**	**8.1Y**	**4.4Y**	**3.8Y**	**8.7Y**	**7.2Y**	**7.4Y**	**17.9Y**	**38.2Y**	**47.9Y**	**56.5Y**	**60.7Y**	**65.6Y**	**83.2Y**	**109.8Y**
Africa	**607**	**.2Y**	**.2Y**	**.9Y**	**.4Y**	**.6Y**	**.4Y**	**.5Y**	**22.3Y**	**24.7Y**	**31.3Y**	**27.0Y**	**24.5Y**	**28.1Y**	**37.0Y**
Algeria	612	.01V	—V	—Y	—Y	—Y	—Y	—Y	—V	—V	—Y	—Y	—Y	—Y	—Y
Benin	638	—V	—V	—V	—V	—V	—Y	—Y	—V	.01V	—V	—V	—V	—Y	—Y
Cameroon	622	—V	—V	—V	—Y	—Y	—Y	—Y	.03V	.02V	—V	—Y	—Y	—Y	—Y
Côte d'Ivoire	662	.01V	—V	—V	—V	—V	—V	—Y	—V	—V	.04V	—V	.02V	—V	—Y
Kenya	664	.01V	—V	—V	—V	—Y	—Y	—Y	4.97V	3.81V	4.45V	5.07V	5.80Y	7.16Y	8.89Y
Madagascar	674	.09V	.03V	.14V	.18Y	.21Y	.26Y	.32Y	2.47V	1.80V	2.30V	3.02Y	3.45Y	4.26Y	5.29Y
Mauritius	684	—V	.07V	.67V	.07V	.01V	.01V	.02V	3.96V	3.52V	5.01V	4.78V	4.12V	4.70V	6.02V
Morocco	686	—V	—V	.01V	.04V	—V	—Y	—Y	.78V	1.15V	1.22V	.83V	1.49V	1.84Y	2.28Y
Niger	692	—V	—V	—V	—V	—Y	—Y	—Y	—V	.01V	—V	.01V	.01Y	.01Y	.01Y
Nigeria	694	.07V	—V	.04V	.05Y	.06Y	.07Y	.09Y	—V	—V	—V	—Y	—Y	—Y	—Y
Senegal	722	—V	—V	—V	.01V	.02V	—V	—Y	—V	—V	—V	—V	—V	.04V	.05Y
South Africa	199	—V	.13V	.04V	.07V	.28V	—V	—V	9.72V	13.88V	17.74V	12.66V	8.24V	9.16V	13.27V
Tanzania	738	—V	—V	—Y	—Y	—Y	—Y	—Y	.02V	.40V	.50Y	.66Y	.75Y	.93Y	1.15Y
Tunisia	744	.01V	.01V	.03V	—V	.01V	.01V	.02Y	.32V	.07V	.01V	—V	.64V	.03V	.04Y
Asia	**507**	**7.4Y**	**3.8Y**	**2.1Y**	**6.1Y**	**4.9Y**	**3.9Y**	**4.4Y**	**10.2Y**	**17.0Y**	**15.0Y**	**19.1Y**	**22.8Y**	**30.7Y**	**43.9Y**
China,P.R.: Mainland	924	.04V	—V	—V	—V	—V	—V	—V	.50V	.84V	.76V	1.48V	2.03V	6.81V	8.41V
China,P.R.:Hong Kong	532	.40V	—V	—V	—V	—V	.13V	.10V	—V	.57V	.05V	.05V	.11V	.28V	2.36V
French Polynesia	887	.01Y	.01Y	.02Y	.02Y	.03Y	.03Y	.04Y	....	....	....	....	....	....	....
India	534	—Y	.42V	.40V	.21V	.79V	.98Y	1.22Y	1.43Y	5.92V	3.37V	2.54V	5.06V	6.25Y	7.76Y
Indonesia	536	.43V	.05V	—V	—V	—V	—V	—V	2.34V	2.44V	1.26V	1.18V	.64V	.70V	1.63V
Korea	542	—V	—V	—V	—V	—V	—V	—V	.01V	.02V	.08V	—V	.04V	.03V	.04V
Malaysia	548	—V	.01V	.01V	—V	.02V	—V	.10V	.22V	.32V	.44V	.41V	.72V	.95V	1.78V
New Caledonia	839	—V	—V	—V	—V	—Y	.01Y	.01Y	....	....	....	....	....	....	....
Pakistan	564	—V	.01V	.02V	.11V	.06V	.07Y	.09Y	.38V	.61V	1.61V	5.43V	7.31V	9.04Y	11.22Y
Philippines	566	—V	—V	.10V	—V	—V	—V	—V	—V	—V	—V	—V	—V	—V	—V
Singapore	576	6.43V	3.17V	1.42V	5.69V	3.93V	2.50V	2.79V	1.38V	1.94V	2.43V	4.65V	3.47V	3.71V	6.03V
Taiwan Province of China	528	—V	.01V	—V	—V	—V	.01V	—V	—V	.01V	.01V	—V	—V	—V	—V
Thailand	578	—V	—V	.02V	—V	—V	.04V	—V	3.67V	4.09V	4.67V	3.03V	3.08V	2.55V	4.34V
Asia n.s.	598	.10Y	.10Y	.10Y	.10Y	.10Y	.10Y	.10Y	.22Y	.25Y	.27Y	.29Y	.32Y	.34Y	.36Y
Europe	**170**	**.4Y**	**.3Y**	**.7Y**	**2.0Y**	**.8Y**	**2.1Y**	**11.8Y**	**.1Y**	**.2Y**	**1.1Y**	**3.5Y**	**3.1Y**	**4.8Y**	**8.4Y**
Belarus	913	—V	—V	—V	—V	.01V	—V	—V	—V	—V	—V	—V	—V	—V	—V
Bulgaria	918	.01V	—V	—V	.01V	—V	.01V	.03V	—V	.10V	.93V	1.16V	.91V	2.28V	1.13V
Czech Republic	935	.05V	.03V	—V	—V	—V	—V	—V	.03V	.03V	.04V	.04V	—V	.04V	.13V
Hungary	944	.01V	.09V	.01V	—V	.01V	—V	—V	—V	—V	—V	—V	—V	—V	—V
Latvia	941	—V	.04V	—V	—V	—V	—V	—V	—Y	—Y	—Y	—Y	.01V	.05V	.02V
Lithuania	946	.01V	.01V	—V	—V	—V	.29V	—V	—Y	—Y	—Y	—Y	.01V	.03V	3.60V
Poland	964	.11V	.13V	.58V	.23V	—V	.06V	—V	—V	—V	—V	—V	—V	—V	.08V
Romania	968	—V	—V	—V	.06V	.06V	—V	—V	.03V	.07V	.08V	.04V	.06V	.17V	.19V
Russia	922	.11V	—V	.04V	.01V	.08V	.03V	.02V	—Y	—Y	.02V	.04Y	.06Y	.08Y	.10Y
Slovak Republic	936	—V	.01V	.01Y	.01Y	—V	—V	—V	—V	—V	—Y	—Y	—V	—V	—V
Turkey	186	.15V	.01V	—V	1.67V	.55V	1.58V	11.58V	.02V	.02V	.05V	2.20V	1.82V	1.85V	2.67V
Ukraine	926	—V	—V	.01V	.02V	.10V	.12Y	.15Y	—V	—V	—V	.06V	.28V	.34Y	.43Y
Middle East	**407**	**—Y**	**—Y**	**.1Y**	**—Y**	**.8Y**	**1.0Y**	**1.2Y**	**5.5Y**	**5.9Y**	**7.2Y**	**9.6Y**	**13.0Y**	**16.3Y**	**19.7Y**
Oman	449	—V	—V	—V	—Y	—Y	—Y	—Y	.06V	.13V	.25V	.34Y	.46Y	.57Y	.69Y
Saudi Arabia	456	.01V	.01V	.14V	.02V	.77V	.95Y	1.23Y	.59Y	.63Y	.76Y	1.01Y	1.37Y	1.72Y	2.08Y
United Arab Emirates	466	—V	—V	—Y	—Y	—Y	—Y	—Y	4.81Y	5.12Y	6.21Y	8.21Y	11.17Y	14.04Y	16.94Y

	Exports							Imports						
	2001	2002	2003	2004	2005	2006	2007	2001	2002	2003	2004	2005	2006	2007
	Millions of U.S. Dollars							*Millions of U.S. Dollars*						
Western Hemisphere................ 207	**—Y**	**—Y**	**—Y**	**.1Y**	**.1Y**	**.1Y**	**—Y**	**.3Y**	**.1Y**	**1.9Y**	**1.5Y**	**2.1Y**	**3.2Y**	**.8Y**
Argentina.................................. 213	—V	—V	—V	.03V	.01V	.04V	—V	—V	—V	—V	.21V	.12V	.38V	.53V
Barbados.................................... 316	—V	—V	—V	—V	—V	—V	—Y	—V	—V	.01V	—V	—V	—V	—Y
Brazil.. 223	.02V	.01V	—V	.10V	.02V	—V	—V	.26V	.09V	1.72V	1.27V	1.91V	2.67V	—V
Colombia.................................... 233	—V	.02V	—V	—V	—V	—V	—V	—V	—V	—V	—V	—V	—V	—V
Mexico....................................... 273	—V	—V	—V	—V	.02V	.03V	.02V	—V	—V	—V	—V	—V	—V	—V
Paraguay.................................... 288	....	....	....	....	....	....	....	—V	—V	.14V	—V	.08V	.13V	.17Y
Trinidad and Tobago.................... 369	—V	—V	—Y	—Y	—Y	—Y	—Y	.01V	.02V	.03Y	.04Y	.04Y	.05Y	.06Y
Countries & Areas n.s.............. 898	**.1Y**	**.1Y**	**.2Y**	**.2Y**	**.3Y**	**.3Y**	**.4Y**	**.8Y**	**.8Y**	**1.0Y**	**1.4Y**	**1.6Y**	**1.9Y**	**2.4Y**
Memorandum Items														
European Union.......................... 998	17.65Y	18.22Y	23.63Y	9.94Y	11.63Y	22.91Y	11.54Y	35.60Y	41.21Y	48.79Y	47.79Y	45.18Y	53.71Y	45.74Y
Oil Exporting Ctys....................... 999	.52Y	.06Y	.17Y	.07Y	.83Y	1.02Y	1.33Y	7.80Y	8.31Y	8.48Y	10.74Y	13.64Y	17.05Y	21.35Y
Non-Oil Develop.Ctys.................. 201	7.57Y	4.31Y	3.65Y	8.65Y	6.34Y	6.34Y	16.61Y	30.44Y	39.56Y	47.98Y	49.99Y	51.94Y	66.18Y	88.44Y
PERCENT DISTRIBUTION														
Industrial Countries................. 101	**78.1**	**84.1**	**87.8**	**74.0**	**69.1**	**75.9**	**39.6**	**52.8**	**49.2**	**53.4**	**44.2**	**41.1**	**39.9**	**28.2**
Developing Countries.............. 202	**21.6**	**15.3**	**11.6**	**25.3**	**29.7**	**23.1**	**59.0**	**46.3**	**49.9**	**45.7**	**54.5**	**57.5**	**58.7**	**70.2**
Africa...................................... 607	**.5**	**.8**	**2.8**	**1.2**	**2.5**	**1.1**	**1.5**	**27.0**	**25.7**	**25.3**	**24.3**	**21.5**	**19.9**	**23.7**
Asia.. 507	**19.7**	**13.3**	**6.4**	**17.8**	**20.5**	**12.1**	**14.6**	**12.3**	**17.7**	**12.1**	**17.1**	**20.0**	**21.6**	**28.1**
Europe.................................... 170	**1.2**	**1.1**	**2.0**	**5.8**	**3.3**	**6.6**	**38.7**	**.1**	**.2**	**.9**	**3.2**	**2.7**	**3.4**	**5.3**
Middle East............................ 407	**—**	**—**	**.4**	**.1**	**3.2**	**3.0**	**4.1**	**6.6**	**6.1**	**5.8**	**8.6**	**11.4**	**11.5**	**12.6**
Western Hemisphere............. 207	**.1**	**.1**	**—**	**.4**	**.2**	**.2**	**.1**	**.3**	**.1**	**1.5**	**1.4**	**1.9**	**2.3**	**.5**
ANNUAL PERCENT CHANGE														
World....................................... 001	**141.1**	**−24.1**	**15.8**	**4.7**	**−30.1**	**32.6**	**−4.8**	**18.5**	**16.0**	**28.9**	**−9.9**	**2.4**	**24.3**	**10.3**
Industrial Countries................. 101	**146.4**	**−18.2**	**20.9**	**−11.8**	**−34.8**	**45.5**	**−50.3**	**46.0**	**8.1**	**40.0**	**−25.4**	**−4.9**	**20.7**	**−22.0**
Developing Countries.............. 202	**128.0**	**−45.9**	**−12.5**	**128.2**	**−17.8**	**2.8**	**143.4**	**−2.4**	**25.2**	**18.0**	**7.6**	**8.0**	**26.9**	**31.9**
Africa...................................... 607	**100.9**	**14.3**	**299.8**	**−53.5**	**40.8**	**−39.4**	**26.5**	**−4.7**	**10.7**	**26.8**	**−13.6**	**−9.3**	**14.7**	**31.5**
Asia.. 507	**136.1**	**−48.8**	**−44.6**	**192.2**	**−19.5**	**−21.5**	**14.5**	**−1.3**	**67.5**	**−12.0**	**27.6**	**19.4**	**34.7**	**43.3**
Europe.................................... 170	**111.2**	**−31.3**	**113.3**	**204.5**	**−60.0**	**161.4**	**460.4**	**30.3**	**148.9**	**400.0**	**216.5**	**−11.6**	**54.4**	**72.6**
Middle East............................ 407	**−55.6**	**−26.5**	**—**	**−85.4**	**—**	**23.5**	**29.5**	**3.8**	**7.5**	**22.9**	**32.3**	**36.0**	**25.7**	**20.7**
Western Hemisphere............. 207	**−70.3**	**44.8**	**−86.3**	**—**	**−58.6**	**40.7**	**−63.9**	**45.5**	**−59.0**	**—**	**−19.7**	**41.0**	**50.4**	**−76.4**

Congo, Democratic Republic of 636

	Exports							Imports						
	2001	2002	2003	2004	2005	2006	2007	2001	2002	2003	2004	2005	2006	2007
	Millions of U.S. Dollars							*Millions of U.S. Dollars*						
IFS World Total	**901.0**	**1,131.7**	**1,374.1**	**1,849.9**	**2,190.0**	**2,320.0**	**2,600.0**	**807.0**	**1,080.9**	**1,594.3**	**1,986.5**	**2,270.0**	**2,740.0**	**2,950.0**
DOTS World Total 001	**1,135.6Y**	**1,333.4Y**	**988.7Y**	**1,122.3Y**	**1,433.8Y**	**1,588.3Y**	**1,931.2Y**	**687.6Y**	**924.4Y**	**1,049.8Y**	**1,384.9Y**	**1,640.6Y**	**2,248.2Y**	**3,040.9Y**
Industrial Countries 101	**1,010.1Y**	**1,287.0Y**	**902.3Y**	**953.7Y**	**1,069.3Y**	**785.5Y**	**1,064.1Y**	**309.4Y**	**449.7Y**	**537.1Y**	**638.5Y**	**778.6Y**	**927.9Y**	**1,174.8Y**
United States 111	151.73V	190.27V	166.55V	120.09V	244.55V	78.18V	189.55V	20.46V	31.02V	33.66V	73.37V	70.84V	77.77V	124.19V
Canada 156	—V	—V	.05V	.20V	.22V	.47V	.28V	3.36V	7.42V	7.66V	7.89V	13.77V	19.51V	40.24V
Australia 193	—V	.02V	1.19V	.61V	.18V	.13V	.38V	.47V	3.01V	.26V	.21V	2.15V	1.07V	6.25V
Japan 158	9.44V	28.43V	12.55V	8.43V	3.03V	2.34V	2.82V	5.39V	13.75V	7.31V	11.03V	18.39V	25.92V	22.26V
New Zealand 196	—V	—V	—V	.08V	—V	—V	—V	—V	.33V	1.35V	2.21V	4.29V	7.98V	5.87V
Austria 122	.04V	—V	.04V	.24V	.26V	.21V	.22V	.75V	1.33V	1.15V	.90V	1.27V	2.80V	4.30V
Belgium 124	705.95V	911.21V	595.59V	525.45V	522.89V	466.27V	456.56V	121.89V	132.38V	156.72V	190.88V	252.65V	246.01V	311.73V
Cyprus 423	.07V	.06V	.03V	.06V	.14Y	.10V	.53V	—V	—V	—V	—V	—V	.02V	.06V
Denmark 128	.01V	.16V	1.02V	.14V	.15V	.17V	.90V	1.37V	1.70V	6.09V	6.33V	5.28V	4.57V	4.89V
Finland 172	82.32V	68.74V	52.61V	230.15V	106.21V	114.05V	176.45V	.52V	.14V	.91V	1.41V	1.53V	.82V	2.50V
France 132	6.04V	33.79V	26.97V	13.15V	109.53V	30.28V	132.18V	44.04V	85.67V	133.14V	133.21V	142.52V	192.36V	206.47V
Germany 134	10.55V	7.45V	11.30V	7.55V	17.71V	15.43V	14.50V	33.17V	68.81V	71.77V	71.89V	72.64V	69.73V	101.91V
Greece 174	.09V	.08V	.12V	.10V	.08V	.11V	.19V	.04V	.44V	.31V	.56V	.64V	.67V	.67V
Ireland 178	—V	—V	—V	.10V	.03V	.04V	.04V	3.43V	5.33V	10.40V	18.06V	18.28V	31.26V	31.04V
Italy 136	20.73V	11.14V	10.87V	13.85V	17.85V	23.21V	28.78V	12.12V	21.63V	28.75V	26.69V	36.09V	54.18V	80.69V
Luxembourg 137	.04V	.01V	.04V	.04V	—V	.12V	—V	.53V	.84V	.92V	1.21V	1.58V	1.52V	1.72V
Malta 181	—Y	—V	—V	—V	—V	—V	—V	—Y	—V	—V	—V	—V	.03V	.51V
Netherlands 138	6.38V	2.23V	3.88V	1.97V	7.69V	23.32V	29.49V	33.27V	48.12V	42.39V	38.49V	64.99V	75.30V	92.88V
Norway 142	.02V	—V	—V	.01V	.06V	—V	—V	2.08V	4.12V	4.03V	6.24V	9.46V	16.25V	27.36V
Portugal 182	14.99V	9.61V	11.13V	20.67V	23.79V	25.25V	23.73V	.89V	4.11V	1.73V	4.53V	5.22V	10.38V	10.53V
Slovenia 961	.05V	.01V	.01V	.01Y	.05V	.10V	.21V	—V	—V	.01V	.01Y	.32V	.15V	.04V
Spain 184	.51V	21.42V	3.00V	2.69V	3.95V	3.92V	4.88V	3.55V	5.29V	8.20V	11.67V	11.22V	21.16V	22.49V
Sweden 144	.04V	.06V	.07V	—V	.32V	.10V	.37V	2.94V	1.63V	1.94V	14.16V	17.34V	30.61V	47.86V
Switzerland 146	.35V	.96V	3.11V	.32V	.44V	.42V	.48V	3.85V	3.47V	3.86V	4.34V	5.16V	3.82V	2.86V
United Kingdom 112	.74V	1.33V	2.15V	7.83V	10.12V	1.31V	1.57V	15.27V	9.15V	14.51V	13.22V	22.93V	34.06V	25.53V
Developing Countries 202	**125.5Y**	**46.4Y**	**86.5Y**	**168.5Y**	**364.6Y**	**802.7Y**	**867.1Y**	**377.8Y**	**474.3Y**	**512.2Y**	**745.8Y**	**861.3Y**	**1,319.4Y**	**1,864.9Y**
Africa 607	**111.4Y**	**27.8Y**	**37.7Y**	**53.0Y**	**126.8Y**	**107.2Y**	**206.6Y**	**313.3Y**	**390.7Y**	**408.2Y**	**610.4Y**	**709.6Y**	**1,108.9Y**	**1,657.7Y**
Benin 638	.07V	.01V	—V	.01V	.01V	.01Y	.02Y	—V	—V	.04V	.28V	.01V	.02Y	.02Y
Burundi 618	.66V	.55V	1.26V	2.01V	.93V	.73V	.91Y	.18V	.57V	.35V	.32V	.66V	.92V	1.15Y
Cameroon 622	—V	—V	.12V	.16Y	.18Y	.22Y	.28Y	29.82V	12.57V	—V	—Y	—Y	—Y	—Y
Central African Rep. 626	1.56Y	1.69Y	2.14Y	2.81Y	3.21Y	3.97Y	4.93Y	2.91Y	3.15Y	3.99Y	5.24Y	5.99Y	7.40Y	9.19Y
Congo, Republic of 634	2.69V	4.99V	5.05V	2.19V	2.51Y	3.10Y	3.85Y	4.11V	4.30V	.88V	.90V	1.03Y	1.27Y	1.57Y
Côte d'Ivoire 662	.01V	.01V	.26V	.05V	.30V	.03V	.03Y	17.34V	31.74V	32.47V	51.54V	67.39V	99.55V	123.54Y
Gabon 646	.02Y	.02Y	.03Y	.04Y	.05Y	.06Y	.07Y	10.76Y	11.68Y	14.78Y	19.41Y	22.18Y	27.41Y	34.02Y
Ghana 652	.01Y	.01Y	.01Y	.02Y	.02Y	.02Y	.03Y	—Y	—Y	—Y	—Y	—Y	—Y	—Y
Guinea 656	—V	—Y	—V	—V	.01Y	.01Y	.01Y	—V	—Y	—V	.02V	.02Y	.02Y	.03Y
Kenya 664	8.82V	4.97V	.69V	4.76V	5.43Y	6.72Y	8.33Y	60.01V	69.16V	77.75V	108.81V	124.32Y	153.65Y	190.68Y
Madagascar 674	.02V	—V	.04V	.05Y	.06Y	.08Y	.09Y	.02V	—V	.17V	.22Y	.25Y	.31Y	.38Y
Malawi 676	.03Y	.03Y	.03Y	.05Y	.05Y	.06Y	.08Y	1.07Y	1.16Y	1.47Y	1.93Y	2.20Y	2.72Y	3.38Y
Mauritania 682	—Y	—Y	—Y	—Y	—Y	—Y	—Y	.21Y	.23Y	.29Y	.38Y	.43Y	.54Y	.67Y
Mauritius 684	—V	—V	—V	—V	.01V	—V	—V	.03V	—V	—V	—V	—V	.01V	—V
Morocco 686	—V	.08V	.03V	1.62V	2.57V	3.18Y	3.94Y	3.05V	5.33V	7.28V	10.06V	11.94V	14.76Y	18.32Y
Mozambique 688	—V	—V	—Y	—Y	—V	—V	—Y	—V	.07V	.33V	.81V	.36V	—V	—Y
Nigeria 694	.68V	.78V	.45V	.58Y	.74Y	.91Y	1.18Y	—V	—V	.22V	.29Y	.39Y	.49Y	.60Y
Rwanda 714	6.26Y	6.79Y	8.59Y	11.29Y	12.90Y	15.94Y	19.78Y	1.24Y	1.35Y	1.71Y	2.24Y	2.56Y	3.17Y	3.93Y
Senegal 722	.13V	.11V	—V	.46V	.01V	.02V	.02Y	.12V	.95V	.47V	.66V	1.13V	2.34V	2.90Y
South Africa 199	2.38V	1.68V	3.96V	6.83V	3.96V	7.03V	7.73V	118.21V	168.40V	178.91V	227.11V	291.83V	400.44V	684.11V
Sacca exc. South Afr. 608	—V	—V	—V	—Y	—Y	—Y	—Y	5.08V	2.13V	.19V	.35V	.40Y	.49Y	.61Y
Sudan 732	—Y	—Y	.01Y	—V	.92V	6.37V	.60V	—Y	—Y	—V	—V	—V	—V	—V
Tanzania 738	.09V	.34V	.43Y	.56Y	.64Y	.79Y	.98Y	9.52V	17.42V	22.05Y	28.96Y	33.08Y	40.89Y	50.74Y
Togo 742	.01V	.01V	.01V	.02V	.02V	.02Y	.03Y	.08V	.17V	.07V	.46V	.20V	.25Y	.31Y
Tunisia 744	—V	—V	—V	—V	.02V	—V	—Y	—V	—V	—V	—V	—V	.01V	.01Y
Uganda 746	.04V	.17V	.27V	.36Y	.41Y	.51Y	.63Y	9.71V	8.31V	14.18V	18.62Y	21.28Y	26.30Y	32.64Y
Zambia 754	.58V	1.41V	10.90V	12.83V	21.21V	27.73V	116.26V	35.50V	32.95V	40.47V	116.39V	112.18V	141.36V	270.20V
Zimbabwe 698	87.34V	4.13V	3.45V	6.27V	70.62V	29.67V	36.81Y	2.94V	17.45V	8.44V	13.61V	7.85V	182.60V	226.61Y
Africa n.s. 799	—Y	—Y	—Y	—Y	—Y	—Y	—Y	1.45Y	1.55Y	1.65Y	1.75Y	1.86Y	1.96Y	2.06Y
Asia 507	**10.1Y**	**13.2Y**	**27.3Y**	**97.9Y**	**169.3Y**	**347.7Y**	**435.1Y**	**48.9Y**	**68.1Y**	**81.2Y**	**85.1Y**	**100.8Y**	**123.1Y**	**150.7Y**
Bangladesh 513	....	....	....	....	....	....	....	.02V	—V	—V	.02V	.69V	.85Y	1.06Y
Brunei Darussalam 516	—Y	—Y	.08V	.10Y	.11Y	.14Y	.17Y	—Y	—Y	—V	—Y	—Y	—Y	—Y
Cambodia 522	—V	—V	—V	—V	.01V	—V	—Y	—V	—Y	—Y	—Y	—Y	—Y	—Y
China,P.R.: Mainland 924	6.62V	11.34V	24.52V	83.15V	159.73V	334.96V	418.41V	14.55V	20.89V	27.96V	35.80V	54.69V	75.64V	102.25V
China,P.R.:Hong Kong 532	.09V	.09V	1.15V	.89V	.19V	.10V	.19V	12.53V	16.75V	30.54V	33.94V	25.45V	22.77V	18.08V
India 534	.28Y	.03V	.06V	1.48V	6.42V	7.94Y	9.85Y	5.59Y	4.56V	10.39V	5.39V	6.88V	8.51Y	10.55Y
Indonesia 536	—V	.02V	—V	—V	—V	—V	—V	5.16V	7.76V	4.17V	3.39V	.48V	.54V	—V
Korea 542	.75V	.56V	—V	—V	—V	—V	—V	1.11V	1.36V	—V	—V	—V	—V	—V
Malaysia 548	1.82V	.72V	.92V	12.20V	2.17V	3.44V	5.45V	1.39V	3.08V	3.16V	5.36V	9.60V	11.49V	14.96V
New Caledonia 839	—V	—V	—V	—V	—Y	—Y	.01Y	....	....	....	....	....	....	....
Pakistan 564	.06V	.37V	.53V	.11V	.68V	.84Y	1.04Y	.25V	.53V	.14V	.24V	1.87V	2.31Y	2.86Y
Philippines 566	—V	.05V	.06V	—V	—V	.27V	—V	.34V	—V	.09V	—V	.01V	.09V	—V

Congo, Democratic Republic of 636

		Exports							Imports						
		2001	2002	2003	2004	2005	2006	2007	2001	2002	2003	2004	2005	2006	2007
		Millions of U.S. Dollars							*Millions of U.S. Dollars*						
Singapore	576	.49V	—V	—V	—V	—V	—V	—V	5.78V	10.88V	—V	—V	—V	—V	—V
Solomon Islands	813	....	....	....	....	....	....	....	.01Y	.01Y	.01Y	.02Y	.02Y	.02Y	.03Y
Sri Lanka	524	—V	—V	—V	—V	—V	—V	—V	—V	.01V	.13V	.17V	.22V	—V	—V
Taiwan Province of China	528	.01V	—V	—V	—V	—V	—V	—V	.41V	.79V	.49V	—V	—V	—V	—V
Thailand	578	—V	—V	.01V	.01V	—V	—V	—V	—V	—V	.30V	.03V	.16V	.09V	.05V
Vietnam	582	—V	—V	—V	—V	—V	—V	—V	1.18V	.84V	3.14V	—V	—V	—V	—V
Asia n.s.	598	—Y	—Y	—Y	—Y	—Y	—Y	—Y	.58Y	.62Y	.66Y	.70Y	.74Y	.78Y	.82Y
Europe	**170**	**1.4Y**	**2.3Y**	**1.7Y**	**5.0Y**	**3.9Y**	**25.1Y**	**46.3Y**	**3.8Y**	**4.5Y**	**6.1Y**	**9.5Y**	**9.7Y**	**14.1Y**	**13.2Y**
Azerbaijan	912	—V	—V	—V	—V	—V	—V	.04V	—V	—V	—V	—V	—V	—V	.09V
Belarus	913	—V	—V	—V	.04V	—V	.01V	—V	—V	—V	—V	—V	.30V	—V	—V
Bulgaria	918	—V	.06V	—V	—V	—V	.01V	.11V	.01V	.14V	.05V	—V	.02V	.04V	1.05V
Czech Republic	935	.13V	.06V	—V	.14V	.15V	.33V	.58V	.29V	.07V	1.66V	2.39V	1.93V	1.54V	1.56V
Estonia	939	—V	.38V	—V	—V	—V	—V	—V	.47V	—V	—V	—V	.04V	—V	—V
Hungary	944	.15V	.10V	.12V	—V	.30V	.01V	.03V	.03V	—V	.24V	.45V	.80V	1.13V	1.85V
Latvia	941	—Y	—Y	—Y	—Y	—V	.28V	.54V	—V	—V	—V	—Y	—V	—V	.01V
Lithuania	946	—V	.01V	.02V	.01V	.43V	1.01V	.09V	—V	—V	—V	.08V	.20V	.12V	—V
Macedonia, FYR	962	—V	—V	.01V	—V	—V	—V	—Y	—V	—V	—V	—V	—V	—V	—Y
Poland	964	.13V	.24V	.31V	1.17V	.62V	19.69V	35.18V	.26V	.54V	.80V	1.16V	.38V	.38V	.86V
Romania	968	.01V	.06V	.13V	1.08V	.05V	.01V	.21V	.03V	.01V	.04V	—V	—V	2.03V	.06V
Russia	922	.18V	.53V	.30V	1.54V	.91V	1.68V	6.49V	—V	.14V	2.13V	2.68V	3.17V	2.90V	2.64V
Slovak Republic	936	—V	—V	—Y	—Y	.10V	.03V	.02V	—V	.01V	.01Y	.01Y	.31V	1.38V	.38V
Turkey	186	.20V	.04V	.03V	.03V	.07V	.50V	1.06V	1.10V	1.19V	1.11V	2.33V	2.38V	4.41V	4.46V
Ukraine	926	.02V	.20V	—V	.01V	.08V	.10Y	.12Y	1.64V	2.45V	—V	.38V	.15V	.18Y	.22Y
Europe n.s.	884	.56Y	.61Y	.77Y	1.01Y	1.15Y	1.43Y	1.77Y	—Y	—Y	—Y	—Y	—Y	—Y	—Y
Middle East	**407**	**—Y**	**—Y**	**.3Y**	**.4Y**	**.5Y**	**.6Y**	**.7Y**	**4.6Y**	**4.6Y**	**4.3Y**	**5.0Y**	**5.1Y**	**7.2Y**	**8.3Y**
Egypt	469	—V	—Y	—Y	—Y	—Y	—Y	—Y	1.60V	1.74Y	2.20Y	2.89Y	3.30Y	4.08Y	5.06Y
Israel	436	—V	—V	—V	—V	—V	—V	—V	2.20V	2.09V	.88V	.55V	—V	.88V	.44V
Jordan	439	—V	—V	—V	—V	—V	—V	—V	—V	—V	—V	.02V	—V	—V	—V
Lebanon	446	—Y	—Y	—Y	—Y	—Y	—Y	—Y	.75Y	.82Y	1.03Y	1.36Y	1.55Y	1.92Y	2.38Y
Oman	449	—V	—V	—V	—Y	—Y	—Y	—Y	—V	—V	.15V	.20Y	.27Y	.34Y	.41Y
Saudi Arabia	456	.04V	—V	.01V	—V	—V	—Y	—Y	—Y	—Y	—Y	—Y	—Y	—Y	—Y
United Arab Emirates	466	—V	—V	.27V	.35Y	.45Y	.56Y	.72Y	—Y	—Y	—Y	—Y	—Y	—Y	—Y
Yemen, Republic of	474	—V	.02V	.02Y	—V	—V	—Y	—Y	—V	—V	—Y	.02V	—V	—Y	—Y
Western Hemisphere	**207**	**2.6Y**	**3.1Y**	**19.4Y**	**12.2Y**	**64.2Y**	**322.2Y**	**178.4Y**	**7.2Y**	**6.4Y**	**12.5Y**	**35.8Y**	**36.2Y**	**66.1Y**	**35.1Y**
Argentina	213	—V	—V	—V	—V	—V	—V	—V	1.85V	2.17V	.52V	18.65V	14.02V	38.85V	30.02V
Brazil	223	.08V	.46V	.22V	.62V	.22V	195.34V	175.29V	4.20V	2.62V	10.09V	14.32V	18.56V	22.22V	—V
Chile	228	—V	—V	.02V	.01V	58.60V	123.82V	—V	—V	—V	.42V	1.00V	1.19V	1.46V	1.92V
Colombia	233	.01V	—V	16.45V	8.73V	2.42V	—V	—V	.02V	—V	—V	.04V	—V	—V	—V
Costa Rica	238	—V	.05V	—V	—V	—V	—Y	—Y	—V	.17V	.02V	.02V	.07V	.08Y	.10Y
Guatemala	258	.03V	—V	—V	.01V	—V	—Y	—Y	—V	.30V	.49V	.36V	.07V	.09Y	.11Y
Jamaica	343	.01V	—V	—V	—V	—V	—V	—V	—V	—V	—V	—V	—V	—V	—V
Peru	293	—V	.02V	.03V	—V	—V	—V	—Y	.04V	—V	.02V	—V	.30V	1.16V	.37Y
St. Vincent & Grens.	364	—V	—V	—V	.02V	—V	—Y	—Y	—V	—V	—V	—V	—V	—Y	—Y
Uruguay	298	—V	—Y	—V	.01V	—V	—Y	—Y	.18V	.19Y	—V	.40V	.85V	1.05Y	1.31Y
Western Hem. n.s.	399	2.48Y	2.59Y	2.70Y	2.80Y	2.91Y	3.02Y	3.13Y	.87Y	.93Y	.99Y	1.05Y	1.11Y	1.17Y	1.24Y
Other Countries n.i.e.	**910**	**—Y**	**—Y**	**—Y**	**—Y**	**—Y**	**—Y**	**—Y**	**.4Y**	**.4Y**	**.5Y**	**.7Y**	**.7Y**	**.9Y**	**1.1Y**
North Korea	954	—Y	—Y	—Y	—Y	—Y	—Y	—Y	.36Y	.39Y	.50Y	.65Y	.74Y	.92Y	1.14Y
Memorandum Items															
European Union	998	848.97Y	1,068.08Y	719.28Y	825.34Y	822.40Y	725.35Y	907.07Y	274.85Y	387.18Y	481.65Y	537.31Y	658.15Y	780.17Y	950.46Y
Oil Exporting Ctys.	999	.73Y	.81Y	.73Y	.94Y	1.19Y	1.47Y	1.91Y	5.16Y	7.76Y	4.54Y	3.88Y	1.14Y	1.37Y	1.00Y
Non-Oil Develop.Ctys.	201	124.81Y	45.59Y	85.74Y	167.57Y	363.39Y	801.25Y	865.21Y	372.65Y	466.57Y	507.65Y	741.89Y	860.20Y	1,317.99Y	1,863.88Y
PERCENT DISTRIBUTION															
Industrial Countries	**101**	**88.9**	**96.5**	**91.3**	**85.0**	**74.6**	**49.5**	**55.1**	**45.0**	**48.6**	**51.2**	**46.1**	**47.5**	**41.3**	**38.6**
Developing Countries	**202**	**11.1**	**3.5**	**8.7**	**15.0**	**25.4**	**50.5**	**44.9**	**54.9**	**51.3**	**48.8**	**53.8**	**52.5**	**58.7**	**61.3**
Africa	**607**	**9.8**	**2.1**	**3.8**	**4.7**	**8.8**	**6.7**	**10.7**	**45.6**	**42.3**	**38.9**	**44.1**	**43.2**	**49.3**	**54.5**
Asia	**507**	**.9**	**1.0**	**2.8**	**8.7**	**11.8**	**21.9**	**22.5**	**7.1**	**7.4**	**7.7**	**6.1**	**6.1**	**5.5**	**5.0**
Europe	**170**	**.1**	**.2**	**.2**	**.4**	**.3**	**1.6**	**2.4**	**.6**	**.5**	**.6**	**.7**	**.6**	**.6**	**.4**
Middle East	**407**	**—**	**—**	**—**	**—**	**—**	**—**	**—**	**.7**	**.5**	**.4**	**.4**	**.3**	**.3**	**.3**
Western Hemisphere	**207**	**.2**	**.2**	**2.0**	**1.1**	**4.5**	**20.3**	**9.2**	**1.0**	**.7**	**1.2**	**2.6**	**2.2**	**2.9**	**1.2**
Other Countries n.i.e.	**910**	**—**	**—**	**—**	**—**	**—**	**—**	**—**	**.1**	**—**	**—**	**—**	**—**	**—**	**—**
ANNUAL PERCENT CHANGE															
World	**001**	**.2**	**17.4**	**–25.8**	**13.5**	**27.8**	**10.8**	**21.6**	**2.8**	**34.4**	**13.6**	**31.9**	**18.5**	**37.0**	**35.3**
Industrial Countries	**101**	**–8.0**	**27.4**	**–29.9**	**5.7**	**12.1**	**–26.5**	**35.5**	**.2**	**45.3**	**19.4**	**18.9**	**21.9**	**19.2**	**26.6**
Developing Countries	**202**	**258.8**	**–63.0**	**86.4**	**94.9**	**116.4**	**120.2**	**8.0**	**5.0**	**25.5**	**8.0**	**45.6**	**15.5**	**53.2**	**41.3**
Africa	**607**	**346.8**	**–75.1**	**35.9**	**40.3**	**139.4**	**–15.5**	**92.8**	**6.8**	**24.7**	**4.5**	**49.5**	**16.3**	**56.3**	**49.5**
Asia	**507**	**105.6**	**30.4**	**107.3**	**258.4**	**72.9**	**105.3**	**25.1**	**–15.5**	**39.2**	**19.2**	**4.8**	**18.5**	**22.1**	**22.4**
Europe	**170**	**–43.1**	**66.4**	**–26.9**	**201.2**	**–23.2**	**547.2**	**84.3**	**33.2**	**18.3**	**33.0**	**56.7**	**2.1**	**45.6**	**–6.4**
Middle East	**407**	**–73.2**	**–42.5**	**—**	**17.1**	**27.3**	**23.5**	**29.5**	**33.6**	**2.0**	**–8.2**	**18.1**	**1.7**	**40.9**	**14.9**
Western Hemisphere	**207**	**1.8**	**19.4**	**522.9**	**–37.1**	**425.7**	**402.2**	**–44.6**	**198.0**	**–10.7**	**96.3**	**185.8**	**.9**	**82.7**	**–46.9**
Other Countries n.i.e.	**910**	**—**	**—**	**....**	**....**	**....**	**....**	**....**	**10.4**	**8.5**	**26.6**	**31.3**	**14.3**	**23.6**	**24.1**

Congo, Republic of 634

	Exports 2001	2002	2003	2004	2005	2006	2007	Imports 2001	2002	2003	2004	2005	2006	2007
	Millions of U.S. Dollars							Millions of U.S. Dollars						
IFS World Total	**2,055.0**	**2,280.0**	**2,677.0**	**3,433.0**	**4,745.0**	**6,300.0**	**6,100.0**	**702.5**	**695.3**	**855.9**	**904.9**	**1,501.2**	**1,909.6**	**2,987.0**
DOTS World Total 001	**1,312.1**	**2,396.1**	**1,709.7**	**838.7**	**5,421.4Y**	**8,163.6Y**	**7,048.9Y**	**537.6**	**630.0**	**858.1**	**325.7**	**1,610.8Y**	**2,006.5Y**	**3,672.8Y**
Industrial Countries 101	**403.8**	**864.0**	**397.0**	**169.4**	**1,901.2Y**	**3,351.5Y**	**3,337.6Y**	**359.7**	**383.6**	**651.3**	**223.9**	**886.5Y**	**1,118.6Y**	**1,868.7Y**
United States 111	273.76	250.92	164.35	61.46	1,542.36V	2,895.00V	2,893.00V	59.22	66.15	69.73	32.88	114.29V	151.80V	154.11V
Canada 156	—	.01	.02	.08	1.10V	1.84V	3.84V	1.50	3.76	2.64	1.24	10.86V	16.50V	26.49V
Australia 193	—	—	.01	.01	3.37V	.37V	60.56V	.58	.30	1.54	1.90	.57V	1.97V	5.12V
Japan 158	1.70	96.57	.44	.26	1.77V	1.48V	4.06V	27.54	21.30	23.22	11.34	7.13V	11.17V	9.49V
New Zealand 196	—	.03	.02	—	.14V	.20V	.11V	.19	.50	1.63	.95	.83V	1.54V	1.68V
Austria 122	—	—	—	—	1.07V	.03V	—V	.30	.32	.42	.37	9.87V	13.75V	14.10V
Belgium 124	—	—	—	—	2.33V	6.73V	14.88V	—	—	—	—	71.55V	106.34V	139.94V
Cyprus 423	—	—	—	.01	—Y	.03V	.06V	.04	—	—	—	.48V	.18V	.29V
Denmark 128	.03	.04	.37	.39	1.69V	2.65V	3.30V	1.25	1.49	3.12	.81	5.26V	4.30V	12.74V
Finland 172	.26	.26	.07	—	.09V	.12V	.19V	.18	.29	.23	.09	1.18V	3.20V	3.44V
France 132	25.16	174.51	67.95	45.92	163.53V	164.00V	113.77V	127.15	165.69	190.78	106.35	363.30V	472.67V	666.11V
Germany 134	4.43	141.91	8.76	5.57	65.66V	50.45V	124.00V	16.33	23.18	35.72	20.21	33.98V	38.89V	68.13V
Greece 174	.80	.95	.71	.46	2.24V	.71V	.58V	.22	.27	.18	.05	1.14V	1.57V	.88V
Iceland 176	—	62.26	45.56	.03	.32V	.04V	—V	.10	.12	—	—	—V	.01V	.01V
Ireland 178	.05	.22	.71	.49	.99V	.87V	1.18V	4.11	5.34	8.56	4.69	13.06V	10.32V	13.59V
Italy 136	38.02	39.07	21.72	6.58	29.18V	139.40V	37.48V	79.61	52.96	43.12	19.62	105.49V	112.28V	378.37V
Luxembourg 137	—	—	—	—	—V	—V	—V	—	—	—	—	1.54V	1.30V	1.89V
Malta 181	—	—	—	—	—V	—V	—V	—	.02	.13	—	.18V	.38V	.43V
Netherlands 138	21.25	35.08	8.52	1.86	6.01V	5.84V	8.22V	29.16	28.91	255.80	14.76	59.10V	65.15V	85.44V
Norway 142	1.52	.03	.01	.11	18.61V	26.40V	5.98V	1.96	2.04	1.93	1.80	5.70V	10.68V	111.37V
Portugal 182	17.70	24.79	38.71	15.78	17.07V	13.99V	13.70V	4.11	4.10	1.71	.95	5.61V	5.95V	6.92V
Slovenia 961	—	—	—	—	—V	—V	.13V	.03	.01	—	.03	—V	.06V	.11V
Spain 184	15.88	18.05	26.53	20.56	29.43V	23.61V	24.13V	4.24	3.94	5.72	3.13	18.24V	20.86V	39.13V
Sweden 144	—	—	.01	.03	.40V	.61V	.39V	.53	1.09	2.18	1.32	13.79V	9.69V	20.21V
Switzerland 146	.51	—	6.48	7.39	.79V	.87V	1.21V	1.30	1.86	2.91	1.46	2.49V	3.52V	7.92V
United Kingdom 112	2.74	19.31	6.06	2.46	13.06V	16.32V	26.86V	—	—	—	—	40.86V	54.55V	100.80V
Developing Countries 202	**700.9**	**1,259.2**	**1,180.9**	**590.2**	**3,429.9Y**	**4,700.4Y**	**3,572.8Y**	**155.9**	**217.7**	**192.9**	**96.2**	**717.9Y**	**880.0Y**	**1,794.4Y**
Africa 607	**24.6**	**92.8**	**34.0**	**40.2**	**97.8Y**	**84.7Y**	**106.4Y**	**77.1**	**68.3**	**89.5**	**36.5**	**184.0Y**	**174.8Y**	**207.7Y**
Algeria 612	—	.18	.03	.01	.02Y	.02Y	.03Y	.01	—	—	—	—Y	—Y	—Y
Angola 614	5.20	9.77	4.82	7.80	8.92Y	11.02Y	13.67Y	5.08	2.70	.47	.27	.30Y	.37Y	.46Y
Benin 638	2.72	4.80	1.00	3.49	1.64V	2.03Y	2.52Y	.37	.30	.27	.10	.35V	.44Y	.54Y
Botswana 616	—	—	—	—	—Y	—Y	—Y	.04	—	—	—	—Y	—Y	—Y
Burkina Faso 748	—	—	—	—	—Y	—Y	—Y	—	—	.30	—	—Y	—Y	—Y
Burundi 618	—	—	—	—	—V	—V	—Y	—	—	—	—	.05V	—V	—Y
Cameroon 622	1.09	26.59	10.18	1.04	1.19Y	1.47Y	1.83Y	22.14	22.88	29.65	11.19	12.78Y	15.80Y	19.61Y
Cape Verde 624	—	.24	.27	—	—Y	—Y	—Y	—	—	—	—	—Y	—Y	—Y
Central African Rep. 626	.95	.66	.93	.19	.22Y	.27Y	.34Y	.13	.13	.21	.17	.19Y	.24Y	.29Y
Chad 628	.02	.11	.08	—	—Y	—Y	—Y	.04	.06	.01	.03	.03Y	.04Y	.05Y
Congo, Dem. Rep. of 636	3.74	3.91	.80	.82	.93Y	1.15Y	1.43Y	2.95	5.49	5.56	2.41	2.76Y	3.41Y	4.23Y
Côte d'Ivoire 662	3.17	20.25	3.98	1.67	10.84V	10.97V	13.61Y	6.94	6.94	10.20	3.91	23.85V	32.56V	40.41Y
Djibouti 611	—	.01	—	—	—Y	—Y	—Y	—	—	—	—	—Y	—Y	—Y
Equatorial Guinea 642	.09	.14	.09	.42	.48Y	.60Y	.74Y	.06	.02	.28	.03	.03Y	.04Y	.05Y
Gabon 646	1.22	2.73	2.66	17.15	19.60Y	24.22Y	30.05Y	9.03	2.93	1.90	.95	1.09Y	1.34Y	1.67Y
Gambia, The 648	—	—	—	—	—Y	—Y	—Y	.03	.04	.10	—	—Y	—Y	—Y
Ghana 652	3.28	8.09	.31	—	—Y	—Y	—Y	.03	.37	.37	.04	.05Y	.06Y	.08Y
Guinea 656	—	—	—	—	—Y	—Y	—Y	.06	.04	—	—	—Y	—Y	—Y
Kenya 664	—	—	—	—	—Y	—Y	—Y	.10	.02	.12	.35	.40Y	.49Y	.61Y
Liberia 668	.01	—	.01	—	—Y	—Y	—Y	—	—	—	.01	.01Y	.01Y	.02Y
Madagascar 674	—	.01	—	—	—Y	—Y	—Y	—	—	.01	—	—Y	—Y	—Y
Mali 678	—	—	—	—	—Y	—Y	—Y	.05	—	.02	—	—Y	—Y	—Y
Mauritania 682	—	—	.02	—	—Y	—Y	—Y	1.08	1.66	7.71	4.09	4.67Y	5.78Y	7.17Y
Mauritius 684	.16	.47	.13	.43	.91V	1.24V	2.09V	.03	.02	.15	.04	.43V	.50V	.70V
Morocco 686	1.47	.40	1.68	4.03	4.74V	5.86Y	7.27Y	2.81	2.15	3.45	1.63	15.95V	19.71Y	24.46Y
Mozambique 688	—	—	—	—	—V	—V	—Y	.01	.14	—	—	—V	—V	—Y
Niger 692	—	—	—	.08	.09Y	.11Y	.13Y	.01	.03	—	—	—Y	—Y	—Y
Nigeria 694	.01	1.97	1.98	.37	.47Y	.59Y	.76Y	3.03	2.17	1.69	.92	1.25Y	1.57Y	1.89Y
Rwanda 714	—	—	.01	—	—Y	—Y	—Y	—	—	—	—	—Y	—Y	—Y
São Tomé & Príncipe 716	—	—	.02	—	—Y	—Y	—Y	—	—	—	—	—Y	—Y	—Y
Senegal 722	.25	8.29	3.87	1.67	12.44V	6.88V	8.54Y	5.05	5.64	9.21	3.27	11.89V	13.92V	17.27Y
Seychelles 718	....	....	....	....	....	....	....	—	—	.01	—	—Y	—Y	—Y
South Africa 199	1.07	1.72	.73	.87	20.76V	2.54V	3.52V	14.74	11.75	15.76	6.34	62.52V	68.70V	76.00V
Sudan 732	—	—	—	—	1.88V	.18V	.73V	—	—	.03	—	—V	—V	—V
Swaziland 734	—	—	—	—	—Y	—Y	—Y	2.32	.46	—	—	—Y	—Y	—Y
Tanzania 738	—	—	—	—	—Y	—Y	—Y	.01	—	.06	—	—Y	—Y	—Y
Togo 742	.01	2.07	.10	—	.08V	.10Y	.12Y	.45	1.60	.80	.28	1.02V	1.26Y	1.57Y
Tunisia 744	.14	.38	.31	.12	1.44V	1.51V	1.87Y	.41	.72	1.12	.46	6.63V	7.66V	9.51Y
Uganda 746	—	—	—	—	—Y	—Y	—Y	.04	.03	—	—	—Y	—Y	—Y
Zambia 754	—	.01	—	—	—V	—V	.09V	—	—	—	—	—V	—V	—V
Zimbabwe 698	—	—	—	—	10.23V	12.90V	16.01Y	.06	—	.05	—	37.78V	.86V	1.06Y
Africa n.s. 799	—	—	—	—	.92Y	1.00Y	1.08Y	—	—	—	—	—Y	—Y	—Y

		Exports							Imports						
		2001	2002	2003	2004	2005	2006	2007	2001	2002	2003	2004	2005	2006	2007
		Millions of U.S. Dollars							*Millions of U.S. Dollars*						
Asia	**507**	**639.4**	**1,070.3**	**1,080.3**	**531.7**	**3,221.2Y**	**4,247.4Y**	**3,261.0Y**	**40.0**	**63.6**	**59.4**	**37.6**	**411.3Y**	**568.1Y**	**1,354.1Y**
Afghanistan, I.S. of	512	....	....	....	....	....	....	....	—	—	.01	—	—Y	—Y	—Y
Bangladesh	513	—	—	—	—	—V	—V	—V	.02	.01	.05	.03	—V	—Y	—Y
Cambodia	522	....	....	....	....	....	....	....	—	.01	.01	.01	.03V	—V	—Y
China,P.R.: Mainland	924	78.09	167.87	373.54	224.94	2,070.92V	2,531.47V	2,571.15V	6.89	25.96	22.83	17.08	159.19V	265.87V	462.11V
China,P.R.:Hong Kong	532	2.43	.49	1.03	4.16	6.14V	3.54V	4.16V	4.94	4.26	6.31	1.84	13.43V	14.01V	14.92V
India	534	20.58	18.66	—	31.35	34.49V	42.63Y	52.91Y	5.98	11.86	10.36	6.44	112.96V	139.61Y	173.26Y
Indonesia	536	—	21.19	24.74	.01	.06V	.08V	.20V	6.17	5.57	2.77	1.40	12.32V	14.15V	16.74V
Korea	542	20.60	173.67	237.63	40.15	380.78V	753.85V	175.49V	.79	.61	.59	.44	18.92V	19.38V	539.06V
Malaysia	548	.10	.21	.03	.09	—V	.31V	13.41V	.46	1.62	3.20	2.66	18.26V	20.10V	41.47V
Pakistan	564	—	—	—	—	.07V	.09Y	.11Y	2.40	.32	.64	.07	11.94V	14.76Y	18.32Y
Philippines	566	—	—	—	—	.01V	—V	—V	.01	.05	.11	.05	.04V	.41V	.35V
Singapore	576	.34	44.07	.09	—	—V	—V	—V	4.62	4.81	4.87	3.92	—V	—V	—V
Sri Lanka	524	—	—	—	—	—Y	—Y	—Y	.03	.01	.01	—	—Y	—Y	—Y
Taiwan Province of China	528	517.28	644.08	443.21	231.05	705.36V	897.10V	375.47V	.49	.50	.40	.16	2.70V	3.06V	1.93V
Thailand	578	—	.01	—	—	22.74V	17.65V	67.37V	7.18	7.51	6.00	2.78	27.16V	39.28V	45.34V
Vietnam	582	—	—	—	—	—V	—V	—V	—	.46	1.24	.72	—V	—V	—V
Asia n.s.	598	—	—	—	—	.67Y	.72Y	.78Y	—	—	—	—	34.33Y	37.46Y	40.58Y
Europe	**170**	**2.9**	**.6**	**2.9**	**1.5**	**16.6Y**	**37.9Y**	**37.3Y**	**25.6**	**28.5**	**24.3**	**15.4**	**28.8Y**	**30.9Y**	**42.2Y**
Albania	914	—	—	—	—	—V	—V	.01V	—	—	—	1.27	.01V	—V	—V
Azerbaijan	912	.01	—	.01	—	.01V	—V	—V	—	—	—	—	—V	—V	—V
Belarus	913	—	—	—	—	—V	.01V	.08V	—	—	—	—	.82V	1.40V	3.41V
Bulgaria	918	—	—	—	—	1.62V	19.91V	18.84V	.02	—	.12	.07	.39V	2.37V	.08V
Croatia	960	—	—	—	—	—V	—V	—V	.04	.03	.05	—	—V	—V	—V
Czech Republic	935	—	—	—	—	.80V	.49V	1.19V	.07	.05	.14	.08	1.70V	1.50V	3.13V
Estonia	939	—	—	—	—	—V	—V	—V	.31	.10	.62	—	—V	.01V	.04V
Hungary	944	—	—	—	—	.05V	.03V	.09V	.15	.20	.37	.21	.22V	.85V	.77V
Kazakhstan	916	—	—	—	—	—Y	—Y	—Y	—	—	.02	—	—Y	—Y	—Y
Latvia	941	—	—	—	—	.56V	.41V	.13V	—	—	—	—	.02V	—V	—V
Lithuania	946	—	.02	.03	.02	.15V	.10V	.08V	—	.01	.04	—	.06V	.23V	.37V
Macedonia, FYR	962	—	—	—	—	—V	—V	—Y	—	—	—	—	—V	.04V	.05Y
Moldova	921	....	....	....	....	....	....	....	—	—	—	—	.28V	.35Y	.43Y
Poland	964	—	—	—	.01	.28V	1.35V	1.04V	.13	.13	.48	.53	2.91V	1.51V	5.45V
Romania	968	—	—	—	—	.18V	.35V	.93V	.29	.86	.51	.29	1.12V	1.20V	1.38V
Russia	922	.04	.04	.27	.20	.41V	.86V	1.06V	.56	.12	.67	.20	.35V	1.79V	1.47V
Slovak Republic	936	—	—	—	—	.03V	.15V	—V	.01	—	.08	—	.81V	.28V	.53V
Turkey	186	2.89	.49	2.58	1.29	12.31V	13.95V	13.48V	1.21	2.22	2.75	2.89	17.56V	16.21V	21.19V
Ukraine	926	—	—	—	—	.23V	.29Y	.36Y	22.83	24.75	18.44	9.86	2.56V	3.16Y	3.92Y
Yugoslavia n.s.	966	—	—	—	—	—Y	—Y	—Y	—	.01	—	—	—Y	—Y	—Y
Middle East	**407**	**1.0**	**36.7**	**4.0**	**4.5**	**5.8Y**	**7.3Y**	**9.9Y**	**8.2**	**50.5**	**8.4**	**3.2**	**6.2Y**	**13.3Y**	**18.2Y**
Bahrain	419	—	—	—	—	—Y	—Y	—Y	—	1.96	.57	.03	.04Y	.05Y	.06Y
Egypt	469	—	.02	.08	.09	.11Y	.13Y	.16Y	.31	.66	1.48	.57	.66Y	.81Y	1.01Y
Iran, I.R. of	429	—	—	—	—	—Y	—Y	—Y	3.68	.59	1.37	—	—Y	—Y	—Y
Israel	436	.78	36.51	2.86	.19	.09V	.18V	.64V	.05	.04	.07	.39	1.76V	7.04V	11.88V
Jordan	439	—	—	—	—	—V	.08V	.07V	—	—	.04	—	.98V	2.00V	1.07V
Kuwait	443	.03	—	.03	—	—Y	—Y	—Y	—	—	—	—	—Y	—Y	—Y
Lebanon	446	—	—	.04	.01	.01Y	.02Y	.02Y	.57	37.92	2.30	1.32	1.51Y	1.87Y	2.32Y
Libya	672	.01	.09	—	—	—Y	.01Y	.01Y	—	—	—	—	—Y	—Y	—Y
Oman	449	—	—	—	—	—Y	—Y	—Y	—	—	—	.04	.06Y	.07Y	.09Y
Qatar	453	—	—	—	—	—V	—V	—Y	.01	.22	.01	.02	—V	—V	—Y
Saudi Arabia	456	.10	.01	.05	.18	.49V	.61Y	.79Y	3.57	9.09	2.49	.72	.99Y	1.24Y	1.50Y
Syrian Arab Republic	463	—	.01	.15	—	—Y	—Y	—Y	—	.02	.07	.13	.17Y	.21Y	.27Y
United Arab Emirates	466	.11	.04	.84	4.01	5.11Y	6.31Y	8.18Y	....	....	....	....	....	....	....
Western Hemisphere	**207**	**32.9**	**58.9**	**59.7**	**12.3**	**88.4Y**	**323.1Y**	**158.2Y**	**5.0**	**6.8**	**11.3**	**3.4**	**87.6Y**	**93.0Y**	**172.2Y**
Argentina	213	—	4.08	2.87	—	.06V	.11V	.04V	2.68	2.52	.03	.01	47.27V	49.23V	60.31V
Bahamas, The	313	—	—	.05	—	—Y	—Y	—Y	—	—	—	—	—Y	—Y	—Y
Belize	339	—	3.50	—	—	—Y	—Y	—Y	—	—	—	—	—Y	—Y	—Y
Bermuda	319	.12	.40	.26	.08	—V	—V	—Y	—	—	—	—	—Y	—Y	—Y
Bolivia	218	—	—	—	.07	—V	—Y	—Y	—	—	—	—	—Y	—Y	—Y
Brazil	223	21.71	16.45	56.21	12.10	66.10V	291.38V	135.82V	1.99	3.06	.30	3.09	39.27V	37.50V	92.46V
Chile	228	10.88	33.42	—	—	1.65V	13.31V	1.73V	.01	.02	.02	—	—V	—V	—V
Colombia	233	—	—	—	—	.01V	.01V	1.34V	.06	.06	.01	.02	.30V	.83V	1.52V
Costa Rica	238	—	—	—	—	—V	—Y	—Y	—	—	.03	.01	.01Y	.01Y	.01Y
Dominican Republic	243	.14	—	—	—	—Y	—Y	—Y	—	—	—	—	—Y	—Y	—Y
Ecuador	248	—	—	—	—	18.45V	14.61V	18.13Y	—	—	—	—	.15V	.28V	.35Y
Greenland	326	....	....	....	....	....	....	....	—	—	.04	—	—Y	—Y	—Y
Guatemala	258	....	....	....	....	....	....	....	—	—	.23	—	—V	.01Y	.01Y
Haiti	263	—	—	—	—	—Y	—Y	—Y	—	—	.01	—	—Y	—Y	—Y
Jamaica	343	—	—	—	—	—V	—V	—V	—	.03	—	—	—V	—V	—V
Mexico	273	.03	1.08	.34	.01	2.12V	3.59V	1.00V	.03	.03	—	.02	.08V	3.29V	14.50V
Netherlands Antilles	353	—	—	—	—	—Y	—Y	—Y	.04	.40	—	.19	.22Y	.27Y	.33Y
Paraguay	288	—	—	—	—	—V	—V	—Y	—	—	3.84	—	.18V	.07V	.09Y
Peru	293	—	—	—	—	—V	—V	—Y	—	.02	6.69	—	.11V	1.51V	2.62Y
Uruguay	298	—	—	—	—	—V	—Y	—Y	.05	.38	—	.09	—V	—Y	—Y
Venezuela, Rep. Bol	299	.01	—	—	.01	—V	—V	—V	—	.28	—	—	—V	—V	—Y
Western Hem. n.s.	399	—	—	—	.02	.04Y	.06Y	.08Y	.14	.02	.10	—	—Y	—Y	—Y

	Exports							Imports						
	2001	2002	2003	2004	2005	2006	2007	2001	2002	2003	2004	2005	2006	2007
	Millions of U.S. Dollars							*Millions of U.S. Dollars*						
Other Countries n.i.e.....910	**207.3**	**270.0**	**130.3**	**70.2**	**80.2Y**	**99.1Y**	**123.0Y**	**—**	**—**	**1.0**	**—**	**—Y**	**—Y**	**—Y**
Cuba.....928	—	—	—	—	—Y	—Y	—Y	—	—	1.00	—	—Y	—Y	—Y
North Korea.....954	207.29	269.95	130.25	70.21	80.22Y	99.15Y	123.04Y	—	—	—	—	—Y	—Y	—Y
Countries & Areas n.s.....898	**—**	**3.0**	**1.5**	**8.8**	**10.1Y**	**12.5Y**	**15.5Y**	**22.1**	**28.6**	**12.9**	**5.5**	**6.3Y**	**7.8Y**	**9.7Y**
Memorandum Items														
European Union.....998	126.33	454.20	180.15	100.14	334.60Y	427.88Y	371.38Y	267.93	288.09	549.42	173.21	750.36Y	925.84Y	1,562.82Y
Oil Exporting Ctys.....999	.27	23.49	27.66	4.61	6.16Y	7.61Y	9.96Y	16.47	17.92	8.34	3.11	14.61Y	17.03Y	20.22Y
Non-Oil Develop.Ctys.....201	700.64	1,235.74	1,153.28	585.62	3,423.76Y	4,692.79Y	3,562.83Y	139.40	199.78	184.53	93.05	703.29Y	863.00Y	1,774.14Y
PERCENT DISTRIBUTION														
Industrial Countries.....101	**30.8**	**36.1**	**23.2**	**20.2**	**35.1**	**41.1**	**47.3**	**66.9**	**60.9**	**75.9**	**68.8**	**55.0**	**55.8**	**50.9**
Developing Countries.....202	**53.4**	**52.6**	**69.1**	**70.4**	**63.3**	**57.6**	**50.7**	**29.0**	**34.6**	**22.5**	**29.5**	**44.6**	**43.9**	**48.9**
Africa.....607	**1.9**	**3.9**	**2.0**	**4.8**	**1.8**	**1.0**	**1.5**	**14.3**	**10.8**	**10.4**	**11.2**	**11.4**	**8.7**	**5.7**
Asia.....507	**48.7**	**44.7**	**63.2**	**63.4**	**59.4**	**52.0**	**46.3**	**7.4**	**10.1**	**6.9**	**11.5**	**25.5**	**28.3**	**36.9**
Europe.....170	**.2**	**—**	**.2**	**.2**	**.3**	**.5**	**.5**	**4.8**	**4.5**	**2.8**	**4.7**	**1.8**	**1.5**	**1.2**
Middle East.....407	**.1**	**1.5**	**.2**	**.5**	**.1**	**.1**	**.1**	**1.5**	**8.0**	**1.0**	**1.0**	**.4**	**.7**	**.5**
Western Hemisphere.....207	**2.5**	**2.5**	**3.5**	**1.5**	**1.6**	**4.0**	**2.2**	**.9**	**1.1**	**1.3**	**1.1**	**5.4**	**4.6**	**4.7**
Other Countries n.i.e.....910	**15.8**	**11.3**	**7.6**	**8.4**	**1.5**	**1.2**	**1.7**	**—**	**—**	**.1**	**—**	**—**	**—**	**—**
ANNUAL PERCENT CHANGE														
World.....001	**–39.1**	**82.6**	**–28.6**	**–50.9**	**546.4**	**50.6**	**–13.7**	**9.2**	**17.2**	**36.2**	**–62.0**	**394.6**	**24.6**	**83.0**
Industrial Countries.....101	**–39.7**	**114.0**	**–54.0**	**–57.3**	**—**	**76.3**	**–.4**	**10.6**	**6.7**	**69.8**	**–65.6**	**295.9**	**26.2**	**67.1**
Developing Countries.....202	**–47.2**	**79.7**	**–6.2**	**–50.0**	**481.1**	**37.0**	**–24.0**	**17.6**	**39.7**	**–11.4**	**–50.1**	**646.6**	**22.6**	**103.9**
Africa.....607	**–65.3**	**277.0**	**–63.3**	**18.1**	**143.4**	**–13.5**	**25.7**	**14.2**	**–11.4**	**31.0**	**–59.2**	**404.4**	**–5.0**	**18.8**
Asia.....507	**–43.5**	**67.4**	**.9**	**–50.8**	**505.8**	**31.9**	**–23.2**	**13.8**	**58.9**	**–6.6**	**–36.7**	**993.9**	**38.1**	**138.4**
Europe.....170	**311.0**	**–81.2**	**421.7**	**–47.2**	**992.6**	**127.9**	**–1.6**	**11.0**	**11.2**	**–14.7**	**–36.6**	**86.9**	**7.3**	**36.8**
Middle East.....407	**–94.8**	**—**	**–89.0**	**11.1**	**29.5**	**25.9**	**34.5**	**79.4**	**517.8**	**–83.4**	**–61.5**	**90.4**	**115.7**	**36.9**
Western Hemisphere.....207	**–68.0**	**79.1**	**1.4**	**–79.4**	**620.3**	**265.3**	**–51.0**	**117.2**	**36.8**	**65.4**	**–69.7**	**—**	**6.2**	**85.2**
Other Countries n.i.e.....910	**32.3**	**30.2**	**–51.7**	**–46.1**	**14.3**	**23.6**	**24.1**	**10.0**	**8.5**	**—**	**31.3**	**....**	**....**	**....**

		Exports							Imports						
		2001	2002	2003	2004	2005	2006	2007	2001	2002	2003	2004	2005	2006	2007
		Millions of U.S. Dollars							*Millions of U.S. Dollars*						
IFS World Total		**5,021.4**	**5,263.5**	**6,102.2**	**6,301.5**	**7,026.4**	**8,215.5**	**9,375.7**	**6,568.6**	**7,187.9**	**7,663.2**	**8,268.0**	**9,812.0**	**11,520.1**	**12,957.4**
DOTS World Total	**001**	**5,005.9**	**5,263.5**	**6,102.2**	**6,301.5**	**7,021.0**	**13,362.7Y**	**14,887.1Y**	**6,564.3**	**7,187.9**	**7,663.2**	**8,268.0**	**9,806.7**	**10,965.9Y**	**12,300.9Y**
Industrial Countries	**101**	**1,375.3**	**1,387.5**	**4,172.7**	**4,106.2**	**4,245.4**	**7,829.5Y**	**8,307.6Y**	**2,435.3**	**2,695.7**	**5,356.4**	**5,302.8**	**6,044.5**	**6,723.5Y**	**7,324.5Y**
United States	111	814.28	807.46	3,013.30	2,956.70	2,991.32	3,712.55V	3,826.00V	1,505.70	1,595.49	3,917.33	3,812.53	4,050.82	4,545.53V	5,038.66V
Canada	156	22.08	25.05	29.50	33.25	54.80	343.29V	341.61V	69.00	68.41	73.28	82.71	90.38	66.93V	84.49V
Australia	193	.98	1.03	7.31	5.72	4.87	34.59V	49.81V	3.74	1.41	2.28	4.14	5.09	12.66V	38.21V
Japan	158	15.25	16.23	58.66	40.69	50.55	260.06V	260.55V	214.63	287.03	308.11	483.72	551.98	542.45V	667.08V
New Zealand	196	.07	.13	.37	.26	.44	2.26V	3.14V	1.71	2.81	2.86	1.50	1.66	1.54V	2.61V
Austria	122	.17	.18	.30	.22	.45	16.57V	2.94V	8.96	10.08	8.56	8.02	11.53	12.86V	14.54V
Belgium	124	—	—	—	—	—	330.61V	526.26V	—	—	—	—	—	39.30V	115.82V
Belgium-Luxembourg n.s.	127	86.86	78.40	91.58	108.13	117.85	—Y	—Y	36.65	37.86	57.42	42.44	40.04	—Y	—Y
Cyprus	423	.01	.08	.01	.01	.03	.01V	.06V	.03	.02	.02	.02	.96	—V	—V
Denmark	128	1.13	1.22	1.47	1.63	1.26	13.10V	2.21V	15.71	7.77	10.34	11.37	6.87	11.08V	13.72V
Finland	172	5.07	2.76	15.37	11.26	4.41	4.14V	1.49V	3.43	3.42	32.63	19.20	14.78	16.40V	14.19V
France	132	30.85	27.07	31.36	34.82	28.39	33.43V	45.58V	74.13	62.53	194.61	90.87	181.45	172.29V	169.80V
Germany	134	106.29	125.90	179.67	235.88	188.52	188.75V	213.88V	126.74	143.89	165.89	176.81	157.16	178.63V	201.74V
Greece	174	1.14	.59	.58	.94	.44	4.93V	4.08V	.29	.45	2.24	.33	.49	9.89V	.84V
Iceland	176	.03	.21	2.06	—	.13	2.20V	3.91V	—	.01	.01	.01	.06	.01V	—V
Ireland	178	.50	11.10	24.87	31.33	37.78	36.47V	10.89V	7.47	14.85	10.35	45.26	420.73	549.02V	282.05V
Italy	136	93.11	73.15	84.71	70.07	63.38	112.68V	148.16V	67.02	80.18	112.08	91.74	88.43	109.91V	148.79V
Luxembourg	137	—	—	—	—	—	.29V	.74V	—	—	—	—	—	2.08V	4.21V
Malta	181	.02	.03	—	.01	.02	.22V	.01V	—	—	—	.04	.03	.06V	.02V
Netherlands	138	84.17	82.34	359.92	331.69	446.77	1,656.20V	1,626.06V	101.95	122.81	162.49	132.07	140.13	174.55V	179.32V
Norway	142	1.36	1.25	.37	.47	.59	45.45V	49.15V	2.63	1.02	1.12	5.73	8.60	7.29V	5.93V
Portugal	182	4.11	3.11	5.94	11.31	14.80	42.52V	57.86V	6.01	2.76	8.31	2.50	2.54	3.95V	5.12V
Slovenia	961	—	.02	.03	.01	.01	.44V	1.15V	.03	.07	.23	.16	3.78	2.12V	.25V
Spain	184	19.82	18.31	31.63	25.86	33.99	37.35V	75.33V	102.54	132.60	131.64	111.32	119.68	116.27V	138.85V
Sweden	144	45.37	55.17	71.62	73.59	73.51	65.48V	64.19V	10.05	13.21	20.88	25.84	21.44	30.61V	41.51V
Switzerland	146	1.61	2.80	5.96	4.23	5.70	49.80V	60.94V	29.93	26.90	53.00	69.92	65.91	49.73V	55.00V
United Kingdom	112	41.05	53.86	156.05	128.18	125.39	836.12V	931.61V	46.96	80.09	80.69	84.52	59.95	68.39V	101.69V
Developing Countries	**202**	**924.0**	**884.4**	**1,916.9**	**2,180.5**	**2,761.3**	**5,515.5Y**	**6,557.5Y**	**1,642.7**	**1,989.3**	**2,268.9**	**2,920.3**	**3,705.1**	**4,171.8Y**	**4,888.9Y**
Africa	**607**	**3.2**	**3.8**	**3.8**	**8.9**	**10.0**	**45.3Y**	**41.2Y**	**1.5**	**1.3**	**5.7**	**6.4**	**3.1**	**15.3Y**	**10.0Y**
Algeria	612	.15	—	.16	.40	.28	.35Y	.45Y	—	.02	—	.02	.01	.02Y	.02Y
Angola	614	—	—	—	—	—	—Y	—Y	.01	—	—	—	.05	.07Y	.08Y
Botswana	616	—	—	—	—	—	—Y	—Y	—	.01	.01	.01	—	.01Y	.01Y
Burkina Faso	748	—	—	—	—	—	—Y	—Y	—	—	.17	—	—	—Y	—Y
Burundi	618	—	—	—	—	.04	—V	—Y	—	—	—	—	—	—Y	—Y
Cameroon	622	1.93	2.33	1.94	5.92	6.06	7.48Y	9.29Y	—	—	—	—	—	—Y	—Y
Central African Rep.	626	—	—	—	.02	.02	.02Y	.02Y	.01	.01	.02	.02	—	—Y	—Y
Chad	628	....	....	....	....	....	....	....	—	—	—	.01	—	—Y	—Y
Comoros	632	....	....	....	....	....	....	....	.01	.03	—	—	—	—Y	—Y
Congo, Dem. Rep. of	636	—	.15	.01	.02	.06	.08Y	.09Y	—	.06	—	—	—	—Y	—Y
Congo, Republic of	634	—	—	—	—	—	.01Y	.01Y	—	—	—	—	—	—Y	—Y
Côte d'Ivoire	662	—	—	.01	—	.03	.08V	.10Y	—	—	—	—	.01	—V	—Y
Equatorial Guinea	642	....	....	....	....	....	....	....	.15	—	—	4.13	—	—Y	—Y
Ethiopia	644	—	—	—	.04	.14	.17Y	.21Y	.01	—	—	—	.01	.01Y	.01Y
Gambia, The	648	....	....	....	....	....	....	....	—	.01	—	.04	—	—Y	—Y
Ghana	652	—	.04	.19	.09	.01	.02Y	.02Y	—	—	—	.04	.03	.03Y	.04Y
Guinea-Bissau	654	....	....	....	....	....	....	....	—	.01	—	—	—	—Y	—Y
Kenya	664	—	.25	.02	.01	.02	.02Y	.02Y	.05	—	.05	.10	.02	.02Y	.03Y
Madagascar	674	—	—	—	—	—	—Y	—Y	—	.01	—	.02	.04	.05Y	.07Y
Malawi	676	....	....	....	....	....	....	....	.27	—	.25	.31	.39	.48Y	.59Y
Mauritania	682	—	—	—	—	—	—Y	—Y	—	—	—	—	.02	.02Y	.03Y
Mauritius	684	—	—	.01	.14	.01	.33V	.28V	.01	.07	.01	.01	.07	.01V	—V
Morocco	686	.26	.26	.36	.48	.66	.82Y	1.01Y	.27	.01	.16	.20	1.33	1.64Y	2.04Y
Mozambique	688	—	—	—	—	—	—V	—Y	.01	—	.02	—	—	—V	—Y
Nigeria	694	.03	.24	.37	.14	—	—Y	—Y	—	.07	.03	—	.06	.07Y	.08Y
Rwanda	714	—	—	—	—	—	—Y	—Y	—	—	—	—	—	—Y	.01Y
São Tomé & Príncipe	716	.04	—	—	.01	.01	.02Y	.02Y	—	—	—	.01	—	—Y	—Y
Senegal	722	—	—	—	—	—	.04V	.05Y	—	—	—	—	—	—V	—Y
Sierra Leone	724	.02	—	—	—	—	—Y	—Y	—	—	—	—	—	—Y	—Y
South Africa	199	.78	.49	.71	1.67	2.63	35.36V	28.97V	.71	.92	.67	1.01	1.06	12.84V	7.03V
Tanzania	738	—	—	—	—	—	—Y	—Y	—	—	—	.01	—	—Y	—Y
Tunisia	744	—	—	—	—	—	.50V	.62Y	—	.04	—	.01	.02	—V	—Y
Uganda	746	—	—	—	—	—	—Y	—Y	—	—	.02	.01	—	—Y	—Y
Zambia	754	—	—	—	.02	.02	—V	—V	—	—	4.33	.38	—	—V	—V
Zimbabwe	698	—	—	—	—	—	—V	—Y	—	.02	—	—	—	—V	—Y
Asia	**507**	**19.9**	**19.1**	**548.1**	**571.6**	**979.7**	**2,731.8Y**	**3,459.0Y**	**159.3**	**371.1**	**438.7**	**637.3**	**948.3**	**1,117.5Y**	**1,326.8Y**
Afghanistan, I.S. of	512	....	....	....	....	....	....	....	.06	.39	.14	.09	.04	.05Y	.07Y
Bangladesh	513	—	—	—	.03	.08	—V	—V	.37	.46	.65	.49	.67	.83Y	1.03Y
Cambodia	522	....	....	....	....	....	....	....	—	—	—	.01	.02	.01V	.01Y
China,P.R.: Mainland	924	3.65	2.65	88.83	163.94	244.91	1,588.44V	2,096.88V	90.45	109.85	160.23	272.54	409.25	449.83V	624.50V

		Exports							Imports						
		2001	2002	2003	2004	2005	2006	2007	2001	2002	2003	2004	2005	2006	2007
		Millions of U.S. Dollars							*Millions of U.S. Dollars*						
China,P.R.:Hong Kong	532	13.69	8.19	132.82	136.96	485.09	319.48V	453.54V	28.01	27.75	49.89	57.71	62.44	36.21V	38.96V
China,P.R.:Macao	546	—	—	—	—	—	.01V	.02V	.01	—	.04	.01	.04	—V	.07V
Fiji	819	—	—	—	—	—	—Y	—Y	—	—	—	—	.29	.36Y	.45Y
French Polynesia	887	—	.32	—	—	.04	.05Y	.06Y	—	.01	.08	—	—	—Y	—Y
Guam	829	—	.02	.03	.03	.06	.07Y	.09Y	—	—	—	.03	—	—Y	—Y
India	534	1.13	3.03	9.28	7.69	7.55	9.33Y	11.58Y	8.32	11.81	13.43	19.10	29.24	36.14Y	44.85Y
Indonesia	536	.04	.03	.97	1.73	1.53	1.79V	1.99V	5.46	3.96	5.10	7.80	11.26	14.51V	20.65V
Kiribati	826	—	—	—	—	—	—Y	—Y	.02	.01	—	—	—	—Y	—Y
Korea	542	.05	1.17	11.31	10.97	20.91	52.79V	103.31V	3.08	133.64	103.58	126.29	177.31	260.46V	270.50V
Lao People's Dem.Rep	544	—	—	—	—	—	—Y	—Y	—	—	—	—	.01	.01Y	.01Y
Malaysia	548	.17	.09	206.38	160.84	89.77	373.52V	392.14V	4.44	4.44	7.35	23.10	50.55	42.22V	57.27V
Mongolia	948	....	....	....	....	....	....	....	—	—	.02	.02	—	—Y	—Y
Myanmar	518	—	—	.27	1.09	1.00	1.23Y	1.53Y	.01	—	—	—	—	—Y	.01Y
Nepal	558	—	—	—	—	—	—Y	—Y	—	.01	.02	.01	.01	.02Y	.02Y
New Caledonia	839	—	—	—	—	—	.10Y	.12Y	.03	—	—	—	.03	.03Y	.04Y
Pakistan	564	.20	.21	.08	.43	.03	.04Y	.05Y	1.16	1.95	1.03	2.50	4.49	5.55Y	6.89Y
Papua New Guinea	853	.01	—	—	.01	.03	.03Y	.04Y	—	—	—	—	—	—Y	—Y
Philippines	566	.12	.29	32.94	23.36	12.23	40.71V	43.13V	.33	.64	5.13	10.26	40.59	47.76V	28.10V
Samoa	862	....	....	....	....	....	....	....	—	—	.02	.03	—	—Y	—Y
Singapore	576	.70	.96	23.58	25.15	23.35	194.77V	209.38V	4.02	3.81	9.52	19.07	28.20	23.95V	19.31V
Sri Lanka	524	—	—	—	.02	.10	.12Y	.15Y	.32	.26	.20	.20	.42	.52Y	.65Y
Taiwan Province of China	528	—	1.91	38.62	34.80	83.42	126.94V	118.53V	—	61.58	66.48	71.10	101.27	168.58V	148.65V
Thailand	578	.16	.09	2.36	3.27	6.28	22.38V	26.51V	9.21	10.23	15.27	24.63	30.56	30.46V	64.74V
Vanuatu	846	.03	.02	—	—	—	—Y	—Y	3.49	—	—	1.45	—	—Y	.01Y
Vietnam	582	—	.16	.66	1.27	3.31	—V	—V	.54	.27	.49	.88	1.62	—V	—V
Europe	**170**	**28.1**	**10.6**	**27.2**	**20.4**	**29.5**	**115.2Y**	**108.3Y**	**37.6**	**43.7**	**45.0**	**73.7**	**95.7**	**74.6Y**	**80.3Y**
Albania	914	—	—	—	—	.12	.60V	.05V	.04	.02	.06	.02	.08	—V	.02V
Armenia	911	—	—	.03	—	—	.76V	.55V	—	—	—	—	—	—V	—V
Azerbaijan	912	—	—	—	—	—	.29V	.47V	.02	—	—	—	—	—V	—V
Belarus	913	—	—	—	—	—	2.54V	3.11V	—	—	.11	—	—	3.03V	1.43V
Bosnia & Herzegovina	963	....	....	....	....	....	....	....	—	—	—	—	.01	.01Y	.01Y
Bulgaria	918	.68	.02	2.61	.28	.02	2.29V	.01V	.09	.41	.08	.70	1.01	.09V	.27V
Croatia	960	—	.02	—	—	—	2.68V	3.57V	—	—	.05	.07	.19	3.48V	1.02V
Czech Republic	935	.15	.16	.15	.20	.26	6.25V	12.35V	1.08	1.22	1.47	.94	2.19	2.57V	7.19V
Estonia	939	—	—	—	—	.07	.06V	.24V	—	1.72	—	.01	.45	.13V	.10V
Georgia	915	—	—	—	—	—	.42V	1.48Y	—	.06	—	.01	—	—V	—Y
Gibraltar	823	.10	—	—	—	—	—Y	—Y	—	—	—	.03	—	—Y	.01Y
Hungary	944	.09	.04	1.50	1.49	1.52	6.11V	4.98V	.25	.21	.29	.62	.61	1.32V	2.07V
Kazakhstan	916	—	—	—	—	—	.56Y	.69Y	—	—	—	—	—	—Y	—Y
Latvia	941	—	—	—	—	—	.05V	—V	3.30	—	.19	.15	2.55	.31V	.31V
Lithuania	946	—	.08	—	.31	—	.16V	.32V	.01	.01	.04	.03	.06	.13V	.23V
Macedonia, FYR	962	—	—	—	—	—	.71V	.88Y	—	—	—	—	—	—V	—Y
Moldova	921	.01	—	.04	—	—	—Y	—Y	—	—	—	—	—	—Y	—Y
Poland	964	1.41	.32	3.48	13.04	4.38	5.54V	5.15V	3.19	3.96	8.83	33.44	7.69	4.60V	5.88V
Romania	968	.02	—	—	.02	—	13.46V	4.01V	.97	4.47	.18	.38	.57	.11V	.13V
Russia	922	23.68	9.88	18.80	4.98	17.55	27.79V	30.74V	9.63	11.48	19.04	16.46	52.12	15.68V	13.76V
Serbia & Montenegro	965	.06	.03	.02	.01	.01	.01Y	.01Y	—	.04	.01	—	.09	.11Y	.14Y
Slovak Republic	936	—	—	—	.01	—	.34V	.76V	.50	.37	.38	.70	1.35	4.67V	2.11V
Turkey	186	.07	.01	.49	.06	4.46	43.24V	37.34V	12.11	7.17	5.20	5.99	4.31	10.60V	11.13V
Ukraine	926	1.86	.02	.05	.02	1.06	1.30Y	1.62Y	6.36	12.48	9.08	14.15	22.44	27.73Y	34.41Y
Uzbekistan	927	....	....	....	....	....	....	....	—	—	—	—	.01	.02Y	.02Y
Europe n.s.	884	—	—	—	—	—	—Y	—Y	.01	.09	—	—	.01	.01Y	.01Y
Middle East	**407**	**3.6**	**2.5**	**4.5**	**9.0**	**9.5**	**7.7Y**	**10.4Y**	**23.2**	**18.8**	**36.8**	**22.3**	**32.4**	**84.7Y**	**41.0Y**
Bahrain	419	.08	.03	—	—	—	—Y	.01Y	.01	.01	—	.01	.02	.02Y	.02Y
Egypt	469	.06	.05	.05	.09	.06	.08Y	.10Y	.28	.17	.16	.29	.45	.56Y	.69Y
Iran, I.R. of	429	—	.05	—	.16	2.60	3.20Y	4.15Y	.03	.04	.01	.01	.19	.23Y	.28Y
Israel	436	2.68	1.49	3.42	7.40	5.17	1.64V	2.18V	15.94	18.20	36.19	21.16	30.51	81.84V	38.06V
Jordan	439	.12	.01	.09	.05	.04	.22V	.60V	—	—	.02	.01	.01	.57V	.16V
Kuwait	443	.05	.04	.08	.03	.02	.03Y	.04Y	—	—	—	—	—	—Y	—Y
Lebanon	446	.14	.03	.07	.25	.19	.24Y	.30Y	.01	.11	.01	—	.03	.03Y	.04Y
Oman	449	.03	.05	.11	.03	—	.01Y	.01Y	—	—	—	—	—	—Y	—Y
Qatar	453	.01	.11	—	—	.04	.58V	.75Y	.10	.04	—	.06	.06	—V	—Y
Saudi Arabia	456	.06	.12	.23	.29	.24	.29Y	.38Y	6.63	.05	.03	.02	.40	.51Y	.61Y
Syrian Arab Republic	463	.12	.16	.13	.02	.05	.06Y	.07Y	.12	.08	.03	.07	.03	.03Y	.04Y
United Arab Emirates	466	.29	.35	.26	.63	1.11	1.37Y	1.78Y	.07	.07	.30	.64	.71	.90Y	1.08Y
Yemen, Republic of	474	—	—	—	—	—	—Y	—Y	—	—	—	.02	—	—Y	—Y
Western Hemisphere	**207**	**869.0**	**848.4**	**1,333.3**	**1,570.6**	**1,732.6**	**2,615.5Y**	**2,938.6Y**	**1,421.1**	**1,554.5**	**1,742.7**	**2,180.6**	**2,625.5**	**2,879.8Y**	**3,430.8Y**
Antigua and Barbuda	311	.12	.23	.31	1.03	.34	.42Y	.52Y	—	—	—	—	—	—	—Y
Argentina	213	1.27	.16	.94	1.74	2.28	19.48V	18.88V	28.30	30.74	37.96	62.86	61.39	109.44V	113.75V
Aruba	314	2.04	1.51	1.46	1.39	1.28	1.50V	3.37V	—	1.87	16.40	62.24	165.51	.02V	.62V
Bahamas, The	313	2.19	2.24	3.78	21.39	5.55	6.86Y	8.51Y	.01	16.54	8.42	7.55	.16	.19Y	.24Y
Barbados	316	2.48	2.43	4.78	6.17	7.46	—V	—Y	.37	.19	.12	.10	.17	.11V	.14Y
Belize	339	2.07	2.06	4.52	4.86	5.59	6.90Y	8.57Y	2.13	.82	.54	.62	.68	.85Y	1.05Y
Bermuda	319	.53	.95	2.04	3.26	2.79	.87V	1.08Y	.69	1.56	4.22	1.39	1.24	1.53Y	1.90Y
Bolivia	218	.21	.12	.31	.62	.80	.99Y	1.23Y	.27	.56	.11	.27	.27	.33Y	.41Y
Brazil	223	4.40	12.06	17.28	19.20	10.58	117.70V	154.84V	105.15	156.10	210.06	350.36	414.79	470.55V	529.86V
Chile	228	3.45	2.76	7.35	11.73	12.75	7.71V	16.93V	55.55	75.06	80.55	109.83	139.25	206.53V	187.79V

		Exports							Imports						
		2001	2002	2003	2004	2005	2006	2007	2001	2002	2003	2004	2005	2006	2007
		Millions of U.S. Dollars							*Millions of U.S. Dollars*						
Colombia	233	13.17	15.52	24.73	30.08	34.89	32.43V	34.93V	143.38	154.13	212.11	279.03	267.39	266.40V	311.40V
Dominica	321	.66	.80	.53	.63	.51	.63Y	.78Y	—	—	—	.02	.03	.04Y	.05Y
Dominican Republic	243	30.27	35.58	67.95	72.71	101.01	124.85Y	154.93Y	3.21	5.12	5.63	12.20	10.73	13.26Y	16.45Y
Ecuador	248	10.46	9.23	11.98	15.81	15.44	18.82V	23.35Y	5.95	8.27	7.39	8.00	24.93	9.63V	11.95Y
El Salvador	253	132.08	111.03	173.63	200.38	209.15	199.56V	225.94V	78.21	84.60	102.02	92.49	98.16	130.67V	150.94V
Grenada	328	.06	.07	.39	.26	.13	.16Y	.20Y	—	7.38	—	—	—	—Y	—Y
Guatemala	258	176.30	169.83	257.76	279.70	297.98	368.28Y	457.04Y	138.06	142.64	154.14	159.11	183.19	226.40Y	280.97Y
Guyana	336	1.17	.84	2.38	3.23	3.86	4.77Y	5.92Y	—	—	.27	.01	—	.01Y	.01Y
Haiti	263	5.77	5.31	7.33	5.91	6.12	7.57Y	9.39Y	—	—	.01	.03	.02	.03Y	.04Y
Honduras	268	99.87	99.36	158.42	194.70	231.62	286.27Y	355.26Y	36.88	31.74	55.81	52.03	64.09	79.21Y	98.30Y
Jamaica	343	30.20	29.13	39.54	38.98	45.32	46.16V	46.28V	.11	4.74	.73	.43	.66	.10V	.93V
Mexico	273	41.38	61.67	133.56	180.50	183.82	789.13V	740.47V	365.39	354.46	379.24	418.55	474.50	573.98V	755.94V
Netherlands Antilles	353	2.26	2.57	6.25	5.90	6.45	7.97Y	9.89Y	4.28	4.21	11.30	36.85	33.51	41.42Y	51.40Y
Nicaragua	278	152.78	143.77	188.50	223.21	268.68	236.54V	276.91V	38.06	48.88	51.14	53.39	58.67	65.92V	95.65V
Panama	283	117.33	109.51	165.31	182.74	206.92	223.86V	296.57V	109.19	116.95	114.77	103.89	121.28	50.17V	62.81V
Paraguay	288	.07	.02	.02	.05	.04	.30V	.37Y	.03	.13	.12	.04	.25	.13V	.16Y
Peru	293	7.22	5.66	10.69	9.52	12.81	12.99V	20.84Y	7.58	8.98	9.73	10.38	13.35	30.34V	30.56Y
St. Kitts and Nevis	361	.04	.10	.08	.12	.12	.15Y	.19Y	—	—	—	—	—	—Y	—Y
St. Lucia	362	.26	.35	.68	.56	.70	.86Y	1.07Y	—	—	—	—	—	—Y	—Y
St. Vincent & Grens.	364	.13	.16	.40	.52	.38	.47Y	.59Y	.13	—	—	.02	—	—Y	—Y
Suriname	366	.89	.22	1.84	2.32	2.90	3.59Y	4.45Y	.05	.31	.01	.04	.01	.01Y	.01Y
Trinidad and Tobago	369	4.33	4.66	14.56	16.46	20.36	25.17Y	31.23Y	9.62	12.86	15.03	18.74	10.21	12.62Y	15.66Y
Uruguay	298	1.42	.61	.70	.55	1.07	1.33Y	1.64Y	3.97	5.07	3.31	11.83	5.26	6.50Y	8.07Y
Venezuela, Rep. Bol.	299	20.96	15.84	22.43	33.77	32.31	60.71V	25.87V	284.45	280.44	258.90	327.91	475.39	582.96V	703.27Y
Western Hem. n.s.	399	1.18	2.08	.91	.59	.58	.56Y	.55Y	.06	.16	2.66	.35	.38	.41Y	.44Y
Other Countries n.i.e.	**910**	**8.6**	**6.9**	**10.8**	**11.5**	**10.7**	**13.2Y**	**16.4Y**	**134.3**	**3.5**	**5.2**	**11.4**	**10.2**	**12.7Y**	**15.7Y**
Cuba	928	7.03	6.30	10.52	11.45	10.62	13.12Y	16.28Y	2.18	1.37	3.54	8.16	7.60	9.40Y	11.66Y
North Korea	954	1.55	.63	.27	.01	.07	.08Y	.10Y	132.10	2.11	1.71	3.24	2.64	3.26Y	4.05Y
Countries & Areas n.s.	**898**	**5.6**	**—**	**1.8**	**3.3**	**3.6**	**4.5Y**	**5.6Y**	**295.1**	**311.6**	**32.6**	**33.6**	**46.8**	**57.9Y**	**71.8Y**
Special Categories	**899**	**2,692.4**	**2,984.7**	**—**	**—**	**—**	**—Y**	**—Y**	**2,056.9**	**2,187.9**	**—**	**—**	**—**	**—Y**	**—Y**
Memorandum Items															
European Union	998	521.32	533.90	1,060.26	1,079.99	1,143.21	3,397.81Y	3,736.31Y	616.30	720.07	1,009.57	878.41	1,284.91	1,511.12Y	1,450.37Y
Oil Exporting Ctys.	999	21.62	16.84	24.62	37.19	38.13	68.32Y	35.42Y	296.74	284.67	264.37	336.46	488.08	599.20Y	726.01Y
Non-Oil Develop.Ctys.	201	902.33	867.56	1,892.25	2,143.30	2,723.14	5,447.18Y	6,522.09Y	1,345.93	1,704.66	2,004.51	2,583.81	3,217.02	3,572.64Y	4,162.85Y
PERCENT DISTRIBUTION															
Industrial Countries	**101**	**27.5**	**26.4**	**68.4**	**65.2**	**60.5**	**58.6**	**55.8**	**37.1**	**37.5**	**69.9**	**64.1**	**61.6**	**61.3**	**59.5**
Developing Countries	**202**	**18.5**	**16.8**	**31.4**	**34.6**	**39.3**	**41.3**	**44.0**	**25.0**	**27.7**	**29.6**	**35.3**	**37.8**	**38.0**	**39.7**
Africa	**607**	**.1**	**.1**	**.1**	**.1**	**.1**	**.3**	**.3**	**—**	**—**	**.1**	**.1**	**—**	**.1**	**.1**
Asia	**507**	**.4**	**.4**	**9.0**	**9.1**	**14.0**	**20.4**	**23.2**	**2.4**	**5.2**	**5.7**	**7.7**	**9.7**	**10.2**	**10.8**
Europe	**170**	**.6**	**.2**	**.4**	**.3**	**.4**	**.9**	**.7**	**.6**	**.6**	**.6**	**.9**	**1.0**	**.7**	**.7**
Middle East	**407**	**.1**	**—**	**.1**	**.1**	**.1**	**.1**	**.1**	**.4**	**.3**	**.5**	**.3**	**.3**	**.8**	**.3**
Western Hemisphere	**207**	**17.4**	**16.1**	**21.9**	**24.9**	**24.7**	**19.6**	**19.7**	**21.6**	**21.6**	**22.7**	**26.4**	**26.8**	**26.3**	**27.9**
Other Countries n.i.e.	**910**	**.2**	**.1**	**.2**	**.2**	**.2**	**.1**	**.1**	**2.0**	**—**	**.1**	**.1**	**.1**	**.1**	**.1**
ANNUAL PERCENT CHANGE															
World	**001**	**−14.4**	**5.1**	**15.9**	**3.3**	**11.4**	**90.3**	**11.4**	**2.8**	**9.5**	**6.6**	**7.9**	**18.6**	**11.8**	**12.2**
Industrial Countries	**101**	**−12.3**	**.9**	**200.7**	**−1.6**	**3.4**	**84.4**	**6.1**	**.2**	**10.7**	**98.7**	**−1.0**	**14.0**	**11.2**	**8.9**
Developing Countries	**202**	**1.8**	**−4.3**	**116.7**	**13.8**	**26.6**	**99.7**	**18.9**	**−.4**	**21.1**	**14.1**	**28.7**	**26.9**	**12.6**	**17.2**
Africa	**607**	**−60.4**	**17.0**	**.7**	**136.0**	**11.7**	**353.2**	**−9.1**	**20.3**	**−15.3**	**344.2**	**10.6**	**−50.6**	**386.6**	**−34.3**
Asia	**507**	**3.2**	**−4.1**	**—**	**4.3**	**71.4**	**178.8**	**26.6**	**17.6**	**132.9**	**18.2**	**45.3**	**48.8**	**17.8**	**18.7**
Europe	**170**	**66.2**	**−62.4**	**157.1**	**−24.8**	**44.1**	**291.0**	**−5.9**	**−12.0**	**16.3**	**3.1**	**63.7**	**29.9**	**−22.1**	**7.6**
Middle East	**407**	**−28.0**	**−31.2**	**78.1**	**100.7**	**6.4**	**−19.0**	**34.2**	**62.0**	**−19.1**	**96.0**	**−39.4**	**45.4**	**161.4**	**−51.6**
Western Hemisphere	**207**	**1.2**	**−2.4**	**57.1**	**17.8**	**10.3**	**51.0**	**12.4**	**−2.4**	**9.4**	**12.1**	**25.1**	**20.4**	**9.7**	**19.1**
Other Countries n.i.e.	**910**	**−30.0**	**−19.3**	**56.0**	**6.1**	**−6.8**	**23.6**	**24.1**	**15.9**	**−97.4**	**50.9**	**117.3**	**−10.2**	**23.6**	**24.1**

	Exports							Imports						
	2001	2002	2003	2004	2005	2006	2007	2001	2002	2003	2004	2005	2006	2007
	Millions of U.S. Dollars							Millions of U.S. Dollars						
IFS World Total	**3,946.2**	**5,275.0**	**5,788.0**	**6,919.0**	**7,697.3**	**8,368.5**	**8,400.0**	**2,418.0**	**2,456.0**	**3,231.1**	**4,291.0**	**5,251.1**	**5,217.5**	**6,100.0**
DOTS World Total 001	**3,887.4**	**4,963.0**	**5,493.2**	**6,545.1**	**7,251.0**	**8,133.7**	**8,294.0Y**	**2,794.3**	**2,595.2**	**3,585.3**	**4,705.6**	**5,872.9**	**5,814.4**	**6,239.6Y**
Industrial Countries 101	**1,989.8**	**2,851.0**	**3,451.7**	**4,057.1**	**4,057.9**	**4,727.4**	**4,179.3Y**	**1,353.2**	**1,332.0**	**2,160.7**	**2,646.0**	**2,686.1**	**2,569.9**	**2,298.0Y**
United States 111	272.33	374.99	388.91	665.81	1,024.36	738.49	580.73V	133.68	89.46	113.89	133.46	119.46	134.64	177.76V
Canada 156	2.76	2.96	12.90	29.88	21.28	127.51	258.03V	10.78	10.58	7.51	103.75	8.51	7.23	18.61V
Australia 193	7.38	10.54	14.24	12.44	8.09	7.18	10.33V	2.76	1.32	1.27	3.13	2.25	2.43	12.94V
Japan 158	5.45	7.64	12.52	10.08	7.81	8.36	16.15V	54.23	70.76	58.00	108.47	79.98	106.39	45.25V
New Zealand 196	.04	.04	.37	.03	.15	.11	.10V	.56	.98	1.68	3.43	5.18	3.74	2.32V
Austria 122	.04	.18	.04	.07	.09	.07	.44V	6.27	6.02	6.40	7.01	6.28	6.76	10.01V
Belgium 124	—	—	—	—	—	—	257.47V	—	—	—	—	—	—	218.01V
Belgium-Luxembourg n.s. 127	79.79	123.23	146.98	217.44	163.15	225.56	—Y	61.94	62.37	80.07	93.03	90.32	79.08	—Y
Cyprus 423	3.44	2.68	2.13	1.93	3.10	2.56	.85V	.02	.01	.01	.07	.13	.04	.03V
Denmark 128	4.15	5.84	3.42	3.30	14.12	4.26	21.63V	6.45	5.19	6.45	10.40	7.85	8.25	6.51V
Finland 172	8.72	1.42	2.60	1.99	7.49	3.10	4.69V	10.83	11.93	8.97	6.58	5.36	8.39	9.19V
France 132	508.30	618.10	1,045.24	1,549.09	1,327.39	1,485.84	606.06V	537.12	556.78	1,148.72	1,538.16	1,626.94	1,476.35	1,044.67V
Germany 134	148.61	137.18	119.79	87.82	84.51	338.50	806.72V	90.40	93.20	100.60	124.45	104.68	145.50	151.39V
Greece 174	27.46	27.92	27.97	34.33	30.41	39.24	52.17V	1.57	2.82	5.32	1.26	20.20	14.09	5.85V
Iceland 176	.40	.27	.18	.27	.91	1.92	.10V	.25	.20	.06	.13	.05	.31	.21V
Ireland 178	9.13	5.03	7.91	10.25	10.43	12.88	9.80V	11.71	12.83	15.37	16.11	16.75	16.12	2.49V
Italy 136	155.64	187.64	188.17	312.51	200.45	318.47	309.36V	115.12	121.18	110.82	128.14	132.39	116.46	152.69V
Luxembourg 137	—	—	—	—	—	—	1.36V	—	—	—	—	—	—	6.24V
Malta 181	2.84	2.03	2.81	3.80	7.43	16.58	.50V	—	—	.10	.23	.13	.05	—V
Netherlands 138	510.90	941.28	973.35	709.54	798.17	788.40	700.27V	101.97	92.74	117.52	118.09	112.97	136.83	141.01V
Norway 142	2.98	.60	1.39	1.44	17.59	2.37	7.01V	3.93	6.13	6.69	12.03	47.03	6.26	7.65V
Portugal 182	9.20	14.83	17.06	24.63	10.03	10.90	21.32V	4.55	6.44	7.55	6.96	9.91	9.26	8.48V
Slovenia 961	—	—	—	—	—	—	4.68V	—	—	—	—	—	—	.32V
Spain 184	146.40	248.29	309.21	191.11	192.68	248.16	301.25V	79.27	83.45	82.62	80.82	70.16	81.96	103.72V
Sweden 144	.41	.60	.84	.50	.77	.65	2.11V	13.24	13.48	11.16	14.77	18.64	38.29	29.80V
Switzerland 146	3.91	6.07	4.72	50.60	23.25	31.16	19.17V	23.83	19.67	23.15	24.45	23.79	36.21	52.06V
United Kingdom 112	79.47	131.60	168.93	138.29	104.27	315.15	187.02V	82.75	64.46	246.73	111.07	177.17	135.27	90.74V
Developing Countries 202	**1,867.1**	**2,046.6**	**1,993.2**	**2,472.5**	**3,181.8**	**3,347.7**	**4,041.8Y**	**1,440.7**	**1,253.3**	**1,418.6**	**2,043.9**	**3,169.1**	**3,228.9**	**3,922.3Y**
Africa 607	**1,238.9**	**1,518.8**	**1,361.6**	**1,790.5**	**2,159.4**	**2,397.7**	**3,008.1Y**	**669.9**	**562.1**	**698.8**	**1,184.0**	**1,722.9**	**1,915.5**	**2,326.6Y**
Algeria 612	19.28	29.75	40.49	52.21	42.48	62.50	80.97Y	.55	19.50	.14	.03	.02	.19	.23Y
Angola 614	60.73	30.10	22.54	14.84	8.70	10.62	13.18Y	.07	.59	.06	.41	.52	.16	.19Y
Benin 638	30.74	41.82	74.18	81.84	149.04	110.40	137.00Y	.37	.57	.67	.92	2.27	8.84	10.97Y
Botswana 616	.03	.02	—	—	—	—	—Y	.01	—	—	.01	—	—	—Y
Burkina Faso 748	122.96	146.91	112.65	191.09	231.13	296.73	368.24Y	.75	1.12	1.36	.34	.87	.88	1.09Y
Burundi 618	.24	—	—	.01	.10	.09	.12Y	—	—	.01	.02	.01	.03	.03Y
Cameroon 622	30.22	41.10	59.60	55.77	40.06	68.35	84.82Y	2.91	15.08	2.97	17.15	25.77	2.12	2.63Y
Cape Verde 624	8.38	8.42	4.20	1.78	10.29	30.30	37.60Y	.01	—	—	—	.01	—	—Y
Central African Rep. 626	1.34	.94	1.51	.76	.80	1.41	1.75Y	.01	—	—	—	—	—	—Y
Chad 628	1.90	3.22	3.71	3.79	4.00	4.58	5.68Y	.02	.01	—	.01	.03	.02	.02Y
Comoros 632	—	—	.04	—	.02	—	—Y	.01	—	—	—	—	—	—Y
Congo, Dem. Rep. of 636	15.77	28.24	29.50	46.64	61.43	90.50	112.31Y	.01	.01	.28	.05	.32	.03	.04Y
Congo, Republic of 634	14.42	41.60	27.24	22.23	21.74	29.60	36.74Y	21.85	8.69	8.12	9.83	11.91	12.07	14.97Y
Djibouti 611	.09	—	.18	—	—	.06	.07Y	—	.02	—	—	—	.01	.01Y
Equatorial Guinea 642	13.55	17.38	130.72	36.12	87.58	115.42	143.23Y	—	—	.29	.43	2.55	11.20	13.90Y
Ethiopia 644	.10	.12	.02	.05	.06	.02	.02Y	.05	.02	.07	.62	.06	.01	.02Y
Gabon 646	17.76	19.08	22.40	27.67	30.43	19.62	24.35Y	1.83	10.98	10.74	1.98	1.52	4.51	5.59Y
Gambia, The 648	12.04	18.06	15.91	17.64	49.50	52.14	64.71Y	—	—	.05	.01	.01	.03	.04Y
Ghana 652	165.06	105.97	124.24	160.94	148.15	159.64	198.11Y	7.57	16.12	9.28	12.41	10.06	30.82	38.25Y
Guinea 656	55.71	40.79	38.14	40.10	88.26	71.40	88.61Y	9.90	3.27	5.31	8.41	9.49	10.24	12.71Y
Guinea-Bissau 654	.40	.74	.83	1.25	8.24	6.14	7.61Y	.76	.98	.14	—	.13	.62	.77Y
Kenya 664	.13	.55	.63	.42	.77	.37	.46Y	1.12	1.17	1.48	1.96	1.01	1.48	1.84Y
Lesotho 666	—	.04	.02	.78	—	—	—Y	.02	—	—	—	—	—	—Y
Liberia 668	36.05	24.91	18.67	42.55	78.74	96.94	120.30Y	2.03	2.95	1.43	5.47	6.21	7.47	9.27Y
Madagascar 674	.40	.41	.50	1.16	2.26	.91	1.13Y	.03	.06	.48	.51	.26	.19	.23Y
Malawi 676	—	.01	.18	.03	.01	—	—Y	—	.02	.06	.04	—	—	—Y
Mali 678	203.11	179.58	97.81	144.23	158.45	224.00	277.98Y	1.91	1.98	.06	.13	.51	.39	.49Y
Mauritania 682	5.18	9.11	6.58	4.05	2.93	18.99	23.56Y	20.58	12.33	26.60	54.66	74.07	71.05	88.17Y
Mauritius 684	1.22	.29	.21	.07	.11	.29	1.82V	.52	.73	.27	.41	.58	.72	.73V
Morocco 686	12.07	12.47	15.81	14.55	11.92	9.98	12.38Y	10.20	12.51	16.35	23.39	28.78	32.65	40.52Y
Mozambique 688	.21	.17	.38	.33	.06	.21	.26Y	—	—	—	—	—	.03	.03Y
Niger 692	41.11	52.06	49.78	39.83	38.86	45.27	56.18Y	.01	.04	.15	.53	1.72	1.30	1.62Y
Nigeria 694	50.92	466.51	164.23	493.95	578.47	588.07	761.79Y	478.42	365.18	507.51	955.06	1,440.17	1,606.06	1,937.52Y
Rwanda 714	.04	.17	—	.10	.13	.06	.08Y	.01	.01	.02	.03	.02	.01	.01Y
St. Helena 856	—	1.15	—	—	—	—	—Y	—	—	—	—	—	—	—Y
São Tomé & Príncipe 716	.28	.05	.01	—	.18	.12	.15Y	—	—	—	—	—	—	—Y
Senegal 722	70.96	57.33	95.58	100.75	131.61	96.30	119.50Y	23.06	26.83	42.77	29.33	36.44	32.04	39.77Y
Seychelles 718	1.01	.17	—	.03	—	—	—Y	2.70	3.23	—	—	4.53	—	—Y
Sierra Leone 724	20.11	27.68	39.24	42.29	61.51	47.15	58.51Y	.16	.36	.01	.59	2.30	.76	.95Y
Somalia 726	.02	—	—	—	—	—	—Y	—	—	.55	1.07	.55	.84	1.04Y

	Exports							Imports						
	2001	2002	2003	2004	2005	2006	2007	2001	2002	2003	2004	2005	2006	2007
	Millions of U.S. Dollars							Millions of U.S. Dollars						
South Africa 199	11.99	14.06	15.59	15.23	17.40	23.98	26.39V	40.66	48.20	52.91	46.13	44.30	51.09	69.49V
Sudan 732	—	.01	—	.02	—	—	—V	—	—	—	—	—	—	—V
Swaziland 734	—	.15	—	—	—	—	—Y	.02	—	—	—	.03	—	—Y
Tanzania 738	.38	.72	1.05	13.72	2.43	1.39	1.72Y	.01	.23	.09	.13	—	.01	.01Y
Togo 742	85.05	81.21	121.10	103.40	73.16	93.06	115.49Y	.31	.31	1.22	1.35	3.22	3.05	3.78Y
Tunisia 744	12.18	13.84	24.08	15.39	14.67	17.29	21.45Y	5.39	8.45	7.27	10.33	12.52	23.88	29.64Y
Uganda 746	.16	.44	.83	1.04	1.47	2.21	2.74Y	.13	.04	—	—	.10	.01	.01Y
Zambia 754	.36	1.35	.35	.90	.56	.62	.17V	—	—	—	.11	—	.63	—V
Zimbabwe 698	.07	.09	.17	.13	—	.02	.03Y	.09	.45	.03	.07	—	—	—Y
Africa n.s. 799	115.12	—	.65	.85	1.60	.96	.84Y	35.89	—	.08	.03	—	—	.01Y
Asia 507	**212.3**	**225.7**	**301.5**	**360.2**	**351.0**	**368.6**	**310.9Y**	**410.7**	**455.1**	**416.8**	**483.3**	**986.9**	**769.3**	**1,024.0Y**
Afghanistan, I.S. of 512	—	.04	—	—	—	.01	.02Y	—	—	—	—	—	.08	.10Y
Bangladesh 513	2.42	5.00	5.34	9.32	4.37	7.48	5.53V	6.03	10.38	4.47	6.36	6.83	20.15	22.93Y
Cambodia 522	—	.02	—	.01	.19	—	—Y	—	.02	.01	.49	.16	—	—Y
China,P.R.: Mainland 924	5.65	11.24	62.17	57.86	81.79	104.34	37.11V	75.76	62.59	122.86	130.42	179.32	252.68	453.77V
China,P.R.:Hong Kong 532	.34	.10	.97	3.96	2.82	.28	.18V	.91	1.27	.76	.70	1.28	1.06	13.35V
China,P.R.:Macao 546	.01	—	—	—	—	—	—V	—	—	—	—	—	—	—V
Fiji 819	—	—	.07	—	—	—	—Y	—	—	—	—	—	.01	.01Y
French Polynesia 887	—	.04	.04	—	—	—	—Y	—	—	—	—	—	—	—Y
India 534	78.76	85.92	75.22	115.30	132.92	110.49	137.11Y	24.16	72.59	69.95	54.60	79.68	107.11	132.92Y
Indonesia 536	40.08	57.07	57.18	70.11	37.82	34.57	28.28V	21.71	17.43	36.15	22.93	29.25	19.51	25.38V
Korea 542	2.56	1.36	5.08	5.20	.96	.90	.48V	26.45	38.08	38.96	40.40	46.30	70.94	63.69V
Lao People's Dem.Rep 544	.02	—	—	—	—	—	—Y	—	—	—	—	—	.01	.01Y
Malaysia 548	4.79	8.22	27.27	48.18	38.47	39.60	72.27V	6.71	5.54	20.92	10.02	10.04	10.74	17.90V
Myanmar 518	—	—	—	—	—	—	—Y	10.68	22.20	3.21	—	—	—	—Y
New Caledonia 839	—	—	.03	—	—	.05	.06Y	—	.03	—	—	—	—	—Y
Pakistan 564	—	10.45	8.98	8.29	4.54	.93	1.16Y	16.90	1.49	.96	4.32	21.05	57.12	70.89Y
Papua New Guinea 853	—	—	—	—	—	—	—Y	—	—	.09	—	—	—	—Y
Philippines 566	1.55	.23	1.14	1.13	2.82	3.39	.41V	.52	.40	.47	.87	.74	4.22	8.29V
Samoa 862	—	—	—	—	—	—	—Y	.01	—	—	—	—	—	—Y
Singapore 576	1.58	6.92	19.73	14.42	8.96	7.66	6.25V	2.69	140.59	7.28	5.67	388.99	7.99	18.83V
Sri Lanka 524	.14	.11	—	—	.10	.04	—V	.63	.23	.68	.69	.73	.92	—V
Taiwan Province of China 528	28.34	22.94	14.78	10.15	10.62	23.67	13.20V	10.49	14.31	9.53	10.23	18.20	11.85	15.02V
Thailand 578	9.49	10.69	16.80	8.87	11.70	20.19	7.42V	70.36	64.29	73.77	133.80	100.97	136.02	180.93V
Vanuatu 846	.48	.58	.27	.31	.17	1.06	1.31Y	—	—	—	—	—	—	—Y
Vietnam 582	5.22	4.76	6.44	7.08	12.73	13.89	—V	18.33	3.70	23.57	61.83	94.74	68.94	—V
Asia n.s. 598	30.91	—	—	—	—	.04	.09Y	118.33	—	3.21	—	8.66	—	.01Y
Europe 170	**236.1**	**246.0**	**248.0**	**252.5**	**249.1**	**316.3**	**583.6Y**	**116.8**	**106.7**	**159.9**	**157.3**	**148.5**	**161.6**	**147.4Y**
Albania 914	—	—	—	—	—	—	—V	.01	.02	.01	.01	.01	.01	—V
Belarus 913	—	—	—	—	—	—	.30V	—	—	—	—	—	—	13.99V
Bulgaria 918	.89	.13	.13	.01	.87	2.24	2.33V	.92	2.21	2.64	3.79	1.76	2.01	.53V
Czech Republic 935	—	.31	.71	.79	4.60	6.68	8.07V	—	—	4.58	4.24	8.69	7.94	2.70V
Estonia 939	—	—	—	—	—	—	3.67V	—	—	—	—	—	—	.41V
Faroe Islands 816	—	—	—	—	—	—	—Y	—	—	—	—	.04	—	—Y
Gibraltar 823	5.55	—	—	.40	.27	.36	.45Y	—	—	—	—	.08	.17	.21Y
Hungary 944	.56	.04	.03	—	.02	.02	5.33V	1.81	2.68	2.47	5.21	6.22	6.95	6.25V
Lithuania 946	—	—	—	—	—	—	.72V	—	—	—	—	—	—	3.87V
Poland 964	50.06	78.14	91.67	81.74	89.21	67.21	94.11V	5.04	8.45	9.06	15.51	12.61	18.82	25.02V
Romania 968	.64	.85	1.49	4.38	2.05	6.54	9.65V	2.95	5.83	5.40	11.51	3.93	4.40	4.75V
Russia 922	—	137.35	116.43	112.29	114.58	14.50	153.78V	—	—	57.34	80.89	65.62	52.06	13.91V
Serbia & Montenegro 965	—	.78	1.08	1.60	2.10	1.77	2.19Y	—	—	—	—	—	.18	.22Y
Slovak Republic 936	—	—	—	—	—	—	—V	—	—	—	—	—	—	1.70V
Turkey 186	13.17	28.01	32.25	46.89	21.03	35.79	78.20V	8.85	10.72	16.46	18.39	34.76	38.25	35.55V
U.S.S.R. n.s. 930	84.57	—	—	—	—	—	—Y	69.80	76.76	57.33	—	—	—	—Y
Europe n.s. 884	80.69	.45	4.20	4.44	14.37	181.15	224.81Y	27.37	—	4.64	17.75	14.74	30.85	38.28Y
Middle East 407	**14.8**	**18.1**	**19.7**	**29.3**	**38.8**	**36.1**	**45.6Y**	**57.7**	**72.4**	**56.6**	**68.9**	**110.7**	**95.4**	**111.8Y**
Bahrain 419	3.13	.54	.01	—	.44	.11	.14Y	15.07	9.18	.04	—	.14	.27	.34Y
Egypt 469	.63	1.19	1.71	3.65	3.96	2.29	2.84Y	7.38	3.45	7.99	24.05	55.03	7.41	9.20Y
Iran, I.R. of 429	.11	.12	2.18	1.66	9.06	4.82	6.25Y	.52	.39	1.73	.91	1.29	3.04	3.67Y
Israel 436	4.62	4.52	6.60	5.63	5.63	4.18	4.55V	2.26	10.93	10.25	8.67	8.64	9.02	8.58V
Jordan 439	.41	.22	.05	.34	.13	.18	.30V	—	.02	—	.10	.02	8.15	.27V
Kuwait 443	.11	.02	.03	.14	.04	.09	.11Y	5.31	1.36	4.16	3.03	4.07	6.23	7.51Y
Lebanon 446	1.05	1.15	1.43	3.50	4.03	2.76	3.43Y	1.49	2.25	3.09	4.43	5.16	6.12	7.59Y
Libya 672	.83	.09	—	.29	.06	.24	.31Y	—	24.94	4.36	—	.01	—	—Y
Oman 449	—	.02	.04	.01	.04	.02	.02Y	.09	.10	.10	.35	.31	.92	1.10Y
Qatar 453	—	.17	.01	—	.26	.64	.83Y	—	1.42	2.51	1.46	3.22	3.70	4.46Y
Saudi Arabia 456	.88	1.30	2.25	4.43	5.18	6.88	8.92Y	23.48	15.61	18.59	19.15	25.32	22.60	27.27Y
Syrian Arab Republic 463	.29	.48	1.22	1.55	3.26	1.81	2.25Y	.33	.60	.47	2.12	.67	.95	1.18Y
United Arab Emirates 466	2.69	8.26	4.18	8.12	6.75	12.09	15.66Y	1.75	2.19	3.22	4.62	6.73	11.70	14.12Y
Yemen, Republic of 474	—	—	—	—	—	—	—Y	—	—	—	.02	—	.09	.11Y
Middle East n.s. 489	—	—	—	—	.01	—	—Y	—	—	.05	.04	.04	15.21	26.43Y
Western Hemisphere 207	**165.0**	**38.0**	**62.4**	**39.9**	**383.5**	**229.0**	**93.7Y**	**185.7**	**57.0**	**86.4**	**150.3**	**200.2**	**287.1**	**312.5Y**
Antigua and Barbuda 311	1.66	.60	.39	1.94	3.89	1.71	2.13Y	—	—	—	—	—	—	—Y
Argentina 213	.69	.88	11.71	.54	1.40	1.69	1.18V	6.98	7.42	5.22	8.19	21.88	14.46	18.95V
Bahamas, The 313	.59	.43	.80	1.19	3.71	1.48	1.84Y	—	1.49	2.23	.01	—	.01	.02Y
Barbados 316	.01	.04	.01	—	.02	—	—Y	—	—	—	—	—	—	—Y
Belize 339	1.43	.65	.84	.75	1.88	.98	1.22Y	1.52	1.27	.81	4.95	8.64	17.10	21.22Y

		Exports							Imports						
		2001	2002	2003	2004	2005	2006	2007	2001	2002	2003	2004	2005	2006	2007
		Millions of U.S. Dollars							*Millions of U.S. Dollars*						
Bermuda	319	—	.01	—	—	—	.13	.16Y	—	—	—	—	—	—	—Y
Bolivia	218	.15	.14	.06	.01	—	—	—Y	—	—	—	—	—	.03	.03Y
Brazil	223	12.74	19.90	31.80	14.64	23.47	26.56	62.66V	20.59	30.94	31.57	54.80	70.55	82.78	66.45V
Chile	228	—	—	.03	7.70	—	—	—V	2.84	1.48	.25	.75	.40	.25	—V
Colombia	233	.28	.40	.71	.60	.52	.84	.77V	.07	.11	.17	.76	.54	.98	1.16V
Costa Rica	238	—	—	—	—	—	—	—Y	.01	.02	.02	.03	.10	.09	.11Y
Dominica	321	.03	—	—	.01	.02	.11	.13Y	.01	—	—	—	—	—	—Y
Dominican Republic	243	.14	.05	.04	.09	.25	.80	1.00Y	—	—	—	—	—	—	—Y
Ecuador	248	.61	.03	.22	.45	1.18	.96	1.19Y	.01	—	.01	.05	—	.37	.46Y
El Salvador	253	.01	—	—	—	—	—	—Y	—	—	—	.04	—	.01	.01Y
Falkland Islands	323	—	—	—	—	—	—	—Y	—	—	—	—	.01	—	—Y
Guatemala	258	.01	—	.26	—	.63	—	—Y	.29	.04	.09	.12	.09	.11	.13Y
Haiti	263	—	.08	.12	.07	.03	.44	.54Y	—	—	—	—	.03	—	—Y
Honduras	268	1.06	.39	.87	.23	1.05	.01	.02Y	—	—	—	.02	—	—	—Y
Jamaica	343	.21	.01	—	.01	.02	.09	—V	.03	—	—	.05	.02	—	—V
Mexico	273	.67	.15	.16	.06	.09	2.63	17.81V	53.71	.81	30.47	1.31	19.86	2.09	.18V
Netherlands Antilles	353	—	—	—	.08	.17	.60	.74Y	1.00	1.20	1.49	1.16	.01	—	—Y
Nicaragua	278	—	—	—	—	—	—	—V	—	—	—	—	.01	—	—Y
Panama	283	123.46	3.27	2.85	4.74	315.62	187.45	—V	.02	—	4.33	.62	.04	2.06	2.55Y
Paraguay	288	—	—	—	—	—	—	—Y	.02	.09	—	.14	.35	.29	.36Y
Peru	293	.35	.16	.11	.38	.31	.22	.51Y	.16	.17	.12	.50	.34	.42	.44Y
St. Vincent & Grens.	364	2.18	.99	.53	.56	.44	.42	.52Y	4.18	.22	—	—	—	—	—Y
Trinidad and Tobago	369	.05	.14	.08	.19	22.84	—	—Y	—	.25	.87	—	—	—	—Y
Uruguay	298	—	—	.03	.03	.07	—	—Y	.04	.12	.33	.58	.79	1.77	2.20Y
Venezuela, Rep. Bol.	299	.34	.23	.16	—	.01	—	—V	21.98	11.01	8.28	75.69	76.47	164.21	198.10Y
Western Hem. n.s.	399	18.28	9.42	10.66	5.71	5.88	1.85	1.23Y	72.19	.39	.12	.56	.08	.04	.09Y
Other Countries n.i.e.	**910**	**.3**	**—**	**1.2**	**—**	**—**	**—**	**—Y**	**.2**	**.1**	**—**	**.3**	**.3**	**—**	**—Y**
Cuba	928	.21	—	—	—	—	—	—Y	.05	.04	.01	.01	.01	.03	.04Y
North Korea	954	.13	—	1.16	—	—	—	—Y	.18	.04	.02	.29	.31	.01	.01Y
Countries & Areas n.s.	**898**	**—**	**65.4**	**47.2**	**15.4**	**11.2**	**58.7**	**72.8Y**	**.1**	**9.8**	**6.0**	**15.4**	**17.3**	**15.6**	**19.3Y**
Special Categories	**899**	**30.3**	**—**	**—**	**—**	**—**	**—**	**—Y**	**.1**	**—**	**—**	**—**	**—**	**—**	**—Y**
Memorandum Items															
European Union	998	1,745.12	2,526.36	3,108.85	3,369.12	3,048.33	3,884.21	3,399.63Y	1,130.04	1,144.03	1,964.52	2,282.11	2,427.41	2,306.43	2,021.10Y
Oil Exporting Ctys.	999	115.24	563.54	270.75	630.92	680.15	709.93	903.15Y	553.82	459.11	586.77	1,083.22	1,586.87	1,838.15	2,219.36Y
Non-Oil Develop.Ctys.	201	1,751.82	1,483.08	1,722.47	1,841.62	2,501.67	2,637.73	3,138.70Y	886.92	794.23	831.82	960.64	1,582.28	1,390.76	1,702.94Y
PERCENT DISTRIBUTION															
Industrial Countries	**101**	**51.2**	**57.4**	**62.8**	**62.0**	**56.0**	**58.1**	**50.4**	**48.4**	**51.3**	**60.3**	**56.2**	**45.7**	**44.2**	**36.8**
Developing Countries	**202**	**48.0**	**41.2**	**36.3**	**37.8**	**43.9**	**41.2**	**48.7**	**51.6**	**48.3**	**39.6**	**43.4**	**54.0**	**55.5**	**62.9**
Africa	**607**	**31.9**	**30.6**	**24.8**	**27.4**	**29.8**	**29.5**	**36.3**	**24.0**	**21.7**	**19.5**	**25.2**	**29.3**	**32.9**	**37.3**
Asia	**507**	**5.5**	**4.5**	**5.5**	**5.5**	**4.8**	**4.5**	**3.7**	**14.7**	**17.5**	**11.6**	**10.3**	**16.8**	**13.2**	**16.4**
Europe	**170**	**6.1**	**5.0**	**4.5**	**3.9**	**3.4**	**3.9**	**7.0**	**4.2**	**4.1**	**4.5**	**3.3**	**2.5**	**2.8**	**2.4**
Middle East	**407**	**.4**	**.4**	**.4**	**.4**	**.5**	**.4**	**.5**	**2.1**	**2.8**	**1.6**	**1.5**	**1.9**	**1.6**	**1.8**
Western Hemisphere	**207**	**4.2**	**.8**	**1.1**	**.6**	**5.3**	**2.8**	**1.1**	**6.6**	**2.2**	**2.4**	**3.2**	**3.4**	**4.9**	**5.0**
ANNUAL PERCENT CHANGE															
World	**001**	**1.0**	**27.7**	**10.7**	**19.1**	**10.8**	**12.2**	**2.0**	**2.2**	**–7.1**	**38.1**	**31.2**	**24.8**	**–1.0**	**7.3**
Industrial Countries	**101**	**2.1**	**43.3**	**21.1**	**17.5**	**—**	**16.5**	**–11.6**	**9.3**	**–1.6**	**62.2**	**22.5**	**1.5**	**–4.3**	**–10.6**
Developing Countries	**202**	**.1**	**9.6**	**–2.6**	**24.0**	**28.7**	**5.2**	**20.7**	**–3.6**	**–13.0**	**13.2**	**44.1**	**55.1**	**1.9**	**21.5**
Africa	**607**	**.1**	**22.6**	**–10.4**	**31.5**	**20.6**	**11.0**	**25.5**	**–15.5**	**–16.1**	**24.3**	**69.4**	**45.5**	**11.2**	**21.5**
Asia	**507**	**–7.8**	**6.3**	**33.6**	**19.5**	**–2.6**	**5.0**	**–15.7**	**22.2**	**10.8**	**–8.4**	**15.9**	**104.2**	**–22.0**	**33.1**
Europe	**170**	**–9.6**	**4.2**	**.8**	**1.8**	**–1.4**	**27.0**	**84.5**	**–33.0**	**–8.6**	**49.9**	**–1.7**	**–5.6**	**8.9**	**–8.8**
Middle East	**407**	**–22.7**	**22.5**	**9.0**	**48.6**	**32.5**	**–7.0**	**26.3**	**–34.4**	**25.5**	**–21.9**	**21.8**	**60.5**	**–13.8**	**17.2**
Western Hemisphere	**207**	**40.0**	**–77.0**	**64.3**	**–36.0**	**860.0**	**–40.3**	**–59.1**	**78.6**	**–69.3**	**51.4**	**74.0**	**33.2**	**43.4**	**8.8**
Other Countries n.i.e.	**910**	**83.9**	**–98.9**	**—**	**31.3**	**....**	**....**	**....**	**–81.9**	**–66.1**	**–70.6**	**—**	**5.0**	**–87.7**	**24.1**

	Exports 2001	2002	2003	2004	2005	2006	2007	Imports 2001	2002	2003	2004	2005	2006	2007
	Millions of U.S. Dollars							*Millions of U.S. Dollars*						
IFS World Total	**4,666**	**4,904**	**6,187**	**8,024**	**8,773**	**10,376**	**12,364**	**9,147**	**10,722**	**14,209**	**16,589**	**18,560**	**21,488**	**25,829**
DOTS World Total 001	**4,543**	**4,834**	**6,054**	**7,859**	**8,733**	**10,304**	**12,130**	**8,918**	**10,464**	**14,044**	**16,433**	**18,355**	**21,405**	**25,629**
Industrial Countries 101	**3,132**	**3,099**	**4,180**	**5,280**	**5,579**	**6,642**	**7,241**	**6,313**	**7,344**	**9,867**	**11,016**	**11,585**	**13,290**	**15,606**
United States 111	81	78	137	211	305	327	347	281	288	343	355	395	364	473
Canada 156	9	7	9	10	10	15	24	12	15	51	19	25	30	42
Australia 193	4	6	7	11	12	11	14	13	13	18	14	8	8	13
Japan 158	36	24	74	48	40	93	68	143	157	243	279	272	320	416
New Zealand 196	—	—	—	3	1	1	1	1	1	4	5	5	5	8
Austria 122	256	353	479	752	624	627	756	615	703	931	1,127	1,062	1,161	1,365
Belgium-Luxembourg n.s. 127	42	51	43	61	63	61	81	136	158	187	209	211	229	296
Cyprus 423	9	31	3	153	84	43	8	2	3	2	2	3	3	3
Denmark 128	16	11	16	20	25	33	33	65	90	117	126	134	134	185
Finland 172	6	5	12	9	10	13	16	55	49	52	60	60	69	90
France 132	160	158	174	184	199	211	275	395	549	744	730	765	840	925
Germany 134	675	607	728	895	936	1,074	1,232	1,526	1,715	2,198	2,543	2,729	3,110	3,694
Greece 174	47	65	37	14	114	34	21	27	24	70	53	84	89	69
Ireland 178	33	37	30	28	22	27	17	35	58	65	96	105	115	121
Italy 136	1,049	1,084	1,581	1,811	1,872	2,382	2,343	1,484	1,756	2,508	2,804	2,910	3,583	4,126
Malta 181	56	1	93	62	114	111	240	1	1	—	1	2	37	118
Netherlands 138	46	42	49	77	78	89	126	161	198	271	294	371	363	436
Norway 142	6	5	8	7	12	17	13	38	40	72	59	59	72	86
Portugal 182	6	1	2	2	6	6	8	5	11	19	25	24	28	33
Slovenia 961	423	385	505	600	711	851	1,019	704	818	1,044	1,174	1,250	1,463	1,528
Spain 184	38	36	39	42	52	72	77	131	188	268	299	281	342	454
Sweden 144	27	23	46	111	80	227	147	109	128	192	225	215	227	263
Switzerland 146	41	31	39	75	83	124	132	149	166	181	201	258	291	400
United Kingdom 112	66	58	71	96	125	192	240	224	216	288	316	355	405	463
Developing Countries 202	**1,126**	**1,468**	**1,592**	**2,143**	**2,681**	**2,854**	**3,459**	**2,509**	**3,007**	**4,042**	**5,198**	**6,532**	**7,735**	**9,538**
Africa 607	**136**	**213**	**124**	**295**	**351**	**192**	**68**	**61**	**106**	**62**	**70**	**105**	**84**	**100**
Algeria 612	4	5	7	4	7	13	6	12	14	3	1	—	—	—
Ghana 652	—	1	—	—	2	10	3	7	12	14	13	13	11	11
Guinea 656	—	—	—	—	1	1	1	—	—	—	—	—	—	—
Liberia 668	115	180	100	232	244	108	9	5	—	—	—	—	5	—
Morocco 686	7	6	1	19	5	3	5	14	40	17	24	25	29	41
Nigeria 694	5	7	6	32	61	9	1	—	—	—	—	—	—	—
South Africa 199	—	5	2	1	13	30	41	18	20	18	18	44	22	27
Sudan 732	—	8	—	6	8	—	2	—	—	1	—	—	—	—
Tunisia 744	4	1	7	1	10	17	1	2	17	7	10	21	17	19
Zimbabwe 698	—	—	—	—	—	—	—	3	4	3	2	1	—	1
Asia 507	**34**	**15**	**31**	**23**	**42**	**59**	**140**	**369**	**557**	**872**	**1,135**	**1,392**	**1,763**	**2,356**
China,P.R.: Mainland 924	2	2	4	7	9	17	20	142	254	404	632	868	1,139	1,589
China,P.R.:Hong Kong 532	3	2	2	3	5	4	3	10	21	27	28	24	33	33
India 534	22	1	8	2	7	4	8	23	28	44	48	59	88	108
Indonesia 536	—	1	2	1	3	4	2	15	28	43	83	36	41	73
Korea 542	2	3	2	2	4	14	12	68	104	147	126	182	203	258
Malaysia 548	1	1	8	1	3	3	4	34	41	44	41	52	57	69
Pakistan 564	1	1	1	2	1	4	2	2	6	6	8	9	14	19
Singapore 576	1	3	2	3	7	6	87	11	15	20	20	25	30	20
Taiwan Province of China 528	—	—	1	1	3	2	3	48	37	105	110	93	109	123
Thailand 578	1	—	1	1	1	2	—	15	24	33	38	44	48	64
Europe 170	**884**	**1,123**	**1,347**	**1,700**	**2,023**	**2,255**	**2,895**	**1,633**	**1,936**	**2,456**	**3,501**	**4,560**	**5,471**	**6,556**
Albania 914	11	17	26	27	20	30	31	1	—	1	1	1	3	4
Belarus 913	3	4	11	8	11	15	11	17	14	21	29	27	30	40
Bosnia & Herzegovina 963	555	698	886	1,051	1,260	1,309	1,691	124	163	229	348	452	596	727
Bulgaria 918	8	12	23	28	39	48	68	12	15	42	50	162	286	164
Czech Republic 935	34	40	46	50	77	117	137	210	264	349	395	434	483	553
Hungary 944	56	82	80	103	138	172	269	234	315	422	508	573	648	755
Kazakhstan 916	3	5	8	8	12	14	11	1	1	1	—	—	—	—
Lithuania 946	8	4	7	6	6	6	12	1	2	4	9	9	12	15
Macedonia, FYR 962	52	59	70	74	81	83	117	62	65	73	116	144	179	221
Poland 964	21	19	31	42	53	108	119	176	146	211	281	332	403	504
Romania 968	5	8	21	69	81	56	74	21	44	132	189	275	173	201
Russia 922	81	83	70	115	112	122	157	650	709	663	1,195	1,667	2,073	2,597
Slovak Republic 936	14	56	23	26	42	79	64	51	96	141	147	159	253	228
Turkey 186	8	10	21	70	70	64	66	41	67	123	158	243	251	447
Turkmenistan 925	—	—	—	—	—	2	—	—	—	—	—	—	—	—
Ukraine 926	12	10	13	13	18	27	69	25	18	35	67	79	80	98
U.S.S.R. n.s. 930	11	18	11	9	3	—	—	7	16	11	7	2	—	—
Middle East 407	**49**	**51**	**73**	**112**	**234**	**279**	**248**	**308**	**251**	**432**	**226**	**157**	**79**	**146**
Egypt 469	12	9	16	15	16	20	24	4	4	5	6	13	16	14
Iran, I.R. of 429	4	5	4	4	3	7	5	1	3	3	3	2	3	3
Iraq 433	—	4	3	11	7	3	—	72	—	12	14	—	—	12

	Exports 2001	Exports 2002	Exports 2003	Exports 2004	Exports 2005	Exports 2006	Exports 2007	Imports 2001	Imports 2002	Imports 2003	Imports 2004	Imports 2005	Imports 2006	Imports 2007
	Millions of U.S. Dollars							*Millions of U.S. Dollars*						
Israel........ 436	4	7	20	5	6	6	5	17	11	15	19	18	26	43
Jordan........ 439	10	6	1	1	1	1	3	—	3	1	1	1	—	—
Lebanon........ 446	5	7	—	1	39	71	34	—	—	—	—	—	—	—
Libya........ 672	3	2	3	3	14	5	17	70	3	61	31	49	8	50
Saudi Arabia........ 456	4	6	6	13	9	15	69	1	2	3	8	13	18	8
Syrian Arab Republic........ 463	2	1	5	5	24	6	6	143	223	330	139	58	3	3
United Arab Emirates........ 466	5	4	16	55	116	144	86	1	1	1	5	2	2	14
Western Hemisphere........ 207	**23**	**66**	**17**	**13**	**31**	**70**	**107**	**138**	**157**	**219**	**266**	**318**	**339**	**380**
Argentina........ 213	1	1	—	—	4	1	1	10	14	15	38	83	43	16
Bahamas, The........ 313	—	—	—	—	—	—	1	—	—	—	—	—	7	1
Barbados........ 316	—	—	—	—	—	—	—	—	—	—	—	10	—	—
Brazil........ 223	2	2	3	1	5	7	8	61	85	112	116	122	145	223
Colombia........ 233	1	—	—	—	1	—	1	6	9	13	13	14	32	27
Costa Rica........ 238	—	1	—	—	3	3	1	2	2	2	3	2	3	4
Ecuador........ 248	1	1	1	2	5	2	3	14	13	16	18	29	20	27
Honduras........ 268	—	—	—	—	—	—	—	—	1	—	1	1	1	1
Panama........ 283	—	55	—	1	2	45	84	—	1	1	2	1	1	2
Peru........ 293	—	—	—	—	—	—	1	6	4	4	3	3	3	3
Venezuela, Rep. Bol........ 299	—	1	1	—	—	—	—	3	2	1	1	6	14	7
Western Hem. n.s........ 399	17	5	12	7	11	10	8	35	27	55	72	46	70	70
Other Countries n.i.e........ 910	**—**	**1**	**—**	**1**	**—**	**2**	**2**	**—**	**5**	**—**	**—**	**—**	**—**	**1**
Cuba........ 928	—	1	—	1	—	2	2	—	5	—	—	—	—	1
Countries & Areas n.s........ 898	**285**	**266**	**282**	**436**	**473**	**806**	**1,429**	**96**	**107**	**135**	**218**	**238**	**379**	**485**
Memorandum Items														
European Union........ 998	3,089	3,150	4,094	5,143	5,432	6,536	7,243	6,347	7,488	10,082	11,424	12,070	13,998	16,224
Oil Exporting Ctys........ 999	26	35	47	124	222	201	186	175	53	127	147	110	88	167
Non-Oil Develop.Ctys........ 201	1,100	1,433	1,545	2,019	2,459	2,653	3,272	2,334	2,955	3,914	5,051	6,422	7,648	9,371
PERCENT DISTRIBUTION														
Industrial Countries........ 101	**68.9**	**64.1**	**69.0**	**67.2**	**63.9**	**64.5**	**59.7**	**70.8**	**70.2**	**70.3**	**67.0**	**63.1**	**62.1**	**60.9**
Developing Countries........ 202	**24.8**	**30.4**	**26.3**	**27.3**	**30.7**	**27.7**	**28.5**	**28.1**	**28.7**	**28.8**	**31.6**	**35.6**	**36.1**	**37.2**
Africa........ 607	**3.0**	**4.4**	**2.0**	**3.8**	**4.0**	**1.9**	**.6**	**.7**	**1.0**	**.4**	**.4**	**.6**	**.4**	**.4**
Asia........ 507	**.7**	**.3**	**.5**	**.3**	**.5**	**.6**	**1.2**	**4.1**	**5.3**	**6.2**	**6.9**	**7.6**	**8.2**	**9.2**
Europe........ 170	**19.5**	**23.2**	**22.2**	**21.6**	**23.2**	**21.9**	**23.9**	**18.3**	**18.5**	**17.5**	**21.3**	**24.8**	**25.6**	**25.6**
Middle East........ 407	**1.1**	**1.1**	**1.2**	**1.4**	**2.7**	**2.7**	**2.0**	**3.5**	**2.4**	**3.1**	**1.4**	**.9**	**.4**	**.6**
Western Hemisphere........ 207	**.5**	**1.4**	**.3**	**.2**	**.4**	**.7**	**.9**	**1.5**	**1.5**	**1.6**	**1.6**	**1.7**	**1.6**	**1.5**
ANNUAL PERCENT CHANGE														
World........ 001	**11.6**	**6.4**	**25.2**	**29.8**	**11.1**	**18.0**	**17.7**	**16.0**	**17.3**	**34.2**	**17.0**	**11.7**	**16.6**	**19.7**
Industrial Countries........ 101	**9.2**	**−1.0**	**34.9**	**26.3**	**5.7**	**19.1**	**9.0**	**14.1**	**16.3**	**34.3**	**11.6**	**5.2**	**14.7**	**17.4**
Developing Countries........ 202	**6.5**	**30.4**	**8.4**	**34.6**	**25.1**	**6.5**	**21.2**	**21.1**	**19.9**	**34.4**	**28.6**	**25.7**	**18.4**	**23.3**
Africa........ 607	**−30.1**	**56.7**	**−42.0**	**138.7**	**18.9**	**−45.2**	**−64.7**	**−27.0**	**74.7**	**−41.5**	**12.2**	**50.3**	**−19.6**	**18.3**
Asia........ 507	**138.1**	**−56.5**	**113.6**	**−26.2**	**84.1**	**38.0**	**138.2**	**33.4**	**50.9**	**56.7**	**30.1**	**22.7**	**26.6**	**33.6**
Europe........ 170	**14.3**	**27.1**	**19.9**	**26.2**	**19.0**	**11.5**	**28.4**	**21.8**	**18.6**	**26.8**	**42.5**	**30.3**	**20.0**	**19.8**
Middle East........ 407	**−14.8**	**4.4**	**42.5**	**54.1**	**109.4**	**18.9**	**−10.9**	**13.9**	**−18.5**	**72.3**	**−47.7**	**−30.8**	**−49.8**	**86.2**
Western Hemisphere........ 207	**29.5**	**182.6**	**−74.0**	**−25.3**	**139.8**	**127.2**	**53.7**	**36.5**	**13.7**	**39.2**	**21.6**	**19.6**	**6.5**	**12.3**
Other Countries n.i.e........ 910	**. . . .**	**332.9**	**−33.2**	**28.4**	**−69.8**	**896.2**	**.6**	**−22.2**	**—**	**−94.0**	**18.4**	**17.2**	**14.9**	**34.3**

		Exports							Imports						
		2001	2002	2003	2004	2005	2006	2007	2001	2002	2003	2004	2005	2006	2007
		Millions of U.S. Dollars							*Millions of U.S. Dollars*						
DOTS World Total	**001**	**1,581.5Y**	**1,515.0Y**	**1,646.9Y**	**2,208.6Y**	**2,171.4Y**	**2,572.2Y**	**3,657.1Y**	**3,548.9Y**	**3,005.1Y**	**2,964.9Y**	**4,765.0Y**	**6,897.8Y**	**9,084.1Y**	**9,630.4Y**
Industrial Countries	**101**	**786.8Y**	**800.1Y**	**907.0Y**	**1,315.8Y**	**1,339.2Y**	**1,430.7Y**	**1,789.2Y**	**1,777.3Y**	**1,606.9Y**	**1,919.9Y**	**2,188.3Y**	**2,792.0Y**	**3,378.7Y**	**3,557.9Y**
United States	111	—V	.18V	.18V	—V	—V	.18V	.27V	7.48V	158.95V	287.10V	440.44V	397.87V	382.47V	491.70V
Canada	156	234.20V	207.45V	266.54V	452.82V	456.25V	555.07V	985.45V	254.26V	176.50V	183.68V	257.45V	407.93V	497.69V	580.52V
Australia	193	4.04V	5.02V	2.93V	3.11V	3.26V	6.70V	7.40V	12.08V	13.01V	3.59V	2.47V	6.90V	6.80V	14.08V
Japan	158	33.98V	25.50V	25.49V	23.99V	28.55V	16.81V	15.16V	29.31V	28.53V	65.09V	115.81V	194.67V	140.62V	195.02V
New Zealand	196	.49V	.53V	.50V	.65V	.79V	.80V	1.07V	50.86V	34.79V	44.12V	60.26V	46.39V	50.70V	92.91V
Austria	122	2.01V	1.25V	2.13V	1.39V	2.01V	1.81V	2.21V	3.12V	2.21V	3.39V	4.43V	3.97V	5.92V	11.61V
Belgium	124	13.40V	9.79V	7.41V	6.73V	5.05V	3.90V	1.82V	26.51V	23.10V	31.34V	36.06V	57.81V	57.16V	49.57V
Cyprus	423	8.73V	6.18V	11.86V	11.92V	1.06V	2.65V	2.87V	—V	—V	.82V	—V	—V	—V	—V
Denmark	128	1.11V	.85V	1.49V	1.88V	1.32V	1.54V	10.87V	14.72V	12.25V	16.70V	23.56V	23.75V	39.94V	33.96V
Finland	172	.31V	.32V	.61V	7.16V	.21V	.43V	7.24V	3.43V	2.06V	1.86V	5.60V	10.71V	9.07V	6.03V
France	132	34.35V	39.25V	25.79V	20.62V	30.87V	32.69V	44.94V	243.01V	217.44V	166.69V	110.30V	142.38V	131.07V	130.67V
Germany	134	28.02V	27.15V	28.64V	41.09V	40.51V	15.37V	25.07V	99.83V	78.50V	124.46V	153.59V	348.73V	568.94V	322.29V
Greece	174	.03V	.14V	.75V	1.66V	2.82V	3.41V	6.32V	1.56V	.40V	.65V	.39V	.80V	.68V	.24V
Iceland	176	.03V	.04V	.04V	.05V	.10V	.08V	.11V	.01V	—V	.02V	.08V	—V	—V	.01V
Ireland	178	.16V	.04V	.09V	.05V	.02V	.05V	.20V	.87V	.20V	.63V	1.08V	.92V	.50V	.91V
Italy	136	12.64V	13.38V	14.13V	14.93V	10.68V	17.97V	24.01V	275.43V	260.33V	289.34V	246.44V	269.53V	389.16V	341.77V
Luxembourg	137	.02V	.01V	.02V	.01V	.01V	.08V	.01V	.21V	2.90V	.22V	.20V	.39V	.26V	.91V
Malta	181	.23Y	.21V	.24V	.10V	.12V	.09V	.11V	.01Y	.08V	.05V	—V	.01V	.32V	—V
Netherlands	138	253.42V	277.23V	330.85V	501.03V	558.54V	560.39V	407.34V	72.69V	64.14V	69.17V	70.93V	143.57V	129.05V	165.01V
Norway	142	.45V	.42V	.35V	.85V	.47V	.62V	15.51V	1.84V	1.44V	.89V	.94V	1.94V	1.11V	.64V
Portugal	182	16.44V	16.93V	20.22V	39.65V	9.26V	21.27V	27.37V	5.98V	4.66V	3.22V	4.13V	5.33V	7.78V	13.35V
Slovenia	961	.89V	.83V	.57V	.75Y	.01V	.01V	.03V	—V	—V	—V	—Y	—V	.22V	.16V
Spain	184	108.56V	138.10V	131.52V	141.38V	148.36V	152.34V	172.69V	615.21V	491.37V	567.07V	590.01V	660.28V	873.24V	1,001.22V
Sweden	144	1.18V	.66V	1.46V	2.39V	2.09V	2.35V	.81V	23.82V	10.93V	21.42V	29.20V	20.26V	22.51V	46.97V
Switzerland	146	16.83V	17.67V	19.67V	21.15V	22.13V	20.63V	21.29V	14.61V	4.16V	7.64V	11.80V	16.60V	21.82V	22.05V
United Kingdom	112	15.23V	10.97V	13.50V	20.39V	14.72V	13.49V	9.03V	20.47V	18.93V	30.73V	23.16V	31.29V	41.72V	36.34V
Developing Countries	**202**	**794.8Y**	**714.9Y**	**739.9Y**	**892.9Y**	**832.1Y**	**1,141.4Y**	**1,867.9Y**	**1,771.6Y**	**1,398.2Y**	**1,045.0Y**	**2,576.7Y**	**4,105.8Y**	**5,705.4Y**	**6,072.5Y**
Africa	**607**	**34.3Y**	**42.5Y**	**46.0Y**	**54.7Y**	**59.9Y**	**74.1Y**	**91.4Y**	**32.2Y**	**20.0Y**	**24.5Y**	**26.6Y**	**32.1Y**	**39.2Y**	**48.6Y**
Algeria	612	3.02V	9.80V	10.89V	14.17Y	18.04Y	22.27Y	28.84Y	.02V	.05V	.06Y	.09Y	.12Y	.15Y	.18Y
Benin	638	—V	.02V	—V	.03V	—V	—Y	—Y	—V	—V	—V	—V	—V	—Y	—Y
Cape Verde	624	.02V	.02Y	.03Y	.04Y	.05Y	.06Y	.07Y	—V	—Y	—Y	—Y	—Y	—Y	—Y
Congo, Republic of	634	—V	—V	.91V	—V	—Y	—Y	—Y	—V	—V	—V	—V	—Y	—Y	—Y
Côte d'Ivoire	662	.05V	.03V	.01V	.01V	.01V	.03V	.04Y	.23V	—V	—V	—V	—V	—V	—Y
Ethiopia	644	—V	—V	—V	.04V	.07V	.08Y	.10Y	—V	—V	.09V	—V	.26V	.32Y	.39Y
Gambia, The	648	.02Y	.03Y	.03Y	.04Y	.05Y	.06Y	.08Y	—Y	—Y	—Y	—Y	—Y	—Y	—Y
Ghana	652	14.38Y	15.60Y	19.75Y	25.94Y	29.64Y	36.63Y	45.46Y	14.52Y	15.76Y	19.94Y	26.19Y	29.93Y	36.99Y	45.90Y
Guinea	656	—V	—Y	.01V	—V	.01Y	.01Y	.01Y	....	....	....	....	....	....	....
Guinea-Bissau	654	2.71Y	2.94Y	3.72Y	4.89Y	5.58Y	6.90Y	8.56Y	—Y	—Y	—Y	—Y	—Y	—Y	—Y
Madagascar	674	.02V	.01V	.01V	.01Y	.01Y	.01Y	.01Y	—V	—V	—V	—Y	—Y	—Y	—Y
Mauritania	682	.02Y	.02Y	.03Y	.04Y	.04Y	.05Y	.06Y	—Y	—Y	—Y	—Y	—Y	—Y	—Y
Mauritius	684	.11V	.06V	.07V	.10V	.10V	.14V	.14V	—V	.05V	—V	—V	—V	—V	—V
Morocco	686	.07V	.45V	.59V	1.48V	2.66V	3.28Y	4.07Y	.17V	.02V	.01V	.02V	1.19V	1.47Y	1.82Y
Nigeria	694	.23V	.01V	.13V	.17Y	.21Y	.27Y	.34Y	—V	—V	—V	—Y	—Y	—Y	—Y
Senegal	722	.09V	.13V	.38V	.29V	.62V	.71V	.88Y	—V	—V	—V	—V	—V	—V	—Y
Seychelles	718	—V	.02V	—V	—Y	—Y	—Y	—Y	—V	—V	—V	—Y	—Y	—Y	—Y
South Africa	199	1.01V	1.00V	1.39V	2.17V	2.65V	3.34V	2.33V	.35V	.31V	.33V	.35V	.59V	.30V	.30V
Sacca exc. South Afr.	608	—Y	—Y	—Y	—Y	—Y	—Y	—Y	—V	.03V	—V	—V	—Y	—Y	—Y
Tanzania	738	—V	—V	—Y	—Y	—Y	—Y	—Y	.13V	—V	—Y	—Y	—Y	—Y	—Y
Togo	742	.05V	.01V	.01V	—V	.02V	.02Y	.02Y	—V	—V	—V	—V	—V	—Y	—Y
Tunisia	744	12.46V	12.34V	8.05V	5.27V	.11V	.26V	.32Y	16.77V	3.81V	4.02V	—V	—V	.02V	.02Y
Zambia	754	—V	—V	—V	—V	—V	—V	—V	.02V	—V	—V	—V	—V	—V	—V
Asia	**507**	**119.1Y**	**130.2Y**	**128.1Y**	**190.1Y**	**240.3Y**	**514.7Y**	**1,047.2Y**	**462.3Y**	**435.2Y**	**378.9Y**	**530.3Y**	**973.6Y**	**1,876.1Y**	**1,582.4Y**
Bangladesh	513	....	....	....	....	....	....	....	—V	1.09V	—V	1.80V	.39V	1.19Y	.36Y
China,P.R.: Mainland	924	103.68V	105.16V	109.76V	169.77V	215.77V	480.28V	1,004.88V	366.49V	341.47V	259.91V	354.52V	698.87V	1,388.18V	1,286.45V
China,P.R.:Hong Kong	532	5.98V	6.63V	7.34V	10.87V	9.97V	13.42V	17.29V	10.79V	6.68V	4.32V	7.18V	7.55V	20.09V	5.07V
China,P.R.:Macao	546	.68V	.71V	1.29V	1.68V	2.69V	3.67V	5.14V	....	....	....	....	....	....	....
India	534	4.92Y	3.34V	2.09V	1.60V	2.65V	3.27Y	4.06Y	5.25Y	5.59V	5.41V	7.07V	11.85V	14.65Y	18.18Y
Indonesia	536	.23V	—V	—V	—V	—V	.01V	.05V	1.61V	.72V	2.02V	1.51V	.88V	.82V	7.12V
Korea	542	—V	—V	.03V	.28V	—V	2.93V	2.73V	—V	—V	1.91V	10.40V	—V	223.57V	235.75V
Malaysia	548	.18V	4.29V	.15V	.10V	.98V	.50V	1.11V	1.74V	1.58V	1.13V	1.92V	2.89V	2.22V	4.44V
Pakistan	564	—V	.38V	.68V	.16V	1.16V	1.44Y	1.78Y	—V	.16V	.58V	1.09V	.55V	.68Y	.84Y
Philippines	566	.12V	—V	.08V	.01V	1.07V	.70V	.55V	.19V	.26V	.02V	.19V	.03V	.48V	.59V
Singapore	576	1.42V	6.89V	1.29V	1.88V	2.19V	2.91V	3.47V	1.50V	1.81V	1.60V	2.19V	2.10V	11.56V	8.39V
Taiwan Province of China	528	.62V	2.01V	4.69V	3.31V	3.01V	4.75V	4.20V	20.83V	19.86V	21.53V	14.84V	9.78V	10.37V	9.65V
Thailand	578	.67V	.60V	.57V	.49V	.84V	.78V	1.90V	5.26V	4.28V	8.62V	11.72V	10.93V	34.20V	5.53V
Vietnam	582	.63V	.14V	.13V	—V	—V	—V	—V	48.65V	51.74V	71.81V	115.83V	227.81V	168.08V	—V
Europe	**170**	**452.0Y**	**346.2Y**	**230.2Y**	**248.4Y**	**107.9Y**	**104.2Y**	**124.8Y**	**106.6Y**	**77.8Y**	**97.4Y**	**104.4Y**	**235.2Y**	**327.6Y**	**416.1Y**
Albania	914	—V	—V	.02V	.02V	.01V	.01V	.08V	—V	—V	—V	—V	—V	—V	—V
Armenia	911	1.62V	—V	—V	.12V	.05V	.21V	.06V	—V	—V	—V	—V	—V	.02V	—V
Azerbaijan	912	—V	.29V	—V	.05V	.06V	—V	—V	1.23V	.78V	1.40V	.78V	.45V	.52V	.29V

	Exports 2001	2002	2003	2004	2005	2006	2007	Imports 2001	2002	2003	2004	2005	2006	2007
	Millions of U.S. Dollars							Millions of U.S. Dollars						
Belarus 913	12.32V	24.32V	16.29V	27.18V	5.19V	10.58V	5.82V	7.86V	5.80V	6.51V	7.58V	14.50V	11.38V	16.29V
Bulgaria 918	8.36V	8.17V	6.31V	5.51V	.55V	10.21V	6.62V	2.29V	1.14V	.25V	.58V	1.31V	8.48V	6.57V
Croatia 960	.13V	4.70V	.28V	.33V	.39V	.45V	.60V	.15V	.67V	.45V	.57V	.17V	1.72V	1.73V
Czech Republic 935	.89V	1.04V	1.77V	2.60V	4.27V	1.48V	1.26V	5.96V	3.56V	8.90V	12.68V	18.08V	33.66V	21.87V
Estonia 939	.20V	.33V	1.51V	.15V	.21V	.31V	.35V	.13V	1.23V	3.21V	.07V	.19V	.65V	.01V
Georgia 915	—V	—V	.05V	.10V	—V	—V	—Y	—V	—V	—V	—V	—V	—V	—Y
Hungary 944	.24V	.26V	.40V	.19V	.25V	.08V	.28V	.20V	.40V	.59V	.65V	.49V	.95V	1.65V
Kazakhstan 916	5.90V	20.30V	12.40V	24.11V	27.54Y	34.04Y	42.25Y	.17V	2.20V	—V	2.88V	3.29Y	4.07Y	5.05Y
Kyrgyz Republic 917	—V	—V	—V	—V	3.53V	—V	—V	—V	—V	—V	—V	—V	—V	—V
Latvia 941	.02V	.02V	.25V	.32V	.22V	.09V	.19V	.02V	.04V	.61V	.05V	—V	.02V	.04V
Lithuania 946	.06V	.07V	.31V	.03V	.06V	.06V	.07V	1.74V	.06V	.05V	.05V	.24V	1.45V	.36V
Macedonia, FYR 962	—V	—V	.06V	.02V	.07V	.05V	.07Y	—V	—V	—V	—V	—V	—V	—Y
Moldova 921	—V	5.73V	.06V	—V	—V	—Y	—Y	—V	—V	—V	—V	—V	—Y	—Y
Poland 964	1.76V	1.12V	1.24V	3.37V	.38V	.47V	.56V	3.48V	10.44V	18.59V	8.44V	15.45V	13.42V	20.61V
Romania 968	16.54V	13.50V	13.14V	8.15V	6.10V	.62V	.83V	1.46V	1.95V	.36V	.35V	2.80V	.08V	1.06V
Russia 922	395.31V	261.82V	162.38V	164.25V	55.80V	42.38V	61.79V	70.78V	37.93V	42.08V	58.31V	137.70V	202.93V	238.63V
Slovak Republic 936	.28V	.39V	.49Y	.65Y	.32V	.48V	.58V	1.20V	.41V	.52Y	.68Y	14.91V	9.29V	30.09V
Turkey 186	.09V	.15V	.06V	.07V	1.61V	.97V	1.34V	4.36V	2.02V	3.60V	2.38V	1.93V	9.66V	35.43V
Ukraine 926	8.27V	4.01V	13.17V	11.20V	1.35V	1.66Y	2.06Y	5.58V	9.21V	10.28V	8.33V	23.73V	29.32Y	36.39Y
Middle East 407	**22.5Y**	**48.3Y**	**55.5Y**	**60.8Y**	**77.1Y**	**95.7Y**	**123.8Y**	**17.1Y**	**18.2Y**	**22.2Y**	**29.2Y**	**39.6Y**	**49.5Y**	**60.1Y**
Bahrain 419	.83Y	.90Y	1.14Y	1.49Y	1.71Y	2.11Y	2.62Y	—Y	—Y	—Y	—Y	—Y	—Y	—Y
Egypt 469	.20V	.22Y	.28Y	.36Y	.41Y	.51Y	.63Y	.10V	.11Y	.14Y	.18Y	.21Y	.26Y	.32Y
Iran, I.R. of 429	13.28V	39.10V	43.46Y	56.52Y	71.96Y	88.84Y	115.08Y	—Y	—Y	—Y	—Y	—Y	—Y	—Y
Jordan 439	.11V	.05V	.02V	.04V	.06V	.05V	.01V	.03V	.06V	.20V	.13V	.15V	—V	.28V
Kuwait 443	.14Y	.14Y	.16Y	.21Y	.26Y	.32Y	.42Y	—Y	—Y	—Y	—Y	—Y	—Y	—Y
Lebanon 446	.18Y	.20Y	.25Y	.33Y	.37Y	.46Y	.57Y	—Y	—Y	—Y	—Y	—Y	—Y	—Y
Libya 672	.28Y	.29Y	.32Y	.42Y	.53Y	.65Y	.85Y	16.41Y	17.45Y	21.16Y	28.00Y	38.08Y	47.88Y	57.76Y
Oman 449	.05V	.01V	—V	—Y	—Y	—Y	—Y	.03V	.01V	—V	—Y	—Y	—Y	—Y
Qatar 453	—V	.02V	.03V	.01V	.27V	.85V	1.11Y	—Y	—Y	—Y	—Y	—V	—V	—Y
Saudi Arabia 456	.74V	.11V	.22V	.41V	.34V	.41Y	.54Y	.33Y	.35Y	.42Y	.56Y	.76Y	.96Y	1.16Y
Syrian Arab Republic 463	6.51Y	7.06Y	8.94Y	—V	—Y	—Y	—Y	.20Y	.22Y	.28Y	.30V	.34Y	.42Y	.52Y
United Arab Emirates 466	.18V	.18V	.73V	.95Y	1.20Y	1.49Y	1.93Y	—Y	—Y	—Y	—Y	—Y	—Y	—Y
Yemen, Republic of 474	.02V	—V	—Y	.07V	.01V	.01Y	.01Y	—V	—V	—Y	—V	.01V	.02Y	.02Y
Western Hemisphere 207	**166.9Y**	**147.8Y**	**280.1Y**	**338.8Y**	**346.9Y**	**352.8Y**	**480.8Y**	**1,153.3Y**	**846.9Y**	**522.1Y**	**1,886.2Y**	**2,825.3Y**	**3,412.9Y**	**3,965.4Y**
Argentina 213	3.02V	1.04V	1.06V	1.37V	1.60V	2.38V	2.74V	53.64V	24.29V	25.58V	100.50V	106.53V	105.38V	110.70V
Aruba 314	.72V	.37V	.28V	.93V	.26V	.92V	1.07V	.66V	.24V	.06V	.18V	.03V	.02V	.06V
Bahamas, The 313	.21Y	.22Y	.28Y	.37Y	.42Y	.52Y	.65Y	—Y	—Y	—Y	—Y	—Y	—Y	—Y
Barbados 316	.23V	.26V	.35V	.38V	.39V	.24V	.29Y	.17V	.05V	.05V	—V	—V	.01V	.01Y
Belize 339	20.24Y	21.96Y	27.80Y	36.51Y	41.71Y	51.55Y	63.98Y	.08Y	.09Y	.11Y	.15Y	.17Y	.21Y	.26Y
Bermuda 319	.43Y	.46Y	.59Y	.77Y	.88V	.42V	.52Y	—Y	—Y	—Y	—Y	—Y	—Y	—Y
Bolivia 218	.68V	.61V	.39V	.33V	1.24V	1.53Y	1.90Y	.23V	—V	.07V	.03V	.04Y	.04Y	.06Y
Brazil 223	10.60V	14.12V	22.38V	45.31V	38.88V	31.60V	88.79V	123.15V	81.28V	76.47V	145.15V	270.05V	377.58V	356.24V
Chile 228	.72V	1.00V	.92V	.72V	1.58V	1.36V	2.64V	40.19V	45.87V	42.02V	51.69V	46.84V	48.74V	70.72V
Colombia 233	12.24V	3.57V	4.27V	6.15V	5.01V	3.70V	7.84V	26.43V	69.31V	66.96V	36.05V	70.06V	53.43V	55.56V
Costa Rica 238	1.98V	1.24V	3.22V	7.42V	6.91V	8.54Y	10.60Y	7.74V	6.92V	11.57V	12.59V	11.68V	14.43Y	17.91Y
Dominican Republic 243	29.89V	32.44Y	41.06Y	53.93Y	61.62Y	76.16Y	94.51Y	12.54V	13.61Y	17.23Y	22.63Y	25.85Y	31.95Y	39.65Y
Ecuador 248	.63V	.75V	.42V	.25V	.27V	.63V	.79Y	6.28V	4.26V	6.08V	15.88V	8.11V	7.46V	9.25Y
El Salvador 253	.15V	.23V	.19V	.25V	.28V	.26V	.31V	.78V	1.38V	1.52V	4.08V	5.94V	8.43V	8.87V
Grenada 328	.02Y	.02Y	.03Y	.04Y	.04Y	.05Y	.07Y	—Y	—Y	—Y	—Y	—Y	—Y	—Y
Guatemala 258	4.91V	3.07V	2.02V	2.16V	3.32V	4.10Y	5.09Y	5.20V	6.32V	11.10V	12.74V	11.70V	14.45Y	17.94Y
Guyana 336	21.16Y	22.96Y	29.06Y	38.17Y	43.61Y	53.90Y	66.89Y	8.06Y	8.75Y	11.07Y	14.54Y	16.61Y	20.53Y	25.48Y
Haiti 263	10.39V	7.50V	10.89V	8.07V	9.22Y	11.40Y	14.15Y	—Y	—Y	—Y	—Y	—Y	—Y	—Y
Honduras 268	2.35V	1.59V	2.35V	3.40V	3.89Y	4.81Y	5.97Y	.13V	.56V	1.51V	1.12V	1.28Y	1.59Y	1.97Y
Jamaica 343	4.19V	3.63V	6.68V	3.45V	3.52V	1.83V	15.21V	.85V	3.59V	2.60V	2.23V	1.70V	5.37V	6.73V
Mexico 273	25.67V	24.29V	20.31V	21.16V	20.30V	43.40V	15.65V	193.11V	157.67V	179.46V	194.60V	243.75V	213.86V	208.51V
Netherlands Antilles 353	.15V	.18V	.17V	.22Y	.25Y	.31Y	.38Y	132.17V	67.69V	35.34V	46.42Y	53.03Y	65.55Y	81.34Y
Nicaragua 278	.62V	.26V	.37V	.55V	.27V	.89V	5.70V	1.24V	1.11V	.43V	.11V	.55V	.41V	.72V
Panama 283	.56V	.13V	.20V	.41V	14.34V	19.77V	23.71V	1.82V	2.18V	.78V	.80V	.52V	.85V	3.37V
Paraguay 288	.32V	.21V	.07V	.13V	.10V	.03V	.03Y	—V	.05V	.05V	.01V	.01V	.05V	.06Y
Peru 293	.46V	.37V	.37V	.41V	.65V	.54V	.59Y	3.25V	.86V	2.57V	2.77V	3.33V	3.70V	4.98Y
St. Lucia 362	.06Y	.07Y	.08Y	.11Y	.12Y	.15Y	.19Y	—Y	—Y	—Y	—Y	—Y	—Y	—Y
St. Vincent & Grens. 364	—V	—V	—V	—V	.01V	.01Y	.01Y	.01V	.04V	.09V	—V	—V	—Y	—Y
Suriname 366	.04Y	.04Y	.05Y	.07Y	.08Y	.09Y	.12Y	.19Y	.21Y	.26Y	.35Y	.40Y	.49Y	.61Y
Trinidad and Tobago 369	.08V	.20V	.25Y	.33Y	.38Y	.47Y	.59Y	14.45V	13.90V	17.60Y	23.11Y	26.41Y	32.64Y	40.50Y
Uruguay 298	.18V	.19Y	.31V	.22V	.32V	.39Y	.49Y	.65V	.70Y	.81V	9.66V	37.04V	45.78Y	56.82Y
Venezuela, Rep. Bol. 299	13.99V	4.80V	103.64V	105.27V	85.43V	30.81V	49.38V	520.30V	335.94V	10.71V	1,188.85V	1,883.66V	2,359.98V	2,847.03V
Memorandum Items														
European Union 998	500.21Y	546.52Y	597.23Y	820.42Y	833.35Y	832.82Y	746.20Y	1,419.63Y	1,205.63Y	1,360.20Y	1,321.69Y	1,769.09Y	2,336.96Y	2,235.63Y
Oil Exporting Ctys 999	32.14Y	54.46Y	159.57Y	178.11Y	178.25Y	145.92Y	198.53Y	538.70Y	354.52Y	34.37Y	1,219.00Y	1,923.50Y	2,409.78Y	2,913.24Y
Non-Oil Develop.Ctys 201	762.63Y	660.48Y	580.34Y	714.75Y	653.89Y	995.51Y	1,669.41Y	1,232.87Y	1,043.66Y	1,010.64Y	1,357.68Y	2,182.28Y	3,295.59Y	3,159.23Y
PERCENT DISTRIBUTION														
Industrial Countries 101	**49.7**	**52.8**	**55.1**	**59.6**	**61.7**	**55.6**	**48.9**	**50.1**	**53.5**	**64.8**	**45.9**	**40.5**	**37.2**	**36.9**
Developing Countries 202	**50.3**	**47.2**	**44.9**	**40.4**	**38.3**	**44.4**	**51.1**	**49.9**	**46.5**	**35.2**	**54.1**	**59.5**	**62.8**	**63.1**
Africa 607	**2.2**	**2.8**	**2.8**	**2.5**	**2.8**	**2.9**	**2.5**	**.9**	**.7**	**.8**	**.6**	**.5**	**.4**	**.5**
Asia 507	**7.5**	**8.6**	**7.8**	**8.6**	**11.1**	**20.0**	**28.6**	**13.0**	**14.5**	**12.8**	**11.1**	**14.1**	**20.7**	**16.4**
Europe 170	**28.6**	**22.9**	**14.0**	**11.2**	**5.0**	**4.0**	**3.4**	**3.0**	**2.6**	**3.3**	**2.2**	**3.4**	**3.6**	**4.3**
Middle East 407	**1.4**	**3.2**	**3.4**	**2.8**	**3.6**	**3.7**	**3.4**	**.5**	**.6**	**.7**	**.6**	**.6**	**.5**	**.6**
Western Hemisphere 207	**10.6**	**9.8**	**17.0**	**15.3**	**16.0**	**13.7**	**13.1**	**32.5**	**28.2**	**17.6**	**39.6**	**41.0**	**37.6**	**41.2**

	Exports							Imports						
	2001	2002	2003	2004	2005	2006	2007	2001	2002	2003	2004	2005	2006	2007
ANNUAL PERCENT CHANGE														
World........ 001	1.0	–4.2	8.7	34.1	–1.7	18.5	42.2	–6.8	–15.3	–1.3	60.7	44.8	31.7	6.0
Industrial Countries........ 101	–13.6	1.7	13.4	45.1	1.8	6.8	25.1	5.1	–9.6	19.5	14.0	27.6	21.0	5.3
Developing Countries........ 202	21.2	–10.0	3.5	20.7	–6.8	37.2	63.7	–16.3	–21.1	–25.3	146.6	59.3	39.0	6.4
Africa........ 607	27.9	24.0	8.3	18.9	9.5	23.8	23.3	15.1	–37.8	22.1	9.0	20.4	22.3	23.9
Asia........ 507	25.6	9.2	–1.6	48.4	26.4	114.2	103.5	32.2	–5.9	–13.0	40.0	83.6	92.7	–15.7
Europe........ 170	22.6	–23.4	–33.5	7.9	–56.5	–3.5	19.8	–23.6	–27.0	25.1	7.2	125.3	39.3	27.0
Middle East........ 407	–14.4	114.6	15.0	9.5	26.9	24.1	29.3	–10.7	6.5	21.9	31.4	35.6	25.2	21.2
Western Hemisphere........ 207	20.0	–11.4	89.5	21.0	2.4	1.7	36.3	–27.0	–26.6	–38.3	261.3	49.8	20.8	16.2

		Exports							Imports						
		2001	2002	2003	2004	2005	2006	2007	2001	2002	2003	2004	2005	2006	2007
		Millions of U.S. Dollars							*Millions of U.S. Dollars*						
IFS World Total		**976.0**	**769.6**	**833.5**	**1,081.5**	**1,303.2**	**1,152.8**	**1,254.3**	**3,922.6**	**3,863.4**	**4,288.1**	**5,658.6**	**6,282.0**	**6,950.7**	**8,686.8**
DOTS World Total	**001**	**974.8**	**849.3**	**925.3**	**1,171.0**	**1,457.5**	**1,329.9**	**1,391.0**	**4,097.8**	**4,086.4**	**4,487.2**	**5,730.1**	**6,296.3**	**6,931.6**	**8,634.8**
Industrial Countries	**101**	**423.0**	**471.6**	**556.9**	**724.5**	**917.4**	**738.1**	**790.4**	**2,875.5**	**2,742.2**	**3,018.8**	**4,166.5**	**4,477.4**	**4,842.2**	**6,165.0**
United States	111	16.68	19.11	17.75	19.23	22.75	9.87	8.57	468.65	199.76	186.65	131.18	98.10	105.13	105.23
Canada	156	1.21	.93	3.07	1.63	2.68	1.63	3.40	9.53	9.74	8.17	14.12	8.29	10.59	12.58
Australia	193	.79	.99	1.53	1.47	1.97	2.48	5.11	9.80	8.36	8.68	9.96	7.56	10.79	14.50
Japan	158	3.50	1.30	2.50	23.66	22.24	16.21	20.04	238.96	274.79	251.18	271.71	177.61	172.32	220.85
New Zealand	196	.05	.14	.26	.22	.45	.51	.68	5.04	6.09	6.75	11.45	12.13	10.58	14.08
Austria	122	3.51	4.67	5.61	11.93	6.66	6.19	6.57	25.59	25.92	27.98	35.14	34.10	43.67	53.39
Belgium	124	18.03	18.46	20.58	10.76	11.07	18.09	21.37	62.07	62.49	70.11	114.90	133.52	151.95	194.89
Denmark	128	3.82	4.09	5.96	11.32	3.75	3.86	5.78	30.25	31.15	37.32	39.94	34.68	33.41	53.32
Finland	172	1.80	1.87	2.16	2.12	2.32	2.80	3.13	28.05	30.20	31.26	83.91	206.07	64.66	31.63
France	132	9.61	11.54	10.89	28.70	256.53	101.35	11.89	264.90	209.34	227.98	358.65	235.70	297.43	466.87
Germany	134	22.06	21.75	27.64	58.56	82.39	64.71	91.63	268.52	359.42	335.94	511.86	528.99	622.57	809.11
Greece	174	82.66	69.57	85.31	139.28	177.12	188.51	293.37	350.15	390.96	536.49	870.27	1,089.16	1,216.93	1,524.13
Iceland	176	.04	.06	.04	.03	.05	.05	.10	.20	.16	.28	.35	.43	.25	.43
Ireland	178	5.00	4.92	5.75	7.95	7.68	15.14	21.06	29.06	29.64	31.53	31.77	35.86	32.46	33.03
Italy	136	6.38	20.44	14.89	20.33	15.00	47.50	40.39	347.02	377.68	439.44	602.48	648.28	790.76	882.75
Luxembourg	137	—	.01	—	.02	.02	.11	.32	.38	.56	1.41	2.28	2.91	3.19	4.85
Malta	181	1.92	2.70	2.36	7.68	3.41	4.54	4.87	18.27	3.00	1.05	.99	8.66	4.01	48.86
Netherlands	138	15.33	21.31	23.09	30.07	31.01	20.35	22.58	82.10	87.11	109.45	188.98	249.99	296.98	351.79
Norway	142	19.49	2.52	2.52	4.55	4.86	3.56	3.37	8.17	11.91	4.53	6.08	9.84	7.06	9.07
Portugal	182	.51	.63	6.17	2.98	.73	.94	.77	14.45	16.82	19.35	26.00	24.98	32.36	39.07
Slovenia	961	3.46	3.19	1.17	1.00	1.10	1.77	1.79	3.16	3.15	3.90	14.05	30.66	3.55	6.74
Spain	184	15.99	12.63	10.40	9.59	6.29	8.87	8.30	150.16	143.39	178.46	208.62	208.54	200.41	308.03
Sweden	144	5.47	5.46	6.90	8.48	7.70	9.15	10.33	66.25	63.25	75.67	81.67	83.55	67.46	84.36
Switzerland	146	3.17	3.14	3.45	4.54	2.73	9.60	6.05	49.22	54.34	54.52	59.83	44.28	46.81	65.05
United Kingdom	112	182.56	240.15	296.87	318.35	246.91	200.37	198.94	345.60	342.99	370.67	490.30	563.56	616.92	830.42
Developing Countries	**202**	**463.0**	**307.7**	**278.1**	**349.1**	**295.8**	**326.0**	**366.9**	**1,058.5**	**1,115.0**	**1,250.5**	**1,477.6**	**1,716.1**	**1,988.3**	**2,446.5**
Africa	**607**	**22.8**	**29.4**	**31.0**	**33.9**	**27.3**	**30.1**	**33.3**	**16.2**	**19.4**	**21.6**	**27.7**	**18.8**	**24.7**	**35.6**
Algeria	612	1.03	3.70	2.78	2.50	3.33	3.42	2.73	.05	.39	1.06	.05	.09	4.88	13.93
Angola	614	.08	.62	.92	.27	.08	.21	.07	—	—	—	—	—	—	—
Benin	638	1.46	.11	.21	.22	—	.21	—	—	—	—	—	—	—	—
Botswana	616	1.22	.60	.38	.61	1.53	.72	.01	—	—	—	—	—	—	—
Burkina Faso	748	—	—	—	—	—	.02	.02	—	—	—	.01	.03	.03	—
Burundi	618	—	.04	.02	.05	.09	.03	.07	—	—	—	—	—	—	—
Cameroon	622	.05	.26	.26	.03	—	.01	.06	.13	.13	.24	.24	.12	.17	.27
Cape Verde	624	—	—	—	.01	—	—	—	—	—	—	—	—	—	—
Central African Rep.	626	.14	.01	.11	.24	—	—	.01	.19	.60	.05	.06	—	—	—
Chad	628	—	—	—	—	—	.04	.01	.01	—	—	.03	—	—	—
Congo, Dem. Rep. of	636	—	—	—	—	—	.01	.06	.08	.06	.03	.07	.15	.11	.59
Congo, Republic of	634	—	—	—	.06	.43	.16	.26	—	—	—	.01	—	.03	.06
Côte d'Ivoire	662	.05	.01	—	.02	.06	.02	.03	.25	.45	.47	.59	1.01	.62	.94
Djibouti	611	.56	.53	2.48	.45	.14	.04	.04	.13	.03	.17	.05	—	—	—
Equatorial Guinea	642	—	.38	.09	—	—	—	—	—	—	—	—	—	—	—
Eritrea	643	.25	.38	.18	.13	.21	.11	.03	—	—	—	—	—	—	—
Ethiopia	644	1.16	2.13	2.44	1.95	2.39	2.66	3.69	.08	.03	.03	.10	.30	.20	.33
Gabon	646	.04	—	—	.01	—	—	—	.42	.39	.10	.52	.58	.22	.99
Gambia, The	648	.07	.11	.13	.08	.11	.17	.15	—	—	.01	—	—	—	—
Ghana	652	.52	1.34	.64	.35	.21	.20	.76	.23	.18	.50	.24	.21	.25	.21
Guinea	656	.50	.27	.08	.16	.15	.30	.09	—	—	—	—	—	—	—
Guinea-Bissau	654	.01	.01	—	.04	—	—	—	—	—	—	—	—	—	—
Kenya	664	.76	.64	1.17	1.30	.84	1.44	1.50	.60	.41	.45	.33	.72	1.27	1.73
Lesotho	666	.17	.08	.18	.31	.28	.71	.51	—	—	—	—	—	—	—
Liberia	668	.05	—	—	—	.10	.03	.11	—	.06	—	—	—	—	—
Madagascar	674	—	—	.01	.02	.08	.12	.16	.02	.03	.02	.02	—	.14	.26
Malawi	676	.07	.07	.53	.19	.26	.14	1.48	.03	.04	.01	—	—	—	—
Mali	678	.03	.04	.17	.06	.06	.10	.07	—	—	.01	.11	.04	.01	.02
Mauritania	682	.11	.08	.22	.02	—	.12	—	.23	.26	.18	.02	—	—	—
Mauritius	684	.20	.06	.28	.26	1.63	1.06	1.31	.37	.27	.31	.29	.03	—	.02
Morocco	686	1.99	1.66	1.75	.73	.38	.89	.76	3.59	4.82	5.91	2.89	.56	.32	.44
Mozambique	688	.07	.04	.04	.05	.06	.09	.82	.02	—	—	—	—	—	—
Namibia	728	.36	.02	.05	.25	.21	.38	.36	.01	.01	.03	.27	.50	.16	.42
Niger	692	.19	.19	—	.07	—	—	—	—	—	—	—	.01	—	—
Nigeria	694	3.41	1.88	2.68	1.92	2.19	2.01	1.73	.01	—	.01	.06	.21	.03	.01
Rwanda	714	—	—	—	—	.07	—	.01	—	—	—	.01	—	—	—
St. Helena	856	—	—	—	—	—	—	.01	—	—	—	—	.01	—	—
Senegal	722	.05	.06	—	.77	.01	.01	.15	.07	.02	—	—	—	.06	.36
Seychelles	718	.09	.26	.16	.16	.08	.09	.07	.16	.12	.12	.33	.13	.15	.23
Sierra Leone	724	—	.14	.05	.01	—	—	.01	—	—	.17	.07	—	.48	.02
Somalia	726	.23	.08	.17	.06	.34	.23	.16	—	—	—	—	—	—	—
South Africa	199	.84	2.46	1.56	1.38	.99	1.15	2.17	7.52	8.63	8.68	9.83	9.52	11.47	10.29

	Exports							Imports						
	2001	2002	2003	2004	2005	2006	2007	2001	2002	2003	2004	2005	2006	2007
	Millions of U.S. Dollars							*Millions of U.S. Dollars*						
Sudan......732	3.66	3.82	5.44	8.98	7.61	8.73	9.66	.07	.18	.13	.71	1.50	.05	.02
Swaziland......734	.17	.30	.59	.65	.70	.55	.15	—	—	.09	.05	—	.09	.46
Tanzania......738	.61	.74	.73	7.86	.98	1.65	1.99	.02	.09	.12	.23	.36	.44	.53
Togo......742	—	—	—	.04	.01	—	.04	—	—	—	—	—	—	—
Tunisia......744	2.20	5.84	4.03	1.11	1.14	1.21	.71	1.63	1.89	2.27	10.31	2.63	3.31	3.18
Uganda......746	.34	.40	.35	.47	.56	.95	.98	.20	.30	.33	.15	—	.20	.31
Zambia......754	.14	.07	.06	.12	.12	.10	.14	.03	.05	.06	—	—	—	—
Zimbabwe......698	.16	.39	.20	.06	.12	.15	.18	.01	—	.03	.06	.04	.01	.01
Asia......507	**23.3**	**25.4**	**26.9**	**37.7**	**46.5**	**49.3**	**54.8**	**395.1**	**403.9**	**478.5**	**527.6**	**507.3**	**570.0**	**815.4**
Afghanistan, I.S. of......512	—	.03	.01	.06	.05	.17	.49	.05	.02	.06	—	.06	.02	.03
American Samoa......859	—	—	—	—	—	—	—	—	—	—	.02	.01	—	—
Bangladesh......513	.25	.34	.57	.50	.51	.97	1.35	1.27	1.12	2.06	2.38	1.96	2.61	2.53
Bhutan......514	.03	—	—	—	.01	.01	—	—	.02	—	—	—	—	—
Brunei Darussalam......516	—	—	.03	.04	.07	.05	.14	.09	—	—	.06	—	—	—
Cambodia......522	.13	.22	.03	.04	.21	.17	.65	.06	.09	.04	.12	.04	.08	.22
China,P.R.: Mainland......924	.76	.76	1.05	2.66	14.01	11.05	10.38	141.56	164.08	219.16	231.07	240.39	291.98	456.63
China,P.R.:Hong Kong......532	4.27	4.45	5.90	6.97	6.53	6.36	7.14	28.17	31.84	35.60	36.13	26.55	24.46	29.46
China,P.R.:Macao......546	.02	.02	.09	.03	.01	.02	—	.54	.60	.75	.50	.19	.25	.29
Fiji......819	.04	.01	.05	—	—	—	—	—	—	—	—	—	—	—
French Polynesia......887	—	—	—	—	.02	—	—	—	—	—	—	—	—	—
Guam......829	—	—	—	—	.01	—	—	—	—	—	—	—	—	—
India......534	2.41	1.79	2.50	5.28	3.62	5.54	5.64	33.27	30.78	33.38	39.05	35.69	43.53	49.13
Indonesia......536	.13	.18	.13	.12	.32	.11	.28	20.36	19.13	17.99	15.60	15.30	14.12	15.90
Korea......542	.44	.93	.42	2.12	2.24	3.17	3.22	37.74	28.45	32.99	32.36	38.54	48.20	56.88
Lao People's Dem.Rep......544	—	—	—	—	—	—	—	—	.05	.04	.01	.02	.05	—
Malaysia......548	3.76	3.46	4.16	4.74	3.60	3.31	3.14	17.20	15.08	16.07	18.79	19.77	22.79	27.34
Maldives......556	.07	—	.02	.11	.03	.01	.11	—	—	—	—	.01	—	—
Mongolia......948	.03	.03	.02	.02	.16	.19	.47	.01	—	.02	—	—	—	—
Myanmar......518	.44	.41	.25	.42	.44	.58	.31	.33	.32	.22	.02	.07	.21	.40
Nauru......836	—	—	—	—	—	—	—	—	—	—	—	.21	—	—
Nepal......558	—	.08	.14	.02	.03	.03	.20	—	.01	.01	.03	.03	.01	.01
Pakistan......564	.62	.77	1.86	1.61	1.63	3.66	4.64	5.90	5.32	6.77	6.64	6.80	6.24	7.25
Papua New Guinea......853	—	—	.01	—	—	—	—	—	.17	.10	—	.17	.11	.05
Philippines......566	.39	.74	.36	.61	.60	1.10	1.17	1.79	2.48	2.23	2.25	2.27	2.15	3.32
Samoa......862	.01	—	—	.03	—	—	—	—	—	—	—	—	—	—
Singapore......576	3.41	3.43	3.36	3.55	2.88	3.14	3.49	7.93	10.47	19.45	39.57	31.59	28.25	45.37
Solomon Islands......813	—	—	—	—	.01	—	—	—	—	—	—	—	—	—
Sri Lanka......524	1.07	2.18	1.34	2.25	1.98	1.81	1.76	3.25	4.88	5.20	3.30	1.32	1.62	1.91
Taiwan Province of China......528	.93	.86	.65	.90	.85	1.10	1.36	42.50	40.45	42.13	42.54	40.93	40.95	51.85
Thailand......578	1.58	1.86	1.14	1.85	1.88	1.52	2.00	48.83	44.33	39.29	52.35	40.88	35.44	58.11
Vietnam......582	2.51	2.81	2.84	3.75	4.80	5.18	6.80	4.21	4.22	4.93	4.77	4.58	6.98	8.75
Europe......170	**137.6**	**74.6**	**60.3**	**90.5**	**83.5**	**87.3**	**142.6**	**240.5**	**275.9**	**309.8**	**352.6**	**364.0**	**455.8**	**439.1**
Albania......914	3.34	4.52	4.01	3.18	2.74	4.20	2.97	—	.04	.06	.09	.01	.01	2.60
Armenia......911	.26	.33	.78	.57	.58	.67	.99	.09	.27	.12	.08	1.16	.08	.19
Azerbaijan......912	—	.16	.10	.22	.36	.42	.46	.46	.05	—	—	1.14	—	—
Belarus......913	.06	.09	.12	.89	1.24	1.74	1.57	.01	.01	.04	1.51	13.40	9.48	3.68
Bosnia & Herzegovina......963	.22	.31	.14	.13	.07	.91	.33	.02	.13	.66	.12	.01	.05	.08
Bulgaria......918	4.99	9.94	4.52	11.46	7.44	4.79	7.60	14.79	12.81	17.02	21.95	43.10	76.70	60.51
Croatia......960	2.08	1.13	1.26	1.45	1.42	1.59	1.47	3.29	3.20	3.70	13.68	9.43	7.94	21.06
Czech Republic......935	4.31	6.79	8.73	9.51	8.54	6.21	10.03	7.04	9.51	11.75	12.00	11.22	15.58	28.46
Estonia......939	.64	.72	.70	1.10	1.23	1.28	2.05	.13	.23	.54	.64	.42	.52	.82
Faroe Islands......816	—	—	—	—	—	—	—	.04	—	.08	.12	.08	.16	—
Georgia......915	.19	.86	.34	.31	.20	.47	.56	.12	.05	8.41	26.98	30.34	65.69	38.30
Gibraltar......823	.01	.74	1.35	1.80	2.12	1.33	3.49	—	—	—	—	.02	—	—
Hungary......944	.84	.89	.67	.44	.60	2.50	2.51	8.72	13.10	9.31	17.89	56.71	39.39	57.73
Kazakhstan......916	2.82	.79	1.24	1.15	1.08	1.31	1.98	.18	.21	.04	—	1.49	4.66	5.83
Kosovo......967	—	—	—	—	.03	.43	.32	—	—	—	—	—	.02	—
Kyrgyz Republic......917	—	—	—	—	—	—	—	—	.01	.06	.01	—	—	—
Latvia......941	1.05	.91	.52	.65	1.06	1.03	1.75	.19	.14	.25	1.50	.79	.41	.53
Lithuania......946	.92	.43	.59	1.21	2.46	2.47	3.39	.40	.61	.93	1.21	1.86	2.89	5.11
Macedonia, FYR......962	1.35	1.22	1.09	1.00	.93	.80	.49	.14	.30	.24	.17	1.92	.85	2.38
Moldova......921	.12	.18	.04	.28	.18	.60	.89	3.34	2.55	6.49	8.72	5.64	2.63	15.07
Montenegro, Rep. of......943	—	—	—	—	—	.16	.17	—	—	—	—	—	—	.03
Poland......964	.29	.33	.64	1.38	1.27	1.78	3.61	9.06	9.65	11.84	13.53	16.61	19.67	34.80
Romania......968	10.07	10.05	8.82	16.49	14.27	17.69	42.72	6.86	8.26	21.88	48.79	13.52	33.66	19.09
Russia......922	84.17	20.58	15.56	23.14	19.64	20.89	26.55	122.66	142.88	138.23	77.43	57.74	53.36	50.87
Serbia, Rep. of......942	—	—	—	—	—	5.17	7.83	—	—	—	—	—	23.99	12.80
Serbia & Montenegro......965	2.59	3.54	1.98	4.37	8.97	—	—	1.68	7.12	2.73	2.85	15.80	—	—
Slovak Republic......936	3.77	2.25	3.95	6.02	3.35	4.61	7.46	5.93	3.98	6.77	6.43	7.50	11.36	13.65
Tajikistan......923	—	—	—	—	—	—	—	—	.16	—	—	—	—	—
Turkey......186	5.19	2.97	.43	.12	.25	.02	1.85	.66	.83	1.28	9.33	15.68	11.39	15.08
Turkmenistan......925	—	—	—	—	—	.08	—	1.14	—	—	.01	—	.01	.01
Ukraine......926	8.18	4.85	2.71	3.64	3.43	4.60	9.78	53.45	59.86	67.34	87.53	58.37	75.35	50.41
Uzbekistan......927	.10	.01	—	—	.09	—	.11	.07	.01	—	—	—	—	—
Europe n.s......884	—	—	—	—	.01	—	—	—	—	.01	—	—	—	.02
Middle East......407	**275.2**	**171.6**	**151.9**	**183.0**	**136.1**	**157.2**	**134.5**	**361.5**	**363.2**	**382.7**	**471.5**	**684.7**	**733.2**	**873.8**
Bahrain......419	1.93	1.81	1.73	1.51	2.59	2.81	3.15	.21	.26	.50	.70	.50	4.41	2.54
Egypt......469	26.13	24.45	22.77	7.35	7.71	11.83	17.10	10.39	22.26	23.12	53.87	65.09	95.55	102.46
Iran, I.R. of......429	5.11	1.36	1.09	1.61	5.30	5.30	7.40	2.55	1.76	2.53	2.67	2.86	4.00	2.84

	Exports 2001	2002	2003	2004	2005	2006	2007	Imports 2001	2002	2003	2004	2005	2006	2007
	Millions of U.S. Dollars							*Millions of U.S. Dollars*						
Iraq.......... 433	14.80	8.89	1.84	19.40	12.01	4.95	4.19	—	.14	—	—	.01	—	.04
Israel.......... 436	14.14	8.06	8.38	11.90	14.42	12.95	11.82	155.04	151.27	169.08	252.04	448.77	432.36	563.17
Jordan.......... 439	16.01	17.29	25.01	16.49	12.90	13.21	14.64	.52	1.02	2.02	2.60	2.94	2.92	3.09
Kuwait.......... 443	6.02	5.60	4.65	5.49	6.06	6.77	6.95	3.78	3.16	1.04	2.03	14.27	17.74	15.37
Lebanon.......... 446	36.18	30.69	31.50	31.44	13.32	14.94	19.82	8.02	9.73	16.93	22.31	24.58	21.26	23.65
Libya.......... 672	4.35	3.04	3.82	5.70	6.69	7.71	5.68	1.34	.58	1.08	—	2.62	3.93	11.19
Oman.......... 449	3.37	3.74	3.17	3.30	2.69	3.19	3.06	.43	.42	1.30	2.35	2.21	1.63	2.72
Qatar.......... 453	2.67	3.10	2.47	1.82	1.74	4.47	4.58	.42	.45	.92	1.72	1.20	.47	.38
Saudi Arabia.......... 456	9.20	8.00	7.01	8.18	11.79	8.21	11.29	16.27	11.26	19.35	18.30	14.83	20.17	62.51
Syrian Arab Republic.......... 463	58.21	25.96	16.80	11.76	2.93	3.31	3.41	150.13	146.00	118.38	71.32	13.46	16.34	11.78
United Arab Emirates.......... 466	76.25	29.08	20.92	55.90	33.44	55.08	18.81	12.43	14.96	26.09	41.51	91.41	97.80	72.06
West Bank/Gaza Strip.......... 487	—	.01	.03	—	—	.29	.10	—	—	—	—	.09	.12	.05
Yemen, Republic of.......... 474	.88	.54	.70	1.09	2.54	2.52	2.67	—	—	.38	.03	—	14.60	.01
Middle East n.s.......... 489	—	—	—	.01	—	—	—	—	—	—	.02	—	—	—
Western Hemisphere.......... 207	**4.1**	**6.7**	**8.1**	**4.0**	**2.3**	**2.0**	**1.6**	**45.3**	**52.4**	**57.9**	**98.3**	**141.3**	**204.6**	**282.5**
Antigua and Barbuda.......... 311	.01	.01	.09	.16	.02	.02	.13	—	—	—	.01	—	—	—
Argentina.......... 213	.07	.11	.15	.02	.08	.02	—	19.57	30.26	28.82	29.16	23.48	23.36	40.04
Aruba.......... 314	.05	.08	.08	.09	.13	.08	—	—	—	—	—	—	—	—
Bahamas, The.......... 313	.15	.12	.29	.17	.16	.12	.09	.32	.31	.34	—	—	.01	—
Barbados.......... 316	.23	.27	.51	.44	.37	.43	.08	—	—	—	—	—	—	—
Belize.......... 339	—	—	.01	—	—	—	—	.03	—	—	.16	.02	—	—
Bermuda.......... 319	.01	—	—	.02	—	—	—	—	—	—	—	.02	—	—
Bolivia.......... 218	—	.01	.02	—	—	—	.04	.01	.01	.01	—	—	.01	.02
Brazil.......... 223	.15	1.63	—	.08	.14	.08	.01	15.79	13.50	19.86	61.76	111.63	175.68	233.12
Chile.......... 228	.77	.85	.46	.12	.14	.29	.02	.42	.33	.46	.64	.87	1.60	2.45
Colombia.......... 233	—	—	—	—	—	—	—	.30	.65	.47	.21	.02	.02	.14
Costa Rica.......... 238	.08	—	—	.45	.42	—	—	.14	.25	.31	.06	.06	.01	.07
Dominica.......... 321	—	—	—	—	—	.02	.01	—	—	—	.01	—	—	.07
Dominican Republic.......... 243	.02	.62	1.03	.07	.02	—	.04	.14	.09	.46	.55	.09	.14	.15
Ecuador.......... 248	.04	.13	.26	.16	.10	.13	.08	.12	.16	.25	.09	.03	.19	.37
El Salvador.......... 253	—	—	—	—	—	—	—	—	—	.07	.02	—	.01	—
Falkland Islands.......... 323	—	.01	—	—	—	—	.01	—	—	—	—	—	—	—
Greenland.......... 326	—	—	.03	.03	.04	.04	.05	.04	.02	.23	.07	.09	—	—
Grenada.......... 328	—	.01	.01	.03	.04	.01	.01	—	—	—	—	—	—	—
Guatemala.......... 258	.03	—	.31	.09	.02	—	—	.03	—	—	.11	.96	—	—
Guyana.......... 336	.06	.09	.06	.11	—	.07	.03	—	—	—	—	—	.02	—
Haiti.......... 263	.28	.22	.38	.35	.18	.01	.06	—	—	—	—	—	—	—
Honduras.......... 268	.01	—	—	—	—	—	—	.09	.03	.02	.03	.08	.10	.10
Jamaica.......... 343	.05	.21	.32	.22	.05	.05	.06	.22	.18	.04	—	.02	.01	.02
Mexico.......... 273	—	.01	—	.20	.04	.04	.17	3.31	2.68	3.38	3.14	2.31	2.29	3.78
Netherlands Antilles.......... 353	.03	.21	.45	.15	.05	.23	.21	—	—	—	—	—	—	—
Nicaragua.......... 278	—	—	—	—	—	—	—	—	—	.04	.02	.02	.02	.03
Panama.......... 283	.53	1.70	2.48	.63	.03	.03	.05	.06	.26	.14	.03	.05	—	—
Paraguay.......... 288	—	.01	.22	.04	—	—	—	—	—	.59	.03	.02	.01	.05
Peru.......... 293	.10	.19	.71	.15	.02	—	—	1.16	.23	.69	1.23	.63	.29	.97
St. Pierre-Miquelon.......... 363	—	—	—	—	—	—	—	.02	.19	.03	—	—	—	—
St. Vincent & Grens.......... 364	—	—	—	—	—	.02	—	—	—	—	—	—	—	—
Suriname.......... 366	.01	—	.07	.02	.05	.14	.16	—	—	—	—	.01	—	.01
Trinidad and Tobago.......... 369	.11	.14	.13	.14	.20	.15	.07	.02	—	.06	—	.02	—	—
Uruguay.......... 298	1.22	.09	.03	.04	.02	.05	.04	.70	1.03	1.23	.47	.76	.84	1.02
Venezuela, Rep. Bol.......... 299	.04	.03	—	—	—	—	—	2.78	2.24	—	—	—	—	.04
Western Hem. n.s.......... 399	—	—	—	—	—	.01	.19	—	—	.38	.42	.08	.02	—
Other Countries n.i.e.......... 910	**—**	**—**	**.8**	**—**	**—**	**—**	**—**	**9.6**	**6.8**	**13.0**	**13.5**	**1.7**	**3.0**	**3.3**
Cuba.......... 928	—	—	.74	—	—	—	—	9.63	6.82	13.04	13.11	1.17	2.91	3.16
North Korea.......... 954	.02	—	.01	—	—	—	—	—	—	—	.35	.50	.10	.16
Countries & Areas n.s.......... 898	**—**	**—**	**—**	**7.5**	**4.5**	**2.8**	**.2**	**152.0**	**221.9**	**204.9**	**72.6**	**74.8**	**98.1**	**20.0**
Special Categories.......... 899	**88.8**	**70.0**	**89.5**	**90.0**	**239.8**	**262.9**	**233.5**	**2.1**	**.6**	**—**	**—**	**26.3**	**—**	**—**
Memorandum Items														
European Union.......... 998	389.93	455.70	541.54	689.44	878.20	714.12	773.89	2,117.44	2,214.27	2,539.38	3,715.04	4,214.32	4,568.53	5,864.34
Oil Exporting Ctys.......... 999	126.37	68.60	50.57	105.94	85.56	101.22	66.68	60.43	54.47	71.37	84.30	145.00	164.76	197.01
Non-Oil Develop.Ctys.......... 201	336.60	239.15	227.56	243.13	210.27	224.76	300.18	998.09	1,060.49	1,179.10	1,393.27	1,571.11	1,823.57	2,249.45
PERCENT DISTRIBUTION														
Industrial Countries.......... 101	**43.4**	**55.5**	**60.2**	**61.9**	**62.9**	**55.5**	**56.8**	**70.2**	**67.1**	**67.3**	**72.7**	**71.1**	**69.9**	**71.4**
Developing Countries.......... 202	**47.5**	**36.2**	**30.1**	**29.8**	**20.3**	**24.5**	**26.4**	**25.8**	**27.3**	**27.9**	**25.8**	**27.3**	**28.7**	**28.3**
Africa.......... 607	**2.3**	**3.5**	**3.3**	**2.9**	**1.9**	**2.3**	**2.4**	**.4**	**.5**	**.5**	**.5**	**.3**	**.4**	**.4**
Asia.......... 507	**2.4**	**3.0**	**2.9**	**3.2**	**3.2**	**3.7**	**3.9**	**9.6**	**9.9**	**10.7**	**9.2**	**8.1**	**8.2**	**9.4**
Europe.......... 170	**14.1**	**8.8**	**6.5**	**7.7**	**5.7**	**6.6**	**10.3**	**5.9**	**6.8**	**6.9**	**6.2**	**5.8**	**6.6**	**5.1**
Middle East.......... 407	**28.2**	**20.2**	**16.4**	**15.6**	**9.3**	**11.8**	**9.7**	**8.8**	**8.9**	**8.5**	**8.2**	**10.9**	**10.6**	**10.1**
Western Hemisphere.......... 207	**.4**	**.8**	**.9**	**.3**	**.2**	**.2**	**.1**	**1.1**	**1.3**	**1.3**	**1.7**	**2.2**	**3.0**	**3.3**
Other Countries n.i.e.......... 910	**—**	**—**	**.1**	**—**	**—**	**—**	**—**	**.2**	**.2**	**.3**	**.2**	**—**	**—**	**—**
ANNUAL PERCENT CHANGE														
World.......... 001	**6.3**	**–12.9**	**8.9**	**26.6**	**24.5**	**–8.8**	**4.6**	**10.4**	**–.3**	**9.8**	**27.7**	**9.9**	**10.1**	**24.6**
Industrial Countries.......... 101	**14.2**	**11.5**	**18.1**	**30.1**	**26.6**	**–19.5**	**7.1**	**10.1**	**–4.6**	**10.1**	**38.0**	**7.5**	**8.1**	**27.3**
Developing Countries.......... 202	**5.9**	**–33.5**	**–9.6**	**25.5**	**–15.3**	**10.2**	**12.5**	**–2.9**	**5.3**	**12.2**	**18.2**	**16.1**	**15.9**	**23.0**

	Exports							Imports						
	2001	2002	2003	2004	2005	2006	2007	2001	2002	2003	2004	2005	2006	2007
Africa.....607	55.8	29.0	5.1	9.5	−19.3	10.2	10.6	−17.9	20.0	11.2	28.2	−32.2	31.3	44.4
Asia.....507	−5.6	9.0	6.1	40.0	23.4	5.9	11.2	−7.4	2.2	18.5	10.3	−3.8	12.4	43.1
Europe.....170	.1	−45.8	−19.2	50.2	−7.7	4.5	63.3	−4.0	14.8	12.3	13.8	3.2	25.2	−3.7
Middle East.....407	6.1	−37.7	−11.5	20.5	−25.6	15.5	−14.4	.3	.5	5.4	23.2	45.2	7.1	19.2
Western Hemisphere.....207	414.5	66.1	20.1	−50.6	−42.1	−12.6	−20.5	38.0	15.8	10.3	69.8	43.8	44.9	38.0
Other Countries n.i.e.....910	−78.7	−85.3	—	31.3	....	....	....	17.3	−29.1	91.1	3.2	−87.6	80.5	9.9

	Exports 2001	2002	2003	2004	2005	2006	2007	Imports 2001	2002	2003	2004	2005	2006	2007
	Millions of U.S. Dollars							Millions of U.S. Dollars						
IFS World Total	**33,399**	**38,486**	**48,709**	**67,194**	**77,985**	**95,140**	**122,618**	**38,307**	**42,773**	**53,801**	**71,619**	**76,340**	**93,433**	**118,367**
DOTS World Total 001	**33,271**	**38,080**	**48,497**	**67,131**	**78,137**	**95,024**	**122,742**	**39,324**	**43,942**	**56,128**	**68,171**	**76,506**	**93,342**	**118,456**
Industrial Countries 101	**25,078**	**28,541**	**36,685**	**49,317**	**56,208**	**67,632**	**85,581**	**28,599**	**30,796**	**38,305**	**48,072**	**51,105**	**64,721**	**81,029**
United States 111	1,000	1,091	1,190	1,520	2,039	2,184	2,368	1,596	1,459	1,753	2,186	2,008	1,270	1,539
Canada 156	61	67	74	103	162	231	157	111	113	142	182	262	227	231
Australia 193	29	47	57	101	104	160	247	73	64	65	91	87	11	19
Japan 158	125	141	162	229	328	407	500	742	923	1,279	2,365	2,392	1,843	2,489
New Zealand 196	3	8	6	14	14	16	25	8	13	13	11	12	4	4
Austria 122	1,921	2,117	3,037	4,036	4,298	4,863	5,628	1,831	1,932	2,409	2,813	3,030	4,700	6,000
Belgium 124	998	905	1,091	1,731	2,106	2,726	3,472	956	1,003	1,148	1,377	1,526	2,694	3,416
Cyprus 423	10	17	23	20	20	34	48	6	12	19	18	17	69	51
Denmark 128	194	225	288	386	589	912	1,067	245	280	367	449	491	785	1,001
Finland 172	142	144	204	273	434	551	701	289	264	309	350	359	444	539
France 132	1,430	1,777	2,301	3,105	4,149	5,210	6,674	1,924	2,134	2,769	3,333	3,474	4,056	4,822
Germany 134	12,736	13,931	17,985	24,282	26,165	30,316	37,695	13,202	14,458	18,308	22,246	22,935	30,349	37,703
Greece 174	134	150	236	258	204	410	463	70	74	79	94	112	110	133
Iceland 176	7	10	10	17	31	37	55	1	4	3	2	7	2	3
Ireland 178	238	244	214	253	353	403	422	228	277	308	380	445	592	793
Italy 136	1,357	1,552	2,161	2,912	3,337	4,398	6,021	2,107	2,405	2,984	3,733	3,640	4,098	5,202
Luxembourg 137	62	63	96	106	112	119	142	65	87	101	148	189	192	209
Malta 181	4	6	5	13	7	14	23	9	14	6	9	21	23	14
Netherlands 138	931	1,489	2,011	2,886	2,927	3,402	4,590	948	1,050	1,231	1,957	3,077	6,358	7,996
Norway 142	136	172	170	232	283	404	638	396	413	476	443	586	52	82
Portugal 182	127	146	142	197	292	364	444	82	101	141	168	173	198	286
Slovenia 961	220	245	320	384	447	486	683	228	266	330	382	379	598	718
Spain 184	598	758	1,023	1,483	1,988	2,555	3,241	754	848	1,020	1,418	1,500	1,612	2,002
Sweden 144	326	425	554	786	1,204	1,561	2,217	477	494	598	781	1,262	1,073	1,370
Switzerland 146	467	603	705	837	987	1,323	1,803	647	714	920	1,102	1,198	776	1,186
United Kingdom 112	1,824	2,207	2,621	3,155	3,629	4,546	6,256	1,602	1,397	1,527	2,034	1,921	2,583	3,219
Developing Countries 202	**8,187**	**9,535**	**11,803**	**17,800**	**21,909**	**27,307**	**37,085**	**10,723**	**13,143**	**17,818**	**20,085**	**25,386**	**28,616**	**37,292**
Africa 607	**110**	**143**	**177**	**273**	**431**	**531**	**740**	**178**	**164**	**187**	**360**	**356**	**135**	**325**
Algeria 612	28	44	67	65	80	64	63	55	18	—	57	62	10	152
Angola 614	1	—	—	2	4	8	8	1	—	—	—	—	—	—
Benin 638	1	1	1	1	2	1	2	2	1	1	1	—	1	—
Botswana 616	2	2	—	—	—	—	—	—	—	—	2	—	—	—
Burkina Faso 748	—	—	—	1	2	1	1	—	—	—	1	—	—	—
Burundi 618	—	—	—	—	1	—	—	—	—	—	—	—	—	—
Cameroon 622	2	1	1	—	2	1	2	4	4	4	5	5	1	—
Cape Verde 624	—	—	—	—	—	1	1	—	—	—	—	—	1	—
Central African Rep. 626	—	—	—	—	—	—	—	1	—	1	1	—	—	—
Chad 628	—	—	—	—	—	1	—	5	3	3	2	2	—	—
Congo, Dem. Rep. of 636	—	—	2	2	2	1	1	—	—	—	—	—	—	1
Congo, Republic of 634	1	1	—	1	2	1	3	—	—	—	2	1	1	1
Côte d'Ivoire 662	1	3	2	3	5	2	2	13	8	17	27	10	5	9
Equatorial Guinea 642	—	—	—	—	1	—	3	—	—	—	—	—	—	—
Ethiopia 644	1	1	2	2	4	3	16	1	1	1	1	2	2	3
Gabon 646	1	—	—	2	1	—	1	—	—	—	—	1	—	—
Gambia, The 648	—	—	—	—	1	—	1	—	—	—	—	—	—	—
Ghana 652	4	3	4	5	6	15	13	1	1	2	3	2	1	5
Guinea 656	1	1	—	2	6	—	1	1	—	1	—	1	—	1
Kenya 664	3	2	4	5	5	5	5	1	1	1	1	2	1	2
Liberia 668	—	—	—	2	—	—	1	—	—	1	10	13	5	3
Madagascar 674	—	—	—	1	—	1	—	1	1	—	1	1	—	1
Malawi 676	—	—	—	—	—	—	—	4	3	5	7	5	5	4
Mali 678	1	1	1	11	19	22	22	5	6	4	5	4	1	2
Mauritania 682	—	—	1	1	3	2	2	—	—	—	—	—	—	—
Mauritius 684	1	—	1	1	1	1	2	1	1	1	2	3	2	6
Morocco 686	11	8	10	24	37	41	154	13	19	25	35	35	3	3
Mozambique 688	—	—	—	—	—	—	—	—	—	1	6	27	3	5
Namibia 728	—	—	—	—	—	—	1	—	—	—	—	1	—	1
Niger 692	—	—	—	—	—	1	1	—	—	—	—	—	—	—
Nigeria 694	13	14	9	17	17	82	35	13	14	15	10	1	3	3
Senegal 722	1	1	1	4	2	4	8	—	—	—	1	1	—	—
Seychelles 718	—	—	—	6	1	6	12	—	—	—	—	—	—	—
Sierra Leone 724	—	1	—	—	2	—	3	1	1	1	7	2	—	—
South Africa 199	18	37	41	74	156	203	316	35	51	69	141	134	80	115
Sudan 732	5	3	2	5	22	11	10	2	1	2	1	—	—	—
Swaziland 734	—	—	—	1	—	—	—	—	—	—	—	—	—	—
Tanzania 738	1	1	1	4	9	4	2	—	1	3	5	4	3	3
Togo 742	—	1	1	1	5	1	3	—	—	—	—	—	—	—
Tunisia 744	9	11	21	24	31	41	40	10	22	24	24	35	7	5
Uganda 746	—	1	1	2	1	2	2	1	1	2	1	1	—	1
Zambia 754	—	1	—	1	—	1	1	—	—	—	—	—	—	—
Zimbabwe 698	—	1	1	—	—	—	—	6	5	3	1	1	—	—

	Exports 2001	2002	2003	2004	2005	2006	2007	Imports 2001	2002	2003	2004	2005	2006	2007
	Millions of U.S. Dollars							Millions of U.S. Dollars						
Asia 507	**518**	**714**	**846**	**1,178**	**1,315**	**1,661**	**2,559**	**2,378**	**3,938**	**6,112**	**7,080**	**7,178**	**5,522**	**9,038**
Afghanistan, I.S. of 512	—	1	1	5	5	4	15	—	—	—	1	—	1	—
Bangladesh 513	8	6	6	15	14	21	22	9	11	16	30	35	22	18
Brunei Darussalam 516	—	—	—	—	—	3	—	—	—	—	—	1	1	—
Cambodia 522	—	—	—	—	—	1	—	1	2	3	5	6	1	2
China,P.R.: Mainland 924	81	147	241	272	298	401	699	1,174	2,061	2,935	3,666	3,921	3,287	5,987
China,P.R.:Hong Kong 532	88	114	132	182	212	213	340	69	71	117	167	175	97	67
China,P.R.:Macao 546	—	4	—	—	—	—	—	2	2	3	10	9	2	4
Fiji 819	—	—	—	—	—	—	4	—	—	—	—	—	—	—
India 534	68	155	120	202	262	399	552	94	110	132	187	240	167	251
Indonesia 536	13	16	18	32	53	41	70	92	126	133	157	169	116	156
Korea 542	47	34	38	58	97	121	232	172	340	414	581	611	387	701
Lao People's Dem.Rep. 544	—	—	—	1	—	—	—	1	—	1	1	2	1	1
Malaysia 548	34	52	31	41	58	56	64	350	511	729	600	426	244	253
Maldives 556	—	—	—	—	—	—	1	—	—	—	—	—	—	—
Mongolia 948	7	4	5	5	6	5	10	—	—	—	—	—	—	—
Myanmar 518	1	1	—	1	—	—	—	1	1	1	4	1	1	1
Nepal 558	1	1	1	1	1	1	1	—	—	1	1	1	1	1
New Caledonia 839	—	—	—	2	—	—	1	—	—	—	—	—	—	—
Pakistan 564	10	12	14	28	27	32	73	19	21	26	30	32	25	32
Papua New Guinea 853	—	—	—	—	—	—	—	—	—	—	—	—	2	1
Philippines 566	10	8	20	26	48	56	67	47	222	352	314	144	31	44
Singapore 576	84	85	118	143	103	136	170	159	249	295	234	184	83	225
Sri Lanka 524	5	1	2	3	2	7	6	7	7	9	14	15	9	10
Taiwan Province of China 528	—	—	37	38	51	56	74	—	—	643	689	716	655	691
Thailand 578	44	59	39	102	57	76	92	125	146	244	306	400	315	495
Vietnam 582	15	15	20	21	18	29	66	55	56	60	82	91	73	97
Europe 170	**6,908**	**7,954**	**10,016**	**15,190**	**18,423**	**23,288**	**31,449**	**7,570**	**8,202**	**10,529**	**11,625**	**16,771**	**22,450**	**27,415**
Albania 914	11	9	14	18	24	20	20	1	1	1	2	1	3	—
Armenia 911	5	4	4	7	8	13	17	—	—	—	2	9	2	5
Azerbaijan 912	15	17	25	26	37	49	60	120	189	259	293	584	972	1,025
Belarus 913	52	47	63	87	98	116	179	39	44	58	62	72	110	96
Bosnia & Herzegovina 963	70	78	86	106	133	145	162	4	5	8	8	27	31	39
Bulgaria 918	100	117	144	237	286	376	540	29	42	66	92	86	77	113
Croatia 960	189	235	288	377	415	480	600	42	50	54	62	73	93	104
Estonia 939	29	37	56	85	105	146	201	15	19	34	31	28	34	88
Faroe Islands 816	—	—	—	—	1	—	—	—	—	—	—	—	—	—
Georgia 915	5	6	11	14	41	40	45	—	—	4	4	8	7	7
Gibraltar 823	7	10	11	6	—	1	—	—	—	—	—	—	—	—
Hungary 944	631	923	1,109	1,826	2,094	2,856	3,846	695	874	1,143	1,476	1,675	2,475	3,536
Kazakhstan 916	34	40	28	50	92	113	140	117	40	66	131	164	263	178
Kosovo 967	—	—	—	—	—	11	8	—	—	—	—	—	—	—
Kyrgyz Republic 917	1	1	1	1	2	3	5	6	4	4	3	2	2	2
Latvia 941	55	60	80	104	141	211	278	15	15	15	19	19	48	59
Lithuania 946	126	149	212	232	245	320	443	22	31	36	49	55	105	147
Macedonia, FYR 962	12	9	11	16	25	37	42	4	3	5	9	11	12	13
Moldova 921	16	11	14	24	36	36	45	1	1	2	20	9	5	7
Montenegro, Rep. of 943	—	—	—	—	—	26	29	—	—	—	—	—	2	5
Poland 964	1,730	1,807	2,330	3,532	4,287	5,412	7,285	1,504	1,784	2,332	3,333	3,789	5,694	7,404
Romania 968	234	284	345	555	831	1,160	1,584	62	84	151	229	351	363	421
Russia 922	487	513	583	946	1,400	1,895	2,870	2,197	2,016	2,565	980	4,353	5,306	5,385
Serbia, Rep. of 942	—	—	—	—	—	257	434	—	—	—	—	—	94	117
Slovak Republic 936	2,680	2,949	3,872	5,692	6,783	8,033	10,653	2,157	2,326	2,914	3,761	4,151	5,782	7,523
Tajikistan 923	1	1	1	3	3	6	2	12	22	17	20	12	3	3
Turkey 186	128	272	328	537	522	544	731	189	256	360	428	534	365	510
Turkmenistan 925	3	3	4	10	4	8	8	7	17	1	2	29	—	—
Ukraine 926	185	211	260	466	701	962	1,190	283	317	382	581	690	596	623
Uzbekistan 927	20	35	9	14	21	21	37	32	33	22	20	12	5	4
Yugoslavia n.s. 966	85	124	127	215	86	—	—	19	29	32	11	27	—	—
Europe n.s. 884	—	—	—	1	1	2	2	—	—	—	—	—	—	—
Middle East 407	**462**	**538**	**570**	**838**	**1,234**	**1,262**	**1,582**	**213**	**262**	**399**	**321**	**302**	**239**	**217**
Bahrain 419	2	2	2	5	6	6	9	—	—	—	—	—	—	—
Egypt 469	55	49	36	69	117	155	168	10	14	27	21	22	8	11
Iran, I.R. of 429	29	40	75	46	90	24	30	8	8	13	14	15	2	3
Iraq 433	—	—	5	21	17	22	76	—	—	—	—	—	—	—
Israel 436	74	73	63	116	194	285	353	57	65	78	101	104	115	147
Jordan 439	12	17	14	22	70	23	25	—	—	—	—	—	—	—
Kuwait 443	7	10	13	19	32	26	37	—	—	—	—	1	—	—
Lebanon 446	33	31	32	37	33	27	32	—	1	1	1	1	1	1
Libya 672	3	2	10	10	11	14	20	107	29	55	68	111	91	26
Oman 449	1	1	1	5	9	11	35	—	—	—	—	—	—	—
Qatar 453	1	4	3	7	23	27	40	—	—	—	1	—	—	—
Saudi Arabia 456	55	34	31	75	103	97	142	1	4	5	8	9	1	1
Syrian Arab Republic 463	39	44	29	30	39	52	62	16	114	156	82	18	3	1
United Arab Emirates 466	146	219	254	371	487	485	543	12	28	64	23	22	16	25
Yemen, Republic of 474	5	12	2	6	4	8	10	—	—	—	—	—	—	—

	Exports							Imports						
	2001	2002	2003	2004	2005	2006	2007	2001	2002	2003	2004	2005	2006	2007
	Millions of U.S. Dollars							*Millions of U.S. Dollars*						
Western Hemisphere.............. 207	**189**	**187**	**194**	**320**	**506**	**565**	**754**	**383**	**578**	**591**	**699**	**779**	**270**	**298**
Antigua and Barbuda.................. 311	—	—	—	—	—	—	—	—	1	—	—	—	—	—
Argentina.................................. 213	10	7	16	23	30	36	42	38	35	39	41	55	15	14
Aruba.. 314	—	—	—	—	—	—	1	—	—	—	—	—	—	—
Bahamas, The............................. 313	1	2	1	3	5	7	1	—	—	1	1	1	—	—
Barbados.................................... 316	2	2	—	1	—	1	—	—	35	13	—	—	—	1
Belize.. 339	1	1	2	—	—	1	1	—	—	—	—	—	—	—
Bermuda..................................... 319	—	—	—	1	—	—	—	—	—	—	—	—	—	—
Bolivia....................................... 218	1	1	1	1	1	2	2	—	—	—	—	—	—	—
Brazil... 223	39	46	52	96	184	186	226	117	102	144	197	194	75	118
Chile.. 228	6	6	5	10	16	21	23	5	8	15	21	33	6	13
Colombia.................................... 233	14	14	8	15	18	18	22	29	32	39	55	50	6	5
Costa Rica.................................. 238	2	2	2	3	3	2	7	35	245	192	160	84	7	14
Dominican Republic.................... 243	12	11	4	5	14	8	10	1	2	5	3	5	3	3
Ecuador..................................... 248	11	11	4	8	11	12	14	19	14	20	25	48	1	1
El Salvador................................ 253	27	17	25	19	14	8	42	52	12	11	31	40	16	15
Falkland Islands......................... 323	—	3	—	—	—	—	—	—	4	5	3	2	—	—
Greenland.................................. 326	—	—	—	—	—	—	1	—	—	—	—	—	—	—
Grenada..................................... 328	1	—	—	—	—	—	—	—	—	—	—	—	—	—
Guatemala................................. 258	2	3	4	4	4	5	6	1	—	—	—	—	—	—
Guyana...................................... 336	—	—	—	—	—	1	—	—	—	—	—	—	—	—
Haiti.. 263	1	1	—	1	1	2	1	—	—	—	—	—	—	—
Honduras................................... 268	1	1	1	2	2	2	3	2	2	2	2	2	2	1
Jamaica...................................... 343	—	—	—	—	—	—	—	—	—	—	—	1	—	—
Mexico....................................... 273	29	29	52	96	129	172	193	55	55	78	111	108	107	102
Netherlands Antilles.................... 353	—	—	—	—	—	—	—	—	—	—	—	3	—	—
Nicaragua.................................. 278	—	—	—	—	—	—	—	1	—	—	—	—	—	—
Panama...................................... 283	11	4	5	4	8	8	84	12	17	13	27	38	—	—
Paraguay.................................... 288	1	1	—	—	1	1	1	—	1	—	—	—	—	—
Peru.. 293	6	5	3	10	6	8	11	11	8	9	10	12	4	7
St. Kitts and Nevis...................... 361	—	—	—	—	—	—	—	—	—	—	1	—	1	1
Suriname.................................... 366	—	—	—	—	—	—	—	—	—	—	1	—	—	—
Trinidad and Tobago................... 369	1	1	1	7	1	2	2	—	—	2	3	8	10	—
Uruguay..................................... 298	1	9	1	1	2	9	6	3	2	3	3	4	1	1
Venezuela, Rep. Bol.................... 299	8	8	2	5	11	21	19	—	—	—	—	6	—	1
Western Hem. n.s........................ 399	—	—	3	4	44	31	33	—	—	—	1	84	13	—
Other Countries n.i.e............... 910	**6**	**4**	**8**	**14**	**17**	**32**	**20**	**2**	**2**	**5**	**13**	**15**	**2**	**1**
Cuba.. 928	5	3	8	12	16	31	20	1	1	2	3	5	2	1
North Korea................................ 954	—	1	—	2	—	1	—	1	1	3	11	10	—	—
Countries & Areas n.s.............. 898	**—**	**—**	**—**	**—**	**—**	**52**	**55**	**—**	**—**	**—**	**—**	**—**	**4**	**134**
Memorandum Items														
European Union.......................... 998	28,502	32,327	41,971	57,737	65,915	79,847	102,492	29,431	32,143	40,128	50,359	54,270	74,673	94,232
Oil Exporting Ctys....................... 999	305	392	488	673	933	914	1,112	289	227	285	339	394	241	367
Non-Oil Develop.Ctys.................. 201	7,881	9,143	11,315	17,126	20,976	26,393	35,974	10,434	12,917	17,532	19,746	24,992	28,375	36,925
PERCENT DISTRIBUTION														
Industrial Countries................. 101	**75.4**	**74.9**	**75.6**	**73.5**	**71.9**	**71.2**	**69.7**	**72.7**	**70.1**	**68.2**	**70.5**	**66.8**	**69.3**	**68.4**
Developing Countries............. 202	**24.6**	**25.0**	**24.3**	**26.5**	**28.0**	**28.7**	**30.2**	**27.3**	**29.9**	**31.7**	**29.5**	**33.2**	**30.7**	**31.5**
Africa...................................... 607	**.3**	**.4**	**.4**	**.4**	**.6**	**.6**	**.6**	**.5**	**.4**	**.3**	**.5**	**.5**	**.1**	**.3**
Asia.. 507	**1.6**	**1.9**	**1.7**	**1.8**	**1.7**	**1.7**	**2.1**	**6.0**	**9.0**	**10.9**	**10.4**	**9.4**	**5.9**	**7.6**
Europe.................................... 170	**20.8**	**20.9**	**20.7**	**22.6**	**23.6**	**24.5**	**25.6**	**19.3**	**18.7**	**18.8**	**17.1**	**21.9**	**24.1**	**23.1**
Middle East............................ 407	**1.4**	**1.4**	**1.2**	**1.2**	**1.6**	**1.3**	**1.3**	**.5**	**.6**	**.7**	**.5**	**.4**	**.3**	**.2**
Western Hemisphere............. 207	**.6**	**.5**	**.4**	**.5**	**.6**	**.6**	**.6**	**1.0**	**1.3**	**1.1**	**1.0**	**1.0**	**.3**	**.3**
ANNUAL PERCENT CHANGE														
World....................................... 001	**15.0**	**14.5**	**27.4**	**38.4**	**16.4**	**21.6**	**29.2**	**13.0**	**11.7**	**27.7**	**21.5**	**12.2**	**22.0**	**26.9**
Industrial Countries................. 101	**15.6**	**13.8**	**28.5**	**34.4**	**14.0**	**20.3**	**26.5**	**12.6**	**7.7**	**24.4**	**25.5**	**6.3**	**26.6**	**25.2**
Developing Countries............. 202	**13.3**	**16.5**	**23.8**	**50.8**	**23.1**	**24.6**	**35.8**	**14.7**	**22.6**	**35.6**	**12.7**	**26.4**	**12.7**	**30.3**
Africa...................................... 607	**26.6**	**29.8**	**24.3**	**53.7**	**58.1**	**23.2**	**39.4**	**–20.8**	**–8.3**	**14.2**	**92.8**	**–1.1**	**–62.3**	**141.4**
Asia.. 507	**–7.0**	**37.9**	**18.4**	**39.3**	**11.7**	**26.3**	**54.1**	**46.6**	**65.6**	**55.2**	**15.8**	**1.4**	**–23.1**	**63.7**
Europe.................................... 170	**15.1**	**15.1**	**25.9**	**51.7**	**21.3**	**26.4**	**35.0**	**7.3**	**8.3**	**28.4**	**10.4**	**44.3**	**33.9**	**22.1**
Middle East............................ 407	**9.7**	**16.5**	**5.8**	**47.1**	**47.2**	**2.3**	**25.3**	**78.7**	**22.9**	**52.2**	**–19.5**	**–5.8**	**–20.8**	**–9.5**
Western Hemisphere............. 207	**17.8**	**–1.2**	**4.2**	**64.8**	**58.0**	**11.7**	**33.5**	**18.2**	**50.7**	**2.3**	**18.4**	**11.4**	**–65.4**	**10.5**
Other Countries n.i.e.............. 910	**–29.8**	**–35.0**	**122.7**	**66.0**	**21.0**	**90.5**	**–37.6**	**1.5**	**35.5**	**132.1**	**174.5**	**8.7**	**–87.3**	**–23.7**

	Exports							Imports						
	2001	2002	2003	2004	2005	2006	2007	2001	2002	2003	2004	2005	2006	2007
	Millions of U.S. Dollars							*Millions of U.S. Dollars*						
IFS World Total........................	**51,068**	**56,304**	**65,267**	**75,620**	**83,562**	**91,713**	**102,847**	**44,124**	**48,886**	**56,216**	**66,886**	**74,259**	**85,100**	**98,821**
DOTS World Total.................... 001	**50,999**	**56,021**	**65,828**	**76,015**	**84,965**	**92,607**	**103,169**	**44,271**	**48,643**	**56,299**	**66,737**	**75,435**	**85,557**	**99,676**
Industrial Countries................. 101	**42,772**	**46,855**	**54,944**	**63,231**	**70,160**	**76,378**	**83,554**	**36,597**	**40,761**	**45,611**	**52,855**	**59,551**	**67,816**	**78,918**
United States.............................. 111	3,525	3,569	4,078	4,380	5,459	5,753	6,279	1,965	1,910	1,828	2,265	2,064	2,488	3,188
Canada....................................... 156	367	433	557	565	732	898	966	260	229	185	230	274	302	517
Australia.................................... 193	312	372	487	689	661	695	772	57	71	106	143	155	155	171
Japan.. 158	1,774	1,704	2,025	2,188	1,945	1,846	1,900	626	660	477	634	814	684	716
New Zealand.............................. 196	47	54	78	135	91	148	100	52	51	100	156	142	127	137
Austria.. 122	445	506	677	684	689	723	820	486	554	707	814	874	936	1,090
Belgium...................................... 124	833	897	1,202	1,296	1,328	1,441	1,603	1,502	1,774	1,969	2,306	2,549	2,850	3,477
Cyprus.. 423	42	37	76	51	53	167	98	3	5	5	10	9	14	17
Finland....................................... 172	1,523	1,754	2,096	2,207	2,353	2,789	2,810	1,186	1,256	1,310	1,458	1,655	1,905	2,152
France.. 132	2,609	2,630	3,350	3,777	4,698	4,531	4,989	2,572	2,921	2,754	3,026	3,180	3,754	4,026
Germany..................................... 134	10,100	10,880	12,292	13,692	14,921	16,052	17,963	9,686	10,824	13,010	14,881	15,468	18,329	21,538
Greece.. 174	407	432	503	606	629	731	816	100	111	137	158	166	171	196
Iceland....................................... 176	226	230	303	348	421	452	558	167	110	137	125	134	121	168
Ireland.. 178	716	839	1,009	1,169	1,202	1,252	1,566	533	600	688	806	937	1,053	1,108
Italy.. 136	1,730	1,798	2,239	2,593	2,919	3,220	3,569	1,938	2,071	2,329	2,718	3,074	3,381	4,061
Luxembourg............................... 137	126	146	48	51	86	52	68	60	62	133	202	295	319	339
Malta.. 181	22	26	27	41	33	43	62	3	2	4	9	6	9	11
Netherlands............................... 138	2,302	2,504	3,121	4,191	4,493	5,006	4,913	3,090	3,328	3,893	4,559	4,934	5,374	7,063
Norway....................................... 142	2,832	3,378	3,727	4,100	4,324	4,990	5,884	2,018	2,266	2,512	3,018	4,988	5,535	6,018
Portugal..................................... 182	245	270	276	534	1,135	701	560	292	296	325	324	356	361	410
Slovenia...................................... 961	45	51	65	85	91	110	113	86	92	117	146	184	242	277
Spain.. 184	1,156	1,576	2,097	2,408	2,454	2,830	3,082	697	802	978	1,100	1,512	1,623	1,810
Sweden....................................... 144	5,854	6,597	8,289	10,040	11,203	13,068	14,979	5,285	5,899	7,302	8,994	10,399	12,109	14,311
Switzerland................................ 146	640	704	746	810	851	792	867	569	555	638	671	929	1,090	849
United Kingdom......................... 112	4,895	5,466	5,576	6,591	7,392	8,086	8,218	3,363	4,311	3,967	4,103	4,451	4,884	5,268
Developing Countries............. 202	**7,994**	**8,946**	**10,531**	**12,303**	**14,139**	**16,092**	**19,554**	**7,616**	**7,826**	**10,611**	**13,824**	**15,791**	**17,736**	**20,744**
Africa....................................... 607	**433**	**500**	**587**	**635**	**603**	**752**	**797**	**193**	**224**	**270**	**583**	**318**	**363**	**424**
Algeria....................................... 612	42	59	39	74	55	75	88	—	—	3	1	—	—	—
Angola.. 614	21	10	11	9	6	9	9	—	1	1	1	—	—	2
Benin.. 638	4	5	3	4	2	2	2	1	—	4	9	1	11	10
Botswana.................................... 616	1	1	1	2	3	3	1	—	—	—	—	—	—	—
Burkina Faso.............................. 748	6	4	4	7	2	3	3	3	1	4	1	1	1	10
Burundi...................................... 618	1	2	2	2	2	2	1	—	—	1	—	2	1	1
Cameroon................................... 622	3	3	4	5	2	3	3	2	1	1	2	3	2	3
Cape Verde................................. 624	1	1	1	1	1	1	1	—	—	—	1	—	—	—
Central African Rep.....................626	—	—	1	1	1	1	2	—	—	—	—	—	—	—
Chad... 628	3	3	2	1	1	2	3	—	—	—	—	—	—	—
Congo, Dem. Rep. of.................. 636	1	2	6	6	5	4	4	—	—	1	—	—	—	1
Congo, Republic of..................... 634	3	2	3	3	5	4	12	1	1	1	1	2	3	4
Côte d'Ivoire.............................. 662	4	4	4	6	7	6	6	5	4	2	3	12	1	24
Djibouti...................................... 611	1	2	3	3	2	1	2	—	—	—	—	—	—	—
Equatorial Guinea....................... 642	—	1	1	3	2	2	2	—	—	—	—	—	—	42
Eritrea.. 643	4	3	4	5	2	2	2	—	1	—	—	—	—	—
Ethiopia..................................... 644	21	9	10	14	11	9	12	—	1	2	2	2	2	2
Gabon... 646	4	1	3	2	2	10	2	—	—	—	1	1	1	1
Gambia, The............................... 648	2	2	2	4	5	3	5	—	—	—	—	—	—	—
Ghana... 652	14	18	16	24	22	14	20	5	6	13	34	14	18	37
Guinea.. 656	3	5	4	3	2	3	3	—	—	—	—	26	—	—
Guinea-Bissau............................. 654	—	1	—	—	1	—	1	—	3	—	—	—	—	—
Kenya.. 664	19	19	16	19	19	17	20	4	3	4	4	3	5	7
Lesotho....................................... 666	1	1	1	1	—	—	—	—	—	—	—	—	—	—
Liberia.. 668	5	5	73	9	11	134	5	—	63	9	296	—	—	—
Madagascar................................ 674	5	3	6	5	5	4	4	4	2	1	3	3	3	2
Malawi.. 676	2	2	3	3	3	3	4	3	3	3	5	7	6	6
Mali.. 678	3	2	3	3	1	1	2	3	—	—	2	1	—	3
Mauritania.................................. 682	—	3	5	1	1	1	—	—	—	—	—	—	—	—
Mauritius.................................... 684	5	5	10	6	11	6	11	2	3	3	3	2	8	3
Morocco...................................... 686	23	59	37	52	28	31	43	6	6	7	5	4	8	4
Mozambique............................... 688	4	5	7	6	3	2	3	—	—	—	—	—	1	5
Namibia...................................... 728	2	2	2	3	3	2	6	2	3	4	2	3	6	8
Niger... 692	1	1	1	2	5	2	1	—	—	—	—	—	—	—
Nigeria....................................... 694	41	51	54	79	97	102	94	2	1	1	1	1	2	2
Rwanda....................................... 714	2	4	3	4	2	2	1	—	1	1	1	1	1	1
Senegal....................................... 722	9	13	6	9	5	4	14	1	—	1	1	1	—	—
Seychelles................................... 718	3	3	3	3	4	2	2	1	1	2	1	1	1	1
Sierra Leone............................... 724	16	15	18	12	6	3	4	1	1	1	—	—	—	—
Somalia....................................... 726	1	—	—	—	—	—	—	—	—	—	—	—	—	—
South Africa............................... 199	101	114	140	162	178	214	264	116	92	172	176	196	262	225
Sudan.. 732	10	9	20	20	26	19	20	—	—	—	1	—	1	1

	Exports 2001	Exports 2002	Exports 2003	Exports 2004	Exports 2005	Exports 2006	Exports 2007	Imports 2001	Imports 2002	Imports 2003	Imports 2004	Imports 2005	Imports 2006	Imports 2007
	Millions of U.S. Dollars							*Millions of U.S. Dollars*						
Swaziland........ 734	1	1	—	—	—	—	—	—	2	—	—	—	1	—
Tanzania........ 738	13	15	13	12	8	8	11	3	2	2	2	1	1	2
Togo........ 742	2	3	4	3	10	3	23	1	—	3	1	12	—	—
Tunisia........ 744	18	19	26	32	23	23	67	5	6	5	6	5	7	7
Uganda........ 746	4	4	6	7	5	8	9	3	3	3	4	3	2	4
Zambia........ 754	3	3	5	5	4	2	3	—	—	—	—	1	4	3
Zimbabwe........ 698	5	4	5	4	3	3	2	14	11	12	14	5	4	5
Asia........ 507	**2,225**	**2,479**	**3,023**	**3,751**	**4,131**	**4,518**	**5,144**	**3,261**	**3,420**	**5,141**	**6,483**	**7,315**	**8,243**	**9,292**
Afghanistan, I.S. of........ 512	1	10	7	20	8	8	13	2	1	2	3	3	6	1
Bangladesh........ 513	30	24	26	31	28	36	47	74	75	105	129	92	137	139
Bhutan........ 514	—	—	—	1	—	—	—	—	—	—	—	—	1	—
Brunei Darussalam........ 516	—	1	—	1	1	1	1	—	—	—	—	—	—	—
Cambodia........ 522	1	1	2	2	2	1	2	4	3	4	4	1	11	12
China,P.R.: Mainland........ 924	435	540	761	975	1,054	1,144	1,761	1,312	1,395	2,069	2,690	3,577	4,288	5,333
China,P.R.:Hong Kong........ 532	451	539	606	743	683	1,129	795	224	221	244	357	473	465	386
China,P.R.:Macao........ 546	2	2	5	6	5	4	3	27	29	34	36	18	22	20
Fiji........ 819	1	1	2	2	2	1	1	—	—	—	—	—	—	—
French Polynesia........ 887	3	2	3	4	4	3	3	—	—	—	—	—	—	—
Guam........ 829	1	2	2	2	1	1	2	—	—	—	—	—	—	—
India........ 534	141	135	232	324	506	333	365	192	210	301	401	497	494	624
Indonesia........ 536	68	64	62	78	90	82	84	160	142	164	177	165	194	213
Kiribati........ 826	1	—	—	—	—	1	—	—	—	—	—	—	—	—
Korea........ 542	302	368	365	504	558	564	696	323	385	642	1,066	682	711	559
Lao People's Dem.Rep........ 544	1	—	5	1	4	—	2	1	1	1	1	1	1	1
Malaysia........ 548	114	112	116	115	125	117	151	183	173	199	243	350	253	322
Maldives........ 556	4	3	3	5	4	4	4	1	—	—	—	—	—	—
Mongolia........ 948	6	2	3	1	1	2	3	—	—	—	—	—	—	—
Myanmar........ 518	1	1	1	1	2	1	1	19	17	16	14	13	8	10
Nepal........ 558	3	2	2	2	2	1	3	1	1	1	2	2	2	2
New Caledonia........ 839	2	2	3	3	3	5	4	—	—	—	—	—	—	—
Pakistan........ 564	24	40	33	54	101	69	69	47	38	50	57	47	56	68
Papua New Guinea........ 853	2	2	3	2	3	3	4	1	1	2	1	3	4	3
Philippines........ 566	58	63	55	76	79	70	85	47	56	63	73	106	96	69
Samoa........ 862	1	—	—	—	—	—	—	—	—	—	—	—	—	—
Singapore........ 576	191	186	282	313	371	344	421	79	96	472	164	222	356	155
Solomon Islands........ 813	—	—	—	—	—	1	—	—	—	—	—	—	—	—
Sri Lanka........ 524	14	16	15	23	37	32	21	10	11	11	12	11	16	23
Taiwan Province of China........ 528	190	184	194	213	207	240	240	319	320	429	660	651	664	734
Thailand........ 578	128	130	166	185	179	212	207	171	169	221	269	275	318	438
Vietnam........ 582	50	43	69	65	71	107	154	64	77	112	123	125	140	180
Europe........ 170	**3,324**	**3,667**	**4,478**	**5,100**	**6,414**	**7,891**	**9,843**	**2,930**	**3,094**	**3,855**	**4,922**	**5,691**	**6,918**	**8,668**
Albania........ 914	3	3	6	6	7	4	7	1	—	—	—	1	—	—
Armenia........ 911	2	2	2	2	2	2	4	—	—	—	—	—	—	—
Azerbaijan........ 912	3	7	11	8	7	5	10	2	—	—	1	1	—	—
Belarus........ 913	25	29	35	40	57	72	68	24	32	27	44	53	101	69
Bosnia & Herzegovina........ 963	19	16	13	17	22	14	23	3	6	1	2	2	2	7
Bulgaria........ 918	56	65	75	87	96	100	111	31	27	30	33	42	36	32
Croatia........ 960	67	84	110	133	127	136	174	10	10	12	19	23	25	31
Czech Republic........ 935	205	238	309	356	620	904	1,063	185	204	269	364	568	793	916
Estonia........ 939	127	148	170	195	212	312	357	168	173	181	196	208	269	289
Faroe Islands........ 816	228	244	276	305	308	360	468	182	170	210	196	229	216	240
Georgia........ 915	9	7	7	10	7	8	10	1	1	1	—	1	1	1
Gibraltar........ 823	9	5	5	5	8	10	8	—	—	—	—	—	—	—
Hungary........ 944	172	223	276	353	446	486	584	137	165	236	340	380	423	786
Kazakhstan........ 916	17	17	26	42	30	40	61	1	1	4	69	5	24	15
Kosovo........ 967	—	—	—	—	5	2	6	—	—	—	—	—	—	—
Kyrgyz Republic........ 917	1	—	1	3	1	2	2	—	1	4	—	—	—	—
Latvia........ 941	137	151	165	225	306	319	418	173	162	230	220	250	295	363
Lithuania........ 946	237	263	300	302	309	504	682	225	253	316	351	347	375	477
Macedonia, FYR........ 962	10	7	12	15	16	15	20	3	8	2	2	3	1	9
Moldova........ 921	3	6	4	4	5	6	8	—	—	—	—	1	—	2
Montenegro, Rep. of........ 943	—	—	—	—	—	1	2	—	—	—	—	—	—	2
Poland........ 964	865	896	1,035	1,186	1,698	1,893	2,357	921	938	1,012	1,191	1,491	1,974	2,431
Romania........ 968	53	77	99	104	133	198	271	37	29	33	42	53	67	61
Russia........ 922	704	687	874	1,006	1,189	1,612	1,873	418	406	605	923	943	1,028	1,234
Serbia, Rep. of........ 942	—	—	—	—	—	49	91	—	—	—	—	—	8	12
Serbia & Montenegro........ 965	41	50	60	63	38	—	—	3	6	6	7	8	—	—
Slovak Republic........ 936	60	67	103	111	140	192	258	69	76	114	157	194	304	486
Tajikistan........ 923	2	2	5	1	3	1	1	—	1	—	—	—	—	—
Turkey........ 186	162	248	309	312	388	380	589	280	387	511	655	757	829	988
Turkmenistan........ 925	1	1	5	2	6	3	7	2	—	—	—	—	—	—
Ukraine........ 926	98	116	176	199	227	257	307	52	37	51	108	131	144	215
Uzbekistan........ 927	9	6	6	5	2	4	6	—	—	—	—	—	1	—
Europe n.s........ 884	1	—	1	1	1	1	2	—	—	—	—	—	—	—
Middle East........ 407	**1,035**	**1,148**	**1,340**	**1,498**	**1,561**	**1,251**	**1,771**	**264**	**162**	**181**	**454**	**938**	**647**	**445**
Bahrain........ 419	18	18	23	21	20	27	27	38	18	1	1	2	2	1
Egypt........ 469	143	102	121	120	118	126	186	5	6	10	11	13	16	27
Iran, I.R. of........ 429	61	91	130	213	212	104	161	9	8	11	15	12	12	14

	Exports							Imports						
	2001	2002	2003	2004	2005	2006	2007	2001	2002	2003	2004	2005	2006	2007
	Millions of U.S. Dollars							*Millions of U.S. Dollars*						
Iraq.. 433	39	36	26	56	36	24	59	—	1	—	1	—	—	—
Israel.. 436	148	197	139	129	195	149	174	84	67	71	81	94	124	127
Jordan... 439	34	29	54	44	38	34	46	—	—	1	1	1	1	2
Kuwait... 443	52	56	91	89	85	50	71	65	17	15	—	43	29	59
Lebanon...................................... 446	38	42	54	60	53	56	83	3	2	4	3	1	1	2
Libya... 672	14	16	30	43	38	8	45	—	8	—	—	—	1	—
Oman.. 449	27	27	50	41	40	33	79	—	—	—	1	1	—	—
Qatar... 453	15	15	19	21	41	35	58	—	3	—	1	4	—	4
Saudi Arabia............................... 456	238	283	334	355	370	281	392	4	5	3	5	12	4	8
Syrian Arab Republic.................... 463	17	18	23	29	33	26	33	3	4	2	3	3	1	2
United Arab Emirates.................. 466	155	179	207	238	240	273	316	51	21	63	332	751	456	195
West Bank/Gaza Strip.................. 487	1	1	1	1	1	—	1	—	—	—	—	—	—	—
Yemen, Republic of...................... 474	36	38	39	39	40	26	40	—	—	—	—	—	—	3
Western Hemisphere................ 207	**978**	**1,152**	**1,104**	**1,319**	**1,431**	**1,681**	**2,000**	**968**	**927**	**1,165**	**1,381**	**1,529**	**1,564**	**1,915**
Antigua and Barbuda.................. 311	2	1	1	1	7	5	23	—	—	—	—	—	5	1
Argentina.................................... 213	78	28	58	96	98	105	135	274	266	302	384	352	354	382
Aruba.. 314	2	2	2	3	3	3	4	—	—	—	—	—	25	2
Bahamas, The.............................. 313	21	104	4	15	7	42	11	—	—	11	—	—	1	—
Barbados..................................... 316	5	5	7	4	5	40	5	—	—	—	—	1	—	—
Belize.. 339	2	4	5	2	3	2	2	—	—	—	—	—	—	—
Bermuda...................................... 319	2	1	2	6	3	43	39	—	—	—	—	1	—	41
Bolivia... 218	2	3	2	4	4	6	6	1	—	1	1	1	2	1
Brazil... 223	180	150	185	213	255	317	360	125	94	137	185	205	285	391
Chile.. 228	58	61	63	67	102	101	128	74	73	87	98	161	156	168
Colombia..................................... 233	33	29	34	23	32	38	44	34	44	113	95	99	128	246
Costa Rica................................... 238	16	10	11	10	7	10	12	3	5	8	10	12	14	2
Dominica..................................... 321	—	—	—	—	—	1	—	—	—	—	—	—	—	—
Dominican Republic..................... 243	59	59	34	52	83	59	99	1	1	1	2	1	1	1
Ecuador....................................... 248	8	8	9	13	10	9	12	2	2	3	7	19	18	25
El Salvador.................................. 253	7	10	12	8	14	9	13	1	1	—	1	1	1	—
Greenland.................................... 326	254	334	341	428	442	453	509	230	272	321	336	348	354	402
Grenada....................................... 328	1	1	1	1	1	1	1	—	—	—	—	—	—	—
Guatemala................................... 258	8	10	11	11	9	9	12	4	3	4	3	3	2	2
Guyana.. 336	1	1	1	1	1	2	2	—	—	—	—	—	—	—
Haiti.. 263	1	2	2	3	2	3	4	—	—	—	—	—	—	—
Honduras..................................... 268	3	7	6	7	7	6	6	4	5	4	4	4	5	4
Jamaica....................................... 343	3	2	8	5	4	6	6	—	—	—	—	1	—	1
Mexico.. 273	135	140	168	162	176	197	238	55	51	61	58	72	98	106
Netherlands Antilles.................... 353	11	6	8	7	7	7	16	—	—	9	1	—	1	—
Nicaragua.................................... 278	1	2	2	5	3	1	3	2	1	1	1	—	—	1
Panama.. 283	11	28	24	67	23	88	71	78	1	27	36	62	1	4
Paraguay..................................... 288	1	1	1	2	2	1	2	—	—	1	1	1	—	1
Peru.. 293	16	19	19	22	22	23	25	14	16	17	28	53	87	110
St. Kitts and Nevis....................... 361	1	11	12	5	3	3	5	1	—	—	—	—	—	—
St. Lucia...................................... 362	1	—	—	1	—	1	1	—	—	—	—	—	—	—
St. Vincent & Grens..................... 364	1	2	2	2	1	1	7	—	—	—	—	—	—	—
Suriname..................................... 366	1	1	2	2	4	1	2	—	—	—	—	—	—	—
Trinidad and Tobago.................... 369	2	3	8	7	9	16	12	—	1	—	1	1	—	—
Uruguay...................................... 298	10	11	9	9	9	15	22	2	2	5	5	5	6	6
Venezuela, Rep. Bol..................... 299	36	28	33	38	42	44	64	62	88	50	125	120	17	13
Western Hem. n.s........................ 399	3	67	18	18	30	15	100	—	—	—	1	3	—	1
Other Countries n.i.e................ 910	**26**	**24**	**28**	**33**	**33**	**41**	**37**	**5**	**4**	**4**	**4**	**3**	**4**	**13**
Cuba... 928	13	11	15	21	22	36	31	1	1	2	2	1	2	12
North Korea................................ 954	13	13	12	11	11	5	6	4	3	2	2	2	3	1
Countries & Areas n.s.............. 898	**169**	**194**	**324**	**416**	**4**	**—**	**9**	**53**	**53**	**73**	**54**	**2**	**—**	**—**
Special Categories................... 899	**—**	**—**	**—**	**—**	**518**	**92**	**13**	**—**	**—**	**—**	**—**	**—**	**—**	**—**
Memorandum Items														
European Union.......................... 998	34,852	38,396	45,301	52,746	59,410	65,412	71,948	32,763	36,881	41,985	48,433	53,487	61,748	72,902
Oil Exporting Ctys....................... 999	787	908	1,074	1,325	1,347	1,110	1,510	353	293	311	658	1,110	716	508
Non-Oil Develop.Ctys.................. 201	7,208	8,038	9,457	10,978	12,793	14,983	18,044	7,262	7,533	10,300	13,166	14,681	17,020	20,235
PERCENT DISTRIBUTION														
Industrial Countries................. 101	**83.9**	**83.6**	**83.5**	**83.2**	**82.6**	**82.5**	**81.0**	**82.7**	**83.8**	**81.0**	**79.2**	**78.9**	**79.3**	**79.2**
Developing Countries.............. 202	**15.7**	**16.0**	**16.0**	**16.2**	**16.6**	**17.4**	**19.0**	**17.2**	**16.1**	**18.8**	**20.7**	**20.9**	**20.7**	**20.8**
Africa..................................... 607	**.8**	**.9**	**.9**	**.8**	**.7**	**.8**	**.8**	**.4**	**.5**	**.5**	**.9**	**.4**	**.4**	**.4**
Asia....................................... 507	**4.4**	**4.4**	**4.6**	**4.9**	**4.9**	**4.9**	**5.0**	**7.4**	**7.0**	**9.1**	**9.7**	**9.7**	**9.6**	**9.3**
Europe.................................. 170	**6.5**	**6.5**	**6.8**	**6.7**	**7.5**	**8.5**	**9.5**	**6.6**	**6.4**	**6.8**	**7.4**	**7.5**	**8.1**	**8.7**
Middle East........................... 407	**2.0**	**2.0**	**2.0**	**2.0**	**1.8**	**1.4**	**1.7**	**.6**	**.3**	**.3**	**.7**	**1.2**	**.8**	**.4**
Western Hemisphere............. 207	**1.9**	**2.1**	**1.7**	**1.7**	**1.7**	**1.8**	**1.9**	**2.2**	**1.9**	**2.1**	**2.1**	**2.0**	**1.8**	**1.9**
Other Countries n.i.e................ 910	**.1**	**—**	**—**	**—**	**—**	**—**	**—**	**—**	**—**	**—**	**—**	**—**	**—**	**—**
ANNUAL PERCENT CHANGE														
World...................................... 001	**.5**	**9.8**	**17.5**	**15.5**	**11.8**	**9.0**	**11.4**	**–2.8**	**9.9**	**15.7**	**18.5**	**13.0**	**13.4**	**16.5**
Industrial Countries................. 101	**–1.1**	**9.5**	**17.3**	**15.1**	**11.0**	**8.9**	**9.4**	**–3.7**	**11.4**	**11.9**	**15.9**	**12.7**	**13.9**	**16.4**
Developing Countries.............. 202	**6.9**	**11.9**	**17.7**	**16.8**	**14.9**	**13.8**	**21.5**	**2.2**	**2.8**	**35.6**	**30.3**	**14.2**	**12.3**	**17.0**
Africa..................................... 607	**18.8**	**15.4**	**17.4**	**8.3**	**–5.2**	**24.8**	**6.0**	**9.4**	**16.1**	**20.7**	**116.1**	**–45.5**	**14.4**	**16.7**
Asia....................................... 507	**2.9**	**11.4**	**21.9**	**24.1**	**10.1**	**9.4**	**13.9**	**–9.4**	**4.9**	**50.3**	**26.1**	**12.8**	**12.7**	**12.7**

Denmark 128

	Exports							Imports						
	2001	2002	2003	2004	2005	2006	2007	2001	2002	2003	2004	2005	2006	2007
Europe.................................... 170	15.9	10.3	22.1	13.9	25.7	23.0	24.7	13.7	5.6	24.6	27.7	15.6	21.6	25.3
Middle East............................ 407	6.0	11.0	16.7	11.8	4.2	−19.8	41.5	19.9	−38.8	12.1	150.5	106.5	−31.0	−31.3
Western Hemisphere.............. 207	−11.7	17.9	−4.2	19.5	8.5	17.5	18.9	10.2	−4.3	25.7	18.6	10.7	2.3	22.4
Other Countries n.i.e................ 910	73.7	−8.7	15.0	18.4	−.1	26.7	−9.8	193.9	−24.8	−.8	11.8	−24.1	41.6	200.9

		Exports							Imports						
		2001	2002	2003	2004	2005	2006	2007	2001	2002	2003	2004	2005	2006	2007
		Millions of U.S. Dollars							Millions of U.S. Dollars						
IFS World Total		**32.0**	**35.6**	**37.2**	**38.0**	**39.5**	**55.2**	**60.0**	**196.0**	**197.1**	**238.2**	**261.4**	**277.3**	**335.7**	**410.0**
DOTS World Total	**001**	**236.3Y**	**202.3Y**	**247.1Y**	**252.3Y**	**274.5Y**	**340.0Y**	**421.5Y**	**719.8Y**	**668.9Y**	**863.8Y**	**895.9Y**	**1,206.4Y**	**1,547.5Y**	**1,911.2Y**
Industrial Countries	**101**	**52.7Y**	**6.7Y**	**7.9Y**	**8.9Y**	**9.1Y**	**11.7Y**	**10.5Y**	**237.5Y**	**248.6Y**	**237.8Y**	**247.0Y**	**253.6Y**	**327.3Y**	**391.6Y**
United States	111	.82V	1.82V	.55V	.91V	.91V	3.09V	4.36V	20.46V	61.60V	37.84V	47.63V	52.58V	52.58V	65.01V
Canada	156	.10V	.42V	.23V	.14V	.03V	.09V	—V	.19V	.70V	.41V	1.66V	1.82V	2.69V	1.18V
Australia	193	—V	—V	—V	—V	.06V	.18V	.10V	.38V	1.43V	.17V	1.64V	1.69V	1.39V	2.67V
Japan	158	—V	.02V	.05V	—V	.18V	—V	.13V	13.10V	16.88V	26.12V	34.20V	50.82V	49.43V	81.15V
New Zealand	196	—V	—V	—V	—V	—V	—V	.01V	.34V	—V	.02V	.06V	.44V	1.10V	1.98V
Austria	122	—V	—V	—V	—V	.01V	—V	.02V	2.84V	1.28V	.30V	.57V	1.12V	5.31V	1.23V
Belgium	124	.21V	.89V	.16V	1.69V	.24V	.17V	.59V	7.63V	9.62V	11.25V	15.79V	6.52V	33.18V	21.79V
Cyprus	423	.12V	.03V	.16V	.04V	.05Y	—V	—V	.62V	.58V	2.72V	.50V	.16V	.05V	.05V
Denmark	128	—V	.03V	.03V	.06V	—V	—V	—V	1.49V	2.31V	2.82V	2.79V	2.52V	1.60V	1.72V
Finland	172	—V	.02V	—V	—V	.07V	—V	—V	.33V	.61V	1.12V	1.95V	5.31V	7.21V	7.24V
France	132	46.34V	1.09V	1.83V	1.28V	.74V	.43V	.83V	101.69V	57.45V	51.17V	55.29V	56.86V	60.98V	73.51V
Germany	134	.72V	.11V	.25V	.22V	.16V	.16V	.21V	15.83V	17.61V	14.13V	12.98V	8.61V	18.43V	31.20V
Greece	174	.06V	.28V	.20V	.10V	.07V	.19V	.23V	.18V	.46V	.53V	1.39V	.35V	2.02V	.23V
Iceland	176	—V	—V	—V	.03V	—V	—V	—V	—V	.09V	.08V	—V	—V	—V	—V
Ireland	178	.01V	.01V	2.04V	—V	.53V	.05V	—V	.12V	.02V	.58V	.10V	.02V	.57V	.46V
Italy	136	1.57V	.96V	.57V	.41V	3.33V	2.70V	2.40V	23.66V	17.79V	17.76V	17.94V	19.30V	29.35V	29.08V
Luxembourg	137	—V	—V	.01V	.04V	—V	—V	—V	—V	.01V	.12V	.03V	.02V	.40V	.02V
Malta	181	—Y	—V	—V	—V	—V	—V	—V	3.93Y	2.23V	2.02V	2.09V	1.61V	2.19V	1.63V
Netherlands	138	2.43V	.29V	.28V	.40V	.33V	.64V	.67V	19.46V	27.65V	20.42V	20.16V	21.74V	36.93V	40.77V
Norway	142	.01V	—V	—V	—V	—V	.09V	—V	.34V	.01V	.68V	.52V	.40V	.18V	.56V
Portugal	182	—V	.11V	—V	—V	—V	—V	—V	.04V	.19V	.13V	.15V	.22V	.41V	.73V
Slovenia	961	—V	—V	—V	—Y	—V	—V	—V	1.59V	1.11V	.13V	.17Y	1.54V	1.33V	.98V
Spain	184	—V	.04V	—V	.32V	.04V	.06V	.15V	2.27V	6.77V	3.04V	2.26V	3.53V	5.39V	4.23V
Sweden	144	.10V	.30V	.31V	.17V	.02V	.03V	.30V	2.52V	.56V	3.81V	4.46V	4.84V	3.63V	10.04V
Switzerland	146	.02V	.10V	—V	—V	.13V	.21V	.13V	.09V	.42V	.44V	1.68V	.30V	.50V	.55V
United Kingdom	112	.16V	.14V	1.19V	3.09V	2.16V	3.62V	.33V	18.40V	21.23V	39.99V	20.99V	11.25V	10.42V	13.55V
Developing Countries	**202**	**183.6Y**	**195.6Y**	**239.3Y**	**243.4Y**	**265.4Y**	**328.3Y**	**411.0Y**	**465.8Y**	**402.5Y**	**603.5Y**	**619.4Y**	**919.1Y**	**1,178.5Y**	**1,467.7Y**
Africa	**607**	**133.5Y**	**151.0Y**	**181.9Y**	**217.5Y**	**241.8Y**	**298.6Y**	**370.8Y**	**163.0Y**	**76.5Y**	**145.6Y**	**47.2Y**	**76.8Y**	**104.7Y**	**118.2Y**
Benin	638	—V	—V	—V	—V	.01V	.01Y	.01Y	—V	—V	—V	.03V	—V	—Y	—Y
Burkina Faso	748	.01Y	.01Y	.02Y	.02Y	.03Y	.03Y	.04Y	—Y	—Y	—Y	—Y	—Y	—Y	—Y
Burundi	618	.07V	—V	—V	—V	—V	.02V	.03Y	—V	—V	—V	—V	—V	—V	—Y
Congo, Republic of	634	—V	—V	—V	—V	—Y	—Y	—Y	—V	.02V	—V	—V	—Y	—Y	—Y
Côte d'Ivoire	662	—V	.02V	—V	—V	—V	.01V	.01Y	.10V	—V	.19V	—V	—V	.07V	.08Y
Ethiopia	644	44.49V	54.85V	60.17V	57.65V	59.01V	72.93Y	90.50Y	133.51V	59.78V	131.81V	29.83V	58.43V	72.22Y	89.62Y
Guinea	656	.01V	.01Y	—V	—V	—Y	—Y	—Y	—V	—Y	—V	—V	—Y	—Y	—Y
Kenya	664	.04V	—V	—V	.01V	.01Y	.01Y	.01Y	11.81V	6.58V	5.48V	7.28V	8.32Y	10.28Y	12.76Y
Madagascar	674	.27V	.01V	.02V	.03Y	.03Y	.04Y	.05Y	.02V	.01V	—V	—Y	—Y	—Y	—Y
Mauritius	684	—V	—V	—V	—V	.06V	—V	—V	.02V	—V	—V	.01V	.22V	—V	—V
Morocco	686	—V	—V	—V	.03V	—V	—Y	—Y	.30V	.31V	.30V	.12V	.12V	.15Y	.19Y
Nigeria	694	.03V	—V	.04V	.05Y	.07Y	.09Y	.11Y	—V	—V	—V	—Y	—Y	—Y	—Y
Senegal	722	—V	.01V	—V	.03V	—V	—V	—Y	—V	.02V	—V	—V	.04V	.02V	.02Y
Somalia	726	88.49Y	96.04Y	121.55Y	159.64Y	182.40Y	225.43Y	279.76Y	.44Y	.47Y	.60Y	.79Y	.90Y	1.11Y	1.38Y
South Africa	199	—Y	—Y	—Y	—Y	—Y	—Y	—Y	7.38V	6.25V	4.46V	6.66V	6.20V	18.12V	11.12V
Sudan	732	—Y	—Y	.02Y	—V	.19V	.02V	.28V	—Y	—Y	.05V	—V	—V	—V	—V
Tanzania	738	—V	—V	—Y	—Y	—Y	.01Y	.01Y	.03V	.06V	.07Y	.09Y	.11Y	.13Y	.16Y
Tunisia	744	—V	—V	.04V	.06V	.04V	.02V	.03Y	8.11V	1.60V	1.11V	.36V	.61V	.77V	.96Y
Zambia	754	.04V	—V	—V	—V	—V	—V	—V	—V	—V	—V	—V	—V	—V	—V
Zimbabwe	698	—V	—V	—V	—V	—V	—V	—Y	—V	—V	—V	.42V	.10V	—V	.01Y
Africa n.s.	799	—Y	—Y	—Y	—Y	—Y	—Y	—Y	1.33Y	1.42Y	1.52Y	1.61Y	1.70Y	1.80Y	1.89Y
Asia	**507**	**3.2Y**	**10.1Y**	**9.0Y**	**4.8Y**	**5.3Y**	**7.5Y**	**12.3Y**	**146.6Y**	**155.8Y**	**245.6Y**	**299.1Y**	**489.8Y**	**624.6Y**	**747.8Y**
Bangladesh	513	—V	—V	—V	—V	—V	—V	—V	1.50V	1.02V	3.72V	1.07V	.70V	.85Y	1.16Y
China,P.R.: Mainland	924	.29V	.02V	.14V	.52V	.49V	.38V	1.61V	52.48V	54.79V	72.78V	79.51V	122.56V	170.58V	180.40V
China,P.R.:Hong Kong	532	.78V	.65V	2.00V	.91V	.65V	.94V	2.00V	1.08V	.80V	1.54V	2.19V	6.53V	3.83V	1.73V
China,P.R.:Macao	546	.02V	.01V	—V	—V	—V	—V	—V	—V	—V	—V	—V	—V	—V	—V
India	534	.43Y	.73V	1.00V	2.37V	2.97V	3.67Y	4.55Y	22.47Y	35.33V	71.07V	122.53V	225.54V	278.75Y	345.93Y
Indonesia	536	—V	.04V	.13V	.02V	—V	.27V	.08V	16.33V	13.84V	17.93V	25.17V	46.69V	49.56V	48.70V
Korea	542	.02V	.09V	.01V	.18V	.06V	.55V	—V	12.16V	8.47V	9.11V	8.75V	16.91V	22.96V	21.25V
Malaysia	548	.03V	.02V	.01V	—V	.01V	.38V	1.96V	5.04V	5.55V	14.07V	14.72V	23.99V	36.27V	87.24V
Pakistan	564	1.43V	8.13V	5.59V	.68V	.82V	1.01Y	1.26Y	1.64V	3.86V	5.03V	2.44V	4.08V	5.04Y	6.25Y
Philippines	566	.17V	—V	—V	—V	—V	—V	—V	—V	.06V	—V	.04V	.15V	.30V	.01V
Singapore	576	.04V	.30V	.15V	.06V	.11V	.27V	.62V	10.16V	13.73V	17.85V	14.58V	11.10V	14.33V	10.01V
Taiwan Province of China	528	—V	—V	—V	—V	—V	.01V	.26V	10.54V	5.70V	15.79V	10.75V	12.23V	14.26V	15.18V
Thailand	578	—V	—V	—V	.07V	.22V	.04V	—V	3.99V	2.62V	6.03V	6.23V	7.60V	15.46V	16.93V
Vietnam	582	—V	.11V	.01V	—V	—V	—V	—V	.04V	.17V	.20V	—V	—V	—V	—V
Asia n.s.	598	—Y	—Y	—Y	—Y	—Y	—Y	—Y	9.19Y	9.83Y	10.48Y	11.12Y	11.76Y	12.41Y	13.05Y
Europe	**170**	**.4Y**	**.2Y**	**.2Y**	**.6Y**	**.1Y**	**.2Y**	**.2Y**	**17.0Y**	**14.9Y**	**18.2Y**	**23.7Y**	**26.3Y**	**39.0Y**	**116.2Y**
Bulgaria	918	—V	—V	—V	—V	—V	—V	—V	.06V	.18V	.07V	.03V	.02V	.02V	.04V
Czech Republic	935	.13V	.12V	.03V	—V	—V	—V	—V	.14V	.13V	.20V	.08V	.09V	.19V	.28V
Hungary	944	—V	—V	—V	—V	—V	—V	—V	.04V	—V	.17V	.01V	1.41V	2.37V	9.29V

	Exports 2001	Exports 2002	Exports 2003	Exports 2004	Exports 2005	Exports 2006	Exports 2007	Imports 2001	Imports 2002	Imports 2003	Imports 2004	Imports 2005	Imports 2006	Imports 2007
	Millions of U.S. Dollars							*Millions of U.S. Dollars*						
Lithuania 946	—V	—V	—V	—V	—V	.01V	—V	—V	—V	—V	.01V	—V	.01V	24.21V
Poland 964	.12V	.09V	.07V	.35V	—V	—V	—V	6.88V	5.68V	8.26V	10.39V	.97V	1.16V	1.21V
Romania 968	—V	—V	—V	—V	—V	—V	—V	.03V	.08V	.08V	.18V	.09V	.15V	—V
Russia 922	—V	—V	—V	—V	—V	—V	—V	.26V	2.39V	.14V	.18V	.14V	4.24V	7.41V
Slovak Republic 936	—V	.01V	.01Y	.01Y	—V	—V	—V	—V	—V	—Y	—Y	.28V	.08V	.04V
Tajikistan 923	.18V	—V	—V	—V	—V	—V	—V	.22V	—V	—V	—V	—V	—V	—V
Turkey 186	.01V	—V	.11V	.21V	.09V	.18V	.18V	7.52V	4.15V	5.90V	9.43V	7.84V	11.62V	49.93V
Ukraine 926	—V	—V	—V	—V	—V	—Y	—Y	.04V	.30V	.93V	.17V	11.76V	14.53Y	18.03Y
Europe n.s. 884	....	....	....	....	....	....	....	1.81Y	1.96Y	2.48Y	3.26Y	3.73Y	4.61Y	5.72Y
Middle East 407	**46.5Y**	**34.3Y**	**48.1Y**	**20.2Y**	**17.6Y**	**21.7Y**	**27.5Y**	**136.4Y**	**150.3Y**	**184.5Y**	**238.1Y**	**318.9Y**	**401.3Y**	**484.5Y**
Bahrain 419	.01Y	.01Y	.01Y	.01Y	.01Y	.01Y	.02Y	—Y	—Y	—Y	—Y	—Y	—Y	—Y
Jordan 439	—V	—V	—V	—V	—V	.01V	—V	.87V	.91V	.57V	.14V	.23V	.89V	1.07V
Lebanon 446	—Y	—Y	—Y	—Y	—Y	—Y	—Y	.13Y	.14Y	.18Y	.24Y	.28Y	.34Y	.42Y
Oman 449	—V	—V	—V	—Y	—Y	—Y	—Y	2.37V	5.79V	9.37V	12.40Y	16.86Y	21.20Y	25.58Y
Qatar 453	—Y	—Y	—Y	—Y	—V	—V	—Y	—V	.02V	.04V	.02V	—V	—V	—Y
Saudi Arabia 456	.32V	.29V	.17V	.26V	.09V	.11Y	.15Y	114.10Y	121.33Y	147.09Y	194.63Y	264.76Y	332.85Y	401.54Y
United Arab Emirates 466	—V	—V	4.91V	6.38Y	8.13Y	10.04Y	13.00Y	11.37Y	12.08Y	14.65Y	19.39Y	26.37Y	33.15Y	40.00Y
Yemen, Republic of 474	46.13V	33.98V	43.01Y	13.57V	9.33V	11.54Y	14.32Y	7.58V	9.98V	12.64Y	11.26V	10.39V	12.84Y	15.93Y
Western Hemisphere 207	**—Y**	**.1Y**	**—Y**	**.3Y**	**.6Y**	**.3Y**	**.2Y**	**2.7Y**	**5.1Y**	**9.5Y**	**11.2Y**	**7.3Y**	**8.9Y**	**1.0Y**
Argentina 213	—V	—V	—V	—V	—V	—V	—V	—V	.08V	—V	.11V	.11V	.18V	.40V
Brazil 223	—V	—V	—V	—V	—V	—V	—V	2.25V	4.59V	8.97V	10.73V	4.55V	8.30V	—V
Colombia 233	—V	.07V	—V	.27V	.57V	.21V	.15V	—V	—V	—V	—V	.66V	—V	.06V
Guatemala 258	—V	—V	—V	—V	.02V	.02Y	.03Y	—V	—V	—V	—V	—V	—Y	—Y
Jamaica 343	—V	—V	.01V	—V	—V	—V	—V	—V	—V	—V	—V	—V	—V	—V
Mexico 273	—V	—V	—V	—V	—V	.04V	.01V	—V	—V	—V	—V	—V	—V	—V
Paraguay 288	....	....	....	....	....	....	....	.06V	.03V	.16V	—V	—V	—V	—Y
Peru 293	—V	—V	—V	—V	—V	—V	—Y	.10V	—V	—V	—V	1.51V	—V	.07Y
St. Kitts and Nevis 361	—Y	—Y	—Y	—Y	—Y	.01Y	.01Y	—Y	—Y	—Y	—Y	—Y	.01Y	.01Y
Western Hem. n.s. 399	—Y	—Y	—Y	—Y	—Y	—Y	—Y	.34Y	.36Y	.38Y	.41Y	.43Y	.45Y	.48Y
Other Countries n.i.e 910	....	....	....	....	....	....	....	**1.5Y**	**1.6Y**	**2.1Y**	**2.7Y**	**3.1Y**	**3.9Y**	**4.8Y**
North Korea 954	....	....	....	....	....	....	....	1.52Y	1.65Y	2.08Y	2.74Y	3.13Y	3.86Y	4.79Y
Countries & Areas n.s. 898	....	....	....	....	....	....	....	**14.4Y**	**15.6Y**	**19.8Y**	**26.0Y**	**29.7Y**	**36.6Y**	**45.5Y**
Special Categories 899	....	....	....	....	....	....	....	**.4Y**	**.4Y**	**.6Y**	**.7Y**	**.8Y**	**1.0Y**	**1.3Y**
Memorandum Items														
European Union 998	51.99Y	4.53Y	7.15Y	8.17Y	7.77Y	8.06Y	5.75Y	209.68Y	173.28Y	180.68Y	170.10Y	148.26Y	223.21Y	273.50Y
Oil Exporting Ctys 999	.35Y	.33Y	5.25Y	6.72Y	8.29Y	10.50Y	13.34Y	144.18Y	153.07Y	189.08Y	251.60Y	354.68Y	436.77Y	515.81Y
Non-Oil Develop.Ctys 201	183.23Y	195.29Y	234.00Y	236.69Y	257.13Y	317.80Y	397.69Y	321.67Y	249.45Y	414.41Y	367.76Y	564.39Y	741.69Y	951.92Y
PERCENT DISTRIBUTION														
Industrial Countries 101	**22.3**	**3.3**	**3.2**	**3.5**	**3.3**	**3.4**	**2.5**	**33.0**	**37.2**	**27.5**	**27.6**	**21.0**	**21.1**	**20.5**
Developing Countries 202	**77.7**	**96.7**	**96.8**	**96.5**	**96.7**	**96.6**	**97.5**	**64.7**	**60.2**	**69.9**	**69.1**	**76.2**	**76.2**	**76.8**
Africa 607	**56.5**	**74.6**	**73.6**	**86.2**	**88.1**	**87.8**	**88.0**	**22.7**	**11.4**	**16.9**	**5.3**	**6.4**	**6.8**	**6.2**
Asia 507	**1.4**	**5.0**	**3.7**	**1.9**	**1.9**	**2.2**	**2.9**	**20.4**	**23.3**	**28.4**	**33.4**	**40.6**	**40.4**	**39.1**
Europe 170	**.2**	**.1**	**.1**	**.2**	**—**	**.1**	**—**	**2.4**	**2.2**	**2.1**	**2.6**	**2.2**	**2.5**	**6.1**
Middle East 407	**19.7**	**16.9**	**19.5**	**8.0**	**6.4**	**6.4**	**6.5**	**19.0**	**22.5**	**21.4**	**26.6**	**26.4**	**25.9**	**25.4**
Western Hemisphere 207	**—**	**—**	**—**	**.1**	**.2**	**.1**	**—**	**.4**	**.8**	**1.1**	**1.3**	**.6**	**.6**	**.1**
Other Countries n.i.e 910	....	....	....	....	....	....	....	**.2**	**.2**	**.2**	**.3**	**.3**	**.2**	**.3**
ANNUAL PERCENT CHANGE														
World 001	**55.9**	**−14.4**	**22.2**	**2.1**	**8.8**	**23.9**	**24.0**	**17.2**	**−7.1**	**29.1**	**3.7**	**34.7**	**28.3**	**23.5**
Industrial Countries 101	**317.0**	**−87.3**	**17.8**	**13.3**	**2.0**	**29.0**	**−10.5**	**5.7**	**4.7**	**−4.3**	**3.9**	**2.7**	**29.1**	**19.6**
Developing Countries 202	**32.2**	**6.6**	**22.3**	**1.7**	**9.0**	**23.7**	**25.2**	**24.3**	**−13.6**	**49.9**	**2.6**	**48.4**	**28.2**	**24.5**
Africa 607	**31.3**	**13.1**	**20.5**	**19.6**	**11.2**	**23.5**	**24.2**	**146.0**	**−53.1**	**90.2**	**−67.6**	**62.6**	**36.4**	**12.9**
Asia 507	**82.2**	**214.8**	**−10.3**	**−46.9**	**10.7**	**41.1**	**64.2**	**−12.5**	**6.3**	**57.7**	**21.8**	**63.8**	**27.5**	**19.7**
Europe 170	**152.7**	**−50.5**	**6.4**	**141.9**	**−84.0**	**106.5**	**−2.7**	**137.5**	**−12.6**	**22.6**	**30.1**	**10.9**	**48.1**	**198.1**
Middle East 407	**32.1**	**−26.2**	**40.3**	**−58.0**	**−13.1**	**23.6**	**26.6**	**3.5**	**10.1**	**22.8**	**29.0**	**33.9**	**25.8**	**20.8**
Western Hemisphere 207	**−97.3**	**—**	**−84.6**	**—**	**111.6**	**−53.7**	**−30.2**	**45.2**	**84.3**	**88.0**	**18.2**	**−35.3**	**23.0**	**−88.7**
Other Countries n.i.e 910	....	....	....	....	....	....	....	**10.4**	**8.5**	**26.6**	**31.3**	**14.3**	**23.6**	**24.1**

		Exports							Imports						
		2001	2002	2003	2004	2005	2006	2007	2001	2002	2003	2004	2005	2006	2007
		Millions of U.S. Dollars							*Millions of U.S. Dollars*						
IFS World Total		**46.0**	**46.3**	**41.4**	**43.7**	**46.5**	**41.5**	**40.0**	**131.0**	**116.0**	**127.9**	**144.4**	**165.5**	**166.9**	**190.0**
DOTS World Total	**001**	**43.5**	**60.9Y**	**63.5Y**	**69.5Y**	**85.8Y**	**96.3Y**	**113.8Y**	**130.9**	**206.8Y**	**203.5Y**	**226.7Y**	**265.8Y**	**298.2Y**	**381.4Y**
Industrial Countries	**101**	**15.3**	**30.4Y**	**25.0Y**	**27.7Y**	**31.9Y**	**31.4Y**	**17.5Y**	**81.1**	**87.8Y**	**85.1Y**	**88.8Y**	**113.3Y**	**117.4Y**	**174.3Y**
United States	111	2.63	4.64V	5.27V	3.18V	3.45V	3.09V	1.64V	47.54	49.50V	37.84V	39.49V	67.43V	74.80V	92.07V
Canada	156	.18	.61V	.25V	.24V	.64V	.22V	.39V	3.86	1.79V	6.06V	4.54V	4.61V	5.94V	5.07V
Australia	193	.05	.11V	.03V	.02V	.03V	.34V	.32V	—	.05V	.04V	.09V	.57V	.81V	.17V
Japan	158	.03	1.12V	4.09V	4.01V	2.26V	1.15V	1.76V	8.31	9.50V	12.75V	9.98V	12.39V	5.61V	42.30V
New Zealand	196	—	—V	—V	—V	—V	.02V	.08V	—	.09V	.01V	—V	.04V	.09V	—V
Austria	122	—	—V	—V	—V	—V	—V	—V	.02	.17V	.69V	.02V	.44V	2.13V	.09V
Belgium	124	—	.09V	—V	.02V	.01V	.05V	.17V	.09	.31V	1.77V	.87V	.60V	.63V	1.14V
Cyprus	423	—	—V	—V	.01V	.01Y	—V	.07V	.04	—V	—V	—V	—V	.03V	.01V
Denmark	128	—	.07V	—V	.02V	—V	—V	.01V	.21	.50V	.38V	.31V	.36V	.90V	.49V
Finland	172	—	—V	—V	—V	—V	—V	—V	.01	.06V	.11V	.04V	.02V	.01V	.29V
France	132	3.24	.79V	1.38V	2.32V	1.76V	2.53V	3.21V	2.34	3.31V	4.42V	6.61V	2.43V	4.06V	7.59V
Germany	134	—	.30V	.22V	.17V	.44V	.06V	.22V	.99	1.05V	1.02V	1.81V	1.89V	2.72V	2.50V
Greece	174	—	.01V	—V	—V	.02V	.01V	.02V	.01	—V	.50V	.02V	.16V	.06V	.16V
Iceland	176	—	—V	—V	—V	—V	—V	—V	—	—V	—V	—V	.03V	.02V	.02V
Ireland	178	—	—V	.01V	.02V	—V	—V	—V	.24	.14V	.07V	.08V	.45V	.13V	.66V
Italy	136	—	.18V	.26V	.31V	.10V	.07V	.08V	.70	1.31V	.88V	2.09V	1.89V	3.57V	2.50V
Luxembourg	137	—	—V	—V	—V	—V	—V	—V	—	—V	.02V	—V	—V	—V	—V
Malta	181	—	—V	—V	—V	—V	—V	—V	—	—V	.04V	.04V	—V	.10V	—V
Netherlands	138	—	.34V	.06V	.01V	.12V	.09V	.04V	2.32	2.75V	2.71V	2.63V	2.50V	2.55V	2.77V
Norway	142	—	—V	—V	—V	.04V	—V	—V	.63	.74V	.38V	1.36V	2.49V	.47V	1.36V
Portugal	182	—	.02V	.04V	—V	—V	—V	—V	.02	.19V	.11V	.03V	.05V	.08V	.56V
Slovenia	961	—	—V	—V	—Y	—V	—V	—V	—	—V	.05V	.06Y	—V	.13V	.02V
Spain	184	—	.08V	.01V	—V	—V	—V	—V	.11	.32V	.31V	.72V	.44V	.19V	.34V
Sweden	144	—	—V	.17V	.12V	—V	.39V	.18V	.20	.09V	2.34V	.39V	1.97V	.18V	1.98V
Switzerland	146	—	.04V	.04V	1.21V	.10V	.04V	.01V	.24	.68V	1.30V	1.53V	.92V	.61V	.63V
United Kingdom	112	9.17	22.05V	13.13V	16.05V	22.94V	23.34V	9.34V	13.26	15.25V	11.35V	16.14V	11.63V	11.58V	11.61V
Developing Countries	**202**	**28.1**	**30.3Y**	**38.3Y**	**41.6Y**	**53.6Y**	**64.5Y**	**95.8Y**	**49.3**	**118.4Y**	**117.7Y**	**137.0Y**	**151.5Y**	**179.5Y**	**205.6Y**
Africa	**607**	**—**	**.5Y**	**.5Y**	**.4Y**	**.7Y**	**.3Y**	**.4Y**	**—**	**.4Y**	**1.8Y**	**.9Y**	**.3Y**	**.6Y**	**.6Y**
Côte d'Ivoire	662	—	—V	—V	—V	—V	—V	—Y	—	—V	—V	.01V	.02V	.12V	.14Y
Ghana	652	—	—Y	—Y	—Y	—Y	—Y	—Y	.01	.01Y	.01Y	.01Y	.01Y	.02Y	.02Y
Guinea	656	—	—Y	.01V	—V	—Y	—Y	—Y	—	—Y	—Y	—Y	—Y	—Y	—Y
Senegal	722	—	—V	—V	—V	—V	—V	—Y	—	—V	—V	—V	—V	.04V	.05Y
South Africa	199	—	.41V	.36V	.27V	.52V	.12V	.21V	—	.41V	1.73V	.77V	.16V	.15V	.03V
Tanzania	738	—	.03V	.03Y	.04Y	.05Y	.06Y	.08Y	—	.02V	.03Y	.03Y	.04Y	.05Y	.06Y
Tunisia	744	—	—V	—V	—V	—V	—V	—Y	—	—V	.03V	—V	.04V	.16V	.20Y
Uganda	746	—	.08V	.09V	.10Y	.11Y	.12Y	.14Y	—	—V	.02V	.03Y	.03Y	.04Y	.05Y
Zambia	754	—	—V	—V	.03V	—V	—V	—V	—	—V	—V	—V	—V	—V	—V
Zimbabwe	698	—	—V	.01V	—V	.02V	—V	—Y	—	—V	—V	—V	—V	—V	—Y
Asia	**507**	**—**	**1.4Y**	**3.7Y**	**3.5Y**	**10.9Y**	**9.9Y**	**31.7Y**	**3.0**	**73.3Y**	**55.0Y**	**64.6Y**	**81.2Y**	**93.7Y**	**101.4Y**
Bangladesh	513	.01	—V	—V	—V	—V	—V	—V	.02	—V	—V	—V	—V	—Y	—Y
China,P.R.: Mainland	924	—	.67V	.69V	1.69V	.86V	7.44V	27.83V	1.02	50.01V	36.95V	47.75V	54.19V	67.08V	80.79V
China,P.R.:Hong Kong	532	—	—V	—V	—V	—V	—V	—V	.19	—V	—V	—V	—V	—V	—V
China,P.R.:Macao	546	—	.03V	.34V	.10V	.09V	.03V	.04V	—	—V	—V	—V	—V	—V	—V
India	534	—	.02V	.08V	.26V	.19V	.24Y	.30Y	.22	2.28V	2.37V	2.22V	2.59V	3.20Y	3.97Y
Indonesia	536	—	.05V	.10V	.14V	.32V	.98V	.19V	.05	1.03V	.65V	1.06V	1.05V	1.31V	2.06V
Korea	542	—	.12V	.15V	.24V	7.60V	.17V	.41V	.21	15.94V	10.93V	10.74V	18.84V	15.31V	6.81V
Malaysia	548	—	.08V	.22V	.63V	.36V	.17V	1.69V	.23	.57V	.48V	.05V	.22V	1.02V	.96V
Mongolia	948	—	—V	—V	.01V	—V	—Y	—Y	—	—Y	—Y	—Y	—Y	—Y	—Y
Pakistan	564	—	—V	—V	—V	—V	—Y	—Y	.02	—V	.04V	.24V	.21V	.25Y	.32Y
Philippines	566	—	.01V	.08V	.01V	—V	—V	—V	—	—V	—V	—V	.01V	.01V	.06V
Sri Lanka	524	—	.05V	—V	.01V	.45V	.03V	.34V	.02	.08V	.02V	.04V	.24V	.26V	.29V
Taiwan Province of China	528	—	.10V	.03V	.03V	.04V	.08V	.21V	.82	1.29V	1.35V	1.66V	2.63V	3.07V	2.11V
Thailand	578	—	.18V	.19V	.38V	1.00V	.76V	.64V	.18	1.13V	1.52V	.85V	1.24V	2.20V	4.08V
Vietnam	582	—	.08V	1.82V	—V	—V	—V	—V	—	1.00V	.72V	—V	—V	—V	—V
Europe	**170**	**—**	**.3Y**	**2.5Y**	**.4Y**	**.3Y**	**.1Y**	**1.7Y**	**.1**	**3.7Y**	**8.0Y**	**8.6Y**	**.6Y**	**2.8Y**	**4.3Y**
Belarus	913	—	—V	—V	.01V	—V	—V	1.26V	—	—V	—V	—V	—V	—V	.68V
Bulgaria	918	—	—V	—V	—V	—V	.01V	.02V	—	—V	—V	.08V	.07V	.46V	.06V
Czech Republic	935	—	—V	—V	.15V	.19V	—V	—V	—	.07V	.08V	—V	—V	.44V	.01V
Czechoslovakia n.s.	937	—	—Y	—Y	—Y	—Y	—Y	—Y	.08	.08Y	.11Y	.14Y	.16Y	.20Y	.25Y
Estonia	939	—	—V	.01V	—V	—V	—V	—V	—	.86V	.74V	.03V	.01V	.01V	.02V
Hungary	944	—	.02V	.02V	—V	—V	.03V	.02V	.01	—V	1.32V	.10V	—V	.05V	.04V
Latvia	941	—	—V	—V	—V	—V	—V	—V	—	.07V	.11V	.02V	.29V	.60V	.64V
Lithuania	946	—	—V	.01V	—V	—V	—V	—V	—	—V	—V	.01V	.02V	—V	.14V
Macedonia, FYR	962	—	—V	—V	—V	—V	.06V	.08Y	—	—V	—V	—V	—V	—V	—Y
Poland	964	—	.05V	2.41V	.13V	.01V	—V	.33V	.01	.19V	5.17V	6.01V	—V	.45V	1.74V
Romania	968	—	—V	—V	.03V	.04V	.02V	—V	—	1.01V	.01V	—V	—V	—V	—V
Russia	922	—	—V	—V	—V	—V	—V	—V	—	.38V	.10V	1.88V	—V	.19V	.32V
Turkey	186	—	.01V	—V	.08V	.09V	—V	—V	.01	1.07V	.11V	.04V	—V	.32V	.33V
Ukraine	926	—	.25V	.01V	—V	—V	—Y	—Y	—	—V	.20V	.33V	.02V	.03Y	.03Y

	Exports 2001	2002	2003	2004	2005	2006	2007	Imports 2001	2002	2003	2004	2005	2006	2007
	Millions of U.S. Dollars							Millions of U.S. Dollars						
Middle East 407	**—**	**.2Y**	**1.0Y**	**.4Y**	**1.1Y**	**1.4Y**	**1.8Y**	**—**	**—Y**	**—Y**	**.7Y**	**.3Y**	**.1Y**	**.2Y**
Egypt 469	—	—Y	—Y	—Y	—Y	—Y	—Y	.01	.02Y	.02Y	.03Y	.03Y	.04Y	.05Y
Jordan 439	—	—V	—V	—V	—V	—V	—V	—	—V	—V	.40V	.17V	—V	—V
Saudi Arabia 456	—	.19V	1.03V	.45V	1.14V	1.40Y	1.82Y	—	—Y	—Y	—Y	—Y	—Y	—Y
Yemen, Republic of 474	—	—V	—Y	—V	—V	—Y	—Y	—	—V	—Y	.23V	.08V	.10Y	.12Y
Western Hemisphere 207	**28.1**	**27.8Y**	**30.6Y**	**36.8Y**	**40.5Y**	**52.7Y**	**60.2Y**	**46.2**	**40.9Y**	**52.9Y**	**62.3Y**	**69.2Y**	**82.4Y**	**99.2Y**
Antigua and Barbuda 311	3.63	3.94Y	4.99Y	6.55Y	7.49Y	9.25Y	11.48Y	.42	.45Y	.57Y	.75Y	.86Y	1.06Y	1.32Y
Argentina 213	—	—V	—V	.03V	—V	.03V	.01V	.01	.08V	.24V	.29V	.75V	.52V	.43V
Aruba 314	—	—V	—V	.15V	.04V	.61V	.09V	.01	—V	—V	.01V	.01V	—V	—V
Bahamas, The 313	.05	.05Y	.07Y	.09Y	.10Y	.13Y	.16Y	.06	.06Y	.08Y	.10Y	.12Y	.14Y	.18Y
Barbados 316	2.08	1.50V	2.11V	1.77V	2.07V	2.36V	2.93Y	3.72	4.50V	5.78V	4.62V	5.83V	5.67V	7.04Y
Belize 339	—	—Y	—Y	—Y	—Y	—Y	—Y	.02	.02Y	.03Y	.04Y	.04Y	.05Y	.07Y
Bermuda 319	.03	.03Y	.04Y	.05Y	—V	—V	—Y	—	—Y	—Y	—Y	—Y	—Y	—Y
Bolivia 218	—	.01V	—V	.05V	—V	.01Y	.01Y	—	—V	.02V	—V	—Y	—Y	—Y
Brazil 223	.02	—V	.01V	.59V	.32V	.22V	—V	.92	1.04V	1.34V	3.25V	2.07V	1.94V	—V
Chile 228	—	—V	.04V	—V	—V	.01V	.13V	.05	—V	.08V	.36V	.10V	.03V	.03V
Colombia 233	—	—V	.01V	—V	.10V	.02V	.28V	.52	1.23V	1.38V	1.29V	1.22V	2.09V	2.88V
Costa Rica 238	—	—V	—V	.01V	.03V	.04Y	.04Y	.76	.88V	.58V	.69V	.56V	.69Y	.86Y
Dominican Republic 243	.05	.05Y	.07Y	.09Y	.10Y	.12Y	.15Y	.84	.92Y	1.16Y	1.52Y	1.74Y	2.15Y	2.67Y
Ecuador 248	—	—V	—V	—V	—V	—V	—Y	.08	.01V	—V	.04V	—V	.02V	.02Y
El Salvador 253	.01	.01V	—V	—V	.02V	.14V	.07V	.01	—V	—V	—V	.01V	.04V	—V
Grenada 328	.31	.34Y	.43Y	.56Y	.64Y	.79Y	.98Y	1.90	2.06Y	2.61Y	3.43Y	3.91Y	4.84Y	6.00Y
Guatemala 258	.01	.04V	.01V	.01V	—V	—Y	—Y	1.06	.45V	1.50V	1.25V	.74V	.91Y	1.13Y
Guyana 336	3.07	3.34Y	4.22Y	5.54Y	6.33Y	7.83Y	9.72Y	1.68	1.82Y	2.31Y	3.03Y	3.46Y	4.28Y	5.31Y
Haiti 263	.09	.03V	—V	.01V	.01Y	.01Y	.02Y	.01	.01Y	.01Y	.01Y	.01Y	.02Y	.02Y
Honduras 268	—	.11V	.23V	.41V	.47Y	.58Y	.72Y	.06	.11V	.11V	.03V	.03Y	.04Y	.05Y
Jamaica 343	10.12	9.53V	8.39V	7.48V	8.55V	11.56V	11.77V	1.85	1.46V	5.57V	2.64V	2.67V	2.60V	2.18V
Mexico 273	.05	.11V	.05V	.15V	.25V	2.21V	.53V	.81	.91V	.77V	1.10V	.92V	1.15V	1.98V
Netherlands Antilles 353	.03	.01V	—V	—Y	—Y	—Y	.01Y	.20	.01V	.04V	.05Y	.05Y	.07Y	.08Y
Panama 283	—	—V	—V	—V	—V	—V	—V	1.21	—V	—V	—V	—V	—V	—V
Paraguay 288	—	—V	.01V	—V	—V	—V	—Y	....	....	....	....	....	....	....
Peru 293	—	.26V	.02V	.03V	.05V	.01V	.02Y	—	.02V	.06V	.28V	.25V	.17V	.24Y
St. Kitts and Nevis 361	1.46	1.58Y	2.00Y	2.63Y	3.01Y	3.71Y	4.61Y	.44	.48Y	.61Y	.80Y	.92Y	1.13Y	1.41Y
St. Lucia 362	1.66	1.80Y	2.28Y	3.00Y	3.42Y	4.23Y	5.25Y	2.27	2.46Y	3.12Y	4.10Y	4.68Y	5.78Y	7.18Y
St. Vincent & Grens. 364	.58	.58V	.44V	.52V	.53V	.66Y	.81Y	1.24	1.46V	1.51V	1.66V	3.15V	3.89Y	4.83Y
Suriname 366	.53	.57Y	.72Y	.95Y	1.08Y	1.34Y	1.66Y	.02	.02Y	.03Y	.04Y	.05Y	.06Y	.07Y
Trinidad and Tobago 369	2.50	2.15V	2.72Y	3.57Y	4.08Y	5.04Y	6.25Y	22.85	17.34V	21.95Y	28.83Y	32.94Y	40.71Y	50.52Y
Uruguay 298	—	—Y	—V	—V	—V	—Y	—Y	—	—Y	.01V	—V	.02V	.02Y	.03Y
Venezuela, Rep. Bol. 299	.08	.07V	.02V	.80V	.05V	.06V	.67V	2.22	2.25V	.66V	1.27V	1.23V	1.40V	1.69Y
Western Hem. n.s. 399	1.72	1.72Y	1.71Y	1.71Y	1.71Y	1.74Y	1.82Y	.92	.82Y	.77Y	.78Y	.82Y	.87Y	.94Y
Other Countries n.i.e. 910	**—**	**—Y**	**—Y**	**—Y**	**—Y**	**—Y**	**—Y**	**—**	**—Y**	**—Y**	**.1Y**	**.1Y**	**.1Y**	**.1Y**
North Korea 954	—	—Y	—Y	—Y	—Y	—Y	—Y	.04	.04Y	.05Y	.06Y	.07Y	.09Y	.11Y
Countries & Areas n.s. 898	**.1**	**.2Y**	**.2Y**	**.3Y**	**.3Y**	**.4Y**	**.5Y**	**.4**	**.5Y**	**.6Y**	**.8Y**	**.9Y**	**1.1Y**	**1.4Y**
Memorandum Items														
European Union 998	12.42	24.00Y	17.75Y	19.34Y	25.60Y	26.58Y	13.69Y	20.57	26.66Y	34.18Y	38.01Y	25.16Y	30.61Y	35.32Y
Oil Exporting Ctys 999	.08	.31Y	1.15Y	1.40Y	1.51Y	2.44Y	2.68Y	2.27	3.28Y	1.31Y	2.34Y	2.28Y	2.71Y	3.75Y
Non-Oil Develop.Ctys 201	28.00	29.98Y	37.15Y	40.18Y	52.06Y	62.03Y	93.15Y	47.01	115.14Y	116.40Y	134.68Y	149.25Y	176.80Y	201.83Y
PERCENT DISTRIBUTION														
Industrial Countries 101	**35.2**	**50.0**	**39.4**	**39.8**	**37.2**	**32.6**	**15.4**	**62.0**	**42.5**	**41.8**	**39.2**	**42.6**	**39.4**	**45.7**
Developing Countries 202	**64.5**	**49.7**	**60.3**	**59.8**	**62.4**	**67.0**	**84.2**	**37.6**	**57.3**	**57.8**	**60.4**	**57.0**	**60.2**	**53.9**
Africa 607	**—**	**.9**	**.8**	**.6**	**.8**	**.3**	**.4**	**—**	**.2**	**.9**	**.4**	**.1**	**.2**	**.1**
Asia 507	**—**	**2.3**	**5.8**	**5.1**	**12.7**	**10.3**	**27.8**	**2.3**	**35.5**	**27.0**	**28.5**	**30.5**	**31.4**	**26.6**
Europe 170	**—**	**.6**	**3.9**	**.6**	**.4**	**.1**	**1.5**	**.1**	**1.8**	**3.9**	**3.8**	**.2**	**.9**	**1.1**
Middle East 407	**—**	**.3**	**1.6**	**.6**	**1.3**	**1.5**	**1.6**	**—**	**—**	**—**	**.3**	**.1**	**—**	**—**
Western Hemisphere 207	**64.5**	**45.7**	**48.2**	**52.8**	**47.2**	**54.8**	**52.9**	**35.3**	**19.8**	**26.0**	**27.5**	**26.0**	**27.6**	**26.0**
ANNUAL PERCENT CHANGE														
World 001	**−19.5**	**39.9**	**4.3**	**9.5**	**23.4**	**12.2**	**18.3**	**−11.1**	**58.0**	**−1.6**	**11.4**	**17.3**	**12.2**	**27.9**
Industrial Countries 101	**−28.6**	**98.9**	**−17.9**	**10.9**	**15.2**	**−1.6**	**−44.2**	**−12.3**	**8.2**	**−3.1**	**4.3**	**27.6**	**3.6**	**48.5**
Developing Countries 202	**−13.8**	**7.9**	**26.4**	**8.6**	**28.8**	**20.4**	**48.6**	**−9.4**	**140.3**	**−.6**	**16.4**	**10.6**	**18.5**	**14.5**
Africa 607	**—**	**....**	**−2.4**	**−12.9**	**58.8**	**−55.5**	**36.2**	**100.0**	**—**	**310.7**	**−53.1**	**−63.6**	**82.6**	**−2.3**
Asia 507	**70.0**	**—**	**160.9**	**−4.9**	**210.7**	**−9.3**	**219.7**	**−6.2**	**—**	**−24.9**	**17.4**	**25.7**	**15.4**	**8.3**
Europe 170	**—**	**....**	**621.4**	**−83.1**	**−18.6**	**−61.0**	**—**	**−63.9**	**—**	**112.7**	**8.6**	**−93.3**	**377.9**	**55.2**
Middle East 407	**—**	**—**	**448.3**	**−56.6**	**153.5**	**23.5**	**29.5**	**−3.8**	**−15.3**	**26.6**	**—**	**−57.5**	**−52.8**	**24.1**
Western Hemisphere 207	**−13.9**	**−.8**	**9.9**	**20.1**	**10.1**	**30.3**	**14.2**	**−9.3**	**−11.4**	**29.3**	**17.8**	**11.1**	**19.1**	**20.4**
Other Countries n.i.e. 910	**—**	**—**	**....**	**....**	**....**	**....**	**....**	**2.2**	**8.5**	**26.6**	**31.3**	**14.3**	**23.6**	**24.1**

		Exports							Imports, f.o.b						
		2001	2002	2003	2004	2005	2006	2007	2001	2002	2003	2004	2005	2006	2007
		Millions of U.S. Dollars							*Millions of U.S. Dollars*						
IFS World Total		**794.7**	**847.7**	**1,064.1**	**1,250.7**	**1,395.2**	**1,931.2**	**2,674.0**	**5,936.9**	**6,037.3**	**5,265.8**	**5,368.1**	**7,206.6**	**8,745.1**	**11,288.7**
DOTS World Total	**001**	**5,332.8**	**4,510.0Y**	**4,878.0Y**	**5,264.0Y**	**5,439.6Y**	**5,825.8Y**	**5,923.1Y**	**8,784.2**	**8,321.7Y**	**7,280.8Y**	**8,351.8Y**	**9,843.8Y**	**11,197.0Y**	**13,232.9Y**
Industrial Countries	**101**	**5,093.6**	**4,347.1Y**	**4,650.3Y**	**4,914.4Y**	**5,007.5Y**	**5,200.9Y**	**5,138.1Y**	**6,341.2**	**5,694.6V**	**5,233.7V**	**5,484.6Y**	**6,149.2V**	**6,910.3V**	**8,147.7V**
United States	111	4,611.20	3,882.82V	4,143.45V	4,216.18V	4,292.18V	4,226.55V	3,934.45V	5,144.04	4,261.50V	4,213.60V	4,342.80V	4,708.40V	5,347.90V	6,090.90V
Canada	156	29.62	74.99V	81.40V	98.35V	99.06V	100.68V	106.06V	51.99	79.50V	59.68V	74.83V	120.51V	144.28V	186.58V
Australia	193	2.68	2.82V	2.52V	4.08V	8.55V	13.54V	18.90V	3.23	10.37V	3.61V	3.00V	4.54V	5.61V	7.11V
Japan	158	26.37	32.06V	40.41V	54.51V	43.38V	46.74V	79.22V	348.52	308.00V	117.80V	151.84V	314.78V	261.16V	303.67V
New Zealand	196	.01	.61V	.49V	.70V	.81V	1.35V	1.72V	17.39	13.73V	12.70V	13.85V	9.76V	14.00V	23.77V
Austria	122	.90	.17V	1.62V	.78V	2.82V	10.12V	10.17V	3.11	6.46V	4.27V	6.51V	8.26V	10.62V	18.05V
Belgium	124	89.32	42.01V	44.32V	76.33V	96.74V	140.78V	219.77V	32.82	39.43V	64.90V	34.39V	41.56V	46.33V	62.26V
Cyprus	423	.18	.09V	.42V	.50V	.10Y	.13V	.13V	—	.62V	1.03V	.07V	.02V	—V	.04V
Denmark	128	.56	.59V	.69V	1.40V	1.34V	1.22V	1.21V	45.33	58.58V	33.61V	51.99V	82.86V	58.95V	98.76V
Finland	172	2.12	10.63V	29.19V	72.36V	67.63V	119.27V	190.84V	4.53	13.86V	8.38V	27.67V	8.12V	26.41V	18.25V
France	132	61.91	39.71V	30.19V	35.39V	23.43V	24.64V	30.40V	58.91	71.15V	58.99V	62.65V	88.77V	86.59V	109.53V
Germany	134	41.66	50.89V	49.55V	53.91V	49.58V	57.40V	57.81V	168.01	153.49V	98.73V	118.80V	136.32V	179.03V	206.80V
Greece	174	2.97	1.26V	1.55V	1.07V	1.54V	1.61V	2.16V	1.50	.33V	1.01V	.25V	1.29V	.76V	.71V
Iceland	176	.23	.05V	.11V	.12V	.09V	.10V	.13V	.24	—V	—V	.02V	—V	—V	—V
Ireland	178	1.68	.46V	1.00V	.15V	1.62V	2.59V	5.95V	3.67	4.69V	6.27V	5.80V	6.75V	10.93V	13.51V
Italy	136	28.11	28.46V	25.53V	32.69V	33.99V	53.15V	46.70V	89.86	136.07V	105.82V	162.13V	150.68V	163.01V	187.24V
Luxembourg	137	—	—V	—V	—V	—V	—V	—V	.08	2.54V	1.52V	2.12V	3.52V	1.20V	2.07V
Malta	181	.01	.06V	.07V	.02V	—V	.01V	.01V	.04	.25V	.70V	3.47V	.88V	1.67V	2.13V
Netherlands	138	94.64	59.79V	62.12V	90.78V	129.27V	122.06V	138.36V	61.83	58.49V	58.60V	53.28V	68.70V	80.60V	76.11V
Norway	142	.16	.99V	2.81V	3.16V	4.18V	3.27V	4.68V	21.24	28.58V	24.10V	31.59V	29.62V	31.81V	166.09V
Portugal	182	.91	.13V	.11V	.08V	.18V	.70V	.44V	1.55	6.04V	3.96V	2.55V	2.69V	5.10V	4.88V
Slovenia	961	—	.15V	.26V	.34Y	.18V	.20V	.14V	—	1.13V	.73V	.96Y	.11V	.17V	.44V
Spain	184	40.68	27.41V	36.09V	87.85V	53.23V	73.75V	122.46V	235.36	327.52V	255.28V	247.81V	222.42V	289.48V	380.51V
Sweden	144	6.51	7.28V	9.81V	2.76V	1.85V	3.05V	2.70V	7.25	18.75V	16.23V	18.65V	30.09V	31.82V	63.00V
Switzerland	146	12.26	11.16V	14.06V	10.44V	8.40V	9.63V	8.99V	10.40	16.34V	15.75V	11.26V	14.50V	17.64V	15.78V
United Kingdom	112	38.91	72.50V	72.52V	70.41V	87.31V	188.42V	154.69V	30.28	77.16V	66.40V	56.30V	94.08V	95.27V	109.48V
Developing Countries	**202**	**227.8**	**150.5Y**	**212.0Y**	**329.0Y**	**408.6Y**	**595.7Y**	**748.8Y**	**2,412.8**	**2,594.4Y**	**2,005.7Y**	**2,812.8Y**	**3,632.4Y**	**4,209.8Y**	**4,989.8Y**
Africa	**607**	**1.5**	**13.3Y**	**6.0Y**	**7.4Y**	**9.9Y**	**13.5Y**	**17.2Y**	**31.1**	**4.8Y**	**33.5Y**	**41.9Y**	**47.5Y**	**58.7Y**	**71.8Y**
Cameroon	622	—	—V	—V	—Y	—Y	—Y	—Y	—	.06V	28.49V	37.41Y	42.75Y	52.83Y	65.56Y
Cape Verde	624	—	—Y	—Y	—Y	—Y	—Y	—Y	.01	.01Y	.02Y	.02Y	.03Y	.03Y	.04Y
Côte d'Ivoire	662	—	—V	—V	—V	—V	—V	—Y	.12	.05V	.04V	.09V	.26V	.80V	1.00Y
Ethiopia	644	—	—Y	—Y	—Y	—Y	—Y	—Y	.03	—V	—V	—V	—V	—Y	—Y
Ghana	652	—	—Y	—Y	—Y	—Y	—Y	—Y	.03	.04Y	.05Y	.06Y	.07Y	.08Y	.10Y
Kenya	664	—	.08V	.07V	.12V	.13Y	.17Y	.21Y	.29	—V	.02V	.30V	.35Y	.43Y	.53Y
Madagascar	674	—	—V	.47V	.62Y	.71Y	.88Y	1.09Y	.10	.02V	—V	—Y	—Y	—Y	—Y
Malawi	676	—	—Y	—Y	—Y	—Y	—Y	—Y	.27	.29Y	.37Y	.48Y	.55Y	.68Y	.85Y
Mauritius	684	—	.05V	.10V	.10V	.07V	.17V	.38V	.01	—V	.03V	—V	—V	—V	—V
Morocco	686	.83	1.08V	1.01V	.96V	.70V	.86Y	1.07Y	27.21	.81V	1.23V	1.32V	.65V	.80Y	1.00Y
Mozambique	688	.01	—V	—Y	—Y	—Y	—Y	—Y	—	—V	—Y	—Y	—Y	—Y	—Y
Nigeria	694	—	10.24V	1.77V	2.30Y	2.93Y	3.62Y	4.68Y	.03	—V	—V	—Y	—Y	—Y	—Y
São Tomé & Príncipe	716	.01	.01Y	.01Y	.02Y	.02Y	.03Y	.03Y	.08	.09Y	.11Y	.15Y	.17Y	.21Y	.26Y
South Africa	199	—	1.00V	1.43V	1.88V	3.63V	5.74V	7.40V	.82	2.53V	2.48V	1.39V	1.92V	2.03V	1.54V
Swaziland	734	—	—Y	—Y	—Y	—Y	—Y	—Y	.09	.10Y	.13Y	.17Y	.19Y	.24Y	.29Y
Tanzania	738	—	—Y	—Y	—Y	—Y	—Y	—Y	1.32	—V	—Y	—Y	—Y	—Y	—Y
Togo	742	—	—V	.03V	—V	—V	—Y	—Y	.04	—V	—V	—V	—V	—Y	—Y
Tunisia	744	.21	.16V	.09V	.09V	.13V	.17V	.21Y	.03	—V	—V	—V	—V	—V	—Y
Uganda	746	—	—Y	—Y	—Y	—Y	—Y	—Y	.07	.23V	—V	—Y	—Y	—Y	—Y
Zimbabwe	698	—	—V	—V	—V	—V	—V	—Y	—	—V	—V	—V	.02V	.01V	.02Y
Africa n.s.	799	.42	.71Y	1.00Y	1.29Y	1.57Y	1.86Y	2.15Y	.55	.55Y	.55Y	.55Y	.55Y	.55Y	.55Y
Asia	**507**	**69.9**	**28.1Y**	**80.1Y**	**150.9Y**	**142.5Y**	**248.3Y**	**319.4Y**	**437.6**	**508.7Y**	**372.3Y**	**475.7Y**	**618.4Y**	**770.0Y**	**927.9Y**
Bangladesh	513	—	—V	—V	—V	—V	1.71V	2.80V	.08	—V	.10V	—V	—V	—Y	—Y
Brunei Darussalam	516	—	—Y	—V	—Y	—Y	.01Y	.01Y	.30	.33Y	—V	—Y	—Y	—Y	—Y
Cambodia	522	.01	—V	—V	—V	.10V	—V	—Y	.01	—V	—V	—V	—V	—V	—Y
China,P.R.: Mainland	924	4.02	1.65V	3.19V	13.66V	26.46V	85.86V	90.77V	90.19	105.50V	148.48V	225.65V	263.98V	401.61V	512.75V
China,P.R.:Hong Kong	532	1.53	1.74V	3.96V	6.19V	9.27V	16.24V	10.91V	40.96	43.19V	27.45V	28.91V	38.07V	33.93V	38.46V
China,P.R.:Macao	546	—	.40V	.63V	.78V	1.02V	1.46V	2.18V	—	—V	—V	—V	—V	.03V	—V
Guam	829	.03	.03Y	.04Y	.05Y	.06Y	.07Y	.09Y	.02	.02Y	.03Y	.04Y	.05Y	.06Y	.07Y
India	534	.02	.08V	1.22V	2.23V	2.42V	2.99Y	3.71Y	16.34	15.35V	13.21V	18.30V	29.13V	36.00Y	44.68Y
Indonesia	536	.09	.02V	—V	.02V	.01V	.04V	7.90V	14.85	15.51V	8.80V	8.63V	14.36V	15.92V	16.16V
Korea	542	42.55	19.83V	65.31V	110.77V	62.31V	79.29V	114.69V	121.78	185.02V	81.53V	73.87V	120.44V	108.86V	120.36V
Lao People's Dem.Rep	544	—	—Y	—Y	—Y	—Y	—Y	—Y	.16	.18Y	.22Y	.29Y	.34Y	.42Y	.52Y
Malaysia	548	.10	.77V	2.20V	3.13V	8.46V	12.97V	9.10V	1.46	4.90V	7.75V	11.07V	11.52V	14.03V	9.53V
Nauru	836	—	—Y	—Y	—Y	—Y	—Y	—Y	.19	.21Y	.27Y	.35Y	.40Y	.49Y	.61Y
New Caledonia	839	—	—V	.04V	.02V	.02Y	.02Y	.03Y	1.00	—V	—Y	—Y	—Y	—Y	—Y
Pakistan	564	.06	.01V	.04V	.04V	.29V	.36Y	.45Y	8.53	4.35V	1.70V	3.99V	5.61V	6.94Y	8.61Y
Philippines	566	.11	.01V	.01V	.02V	.01V	.06V	.08V	1.17	1.64V	1.10V	1.02V	3.12V	2.41V	3.05V
Singapore	576	.90	1.56V	.95V	1.99V	11.29V	18.94V	18.01V	2.67	3.70V	3.41V	4.80V	7.18V	10.95V	11.25V
Solomon Islands	813	—	—Y	—Y	—Y	—Y	—Y	—Y	—	—Y	—Y	.01Y	.01Y	.01Y	.01Y
Sri Lanka	524	18.52	—V	—Y	—Y	—Y	—Y	—Y	.01	—V	—Y	—Y	—Y	—Y	—Y

	Exports							Imports, f.o.b						
	2001	2002	2003	2004	2005	2006	2007	2001	2002	2003	2004	2005	2006	2007
	Millions of U.S. Dollars							*Millions of U.S. Dollars*						
Taiwan Province of China............ 528	1.49	1.21V	2.14V	10.18V	16.41V	25.52V	48.43V	121.53	83.59V	56.75V	67.25V	77.51V	85.18V	84.93V
Thailand.................................. 578	.42	.19V	.31V	1.82V	4.40V	2.79V	10.25V	13.65	43.23V	19.16V	29.03V	43.80V	49.61V	72.55V
Vietnam.................................... 582	—	.63V	.08V	—V	—V	—V	—V	1.27	.43V	.43V	—V	—V	—V	—V
Europe.................................... 170	**.4**	**7.3Y**	**13.2Y**	**15.9Y**	**13.5Y**	**22.0Y**	**29.0Y**	**53.8**	**85.5Y**	**40.5Y**	**96.9Y**	**92.3Y**	**108.4Y**	**88.7Y**
Belarus.................................... 913	—	.01V	.01V	.09V	.09V	.33V	.31V	—	.01V	—V	—V	.10V	.30V	.38V
Bulgaria.................................... 918	—	.02V	.05V	.13V	.24V	.40V	.23V	1.55	1.73V	1.64V	.51V	1.29V	1.13V	.29V
Czech Republic.......................... 935	.09	1.56V	4.78V	3.07V	4.65V	2.37V	2.69V	9.42	11.21V	4.38V	5.16V	14.15V	8.02V	9.80V
Estonia.................................... 939	—	.18V	.19V	.30V	.18V	.07V	.11V	—	.75V	.50V	.17V	.25V	.01V	—V
Faroe Islands............................ 816	—	—Y	—Y	—Y	—Y	—Y	—Y	.07	.07Y	.09Y	.12Y	.14Y	.17Y	.21Y
Georgia.................................... 915	—	.11V	.44V	2.26V	1.46V	—V	—Y	—	—Y	—Y	—Y	—Y	—Y	—Y
Hungary.................................... 944	.12	.38V	.79V	.09V	.10V	.10V	.12V	.25	1.02V	.71V	1.00V	1.54V	1.41V	1.56V
Kazakhstan................................ 916	—	.02V	—V	.01V	.01Y	.01Y	.01Y	—	1.64V	2.54V	3.42V	3.91Y	4.83Y	6.00Y
Latvia...................................... 941	—	.02V	.06V	.03V	.03V	.08V	.07V	—	.17V	—V	.03V	.17V	.20V	.46V
Lithuania.................................. 946	—	.08V	.16V	.11V	.01V	.02V	.03V	—	.20V	.02V	.05V	.02V	.07V	3.17V
Macedonia, FYR........................ 962	—	.01V	.03V	.02V	.03V	.02V	.03Y	—	—V	—V	—V	—V	.06V	.07Y
Moldova.................................... 921	—	—V	.02V	.01V	—V	—Y	.01Y	....	....	....	....	....	....	....
Poland...................................... 964	.02	3.17V	3.78V	3.00V	1.14V	10.95V	7.90V	1.97	5.74V	10.07V	16.99V	24.40V	5.53V	23.53V
Romania.................................... 968	—	.33V	.22V	.88V	.75V	.80V	1.52V	.17	1.00V	.17V	.56V	2.68V	.87V	4.70V
Russia...................................... 922	.05	.43V	1.03V	1.34V	1.28V	3.05V	11.41V	24.50	13.55V	4.52V	27.12V	25.65V	63.94V	15.46V
Slovak Republic......................... 936	—	.45V	.57Y	.74Y	.22V	.27V	.19V	—	.21V	.27Y	.35Y	4.91V	5.44V	5.28V
Turkey...................................... 186	.06	.49V	.95V	3.00V	2.85V	3.00V	3.67V	10.96	14.98V	3.75V	17.46V	6.00V	7.73V	6.91V
Ukraine.................................... 926	—	.02V	—V	.76V	.32V	.40Y	.50Y	4.84	33.14V	11.73V	23.77V	6.87V	8.49Y	10.54Y
Europe n.s................................ 884	.05	.06Y	.07Y	.09Y	.11Y	.13Y	.17Y	.09	.10Y	.13Y	.17Y	.19Y	.24Y	.30Y
Middle East............................ 407	**.6**	**.3Y**	**1.9Y**	**1.6Y**	**2.0Y**	**2.7Y**	**3.5Y**	**12.0**	**21.8Y**	**13.9Y**	**12.8Y**	**19.9Y**	**24.8Y**	**28.6Y**
Egypt.. 469	.05	.05Y	.07Y	.09Y	.10Y	.12Y	.15Y	.09	.09Y	.12Y	.16Y	.18Y	.22Y	.27Y
Iraq.. 433	—	—Y	—Y	—Y	—Y	—Y	—Y	.10	.11Y	.13Y	.17Y	.24Y	.30Y	.36Y
Israel.. 436	.14	.09V	.36V	.18V	.18V	.64V	.82V	7.50	20.10V	11.80V	10.40V	15.90V	20.50V	23.40V
Jordan...................................... 439	—	—V	—V	—V	—V	—V	.04V	.23	.29V	.35V	.05V	.45V	.32V	.47V
Kuwait...................................... 443	—	—Y	—Y	—Y	—Y	—Y	—Y	.02	.02Y	.02Y	.03Y	.04Y	.05Y	.06Y
Lebanon.................................... 446	.02	.02Y	.02Y	.03Y	.03Y	.04Y	.05Y	.04	.05Y	.06Y	.08Y	.09Y	.11Y	.13Y
Libya.. 672	.01	.01Y	.01Y	.01Y	.01Y	.01Y	.02Y	—	—Y	—Y	—Y	—Y	—Y	—Y
Oman....................................... 449	—	.01V	—V	—Y	—Y	—Y	—Y	—	—V	—V	—Y	—Y	—Y	—Y
Qatar.. 453	.05	—V	—V	.51V	.10V	—V	—Y	.46	—V	.02V	—V	.42V	.03V	.03Y
Saudi Arabia.............................. 456	.06	.02V	1.32V	.65V	1.37V	1.69Y	2.19Y	.54	.58Y	.70Y	.92Y	1.26Y	1.58Y	1.91Y
Syrian Arab Republic.................. 463	—	—Y	—Y	—V	—Y	—Y	—Y	.03	.03Y	.04Y	.05Y	.05Y	.07Y	.08Y
United Arab Emirates.................. 466	.27	.09V	.10Y	.13Y	.17Y	.21Y	.27Y	.53	.57Y	.69Y	.91Y	1.23Y	1.55Y	1.87Y
Yemen, Republic of..................... 474	—	—Y	—Y	—Y	—Y	—Y	—Y	2.49	—V	—Y	—V	.04V	.05Y	.06Y
Western Hemisphere............... 207	**155.5**	**101.4Y**	**110.8Y**	**153.1Y**	**240.7Y**	**309.2Y**	**379.6Y**	**1,878.3**	**1,973.5Y**	**1,545.5Y**	**2,185.5Y**	**2,854.3Y**	**3,247.8Y**	**3,872.9Y**
Antigua and Barbuda.................. 311	.51	.55Y	.69Y	.91Y	1.04Y	1.29Y	1.60Y	—	—Y	—Y	—Y	—Y	.01Y	.01Y
Argentina.................................. 213	2.64	.40V	.49V	.83V	1.12V	2.26V	3.85V	40.45	69.77V	69.67V	108.08V	123.27V	149.03V	197.49V
Aruba.. 314	1.45	1.09V	1.85V	1.45V	2.19V	4.74V	4.81V	15.38	.02V	.13V	.05V	.10V	.11V	.09V
Bahamas, The............................ 313	.69	.75Y	.95Y	1.25Y	1.43Y	1.77Y	2.19Y	.71	.77Y	.97Y	1.28Y	1.46Y	1.81Y	2.24Y
Barbados................................... 316	2.04	2.73V	2.82V	2.88V	3.64V	5.44V	6.76Y	1.12	1.48V	.94V	.72V	1.27V	1.50V	1.86Y
Belize.. 339	.05	.06Y	.07Y	.10Y	.11Y	.13Y	.17Y	3.25	3.53Y	4.47Y	5.87Y	6.70Y	8.28Y	10.28Y
Bermuda.................................... 319	.05	.06Y	.07Y	.10Y	.04V	.13V	.16Y	.52	.57Y	.72Y	.95Y	1.08Y	1.34Y	1.66Y
Bolivia...................................... 218	.02	.03V	.23V	.64V	.28V	.35Y	.43Y	.29	1.10V	1.18V	1.66V	1.89Y	2.34Y	2.90Y
Brazil.. 223	1.06	1.64V	1.71V	2.37V	3.45V	4.47V	12.78V	116.01	209.20V	226.46V	267.68V	331.87V	364.13V	458.99V
Chile... 228	2.22	.82V	1.45V	2.57V	3.21V	4.51V	7.54V	28.90	34.70V	27.07V	28.60V	35.72V	35.05V	41.10V
Colombia................................... 233	1.66	2.78V	2.43V	2.95V	2.89V	7.54V	8.72V	86.04	169.66V	342.81V	436.91V	583.27V	583.40V	621.61V
Costa Rica................................. 238	4.94	4.66V	5.12V	11.09V	9.75V	12.05Y	14.96Y	87.91	35.58V	67.95V	72.71V	101.01V	124.85Y	154.93Y
Dominica.................................. 321	.76	.82Y	1.04Y	1.37Y	1.56Y	1.93Y	2.40Y	.04	.04Y	.05Y	.07Y	.08Y	.10Y	.12Y
Ecuador.................................... 248	.08	.43V	.86V	.64V	4.79V	5.38V	6.68Y	24.87	19.78V	10.70V	23.05V	18.92V	19.45V	24.13Y
El Salvador................................ 253	3.92	1.61V	3.82V	3.39V	3.90V	4.87V	5.87V	15.55	20.83V	22.20V	25.24V	39.09V	50.65V	63.39V
Grenada.................................... 328	.09	.10Y	.13Y	.16Y	.19Y	.23Y	.29Y	—	—Y	—Y	—Y	—Y	—Y	.01Y
Guatemala................................. 258	2.67	14.71V	15.82V	10.29V	18.04V	22.30Y	27.67Y	30.39	51.23V	40.53V	39.92V	49.13V	60.72Y	75.36Y
Guyana..................................... 336	.09	.10Y	.12Y	.16Y	.18Y	.23Y	.28Y	—	—Y	—Y	—Y	—Y	—Y	—Y
Haiti.. 263	53.57	9.11V	6.78V	4.96V	5.67Y	7.00Y	8.69Y	17.32	18.79Y	23.78Y	31.24Y	35.69Y	44.11Y	54.74Y
Honduras................................... 268	21.15	7.15V	3.94V	8.52V	9.74Y	12.03Y	14.93Y	6.63	6.85V	5.70V	6.79V	7.75Y	9.58Y	11.89Y
Jamaica..................................... 343	9.13	10.97V	16.16V	14.54V	21.14V	41.74V	37.00V	9.85	3.03V	9.19V	4.79V	5.13V	8.45V	4.63V
Mexico...................................... 273	6.45	17.83V	16.51V	37.85V	102.06V	113.97V	142.90V	392.01	425.86V	366.87V	430.01V	542.73V	649.79V	782.64V
Netherlands Antilles................... 353	4.86	1.52V	4.26V	5.60Y	6.40Y	7.91Y	9.81Y	36.09	15.63V	3.37V	4.43Y	5.06Y	6.25Y	7.76Y
Nicaragua.................................. 278	1.33	1.50V	1.34V	3.09V	3.09V	4.92V	4.05V	4.08	3.49V	5.79V	6.40V	7.00V	8.63V	4.83V
Panama..................................... 283	14.40	3.23V	5.89V	14.09V	9.04V	8.81V	13.71V	143.85	15.79V	8.24V	9.74V	16.44V	16.03V	13.44V
Paraguay................................... 288	—	—V	—V	.02V	1.13V	—V	—Y	.23	.12V	.35V	.63V	.57V	.18V	.23Y
Peru.. 293	.22	.19V	.22V	1.92V	2.09V	2.41V	3.25Y	12.36	17.26V	16.70V	19.87V	21.33V	28.56V	34.97Y
St. Kitts and Nevis...................... 361	.49	.53Y	.68Y	.89Y	1.01Y	1.25Y	1.56Y	.01	.02Y	.02Y	.03Y	.03Y	.04Y	.05Y
St. Lucia.................................... 362	.83	.90Y	1.14Y	1.49Y	1.70Y	2.11Y	2.61Y	.03	.04Y	.04Y	.06Y	.07Y	.08Y	.10Y
St. Vincent & Grens.................... 364	.21	.91V	.81V	.70V	1.08V	1.33Y	1.65Y	—	—V	—V	—V	—V	—Y	—Y
Suriname................................... 366	2.33	2.53Y	3.20Y	4.20Y	4.80Y	5.93Y	7.36Y	.02	.03Y	.03Y	.04Y	.05Y	.06Y	.08Y
Trinidad and Tobago................... 369	4.75	4.02V	5.09Y	6.69Y	7.64Y	9.44Y	11.72Y	46.77	78.31V	99.11Y	130.17Y	148.72Y	183.81Y	228.11Y
Uruguay..................................... 298	.86	.94Y	.12V	.11V	.07V	.08Y	.10Y	11.34	12.30Y	2.50V	2.94V	3.65V	4.50Y	5.59Y
Venezuela, Rep. Bol.................... 299	8.15	4.92V	3.22V	3.52V	4.42V	8.79V	11.34V	746.15	757.61V	187.76V	525.40V	765.06V	884.85V	1,067.47Y
Western Hem. n.s....................... 399	1.80	1.80Y	1.80Y	1.80Y	1.80Y	1.80Y	1.80Y	.15	.15Y	.15Y	.15Y	.15Y	.15Y	.15Y
Other Countries n.i.e............... 910	**11.4**	**12.4Y**	**15.7Y**	**20.6Y**	**23.5Y**	**29.0Y**	**36.0Y**	**29.9**	**32.4Y**	**41.1Y**	**53.9Y**	**61.6Y**	**76.2Y**	**94.5Y**
Cuba... 928	11.40	12.38Y	15.66Y	20.57Y	23.50Y	29.05Y	36.05Y	29.89	32.44Y	41.06Y	53.93Y	61.62Y	76.16Y	94.51Y
Countries & Areas n.s.............. 898	**.1**	**.1Y**	**.1Y**	**.1Y**	**.1Y**	**.1Y**	**.2Y**	**—**	**—Y**	**—Y**	**—Y**	**—Y**	**—Y**	**—Y**

	Exports 2001	Exports 2002	Exports 2003	Exports 2004	Exports 2005	Exports 2006	Exports 2007	Imports, f.o.b 2001	Imports, f.o.b 2002	Imports, f.o.b 2003	Imports, f.o.b 2004	Imports, f.o.b 2005	Imports, f.o.b 2006	Imports, f.o.b 2007
Memorandum Items														
European Union.......... 998	411.29	347.40Y	375.37Y	534.18Y	557.15Y	812.95Y	995.04Y	755.78	995.87V	802.39Y	879.14Y	992.56V	1,108.61V	1,397.60V
Oil Exporting Ctys.......... 999	8.63	15.31Y	6.42Y	7.13Y	9.01Y	14.36Y	26.40Y	762.68	774.38Y	198.11Y	536.07Y	782.60Y	904.28Y	1,087.86Y
Non-Oil Develop.Ctys.......... 201	219.17	135.14Y	205.56Y	321.82Y	399.55Y	581.34Y	722.35Y	1,650.16	1,819.97Y	1,807.61Y	2,276.70Y	2,849.75Y	3,305.47Y	3,901.99Y
PERCENT DISTRIBUTION														
Industrial Countries.......... 101	95.5	96.4	95.3	93.4	92.1	89.3	86.7	72.2	68.4	71.9	65.7	62.5	61.7	61.6
Developing Countries.......... 202	4.3	3.3	4.3	6.2	7.5	10.2	12.6	27.5	31.2	27.5	33.7	36.9	37.6	37.7
Africa.......... 607	—	.3	.1	.1	.2	.2	.3	.4	.1	.5	.5	.5	.5	.5
Asia.......... 507	1.3	.6	1.6	2.9	2.6	4.3	5.4	5.0	6.1	5.1	5.7	6.3	6.9	7.0
Europe.......... 170	—	.2	.3	.3	.2	.4	.5	.6	1.0	.6	1.2	.9	1.0	.7
Middle East.......... 407	—	—	—	—	—	—	.1	.1	.3	.2	.2	.2	.2	.2
Western Hemisphere.......... 207	2.9	2.2	2.3	2.9	4.4	5.3	6.4	21.4	23.7	21.2	26.2	29.0	29.0	29.3
Other Countries n.i.e.......... 910	.2	.3	.3	.4	.4	.5	.6	.3	.4	.6	.6	.6	.7	.7
ANNUAL PERCENT CHANGE														
World.......... 001	−7.0	−15.4	8.2	7.9	3.3	7.1	1.7	−7.3	−5.3	−12.5	14.7	17.9	13.7	18.2
Industrial Countries.......... 101	−6.0	−14.7	7.0	5.7	1.9	3.9	−1.2	−7.3	−10.2	−8.1	4.8	12.1	12.4	17.9
Developing Countries.......... 202	−23.9	−34.0	40.9	55.2	24.2	45.8	25.7	−7.9	7.5	−22.7	40.2	29.1	15.9	18.5
Africa.......... 607	−64.6	801.3	−55.2	23.4	34.3	36.2	27.7	−1.6	−84.6	599.7	25.1	13.3	23.6	22.2
Asia.......... 507	8.6	−59.8	185.1	88.3	−5.6	74.2	28.6	−13.1	16.2	−26.8	27.8	30.0	24.5	20.5
Europe.......... 170	−21.4	—	79.5	21.0	−15.4	63.4	31.6	4.9	58.9	−52.6	139.1	−4.8	17.5	−18.2
Middle East.......... 407	−39.8	−50.6	540.5	−15.1	23.0	37.8	30.5	13.7	81.4	−36.2	−8.3	55.9	24.5	15.6
Western Hemisphere.......... 207	−32.2	−34.8	9.3	38.2	57.2	28.4	22.8	−7.1	5.1	−21.7	41.4	30.6	13.8	19.2
Other Countries n.i.e.......... 910	−27.2	8.5	26.6	31.3	14.3	23.6	24.1	176.4	8.5	26.6	31.3	14.3	23.6	24.1

		Exports							Imports						
		2001	2002	2003	2004	2005	2006	2007	2001	2002	2003	2004	2005	2006	2007
		Millions of U.S. Dollars							*Millions of U.S. Dollars*						
IFS World Total		**4,678.4**	**5,041.5**	**6,222.7**	**7,752.9**	**10,100.0**	**12,728.2**	**13,852.4**	**5,362.9**	**6,431.1**	**6,702.7**	**8,226.3**	**10,286.9**	**12,113.6**	**13,565.3**
DOTS World Total	**001**	**4,680.3**	**5,038.0**	**6,224.7**	**7,754.9**	**10,102.0**	**12,730.1**	**14,191.6Y**	**4,936.0**	**5,952.7**	**6,102.0**	**7,282.4**	**9,549.4**	**11,266.0**	**13,659.3Y**
Industrial Countries	**101**	**2,621.0**	**3,025.9**	**3,748.0**	**4,463.4**	**6,489.6**	**8,488.3**	**8,550.1Y**	**2,283.9**	**2,675.8**	**2,464.8**	**2,701.2**	**3,358.7**	**4,280.7**	**5,471.6Y**
United States	111	1,789.73	2,086.81	2,530.90	3,298.25	5,050.11	6,825.12	5,945.18V	1,229.05	1,376.15	1,323.56	1,526.57	1,922.30	2,597.24	3,230.59V
Canada	156	22.18	25.15	31.82	30.10	59.84	39.36	206.43V	76.89	64.21	87.46	89.15	98.93	131.94	251.40V
Australia	193	1.26	1.60	2.42	4.44	5.25	5.92	13.75V	7.04	5.54	9.58	13.77	5.11	5.21	7.83V
Japan	158	122.79	97.85	89.34	78.93	73.08	122.51	185.54V	327.35	363.97	258.44	283.86	338.19	429.93	582.78V
New Zealand	196	14.99	15.25	10.86	10.25	10.10	11.32	20.32V	.94	1.37	3.13	.97	1.19	1.14	2.31V
Austria	122	.22	.44	.46	.42	.67	.99	5.12V	4.40	3.69	4.37	5.07	7.40	9.90	28.15V
Belgium	124	81.16	71.70	75.27	75.71	78.15	103.13	398.15V	93.50	137.65	93.20	82.89	97.00	97.02	64.13V
Cyprus	423	—	—	—	—	—	—	.34V	—	—	—	—	—	—	.09V
Denmark	128	.36	.68	.95	3.98	5.02	7.94	22.76V	4.84	4.67	7.55	8.67	8.80	9.81	12.78V
Finland	172	1.53	.86	.94	1.10	1.02	1.25	.96V	3.00	69.72	53.05	20.61	66.88	50.87	47.17V
France	132	32.07	44.70	57.77	61.64	91.48	108.98	135.06V	38.68	55.59	46.90	46.03	59.14	65.04	98.26V
Germany	134	153.03	172.17	215.69	198.20	201.37	223.22	291.52V	165.66	170.26	167.17	195.69	219.16	223.31	350.37V
Greece	174	.55	1.09	.86	10.27	.74	1.85	27.77V	8.41	.83	7.31	.63	1.23	1.23	2.25V
Iceland	176	.02	.40	.48	.02	.05	.05	1.03V	—	.32	—	—	—	—	.34V
Ireland	178	.28	.21	.45	.60	.88	1.33	2.04V	1.75	4.99	4.51	7.10	14.29	11.40	8.45V
Italy	136	203.31	289.62	380.81	355.98	386.16	426.73	375.81V	100.75	131.97	104.49	90.30	107.04	157.54	222.84V
Luxembourg	137	.19	.28	.40	.15	.13	.41	.67V	—	.09	2.06	.49	.07	.03	9.35V
Malta	181	—	—	—	.04	.04	—	.10V	.04	.04	.04	.07	.05	2.34	.03V
Netherlands	138	77.21	86.87	120.58	130.28	204.35	203.68	296.72V	39.13	46.67	64.28	107.15	148.37	206.56	125.74V
Norway	142	—	—	—	—	—	—	21.64V	—	—	—	—	—	—	6.45V
Portugal	182	6.07	5.90	4.21	3.28	5.28	8.24	13.37V	1.16	2.83	3.45	3.34	4.89	5.83	4.95V
Slovenia	961	—	—	—	—	—	—	5.46V	—	—	—	—	—	—	3.43V
Spain	184	70.92	65.75	154.16	114.72	217.70	296.45	369.34V	92.16	127.11	129.94	114.64	130.17	135.92	241.99V
Sweden	144	2.10	2.12	1.56	1.98	3.27	4.18	15.07V	18.65	15.74	24.89	16.85	15.69	22.06	25.91V
Switzerland	146	3.67	4.31	5.58	6.92	21.40	26.85	73.68V	29.08	31.68	24.44	37.02	46.74	53.11	66.35V
United Kingdom	112	37.33	52.11	62.54	76.12	73.51	68.80	122.28V	41.39	60.73	44.95	50.38	66.04	63.23	77.67V
Developing Countries	**202**	**1,985.9**	**1,958.2**	**2,418.5**	**3,174.5**	**3,564.4**	**3,988.6**	**5,327.3Y**	**2,438.5**	**2,984.1**	**3,302.2**	**4,084.4**	**5,558.2**	**6,181.4**	**7,190.0Y**
Africa	**607**	**2.1**	**2.8**	**26.0**	**11.5**	**7.8**	**5.7**	**108.3Y**	**29.3**	**10.3**	**6.0**	**3.2**	**97.1**	**109.6**	**134.2Y**
Algeria	612	.03	1.12	22.05	9.41	4.04	.07	.09Y	14.70	5.38	—	.01	21.46	—	—Y
Angola	614	.01	.60	2.01	.03	.43	.59	.73Y	—	.07	—	—	22.62	35.64	44.23Y
Benin	638	—	—	—	.03	—	—	—Y	—	—	—	—	—	—	—Y
Burundi	618	....	....	....	....	....	....	....	.02	—	—	—	—	—	—Y
Cameroon	622	—	.02	—	—	.02	.03	.04Y	2.85	.02	—	—	—	.03	.03Y
Cape Verde	624	.29	.04	—	—	—	—	—Y	.02	—	—	—	—	.03	.04Y
Central African Rep.	626	.07	—	—	.01	.02	.02	.03Y	—	—	—	—	—	—	—Y
Chad	628	.07	—	—	—	—	—	—Y	.05	.02	—	—	—	—	—Y
Congo, Republic of	634	—	—	.08	.21	.14	.25	.31Y	7.19	—	3.29	—	20.30	16.07	19.94Y
Côte d'Ivoire	662	.01	—	—	—	—	—	—Y	.10	.02	.02	.03	.23	.65	.81Y
Equatorial Guinea	642	....	....	....	....	....	....	....	—	.51	—	.01	1.48	—	—Y
Gabon	646	—	—	—	—	.02	.03	.04Y	—	—	—	—	—	—	—Y
Ghana	652	.05	.18	.28	.33	.17	.73	.90Y	.04	—	.02	.01	.06	—	—Y
Guinea	656	—	.01	—	—	—	.01	.02Y	—	—	—	—	—	—	—Y
Kenya	664	—	—	—	.08	.08	.07	.08Y	—	.05	—	.67	1.04	—	.01Y
Liberia	668	—	—	.03	—	.27	.03	.03Y	.04	—	—	—	—	—	—Y
Madagascar	674	.19	.07	.11	.16	.13	.12	.15Y	.01	—	—	—	—	—	—Y
Mauritius	684	—	—	—	—	—	—	.08V	.01	—	—	—	—	—	.75V
Morocco	686	.15	.15	.10	.21	.53	.80	1.00Y	.60	—	—	—	—	.01	.01Y
Mozambique	688	—	—	—	.09	.02	—	—Y	—	—	—	—	—	—	—Y
Nigeria	694	.06	.09	.09	—	—	.08	.10Y	.06	—	.10	.04	26.90	53.45	64.48Y
São Tomé & Príncipe	716	....	....	....	....	....	....	....	—	.04	—	—	—	—	—Y
Senegal	722	.06	.12	.09	—	.02	—	—Y	—	—	—	—	.05	—	—Y
Sierra Leone	724	—	—	—	.01	—	—	—Y	....	....	....	....	....	....	....
South Africa	199	.26	.35	.98	.91	1.49	2.80	72.56V	2.57	4.15	2.54	2.31	2.97	3.55	3.69V
Sudan	732	—	—	—	.03	.26	—	32.05V	—	—	—	—	—	—	—V
Tanzania	738	—	—	—	—	.10	.04	.05Y	—	—	—	—	—	—	—Y
Togo	742	—	—	—	.01	.03	—	—Y	1.04	.01	—	—	—	.13	.17Y
Tunisia	744	.80	.04	.16	.01	.01	.01	.01Y	—	—	.02	.06	—	—	—Y
Uganda	746	—	—	—	.01	—	—	—Y	—	—	—	.09	—	—	—Y
Zambia	754	—	—	—	—	—	—	—V	.02	—	—	—	—	—	—V
Asia	**507**	**277.0**	**307.0**	**252.9**	**180.6**	**51.2**	**73.1**	**267.5Y**	**236.1**	**264.0**	**318.3**	**329.7**	**840.8**	**797.1**	**2,089.3Y**
Afghanistan, I.S. of	512	.28	.11	—	.20	.15	.09	.11Y	1.39	.17	—	—	—	—	—Y
Bangladesh	513	—	—	—	—	.18	1.24	—V	—	—	.17	—	—	.11	.07Y
Brunei Darussalam	516	—	—	—	—	—	—	—Y	.09	—	—	—	.01	—	—Y
Cambodia	522	....	....	....	....	....	....	....	—	—	—	—	.02	.16	.20Y
China,P.R.: Mainland	924	—	—	—	—	—	—	128.35V	—	—	—	—	—	—	1,036.03V
China,P.R.:Hong Kong	532	—	—	—	—	—	—	19.97V	—	—	—	—	—	—	59.01V
China,P.R.:Macao	546	—	—	—	—	—	—	.03V	—	—	—	—	—	—	—V
Fiji	819	.01	.22	—	—	.02	—	—Y	.02	—	.03	—	.01	—	—Y
India	534	1.06	.70	1.03	22.54	36.09	50.77	63.00Y	10.11	15.56	14.66	18.84	30.13	45.39	56.32Y

		Exports							Imports						
		2001	2002	2003	2004	2005	2006	2007	2001	2002	2003	2004	2005	2006	2007
		Millions of U.S. Dollars							*Millions of U.S. Dollars*						
Indonesia	536	1.95	1.40	.99	1.41	2.16	2.59	4.46V	9.32	11.77	8.39	16.05	18.59	22.72	43.28V
Korea	542	238.24	296.11	241.91	146.94	3.57	6.11	21.16V	123.70	136.08	188.26	170.72	486.77	442.46	471.45V
Lao People's Dem.Rep.	544	.03	—	—	—	—	—	—Y	—	—	.04	—	—	—	—Y
Malaysia	548	.09	.01	.06	.26	.22	.21	4.71V	10.19	5.88	6.19	10.29	9.09	14.45	14.13V
Nepal	558	....	....	....	....	....	....	....	—	—	.01	.01	—	—	—Y
New Caledonia	839	.16	—	.09	—	—	.04	.04Y	—	—	—	.01	—	—	—Y
Pakistan	564	—	.01	.08	.14	.28	.32	.39Y	2.10	3.28	1.15	1.71	3.26	2.63	3.27Y
Papua New Guinea	853	—	—	—	—	—	—	—Y	—	—	—	—	—	.01	.02Y
Philippines	566	.25	.16	.36	.37	.11	.88	.11V	.29	1.31	1.81	2.91	19.52	2.88	2.55V
Samoa	862	4.55	—	—	.78	—	.02	.03Y	.02	.05	.08	.06	.07	.08	.10Y
Singapore	576	1.20	.26	1.04	.76	1.05	1.68	5.45V	6.16	4.91	5.16	4.73	7.59	9.10	16.01V
Sri Lanka	524	.77	.90	1.37	1.19	.86	1.43	.10V	1.50	1.77	1.55	2.26	2.21	3.10	4.16V
Taiwan Province of China	528	19.87	6.69	3.82	4.36	5.41	5.66	16.41V	56.85	60.65	68.40	61.18	140.05	100.89	130.89V
Thailand	578	8.39	.18	1.76	1.24	.65	1.04	3.12V	12.90	22.51	21.04	39.06	117.59	147.65	246.59V
Vanuatu	846	.08	.08	—	—	—	—	—Y	—	.05	.24	.24	.12	.02	.03Y
Vietnam	582	.06	.15	.36	.36	.49	1.05	—V	1.41	—	1.18	1.68	5.77	5.39	—V
Asia n.s.	598	—	—	—	—	—	—	.04Y	—	—	—	—	—	—	5.15Y
Europe	**170**	**184.6**	**248.0**	**288.4**	**290.1**	**349.1**	**408.0**	**996.1Y**	**89.6**	**69.3**	**62.9**	**148.3**	**163.7**	**249.7**	**161.8Y**
Albania	914	.47	—	.03	.02	—	.24	14.76V	—	.03	.03	—	—	—	—V
Armenia	911	—	.02	—	—	—	—	9.20V	—	—	—	—	—	—	—V
Azerbaijan	912	.02	.03	.04	.07	.09	.18	3.45V	—	—	—	—	—	.01	—V
Belarus	913	—	—	—	—	—	.14	14.47V	—	—	—	—	—	—	9.12V
Bosnia & Herzegovina	963	....	....	....	....	....	....	....	—	.05	—	—	—	—	—Y
Bulgaria	918	.61	.07	1.25	.05	.12	.37	13.17V	.37	.33	.39	.24	.53	.58	.54V
Croatia	960	.17	1.40	.36	.26	.33	.73	24.09V	.07	.04	—	—	.01	.01	3.00V
Czech Republic	935	.34	.28	.40	1.28	1.58	.46	.73V	1.78	.89	.76	.94	1.82	2.51	15.66V
Estonia	939	.02	—	.07	.26	.22	.10	.02V	.28	.33	—	3.50	6.98	16.83	.10V
Faroe Islands	816	—	.02	—	—	—	—	—Y	—	—	.01	—	—	—	—Y
Georgia	915	.03	.08	.07	.01	.94	.11	1.88Y	—	—	—	9.42	—	.02	.16Y
Gibraltar	823	—	.01	—	—	—	—	.01Y	—	—	—	—	—	—	—Y
Hungary	944	.18	.09	.04	.06	.01	.03	.84V	.48	.38	.47	.27	.22	.42	1.10V
Kyrgyz Republic	917	—	—	—	—	—	—	1.04V	....	....	....	....	....	....	....
Latvia	941	—	—	—	—	—	—	1.15V	—	—	—	—	—	—	.64V
Lithuania	946	1.04	.02	.05	.18	.18	.45	.57V	1.85	1.18	2.39	16.33	.09	9.57	.22V
Macedonia, FYR	962	—	—	—	.07	.01	.03	.04Y	—	—	—	—	—	.09	.11Y
Moldova	921	—	.09	—	—	—	—	—Y	.02	.04	—	—	—	—	—Y
Poland	964	25.32	11.60	20.22	10.18	15.54	19.22	38.50V	4.18	8.30	5.56	6.47	8.59	6.31	5.92V
Romania	968	.32	1.66	.24	.20	.23	5.82	74.96V	.42	.33	1.31	.49	2.33	1.31	.86V
Russia	922	144.30	219.66	263.02	272.16	308.69	337.98	685.93V	42.71	29.49	32.16	45.92	82.58	142.53	46.23V
Slovak Republic	936	—	—	—	—	—	—	.78V	—	—	—	—	—	—	.50V
Turkey	186	9.75	10.48	1.61	3.83	14.99	24.33	88.37V	9.46	6.48	1.79	24.06	15.72	28.95	27.27V
Ukraine	926	1.96	2.41	.96	1.48	6.08	5.83	7.24Y	27.66	21.29	17.89	40.59	44.79	40.57	50.35Y
Uzbekistan	927	—	.04	—	—	.04	.07	.09Y	....	....	....	....	....	....	....
Yugoslavia n.s.	966	—	.01	—	—	—	11.90	14.77Y	.25	.14	.03	.08	—	—	—Y
Europe n.s.	884	.06	—	—	—	—	—	—Y	.03	.05	.07	.02	.04	—	—Y
Middle East	**407**	**27.4**	**18.7**	**28.1**	**33.6**	**39.6**	**22.9**	**29.9Y**	**27.8**	**12.8**	**23.3**	**37.1**	**74.7**	**122.0**	**144.0Y**
Bahrain	419	.01	.01	.03	.02	.07	.10	.13Y	.02	—	—	—	—	—	—Y
Egypt	469	.49	.09	1.93	.08	.10	.27	.34Y	.35	.60	.21	.38	.81	.50	.62Y
Iran, I.R. of	429	.01	.01	2.56	.10	.87	—	—Y	.28	.15	.02	.03	.07	.03	.03Y
Iraq	433	—	.02	—	—	—	—	—Y	1.31	—	—	—	—	—	—Y
Israel	436	4.15	2.56	2.30	4.77	6.89	3.51	3.18V	10.54	10.58	13.69	17.12	28.80	31.39	34.32V
Jordan	439	.14	.05	.15	.03	.04	.05	2.01V	—	.04	—	—	.05	.19	.52V
Kuwait	443	.08	.18	.07	.25	.38	.63	.82Y	—	—	.02	—	—	.01	.01Y
Lebanon	446	.11	.16	.15	.08	.05	.17	.21Y	—	—	.01	.04	.17	.44	.55Y
Libya	672	.02	—	—	—	.03	.04	.05Y	.03	—	—	—	—	—	—Y
Oman	449	.01	.03	—	—	.04	.11	.14Y	—	—	.02	.02	—	.02	.02Y
Qatar	453	.06	.01	—	.01	.11	.23	.30Y	—	.03	—	.16	.07	28.86	34.81Y
Saudi Arabia	456	22.09	14.15	19.87	16.86	16.81	14.09	18.26Y	14.08	.10	.34	17.94	42.79	58.39	70.44Y
Syrian Arab Republic	463	.24	1.48	1.06	11.36	14.18	3.64	4.52Y	1.19	1.27	.93	1.39	1.91	2.18	2.71Y
Yemen, Republic of	474	—	—	.01	—	—	—	—Y	.01	.07	8.02	—	—	—	—Y
Western Hemisphere	**207**	**1,494.9**	**1,381.7**	**1,823.2**	**2,658.7**	**3,116.7**	**3,479.0**	**3,925.5Y**	**2,055.7**	**2,627.7**	**2,891.7**	**3,566.0**	**4,381.9**	**4,903.0**	**4,660.8Y**
Antigua and Barbuda	311	—	.03	—	.02	.15	.05	.06Y	—	—	—	—	—	.18	.22Y
Argentina	213	72.27	15.26	35.40	34.58	42.93	44.16	100.01V	84.31	152.12	156.50	219.91	302.98	365.90	379.80V
Aruba	314	.14	.20	.13	.13	12.56	.15	.15V	.04	4.27	7.25	10.87	—	47.51	—V
Bahamas, The	313	2.56	8.83	2.74	1.41	1.76	1.54	1.92Y	10.25	.07	37.64	—	.99	.33	.41Y
Barbados	316	.19	.35	.36	.81	.55	.59	.74Y	.08	—	.01	.04	.01	—	—Y
Belize	339	.05	.07	.01	.39	.08	.06	.07Y	.01	.05	—	—	.01	—	—Y
Bermuda	319	—	.03	—	—	—	—	—Y	.21	.18	.08	—	—	—	—Y
Bolivia	218	5.49	4.93	5.55	7.54	9.43	9.29	11.53Y	6.57	5.46	8.96	1.71	2.37	4.94	6.13Y
Brazil	223	15.10	15.02	20.59	74.85	91.18	26.51	30.28V	177.42	374.50	335.51	434.70	621.42	824.04	727.90V
Chile	228	91.03	74.45	75.70	125.80	305.23	554.36	689.01V	241.25	273.73	326.05	378.44	373.28	447.03	506.73V
Colombia	233	324.31	362.53	375.58	334.82	511.03	715.26	666.17V	738.78	865.78	900.01	1,107.20	1,345.75	1,493.99	1,403.64V
Costa Rica	238	5.17	8.82	6.57	7.24	32.73	8.76	10.87Y	10.22	13.64	18.27	17.33	19.81	20.70	25.69Y
Dominica	321	.05	.01	—	.04	—	.02	.02Y	.01	—	—	—	—	—	—Y
Dominican Republic	243	14.71	19.78	10.70	23.05	18.92	19.45	24.13Y	.96	.47	.95	.71	5.27	5.92	7.35Y
El Salvador	253	64.27	81.79	113.11	68.85	72.22	72.50	202.37V	15.03	.29	7.30	.45	.32	.35	1.41V
Guatemala	258	12.39	45.82	54.57	36.16	153.56	195.38	242.46Y	2.85	2.16	11.08	16.58	76.80	29.17	36.20Y

	Exports							Imports						
	2001	2002	2003	2004	2005	2006	2007	2001	2002	2003	2004	2005	2006	2007
	Millions of U.S. Dollars							*Millions of U.S. Dollars*						
Guyana.......336	—	.03	.03	.01	.01	.03	.03Y	.39	.74	.53	.16	.59	.56	.70Y
Haiti.......263	.45	.32	.53	1.13	.58	.71	.88Y	.04	.03	—	—	.01	—	—Y
Honduras.......268	5.29	20.21	28.00	9.37	7.06	16.52	20.51Y	.44	.51	.75	.35	.72	5.76	7.15Y
Jamaica.......343	9.27	61.68	64.94	37.04	2.16	3.51	3.22V	.34	.34	.16	.31	.21	.94	.16V
Mexico.......273	49.97	25.68	49.56	42.28	61.73	58.38	123.16V	156.75	179.05	171.69	223.97	288.36	340.38	493.23V
Netherlands Antilles.......353	.76	.69	4.16	3.34	2.46	1.84	2.29Y	16.41	11.11	18.23	31.81	60.69	30.21	37.49Y
Nicaragua.......278	10.09	26.51	23.75	25.04	60.37	48.80	127.75V	.15	.10	.07	.03	.06	.35	.56V
Panama.......283	297.30	163.64	244.91	1,088.94	679.55	337.26	13.31V	218.76	258.64	330.09	359.24	436.35	451.07	1.92V
Paraguay.......288	.58	3.71	.45	1.20	.51	.95	1.17Y	2.99	3.67	5.32	4.91	4.35	8.26	10.25Y
Peru.......293	341.62	374.51	642.46	605.77	876.06	1,039.36	1,207.26Y	95.53	144.07	167.08	228.85	358.56	325.96	407.56Y
St. Pierre-Miquelon.......363	—	—	—	—	—	—	—Y	.01	.08	—	—	—	—	—Y
St. Vincent & Grens.......364	—	—	—	—	—	—	.13Y	—	—	—	—	—	—	—Y
Suriname.......366	.04	—	.09	.04	.17	.20	.25Y	—	—	.02	.02	.05	—	—Y
Trinidad and Tobago.......369	.71	.88	2.83	1.30	30.46	1.41	1.75Y	.65	2.82	22.25	7.41	12.20	48.79	60.55Y
Uruguay.......298	5.36	1.20	1.12	1.21	3.47	3.00	3.72Y	15.50	23.39	31.27	40.11	57.76	58.77	72.93Y
Venezuela, Rep. Bol.......299	165.69	64.75	59.30	126.35	139.76	318.90	440.26V	259.67	310.25	334.68	480.74	412.96	391.93	472.81Y
Western Hem. n.s.......399	.01	.01	.01	.02	.04	.05	.05Y	.07	.15	—	.13	—	—	—Y
Other Countries n.i.e.......910	**7.3**	**4.6**	**5.8**	**36.5**	**7.7**	**6.8**	**8.4Y**	**.8**	**1.0**	**.5**	**.3**	**.3**	**.7**	**.9Y**
Cuba.......928	5.71	3.87	5.53	14.44	7.38	6.78	8.41Y	.70	.82	.46	.27	.29	.70	.87Y
North Korea.......954	1.60	.77	.26	22.09	.28	—	—Y	.09	.15	—	—	—	—	—Y
Countries & Areas n.s.......898	**66.0**	**49.3**	**52.3**	**80.5**	**40.4**	**246.4**	**305.8Y**	**212.8**	**290.3**	**334.5**	**496.4**	**632.2**	**803.3**	**996.9Y**
Memorandum Items														
European Union.......998	693.24	806.49	1,097.41	1,046.44	1,287.31	1,477.43	2,125.15Y	622.10	843.66	767.35	777.43	963.91	1,097.74	1,347.69Y
Oil Exporting Ctys.......999	189.99	81.75	104.92	154.40	164.20	336.74	464.47Y	299.45	327.68	343.57	514.99	522.84	555.40	685.89Y
Non-Oil Develop.Ctys.......201	1,795.91	1,876.44	2,313.60	3,020.10	3,400.19	3,651.90	4,862.81Y	2,139.00	2,656.41	2,958.65	3,569.44	5,035.35	5,625.99	6,504.13Y
PERCENT DISTRIBUTION														
Industrial Countries.......101	56.0	60.1	60.2	57.6	64.2	66.7	60.2	46.3	45.0	40.4	37.1	35.2	38.0	40.1
Developing Countries.......202	42.4	38.9	38.9	40.9	35.3	31.3	37.5	49.4	50.1	54.1	56.1	58.2	54.9	52.6
Africa.......607	—	.1	.4	.1	.1	—	.8	.6	.2	.1	—	1.0	1.0	1.0
Asia.......507	5.9	6.1	4.1	2.3	.5	.6	1.9	4.8	4.4	5.2	4.5	8.8	7.1	15.3
Europe.......170	3.9	4.9	4.6	3.7	3.5	3.2	7.0	1.8	1.2	1.0	2.0	1.7	2.2	1.2
Middle East.......407	.6	.4	.5	.4	.4	.2	.2	.6	.2	.4	.5	.8	1.1	1.1
Western Hemisphere.......207	31.9	27.4	29.3	34.3	30.9	27.3	27.7	41.6	44.1	47.4	49.0	45.9	43.5	34.1
Other Countries n.i.e.......910	.2	.1	.1	.5	.1	.1	.1	—	—	—	—	—	—	—
ANNUAL PERCENT CHANGE														
World.......001	–5.0	7.6	23.6	24.6	30.3	26.0	11.5	45.1	20.6	2.5	19.3	31.1	18.0	21.2
Industrial Countries.......101	–1.2	15.4	23.9	19.1	45.4	30.8	.7	42.3	17.2	–7.9	9.6	24.3	27.5	27.8
Developing Countries.......202	–5.2	–1.4	23.5	31.3	12.3	11.9	33.6	45.1	22.4	10.7	23.7	36.1	11.2	16.3
Africa.......607	53.8	34.3	833.9	–55.5	–32.5	–27.1	—	–10.0	–65.0	–41.5	–45.9	—	12.8	22.4
Asia.......507	–21.7	10.8	–17.6	–28.6	–71.6	42.7	265.8	97.5	11.8	20.6	3.6	155.0	–5.2	162.1
Europe.......170	15.5	34.3	16.3	.6	20.3	16.9	144.1	8.4	–22.6	–9.3	135.9	10.3	52.5	–35.2
Middle East.......407	–5.9	–31.6	50.1	19.3	17.9	–42.2	31.1	126.2	–53.8	81.3	59.4	101.3	63.4	18.1
Western Hemisphere.......207	–3.7	–7.6	31.9	45.8	17.2	11.6	12.8	43.4	27.8	10.1	23.3	22.9	11.9	–4.9
Other Countries n.i.e.......910	–.1	–36.5	24.6	531.2	–79.1	–11.4	24.1	72.3	23.7	–52.4	–41.6	8.2	138.8	24.1

		Exports							Imports						
		2001	2002	2003	2004	2005	2006	2007	2001	2002	2003	2004	2005	2006	2007
		Millions of U.S. Dollars							*Millions of U.S. Dollars*						
IFS World Total		**4,128**	**4,708**	**6,311**	**7,530**	**10,672**	**13,736**	**16,218**	**12,756**	**12,552**	**11,139**	**12,859**	**19,851**	**17,644**	**27,092**
DOTS World Total	**001**	**4,140**	**7,049Y**	**8,499Y**	**12,187Y**	**15,593Y**	**20,759Y**	**23,853Y**	**12,720**	**19,888Y**	**21,351Y**	**27,936Y**	**33,181Y**	**40,037Y**	**50,470Y**
Industrial Countries	**101**	**1,775**	**4,252Y**	**4,698Y**	**6,357Y**	**8,136Y**	**11,607Y**	**11,869Y**	**6,979**	**11,346Y**	**12,055Y**	**15,239Y**	**16,325Y**	**18,655Y**	**23,230Y**
United States	111	345	1,288V	1,108V	1,308V	2,019V	2,340V	2,314V	1,832	3,153V	2,926V	3,415V	3,486V	4,514V	5,882V
Canada	156	10	37V	83V	153V	118V	123V	153V	115	123V	180V	164V	286V	411V	360V
Australia	193	2	15V	10V	26V	10V	13V	15V	524	395V	174V	525V	290V	346V	335V
Japan	158	67	63V	60V	52V	107V	412V	766V	366	559V	804V	840V	867V	1,254V	1,419V
New Zealand	196	—	1V	2V	4V	2V	3V	5V	51	74V	73V	68V	92V	114V	142V
Austria	122	2	9V	10V	11V	13V	13V	15V	43	133V	132V	151V	184V	234V	296V
Belgium	124	42	61V	107V	186V	278V	454V	439V	198	337V	375V	495V	641V	674V	857V
Cyprus	423	4	20V	21V	49V	59V	87V	93V	9	27V	25V	8V	8V	13V	19V
Denmark	128	2	6V	9V	10V	12V	14V	24V	139	112V	133V	132V	130V	138V	204V
Finland	172	1	7V	4V	5V	6V	8V	14V	151	165V	140V	211V	286V	331V	401V
France	132	163	276V	381V	460V	755V	1,111V	929V	507	1,217V	1,417V	1,580V	2,072V	1,827V	1,811V
Germany	134	111	236V	387V	573V	744V	857V	908V	960	1,458V	1,595V	1,952V	2,321V	2,555V	3,198V
Greece	174	47	145V	138V	177V	179V	202V	387V	95	66V	82V	157V	157V	161V	157V
Iceland	176	—	—V	3V	1V	1V	1V	2V	2	—V	—V	—V	—V	—V	—V
Ireland	178	6	13V	23V	8V	23V	31V	47V	78	99V	66V	94V	73V	93V	126V
Italy	136	379	959V	1,017V	1,446V	1,444V	2,477V	2,260V	642	1,252V	1,497V	1,845V	1,898V	2,135V	3,247V
Luxembourg	137	1	—V	—V	—V	—V	—V	—V	—	6V	9V	6V	11V	11V	12V
Malta	181	20	2V	7V	41V	10V	7V	5V	12	7V	4V	6V	8V	11V	6V
Netherlands	138	278	218V	240V	372V	423V	357V	462V	258	427V	442V	593V	884V	992V	1,191V
Norway	142	4	8V	8V	18V	22V	21V	50V	23	44V	31V	31V	60V	47V	68V
Portugal	182	16	54V	75V	60V	41V	104V	98V	13	26V	25V	24V	48V	34V	55V
Slovenia	961	6	5V	6V	7Y	9V	11V	14V	68	34V	38V	50Y	52V	56V	69V
Spain	184	153	221V	315V	508V	1,192V	1,787V	1,816V	175	343V	448V	906V	562V	573V	677V
Sweden	144	3	5V	7V	10V	21V	14V	25V	194	192V	269V	336V	474V	575V	716V
Switzerland	146	16	14V	19V	26V	27V	25V	21V	224	332V	339V	347V	345V	367V	429V
United Kingdom	112	98	590V	658V	848V	621V	1,137V	1,008V	300	767V	831V	1,303V	1,093V	1,188V	1,554V
Developing Countries	**202**	**1,567**	**1,930Y**	**2,704Y**	**4,389Y**	**5,812Y**	**7,118Y**	**9,459Y**	**4,869**	**7,596Y**	**8,098Y**	**11,124Y**	**15,057Y**	**19,160Y**	**24,482Y**
Africa	**607**	**168**	**329Y**	**534Y**	**677Y**	**1,007Y**	**1,209Y**	**1,379Y**	**307**	**452Y**	**508Y**	**658Y**	**874Y**	**1,113Y**	**1,372Y**
Algeria	612	12	53V	59Y	76Y	97Y	120Y	155Y	4	171V	207Y	274Y	373Y	469Y	566Y
Angola	614	1	1Y	1Y	1Y	1Y	1Y	2Y	—	—Y	—Y	—Y	—Y	—Y	—Y
Benin	638	—	4V	1V	1V	4V	5Y	6Y	—	—V	—V	—V	—V	—Y	—Y
Burundi	618	—	—V	—V	—V	—V	—V	—Y	—	—V	—V	3V	2V	3V	3Y
Cameroon	622	3	9V	11V	14Y	16Y	20Y	24Y	—	—V	1V	2Y	2Y	2Y	3Y
Chad	628	—	—Y	—Y	—Y	—Y	—Y	—Y	—	—Y	—Y	—Y	—Y	—Y	1Y
Congo, Dem. Rep. of	636	1	2Y	2Y	3Y	3Y	4Y	5Y	—	—Y	—Y	—Y	—Y	—Y	—Y
Congo, Republic of	634	—	1V	1V	1V	1Y	1Y	1Y	—	—V	—V	—V	—Y	—Y	—Y
Côte d'Ivoire	662	5	3V	7V	22V	49V	7V	8Y	—	1V	2V	4V	4V	3V	3Y
Eritrea	643	—	—Y	1Y	1Y	1Y	1Y	1Y	—	—Y	—Y	—Y	—Y	—Y	—Y
Ethiopia	644	3	18V	21V	28V	47V	57Y	71Y	4	5V	3V	3V	15V	18Y	23Y
Gabon	646	—	—Y	—Y	1Y	1Y	1Y	1Y	—	—Y	—Y	—Y	—Y	—Y	—Y
Gambia, The	648	1	1Y	2Y	2Y	3Y	3Y	4Y	—	—Y	—Y	—Y	—Y	—Y	—Y
Ghana	652	4	4Y	5Y	7Y	8Y	10Y	12Y	1	1Y	1Y	2Y	2Y	2Y	3Y
Guinea	656	3	3Y	3V	4V	5Y	6Y	8Y	—	—Y	—V	—V	—Y	—Y	—Y
Kenya	664	20	33V	58V	74V	84Y	104Y	129Y	95	94V	79V	96V	110Y	136Y	168Y
Madagascar	674	1	2V	8V	10Y	12Y	14Y	18Y	—	—V	—V	1Y	1Y	1Y	1Y
Malawi	676	—	—Y	—Y	—Y	—Y	—Y	—Y	25	28Y	35Y	46Y	52Y	65Y	80Y
Mali	678	1	1Y	1Y	1Y	1Y	2Y	2Y	1	1Y	1Y	1Y	1Y	1Y	2Y
Mauritania	682	1	2Y	2Y	3Y	3Y	4Y	5Y	2	3Y	3Y	4Y	5Y	6Y	8Y
Mauritius	684	5	9V	13V	17V	19V	25V	25V	—	1V	1V	—V	—V	—V	—V
Morocco	686	26	50V	112V	88V	146V	180Y	224Y	21	22V	27V	26V	25V	31Y	38Y
Mozambique	688	1	—V	—V	—V	2V	—V	—Y	2	—V	—Y	—Y	—Y	—Y	—Y
Niger	692	—	—V	—V	1V	2Y	2Y	2Y	—	—V	—V	—V	—Y	—Y	—Y
Nigeria	694	7	12V	6V	8Y	11Y	13Y	17Y	1	—V	—V	—Y	—Y	—Y	—Y
Senegal	722	5	10V	11V	18V	36V	11V	14Y	—	—V	—V	—V	—V	—V	—Y
Sierra Leone	724	2	2Y	3Y	4Y	4Y	5Y	6Y	—	—Y	—Y	—Y	—Y	—Y	—Y
Somalia	726	—	—Y	—Y	—Y	—Y	—Y	—Y	—	—Y	1Y	1Y	1Y	1Y	1Y
South Africa	199	5	10V	47V	17V	27V	95V	29V	19	19V	39V	27V	42V	35V	74V
Sacca exc. South Afr.	608	—	1V	1V	2Y	2Y	3Y	3Y	—	—V	—V	—V	—Y	—Y	—Y
Sudan	732	33	36Y	95Y	190V	336V	389V	448V	64	70Y	69V	119V	87V	107V	60V
Tanzania	738	4	5V	6Y	8Y	9Y	11Y	14Y	3	2V	2Y	3Y	3Y	4Y	5Y
Togo	742	—	6V	3V	6V	—V	1Y	1Y	2	—V	—V	—V	—V	—Y	—Y
Tunisia	744	22	43V	44V	57V	62V	97V	120Y	16	28V	31V	34V	53V	55V	68Y
Uganda	746	1	4V	6V	8Y	9Y	11Y	13Y	3	2V	3V	4Y	4Y	5Y	7Y
Zambia	754	1	—V	2V	3V	6V	6V	8V	43	—V	1V	1V	87V	166V	255V
Zimbabwe	698	1	3V	1V	2V	1V	1V	1Y	2	3V	3V	6V	2V	1V	1Y
Asia	**507**	**497**	**596Y**	**781Y**	**1,088Y**	**1,253Y**	**1,384Y**	**1,983Y**	**1,689**	**2,922Y**	**3,323Y**	**4,079Y**	**5,454Y**	**7,502Y**	**10,054Y**
Afghanistan, I.S. of	512	—	—Y	—Y	—Y	—Y	—Y	—Y	1	1Y	2Y	2Y	3Y	3Y	4Y
Bangladesh	513	—	7V	9V	6V	19V	23V	17V	4	13V	7V	10V	13V	13Y	14Y
Cambodia	522	—	—V	—V	—V	2V	—V	—Y	—	—V	—V	—V	—V	—V	—Y

		Exports							Imports						
		2001	2002	2003	2004	2005	2006	2007	2001	2002	2003	2004	2005	2006	2007
		Millions of U.S. Dollars							Millions of U.S. Dollars						
China,P.R.: Mainland	924	40	84V	138V	173V	192V	197V	216V	513	938V	1,032V	1,519V	2,129V	3,274V	4,876V
China,P.R.:Hong Kong	532	8	29V	36V	58V	123V	80V	115V	42	146V	142V	145V	145V	167V	192V
India	534	252	177V	118V	116V	183V	227Y	281Y	284	373V	385V	450V	670V	828Y	1,028Y
Indonesia	536	9	19V	28V	17V	36V	46V	45V	158	198V	187V	217V	320V	511V	649V
Korea	542	51	122V	177V	306V	183V	409V	558V	269	353V	468V	592V	777V	939V	1,283V
Malaysia	548	10	15V	21V	28V	34V	44V	78V	112	325V	500V	402V	503V	376V	525V
Maldives	556	—	—V	—V	—V	—V	—Y	1Y	—	—Y	—Y	—Y	—Y	—Y	—Y
Myanmar	518	—	—Y	—Y	—Y	—Y	—Y	—Y	2	3Y	3Y	4Y	5Y	6Y	8Y
Pakistan	564	21	36V	32V	50V	113V	140Y	174Y	10	59V	45V	53V	57V	71Y	88Y
Philippines	566	—	1V	2V	4V	9V	11V	13V	2	8V	5V	7V	9V	10V	19V
Singapore	576	86	77V	113V	230V	261V	77V	60V	40	140V	121V	142V	168V	321V	364V
Sri Lanka	524	1	—V	4V	1V	2V	8V	10V	9	—V	12V	14V	16V	20V	20V
Taiwan Province of China	528	9	19V	46V	21V	19V	99V	409V	126	202V	206V	237V	296V	489V	454V
Thailand	578	9	10V	48V	76V	59V	15V	6V	106	138V	191V	239V	292V	418V	527V
Vanuatu	846	—	—Y	—Y	—Y	—Y	—Y	—Y	1	1Y	1Y	1Y	1Y	2Y	2Y
Vietnam	582	1	1V	6V	2V	17V	7V	—V	8	24V	16V	44V	50V	54V	—V
Europe	**170**	**147**	**210Y**	**323Y**	**433Y**	**533Y**	**802Y**	**1,132Y**	**1,285**	**1,906Y**	**1,837Y**	**2,758Y**	**4,067Y**	**4,847Y**	**6,377Y**
Albania	914	1	4V	10V	8V	10V	17V	22V	8	—V	—V	—V	—V	—V	—V
Armenia	911	1	—V	—V	—V	1V	2V	4V	—	—V	—V	—V	—V	—V	—V
Azerbaijan	912	1	—V	—V	1V	1V	1V	2V	—	—V	—V	1V	43V	—V	—V
Belarus	913	1	—V	1V	2V	5V	8V	13V	1	13V	9V	25V	36V	41V	63V
Bosnia & Herzegovina	963	—	—Y	1Y	1Y	1Y	1Y	1Y	13	14Y	18Y	23Y	26Y	33Y	40Y
Bulgaria	918	5	4V	4V	7V	10V	15V	26V	19	31V	48V	57V	73V	51V	71V
Croatia	960	5	4V	4V	6V	12V	15V	12V	35	10V	17V	16V	17V	22V	26V
Czech Republic	935	3	12V	25V	19V	20V	7V	10V	28	54V	40V	76V	128V	171V	185V
Estonia	939	—	1V	1V	—V	—V	—V	2V	11	11V	16V	8V	7V	68V	20V
Georgia	915	—	—V	—V	—V	2V	7V	10Y	—	—V	—V	—V	1V	1V	4Y
Gibraltar	823	1	2Y	2Y	3Y	3Y	4Y	5Y	1	1Y	1Y	2Y	2Y	2Y	3Y
Hungary	944	3	5V	7V	4V	8V	8V	9V	17	26V	45V	68V	123V	208V	301V
Kazakhstan	916	1	3V	3V	4V	5Y	6Y	8Y	6	3V	3V	10V	11Y	14Y	17Y
Latvia	941	—	1V	1V	1V	1V	6V	7V	9	24V	14V	6V	6V	20V	17V
Lithuania	946	—	—V	1V	3V	2V	4V	5V	1	1V	1V	1V	1V	1V	2V
Macedonia, FYR	962	—	4V	2V	1V	2V	3V	4Y	10	5V	4V	1V	1V	3V	3Y
Moldova	921	—	1V	1V	2V	4V	5Y	6Y	—	—V	—V	1V	1V	1Y	1Y
Poland	964	1	10V	11V	17V	16V	22V	31V	41	98V	77V	63V	139V	183V	166V
Romania	968	23	19V	26V	41V	67V	138V	110V	131	130V	131V	227V	207V	240V	259V
Russia	922	8	19V	35V	51V	75V	120V	157V	291	538V	412V	854V	1,155V	1,363V	2,147V
Serbia & Montenegro	965	1	1Y	1Y	1Y	2Y	2Y	3Y	3	3Y	4Y	5Y	6Y	7Y	9Y
Slovak Republic	936	1	2V	2Y	3Y	4V	4V	6V	3	15V	19Y	25Y	33V	38V	62V
Turkey	186	77	107V	172V	232V	243V	357V	618V	244	359V	380V	520V	756V	780V	993V
Ukraine	926	10	7V	8V	18V	34V	42Y	52Y	211	350V	321V	404V	879V	1,086Y	1,348Y
Europe n.s.	884	3	4Y	5Y	6Y	7Y	8Y	11Y	202	219Y	277Y	364Y	416Y	514Y	638Y
Middle East	**407**	**722**	**744Y**	**998Y**	**2,112Y**	**2,825Y**	**3,562Y**	**4,498Y**	**1,043**	**1,404Y**	**1,383Y**	**2,204Y**	**2,958Y**	**3,683Y**	**4,480Y**
Bahrain	419	2	3Y	3Y	4Y	5Y	6Y	7Y	15	16Y	20Y	27Y	30Y	37Y	47Y
Iran, I.R. of	429	4	13V	15Y	19Y	24Y	30Y	39Y	11	11Y	14Y	18Y	25Y	31Y	37Y
Iraq	433	91	94Y	104Y	135Y	172Y	213Y	276Y	1	1Y	1Y	2Y	2Y	3Y	3Y
Israel	436	190	18V	20V	26V	45V	70V	85V	19	29V	29V	32V	103V	138V	169V
Jordan	439	25	69V	107V	275V	335V	444V	537V	21	21V	30V	33V	50V	62V	80V
Kuwait	443	17	17Y	19Y	25Y	32Y	39Y	51Y	50	54Y	65Y	86Y	117Y	147Y	177Y
Lebanon	446	53	57Y	73Y	96Y	109Y	135Y	167Y	23	25Y	32Y	42Y	48Y	60Y	74Y
Libya	672	45	47Y	52Y	68Y	86Y	106Y	138Y	40	42Y	51Y	68Y	92Y	116Y	140Y
Oman	449	4	16V	21V	27Y	34Y	42Y	54Y	4	6V	9V	13Y	17Y	21Y	26Y
Qatar	453	5	14V	26V	18V	43V	82V	106Y	12	290V	27V	20V	42V	23V	27Y
Saudi Arabia	456	147	197V	275V	385V	725V	895Y	1,160Y	679	722Y	875Y	1,158Y	1,575Y	1,980Y	2,388Y
Syrian Arab Republic	463	56	61Y	77Y	752V	859Y	1,062Y	1,318Y	49	53Y	67Y	503V	575Y	711Y	882Y
United Arab Emirates	466	59	93V	152V	198Y	252Y	311Y	403Y	111	118Y	143Y	189Y	258Y	324Y	391Y
Yemen, Republic of	474	18	40V	50Y	81V	101V	125Y	155Y	9	16V	20Y	14V	25V	30Y	38Y
Middle East n.s.	489	6	4Y	3Y	3Y	3Y	3Y	3Y	—	—Y	—Y	—Y	—Y	—Y	—Y
Western Hemisphere	**207**	**34**	**50Y**	**68Y**	**80Y**	**194Y**	**161Y**	**468Y**	**545**	**912Y**	**1,047Y**	**1,425Y**	**1,704Y**	**2,015Y**	**2,200Y**
Argentina	213	1	2V	6V	16V	4V	14V	36V	257	446V	491V	657V	615V	357V	635V
Bolivia	218	—	—V	—V	—V	—V	—Y	—Y	—	1V	1V	3V	3Y	4Y	5Y
Brazil	223	26	25V	35V	33V	31V	38V	53V	252	425V	508V	686V	955V	1,484V	1,362V
Chile	228	—	1V	1V	1V	—V	—V	—V	9	—V	3V	5V	10V	6V	14V
Colombia	233	—	1V	2V	2V	3V	4V	5V	—	1V	13V	1V	1V	2V	1V
Costa Rica	238	—	—V	—V	—V	—V	1Y	1Y	—	—V	—V	—V	—V	—Y	—Y
Ecuador	248	—	1V	—V	—V	1V	—V	1Y	2	—V	2V	—V	—V	—V	—Y
El Salvador	253	—	—V	2V	—V	—V	—V	1V	—	—V	—V	—V	—V	—V	—V
Guatemala	258	—	—V	—V	—V	1V	1Y	1Y	1	12V	—V	1V	5V	7Y	8Y
Honduras	268	—	1V	—V	—V	—Y	—Y	—Y	—	—V	—V	—V	—Y	—Y	—Y
Jamaica	343	—	1V	6V	1V	—V	—V	—V	—	—V	—V	—V	—V	—V	—V
Mexico	273	—	3V	3V	4V	134V	76V	340V	16	19V	19V	33V	48V	67V	67V
Paraguay	288	—	—V	—V	—V	—V	—V	—Y	—	—V	—V	—V	5V	1V	1Y
Peru	293	—	—V	1V	—V	1V	1V	1Y	1	3V	3V	3V	4V	7V	7Y
Trinidad and Tobago	369	—	8V	10Y	13Y	15Y	19Y	23Y	—	—V	1Y	1Y	1Y	1Y	1Y
Uruguay	298	6	7Y	1V	5V	3V	4Y	4Y	4	4Y	4V	10V	31V	38Y	48Y
Venezuela, Rep. Bol.	299	1	1V	—V	1V	1V	3V	2V	3	2V	1V	24V	26V	42V	50Y
Other Countries n.i.e.	**910**	**—**	**—Y**	**—Y**	**—Y**	**—Y**	**—Y**	**—Y**	**2**	**2Y**	**2Y**	**3Y**	**3Y**	**4Y**	**5Y**
Cuba	928	—	—Y	—Y	—Y	—Y	—Y	—Y	—	—Y	—Y	—Y	—Y	1Y	1Y
North Korea	954	—	—Y	—Y	—Y	—Y	—Y	—Y	1	1Y	2Y	2Y	3Y	3Y	4Y

	Exports 2001	2002	2003	2004	2005	2006	2007	Imports 2001	2002	2003	2004	2005	2006	2007
	Millions of U.S. Dollars							Millions of U.S. Dollars						
Special Categories 899	**798**	**866Y**	**1,097Y**	**1,440Y**	**1,646Y**	**2,034Y**	**2,524Y**	**871**	**945Y**	**1,196Y**	**1,571Y**	**1,795Y**	**2,218Y**	**2,753Y**
Memorandum Items														
European Union 998	1,339	2,860Y	3,453Y	4,817Y	5,881Y	8,722Y	8,613Y	3,952	6,895Y	7,739Y	10,095Y	11,336Y	12,290Y	15,349Y
Oil Exporting Ctys 999	400	577Y	758Y	977Y	1,514Y	1,899Y	2,445Y	1,073	1,614Y	1,581Y	2,068Y	2,846Y	3,666Y	4,455Y
Non-Oil Develop.Ctys 201	1,166	1,353Y	1,946Y	3,412Y	4,297Y	5,219Y	7,014Y	3,796	5,981Y	6,517Y	9,055Y	12,211Y	15,494Y	20,026Y
PERCENT DISTRIBUTION														
Industrial Countries 101	**42.9**	**60.3**	**55.3**	**52.2**	**52.2**	**55.9**	**49.8**	**54.9**	**57.0**	**56.5**	**54.5**	**49.2**	**46.6**	**46.0**
Developing Countries 202	**37.8**	**27.4**	**31.8**	**36.0**	**37.3**	**34.3**	**39.7**	**38.3**	**38.2**	**37.9**	**39.8**	**45.4**	**47.9**	**48.5**
Africa 607	**4.0**	**4.7**	**6.3**	**5.6**	**6.5**	**5.8**	**5.8**	**2.4**	**2.3**	**2.4**	**2.4**	**2.6**	**2.8**	**2.7**
Asia 507	**12.0**	**8.5**	**9.2**	**8.9**	**8.0**	**6.7**	**8.3**	**13.3**	**14.7**	**15.6**	**14.6**	**16.4**	**18.7**	**19.9**
Europe 170	**3.5**	**3.0**	**3.8**	**3.6**	**3.4**	**3.9**	**4.7**	**10.1**	**9.6**	**8.6**	**9.9**	**12.3**	**12.1**	**12.6**
Middle East 407	**17.4**	**10.5**	**11.7**	**17.3**	**18.1**	**17.2**	**18.9**	**8.2**	**7.1**	**6.5**	**7.9**	**8.9**	**9.2**	**8.9**
Western Hemisphere 207	**.8**	**.7**	**.8**	**.7**	**1.2**	**.8**	**2.0**	**4.3**	**4.6**	**4.9**	**5.1**	**5.1**	**5.0**	**4.4**
ANNUAL PERCENT CHANGE														
World 001	**–34.8**	**70.2**	**20.6**	**43.4**	**27.9**	**33.1**	**14.9**	**–42.3**	**56.3**	**7.4**	**30.8**	**18.8**	**20.7**	**26.1**
Industrial Countries 101	**–55.6**	**139.6**	**10.5**	**35.3**	**28.0**	**42.7**	**2.3**	**–48.2**	**62.6**	**6.3**	**26.4**	**7.1**	**14.3**	**24.5**
Developing Countries 202	**–10.2**	**23.1**	**40.2**	**62.3**	**32.4**	**22.5**	**32.9**	**–32.7**	**56.0**	**6.6**	**37.4**	**35.4**	**27.2**	**27.8**
Africa 607	**–18.6**	**96.4**	**62.3**	**26.7**	**48.9**	**20.0**	**14.0**	**7.4**	**47.1**	**12.4**	**29.4**	**32.8**	**27.4**	**23.2**
Asia 507	**–17.6**	**20.0**	**31.0**	**39.4**	**15.1**	**10.4**	**43.3**	**–47.3**	**73.0**	**13.7**	**22.7**	**33.7**	**37.6**	**34.0**
Europe 170	**–28.6**	**43.5**	**53.3**	**34.1**	**23.1**	**50.6**	**41.1**	**–29.2**	**48.3**	**–3.6**	**50.1**	**47.5**	**19.2**	**31.6**
Middle East 407	**6.4**	**3.1**	**34.3**	**111.5**	**33.8**	**26.1**	**26.3**	**–16.7**	**34.5**	**–1.5**	**59.4**	**34.2**	**24.5**	**21.6**
Western Hemisphere 207	**–35.6**	**46.0**	**35.9**	**17.3**	**142.3**	**–17.2**	**190.7**	**–19.9**	**67.3**	**14.8**	**36.2**	**19.6**	**18.2**	**9.2**
Other Countries n.i.e. 910	**–97.6**	**8.5**	**26.6**	**31.3**	**14.3**	**23.6**	**24.1**	**–74.4**	**8.5**	**26.6**	**31.3**	**14.3**	**23.6**	**24.1**

	Exports							Imports						
	2001	2002	2003	2004	2005	2006	2007	2001	2002	2003	2004	2005	2006	2007
	Millions of U.S. Dollars							*Millions of U.S. Dollars*						
IFS World Total	**2,863.8**	**2,995.0**	**3,128.0**	**3,304.6**	**3,386.5**	**3,513.3**	**3,976.8**	**5,026.8**	**5,184.5**	**5,754.3**	**6,328.9**	**6,834.3**	**7,627.8**	**8,676.6**
DOTS World Total...... 001	**2,863.8**	**2,995.0**	**3,128.0**	**3,304.6**	**3,418.2**	**3,706.5**	**3,979.9**	**5,026.8**	**5,184.5**	**5,754.3**	**6,328.9**	**6,689.7**	**7,670.6**	**8,676.6**
Industrial Countries...... 101	**1,968.6**	**2,099.2**	**2,208.8**	**2,304.9**	**2,040.8**	**2,252.4**	**2,311.1**	**3,028.7**	**3,097.7**	**3,448.1**	**3,640.3**	**3,207.9**	**3,588.4**	**4,008.1**
United States...... 111	1,878.09	2,009.52	2,116.87	2,171.50	1,828.69	1,992.25	2,029.98	2,485.17	2,590.87	2,873.08	2,971.60	2,470.89	2,721.44	3,097.54
Canada...... 156	4.99	4.34	6.13	13.81	22.33	26.32	11.96	36.82	34.25	48.79	46.51	54.46	62.35	55.52
Australia...... 193	.04	.06	.10	.21	.52	1.13	1.53	6.23	5.79	6.70	7.80	10.74	19.49	34.19
Japan...... 158	5.60	6.07	8.81	7.63	16.84	17.63	15.51	124.65	136.29	132.27	134.06	127.72	157.53	184.72
New Zealand...... 196	.01	.01	.01	.04	—	.40	.41	15.41	11.41	11.41	12.81	13.24	18.96	18.67
Austria...... 122	.27	.55	.49	.55	.28	.70	.17	9.78	4.16	5.39	5.55	6.65	5.30	6.63
Belgium-Luxembourg n.s...... 127	4.75	4.98	6.58	8.01	18.08	15.96	19.54	19.83	18.88	35.01	37.01	41.26	38.48	41.05
Cyprus...... 423	—	—	—	—	—	.02	—	—	—	—	—	—	—	—
Denmark...... 128	.06	.13	.14	.52	.46	.44	.24	6.55	8.96	16.46	10.15	18.07	11.08	11.30
Finland...... 172	1.05	1.80	1.03	.40	.68	.18	.10	29.33	13.70	7.70	9.00	9.30	35.12	29.36
France...... 132	10.15	10.51	7.91	9.81	14.01	11.55	3.86	31.97	29.86	33.64	66.87	81.69	47.44	58.01
Germany...... 134	48.81	36.38	31.30	34.20	45.22	96.49	105.20	88.95	81.04	91.61	92.69	118.71	126.60	130.57
Greece...... 174	.01	.11	.06	.10	.15	.14	.11	.55	1.29	.64	.59	.98	.57	.50
Iceland...... 176	—	—	—	—	—	—	.01	—	.03	—	—	—	—	.13
Ireland...... 178	—	.06	.03	.02	—	—	.84	1.30	1.62	3.20	3.86	5.11	5.94	4.80
Italy...... 136	2.14	6.96	4.25	4.75	7.00	7.14	9.40	41.75	42.67	45.67	36.16	38.74	70.02	63.45
Malta...... 181	—	—	—	—	—	—	—	—	—	—	—	.03	—	—
Netherlands...... 138	1.09	2.95	3.15	5.53	8.46	7.47	4.60	13.63	11.18	10.42	6.80	10.13	29.80	33.73
Norway...... 142	.08	.51	.16	.15	.48	.28	.19	.29	.83	.42	9.94	19.53	19.58	19.86
Portugal...... 182	.67	1.34	1.04	1.04	1.04	1.33	2.44	3.19	2.55	1.46	2.15	4.98	11.89	13.14
Spain...... 184	3.92	5.81	14.57	37.71	64.71	60.23	93.65	54.85	61.89	66.53	104.66	71.73	86.88	76.34
Sweden...... 144	.27	.30	.46	1.69	2.31	3.02	2.60	19.08	11.73	11.55	36.16	28.25	43.76	77.69
Switzerland...... 146	.05	.46	.13	.27	.56	.66	.35	24.57	13.29	22.09	25.13	24.31	33.70	29.76
United Kingdom...... 112	6.53	6.37	5.54	7.00	8.99	9.10	8.41	14.79	15.46	24.05	20.80	51.37	42.45	21.10
Developing Countries...... 202	**893.9**	**894.5**	**917.9**	**995.8**	**1,371.4**	**1,446.4**	**1,660.1**	**1,991.4**	**2,085.2**	**2,305.3**	**2,687.1**	**3,479.1**	**4,077.9**	**4,663.4**
Africa...... 607	**.1**	**1.1**	**.4**	**3.0**	**1.4**	**1.8**	**1.5**	**2.6**	**7.4**	**2.8**	**1.8**	**6.3**	**17.9**	**20.4**
Algeria...... 612	—	.69	—	—	—	—	—	—	—	—	—	—	—	—
Angola...... 614	.01	—	—	—	—	—	—	.07	—	—	.03	—	—	—
Cameroon...... 622	—	.02	.03	—	—	—	—	.03	.01	.02	—	—	.02	—
Central African Rep...... 626	—	—	—	—	—	—	—	—	—	—	—	.02	—	—
Ghana...... 652	—	—	.14	.65	—	—	—	—	—	—	—	—	—	—
Kenya...... 664	—	—	—	—	—	—	—	.04	.04	.03	.40	.24	—	—
Madagascar...... 674	—	—	—	—	—	.03	—	—	—	.01	—	.42	1.07	—
Mauritania...... 682	—	—	.01	—	—	—	—	—	—	—	—	—	—	—
Mauritius...... 684	—	—	—	—	—	—	—	—	—	—	—	—	.03	—
Morocco...... 686	.10	—	.08	.09	.05	.33	.20	.05	3.26	.40	.43	1.82	.38	1.37
Mozambique...... 688	—	—	—	—	—	—	—	—	—	—	—	—	.01	—
Nigeria...... 694	—	—	—	—	.02	—	—	—	—	—	—	—	5.08	6.78
Rwanda...... 714	....	....	....	....	....	....	....	—	—	—	.01	—	3.21	—
South Africa...... 199	.02	.03	.10	.03	1.01	1.37	.95	2.34	2.76	1.00	.65	3.73	.72	.36
Sudan...... 732	—	—	—	—	—	—	—	—	—	—	—	—	.05	—
Zambia...... 754	—	—	—	—	.18	—	—	—	—	—	—	—	—	—
Zimbabwe...... 698	—	—	—	—	—	—	—	—	—	—	—	—	—	.05
Africa n.s...... 799	—	.33	—	2.26	.15	.05	.34	.10	1.30	1.36	.31	.09	7.38	11.85
Asia...... 507	**3.0**	**12.7**	**11.6**	**11.7**	**20.2**	**49.3**	**29.0**	**187.7**	**216.4**	**271.6**	**315.4**	**654.2**	**802.1**	**864.4**
Afghanistan, I.S. of...... 512	—	—	—	—	—	—	—	.15	—	—	—	.08	.33	.01
Bangladesh...... 513	—	—	—	—	—	—	—	.39	.12	.77	.38	.58	.67	.73
Cambodia...... 522	—	—	—	—	2.43	.37	.69	.01	—	.01	—	.10	.02	.13
China,P.R.: Mainland...... 924	.13	.95	5.12	3.62	2.96	6.68	6.98	49.75	68.93	89.08	108.07	218.93	332.46	409.68
China,P.R.:Hong Kong...... 532	1.68	1.29	1.95	2.06	3.01	2.19	3.65	29.58	24.80	23.15	27.74	133.17	150.32	114.66
China,P.R.:Macao...... 546	—	—	—	—	—	.06	—	—	—	—	—	—	.01	—
India...... 534	.52	.64	.79	1.37	1.06	1.61	3.00	3.96	6.73	7.78	12.90	14.67	21.38	25.08
Indonesia...... 536	—	.01	.13	.52	1.13	10.17	.06	3.94	6.48	4.49	4.56	8.00	8.02	7.75
Korea...... 542	.26	2.76	1.10	.90	2.87	3.92	3.10	43.10	50.14	59.41	66.63	111.43	123.37	104.85
Malaysia...... 548	—	.01	.07	.01	.06	16.53	.13	3.55	3.46	5.05	7.53	11.79	18.31	21.19
Pakistan...... 564	—	—	—	—	.05	.18	.49	.87	1.16	1.46	1.25	16.70	19.92	22.47
Philippines...... 566	—	—	.01	—	.25	—	.15	.39	.34	.34	4.41	1.14	.94	1.54
Singapore...... 576	.02	—	.05	.05	.04	.38	.50	3.98	1.47	4.86	11.23	21.46	7.94	19.61
Sri Lanka...... 524	—	—	—	.17	.03	.42	.34	.41	.60	.48	.74	.71	1.02	1.21
Thailand...... 578	.01	.42	—	.04	.24	.15	.41	9.11	11.67	14.70	16.01	17.76	22.57	36.60
Vietnam...... 582	—	—	—	.94	.94	.65	3.28	.05	.28	.51	.60	1.46	1.93	1.74
Asia n.s...... 598	.34	6.60	2.38	1.99	5.14	5.96	6.28	38.49	40.20	59.48	53.35	96.19	92.86	97.12
Europe...... 170	**49.1**	**18.7**	**26.2**	**25.7**	**23.4**	**14.4**	**39.2**	**64.6**	**48.2**	**53.3**	**67.4**	**78.4**	**97.2**	**107.8**
Albania...... 914	—	—	—	—	—	—	—	.01	—	—	—	—	.01	—
Bulgaria...... 918	—	.01	—	—	.03	—	—	.52	.76	1.13	2.42	1.21	.14	.09
Czechoslovakia n.s...... 937	.14	.14	.23	.13	.26	.42	.12	6.12	1.69	2.11	1.49	8.61	4.93	31.34
Hungary...... 944	—	—	—	—	—	—	—	.09	.02	.04	.02	.04	.30	.17
Poland...... 964	—	.01	.01	—	—	—	.02	.21	.33	.20	.58	.40	.31	.77
Romania...... 968	—	—	.03	.04	.05	—	—	.01	—	.51	.58	—	—	.04

		Exports							Imports						
		2001	2002	2003	2004	2005	2006	2007	2001	2002	2003	2004	2005	2006	2007
		Millions of U.S. Dollars							*Millions of U.S. Dollars*						
Russia	922	48.88	18.53	25.93	25.10	22.63	13.68	38.17	48.55	25.37	21.53	28.10	48.45	80.65	50.84
Turkey	186	—	.01	.01	.33	.36	.02	.36	3.01	2.19	1.52	1.27	2.07	3.50	1.78
Yugoslavia n.s.	966	—	—	—	—	—	—	—	.17	—	—	—	—	—	—
Europe n.s.	884	.03	—	—	.06	.06	.27	.51	5.88	17.88	26.31	32.99	17.63	7.33	22.73
Middle East	**407**	**.4**	**1.4**	**1.7**	**.2**	**.3**	**2.3**	**1.4**	**2.1**	**3.8**	**16.2**	**5.7**	**5.8**	**11.6**	**22.6**
Egypt	469	—	—	—	—	.10	.03	.28	.03	.26	2.24	.16	.09	.04	.56
Iran, I.R. of	429	.01	—	1.46	—	—	—	.01	.04	—	.02	—	.02	—	10.89
Iraq	433	—	—	—	—	—	—	—	.04	—	—	—	—	—	—
Israel	436	.29	1.20	.18	.05	.10	1.54	.76	1.93	3.25	12.46	5.32	5.22	11.28	10.43
Jordan	439	.03	—	.02	.02	.01	.01	.03	.04	—	.05	.05	.08	.07	.15
Kuwait	443	.08	—	—	.01	—	—	—	—	—	—	—	—	—	—
Lebanon	446	—	—	—	.01	—	—	—	—	—	.03	—	.01	—	—
Libya	672	—	—	—	—	—	.70	—	—	—	—	—	.09	—	—
Oman	449	—	—	—	—	—	—	—	—	—	—	—	—	—	.14
Saudi Arabia	456	.03	.07	—	—	—	.03	.14	.05	.08	.01	—	.05	—	.14
United Arab Emirates	466	—	.10	—	.08	.07	.03	.21	—	.24	1.39	.18	.21	.18	.25
Western Hemisphere	**207**	**841.4**	**860.7**	**878.1**	**955.3**	**1,326.1**	**1,378.6**	**1,589.0**	**1,734.4**	**1,809.4**	**1,961.4**	**2,296.7**	**2,734.4**	**3,149.2**	**3,648.2**
Argentina	213	.10	.04	.27	.08	.19	.08	.18	11.69	13.63	27.22	73.60	70.46	126.08	116.22
Bahamas, The	313	.86	.67	.97	1.30	.95	.63	.86	9.49	13.78	2.88	4.40	—	—	3.54
Barbados	316	1.24	2.22	.95	.47	.08	.08	.23	.03	3.90	.02	.17	.09	1.23	.20
Belize	339	7.17	7.54	8.62	8.76	9.54	11.93	12.74	.40	1.10	.40	.68	.73	2.74	2.85
Bermuda	319	.11	.11	.12	.27	.05	.02	.03	.06	—	—	—	—	—	—
Bolivia	218	.18	.01	.03	.13	.03	.03	.10	.02	.01	.23	2.27	.28	.28	.11
Brazil	223	6.42	.16	.14	.32	1.33	2.18	4.22	52.61	82.18	116.71	168.42	263.15	283.78	291.10
Chile	228	1.86	.28	.67	2.57	1.87	.67	2.55	15.99	22.95	43.82	73.73	100.57	133.16	140.67
Colombia	233	.24	.52	.76	.90	1.73	2.45	5.52	35.06	40.12	64.97	58.22	61.66	85.36	83.19
Costa Rica	238	94.62	106.63	102.03	100.39	111.43	118.79	137.22	163.46	149.32	157.36	174.46	180.51	219.51	248.53
Dominica	321	—	—	—	—	.01	.04	—	—	.01	—	—	.02	.16	.08
Dominican Republic	243	12.40	20.83	22.20	25.24	39.09	50.65	63.39	1.28	1.78	4.21	3.73	4.29	5.36	6.46
Ecuador	248	.52	.40	.35	.69	.56	.46	1.28	127.41	152.49	168.26	94.72	115.36	155.88	222.61
Greenland	326	—	—	—	—	—	—	—	—	—	—	—	—	.01	—
Grenada	328	—	—	—	—	—	.12	—	—	—	—	—	—	—	—
Guatemala	258	323.38	343.97	361.25	386.80	417.73	468.80	539.72	435.19	418.70	463.60	505.98	567.52	631.01	741.78
Guyana	336	—	.03	.03	.02	.34	.03	.16	.01	—	—	—	.02	—	—
Haiti	263	.55	.87	.59	.88	2.47	3.84	2.33	.06	.11	.08	.01	.93	.02	.07
Honduras	268	184.46	176.61	184.89	205.52	476.67	404.75	445.70	133.85	155.26	134.94	153.10	175.66	277.62	299.19
Jamaica	343	4.20	2.19	4.55	4.17	3.16	2.40	3.22	.47	.16	.16	.31	.58	.17	.16
Mexico	273	24.63	31.91	37.38	35.80	41.96	44.15	47.49	313.77	294.58	315.63	374.15	510.26	600.71	850.70
Netherlands Antilles	353	1.00	.94	1.34	1.35	.73	.17	.20	42.51	64.07	24.65	62.65	90.37	62.04	61.39
Nicaragua	278	120.26	113.22	98.05	128.63	158.10	195.38	220.38	87.94	97.52	111.57	111.49	127.39	152.07	164.44
Panama	283	48.88	45.03	46.26	46.14	51.95	63.63	90.58	135.14	156.17	126.01	146.31	165.65	206.69	187.79
Paraguay	288	.09	.04	.28	.13	.04	.18	.12	.03	.08	.14	.21	.35	1.08	1.62
Peru	293	.18	.40	.47	.20	.44	.93	3.17	13.12	24.78	12.90	20.66	55.22	28.23	62.38
Suriname	366	.06	.02	—	—	—	.11	.22	—	—	—	—	—	—	—
Trinidad and Tobago	369	.59	.55	.91	.98	1.11	1.02	1.03	11.16	19.30	45.23	14.31	14.47	13.53	19.20
Uruguay	298	.05	.02	—	.12	.01	.01	.13	1.33	1.10	5.49	3.03	4.68	26.02	30.67
Venezuela, Rep. Bol.	299	6.65	4.57	3.87	2.28	3.76	4.70	5.45	82.30	78.70	134.85	244.58	223.55	135.13	112.51
Western Hem. n.s.	399	.64	.92	1.08	1.17	.75	.39	.76	59.99	17.55	.01	5.52	.67	1.30	.77
Other Countries n.i.e.	**910**	**.7**	**1.3**	**1.4**	**3.7**	**5.4**	**7.7**	**8.2**	**.2**	**.3**	**.2**	**.3**	**.3**	**.9**	**.3**
Cuba	928	.71	1.25	1.38	3.71	5.40	7.66	8.07	.16	.25	.20	.27	.31	.29	.34
North Korea	954	—	—	—	—	—	—	.14	—	—	—	—	.02	.63	—
Countries & Areas n.s.	**898**	**.5**	**.1**	**—**	**.1**	**.5**	**—**	**.4**	**6.4**	**1.2**	**.6**	**1.2**	**2.3**	**3.4**	**3.5**
Memorandum Items															
European Union	998	79.73	78.26	76.57	111.34	171.41	213.75	251.18	335.87	305.33	353.58	433.03	487.44	555.96	568.61
Oil Exporting Ctys	999	6.76	5.43	5.46	2.89	4.99	15.63	5.86	86.37	85.50	140.76	249.33	231.92	148.41	138.47
Non-Oil Develop.Ctys	201	887.17	889.07	912.41	992.96	1,366.42	1,430.76	1,654.28	1,905.07	1,999.69	2,164.55	2,437.81	3,247.15	3,929.51	4,524.88
PERCENT DISTRIBUTION															
Industrial Countries	**101**	**68.7**	**70.1**	**70.6**	**69.7**	**59.7**	**60.8**	**58.1**	**60.3**	**59.8**	**59.9**	**57.5**	**48.0**	**46.8**	**46.2**
Developing Countries	**202**	**31.2**	**29.9**	**29.3**	**30.1**	**40.1**	**39.0**	**41.7**	**39.6**	**40.2**	**40.1**	**42.5**	**52.0**	**53.2**	**53.7**
Africa	**607**	**—**	**—**	**—**	**.1**	**—**	**—**	**—**	**.1**	**.1**	**—**	**—**	**.1**	**.2**	**.2**
Asia	**507**	**.1**	**.4**	**.4**	**.4**	**.6**	**1.3**	**.7**	**3.7**	**4.2**	**4.7**	**5.0**	**9.8**	**10.5**	**10.0**
Europe	**170**	**1.7**	**.6**	**.8**	**.8**	**.7**	**.4**	**1.0**	**1.3**	**.9**	**.9**	**1.1**	**1.2**	**1.3**	**1.2**
Middle East	**407**	**—**	**—**	**.1**	**—**	**—**	**.1**	**—**	**—**	**.1**	**.3**	**.1**	**.1**	**.2**	**.3**
Western Hemisphere	**207**	**29.4**	**28.7**	**28.1**	**28.9**	**38.8**	**37.2**	**39.9**	**34.5**	**34.9**	**34.1**	**36.3**	**40.9**	**41.1**	**42.0**
Other Countries n.i.e.	**910**	**—**	**—**	**—**	**.1**	**.2**	**.2**	**.2**	**—**	**—**	**—**	**—**	**—**	**—**	**—**
ANNUAL PERCENT CHANGE															
World	**001**	**–2.6**	**4.6**	**4.4**	**5.6**	**3.4**	**8.4**	**7.4**	**1.6**	**3.1**	**11.0**	**10.0**	**5.7**	**14.7**	**13.1**
Industrial Countries	**101**	**–5.9**	**6.6**	**5.2**	**4.4**	**–11.5**	**10.4**	**2.6**	**.8**	**2.3**	**11.3**	**5.6**	**–11.9**	**11.9**	**11.7**
Developing Countries	**202**	**5.4**	**.1**	**2.6**	**8.5**	**37.7**	**5.5**	**14.8**	**2.7**	**4.7**	**10.6**	**16.6**	**29.5**	**17.2**	**14.4**
Africa	**607**	**–98.6**	**779.7**	**–66.9**	**757.2**	**–53.1**	**25.3**	**–16.5**	**–54.3**	**181.7**	**–61.8**	**–34.9**	**244.2**	**184.1**	**13.8**
Asia	**507**	**44.4**	**326.6**	**–8.5**	**.7**	**73.2**	**143.8**	**–41.0**	**25.4**	**15.2**	**25.5**	**16.1**	**107.4**	**22.6**	**7.8**
Europe	**170**	**178.7**	**–61.9**	**40.1**	**–2.1**	**–8.8**	**–38.5**	**172.3**	**36.2**	**–25.3**	**10.6**	**26.4**	**16.2**	**23.9**	**10.9**
Middle East	**407**	**242.0**	**220.1**	**21.2**	**–89.8**	**71.3**	**702.2**	**–39.2**	**–73.9**	**80.1**	**321.3**	**–64.8**	**1.1**	**100.6**	**95.1**
Western Hemisphere	**207**	**2.6**	**2.3**	**2.0**	**8.8**	**38.8**	**4.0**	**15.3**	**.4**	**4.3**	**8.4**	**17.1**	**19.1**	**15.2**	**15.8**
Other Countries n.i.e.	**910**	**75.3**	**76.8**	**10.5**	**168.2**	**45.8**	**41.8**	**7.1**	**–56.8**	**52.6**	**–18.5**	**35.2**	**18.2**	**179.7**	**–62.4**

		Exports							Imports						
		2001	2002	2003	2004	2005	2006	2007	2001	2002	2003	2004	2005	2006	2007
		Millions of U.S. Dollars							Millions of U.S. Dollars						
IFS World Total		**1,735.0**	**2,117.0**	**2,801.0**	**4,598.8**	**6,990.6**	**8,216.0**	**10,100.0**	**813.0**	**507.0**	**1,236.0**	**1,567.0**	**2,109.0**	**2,621.0**	**3,100.0**
DOTS World Total	**001**	**1,558.9Y**	**1,736.4Y**	**2,640.2Y**	**3,935.0Y**	**6,195.8Y**	**7,466.9Y**	**8,203.9Y**	**318.0Y**	**442.9Y**	**1,224.1Y**	**737.2Y**	**1,117.5Y**	**1,614.0Y**	**1,325.6Y**
Industrial Countries	**101**	**1,135.6Y**	**1,384.6Y**	**2,211.6Y**	**2,412.1Y**	**4,079.2Y**	**4,193.1Y**	**5,446.4Y**	**274.1Y**	**397.8Y**	**1,038.0Y**	**620.6Y**	**919.0Y**	**1,175.6Y**	**924.5Y**
United States	111	433.73V	503.27V	875.36V	1,144.55V	1,523.00V	1,659.36V	1,692.64V	88.33V	119.57V	370.04V	236.83V	274.01V	606.76V	260.04V
Canada	156	70.42V	188.24V	335.36V	265.66V	453.66V	205.70V	224.72V	2.08V	1.48V	2.51V	1.58V	2.28V	1.48V	2.64V
Australia	193	—V	—V	.02V	—V	.01V	—V	.01V	.01V	.01V	.20V	.11V	.03V	.79V	.25V
Japan	158	13.75V	45.82V	.02V	44.28V	202.76V	290.62V	533.20V	1.08V	1.59V	4.00V	8.55V	6.48V	17.91V	8.47V
New Zealand	196	—V	—V	—V	7.46V	—V	—V	—V	—V	—V	.04V	.30V	.02V	.13V	—V
Austria	122	—V	—V	—V	—V	—V	—V	—V	.01V	—V	.02V	.09V	1.50V	1.03V	2.49V
Belgium	124	—V	.24V	1.17V	2.22V	1.16V	1.29V	4.08V	3.11V	9.46V	14.38V	18.24V	17.68V	31.24V	45.78V
Cyprus	423	—V	—V	—V	—V	—Y	—V	—V	—V	.42V	.09V	.01V	—V	—V	—V
Denmark	128	.10V	.06V	.14V	.29V	.06V	—V	37.78V	.48V	1.25V	1.40V	3.25V	2.19V	1.79V	2.54V
Finland	172	—V	—V	.05V	—V	—V	—V	—V	.07V	2.11V	.70V	.19V	.04V	.08V	.20V
France	132	36.33V	87.70V	94.69V	82.26V	248.75V	169.83V	617.83V	27.59V	42.61V	182.09V	77.38V	135.08V	98.58V	127.52V
Germany	134	4.38V	5.86V	3.39V	7.60V	32.90V	70.12V	100.02V	4.99V	5.55V	8.58V	5.62V	8.48V	21.80V	41.21V
Greece	174	—V	—V	—V	.26V	1.46V	1.33V	.70V	.04V	.01V	.50V	.22V	.07V	—V	—V
Iceland	176	—V	—V	—V	5.86V	—V	2.71V	—V	—V	—V	—V	—V	—V	—V	—V
Ireland	178	.15V	—V	—V	.10V	.64V	.50V	.02V	1.33V	.02V	.24V	.05V	.06V	.09V	.05V
Italy	136	.63V	24.61V	165.94V	154.73V	224.11V	172.15V	158.49V	25.65V	19.46V	64.26V	38.48V	230.21V	79.70V	87.68V
Luxembourg	137	—V	—V	—V	—V	—V	—V	—V	15.13V	.08V	.01V	.91V	.13V	.66V	1.19V
Malta	181	—Y	—V	—V	—V	—V	—V	—V	—Y	—V	—V	—V	—V	.10V	.01V
Netherlands	138	30.68V	18.12V	49.49V	49.36V	324.60V	142.68V	305.63V	13.50V	19.61V	22.78V	25.85V	27.34V	43.70V	54.13V
Norway	142	.04V	.04V	.04V	1.25V	26.76V	52.09V	84.84V	1.94V	45.62V	71.44V	8.28V	9.51V	4.89V	3.80V
Portugal	182	2.05V	51.41V	3.51V	3.28V	337.68V	452.86V	527.43V	.03V	.62V	.80V	3.42V	1.89V	14.06V	17.82V
Slovenia	961	—V	—V	—V	—Y	—V	—V	—V	—V	—V	—V	—Y	—V	.03V	—V
Spain	184	535.93V	449.92V	670.21V	624.02V	672.10V	943.16V	1,140.11V	49.00V	65.40V	99.26V	121.51V	121.19V	157.42V	181.89V
Sweden	144	—V	—V	—V	—V	—V	—V	.01V	.10V	1.76V	.32V	.50V	.28V	.08V	.55V
Switzerland	146	—V	.12V	.37V	.09V	2.19V	—V	—V	.32V	.40V	.41V	.21V	2.87V	.41V	.80V
United Kingdom	112	7.41V	9.22V	11.84V	18.81V	27.30V	28.73V	18.85V	39.34V	60.81V	193.89V	69.02V	77.63V	92.86V	85.43V
Developing Countries	**202**	**423.3Y**	**351.7Y**	**428.6Y**	**1,522.9Y**	**2,116.7Y**	**3,273.7Y**	**2,757.5Y**	**43.8Y**	**45.1Y**	**186.2Y**	**116.6Y**	**198.5Y**	**438.4Y**	**401.1Y**
Africa	**607**	**39.3Y**	**2.1Y**	**3.1Y**	**3.7Y**	**10.1Y**	**28.2Y**	**35.1Y**	**36.2Y**	**33.0Y**	**172.0Y**	**76.0Y**	**131.9Y**	**163.4Y**	**201.3Y**
Benin	638	—V	—V	—V	—V	—V	—Y	—Y	.12V	—V	.03V	1.40V	.83V	1.02Y	1.27Y
Cameroon	622	36.31V	—V	—V	—Y	—Y	—Y	—Y	11.00V	—V	—V	—Y	—Y	—Y	—Y
Congo, Republic of	634	.06V	.02V	.25V	.03V	.03Y	.04Y	.05Y	.10V	.16V	.10V	.47V	.53Y	.66Y	.82Y
Côte d'Ivoire	662	—V	—V	.26V	.38V	2.22V	10.18V	12.63Y	14.99V	19.27V	148.12V	39.78V	96.27V	126.96V	157.56Y
Gabon	646	.12Y	.13Y	.17Y	.22Y	.25Y	.31Y	.39Y	1.82Y	1.98Y	2.50Y	3.29Y	3.76Y	4.65Y	5.77Y
Ghana	652	.02Y	.02Y	.02Y	.03Y	.03Y	.04Y	.05Y	....	....	....	....	....	....	....
Guinea	656	—V	—Y	—V	.03V	.04Y	.04Y	.06Y	....	....	....	....	....	....	....
Kenya	664	—V	—V	—V	—V	—Y	—Y	—Y	—V	.01V	.17V	.10V	.11Y	.14Y	.17Y
Madagascar	674	—V	—V	.58V	.76Y	.87Y	1.07Y	1.33Y	.16V	—V	—V	—Y	—Y	—Y	—Y
Mauritania	682	—Y	—Y	—Y	—Y	—Y	—Y	—Y	.56Y	.61Y	.77Y	1.01Y	1.15Y	1.43Y	1.77Y
Mauritius	684	—V	—V	—V	—V	—V	—V	—V	—V	—V	—V	—V	.23V	—V	—V
Morocco	686	2.54V	1.87V	1.77V	1.51V	2.89V	3.58Y	4.44Y	4.87V	6.59V	11.12V	12.68V	9.40V	11.61Y	14.41Y
Niger	692	—V	—V	—V	.02V	.03Y	.03Y	.04Y	—V	—V	—V	.14V	.15Y	.19Y	.24Y
Nigeria	694	.20V	—V	.04V	.05Y	.06Y	.08Y	.10Y	—V	.01V	—V	—Y	—Y	—Y	—Y
Senegal	722	.07V	—V	—V	.58V	3.66V	12.86V	15.97Y	.36V	.37V	2.99V	3.17V	4.54V	1.28V	1.58Y
South Africa	199	—Y	—Y	—Y	—Y	—Y	—Y	—Y	1.26V	3.52V	5.32V	11.03V	13.95V	13.02V	14.67V
Togo	742	—V	—V	—V	.04V	—V	—Y	—Y	.03V	—V	.01V	—V	.06V	.08Y	.10Y
Tunisia	744	—V	—V	—V	—V	—V	—V	—Y	.96V	.44V	.81V	2.96V	.88V	2.34V	2.91Y
Zimbabwe	698	....	....	....	....	....	....	....	—V	—V	.02V	—V	—V	—V	—Y
Asia	**507**	**357.3Y**	**332.9Y**	**423.6Y**	**1,499.7Y**	**1,795.7Y**	**3,098.4Y**	**2,639.7Y**	**3.9Y**	**5.8Y**	**9.1Y**	**21.0Y**	**34.3Y**	**219.7Y**	**120.6Y**
Bangladesh	513	—Y	—Y	—Y	—Y	—V	—V	—V	—V	.06V	—V	—V	—V	—Y	—Y
China,P.R.: Mainland	924	338.49V	309.99V	374.44V	889.28V	1,350.97V	2,306.90V	1,542.98V	2.80V	3.31V	5.58V	11.20V	20.68V	45.13V	102.18V
China,P.R.:Hong Kong	532	—V	—V	—V	—V	—V	—V	.03V	.23V	1.13V	1.26V	3.58V	2.61V	2.67V	1.73V
India	534	—Y	.01V	.18V	.55V	.21V	.27Y	.33Y	.27Y	.22V	.73V	3.14V	6.34V	7.83Y	9.72Y
Indonesia	536	—V	—V	—V	—V	—V	.03V	.01V	.39V	.52V	.70V	1.31V	2.18V	3.69V	2.60V
Korea	542	.76V	.37V	—V	27.82V	—V	—V	—V	.07V	—V	.31V	.53V	.50V	97.72V	1.03V
Malaysia	548	—V	—V	—V	—V	—V	—V	—V	—V	—V	.16V	.32V	.79V	59.61V	1.40V
Pakistan	564	—V	.24V	.50V	—V	.04V	.04Y	.05Y	.04V	.33V	.29V	.80V	1.03V	1.28Y	1.58Y
Philippines	566	.01V	.04V	.01V	—V	—V	—V	—V	.07V	—V	—V	—V	—V	.26V	—V
Taiwan Province of China	528	18.06V	22.11V	48.41V	582.02V	444.50V	791.17V	1,096.25V	.02V	.22V	.12V	.13V	.19V	1.54V	.37V
Vietnam	582	—V	.11V	.01V	—V	—V	—V	—V	—V	—V	.01V	—V	—V	—V	—V
Europe	**170**	**.2Y**	**1.2Y**	**1.9Y**	**2.2Y**	**5.4Y**	**30.7Y**	**41.9Y**	**1.4Y**	**1.6Y**	**1.1Y**	**8.1Y**	**8.9Y**	**28.3Y**	**22.9Y**
Azerbaijan	912	.01V	—V	—V	—V	—V	.02V	—V	—V	.29V	.11V	—V	—V	—V	—V
Bulgaria	918	—V	—V	—V	.10V	—V	—V	—V	.19V	.03V	—V	.21V	—V	—V	.49V
Czech Republic	935	.05V	.09V	.04V	—V	—V	—V	.01V	.06V	.10V	.11V	.13V	1.28V	.04V	2.95V
Hungary	944	—V	—V	—V	—V	.05V	—V	.06V	—V	.01V	.02V	.04V	.09V	.02V	.13V
Latvia	941	—V	—V	—Y	—V	—V	—V	—V	—V	—V	—Y	—V	—V	—V	.08V
Macedonia, FYR	962	—V	.01V	—V	—V	.01V	.02V	.02Y	—V	—V	—V	—V	—V	—V	—Y
Poland	964	—V	.18V	—V	—V	—V	—V	—V	—V	.04V	.02V	.17V	.20V	2.94V	.61V
Romania	968	—V	—V	—V	—V	—V	—V	—V	.13V	.02V	—V	.58V	—V	.05V	.11V
Russia	922	.02V	.02V	—V	—V	—V	—V	—V	.17V	.12V	.24V	2.63V	1.54V	12.83V	7.24V

	Exports 2001	Exports 2002	Exports 2003	Exports 2004	Exports 2005	Exports 2006	Exports 2007	Imports 2001	Imports 2002	Imports 2003	Imports 2004	Imports 2005	Imports 2006	Imports 2007
	Millions of U.S. Dollars							*Millions of U.S. Dollars*						
Slovak Republic 936	—V	—V	—Y	—Y	—V	—V	—V	—V	—V	—Y	—Y	.01V	—V	.04V
Turkey 186	.14V	.85V	1.82V	2.06V	5.34V	30.66V	41.80V	.19V	.22V	.55V	2.59V	5.39V	11.90V	10.55V
Ukraine 926	—V	.01V	.02V	—V	—V	—Y	—Y	.67V	.78V	.02V	1.74V	.44V	.55Y	.68Y
Middle East 407	**.8Y**	**.2Y**	**—Y**	**.1Y**	**.1Y**	**.1Y**	**.1Y**	**.1Y**	**.1Y**	**—Y**	**6.3Y**	**13.1Y**	**11.3Y**	**14.4Y**
Israel 436	.73V	.18V	—V	—V	—V	—V	—V	.11V	.11V	—V	6.27V	13.09V	11.22V	14.41V
Lebanon 446	.03Y	.03Y	.04Y	.05Y	.06Y	.08Y	.10Y	.01Y	.01Y	.02Y	.02Y	.03Y	.03Y	.04Y
Yemen, Republic of 474	—V	—V	—Y	.01V	—V	—Y	—Y	—V	—V	—Y	—V	—V	—Y	—Y
Western Hemisphere 207	**25.7Y**	**15.5Y**	**—Y**	**17.4Y**	**305.4Y**	**116.3Y**	**40.8Y**	**2.2Y**	**4.6Y**	**4.0Y**	**5.2Y**	**10.2Y**	**15.7Y**	**41.9Y**
Argentina 213	—V	—V	—V	—V	—V	—V	—V	1.41V	.69V	.85V	.83V	1.75V	1.35V	2.96V
Bolivia 218	—V	—V	—V	.03V	—V	—Y	—Y	—V	—V	—V	—V	—Y	—Y	—Y
Brazil 223	10.39V	4.17V	—V	13.60V	285.30V	93.09V	—V	.33V	3.84V	2.91V	3.94V	7.55V	11.61V	37.95V
Chile 228	5.18V	—V	—V	—V	—V	—V	—V	.44V	—V	—V	.13V	.19V	.86V	.61V
Colombia 233	.01V	—V	—V	—V	.01V	.03V	—V	—V	.03V	.17V	—V	—V	.03V	.01V
Costa Rica 238	.14V	—V	—V	3.76V	—V	—Y	—Y	....	....	....	....	....	....	....
Ecuador 248	—V	.47V	—V	.01V	1.35V	—V	—Y	—Y	—Y	—Y	—Y	—Y	—Y	—Y
Mexico 273	—V	—V	—V	—V	—V	—V	4.74V	—V	—V	—V	—V	—V	1.66V	—V
Paraguay 288	—V	—V	—V	—V	—V	—V	—Y	—V	—V	—V	.27V	.71V	.09V	.12Y
Peru 293	—V	—V	.01V	—V	—V	—V	7.27Y	—V	—V	.01V	—V	.01V	.10V	.21Y
Uruguay 298	9.97V	10.82Y	—V	—V	18.76V	23.18Y	28.77Y	—Y	—Y	—Y	—Y	—Y	—Y	—Y
Memorandum Items														
European Union 998	617.72Y	647.42Y	1,000.47Y	942.93Y	1,870.82Y	1,982.65Y	2,911.03Y	180.43Y	229.32Y	589.50Y	365.07Y	625.36Y	546.23Y	652.29Y
Oil Exporting Ctys 999	.20Y	—Y	.04Y	.05Y	.06Y	.10Y	.11Y	.39Y	.53Y	.70Y	1.31Y	2.18Y	3.69Y	2.60Y
Non-Oil Develop.Ctys 201	423.11Y	351.75Y	428.54Y	1,522.88Y	2,116.63Y	3,273.62Y	2,757.37Y	43.43Y	44.52Y	185.45Y	115.29Y	196.29Y	434.68Y	398.46Y
PERCENT DISTRIBUTION														
Industrial Countries 101	**72.8**	**79.7**	**83.8**	**61.3**	**65.8**	**56.2**	**66.4**	**86.2**	**89.8**	**84.8**	**84.2**	**82.2**	**72.8**	**69.7**
Developing Countries 202	**27.2**	**20.3**	**16.2**	**38.7**	**34.2**	**43.8**	**33.6**	**13.8**	**10.2**	**15.2**	**15.8**	**17.8**	**27.2**	**30.3**
Africa 607	**2.5**	**.1**	**.1**	**.1**	**.2**	**.4**	**.4**	**11.4**	**7.4**	**14.0**	**10.3**	**11.8**	**10.1**	**15.2**
Asia 507	**22.9**	**19.2**	**16.0**	**38.1**	**29.0**	**41.5**	**32.2**	**1.2**	**1.3**	**.7**	**2.9**	**3.1**	**13.6**	**9.1**
Europe 170	**—**	**.1**	**.1**	**.1**	**.1**	**.4**	**.5**	**.4**	**.4**	**.1**	**1.1**	**.8**	**1.8**	**1.7**
Middle East 407	**—**	**—**	**—**	**—**	**—**	**—**	**—**	**—**	**—**	**—**	**.9**	**1.2**	**.7**	**1.1**
Western Hemisphere 207	**1.6**	**.9**	**—**	**.4**	**4.9**	**1.6**	**.5**	**.7**	**1.0**	**.3**	**.7**	**.9**	**1.0**	**3.2**
ANNUAL PERCENT CHANGE														
World 001	**44.5**	**11.4**	**52.1**	**49.0**	**57.5**	**20.5**	**9.9**	**1.1**	**39.3**	**176.4**	**–39.8**	**51.6**	**44.4**	**–17.9**
Industrial Countries 101	**43.6**	**21.9**	**59.7**	**9.1**	**69.1**	**2.8**	**29.9**	**6.2**	**45.1**	**160.9**	**–40.2**	**48.1**	**27.9**	**–21.4**
Developing Countries 202	**47.2**	**–16.9**	**21.8**	**255.3**	**39.0**	**54.7**	**–15.8**	**–22.0**	**2.8**	**313.2**	**–37.4**	**70.2**	**120.9**	**–8.5**
Africa 607	**89.3**	**–94.8**	**50.7**	**18.2**	**176.1**	**180.0**	**24.1**	**–11.1**	**–9.0**	**421.8**	**–55.8**	**73.5**	**23.9**	**23.2**
Asia 507	**47.6**	**–6.8**	**27.2**	**254.1**	**19.7**	**72.5**	**–14.8**	**–45.2**	**49.3**	**57.7**	**130.0**	**63.2**	**540.4**	**–45.1**
Europe 170	**–73.5**	**442.5**	**62.7**	**14.5**	**150.5**	**467.9**	**36.5**	**–46.4**	**14.0**	**–33.2**	**649.3**	**10.5**	**216.5**	**–19.2**
Middle East 407	**—**	**–71.7**	**–80.7**	**49.1**	**.6**	**23.6**	**24.1**	**–61.5**	**.8**	**–86.5**	**—**	**108.4**	**–14.2**	**28.4**
Western Hemisphere 207	**7.1**	**–39.8**	**–99.9**	**—**	**—**	**–61.9**	**–64.9**	**–59.6**	**108.6**	**–13.3**	**30.8**	**97.7**	**53.6**	**166.6**

		Exports							Imports						
		2001	2002	2003	2004	2005	2006	2007	2001	2002	2003	2004	2005	2006	2007
		Millions of U.S. Dollars							*Millions of U.S. Dollars*						
IFS World Total		**3,313.8**	**3,448.0**	**4,538.9**	**5,933.9**	**7,675.0**	**8,755.3**	**10,957.5**	**4,300.3**	**4,810.5**	**6,480.5**	**8,334.0**	**10,186.9**	**11,884.1**	**15,061.2**
DOTS World Total	**001**	**4,017.8**	**4,342.0**	**5,622.5**	**5,905.9**	**7,694.5**	**9,700.6**	**11,006.5**	**5,230.8**	**5,865.4**	**7,966.6**	**8,362.1**	**10,208.0**	**13,454.6**	**15,525.3**
Industrial Countries	**101**	**2,705.0**	**2,824.1**	**3,701.7**	**4,153.5**	**5,223.9**	**5,689.0**	**6,561.0**	**3,202.0**	**3,679.3**	**4,895.2**	**5,506.8**	**6,589.4**	**8,027.2**	**9,367.8**
United States	111	86.60	93.62	131.84	189.26	239.32	637.15	455.18	122.14	166.62	232.15	98.31	153.86	156.10	183.51
Canada	156	14.67	15.58	19.43	13.81	53.56	56.46	93.39	10.65	9.86	22.08	6.26	15.19	14.49	25.24
Australia	193	1.79	2.15	4.13	9.53	11.20	6.69	4.93	1.32	1.52	2.16	1.14	2.29	3.50	1.98
Japan	158	38.36	27.52	20.71	17.17	25.33	55.80	57.41	230.17	225.57	326.21	114.39	202.31	144.02	125.38
New Zealand	196	.33	.11	1.20	.14	.18	.22	.20	6.49	1.67	8.18	2.43	2.02	2.02	1.47
Austria	122	19.65	21.13	28.13	26.29	35.42	46.54	69.96	49.71	57.46	72.97	79.85	120.00	143.41	160.59
Belgium	124	37.34	36.04	75.57	51.67	101.76	99.57	110.38	86.93	113.10	130.15	155.58	184.48	240.41	313.72
Cyprus	423	11.42	18.21	21.89	14.12	3.39	3.20	2.70	.59	.79	.96	2.35	4.62	6.96	6.27
Denmark	128	118.49	167.09	179.35	195.15	242.94	248.47	307.87	121.70	133.12	157.10	217.12	243.79	314.35	366.40
Finland	172	1,142.69	883.41	1,231.07	1,364.84	2,025.10	1,765.03	1,971.90	839.21	912.27	1,264.51	1,852.26	2,011.10	2,466.33	2,468.21
France	132	41.76	50.24	85.42	88.64	94.93	125.72	149.32	127.06	154.34	245.95	164.47	208.33	250.17	321.78
Germany	134	249.73	360.42	469.83	494.79	471.24	484.38	576.96	532.78	652.93	881.93	1,076.66	1,427.28	1,666.14	1,986.17
Greece	174	4.81	6.62	8.76	9.17	20.30	17.03	19.77	4.96	6.88	8.74	6.85	7.91	9.91	12.28
Iceland	176	4.18	5.05	10.03	11.87	19.24	22.84	22.44	.82	1.44	1.94	1.79	.35	1.03	1.19
Ireland	178	12.99	23.03	40.46	34.89	30.31	37.64	40.00	43.26	34.08	36.39	26.91	25.38	30.20	61.33
Italy	136	36.69	42.49	62.83	53.26	61.26	69.99	117.52	166.05	239.20	283.93	200.47	260.43	344.32	437.55
Luxembourg	137	.27	1.37	1.17	.44	.20	.45	1.90	2.88	2.79	4.59	6.32	11.46	16.12	16.95
Malta	181	13.14	17.74	13.34	1.44	.92	.81	1.33	2.58	2.92	3.20	4.15	.32	.92	.39
Netherlands	138	102.71	129.52	160.22	178.51	185.88	219.64	296.29	117.94	144.40	161.58	300.53	348.38	467.39	529.82
Norway	142	104.75	130.96	170.35	192.74	221.13	257.17	372.66	62.70	69.78	83.86	64.83	75.21	80.72	85.31
Portugal	182	4.87	3.78	7.41	7.83	11.39	7.32	11.35	11.58	11.11	13.68	8.70	9.76	12.06	17.02
Slovenia	961	.48	.96	1.00	1.51	2.86	2.96	6.52	7.41	7.29	10.94	10.20	15.05	18.49	26.84
Spain	184	10.57	33.56	24.93	54.77	56.38	58.80	67.74	45.06	49.90	86.68	51.99	72.21	87.67	109.93
Sweden	144	476.68	539.57	700.77	906.28	1,009.65	1,186.22	1,456.90	433.76	494.74	610.16	815.07	899.10	1,224.12	1,572.86
Switzerland	146	23.07	29.17	31.97	25.63	26.09	30.19	36.92	45.70	49.99	67.64	52.56	51.81	56.52	50.94
United Kingdom	112	146.98	184.72	199.86	209.71	273.88	248.74	309.47	128.52	135.48	177.50	185.61	236.78	269.83	484.63
Developing Countries	**202**	**1,172.9**	**1,404.1**	**1,897.1**	**1,711.8**	**2,438.5**	**3,960.8**	**4,370.5**	**2,028.2**	**2,185.7**	**3,069.4**	**2,854.7**	**3,618.2**	**5,427.0**	**6,148.4**
Africa	**607**	**22.4**	**20.1**	**26.5**	**11.4**	**36.2**	**168.8**	**388.0**	**80.2**	**119.5**	**147.0**	**10.0**	**6.4**	**5.7**	**11.9**
Algeria	612	3.24	1.33	.64	2.19	3.49	2.31	1.27	—	—	—	—	—	—	—
Angola	614	.12	1.06	.29	.15	.08	.27	3.69	—	—	—	—	—	—	—
Benin	638	.38	.40	—	.09	2.09	.03	.27	—	—	—	—	—	—	—
Botswana	616	—	—	—	.03	.01	—	—	—	—	—	—	—	—	—
Burkina Faso	748	—	—	—	—	—	.02	.04	—	—	—	—	—	—	—
Burundi	618	—	.01	—	—	—	—	—	—	—	—	—	—	—	—
Cameroon	622	.98	.47	.30	.56	.94	.13	.16	.01	—	.20	—	—	—	—
Cape Verde	624	.18	—	—	—	—	—	—	—	—	—	—	—	—	—
Central African Rep.	626	—	—	—	.01	—	—	—	—	—	—	—	—	—	—
Chad	628	.05	—	—	—	—	—	—	—	—	—	—	—	—	—
Comoros	632	—	—	—	.01	.01	—	—	.01	.01	.01	—	—	—	—
Congo, Dem. Rep. of	636	.43	—	—	—	.03	—	—	—	.42	—	—	—	—	—
Congo, Republic of	634	—	—	—	—	—	.01	.04	—	—	—	—	—	—	—
Côte d'Ivoire	662	.96	.90	1.11	.40	.44	.34	.37	61.62	82.55	104.91	—	.53	.76	4.04
Eritrea	643	—	.03	—	—	—	—	—	—	—	—	—	—	—	—
Ethiopia	644	—	—	6.69	.21	.22	.06	1.29	—	.02	.42	—	—	—	—
Gabon	646	—	—	—	—	—	—	—	—	.01	.01	—	—	—	—
Gambia, The	648	—	.01	—	.01	—	—	.04	—	—	—	—	—	—	—
Ghana	652	.96	.66	1.39	.01	.62	.32	.17	8.72	17.37	25.00	2.11	1.59	1.81	1.79
Guinea	656	—	.03	.03	.08	—	.03	.01	—	.04	.04	—	—	—	—
Kenya	664	.28	.08	.02	.46	.06	.14	.01	.18	.27	.21	.01	—	.03	.09
Liberia	668	4.57	8.07	8.87	.68	1.45	18.32	.08	—	—	—	—	—	—	—
Madagascar	674	—	.01	—	.27	—	—	—	.13	.13	.11	.01	.01	—	.01
Malawi	676	—	.05	.05	.11	—	.01	.01	—	—	—	—	—	—	—
Mali	678	—	—	—	—	.01	—	.04	.03	.75	.01	—	—	—	—
Mauritania	682	.61	1.05	.36	.25	.14	.14	.05	.12	.07	.01	.13	—	.13	.42
Mauritius	684	.10	.06	—	.74	.06	.02	.02	.04	.16	.09	.03	—	—	.01
Morocco	686	3.28	3.50	2.60	1.43	2.01	2.44	5.35	1.44	1.31	2.63	.05	.25	.48	1.68
Mozambique	688	—	.02	.06	.15	.02	.01	.01	—	—	—	—	—	—	—
Namibia	728	.02	.10	.14	—	—	—	.06	.01	—	.13	.11	.11	.02	—
Niger	692	.10	—	—	—	.06	.18	—	—	—	—	—	—	—	—
Nigeria	694	2.22	.89	.75	1.18	17.26	35.20	9.31	3.23	12.37	6.34	—	.17	.08	.02
Rwanda	714	.05	—	—	—	—	—	—	.01	—	—	—	—	—	—
St. Helena	856	—	—	—	—	—	—	—	—	.01	.01	—	—	—	—
São Tomé & Príncipe	716	.07	—	—	—	—	—	—	—	—	—	—	—	—	—
Senegal	722	.02	—	—	.01	.18	—	.32	—	—	.01	—	—	—	—
Seychelles	718	.01	.05	.05	.04	1.40	.15	.03	—	—	—	.01	.01	—	—
Sierra Leone	724	—	—	—	—	.04	—	—	.28	.08	.23	—	—	—	.04
South Africa	199	1.00	.68	.41	.84	1.88	4.87	2.22	3.83	2.55	4.87	7.58	3.74	2.41	3.51
Sudan	732	.41	.28	2.56	.45	—	—	—	.01	—	.01	—	.02	—	—
Swaziland	734	—	—	.01	.01	.01	.01	.01	.01	.01	—	—	—	—	—

		Exports							Imports						
		2001	2002	2003	2004	2005	2006	2007	2001	2002	2003	2004	2005	2006	2007
		Millions of U.S. Dollars							*Millions of U.S. Dollars*						
Tanzania	738	—	—	—	.06	—	3.05	.52	.03	.03	—	—	—	—	.14
Togo	742	2.35	.24	—	.03	2.13	98.51	362.24	—	—	—	—	—	—	—
Tunisia	744	.02	.13	.06	.98	1.55	2.22	.26	.48	1.32	1.68	—	—	.01	.10
Uganda	746	—	—	.05	—	.04	.02	—	.03	—	—	—	—	—	—
Zambia	754	—	—	—	—	—	—	.14	—	—	—	—	—	—	—
Zimbabwe	698	—	.02	.02	—	—	.01	—	.01	.01	.03	—	—	—	—
Asia	**507**	**67.5**	**97.6**	**108.6**	**112.7**	**134.9**	**357.7**	**201.5**	**581.8**	**541.1**	**700.5**	**401.0**	**627.5**	**710.1**	**684.7**
Afghanistan, I.S. of	512	—	—	.09	.01	.02	1.00	2.14	.01	—	.01	.01	—	—	.02
Bangladesh	513	.63	.22	.07	.11	.26	.11	.08	2.09	2.65	3.54	.05	.28	.99	.67
Brunei Darussalam	516	—	—	—	—	—	—	—	—	—	.01	—	—	—	—
Cambodia	522	.89	1.60	1.13	.04	.02	.07	.02	.18	.34	.33	—	—	.82	.67
China,P.R.: Mainland	924	15.96	22.49	35.11	35.58	41.51	268.43	88.32	383.80	272.27	331.54	158.80	373.54	417.37	411.06
China,P.R.:Hong Kong	532	6.27	9.03	10.86	6.24	8.91	7.64	12.42	11.26	23.96	23.94	81.86	36.71	42.93	40.45
China,P.R.:Macao	546	—	—	—	—	—	.02	2.41	.62	1.15	1.28	—	.01	—	—
Fiji	819	.01	—	—	—	—	—	.01	—	—	—	—	—	—	—
French Polynesia	887	—	—	—	—	.02	—	.01	—	—	—	—	—	—	—
Guam	829	—	—	—	—	—	—	—	—	—	—	.01	—	—	—
India	534	1.79	2.01	6.74	2.93	15.97	14.76	20.66	9.07	11.59	14.09	5.23	8.73	10.68	22.14
Indonesia	536	1.26	1.52	3.06	.56	4.17	1.34	5.03	18.53	25.29	18.91	2.87	3.10	4.53	8.79
Korea	542	22.02	28.26	29.66	50.33	43.31	24.04	26.45	39.94	42.37	76.12	30.23	45.48	43.67	59.83
Lao People's Dem.Rep	544	—	—	—	.07	—	—	.01	.10	.09	.08	—	—	—	—
Malaysia	548	6.12	7.65	2.18	2.72	3.13	5.89	7.42	34.97	38.77	54.55	7.76	22.59	16.83	20.67
Maldives	556	—	—	—	—	—	.01	—	—	—	—	—	—	—	—
Mongolia	948	—	.04	.33	.02	.03	.07	.13	—	—	—	.01	—	—	—
Myanmar	518	.01	.02	.08	.01	.01	—	—	.13	.13	.30	—	.06	—	—
Nepal	558	—	—	.01	.01	—	—	—	.01	.01	.03	—	.01	.03	.02
New Caledonia	839	—	—	—	—	.02	.02	.01	—	—	—	—	—	—	—
Pakistan	564	2.47	5.84	1.34	.85	2.77	7.34	1.96	7.94	13.22	15.32	11.46	9.53	11.25	10.34
Papua New Guinea	853	—	—	—	—	—	—	—	—	—	.03	—	—	—	—
Philippines	566	1.03	.25	.77	.09	.15	.53	.19	4.22	20.25	29.68	.91	2.82	4.64	3.33
Samoa	862	—	—	.11	—	—	—	—	—	—	—	—	—	—	—
Singapore	576	1.22	5.14	1.64	1.19	4.77	3.43	2.00	6.34	12.07	19.46	36.54	40.96	28.64	5.45
Sri Lanka	524	.96	2.13	2.71	1.55	.46	.37	.62	1.68	2.04	2.38	.56	1.46	1.89	1.88
Taiwan Province of China	528	2.90	5.89	7.32	4.77	4.56	7.33	25.15	38.32	42.86	60.87	51.17	68.51	108.65	75.62
Thailand	578	3.69	4.70	3.54	3.93	2.71	13.77	2.38	16.27	26.47	41.10	12.58	11.90	12.85	18.81
Tuvalu	869	—	—	—	—	.03	—	—	—	—	—	—	—	—	—
Vanuatu	846	.02	.22	.09	.01	.04	—	—	—	—	—	—	—	—	.02
Vietnam	582	.28	.54	1.75	1.72	2.06	1.53	4.07	6.28	5.55	6.96	.95	1.85	4.30	4.94
Europe	**170**	**1,017.7**	**1,218.3**	**1,692.1**	**1,550.0**	**2,210.5**	**3,264.0**	**3,598.2**	**1,333.2**	**1,480.2**	**2,160.8**	**2,380.2**	**2,936.8**	**4,668.2**	**5,397.5**
Albania	914	—	—	—	—	.18	—	.05	.02	.03	.01	—	—	.01	—
Armenia	911	.35	.24	.46	.45	.98	1.79	1.36	.06	.18	.12	.01	.02	.05	.07
Azerbaijan	912	.19	.20	1.60	1.61	5.82	2.66	7.82	.78	.28	.19	.17	.60	6.00	.51
Belarus	913	20.03	17.78	19.64	13.67	19.90	55.67	50.09	61.36	49.00	110.68	101.43	128.78	185.30	229.22
Bosnia & Herzegovina	963	—	.08	.09	.01	.38	1.71	1.52	.12	.11	.11	—	—	.05	.35
Bulgaria	918	.48	.75	1.20	2.25	2.02	3.48	7.61	4.64	3.50	5.87	7.48	7.17	4.93	3.17
Croatia	960	.21	.61	1.54	2.56	3.52	3.80	4.11	.90	1.88	1.04	2.67	1.40	3.28	1.29
Czech Republic	935	8.76	12.99	27.59	25.04	28.66	35.99	38.02	78.14	52.34	80.19	85.15	86.68	126.00	162.79
Faroe Islands	816	.29	.16	.30	.57	.76	.72	2.15	.12	.18	—	—	.08	.25	.34
Georgia	915	.87	.57	.67	.11	1.00	.71	3.73	.37	.18	.18	.34	2.85	2.20	1.27
Gibraltar	823	.04	1.06	2.93	9.78	117.84	441.86	2.56	.01	.01	—	—	—	—	—
Hungary	944	31.08	44.28	57.37	216.31	174.64	175.05	51.40	45.56	40.17	66.72	118.55	109.76	124.91	127.70
Kazakhstan	916	4.46	5.54	6.34	5.78	22.99	26.54	38.04	19.00	24.33	26.53	15.02	16.90	62.79	58.66
Kosovo	967	—	—	—	—	.10	—	—	—	—	—	—	—	—	—
Kyrgyz Republic	917	.04	.06	.17	.47	1.02	1.82	3.46	.60	1.33	.71	2.53	1.62	.26	.03
Latvia	941	298.89	335.32	417.62	464.60	698.92	880.66	1,255.66	110.86	135.64	191.11	395.60	493.69	788.04	1,182.57
Lithuania	946	143.70	179.06	226.61	258.61	355.90	467.21	637.10	117.71	164.96	228.03	442.43	612.06	867.99	1,066.10
Macedonia, FYR	962	.05	.17	.09	.16	.08	.01	.08	.25	.21	.19	.04	.03	.03	.15
Moldova	921	3.69	3.30	3.40	2.61	3.63	4.01	6.86	1.85	1.70	1.42	1.15	.77	.73	1.32
Montenegro, Rep. of	943	—	—	—	—	—	.17	.05	—	—	—	—	—	—	.01
Poland	964	27.23	36.62	54.45	60.19	90.18	115.79	159.26	104.82	142.70	199.31	273.78	372.85	506.88	699.75
Romania	968	.46	.90	1.09	2.59	3.35	6.48	11.05	2.67	3.72	6.31	3.09	4.48	6.15	11.93
Russia	922	344.19	432.83	643.17	334.56	496.94	763.67	976.22	653.24	704.13	811.13	769.00	936.84	1,739.31	1,558.79
Serbia, Rep. of	942	—	—	—	—	—	2.73	4.54	—	—	—	—	—	2.50	2.94
Serbia & Montenegro	965	—	—	—	2.16	2.06	—	—	—	—	—	1.01	1.05	—	—
Slovak Republic	936	1.12	4.15	5.05	5.14	7.44	11.02	20.69	7.98	10.50	22.64	15.68	14.46	27.45	47.46
Tajikistan	923	.30	.10	.09	.06	.07	.39	.34	4.85	10.62	16.26	7.04	3.31	15.90	5.65
Turkey	186	6.44	6.03	13.96	36.89	61.98	104.74	140.84	20.74	29.73	38.78	25.32	45.45	82.39	75.79
Turkmenistan	925	1.10	1.05	2.15	.09	.25	2.83	1.64	3.15	6.32	.15	.02	.25	.88	.72
Ukraine	926	120.15	129.88	200.51	99.82	105.56	148.21	163.14	68.57	77.84	340.21	111.91	92.67	104.63	153.48
Uzbekistan	927	3.21	3.18	3.06	3.91	4.36	4.33	8.77	24.05	16.76	11.26	.80	3.06	9.27	5.38
Yugoslavia n.s.	966	.11	1.24	.94	—	—	—	—	.78	1.84	1.64	—	—	—	—
Europe n.s.	884	.23	.18	.01	—	.07	—	—	—	.01	—	—	—	—	.05
Middle East	**407**	**20.6**	**26.0**	**26.8**	**17.7**	**21.7**	**91.4**	**126.9**	**5.3**	**8.3**	**11.6**	**6.5**	**6.1**	**10.7**	**17.9**
Bahrain	419	.26	.01	.05	.04	.04	2.83	.09	—	—	—	—	.11	.06	.59
Egypt	469	9.69	10.42	14.20	6.87	6.21	61.45	18.00	.74	1.01	1.08	.23	.12	.51	2.59
Iran, I.R. of	429	.43	.10	.11	.18	2.07	1.00	1.53	.40	.83	1.59	.64	.36	.38	.20
Iraq	433	1.85	7.26	—	—	.76	.16	.61	—	.28	—	—	—	—	—

		Exports							Imports						
		2001	2002	2003	2004	2005	2006	2007	2001	2002	2003	2004	2005	2006	2007
		Millions of U.S. Dollars							*Millions of U.S. Dollars*						
Israel	436	1.97	2.77	3.23	4.29	3.21	3.68	3.66	2.71	2.88	7.75	3.39	4.22	8.95	11.33
Jordan	439	.01	.01	.08	.16	.64	.71	1.03	—	.03	.03	—	.01	—	.01
Kuwait	443	.24	.26	.26	.29	.29	.46	.78	.02	—	—	—	—	—	—
Lebanon	446	.14	.10	.23	.11	.09	.17	.24	.60	—	.09	.66	.81	.19	.18
Libya	672	.10	1.06	.66	.17	.13	.13	.44	—	.01	—	—	—	—	—
Oman	449	.11	.13	.16	.27	.24	.36	.44	—	—	—	—	—	—	.02
Qatar	453	—	—	—	.04	.05	.13	.19	—	—	—	—	—	—	—
Saudi Arabia	456	1.84	2.40	2.82	2.22	4.48	12.85	52.99	.09	.21	.53	—	.26	.27	.76
Syrian Arab Republic	463	1.22	.73	1.10	1.29	.07	.84	.97	.01	2.10	.05	—	.03	—	—
United Arab Emirates	466	.73	.76	3.87	1.73	3.22	6.01	43.92	.69	.94	.51	1.61	.17	.37	2.21
Yemen, Republic of	474	2.00	.03	—	—	.22	.59	1.99	—	—	—	—	.03	—	—
Middle East n.s.	489	—	—	—	—	—	—	—	.01	—	—	—	—	—	—
Western Hemisphere	**207**	**44.7**	**42.1**	**43.2**	**19.9**	**35.2**	**78.8**	**55.9**	**27.7**	**36.6**	**49.5**	**56.9**	**41.3**	**32.3**	**36.4**
Antigua and Barbuda	311	.52	3.29	1.83	.09	1.87	.04	.04	.01	—	—	—	—	3.59	—
Argentina	213	.81	.04	.05	.56	.67	.55	.69	1.73	4.64	6.48	3.93	4.26	5.35	5.39
Aruba	314	—	—	—	.24	—	—	—	—	.07	—	—	—	—	—
Bahamas, The	313	2.22	3.92	4.67	.10	.19	.26	.08	.11	.07	.26	—	—	—	—
Barbados	316	.07	.02	—	.06	—	—	—	—	—	—	.04	—	—	—
Belize	339	.34	1.69	1.23	2.28	.07	.35	1.01	.01	—	—	.01	—	—	—
Bermuda	319	.15	.23	.03	2.61	—	—	—	.02	—	4.36	31.78	—	—	—
Bolivia	218	.02	.05	.02	—	.11	.27	.39	.02	.01	.03	—	.08	.14	.09
Brazil	223	7.97	9.24	13.34	9.81	14.51	23.47	27.51	10.17	13.58	17.07	12.15	21.31	11.91	18.94
Chile	228	3.56	.27	.89	.77	3.94	6.91	1.47	3.98	5.74	4.91	3.04	5.34	6.24	7.20
Colombia	233	.08	1.90	.89	.15	.15	.08	.07	1.55	1.22	1.06	.26	.45	.49	.34
Costa Rica	238	.10	—	—	.14	.03	.12	.09	.73	1.68	1.64	1.11	1.09	.06	.26
Dominica	321	—	.78	.67	.03	.01	.01	.02	.01	—	.01	—	—	—	—
Dominican Republic	243	—	.75	.50	.17	.25	.01	—	.13	.20	.21	.33	.19	.08	.12
Ecuador	248	—	1.43	.01	.25	.19	.02	.09	2.91	2.50	3.28	.26	.75	.11	.02
El Salvador	253	.84	—	.35	.09	—	.01	.01	.01	.02	.04	—	—	.01	—
Falkland Islands	323	—	—	—	—	—	—	—	—	—	.04	—	—	—	—
Greenland	326	—	—	.05	—	—	—	—	.24	.35	.62	—	—	—	—
Grenada	328	—	.02	—	—	—	—	—	.05	—	.05	—	—	—	—
Guatemala	258	.46	1.12	.04	.01	.01	.26	.05	.17	.15	.41	—	—	—	—
Guyana	336	.04	.01	.06	—	—	—	.11	—	—	.01	—	—	—	.02
Haiti	263	—	—	—	—	.75	.91	.04	—	—	—	—	—	—	—
Honduras	268	.02	—	—	—	—	.12	.01	.06	.05	.30	—	.01	—	—
Jamaica	343	.27	.63	.23	—	—	.33	—	.05	.09	.12	—	—	—	—
Mexico	273	7.42	4.87	3.03	1.23	3.37	1.56	9.23	3.25	4.41	4.64	.60	2.04	3.02	2.55
Netherlands Antilles	353	.06	.37	1.14	.01	5.16	37.28	.04	—	—	—	—	—	—	—
Nicaragua	278	—	—	.08	.02	1.57	—	.01	.03	—	.01	—	.04	.02	.02
Panama	283	8.89	6.71	3.81	.69	.57	.22	.37	1.19	.65	2.07	2.47	4.24	.07	.05
Paraguay	288	—	.03	—	.01	—	—	.09	—	—	—	—	—	—	—
Peru	293	1.09	.03	.03	.31	.04	.30	.51	.99	.90	1.30	.49	.78	.87	1.41
St. Kitts and Nevis	361	.02	.03	.03	—	—	—	—	—	—	—	—	—	—	—
St. Vincent & Grens.	364	1.80	2.65	3.32	—	.25	.07	.16	—	.02	—	—	—	—	—
Suriname	366	.01	—	—	—	—	—	.02	.01	—	—	—	—	—	—
Trinidad and Tobago	369	.01	.34	.09	.07	.83	.02	—	—	—	—	—	—	.01	—
Uruguay	298	.10	.01	—	.06	.02	4.00	.29	.28	.25	.42	.26	.64	.06	—
Venezuela, Rep. Bol.	299	1.55	.52	1.45	.16	.13	.30	4.33	—	—	.01	—	.01	.01	.02
Western Hem. n.s.	399	6.23	1.15	5.35	.01	.49	1.36	9.15	—	—	.15	.21	.05	.26	—
Other Countries n.i.e.	**910**	**1.1**	**1.1**	**2.9**	**.1**	**.2**	**.6**	**—**	**.4**	**.4**	**1.9**	**.2**	**.2**	**.3**	**.4**
Cuba	928	.12	1.12	2.92	.06	.18	.59	.01	.22	.36	1.66	.16	.23	.34	.39
North Korea	954	.94	—	.01	.01	—	.04	—	.15	.07	.23	.01	—	—	—
Countries & Areas n.s.	**898**	**137.1**	**110.3**	**17.2**	**40.4**	**—**	**—**	**—**	**.1**	**—**	**—**	**.3**	**.1**	**—**	**8.8**
Special Categories	**899**	**—**	**—**	**—**	**—**	**31.9**	**50.1**	**73.9**	**—**	**—**	**—**	**—**	**—**	**—**	**—**
Memorandum Items															
European Union	998	2,942.05	3,132.32	4,100.70	4,723.20	5,983.59	6,308.24	7,679.98	3,187.05	3,699.11	4,938.96	6,496.28	7,775.88	10,010.08	12,179.11
Oil Exporting Ctys.	999	13.57	16.23	13.78	8.99	36.28	60.24	120.85	22.96	39.93	27.89	5.12	4.08	5.63	12.01
Non-Oil Develop.Ctys.	201	1,159.28	1,387.89	1,883.33	1,702.78	2,402.24	3,900.51	4,249.62	2,005.21	2,145.73	3,041.52	2,849.61	3,614.17	5,421.41	6,136.34
PERCENT DISTRIBUTION															
Industrial Countries	**101**	**67.3**	**65.0**	**65.8**	**70.3**	**67.9**	**58.6**	**59.6**	**61.2**	**62.7**	**61.4**	**65.9**	**64.6**	**59.7**	**60.3**
Developing Countries	**202**	**29.2**	**32.3**	**33.7**	**29.0**	**31.7**	**40.8**	**39.7**	**38.8**	**37.3**	**38.5**	**34.1**	**35.4**	**40.3**	**39.6**
Africa	**607**	**.6**	**.5**	**.5**	**.2**	**.5**	**1.7**	**3.5**	**1.5**	**2.0**	**1.8**	**.1**	**.1**	**—**	**.1**
Asia	**507**	**1.7**	**2.2**	**1.9**	**1.9**	**1.8**	**3.7**	**1.8**	**11.1**	**9.2**	**8.8**	**4.8**	**6.1**	**5.3**	**4.4**
Europe	**170**	**25.3**	**28.1**	**30.1**	**26.2**	**28.7**	**33.6**	**32.7**	**25.5**	**25.2**	**27.1**	**28.5**	**28.8**	**34.7**	**34.8**
Middle East	**407**	**.5**	**.6**	**.5**	**.3**	**.3**	**.9**	**1.2**	**.1**	**.1**	**.1**	**.1**	**.1**	**.1**	**.1**
Western Hemisphere	**207**	**1.1**	**1.0**	**.8**	**.3**	**.5**	**.8**	**.5**	**.5**	**.6**	**.6**	**.7**	**.4**	**.2**	**.2**
Other Countries n.i.e.	**910**	**—**	**—**	**.1**	**—**	**—**	**—**	**—**	**—**	**—**	**—**	**—**	**—**	**—**	**—**
ANNUAL PERCENT CHANGE															
World	**001**	**4.9**	**8.1**	**29.5**	**5.0**	**30.3**	**26.1**	**13.5**	**−1.9**	**12.1**	**35.8**	**5.0**	**22.1**	**31.8**	**15.4**
Industrial Countries	**101**	**−5.8**	**4.4**	**31.1**	**12.2**	**25.8**	**8.9**	**15.3**	**−4.6**	**14.9**	**33.0**	**12.5**	**19.7**	**21.8**	**16.7**
Developing Countries	**202**	**22.4**	**19.7**	**35.1**	**−9.8**	**42.5**	**62.4**	**10.3**	**3.1**	**7.8**	**40.4**	**−7.0**	**26.7**	**50.0**	**13.3**
Africa	**607**	**37.7**	**−10.3**	**31.6**	**−56.8**	**216.6**	**366.1**	**129.9**	**14.5**	**48.9**	**23.0**	**−93.2**	**−35.9**	**−10.7**	**106.2**
Asia	**507**	**.9**	**44.5**	**11.3**	**3.8**	**19.7**	**165.1**	**−43.7**	**90.0**	**−7.0**	**29.5**	**−42.8**	**56.5**	**13.1**	**−3.6**
Europe	**170**	**22.4**	**19.7**	**38.9**	**−8.4**	**42.6**	**47.7**	**10.2**	**4.2**	**11.0**	**46.0**	**10.2**	**23.4**	**59.0**	**15.6**
Middle East	**407**	**7.5**	**26.5**	**2.8**	**−34.0**	**23.1**	**320.5**	**38.9**	**−98.2**	**57.3**	**40.3**	**−43.9**	**−6.2**	**75.2**	**66.8**
Western Hemisphere	**207**	**80.8**	**−5.7**	**2.6**	**−53.9**	**76.5**	**124.2**	**−29.1**	**16.3**	**32.1**	**35.2**	**15.0**	**−27.4**	**−21.8**	**12.8**
Other Countries n.i.e.	**910**	**82.8**	**5.7**	**161.6**	**−97.6**	**150.3**	**262.7**	**−98.7**	**−96.0**	**16.2**	**339.5**	**−91.0**	**33.5**	**51.0**	**13.7**

		Exports							Imports						
		2001	2002	2003	2004	2005	2006	2007	2001	2002	2003	2004	2005	2006	2007
		Millions of U.S. Dollars							Millions of U.S. Dollars						
IFS World Total		**455.2**	**480.2**	**496.4**	**678.3**	**903.1**	**1,036.2**	**1,290.0**	**1,808.7**	**1,622.2**	**2,119.0**	**3,087.4**	**4,126.9**	**4,805.0**	**5,320.0**
DOTS World Total	**001**	**285.9**	**421.5**	**467.9**	**570.4**	**781.9**	**1,091.2Y**	**1,225.6Y**	**1,782.6**	**1,567.6**	**2,102.1**	**2,557.3**	**4,081.6**	**4,246.9Y**	**5,363.6Y**
Industrial Countries	**101**	**100.1**	**254.9**	**242.8**	**362.6**	**455.4**	**517.3Y**	**580.9Y**	**803.1**	**748.6**	**840.9**	**971.6**	**1,588.6**	**1,139.9Y**	**1,412.3Y**
United States	111	3.56	16.43	22.84	36.90	43.13	77.64V	84.64V	167.04	126.05	185.19	282.74	507.52	151.03V	184.47V
Canada	156	.11	1.63	1.69	2.66	5.32	6.15V	8.05V	14.22	6.46	6.21	6.13	23.89	14.93V	16.26V
Australia	193	1.17	.90	1.27	1.41	2.22	2.81V	3.93V	6.43	4.72	9.28	11.19	5.20	2.85V	2.21V
Japan	158	.28	37.34	44.05	63.07	66.24	84.86V	71.77V	78.61	112.99	78.68	111.38	135.38	127.36V	140.05V
New Zealand	196	—	—	—	—	—	.63V	1.07V	—	—	—	—	—	.56V	.10V
Austria	122	—	.02	.01	.41	.01	.44V	.23V	6.84	5.78	5.28	8.37	5.54	7.87V	23.36V
Belgium	124	—	12.39	15.00	20.79	23.88	32.89V	38.73V	38.01	40.95	46.35	42.04	91.69	71.26V	136.58V
Cyprus	423	—	.03	.03	.07	.05	.18V	.30V	1.04	1.96	1.43	1.19	2.31	2.92V	4.06V
Denmark	128	—	.26	.50	1.30	2.36	1.56V	1.69V	21.06	10.34	12.83	2.65	47.63	9.84V	13.65V
Finland	172	—	.88	.39	.43	.45	4.34V	6.07V	1.90	2.51	5.50	23.72	33.03	18.86V	11.53V
France	132	26.98	11.00	8.75	11.59	16.44	25.97V	26.51V	58.29	25.71	42.18	38.30	68.01	94.18V	92.50V
Germany	134	7.19	49.51	57.65	77.48	121.46	98.71V	100.98V	87.16	83.65	82.66	105.95	151.70	151.38V	177.99V
Greece	174	—	4.79	3.19	4.29	4.39	5.70V	11.80V	15.16	16.25	7.31	6.22	6.51	5.65V	9.26V
Iceland	176	—	—	—	—	—	.15V	.20V	—	—	—	—	—	—V	—V
Ireland	178	—	.02	.26	.13	—	.03V	.85V	2.61	4.40	4.89	8.00	9.02	8.48V	10.20V
Italy	136	14.58	40.97	30.85	39.36	46.50	56.47V	79.12V	135.44	140.61	162.88	126.23	186.16	213.57V	271.56V
Luxembourg	137	—	—	—	—	—	—V	—V	—	—	—	—	—	1.94V	1.66V
Malta	181	—	—	—	—	—	.03V	—V	—	—	—	—	—	.62V	.48V
Netherlands	138	—	4.16	5.68	18.53	33.07	37.33V	58.63V	41.91	38.98	51.53	44.99	73.99	51.57V	60.09V
Norway	142	—	.48	1.45	.92	1.22	12.87V	7.83V	1.64	1.12	2.23	4.33	10.63	2.18V	4.18V
Portugal	182	—	7.79	9.90	.89	8.93	8.43V	16.76V	.83	.46	1.08	.46	.33	1.11V	2.06V
Slovenia	961	—	—	—	—	—	.41V	.07V	—	—	—	—	—	1.31V	1.33V
Spain	184	—	3.47	1.64	2.08	2.22	4.22V	6.53V	6.82	9.42	13.89	9.57	14.35	71.72V	54.65V
Sweden	144	.07	.89	2.05	4.05	3.15	14.46V	14.10V	38.51	30.12	23.11	35.53	101.38	26.56V	45.86V
Switzerland	146	34.85	44.62	20.09	53.02	50.01	4.77V	8.22V	17.75	13.05	12.88	15.11	19.81	24.32V	26.78V
United Kingdom	112	11.32	17.34	15.54	23.26	24.37	36.28V	32.78V	61.81	73.05	85.46	87.49	94.57	77.79V	121.39V
Developing Countries	**202**	**185.8**	**165.0**	**223.7**	**201.4**	**322.8**	**569.3Y**	**639.0Y**	**971.2**	**808.0**	**1,237.4**	**1,565.8**	**2,483.5**	**3,095.4Y**	**3,936.8Y**
Africa	**607**	**121.4**	**56.7**	**128.1**	**42.1**	**77.3**	**98.7Y**	**120.3Y**	**65.4**	**78.8**	**93.6**	**85.4**	**138.4**	**229.3Y**	**236.8Y**
Côte d'Ivoire	662	—	—	—	—	—	.01V	.01Y	—	—	—	—	—	.02V	.03Y
Djibouti	611	121.38	54.35	119.83	27.12	53.12	65.65Y	81.47Y	48.94	60.33	66.18	63.42	64.91	80.22Y	99.55Y
Ghana	652	—	—	—	.01	.12	.15Y	.18Y	.04	.03	.02	.01	.07	.09Y	.11Y
Kenya	664	—	.02	.82	1.06	2.44	3.01Y	3.74Y	15.15	17.44	20.40	20.91	25.75	31.82Y	39.49Y
Mauritius	684	—	—	—	—	—	.07V	.54V	—	—	—	—	—	.58V	.12V
Nigeria	694	—	.09	—	.03	—	—Y	—Y	.20	.06	.12	.14	.03	.04Y	.04Y
Rwanda	714	—	—	—	—	—	—Y	—Y	.16	.02	.03	.07	.08	.10Y	.12Y
Senegal	722	—	—	—	—	—	.01V	.01Y	—	—	—	—	—	.08V	.10Y
South Africa	199	—	—	—	—	—	3.55V	4.48V	—	—	—	—	—	37.30V	37.43V
Sudan	732	—	2.26	7.42	12.54	20.01	12.23V	14.51V	.88	.81	6.52	.58	47.00	55.34V	31.36V
Tanzania	738	—	.01	—	.99	1.26	1.56Y	1.93Y	—	—	—	—	—	—Y	—Y
Tunisia	744	—	—	—	—	—	.25V	.31Y	—	—	—	—	—	19.91V	24.71Y
Uganda	746	—	—	—	.17	.01	.01Y	.02Y	—	—	—	—	—	—Y	—Y
Zambia	754	—	—	—	.15	.31	.14V	.11V	—	.09	.35	.24	.60	.20V	.03V
Zimbabwe	698	—	—	—	—	—	.01V	.01Y	—	—	—	—	—	.24V	.30Y
Africa n.s.	799	—	—	—	—	—	12.07Y	12.97Y	—	—	—	—	—	3.39Y	3.39Y
Asia	**507**	**21.7**	**40.6**	**22.9**	**40.7**	**113.6**	**291.4Y**	**280.5Y**	**301.1**	**303.5**	**472.8**	**537.4**	**953.5**	**1,141.6Y**	**1,611.1Y**
Bangladesh	513	—	—	—	—	—	—V	9.67V	—	—	—	—	—	.26Y	.29Y
Cambodia	522	—	—	—	—	—	—V	—Y	—	—	—	—	—	.14V	.18Y
China,P.R.: Mainland	924	1.67	7.41	5.14	15.74	82.42	119.81V	79.13V	135.96	144.85	228.16	290.53	514.12	474.83V	852.23V
China,P.R.:Hong Kong	532	—	1.29	2.27	2.63	2.85	2.09V	2.33V	.27	.62	12.38	7.14	7.54	4.91V	6.04V
China,P.R.:Macao	546	—	—	—	—	—	.07V	.10V	—	—	—	—	—	—Y	—Y
India	534	9.70	10.97	7.59	9.45	9.14	11.29Y	14.01Y	91.25	93.56	141.43	149.94	274.04	338.70Y	420.32Y
Indonesia	536	—	—	—	—	—	3.59V	.83V	—	—	—	—	—	34.29V	16.28V
Korea	542	—	—	.76	.90	1.03	2.40V	4.48V	42.83	21.48	26.54	27.64	57.09	69.31V	80.57V
Malaysia	548	—	4.27	1.94	3.45	5.80	3.52V	2.13V	12.14	7.32	16.26	14.49	29.84	13.72V	13.95V
New Caledonia	839	—	—	—	—	—	.06Y	.08Y	....	....	....	....	....	....	....
Pakistan	564	—	13.78	1.25	3.47	2.88	3.56Y	4.42Y	1.21	3.27	3.27	2.52	4.95	6.11Y	7.59Y
Philippines	566	—	—	—	—	—	.62V	.68V	—	—	—	—	—	16.88V	.38V
Singapore	576	—	1.42	1.15	2.29	7.63	.29V	2.78V	—	11.62	12.44	13.16	21.80	9.12V	17.76V
Sri Lanka	524	—	—	—	—	—	—V	.38V	—	—	—	—	—	.38V	.25V
Taiwan Province of China	528	.24	.37	1.72	.68	.56	.96V	1.52V	9.59	6.50	16.84	14.68	13.24	4.59V	5.05V
Thailand	578	10.14	1.07	1.03	2.03	1.31	1.86V	1.04V	7.79	14.28	15.50	17.33	30.83	32.76V	45.37V
Asia n.s.	598	—	—	—	—	—	141.28Y	156.90Y	—	—	—	—	—	135.56Y	144.83Y
Europe	**170**	**3.2**	**10.5**	**15.4**	**41.2**	**18.7**	**35.0Y**	**58.9Y**	**77.1**	**82.0**	**105.2**	**173.0**	**238.0**	**315.6Y**	**423.9Y**
Albania	914	—	—	—	—	—	.06V	.07V	—	—	—	—	—	—V	—V
Belarus	913	—	—	—	—	—	.22V	.26V	—	—	—	—	—	8.76V	1.75V
Bulgaria	918	—	.18	.23	.55	.34	.08V	.15V	2.02	1.23	2.33	.86	1.09	1.50V	3.54V
Czech Republic	935	—	.19	—	.30	.49	1.99V	2.80V	1.17	3.05	2.24	.64	11.70	3.65V	17.83V
Estonia	939	—	—	—	—	—	—V	—V	—	—	—	—	—	.07V	1.42V
Hungary	944	—	.28	.35	.48	.36	.99V	1.12V	11.81	2.67	1.08	.92	1.54	1.59V	1.57V

	Exports 2001	2002	2003	2004	2005	2006	2007	Imports 2001	2002	2003	2004	2005	2006	2007
	Millions of U.S. Dollars							*Millions of U.S. Dollars*						
Kazakhstan.......916	—	—	—	—	—	—Y	—Y	—	—	—	—	—	1.77Y	2.20Y
Latvia.......941	—	—	—	—	—	—V	.01V	—	—	—	—	—	.57V	.10V
Lithuania.......946	—	—	—	—	—	.09V	.24V	—	—	—	—	—	13.81V	6.77V
Macedonia, FYR.......962	—	—	—	—	—	.04V	.05Y	—	—	—	—	—	—V	—Y
Poland.......964	—	.24	1.66	.57	.45	1.64V	3.35V	2.38	1.72	3.16	2.87	4.11	5.65V	3.93V
Romania.......968	—	1.08	1.15	1.75	1.08	1.72V	1.57V	1.17	2.02	1.42	.73	.84	.79V	.45V
Russia.......922	.09	.33	.54	1.45	2.05	4.30V	7.04V	8.80	15.75	25.86	31.90	22.57	11.89V	25.23V
Slovak Republic.......936	—	—	—	—	—	.57V	1.16V	—	—	—	—	—	7.43V	3.75V
Turkey.......186	.10	5.57	11.07	16.05	12.66	21.53V	38.86V	22.87	35.09	42.71	73.79	112.80	101.14V	160.52V
Ukraine.......926	—	—	—	—	—	.13Y	.17Y	—	—	—	—	—	54.02Y	67.04Y
Europe n.s.......884	2.99	2.59	.35	20.01	1.31	1.62Y	2.02Y	26.93	20.49	26.43	61.25	83.34	103.00Y	127.83Y
Middle East.......407	**39.5**	**55.9**	**55.9**	**75.9**	**111.4**	**140.9Y**	**176.6Y**	**515.9**	**319.4**	**547.5**	**739.6**	**1,110.3**	**1,336.9Y**	**1,608.8Y**
Egypt.......469	.02	4.89	2.37	2.40	13.56	16.76Y	20.80Y	17.80	19.37	22.74	30.48	51.16	63.23Y	78.47Y
Israel.......436	1.75	15.14	1.51	16.44	21.81	20.09V	23.64V	2.66	2.89	7.17	13.99	56.55	11.66V	13.20V
Jordan.......439	—	—	—	—	—	10.16V	11.93V	—	—	—	—	—	4.00V	12.66V
Kuwait.......443	—	—	.05	.04	.11	.14Y	.18Y	.97	.29	46.42	.59	1.40	1.75Y	2.12Y
Lebanon.......446	—	.16	—	.38	.02	.03Y	.03Y	.28	.46	.32	.32	.44	.54Y	.67Y
Libya.......672	—	—	—	.19	.28	.34Y	.45Y	—	5.14	.02	—	.01	.01Y	.01Y
Qatar.......453	—	—	—	—	—	—V	—Y	—	—	—	—	—	13.57V	16.37Y
Saudi Arabia.......456	.16	28.07	35.77	40.97	53.79	66.40Y	86.01Y	201.40	111.07	254.44	380.95	600.07	754.40Y	910.10Y
Yemen, Republic of.......474	37.53	7.65	16.17	15.52	21.85	27.01Y	33.52Y	132.56	7.94	10.08	6.23	8.61	10.64Y	13.21Y
Middle East n.s.......489	—	—	—	—	—	—Y	—Y	160.23	172.18	206.36	307.09	392.08	477.07Y	562.06Y
Western Hemisphere.......207	**—**	**1.4**	**1.6**	**1.6**	**1.7**	**3.3Y**	**2.8Y**	**11.7**	**24.3**	**18.2**	**30.4**	**43.3**	**71.9Y**	**56.2Y**
Argentina.......213	—	—	—	—	—	.02V	.01V	—	—	—	—	—	.17V	.56V
Bolivia.......218	—	—	—	—	—	—Y	—Y	—	—	—	—	—	.03Y	.04Y
Brazil.......223	—	—	.10	.78	.45	.06V	—V	9.13	9.01	15.47	15.42	29.41	59.96V	41.15V
Chile.......228	—	—	—	—	—	.42V	.01V	—	—	—	—	—	.03V	.30V
Colombia.......233	—	—	—	—	—	—V	.02V	—	—	—	—	—	.02V	.25V
Honduras.......268	—	—	—	—	—	.17Y	.22Y	....	....	....	....	....	....	....
Mexico.......273	—	—	.16	.55	.49	1.30V	.75V	.11	.01	.52	—	.59	.07V	2.93V
Peru.......293	—	—	—	—	—	—V	—Y	—	—	—	—	—	.04V	—Y
Western Hem. n.s.......399	—	1.35	1.32	.29	.79	1.29Y	1.79Y	2.46	15.26	2.24	14.99	13.30	11.62Y	10.92Y
Other Countries n.i.e.......910	**—**	**.4**	**.1**	**.1**	**1.4**	**1.7Y**	**2.1Y**	**.9**	**2.1**	**1.6**	**5.4**	**5.8**	**7.2Y**	**8.9Y**
Cuba.......928	—	—	.09	—	.23	.29Y	.36Y	—	—	—	.04	.07	.09Y	.11Y
North Korea.......954	.01	.35	.03	.10	1.13	1.39Y	1.73Y	.91	2.09	1.58	5.37	5.76	7.11Y	8.83Y
Countries & Areas n.s.......898	**.1**	**1.2**	**1.2**	**6.2**	**2.3**	**2.9Y**	**3.6Y**	**7.4**	**9.0**	**22.2**	**14.5**	**3.6**	**4.5Y**	**5.6Y**
Memorandum Items														
European Union.......998	60.14	154.23	153.42	206.00	288.58	332.73Y	403.85Y	532.76	491.66	552.86	545.16	903.56	849.40Y	1,073.57Y
Oil Exporting Ctys.......999	.16	28.16	35.82	41.22	54.18	70.47Y	87.47Y	202.57	116.56	301.00	381.68	601.50	804.05Y	944.91Y
Non-Oil Develop.Ctys.......201	185.61	136.88	187.91	160.22	268.60	498.82Y	551.55Y	768.60	691.39	936.45	1,184.14	1,881.98	2,291.31Y	2,991.91Y
PERCENT DISTRIBUTION														
Industrial Countries.......101	**35.0**	**60.5**	**51.9**	**63.6**	**58.2**	**47.4**	**47.4**	**45.1**	**47.8**	**40.0**	**38.0**	**38.9**	**26.8**	**26.3**
Developing Countries.......202	**65.0**	**39.2**	**47.8**	**35.3**	**41.3**	**52.2**	**52.1**	**54.5**	**51.5**	**58.9**	**61.2**	**60.8**	**72.9**	**73.4**
Africa.......607	**42.4**	**13.5**	**27.4**	**7.4**	**9.9**	**9.0**	**9.8**	**3.7**	**5.0**	**4.5**	**3.3**	**3.4**	**5.4**	**4.4**
Asia.......507	**7.6**	**9.6**	**4.9**	**7.1**	**14.5**	**26.7**	**22.9**	**16.9**	**19.4**	**22.5**	**21.0**	**23.4**	**26.9**	**30.0**
Europe.......170	**1.1**	**2.5**	**3.3**	**7.2**	**2.4**	**3.2**	**4.8**	**4.3**	**5.2**	**5.0**	**6.8**	**5.8**	**7.4**	**7.9**
Middle East.......407	**13.8**	**13.3**	**11.9**	**13.3**	**14.2**	**12.9**	**14.4**	**28.9**	**20.4**	**26.0**	**28.9**	**27.2**	**31.5**	**30.0**
Western Hemisphere.......207	**—**	**.3**	**.3**	**.3**	**.2**	**.3**	**.2**	**.7**	**1.5**	**.9**	**1.2**	**1.1**	**1.7**	**1.0**
Other Countries n.i.e.......910	**—**	**.1**	**—**	**—**	**.2**	**.2**	**.2**	**.1**	**.1**	**.1**	**.2**	**.1**	**.2**	**.2**
ANNUAL PERCENT CHANGE														
World.......001	**–34.9**	**47.4**	**11.0**	**21.9**	**37.1**	**39.6**	**12.3**	**45.4**	**–12.1**	**34.1**	**21.7**	**59.6**	**4.1**	**26.3**
Industrial Countries.......101	**–65.9**	**154.7**	**–4.7**	**49.3**	**25.6**	**13.6**	**12.3**	**56.0**	**–6.8**	**12.3**	**15.5**	**63.5**	**–28.2**	**23.9**
Developing Countries.......202	**27.6**	**–11.2**	**35.6**	**–10.0**	**60.2**	**76.4**	**12.2**	**36.9**	**–16.8**	**53.2**	**26.5**	**58.6**	**24.6**	**27.2**
Africa.......607	**131.8**	**–53.3**	**125.7**	**–67.1**	**83.7**	**27.8**	**21.9**	**48.6**	**20.5**	**18.8**	**–8.8**	**62.2**	**65.7**	**3.3**
Asia.......507	**7.5**	**86.6**	**–43.7**	**77.8**	**179.5**	**156.5**	**–3.7**	**40.8**	**.8**	**55.8**	**13.7**	**77.4**	**19.7**	**41.1**
Europe.......170	**–32.1**	**229.4**	**46.6**	**168.2**	**–54.5**	**86.7**	**68.3**	**51.5**	**6.3**	**28.3**	**64.4**	**37.6**	**32.6**	**34.3**
Middle East.......407	**–41.9**	**41.7**	**—**	**35.9**	**46.7**	**26.5**	**25.3**	**30.4**	**–38.1**	**71.5**	**35.1**	**50.1**	**20.4**	**20.3**
Western Hemisphere.......207	**–10.1**	**32.0**	**16.5**	**2.6**	**6.5**	**89.3**	**–14.4**	**136.0**	**107.4**	**–25.0**	**66.9**	**42.4**	**66.1**	**–21.9**
Other Countries n.i.e.......910	**10.4**	**—**	**–66.3**	**–17.5**	**—**	**23.6**	**24.1**	**–5.8**	**128.6**	**–24.4**	**243.1**	**7.6**	**23.6**	**24.1**

Faroe Islands 816

		Exports							Imports						
		2001	2002	2003	2004	2005	2006	2007	2001	2002	2003	2004	2005	2006	2007
		Millions of U.S. Dollars							*Millions of U.S. Dollars*						
DOTS World Total	**001**	**424.0Y**	**427.3Y**	**519.3Y**	**533.5Y**	**545.5Y**	**633.7Y**	**735.8Y**	**509.4Y**	**466.2Y**	**578.8Y**	**639.5Y**	**725.2Y**	**751.4Y**	**991.3Y**
Industrial Countries	**101**	**408.8Y**	**395.8Y**	**476.3Y**	**460.8Y**	**469.2Y**	**524.4Y**	**603.3Y**	**497.2Y**	**455.5Y**	**564.3Y**	**581.7Y**	**709.4Y**	**730.4Y**	**961.1Y**
United States	111	13.09V	15.18V	16.82V	6.82V	4.27V	4.36V	8.45V	21.89V	5.28V	14.85V	10.12V	2.64V	4.40V	3.08V
Canada	156	—V	10.74V	5.80V	2.41V	6.80V	7.60V	2.53V	.16V	.15V	.17V	1.75V	2.16V	2.35V	1.90V
Australia	193	—V	—V	—V	—V	—V	.19V	—V	—V	—V	—V	—V	—V	—V	—V
New Zealand	196	—V	—V	—V	—V	—V	—V	.01V	.71V	.88V	.98V	1.37V	1.76V	1.90V	2.54V
Austria	122	—V	—V	.03V	.02V	—V	—V	—V	.38V	.31V	.89V	.50V	.47V	2.85V	3.68V
Belgium	124	.04V	.02V	.38V	.83V	—V	.01V	.01V	1.34V	1.36V	1.06V	1.50V	2.13V	1.94V	4.18V
Cyprus	423	.04V	—V	.07V	.11V	.13Y	.14V	—V	—V	—V	—V	—V	—V	—V	—V
Denmark	128	165.59V	154.15V	190.63V	178.49V	208.37V	196.37V	218.09V	251.29V	268.52V	303.83V	335.80V	338.68V	395.45V	514.46V
Finland	172	.23V	1.52V	2.99V	2.65V	2.07V	1.49V	.10V	1.53V	3.80V	1.77V	3.30V	1.71V	1.73V	4.04V
France	132	1.69V	.69V	3.41V	6.52V	2.44V	3.99V	.35V	1.05V	1.08V	1.22V	1.65V	1.21V	1.80V	1.90V
Germany	134	18.65V	11.59V	13.66V	13.48V	7.14V	9.30V	10.16V	12.86V	7.48V	24.33V	10.58V	60.13V	18.43V	34.45V
Greece	174	.09V	.06V	—V	3.35V	7.74V	4.13V	3.23V	.01V	.02V	.01V	.02V	.01V	.01V	.01V
Iceland	176	5.06V	5.15V	11.27V	18.26V	7.58V	14.23V	21.39V	28.75V	26.29V	27.29V	31.68V	35.35V	45.54V	37.71V
Ireland	178	.10V	.24V	.61V	.66V	.28V	.15V	1.36V	.12V	.05V	.06V	5.99V	.36V	.37V	.21V
Italy	136	—V	.12V	.24V	.25V	.01V	.34V	.45V	.78V	1.43V	1.66V	6.93V	1.56V	11.53V	2.57V
Luxembourg	137	—V	—V	—V	—V	—V	—V	—V	.77V	.11V	.56V	.09V	.03V	.13V	.72V
Netherlands	138	26.61V	26.24V	31.72V	19.12V	23.70V	35.17V	49.97V	2.56V	2.27V	9.43V	9.45V	6.16V	24.06V	16.78V
Norway	142	30.30V	27.35V	28.37V	44.75V	33.57V	65.43V	98.22V	109.01V	98.28V	129.81V	116.52V	144.15V	156.08V	214.47V
Portugal	182	.22V	.14V	.01V	.10V	.01V	.01V	—V	1.47V	1.89V	2.09V	2.65V	4.21V	3.12V	3.35V
Slovenia	961	—V	.01V	—V	—Y	—V	—V	—V	—V	—V	—V	—Y	—V	—V	.48V
Spain	184	1.27V	1.04V	.61V	1.43V	.53V	2.20V	2.58V	1.89V	8.45V	.93V	.95V	55.48V	1.34V	9.94V
Sweden	144	2.23V	1.94V	1.62V	1.46V	2.33V	3.65V	4.21V	16.25V	16.47V	19.94V	26.78V	28.25V	32.59V	50.02V
Switzerland	146	1.09V	1.47V	1.06V	1.58V	.88V	1.99V	2.11V	.16V	.21V	.05V	.31V	9.55V	1.19V	8.99V
United Kingdom	112	142.51V	138.19V	166.97V	158.52V	161.31V	173.63V	180.08V	44.20V	11.13V	23.34V	13.78V	13.37V	23.62V	45.65V
Developing Countries	**202**	**14.6Y**	**30.9Y**	**42.2Y**	**71.6Y**	**75.1Y**	**107.9Y**	**130.7Y**	**10.3Y**	**8.8Y**	**12.0Y**	**54.4Y**	**12.0Y**	**16.2Y**	**24.3Y**
Africa	**607**	**5.1Y**	**20.5Y**	**29.3Y**	**38.3Y**	**48.7Y**	**60.5Y**	**77.8Y**	**—Y**	**.1Y**	**—Y**	**.1Y**	**—Y**	**—Y**	**—Y**
Benin	638	.01V	—V	—V	—V	—V	—Y	—Y	....	....	....	....	....	....	....
Côte d'Ivoire	662	—V	—V	—V	—V	.03V	—V	—Y	—V	—V	—V	—V	—V	—V	—Y
Kenya	664	—V	—V	—V	.03V	.04Y	.05Y	.06Y	—V	—V	—V	—V	—Y	—Y	—Y
Madagascar	674	.05V	—V	—V	—Y	—Y	—Y	—Y	—V	—V	—V	—Y	—Y	—Y	—Y
Mauritius	684	—V	—V	—V	—V	—V	—V	—V	—V	—V	—V	.01V	—V	—V	—V
Morocco	686	—V	—V	—V	—V	.06V	.07Y	.09Y	—V	—V	—V	—V	—V	—Y	—Y
Nigeria	694	5.02V	20.43V	29.30V	38.11Y	48.53Y	59.91Y	77.60Y	—V	.02V	—V	—Y	—Y	—Y	—Y
Senegal	722	.01V	—V	—V	—V	—V	—V	—Y	—Y	—Y	—V	—V	—V	—V	—Y
South Africa	199	.03V	.03V	—V	.11V	—V	.44V	—V	—Y	—Y	—Y	—Y	—V	—V	—V
Tunisia	744	.01V	—V	—V	—V	—V	—V	—Y	—V	.01V	—V	.07V	.04V	—V	—Y
Zambia	754	—V	—V	—V	.01V	—V	—V	—V	—V	—V	—V	—V	—V	—V	—V
Zimbabwe	698	—V	—V	—V	—V	—V	—V	—Y	—V	.06V	—V	—V	—V	—V	—Y
Asia	**507**	**3.4Y**	**4.2Y**	**6.8Y**	**6.7Y**	**5.7Y**	**9.2Y**	**12.3Y**	**3.7Y**	**2.9Y**	**5.0Y**	**4.1Y**	**1.8Y**	**.7Y**	**1.2Y**
China,P.R.: Mainland	924	—V	—V	—Y	—Y	—Y	3.14V	6.26V	—V	—V	—V	—V	—V	.03V	.56Y
India	534	—Y	.01V	—V	—V	.02V	.02Y	.02Y	.03Y	.06V	.43V	.26V	.22V	.27Y	.34Y
Indonesia	536	.13V	.04V	—V	—V	—V	—V	—V	3.05V	1.88V	3.12V	3.30V	.58V	—V	—V
Korea	542	.22V	—V	.05V	.11V	.19V	.10V	.32V	.04V	.22V	.37V	.22V	.47V	.10V	.07V
Malaysia	548	—V	—V	—V	—V	—V	—V	—V	—V	—V	.08V	.04V	—V	—V	.04V
New Caledonia	839	.01V	—V	—V	.03V	.04Y	.05Y	.06Y	....	....	....	....	....	....	....
Pakistan	564	—V	—V	—V	—V	—V	.01Y	.01Y	—V	—V	.09V	—V	.01V	.01Y	.02Y
Philippines	566	—V	—V	—V	—V	—V	—V	—V	—V	—V	—V	—V	.12V	—V	—V
Thailand	578	.68V	1.46V	3.74V	3.29V	1.84V	1.99V	1.47V	.39V	.54V	.75V	.10V	.20V	.06V	—V
Asia n.s.	598	2.41Y	2.71Y	3.01Y	3.30Y	3.60Y	3.90Y	4.20Y	.20Y	.20Y	.20Y	.20Y	.20Y	.20Y	.20Y
Europe	**170**	**5.2Y**	**6.0Y**	**5.9Y**	**26.4Y**	**20.5Y**	**37.9Y**	**39.2Y**	**4.0Y**	**3.0Y**	**3.4Y**	**28.5Y**	**4.9Y**	**8.9Y**	**14.4Y**
Belarus	913	—V	1.30V	2.58V	1.88V	5.33V	5.31V	6.75V	—V	—V	—V	—V	—V	—V	—V
Bulgaria	918	—V	—V	—V	—V	—V	—V	—V	—V	.01V	—V	—V	—V	—V	—V
Czech Republic	935	.05V	—V	—V	.04V	.30V	—V	—V	.03V	.10V	.08V	.08V	.59V	.22V	.46V
Czechoslovakia n.s.	937	....	....	....	....	....	....	....	.35Y	.38Y	.49Y	.64Y	.73Y	.90Y	1.12Y
Estonia	939	.11V	.16V	—V	—V	.08V	.23V	.31V	.32V	.18V	.33V	.63V	.83V	.79V	2.37V
Hungary	944	—V	—V	—Y	—Y	—V	—V	—V	—V	—V	—Y	—V	—V	.02V	.01V
Lithuania	946	1.26V	1.69V	.20V	8.00V	2.95V	2.71V	1.56V	—V	.38V	.14V	11.13V	.32V	1.48V	1.83V
Moldova	921	—V	—V	.01V	.01V	.04V	.05Y	.07Y	....	....	....	....	....	....	....
Poland	964	3.59V	2.29V	1.91V	12.36V	4.27V	1.99V	2.66V	1.68V	.11V	.21V	13.87V	.25V	2.46V	4.53V
Romania	968	—V	.03V	.01V	.74V	.34V	.03V	.13V	—V	.10V	.13V	.04V	.05V	.01V	.27V
Russia	922	—V	.23V	.60V	2.34V	2.88V	22.21V	21.11V	.02V	.52V	.67V	.05V	—V	.45V	.60V
Slovak Republic	936	.06V	.04V	.05Y	.07Y	—V	—V	.01V	.39V	.02V	.03Y	.04Y	.06V	.06Y	.19V
Turkey	186	.08V	.20V	.20V	.14V	—V	—V	.01V	.46V	.37V	.24V	.60V	.45V	.53V	.63V
Ukraine	926	.01V	—V	.36V	.80V	4.33V	5.35Y	6.64Y	—V	—V	—V	—V	—V	—Y	—Y
Europe n.s.	884	—Y	—Y	—Y	—Y	—Y	—Y	—Y	.77Y	.83Y	1.05Y	1.38Y	1.58Y	1.95Y	2.42Y
Western Hemisphere	**207**	**.9Y**	**.2Y**	**.2Y**	**.2Y**	**.3Y**	**.3Y**	**1.4Y**	**2.6Y**	**2.8Y**	**3.6Y**	**21.7Y**	**5.3Y**	**6.7Y**	**8.6Y**
Brazil	223	.71V	.02V	—V	—V	—V	—V	—V	—V	—V	.07V	17.14V	.08V	.22V	—V
Colombia	233	.03V	.02V	—V	.02V	—V	—V	—V	.07V	—V	—V	—V	—V	—V	—V
Dominican Republic	243	.07V	.07Y	.09Y	.12Y	.14Y	.17Y	.21Y	....	....	....	....	....	....	....

	Exports							Imports						
	2001	2002	2003	2004	2005	2006	2007	2001	2002	2003	2004	2005	2006	2007
	Millions of U.S. Dollars							Millions of U.S. Dollars						
Ecuador.......248	—V	—V	.01V	—V	—V	—V	—Y	—V	.02V	—V	—V	—V	—V	—Y
Falkland Islands.......323	—Y	—Y	—Y	—Y	—Y	—Y	—Y	2.15Y	2.33Y	2.95Y	3.88Y	4.43Y	5.48Y	6.80Y
Greenland.......326	.05Y	.06Y	.07Y	.09Y	.11Y	.13Y	.16Y	.38Y	.41Y	.52Y	.69Y	.79Y	.97Y	1.21Y
Guatemala.......258	—V	.07V	—V	—V	.01V	.02Y	.02Y	....	....	....	....	....	....	....
Jamaica.......343	—V	—V	—V	—V	—V	—V	.96V	—V	—V	—V	—V	—V	—V	—V
Panama.......283	—V	—V	—V	—V	—V	—V	—V	—V	—V	—V	—V	—V	—V	.61V
Peru.......293	—V	—V	—V	—V	—V	—V	—Y	—V	—V	.02V	—V	—V	—V	—Y
Uruguay.......298	—V	—Y	—V	—V	—V	—Y	—Y	—V	—Y	—V	.04V	—V	—Y	—Y
Countries & Areas n.s.......898	**.6Y**	**.6Y**	**.8Y**	**1.0Y**	**1.2Y**	**1.5Y**	**1.8Y**	**1.8Y**	**2.0Y**	**2.5Y**	**3.3Y**	**3.7Y**	**4.6Y**	**5.7Y**
Memorandum Items														
European Union.......998	364.34Y	340.14Y	415.11Y	407.45Y	423.67Y	435.54Y	475.14Y	338.93Y	325.16Y	391.94Y	445.75Y	515.81Y	524.02Y	701.83Y
Oil Exporting Ctys.......999	5.15Y	20.47Y	29.31Y	38.11Y	48.53Y	59.91Y	77.60Y	3.05Y	1.90Y	3.12Y	3.30Y	.58Y	—Y	—Y
Non-Oil Develop.Ctys.......201	9.45Y	10.40Y	12.89Y	33.50Y	26.60Y	47.96Y	53.09Y	7.29Y	6.86Y	8.86Y	51.10Y	11.43Y	16.24Y	24.28Y
PERCENT DISTRIBUTION														
Industrial Countries.......101	**96.4**	**92.6**	**91.7**	**86.4**	**86.0**	**82.7**	**82.0**	**97.6**	**97.7**	**97.5**	**91.0**	**97.8**	**97.2**	**97.0**
Developing Countries.......202	**3.4**	**7.2**	**8.1**	**13.4**	**13.8**	**17.0**	**17.8**	**2.0**	**1.9**	**2.1**	**8.5**	**1.7**	**2.2**	**2.4**
Africa.......607	**1.2**	**4.8**	**5.6**	**7.2**	**8.9**	**9.5**	**10.6**	**—**	**—**	**—**	**—**	**—**	**—**	**—**
Asia.......507	**.8**	**1.0**	**1.3**	**1.3**	**1.0**	**1.5**	**1.7**	**.7**	**.6**	**.9**	**.6**	**.2**	**.1**	**.1**
Europe.......170	**1.2**	**1.4**	**1.1**	**4.9**	**3.8**	**6.0**	**5.3**	**.8**	**.6**	**.6**	**4.5**	**.7**	**1.2**	**1.5**
Western Hemisphere.......207	**.2**	**.1**	**—**	**—**	**—**	**.1**	**.2**	**.5**	**.6**	**.6**	**3.4**	**.7**	**.9**	**.9**
ANNUAL PERCENT CHANGE														
World.......001	**7.4**	**.8**	**21.5**	**2.7**	**2.3**	**16.2**	**16.1**	**11.9**	**–8.5**	**24.2**	**10.5**	**13.4**	**3.6**	**31.9**
Industrial Countries.......101	**5.9**	**–3.2**	**20.3**	**–3.2**	**1.8**	**11.8**	**15.0**	**12.4**	**–8.4**	**23.9**	**3.1**	**21.9**	**3.0**	**31.6**
Developing Countries.......202	**82.4**	**111.3**	**36.7**	**69.7**	**4.9**	**43.6**	**21.2**	**–8.5**	**–15.3**	**36.8**	**354.0**	**–77.9**	**35.2**	**49.6**
Africa.......607	**101.1**	**298.5**	**43.3**	**30.5**	**27.2**	**24.3**	**28.6**	**—**	**....**	**–95.4**	**—**	**–40.3**	**–95.7**	**–50.3**
Asia.......507	**44.4**	**22.6**	**61.0**	**–.9**	**–15.5**	**61.6**	**34.2**	**–30.2**	**–22.1**	**73.9**	**–18.3**	**–56.2**	**–62.1**	**80.9**
Europe.......170	**78.2**	**15.1**	**–.6**	**346.1**	**–22.2**	**84.6**	**3.6**	**15.0**	**–25.4**	**12.6**	**742.6**	**–82.9**	**82.6**	**62.4**
Western Hemisphere.......207	**412.4**	**–72.8**	**–24.6**	**33.5**	**9.5**	**23.6**	**326.1**	**4.9**	**6.7**	**28.5**	**509.7**	**–75.6**	**25.8**	**29.3**

	Exports 2001	2002	2003	2004	2005	2006	2007	Imports 2001	2002	2003	2004	2005	2006	2007
	Millions of U.S. Dollars							Millions of U.S. Dollars						
IFS World Total	**533.9**	**519.4**	**673.5**	**693.3**	**700.9**	**678.9**	**754.7**	**886.0**	**905.5**	**1,209.5**	**1,445.6**	**1,607.2**	**1,801.7**	**1,800.7**
DOTS World Total 001	**639.7Y**	**620.9Y**	**738.2Y**	**881.1Y**	**868.0Y**	**927.4Y**	**1,003.4Y**	**754.6Y**	**845.2Y**	**995.4Y**	**1,230.9Y**	**1,451.0Y**	**1,588.3Y**	**1,566.9Y**
Industrial Countries 101	**444.9Y**	**420.8Y**	**483.3Y**	**557.4Y**	**519.5Y**	**510.6Y**	**492.1Y**	**537.0Y**	**540.5Y**	**620.9Y**	**713.9Y**	**777.9Y**	**797.0Y**	**750.1Y**
United States 111	181.00V	154.91V	168.73V	206.64V	170.64V	156.82V	173.09V	21.34V	18.59V	21.56V	27.83V	30.91V	35.86V	33.00V
Canada 156	1.81V	3.78V	2.86V	4.26V	5.90V	7.61V	6.86V	1.95V	4.50V	4.43V	3.28V	8.37V	3.52V	5.21V
Australia 193	123.87V	119.88V	139.37V	164.01V	146.89V	129.52V	100.81V	333.41V	312.56V	347.47V	319.26V	344.11V	371.14V	338.42V
Japan 158	31.22V	38.99V	34.41V	35.31V	47.11V	49.26V	40.67V	28.70V	35.47V	48.18V	47.89V	51.20V	51.65V	44.35V
New Zealand 196	21.75V	23.18V	27.69V	30.03V	32.79V	34.62V	45.54V	112.07V	143.65V	169.81V	261.13V	275.13V	267.47V	277.67V
Austria 122	.38V	.04V	—V	.02V	.10V	.21V	.17V	.03V	.04V	.12V	.03V	.08V	.81V	.06V
Belgium 124	—V	—V	.44V	.04V	2.71V	1.01V	3.79V	—V	1.88V	1.63V	1.50V	1.09V	1.09V	3.52V
Cyprus 423	—V	—V	—V	—V	—Y	—V	—V	.04V	.01V	.05V	—V	—V	—V	—V
Denmark 128	.19V	.07V	.06V	.03V	.30V	.04V	.03V	1.14V	1.14V	1.80V	1.95V	1.89V	1.52V	1.44V
Finland 172	.01V	.02V	.01V	.01V	.03V	.01V	.01V	6.49V	.12V	.23V	.10V	.37V	.18V	.33V
France 132	.71V	.59V	.76V	.15V	2.35V	.79V	1.70V	15.01V	6.76V	4.14V	14.32V	12.97V	11.60V	7.18V
Germany 134	3.74V	1.68V	4.20V	2.33V	2.20V	2.90V	1.78V	2.66V	3.30V	3.47V	6.89V	19.09V	14.07V	6.32V
Greece 174	—V	—V	—V	—V	.01V	.01V	—V	.75V	—V	—V	—V	.01V	.01V	—V
Ireland 178	.02V	.02V	.03V	.02V	.01V	.04V	.07V	.08V	.18V	.28V	1.14V	1.98V	2.64V	2.79V
Italy 136	.21V	.23V	.40V	.32V	.28V	.42V	.35V	1.68V	2.84V	2.62V	3.22V	8.20V	4.63V	5.35V
Luxembourg 137	—V	—V	—V	—V	—V	—V	—V	.01V	—V	.14V	.04V	.02V	.14V	.05V
Malta 181	—Y	—V	—V	—V	—V	—V	—V	.03Y	—V	—V	—V	—V	—V	—V
Netherlands 138	.49V	3.29V	1.04V	1.12V	1.39V	.83V	1.62V	4.88V	2.48V	3.60V	5.84V	4.57V	16.49V	4.66V
Norway 142	.02V	.02V	.02V	—V	.07V	.06V	.02V	.05V	.03V	.03V	2.34V	.46V	.12V	.14V
Portugal 182	12.15V	8.48V	5.38V	4.37V	—V	—V	—V	.10V	.16V	.02V	.02V	.01V	.02V	.28V
Slovenia 961	.02V	.01V	.01V	.01Y	—V	—V	—V	—V	.02V	—V	—Y	.02V	.02V	—V
Spain 184	.10V	.04V	.91V	.05V	.07V	.05V	1.57V	.58V	.64V	.69V	1.23V	1.42V	.66V	.97V
Sweden 144	.07V	.12V	.04V	.04V	.05V	.07V	.11V	.38V	.57V	.45V	.61V	4.52V	1.82V	5.89V
Switzerland 146	.02V	.03V	.04V	.02V	.18V	.20V	.07V	.18V	.46V	1.18V	2.53V	2.11V	1.00V	1.81V
United Kingdom 112	67.11V	65.42V	96.89V	108.65V	106.39V	126.10V	113.79V	5.42V	5.08V	8.99V	12.79V	9.36V	10.58V	10.70V
Developing Countries 202	**123.6Y**	**122.8Y**	**157.1Y**	**195.3Y**	**201.8Y**	**235.5Y**	**286.3Y**	**209.0Y**	**295.4Y**	**362.7Y**	**501.4Y**	**655.2Y**	**769.2Y**	**789.4Y**
Africa 607	**.1Y**	**.2Y**	**.2Y**	**.2Y**	**.1Y**	**.1Y**	**1.5Y**	**1.2Y**	**1.9Y**	**2.9Y**	**4.3Y**	**4.7Y**	**22.0Y**	**3.5Y**
Côte d'Ivoire 662	—V	—V	—V	—V	—V	.01V	.01Y	—V	—V	.07V	—V	—V	—V	—Y
Liberia 668	—Y	—Y	—Y	—Y	—Y	—Y	—Y	—Y	—Y	—Y	—Y	—Y	.01Y	.01Y
Madagascar 674	.01V	—V	—V	—Y	—Y	—Y	—Y	—V	—V	—V	—Y	—Y	—Y	—Y
Malawi 676	—Y	—Y	—Y	—Y	—Y	—Y	—Y	.29Y	.32Y	.40Y	.53Y	.60Y	.75Y	.93Y
Mali 678	.01Y	.01Y	.01Y	.02Y	.02Y	.02Y	.03Y	.02Y	.02Y	.02Y	.03Y	.03Y	.04Y	.05Y
Mauritius 684	—V	.10V	.16V	.14V	.11V	.02V	.03V	—V	—V	—V	.09V	—V	16.69V	.68V
Nigeria 694	.08V	.02V	.01V	.01Y	.01Y	.02Y	.02Y	—V	—V	—V	—Y	—Y	—Y	—Y
Seychelles 718	.03V	—V	—V	—Y	—Y	—Y	—Y	.04V	—V	—V	—Y	—Y	—Y	—Y
South Africa 199	—V	.02V	.03V	—V	—V	—V	1.44V	.78V	1.48V	2.35V	3.48V	3.90V	4.39V	1.67V
Swaziland 734	—Y	—Y	—Y	—Y	—Y	—Y	—Y	.05Y	.06Y	.07Y	.10Y	.11Y	.14Y	.17Y
Tunisia 744	—V	—V	—V	—V	—V	—V	—Y	—V	—V	—V	—V	.04V	—V	—Y
Zimbabwe 698	—V	—V	—V	—V	—V	—V	—Y	—V	—V	—V	.03V	—V	—V	—Y
Asia 507	**123.2Y**	**122.5Y**	**156.5Y**	**194.0Y**	**196.5Y**	**226.5Y**	**276.1Y**	**205.7Y**	**290.7Y**	**354.7Y**	**492.3Y**	**645.7Y**	**739.6Y**	**771.1Y**
Bangladesh 513	1.53V	—V	—V	—V	—V	—V	—V	.03V	.06V	—V	—V	—V	—Y	—Y
Brunei Darussalam 516	—Y	—Y	—V	—Y	—Y	—Y	—Y	.04Y	.04Y	—V	—Y	—Y	—Y	—Y
China,P.R.: Mainland 924	.22V	1.27V	4.87V	4.26V	2.07V	1.12V	2.34V	28.69V	33.62V	28.58V	35.48V	47.41V	74.79V	70.05V
China,P.R.:Hong Kong 532	11.47V	6.16V	6.43V	7.30V	4.51V	5.64V	8.11V	21.59V	19.93V	25.75V	20.74V	9.52V	12.56V	9.24V
China,P.R.:Macao 546	—V	—V	—V	—V	—V	—V	.02V	—V	—V	—V	.03V	.01V	.10V	.02V
French Polynesia 887	7.68Y	8.33Y	10.54Y	13.85Y	15.82Y	19.56Y	24.27Y	.01Y	.01Y	.02Y	.02Y	.03Y	.03Y	.04Y
Guam 829	.01Y	.01Y	.02Y	.02Y	.03Y	.03Y	.04Y	.01Y	.01Y	.02Y	.02Y	.03Y	.03Y	.04Y
India 534	—Y	.01V	1.17V	.59V	.65V	.80Y	1.00Y	15.18Y	24.87V	23.83V	28.79V	31.68V	39.16Y	48.59Y
Indonesia 536	1.77V	2.20V	2.39V	.16V	7.21V	.01V	.01V	15.27V	15.92V	16.08V	19.70V	22.22V	20.50V	20.62V
Kiribati 826	9.28Y	10.07Y	12.74Y	16.74Y	19.12Y	23.64Y	29.33Y	.03Y	.04Y	.05Y	.06Y	.07Y	.09Y	.11Y
Korea 542	1.03V	.81V	.94V	.62V	2.26V	3.18V	1.79V	10.77V	11.79V	12.69V	25.44V	21.45V	22.30V	27.41V
Lao People's Dem.Rep. 544	.03Y	.03Y	.04Y	.05Y	.05Y	.07Y	.08Y	—Y	—Y	—Y	—Y	—Y	—Y	—Y
Malaysia 548	.19V	.08V	.34V	.07V	.38V	1.85V	.10V	11.38V	11.15V	17.27V	22.41V	27.23V	31.78V	27.72V
Mongolia 948	—V	—V	—V	—V	.06V	—Y	—Y	—V	—Y	—Y	—Y	—Y	—Y	—Y
Myanmar 518	—Y	—Y	—Y	—Y	—Y	—Y	—Y	.02Y	.02Y	.03Y	.04Y	.04Y	.05Y	.06Y
Nauru 836	.29Y	.31Y	.40Y	.52Y	.60Y	.74Y	.92Y	—Y	—Y	—Y	—Y	—Y	—Y	—Y
New Caledonia 839	1.14V	1.68V	1.52V	1.95V	2.22Y	2.75Y	3.41Y	.67V	.84V	.79V	.38V	.44Y	.54Y	.67Y
Pakistan 564	—V	—V	—V	—V	.04V	.05Y	.06Y	1.81V	.97V	1.26V	1.32V	1.01V	1.25Y	1.55Y
Papua New Guinea 853	2.98Y	3.24Y	4.10Y	5.38Y	6.15Y	7.60Y	9.43Y	1.50Y	1.63Y	2.06Y	2.71Y	3.10Y	3.83Y	4.75Y
Philippines 566	.07V	.10V	.19V	.69V	.10V	.02V	.02V	1.93V	1.17V	.72V	2.88V	2.01V	1.85V	1.85V
Samoa 862	30.97Y	33.62Y	42.55Y	55.88Y	35.19V	43.49Y	53.98Y	.31Y	.33Y	.42Y	.55Y	.70V	.87Y	1.08Y
Singapore 576	.54V	1.07V	.93V	2.01V	4.13V	3.87V	5.81V	63.60V	134.45V	190.01V	285.21V	398.90V	459.00V	476.19V
Solomon Islands 813	3.88Y	4.21Y	5.33Y	7.00Y	7.99Y	9.88Y	12.26Y	.13Y	.14Y	.17Y	.23Y	.26Y	.32Y	.40Y
Sri Lanka 524	—V	—V	—V	.34V	.02V	.08V	.03V	1.17V	1.17V	1.59V	1.60V	2.27V	2.17V	1.96V
Taiwan Province of China 528	4.08V	.17V	2.03V	2.25V	1.97V	.70V	2.18V	14.00V	12.93V	9.83V	10.10V	10.70V	12.64V	20.64V
Thailand 578	1.28V	.11V	.49V	.06V	2.06V	1.17V	.30V	16.24V	17.95V	21.93V	33.53V	65.45V	54.27V	56.33V
Tonga 866	15.01Y	16.29Y	20.62Y	27.08Y	30.94Y	38.24Y	47.45Y	.37Y	.40Y	.51Y	.67Y	.77Y	.95Y	1.18Y
Tuvalu 869	7.83Y	8.50Y	10.75Y	14.12Y	16.14Y	19.95Y	24.75Y	.10Y	.11Y	.13Y	.18Y	.20Y	.25Y	.31Y
Vanuatu 846	7.43Y	8.06Y	10.20Y	13.40Y	15.31Y	18.93Y	23.49Y	.07Y	.07Y	.09Y	.12Y	.14Y	.17Y	.21Y
Vietnam 582	—V	—V	—V	—V	—V	—V	—V	.70V	.99V	.72V	—V	—V	—V	—V
Asia n.s. 598	14.45Y	16.20Y	17.95Y	19.69Y	21.44Y	23.19Y	24.94Y	.07Y	.08Y	.09Y	.09Y	.10Y	.11Y	.11Y

	Exports 2001	Exports 2002	Exports 2003	Exports 2004	Exports 2005	Exports 2006	Exports 2007	Imports 2001	Imports 2002	Imports 2003	Imports 2004	Imports 2005	Imports 2006	Imports 2007
	Millions of U.S. Dollars							Millions of U.S. Dollars						
Europe 170	—Y	—Y	—Y	.1Y	.1Y	.2Y	.3Y	.6Y	.3Y	.5Y	.8Y	1.0Y	2.1Y	10.2Y
Bulgaria 918	—V	—V	—V	—V	—V	—V	—V	—V	.02V	.08V	.04V	.02V	1.04V	.06V
Czech Republic 935	—V	—V	—V	—V	.04V	.06V	.09V	.23V	.07V	.08V	.23V	.36V	.41V	4.53V
Estonia 939	—V	—V	—V	—V	—V	—V	—V	.01V	—V	—V	—V	—V	—V	.01V
Hungary 944	—V	—V	.03V	.01V	.02V	.01V	—V	—V	—V	.02V	.01V	.03V	.06V	.01V
Poland 964	—V	—V	—V	.02V	—V	.02V	—V	.14V	.01V	.01V	.08V	.04V	.18V	.05V
Romania 968	—V	—V	—V	—V	—V	.01V	—V	—V	—V	—V	—V	—V	—V	—V
Russia 922	—V	—V	.01V	.05V	.02V	.11V	.24V	—V	—V	—Y	—Y	—Y	—Y	5.13V
Slovak Republic 936	—V	—V	—Y	—Y	—V	—V	—V	.06V	.01V	.02Y	.02Y	—V	—V	—V
Turkey 186	—V	—V	.01V	—V	.02V	—V	—V	.11V	.14V	.21V	.28V	.46V	.30V	.26V
U.S.S.R. n.s. 930	—Y	—Y	—Y	—Y	—Y	—Y	—Y	.06Y	.06Y	.08Y	.10Y	.11Y	.14Y	.18Y
Middle East 407	.2Y	—Y	.2Y	.6Y	1.2Y	1.5Y	2.0Y	.2Y	—Y	.1Y	.1Y	.3Y	.9Y	.1Y
Israel 436	—V	—V	—V	—V	—V	—V	—V	.11V	—V	.11V	.11V	.33V	.88V	.11V
Jordan 439	—V	—V	—V	—V	—V	—V	—V	—V	—V	—V	—V	—V	—V	.02V
Kuwait 443	.01Y	.01Y	.01Y	.01Y	.02Y	.02Y	.03Y	—Y	—Y	—Y	—Y	—Y	—Y	—Y
Oman 449	....	....	....	....	....	....	....	.06V	—V	—V	—Y	—Y	—Y	—Y
Saudi Arabia 456	.20V	.02V	.21V	.60V	1.23V	1.52Y	1.96Y	—Y	—Y	—Y	—Y	—Y	—Y	—Y
Yemen, Republic of 474	—V	.01V	.01Y	—V	—V	—Y	—Y	—V	—V	—Y	—V	—V	—Y	—Y
Western Hemisphere 207	.1Y	—Y	.1Y	.4Y	3.8Y	7.1Y	6.3Y	1.3Y	2.4Y	4.5Y	3.9Y	3.5Y	4.6Y	4.4Y
Argentina 213	—V	—V	—V	—V	—V	—V	—V	.13V	1.31V	2.19V	.06V	.09V	.12V	.22V
Barbados 316	—V	.01V	—V	—V	—V	.14V	.18Y	—V	—V	—V	—V	—V	—V	—Y
Bermuda 319	—Y	—Y	—Y	—Y	—V	.08V	.10Y	—Y	—Y	—Y	—Y	—Y	—Y	—Y
Brazil 223	.01V	—V	.01V	.02V	.09V	.03V	—V	.41V	.76V	1.19V	2.24V	1.12V	.89V	—V
Chile 228	—V	—V	—V	.03V	—V	—V	—V	—V	—V	.77V	1.38V	1.60V	2.47V	2.65V
Colombia 233	.02V	—V	.01V	.05V	—V	—V	.25V	.48V	.07V	.31V	.20V	.12V	.36V	.11V
Costa Rica 238	—V	—V	—V	—V	.27V	.33Y	.41Y	—V	—Y	—Y	—Y	—Y	—Y	—Y
Ecuador 248	.02V	—V	.02V	—V	.01V	—V	—Y	.02V	.24V	—V	—V	.02V	—V	—Y
Guatemala 258	—V	—V	.03V	—V	—V	—Y	—Y	—V	—V	—V	.02V	—V	—Y	—Y
Honduras 268	—V	—V	—V	.21V	.24Y	.30Y	.37Y	—V	—V	—V	—V	—Y	—Y	—Y
Jamaica 343	—V	—V	—V	.02V	1.29V	3.80V	3.40V	—V	—V	—V	—V	—V	—V	—V
Mexico 273	—V	—V	—V	—V	1.83V	2.32V	1.50V	—V	—V	—V	—V	.51V	.14V	.18V
Paraguay 288	—V	—V	—V	—V	—V	—V	—Y	.03V	.01V	—V	—V	—V	—V	—Y
Peru 293	—V	—V	—V	—V	—V	.03V	—Y	.22V	.05V	.02V	—V	—V	.63V	1.28Y
Trinidad and Tobago 369	—V	.03V	.04Y	.06Y	.07Y	.08Y	.10Y	—V	—V	—Y	—Y	—Y	—Y	—Y
Other Countries n.i.e. 910	—Y	—Y	—Y	—Y	.1Y	.1Y	.1Y	.4Y	.4Y	.6Y	.7Y	.8Y	1.0Y	1.3Y
North Korea 954	.03Y	.03Y	.04Y	.05Y	.05Y	.07Y	.08Y	.40Y	.44Y	.55Y	.73Y	.83Y	1.03Y	1.27Y
Countries & Areas n.s. 898	60.4Y	65.5Y	82.9Y	108.9Y	124.4Y	153.8Y	190.8Y	8.2Y	8.9Y	11.2Y	14.8Y	16.9Y	20.9Y	25.9Y
Memorandum Items														
European Union 998	85.20Y	80.02Y	110.18Y	117.20Y	115.96Y	132.56Y	125.08Y	39.72Y	25.32Y	28.35Y	50.04Y	66.04Y	66.94Y	54.14Y
Oil Exporting Ctys 999	2.06Y	2.25Y	2.62Y	.78Y	8.47Y	1.57Y	2.03Y	15.33Y	15.92Y	16.08Y	19.70Y	22.22Y	20.50Y	20.62Y
Non-Oil Develop.Ctys 201	121.53Y	120.55Y	154.50Y	194.48Y	193.28Y	233.89Y	284.26Y	193.63Y	279.43Y	346.57Y	481.66Y	633.02Y	748.73Y	768.82Y
PERCENT DISTRIBUTION														
Industrial Countries 101	69.5	67.8	65.5	63.3	59.8	55.1	49.0	71.2	63.9	62.4	58.0	53.6	50.2	47.9
Developing Countries 202	19.3	19.8	21.3	22.2	23.2	25.4	28.5	27.7	34.9	36.4	40.7	45.2	48.4	50.4
Africa 607	—	—	—	—	—	—	.2	.2	.2	.3	.3	.3	1.4	.2
Asia 507	19.3	19.7	21.2	22.0	22.6	24.4	27.5	27.3	34.4	35.6	40.0	44.5	46.6	49.2
Europe 170	—	—	—	—	—	—	—	.1	—	—	.1	.1	.1	.7
Middle East 407	—	—	—	.1	.1	.2	.2	—	—	—	—	—	.1	—
Western Hemisphere 207	—	—	—	—	.4	.8	.6	.2	.3	.4	.3	.2	.3	.3
Other Countries n.i.e. 910	—	—	—	—	—	—	—	.1	.1	.1	.1	.1	.1	.1
ANNUAL PERCENT CHANGE														
World 001	-6.6	-2.9	18.9	19.4	-1.5	6.8	8.2	-1.0	12.0	17.8	23.7	17.9	9.5	-1.3
Industrial Countries 101	-8.2	-5.4	14.8	15.3	-6.8	-1.7	-3.6	-3.7	.7	14.9	15.0	9.0	2.5	-5.9
Developing Countries 202	-9.1	-.6	28.0	24.3	3.3	16.7	21.6	6.0	41.3	22.8	38.2	30.7	17.4	2.6
Africa 607	33.6	23.5	33.0	-20.2	-13.4	-52.5	—	21.4	58.6	55.4	45.6	10.0	369.1	-84.1
Asia 507	-8.5	-.5	27.7	24.0	1.3	15.3	21.9	6.4	41.3	22.0	38.8	31.2	14.5	4.3
Europe 170	-83.5	-46.9	595.4	50.2	39.9	110.9	60.3	63.3	-47.0	53.7	58.5	32.6	108.5	378.5
Middle East 407	-77.2	-83.3	546.6	162.7	103.9	23.5	29.5	—	-99.9	—	—	202.5	165.2	-84.5
Western Hemisphere 207	-46.8	-4.0	117.2	258.3	884.5	86.9	-11.3	-45.6	89.3	82.6	-12.7	-11.2	32.9	-3.5
Other Countries n.i.e. 910	10.4	8.5	26.6	31.3	14.3	23.6	24.1	10.4	8.5	26.6	31.3	14.3	23.6	24.1

	Exports							Imports						
	2001	2002	2003	2004	2005	2006	2007	2001	2002	2003	2004	2005	2006	2007
	Millions of U.S. Dollars							*Millions of U.S. Dollars*						
IFS World Total........................	**42,794**	**44,650**	**52,504**	**60,895**	**65,234**	**77,284**	**90,091**	**32,108**	**33,627**	**41,592**	**50,661**	**58,469**	**69,445**	**81,757**
DOTS World Total.................... 001	**43,258**	**44,836**	**53,224**	**61,589**	**65,432**	**77,287**	**90,081**	**32,653**	**33,368**	**42,509**	**51,452**	**58,692**	**69,448**	**81,762**
Industrial Countries................ 101	**30,625**	**31,520**	**36,629**	**40,228**	**41,020**	**48,554**	**56,431**	**21,648**	**21,987**	**31,497**	**37,026**	**40,328**	**47,358**	**55,138**
United States.............................. 111	4,224	4,042	4,344	3,949	3,874	5,022	5,731	1,372	1,240	1,561	1,677	1,634	1,738	1,830
Canada.. 156	351	376	579	611	688	658	696	162	128	131	174	271	357	771
Australia..................................... 193	355	352	378	498	546	544	659	224	215	320	462	410	866	1,270
Japan.. 158	810	998	1,132	1,227	1,101	1,273	1,609	997	952	1,180	1,259	1,269	1,247	1,340
New Zealand............................... 196	64	47	64	104	97	82	84	8	10	9	10	11	14	18
Austria.. 122	456	442	527	548	484	591	640	370	421	571	556	568	608	722
Belgium....................................... 124	1,060	1,208	1,468	1,612	1,529	1,772	2,194	743	778	1,233	1,607	1,793	2,036	2,381
Cyprus.. 423	15	14	15	80	174	63	41	2	2	3	3	3	4	4
Denmark...................................... 128	1,052	1,077	1,170	1,360	1,545	1,640	1,775	1,172	1,386	2,444	2,660	2,729	3,107	2,918
France... 132	1,990	2,031	1,990	2,187	2,244	2,594	3,220	1,462	1,422	1,855	2,191	2,171	2,270	2,811
Germany...................................... 134	5,343	5,284	6,258	6,565	6,924	8,730	9,810	4,685	4,853	6,914	8,322	9,645	10,840	12,886
Greece... 174	326	366	443	383	333	406	506	72	73	108	124	130	166	260
Iceland.. 176	33	32	40	81	57	65	78	16	19	19	13	12	14	20
Ireland.. 178	339	340	268	283	408	289	316	351	342	367	385	446	695	708
Italy.. 136	1,568	1,494	2,110	1,837	2,011	2,465	2,532	1,143	1,207	1,467	1,896	1,908	2,128	2,578
Luxembourg................................ 137	34	36	48	72	82	51	48	37	33	55	60	55	72	119
Malta... 181	4	40	5	4	8	18	8	23	25	12	19	8	72	97
Netherlands................................ 138	1,685	2,043	2,564	3,170	3,151	3,971	5,004	1,186	1,239	2,678	3,262	3,639	4,501	5,531
Norway....................................... 142	1,112	1,104	1,306	1,894	1,687	2,011	2,809	1,017	1,055	1,104	1,164	1,184	1,977	1,560
Portugal...................................... 182	239	271	309	310	351	251	319	152	148	164	235	245	331	284
Slovenia...................................... 961	29	37	38	49	74	141	145	30	30	33	50	56	79	103
Spain... 184	1,073	1,146	1,469	1,614	1,603	1,926	2,474	597	482	576	692	787	878	1,152
Sweden....................................... 144	3,671	3,826	5,274	6,826	7,058	8,123	9,645	3,321	3,643	6,026	7,382	8,342	9,668	11,241
Switzerland................................. 146	641	625	580	660	619	840	849	415	381	404	447	464	457	499
United Kingdom.......................... 112	4,152	4,287	4,249	4,304	4,372	5,028	5,237	2,092	1,902	2,262	2,375	2,548	3,234	4,036
Developing Countries............. 202	**12,377**	**13,061**	**16,592**	**21,356**	**24,349**	**28,654**	**33,585**	**7,653**	**7,835**	**11,011**	**14,418**	**18,364**	**22,090**	**26,616**
Africa....................................... 607	**547**	**540**	**712**	**1,037**	**1,164**	**1,469**	**1,862**	**202**	**166**	**188**	**388**	**237**	**374**	**401**
Algeria.. 612	66	73	93	121	90	131	205	—	—	2	—	—	61	—
Angola.. 614	1	1	1	3	1	3	12	—	—	—	—	—	—	—
Benin... 638	1	1	1	3	1	1	1	—	—	—	—	—	—	—
Botswana.................................... 616	2	2	1	3	1	1	9	—	—	—	19	8	—	18
Burkina Faso............................... 748	—	2	1	8	1	3	2	—	—	—	—	—	—	—
Burundi....................................... 618	—	—	—	—	—	—	—	—	—	1	—	2	1	1
Cameroon.................................... 622	8	5	48	10	5	5	8	—	—	—	—	—	5	1
Chad... 628	—	—	1	—	9	—	1	—	—	—	—	—	—	—
Congo, Dem. Rep. of.................. 636	—	—	1	1	1	1	2	91	76	58	253	117	125	194
Congo, Republic of..................... 634	1	1	1	1	1	3	3	—	—	—	—	—	—	—
Côte d'Ivoire............................... 662	10	9	8	5	6	7	8	11	2	3	3	8	3	5
Djibouti....................................... 611	—	1	1	2	5	7	7	—	—	—	—	—	—	—
Equatorial Guinea....................... 642	—	2	1	—	—	—	—	—	—	—	—	—	—	—
Eritrea... 643	1	1	1	1	1	—	—	—	—	—	—	—	—	—
Ethiopia...................................... 644	4	3	10	31	14	17	10	2	1	3	3	4	5	7
Gabon... 646	—	1	1	1	—	7	2	—	—	—	—	—	—	—
Ghana... 652	7	6	9	18	12	22	18	1	2	1	3	4	2	1
Guinea.. 656	—	1	6	24	7	4	2	—	—	—	—	—	—	—
Kenya.. 664	14	14	8	20	14	31	59	7	6	10	9	19	14	17
Liberia... 668	—	—	—	—	—	1	1	—	—	—	—	—	—	—
Madagascar................................ 674	1	—	1	1	—	6	31	1	—	—	—	1	1	—
Malawi.. 676	2	1	1	2	4	3	8	1	1	—	—	—	7	1
Mali.. 678	2	3	2	6	—	—	2	—	—	—	—	—	—	—
Mauritania.................................. 682	—	—	—	—	3	2	4	7	3	—	2	6	3	24
Mauritius.................................... 684	3	5	13	84	180	95	29	2	1	1	1	1	—	—
Morocco...................................... 686	69	61	61	105	83	96	142	8	5	2	4	4	16	22
Mozambique............................... 688	2	2	3	2	7	8	10	—	—	—	—	—	9	3
Namibia....................................... 728	1	1	1	2	1	8	18	—	—	—	—	—	—	—
Niger... 692	2	—	—	—	2	1	—	—	—	—	9	—	—	—
Nigeria.. 694	20	20	15	35	61	123	143	—	—	—	—	—	—	—
Rwanda....................................... 714	1	—	—	—	—	—	3	—	—	—	—	—	—	—
Senegal....................................... 722	2	16	3	4	17	50	15	—	—	—	—	—	—	—
Seychelles................................... 718	—	7	—	1	1	6	17	3	2	1	2	—	—	—
Sierra Leone................................ 724	—	1	—	1	—	1	4	—	—	—	—	—	—	—
South Africa................................ 199	240	221	303	372	474	675	749	48	42	53	44	36	98	92
Sudan.. 732	16	3	20	58	61	10	38	—	9	11	1	2	2	2
Swaziland................................... 734	—	1	—	—	—	—	—	7	6	12	10	9	6	1
Tanzania..................................... 738	9	11	15	18	15	19	106	2	2	1	1	1	2	6
Togo.. 742	—	—	—	—	—	—	—	—	—	—	—	5	—	—
Tunisia.. 744	44	47	60	72	58	59	89	2	6	2	4	5	3	1
Uganda....................................... 746	2	2	4	6	11	23	59	—	1	—	—	1	—	—
Zambia.. 754	10	10	11	11	10	36	32	1	1	22	17	3	6	2
Zimbabwe................................... 698	5	7	8	5	4	4	8	8	2	1	1	1	4	—

	Exports 2001	2002	2003	2004	2005	2006	2007	Imports 2001	2002	2003	2004	2005	2006	2007
	Millions of U.S. Dollars							*Millions of U.S. Dollars*						
Asia.................................... 507	**3,575**	**3,170**	**3,761**	**5,246**	**4,625**	**5,496**	**6,727**	**1,687**	**1,790**	**2,437**	**3,073**	**4,142**	**5,948**	**7,324**
Afghanistan, I.S. of.................... 512	—	—	1	—	1	3	4	7	7	7	6	11	13	11
Bangladesh.............................. 513	16	12	15	24	17	29	45	22	24	24	29	22	25	27
Brunei Darussalam...................... 516	—	—	2	—	—	—	—	—	—	—	—	—	—	—
Cambodia................................ 522	—	—	—	11	18	10	—	1	2	1	1	1	—	1
China,P.R.: Mainland.................. 924	1,132	1,151	1,485	2,455	1,945	2,483	2,962	774	907	1,287	1,712	2,416	3,716	4,518
China,P.R.:Hong Kong................. 532	423	510	463	463	407	415	337	83	64	121	97	76	77	73
China,P.R.:Macao....................... 546	1	3	2	1	2	1	2	4	4	3	4	2	3	4
Fiji.. 819	6	—	—	—	—	—	—	—	—	—	—	—	—	—
French Polynesia....................... 887	—	11	1	2	1	1	5	—	—	—	—	—	—	—
India...................................... 534	196	182	237	329	344	413	624	61	60	75	105	118	143	195
Indonesia................................ 536	82	69	85	159	238	235	227	127	109	164	112	162	137	89
Korea..................................... 542	347	358	360	386	517	489	799	116	97	136	180	323	548	884
Lao People's Dem.Rep................ 544	1	—	—	15	—	—	1	2	1	1	—	1	—	1
Malaysia................................. 548	144	122	118	171	188	220	274	159	170	165	227	246	298	316
Maldives................................. 556	4	1	—	2	1	—	—	—	—	—	—	—	—	—
Mongolia................................. 948	3	2	2	2	2	3	8	—	—	—	—	—	—	—
Myanmar................................. 518	1	1	—	1	1	—	—	1	—	—	—	—	1	2
Nepal..................................... 558	2	1	1	1	1	1	1	—	—	—	—	—	—	—
New Caledonia.......................... 839	1	1	2	2	3	4	3	16	13	7	—	—	—	—
Pakistan................................. 564	18	29	38	110	117	123	162	15	16	19	23	20	23	28
Papua New Guinea..................... 853	2	2	1	—	—	—	1	—	1	—	1	—	—	—
Philippines.............................. 566	335	113	172	146	88	127	121	29	29	27	61	101	74	58
Samoa.................................... 862	1	—	—	—	—	—	—	—	—	—	—	—	—	—
Singapore............................... 576	253	167	208	290	219	291	354	35	46	63	84	64	73	100
Sri Lanka................................ 524	11	13	37	41	10	26	11	3	3	4	5	6	7	8
Taiwan Province of China............ 528	212	135	337	364	263	352	493	146	144	203	252	348	540	702
Thailand................................. 578	356	254	153	199	196	213	208	65	66	102	137	184	214	239
Vietnam.................................. 582	28	35	42	73	45	54	85	21	24	28	37	42	53	68
Europe.................................. 170	**6,038**	**6,834**	**8,717**	**11,262**	**13,562**	**16,194**	**19,038**	**5,222**	**5,352**	**7,680**	**10,022**	**12,838**	**14,110**	**16,923**
Albania.................................. 914	23	3	3	12	4	5	5	—	—	—	—	—	—	—
Armenia................................. 911	2	2	3	5	5	5	6	—	—	—	—	5	7	—
Azerbaijan.............................. 912	5	7	9	17	62	188	113	—	—	—	15	21	—	—
Belarus.................................. 913	22	23	32	46	46	72	87	5	9	12	35	27	34	69
Bosnia & Herzegovina................. 963	1	2	5	3	5	12	6	9	—	1	—	—	—	2
Bulgaria................................. 918	40	29	28	32	38	77	114	6	10	9	10	14	67	50
Croatia.................................. 960	31	32	36	41	33	48	67	3	4	6	8	12	16	21
Czech Republic......................... 935	212	201	245	263	275	406	501	203	187	227	239	343	361	556
Estonia.................................. 939	981	1,183	1,322	1,739	1,688	2,225	2,392	1,081	926	1,189	1,287	1,836	1,626	1,780
Faroe Islands........................... 816	1	3	2	3	2	2	4	—	2	3	3	2	2	—
Georgia.................................. 915	10	4	3	8	22	22	21	—	—	—	—	—	9	8
Gibraltar................................ 823	—	—	—	10	1	—	8	—	—	—	—	—	—	—
Hungary.................................. 944	288	323	418	561	430	528	485	125	147	271	489	839	451	433
Kazakhstan.............................. 916	88	68	91	188	219	283	464	155	142	199	229	224	372	423
Kosovo................................... 967	—	—	—	—	—	—	1	—	—	—	—	—	—	—
Kyrgyz Republic........................ 917	4	3	2	5	3	14	16	—	—	—	—	—	—	—
Latvia.................................... 941	269	303	364	424	517	589	649	57	69	90	119	164	164	301
Lithuania................................ 946	212	254	301	332	386	467	566	56	59	83	73	106	103	179
Macedonia, FYR........................ 962	6	5	8	8	8	8	12	2	1	—	—	—	—	—
Moldova.................................. 921	4	9	32	13	19	11	14	—	—	—	—	—	—	—
Montenegro, Rep. of................... 943	—	—	—	—	—	1	9	—	—	—	—	—	—	—
Poland.................................... 964	807	752	979	1,030	1,279	1,577	2,128	287	282	341	487	610	727	946
Romania.................................. 968	30	39	57	59	114	164	229	6	8	17	26	33	44	66
Russia.................................... 922	2,529	2,978	3,978	5,458	7,136	7,823	9,250	3,076	3,317	4,940	6,598	8,129	9,645	11,409
Serbia, Rep. of......................... 942	—	—	—	—	—	23	60	—	—	—	—	—	6	12
Serbia & Montenegro.................. 965	5	8	18	21	17	—	—	2	2	3	4	5	—	—
Slovak Republic........................ 936	69	81	101	90	77	135	165	49	53	58	102	133	190	226
Tajikistan............................... 923	1	—	1	1	—	2	2	—	—	—	—	—	—	—
Turkey.................................... 186	235	330	427	553	765	900	914	80	113	200	265	300	246	369
Turkmenistan........................... 925	2	2	4	3	4	6	8	—	—	—	—	—	—	—
Ukraine.................................. 926	138	177	236	322	386	583	714	17	21	29	32	35	39	64
Uzbekistan.............................. 927	19	14	12	12	19	18	28	—	—	—	—	—	1	9
Europe n.s............................... 884	1	—	—	—	—	1	—	—	—	—	—	—	1	1
Middle East............................ 407	**1,165**	**1,555**	**2,398**	**2,561**	**3,582**	**3,682**	**4,170**	**121**	**85**	**82**	**114**	**135**	**123**	**146**
Bahrain................................... 419	10	17	26	66	49	57	120	9	—	1	3	5	7	10
Egypt..................................... 469	142	150	127	192	260	301	364	6	8	5	5	6	9	15
Iran, I.R. of............................. 429	97	75	169	186	199	248	172	1	1	2	2	2	9	1
Iraq....................................... 433	9	8	26	23	169	117	153	—	—	—	—	—	—	—
Israel.................................... 436	164	180	156	172	197	225	237	58	65	67	90	110	79	89
Jordan................................... 439	29	31	33	86	171	243	322	7	5	4	5	3	7	8
Kuwait................................... 443	33	57	60	103	130	141	174	14	1	—	1	1	1	—
Lebanon.................................. 446	34	40	31	70	49	49	84	18	—	—	—	—	—	1
Libya..................................... 672	4	10	9	9	17	20	19	—	—	—	—	—	—	—
Oman..................................... 449	14	17	15	19	21	35	74	—	—	—	—	—	—	—
Qatar..................................... 453	5	9	8	31	46	95	145	—	—	—	—	—	—	1
Saudi Arabia............................ 456	241	358	432	252	800	1,043	1,078	1	1	1	1	1	1	7

	Exports							Imports						
	2001	2002	2003	2004	2005	2006	2007	2001	2002	2003	2004	2005	2006	2007
	Millions of U.S. Dollars							Millions of U.S. Dollars						
Syrian Arab Republic 463	25	29	37	37	48	45	61	—	—	—	—	—	—	1
United Arab Emirates 466	355	548	1,262	1,250	1,406	1,041	1,153	7	4	2	6	6	8	12
West Bank/Gaza Strip 487	—	—	—	—	—	—	1	—	—	—	—	—	—	—
Yemen, Republic of 474	3	26	7	65	20	23	14	—	—	—	—	—	—	—
Western Hemisphere 207	**1,053**	**961**	**1,005**	**1,250**	**1,416**	**1,814**	**1,788**	**421**	**442**	**625**	**822**	**1,011**	**1,536**	**1,821**
Antigua and Barbuda 311	1	1	14	2	1	17	10	—	—	—	—	—	—	2
Argentina 213	66	24	58	65	108	97	106	52	46	79	94	56	102	132
Aruba 314	—	—	—	—	1	12	1	—	—	—	—	—	—	—
Bahamas, The 313	—	2	17	4	2	6	7	—	—	5	1	—	—	—
Barbados 316	1	—	—	1	1	1	—	—	—	—	—	—	—	—
Belize 339	—	—	—	—	1	9	—	—	—	—	—	—	9	16
Bermuda 319	—	10	1	1	3	1	—	—	—	—	—	—	—	—
Bolivia 218	4	4	1	3	5	7	8	—	—	1	—	1	—	—
Brazil 223	387	335	244	390	299	541	656	151	149	214	256	405	529	563
Chile 228	74	112	193	157	391	212	199	66	67	93	141	179	291	314
Colombia 233	42	43	69	72	147	135	97	56	55	68	70	29	64	51
Costa Rica 238	9	16	27	26	15	15	13	15	7	20	18	18	5	2
Dominica 321	1	—	—	—	—	—	—	—	—	—	—	—	—	—
Dominican Republic 243	9	14	8	28	8	26	18	2	12	32	80	74	131	210
Ecuador 248	14	57	68	41	55	28	43	3	4	7	5	3	1	1
El Salvador 253	26	8	9	10	10	32	15	2	3	2	1	1	1	1
Greenland 326	2	2	2	2	3	4	6	—	—	—	—	—	—	—
Grenada 328	—	—	—	—	4	—	1	—	—	—	—	—	—	—
Guatemala 258	8	103	10	16	17	12	19	12	5	7	5	8	12	15
Guyana 336	—	—	—	1	—	6	1	7	1	4	—	—	—	—
Haiti 263	1	1	1	—	1	1	—	—	—	—	—	—	—	—
Honduras 268	2	—	13	125	8	22	11	4	5	4	6	6	6	6
Jamaica 343	5	1	10	7	6	29	5	1	2	1	4	7	—	14
Mexico 273	218	107	157	166	168	228	273	22	22	29	41	87	139	137
Netherlands Antilles 353	6	2	3	3	6	4	5	—	—	—	2	—	—	11
Nicaragua 278	1	1	1	2	2	2	2	3	4	4	6	9	9	12
Panama 283	8	11	6	9	13	11	22	3	1	1	—	1	—	—
Paraguay 288	—	1	1	2	3	2	4	—	—	—	—	—	—	—
Peru 293	41	34	30	48	61	60	67	14	51	41	75	113	207	284
St. Kitts and Nevis 361	—	6	—	—	3	3	1	—	—	—	—	—	—	—
St. Lucia 362	1	—	1	26	17	—	—	—	—	—	—	—	—	—
St. Vincent & Grens 364	—	—	10	—	1	—	—	—	—	—	—	—	—	—
Suriname 366	1	5	—	1	1	1	1	—	—	—	—	—	—	—
Trinidad and Tobago 369	5	2	3	1	1	3	9	3	—	—	—	—	—	—
Uruguay 298	9	4	5	7	12	202	93	2	6	10	14	12	21	51
Venezuela, Rep. Bol. 299	103	52	23	30	43	74	79	1	2	3	—	—	7	—
Western Hem. n.s. 399	9	4	18	4	1	11	11	—	—	—	—	—	—	—
Other Countries n.i.e. 910	**4**	**2**	**3**	**5**	**12**	**8**	**6**	**1**	**—**	**1**	**8**	**—**	**1**	**8**
Cuba 928	3	2	2	5	10	8	5	—	—	1	8	—	—	8
North Korea 954	1	—	1	—	2	—	—	—	—	—	—	—	—	—
Special Categories 899	**251**	**254**	**—**	**—**	**51**	**70**	**59**	**3,352**	**3,546**	**—**	**1**	**—**	**—**	**—**
Memorandum Items														
European Union 998	25,874	27,039	31,936	35,643	37,003	43,988	50,801	19,297	19,710	29,029	34,615	39,104	44,311	52,250
Oil Exporting Ctys 999	1,028	1,297	2,197	2,218	3,219	3,302	3,623	152	117	175	122	173	224	110
Non-Oil Develop.Ctys 201	11,349	11,763	14,396	19,138	21,130	25,352	29,962	7,502	7,718	10,836	14,296	18,191	21,865	26,505
PERCENT DISTRIBUTION														
Industrial Countries 101	**70.8**	**70.3**	**68.8**	**65.3**	**62.7**	**62.8**	**62.6**	**66.3**	**65.9**	**74.1**	**72.0**	**68.7**	**68.2**	**67.4**
Developing Countries 202	**28.6**	**29.1**	**31.2**	**34.7**	**37.2**	**37.1**	**37.3**	**23.4**	**23.5**	**25.9**	**28.0**	**31.3**	**31.8**	**32.6**
Africa 607	**1.3**	**1.2**	**1.3**	**1.7**	**1.8**	**1.9**	**2.1**	**.6**	**.5**	**.4**	**.8**	**.4**	**.5**	**.5**
Asia 507	**8.3**	**7.1**	**7.1**	**8.5**	**7.1**	**7.1**	**7.5**	**5.2**	**5.4**	**5.7**	**6.0**	**7.1**	**8.6**	**9.0**
Europe 170	**14.0**	**15.2**	**16.4**	**18.3**	**20.7**	**21.0**	**21.1**	**16.0**	**16.0**	**18.1**	**19.5**	**21.9**	**20.3**	**20.7**
Middle East 407	**2.7**	**3.5**	**4.5**	**4.2**	**5.5**	**4.8**	**4.6**	**.4**	**.3**	**.2**	**.2**	**.2**	**.2**	**.2**
Western Hemisphere 207	**2.4**	**2.1**	**1.9**	**2.0**	**2.2**	**2.3**	**2.0**	**1.3**	**1.3**	**1.5**	**1.6**	**1.7**	**2.2**	**2.2**
ANNUAL PERCENT CHANGE														
World 001	**–5.7**	**3.7**	**18.7**	**15.7**	**6.2**	**18.1**	**16.6**	**–4.8**	**2.2**	**27.4**	**21.0**	**14.1**	**18.3**	**17.7**
Industrial Countries 101	**–5.5**	**2.9**	**16.2**	**9.8**	**2.0**	**18.4**	**16.2**	**–15.5**	**1.6**	**43.3**	**17.6**	**8.9**	**17.4**	**16.4**
Developing Countries 202	**–6.4**	**5.5**	**27.0**	**28.7**	**14.0**	**17.7**	**17.2**	**–3.1**	**2.4**	**40.5**	**30.9**	**27.4**	**20.3**	**20.5**
Africa 607	**–14.5**	**–1.1**	**31.7**	**45.7**	**12.2**	**26.3**	**26.7**	**5.4**	**–18.0**	**13.4**	**106.4**	**–38.9**	**57.7**	**7.3**
Asia 507	**–11.0**	**–11.3**	**18.6**	**39.5**	**–11.8**	**18.8**	**22.4**	**–20.0**	**6.1**	**36.2**	**26.1**	**34.8**	**43.6**	**23.1**
Europe 170	**–2.7**	**13.2**	**27.5**	**29.2**	**20.4**	**19.4**	**17.6**	**3.1**	**2.5**	**43.5**	**30.5**	**28.1**	**9.9**	**19.9**
Middle East 407	**2.8**	**33.4**	**54.3**	**6.8**	**39.9**	**2.8**	**13.3**	**124.8**	**–30.2**	**–3.6**	**39.2**	**19.1**	**–9.3**	**19.0**
Western Hemisphere 207	**–14.4**	**–8.8**	**4.6**	**24.4**	**13.3**	**28.0**	**–1.4**	**–12.2**	**5.0**	**41.4**	**31.5**	**23.0**	**51.9**	**18.6**
Other Countries n.i.e. 910	**5.4**	**–51.4**	**47.9**	**71.3**	**135.2**	**–30.0**	**–33.2**	**–91.6**	**–29.2**	**96.9**	**—**	**–97.1**	**176.4**	**—**

	Exports 2001	Exports 2002	Exports 2003	Exports 2004	Exports 2005	Exports 2006	Exports 2007	Imports 2001	Imports 2002	Imports 2003	Imports 2004	Imports 2005	Imports 2006	Imports 2007
	Millions of U.S. Dollars							Millions of U.S. Dollars						
IFS World Total	**297,225**	**311,966**	**365,646**	**424,910**	**443,771**	**488,063**	**541,900**	**301,962**	**312,024**	**370,494**	**441,909**	**484,493**	**536,309**	**616,890**
DOTS World Total............ 001	**322,885**	**331,109**	**392,069**	**451,741**	**462,851**	**495,509**	**553,257**	**328,592**	**328,309**	**398,661**	**470,873**	**503,791**	**541,802**	**615,793**
Industrial Countries............ 101	**247,591**	**251,982**	**299,523**	**340,409**	**337,956**	**363,051**	**397,767**	**263,642**	**262,918**	**317,929**	**370,351**	**381,218**	**412,156**	**463,340**
United States............ 111	27,730	25,953	26,297	30,326	32,956	32,631	34,011	24,174	22,277	21,026	23,747	25,489	24,762	26,912
Canada............ 156	2,954	2,779	2,820	3,251	3,189	3,445	3,602	1,900	2,095	2,244	2,252	2,443	2,323	3,019
Australia............ 193	1,252	1,629	2,218	3,094	3,070	2,745	3,181	707	793	1,046	1,161	1,220	1,294	1,230
Japan............ 158	4,920	5,318	6,085	6,773	6,817	7,143	7,909	6,562	6,314	7,433	8,520	7,919	7,821	8,316
New Zealand............ 196	209	234	469	606	605	393	363	175	194	222	239	227	202	271
Austria............ 122	3,120	3,274	3,656	4,551	4,268	4,628	4,978	3,270	3,647	4,148	4,472	4,614	4,739	5,520
Belgium............ 124	21,882	22,726	28,662	32,638	33,043	35,926	40,441	28,977	30,203	37,804	46,641	54,082	60,179	69,900
Cyprus............ 423	499	455	464	389	305	494	504	279	130	188	46	40	177	41
Denmark............ 128	2,413	2,664	3,164	3,411	3,278	3,651	3,940	2,627	2,816	3,420	3,954	3,996	3,993	4,118
Finland............ 172	1,700	1,540	2,124	2,322	2,129	2,396	2,758	2,035	2,111	2,288	2,482	2,479	2,686	3,282
Germany............ 134	48,129	49,656	60,115	67,934	68,125	77,062	82,320	61,466	63,642	78,101	90,443	95,345	102,439	116,530
Greece............ 174	2,430	2,512	3,395	4,347	3,892	4,128	5,194	626	641	1,116	755	659	953	836
Iceland............ 176	99	61	120	97	128	168	136	70	88	89	60	48	36	32
Ireland............ 178	2,833	2,881	2,703	3,426	3,512	3,406	4,001	4,840	4,726	5,833	6,428	7,395	7,242	8,023
Italy............ 136	27,300	29,739	36,318	40,560	40,341	44,054	49,348	28,379	28,968	36,389	41,486	41,789	45,242	51,718
Luxembourg............ 137	2,361	1,972	3,151	3,247	2,141	2,292	2,585	2,442	1,918	3,335	3,997	2,888	3,325	3,567
Malta............ 181	431	549	678	820	593	724	970	219	200	244	366	362	426	375
Netherlands............ 138	12,748	12,761	14,843	17,227	18,008	19,942	22,609	23,175	23,049	27,839	31,729	33,033	36,738	42,828
Norway............ 142	1,101	1,214	1,419	1,666	1,762	1,968	2,252	5,838	5,134	6,107	7,890	7,171	7,533	7,445
Portugal............ 182	6,689	5,641	7,181	7,722	5,822	6,123	6,826	5,493	4,315	6,054	6,995	4,608	4,970	5,612
Slovenia............ 961	980	1,101	1,382	1,707	1,647	1,623	1,657	607	772	1,140	1,193	1,313	1,258	1,595
Spain............ 184	28,585	29,760	37,605	42,797	44,672	47,655	51,532	21,045	22,133	29,397	34,724	35,231	37,827	44,022
Sweden............ 144	4,420	4,454	5,040	5,850	5,494	6,311	7,337	4,055	4,178	4,985	5,893	6,184	6,756	8,150
Switzerland............ 146	11,429	10,526	12,687	13,281	13,585	13,034	14,240	9,243	8,550	9,835	11,924	12,899	13,401	15,293
United Kingdom............ 112	31,377	32,583	36,925	42,367	38,573	41,111	45,071	25,438	24,026	27,644	32,956	29,783	35,832	34,705
Developing Countries............ 202	**71,582**	**73,551**	**87,571**	**102,716**	**117,223**	**124,146**	**143,404**	**62,976**	**62,900**	**77,788**	**97,087**	**118,689**	**126,700**	**147,860**
Africa............ 607	**16,971**	**17,149**	**20,011**	**22,465**	**27,050**	**24,139**	**27,886**	**13,704**	**13,352**	**16,076**	**17,151**	**22,539**	**21,128**	**23,482**
Algeria............ 612	3,444	3,687	4,301	5,700	5,986	5,040	5,644	3,067	2,762	3,776	3,986	4,795	5,178	4,636
Angola............ 614	148	180	265	279	374	632	745	664	635	694	821	1,743	1,553	2,374
Benin............ 638	207	215	237	239	213	234	361	3	4	5	5	7	10	6
Botswana............ 616	34	15	27	13	7	7	10	4	4	3	6	6	4	5
Burkina Faso............ 748	117	160	240	271	237	261	294	13	15	14	8	9	7	7
Burundi............ 618	13	9	10	16	13	13	21	1	2	2	1	3	2	4
Cameroon............ 622	553	552	715	578	556	624	768	276	281	281	347	379	598	647
Cape Verde............ 624	13	10	14	10	21	13	50	1	5	8	—	—	—	—
Central African Rep............ 626	37	38	37	32	34	42	52	5	5	10	9	12	10	10
Chad............ 628	95	128	90	81	94	90	133	6	4	6	9	16	14	8
Comoros............ 632	21	28	34	25	23	32	26	8	10	17	7	7	6	9
Congo, Dem. Rep. of............ 636	40	78	121	121	130	175	188	7	37	30	14	120	33	145
Congo, Republic of............ 634	194	223	259	266	330	430	606	74	129	86	106	180	180	125
Côte d'Ivoire............ 662	637	634	637	785	699	752	950	576	760	691	627	598	804	667
Djibouti............ 611	92	52	47	50	52	55	67	51	1	2	1	1	—	1
Equatorial Guinea............ 642	25	39	166	70	123	90	116	40	96	104	90	274	187	680
Eritrea............ 643	14	8	10	4	13	4	5	1	—	—	—	2	2	1
Ethiopia............ 644	32	31	68	45	91	86	84	15	15	13	18	27	29	29
Gabon............ 646	825	530	629	643	624	626	694	848	416	351	363	354	402	646
Gambia, The............ 648	19	14	14	13	20	17	14	1	7	—	6	—	3	3
Ghana............ 652	129	106	156	234	187	253	309	77	106	166	171	147	138	222
Guinea............ 656	109	144	132	137	122	165	184	86	65	76	61	84	116	129
Guinea-Bissau............ 654	3	2	4	4	6	6	13	—	—	—	—	—	—	—
Kenya............ 664	119	193	102	134	131	127	218	116	68	75	95	101	99	80
Lesotho............ 666	—	2	—	1	—	1	1	4	1	—	1	—	—	—
Liberia............ 668	1,060	427	22	61	33	13	20	44	98	54	12	16	19	16
Madagascar............ 674	250	168	273	270	288	269	347	308	311	391	424	349	379	428
Malawi............ 676	6	10	9	12	12	12	17	12	10	8	8	11	7	11
Mali............ 678	180	175	213	244	244	275	330	5	7	8	8	12	9	12
Mauritania............ 682	142	137	151	145	227	159	279	81	83	95	96	123	161	176
Mauritius............ 684	417	371	750	325	358	518	485	406	468	750	472	414	341	328
Morocco............ 686	2,525	2,567	3,179	3,578	6,842	4,007	4,773	2,278	2,352	2,764	2,998	5,775	2,986	3,335
Mozambique............ 688	28	125	37	42	32	28	40	1	5	2	15	15	14	16
Namibia............ 728	55	53	66	91	65	9	9	56	101	114	228	141	79	65
Niger............ 692	73	77	85	102	110	111	159	91	59	75	136	156	164	241
Nigeria............ 694	757	979	1,063	1,011	1,323	1,484	1,537	1,180	1,072	1,367	1,201	1,473	2,488	1,759
Rwanda............ 714	8	10	16	22	10	11	12	1	1	1	1	3	6	3
St. Helena............ 856	1	—	—	—	—	16	—	—	—	—	—	—	—	—
São Tomé & Príncipe............ 716	2	2	2	2	2	14	1	—	—	1	1	—	—	1
Senegal............ 722	462	521	574	711	990	840	1,000	182	137	128	155	415	124	172
Seychelles............ 718	38	42	60	52	50	59	75	40	65	68	64	54	68	73
Sierra Leone............ 724	15	14	39	19	13	21	16	1	2	1	1	—	1	2

		Exports							Imports						
		2001	2002	2003	2004	2005	2006	2007	2001	2002	2003	2004	2005	2006	2007
		Millions of U.S. Dollars							*Millions of U.S. Dollars*						
Somalia	726	3	1	1	1	1	2	4	1	—	—	—	—	—	—
South Africa	199	1,061	1,324	1,710	2,132	2,423	2,104	2,207	838	768	936	1,086	1,111	995	1,220
Sudan	732	101	75	132	164	220	320	185	104	45	39	136	87	14	32
Swaziland	734	2	2	1	2	2	2	1	35	32	23	58	35	21	23
Tanzania	738	50	49	58	72	78	50	141	9	7	7	16	15	16	19
Togo	742	99	174	178	179	213	211	265	12	9	10	15	18	16	11
Tunisia	744	2,673	2,718	3,006	3,406	3,375	3,755	4,339	2,039	2,257	2,785	3,212	3,378	3,771	5,020
Uganda	746	27	31	46	35	39	51	58	10	12	15	33	61	60	68
Zambia	754	11	13	18	26	17	17	27	1	3	3	1	3	4	3
Zimbabwe	698	20	15	21	12	11	11	16	23	17	19	18	10	10	15
Asia	**507**	**18,343**	**17,452**	**20,788**	**25,366**	**30,668**	**33,394**	**39,765**	**19,289**	**19,647**	**24,439**	**30,440**	**36,314**	**38,892**	**46,343**
Afghanistan, I.S. of	512	5	14	34	53	31	47	65	—	1	41	5	—	1	2
American Samoa	859	—	—	—	—	2	—	—	—	—	—	—	—	—	—
Bangladesh	513	84	96	118	82	72	116	87	341	351	447	573	569	698	757
Bhutan	514	—	—	—	1	5	—	—	—	—	—	—	—	—	1
Brunei Darussalam	516	8	11	118	10	6	19	9	—	—	—	1	1	1	2
Cambodia	522	48	57	49	50	56	64	75	42	43	45	44	39	49	55
China,P.R.: Mainland	924	3,175	3,524	5,311	6,673	7,806	10,124	12,417	7,471	8,118	10,862	14,494	17,936	19,915	24,687
China,P.R.:Hong Kong	532	3,557	2,633	2,523	2,699	3,420	3,361	3,250	470	412	389	456	519	573	559
China,P.R.:Macao	546	16	21	21	20	15	39	50	114	89	104	98	66	92	75
Fiji	819	14	6	4	13	12	11	7	1	1	1	—	3	1	2
French Polynesia	887	479	700	918	605	896	618	675	93	98	362	155	228	13	17
Guam	829	—	—	—	—	15	17	18	—	—	—	—	—	1	—
India	534	979	1,067	1,229	1,807	2,450	3,315	4,608	1,151	1,200	1,406	1,807	2,245	2,281	2,792
Indonesia	536	454	535	578	522	570	566	754	800	811	903	946	948	1,092	1,191
Kiribati	826	—	23	1	2	—	—	—	—	—	—	9	—	—	—
Korea	542	2,184	2,324	2,304	2,654	2,965	3,625	4,115	1,751	1,771	1,977	2,860	3,415	3,851	3,707
Lao People's Dem.Rep	544	8	8	11	10	12	10	11	37	37	37	48	46	32	29
Malaysia	548	878	774	808	1,023	1,393	1,786	1,959	1,234	1,429	1,452	1,548	1,332	1,474	1,646
Maldives	556	4	7	10	13	20	15	13	—	—	1	4	6	13	16
Mongolia	948	8	6	8	25	15	12	17	2	1	1	3	2	7	14
Myanmar	518	11	29	11	36	14	9	38	79	87	62	78	44	37	20
Nepal	558	15	16	16	11	34	10	12	9	7	9	16	12	14	17
New Caledonia	839	434	564	671	727	640	723	868	140	109	199	175	189	241	301
Pakistan	564	275	296	324	583	542	507	479	287	306	365	434	393	356	408
Papua New Guinea	853	1	2	2	7	2	2	2	1	2	17	9	6	5	7
Philippines	566	462	374	382	444	540	445	864	263	282	267	286	295	324	322
Samoa	862	—	—	—	2	—	—	—	—	—	1	—	—	—	—
Singapore	576	1,878	1,865	2,443	3,550	3,910	4,348	4,952	1,583	1,518	2,176	2,305	3,970	3,222	4,591
Solomon Islands	813	—	—	1	—	1	—	—	—	—	—	—	—	—	—
Sri Lanka	524	178	96	125	149	129	123	171	155	79	81	87	93	122	163
Taiwan Province of China	528	1,974	1,303	1,540	2,136	2,679	2,226	2,260	1,596	1,364	1,519	1,912	1,762	1,908	2,058
Thailand	578	803	757	783	1,012	2,024	841	1,351	1,029	976	1,078	1,374	1,438	1,610	1,849
Tonga	866	2	1	1	—	1	7	1	—	—	—	—	—	—	—
Vanuatu	846	7	3	3	4	3	5	5	—	1	1	2	1	1	1
Vietnam	582	403	341	444	442	389	402	630	638	553	638	712	754	960	1,053
Wallis-Futuna	857	236	11	8	12	10	10	12	—	—	—	—	—	—	—
Europe	**170**	**15,254**	**17,651**	**22,674**	**28,431**	**31,320**	**38,798**	**44,258**	**14,377**	**15,912**	**20,907**	**28,261**	**33,797**	**41,119**	**51,321**
Albania	914	14	14	26	25	21	20	30	2	3	3	4	5	6	6
Armenia	911	11	15	18	54	47	53	77	—	1	1	6	44	2	3
Azerbaijan	912	31	108	56	96	181	59	147	122	155	170	109	492	1,131	2,276
Belarus	913	62	71	98	128	122	158	208	60	96	346	305	459	363	459
Bosnia & Herzegovina	963	48	49	64	58	103	83	89	25	22	46	47	57	85	71
Bulgaria	918	416	407	490	563	627	804	785	333	307	403	505	518	585	599
Croatia	960	325	436	549	550	547	588	587	145	143	154	137	140	142	152
Czech Republic	935	1,954	2,023	2,451	2,923	3,226	3,943	4,567	1,279	1,505	1,765	2,234	3,566	4,753	6,132
Estonia	939	129	155	214	205	229	393	385	83	50	87	312	199	356	319
Faroe Islands	816	1	1	1	2	1	2	2	2	1	4	7	3	4	—
Georgia	915	24	42	72	49	56	52	91	18	2	11	15	16	32	65
Gibraltar	823	82	59	91	114	311	161	83	24	9	71	58	4	—	21
Hungary	944	1,671	1,858	2,220	2,609	2,882	3,382	3,803	1,470	1,548	1,922	2,254	2,557	3,057	3,732
Kazakhstan	916	130	232	309	770	581	840	634	286	484	508	1,502	2,236	2,507	2,783
Kosovo	967	—	—	—	—	8	8	17	—	—	—	—	1	1	—
Kyrgyz Republic	917	3	5	3	5	6	16	14	1	1	1	1	—	2	4
Latvia	941	128	133	163	174	190	288	368	150	71	79	309	427	307	221
Lithuania	946	214	269	366	393	400	540	700	307	315	460	737	822	539	703
Macedonia, FYR	962	54	59	59	58	55	51	61	16	12	10	15	15	12	23
Moldova	921	28	29	132	178	117	51	84	9	11	81	91	84	29	32
Montenegro, Rep. of	943	—	—	—	—	—	14	12	—	—	—	—	—	2	1
Poland	964	3,141	3,605	4,474	5,357	5,854	8,730	8,661	1,735	1,995	2,670	3,706	4,924	6,605	7,884
Romania	968	957	1,116	1,696	2,063	2,471	2,879	3,384	939	1,135	1,459	1,762	1,864	2,129	2,414
Russia	922	2,184	2,266	3,203	4,058	4,600	5,931	7,692	4,470	4,789	6,763	9,016	9,932	11,852	14,393
Serbia, Rep. of	942	—	—	—	—	—	274	401	—	—	—	—	—	195	241
Serbia & Montenegro	965	134	178	248	311	326	—	—	53	70	114	122	146	—	—
Slovak Republic	936	477	596	738	807	1,030	1,396	2,551	310	379	551	632	802	1,236	2,301
Tajikistan	923	1	1	1	3	9	7	6	12	9	11	9	4	14	12
Turkey	186	2,275	3,067	3,862	5,599	5,980	6,539	7,136	2,267	2,541	2,933	3,934	4,101	4,699	5,715
Turkmenistan	925	46	95	79	124	88	87	51	16	10	2	6	25	43	2
Ukraine	926	335	428	586	723	802	996	1,227	182	197	238	361	287	345	531
Uzbekistan	927	108	35	44	39	50	55	70	49	32	25	38	44	63	209
Europe n.s.	884	273	299	358	394	409	405	352	12	19	20	28	24	21	19

	Exports 2001	2002	2003	2004	2005	2006	2007	Imports 2001	2002	2003	2004	2005	2006	2007
	Millions of U.S. Dollars							Millions of U.S. Dollars						
Middle East.......... 407	**10,728**	**11,811**	**14,284**	**16,668**	**17,118**	**17,292**	**18,712**	**7,894**	**7,090**	**8,241**	**10,906**	**15,497**	**15,654**	**16,576**
Bahrain.......... 419	97	95	145	255	115	131	170	108	72	36	133	65	38	86
Egypt.......... 469	997	1,106	1,288	1,437	1,883	1,661	1,646	308	303	420	506	831	1,222	1,022
Iran, I.R. of.......... 429	1,072	1,496	2,362	2,902	2,490	2,385	2,059	737	792	1,186	1,775	2,675	2,979	3,376
Iraq.......... 433	591	443	176	291	263	169	272	887	762	190	343	515	914	1,409
Israel.......... 436	1,263	1,124	1,160	1,248	1,301	1,336	1,542	744	676	732	862	1,011	985	1,233
Jordan.......... 439	244	420	302	322	371	404	319	25	49	74	33	60	15	19
Kuwait.......... 443	319	404	428	529	672	473	646	353	344	579	581	1,042	719	950
Lebanon.......... 446	560	610	934	883	805	767	980	107	25	30	81	44	45	62
Libya.......... 672	237	280	324	279	374	540	679	678	393	920	1,328	1,982	2,410	3,006
Oman.......... 449	166	151	142	131	240	198	485	16	66	13	37	40	22	16
Qatar.......... 453	656	656	913	1,659	1,092	1,914	1,632	465	133	481	31	230	187	47
Saudi Arabia.......... 456	1,566	2,076	2,022	1,846	2,471	2,272	2,659	2,359	2,443	2,644	3,915	4,666	4,869	3,708
Syrian Arab Republic.......... 463	354	285	446	383	569	644	426	589	484	368	439	558	524	783
United Arab Emirates.......... 466	2,455	2,501	3,478	4,113	4,253	4,250	4,966	484	534	545	822	1,683	701	793
West Bank/Gaza Strip.......... 487	6	5	3	7	9	11	11	—	—	1	1	3	6	5
Yemen, Republic of.......... 474	153	164	163	390	219	148	232	36	14	23	22	94	23	68
Western Hemisphere.......... 207	**10,286**	**9,488**	**9,814**	**9,786**	**11,067**	**10,523**	**12,782**	**7,711**	**6,899**	**8,125**	**10,330**	**10,543**	**9,906**	**10,138**
Antigua and Barbuda.......... 311	122	144	7	13	9	15	5	120	520	2	7	4	1	2
Argentina.......... 213	728	324	413	699	770	1,001	1,307	378	383	475	427	486	671	678
Aruba.......... 314	5	5	6	7	16	58	33	29	29	40	140	144	118	183
Bahamas, The.......... 313	62	26	474	53	28	134	30	142	90	109	71	53	46	40
Barbados.......... 316	18	30	26	19	16	37	20	11	11	6	4	15	3	3
Belize.......... 339	2	1	15	1	19	2	8	—	—	10	—	16	1	2
Bermuda.......... 319	1,220	1,059	1,529	1,192	1,229	36	150	1,085	750	915	1,184	1,281	22	24
Bolivia.......... 218	20	18	18	21	18	23	22	29	16	7	12	11	14	15
Brazil.......... 223	2,965	2,749	1,865	2,294	2,844	3,187	4,236	2,617	2,174	2,614	2,810	3,110	3,231	4,114
Chile.......... 228	884	670	476	446	560	554	823	766	670	798	1,363	1,372	2,449	2,449
Colombia.......... 233	296	246	419	290	339	457	538	143	138	188	424	243	233	293
Costa Rica.......... 238	101	123	185	72	144	157	154	42	43	38	61	40	37	50
Dominica.......... 321	4	3	4	6	2	4	7	1	1	2	3	2	3	4
Dominican Republic.......... 243	68	71	59	63	89	87	110	30	44	33	39	26	27	33
Ecuador.......... 248	90	107	217	60	80	75	89	40	81	123	79	114	122	149
El Salvador.......... 253	302	171	175	158	101	143	201	10	12	10	65	61	16	7
Falkland Islands.......... 323	8	—	—	3	—	—	—	—	—	—	—	—	—	—
Greenland.......... 326	—	1	—	—	5	5	6	—	—	—	—	—	—	—
Grenada.......... 328	2	4	4	3	5	5	3	16	2	2	2	2	2	1
Guatemala.......... 258	39	40	37	47	52	89	67	19	15	25	15	31	43	27
Guyana.......... 336	9	9	6	5	5	6	2	10	13	8	13	9	29	42
Haiti.......... 263	25	22	24	20	30	34	24	4	4	4	6	7	7	10
Honduras.......... 268	26	32	21	35	37	23	28	36	26	54	42	53	21	25
Jamaica.......... 343	51	112	165	206	197	25	32	71	57	139	256	358	77	87
Mexico.......... 273	1,358	1,451	1,605	1,928	2,145	2,100	2,557	561	468	520	634	697	715	788
Netherlands Antilles.......... 353	48	45	58	45	48	73	51	27	14	15	7	43	7	10
Nicaragua.......... 278	7	4	4	6	9	9	6	12	11	6	8	5	8	20
Panama.......... 283	181	169	426	489	228	764	889	26	9	17	17	17	20	11
Paraguay.......... 288	22	19	17	24	35	32	33	9	11	13	17	14	20	15
Peru.......... 293	104	106	106	108	105	111	165	111	106	115	122	156	228	237
St. Kitts and Nevis.......... 361	2	2	3	1	12	3	8	—	—	—	—	—	—	—
St. Lucia.......... 362	6	7	6	7	27	85	19	20	1	—	—	56	221	34
St. Pierre-Miquelon.......... 363	20	21	24	24	23	26	27	—	1	1	1	1	1	1
St. Vincent & Grens.......... 364	62	116	140	85	229	21	10	78	59	117	87	187	56	21
Suriname.......... 366	6	42	6	8	11	10	11	56	45	64	82	82	116	110
Trinidad and Tobago.......... 369	36	38	39	44	87	45	53	189	205	251	338	268	368	281
Uruguay.......... 298	108	59	73	83	98	132	141	25	26	31	37	41	46	45
Venezuela, Rep. Bol.......... 299	363	318	297	285	389	551	606	264	250	363	271	434	703	250
Western Hem. n.s.......... 399	915	1,124	866	937	1,026	407	309	729	612	1,007	1,686	1,106	226	79
Other Countries n.i.e.......... 910	**228**	**205**	**156**	**107**	**137**	**123**	**122**	**41**	**45**	**29**	**24**	**35**	**38**	**51**
Cuba.......... 928	221	198	152	100	129	119	119	38	43	28	23	34	36	49
North Korea.......... 954	7	7	4	7	8	4	3	3	1	1	1	1	2	1
Countries & Areas n.s.......... 898	**2,797**	**4,337**	**3,681**	**6,753**	**6,542**	**6,101**	**9,875**	**1,550**	**1,888**	**2,155**	**2,499**	**3,696**	**2,906**	**4,529**
Special Categories.......... 899	**686**	**1,018**	**1,131**	**1,737**	**839**	**2,081**	**2,083**	**383**	**558**	**737**	**897**	**—**	**—**	**—**
Memorandum Items														
European Union.......... 998	205,611	212,907	258,032	293,782	289,654	320,196	353,108	220,309	223,337	277,460	324,742	337,099	371,637	422,113
Oil Exporting Ctys.......... 999	12,079	13,525	16,084	19,268	20,123	19,842	21,938	11,290	10,362	12,968	15,236	20,484	22,262	21,139
Non-Oil Develop.Ctys.......... 201	59,504	60,026	71,487	83,448	97,100	104,303	121,466	51,686	52,538	64,820	81,851	98,205	104,437	126,722
PERCENT DISTRIBUTION														
Industrial Countries.......... 101	**76.7**	**76.1**	**76.4**	**75.4**	**73.0**	**73.3**	**71.9**	**80.2**	**80.1**	**79.7**	**78.7**	**75.7**	**76.1**	**75.2**
Developing Countries.......... 202	**22.2**	**22.2**	**22.3**	**22.7**	**25.3**	**25.1**	**25.9**	**19.2**	**19.2**	**19.5**	**20.6**	**23.6**	**23.4**	**24.0**
Africa.......... 607	**5.3**	**5.2**	**5.1**	**5.0**	**5.8**	**4.9**	**5.0**	**4.2**	**4.1**	**4.0**	**3.6**	**4.5**	**3.9**	**3.8**
Asia.......... 507	**5.7**	**5.3**	**5.3**	**5.6**	**6.6**	**6.7**	**7.2**	**5.9**	**6.0**	**6.1**	**6.5**	**7.2**	**7.2**	**7.5**
Europe.......... 170	**4.7**	**5.3**	**5.8**	**6.3**	**6.8**	**7.8**	**8.0**	**4.4**	**4.8**	**5.2**	**6.0**	**6.7**	**7.6**	**8.3**
Middle East.......... 407	**3.3**	**3.6**	**3.6**	**3.7**	**3.7**	**3.5**	**3.4**	**2.4**	**2.2**	**2.1**	**2.3**	**3.1**	**2.9**	**2.7**
Western Hemisphere.......... 207	**3.2**	**2.9**	**2.5**	**2.2**	**2.4**	**2.1**	**2.3**	**2.3**	**2.1**	**2.0**	**2.2**	**2.1**	**1.8**	**1.6**
Other Countries n.i.e.......... 910	**.1**	**.1**	**—**	**—**	**—**	**—**	**—**	**—**	**—**	**—**	**—**	**—**	**—**	**—**

	Exports							Imports						
	2001	2002	2003	2004	2005	2006	2007	2001	2002	2003	2004	2005	2006	2007
ANNUAL PERCENT CHANGE														
World.......... 001	–.2	2.5	18.4	15.2	2.5	7.1	11.7	–1.0	–.1	21.4	18.1	7.0	7.5	13.7
Industrial Countries.......... 101	–1.4	1.8	18.9	13.7	–.7	7.4	9.6	–1.2	–.3	20.9	16.5	2.9	8.1	12.4
Developing Countries.......... 202	4.4	2.8	19.1	17.3	14.1	5.9	15.5	–.1	–.1	23.7	24.8	22.2	6.7	16.7
Africa.......... 607	—	1.0	16.7	12.3	20.4	–10.8	15.5	13.9	–2.6	20.4	6.7	31.4	–6.3	11.1
Asia.......... 507	3.6	–4.9	19.1	22.0	20.9	8.9	19.1	–9.6	1.9	24.4	24.6	19.3	7.1	19.2
Europe.......... 170	2.0	15.7	28.5	25.4	10.2	23.9	14.1	8.3	10.7	31.4	35.2	19.6	21.7	24.8
Middle East.......... 407	14.8	10.1	20.9	16.7	2.7	1.0	8.2	–14.0	–10.2	16.2	32.3	42.1	1.0	5.9
Western Hemisphere.......... 207	7.6	–7.8	3.4	–.3	13.1	–4.9	21.5	6.4	–10.5	17.8	27.1	2.1	–6.0	2.3
Other Countries n.i.e.......... 910	–8.1	–9.9	–24.0	–31.5	28.3	–10.3	–.8	7.5	8.9	–34.2	–19.3	49.6	6.7	34.4

	Exports							Imports						
	2001	2002	2003	2004	2005	2006	2007	2001	2002	2003	2004	2005	2006	2007
	Millions of U.S. Dollars							Millions of U.S. Dollars						
IFS World Total	**443.6**	**495.0**	**787.6**	**1,035.6**	**1,089.9**	**1,349.2**	**2,165.0**	**931.8**	**1,012.6**	**1,532.2**	**1,641.5**	**1,774.0**	**2,117.4**	**2,836.0**
DOTS World Total 001	**425.0**	**448.0**	**731.1**	**999.4**	**996.2Y**	**1,377.7Y**	**2,369.4Y**	**931.4**	**1,007.5**	**1,541.0**	**1,636.3**	**1,790.5Y**	**2,014.7Y**	**2,603.8Y**
Industrial Countries 101	**311.7**	**316.6**	**479.5**	**580.9**	**613.3Y**	**890.8Y**	**1,441.2Y**	**777.6**	**800.5**	**1,238.4**	**1,243.0**	**1,321.2Y**	**1,482.5Y**	**1,893.9Y**
United States 111	10.70	9.52	10.36	27.35	25.00V	47.09V	73.09V	36.47	44.10	55.88	51.43	42.13V	48.18V	63.58V
Canada 156	.63	—	.03	.03	.65V	.41V	.20V	2.72	2.12	2.99	4.76	11.24V	6.84V	24.00V
Australia 193	32.70	38.01	52.43	61.38	37.33V	63.54V	91.75V	150.79	129.22	145.94	148.40	234.91V	227.60V	313.94V
Japan 158	94.59	89.69	156.57	219.88	210.32V	239.27V	477.05V	28.92	32.84	40.26	50.16	39.72V	45.87V	51.31V
New Zealand 196	.33	.50	.48	.64	.52V	.43V	.97V	45.86	51.12	65.74	79.95	94.92V	96.68V	134.28V
Austria 122	—	—	—	—	.04V	.02V	.03V	4.99	2.51	2.53	10.39	2.72V	2.98V	6.84V
Belgium 124	9.52	2.47	.02	19.53	44.52V	100.35V	245.41V	12.50	15.24	21.18	24.81	29.20V	64.47V	43.93V
Cyprus 423	—	—	—	—	—Y	—V	—V	.01	.01	.01	.04	—V	—V	—V
Denmark 128	—	.01	—	—	.04V	—V	.01V	3.50	3.82	4.63	5.57	3.63V	5.17V	4.36V
Finland 172	10.33	8.43	5.66	—	—V	—V	.01V	1.47	.86	2.06	3.96	3.06V	4.91V	3.21V
France 132	109.97	102.66	138.30	164.97	171.48V	218.71V	273.96V	373.05	399.60	710.39	659.82	704.30V	795.28V	954.55V
Germany 134	.04	.10	.06	.19	.88V	2.05V	.29V	29.93	30.23	54.02	63.18	50.32V	61.40V	119.21V
Greece 174	—	—	—	—	.02V	—V	—V	.38	.43	.85	.74	.03V	.16V	.26V
Iceland 176	—	—	—	—	—V	—V	—V	.06	.06	.07	.07	.01V	—V	—V
Ireland 178	—	—	—	—	.22V	.41V	.23V	2.15	1.67	2.32	2.68	2.02V	2.30V	4.11V
Italy 136	9.40	26.31	36.65	12.76	31.85V	82.72V	72.76V	27.14	28.76	48.70	46.08	35.61V	46.07V	60.90V
Luxembourg 137	—	—	—	—	.01V	.01V	—V	1.59	.61	.90	.75	.46V	.47V	.97V
Malta 181	—	—	—	—	—V	—V	—V	.02	.05	.04	.01	—V	—V	—V
Netherlands 138	.01	.01	.05	.05	.22V	.37V	1.52V	6.25	7.10	9.19	9.23	14.86V	17.59V	17.97V
Norway 142	—	—	—	—	—V	—V	.08V	1.50	2.40	2.65	2.37	3.34V	3.69V	5.82V
Portugal 182	—	—	—	.02	—V	—V	—V	3.21	1.77	2.51	2.51	.98V	2.13V	1.56V
Slovenia 961	—	—	—	—	—V	—V	—V	.08	.10	.14	.27	.83V	.18V	2.45V
Spain 184	33.32	38.88	78.72	63.31	88.24V	129.54V	203.26V	18.65	18.53	21.69	29.46	20.11V	24.81V	27.11V
Sweden 144	.01	—	.10	10.69	1.09V	4.43V	.06V	1.87	2.50	15.75	10.55	3.94V	3.56V	14.71V
Switzerland 146	.03	—	.01	—	—V	.03V	.20V	3.49	4.84	4.71	6.00	2.70V	2.48V	6.20V
United Kingdom 112	.15	.01	.03	.05	.84V	1.40V	.28V	20.97	19.99	23.26	29.80	20.17V	19.66V	32.66V
Developing Countries 202	**110.9**	**129.1**	**240.6**	**410.2**	**373.4Y**	**475.2Y**	**913.6Y**	**144.3**	**199.3**	**281.7**	**374.5**	**447.8Y**	**505.6Y**	**676.9Y**
Africa 607	**—**	**2.5**	**26.7**	**44.6**	**44.0Y**	**47.3Y**	**162.9Y**	**4.1**	**5.6**	**5.5**	**6.0**	**1.9Y**	**4.0Y**	**4.8Y**
Algeria 612	—	—	—	—	—Y	—Y	—Y	.01	.01	.01	.02	.03Y	.04Y	.05Y
Cameroon 622	—	—	—	—	—Y	—Y	—Y	.01	.01	.01	—	—Y	—Y	.01Y
Central African Rep. 626	—	—	—	—	—Y	—Y	—Y	—	—	.01	—	—Y	—Y	—Y
Comoros 632	....	....	....	....	....	....	....	—	—	—	—	.01Y	.01Y	.01Y
Congo, Dem. Rep. of 636	....	....	....	....	....	....	....	—	—	—	—	—Y	—Y	.01Y
Côte d'Ivoire 662	—	—	—	—	—V	—V	—Y	.17	.11	.15	.16	—V	.05V	.06Y
Djibouti 611	....	....	....	....	....	....	....	.01	—	—	—	—Y	—Y	—Y
Ethiopia 644	....	....	....	....	....	....	....	.01	.04	.05	.05	.06Y	.07Y	.09Y
Gabon 646	....	....	....	....	....	....	....	.01	.03	.03	.01	.01Y	.01Y	.02Y
Gambia, The 648	....	....	....	....	....	....	....	—	.07	.04	—	—Y	—Y	—Y
Kenya 664	—	—	—	—	—Y	—Y	—Y	.02	.01	.01	.02	.02Y	.02Y	.03Y
Liberia 668	—	—	—	—	—Y	—Y	—Y	.04	.01	.02	.01	.02Y	.02Y	.02Y
Madagascar 674	—	—	.05	—	—Y	—Y	—Y	.10	.08	.07	.10	.12Y	.15Y	.18Y
Mauritania 682	—	—	—	—	—Y	—Y	—Y	.01	—	.01	.01	.01Y	.01Y	.01Y
Mauritius 684	—	—	—	—	—V	.02V	—V	.17	.13	.19	.28	—V	.02V	.02V
Morocco 686	—	—	—	—	—V	—Y	—Y	1.87	1.79	2.15	2.07	.96V	1.19Y	1.47Y
Nigeria 694	—	—	—	—	—Y	—Y	—Y	—	—	—	—	.01Y	.01Y	.01Y
Senegal 722	—	—	—	—	—V	.01V	.01Y	.15	.15	.29	.23	—V	.03V	.04Y
Seychelles 718	—	—	—	—	—Y	—Y	—Y	—	.01	.03	.03	.03Y	.04Y	.04Y
Sierra Leone 724	....	....	....	....	....	....	....	—	—	.01	—	—Y	—Y	—Y
South Africa 199	—	2.49	26.67	44.57	43.88V	47.28V	162.93V	.48	1.50	1.27	1.41	.34V	1.55V	1.77V
Swaziland 734	....	....	....	....	....	....	....	.21	.78	.03	.23	.27Y	.33Y	.41Y
Togo 742	—	—	—	—	—V	—Y	—Y	—	—	—	—	—Y	.01Y	.01Y
Tunisia 744	—	—	—	—	.08V	—V	—Y	.78	.87	1.12	1.31	.03V	.40V	.50Y
Zimbabwe 698	—	—	—	—	—V	—V	—Y	.02	—	—	—	—V	—V	—Y
Asia 507	**107.7**	**126.6**	**202.5**	**326.0**	**314.6Y**	**409.6Y**	**728.0Y**	**127.2**	**182.9**	**259.3**	**342.0**	**427.9Y**	**487.1Y**	**656.1Y**
Afghanistan, I.S. of 512	....	....	....	....	....	....	....	—	—	—	.01	.01Y	.01Y	.01Y
Bangladesh 513	—	—	—	—	—V	—V	—V	.59	.57	.69	.67	—V	—Y	—Y
Cambodia 522	—	—	—	—	—V	—V	—Y	.04	.06	.06	.10	.03V	.01V	.01Y
China,P.R.: Mainland 924	2.11	.67	9.55	48.04	71.28V	148.79V	343.67V	22.25	27.46	43.06	58.69	16.66V	20.98V	33.83V
China,P.R.:Hong Kong 532	1.33	.93	1.05	1.55	—V	—V	—V	3.59	4.07	4.59	5.35	—V	—V	—V
China,P.R.:Macao 546	—	—	—	—	—V	—V	—V	.05	.03	.06	.10	—V	—V	—V
Fiji 819	.61	.76	.72	.35	.40Y	.49Y	.61Y	1.25	1.85	1.67	2.14	2.45Y	3.02Y	3.75Y
French Polynesia 887	—	1.26	9.28	1.79	2.05Y	2.53Y	3.14Y	—	2.14	1.65	1.66	1.89Y	2.34Y	2.90Y
India 534	1.49	11.51	9.56	14.14	4.21V	5.20Y	6.45Y	2.10	2.08	2.98	3.22	1.21V	1.49Y	1.85Y
Indonesia 536	.14	.04	1.66	.02	.23V	—V	.06V	6.38	7.28	8.30	9.98	11.89V	9.53V	.02V
Kiribati 826	—	—	—	.07	.08Y	.10Y	.12Y	—	—	—	—	—Y	—Y	—Y
Korea 542	18.69	25.86	60.53	120.13	99.41V	23.03V	1.28V	10.84	11.05	17.70	24.16	43.51V	52.51V	67.31V
Lao People's Dem.Rep 544	....	....	....	....	....	....	....	.03	.03	.04	.03	.04Y	.04Y	.06Y
Malaysia 548	—	.01	—	—	.25V	.09V	.01V	3.84	4.08	4.24	7.11	2.96V	26.89V	7.58V
Mongolia 948	....	....	....	....	....	....	....	.05	.20	.19	.18	.21Y	.26Y	.32Y

		Exports							Imports						
		2001	2002	2003	2004	2005	2006	2007	2001	2002	2003	2004	2005	2006	2007
		Millions of U.S. Dollars							*Millions of U.S. Dollars*						
Myanmar	518	....	....	....	....	....	....	....	.06	.06	.06	.03	.04Y	.05Y	.06Y
Nepal	558	....	....	....	....	....	....	....	—	—	.02	.02	.02Y	.03Y	.03Y
Pakistan	564	—	—	—	—	4.47V	5.52Y	6.85Y	.49	.55	.67	.57	.16V	.19Y	.24Y
Papua New Guinea	853	—	.01	.03	—	—Y	—Y	—Y	1.62	1.40	1.30	1.32	1.51Y	1.86Y	2.31Y
Philippines	566	—	—	—	—	—V	—V	.01V	.78	.89	.77	6.26	.83V	22.36V	102.32V
Samoa	862	.37	.55	.41	1.44	1.64Y	2.03Y	2.52Y	.01	—	.01	—	.01V	.01Y	.02Y
Singapore	576	.68	.15	.22	.46	.20V	.24V	.22V	56.76	100.39	143.11	178.13	313.50V	305.07V	382.55V
Solomon Islands	813	.06	.06	—	—	—Y	—Y	—Y	.15	.12	.24	.24	.28Y	.34Y	.43Y
Sri Lanka	524	—	—	—	—	—Y	—Y	—Y	.16	.16	.13	.20	.23Y	.28Y	.35Y
Taiwan Province of China	528	78.12	81.04	102.41	130.58	121.65V	210.90V	349.65V	5.07	6.08	10.04	8.89	4.95V	5.81V	8.86V
Thailand	578	—	—	—	—	.19V	.13V	.32V	7.09	8.45	12.49	24.07	23.48V	31.46V	38.15V
Tonga	866	—	.01	—	.01	.01Y	.01Y	.02Y	—	.01	—	—	—Y	—Y	.01Y
Vanuatu	846	4.09	3.68	7.06	7.47	8.53Y	10.54Y	13.08Y	1.14	1.17	1.56	1.77	2.03Y	2.51Y	3.11Y
Vietnam	582	—	—	—	—	—V	—V	—V	2.87	2.70	3.69	7.09	—V	—V	—V
Wallis-Futuna	857	3.66	9.55	7.43	7.96	9.10Y	11.25Y	13.96Y	.01	.11	.01	—	.01Y	.01Y	.01Y
Europe	**170**	**3.2**	**—**	**11.4**	**39.6**	**14.6Y**	**18.1Y**	**22.4Y**	**7.3**	**6.0**	**8.3**	**11.9**	**8.1Y**	**6.2Y**	**11.6Y**
Albania	914	—	—	—	—	—V	—V	—V	.01	.01	.04	.01	—V	—V	—V
Azerbaijan	912	—	—	—	—	—V	.02V	—V	—	—	—	—	—Y	—Y	—Y
Belarus	913	—	—	—	—	—V	—V	—V	—	.03	—	—	—V	—V	—V
Bosnia & Herzegovina	963	....	....	....	....	....	....	....	—	—	—	.02	.03Y	.03Y	.04Y
Bulgaria	918	—	—	—	—	—V	—V	—V	.10	.12	.21	.26	.05V	.06V	.07V
Croatia	960	—	—	—	—	—V	—V	—V	.01	—	.12	.08	—V	—V	—V
Czech Republic	935	—	—	—	—	—V	—V	.01V	.36	.61	.91	.82	.27V	.28V	.59V
Czechoslovakia n.s.	937	—	—	—	—	—Y	—Y	—Y	.12	.15	.12	.06	.06Y	.08Y	.10Y
Estonia	939	—	—	—	—	—V	—V	—V	.01	.02	.05	.02	.02V	.02V	.01V
Faroe Islands	816	....	....	....	....	....	....	....	.01	.01	—	.04	.04Y	.05Y	.06Y
Hungary	944	—	—	—	—	—V	—V	—V	1.06	1.05	1.54	2.39	.03V	.02V	.20V
Latvia	941	—	—	—	—	—V	—V	—V	.02	.05	.06	.06	—V	—V	—V
Lithuania	946	—	—	—	—	—V	—V	—V	.09	.10	.10	.08	—V	—V	—V
Macedonia, FYR	962	—	—	—	—	—Y	—Y	—Y	—	.01	—	—	—Y	—Y	—Y
Poland	964	—	—	—	—	—V	—V	—V	1.24	1.65	2.09	1.87	.49V	.81V	1.58V
Romania	968	—	—	—	—	—V	—V	—V	.18	.33	.75	.72	3.66V	1.12V	4.54V
Russia	922	—	—	—	—	—V	.02V	.02V	.06	.06	.05	.21	.24Y	.29Y	.18V
Serbia & Montenegro	965	—	—	—	—	—Y	—Y	—Y	—	—	.02	.09	.10Y	.13Y	.16Y
Slovak Republic	936	—	—	—	—	—V	—V	—V	.14	.19	.29	1.29	2.19V	2.24V	2.24V
Turkey	186	—	—	—	—	—V	.02V	.01V	3.87	1.59	1.83	3.66	.91V	1.10V	1.76V
Turkmenistan	925	—	—	—	—	—Y	—Y	—Y	—	—	.01	—	—Y	.01Y	.01Y
Ukraine	926	3.20	—	11.36	39.59	14.57V	18.01Y	22.34Y	.03	.03	.06	.21	—V	—Y	—Y
Europe n.s.	884	....	....	....	....	....	....	....	—	.02	—	—	—Y	—Y	—Y
Middle East	**407**	**—**	**—**	**—**	**—**	**—Y**	**—Y**	**—Y**	**1.6**	**1.1**	**1.2**	**1.4**	**.7Y**	**.9Y**	**1.1Y**
Bahrain	419	—	—	—	—	—Y	—Y	—Y	—	—	.01	—	—Y	—Y	—Y
Egypt	469	—	—	—	—	—Y	—Y	—Y	.13	.18	.20	.21	.23Y	.29Y	.36Y
Iran, I.R. of	429	—	—	—	—	—Y	—Y	—Y	.04	.06	.06	.05	.06Y	.08Y	.10Y
Iraq	433	—	—	—	—	—Y	—Y	—Y	—	—	.01	—	—Y	—Y	—Y
Israel	436	—	—	—	.01	—V	—V	—V	1.08	.58	.73	.81	—V	—V	—V
Lebanon	446	—	—	—	—	—Y	—Y	—Y	.03	.01	.03	.03	.04Y	.05Y	.06Y
Qatar	453	—	—	—	—	—Y	—Y	—Y	.01	—	—	—	—V	—V	—Y
Saudi Arabia	456	—	.05	—	.01	—V	—Y	—Y	.21	—	.01	—	—Y	—Y	.01Y
Syrian Arab Republic	463	....	....	....	....	....	....	....	—	.01	.01	.01	.01Y	.01Y	.01Y
United Arab Emirates	466	....	....	....	....	....	....	....	.07	.26	.15	.29	.39Y	.49Y	.59Y
Western Hemisphere	**207**	**—**	**—**	**—**	**—**	**.3Y**	**.2Y**	**.2Y**	**4.1**	**3.6**	**7.4**	**13.3**	**9.1Y**	**7.4Y**	**3.4Y**
Argentina	213	—	—	—	—	—V	—V	—V	.06	.07	.39	.90	—V	—V	—V
Bahamas, The	313	....	....	....	....	....	....	....	.03	—	—	—	—Y	—Y	—Y
Bermuda	319	—	—	—	—	.01V	.01V	.01Y	—	.02	.01	—	—Y	—Y	—Y
Bolivia	218	—	—	—	—	.01V	.01Y	.01Y	—	—	—	—	—Y	—Y	—Y
Brazil	223	—	—	—	—	.05V	.01V	—V	1.12	1.56	4.95	8.29	6.07V	5.43V	—V
Chile	228	....	....	....	....	....	....	....	.99	.87	.77	.87	.99Y	1.23Y	1.53Y
Colombia	233	—	—	—	—	—V	—V	.01V	.08	.09	.06	.06	.18V	—V	.17V
Costa Rica	238	—	—	—	—	.02V	.03Y	.04Y	.05	.06	.04	.08	.09Y	.11Y	.14Y
Dominica	321	....	....	....	....	....	....	....	—	—	—	—	—Y	—Y	.01Y
Dominican Republic	243	—	—	—	—	—Y	—Y	—Y	—	—	.04	.02	.02Y	.03Y	.03Y
Ecuador	248	—	—	—	—	—V	—V	—Y	.03	.03	.04	.06	—V	.04V	.05Y
Greenland	326	....	....	....	....	....	....	....	—	—	.01	.02	.02Y	.03Y	.04Y
Guatemala	258	—	—	—	—	—V	—Y	—Y	—	.02	.01	—	—V	—Y	.01Y
Honduras	268	....	....	....	....	....	....	....	—	.01	—	—	—Y	—Y	—Y
Jamaica	343	—	—	—	—	—Y	—Y	—Y	—	.01	—	—	—Y	—Y	—Y
Mexico	273	—	—	—	—	.18V	.13V	.17V	.67	.51	.60	1.26	.71V	.04V	.19V
Netherlands Antilles	353	—	—	—	—	—Y	—Y	—Y	.01	—	.01	—	—Y	—Y	—Y
Nicaragua	278	—	—	—	—	—V	—V	—V	.01	—	—	—	—V	—V	—V
Panama	283	—	—	—	—	—Y	—Y	—Y	.05	—	—	.04	.04Y	.05Y	.06Y
Peru	293	—	—	—	—	—V	—V	—Y	.98	.35	.42	1.60	.91V	.37V	1.02Y
Venezuela, Rep. Bol.	299	—	—	—	—	—V	—V	—V	—	—	.01	.05	.07Y	.09Y	.11Y
Other Countries n.i.e.	**910**	....	....	....	....	....	....	....	**—**	**.2**	**.3**	**.1**	**.1Y**	**.1Y**	**.1Y**
North Korea	954	....	....	....	....	....	....	....	.02	.17	.30	.07	.08Y	.10Y	.13Y
Countries & Areas n.s.	**898**	**—**	**.9**	**11.0**	**8.2**	**9.4Y**	**11.6Y**	**14.4Y**	**8.4**	**7.4**	**20.5**	**18.6**	**21.3Y**	**26.3Y**	**32.6Y**
Special Categories	**899**	**.1**	**.1**	**.1**	**.1**	**.2Y**	**.2Y**	**.3Y**	**1.1**	**.1**	**.1**	**.1**	**.1Y**	**.1Y**	**.1Y**

Exports

	2001	2002	2003	2004	2005	2006	2007
Memorandum Items							
European Union.......................... 998	172.76	178.87	259.59	271.59	339.45Y	540.02Y	797.86Y
Oil Exporting Ctys........................ 999	.14	.09	1.66	.03	.23Y	—Y	.06Y
Non-Oil Develop.Ctys.................... 201	110.76	129.01	238.90	410.20	373.18Y	475.18Y	913.54Y
PERCENT DISTRIBUTION							
Industrial Countries................. 101	73.3	70.7	65.6	58.1	61.6	64.7	60.8
Developing Countries.............. 202	26.1	28.8	32.9	41.0	37.5	34.5	38.6
Africa...................................... 607	—	.6	3.7	4.5	4.4	3.4	6.9
Asia... 507	25.3	28.2	27.7	32.6	31.6	29.7	30.7
Europe.................................... 170	.8	—	1.6	4.0	1.5	1.3	.9
Middle East............................ 407	—	—	—	—	—	—	—
Western Hemisphere.............. 207	—	—	—	—	—	—	—
ANNUAL PERCENT CHANGE							
World.. 001	–25.9	5.4	63.2	36.7	–.3	38.3	72.0
Industrial Countries................. 101	–28.3	1.6	51.4	21.2	5.6	45.3	61.8
Developing Countries.............. 202	–19.4	16.4	86.3	70.5	–9.0	27.3	92.3
Africa...................................... 607	–98.9	—	970.8	66.8	–1.4	7.6	244.4
Asia... 507	–21.7	17.5	60.0	61.0	–3.5	30.2	77.7
Europe.................................... 170	—	—	—	248.5	–63.2	24.0	23.9
Middle East............................ 407	....	—	–100.2	....	–16.8	....	....
Western Hemisphere.............. 207	–97.6	—	—	....	—	–29.6	23.5
Other Countries n.i.e............... 910	....	....	....	....	....	....	....

Imports

	2001	2002	2003	2004	2005	2006	2007
Memorandum Items							
European Union.......................... 998	510.67	537.45	925.21	906.36	895.25Y	1,054.52Y	1,299.43Y
Oil Exporting Ctys........................ 999	6.73	7.62	8.56	10.40	12.46Y	10.25Y	.89Y
Non-Oil Develop.Ctys.................... 201	137.53	191.65	273.10	364.09	435.32Y	495.39Y	675.98Y
PERCENT DISTRIBUTION							
Industrial Countries................. 101	83.5	79.5	80.4	76.0	73.8	73.6	72.7
Developing Countries.............. 202	15.5	19.8	18.3	22.9	25.0	25.1	26.0
Africa...................................... 607	.4	.6	.4	.4	.1	.2	.2
Asia... 507	13.7	18.2	16.8	20.9	23.9	24.2	25.2
Europe.................................... 170	.8	.6	.5	.7	.5	.3	.4
Middle East............................ 407	.2	.1	.1	.1	—	—	—
Western Hemisphere.............. 207	.4	.4	.5	.8	.5	.4	.1
ANNUAL PERCENT CHANGE							
World.. 001	.8	8.2	53.0	6.2	9.4	12.5	29.2
Industrial Countries................. 101	1.1	2.9	54.7	.4	6.3	12.2	27.8
Developing Countries.............. 202	–2.3	38.1	41.3	33.0	19.6	12.9	33.9
Africa...................................... 607	47.7	38.3	–2.0	8.3	–68.0	107.2	19.9
Asia... 507	–5.7	43.8	41.8	31.9	25.1	13.8	34.7
Europe.................................... 170	90.2	–17.5	36.9	43.8	–31.7	–23.1	85.2
Middle East............................ 407	–16.2	–29.5	9.1	14.9	–46.8	24.9	21.9
Western Hemisphere.............. 207	–4.7	–11.7	104.3	79.4	–31.1	–18.5	–54.9
Other Countries n.i.e............... 910	5.2	636.8	79.7	–75.6	14.3	23.6	24.1

		Exports							Imports						
		2001	2002	2003	2004	2005	2006	2007	2001	2002	2003	2004	2005	2006	2007
		Millions of U.S. Dollars							*Millions of U.S. Dollars*						
IFS World Total		**2,522.0**	**2,411.0**	**2,826.0**	**3,620.0**	**4,860.0**	**5,250.0**	**5,950.0**	**859.0**	**942.0**	**1,043.0**	**1,216.0**	**1,471.9**	**1,724.9**	**2,200.0**
DOTS World Total	**001**	**3,502.3Y**	**3,061.4Y**	**3,673.7Y**	**4,498.9Y**	**5,108.8Y**	**4,665.9Y**	**6,271.7Y**	**1,447.2Y**	**1,143.4Y**	**1,356.8Y**	**1,609.6Y**	**1,698.7Y**	**1,949.2Y**	**2,752.6Y**
Industrial Countries	**101**	**2,560.1Y**	**2,104.0Y**	**2,600.5Y**	**3,054.9Y**	**3,488.5Y**	**2,073.4Y**	**3,158.8Y**	**1,266.1Y**	**949.2Y**	**1,108.5Y**	**1,285.2Y**	**1,271.0Y**	**1,405.1Y**	**2,026.5Y**
United States	111	1,577.18V	1,514.00V	1,885.82V	2,381.73V	2,686.55V	1,287.64V	2,039.45V	81.95V	71.94V	69.30V	102.30V	108.02V	148.72V	525.36V
Canada	156	1.38V	1.67V	1.76V	.64V	1.12V	1.06V	1.60V	2.97V	4.51V	2.33V	9.35V	10.08V	16.96V	20.83V
Australia	193	.07V	30.85V	.14V	.14V	101.16V	.47V	.10V	.80V	.32V	.27V	.60V	.60V	1.00V	1.03V
Japan	158	10.95V	32.74V	147.31V	7.31V	12.27V	69.47V	140.77V	31.28V	30.48V	32.89V	26.75V	44.59V	47.98V	53.54V
New Zealand	196	.01V	—V	.01V	.03V	—V	—V	.03V	.28V	.52V	.29V	.56V	.20V	.88V	3.63V
Austria	122	—V	—V	.01V	.07V	.03V	.01V	.20V	7.38V	15.14V	18.06V	19.68V	22.77V	17.35V	43.78V
Belgium	124	12.94V	11.44V	12.19V	13.15V	14.46V	18.41V	21.32V	37.86V	34.57V	45.34V	51.03V	67.21V	84.53V	148.87V
Cyprus	423	.38V	.36V	.09V	.47V	.58V	.20V	.90V	.05V	—V	—V	.01V	—V	—V	—V
Denmark	128	.32V	.22V	.39V	.91V	.73V	.56V	1.11V	4.15V	1.41V	2.99V	2.20V	1.89V	10.73V	2.74V
Finland	172	.11V	.03V	—V	—V	—V	—V	.32V	.49V	.66V	.72V	1.03V	.23V	7.18V	2.16V
France	132	770.78V	378.01V	319.47V	330.45V	321.74V	365.53V	587.14V	907.47V	583.37V	691.37V	706.83V	686.30V	688.62V	763.64V
Germany	134	9.14V	7.55V	20.03V	15.21V	18.59V	20.32V	71.13V	28.92V	28.96V	35.88V	44.47V	43.05V	73.03V	68.21V
Greece	174	12.48V	9.70V	11.53V	15.54V	17.66V	17.02V	11.29V	.55V	3.26V	1.56V	5.39V	11.53V	.24V	17.85V
Iceland	176	—V	—V	—V	—V	—V	.01V	.16V	.02V	.08V	.14V	.14V	.06V	—V	—V
Ireland	178	2.95V	—V	.04V	.01V	.03V	.02V	.04V	2.31V	2.85V	2.53V	2.20V	4.47V	3.27V	5.66V
Italy	136	33.61V	36.47V	51.42V	80.58V	82.36V	80.24V	88.40V	30.49V	38.75V	36.26V	46.50V	48.50V	60.60V	65.65V
Luxembourg	137	—V	—V	—V	—V	—V	.04V	—V	.49V	.64V	.60V	1.09V	.59V	1.02V	1.54V
Malta	181	—Y	—V	—V	—V	—V	—V	—V	.02Y	—V	—V	.17V	.33V	.33V	.24V
Netherlands	138	13.55V	12.83V	10.90V	9.56V	42.04V	17.50V	29.62V	35.62V	41.67V	49.30V	64.27V	64.58V	107.80V	129.28V
Norway	142	8.50V	12.66V	15.61V	29.28V	37.42V	22.63V	31.83V	3.93V	4.33V	2.92V	3.78V	11.91V	2.78V	7.47V
Portugal	182	52.33V	20.60V	61.89V	83.69V	17.70V	10.76V	14.26V	2.73V	4.75V	22.26V	50.89V	2.30V	2.90V	2.56V
Slovenia	961	—V	—V	.01V	.01Y	.09V	—V	.01V	—V	.02V	—V	—Y	.54V	.87V	.01V
Spain	184	47.25V	26.80V	26.63V	67.59V	116.40V	150.45V	107.20V	21.76V	31.79V	22.05V	27.98V	63.45V	44.44V	62.32V
Sweden	144	.06V	.03V	—V	.12V	.23V	.03V	.02V	3.81V	3.23V	4.99V	11.83V	9.22V	19.79V	27.24V
Switzerland	146	.49V	.14V	.23V	7.19V	.63V	.29V	1.03V	5.47V	5.06V	6.42V	10.79V	9.94V	6.44V	3.84V
United Kingdom	112	5.66V	7.90V	35.04V	11.17V	16.71V	10.72V	10.83V	55.32V	40.90V	60.05V	95.34V	58.62V	57.64V	69.06V
Developing Countries	**202**	**722.6Y**	**719.2Y**	**771.7Y**	**1,048.1Y**	**1,168.0Y**	**2,033.5Y**	**2,419.2Y**	**174.5Y**	**187.0Y**	**239.2Y**	**312.5Y**	**414.1Y**	**527.2Y**	**705.1Y**
Africa	**607**	**129.4Y**	**138.7Y**	**88.3Y**	**121.1Y**	**212.4Y**	**331.8Y**	**220.8Y**	**78.7Y**	**99.6Y**	**125.0Y**	**179.2Y**	**209.0Y**	**251.8Y**	**298.7Y**
Algeria	612	3.20V	.59V	.66Y	.85Y	1.09Y	1.34Y	1.74Y	—V	5.04V	6.11Y	8.09Y	11.01Y	13.84Y	16.69Y
Angola	614	1.21Y	1.31Y	1.66Y	2.18Y	2.49Y	3.08Y	3.82Y	.56Y	.61Y	.77Y	1.02Y	1.16Y	1.43Y	1.78Y
Benin	638	.06V	.28V	1.79V	.07V	.81V	1.00Y	1.25Y	.19V	.34V	.30V	1.81V	.46V	.57Y	.71Y
Burkina Faso	748	.01Y	.01Y	.02Y	.02Y	.02Y	.03Y	.04Y	.01Y	.01Y	.02Y	.02Y	.02Y	.03Y	.04Y
Cameroon	622	3.13V	2.84V	2.06V	2.70Y	3.09Y	3.82Y	4.74Y	17.22V	20.51V	47.06V	61.81Y	70.62Y	87.28Y	108.32Y
Central African Rep.	626	.04V	.04V	.05Y	.07Y	.08Y	.10Y	.12Y	.02Y	.02Y	.03Y	.04Y	.04Y	.05Y	.06Y
Chad	628	—Y	—Y	—Y	—Y	—Y	—Y	—Y	.01Y	.01Y	.01Y	.02Y	.02Y	.02Y	.03Y
Congo, Dem. Rep. of	636	9.26Y	10.05Y	12.72Y	16.70Y	19.08Y	23.59Y	29.27Y	.03Y	.03Y	.04Y	.05Y	.05Y	.07Y	.08Y
Congo, Republic of	634	8.20V	2.66V	1.73V	.87V	.99Y	1.22Y	1.52Y	1.34V	3.00V	2.92V	18.86V	21.55Y	26.64Y	33.06Y
Côte d'Ivoire	662	1.65V	10.29V	9.54V	1.79V	1.38V	4.10V	5.09Y	19.60V	20.86V	24.34V	30.68V	34.13V	21.58V	26.78Y
Equatorial Guinea	642	1.57Y	1.70Y	2.16Y	2.83Y	3.23Y	4.00Y	4.96Y	.14Y	.16Y	.20Y	.26Y	.29Y	.36Y	.45Y
Ethiopia	644	....	....	....	....	....	....	....	.01Y	.01Y	.01Y	.02Y	.02Y	.02Y	.03Y
Ghana	652	—Y	—Y	—Y	—Y	—Y	—Y	—Y	.01Y	.01Y	.01Y	.02Y	.02Y	.02Y	.03Y
Guinea	656	3.26V	3.54Y	2.03V	6.04V	6.90Y	8.52Y	10.58Y	.01V	.01Y	—V	—V	—Y	—Y	—Y
Kenya	664	—V	—V	.02V	.05V	.05Y	.07Y	.08Y	—V	.01V	.01V	.08V	.09Y	.12Y	.15Y
Madagascar	674	.22V	.04V	—V	—Y	—Y	—Y	—Y	.02V	—V	.02V	.02Y	.03Y	.03Y	.04Y
Malawi	676	—Y	—Y	—Y	—Y	—Y	—Y	—Y	.42Y	.45Y	.57Y	.75Y	.86Y	1.06Y	1.31Y
Mali	678	.08Y	.09Y	.11Y	.14Y	.16Y	.20Y	.25Y	.04Y	.04Y	.06Y	.07Y	.08Y	.10Y	.13Y
Mauritania	682	.01Y	.01Y	.01Y	.01Y	.01Y	.02Y	.02Y	.51Y	.56Y	.71Y	.93Y	1.06Y	1.31Y	1.63Y
Mauritius	684	—V	—V	.02V	—V	—V	—V	—V	.09V	2.89V	.02V	.10V	.21V	.03V	.01V
Morocco	686	18.77V	18.22V	24.86V	34.88V	24.62V	30.42Y	37.76Y	8.73V	10.82V	10.84V	10.12V	12.51V	15.46Y	19.19Y
Niger	692	—V	—V	.04V	.01V	.01Y	.01Y	.02Y	.02V	—V	—V	—V	—Y	—Y	—Y
Nigeria	694	5.37V	7.36V	10.11V	13.15Y	16.75Y	20.68Y	26.78Y	—V	1.19V	6.31V	8.35Y	11.35Y	14.28Y	17.22Y
Rwanda	714	.02Y	.02Y	.03Y	.04Y	.04Y	.05Y	.06Y	—Y	—Y	—Y	—Y	—Y	—Y	—Y
São Tomé & Príncipe	716	1.04Y	1.13Y	1.43Y	1.88Y	2.15Y	2.65Y	3.29Y	.01Y	.01Y	.01Y	.02Y	.02Y	.02Y	.03Y
Senegal	722	3.59V	5.94V	5.12V	9.04V	18.39V	46.82V	58.10Y	10.43V	9.24V	4.04V	5.48V	4.97V	7.93V	9.84Y
Seychelles	718	....	....	....	....	....	....	....	.01Y	.01Y	.01Y	.02Y	.02Y	.03Y	.03Y
South Africa	199	66.16V	66.90V	6.94V	25.45V	104.73V	175.04V	24.86V	16.41V	20.63V	16.62V	24.81V	31.50V	49.74V	48.89V
Tanzania	738	.20V	.09V	.11Y	.15Y	.17Y	.21Y	.26Y	—V	.05V	.07Y	.09Y	.10Y	.12Y	.15Y
Togo	742	.54V	.04V	3.35V	.05V	1.88V	2.33Y	2.89Y	.74V	.48V	.57V	.70V	.68V	.84Y	1.04Y
Tunisia	744	1.52V	5.55V	1.63V	2.14V	4.27V	2.50V	3.10Y	2.06V	2.62V	3.22V	4.46V	5.99V	8.55V	10.62Y
Zambia	754	—V	—V	.10V	—V	—V	—V	.17V	—V	—V	—V	—V	—V	—V	—V
Zimbabwe	698	.32V	.01V	—V	—V	.01V	—V	—Y	—V	—V	.12V	.54V	.08V	.26V	.32Y
Asia	**507**	**446.5Y**	**398.6Y**	**492.3Y**	**597.0Y**	**636.4Y**	**1,268.2Y**	**1,719.6Y**	**69.8Y**	**64.4Y**	**78.3Y**	**81.6Y**	**130.0Y**	**185.9Y**	**278.9Y**
Bangladesh	513	—V	—V	—V	—V	—V	—V	—V	—V	—V	—V	—V	.33V	.41Y	.51Y
China,P.R.: Mainland	924	235.80V	210.84V	273.79V	381.35V	316.33V	742.63V	993.14V	6.48V	5.17V	9.78V	15.38V	45.40V	70.29V	112.95V
China,P.R.:Hong Kong	532	23.51V	8.98V	7.78V	1.24V	1.00V	1.47V	3.11V	9.18V	6.46V	5.90V	4.07V	5.52V	5.63V	8.67V
China,P.R.:Macao	546	—V	—V	—V	—V	—V	—V	—V	.03V	—V	—V	—V	—V	—V	—V
India	534	12.24Y	16.66V	20.08V	32.56V	38.18V	47.19V	58.56Y	5.86Y	16.10V	13.56V	10.91V	16.29V	20.14Y	24.99Y
Indonesia	536	.03V	.10V	.04V	.63V	.17V	.09V	.03V	3.11V	2.10V	2.18V	3.80V	5.46V	6.16V	28.21V
Korea	542	122.90V	46.09V	109.10V	38.37V	78.14V	14.79V	23.41V	3.91V	3.66V	3.04V	3.36V	3.58V	6.02V	22.62V

	Exports							Imports						
	2001	2002	2003	2004	2005	2006	2007	2001	2002	2003	2004	2005	2006	2007
	Millions of U.S. Dollars							*Millions of U.S. Dollars*						
Malaysia........ 548	.77V	.60V	.02V	.03V	.87V	77.88V	376.52V	.85V	1.09V	.41V	1.37V	5.08V	7.81V	8.25V
New Caledonia........ 839	.01V	.03V	.03V	.01V	.01Y	.01Y	.01Y	....	....	....	....	....	....	....
Pakistan........ 564	—V	.03V	.03V	.02V	.11V	.14Y	.17Y	1.71V	.62V	.23V	.49V	.15V	.19Y	.23Y
Philippines........ 566	.03V	.04V	.05V	.02V	.04V	—V	.15V	.04V	—V	.20V	—V	.12V	—V	—V
Singapore........ 576	6.83V	69.69V	28.56V	7.62V	38.71V	116.71V	86.15V	5.25V	4.52V	5.41V	6.48V	9.40V	15.24V	19.28V
Taiwan Province of China........ 528	11.67V	6.63V	7.74V	49.39V	14.57V	9.02V	16.29V	1.25V	.86V	.91V	.85V	.67V	.61V	1.75V
Thailand........ 578	1.28V	2.25V	3.11V	38.62V	95.91V	200.59V	99.14V	17.06V	9.85V	13.98V	16.93V	18.06V	31.37V	27.43V
Vanuatu........ 846	—Y	—Y	—Y	—Y	—Y	—Y	—Y	.16Y	.17Y	.22Y	.29Y	.33Y	.40Y	.50Y
Vietnam........ 582	—V	—V	—V	—V	—V	—V	—V	3.18V	.07V	6.78V	—V	—V	—V	—V
Asia n.s........ 598	31.45Y	36.69Y	41.93Y	47.17Y	52.41Y	57.65Y	62.89Y	11.77Y	13.73Y	15.69Y	17.65Y	19.61Y	21.57Y	23.53Y
Europe........ 170	**8.1Y**	**10.7Y**	**22.4Y**	**75.2Y**	**93.6Y**	**106.0Y**	**137.1Y**	**3.6Y**	**6.6Y**	**7.2Y**	**9.9Y**	**12.2Y**	**14.7Y**	**34.2Y**
Albania........ 914	—V	—V	—V	—V	—V	—V	—V	—V	—V	—V	—V	.57V	—V	—V
Belarus........ 913	.01V	.04V	—V	—V	.18V	—V	—V	—V	—V	—V	—V	—V	—V	.03V
Bosnia & Herzegovina........ 963	....	....	....	....	....	....	....	.01Y	.01Y	.01Y	.01Y	.01Y	.02Y	.02Y
Bulgaria........ 918	.07V	.04V	.02V	—V	—V	—V	2.12V	—V	.04V	—V	.03V	.14V	.01V	.11V
Czech Republic........ 935	.03V	.06V	.33V	.14V	.72V	—V	.04V	.75V	.40V	.47V	2.22V	1.42V	.17V	1.08V
Estonia........ 939	—V	.01V	.01V	—V	—V	—V	—V	—V	—V	—V	—V	—V	—V	—V
Hungary........ 944	.11V	—V	.05V	.07V	.06V	.03V	.15V	.08V	—V	.11V	.56V	.61V	.81V	.62V
Latvia........ 941	—V	—V	—Y	—V	—V	.19V	.09V	—V	—V	—Y	—V	—V	.02V	.52V
Lithuania........ 946	—V	.02V	—V	.02V	—V	—V	.03V	.02Y	.02Y	.02Y	.02Y	.04V	.11V	.12V
Macedonia, FYR........ 962	—V	.02V	—V	—V	—V	4.58V	5.68Y	—V	—V	—V	—V	—V	—V	—Y
Poland........ 964	1.30V	1.04V	1.87V	1.74V	.29V	1.67V	.52V	.26V	.56V	2.04V	.85V	1.71V	2.69V	3.29V
Romania........ 968	—V	.02V	.03V	.85V	3.15V	.54V	.94V	.01V	.31V	.95V	1.30V	.94V	1.56V	1.22V
Russia........ 922	—V	—V	.02V	—V	.03V	.75V	.78V	.03V	—V	—V	—V	.22V	.15V	.32V
Slovak Republic........ 936	.05V	.03V	.04Y	.06Y	.02V	—V	—V	.03V	.10V	.12Y	.16Y	.57V	1.45V	.64V
Turkey........ 186	6.56V	6.79V	7.54V	16.78V	20.67V	13.58V	21.65V	2.04V	4.83V	2.82V	3.62V	5.18V	6.72V	25.05V
Ukraine........ 926	—V	2.62V	12.45V	55.52V	68.50V	84.66Y	105.06Y	.41V	.37V	.61V	1.16V	.79V	.97Y	1.21Y
Middle East........ 407	**4.3Y**	**1.3Y**	**2.5Y**	**1.9Y**	**1.5Y**	**1.5Y**	**.4Y**	**3.5Y**	**3.3Y**	**3.9Y**	**4.9Y**	**6.7Y**	**8.8Y**	**10.2Y**
Egypt........ 469	—V	—Y	—Y	—Y	—Y	—Y	—Y	.34V	.37Y	.47Y	.62Y	.71Y	.87Y	1.09Y
Israel........ 436	4.27V	1.27V	2.45V	1.64V	1.36V	1.36V	.18V	.77V	.33V	.11V	—V	.88V	1.54V	1.21V
Jordan........ 439	—V	—V	—V	—V	—V	—V	—V	.03V	.07V	.09V	.07V	.01V	.09V	.12V
Kuwait........ 443	—Y	.01Y	.01Y	.01Y	.01Y	.01Y	.02Y	.02Y	.03Y	.03Y	.04Y	.06Y	.07Y	.09Y
Lebanon........ 446	.05Y	.05Y	.07Y	.09Y	.10Y	.13Y	.16Y	1.82Y	1.98Y	2.50Y	3.29Y	3.75Y	4.64Y	5.76Y
Oman........ 449	—V	—V	—V	—Y	—Y	—Y	—Y	.04V	.01V	.12V	.15Y	.21Y	.26Y	.32Y
Saudi Arabia........ 456	.02V	—V	—V	.08V	.01V	.01Y	.01Y	—Y	—Y	—Y	—Y	—Y	—Y	—Y
United Arab Emirates........ 466	—Y	—Y	—Y	—Y	.01Y	.01Y	.01Y	.46Y	.49Y	.59Y	.78Y	1.06Y	1.33Y	1.61Y
Yemen, Republic of........ 474	—V	—V	—Y	.03V	—V	—Y	—Y	—Y	—Y	—Y	—Y	—Y	—Y	—Y
Western Hemisphere........ 207	**134.2Y**	**169.9Y**	**166.3Y**	**252.9Y**	**224.0Y**	**326.0Y**	**341.4Y**	**18.8Y**	**13.1Y**	**24.8Y**	**36.8Y**	**56.2Y**	**66.0Y**	**83.1Y**
Argentina........ 213	—V	—V	—V	—V	—V	.72V	—V	5.12V	2.38V	5.98V	6.31V	9.11V	13.54V	11.28V
Aruba........ 314	7.82Y	8.49Y	10.75Y	14.12Y	16.13Y	19.93Y	24.74Y	6.42Y	6.97Y	8.82Y	11.58Y	13.23Y	16.35Y	20.30Y
Bahamas, The........ 313	—Y	—Y	—Y	—Y	—Y	.01Y	.01Y	—Y	—Y	—Y	—Y	—Y	—Y	—Y
Barbados........ 316	—V	—V	—V	.07V	.01V	—V	—Y	.01V	—V	—V	—V	.01V	—V	—Y
Bermuda........ 319	—Y	—Y	—Y	—Y	—V	.03V	.03Y	....	....	....	....	....	....	....
Bolivia........ 218	—V	—V	—V	—V	—V	—Y	—Y	—V	—V	—V	.01V	.01Y	.01Y	.01Y
Brazil........ 223	62.31V	54.27V	—V	—V	—V	—V	—V	6.55V	3.30V	8.46V	16.39V	30.18V	29.63V	44.82V
Chile........ 228	.06V	—V	20.06V	60.96V	.40V	52.35V	—V	.09V	—V	.40V	.88V	.34V	.25V	.36V
Colombia........ 233	.04V	.10V	.05V	.08V	.03V	.01V	—V	.04V	.07V	.07V	.16V	.11V	.18V	.04V
Ecuador........ 248	—V	—V	—V	—V	—V	—V	—Y	—V	—V	—V	—V	.02V	.03V	.04Y
Guatemala........ 258	.02V	—V	.05V	—V	—V	—Y	—Y	.32Y	.33Y	.37Y	.47Y	.60Y	.75Y	.97Y
Haiti........ 263	—V	—V	.05V	—V	—Y	—Y	—Y	—Y	—Y	—Y	—Y	—Y	—Y	—Y
Mexico........ 273	—V	—V	—V	—V	4.31V	1.99V	5.20V	—V	—V	—V	—V	.53V	1.14V	.24V
Netherlands Antilles........ 353	.06V	.08V	—V	—Y	—Y	—Y	—Y	—V	.02V	—V	—Y	—Y	—Y	—Y
Paraguay........ 288	—V	—V	—V	—V	—V	—V	—Y	.14V	—V	.09V	—V	.10V	1.04V	1.29Y
Peru........ 293	.04V	—V	—V	—V	.01V	—V	—Y	.14V	—V	.05V	.05V	.14V	.82V	.95Y
St. Lucia........ 362	.02Y	.02Y	.02Y	.03Y	.03Y	.04Y	.05Y	—Y	—Y	—Y	—Y	—Y	—Y	—Y
St. Vincent & Grens........ 364	—V	.01V	.01V	—V	—V	—Y	—Y	—V	—V	—V	—V	—V	—Y	—Y
Trinidad and Tobago........ 369	63.86V	106.90V	135.30Y	177.69Y	203.02Y	250.92Y	311.39Y	—V	.01V	.01Y	.01Y	.01Y	.01Y	.02Y
Uruguay........ 298	—V	—Y	—V	—V	—V	—Y	—Y	—V	—Y	.60V	.91V	1.82V	2.25Y	2.80Y
Other Countries n.i.e........ 910	**1.3Y**	**1.4Y**	**1.7Y**	**2.3Y**	**2.6Y**	**3.2Y**	**4.0Y**	**.2Y**	**.3Y**	**.3Y**	**.4Y**	**.5Y**	**.6Y**	**.7Y**
North Korea........ 954	1.27Y	1.37Y	1.74Y	2.29Y	2.61Y	3.23Y	4.00Y	.23Y	.25Y	.32Y	.42Y	.48Y	.59Y	.73Y
Countries & Areas n.s........ 898	**218.2Y**	**236.8Y**	**299.7Y**	**393.6Y**	**449.7Y**	**555.8Y**	**689.8Y**	**6.4Y**	**6.9Y**	**8.8Y**	**11.5Y**	**13.2Y**	**16.3Y**	**20.2Y**
Memorandum Items														
European Union........ 998	963.05Y	513.10Y	551.95Y	630.57Y	650.44Y	693.70Y	944.60Y	1,140.57Y	833.04Y	996.72Y	1,134.74Y	1,089.93Y	1,185.62Y	1,417.06Y
Oil Exporting Ctys........ 999	8.63Y	8.06Y	10.83Y	14.73Y	18.03Y	22.13Y	28.59Y	3.64Y	8.84Y	15.34Y	21.21Y	29.14Y	35.93Y	64.14Y
Non-Oil Develop.Ctys........ 201	714.02Y	711.18Y	760.90Y	1,033.42Y	1,149.92Y	2,011.35Y	2,390.60Y	170.82Y	178.18Y	223.86Y	291.26Y	384.95Y	491.29Y	640.98Y
PERCENT DISTRIBUTION														
Industrial Countries........ 101	**73.1**	**68.7**	**70.8**	**67.9**	**68.3**	**44.4**	**50.4**	**87.5**	**83.0**	**81.7**	**79.8**	**74.8**	**72.1**	**73.6**
Developing Countries........ 202	**20.6**	**23.5**	**21.0**	**23.3**	**22.9**	**43.6**	**38.6**	**12.1**	**16.4**	**17.6**	**19.4**	**24.4**	**27.0**	**25.6**
Africa........ 607	**3.7**	**4.5**	**2.4**	**2.7**	**4.2**	**7.1**	**3.5**	**5.4**	**8.7**	**9.2**	**11.1**	**12.3**	**12.9**	**10.8**
Asia........ 507	**12.7**	**13.0**	**13.4**	**13.3**	**12.5**	**27.2**	**27.4**	**4.8**	**5.6**	**5.8**	**5.1**	**7.7**	**9.5**	**10.1**
Europe........ 170	**.2**	**.3**	**.6**	**1.7**	**1.8**	**2.3**	**2.2**	**.3**	**.6**	**.5**	**.6**	**.7**	**.8**	**1.2**
Middle East........ 407	**.1**	**—**	**.1**	**—**	**—**	**—**	**—**	**.2**	**.3**	**.3**	**.3**	**.4**	**.5**	**.4**
Western Hemisphere........ 207	**3.8**	**5.5**	**4.5**	**5.6**	**4.4**	**7.0**	**5.4**	**1.3**	**1.1**	**1.8**	**2.3**	**3.3**	**3.4**	**3.0**
Other Countries n.i.e........ 910	**—**	**—**	**—**	**.1**	**.1**	**.1**	**.1**	**—**	**—**	**—**	**—**	**—**	**—**	**—**
ANNUAL PERCENT CHANGE														
World........ 001	**–7.7**	**–12.6**	**20.0**	**22.5**	**13.6**	**–8.7**	**34.4**	**3.7**	**–21.0**	**18.7**	**18.6**	**5.5**	**14.7**	**41.2**

Gabon 646

	Exports							Imports						
	2001	2002	2003	2004	2005	2006	2007	2001	2002	2003	2004	2005	2006	2007
Industrial Countries................. 101	−10.8	−17.8	23.6	17.5	14.2	−40.6	52.3	2.8	−25.0	16.8	15.9	−1.1	10.6	44.2
Developing Countries.............. 202	−.3	−.5	7.3	35.8	11.4	74.1	19.0	10.7	7.2	27.9	30.6	32.5	27.3	33.7
Africa..................................... 607	108.1	7.2	−36.4	37.2	75.4	56.2	−33.5	.4	26.7	25.5	43.4	16.6	20.5	18.6
Asia.. 507	−18.9	−10.7	23.5	21.3	6.6	99.3	35.6	21.1	−7.8	21.6	4.2	59.4	43.0	50.1
Europe.................................... 170	−44.1	31.6	109.1	236.3	24.5	13.2	29.3	−49.2	82.3	7.8	39.0	22.8	20.3	132.9
Middle East............................ 407	−59.8	−69.2	89.6	−26.9	−19.6	2.0	−75.0	−12.9	−6.3	19.6	26.4	35.1	31.9	15.5
Western Hemisphere.............. 207	55.8	26.5	−2.1	52.1	−11.5	45.6	4.7	82.6	−30.5	89.9	48.0	52.9	17.5	25.9
Other Countries n.i.e................ 910	10.4	8.5	26.6	31.3	14.3	23.6	24.1	10.4	8.5	26.6	31.3	14.3	23.6	24.1

	Exports 2001	2002	2003	2004	2005	2006	2007	Imports 2001	2002	2003	2004	2005	2006	2007
	Millions of U.S. Dollars							*Millions of U.S. Dollars*						
IFS World Total	**10.0**	**12.7**	**7.6**	**10.0**	**8.0**	**11.5**	**13.0**	**134.0**	**159.6**	**156.0**	**229.0**	**237.0**	**259.3**	**305.0**
DOTS World Total 001	**27.4Y**	**31.2Y**	**18.5Y**	**37.9Y**	**27.9Y**	**34.1Y**	**46.4Y**	**398.6Y**	**412.2Y**	**505.7Y**	**576.6Y**	**638.3Y**	**708.8Y**	**861.8Y**
Industrial Countries 101	**21.0Y**	**21.3Y**	**8.8Y**	**20.9Y**	**8.3Y**	**13.8Y**	**14.4Y**	**156.0Y**	**147.8Y**	**177.6Y**	**168.0Y**	**184.2Y**	**174.5Y**	**189.9Y**
United States 111	.55V	.27V	—V	.45V	.27V	.18V	.09V	9.35V	10.45V	29.26V	25.41V	33.55V	23.32V	22.00V
Canada 156	2.08V	.03V	.08V	.05V	.03V	.06V	.08V	.40V	.37V	.22V	.20V	.28V	.62V	.77V
Australia 193	—V	.01V	—V	.01V	.01V	.04V	.03V	.03V	.12V	.24V	.21V	5.40V	.19V	.05V
Japan 158	.55V	.14V	.29V	.82V	.63V	.68V	1.21V	5.33V	6.67V	5.42V	3.51V	4.07V	5.27V	4.85V
New Zealand 196	—V	—V	—V	—V	—V	—V	—V	.02V	.18V	.72V	.70V	.54V	.66V	.55V
Austria 122	.02V	.01V	.01V	.01V	.01V	.01V	.02V	1.31V	1.67V	.80V	.70V	.49V	.66V	1.15V
Belgium 124	2.72V	1.82V	.89V	.96V	1.21V	.87V	1.94V	27.73V	18.83V	13.37V	15.33V	14.73V	19.93V	22.61V
Cyprus 423	—V	—V	.01V	—V	—Y	—V	—V	.07V	.12V	.14V	.09V	.12V	.19V	.17V
Denmark 128	.01V	.02V	.22V	—V	.01V	.01V	—V	2.30V	1.70V	2.69V	4.31V	5.79V	2.79V	5.14V
Finland 172	—V	.02V	.02V	—V	.01V	.01V	.03V	.11V	.11V	.07V	.10V	.17V	.34V	.53V
France 132	1.33V	6.28V	.17V	5.25V	.26V	2.56V	2.35V	20.36V	15.28V	15.88V	14.56V	22.07V	18.44V	14.86V
Germany 134	1.20V	2.14V	1.29V	3.52V	.27V	.17V	.12V	13.06V	15.64V	15.87V	18.83V	13.06V	13.97V	11.77V
Greece 174	.01V	.01V	.01V	—V	—V	.03V	1.61V	.17V	.03V	2.20V	2.00V	.66V	.31V	.14V
Iceland 176	—V	—V	—V	—V	—V	—V	—V	—V	.01V	—V	—V	.03V	—V	.01V
Ireland 178	.14V	.02V	.01V	—V	—V	—V	.10V	.83V	.53V	.70V	.66V	1.07V	1.19V	.35V
Italy 136	.05V	3.16V	.80V	3.05V	—V	1.67V	—V	10.45V	11.94V	13.86V	8.81V	7.73V	8.50V	5.10V
Luxembourg 137	.04V	—V	—V	—V	—V	—V	—V	.22V	.11V	.14V	.02V	.03V	.02V	.19V
Malta 181	—Y	—V	—V	—V	—V	—V	—V	—Y	.42V	.38V	.49V	.72V	.34V	.39V
Netherlands 138	1.25V	.57V	.41V	.53V	.32V	1.28V	1.51V	24.43V	22.39V	26.98V	26.37V	26.30V	31.74V	45.19V
Norway 142	—V	—V	.01V	.03V	.05V	.03V	.06V	.46V	.41V	.32V	.13V	.21V	.25V	.39V
Portugal 182	.13V	.14V	.09V	.12V	.02V	—V	.29V	1.16V	.46V	.58V	.66V	1.06V	2.76V	1.52V
Slovenia 961	.01V	.01V	.12V	.16Y	—V	—V	—V	.06V	.18V	.24V	.32Y	.04V	—V	—V
Spain 184	.78V	1.14V	.28V	.33V	.02V	.39V	.94V	6.81V	8.72V	10.80V	10.05V	10.02V	9.45V	12.84V
Sweden 144	.03V	.01V	.03V	.01V	.01V	.02V	.01V	1.10V	1.35V	1.74V	1.74V	1.91V	4.16V	4.30V
Switzerland 146	—V	.04V	.01V	.04V	—V	.02V	.02V	.93V	2.98V	.86V	1.15V	1.24V	.97V	4.65V
United Kingdom 112	10.09V	5.45V	4.08V	5.58V	5.13V	5.81V	4.03V	29.30V	27.14V	34.09V	31.62V	32.93V	28.44V	30.37V
Developing Countries 202	**6.4Y**	**9.9Y**	**9.6Y**	**17.0Y**	**19.6Y**	**20.3Y**	**32.0Y**	**242.6Y**	**264.3Y**	**328.2Y**	**408.6Y**	**454.1Y**	**534.2Y**	**671.9Y**
Africa 607	**2.8Y**	**2.3Y**	**1.6Y**	**3.8Y**	**3.5Y**	**2.5Y**	**3.9Y**	**56.7Y**	**70.0Y**	**80.4Y**	**113.5Y**	**150.6Y**	**169.0Y**	**203.9Y**
Benin 638	.12V	.13V	.07V	—V	.10V	.12Y	.15Y	—V	—V	.06V	.01V	.02V	.03Y	.04Y
Cameroon 622	—V	.01V	.04V	.05Y	.06Y	.07Y	.09Y	—V	.07V	1.63V	2.15Y	2.45Y	3.03Y	3.76Y
Congo, Republic of 634	.03V	.03V	.09V	—V	—Y	—Y	—Y	—V	—V	—V	—V	—Y	—Y	—Y
Côte d'Ivoire 662	—V	—V	.05V	.01V	.01V	.03V	.04Y	13.19V	20.01V	17.40V	19.22V	54.18V	57.36V	71.18Y
Ghana 652	.18Y	.20Y	.25Y	.33Y	.38Y	.47Y	.58Y	.91Y	.99Y	1.26Y	1.65Y	1.88Y	2.33Y	2.89Y
Guinea 656	.02V	.03Y	.08V	.24V	.28Y	.34Y	.42Y	—V	—Y	—V	.04V	.05Y	.06Y	.07Y
Guinea-Bissau 654	.29Y	.32Y	.40Y	.53Y	.60Y	.75Y	.92Y	.10Y	.11Y	.14Y	.18Y	.21Y	.26Y	.32Y
Kenya 664	.69V	.59V	.09V	.11V	.12Y	.15Y	.18Y	.02V	.03V	.10V	.16V	.18Y	.22Y	.28Y
Liberia 668	—Y	—Y	—Y	—Y	—Y	—Y	—Y	.18Y	.20Y	.25Y	.33Y	.38Y	.47Y	.58Y
Madagascar 674	—V	—V	—V	—Y	.01Y	.01Y	.01Y	.07V	—V	—V	—Y	—Y	—Y	—Y
Malawi 676	—Y	—Y	—Y	—Y	—Y	—Y	—Y	.02Y	.02Y	.03Y	.04Y	.04Y	.05Y	.07Y
Mali 678	.03Y	.04Y	.05Y	.06Y	.07Y	.09Y	.11Y	.01Y	.01Y	.01Y	.01Y	.01Y	.01Y	.02Y
Mauritania 682	.10Y	.11Y	.13Y	.18Y	.20Y	.25Y	.31Y	.16Y	.17Y	.22Y	.28Y	.32Y	.40Y	.50Y
Mauritius 684	.03V	—V	—V	—V	—V	—V	—V	—V	—V	.07V	.08V	.15V	.13V	—V
Morocco 686	—V	—V	—V	—V	.01V	.01Y	.01Y	4.00V	6.98V	7.59V	7.83V	9.73V	12.03Y	14.92Y
Mozambique 688	—V	—V	—Y	—Y	—Y	—V	—Y	—V	—V	—V	.13V	—V	—V	—Y
Niger 692	—V	—V	.03V	—V	—Y	—Y	—Y	—V	—V	.01V	—V	—Y	—Y	—Y
Nigeria 694	.01V	.05V	—V	—Y	—Y	—Y	—Y	—V	—V	—V	—Y	—Y	—Y	—Y
Senegal 722	—V	.17V	.01V	1.39V	1.30V	.02V	.03Y	29.56V	36.90V	45.82V	71.23V	72.92V	79.95V	99.22Y
Sierra Leone 724	.03Y	.03Y	.04Y	.05Y	.06Y	.08Y	.09Y	.31Y	.34Y	.43Y	.57Y	.65Y	.80Y	.99Y
South Africa 199	1.08V	.10V	.04V	.35V	.05V	.03V	.79V	7.48V	3.17V	4.58V	8.89V	6.67V	10.80V	7.79V
Tanzania 738	.15V	.04V	.05Y	.07Y	.08Y	.10Y	.12Y	.10V	.10V	.13Y	.17Y	.20Y	.24Y	.30Y
Togo 742	.01V	—V	.01V	.11V	.02V	.03Y	.03Y	.02V	.02V	.10V	.06V	—V	—Y	—Y
Tunisia 744	—V	.02V	.05V	.01V	—V	—V	—Y	.57V	.85V	.56V	.50V	.47V	.80V	1.00Y
Zambia 754	.03V	.03V	—V	—V	.07V	—V	—V	—V	—V	—V	—V	.08V	.01V	—V
Zimbabwe 698	.01V	.42V	.06V	.31V	.08V	—V	—Y	—V	.01V	—V	—V	—V	—V	—Y
Asia 507	**2.7Y**	**7.3Y**	**7.5Y**	**12.6Y**	**15.4Y**	**16.7Y**	**27.2Y**	**136.7Y**	**143.5Y**	**184.3Y**	**202.8Y**	**215.8Y**	**258.8Y**	**318.4Y**
Bangladesh 513	—V	—V	—V	—V	—V	—V	—V	—V	.07V	—V	—V	—V	—Y	—Y
China,P.R.: Mainland 924	—V	—V	1.42V	.10V	.16V	.40V	8.13V	79.76V	90.06V	128.00V	136.54V	137.41V	178.96V	203.86V
China,P.R.:Hong Kong 532	.24V	.26V	.34V	.11V	.16V	.12V	.35V	17.04V	14.17V	15.30V	13.17V	9.51V	6.93V	6.67V
India 534	.30Y	3.20V	3.60V	8.68V	11.42V	14.11Y	17.51Y	18.88Y	15.33V	15.14V	15.41V	18.48V	22.85Y	28.35Y
Indonesia 536	.05V	—V	—V	.01V	2.34V	.02V	.07V	6.36V	6.56V	5.65V	5.74V	2.79V	2.34V	4.69V
Korea 542	.21V	.07V	.28V	.02V	.01V	.10V	.10V	2.13V	2.19V	1.10V	1.41V	2.58V	5.40V	2.60V
Malaysia 548	.87V	3.32V	.89V	1.51V	.21V	1.43V	.15V	.95V	3.93V	9.73V	16.57V	17.44V	18.91V	33.41V
Pakistan 564	—V	.02V	.12V	.05V	.02V	.03Y	.04Y	.84V	2.36V	2.80V	5.97V	9.18V	11.35Y	14.08Y
Philippines 566	.03V	—V	—V	—V	—V	—V	—V	—V	—V	—V	—V	—V	.28V	.11V
Singapore 576	—Y	—Y	—Y	—Y	—Y	—Y	—Y	.52Y	.57Y	.72Y	.95Y	1.08Y	1.34Y	1.66Y
Taiwan Province of China 528	.01V	.19V	.23V	—V	—V	—V	.66V	1.01V	.92V	1.00V	1.24V	1.33V	1.78V	.98V
Thailand 578	.83V	.18V	.59V	2.17V	1.04V	.46V	.21V	8.42V	5.32V	3.93V	5.79V	15.94V	8.70V	21.99V
Vietnam 582	.16V	.05V	—V	—V	—V	—V	—V	.83V	2.08V	.93V	—V	—V	—V	—V
Europe 170	**.8Y**	**.2Y**	**.6Y**	**.3Y**	**.2Y**	**.3Y**	**.2Y**	**7.0Y**	**12.1Y**	**14.1Y**	**32.5Y**	**19.5Y**	**19.0Y**	**28.7Y**
Belarus 913	—V	.02V	—V	—V	.03V	.01V	—V	—V	—V	.03V	—V	—V	—V	—V
Bulgaria 918	.59V	.18V	.21V	.22V	.01V	.19V	.03V	2.13V	.32V	.86V	1.61V	2.38V	.14V	—V
Czech Republic 935	—V	—V	—V	—V	—V	—V	—V	.12V	.07V	.12V	.26V	.64V	.48V	1.04V

	Exports							Imports						
	2001	2002	2003	2004	2005	2006	2007	2001	2002	2003	2004	2005	2006	2007
	Millions of U.S. Dollars							*Millions of U.S. Dollars*						
Estonia........ 939	—V	—V	—V	—V	—V	—V	—V	—V	.01V	—V	.01V	—V	—V	.05V
Georgia........ 915	—V	—V	—V	—V	—V	—V	—Y	.01V	2.69V	—V	—V	—V	—V	—Y
Hungary........ 944	—V	—V	.01V	—V	—V	—V	.02V	—V	—V	—V	.05V	.13V	.31V	.81V
Kazakhstan........ 916	—V	.01V	—V	.01V	.01Y	.02Y	.02Y	—V	—V	—V	—V	—Y	—Y	—Y
Latvia........ 941	—V	—V	—V	—V	—V	.01V	—V	.13V	.22V	.31V	.26V	.15V	.37V	.22V
Lithuania........ 946	—V	—V	—V	—V	—V	—V	—V	—V	.04V	.18V	.20V	.22V	.32V	.57V
Macedonia, FYR........ 962	—V	—V	.04V	.02V	—V	—V	—Y	—V	—V	—V	—V	—V	—V	—Y
Poland........ 964	—V	.02V	—V	—V	—V	.01V	—V	.23V	.15V	.18V	.51V	.48V	.89V	.57V
Romania........ 968	.05V	—V	—V	—V	—V	—V	—V	.08V	.69V	.76V	6.73V	.51V	.25V	.07V
Russia........ 922	—V	.01V	—V	.01V	—V	—V	—V	.12V	.02V	.15V	.04V	—V	—V	—V
Slovak Republic........ 936	—V	—V	—Y	—Y	—V	.02V	—V	.27V	—V	—Y	—Y	.35V	.07V	.94V
Turkey........ 186	.11V	—V	.30V	.01V	.17V	—V	.11V	3.67V	6.73V	11.03V	15.80V	11.38V	12.13V	19.43V
Ukraine........ 926	—V	—V	—V	.01V	.01V	.01Y	.01Y	.20V	1.14V	.49V	7.00V	3.24V	4.00Y	4.97Y
Middle East........ 407	**.1Y**	**—Y**	**—Y**	**.1Y**	**—Y**	**—Y**	**—Y**	**12.5Y**	**13.4Y**	**17.1Y**	**22.6Y**	**28.9Y**	**36.1Y**	**43.7Y**
Egypt........ 469	—V	—Y	—Y	—Y	—Y	—Y	—Y	1.39V	1.51Y	1.91Y	2.51Y	2.86Y	3.54Y	4.39Y
Iran, I.R. of........ 429	—V	—V	—Y	—Y	—Y	—Y	—Y	1.15Y	1.23Y	1.49Y	1.97Y	2.68Y	3.37Y	4.06Y
Israel........ 436	—V	—V	—V	—V	—V	—V	—V	—V	—V	—V	—V	.22V	.22V	—V
Jordan........ 439	—V	—V	—V	—V	—V	—V	—V	.01V	.04V	.01V	.01V	—V	—V	—V
Kuwait........ 443	—Y	—Y	—Y	—Y	—Y	—Y	—Y	—Y	—Y	.01Y	.01Y	.01Y	.01Y	.01Y
Lebanon........ 446	—Y	—Y	—Y	—Y	—Y	—Y	—Y	4.34Y	4.71Y	5.96Y	7.82Y	8.94Y	11.04Y	13.71Y
Oman........ 449	—V	—V	—V	—Y	—Y	—Y	—Y	—V	—V	.59V	.77Y	1.05Y	1.32Y	1.60Y
Saudi Arabia........ 456	.09V	.03V	—V	.07V	—V	—Y	—Y	2.62Y	2.79Y	3.38Y	4.47Y	6.08Y	7.64Y	9.22Y
United Arab Emirates........ 466	—V	—V	—Y	—Y	—Y	—Y	—Y	2.95Y	3.14Y	3.81Y	5.04Y	6.85Y	8.61Y	10.39Y
Yemen, Republic of........ 474	—V	—V	—Y	.01V	—V	—Y	—Y	—V	—V	—Y	.02V	.24V	.30Y	.37Y
Western Hemisphere........ 207	**—Y**	**—Y**	**—Y**	**.2Y**	**.5Y**	**.8Y**	**.7Y**	**29.7Y**	**25.3Y**	**32.2Y**	**37.2Y**	**39.3Y**	**51.4Y**	**77.1Y**
Argentina........ 213	—V	—V	—V	—V	—V	—V	—V	—V	.76V	1.09V	2.05V	1.32V	2.36V	4.77V
Barbados........ 316	—V	—V	—V	—V	.01V	.01V	.01Y	.01V	.01V	—V	—V	.01V	—V	—Y
Bermuda........ 319	—Y	—Y	—Y	—Y	.34V	.24V	.30Y	....	....	....	....	....	....	....
Brazil........ 223	.01V	—V	—V	—V	—V	—V	—V	29.55V	24.28V	29.89V	34.04V	35.72V	46.49V	69.03V
Chile........ 228	—V	—V	—V	—V	—V	—V	—V	.02V	—V	.05V	.01V	—V	—V	—V
Colombia........ 233	—V	.01V	—V	.02V	—V	.25V	.09V	.04V	.10V	.63V	.17V	.01V	.15V	.04V
Costa Rica........ 238	—V	.01V	—V	.03V	—V	—Y	—Y	....	....	....	....	....	....	....
Honduras........ 268	—V	—V	—V	.04V	.05Y	.06Y	.08Y	—V	—V	—V	—V	—Y	—Y	—Y
Mexico........ 273	—V	—V	—V	—V	.08V	.14V	.08V	—V	—V	—V	—V	.12V	.01V	.01V
Paraguay........ 288	—V	—V	.01V	—V	—V	—V	—Y	....	....	....	....	....	....	....
Peru........ 293	—V	—V	—V	—V	—V	—V	—Y	.02V	—V	.34V	.74V	1.84V	2.07V	2.85Y
St. Lucia........ 362	.03Y	.03Y	.04Y	.05Y	.06Y	.07Y	.09Y	.02Y	.02Y	.03Y	.04Y	.05Y	.06Y	.07Y
Trinidad and Tobago........ 369	—V	—V	—Y	—Y	—Y	—Y	—Y	.03V	.11V	.14Y	.18Y	.21Y	.26Y	.32Y
Uruguay........ 298	—V	—Y	—V	—V	—V	—Y	—Y	—V	—Y	.04V	—V	—V	—Y	—Y
Other Countries n.i.e........ 910	**—Y**	**—Y**	**—Y**	**—Y**	**—Y**	**—Y**	**—Y**	**—Y**	**—Y**	**—Y**	**—Y**	**.1Y**	**.1Y**	**.1Y**
Cuba........ 928	—Y	—Y	—Y	—Y	—Y	—Y	—Y	.03Y	.03Y	.04Y	.05Y	.06Y	.07Y	.09Y
Memorandum Items														
European Union........ 998	17.80Y	20.81Y	8.46Y	19.51Y	7.26Y	12.87Y	12.98Y	140.22Y	127.12Y	141.32Y	137.96Y	140.87Y	145.68Y	160.82Y
Oil Exporting Ctys........ 999	.15Y	.09Y	.01Y	.08Y	2.35Y	.02Y	.08Y	13.09Y	13.72Y	14.91Y	17.99Y	19.46Y	23.29Y	29.97Y
Non-Oil Develop.Ctys........ 201	6.26Y	9.83Y	9.62Y	16.89Y	17.29Y	20.23Y	31.90Y	229.47Y	250.60Y	313.24Y	390.63Y	434.59Y	510.95Y	641.90Y
PERCENT DISTRIBUTION														
Industrial Countries........ 101	**76.6**	**68.2**	**47.9**	**55.2**	**29.6**	**40.6**	**31.1**	**39.1**	**35.9**	**35.1**	**29.1**	**28.9**	**24.6**	**22.0**
Developing Countries........ 202	**23.4**	**31.8**	**52.1**	**44.8**	**70.4**	**59.4**	**68.9**	**60.9**	**64.1**	**64.9**	**70.9**	**71.1**	**75.4**	**78.0**
Africa........ 607	**10.3**	**7.4**	**8.4**	**10.1**	**12.6**	**7.5**	**8.4**	**14.2**	**17.0**	**15.9**	**19.7**	**23.6**	**23.8**	**23.7**
Asia........ 507	**9.8**	**23.3**	**40.5**	**33.4**	**55.1**	**48.9**	**58.6**	**34.3**	**34.8**	**36.4**	**35.2**	**33.8**	**36.5**	**36.9**
Europe........ 170	**2.8**	**.8**	**3.0**	**.7**	**.8**	**.8**	**.4**	**1.7**	**2.9**	**2.8**	**5.6**	**3.1**	**2.7**	**3.3**
Middle East........ 407	**.3**	**.1**	**—**	**.2**	**—**	**—**	**—**	**3.1**	**3.3**	**3.4**	**3.9**	**4.5**	**5.1**	**5.1**
Western Hemisphere........ 207	**.1**	**.2**	**.3**	**.4**	**1.9**	**2.3**	**1.4**	**7.4**	**6.1**	**6.4**	**6.5**	**6.2**	**7.3**	**8.9**
ANNUAL PERCENT CHANGE														
World........ 001	**–40.6**	**13.9**	**–40.8**	**105.2**	**–26.4**	**22.2**	**36.1**	**19.2**	**3.4**	**22.7**	**14.0**	**10.7**	**11.0**	**21.6**
Industrial Countries........ 101	**–33.2**	**1.4**	**–58.5**	**136.6**	**–60.5**	**67.5**	**4.3**	**33.1**	**–5.2**	**20.1**	**–5.4**	**9.7**	**–5.3**	**8.8**
Developing Countries........ 202	**–56.3**	**54.8**	**–3.0**	**76.3**	**15.7**	**3.1**	**57.8**	**11.7**	**9.0**	**24.1**	**24.5**	**11.1**	**17.7**	**25.8**
Africa........ 607	**–66.0**	**–17.9**	**–33.2**	**145.8**	**–8.0**	**–27.4**	**53.7**	**–1.1**	**23.4**	**14.9**	**41.2**	**32.7**	**12.2**	**20.7**
Asia........ 507	**3.1**	**170.0**	**2.6**	**69.3**	**21.5**	**8.5**	**63.3**	**6.7**	**5.0**	**28.4**	**10.0**	**6.4**	**20.0**	**23.0**
Europe........ 170	**58.8**	**–68.8**	**136.4**	**–51.2**	**–15.0**	**15.4**	**–29.4**	**146.4**	**73.5**	**16.7**	**130.2**	**–40.0**	**–2.6**	**51.1**
Middle East........ 407	**–79.2**	**–65.5**	**....**	**....**	**–97.5**	**23.5**	**29.5**	**14.2**	**7.6**	**27.9**	**31.9**	**28.0**	**24.6**	**21.3**
Western Hemisphere........ 207	**–98.7**	**35.0**	**1.1**	**218.7**	**249.5**	**43.6**	**–16.0**	**65.8**	**–14.8**	**27.4**	**15.6**	**5.5**	**30.9**	**50.0**
Other Countries n.i.e........ 910	**—**	**—**	**....**	**....**	**....**	**....**	**....**	**10.4**	**8.5**	**26.6**	**31.3**	**14.3**	**23.6**	**24.1**

		Exports							Imports						
		2001	2002	2003	2004	2005	2006	2007	2001	2002	2003	2004	2005	2006	2007
		Millions of U.S. Dollars							*Millions of U.S. Dollars*						
IFS World Total		**317.6**	**345.9**	**461.4**	**646.9**	**865.5**	**992.5**	**1,240.2**	**753.2**	**795.5**	**1,141.2**	**1,845.6**	**2,490.0**	**3,677.8**	**5,216.7**
DOTS World Total	**001**	**317.3**	**349.4**	**465.3**	**644.8**	**851.0**	**980.9**	**1,529.0Y**	**753.6**	**792.3**	**1,141.2**	**1,847.6**	**2,490.7**	**3,677.5**	**5,320.1Y**
Industrial Countries	**101**	**82.8**	**100.6**	**127.4**	**146.3**	**216.6**	**279.9**	**661.5Y**	**307.6**	**308.0**	**519.1**	**730.3**	**796.2**	**1,073.1**	**1,502.4Y**
United States	111	9.05	13.98	15.36	21.23	26.75	58.86	171.99S	63.99	68.04	90.77	110.91	148.31	129.76	267.04S
Canada	156	.04	.07	.20	3.69	35.64	48.87	64.53S	1.58	.46	1.42	4.34	7.11	14.29	15.70S
Australia	193	.02	.05	.03	.19	.03	.05	3.34S	.43	.56	.43	1.06	2.60	1.64	2.13S
Japan	158	1.04	.69	.22	.63	1.44	.52	.50S	3.18	3.95	2.49	5.93	8.34	39.54	97.63S
New Zealand	196	—	—	.02	.02	—	—	.02S	.49	.84	.44	.57	2.10	7.93	10.67S
Austria	122	.72	.47	.30	.31	1.05	1.80	3.31S	9.58	10.21	11.28	22.26	19.01	36.62	63.23S
Belgium	124	6.75	1.31	3.11	5.07	5.08	11.01	21.75S	7.98	7.12	9.95	15.52	25.58	37.16	46.91S
Cyprus	423	.10	.09	.55	.43	.24	.80	23.46S	2.57	1.08	1.49	8.06	1.73	2.88	2.65S
Denmark	128	.51	.32	.63	.75	.22	.65	.82S	6.90	9.72	11.04	8.38	7.07	10.66	12.69S
Finland	172	.06	—	—	—	—	.18	7.27S	10.53	2.81	2.68	6.34	13.25	26.56	29.42S
France	132	.35	3.03	4.92	9.56	11.55	30.88	40.04S	19.14	15.60	55.84	63.24	97.38	68.74	106.79S
Germany	134	7.69	7.69	9.80	15.85	28.46	45.38	57.59S	76.19	59.86	82.51	151.07	206.76	351.15	361.65S
Greece	174	2.91	2.89	5.20	7.33	10.41	5.50	59.05S	4.72	8.51	9.43	14.49	18.59	22.87	49.95S
Iceland	176	.02	—	—	—	—	—	.03S	.03	.73	1.51	2.94	.06	—	.02S
Ireland	178	—	.12	.04	.06	.94	.05	.14S	.76	.66	1.65	2.18	4.33	6.68	5.68S
Italy	136	8.59	7.57	8.68	11.59	33.55	24.05	54.44S	37.67	41.76	36.50	61.63	64.43	102.13	167.28S
Luxembourg	137	—	—	—	.12	.03	.34	—S	.15	.23	.41	.47	.94	.93	2.69S
Malta	181	—	.03	—	.45	.01	—	.57S	.03	—	—	—	—	.80	1.52S
Netherlands	138	3.49	4.38	9.89	9.84	11.33	6.56	11.65S	10.50	15.08	23.88	34.60	53.09	75.62	82.80S
Norway	142	—	—	.01	.09	.04	.43	.16S	.20	.26	.59	1.01	2.46	4.03	2.76S
Portugal	182	.09	.10	.25	.14	.21	.96	2.77S	1.33	1.40	1.39	2.16	3.14	2.88	12.10S
Slovenia	961	—	—	.02	—	.02	.01	.09S	5.76	2.71	3.25	3.97	4.05	5.55	8.39S
Spain	184	1.96	.68	6.99	9.50	14.24	16.64	53.64S	1.98	2.85	3.63	6.41	8.45	15.28	31.06S
Sweden	144	.25	.02	.04	.06	.15	.01	.13S	1.13	7.87	6.38	4.81	9.62	13.61	37.72S
Switzerland	146	16.33	24.31	33.25	17.75	3.26	1.94	1.04S	14.80	18.52	14.50	26.18	17.57	32.71	27.10S
United Kingdom	112	22.87	32.77	27.93	31.67	31.93	24.41	83.15S	26.00	27.16	145.62	171.81	70.21	63.01	56.83S
Developing Countries	**202**	**234.5**	**248.8**	**337.8**	**498.2**	**634.4**	**698.6**	**865.2Y**	**443.5**	**482.1**	**619.7**	**1,116.7**	**1,694.4**	**2,604.0**	**3,817.2Y**
Africa	**607**	**.5**	**2.8**	**.1**	**—**	**.1**	**5.8**	**5.8Y**	**1.5**	**1.6**	**.4**	**8.9**	**2.4**	**2.0**	**12.6Y**
Algeria	612	.24	—	—	—	—	3.94	4.35S	—	—	—	.16	—	.01	.01S
Angola	614	—	—	—	—	—	1.78	1.19S	—	.03	—	—	—	—	—S
Botswana	616	—	.02	—	—	—	—	—S	—	.01	—	—	—	—	—S
Cameroon	622	—	—	—	—	—	—	—S	—	—	.01	.10	.12	—	—S
Central African Rep.	626	—	—	—	—	—	—	—S	.01	—	—	—	—	—	—S
Côte d'Ivoire	662	—	—	—	—	—	—	—S	—	—	—	.01	—	.03	4.96S
Djibouti	611	—	.07	—	—	—	—	—S	....	....	....	....	....	....	....
Equatorial Guinea	642	....	....	....	....	....	....	....	.04	—	—	—	—	—	—S
Ethiopia	644	.01	—	—	—	—	—	—S	—	—	.01	.01	—	—	—S
Gambia, The	648	.01	2.45	—	—	—	—	—S	—	—	—	—	—	—	—S
Ghana	652	.10	—	.06	—	—	—	—S	—	—	—	—	—	—	1.84S
Guinea	656	.07	.03	—	—	—	—	—S	—	—	—	.03	.04	—	—S
Kenya	664	—	—	—	—	—	—	—S	—	.09	—	—	.12	—	—S
Liberia	668	—	—	—	.01	.01	.01	—S	—	—	—	—	—	—	—S
Malawi	676	....	....	....	....	....	....	....	.30	.33	—	—	—	—	.13S
Mauritania	682	—	—	—	—	—	—	—S	.04	.17	—	—	—	—	.04S
Mauritius	684	—	—	—	—	—	—	.01S	—	—	—	—	—	—	—S
Morocco	686	—	—	—	—	—	.02	.01S	.02	—	—	—	.05	.13	.49S
Mozambique	688	.01	—	—	.01	—	—	—S	—	—	—	—	—	—	—S
Namibia	728	....	....	....	....	....	....	....	—	—	.01	.01	—	—	—S
Nigeria	694	—	—	—	—	—	—	—S	—	—	—	—	.01	—	—S
Seychelles	718	....	....	....	....	....	....	....	—	—	.04	4.63	.14	.13	.09S
Somalia	726	....	....	....	....	....	....	....	—	—	—	.01	—	—	—S
South Africa	199	.06	.01	—	—	.04	—	.20S	.02	.24	.34	3.90	1.93	1.58	4.96S
Tanzania	738	—	—	—	—	—	—	—S	—	—	—	—	—	—	.01S
Tunisia	744	—	.01	—	—	.03	—	—S	—	—	—	.01	—	—	—S
Uganda	746	—	.21	.02	—	—	—	—S	—	—	—	—	—	—	—S
Zimbabwe	698	—	—	—	—	—	—	—S	1.04	.68	—	—	—	.12	.09S
Africa n.s.	799	—	—	—	—	—	—	—S	—	—	—	.01	—	—	—S
Asia	**507**	**6.3**	**5.8**	**10.7**	**15.5**	**19.0**	**22.6**	**33.7Y**	**10.4**	**15.2**	**33.5**	**45.0**	**69.3**	**146.8**	**302.9Y**
Afghanistan, I.S. of	512	.01	.13	.03	—	.89	.75	.78S	—	—	—	—	—	.06	.05S
Bangladesh	513	—	—	—	—	—	—	—S	—	—	—	—	—	.03	1.44S
Bhutan	514	—	.01	.09	—	—	—	—S	.01	—	—	—	—	—	—S
Cambodia	522	—	—	—	—	—	—	—S	—	—	—	.03	—	.02	.03S
China,P.R.: Mainland	924	1.05	1.18	1.17	3.31	5.60	10.35	13.22S	3.83	8.72	23.17	28.90	46.71	103.33	203.87S
China,P.R.:Hong Kong	532	—	.11	.67	.02	.01	.98	.40S	.35	.25	.25	.51	1.25	2.29	9.73S
India	534	4.44	2.13	6.35	6.03	2.26	8.69	10.55S	2.08	4.19	6.02	5.77	8.34	11.84	16.57S
Indonesia	536	.10	.05	—	.39	—	.03	.14S	2.60	.20	.44	1.49	1.72	2.33	14.09S
Korea	542	.09	1.54	.34	.60	8.01	.74	2.88S	.85	.33	.82	2.62	5.12	12.42	30.86S
Malaysia	548	.02	—	—	—	—	.02	2.95S	.05	—	.10	.27	.42	.75	5.83S
Mongolia	948	.30	.44	.50	.76	.39	.45	.58S	—	—	—	—	—	—	—S

		Exports							Imports						
		2001	2002	2003	2004	2005	2006	2007	2001	2002	2003	2004	2005	2006	2007
		Millions of U.S. Dollars							*Millions of U.S. Dollars*						
Pakistan	564	—	—	.03	—	.04	.07	.09S	—	—	.02	.61	.09	.45	.43S
Philippines	566	.02	.01	—	—	—	—	.20S	—	.06	.03	.01	—	.05	—S
Singapore	576	.24	.23	1.11	2.94	1.27	.47	.55S	.20	.47	1.05	.89	.95	2.24	4.61S
Sri Lanka	524	—	—	—	—	—	—	—S	.07	.06	.09	.30	.54	.46	.94S
Taiwan Province of China	528	—	.01	—	.07	.26	.01	1.31S	.27	.50	.43	1.35	2.49	4.75	7.16S
Thailand	578	.02	—	.10	—	—	—	—S	.10	.32	.89	1.81	1.18	3.97	5.86S
Tonga	866	—	—	—	—	—	—	—S	.01	—	—	—	—	—	—S
Tuvalu	869	....	....	....	....	....	....	....	—	.01	—	—	—	—	—S
Vietnam	582	—	—	.25	1.36	.28	—	—S	.02	.05	.19	.44	.47	1.83	1.38S
Europe	**170**	**220.2**	**232.1**	**317.5**	**472.6**	**598.5**	**622.7**	**733.4Y**	**408.6**	**420.9**	**538.3**	**956.2**	**1,464.4**	**2,211.3**	**3,106.8Y**
Albania	914	.18	—	.01	.12	—	—	9.31S	—	—	—	—	.02	5.17	1.54S
Armenia	911	12.51	20.99	30.76	54.46	39.93	73.62	72.87S	10.29	8.56	11.20	26.23	39.29	40.25	82.06S
Azerbaijan	912	9.98	29.25	16.62	25.33	83.45	92.17	96.22S	73.19	79.89	93.79	156.40	233.42	318.53	386.98S
Belarus	913	1.52	2.46	1.99	2.72	2.45	3.26	4.20S	1.62	.65	1.95	2.86	6.77	25.68	31.44S
Bosnia & Herzegovina	963	—	—	—	—	—	—	—S	—	.06	.16	—	1.45	.53	.38S
Bulgaria	918	.58	.14	.15	15.55	42.84	62.31	77.44S	10.68	13.76	19.31	38.88	72.28	115.54	245.26S
Croatia	960	—	—	—	—	—	—	—S	.59	2.55	.60	1.87	4.25	14.80	5.98S
Czech Republic	935	.65	.85	.85	1.62	6.63	6.21	6.08S	2.93	5.39	6.18	12.35	20.55	42.69	46.96S
Estonia	939	—	.06	.01	.87	2.78	1.88	1.15S	.15	.14	.04	.44	1.14	1.01	4.33S
Gibraltar	823	.46	4.78	1.80	.19	.37	7.77	10.44S	.45	1.39	.45	.22	.01	.56	.73S
Hungary	944	.31	.11	.53	.08	.03	.14	.04S	5.06	5.26	7.66	10.15	14.34	20.17	33.63S
Kazakhstan	916	4.30	2.97	4.33	7.57	9.80	15.43	28.43S	5.26	5.28	9.76	21.42	11.55	25.38	48.29S
Kyrgyz Republic	917	—	.08	.52	.64	.25	.49	.26S	.23	.19	.29	.68	.48	1.86	1.21S
Latvia	941	.53	.42	.82	1.03	1.75	3.69	4.02S	.98	.92	3.99	2.91	6.20	6.37	7.94S
Lithuania	946	2.93	1.63	.72	.87	.97	2.94	5.68S	4.51	1.25	1.41	4.55	5.01	9.32	16.05S
Macedonia, FYR	962	—	—	.01	.19	.04	—	—S	.06	.13	.05	.27	.02	.09	.06S
Moldova	921	.15	.13	.17	.12	.24	.22	.70S	.23	.34	1.00	1.76	4.02	3.52	4.14S
Poland	964	.94	1.02	.23	1.52	.74	3.07	3.69S	3.54	2.98	3.64	8.43	13.66	20.63	66.57S
Romania	968	.07	.07	.97	1.29	8.75	5.65	1.53S	16.93	5.19	10.53	14.02	40.69	40.77	122.28S
Russia	922	74.40	60.96	83.94	104.53	153.92	75.66	53.55S	93.47	121.62	161.09	257.77	384.35	558.77	655.03S
Serbia & Montenegro	965	.12	.02	.05	.32	.94	8.02	5.44S	.43	.97	.88	1.47	1.17	5.00	4.47S
Slovak Republic	936	.18	—	.11	2.63	2.90	1.33	1.82S	.76	.74	.91	1.34	2.95	4.56	4.79S
Tajikistan	923	.32	.52	.55	1.06	2.67	2.59	2.86S	.12	—	.03	.07	.04	.09	.03S
Turkey	186	68.57	53.74	82.55	118.61	121.81	124.92	199.54S	107.14	89.68	112.14	202.09	283.01	522.56	746.08S
Turkmenistan	925	28.88	36.73	58.40	113.44	75.83	71.81	69.41S	17.64	14.62	9.91	32.67	95.07	101.06	126.63S
Ukraine	926	11.51	12.65	30.22	15.61	37.27	56.96	76.18S	50.84	58.97	80.27	142.38	219.37	320.09	453.23S
Uzbekistan	927	1.14	2.57	1.14	2.21	2.14	2.55	2.57S	1.50	.38	1.02	14.99	3.33	6.29	10.73S
Middle East	**407**	**6.9**	**7.0**	**5.8**	**9.9**	**11.8**	**35.2**	**55.0Y**	**17.6**	**16.8**	**30.3**	**70.0**	**113.9**	**183.2**	**289.8Y**
Egypt	469	—	.02	.05	.42	1.22	.91	3.40S	.41	.07	.10	.47	1.73	7.69	10.46S
Iran, I.R. of	429	4.31	3.32	3.43	4.50	4.68	2.70	4.02S	6.32	8.10	7.00	15.16	26.00	40.30	48.96S
Iraq	433	.07	—	.26	.68	.64	.79	1.10S	—	.01	.11	.01	—	.13	.09S
Israel	436	.54	.78	.96	1.45	1.01	2.34	11.85S	.80	1.30	1.75	4.92	9.66	22.31	62.16S
Jordan	439	.10	.04	—	—	—	—	.01S	.01	—	.08	.25	.16	.06	.41S
Kuwait	443	—	—	.01	—	—	—	—S	—	—	—	.06	.04	.23	.39S
Lebanon	446	.08	.19	.04	—	—	.02	.01S	1.36	.22	.37	.11	.27	.26	.28S
Libya	672	.02	—	—	—	—	—	—S	—	—	—	—	—	—	—S
Oman	449	—	—	—	—	.03	—	—S	—	.28	.37	.40	.52	.38	.42S
Qatar	453	—	—	—	—	.15	—	—S	....	....	....	....	....	....	....
Saudi Arabia	456	.02	—	—	.02	.01	—	.01S	—	.14	.18	1.09	.02	.19	.14S
Syrian Arab Republic	463	.53	.60	—	.02	.07	—	.01S	.42	.37	.42	.85	2.54	2.53	3.14S
United Arab Emirates	466	1.25	2.06	1.01	2.79	3.94	22.88	28.76S	8.25	6.36	19.90	46.71	72.99	109.12	163.34S
Yemen, Republic of	474	—	—	—	—	—	5.57	5.80S	—	—	—	—	—	—	—S
Western Hemisphere	**207**	**.6**	**1.0**	**3.8**	**.3**	**5.0**	**12.4**	**37.4Y**	**5.4**	**27.6**	**17.2**	**36.5**	**44.3**	**60.7**	**105.1Y**
Argentina	213	—	—	—	—	—	—	—S	.01	—	.13	.22	1.05	.94	2.68S
Bahamas, The	313	.53	—	.20	—	.16	—	—S	.31	3.17	.02	—	—	.06	.04S
Barbados	316	—	—	—	—	—	—	.02S	—	—	.01	—	—	—	—S
Belize	339	—	.18	.56	.25	.09	.07	1.10S	—	—	.04	—	.05	.40	.35S
Bermuda	319	....	....	....	....	....	....	....	—	—	—	—	.07	—	—S
Bolivia	218	—	.15	—	—	—	—	—S	....	....	....	....	....	....	....
Brazil	223	—	—	—	—	—	3.40	19.07S	3.98	18.45	11.21	23.66	33.03	52.27	71.31S
Chile	228	—	—	—	—	—	.05	.19S	—	—	—	—	.04	.65	.30S
Colombia	233	—	—	—	—	—	.06	.41S	.02	.22	.04	4.41	3.98	.10	.10S
Costa Rica	238	—	—	—	—	—	—	—S	—	.13	—	—	—	.46	1.63S
Dominica	321	....	....	....	....	....	....	....	—	.09	.08	.35	.56	.01	—S
Dominican Republic	243	....	....	....	....	....	....	....	—	.12	.49	2.48	1.61	—	—S
Ecuador	248	—	.01	—	—	—	.02	.14S	.56	.83	1.52	1.51	2.24	1.81	3.28S
El Salvador	253	—	—	—	—	—	—	—S	—	—	.09	.20	.19	—	.17S
Grenada	328	—	—	—	—	—	—	—S	—	—	—	.03	.02	—	—S
Guatemala	258	—	—	—	—	—	—	.18S	—	—	—	—	—	—	—S
Honduras	268	—	—	—	—	—	—	—S	.15	—	.01	.17	.04	.11	.08S
Jamaica	343	—	—	—	—	—	—	—S	—	.08	—	—	—	—	19.85S
Mexico	273	—	—	—	—	3.35	5.24	13.06S	—	—	.13	.06	.01	—	—S
Nicaragua	278	—	—	—	—	—	.01	.01S	....	....	....	....	....	....	....
Panama	283	—	.67	1.06	.01	.01	.54	.01S	—	.05	.19	.23	.24	.16	.44S
Peru	293	—	.01	—	—	—	.21	.71S	—	.05	.04	—	—	.31	1.26S
St. Kitts and Nevis	361	—	—	—	—	—	—	—S	.04	—	—	.01	—	—	—S
Trinidad and Tobago	369	—	—	1.98	—	—	—	—S	—	—	—	—	—	—	—S

	Exports							Imports						
	2001	2002	2003	2004	2005	2006	2007	2001	2002	2003	2004	2005	2006	2007
	Millions of U.S. Dollars							*Millions of U.S. Dollars*						
Uruguay........ 298	—	—	—	—	.02	.16	.10S	—	.01	.05	—	—	.39	.53S
Venezuela, Rep. Bol........ 299	—	—	—	—	—	—	—S	—	—	—	—	.01	—	—S
Western Hem. n.s........ 399	.02	—	.03	—	1.41	2.66	2.40S	.32	4.43	3.18	3.20	1.14	3.01	3.11S
Other Countries n.i.e........ 910	**—**	**—**	**—**	**.2**	**—**	**2.4**	**2.3Y**	**.1**	**.4**	**.1**	**.2**	**.1**	**.4**	**.4Y**
Cuba........ 928	—	—	—	—	—	—	—S	—	—	.06	.11	—	—	—S
North Korea........ 954	—	.04	.02	.23	.05	2.38	2.30S	.11	.38	.05	.04	.10	.35	.41S
Memorandum Items														
European Union........ 998	61.89	65.53	81.64	111.37	165.22	188.49	442.36Y	240.85	231.32	430.78	617.57	671.50	947.90	1,259.62Y
Oil Exporting Ctys........ 999	6.01	5.44	4.72	8.38	9.45	30.35	38.38Y	17.17	15.08	27.99	65.08	101.31	152.70	227.44Y
Non-Oil Develop.Ctys........ 201	228.49	243.37	333.07	489.86	624.92	668.25	826.86Y	426.31	467.01	591.66	1,051.60	1,593.08	2,451.27	3,589.78Y
PERCENT DISTRIBUTION														
Industrial Countries........ 101	**26.1**	**28.8**	**27.4**	**22.7**	**25.4**	**28.5**	**43.3**	**40.8**	**38.9**	**45.5**	**39.5**	**32.0**	**29.2**	**28.2**
Developing Countries........ 202	**73.9**	**71.2**	**72.6**	**77.3**	**74.5**	**71.2**	**56.6**	**58.9**	**60.8**	**54.3**	**60.4**	**68.0**	**70.8**	**71.8**
Africa........ 607	**.2**	**.8**	**—**	**—**	**—**	**.6**	**.4**	**.2**	**.2**	**—**	**.5**	**.1**	**.1**	**.2**
Asia........ 507	**2.0**	**1.7**	**2.3**	**2.4**	**2.2**	**2.3**	**2.2**	**1.4**	**1.9**	**2.9**	**2.4**	**2.8**	**4.0**	**5.7**
Europe........ 170	**69.4**	**66.4**	**68.2**	**73.3**	**70.3**	**63.5**	**48.0**	**54.2**	**53.1**	**47.2**	**51.8**	**58.8**	**60.1**	**58.4**
Middle East........ 407	**2.2**	**2.0**	**1.2**	**1.5**	**1.4**	**3.6**	**3.6**	**2.3**	**2.1**	**2.7**	**3.8**	**4.6**	**5.0**	**5.4**
Western Hemisphere........ 207	**.2**	**.3**	**.8**	**—**	**.6**	**1.3**	**2.4**	**.7**	**3.5**	**1.5**	**2.0**	**1.8**	**1.6**	**2.0**
Other Countries n.i.e........ 910	**—**	**—**	**—**	**—**	**—**	**.2**	**.2**	**—**	**—**	**—**	**—**	**—**	**—**	**—**
ANNUAL PERCENT CHANGE														
World........ 001	**–2.7**	**10.1**	**33.2**	**38.6**	**32.0**	**15.3**	**55.9**	**4.4**	**5.1**	**44.0**	**61.9**	**34.8**	**47.6**	**44.7**
Industrial Countries........ 101	**–9.3**	**21.4**	**26.7**	**14.8**	**48.0**	**29.2**	**136.3**	**10.3**	**.1**	**68.5**	**40.7**	**9.0**	**34.8**	**40.0**
Developing Countries........ 202	**—**	**6.1**	**35.8**	**47.5**	**27.3**	**10.1**	**23.9**	**1.5**	**8.7**	**28.5**	**80.2**	**51.7**	**53.7**	**46.6**
Africa........ 607	**–89.5**	**477.2**	**–96.9**	**–62.4**	**150.6**	**—**	**.2**	**201.5**	**4.5**	**–74.1**	**—**	**–72.6**	**–17.5**	**528.8**
Asia........ 507	**126.0**	**–7.3**	**82.6**	**45.3**	**22.7**	**18.7**	**49.2**	**–8.5**	**45.1**	**121.0**	**34.4**	**53.9**	**111.9**	**106.3**
Europe........ 170	**3.6**	**5.4**	**36.8**	**48.9**	**26.6**	**4.0**	**17.8**	**3.4**	**3.0**	**27.9**	**77.6**	**53.1**	**51.0**	**40.5**
Middle East........ 407	**–42.1**	**1.4**	**–17.8**	**71.2**	**19.0**	**199.5**	**56.1**	**–19.8**	**–4.2**	**79.7**	**131.4**	**62.7**	**60.8**	**58.2**
Western Hemisphere........ 207	**–79.0**	**82.8**	**275.7**	**–93.0**	**—**	**146.7**	**201.1**	**–29.8**	**413.8**	**–37.6**	**112.1**	**21.2**	**37.0**	**73.3**
Other Countries n.i.e........ 910	**—**	**....**	**–49.2**	**961.2**	**–79.4**	**—**	**–3.4**	**–9.1**	**239.1**	**–70.2**	**34.9**	**–35.3**	**262.1**	**18.0**

		Exports							Imports						
		2001	2002	2003	2004	2005	2006	2007	2001	2002	2003	2004	2005	2006	2007
		Millions of U.S. Dollars							*Millions of U.S. Dollars*						
IFS World Total		**571,357**	**615,446**	**751,679**	**911,582**	**977,881**	**1,122,066**	**1,329,053**	**485,969**	**489,949**	**604,613**	**718,045**	**780,444**	**922,338**	**1,059,643**
DOTS World Total	**001**	**570,419**	**613,034**	**742,149**	**911,777**	**977,049**	**1,108,781**	**1,327,220**	**492,657**	**493,636**	**596,481**	**718,241**	**776,934**	**907,439**	**1,059,479**
Industrial Countries	**101**	**427,561**	**452,347**	**543,482**	**662,007**	**702,727**	**772,157**	**913,955**	**353,828**	**346,889**	**410,716**	**487,405**	**520,029**	**611,640**	**716,010**
United States	111	60,266	62,926	69,009	80,552	86,071	95,712	100,128	40,710	37,803	43,626	50,017	51,367	42,441	47,637
Canada	156	4,564	5,263	5,434	6,050	6,834	7,731	8,653	2,977	2,690	2,686	2,971	3,260	3,494	3,615
Australia	193	3,237	3,709	4,719	5,768	6,263	6,807	7,943	1,111	1,181	1,175	1,600	1,563	1,326	1,427
Japan	158	11,709	11,524	13,281	15,789	16,603	17,156	17,872	20,251	18,083	21,455	26,233	26,606	21,913	24,943
New Zealand	196	506	557	687	834	865	872	1,031	502	550	589	668	746	611	630
Austria	122	29,241	31,540	39,503	49,044	52,831	61,656	72,321	18,584	20,066	23,601	30,118	31,406	39,235	47,125
Belgium	124	28,124	29,476	37,477	51,173	54,672	58,315	70,351	25,482	25,337	28,939	35,439	38,710	66,465	82,110
Cyprus	423	338	412	505	628	833	913	1,191	137	54	123	143	120	517	705
Denmark	128	9,262	10,345	12,698	14,032	15,304	17,915	21,039	8,162	8,688	10,066	11,622	11,899	14,351	16,401
Finland	172	6,065	6,282	7,604	9,259	10,226	11,487	14,090	5,679	5,238	5,910	7,519	9,263	9,447	11,273
France	132	63,312	65,803	78,504	93,608	99,425	106,179	128,610	46,260	46,543	54,764	64,900	67,876	78,007	91,193
Greece	174	4,584	4,696	6,294	7,836	8,101	8,339	10,421	1,517	1,471	1,681	1,830	2,014	2,485	2,718
Iceland	176	267	245	304	427	574	834	855	332	436	468	541	529	513	598
Ireland	178	3,550	3,745	4,138	5,418	6,057	7,246	8,667	14,833	12,461	15,593	18,737	19,161	10,481	12,327
Italy	136	42,578	44,898	54,757	65,252	67,657	73,952	89,213	31,938	31,795	37,795	43,492	44,280	51,524	60,942
Luxembourg	137	2,493	2,759	3,399	4,345	4,752	5,430	6,296	1,642	1,723	2,182	2,734	3,202	4,450	5,203
Malta	181	285	243	325	485	402	421	469	328	253	287	272	251	374	513
Netherlands	138	35,203	37,475	46,035	56,580	59,411	70,050	85,178	41,470	40,577	49,858	59,607	66,313	108,183	126,881
Norway	142	4,379	4,322	5,040	6,424	7,106	8,214	10,332	10,296	10,854	14,867	16,372	18,604	21,556	21,829
Portugal	182	5,734	6,418	7,074	8,455	9,230	9,179	10,744	4,892	4,821	5,793	5,761	5,065	5,027	5,652
Slovenia	961	2,151	2,231	2,739	3,327	3,657	4,334	5,692	2,320	2,451	2,722	2,929	3,151	3,791	4,934
Spain	184	25,434	28,070	36,515	45,777	50,268	52,121	65,917	13,986	14,880	18,429	21,539	22,405	24,118	28,615
Sweden	144	11,593	12,759	16,045	19,721	21,440	23,469	29,703	8,171	8,457	10,624	12,639	14,048	16,147	19,144
Switzerland	146	24,995	25,462	29,424	35,327	37,377	43,378	50,112	18,026	18,700	21,702	27,037	29,263	33,541	40,123
United Kingdom	112	47,692	51,188	61,973	75,897	76,769	80,446	97,128	34,223	31,776	35,781	42,685	48,927	51,643	59,472
Developing Countries	**202**	**141,169**	**158,681**	**196,761**	**247,760**	**272,116**	**330,822**	**407,719**	**138,110**	**146,068**	**184,887**	**229,990**	**256,022**	**294,473**	**342,432**
Africa	**607**	**8,925**	**9,728**	**11,493**	**14,302**	**15,418**	**17,126**	**20,111**	**7,870**	**8,288**	**8,541**	**8,905**	**10,751**	**11,933**	**12,684**
Algeria	612	705	849	767	1,215	1,344	1,346	1,611	845	862	976	1,028	2,019	1,415	1,376
Angola	614	39	53	95	97	143	251	509	54	209	60	4	77	76	196
Benin	638	51	47	52	46	42	56	69	4	2	2	3	3	9	7
Botswana	616	15	14	13	10	25	24	36	12	8	8	11	13	11	24
Burkina Faso	748	10	10	23	20	17	23	22	2	2	3	5	3	3	3
Burundi	618	7	4	6	9	8	10	19	8	8	8	11	25	15	31
Cameroon	622	120	94	83	94	98	94	128	81	86	64	70	89	60	79
Cape Verde	624	5	17	7	7	7	9	17	—	—	1	—	1	—	—
Central African Rep.	626	5	4	2	3	4	6	5	3	2	3	3	1	5	3
Chad	628	9	22	12	24	14	35	49	13	11	16	12	12	11	12
Comoros	632	2	1	1	1	1	1	1	4	6	7	2	4	1	1
Congo, Dem. Rep. of	636	30	63	65	65	66	63	93	12	8	12	8	19	17	16
Congo, Republic of	634	20	25	23	27	31	35	62	172	145	6	9	72	55	136
Côte d'Ivoire	662	79	84	89	98	102	130	138	235	296	355	311	336	549	887
Djibouti	611	14	16	13	12	8	17	28	1	—	—	—	—	—	—
Equatorial Guinea	642	5	5	8	5	8	20	37	5	6	4	8	36	77	110
Eritrea	643	17	14	8	9	13	13	17	1	1	1	1	2	—	—
Ethiopia	644	63	66	76	78	136	138	162	37	47	76	88	118	109	111
Gabon	646	26	26	33	40	39	66	62	10	8	22	17	20	22	78
Gambia, The	648	12	14	14	17	12	13	11	1	2	1	4	—	—	—
Ghana	652	118	138	165	177	176	199	271	123	119	136	113	116	120	164
Guinea	656	20	26	30	24	21	26	39	47	46	49	63	74	81	137
Guinea-Bissau	654	2	3	1	1	1	2	2	—	—	—	—	—	—	—
Kenya	664	124	125	159	167	192	241	286	92	84	92	104	110	105	124
Lesotho	666	1	3	21	9	13	16	12	—	—	—	—	—	—	—
Liberia	668	217	735	385	187	66	108	269	429	626	446	189	47	683	129
Madagascar	674	30	16	27	34	33	32	43	66	52	71	107	97	71	82
Malawi	676	16	13	10	27	11	33	26	62	62	69	63	48	65	102
Mali	678	59	49	50	67	58	62	79	7	9	8	18	11	106	2
Mauritania	682	34	39	44	44	47	46	62	33	63	47	84	85	45	56
Mauritius	684	106	77	124	122	155	137	109	63	56	59	52	38	39	56
Morocco	686	621	686	1,008	1,221	1,151	1,362	1,751	480	514	546	565	564	517	547
Mozambique	688	12	39	33	22	25	54	32	58	85	96	152	154	22	51
Namibia	728	34	44	35	51	50	73	68	42	42	38	57	63	112	122
Niger	692	36	50	46	42	34	27	28	—	1	1	2	1	—	—
Nigeria	694	883	737	715	894	938	1,194	1,482	689	537	749	374	885	1,744	1,239
Rwanda	714	6	18	24	32	27	44	43	31	5	8	12	20	21	18
São Tomé & Príncipe	716	1	6	7	6	—	1	1	—	1	1	1	1	—	—
Senegal	722	52	47	59	62	64	73	86	15	18	7	8	9	6	6
Seychelles	718	6	7	6	12	23	27	99	17	25	38	22	27	3	7
Sierra Leone	724	22	117	125	67	104	13	18	4	35	20	24	29	3	2
Somalia	726	1	1	3	2	1	1	2	1	—	—	1	—	1	4

		Exports							Imports						
		2001	2002	2003	2004	2005	2006	2007	2001	2002	2003	2004	2005	2006	2007
		Millions of U.S. Dollars							Millions of U.S. Dollars						
South Africa	199	3,959	4,122	5,663	7,541	8,303	8,814	9,727	2,931	3,039	3,172	3,997	4,199	4,339	4,987
Sudan	732	131	106	124	177	284	405	318	32	36	36	41	42	30	23
Swaziland	734	2	3	5	12	7	7	8	2	3	3	3	3	1	6
Tanzania	738	66	51	83	94	111	155	165	61	40	55	53	72	72	123
Togo	742	35	42	52	55	48	51	49	5	5	3	6	28	34	71
Tunisia	744	1,024	932	1,002	1,176	1,253	1,417	1,766	898	891	974	1,026	1,026	1,106	1,372
Uganda	746	25	27	35	40	53	67	88	26	28	34	33	44	58	74
Zambia	754	13	12	21	15	26	34	71	17	11	12	21	22	25	36
Zimbabwe	698	55	42	52	55	37	67	51	141	144	145	119	87	90	71
Asia	**507**	**36,215**	**41,507**	**52,907**	**66,377**	**68,781**	**83,479**	**99,182**	**48,251**	**50,678**	**65,027**	**86,872**	**96,759**	**102,794**	**115,197**
Afghanistan, I.S. of	512	14	52	94	118	152	250	186	7	5	5	11	4	3	6
American Samoa	859	1	3	1	16	—	1	1	—	—	—	—	—	—	—
Bangladesh	513	178	153	193	277	321	343	295	803	780	1,162	1,536	1,455	1,771	1,858
Bhutan	514	3	3	2	99	6	5	3	—	—	—	—	—	—	—
Brunei Darussalam	516	22	34	120	57	27	34	37	4	2	3	2	2	—	3
Cambodia	522	8	10	9	10	13	15	28	152	176	235	333	326	369	328
China,P.R.: Mainland	924	10,793	13,761	20,453	26,072	26,396	34,144	41,045	17,692	20,002	28,094	40,444	49,415	54,249	65,725
China,P.R.:Hong Kong	532	3,781	4,010	4,448	5,024	5,088	5,918	6,223	2,146	2,049	2,291	2,473	2,464	2,768	2,459
China,P.R.:Macao	546	55	233	236	51	61	43	79	239	236	250	315	173	217	217
Fiji	819	2	3	3	6	17	13	6	4	2	5	3	2	3	2
French Polynesia	887	19	22	30	32	26	28	31	7	5	4	7	5	5	8
Guam	829	—	3	4	8	7	9	7	—	—	—	1	1	—	—
India	534	2,065	2,283	2,745	4,095	5,219	7,690	10,086	2,240	2,380	2,924	3,647	4,218	4,692	5,941
Indonesia	536	1,328	1,414	1,411	2,101	1,798	1,858	2,177	2,143	2,123	2,371	2,816	2,984	2,886	3,548
Kiribati	826	—	1	—	1	—	2	1	—	1	—	—	—	—	—
Korea	542	4,120	4,610	6,255	7,945	8,806	10,212	11,723	4,182	4,927	6,404	9,521	11,215	12,986	10,698
Lao People's Dem.Rep	544	7	4	7	25	10	11	32	28	24	26	32	35	38	47
Malaysia	548	2,270	2,422	3,583	3,948	3,981	4,543	5,735	3,095	3,216	3,920	4,617	4,625	3,771	4,719
Maldives	556	6	8	9	13	16	21	33	6	4	1	2	3	4	6
Mongolia	948	30	35	41	48	52	52	75	2	4	7	13	17	10	13
Myanmar	518	17	18	14	25	33	40	53	110	80	103	130	112	126	121
Nauru	836	—	1	—	1	1	1	1	—	—	—	4	—	—	—
Nepal	558	21	30	25	19	24	29	40	72	45	47	58	49	46	45
New Caledonia	839	28	30	52	47	46	56	108	1	2	3	3	1	2	—
Pakistan	564	460	533	612	832	1,186	1,268	1,241	522	543	665	782	720	703	802
Palau	565	9	—	3	—	1	1	1	—	—	—	—	—	—	—
Papua New Guinea	853	7	8	6	5	5	16	11	117	85	149	222	228	267	269
Philippines	566	979	766	1,053	1,389	1,338	1,632	1,293	1,800	2,083	2,398	2,511	2,350	1,983	1,937
Samoa	862	1	1	1	1	1	1	1	2	2	1	2	2	—	—
Singapore	576	3,755	3,848	4,284	5,022	5,305	5,812	6,850	3,467	3,434	3,813	5,472	4,860	4,710	3,364
Solomon Islands	813	2	1	1	1	2	2	3	—	1	1	4	4	—	—
Sri Lanka	524	143	132	179	309	281	221	201	233	221	256	316	322	330	420
Taiwan Province of China	528	3,733	4,575	4,257	5,308	5,336	5,573	6,560	5,827	4,926	6,080	6,889	6,415	6,379	6,786
Thailand	578	1,964	1,991	2,108	2,513	2,547	2,739	3,326	2,262	2,216	2,508	3,025	3,027	2,504	3,296
Timor-Leste	537	—	1	3	4	4	7	5	—	—	1	1	—	4	2
Tonga	866	—	—	2	3	1	2	1	—	1	—	—	—	—	—
Tuvalu	869	—	1	2	1	—	5	1	—	—	—	1	2	—	—
Vanuatu	846	16	1	—	—	—	—	1	2	1	1	6	4	—	—
Vietnam	582	383	506	666	955	679	890	1,691	1,084	1,101	1,299	1,674	1,719	1,969	2,576
Wallis-Futuna	857	—	—	—	—	—	1	—	—	—	—	—	—	—	—
Europe	**170**	**66,961**	**77,695**	**98,792**	**125,065**	**139,418**	**176,866**	**224,763**	**66,221**	**72,295**	**93,138**	**110,921**	**120,668**	**148,167**	**179,281**
Albania	914	64	67	90	111	142	150	194	18	21	23	25	28	26	30
Armenia	911	34	41	73	62	121	102	135	13	25	30	78	152	145	173
Azerbaijan	912	81	122	211	299	548	609	610	246	272	216	214	388	785	1,509
Belarus	913	705	826	944	1,158	1,358	1,945	2,119	282	332	400	463	451	536	559
Bosnia & Herzegovina	963	364	418	495	656	719	788	893	125	119	214	343	315	373	462
Bulgaria	918	929	1,107	1,445	1,948	2,283	2,720	3,178	621	692	926	1,196	1,326	1,633	1,870
Croatia	960	1,385	1,721	2,271	2,687	2,798	3,235	3,775	608	579	655	789	815	932	997
Czech Republic	935	13,370	15,124	18,768	22,135	23,404	28,163	35,711	12,987	15,362	19,660	21,147	21,936	27,530	36,494
Estonia	939	471	589	802	960	1,196	1,637	2,004	271	360	557	535	426	449	581
Faroe Islands	816	12	7	22	10	55	17	31	21	13	15	15	8	10	11
Georgia	915	74	71	78	113	143	238	289	22	20	28	28	49	42	74
Gibraltar	823	204	435	78	202	109	192	1,141	—	15	74	30	54	26	30
Hungary	944	9,416	10,560	13,327	15,539	16,862	20,061	23,707	10,722	11,450	13,721	16,665	17,765	19,726	24,774
Kazakhstan	916	490	596	774	1,108	1,295	1,816	2,683	1,050	1,110	1,571	2,516	3,108	4,087	4,746
Kosovo	967	—	—	—	—	—	79	121	—	—	—	—	—	5	12
Kyrgyz Republic	917	29	31	35	47	50	67	97	97	4	4	4	4	6	9
Latvia	941	727	829	1,003	1,034	1,098	1,704	2,288	415	413	495	492	472	609	647
Lithuania	946	1,115	1,442	1,806	1,842	1,866	2,567	3,276	635	659	823	890	796	1,037	1,591
Macedonia, FYR	962	224	244	258	322	352	427	546	250	225	287	335	386	452	576
Moldova	921	136	143	179	235	247	277	371	65	74	103	137	102	117	164
Montenegro, Rep. of	943	—	—	—	—	—	85	139	—	—	—	—	—	5	10
Poland	964	13,531	15,193	18,393	23,373	27,171	36,389	49,546	12,002	13,413	17,741	19,827	19,979	26,662	33,504
Romania	968	2,765	3,100	3,963	5,472	6,598	8,991	10,385	2,057	2,325	2,972	3,861	4,252	5,180	5,205
Russia	922	9,165	10,761	13,633	18,645	21,420	29,160	38,635	13,007	12,362	15,019	20,243	26,872	36,122	37,961
Serbia, Rep. of	942	—	—	—	—	—	1,496	1,999	—	—	—	—	—	627	842
Serbia & Montenegro	965	592	824	1,004	1,286	1,328	—	—	273	307	330	408	463	—	—
Slovak Republic	936	3,511	3,857	5,834	6,944	7,353	9,576	11,728	3,738	4,828	8,249	9,471	8,811	9,206	12,372

		Exports							Imports						
		2001	2002	2003	2004	2005	2006	2007	2001	2002	2003	2004	2005	2006	2007
		Millions of U.S. Dollars							Millions of U.S. Dollars						
Tajikistan	923	9	12	20	23	21	34	37	8	5	6	10	5	24	51
Turkey	186	5,380	7,018	9,960	14,692	15,889	17,721	20,495	5,860	6,522	8,065	9,871	10,265	10,240	12,086
Turkmenistan	925	128	154	161	200	133	196	217	6	20	76	46	51	45	4
Ukraine	926	1,810	2,161	2,920	3,700	4,527	6,185	8,120	756	717	834	1,210	1,311	1,468	1,842
Uzbekistan	927	207	204	214	221	285	279	360	62	48	38	66	58	54	87
Europe n.s.	884	33	40	33	41	46	40	53	5	3	3	4	18	12	20
Middle East	**407**	**14,247**	**15,724**	**19,059**	**23,690**	**27,523**	**29,783**	**35,122**	**6,759**	**5,889**	**7,158**	**9,289**	**11,203**	**13,264**	**12,975**
Bahrain	419	176	235	241	328	414	400	445	23	14	102	34	45	55	115
Egypt	469	1,317	1,325	1,450	1,774	2,110	2,323	2,908	265	260	426	630	819	943	999
Iran, I.R. of	429	1,720	2,122	3,016	4,454	5,516	5,158	4,950	363	301	321	487	575	453	683
Iraq	433	301	380	230	455	343	458	438	—	5	11	3	2	14	57
Israel	436	2,402	2,190	2,639	3,063	3,070	3,316	3,566	1,780	1,432	1,340	1,561	1,540	1,463	1,753
Jordan	439	387	402	502	595	688	1,007	993	30	29	22	57	29	31	35
Kuwait	443	668	772	978	1,410	1,510	1,168	1,434	34	55	89	79	29	35	61
Lebanon	446	492	475	816	720	566	601	632	14	17	26	28	21	21	36
Libya	672	489	492	584	815	817	729	916	1,923	1,530	2,032	3,527	4,821	6,201	5,786
Oman	449	240	257	259	359	506	568	749	12	9	10	14	17	30	26
Qatar	453	284	325	478	671	790	1,118	1,505	4	15	27	38	28	20	46
Saudi Arabia	456	2,683	3,250	3,570	3,802	5,023	5,473	7,288	857	799	1,046	1,318	1,688	1,683	1,221
Syrian Arab Republic	463	401	478	544	647	654	819	1,000	1,280	1,247	1,439	1,103	1,119	1,631	1,537
United Arab Emirates	466	2,580	2,901	3,621	4,418	5,351	6,422	7,898	171	172	262	400	463	678	500
West Bank/Gaza Strip	487	9	11	14	19	21	18	27	—	—	1	1	1	—	—
Yemen, Republic of	474	104	120	130	177	166	225	399	2	4	5	8	7	7	120
Middle East n.s.	489	3	—	—	—	—	—	—	—	—	—	—	—	—	—
Western Hemisphere	**207**	**14,821**	**14,027**	**14,510**	**18,326**	**20,976**	**23,567**	**28,541**	**9,009**	**8,919**	**11,023**	**14,003**	**16,640**	**18,316**	**22,296**
Antigua and Barbuda	311	22	94	29	24	120	141	93	184	201	340	21	41	184	35
Argentina	213	1,015	557	771	1,163	1,297	1,629	2,349	736	878	1,073	1,230	1,207	1,212	1,555
Aruba	314	8	5	18	5	7	54	52	—	1	—	6	1	—	2
Bahamas, The	313	75	555	56	11	420	19	51	130	150	111	97	130	262	170
Barbados	316	22	20	18	19	22	19	30	3	2	4	3	4	2	4
Belize	339	19	7	5	5	10	7	11	3	2	2	1	1	—	—
Bermuda	319	411	100	7	17	66	612	557	—	—	—	—	6	23	73
Bolivia	218	33	32	30	35	54	65	69	11	11	12	19	27	27	27
Brazil	223	5,104	4,624	4,566	5,776	6,780	7,056	9,371	3,653	3,579	4,317	5,695	7,091	6,482	8,490
Chile	228	704	687	810	1,147	1,227	1,583	1,595	606	559	798	1,547	1,618	2,143	2,304
Colombia	233	499	456	616	749	855	911	1,227	482	477	492	630	736	470	695
Costa Rica	238	131	144	145	205	148	162	183	269	282	321	437	476	208	235
Dominica	321	12	1	1	2	2	2	2	—	—	—	—	—	—	—
Dominican Republic	243	162	153	99	119	136	179	207	47	56	55	59	55	63	64
Ecuador	248	204	200	176	211	269	267	319	273	321	400	453	532	288	321
El Salvador	253	65	66	148	117	111	421	231	54	44	44	61	71	94	109
Falkland Islands	323	1	—	—	—	—	1	3	—	—	—	—	1	—	2
Greenland	326	14	3	3	2	3	3	4	7	15	12	16	18	1	4
Grenada	328	2	4	2	2	3	4	4	8	6	7	3	4	—	—
Guatemala	258	137	133	137	158	165	203	194	86	65	64	66	78	80	83
Guyana	336	4	4	5	5	7	4	6	5	5	6	4	6	3	4
Haiti	263	12	14	10	15	20	36	11	2	3	2	2	2	2	2
Honduras	268	40	37	48	126	190	84	128	73	79	82	114	138	173	191
Jamaica	343	98	41	206	36	39	49	44	105	108	110	117	116	103	94
Mexico	273	4,767	4,904	5,434	6,073	7,347	7,946	8,999	1,390	1,228	1,730	2,021	2,560	3,417	4,694
Netherlands Antilles	353	24	49	36	41	28	32	64	67	7	10	14	27	264	29
Nicaragua	278	25	21	31	35	37	33	33	39	15	12	23	21	34	33
Panama	283	107	114	160	120	128	155	329	89	161	185	188	164	236	270
Paraguay	288	49	34	38	43	48	63	99	36	22	80	86	96	81	186
Peru	293	204	203	217	276	326	435	620	222	287	292	465	645	812	1,036
St. Kitts and Nevis	361	1	2	3	7	5	5	8	2	2	3	2	3	1	1
St. Lucia	362	5	5	4	4	6	6	16	—	—	—	—	1	—	1
St. Pierre-Miquelon	363	2	—	—	1	—	1	1	—	—	—	—	—	—	—
St. Vincent & Grens.	364	2	2	1	2	10	23	3	1	—	—	1	1	—	7
Suriname	366	7	11	19	16	22	15	22	—	4	2	2	3	—	1
Trinidad and Tobago	369	142	85	222	567	123	132	167	25	12	13	36	14	19	24
Uruguay	298	98	74	73	92	107	182	180	73	131	164	225	169	224	270
Venezuela, Rep. Bol.	299	570	546	341	568	704	810	1,049	324	204	277	338	572	715	1,240
Western Hem. n.s.	399	25	40	22	530	137	216	209	1	2	5	21	5	693	36
Other Countries n.i.e.	**910**	**173**	**213**	**183**	**208**	**381**	**577**	**330**	**53**	**59**	**56**	**68**	**78**	**33**	**42**
Cuba	928	91	71	113	140	317	517	293	31	30	32	45	45	17	28
North Korea	954	82	141	70	69	64	59	37	23	29	24	23	34	16	14
Countries & Areas n.s.	**898**	**817**	**974**	**1,040**	**1,120**	**1,129**	**4,198**	**3,811**	**572**	**607**	**792**	**771**	**800**	**874**	**932**
Special Categories	**899**	**555**	**568**	**594**	**590**	**679**	**946**	**996**	**26**	**—**	**1**	**1**	**—**	**—**	**—**
Memorandum Items															
European Union	998	359,781	385,934	475,517	582,662	619,986	691,549	845,290	300,394	303,076	365,394	430,993	458,276	571,465	685,170
Oil Exporting Ctys	999	12,452	14,045	15,970	21,163	24,639	26,302	31,499	7,366	6,612	8,171	10,422	14,084	15,873	15,782
Non-Oil Develop.Ctys	201	128,717	144,636	180,791	226,597	247,476	304,520	376,220	130,744	139,456	176,716	219,568	241,938	278,600	326,650
PERCENT DISTRIBUTION															
Industrial Countries	**101**	**75.0**	**73.8**	**73.2**	**72.6**	**71.9**	**69.6**	**68.9**	**71.8**	**70.3**	**68.9**	**67.9**	**66.9**	**67.4**	**67.6**
Developing Countries	**202**	**24.7**	**25.9**	**26.5**	**27.2**	**27.9**	**29.8**	**30.7**	**28.0**	**29.6**	**31.0**	**32.0**	**33.0**	**32.5**	**32.3**
Africa	**607**	**1.6**	**1.6**	**1.5**	**1.6**	**1.6**	**1.5**	**1.5**	**1.6**	**1.7**	**1.4**	**1.2**	**1.4**	**1.3**	**1.2**

	Exports							Imports						
	2001	2002	2003	2004	2005	2006	2007	2001	2002	2003	2004	2005	2006	2007
Asia........ 507	6.3	6.8	7.1	7.3	7.0	7.5	7.5	9.8	10.3	10.9	12.1	12.5	11.3	10.9
Europe........ 170	11.7	12.7	13.3	13.7	14.3	16.0	16.9	13.4	14.6	15.6	15.4	15.5	16.3	16.9
Middle East........ 407	2.5	2.6	2.6	2.6	2.8	2.7	2.6	1.4	1.2	1.2	1.3	1.4	1.5	1.2
Western Hemisphere........ 207	2.6	2.3	2.0	2.0	2.1	2.1	2.2	1.8	1.8	1.8	1.9	2.1	2.0	2.1
Other Countries n.i.e........ 910	—	—	—	—	—	.1	—	—	—	—	—	—	—	—
ANNUAL PERCENT CHANGE														
World........ 001	3.9	7.5	21.1	22.9	7.2	13.5	19.7	–1.5	.2	20.8	20.4	8.2	16.8	16.8
Industrial Countries........ 101	2.6	5.8	20.1	21.8	6.2	9.9	18.4	–2.1	–2.0	18.4	18.7	6.7	17.6	17.1
Developing Countries........ 202	8.4	12.4	24.0	25.9	9.8	21.6	23.2	—	5.8	26.6	24.4	11.3	15.0	16.3
Africa........ 607	15.1	9.0	18.1	24.4	7.8	11.1	17.4	–3.0	5.3	3.0	4.3	20.7	11.0	6.3
Asia........ 507	7.0	14.6	27.5	25.5	3.6	21.4	18.8	–3.9	5.0	28.3	33.6	11.4	6.2	12.1
Europe........ 170	8.6	16.0	27.2	26.6	11.5	26.9	27.1	6.3	9.2	28.8	19.1	8.8	22.8	21.0
Middle East........ 407	8.0	10.4	21.2	24.3	16.2	8.2	17.9	–17.9	–12.9	21.5	29.8	20.6	18.4	–2.2
Western Hemisphere........ 207	7.4	–5.4	3.4	26.3	14.5	12.4	21.1	–2.9	–1.0	23.6	27.0	18.8	10.1	21.7
Other Countries n.i.e........ 910	46.9	23.0	–13.9	13.7	82.8	51.5	–42.7	–26.6	10.5	–5.6	21.7	15.7	–57.8	27.0

	Exports							Imports						
	2001	2002	2003	2004	2005	2006	2007	2001	2002	2003	2004	2005	2006	2007
	Millions of U.S. Dollars							Millions of U.S. Dollars						
IFS World Total	**1,716.0**	**1,850.0**	**2,324.3**	**2,450.0**	**2,802.0**	**3,735.1**	**4,320.0**	**3,154.0**	**2,720.1**	**3,210.2**	**4,073.9**	**5,753.9**	**6,497.6**	**7,980.0**
DOTS World Total ... 001	**1,481.9Y**	**1,654.5Y**	**1,990.4Y**	**2,284.5Y**	**2,370.0Y**	**2,850.8Y**	**3,241.9Y**	**2,685.5Y**	**3,011.4Y**	**3,848.6Y**	**5,191.9Y**	**5,932.4Y**	**6,866.4Y**	**9,033.6Y**
Industrial Countries ... 101	**1,032.7Y**	**1,103.8Y**	**1,267.7Y**	**1,400.2Y**	**1,372.2Y**	**1,621.9Y**	**1,793.6Y**	**1,308.7Y**	**1,434.5Y**	**1,654.5Y**	**2,227.0Y**	**2,361.0Y**	**2,633.9Y**	**3,391.6Y**
United States ... 111	186.55V	116.91V	84.91V	145.27V	157.64V	190.55V	192.73V	219.89V	211.86V	230.23V	337.04V	371.36V	318.56V	457.49V
Canada ... 156	13.88V	26.25V	34.83V	23.70V	23.97V	47.72V	20.40V	47.28V	48.04V	46.46V	55.15V	85.64V	106.49V	163.80V
Australia ... 193	1.93V	2.51V	2.64V	3.39V	4.99V	7.74V	7.02V	37.45V	34.44V	48.31V	75.61V	82.96V	77.44V	96.82V
Japan ... 158	44.94V	62.94V	104.46V	95.40V	70.38V	72.97V	113.65V	54.52V	51.69V	79.24V	105.61V	108.46V	99.85V	125.00V
New Zealand ... 196	.39V	.61V	.80V	.69V	1.19V	1.53V	2.34V	3.09V	2.03V	5.50V	5.69V	7.51V	25.33V	37.60V
Austria ... 122	7.07V	.94V	.83V	.68V	1.14V	.87V	.46V	19.97V	13.71V	9.41V	57.79V	9.90V	12.07V	17.62V
Belgium ... 124	45.85V	73.64V	71.41V	106.91V	136.08V	146.56V	141.81V	50.46V	67.18V	91.27V	118.88V	134.95V	322.04V	336.27V
Cyprus ... 423	.20V	.17V	.46V	.22V	.23Y	.22V	.19V	.57V	1.47V	.71V	.39V	.23V	.22V	.84V
Denmark ... 128	4.93V	5.29V	11.81V	30.59V	13.14V	16.68V	33.70V	14.99V	19.55V	18.08V	25.91V	23.67V	15.49V	21.62V
Finland ... 172	.99V	1.99V	.99V	3.03V	3.97V	2.24V	.98V	7.28V	6.77V	9.37V	20.18V	13.50V	24.46V	20.18V
France ... 132	70.05V	96.49V	150.99V	155.64V	133.42V	125.85V	202.12V	142.43V	117.10V	171.13V	257.50V	205.26V	278.74V	339.62V
Germany ... 134	111.90V	108.03V	123.60V	103.05V	105.12V	109.16V	148.79V	129.56V	152.27V	181.55V	194.50V	194.08V	218.36V	297.74V
Greece ... 174	4.16V	4.62V	7.70V	18.86V	12.41V	10.86V	20.31V	.38V	.97V	1.86V	3.22V	91.67V	2.88V	3.32V
Iceland ... 176	.05V	.02V	.07V	.05V	.24V	.17V	.43V	—V	—V	.04V	—V	.05V	.01V	.03V
Ireland ... 178	22.15V	24.68V	22.36V	14.61V	20.55V	14.04V	18.84V	19.99V	15.95V	20.45V	21.55V	26.25V	24.57V	32.59V
Italy ... 136	61.86V	69.05V	91.53V	81.60V	87.15V	80.31V	81.93V	105.60V	198.30V	142.59V	169.18V	178.44V	212.35V	251.10V
Luxembourg ... 137	1.90V	1.75V	4.04V	3.23V	2.60V	2.60V	1.37V	1.65V	2.24V	5.82V	4.46V	4.97V	2.73V	3.75V
Malta ... 181	.06Y	.08V	.20V	.24V	.38V	.65V	.36V	.35Y	1.77V	1.79V	.56V	.86V	.35V	11.54V
Netherlands ... 138	214.46V	246.87V	224.94V	279.22V	295.77V	320.61V	357.18V	111.27V	127.79V	148.96V	219.47V	237.11V	268.56V	351.61V
Norway ... 142	5.09V	4.05V	4.39V	5.97V	7.00V	9.89V	12.53V	4.40V	8.35V	12.30V	18.37V	32.67V	13.98V	15.23V
Portugal ... 182	2.89V	5.82V	2.65V	9.25V	6.25V	8.23V	5.46V	4.53V	4.48V	4.88V	3.85V	4.90V	12.83V	10.09V
Slovenia ... 961	.16V	.10V	.35V	.46Y	.07V	.14V	.14V	1.18V	1.44V	1.88V	2.47Y	2.19V	3.53V	4.86V
Spain ... 184	38.46V	60.58V	74.97V	65.32V	57.97V	161.89V	91.58V	53.86V	62.57V	74.13V	94.42V	93.66V	73.53V	139.75V
Sweden ... 144	1.75V	7.47V	3.63V	1.16V	1.43V	7.05V	.35V	37.10V	40.32V	60.90V	66.39V	120.07V	112.95V	162.84V
Switzerland ... 146	16.18V	18.77V	30.32V	24.67V	32.99V	37.11V	45.86V	11.89V	12.42V	13.24V	23.53V	21.18V	20.03V	22.03V
United Kingdom ... 112	174.86V	164.15V	212.84V	227.01V	196.11V	246.24V	293.07V	229.03V	231.84V	274.40V	345.32V	309.50V	386.50V	468.24V
Developing Countries ... 202	**299.7Y**	**388.4Y**	**517.3Y**	**614.5Y**	**689.7Y**	**848.1Y**	**975.7Y**	**1,324.6Y**	**1,520.2Y**	**2,122.5Y**	**2,870.8Y**	**3,463.9Y**	**4,099.7Y**	**5,477.2Y**
Africa ... 607	**93.3Y**	**140.4Y**	**164.2Y**	**196.1Y**	**210.2Y**	**265.5Y**	**330.5Y**	**682.6Y**	**777.9Y**	**966.1Y**	**1,234.2Y**	**1,540.5Y**	**1,849.2Y**	**2,246.8Y**
Algeria ... 612	.13V	.03V	.03Y	.04Y	.05Y	.06Y	.08Y	.51V	—V	.01Y	.01Y	.01Y	.01Y	.01Y
Angola ... 614	16.79Y	18.22Y	23.07Y	30.29Y	34.61Y	42.78Y	53.09Y	1.60Y	1.73Y	2.20Y	2.88Y	3.29Y	4.07Y	5.05Y
Benin ... 638	26.71V	36.44V	49.48V	58.40V	58.04V	71.73V	89.01Y	16.67V	14.81V	5.32V	6.03V	3.79V	4.68Y	5.81Y
Burkina Faso ... 748	7.04Y	7.64Y	9.67Y	12.70Y	14.51Y	17.93Y	22.25Y	10.69Y	11.60Y	14.69Y	19.29Y	22.04Y	27.24Y	33.80Y
Cameroon ... 622	.56V	16.43V	9.10V	11.95Y	13.65Y	16.87Y	20.93Y	.24V	11.96V	35.93V	47.18Y	53.91Y	66.63Y	82.69Y
Chad ... 628	....	....	....	....	....	....	....	.04Y	.05Y	.06Y	.08Y	.09Y	.11Y	.14Y
Congo, Dem. Rep. of ... 636	—Y	—Y	—Y	—Y	—Y	—Y	—Y	.01Y	.01Y	.01Y	.02Y	.02Y	.03Y	.03Y
Congo, Republic of ... 634	.03V	.34V	.34V	.04V	.05Y	.06Y	.07Y	3.61V	8.90V	.35V	—V	—Y	—Y	—Y
Côte d'Ivoire ... 662	6.89V	14.87V	8.41V	11.29V	9.16V	28.02V	34.77Y	181.23V	116.65V	137.26V	176.64V	162.80V	175.61V	217.93Y
Equatorial Guinea ... 642	....	....	....	....	....	....	....	.02Y	.02Y	.02Y	.03Y	.04Y	.04Y	.05Y
Ethiopia ... 644	.03V	.03V	.02V	.01V	.07V	.08Y	.10Y	—V	—V	—V	.01V	.13V	.16Y	.20Y
Gabon ... 646	.01Y	.01Y	.01Y	.01Y	.02Y	.02Y	.02Y	—Y	—Y	—Y	—Y	—Y	—Y	—Y
Gambia, The ... 648	.83Y	.90Y	1.14Y	1.50Y	1.71Y	2.12Y	2.63Y	.20Y	.22Y	.28Y	.37Y	.42Y	.52Y	.64Y
Guinea ... 656	.11V	.12Y	.36V	.83V	.95Y	1.18Y	1.46Y	.05V	.06Y	.01V	.11V	.13Y	.16Y	.20Y
Kenya ... 664	.05V	.02V	.03V	.16V	.19Y	.23Y	.29Y	.81V	1.24V	4.86V	2.80V	3.20Y	3.96Y	4.91Y
Liberia ... 668	.08Y	.09Y	.11Y	.14Y	.16Y	.20Y	.25Y	.53Y	.58Y	.73Y	.97Y	1.10Y	1.36Y	1.69Y
Madagascar ... 674	.01V	—V	.02V	.02Y	.03Y	.03Y	.04Y	—V	—V	.03V	.04Y	.04Y	.05Y	.07Y
Malawi ... 676	.05Y	.06Y	.07Y	.10Y	.11Y	.14Y	.17Y	—Y	—Y	—Y	—Y	—Y	—Y	—Y
Mali ... 678	.01Y	.01Y	.01Y	.02Y	.02Y	.03Y	.03Y	.01Y	.01Y	.02Y	.02Y	.03Y	.03Y	.04Y
Mauritania ... 682	—Y	—Y	—Y	—Y	—Y	—Y	—Y	2.07Y	2.25Y	2.85Y	3.74Y	4.27Y	5.28Y	6.55Y
Mauritius ... 684	—V	—V	—V	.03V	1.36V	—V	.06V	.34V	.14V	.30V	.33V	.77V	2.09V	1.24V
Morocco ... 686	1.07V	.65V	1.18V	1.69V	1.67V	2.06Y	2.56Y	4.53V	9.49V	10.01V	14.36V	14.12V	17.45Y	21.66Y
Niger ... 692	5.78V	7.16V	7.19V	4.61V	5.27Y	6.51Y	8.08Y	3.69V	9.81V	11.40V	9.83V	11.24Y	13.89Y	17.23Y
Nigeria ... 694	10.89V	16.00V	20.35V	26.47Y	33.70Y	41.60Y	53.89Y	298.24V	417.42V	499.88V	661.45Y	899.77Y	1,131.18Y	1,364.63Y
Rwanda ... 714	—Y	—Y	—Y	—Y	—Y	—Y	—Y	.01Y	.01Y	.01Y	.01Y	.01Y	.02Y	.02Y
St. Helena ... 856	....	....	....	....	....	....	....	.01Y	.01Y	.01Y	.02Y	.02Y	.03Y	.03Y
São Tomé & Príncipe ... 716	.01Y	.01Y	.01Y	.01Y	.01Y	.02Y	.02Y	—Y	—Y	—Y	—Y	—Y	—Y	—Y
Senegal ... 722	4.87V	6.35V	12.37V	13.51V	13.30V	10.86V	13.48Y	3.90V	5.65V	3.79V	4.36V	3.94V	3.70V	4.59V
Seychelles ... 718	—V	—V	—V	—Y	—Y	—Y	—Y	—V	—V	.10V	.13Y	.15Y	.19Y	.23Y
Sierra Leone ... 724	.14Y	.15Y	.19Y	.26Y	.29Y	.36Y	.45Y	—Y	—Y	—Y	—Y	—Y	—Y	—Y
Somalia ... 726	—Y	—Y	—Y	—Y	—Y	—Y	—Y	.12Y	.13Y	.17Y	.22Y	.25Y	.31Y	.39Y
South Africa ... 199	3.12V	6.74V	6.83V	9.85V	11.50V	12.01V	13.69V	95.16V	102.25V	161.90V	206.80V	264.65V	279.00V	339.19V
Sacca exc. South Afr. ... 608	—Y	—Y	—Y	—Y	—Y	—Y	—Y	.03V	.28V	—V	.14V	.16Y	.19Y	.24Y
Sudan ... 732	—Y	—Y	—Y	—V	—V	—V	—V	.05Y	.05Y	—V	—V	—V	—V	—V
Tanzania ... 738	.38V	.35V	.44Y	.58Y	.66Y	.82Y	1.01Y	.11V	—V	.01Y	.01Y	.01Y	.01Y	.01Y
Togo ... 742	6.54V	7.36V	12.31V	8.85V	7.31V	9.03Y	11.21Y	54.40V	58.82V	69.99V	71.26V	84.44V	104.36Y	129.51Y
Tunisia ... 744	.90V	.26V	1.39V	2.47V	.15V	.49V	.60Y	2.68V	3.03V	3.41V	4.50V	5.34V	6.02V	7.48Y
Uganda ... 746	.01V	.05V	.05V	.07Y	.08Y	.09Y	.12Y	—V	.02V	.19V	.24Y	.28Y	.35Y	.43Y
Zambia ... 754	.06V	.04V	.04V	.09V	1.60V	.23V	.11V	—V	.05V	—V	.01V	.01V	.46V	.10V
Zimbabwe ... 698	.18V	.10V	.01V	.06V	—V	—V	—Y	.96V	.62V	.36V	.31V	.05V	.01V	.01Y
Asia ... 507	**86.3Y**	**84.4Y**	**106.5Y**	**167.9Y**	**224.8Y**	**324.2Y**	**351.0Y**	**475.2Y**	**540.9Y**	**889.6Y**	**1,267.0Y**	**1,436.1Y**	**1,750.8Y**	**2,483.4Y**
Bangladesh ... 513	—V	—V	—V	—V	—V	—V	1.21V	.94V	2.19V	.69V	4.76V	1.88V	2.39Y	7.62Y
Bhutan ... 514	....	....	....	....	....	....	....	—Y	—Y	—Y	.01Y	.01Y	.01Y	.01Y
Brunei Darussalam ... 516	—Y	—Y	—V	—Y	—Y	—Y	—Y	—Y	—Y	.04V	.05Y	.06Y	.07Y	.09Y

		Exports							Imports						
		2001	2002	2003	2004	2005	2006	2007	2001	2002	2003	2004	2005	2006	2007
		Millions of U.S. Dollars							*Millions of U.S. Dollars*						
China,P.R.: Mainland	924	33.27V	27.41V	31.15V	69.95V	86.87V	72.67V	48.16V	160.55V	200.50V	354.19V	597.85V	740.07V	883.23V	1,346.51V
China,P.R.:Hong Kong	532	1.00V	.66V	.46V	.65V	1.53V	1.99V	3.77V	24.55V	22.64V	28.53V	26.25V	19.20V	21.10V	29.85V
French Polynesia	887	—Y	—Y	—Y	—Y	—Y	—Y	—Y	.14Y	.16Y	.20Y	.26Y	.30Y	.37Y	.46Y
India	534	23.23Y	17.23V	26.69V	41.32V	65.34V	80.76Y	100.22Y	72.47Y	105.96V	179.76V	193.56V	215.37V	266.18Y	330.33Y
Indonesia	536	5.18V	8.71V	4.53V	6.00V	3.31V	12.11V	4.65V	17.58V	26.06V	35.75V	51.63V	58.48V	98.93V	130.75V
Korea	542	4.32V	9.12V	9.80V	6.36V	6.28V	14.01V	16.18V	98.75V	46.48V	77.61V	82.87V	97.69V	103.65V	160.35V
Malaysia	548	3.37V	8.17V	16.54V	21.83V	45.05V	101.67V	106.80V	22.28V	29.19V	51.48V	61.23V	74.00V	95.13V	131.86V
Maldives	556	—V	—V	—V	—V	—V	—Y	—Y	.25Y	.28Y	.35Y	.46Y	.52Y	.65Y	.80Y
Myanmar	518	—Y	—Y	—Y	—Y	—Y	—Y	—Y	2.83Y	3.07Y	3.89Y	5.10Y	5.83Y	7.21Y	8.94Y
Nauru	836	—Y	—Y	—Y	.01Y	.01Y	.01Y	.01Y	—Y	—Y	—Y	—Y	—Y	—Y	—Y
New Caledonia	839	—V	—V	—V	—V	—Y	—Y	—Y	.06Y	.07Y	.08Y	.11Y	.13Y	.16Y	.20Y
Pakistan	564	.13V	.06V	.05V	.05V	.83V	1.03Y	1.28Y	1.51V	1.35V	5.57V	4.26V	29.73V	36.74Y	45.60Y
Philippines	566	—V	.02V	.06V	—V	.02V	.04V	.02V	.46V	.29V	.57V	2.91V	1.09V	3.64V	10.98V
Samoa	862	.22Y	.24Y	.30Y	.40Y	.46Y	.56Y	.70Y	—Y	—Y	—Y	—Y	—Y	—Y	—Y
Singapore	576	2.26V	3.95V	5.18V	4.17V	8.07V	27.81V	48.23V	20.08V	33.80V	41.21V	46.37V	43.96V	52.62V	67.45V
Sri Lanka	524	—V	—V	—V	.07V	.08V	.79V	.70V	.16V	.33V	1.07V	1.87V	2.64V	2.73V	3.30V
Taiwan Province of China	528	8.19V	3.04V	1.69V	2.84V	1.40V	2.42V	2.93V	10.35V	11.40V	17.80V	23.98V	27.60V	28.19V	25.17V
Thailand	578	5.10V	5.75V	9.23V	14.22V	5.61V	8.31V	16.17V	36.85V	47.37V	73.70V	128.15V	91.45V	105.42V	182.72V
Tuvalu	869	....	....	....	....	....	....	....	.02Y	.02Y	.03Y	.04Y	.04Y	.05Y	.06Y
Vietnam	582	.01V	.02V	.81V	—V	—V	—V	—V	5.13V	9.46V	16.79V	34.98V	25.74V	42.02V	—V
Asia n.s.	598	—Y	—Y	—Y	—Y	—Y	—Y	—Y	.27Y	.29Y	.31Y	.33Y	.35Y	.37Y	.39Y
Europe	**170**	**108.1Y**	**127.1Y**	**223.8Y**	**192.6Y**	**190.4Y**	**202.7Y**	**224.9Y**	**67.2Y**	**68.8Y**	**91.1Y**	**119.7Y**	**147.5Y**	**153.6Y**	**253.0Y**
Albania	914	—V	.02V	—V	.01V	.05V	.02V	.03V	—V	—V	—V	—V	—V	—V	—V
Azerbaijan	912	—V	—V	—V	—V	—V	—V	—V	—V	4.15V	—V	—V	—V	—V	—V
Belarus	913	4.17V	7.86V	5.73V	10.66V	9.80V	10.54V	14.48V	.32V	.38V	.75V	.31V	.40V	.16V	10.03V
Bulgaria	918	.32V	.16V	.39V	.72V	.39V	.35V	.26V	2.35V	1.44V	.82V	2.01V	2.81V	4.57V	5.00V
Croatia	960	6.02V	10.63V	12.49V	12.03V	12.07V	9.65V	9.97V	.11V	1.09V	—V	.27V	2.29V	11.51V	3.77V
Czech Republic	935	.97V	1.07V	1.91V	2.42V	1.57V	.61V	4.49V	4.51V	3.39V	3.97V	5.56V	6.28V	16.13V	14.28V
Estonia	939	7.93V	15.79V	22.73V	1.92V	1.45V	1.65V	1.62V	1.06V	.73V	1.53V	.01V	.68V	.35V	.19V
Faroe Islands	816	.10Y	.11Y	.14Y	.18Y	.21Y	.26Y	.32Y	....	....	....	....	....	....	....
Georgia	915	—V	—V	—V	—V	—V	—V	1.67Y	.11V	—V	.07V	—V	—V	—V	—Y
Gibraltar	823	—Y	—Y	—Y	—Y	—Y	—Y	—Y	.15Y	.16Y	.21Y	.27Y	.31Y	.38Y	.48Y
Hungary	944	.33V	1.10V	.82V	.10V	.02V	.37V	.19V	.85V	2.30V	8.15V	4.96V	21.26V	11.47V	15.57V
Kazakhstan	916	1.45V	1.89V	5.10V	7.43V	8.49Y	10.50Y	13.03Y	.02V	.32V	.32V	2.22V	2.53Y	3.13Y	3.89Y
Latvia	941	—V	.26V	.09V	.01V	.42V	2.49V	3.06V	.02V	.01V	.01V	.03V	.38V	.06V	.36V
Lithuania	946	.14V	.19V	.59V	.07V	.38V	.58V	.35V	.04V	.06V	.06V	.40V	.46V	.27V	.20V
Macedonia, FYR	962	.71V	.99V	.48V	.72V	2.57V	.68V	.85Y	.01V	—V	—V	—V	—V	—V	—Y
Poland	964	4.17V	4.98V	5.40V	9.11V	7.98V	19.17V	18.41V	11.18V	10.86V	10.43V	18.83V	16.23V	13.51V	17.20V
Romania	968	.38V	2.01V	2.19V	1.51V	2.38V	3.88V	1.21V	1.45V	.80V	2.56V	3.96V	11.11V	2.13V	2.11V
Russia	922	12.12V	15.66V	16.93V	21.70V	25.60V	27.32V	40.16V	4.53V	5.58V	6.57V	20.63V	17.81V	17.32V	38.85V
Slovak Republic	936	.29V	.18V	.22Y	.29Y	.01V	.02V	.11V	1.30V	1.37V	1.73Y	2.28Y	3.36V	3.16V	7.28V
Turkey	186	32.34V	35.66V	86.55V	73.27V	66.54V	52.24V	37.33V	19.51V	24.92V	40.55V	34.90V	34.76V	36.26V	92.54V
Ukraine	926	36.70V	28.54V	62.00V	50.44V	50.44V	62.34Y	77.37Y	19.66V	11.23V	13.32V	23.08V	26.88V	33.22Y	41.22Y
Middle East	**407**	**7.8Y**	**8.9Y**	**19.8Y**	**28.8Y**	**39.1Y**	**49.5Y**	**62.5Y**	**17.9Y**	**20.0Y**	**36.0Y**	**38.6Y**	**53.3Y**	**55.8Y**	**73.0Y**
Bahrain	419	.01Y	.01Y	.01Y	.01Y	.01Y	.02Y	.02Y	.56Y	.61Y	.77Y	1.01Y	1.16Y	1.43Y	1.77Y
Egypt	469	.76V	.83Y	1.05Y	1.38Y	1.57Y	1.94Y	2.41Y	4.33V	4.70Y	5.95Y	7.81Y	8.92Y	11.03Y	13.69Y
Iran, I.R. of	429	.08V	—V	—Y	—Y	—Y	—Y	—Y	—Y	—Y	—Y	—Y	—Y	—Y	—Y
Israel	436	.36V	.82V	.36V	1.00V	1.55V	3.00V	3.09V	4.73V	5.94V	18.37V	12.21V	21.12V	15.51V	23.76V
Jordan	439	—V	.02V	.13V	.15V	.31V	.22V	.25V	.77V	.16V	.07V	.23V	.23V	.39V	.30V
Kuwait	443	.44Y	.45Y	.50Y	.65Y	.83Y	1.03Y	1.33Y	—Y	—Y	—Y	—Y	—Y	—Y	—Y
Lebanon	446	2.30Y	2.49Y	3.16Y	4.15Y	4.74Y	5.86Y	7.27Y	2.36Y	2.56Y	3.24Y	4.25Y	4.86Y	6.00Y	7.45Y
Libya	672	.29Y	.30Y	.33Y	.43Y	.54Y	.67Y	.87Y	—Y	—Y	—Y	—Y	—Y	—Y	—Y
Oman	449	.01V	.03V	.07V	.09Y	.12Y	.14Y	.19Y	.43V	.92V	1.42V	1.88Y	2.56Y	3.21Y	3.88Y
Qatar	453	—V	.04V	.05V	.06V	.13V	.41V	.53Y	.04V	.01V	.04V	.12V	.34V	.53V	.63Y
Saudi Arabia	456	3.35V	3.94V	3.52V	2.36V	6.38V	7.88Y	10.21Y	2.45Y	2.61Y	3.16Y	4.19Y	5.69Y	7.16Y	8.64Y
Syrian Arab Republic	463	—Y	—Y	—Y	4.68V	5.34Y	6.60Y	8.19Y	—Y	—Y	—Y	2.53V	2.90Y	3.58Y	4.44Y
United Arab Emirates	466	—V	—V	10.64V	13.83Y	17.61Y	21.74Y	28.17Y	2.20Y	2.34Y	2.84Y	3.76Y	5.12Y	6.43Y	7.76Y
Yemen, Republic of	474	.16V	—V	—Y	—V	—V	—Y	—Y	.03V	.09V	.12Y	.57V	.43V	.53Y	.65Y
Middle East n.s.	489	—Y	—Y	—Y	—Y	—Y	—Y	—Y	.01Y	.01Y	.01Y	.01Y	.01Y	.01Y	.01Y
Western Hemisphere	**207**	**4.2Y**	**27.6Y**	**3.0Y**	**29.2Y**	**25.1Y**	**6.2Y**	**6.8Y**	**81.7Y**	**112.7Y**	**139.7Y**	**211.3Y**	**286.3Y**	**290.2Y**	**421.0Y**
Antigua and Barbuda	311	—Y	—Y	—Y	—Y	—Y	—Y	—Y	.01Y	.01Y	.01Y	.02Y	.02Y	.03Y	.03Y
Argentina	213	.01V	.07V	1.05V	27.99V	14.98V	.79V	—V	2.49V	7.91V	11.41V	14.49V	28.75V	22.56V	35.59V
Barbados	316	.01V	.07V	.01V	—V	—V	.02V	.03Y	—V	—V	—V	.05V	—V	.01V	.01Y
Bolivia	218	.04V	.01V	—V	—V	—V	—Y	—Y	—V	—V	.11V	.43V	.49Y	.60Y	.75Y
Brazil	223	.67V	26.90V	1.51V	.45V	.52V	2.12V	2.93V	25.94V	63.16V	115.23V	186.30V	240.76V	245.22V	352.64V
Chile	228	.02V	.09V	.02V	.12V	.01V	.03V	.07V	1.95V	.88V	2.98V	3.28V	5.12V	7.72V	12.23V
Colombia	233	.10V	.02V	.02V	.10V	.01V	.04V	.01V	.07V	.24V	2.48V	1.26V	2.33V	1.79V	2.55V
Costa Rica	238	—V	—V	—V	.03V	.03V	.03Y	.04Y	—V	.04V	.21V	.09V	.02V	.02Y	.02Y
Dominica	321	.01V	.01Y	.01Y	.01Y	.01Y	.01Y	.02Y	—V	—Y	—Y	—Y	—Y	—Y	—Y
Dominican Republic	243	.03V	.04Y	.05Y	.06Y	.07Y	.08Y	.10Y	—V	—Y	—Y	—Y	—Y	—Y	—Y
Ecuador	248	.04V	—V	.02V	.01V	.05V	—V	—Y	.06V	.19V	.31V	.36V	.19V	.80V	.99Y
El Salvador	253	—V	—V	—V	—V	—V	—V	—V	—V	—V	.15V	.71V	—V	—V	—V
Greenland	326	—Y	—Y	—Y	—Y	—Y	.01Y	.01Y	—Y	—Y	—Y	—Y	—Y	—Y	—Y
Guatemala	258	—V	.06V	—V	—V	—V	—Y	—Y	—V	—V	.15V	.91V	.01V	.01Y	.02Y

Exports

	2001	2002	2003	2004	2005	2006	2007
	Millions of U.S. Dollars						
Guyana........ 336	.02Y	.02Y	.02Y	.03Y	.04Y	.04Y	.05Y
Honduras........ 268	1.11V	.06V	—V	.03V	.04Y	.05Y	.06Y
Jamaica........ 343	.03V	.09V	.11V	.11V	.18V	.10V	.19V
Mexico........ 273	—V	—V	—V	—V	6.23V	2.37V	2.70V
Netherlands Antilles........ 353	—V	—V	—V	—Y	—Y	—Y	—Y
Panama........ 283	.13Y	.15Y	.19Y	.24Y	.28Y	.34Y	.43Y
Paraguay........ 288	—V	—V	—V	—V	—V	—V	—Y
Peru........ 293	.15V	.01V	.01V	.02V	.09V	—V	—Y
St. Vincent & Grens........ 364	—V	—V	—V	.01V	—V	—Y	—Y
Suriname........ 366	—Y	—Y	—Y	—Y	—Y	—Y	—Y
Trinidad and Tobago........ 369	.03V	—V	—Y	—Y	—Y	—Y	—Y
Uruguay........ 298	—V	—Y	—V	—V	.09V	.11Y	.13Y
Venezuela, Rep. Bol........ 299	1.82V	—V	—V	—V	2.53V	—V	—V
Western Hem. n.s........ 399	—Y	—Y	—Y	—Y	—Y	—Y	—Y
Other Countries n.i.e........ 910	**13.4Y**	**14.5Y**	**18.3Y**	**24.1Y**	**27.5Y**	**34.0Y**	**42.2Y**
Cuba........ 928	13.31Y	14.45Y	18.29Y	24.02Y	27.44Y	33.91Y	42.09Y
North Korea........ 954	.04Y	.05Y	.06Y	.08Y	.09Y	.11Y	.14Y
Countries & Areas n.s........ 898	**136.1Y**	**147.8Y**	**187.0Y**	**245.6Y**	**280.6Y**	**346.8Y**	**430.4Y**
Memorandum Items							
European Union........ 998	777.52Y	895.28Y	1,037.07Y	1,115.02Y	1,085.63Y	1,279.11Y	1,426.87Y
Oil Exporting Ctys........ 999	22.19Y	29.49Y	40.02Y	49.93Y	65.21Y	85.65Y	99.91Y
Non-Oil Develop.Ctys........ 201	277.49Y	358.94Y	477.29Y	564.61Y	624.48Y	762.44Y	875.79Y
PERCENT DISTRIBUTION							
Industrial Countries........ 101	69.7	66.7	63.7	61.3	57.9	56.9	55.3
Developing Countries........ 202	20.2	23.5	26.0	26.9	29.1	29.7	30.1
Africa........ 607	6.3	8.5	8.3	8.6	8.9	9.3	10.2
Asia........ 507	5.8	5.1	5.4	7.3	9.5	11.4	10.8
Europe........ 170	7.3	7.7	11.2	8.4	8.0	7.1	6.9
Middle East........ 407	.5	.5	1.0	1.3	1.7	1.7	1.9
Western Hemisphere........ 207	.3	1.7	.2	1.3	1.1	.2	.2
Other Countries n.i.e........ 910	.9	.9	.9	1.1	1.2	1.2	1.3
ANNUAL PERCENT CHANGE							
World........ 001	–.7	11.6	20.3	14.8	3.7	20.3	13.7
Industrial Countries........ 101	–3.5	6.9	14.9	10.5	–2.0	18.2	10.6
Developing Countries........ 202	4.8	29.6	33.2	18.8	12.2	23.0	15.0
Africa........ 607	14.7	50.5	17.0	19.4	7.2	26.3	24.5
Asia........ 507	–2.4	–2.2	26.2	57.6	34.0	44.2	8.3
Europe........ 170	6.0	17.5	76.1	–13.9	–1.2	6.5	11.0
Middle East........ 407	–39.2	15.0	122.1	45.3	36.0	26.5	26.3
Western Hemisphere........ 207	178.8	556.5	–89.1	874.2	–14.0	–75.5	10.1
Other Countries n.i.e........ 910	10.4	8.5	26.6	31.3	14.3	23.6	24.1

Imports

	2001	2002	2003	2004	2005	2006	2007
	Millions of U.S. Dollars						
Guyana........ 336	.28Y	.31Y	.39Y	.51Y	.58Y	.72Y	.89Y
Honduras........ 268	—V	.01V	—V	.02V	.03Y	.03Y	.04Y
Jamaica........ 343	21.53V	26.21V	3.65V	.01V	—V	.08V	.14V
Mexico........ 273	—V	—V	—V	—V	1.11V	.50V	2.25V
Netherlands Antilles........ 353	8.86V	—V	—V	—Y	—Y	—Y	—Y
Panama........ 283	.65Y	.70Y	.89Y	1.17Y	1.34Y	1.65Y	2.05Y
Paraguay........ 288	.19V	—V	.17V	.07V	.28V	.50V	.62Y
Peru........ 293	.90V	.28V	.66V	.17V	.77V	2.37V	3.29Y
St. Vincent & Grens........ 364	—V	—V	—V	—V	—V	—Y	—Y
Suriname........ 366	.04Y	.05Y	.06Y	.08Y	.09Y	.11Y	.14Y
Trinidad and Tobago........ 369	.29V	.16V	.20Y	.26Y	.29Y	.36Y	.45Y
Uruguay........ 298	.79V	.86Y	.32V	.71V	3.83V	4.73Y	5.87Y
Venezuela, Rep. Bol........ 299	17.40V	11.42V	.01V	.02V	—V	.05V	.06Y
Western Hem. n.s........ 399	.26Y	.28Y	.30Y	.32Y	.34Y	.36Y	.38Y
Other Countries n.i.e........ 910	**25.2Y**	**27.3Y**	**34.6Y**	**45.4Y**	**51.9Y**	**64.1Y**	**79.6Y**
Cuba........ 928	15.68Y	17.02Y	21.54Y	28.29Y	32.32Y	39.95Y	49.58Y
North Korea........ 954	9.49Y	10.30Y	13.03Y	17.12Y	19.56Y	24.17Y	30.00Y
Countries & Areas n.s........ 898	**26.7Y**	**29.0Y**	**36.6Y**	**48.1Y**	**55.0Y**	**68.0Y**	**84.3Y**
Memorandum Items							
European Union........ 998	949.15Y	1,084.42Y	1,245.07Y	1,638.09Y	1,699.86Y	2,017.12Y	2,528.67Y
Oil Exporting Ctys........ 999	338.86Y	460.78Y	543.11Y	723.07Y	971.97Y	1,247.50Y	1,516.37Y
Non-Oil Develop.Ctys........ 201	985.75Y	1,059.45Y	1,579.38Y	2,147.74Y	2,491.91Y	2,852.22Y	3,960.86Y
PERCENT DISTRIBUTION							
Industrial Countries........ 101	48.7	47.6	43.0	42.9	39.8	38.4	37.5
Developing Countries........ 202	49.3	50.5	55.1	55.3	58.4	59.7	60.6
Africa........ 607	25.4	25.8	25.1	23.8	26.0	26.9	24.9
Asia........ 507	17.7	18.0	23.1	24.4	24.2	25.5	27.5
Europe........ 170	2.5	2.3	2.4	2.3	2.5	2.2	2.8
Middle East........ 407	.7	.7	.9	.7	.9	.8	.8
Western Hemisphere........ 207	3.0	3.7	3.6	4.1	4.8	4.2	4.7
Other Countries n.i.e........ 910	.9	.9	.9	.9	.9	.9	.9
ANNUAL PERCENT CHANGE							
World........ 001	–6.5	12.1	27.8	34.9	14.3	15.7	31.6
Industrial Countries........ 101	–19.2	9.6	15.3	34.6	6.0	11.6	28.8
Developing Countries........ 202	9.9	14.8	39.6	35.3	20.7	18.4	33.6
Africa........ 607	5.3	14.0	24.2	27.7	24.8	20.0	21.5
Asia........ 507	18.6	13.8	64.5	42.4	13.3	21.9	41.8
Europe........ 170	24.6	2.4	32.4	31.5	23.2	4.1	64.6
Middle East........ 407	–.1	11.4	80.4	7.2	38.2	4.7	30.8
Western Hemisphere........ 207	–2.9	37.9	23.9	51.2	35.5	1.4	45.1
Other Countries n.i.e........ 910	10.4	8.5	26.6	31.3	14.3	23.6	24.1

		Exports							Imports						
		2001	2002	2003	2004	2005	2006	2007	2001	2002	2003	2004	2005	2006	2007
		Millions of U.S. Dollars							Millions of U.S. Dollars						
IFS World Total		**9,483**	**10,315**	**13,195**	**14,996**	**15,511**	**20,180**	**23,472**	**29,928**	**31,164**	**44,375**	**51,559**	**49,817**	**59,121**	**75,100**
DOTS World Total	**001**	**9,710**	**10,332**	**13,379**	**15,336**	**17,344**	**20,759**	**23,512**	**28,161**	**31,319**	**44,853**	**52,633**	**54,456**	**63,621**	**76,254**
Industrial Countries	**101**	**5,709**	**5,426**	**8,369**	**9,367**	**10,154**	**12,072**	**13,668**	**17,895**	**19,597**	**29,729**	**34,706**	**33,797**	**37,555**	**45,982**
United States	111	543	542	758	812	912	911	980	992	1,478	2,282	2,335	1,912	1,139	1,727
Canada	156	72	70	80	92	108	99	102	89	92	138	165	132	120	211
Australia	193	56	60	88	98	98	99	97	36	32	27	45	32	35	99
Japan	158	60	51	82	74	55	72	173	864	951	1,908	1,542	1,160	1,611	1,694
New Zealand	196	3	5	6	7	10	5	8	35	33	42	41	55	44	48
Austria	122	66	74	118	158	154	169	202	223	243	444	558	568	730	983
Belgium	124	98	110	204	242	234	271	383	813	1,349	1,631	1,954	1,952	2,222	2,923
Cyprus	423	459	489	625	707	893	1,123	1,547	86	77	133	253	368	525	841
Denmark	128	81	69	107	133	154	159	179	338	315	398	493	487	638	656
Finland	172	49	36	85	124	113	125	133	279	294	537	519	485	702	716
France	132	371	369	581	643	718	921	987	1,780	1,779	3,002	3,353	3,118	3,780	4,241
Germany	134	1,113	1,077	1,756	2,000	2,138	2,356	2,722	3,854	3,804	5,663	7,009	6,982	7,987	9,813
Iceland	176	10	2	2	3	3	2	3	5	8	18	10	15	24	15
Ireland	178	35	26	52	58	49	85	82	249	203	371	445	489	545	722
Italy	136	836	881	1,466	1,571	1,801	2,343	2,547	3,387	3,604	5,619	6,737	6,740	7,315	8,926
Luxembourg	137	5	2	6	10	5	5	5	20	31	156	230	322	376	383
Malta	181	151	103	68	33	19	31	41	10	30	2	23	10	4	7
Netherlands	138	240	245	357	409	412	451	477	1,579	1,753	2,378	2,911	2,993	3,276	3,810
Norway	142	39	34	43	72	39	42	46	104	76	114	107	158	140	173
Portugal	182	68	64	88	109	101	119	163	79	79	114	140	141	140	161
Slovenia	961	29	25	38	62	47	255	287	27	30	45	56	64	97	119
Spain	184	322	261	501	509	618	839	802	938	1,208	1,634	2,002	2,143	2,258	2,760
Sweden	144	94	93	141	159	175	203	245	408	370	581	835	689	731	759
Switzerland	146	100	86	119	136	139	137	173	441	476	636	754	749	752	1,445
United Kingdom	112	808	650	996	1,146	1,160	1,246	1,285	1,259	1,278	1,856	2,188	2,034	2,366	2,751
Developing Countries	**202**	**3,979**	**4,253**	**4,871**	**5,802**	**6,941**	**8,541**	**9,182**	**10,230**	**11,615**	**15,015**	**17,836**	**20,566**	**25,082**	**29,591**
Africa	**607**	**227**	**245**	**270**	**315**	**458**	**530**	**543**	**458**	**366**	**460**	**471**	**440**	**531**	**703**
Algeria	612	47	42	39	47	49	219	111	90	81	99	85	114	188	210
Angola	614	—	1	1	1	2	2	2	—	—	—	—	—	—	—
Benin	638	1	—	—	1	3	3	7	—	—	—	—	—	—	—
Botswana	616	—	—	—	—	—	—	—	3	3	4	5	6	4	9
Burkina Faso	748	—	—	—	—	—	—	—	—	—	1	—	—	—	—
Cameroon	622	5	4	8	4	8	3	11	7	7	11	8	10	7	9
Cape Verde	624	—	—	—	—	—	—	—	—	—	—	—	—	1	—
Comoros	632	1	—	—	—	1	2	1	—	1	1	1	—	—	1
Congo, Dem. Rep. of	636	—	—	—	1	1	1	1	—	—	—	—	—	—	—
Congo, Republic of	634	—	1	—	1	1	1	1	2	2	1	2	2	1	1
Côte d'Ivoire	662	2	1	1	1	3	1	5	42	53	32	39	36	43	57
Djibouti	611	—	—	—	1	—	2	—	—	—	—	—	—	—	—
Equatorial Guinea	642	—	—	—	—	—	—	—	—	—	—	—	2	1	1
Eritrea	643	1	1	1	—	—	—	—	1	—	—	—	—	—	—
Ethiopia	644	5	4	4	5	10	5	8	3	4	7	5	11	6	13
Gabon	646	—	3	1	5	10	—	16	14	11	13	17	19	19	12
Gambia, The	648	—	—	2	2	1	—	—	—	—	—	—	—	—	2
Ghana	652	—	1	2	3	83	3	3	5	5	8	21	14	12	22
Guinea	656	5	9	11	4	1	1	—	5	2	3	2	1	2	4
Kenya	664	1	1	3	8	14	12	11	4	5	6	5	5	3	5
Liberia	668	24	12	6	11	11	25	27	103	34	93	80	1	9	1
Madagascar	674	1	4	5	4	7	3	3	—	1	1	—	1	1	3
Malawi	676	—	—	1	—	3	—	9	2	4	5	7	7	5	4
Mali	678	1	—	—	—	—	6	7	—	—	—	—	—	—	—
Mauritania	682	4	13	26	38	36	19	25	3	4	8	3	6	5	6
Mauritius	684	1	1	1	2	1	—	1	—	1	1	1	1	2	3
Morocco	686	15	30	32	41	29	56	65	48	44	41	44	51	49	88
Mozambique	688	—	1	—	1	—	—	—	—	—	—	1	2	2	2
Namibia	728	—	—	—	—	—	—	—	1	2	2	2	2	1	6
Niger	692	7	10	11	7	11	5	12	—	—	—	—	—	—	—
Nigeria	694	40	34	41	41	82	45	52	—	—	5	16	25	18	61
São Tomé & Príncipe	716	1	—	—	—	—	—	—	—	—	—	—	—	—	—
Senegal	722	4	2	5	2	1	1	2	18	19	23	23	26	22	27
Seychelles	718	—	—	—	—	—	—	—	1	1	1	1	—	—	—
Sierra Leone	724	5	5	3	3	1	1	—	1	—	—	—	—	—	—
South Africa	199	9	12	16	21	30	33	78	55	40	46	51	46	76	90
Sudan	732	5	5	5	6	6	7	9	13	6	6	10	3	9	9
Tanzania	738	1	2	2	2	2	6	1	6	6	9	8	11	13	11
Togo	742	—	1	—	4	—	1	21	5	7	4	1	—	—	—
Tunisia	744	37	47	38	45	39	62	49	10	12	17	23	27	23	36
Uganda	746	1	—	—	2	7	2	2	2	2	2	2	3	3	5
Zambia	754	—	—	—	—	—	—	—	—	1	—	—	—	1	—
Zimbabwe	698	—	—	—	—	1	1	1	17	9	8	8	5	2	4

	Exports 2001	2002	2003	2004	2005	2006	2007	Imports 2001	2002	2003	2004	2005	2006	2007
	Millions of U.S. Dollars							*Millions of U.S. Dollars*						
Asia.......... 507	**263**	**398**	**359**	**399**	**539**	**551**	**509**	**2,568**	**3,748**	**4,988**	**5,421**	**5,063**	**6,613**	**8,533**
Afghanistan, I.S. of.......... 512	—	—	—	—	1	1	—	—	—	1	—	—	2	—
Bangladesh.......... 513	6	5	7	4	3	7	4	6	10	11	17	18	26	33
Cambodia.......... 522	3	3	1	1	1	1	1	1	1	1	5	2	3	4
China,P.R.: Mainland.......... 924	42	56	61	75	97	157	152	842	969	1,389	1,767	2,117	2,279	3,828
China,P.R.:Hong Kong.......... 532	64	50	36	48	56	43	39	51	80	95	84	133	88	138
China,P.R.:Macao.......... 546	1	—	—	1	1	—	1	4	5	8	13	2	2	3
Fiji.......... 819	1	—	—	—	—	—	—	—	—	—	—	—	—	—
India.......... 534	32	128	53	27	42	62	64	146	176	219	357	397	607	628
Indonesia.......... 536	15	15	19	24	26	27	38	114	103	122	127	133	122	215
Korea.......... 542	32	30	73	50	60	42	45	852	1,880	2,474	2,148	1,470	2,658	2,550
Malaysia.......... 548	5	6	4	5	6	10	9	97	80	104	114	85	110	146
Maldives.......... 556	—	—	—	—	1	1	1	1	1	1	2	1	1	—
Mongolia.......... 948	—	—	1	1	1	1	1	—	—	—	—	—	—	—
Myanmar.......... 518	—	—	—	—	—	—	—	—	—	1	2	1	1	1
Nepal.......... 558	1	—	—	—	—	—	—	—	—	1	—	—	—	—
Pakistan.......... 564	7	9	13	19	21	31	32	48	59	78	99	82	74	89
Papua New Guinea.......... 853	—	—	—	—	—	—	—	1	1	4	6	7	7	11
Philippines.......... 566	4	11	6	7	8	10	7	10	14	19	22	16	37	27
Singapore.......... 576	24	56	54	99	157	107	61	30	25	45	134	28	29	46
Sri Lanka.......... 524	1	1	2	2	2	2	2	4	4	5	6	5	5	8
Taiwan Province of China.......... 528	12	13	14	17	24	23	14	164	154	180	218	205	245	298
Thailand.......... 578	11	11	13	18	26	25	31	157	141	169	234	287	233	398
Tonga.......... 866	—	1	—	—	—	—	—	—	1	3	—	—	—	—
Vanuatu.......... 846	—	—	—	—	1	1	—	9	—	—	3	—	—	—
Vietnam.......... 582	2	2	1	2	4	1	4	31	45	58	62	71	81	107
Europe.......... 170	**2,779**	**2,823**	**3,498**	**4,094**	**4,422**	**5,760**	**6,760**	**3,937**	**4,890**	**5,961**	**7,032**	**8,838**	**10,747**	**12,716**
Albania.......... 914	330	322	353	428	430	471	621	58	10	20	23	24	42	94
Armenia.......... 911	12	13	25	28	31	23	27	2	1	1	1	1	1	2
Azerbaijan.......... 912	10	7	12	9	4	5	10	12	6	37	30	35	71	50
Belarus.......... 913	2	3	3	5	8	8	12	3	3	6	3	15	2	2
Bosnia & Herzegovina.......... 963	9	12	19	25	26	23	36	16	39	27	8	10	11	8
Bulgaria.......... 918	544	555	829	970	1,009	1,324	1,523	423	312	423	577	731	978	1,188
Croatia.......... 960	22	25	45	51	43	106	156	22	16	81	88	83	27	23
Czech Republic.......... 935	54	59	69	61	72	106	123	145	170	249	233	238	304	394
Estonia.......... 939	4	7	8	6	8	10	11	4	4	7	4	15	8	15
Faroe Islands.......... 816	—	—	—	—	—	—	—	—	—	—	4	9	5	4
Georgia.......... 915	9	15	12	17	21	28	50	11	51	88	56	37	54	66
Gibraltar.......... 823	65	50	7	1	49	139	167	1	5	8	20	—	15	18
Hungary.......... 944	55	66	70	68	70	84	133	116	127	182	243	302	355	522
Kazakhstan.......... 916	56	16	5	7	10	10	14	128	228	93	132	403	688	1,014
Kosovo.......... 967	—	—	—	—	9	18	95	—	—	—	—	—	—	—
Kyrgyz Republic.......... 917	—	—	—	—	—	—	1	—	—	—	—	—	—	1
Latvia.......... 941	5	7	7	10	10	16	17	12	8	4	4	5	8	6
Lithuania.......... 946	6	8	8	12	13	21	24	4	2	4	4	8	13	17
Macedonia, FYR.......... 962	350	328	354	386	405	471	535	78	54	107	152	236	291	413
Moldova.......... 921	8	13	10	8	8	18	20	8	15	16	15	5	16	23
Montenegro, Rep. of.......... 943	—	—	—	—	—	78	63	—	—	—	—	—	77	67
Poland.......... 964	105	116	130	139	167	237	321	118	135	158	162	188	311	494
Romania.......... 968	316	280	347	477	504	752	1,056	340	322	443	625	540	635	734
Russia.......... 922	270	296	325	335	336	404	494	1,606	2,301	2,678	2,876	4,213	4,493	4,295
Serbia, Rep. of.......... 942	—	—	—	—	—	239	301	—	—	—	—	—	165	191
Serbia & Montenegro.......... 965	156	180	241	272	227	—	—	91	106	111	175	174	—	—
Slovak Republic.......... 936	17	20	25	33	20	36	57	57	50	75	87	88	164	244
Tajikistan.......... 923	—	—	—	—	—	—	—	—	—	8	7	5	41	43
Turkey.......... 186	330	346	534	691	880	1,063	848	492	601	886	1,236	1,191	1,671	2,291
Turkmenistan.......... 925	—	2	—	—	—	—	1	5	3	33	34	54	11	28
Ukraine.......... 926	40	72	55	53	67	87	135	152	308	187	201	194	267	389
Uzbekistan.......... 927	1	4	4	3	2	1	2	33	11	27	31	35	27	82
Middle East.......... 407	**552**	**632**	**648**	**881**	**1,236**	**1,476**	**1,093**	**2,827**	**2,057**	**3,096**	**4,056**	**5,396**	**6,396**	**6,328**
Bahrain.......... 419	5	3	3	4	5	5	13	9	14	2	2	2	6	25
Egypt.......... 469	76	60	75	143	142	146	143	101	159	152	194	197	222	425
Iran, I.R. of.......... 429	18	8	10	21	60	24	14	967	457	970	1,426	1,847	2,272	2,719
Iraq.......... 433	5	45	8	8	16	27	6	231	117	57	62	34	—	47
Israel.......... 436	109	121	118	121	134	294	166	146	155	210	218	211	222	291
Jordan.......... 439	20	28	22	10	47	16	17	4	4	2	4	3	4	14
Kuwait.......... 443	8	8	13	14	16	19	15	3	4	8	17	4	41	2
Lebanon.......... 446	73	47	46	43	71	122	65	12	9	8	32	17	20	43
Libya.......... 672	38	95	79	211	199	280	154	274	229	367	359	759	1,042	1,381
Oman.......... 449	2	16	11	2	9	11	27	4	4	12	7	7	7	6
Qatar.......... 453	6	2	3	5	9	18	10	—	4	16	67	24	28	10
Saudi Arabia.......... 456	63	83	61	65	75	67	73	1,044	879	1,232	1,600	2,226	2,420	1,270
Syrian Arab Republic.......... 463	42	33	86	97	194	202	89	17	13	22	22	24	24	35
United Arab Emirates.......... 466	79	75	103	130	257	240	277	13	9	37	44	41	56	60
West Bank/Gaza Strip.......... 487	—	—	—	—	—	1	—	—	—	—	—	—	—	—
Yemen, Republic of.......... 474	9	8	9	5	3	4	24	1	1	—	—	1	32	1

	Exports							Imports						
	2001	2002	2003	2004	2005	2006	2007	2001	2002	2003	2004	2005	2006	2007
	Millions of U.S. Dollars							Millions of U.S. Dollars						
Western Hemisphere................207	**159**	**154**	**97**	**113**	**285**	**224**	**276**	**439**	**554**	**510**	**856**	**830**	**794**	**1,311**
Antigua and Barbuda..................311	3	5	4	1	3	3	7	3	—	—	—	—	1	—
Argentina.................................. 213	5	3	5	10	11	7	7	71	83	113	167	105	104	159
Aruba..314	—	—	—	—	—	—	—	1	—	—	—	—	8	6
Bahamas, The.............................313	19	15	5	5	9	13	8	10	27	23	1	32	1	86
Barbados....................................316	—	—	—	—	1	1	—	—	—	—	—	—	1	1
Belize...339	—	—	—	—	1	—	—	2	1	1	—	—	—	—
Bermuda.....................................319	1	—	—	—	1	2	—	1	1	4	—	1	1	1
Brazil...223	16	19	24	29	28	56	49	166	94	136	338	301	203	328
Chile..228	4	12	3	4	25	9	9	43	59	79	146	115	214	379
Colombia....................................233	2	2	1	—	9	1	3	13	4	6	6	9	13	16
Costa Rica..................................238	—	—	2	—	—	9	1	1	2	8	7	2	5	4
Dominican Republic.....................243	1	—	1	—	1	1	1	2	1	2	1	2	2	2
Ecuador......................................248	—	1	8	2	1	1	2	14	28	22	28	41	28	31
El Salvador.................................253	—	1	1	—	1	1	1	—	—	—	—	—	—	—
Greenland...................................326	1	—	—	—	—	—	—	—	—	—	—	—	—	—
Grenada......................................328	—	—	—	—	—	—	1	—	—	—	—	—	—	—
Guatemala...................................258	—	—	—	—	1	1	3	—	—	1	—	—	—	1
Haiti...263	1	—	1	—	—	—	—	—	—	—	—	—	—	—
Honduras....................................268	1	—	—	4	1	1	—	—	—	—	—	1	—	—
Jamaica.......................................343	—	—	—	—	—	2	—	—	—	—	—	—	—	—
Mexico..273	17	25	15	25	20	33	59	11	16	28	24	30	37	60
Netherlands Antilles.....................353	—	—	—	—	1	1	29	—	—	—	—	—	—	—
Nicaragua...................................278	—	—	—	—	—	—	—	—	—	—	1	1	1	—
Panama.......................................283	63	42	14	11	35	57	74	62	145	33	37	79	25	63
Paraguay....................................288	2	1	1	1	1	—	—	—	—	2	17	23	23	25
Peru...293	1	—	3	2	3	3	6	9	16	19	6	13	21	29
St. Kitts and Nevis.......................361	—	—	—	—	—	—	—	—	—	—	—	—	—	2
St. Vincent & Grens......................364	9	15	2	3	4	11	3	18	45	14	39	41	45	49
Trinidad and Tobago....................369	1	1	—	1	1	2	2	—	1	—	1	1	2	1
Uruguay......................................298	3	3	2	2	4	2	2	1	4	3	3	1	3	2
Venezuela, Rep. Bol.....................299	4	3	1	7	5	3	4	8	25	16	28	28	53	48
Western Hem. n.s.........................399	2	4	1	2	118	2	2	1	1	—	5	3	5	16
Other Countries n.i.e................910	**3**	**9**	**1**	**1**	**2**	**2**	**1**	**—**	**—**	**1**	**4**	**4**	**90**	**7**
Cuba...928	1	—	1	—	1	1	—	—	—	1	2	3	4	7
North Korea.................................954	1	8	1	—	1	1	—	—	—	—	3	1	86	—
Countries & Areas n.s..............898	**13**	**—**	**15**	**15**	**177**	**134**	**631**	**—**	**—**	**60**	**83**	**89**	**795**	**535**
Special Categories...................899	**1**	**627**	**120**	**143**	**58**	**—**	**—**	**—**	**16**	**—**	**—**	**—**	**—**	**—**
Memorandum Items														
European Union...........................998	5,072	4,857	7,508	8,403	9,152	11,213	12,774	15,783	16,945	25,242	30,444	30,429	34,853	42,261
Oil Exporting Ctys........................999	325	428	389	576	803	980	781	2,749	1,911	2,941	3,839	5,242	6,246	6,028
Non-Oil Develop.Ctys...................201	3,654	3,826	4,482	5,226	6,138	7,560	8,401	7,481	9,704	12,074	13,997	15,323	18,836	23,563
PERCENT DISTRIBUTION														
Industrial Countries.................101	**58.8**	**52.5**	**62.6**	**61.1**	**58.5**	**58.2**	**58.1**	**63.5**	**62.6**	**66.3**	**65.9**	**62.1**	**59.0**	**60.3**
Developing Countries..............202	**41.0**	**41.2**	**36.4**	**37.8**	**40.0**	**41.1**	**39.1**	**36.3**	**37.1**	**33.5**	**33.9**	**37.8**	**39.4**	**38.8**
Africa....................................607	**2.3**	**2.4**	**2.0**	**2.1**	**2.6**	**2.6**	**2.3**	**1.6**	**1.2**	**1.0**	**.9**	**.8**	**.8**	**.9**
Asia.......................................507	**2.7**	**3.9**	**2.7**	**2.6**	**3.1**	**2.7**	**2.2**	**9.1**	**12.0**	**11.1**	**10.3**	**9.3**	**10.4**	**11.2**
Europe...................................170	**28.6**	**27.3**	**26.1**	**26.7**	**25.5**	**27.7**	**28.8**	**14.0**	**15.6**	**13.3**	**13.4**	**16.2**	**16.9**	**16.7**
Middle East............................407	**5.7**	**6.1**	**4.8**	**5.7**	**7.1**	**7.1**	**4.7**	**10.0**	**6.6**	**6.9**	**7.7**	**9.9**	**10.1**	**8.3**
Western Hemisphere.............207	**1.6**	**1.5**	**.7**	**.7**	**1.6**	**1.1**	**1.2**	**1.6**	**1.8**	**1.1**	**1.6**	**1.5**	**1.2**	**1.7**
Other Countries n.i.e...............910	**—**	**.1**	**—**	**—**	**—**	**—**	**—**	**—**	**—**	**—**	**—**	**—**	**.1**	**—**
ANNUAL PERCENT CHANGE														
World......................................001	**–11.5**	**6.4**	**29.5**	**14.6**	**13.1**	**19.7**	**13.3**	**–.6**	**11.2**	**43.2**	**17.3**	**3.5**	**16.8**	**19.9**
Industrial Countries.................101	**–9.9**	**–5.0**	**54.2**	**11.9**	**8.4**	**18.9**	**13.2**	**–6.8**	**9.5**	**51.7**	**16.7**	**–2.6**	**11.1**	**22.4**
Developing Countries..............202	**–13.4**	**6.9**	**14.5**	**19.1**	**19.6**	**23.1**	**7.5**	**12.2**	**13.5**	**29.3**	**18.8**	**15.3**	**22.0**	**18.0**
Africa....................................607	**–21.5**	**8.2**	**9.9**	**16.6**	**45.6**	**15.6**	**2.5**	**–10.4**	**–20.2**	**25.9**	**2.3**	**–6.5**	**20.7**	**32.4**
Asia.......................................507	**–1.7**	**51.6**	**–9.9**	**11.4**	**34.9**	**2.3**	**–7.6**	**22.6**	**46.0**	**33.1**	**8.7**	**–6.6**	**30.6**	**29.0**
Europe...................................170	**–9.8**	**1.6**	**23.9**	**17.0**	**8.0**	**30.3**	**17.4**	**26.9**	**24.2**	**21.9**	**18.0**	**25.7**	**21.6**	**18.3**
Middle East............................407	**–24.8**	**14.4**	**2.4**	**36.0**	**40.4**	**19.4**	**–25.9**	**–8.7**	**–27.2**	**50.5**	**31.0**	**33.0**	**18.5**	**–1.1**
Western Hemisphere.............207	**–29.1**	**–2.7**	**–37.3**	**17.2**	**151.5**	**–21.6**	**23.5**	**41.3**	**26.1**	**–7.9**	**67.8**	**–3.0**	**–4.2**	**65.0**
Other Countries n.i.e...............910	**42.7**	**197.6**	**–85.4**	**–31.7**	**133.2**	**.7**	**–67.6**	**–83.2**	**87.8**	**166.9**	**385.0**	**–10.3**	**—**	**–91.8**

	Exports							Imports						
	2001	2002	2003	2004	2005	2006	2007	2001	2002	2003	2004	2005	2006	2007
	Millions of U.S. Dollars							*Millions of U.S. Dollars*						
DOTS World Total.................... 001	**367.0Y**	**389.1Y**	**451.4Y**	**483.2Y**	**512.7Y**	**479.7Y**	**591.7Y**	**422.7Y**	**443.8Y**	**452.9Y**	**600.5Y**	**724.8Y**	**712.4Y**	**822.2Y**
Industrial Countries................ 101	**323.4Y**	**350.1Y**	**390.2Y**	**431.8Y**	**450.7Y**	**419.2Y**	**519.0Y**	**417.8Y**	**432.8Y**	**448.0Y**	**593.3Y**	**717.3Y**	**705.0Y**	**812.2Y**
United States.............................. 111	27.55V	21.36V	13.09V	13.91V	16.27V	10.64V	9.36V	5.17V	4.40V	3.52V	3.96V	5.61V	3.30V	4.95V
Canada....................................... 156	4.19V	.79V	.77V	.78V	.44V	.45V	43.19V	5.83V	3.20V	3.63V	11.44V	18.37V	23.65V	20.74V
Australia.................................... 193	—V	—V	—V	—V	—V	.09V	—V	—V	—V	—V	—V	—V	—V	—V
Japan... 158	56.43V	55.64V	64.37V	60.51V	62.78V	58.15V	58.73V	.48V	.30V	.38V	.08V	.28V	.32V	.81V
New Zealand.............................. 196	—V	—V	—V	—V	—V	—V	—V	.21V	.08V	.22V	.12V	.15V	.07V	.01V
Austria....................................... 122	—V	—V	—V	—V	—V	—V	.01V	.03V	.13V	.07V	.04V	.03V	.03V	.13V
Belgium...................................... 124	.08V	.04V	.02V	.03V	.01V	—V	.42V	6.78V	3.19V	1.05V	1.82V	1.76V	2.95V	1.20V
Belgium-Luxembourg n.s............. 127	....	....	....	....	....	....	....	1.32Y	1.31Y	1.55Y	1.86Y	1.95Y	2.19Y	2.60Y
Cyprus.. 423	.04V	.02V	.21V	.06V	.13Y	—V	—V	—V	—V	.03V	.04V	.04V	.04V	.05V
Denmark..................................... 128	209.29V	247.20V	292.12V	305.67V	316.56V	321.59V	365.39V	279.80V	367.28V	374.72V	470.97V	485.93V	497.75V	559.91V
Finland....................................... 172	.02V	.05V	.02V	.02V	—V	.12V	.08V	1.82V	2.09V	2.46V	1.99V	2.81V	4.77V	6.15V
France.. 132	.02V	.04V	.11V	.02V	.04V	.09V	.02V	.32V	.63V	.46V	.26V	5.01V	5.47V	6.78V
Germany..................................... 134	6.52V	13.33V	10.46V	14.20V	16.17V	1.02V	3.62V	15.89V	2.88V	3.49V	2.70V	3.42V	3.54V	4.12V
Greece.. 174	—V	—V	—V	—V	—V	—V	.02V	1.37V	.03V	—V	.01V	—V	.07V	.09V
Iceland....................................... 176	2.44V	3.16V	4.10V	11.14V	7.63V	5.21V	5.52V	9.11V	5.24V	3.54V	6.15V	8.09V	6.47V	17.51V
Ireland.. 178	.09V	—V	—V	—V	—V	—V	.01V	1.97V	.03V	.27V	.62V	25.60V	2.90V	.07V
Italy.. 136	.02V	.04V	.01V	.12V	—V	—V	.05V	.39V	.11V	.22V	.12V	.05V	.12V	1.00V
Luxembourg................................ 137	.08V	.03V	.03V	.01V	.32V	.01V	.01V	—V	—V	.38V	.05V	—V	1.54V	—V
Netherlands................................ 138	.86V	1.40V	1.33V	.30V	1.44V	3.83V	5.98V	.17V	.30V	.50V	.94V	2.32V	4.90V	2.56V
Norway....................................... 142	11.17V	3.02V	2.10V	6.12V	4.85V	6.97V	3.01V	50.00V	38.44V	33.91V	16.05V	15.75V	26.63V	19.41V
Portugal...................................... 182	—V	.38V	.39V	—V	—V	—V	—V	.07V	—V	.01V	.04V	—V	.12V	.27V
Slovenia...................................... 961	.01V	.01V	.01V	.01Y	—V	—V	—V	—V	—V	—V	—Y	—V	—V	—V
Spain.. 184	.11V	.11V	.19V	17.94V	23.84V	8.26V	.17V	29.89V	.04V	.32V	.10V	.11V	.11V	.10V
Sweden....................................... 144	.31V	1.90V	.65V	.33V	.11V	1.79V	14.64V	2.44V	2.38V	15.83V	71.33V	139.06V	116.26V	158.57V
Switzerland................................. 146	.02V	—V	—V	.31V	—V	—V	—V	.01V	.14V	.19V	.05V	.02V	.09V	2.21V
United Kingdom........................... 112	4.15V	1.60V	.23V	.32V	.11V	.96V	8.77V	4.75V	.57V	1.20V	2.55V	.93V	1.69V	2.98V
Developing Countries............. 202	**37.6Y**	**32.4Y**	**52.9Y**	**40.6Y**	**49.7Y**	**45.2Y**	**53.7Y**	**2.9Y**	**8.9Y**	**2.3Y**	**3.8Y**	**3.6Y**	**2.5Y**	**4.0Y**
Africa....................................... 607	**2.4Y**	**.4Y**	**.6Y**	**.8Y**	**1.1Y**	**1.3Y**	**1.7Y**	**—Y**	**—Y**	**—Y**	**—Y**	**.1Y**	**.2Y**	**.2Y**
Benin.. 638	—V	—V	—V	—V	.05V	.06Y	.07Y	—V	—V	—V	—V	—V	—Y	—Y
Congo, Republic of..................... 634	—V	—V	.04V	—V	—Y	—Y	—Y	....	....	....	....	....	....	....
Ghana... 652	—Y	—Y	—Y	—Y	—Y	—Y	—Y	—Y	—Y	—Y	—Y	—Y	.01Y	.01Y
Guinea.. 656	—V	—Y	.01V	.08V	.09Y	.11Y	.14Y	—Y	—Y	—Y	—Y	—Y	—Y	—Y
Kenya.. 664	—V	—V	—V	.01V	.01Y	.01Y	.01Y	—V	—V	—V	—V	—Y	—Y	—Y
Madagascar................................ 674	—V	.01V	—V	—Y	—Y	—Y	.01Y	—Y	—Y	—V	—Y	—Y	—Y	—Y
Mauritius.................................... 684	—V	.02V	—V	—V	—V	—V	—V	—V	—V	—V	—V	—V	—V	—V
Nigeria.. 694	2.38V	.40V	.54V	.71Y	.90Y	1.11Y	1.44Y	—V	—V	—V	—Y	—Y	—Y	—Y
Senegal....................................... 722	—V	—V	—V	—V	—V	—V	—Y	—V	—V	—V	—V	.03V	—V	—Y
South Africa................................ 199	—Y	—Y	—Y	—Y	—V	—V	—V	—Y	—Y	—Y	—Y	.11V	—V	—V
Togo... 742	—V	—V	.01V	—V	—V	—Y	—Y	—V	.01V	—V	—V	—V	—Y	—Y
Tunisia.. 744	—V	—V	—V	—V	—V	—V	—Y	—V	—V	—V	—V	—V	.17V	.21Y
Asia.. 507	**33.3Y**	**30.3Y**	**48.1Y**	**35.5Y**	**46.6Y**	**41.0Y**	**42.9Y**	**2.4Y**	**.7Y**	**1.7Y**	**1.4Y**	**2.4Y**	**1.3Y**	**2.5Y**
Bangladesh................................. 513	.17V	—V	—V	—V	—V	—V	—V	—V	—V	—V	—V	—V	—Y	—Y
China,P.R.: Mainland.................. 924	9.51V	11.27V	20.16V	18.89V	26.81V	26.97V	34.54V	.47V	.16V	.63V	.45V	1.83V	.54V	.69V
China,P.R.:Hong Kong................ 532	—V	—V	—V	—V	—V	—V	—V	—V	—V	.44V	.49V	.27V	.34V	1.08V
China,P.R.:Macao....................... 546	—V	—V	—V	.01V	—V	—V	.01V	—V	.05V	.02V	—V	—V	—V	—V
India... 534	.08Y	.01V	—V	.01V	—V	—Y	—Y	.33Y	.08V	.14V	.11V	.01V	.02Y	.02Y
Indonesia.................................... 536	.11V	.01V	.09V	—V	—V	—V	—V	.05V	—V	.01V	—V	—V	—V	.04V
Korea.. 542	.42V	.82V	.92V	1.13V	1.66V	2.25V	1.10V	—V	.01V	.02V	—V	—V	—V	.17V
Lao People's Dem.Rep................ 544	....	....	....	....	....	....	....	.01Y	.01Y	.01Y	.01Y	.01Y	.02Y	.02Y
Malaysia..................................... 548	—V	—V	11.65V	2.24V	1.80V	—V	.03V	—V	—V	—V	—V	—V	—V	—V
Myanmar..................................... 518	—Y	—Y	—Y	—Y	—Y	—Y	—Y	.01Y	.01Y	.01Y	.01Y	.01Y	.01Y	.02Y
New Caledonia............................ 839	—V	—V	.01V	.02V	.02Y	.03Y	.03Y	—Y	—Y	—Y	—Y	—Y	—Y	—Y
Pakistan...................................... 564	.29V	.02V	.38V	.05V	1.51V	1.87Y	2.32Y	1.03V	.32V	.20V	.01V	.24V	.30Y	.37Y
Philippines.................................. 566	—V	—V	—V	—V	—V	—V	—V	—V	.01V	—V	.01V	—V	—V	—V
Thailand...................................... 578	22.72V	18.14V	14.85V	13.14V	14.83V	9.93V	4.84V	.08V	—V	.20V	.29V	.04V	.02V	.05V
Vietnam...................................... 582	....	....	....	....	....	....	....	.46V	.09V	.06V	—V	—V	—V	—V
Europe..................................... 170	**1.9Y**	**1.7Y**	**4.2Y**	**4.3Y**	**1.9Y**	**2.9Y**	**9.1Y**	**.4Y**	**8.1Y**	**.5Y**	**2.3Y**	**1.0Y**	**1.0Y**	**1.2Y**
Belarus....................................... 913	—V	—V	—V	—V	—V	—V	.01V	—V	—Y	—Y	—Y	—Y	—Y	—Y
Bulgaria...................................... 918	—V	—V	.02V	.02V	.05V	.06V	—V	—V	.01V	—V	—V	—V	.01V	—V
Czech Republic........................... 935	.21V	.15V	.03V	—V	—V	—V	—V	.23V	.17V	.24V	.42V	.23V	.32V	.64V
Estonia....................................... 939	.22V	.32V	.56V	—V	—V	—V	—V	—V	—V	.06V	—V	—V	—V	—V
Faroe Islands.............................. 816	.35Y	.38Y	.48Y	.63Y	.71Y	.88Y	1.10Y	.06Y	.06Y	.08Y	.10Y	.12Y	.14Y	.18Y
Hungary...................................... 944	—V	—V	—Y	—Y	—V	—V	—V	—V	—V	—Y	—V	—V	.14V	—V
Kazakhstan.................................. 916	.02V	—V	—V	.01V	.01Y	.01Y	.01Y	—V	—V	—V	—V	—Y	—Y	—Y
Kyrgyz Republic.......................... 917	....	....	....	....	....	....	....	.01Y	.01Y	.01Y	.02Y	.02Y	.02Y	.03Y
Latvia... 941	—V	—V	—Y	—V	—V	—V	—V	—V	—V	—Y	—V	—V	.01V	.01V
Lithuania.................................... 946	.03V	.04V	.02V	.88V	—V	—V	.05V	—V	—V	—V	1.57V	.35V	.09V	.19V
Poland.. 964	1.03V	.65V	1.54V	2.02V	—V	—V	—V	.11V	.02V	.07V	.06V	.02V	.25V	.07V
Romania..................................... 968	—V	—V	—V	—V	.03V	.01V	—V	—V	—V	—V	—V	—V	—V	—V
Russia... 922	.02V	.21V	1.47V	.61V	.88V	1.51V	7.54V	.01V	7.84V	—V	—V	—V	—V	—V

	Exports							Imports						
	2001	2002	2003	2004	2005	2006	2007	2001	2002	2003	2004	2005	2006	2007
	Millions of U.S. Dollars							*Millions of U.S. Dollars*						
Turkey.. 186	—V	—V	.05V	.12V	.03V	.11V	.09V	—V	.01V	—V	.12V	.22V	—V	.05V
Ukraine....................................... 926	—V	—V	.04V	—V	.23V	.28Y	.35Y	—V	—V	—V	—V	—V	—Y	—Y
Uzbekistan.................................. 927	—Y	—Y	—Y	—Y	—Y	—Y	—Y	—Y	—Y	—Y	—Y	.01Y	.01Y	.01Y
Middle East............................. 407	**—Y**	**—Y**	**—Y**	**—Y**	**—Y**	**—Y**	**—Y**	**—Y**	**—Y**	**—Y**	**—Y**	**—Y**	**—Y**	**—Y**
United Arab Emirates.................. 466	—V	—V	—V	—Y	—Y	—Y	—Y	—Y	—Y	.01Y	.01Y	.01Y	.01Y	.02Y
Western Hemisphere................ 207	**.1Y**	**—Y**	**—Y**	**—Y**	**—Y**	**—Y**	**—Y**	**.1Y**	**.1Y**	**.1Y**	**.1Y**	**.1Y**	**.1Y**	**.1Y**
Bahamas, The............................. 313	—Y	—Y	—Y	—Y	—Y	—Y	—Y	.03Y	.03Y	.04Y	.05Y	.06Y	.07Y	.08Y
Brazil... 223	—V	—V	—V	—V	—V	.01V	—V	—V	—V	—V	—V	—V	—V	—V
Colombia.................................... 233	—V	—V	.05V	—V	—V	—V	—V	—V	—V	.02V	—V	—V	—V	.01V
Guatemala.................................. 258	.07V	—V	—V	—V	—V	—Y	—Y	—V	—V	—V	—V	—V	—Y	—Y
Netherlands Antilles..................... 353	—V	—V	—V	—Y	—Y	—Y	—Y	.03V	—V	—V	—Y	—Y	—Y	—Y
Panama...................................... 283	—V	—V	—V	—V	—V	—V	—V	—V	.02V	—V	—V	—V	—V	—V
Peru.. 293	—V	—V	—V	—V	—V	—V	—Y	—V	—V	—V	.03V	—V	—V	—Y
St. Pierre-Miquelon...................... 363	—Y	—Y	—Y	—Y	—Y	—Y	—Y	—Y	.01Y	.01Y	.01Y	.01Y	.01Y	.02Y
Venezuela, Rep. Bol..................... 299	—V	—V	—V	—V	.05V	—V	—V	—V	—V	—V	—V	—V	—V	—Y
Other Countries n.i.e................ 910	**—Y**	**—Y**	**—Y**	**—Y**	**—Y**	**—Y**	**—Y**	**—Y**	**—Y**	**—Y**	**—Y**	**—Y**	**—Y**	**—Y**
North Korea................................ 954	—Y	—Y	—Y	—Y	—Y	—Y	—Y	.01Y	.01Y	.02Y	.02Y	.02Y	.03Y	.04Y
Countries & Areas n.s.............. 898	**6.0Y**	**6.5Y**	**8.2Y**	**10.8Y**	**12.4Y**	**15.3Y**	**19.0Y**	**1.9Y**	**2.1Y**	**2.6Y**	**3.4Y**	**3.9Y**	**4.8Y**	**6.0Y**
Memorandum Items														
European Union........................... 998	223.10Y	267.31Y	307.91Y	341.93Y	358.73Y	337.67Y	399.24Y	347.35Y	381.18Y	402.93Y	557.48Y	669.63Y	645.27Y	747.50Y
Oil Exporting Ctys........................ 999	2.49Y	.40Y	.63Y	.71Y	.94Y	1.11Y	1.44Y	.05Y	—Y	.02Y	.01Y	.01Y	.01Y	.05Y
Non-Oil Develop.Ctys.................. 201	35.14Y	32.03Y	52.30Y	39.86Y	48.72Y	44.11Y	52.26Y	2.88Y	8.93Y	2.25Y	3.78Y	3.60Y	2.51Y	3.92Y
PERCENT DISTRIBUTION														
Industrial Countries................. 101	**88.1**	**90.0**	**86.4**	**89.4**	**87.9**	**87.4**	**87.7**	**98.9**	**97.5**	**98.9**	**98.8**	**99.0**	**99.0**	**98.8**
Developing Countries.............. 202	**10.3**	**8.3**	**11.7**	**8.4**	**9.7**	**9.4**	**9.1**	**.7**	**2.0**	**.5**	**.6**	**.5**	**.4**	**.5**
Africa.................................... 607	**.6**	**.1**	**.1**	**.2**	**.2**	**.3**	**.3**	**—**	**—**	**—**	**—**	**—**	**—**	**—**
Asia....................................... 507	**9.1**	**7.8**	**10.6**	**7.3**	**9.1**	**8.6**	**7.2**	**.6**	**.2**	**.4**	**.2**	**.3**	**.2**	**.3**
Europe................................... 170	**.5**	**.4**	**.9**	**.9**	**.4**	**.6**	**1.5**	**.1**	**1.8**	**.1**	**.4**	**.1**	**.1**	**.1**
ANNUAL PERCENT CHANGE														
World...................................... 001	**10.6**	**6.0**	**16.0**	**7.0**	**6.1**	**–6.4**	**23.3**	**2.4**	**5.0**	**2.0**	**32.6**	**20.7**	**–1.7**	**15.4**
Industrial Countries................. 101	**7.2**	**8.3**	**11.4**	**10.7**	**4.4**	**–7.0**	**23.8**	**4.2**	**3.6**	**3.5**	**32.4**	**20.9**	**–1.7**	**15.2**
Developing Countries.............. 202	**51.6**	**–13.8**	**63.2**	**–23.4**	**22.4**	**–8.9**	**18.7**	**–71.2**	**204.3**	**–74.6**	**66.5**	**–4.6**	**–30.3**	**57.7**
Africa.................................... 607	**558.2**	**–82.2**	**44.7**	**29.5**	**32.4**	**23.0**	**28.8**	**–91.7**	**180.6**	**–78.9**	**31.3**	**—**	**15.6**	**24.1**
Asia....................................... 507	**46.4**	**–9.1**	**58.8**	**–26.2**	**31.4**	**–12.0**	**4.5**	**73.5**	**–69.6**	**134.3**	**–19.7**	**74.0**	**–48.2**	**95.4**
Europe................................... 170	**15.2**	**–7.5**	**141.2**	**1.5**	**–54.7**	**47.9**	**219.1**	**–95.1**	**—**	**–94.4**	**404.0**	**–58.3**	**3.7**	**18.1**
Middle East........................... 407	**—**	**—**	**....**	**....**	**....**	**....**	**....**	**7.9**	**6.3**	**21.2**	**32.3**	**36.0**	**25.7**	**20.6**
Western Hemisphere............. 207	**–13.3**	**–99.7**	**—**	**–91.1**	**986.0**	**–59.6**	**–77.5**	**–35.7**	**–12.0**	**40.7**	**20.1**	**–20.4**	**23.6**	**35.9**
Other Countries n.i.e.............. 910	**—**	**—**	**....**	**....**	**....**	**....**	**....**	**10.4**	**8.5**	**26.6**	**31.3**	**14.3**	**23.6**	**24.1**

		Exports							Imports						
		2001	2002	2003	2004	2005	2006	2007	2001	2002	2003	2004	2005	2006	2007
		Millions of U.S. Dollars							*Millions of U.S. Dollars*						
IFS World Total		**59.5**	**58.3**	**41.7**	**30.4**	**39.4**	**20.0**	**. . . .**	**219.2**	**202.0**	**254.4**	**233.5**	**318.5**	**280.3**	**. . . .**
DOTS World Total	**001**	**75.0Y**	**50.9Y**	**45.0Y**	**40.1Y**	**48.0Y**	**38.3Y**	**697.9Y**	**204.0Y**	**202.8Y**	**243.8Y**	**272.5Y**	**339.2Y**	**344.0Y**	**393.3Y**
Industrial Countries	**101**	**57.1Y**	**23.8Y**	**26.6Y**	**18.0Y**	**21.3Y**	**10.0Y**	**14.7Y**	**101.7Y**	**102.1Y**	**128.2Y**	**129.1Y**	**163.9Y**	**145.3Y**	**164.7Y**
United States	111	22.73V	6.64V	7.36V	4.91V	5.45V	4.36V	8.09V	65.89V	62.26V	75.13V	76.78V	90.64V	83.16V	91.52V
Canada	156	.67V	.85V	.76V	.97V	.79V	.84V	.64V	2.26V	2.84V	4.29V	5.38V	7.21V	7.19V	7.39V
Australia	193	—V	.01V	.03V	—V	—V	.09V	—V	.73V	.83V	1.86V	1.10V	.29V	.13V	.31V
Japan	158	.14V	.19V	.18V	.28V	—V	.07V	—V	6.91V	5.95V	10.77V	9.96V	12.58V	9.21V	8.62V
New Zealand	196	—V	—V	—V	—V	.01V	.01V	—V	1.76V	2.20V	1.55V	1.92V	2.16V	1.87V	2.26V
Austria	122	—V	.04V	—V	—V	—V	—V	—V	.04V	.02V	.04V	.09V	.03V	.24V	.39V
Belgium	124	.40V	1.13V	1.54V	1.56V	.86V	.74V	.36V	.30V	.62V	.62V	.49V	.57V	.91V	1.11V
Cyprus	423	—V	—V	—V	—V	—Y	—V	—V	—V	.01V	.01V	.03V	.04V	.01V	.01V
Denmark	128	—V	—V	—V	.08V	—V	—V	.01V	.96V	1.50V	1.44V	1.41V	1.49V	1.45V	1.55V
Finland	172	—V	—V	.01V	—V	—V	.03V	.03V	.21V	.09V	.15V	.52V	4.76V	.14V	.72V
France	132	14.17V	2.02V	1.80V	1.86V	2.02V	1.52V	1.06V	1.93V	4.05V	3.88V	3.15V	5.64V	5.25V	3.64V
Germany	134	7.60V	5.75V	6.33V	2.87V	3.84V	.38V	.11V	2.26V	4.75V	2.64V	1.69V	3.24V	4.77V	3.94V
Greece	174	—V	—V	—V	—V	.01V	—V	—V	.05V	.03V	.06V	.09V	.03V	.04V	.67V
Iceland	176	—V	—V	—V	—V	—V	—V	—V	.04V	—V	—V	—V	—V	—V	—V
Ireland	178	—V	—V	.01V	—V	—V	—V	—V	.26V	.27V	.33V	.36V	.24V	.27V	.28V
Italy	136	.35V	.11V	.09V	.05V	.97V	.01V	2.19V	.89V	1.52V	.87V	6.42V	7.01V	7.43V	16.01V
Luxembourg	137	.02V	—V	—V	—V	—V	—V	—V	—V	.02V	—V	—V	.82V	—V	.25V
Netherlands	138	5.84V	4.16V	4.39V	3.19V	3.77V	1.33V	1.34V	2.82V	2.93V	5.61V	3.99V	4.55V	4.95V	6.96V
Norway	142	.08V	.12V	.12V	.10V	.09V	.09V	.11V	2.08V	.98V	.79V	.79V	1.28V	1.60V	1.66V
Portugal	182	—V	—V	—V	—V	—V	—V	—V	.02V	.01V	.02V	.01V	.05V	.05V	.46V
Slovenia	961	1.88V	.28V	.06V	.08Y	—V	—V	—V	.04V	.03V	.03V	.04Y	.02V	—V	—V
Spain	184	1.76V	.29V	.02V	—V	—V	—V	.08V	.87V	.56V	.46V	.45V	.53V	.76V	.52V
Sweden	144	—V	—V	—V	—V	.19V	.05V	—V	.12V	1.55V	4.16V	1.09V	.59V	1.14V	2.49V
Switzerland	146	.43V	.43V	1.36V	1.42V	—V	.19V	.27V	.26V	.04V	.14V	.08V	.08V	.15V	.57V
United Kingdom	112	1.08V	1.81V	2.58V	.62V	3.27V	.27V	.44V	11.02V	9.01V	13.40V	13.24V	20.06V	14.62V	13.36V
Developing Countries	**202**	**17.7Y**	**26.9Y**	**18.2Y**	**21.8Y**	**26.4Y**	**28.0Y**	**682.7Y**	**102.2Y**	**100.7Y**	**115.5Y**	**143.3Y**	**175.2Y**	**198.6Y**	**228.5Y**
Africa	**607**	**.1Y**	**—Y**	**.2Y**	**.1Y**	**.2Y**	**.2Y**	**.3Y**	**.1Y**	**.2Y**	**.2Y**	**.2Y**	**.2Y**	**—Y**	**—Y**
Benin	638	—V	—V	—V	—V	—V	—Y	—Y	—V	.03V	—V	—V	—V	—Y	—Y
Guinea	656	—V	—Y	.01V	.02V	.03Y	.03Y	.04Y	—V	—Y	—V	—V	—Y	—Y	—Y
South Africa	199	—V	—V	.05V	—V	—V	—V	—V	.12V	.15V	.20V	.12V	.21V	—V	—V
Tanzania	738	—V	.04V	.05Y	.06Y	.07Y	.09Y	.11Y	.03V	—V	—Y	—Y	—Y	—Y	—Y
Tunisia	744	.02V	—V	.09V	—V	.01V	—V	—Y	—V	—V	—V	—V	—V	—V	—Y
Uganda	746	.03V	—V	.02V	.04Y	.06Y	.07Y	.09Y	—V	—V	.02V	.03Y	.03Y	.04Y	.05Y
Zambia	754	—V	.01V	—V	—V	—V	—V	—V	—V	—V	—V	—V	—V	—V	—V
Zimbabwe	698	—V	—V	—V	—V	—V	.01V	.02Y	—V	—V	—V	—V	—V	—V	—Y
Asia	**507**	**2.4Y**	**5.1Y**	**.4Y**	**.3Y**	**.3Y**	**.3Y**	**1.0Y**	**2.7Y**	**2.4Y**	**3.3Y**	**4.1Y**	**11.2Y**	**11.0Y**	**10.3Y**
Bangladesh	513	2.14V	4.71V	—V	—V	—V	—V	—V	—V	—V	—V	—V	—V	—Y	—Y
China,P.R.: Mainland	924	—V	—V	.28V	—V	—V	.02V	.04Y	.28V	.34V	.43V	.98V	3.00V	4.50V	3.29V
China,P.R.:Hong Kong	532	—V	.02V	—V	—V	—V	—V	—V	.25V	.11V	.22V	.18V	.16V	.35V	.31V
India	534	—Y	.19V	.14V	.05V	.11V	.14Y	.18Y	—Y	.50V	.61V	.33V	.72V	.89Y	1.11Y
Indonesia	536	—V	.05V	—V	—V	—V	.01V	.04V	.39V	.17V	.25V	.06V	.23V	.21V	.42V
Korea	542	.05V	.01V	—V	—V	.04V	—V	.30V	.85V	.74V	.94V	1.55V	3.67V	2.22V	1.99V
Malaysia	548	.16V	.01V	—V	.05V	.01V	.05V	.14V	.10V	.06V	—V	.42V	.07V	.19V	.16V
Pakistan	564	—Y	—Y	—V	—V	—V	—Y	—Y	—V	—V	—V	.02V	.34V	.43Y	.53Y
Philippines	566	—V	—V	—V	.03V	—V	—V	—V	.04V	—V	—V	—V	—V	—V	.01V
Taiwan Province of China	528	—V	—V	—V	.02V	.13V	.04V	.25V	.45V	.19V	.39V	.35V	2.01V	.76V	1.40V
Thailand	578	.01V	.07V	.01V	.11V	.03V	.02V	.10V	.36V	.24V	.47V	.25V	.99V	1.41V	1.04V
Vietnam	582	. . . .	. . . .	. . . .	. . . .	. . . .	. . . .	. . . .	.02V	.04V	.01V	—V	—V	—V	—V
Europe	**170**	**.3Y**	**.2Y**	**.3Y**	**.4Y**	**.3Y**	**.4Y**	**.5Y**	**.9Y**	**.1Y**	**.2Y**	**.2Y**	**.4Y**	**.4Y**	**.3Y**
Belarus	913	.02V	—V	—V	.05V	—V	—V	—V	—V	—V	—V	—V	—V	—V	—V
Bulgaria	918	—V	—V	—V	—V	.01V	—V	—V	—V	—V	—V	—V	—V	—V	—V
Czech Republic	935	.03V	.03V	—V	—V	.04V	—V	—V	.75V	.03V	.04V	—V	—V	.01V	.02V
Estonia	939	.05V	—V	.05V	—V	—V	—V	—V	—V	.02V	—V	—V	—V	—V	—V
Georgia	915	—V	—V	—V	.03V	.02V	—V	—Y	. . . .	. . . .	. . . .	. . . .	. . . .	. . . .	. . . .
Hungary	944	.01V	—V	.01V	.01V	—V	—V	—V	.11V	—V	—V	.08V	—V	.01V	—V
Lithuania	946	—V	.01V	—V	—V	—V	—V	—V	—V	—V	.08V	.01V	—V	—V	—V
Moldova	921	.01V	—V	—V	—V	—V	—Y	—Y	. . . .	. . . .	. . . .	. . . .	. . . .	. . . .	. . . .
Poland	964	.01V	.03V	.01V	.02V	—V	—V	—V	.03V	.01V	.05V	.03V	.33V	.25V	.26V
Romania	968	.01V	.01V	.01V	—V	—V	—V	—V	—V	—V	—V	—V	.01V	—V	—V
Russia	922	.01V	.02V	.02V	.03V	—V	.03V	—V	—V	—V	—V	—V	—V	—V	—V
Turkey	186	—V	—V	—V	—V	—V	.01V	.08V	.01V	.02V	.03V	.09V	.09V	.15V	.06V
Ukraine	926	.01V	—V	.01V	—V	.01V	.01Y	.01Y	—V	—V	—V	—V	—V	—Y	—Y
Europe n.s.	884	.12Y	.13Y	.17Y	.22Y	.25Y	.31Y	.38Y	—Y	—Y	—Y	—Y	—Y	—Y	—Y
Middle East	**407**	**—Y**	**—Y**	**—Y**	**.4Y**	**.1Y**	**.1Y**	**.1Y**	**—Y**	**—Y**	**—Y**	**—Y**	**—Y**	**—Y**	**—Y**
Saudi Arabia	456	—V	—V	—V	—V	.06V	.08Y	.10Y	—Y	—Y	—Y	—Y	—Y	—Y	—Y
Yemen, Republic of	474	—V	—V	—Y	.36V	—V	—Y	—Y	—V	—V	—Y	—V	—V	—Y	—Y
Western Hemisphere	**207**	**15.0Y**	**21.5Y**	**17.2Y**	**20.7Y**	**25.5Y**	**27.0Y**	**680.8Y**	**98.4Y**	**98.1Y**	**111.8Y**	**138.8Y**	**163.4Y**	**187.2Y**	**217.8Y**
Antigua and Barbuda	311	1.93Y	2.09Y	2.65Y	3.48Y	3.98Y	4.91Y	6.10Y	.28Y	.31Y	.39Y	.51Y	.58Y	.72Y	.90Y
Argentina	213	.97V	.45V	.60V	.50V	.68V	.04V	—V	.22V	.26V	.43V	.65V	.78V	.87V	.62V
Aruba	314	—V	—V	—V	—V	—V	—V	—V	.06V	.06V	.05V	.01V	.02V	.03V	—V

	Exports							Imports						
	2001	2002	2003	2004	2005	2006	2007	2001	2002	2003	2004	2005	2006	2007
	Millions of U.S. Dollars							*Millions of U.S. Dollars*						
Bahamas, The....... 313	—Y	—Y	—Y	—Y	—Y	—Y	—Y	.11Y	.12Y	.15Y	.19Y	.22Y	.27Y	.34Y
Barbados....... 316	1.37V	1.25V	1.19V	1.22V	1.54V	1.38V	1.71Y	8.11V	7.32V	8.12V	8.86V	13.29V	9.67V	12.00Y
Belize....... 339	—Y	—Y	—Y	—Y	—Y	—Y	—Y	.01Y	.01Y	.01Y	.01Y	.01Y	.01Y	.02Y
Brazil....... 223	.15V	.09V	.08V	.10V	—V	—V	—V	1.74V	2.03V	2.53V	3.45V	5.63V	5.18V	—V
Chile....... 228	—V	—V	—V	—V	—V	—V	—V	.15V	—V	.13V	.15V	.15V	.41V	.25V
Colombia....... 233	.26V	.18V	—V	—V	.11V	—V	—V	.57V	.25V	.44V	.25V	.22V	1.20V	.33V
Costa Rica....... 238	—V	6.71V	—V	—V	—V	—Y	—Y	.06V	.08V	.43V	.29V	.14V	.18Y	.22Y
Dominica....... 321	1.73V	1.87Y	2.37Y	3.11Y	3.56Y	4.40Y	5.46Y	.34V	.37Y	.47Y	.61Y	.70Y	.87Y	1.08Y
Dominican Republic....... 243	—V	—Y	—Y	—Y	—Y	—Y	.01Y	.10V	.11Y	.14Y	.18Y	.21Y	.26Y	.32Y
El Salvador....... 253	—V	—V	—V	—V	—V	—V	—V	—V	—V	—V	—V	—V	.13V	—V
Guatemala....... 258	—Y	—Y	—Y	—Y	—Y	—Y	—Y	.05V	.05V	.06V	.04V	.03V	.03Y	.04Y
Guyana....... 336	.12Y	.13Y	.17Y	.22Y	.25Y	.31Y	.38Y	2.62Y	2.84Y	3.59Y	4.72Y	5.39Y	6.66Y	8.27Y
Jamaica....... 343	.59V	.65V	.44V	.43V	.64V	.52V	647.88V	1.64V	1.57V	1.87V	1.53V	2.22V	1.79V	1.84V
Mexico....... 273	—V	—V	—V	—V	.23V	.05V	.69V	—V	—V	—V	—V	1.43V	.65V	.51V
Netherlands Antilles....... 353	—V	.01V	—V	—Y	—Y	—Y	—Y	7.28V	4.80V	.22V	.29Y	.33Y	.40Y	.50Y
Panama....... 283	—V	—V	—V	—V	—V	—V	—V	—V	—V	—V	—V	.01V	.03V	—V
Paraguay....... 288	—V	—V	—V	—V	—V	.01V	.01Y	—V	—V	—V	—V	—V	—V	—Y
Peru....... 293	.01V	—V	—V	—V	—V	—V	—Y	—V	—V	.03V	.04V	.02V	.04V	.03Y
St. Kitts and Nevis....... 361	1.73Y	1.88Y	2.38Y	3.12Y	3.57Y	4.41Y	5.47Y	.12Y	.13Y	.16Y	.21Y	.24Y	.30Y	.37Y
St. Lucia....... 362	2.84Y	3.08Y	3.90Y	5.12Y	5.85Y	7.23Y	8.97Y	1.73Y	1.88Y	2.38Y	3.12Y	3.57Y	4.41Y	5.47Y
St. Vincent & Grens....... 364	.51V	.49V	.67V	.50V	.49V	.60Y	.75Y	1.32V	1.40V	1.44V	2.15V	3.00V	3.71Y	4.61Y
Suriname....... 366	.03Y	.04Y	.05Y	.06Y	.07Y	.08Y	.10Y	.07Y	.07Y	.09Y	.12Y	.14Y	.17Y	.21Y
Trinidad and Tobago....... 369	.22V	.13V	.16Y	.21Y	.24Y	.30Y	.37Y	50.22V	49.21V	62.29Y	81.80Y	93.46Y	115.51Y	143.35Y
Uruguay....... 298	.05V	.06Y	.05V	.05V	.01V	.01Y	.01Y	—V	—Y	.03V	—V	—V	—Y	—Y
Venezuela, Rep. Bol....... 299	.19V	—V	.02V	.01V	1.60V	.04V	.04V	2.20V	3.01V	1.39V	1.98V	1.17V	.56V	.67Y
Western Hem. n.s....... 399	2.33Y	2.41Y	2.49Y	2.57Y	2.65Y	2.73Y	2.81Y	19.45Y	22.19Y	24.93Y	27.67Y	30.41Y	33.15Y	35.89Y
Other Countries n.i.e....... 910	**—Y**	**—Y**	**—Y**	**—Y**	**—Y**	**—Y**	**—Y**	**—Y**	**—Y**	**—Y**	**—Y**	**—Y**	**.1Y**	**.1Y**
Cuba....... 928	—Y	—Y	—Y	—Y	—Y	—Y	—Y	.02Y	.02Y	.03Y	.04Y	.05Y	.06Y	.07Y
Countries & Areas n.s....... 898	**.2Y**	**.2Y**	**.2Y**	**.3Y**	**.3Y**	**.4Y**	**.5Y**	**—Y**	**—Y**	**—Y**	**—Y**	**—Y**	**—Y**	**—Y**
Memorandum Items														
European Union....... 998	33.19Y	15.66Y	16.90Y	10.33Y	14.97Y	4.31Y	5.62Y	22.68Y	27.05Y	33.87Y	33.19Y	49.99Y	42.29Y	52.64Y
Oil Exporting Ctys....... 999	.19Y	.05Y	.02Y	.01Y	1.66Y	.12Y	.18Y	2.59Y	3.18Y	1.64Y	2.04Y	1.40Y	.77Y	1.10Y
Non-Oil Develop.Ctys....... 201	17.53Y	26.81Y	18.13Y	21.83Y	24.70Y	27.84Y	682.48Y	99.64Y	97.52Y	113.87Y	141.30Y	173.84Y	197.86Y	227.41Y
PERCENT DISTRIBUTION														
Industrial Countries....... 101	**76.2**	**46.8**	**59.2**	**44.8**	**44.3**	**26.0**	**2.1**	**49.9**	**50.3**	**52.6**	**47.4**	**48.3**	**42.2**	**41.9**
Developing Countries....... 202	**23.6**	**52.8**	**40.3**	**54.4**	**54.9**	**72.9**	**97.8**	**50.1**	**49.7**	**47.4**	**52.6**	**51.7**	**57.7**	**58.1**
Africa....... 607	**.1**	**.1**	**.5**	**.3**	**.4**	**.6**	**—**	**.1**	**.1**	**.1**	**.1**	**.1**	**—**	**—**
Asia....... 507	**3.1**	**9.9**	**1.0**	**.7**	**.7**	**.7**	**.1**	**1.3**	**1.2**	**1.4**	**1.5**	**3.3**	**3.2**	**2.6**
Europe....... 170	**.4**	**.5**	**.6**	**.9**	**.7**	**.9**	**.1**	**.4**	**—**	**.1**	**.1**	**.1**	**.1**	**.1**
Middle East....... 407	**—**	**—**	**—**	**.9**	**.1**	**.2**	**—**	**—**	**—**	**—**	**—**	**—**	**—**	**—**
Western Hemisphere....... 207	**20.0**	**42.3**	**38.3**	**51.6**	**53.1**	**70.5**	**97.5**	**48.3**	**48.4**	**45.8**	**51.0**	**48.2**	**54.4**	**55.4**
ANNUAL PERCENT CHANGE														
World....... 001	**–2.8**	**–32.2**	**–11.5**	**–10.9**	**19.6**	**–20.1**	**—**	**–17.0**	**–.6**	**20.2**	**11.8**	**24.5**	**1.4**	**14.3**
Industrial Countries....... 101	**–8.1**	**–58.3**	**11.8**	**–32.5**	**18.3**	**–53.2**	**48.1**	**–37.8**	**.4**	**25.6**	**.7**	**27.0**	**–11.3**	**13.3**
Developing Countries....... 202	**19.1**	**51.6**	**–32.4**	**20.3**	**20.7**	**6.1**	**—**	**24.4**	**–1.5**	**14.7**	**24.1**	**22.3**	**13.3**	**15.0**
Africa....... 607	**. . . .**	**–8.4**	**340.2**	**–40.9**	**33.3**	**24.5**	**24.4**	**. . . .**	**21.5**	**20.2**	**–30.3**	**56.4**	**–83.4**	**24.1**
Asia....... 507	**. . . .**	**114.2**	**–91.5**	**–38.5**	**22.0**	**–12.9**	**270.7**	**–20.9**	**–13.7**	**40.2**	**24.7**	**170.0**	**–2.1**	**–6.3**
Europe....... 170	**147.0**	**–12.9**	**14.3**	**36.7**	**–11.2**	**9.5**	**33.1**	**. . . .**	**–90.1**	**121.7**	**8.5**	**95.5**	**–1.1**	**–17.7**
Middle East....... 407	**—**	**—**	**. . . .**	**. . . .**	**–82.9**	**23.5**	**29.5**	**—**	**—**	**. . . .**	**. . . .**	**. . . .**	**. . . .**	**. . . .**
Western Hemisphere....... 207	**1.8**	**43.2**	**–19.9**	**20.2**	**23.0**	**6.1**	**—**	**25.1**	**–.4**	**14.0**	**24.2**	**17.7**	**14.6**	**16.4**
Other Countries n.i.e....... 910	**—**	**—**	**. . . .**	**. . . .**	**. . . .**	**. . . .**	**. . . .**	**10.4**	**8.5**	**26.6**	**31.3**	**14.3**	**23.6**	**24.1**

	Exports							Imports						
	2001	2002	2003	2004	2005	2006	2007	2001	2002	2003	2004	2005	2006	2007
	Millions of U.S. Dollars							Millions of U.S. Dollars						
IFS World Total	**2,463.6**	**2,473.2**	**2,631.7**	**2,938.7**	**3,476.9**	**3,664.9**	**4,489.5**	**5,606.4**	**6,304.1**	**6,721.5**	**7,811.6**	**8,809.8**	**10,156.5**	**11,860.6**
DOTS World Total....001	**2,412.4**	**4,162.0**	**4,459.4**	**5,035.6**	**5,380.9**	**6,468.3Y**	**7,040.2Y**	**5,606.4**	**7,658.6**	**8,127.6**	**9,470.4**	**10,500.9**	**11,505.8Y**	**12,837.8Y**
Industrial Countries....101	**898.2**	**2,479.3**	**2,666.4**	**2,998.8**	**3,145.6**	**3,743.4Y**	**3,705.6Y**	**2,969.1**	**4,379.3**	**4,459.4**	**4,721.6**	**5,514.8**	**5,486.3Y**	**6,115.4Y**
United States....111	644.95	2,225.40	2,392.49	2,668.83	2,694.24	3,023.91V	2,972.09V	1,969.81	3,274.22	3,375.58	3,219.02	4,001.27	3,870.02V	4,483.71V
Canada....156	42.74	40.93	43.61	59.83	73.25	205.72V	204.10V	140.58	73.15	59.46	147.68	141.25	177.21V	133.52V
Australia....193	.24	1.11	.86	1.74	1.46	3.94V	4.56V	6.20	8.74	6.85	10.32	12.21	18.97V	30.08V
Japan....158	42.29	33.66	25.32	27.85	38.47	86.24V	89.40V	289.73	209.25	253.81	417.19	275.25	319.70V	347.29V
New Zealand....196	.11	.17	.18	.38	1.11	1.46V	1.52V	26.15	19.03	19.26	27.72	23.48	25.49V	27.31V
Austria....122	.47	.67	.59	.66	.71	1.98V	1.70V	10.32	7.84	8.25	8.60	6.13	19.09V	19.11V
Belgium....124	11.95	11.93	13.72	14.76	23.04	20.27V	18.32V	25.64	27.39	34.80	39.39	51.22	56.20V	50.78V
Cyprus....423	.02	—	—	—	—	—V	—V	.04	—	—	—	.03	—V	—V
Denmark....128	1.81	2.07	2.35	2.31	1.47	2.04V	2.25V	9.96	12.56	11.27	12.64	9.82	10.38V	13.69V
Finland....172	7.22	4.00	5.30	4.60	7.21	10.90V	13.48V	7.11	84.63	34.78	13.49	17.25	13.43V	20.82V
France....132	7.18	8.66	10.98	8.57	11.28	39.21V	24.12V	35.48	47.79	61.99	83.89	72.28	97.77V	73.80V
Germany....134	58.30	54.63	53.64	60.92	73.83	72.29V	75.06V	158.86	165.62	166.43	190.34	208.24	223.06V	212.90V
Greece....174	.12	.02	.04	.08	.05	.21V	.80V	.36	.12	.35	.90	.73	1.09V	3.04V
Iceland....176	.02	.10	.02	.05	.09	.24V	.27V	.02	.02	—	.01	.03	—V	—V
Ireland....178	.04	.09	.73	1.40	.09	.94V	1.52V	7.84	3.58	5.94	5.41	3.89	5.44V	9.34V
Italy....136	16.44	15.03	21.06	28.69	32.02	40.38V	46.52V	56.92	84.43	75.80	109.74	90.28	133.75V	180.79V
Luxembourg....137	—	—	—	—	.03	—V	—V	.28	.32	.13	.02	.42	.16V	.06V
Malta....181	—	.02	—	.03	—	.02V	—V	3.87	.05	.02	.03	.03	.01V	.88V
Netherlands....138	15.83	23.37	37.29	41.77	47.48	104.54V	107.77V	16.04	37.16	36.79	33.70	77.59	76.69V	89.90V
Norway....142	4.83	3.11	4.56	5.24	7.53	12.67V	14.91V	4.14	1.03	1.47	69.16	38.27	119.04V	83.79V
Portugal....182	1.22	.96	1.89	2.47	2.41	3.83V	4.87V	1.95	2.30	1.91	3.28	1.61	3.30V	3.73V
Slovenia....961	—	—	—	—	—	.01V	.11V	—	—	—	—	—	.37V	.51V
Spain....184	13.01	8.88	13.96	19.68	30.31	60.03V	62.25V	83.66	103.66	95.14	126.34	121.13	137.95V	147.44V
Sweden....144	8.62	6.13	6.41	3.69	5.76	7.85V	11.90V	22.51	31.06	27.56	65.29	53.91	94.65V	103.14V
Switzerland....146	11.69	26.84	18.30	31.73	80.60	13.38V	18.88V	52.69	130.78	144.72	80.01	262.17	23.74V	25.87V
United Kingdom....112	9.12	11.51	13.09	13.49	13.19	31.32V	29.21V	38.96	54.53	37.06	57.45	46.29	58.78V	53.90V
Developing Countries....202	**1,497.6**	**1,657.8**	**1,756.3**	**1,964.8**	**2,149.5**	**2,618.9Y**	**3,203.1Y**	**2,595.1**	**3,219.4**	**3,577.6**	**4,708.9**	**4,839.4**	**5,838.1Y**	**6,497.3Y**
Africa....607	**3.7**	**7.9**	**13.0**	**5.6**	**10.5**	**12.7Y**	**15.3Y**	**3.7**	**2.9**	**2.1**	**7.6**	**2.2**	**8.6Y**	**3.3Y**
Algeria....612	—	3.10	4.13	—	3.64	4.50Y	5.83Y	—	—	—	—	.01	.01Y	.01Y
Angola....614	—	—	.03	—	—	—Y	—Y	—	—	—	—	—	—Y	—Y
Benin....638	—	—	—	—	—	—Y	—Y	—	.03	—	.27	—	—Y	—Y
Cameroon....622	.01	—	—	—	.16	.20Y	.25Y	.16	—	—	.01	—	—Y	—Y
Cape Verde....624	—	—	—	—	—	—Y	—Y	—	.05	—	—	—	—Y	—Y
Central African Rep....626	.02	.06	—	—	.04	.05Y	.07Y	—	—	—	—	—	—Y	—Y
Congo, Dem. Rep. of....636	—	.28	.44	.33	.07	.08Y	.10Y	.03	—	—	.01	—	—Y	—Y
Congo, Republic of....634	—	.04	—	—	—	.01Y	.01Y	....	....	....	....	....	....	....
Côte d'Ivoire....662	—	.12	.04	.18	.08	.10V	.12Y	.01	—	—	.36	.08	—V	—Y
Djibouti....611	—	—	—	—	—	—Y	—Y	—	—	—	.01	.02	.02Y	.03Y
Ethiopia....644	—	—	—	—	—	—Y	—Y	.03	—	.13	.11	.22	.27Y	.33Y
Gabon....646	....	....	....	....	....	....	....	.02	—	.05	—	—	—Y	—Y
Gambia, The....648	....	....	....	....	....	....	....	—	—	—	—	.02	.03Y	.03Y
Ghana....652	—	—	.14	.83	.01	.01Y	.01Y	—	.07	—	—	—	—Y	—Y
Kenya....664	—	—	.03	—	.12	.15Y	.19Y	—	.12	—	—	.13	.16Y	.20Y
Malawi....676	....	....	....	....	....	....	....	.18	—	—	—	—	—Y	—Y
Mali....678	....	....	....	....	....	....	....	.58	—	—	—	.01	.02Y	.02Y
Mauritania....682	....	....	....	....	....	....	....	—	—	—	.01	—	—Y	—Y
Mauritius....684	.02	—	—	—	—	.07V	.12V	—	—	—	—	—	—V	—V
Morocco....686	.12	.32	4.63	.39	.37	.45Y	.56Y	.02	.02	—	.04	.02	.03Y	.03Y
Mozambique....688	....	....	....	....	....	....	....	—	—	.01	.04	—	—Y	—Y
Niger....692	—	.02	.07	—	.05	.06Y	.07Y	—	.09	—	—	.02	.02Y	.03Y
Nigeria....694	—	—	—	—	—	—Y	—Y	—	.01	—	—	.02	.03Y	.04Y
Rwanda....714	—	—	—	—	—	—Y	—Y	—	—	—	—	.04	.04Y	.06Y
São Tomé & Príncipe....716	—	.13	—	—	.24	.30Y	.37Y	—	.08	—	—	—	—Y	—Y
Senegal....722	—	—	—	—	.01	—V	—Y	.01	—	—	—	.01	—V	—Y
Seychelles....718	....	....	....	....	....	....	....	—	.03	—	—	.29	.36Y	.45Y
Sierra Leone....724	1.95	—	—	—	—	—Y	—Y	—	—	—	.01	—	—Y	—Y
South Africa....199	1.04	.46	.37	3.06	1.73	1.81V	1.55V	1.58	1.68	1.09	2.69	1.15	7.38V	1.83V
Sudan....732	.14	.34	.09	.34	.09	—V	—V	.03	—	.08	3.89	—	—V	—V
Swaziland....734	.40	.01	—	—	.20	.25Y	.31Y	.82	.66	.38	—	.15	.19Y	.24Y
Tanzania....738	—	—	—	—	3.71	4.59Y	5.69Y	.01	—	.06	—	—	—Y	—Y
Togo....742	—	—	.04	—	—	—Y	—Y	—	—	—	—	—	—Y	—Y
Tunisia....744	—	3.00	2.50	—	—	.03V	.04Y	.07	—	.20	.14	—	—V	—Y
Uganda....746	—	.02	.46	.43	.01	.01Y	.02Y	.05	.02	.07	—	.01	.01Y	.01Y
Zambia....754	—	—	—	—	—	—V	—V	—	.04	—	—	—	—V	—V
Zimbabwe....698	—	—	—	.01	—	—V	—Y	.07	—	.04	.01	—	—V	—Y
Asia....507	**112.3**	**120.2**	**101.0**	**88.3**	**89.7**	**311.1Y**	**329.8Y**	**341.9**	**935.6**	**1,007.9**	**1,687.1**	**1,250.5**	**1,768.0Y**	**1,727.5Y**
Afghanistan, I.S. of....512	—	.01	.20	—	.03	.04Y	.05Y	.06	.09	.58	.11	.18	.23Y	.28Y
Bangladesh....513	—	—	.28	.46	4.08	2.25V	1.41V	.09	.17	.03	.49	.09	.12Y	.14Y
Cambodia....522	—	—	—	—	—	—Y	—Y	—	.03	.03	.03	—	—V	—Y

	Exports 2001	2002	2003	2004	2005	2006	2007	Imports 2001	2002	2003	2004	2005	2006	2007
	Millions of U.S. Dollars							Millions of U.S. Dollars						
China,P.R.: Mainland.................. 924	.45	.58	4.60	20.00	36.68	39.76V	42.80V	123.67	118.37	167.64	627.09	331.96	756.08V	876.35V
China,P.R.:Hong Kong................ 532	.52	2.02	1.42	1.40	3.88	3.72V	5.41V	25.50	98.54	123.41	85.98	179.90	86.65V	79.79V
China,P.R.:Macao....................... 546	—	—	—	.01	—	.01V	.01V	—	.22	—	.06	.33	—V	—V
Fiji.. 819	—	—	—	.02	—	—Y	—Y	—	—	.03	—	—	—Y	—Y
French Polynesia......................... 887	—	—	.02	—	.07	.09Y	.11Y	—	—	.03	—	—	—Y	—Y
India... 534	.82	1.19	2.50	2.30	2.84	3.51Y	4.35Y	14.69	17.94	22.81	47.03	41.49	51.28Y	63.63Y
Indonesia.................................... 536	—	.03	.17	.28	7.62	12.11V	30.53V	9.16	12.77	8.97	19.55	6.28	12.76V	12.59V
Korea.. 542	93.95	87.19	62.50	39.50	8.36	87.37V	77.91V	77.09	535.74	538.69	648.20	499.88	600.61V	430.51V
Lao People's Dem.Rep................ 544	—	—	—	—	—	—Y	—Y	—	—	—	.03	—	—Y	—Y
Malaysia..................................... 548	5.77	13.37	18.36	10.95	7.25	12.57V	12.20V	9.87	11.45	22.52	30.04	18.45	20.97V	21.53V
Mongolia..................................... 948	....	....	....	....	....	....	....	.01	—	—	—	—	—Y	—Y
Myanmar..................................... 518	—	—	.08	—	—	—Y	—Y	.01	—	.03	—	—	—Y	—Y
Nauru.. 836	....	....	....	....	....	....	....	—	.02	.01	—	—	—Y	—Y
Nepal... 558	—	.43	.74	—	.43	.54Y	.66Y	—	—	—	—	—	—Y	.01Y
New Caledonia............................ 839	—	—	—	.03	—	—Y	—Y	.02	—	—	.03	—	—Y	—Y
Pakistan...................................... 564	.75	2.20	4.01	3.17	2.92	3.61Y	4.48Y	1.46	21.82	6.85	18.14	10.17	12.57Y	15.60Y
Philippines.................................. 566	.03	.08	.02	.02	.03	.09V	.21V	1.26	.51	.81	2.37	1.34	4.31V	2.66V
Samoa.. 862	—	—	—	—	—	—Y	—Y	—	—	.03	—	—	—Y	—Y
Singapore.................................... 576	4.16	7.18	5.75	4.86	2.69	3.31V	7.38V	4.65	2.92	4.17	22.99	24.99	4.83V	6.26V
Sri Lanka..................................... 524	.01	—	—	3.57	.20	—V	—V	.78	.82	1.00	1.70	1.02	2.69V	2.33V
Taiwan Province of China............ 528	5.38	4.68	.30	1.70	12.36	40.38V	29.80V	58.85	102.02	101.77	136.66	117.78	135.83V	104.19V
Thailand...................................... 578	.44	1.22	.01	.03	.01	1.12V	1.95V	14.28	10.23	6.56	44.46	15.90	57.32V	87.77V
Vietnam....................................... 582	—	.03	.04	.02	.19	—V	—V	.38	1.92	1.92	2.13	.67	—V	—V
Asia n.s....................................... 598	—	—	—	—	—	100.68Y	110.49Y	—	—	—	—	—	21.78Y	23.88Y
Europe...................................... 170	**33.1**	**27.0**	**53.4**	**13.4**	**4.4**	**24.0Y**	**33.1Y**	**86.3**	**25.3**	**24.4**	**140.8**	**25.5**	**99.8Y**	**90.0Y**
Albania.. 914	—	—	—	.15	—	.11V	.01V	—	.01	.01	.06	.17	.04V	—V
Azerbaijan................................... 912	.08	—	—	—	—	.05V	—V	—	—	—	—	—	—V	—V
Belarus.. 913	—	—	—	—	—	.09V	.04V	—	.01	—	.04	.04	1.80V	.01V
Bosnia & Herzegovina................. 963	....	....	....	....	....	....	....	—	—	.06	—	—	—Y	—Y
Bulgaria...................................... 918	.02	3.46	3.61	.02	.05	.12V	.87V	.83	.18	.36	.61	.44	1.12V	.44V
Croatia.. 960	—	1.91	—	.02	.10	—V	—V	.19	.01	.01	.13	.02	—V	—V
Czech Republic............................ 935	—	.34	.07	.02	.02	.09V	.16V	2.47	3.23	3.99	6.55	2.30	5.61V	6.85V
Estonia.. 939	—	—	—	—	.66	—V	—V	.01	.08	.11	3.66	.02	.29V	.06V
Faroe Islands.............................. 816	....	....	....	....	....	....	....	—	.07	—	—	.01	.02Y	.02Y
Georgia....................................... 915	—	—	—	—	—	—V	—Y	—	—	—	—	.12	.15Y	.19Y
Gibraltar..................................... 823	—	—	1.63	—	.55	.68Y	.85Y	.06	—	—	—	—	—Y	—Y
Hungary....................................... 944	—	—	—	—	—	.17V	.06V	.67	.31	.32	2.32	.25	1.05V	1.80V
Kazakhstan.................................. 916	—	—	—	—	—	3.79Y	4.71Y	—	.16	—	—	—	1.69Y	2.10Y
Kyrgyz Republic........................... 917	.01	—	—	—	—	—V	—V	—	—	—	—	—	—Y	—Y
Latvia.. 941	—	—	—	—	—	—V	—V	2.86	.34	—	.40	.18	.13V	.19V
Lithuania..................................... 946	—	—	—	—	.01	4.25V	.13V	.22	—	.10	.24	.02	.11V	.16V
Macedonia, FYR.......................... 962	—	—	—	—	—	.45V	.56Y	.05	—	—	—	—	—V	—Y
Poland... 964	1.37	1.94	.81	.31	.27	2.15V	4.79V	3.03	1.11	.40	3.83	.24	3.48V	4.98V
Romania...................................... 968	.22	.12	.04	.01	.16	3.31V	9.18V	.32	.12	.10	2.26	.26	3.37V	1.66V
Russia.. 922	31.32	19.04	46.81	11.93	1.27	5.78V	7.94V	43.32	12.78	8.67	92.12	11.38	60.31V	53.38V
Serbia & Montenegro.................. 965	....	....	....	....	....	....	....	—	—	—	—	.17	.22Y	.27Y
Slovak Republic........................... 936	—	—	.01	.82	.02	.04V	.15V	.84	.78	.77	1.66	.41	3.01V	2.35V
Turkey... 186	.04	.12	.25	.07	1.15	2.82V	3.47V	6.34	4.78	4.47	6.21	6.48	13.66V	10.96V
Ukraine.. 926	—	.08	.19	.02	.07	.09Y	.11Y	25.02	1.29	5.02	20.64	2.74	3.38Y	4.20Y
Uzbekistan................................... 927	—	—	—	—	.01	.02Y	.02Y	—	—	.05	—	.14	.17Y	.21Y
Yugoslavia n.s............................. 966	—	—	—	—	—	—Y	—Y	—	—	—	.03	.11	.13Y	.16Y
Middle East.............................. 407	**81.5**	**89.5**	**60.7**	**58.8**	**63.1**	**74.6Y**	**97.2Y**	**16.7**	**17.7**	**13.9**	**25.7**	**22.8**	**32.9Y**	**37.1Y**
Bahrain.. 419	.49	.47	.30	.46	.41	.50Y	.63Y	—	—	—	—	—	—Y	—Y
Egypt... 469	1.28	10.45	.41	.76	4.85	5.99Y	7.43Y	.09	.32	.28	.33	.73	.90Y	1.12Y
Iran, I.R. of................................. 429	—	5.54	.01	—	.57	.70Y	.91Y	.08	.05	.01	.11	—	—Y	—Y
Iraq... 433	—	—	—	—	1.30	1.60Y	2.08Y	—	—	—	—	—	—Y	—Y
Israel... 436	3.31	2.47	2.55	1.58	2.30	.91V	3.09V	16.00	14.63	11.70	22.60	17.85	26.62V	28.71V
Jordan... 439	1.38	3.05	3.12	5.22	3.12	2.32V	2.42V	.04	.69	—	.28	.07	.12V	.97V
Kuwait... 443	2.90	2.67	2.71	2.10	1.60	1.97Y	2.56Y	—	—	—	—	—	—Y	—Y
Lebanon....................................... 446	.79	1.05	.56	.75	.34	.42Y	.52Y	—	.01	.01	.01	.01	.02Y	.02Y
Libya.. 672	.07	—	—	—	—	—Y	—Y	—	—	—	—	—	—Y	—Y
Oman... 449	.29	.45	.46	.29	.39	.48Y	.62Y	.01	—	—	—	—	—Y	—Y
Qatar.. 453	.74	.81	.23	.36	.45	.68V	.89Y	....	....	....	....	....	....	....
Saudi Arabia................................ 456	55.85	46.25	35.95	33.72	33.13	40.90Y	52.98Y	.08	.06	.36	1.72	.81	1.02Y	1.23Y
Syrian Arab Republic.................. 463	4.85	4.80	4.56	6.40	5.22	6.45Y	8.00Y	.15	.13	.05	.02	.07	.08Y	.11Y
United Arab Emirates.................. 466	9.50	11.28	9.80	7.03	9.42	11.62Y	15.06Y	.30	1.82	1.48	.58	3.27	4.11Y	4.96Y
Yemen, Republic of...................... 474	.08	.19	.06	.07	—	.01Y	.01Y	—	—	—	—	—	—Y	—Y
Western Hemisphere............... 207	**1,267.0**	**1,413.2**	**1,528.2**	**1,798.8**	**1,981.9**	**2,196.5Y**	**2,727.7Y**	**2,146.6**	**2,237.9**	**2,529.3**	**2,847.8**	**3,538.3**	**3,928.8Y**	**4,639.4Y**
Antigua and Barbuda................... 311	—	.02	.09	.04	.05	.07Y	.08Y	.06	—	.02	—	—	—Y	—Y
Argentina..................................... 213	.53	.53	.14	1.39	1.90	1.20V	2.31V	53.99	28.67	30.49	104.63	63.00	188.99V	169.73V
Aruba... 314	.14	1.06	.11	.35	.53	.04V	.10V	1.47	—	.01	1.28	.03	—V	—V
Bahamas, The.............................. 313	.21	.61	.07	1.73	1.22	1.51Y	1.88Y	3.29	29.31	66.66	.02	95.29	117.78Y	146.16Y
Barbados...................................... 316	1.38	1.29	.63	2.00	2.62	.98V	1.22Y	32.82	116.99	167.79	5.16	258.49	.02V	.02Y
Belize... 339	13.76	21.39	31.67	37.39	39.05	48.26Y	59.89Y	1.64	1.95	30.10	1.75	2.50	3.09Y	3.84Y
Bermuda...................................... 319	—	.05	.03	.12	.21	.06V	.07Y	3.10	7.65	8.55	.68	10.20	12.61Y	15.65Y
Bolivia... 218	.06	.10	.10	.35	.27	.34Y	.42Y	.14	.51	2.83	2.65	.27	.33Y	.41Y
Brazil... 223	.25	.71	.56	.96	2.18	6.18V	12.00V	84.27	87.49	124.05	305.63	234.65	351.28V	281.75V

		Exports							Imports						
		2001	2002	2003	2004	2005	2006	2007	2001	2002	2003	2004	2005	2006	2007
		Millions of U.S. Dollars							Millions of U.S. Dollars						
Chile	228	1.78	9.54	4.60	8.63	11.56	5.93V	40.56V	43.06	38.04	46.44	153.39	65.09	166.88V	274.02V
Colombia	233	7.13	9.38	10.37	12.64	15.02	18.76V	22.78V	98.01	90.52	101.01	157.45	166.73	172.97V	176.62V
Costa Rica	238	156.34	150.18	158.72	182.05	205.18	253.58Y	314.70Y	232.20	288.24	303.54	233.69	339.32	419.38Y	520.45Y
Dominica	321	.27	.40	1.36	1.13	.67	.83Y	1.02Y	—	.04	.02	.01	—	—Y	—Y
Dominican Republic	243	19.93	51.23	40.53	39.92	49.13	60.72Y	75.36Y	2.43	16.18	17.40	11.31	19.85	24.53Y	30.44Y
Ecuador	248	.81	3.19	3.39	9.22	5.53	26.51V	32.90Y	36.39	8.16	11.39	45.04	24.21	214.91V	266.71Y
El Salvador	253	477.15	471.13	518.80	573.89	653.00	573.65V	674.35V	385.02	397.68	410.05	336.29	502.80	515.68V	593.69V
Greenland	326	—	—	—	—	—	—Y	—Y	.08	—	—	—	—	—Y	—Y
Grenada	328	.04	.05	.06	.03	.03	.03Y	.04Y	....	....	....	....	....	....	....
Guyana	336	.27	.48	.35	.69	.66	.81Y	1.01Y	—	—	.01	.09	—	—Y	—Y
Haiti	263	10.60	9.99	10.79	6.73	11.54	14.26Y	17.70Y	.01	.08	.71	.22	.25	.31Y	.38Y
Honduras	268	295.31	280.84	288.66	359.41	394.04	487.01Y	604.37Y	129.32	112.05	114.96	92.82	156.63	193.58Y	240.24Y
Jamaica	343	6.25	20.54	29.52	15.53	22.93	12.51V	28.44V	.76	.90	.90	1.16	.97	.27V	.53V
Mexico	273	79.05	133.76	156.43	208.36	215.84	355.57V	456.70V	594.59	580.43	585.44	770.77	794.24	1,028.99V	1,267.64V
Netherlands Antilles	353	3.60	.40	.47	1.41	2.03	2.51Y	3.12Y	39.36	1.53	11.08	201.37	96.35	119.08Y	147.77Y
Nicaragua	278	130.61	137.39	156.23	177.47	213.22	179.84V	203.30V	30.39	28.23	30.88	29.95	40.32	53.01V	72.39V
Panama	283	43.39	78.01	104.10	125.70	80.52	77.14V	97.61V	69.55	313.59	373.99	131.37	461.49	36.32V	18.38V
Paraguay	288	.05	—	.02	.05	.30	.01V	.01Y	.53	.50	.95	12.18	.39	.29V	.36Y
Peru	293	6.51	6.50	1.89	7.87	11.34	29.94V	32.27Y	15.17	19.53	20.97	77.21	36.83	76.16V	83.04Y
St. Kitts and Nevis	361	—	—	.07	.01	.01	.01Y	.01Y	.02	—	—	—	—	—Y	—Y
St. Lucia	362	.01	.15	.10	.03	.05	.06Y	.07Y	—	—	—	—	—	—Y	—Y
St. Pierre-Miquelon	363	—	—	—	—	—	—Y	—Y	—	.02	—	—	—	—Y	—Y
St. Vincent & Grens.	364	.07	.13	.13	.03	—	—Y	—Y	—	.01	.02	—	—	—Y	—Y
Suriname	366	.81	.80	.35	.46	.57	.71Y	.88Y	—	—	.02	—	—	—Y	—Y
Trinidad and Tobago	369	2.03	3.07	2.00	5.27	11.16	13.79Y	17.11Y	13.75	1.62	2.79	16.85	1.38	1.70Y	2.12Y
Uruguay	298	.07	.41	.30	.06	.14	.18Y	.22Y	2.67	9.90	20.87	14.82	29.45	36.40Y	45.17Y
Venezuela, Rep. Bol.	299	7.70	17.76	4.24	17.85	27.44	19.70V	19.54V	271.83	45.44	30.21	138.01	54.11	29.19V	35.21Y
Western Hem. n.s.	399	.83	2.08	1.29	.04	1.92	3.81Y	5.70Y	.67	12.61	15.09	1.95	83.51	165.08Y	246.65Y
Other Countries n.i.e.	**910**	**4.7**	**5.8**	**10.1**	**11.6**	**34.4**	**42.5Y**	**52.7Y**	**17.5**	**9.4**	**7.4**	**10.6**	**8.7**	**10.8Y**	**13.4Y**
Cuba	928	4.73	5.75	10.09	11.58	10.63	13.14Y	16.31Y	5.40	3.38	2.22	2.37	3.65	4.51Y	5.60Y
North Korea	954	—	.05	—	—	23.74	29.35Y	36.42Y	12.09	6.05	5.17	8.25	5.06	6.26Y	7.77Y
Countries & Areas n.s.	**898**	**7.7**	**19.2**	**26.6**	**56.9**	**51.4**	**63.5Y**	**78.8Y**	**3.7**	**50.4**	**83.2**	**28.4**	**138.0**	**170.6Y**	**211.7Y**
Special Categories	**899**	**4.2**	**—**	**—**	**—**	**—**	**—Y**	**—Y**	**21.0**	**—**	**—**	**.8**	**—**	**—Y**	**—Y**
Memorandum Items															
European Union	998	152.71	150.27	181.95	204.28	249.89	402.50Y	405.16Y	489.90	668.90	603.90	769.18	764.32	945.81Y	1,000.22Y
Oil Exporting Ctys.	999	77.06	87.90	57.70	61.64	85.55	94.28Y	130.98Y	281.46	60.15	41.03	159.98	64.51	47.12Y	54.04Y
Non-Oil Develop.Ctys.	201	1,420.49	1,569.87	1,698.62	1,903.17	2,063.93	2,524.63Y	3,072.08Y	2,313.64	3,159.22	3,536.61	4,548.91	4,774.85	5,790.95Y	6,443.27Y
PERCENT DISTRIBUTION															
Industrial Countries	**101**	**37.2**	**59.6**	**59.8**	**59.6**	**58.5**	**57.9**	**52.6**	**53.0**	**57.2**	**54.9**	**49.9**	**52.5**	**47.7**	**47.6**
Developing Countries	**202**	**62.1**	**39.8**	**39.4**	**39.0**	**39.9**	**40.5**	**45.5**	**46.3**	**42.0**	**44.0**	**49.7**	**46.1**	**50.7**	**50.6**
Africa	**607**	**.2**	**.2**	**.3**	**.1**	**.2**	**.2**	**.2**	**.1**	**—**	**—**	**.1**	**—**	**.1**	**—**
Asia	**507**	**4.7**	**2.9**	**2.3**	**1.8**	**1.7**	**4.8**	**4.7**	**6.1**	**12.2**	**12.4**	**17.8**	**11.9**	**15.4**	**13.5**
Europe	**170**	**1.4**	**.6**	**1.2**	**.3**	**.1**	**.4**	**.5**	**1.5**	**.3**	**.3**	**1.5**	**.2**	**.9**	**.7**
Middle East	**407**	**3.4**	**2.1**	**1.4**	**1.2**	**1.2**	**1.2**	**1.4**	**.3**	**.2**	**.2**	**.3**	**.2**	**.3**	**.3**
Western Hemisphere	**207**	**52.5**	**34.0**	**34.3**	**35.7**	**36.8**	**34.0**	**38.7**	**38.3**	**29.2**	**31.1**	**30.1**	**33.7**	**34.1**	**36.1**
Other Countries n.i.e.	**910**	**.2**	**.1**	**.2**	**.2**	**.6**	**.7**	**.7**	**.3**	**.1**	**.1**	**.1**	**.1**	**.1**	**.1**
ANNUAL PERCENT CHANGE															
World	**001**	**−10.6**	**72.5**	**7.1**	**12.9**	**6.9**	**20.2**	**8.8**	**8.4**	**36.6**	**6.1**	**16.5**	**10.9**	**9.6**	**11.6**
Industrial Countries	**101**	**−36.0**	**176.0**	**7.5**	**12.5**	**4.9**	**19.0**	**−1.0**	**5.3**	**47.5**	**1.8**	**5.9**	**16.8**	**−.5**	**11.5**
Developing Countries	**202**	**16.8**	**10.7**	**5.9**	**11.9**	**9.4**	**21.8**	**22.3**	**12.8**	**24.1**	**11.1**	**31.6**	**2.8**	**20.6**	**11.3**
Africa	**607**	**−81.3**	**112.3**	**64.3**	**−57.2**	**89.2**	**20.4**	**20.8**	**23.5**	**−20.5**	**−26.9**	**256.0**	**−70.8**	**287.8**	**−61.3**
Asia	**507**	**144.4**	**7.1**	**−16.0**	**−12.6**	**1.5**	**247.0**	**6.0**	**52.8**	**173.7**	**7.7**	**67.4**	**−25.9**	**41.4**	**−2.3**
Europe	**170**	**−28.0**	**−18.3**	**97.9**	**−75.0**	**−67.4**	**451.4**	**37.6**	**44.8**	**−70.7**	**−3.3**	**476.1**	**−81.9**	**290.8**	**−9.8**
Middle East	**407**	**19.8**	**9.7**	**−32.1**	**−3.2**	**7.4**	**18.2**	**30.4**	**94.4**	**5.8**	**−21.5**	**84.7**	**−11.1**	**44.1**	**12.9**
Western Hemisphere	**207**	**15.0**	**11.5**	**8.1**	**17.7**	**10.2**	**10.8**	**24.2**	**7.1**	**4.3**	**13.0**	**12.6**	**24.2**	**11.0**	**18.1**
Other Countries n.i.e.	**910**	**112.9**	**22.6**	**74.1**	**14.8**	**196.8**	**23.6**	**24.1**	**485.0**	**−46.1**	**−21.6**	**43.8**	**−18.0**	**23.6**	**24.1**

	Exports 2001	Exports 2002	Exports 2003	Exports 2004	Exports 2005	Exports 2006	Exports 2007	Imports 2001	Imports 2002	Imports 2003	Imports 2004	Imports 2005	Imports 2006	Imports 2007
	Millions of U.S. Dollars							*Millions of U.S. Dollars*						
IFS World Total	**731.0**	**709.0**	**609.0**	**744.2**	**852.7**	**1,010.0**	**1,100.0**	**601.0**	**667.0**	**640.0**	**780.0**	**820.0**	**930.0**	**1,190.0**
DOTS World Total 001	**542.7**	**828.1Y**	**628.7**	**559.6**	**1,328.3Y**	**1,365.0Y**	**1,676.8Y**	**498.8**	**876.9Y**	**694.0**	**1,140.5**	**1,879.5Y**	**2,263.9Y**	**2,904.4Y**
Industrial Countries 101	**457.7**	**476.6Y**	**485.4**	**369.0**	**575.5Y**	**574.1Y**	**754.0Y**	**292.7**	**570.4Y**	**385.5**	**366.6**	**675.7Y**	**749.4Y**	**912.0Y**
United States 111	95.86	76.82V	59.82	5.93	81.36V	104.82V	126.45V	35.57	69.19V	26.00	38.22	137.39V	71.28V	81.07V
Canada 156	15.43	25.95V	.04	.04	24.20V	29.74V	41.82V	1.45	4.38V	1.41	2.47	7.79V	7.82V	10.80V
Australia 193	—	.01V	.01	6.37	.01V	.33V	.05V	10.75	3.95V	18.90	11.57	6.58V	14.58V	29.33V
Japan 158	—	.52V	.32	.01	1.10V	.60V	.29V	26.22	22.16V	28.02	25.36	15.06V	52.50V	11.30V
New Zealand 196	—	—V	—	—	.01V	.04V	.04V	—	.17V	.56	.67	.04V	.46V	.48V
Austria 122	—	.44V	—	—	.38V	.10V	.08V	—	15.72V	—	.61	9.89V	19.15V	14.64V
Belgium 124	11.91	80.28V	72.33	82.32	59.78V	43.84V	49.43V	43.41	64.01V	46.79	67.77	77.04V	98.60V	100.46V
Cyprus 423	—	—V	4.62	—	—Y	—V	—V	.32	.30V	.37	.07	.17V	.33V	.10V
Denmark 128	—	.12V	.02	—	23.69V	.13V	.26V	3.87	5.74V	2.55	3.25	2.72V	2.96V	3.62V
Finland 172	—	—V	—	—	.03V	.25V	—V	.19	1.01V	—	13.41	7.44V	4.17V	2.10V
France 132	114.99	59.06V	90.98	99.16	76.16V	105.01V	117.23V	96.24	158.37V	103.72	99.70	134.73V	181.06V	202.62V
Germany 134	37.38	41.54V	1.42	.58	66.87V	73.33V	124.71V	12.57	28.73V	25.81	19.44	22.98V	28.62V	43.19V
Greece 174	1.35	2.17V	.06	.03	1.03V	1.84V	3.44V	2.25	9.42V	3.25	3.03	1.36V	1.26V	.51V
Iceland 176	—	—V	.13	.05	—V	—V	—V	—	—V	.03	.02	—V	—V	—V
Ireland 178	60.52	71.38V	6.54	5.23	79.70V	69.21V	91.50V	.23	.90V	.61	.59	1.00V	2.85V	1.47V
Italy 136	.77	22.23V	2.61	2.90	7.81V	11.75V	12.70V	14.65	75.28V	23.52	19.50	88.08V	35.83V	22.86V
Luxembourg 137	—	—V	—	—	—V	—V	—V	3.05	4.44V	4.47	1.50	3.86V	5.36V	3.51V
Malta 181	—	—V	—	—	—V	—V	—V	.05	—V	1.50	.05	3.10V	1.37V	4.58V
Netherlands 138	7.17	4.92V	1.48	5.65	6.24V	4.74V	34.62V	10.18	24.95V	17.10	22.57	59.58V	107.15V	181.78V
Norway 142	—	.21V	—	—	.06V	—V	.14V	.03	.25V	.18	.86	.86V	2.03V	1.79V
Portugal 182	.01	1.90V	.04	.01	2.73V	2.69V	.24V	.45	.73V	.64	1.21	8.59V	7.19V	5.96V
Slovenia 961	—	.03V	—	—	.31V	—V	—V	—	2.69V	—	—	—V	—V	—V
Spain 184	55.85	83.90V	7.10	4.62	134.97V	122.42V	147.91V	13.20	18.00V	13.10	13.24	29.46V	22.81V	93.71V
Sweden 144	—	1.19V	3.24	2.02	—V	.23V	.24V	.32	1.55V	.87	.81	5.09V	9.34V	38.60V
Switzerland 146	12.72	.09V	83.67	71.79	1.55V	.11V	.14V	8.04	14.40V	27.30	10.22	8.37V	6.52V	4.20V
United Kingdom 112	43.77	3.87V	150.98	82.29	7.53V	2.85V	2.69V	9.63	44.04V	38.75	10.43	44.53V	66.15V	53.31V
Developing Countries 202	**84.9**	**351.4Y**	**78.6**	**34.1**	**573.9Y**	**569.9Y**	**648.5Y**	**205.7**	**306.1Y**	**306.5**	**742.2**	**1,167.6Y**	**1,469.7Y**	**1,936.8Y**
Africa 607	**80.2**	**31.5Y**	**68.2**	**8.5**	**25.3Y**	**29.2Y**	**36.7Y**	**109.8**	**103.3Y**	**93.4**	**256.0**	**223.0Y**	**212.2Y**	**257.2Y**
Algeria 612	.03	.20V	.37	—	—Y	—Y	—Y	—	—V	.03	.01	.01Y	.01Y	.02Y
Angola 614	—	—Y	.01	—	—Y	—Y	—Y	.01	.01Y	—	—	—Y	—Y	—Y
Benin 638	—	.01V	.03	—	.12V	.15Y	.18Y	—	.01V	—	.07	.08V	.10Y	.12Y
Botswana 616	....	....	....	....	....	....	....	.04	.04Y	.02	.13	.15Y	.18Y	.23Y
Cameroon 622	74.27	12.41V	9.14	.01	.01Y	.01Y	.01Y	.03	.83V	2.60	1.13	1.29Y	1.59Y	1.98Y
Cape Verde 624	—	—Y	—	—	—Y	—Y	—Y	.01	.01Y	.07	.02	.02Y	.02Y	.03Y
Central African Rep. 626	—	—Y	—	—	—Y	—Y	—Y	—	—Y	.01	—	—Y	—Y	—Y
Chad 628	—	.01Y	—	—	—Y	—Y	—Y	—	—Y	.01	.01	.01Y	.01Y	.01Y
Congo, Dem. Rep. of 636	—	—Y	—	.02	.02Y	.02Y	.03Y	—	—Y	—	.01	.01Y	.01Y	.01Y
Congo, Republic of 634	.01	.03V	—	.01	.01Y	.01Y	.01Y	.03	—V	—	—	.01Y	.01Y	.01Y
Côte d'Ivoire 662	.04	2.95V	53.18	.10	8.61V	9.31V	11.55Y	86.22	44.42V	48.89	172.28	96.79V	78.54V	97.47Y
Djibouti 611	—	—Y	—	—	—Y	—Y	—Y	.01	.02Y	—	—	—Y	—Y	—Y
Equatorial Guinea 642	.01	.01Y	—	.01	.01Y	.01Y	.01Y	—	—Y	—	.03	.04Y	.05Y	.06Y
Ethiopia 644	—	—Y	—	.01	.01Y	.01Y	.01Y	—	—V	.06	—	—V	—Y	—Y
Gabon 646	.01	.01Y	—	—	—Y	—Y	—Y	3.58	3.89Y	2.23	6.64	7.59Y	9.38Y	11.63Y
Gambia, The 648	—	—Y	—	.04	.04Y	.05Y	.07Y	.03	.03Y	.09	.27	.30Y	.38Y	.47Y
Ghana 652	.05	.05Y	.01	.10	.12Y	.15Y	.18Y	.12	.13Y	.39	.92	1.05Y	1.29Y	1.61Y
Guinea-Bissau 654	.20	.21Y	.31	.23	.26Y	.32Y	.40Y	.75	.81Y	1.58	.28	.33Y	.40Y	.50Y
Kenya 664	—	—V	.04	—	—Y	—Y	—Y	—	.45V	.53	1.26	1.44Y	1.77Y	2.20Y
Lesotho 666	....	....	....	....	....	....	....	.01	.01Y	.99	.38	.43Y	.53Y	.66Y
Liberia 668	1.91	2.07Y	.27	.72	.83Y	1.02Y	1.27Y	.01	.01Y	1.80	.06	.07Y	.08Y	.10Y
Madagascar 674	.05	—V	—	—	—Y	—Y	—Y	.01	—V	—	—	—Y	—Y	.01Y
Malawi 676	.01	.01Y	—	—	—Y	—Y	—Y	—	—Y	—	.11	.13Y	.16Y	.19Y
Mali 678	.72	.79Y	1.01	1.86	2.13Y	2.63Y	3.26Y	.02	.02Y	.01	.07	.08Y	.10Y	.12Y
Mauritania 682	.02	.02Y	.19	.05	.05Y	.07Y	.08Y	—	—Y	.04	.03	.03Y	.04Y	.05Y
Mauritius 684	—	—V	—	—	.12V	.12V	.08V	.04	.17V	.11	.06	.53V	.39V	.49V
Morocco 686	.75	5.33V	.91	.93	6.61V	8.18Y	10.15Y	3.13	9.78V	4.70	3.91	20.19V	24.95Y	30.97Y
Mozambique 688	—	—V	—	—	—Y	—Y	—Y	—	—V	.01	.17	.19Y	.24Y	.29Y
Namibia 728	....	....	....	....	....	....	....	—	—Y	.01	—	—Y	—Y	—Y
Niger 692	.03	.01V	.07	.04	.04Y	.05Y	.06Y	—	—V	.01	—	—Y	—Y	—Y
Nigeria 694	.17	5.17V	.08	.05	.06Y	.07Y	.09Y	1.22	9.71V	1.64	4.01	5.46Y	6.86Y	8.28Y
Rwanda 714	—	—Y	—	—	—Y	—Y	—Y	—	—Y	—	.02	.03Y	.03Y	.04Y
São Tomé & Príncipe 716	....	....	....	....	....	....	....	—	—Y	.02	—	—Y	—Y	—Y
Senegal 722	.23	.59V	.33	1.38	2.05V	2.10V	2.60Y	4.31	18.17V	4.52	5.27	43.90V	40.75V	50.57Y
Seychelles 718	.62	—V	.26	—	—Y	—Y	—Y	—	—V	.01	—	—Y	—Y	—Y
Sierra Leone 724	1.09	1.18Y	1.62	2.01	2.29Y	2.83Y	3.51Y	.01	.01Y	.19	.59	.67Y	.83Y	1.03Y
Somalia 726	—	—Y	—	—	—Y	—Y	—Y	.02	.02Y	—	.03	.04Y	.05Y	.06Y
South Africa 199	—	.42V	.30	.92	1.77V	1.96V	2.92V	9.26	12.24V	18.81	52.90	41.02V	41.36V	45.48V
Sudan 732	....	....	....	....	....	....	....	—	—Y	—	—	.01Y	.01Y	.01Y
Tanzania 738	—	.04V	.05	.04	.04Y	.05Y	.07Y	.02	.12V	.12	—	—Y	—Y	—Y
Togo 742	—	—V	.01	.01	.04V	.05Y	.06Y	.06	.56V	1.83	4.16	.07V	.09Y	.11Y

	Exports							Imports						
	2001	2002	2003	2004	2005	2006	2007	2001	2002	2003	2004	2005	2006	2007
	Millions of U.S. Dollars							Millions of U.S. Dollars						
Tunisia 744	—	—V	—	—	.02V	.01V	.02Y	.87	1.69V	2.09	1.13	1.05V	1.95V	2.41Y
Uganda 746	—	.01V	—	—	—Y	—Y	—Y	—	—V	—	—	—Y	—Y	.01Y
Zambia 754	—	—V	—	—	—V	—V	.02V	—	—V	—	—	—V	—V	—V
Zimbabwe 698	—	—V	—	—	—V	—V	—Y	—	.09V	—	—	.01V	—V	—Y
Asia 507	**.3**	**176.3Y**	**1.3**	**1.6**	**179.6Y**	**166.5Y**	**253.5Y**	**72.4**	**154.5Y**	**150.7**	**150.1**	**324.6Y**	**376.1Y**	**514.3Y**
Bangladesh 513	—	—V	—	—	—V	—V	—V	.06	.04V	.24	.18	.56V	.87Y	1.37Y
China,P.R.: Mainland 924	.01	10.49V	.01	.12	2.74V	11.08V	83.95V	31.25	47.71V	79.90	67.32	158.70V	193.06V	289.31V
China,P.R.:Hong Kong 532	—	1.93V	.76	.87	3.10V	3.25V	3.37V	5.58	20.12V	7.52	5.58	15.29V	14.31V	12.48V
Fiji 819	—	—Y	—	—	—Y	—Y	—Y	—	—Y	—	.03	.03Y	.04Y	.05Y
French Polynesia 887	—	—Y	—	—	—Y	—Y	—Y	.02	.02Y	—	—	—Y	—Y	—Y
India 534	.24	13.74V	.04	.09	21.29V	26.31Y	32.65Y	9.51	35.12V	23.16	26.16	58.71V	72.56Y	90.05Y
Indonesia 536	—	.44V	—	—	.11V	.26V	.21V	6.55	20.96V	15.32	6.60	18.09V	18.45V	22.45V
Korea 542	.09	147.88V	.38	.32	149.92V	120.41V	120.07V	1.33	10.26V	3.43	2.68	20.22V	9.20V	15.73V
Malaysia 548	—	.04V	.09	.06	.22V	.10V	1.81V	2.02	1.03V	3.27	8.25	3.67V	9.73V	14.91V
Myanmar 518	....	....	....	....	....	....	....	—	—Y	.37	—	—Y	—Y	—Y
Nepal 558	....	....	....	....	....	....	....	.04	.04Y	—	.03	.04Y	.05Y	.06Y
New Caledonia 839	.01	—V	—	—	—Y	—Y	—Y	—	—V	—	—	—Y	—Y	—Y
Pakistan 564	—	.02V	—	—	1.08V	1.33Y	1.65Y	—	.54V	.35	.54	12.89V	15.93Y	19.77Y
Philippines 566	—	.15V	—	—	—V	—V	—V	—	.01V	3.03	6.68	.13V	.13V	5.60V
Singapore 576	—	.10V	.02	.07	.16V	.49V	1.06V	3.04	9.12V	4.62	3.62	9.90V	10.73V	21.89V
Sri Lanka 524	—	—V	—	—	—V	1.47V	7.30V	.35	1.55V	.99	.62	.76V	.90V	1.53V
Taiwan Province of China 528	—	1.38V	—	.09	.56V	.42V	1.35V	.54	4.70V	2.27	.95	3.71V	3.67V	5.82V
Thailand 578	—	.04V	.01	—	.44V	1.39V	.09V	10.70	2.66V	4.55	14.46	14.60V	10.50V	13.31V
Vietnam 582	—	.07V	—	—	—V	—V	—V	1.45	.59V	1.67	6.36	7.26V	15.95V	—V
Europe 170	**4.3**	**143.5Y**	**5.4**	**23.9**	**368.7Y**	**373.0Y**	**358.0Y**	**9.2**	**19.3Y**	**17.2**	**36.8**	**51.5Y**	**45.6Y**	**51.9Y**
Azerbaijan 912	—	—V	—	—	29.52V	36.76V	10.61V	—	—V	—	—	.75V	—V	—V
Belarus 913	—	.05V	—	—	.32V	.03V	—V	.02	.33V	.03	—	5.56V	3.09V	2.17V
Bulgaria 918	—	—V	.02	—	.07V	.03V	—V	.06	.08V	.02	.30	.41V	.44V	.39V
Croatia 960	—	.08V	—	—	.06V	.15V	.24V	—	.15V	—	—	1.44V	.71V	.63V
Czech Republic 935	.01	.27V	—	—	.83V	.07V	.59V	.56	.71V	.09	.16	6.07V	.32V	1.08V
Estonia 939	—	.04V	—	—	—V	—V	—V	—	.03V	—	—	—V	.03V	.02V
Georgia 915	—	—V	—	—	.03V	—V	—Y	—	.03V	—	—	—V	—V	—Y
Gibraltar 823	....	....	....	....	....	....	....	—	—Y	.14	—	—Y	—Y	—Y
Hungary 944	.01	.22V	—	.02	.04V	.11V	.26V	.15	—V	.01	.04	.16V	.28V	.75V
Kazakhstan 916	—	—V	—	—	.01Y	.02Y	.02Y	—	—V	—	—	—Y	—Y	—Y
Latvia 941	—	.01V	—	—	—V	—V	.32V	—	—V	—	—	—V	—V	.03V
Lithuania 946	—	—V	—	—	.06V	.07V	—V	—	.04V	—	—	.26V	.17V	.25V
Poland 964	—	1.52V	3.75	.33	.93V	2.43V	2.00V	.19	1.02V	.24	.55	1.46V	.76V	.72V
Romania 968	—	20.92V	.07	—	37.09V	24.14V	1.43V	.08	.81V	1.27	4.23	.20V	.23V	.43V
Russia 922	—	56.35V	—	—	194.23V	157.48V	180.34V	—	2.76V	—	—	10.82V	6.97V	8.49V
Serbia & Montenegro 965	2.73	2.97Y	—	—	—Y	—Y	—Y	.44	.48Y	—	.02	.02Y	.03Y	.03Y
Slovak Republic 936	—	—V	—	—	.02V	.01V	—V	—	.07V	—	—	.02V	.22V	.09V
Tajikistan 923	—	5.36V	—	—	—V	21.18V	—V	—	—Y	—	—	—Y	—Y	—Y
Turkey 186	.01	.27V	.03	—	.16V	.36V	.65V	2.20	6.70V	4.98	5.49	13.37V	18.78V	20.00V
Ukraine 926	1.55	55.44V	1.55	23.55	105.33V	130.18Y	161.56Y	4.12	4.57V	10.47	25.98	10.99V	13.58Y	16.86Y
U.S.S.R. n.s. 930	—	—Y	—	—	—Y	—Y	—Y	1.41	1.53Y	—	—	—Y	—Y	—Y
Europe n.s. 884	—	—Y	—	—	—Y	—Y	—Y	.01	.01Y	—	—	—Y	—Y	—Y
Middle East 407	**.1**	**—Y**	**—**	**.1**	**.2Y**	**.8Y**	**.2Y**	**10.6**	**11.2Y**	**15.4**	**19.6**	**25.4Y**	**31.4Y**	**48.4Y**
Egypt 469	—	—Y	—	—	—Y	—Y	—Y	1.41	1.53Y	3.61	4.73	5.40Y	6.67Y	8.28Y
Iran, I.R. of 429	—	—V	.01	—	—Y	—Y	—Y	1.01	1.08Y	.40	.84	1.15Y	1.44Y	1.74Y
Iraq 433	.01	.01Y	—	—	—Y	—Y	—Y	.03	.03Y	.03	—	—Y	—Y	—Y
Israel 436	.02	—V	—	—	.09V	.55V	—V	.19	—V	.02	.10	.22V	.44V	10.56V
Jordan 439	—	—V	—	—	—V	.03V	—V	.01	.03V	.02	—	.43V	.01V	.10V
Kuwait 443	—	—Y	—	—	—Y	—Y	—Y	.79	.84Y	.02	.16	.22Y	.27Y	.33Y
Lebanon 446	—	—Y	—	—	—Y	—Y	—Y	.94	1.02Y	1.28	3.50	3.99Y	4.94Y	6.13Y
Libya 672	—	—Y	—	—	—Y	—Y	—Y	—	—Y	.01	—	—Y	—Y	—Y
Oman 449	—	—V	—	—	—Y	—Y	—Y	—	.21V	.02	.02	.03Y	.04Y	.04Y
Saudi Arabia 456	.01	.01V	.01	—	.05V	.06Y	.08Y	.84	.90Y	2.79	1.34	1.83Y	2.29Y	2.77Y
United Arab Emirates 466	.04	—V	—	.07	.09Y	.11Y	.14Y	5.21	5.54Y	7.17	8.81	11.98Y	15.07Y	18.18Y
Yemen, Republic of 474	—	—V	—	—	.01V	.01Y	.01Y	.18	.02V	.01	.15	.20V	.24Y	.30Y
Western Hemisphere 207	**—**	**.1Y**	**3.6**	**—**	**.1Y**	**.4Y**	**.1Y**	**3.6**	**17.8Y**	**29.7**	**279.7**	**543.0Y**	**804.4Y**	**1,064.9Y**
Antigua and Barbuda 311	—	—Y	—	—	—Y	—Y	—Y	.01	.01Y	—	—	—Y	—Y	—Y
Argentina 213	—	—V	—	—	—V	—V	—V	.01	.55V	.04	.64	1.92V	2.34V	3.77V
Barbados 316	—	—V	—	—	.01V	—V	—Y	.03	.01V	.03	—	—V	—V	—Y
Brazil 223	—	.01V	—	—	—V	.38V	—V	2.43	15.30V	14.53	14.58	22.42V	32.46V	34.89V
Chile 228	—	—V	1.57	—	—V	—V	—V	.04	—V	.01	.35	1.00V	.35V	.70V
Colombia 233	—	.04V	—	—	—V	.01V	—V	—	.12V	3.18	.12	.02V	.01V	.37V
Dominica 321	—	—Y	—	—	—Y	—Y	—Y	—	—Y	.01	—	—Y	—Y	—Y
Ecuador 248	—	—V	—	—	—V	—V	—Y	—	.01V	—	—	—V	.01V	.02Y
El Salvador 253	—	—V	—	—	—V	—V	—V	.01	.01Y	—	—	—Y	—Y	—Y
Falkland Islands 323	....	....	....	....	....	....	....	—	—Y	—	.02	.02Y	.02Y	.03Y
Greenland 326	....	....	....	....	....	....	....	—	—Y	.01	.09	.10Y	.12Y	.15Y
Grenada 328	—	—Y	—	—	—Y	—Y	—Y	—	—Y	.01	.03	.03Y	.04Y	.05Y
Guyana 336	....	....	....	....	....	....	....	—	.01Y	—	.17	.19Y	.24Y	.29Y
Honduras 268	—	.03V	—	—	—Y	—Y	—Y	—	—V	.01	.08	.09Y	.12Y	.14Y
Jamaica 343	—	—V	—	.02	.03Y	.03Y	.04Y	—	—V	.01	—	—V	—V	—V
Mexico 273	—	—V	1.18	—	.05V	.01V	.03V	.03	—V	.13	.02	.32V	.15V	4.12V

	Exports							Imports						
	2001	2002	2003	2004	2005	2006	2007	2001	2002	2003	2004	2005	2006	2007
	Millions of U.S. Dollars							*Millions of U.S. Dollars*						
Netherlands Antilles..................... 353	—	—V	.87	—	—Y	—Y	—Y	.09	.03V	—	.05	.06Y	.07Y	.09Y
Paraguay..................................... 288	....	....	....	....	....	....	....	.02	.02Y	—	—	—Y	—Y	—Y
Peru.. 293	—	—V	—	—	—V	—V	—Y	—	—V	.44	.56	1.94V	1.72V	1.74Y
Uruguay...................................... 298	—	—Y	—	—	—V	—Y	—Y	—	—Y	—	—	.14V	.17Y	.21Y
Venezuela, Rep. Bol..................... 299	—	—V	—	—	—V	—V	—V	—	—V	—	—	.01V	.11V	.14Y
Western Hem. n.s........................ 399	—	—Y	—	—	—Y	—Y	—Y	.89	1.75Y	11.30	263.02	514.73Y	766.45Y	1,018.17Y
Other Countries n.i.e............... 910	**—**	**—Y**	**.1**	**—**	**—Y**	**—Y**	**—Y**	**.3**	**.4Y**	**1.4**	**.3**	**.3Y**	**.4Y**	**.5Y**
Cuba... 928	....	....	....	....	....	....	....	—	—Y	.01	.01	.01Y	.01Y	.01Y
North Korea................................ 954	.01	.01Y	.05	.01	.01Y	.02Y	.02Y	.32	.35Y	1.37	.30	.34Y	.42Y	.52Y
Countries & Areas n.s.............. 898	**—**	**—Y**	**64.7**	**156.5**	**178.8Y**	**221.0Y**	**274.3Y**	**—**	**—Y**	**.7**	**4.5**	**5.1Y**	**6.3Y**	**7.9Y**
Memorandum Items														
European Union.......................... 998	333.75	375.10Y	345.18	285.14	469.11Y	441.08Y	588.24Y	211.53	457.75Y	283.38	277.94	507.62Y	595.99Y	775.97Y
Oil Exporting Ctys....................... 999	.26	5.82Y	.47	.12	.31Y	.51Y	.52Y	15.66	39.27Y	27.42	21.80	38.78Y	44.55Y	53.94Y
Non-Oil Develop.Ctys.................. 201	84.69	345.60Y	78.09	34.01	573.58Y	569.39Y	647.98Y	190.06	266.84Y	279.04	720.36	1,128.78Y	1,425.12Y	1,882.87Y
PERCENT DISTRIBUTION														
Industrial Countries................. 101	**84.3**	**57.6**	**77.2**	**65.9**	**43.3**	**42.1**	**45.0**	**58.7**	**65.0**	**55.5**	**32.1**	**36.0**	**33.1**	**31.4**
Developing Countries.............. 202	**15.7**	**42.4**	**12.5**	**6.1**	**43.2**	**41.8**	**38.7**	**41.2**	**34.9**	**44.2**	**65.1**	**62.1**	**64.9**	**66.7**
Africa..................................... 607	**14.8**	**3.8**	**10.8**	**1.5**	**1.9**	**2.1**	**2.2**	**22.0**	**11.8**	**13.5**	**22.4**	**11.9**	**9.4**	**8.9**
Asia....................................... 507	**.1**	**21.3**	**.2**	**.3**	**13.5**	**12.2**	**15.1**	**14.5**	**17.6**	**21.7**	**13.2**	**17.3**	**16.6**	**17.7**
Europe.................................... 170	**.8**	**17.3**	**.9**	**4.3**	**27.8**	**27.3**	**21.4**	**1.9**	**2.2**	**2.5**	**3.2**	**2.7**	**2.0**	**1.8**
Middle East............................ 407	**—**	**—**	**—**	**—**	**—**	**.1**	**—**	**2.1**	**1.3**	**2.2**	**1.7**	**1.4**	**1.4**	**1.7**
Western Hemisphere.............. 207	**—**	**—**	**.6**	**—**	**—**	**—**	**—**	**.7**	**2.0**	**4.3**	**24.5**	**28.9**	**35.5**	**36.7**
Other Countries n.i.e............... 910	**—**	**—**	**—**	**—**	**—**	**—**	**—**	**.1**	**—**	**.2**	**—**	**—**	**—**	**—**
ANNUAL PERCENT CHANGE														
World...................................... 001	**–12.1**	**52.6**	**–24.1**	**–11.0**	**137.3**	**2.8**	**22.8**	**–6.4**	**75.8**	**–20.9**	**64.3**	**64.8**	**20.4**	**28.3**
Industrial Countries................. 101	**–6.8**	**4.1**	**1.8**	**–24.0**	**56.0**	**–.3**	**31.3**	**–5.3**	**94.9**	**–32.4**	**–4.9**	**84.3**	**10.9**	**21.7**
Developing Countries.............. 202	**–32.6**	**313.7**	**–77.6**	**–56.6**	**—**	**–.7**	**13.8**	**–7.8**	**48.8**	**.1**	**142.2**	**57.3**	**25.9**	**31.8**
Africa..................................... 607	**72.0**	**–60.7**	**116.2**	**–87.5**	**196.5**	**15.6**	**25.6**	**–17.4**	**–6.0**	**–9.5**	**174.0**	**–12.9**	**–4.9**	**21.2**
Asia....................................... 507	**–49.6**	**—**	**–99.3**	**24.9**	**—**	**–7.3**	**52.2**	**3.5**	**113.3**	**–2.4**	**–.4**	**116.3**	**15.9**	**36.8**
Europe.................................... 170	**–94.5**	**—**	**–96.2**	**340.5**	**—**	**1.2**	**–4.0**	**10.2**	**109.1**	**–10.8**	**113.2**	**40.2**	**–11.5**	**13.9**
Middle East............................ 407	**67.9**	**–75.3**	**–20.3**	**391.0**	**217.0**	**219.4**	**–69.5**	**42.8**	**5.4**	**37.2**	**27.8**	**29.5**	**23.5**	**54.2**
Western Hemisphere.............. 207	**—**	**....**	**—**	**–99.3**	**277.6**	**396.5**	**–80.4**	**–15.1**	**399.1**	**66.7**	**840.9**	**94.1**	**48.1**	**32.4**
Other Countries n.i.e............... 910	**....**	**8.5**	**677.7**	**–78.0**	**14.3**	**23.6**	**24.1**	**–51.5**	**8.5**	**292.0**	**–78.2**	**14.3**	**23.6**	**24.1**

		Exports							Imports						
		2001	2002	2003	2004	2005	2006	2007	2001	2002	2003	2004	2005	2006	2007
		Millions of U.S. Dollars							*Millions of U.S. Dollars*						
IFS World Total		**62.9**	**53.9**	**65.2**	**76.0**	**89.5**	**64.1**	**70.0**	**61.9**	**58.0**	**65.0**	**83.0**	**105.8**	**98.1**	**110.0**
DOTS World Total	**001**	**124.6Y**	**95.5Y**	**70.7Y**	**110.0Y**	**108.8Y**	**132.7Y**	**372.8Y**	**108.4Y**	**101.9Y**	**158.9Y**	**135.7Y**	**213.0Y**	**201.4Y**	**240.2Y**
Industrial Countries	**101**	**4.7Y**	**9.4Y**	**9.7Y**	**31.6Y**	**4.0Y**	**3.9Y**	**1.7Y**	**45.0Y**	**47.0Y**	**58.6Y**	**57.5Y**	**117.9Y**	**99.5Y**	**108.1Y**
United States	111	—V	—V	1.91V	25.64V	.18V	.45V	—V	.88V	2.64V	1.32V	1.32V	2.42V	6.27V	7.48V
Canada	156	.01V	—V	—V	—V	—V	—V	—V	.05V	.03V	.13V	.01V	.03V	.07V	.12V
Australia	193	—V	—V	—V	—V	—V	—V	—V	.03V	.03V	.22V	.02V	.04V	.67V	.15V
Japan	158	.90V	—V	.07V	.43V	.05V	.03V	—V	1.37V	1.52V	1.32V	.25V	.34V	.24V	.50V
New Zealand	196	—V	—V	—V	—V	—V	—V	—V	—V	—V	—V	—V	—V	.12V	—V
Austria	122	—V	—V	.02V	—V	—V	—V	—V	—V	.02V	—V	.04V	.12V	.01V	.07V
Belgium	124	—V	—V	—V	—V	—V	.03V	—V	3.25V	3.07V	2.39V	4.46V	6.51V	4.50V	1.80V
Cyprus	423	—V	—V	—V	—V	—Y	—V	—V	.01V	.01V	—V	.05V	—V	—V	—V
Denmark	128	.05V	2.74V	—V	.02V	—V	—V	—V	.46V	.74V	.43V	.42V	.65V	.37V	1.14V
Finland	172	—V	—V	.02V	—V	—V	—V	—V	—V	—V	.01V	—V	.06V	.03V	.14V
France	132	—V	.24V	.21V	.02V	.01V	.04V	.13V	2.82V	2.51V	4.25V	3.93V	6.49V	6.08V	14.50V
Germany	134	.04V	.14V	—V	.12V	.08V	.03V	—V	1.86V	2.77V	1.10V	1.05V	1.31V	1.88V	1.84V
Greece	174	—V	.06V	—V	—V	.03V	—V	—V	.06V	.10V	—V	.01V	—V	.01V	.21V
Ireland	178	—V	—V	—V	—V	.01V	—V	—V	—V	—V	—V	.02V	.01V	—V	—V
Italy	136	1.43V	3.12V	5.39V	3.89V	2.38V	1.82V	.15V	2.30V	3.48V	12.75V	6.49V	52.83V	25.98V	5.04V
Luxembourg	137	—V	—V	—V	—V	—V	—V	—V	.01V	.01V	.02V	.01V	.01V	—V	—V
Malta	181	—Y	—V	—V	—V	—V	—V	—V	—Y	.12V	.42V	.45V	.73V	1.07V	1.48V
Netherlands	138	.02V	—V	.13V	.43V	.14V	.02V	.28V	3.74V	3.63V	4.64V	6.98V	7.78V	7.54V	9.35V
Norway	142	—V	—V	—V	—V	—V	—V	—V	.02V	.01V	—V	.06V	.01V	—V	—V
Portugal	182	2.21V	2.81V	1.93V	.89V	1.11V	1.34V	.63V	22.46V	21.31V	21.15V	24.42V	32.88V	37.54V	52.12V
Slovenia	961	—V	—V	—V	—Y	—V	—V	—V	—V	—V	—V	—Y	—V	.03V	.10V
Spain	184	.01V	.30V	.07V	.05V	.02V	.03V	.46V	1.91V	2.53V	6.91V	4.05V	3.15V	3.57V	6.11V
Sweden	144	—V	—V	—V	.12V	—V	—V	—V	.46V	.24V	.02V	1.66V	.14V	.99V	4.16V
Switzerland	146	.01V	—V	—V	—V	—V	—V	.01V	.96V	.47V	.09V	.32V	1.56V	1.19V	1.30V
United Kingdom	112	—V	—V	—V	—V	—V	.14V	—V	2.41V	1.79V	1.45V	1.46V	.79V	1.39V	.44V
Developing Countries	**202**	**120.0Y**	**86.1Y**	**61.0Y**	**78.4Y**	**104.8Y**	**128.7Y**	**371.1Y**	**51.1Y**	**41.7Y**	**83.5Y**	**56.3Y**	**70.0Y**	**70.8Y**	**93.6Y**
Africa	**607**	**3.0Y**	**4.3Y**	**14.3Y**	**16.0Y**	**20.4Y**	**25.6Y**	**33.0Y**	**18.0Y**	**25.2Y**	**60.6Y**	**41.3Y**	**50.7Y**	**44.4Y**	**55.9Y**
Angola	614	—Y	.01Y	.01Y	.01Y	.01Y	.01Y	.02Y	—Y	—Y	—Y	—Y	—Y	—Y	—Y
Benin	638	—V	—V	—V	—V	.01V	.01Y	.01Y	—V	—V	—V	.01V	—V	—Y	—Y
Burkina Faso	748	.01Y	.01Y	.01Y	.01Y	.01Y	.01Y	.02Y	.03Y	.03Y	.04Y	.05Y	.06Y	.07Y	.09Y
Cameroon	622	.98V	.19V	—V	—Y	—Y	—Y	—Y	—V	—V	—V	—Y	—Y	—Y	—Y
Cape Verde	624	.05V	.05Y	.07Y	.09Y	.10Y	.13Y	.16Y	—V	—Y	—Y	—Y	—Y	—Y	—Y
Côte d'Ivoire	662	.70V	.86V	.12V	—V	.11V	.56V	.70Y	.44V	.83V	.91V	1.37V	8.96V	6.75V	8.38Y
Gambia, The	648	.09Y	.10Y	.13Y	.17Y	.19Y	.24Y	.29Y	.32Y	.35Y	.44Y	.58Y	.66Y	.82Y	1.02Y
Guinea	656	.68V	.74Y	1.43V	.26V	.30Y	.37Y	.45Y	.22V	.24Y	.34V	.25V	.28Y	.35Y	.44Y
Madagascar	674	—V	—V	.01V	.01Y	.01Y	.01Y	.02Y	—V	—V	.02V	.02Y	.03Y	.03Y	.04Y
Malawi	676	—Y	—Y	—Y	—Y	—Y	—Y	—Y	.14Y	.16Y	.20Y	.26Y	.30Y	.37Y	.46Y
Mauritania	682	—Y	—Y	—Y	—Y	—Y	—Y	—Y	.01Y	.01Y	.01Y	.01Y	.01Y	.02Y	.02Y
Morocco	686	.03V	—V	—V	—V	—V	—Y	—Y	.80V	1.49V	.79V	.28V	.93V	1.14Y	1.42Y
Nigeria	694	.45V	2.34V	11.73V	15.25Y	19.42Y	23.98Y	31.06Y	—V	—V	—V	—Y	—Y	—Y	—Y
Senegal	722	.01V	—V	.66V	.17V	—V	—V	—Y	15.81V	21.86V	57.57V	37.83V	38.84V	32.58V	40.44Y
South Africa	199	—V	—V	—V	—V	—V	—V	—V	.20V	.21V	.23V	.64V	.60V	2.14V	3.54V
Togo	742	—V	—V	.10V	—V	.19V	.24Y	.29Y	—V	—V	.02V	—V	—V	—Y	—Y
Tunisia	744	—V	—V	.01V	.07V	.02V	.01V	.01Y	.03V	.03V	.03V	.04V	.06V	.09V	.11Y
Zimbabwe	698	—V	—V	—V	—V	—V	—V	—Y	—V	.01V	—V	—V	—V	—V	—Y
Asia	**507**	**95.9Y**	**59.0Y**	**46.7Y**	**62.4Y**	**84.4Y**	**103.1Y**	**128.4Y**	**32.6Y**	**15.5Y**	**21.9Y**	**14.4Y**	**17.3Y**	**21.1Y**	**35.5Y**
Bangladesh	513	—Y	—Y	—Y	—Y	—V	—V	—V	—V	—V	—V	—V	.41V	.51Y	.90Y
China,P.R.: Mainland	924	—V	—V	—V	.05V	—V	—V	.16Y	6.13V	4.26V	13.59V	7.34V	6.37V	6.24V	7.56V
China,P.R.:Hong Kong	532	—V	.01V	.09V	—V	.23V	.02V	.77V	.53V	.51V	.06V	.14V	.06V	.06V	4.81V
India	534	55.50Y	34.51V	46.54V	60.24V	81.64V	100.90Y	125.21Y	15.85Y	6.30V	3.19V	1.34V	.85V	1.05Y	1.30Y
Indonesia	536	—V	—V	—V	—V	.06V	.14V	—V	.03V	.01V	.03V	—V	.03V	1.12V	3.83V
Korea	542	1.49V	1.65V	—V	1.26V	1.42V	1.16V	1.06V	.21V	—V	.01V	.15V	.17V	.28V	.20V
Malaysia	548	—V	.03V	—V	—V	—V	—V	.04V	—V	—V	.17V	.02V	—V	.19V	1.80V
Pakistan	564	—V	.04V	.02V	.54V	.73V	.91Y	1.13Y	.09V	.21V	.41V	3.27V	7.36V	9.09Y	11.29Y
Philippines	566	—V	—V	.01V	—V	—V	—V	—V	—V	—V	1.81V	—V	.07V	.36V	1.46V
Singapore	576	—V	—V	—V	—V	—V	—V	—V	.02V	—V	.03V	.04V	.33V	.84V	1.76V
Taiwan Province of China	528	—V	—V	—V	.05V	.28V	—V	.04V	5.28V	—V	.03V	—V	.01V	.27V	.03V
Thailand	578	38.92V	22.74V	.03V	.25V	—V	—V	—V	4.43V	4.14V	2.59V	2.14V	1.69V	1.13V	.61V
Vietnam	582	—V	—V	—V	—V	—V	—V	—V	—V	.02V	.01V	—V	—V	—V	—V
Europe	**170**	**—Y**	**—Y**	**—Y**	**—Y**	**—Y**	**—Y**	**.1Y**	**.3Y**	**.8Y**	**.7Y**	**.1Y**	**.3Y**	**.5Y**	**1.4Y**
Belarus	913	—V	—V	—V	—V	—V	—V	—V	—V	—V	.16V	—V	—V	—V	—V
Bulgaria	918	—V	—V	—V	.01V	—V	—V	—V	—V	—V	.02V	—V	—V	—V	—V
Czech Republic	935	—V	—V	—V	—V	.04V	—V	—V	—V	—V	—V	—V	—V	.11V	.01V
Hungary	944	—V	—V	—V	—V	—V	—V	—V	—V	—V	—V	—V	.02V	.08V	.16V
Lithuania	946	—V	—V	—V	—V	—V	—V	—V	—V	—V	—V	—V	.02V	.02V	.02V
Poland	964	.01V	—V	.04V	.01V	—V	—V	—V	—V	—V	—V	—V	—V	.05V	—V
Romania	968	—V	—V	—V	—V	—V	—V	—V	—V	.32V	.09V	—V	—V	.04V	—V
Russia	922	—V	—V	—V	—V	—V	—V	—V	.09V	.02V	.04V	—V	—V	—V	—V
Slovak Republic	936	—V	—V	—Y	—Y	—V	—V	—V	—V	—V	—Y	—Y	.01V	—V	—V
Turkey	186	.04V	—V	—V	—V	—V	—V	.15V	.11V	—V	.34V	.06V	.20V	.18V	1.16V
Ukraine	926	—V	—V	—V	—V	—V	—Y	—Y	.06V	.43V	.03V	—V	—V	—Y	—Y

	Exports							Imports						
	2001	2002	2003	2004	2005	2006	2007	2001	2002	2003	2004	2005	2006	2007
	Millions of U.S. Dollars							*Millions of U.S. Dollars*						
Western Hemisphere................ 207	**21.0Y**	**22.8Y**	**—Y**	**—Y**	**—Y**	**—Y**	**209.5Y**	**.3Y**	**.2Y**	**.3Y**	**.4Y**	**1.6Y**	**4.8Y**	**.7Y**
Argentina.................................. 213	—V	—V	—V	—V	—V	—V	—V	—V	—V	—V	.06V	.32V	.51V	.52V
Brazil.. 223	—V	—V	—V	—V	—V	—V	209.45V	.30V	.20V	.28V	.31V	1.15V	4.16V	—V
Colombia.................................... 233	—V	—V	—V	—V	—V	—V	—V	—V	—V	.03V	.03V	—V	—V	.04V
Costa Rica.................................. 238	—V	.01V	—V	—V	—V	—Y	—Y	....	....	....	....	....	....	....
Mexico....................................... 273	—V	—V	—V	—V	.04V	.04V	.03V	—V	—V	—V	—V	.07V	—V	.02V
Paraguay.................................... 288	—V	—V	—V	—V	—V	—V	—Y	—V	—V	—V	—V	—V	.05V	.06Y
Peru... 293	—V	—V	—V	—V	—V	—V	—Y	—V	—V	—V	.02V	.11V	.08V	.10Y
Uruguay..................................... 298	20.99V	22.78Y	—V	—V	—V	—Y	—Y	—V	—Y	—V	—V	—V	—Y	—Y
Other Countries n.i.e................ 910	**—Y**	**—Y**	**—Y**	**—Y**	**—Y**	**—Y**	**—Y**	**3.0Y**	**3.2Y**	**4.1Y**	**5.3Y**	**6.1Y**	**7.5Y**	**9.3Y**
Cuba.. 928	—Y	—Y	—Y	—Y	—Y	—Y	—Y	2.95Y	3.21Y	4.06Y	5.33Y	6.09Y	7.52Y	9.34Y
Countries & Areas n.s............... 898	**—Y**	**—Y**	**—Y**	**—Y**	**—Y**	**—Y**	**—Y**	**9.2Y**	**10.0Y**	**12.7Y**	**16.7Y**	**19.0Y**	**23.5Y**	**29.2Y**
Memorandum Items														
European Union.......................... 998	3.77Y	9.40Y	7.79Y	5.54Y	3.83Y	3.46Y	1.66Y	41.74Y	42.33Y	55.53Y	55.50Y	113.51Y	91.23Y	98.72Y
Oil Exporting Ctys....................... 999	.45Y	2.34Y	11.73Y	15.25Y	19.48Y	24.11Y	31.06Y	.03Y	.01Y	.03Y	—Y	.03Y	1.12Y	3.83Y
Non-Oil Develop.Ctys.................. 201	119.51Y	83.72Y	49.27Y	63.19Y	85.34Y	104.62Y	340.02Y	51.11Y	41.64Y	83.49Y	56.27Y	69.95Y	69.66Y	89.77Y
PERCENT DISTRIBUTION														
Industrial Countries................. 101	**3.8**	**9.8**	**13.8**	**28.7**	**3.7**	**3.0**	**.4**	**41.6**	**46.1**	**36.9**	**42.3**	**55.3**	**49.4**	**45.0**
Developing Countries............. 202	**96.2**	**90.2**	**86.2**	**71.3**	**96.3**	**97.0**	**99.6**	**47.2**	**40.9**	**52.6**	**41.5**	**32.9**	**35.1**	**39.0**
Africa..................................... 607	**2.4**	**4.5**	**20.2**	**14.6**	**18.7**	**19.3**	**8.9**	**16.6**	**24.7**	**38.2**	**30.5**	**23.8**	**22.0**	**23.3**
Asia....................................... 507	**77.0**	**61.8**	**66.0**	**56.7**	**77.5**	**77.7**	**34.5**	**30.0**	**15.2**	**13.8**	**10.6**	**8.1**	**10.5**	**14.8**
Europe.................................. 170	**—**	**—**	**.1**	**—**	**—**	**—**	**—**	**.3**	**.8**	**.4**	**—**	**.1**	**.2**	**.6**
Western Hemisphere............. 207	**16.8**	**23.9**	**—**	**—**	**—**	**—**	**56.2**	**.3**	**.2**	**.2**	**.3**	**.8**	**2.4**	**.3**
Other Countries n.i.e............... 910	**—**	**—**	**—**	**—**	**—**	**—**	**—**	**2.7**	**3.1**	**2.6**	**3.9**	**2.9**	**3.7**	**3.9**
ANNUAL PERCENT CHANGE														
World...................................... 001	**11.5**	**−23.4**	**−25.9**	**55.6**	**−1.1**	**21.9**	**181.0**	**2.7**	**−6.0**	**55.9**	**−14.6**	**56.9**	**−5.4**	**19.3**
Industrial Countries................. 101	**−.6**	**100.9**	**3.6**	**224.5**	**−87.2**	**−2.1**	**−57.6**	**−9.6**	**4.4**	**24.6**	**−2.0**	**105.1**	**−15.5**	**8.6**
Developing Countries............. 202	**12.0**	**−28.3**	**−29.1**	**28.6**	**33.6**	**22.8**	**188.3**	**14.5**	**−18.5**	**100.5**	**−32.6**	**24.4**	**1.1**	**32.2**
Africa..................................... 607	**76.6**	**43.7**	**231.9**	**12.3**	**27.1**	**25.4**	**29.2**	**20.7**	**40.1**	**140.4**	**−31.8**	**22.7**	**−12.5**	**26.1**
Asia....................................... 507	**78.6**	**−38.5**	**−20.8**	**33.6**	**35.2**	**22.2**	**24.5**	**11.7**	**−52.5**	**41.7**	**−34.1**	**20.0**	**21.9**	**68.2**
Europe.................................. 170	**328.8**	**−83.0**	**342.1**	**−46.5**	**120.0**	**−89.8**	**—**	**−19.8**	**180.9**	**−12.7**	**−91.2**	**326.5**	**86.0**	**190.1**
Middle East........................... 407	**—**	**—**	**....**	**....**	**....**	**....**	**....**	**−766.7**	**—**	**100.0**	**−36.4**	**33.3**	**25.0**	**....**
Western Hemisphere............. 207	**−59.4**	**8.5**	**—**	**1.5**	**14.3**	**1.8**	**—**	**119.2**	**−33.8**	**58.9**	**32.9**	**291.7**	**191.0**	**−84.6**
Other Countries n.i.e............... 910	**—**	**—**	**....**	**....**	**....**	**....**	**....**	**10.4**	**8.5**	**26.6**	**31.3**	**14.3**	**23.6**	**24.1**

		Exports							Imports						
		2001	2002	2003	2004	2005	2006	2007	2001	2002	2003	2004	2005	2006	2007
		Millions of U.S. Dollars							Millions of U.S. Dollars						
IFS World Total		**489.8**	**495.5**	**513.3**	**593.1**	**553.1**	**588.2**	**678.6**	**583.3**	**576.2**	**576.1**	**651.3**	**788.3**	**889.4**	**1,059.4**
DOTS World Total	**001**	**574.5Y**	**543.8Y**	**578.3Y**	**648.3Y**	**645.4Y**	**683.8Y**	**807.9Y**	**708.7Y**	**563.1Y**	**584.3Y**	**609.6Y**	**724.2Y**	**944.0Y**	**1,009.1Y**
Industrial Countries	**101**	**453.9Y**	**431.5Y**	**458.7Y**	**496.1Y**	**447.3Y**	**459.4Y**	**545.4Y**	**257.7Y**	**276.2Y**	**312.7Y**	**260.1Y**	**321.4Y**	**376.8Y**	**384.8Y**
United States	111	146.00V	121.64V	123.64V	125.55V	121.00V	127.91V	133.18V	155.21V	141.13V	128.92V	149.16V	192.83V	197.23V	206.80V
Canada	156	135.26V	143.65V	144.52V	151.42V	121.10V	125.46V	151.45V	5.88V	7.44V	7.07V	9.66V	14.94V	23.69V	27.83V
Australia	193	.72V	.30V	.15V	.78V	.91V	.53V	.72V	1.53V	1.25V	4.08V	.94V	1.18V	1.62V	5.98V
Japan	158	3.62V	2.90V	2.92V	3.07V	4.08V	6.52V	5.64V	13.72V	13.48V	16.17V	17.89V	24.37V	31.07V	27.25V
New Zealand	196	.47V	.11V	.15V	.39V	.86V	.24V	.84V	3.95V	4.52V	4.48V	4.34V	5.54V	6.04V	7.69V
Austria	122	.02V	—V	—V	—V	—V	—V	—V	.38V	.06V	.10V	.15V	.24V	.09V	.81V
Belgium	124	33.62V	22.58V	36.99V	41.52V	23.94V	29.25V	26.59V	1.77V	2.98V	2.20V	2.33V	2.21V	2.94V	4.65V
Cyprus	423	—V	—V	—V	—V	—Y	.02V	—V	.07V	.10V	.07V	.12V	—V	.08V	.03V
Denmark	128	.08V	—V	.03V	.14V	.18V	.16V	.24V	.90V	.79V	1.27V	1.19V	1.35V	1.95V	2.07V
Finland	172	6.71V	.95V	3.71V	—V	.04V	.02V	.01V	.16V	.31V	.21V	1.46V	.20V	6.87V	1.57V
France	132	8.84V	11.99V	7.45V	12.22V	8.24V	25.96V	38.18V	9.71V	10.02V	6.81V	5.72V	5.38V	6.14V	2.25V
Germany	134	4.44V	4.15V	5.45V	3.49V	5.25V	3.03V	4.02V	4.20V	4.74V	5.82V	5.90V	7.41V	4.91V	6.86V
Greece	174	—V	—V	—V	.02V	—V	—V	—V	.06V	.05V	.23V	.10V	.05V	.10V	.07V
Iceland	176	—V	—V	—V	—V	—V	—V	.02V	—V	—V	—V	—V	—V	—V	—V
Ireland	178	.05V	—V	—V	—V	.01V	—V	.03V	.61V	.56V	5.11V	1.78V	1.13V	.78V	1.65V
Italy	136	2.02V	2.05V	1.68V	2.33V	5.89V	1.51V	5.46V	4.84V	37.32V	64.00V	3.64V	3.71V	8.09V	9.20V
Luxembourg	137	—V	—V	—V	—V	—V	—V	—V	2.34V	.78V	2.93V	1.68V	3.12V	1.18V	.18V
Malta	181	—Y	.01V	.01V	—V	—V	—V	—V	.10Y	.08V	.14V	.06V	.05V	—V	—V
Netherlands	138	11.94V	10.03V	13.40V	18.51V	23.09V	29.31V	37.48V	13.46V	14.67V	16.76V	15.33V	17.37V	29.61V	17.52V
Norway	142	—V	.02V	—V	.03V	—V	.08V	.05V	—V	1.72V	.65V	.66V	.23V	.38V	.14V
Portugal	182	19.90V	28.34V	37.64V	59.29V	51.77V	44.44V	61.48V	.03V	.02V	.04V	.04V	.05V	.12V	.20V
Slovenia	961	—V	.06V	—V	—Y	—V	—V	.01V	—V	—V	—V	—Y	—V	.25V	.09V
Spain	184	.40V	12.07V	3.69V	5.70V	3.95V	4.01V	4.32V	1.25V	1.53V	1.50V	1.98V	1.47V	1.32V	2.69V
Sweden	144	.02V	—V	.01V	.01V	.43V	1.59V	1.71V	1.10V	1.29V	1.82V	2.23V	1.30V	10.03V	4.46V
Switzerland	146	.24V	.12V	.13V	.53V	1.22V	.20V	.18V	.56V	.80V	.89V	.83V	.99V	.91V	.57V
United Kingdom	112	79.57V	70.56V	77.10V	71.12V	75.36V	59.14V	73.77V	35.86V	30.56V	41.46V	32.93V	36.26V	41.45V	54.22V
Developing Countries	**202**	**111.0Y**	**101.9Y**	**106.5Y**	**135.0Y**	**178.3Y**	**200.1Y**	**232.2Y**	**422.5Y**	**255.9Y**	**232.4Y**	**298.1Y**	**344.0Y**	**494.5Y**	**534.1Y**
Africa	**607**	**1.4Y**	**.9Y**	**1.8Y**	**2.4Y**	**2.9Y**	**3.5Y**	**4.3Y**	**.6Y**	**.3Y**	**5.1Y**	**2.6Y**	**1.9Y**	**2.1Y**	**3.3Y**
Benin	638	.08V	—V	.02V	—V	—V	—Y	—Y	—V	—V	—V	.22V	—V	—Y	—Y
Cape Verde	624	.01V	.01Y	.02Y	.02Y	.03Y	.03Y	.04Y	....	....	....	....	....	....	....
Ghana	652	.26Y	.28Y	.35Y	.46Y	.53Y	.65Y	.81Y	.02Y	.02Y	.03Y	.03Y	.04Y	.05Y	.06Y
Guinea	656	—V	—Y	—V	.15V	.17Y	.22Y	.27Y	....	....	....	....	....	....	....
Kenya	664	.01V	.01V	—V	.18V	.20Y	.25Y	.31Y	—V	—V	.11V	.49V	.56Y	.70Y	.86Y
Madagascar	674	—V	—V	.01V	.01Y	.01Y	.01Y	.01Y	.02V	.01V	—V	—Y	.01Y	.01Y	.01Y
Mauritius	684	—V	—V	—V	—V	—V	—V	.12V	—V	—V	—V	—V	.31V	.02V	.04V
Morocco	686	—V	.03V	—V	—V	—V	—Y	—Y	.09V	—V	—V	.02V	.12V	.15Y	.19Y
Namibia	728	.36Y	.38Y	.41Y	.43Y	.46Y	.48Y	.51Y	—Y	—Y	—Y	—Y	—Y	—Y	—Y
Nigeria	694	.36V	.05V	.70V	.91Y	1.16Y	1.43Y	1.85Y	—V	—V	—V	—Y	—Y	—Y	—Y
South Africa	199	—V	.06V	.10V	—V	.04V	.14V	—V	.32V	.23V	.65V	1.28V	.70V	.89V	1.78V
Sudan	732	—Y	—Y	—Y	—V	—V	—V	—V	.01Y	.01Y	—V	—V	—V	—V	—V
Tanzania	738	.01V	.09V	.12Y	.15Y	.17Y	.21Y	.26Y	.10V	.05V	.06Y	.08Y	.09Y	.11Y	.14Y
Togo	742	.16V	.02V	.04V	—V	.03V	.04Y	.05Y	....	....	....	....	....	....	....
Tunisia	744	.10V	—V	—V	.05V	.08V	—V	—Y	—V	—V	4.26V	.45V	.05V	.15V	.18Y
Uganda	746	.01V	—V	.02V	.03Y	.03Y	.04Y	.05Y	—Y	—Y	—Y	—Y	—Y	—Y	—Y
Asia	**507**	**7.4Y**	**11.7Y**	**13.0Y**	**18.1Y**	**37.9Y**	**51.7Y**	**53.4Y**	**30.6Y**	**31.8Y**	**38.8Y**	**44.9Y**	**64.1Y**	**137.7Y**	**116.4Y**
Bangladesh	513	—V	—V	—V	—V	—V	1.34V	—V	—V	—V	—V	—V	—V	—Y	—Y
China,P.R.: Mainland	924	2.16V	3.63V	.27V	1.01V	6.82V	16.29V	16.50V	13.67V	15.09V	21.25V	23.09V	29.93V	89.67V	72.02V
China,P.R.:Hong Kong	532	1.90V	3.23V	3.17V	5.00V	5.07V	4.16V	6.39V	2.32V	2.68V	2.00V	1.55V	1.92V	2.33V	.60V
China,P.R.:Macao	546	—V	.01V	—V	—V	—V	—V	—V	—V	—V	—Y	—Y	—Y	—Y	—Y
India	534	1.41Y	1.94V	8.63V	7.46V	16.39V	20.26Y	25.14Y	5.37Y	3.48V	4.90V	6.68V	11.03V	13.63Y	16.92Y
Indonesia	536	—V	—V	.05V	.30V	.30V	.06V	.05V	1.00V	.95V	.94V	.80V	.76V	1.84V	1.27V
Korea	542	1.34V	2.58V	.03V	1.26V	1.83V	1.28V	.11V	2.33V	1.49V	2.02V	3.76V	3.34V	6.46V	5.91V
Malaysia	548	.24V	.16V	.04V	.32V	.36V	.35V	.60V	.34V	1.52V	.60V	1.38V	7.83V	11.73V	4.95V
Pakistan	564	.02V	.05V	.02V	.06V	.08V	.09Y	.12Y	.07V	.35V	.63V	.67V	.94V	1.16Y	1.44Y
Papua New Guinea	853	—Y	—Y	—Y	.01Y	.01Y	.01Y	.01Y	—Y	—Y	—Y	—Y	—Y	—Y	—Y
Philippines	566	—V	—V	—V	—V	—V	—V	—V	.03V	.28V	.14V	—V	—V	—V	—V
Singapore	576	.02V	—V	.11V	.13V	.80V	.38V	.21V	1.33V	1.31V	.65V	1.43V	2.19V	4.32V	5.93V
Sri Lanka	524	—V	—V	—V	—V	—V	—V	—V	—V	—V	1.98V	.08V	—V	.02V	.05V
Taiwan Province of China	528	.35V	.07V	.30V	2.49V	4.47V	6.74V	3.51V	1.73V	2.46V	2.06V	3.15V	2.66V	2.34V	3.64V
Thailand	578	—V	—V	.08V	.09V	1.83V	.72V	.73V	2.33V	2.04V	1.53V	2.28V	3.53V	4.19V	3.70V
Vietnam	582	—V	.03V	.26V	—V	—V	—V	—V	.11V	.15V	.14V	—V	—V	—V	—V
Europe	**170**	**18.9Y**	**4.1Y**	**2.7Y**	**1.4Y**	**.2Y**	**.2Y**	**.7Y**	**3.6Y**	**3.5Y**	**2.9Y**	**4.8Y**	**3.3Y**	**3.9Y**	**4.1Y**
Bulgaria	918	—V	—V	—V	—V	.01V	—V	—V	—V	—V	—V	—V	—V	—V	.01V
Czech Republic	935	.11V	.15V	.18V	.22V	.04V	—V	.13V	.20V	.27V	.46V	.38V	.04V	.57V	.36V
Estonia	939	—V	—V	.01V	—V	—V	—V	.02V	.04V	.01V	.07V	—V	—V	—V	.12V
Hungary	944	.01V	.01V	.04V	.01V	.01V	—V	—V	.01V	—V	.03V	—V	.02V	.02V	.01V
Latvia	941	—V	—V	—Y	—V	—V	—V	—V	—Y	—Y	—Y	—Y	—V	.01V	.01V
Lithuania	946	—V	—V	—V	.06V	.01V	—V	—V	.04V	—V	—V	—V	—V	—V	—V
Macedonia, FYR	962	—V	—V	—V	—V	—V	—V	—Y	—V	.04V	—V	—V	—V	—V	—Y

		Exports							Imports						
		2001	2002	2003	2004	2005	2006	2007	2001	2002	2003	2004	2005	2006	2007
		Millions of U.S. Dollars							Millions of U.S. Dollars						
Poland	964	.29V	.22V	.41V	.61V	—V	—V	—V	.10V	.42V	.30V	.14V	.19V	.47V	.25V
Romania	968	5.25V	.03V	—V	—V	—V	.01V	—V	.04V	.02V	.01V	.02V	—V	.27V	—V
Russia	922	.05V	1.76V	.01V	.03V	.02V	.06V	.33V	.22V	.64V	.07V	2.25V	.67V	.09V	.06V
Slovak Republic	936	.01V	.02V	.03Y	.03Y	—V	—V	—V	.02V	—V	—Y	—Y	.64V	.04V	1.08V
Turkey	186	—V	—V	.02V	.37V	.06V	.12V	.22V	2.88V	2.07V	1.96V	1.91V	1.66V	2.29V	2.04V
Ukraine	926	13.22V	1.92V	2.02V	.03V	.01V	.02Y	.02Y	—V	.01V	—V	.07V	.09V	.11Y	.13Y
Middle East	**407**	**.4Y**	**.2Y**	**.1Y**	**.2Y**	**10.2Y**	**7.5Y**	**5.5Y**	**.4Y**	**.4Y**	**.5Y**	**1.0Y**	**1.0Y**	**1.2Y**	**1.8Y**
Egypt	469	—V	—Y	—Y	—Y	—Y	—Y	—Y	.04V	.04Y	.05Y	.07Y	.08Y	.09Y	.12Y
Iran, I.R. of	429	—V	.01V	.01Y	.01Y	.01Y	.02Y	.02Y	—Y	—Y	—Y	—Y	—Y	—Y	—Y
Israel	436	.09V	—V	—V	—V	10.09V	7.45V	5.36V	—V	—V	—V	.33V	.11V	.11V	.55V
Lebanon	446	—Y	—Y	—Y	—Y	—Y	—Y	—Y	.01Y	.01Y	.02Y	.02Y	.03Y	.03Y	.04Y
Oman	449	.01V	.16V	—V	—Y	—Y	—Y	—Y	.03V	—V	—V	—Y	—Y	—Y	—Y
Saudi Arabia	456	.27V	—V	.08V	.17V	.05V	.06Y	.08Y	.32Y	.34Y	.41Y	.54Y	.74Y	.93Y	1.12Y
Western Hemisphere	**207**	**82.9Y**	**85.0Y**	**89.0Y**	**112.9Y**	**127.1Y**	**137.1Y**	**168.4Y**	**387.3Y**	**219.9Y**	**185.1Y**	**244.9Y**	**273.7Y**	**349.7Y**	**408.5Y**
Antigua and Barbuda	311	4.83Y	5.24Y	6.63Y	8.71Y	9.95Y	12.30Y	15.26Y	1.53Y	1.66Y	2.11Y	2.77Y	3.16Y	3.91Y	4.85Y
Argentina	213	.25V	.05V	—V	—V	—V	—V	—V	.18V	.72V	1.62V	1.33V	1.75V	2.47V	2.17V
Aruba	314	3.84V	2.43V	1.78V	1.26V	.75V	.88V	1.09V	—V	—V	—V	—V	—V	—V	—V
Bahamas, The	313	—Y	—Y	—Y	—Y	—Y	—Y	—Y	.01Y	.01Y	.01Y	.02Y	.02Y	.02Y	.03Y
Barbados	316	9.30V	9.61V	11.16V	14.18V	13.58V	15.83V	19.64Y	6.99V	9.38V	6.81V	7.84V	6.81V	7.12V	8.83Y
Belize	339	.35Y	.38Y	.48Y	.63Y	.72Y	.89Y	1.10Y	.52Y	.56Y	.71Y	.94Y	1.07Y	1.32Y	1.64Y
Bermuda	319	.01Y	.01Y	.01Y	.01Y	.01V	.02V	.02Y	—Y	—Y	—Y	—Y	—Y	—Y	—Y
Bolivia	218	.02V	—V	—V	—V	—V	—Y	—Y	—V	—V	.08V	.10V	.12Y	.15Y	.18Y
Brazil	223	.03V	.03V	—V	.01V	.01V	.56V	—V	6.79V	9.60V	10.62V	14.95V	18.19V	22.09V	—V
Chile	228	2.61V	8.09V	.26V	.30V	1.00V	1.37V	.65V	105.66V	—V	.50V	.45V	.57V	1.10V	.93V
Colombia	233	.79V	.21V	.09V	1.39V	1.05V	.95V	.89V	2.79V	3.31V	3.55V	4.25V	5.40V	6.34V	8.31V
Costa Rica	238	—V	—V	.24V	.01V	—V	—Y	.01Y	1.29V	.92V	2.62V	3.55V	4.25V	5.25Y	6.52Y
Dominica	321	1.53V	1.66Y	2.10Y	2.75Y	3.15Y	3.89Y	4.83Y	3.38V	3.67Y	4.64Y	6.10Y	6.97Y	8.61Y	10.69Y
Dominican Republic	243	—V	—Y	—Y	—Y	—Y	—Y	—Y	.10V	.11Y	.14Y	.18Y	.20Y	.25Y	.31Y
Ecuador	248	.36V	.67V	.49V	.15V	.54V	.51V	.63Y	—V	.03V	.03V	.01V	.01V	.03V	.03Y
El Salvador	253	.01V	—V	—V	—V	.01V	—V	—V	—V	.03V	.03V	.02V	.38V	.03V	.18V
Grenada	328	2.38Y	2.58Y	3.27Y	4.29Y	4.90Y	6.06Y	7.52Y	.13Y	.15Y	.18Y	.24Y	.28Y	.34Y	.42Y
Guatemala	258	—V	—V	.01V	.09V	—V	—Y	—Y	.29V	.52V	.39V	.76V	.72V	.90Y	1.11Y
Haiti	263	.27V	.36V	2.02V	2.38V	2.71Y	3.36Y	4.16Y	—Y	—Y	—Y	—Y	—Y	—Y	—Y
Jamaica	343	28.06V	27.78V	26.06V	29.25V	34.01V	28.04V	32.60V	4.36V	3.12V	3.76V	4.22V	3.03V	4.12V	5.50V
Mexico	273	.69V	.06V	.59V	2.25V	4.59V	1.37V	3.38V	1.58V	3.07V	2.15V	2.68V	2.78V	2.05V	5.67V
Netherlands Antilles	353	.87V	.06V	3.49V	4.58Y	5.23Y	6.47Y	8.02Y	132.12V	76.66V	12.70V	16.68Y	19.06Y	23.56Y	29.23Y
Panama	283	.05V	.07V	.01V	.54V	.49V	.11V	.07V	.21V	.22V	.08V	.16V	.14V	.18V	.12V
Paraguay	288	—V	—V	—V	—V	—V	—V	—Y	—V	—V	—V	.48V	.06V	—V	—Y
Peru	293	.21V	.03V	.03V	.02V	.22V	.16V	.05Y	1.03V	1.12V	1.50V	1.93V	1.64V	2.13V	2.87Y
St. Kitts and Nevis	361	.14Y	.15Y	.20Y	.26Y	.29Y	.36Y	.45Y	.01Y	.02Y	.02Y	.03Y	.03Y	.04Y	.05Y
St. Lucia	362	3.90Y	4.23Y	5.35Y	7.03Y	8.03Y	9.93Y	12.32Y	.42Y	.45Y	.58Y	.76Y	.86Y	1.07Y	1.32Y
St. Pierre-Miquelon	363	.01Y	.01Y	.01Y	.01Y	.01Y	.01Y	.02Y	.04Y	.05Y	.06Y	.08Y	.09Y	.11Y	.13Y
St. Vincent & Grens	364	1.96V	1.91V	1.50V	2.32V	1.77V	2.19Y	2.72Y	.29V	.19V	.15V	.13V	.17V	.21Y	.26Y
Suriname	366	2.87Y	3.11Y	3.94Y	5.17Y	5.91Y	7.30Y	9.06Y	6.91Y	7.50Y	9.49Y	12.46Y	14.24Y	17.60Y	21.84Y
Trinidad and Tobago	369	14.77V	14.31V	18.12Y	23.79Y	27.18Y	33.60Y	41.69Y	101.90V	90.73V	114.84Y	150.82Y	172.33Y	212.98Y	264.31Y
Uruguay	298	—V	—Y	—V	—V	.04V	.05Y	.07Y	—V	—Y	—V	—V	—V	—Y	—Y
Venezuela, Rep. Bol.	299	2.52V	1.59V	.75V	1.09V	.54V	.45V	1.61V	8.80V	6.10V	5.68V	10.91V	9.41V	25.67V	30.97Y
Western Hem. n.s.	399	.33Y	.36Y	.38Y	.41Y	.43Y	.45Y	.48Y	.01Y	.01Y	.01Y	.01Y	.01Y	.01Y	.01Y
Other Countries n.i.e.	**910**	**7.5Y**	**8.2Y**	**10.3Y**	**13.6Y**	**15.5Y**	**19.2Y**	**23.8Y**	**28.5Y**	**31.0Y**	**39.2Y**	**51.5Y**	**58.8Y**	**72.7Y**	**90.2Y**
Cuba	928	7.39Y	8.02Y	10.15Y	13.33Y	15.23Y	18.83Y	23.36Y	23.08Y	25.05Y	31.70Y	41.63Y	47.57Y	58.79Y	72.96Y
North Korea	954	.14Y	.15Y	.20Y	.26Y	.29Y	.36Y	.45Y	5.45Y	5.91Y	7.48Y	9.82Y	11.22Y	13.87Y	17.22Y
Special Categories	**899**	**2.0Y**	**2.2Y**	**2.8Y**	**3.7Y**	**4.2Y**	**5.2Y**	**6.4Y**	**—Y**	**—Y**	**—Y**	**—Y**	**—Y**	**—Y**	**—Y**
Memorandum Items															
European Union	998	168.01Y	163.18Y	187.83Y	215.28Y	198.20Y	198.43Y	253.44Y	77.27Y	106.55Y	151.32Y	77.16Y	82.20Y	117.01Y	110.35Y
Oil Exporting Ctys	999	3.16Y	1.80Y	1.59Y	2.47Y	2.06Y	2.02Y	3.62Y	10.16Y	7.39Y	7.03Y	12.26Y	10.91Y	28.44Y	33.36Y
Non-Oil Develop.Ctys	201	107.86Y	100.12Y	104.91Y	132.48Y	176.27Y	198.03Y	228.60Y	412.33Y	248.53Y	225.35Y	285.80Y	333.11Y	466.01Y	500.75Y
PERCENT DISTRIBUTION															
Industrial Countries	**101**	**79.0**	**79.3**	**79.3**	**76.5**	**69.3**	**67.2**	**67.5**	**36.4**	**49.1**	**53.5**	**42.7**	**44.4**	**39.9**	**38.1**
Developing Countries	**202**	**19.3**	**18.7**	**18.4**	**20.8**	**27.6**	**29.3**	**28.7**	**59.6**	**45.4**	**39.8**	**48.9**	**47.5**	**52.4**	**52.9**
Africa	**607**	**.2**	**.2**	**.3**	**.4**	**.5**	**.5**	**.5**	**.1**	**.1**	**.9**	**.4**	**.3**	**.2**	**.3**
Asia	**507**	**1.3**	**2.2**	**2.2**	**2.8**	**5.9**	**7.6**	**6.6**	**4.3**	**5.6**	**6.6**	**7.4**	**8.9**	**14.6**	**11.5**
Europe	**170**	**3.3**	**.8**	**.5**	**.2**	**—**	**—**	**.1**	**.5**	**.6**	**.5**	**.8**	**.5**	**.4**	**.4**
Middle East	**407**	**.1**	**—**	**—**	**—**	**1.6**	**1.1**	**.7**	**.1**	**.1**	**.1**	**.2**	**.1**	**.1**	**.2**
Western Hemisphere	**207**	**14.4**	**15.6**	**15.4**	**17.4**	**19.7**	**20.1**	**20.8**	**54.7**	**39.1**	**31.7**	**40.2**	**37.8**	**37.0**	**40.5**
Other Countries n.i.e.	**910**	**1.3**	**1.5**	**1.8**	**2.1**	**2.4**	**2.8**	**2.9**	**4.0**	**5.5**	**6.7**	**8.4**	**8.1**	**7.7**	**8.9**
ANNUAL PERCENT CHANGE															
World	**001**	**–3.6**	**–5.3**	**6.3**	**12.1**	**–.5**	**6.0**	**18.1**	**8.9**	**–20.5**	**3.8**	**4.3**	**18.8**	**30.3**	**6.9**
Industrial Countries	**101**	**–1.1**	**–4.9**	**6.3**	**8.2**	**–9.8**	**2.7**	**18.7**	**–5.5**	**7.2**	**13.2**	**–16.8**	**23.6**	**17.3**	**2.1**
Developing Countries	**202**	**–13.3**	**–8.2**	**4.5**	**26.7**	**32.1**	**12.2**	**16.1**	**19.9**	**–39.4**	**–9.2**	**28.3**	**15.4**	**43.7**	**8.0**
Africa	**607**	**–9.8**	**–30.5**	**88.3**	**35.3**	**21.5**	**20.5**	**22.2**	**59.2**	**–42.1**	**—**	**–49.7**	**–26.9**	**10.2**	**57.5**
Asia	**507**	**–58.0**	**57.5**	**10.7**	**39.9**	**109.3**	**36.2**	**3.3**	**9.4**	**3.8**	**22.1**	**15.6**	**42.9**	**114.7**	**–15.4**
Europe	**170**	**–26.2**	**–78.3**	**–34.1**	**–49.4**	**–88.4**	**35.7**	**236.8**	**191.4**	**–1.8**	**–17.1**	**65.4**	**–30.7**	**16.7**	**5.5**
Middle East	**407**	**281.7**	**–55.0**	**–44.8**	**92.6**	**—**	**–25.8**	**–27.5**	**–19.2**	**–2.1**	**22.0**	**101.1**	**–1.2**	**22.5**	**56.8**
Western Hemisphere	**207**	**–.2**	**2.5**	**4.7**	**26.9**	**12.7**	**7.8**	**22.8**	**20.2**	**–43.2**	**–15.8**	**32.3**	**11.8**	**27.7**	**16.8**
Other Countries n.i.e.	**910**	**10.4**	**8.5**	**26.6**	**31.3**	**14.3**	**23.6**	**24.1**	**10.4**	**8.5**	**26.6**	**31.3**	**14.3**	**23.6**	**24.1**

		Exports							Imports						
		2001	2002	2003	2004	2005	2006	2007	2001	2002	2003	2004	2005	2006	2007
		Millions of U.S. Dollars							*Millions of U.S. Dollars*						
IFS World Total		**274.3**	**280.4**	**346.6**	**391.3**	**470.2**	**475.8**	**521.8**	**1,013.0**	**1,130.3**	**1,187.8**	**1,306.0**	**1,453.7**	**1,875.3**	**1,681.5**
DOTS World Total	**001**	**293.7Y**	**284.3Y**	**372.7Y**	**425.3Y**	**515.6Y**	**578.7Y**	**623.5Y**	**748.5**	**757.8**	**744.9**	**897.5**	**1,529.4Y**	**1,935.7Y**	**1,897.0Y**
Industrial Countries	**101**	**270.4Y**	**260.5Y**	**340.6Y**	**381.0Y**	**459.2Y**	**506.0Y**	**516.9Y**	**380.6**	**354.5**	**336.7**	**408.1**	**967.6Y**	**1,179.0Y**	**1,005.6Y**
United States	111	247.27V	239.82V	310.36V	346.09V	416.82V	462.27V	454.73V	247.44	227.29	214.17	312.35	756.91V	890.23V	781.77V
Canada	156	6.95V	6.78V	13.48V	17.48V	20.66V	17.41V	20.86V	24.39	27.51	19.60	13.49	30.75V	30.09V	32.72V
Australia	193	.01V	.02V	.62V	.77V	1.19V	1.02V	1.64V	1.90	.05	.01	.21	.30V	.41V	1.22V
Japan	158	.44V	.42V	.55V	.83V	1.08V	1.29V	.84V	26.17	24.74	26.97	29.33	27.54V	34.46V	42.52V
New Zealand	196	.01V	—V	.01V	.06V	.13V	.15V	.31V	.24	.27	.17	.42	1.40V	.39V	.25V
Austria	122	.01V	.01V	.08V	.03V	.01V	.12V	.01V	1.37	1.14	.54	.12	1.32V	1.53V	2.05V
Belgium	124	5.07V	1.71V	2.35V	2.57V	5.00V	7.76V	12.89V	3.80	7.22	5.20	2.68	6.49V	5.53V	6.99V
Cyprus	423	—V	—V	—V	—V	—Y	—V	—V	—	—	—	—	.20V	.02V	.07V
Denmark	128	.01V	—V	—V	—V	—V	—V	.02V	1.22	1.38	4.06	1.20	2.39V	3.35V	4.56V
Finland	172	—V	.01V	.01V	—V	.01V	.01V	.01V	.18	.16	.37	—	.64V	.75V	.36V
France	132	3.87V	3.80V	3.89V	5.08V	6.23V	6.80V	8.84V	14.09	19.96	24.14	14.86	33.11V	37.56V	26.90V
Germany	134	1.82V	2.82V	2.06V	2.18V	2.22V	2.09V	2.12V	14.86	11.11	8.80	7.87	21.45V	39.91V	12.28V
Greece	174	—V	.01V	—V	.02V	.01V	—V	.01V	.33	.68	.54	—	—V	.13V	.01V
Iceland	176	—V	—V	—V	—V	—V	—V	—V	.02	.11	.15	.61	—V	—V	—V
Ireland	178	—V	.03V	.02V	.09V	.05V	.07V	.08V	.46	.45	.30	.65	.80V	2.74V	1.01V
Italy	136	1.31V	1.04V	1.04V	1.28V	.70V	.67V	.91V	3.65	3.25	3.69	3.07	15.24V	13.44V	17.72V
Luxembourg	137	—V	—V	—V	—V	—V	—V	—V	.66	.55	—	.01	.12V	.01V	.17V
Malta	181	—Y	—V	—V	—V	—V	—V	—V	—	—	.01	.02	2.38V	—V	—V
Netherlands	138	1.39V	.64V	1.90V	1.04V	.80V	.85V	.69V	25.07	17.52	14.16	12.21	16.18V	25.68V	21.37V
Norway	142	.07V	.02V	.07V	.02V	.03V	.01V	.03V	1.61	2.67	2.43	2.21	2.37V	6.59V	1.80V
Portugal	182	—V	—V	—V	—V	—V	—V	.01V	.08	.21	.25	.35	.48V	.22V	.14V
Slovenia	961	—V	—V	—V	—Y	—V	—V	—V	.06	.09	—	—	—V	.01V	.02V
Spain	184	.65V	.93V	1.42V	1.24V	1.69V	2.46V	2.69V	7.97	6.80	5.55	5.49	18.87V	15.86V	9.90V
Sweden	144	.01V	.02V	.03V	.02V	.04V	.05V	.02V	.89	.38	.74	.21	17.86V	54.46V	30.21V
Switzerland	146	1.01V	1.00V	2.12V	1.39V	1.55V	2.28V	2.69V	.39	.97	.59	.72	1.55V	1.28V	1.18V
United Kingdom	112	.51V	1.39V	.56V	.82V	.94V	.67V	7.52V	3.80	—	4.23	—	9.25V	14.42V	10.35V
Developing Countries	**202**	**23.3Y**	**23.8Y**	**32.1Y**	**44.3Y**	**56.5Y**	**72.8Y**	**106.6Y**	**356.5**	**395.1**	**395.9**	**480.5**	**551.6Y**	**744.1Y**	**875.8Y**
Africa	**607**	**.1Y**	**.1Y**	**.1Y**	**.1Y**	**.1Y**	**.1Y**	**.1Y**	**1.1**	**1.3**	**.4**	**.1**	**4.4Y**	**2.0Y**	**3.3Y**
Algeria	612	—V	.02V	.02Y	.02Y	.03Y	.04Y	.05Y	—	—	.05	—	—Y	—Y	—Y
Côte d'Ivoire	662	—V	—V	—V	—V	.02V	—V	—Y	—	—	.01	.01	.03V	.48V	.59Y
Gabon	646	—Y	—Y	—Y	—Y	—Y	—Y	—Y	—	—	.05	—	—Y	—Y	—Y
Madagascar	674	—V	.01V	—V	—Y	—Y	—Y	—Y	—	—	—	—	—Y	—Y	—Y
Mauritania	682	....	....	....	....	....	....	....	—	—	.09	—	—Y	—Y	—Y
Mauritius	684	.01V	.04V	.03V	.04V	.02V	.02V	.03V	—	—	—	—	—V	.02V	—V
Morocco	686	.04V	—V	—V	—V	—V	—Y	—Y	.05	.08	.05	.04	.90V	1.11Y	1.37Y
Mozambique	688	—V	—V	—Y	—Y	—Y	—Y	—Y	.02	.01	—	—	—Y	—Y	—Y
Niger	692	—V	.01V	—V	—V	—Y	—Y	—Y	....	....	....	....	....	....	....
Nigeria	694	.03V	—V	.02V	.02Y	.03Y	.03Y	.04Y	—	—	—	—	—Y	—Y	—Y
Senegal	722	—V	—V	.03V	—V	—V	—V	—Y	.01	.01	—	—	2.79V	—V	—Y
Sierra Leone	724	....	....	....	....	....	....	....	.27	—	—	—	—Y	—Y	—Y
South Africa	199	—Y	—Y	—Y	—Y	—V	—V	—V	.10	.01	.09	.05	.63V	.39V	1.28V
Tanzania	738	—V	—V	—Y	—Y	—Y	—Y	—Y	—	—	.02	—	—Y	—Y	—Y
Tunisia	744	—V	—V	—V	—V	—V	—V	—Y	—	—	—	.02	—V	—V	—Y
Zimbabwe	698	—V	—V	—V	—V	—V	—V	—Y	.64	1.22	—	—	.01V	—V	—Y
Asia	**507**	**.9Y**	**.9Y**	**1.8Y**	**3.7Y**	**6.7Y**	**8.5Y**	**23.8Y**	**37.1**	**49.0**	**68.0**	**107.2**	**130.5Y**	**177.7Y**	**251.4Y**
Bangladesh	513	—V	—V	—V	—V	—V	—V	—V	.03	—	—	—	—V	—Y	—Y
Cambodia	522	—V	—V	—V	—V	—V	—V	—Y	—	—	—	—	.16V	—V	—Y
China,P.R.: Mainland	924	.02V	—V	.02V	.23V	.25V	1.24V	5.76V	8.86	15.84	15.74	20.77	33.24V	65.75V	89.76V
China,P.R.:Hong Kong	532	.08V	.74V	.35V	.82V	.20V	.82V	.68V	5.84	6.06	6.16	3.52	3.49V	1.94V	3.35V
India	534	—Y	.03V	.34V	.80V	.43V	.53Y	.66Y	4.41	6.04	7.83	6.73	15.72V	19.43Y	24.11Y
Indonesia	536	—V	—V	.01V	.01V	—V	—V	—V	4.21	4.96	3.76	3.69	5.45V	7.33V	9.80V
Korea	542	—V	—V	.04V	.34V	.47V	.01V	.31V	6.06	4.45	5.21	6.53	16.57V	15.31V	56.66V
Malaysia	548	—V	—V	—V	.03V	.04V	.15V	.28V	1.08	4.93	21.08	45.70	39.41V	49.55V	45.56V
Pakistan	564	.05V	—V	—V	.01V	—V	—Y	—Y	.09	.11	.24	.22	2.80V	3.46Y	4.29Y
Philippines	566	.51V	.01V	.15V	—V	.02V	.02V	.01V	.05	.16	.90	1.70	.13V	.05V	.11V
Samoa	862	....	....	....	....	....	....	....	—	—	—	.07	.08Y	.10Y	.13Y
Singapore	576	—V	—V	—V	—V	—V	—V	—V	.31	.30	.23	1.24	—V	—V	—V
Solomon Islands	813	....	....	....	....	....	....	....	—	—	—	.03	.03Y	.04Y	.05Y
Taiwan Province of China	528	.01V	.06V	.05V	1.02V	3.68V	3.94V	5.69V	3.95	3.22	4.97	4.65	7.11V	4.86V	5.94V
Thailand	578	—V	.04V	.07V	.45V	1.57V	1.80V	10.39V	1.94	2.94	1.82	12.26	4.02V	7.44V	9.10V
Vietnam	582	.19V	—V	.76V	—V	—V	—V	—V	.31	.02	.05	.06	—V	—V	—V
Asia n.s.	598	—Y	—Y	—Y	—Y	—Y	—Y	—Y	—	—	—	—	2.28Y	2.41Y	2.53Y
Europe	**170**	**.1Y**	**.1Y**	**.2Y**	**.1Y**	**.1Y**	**.1Y**	**.1Y**	**11.1**	**18.9**	**9.8**	**8.2**	**9.9Y**	**14.3Y**	**11.9Y**
Belarus	913	—Y	—Y	—Y	—Y	—Y	—Y	—V	—	—	—	—	—Y	—Y	.22V
Bulgaria	918	—V	—V	—V	—V	—V	—V	—V	.04	.05	.74	.01	.03V	.70V	.22V
Czech Republic	935	—V	.03V	—V	—V	—V	.01V	.02V	.03	—	—	—	1.10V	1.81V	1.52V
Estonia	939	—V	—V	—V	—V	—V	—V	—V	—	—	—	—	.82V	1.00V	.04V
Georgia	915	—V	—V	—V	—V	—V	—V	—Y	.02	.02	—	—	—V	—V	—Y
Gibraltar	823	—Y	—Y	—Y	—Y	—Y	—Y	—Y	.03	.03	.02	—	—Y	—Y	—Y

	Exports 2001	2002	2003	2004	2005	2006	2007	Imports 2001	2002	2003	2004	2005	2006	2007
	Millions of U.S. Dollars							Millions of U.S. Dollars						
Hungary 944	.01V	—V	.06V	—V	—V	—V	—V	.02	.02	.02	—	.35V	.49V	.49V
Latvia 941	—V	—V	—V	—V	—V	—V	—V	.26	.22	—	—	.01V	.02V	.01V
Lithuania 946	—V	—V	—V	—V	—V	—V	—V	—	—	—	—	—V	.09V	—V
Poland 964	.04V	.09V	.09V	.09V	.01V	—V	.01V	.31	.04	.02	.13	1.06V	1.01V	.44V
Romania 968	—V	—V	—V	—V	.02V	.01V	—V	.02	.02	.16	—	.16V	.12V	.33V
Russia 922	—V	—V	—V	—V	—V	.01V	.01V	.07	.06	.35	—	1.26V	2.61V	1.23V
Slovak Republic 936	.03V	—V	—Y	—Y	—V	—V	—V	.01	.02	—	—	.01V	—V	.02V
Turkey 186	—V	—V	—V	—V	.02V	.04V	.02V	10.22	12.38	8.46	5.50	5.07V	6.47V	7.38V
Ukraine 926	—V	—V	—V	—V	—V	.01Y	.01Y	.03	6.10	—	2.60	—V	—Y	—Y
Middle East 407	**2.0Y**	**2.1Y**	**2.3Y**	**3.0Y**	**3.9Y**	**4.9Y**	**6.3Y**	**3.4**	**3.6**	**2.9**	**2.8**	**8.7Y**	**10.5Y**	**8.0Y**
Egypt 469	—V	—Y	—Y	—Y	—Y	—Y	—Y	.01	.01	.03	.06	.06Y	.08Y	.10Y
Israel 436	—V	—V	—V	—V	—V	—V	—V	2.91	3.57	2.75	2.14	4.62V	8.69V	6.49V
Jordan 439	—V	—V	—V	—V	—V	—V	—V	—	—	—	—	3.31V	.79V	.29V
Kuwait 443	.02Y	.02Y	.02Y	.03Y	.04Y	.05Y	.06Y	—	—	—	—	—Y	—Y	—Y
Lebanon 446	.09Y	.10Y	.12Y	.16Y	.19Y	.23Y	.29Y	.01	.01	.02	.06	.07Y	.08Y	.10Y
Libya 672	1.89Y	1.95Y	2.17Y	2.82Y	3.60Y	4.44Y	5.75Y	—	—	—	—	—Y	—Y	—Y
Saudi Arabia 456	—V	—V	—V	—V	.12V	.15Y	.19Y	.01	.01	.09	.12	.17Y	.21Y	.25Y
United Arab Emirates 466	—V	—V	—V	—Y	—Y	—Y	—Y	.44	—	.02	.37	.50Y	.63Y	.76Y
Yemen, Republic of 474	—V	—V	—Y	.01V	—V	—Y	—Y	—	—	—	—	—Y	—Y	—Y
Western Hemisphere 207	**20.2Y**	**20.7Y**	**27.8Y**	**37.3Y**	**45.7Y**	**59.2Y**	**76.3Y**	**303.8**	**322.2**	**314.9**	**362.2**	**398.1Y**	**539.6Y**	**601.3Y**
Antigua and Barbuda 311	—Y	—Y	—Y	—Y	—Y	—Y	—Y	.07	.04	—	—	—Y	—Y	—Y
Argentina 213	.02V	.01V	.01V	.04V	.02V	.02V	.03V	26.30	15.06	9.59	15.69	12.71V	23.66V	16.08V
Aruba 314	.07V	.08V	.09V	.03V	.01V	.01V	.05V	1.13	.03	—	—	.03V	.08V	.08V
Bahamas, The 313	.01Y	.01Y	.02Y	.02Y	.02Y	.03Y	.04Y	.05	.69	.15	.05	.06Y	.07Y	.09Y
Barbados 316	.18V	—V	.09V	.10V	—V	.08V	.10Y	.25	.29	.18	.40	.98V	1.37V	1.71Y
Belize 339	—Y	—Y	—Y	—Y	—Y	—Y	—Y	—	—	—	.02	.02Y	.02Y	.03Y
Bermuda 319	—Y	—Y	—Y	—Y	—V	.01V	.01Y	1.32	—	—	—	—Y	—Y	—Y
Bolivia 218	.01V	—V	—V	—V	—V	—Y	—Y	—	—	—	—	—Y	—Y	—Y
Brazil 223	.01V	.05V	.16V	.18V	.18V	.33V	—V	24.41	28.92	24.84	27.13	50.54V	72.99V	84.27V
Chile 228	—V	—V	—V	.06V	.05V	.07V	.13V	4.20	4.96	3.19	4.47	6.68V	5.88V	4.49V
Colombia 233	.06V	.01V	.05V	.03V	.42V	.39V	6.13V	25.89	31.57	49.56	42.44	48.82V	74.90V	60.13V
Costa Rica 238	—V	—V	.01V	.03V	.02V	.03Y	.03Y	5.45	7.13	4.76	4.97	6.73V	8.32Y	10.33Y
Dominica 321	.01V	.01Y	.01Y	.01Y	.01Y	.01Y	.02Y	.04	.03	—	.01	.01Y	.01Y	.02Y
Dominican Republic 243	17.32V	18.79Y	23.78Y	31.24Y	35.69Y	44.11Y	54.74Y	6.62	10.03	7.46	5.46	6.23Y	7.70Y	9.56Y
Ecuador 248	.03V	.03V	—V	—V	.01V	—V	—Y	.24	.39	.36	.44	.64V	.78V	.97Y
El Salvador 253	.05V	.10V	.07V	.01V	.84V	.02V	.06V	.28	.42	.32	.27	2.72V	4.23V	2.56V
Guatemala 258	.01V	.07V	.64V	.20V	.23V	.28Y	.35Y	17.97	9.80	9.45	8.46	12.69V	15.69Y	19.47Y
Guyana 336	—Y	—Y	—Y	—Y	—Y	—Y	—Y	.30	.39	2.22	2.61	2.99Y	3.69Y	4.58Y
Honduras 268	.03V	.04V	—V	.07V	.08Y	.10Y	.12Y	4.10	.49	1.49	1.95	2.23Y	2.75Y	3.41Y
Jamaica 343	.01V	.06V	.05V	.09V	.03V	.07V	.13V	1.93	1.60	2.69	2.38	.57V	1.23V	.34V
Mexico 273	1.53V	.38V	1.63V	3.86V	6.49V	11.89V	12.26V	6.28	18.84	5.73	4.80	12.34V	13.33V	14.60V
Netherlands Antilles 353	.02V	.01V	.01V	.01Y	.01Y	.02Y	.02Y	121.73	128.21	139.50	161.47	184.49Y	228.01Y	282.96Y
Nicaragua 278	—V	—V	—V	—V	—V	—V	—V	.01	.01	—	4.34	—V	—V	—V
Panama 283	—V	—V	—V	.01V	.01V	—V	.05V	22.10	19.68	18.25	23.25	4.20V	1.90V	.39V
Paraguay 288	—V	—V	—V	—V	—V	—V	—Y	.03	.03	—	—	—V	—V	—Y
Peru 293	—V	—V	—V	—V	.01V	.02V	.13Y	6.19	11.19	9.91	19.78	24.59V	43.52V	49.13Y
St. Kitts and Nevis 361	.02Y	.02Y	.02Y	.03Y	.03Y	.04Y	.05Y	—	—	.01	—	—Y	—Y	—Y
St. Lucia 362	.02Y	.02Y	.02Y	.03Y	.03Y	.04Y	.05Y	—	—	—	—	—Y	—Y	—Y
St. Vincent & Grens 364	.02V	.02V	.02V	.02V	.02V	.02Y	.03Y	—	—	—	—	—V	—Y	—Y
Suriname 366	—Y	—Y	—Y	—Y	—Y	—Y	—Y	.14	.05	—	.02	.02Y	.03Y	.03Y
Trinidad and Tobago 369	.15V	.14V	.18Y	.23Y	.27Y	.33Y	.41Y	4.92	7.32	6.11	7.71	8.81Y	10.89Y	13.52Y
Uruguay 298	—V	—Y	—V	—V	—V	—Y	—Y	5.18	5.75	.11	.02	2.90V	3.59Y	4.45Y
Venezuela, Rep. Bol 299	.02V	.02V	—V	—V	.09V	.01V	.01V	16.67	19.25	13.96	24.06	6.09V	14.98V	18.07Y
Western Hem. n.s. 399	.66Y	.78Y	.90Y	1.03Y	1.15Y	1.27Y	1.39Y	—	—	5.05	—	—Y	—Y	—Y
Other Countries n.i.e. 910	**—Y**	**—Y**	**—Y**	**—Y**	**—Y**	**—Y**	**—Y**	**11.4**	**8.2**	**12.0**	**8.9**	**10.1Y**	**12.5Y**	**15.6Y**
Cuba 928	—Y	—Y	—Y	—Y	—Y	—Y	—Y	11.43	8.25	11.98	8.88	10.15Y	12.54Y	15.56Y
Memorandum Items														
European Union 998	14.75Y	12.53Y	13.52Y	14.46Y	17.72Y	21.57Y	35.85Y	79.10	71.19	72.62	48.88	150.13Y	220.02Y	146.62Y
Oil Exporting Ctys 999	1.96Y	2.02Y	2.24Y	2.91Y	3.90Y	4.72Y	6.10Y	21.34	24.22	17.87	28.24	12.21Y	23.15Y	28.88Y
Non-Oil Develop.Ctys 201	21.32Y	21.83Y	29.90Y	41.35Y	52.58Y	68.04Y	100.50Y	335.13	370.86	378.05	452.22	539.35Y	720.93Y	846.91Y
PERCENT DISTRIBUTION														
Industrial Countries 101	**92.1**	**91.6**	**91.4**	**89.6**	**89.0**	**87.4**	**82.9**	**50.9**	**46.8**	**45.2**	**45.5**	**63.3**	**60.9**	**53.0**
Developing Countries 202	**7.9**	**8.4**	**8.6**	**10.4**	**11.0**	**12.6**	**17.1**	**47.6**	**52.1**	**53.1**	**53.5**	**36.1**	**38.4**	**46.2**
Africa 607	**—**	**—**	**—**	**—**	**—**	**—**	**—**	**.1**	**.2**	**—**	**—**	**.3**	**.1**	**.2**
Asia 507	**.3**	**.3**	**.5**	**.9**	**1.3**	**1.5**	**3.8**	**5.0**	**6.5**	**9.1**	**11.9**	**8.5**	**9.2**	**13.3**
Europe 170	**—**	**—**	**—**	**—**	**—**	**—**	**—**	**1.5**	**2.5**	**1.3**	**.9**	**.6**	**.7**	**.6**
Middle East 407	**.7**	**.7**	**.6**	**.7**	**.8**	**.8**	**1.0**	**.5**	**.5**	**.4**	**.3**	**.6**	**.5**	**.4**
Western Hemisphere 207	**6.9**	**7.3**	**7.5**	**8.8**	**8.9**	**10.2**	**12.2**	**40.6**	**42.5**	**42.3**	**40.4**	**26.0**	**27.9**	**31.7**
Other Countries n.i.e. 910	**—**	**—**	**—**	**—**	**—**	**—**	**—**	**1.5**	**1.1**	**1.6**	**1.0**	**.7**	**.6**	**.8**
ANNUAL PERCENT CHANGE														
World 001	**-9.5**	**-3.2**	**31.1**	**14.1**	**21.3**	**12.2**	**7.7**	**1.6**	**1.2**	**-1.7**	**20.5**	**70.4**	**26.6**	**-2.0**
Industrial Countries 101	**-11.8**	**-3.7**	**30.8**	**11.9**	**20.5**	**10.2**	**2.2**	**-5.0**	**-6.9**	**-5.0**	**21.2**	**137.1**	**21.9**	**-14.7**
Developing Countries 202	**29.9**	**2.5**	**34.8**	**37.7**	**27.6**	**28.8**	**46.5**	**10.2**	**10.8**	**.2**	**21.4**	**14.8**	**34.9**	**17.7**
Africa 607	**-52.5**	**1.3**	**19.3**	**-18.3**	**19.8**	**-1.4**	**24.0**	**-65.2**	**23.6**	**-72.9**	**-66.5**	**—**	**-54.4**	**63.4**
Asia 507	**872.3**	**1.0**	**101.7**	**108.8**	**79.2**	**27.8**	**179.4**	**-6.1**	**32.1**	**38.6**	**57.6**	**21.8**	**36.1**	**41.5**
Europe 170	**-82.9**	**59.9**	**22.8**	**-34.1**	**-43.1**	**46.0**	**-15.2**	**18.1**	**71.4**	**-48.4**	**-15.6**	**19.8**	**45.1**	**-16.9**
Middle East 407	**—**	**3.7**	**11.9**	**30.4**	**30.3**	**23.5**	**29.3**	**5.9**	**6.3**	**-19.1**	**-5.4**	**217.2**	**20.1**	**-23.8**
Western Hemisphere 207	**33.5**	**2.2**	**34.4**	**34.4**	**22.5**	**29.5**	**29.0**	**13.2**	**6.0**	**-2.3**	**15.0**	**9.9**	**35.6**	**11.4**
Other Countries n.i.e. 910	**10.4**	**8.5**	**26.6**	**31.3**	**14.3**	**23.6**	**24.1**	**-2.5**	**-27.9**	**45.3**	**-25.9**	**14.3**	**23.6**	**24.1**

		Exports							Imports						
		2001	2002	2003	2004	2005	2006	2007	2001	2002	2003	2004	2005	2006	2007
		Millions of U.S. Dollars							Millions of U.S. Dollars						
IFS World Total		**1,263.9**	**1,239.8**	**1,358.6**	**1,640.4**	**1,892.4**	**2,053.9**	**2,120.1**	**3,069.4**	**3,081.9**	**3,447.6**	**4,212.3**	**4,852.5**	**5,694.6**	**6,761.8**
DOTS World Total	**001**	**1,125.9**	**1,177.7**	**1,323.0**	**1,704.7**	**4,890.9Y**	**5,101.4Y**	**5,549.5Y**	**2,956.9**	**2,943.2**	**3,318.9**	**3,984.8**	**6,903.7Y**	**7,777.9Y**	**9,367.0Y**
Industrial Countries	**101**	**786.8**	**820.1**	**901.1**	**1,230.5**	**4,175.4Y**	**4,191.0Y**	**4,425.2Y**	**1,643.1**	**1,553.2**	**1,781.5**	**2,127.2**	**4,212.9Y**	**4,635.6Y**	**5,689.3Y**
United States	111	616.99	587.17	656.68	927.15	3,563.45V	3,539.18V	3,728.45V	1,337.11	1,198.87	1,331.49	1,493.94	3,568.29V	4,062.74V	4,908.42V
Canada	156	29.48	10.21	3.81	9.12	106.78V	104.52V	115.83V	16.84	19.93	22.31	21.09	40.06V	36.09V	52.49V
Australia	193	.83	1.64	1.12	1.24	7.83V	8.48V	9.21V	5.64	12.45	7.97	5.92	4.36V	6.00V	12.13V
Japan	158	24.20	17.11	15.93	14.61	25.84V	26.75V	23.97V	115.57	105.70	128.13	92.94	103.29V	116.02V	161.18V
New Zealand	196	.01	.03	.05	.06	.49V	.65V	.78V	11.55	11.55	10.86	5.20	.51V	2.16V	.64V
Austria	122	.06	1.54	.12	.21	3.18V	1.79V	.99V	3.01	2.83	3.35	4.70	5.46V	4.10V	4.43V
Belgium	124	19.87	23.87	29.81	44.39	94.75V	116.89V	97.85V	13.50	25.04	25.85	33.71	12.17V	11.73V	13.99V
Cyprus	423	—	—	—	—	.07V	.09V	.09V	—	—	—	—	—V	—V	—V
Denmark	128	2.97	3.56	3.18	3.21	3.66V	4.44V	4.01V	1.89	6.84	4.21	5.41	7.65V	6.69V	7.03V
Finland	172	3.28	3.59	3.03	4.65	5.14V	5.65V	5.33V	.70	.11	9.21	113.27	8.63V	24.71V	12.29V
France	132	11.16	12.47	13.04	13.87	47.86V	19.43V	23.17V	22.87	22.24	22.60	25.54	40.97V	25.51V	30.78V
Germany	134	—	57.33	61.89	100.10	125.06V	157.23V	173.99V	—	40.58	53.55	157.81	208.59V	92.16V	140.33V
Greece	174	.01	1.08	—	—	.79V	.02V	.37V	.02	.16	8.76	1.03	1.31V	.70V	.19V
Iceland	176	.02	—	—	—	.22V	.15V	.18V	.04	.12	.04	.16	.01V	.03V	—V
Ireland	178	1.30	1.66	1.10	1.14	1.05V	1.13V	6.45V	1.45	2.60	2.46	1.62	1.40V	.93V	.82V
Italy	136	14.90	11.18	6.89	16.55	29.73V	18.32V	20.87V	17.92	15.94	18.28	22.34	30.14V	54.23V	80.02V
Luxembourg	137	—	—	—	—	—V	—V	.06V	.10	.04	.01	.02	6.88V	.03V	.40V
Malta	181	—	—	—	—	—V	—V	.01V	.02	.12	—	.04	.01V	—V	—V
Netherlands	138	18.98	30.29	31.19	26.07	40.36V	70.42V	71.52V	15.65	15.08	9.61	13.69	29.08V	40.86V	35.50V
Norway	142	.28	.28	1.02	1.40	5.34V	2.70V	2.25V	.16	.50	2.44	1.59	1.22V	1.15V	10.92V
Portugal	182	1.57	2.86	3.05	4.51	6.61V	8.15V	13.67V	.40	.24	.54	.95	2.90V	2.52V	.89V
Slovenia	961	—	—	.05	—	.24V	.38V	.02V	—	—	.04	.02	.08V	.07V	.09V
Spain	184	12.59	33.09	36.72	32.65	47.14V	52.27V	61.52V	55.30	46.26	62.92	68.34	69.47V	70.43V	93.39V
Sweden	144	1.56	4.30	4.68	4.63	8.01V	10.63V	8.64V	5.83	6.01	32.01	30.26	39.43V	43.46V	78.57V
Switzerland	146	.92	1.76	2.75	2.58	12.99V	11.53V	12.32V	7.17	11.14	13.79	14.68	11.90V	17.70V	23.41V
United Kingdom	112	25.77	15.10	25.04	22.39	38.76V	30.18V	43.62V	10.35	8.84	11.15	12.94	19.10V	15.64V	21.39V
Developing Countries	**202**	**324.1**	**347.6**	**409.7**	**462.4**	**702.1Y**	**893.7Y**	**1,103.6Y**	**1,282.4**	**1,376.9**	**1,523.0**	**1,833.1**	**2,662.8Y**	**3,107.7Y**	**3,634.8Y**
Africa	**607**	**.6**	**.5**	**.7**	**.1**	**.8Y**	**.8Y**	**1.0Y**	**4.3**	**3.8**	**4.5**	**9.1**	**10.7Y**	**11.6Y**	**14.7Y**
Algeria	612	—	—	—	—	—Y	—Y	—Y	—	.03	.01	.15	.20Y	.25Y	.30Y
Benin	638	—	—	—	—	—V	—Y	—Y	—	—	—	—	.03V	.04Y	.05Y
Burundi	618	....	....	....	....	....	....	....	—	—	.04	.49	—V	—V	—Y
Cameroon	622	—	—	—	—	—Y	—Y	—Y	.07	—	.01	.29	.34Y	.42Y	.52Y
Cape Verde	624	—	—	—	—	—Y	—Y	—Y	—	.06	—	.18	.21Y	.26Y	.32Y
Central African Rep.	626	....	....	....	....	....	....	....	—	.04	.07	.29	.34Y	.41Y	.51Y
Congo, Republic of	634	.44	—	—	.04	.04Y	.05Y	.06Y	.01	.25	—	.27	.31Y	.38Y	.47Y
Côte d'Ivoire	662	—	—	—	—	—V	—V	—Y	—	—	—	—	1.18V	.01V	.02Y
Ethiopia	644	....	....	....	....	....	....	....	.02	.02	.02	.14	.16Y	.19Y	.24Y
Gambia, The	648	—	—	—	—	—Y	—Y	—Y	—	—	—	.05	.06Y	.07Y	.09Y
Ghana	652	—	.01	—	.02	.02Y	.03Y	.04Y	1.22	.07	—	.04	.04Y	.05Y	.06Y
Guinea	656	—	—	—	—	—Y	—Y	—Y	—	.04	—	.05	.05Y	.07Y	.08Y
Kenya	664	—	.01	—	—	—Y	—Y	—Y	—	.03	.84	.98	1.11Y	1.38Y	1.71Y
Liberia	668	—	—	—	—	—Y	—Y	—Y	2.22	.01	—	.03	.04Y	.05Y	.06Y
Madagascar	674	—	—	—	—	—Y	—Y	.01Y	—	.02	.02	.03	.03Y	.04Y	.05Y
Mauritius	684	—	—	—	—	.02V	.01V	.02V	—	.43	.05	.03	—V	—V	.14V
Morocco	686	.11	.02	.14	.01	—V	—Y	.01Y	.05	.15	.15	1.03	.62V	.76Y	.95Y
Mozambique	688	—	—	—	—	—Y	—Y	—Y	.02	.01	.02	.01	—V	—V	—Y
Nigeria	694	—	—	—	—	—Y	—Y	—Y	.58	1.42	1.95	3.44	4.67Y	5.88Y	7.09Y
Senegal	722	—	.02	.01	—	—V	—V	—Y	—	—	—	.10	.13V	.01V	.02Y
South Africa	199	—	.39	.56	.01	.69V	.63V	.80V	—	1.01	.90	1.19	.93V	.48V	.99V
Sudan	732	—	—	—	—	—V	—V	—V	—	.02	.02	—	—V	—V	—V
Tanzania	738	—	—	—	—	—Y	—Y	—Y	—	.05	.01	—	—Y	—Y	—Y
Togo	742	—	—	—	—	.01V	.01Y	.01Y	—	—	—	—	.02V	.02Y	.03Y
Tunisia	744	—	.02	—	—	—V	.02V	.02Y	.04	.02	—	.04	—V	.50V	.62Y
Uganda	746	—	—	—	—	.02Y	.03Y	.04Y	—	.09	.30	.21	.24Y	.30Y	.37Y
Zambia	754	.09	—	—	—	—V	—V	—V	.04	—	—	.04	—V	—V	—V
Zimbabwe	698	—	—	—	—	—V	—V	—Y	—	—	.06	.04	—V	—V	—Y
Asia	**507**	**9.7**	**5.8**	**13.2**	**18.4**	**50.8Y**	**66.4Y**	**94.5Y**	**146.8**	**96.2**	**128.1**	**185.2**	**478.7Y**	**624.7Y**	**715.5Y**
Afghanistan, I.S. of	512	—	—	.02	—	—Y	—Y	—Y	.06	.14	.34	2.58	2.94Y	3.64Y	4.51Y
Bangladesh	513	.01	—	—	—	—V	—V	—V	.20	.09	.20	1.08	.07V	.09Y	.11Y
Brunei Darussalam	516	—	—	—	—	.02Y	.03Y	.03Y	....	....	....	....	....	....	....
China,P.R.: Mainland	924	.57	.52	2.68	8.47	12.88V	16.93V	14.28V	22.06	23.43	37.54	66.62	147.29V	245.96V	300.20V
China,P.R.:Hong Kong	532	.63	.79	1.28	.69	1.59V	1.89V	2.01V	11.00	13.96	14.16	18.28	59.00V	55.70V	45.76V
China,P.R.:Macao	546	—	—	—	—	.12V	.04V	.05V	—	—	—	—	—V	—V	—V
Fiji	819	—	—	—	—	—Y	—Y	—Y	—	—	—	.23	.27Y	.33Y	.41Y
India	534	.01	.05	.62	3.79	.09V	.11Y	.14Y	7.23	8.89	10.18	13.32	33.88V	41.87Y	51.96Y
Indonesia	536	—	.03	.07	.10	—V	.01V	.14V	3.11	3.70	2.91	3.78	7.03V	6.39V	5.65V
Korea	542	7.62	3.84	6.73	3.55	20.29V	21.08V	53.76V	10.99	16.12	21.82	26.27	131.62V	152.80V	144.74V
Malaysia	548	—	.02	1.02	—	.23V	11.33V	1.04V	2.29	2.33	7.40	13.04	10.58V	9.95V	20.31V
Mongolia	948	—	—	.02	—	—Y	—Y	—Y	—	.01	—	.01	.01Y	.02Y	.02Y

	Exports 2001	Exports 2002	Exports 2003	Exports 2004	Exports 2005	Exports 2006	Exports 2007	Imports 2001	Imports 2002	Imports 2003	Imports 2004	Imports 2005	Imports 2006	Imports 2007
	Millions of U.S. Dollars							*Millions of U.S. Dollars*						
Pakistan 564	—	—	—	.32	.55V	.68Y	.84Y	.48	.81	2.38	1.93	11.08V	13.69Y	16.99Y
Philippines 566	—	.01	—	—	.50V	.07V	.24V	.20	.11	1.43	4.35	2.29V	2.27V	2.40V
Singapore 576	—	—	.01	.01	.07V	.96V	.23V	.42	.37	.32	.60	8.36V	10.68V	6.36V
Sri Lanka 524	—	—	—	.01	.01Y	.01Y	.02Y	.28	.34	.33	.24	.43V	.92V	1.00V
Taiwan Province of China 528	.28	.41	.73	1.39	13.56V	13.09V	20.75V	16.65	20.80	21.36	26.00	36.14V	39.60V	47.45V
Thailand 578	.01	.08	.05	.04	.88V	.15V	.91V	3.00	4.90	7.60	6.72	27.71V	40.77V	67.63V
Vietnam 582	.61	—	—	.03	—V	—V	—V	68.86	.18	.09	.13	—V	—V	—V
Europe 170	**47.6**	**8.4**	**14.9**	**11.7**	**31.9Y**	**17.3Y**	**16.2Y**	**50.7**	**26.9**	**51.4**	**67.1**	**38.5Y**	**63.7Y**	**71.2Y**
Albania 914	—	.09	1.81	.54	.02V	—V	—V	.01	.34	.75	3.12	—V	—V	—V
Armenia 911	—	—	—	—	—Y	.01V	.04V	....	....	....	....	....	....	....
Belarus 913	—	—	—	—	4.45V	.25V	.07V	—	—	—	—	—V	—V	—V
Bulgaria 918	—	.09	—	—	.20V	.08V	.16V	1.32	.91	.87	2.01	.59V	.47V	.50V
Croatia 960	—	.03	.01	.04	.70V	1.05V	1.20V	—	.05	.01	.24	.27V	.01V	.01V
Czech Republic 935	—	.17	.59	.46	2.01V	2.19V	1.32V	.05	.42	1.37	2.09	2.03V	2.32V	3.37V
Estonia 939	—	—	—	—	.01V	—V	—V	—	1.15	.74	2.07	—V	.13V	.01V
Georgia 915	—	—	—	.04	.03V	.10V	.07Y	—	.04	—	.20	—V	—V	—Y
Hungary 944	.07	.10	.68	.12	1.49V	1.30V	2.07V	—	.15	.04	1.23	.15V	.52V	.40V
Kazakhstan 916	—	—	—	—	—Y	—Y	—Y	—	—	—	—	.32Y	.40Y	.50Y
Latvia 941	—	—	—	—	—V	—V	—V	—	—	—	—	.05V	.10V	.16V
Lithuania 946	—	—	—	—	.04V	.02V	.02V	—	—	—	.03	.01V	.02V	.01V
Macedonia, FYR 962	—	—	—	—	.07V	—V	—Y	—	.01	—	.02	—V	—V	—Y
Moldova 921	—	—	—	—	.02V	.03Y	.03Y	....	....	....	....	....	....	....
Poland 964	4.26	4.08	5.03	.37	.77V	1.96V	1.78V	.30	1.08	.50	1.46	2.55V	1.82V	1.53V
Romania 968	1.76	2.08	1.47	4.38	1.56V	2.54V	.62V	2.41	.08	.17	.25	1.08V	.90V	—V
Russia 922	—	.49	.72	1.98	12.55V	1.94V	2.62V	—	10.80	12.16	31.05	13.69V	33.33V	40.92V
Slovak Republic 936	—	—	.01	—	.01V	.09V	.39V	—	.03	.11	.10	1.01V	1.14V	1.30V
Turkey 186	—	1.20	.04	—	4.70V	1.72V	.83V	.13	3.75	2.03	2.52	4.13V	6.94V	3.10V
Ukraine 926	.03	.01	.19	1.71	.93V	1.15Y	1.43Y	.01	7.50	30.89	17.06	8.43V	10.42Y	12.93Y
Europe n.s. 884	41.50	.05	4.32	2.01	2.30Y	2.84Y	3.52Y	46.46	.57	1.75	3.69	4.22Y	5.21Y	6.47Y
Middle East 407	**.9**	**1.2**	**1.4**	**1.3**	**1.9Y**	**2.5Y**	**3.3Y**	**4.0**	**7.1**	**6.1**	**12.4**	**12.5Y**	**16.4Y**	**21.1Y**
Egypt 469	—	—	—	—	—Y	—Y	—Y	—	.80	.19	.15	.17Y	.21Y	.26Y
Iran, I.R. of 429	—	.33	.25	.02	.02Y	.03Y	.03Y	.08	.17	.03	.14	.19Y	.24Y	.29Y
Iraq 433	—	—	—	—	—Y	—Y	—Y	—	.02	.01	.08	.11Y	.13Y	.16Y
Israel 436	.69	.59	.21	1.08	.18V	.18V	.45V	2.84	3.35	4.07	8.54	7.59V	10.23V	13.64V
Jordan 439	.12	.27	.17	—	—V	.09V	.02V	.04	.13	.18	.15	.05V	.04V	—V
Kuwait 443	—	—	.01	—	—Y	—Y	—Y	—	.02	.01	.15	.21Y	.26Y	.32Y
Lebanon 446	—	—	.02	.06	.07Y	.09Y	.11Y	—	.03	.50	.02	.03Y	.03Y	.04Y
Libya 672	—	—	—	—	—Y	—Y	—Y	—	1.71	—	.07	.09Y	.12Y	.14Y
Oman 449	—	—	—	—	.03Y	.04Y	.06Y	—	—	—	—	.01Y	.02Y	.02Y
Qatar 453	—	—	.05	—	.02V	.05V	.07Y	—	—	—	—	—V	—V	—Y
Saudi Arabia 456	.01	.01	—	.03	.96V	1.19Y	1.54Y	.20	.12	.33	.08	.10Y	.13Y	.16Y
Syrian Arab Republic 463	.03	.01	.02	.04	.04Y	.05Y	.06Y	.23	.19	.20	.23	.27Y	.33Y	.41Y
United Arab Emirates 466	.08	—	.70	.06	.08Y	.09Y	.12Y	.59	.55	.62	2.73	3.72Y	4.67Y	5.64Y
Yemen, Republic of 474	—	—	.02	—	.54V	.67Y	.83Y	.01	.01	—	.01	—V	.01Y	.01Y
Western Hemisphere 207	**265.2**	**331.8**	**379.5**	**431.0**	**616.7Y**	**806.8Y**	**988.7Y**	**1,076.6**	**1,243.1**	**1,332.9**	**1,559.3**	**2,122.3Y**	**2,391.3Y**	**2,812.3Y**
Antigua and Barbuda 311	—	.46	.75	1.74	1.99Y	2.46Y	3.06Y	.01	.12	.70	2.28	2.61Y	3.23Y	4.00Y
Argentina 213	.03	.04	.58	1.06	.09V	.08V	.25V	8.68	10.40	14.17	46.25	52.33V	94.26V	67.62V
Aruba 314	—	.52	.17	.40	1.62V	1.86V	2.00V	2.48	1.28	11.68	3.88	.05V	.10V	—V
Bahamas, The 313	.39	.54	.27	.23	.26Y	.32Y	.40Y	.04	3.01	.38	.65	.74Y	.92Y	1.14Y
Barbados 316	2.01	1.93	3.04	1.99	6.84V	5.80V	7.19Y	27.64	3.75	.04	1.56	—V	.04V	.05Y
Belize 339	2.37	2.97	5.85	6.05	6.92Y	8.55Y	10.61Y	.06	.73	.18	.56	.64Y	.79Y	.98Y
Bermuda 319	—	—	—	—	.04V	.19V	.23Y	—	—	—	—	—Y	—Y	—Y
Bolivia 218	—	.01	.03	—	.02V	.03Y	.03Y	.12	.16	.24	.69	.79Y	.98Y	1.21Y
Brazil 223	.92	.51	1.51	1.79	1.88V	2.48V	4.61V	32.69	50.52	76.60	91.92	152.89V	154.74V	144.27V
Chile 228	.91	.67	.52	.63	.87V	1.05V	.50V	17.87	17.45	24.62	61.21	57.53V	53.18V	45.39V
Colombia 233	2.58	5.81	8.87	2.66	5.06V	3.07V	3.44V	30.98	37.19	46.96	51.02	51.06V	47.91V	63.85V
Costa Rica 238	4.85	27.63	32.24	27.68	58.26V	72.01Y	89.36Y	111.35	132.40	142.39	170.87	254.79V	314.90Y	390.78Y
Dominica 321	—	.10	.10	.03	.03Y	.04Y	.05Y	.02	.12	.26	.45	.52Y	.64Y	.79Y
Dominican Republic 243	3.75	6.85	5.70	6.79	7.75Y	9.58Y	11.89Y	4.65	7.86	4.33	9.37	10.71Y	13.24Y	16.42Y
Ecuador 248	.48	.47	.62	.94	.66V	5.24V	6.50Y	13.49	11.11	16.40	21.56	7.76V	18.18V	22.56Y
El Salvador 253	128.52	138.50	130.81	138.71	159.69V	252.38V	271.99V	147.74	148.79	154.75	160.11	524.33V	445.22V	490.27V
Guatemala 258	78.00	77.83	88.91	92.18	142.39V	175.98Y	218.40Y	229.61	236.82	246.50	273.83	433.45V	535.71Y	664.81Y
Haiti 263	2.67	.83	1.80	16.93	19.35Y	23.91Y	29.67Y	.03	.04	—	.08	.09Y	.11Y	.13Y
Jamaica 343	7.97	16.03	13.36	16.77	23.04V	22.99V	12.39V	12.97	6.57	2.21	1.33	.66V	.62V	.73V
Mexico 273	8.93	12.24	30.57	42.08	104.51V	122.93V	183.25V	152.92	186.86	202.33	216.31	263.57V	312.98V	420.64V
Netherlands Antilles 353	.20	.68	.03	.24	.27Y	.33Y	.41Y	61.60	32.58	62.31	96.48	110.24Y	136.25Y	169.08Y
Nicaragua 278	10.12	17.93	34.53	54.43	55.64V	68.77V	94.69V	29.45	34.39	42.04	56.00	74.91V	107.97V	122.34V
Panama 283	3.73	6.87	6.99	8.38	9.06V	13.70V	20.27V	133.27	154.16	121.48	104.19	17.18V	19.70V	23.02V
Paraguay 288	—	—	.02	—	.01V	.03V	.03Y	.09	.14	.15	.20	.08V	.11V	.14Y
Peru 293	.14	.34	.23	.95	.29V	.18V	.25Y	8.28	8.33	9.38	27.02	12.79V	15.26V	21.14Y
St. Kitts and Nevis 361	—	—	—	—	.04Y	.05Y	.06Y	....	....	....	....	....	....	....
St. Lucia 362	—	1.82	1.82	1.46	1.66Y	2.06Y	2.55Y	—	.04	.01	.03	.03Y	.04Y	.05Y
St. Vincent & Grens. 364	—	.91	1.49	.91	1.65V	2.03Y	2.53Y	—	.01	.61	.01	—V	—Y	—Y
Suriname 366	—	.01	.35	.82	.93Y	1.15Y	1.43Y	—	.04	—	—	—Y	—Y	.01Y
Trinidad and Tobago 369	6.60	7.00	6.17	4.36	4.98Y	6.16Y	7.64Y	41.17	77.05	63.88	63.66	72.73Y	89.89Y	111.56Y
Uruguay 298	—	.23	.87	.05	.08V	.10Y	.12Y	9.43	.77	2.52	1.27	.52V	.64Y	.79Y
Venezuela, Rep. Bol. 299	—	2.08	1.28	.71	.77V	1.29V	2.90V	—	80.36	85.76	96.53	19.28V	23.68V	28.57Y

	Exports							Imports						
	2001	2002	2003	2004	2005	2006	2007	2001	2002	2003	2004	2005	2006	2007
	Millions of U.S. Dollars							*Millions of U.S. Dollars*						
Other Countries n.i.e................910	**3.1**	**4.7**	**8.3**	**9.2**	**10.5Y**	**13.0Y**	**16.1Y**	**10.4**	**4.9**	**8.3**	**7.4**	**8.5Y**	**10.5Y**	**13.0Y**
Cuba................928	.11	.51	1.37	1.02	1.17Y	1.44Y	1.79Y	2.58	1.75	2.59	3.75	4.28Y	5.29Y	6.56Y
North Korea................954	2.97	4.24	6.95	8.16	9.33Y	11.53Y	14.30Y	7.80	3.11	5.72	3.70	4.22Y	5.22Y	6.48Y
Countries & Areas n.s..............898	**12.0**	**5.2**	**3.8**	**2.6**	**3.0Y**	**3.7Y**	**4.6Y**	**21.0**	**8.2**	**6.1**	**17.0**	**19.5Y**	**24.1Y**	**29.9Y**
Memorandum Items														
European Union................998	118.38	206.29	226.11	275.34	456.75Y	502.58Y	537.75Y	149.36	195.75	267.29	498.65	489.09Y	399.80Y	526.88Y
Oil Exporting Ctys................999	.09	2.46	2.36	.91	1.88Y	2.70Y	4.85Y	4.56	88.08	91.62	107.15	35.61Y	41.77Y	48.34Y
Non-Oil Develop.Ctys................201	324.02	345.16	407.37	461.49	700.20Y	891.01Y	1,098.79Y	1,277.88	1,288.84	1,431.34	1,725.98	2,627.16Y	3,065.89Y	3,586.49Y
PERCENT DISTRIBUTION														
Industrial Countries................101	**69.9**	**69.6**	**68.1**	**72.2**	**85.4**	**82.2**	**79.7**	**55.6**	**52.8**	**53.7**	**53.4**	**61.0**	**59.6**	**60.7**
Developing Countries................202	**28.8**	**29.5**	**31.0**	**27.1**	**14.4**	**17.5**	**19.9**	**43.4**	**46.8**	**45.9**	**46.0**	**38.6**	**40.0**	**38.8**
Africa................607	**.1**	**—**	**.1**	**—**	**—**	**—**	**—**	**.1**	**.1**	**.1**	**.2**	**.2**	**.1**	**.2**
Asia................507	**.9**	**.5**	**1.0**	**1.1**	**1.0**	**1.3**	**1.7**	**5.0**	**3.3**	**3.9**	**4.6**	**6.9**	**8.0**	**7.6**
Europe................170	**4.2**	**.7**	**1.1**	**.7**	**.7**	**.3**	**.3**	**1.7**	**.9**	**1.5**	**1.7**	**.6**	**.8**	**.8**
Middle East................407	**.1**	**.1**	**.1**	**.1**	**—**	**—**	**.1**	**.1**	**.2**	**.2**	**.3**	**.2**	**.2**	**.2**
Western Hemisphere................207	**23.6**	**28.2**	**28.7**	**25.3**	**12.6**	**15.8**	**17.8**	**36.4**	**42.2**	**40.2**	**39.1**	**30.7**	**30.7**	**30.0**
Other Countries n.i.e................910	**.3**	**.4**	**.6**	**.5**	**.2**	**.3**	**.3**	**.4**	**.2**	**.3**	**.2**	**.1**	**.1**	**.1**
ANNUAL PERCENT CHANGE														
World................001	**–19.8**	**4.6**	**12.3**	**28.9**	**186.9**	**4.3**	**8.8**	**3.6**	**–.5**	**12.8**	**20.1**	**73.2**	**12.7**	**20.4**
Industrial Countries................101	**–16.6**	**4.2**	**9.9**	**36.6**	**239.3**	**.4**	**5.6**	**.2**	**–5.5**	**14.7**	**19.4**	**98.1**	**10.0**	**22.7**
Developing Countries................202	**–27.2**	**7.3**	**17.9**	**12.9**	**51.8**	**27.3**	**23.5**	**7.9**	**7.4**	**10.6**	**20.4**	**45.3**	**16.7**	**17.0**
Africa................607	**64.6**	**–24.8**	**47.7**	**–87.7**	**854.3**	**–4.2**	**26.9**	**302.6**	**–12.3**	**19.0**	**103.8**	**17.3**	**8.1**	**26.8**
Asia................507	**–49.2**	**–40.9**	**129.7**	**39.2**	**175.9**	**30.6**	**42.3**	**16.4**	**–34.5**	**33.2**	**44.6**	**158.5**	**30.5**	**14.5**
Europe................170	**–33.4**	**–82.4**	**77.4**	**–21.7**	**173.4**	**–45.8**	**–6.3**	**25.1**	**–47.0**	**91.3**	**30.6**	**–42.6**	**65.4**	**11.7**
Middle East................407	**–11.7**	**29.6**	**18.9**	**–11.5**	**52.0**	**27.6**	**32.6**	**–6.8**	**77.6**	**–13.3**	**101.2**	**1.5**	**31.0**	**28.4**
Western Hemisphere................207	**–25.0**	**25.1**	**14.4**	**13.6**	**43.1**	**30.8**	**22.5**	**5.9**	**15.5**	**7.2**	**17.0**	**36.1**	**12.7**	**17.6**
Other Countries n.i.e................910	**–20.1**	**53.6**	**75.4**	**10.3**	**14.3**	**23.6**	**24.1**	**1.3**	**–53.1**	**70.6**	**–10.4**	**14.3**	**23.6**	**24.1**

	Exports 2001	Exports 2002	Exports 2003	Exports 2004	Exports 2005	Exports 2006	Exports 2007	Imports 2001	Imports 2002	Imports 2003	Imports 2004	Imports 2005	Imports 2006	Imports 2007
	Millions of U.S. Dollars							Millions of U.S. Dollars						
IFS World Total	**30,530**	**34,512**	**42,532**	**54,892**	**62,179**	**74,216**	**93,985**	**33,724**	**37,787**	**47,602**	**59,637**	**65,783**	**77,206**	**94,397**
DOTS World Total 001	**30,155**	**33,960**	**42,480**	**54,784**	**62,806**	**75,358**	**95,553**	**33,474**	**37,322**	**47,526**	**59,479**	**66,412**	**78,366**	**95,715**
Industrial Countries 101	**24,932**	**27,790**	**34,053**	**42,290**	**45,371**	**50,685**	**62,364**	**23,138**	**24,810**	**30,902**	**41,547**	**42,894**	**48,655**	**58,759**
United States 111	1,495	1,181	1,342	1,649	1,893	2,048	2,232	1,410	1,373	1,524	989	1,095	1,105	1,312
Canada 156	43	63	65	69	88	140	178	68	101	128	84	140	114	127
Australia 193	24	103	51	67	92	127	139	29	21	35	33	19	15	18
Japan 158	169	192	302	322	361	386	403	1,536	1,566	1,981	1,816	2,071	2,031	2,500
New Zealand 196	3	3	6	11	10	13	16	3	4	11	4	2	3	2
Austria 122	2,359	2,406	3,379	3,721	3,525	3,715	4,359	2,479	2,580	2,982	4,956	4,368	4,859	5,830
Belgium 124	982	917	982	1,278	1,342	1,457	1,472	753	717	837	1,203	1,471	1,613	1,904
Cyprus 423	21	7	14	34	57	59	77	1	3	2	11	12	25	41
Denmark 128	154	203	330	403	502	463	688	194	254	299	369	436	478	641
Finland 172	174	227	344	1,191	655	423	451	351	400	473	571	586	568	710
France 132	1,797	1,924	2,414	3,119	3,316	3,722	4,504	1,565	1,798	2,283	2,776	3,264	3,685	4,146
Germany 134	10,843	12,048	14,489	17,210	18,850	22,012	26,886	8,391	9,045	11,663	17,357	18,265	21,176	25,454
Greece 174	117	131	174	328	427	400	779	57	65	74	76	74	78	102
Iceland 176	2	3	6	14	28	15	15	—	2	1	3	2	5	5
Ireland 178	329	144	150	208	185	345	563	186	200	225	225	300	396	466
Italy 136	1,888	1,953	2,478	3,094	3,559	4,211	5,395	2,636	2,814	3,352	3,242	3,224	3,569	4,318
Luxembourg 137	17	19	40	54	36	32	79	24	34	53	83	73	75	113
Malta 181	6	4	5	3	7	6	12	31	26	57	94	169	79	26
Netherlands 138	1,367	1,437	1,731	2,009	2,418	2,294	2,769	686	767	1,023	2,940	2,875	3,372	4,114
Norway 142	51	59	110	187	182	198	258	45	56	70	52	43	23	51
Portugal 182	193	217	263	335	381	434	658	112	116	141	101	126	167	193
Slovenia 961	306	300	350	540	734	778	1,049	168	206	278	436	363	467	875
Spain 184	621	810	1,158	1,579	2,004	2,529	2,977	611	685	917	830	917	1,088	1,451
Sweden 144	298	1,474	1,385	1,443	837	823	1,051	347	435	558	758	746	1,115	1,302
Switzerland 146	377	381	556	623	718	727	1,070	467	481	649	963	604	660	678
United Kingdom 112	1,295	1,586	1,931	2,796	3,163	3,330	4,281	987	1,062	1,289	1,576	1,648	1,889	2,381
Developing Countries 202	**5,221**	**6,168**	**8,425**	**12,493**	**17,434**	**24,648**	**33,179**	**10,335**	**12,510**	**16,622**	**17,930**	**23,517**	**29,711**	**36,955**
Africa 607	**79**	**140**	**222**	**243**	**532**	**791**	**989**	**135**	**131**	**126**	**39**	**61**	**44**	**68**
Algeria 612	11	15	25	22	49	72	62	—	—	—	—	—	—	—
Angola 614	—	—	1	1	4	5	5	—	—	—	—	—	—	—
Benin 638	—	—	1	—	1	2	6	—	—	—	—	—	—	—
Botswana 616	—	—	1	2	4	4	2	2	4	3	—	—	—	—
Burkina Faso 748	—	—	—	—	—	1	—	—	—	—	—	—	—	—
Burundi 618	—	—	—	—	—	—	—	1	—	1	—	—	—	—
Cameroon 622	—	1	3	1	2	2	2	1	2	2	1	1	1	—
Chad 628	—	2	—	—	—	—	—	—	—	—	—	—	—	—
Congo, Dem. Rep. of 636	—	—	—	—	1	1	2	—	—	—	—	—	—	—
Congo, Republic of 634	—	—	1	—	—	1	1	—	—	—	—	—	—	—
Côte d'Ivoire 662	—	1	1	1	2	2	6	5	7	7	4	6	5	6
Djibouti 611	—	—	—	—	1	2	8	—	—	—	—	—	—	—
Ethiopia 644	2	2	2	2	1	1	1	—	1	2	1	1	1	1
Gabon 646	—	—	—	1	1	1	1	—	—	—	—	—	—	—
Gambia, The 648	—	—	—	—	—	—	1	—	—	—	—	—	—	—
Ghana 652	1	2	7	5	19	10	14	—	1	1	—	—	—	—
Guinea 656	—	—	—	—	—	—	1	2	—	2	1	—	—	—
Kenya 664	1	2	3	4	5	15	37	1	—	1	—	—	—	1
Liberia 668	—	1	—	—	—	1	1	—	—	—	—	—	—	—
Madagascar 674	—	—	—	—	—	1	2	—	—	1	—	—	—	—
Malawi 676	—	—	—	1	—	1	1	7	5	5	1	1	1	1
Mali 678	—	—	—	—	—	—	—	—	1	1	—	—	—	—
Mauritania 682	1	—	—	—	—	1	2	—	—	—	—	—	—	—
Mauritius 684	1	2	8	15	54	78	16	—	—	—	2	1	2	1
Morocco 686	10	13	16	16	46	61	73	12	16	17	3	6	3	5
Mozambique 688	—	—	—	—	1	2	3	—	—	—	—	—	—	1
Namibia 728	—	—	—	—	—	—	1	—	—	—	—	—	—	—
Nigeria 694	6	15	16	6	38	152	194	—	1	—	—	—	—	—
Rwanda 714	—	—	—	—	—	—	2	—	—	—	—	1	—	1
Senegal 722	1	2	1	1	1	3	3	—	2	—	—	—	—	—
Seychelles 718	1	2	8	3	4	3	6	1	—	—	6	3	1	—
Sierra Leone 724	1	—	—	—	1	4	5	—	—	—	—	—	—	—
Somalia 726	—	—	—	—	—	2	—	—	—	—	—	—	—	—
South Africa 199	31	62	98	134	253	275	398	69	58	52	9	16	19	34
Sudan 732	—	1	3	—	1	3	24	1	—	—	—	—	—	—
Tanzania 738	—	—	—	—	1	2	19	4	3	5	3	17	2	3
Togo 742	—	—	—	—	1	1	2	—	—	—	—	—	—	—
Tunisia 744	9	14	25	23	34	56	53	19	20	16	1	2	4	6
Uganda 746	—	1	1	2	5	23	31	7	7	7	4	4	3	3
Zambia 754	—	—	—	—	1	2	3	—	—	—	—	—	—	—
Zimbabwe 698	—	—	—	—	—	—	1	2	2	2	1	1	1	6

	Exports							Imports						
	2001	2002	2003	2004	2005	2006	2007	2001	2002	2003	2004	2005	2006	2007
	Millions of U.S. Dollars							*Millions of U.S. Dollars*						
Asia.......... 507	**564**	**668**	**526**	**897**	**1,144**	**1,825**	**2,135**	**4,036**	**5,505**	**7,319**	**6,582**	**8,553**	**10,022**	**13,762**
Afghanistan, I.S. of.......... 512	—	—	3	3	3	6	7	—	—	—	—	—	—	—
American Samoa.......... 859	—	—	—	—	1	—	—	—	—	—	—	—	—	—
Bangladesh.......... 513	4	3	4	4	15	3	4	8	9	13	7	8	13	5
Brunei Darussalam.......... 516	—	—	—	—	—	—	—	—	—	—	—	5	1	—
Cambodia.......... 522	—	—	—	—	—	—	—	—	1	1	—	—	1	—
China,P.R.: Mainland.......... 924	110	153	177	390	409	774	1,030	1,318	2,079	3,285	2,872	4,737	5,423	7,427
China,P.R.:Hong Kong.......... 532	35	38	53	79	121	138	172	123	207	298	660	101	85	93
China,P.R.:Macao.......... 546	—	—	—	—	2	—	2	1	2	3	1	2	8	1
India.......... 534	26	25	35	35	45	133	102	69	79	130	120	117	149	303
Indonesia.......... 536	9	12	16	11	16	14	21	124	160	200	115	141	153	151
Korea.......... 542	36	53	40	99	128	205	259	414	587	1,018	901	1,252	1,450	2,088
Lao People's Dem.Rep.......... 544	—	—	—	—	—	—	—	1	1	1	—	—	—	—
Malaysia.......... 548	52	69	20	36	42	36	50	477	612	693	618	543	456	502
Mongolia.......... 948	2	2	3	5	3	3	4	—	—	—	—	9	—	—
Myanmar.......... 518	—	3	—	—	—	—	—	1	1	1	—	1	—	—
Pakistan.......... 564	7	22	30	46	130	200	153	17	21	25	21	18	23	22
Philippines.......... 566	55	33	33	23	25	15	15	189	431	199	94	226	378	365
Singapore.......... 576	148	119	45	57	88	134	179	516	437	366	530	455	457	492
Sri Lanka.......... 524	1	2	1	2	2	2	2	5	5	8	3	3	3	3
Taiwan Province of China.......... 528	47	40	25	63	58	56	54	479	580	744	485	677	1,097	1,828
Thailand.......... 578	16	28	22	20	34	76	49	260	254	286	133	235	297	421
Tuvalu.......... 869	—	49	—	—	—	—	—	—	—	—	—	—	—	—
Vietnam.......... 582	15	17	19	21	22	28	32	34	37	47	21	24	30	60
Europe.......... 170	**4,112**	**4,736**	**6,667**	**9,954**	**13,990**	**19,970**	**27,674**	**5,656**	**6,345**	**8,517**	**10,961**	**14,452**	**19,220**	**22,501**
Albania.......... 914	9	8	12	19	32	56	55	—	—	—	—	1	—	—
Armenia.......... 911	2	2	3	5	7	8	12	—	—	—	—	—	—	1
Azerbaijan.......... 912	4	3	6	10	16	29	46	—	—	—	—	—	—	—
Belarus.......... 913	23	23	35	52	95	136	156	100	94	119	153	143	111	156
Bosnia & Herzegovina.......... 963	210	231	283	270	289	284	371	5	9	23	79	129	160	197
Bulgaria.......... 918	105	125	157	275	406	584	816	42	45	69	91	108	153	129
Croatia.......... 960	225	307	424	703	897	1,125	1,423	60	78	77	133	140	184	288
Czech Republic.......... 935	547	643	867	1,821	1,915	2,557	3,607	710	868	1,144	1,753	1,891	2,405	3,376
Estonia.......... 939	30	25	46	77	83	119	139	19	43	56	90	141	108	55
Georgia.......... 915	6	6	7	10	16	24	33	—	—	—	—	—	—	2
Gibraltar.......... 823	—	1	1	—	—	1	1	—	—	—	1	—	—	1
Kazakhstan.......... 916	27	33	38	69	101	161	280	14	25	31	58	66	59	127
Kosovo.......... 967	—	—	—	—	3	13	18	—	—	—	—	—	—	—
Kyrgyz Republic.......... 917	2	1	2	3	3	6	9	1	1	—	—	—	—	—
Latvia.......... 941	31	30	36	61	86	107	248	4	5	8	15	14	12	21
Lithuania.......... 946	58	58	77	104	150	202	257	13	24	48	41	39	44	63
Macedonia, FYR.......... 962	37	45	50	72	78	99	162	4	2	3	3	3	8	9
Moldova.......... 921	21	19	22	35	60	50	72	4	2	3	12	14	11	19
Montenegro, Rep. of.......... 943	—	—	—	—	—	25	25	—	—	—	—	—	26	120
Poland.......... 964	601	717	953	1,529	2,037	3,048	3,982	774	946	1,321	1,947	2,503	3,322	3,765
Romania.......... 968	754	775	1,104	1,745	2,372	3,109	4,323	361	426	600	902	1,329	2,166	2,068
Russia.......... 922	465	444	651	908	1,167	2,042	3,072	2,367	2,280	2,958	3,387	4,931	6,429	6,578
Serbia, Rep. of.......... 942	—	—	—	—	—	732	1,197	—	—	—	—	—	183	316
Serbia & Montenegro.......... 965	192	221	313	—	623	—	—	56	67	75	—	149	—	—
Slovak Republic.......... 936	405	493	843	1,045	1,791	2,925	4,004	601	677	929	1,179	1,491	2,124	2,895
Tajikistan.......... 923	1	1	3	1	1	7	9	41	72	81	36	3	2	5
Turkey.......... 186	146	260	289	506	926	1,163	1,410	180	242	376	352	458	498	585
Turkmenistan.......... 925	1	1	1	2	3	11	17	—	—	—	62	330	175	—
Ukraine.......... 926	204	262	438	613	825	1,342	1,926	294	435	589	645	549	886	1,330
Uzbekistan.......... 927	6	4	9	15	10	19	23	8	5	7	22	19	155	394
Middle East.......... 407	**301**	**440**	**840**	**1,137**	**1,461**	**1,712**	**1,963**	**108**	**87**	**112**	**107**	**120**	**142**	**304**
Bahrain.......... 419	1	3	7	11	14	31	26	—	—	—	—	—	5	14
Egypt.......... 469	26	23	41	62	112	189	274	4	6	8	5	9	8	10
Iran, I.R. of.......... 429	46	41	16	20	78	51	31	6	8	8	7	4	4	5
Iraq.......... 433	3	3	6	14	115	76	117	—	—	—	—	—	—	—
Israel.......... 436	85	80	100	154	168	386	260	92	68	83	84	84	99	116
Jordan.......... 439	6	12	19	46	55	88	172	—	—	2	—	3	3	4
Kuwait.......... 443	18	9	26	40	31	50	78	—	—	—	—	—	—	—
Lebanon.......... 446	15	18	19	47	34	21	47	1	—	—	3	1	1	2
Libya.......... 672	5	3	5	3	19	39	25	—	—	1	—	—	—	34
Oman.......... 449	2	4	7	6	8	7	27	—	—	—	—	—	—	—
Qatar.......... 453	1	5	3	9	14	16	33	—	—	—	—	—	—	—
Saudi Arabia.......... 456	39	84	99	109	198	240	277	2	3	4	1	1	—	1
Syrian Arab Republic.......... 463	19	20	24	21	58	47	59	1	1	1	3	6	3	89
United Arab Emirates.......... 466	32	132	462	590	556	456	533	1	1	4	5	12	17	28
Yemen, Republic of.......... 474	2	4	7	5	3	16	5	—	—	—	—	—	—	—
Western Hemisphere.......... 207	**165**	**185**	**169**	**262**	**307**	**349**	**419**	**400**	**443**	**548**	**241**	**332**	**282**	**321**
Antigua and Barbuda.......... 311	—	—	—	—	—	—	—	—	1	1	—	3	—	—
Argentina.......... 213	8	3	8	9	11	15	27	21	30	27	17	13	16	17
Bahamas, The.......... 313	1	1	—	—	—	—	—	—	—	1	3	—	—	—
Barbados.......... 316	—	—	—	—	1	—	1	—	—	—	—	—	—	—
Belize.......... 339	—	—	—	1	—	—	—	—	—	1	2	—	—	—

	Exports							Imports						
	2001	2002	2003	2004	2005	2006	2007	2001	2002	2003	2004	2005	2006	2007
	Millions of U.S. Dollars							Millions of U.S. Dollars						
Bermuda....319	1	1	5	6	—	—	—	—	—	—	—	—	—	—
Bolivia....218	—	—	—	—	—	4	8	—	—	—	—	—	—	—
Brazil....223	55	51	64	98	92	88	91	226	231	277	140	215	138	139
Chile....228	3	3	6	6	8	10	13	2	4	4	2	3	2	3
Colombia....233	2	2	3	5	6	8	11	3	5	13	4	9	3	3
Costa Rica....238	—	1	—	1	3	1	2	2	20	62	3	13	7	5
Dominica....321	—	—	1	—	—	—	—	—	—	—	—	—	—	—
Dominican Republic....243	1	1	1	1	2	1	2	—	—	1	—	—	—	—
Ecuador....248	1	2	1	—	—	1	1	5	12	14	2	5	1	1
Falkland Islands....323	—	—	—	—	—	—	—	—	—	—	1	—	—	—
Guatemala....258	—	—	—	1	1	1	2	1	—	—	—	—	—	—
Haiti....263	—	—	1	—	—	—	—	—	—	—	—	—	—	—
Honduras....268	—	—	—	—	—	—	—	1	1	2	1	2	1	2
Jamaica....343	3	2	3	4	4	4	6	—	—	—	1	—	—	—
Mexico....273	81	108	67	120	169	196	227	120	119	125	57	65	110	143
Netherlands Antilles....353	1	1	—	—	1	1	2	—	—	—	1	—	—	—
Panama....283	1	1	1	1	1	2	2	1	3	5	2	—	—	—
Paraguay....288	—	—	—	1	—	—	—	1	—	—	—	—	—	—
Peru....293	1	6	2	2	2	3	9	17	14	12	2	1	2	2
St. Kitts and Nevis....361	—	—	—	—	—	—	—	—	—	—	2	—	—	—
Trinidad and Tobago....369	—	—	1	1	1	1	3	—	—	—	—	—	—	—
Uruguay....298	1	1	1	1	1	2	2	—	1	1	1	—	—	—
Venezuela, Rep. Bol....299	4	3	3	4	3	6	8	—	—	—	—	1	1	3
Western Hem. n.s....399	—	—	—	—	1	2	1	—	—	—	—	—	—	1
Other Countries n.i.e....910	**1**	**—**	**1**	**1**	**1**	**1**	**4**	**1**	**1**	**2**	**1**	**—**	**—**	**1**
Cuba....928	—	—	1	1	—	1	1	—	—	—	—	—	—	—
North Korea....954	—	—	—	—	—	—	3	—	1	2	—	—	—	—
Countries & Areas n.s....898	**—**	**—**	**—**	**—**	**—**	**24**	**5**	**—**	**—**	**—**	**—**	**—**	**—**	**—**
Memorandum Items														
European Union....998	24,440	27,771	34,438	43,984	48,060	55,988	70,289	21,699	23,770	30,010	42,628	44,997	52,713	64,244
Oil Exporting Ctys....999	175	325	684	834	1,123	1,178	1,406	134	174	218	128	159	176	224
Non-Oil Develop.Ctys....201	5,046	5,843	7,740	11,658	16,310	23,471	31,774	10,201	12,337	16,404	17,802	23,358	29,535	36,732
PERCENT DISTRIBUTION														
Industrial Countries....101	**82.7**	**81.8**	**80.2**	**77.2**	**72.2**	**67.3**	**65.3**	**69.1**	**66.5**	**65.0**	**69.9**	**64.6**	**62.1**	**61.4**
Developing Countries....202	**17.3**	**18.2**	**19.8**	**22.8**	**27.8**	**32.7**	**34.7**	**30.9**	**33.5**	**35.0**	**30.1**	**35.4**	**37.9**	**38.6**
Africa....607	**.3**	**.4**	**.5**	**.4**	**.8**	**1.0**	**1.0**	**.4**	**.4**	**.3**	**.1**	**.1**	**.1**	**.1**
Asia....507	**1.9**	**2.0**	**1.2**	**1.6**	**1.8**	**2.4**	**2.2**	**12.1**	**14.7**	**15.4**	**11.1**	**12.9**	**12.8**	**14.4**
Europe....170	**13.6**	**13.9**	**15.7**	**18.2**	**22.3**	**26.5**	**29.0**	**16.9**	**17.0**	**17.9**	**18.4**	**21.8**	**24.5**	**23.5**
Middle East....407	**1.0**	**1.3**	**2.0**	**2.1**	**2.3**	**2.3**	**2.1**	**.3**	**.2**	**.2**	**.2**	**.2**	**.2**	**.3**
Western Hemisphere....207	**.5**	**.5**	**.4**	**.5**	**.5**	**.5**	**.4**	**1.2**	**1.2**	**1.2**	**.4**	**.5**	**.4**	**.3**
ANNUAL PERCENT CHANGE														
World....001	**7.4**	**12.6**	**25.1**	**29.0**	**14.6**	**20.0**	**26.8**	**4.0**	**11.5**	**27.3**	**25.1**	**11.7**	**18.0**	**22.1**
Industrial Countries....101	**6.1**	**11.5**	**22.5**	**24.2**	**7.3**	**11.7**	**23.0**	**3.0**	**7.2**	**24.6**	**34.4**	**3.2**	**13.4**	**20.8**
Developing Countries....202	**13.7**	**18.1**	**36.6**	**48.3**	**39.6**	**41.4**	**34.6**	**7.5**	**21.0**	**32.9**	**7.9**	**31.2**	**26.3**	**24.4**
Africa....607	**5.3**	**77.0**	**58.2**	**9.4**	**119.2**	**48.6**	**25.0**	**12.7**	**–2.9**	**–4.3**	**–69.2**	**58.6**	**–28.3**	**55.5**
Asia....507	**3.6**	**18.5**	**–21.2**	**70.4**	**27.6**	**59.5**	**17.0**	**13.5**	**36.4**	**33.0**	**–10.1**	**29.9**	**17.2**	**37.3**
Europe....170	**14.8**	**15.2**	**40.8**	**49.3**	**40.5**	**42.8**	**38.6**	**4.2**	**12.2**	**34.2**	**28.7**	**31.9**	**33.0**	**17.1**
Middle East....407	**30.1**	**46.0**	**91.0**	**35.4**	**28.5**	**17.2**	**14.7**	**24.5**	**–19.6**	**29.0**	**–4.4**	**11.6**	**18.4**	**114.8**
Western Hemisphere....207	**4.7**	**11.9**	**–8.4**	**55.1**	**16.9**	**13.9**	**19.9**	**–5.3**	**10.6**	**23.9**	**–56.0**	**37.4**	**–14.8**	**13.5**
Other Countries n.i.e....910	**–34.7**	**–39.2**	**100.0**	**20.9**	**–34.6**	**52.7**	**329.2**	**–65.6**	**120.5**	**70.2**	**–72.2**	**–21.3**	**–21.2**	**42.8**

		Exports							Imports						
		2001	2002	2003	2004	2005	2006	2007	2001	2002	2003	2004	2005	2006	2007
		Millions of U.S. Dollars							*Millions of U.S. Dollars*						
IFS World Total		**2,021.8**	**2,227.3**	**2,385.4**	**2,895.9**	**2,942.4**	**3,239.2**	**4,349.6**	**2,253.3**	**2,273.7**	**2,789.1**	**3,553.0**	**4,556.6**	**5,083.4**	**6,105.5**
DOTS World Total	**001**	**2,015.7**	**2,231.2**	**2,396.9**	**2,877.0**	**2,980.9**	**3,453.3**	**4,783.5**	**2,275.2**	**2,275.1**	**2,829.0**	**3,707.1**	**4,848.0**	**6,140.3**	**6,630.0**
Industrial Countries	**101**	**1,858.4**	**2,052.4**	**2,211.9**	**2,613.6**	**2,662.5**	**3,049.9**	**4,308.9**	**1,881.7**	**1,814.3**	**2,233.0**	**3,025.7**	**3,872.1**	**4,977.6**	**5,362.1**
United States	111	212.35	242.57	236.32	267.75	241.19	372.01	346.83	259.63	247.10	211.67	373.78	440.44	783.21	905.66
Canada	156	21.47	18.71	18.01	24.95	30.85	19.68	23.07	22.99	17.91	24.02	42.42	75.13	175.05	117.85
Australia	193	2.26	4.74	3.07	7.67	4.01	3.84	4.72	63.57	66.11	33.62	16.44	5.11	6.93	50.43
Japan	158	69.63	74.61	77.42	85.63	99.23	70.54	206.34	75.23	71.44	107.99	142.50	225.83	251.95	245.48
New Zealand	196	1.26	.88	1.42	2.12	.76	.55	2.13	.95	1.23	1.36	1.91	2.08	3.44	3.15
Austria	122	2.76	2.43	3.52	5.25	8.26	7.07	11.75	14.01	12.32	17.60	21.84	32.09	35.67	45.33
Belgium	124	28.52	34.36	41.98	52.40	65.12	67.44	78.28	42.19	41.04	62.43	65.63	78.58	94.32	105.67
Cyprus	423	.16	1.66	2.04	.36	.93	.70	.63	.07	.11	9.55	.22	.41	2.12	4.09
Denmark	128	83.87	103.23	121.18	137.16	128.26	121.16	157.84	196.02	194.17	227.07	282.53	354.79	373.73	497.23
Finland	172	13.88	19.58	17.38	14.51	12.31	11.24	16.84	38.30	39.11	41.88	53.55	66.21	84.04	96.45
France	132	78.77	81.29	96.28	116.97	107.26	117.17	122.97	71.74	70.50	90.57	112.52	169.31	239.54	191.30
Germany	134	302.15	412.08	415.55	498.83	488.85	517.18	638.11	276.80	243.12	334.69	467.26	647.96	753.99	809.19
Greece	174	12.31	16.24	27.43	39.87	21.49	31.65	29.86	1.31	1.39	1.58	17.77	3.71	2.19	2.98
Ireland	178	2.86	3.57	4.41	4.95	33.61	17.16	368.50	25.65	30.99	66.92	94.83	96.28	120.55	79.25
Italy	136	25.77	29.75	32.38	31.32	30.02	25.79	31.58	69.62	68.47	132.02	145.60	180.13	199.65	228.56
Luxembourg	137	.57	.71	.71	2.64	1.08	1.11	1.45	2.41	2.24	2.73	9.23	11.40	105.46	10.88
Malta	181	.32	.16	1.10	2.57	3.85	2.85	2.06	.28	1.06	1.00	3.46	4.07	5.34	1.66
Netherlands	138	221.49	253.55	269.01	308.45	386.48	570.20	1,016.64	149.91	137.55	174.31	212.02	240.23	297.29	374.71
Norway	142	103.99	93.03	109.16	86.46	82.28	137.23	182.80	178.34	182.96	196.57	353.69	347.12	434.19	306.26
Portugal	182	112.02	96.05	90.14	95.87	82.49	76.89	117.58	12.62	11.12	13.35	12.63	18.95	24.61	15.87
Slovenia	961	.16	.10	.11	.23	.48	.21	.53	2.90	2.74	2.95	6.22	7.20	13.31	15.35
Spain	184	108.41	115.70	150.50	200.60	229.61	220.28	221.29	44.34	41.82	51.48	61.68	65.84	82.98	89.72
Sweden	144	21.45	23.61	30.56	31.88	33.23	31.51	34.19	130.69	135.14	182.90	232.30	418.81	426.34	674.37
Switzerland	146	64.89	32.89	46.09	45.51	38.75	84.75	60.49	31.54	24.97	34.16	42.07	92.65	138.01	131.72
United Kingdom	112	367.11	390.91	416.15	549.67	532.11	541.66	632.48	170.52	169.72	210.58	253.63	287.76	323.72	358.96
Developing Countries	**202**	**157.2**	**178.7**	**184.8**	**263.3**	**318.2**	**403.3**	**474.6**	**393.5**	**460.7**	**595.8**	**681.3**	**975.8**	**1,162.6**	**1,267.6**
Africa	**607**	**36.6**	**44.1**	**43.7**	**54.3**	**56.6**	**59.4**	**65.5**	**4.5**	**5.4**	**6.5**	**17.3**	**19.4**	**26.8**	**29.7**
Algeria	612	.33	—	—	—	—	—	—	.01	—	.01	.01	.01	.02	—
Botswana	616	—	—	—	—	—	—	.05	—	—	—	—	—	—	—
Burkina Faso	748	—	.91	—	—	—	—	—	—	—	.01	—	—	.01	.02
Cameroon	622	—	—	—	—	—	—	—	.04	.03	.03	.04	.22	—	.02
Central African Rep.	626	—	—	—	—	—	.01	.01	—	—	—	—	—	.01	—
Congo, Republic of	634	—	—	—	—	—	—	.01	—	—	.04	.48	.35	.04	—
Côte d'Ivoire	662	—	—	.01	—	.01	.01	.19	.07	.11	.08	.05	.03	.07	.11
Djibouti	611	—	.08	.07	—	—	—	—	—	—	—	.03	—	—	—
Equatorial Guinea	642	—	—	—	—	—	—	—	—	—	—	6.45	—	2.98	—
Eritrea	643	—	.02	—	.03	—	—	.01	—	—	—	—	—	—	—
Ethiopia	644	—	—	—	—	—	—	—	.03	.04	.03	.06	.04	.17	.22
Gabon	646	.02	.07	.13	.13	.06	—	—	—	—	—	—	—	.01	.18
Gambia, The	648	—	—	—	—	.03	—	.01	—	—	—	—	—	—	—
Ghana	652	—	—	.04	—	.05	—	.03	.05	.02	.08	.05	.26	.18	.47
Kenya	664	—	—	—	.01	.02	.03	.02	.06	.13	.20	.21	.38	.32	.40
Liberia	668	—	—	—	—	—	.04	—	—	.01	—	—	6.32	4.91	—
Madagascar	674	—	.01	.01	.01	.04	—	—	.03	.03	.02	.04	.05	.07	.08
Malawi	676	—	—	—	—	—	—	—	—	.01	—	—	—	.01	.04
Mali	678	—	—	—	—	—	—	—	—	.01	—	—	—	—	.08
Mauritania	682	—	—	—	—	.03	—	.67	.01	.02	.03	.02	.02	.03	.03
Mauritius	684	.01	—	—	.04	.01	—	—	.14	.15	.23	.29	.38	.40	.49
Morocco	686	2.88	.23	.09	1.05	.21	1.02	2.29	.90	1.16	1.59	1.74	2.01	3.32	3.41
Mozambique	688	—	.02	—	—	—	—	.01	—	—	—	—	.03	—	—
Namibia	728	3.93	3.84	.87	.46	.54	1.21	.94	—	.10	—	.03	.05	.05	.10
Niger	692	—	—	—	—	.05	.01	—	—	—	—	—	—	—	—
Nigeria	694	23.19	33.40	38.92	49.52	51.24	54.57	58.18	—	—	—	.01	.01	.01	.02
Rwanda	714	—	—	—	—	—	—	—	.03	—	—	—	—	—	—
St. Helena	856	—	—	—	—	—	—	—	—	—	—	—	.02	.01	—
São Tomé & Príncipe	716	—	—	—	—	—	—	—	—	—	—	—	—	—	.01
Senegal	722	—	.02	.03	.04	—	—	.11	.01	—	.01	.02	.04	.05	.03
Seychelles	718	—	.05	.78	.40	.01	.01	.02	—	—	—	—	.08	—	—
Sierra Leone	724	—	—	—	.01	.02	—	—	—	—	—	—	—	—	—
South Africa	199	6.23	4.32	2.03	2.46	3.59	2.32	2.96	2.12	2.45	2.86	4.51	4.04	9.54	16.62
Sudan	732	—	—	—	—	—	.02	—	.12	.13	.14	.33	.71	.28	.33
Swaziland	734	—	—	—	—	—	—	—	—	—	—	.06	.01	—	—
Tanzania	738	.02	.07	.05	.06	.09	.06	—	.03	.08	.14	.10	.24	.08	.02
Tunisia	744	—	—	—	.10	.01	—	.01	.74	.82	.95	2.29	3.97	3.66	6.79
Uganda	746	—	1.11	.68	—	.63	.02	—	.04	.02	.01	—	.05	.10	.09
Zambia	754	—	—	—	—	—	—	—	.02	.03	.03	.04	—	—	.02
Zimbabwe	698	—	—	—	—	—	—	—	.07	.06	.04	.04	.05	.10	.11
Africa n.s.	799	—	—	—	—	—	—	—	—	—	—	.41	—	.36	—
Asia	**507**	**32.9**	**42.5**	**45.1**	**46.7**	**50.3**	**64.7**	**73.7**	**142.2**	**168.8**	**217.0**	**268.6**	**424.7**	**503.2**	**555.8**
Afghanistan, I.S. of	512	—	—	—	—	—	—	—	.01	—	—	—	.01	—	—
American Samoa	859	—	—	—	—	—	.01	—	—	—	—	—	—	—	—
Bangladesh	513	.01	.01	.01	.05	—	.07	.04	1.42	1.52	2.50	3.05	2.66	3.47	3.31

	Exports							Imports						
	2001	2002	2003	2004	2005	2006	2007	2001	2002	2003	2004	2005	2006	2007
	Millions of U.S. Dollars							*Millions of U.S. Dollars*						
Brunei Darussalam........ 516	—	—	—	—	—	.06	—	—	—	—	—	—	—	—
Cambodia........ 522	—	—	—	—	—	.01	—	.17	.19	.25	.44	.58	.70	.74
China,P.R.: Mainland........ 924	8.98	14.48	17.47	15.87	26.87	38.75	37.43	63.97	66.28	101.11	140.28	255.14	323.63	338.61
China,P.R.:Hong Kong........ 532	.77	1.88	2.47	2.54	3.07	8.51	6.30	7.45	7.56	7.81	8.49	11.14	14.68	23.59
China,P.R.:Macao........ 546	—	—	—	—	—	—	.01	.53	.32	.29	.47	.37	.63	.70
French Polynesia........ 887	—	.04	—	—	—	—	—	—	—	—	—	.01	—	—
Guam........ 829	—	—	—	—	—	—	—	—	—	—	.02	.01	.01	.01
India........ 534	.47	.47	.76	.89	1.13	.81	1.27	12.69	26.82	23.10	16.13	18.94	22.20	26.72
Indonesia........ 536	.21	.29	.33	.14	.04	.05	.39	4.42	4.97	5.16	7.26	7.00	6.96	7.73
Kiribati........ 826	—	—	.05	.03	—	—	—	—	—	—	—	—	—	—
Korea........ 542	3.29	4.36	2.95	5.07	6.55	11.34	19.88	14.09	18.44	25.17	29.53	58.31	54.34	60.61
Lao People's Dem.Rep........ 544	.01	—	—	—	—	.02	—	.09	.04	.05	.08	.08	.06	.05
Malaysia........ 548	.34	.46	.53	1.26	.98	.48	.60	4.94	6.74	8.70	9.65	11.14	11.51	12.65
Maldives........ 556	—	.30	—	—	—	—	—	—	—	—	—	—	.01	.01
Mongolia........ 948	—	—	—	.02	—	.01	.01	—	—	—	—	—	.01	.09
Myanmar........ 518	—	—	—	—	—	—	—	.10	.14	.43	.41	.19	.32	.21
Nepal........ 558	—	—	—	—	—	—	.01	—	—	.01	.04	.12	.10	.09
New Caledonia........ 839	—	—	—	.01	.01	—	—	—	—	—	—	—	—	—
Pakistan........ 564	—	—	—	.20	—	—	—	1.04	1.11	1.49	2.28	2.28	2.98	3.17
Papua New Guinea........ 853	—	—	—	—	—	—	.01	.01	.01	—	.01	.05	—	.07
Philippines........ 566	.03	.06	.01	.02	.17	.10	.25	.84	.83	1.20	1.71	1.63	1.52	2.35
Singapore........ 576	.22	.15	.46	.53	.77	.32	.29	3.04	3.33	4.01	4.94	5.30	5.30	7.24
Sri Lanka........ 524	—	—	—	.06	.08	—	.02	.50	.59	.87	1.31	1.10	1.31	1.62
Taiwan Province of China........ 528	17.86	18.40	17.50	16.28	8.93	2.44	3.77	18.13	20.77	21.34	23.42	25.41	30.02	34.98
Thailand........ 578	.67	1.42	2.36	3.34	1.54	1.57	3.05	6.47	6.87	10.27	14.38	18.09	17.58	23.12
Tonga........ 866	—	—	—	—	—	—	—	—	.03	—	—	—	—	—
Vietnam........ 582	.01	.20	.14	.42	.15	.18	.41	2.24	2.22	3.20	4.71	5.11	5.86	8.15
Asia n.s........ 598	—	—	—	—	—	—	—	—	—	—	.01	—	—	—
Europe........ 170	**70.0**	**76.5**	**86.0**	**148.4**	**194.8**	**217.2**	**228.6**	**138.0**	**231.9**	**302.1**	**307.1**	**417.9**	**468.6**	**568.7**
Albania........ 914	—	—	—	—	—	—	—	.02	.03	.02	.01	.03	.02	.03
Azerbaijan........ 912	—	—	—	—	.01	.02	7.72	—	—	—	—	—	—	—
Belarus........ 913	1.83	1.05	3.34	4.70	7.51	4.58	13.93	.26	1.23	1.18	.57	.72	10.02	3.73
Bosnia & Herzegovina........ 963	.08	.03	—	—	—	.05	.02	.04	.04	.05	.07	.12	.19	.25
Bulgaria........ 918	.13	.16	.19	.72	1.90	2.21	3.21	.68	.89	1.21	1.34	1.56	2.01	3.15
Croatia........ 960	.16	.32	.73	1.05	1.88	3.28	2.71	.23	.42	.79	.76	3.44	7.18	2.43
Czech Republic........ 935	.41	.18	.39	.27	.98	1.28	1.37	7.09	8.68	18.14	25.65	39.76	45.23	59.63
Estonia........ 939	3.78	.97	3.08	.71	.39	1.59	.83	37.10	71.32	83.38	53.29	44.15	49.78	49.64
Faroe Islands........ 816	26.14	23.90	24.81	28.80	32.14	41.40	34.28	5.56	5.66	12.40	20.08	8.33	15.65	23.53
Georgia........ 915	—	—	—	—	.01	—	.01	—	—	—	—	.02	—	.03
Gibraltar........ 823	.07	—	—	.08	—	—	.81	—	—	—	—	.11	—	—
Hungary........ 944	.04	.31	.19	2.58	2.12	2.97	3.12	4.20	7.83	10.21	20.91	40.09	30.42	27.73
Kazakhstan........ 916	.02	—	—	—	—	—	.18	—	—	—	—	—	—	—
Latvia........ 941	7.21	5.82	2.54	3.55	4.48	3.20	1.07	8.56	11.47	28.11	50.76	37.87	46.05	63.71
Lithuania........ 946	8.11	15.62	17.02	28.11	40.07	47.41	43.70	7.11	6.84	13.93	29.16	75.26	109.04	81.17
Macedonia, FYR........ 962	—	—	—	—	—	.03	.04	.03	.04	.06	.15	.23	.32	.51
Moldova........ 921	—	—	.11	.18	—	—	.09	.04	.03	.03	.03	.05	.05	.05
Poland........ 964	10.14	14.03	14.80	35.40	63.09	27.89	29.78	18.55	14.64	24.71	30.34	75.53	66.98	114.59
Romania........ 968	.08	.13	.75	1.05	.23	2.34	2.07	2.23	3.11	3.81	5.34	20.94	9.66	11.08
Russia........ 922	7.34	8.67	13.42	33.39	31.79	66.26	65.14	36.28	87.53	78.61	38.45	23.91	21.39	78.09
Serbia & Montenegro........ 965	—	.02	.07	.05	.05	.28	.75	—	.24	.08	.18	.51	.85	.40
Slovak Republic........ 936	.30	.20	.20	.14	.27	1.81	2.36	1.65	2.34	2.96	4.56	5.22	7.86	10.98
Turkey........ 186	.78	.93	1.28	2.54	3.96	3.53	3.74	7.22	8.99	21.81	23.82	39.07	44.95	35.84
Turkmenistan........ 925	—	—	—	—	—	—	—	—	—	—	.02	.04	.03	.01
Ukraine........ 926	3.33	4.10	3.05	5.07	3.88	7.00	11.67	1.07	.32	.60	1.53	.93	.87	2.10
Yugoslavia n.s........ 966	.05	.03	—	.01	—	—	—	.12	.21	—	.02	—	—	—
Europe n.s........ 884	—	—	—	—	—	.02	—	—	—	—	—	.01	.05	—
Middle East........ 407	**2.7**	**4.1**	**3.0**	**2.1**	**3.6**	**41.9**	**76.6**	**4.4**	**5.4**	**10.6**	**8.6**	**17.2**	**42.2**	**20.1**
Bahrain........ 419	.12	.01	—	.04	—	—	—	.10	—	—	—	5.86	32.73	6.51
Egypt........ 469	.59	.01	.04	.04	.08	.07	.31	.23	.16	2.89	.73	.94	1.02	2.68
Iran, I.R. of........ 429	—	.10	.07	.21	.62	.16	.05	.13	.17	.20	.30	.43	.50	.49
Israel........ 436	1.35	3.05	2.02	1.02	.97	.85	.80	3.68	4.96	5.33	7.11	9.14	7.32	8.81
Jordan........ 439	.03	—	—	.03	.01	—	.01	—	—	—	.01	—	.01	.01
Kuwait........ 443	.05	.02	.03	.21	.08	.08	.01	—	—	—	—	—	—	—
Lebanon........ 446	.02	.01	—	.03	.01	—	.50	.01	.01	.03	.06	.05	.06	.12
Libya........ 672	—	—	—	—	—	.01	.02	—	—	—	—	—	—	—
Oman........ 449	.02	.03	.03	.03	.01	.01	—	—	—	—	—	—	—	—
Qatar........ 453	—	—	—	—	.06	—	—	.04	.03	.01	—	—	—	—
Saudi Arabia........ 456	.29	.71	.06	.09	.07	.14	.22	—	—	1.39	.17	.40	.41	.83
Syrian Arab Republic........ 463	—	—	—	.09	1.06	.01	.02	.01	.01	.02	.01	.02	.02	.01
United Arab Emirates........ 466	.15	.05	.63	.22	.13	40.52	74.65	.23	.08	.72	.19	.35	.18	.60
Yemen, Republic of........ 474	.03	.10	.14	.06	.47	—	.01	—	—	—	—	—	—	.03
Western Hemisphere........ 207	**15.0**	**11.4**	**7.1**	**11.8**	**13.0**	**20.2**	**30.1**	**104.4**	**49.2**	**59.7**	**79.7**	**96.6**	**121.7**	**93.4**
Antigua and Barbuda........ 311	—	.06	.03	—	.09	.10	—	—	—	—	—	—	—	—
Argentina........ 213	.62	.76	.31	.22	.16	.50	.48	.22	.30	.65	.85	2.34	2.25	4.12
Bahamas, The........ 313	—	.09	—	—	—	.71	.69	1.83	1.30	2.13	.34	1.81	1.35	1.04

	Exports							Imports						
	2001	2002	2003	2004	2005	2006	2007	2001	2002	2003	2004	2005	2006	2007
	Millions of U.S. Dollars							Millions of U.S. Dollars						
Barbados 316	—	—	.01	—	.01	—	—	—	—	.07	.19	.14	.29	.31
Belize 339	.04	.02	—	.01	—	—	.02	—	—	—	—	.02	—	—
Bermuda 319	—	—	—	—	—	5.43	.02	—	—	—	—	—	—	—
Bolivia 218	—	—	.04	—	—	—	—	—	.01	—	—	.55	.02	.02
Brazil 223	.95	.88	.48	1.85	1.22	2.44	4.16	4.66	2.03	13.17	12.77	9.93	6.11	8.28
Chile 228	3.47	2.27	1.74	3.05	2.63	2.73	5.68	39.97	1.80	1.75	2.76	3.63	4.91	6.42
Colombia 233	.16	.37	.14	.08	.12	.23	.20	.29	.19	.43	.62	1.05	4.28	2.55
Costa Rica 238	—	.03	—	.06	.13	.01	—	.90	1.67	2.19	1.99	2.22	2.42	4.30
Dominica 321	—	—	—	—	.03	.02	.01	—	—	—	—	—	—	—
Dominican Republic 243	—	—	—	.02	—	—	—	.07	.06	.12	.13	.10	.11	.15
Ecuador 248	.07	.34	—	.01	.02	.01	.31	.58	.53	.39	.45	.78	.62	1.14
El Salvador 253	—	—	—	.01	.16	.48	.98	—	.01	.01	.01	.02	.07	.04
Falkland Islands 323	.02	.70	—	.02	.01	—	.02	.81	—	—	.01	—	.01	—
Greenland 326	8.28	4.76	3.22	5.59	7.35	5.88	15.92	2.68	3.48	4.51	12.26	8.39	5.73	6.07
Grenada 328	.04	—	—	—	—	—	—	—	—	—	—	—	—	—
Guatemala 258	—	—	—	—	—	—	—	.16	.11	.11	.33	.35	.26	.30
Guyana 336	—	—	—	—	—	—	—	—	—	—	—	—	—	.02
Haiti 263	—	—	—	.03	—	—	—	—	—	—	—	—	—	—
Honduras 268	—	—	—	.01	.01	.02	—	.05	.07	.11	.11	.24	.17	.19
Jamaica 343	.09	.18	—	.08	.04	—	—	.35	.19	.20	.07	.08	12.84	24.40
Mexico 273	.71	.24	.11	.34	.37	.39	.31	2.40	2.00	2.11	3.06	4.11	4.66	6.43
Netherlands Antilles 353	.02	—	—	—	—	—	—	—	—	—	—	—	—	—
Nicaragua 278	—	—	—	.03	—	—	—	.01	.01	.01	.06	.08	.28	.44
Panama 283	—	.55	.57	—	—	.39	.42	2.66	1.43	1.67	2.85	3.21	.80	2.08
Paraguay 288	—	—	—	—	—	—	—	.05	.09	.11	.21	.13	.04	.06
Peru 293	.01	.02	.02	—	.06	.03	.14	.06	.13	.14	.25	.31	.43	1.01
St. Pierre-Miquelon 363	.01	—	—	—	—	—	—	—	—	—	.20	.13	.25	—
Suriname 366	—	.01	—	—	—	.02	—	35.49	32.87	29.17	37.71	29.62	56.64	21.94
Trinidad and Tobago 369	—	—	—	.01	—	—	.01	—	—	—	—	—	—	—
Uruguay 298	.19	.15	.38	.25	.44	.63	.45	.04	.03	.05	.06	.36	.12	.29
Venezuela, Rep. Bol 299	.01	—	.01	—	.04	.01	.13	11.06	.89	.57	.91	26.38	10.25	1.82
Western Hem. n.s. 399	.35	—	—	.10	.08	.14	.17	.03	.04	.02	1.51	.60	6.81	—
Other Countries n.i.e. 910	**—**	**—**	**.2**	**.1**	**—**	**—**	**—**	**—**	**—**	**—**	**.1**	**.1**	**.1**	**.1**
Cuba 928	.01	—	.02	.07	—	—	.01	.03	.04	.05	.05	.11	.08	.12
North Korea 954	—	—	.19	—	—	—	—	—	—	—	—	—	—	—
Memorandum Items														
European Union 998	1,412.57	1,622.12	1,758.65	2,164.28	2,276.84	2,447.45	3,564.79	1,333.67	1,325.70	1,805.06	2,267.56	3,001.61	3,540.20	4,009.01
Oil Exporting Ctys 999	24.26	34.61	40.08	50.42	52.30	95.57	133.66	15.89	6.14	8.06	8.86	34.60	18.32	11.49
Non-Oil Develop.Ctys 201	132.92	144.08	144.74	212.87	265.92	307.69	340.92	377.64	454.59	587.78	672.42	941.16	1,144.24	1,256.15
PERCENT DISTRIBUTION														
Industrial Countries 101	**92.2**	**92.0**	**92.3**	**90.8**	**89.3**	**88.3**	**90.1**	**82.7**	**79.7**	**78.9**	**81.6**	**79.9**	**81.1**	**80.9**
Developing Countries 202	**7.8**	**8.0**	**7.7**	**9.2**	**10.7**	**11.7**	**9.9**	**17.3**	**20.3**	**21.1**	**18.4**	**20.1**	**18.9**	**19.1**
Africa 607	**1.8**	**2.0**	**1.8**	**1.9**	**1.9**	**1.7**	**1.4**	**.2**	**.2**	**.2**	**.5**	**.4**	**.4**	**.4**
Asia 507	**1.6**	**1.9**	**1.9**	**1.6**	**1.7**	**1.9**	**1.5**	**6.2**	**7.4**	**7.7**	**7.2**	**8.8**	**8.2**	**8.4**
Europe 170	**3.5**	**3.4**	**3.6**	**5.2**	**6.5**	**6.3**	**4.8**	**6.1**	**10.2**	**10.7**	**8.3**	**8.6**	**7.6**	**8.6**
Middle East 407	**.1**	**.2**	**.1**	**.1**	**.1**	**1.2**	**1.6**	**.2**	**.2**	**.4**	**.2**	**.4**	**.7**	**.3**
Western Hemisphere 207	**.7**	**.5**	**.3**	**.4**	**.4**	**.6**	**.6**	**4.6**	**2.2**	**2.1**	**2.2**	**2.0**	**2.0**	**1.4**
ANNUAL PERCENT CHANGE														
World 001	**6.3**	**10.7**	**7.4**	**20.0**	**3.6**	**15.8**	**38.5**	**–12.0**	**—**	**24.3**	**31.0**	**30.8**	**26.7**	**8.0**
Industrial Countries 101	**4.7**	**10.4**	**7.8**	**18.2**	**1.9**	**14.5**	**41.3**	**–15.2**	**–3.6**	**23.1**	**35.5**	**28.0**	**28.6**	**7.7**
Developing Countries 202	**30.4**	**13.7**	**3.4**	**42.5**	**20.9**	**26.7**	**17.7**	**7.1**	**17.1**	**29.3**	**14.3**	**43.2**	**19.1**	**9.0**
Africa 607	**77.4**	**20.6**	**–1.0**	**24.3**	**4.3**	**4.8**	**10.4**	**–37.9**	**19.9**	**20.6**	**165.3**	**11.9**	**38.3**	**10.7**
Asia 507	**–6.5**	**29.3**	**6.0**	**3.7**	**7.6**	**28.7**	**13.9**	**3.9**	**18.7**	**28.5**	**23.8**	**58.1**	**18.5**	**10.4**
Europe 170	**27.0**	**9.3**	**12.4**	**72.6**	**31.2**	**11.5**	**5.3**	**–9.3**	**68.0**	**30.3**	**1.6**	**36.1**	**12.1**	**21.4**
Middle East 407	**28.7**	**54.3**	**–26.3**	**–32.0**	**73.5**	**—**	**83.0**	**–52.4**	**22.2**	**95.7**	**–19.0**	**100.5**	**145.6**	**–52.5**
Western Hemisphere 207	**99.2**	**–24.0**	**–38.2**	**66.5**	**10.2**	**55.5**	**49.4**	**69.0**	**–52.8**	**21.2**	**33.6**	**21.1**	**26.0**	**–23.3**
Other Countries n.i.e. 910	**. . . .**	**—**	**. . . .**	**–64.1**	**. . . .**	**. . . .**	**. . . .**	**–47.7**	**37.9**	**11.8**	**13.4**	**105.7**	**–25.2**	**43.5**

	Exports 2001	Exports 2002	Exports 2003	Exports 2004	Exports 2005	Exports 2006	Exports 2007	Imports 2001	Imports 2002	Imports 2003	Imports 2004	Imports 2005	Imports 2006	Imports 2007
	Millions of U.S. Dollars							*Millions of U.S. Dollars*						
IFS World Total	**43,361**	**50,372**	**58,963**	**76,649**	**99,620**	**120,861**	**145,515**	**50,392**	**56,517**	**72,558**	**99,775**	**142,842**	**175,242**	**215,717**
DOTS World Total 001	**45,513Y**	**50,496**	**61,119**	**75,385**	**97,918**	**122,354Y**	**152,691Y**	**59,151Y**	**58,912**	**74,070**	**99,835**	**134,690**	**186,618Y**	**249,576Y**
Industrial Countries 101	**23,781Y**	**24,960**	**28,498**	**33,054**	**42,555**	**53,209Y**	**62,014Y**	**20,624Y**	**22,647**	**28,006**	**35,479**	**44,824**	**59,925Y**	**82,596Y**
United States 111	9,355V	10,308	11,364	12,839	16,362	20,902V	22,831V	4,141V	4,129	4,890	5,981	7,591	11,100V	19,352V
Canada 156	745V	670	747	803	973	1,691V	1,852V	408V	557	686	735	865	1,625V	1,841V
Australia 193	409V	483	564	661	789	961V	1,225V	1,367V	1,329	2,321	3,333	4,594	7,413V	8,552V
Japan 158	2,011V	1,776	1,748	1,911	2,376	3,743V	3,781V	2,134V	1,914	2,460	2,921	3,473	4,935V	6,782V
New Zealand 196	72V	66	81	88	129	148V	180V	72V	78	78	100	179	240V	297V
Austria 122	103V	80	100	111	127	202V	250V	152V	143	192	246	322	564V	812V
Belgium 124	1,371V	1,594	1,770	2,283	2,767	3,451V	4,121V	2,966V	3,475	3,910	4,419	4,676	6,392V	8,135V
Cyprus 423	30V	25	27	28	31	40V	45V	3V	4	3	4	6	6V	6V
Denmark 128	174V	176	227	276	378	449V	567V	155V	138	205	251	357	366V	402V
Finland 172	56V	71	101	130	188	130V	178V	216V	190	252	350	532	454V	687V
France 132	1,047V	1,054	1,243	1,538	1,971	2,073V	2,538V	1,077V	1,032	1,092	1,311	1,801	3,646V	5,069V
Germany 134	2,037V	2,027	2,435	2,619	3,344	4,265V	5,401V	2,272V	2,310	2,790	3,631	5,368	8,459V	11,094V
Greece 174	132V	138	187	267	496	552V	571V	35V	25	41	29	39	69V	71V
Iceland 176	12V	7	15	14	13	20V	24V	1V	11	11	4	5	1V	1V
Ireland 178	107V	127	147	180	259	226V	302V	105V	95	123	131	167	214V	257V
Italy 136	1,357V	1,319	1,636	2,053	2,439	3,396V	4,220V	1,017V	785	1,006	1,260	1,715	3,006V	4,562V
Luxembourg 137	8V	8	13	12	11	15V	27V	12V	16	38	18	14	35V	45V
Malta 181	16Y	27	97	53	98	19V	25V	—Y	—	1	1	10	2V	5V
Netherlands 138	811V	1,002	1,229	1,461	2,243	2,156V	2,603V	540V	406	498	703	977	1,562V	2,414V
Norway 142	88V	67	74	94	121	212V	264V	53V	85	252	222	260	370V	653V
Portugal 182	146V	159	168	197	244	271V	436V	16V	15	14	17	27	40V	48V
Slovenia 961	28V	25	33	56	73	63V	107V	17V	59	63	31	23	48V	63V
Spain 184	700V	778	955	1,236	1,550	1,959V	2,528V	220V	175	238	344	530	751V	1,100V
Sweden 144	183V	171	209	226	301	403V	563V	395V	489	653	863	1,099	1,481V	1,738V
Switzerland 146	315V	389	434	504	491	534V	719V	427V	2,465	3,067	5,192	6,380	1,656V	2,111V
United Kingdom 112	2,467V	2,413	2,892	3,415	4,780	5,325V	6,655V	2,824V	2,724	3,120	3,382	3,815	5,492V	6,499V
Developing Countries 202	**20,043Y**	**24,647**	**32,229**	**41,891**	**55,035**	**68,740Y**	**90,174Y**	**25,516Y**	**19,401**	**26,041**	**36,520**	**49,043**	**76,239Y**	**104,367Y**
Africa 607	**1,700Y**	**2,709**	**3,294**	**4,434**	**5,973**	**7,387Y**	**9,111Y**	**3,712Y**	**3,030**	**3,119**	**3,469**	**4,297**	**2,955Y**	**3,948Y**
Algeria 612	35V	57	108	198	259	320Y	414Y	20V	1	4	6	13	16Y	19Y
Angola 614	14Y	34	62	68	131	162Y	201Y	—Y	5	2	1	3	3Y	4Y
Benin 638	8V	62	56	46	98	121Y	150Y	67V	39	49	72	78	96Y	119Y
Botswana 616	5Y	4	6	7	11	14Y	17Y	—Y	—	—	—	—	—Y	—Y
Burkina Faso 748	7Y	15	22	21	20	24Y	30Y	12Y	10	10	9	4	5Y	6Y
Burundi 618	5V	4	5	7	10	13V	17Y	—V	—	—	—	—	—V	—Y
Cameroon 622	10V	19	23	25	35	43Y	53Y	17V	7	9	11	12	15Y	18Y
Central African Rep. 626	1Y	2	1	1	1	2Y	2Y	—Y	1	—	—	—	—Y	1Y
Chad 628	3Y	2	2	3	4	5Y	6Y	—Y	1	3	2	—	1Y	1Y
Comoros 632	1Y	5	3	2	5	6Y	7Y	—Y	—	—	—	1	1Y	1Y
Congo, Dem. Rep. of 636	5Y	4	9	5	6	8Y	10Y	—Y	—	—	2	7	9Y	11Y
Congo, Republic of 634	5V	50	59	80	103	127Y	158Y	23V	3	5	17	38	47Y	58Y
Côte d'Ivoire 662	22V	50	86	99	134	97V	121Y	84V	84	96	143	185	122V	151Y
Djibouti 611	20Y	32	65	111	205	253Y	314Y	—Y	1	1	3	3	4Y	5Y
Equatorial Guinea 642	—Y	—	1	3	6	7Y	9Y	—Y	—	—	1	—	—Y	—Y
Ethiopia 644	83V	69	76	60	69	85Y	106Y	11V	13	8	9	9	11Y	14Y
Gabon 646	5Y	15	12	10	15	18Y	23Y	13Y	18	22	36	42	52Y	64Y
Gambia, The 648	17Y	14	14	14	17	21Y	26Y	—Y	4	4	10	13	16Y	19Y
Ghana 652	66Y	96	163	176	196	242Y	300Y	26Y	19	29	45	72	89Y	110Y
Guinea 656	9V	32	35	46	53	66Y	82Y	—V	15	7	21	23	29Y	36Y
Guinea-Bissau 654	14Y	6	3	1	1	1Y	1Y	61Y	38	51	66	90	111Y	138Y
Kenya 664	148V	192	223	368	533	659Y	818Y	33V	33	40	44	48	59Y	73Y
Lesotho 666	—Y	3	5	10	13	16Y	20Y	—Y	—	—	—	—	—Y	—Y
Liberia 668	13Y	8	13	17	22	28Y	34Y	9Y	12	4	6	17	22Y	27Y
Madagascar 674	17V	14	33	35	45	56Y	69Y	2V	4	5	7	14	17Y	22Y
Malawi 676	21Y	28	36	52	47	58Y	72Y	—Y	2	4	5	3	3Y	4Y
Mali 678	18Y	25	39	27	25	31Y	38Y	13Y	15	28	17	5	6Y	8Y
Mauritania 682	14Y	20	19	22	40	49Y	61Y	—Y	—	—	1	1	1Y	2Y
Mauritius 684	145V	164	193	237	211	450V	744V	2V	13	10	7	7	13V	12V
Morocco 686	61V	109	98	103	122	151Y	188Y	269V	216	242	256	414	512Y	635Y
Mozambique 688	23V	43	64	76	124	84V	104Y	4V	22	25	37	48	33V	41Y
Namibia 728	1Y	6	7	7	13	18Y	24Y	1Y	2	1	—	15	30Y	45Y
Niger 692	2V	49	41	36	21	26Y	32Y	—V	—	2	1	1	1Y	1Y
Nigeria 694	287V	478	536	601	842	1,039Y	1,346Y	2,291V	80	76	55	66	83Y	100Y
Rwanda 714	4Y	6	5	7	10	12Y	15Y	—Y	—	—	1	—	—Y	—Y
St. Helena 856	—Y	1	1	—	—	1Y	1Y	—Y	—	—	—	—	—Y	1Y
São Tomé & Príncipe 716	—Y	—	1	1	—	—Y	—Y	—Y	—	—	—	—	—Y	—Y
Senegal 722	18V	44	33	57	102	81V	100Y	107V	163	152	163	259	87V	108Y
Seychelles 718	6V	6	9	10	11	13Y	16Y	—V	—	—	—	1	1Y	2Y
Sierra Leone 724	4Y	13	12	13	18	22Y	27Y	1Y	3	6	3	3	4Y	5Y
Somalia 726	8Y	19	35	45	48	59Y	73Y	3Y	24	14	7	11	13Y	16Y

	Exports							Imports						
	2001	2002	2003	2004	2005	2006	2007	2001	2002	2003	2004	2005	2006	2007
	Millions of U.S. Dollars							Millions of U.S. Dollars						
South Africa.......... 199	245V	451	526	854	1,410	1,586V	1,776V	398V	1,930	1,948	2,085	2,386	860V	1,486V
Sacca exc. South Afr.......... 608	12V	—	—	—	—	3Y	3Y	—V	—	—	—	—	—Y	1Y
Sudan.......... 732	101Y	109	107	255	314	545V	497V	8Y	22	30	25	29	25V	18V
Swaziland.......... 734	2Y	10	25	24	9	11Y	14Y	1Y	—	1	3	18	23Y	28Y
Tanzania.......... 738	80V	109	161	170	223	276Y	343Y	90V	87	105	124	122	151Y	188Y
Togo.......... 742	5V	66	53	207	141	174Y	216Y	5V	12	19	34	69	85Y	105Y
Tunisia.......... 744	40V	56	66	69	78	101V	125Y	90V	96	72	82	100	144V	179Y
Uganda.......... 746	61V	63	82	77	87	108Y	134Y	—V	2	2	5	4	5Y	6Y
Zambia.......... 754	17V	30	38	46	61	78V	150V	35V	14	18	22	36	147V	57V
Zimbabwe.......... 698	11V	15	22	23	24	19V	23Y	13V	15	16	24	26	2V	2Y
Asia.......... 507	**10,870Y**	**12,363**	**16,568**	**21,137**	**28,265**	**34,491Y**	**45,888Y**	**13,124Y**	**11,104**	**15,907**	**21,256**	**28,980**	**49,545Y**	**70,449Y**
Afghanistan, I.S. of.......... 512	31Y	52	124	154	144	178Y	221Y	28Y	18	35	43	56	69Y	85Y
American Samoa.......... 859	1Y	—	—	1	1	1Y	1Y	—Y	—	—	—	4	4Y	5Y
Bangladesh.......... 513	1,087V	1,133	1,600	1,625	1,632	1,874V	2,406V	67V	61	74	61	104	152Y	211Y
Bhutan.......... 514	3Y	31	77	85	96	118Y	146Y	22Y	30	47	51	84	104Y	129Y
Brunei Darussalam.......... 516	3Y	4	5	5	33	41Y	51Y	—Y	—	—	—	1	1Y	1Y
Cambodia.......... 522	3V	18	19	17	22	25V	31Y	—V	1	—	—	1	1V	1Y
China,P.R.: Mainland.......... 924	1,545V	1,720	2,710	4,178	6,445	9,518V	13,326V	2,094V	2,603	3,738	6,073	9,829	16,047V	26,440V
China,P.R.:Hong Kong.......... 532	2,088V	2,552	3,100	3,554	4,266	4,311V	5,574V	1,322V	912	1,363	1,656	2,058	3,253V	4,914V
China,P.R.:Macao.......... 546	3V	3	4	2	2	5V	4V	—V	10	5	1	—	—V	1V
Fiji.......... 819	14Y	23	22	26	29	36Y	44Y	—Y	—	1	1	1	1Y	1Y
French Polynesia.......... 887	—Y	—	—	1	1	1Y	1Y	—Y	—	—	—	—	—Y	—Y
Guam.......... 829	—Y	—	1	—	—	—Y	1Y	—Y	—	—	—	1	1Y	1Y
Indonesia.......... 536	442V	754	1,053	1,251	1,362	1,279V	1,463V	1,159V	1,295	1,937	2,412	2,855	3,730V	5,438V
Korea.......... 542	1,005V	601	735	913	1,625	3,310V	4,204V	1,549V	1,427	2,502	3,103	4,135	6,086V	7,260V
Lao People's Dem.Rep.......... 544	6Y	2	1	2	5	6Y	7Y	—Y	—	—	—	—	—Y	—Y
Malaysia.......... 548	702V	755	857	970	1,135	1,212V	1,873V	1,735V	1,382	1,901	2,177	2,366	5,641V	6,472V
Maldives.......... 556	37V	30	40	42	62	77Y	96Y	1V	—	—	1	2	2Y	3Y
Mongolia.......... 948	1V	1	1	1	1	1Y	1Y	—V	—	1	—	1	1Y	2Y
Myanmar.......... 518	53Y	72	86	105	111	137Y	170Y	198Y	346	391	400	494	611Y	758Y
Nauru.......... 836	—Y	—	—	—	—	—Y	—Y	8Y	2	3	2	1	1Y	1Y
Nepal.......... 558	557V	316	590	714	830	1,347V	1,671Y	388V	300	285	327	371	619V	769Y
New Caledonia.......... 839	2V	1	2	1	1	1Y	2Y	2V	1	9	9	5	6Y	7Y
Pakistan.......... 564	219V	191	267	451	642	793Y	984Y	73V	50	54	86	157	194Y	241Y
Papua New Guinea.......... 853	5Y	6	5	11	10	13Y	16Y	1Y	—	1	70	72	89Y	110Y
Philippines.......... 566	226V	416	359	376	471	364V	445V	78V	117	123	167	198	131V	268V
Samoa.......... 862	1Y	1	—	—	—	—Y	1Y	—Y	—	—	—	—	—Y	—Y
Singapore.......... 576	1,017V	1,309	1,949	3,378	5,178	4,440V	5,335V	3,018V	1,402	1,923	2,458	3,086	8,440V	11,000V
Solomon Islands.......... 813	1Y	—	5	2	—	—Y	—Y	3Y	2	2	1	2	3Y	3Y
Sri Lanka.......... 524	547V	848	1,220	1,345	1,867	1,975V	2,373V	79V	85	169	322	523	538V	567V
Taiwan Province of China.......... 528	448V	524	544	574	617	1,132V	2,307V	693V	637	742	984	1,301	1,618V	2,576V
Thailand.......... 578	612V	692	802	850	1,022	1,491V	1,895V	530V	390	552	777	1,118	2,004V	2,931V
Tonga.......... 866	—Y	—	1	1	1	1Y	1Y	—Y	1	1	—	—	—Y	—Y
Vanuatu.......... 846	6Y	—	—	1	2	2Y	3Y	26Y	3	11	4	36	45Y	55Y
Vietnam.......... 582	207V	308	392	497	654	800V	1,234V	50V	27	36	70	119	152V	198V
Europe.......... 170	**1,532Y**	**1,561**	**2,030**	**2,273**	**2,779**	**3,996Y**	**5,749Y**	**1,510Y**	**1,095**	**1,619**	**2,285**	**3,552**	**5,725Y**	**7,880Y**
Albania.......... 914	4V	4	5	5	5	6V	14V	—V	—	—	—	—	—V	9V
Armenia.......... 911	5V	2	3	6	7	21V	20V	—V	—	1	1	2	1V	4V
Azerbaijan.......... 912	14V	9	11	23	29	52V	65V	1V	1	3	6	6	1V	159V
Belarus.......... 913	13V	5	6	9	12	53V	74V	71V	7	7	11	31	124V	112V
Bosnia & Herzegovina.......... 963	—Y	2	3	3	2	2Y	3Y	—Y	2	2	1	—	—Y	—Y
Bulgaria.......... 918	17V	10	22	24	24	43V	77V	12V	10	10	16	22	36V	86V
Croatia.......... 960	21V	9	15	21	27	80V	98V	25V	1	6	3	23	5V	8V
Czech Republic.......... 935	85V	—	64	—	94	152V	228V	75V	—	105	—	233	439V	608V
Czechoslovakia n.s.......... 937	51Y	53	80	84	—	—Y	—Y	50Y	74	105	154	—	—Y	—Y
Estonia.......... 939	8V	4	6	9	13	10V	20V	2V	2	—	1	6	16V	23V
Georgia.......... 915	2V	16	30	28	32	11V	15Y	5V	5	6	13	16	10V	12Y
Gibraltar.......... 823	1Y	1	1	1	—	1Y	1Y	—Y	—	—	—	—	—Y	—Y
Hungary.......... 944	63V	48	81	101	90	135V	276V	28V	21	26	30	31	146V	112V
Kazakhstan.......... 916	41V	47	68	78	87	108Y	134Y	11V	11	10	14	23	29Y	36Y
Kyrgyz Republic.......... 917	2V	14	32	46	33	6V	8V	1V	—	1	1	1	4V	1V
Latvia.......... 941	4V	8	14	16	25	26V	27V	1V	2	1	1	3	9V	13V
Lithuania.......... 946	17V	9	16	27	32	22V	28V	4V	4	9	16	25	21V	14V
Macedonia, FYR.......... 962	4V	1	2	2	4	13V	16Y	—V	1	—	—	3	—V	—Y
Moldova.......... 921	4V	2	4	5	5	7Y	8Y	—V	1	—	—	—	—Y	—Y
Poland.......... 964	143V	106	127	159	211	322V	490V	104V	37	47	78	102	223V	180V
Romania.......... 968	29V	23	43	91	89	197V	322V	43V	46	65	143	230	265V	498V
Russia.......... 922	492V	728	711	627	705	879V	1,197V	765V	578	868	1,189	1,825	3,198V	4,412V
Serbia & Montenegro.......... 965	—Y	5	14	11	8	10Y	13Y	—Y	1	3	4	3	3Y	4Y
Slovak Republic.......... 936	27V	10	15	21	22	45V	81V	47V	12	11	19	36	29V	63V
Tajikistan.......... 923	31V	7	6	6	6	9V	8V	—V	—	3	4	5	—V	—V
Turkey.......... 186	323V	331	515	657	931	1,435V	2,090V	82V	62	70	115	178	244V	382V
Turkmenistan.......... 925	7V	9	17	16	18	22Y	27Y	2V	5	8	10	12	15Y	18Y
Ukraine.......... 926	87V	91	106	179	244	301Y	374Y	143V	188	225	427	706	872Y	1,082Y
Uzbekistan.......... 927	11Y	5	13	19	23	29Y	36Y	12Y	20	26	29	27	34Y	42Y
Yugoslavia n.s.......... 966	28Y	—	—	—	—	—Y	—Y	26Y	—	—	—	—	—Y	—Y
Middle East.......... 407	**4,477Y**	**6,759**	**9,142**	**12,203**	**15,268**	**18,786Y**	**24,155Y**	**5,988Y**	**3,147**	**4,245**	**7,754**	**9,890**	**13,184Y**	**15,990Y**
Bahrain.......... 419	82Y	94	109	134	181	224Y	278Y	271Y	124	86	103	171	211Y	262Y
Egypt.......... 469	258V	339	350	409	609	753Y	935Y	277V	195	130	127	202	249Y	309Y
Iran, I.R. of.......... 429	510V	554	852	1,139	1,190	1,469Y	1,903Y	508Y	265	265	366	617	776Y	936Y

		Exports							Imports						
		2001	2002	2003	2004	2005	2006	2007	2001	2002	2003	2004	2005	2006	2007
		Millions of U.S. Dollars							Millions of U.S. Dollars						
Iraq	433	75Y	213	110	115	142	175Y	227Y	59Y	—	—	1	2	2Y	3Y
Israel	436	390V	583	702	923	1,162	1,303V	1,536V	519V	559	653	897	1,041	1,397V	1,775V
Jordan	439	67V	97	139	128	168	162V	275V	226V	221	229	305	416	437V	505V
Kuwait	443	187Y	239	302	383	486	600Y	777Y	607Y	153	152	256	422	530Y	640Y
Lebanon	446	48Y	48	57	64	70	87Y	108Y	9Y	13	9	17	19	23Y	29Y
Libya	672	12Y	16	18	132	121	149Y	193Y	12Y	5	9	13	12	15Y	19Y
Oman	449	206V	186	244	257	370	457Y	592Y	157V	12	42	28	198	248Y	300Y
Qatar	453	79V	84	120	135	241	410V	531Y	172V	108	169	526	839	1,812V	2,186Y
Saudi Arabia	456	681V	912	1,078	1,308	1,708	2,109Y	2,732Y	1,316Y	495	680	1,130	1,538	1,934Y	2,333Y
Syrian Arab Republic	463	79Y	116	181	236	269	332Y	412Y	9Y	8	6	4	5	6Y	7Y
United Arab Emirates	466	1,679V	3,119	4,676	6,605	8,282	10,224Y	13,244Y	1,163Y	947	1,784	3,951	4,394	5,525Y	6,665Y
Yemen, Republic of	474	123V	160	204	233	269	333Y	413Y	680V	44	33	30	15	19Y	23Y
Western Hemisphere	**207**	**1,463Y**	**1,255**	**1,195**	**1,844**	**2,749**	**4,079Y**	**5,270Y**	**1,182Y**	**1,025**	**1,152**	**1,756**	**2,325**	**4,830Y**	**6,101Y**
Antigua and Barbuda	311	—Y	—	3	2	1	1Y	2Y	—Y	—	—	—	—	—Y	—Y
Argentina	213	137V	61	81	156	193	276V	349V	479V	412	494	518	662	1,001V	945V
Aruba	314	1V	—	—	—	—	1V	2V	—V	—	—	—	—	—V	—V
Bahamas, The	313	2Y	3	3	5	8	10Y	13Y	—Y	—	—	—	12	14Y	18Y
Barbados	316	2V	2	2	2	2	5V	6Y	—V	—	—	—	—	—V	—Y
Belize	339	1Y	1	2	1	2	3Y	3Y	—Y	—	—	—	—	—Y	—Y
Bermuda	319	1Y	—	—	1	—	1V	2Y	—Y	—	—	1	—	—Y	1Y
Bolivia	218	4V	2	3	4	6	7Y	9Y	3V	1	2	1	1	1Y	1Y
Brazil	223	543V	414	326	561	982	1,474V	2,165V	314V	315	314	650	846	1,030V	1,054V
Chile	228	68V	75	80	99	140	150V	189V	122V	149	159	296	411	1,638V	2,433V
Colombia	233	66V	60	87	267	420	315V	433V	3V	6	9	13	10	69V	85V
Costa Rica	238	8V	10	18	17	16	20Y	25Y	1V	4	21	32	37	46Y	57Y
Dominica	321	—V	2	2	2	2	3Y	4Y	—V	—	—	—	—	—Y	—Y
Dominican Republic	243	16V	15	13	18	29	36Y	45Y	—V	—	1	2	3	3Y	4Y
Ecuador	248	9V	12	14	20	25	41V	51Y	1V	3	5	18	20	56V	69Y
El Salvador	253	4V	4	6	8	11	19V	23V	1V	1	1	2	2	2V	3V
Grenada	328	—Y	—	1	—	1	1Y	1Y	—Y	—	—	—	—	—Y	—Y
Guatemala	258	13V	17	24	33	43	53Y	66Y	1V	2	1	1	2	2Y	2Y
Guyana	336	5Y	3	4	6	10	12Y	15Y	2Y	2	9	8	18	22Y	28Y
Haiti	263	4V	10	9	14	14	18Y	22Y	—Y	—	—	1	—	1Y	1Y
Honduras	268	7V	19	14	18	31	38Y	47Y	—V	—	—	—	—	—Y	—Y
Jamaica	343	6V	9	9	12	23	23V	26V	—V	—	1	2	2	—V	1V
Mexico	273	392V	256	264	330	418	1,126V	1,207V	176V	65	72	78	93	748V	1,150V
Netherlands Antilles	353	6V	28	16	7	9	11Y	14Y	—V	—	—	—	—	—Y	—Y
Nicaragua	278	—V	5	6	10	11	—V	—V	—V	1	—	—	—	—V	—V
Panama	283	3V	59	58	54	64	10V	11V	—V	20	11	76	147	7V	9V
Paraguay	288	7V	7	10	11	15	23V	28Y	31V	5	1	2	4	3V	4Y
Peru	293	41V	46	41	59	80	138V	183Y	40V	26	29	32	26	113V	148Y
St. Kitts and Nevis	361	—Y	—	—	—	—	1Y	1Y	—Y	—	—	—	—	—Y	—Y
St. Lucia	362	—Y	—	—	—	1	1Y	1Y	—Y	—	—	—	—	—Y	—Y
St. Pierre-Miquelon	363	—Y	—	—	2	2	2Y	3Y	—Y	—	—	—	3	3Y	4Y
St. Vincent & Grens	364	—V	—	—	—	—	—Y	1Y	—V	2	2	2	1	1Y	1Y
Suriname	366	1Y	2	3	14	16	20Y	25Y	—Y	3	1	1	5	6Y	8Y
Trinidad and Tobago	369	15V	19	20	26	57	70Y	87Y	—V	—	6	10	5	6Y	7Y
Uruguay	298	21V	19	19	22	27	33Y	41Y	2V	4	9	6	4	5Y	6Y
Venezuela, Rep. Bol.	299	48V	44	26	57	88	135V	172V	4V	3	3	4	8	45V	54Y
Western Hem. n.s.	399	31Y	50	28	6	2	2Y	2Y	—Y	—	—	—	3	6Y	8Y
Other Countries n.i.e.	**910**	**165Y**	**182**	**170**	**138**	**81**	**100Y**	**125Y**	**26Y**	**8**	**4**	**5**	**48**	**59Y**	**73Y**
Cuba	928	5Y	5	5	6	11	13Y	17Y	5Y	4	2	2	3	4Y	4Y
North Korea	954	160Y	177	165	131	70	87Y	108Y	21Y	4	2	3	45	55Y	69Y
Countries & Areas n.s.	**898**	**1,523Y**	**680**	**210**	**301**	**236**	**292Y**	**362Y**	**12,984Y**	**16,857**	**20,011**	**27,829**	**40,775**	**50,395Y**	**62,539Y**
Memorandum Items															
European Union	998	11,122Y	11,380	13,794	16,473	21,787	25,707Y	32,288Y	12,282Y	12,158	14,440	17,136	21,914	33,469Y	44,020Y
Oil Exporting Ctys	999	4,242Y	6,657	9,125	12,181	15,090	18,367Y	23,596Y	7,471Y	3,363	5,118	8,747	10,963	14,716Y	18,692Y
Non-Oil Develop.Ctys	201	15,801Y	17,991	23,105	29,710	39,945	50,373Y	66,579Y	18,045Y	16,038	20,923	27,773	38,080	61,523Y	85,676Y
PERCENT DISTRIBUTION															
Industrial Countries	**101**	**52.3**	**49.4**	**46.6**	**43.8**	**43.5**	**43.5**	**40.6**	**34.9**	**38.4**	**37.8**	**35.5**	**33.3**	**32.1**	**33.1**
Developing Countries	**202**	**44.0**	**48.8**	**52.7**	**55.6**	**56.2**	**56.2**	**59.1**	**43.1**	**32.9**	**35.2**	**36.6**	**36.4**	**40.9**	**41.8**
Africa	**607**	**3.7**	**5.4**	**5.4**	**5.9**	**6.1**	**6.0**	**6.0**	**6.3**	**5.1**	**4.2**	**3.5**	**3.2**	**1.6**	**1.6**
Asia	**507**	**23.9**	**24.5**	**27.1**	**28.0**	**28.9**	**28.2**	**30.1**	**22.2**	**18.8**	**21.5**	**21.3**	**21.5**	**26.5**	**28.2**
Europe	**170**	**3.4**	**3.1**	**3.3**	**3.0**	**2.8**	**3.3**	**3.8**	**2.6**	**1.9**	**2.2**	**2.3**	**2.6**	**3.1**	**3.2**
Middle East	**407**	**9.8**	**13.4**	**15.0**	**16.2**	**15.6**	**15.4**	**15.8**	**10.1**	**5.3**	**5.7**	**7.8**	**7.3**	**7.1**	**6.4**
Western Hemisphere	**207**	**3.2**	**2.5**	**2.0**	**2.4**	**2.8**	**3.3**	**3.5**	**2.0**	**1.7**	**1.6**	**1.8**	**1.7**	**2.6**	**2.4**
Other Countries n.i.e.	**910**	**.4**	**.4**	**.3**	**.2**	**.1**	**.1**	**.1**	—	—	—	—	—	—	—
ANNUAL PERCENT CHANGE															
World	**001**	**6.8**	**10.9**	**21.0**	**23.3**	**29.9**	**25.0**	**24.8**	**17.5**	**–.4**	**25.7**	**34.8**	**34.9**	**38.6**	**33.7**
Industrial Countries	**101**	**5.0**	**5.0**	**14.2**	**16.0**	**28.7**	**25.0**	**16.5**	**1.1**	**9.8**	**23.7**	**26.7**	**26.3**	**33.7**	**37.8**
Developing Countries	**202**	**8.7**	**23.0**	**30.8**	**30.0**	**31.4**	**24.9**	**31.2**	**40.6**	**–24.0**	**34.2**	**40.2**	**34.3**	**55.5**	**36.9**
Africa	**607**	**–11.3**	**59.4**	**21.6**	**34.6**	**34.7**	**23.7**	**23.3**	**21.5**	**–18.4**	**2.9**	**11.2**	**23.9**	**–31.2**	**33.6**
Asia	**507**	**23.6**	**13.7**	**34.0**	**27.6**	**33.7**	**22.0**	**33.0**	**51.6**	**–15.4**	**43.3**	**33.6**	**36.3**	**71.0**	**42.2**
Europe	**170**	**–4.9**	**1.9**	**30.1**	**12.0**	**22.3**	**43.8**	**43.9**	**60.1**	**–27.5**	**47.9**	**41.2**	**55.4**	**61.2**	**37.6**
Middle East	**407**	**–13.3**	**51.0**	**35.3**	**33.5**	**25.1**	**23.0**	**28.6**	**26.7**	**–47.4**	**34.9**	**82.7**	**27.5**	**33.3**	**21.3**
Western Hemisphere	**207**	**53.2**	**–14.2**	**–4.8**	**54.3**	**49.1**	**48.4**	**29.2**	**54.8**	**–13.3**	**12.3**	**52.4**	**32.4**	**107.7**	**26.3**
Other Countries n.i.e.	**910**	**10.4**	**10.9**	**–7.0**	**–18.9**	**–41.0**	**23.6**	**24.1**	**10.4**	**–69.2**	**–46.5**	**14.1**	**875.1**	**23.6**	**24.1**

	Exports							Imports						
	2001	2002	2003	2004	2005	2006	2007	2001	2002	2003	2004	2005	2006	2007
	Millions of U.S. Dollars							Millions of U.S. Dollars						
IFS World Total	**57,360**	**59,164**	**64,107**	**70,767**	**86,996**	**103,486**	**118,728**	**37,534**	**38,340**	**42,244**	**54,877**	**75,533**	**80,333**	**93,088**
DOTS World Total............ 001	**56,318**	**57,154**	**61,013**	**71,550**	**85,623**	**100,797**	**114,098**	**30,961**	**31,289**	**32,549**	**46,524**	**57,700**	**61,065**	**74,473**
Industrial Countries............ 101	**31,101**	**30,120**	**31,487**	**36,230**	**41,105**	**48,596**	**52,843**	**14,539**	**13,309**	**12,888**	**17,946**	**20,436**	**19,867**	**23,781**
United States............ 111	7,761	7,570	7,386	8,787	9,889	11,259	11,644	3,210	2,644	2,702	3,236	3,886	4,066	4,797
Canada............ 156	390	378	382	437	464	551	551	357	412	322	552	698	667	1,056
Australia............ 193	1,845	1,924	1,792	1,887	2,228	2,771	3,395	1,814	1,587	1,648	2,215	2,567	2,986	3,004
Japan............ 158	13,010	12,045	13,603	15,962	18,049	21,732	23,633	4,689	4,409	4,228	6,082	6,906	5,516	6,527
New Zealand............ 196	145	150	156	187	275	320	362	211	156	154	224	263	334	503
Austria............ 122	27	28	26	23	24	24	24	103	75	66	78	107	89	128
Belgium............ 124	762	783	903	916	997	1,136	1,332	212	189	189	264	317	306	338
Cyprus............ 423	17	13	11	11	17	11	12	—	4	—	—	1	—	—
Denmark............ 128	109	103	96	112	127	143	141	58	45	41	74	74	81	101
Finland............ 172	116	145	132	148	183	177	121	89	63	89	211	329	373	327
France............ 132	690	673	666	675	643	744	828	398	407	454	547	708	955	1,447
Germany............ 134	1,297	1,270	1,417	1,655	1,782	2,026	2,316	1,301	1,224	1,181	1,734	1,781	1,457	1,982
Greece............ 174	94	88	95	92	105	126	233	18	16	16	22	28	28	29
Iceland............ 176	2	2	2	2	2	2	1	—	1	1	—	—	1	1
Ireland............ 178	67	55	62	55	93	103	78	42	42	45	107	81	148	171
Italy............ 136	622	721	845	924	1,009	1,213	1,387	409	402	324	473	569	551	668
Luxembourg............ 137	10	11	9	11	25	14	—	4	2	2	2	8	9	36
Malta............ 181	2	3	4	4	13	5	24	1	—	5	—	1	3	—
Netherlands............ 138	1,498	1,618	1,401	1,798	2,234	2,518	2,749	344	352	370	475	369	515	504
Norway............ 142	35	32	38	45	54	52	57	30	28	46	124	53	58	76
Portugal............ 182	76	52	50	73	89	114	95	2	2	2	2	5	8	10
Slovenia............ 961	27	23	26	31	68	107	74	2	3	3	3	5	4	6
Spain............ 184	904	996	1,022	837	1,205	1,641	1,906	178	130	121	183	214	207	286
Sweden............ 144	118	128	110	115	108	135	110	249	266	191	380	500	646	773
Switzerland............ 146	95	55	117	148	131	237	314	174	193	222	255	321	307	355
United Kingdom............ 112	1,383	1,252	1,136	1,295	1,291	1,432	1,454	643	656	464	703	645	553	654
Developing Countries............ 202	**25,141**	**26,974**	**29,504**	**35,311**	**44,509**	**52,143**	**61,236**	**16,152**	**17,744**	**19,354**	**28,371**	**36,953**	**40,782**	**50,679**
Africa............ 607	**972**	**1,038**	**1,063**	**1,136**	**1,346**	**1,472**	**1,867**	**1,209**	**1,642**	**1,499**	**2,305**	**1,482**	**709**	**1,614**
Algeria............ 612	47	58	55	72	127	106	146	437	154	176	144	59	137	186
Angola............ 614	16	12	14	21	32	44	43	—	—	95	333	1	—	1
Benin............ 638	15	16	16	24	41	53	58	12	18	13	16	8	3	9
Botswana............ 616	—	—	1	1	1	—	—	—	—	—	—	—	—	—
Burkina Faso............ 748	1	1	2	2	4	2	2	3	4	4	11	8	12	16
Burundi............ 618	1	2	—	1	—	—	—	—	—	—	—	—	—	—
Cameroon............ 622	7	11	14	16	14	16	17	2	4	3	9	7	11	6
Cape Verde............ 624	1	—	—	—	—	—	—	—	—	—	—	—	—	—
Central African Rep............ 626	1	—	1	1	1	—	—	4	4	9	8	8	8	26
Chad............ 628	—	—	—	—	—	—	—	—	—	1	—	1	2	7
Comoros............ 632	2	2	1	1	1	1	1	—	—	—	—	—	—	—
Congo, Dem. Rep. of............ 636	5	7	4	3	—	—	—	—	—	—	—	—	—	—
Congo, Republic of............ 634	14	17	11	10	11	13	15	1	25	1	—	—	—	—
Côte d'Ivoire............ 662	17	16	19	13	9	16	23	32	39	41	48	37	28	31
Djibouti............ 611	15	13	16	23	42	45	44	—	—	—	—	—	—	—
Equatorial Guinea............ 642	—	—	1	1	2	3	2	—	—	—	—	—	—	—
Eritrea............ 643	3	4	2	6	1	1	2	1	—	—	—	—	—	—
Ethiopia............ 644	6	12	20	31	44	31	15	3	1	2	4	1	4	1
Gabon............ 646	3	2	2	3	5	6	26	—	—	—	1	—	—	—
Gambia, The............ 648	6	6	5	5	3	2	4	—	—	—	—	3	—	—
Ghana............ 652	16	24	33	47	53	90	119	6	10	5	7	4	13	5
Guinea............ 656	15	19	16	17	16	17	20	—	—	—	—	—	—	—
Guinea-Bissau............ 654	—	—	—	—	—	1	3	—	—	—	—	—	—	—
Kenya............ 664	25	23	28	35	43	36	54	7	7	8	8	10	8	9
Lesotho............ 666	—	1	1	2	3	2	4	—	—	—	—	—	—	—
Liberia............ 668	1	2	3	4	5	4	10	128	5	—	2	—	12	26
Madagascar............ 674	19	14	15	10	21	17	33	10	1	—	1	1	2	2
Malawi............ 676	1	1	1	2	3	4	6	—	—	—	—	2	5	6
Mali............ 678	9	9	5	5	3	2	3	5	4	5	8	7	9	12
Mauritania............ 682	18	13	9	14	14	11	12	—	—	—	—	—	—	—
Mauritius............ 684	37	33	32	35	42	54	67	2	—	—	2	—	2	3
Morocco............ 686	24	23	32	36	32	55	47	13	7	4	13	26	57	27
Mozambique............ 688	8	10	22	34	24	33	36	—	4	5	3	7	9	15
Namibia............ 728	4	2	1	2	1	3	4	—	—	—	2	2	20	7
Niger............ 692	7	6	8	11	7	8	3	—	5	1	—	—	—	—
Nigeria............ 694	283	294	247	177	169	158	196	445	1,132	862	1,077	953	5	607
Rwanda............ 714	—	1	—	—	—	1	1	—	59	66	272	—	—	—
St. Helena............ 856	1	1	1	1	—	—	—	—	1	2	—	—	—	—
São Tomé & Príncipe............ 716	1	1	1	1	1	1	1	—	—	—	—	—	—	—
Senegal............ 722	21	11	15	11	14	11	11	—	—	1	1	1	2	1
Seychelles............ 718	2	2	2	2	3	5	3	2	—	1	—	—	—	—

	Exports 2001	2002	2003	2004	2005	2006	2007	Imports 2001	2002	2003	2004	2005	2006	2007
	Millions of U.S. Dollars							*Millions of U.S. Dollars*						
Sierra Leone......724	5	4	4	8	6	12	18	—	—	—	—	—	—	—
Somalia......726	13	3	1	1	9	6	8	—	—	—	—	—	—	—
South Africa......199	160	167	233	260	314	382	557	—	126	158	229	263	226	253
Sudan......732	62	93	48	55	78	85	85	34	—	1	48	1	69	280
Swaziland......734	1	1	1	1	3	1	1	4	1	3	5	13	10	21
Tanzania......738	36	57	71	80	84	80	63	13	7	12	13	9	9	16
Togo......742	24	28	21	31	31	34	47	18	5	6	13	10	4	5
Tunisia......744	13	10	14	13	18	14	41	7	2	6	3	13	16	11
Uganda......746	2	2	3	3	2	3	4	3	1	3	5	8	5	5
Zambia......754	1	2	6	5	1	2	4	—	—	—	6	6	3	4
Zimbabwe......698	6	6	5	5	6	3	5	16	12	3	16	12	14	14
Africa n.s......799	—	—	—	—	—	—	—	1	—	—	—	—	—	—
Asia......507	**20,668**	**22,319**	**24,848**	**29,909**	**37,894**	**44,114**	**50,958**	**11,563**	**12,926**	**14,186**	**20,312**	**28,589**	**31,855**	**39,250**
Afghanistan, I.S. of......512	7	9	17	14	6	6	7	1	1	1	—	—	—	—
American Samoa......859	3	3	—	—	—	1	1	8	23	—	—	4	5	15
Bangladesh......513	216	246	266	282	353	428	634	5	5	5	7	19	19	20
Bhutan......514	—	—	—	—	1	1	—	—	—	—	—	—	—	—
Brunei Darussalam......516	22	32	30	32	39	38	43	37	35	117	295	1,197	1,607	1,865
Cambodia......522	72	69	80	72	94	104	122	—	1	1	1	1	1	1
China,P.R.: Mainland......924	2,201	2,903	3,803	4,605	6,662	8,344	9,676	1,843	2,427	2,957	4,101	5,843	6,637	8,558
China,P.R.:Hong Kong......532	1,290	1,242	1,183	1,387	1,492	1,703	1,687	257	241	222	267	291	346	443
China,P.R.:Macao......546	4	2	8	8	4	13	4	—	—	—	1	1	—	1
Fiji......819	14	14	15	18	20	19	19	2	2	3	—	8	—	—
French Polynesia......887	7	6	6	7	8	9	11	—	—	—	—	—	—	—
Guam......829	1	1	2	2	1	4	1	—	—	—	—	—	—	—
India......534	1,054	1,302	1,742	2,171	2,878	3,391	4,944	486	638	666	1,102	1,052	1,407	1,610
Korea......542	3,772	4,107	4,324	4,830	7,086	7,694	7,583	2,209	1,647	1,528	1,943	2,869	2,876	3,197
Lao People's Dem.Rep......544	1	1	—	2	2	4	4	—	—	3	—	—	—	3
Malaysia......548	1,779	2,030	2,364	3,016	3,431	4,111	5,096	1,005	1,037	1,138	1,682	2,149	3,193	6,412
Maldives......556	11	10	10	15	17	20	24	—	—	—	—	—	—	2
Mongolia......948	3	3	4	3	2	3	6	—	—	—	—	—	—	—
Myanmar......518	69	54	46	60	78	138	262	21	31	15	17	14	20	30
Nauru......836	1	1	3	1	—	—	11	2	—	—	—	—	—	—
Nepal......558	8	6	5	6	15	9	12	—	—	—	—	—	—	—
New Caledonia......839	5	5	8	7	11	9	—	—	—	—	—	—	—	—
Pakistan......564	179	265	265	416	634	734	935	193	85	47	51	46	36	47
Palau......565	—	1	—	—	—	—	—	—	—	—	—	—	—	—
Papua New Guinea......853	28	30	34	36	49	66	70	12	66	118	93	50	184	14
Philippines......566	815	778	945	1,238	1,419	1,406	1,854	94	114	183	229	322	285	360
Samoa......862	6	5	6	6	7	10	17	—	—	17	6	—	—	—
Singapore......576	5,364	5,349	5,400	6,001	7,837	8,930	10,502	3,147	4,100	4,155	6,083	9,471	10,035	9,840
Solomon Islands......813	1	2	2	2	4	4	6	—	—	1	—	—	—	1
Sri Lanka......524	159	153	185	238	338	424	415	7	6	3	6	23	47	42
Taiwan Province of China......528	2,188	2,067	2,233	2,854	2,475	2,735	2,597	1,071	1,010	877	1,240	1,338	1,322	1,495
Thailand......578	1,064	1,227	1,393	1,976	2,246	2,702	3,054	986	1,191	1,702	2,772	3,447	2,983	4,287
Timor-Leste......537	—	—	43	28	35	—	—	—	—	1	1	1	—	—
Tonga......866	—	1	1	2	2	2	2	—	—	—	—	—	—	—
Tuvalu......869	—	—	—	—	1	—	1	—	—	—	—	—	2	—
Vanuatu......846	—	—	—	2	2	2	4	—	6	11	—	—	—	—
Vietnam......582	322	393	468	601	678	1,052	1,355	171	259	416	416	439	847	994
Asia n.s......598	—	—	—	—	—	—	—	3	1	—	—	3	2	11
Europe......170	**515**	**693**	**842**	**973**	**1,362**	**1,643**	**2,328**	**502**	**383**	**469**	**1,045**	**1,022**	**1,065**	**2,104**
Albania......914	1	2	1	1	—	—	1	—	—	—	—	—	—	—
Armenia......911	—	—	—	—	—	1	1	—	—	—	—	—	—	—
Azerbaijan......912	—	—	1	1	2	2	3	—	—	—	169	—	65	99
Belarus......913	—	—	2	3	5	6	5	1	—	—	—	9	16	27
Bosnia & Herzegovina......963	—	—	1	1	—	—	1	—	1	—	2	—	—	—
Bulgaria......918	77	72	103	48	51	19	38	4	7	9	20	19	20	12
Croatia......960	2	5	8	18	9	14	27	—	1	1	2	2	3	3
Czech Republic......935	13	26	26	23	20	39	71	11	15	22	23	34	28	61
Czechoslovakia n.s......937	4	2	2	8	—	15	31	1	3	1	—	—	—	—
Estonia......939	3	10	4	6	6	6	19	143	1	—	1	2	2	5
Faroe Islands......816	3	2	3	3	1	—	—	—	—	—	—	—	—	—
Georgia......915	5	5	7	6	8	15	21	1	—	2	—	1	1	—
Hungary......944	40	70	98	96	63	66	37	6	11	12	12	22	13	26
Kazakhstan......916	2	5	2	3	4	1	6	5	5	76	13	23	—	9
Kyrgyz Republic......917	1	1	1	—	—	1	1	—	—	2	2	4	2	1
Latvia......941	1	1	2	3	11	7	11	—	3	1	—	1	1	—
Lithuania......946	5	6	6	5	7	10	20	1	6	6	—	—	5	2
Macedonia, FYR......962	—	—	—	—	—	—	2	—	—	—	—	1	—	—
Moldova......921	—	—	—	—	—	—	—	—	—	—	—	—	1	1
Poland......964	82	111	96	102	115	144	191	8	18	14	26	25	45	93
Romania......968	9	14	23	25	33	48	59	7	11	6	22	12	7	11
Russia......922	62	66	110	154	245	273	338	141	151	100	234	436	416	440
Slovak Republic......936	1	1	2	27	44	40	46	19	2	1	2	3	3	11
Tajikistan......923	—	—	1	—	—	—	—	—	—	—	—	—	—	1
Turkey......186	176	238	264	356	566	724	1,045	28	23	49	54	69	79	735
Turkmenistan......925	1	1	1	1	1	—	1	—	—	—	—	—	1	—

		Exports							Imports						
		2001	2002	2003	2004	2005	2006	2007	2001	2002	2003	2004	2005	2006	2007
		Millions of U.S. Dollars							Millions of U.S. Dollars						
Ukraine	926	25	52	76	78	166	207	351	116	122	165	421	350	345	538
U.S.S.R. n.s.	930	—	—	—	—	—	—	—	3	—	—	33	—	—	—
Uzbekistan	927	—	1	1	1	1	1	2	3	3	3	3	10	9	27
Yugoslavia n.s.	966	1	1	2	3	3	2	3	1	1	1	3	1	—	1
Europe n.s.	884	—	1	2	1	—	—	1	—	—	—	2	—	4	1
Middle East	**407**	**2,037**	**1,970**	**1,910**	**2,190**	**2,611**	**3,233**	**4,154**	**2,439**	**2,259**	**2,636**	**3,697**	**4,699**	**5,903**	**6,165**
Bahrain	419	18	17	17	20	18	26	35	24	43	47	108	138	40	30
Egypt	469	197	180	170	197	290	464	590	16	21	31	18	40	50	49
Iran, I.R. of	429	121	129	185	188	290	313	473	132	67	97	71	79	91	80
Iraq	433	83	63	12	43	85	66	12	—	102	—	71	—	—	—
Jordan	439	69	91	89	311	157	181	129	28	17	27	22	21	18	44
Kuwait	443	75	74	73	63	84	91	—	708	675	687	1,066	1,275	1,506	1,706
Lebanon	446	41	31	29	29	24	23	44	—	34	31	1	1	1	1
Libya	672	3	6	5	7	18	34	34	4	—	55	12	74	423	643
Oman	449	20	19	17	21	29	45	98	1	2	3	1	—	13	5
Qatar	453	21	24	25	35	62	102	146	22	9	10	11	3	24	42
Saudi Arabia	456	482	475	435	418	524	672	944	1,314	1,104	1,498	1,967	2,712	3,384	3,373
Syrian Arab Republic	463	60	59	40	48	48	56	79	15	15	7	8	12	7	—
United Arab Emirates	466	757	720	760	745	907	1,068	1,325	174	115	113	340	343	345	190
Yemen, Republic of	474	89	82	52	64	75	90	243	1	55	29	—	—	—	1
Middle East n.s.	489	2	1	1	—	—	1	—	—	—	—	—	—	—	—
Western Hemisphere	**207**	**950**	**955**	**841**	**1,103**	**1,296**	**1,680**	**1,930**	**439**	**533**	**564**	**1,013**	**1,160**	**1,249**	**1,546**
Antigua and Barbuda	311	1	1	2	2	1	1	1	—	—	—	—	—	—	—
Argentina	213	72	21	56	83	119	164	180	30	82	72	330	379	363	453
Aruba	314	1	—	1	1	1	1	1	—	—	—	—	—	—	—
Bahamas, The	313	1	1	1	1	1	1	1	—	14	—	—	6	—	—
Barbados	316	1	1	1	1	3	6	5	—	—	—	—	—	—	—
Belize	339	3	1	—	1	—	1	—	—	1	—	—	—	—	—
Bermuda	319	—	—	—	1	2	1	7	—	—	—	—	—	—	—
Bolivia	218	—	1	1	4	2	1	1	—	—	—	—	—	—	—
Brazil	223	202	327	244	330	403	626	786	170	274	332	442	454	515	687
Chile	228	85	66	68	91	114	153	135	57	52	62	110	136	198	203
Colombia	233	35	36	46	68	85	100	108	2	3	1	3	4	3	5
Costa Rica	238	5	9	15	9	10	13	19	—	1	1	2	3	2	2
Dominica	321	1	1	1	1	1	1	2	1	—	—	—	—	1	—
Dominican Republic	243	14	16	9	9	14	16	16	—	—	—	—	—	—	9
Ecuador	248	18	12	12	22	29	48	39	3	1	1	2	3	3	5
El Salvador	253	6	6	8	5	7	8	7	—	—	—	—	1	13	—
Falkland Islands	323	2	—	—	—	—	—	—	—	—	—	—	—	—	—
Guatemala	258	11	14	8	8	10	12	11	—	—	—	1	2	13	34
Guyana	336	1	1	1	1	1	2	1	—	—	—	—	—	—	—
Haiti	263	4	7	4	6	5	7	9	—	—	—	—	—	—	—
Honduras	268	4	6	5	6	6	6	5	—	—	—	—	—	—	—
Jamaica	343	6	4	4	7	7	8	15	—	—	—	—	—	—	1
Mexico	273	230	264	238	279	277	318	361	25	24	31	30	46	60	68
Netherlands Antilles	353	13	9	5	9	11	6	8	10	13	9	5	4	9	1
Nicaragua	278	5	8	3	3	5	5	5	26	—	—	—	—	—	—
Panama	283	147	78	43	54	77	57	57	56	20	19	18	39	22	1
Paraguay	288	3	2	1	3	3	4	7	3	1	1	11	5	—	—
Peru	293	21	25	22	25	28	34	42	46	28	19	26	36	31	28
St. Kitts and Nevis	361	1	1	—	—	—	—	—	—	—	—	—	—	—	—
St. Lucia	362	—	—	—	—	1	1	1	—	—	—	—	—	—	—
St. Vincent & Grens.	364	—	—	—	—	—	—	—	—	8	2	—	—	3	—
Suriname	366	2	2	2	3	2	3	3	—	—	—	—	—	—	—
Trinidad and Tobago	369	3	3	2	6	4	8	6	—	3	7	18	11	7	43
Uruguay	298	20	4	4	4	5	5	7	1	4	2	2	1	1	1
Venezuela, Rep. Bol.	299	26	22	24	55	61	62	78	7	3	—	9	20	1	4
Western Hem. n.s.	399	4	4	7	4	3	1	2	—	1	1	2	10	1	3
Other Countries n.i.e.	**910**	**5**	**2**	**4**	**5**	**7**	**14**	**7**	**2**	**3**	—	**7**	**9**	**1**	**3**
Cuba	928	1	1	2	1	1	1	6	—	—	—	—	—	—	—
North Korea	954	4	2	2	4	7	13	—	2	3	—	7	9	1	3
Countries & Areas n.s.	**898**	**1**	**9**	**1**	—	—	—	—	—	—	**1**	**5**	—	—	—
Special Categories	**899**	**53**	**39**	—	—	—	—	—	**266**	**229**	**300**	**192**	**290**	**409**	—
Memorandum Items															
European Union	998	7,963	8,187	8,244	9,037	10,278	11,983	13,280	4,241	3,935	3,619	5,324	5,828	6,029	7,660
Oil Exporting Ctys.	999	1,919	1,883	1,838	1,826	2,355	2,717	3,454	3,244	3,363	3,502	4,769	5,520	5,930	6,837
Non-Oil Develop.Ctys.	201	23,223	25,091	27,666	33,486	42,154	49,425	57,782	12,908	14,381	15,852	23,602	31,433	34,852	43,842
PERCENT DISTRIBUTION															
Industrial Countries	**101**	**55.2**	**52.7**	**51.6**	**50.6**	**48.0**	**48.2**	**46.3**	**47.0**	**42.5**	**39.6**	**38.6**	**35.4**	**32.5**	**31.9**
Developing Countries	**202**	**44.6**	**47.2**	**48.4**	**49.4**	**52.0**	**51.7**	**53.7**	**52.2**	**56.7**	**59.5**	**61.0**	**64.0**	**66.8**	**68.0**
Africa	**607**	**1.7**	**1.8**	**1.7**	**1.6**	**1.6**	**1.5**	**1.6**	**3.9**	**5.2**	**4.6**	**5.0**	**2.6**	**1.2**	**2.2**
Asia	**507**	**36.7**	**39.1**	**40.7**	**41.8**	**44.3**	**43.8**	**44.7**	**37.3**	**41.3**	**43.6**	**43.7**	**49.5**	**52.2**	**52.7**
Europe	**170**	**.9**	**1.2**	**1.4**	**1.4**	**1.6**	**1.6**	**2.0**	**1.6**	**1.2**	**1.4**	**2.2**	**1.8**	**1.7**	**2.8**
Middle East	**407**	**3.6**	**3.4**	**3.1**	**3.1**	**3.0**	**3.2**	**3.6**	**7.9**	**7.2**	**8.1**	**7.9**	**8.1**	**9.7**	**8.3**
Western Hemisphere	**207**	**1.7**	**1.7**	**1.4**	**1.5**	**1.5**	**1.7**	**1.7**	**1.4**	**1.7**	**1.7**	**2.2**	**2.0**	**2.0**	**2.1**
ANNUAL PERCENT CHANGE															

Indonesia 536

	Exports							Imports						
	2001	2002	2003	2004	2005	2006	2007	2001	2002	2003	2004	2005	2006	2007
World.. 001	–9.3	1.5	6.8	17.3	19.7	17.7	13.2	–7.6	1.1	4.0	42.9	24.0	5.8	22.0
Industrial Countries................. 101	–8.0	–3.2	4.5	15.1	13.5	18.2	8.7	–7.7	–8.5	–3.2	39.2	13.9	–2.8	19.7
Developing Countries.............. 202	–11.0	7.3	9.4	19.7	26.0	17.2	17.4	–7.5	9.9	9.1	46.6	30.2	10.4	24.3
Africa.......................................607	10.0	6.8	2.4	6.9	18.4	9.4	26.8	51.3	35.8	–8.7	53.7	–35.7	–52.1	127.5
Asia... 507	–12.9	8.0	11.3	20.4	26.7	16.4	15.5	–10.5	11.8	9.7	43.2	40.7	11.4	23.2
Europe.....................................170	–.5	34.4	21.6	15.6	40.0	20.7	41.7	57.7	–23.7	22.5	122.6	–2.1	4.2	97.5
Middle East............................ 407	–1.2	–3.3	–3.0	14.6	19.2	23.8	28.5	–13.7	–7.4	16.7	40.3	27.1	25.6	4.4
Western Hemisphere.............207	–9.6	.5	–11.9	31.1	17.5	29.6	14.9	–26.2	21.4	5.8	79.4	14.6	7.7	23.8
Other Countries n.i.e................910	–69.2	–55.5	73.1	32.2	46.2	90.5	–51.1	92.7	20.9	–85.9	—	28.1	–93.6	390.3

		Exports							Imports						
		2001	2002	2003	2004	2005	2006	2007	2001	2002	2003	2004	2005	2006	2007
		Millions of U.S. Dollars							*Millions of U.S. Dollars*						
IFS World Total		**25,689**	**24,440**	**33,750**	**41,697**	**56,252**	**77,012**	**83,000**	**16,709**	**20,617**	**24,798**	**31,976**	**40,041**	**40,772**	**45,000**
DOTS World Total	**001**	**24,337Y**	**22,176Y**	**31,782Y**	**40,998Y**	**55,403Y**	**71,051Y**	**80,948Y**	**17,690**	**22,324**	**30,646Y**	**38,546Y**	**43,587Y**	**46,984Y**	**56,642Y**
Industrial Countries	**101**	**10,306Y**	**9,474Y**	**14,197Y**	**17,194Y**	**22,555Y**	**26,358Y**	**28,619Y**	**8,765**	**12,537**	**14,550Y**	**18,392Y**	**20,129Y**	**18,085Y**	**17,816Y**
United States	111	135V	148V	152V	142V	163V	147V	162V	74	68	109V	94V	105V	94V	160V
Canada	156	29V	35V	45V	62V	37V	39V	41V	382	199	179V	157V	251V	299V	280V
Australia	193	14V	21V	34V	21V	26V	29V	30V	455	357	186V	123V	146V	342V	179V
Japan	158	4,561V	4,311V	6,764V	7,515V	9,362V	9,887V	11,599V	787	714	1,236V	1,231V	1,474V	1,291V	1,465V
New Zealand	196	9V	35V	22V	26V	8V	103V	4V	22	35	70V	72V	60V	93V	116V
Austria	122	11V	13V	10V	67V	209V	162V	276V	239	252	408V	494V	604V	508V	525V
Belgium	124	31V	20V	26V	97V	114V	152V	248V	440	396	537V	686V	638V	608V	605V
Cyprus	423	2V	2V	2V	2V	3V	4V	3V	18	17	1V	2V	6V	6V	8V
Denmark	128	8V	8V	10V	14V	11V	11V	13V	87	95	143V	234V	234V	114V	177V
Finland	172	1V	1V	2V	2V	2V	8V	1V	77	69	186V	204V	219V	272V	189V
France	132	670V	720V	1,078V	1,614V	2,432V	2,708V	3,069V	1,109	1,318	2,598V	3,192V	2,739V	2,624V	2,265V
Germany	134	330V	273V	292V	443V	523V	412V	621V	1,807	3,777	3,318V	4,900V	6,067V	5,674V	5,445V
Greece	174	879V	415V	882V	1,296V	1,679V	2,066V	2,471V	19	8	12V	24V	66V	26V	15V
Iceland	176	—V	—V	—V	—V	—V	—V	—V	—	—	—V	—V	1V	—V	—V
Ireland	178	1V	1V	1V	17V	1V	1V	—V	22	38	21V	21V	31V	33V	42V
Italy	136	1,920V	1,620V	1,946V	2,466V	3,316V	4,467V	5,215V	996	1,389	2,442V	2,963V	3,079V	2,519V	2,824V
Luxembourg	137	5V	9V	4V	5V	8V	4V	3V	41	14	14V	25V	12V	11V	9V
Malta	181	5Y	—V	—V	—V	3V	—V	1V	—	—	—V	1V	1V	3V	3V
Netherlands	138	206V	620V	1,171V	1,660V	2,524V	3,249V	2,307V	346	308	465V	711V	1,000V	920V	742V
Norway	142	7V	7V	8V	9V	8V	11V	10V	12	9	27V	69V	38V	47V	31V
Portugal	182	82V	132V	55V	132V	125V	337V	365V	12	15	26V	24V	24V	21V	21V
Slovenia	961	1V	2V	2V	2Y	1V	3V	5V	33	53	76V	99Y	73V	60V	94V
Spain	184	752V	639V	948V	979V	1,737V	2,278V	1,903V	308	300	505V	607V	513V	453V	660V
Sweden	144	510V	300V	581V	415V	159V	135V	126V	377	350	699V	1,045V	1,162V	539V	379V
Switzerland	146	96V	93V	115V	135V	43V	26V	29V	435	1,989	443V	517V	659V	659V	704V
United Kingdom	112	39V	49V	46V	72V	64V	119V	117V	666	769	852V	897V	926V	872V	876V
Developing Countries	**202**	**10,388Y**	**8,829Y**	**12,890Y**	**17,590Y**	**24,395Y**	**34,066Y**	**39,509Y**	**8,790**	**9,673**	**15,969Y**	**19,990Y**	**23,248Y**	**28,639Y**	**38,491Y**
Africa	**607**	**1,323Y**	**1,207Y**	**1,422Y**	**2,802Y**	**3,019Y**	**3,647Y**	**4,080Y**	**153**	**119**	**154Y**	**155Y**	**240Y**	**364Y**	**403Y**
Benin	638	—V	—V	—V	1V	—V	—Y	—Y	—	—	—V	—V	—V	—Y	—Y
Burundi	618	1V	—V	—V	—V	—V	—V	—Y	—	—	—V	—V	—V	—V	—Y
Cameroon	622	1V	1V	2V	2Y	3Y	4Y	5Y	—	—	—V	—Y	—Y	—Y	—Y
Congo, Republic of	634	3V	1V	1V	—V	—Y	—Y	—Y	—	—	—V	—V	—Y	—Y	—Y
Côte d'Ivoire	662	—V	—V	2V	1V	1V	3V	3Y	—	—	2V	2V	10V	5V	7Y
Guinea	656	1V	1Y	—V	1V	1Y	1Y	2Y	—	—	—V	—V	—Y	—Y	—Y
Kenya	664	9V	3V	30V	24V	32Y	41Y	49Y	2	—	1V	2V	2Y	3Y	4Y
Madagascar	674	2V	3V	76V	101Y	137Y	172Y	208Y	—	—	—V	—Y	—Y	—Y	—Y
Mali	678	—Y	—Y	—Y	—Y	—Y	—Y	—Y	—	—	—Y	—Y	—Y	—Y	1Y
Mauritius	684	6V	5V	1V	6V	2V	2V	3V	—	—	—V	—V	—V	—V	—V
Morocco	686	256V	263V	41V	252V	514V	646Y	779Y	26	28	35V	43V	43V	53Y	69Y
Niger	692	—V	1V	1V	3V	3Y	4Y	5Y	—	—	—V	—V	—Y	—Y	—Y
Nigeria	694	1V	3V	1V	1Y	1Y	1Y	2Y	—	—	—V	—Y	—Y	—Y	—Y
Senegal	722	1V	—V	1V	1V	1V	1V	1Y	—	—	—V	—V	—V	—V	—Y
Seychelles	718	—V	—V	—V	—Y	—Y	—Y	—Y	—	4	—V	—Y	—Y	—Y	—Y
South Africa	199	1,027V	917V	1,238V	2,357V	2,257V	2,710V	2,957V	73	36	44V	59V	142V	234V	235V
Sudan	732	—Y	—Y	14Y	25V	51V	43V	45V	—	2	6V	—V	—V	—V	—V
Tanzania	738	5V	4V	4Y	6Y	8Y	10Y	12Y	—	—	—Y	—Y	1Y	1Y	1Y
Togo	742	1V	—V	—V	—V	—V	—Y	—Y	2	—	—V	—V	—V	—Y	—Y
Tunisia	744	5V	2V	8V	1V	2V	2V	3Y	44	47	45V	48V	41V	67V	87Y
Uganda	746	1V	1V	2V	2Y	3Y	4Y	5Y	—	—	—V	—Y	—Y	—Y	—Y
Zambia	754	1V	—V	—V	1V	—V	1V	2V	—	—	1V	—V	—V	—V	—V
Zimbabwe	698	1V	1V	—V	19V	2V	—V	—Y	5	1	19V	2V	—V	—V	1Y
Asia	**507**	**7,401Y**	**5,929Y**	**8,798Y**	**11,210Y**	**15,724Y**	**22,121Y**	**25,248Y**	**3,219**	**3,740**	**7,289Y**	**8,732Y**	**9,805Y**	**12,457Y**	**17,703Y**
Afghanistan, I.S. of	512	—Y	—Y	—Y	—Y	—Y	—Y	—Y	1	—	—Y	—Y	—Y	—Y	—Y
Bangladesh	513	9V	9V	18V	15V	21V	40V	35V	39	49	40V	38V	51V	59Y	72Y
Brunei Darussalam	516	—Y	—Y	1V	1Y	1Y	1Y	1Y	—	—	—V	—Y	—Y	—Y	—Y
Cambodia	522	—V	—V	—V	—V	—V	1V	2Y	—	—	—V	—V	—V	—V	—Y
China,P.R.: Mainland	924	2,203V	2,133V	3,014V	3,961V	6,178V	9,042V	12,118V	887	1,046	2,550V	2,762V	3,628V	4,927V	8,017V
China,P.R.:Hong Kong	532	52V	94V	146V	115V	173V	153V	172V	10	13	41V	55V	68V	94V	92V
India	534	462Y	241V	241V	333V	561V	705Y	851Y	561	717	937V	1,253V	1,309V	1,616Y	2,094Y
Indonesia	536	120V	61V	88V	64V	72V	83V	73V	92	103	204V	207V	318V	344V	520V
Korea	542	1,908V	1,214V	1,677V	2,214V	3,214V	4,590V	5,893V	958	894	1,956V	2,348V	2,355V	2,815V	3,592V
Malaysia	548	136V	118V	91V	235V	316V	528V	389V	189	195	361V	380V	395V	486V	679V
Myanmar	518	—Y	—Y	—Y	—Y	—Y	—Y	—Y	—	—	—Y	—Y	—Y	—Y	1Y
Nepal	558	—V	—V	1V	1V	2V	4V	4Y	—	—	—V	—V	—V	—V	—Y
Pakistan	564	198V	186V	274V	247V	330V	415Y	500Y	—	88	90V	113V	196V	242Y	314Y
Philippines	566	690V	394V	539V	770V	912V	1,536V	176V	7	6	14V	38V	44V	76V	104V
Samoa	862	—Y	—Y	—Y	—Y	1V	1Y	1Y	—	—	—Y	—Y	—Y	—Y	—Y
Singapore	576	519V	543V	686V	933V	1,167V	1,588V	1,223V	159	321	434V	587V	543V	502V	587V
Sri Lanka	524	212V	167V	227V	381V	476V	690V	767V	15	1	39V	64V	82V	92V	129V

	Exports 2001	2002	2003	2004	2005	2006	2007	Imports 2001	2002	2003	2004	2005	2006	2007
	Millions of U.S. Dollars							Millions of U.S. Dollars						
Taiwan Province of China............ 528	808V	694V	1,709V	1,867V	2,243V	2,643V	2,964V	195	179	278V	367V	379V	563V	649V
Thailand.................................... 578	69V	56V	65V	36V	37V	52V	80V	108	123	328V	497V	346V	622V	853V
Vietnam..................................... 582	13V	18V	21V	37V	20V	50V	—V	—	4	15V	22V	91V	18V	—V
Europe.................................... 170	**1,106Y**	**1,170Y**	**2,073Y**	**2,227Y**	**3,821Y**	**6,044Y**	**7,436Y**	**2,082**	**2,062**	**3,923Y**	**5,582Y**	**6,570Y**	**7,389Y**	**10,156Y**
Albania...................................... 914	—V	1V	2V	1V	2V	1V	1V	—	—	—V	—V	1V	—V	—V
Armenia..................................... 911	71V	57V	47V	57V	81V	—V	—V	42	49	25V	34V	31V	33V	42V
Azerbaijan.................................. 912	50V	53V	46V	41V	69V	78V	96V	21	25	54V	169V	183V	325V	478V
Belarus...................................... 913	1V	1V	1V	3V	3V	4V	9V	28	5	23V	37V	39V	35V	73V
Bulgaria..................................... 918	1V	1V	2V	2V	6V	9V	11V	23	6	21V	13V	17V	49V	43V
Croatia...................................... 960	1V	3V	3V	3V	2V	3V	3V	10	11	4V	4V	4V	7V	5V
Czech Republic........................... 935	7V	8V	12V	13V	13V	2V	3V	77	35	84V	51V	99V	26V	33V
Estonia...................................... 939	—V	1V	1V	1V	—V	—V	—V	—	—	—V	—V	2V	1V	2V
Georgia...................................... 915	6V	7V	6V	14V	24V	37V	45Y	14	18	4V	5V	5V	3V	4Y
Hungary..................................... 944	6V	7V	7V	6V	4V	4V	5V	58	28	18V	22V	86V	56V	35V
Kazakhstan................................ 916	10V	11V	12V	12V	16Y	20Y	24Y	270	262	452V	783V	997Y	1,231Y	1,595Y
Kyrgyz Republic.......................... 917	6V	4V	5V	6V	5V	7V	5V	12	9	2V	4V	4V	8V	11V
Latvia.. 941	—V	1V	1V	1V	1V	1V	1V	2	—	5V	11V	1V	—V	1V
Lithuania.................................... 946	3V	3V	4V	3V	4V	7V	13V	8	7	1V	1V	1V	1V	1V
Macedonia, FYR.......................... 962	2V	3V	1V	1V	1V	2V	2Y	1	—	2V	1V	—V	1V	2Y
Moldova..................................... 921	—V	—V	—V	—V	—V	1Y	1Y	—	—	—V	—V	—V	—Y	—Y
Poland....................................... 964	15V	24V	48V	17V	9V	14V	10V	68	29	81V	71V	137V	118V	117V
Romania..................................... 968	7V	4V	7V	9V	90V	274V	561V	44	43	93V	65V	103V	69V	152V
Russia.. 922	31V	45V	56V	101V	128V	216V	317V	914	874	1,451V	2,081V	2,123V	2,085V	3,253V
Slovak Republic.......................... 936	3V	4V	5Y	7Y	11V	4V	5V	3	3	4Y	5Y	9V	7V	12V
Tajikistan................................... 923	9V	14V	22V	24V	28V	31V	55V	1	8	57V	33V	40V	84V	83V
Turkey....................................... 186	763V	837V	1,692V	1,783V	3,154V	5,115V	6,013V	291	369	587V	891V	1,004V	1,173V	1,526V
Turkmenistan............................. 925	110V	74V	85V	112Y	153Y	192Y	231Y	16	19	559V	727Y	925Y	1,142Y	1,480Y
Ukraine...................................... 926	3V	6V	8V	8V	17V	21Y	25Y	111	195	325V	478V	635V	783Y	1,015Y
Uzbekistan.................................. 927	—Y	—Y	—Y	—Y	—Y	—Y	—Y	44	57	64Y	83Y	105Y	130Y	168Y
Yugoslavia n.s............................ 966	—Y	—Y	—Y	—Y	—Y	—Y	—Y	10	3	3Y	4Y	5Y	7Y	9Y
Europe n.s................................. 884	—Y	—Y	—Y	—Y	—Y	—Y	—Y	13	6	7Y	9Y	11Y	14Y	18Y
Middle East............................. 407	**541Y**	**506Y**	**575Y**	**1,235Y**	**1,804Y**	**2,175Y**	**2,587Y**	**2,015**	**2,704**	**3,467Y**	**4,071Y**	**5,266Y**	**6,337Y**	**7,458Y**
Bahrain...................................... 419	—Y	—Y	—Y	—Y	—Y	—Y	—Y	72	56	63Y	82Y	104Y	128Y	166Y
Egypt... 469	10V	10Y	12Y	16Y	22Y	28Y	34Y	10	15	16Y	21Y	27Y	33Y	43Y
Iraq... 433	—Y	—Y	—Y	—Y	—Y	—Y	—Y	24	15	17Y	19Y	25Y	31Y	36Y
Jordan.. 439	11V	11V	14V	8V	21V	8V	7V	10	21	29V	57V	41V	72V	36V
Kuwait.. 443	—Y	—Y	—Y	—Y	—Y	—Y	—Y	11	14	15Y	18Y	23Y	28Y	33Y
Lebanon..................................... 446	27Y	29Y	35Y	46Y	63Y	79Y	96Y	17	33	36Y	47Y	60Y	74Y	96Y
Oman... 449	42V	20V	42V	48Y	64Y	76Y	90Y	3	3	472V	544Y	722Y	864Y	1,020Y
Qatar... 453	22V	17V	16V	12V	47V	48V	57Y	10	26	12V	67V	—V	—V	—Y
Saudi Arabia............................... 456	108V	82V	105V	249V	443V	530Y	625Y	222	335	372Y	429Y	569Y	682Y	804Y
Syrian Arab Republic.................. 463	—Y	—Y	—Y	449V	610Y	767Y	925Y	2	35	39Y	28V	35Y	43Y	56Y
United Arab Emirates.................. 466	316V	332V	346V	398Y	529Y	633Y	747Y	1,633	2,152	2,395Y	2,757Y	3,659Y	4,381Y	5,168Y
Yemen, Republic of..................... 474	4V	5V	5Y	8V	4V	5Y	6Y	1	—	—Y	3V	—V	—Y	—Y
Western Hemisphere................ 207	**18Y**	**16Y**	**22Y**	**116Y**	**27Y**	**80Y**	**158Y**	**1,321**	**1,049**	**1,136Y**	**1,451Y**	**1,367Y**	**2,093Y**	**2,771Y**
Argentina.................................. 213	2V	—V	—V	1V	1V	1V	1V	319	95	51V	1V	—V	7V	351V
Aruba.. 314	—V	—V	—V	—V	—V	—V	—V	5	3	3Y	4Y	5Y	6Y	8Y
Brazil... 223	3V	9V	14V	3V	3V	31V	11V	896	843	956V	1,246V	1,065V	1,725V	2,021V
Chile.. 228	2V	1V	1V	1V	1V	2V	1V	—	2	61V	92V	163V	195V	200V
Colombia.................................... 233	—V	—V	1V	1V	—V	1V	3V	—	—	3V	3V	5V	4V	—V
Costa Rica.................................. 238	—V	—V	—V	—V	—V	—Y	—Y	—	—	—V	—V	3V	4Y	5Y
Ecuador..................................... 248	—V	—V	—V	—V	—V	—V	—Y	—	2	3V	—V	1V	—V	—Y
El Salvador................................ 253	—V	—V	—V	—V	—V	—V	10V	—	—	2V	—V	—V	—V	—V
Guatemala.................................. 258	—V	—V	—V	—V	—V	—Y	—Y	—	—	—V	—V	1V	1Y	1Y
Jamaica...................................... 343	—V	—V	—V	—V	—V	—V	—V	—	—	—V	6V	—V	—V	—V
Mexico....................................... 273	9V	5V	4V	4V	4V	6V	43V	41	34	24V	41V	29V	26V	21V
Panama...................................... 283	—V	—V	—V	—V	—V	—V	—V	—	—	—V	—V	1V	—V	—V
Paraguay.................................... 288	—V	—V	—V	—V	—V	—V	—Y	13	—	—V	—V	—V	—V	—Y
Peru... 293	—V	—V	—V	1V	1V	1V	46Y	19	26	15V	9V	5V	2V	4Y
Trinidad and Tobago................... 369	—V	—V	—Y	—Y	1Y	1Y	1Y	—	—	—Y	—Y	—Y	—Y	—Y
Uruguay..................................... 298	—V	—Y	—V	104V	1V	1Y	1Y	28	43	17V	48V	89V	110Y	142Y
Venezuela, Rep. Bol.................... 299	—V	—V	—V	—V	15V	37V	40V	—	—	—V	1V	—V	15V	18Y
Other Countries n.i.e............... 910	**—Y**	**—Y**	**—Y**	**—Y**	**—Y**	**—Y**	**—Y**	**15**	**43**	**48Y**	**62Y**	**79Y**	**98Y**	**127Y**
Cuba.. 928	—Y	—Y	—Y	—Y	—Y	—Y	—Y	15	43	48Y	62Y	79Y	98Y	127Y
Countries & Areas n.s.............. 898	**3,643Y**	**3,874Y**	**4,696Y**	**6,214Y**	**8,453Y**	**10,627Y**	**12,820Y**	**113**	**52**	**58Y**	**75Y**	**96Y**	**118Y**	**153Y**
Special Categories.................. 899	**—Y**	**—Y**	**—Y**	**—Y**	**—Y**	**—Y**	**—Y**	**7**	**19**	**21Y**	**27Y**	**35Y**	**43Y**	**56Y**
Memorandum Items														
European Union.......................... 998	5,490Y	4,871Y	7,136Y	9,332Y	12,951Y	16,149Y	16,781Y	6,814	9,269	12,493Y	16,290Y	17,729Y	15,471Y	15,079Y
Oil Exporting Ctys....................... 999	610Y	515Y	598Y	773Y	1,171Y	1,409Y	1,633Y	1,994	2,647	3,487Y	4,041Y	5,318Y	6,345Y	7,598Y
Non-Oil Develop.Ctys.................. 201	9,778Y	8,314Y	12,292Y	16,817Y	23,224Y	32,657Y	37,876Y	6,796	7,026	12,482Y	15,948Y	17,930Y	22,295Y	30,893Y
PERCENT DISTRIBUTION														
Industrial Countries................. 101	**42.3**	**42.7**	**44.7**	**41.9**	**40.7**	**37.1**	**35.4**	**49.6**	**56.2**	**47.5**	**47.7**	**46.2**	**38.5**	**31.5**
Developing Countries.............. 202	**42.7**	**39.8**	**40.6**	**42.9**	**44.0**	**47.9**	**48.8**	**49.7**	**43.3**	**52.1**	**51.9**	**53.3**	**61.0**	**68.0**
Africa.................................... 607	**5.4**	**5.4**	**4.5**	**6.8**	**5.4**	**5.1**	**5.0**	**.9**	**.5**	**.5**	**.4**	**.6**	**.8**	**.7**
Asia....................................... 507	**30.4**	**26.7**	**27.7**	**27.3**	**28.4**	**31.1**	**31.2**	**18.2**	**16.8**	**23.8**	**22.7**	**22.5**	**26.5**	**31.3**
Europe.................................... 170	**4.5**	**5.3**	**6.5**	**5.4**	**6.9**	**8.5**	**9.2**	**11.8**	**9.2**	**12.8**	**14.5**	**15.1**	**15.7**	**17.9**

Iran, Islamic Republic of 429

	Exports							Imports						
	2001	2002	2003	2004	2005	2006	2007	2001	2002	2003	2004	2005	2006	2007
Middle East........................... 407	2.2	2.3	1.8	3.0	3.3	3.1	3.2	11.4	12.1	11.3	10.6	12.1	13.5	13.2
Western Hemisphere............. 207	.1	.1	.1	.3	—	.1	.2	7.5	4.7	3.7	3.8	3.1	4.5	4.9
Other Countries n.i.e............... 910	—	—	—	—	—	—	—	.1	.2	.2	.2	.2	.2	.2
ANNUAL PERCENT CHANGE														
World....................................... 001	–9.9	–8.9	43.3	29.0	35.1	28.2	13.9	23.3	26.2	37.3	25.8	13.1	7.8	20.6
Industrial Countries................. 101	–16.2	–8.1	49.9	21.1	31.2	16.9	8.6	18.5	43.0	16.1	26.4	9.4	–10.2	–1.5
Developing Countries............. 202	–8.3	–15.0	46.0	36.5	38.7	39.6	16.0	28.3	10.0	65.1	25.2	16.3	23.2	34.4
Africa..................................... 607	–18.2	–8.7	17.8	97.1	7.7	20.8	11.9	–26.6	–21.9	29.2	.8	54.4	51.7	10.8
Asia....................................... 507	–8.2	–19.9	48.4	27.4	40.3	40.7	14.1	30.8	16.2	94.9	19.8	12.3	27.0	42.1
Europe.................................... 170	.5	5.8	77.1	7.4	71.6	58.2	23.0	6.9	–1.0	90.2	42.3	17.7	12.5	37.5
Middle East........................... 407	10.9	–6.3	13.6	114.6	46.1	20.6	18.9	56.2	34.2	28.2	17.4	29.4	20.3	17.7
Western Hemisphere............. 207	–69.1	–6.8	32.7	432.2	–76.6	194.1	97.6	39.8	–20.6	8.4	27.7	–5.7	53.1	32.4
Other Countries n.i.e............... 910	—	—	....	....	....	....	....	–5.7	194.5	11.2	30.1	27.3	23.5	29.5

		Exports							Imports						
		2001	2002	2003	2004	2005	2006	2007	2001	2002	2003	2004	2005	2006	2007
		Millions of U.S. Dollars							*Millions of U.S. Dollars*						
DOTS World Total	**001**	**11,065Y**	**9,134Y**	**8,141Y**	**16,119Y**	**17,657Y**	**23,907Y**	**29,385Y**	**5,619Y**	**6,067Y**	**4,453Y**	**10,241Y**	**12,914Y**	**13,555Y**	**15,656Y**
Industrial Countries	**101**	**9,217Y**	**6,668Y**	**6,955Y**	**13,139Y**	**14,204Y**	**19,409Y**	**21,769Y**	**2,714Y**	**2,683Y**	**1,808Y**	**3,353Y**	**3,938Y**	**3,687Y**	**4,007Y**
United States	111	5,725V	3,453V	4,466V	8,367V	8,770V	11,119V	10,813V	51V	35V	347V	942V	1,509V	1,643V	1,732V
Canada	156	524V	695V	798V	843V	995V	1,473V	1,396V	4V	10V	4V	27V	69V	141V	271V
Australia	193	—V	21V	28V	4V	—V	116V	—V	483V	399V	179V	380V	240V	101V	9V
Japan	158	128V	96V	100V	1,066V	402V	940V	992V	209V	311V	84V	77V	143V	219V	133V
New Zealand	196	—V	—V	—V	—V	—V	—V	—V	—V	—V	—V	—V	1V	—V	—V
Austria	122	155V	171V	35V	42V	—V	52V	463V	84V	90V	25V	57V	54V	40V	60V
Belgium	124	—V	1V	—V	1V	—V	1V	1V	97V	119V	65V	100V	74V	81V	71V
Cyprus	423	—V	—V	—V	—V	—Y	—V	—V	16V	10V	2V	21V	13V	5V	5V
Denmark	128	—V	1V	—V	1V	—V	—V	—V	43V	40V	29V	61V	39V	26V	65V
Finland	172	—V	—V	—V	—V	—V	—V	—V	10V	9V	29V	26V	186V	128V	169V
France	132	806V	693V	173V	311V	469V	831V	1,281V	650V	487V	194V	321V	290V	186V	299V
Germany	134	—V	5V	10V	2V	2V	13V	52V	332V	418V	253V	501V	378V	504V	482V
Greece	174	210V	106V	52V	56V	31V	—V	42V	6V	49V	9V	9V	18V	30V	7V
Ireland	178	—V	—V	—V	—V	—V	—V	—V	—V	1V	1V	7V	14V	19V	15V
Italy	136	552V	452V	721V	914V	1,834V	2,537V	3,698V	359V	354V	183V	274V	398V	180V	145V
Luxembourg	137	—V	—V	—V	—V	—V	—V	—V	—V	4V	—V	—V	1V	1V	3V
Malta	181	—Y	—V	—V	—V	—V	—V	—V	—Y	—V	2V	7V	2V	1V	1V
Netherlands	138	719V	540V	270V	250V	294V	535V	1,234V	42V	38V	42V	105V	83V	70V	77V
Norway	142	—V	—V	—V	—V	—V	—V	—V	—V	—V	1V	4V	5V	2V	4V
Portugal	182	47V	62V	—V	110V	293V	310V	274V	1V	—V	—V	2V	12V	1V	—V
Slovenia	961	—V	—V	—V	—Y	—V	—V	—V	—V	4V	12V	15Y	12V	3V	1V
Spain	184	348V	374V	302V	1,171V	1,112V	1,479V	1,518V	102V	75V	57V	51V	33V	29V	33V
Sweden	144	—V	—V	—V	—V	—V	—V	1V	80V	63V	22V	100V	64V	55V	56V
Switzerland	146	—V	—V	—V	—V	—V	—V	—V	48V	87V	31V	89V	43V	67V	77V
United Kingdom	112	1V	—V	—V	1V	2V	3V	6V	95V	78V	238V	175V	256V	157V	293V
Developing Countries	**202**	**1,848Y**	**2,466Y**	**1,185Y**	**2,980Y**	**3,453Y**	**4,498Y**	**7,616Y**	**2,905Y**	**3,384Y**	**2,646Y**	**6,887Y**	**8,975Y**	**9,868Y**	**11,649Y**
Africa	**607**	**449Y**	**337Y**	**6Y**	**63Y**	**58Y**	**227Y**	**345Y**	**172Y**	**164Y**	**91Y**	**119Y**	**114Y**	**150Y**	**188Y**
Algeria	612	1V	—V	—Y	—Y	—Y	—Y	—Y	44V	55V	61Y	70Y	93Y	112Y	132Y
Morocco	686	373V	248V	—V	61V	57V	72Y	87Y	39V	15V	1V	—V	—V	—Y	1Y
South Africa	199	63V	87V	—V	—V	—V	155V	258V	3V	1V	4V	18V	13V	36V	53V
Tunisia	744	12V	2V	6V	2V	—V	—V	—Y	86V	93V	25V	30V	7V	2V	3Y
Asia	**507**	**423Y**	**963Y**	**422Y**	**1,553Y**	**1,897Y**	**2,552Y**	**5,457Y**	**1,288Y**	**1,574Y**	**552Y**	**957Y**	**1,114Y**	**1,364Y**	**1,583Y**
Bangladesh	513	—V	—V	—V	—V	—V	—V	—V	3V	—V	—V	—V	—V	—Y	—Y
China,P.R.: Mainland	924	66V	87V	—V	377V	378V	594V	693V	438V	463V	62V	169V	449V	540V	755V
China,P.R.:Hong Kong	532	—V	—V	—V	—V	—V	—V	—V	2V	2V	—V	2V	2V	4V	6V
India	534	54Y	—V	—V	1V	2V	2Y	3Y	83Y	234V	121V	127V	156V	193Y	250Y
Indonesia	536	—V	93V	—V	65V	—V	—V	—V	91V	69V	14V	47V	94V	72V	13V
Korea	542	25V	35V	52V	371V	614V	823V	2,800V	81V	95V	39V	138V	75V	120V	231V
Malaysia	548	—V	—V	—V	141V	27V	35V	43V	36V	82V	14V	66V	26V	30V	23V
Pakistan	564	3V	—V	—V	—V	1V	2Y	2Y	25V	36V	4V	5V	19V	24Y	31Y
Philippines	566	—V	—V	—V	—V	—V	—V	—V	—V	—V	—V	—V	—V	—V	1V
Sri Lanka	524	—V	—V	—V	—V	—V	—V	—V	21V	25V	10V	12V	22V	27V	29V
Taiwan Province of China	528	201V	710V	344V	494V	666V	797V	1,861V	—V	1V	1V	1V	3V	6V	6V
Thailand	578	70V	37V	24V	104V	209V	300V	57V	64V	83V	122V	186V	157V	219V	223V
Vietnam	582	3V	—V	1V	—V	—V	—V	—V	446V	484V	166V	203V	111V	129V	16V
Europe	**170**	**113Y**	**1Y**	**117Y**	**440Y**	**418Y**	**447Y**	**727Y**	**585Y**	**633Y**	**1,158Y**	**2,431Y**	**3,557Y**	**3,373Y**	**3,702Y**
Armenia	911	—V	—V	—V	—V	—V	104V	129V	—V	—V	—V	—V	—V	—V	—V
Azerbaijan	912	—V	—V	—V	—V	1V	—V	—V	—V	—V	2V	4V	11V	13V	37V
Belarus	913	—V	—V	—V	—V	—V	—V	—V	29V	36V	9V	1V	—V	1V	—V
Bulgaria	918	—V	—V	1V	—V	—V	—V	—V	6V	1V	1V	9V	22V	9V	18V
Croatia	960	65V	—V	11V	13V	—V	—V	11V	—V	5V	3V	12V	8V	3V	—V
Czech Republic	935	—V	—V	1V	—V	—V	—V	—V	—V	1V	5V	23V	19V	24V	83V
Estonia	939	—V	—V	—V	—V	—V	—V	—V	2V	8V	—V	—V	1V	—V	1V
Georgia	915	—V	—V	—V	—V	—V	—V	—Y	—V	—V	—V	1V	1V	1V	1Y
Hungary	944	—V	—V	—V	—V	—V	—V	—V	4V	3V	7V	16V	126V	83V	129V
Kazakhstan	916	—Y	—Y	—Y	—Y	—Y	—Y	—Y	—V	7V	—V	—V	—Y	—Y	—Y
Kyrgyz Republic	917	—V	—V	—V	—V	—V	—V	—V	—V	—V	—V	—V	—V	1V	1V
Latvia	941	—V	—V	—V	—V	—V	—V	—V	—V	—V	—V	—V	1V	—V	—V
Lithuania	946	—Y	—Y	—Y	—Y	—V	—V	—V	—V	—V	—V	—V	1V	1V	27V
Macedonia, FYR	962	—V	—V	—V	—V	—V	—V	—Y	—V	—V	—V	—V	1V	—V	—Y
Poland	964	—V	—V	—V	—V	—V	—V	—V	—V	1V	8V	23V	103V	83V	79V
Romania	968	47V	—V	1V	2V	—V	—V	—V	14V	33V	12V	22V	29V	71V	30V
Russia	922	—V	—V	—V	—V	—V	—V	—V	206V	403V	184V	226V	118V	125V	57V
Slovak Republic	936	—V	—V	—Y	—Y	—V	—V	—V	1V	—V	1Y	1Y	8V	3V	8V
Tajikistan	923	—V	—V	—V	—V	—V	—V	—V	—V	—V	—V	—V	—V	1V	—V
Turkey	186	—V	—V	102V	425V	417V	342V	586V	—V	—V	912V	1,997V	3,023V	2,848V	3,093V
Ukraine	926	—V	—V	—V	—V	—V	—Y	—Y	322V	135V	15V	97V	85V	105Y	136Y
Middle East	**407**	**646Y**	**699Y**	**360Y**	**450Y**	**557Y**	**673Y**	**815Y**	**747Y**	**881Y**	**782Y**	**3,271Y**	**4,110Y**	**4,771Y**	**6,055Y**
Egypt	469	1V	1Y	1Y	2Y	2Y	3Y	3Y	100V	103Y	115Y	149Y	190Y	234Y	303Y
Iran, I.R. of	429	22V	14V	15Y	17Y	23Y	28Y	33Y	—Y	—Y	—Y	—Y	—Y	—Y	—Y
Jordan	439	623V	684V	341V	58V	25V	7V	11V	587V	664V	597V	684V	809V	698V	784V

	Exports							Imports						
	2001	2002	2003	2004	2005	2006	2007	2001	2002	2003	2004	2005	2006	2007
	Millions of U.S. Dollars							*Millions of U.S. Dollars*						
Lebanon.......... 446	1Y	1Y	1Y	2Y	2Y	3Y	3Y	31Y	33Y	36Y	47Y	60Y	74Y	96Y
Oman.......... 449	—V	—V	—V	—Y	—Y	—Y	—Y	23V	77V	26V	30Y	40Y	47Y	56Y
Qatar.......... 453	—V	—V	—V	—V	—V	—V	—Y	—V	—V	4V	3V	—V	1V	1Y
Syrian Arab Republic.......... 463	—Y	—Y	—Y	368V	500Y	629Y	758Y	—Y	—Y	—Y	2,346V	2,987Y	3,688Y	4,778Y
United Arab Emirates.......... 466	—V	—V	2V	2Y	3Y	4Y	4Y	—Y	—Y	—Y	—Y	—Y	—Y	—Y
Yemen, Republic of.......... 474	—V	—V	—Y	1V	1V	1Y	1Y	5V	4V	4Y	12V	23V	29Y	37Y
Western Hemisphere.......... 207	**217Y**	**466Y**	**280Y**	**473Y**	**523Y**	**599Y**	**273Y**	**112Y**	**133Y**	**64Y**	**110Y**	**80Y**	**210Y**	**121Y**
Argentina.......... 213	—V	—V	—V	—V	—V	—V	—V	59V	55V	17V	38V	21V	34V	19V
Brazil.......... 223	26V	329V	280V	473V	523V	597V	272V	7V	78V	47V	68V	55V	174V	99V
Chile.......... 228	—V	—V	—V	—V	—V	—V	—V	—V	—V	—V	—V	1V	—V	—V
Colombia.......... 233	—V	—V	—V	—V	—V	—V	—V	—V	—V	—V	1V	1V	—V	1V
Ecuador.......... 248	1V	—V	—V	—V	—V	—V	—Y	—V	—V	—V	—V	—V	—V	—Y
Guatemala.......... 258	—V	—V	—V	—Y	—V	—Y	—Y	—V	—V	—V	—V	1V	2Y	2Y
Mexico.......... 273	—V	—V	—V	—V	1V	—V	—V	—V	—V	—V	—V	2V	—V	—V
Netherlands Antilles.......... 353	189V	137V	—V	—Y	—Y	—Y	—Y	....	....	....	....	....	....	....
Uruguay.......... 298	—V	—Y	—V	—V	—V	—Y	—Y	—V	—Y	—V	3V	—V	—Y	—Y
Venezuela, Rep. Bol.......... 299	—V	—V	—V	—V	—V	2V	—V	46V	—V	—V	—V	—V	—V	—Y
Memorandum Items														
European Union.......... 998	2,840Y	2,404Y	1,565Y	2,859Y	4,037Y	5,761Y	8,568Y	1,926Y	1,854Y	1,182Y	1,896Y	2,185Y	1,708Y	2,108Y
Oil Exporting Ctys.......... 999	22Y	107Y	17Y	85Y	27Y	34Y	38Y	205Y	201Y	105Y	151Y	227Y	232Y	202Y
Non-Oil Develop.Ctys.......... 201	1,825Y	2,359Y	1,168Y	2,895Y	3,427Y	4,464Y	7,578Y	2,700Y	3,183Y	2,541Y	6,736Y	8,748Y	9,635Y	11,447Y
PERCENT DISTRIBUTION														
Industrial Countries.......... 101	**83.3**	**73.0**	**85.4**	**81.5**	**80.4**	**81.2**	**74.1**	**48.3**	**44.2**	**40.6**	**32.7**	**30.5**	**27.2**	**25.6**
Developing Countries.......... 202	**16.7**	**27.0**	**14.6**	**18.5**	**19.6**	**18.8**	**25.9**	**51.7**	**55.8**	**59.4**	**67.3**	**69.5**	**72.8**	**74.4**
Africa.......... 607	**4.1**	**3.7**	**.1**	**.4**	**.3**	**.9**	**1.2**	**3.1**	**2.7**	**2.0**	**1.2**	**.9**	**1.1**	**1.2**
Asia.......... 507	**3.8**	**10.5**	**5.2**	**9.6**	**10.7**	**10.7**	**18.6**	**22.9**	**25.9**	**12.4**	**9.3**	**8.6**	**10.1**	**10.1**
Europe.......... 170	**1.0**	**—**	**1.4**	**2.7**	**2.4**	**1.9**	**2.5**	**10.4**	**10.4**	**26.0**	**23.7**	**27.5**	**24.9**	**23.6**
Middle East.......... 407	**5.8**	**7.7**	**4.4**	**2.8**	**3.2**	**2.8**	**2.8**	**13.3**	**14.5**	**17.6**	**31.9**	**31.8**	**35.2**	**38.7**
Western Hemisphere.......... 207	**2.0**	**5.1**	**3.4**	**2.9**	**3.0**	**2.5**	**.9**	**2.0**	**2.2**	**1.4**	**1.1**	**.6**	**1.5**	**.8**
ANNUAL PERCENT CHANGE														
World.......... 001	**–25.8**	**–17.4**	**–10.9**	**98.0**	**9.5**	**35.4**	**22.9**	**64.6**	**8.0**	**–26.6**	**130.0**	**26.1**	**5.0**	**15.5**
Industrial Countries.......... 101	**–22.2**	**–27.7**	**4.3**	**88.9**	**8.1**	**36.6**	**12.2**	**59.7**	**–1.1**	**–32.6**	**85.5**	**17.4**	**–6.4**	**8.7**
Developing Countries.......... 202	**–39.7**	**33.5**	**–51.9**	**151.4**	**15.9**	**30.2**	**69.3**	**69.3**	**16.5**	**–21.8**	**160.3**	**30.3**	**9.9**	**18.0**
Africa.......... 607	**–2.5**	**–25.1**	**–98.3**	**982.5**	**–8.2**	**291.1**	**51.9**	**125.7**	**–5.0**	**–44.7**	**31.4**	**–4.4**	**31.5**	**25.3**
Asia.......... 507	**–73.1**	**127.8**	**–56.2**	**267.8**	**22.1**	**34.5**	**113.8**	**24.3**	**22.1**	**–64.9**	**73.4**	**16.5**	**22.4**	**16.0**
Europe.......... 170	**16.4**	**–99.5**	**—**	**276.3**	**–5.0**	**6.8**	**62.7**	**195.1**	**8.2**	**82.8**	**110.0**	**46.3**	**–5.2**	**9.8**
Middle East.......... 407	**3.9**	**8.2**	**–48.5**	**24.9**	**23.8**	**20.9**	**21.0**	**153.1**	**18.0**	**–11.2**	**318.2**	**25.6**	**16.1**	**26.9**
Western Hemisphere.......... 207	**–30.1**	**115.3**	**–39.9**	**69.0**	**10.6**	**14.4**	**–54.5**	**2.9**	**18.3**	**–52.1**	**72.5**	**–26.7**	**161.0**	**–42.3**

	Exports							Imports						
	2001	2002	2003	2004	2005	2006	2007	2001	2002	2003	2004	2005	2006	2007
	Millions of U.S. Dollars							*Millions of U.S. Dollars*						
IFS World Total	**83,004**	**87,418**	**92,411**	**104,180**	**109,604**	**104,866**	**122,630**	**51,295**	**51,460**	**53,304**	**61,395**	**69,163**	**83,670**	**85,619**
DOTS World Total....001	**82,925**	**87,786**	**92,830**	**104,415**	**109,616**	**108,853**	**121,258**	**50,652**	**51,427**	**53,866**	**61,344**	**68,530**	**73,063**	**83,097**
Industrial Countries....101	**71,209**	**77,375**	**83,537**	**93,489**	**98,165**	**95,721**	**105,787**	**41,484**	**43,608**	**44,551**	**50,904**	**57,627**	**60,424**	**68,920**
United States....111	13,948	14,641	19,061	20,491	20,314	20,383	21,675	7,607	7,889	8,428	8,406	9,467	8,401	9,377
Canada....156	529	474	530	405	420	469	535	571	391	507	328	370	458	443
Australia....193	749	631	731	916	909	1,010	1,126	83	110	122	196	144	155	208
Japan....158	2,835	2,322	2,407	2,922	2,892	2,509	2,378	1,452	1,457	2,013	1,848	1,818	1,318	1,347
New Zealand....196	42	45	48	71	88	87	109	17	14	21	25	33	38	47
Austria....122	361	315	375	454	516	528	697	140	206	213	180	232	207	251
Belgium....124	3,962	12,803	11,713	15,285	16,803	15,559	17,537	919	934	1,082	1,428	1,574	1,799	2,002
Cyprus....423	28	28	27	30	34	37	47	5	7	8	8	25	21	33
Denmark....128	540	502	571	630	740	748	785	599	638	952	990	1,026	815	914
Finland....172	355	287	335	372	422	573	570	266	355	272	260	343	335	301
France....132	5,009	4,412	5,679	6,269	7,080	6,337	7,067	2,429	1,961	2,000	2,625	2,512	2,660	3,457
Germany....134	10,556	6,378	7,711	8,079	8,055	8,439	8,922	3,194	3,506	4,377	5,486	6,288	7,032	8,057
Greece....174	290	310	352	411	418	464	574	36	37	47	41	43	52	53
Iceland....176	25	33	48	56	56	71	48	4	4	5	6	9	19	13
Italy....136	2,966	3,390	4,259	4,742	4,570	4,539	4,324	963	838	1,045	1,229	1,372	1,732	1,795
Luxembourg....137	81	73	120	128	230	192	218	12	23	44	62	73	80	86
Malta....181	15	16	17	13	15	19	23	2	5	4	3	4	2	8
Netherlands....138	3,841	3,222	4,733	4,787	5,118	4,253	4,774	1,903	1,914	2,203	2,656	3,071	3,363	4,144
Norway....142	526	485	594	606	774	778	798	712	586	718	1,007	1,423	1,761	1,705
Portugal....182	261	346	351	422	471	528	571	114	127	130	163	163	177	177
Slovenia....961	26	33	33	33	26	30	38	11	11	15	15	17	22	24
Spain....184	2,062	2,136	2,678	3,045	3,693	4,083	4,452	547	568	668	733	949	1,106	1,287
Sweden....144	1,202	1,110	1,332	1,209	1,334	1,364	1,366	398	353	454	580	598	748	693
Switzerland....146	2,593	2,910	3,006	3,499	4,066	3,204	4,448	412	544	503	610	625	727	682
United Kingdom....112	18,409	20,475	16,825	18,614	19,121	19,517	22,705	19,088	21,132	18,721	22,018	25,447	27,398	31,816
Developing Countries....202	**8,984**	**8,714**	**8,718**	**10,336**	**11,034**	**12,689**	**14,971**	**6,200**	**5,977**	**7,898**	**8,850**	**9,469**	**11,164**	**12,498**
Africa....607	**788**	**729**	**825**	**905**	**920**	**1,038**	**1,295**	**298**	**271**	**344**	**368**	**400**	**427**	**425**
Algeria....612	21	17	22	42	65	59	42	1	—	—	—	—	40	1
Angola....614	3	7	8	9	8	15	13	—	—	—	—	—	—	—
Benin....638	7	5	4	4	3	2	3	—	—	—	—	—	—	—
Botswana....616	2	1	3	—	1	1	1	—	—	—	—	—	—	—
Burkina Faso....748	2	1	1	1	1	2	3	—	—	—	—	—	—	—
Cameroon....622	6	6	7	13	9	9	10	14	10	17	33	37	16	25
Cape Verde....624	—	—	—	1	1	2	1	—	—	—	—	—	—	—
Central African Rep....626	—	—	—	1	—	—	—	—	—	—	—	—	—	—
Chad....628	—	—	1	—	—	—	1	—	—	—	—	—	—	—
Comoros....632	1	—	—	1	1	1	2	—	—	—	—	—	—	—
Congo, Dem. Rep. of....636	3	5	9	16	17	28	28	—	—	—	—	—	—	—
Congo, Republic of....634	6	9	10	15	12	9	12	—	—	1	1	1	1	1
Côte d'Ivoire....662	7	7	8	6	4	4	2	11	7	13	10	10	11	11
Djibouti....611	—	—	1	—	—	1	—	—	—	2	—	1	—	—
Equatorial Guinea....642	1	—	—	—	—	—	—	—	—	—	—	1	1	—
Eritrea....643	10	2	—	23	—	1	—	—	—	—	—	1	—	—
Ethiopia....644	9	9	10	8	8	8	9	—	—	—	—	—	—	1
Gabon....646	2	3	2	2	4	3	5	3	—	—	—	—	—	—
Gambia, The....648	1	—	1	1	1	1	—	—	—	—	—	—	—	—
Ghana....652	18	15	19	20	24	22	30	24	27	25	16	23	15	21
Guinea....656	1	1	1	1	1	3	1	96	79	68	87	88	76	101
Kenya....664	10	17	12	12	13	13	32	11	12	13	14	14	19	14
Liberia....668	1	—	2	6	11	4	1	—	—	—	2	8	6	—
Madagascar....674	—	—	—	—	1	—	—	1	—	4	—	—	—	1
Malawi....676	1	2	2	5	6	14	8	—	—	—	—	—	—	—
Mali....678	7	11	3	8	12	12	16	—	—	—	—	—	—	—
Mauritania....682	2	1	—	1	—	—	1	—	—	—	—	—	—	—
Mauritius....684	7	3	5	4	3	3	5	3	3	4	2	2	2	2
Morocco....686	108	102	121	157	135	110	104	29	27	26	19	21	15	16
Mozambique....688	1	1	—	—	1	—	1	—	—	—	—	1	—	—
Namibia....728	3	3	2	1	2	2	5	—	—	—	—	—	—	—
Niger....692	—	—	1	—	1	2	2	—	—	—	—	—	—	—
Nigeria....694	115	129	144	151	136	188	256	1	1	1	1	1	1	1
Rwanda....714	1	—	—	1	1	—	1	—	—	—	—	—	—	—
Senegal....722	36	36	40	49	51	40	62	—	—	—	—	—	—	—
Seychelles....718	1	1	1	1	2	2	2	—	—	—	—	1	2	3
Sierra Leone....724	4	4	2	1	1	1	1	1	1	—	—	—	—	—
South Africa....199	357	288	309	318	331	402	504	81	91	155	165	172	203	203
Sudan....732	12	13	21	14	21	20	16	1	1	1	—	2	2	3
Swaziland....734	—	—	—	—	—	—	1	1	—	—	1	1	1	1
Tanzania....738	5	8	7	9	9	14	12	3	—	—	—	—	—	—
Togo....742	1	2	4	4	6	7	13	—	—	—	—	2	2	—

	Exports							Imports						
	2001	2002	2003	2004	2005	2006	2007	2001	2002	2003	2004	2005	2006	2007
	Millions of U.S. Dollars							*Millions of U.S. Dollars*						
Tunisia.. 744	11	9	29	11	8	15	61	11	10	11	14	14	14	17
Uganda.. 746	4	4	5	4	4	6	11	—	—	—	—	—	—	—
Zambia.. 754	3	4	6	6	4	10	14	—	—	—	—	—	—	—
Zimbabwe.................................... 698	6	3	3	2	2	2	1	3	1	1	—	—	—	—
Asia.. 507	**4,499**	**4,040**	**4,434**	**5,449**	**5,617**	**6,002**	**6,967**	**4,501**	**4,526**	**5,864**	**6,747**	**7,257**	**8,340**	**9,141**
Afghanistan, I.S. of...................... 512	1	2	3	3	3	7	10	—	—	—	—	3	—	—
Bangladesh.................................. 513	3	2	1	1	2	1	1	25	28	29	41	41	49	47
Bhutan.. 514	1	—	—	—	—	—	—	—	—	—	—	—	—	—
Brunei Darussalam...................... 516	7	1	2	1	1	—	3	—	—	—	—	—	—	—
Cambodia.................................... 522	—	—	1	1	1	3	3	13	15	11	13	10	16	19
China,P.R.: Mainland.................. 924	317	518	663	796	1,125	1,097	1,772	656	718	1,243	1,610	1,916	2,223	2,780
China,P.R.:Hong Kong................ 532	601	521	795	1,046	804	814	914	300	241	381	410	348	329	364
China,P.R.:Macao........................ 546	1	2	2	—	—	6	4	3	4	3	3	3	4	3
Fiji... 819	—	—	—	1	2	2	3	—	—	—	—	—	—	—
French Polynesia......................... 887	1	—	1	—	3	3	3	—	—	—	—	—	—	—
India... 534	95	121	105	135	161	194	233	118	129	133	166	234	248	333
Indonesia.................................... 536	70	51	53	117	117	122	99	60	77	121	156	156	112	116
Korea.. 542	615	599	571	731	674	632	658	611	640	764	546	407	354	477
Lao People's Dem.Rep................. 544	1	1	1	5	2	2	2	1	1	2	3	2	1	2
Malaysia...................................... 548	1,021	721	653	555	689	1,200	954	503	500	410	482	728	608	508
Maldives..................................... 556	1	—	1	1	—	—	—	—	1	1	—	—	1	—
Mongolia..................................... 948	—	—	—	1	—	—	—	1	—	—	—	—	—	—
Myanmar..................................... 518	1	1	—	2	4	—	1	2	1	1	2	—	—	—
Nauru.. 836	—	2	—	—	—	—	—	—	—	—	—	—	—	—
New Caledonia............................ 839	—	1	—	—	2	2	4	—	—	—	—	—	—	—
Pakistan...................................... 564	17	23	19	62	31	35	39	27	35	34	39	38	42	40
Papua New Guinea...................... 853	—	1	—	1	8	8	8	1	—	1	1	2	1	1
Philippines.................................. 566	693	322	235	242	407	534	962	160	172	142	104	149	146	98
Samoa... 862	—	—	—	—	—	1	—	—	—	—	—	—	—	—
Singapore.................................... 576	571	697	822	1,070	948	779	689	927	683	701	936	905	1,602	1,274
Sri Lanka..................................... 524	5	7	5	18	16	10	7	13	12	12	13	15	15	14
Taiwan Province of China............ 528	336	324	320	441	408	364	336	911	1,011	1,529	1,820	1,892	2,145	2,641
Thailand...................................... 578	128	106	163	198	179	147	196	145	230	322	370	370	391	348
Vietnam...................................... 582	13	15	18	19	30	39	65	25	27	22	31	37	53	76
Europe.................................... 170	**1,446**	**1,423**	**1,577**	**1,764**	**1,983**	**2,628**	**3,436**	**755**	**670**	**904**	**954**	**1,057**	**1,664**	**1,966**
Albania....................................... 914	3	5	6	8	8	7	9	—	—	—	—	—	—	—
Armenia...................................... 911	—	—	1	1	1	1	1	—	—	—	—	—	—	—
Azerbaijan................................... 912	7	7	6	6	13	5	5	—	—	—	—	—	—	—
Belarus....................................... 913	2	3	4	8	11	10	8	1	5	2	9	6	5	1
Bosnia & Herzegovina................. 963	5	5	4	10	9	20	16	—	—	—	—	—	1	1
Bulgaria...................................... 918	18	17	17	34	39	44	54	5	6	7	10	8	10	4
Croatia....................................... 960	25	33	39	40	40	51	57	24	36	28	20	17	22	9
Czech Republic........................... 935	233	187	201	247	334	450	539	93	111	228	123	181	329	368
Estonia....................................... 939	37	30	27	16	20	31	56	15	22	35	26	22	23	9
Faroe Islands.............................. 816	—	—	—	5	—	—	—	—	—	1	1	—	—	2
Georgia....................................... 915	—	2	3	10	6	5	5	3	—	—	—	—	—	7
Gibraltar..................................... 823	3	3	4	5	4	3	4	—	—	—	—	—	—	—
Hungary...................................... 944	152	135	154	187	154	299	290	282	132	95	177	192	379	418
Kazakhstan.................................. 916	2	3	5	5	10	16	29	4	4	3	2	—	—	1
Kosovo.. 967	—	—	—	—	1	2	3	—	—	—	—	—	—	—
Latvia.. 941	16	15	22	20	8	7	14	23	25	50	40	49	75	55
Lithuania..................................... 946	18	16	15	9	18	24	29	13	25	24	31	25	34	42
Macedonia, FYR.......................... 962	10	4	5	7	8	14	18	—	—	—	—	—	—	—
Moldova...................................... 921	1	1	—	—	1	1	—	—	—	—	2	—	—	—
Montenegro, Rep. of................... 943	—	—	—	—	—	—	—	—	—	—	—	—	—	1
Poland... 964	291	269	294	328	362	526	812	101	107	152	125	136	210	330
Romania...................................... 968	46	54	59	91	159	199	244	47	14	23	30	19	24	21
Russia... 922	216	246	285	266	293	357	426	20	29	47	65	75	87	103
Serbia, Rep. of............................ 942	—	—	—	—	—	5	103	—	—	—	—	—	2	6
Serbia & Montenegro.................. 965	13	9	10	18	9	—	—	—	—	2	2	2	—	—
Slovak Republic........................... 936	35	38	46	46	50	57	101	10	14	19	20	8	15	33
Turkey... 186	280	319	342	373	400	463	562	108	136	187	268	307	435	541
Turkmenistan.............................. 925	—	—	—	—	—	—	1	—	—	—	—	—	—	—
Ukraine....................................... 926	29	21	23	19	28	30	52	4	1	1	2	9	10	14
Uzbekistan.................................. 927	1	1	2	2	1	2	2	1	—	—	—	—	—	—
Europe n.s................................... 884	1	1	—	—	1	—	—	—	—	—	—	—	—	—
Middle East............................. 407	**1,178**	**1,737**	**914**	**1,174**	**1,229**	**1,354**	**1,683**	**273**	**147**	**157**	**244**	**222**	**214**	**315**
Bahrain.. 419	20	21	13	12	13	17	32	4	1	—	1	2	8	11
Egypt... 469	109	90	60	85	67	85	115	22	14	25	9	25	34	52
Iran, I.R. of................................. 429	7	17	19	19	28	30	38	1	1	1	19	1	2	—
Iraq.. 433	—	1	1	7	13	17	13	—	—	—	—	—	—	—
Israel... 436	313	230	226	378	362	284	298	209	72	87	126	144	107	102
Jordan.. 439	34	27	30	28	34	38	53	3	3	3	3	3	4	3
Kuwait.. 443	57	46	54	61	62	79	76	—	—	—	—	1	1	—
Lebanon....................................... 446	39	45	43	36	30	38	42	2	1	2	1	2	5	3
Libya.. 672	7	6	4	15	22	24	41	—	—	—	26	—	—	86
Oman... 449	34	20	17	18	24	26	30	2	1	1	2	2	3	3

	Exports							Imports						
	2001	2002	2003	2004	2005	2006	2007	2001	2002	2003	2004	2005	2006	2007
	Millions of U.S. Dollars							*Millions of U.S. Dollars*						
Qatar.......453	19	16	12	15	18	26	29	—	6	1	1	4	1	6
Saudi Arabia.......456	343	1,044	297	300	353	400	489	1	23	4	2	2	4	7
Syrian Arab Republic.......463	9	6	8	16	11	17	24	1	2	—	3	1	1	1
United Arab Emirates.......466	177	167	127	179	189	270	394	28	23	30	50	35	44	40
Yemen, Republic of.......474	9	4	3	3	3	4	6	—	—	—	—	—	—	—
Western Hemisphere.......207	**1,073**	**785**	**967**	**1,044**	**1,285**	**1,667**	**1,591**	**374**	**363**	**630**	**538**	**532**	**518**	**651**
Antigua and Barbuda.......311	—	1	1	1	—	1	—	—	—	—	—	—	—	2
Argentina.......213	52	24	24	30	43	44	41	26	44	47	44	84	87	121
Aruba.......314	—	—	—	10	2	—	—	—	—	—	—	—	—	—
Bahamas, The.......313	3	3	3	3	3	3	4	—	—	—	—	—	—	—
Barbados.......316	1	1	2	5	2	3	2	—	—	—	—	—	—	—
Belize.......339	—	—	—	1	4	—	1	2	4	6	—	4	2	5
Bermuda.......319	1	1	2	1	2	1	1	—	—	—	—	—	—	—
Bolivia.......218	—	—	—	—	—	1	1	—	—	—	—	—	—	—
Brazil.......223	201	128	161	188	182	186	223	92	111	206	247	220	186	240
Chile.......228	34	34	48	36	61	59	51	25	30	38	44	48	52	62
Colombia.......233	29	34	32	28	28	36	47	4	4	3	6	5	5	10
Costa Rica.......238	103	8	9	30	223	499	256	15	44	28	31	35	40	12
Dominica.......321	—	—	—	—	—	—	1	—	—	—	—	—	—	—
Dominican Republic.......243	5	5	6	6	7	11	14	—	1	1	—	2	3	7
Ecuador.......248	5	13	4	7	16	14	8	—	—	—	1	1	2	2
El Salvador.......253	20	5	1	1	2	1	4	—	—	—	—	—	—	2
Greenland.......326	2	—	—	1	23	3	—	—	—	—	—	—	—	—
Guatemala.......258	6	1	1	1	4	5	8	—	—	1	—	—	1	2
Guyana.......336	1	1	5	2	1	1	1	—	—	—	—	—	—	—
Haiti.......263	1	—	1	—	1	2	1	—	—	—	—	—	—	—
Honduras.......268	1	2	2	1	1	1	1	21	3	1	1	1	1	7
Jamaica.......343	9	3	4	5	6	6	11	—	—	—	—	—	—	—
Mexico.......273	498	440	579	578	578	671	767	174	117	290	156	124	126	169
Netherlands Antilles.......353	3	1	1	2	—	—	—	—	—	—	—	—	—	—
Nicaragua.......278	1	—	1	1	2	3	4	—	—	—	—	—	—	—
Panama.......283	9	15	19	21	15	19	16	—	—	—	2	—	2	—
Paraguay.......288	21	9	—	—	2	—	2	—	—	—	—	—	—	—
Peru.......293	8	9	8	21	14	12	28	1	2	3	3	4	4	4
St. Kitts and Nevis.......361	—	—	—	—	—	—	1	—	—	—	—	—	—	—
St. Lucia.......362	—	1	—	—	—	—	—	—	—	—	—	—	—	—
St. Pierre-Miquelon.......363	—	—	2	16	—	—	—	—	—	—	—	—	—	—
St. Vincent & Grens.......364	—	1	—	—	—	—	1	—	—	—	—	—	—	—
Suriname.......366	—	—	—	1	1	1	1	—	—	—	—	—	—	—
Trinidad and Tobago.......369	17	11	19	15	12	15	20	—	—	—	—	—	1	1
Uruguay.......298	3	5	6	4	7	7	13	—	1	—	1	1	6	2
Venezuela, Rep. Bol.......299	36	27	23	26	39	58	62	12	1	3	—	—	1	1
Western Hem. n.s.......399	—	—	1	1	2	1	1	—	—	—	1	—	—	1
Other Countries n.i.e.......910	**14**	**—**	**1**	**1**	**1**	**—**	**1**	**8**	**1**	**5**	**6**	**4**	**—**	**—**
Cuba.......928	1	—	1	1	1	—	1	—	—	—	—	—	—	—
North Korea.......954	14	—	—	—	—	—	—	8	1	5	6	4	—	—
Countries & Areas n.s.......898	**373**	**426**	**540**	**495**	**414**	**442**	**499**	**431**	**348**	**456**	**413**	**1,430**	**1,475**	**1,678**
Special Categories.......899	**2,345**	**1,270**	**34**	**94**	**—**	**—**	**—**	**2,529**	**1,493**	**956**	**1,171**	**—**	**—**	**—**
Memorandum Items														
European Union.......998	50,746	56,527	57,872	65,377	69,591	68,604	76,512	31,162	33,051	32,836	39,020	44,351	48,613	56,354
Oil Exporting Ctys.......999	887	1,539	774	951	1,066	1,299	1,570	106	133	164	259	202	209	263
Non-Oil Develop.Ctys.......201	8,097	7,175	7,944	9,385	9,969	11,390	13,401	6,094	5,844	7,734	8,591	9,267	10,956	12,235
PERCENT DISTRIBUTION														
Industrial Countries.......101	**85.9**	**88.1**	**90.0**	**89.5**	**89.6**	**87.9**	**87.2**	**81.9**	**84.8**	**82.7**	**83.0**	**84.1**	**82.7**	**82.9**
Developing Countries.......202	**10.8**	**9.9**	**9.4**	**9.9**	**10.1**	**11.7**	**12.3**	**12.2**	**11.6**	**14.7**	**14.4**	**13.8**	**15.3**	**15.0**
Africa.......607	**.9**	**.8**	**.9**	**.9**	**.8**	**1.0**	**1.1**	**.6**	**.5**	**.6**	**.6**	**.6**	**.6**	**.5**
Asia.......507	**5.4**	**4.6**	**4.8**	**5.2**	**5.1**	**5.5**	**5.7**	**8.9**	**8.8**	**10.9**	**11.0**	**10.6**	**11.4**	**11.0**
Europe.......170	**1.7**	**1.6**	**1.7**	**1.7**	**1.8**	**2.4**	**2.8**	**1.5**	**1.3**	**1.7**	**1.6**	**1.5**	**2.3**	**2.4**
Middle East.......407	**1.4**	**2.0**	**1.0**	**1.1**	**1.1**	**1.2**	**1.4**	**.5**	**.3**	**.3**	**.4**	**.3**	**.3**	**.4**
Western Hemisphere.......207	**1.3**	**.9**	**1.0**	**1.0**	**1.2**	**1.5**	**1.3**	**.7**	**.7**	**1.2**	**.9**	**.8**	**.7**	**.8**
ANNUAL PERCENT CHANGE														
World.......001	**8.6**	**5.9**	**5.7**	**12.5**	**5.0**	**–.7**	**11.4**	**—**	**1.5**	**4.7**	**13.9**	**11.7**	**6.6**	**13.7**
Industrial Countries.......101	**9.3**	**8.7**	**8.0**	**11.9**	**5.0**	**–2.5**	**10.5**	**2.6**	**5.1**	**2.2**	**14.3**	**13.2**	**4.9**	**14.1**
Developing Countries.......202	**5.6**	**–3.0**	**.1**	**18.6**	**6.8**	**15.0**	**18.0**	**–13.4**	**–3.6**	**32.1**	**12.1**	**7.0**	**17.9**	**11.9**
Africa.......607	**12.6**	**–7.5**	**13.3**	**9.7**	**1.6**	**12.8**	**24.7**	**–1.9**	**–9.0**	**27.0**	**7.1**	**8.7**	**6.8**	**–.4**
Asia.......507	**11.3**	**–10.2**	**9.7**	**22.9**	**3.1**	**6.9**	**16.1**	**–17.8**	**.5**	**29.6**	**15.1**	**7.6**	**14.9**	**9.6**
Europe.......170	**–14.3**	**–1.6**	**10.8**	**11.8**	**12.4**	**32.5**	**30.7**	**3.1**	**–11.3**	**35.0**	**5.5**	**10.9**	**57.4**	**18.1**
Middle East.......407	**–12.9**	**47.5**	**–47.4**	**28.4**	**4.7**	**10.2**	**24.3**	**–15.0**	**–46.1**	**6.3**	**55.6**	**–8.9**	**–3.6**	**46.9**
Western Hemisphere.......207	**48.6**	**–26.9**	**23.3**	**8.0**	**23.1**	**29.7**	**–4.5**	**14.1**	**–2.8**	**73.2**	**–14.6**	**–1.0**	**–2.7**	**25.6**
Other Countries n.i.e.......910	**299.0**	**–98.0**	**105.9**	**77.6**	**7.9**	**–59.3**	**80.9**	**127.8**	**–85.0**	**280.4**	**20.3**	**–21.8**	**–95.3**	**46.5**

Israel 436

		Exports							Imports						
		2001	2002	2003	2004	2005	2006	2007	2001	2002	2003	2004	2005	2006	2007
		Millions of U.S. Dollars							*Millions of U.S. Dollars*						
IFS World Total		**29,081**	**29,347**	**31,784**	**38,618**	**42,770**	**46,789**	**54,065**	**35,449**	**35,517**	**36,303**	**42,864**	**47,142**	**50,334**	**59,039**
DOTS World Total	001	**29,046**	**29,512**	**31,291**	**38,520**	**42,514**	**46,449**	**54,049**	**33,299**	**33,106**	**34,213**	**41,101**	**44,942**	**47,751**	**56,597**
Industrial Countries	101	**20,713**	**21,094**	**22,474**	**27,031**	**30,095**	**32,812**	**37,171**	**23,988**	**23,140**	**22,856**	**26,958**	**27,243**	**27,778**	**33,007**
United States	111	11,103	11,870	12,017	14,163	15,498	17,847	18,907	6,704	6,134	5,331	6,148	6,042	5,917	7,848
Canada	156	288	297	318	392	478	582	714	286	376	233	251	320	369	433
Australia	193	231	268	278	382	419	437	520	145	118	127	74	116	109	139
Japan	158	800	650	624	771	792	809	769	1,012	782	846	1,204	1,238	1,292	1,882
New Zealand	196	27	23	25	63	30	41	44	6	7	5	8	10	9	11
Austria	122	83	74	68	83	80	84	118	119	128	154	204	203	215	297
Belgium	124	1,575	1,863	2,322	2,900	3,679	3,034	4,070	2,633	3,028	3,177	4,135	4,558	3,921	4,454
Cyprus	423	171	191	208	346	543	472	623	28	23	111	122	25	32	65
Denmark	128	72	64	72	84	97	92	108	155	194	147	141	187	175	186
Finland	172	63	83	89	128	121	125	155	295	264	242	315	263	290	339
France	132	714	653	684	774	886	1,097	1,315	1,256	1,187	1,182	1,266	1,204	1,302	1,480
Germany	134	1,288	1,030	1,111	1,358	1,353	1,750	1,913	2,615	2,348	2,730	3,103	2,895	3,201	3,484
Greece	174	165	157	219	243	203	273	290	139	136	155	174	227	249	284
Iceland	176	3	4	6	4	7	5	5	10	10	12	14	14	15	13
Ireland	178	163	61	85	138	160	109	118	298	252	252	370	367	353	367
Italy	136	768	694	792	832	878	1,066	1,284	1,651	1,531	1,398	1,572	1,733	1,839	2,301
Luxembourg	137	4	4	4	9	11	9	15	21	29	30	21	31	46	92
Malta	181	21	26	6	36	23	57	90	4	3	37	12	12	5	26
Netherlands	138	829	909	1,084	1,233	1,249	1,309	1,609	1,354	1,178	1,197	1,485	1,627	1,787	2,090
Norway	142	50	47	46	53	63	59	63	75	70	79	80	67	72	64
Portugal	182	55	44	49	76	73	89	91	81	70	66	70	78	87	126
Slovenia	961	33	30	31	23	66	47	100	24	22	27	28	32	39	96
Spain	184	504	400	509	587	705	878	1,106	674	638	625	654	614	749	812
Sweden	144	140	105	91	111	140	127	171	423	314	314	331	365	443	556
Switzerland	146	343	385	505	783	898	797	1,036	1,774	2,075	2,085	2,685	2,465	2,803	2,882
United Kingdom	112	1,220	1,165	1,230	1,461	1,643	1,618	1,938	2,209	2,227	2,293	2,490	2,552	2,459	2,681
Developing Countries	202	**7,011**	**6,948**	**7,308**	**9,987**	**10,986**	**12,500**	**14,784**	**6,078**	**6,861**	**7,484**	**9,508**	**11,277**	**12,758**	**15,699**
Africa	607	**408**	**392**	**357**	**489**	**606**	**882**	**1,032**	**408**	**292**	**354**	**356**	**253**	**193**	**241**
Botswana	616	17	10	1	14	11	16	39	1	1	—	—	—	—	—
Burkina Faso	748	—	3	1	2	1	—	1	—	—	—	—	—	—	—
Cameroon	622	9	5	3	4	6	14	9	1	—	—	—	—	—	—
Central African Rep.	626	—	—	—	—	—	—	—	—	—	2	—	—	—	—
Chad	628	—	—	—	—	1	1	2	—	—	—	—	—	—	—
Congo, Dem. Rep. of	636	2	2	1	1	—	1	—	—	—	—	—	—	—	—
Congo, Republic of	634	—	5	1	1	2	6	11	—	—	—	—	—	—	1
Côte d'Ivoire	662	2	8	8	11	9	9	8	3	3	3	4	6	2	5
Equatorial Guinea	642	—	—	—	6	12	10	13	1	—	—	—	—	—	—
Eritrea	643	1	1	1	—	1	—	—	—	—	—	—	—	—	—
Ethiopia	644	6	3	11	14	42	11	12	15	16	16	25	23	22	26
Gabon	646	1	—	—	—	1	1	1	5	1	3	2	2	2	—
Ghana	652	4	5	17	11	19	14	22	—	1	—	1	2	3	3
Guinea	656	—	—	—	1	—	—	10	—	—	—	—	—	1	—
Kenya	664	24	28	36	47	49	50	97	25	20	21	15	21	18	22
Liberia	668	—	—	—	2	2	3	3	—	—	—	—	—	—	—
Mali	678	—	—	—	—	2	1	1	—	—	—	—	—	—	—
Mauritius	684	6	6	6	8	6	4	10	—	—	1	1	1	2	2
Morocco	686	10	7	7	9	12	11	16	1	1	1	2	1	2	3
Namibia	728	8	1	2	6	25	47	77	—	—	—	—	—	1	1
Niger	692	1	2	—	1	6	1	1	—	—	—	—	—	—	—
Nigeria	694	25	33	28	33	47	77	204	1	—	5	3	1	—	—
Rwanda	714	11	4	3	3	20	13	6	—	—	—	—	—	—	—
Senegal	722	2	3	2	5	5	6	7	—	—	—	—	—	—	1
Sierra Leone	724	—	—	—	1	3	—	—	—	—	—	—	—	—	—
South Africa	199	166	164	175	234	271	329	393	346	235	288	293	183	119	158
Tanzania	738	4	3	5	9	9	19	15	3	5	5	5	6	7	7
Togo	742	—	—	—	—	—	3	5	1	—	1	—	—	—	—
Zambia	754	1	1	2	2	2	2	2	—	1	2	3	2	3	1
Zimbabwe	698	6	9	5	8	2	3	3	2	—	—	1	—	—	1
Africa n.s.	799	101	90	44	59	44	230	65	4	5	6	3	5	11	10
Asia	507	**4,311**	**4,220**	**4,393**	**6,022**	**6,578**	**7,376**	**8,447**	**3,624**	**4,199**	**4,432**	**5,798**	**6,804**	**7,956**	**9,943**
Bangladesh	513	—	—	—	—	—	2	—	—	—	—	—	—	—	—
Cambodia	522	1	1	—	—	—	—	—	—	—	—	—	—	—	—
China,P.R.: Mainland	924	350	427	606	790	743	958	1,040	737	793	1,008	1,419	1,888	2,428	3,476
China,P.R.:Hong Kong	532	1,254	1,373	1,494	1,907	2,373	2,721	3,118	806	1,194	889	1,179	1,278	1,525	1,747
China,P.R.:Macao	546	1	—	1	—	—	—	—	—	—	—	—	—	2	3
Fiji	819	—	—	—	—	—	1	—	—	—	—	—	—	—	—
India	534	472	614	720	1,036	1,224	1,270	1,613	430	653	874	1,109	1,276	1,433	1,689
Indonesia	536	24	10	10	11	13	13	17	56	57	33	28	44	87	89
Korea	542	322	318	—	413	446	642	746	524	512	578	760	853	839	945

	Exports 2001	Exports 2002	Exports 2003	Exports 2004	Exports 2005	Exports 2006	Exports 2007	Imports 2001	Imports 2002	Imports 2003	Imports 2004	Imports 2005	Imports 2006	Imports 2007
	Millions of U.S. Dollars							Millions of U.S. Dollars						
Malaysia....548	616	290	275	203	130	68	70	27	17	26	33	41	54	63
Myanmar....518	—	1	2	2	2	1	1	—	—	—	—	—	—	1
Nepal....558	—	2	4	1	1	2	4	—	—	—	—	—	—	—
Papua New Guinea....853	—	—	—	1	—	1	2	—	—	—	—	—	—	—
Philippines....566	243	96	171	165	153	140	204	31	25	37	45	54	77	85
Singapore....576	262	277	282	358	366	410	416	218	216	199	246	331	434	558
Sri Lanka....524	57	47	41	45	37	45	60	30	32	33	37	32	35	37
Taiwan Province of China....528	330	332	296	581	601	596	562	430	369	386	499	553	617	708
Thailand....578	330	394	454	462	448	420	457	314	303	336	402	409	371	463
Vietnam....582	17	11	17	29	35	37	71	18	20	24	33	37	45	64
Asia n.s....598	31	29	20	20	7	50	66	4	7	11	10	8	9	15
Europe....170	**1,097**	**1,191**	**1,362**	**1,959**	**2,271**	**2,598**	**3,262**	**1,622**	**1,878**	**2,213**	**2,667**	**3,095**	**3,486**	**4,149**
Armenia....911	20	80	123	100	100	86	34	14	63	97	90	103	56	15
Azerbaijan....912	6	7	3	5	5	27	82	—	—	1	—	—	1	—
Belarus....913	7	5	7	6	8	10	14	—	—	1	1	1	1	5
Bosnia & Herzegovina....963	2	2	1	3	2	1	2	1	1	—	1	—	1	2
Bulgaria....918	19	21	24	30	41	47	54	23	32	35	46	48	48	64
Croatia....960	11	8	10	16	10	12	27	3	3	6	5	6	4	3
Czech Republic....935	35	42	53	73	66	107	132	54	76	77	105	97	112	136
Estonia....939	3	2	5	4	8	14	17	2	2	2	3	2	2	4
Georgia....915	4	1	2	5	8	16	54	1	1	1	1	1	1	2
Gibraltar....823	14	7	21	30	40	88	25	1	1	3	1	3	1	1
Hungary....944	79	51	63	78	75	97	116	76	77	110	171	144	399	195
Kazakhstan....916	21	27	28	41	48	64	99	—	1	1	1	4	2	3
Latvia....941	13	12	14	15	21	33	32	2	2	4	4	7	9	259
Lithuania....946	4	5	5	9	14	19	26	4	3	4	3	10	15	22
Macedonia, FYR....962	4	1	1	4	4	7	6	—	—	—	—	—	—	—
Moldova....921	4	3	2	4	5	6	10	1	1	6	8	1	1	1
Poland....964	117	88	95	121	145	178	237	53	68	60	79	94	110	128
Romania....968	128	112	120	135	187	220	240	88	79	77	98	101	103	119
Russia....922	172	211	219	318	416	521	611	507	520	616	683	1,056	1,141	1,398
Serbia & Montenegro....965	4	7	13	24	16	22	21	4	5	4	12	15	13	11
Slovak Republic....936	12	8	10	11	12	12	18	5	9	14	12	24	21	17
Tajikistan....923	—	—	—	—	—	1	1	—	—	—	—	—	—	—
Turkey....186	320	383	453	809	919	859	1,195	684	814	952	1,167	1,221	1,273	1,606
Turkmenistan....925	5	—	7	9	3	—	2	2	1	1	2	2	1	1
Ukraine....926	57	70	75	97	108	128	162	86	110	139	173	157	170	155
Uzbekistan....927	18	38	6	10	6	12	25	2	3	2	1	1	1	2
Europe n.s....884	22	2	3	4	6	10	20	9	7	3	—	—	—	—
Middle East....407	**112**	**95**	**113**	**162**	**209**	**263**	**404**	**62**	**68**	**67**	**80**	**110**	**115**	**148**
Egypt....469	47	26	26	29	93	126	153	20	20	22	29	49	77	94
Jordan....439	65	69	87	133	116	137	250	42	48	45	51	61	38	54
Western Hemisphere....207	**1,083**	**1,050**	**1,083**	**1,354**	**1,323**	**1,382**	**1,639**	**361**	**424**	**419**	**606**	**1,015**	**1,007**	**1,219**
Argentina....213	61	15	31	55	69	81	126	58	48	75	136	137	134	154
Bahamas, The....313	2	1	9	2	1	2	1	—	1	1	—	—	—	—
Barbados....316	1	—	3	—	3	1	4	—	—	—	—	—	—	—
Bermuda....319	—	1	1	—	—	—	—	—	—	—	—	—	—	6
Bolivia....218	3	2	1	5	2	5	5	—	—	—	—	1	2	2
Brazil....223	392	322	346	479	469	468	671	123	117	128	208	167	209	270
Chile....228	45	32	43	46	74	81	78	6	9	13	13	19	15	15
Colombia....233	52	60	68	86	84	123	152	83	139	107	121	535	473	584
Costa Rica....238	150	246	202	152	170	74	35	2	2	2	9	5	2	2
Dominican Republic....243	13	20	12	10	16	21	23	—	—	—	—	—	1	1
Ecuador....248	45	12	17	19	35	39	31	6	4	4	6	7	3	4
El Salvador....253	3	3	13	6	5	9	8	—	—	—	—	—	1	1
Guatemala....258	14	14	12	22	31	24	26	2	1	3	2	1	1	3
Guyana....336	—	—	—	—	—	—	1	—	—	—	—	11	8	6
Haiti....263	5	4	4	4	4	8	6	—	—	—	—	—	—	—
Honduras....268	3	4	6	6	7	9	12	1	—	1	1	—	—	1
Jamaica....343	4	5	5	6	12	15	13	—	—	—	—	—	—	—
Mexico....273	156	192	228	341	214	286	289	14	20	18	22	22	33	57
Nicaragua....278	2	8	2	7	4	7	5	—	—	—	—	—	—	—
Panama....283	12	15	10	8	10	11	18	1	4	11	8	7	15	10
Paraguay....288	3	1	1	3	4	7	11	1	1	1	13	18	19	23
Peru....293	15	15	11	17	25	30	39	7	4	4	4	7	4	3
Trinidad and Tobago....369	11	14	2	3	9	6	4	—	—	—	—	—	—	—
Uruguay....298	12	8	7	7	12	7	8	46	65	45	30	50	71	68
Venezuela, Rep. Bol....299	55	26	26	47	41	38	48	9	10	4	10	2	10	5
Western Hem. n.s....399	25	31	23	22	21	30	26	5	1	3	22	27	6	4
Countries & Areas n.s....898	**1,321**	**1,467**	**1,508**	**1,501**	**1,432**	**1,133**	**2,092**	**3,234**	**3,105**	**3,871**	**4,635**	**6,422**	**7,215**	**7,890**
Memorandum Items														
European Union....998	8,128	7,759	8,899	10,730	12,251	12,696	15,692	14,174	13,806	14,407	16,870	17,348	17,860	20,495
Oil Exporting Ctys....999	104	70	63	91	101	128	270	66	67	42	40	46	97	94
Non-Oil Develop.Ctys....201	6,907	6,878	7,244	9,896	10,885	12,372	14,514	6,012	6,794	7,443	9,468	11,231	12,661	15,605
PERCENT DISTRIBUTION														
Industrial Countries....101	**71.3**	**71.5**	**71.8**	**70.2**	**70.8**	**70.6**	**68.8**	**72.0**	**69.9**	**66.8**	**65.6**	**60.6**	**58.2**	**58.3**
Developing Countries....202	**24.1**	**23.5**	**23.4**	**25.9**	**25.8**	**26.9**	**27.4**	**18.3**	**20.7**	**21.9**	**23.1**	**25.1**	**26.7**	**27.7**
Africa....607	**1.4**	**1.3**	**1.1**	**1.3**	**1.4**	**1.9**	**1.9**	**1.2**	**.9**	**1.0**	**.9**	**.6**	**.4**	**.4**

	Exports 2001	2002	2003	2004	2005	2006	2007	Imports 2001	2002	2003	2004	2005	2006	2007
Asia.......... 507	14.8	14.3	14.0	15.6	15.5	15.9	15.6	10.9	12.7	13.0	14.1	15.1	16.7	17.6
Europe.......... 170	3.8	4.0	4.4	5.1	5.3	5.6	6.0	4.9	5.7	6.5	6.5	6.9	7.3	7.3
Middle East.......... 407	.4	.3	.4	.4	.5	.6	.7	.2	.2	.2	.2	.2	.2	.3
Western Hemisphere.......... 207	3.7	3.6	3.5	3.5	3.1	3.0	3.0	1.1	1.3	1.2	1.5	2.3	2.1	2.2
ANNUAL PERCENT CHANGE														
World.......... 001	−9.0	1.6	6.0	23.1	10.4	9.3	16.4	−9.5	−.6	3.3	20.1	9.3	6.2	18.5
Industrial Countries.......... 101	−7.8	1.8	6.5	20.3	11.3	9.0	13.3	−7.1	−3.5	−1.2	17.9	1.1	2.0	18.8
Developing Countries.......... 202	−6.6	−.9	5.2	36.7	10.0	13.8	18.3	−1.1	12.9	9.1	27.0	18.6	13.1	23.1
Africa.......... 607	−16.1	−4.0	−8.9	37.1	23.8	45.6	17.1	16.0	−28.6	21.2	.8	−28.9	−23.8	24.8
Asia.......... 507	−11.9	−2.1	4.1	37.1	9.2	12.1	14.5	−8.6	15.8	5.6	30.8	17.4	16.9	25.0
Europe.......... 170	−1.5	8.6	14.3	43.9	15.9	14.4	25.6	12.9	15.8	17.8	20.5	16.0	12.6	19.0
Middle East.......... 407	14.9	−15.2	18.6	43.5	29.1	25.4	53.7	8.0	10.0	−2.1	20.4	36.8	4.9	27.9
Western Hemisphere.......... 207	18.2	−3.0	3.2	25.0	−2.3	4.5	18.6	6.8	17.5	−1.2	44.5	67.6	−.7	21.0

		Exports							Imports						
		2001	2002	2003	2004	2005	2006	2007	2001	2002	2003	2004	2005	2006	2007
		Millions of U.S. Dollars							Millions of U.S. Dollars						
IFS World Total		**244,210**	**254,097**	**299,412**	**353,434**	**372,928**	**416,127**	**499,909**	**236,086**	**246,496**	**297,348**	**355,158**	**384,802**	**440,751**	**509,898**
DOTS World Total	**001**	**240,773**	**251,159**	**299,796**	**353,472**	**372,847**	**417,098**	**492,000**	**232,738**	**242,996**	**297,919**	**355,285**	**384,682**	**442,579**	**504,827**
Industrial Countries	**101**	**174,487**	**180,319**	**216,101**	**252,269**	**262,232**	**286,248**	**327,317**	**162,620**	**170,648**	**208,097**	**239,363**	**245,375**	**270,087**	**302,791**
United States	111	23,467	24,500	24,870	27,806	29,740	30,852	33,460	11,465	11,819	11,583	12,437	13,360	13,462	15,198
Canada	156	2,307	2,337	2,729	3,007	3,020	3,377	3,798	1,390	1,163	1,417	1,667	1,726	1,688	2,346
Australia	193	1,764	2,121	2,605	3,160	3,111	3,190	3,822	1,364	1,230	1,231	1,355	1,439	1,570	1,757
Japan	158	4,212	4,251	4,898	5,390	5,642	5,634	5,939	5,618	5,009	5,967	6,854	6,208	6,822	7,332
New Zealand	196	244	303	358	434	484	419	536	271	250	288	297	342	361	350
Austria	122	5,183	5,508	7,033	8,684	9,224	10,362	11,620	5,629	6,581	8,587	9,703	9,680	11,594	11,896
Belgium	124	7,313	7,669	8,140	8,848	10,012	12,003	14,515	10,146	10,587	12,801	15,834	17,187	18,691	21,728
Cyprus	423	342	366	496	805	910	1,058	1,107	15	19	21	30	70	65	87
Denmark	128	1,885	1,921	2,234	2,670	3,258	3,333	3,832	1,653	1,675	2,190	2,624	2,786	2,999	3,142
Finland	172	1,133	1,311	1,485	1,790	1,926	2,020	2,656	1,529	1,540	2,058	1,933	2,245	2,811	2,800
France	132	29,524	30,518	37,428	43,800	45,890	49,082	56,233	25,954	27,478	33,982	38,923	38,413	41,093	45,511
Germany	134	35,093	34,346	42,177	48,176	49,162	55,169	63,266	41,313	43,208	53,933	63,823	66,706	74,199	85,398
Greece	174	4,689	5,232	6,630	8,051	7,511	8,581	10,109	1,184	1,160	1,658	1,868	1,926	2,497	2,632
Iceland	176	54	50	100	102	128	150	170	11	15	5	4	4	2	7
Ireland	178	1,398	1,355	1,571	1,730	1,807	2,172	2,321	3,141	3,364	4,626	5,205	5,077	4,718	4,635
Luxembourg	137	470	381	477	793	675	734	771	775	754	1,241	1,422	1,590	1,567	2,298
Malta	181	723	832	954	889	853	1,112	1,112	150	164	84	144	250	251	229
Netherlands	138	6,388	6,423	7,233	8,335	9,049	10,026	11,571	14,355	14,259	17,433	21,004	21,744	24,768	27,709
Norway	142	964	1,098	1,250	1,404	1,449	1,736	2,164	943	1,930	2,413	2,207	2,590	3,700	3,558
Portugal	182	3,181	3,089	3,748	4,249	4,127	4,679	4,670	1,112	1,254	1,500	1,658	1,720	1,992	2,029
Slovenia	961	2,008	2,085	2,642	3,098	3,379	3,974	4,925	1,275	1,376	1,843	2,023	2,156	2,463	3,014
Spain	184	14,895	15,961	21,479	25,789	27,977	30,761	36,309	9,763	11,146	14,462	16,554	16,391	18,864	21,440
Sweden	144	2,225	2,403	3,034	3,540	3,830	4,580	5,436	3,093	3,265	4,027	4,778	4,598	4,986	5,650
Switzerland	146	8,860	8,907	11,345	14,685	14,540	15,903	18,450	8,648	9,232	10,331	11,716	11,638	13,087	15,357
United Kingdom	112	16,163	17,350	21,184	25,035	24,529	25,342	28,527	11,823	12,170	14,417	15,300	15,529	15,839	16,687
Developing Countries	**202**	**65,289**	**69,464**	**82,045**	**99,346**	**108,587**	**128,745**	**161,509**	**70,019**	**72,051**	**89,474**	**115,580**	**138,948**	**172,056**	**201,208**
Africa	**607**	**6,441**	**6,958**	**8,070**	**9,352**	**10,746**	**12,134**	**14,894**	**10,830**	**10,203**	**12,003**	**14,425**	**16,874**	**20,775**	**21,962**
Algeria	612	928	1,184	1,330	1,544	1,656	1,956	2,556	4,789	4,010	5,280	6,023	7,645	10,039	8,667
Angola	614	106	105	104	124	165	188	274	55	289	196	36	82	51	198
Benin	638	50	57	52	41	46	35	42	28	26	13	5	5	4	6
Botswana	616	11	4	3	6	3	4	9	6	3	5	4	3	2	1
Burkina Faso	748	16	20	24	34	28	29	36	24	22	17	16	9	10	13
Burundi	618	3	4	4	12	19	42	6	1	—	1	1	3	4	1
Cameroon	622	75	85	93	83	82	81	125	565	367	404	468	549	796	868
Cape Verde	624	14	10	11	17	35	32	36	—	—	—	—	—	—	1
Central African Rep.	626	2	2	2	2	2	4	2	7	8	14	12	10	6	10
Chad	628	7	8	8	7	7	6	12	1	—	1	1	—	—	—
Comoros	632	1	1	1	5	4	5	1	—	—	—	—	—	4	1
Congo, Dem. Rep. of	636	11	20	26	24	33	49	73	23	12	12	15	20	26	32
Congo, Republic of	634	103	87	73	84	96	102	344	58	61	34	64	32	153	41
Côte d'Ivoire	662	108	116	113	122	140	110	139	201	197	267	365	274	300	340
Djibouti	611	22	16	16	16	18	27	26	2	1	1	—	4	3	3
Equatorial Guinea	642	23	18	58	35	209	72	80	1	27	183	170	247	189	174
Eritrea	643	39	50	42	48	82	38	36	4	3	1	2	2	3	5
Ethiopia	644	105	94	97	112	183	194	247	46	47	43	41	59	62	87
Gabon	646	28	35	33	42	44	55	60	37	40	57	89	91	88	97
Gambia, The	648	9	11	13	8	7	8	5	—	3	1	3	—	2	—
Ghana	652	96	180	130	154	162	193	228	68	76	101	90	96	88	90
Guinea	656	27	68	52	44	80	33	21	10	24	8	9	9	13	14
Guinea-Bissau	654	2	3	12	6	48	24	5	2	3	6	4	3	2	—
Kenya	664	70	65	82	117	112	185	200	45	40	42	60	69	68	91
Lesotho	666	1	1	—	6	2	—	—	—	—	—	—	—	—	—
Liberia	668	58	66	34	42	64	72	112	60	51	40	7	21	13	4
Madagascar	674	30	13	28	26	26	25	34	28	26	37	48	36	59	59
Malawi	676	2	3	3	7	6	6	8	5	2	9	9	2	4	6
Mali	678	20	20	22	20	25	26	32	11	19	18	25	14	8	8
Mauritania	682	35	28	33	33	27	79	31	81	85	66	83	154	180	159
Mauritius	684	60	65	67	81	86	80	98	65	62	65	78	107	85	110
Morocco	686	736	779	1,010	1,176	1,253	1,443	1,994	521	496	519	581	616	680	856
Mozambique	688	16	18	26	26	24	30	44	36	41	113	211	233	425	584
Namibia	728	8	8	9	22	18	9	10	25	25	39	68	128	268	412
Niger	692	9	11	14	50	51	26	24	1	1	1	—	—	—	1
Nigeria	694	496	525	740	740	705	972	1,147	413	464	525	592	750	1,028	1,210
Rwanda	714	4	3	3	5	4	10	6	1	1	1	—	—	1	1
St. Helena	856	7	5	3	—	—	—	—	—	—	—	—	—	—	—
São Tomé & Príncipe	716	—	—	3	—	—	—	—	—	—	—	—	—	—	—
Senegal	722	83	114	110	99	132	131	140	81	112	115	89	72	91	113
Seychelles	718	27	32	41	34	40	36	30	25	28	47	30	35	46	21
Sierra Leone	724	20	19	19	17	8	16	11	—	3	2	2	—	1	—

		Exports							Imports						
		2001	2002	2003	2004	2005	2006	2007	2001	2002	2003	2004	2005	2006	2007
		Millions of U.S. Dollars							*Millions of U.S. Dollars*						
Somalia	726	4	8	5	6	2	3	3	2	2	1	—	—	1	1
South Africa	199	961	951	1,094	1,428	1,617	1,997	2,128	1,810	1,910	1,732	2,501	2,971	2,886	3,746
Sudan	732	45	70	83	144	265	229	236	38	68	62	26	21	31	54
Swaziland	734	2	4	4	4	4	4	6	6	5	5	5	4	8	12
Tanzania	738	46	40	50	55	72	129	112	11	14	13	17	32	39	49
Togo	742	44	36	59	52	69	54	84	7	9	13	7	10	8	9
Tunisia	744	1,883	1,914	2,237	2,602	3,025	3,262	4,001	1,499	1,444	1,810	2,427	2,310	2,646	3,364
Uganda	746	11	12	19	18	22	27	48	16	15	22	17	17	16	34
Zambia	754	4	6	4	6	12	25	19	30	7	4	13	41	243	300
Zimbabwe	698	13	12	11	14	10	9	10	92	53	60	110	90	96	113
Asia	**507**	**14,254**	**15,249**	**17,223**	**20,533**	**21,313**	**24,774**	**29,958**	**16,012**	**17,280**	**22,787**	**29,971**	**34,166**	**41,652**	**51,110**
Afghanistan, I.S. of	512	1	8	20	25	27	16	31	1	—	1	4	2	1	1
Bangladesh	513	156	108	127	168	186	211	257	293	263	290	376	392	533	528
Bhutan	514	1	—	1	—	2	—	1	—	—	—	—	—	—	—
Brunei Darussalam	516	14	8	44	12	11	32	10	1	—	—	1	—	—	—
Cambodia	522	12	10	9	12	10	15	21	5	6	6	11	9	12	26
China,P.R.: Mainland	924	2,921	3,826	4,362	5,525	5,713	7,160	8,672	6,699	7,852	10,794	14,686	17,575	22,517	29,802
China,P.R.:Hong Kong	532	2,931	2,925	3,058	3,662	3,746	4,017	4,547	353	403	552	699	641	728	658
China,P.R.:Macao	546	21	16	21	20	16	18	22	36	35	68	118	43	55	62
Fiji	819	2	3	2	3	7	4	5	—	—	—	—	—	—	—
French Polynesia	887	23	24	30	29	32	30	29	2	1	1	5	2	3	3
India	534	925	981	1,249	1,590	2,082	2,732	4,148	1,492	1,493	1,896	2,521	2,746	3,736	4,642
Indonesia	536	473	464	455	611	610	742	770	860	938	1,204	1,479	1,528	1,779	1,983
Korea	542	1,821	2,061	2,301	2,312	2,539	2,769	3,488	2,113	2,261	2,907	3,965	4,887	4,674	4,374
Lao People's Dem.Rep	544	2	1	1	2	1	1	2	12	11	11	13	10	7	8
Malaysia	548	1,000	873	992	1,115	971	928	1,003	584	537	642	803	846	1,177	1,268
Maldives	556	5	6	7	14	13	14	22	—	—	1	2	2	4	7
Mongolia	948	5	3	4	10	6	8	23	17	9	12	12	24	40	52
Myanmar	518	11	3	5	11	5	17	96	34	37	44	61	36	38	50
Nepal	558	5	3	7	4	4	4	6	9	9	8	10	11	10	10
New Caledonia	839	17	18	40	30	32	42	55	14	28	34	31	35	91	80
Pakistan	564	268	295	333	473	566	678	712	262	289	420	526	509	535	626
Papua New Guinea	853	1	2	1	2	2	2	3	31	51	55	41	42	65	95
Philippines	566	226	249	272	314	283	267	327	153	132	164	202	224	335	260
Samoa	862	1	1	—	—	—	—	1	—	—	1	1	1	—	—
Singapore	576	1,519	1,365	1,593	1,977	1,881	2,114	2,400	367	293	329	335	379	330	371
Solomon Islands	813	—	—	1	1	1	3	—	—	—	—	5	10	12	13
Sri Lanka	524	71	93	130	153	155	188	204	69	65	105	140	170	274	386
Taiwan Province of China	528	985	995	1,078	1,179	1,221	1,377	1,281	1,493	1,366	1,710	1,934	2,057	2,372	2,754
Thailand	578	585	619	710	926	920	1,005	1,111	778	829	1,086	1,490	1,399	1,559	2,099
Tonga	866	—	1	—	—	—	—	—	—	—	1	—	—	—	—
Tuvalu	869	—	—	—	—	—	—	—	—	—	—	—	1	1	—
Vanuatu	846	—	—	1	—	1	1	1	—	—	—	—	—	—	—
Vietnam	582	251	286	368	353	271	379	712	336	371	446	501	585	764	951
Europe	**170**	**24,678**	**27,458**	**35,265**	**43,668**	**48,432**	**59,476**	**72,726**	**24,869**	**26,764**	**33,019**	**42,865**	**50,738**	**63,431**	**73,530**
Albania	914	418	518	627	726	758	848	1,121	229	271	337	422	439	518	631
Armenia	911	30	36	51	66	82	109	129	7	7	10	16	15	20	21
Azerbaijan	912	38	55	121	156	124	190	241	548	529	715	700	1,189	2,894	3,729
Belarus	913	135	175	209	230	287	351	459	83	98	96	124	137	137	152
Bosnia & Herzegovina	963	348	387	439	503	578	545	708	242	287	360	366	420	466	558
Bulgaria	918	679	811	1,058	1,316	1,532	1,978	2,258	851	924	1,169	1,346	1,525	1,607	1,557
Croatia	960	1,511	1,949	2,414	2,743	2,894	3,417	3,853	854	922	1,248	1,669	1,634	1,972	1,922
Czech Republic	935	1,917	2,050	2,863	3,403	3,634	4,206	5,192	1,250	1,452	1,844	2,229	3,005	3,956	5,447
Estonia	939	147	202	192	230	280	429	509	48	48	63	57	57	84	99
Faroe Islands	816	1	1	2	6	1	10	2	—	—	—	—	—	—	—
Georgia	915	40	51	63	62	95	163	186	77	73	17	25	41	34	81
Gibraltar	823	77	127	113	220	415	968	633	23	4	2	7	27	7	8
Hungary	944	2,674	2,576	3,264	3,473	3,636	4,213	4,921	1,733	1,812	2,107	3,079	3,516	4,259	5,416
Kazakhstan	916	237	189	231	415	505	791	793	508	660	577	932	2,316	3,456	2,986
Kosovo	967	—	—	—	—	25	50	58	—	—	—	—	3	18	16
Kyrgyz Republic	917	3	6	8	7	13	8	11	2	1	1	2	1	1	3
Latvia	941	195	219	307	285	313	425	551	45	59	71	70	63	82	95
Lithuania	946	335	418	564	494	483	740	934	101	111	159	191	198	268	339
Macedonia, FYR	962	154	116	128	170	192	206	259	103	108	156	232	265	302	401
Moldova	921	76	94	111	138	152	193	242	67	94	104	142	110	157	194
Montenegro, Rep. of	943	—	—	—	—	—	177	208	—	—	—	—	—	224	217
Poland	964	3,797	4,053	5,202	6,388	6,999	8,970	11,931	1,969	2,265	3,061	4,435	5,166	7,032	8,751
Romania	968	2,996	3,423	4,385	5,325	5,792	6,963	7,489	3,012	3,609	4,411	5,028	5,077	5,411	5,562
Russia	922	3,166	3,597	4,360	6,178	7,530	9,615	13,187	7,646	7,493	9,285	12,064	14,542	17,038	19,682
Serbia, Rep. of	942	—	—	—	—	—	1,177	1,641	—	—	—	—	—	919	1,101
Serbia & Montenegro	965	657	742	872	1,145	1,136	—	—	379	486	596	712	850	—	—
Slovak Republic	936	815	965	1,195	1,366	1,618	2,042	2,520	1,102	1,102	1,199	1,662	2,048	2,654	3,522
Tajikistan	923	6	4	7	9	22	16	13	22	26	51	60	40	52	109
Turkey	186	3,516	3,868	5,358	7,062	7,644	8,509	9,891	2,706	2,783	3,772	4,941	5,426	6,788	7,328
Turkmenistan	925	14	16	57	74	25	32	20	71	106	138	174	221	243	217
Ukraine	926	630	724	984	1,367	1,583	2,100	2,713	1,022	1,285	1,407	2,124	2,338	2,722	3,287
Uzbekistan	927	41	63	44	69	62	41	67	171	147	60	54	68	127	111
Europe n.s.	884	24	25	36	41	47	44	40	2	2	3	4	3	1	3

	Code	Exports 2001	2002	2003	2004	2005	2006	2007	Imports 2001	2002	2003	2004	2005	2006	2007
		Millions of U.S. Dollars							Millions of U.S. Dollars						
Middle East	407	**11,146**	**11,826**	**13,550**	**16,355**	**17,752**	**20,292**	**27,745**	**12,781**	**11,933**	**14,659**	**19,474**	**27,571**	**34,449**	**40,042**
Bahrain	419	100	110	130	154	174	241	252	58	47	63	46	65	48	104
Egypt	469	1,334	1,138	1,361	1,678	1,726	1,941	2,951	975	1,055	1,119	1,590	1,589	2,725	2,486
Iran, I.R. of	429	1,045	1,708	2,220	2,693	2,799	2,290	2,567	2,112	1,782	2,140	2,713	3,648	4,914	5,737
Iraq	433	326	322	166	250	362	163	131	607	497	794	1,005	2,017	2,791	4,068
Israel	436	1,605	1,451	1,374	1,667	1,913	2,055	2,464	763	754	912	1,121	1,079	1,246	1,325
Jordan	439	244	245	335	400	404	468	554	9	10	13	25	29	37	36
Kuwait	443	387	420	512	589	521	691	1,130	140	27	53	50	146	91	166
Lebanon	446	652	645	749	946	974	973	1,004	22	24	41	25	29	30	40
Libya	672	1,152	1,257	1,549	1,863	1,691	1,759	2,255	4,897	4,650	5,902	7,920	12,119	15,895	19,278
Oman	449	115	185	212	423	173	247	414	9	12	15	17	22	39	30
Qatar	453	314	248	287	400	617	1,272	2,233	5	16	29	52	57	70	61
Saudi Arabia	456	1,591	1,736	1,814	1,832	2,238	3,066	4,171	1,914	1,802	2,493	3,651	5,248	5,321	4,966
Syrian Arab Republic	463	487	520	535	687	840	835	1,290	1,105	1,131	864	927	1,139	891	1,279
United Arab Emirates	466	1,701	1,742	2,206	2,655	3,192	4,170	6,108	150	114	208	315	325	334	446
West Bank/Gaza Strip	487	3	7	2	3	2	2	3	1	2	1	1	1	1	2
Yemen, Republic of	474	90	99	98	117	128	120	221	14	12	13	17	58	17	20
Western Hemisphere	207	**8,770**	**7,972**	**7,937**	**9,438**	**10,343**	**12,068**	**16,187**	**5,526**	**5,872**	**7,005**	**8,845**	**9,599**	**11,748**	**14,564**
Antigua and Barbuda	311	4	4	5	8	10	10	67	—	9	4	—	14	1	2
Argentina	213	814	293	486	707	786	965	1,182	899	1,014	1,110	1,207	1,184	1,272	1,574
Aruba	314	12	10	8	13	13	14	16	—	—	8	21	—	27	11
Bahamas, The	313	231	348	594	411	62	62	691	4	8	33	4	7	44	6
Barbados	316	8	17	23	13	9	11	16	2	2	1	1	1	1	1
Belize	339	2	1	2	4	11	3	19	3	—	4	—	—	—	—
Bermuda	319	479	451	10	47	72	512	500	10	5	—	20	31	—	3
Bolivia	218	23	23	19	22	22	24	31	15	20	18	23	23	34	43
Brazil	223	2,341	1,894	1,829	2,245	2,523	2,801	3,540	2,055	2,041	2,443	3,313	3,586	4,319	5,192
Chile	228	374	328	375	426	506	587	716	878	913	1,151	1,598	1,784	2,857	3,588
Colombia	233	271	258	270	287	314	393	492	267	322	404	561	638	617	760
Costa Rica	238	85	94	110	87	90	100	135	85	93	119	126	119	124	163
Dominica	321	2	1	1	2	2	3	2	1	—	—	—	—	—	—
Dominican Republic	243	130	136	106	162	151	163	187	23	31	28	36	37	58	51
Ecuador	248	113	139	108	112	119	153	203	201	272	282	294	390	393	413
El Salvador	253	44	38	51	35	41	64	49	3	7	5	5	9	7	13
Falkland Islands	323	5	8	2	—	—	—	—	—	—	—	—	—	—	—
Greenland	326	—	—	—	—	—	—	1	—	—	—	—	—	—	—
Grenada	328	1	1	1	6	6	7	15	—	—	—	—	1	—	2
Guatemala	258	89	87	92	100	103	122	164	29	23	32	38	38	44	51
Guyana	336	4	34	58	3	3	7	8	2	2	2	3	6	2	6
Haiti	263	6	7	7	5	14	12	16	1	1	1	1	1	1	1
Honduras	268	25	21	28	28	27	49	73	19	13	12	23	33	20	23
Jamaica	343	14	22	14	13	14	20	33	10	15	12	14	3	1	—
Mexico	273	1,761	1,827	2,052	2,258	2,689	3,235	4,718	283	247	347	370	344	366	590
Netherlands Antilles	353	173	118	79	77	261	532	139	2	15	13	16	2	47	100
Nicaragua	278	8	8	8	6	10	10	9	6	6	7	7	8	10	15
Panama	283	319	646	622	832	596	247	873	50	53	67	63	62	123	114
Paraguay	288	50	44	32	34	39	41	48	40	39	98	148	92	102	114
Peru	293	124	158	158	153	210	280	318	138	177	199	307	379	699	985
St. Kitts and Nevis	361	—	—	36	3	1	5	6	—	—	—	1	—	—	—
St. Lucia	362	2	2	2	2	20	65	9	—	—	—	1	—	—	—
St. Pierre-Miquelon	363	—	—	6	3	2	1	—	—	—	—	—	—	—	—
St. Vincent & Grens.	364	9	4	25	50	75	58	70	2	1	6	51	78	40	25
Suriname	366	3	4	8	4	8	8	38	—	1	28	9	7	1	17
Trinidad and Tobago	369	118	49	83	257	81	84	134	8	21	24	15	15	20	33
Uruguay	298	149	81	78	105	106	121	121	95	100	125	119	113	134	127
Venezuela, Rep. Bol.	299	758	595	306	549	633	880	1,075	350	367	326	304	321	369	472
Western Hem. n.s.	399	216	221	241	364	714	421	471	41	52	96	145	271	16	68
Other Countries n.i.e.	910	**260**	**252**	**291**	**235**	**257**	**365**	**320**	**17**	**45**	**19**	**20**	**12**	**21**	**27**
Cuba	928	250	237	263	224	245	354	311	14	15	16	16	12	20	26
North Korea	954	10	16	28	11	12	12	10	3	30	4	4	1	2	1
Countries & Areas n.s.	898	**432**	**754**	**909**	**1,055**	**1,161**	**1,180**	**1,794**	**83**	**252**	**319**	**312**	**346**	**385**	**797**
Special Categories	899	**291**	**361**	**406**	**485**	**547**	**532**	**888**	—	—	—	—	—	—	—
Memorandum Items															
European Union	998	142,494	147,234	181,531	211,921	221,081	246,012	285,537	139,157	146,848	183,366	214,550	222,123	247,731	280,554
Oil Exporting Ctys.	999	9,289	10,388	11,799	14,150	15,197	18,208	24,557	16,246	14,679	18,969	24,120	33,826	42,670	47,084
Non-Oil Develop.Ctys.	201	56,000	59,076	70,245	85,196	93,389	110,537	136,952	53,773	57,372	70,505	91,460	105,122	129,386	154,124
PERCENT DISTRIBUTION															
Industrial Countries	101	**72.5**	**71.8**	**72.1**	**71.4**	**70.3**	**68.6**	**66.5**	**69.9**	**70.2**	**69.9**	**67.4**	**63.8**	**61.0**	**60.0**
Developing Countries	202	**27.1**	**27.7**	**27.4**	**28.1**	**29.1**	**30.9**	**32.8**	**30.1**	**29.7**	**30.0**	**32.5**	**36.1**	**38.9**	**39.9**
Africa	607	**2.7**	**2.8**	**2.7**	**2.6**	**2.9**	**2.9**	**3.0**	**4.7**	**4.2**	**4.0**	**4.1**	**4.4**	**4.7**	**4.4**
Asia	507	**5.9**	**6.1**	**5.7**	**5.8**	**5.7**	**5.9**	**6.1**	**6.9**	**7.1**	**7.6**	**8.4**	**8.9**	**9.4**	**10.1**
Europe	170	**10.2**	**10.9**	**11.8**	**12.4**	**13.0**	**14.3**	**14.8**	**10.7**	**11.0**	**11.1**	**12.1**	**13.2**	**14.3**	**14.6**
Middle East	407	**4.6**	**4.7**	**4.5**	**4.6**	**4.8**	**4.9**	**5.6**	**5.5**	**4.9**	**4.9**	**5.5**	**7.2**	**7.8**	**7.9**
Western Hemisphere	207	**3.6**	**3.2**	**2.6**	**2.7**	**2.8**	**2.9**	**3.3**	**2.4**	**2.4**	**2.4**	**2.5**	**2.5**	**2.7**	**2.9**
Other Countries n.i.e.	910	**.1**	**.1**	**.1**	**.1**	**.1**	**.1**	**.1**	—	—	—	—	—	—	—

	Exports 2001	2002	2003	2004	2005	2006	2007	Imports 2001	2002	2003	2004	2005	2006	2007
ANNUAL PERCENT CHANGE														
World.......................................001	1.8	4.3	19.4	17.9	5.5	11.9	18.0	−1.1	4.4	22.6	19.3	8.3	15.1	14.1
Industrial Countries.................101	−.1	3.3	19.8	16.7	3.9	9.2	14.3	−.9	4.9	21.9	15.0	2.5	10.1	12.1
Developing Countries..............202	8.1	6.4	18.1	21.1	9.3	18.6	25.4	−1.4	2.9	24.2	29.2	20.2	23.8	16.9
Africa.......................................607	7.5	8.0	16.0	15.9	14.9	12.9	22.7	−5.1	−5.8	17.6	20.2	17.0	23.1	5.7
Asia...507	7.5	7.0	12.9	19.2	3.8	16.2	20.9	−2.3	7.9	31.9	31.5	14.0	21.9	22.7
Europe.....................................170	13.4	11.3	28.4	23.8	10.9	22.8	22.3	11.2	7.6	23.4	29.8	18.4	25.0	15.9
Middle East............................407	9.4	6.1	14.6	20.7	8.5	14.3	36.7	−14.2	−6.6	22.8	32.8	41.6	24.9	16.2
Western Hemisphere..............207	−4.8	−9.1	−.4	18.9	9.6	16.7	34.1	−7.3	6.3	19.3	26.3	8.5	22.4	24.0
Other Countries n.i.e.................910	−1.0	−3.0	15.4	−19.3	9.4	42.2	−12.4	−46.7	169.4	−57.3	6.0	−38.6	71.2	27.1

		Exports							Imports						
		2001	2002	2003	2004	2005	2006	2007	2001	2002	2003	2004	2005	2006	2007
		Millions of U.S. Dollars							*Millions of U.S. Dollars*						
IFS World Total		**1,220.2**	**1,113.6**	**1,179.5**	**1,390.2**	**1,499.5**	**1,874.1**	**2,074.2**	**3,360.2**	**3,533.0**	**3,638.6**	**3,772.2**	**4,460.3**	**5,312.9**	**6,415.1**
DOTS World Total	**001**	**1,227.7**	**1,118.7**	**1,194.8**	**1,405.4**	**1,531.7**	**1,983.5**	**2,218.6**	**3,402.4**	**3,566.3**	**3,672.2**	**3,952.9**	**4,736.1**	**5,646.4**	**7,322.5**
Industrial Countries	**101**	**1,059.7**	**949.3**	**965.0**	**1,095.4**	**1,263.6**	**1,527.5**	**1,911.1**	**2,223.7**	**2,346.4**	**2,350.9**	**2,291.4**	**2,717.9**	**3,135.6**	**3,498.1**
United States	111	382.00	315.23	341.70	302.57	395.81	599.99	825.85	1,544.30	1,564.79	1,619.10	1,622.87	1,962.20	2,219.10	2,724.42
Canada	156	191.12	157.17	192.41	273.52	294.96	309.44	333.30	97.64	112.64	97.99	103.71	109.56	123.66	.14
Australia	193	.10	.01	.18	.32	4.75	.42	.25	18.93	17.56	17.43	21.30	18.20	21.19	30.19
Japan	158	27.85	28.21	25.19	34.84	15.97	28.72	28.12	187.52	214.92	175.59	172.43	217.79	211.58	227.86
New Zealand	196	2.62	2.05	2.25	2.57	3.74	3.75	3.42	21.22	18.27	12.71	18.56	26.55	23.88	32.55
Austria	122	.05	.26	.05	.07	.06	.04	.10	1.80	3.57	2.94	4.98	7.56	18.08	20.06
Belgium	124	1.36	1.08	1.48	.76	.56	1.21	1.24	25.68	25.96	18.36	19.06	22.47	23.07	51.75
Cyprus	423	—	—	—	—	—	—	.09	.14	.11	.09	.02	.12	.07	.06
Denmark	128	.47	1.13	.06	.11	—	.19	1.12	6.55	4.56	6.10	4.75	4.72	28.43	18.54
Finland	172	.06	.01	.09	7.71	.07	—	13.25	4.57	2.72	3.77	2.43	3.56	40.21	4.11
France	132	42.26	41.55	46.01	44.18	54.59	59.87	79.98	22.20	22.14	47.56	40.15	28.70	33.51	35.73
Germany	134	3.59	3.18	72.60	79.14	86.14	71.53	56.16	33.33	63.13	44.19	43.19	54.05	57.78	67.93
Greece	174	.05	—	—	—	—	—	—	.07	.05	.05	.11	.19	.19	.30
Iceland	176	—	4.14	—	—	6.13	15.84	68.12	.42	.18	.04	.11	.04	—	.01
Ireland	178	—	.13	—	—	.12	.17	.81	12.73	21.15	7.82	10.09	8.99	8.76	10.44
Italy	136	.74	.92	1.02	.45	.56	.50	.41	16.00	17.81	23.09	14.44	18.45	19.78	15.97
Luxembourg	137	—	—	—	—	—	—	—	.18	.23	.87	.29	.60	.33	.01
Malta	181	—	—	—	—	—	—	—	.57	.59	.58	.21	.58	.33	.47
Netherlands	138	135.98	135.09	62.62	117.05	131.00	138.85	201.11	23.45	24.14	25.04	36.11	23.46	21.91	18.78
Norway	142	91.56	93.50	44.48	49.85	98.23	90.40	53.97	13.50	17.05	15.18	14.61	16.91	15.78	16.25
Portugal	182	7.70	7.97	—	—	—	—	.28	.56	1.32	1.38	2.25	.53	.44	.60
Slovenia	961	—	—	—	.02	.02	—	—	.52	.52	.40	.51	.48	.20	.22
Spain	184	.82	.53	.47	.66	.55	.65	.38	13.34	16.15	18.85	16.45	24.64	42.84	42.91
Sweden	144	14.21	22.09	20.97	31.38	6.15	.28	8.33	54.02	78.62	38.15	26.28	29.71	38.40	19.91
Switzerland	146	.07	.58	.35	.64	.78	1.01	18.82	21.96	25.12	24.44	23.23	25.45	53.01	29.57
United Kingdom	112	157.06	134.53	153.02	149.55	163.40	204.67	215.99	102.48	93.07	149.23	93.21	112.36	133.05	129.29
Developing Countries	**202**	**167.3**	**165.8**	**227.1**	**307.9**	**266.5**	**451.1**	**301.3**	**1,073.9**	**1,148.5**	**1,242.4**	**1,569.2**	**1,940.0**	**2,426.5**	**3,707.9**
Africa	**607**	**19.8**	**24.1**	**3.4**	**.3**	**.4**	**.2**	**.2**	**3.1**	**3.7**	**2.0**	**2.3**	**26.3**	**5.5**	**33.1**
Cameroon	622	—	—	—	—	—	—	—	—	—	.06	—	.07	—	.04
Congo, Dem. Rep. of	636	—	—	—	—	—	—	—	.01	—	—	—	—	—	—
Côte d'Ivoire	662	—	—	—	—	—	—	—	—	—	—	—	.01	—	—
Djibouti	611	—	—	—	—	—	—	—	—	—	.01	—	—	—	—
Ethiopia	644	—	—	—	—	—	—	—	—	.07	—	—	—	—	—
Ghana	652	19.58	23.83	3.32	.01	—	.08	.12	.03	.10	.12	.12	.20	.11	.21
Guinea	656	—	—	—	.03	—	—	—	—	—	—	—	—	—	—
Kenya	664	.06	—	—	—	.04	—	—	—	.13	.21	—	.36	—	—
Liberia	668	—	—	—	—	—	—	—	—	—	—	—	—	—	.02
Madagascar	674	—	—	—	.17	—	—	—	.01	—	—	—	—	—	—
Malawi	676	—	—	—	—	—	—	—	—	.01	—	—	.03	—	—
Morocco	686	—	—	—	—	—	—	—	—	.06	.09	.14	.49	.06	.12
Nigeria	694	—	.14	.01	.01	.01	—	.01	—	—	—	.07	21.48	3.00	31.03
Senegal	722	—	—	—	—	—	—	—	—	—	—	—	—	.04	.07
Seychelles	718	—	—	—	—	—	—	—	—	—	—	—	.04	—	—
Sierra Leone	724	.01	—	—	—	—	.05	—	.01	—	—	—	—	—	—
South Africa	199	.17	.11	.04	—	—	.05	.06	2.92	3.31	1.45	1.95	3.47	2.19	1.63
Sudan	732	—	—	—	—	—	—	—	—	—	—	—	.01	—	—
Tanzania	738	—	—	—	—	—	—	—	—	—	—	—	.01	—	—
Tunisia	744	—	—	—	—	—	—	—	.06	—	—	—	—	—	—
Uganda	746	—	—	—	.04	.04	—	—	—	—	—	—	.08	—	—
Zambia	754	—	—	—	—	.30	—	—	.02	—	—	—	—	—	—
Zimbabwe	698	—	—	—	—	—	—	—	—	.03	.04	.02	.01	.04	.02
Asia	**507**	**35.3**	**43.9**	**97.5**	**188.8**	**115.0**	**309.5**	**84.7**	**145.2**	**160.6**	**184.3**	**231.5**	**275.9**	**372.5**	**408.9**
Bangladesh	513	—	—	—	.01	.32	.08	1.84	.03	.07	.29	.27	.96	1.16	.67
Cambodia	522	—	—	—	—	—	—	—	—	—	—	—	—	.14	—
China,P.R.: Mainland	924	34.87	43.43	96.58	169.82	107.52	300.59	69.61	62.21	60.49	83.20	115.45	141.33	206.72	227.57
China,P.R.:Hong Kong	532	.07	.10	.10	.19	.07	.17	.29	7.90	10.97	12.84	16.00	14.75	23.64	25.37
China,P.R.:Macao	546	—	—	—	.01	—	—	—	—	—	.01	—	—	—	—
Fiji	819	—	—	—	—	—	—	—	—	—	—	.03	1.42	4.18	3.74
Guam	829	—	—	—	—	—	—	.02	—	—	—	—	—	—	—
India	534	—	.04	.24	3.53	3.54	.44	.80	6.48	8.31	10.54	15.94	15.94	25.54	28.96
Indonesia	536	—	—	—	—	—	—	.33	9.15	7.49	6.26	8.56	10.02	10.40	8.93
Korea	542	.16	.14	.18	.06	.11	.14	.35	15.60	14.32	11.41	17.53	21.72	21.38	26.91
Malaysia	548	—	—	—	—	—	—	—	5.14	7.81	9.16	8.87	10.02	9.96	18.10
Pakistan	564	.01	—	.08	.01	—	.34	.02	.66	.93	.87	.86	.70	4.37	1.21
Philippines	566	.01	—	—	.01	.02	.02	.01	2.60	15.42	9.54	3.24	1.65	1.08	1.75
Singapore	576	.13	.13	.17	.25	.12	.27	2.40	2.79	3.69	3.58	5.20	5.47	5.45	5.32
Sri Lanka	524	—	—	—	—	—	—	—	1.00	1.22	.60	.84	1.16	1.29	1.17
Taiwan Province of China	528	.01	.09	.14	14.65	2.37	6.55	8.84	17.21	18.20	22.09	24.94	21.44	21.07	21.86

	Exports 2001	2002	2003	2004	2005	2006	2007	Imports 2001	2002	2003	2004	2005	2006	2007
	Millions of U.S. Dollars							*Millions of U.S. Dollars*						
Thailand.......... 578	—	—	—	.23	.95	.81	.21	14.24	11.41	13.83	13.61	28.97	35.49	35.93
Vietnam.......... 582	—	—	—	—	—	.13	.02	.19	.24	.14	.20	.34	.65	1.43
Europe.......... 170	**22.8**	**15.8**	**42.4**	**23.2**	**35.9**	**49.5**	**127.9**	**26.1**	**20.4**	**27.6**	**26.3**	**24.7**	**34.4**	**35.2**
Bulgaria.......... 918	—	—	—	.03	—	—	—	.09	.05	.03	.01	.02	—	.11
Croatia.......... 960	—	—	—	—	—	—	—	—	—	—	.02	.02	—	—
Czech Republic.......... 935	—	—	—	—	—	—	—	.51	1.13	.51	.15	.10	.24	.10
Estonia.......... 939	—	—	—	.02	—	—	.02	.11	.09	.06	—	.01	.12	.01
Faroe Islands.......... 816	—	—	—	—	—	—	—	—	—	—	—	—	—	1.05
Georgia.......... 915	—	—	—	—	—	19.89	38.62	—	—	—	—	—	—	—
Hungary.......... 944	—	—	—	—	—	—	—	.12	.52	3.12	.78	6.05	6.25	7.32
Latvia.......... 941	—	.07	—	—	—	—	—	.05	—	—	—	—	—	.02
Lithuania.......... 946	—	—	—	—	—	—	—	.43	.27	.19	.01	—	.09	.02
Poland.......... 964	—	—	—	3.10	—	—	.02	1.66	1.09	.93	1.44	2.15	3.64	6.44
Romania.......... 968	—	6.93	15.62	—	—	—	13.31	.24	2.36	.03	.03	.04	.10	.03
Russia.......... 922	22.79	8.61	18.35	—	21.65	24.70	75.90	2.79	.62	1.04	.85	1.74	1.61	.27
Slovak Republic.......... 936	—	—	8.42	20.03	14.29	4.85	.01	.38	.37	.20	.03	.10	.83	.09
Turkey.......... 186	—	—	—	—	—	—	—	19.41	13.63	18.91	22.23	13.35	21.54	19.72
Ukraine.......... 926	—	.16	—	—	—	—	—	.31	.26	2.55	.74	1.09	—	.08
Middle East.......... 407	**.2**	**.1**	**—**	**5.2**	**26.8**	**.1**	**.1**	**6.3**	**4.3**	**13.0**	**9.7**	**16.6**	**16.9**	**18.7**
Egypt.......... 469	—	—	—	—	—	—	—	.14	1.26	6.90	1.34	.19	.13	.10
Iran, I.R. of.......... 429	—	—	—	5.03	—	—	—	—	—	.06	.15	.04	.15	.08
Iraq.......... 433	—	—	—	—	—	—	—	—	—	—	—	—	—	.02
Israel.......... 436	.01	.07	.02	.19	.05	.06	.04	5.73	2.63	5.23	7.30	15.62	15.53	17.91
Jordan.......... 439	—	—	—	—	.01	—	—	.02	—	—	.02	.08	.48	.01
Lebanon.......... 446	.04	—	—	—	—	—	—	.01	.12	.02	.07	.06	.02	.01
Qatar.......... 453	—	—	—	—	—	—	—	—	—	—	—	—	.19	—
Saudi Arabia.......... 456	.09	—	—	—	—	—	—	—	—	.04	—	.11	.02	.01
Syrian Arab Republic.......... 463	—	—	—	—	—	—	—	.06	.02	.01	.01	.05	—	—
United Arab Emirates.......... 466	.04	.03	.03	.02	26.71	.04	.02	.32	.26	.71	.84	.40	.35	.58
Western Hemisphere.......... 207	**89.2**	**81.9**	**83.8**	**90.4**	**88.4**	**91.8**	**88.4**	**893.2**	**959.5**	**1,015.6**	**1,299.3**	**1,596.6**	**1,997.2**	**3,211.8**
Antigua and Barbuda.......... 311	3.12	5.22	3.10	3.79	3.50	3.79	4.62	.14	—	.14	.01	.05	.14	.54
Argentina.......... 213	.59	—	—	—	.02	—	.02	6.15	4.51	6.99	6.96	13.30	23.35	16.64
Aruba.......... 314	.17	.15	.61	.38	.72	1.56	1.05	.14	.03	1.68	.92	1.65	.79	1.88
Bahamas, The.......... 313	3.05	2.40	2.01	1.87	1.60	1.81	2.15	.88	.89	5.83	.87	1.21	1.93	1.52
Barbados.......... 316	8.74	9.58	8.54	11.46	10.00	10.70	9.80	16.35	14.50	15.60	17.22	18.01	17.87	58.22
Belize.......... 339	3.22	3.83	3.56	3.49	3.31	3.78	3.02	4.24	6.13	10.58	32.18	13.45	13.21	6.15
Bermuda.......... 319	.97	.95	3.82	.68	.91	.93	1.38	.14	.39	.51	.80	.80	.65	.32
Bolivia.......... 218	—	—	—	—	—	—	—	.03	.09	.12	.04	.09	—	—
Brazil.......... 223	.04	.05	.05	.15	5.99	—	.84	68.81	83.80	85.48	151.31	160.03	145.90	305.06
Chile.......... 228	.68	.84	.03	.03	.10	1.40	.10	6.84	8.48	14.89	10.89	11.00	11.93	11.60
Colombia.......... 233	1.90	1.21	.64	.86	.75	1.11	.84	28.48	26.98	35.95	55.30	58.56	126.72	51.50
Costa Rica.......... 238	.09	.24	.39	.08	.20	.09	.84	32.42	33.82	49.11	38.79	49.57	50.78	50.91
Dominica.......... 321	1.67	1.33	5.07	2.40	2.43	2.36	1.98	13.43	10.48	9.23	8.23	9.41	12.72	12.95
Dominican Republic.......... 243	4.23	3.03	9.19	4.79	5.13	8.45	4.63	9.30	12.06	17.77	16.00	23.25	45.91	40.70
Ecuador.......... 248	.27	.20	.22	.20	.40	.19	.15	8.82	55.06	89.61	53.95	30.58	3.40	3.54
El Salvador.......... 253	.06	.15	.18	.05	.09	.11	.14	1.13	1.16	2.74	2.12	2.71	2.77	3.50
Grenada.......... 328	1.49	1.42	1.70	1.39	2.02	1.62	1.67	.64	.72	.48	.48	.70	.57	712.67
Guatemala.......... 258	.61	.75	.66	.93	.83	.25	.48	9.72	11.84	8.96	15.67	18.56	13.76	31.29
Guyana.......... 336	3.96	2.84	3.42	3.84	2.75	3.74	5.00	30.87	30.56	28.67	32.18	37.41	30.84	35.86
Haiti.......... 263	.56	.67	.56	.70	.52	1.11	.30	.02	.06	.05	.10	.03	.08	.14
Honduras.......... 268	5.41	.53	.05	.53	.60	.56	.67	11.51	20.11	16.35	27.20	25.35	25.29	13.63
Mexico.......... 273	5.78	7.79	2.75	5.40	4.83	5.12	4.91	131.91	111.02	103.40	126.29	103.06	81.84	100.20
Netherlands Antilles.......... 353	1.05	5.69	.84	2.68	1.93	1.49	2.67	10.72	4.54	6.68	14.16	18.16	10.47	6.65
Nicaragua.......... 278	.05	.06	1.33	.01	—	—	.02	—	.05	.24	.13	.12	5.47	3.25
Panama.......... 283	.65	.91	1.69	7.47	1.04	1.11	2.14	27.26	33.25	35.51	42.33	52.15	46.13	48.16
Paraguay.......... 288	—	—	—	—	—	—	—	.03	.01	.01	1.82	.03	—	.02
Peru.......... 293	.69	.78	.57	.66	.67	.70	.68	2.61	.68	.71	2.17	.23	3.19	3.56
St. Kitts and Nevis.......... 361	1.63	1.56	1.72	2.21	2.14	2.39	2.37	.01	.07	—	—	.15	.57	.24
St. Lucia.......... 362	2.41	3.66	3.56	3.29	4.11	3.77	3.61	.06	.26	.13	.25	.59	.70	.94
St. Vincent & Grens.......... 364	1.81	1.36	1.37	1.17	1.33	1.31	2.02	2.21	1.84	.78	.20	.33	.20	.38
Suriname.......... 366	.86	.72	.97	1.59	1.07	1.77	2.29	7.12	8.52	7.98	8.60	11.74	13.91	15.95
Trinidad and Tobago.......... 369	21.57	17.27	17.83	17.58	17.60	18.09	20.08	357.95	322.41	408.63	482.64	660.51	767.14	1,059.45
Uruguay.......... 298	—	—	—	—	—	—	—	.31	.79	.77	.92	7.31	1.65	8.01
Venezuela, Rep. Bol.......... 299	1.29	.52	.19	.22	.20	.07	—	102.44	153.27	49.00	146.73	262.82	535.59	605.58
Western Hem. n.s.......... 399	10.59	6.18	7.16	10.50	11.58	12.41	7.89	.48	1.17	.96	1.88	3.72	1.76	.84
Other Countries n.i.e.......... 910	**.8**	**3.3**	**2.4**	**2.1**	**1.6**	**4.9**	**6.3**	**5.6**	**4.5**	**8.1**	**4.2**	**5.7**	**4.3**	**19.9**
Cuba.......... 928	.78	3.26	2.37	2.02	1.54	4.88	6.12	4.61	3.99	7.35	3.79	3.87	2.01	16.73
North Korea.......... 954	—	.02	.01	.09	.02	.03	.15	1.00	.56	.75	.41	1.79	2.33	3.16
Countries & Areas n.s.......... 898	**—**	**.3**	**.4**	**—**	**—**	**—**	**—**	**99.3**	**66.9**	**70.8**	**88.1**	**72.5**	**80.0**	**96.7**
Memorandum Items														
European Union.......... 998	364.37	348.53	366.82	454.23	457.52	482.81	579.31	321.44	379.30	393.48	316.96	349.58	478.57	451.07
Oil Exporting Ctys.......... 999	1.43	.69	.22	5.28	26.92	.11	.35	111.93	161.02	56.06	156.34	294.88	549.70	646.23
Non-Oil Develop.Ctys.......... 201	165.83	165.11	226.87	302.57	239.58	450.97	300.91	961.94	987.49	1,186.33	1,412.83	1,645.11	1,876.79	3,061.66
PERCENT DISTRIBUTION														
Industrial Countries.......... 101	**86.3**	**84.9**	**80.8**	**77.9**	**82.5**	**77.0**	**86.1**	**65.4**	**65.8**	**64.0**	**58.0**	**57.4**	**55.5**	**47.8**
Developing Countries.......... 202	**13.6**	**14.8**	**19.0**	**21.9**	**17.4**	**22.7**	**13.6**	**31.6**	**32.2**	**33.8**	**39.7**	**41.0**	**43.0**	**50.6**
Africa.......... 607	**1.6**	**2.2**	**.3**	**—**	**—**	**—**	**—**	**.1**	**.1**	**.1**	**.1**	**.6**	**.1**	**.5**

	Exports 2001	2002	2003	2004	2005	2006	2007	Imports 2001	2002	2003	2004	2005	2006	2007
Asia.. 507	2.9	3.9	8.2	13.4	7.5	15.6	3.8	4.3	4.5	5.0	5.9	5.8	6.6	5.6
Europe.................................... 170	1.9	1.4	3.5	1.6	2.3	2.5	5.8	.8	.6	.8	.7	.5	.6	.5
Middle East............................ 407	—	—	—	.4	1.7	—	—	.2	.1	.4	.2	.3	.3	.3
Western Hemisphere.............. 207	7.3	7.3	7.0	6.4	5.8	4.6	4.0	26.3	26.9	27.7	32.9	33.7	35.4	43.9
Other Countries n.i.e................ 910	.1	.3	.2	.2	.1	.2	.3	.2	.1	.2	.1	.1	.1	.3
ANNUAL PERCENT CHANGE														
World.. 001	−5.6	−8.9	6.8	17.6	9.0	29.5	11.9	2.9	4.8	3.0	7.6	19.8	19.2	29.7
Industrial Countries................. 101	−9.9	−10.4	1.6	13.5	15.4	20.9	25.1	1.9	5.5	.2	−2.5	18.6	15.4	11.6
Developing Countries.............. 202	35.4	−.9	37.0	35.6	−13.4	69.3	−33.2	4.9	7.0	8.2	26.3	23.6	25.1	52.8
Africa...................................... 607	−4.3	21.5	−86.0	−92.1	47.5	−55.7	16.2	67.6	20.8	−46.9	16.6	—	−79.2	507.9
Asia.. 507	175.5	24.6	121.9	93.6	−39.1	169.1	−72.6	12.3	10.6	14.8	25.6	19.2	35.0	9.8
Europe.................................... 170	—	−30.8	168.9	−45.3	55.1	37.6	158.6	−14.5	−21.9	35.3	−4.7	−6.1	39.5	2.4
Middle East............................ 407	−97.0	−45.4	−53.1	—	411.0	−99.7	−34.3	38.5	−31.6	202.2	−25.0	70.3	1.8	11.1
Western Hemisphere.............. 207	6.8	−8.2	2.3	7.9	−2.2	3.9	−3.7	4.1	7.4	5.8	27.9	22.9	25.1	60.8
Other Countries n.i.e................ 910	−33.6	323.4	−27.7	−10.8	−26.2	214.2	27.7	12.3	−18.9	78.2	−48.2	34.8	−23.4	358.7

	Exports 2001	Exports 2002	Exports 2003	Exports 2004	Exports 2005	Exports 2006	Exports 2007	Imports 2001	Imports 2002	Imports 2003	Imports 2004	Imports 2005	Imports 2006	Imports 2007
	Millions of U.S. Dollars							*Millions of U.S. Dollars*						
IFS World Total	**403,496**	**416,726**	**471,817**	**565,675**	**594,905**	**649,931**	**700,538**	**349,089**	**337,194**	**382,930**	**454,542**	**514,922**	**579,574**	**619,829**
DOTS World Total 001	**403,517**	**416,789**	**471,906**	**565,811**	**594,887**	**646,787**	**714,254**	**349,081**	**337,172**	**382,953**	**454,809**	**515,194**	**578,696**	**621,870**
Industrial Countries 101	**206,105**	**201,664**	**212,314**	**239,184**	**245,231**	**264,333**	**275,032**	**136,963**	**130,005**	**138,837**	**156,717**	**164,954**	**173,607**	**185,901**
United States 111	122,701	120,198	117,384	128,606	136,002	147,230	145,575	63,713	58,589	59,891	63,605	65,447	69,329	72,264
Canada 156	6,563	7,326	7,370	7,647	8,909	9,958	10,538	7,752	7,153	7,511	8,384	8,905	9,565	9,922
Australia 193	7,693	8,318	9,966	11,818	12,513	12,579	14,223	14,385	13,986	15,005	19,404	24,406	27,776	31,060
New Zealand 196	1,181	1,445	1,825	2,292	2,440	2,094	2,495	2,051	1,898	2,055	2,464	2,512	2,530	2,681
Austria 122	860	868	1,158	1,253	1,074	1,193	1,293	899	917	1,055	1,306	1,326	1,511	1,597
Belgium 124	4,576	4,588	5,774	7,219	7,135	7,150	7,913	1,474	1,482	1,847	2,089	2,126	1,822	1,930
Cyprus 423	381	491	285	531	294	418	731	5	3	4	11	19	25	19
Denmark 128	631	600	662	818	868	886	767	2,115	2,169	2,378	2,792	2,381	2,022	2,023
Finland 172	962	1,090	1,375	1,688	1,883	2,405	2,523	875	1,035	1,223	1,388	1,235	1,359	1,682
France 132	6,287	6,064	7,081	8,416	7,820	7,665	8,506	6,183	6,533	7,235	8,359	8,507	8,972	10,028
Germany 134	15,652	14,126	16,412	18,972	18,742	20,415	22,629	12,391	12,437	14,227	17,086	17,870	18,311	19,431
Greece 174	821	626	1,340	1,321	880	1,281	1,301	71	77	110	125	118	62	56
Iceland 176	30	35	61	91	138	154	152	108	103	116	124	138	133	128
Ireland 178	1,335	1,452	1,903	1,988	1,936	1,637	1,601	3,631	3,195	3,551	3,790	3,771	3,537	4,079
Italy 136	4,819	4,476	5,495	6,460	5,745	6,424	6,720	5,388	5,432	6,100	6,897	6,888	7,052	7,249
Luxembourg 137	245	120	152	215	226	202	193	50	47	52	51	43	33	46
Malta 181	315	226	279	113	83	163	190	29	46	44	63	69	124	92
Netherlands 138	11,489	10,587	11,756	13,386	12,080	14,726	18,551	1,867	1,798	1,864	1,989	2,132	2,190	2,807
Norway 142	717	666	797	1,132	1,093	1,626	1,123	1,037	1,071	1,285	1,224	1,134	1,223	1,663
Portugal 182	582	560	652	948	749	777	828	140	144	167	199	196	189	137
Slovenia 961	48	71	97	118	128	122	199	24	27	32	38	50	43	50
Spain 184	2,717	2,711	3,675	4,970	5,185	5,739	5,686	1,295	1,129	1,385	1,747	1,765	1,871	1,976
Sweden 144	1,388	1,449	1,653	1,858	1,961	1,845	1,967	2,195	2,037	1,977	2,113	2,170	2,182	2,237
Switzerland 146	1,966	1,609	1,957	2,190	2,170	2,418	3,023	3,283	3,302	3,875	4,813	5,036	5,078	5,218
United Kingdom 112	12,146	11,961	13,204	15,136	15,177	15,226	16,304	6,002	5,395	5,849	6,655	6,711	6,667	7,529
Developing Countries 202	**196,184**	**214,786**	**259,281**	**326,068**	**349,074**	**381,865**	**438,402**	**211,835**	**206,875**	**243,892**	**297,853**	**350,025**	**404,937**	**435,894**
Africa 607	**3,752**	**4,007**	**4,545**	**6,598**	**7,340**	**7,932**	**9,943**	**4,432**	**5,595**	**6,334**	**8,596**	**9,710**	**12,858**	**14,135**
Algeria 612	161	193	276	522	535	434	853	62	40	59	118	43	126	390
Angola 614	31	35	53	310	119	187	186	22	392	82	9	19	598	193
Benin 638	9	8	14	13	19	16	20	—	—	—	—	—	—	—
Botswana 616	2	1	3	6	6	10	15	—	—	20	25	27	26	29
Burkina Faso 748	7	9	7	4	4	7	6	5	8	9	11	9	9	16
Burundi 618	1	1	3	9	8	2	2	4	—	—	—	—	—	—
Cameroon 622	25	19	21	20	18	18	24	4	5	7	7	6	21	3
Cape Verde 624	—	—	3	1	—	—	1	—	—	—	—	—	—	—
Central African Rep. 626	3	2	2	2	1	1	1	2	1	2	2	2	2	2
Chad 628	2	1	1	1	1	1	5	1	—	—	—	—	12	94
Comoros 632	6	5	15	—	—	2	1	2	1	1	1	4	—	—
Congo, Dem. Rep. of 636	5	13	7	10	17	24	20	10	31	14	9	3	3	3
Congo, Republic of 634	7	7	8	10	6	10	9	9	81	11	9	2	2	4
Côte d'Ivoire 662	22	31	22	38	23	23	41	9	12	20	18	20	19	18
Djibouti 611	12	15	24	31	46	45	74	—	—	—	—	—	—	—
Equatorial Guinea 642	1	1	4	8	6	16	8	15	50	—	49	223	320	587
Ethiopia 644	51	54	65	93	79	116	127	45	43	45	74	74	93	79
Gabon 646	28	28	30	24	41	44	49	12	36	162	8	13	76	155
Gambia, The 648	5	6	5	3	4	5	4	1	—	—	1	1	1	1
Ghana 652	50	47	72	96	99	91	114	49	69	115	105	77	80	125
Guinea 656	17	20	16	14	14	48	10	8	1	1	1	1	1	—
Guinea-Bissau 654	1	1	1	—	—	—	—	1	—	—	—	—	—	—
Kenya 664	144	167	186	258	251	353	553	24	28	25	36	32	29	29
Lesotho 666	1	—	1	3	1	2	1	—	—	1	—	—	—	1
Liberia 668	610	897	632	933	1,104	831	1,194	—	—	—	—	—	11	—
Madagascar 674	21	10	20	26	18	21	52	35	36	32	32	29	30	24
Malawi 676	12	15	19	9	5	9	8	36	26	28	13	33	21	26
Mali 678	6	6	5	5	5	5	5	—	1	—	—	—	—	—
Mauritania 682	16	28	38	29	29	16	19	43	42	79	113	126	83	103
Mauritius 684	56	52	56	70	67	65	84	21	14	12	9	10	12	11
Morocco 686	120	137	183	225	445	248	371	293	321	212	139	165	196	319
Mozambique 688	13	84	21	28	40	45	65	22	20	14	18	17	16	10
Namibia 728	—	—	4	3	—	—	1	—	—	4	3	—	—	—
Niger 692	2	3	3	3	4	4	8	3	—	6	25	2	—	—
Nigeria 694	442	260	359	385	519	562	733	276	749	887	1,428	993	961	678
Rwanda 714	6	5	7	4	13	7	14	2	—	—	—	—	—	1
St. Helena 856	—	—	—	—	—	—	23	3	4	1	2	3	4	3
São Tomé & Príncipe 716	1	1	—	2	1	—	—	—	—	—	—	—	—	—
Senegal 722	17	19	20	21	26	35	30	3	12	12	18	16	9	14
Seychelles 718	5	3	5	4	6	11	16	16	22	18	35	45	32	31
Sierra Leone 724	5	5	5	4	7	2	3	3	1	—	—	—	1	3
Somalia 726	—	—	—	—	—	—	1	—	—	—	1	1	1	—

	Exports							Imports						
	2001	2002	2003	2004	2005	2006	2007	2001	2002	2003	2004	2005	2006	2007
	Millions of U.S. Dollars							*Millions of U.S. Dollars*						
South Africa......199	1,496	1,558	2,036	2,917	3,277	4,067	4,618	2,797	2,912	3,592	4,606	5,532	6,695	7,742
Sudan......732	35	49	62	124	178	208	130	293	291	503	1,291	1,831	3,009	2,896
Swaziland......734	6	4	4	5	5	6	6	7	5	6	6	7	5	5
Tanzania......738	75	69	77	79	95	115	166	63	106	99	79	75	92	76
Togo......742	22	19	20	17	14	13	22	—	—	1	—	—	—	—
Tunisia......744	139	51	63	104	88	85	77	24	23	31	58	63	74	104
Uganda......746	25	30	36	63	61	82	125	9	15	10	9	8	7	11
Zambia......754	18	19	15	16	17	24	26	60	66	68	102	61	48	124
Zimbabwe......698	13	15	17	16	18	13	22	131	124	141	124	134	130	224
Africa n.s......799	1	—	—	30	—	1	—	4	7	1	1	—	1	—
Asia......507	**161,692**	**179,897**	**219,481**	**274,337**	**289,185**	**308,160**	**344,362**	**148,432**	**147,043**	**170,996**	**206,006**	**229,744**	**253,746**	**269,464**
Afghanistan, I.S. of......512	45	84	104	66	77	68	89	—	2	2	1	3	1	—
American Samoa......859	9	4	4	30	4	3	19	—	2	3	2	2	1	1
Bangladesh......513	447	429	428	451	526	573	599	115	112	131	141	153	160	174
Bhutan......514	7	10	10	22	13	9	15	—	—	—	3	—	—	1
Brunei Darussalam......516	56	319	97	108	105	101	123	1,696	1,515	1,826	1,892	2,282	2,273	2,503
Cambodia......522	50	70	54	80	79	82	111	66	75	89	100	106	119	139
China,P.R.: Mainland......924	30,948	39,958	57,480	73,917	80,005	92,789	109,297	57,780	61,792	75,559	94,335	108,439	118,444	127,760
China,P.R.:Hong Kong......532	23,252	25,432	29,918	35,414	36,019	36,437	38,909	1,459	1,419	1,348	1,624	1,571	1,556	1,449
China,P.R.:Macao......546	91	92	88	113	122	141	234	22	20	27	27	30	28	35
Fiji......819	26	32	44	44	47	47	40	34	43	38	39	52	54	45
French Polynesia......887	21	24	33	35	28	27	31	75	93	88	96	102	142	137
Guam......829	118	88	112	121	123	165	221	55	34	52	32	32	52	46
India......534	1,940	1,869	2,396	3,044	3,524	4,486	6,165	2,212	2,090	2,174	2,611	3,194	4,117	4,159
Indonesia......536	6,405	6,235	7,177	9,074	9,332	7,371	9,067	14,883	14,174	16,352	18,652	20,768	24,216	26,263
Kiribati......826	2	8	3	6	13	3	6	20	21	20	5	1	2	2
Korea......542	25,292	28,612	34,823	44,247	46,678	50,290	54,269	17,221	15,497	17,931	22,063	24,398	27,385	27,300
Lao People's Dem.Rep......544	12	18	14	14	19	21	38	7	7	7	8	8	12	12
Malaysia......548	11,012	11,016	11,250	12,565	12,624	13,211	15,057	12,824	11,173	12,593	14,093	14,686	15,587	17,353
Maldives......556	3	4	6	7	11	22	14	5	18	15	19	20	19	11
Mongolia......948	37	31	45	74	73	106	154	11	7	7	8	6	9	16
Myanmar......518	187	115	125	105	92	104	176	102	110	140	180	203	248	296
Nauru......836	—	—	—	—	—	—	—	1	—	12	1	—	—	—
Nepal......558	22	17	13	23	19	22	44	11	6	7	8	10	9	8
New Caledonia......839	16	19	27	33	36	42	47	124	110	149	229	231	263	525
Pakistan......564	501	720	905	1,241	1,510	1,760	1,560	221	151	134	170	143	206	250
Palau......565	7	6	5	8	6	10	6	11	8	11	14	24	38	24
Papua New Guinea......853	47	46	43	63	80	93	152	307	278	293	272	495	563	774
Philippines......566	8,188	8,457	9,011	9,598	9,154	9,007	9,480	6,418	6,498	7,033	8,243	7,717	7,907	8,692
Samoa......862	25	22	27	20	21	25	21	1	3	1	1	3	1	—
Singapore......576	14,713	14,183	14,858	17,976	18,529	19,492	21,821	5,382	5,001	5,493	6,283	6,697	7,439	7,047
Solomon Islands......813	4	2	4	5	7	18	14	19	21	18	18	15	23	20
Sri Lanka......524	269	285	375	339	354	427	396	203	165	193	197	178	205	201
Taiwan Province of China......528	24,256	26,312	31,320	42,015	43,759	44,106	44,874	14,180	13,553	14,264	16,663	18,064	20,270	19,822
Thailand......578	11,873	13,217	16,043	20,274	22,563	22,907	25,610	10,353	10,507	11,890	14,098	15,574	17,037	18,289
Tonga......866	3	2	2	3	3	2	3	13	12	11	14	9	7	4
Tuvalu......869	—	9	2	5	7	14	18	—	—	—	—	—	—	—
Vanuatu......846	40	23	21	24	41	49	5	7	4	8	17	18	31	34
Vietnam......582	1,777	2,135	2,623	3,181	3,590	4,140	5,682	2,604	2,529	3,088	3,858	4,534	5,358	6,094
Europe......170	**3,232**	**3,821**	**6,329**	**9,856**	**12,508**	**16,606**	**23,261**	**5,310**	**4,785**	**5,923**	**7,857**	**8,713**	**9,599**	**14,109**
Albania......914	6	2	2	1	1	2	2	1	—	1	1	1	1	1
Armenia......911	—	1	4	1	1	2	4	1	3	2	1	1	—	5
Azerbaijan......912	63	30	72	78	53	157	96	4	1	3	1	1	2	183
Belarus......913	3	8	15	14	18	36	37	14	5	8	6	6	7	44
Bosnia & Herzegovina......963	1	2	1	1	4	2	5	—	—	1	1	2	3	4
Bulgaria......918	22	11	16	28	33	81	134	17	21	25	28	39	45	52
Croatia......960	8	10	24	27	30	36	47	28	57	64	65	58	103	96
Czech Republic......935	262	334	600	1,247	1,436	1,941	2,625	172	182	215	275	391	416	480
Estonia......939	48	85	121	145	251	164	134	14	18	24	22	27	59	78
Georgia......915	6	6	13	10	13	46	114	11	5	3	8	4	12	5
Gibraltar......823	27	40	67	84	54	53	93	—	—	—	—	—	—	—
Hungary......944	740	806	1,112	1,461	1,820	1,756	2,384	392	387	430	509	564	574	622
Kazakhstan......916	73	91	99	186	178	250	215	105	99	154	246	334	328	401
Kyrgyz Republic......917	1	1	6	4	2	11	34	1	10	17	1	—	—	—
Latvia......941	7	12	20	53	60	63	93	14	18	27	37	39	43	44
Lithuania......946	14	26	27	42	56	73	110	23	18	22	19	20	20	22
Macedonia, FYR......962	12	1	2	2	2	2	5	4	7	4	7	12	6	6
Moldova......921	5	—	1	1	3	2	4	—	—	1	—	1	3	4
Montenegro, Rep. of......943	—	—	—	—	—	—	2	—	—	—	—	—	—	—
Poland......964	348	403	584	833	1,005	1,057	1,640	92	82	128	211	228	267	380
Romania......968	10	19	65	88	179	188	256	46	51	63	105	155	189	223
Russia......922	715	944	1,770	3,157	4,459	7,058	10,766	3,854	3,276	4,235	5,693	6,165	6,675	10,560
Serbia, Rep. of......942	—	—	—	—	—	8	27	—	—	—	—	—	2	10
Serbia & Montenegro......965	4	6	19	12	10	5	—	3	2	2	2	3	1	—
Slovak Republic......936	31	48	65	106	231	487	438	170	153	74	127	108	168	204
Tajikistan......923	—	1	—	—	1	1	3	—	2	7	9	4	1	—
Turkey......186	737	850	1,396	1,911	2,174	2,383	2,751	154	166	209	266	285	329	367
Turkmenistan......925	33	5	26	51	15	52	92	—	1	2	—	—	—	—

	Exports							Imports						
	2001	2002	2003	2004	2005	2006	2007	2001	2002	2003	2004	2005	2006	2007
	Millions of U.S. Dollars							Millions of U.S. Dollars						
Ukraine........ 926	37	58	148	257	383	675	1,084	141	148	111	134	141	169	157
Uzbekistan........ 927	18	17	43	52	35	16	65	53	73	93	86	124	178	162
Europe n.s........ 884	2	1	10	4	1	1	1	—	—	—	—	—	—	—
Middle East........ 407	**11,144**	**12,256**	**13,834**	**15,424**	**17,411**	**20,506**	**27,776**	**44,415**	**40,822**	**51,184**	**62,824**	**87,285**	**110,159**	**115,631**
Bahrain........ 419	165	256	346	391	428	540	678	223	160	142	276	315	508	430
Egypt........ 469	575	508	731	764	788	1,140	1,290	76	69	66	58	118	453	843
Iran, I.R. of........ 429	793	779	1,124	1,119	1,340	1,173	1,332	5,017	4,742	7,441	8,267	10,298	10,875	12,758
Iraq........ 433	190	283	76	70	130	199	121	141	106	109	1,172	442	1,034	1,092
Israel........ 436	935	772	849	1,162	1,219	1,205	1,900	831	752	694	788	837	829	900
Jordan........ 439	154	147	196	214	238	290	375	62	80	74	94	111	111	122
Kuwait........ 443	658	865	1,052	936	1,179	1,189	1,670	4,430	4,207	4,563	5,751	7,627	9,481	10,221
Lebanon........ 446	103	132	146	178	160	167	304	5	5	5	6	3	7	5
Libya........ 672	72	313	199	180	138	190	254	5	6	5	7	10	21	4
Oman........ 449	787	859	969	1,162	1,385	1,730	2,531	2,356	2,101	2,513	1,624	2,722	2,825	3,583
Qatar........ 453	305	370	476	593	988	1,458	1,844	6,030	5,251	6,516	7,887	10,629	15,049	16,964
Saudi Arabia........ 456	3,593	3,766	3,733	3,677	4,168	4,639	6,725	12,316	11,638	14,565	18,484	28,575	36,986	35,593
Syrian Arab Republic........ 463	183	181	184	228	252	341	480	16	22	48	17	17	10	23
United Arab Emirates........ 466	2,563	2,950	3,638	4,610	4,842	6,041	8,062	12,850	11,607	14,327	18,324	25,175	31,720	32,550
West Bank/Gaza Strip........ 487	—	—	—	1	—	—	—	—	—	—	—	—	—	—
Yemen, Republic of........ 474	68	74	116	142	154	204	210	58	75	118	71	405	250	543
Western Hemisphere........ 207	**16,365**	**14,806**	**15,092**	**19,853**	**22,630**	**28,661**	**33,060**	**9,245**	**8,630**	**9,454**	**12,570**	**14,572**	**18,576**	**22,555**
Antigua and Barbuda........ 311	—	—	6	4	—	—	4	—	—	—	—	—	—	—
Argentina........ 213	501	189	267	436	542	663	843	400	444	437	444	327	511	791
Bahamas, The........ 313	154	480	294	418	221	1,216	1,251	3	2	—	1	1	85	3
Barbados........ 316	25	30	38	56	58	40	49	—	—	1	—	—	—	1
Belize........ 339	25	23	15	21	10	7	4	35	8	9	10	8	5	7
Bermuda........ 319	221	22	19	961	26	30	16	2	4	4	4	5	—	—
Bolivia........ 218	23	31	31	28	38	40	64	29	39	26	88	81	192	290
Brazil........ 223	2,476	1,815	1,874	2,347	2,713	3,047	3,997	2,542	2,668	2,884	3,650	4,404	5,048	6,018
Chile........ 228	468	496	575	723	942	1,086	1,585	2,517	2,131	2,595	4,113	4,988	6,703	7,855
Colombia........ 233	620	585	575	740	794	1,024	1,318	196	226	224	290	371	356	426
Costa Rica........ 238	250	378	427	449	480	493	606	170	134	208	175	221	286	287
Dominica........ 321	10	9	12	9	11	5	38	3	1	5	4	2	1	2
Dominican Republic........ 243	285	308	118	152	315	261	304	27	35	44	60	48	51	87
Ecuador........ 248	411	340	257	284	340	434	530	227	182	172	169	138	197	204
El Salvador........ 253	87	104	109	105	123	122	140	12	12	14	13	20	26	20
Falkland Islands........ 323	—	—	—	—	—	—	—	1	3	1	1	2	1	1
Greenland........ 326	—	—	—	—	—	—	1	62	61	71	67	69	64	65
Grenada........ 328	6	5	10	9	11	8	8	—	—	—	—	—	—	—
Guatemala........ 258	155	190	227	237	213	291	316	72	73	67	78	115	95	98
Guyana........ 336	12	12	15	16	22	28	25	4	3	3	3	4	7	6
Haiti........ 263	20	28	26	36	25	31	39	—	—	1	1	1	1	1
Honduras........ 268	84	85	101	91	94	105	147	52	45	30	49	28	29	26
Jamaica........ 343	121	150	154	173	126	168	176	33	34	33	36	24	31	29
Mexico........ 273	4,087	3,766	3,643	5,190	6,881	9,280	10,176	2,008	1,791	1,781	2,174	2,542	2,838	3,169
Netherlands Antilles........ 353	120	49	56	49	49	65	67	12	3	1	1	5	7	52
Nicaragua........ 278	36	49	53	59	75	65	83	7	7	5	8	12	10	16
Panama........ 283	4,773	4,576	5,397	6,059	6,895	7,998	8,616	56	77	103	114	44	26	13
Paraguay........ 288	44	22	29	46	48	49	76	21	24	28	18	18	29	34
Peru........ 293	277	274	233	230	274	381	550	427	429	426	668	695	1,297	2,214
St. Kitts and Nevis........ 361	4	7	7	9	11	12	14	—	—	—	1	—	1	—
St. Lucia........ 362	10	6	9	12	16	23	24	—	—	—	—	—	—	—
St. Pierre-Miquelon........ 363	8	—	—	—	—	—	—	8	—	—	—	—	—	—
St. Vincent & Grens........ 364	6	5	7	29	18	13	21	—	—	—	—	—	—	—
Suriname........ 366	22	32	39	45	43	44	58	19	19	13	13	12	8	9
Trinidad and Tobago........ 369	105	108	144	174	288	203	225	9	2	15	17	4	197	246
Uruguay........ 298	56	30	43	54	54	68	79	46	52	58	63	80	116	93
Venezuela, Rep. Bol........ 299	742	415	187	494	772	1,143	1,310	244	117	193	236	301	351	492
Western Hem. n.s........ 399	119	184	95	108	100	214	303	1	1	—	—	2	1	1
Other Countries n.i.e........ 910	**1,090**	**158**	**151**	**194**	**239**	**172**	**187**	**256**	**258**	**202**	**190**	**164**	**93**	**17**
Cuba........ 928	27	26	59	105	177	128	177	37	28	28	26	31	18	17
North Korea........ 954	1,063	133	91	89	62	44	9	219	230	174	163	132	74	—
Countries & Areas n.s........ 898	—	—	—	—	**2**	—	—	**2**	**10**	**2**	**1**	**22**	**29**	**40**
Special Categories........ 899	**3**	—	**4**	**39**	**90**	**19**	**5**	—	—	**1**	—	—	—	—
Memorandum Items														
European Union........ 998	66,704	63,782	75,481	89,296	86,826	93,813	105,326	45,508	44,760	50,019	57,897	58,753	59,520	64,795
Oil Exporting Ctys........ 999	16,711	17,289	19,265	22,821	25,330	26,130	34,501	58,609	54,739	67,531	81,950	107,584	133,646	140,589
Non-Oil Develop.Ctys........ 201	179,473	197,497	240,016	303,247	323,744	355,735	403,901	153,226	152,136	176,361	215,903	242,441	271,291	295,305
PERCENT DISTRIBUTION														
Industrial Countries........ 101	**51.1**	**48.4**	**45.0**	**42.3**	**41.2**	**40.9**	**38.5**	**39.2**	**38.6**	**36.3**	**34.5**	**32.0**	**30.0**	**29.9**
Developing Countries........ 202	**48.6**	**51.5**	**54.9**	**57.6**	**58.7**	**59.0**	**61.4**	**60.7**	**61.4**	**63.7**	**65.5**	**67.9**	**70.0**	**70.1**
Africa........ 607	**.9**	**1.0**	**1.0**	**1.2**	**1.2**	**1.2**	**1.4**	**1.3**	**1.7**	**1.7**	**1.9**	**1.9**	**2.2**	**2.3**
Asia........ 507	**40.1**	**43.2**	**46.5**	**48.5**	**48.6**	**47.6**	**48.2**	**42.5**	**43.6**	**44.7**	**45.3**	**44.6**	**43.8**	**43.3**
Europe........ 170	**.8**	**.9**	**1.3**	**1.7**	**2.1**	**2.6**	**3.3**	**1.5**	**1.4**	**1.5**	**1.7**	**1.7**	**1.7**	**2.3**
Middle East........ 407	**2.8**	**2.9**	**2.9**	**2.7**	**2.9**	**3.2**	**3.9**	**12.7**	**12.1**	**13.4**	**13.8**	**16.9**	**19.0**	**18.6**
Western Hemisphere........ 207	**4.1**	**3.6**	**3.2**	**3.5**	**3.8**	**4.4**	**4.6**	**2.6**	**2.6**	**2.5**	**2.8**	**2.8**	**3.2**	**3.6**

	Exports 2001	2002	2003	2004	2005	2006	2007	Imports 2001	2002	2003	2004	2005	2006	2007
Other Countries n.i.e.............910	.3	—	—	—	—	—	—	.1	.1	.1	—	—	—	—
ANNUAL PERCENT CHANGE														
World.......................................001	−15.6	3.3	13.2	19.9	5.1	8.7	10.4	−8.0	−3.4	13.6	18.8	13.3	12.3	7.5
Industrial Countries.................101	−15.5	−2.2	5.3	12.7	2.5	7.8	4.0	−8.5	−5.1	6.8	12.9	5.3	5.2	7.1
Developing Countries..............202	−16.2	9.5	20.7	25.8	7.1	9.4	14.8	−7.7	−2.3	17.9	22.1	17.5	15.7	7.6
Africa.....................................607	−8.1	6.8	13.4	45.2	11.2	8.1	25.4	−7.3	26.2	13.2	35.7	13.0	32.4	9.9
Asia..507	−18.1	11.3	22.0	25.0	5.4	6.6	11.7	−6.6	−.9	16.3	20.5	11.5	10.4	6.2
Europe...................................170	−15.1	18.2	65.6	55.7	26.9	32.8	40.1	−10.9	−9.9	23.8	32.6	10.9	10.2	47.0
Middle East............................407	6.0	10.0	12.9	11.5	12.9	17.8	35.5	−10.0	−8.1	25.4	22.7	38.9	26.2	5.0
Western Hemisphere.............207	−11.4	−9.5	1.9	31.5	14.0	26.6	15.3	−13.3	−6.6	9.5	33.0	15.9	27.5	21.4
Other Countries n.i.e.............910	371.9	−85.5	−5.0	29.2	23.1	−28.3	8.7	−11.9	.6	−21.7	−6.1	−13.7	−43.4	−82.0

	Exports 2001	Exports 2002	Exports 2003	Exports 2004	Exports 2005	Exports 2006	Exports 2007	Imports 2001	Imports 2002	Imports 2003	Imports 2004	Imports 2005	Imports 2006	Imports 2007
	Millions of U.S. Dollars							*Millions of U.S. Dollars*						
IFS World Total	**2,294.1**	**2,769.9**	**3,081.6**	**3,921.7**	**4,301.8**	**5,174.7**	**5,725.3**	**4,871.4**	**5,076.4**	**5,743.3**	**8,128.2**	**10,506.1**	**11,446.8**	**13,510.9**
DOTS World Total 001	**2,291.5**	**2,769.5**	**3,081.1**	**3,530.4**	**4,300.6**	**5,203.6**	**5,534.0**	**4,871.4**	**5,076.4**	**5,743.2**	**8,163.7**	**10,497.2**	**11,547.5**	**13,530.9**
Industrial Countries 101	**350.3**	**686.7**	**975.0**	**1,176.6**	**1,289.5**	**1,775.1**	**1,502.9**	**2,118.0**	**2,180.2**	**2,238.1**	**2,886.5**	**3,546.8**	**3,679.4**	**4,333.1**
United States 111	234.77	431.72	662.95	1,019.61	1,125.65	1,302.61	1,242.34	395.95	392.96	389.59	552.42	588.14	554.72	630.07
Canada 156	1.17	1.96	3.00	3.07	4.63	10.69	10.47	17.10	15.32	12.77	20.83	33.71	39.21	55.71
Australia 193	1.27	1.30	2.22	1.66	2.06	1.04	1.68	74.68	68.03	70.82	74.84	44.73	66.90	68.58
Japan 158	12.98	11.97	13.98	16.85	26.46	42.15	48.74	175.05	158.60	199.61	266.56	296.77	357.36	411.82
New Zealand 196	.01	.01	.16	.18	1.03	.35	.21	12.56	17.60	34.00	19.29	25.22	32.65	26.94
Austria 122	.35	.45	.79	.67	.74	2.09	2.52	19.05	18.33	20.74	25.20	32.02	31.52	48.29
Belgium 124	1.36	4.57	10.46	12.67	15.54	16.84	14.98	43.05	63.49	58.21	65.26	78.48	79.56	96.86
Cyprus 423	.61	.90	1.64	1.19	1.70	1.66	1.55	5.94	6.94	6.26	5.46	5.43	11.24	8.54
Denmark 128	.45	.27	.19	.31	.34	.38	1.49	24.08	23.36	37.26	30.02	37.45	23.95	36.10
Finland 172	3.24	4.29	3.05	5.14	2.79	6.29	1.58	18.90	27.74	33.53	76.21	147.22	173.29	273.94
France 132	3.01	3.62	6.24	2.23	6.08	5.92	5.73	185.94	208.50	181.06	225.44	250.26	279.83	331.91
Germany 134	25.98	12.88	12.54	6.83	10.64	8.71	14.91	447.25	464.97	451.65	556.11	842.26	909.97	1,020.64
Greece 174	3.08	1.99	1.34	1.65	1.75	2.97	7.53	35.66	35.97	10.15	9.90	41.39	14.38	14.60
Iceland 176	.03	.02	—	—	—	.01	.07	—	—	—	.01	—	.08	—
Ireland 178	.92	.38	.34	.09	.47	1.25	.37	24.49	28.83	27.78	32.79	45.46	38.81	53.34
Italy 136	8.37	7.78	10.71	21.05	23.10	28.52	31.62	160.78	177.90	216.13	313.18	352.19	421.54	448.54
Luxembourg 137	—	—	—	—	.01	.01	—	.83	.83	.23	.56	.51	10.05	.40
Malta 181	.15	.19	.27	.64	.08	.05	.07	.33	.35	.39	.54	.44	.72	.83
Netherlands 138	2.63	13.24	16.79	16.28	13.23	17.33	18.17	67.41	96.50	83.59	104.47	136.24	114.35	158.09
Norway 142	.01	.02	.04	—	.03	.02	.02	3.71	11.09	4.76	5.25	2.45	3.72	3.89
Portugal 182	3.85	3.56	3.42	3.48	4.33	3.53	3.84	7.62	8.32	8.82	14.34	13.63	12.10	11.29
Slovenia 961	.03	—	.01	.01	.07	.06	.07	1.79	1.44	1.66	1.55	2.38	2.72	3.18
Spain 184	8.61	6.72	12.38	18.06	27.03	28.46	19.48	84.15	63.40	64.52	95.99	73.30	80.77	120.90
Sweden 144	.16	.15	.29	.27	.20	.34	.66	79.82	48.31	51.70	64.48	61.81	65.00	107.46
Switzerland 146	11.79	48.74	201.37	33.95	4.66	273.51	45.83	56.56	54.25	75.04	113.03	140.22	93.17	117.39
United Kingdom 112	25.52	129.93	10.80	10.73	16.93	20.31	29.00	175.37	187.15	197.84	212.78	295.12	261.75	283.81
Developing Countries 202	**1,657.9**	**1,865.3**	**1,885.3**	**2,224.3**	**2,677.1**	**3,037.3**	**3,508.8**	**2,552.8**	**2,844.7**	**3,478.4**	**5,268.2**	**6,944.7**	**7,858.4**	**9,195.5**
Africa 607	**86.0**	**125.1**	**116.5**	**220.2**	**202.9**	**177.3**	**204.5**	**61.4**	**51.1**	**61.1**	**82.8**	**115.4**	**96.5**	**107.7**
Algeria 612	30.25	44.45	57.51	69.15	85.08	69.55	87.37	.39	.07	.73	1.00	23.02	.27	.13
Angola 614	.03	.11	.08	.16	.13	1.71	1.81	—	—	—	—	—	—	—
Burkina Faso 748	—	—	—	—	—	—	—	—	—	—	.04	—	—	—
Burundi 618	.02	—	—	—	—	—	—	.01	.03	—	—	—	.10	—
Cameroon 622	—	.03	—	—	—	—	.04	.05	.12	.19	.19	.17	.11	.40
Chad 628	.04	.01	—	.06	.04	.06	.70	—	—	—	—	—	—	—
Congo, Dem. Rep. of 636	—	—	—	.02	—	—	—	—	—	—	—	—	—	—
Congo, Republic of 634	—	.01	.64	—	.89	1.82	.97	—	.03	.01	.03	—	.08	.07
Côte d'Ivoire 662	.02	.01	.05	—	3.86	5.72	.25	.07	.11	.17	.32	.28	.25	.33
Djibouti 611	.79	.83	.52	.12	.21	.81	.97	—	—	—	—	—	.01	—
Eritrea 643	2.96	.52	.50	.62	.59	.79	.63	—	—	.07	—	.51	—	.14
Ethiopia 644	5.91	16.61	7.14	74.32	36.79	3.64	11.51	2.01	1.62	5.08	4.62	9.40	11.18	13.12
Gabon 646	.03	.07	.08	.06	.01	.08	.11	—	—	—	—	—	—	—
Gambia, The 648	.01	.03	.01	.01	—	—	—	—	—	—	—	—	—	—
Ghana 652	.70	.14	.07	.21	.21	.35	.28	—	.02	.15	.17	.34	.24	.28
Guinea 656	.01	.03	.01	—	.39	.01	.09	—	—	—	—	—	.03	—
Kenya 664	3.39	1.99	2.23	11.02	1.26	8.56	7.40	1.08	1.53	1.26	.68	1.79	1.48	2.10
Liberia 668	—	.01	.01	.06	.03	.03	.16	—	.05	.03	—	—	—	—
Madagascar 674	—	—	.05	—	—	.01	.63	—	—	.03	—	—	.02	.49
Malawi 676	—	—	—	.56	2.13	—	3.05	1.87	1.88	2.53	.67	—	—	.28
Mali 678	—	—	—	—	.01	—	—	—	—	—	—	—	—	—
Mauritania 682	.03	.15	1.03	.28	.27	.35	.12	—	.06	.11	.43	.16	.21	.20
Mauritius 684	—	.80	.55	1.04	2.45	2.43	.82	—	.01	.09	—	—	.01	.06
Morocco 686	3.39	2.39	1.67	2.38	5.35	4.01	6.64	11.23	11.18	14.72	14.11	15.74	18.52	26.45
Mozambique 688	—	3.08	—	3.65	.74	2.87	2.06	—	—	—	.20	.27	.50	.59
Namibia 728	.02	—	—	—	—	—	—	.61	.52	.75	1.25	.58	.63	.54
Niger 692	.12	.07	—	.09	.03	.03	.19	—	—	—	—	—	—	—
Nigeria 694	4.81	2.23	.40	.73	1.79	.89	2.07	.01	—	—	.04	.04	—	.02
Rwanda 714	—	—	.03	.02	.09	.05	.12	—	—	—	—	—	—	—
Senegal 722	.25	.17	.10	.13	.21	.01	.03	.06	.19	.01	.11	.06	.03	—
Seychelles 718	—	—	—	—	—	.03	—	—	—	—	—	—	—	—
Sierra Leone 724	.01	.02	.06	.01	.38	—	.04	—	—	—	—	—	—	—
Somalia 726	.50	.93	.93	.95	.38	.58	.51	.96	.27	.45	.52	.67	.57	.47
South Africa 199	4.59	7.82	5.89	6.05	4.34	7.30	6.92	17.48	12.72	7.78	16.84	24.35	28.34	22.45
Sudan 732	24.26	34.93	28.66	34.01	43.64	54.51	54.30	16.38	11.19	8.56	18.02	4.84	2.90	7.13
Tanzania 738	.32	.30	1.10	4.73	1.86	1.53	3.07	.45	.07	.05	.06	.11	.09	.09
Tunisia 744	6.38	7.54	7.00	9.97	9.95	9.63	11.65	1.32	1.60	1.69	2.83	5.25	4.62	5.14
Uganda 746	.09	.06	.04	.16	.32	.60	.55	.09	.16	—	—	.27	.50	.71
Zambia 754	.05	.27	.54	.19	.07	.10	.01	—	—	.08	—	—	—	—
Zimbabwe 698	.01	—	.03	.04	.02	—	.01	7.35	7.71	16.60	20.64	28.05	25.79	26.67
Asia 507	**372.2**	**384.8**	**352.9**	**406.7**	**502.2**	**572.9**	**714.4**	**754.1**	**925.7**	**1,120.6**	**1,709.3**	**2,095.7**	**2,403.1**	**2,798.3**
Afghanistan, I.S. of 512	—	.02	.21	.74	.52	.27	.79	.30	.63	.92	1.26	.79	1.32	1.02
Bangladesh 513	.66	2.06	1.77	1.07	1.29	5.05	2.04	1.26	1.36	1.23	1.35	1.75	1.48	2.24
Brunei Darussalam 516	.02	.01	.02	.01	.03	.20	.01	.01	—	—	—	—	.01	—

	Exports 2001	2002	2003	2004	2005	2006	2007	Imports 2001	2002	2003	2004	2005	2006	2007
	Millions of U.S. Dollars							*Millions of U.S. Dollars*						
Cambodia........ 522	—	—	.12	—	—	.57	2.60	—	—	—	—	—	—	—
China,P.R.: Mainland........ 924	42.09	52.02	36.23	34.80	41.50	38.07	61.99	237.84	334.07	454.78	687.83	968.54	1,213.53	1,308.24
China,P.R.:Hong Kong........ 532	2.95	2.57	.81	.32	2.05	1.69	5.44	30.85	42.45	38.35	46.88	64.91	74.39	49.68
Fiji........ 819	—	—	—	—	—	—	.02	—	—	—	—	—	—	—
India........ 534	205.21	226.39	199.00	249.97	348.97	396.85	459.01	73.42	82.19	85.03	144.85	147.20	177.84	302.54
Indonesia........ 536	29.98	20.85	27.11	34.53	13.52	21.58	31.19	59.65	78.77	86.22	174.36	146.51	145.10	119.95
Korea........ 542	7.20	7.89	5.55	6.75	13.64	14.53	17.72	140.49	131.96	143.91	256.90	373.87	362.24	423.25
Malaysia........ 548	23.54	17.26	19.46	23.08	24.11	44.90	54.18	48.10	52.16	69.04	95.93	74.48	70.73	118.05
Maldives........ 556	—	—	—	—	.09	.09	.10	....	....	....	....	....	....	....
Mongolia........ 948	—	—	—	—	—	—	—	—	—	.14	—	—	—	—
Myanmar........ 518	—	.02	—	—	—	—	—	.03	.01	.01	.09	.29	.34	.87
Nepal........ 558	.01	—	—	.01	—	—	—	—	—	—	—	—	—	—
Pakistan........ 564	25.62	31.38	22.98	20.99	21.77	7.14	33.72	22.15	18.95	22.08	24.76	22.52	22.77	21.07
Philippines........ 566	15.38	8.17	8.69	7.68	8.10	5.27	5.59	1.15	2.35	3.74	3.83	3.57	4.43	4.58
Singapore........ 576	1.81	1.99	.56	2.07	1.91	.57	3.41	5.82	10.26	7.24	12.26	12.76	18.73	85.72
Sri Lanka........ 524	1.34	1.85	2.33	3.49	2.56	2.08	1.71	15.09	14.64	12.47	17.14	18.71	19.85	18.25
Taiwan Province of China........ 528	7.97	5.94	9.34	4.76	10.61	7.53	12.89	84.85	110.34	137.66	161.39	167.68	175.63	175.71
Thailand........ 578	5.39	3.71	8.06	7.59	6.55	5.45	6.11	31.76	44.29	56.30	76.98	87.73	108.26	149.48
Vietnam........ 582	3.01	2.65	10.64	8.91	4.99	21.01	15.90	1.36	1.32	1.46	3.54	4.42	6.48	17.64
Europe........ 170	**27.5**	**37.7**	**46.0**	**52.3**	**72.7**	**58.2**	**68.7**	**334.6**	**334.3**	**416.9**	**667.2**	**868.0**	**892.9**	**1,370.2**
Albania........ 914	.87	.13	.22	.22	.27	.43	.49	—	—	—	—	—	—	.06
Armenia........ 911	—	—	.01	.03	.01	.01	.05	.04	—	—	—	—	—	—
Azerbaijan........ 912	.02	.07	.40	1.10	1.37	1.60	.76	—	—	.04	—	—	—	.06
Belarus........ 913	—	.14	—	—	—	—	—	—	—	—	—	1.24	—	1.84
Bosnia & Herzegovina........ 963	.17	.50	1.29	2.88	1.05	1.66	2.01	.01	—	—	.04	.06	.04	.28
Bulgaria........ 918	3.14	1.52	9.76	10.13	8.50	2.76	4.71	5.97	3.43	3.33	7.29	12.73	6.93	6.44
Croatia........ 960	—	2.79	—	.17	.38	.12	.17	1.96	1.61	.25	.15	.52	1.02	2.94
Czech Republic........ 935	.10	.14	.06	.13	.20	.22	.32	11.42	14.42	30.54	17.78	18.12	14.77	13.96
Estonia........ 939	—	—	—	—	.06	—	.04	—	.01	.10	.11	.15	.39	.71
Georgia........ 915	—	.12	.01	—	.13	.11	.25	.03	—	.01	.06	.16	.02	—
Hungary........ 944	.09	.05	.33	.28	3.34	3.94	5.62	7.84	17.26	39.08	55.16	78.00	105.39	226.37
Kazakhstan........ 916	.06	.23	.53	.43	.38	.04	.85	2.60	10.08	5.14	16.60	24.90	10.21	12.28
Kyrgyz Republic........ 917	—	—	—	.02	—	.01	.01	—	—	—	—	—	—	—
Latvia........ 941	—	—	—	—	.02	.06	.08	.33	.34	.08	.56	.63	.33	.40
Lithuania........ 946	1.66	—	2.23	1.38	3.37	.16	.17	.20	.09	.09	.02	9.65	.10	.24
Macedonia, FYR........ 962	—	—	.02	.53	.01	.04	—	.43	.04	.01	—	.27	.03	.10
Moldova........ 921	—	.07	.01	.05	1.01	.77	.38	.55	1.31	2.95	3.41	7.97	2.72	8.22
Poland........ 964	2.77	6.27	9.73	9.41	8.52	7.69	2.20	3.59	4.64	6.23	11.45	12.56	21.09	14.07
Romania........ 968	1.28	1.88	1.40	1.91	5.59	8.88	12.54	31.38	41.15	31.85	71.22	38.83	37.23	50.40
Russia........ 922	1.09	1.34	.83	.71	2.73	2.77	4.11	59.98	31.34	61.22	47.97	132.97	102.95	312.46
Serbia & Montenegro........ 965	.11	.05	.02	.03	.22	—	—	.65	.32	.34	.31	5.81	—	—
Slovak Republic........ 936	.69	.33	.31	.69	1.02	1.47	1.23	3.02	1.38	2.21	1.32	1.41	1.86	4.37
Tajikistan........ 923	—	—	—	—	—	.05	.02	—	.01	—	—	—	—	—
Turkey........ 186	13.90	20.14	14.21	15.91	24.82	17.47	23.68	121.89	123.33	139.19	187.81	256.19	304.88	385.40
Turkmenistan........ 925	—	.15	.37	—	.20	.04	.35	.77	—	—	—	.04	.07	—
Ukraine........ 926	1.52	1.70	4.24	6.28	9.50	6.43	7.67	81.83	83.18	93.89	245.94	265.17	280.78	328.06
Uzbekistan........ 927	—	.07	—	—	—	.01	—	.12	.40	.37	.02	.66	.65	.78
Yugoslavia n.s........ 966	—	—	—	—	—	1.47	1.01	—	—	—	—	—	1.47	.81
Middle East........ 407	**1,166.7**	**1,314.3**	**1,367.1**	**1,541.2**	**1,886.2**	**2,216.1**	**2,504.1**	**1,254.0**	**1,394.3**	**1,705.0**	**2,640.7**	**3,678.6**	**4,254.0**	**4,684.1**
Bahrain........ 419	18.67	19.26	18.25	19.18	20.63	23.06	44.95	7.88	10.43	18.75	5.67	6.05	34.09	75.14
Egypt........ 469	23.43	18.98	26.90	29.81	45.47	56.02	72.97	51.62	76.08	117.89	302.36	368.10	488.59	590.69
Iran, I.R. of........ 429	9.22	11.41	26.71	51.45	37.22	65.69	33.05	11.81	12.39	15.08	9.09	23.49	8.70	7.41
Iraq........ 433	533.84	603.97	542.52	621.52	735.58	634.39	712.29	684.91	750.98	374.64	64.31	27.76	7.26	12.37
Israel........ 436	111.97	136.70	108.03	108.90	118.30	132.53	158.53	111.43	125.84	133.90	164.67	156.19	139.42	148.43
Kuwait........ 443	36.95	36.25	39.69	53.11	72.52	97.26	71.87	18.34	17.64	20.75	28.95	61.20	35.19	136.59
Lebanon........ 446	43.10	53.40	50.55	59.54	67.98	75.09	97.59	44.38	42.97	46.81	62.29	74.66	79.98	104.67
Libya........ 672	30.40	22.80	18.84	25.98	26.25	26.20	33.33	.80	3.41	.38	1.87	3.53	.47	.90
Oman........ 449	13.91	15.18	16.92	15.52	27.65	21.72	22.95	10.33	8.61	7.96	9.31	12.02	14.42	15.93
Qatar........ 453	25.63	28.39	26.46	23.08	34.59	52.81	58.80	15.67	12.16	11.04	5.49	6.07	6.23	8.15
Saudi Arabia........ 456	142.12	156.48	161.72	198.99	252.83	396.68	414.38	156.49	144.57	647.93	1,616.83	2,480.06	2,935.09	2,847.85
Syrian Arab Republic........ 463	39.86	69.75	97.10	137.90	202.65	269.50	268.49	66.47	96.93	153.24	207.81	227.92	262.04	364.02
United Arab Emirates........ 466	91.69	95.88	117.27	114.60	171.14	291.39	429.63	58.75	78.44	143.97	145.20	211.76	214.92	287.31
Yemen, Republic of........ 474	17.66	18.53	22.65	26.49	33.48	36.17	42.80	1.87	1.89	2.16	3.64	3.93	4.21	53.66
Middle East n.s........ 489	28.23	27.33	93.53	55.16	39.94	37.55	42.44	13.25	11.97	10.47	13.24	15.89	23.38	30.95
Western Hemisphere........ 207	**5.4**	**3.4**	**2.8**	**3.8**	**13.0**	**12.8**	**17.1**	**148.7**	**139.1**	**174.8**	**168.1**	**186.9**	**211.9**	**235.2**
Argentina........ 213	.15	.18	.02	.01	.04	.08	.05	102.92	104.26	126.34	80.86	88.90	68.03	67.81
Bolivia........ 218	—	—	—	—	—	—	.06	—	—	—	—	.06	—	—
Brazil........ 223	3.40	1.35	.62	.65	2.86	4.79	7.20	37.53	24.75	29.91	65.79	78.21	109.69	124.59
Chile........ 228	—	.10	.06	.13	.14	.16	.14	1.14	.99	1.98	1.10	1.32	2.17	4.71
Colombia........ 233	.06	.03	.05	.07	—	.31	.55	.45	.62	.52	.30	.48	.96	1.24
Costa Rica........ 238	—	—	—	—	.10	.52	.15	.07	.01	.14	.04	.15	.24	.66
Dominica........ 321	—	—	—	.36	—	—	—	—	—	—	—	—	—	—
Dominican Republic........ 243	.30	.29	.35	.05	.45	.32	.47	—	—	—	—	—	—	.05
Ecuador........ 248	—	—	—	.05	—	.48	.48	1.08	.51	.47	1.65	.81	.44	2.21

	Exports							Imports						
	2001	2002	2003	2004	2005	2006	2007	2001	2002	2003	2004	2005	2006	2007
	Millions of U.S. Dollars							*Millions of U.S. Dollars*						
El Salvador.......... 253	—	.01	.03	.02	.08	.09	.18	.13	—	—	.02	—	—	.02
Guatemala.......... 258	.05	.49	.04	.06	.20	.11	.88	1.68	2.57	3.13	2.95	2.47	2.55	2.66
Haiti.......... 263	—	—	—	.01	3.01	.72	.26	—	—	—	—	—	—	—
Honduras.......... 268	—	—	.02	—	.04	.04	—	.03	.05	.09	.02	—	.10	.03
Jamaica.......... 343	.09	.09	.08	.12	.24	.19	.29	—	.01	—	—	.01	—	.03
Mexico.......... 273	.40	.33	.70	.96	3.95	3.60	2.75	1.83	3.65	6.82	5.62	7.47	11.87	16.71
Nicaragua.......... 278	—	—	—	—	—	.15	—	.02	.02	—	.01	—	—	.10
Panama.......... 283	.58	—	.01	.15	.55	.55	1.27	.34	.01	.39	.06	.01	.12	.04
Paraguay.......... 288	—	—	—	—	.12	—	.03	—	—	—	—	.02	.06	.01
Peru.......... 293	.40	.53	.82	1.02	.88	.46	1.06	1.04	.96	.83	1.41	1.49	.53	.49
Uruguay.......... 298	—	—	—	.03	.11	.08	.21	.17	.72	4.16	8.28	5.46	15.08	13.61
Venezuela, Rep. Bol.......... 299	.02	.04	.04	.09	.16	.21	1.11	.23	.01	.06	—	.04	.07	.20
Other Countries n.i.e.......... 910	**—**	**.1**	**.2**	**.4**	**.1**	**—**	**.3**	**.1**	**.2**	**.6**	**.2**	**.3**	**.3**	**—**
Cuba.......... 928	.03	.06	.18	.12	.13	—	.25	.12	.06	.03	.04	.06	.06	.01
North Korea.......... 954	—	—	—	.23	—	—	—	—	.11	.52	.16	.21	.26	—
Countries & Areas n.s.......... 898	**23.9**	**14.6**	**9.2**	**—**	**—**	**—**	**—**	**29.2**	**46.7**	**20.8**	**2.1**	**—**	**—**	**—**
Special Categories.......... 899	**259.3**	**202.8**	**211.4**	**129.2**	**333.9**	**391.2**	**522.0**	**171.2**	**4.7**	**5.4**	**6.7**	**5.4**	**9.4**	**2.3**
Memorandum Items														
European Union.......... 998	93.61	197.70	103.93	113.20	141.55	158.27	163.23	1,408.83	1,500.49	1,529.84	1,920.69	2,536.12	2,675.46	3,278.83
Oil Exporting Ctys.......... 999	948.83	1,037.94	1,035.17	1,208.76	1,458.34	1,678.38	1,898.05	1,017.39	1,107.06	1,308.76	2,056.45	2,995.51	3,367.72	3,436.79
Non-Oil Develop.Ctys.......... 201	709.03	827.37	850.11	1,015.51	1,218.73	1,358.89	1,610.73	1,535.42	1,737.60	2,169.61	3,211.72	3,949.21	4,490.72	5,758.71
PERCENT DISTRIBUTION														
Industrial Countries.......... 101	**15.3**	**24.8**	**31.6**	**33.3**	**30.0**	**34.1**	**27.2**	**43.5**	**42.9**	**39.0**	**35.4**	**33.8**	**31.9**	**32.0**
Developing Countries.......... 202	**72.3**	**67.4**	**61.2**	**63.0**	**62.2**	**58.4**	**63.4**	**52.4**	**56.0**	**60.6**	**64.5**	**66.2**	**68.1**	**68.0**
Africa.......... 607	**3.8**	**4.5**	**3.8**	**6.2**	**4.7**	**3.4**	**3.7**	**1.3**	**1.0**	**1.1**	**1.0**	**1.1**	**.8**	**.8**
Asia.......... 507	**16.2**	**13.9**	**11.5**	**11.5**	**11.7**	**11.0**	**12.9**	**15.5**	**18.2**	**19.5**	**20.9**	**20.0**	**20.8**	**20.7**
Europe.......... 170	**1.2**	**1.4**	**1.5**	**1.5**	**1.7**	**1.1**	**1.2**	**6.9**	**6.6**	**7.3**	**8.2**	**8.3**	**7.7**	**10.1**
Middle East.......... 407	**50.9**	**47.5**	**44.4**	**43.7**	**43.9**	**42.6**	**45.2**	**25.7**	**27.5**	**29.7**	**32.3**	**35.0**	**36.8**	**34.6**
Western Hemisphere.......... 207	**.2**	**.1**	**.1**	**.1**	**.3**	**.2**	**.3**	**3.1**	**2.7**	**3.0**	**2.1**	**1.8**	**1.8**	**1.7**
ANNUAL PERCENT CHANGE														
World.......... 001	**78.4**	**20.9**	**11.3**	**14.6**	**21.8**	**21.0**	**6.4**	**6.0**	**4.2**	**13.1**	**42.1**	**28.6**	**10.0**	**17.2**
Industrial Countries.......... 101	**169.8**	**96.0**	**42.0**	**20.7**	**9.6**	**37.7**	**–15.3**	**–4.9**	**2.9**	**2.7**	**29.0**	**22.9**	**3.7**	**17.8**
Developing Countries.......... 202	**47.5**	**12.5**	**1.1**	**18.0**	**20.4**	**13.5**	**15.5**	**13.6**	**11.4**	**22.3**	**51.5**	**31.8**	**13.2**	**17.0**
Africa.......... 607	**36.2**	**45.4**	**–6.9**	**89.1**	**–7.8**	**–12.6**	**15.3**	**46.6**	**–16.7**	**19.4**	**35.6**	**39.4**	**–16.4**	**11.7**
Asia.......... 507	**–11.0**	**3.4**	**–8.3**	**15.3**	**23.5**	**14.1**	**24.7**	**14.9**	**22.8**	**21.0**	**52.5**	**22.6**	**14.7**	**16.4**
Europe.......... 170	**28.2**	**37.3**	**22.0**	**13.7**	**39.0**	**–19.9**	**18.0**	**20.3**	**–.1**	**24.7**	**60.0**	**30.1**	**2.9**	**53.5**
Middle East.......... 407	**89.3**	**12.7**	**4.0**	**12.7**	**22.4**	**17.5**	**13.0**	**9.4**	**11.2**	**22.3**	**54.9**	**39.3**	**15.6**	**10.1**
Western Hemisphere.......... 207	**15.5**	**–36.8**	**–17.7**	**33.7**	**242.5**	**–.8**	**33.3**	**19.3**	**–6.4**	**25.7**	**–3.9**	**11.2**	**13.4**	**11.0**
Other Countries n.i.e.......... 910	**....**	**115.8**	**204.7**	**98.2**	**–62.5**	**23.7**	**....**	**–69.3**	**36.1**	**229.8**	**–63.3**	**34.8**	**16.3**	**–97.1**

	Exports 2001	Exports 2002	Exports 2003	Exports 2004	Exports 2005	Exports 2006	Exports 2007	Imports 2001	Imports 2002	Imports 2003	Imports 2004	Imports 2005	Imports 2006	Imports 2007
	Millions of U.S. Dollars							*Millions of U.S. Dollars*						
IFS World Total	**8,639**	**9,670**	**12,927**	**20,093**	**27,849**	**40,470**	**46,540**	**6,446**	**6,584**	**8,409**	**12,781**	**17,353**	**24,956**	**32,940**
DOTS World Total 001	**9,085**	**9,670**	**12,927**	**20,095**	**23,508Y**	**30,110Y**	**37,552Y**	**6,478**	**6,584**	**8,409**	**12,780**	**20,156Y**	**27,106Y**	**37,063Y**
Industrial Countries 101	**2,602**	**2,489**	**3,848**	**10,767**	**11,151Y**	**14,554Y**	**16,753Y**	**2,184**	**2,337**	**2,922**	**4,230**	**5,196Y**	**7,174Y**	**8,953Y**
United States 111	159	117	99	274	1,059V	908V	1,173V	349	461	471	563	592V	711V	828V
Canada 156	17	9	11	246	30V	33V	27V	39	47	56	97	105V	117V	189V
Australia 193	—	—	1	1	6V	8V	7V	14	6	19	20	9V	6V	13V
Japan 158	19	23	10	30	303V	298V	365V	142	165	212	398	195V	275V	237V
New Zealand 196	—	—	1	1	4V	1V	3V	1	6	1	3	2V	4V	1V
Austria 122	3	3	1	1	574V	744V	988V	31	46	82	142	190V	240V	348V
Belgium 124	4	7	9	11	31V	50V	157V	51	40	59	108	109V	163V	177V
Cyprus 423	—	4	62	139	1V	4V	5V	2	3	2	2	1V	1V	2V
Denmark 128	—	1	5	26	5V	21V	14V	15	27	30	34	33V	44V	68V
Finland 172	56	49	110	167	204V	338V	384V	71	73	97	152	241V	311V	511V
France 132	10	27	278	1,468	2,033V	2,279V	2,530V	142	110	197	314	639V	924V	698V
Germany 134	502	220	146	213	2,825V	3,716V	4,315V	490	586	734	1,053	1,425V	1,998V	2,951V
Greece 174	4	31	11	6	366V	625V	922V	63	14	6	9	11V	11V	16V
Iceland 176	—	—	—	—	—Y	—Y	—Y	—	1	1	1	—V	—V	—V
Ireland 178	—	8	7	—	—V	—V	1V	13	20	15	27	11V	18V	32V
Italy 136	956	904	1,013	3,109	2,105V	3,142V	2,714V	269	219	250	426	556V	871V	872V
Luxembourg 137	—	—	—	—	—V	1V	—V	18	6	3	5	9V	5V	11V
Malta 181	—	—	—	—	—V	—V	—V	—	—	—	—	—V	10V	1V
Netherlands 138	144	124	186	465	393V	423V	785V	85	87	128	179	388V	448V	613V
Norway 142	6	6	3	6	6V	4V	10V	6	5	16	18	22V	16V	98V
Portugal 182	1	5	54	319	287V	378V	394V	1	—	1	2	1V	2V	3V
Slovenia 961	—	—	—	—	16V	18V	17V	8	11	22	35	50V	83V	80V
Spain 184	7	12	18	281	579V	944V	719V	13	29	72	65	43V	57V	93V
Sweden 144	9	13	1	5	105V	131V	188V	43	55	139	167	181V	243V	293V
Switzerland 146	409	792	1,680	3,760	144V	351V	604V	68	61	62	107	74V	191V	168V
United Kingdom 112	294	132	143	240	74V	137V	433V	249	260	249	301	308V	426V	650V
Developing Countries 202	**6,041**	**7,011**	**8,467**	**9,316**	**12,343Y**	**15,539Y**	**20,777Y**	**4,287**	**4,224**	**5,472**	**8,522**	**14,930Y**	**19,894Y**	**28,063Y**
Africa 607	**8**	**44**	**29**	**6**	**14Y**	**38Y**	**36Y**	**23**	**17**	**20**	**40**	**35Y**	**50Y**	**70Y**
Algeria 612	5	—	3	—	—Y	—Y	—Y	—	—	—	—	—Y	—Y	—Y
Burkina Faso 748	—	—	—	—	1Y	1Y	1Y	—	—	—	—	—Y	—Y	—Y
Côte d'Ivoire 662	—	—	—	—	—Y	—Y	—Y	1	5	2	3	3Y	4Y	5Y
Ethiopia 644	1	—	2	1	1Y	2Y	2Y	—	—	—	—	—Y	—Y	—Y
Ghana 652	—	—	—	2	2Y	3Y	4Y	2	2	6	8	9Y	12Y	14Y
Kenya 664	—	—	—	—	—Y	—Y	—Y	—	1	5	16	18Y	22Y	28Y
Morocco 686	—	6	—	—	—V	—Y	—Y	—	1	1	1	—V	—Y	—Y
Nigeria 694	2	3	6	1	2Y	2Y	3Y	4	—	—	—	—Y	—Y	—Y
Rwanda 714	—	—	—	—	—Y	—Y	—Y	7	5	—	1	1Y	1Y	1Y
South Africa 199	—	1	—	—	—V	9V	—V	7	2	3	7	1V	10V	19V
Sudan 732	—	9	1	—	—Y	—Y	—Y	—	—	—	—	—Y	—Y	—Y
Tunisia 744	—	24	15	—	8V	21V	26Y	—	—	—	—	—V	—V	—Y
Zimbabwe 698	—	—	—	—	—V	—V	—Y	—	1	3	3	—V	—V	—Y
Africa n.s. 799	—	—	1	—	—Y	—Y	—Y	1	—	1	—	—Y	—Y	—Y
Asia 507	**796**	**1,183**	**1,861**	**2,385**	**3,127Y**	**3,777Y**	**6,380Y**	**362**	**518**	**801**	**1,194**	**4,818Y**	**5,830Y**	**9,127Y**
Afghanistan, I.S. of 512	18	31	49	86	99Y	122Y	151Y	—	—	—	—	—Y	—Y	—Y
Bangladesh 513	3	1	2	3	18V	16V	16V	1	2	1	1	2V	1Y	2Y
China,P.R.: Mainland 924	660	1,023	1,653	1,967	2,638V	3,279V	5,836V	172	313	524	758	4,289V	5,227V	8,192V
China,P.R.:Hong Kong 532	3	1	1	—	1V	2V	2V	1	—	1	2	9V	12V	21V
India 534	10	5	6	11	21V	26Y	32Y	45	55	73	86	96V	119Y	147Y
Indonesia 536	2	6	9	7	21V	—V	8V	3	4	11	12	5V	1V	6V
Korea 542	43	49	55	163	220V	251V	233V	111	110	115	248	300V	356V	601V
Malaysia 548	1	3	2	7	9V	—V	—V	10	10	34	23	53V	23V	20V
Mongolia 948	10	8	12	29	35V	28Y	34Y	—	1	—	1	1V	—Y	—Y
Pakistan 564	—	—	1	1	1V	1Y	1Y	1	1	2	2	11V	14Y	17Y
Philippines 566	2	3	6	24	1V	—V	1V	—	—	1	2	—V	—V	—V
Singapore 576	26	6	—	—	—V	1V	2V	6	8	13	18	20V	20V	30V
Sri Lanka 524	—	—	—	—	—Y	—Y	—Y	3	3	3	3	4Y	5Y	6Y
Taiwan Province of China 528	1	3	4	12	16V	33V	46V	6	6	10	18	13V	22V	40V
Thailand 578	3	18	16	19	48V	17V	18V	2	4	15	17	16V	29V	44V
Vietnam 582	13	27	43	54	—V	—V	—V	—	—	1	2	—V	—V	—V
Europe 170	**2,984**	**2,889**	**3,599**	**5,009**	**6,536Y**	**8,031Y**	**9,537Y**	**3,652**	**3,486**	**4,432**	**7,004**	**9,882Y**	**13,748Y**	**18,533Y**
Albania 914	—	—	—	—	1V	2V	2V	—	—	—	—	—V	—V	—V
Armenia 911	2	2	6	14	1V	145V	219V	1	1	1	2	3V	4V	8V
Azerbaijan 912	69	113	114	287	87V	116V	202V	11	15	14	16	19V	116V	140V
Belarus 913	5	12	13	18	28V	68V	138V	46	55	95	144	202V	285V	397V
Bulgaria 918	2	18	15	17	177V	17V	4V	6	6	9	15	12V	26V	69V
Croatia 960	—	4	23	102	—V	—V	—V	2	5	8	8	13V	16V	12V
Czech Republic 935	4	15	30	50	149V	239V	161V	46	53	38	99	101V	125V	154V
Estonia 939	6	8	9	42	15V	57V	53V	2	5	5	80	25V	29V	42V
Georgia 915	3	5	12	32	11V	23V	44Y	4	4	7	7	11V	17V	31Y

	Exports							Imports						
	2001	2002	2003	2004	2005	2006	2007	2001	2002	2003	2004	2005	2006	2007
	Millions of U.S. Dollars							*Millions of U.S. Dollars*						
Gibraltar......823	—	6	28	69	79Y	98Y	121Y	—	1	—	1	1Y	2Y	2Y
Hungary......944	8	13	20	39	60V	53V	116V	33	39	42	58	111V	177V	308V
Kyrgyz Republic......917	87	109	156	222	159V	182V	261V	33	32	55	91	128V	179V	209V
Latvia......941	45	62	77	98	19V	46V	50V	9	14	13	29	19V	28V	53V
Lithuania......946	8	4	5	19	28V	45V	76V	8	9	13	20	120V	239V	365V
Macedonia, FYR......962	—	—	—	1	18V	20V	24Y	—	1	—	—	—V	1V	1Y
Moldova......921	3	3	35	45	61V	75Y	93Y	6	7	9	16	19V	24Y	29Y
Poland......964	164	320	201	189	433V	266V	371V	61	75	117	170	233V	385V	527V
Romania......968	8	121	33	33	1,194V	1,484V	1,236V	16	42	23	37	39V	39V	100V
Russia......922	1,760	1,498	1,968	2,838	2,918V	3,476V	4,202V	2,892	2,549	3,282	4,813	7,182V	9,867V	13,127V
Serbia & Montenegro......965	2	—	1	—	—Y	—Y	—Y	1	2	1	2	2Y	2Y	3Y
Slovak Republic......936	18	26	77	106	9V	16V	35V	21	18	22	24	34V	55V	84V
Tajikistan......923	61	46	76	136	153V	170V	303V	2	3	7	3	22V	31V	26V
Turkey......186	74	97	99	147	507V	903V	1,167V	137	174	209	342	506V	767V	1,188V
Turkmenistan......925	14	15	37	26	30Y	37Y	46Y	77	75	49	76	86Y	107Y	132Y
Ukraine......926	490	291	426	278	169V	209Y	260Y	155	217	324	723	734V	907Y	1,126Y
Uzbekistan......927	150	101	138	202	230Y	285Y	353Y	81	87	90	228	260Y	321Y	399Y
Middle East......407	**563**	**841**	**771**	**1,105**	**1,068Y**	**1,298Y**	**1,679Y**	**75**	**93**	**81**	**86**	**110Y**	**142Y**	**197Y**
Egypt......469	4	3	3	9	10Y	13Y	16Y	2	3	3	5	5Y	7Y	8Y
Iran, I.R. of......429	209	310	411	712	907Y	1,119Y	1,450Y	11	12	13	13	18Y	22Y	27Y
Iraq......433	—	6	—	—	—Y	—Y	—Y	....	....	....	....	....	....	....
Israel......436	4	6	60	322	3V	2V	3V	24	30	36	42	53V	71V	109V
Jordan......439	2	21	43	18	23V	9V	11V	—	—	—	1	—V	—V	1V
Kuwait......443	—	—	—	—	—Y	—Y	1Y	—	—	—	—	—Y	—Y	—Y
Lebanon......446	—	1	3	1	1Y	1Y	2Y	—	3	—	2	3Y	3Y	4Y
Oman......449	1	—	—	—	—Y	—Y	—Y	1	2	2	2	2Y	3Y	4Y
Qatar......453	1	—	—	—	—V	—V	—Y	—	—	—	—	—V	—V	1Y
Saudi Arabia......456	3	14	28	2	68V	84Y	109Y	2	2	1	—	1Y	1Y	1Y
Syrian Arab Republic......463	8	8	9	9	10Y	13Y	16Y	—	—	—	—	—Y	—Y	1Y
United Arab Emirates......466	330	472	215	32	40Y	50Y	65Y	34	39	25	20	28Y	35Y	42Y
Yemen, Republic of......474	—	—	—	—	5V	6Y	7Y	—	—	—	—	—V	—Y	—Y
Western Hemisphere......207	**1,691**	**2,054**	**2,208**	**811**	**1,597Y**	**2,395Y**	**3,144Y**	**174**	**111**	**137**	**198**	**85Y**	**123Y**	**137Y**
Argentina......213	5	—	—	1	19V	16V	10V	4	6	1	4	4V	19V	18V
Bahamas, The......313	—	29	10	30	34Y	42Y	52Y	1	2	1	—	—Y	1Y	1Y
Bermuda......319	1,221	2,011	2,193	—	—Y	—Y	—Y	....	....	....	....	....	....	....
Bolivia......218	....	....	....	....	....	....	....	—	—	2	—	—Y	—Y	—Y
Brazil......223	—	—	—	1	9V	37V	11V	68	72	88	116	35V	46V	45V
Chile......228	—	—	1	—	2V	1V	—V	—	—	—	1	—V	—V	—V
Colombia......233	—	1	—	2	1V	1V	7V	—	—	—	—	—V	—V	—V
Costa Rica......238	—	—	—	—	—Y	—Y	—Y	—	—	—	—	—Y	1Y	1Y
Dominican Republic......243	—	2	3	3	4Y	5Y	6Y	—	—	—	—	—Y	—Y	—Y
Ecuador......248	—	1	—	4	—V	—V	—Y	1	2	4	7	—V	—V	—Y
El Salvador......253	—	1	—	3	—V	—V	—V	7	—	14	9	10Y	13Y	16Y
Guatemala......258	—	—	—	1	1Y	2Y	2Y	27	5	10	3	3Y	4Y	5Y
Mexico......273	—	—	—	—	—Y	—Y	—Y	5	10	5	23	27Y	33Y	41Y
Nicaragua......278	—	1	—	—	—V	—V	—V	3	1	3	—	—Y	—Y	—Y
Panama......283	12	5	—	1	—V	—V	—V	—	—	—	—	—Y	—Y	—Y
Peru......293	6	2	—	—	—V	—V	—Y	26	13	10	31	—V	—V	—Y
Trinidad and Tobago......369	—	—	—	1	1Y	1Y	1Y	—	—	—	—	—Y	—Y	—Y
Western Hem. n.s......399	446	—	—	763	1,527Y	2,290Y	3,054Y	32	—	—	2	5Y	7Y	9Y
Other Countries n.i.e......910	**—**	**2**	**10**	**13**	**14Y**	**18Y**	**22Y**	**7**	**23**	**14**	**27**	**31Y**	**38Y**	**48Y**
Cuba......928	—	2	—	3	3Y	4Y	5Y	6	22	14	27	30Y	37Y	46Y
North Korea......954	—	—	10	10	11Y	14Y	17Y	—	—	—	1	1Y	1Y	1Y
Countries & Areas n.s......898	**441**	**168**	**602**	**—**	**—Y**	**—Y**	**—Y**	**—**	**—**	**—**	**—**	**—Y**	**—Y**	**—Y**
Memorandum Items														
European Union......998	2,244	1,988	2,461	6,992	10,312Y	13,674Y	15,428Y	1,745	1,799	2,335	3,501	4,839Y	6,892Y	8,951Y
Oil Exporting Ctys......999	552	812	673	755	1,038Y	1,257Y	1,635Y	55	60	52	48	53Y	63Y	81Y
Non-Oil Develop.Ctys......201	5,489	6,199	7,794	8,561	11,304Y	14,282Y	19,142Y	4,231	4,164	5,420	8,474	14,877Y	19,831Y	27,983Y
PERCENT DISTRIBUTION														
Industrial Countries......101	**28.6**	**25.7**	**29.8**	**53.6**	**47.4**	**48.3**	**44.6**	**33.7**	**35.5**	**34.8**	**33.1**	**25.8**	**26.5**	**24.2**
Developing Countries......202	**66.5**	**72.5**	**65.5**	**46.4**	**52.5**	**51.6**	**55.3**	**66.2**	**64.2**	**65.1**	**66.7**	**74.1**	**73.4**	**75.7**
Africa......607	**.1**	**.5**	**.2**	**—**	**.1**	**.1**	**.1**	**.4**	**.3**	**.2**	**.3**	**.2**	**.2**	**.2**
Asia......507	**8.8**	**12.2**	**14.4**	**11.9**	**13.3**	**12.5**	**17.0**	**5.6**	**7.9**	**9.5**	**9.3**	**23.9**	**21.5**	**24.6**
Europe......170	**32.8**	**29.9**	**27.8**	**24.9**	**27.8**	**26.7**	**25.4**	**56.4**	**52.9**	**52.7**	**54.8**	**49.0**	**50.7**	**50.0**
Middle East......407	**6.2**	**8.7**	**6.0**	**5.5**	**4.5**	**4.3**	**4.5**	**1.2**	**1.4**	**1.0**	**.7**	**.5**	**.5**	**.5**
Western Hemisphere......207	**18.6**	**21.2**	**17.1**	**4.0**	**6.8**	**8.0**	**8.4**	**2.7**	**1.7**	**1.6**	**1.5**	**.4**	**.5**	**.4**
Other Countries n.i.e......910	**—**	**—**	**.1**	**.1**	**.1**	**.1**	**.1**	**.1**	**.3**	**.2**	**.2**	**.2**	**.1**	**.1**
ANNUAL PERCENT CHANGE														
World......001	**–8.0**	**6.4**	**33.7**	**55.5**	**17.0**	**28.1**	**24.7**	**28.3**	**1.6**	**27.7**	**52.0**	**57.7**	**34.5**	**36.7**
Industrial Countries......101	**–5.8**	**–4.3**	**54.6**	**179.8**	**3.6**	**30.5**	**15.1**	**45.2**	**7.0**	**25.1**	**44.8**	**22.8**	**38.1**	**24.8**
Developing Countries......202	**–.7**	**16.0**	**20.8**	**10.0**	**32.5**	**25.9**	**33.7**	**22.1**	**–1.5**	**29.5**	**55.7**	**75.2**	**33.2**	**41.1**
Africa......607	**–38.6**	**452.6**	**–34.2**	**–80.8**	**155.0**	**169.9**	**–4.0**	**–4.1**	**–27.6**	**17.6**	**101.9**	**–13.7**	**45.8**	**37.9**
Asia......507	**–11.7**	**48.6**	**57.2**	**28.2**	**31.1**	**20.8**	**68.9**	**17.7**	**43.0**	**54.7**	**49.0**	**303.5**	**21.0**	**56.6**
Europe......170	**14.4**	**–3.2**	**24.6**	**39.2**	**30.5**	**22.9**	**18.8**	**20.0**	**–4.6**	**27.2**	**58.0**	**41.1**	**39.1**	**34.8**
Middle East......407	**133.1**	**49.6**	**–8.3**	**43.3**	**–3.3**	**21.5**	**29.4**	**34.2**	**24.0**	**–12.4**	**6.0**	**28.1**	**29.0**	**38.4**
Western Hemisphere......207	**–27.1**	**21.5**	**7.5**	**–63.2**	**96.8**	**49.9**	**31.3**	**120.5**	**–36.5**	**24.1**	**43.9**	**–57.0**	**44.8**	**10.9**
Other Countries n.i.e......910	**192.8**	**601.6**	**341.1**	**26.2**	**14.3**	**23.6**	**24.1**	**–78.7**	**234.9**	**–39.7**	**98.8**	**14.3**	**23.6**	**24.1**

		Exports							Imports						
		2001	2002	2003	2004	2005	2006	2007	2001	2002	2003	2004	2005	2006	2007
		Millions of U.S. Dollars							Millions of U.S. Dollars						
IFS World Total		**1,944.0**	**2,116.2**	**2,411.2**	**2,684.0**	**3,292.8**	**3,436.9**	**4,079.9**	**3,191.9**	**3,244.8**	**3,725.3**	**4,552.7**	**6,148.9**	**7,311.4**	**8,989.4**
DOTS World Total	**001**	**1,872.6**	**2,144.0**	**2,403.7**	**2,702.8**	**3,544.7Y**	**4,102.8Y**	**4,843.6Y**	**3,693.3**	**3,270.2**	**3,709.7**	**4,591.2**	**6,826.6Y**	**8,227.5Y**	**10,319.3Y**
Industrial Countries	**101**	**533.6**	**691.1**	**793.3**	**830.3**	**1,465.1Y**	**1,584.8Y**	**1,716.0Y**	**1,722.1**	**1,547.2**	**1,417.0**	**1,679.8**	**2,412.2Y**	**2,725.2Y**	**3,374.4Y**
United States	111	43.46	42.89	36.84	56.84	334.64V	340.64V	311.27V	496.00	186.07	189.69	182.04	695.64V	578.49V	642.62V
Canada	156	4.56	5.58	5.73	5.82	13.22V	12.93V	15.59V	20.35	15.02	27.01	27.75	36.99V	54.25V	70.20V
Australia	193	10.00	5.98	8.77	6.64	11.38V	12.16V	12.73V	40.91	23.86	20.57	15.21	35.51V	47.46V	48.76V
Japan	158	16.96	22.26	16.00	20.12	29.00V	26.58V	26.79V	183.75	218.95	245.09	304.87	276.39V	388.84V	608.15V
New Zealand	196	.63	.97	.62	.77	1.67V	1.70V	2.23V	2.54	1.26	1.24	1.87	3.04V	4.38V	6.23V
Austria	122	1.26	1.07	5.06	.63	1.13V	1.29V	.84V	5.28	6.50	5.76	5.84	10.09V	24.94V	18.61V
Belgium	124	25.45	29.10	30.71	31.24	31.71V	45.25V	72.96V	97.66	88.19	88.99	122.34	104.92V	117.28V	174.01V
Cyprus	423	.29	.32	.21	.57	.66V	1.16V	1.57V	1.51	1.78	1.04	1.28	.93V	1.59V	1.65V
Denmark	128	3.89	2.51	3.08	2.33	2.97V	4.35V	6.31V	15.39	14.83	11.72	18.69	21.13V	18.51V	21.67V
Finland	172	4.24	5.14	7.23	6.50	17.24V	12.61V	15.46V	13.78	18.32	9.19	22.36	15.91V	33.80V	65.11V
France	132	32.70	34.50	45.89	55.77	91.42V	89.93V	72.65V	136.27	123.50	118.09	154.11	143.76V	139.91V	239.82V
Germany	134	65.39	55.59	70.19	57.77	100.26V	95.08V	112.37V	149.06	164.34	144.35	165.80	210.88V	264.98V	314.85V
Greece	174	3.11	3.78	4.21	3.20	4.35V	2.36V	4.80V	1.31	1.43	2.85	8.20	15.62V	13.34V	12.05V
Iceland	176	—	—	.05	.37	.34V	.29V	.36V	1.35	.57	.57	1.13	.02V	.03V	.02V
Ireland	178	6.40	7.42	10.03	8.14	12.99V	17.12V	12.99V	7.58	52.04	5.56	7.33	13.79V	14.51V	35.03V
Italy	136	14.23	39.21	24.48	24.42	63.00V	62.26V	82.35V	89.07	52.72	76.91	90.25	123.34V	203.49V	220.36V
Luxembourg	137	.04	.03	—	.02	3.83V	4.05V	.30V	1.16	.27	.90	.61	1.34V	.80V	.98V
Malta	181	.21	.50	.08	.02	.38V	2.50V	1.94V	.06	.05	.02	.05	.31V	.23V	.42V
Netherlands	138	135.53	140.04	186.20	215.91	287.17V	327.57V	396.10V	67.79	68.69	82.39	92.31	172.40V	172.89V	200.91V
Norway	142	2.29	3.88	3.84	3.10	11.31V	9.90V	10.92V	7.79	3.98	4.71	4.96	24.06V	10.07V	10.74V
Portugal	182	3.60	3.15	2.34	3.01	3.33V	7.66V	8.46V	3.84	1.48	19.28	8.72	3.01V	4.52V	8.11V
Slovenia	961	.01	.05	.10	.09	.12V	.12V	.31V	.31	1.13	1.04	.47	.36V	2.15V	1.36V
Spain	184	8.52	11.91	13.22	14.70	23.97V	29.04V	33.17V	28.10	37.57	28.37	25.12	46.40V	94.22V	70.50V
Sweden	144	8.74	11.68	8.31	13.68	25.30V	25.81V	34.02V	20.64	155.67	21.27	25.34	43.62V	51.73V	65.30V
Switzerland	146	15.75	14.24	26.65	15.57	23.48V	23.79V	27.71V	50.67	40.56	52.01	50.52	28.38V	46.97V	62.90V
United Kingdom	112	126.33	249.28	283.46	283.09	370.26V	428.63V	451.82V	279.88	268.42	258.39	342.59	384.36V	435.87V	474.02V
Developing Countries	**202**	**1,280.9**	**1,371.0**	**1,484.6**	**1,716.1**	**1,900.9Y**	**2,297.2Y**	**2,853.6Y**	**1,962.1**	**1,708.6**	**2,278.7**	**2,889.0**	**4,388.7Y**	**5,470.5Y**	**6,905.5Y**
Africa	**607**	**841.5**	**955.8**	**1,032.4**	**1,186.4**	**1,297.0Y**	**1,576.0Y**	**1,968.2Y**	**358.4**	**329.4**	**427.4**	**580.7**	**709.9Y**	**790.6Y**	**1,030.8Y**
Algeria	612	1.36	7.06	.07	.28	.35Y	.44Y	.57Y	14.70	—	—	.56	.77Y	.96Y	1.16Y
Angola	614	.39	.82	3.42	1.51	1.73Y	2.14Y	2.65Y	.06	.31	.01	—	—Y	—Y	—Y
Benin	638	.37	.48	.47	.28	.02V	.03Y	.03Y	—	—	—	—	.01V	.01Y	.01Y
Botswana	616	.16	.11	.43	.15	.17Y	.21Y	.27Y	.07	.16	.06	.04	.05Y	.06Y	.07Y
Burkina Faso	748	.19	2.05	2.06	1.07	1.23Y	1.52Y	1.88Y	.03	—	.06	—	—Y	.01Y	.01Y
Burundi	618	23.50	22.83	36.24	37.54	30.95V	32.22V	39.99Y	.86	.01	.03	.04	.41V	1.30V	1.62Y
Cameroon	622	.23	.15	.38	1.78	2.03Y	2.51Y	3.12Y	.06	.02	—	.09	.10Y	.13Y	.16Y
Cape Verde	624	—	—	—	.62	.70Y	.87Y	1.08Y	—	—	.01	—	—Y	—Y	—Y
Central African Rep.	626	—	—	—	.01	.02Y	.02Y	.02Y	—	.06	.16	.04	.04Y	.05Y	.06Y
Chad	628	—	.03	.05	.15	.17Y	.21Y	.26Y	—	—	—	—	—Y	—Y	—Y
Comoros	632	4.51	3.46	4.05	4.61	5.27Y	6.51Y	8.08Y	.01	—	—	—	—Y	—Y	—Y
Congo, Dem. Rep. of	636	54.55	62.87	70.68	98.92	113.02Y	139.68Y	173.35Y	9.70	5.47	.76	5.23	5.98Y	7.39Y	9.17Y
Congo, Republic of	634	5.86	3.90	9.79	2.44	2.78Y	3.44Y	4.27Y	.09	.06	.36	.06	.07Y	.08Y	.10Y
Côte d'Ivoire	662	.43	.41	.36	1.57	.92V	1.35V	1.67Y	.22	.01	.08	.02	.83V	.41V	.51Y
Djibouti	611	10.74	5.98	4.98	6.62	7.56Y	9.35Y	11.60Y	.05	—	—	.01	.01Y	.01Y	.02Y
Equatorial Guinea	642	—	.01	.16	.09	.10Y	.12Y	.15Y	—	—	—	—	—Y	—Y	—Y
Eritrea	643	6.04	5.48	5.41	2.58	2.95Y	3.65Y	4.53Y	.05	—	.04	.01	.02Y	.02Y	.02Y
Ethiopia	644	27.41	25.15	21.39	28.01	23.41V	28.93Y	35.90Y	.79	.14	.20	1.30	2.68V	3.31Y	4.11Y
Gabon	646	—	.01	.01	.08	.09Y	.11Y	.13Y	—	—	.02	.05	.06Y	.07Y	.09Y
Gambia, The	648	.02	.03	.09	.14	.16Y	.20Y	.25Y	.76	.64	.09	.12	.13Y	.16Y	.20Y
Ghana	652	.74	1.12	4.42	2.55	2.91Y	3.60Y	4.46Y	.05	.03	.04	.18	.20Y	.25Y	.31Y
Guinea	656	.11	.41	1.06	1.17	1.34Y	1.66Y	2.06Y	.01	—	.05	.07	.09Y	.11Y	.13Y
Lesotho	666	—	.01	—	.02	.02Y	.03Y	.04Y	.01	—	—	—	—Y	—Y	—Y
Liberia	668	.01	.07	.42	.91	1.04Y	1.29Y	1.60Y	—	—	—	—	—Y	—Y	—Y
Madagascar	674	3.27	8.33	6.24	3.55	4.05Y	5.01Y	6.21Y	.07	.19	—	.01	.01Y	.01Y	.02Y
Malawi	676	4.78	9.62	10.00	14.32	16.36Y	20.21Y	25.09Y	12.12	11.75	14.78	8.17	9.34Y	11.54Y	14.32Y
Mali	678	.48	.44	1.04	2.24	2.56Y	3.16Y	3.92Y	3.22	.13	.07	.32	.37Y	.46Y	.57Y
Mauritania	682	.06	.08	.07	.22	.25Y	.31Y	.39Y	—	.04	2.34	—	—Y	—Y	—Y
Mauritius	684	4.32	2.07	9.79	7.68	8.73V	12.05V	11.66V	7.22	5.57	6.45	15.77	7.72V	4.79V	8.41V
Morocco	686	.26	.69	1.09	.85	1.03V	1.28Y	1.58Y	.70	.63	.78	1.37	10.07V	12.45Y	15.45Y
Mozambique	688	3.77	4.23	2.97	7.21	3.22V	2.82V	3.50Y	1.14	2.52	2.51	1.22	2.32V	1.54V	1.92Y
Namibia	728	.03	.02	.29	.25	.21Y	.17Y	.14Y	4.23	1.15	1.00	.30	.30Y	.30Y	.30Y
Niger	692	.08	.15	.21	1.96	2.23Y	2.76Y	3.43Y	.27	.18	.50	.87	.99Y	1.23Y	1.53Y
Nigeria	694	8.37	14.56	14.31	15.38	19.58Y	24.17Y	31.31Y	1.07	1.38	1.83	1.90	2.58Y	3.24Y	3.91Y
Rwanda	714	44.75	54.77	79.17	78.18	89.33Y	110.40Y	137.01Y	.04	.07	.06	.21	.24Y	.29Y	.36Y
São Tomé & Príncipe	716	—	.03	—	—	—Y	—Y	—Y	.11	.04	.01	.11	.13Y	.16Y	.20Y
Senegal	722	.36	1.15	.64	1.38	1.08V	.72V	.89Y	.24	.15	.36	.39	.82V	.91V	1.13Y
Seychelles	718	2.71	3.11	2.62	3.06	3.49Y	4.32Y	5.36Y	.04	.10	—	.04	.05Y	.06Y	.07Y
Sierra Leone	724	.46	.01	.21	.37	.42Y	.52Y	.65Y	.14	1.07	.70	.54	.62Y	.76Y	.95Y
Somalia	726	30.88	57.86	49.30	41.37	47.27Y	58.42Y	72.50Y	.12	.03	.12	1.13	1.30Y	1.60Y	1.99Y
South Africa	199	5.39	6.58	14.04	20.84	31.14V	23.87V	28.23V	97.20	87.15	129.27	437.35	505.25V	524.46V	707.81V

	Exports 2001	2002	2003	2004	2005	2006	2007	Imports 2001	2002	2003	2004	2005	2006	2007
	Millions of U.S. Dollars							Millions of U.S. Dollars						
Sacca exc. South Afr. 608	—	—	—	—	—Y	—Y	—Y	—	—	—	—	44.68Y	55.22Y	68.53Y
Sudan 732	31.15	35.79	57.66	70.41	36.97V	36.23V	52.03V	13.11	3.22	7.46	2.96	2.44V	—V	—V
Swaziland 734	.11	.04	.95	.04	.05Y	.06Y	.08Y	11.28	25.77	23.04	42.19	48.20Y	59.58Y	73.93Y
Tanzania 738	171.98	180.08	192.11	226.35	258.62Y	319.64Y	396.67Y	7.44	10.19	18.01	25.38	29.00Y	35.84Y	44.48Y
Togo 742	.13	.07	.10	.11	.01V	.01Y	.02Y	—	—	—	—	—V	—Y	—Y
Tunisia 744	1.67	.17	.07	.05	.09V	.12V	.15Y	.07	.04	.09	5.66	.11V	9.24V	11.47Y
Uganda 746	382.37	397.21	403.87	468.09	534.83Y	661.01Y	820.31Y	8.70	8.44	13.66	12.77	14.59Y	18.03Y	22.37Y
Zambia 754	5.17	21.55	21.67	29.71	34.55V	50.35V	71.25V	12.19	4.38	5.13	8.14	15.21V	33.82V	32.45V
Zimbabwe 698	2.32	5.62	3.18	2.24	4.93V	1.92V	2.38Y	1.47	19.18	19.66	6.04	2.15V	.69V	.86Y
Africa n.s. 799	5.99	14.60	.22	—	—Y	—Y	—Y	148.71	139.06	177.69	.02	.02Y	.02Y	.02Y
Asia 507	**216.1**	**216.0**	**259.5**	**302.5**	**354.7Y**	**426.1Y**	**501.7Y**	**588.1**	**622.8**	**681.6**	**774.9**	**1,598.0Y**	**2,119.9Y**	**2,709.7Y**
Afghanistan, I.S. of 512	36.18	46.18	64.48	36.75	41.99Y	51.90Y	64.41Y	.22	.04	—	.09	.10Y	.13Y	.16Y
Bangladesh 513	.36	.35	.38	1.28	—V	—V	—V	2.60	1.25	1.90	2.12	3.22V	3.87Y	4.62Y
Brunei Darussalam 516	—	—	.01	.01	.01Y	.01Y	.01Y	—	—	—	—	—Y	—Y	—Y
Cambodia 522	....	....	....	....	....	....	....	—	—	—	—	.01V	—V	—Y
China,P.R.: Mainland 924	3.15	4.76	6.71	11.40	16.05V	22.19V	25.74V	86.46	76.85	105.65	161.48	502.74V	683.82V	1,025.60V
China,P.R.:Hong Kong 532	8.49	6.78	9.85	15.21	34.38V	38.64V	37.63V	13.05	10.54	14.10	12.77	71.91V	74.68V	91.15V
China,P.R.:Macao 546	—	—	.08	.32	.31V	.32V	.27V	.01	—	—	—	—V	—V	—V
India 534	30.06	32.29	32.89	52.37	43.48V	53.74Y	66.69Y	163.31	175.36	195.05	285.82	586.83V	725.27Y	900.06Y
Indonesia 536	.91	2.43	2.99	6.00	8.97V	7.54V	8.12V	97.75	166.09	164.58	97.14	47.08V	39.28V	59.74V
Korea 542	.70	.66	.90	1.16	3.96V	4.65V	7.08V	49.97	34.99	39.06	41.51	78.14V	225.34V	150.42V
Malaysia 548	3.14	3.97	4.42	5.47	6.43V	11.01V	11.38V	25.20	16.62	18.98	20.40	57.04V	86.16V	112.11V
Maldives 556	.03	—	.01	—	.01V	.01Y	.01Y	.02	—	.17	.21	.24Y	.30Y	.38Y
Myanmar 518	1.14	.99	—	—	—Y	—Y	—Y	—	—	—	—	—Y	—Y	—Y
New Caledonia 839	—	—	.03	—	—Y	—Y	—Y	....	....	....	....	....	....	....
Pakistan 564	112.99	105.91	120.53	143.47	164.71V	203.57Y	252.63Y	26.55	51.05	58.69	41.01	73.08V	90.32Y	112.08Y
Papua New Guinea 853	—	—	.07	.19	.21Y	.27Y	.33Y	.09	—	.23	.18	.20Y	.25Y	.31Y
Philippines 566	1.19	1.27	1.79	4.93	3.06V	.86V	1.49V	.13	1.32	.47	.34	1.20V	4.86V	9.44V
Singapore 576	6.75	3.35	2.30	2.43	9.11V	9.84V	8.90V	71.98	53.18	30.97	56.23	45.07V	53.59V	52.94V
Sri Lanka 524	2.44	1.89	3.44	4.88	6.28V	6.33V	.48V	.91	1.80	1.35	3.24	4.84V	4.76V	4.84V
Taiwan Province of China 528	.12	.20	.18	.40	.60V	1.96V	3.74V	19.59	13.75	17.83	14.26	54.08V	47.83V	70.06V
Thailand 578	7.04	4.04	7.66	13.03	15.14V	13.20V	12.74V	22.78	18.51	27.51	33.67	72.20V	79.44V	115.75V
Vietnam 582	1.31	.87	.75	3.17	—V	—V	—V	7.47	1.43	5.08	4.50	—V	—V	—V
Asia n.s. 598	.12	—	—	—	—Y	—Y	—Y	.03	—	—	—	—Y	—Y	—Y
Europe 170	**13.4**	**21.2**	**27.0**	**34.5**	**50.2Y**	**60.6Y**	**83.7Y**	**38.3**	**28.7**	**91.2**	**93.7**	**178.9Y**	**270.3Y**	**319.9Y**
Azerbaijan 912	—	—	.02	.06	.09V	.17V	.24V	—	—	—	—	—V	—V	—V
Belarus 913	—	—	.02	.01	.02V	.19V	.36V	—	.13	.01	—	.44V	.01V	1.21V
Bosnia & Herzegovina 963	.01	.01	.01	.10	.12Y	.14Y	.18Y	....	....	....	....	....	....	....
Bulgaria 918	.16	.30	1.18	.84	.15V	.22V	.25V	1.45	.55	2.59	7.27	17.38V	5.85V	2.21V
Croatia 960	—	.02	.01	.04	—V	—V	—V	.08	.06	.25	.24	—V	—V	—V
Czech Republic 935	.11	.10	.17	.07	1.41V	1.06V	1.42V	1.63	3.69	10.30	2.87	5.41V	5.51V	6.04V
Czechoslovakia n.s. 937	.13	.02	.03	.04	.05Y	.06Y	.08Y	1.65	.05	.23	.01	.01Y	.01Y	.01Y
Estonia 939	—	—	.01	.01	—V	.02V	.08V	.06	.06	.03	.24	.06V	.15V	.01V
Faroe Islands 816	—	—	—	—	—Y	—Y	—Y	—	—	—	.04	.04Y	.05Y	.06Y
Georgia 915	—	—	—	—	.11V	—V	—Y	2.07	.67	4.24	.74	—V	—V	—Y
Hungary 944	.08	.67	2.30	.14	.11V	.43V	.51V	1.45	1.58	2.92	1.45	5.10V	16.95V	40.92V
Kazakhstan 916	—	.71	2.51	8.72	9.96Y	12.31Y	15.27Y	—	.12	3.22	—	—Y	—Y	—Y
Kyrgyz Republic 917	—	—	—	.28	.15V	.36V	1.05V	.05	—	.08	.14	—V	—V	—V
Latvia 941	.49	1.52	.22	.82	—V	.15V	.10V	.01	—	—	.08	.63V	.58V	.56V
Lithuania 946	—	—	—	—	.01V	—V	—V	—	—	.85	.02	.06V	.13V	10.79V
Macedonia, FYR 962	1.94	.39	—	.02	.01V	.01V	.01Y	.53	—	—	—	—V	—V	—Y
Poland 964	7.07	7.36	7.12	7.56	10.70V	10.99V	9.04V	.58	.26	.91	.83	4.86V	8.03V	7.90V
Romania 968	—	.02	.39	.01	1.77V	2.50V	2.04V	1.89	.46	16.29	17.20	10.17V	38.86V	5.79V
Russia 922	.70	7.14	10.56	13.02	23.34V	27.27V	40.52V	14.18	7.59	28.43	32.05	46.54V	60.14V	88.00V
Serbia & Montenegro 965	.12	1.29	—	—	—Y	—Y	.01Y	.14	.23	.25	—	—Y	—Y	—Y
Slovak Republic 936	—	.08	.12	.04	.14V	.46V	.48V	.03	.56	1.03	.77	2.72V	3.21V	2.86V
Turkey 186	2.40	1.43	1.91	1.83	1.57V	3.63V	11.21V	10.68	7.23	11.05	15.27	55.66V	93.96V	107.85V
Ukraine 926	.19	.13	.47	.91	.53V	.65Y	.81Y	1.79	5.31	8.38	13.95	29.22V	36.11Y	44.81Y
Europe n.s. 884	....	....	....	....	....	....	....	.07	.07	.17	.51	.58Y	.72Y	.89Y
Middle East 407	**203.9**	**174.6**	**158.5**	**181.7**	**189.4Y**	**224.3Y**	**281.4Y**	**916.6**	**686.2**	**1,056.4**	**1,348.8**	**1,785.6Y**	**2,210.2Y**	**2,718.0Y**
Bahrain 419	.44	6.91	.57	2.30	2.63Y	3.25Y	4.03Y	78.73	35.93	160.50	200.92	229.57Y	283.73Y	352.11Y
Egypt 469	90.64	85.74	71.81	87.37	99.83Y	123.38Y	153.12Y	41.47	36.39	63.94	81.17	92.74Y	114.62Y	142.24Y
Iran, I.R. of 429	5.31	1.82	.97	1.59	2.02Y	2.49Y	3.23Y	10.01	3.07	32.93	26.18	35.61Y	44.77Y	54.01Y
Iraq 433	—	—	.04	.01	.01Y	.01Y	.02Y	—	—	—	—	—Y	—Y	—Y
Israel 436	15.41	15.93	16.32	11.17	18.64V	16.45V	19.82V	23.50	19.08	26.06	25.14	53.68V	54.56V	106.92V
Jordan 439	1.35	1.54	1.38	.46	1.62V	1.34V	1.91V	1.91	.87	4.31	14.98	1.38V	9.42V	8.14V
Kuwait 443	.42	.85	.73	.26	.33Y	.40Y	.52Y	6.88	19.84	9.96	12.66	17.22Y	21.65Y	26.12Y
Lebanon 446	1.08	.83	1.06	1.03	1.17Y	1.45Y	1.80Y	.07	.01	.01	.04	.04Y	.05Y	.07Y
Libya 672	.01	—	.01	.02	.02Y	.03Y	.04Y	—	—	.01	.06	.08Y	.10Y	.12Y
Oman 449	.04	.42	.68	.77	.99Y	1.22Y	1.58Y	.59	6.25	.92	1.30	1.76Y	2.22Y	2.68Y
Qatar 453	.05	.01	.14	.22	3.26V	1.53V	1.98Y	4.90	4.66	9.12	14.13	38.10V	25.36V	30.59Y
Saudi Arabia 456	7.36	5.73	5.10	18.84	7.51V	9.27Y	12.01Y	200.77	170.74	320.07	398.22	541.70Y	681.02Y	821.57Y
Syrian Arab Republic 463	.44	.35	.46	.42	.48Y	.60Y	.74Y	—	.01	.01	.03	.04Y	.05Y	.06Y
United Arab Emirates 466	64.09	31.34	27.76	30.26	38.54Y	47.57Y	61.63Y	527.79	369.01	420.33	568.52	773.35Y	972.24Y	1,172.90Y
Yemen, Republic of 474	17.27	23.16	31.48	26.95	12.36V	15.28Y	18.96Y	20.01	20.32	8.19	5.42	.31V	.38Y	.47Y
Western Hemisphere 207	**5.9**	**3.4**	**7.2**	**11.1**	**9.6Y**	**10.3Y**	**18.7Y**	**60.6**	**41.5**	**22.0**	**90.9**	**116.4Y**	**79.5Y**	**127.2Y**
Argentina 213	.30	.15	.33	.15	.23V	.25V	.37V	42.28	27.10	5.66	56.34	28.08V	16.84V	55.54V
Aruba 314	—	.01	—	—	—V	—V	—V	....	....	....	....	....	....	....
Bahamas, The 313	—	.06	.03	.16	.18Y	.22Y	.28Y	.71	.13	.01	.02	.03Y	.03Y	.04Y

	Exports 2001	2002	2003	2004	2005	2006	2007	Imports 2001	2002	2003	2004	2005	2006	2007
	Millions of U.S. Dollars							Millions of U.S. Dollars						
Barbados 316	—	—	.03	.01	.01V	.01V	.02Y	—	—	.01	11.32	—V	.01V	.01Y
Belize 339	—	.01	—	—	—Y	—Y	—Y	.01	.05	.01	.05	.06Y	.07Y	.09Y
Bermuda 319	—	.01	—	—	—V	.01V	.01Y	1.20	—	—	—	—Y	—Y	—Y
Bolivia 218	—	—	—	—	—V	—Y	.01Y	—	.02	—	—	—Y	—Y	—Y
Brazil 223	.41	.09	.33	.36	.20V	.79V	3.42V	11.91	12.38	13.21	17.94	83.95V	52.42V	65.06V
Chile 228	.30	.46	.86	.40	.94V	1.74V	.73V	.02	.14	.64	.90	2.01V	2.22V	3.70V
Colombia 233	.06	.49	.93	3.60	.09V	.24V	—V	3.28	.06	.16	.35	.19V	.41V	.79V
Costa Rica 238	.10	.06	.14	.01	.02V	.02Y	.02Y	—	.13	—	.14	.02V	.02Y	.03Y
Dominican Republic 243	.20	—	.02	.30	.35Y	.43Y	.53Y	.07	.09	.08	.13	.15Y	.18Y	.23Y
Ecuador 248	—	.30	.04	1.85	.95V	—V	—Y	.01	—	—	.15	.09V	.07V	.09Y
El Salvador 253	.01	.01	.37	.19	.22V	—V	—V	—	—	.03	.01	—V	—V	—V
Greenland 326	—	—	—	—	—Y	—Y	—Y	—	—	—	.01	.01Y	.01Y	.01Y
Guatemala 258	.02	.01	.01	.10	.12V	.15Y	.18Y	.01	—	—	.01	.14V	.17Y	.21Y
Guyana 336	—	—	.10	.45	.51Y	.63Y	.79Y	.01	.02	—	.19	.22Y	.28Y	.34Y
Honduras 268	—	.07	.83	1.41	1.62Y	2.00Y	2.48Y	—	—	—	.06	.07Y	.08Y	.10Y
Jamaica 343	.02	.24	.26	.59	.33V	—V	—V	—	.02	.01	.03	.04V	—V	—V
Mexico 273	2.99	.37	2.58	.41	3.37V	3.42V	9.47V	.61	.26	.35	.53	.96V	6.49V	.64V
Nicaragua 278	....	....	....	....	....	....	....	.03	—	—	—	—V	—V	—V
Panama 283	.05	—	—	.16	—V	—V	—V	.03	.06	—	.10	—V	—V	—V
Paraguay 288	—	—	—	—	—V	—V	—Y	—	—	.04	.02	—V	—V	—Y
Peru 293	.03	.07	—	.08	—V	—V	—Y	.23	.99	1.51	2.01	.04V	—V	—Y
St. Kitts and Nevis 361	—	.09	.01	.02	.02Y	.03Y	.03Y	....	....	....	....	....	....	....
St. Lucia 362	—	.01	—	—	—Y	—Y	—Y	—	—	—	—	—Y	—Y	—Y
St. Vincent & Grens 364	—	—	—	.37	—V	—Y	—Y	—	—	—	—	—V	—Y	—Y
Trinidad and Tobago 369	.04	.22	—	.02	.02Y	.03Y	.03Y	—	—	.01	.02	.03Y	.03Y	.04Y
Uruguay 298	.06	—	—	.01	.01V	.01Y	.01Y	.07	.06	.11	.56	.13V	.16Y	.20Y
Venezuela, Rep. Bol 299	1.29	.57	.01	.12	.11V	.02V	.04V	.03	—	.06	.01	.14V	.01V	.01Y
Western Hem. n.s. 399	.04	.09	.29	.28	.27Y	.26Y	.25Y	.11	.03	.12	.03	.03Y	.03Y	.03Y
Other Countries n.i.e. 910	**.1**	**.1**	**.1**	**—**	**—Y**	**—Y**	**.1Y**	**3.4**	**3.3**	**2.5**	**3.3**	**3.8Y**	**4.7Y**	**5.8Y**
North Korea 954	.07	.10	.06	.03	.04Y	.05Y	.06Y	3.39	3.34	2.53	3.33	3.81Y	4.70Y	5.84Y
Countries & Areas n.s. 898	**—**	**.2**	**.2**	**—**	**—Y**	**—Y**	**—Y**	**—**	**1.4**	**—**	**.1**	**.1Y**	**.1Y**	**.2Y**
Special Categories 899	**57.9**	**44.8**	**62.0**	**107.2**	**122.5Y**	**151.4Y**	**187.9Y**	**5.7**	**8.8**	**10.0**	**11.8**	**13.5Y**	**16.7Y**	**20.7Y**
Memorandum Items														
European Union 998	447.70	605.02	704.72	729.73	1,052.45Y	1,169.90Y	1,320.06Y	922.47	1,063.08	892.16	1,097.66	1,331.00Y	1,629.31Y	1,993.85Y
Oil Exporting Ctys 999	89.20	64.79	52.82	73.75	81.69Y	94.69Y	121.03Y	864.47	741.05	959.81	1,120.68	1,458.40Y	1,790.85Y	2,172.81Y
Non-Oil Develop.Ctys 201	1,191.67	1,306.21	1,431.77	1,642.37	1,819.25Y	2,202.53Y	2,732.54Y	1,097.62	967.51	1,318.87	1,768.28	2,930.35Y	3,679.60Y	4,732.72Y
PERCENT DISTRIBUTION														
Industrial Countries 101	**28.5**	**32.2**	**33.0**	**30.7**	**41.3**	**38.6**	**35.4**	**46.6**	**47.3**	**38.2**	**36.6**	**35.3**	**33.1**	**32.7**
Developing Countries 202	**68.4**	**63.9**	**61.8**	**63.5**	**53.6**	**56.0**	**58.9**	**53.1**	**52.2**	**61.4**	**62.9**	**64.3**	**66.5**	**66.9**
Africa 607	**44.9**	**44.6**	**42.9**	**43.9**	**36.6**	**38.4**	**40.6**	**9.7**	**10.1**	**11.5**	**12.6**	**10.4**	**9.6**	**10.0**
Asia 507	**11.5**	**10.1**	**10.8**	**11.2**	**10.0**	**10.4**	**10.4**	**15.9**	**19.0**	**18.4**	**16.9**	**23.4**	**25.8**	**26.3**
Europe 170	**.7**	**1.0**	**1.1**	**1.3**	**1.4**	**1.5**	**1.7**	**1.0**	**.9**	**2.5**	**2.0**	**2.6**	**3.3**	**3.1**
Middle East 407	**10.9**	**8.1**	**6.6**	**6.7**	**5.3**	**5.5**	**5.8**	**24.8**	**21.0**	**28.5**	**29.4**	**26.2**	**26.9**	**26.3**
Western Hemisphere 207	**.3**	**.2**	**.3**	**.4**	**.3**	**.3**	**.4**	**1.6**	**1.3**	**.6**	**2.0**	**1.7**	**1.0**	**1.2**
Other Countries n.i.e. 910	**—**	**—**	**—**	**—**	**—**	**—**	**—**	**.1**	**.1**	**.1**	**.1**	**.1**	**.1**	**.1**
ANNUAL PERCENT CHANGE														
World 001	**6.4**	**14.5**	**12.1**	**12.4**	**31.2**	**15.7**	**18.1**	**13.5**	**−11.5**	**13.4**	**23.8**	**48.7**	**20.5**	**25.4**
Industrial Countries 101	**−13.3**	**29.5**	**14.8**	**4.7**	**76.5**	**8.2**	**8.3**	**24.9**	**−10.2**	**−8.4**	**18.5**	**43.6**	**13.0**	**23.8**
Developing Countries 202	**14.7**	**7.0**	**8.3**	**15.6**	**10.8**	**20.8**	**24.2**	**5.3**	**−12.9**	**33.4**	**26.8**	**51.9**	**24.6**	**26.2**
Africa 607	**19.1**	**13.6**	**8.0**	**14.9**	**9.3**	**21.5**	**24.9**	**30.2**	**−8.1**	**29.8**	**35.8**	**22.3**	**11.4**	**30.4**
Asia 507	**−.2**	**−.1**	**20.1**	**16.6**	**17.3**	**20.1**	**17.7**	**22.5**	**5.9**	**9.4**	**13.7**	**106.2**	**32.7**	**27.8**
Europe 170	**35.0**	**57.8**	**27.6**	**27.7**	**45.5**	**20.7**	**38.0**	**−47.9**	**−25.3**	**218.4**	**2.7**	**91.0**	**51.1**	**18.4**
Middle East 407	**13.5**	**−14.4**	**−9.2**	**14.6**	**4.3**	**18.4**	**25.5**	**−6.9**	**−25.1**	**53.9**	**27.7**	**32.4**	**23.8**	**23.0**
Western Hemisphere 207	**44.9**	**−43.0**	**112.6**	**53.8**	**−13.4**	**7.3**	**81.8**	**24.3**	**−31.5**	**−47.0**	**312.9**	**28.0**	**−31.7**	**59.9**
Other Countries n.i.e. 910	**−65.2**	**30.3**	**−38.3**	**−41.1**	**14.3**	**23.6**	**24.1**	**196.6**	**−1.5**	**−24.3**	**31.7**	**14.3**	**23.6**	**24.1**

		Exports							Imports						
		2001	2002	2003	2004	2005	2006	2007	2001	2002	2003	2004	2005	2006	2007
		Millions of U.S. Dollars							*Millions of U.S. Dollars*						
IFS World Total		**150,439**	**162,471**	**193,817**	**253,845**	**284,419**	**325,465**	**371,489**	**141,098**	**152,126**	**178,827**	**224,463**	**261,238**	**309,383**	**356,846**
DOTS World Total	**001**	**150,436**	**162,308**	**197,308**	**253,744**	**284,337**	**325,386**	**371,445**	**141,098**	**152,125**	**180,900**	**224,425**	**261,211**	**309,381**	**356,845**
Industrial Countries	**101**	**73,624**	**76,782**	**84,823**	**108,428**	**114,843**	**123,214**	**127,941**	**73,411**	**80,355**	**91,223**	**111,151**	**121,176**	**132,524**	**150,436**
United States	111	31,358	32,943	34,369	43,027	41,500	43,321	45,884	22,431	23,111	24,935	28,919	30,788	33,797	37,393
Canada	156	2,036	2,341	2,682	3,383	3,446	3,620	3,506	1,821	1,846	1,860	2,189	2,604	3,091	3,254
Australia	193	2,173	2,340	3,272	3,378	3,812	4,692	4,691	5,534	5,973	5,916	7,438	9,860	11,309	13,232
Japan	158	16,506	15,143	17,276	21,701	24,027	26,534	26,370	26,633	29,856	36,313	46,144	48,403	51,926	56,250
New Zealand	196	272	322	433	620	670	673	699	743	753	708	880	891	967	1,171
Austria	122	224	398	416	670	971	887	771	285	333	380	454	645	738	873
Belgium	124	765	800	1,295	1,436	1,817	2,186	2,582	571	642	767	910	967	939	1,180
Cyprus	423	413	554	320	1,092	884	1,153	1,073	1	3	9	27	4	5	20
Denmark	128	220	292	335	639	621	653	463	333	425	404	471	560	575	702
Finland	172	529	707	1,074	1,696	2,012	1,897	1,293	381	411	379	441	659	513	963
France	132	1,599	1,665	1,805	2,708	3,287	3,507	3,571	2,096	2,125	2,228	2,492	2,768	3,245	4,051
Germany	134	4,322	4,287	5,603	8,334	10,304	10,056	11,543	4,473	5,472	6,822	8,486	9,774	11,365	13,534
Greece	174	1,222	1,654	1,765	1,773	1,793	2,768	1,661	39	36	104	109	93	83	60
Iceland	176	28	14	16	24	42	36	38	6	4	6	19	9	13	21
Ireland	178	576	560	646	677	651	545	888	743	754	664	829	835	836	835
Italy	136	2,063	2,218	2,561	3,408	4,297	4,286	4,152	1,788	2,277	2,386	2,500	2,778	2,916	3,583
Luxembourg	137	5	152	6	10	14	80	24	11	19	34	55	71	80	62
Malta	181	312	514	273	570	418	515	574	51	61	78	80	53	45	145
Netherlands	138	2,532	2,567	2,535	3,007	3,647	3,609	4,489	1,017	1,150	1,372	1,729	2,759	3,026	3,703
Norway	142	357	378	739	323	468	851	596	402	610	538	560	639	857	1,536
Portugal	182	222	228	240	303	381	380	414	21	28	39	65	48	104	202
Slovenia	961	52	54	71	75	92	148	426	13	15	22	21	20	25	35
Spain	184	1,518	1,552	2,016	2,809	2,867	3,479	3,925	327	429	446	562	653	778	856
Sweden	144	396	395	546	732	904	858	950	486	578	665	762	977	988	1,193
Switzerland	146	432	449	434	516	580	844	488	851	1,004	1,444	1,214	1,170	1,325	1,997
United Kingdom	112	3,490	4,255	4,094	5,516	5,339	5,635	6,870	2,354	2,437	2,703	3,793	3,149	2,977	3,581
Developing Countries	**202**	**76,027**	**84,698**	**107,653**	**144,328**	**167,930**	**200,621**	**240,497**	**67,650**	**71,737**	**87,572**	**113,226**	**139,956**	**176,747**	**206,335**
Africa	**607**	**3,336**	**3,251**	**3,580**	**6,289**	**6,960**	**8,636**	**9,670**	**1,944**	**2,022**	**2,323**	**3,315**	**3,317**	**5,288**	**5,432**
Algeria	612	153	186	225	355	340	391	768	115	205	192	240	166	578	647
Angola	614	696	19	25	1,814	1,517	1,037	174	220	178	268	137	1	219	343
Benin	638	15	16	15	13	15	21	35	—	1	1	—	—	—	2
Botswana	616	3	2	3	5	5	4	3	—	—	1	1	1	1	1
Burkina Faso	748	1	—	1	1	1	3	7	2	5	4	7	3	—	—
Burundi	618	—	1	1	1	1	1	1	—	—	—	—	—	—	—
Cameroon	622	7	11	10	15	13	11	25	2	2	56	269	324	426	520
Cape Verde	624	—	—	—	—	—	1	1	—	—	—	—	—	—	—
Central African Rep.	626	—	—	1	—	1	—	—	—	—	—	—	—	—	—
Chad	628	—	1	1	—	—	1	—	—	—	1	30	53	58	1
Congo, Dem. Rep. of	636	1	1	—	—	—	—	—	1	1	—	—	—	—	—
Congo, Republic of	634	17	9	11	14	17	18	490	389	509	369	284	419	829	193
Côte d'Ivoire	662	21	26	26	25	31	49	58	3	1	4	8	1	—	1
Djibouti	611	11	8	8	8	15	21	19	—	—	—	—	—	1	—
Equatorial Guinea	642	—	—	—	—	—	89	1	1	—	—	31	—	—	—
Eritrea	643	3	7	2	3	1	2	5	—	—	—	—	—	—	—
Ethiopia	644	21	18	19	19	36	63	73	1	1	2	1	17	3	5
Gabon	646	4	3	3	3	3	5	21	135	51	120	42	86	16	26
Gambia, The	648	2	2	1	1	2	5	2	—	—	—	—	—	—	—
Ghana	652	90	42	71	75	89	94	146	5	10	11	7	7	15	18
Guinea	656	7	9	8	6	18	8	14	44	163	128	117	165	132	132
Guinea-Bissau	654	—	—	—	—	—	—	—	2	2	—	1	2	1	1
Kenya	664	46	45	49	62	71	205	137	1	2	2	2	4	5	8
Lesotho	666	6	5	3	10	4	11	46	—	—	—	—	—	—	—
Liberia	668	987	1,427	1,526	1,708	1,987	3,207	2,511	9	1	5	26	8	54	1
Madagascar	674	13	5	13	15	14	16	27	1	—	—	1	1	2	2
Malawi	676	2	2	3	6	6	7	8	—	—	1	1	1	4	20
Mali	678	3	1	2	2	2	2	1	8	4	2	1	1	—	1
Mauritania	682	2	2	4	2	3	2	12	—	1	1	—	—	1	2
Mauritius	684	22	17	19	21	22	29	36	2	1	1	1	1	2	3
Morocco	686	106	95	128	162	208	223	390	35	50	35	41	56	87	105
Mozambique	688	7	5	5	18	9	15	23	—	4	—	—	—	1	2
Namibia	728	2	2	1	2	5	2	2	4	2	2	2	26	81	98
Niger	692	1	3	5	4	3	6	3	51	—	—	61	1	1	5
Nigeria	694	415	687	599	680	831	809	2,375	76	73	108	551	366	626	443
Rwanda	714	1	—	—	—	2	1	1	—	—	—	—	—	—	—
St. Helena	856	—	—	—	—	—	—	—	—	—	—	1	—	1	—
São Tomé & Príncipe	716	—	—	—	—	—	—	—	—	—	—	—	1	—	—
Senegal	722	9	13	12	13	17	23	33	1	3	3	3	3	5	9
Seychelles	718	—	1	1	4	5	6	8	—	—	—	—	—	1	—
Sierra Leone	724	7	4	2	2	2	3	5	1	1	—	—	—	1	1

Korea, Republic of 542

		Exports							Imports						
		2001	2002	2003	2004	2005	2006	2007	2001	2002	2003	2004	2005	2006	2007
		Millions of U.S. Dollars							*Millions of U.S. Dollars*						
Somalia	726	2	1	1	1	2	1	—	—	—	—	—	—	—	—
South Africa	199	423	394	530	959	1,320	1,794	1,753	689	603	782	999	1,094	1,385	1,767
Sudan	732	72	71	87	100	165	260	212	112	80	89	180	139	236	343
Swaziland	734	26	12	54	16	18	18	16	24	54	55	87	90	37	45
Tanzania	738	15	18	31	26	31	42	68	1	1	18	1	2	8	3
Togo	742	41	16	19	22	17	19	23	—	1	—	—	—	3	2
Tunisia	744	61	51	43	70	80	80	101	3	2	3	7	10	14	25
Uganda	746	2	5	3	5	6	9	11	1	—	3	2	3	2	3
Zambia	754	4	3	5	11	12	8	15	2	5	46	151	251	433	605
Zimbabwe	698	12	11	8	10	10	15	14	6	6	11	17	13	19	50
Asia	**507**	**53,182**	**61,956**	**81,623**	**107,272**	**122,307**	**141,150**	**161,097**	**36,385**	**42,373**	**50,656**	**64,956**	**77,546**	**93,949**	**113,767**
Afghanistan, I.S. of	512	95	128	125	77	60	79	109	—	—	—	—	—	—	—
American Samoa	859	26	18	3	3	3	2	13	—	1	—	—	—	—	7
Bangladesh	513	655	506	544	620	611	648	612	28	22	29	42	45	69	142
Bhutan	514	1	1	2	2	3	2	3	—	—	—	—	—	—	—
Brunei Darussalam	516	16	27	30	32	61	22	27	452	462	501	693	787	1,206	935
Cambodia	522	102	115	106	126	144	205	281	7	3	4	7	6	5	9
China,P.R.: Mainland	924	18,190	23,754	35,110	49,763	61,915	69,459	81,985	13,303	17,400	21,909	29,585	38,648	48,557	63,028
China,P.R.:Hong Kong	532	9,452	10,146	14,654	18,127	15,531	18,979	18,654	1,228	1,695	2,735	3,268	2,043	2,101	2,142
China,P.R.:Macao	546	52	40	33	36	26	28	30	2	5	5	5	6	6	9
Fiji	819	10	11	12	23	19	20	25	1	1	1	1	2	3	2
French Polynesia	887	5	4	6	9	17	14	19	—	—	—	1	—	—	—
Guam	829	181	88	88	133	188	247	107	1	3	13	5	2	1	1
India	534	1,408	1,384	2,853	3,632	4,598	5,533	6,600	1,106	1,249	1,233	1,850	2,112	3,641	4,624
Indonesia	536	3,280	3,146	3,378	3,678	5,046	4,874	5,771	4,474	4,723	5,212	6,368	8,184	8,849	9,114
Kiribati	826	2	2	—	—	—	—	—	5	6	—	—	—	—	—
Lao People's Dem.Rep	544	6	4	8	9	14	23	56	—	—	—	1	2	18	70
Malaysia	548	2,628	3,218	3,852	4,480	4,608	5,227	5,704	4,126	4,041	4,249	5,679	6,012	7,242	8,442
Maldives	556	1	2	1	2	2	3	5	—	—	—	—	—	—	—
Mongolia	948	77	87	100	75	78	110	170	2	6	4	5	5	6	21
Myanmar	518	232	143	184	162	120	121	292	51	56	29	30	56	96	81
Nauru	836	—	—	—	—	12	11	16	1	4	2	—	1	2	10
Nepal	558	15	18	30	23	14	12	19	1	1	1	1	1	1	1
New Caledonia	839	8	8	16	22	40	48	61	24	29	47	101	109	25	1
Pakistan	564	355	405	447	591	662	673	678	320	267	231	281	316	341	491
Palau	565	—	7	4	6	3	2	2	—	—	1	—	—	—	—
Papua New Guinea	853	9	9	8	14	17	17	18	86	32	53	39	72	95	137
Philippines	566	2,535	2,950	2,975	3,379	3,220	3,931	4,420	1,819	1,867	1,964	2,120	2,316	2,187	2,438
Samoa	862	4	5	4	5	6	7	6	—	—	—	—	—	—	—
Singapore	576	4,080	4,222	4,636	5,654	7,407	9,489	11,949	3,011	3,430	4,090	4,461	5,318	5,887	6,860
Solomon Islands	813	1	1	1	1	2	1	1	17	16	24	32	31	28	25
Sri Lanka	524	335	305	287	243	205	193	186	41	39	31	45	38	39	47
Taiwan Province of China	528	5,835	6,632	7,045	9,844	10,863	12,996	13,027	4,301	4,832	5,880	7,312	8,050	9,288	9,967
Thailand	578	1,848	2,335	2,524	3,249	3,381	4,246	4,488	1,589	1,703	1,898	2,351	2,689	3,328	3,769
Timor-Leste	537	—	—	1	—	—	1	1	—	—	—	36	26	—	—
Tonga	866	—	—	—	—	1	—	—	—	—	—	—	—	2	1
Vanuatu	846	1	1	1	2	3	2	3	1	9	—	—	1	—	—
Vietnam	582	1,732	2,240	2,561	3,256	3,432	3,927	5,760	386	470	511	673	694	925	1,392
Asia n.s.	598	7	—	—	—	—	—	—	—	—	—	—	—	—	—
Europe	**170**	**3,204**	**3,719**	**5,722**	**9,101**	**12,438**	**17,128**	**26,093**	**2,811**	**3,158**	**3,509**	**5,244**	**5,254**	**6,308**	**9,570**
Albania	914	2	3	5	8	6	25	8	—	—	—	—	6	—	1
Armenia	911	1	2	3	2	3	7	13	—	—	—	—	—	4	3
Azerbaijan	912	4	4	11	19	32	47	130	—	—	—	1	—	—	316
Belarus	913	8	7	10	17	18	31	35	12	17	10	4	4	7	13
Bosnia & Herzegovina	963	5	3	5	43	7	14	21	—	—	—	—	—	1	—
Bulgaria	918	22	29	58	279	193	181	191	10	15	18	20	24	57	37
Croatia	960	30	61	50	74	83	80	178	3	3	2	6	4	17	21
Czech Republic	935	73	109	158	313	339	564	966	99	100	105	108	150	259	369
Estonia	939	16	20	29	37	48	64	96	22	15	10	43	33	19	67
Georgia	915	—	—	4	6	9	16	40	—	—	11	4	11	6	4
Gibraltar	823	—	—	1	2	13	1	1	—	—	—	—	—	—	—
Hungary	944	228	364	661	807	1,099	1,201	1,890	99	105	87	123	151	229	258
Kazakhstan	916	108	126	217	314	273	324	546	56	72	153	204	242	276	257
Kyrgyz Republic	917	20	28	32	50	67	82	126	1	—	—	3	2	1	1
Latvia	941	10	17	26	41	45	96	93	1	1	2	4	4	13	61
Lithuania	946	18	40	63	77	78	92	101	7	20	20	19	5	9	10
Macedonia, FYR	962	—	—	3	4	3	6	10	—	—	—	2	2	—	2
Moldova	921	1	2	2	3	3	5	11	—	13	—	—	1	1	2
Poland	964	337	349	382	807	1,175	2,613	3,509	46	47	74	89	116	271	301
Romania	968	127	160	171	254	387	609	855	34	57	65	146	87	51	79
Russia	922	938	1,066	1,659	2,339	3,864	5,179	8,088	1,929	2,218	2,522	3,671	3,937	4,573	6,977
Serbia & Montenegro	965	—	—	39	18	18	32	65	—	—	3	—	3	1	2
Slovak Republic	936	10	17	110	357	692	1,267	2,707	10	13	18	23	31	50	71
Tajikistan	923	2	5	4	5	13	14	23	7	6	5	5	2	8	36
Turkey	186	697	866	1,375	2,356	2,782	3,036	4,087	130	125	78	104	127	194	282
Turkmenistan	925	15	22	36	14	6	6	7	2	1	1	—	1	2	1
Ukraine	926	173	220	358	493	687	884	1,546	195	230	243	584	280	218	295
Uzbekistan	927	346	188	247	359	493	649	748	137	97	79	77	29	40	104

	Exports							Imports						
	2001	2002	2003	2004	2005	2006	2007	2001	2002	2003	2004	2005	2006	2007
	Millions of U.S. Dollars							*Millions of U.S. Dollars*						
Yugoslavia n.s. 966	11	11	—	—	—	—	—	—	—	—	—	—	—	—
Europe n.s. 884	2	—	1	1	1	1	1	11	3	3	3	1	2	1
Middle East 407	**6,743**	**7,093**	**8,105**	**10,317**	**11,444**	**13,507**	**18,238**	**23,121**	**20,544**	**26,610**	**33,197**	**47,024**	**61,615**	**66,419**
Bahrain 419	47	61	53	82	118	125	202	129	155	251	288	308	341	320
Egypt 469	431	321	425	538	707	853	1,167	139	134	195	337	201	450	614
Iran, I.R. of 429	875	1,227	1,778	2,134	2,141	2,559	3,266	2,099	1,335	1,845	2,435	3,535	5,049	6,482
Iraq 433	73	86	36	125	68	109	210	28	39	57	408	675	906	3,080
Israel 436	450	501	578	851	850	746	970	341	322	318	477	504	542	737
Jordan 439	185	195	321	526	468	359	386	11	11	15	30	40	43	48
Kuwait 443	178	184	294	419	458	670	1,306	2,251	2,230	3,191	3,832	5,977	8,133	8,747
Lebanon 446	106	65	71	89	92	90	142	5	8	6	10	12	18	33
Libya 672	202	323	136	447	365	434	402	5	18	4	10	3	2	6
Oman 449	155	102	104	157	304	344	542	2,311	1,896	2,323	2,475	3,705	5,129	3,814
Qatar 453	221	148	357	226	521	760	1,163	2,572	2,173	3,140	3,650	5,599	6,985	8,454
Saudi Arabia 456	1,274	1,259	1,409	1,708	2,093	2,978	4,026	8,058	7,551	9,268	11,800	16,106	20,552	21,164
Syrian Arab Republic 463	329	298	274	356	400	484	608	3	13	2	12	12	30	7
United Arab Emirates 466	2,169	2,269	2,208	2,587	2,733	2,896	3,705	4,633	4,210	5,756	7,290	10,018	12,931	12,656
Yemen, Republic of 474	46	52	60	67	115	94	123	434	429	238	143	326	499	255
Middle East n.s. 489	1	—	1	3	10	5	20	103	19	—	1	4	5	4
Western Hemisphere 207	**9,562**	**8,679**	**8,624**	**11,349**	**14,780**	**20,201**	**25,399**	**3,389**	**3,640**	**4,473**	**6,515**	**6,815**	**9,586**	**11,147**
Antigua and Barbuda 311	31	51	3	3	5	6	4	—	—	1	—	—	—	—
Argentina 213	302	51	161	239	309	331	489	374	376	436	421	372	556	732
Aruba 314	6	6	9	11	15	13	13	—	—	—	—	—	—	1
Bahamas, The 313	505	967	909	998	1,583	1,123	1,308	11	—	—	13	29	—	—
Barbados 316	3	3	33	23	10	12	11	—	—	—	—	—	—	—
Belize 339	12	5	4	14	4	4	5	10	3	1	5	5	1	5
Bermuda 319	36	361	163	646	661	1,144	1,535	—	—	5	5	—	—	—
Bolivia 218	7	8	7	6	8	8	10	13	8	23	43	34	162	182
Brazil 223	1,611	1,247	1,137	1,785	2,411	3,063	3,487	1,126	1,248	1,619	2,195	2,501	2,707	2,794
Chile 228	573	454	517	708	1,151	1,566	3,115	696	754	1,058	1,934	2,279	3,813	4,184
Colombia 233	226	272	297	459	624	913	1,121	42	49	76	106	137	206	116
Costa Rica 238	111	111	81	122	164	237	246	34	39	66	29	35	58	114
Dominica 321	12	14	10	10	17	14	6	1	—	—	—	8	—	—
Dominican Republic 243	131	185	82	74	120	109	120	38	22	72	122	69	87	126
Ecuador 248	168	167	178	263	344	386	429	297	315	258	444	29	13	23
El Salvador 253	87	73	74	69	74	87	86	1	2	8	3	3	6	6
Greenland 326	—	—	—	—	—	—	—	—	1	1	1	2	2	1
Grenada 328	1	1	1	1	3	2	2	—	—	—	—	—	—	—
Guatemala 258	471	501	523	550	499	546	391	149	106	66	62	83	96	86
Guyana 336	2	1	2	3	3	6	5	1	3	—	1	2	1	—
Haiti 263	9	16	18	12	15	14	52	—	—	—	—	1	—	—
Honduras 268	136	138	133	144	120	139	132	15	11	12	15	22	23	59
Jamaica 343	14	13	12	13	17	19	25	1	5	1	1	1	1	3
Mexico 273	2,149	2,231	2,455	2,994	3,789	6,285	7,482	267	295	334	411	460	798	1,013
Netherlands Antilles 353	3	3	2	7	11	14	14	3	1	—	—	—	1	—
Nicaragua 278	59	85	74	117	130	144	175	—	—	—	4	1	—	1
Panama 283	1,719	1,184	1,252	1,264	1,623	2,227	3,145	142	143	179	294	248	241	334
Paraguay 288	32	21	27	38	51	68	65	—	1	1	5	4	6	2
Peru 293	188	196	204	245	282	359	466	116	205	194	283	249	676	1,040
St. Kitts and Nevis 361	—	—	—	—	1	1	2	—	—	—	—	—	—	—
St. Lucia 362	—	1	1	1	2	2	4	—	—	—	—	—	—	—
St. Vincent & Grens 364	23	—	1	27	1	1	1	—	—	—	—	—	—	—
Suriname 366	3	2	3	4	5	7	9	—	—	—	—	—	—	—
Trinidad and Tobago 369	20	23	19	23	36	47	64	1	1	—	7	—	26	181
Uruguay 298	78	35	44	40	57	54	72	8	6	12	15	26	30	41
Venezuela, Rep. Bol. 299	555	247	107	230	571	996	1,233	42	46	50	94	212	76	100
Western Hem. n.s. 399	279	3	81	205	65	255	78	—	—	—	—	—	—	3
Other Countries n.i.e. 910	**—**	**—**	**2**	**9**	**—**	**203**	**214**	**12**	**22**	**—**	**—**	**—**	**3**	**3**
Cuba 928	—	—	2	9	—	203	214	—	—	—	—	—	3	3
North Korea 954	—	—	—	—	—	—	—	12	22	—	—	—	—	—
Countries & Areas n.s. 898	**—**	**—**	**2**	**3**	**3**	**9**	**22**	**—**	**—**	**1**	**1**	**—**	**—**	**6**
Special Categories 899	**186**	**—**	**286**	**360**	**415**	**368**	**486**	**22**	**10**	**30**	**47**	**78**	**106**	**63**
Memorandum Items														
European Union 998	21,154	23,768	27,030	37,894	43,773	48,541	55,030	15,274	17,498	19,817	24,196	27,304	30,087	36,717
Oil Exporting Ctys 999	9,551	9,865	10,629	12,746	15,471	17,820	24,766	26,664	24,499	31,147	39,153	54,547	69,815	74,705
Non-Oil Develop.Ctys 201	66,476	74,833	97,024	131,582	152,459	182,802	215,731	40,987	47,238	56,426	74,073	85,409	106,932	131,630
PERCENT DISTRIBUTION														
Industrial Countries 101	**48.9**	**47.3**	**43.0**	**42.7**	**40.4**	**37.9**	**34.4**	**52.0**	**52.8**	**50.4**	**49.5**	**46.4**	**42.8**	**42.2**
Developing Countries 202	**50.5**	**52.2**	**54.6**	**56.9**	**59.1**	**61.7**	**64.7**	**47.9**	**47.2**	**48.4**	**50.5**	**53.6**	**57.1**	**57.8**
Africa 607	**2.2**	**2.0**	**1.8**	**2.5**	**2.4**	**2.7**	**2.6**	**1.4**	**1.3**	**1.3**	**1.5**	**1.3**	**1.7**	**1.5**
Asia 507	**35.4**	**38.2**	**41.4**	**42.3**	**43.0**	**43.4**	**43.4**	**25.8**	**27.9**	**28.0**	**28.9**	**29.7**	**30.4**	**31.9**
Europe 170	**2.1**	**2.3**	**2.9**	**3.6**	**4.4**	**5.3**	**7.0**	**2.0**	**2.1**	**1.9**	**2.3**	**2.0**	**2.0**	**2.7**
Middle East 407	**4.5**	**4.4**	**4.1**	**4.1**	**4.0**	**4.2**	**4.9**	**16.4**	**13.5**	**14.7**	**14.8**	**18.0**	**19.9**	**18.6**
Western Hemisphere 207	**6.4**	**5.3**	**4.4**	**4.5**	**5.2**	**6.2**	**6.8**	**2.4**	**2.4**	**2.5**	**2.9**	**2.6**	**3.1**	**3.1**
Other Countries n.i.e. 910	**—**	**—**	**—**	**—**	**—**	**.1**	**.1**	**—**	**—**	**—**	**—**	**—**	**—**	**—**
ANNUAL PERCENT CHANGE														

Korea, Republic of 542

	Exports							Imports						
	2001	2002	2003	2004	2005	2006	2007	2001	2002	2003	2004	2005	2006	2007
World.. 001	−12.7	7.9	21.6	28.6	12.1	14.4	14.2	−12.1	7.8	18.9	24.1	16.4	18.4	15.3
Industrial Countries.................. 101	−16.8	4.3	10.5	27.8	5.9	7.3	3.8	−15.7	9.5	13.5	21.8	9.0	9.4	13.5
Developing Countries.............. 202	−8.4	11.4	27.1	34.1	16.4	19.5	19.9	−7.7	6.0	22.1	29.3	23.6	26.3	16.7
Africa...................................... 607	27.2	−2.5	10.1	75.7	10.7	24.1	12.0	−36.3	4.0	14.9	42.7	—	59.4	2.7
Asia... 507	−12.1	16.5	31.7	31.4	14.0	15.4	14.1	−5.5	16.5	19.5	28.2	19.4	21.2	21.1
Europe.................................... 170	−10.6	16.1	53.9	59.1	36.7	37.7	52.3	−6.0	12.4	11.1	49.4	.2	20.1	51.7
Middle East............................ 407	−5.9	5.2	14.3	27.3	10.9	18.0	35.0	−9.5	−11.1	29.5	24.8	41.7	31.0	7.8
Western Hemisphere.............. 207	4.5	−9.2	−.6	31.6	30.2	36.7	25.7	5.3	7.4	22.9	45.6	4.6	40.7	16.3
Other Countries n.i.e................ 910	—	—	....	445.0	....	....	5.5	−15.2	75.9	−99.9	—	—	−92.2	−6.8

		Exports							Imports						
		2001	2002	2003	2004	2005	2006	2007	2001	2002	2003	2004	2005	2006	2007
		Millions of U.S. Dollars							Millions of U.S. Dollars						
IFS World Total		**16,203**	**15,363**	**20,677**	**28,599**	**44,868**	**57,266**	**62,161**	**7,869**	**9,007**	**10,992**	**12,630**	**15,801**	**15,960**	**19,416**
DOTS World Total	**001**	**16,155Y**	**15,526Y**	**18,746Y**	**25,520Y**	**35,191Y**	**42,325Y**	**46,789Y**	**7,724Y**	**8,799Y**	**11,406Y**	**12,834Y**	**15,285Y**	**16,645Y**	**21,602Y**
Industrial Countries	**101**	**8,199Y**	**7,425Y**	**8,574Y**	**11,042Y**	**15,122Y**	**17,231Y**	**18,389Y**	**4,898Y**	**5,665Y**	**7,350Y**	**8,150Y**	**9,444Y**	**9,454Y**	**11,992Y**
United States	111	2,010V	1,866V	2,253V	3,157V	4,195V	3,802V	3,921V	996V	1,116V	1,660V	1,671V	2,172V	2,348V	2,734V
Canada	156	12V	16V	33V	—V	51V	56V	1V	41V	52V	60V	63V	108V	87V	117V
Australia	193	63V	87V	89V	83V	181V	165V	247V	277V	315V	401V	422V	396V	447V	492V
Japan	158	4,027V	3,825V	4,148V	5,228V	6,934V	8,619V	9,292V	724V	952V	1,157V	1,029V	1,296V	1,308V	1,837V
New Zealand	196	87V	16V	63V	16V	65V	71V	87V	20V	21V	32V	25V	43V	51V	78V
Austria	122	—V	—V	1V	—V	—V	—V	—V	32V	45V	83V	81V	90V	121V	155V
Belgium	124	36V	31V	19V	17V	102V	29V	45V	93V	108V	149V	159V	179V	213V	274V
Cyprus	423	3V	3V	1V	2V	13V	16V	14V	7V	6V	5V	6V	7V	7V	8V
Denmark	128	59V	16V	14V	—V	39V	27V	54V	57V	61V	100V	97V	94V	55V	78V
Finland	172	13V	1V	—V	—V	1V	—V	—V	36V	63V	66V	113V	143V	155V	192V
France	132	321V	313V	526V	529V	947V	654V	863V	351V	444V	471V	582V	739V	520V	710V
Germany	134	31V	50V	81V	72V	26V	31V	56V	735V	849V	1,076V	1,551V	1,661V	1,285V	1,577V
Greece	174	3V	3V	8V	15V	3V	37V	2V	9V	9V	14V	15V	17V	21V	17V
Ireland	178	—V	—V	—V	—V	1V	1V	—V	63V	50V	59V	67V	69V	87V	84V
Italy	136	127V	24V	48V	45V	133V	83V	151V	426V	462V	564V	648V	573V	760V	1,243V
Luxembourg	137	—V	—V	—V	1V	5V	—V	—V	2V	3V	6V	6V	11V	5V	3V
Malta	181	6Y	—V	—V	1V	—V	—V	—V	2Y	2V	5V	3V	3V	3V	3V
Netherlands	138	954V	701V	697V	1,012V	1,660V	2,224V	2,252V	163V	203V	268V	337V	341V	375V	564V
Norway	142	1V	—V	—V	—V	1V	2V	1V	6V	9V	7V	7V	28V	46V	14V
Portugal	182	7V	20V	29V	33V	19V	—V	53V	9V	10V	30V	33V	64V	12V	15V
Slovenia	961	1V	1V	1V	2Y	—V	—V	—V	1V	3V	2V	3Y	15V	17V	20V
Spain	184	13V	23V	20V	83V	50V	62V	66V	125V	139V	158V	177V	166V	184V	252V
Sweden	144	4V	—V	—V	15V	1V	—V	11V	46V	65V	96V	123V	112V	141V	185V
Switzerland	146	14V	35V	36V	35V	42V	59V	52V	114V	162V	200V	210V	248V	297V	349V
United Kingdom	112	408V	394V	507V	695V	653V	1,290V	1,219V	566V	515V	683V	719V	871V	907V	992V
Developing Countries	**202**	**7,956Y**	**8,101Y**	**10,172Y**	**14,478Y**	**20,069Y**	**25,094Y**	**28,400Y**	**2,824Y**	**3,132Y**	**4,054Y**	**4,681Y**	**5,838Y**	**7,188Y**	**9,605Y**
Africa	**607**	**134Y**	**247Y**	**179Y**	**176Y**	**222Y**	**226Y**	**229Y**	**29Y**	**38Y**	**54Y**	**58Y**	**79Y**	**90Y**	**122Y**
Algeria	612	2V	1V	1Y	1Y	2Y	2Y	3Y	2V	17V	19Y	21Y	28Y	34Y	40Y
Benin	638	—V	5V	—V	1V	1V	2Y	2Y	1Y	1Y	1Y	—V	—V	—Y	—Y
Cameroon	622	—V	—V	—V	—Y	—Y	—Y	—Y	—V	—V	—V	—Y	—Y	—Y	1Y
Côte d'Ivoire	662	5V	1V	4V	3V	4V	6V	7Y	—V	—V	—V	—V	—V	—V	—Y
Ethiopia	644	1V	—V	42V	1V	1V	2Y	2Y	—V	—V	—V	—V	—V	—Y	—Y
Ghana	652	—Y	—Y	—Y	—Y	—Y	—Y	—Y	—Y	—Y	1Y	1Y	1Y	1Y	1Y
Guinea	656	1V	1Y	—V	—V	—Y	—Y	—Y	—V	—Y	—Y	—Y	—Y	—Y	—Y
Kenya	664	6V	18V	9V	12V	16Y	20Y	24Y	—V	1V	1V	—V	—Y	—Y	1Y
Madagascar	674	—V	2V	—V	—Y	—Y	—Y	—Y	—V	—V	—V	—Y	—Y	—Y	—Y
Mauritius	684	—V	1V	1V	7V	1V	1V	1V	—V	—V	—V	—V	—V	—V	—V
Morocco	686	5V	10V	11V	20V	24V	30Y	36Y	3V	2V	4V	4V	7V	8Y	11Y
Niger	692	—V	—V	—V	2V	2Y	3Y	3Y	—V	—V	—V	—V	—Y	—Y	—Y
Nigeria	694	2V	3V	2V	2Y	2Y	3Y	3Y	—V	—V	—V	—Y	—Y	—Y	—Y
Somalia	726	—Y	—Y	—Y	—Y	—Y	—Y	—Y	3Y	3Y	4Y	5Y	6Y	8Y	10Y
South Africa	199	94V	18V	83V	53V	47V	22V	1V	16V	10V	21V	25V	32V	26V	44V
Sudan	732	—Y	—Y	3Y	9V	15V	28V	16V	1Y	1Y	2V	1V	2V	2V	1V
Tanzania	738	2V	1V	2Y	2Y	3Y	3Y	4Y	—V	—V	—Y	—Y	—Y	—Y	—Y
Togo	742	—V	2V	—V	4V	9V	12Y	14Y	—V	—V	—V	—V	—V	—Y	—Y
Tunisia	744	8V	7V	11V	17V	14V	36V	43Y	2V	1V	1V	1V	1V	9V	11Y
Uganda	746	1V	1V	2V	3Y	3Y	4Y	5Y	—V	—V	—V	—Y	—Y	—Y	—Y
Zimbabwe	698	7V	175V	8V	39V	76V	52V	63Y	—V	—V	—V	—V	—V	—V	—Y
Asia	**507**	**7,146Y**	**7,266Y**	**9,244Y**	**13,270Y**	**18,466Y**	**23,127Y**	**25,993Y**	**1,125Y**	**1,298Y**	**2,036Y**	**2,083Y**	**2,566Y**	**3,326Y**	**4,877Y**
Bangladesh	513	26V	107V	158V	581V	1,072V	1,126V	1,397V	3V	4V	3V	4V	6V	7Y	9Y
China,P.R.: Mainland	924	412V	422V	467V	727V	928V	1,749V	2,080V	212V	289V	744V	536V	691V	948V	1,472V
China,P.R.:Hong Kong	532	43V	67V	77V	375V	203V	189V	65V	55V	57V	55V	57V	58V	62V	63V
India	534	552Y	139V	138V	233V	384V	482Y	582Y	206Y	263V	332V	421V	535V	660Y	855Y
Indonesia	536	644V	614V	624V	969V	1,159V	1,369V	1,551V	82V	82V	80V	70V	92V	100V	—V
Korea	542	2,046V	2,028V	2,901V	3,484V	5,434V	7,394V	7,952V	196V	202V	323V	461V	504V	737V	1,436V
Lao People's Dem.Rep.	544	—Y	—Y	—Y	—Y	—Y	—Y	—Y	—Y	—Y	—Y	—Y	—Y	1Y	1Y
Malaysia	548	61V	42V	49V	61V	247V	279V	547V	70V	78V	99V	119V	134V	176V	185V
Maldives	556	—V	—V	—V	—V	2V	2Y	3Y	—V	—V	—V	—V	—V	—Y	—Y
Mongolia	948	—V	—V	—V	—V	—V	—Y	1Y	—V	1V	1V	1V	1V	1Y	2Y
Myanmar	518	—Y	—Y	—Y	—Y	—Y	—Y	—Y	2Y	2Y	3Y	3Y	4Y	5Y	7Y
Nepal	558	9V	13V	—V	—V	—V	—V	—Y	—V	—V	—V	—V	—V	—V	—Y
Pakistan	564	721V	689V	756V	909V	1,149V	1,444Y	1,743Y	58V	66V	85V	83V	85V	105Y	136Y
Philippines	566	13V	44V	9V	12V	16V	41V	53V	13V	12V	17V	16V	22V	33V	32V
Singapore	576	1,237V	1,587V	1,921V	2,872V	3,352V	4,098V	4,625V	73V	74V	98V	84V	112V	133V	274V
Sri Lanka	524	6V	88V	16V	14V	7V	7V	7V	10V	11V	11V	11V	13V	14V	15V
Taiwan Province of China	528	1,028V	1,172V	1,820V	2,518V	3,905V	4,553V	5,221V	69V	80V	87V	109V	126V	120V	141V
Thailand	578	307V	118V	152V	282V	283V	259V	148V	72V	74V	90V	103V	168V	213V	248V
Vietnam	582	42V	137V	157V	233V	326V	132V	20V	3V	3V	8V	4V	13V	12V	—V
Europe	**170**	**113Y**	**25Y**	**16Y**	**25Y**	**40Y**	**160Y**	**86Y**	**174Y**	**319Y**	**283Y**	**414Y**	**433Y**	**472Y**	**554Y**
Belarus	913	—V	—V	—V	—V	—V	—V	—V	2V	—V	—V	—V	—V	—V	—V
Bulgaria	918	—V	—V	—V	—V	—V	—V	1V	1V	1V	2V	3V	17V	4V	4V
Czech Republic	935	—V	—V	—V	—V	1V	—V	—V	8V	11V	14V	21V	35V	29V	41V

	Exports 2001	Exports 2002	Exports 2003	Exports 2004	Exports 2005	Exports 2006	Exports 2007	Imports 2001	Imports 2002	Imports 2003	Imports 2004	Imports 2005	Imports 2006	Imports 2007
	Millions of U.S. Dollars							Millions of U.S. Dollars						
Estonia........ 939	—V	—V	—V	—V	—V	—V	—V	—V	—V	—V	—V	—V	1V	1V
Hungary........ 944	—V	—V	—V	—V	—V	—V	—V	20V	10V	29V	44V	34V	55V	85V
Kazakhstan........ 916	—V	—V	—V	—V	—Y	—Y	—Y	—V	—V	—V	—V	—Y	—Y	1Y
Latvia........ 941	—V	—V	—V	—V	—V	—V	—V	—V	—V	1V	1V	1V	—V	1V
Lithuania........ 946	—V	—V	—V	—V	—V	—V	—V	—V	—V	—V	—V	1V	1V	2V
Poland........ 964	—V	—V	—V	—V	—V	108V	—V	8V	11V	11V	13V	23V	25V	36V
Romania........ 968	—V	—V	—V	—V	—V	—V	—V	8V	29V	20V	17V	29V	52V	68V
Russia........ 922	—V	—V	—V	1V	—V	—V	—V	10V	90V	4V	1V	26V	11V	20V
Slovak Republic........ 936	—V	—V	—Y	—Y	—V	—V	—V	1V	1V	1Y	2Y	16V	30V	22V
Turkey........ 186	112V	24V	14V	23V	38V	51V	82V	115V	153V	183V	292V	231V	241V	243V
Ukraine........ 926	—V	—V	—V	—V	1V	1Y	1Y	1V	11V	18V	18V	18V	22Y	29Y
Yugoslavia n.s........ 966	....	....	....	....	....	....	....	—Y	—Y	—Y	1Y	1Y	1Y	1Y
Middle East........ 407	**486Y**	**530Y**	**655Y**	**978Y**	**1,284Y**	**1,570Y**	**1,961Y**	**1,378Y**	**1,386Y**	**1,554Y**	**1,924Y**	**2,481Y**	**3,007Y**	**3,594Y**
Bahrain........ 419	15Y	16Y	19Y	25Y	35Y	44Y	53Y	62Y	64Y	71Y	92Y	117Y	145Y	188Y
Egypt........ 469	46V	49Y	59Y	78Y	106Y	134Y	161Y	18V	19Y	21Y	28Y	35Y	43Y	56Y
Iran, I.R. of........ 429	10V	12V	14Y	16Y	21Y	25Y	30Y	130Y	123Y	137Y	157Y	209Y	250Y	295Y
Jordan........ 439	17V	16V	19V	26V	56V	32V	124V	41V	40V	44V	58V	80V	107V	79V
Lebanon........ 446	16Y	17Y	20Y	27Y	37Y	46Y	55Y	29Y	30Y	33Y	43Y	55Y	68Y	88Y
Oman........ 449	38V	25V	32V	36Y	48Y	58Y	68Y	28V	29V	49V	56Y	75Y	89Y	105Y
Qatar........ 453	14V	26V	19V	26V	43V	78V	92Y	19V	36V	36V	85V	18V	22V	26Y
Saudi Arabia........ 456	100V	114V	119V	186V	203V	243Y	287Y	594Y	560Y	623Y	718Y	952Y	1,140Y	1,345Y
Syrian Arab Republic........ 463	19Y	20Y	25Y	146V	199Y	250Y	301Y	84Y	87Y	96Y	256V	326Y	402Y	521Y
United Arab Emirates........ 466	95V	95V	161V	186Y	247Y	295Y	348Y	303Y	285Y	318Y	366Y	485Y	581Y	686Y
Yemen, Republic of........ 474	117V	139V	168Y	224V	290V	365Y	440Y	71V	114V	126Y	65V	129V	159Y	206Y
Western Hemisphere........ 207	**77Y**	**34Y**	**78Y**	**28Y**	**56Y**	**11Y**	**132Y**	**117Y**	**92Y**	**127Y**	**201Y**	**278Y**	**293Y**	**459Y**
Argentina........ 213	2V	3V	4V	5V	—V	9V	18V	29V	19V	29V	27V	33V	70V	44V
Brazil........ 223	55V	28V	74V	22V	33V	1V	114V	72V	65V	81V	141V	211V	184V	254V
Chile........ 228	—V	—V	—V	—V	—V	—V	—V	2V	—V	8V	11V	10V	10V	15V
Colombia........ 233	—V	—V	—V	—V	—V	—V	—V	1V	1V	1V	2V	1V	1V	2V
Ecuador........ 248	—V	—V	—V	—V	—V	—V	—Y	—V	—V	—V	—V	—V	1V	1Y
Guatemala........ 258	—V	—V	—V	—V	—V	—Y	—Y	3V	3V	3V	2V	2V	2Y	3Y
Mexico........ 273	18V	—V	—V	1V	1V	—V	—V	9V	4V	3V	14V	18V	22V	137V
Paraguay........ 288	—V	—V	—V	—V	—V	—V	—Y	—V	—V	—V	—V	1V	—V	—Y
Peru........ 293	—V	—V	—V	—V	22V	—V	—Y	1V	—V	1V	1V	1V	1V	1Y
Uruguay........ 298	2V	3Y	—V	—V	—V	—Y	—Y	—V	—Y	—V	1V	2V	2Y	2Y
Countries & Areas n.s........ 898	**—Y**	**—Y**	**—Y**	**—Y**	**—Y**	**—Y**	**—Y**	**1Y**	**1Y**	**2Y**	**2Y**	**3Y**	**3Y**	**4Y**
Memorandum Items														
European Union........ 998	1,987Y	1,581Y	1,954Y	2,523Y	3,654Y	4,564Y	4,788Y	2,757Y	3,073Y	3,890Y	4,804Y	5,264Y	5,010Y	6,559Y
Oil Exporting Ctys........ 999	905Y	891Y	971Y	1,423Y	1,726Y	2,075Y	2,383Y	1,158Y	1,132Y	1,261Y	1,473Y	1,860Y	2,217Y	2,497Y
Non-Oil Develop.Ctys........ 201	7,051Y	7,210Y	9,201Y	13,055Y	18,342Y	23,019Y	26,017Y	1,666Y	2,000Y	2,792Y	3,208Y	3,978Y	4,971Y	7,108Y
PERCENT DISTRIBUTION														
Industrial Countries........ 101	**50.8**	**47.8**	**45.7**	**43.3**	**43.0**	**40.7**	**39.3**	**63.4**	**64.4**	**64.4**	**63.5**	**61.8**	**56.8**	**55.5**
Developing Countries........ 202	**49.2**	**52.2**	**54.3**	**56.7**	**57.0**	**59.3**	**60.7**	**36.6**	**35.6**	**35.5**	**36.5**	**38.2**	**43.2**	**44.5**
Africa........ 607	**.8**	**1.6**	**1.0**	**.7**	**.6**	**.5**	**.5**	**.4**	**.4**	**.5**	**.5**	**.5**	**.5**	**.6**
Asia........ 507	**44.2**	**46.8**	**49.3**	**52.0**	**52.5**	**54.6**	**55.6**	**14.6**	**14.7**	**17.9**	**16.2**	**16.8**	**20.0**	**22.6**
Europe........ 170	**.7**	**.2**	**.1**	**.1**	**.1**	**.4**	**.2**	**2.3**	**3.6**	**2.5**	**3.2**	**2.8**	**2.8**	**2.6**
Middle East........ 407	**3.0**	**3.4**	**3.5**	**3.8**	**3.6**	**3.7**	**4.2**	**17.8**	**15.8**	**13.6**	**15.0**	**16.2**	**18.1**	**16.6**
Western Hemisphere........ 207	**.5**	**.2**	**.4**	**.1**	**.2**	**—**	**.3**	**1.5**	**1.0**	**1.1**	**1.6**	**1.8**	**1.8**	**2.1**
ANNUAL PERCENT CHANGE														
World........ 001	**–13.9**	**–3.9**	**20.7**	**36.1**	**37.9**	**20.3**	**10.5**	**5.0**	**13.9**	**29.6**	**12.5**	**19.1**	**8.9**	**29.8**
Industrial Countries........ 101	**–17.5**	**–9.4**	**15.5**	**28.8**	**36.9**	**13.9**	**6.7**	**14.9**	**15.7**	**29.7**	**10.9**	**15.9**	**.1**	**26.8**
Developing Countries........ 202	**–9.8**	**1.8**	**25.6**	**42.3**	**38.6**	**25.0**	**13.2**	**–8.8**	**10.9**	**29.4**	**15.5**	**24.7**	**23.1**	**33.6**
Africa........ 607	**–19.1**	**84.1**	**–27.5**	**–1.4**	**25.7**	**1.7**	**1.5**	**–14.6**	**28.3**	**41.6**	**9.2**	**35.6**	**13.2**	**35.8**
Asia........ 507	**–10.9**	**1.7**	**27.2**	**43.5**	**39.2**	**25.2**	**12.4**	**–17.2**	**15.4**	**56.9**	**2.3**	**23.2**	**29.6**	**46.6**
Europe........ 170	**–23.8**	**–78.1**	**–35.4**	**59.9**	**59.0**	**296.1**	**–46.7**	**28.9**	**83.1**	**–11.1**	**46.3**	**4.5**	**9.0**	**17.3**
Middle East........ 407	**23.8**	**8.9**	**23.6**	**49.3**	**31.4**	**22.2**	**24.9**	**–5.5**	**.6**	**12.1**	**23.9**	**28.9**	**21.2**	**19.5**
Western Hemisphere........ 207	**–11.8**	**–55.6**	**128.7**	**–63.6**	**97.5**	**–80.0**	**—**	**8.8**	**–21.9**	**38.4**	**58.4**	**38.4**	**5.4**	**56.4**
Other Countries n.i.e........ 910	**—**	**—**	**....**	**....**	**....**	**....**	**....**	**–.4**	**3.4**	**11.2**	**30.1**	**27.3**	**23.5**	**29.5**

	Exports 2001	Exports 2002	Exports 2003	Exports 2004	Exports 2005	Exports 2006	Exports 2007	Imports 2001	Imports 2002	Imports 2003	Imports 2004	Imports 2005	Imports 2006	Imports 2007
	Millions of U.S. Dollars							*Millions of U.S. Dollars*						
IFS World Total	**476.1**	**485.5**	**581.7**	**733.2**	**671.6**	**795.5**	**1,105.0**	**467.2**	**586.7**	**717.0**	**941.0**	**1,102.2**	**1,847.8**	**2,475.0**
DOTS World Total 001	**476.1**	**485.5**	**580.7**	**705.3**	**633.8**	**796.1**	**1,134.1**	**471.6**	**587.2**	**717.0**	**940.9**	**1,111.6**	**1,710.6**	**2,415.2**
Industrial Countries 101	**250.3**	**156.3**	**173.1**	**163.5**	**70.8**	**244.1**	**271.9**	**99.8**	**144.9**	**152.8**	**172.4**	**199.9**	**331.0**	**339.9**
United States 111	7.08	36.06	6.52	3.23	3.28	9.60	4.09	26.71	47.38	47.93	44.61	67.24	97.52	95.79
Canada 156	1.13	4.91	30.98	42.74	22.50	.20	.80	10.89	9.05	8.30	12.60	14.98	32.16	23.04
Australia 193	.01	.02	.03	.06	—	.05	.22	.19	.35	.12	.19	2.48	4.18	3.54
Japan 158	.38	.19	.09	.01	.39	.99	1.67	5.88	6.42	11.83	11.60	11.69	13.30	17.92
New Zealand 196	—	—	—	—	—	—	—	.02	.01	.04	.01	—	1.19	1.23
Austria 122	1.42	1.49	1.85	2.85	.20	—	.14	.61	1.22	3.28	1.83	3.41	2.26	3.77
Belgium 124	.89	3.22	4.91	3.89	2.93	5.16	11.50	8.43	1.58	3.32	2.26	4.49	16.77	8.03
Cyprus 423	—	—	—	.01	—	—	—	—	.61	.01	—	—	.16	.08
Denmark 128	—	—	—	.05	—	.31	—	1.88	.84	1.13	1.02	3.02	1.74	3.09
Finland 172	.12	.17	.01	.38	.20	.21	.10	1.39	4.53	4.54	2.46	6.61	18.85	26.36
France 132	1.83	5.60	.21	.25	.92	.21	.37	4.43	5.17	3.84	6.16	6.15	24.84	17.58
Germany 134	94.47	1.76	3.01	3.10	4.10	2.18	6.41	24.30	31.40	38.22	52.55	37.59	39.92	54.20
Greece 174	—	—	—	.09	.11	—	—	.34	.50	1.09	.36	.78	.45	.52
Iceland 176	—	—	—	—	—	—	—	—	—	.72	.61	.51	.84	.43
Ireland 178	—	—	.03	.31	.14	—	.07	.03	.11	.13	.61	.45	.86	.35
Italy 136	1.37	1.00	.43	.09	.90	6.45	6.66	2.97	3.59	5.81	4.97	5.61	13.82	8.93
Luxembourg 137	—	—	.67	.79	—	—	.09	.01	.02	.09	.02	—	.42	.20
Netherlands 138	1.57	4.20	5.28	1.31	3.20	3.19	3.44	3.89	16.10	12.31	15.71	18.90	27.69	36.41
Norway 142	—	.04	—	—	—	—	—	.05	.25	1.23	.34	.26	.89	1.58
Portugal 182	—	.35	.61	1.43	1.46	1.88	1.02	.01	.17	.11	.22	—	.08	.27
Slovenia 961	—	—	—	—	—	—	.02	.33	1.10	.62	.94	1.81	2.37	3.90
Spain 184	.11	.03	.28	.10	.13	.37	.19	.56	.74	1.16	1.63	1.28	2.05	2.19
Sweden 144	1.64	.04	—	—	—	.36	.02	.91	7.40	2.05	4.58	3.57	16.76	7.94
Switzerland 146	124.16	96.37	118.12	101.99	28.04	207.70	226.13	1.18	3.54	2.49	2.96	4.36	6.49	12.45
United Kingdom 112	14.10	.86	.08	.84	2.27	5.19	8.95	4.82	2.78	2.50	4.18	4.66	5.41	10.08
Developing Countries 202	**225.8**	**329.2**	**407.3**	**541.3**	**562.3**	**552.1**	**862.2**	**371.7**	**442.3**	**564.1**	**768.5**	**906.8**	**1,379.6**	**2,075.3**
Africa 607	**—**	**—**	**—**	**.1**	**.1**	**—**	**.1**	**.2**	**.1**	**.5**	**.1**	**11.7**	**1.2**	**1.6**
Algeria 612	—	—	—	.05	—	—	—	—	—	.01	—	—	—	—
Benin 638	—	—	—	—	—	—	.03	—	—	—	—	—	—	—
Central African Rep. 626	—	.01	—	—	—	—	.03	....	....	....	....	....	....	....
Congo, Dem. Rep. of 636	—	—	.02	—	—	—	—	....	....	....	....	....	....	....
Congo, Republic of 634	—	—	—	—	.05	—	—	—	—	—	—	—	—	—
Gabon 646	—	—	—	.07	—	—	—	....	....	....	....	....	....	....
Kenya 664	—	—	—	—	—	—	—	—	—	—	.05	.17	.39	1.06
Malawi 676	....	....	....	....	....	....	....	.14	.03	.04	.01	—	—	—
Mali 678	....	....	....	....	....	....	....	—	.01	—	—	—	—	—
Mauritania 682	....	....	....	....	....	....	....	—	—	—	—	—	—	.01
Morocco 686	....	....	....	....	....	....	....	.01	.02	.06	.01	9.30	—	.08
Nigeria 694	....	....	....	....	....	....	....	—	—	—	—	—	—	.01
Senegal 722	....	....	....	....	....	....	....	—	—	—	—	—	—	.06
Somalia 726	....	....	....	....	....	....	....	—	—	—	.02	—	—	.11
South Africa 199	—	—	—	—	—	—	—	.02	.06	.37	.03	.35	.46	.23
Tunisia 744	—	—	—	—	—	—	—	—	—	—	—	—	—	.01
Zimbabwe 698	....	....	....	....	....	....	....	.01	—	—	—	1.89	.33	—
Asia 507	**24.0**	**54.4**	**31.5**	**41.7**	**52.1**	**120.0**	**189.4**	**63.9**	**72.8**	**96.7**	**113.8**	**142.8**	**283.7**	**417.6**
Afghanistan, I.S. of 512	1.58	4.41	6.13	—	12.38	74.75	118.37	—	—	.06	.26	.17	—	.22
Bangladesh 513	—	—	—	—	—	—	—	—	.03	.05	.09	.60	.19	.36
Brunei Darussalam 516	....	....	....	....	....	....	....	—	—	.01	—	—	—	—
Cambodia 522	—	—	—	—	—	—	—	—	—	—	—	—	—	.44
China,P.R.: Mainland 924	19.38	41.26	23.34	39.34	26.57	38.12	61.88	48.55	59.12	77.69	80.08	102.92	245.64	355.56
China,P.R.:Hong Kong 532	—	—	—	—	—	—	—	—	—	—	.01	—	—	.03
India 534	1.27	6.11	.67	.58	10.16	3.70	.83	2.73	3.36	3.73	4.02	3.86	6.22	8.71
Indonesia 536	—	—	—	—	—	—	—	.18	.20	.24	.30	.17	.88	.63
Korea 542	.59	1.07	.38	.48	1.72	2.05	3.12	7.83	6.96	11.67	25.07	27.81	24.30	39.06
Malaysia 548	—	—	—	—	—	—	—	.47	.65	.23	.76	1.45	1.31	2.37
Mongolia 948	1.14	1.10	.96	1.21	1.16	1.19	1.79	—	.03	.01	.02	—	.13	1.99
Pakistan 564	.03	.03	.02	—	—	—	.29	.24	.35	.52	.39	1.25	.86	2.97
Philippines 566	—	—	—	.04	.05	—	—	.01	.02	.01	.05	—	.17	.70
Singapore 576	—	.39	—	—	—	—	—	.09	.25	.26	.19	.28	.34	.78
Sri Lanka 524	—	—	—	—	—	—	—	3.45	1.46	1.74	1.87	1.45	1.35	1.00
Taiwan Province of China 528	—	—	—	—	—	—	3.04	.18	.15	.14	.31	1.54	1.43	1.29
Thailand 578	—	—	—	.05	.07	.17	—	.13	.18	.31	.30	1.28	.78	1.16
Vietnam 582	—	—	—	—	—	—	.08	—	.02	.02	.10	.06	.05	.33
Europe 170	**192.3**	**200.8**	**228.1**	**305.6**	**333.0**	**415.1**	**646.1**	**283.3**	**351.6**	**450.8**	**636.1**	**736.3**	**1,064.0**	**1,621.2**
Albania 914	.01	.01	.01	—	—	—	.02	—	—	—	—	—	—	—
Armenia 911	—	.06	—	.86	—	—	—	.02	.45	.01	.02	—	—	.09
Azerbaijan 912	2.15	5.56	2.05	1.77	1.91	1.89	2.70	.39	2.37	.35	.39	1.80	7.65	1.99
Belarus 913	3.25	1.34	1.51	1.97	1.41	.88	1.80	5.95	5.07	5.89	4.21	7.08	18.70	23.83
Bosnia & Herzegovina 963	—	—	—	.05	—	.18	.05	—	—	—	—	—	—	—

	Exports							Imports						
	2001	2002	2003	2004	2005	2006	2007	2001	2002	2003	2004	2005	2006	2007
	Millions of U.S. Dollars							Millions of U.S. Dollars						
Bulgaria 918	.15	.11	.39	3.15	2.45	1.89	7.99	.35	.31	.68	.77	1.23	1.03	1.62
Croatia 960	.02	—	—	—	—	—	.10	—	2.36	.02	.06	.15	.82	.98
Czech Republic 935	2.07	1.94	2.33	1.34	1.79	.51	.08	1.91	1.94	1.78	2.48	1.71	2.44	4.02
Estonia 939	.38	.17	.80	1.05	.35	.09	3.66	.17	.11	1.04	.68	1.20	2.20	3.49
Georgia 915	.26	.14	.34	.40	.48	1.31	.62	—	.11	.49	.44	.16	.26	.33
Gibraltar 823	....	....	....	....	....	....	....	—	.01	—	—	—	—	—
Hungary 944	1.14	1.37	.25	.21	—	—	—	1.54	1.32	2.39	2.54	2.85	5.86	5.39
Kazakhstan 916	39.04	36.83	57.13	87.31	116.14	162.64	204.58	81.87	123.90	170.93	202.90	174.40	199.80	312.41
Latvia 941	3.40	8.66	8.38	3.04	4.21	1.96	16.55	.56	.93	.90	1.69	1.26	2.50	6.88
Lithuania 946	.82	.06	.15	.08	.06	1.23	4.22	.72	.27	.48	.78	1.53	2.30	3.54
Macedonia, FYR 962	—	—	—	—	—	.07	.75	—	—	—	—	—	—	—
Moldova 921	.36	.10	.46	.46	.09	.36	.90	.18	.70	1.45	1.60	1.88	.86	2.85
Poland 964	.42	.27	.20	.40	1.28	1.09	1.67	4.88	3.86	6.07	10.34	11.59	13.39	16.93
Romania 968	1.37	2.62	2.63	2.90	1.29	.75	.44	.09	.31	.29	.14	.87	.41	.38
Russia 922	64.56	80.04	97.02	137.73	134.39	153.78	234.63	85.10	116.71	176.13	293.66	378.95	652.31	978.75
Serbia & Montenegro 965	.01	.03	.06	.15	—	—	.10	—	.19	.26	.37	—	—	.93
Slovak Republic 936	—	.64	.53	.65	.14	1.17	.40	.27	.51	.44	.90	.94	2.51	1.99
Tajikistan 923	6.70	10.19	18.86	22.07	22.90	23.93	28.15	1.51	3.48	3.07	2.37	2.01	2.82	2.31
Turkey 186	13.76	16.40	11.00	17.05	18.17	27.22	42.96	15.77	17.01	25.99	33.24	33.41	39.47	50.92
Turkmenistan 925	1.54	2.41	2.34	4.04	2.83	2.14	1.92	9.02	1.73	.40	1.37	13.04	1.77	1.29
Ukraine 926	2.92	3.97	5.42	4.24	6.01	4.13	6.13	6.25	7.84	12.56	23.29	40.09	41.88	79.46
Uzbekistan 927	47.94	27.84	16.26	14.69	17.10	27.86	85.67	66.75	60.14	39.21	51.88	60.11	65.00	120.86
Middle East 407	**9.5**	**74.1**	**147.7**	**193.7**	**177.2**	**17.0**	**26.7**	**20.8**	**12.2**	**14.3**	**15.4**	**12.6**	**20.1**	**22.3**
Bahrain 419	—	—	—	—	—	—	—	—	—	—	—	—	—	.03
Egypt 469	.02	—	—	—	—	—	—	—	.01	.05	.05	—	—	.17
Iran, I.R. of 429	8.24	4.74	2.15	3.47	3.90	7.34	10.97	6.71	4.34	5.95	7.01	5.61	8.11	5.69
Iraq 433	.04	.14	.14	.26	—	.50	1.13	6.66	—	—	.03	—	—	—
Israel 436	.24	.06	—	—	—	—	—	.23	.33	.26	.55	1.26	.99	1.19
Jordan 439	—	—	.34	.02	—	—	.02	—	.02	.02	.04	—	—	.08
Kuwait 443	....	....	....	....	....	....	....	—	—	.05	—	—	—	—
Lebanon 446	—	—	.06	.04	—	—	—	—	—	—	.01	—	—	.20
Oman 449	—	—	—	—	—	—	—	—	—	.01	—	—	—	—
Qatar 453	—	—	—	.01	—	—	—	—	—	—	—	—	—	.01
Saudi Arabia 456	.12	.10	.18	.03	—	—	.02	.24	.02	.01	.02	.34	—	.13
Syrian Arab Republic 463	.30	.20	.44	.61	.20	.20	.17	.19	.13	.15	.12	.09	—	.02
United Arab Emirates 466	.55	68.82	144.34	189.31	173.06	8.95	14.37	6.74	7.35	7.79	7.62	5.25	10.97	14.74
Western Hemisphere 207	**—**	**—**	**—**	**.1**	**—**	**—**	**—**	**3.5**	**5.6**	**1.7**	**2.9**	**3.5**	**10.7**	**12.6**
Argentina 213	—	—	—	—	—	—	—	.07	.09	.03	.02	.52	1.83	.77
Bermuda 319	—	—	—	.12	—	—	—	....	....	....	....	....	....	....
Brazil 223	—	—	—	—	—	—	—	1.68	.22	.32	2.03	1.97	7.38	9.55
Chile 228	—	—	—	—	—	—	—	1.51	2.28	.75	.03	—	.23	.10
Colombia 233	....	....	....	....	....	....	....	—	—	—	.04	—	—	.01
Costa Rica 238	....	....	....	....	....	....	....	.01	—	.11	.03	—	—	—
Dominican Republic 243	....	....	....	....	....	....	....	—	—	—	—	—	—	.02
Ecuador 248	—	—	—	—	—	—	—	.20	.23	.38	.54	.71	.74	1.15
Guatemala 258	—	—	—	—	—	—	—	.02	2.69	—	.03	—	—	.01
Honduras 268	....	....	....	....	....	....	....	—	—	—	—	—	—	.02
Mexico 273	.01	—	—	—	—	—	.02	—	.04	.15	.20	.28	.49	.85
Panama 283	—	—	—	—	—	—	—	—	—	—	.03	—	—	.02
Peru 293	—	—	—	—	—	—	—	.05	—	—	—	—	—	—
St. Kitts and Nevis 361	....	....	....	....	....	....	....	—	.02	—	—	—	—	—
Western Hem. n.s. 399	—	—	—	—	—	—	—	—	—	—	—	—	—	.08
Other Countries n.i.e. 910	**—**	**—**	**.3**	**.5**	**.7**	**—**	**—**	**.1**	**—**	**.1**	**—**	**4.9**	**—**	**.1**
Cuba 928	—	—	—	—	—	—	—	.07	—	—	—	3.88	—	.01
North Korea 954	—	—	.27	.50	.68	—	—	—	—	.06	.02	1.02	—	.05
Memorandum Items														
European Union 998	125.75	31.83	30.00	22.27	24.39	31.56	65.56	64.96	86.80	93.28	118.91	119.41	205.65	226.14
Oil Exporting Ctys 999	8.95	73.80	146.82	193.13	176.96	16.79	26.49	20.53	11.91	14.06	14.98	11.37	19.96	21.22
Non-Oil Develop.Ctys 201	216.83	255.40	260.48	348.19	385.36	535.26	835.74	351.12	430.39	550.00	753.48	895.47	1,359.59	2,054.05
PERCENT DISTRIBUTION														
Industrial Countries 101	**52.6**	**32.2**	**29.8**	**23.2**	**11.2**	**30.7**	**24.0**	**21.2**	**24.7**	**21.3**	**18.3**	**18.0**	**19.4**	**14.1**
Developing Countries 202	**47.4**	**67.8**	**70.1**	**76.7**	**88.7**	**69.3**	**76.0**	**78.8**	**75.3**	**78.7**	**81.7**	**81.6**	**80.6**	**85.9**
Africa 607	**—**	**—**	**—**	**—**	**—**	**—**	**—**	**—**	**—**	**.1**	**—**	**1.1**	**.1**	**.1**
Asia 507	**5.0**	**11.2**	**5.4**	**5.9**	**8.2**	**15.1**	**16.7**	**13.5**	**12.4**	**13.5**	**12.1**	**12.9**	**16.6**	**17.3**
Europe 170	**40.4**	**41.4**	**39.3**	**43.3**	**52.5**	**52.1**	**57.0**	**60.1**	**59.9**	**62.9**	**67.6**	**66.2**	**62.2**	**67.1**
Middle East 407	**2.0**	**15.3**	**25.4**	**27.5**	**28.0**	**2.1**	**2.4**	**4.4**	**2.1**	**2.0**	**1.6**	**1.1**	**1.2**	**.9**
Western Hemisphere 207	**—**	**—**	**—**	**—**	**—**	**—**	**—**	**.8**	**.9**	**.2**	**.3**	**.3**	**.6**	**.5**
Other Countries n.i.e. 910	**—**	**—**	**—**	**.1**	**.1**	**—**	**—**	**—**	**—**	**—**	**—**	**.4**	**—**	**—**
ANNUAL PERCENT CHANGE														
World 001	**–5.1**	**2.0**	**19.6**	**21.5**	**–10.1**	**25.6**	**42.5**	**–14.7**	**24.5**	**22.1**	**31.2**	**18.1**	**53.9**	**41.2**
Industrial Countries 101	**19.9**	**–37.5**	**10.7**	**–5.5**	**–56.7**	**244.8**	**11.4**	**–32.2**	**45.1**	**5.5**	**12.8**	**15.9**	**65.6**	**2.7**
Developing Countries 202	**–22.9**	**45.8**	**23.7**	**32.9**	**3.9**	**–1.8**	**56.2**	**–8.4**	**19.0**	**27.5**	**36.2**	**18.0**	**52.1**	**50.4**
Africa 607	**....**	**....**	**....**	**....**	**....**	**....**	**....**	**....**	**–33.3**	**298.8**	**–71.9**	**—**	**–89.9**	**34.0**
Asia 507	**–53.8**	**126.6**	**–42.1**	**32.4**	**25.0**	**130.2**	**57.9**	**17.2**	**14.0**	**32.9**	**17.7**	**25.5**	**98.6**	**47.2**
Europe 170	**–17.3**	**4.4**	**13.6**	**34.0**	**9.0**	**24.6**	**55.7**	**–15.4**	**24.1**	**28.2**	**41.1**	**15.7**	**44.5**	**52.4**
Middle East 407	**14.6**	**678.8**	**99.4**	**31.2**	**–8.6**	**–90.4**	**57.1**	**29.0**	**–41.3**	**17.1**	**8.2**	**–18.8**	**59.9**	**10.9**
Western Hemisphere 207	**....**	**—**	**....**	**222.7**	**135.7**	**23.6**	**....**	**—**	**57.3**	**–68.7**	**68.5**	**18.6**	**206.6**	**18.0**
Other Countries n.i.e. 910	**—**	**....**	**—**	**86.5**	**35.5**	**–40.0**	**46.0**	**....**	**100.0**	**—**	**–64.8**	**—**	**23.6**	**....**

		Exports							Imports						
		2001	2002	2003	2004	2005	2006	2007	2001	2002	2003	2004	2005	2006	2007
		Millions of U.S. Dollars							*Millions of U.S. Dollars*						
IFS World Total		**319.5**	**300.6**	**335.5**	**363.3**	**553.1**	**882.0**	**841.6**	**510.3**	**446.9**	**462.1**	**712.7**	**882.0**	**1,059.5**	**1,066.9**
DOTS World Total	**001**	**375.7Y**	**386.0Y**	**437.7Y**	**535.4Y**	**696.8Y**	**1,178.2Y**	**1,320.6Y**	**719.5Y**	**722.2Y**	**808.9Y**	**1,055.8Y**	**1,270.2Y**	**1,655.3Y**	**2,106.1Y**
Industrial Countries	**101**	**126.0Y**	**127.1Y**	**139.3Y**	**169.1Y**	**158.9Y**	**164.2Y**	**196.9Y**	**59.6Y**	**77.8Y**	**76.1Y**	**126.3Y**	**107.0Y**	**93.7Y**	**164.4Y**
United States	111	3.64V	2.64V	4.00V	3.36V	4.09V	8.45V	19.09V	3.96V	4.62V	4.95V	6.60V	10.78V	7.37V	14.63V
Canada	156	1.85V	2.15V	4.32V	6.66V	5.73V	4.87V	6.13V	.05V	.03V	—V	.61V	.74V	.88V	.71V
Australia	193	.90V	.31V	.32V	.41V	6.69V	26.59V	4.79V	8.26V	12.62V	7.93V	18.31V	19.88V	20.58V	24.13V
Japan	158	6.30V	6.11V	6.71V	7.29V	7.30V	11.27V	10.85V	12.97V	19.63V	15.02V	15.40V	21.33V	22.55V	41.70V
New Zealand	196	.04V	.02V	.14V	.11V	.06V	.06V	.04V	.62V	.14V	.31V	.83V	.18V	.38V	.61V
Austria	122	.25V	.10V	.20V	.42V	.81V	.59V	.50V	.07V	.04V	.03V	.77V	.04V	.03V	.58V
Belgium	124	10.36V	13.55V	17.96V	13.37V	15.61V	16.66V	11.18V	3.01V	2.78V	3.30V	11.24V	12.37V	7.17V	10.19V
Cyprus	423	—V	.05V	.04V	.01V	.02Y	.04V	—V	—V	—V	—V	—V	—V	—V	—V
Denmark	128	.58V	.61V	.50V	.70V	.59V	1.02V	1.35V	.56V	.46V	5.39V	.59V	4.31V	.29V	2.46V
Finland	172	1.71V	.91V	.69V	.40V	.46V	.39V	.74V	1.31V	.34V	.09V	16.08V	.32V	.54V	.76V
France	132	33.71V	33.82V	33.61V	43.36V	41.91V	29.11V	26.09V	8.47V	8.93V	11.78V	10.52V	13.48V	11.24V	12.64V
Germany	134	25.47V	22.01V	23.63V	28.75V	31.57V	34.58V	43.01V	7.38V	4.11V	7.54V	27.99V	11.30V	11.99V	34.78V
Greece	174	.42V	.29V	.26V	.30V	.40V	.23V	.18V	.01V	—V	.02V	—V	—V	—V	—V
Iceland	176	.08V	.03V	.05V	.07V	.08V	.06V	.04V	.01V	—V	—V	—V	—V	.02V	—V
Ireland	178	1.01V	1.24V	1.49V	2.78V	1.42V	1.07V	1.87V	.93V	1.25V	1.27V	5.41V	1.67V	1.75V	2.53V
Italy	136	10.85V	10.06V	10.26V	11.85V	8.89V	6.62V	7.31V	1.67V	1.30V	1.62V	1.99V	1.50V	1.03V	1.88V
Luxembourg	137	.13V	.16V	.02V	—V	—V	—V	.04V	.31V	.01V	.03V	.04V	.05V	.09V	.16V
Malta	181	.01Y	.06V	.05V	.01V	—V	—V	—V	—Y	—V	—V	—V	—V	—V	—V
Netherlands	138	9.65V	10.58V	10.35V	10.89V	13.38V	13.98V	10.60V	2.34V	5.59V	2.24V	1.26V	1.03V	.43V	1.35V
Norway	142	2.71V	2.40V	1.56V	2.26V	1.36V	.63V	.78V	2.19V	1.55V	.17V	.26V	.80V	1.52V	.91V
Portugal	182	.18V	.17V	.22V	.50V	.79V	.72V	1.28V	—V	—V	—V	—V	—V	.02V	.05V
Slovenia	961	.03V	.11V	.15V	.19Y	—V	—V	—V	—V	—V	—V	—Y	—V	.08V	.02V
Spain	184	3.69V	4.17V	2.42V	3.14V	3.52V	2.60V	3.80V	.24V	1.31V	.49V	.13V	.43V	.16V	.52V
Sweden	144	.88V	.68V	3.69V	2.46V	2.25V	1.85V	2.67V	1.24V	9.68V	7.27V	4.60V	2.00V	1.74V	4.61V
Switzerland	146	2.25V	1.54V	2.61V	3.00V	3.62V	1.46V	2.30V	.36V	.79V	.63V	1.18V	1.71V	1.94V	1.91V
United Kingdom	112	9.30V	13.36V	14.09V	26.82V	8.32V	1.36V	42.30V	3.65V	2.60V	6.01V	2.47V	3.08V	1.87V	7.27V
Developing Countries	**202**	**159.0Y**	**160.4Y**	**173.9Y**	**202.8Y**	**351.0Y**	**783.0Y**	**837.0Y**	**648.0Y**	**631.5Y**	**716.4Y**	**908.0Y**	**1,138.6Y**	**1,531.3Y**	**1,904.1Y**
Africa	**607**	**.6Y**	**.3Y**	**.3Y**	**.6Y**	**.6Y**	**.7Y**	**.9Y**	**.2Y**	**2.1Y**	**.7Y**	**3.8Y**	**3.1Y**	**3.4Y**	**.6Y**
Algeria	612	.35V	.02V	.02Y	.02Y	.03Y	.04Y	.05Y	—V	—V	—Y	—Y	—Y	—Y	—Y
Benin	638	.03V	—V	—V	—V	—V	—Y	—Y	—Y	—Y	—Y	—V	—V	—Y	—Y
Côte d'Ivoire	662	—V	—V	—V	—V	—V	.01V	.01Y	.02V	—V	—V	—V	—V	—V	—Y
Mauritius	684	—V	.01V	—V	—V	—V	—V	—V	—V	—V	—V	—V	—V	—V	—V
Nigeria	694	.22V	.19V	.27V	.36Y	.45Y	.56Y	.72Y	—V	—V	—V	—Y	—Y	—Y	—Y
Senegal	722	—V	—V	.03V	.02V	—V	.01V	.01Y	.16V	—V	—V	—V	—V	.13V	.16Y
South Africa	199	.03V	.03V	—V	.04V	.07V	.09V	.10V	.04V	2.13V	.66V	3.76V	3.11V	3.23V	.45V
Tunisia	744	—V	.01V	—V	.13V	.02V	.01V	.01Y	—V	—V	—V	—V	—V	—V	—Y
Uganda	746	—Y	—Y	—Y	—Y	—Y	—Y	—Y	—V	—V	—V	.01Y	.01Y	.01Y	.01Y
Asia	**507**	**155.3Y**	**155.3Y**	**165.5Y**	**191.3Y**	**340.1Y**	**771.0Y**	**822.3Y**	**641.4Y**	**622.8Y**	**712.2Y**	**893.7Y**	**1,123.2Y**	**1,522.8Y**	**1,896.8Y**
Bangladesh	513	.42V	.22V	—V	—V	—V	—V	—V	.05V	—V	—V	—V	—V	—Y	—Y
Cambodia	522	.02V	—V	—V	—V	.18V	.87V	1.08Y	.88V	—V	—V	—V	.23V	.30V	.38Y
China,P.R.: Mainland	924	6.78V	8.77V	10.19V	11.36V	23.22V	45.12V	77.26V	59.85V	59.69V	108.06V	108.80V	115.87V	185.59V	195.15V
China,P.R.:Hong Kong	532	.11V	.06V	.13V	.02V	.03V	.40V	.09V	10.13V	6.13V	8.15V	7.99V	8.27V	15.47V	14.75V
China,P.R.:Macao	546	—V	—V	—V	—V	—V	—V	—V	.05V	—V	—V	—V	—V	—V	—V
India	534	—Y	.11V	.12V	.06V	.08V	.10Y	.13Y	6.07Y	2.17V	.79V	2.28V	5.15V	6.37Y	7.90Y
Indonesia	536	.18V	.16V	3.02V	—V	.06V	.15V	2.67V	1.58V	.78V	.52V	1.73V	1.93V	4.78V	4.08V
Korea	542	.44V	.10V	.14V	1.31V	1.92V	16.15V	63.94V	6.88V	4.95V	8.68V	9.88V	15.32V	25.66V	61.22V
Malaysia	548	.28V	.35V	.15V	.13V	11.78V	44.65V	32.39V	1.88V	3.21V	3.30V	2.76V	6.90V	6.23V	10.23V
New Caledonia	839	.03V	.03V	.04V	.03V	.03Y	.04Y	.05Y	....	....	....	....	....	....	....
Pakistan	564	.02V	.01V	—V	.33V	.14V	.17Y	.21Y	.04V	.13V	.08V	.14V	.05V	.06Y	.08Y
Philippines	566	.01V	.02V	.05V	—V	—V	—V	—V	.09V	.02V	.14V	.26V	.79V	.50V	.49V
Singapore	576	.39V	.45V	.23V	.59V	1.32V	.51V	1.17V	28.86V	29.09V	22.40V	42.30V	44.09V	45.19V	42.95V
Taiwan Province of China	528	3.79V	3.13V	1.88V	5.61V	8.26V	35.93V	22.78V	2.56V	1.44V	1.54V	2.79V	2.21V	2.76V	1.88V
Thailand	578	81.02V	85.01V	94.35V	104.28V	204.39V	475.45V	431.49V	451.70V	444.00V	501.54V	639.55V	846.24V	1,125.43V	1,442.82V
Vietnam	582	61.85V	56.89V	55.22V	67.55V	88.64V	151.45V	189.00V	70.78V	71.15V	56.95V	75.24V	76.12V	104.50V	114.84V
Europe	**170**	**2.2Y**	**4.0Y**	**6.8Y**	**9.5Y**	**8.4Y**	**9.1Y**	**10.9Y**	**6.2Y**	**6.5Y**	**3.3Y**	**10.2Y**	**12.2Y**	**4.9Y**	**6.5Y**
Azerbaijan	912	—V	—V	—V	—V	—V	—V	—V	—V	.12V	—V	.25V	—V	—V	—V
Bulgaria	918	.01V	.16V	.01V	.02V	.06V	.08V	.10V	—V	—V	—V	—V	—V	.01V	.02V
Czech Republic	935	.53V	.37V	.82V	1.11V	1.67V	.75V	.79V	.17V	.10V	.08V	.68V	—V	.03V	.02V
Estonia	939	.09V	.08V	.07V	—V	—V	—V	—V	—V	—V	—V	.08V	—V	—V	.01V
Hungary	944	.47V	.84V	.69V	—V	.10V	.11V	.39V	.04V	—V	—V	.02V	—V	—V	.03V
Latvia	941	—V	—V	.04V	.11V	.13V	.02V	.08V	—V	—V	—V	.01V	.03V	.04V	.09V
Lithuania	946	.01V	.01V	.01V	—V	.06V	—V	—V	—V	—V	—V	—V	—V	—V	—V
Macedonia, FYR	962	—V	—V	—V	—V	—V	.01V	.01Y	—V	—V	—V	.01V	—V	—V	—Y
Poland	964	.62V	1.98V	4.33V	6.96V	5.11V	6.20V	7.36V	.04V	.03V	.04V	.94V	.17V	.22V	3.65V
Romania	968	.05V	.05V	.12V	.38V	.14V	.08V	.02V	—V	—V	—V	.29V	—V	—V	—V
Russia	922	.03V	.15V	.14V	.22V	.34V	.50V	.97V	4.13V	4.41V	2.45V	7.13V	11.98V	3.94V	2.38V
Slovak Republic	936	.30V	.14V	.18Y	.24Y	—V	.32V	—V	—V	.03V	.04Y	.05Y	.01V	.42V	.30V
Turkey	186	.04V	.22V	.42V	.42V	.50V	.58V	.67V	1.13V	1.62V	.73V	.78V	—V	.26V	.02V
Ukraine	926	.01V	.02V	.01V	.01V	.33V	.41Y	.51Y	.66V	.23V	—V	—V	—V	—Y	—Y

Lao People's Democratic Republic 544

	Exports							Imports						
	2001	2002	2003	2004	2005	2006	2007	2001	2002	2003	2004	2005	2006	2007
	Millions of U.S. Dollars							*Millions of U.S. Dollars*						
Middle East.......... 407	**.5Y**	**.5Y**	**.8Y**	**.9Y**	**1.0Y**	**1.2Y**	**1.5Y**	**—Y**	**—Y**	**—Y**	**—Y**	**—Y**	**—Y**	**—Y**
Egypt.......... 469	.13V	.14Y	.18Y	.24Y	.27Y	.34Y	.42Y	—V	—Y	—Y	—Y	—Y	—Y	—Y
Kuwait.......... 443	.22Y	.22Y	.25Y	.32Y	.41Y	.51Y	.66Y	....	....	....	....	....	....	....
Lebanon.......... 446	.04Y	.04Y	.06Y	.07Y	.08Y	.10Y	.13Y	—Y	—Y	—Y	—Y	—Y	—Y	—Y
Saudi Arabia.......... 456	.15V	.09V	.34V	.22V	.19V	.24Y	.31Y	—Y	—Y	—Y	—Y	—Y	—Y	—Y
Yemen, Republic of.......... 474	—V	—V	—Y	—V	.01V	.01Y	.02Y	—Y	—Y	—Y	—Y	—Y	—Y	—Y
Western Hemisphere.......... 207	**.3Y**	**.3Y**	**.3Y**	**.6Y**	**1.0Y**	**1.0Y**	**1.4Y**	**.2Y**	**—Y**	**.3Y**	**.3Y**	**.2Y**	**.1Y**	**.2Y**
Argentina.......... 213	—V	—V	—V	.03V	.10V	.01V	.31V	—V	—V	—V	.06V	—V	—V	.05V
Barbados.......... 316	.02V	.01V	.01V	.01V	.01V	—V	—Y	....	....	....	....	....	....	....
Bermuda.......... 319	—Y	—Y	—Y	—Y	.02V	—V	—Y	—Y	—Y	—Y	—Y	—Y	—Y	—Y
Brazil.......... 223	—V	.04V	.01V	.18V	.10V	.09V	—V	—V	.01V	.25V	.23V	.14V	.13V	—V
Chile.......... 228	.05V	—V	.02V	—V	—V	.01V	.02V	.10V	—V	—V	—V	—V	—V	—V
Colombia.......... 233	.02V	.05V	.02V	.03V	.06V	.01V	.01V	—V	—V	—V	.01V	—V	—V	—V
Costa Rica.......... 238	—V	—V	—V	—V	—V	.01Y	.01Y	—V	—V	—V	—V	—V	—Y	—Y
Dominican Republic.......... 243	.16V	.18Y	.22Y	.29Y	.34Y	.42Y	.52Y	....	....	....	....	....	....	....
Ecuador.......... 248	—V	—V	.04V	—V	—V	—V	—Y	.03V	—V	—V	—V	—V	—V	—Y
Greenland.......... 326	.01Y	.01Y	.01Y	.01Y	.01Y	.02Y	.02Y	....	....	....	....	....	....	....
Guatemala.......... 258	—V	—V	—V	.02V	—V	—Y	—Y	—V	—V	—V	—V	—V	—Y	—Y
Mexico.......... 273	—V	—V	—V	—V	.25V	.43V	.50V	—V	—V	—V	—V	.01V	.01V	.14V
Peru.......... 293	.08V	—V	—V	—V	.08V	.01V	.01Y	.02V	—V	.04V	—V	.02V	.01V	—Y
Uruguay.......... 298	—V	—Y	—V	.01V	—V	—Y	—Y	....	....	....	....	....	....	....
Countries & Areas n.s.......... 898	**90.7Y**	**98.4Y**	**124.5Y**	**163.6Y**	**186.9Y**	**231.0Y**	**286.7Y**	**11.9Y**	**12.9Y**	**16.3Y**	**21.5Y**	**24.5Y**	**30.3Y**	**37.6Y**
Memorandum Items														
European Union.......... 998	110.25Y	115.36Y	125.77Y	154.37Y	137.01Y	118.24Y	161.54Y	31.45Y	38.57Y	47.25Y	84.86Y	51.77Y	39.14Y	83.90Y
Oil Exporting Ctys.......... 999	1.12Y	.68Y	3.90Y	.93Y	1.15Y	1.50Y	4.41Y	1.58Y	.78Y	.52Y	1.73Y	1.93Y	4.78Y	4.08Y
Non-Oil Develop.Ctys.......... 201	157.91Y	159.74Y	169.95Y	201.82Y	349.89Y	781.53Y	832.63Y	646.41Y	630.69Y	715.93Y	906.30Y	1,136.71Y	1,526.51Y	1,900.03Y
PERCENT DISTRIBUTION														
Industrial Countries.......... 101	33.5	32.9	31.8	31.6	22.8	13.9	14.9	8.3	10.8	9.4	12.0	8.4	5.7	7.8
Developing Countries.......... 202	42.3	41.6	39.7	37.9	50.4	66.5	63.4	90.1	87.4	88.6	86.0	89.6	92.5	90.4
Africa.......... 607	.2	.1	.1	.1	.1	.1	.1	—	.3	.1	.4	.2	.2	—
Asia.......... 507	41.3	40.2	37.8	35.7	48.8	65.4	62.3	89.1	86.2	88.0	84.7	88.4	92.0	90.1
Europe.......... 170	.6	1.0	1.6	1.8	1.2	.8	.8	.9	.9	.4	1.0	1.0	.3	.3
Middle East.......... 407	.1	.1	.2	.2	.1	.1	.1	—	—	—	—	—	—	—
Western Hemisphere.......... 207	.1	.1	.1	.1	.1	.1	.1	—	—	—	—	—	—	—
ANNUAL PERCENT CHANGE														
World.......... 001	–4.0	2.7	13.4	22.3	30.1	69.1	12.1	4.3	.4	12.0	30.5	20.3	30.3	27.2
Industrial Countries.......... 101	–1.2	.9	9.6	21.4	–6.1	3.4	19.9	–25.2	30.5	–2.2	65.9	–15.3	–12.4	75.5
Developing Countries.......... 202	–12.4	.9	8.4	16.6	73.1	123.1	6.9	8.1	–2.5	13.5	26.7	25.4	34.5	24.3
Africa.......... 607	–.7	–58.9	24.4	72.8	1.6	24.3	26.1	401.1	853.4	–68.7	464.5	–17.5	8.4	–81.5
Asia.......... 507	–12.1	—	6.6	15.6	77.8	126.7	6.7	7.5	–2.9	14.3	25.5	25.7	35.6	24.6
Europe.......... 170	–41.1	86.7	69.1	38.6	–10.8	7.4	20.1	171.7	5.8	–49.1	206.9	19.1	–59.6	32.5
Middle East.......... 407	16.5	–7.2	64.9	3.8	13.9	23.5	27.5	—	—	....	....	....	23.6	....
Western Hemisphere.......... 207	317.7	–16.4	15.5	74.9	66.3	4.5	38.9	–38.3	–92.8	—	4.6	–46.2	–12.6	29.0

	Exports							Imports						
	2001	2002	2003	2004	2005	2006	2007	2001	2002	2003	2004	2005	2006	2007
	Millions of U.S. Dollars							Millions of U.S. Dollars						
IFS World Total	**2,000.7**	**2,283.7**	**2,892.8**	**3,982.3**	**5,108.5**	**5,895.8**	**7,889.8**	**3,504.5**	**4,052.6**	**5,242.3**	**7,048.4**	**8,591.7**	**11,430.4**	**15,176.7**
DOTS World Total 001	**2,039.9**	**2,312.7**	**2,892.9**	**3,978.9**	**5,144.4**	**6,145.3**	**8,293.0**	**3,507.1**	**4,040.7**	**5,244.2**	**7,039.4**	**8,660.4**	**11,580.8**	**15,347.7**
Industrial Countries 101	**1,345.8**	**1,568.2**	**2,003.5**	**2,437.9**	**2,908.7**	**3,046.4**	**3,715.0**	**2,042.9**	**2,361.9**	**2,979.7**	**3,488.7**	**4,143.6**	**5,759.7**	**7,476.9**
United States 111	57.38	98.60	83.79	116.86	140.15	112.98	112.06	64.68	63.53	91.26	92.51	92.01	107.00	174.46
Canada 156	4.61	9.97	12.34	16.30	21.08	27.52	22.44	8.42	6.37	10.41	12.98	19.16	19.57	25.07
Australia 193	.89	2.85	1.65	1.80	2.71	2.22	2.66	4.73	3.84	1.81	2.72	2.81	3.77	4.52
Japan 158	12.36	18.11	25.96	36.52	44.24	42.98	39.36	4.04	6.46	11.32	7.40	22.13	32.55	55.24
New Zealand 196	.16	.14	.32	.55	1.06	1.64	2.47	.36	.56	1.36	1.43	1.66	2.18	2.58
Austria 122	12.15	13.72	14.33	17.69	21.52	25.80	45.38	40.33	56.30	81.90	102.36	139.92	178.68	225.47
Belgium 124	25.33	24.83	30.34	34.31	36.45	84.10	81.61	64.28	79.04	91.99	110.15	141.34	196.73	291.70
Cyprus 423	1.03	3.86	2.34	7.79	21.75	17.40	26.35	.35	.25	5.61	3.96	8.43	20.45	129.84
Denmark 128	115.66	130.09	173.67	213.55	274.07	297.29	315.80	130.45	137.22	178.87	207.96	251.90	313.51	407.83
Finland 172	45.67	53.10	77.67	98.29	180.02	174.05	249.36	281.02	323.78	387.50	446.74	506.85	657.13	778.84
France 132	38.68	46.37	64.07	73.93	92.20	102.75	123.92	84.89	105.77	147.83	163.01	178.59	283.02	352.82
Germany 134	333.64	353.08	428.94	475.69	527.09	600.00	692.31	596.99	694.70	842.33	978.97	1,205.92	1,789.97	2,311.74
Greece 174	.80	3.47	4.17	4.45	5.38	5.95	17.19	6.66	6.11	5.95	7.46	8.41	11.46	16.55
Iceland 176	7.14	9.31	16.63	27.96	31.82	43.12	56.81	3.61	3.44	2.94	3.53	3.24	2.97	3.05
Ireland 178	22.94	21.49	34.57	57.22	77.79	86.39	86.17	19.79	19.09	23.04	27.80	23.10	29.58	30.29
Italy 136	36.64	49.16	75.96	68.76	83.91	122.52	121.07	144.29	168.90	228.80	233.62	290.61	392.84	561.56
Luxembourg 137	.51	.07	.28	.13	.52	.76	3.46	1.76	2.63	3.33	4.74	6.31	21.85	24.58
Malta 181	.44	.47	.40	.85	24.35	10.76	7.87	.09	.13	.07	.11	1.24	.35	.41
Netherlands 138	73.74	86.99	93.87	97.22	109.45	139.30	167.10	113.85	136.51	162.47	236.15	304.91	372.78	491.29
Norway 142	28.16	37.62	56.25	75.33	101.87	142.95	203.63	44.11	50.77	67.92	70.29	101.67	232.48	159.53
Portugal 182	.96	5.85	11.13	24.18	32.43	11.65	8.43	4.83	7.78	8.49	15.86	17.07	28.38	33.15
Slovenia 961	1.79	1.92	2.60	2.46	3.20	4.15	5.53	8.04	10.28	13.87	13.73	17.36	20.35	27.21
Spain 184	13.74	15.50	24.22	21.09	66.21	69.03	112.53	41.54	49.72	64.77	65.97	105.96	108.10	210.88
Sweden 144	191.28	240.34	305.38	398.69	403.06	384.21	615.23	227.82	257.93	328.44	430.52	443.22	580.55	745.46
Switzerland 146	6.70	8.93	12.76	58.91	84.16	72.27	54.99	61.42	77.18	99.43	107.28	91.57	127.36	164.04
United Kingdom 112	313.39	332.34	449.89	507.41	522.24	464.58	541.24	84.59	93.62	117.98	141.48	158.22	226.07	248.78
Developing Countries 202	**688.6**	**736.9**	**880.4**	**1,412.1**	**2,220.2**	**3,094.0**	**4,566.1**	**1,435.0**	**1,647.9**	**2,241.4**	**3,375.3**	**4,516.4**	**5,821.0**	**7,870.6**
Africa 607	**50.5**	**50.8**	**18.0**	**11.1**	**28.5**	**54.5**	**75.6**	**3.0**	**3.1**	**4.2**	**2.4**	**4.2**	**9.8**	**11.4**
Algeria 612	41.64	47.85	9.02	2.08	8.62	31.85	25.98	—	—	—	—	—	—	—
Angola 614	.01	—	—	—	—	—	—	—	—	—	—	—	—	—
Benin 638	.02	.04	.01	1.28	—	.22	.19	—	—	—	—	—	—	—
Botswana 616	—	—	—	—	—	—	.04	—	—	—	—	—	—	—
Burundi 618	—	—	—	.02	.51	.12	—	—	—	—	—	—	—	—
Cameroon 622	.01	—	1.04	—	—	.01	.05	.02	—	—	—	—	—	—
Cape Verde 624	—	—	—	—	—	—	.11	—	—	—	—	—	—	.01
Central African Rep. 626	—	—	—	—	—	—	.04	—	—	—	—	—	.32	.13
Comoros 632	—	—	—	—	.01	.04	.02	—	.04	—	—	—	—	—
Congo, Dem. Rep. of 636	—	—	—	—	—	—	.01	—	—	—	—	—	.31	.59
Congo, Republic of 634	—	—	.05	—	.02	—	—	—	—	—	—	.61	.45	.14
Côte d'Ivoire 662	—	—	.01	—	.01	—	—	—	—	—	.02	—	—	—
Equatorial Guinea 642	—	—	—	—	—	—	.07	—	—	—	—	—	—	—
Eritrea 643	.10	.06	.02	.03	.03	.03	—	—	—	—	—	—	—	—
Ethiopia 644	—	—	—	—	.23	.52	.09	.04	.04	—	—	.01	—	.01
Gabon 646	—	—	—	—	—	.02	.48	—	—	—	—	—	.21	.10
Gambia, The 648	.24	.20	.28	.24	.14	.33	.20	—	—	—	—	—	.01	—
Ghana 652	.04	.01	.01	.03	.35	.05	.32	.01	.29	.10	.01	.47	2.74	3.36
Guinea 656	.04	—	—	—	—	—	.02	.01	.01	—	—	—	—	.35
Kenya 664	.02	.01	.11	.27	.57	.53	.51	.02	—	—	—	—	.16	.11
Liberia 668	.64	.67	.47	.80	2.75	4.44	4.72	.01	—	.14	.08	—	—	.01
Madagascar 674	—	—	.04	.04	.37	.04	—	.07	—	.02	.01	.04	.04	.06
Malawi 676	—	—	—	—	—	.02	.04	.07	.17	.09	—	.41	.21	.14
Mali 678	—	.02	—	—	.02	.27	.03	—	—	—	—	—	—	—
Mauritania 682	—	.01	.14	—	—	—	—	1.20	.66	.35	.02	—	.07	.07
Mauritius 684	—	—	—	—	—	—	—	.03	.03	.02	.22	.15	.10	.01
Morocco 686	2.04	1.31	2.67	.96	2.17	1.81	23.32	.32	.67	.68	.20	.50	3.51	3.94
Mozambique 688	—	—	—	—	.01	.02	.04	—	—	—	—	—	—	—
Namibia 728	—	—	.09	.03	.03	.01	—	.03	.05	—	—	.01	.02	.03
Niger 692	—	—	—	—	—	.15	—	—	—	—	—	—	—	—
Nigeria 694	4.64	.18	.08	1.85	7.69	2.57	1.80	.01	—	.06	—	.05	.02	.01
Rwanda 714	—	—	—	—	—	.76	—	—	—	—	—	—	—	—
Senegal 722	.02	—	—	.29	.01	.01	.03	—	—	—	—	—	—	—
Seychelles 718	.41	.12	—	.13	.05	.11	.74	—	—	—	—	.01	.01	—
Sierra Leone 724	—	—	—	—	—	—	.02	—	—	—	—	—	—	.14
South Africa 199	.29	.19	3.28	.72	1.27	1.73	3.74	.28	.30	.64	.88	1.39	1.26	2.13
Sudan 732	.13	.15	.16	.01	—	.57	.66	—	—	—	—	—	—	—
Tanzania 738	.34	.02	.28	.06	.73	.54	.06	—	—	.14	.14	—	.01	—
Togo 742	—	—	—	—	.04	.01	.50	—	—	—	.01	.01	—	—
Tunisia 744	.01	.07	.22	2.29	2.82	7.51	11.33	.36	.52	.81	.48	.18	.05	.03
Uganda 746	—	—	—	—	—	.07	.31	—	.01	—	—	.18	.04	—
Zambia 754	—	—	—	—	.05	.16	.09	—	—	—	—	—	.08	—
Zimbabwe 698	—	—	—	.03	—	—	.03	.54	.26	1.13	.28	.21	.16	.05

		Exports							Imports						
		2001	2002	2003	2004	2005	2006	2007	2001	2002	2003	2004	2005	2006	2007
		Millions of U.S. Dollars							Millions of U.S. Dollars						
Asia	**507**	**16.7**	**17.5**	**27.2**	**29.7**	**36.1**	**59.3**	**85.9**	**58.7**	**82.3**	**136.5**	**172.5**	**247.1**	**373.4**	**585.6**
Afghanistan, I.S. of	512	.19	.39	.38	.27	.30	.42	1.08	—	—	.02	—	—	—	—
Bangladesh	513	—	—	.02	.36	.63	.06	.25	.11	.39	.64	.53	.10	.27	.32
Brunei Darussalam	516	—	—	—	—	—	—	—	—	—	—	—	.07	—	—
Cambodia	522	.03	.03	.04	.02	.15	.28	.34	—	.02	.02	.01	.02	—	.09
China,P.R.: Mainland	924	1.65	2.92	16.80	10.67	10.29	19.69	22.86	27.07	42.60	67.47	88.64	129.95	193.26	353.58
China,P.R.:Hong Kong	532	4.34	6.06	1.84	1.87	3.56	2.67	4.58	2.22	2.95	5.96	8.44	10.43	16.93	22.49
China,P.R.:Macao	546	—	—	—	—	—	—	—	.11	.15	.27	.34	.09	.14	.06
Fiji	819	—	—	—	—	.04	.03	.03	—	—	—	—	—	—	—
French Polynesia	887	—	—	—	—	—	—	.01	—	—	—	—	—	—	—
India	534	.81	1.18	.86	2.40	3.15	8.14	11.42	4.84	7.64	9.25	10.70	18.57	28.12	30.21
Indonesia	536	—	.01	.06	.34	.14	.68	1.08	.94	1.29	2.30	1.72	2.51	4.63	8.71
Kiribati	826	3.93	—	—	—	—	—	—	.50	—	—	—	—	—	—
Korea	542	.54	1.41	2.51	5.87	7.55	11.41	17.96	7.15	8.18	17.99	25.41	40.17	57.47	74.14
Lao People's Dem.Rep	544	—	—	—	.01	.02	.04	.09	—	—	.04	.12	.14	.02	.09
Malaysia	548	.08	1.42	.07	.43	1.23	1.42	1.01	1.66	1.13	1.20	2.13	2.88	5.27	15.21
Mongolia	948	.17	.64	.69	.15	.29	.25	.95	—	—	—	—	—	—	.11
Myanmar	518	—	—	.01	—	—	—	—	.08	.05	.07	.04	—	.03	—
Nepal	558	—	—	—	—	—	—	.01	—	—	.01	.01	.06	.03	.03
Pakistan	564	.05	.16	.22	.33	.93	2.69	2.59	.14	.55	.71	.83	1.12	2.89	4.25
Philippines	566	—	.01	—	.04	.15	.09	.02	.10	.14	.35	.44	.66	.55	.85
Singapore	576	.12	1.70	.16	.93	4.05	5.12	4.01	1.41	1.43	3.52	4.02	2.14	5.27	3.41
Sri Lanka	524	.19	.18	.22	.16	.11	.27	.40	1.07	1.20	1.34	1.35	1.15	1.46	1.45
Taiwan Province of China	528	4.19	.93	1.91	2.75	1.96	1.97	5.69	7.77	10.61	19.12	21.08	26.09	41.81	49.27
Thailand	578	.28	.22	1.27	2.67	1.17	.75	1.41	1.98	2.40	3.86	3.90	7.60	11.35	16.02
Vanuatu	846	—	—	—	—	—	.19	—	—	—	—	—	—	—	—
Vietnam	582	.17	.20	.14	.39	.37	3.17	10.06	1.54	1.61	2.32	2.82	3.37	3.90	5.25
Europe	**170**	**555.0**	**623.5**	**791.7**	**1,316.7**	**2,097.6**	**2,918.5**	**4,308.7**	**1,352.6**	**1,538.2**	**2,070.1**	**3,166.8**	**4,222.0**	**5,378.2**	**7,213.8**
Albania	914	.02	.01	—	.01	.11	.04	.07	—	—	.01	—	—	—	—
Armenia	911	.57	.55	.64	1.50	1.91	2.05	2.43	.37	.56	.54	.94	.68	1.29	1.15
Azerbaijan	912	.64	.56	1.31	3.04	4.17	8.65	9.71	.46	1.53	.76	.91	2.46	1.96	1.99
Belarus	913	35.84	34.25	42.10	83.55	102.28	141.98	190.82	135.89	110.34	194.57	335.94	502.51	542.69	505.78
Bosnia & Herzegovina	963	.07	.10	.14	.12	.30	.06	.71	—	.01	—	.07	.07	.97	—
Bulgaria	918	.19	.62	.92	1.98	4.12	7.08	7.76	8.42	8.71	9.00	9.66	7.39	10.58	17.70
Croatia	960	.10	.93	1.18	1.36	3.03	1.63	2.64	1.62	2.89	2.31	5.03	6.40	6.25	12.30
Czech Republic	935	14.99	13.30	13.83	16.33	21.77	38.54	46.76	49.76	55.70	73.42	106.40	121.83	202.54	284.28
Estonia	939	114.80	136.66	190.47	316.45	555.77	758.40	1,141.93	221.55	248.91	336.49	489.83	681.63	895.30	1,234.07
Faroe Islands	816	—	—	—	—	.12	.22	.34	—	—	—	—	.02	.14	.10
Georgia	915	3.93	.92	1.73	4.06	4.70	5.52	7.17	.50	.59	.58	1.30	.99	2.95	4.43
Gibraltar	823	.58	.30	.22	.55	1.05	1.84	1.43	.18	.11	.52	.07	—	—	—
Hungary	944	3.38	3.90	6.25	11.22	26.57	25.64	27.03	35.79	36.44	41.22	62.51	100.38	115.61	163.49
Kazakhstan	916	7.49	9.34	10.61	20.72	16.89	25.30	48.54	2.87	2.93	2.74	3.09	20.66	50.12	54.54
Kosovo	967	—	—	—	—	.08	.03	.04	—	—	—	—	.01	.01	—
Kyrgyz Republic	917	.70	.60	.86	.70	1.32	2.91	4.10	.16	.40	.31	.22	.23	.45	.87
Lithuania	946	162.40	190.42	237.20	361.34	564.12	873.65	1,255.56	296.83	397.60	508.09	857.88	1,180.61	1,498.43	2,125.17
Macedonia, FYR	962	.01	—	—	—	.01	.07	.04	—	.01	—	.11	.34	.36	.90
Moldova	921	.95	1.58	4.50	8.45	9.09	10.26	10.55	1.92	2.03	2.69	4.02	3.99	4.51	5.79
Montenegro, Rep. of	943	—	—	—	—	—	—	.03	—	—	—	—	—	—	—
Poland	964	38.38	35.64	43.07	143.92	272.40	143.91	285.49	175.52	203.44	268.06	383.33	551.03	831.93	1,066.65
Romania	968	.22	.29	2.32	1.99	5.33	4.44	13.63	.82	1.18	1.94	3.51	2.33	5.61	10.93
Russia	922	117.06	133.53	155.81	254.46	405.66	707.64	1,074.67	321.94	353.85	455.45	614.61	740.42	921.09	1,337.48
Serbia, Rep. of	942	—	—	—	—	—	1.03	1.43	—	—	—	—	—	7.12	14.52
Serbia & Montenegro	965	—	—	—	—	1.18	—	—	—	—	—	—	.69	—	—
Slovak Republic	936	9.53	8.51	9.42	9.97	9.17	15.48	28.46	25.60	27.77	33.72	50.79	60.15	76.87	96.30
Tajikistan	923	.01	.25	2.22	.61	1.39	1.57	2.55	.59	.36	.50	1.03	.76	.37	.91
Turkey	186	2.98	4.74	.91	2.05	4.02	19.05	5.49	17.62	23.91	35.15	43.24	54.44	68.13	91.54
Turkmenistan	925	.52	.08	.17	.34	1.13	.77	1.09	.72	.01	—	.24	.35	1.04	.84
Ukraine	926	33.31	41.72	60.29	63.24	70.95	109.42	124.24	49.64	54.92	96.17	184.59	166.65	122.22	171.01
Uzbekistan	927	5.96	4.10	4.90	8.78	8.99	11.31	13.94	2.28	2.23	5.02	7.41	14.83	9.61	10.99
Yugoslavia n.s.	966	.36	.56	.64	—	—	—	—	1.51	1.72	.66	—	—	—	—
Europe n.s.	884	.01	—	—	—	—	.03	.02	.09	.03	.16	.07	.17	.04	.04
Middle East	**407**	**45.6**	**31.9**	**24.5**	**26.3**	**20.0**	**40.9**	**53.4**	**13.0**	**14.1**	**15.9**	**18.5**	**21.8**	**31.2**	**29.0**
Bahrain	419	.03	.02	.05	.02	.08	.06	.14	—	.01	.07	—	—	—	—
Egypt	469	25.05	21.50	12.65	5.43	5.03	18.34	15.67	.41	.88	1.26	.81	1.23	6.75	7.26
Iran, I.R. of	429	16.59	4.01	4.40	10.10	.85	.10	.78	.38	.81	1.30	1.52	.72	1.53	.71
Iraq	433	—	.18	.04	.28	.57	.29	.34	—	—	—	—	.01	—	—
Israel	436	1.34	1.91	2.92	3.99	6.93	8.99	10.10	9.75	9.74	11.06	10.74	14.64	17.94	17.55
Jordan	439	.22	.18	.24	.39	.38	.35	.58	—	—	—	—	.05	.10	.04
Kuwait	443	.01	.13	.47	1.27	.50	.42	.56	—	—	—	—	—	—	—
Lebanon	446	.02	.08	.21	.59	1.07	1.19	.93	.05	.34	—	.07	.06	.22	.13
Libya	672	—	—	—	—	.07	4.35	7.16	—	—	—	—	—	—	—
Oman	449	.02	.01	.06	.19	.20	.36	.48	—	—	—	—	.06	.48	.46
Qatar	453	—	—	—	—	.09	.12	.19	—	—	—	.10	—	—	—
Saudi Arabia	456	.89	2.45	1.88	1.96	1.14	2.09	7.19	.02	—	.04	.03	.11	.17	.16
Syrian Arab Republic	463	—	—	.14	—	—	.01	.06	—	—	—	.07	.11	—	.01
United Arab Emirates	466	.07	.25	.46	1.57	2.19	3.06	8.10	2.36	2.35	2.13	5.22	4.85	3.97	2.65
Yemen, Republic of	474	1.36	1.16	.94	.47	.88	1.20	1.09	—	—	—	—	—	—	—

	Exports 2001	Exports 2002	Exports 2003	Exports 2004	Exports 2005	Exports 2006	Exports 2007	Imports 2001	Imports 2002	Imports 2003	Imports 2004	Imports 2005	Imports 2006	Imports 2007
	Millions of U.S. Dollars							*Millions of U.S. Dollars*						
Western Hemisphere................207	**20.7**	**13.3**	**19.1**	**28.3**	**38.1**	**20.7**	**42.6**	**7.7**	**10.2**	**14.8**	**15.0**	**21.2**	**28.4**	**30.9**
Antigua and Barbuda..................311	—	.01	.07	.29	2.13	1.23	.93	—	—	—	—	—	—	—
Argentina..................................213	—	.01	.01	.08	.21	.71	1.85	.98	1.13	2.35	1.85	3.15	5.62	4.59
Bahamas, The............................313	.05	.25	1.27	.26	1.14	1.22	1.77	—	—	—	—	—	—	—
Barbados...................................316	—	—	—	.01	.21	.23	.23	—	.01	.03	.02	—	—	—
Belize...339	.31	.02	.04	.17	.69	.74	.89	—	1.04	1.28	.12	1.75	.12	—
Bermuda.....................................319	.03	.02	—	—	—	—	.04	—	—	—	—	—	—	—
Bolivia..218	—	—	—	.02	.01	.02	.07	—	.04	.24	.05	.05	.06	.38
Brazil...223	.61	.54	.20	.27	.52	.87	1.66	2.41	3.37	6.18	8.55	8.30	12.49	12.58
Chile..228	2.82	1.14	2.00	6.97	6.53	2.74	.78	1.77	2.83	2.36	1.80	2.29	3.22	4.55
Colombia...................................233	.01	—	1.06	2.05	2.48	1.77	1.38	.11	.14	.27	.17	.51	1.58	2.58
Costa Rica.................................238	3.69	.10	.13	4.14	.35	.28	.29	.01	—	.01	.03	.05	.06	—
Dominica...................................321	.40	.06	.10	.02	.27	.55	.59	—	—	—	—	.01	—	—
Dominican Republic....................243	—	.17	—	.03	.17	.20	.46	—	.02	.07	.04	.03	.09	.07
Ecuador......................................248	.84	—	.01	.01	—	.25	.58	.38	.31	.30	.52	2.27	.97	1.26
El Salvador.................................253	.08	—	—	—	.01	.09	.10	—	—	—	—	—	—	—
Greenland...................................326	—	—	—	—	—	.01	.01	—	—	—	—	—	—	—
Guatemala..................................258	3.97	1.20	.08	.32	.21	.12	.17	.03	.01	—	.01	—	—	—
Guyana.......................................336	—	—	—	—	—	.01	.01	—	—	—	—	—	—	—
Haiti...263	—	.70	.01	.01	.01	.02	.01	—	—	—	—	—	—	—
Honduras...................................268	.57	—	—	—	.04	.09	.14	.07	—	.01	.01	—	—	—
Jamaica......................................343	.03	—	—	.01	—	—	—	.04	.04	.04	.01	—	—	—
Mexico..273	.93	.20	.23	1.16	1.17	1.86	2.41	.64	.65	.93	1.21	1.78	2.62	3.77
Netherlands Antilles....................353	—	—	—	.04	.47	.22	.35	—	—	—	—	—	—	—
Nicaragua...................................278	.61	—	—	—	.01	—	—	—	—	—	.01	.02	.02	.01
Panama......................................283	2.05	1.51	2.90	7.49	6.97	3.07	8.75	.11	.01	.26	.08	.07	.12	.03
Paraguay....................................288	.01	.05	.02	.24	.40	.12	.07	—	—	—	—	.02	—	.08
Peru...293	3.16	5.84	10.56	3.10	10.09	.72	16.44	.71	.11	.01	.03	.77	.88	.25
St. Kitts and Nevis.......................361	—	—	.01	1.12	.57	.01	.19	—	—	—	—	—	—	—
St. Vincent & Grens.....................364	.04	.03	.09	.25	1.61	2.82	.84	—	—	—	—	—	—	—
Suriname....................................366	—	—	—	—	.04	.02	.03	—	—	—	—	—	—	—
Trinidad and Tobago...................369	—	—	.01	.10	.14	.04	.02	—	—	—	—	—	—	—
Uruguay.....................................298	.01	.01	.02	.03	.03	.05	.32	43	.46	.34	.12	.07	.02	.06
Venezuela, Rep. Bol....................299	—	.06	.03	.10	.22	.10	.34	.02	—	.01	.40	—	—	—
Western Hem. n.s.......................399	.46	1.34	.20	—	1.42	.55	.87	—	.02	.05	—	.05	.54	.65
Other Countries n.i.e...............910	—	—	**.6**	—	—	—	—	—	—	**.3**	**.4**	**.2**	**.1**	**.2**
Cuba..928	.02	.04	.55	.04	—	.02	.04	.03	.02	.27	.36	.24	.10	.21
North Korea................................954	—	—	—	—	—	—	—	—	—	.01	—	—	—	—
Countries & Areas n.s..............898	**5.5**	**7.6**	**8.3**	**128.8**	**14.6**	**3.7**	**10.1**	**29.1**	**30.9**	**22.8**	**175.0**	**.1**	—	—
Memorandum Items														
European Union..........................998	1,571.89	1,771.08	2,294.07	2,962.93	3,931.44	4,456.33	6,005.82	2,656.61	3,119.62	3,954.24	5,141.33	6,504.98	8,852.49	11,858.37
Oil Exporting Ctys.......................999	63.85	55.12	16.52	19.73	22.28	45.98	54.00	3.73	4.45	5.83	8.98	8.31	10.80	12.72
Non-Oil Develop.Ctys..................201	624.77	681.82	863.89	1,392.33	2,197.94	3,047.99	4,512.09	1,431.31	1,643.43	2,235.55	3,366.29	4,508.06	5,810.16	7,857.90
PERCENT DISTRIBUTION														
Industrial Countries.................101	**66.0**	**67.8**	**69.3**	**61.3**	**56.5**	**49.6**	**44.8**	**58.3**	**58.5**	**56.8**	**49.6**	**47.8**	**49.7**	**48.7**
Developing Countries.............202	**33.8**	**31.9**	**30.4**	**35.5**	**43.2**	**50.3**	**55.1**	**40.9**	**40.8**	**42.7**	**47.9**	**52.1**	**50.3**	**51.3**
Africa.....................................607	**2.5**	**2.2**	**.6**	**.3**	**.6**	**.9**	**.9**	**.1**	**.1**	**.1**	—	—	**.1**	**.1**
Asia..507	**.8**	**.8**	**.9**	**.7**	**.7**	**1.0**	**1.0**	**1.7**	**2.0**	**2.6**	**2.5**	**2.9**	**3.2**	**3.8**
Europe....................................170	**27.2**	**27.0**	**27.4**	**33.1**	**40.8**	**47.5**	**52.0**	**38.6**	**38.1**	**39.5**	**45.0**	**48.8**	**46.4**	**47.0**
Middle East.............................407	**2.2**	**1.4**	**.8**	**.7**	**.4**	**.7**	**.6**	**.4**	**.3**	**.3**	**.3**	**.3**	**.3**	**.2**
Western Hemisphere.............207	**1.0**	**.6**	**.7**	**.7**	**.7**	**.3**	**.5**	**.2**	**.3**	**.3**	**.2**	**.2**	**.2**	**.2**
ANNUAL PERCENT CHANGE														
World.......................................001	**9.4**	**13.4**	**25.1**	**37.5**	**29.3**	**19.5**	**34.9**	**10.1**	**15.2**	**29.8**	**34.2**	**23.0**	**33.7**	**32.5**
Industrial Countries.................101	**.4**	**16.5**	**27.8**	**21.7**	**19.3**	**4.7**	**21.9**	**10.2**	**15.6**	**26.2**	**17.1**	**18.8**	**39.0**	**29.8**
Developing Countries.............202	**32.5**	**7.0**	**19.5**	**60.4**	**57.2**	**39.4**	**47.6**	**9.0**	**14.8**	**36.0**	**50.6**	**33.8**	**28.9**	**35.2**
Africa.....................................607	**76.1**	**.6**	**–64.7**	**–38.0**	**155.4**	**91.4**	**38.8**	**10.5**	**.7**	**37.5**	**–43.9**	**78.9**	**132.0**	**16.9**
Asia..507	**247.6**	**4.3**	**55.7**	**9.1**	**21.6**	**64.4**	**44.8**	**13.3**	**40.3**	**65.7**	**26.4**	**43.2**	**51.1**	**56.8**
Europe....................................170	**21.7**	**12.3**	**27.0**	**66.3**	**59.3**	**39.1**	**47.6**	**8.9**	**13.7**	**34.6**	**53.0**	**33.3**	**27.4**	**34.1**
Middle East.............................407	**83.6**	**–30.1**	**–23.2**	**7.3**	**–23.8**	**104.7**	**30.4**	**–13.9**	**9.0**	**12.3**	**16.9**	**17.7**	**42.7**	**–7.0**
Western Hemisphere.............207	**288.6**	**–35.9**	**43.4**	**48.4**	**34.7**	**–45.6**	**105.5**	**51.3**	**32.3**	**44.7**	**1.8**	**41.1**	**34.1**	**8.7**
Other Countries n.i.e...............910	**. . . .**	**66.9**	—	**–92.3**	**–98.8**	—	**74.1**	**734.0**	**1.6**	**912.5**	**27.6**	**–31.7**	**–57.8**	**108.7**

		Exports							Imports						
		2001	2002	2003	2004	2005	2006	2007	2001	2002	2003	2004	2005	2006	2007
		Millions of U.S. Dollars							*Millions of U.S. Dollars*						
IFS World Total		**1,093.0**	**1,238.0**	**1,813.0**	**2,199.0**	**2,337.0**	**2,814.0**	**3,574.0**	**7,380.0**	**6,560.0**	**7,315.0**	**9,609.0**	**9,633.0**	**9,647.0**	**12,251.0**
DOTS World Total	**001**	**1,023.5Y**	**1,018.0Y**	**1,194.0Y**	**1,926.7Y**	**2,183.2Y**	**2,543.5Y**	**3,341.6Y**	**6,376.5Y**	**6,312.7Y**	**7,705.0Y**	**9,380.1Y**	**9,630.6Y**	**10,915.9Y**	**13,035.6Y**
Industrial Countries	**101**	**455.6Y**	**340.5Y**	**453.6Y**	**504.2Y**	**520.1Y**	**510.4Y**	**780.4Y**	**3,830.1Y**	**3,869.9Y**	**4,907.9Y**	**5,358.3Y**	**5,047.1Y**	**5,661.6Y**	**6,337.3Y**
United States	111	84.09V	59.91V	87.18V	71.00V	82.91V	84.27V	100.09V	459.91V	349.80V	345.73V	509.30V	510.18V	1,026.96V	908.71V
Canada	156	5.28V	5.20V	7.06V	7.64V	8.98V	10.31V	14.55V	22.73V	26.33V	22.90V	38.40V	45.29V	58.68V	70.99V
Australia	193	2.80V	4.17V	7.12V	6.26V	8.40V	8.43V	11.96V	24.93V	16.78V	14.69V	29.58V	22.32V	20.55V	18.72V
Japan	158	4.15V	4.51V	4.14V	5.72V	2.89V	6.28V	4.68V	113.13V	145.37V	160.06V	195.50V	176.13V	183.40V	334.23V
New Zealand	196	.12V	.21V	.20V	.07V	.23V	.09V	.49V	3.72V	3.13V	5.17V	7.30V	7.96V	6.14V	5.41V
Austria	122	.84V	.40V	.56V	.64V	.93V	2.65V	2.11V	30.16V	28.95V	34.42V	37.78V	40.16V	45.75V	56.77V
Belgium	124	27.77V	30.31V	29.64V	25.15V	31.07V	30.72V	44.84V	244.35V	284.16V	269.72V	294.63V	274.98V	264.28V	318.14V
Cyprus	423	7.23V	8.85V	15.39V	20.28V	22.34V	19.33V	21.50V	39.88V	33.73V	34.65V	34.59V	14.65V	16.43V	21.80V
Denmark	128	2.62V	2.25V	3.48V	3.00V	1.32V	1.14V	1.69V	41.57V	45.79V	59.78V	65.79V	57.77V	61.81V	91.59V
Finland	172	16.22V	.31V	.11V	.19V	.35V	.22V	.96V	37.27V	43.79V	34.32V	77.23V	53.87V	53.81V	92.00V
France	132	97.03V	22.32V	27.34V	73.19V	39.58V	41.12V	56.21V	615.48V	671.07V	1,027.08V	971.79V	885.28V	843.24V	1,077.50V
Germany	134	12.91V	15.32V	23.78V	25.76V	19.38V	19.50V	32.31V	540.81V	522.85V	898.00V	792.55V	622.33V	660.69V	695.16V
Greece	174	11.27V	8.32V	7.45V	29.54V	15.37V	18.45V	39.09V	80.58V	51.26V	50.74V	47.48V	78.58V	134.52V	71.84V
Iceland	176	.01V	.01V	.03V	.06V	.04V	.06V	.10V	.03V	.01V	—V	.03V	.01V	—V	.55V
Ireland	178	1.47V	.90V	2.08V	1.19V	1.75V	4.76V	2.70V	43.08V	49.65V	46.91V	39.56V	33.41V	41.30V	46.58V
Italy	136	20.29V	21.63V	37.31V	22.86V	25.98V	27.66V	36.27V	716.82V	709.33V	824.30V	1,041.03V	1,071.23V	1,070.32V	1,103.99V
Luxembourg	137	.38V	.01V	.08V	.07V	.02V	.03V	.07V	.85V	1.40V	2.47V	2.31V	1.38V	.52V	1.67V
Malta	181	12.19Y	.25V	.33V	.23V	.33V	.63V	.28V	11.86Y	1.34V	1.43V	2.58V	.59V	.67V	.72V
Netherlands	138	12.17V	11.45V	8.60V	15.31V	17.64V	24.40V	35.69V	146.28V	165.67V	190.52V	222.88V	224.47V	246.07V	283.69V
Norway	142	1.41V	1.63V	3.32V	.93V	.94V	.55V	1.40V	12.33V	5.43V	4.74V	7.41V	6.37V	6.03V	5.08V
Portugal	182	1.86V	.59V	.66V	1.58V	3.17V	.19V	.51V	19.49V	12.36V	12.33V	13.12V	11.83V	10.11V	14.43V
Slovenia	961	.02V	.07V	.54V	.71Y	2.66V	2.36V	3.62V	2.31V	2.01V	2.09V	2.75Y	5.71V	3.19V	7.93V
Spain	184	16.53V	19.15V	21.18V	16.55V	15.55V	11.71V	12.48V	171.84V	194.73V	224.65V	185.95V	169.47V	176.43V	212.59V
Sweden	144	3.11V	5.44V	5.22V	8.00V	9.15V	8.96V	11.73V	38.25V	36.33V	56.53V	51.69V	45.76V	48.08V	51.67V
Switzerland	146	92.93V	89.80V	136.01V	139.99V	175.87V	152.28V	275.25V	124.89V	205.77V	205.75V	262.01V	264.00V	259.78V	355.19V
United Kingdom	112	20.93V	27.46V	24.76V	28.31V	33.22V	34.27V	69.79V	287.57V	262.90V	378.92V	425.08V	423.45V	422.84V	490.33V
Developing Countries	**202**	**557.6Y**	**666.4Y**	**726.3Y**	**1,403.9Y**	**1,641.9Y**	**2,006.9Y**	**2,528.7Y**	**2,427.3Y**	**2,313.5Y**	**2,633.5Y**	**3,807.0Y**	**4,338.0Y**	**4,950.9Y**	**6,321.9Y**
Africa	**607**	**71.1Y**	**134.2Y**	**93.3Y**	**124.7Y**	**158.7Y**	**189.0Y**	**244.5Y**	**56.0Y**	**64.0Y**	**76.6Y**	**97.3Y**	**131.0Y**	**119.0Y**	**162.4Y**
Algeria	612	15.47V	23.91V	26.57Y	34.56Y	44.00Y	54.32Y	70.37Y	8.79V	11.32V	13.73Y	18.16Y	24.71Y	31.06Y	37.47Y
Angola	614	2.52Y	2.73Y	3.46Y	4.54Y	5.19Y	6.41Y	7.96Y	.01Y	.01Y	.02Y	.02Y	.02Y	.03Y	.03Y
Benin	638	.21V	.20V	.36V	2.14V	1.02V	1.27Y	1.57Y	.03V	.05V	.04V	.02V	.03V	.04Y	.05Y
Burkina Faso	748	.40Y	.43Y	.55Y	.72Y	.82Y	1.01Y	1.26Y	.02Y	.02Y	.03Y	.04Y	.05Y	.06Y	.07Y
Cameroon	622	4.23V	1.37V	.86V	1.14Y	1.30Y	1.60Y	1.99Y	.64V	.55V	3.33V	4.37Y	5.00Y	6.18Y	7.67Y
Central African Rep.	626	1.10Y	1.20Y	1.52Y	1.99Y	2.28Y	2.81Y	3.49Y	.10Y	.11Y	.14Y	.18Y	.20Y	.25Y	.31Y
Chad	628	.03Y	.04Y	.05Y	.06Y	.07Y	.08Y	.10Y	—Y	—Y	—Y	—Y	—Y	—Y	—Y
Congo, Dem. Rep. of	636	.68Y	.74Y	.94Y	1.23Y	1.41Y	1.74Y	2.16Y	—Y	—Y	—Y	—Y	—Y	—Y	—Y
Congo, Republic of	634	.51V	34.48V	2.09V	1.20V	1.37Y	1.70Y	2.10Y	—V	—V	.04V	.01V	.01Y	.02Y	.02Y
Côte d'Ivoire	662	1.36V	2.06V	2.85V	4.03V	4.67V	5.56V	6.90Y	1.16V	1.28V	1.58V	3.88V	4.47V	3.04V	3.77Y
Djibouti	611	.12Y	.13Y	.17Y	.22Y	.25Y	.31Y	.38Y	—Y	—Y	—Y	—Y	—Y	—Y	—Y
Equatorial Guinea	642	.01Y	.01Y	.02Y	.02Y	.02Y	.03Y	.03Y	.03Y	.04Y	.05Y	.06Y	.07Y	.08Y	.10Y
Eritrea	643	.03Y	.04Y	.05Y	.06Y	.07Y	.08Y	.10Y	—Y	—Y	—Y	—Y	—Y	—Y	—Y
Ethiopia	644	.26V	.42V	.29V	.29V	.40V	.49Y	.61Y	—V	.18V	—V	.42V	.02V	.03Y	.04Y
Gabon	646	1.66Y	1.80Y	2.27Y	2.99Y	3.41Y	4.22Y	5.24Y	.06Y	.06Y	.08Y	.10Y	.11Y	.14Y	.17Y
Gambia, The	648	3.94Y	4.28Y	5.41Y	7.11Y	8.12Y	10.04Y	12.46Y	—Y	—Y	—Y	—Y	—Y	—Y	—Y
Ghana	652	2.14Y	2.32Y	2.94Y	3.86Y	4.41Y	5.46Y	6.77Y	2.53Y	2.74Y	3.47Y	4.56Y	5.21Y	6.44Y	7.99Y
Guinea	656	.85V	.93Y	1.16V	3.18V	3.63Y	4.49Y	5.57Y	—V	—Y	—V	—V	—Y	—Y	—Y
Kenya	664	.06V	.01V	.01V	.03V	.04Y	.05Y	.06Y	1.19V	.92V	1.16V	1.13V	1.29Y	1.60Y	1.98Y
Liberia	668	2.90Y	3.15Y	3.99Y	5.24Y	5.98Y	7.40Y	9.18Y	.10Y	.11Y	.14Y	.18Y	.20Y	.25Y	.31Y
Madagascar	674	.02V	.01V	—V	—Y	—Y	—Y	—Y	—V	.01V	—V	—Y	—Y	—Y	—Y
Malawi	676	—Y	—Y	—Y	—Y	—Y	—Y	—Y	.51Y	.55Y	.70Y	.92Y	1.05Y	1.29Y	1.61Y
Mali	678	.22Y	.24Y	.30Y	.40Y	.46Y	.56Y	.70Y	.04Y	.05Y	.06Y	.08Y	.09Y	.11Y	.14Y
Mauritania	682	2.04Y	2.22Y	2.81Y	3.68Y	4.21Y	5.20Y	6.46Y	1.90Y	2.06Y	2.61Y	3.43Y	3.91Y	4.84Y	6.00Y
Mauritius	684	.04V	1.85V	1.77V	.08V	.14V	.15V	.25V	—V	.05V	.04V	.25V	.03V	.01V	—V
Morocco	686	6.44V	6.03V	6.50V	7.97V	12.58V	15.55Y	19.29Y	6.32V	9.87V	14.40V	16.63V	19.99V	24.71Y	30.66Y
Mozambique	688	—V	—V	—V	—V	.60V	—V	—Y	—V	—V	—V	—V	.19V	—V	—Y
Namibia	728	—Y	—Y	—Y	—Y	—Y	—Y	—Y	.08Y	.08Y	.08Y	.08Y	.08Y	.08Y	.08Y
Niger	692	.02V	.02V	—V	.03V	.03Y	.04Y	.05Y	—V	—V	—V	—V	—Y	—Y	—Y
Nigeria	694	8.05V	28.27V	7.40V	9.62Y	12.26Y	15.13Y	19.60Y	—V	—V	.70V	.92Y	1.25Y	1.58Y	1.90Y
São Tomé & Príncipe	716	—Y	—Y	—Y	—Y	—Y	—Y	—Y	.01Y	.01Y	.02Y	.02Y	.02Y	.03Y	.03Y
Senegal	722	1.35V	3.38V	2.59V	4.70V	5.39V	7.90V	9.81Y	1.91V	1.01V	2.55V	2.13V	1.45V	1.34V	1.66Y
Sierra Leone	724	1.56Y	1.69Y	2.14Y	2.81Y	3.21Y	3.97Y	4.92Y	.01Y	.01Y	.02Y	.02Y	.02Y	.03Y	.03Y
Somalia	726	—Y	—Y	—Y	—Y	—Y	—Y	—Y	.43Y	.47Y	.59Y	.78Y	.89Y	1.10Y	1.36Y
South Africa	199	.07V	.05V	.08V	.98V	2.18V	—V	—V	5.89V	7.46V	6.90V	6.81V	8.37V	7.26V	29.54V
Sudan	732	2.95Y	3.20Y	5.16Y	8.40V	12.02V	15.65V	24.37V	16.90Y	18.34Y	19.98V	27.48V	46.79V	19.00V	18.94V
Swaziland	734	—Y	—Y	—Y	—Y	—Y	—Y	—Y	.02Y	.02Y	.03Y	.04Y	.05Y	.06Y	.07Y
Tanzania	738	.15V	.29V	.37Y	.48Y	.55Y	.68Y	.84Y	.36V	—V	—Y	—Y	—Y	—Y	—Y
Togo	742	.09V	.11V	.38V	.26V	.31V	.38Y	.47Y	—V	—V	—V	.01V	.01V	.01Y	.02Y
Tunisia	744	7.47V	3.72V	4.81V	6.03V	9.64V	8.46V	10.50Y	6.87V	5.93V	3.89V	4.26V	5.10V	7.95V	9.86Y
Uganda	746	.14V	.03V	.06V	.08Y	.10Y	.12Y	.15Y	.06V	.05V	.19V	.25Y	.28Y	.35Y	.43Y

		Exports							Imports						
		2001	2002	2003	2004	2005	2006	2007	2001	2002	2003	2004	2005	2006	2007
		Millions of U.S. Dollars							Millions of U.S. Dollars						
Zambia	754	.06V	.14V	.21V	.46V	2.08V	1.08V	3.08V	.02V	—V	—V	.11V	—V	—V	.02V
Zimbabwe	698	.04V	.18V	.05V	.37V	.19V	.17V	.21Y	—V	.62V	.01V	—V	.01V	—V	—Y
Africa n.s.	799	1.95Y	2.55Y	3.15Y	3.75Y	4.35Y	4.95Y	5.55Y	—Y	—Y	—Y	—Y	—Y	—Y	—Y
Asia	**507**	**32.3Y**	**62.4Y**	**57.3Y**	**57.5Y**	**58.9Y**	**86.1Y**	**117.6Y**	**792.1Y**	**715.8Y**	**823.6Y**	**1,020.9Y**	**1,007.2Y**	**1,086.9Y**	**1,497.9Y**
Afghanistan, I.S. of	512	—Y	—Y	—Y	—Y	—Y	—Y	—Y	1.09Y	1.19Y	1.50Y	1.97Y	2.25Y	2.78Y	3.46Y
Bangladesh	513	—V	—V	—V	—V	—V	6.23V	5.30V	.63V	.82V	.52V	.69V	.43V	.30Y	.37Y
Brunei Darussalam	516	—Y	—Y	.01V	.01Y	.01Y	.02Y	.02Y	—Y	—Y	—V	—Y	—Y	—Y	—Y
Cambodia	522	—V	—Y	—Y	—Y	—Y	—Y	—Y	—V	—V	—V	—V	.03V	.10V	.12Y
China,P.R.: Mainland	924	2.36V	3.82V	4.26V	8.19V	3.81V	7.82V	16.93V	260.06V	303.68V	402.03V	532.17V	519.34V	549.60V	775.17V
China,P.R.:Hong Kong	532	6.74V	6.95V	6.00V	7.28V	5.36V	3.81V	4.47V	73.70V	62.56V	48.94V	51.09V	44.45V	62.36V	48.35V
China,P.R.:Macao	546	—V	—V	—V	—V	—V	—V	—V	—V	.03V	.06V	.09V	.05V	.06V	.08V
India	534	15.30Y	11.58V	8.20V	15.45V	17.22V	21.28Y	26.41Y	67.58Y	52.79V	62.71V	70.60V	77.13V	95.33Y	118.30Y
Indonesia	536	.43V	30.56V	28.55V	.81V	.68V	.74V	.59V	44.84V	34.25V	31.60V	32.02V	26.78V	24.94V	48.75V
Korea	542	4.18V	6.87V	5.01V	9.30V	10.88V	16.22V	30.05V	116.43V	71.13V	78.52V	97.74V	101.50V	99.10V	156.60V
Lao People's Dem.Rep	544	—Y	—Y	—Y	—Y	—Y	—Y	—Y	.04Y	.05Y	.06Y	.08Y	.09Y	.11Y	.14Y
Malaysia	548	.31V	.31V	.62V	2.36V	1.87V	3.46V	6.76V	33.83V	35.03V	44.95V	48.59V	48.27V	42.96V	67.85V
Maldives	556	—V	—V	.02V	.28V	.03V	.04Y	.05Y	.04Y	.05Y	.06Y	.08Y	.09Y	.11Y	.14Y
Mongolia	948	—V	—V	—V	—V	—V	—Y	—Y	.86V	.64V	.57V	.86V	.17V	.03Y	.04Y
Myanmar	518	—Y	—Y	—Y	—Y	—Y	—Y	—Y	.39Y	.42Y	.53Y	.70Y	.80Y	.98Y	1.22Y
Nepal	558	—Y	—Y	—Y	—Y	—Y	—Y	—Y	.06Y	.06Y	.08Y	.10Y	.11Y	.14Y	.17Y
New Caledonia	839	.03V	.01V	.02V	.03V	.04Y	.04Y	.05Y	—V	—V	—Y	—Y	—Y	—Y	—Y
Pakistan	564	.49V	.21V	.66V	4.53V	13.39V	16.55Y	20.53Y	13.46V	10.36V	11.71V	16.35V	23.44V	28.97Y	35.95Y
Papua New Guinea	853	.02Y	.02Y	.03Y	.04Y	.05Y	.06Y	.07Y	—Y	—Y	—Y	—Y	—Y	—Y	—Y
Philippines	566	.03V	.09V	.05V	.03V	.11V	.45V	.10V	3.66V	3.52V	5.53V	5.75V	3.73V	4.88V	4.15V
Samoa	862	—Y	—Y	—Y	—Y	—Y	—Y	—Y	.01Y	.01Y	.02Y	.02Y	.02Y	.03Y	.03Y
Singapore	576	.44V	.79V	.53V	.85V	.89V	.89V	1.28V	43.18V	24.68V	19.44V	22.19V	23.86V	26.11V	29.70V
Sri Lanka	524	.84V	.10V	.28V	.63V	.18V	.08V	.54V	8.41V	6.14V	7.93V	7.23V	6.75V	6.64V	11.07V
Taiwan Province of China	528	.45V	.40V	.56V	2.81V	3.03V	6.76V	2.17V	61.90V	49.17V	48.51V	60.36V	51.12V	58.00V	72.33V
Thailand	578	.65V	.52V	2.41V	4.84V	1.33V	1.66V	2.27V	58.56V	54.88V	53.40V	72.15V	76.71V	83.37V	123.90V
Tonga	866	—Y	—Y	—Y	—Y	—Y	—Y	—Y	.01Y	.01Y	.02Y	.02Y	.02Y	.03Y	.03Y
Vietnam	582	.06V	.17V	.05V	—V	—V	—V	—V	3.36V	4.32V	4.92V	—V	—V	—V	—V
Europe	**170**	**41.7Y**	**56.1Y**	**83.1Y**	**158.5Y**	**153.8Y**	**147.4Y**	**146.8Y**	**726.7Y**	**590.3Y**	**603.9Y**	**840.0Y**	**988.6Y**	**995.4Y**	**1,258.3Y**
Albania	914	.04V	4.60V	8.71V	.03V	1.39V	.12V	2.94V	.11V	—V	.98V	—V	—V	.02V	—V
Armenia	911	5.44V	1.38V	.70V	.88V	1.60V	5.30V	7.52V	.23V	.46V	.23V	.54V	.16V	.40V	.31V
Azerbaijan	912	.04V	.01V	.25V	.11V	.03V	.08V	.18V	9.43V	2.83V	7.38V	.02V	4.90V	16.69V	6.60V
Belarus	913	.11V	.24V	.06V	.07V	.09V	.54V	1.05V	11.99V	1.38V	.06V	4.67V	11.03V	3.66V	3.57V
Bosnia & Herzegovina	963	.12Y	.13Y	.17Y	.22Y	.25Y	.31Y	.38Y	.04Y	.05Y	.06Y	.08Y	.09Y	.11Y	.14Y
Bulgaria	918	.27V	.53V	.52V	.67V	.36V	.32V	1.26V	19.83V	13.19V	12.65V	75.04V	48.92V	68.40V	100.62V
Croatia	960	.01V	.36V	.36V	.04V	.22V	.10V	.28V	5.10V	7.38V	.36V	1.22V	42.47V	78.63V	37.30V
Czech Republic	935	.24V	.46V	.83V	.96V	.90V	1.09V	1.09V	36.70V	33.77V	35.15V	40.58V	35.93V	29.80V	34.92V
Estonia	939	.55V	—V	.08V	.60V	.74V	.17V	.16V	.15V	.11V	.25V	.12V	.10V	.19V	.26V
Georgia	915	1.24V	.20V	.34V	.10V	.25V	.24V	.26Y	.08V	.21V	.04V	—V	—V	.02V	.02Y
Gibraltar	823	—Y	—Y	—Y	—Y	—Y	—Y	—Y	.01Y	.01Y	.02Y	.02Y	.02Y	.03Y	.03Y
Hungary	944	1.34V	.01V	.29V	3.11V	.97V	.89V	1.48V	16.99V	19.46V	20.94V	51.62V	36.93V	23.27V	51.89V
Kazakhstan	916	.17V	3.12V	.03V	2.01V	2.30Y	2.84Y	3.53Y	.26V	.94V	2.98V	.99V	1.13Y	1.40Y	1.73Y
Kyrgyz Republic	917	—V	—V	—V	—V	—V	—V	.13V	—V	—V	.06V	.01V	—V	—V	—V
Latvia	941	.05V	.31V	—V	.06V	.06V	.20V	.12V	.02V	.09V	.24V	.65V	1.18V	1.31V	1.03V
Lithuania	946	.02V	.04V	.06V	.29V	.44V	.58V	.51V	.16V	.27V	.40V	.51V	.20V	.31V	.36V
Macedonia, FYR	962	.01V	—V	—V	.01V	.01V	.01V	.02Y	.25V	.10V	.35V	.03V	—V	.06V	.07Y
Moldova	921	.05V	.07V	.23V	.02V	.33V	.41Y	.51Y	.17V	1.57V	2.19V	2.60V	1.70V	2.10Y	2.61Y
Poland	964	1.33V	.80V	.59V	6.09V	1.18V	2.35V	2.79V	12.67V	9.34V	6.35V	14.71V	14.36V	21.96V	23.49V
Romania	968	.98V	.82V	1.14V	2.65V	2.18V	3.69V	5.44V	35.20V	84.27V	77.65V	107.43V	173.34V	156.97V	137.95V
Russia	922	4.56V	3.82V	1.92V	5.44V	7.05V	10.13V	8.13V	250.38V	122.72V	150.90V	164.25V	261.12V	156.29V	216.02V
Slovak Republic	936	—V	.01V	.02Y	.02Y	.03V	.10V	.05V	8.08V	12.30V	15.57Y	20.45Y	11.82V	11.33V	11.14V
Tajikistan	923	—V	—V	—V	—V	—V	—V	.09V	—V	—V	—V	—V	—V	—V	—V
Turkey	186	23.66V	38.11V	65.19V	132.86V	131.24V	115.17V	105.43V	202.27V	206.07V	162.94V	257.84V	215.50V	264.66V	432.42V
Turkmenistan	925	—V	—V	—V	—Y	—Y	—Y	—Y	—V	.01V	—V	—Y	—Y	—Y	—Y
Ukraine	926	1.29V	.80V	1.28V	1.93V	1.79V	2.21Y	2.74Y	109.29V	65.89V	96.08V	83.49V	112.64V	139.22Y	172.77Y
Uzbekistan	927	.03Y	.04Y	.05Y	.06Y	.07Y	.08Y	.10Y	.26Y	.29Y	.36Y	.48Y	.55Y	.67Y	.84Y
Yugoslavia n.s.	966	.18Y	.19Y	.24Y	.32Y	.36Y	.45Y	.56Y	2.98Y	3.23Y	4.09Y	5.38Y	6.14Y	7.59Y	9.42Y
Europe n.s.	884	—Y	—Y	—Y	—Y	—Y	—Y	—Y	4.05Y	4.40Y	5.57Y	7.31Y	8.35Y	10.32Y	12.81Y
Middle East	**407**	**408.5Y**	**406.0Y**	**483.6Y**	**1,049.7Y**	**1,263.1Y**	**1,574.1Y**	**1,998.8Y**	**775.1Y**	**843.5Y**	**1,020.5Y**	**1,690.4Y**	**2,019.5Y**	**2,502.3Y**	**3,080.6Y**
Bahrain	419	6.24Y	6.77Y	8.57Y	11.25Y	12.86Y	15.89Y	19.72Y	54.21Y	58.83Y	74.46Y	97.79Y	111.73Y	138.09Y	171.37Y
Egypt	469	21.35V	23.17Y	29.33Y	38.52Y	44.01Y	54.39Y	67.50Y	58.24Y	63.21Y	80.00Y	105.07Y	120.05Y	148.37Y	184.12Y
Iran, I.R. of	429	15.33V	29.69V	33.00Y	42.92Y	54.65Y	67.47Y	87.40Y	29.88Y	31.77Y	38.51Y	50.96Y	69.33Y	87.15Y	105.14Y
Iraq	433	28.63Y	29.61Y	32.91Y	42.81Y	54.51Y	67.29Y	87.17Y	.98Y	1.04Y	1.27Y	1.67Y	2.28Y	2.86Y	3.46Y
Jordan	439	40.35V	39.06V	42.56V	56.63V	67.87V	72.71V	95.16V	47.41V	58.74V	55.60V	65.49V	74.78V	82.60V	107.35V
Kuwait	443	26.19Y	27.09Y	30.11Y	39.16Y	49.86Y	61.55Y	79.74Y	17.34Y	18.44Y	22.35Y	29.58Y	40.23Y	50.58Y	61.02Y
Libya	672	6.06Y	6.27Y	6.97Y	9.07Y	11.55Y	14.25Y	18.46Y	10.49Y	11.15Y	13.52Y	17.89Y	24.34Y	30.59Y	36.91Y
Oman	449	3.98V	15.16V	4.86V	6.32Y	8.05Y	9.94Y	12.87Y	5.19V	2.80V	4.28V	5.66Y	7.70Y	9.68Y	11.68Y
Qatar	453	8.54V	9.05V	12.20V	21.41V	37.70V	71.62V	92.78Y	8.68V	13.67V	4.54V	21.13V	3.36V	5.97V	7.21Y
Saudi Arabia	456	114.12V	79.23V	90.72V	101.52V	117.27V	144.77V	187.54Y	177.99Y	189.26Y	229.45Y	303.61Y	413.00Y	519.22Y	626.37Y
Syrian Arab Republic	463	28.45Y	30.88Y	39.08Y	480.56V	549.07Y	678.61Y	842.15Y	312.72Y	339.39Y	429.55Y	903.44V	1,032.25Y	1,275.79Y	1,583.24Y
United Arab Emirates	466	103.64V	106.64V	149.00V	193.78Y	246.74Y	304.60Y	394.59Y	51.57Y	54.83Y	66.47Y	87.96Y	119.65Y	150.42Y	181.46Y
Yemen, Republic of	474	5.60V	3.41V	4.32Y	5.74V	8.93V	11.03Y	13.69Y	.38V	.42V	.53Y	.20V	.81V	1.00Y	1.24Y
Western Hemisphere	**207**	**4.0Y**	**7.7Y**	**9.0Y**	**13.6Y**	**7.5Y**	**10.3Y**	**21.1Y**	**77.5Y**	**99.9Y**	**109.0Y**	**158.3Y**	**191.7Y**	**247.3Y**	**322.7Y**
Antigua and Barbuda	311	.01Y	.01Y	.02Y	.02Y	.02Y	.03Y	.03Y	—Y	—Y	—Y	—Y	—Y	—Y	—Y
Argentina	213	.13V	—V	.08V	.14V	.11V	.18V	.27V	18.32V	35.84V	34.19V	36.70V	30.65V	30.27V	50.54V
Aruba	314	.07V	.02V	.03V	.02V	.04V	.03V	.02V	—V	—V	—V	—V	—V	—V	.03V

	Exports							Imports						
	2001	2002	2003	2004	2005	2006	2007	2001	2002	2003	2004	2005	2006	2007
	Millions of U.S. Dollars							*Millions of U.S. Dollars*						
Bahamas, The..........313	—Y	—Y	—Y	—Y	—Y	—Y	—Y	.04Y	.05Y	.06Y	.08Y	.09Y	.11Y	.14Y
Barbados..........316	.06V	.03V	.06V	1.46V	.03V	.01V	.01Y	—V	—V	—V	—V	.01V	—V	—Y
Belize..........339	—Y	—Y	—Y	—Y	—Y	—Y	—Y	.04Y	.05Y	.06Y	.08Y	.09Y	.11Y	.14Y
Bermuda..........319	.07Y	.07Y	.09Y	.12Y	—V	—V	—Y	—Y	—Y	—Y	—Y	—Y	—Y	—Y
Bolivia..........218	—V	—V	—V	—V	—V	—Y	—Y	.12V	—V	.05V	.08V	.09Y	.12Y	.14Y
Brazil..........223	1.47V	5.18V	6.86V	10.20V	5.50V	7.29V	14.88V	50.68V	50.81V	60.28V	98.62V	136.46V	195.95V	248.61V
Chile..........228	.15V	.09V	.27V	.13V	.18V	.15V	.06V	1.32V	1.32V	1.02V	1.14V	1.28V	1.05V	2.26V
Colombia..........233	.38V	.44V	.25V	.10V	.06V	.06V	.23V	.98V	4.73V	.91V	1.56V	2.07V	1.62V	2.82V
Costa Rica..........238	.01V	.10V	.01V	—V	.02V	.03Y	.04Y	.15V	.04V	.08V	.27V	.21V	.26Y	.33Y
Dominican Republic..........243	.04V	.05Y	.06Y	.08Y	.09Y	.11Y	.13Y	.02V	.02Y	.02Y	.03Y	.04Y	.04Y	.06Y
Ecuador..........248	—V	—V	.01V	.04V	.15V	.40V	.50Y	.13V	.18V	.16V	.08V	.06V	.19V	.23Y
El Salvador..........253	—V	—V	.02V	—V	.01V	—V	—V	—V	—V	—V	.01V	—V	—V	—V
Guatemala..........258	—V	—V	.01V	.01V	.01V	.01Y	.02Y	.87V	1.15V	.61V	.83V	.37V	.46Y	.57Y
Guyana..........336	.01Y	.01Y	.02Y	.02Y	.02Y	.03Y	.03Y	—Y	—Y	—Y	—Y	—Y	—Y	—Y
Haiti..........263	.01V	.01V	.02V	.05V	.06Y	.07Y	.09Y	.10Y	.11Y	.14Y	.18Y	.20Y	.25Y	.31Y
Honduras..........268	—V	.03V	.46V	.02V	.03Y	.03Y	.04Y	—V	—V	.02V	.07V	.08Y	.09Y	.12Y
Jamaica..........343	.01V	.11V	.02V	.06V	.06V	.01V	.01V	.05V	—V	—V	—V	—V	—V	—V
Mexico..........273	.21V	.19V	.16V	.28V	.20V	.48V	1.95V	3.17V	3.72V	6.25V	5.66V	4.15V	6.85V	4.99V
Netherlands Antilles..........353	.06V	.20V	.04V	.06Y	.07Y	.08Y	.10Y	—V	.08V	—V	—Y	—Y	—Y	—Y
Panama..........283	.02V	.02V	—V	.01V	.07V	.01V	.03V	—V	—V	—V	—V	—V	—V	—V
Paraguay..........288	.11V	.13V	.08V	.02V	.08V	.05V	.07Y	.03V	.11V	3.16V	10.84V	13.95V	6.91V	8.58Y
Peru..........293	—V	—V	.01V	—V	.06V	—V	—Y	1.29V	1.18V	1.54V	1.23V	.80V	1.61V	1.11Y
St. Kitts and Nevis..........361	.10Y	.11Y	.14Y	.18Y	.20Y	.25Y	.31Y	.02Y	.02Y	.03Y	.04Y	.05Y	.06Y	.07Y
Suriname..........366	—Y	—Y	—Y	—Y	—Y	—Y	—Y	.01Y	.01Y	.02Y	.02Y	.02Y	.03Y	.03Y
Trinidad and Tobago..........369	—V	—V	—Y	.01Y	.01Y	.01Y	.01Y	.01V	—V	.01Y	.01Y	.01Y	.01Y	.01Y
Uruguay..........298	.66V	.71Y	.01V	.24V	.01V	.02Y	.02Y	.01V	.01Y	.32V	.68V	.97V	1.20Y	1.49Y
Venezuela, Rep. Bol..........299	.40V	.20V	.34V	.36V	.38V	.96V	2.27V	.06V	.42V	.01V	.07V	.04V	.08V	.10Y
Western Hem. n.s..........399	—Y	—Y	—Y	—Y	—Y	—Y	—Y	.03Y	.03Y	.03Y	.03Y	.03Y	.03Y	.03Y
Other Countries n.i.e..........910	**4.0Y**	**4.3Y**	**5.4Y**	**7.1Y**	**8.2Y**	**10.1Y**	**12.5Y**	**28.2Y**	**30.6Y**	**38.7Y**	**50.8Y**	**58.1Y**	**71.8Y**	**89.1Y**
Cuba..........928	—Y	—Y	—Y	—Y	—Y	—Y	—Y	.20Y	.22Y	.27Y	.36Y	.41Y	.51Y	.63Y
North Korea..........954	3.96Y	4.30Y	5.44Y	7.15Y	8.17Y	10.10Y	12.53Y	27.99Y	30.37Y	38.44Y	50.49Y	57.69Y	71.30Y	88.48Y
Countries & Areas n.s..........898	**.2Y**	**.2Y**	**.2Y**	**.3Y**	**.4Y**	**.4Y**	**.6Y**	**80.6Y**	**87.5Y**	**110.8Y**	**145.5Y**	**166.2Y**	**205.4Y**	**254.9Y**
Special Categories..........899	**6.2Y**	**6.7Y**	**8.5Y**	**11.1Y**	**12.7Y**	**15.7Y**	**19.5Y**	**10.3Y**	**11.1Y**	**14.1Y**	**18.5Y**	**21.2Y**	**26.2Y**	**32.5Y**
Memorandum Items														
European Union..........998	268.35Y	176.64Y	210.39Y	283.68Y	244.12Y	253.46Y	378.06Y	3,143.22Y	3,192.65Y	4,227.77Y	4,437.40Y	4,115.43Y	4,188.22Y	4,761.46Y
Oil Exporting Ctys..........999	330.85Y	385.67Y	422.63Y	502.34Y	637.64Y	812.64Y	1,053.36Y	355.81Y	368.96Y	426.42Y	569.63Y	732.65Y	914.14Y	1,121.47Y
Non-Oil Develop.Ctys..........201	226.79Y	280.69Y	303.65Y	901.61Y	1,004.29Y	1,194.25Y	1,475.34Y	2,071.52Y	1,944.56Y	2,207.07Y	3,237.36Y	3,605.32Y	4,036.80Y	5,200.41Y
PERCENT DISTRIBUTION														
Industrial Countries..........101	44.5	33.4	38.0	26.2	23.8	20.1	23.4	60.1	61.3	63.7	57.1	52.4	51.9	48.6
Developing Countries..........202	54.5	65.5	60.8	72.9	75.2	78.9	75.7	38.1	36.6	34.2	40.6	45.0	45.4	48.5
Africa..........607	6.9	13.2	7.8	6.5	7.3	7.4	7.3	.9	1.0	1.0	1.0	1.4	1.1	1.2
Asia..........507	3.2	6.1	4.8	3.0	2.7	3.4	3.5	12.4	11.3	10.7	10.9	10.5	10.0	11.5
Europe..........170	4.1	5.5	7.0	8.2	7.0	5.8	4.4	11.4	9.4	7.8	9.0	10.3	9.1	9.7
Middle East..........407	39.9	39.9	40.5	54.5	57.9	61.9	59.8	12.2	13.4	13.2	18.0	21.0	22.9	23.6
Western Hemisphere..........207	.4	.8	.8	.7	.3	.4	.6	1.2	1.6	1.4	1.7	2.0	2.3	2.5
Other Countries n.i.e..........910	.4	.4	.5	.4	.4	.4	.4	.4	.5	.5	.5	.6	.7	.7
ANNUAL PERCENT CHANGE														
World..........001	43.3	–.5	17.3	61.4	13.3	16.5	31.4	2.4	–1.0	22.1	21.7	2.7	13.3	19.4
Industrial Countries..........101	62.7	–25.3	33.2	11.2	3.1	–1.9	52.9	–2.6	1.0	26.8	9.2	–5.8	12.2	11.9
Developing Countries..........202	31.3	19.5	9.0	93.3	17.0	22.2	26.0	11.0	–4.7	13.8	44.6	13.9	14.1	27.7
Africa..........607	48.8	88.6	–30.5	33.6	27.3	19.1	29.4	–27.5	14.3	19.6	27.2	34.6	–9.2	36.5
Asia..........507	9.2	92.9	–8.2	.3	2.5	46.2	36.6	23.2	–9.6	15.1	23.9	–1.3	7.9	37.8
Europe..........170	49.2	34.4	48.2	90.9	–3.0	–4.2	–.4	18.2	–18.8	2.3	39.1	17.7	.7	26.4
Middle East..........407	29.5	–.6	19.1	117.0	20.3	24.6	27.0	5.1	8.8	21.0	65.6	19.5	23.9	23.1
Western Hemisphere..........207	–2.5	94.6	17.2	50.4	–45.1	37.9	105.2	–33.0	28.9	9.1	45.3	21.1	29.0	30.5
Other Countries n.i.e..........910	10.4	8.5	26.6	31.3	14.3	23.6	24.1	10.4	8.5	26.6	31.3	14.3	23.6	24.1

	Exports							Imports						
	2001	2002	2003	2004	2005	2006	2007	2001	2002	2003	2004	2005	2006	2007
	Millions of U.S. Dollars							*Millions of U.S. Dollars*						
DOTS World Total.................... 001	**968.2Y**	**1,072.4Y**	**922.0Y**	**951.1Y**	**987.5Y**	**1,563.3Y**	**1,023.4Y**	**4,404.5Y**	**5,034.5Y**	**4,284.5Y**	**4,863.0Y**	**5,751.5Y**	**7,582.1Y**	**8,803.2Y**
Industrial Countries................ 101	**691.5Y**	**879.8Y**	**697.8Y**	**656.5Y**	**755.5Y**	**1,016.4Y**	**453.2Y**	**2,379.6Y**	**2,494.0Y**	**1,648.1Y**	**1,585.2Y**	**1,824.0Y**	**1,669.0Y**	**2,259.8Y**
United States.............................. 111	40.64V	43.18V	56.36V	81.27V	88.27V	131.18V	107.55V	40.48V	30.58V	36.63V	66.55V	82.50V	74.69V	83.38V
Canada....................................... 156	1.09V	1.20V	2.54V	6.66V	11.09V	17.26V	18.45V	1.50V	1.15V	.79V	2.19V	3.90V	4.87V	8.73V
Australia..................................... 193	—V	—V	.03V	—V	—V	.98V	.06V	.29V	.07V	.31V	4.57V	3.86V	.58V	2.18V
Japan.. 158	.11V	.05V	.02V	.07V	.23V	9.61V	.13V	670.48V	987.07V	694.98V	1,026.62V	1,214.67V	914.34V	1,313.05V
New Zealand................................ 196	—V	—V	—V	.02V	.04V	—V	.06V	—V	—V	.02V	.35V	.68V	.90V	.35V
Austria....................................... 122	1.03V	—V	.04V	.05V	—V	—V	—V	.73V	.23V	.44V	2.21V	2.50V	1.74V	3.49V
Belgium...................................... 124	2.70V	.78V	1.69V	.21V	402.59V	22.48V	28.19V	9.54V	4.78V	12.10V	13.05V	10.96V	11.28V	13.07V
Cyprus.. 423	—V	.05V	—V	—V	—Y	—V	—V	.05V	—V	—V	—V	.11V	.04V	.12V
Denmark..................................... 128	.02V	57.05V	7.87V	268.73V	.01V	—V	.01V	5.39V	5.07V	80.17V	9.86V	12.13V	147.88V	5.37V
Finland.. 172	—V	—V	—V	—V	—V	.03V	—V	.36V	.04V	.30V	.38V	.19V	1.14V	1.11V
France.. 132	39.99V	88.65V	48.66V	11.16V	14.46V	17.61V	14.82V	1,166.27V	469.38V	24.73V	66.84V	35.93V	14.48V	22.11V
Germany..................................... 134	390.05V	569.37V	405.69V	172.19V	42.72V	621.27V	117.31V	238.48V	809.02V	423.56V	205.45V	72.82V	118.28V	295.97V
Greece.. 174	93.22V	30.57V	84.86V	73.02V	.98V	8.31V	.70V	26.72V	13.34V	6.74V	12.05V	11.96V	27.38V	29.89V
Iceland.. 176	—V	.01V	—V	—V	5.74V	4.46V	—V	—V	—V	—V	—V	—V	.04V	—V
Ireland.. 178	—V	.10V	—V	1.66V	7.21V	5.09V	—V	.63V	.08V	1.73V	6.43V	11.99V	4.53V	1.60V
Italy.. 136	54.19V	46.81V	36.75V	6.36V	19.09V	11.81V	3.43V	64.22V	73.01V	36.99V	45.85V	70.18V	79.37V	122.88V
Luxembourg................................ 137	—V	—V	—V	—V	—V	—V	—V	.29V	.25V	.20V	.03V	.02V	.02V	.02V
Malta.. 181	—Y	—V	—V	—V	—V	.03V	—V	.02V	—V	.03V	.17V	.32V	.28V	.56V
Netherlands................................ 138	3.39V	1.76V	2.48V	6.12V	6.66V	.81V	.47V	13.61V	9.57V	13.56V	34.98V	30.31V	31.58V	53.46V
Norway....................................... 142	38.09V	26.00V	6.60V	23.70V	.04V	17.24V	55.86V	101.19V	64.25V	121.35V	30.59V	73.56V	4.91V	206.10V
Portugal..................................... 182	1.59V	.55V	.76V	.14V	.05V	.22V	.03V	.91V	.40V	.52V	3.60V	.58V	.72V	.25V
Slovenia..................................... 961	.03V	.80V	2.27V	2.98Y	1.05V	3.26V	5.33V	.25V	.20V	.31V	.41Y	.10V	.27V	.04V
Spain.. 184	9.44V	8.16V	18.99V	.20V	150.20V	127.10V	83.74V	10.02V	3.83V	173.62V	20.11V	137.01V	179.68V	33.00V
Sweden....................................... 144	.01V	—V	.02V	.01V	.04V	.01V	.03V	.88V	.24V	1.58V	3.90V	12.13V	11.11V	20.61V
Switzerland................................. 146	.20V	.43V	.41V	.88V	.45V	1.05V	.56V	10.79V	10.96V	8.46V	11.67V	12.97V	14.92V	11.64V
United Kingdom.......................... 112	15.68V	4.25V	21.75V	1.03V	4.61V	16.55V	16.51V	16.49V	10.44V	8.99V	17.36V	22.60V	24.01V	30.78V
Developing Countries............. 202	**276.7Y**	**192.6Y**	**224.2Y**	**294.6Y**	**232.0Y**	**546.9Y**	**570.2Y**	**2,024.9Y**	**2,540.5Y**	**2,636.4Y**	**3,277.8Y**	**3,927.5Y**	**5,913.1Y**	**6,543.5Y**
Africa....................................... 607	**9.9Y**	**11.2Y**	**13.6Y**	**14.7Y**	**14.5Y**	**202.9Y**	**25.3Y**	**57.0Y**	**52.8Y**	**61.7Y**	**93.3Y**	**141.7Y**	**181.5Y**	**220.4Y**
Algeria.. 612	.54V	.28V	.31Y	.40Y	.51Y	.63Y	.81Y	.01V	.01V	.02Y	.02Y	.03Y	.03Y	.04Y
Benin.. 638	.10V	.03V	.02V	2.40V	—V	—Y	—Y	—V	—V	.01V	.02V	—V	—Y	—Y
Burkina Faso............................... 748	—Y	—Y	—Y	.01Y	.01Y	.01Y	.01Y	—Y	—Y	—Y	—Y	—Y	—Y	—Y
Cameroon................................... 622	—V	—V	—V	—Y	—Y	—Y	—Y	—V	—V	3.07V	4.03Y	4.60Y	5.69Y	7.06Y
Congo, Republic of...................... 634	—V	—V	—V	.01V	.01Y	.01Y	.02Y	.01V	—V	.02V	—V	—Y	—Y	—Y
Côte d'Ivoire............................... 662	1.84V	2.72V	1.33V	4.99V	5.66V	6.79V	8.43Y	34.03V	27.54V	20.64V	47.01V	86.29V	106.63V	132.33Y
Gambia, The................................ 648	.17Y	.18Y	.23Y	.30Y	.35Y	.43Y	.53Y	—Y	—Y	—Y	—Y	—Y	—Y	—Y
Ghana... 652	.49Y	.53Y	.67Y	.88Y	1.00Y	1.24Y	1.54Y	.09Y	.09Y	.12Y	.16Y	.18Y	.22Y	.28Y
Guinea.. 656	—V	.01Y	1.64V	.05V	.06Y	.08Y	.09Y	2.10V	2.28Y	.30V	.80V	.91Y	1.12Y	1.39Y
Kenya.. 664	—V	—V	—V	—V	—Y	—Y	—Y	.01V	.08V	.46V	1.00V	1.15Y	1.42Y	1.76Y
Madagascar................................ 674	.04V	—V	.33V	.43Y	.49Y	.60Y	.75Y	—V	—V	.15V	.19Y	.22Y	.27Y	.34Y
Mauritania................................... 682	—Y	—Y	—Y	—Y	—Y	—Y	—Y	13.09Y	14.21Y	17.98Y	23.62Y	26.98Y	33.35Y	41.39Y
Mauritius.................................... 684	—V	—V	.58V	—V	—V	—V	—V	—V	.01V	—V	—V	—V	—V	.02V
Morocco...................................... 686	1.34V	1.50V	1.10V	.49V	1.73V	2.14Y	2.66Y	3.14V	3.02V	4.28V	3.93V	5.69V	7.03Y	8.73Y
Niger... 692	—V	.01V	—V	.05V	.05Y	.07Y	.08Y	—V	—V	—V	—V	—Y	—Y	—Y
Nigeria.. 694	.04V	.48V	.70V	.92Y	1.17Y	1.44Y	1.86Y	—V	—V	—V	—Y	—Y	—Y	—Y
Senegal....................................... 722	2.76V	2.78V	3.19V	—V	—V	.02V	.02Y	2.38V	2.78V	8.58V	4.65V	7.90V	4.31V	5.35Y
Sierra Leone................................ 724	1.31Y	1.42Y	1.80Y	2.36Y	2.70Y	3.34Y	4.14Y	—Y	—Y	—Y	—Y	—Y	—Y	—Y
South Africa................................ 199	.60V	.79V	.83V	1.35V	.71V	186.00V	4.19V	1.48V	1.87V	4.29V	5.68V	6.98V	19.41V	20.73V
Sudan.. 732	....	....	....	....	....	....	....	—Y	—Y	—V	—V	—V	1.15V	—V
Togo.. 742	.15V	.16V	.09V	.10V	.09V	.12Y	.14Y	.37V	.07V	.15V	.70V	.41V	.51Y	.63Y
Tunisia.. 744	.47V	.33V	.80V	—V	—V	—V	—Y	.04V	.07V	1.62V	1.54V	.37V	.29V	.36Y
Uganda....................................... 746	.01V	—V	—V	—Y	—Y	—Y	—Y	.23V	.82V	—V	—Y	—Y	—Y	—Y
Zambia.. 754	—V	—V	—V	—V	—V	—V	.01V	—V	—V	—V	—V	.01V	—V	—V
Zimbabwe................................... 698	—V	—V	—V	—V	—V	—V	—Y	—V	.01V	—V	—V	—V	.02V	.03Y
Asia.. 507	**166.2Y**	**74.3Y**	**93.6Y**	**98.4Y**	**138.5Y**	**144.7Y**	**337.9Y**	**1,611.8Y**	**2,039.0Y**	**2,270.5Y**	**2,672.5Y**	**3,223.8Y**	**5,243.6Y**	**5,696.7Y**
Bangladesh.................................. 513	4.20V	—V	—V	—V	—V	—V	—V	—V	.13V	.06V	.16V	.03V	.04Y	.05Y
China,P.R.: Mainland.................. 924	26.17V	50.53V	38.14V	11.31V	12.78V	1.75V	3.31Y	124.03V	33.12V	28.82V	151.24V	164.60V	582.80V	886.29V
China,P.R.:Hong Kong................. 532	.29V	2.27V	.09V	.05V	.39V	.31V	.83V	6.76V	5.41V	6.45V	10.26V	8.52V	6.39V	7.91V
Fiji.. 819	—Y	—Y	—Y	—Y	—Y	—Y	.01Y	—Y	—Y	—Y	—Y	—Y	—Y	—Y
India... 534	7.90Y	11.31V	3.25V	5.01V	15.90V	19.66Y	24.39Y	14.03Y	8.47V	14.53V	18.74V	24.70V	30.52Y	37.88Y
Indonesia.................................... 536	116.17V	4.15V	.05V	1.79V	—V	11.19V	23.54V	1.37V	1.74V	2.95V	4.48V	5.66V	4.31V	11.05V
Korea.. 542	8.34V	1.06V	4.85V	23.97V	6.92V	48.86V	.55V	1,085.72V	1,569.31V	1,678.23V	1,878.86V	2,185.77V	3,527.58V	2,762.13V
Malaysia..................................... 548	1.34V	.07V	1.03V	4.93V	53.73V	10.52V	281.14V	.58V	1.74V	3.95V	7.05V	9.31V	8.50V	13.52V
New Caledonia............................ 839	.04V	.01V	.02V	.01V	.01Y	.02Y	.02Y	—V	—V	—V	—V	—Y	—Y	—Y
Pakistan...................................... 564	.01V	4.37V	.04V	—V	1.28V	1.58Y	1.96Y	.23V	.56V	1.63V	5.90V	2.08V	2.57Y	3.19Y
Papua New Guinea...................... 853	—Y	—Y	.01Y	.01Y	.01Y	.01Y	.01Y	—Y	—Y	—Y	—Y	—Y	—Y	—Y
Philippines.................................. 566	—V	.01V	.03V	—V	.01V	.10V	—V	.26V	.06V	.24V	.01V	.42V	.11V	4.57V
Singapore.................................... 576	.36V	.01V	.09V	.21V	2.16V	.12V	2.10V	366.11V	409.24V	530.87V	592.77V	816.81V	1,074.23V	1,947.56V
Taiwan Province of China............ 528	.02V	.06V	—V	.01V	.05V	.04V	.05V	9.38V	7.64V	1.01V	1.00V	2.73V	.98V	16.90V
Thailand...................................... 578	1.23V	.08V	45.91V	46.05V	44.98V	46.86V	.02V	2.27V	.97V	1.54V	2.04V	3.14V	5.61V	5.63V
Vietnam...................................... 582	.11V	.41V	.06V	5.09V	.27V	3.64V	—V	1.08V	.60V	.25V	—V	—V	—V	—V

	Exports							Imports						
	2001	2002	2003	2004	2005	2006	2007	2001	2002	2003	2004	2005	2006	2007
	Millions of U.S. Dollars							Millions of U.S. Dollars						
Europe....170	**98.2Y**	**106.5Y**	**109.5Y**	**170.8Y**	**77.7Y**	**196.1Y**	**204.6Y**	**334.4Y**	**428.8Y**	**255.1Y**	**428.8Y**	**495.2Y**	**407.2Y**	**529.3Y**
Belarus....913	—V	—V	—V	.46V	.57V	.07V	—V	.03V	—V	—V	—V	—V	.08V	—V
Bulgaria....918	.01V	.02V	.67V	2.73V	6.47V	.02V	.04V	.20V	.30V	.57V	1.99V	9.43V	2.19V	1.48V
Croatia....960	4.11V	.01V	.03V	.13V	.05V	4.57V	.07V	126.60V	198.52V	110.38V	255.63V	268.77V	118.39V	9.60V
Czech Republic....935	.13V	.09V	.68V	8.93V	11.79V	4.63V	2.56V	.20V	.40V	.08V	1.76V	.46V	.53V	1.11V
Estonia....939	—V	—V	—V	—V	—V	—V	—V	5.03V	8.88V	9.76V	.75V	1.60V	20.15V	.09V
Georgia....915	—V	—V	—V	—V	—V	—V	—Y	—V	—V	—V	.02V	.01V	.01V	—Y
Hungary....944	.01V	.02V	.08V	—V	—V	.03V	.09V	.54V	.63V	.12V	.05V	.12V	1.57V	1.30V
Kazakhstan....916	—V	—V	—V	.04V	.04Y	.05Y	.06Y	—V	—V	—V	—V	—Y	—Y	—Y
Latvia....941	—V	—V	.13V	.07V	—V	—V	.01V	.35V	.73V	.52V	.88V	3.02V	4.88V	5.20V
Lithuania....946	.12V	15.48V	.02V	4.90V	2.16V	1.38V	—V	.49V	1.22V	.14V	7.34V	12.17V	.08V	7.13V
Macedonia, FYR....962	—V	—V	—V	—V	—V	—V	—Y	—V	—V	—V	—V	.01V	—V	—Y
Moldova....921	—V	—V	—V	—V	—V	—Y	—Y	.01V	.09V	—V	.24V	—V	—Y	—Y
Poland....964	85.67V	72.87V	102.49V	130.27V	44.81V	181.04V	189.56V	174.57V	70.09V	65.54V	73.17V	77.02V	117.94V	232.66V
Romania....968	.14V	.10V	—V	.14V	—V	—V	—V	1.01V	.32V	.26V	3.69V	29.15V	58.29V	104.56V
Russia....922	.04V	.01V	—V	.63V	.36V	.57V	9.35V	11.26V	141.68V	44.10V	30.46V	39.41V	70.49V	53.23V
Slovak Republic....936	.04V	—V	—Y	—Y	—V	—V	—V	.38V	.04V	.05Y	.06Y	.10V	.10V	.02V
Turkey....186	6.75V	17.32V	5.39V	22.24V	10.14V	2.16V	.89V	9.81V	2.38V	21.86V	51.44V	52.36V	10.49V	110.44V
Ukraine....926	1.18V	.56V	.04V	.23V	1.30V	1.61Y	2.00Y	3.90V	3.51V	1.75V	1.35V	1.59V	1.97Y	2.45Y
Middle East....407	**.2Y**	**.2Y**	**.3Y**	**.2Y**	**.3Y**	**.3Y**	**.4Y**	**3.8Y**	**3.8Y**	**5.2Y**	**9.1Y**	**9.8Y**	**13.0Y**	**15.3Y**
Egypt....469	—V	—Y	—Y	—Y	—Y	—Y	—Y	.11V	.12Y	.15Y	.20Y	.23Y	.29Y	.35Y
Israel....436	—V	—V	—V	—V	—V	—V	—V	—V	—V	—V	2.09V	1.76V	2.97V	2.75V
Jordan....439	—V	.04V	.02V	—V	—V	—V	—V	—V	.01V	.01V	.07V	.03V	.03V	.17V
Kuwait....443	.01Y	.01Y	.01Y	.01Y	.02Y	.02Y	.03Y	—Y	—Y	—Y	—Y	—Y	—Y	—Y
Lebanon....446	.09Y	.10Y	.12Y	.16Y	.19Y	.23Y	.29Y	3.19Y	3.47Y	4.39Y	5.76Y	6.58Y	8.14Y	10.10Y
Oman....449	—V	—V	.03V	.04V	.06Y	.07Y	.09Y	.51V	.19V	.66V	.88Y	1.20Y	1.50Y	1.81Y
Saudi Arabia....456	.02V	.01V	.07V	.01V	.01V	.01Y	.01Y	—Y	—Y	—Y	—Y	—Y	—Y	—Y
Yemen, Republic of....474	.09V	—V	—Y	—V	—V	—Y	—Y	—V	—V	—Y	.09V	.04V	.05Y	.06Y
Western Hemisphere....207	**2.3Y**	**.4Y**	**7.3Y**	**10.4Y**	**1.0Y**	**2.9Y**	**1.9Y**	**17.9Y**	**16.1Y**	**43.8Y**	**74.0Y**	**57.0Y**	**67.8Y**	**81.8Y**
Argentina....213	—V	—V	—V	.02V	.06V	—V	.08V	.06V	.48V	6.07V	3.91V	3.41V	3.83V	15.17V
Aruba....314	—V	—V	.57V	.10V	—V	.40V	.02V	—V	—V	.03V	.10V	—V	—V	.17V
Bahamas, The....313	.01Y	.02Y	.02Y	.03Y	.03Y	.04Y	.04Y	—Y	—Y	—Y	—Y	—Y	—Y	—Y
Barbados....316	—V	—V	.01V	—V	—V	—V	—Y	.04V	—V	—V	—V	—V	.03V	.04Y
Brazil....223	.02V	.09V	—V	.11V	.11V	.12V	—V	2.17V	1.61V	2.49V	30.81V	9.66V	12.57V	—V
Chile....228	—V	—V	—V	.01V	—V	—V	—V	1.47V	2.09V	1.74V	1.31V	.04V	—V	.02V
Colombia....233	.04V	.01V	—V	.01V	.01V	—V	.85V	.80V	.54V	4.48V	.62V	.70V	.19V	.68V
Ecuador....248	.03V	—V	—V	—V	—V	—V	—Y	—V	—V	.04V	—V	.30V	.03V	.03Y
Honduras....268	2.02V	.01V	—V	.03V	.03Y	.04Y	.05Y	—V	—V	—V	—V	—Y	—Y	—Y
Jamaica....343	—V	—V	—V	—V	—V	—V	.01V	—V	—V	—V	—V	—V	—V	—V
Mexico....273	.07V	.11V	—V	—V	.44V	2.16V	.75V	.97V	2.35V	2.54V	1.66V	2.39V	1.04V	3.52V
Netherlands Antilles....353	—V	—V	—V	—Y	—Y	—Y	—Y	1.18V	—V	14.69V	19.29Y	22.04Y	27.25Y	33.81Y
Paraguay....288	—V	—V	—V	—V	—V	—V	—Y	—V	—V	—V	—V	.39V	.25V	.31Y
Peru....293	.01V	.18V	—V	—V	—V	—V	—Y	.04V	—V	.09V	.44V	.52V	.97V	1.23Y
Suriname....366	.04Y	.04Y	.05Y	.07Y	.08Y	.09Y	.12Y	8.34Y	9.05Y	11.46Y	15.05Y	17.19Y	21.25Y	26.37Y
Trinidad and Tobago....369	.03V	—V	—Y	—Y	—Y	—Y	—Y	2.83V	—V	—Y	—Y	—Y	—Y	—Y
Uruguay....298	—V	—Y	—V	—V	—V	—Y	—Y	—V	—Y	.22V	.80V	.33V	.41Y	.51Y
Venezuela, Rep. Bol....299	.07V	—V	6.62V	10.08V	.21V	—V	—V	—V	—V	—V	—V	—V	—V	—Y
Memorandum Items														
European Union....998	697.31Y	897.37Y	735.22Y	688.03Y	708.40Y	1,021.66Y	462.79Y	1,736.43Y	1,481.87Y	861.80Y	526.70Y	526.32Y	799.04Y	881.85Y
Oil Exporting Ctys....999	116.84Y	4.92Y	7.80Y	13.25Y	1.97Y	13.36Y	26.35Y	1.89Y	1.94Y	3.63Y	5.37Y	6.88Y	5.85Y	12.90Y
Non-Oil Develop.Ctys....201	159.90Y	187.72Y	216.45Y	281.38Y	230.01Y	533.56Y	543.85Y	2,023.03Y	2,538.60Y	2,632.75Y	3,272.38Y	3,920.64Y	5,907.23Y	6,530.56Y
PERCENT DISTRIBUTION														
Industrial Countries....101	71.4	82.0	75.7	69.0	76.5	65.0	44.3	54.0	49.5	38.5	32.6	31.7	22.0	25.7
Developing Countries....202	28.6	18.0	24.3	31.0	23.5	35.0	55.7	46.0	50.5	61.5	67.4	68.3	78.0	74.3
Africa....607	1.0	1.0	1.5	1.5	1.5	13.0	2.5	1.3	1.0	1.4	1.9	2.5	2.4	2.5
Asia....507	17.2	6.9	10.1	10.4	14.0	9.3	33.0	36.6	40.5	53.0	55.0	56.1	69.2	64.7
Europe....170	10.1	9.9	11.9	18.0	7.9	12.5	20.0	7.6	8.5	6.0	8.8	8.6	5.4	6.0
Middle East....407	—	—	—	—	—	—	—	.1	.1	.1	.2	.2	.2	.2
Western Hemisphere....207	.2	—	.8	1.1	.1	.2	.2	.4	.3	1.0	1.5	1.0	.9	.9
ANNUAL PERCENT CHANGE														
World....001	66.4	10.8	-14.0	3.2	3.8	58.3	-34.5	-19.8	14.3	-14.9	13.5	18.3	31.8	16.1
Industrial Countries....101	54.2	27.2	-20.7	-5.9	15.1	34.5	-55.4	-22.4	4.8	-33.9	-3.8	15.1	-8.5	35.4
Developing Countries....202	107.8	-30.4	16.4	31.4	-21.3	135.8	4.3	-16.6	25.5	3.8	24.3	19.8	50.6	10.7
Africa....607	22.6	13.8	21.4	8.3	-1.3	—	-87.5	-64.8	-7.3	16.7	51.3	51.8	28.0	21.5
Asia....507	99.6	-55.3	25.9	5.2	40.7	4.5	133.6	-13.9	26.5	11.4	17.7	20.6	62.7	8.6
Europe....170	331.2	8.5	2.8	55.9	-54.5	152.5	4.3	-.1	28.2	-40.5	68.1	15.5	-17.8	30.0
Middle East....407	-94.9	-27.2	72.8	-14.9	17.2	23.6	25.7	5.9	-1.0	37.8	74.4	8.2	31.9	17.5
Western Hemisphere....207	-84.5	-81.1	—	43.7	-90.6	192.7	-32.4	-66.9	-10.0	172.0	68.8	-23.0	19.0	20.7

Libya 672

		Exports							Imports						
		2001	2002	2003	2004	2005	2006	2007	2001	2002	2003	2004	2005	2006	2007
		Millions of U.S. Dollars							Millions of U.S. Dollars						
IFS World Total		**11,014**	**9,803**	**14,647**	**20,410**	**30,948**	**39,200**	**45,000**	**4,397**	**4,396**	**4,330**	**6,326**	**6,079**	**6,950**	**8,600**
DOTS World Total	**001**	**11,337Y**	**9,883Y**	**13,761Y**	**19,361Y**	**29,013Y**	**39,684Y**	**43,275Y**	**4,423Y**	**5,515Y**	**6,103Y**	**8,164Y**	**8,757Y**	**10,281Y**	**13,091Y**
Industrial Countries	**101**	**9,713Y**	**8,509Y**	**11,742Y**	**16,388Y**	**24,735Y**	**33,396Y**	**38,538Y**	**3,160Y**	**3,915Y**	**4,317Y**	**5,332Y**	**5,322Y**	**5,968Y**	**7,458Y**
United States	111	—V	—V	—V	314V	1,506V	2,390V	3,218V	10V	20V	—V	43V	92V	479V	561V
Canada	156	—V	—V	6V	70V	77V	58V	—V	13V	32V	29V	83V	77V	65V	210V
Australia	193	—V	—V	—V	—V	33V	—V	—V	23V	54V	7V	11V	13V	9V	16V
Japan	158	4V	6V	5V	7V	9V	19V	4V	79V	344V	219V	198V	152V	209V	279V
New Zealand	196	—V	—V	—V	—V	24V	—V	4V	1V	—V	2V	3V	2V	6V	6V
Austria	122	225V	125V	178V	259V	126V	538V	878V	51V	63V	54V	98V	85V	83V	109V
Belgium	124	25V	54V	53V	75V	53V	110V	170V	123V	143V	110V	169V	165V	237V	184V
Cyprus	423	1V	1V	1V	—V	2Y	4V	10V	5V	3V	4V	6V	7V	8V	6V
Denmark	128	—V	7V	—V	—V	—V	1V	—V	15V	18V	33V	48V	42V	8V	50V
Finland	172	—V	—V	—V	—V	—V	—V	—V	5V	11V	10V	10V	19V	22V	21V
France	132	616V	357V	837V	1,207V	1,802V	2,191V	2,732V	261V	309V	357V	307V	411V	594V	746V
Germany	134	1,748V	1,391V	1,847V	3,207V	4,383V	5,637V	5,260V	538V	541V	643V	896V	898V	802V	1,008V
Greece	174	249V	208V	333V	327V	690V	947V	1,255V	42V	105V	87V	232V	218V	308V	169V
Ireland	178	—V	—V	—V	24V	—V	—V	78V	8V	6V	4V	17V	24V	26V	45V
Italy	136	4,452V	4,228V	5,366V	7,200V	11,017V	14,450V	17,526V	1,268V	1,382V	1,704V	2,049V	1,860V	1,935V	2,480V
Luxembourg	137	—V	—V	—V	—V	—V	—V	—V	1V	1V	—V	1V	3V	—V	1V
Malta	181	37Y	17V	3V	9V	3V	3V	5V	39Y	82V	64V	102V	104V	78V	82V
Netherlands	138	51V	82V	71V	79V	370V	863V	854V	158V	177V	168V	181V	190V	194V	349V
Norway	142	—V	—V	—V	—V	—V	—V	11V	3V	2V	2V	6V	6V	14V	4V
Portugal	182	57V	51V	371V	407V	346V	530V	985V	3V	5V	3V	16V	10V	8V	14V
Slovenia	961	1V	—V	1V	1Y	—V	—V	23V	6V	6V	4V	6Y	12V	24V	37V
Spain	184	1,576V	1,346V	1,854V	2,292V	2,706V	3,407V	3,190V	84V	100V	156V	151V	236V	117V	167V
Sweden	144	—V	24V	7V	—V	22V	33V	30V	62V	59V	122V	96V	106V	117V	159V
Switzerland	146	421V	384V	510V	580V	986V	1,216V	1,256V	73V	97V	100V	168V	165V	210V	255V
United Kingdom	112	250V	229V	299V	329V	581V	998V	1,053V	292V	354V	433V	435V	422V	414V	498V
Developing Countries	**202**	**1,609Y**	**1,357Y**	**2,000Y**	**2,947Y**	**4,242Y**	**6,243Y**	**4,684Y**	**1,263Y**	**1,600Y**	**1,786Y**	**2,832Y**	**3,434Y**	**4,313Y**	**5,631Y**
Africa	**607**	**379Y**	**385Y**	**408Y**	**455Y**	**578Y**	**788Y**	**971Y**	**353Y**	**453Y**	**474Y**	**458Y**	**593Y**	**756Y**	**969Y**
Algeria	612	3V	2V	2Y	2Y	3Y	3Y	4Y	1V	10V	11Y	13Y	17Y	20Y	24Y
Burkina Faso	748	15Y	16Y	19Y	25Y	34Y	43Y	52Y	—Y	—Y	—Y	—Y	—Y	—Y	—Y
Côte d'Ivoire	662	—V	21V	4V	—V	—V	—V	—Y	1V	—V	—V	—V	—V	—V	—Y
Ethiopia	644	—V	5V	—V	—V	—V	—Y	—Y	—V	—V	—V	—V	—V	—Y	—Y
Ghana	652	—Y	—Y	—Y	—Y	—Y	—Y	—Y	—Y	—Y	—Y	—Y	1Y	1Y	1Y
Morocco	686	63V	75V	55V	42V	63V	80Y	96Y	64V	75V	51V	36V	21V	26Y	34Y
Niger	692	1V	—V	1V	—V	—Y	—Y	—Y	—V	1V	1V	—V	—Y	1Y	1Y
Nigeria	694	1V	—V	—V	—Y	—Y	—Y	—Y	—V	—V	—V	—Y	—Y	—Y	—Y
Senegal	722	—V	—V	—V	—V	2V	1V	1Y	—V	—V	—V	—V	—V	—V	—Y
South Africa	199	—V	—V	—V	—V	—V	—V	—V	5V	7V	6V	8V	7V	—V	—V
Sudan	732	2Y	2Y	1Y	—V	11V	1V	22V	—Y	—Y	5V	4V	2V	6V	3V
Togo	742	—V	2V	1V	—V	—V	—Y	—Y	—V	—V	—V	—V	—V	—Y	—Y
Tunisia	744	295V	262V	325V	385V	464V	660V	796Y	273V	348V	387V	382V	528V	682V	884Y
Zimbabwe	698	—V	—V	—V	—V	—V	—V	—Y	—V	1V	—V	—V	—V	—V	—Y
Africa n.s.	799	—Y	—Y	—Y	—Y	—Y	—Y	—Y	8Y	10Y	12Y	14Y	17Y	19Y	21Y
Asia	**507**	**78Y**	**42Y**	**132Y**	**418Y**	**949Y**	**1,946Y**	**2,070Y**	**380Y**	**594Y**	**551Y**	**1,111Y**	**1,171Y**	**1,709Y**	**2,118Y**
Bangladesh	513	—V	—V	—V	—V	—V	—V	—V	—V	—V	1V	1V	—V	—Y	1Y
China,P.R.: Mainland	924	49V	1V	37V	379V	856V	1,540V	1,407V	45V	123V	203V	258V	396V	774V	950V
China,P.R.:Hong Kong	532	—V	—V	—V	—V	—V	—V	—V	3V	2V	2V	1V	2V	2V	4V
India	534	11Y	4V	8V	12V	11V	14Y	17Y	13Y	17V	20V	146V	133V	164Y	212Y
Indonesia	536	3V	—V	50V	11V	67V	384V	585V	4V	6V	6V	8V	20V	38V	38V
Korea	542	5V	16V	4V	9V	3V	2V	6V	222V	355V	150V	492V	401V	477V	442V
Malaysia	548	1V	—V	1V	6V	10V	—V	22V	4V	10V	23V	34V	18V	35V	83V
Pakistan	564	—V	—V	—V	—V	1V	1Y	2Y	4V	3V	3V	3V	4V	5Y	6Y
Philippines	566	1V	—V	—V	—V	—V	—V	—V	—V	—V	—V	—V	1V	2V	1V
Singapore	576	2V	5V	18V	—V	—V	—V	21V	17V	19V	25V	25V	33V	27V	43V
Sri Lanka	524	—V	—V	—V	—V	—V	—V	—V	41V	11V	38V	3V	24V	12V	25V
Taiwan Province of China	528	2V	13V	—V	—V	—V	4V	—V	8V	13V	14V	16V	15V	20V	20V
Thailand	578	4V	2V	14V	—V	—V	1V	11V	19V	34V	66V	124V	124V	153V	294V
Vietnam	582	—V	—V	—V	—V	—V	—V	—V	—V	—V	1V	—V	—V	—V	—V
Europe	**170**	**1,052Y**	**841Y**	**1,233Y**	**1,664Y**	**2,221Y**	**2,527Y**	**957Y**	**258Y**	**301Y**	**446Y**	**640Y**	**843Y**	**876Y**	**1,294Y**
Albania	914	—V	1V	—V	—V	—V	—V	1V	—V	—V	—V	—V	—V	—V	—V
Azerbaijan	912	—V	—V	—V	—V	—V	—V	—V	—V	—V	1V	—V	—V	—V	—V
Belarus	913	—V	—V	—V	—V	—V	1V	—V	—V	5V	1V	16V	17V	2V	4V
Bulgaria	918	—V	1V	—V	—V	—V	1V	3V	3V	1V	3V	7V	24V	4V	3V
Croatia	960	63V	3V	56V	29V	45V	7V	46V	3V	2V	3V	4V	16V	5V	19V
Czech Republic	935	98V	26V	51V	62V	101V	83V	24V	4V	2V	11V	10V	12V	15V	22V
Estonia	939	—V	—V	—V	—V	—V	—V	—V	—V	1V	1V	—V	—V	—V	—V
Hungary	944	—V	—V	—V	—V	—V	—V	31V	5V	3V	6V	3V	21V	42V	27V
Latvia	941	—V	—V	—V	—V	—V	—V	—V	—Y	—Y	—Y	—Y	—V	5V	8V
Lithuania	946	—V	—V	—V	—V	—V	—V	—V	—V	—V	—V	—V	—V	—V	18V
Macedonia, FYR	962	—V	—V	—V	—V	—V	—V	—Y	—V	1V	—V	1V	—V	—V	—Y

	Exports							Imports						
	2001	2002	2003	2004	2005	2006	2007	2001	2002	2003	2004	2005	2006	2007
	Millions of U.S. Dollars							*Millions of U.S. Dollars*						
Poland 964	4V	2V	2V	1V	3V	3V	14V	7V	6V	11V	10V	14V	27V	41V
Romania 968	—V	—V	—V	—V	—V	6V	67V	11V	10V	21V	13V	24V	22V	13V
Russia 922	—V	—V	—V	—V	—V	—V	—V	12V	27V	60V	131V	183V	79V	255V
Serbia & Montenegro 965	115Y	122Y	148Y	196Y	267Y	335Y	404Y	20Y	20Y	23Y	29Y	37Y	46Y	60Y
Slovak Republic 936	—V	—V	—Y	—Y	—V	—V	1V	3V	5V	6Y	7Y	1V	3V	3V
Turkey 186	771V	685V	975V	1,376V	1,804V	2,089V	363V	74V	182V	280V	371V	423V	538V	708V
Ukraine 926	—V	—V	—V	—V	1V	1Y	2Y	115V	36V	20V	37V	70V	86Y	112Y
Middle East 407	**78Y**	**84Y**	**180Y**	**338Y**	**456Y**	**568Y**	**681Y**	**203Y**	**197Y**	**231Y**	**429Y**	**519Y**	**617Y**	**777Y**
Bahrain 419	—Y	—Y	—Y	—Y	—Y	—Y	—Y	3Y	3Y	3Y	4Y	6Y	7Y	9Y
Egypt 469	36V	38Y	46Y	62Y	84Y	105Y	127Y	50V	52Y	57Y	74Y	95Y	117Y	152Y
Jordan 439	1V	3V	—V	2V	3V	—V	1V	33V	25V	21V	29V	29V	29V	37V
Lebanon 446	10Y	10Y	12Y	16Y	22Y	28Y	34Y	7Y	7Y	8Y	10Y	13Y	16Y	20Y
Oman 449	—V	—V	—V	—Y	—Y	—Y	—Y	20V	21V	42V	49Y	65Y	78Y	91Y
Qatar 453	—V	2V	—V	5V	—V	7V	9Y	—V	1V	1V	24V	9V	1V	1Y
Saudi Arabia 456	1V	—V	—V	—V	6V	7Y	9Y	26Y	25Y	28Y	32Y	42Y	50Y	60Y
Syrian Arab Republic 463	24Y	25Y	31Y	150V	204Y	256Y	309Y	34Y	36Y	39Y	167V	212Y	262Y	339Y
United Arab Emirates 466	7V	4V	90V	103Y	137Y	164Y	193Y	30Y	28Y	31Y	36Y	48Y	57Y	67Y
Yemen, Republic of 474	—V	—V	—Y	1V	—V	—Y	—Y	—V	—V	—Y	4V	1V	1Y	1Y
Western Hemisphere 207	**22Y**	**6Y**	**47Y**	**73Y**	**39Y**	**413Y**	**5Y**	**69Y**	**55Y**	**84Y**	**194Y**	**309Y**	**355Y**	**473Y**
Argentina 213	5V	—V	—V	—V	—V	7V	5V	26V	20V	24V	59V	66V	92V	135V
Brazil 223	8V	2V	26V	57V	34V	401V	—V	39V	33V	58V	128V	234V	225V	263V
Chile 228	—V	—V	—V	—V	—V	—V	—V	1V	—V	—V	—V	—V	—V	—V
Colombia 233	—V	—V	8V	9V	4V	4V	—V	—V	—V	—V	—V	—V	—V	—V
El Salvador 253	—V	—V	—V	—V	—V	—V	—V	—V	—V	—V	—V	—V	1V	—V
Haiti 263	—V	—V	—V	—V	—Y	—Y	—Y	2Y	2Y	2Y	3Y	4Y	5Y	6Y
Honduras 268	—V	2V	—V	—V	—Y	—Y	—Y	—V	—V	—V	—V	—Y	—Y	—Y
Mexico 273	7V	—V	13V	7V	—V	1V	—V	—V	—V	—V	3V	4V	32V	67V
Peru 293	—V	—V	—V	—V	—V	—V	—Y	—V	—V	—V	—V	—V	—V	1Y
Venezuela, Rep. Bol. 299	2V	2V	—V	—V	—V	—V	—V	1V	—V	—V	—V	—V	—V	—Y
Other Countries n.i.e. 910	**15Y**	**16Y**	**20Y**	**26Y**	**35Y**	**44Y**	**54Y**	**—Y**	**—Y**	**—Y**	**1Y**	**1Y**	**1Y**	**1Y**
Cuba 928	15Y	16Y	20Y	26Y	35Y	44Y	54Y	—Y	—Y	—Y	—Y	1Y	1Y	1Y
Memorandum Items														
European Union 998	9,390Y	8,148Y	11,274Y	15,478Y	22,205Y	29,799Y	34,119Y	2,977Y	3,383Y	3,991Y	4,851Y	4,862Y	5,068Y	6,246Y
Oil Exporting Ctys 999	17Y	11Y	142Y	122Y	213Y	566Y	800Y	81Y	91Y	119Y	162Y	201Y	244Y	282Y
Non-Oil Develop.Ctys 201	1,591Y	1,347Y	1,858Y	2,826Y	4,029Y	5,677Y	3,884Y	1,182Y	1,509Y	1,666Y	2,670Y	3,234Y	4,069Y	5,350Y
PERCENT DISTRIBUTION														
Industrial Countries 101	**85.7**	**86.1**	**85.3**	**84.6**	**85.3**	**84.2**	**89.1**	**71.4**	**71.0**	**70.7**	**65.3**	**60.8**	**58.0**	**57.0**
Developing Countries 202	**14.2**	**13.7**	**14.5**	**15.2**	**14.6**	**15.7**	**10.8**	**28.5**	**29.0**	**29.3**	**34.7**	**39.2**	**41.9**	**43.0**
Africa 607	**3.3**	**3.9**	**3.0**	**2.3**	**2.0**	**2.0**	**2.2**	**8.0**	**8.2**	**7.8**	**5.6**	**6.8**	**7.4**	**7.4**
Asia 507	**.7**	**.4**	**1.0**	**2.2**	**3.3**	**4.9**	**4.8**	**8.6**	**10.8**	**9.0**	**13.6**	**13.4**	**16.6**	**16.2**
Europe 170	**9.3**	**8.5**	**9.0**	**8.6**	**7.7**	**6.4**	**2.2**	**5.8**	**5.5**	**7.3**	**7.8**	**9.6**	**8.5**	**9.9**
Middle East 407	**.7**	**.8**	**1.3**	**1.7**	**1.6**	**1.4**	**1.6**	**4.6**	**3.6**	**3.8**	**5.3**	**5.9**	**6.0**	**5.9**
Western Hemisphere 207	**.2**	**.1**	**.3**	**.4**	**.1**	**1.0**	**—**	**1.6**	**1.0**	**1.4**	**2.4**	**3.5**	**3.5**	**3.6**
Other Countries n.i.e. 910	**.1**	**.2**	**.1**	**.1**	**.1**	**.1**	**.1**	**—**	**—**	**—**	**—**	**—**	**—**	**—**
ANNUAL PERCENT CHANGE														
World 001	**–10.9**	**–12.8**	**39.2**	**40.7**	**49.9**	**36.8**	**9.1**	**10.1**	**24.7**	**10.7**	**33.8**	**7.3**	**17.4**	**27.3**
Industrial Countries 101	**–13.5**	**–12.4**	**38.0**	**39.6**	**50.9**	**35.0**	**15.4**	**12.1**	**23.9**	**10.3**	**23.5**	**–.2**	**12.1**	**25.0**
Developing Countries 202	**9.6**	**–15.6**	**47.4**	**47.4**	**43.9**	**47.2**	**–25.0**	**5.4**	**26.7**	**11.6**	**58.6**	**21.3**	**25.6**	**30.6**
Africa 607	**3.3**	**1.6**	**6.0**	**11.3**	**27.1**	**36.4**	**23.2**	**–4.2**	**28.5**	**4.6**	**–3.4**	**29.5**	**27.5**	**28.2**
Asia 507	**3.9**	**–46.7**	**216.7**	**217.3**	**127.1**	**105.2**	**6.3**	**20.5**	**56.5**	**–7.2**	**101.6**	**5.3**	**46.0**	**23.9**
Europe 170	**16.2**	**–20.1**	**46.6**	**35.0**	**33.5**	**13.8**	**–62.2**	**25.1**	**16.8**	**47.9**	**43.6**	**31.8**	**3.9**	**47.7**
Middle East 407	**–19.8**	**7.8**	**114.7**	**87.9**	**34.8**	**24.7**	**19.8**	**3.8**	**–3.3**	**17.2**	**86.0**	**20.9**	**19.0**	**25.9**
Western Hemisphere 207	**–6.9**	**–74.9**	**750.1**	**54.7**	**–46.3**	**959.1**	**–98.7**	**–38.4**	**–20.3**	**53.3**	**129.5**	**59.7**	**14.8**	**33.2**
Other Countries n.i.e. 910	**7.9**	**6.3**	**21.2**	**32.3**	**36.0**	**25.7**	**20.6**	**–.4**	**3.4**	**11.2**	**30.1**	**27.3**	**23.5**	**29.5**

		Exports							Imports						
		2001	2002	2003	2004	2005	2006	2007	2001	2002	2003	2004	2005	2006	2007
		Millions of U.S. Dollars							*Millions of U.S. Dollars*						
IFS World Total		**4,279.3**	**5,232.1**	**6,970.3**	**9,306.9**	**11,781.8**	**14,153.3**	**17,162.4**	**6,060.3**	**7,526.4**	**9,668.4**	**12,385.7**	**15,510.5**	**19,412.6**	**24,445.2**
DOTS World Total	**001**	**4,583.8**	**5,476.9**	**7,162.4**	**9,296.7**	**11,764.1**	**14,153.5**	**17,169.4**	**6,353.4**	**7,709.4**	**9,803.8**	**12,379.1**	**15,488.2**	**19,413.1**	**24,455.9**
Industrial Countries	**101**	**2,489.5**	**3,184.4**	**4,352.8**	**5,437.3**	**6,259.5**	**6,778.3**	**7,593.0**	**3,281.9**	**4,133.2**	**5,206.4**	**6,116.5**	**6,977.9**	**8,841.2**	**12,018.1**
United States	111	174.96	195.59	200.74	440.56	554.97	605.34	439.61	194.18	219.24	291.16	195.52	305.45	313.89	538.79
Canada	156	15.69	28.91	30.20	85.27	333.53	279.29	76.03	16.26	12.65	17.35	14.58	13.69	16.68	23.04
Australia	193	.63	1.60	4.09	4.77	7.06	4.85	4.11	5.21	4.81	5.40	3.46	8.19	2.43	4.15
Japan	158	18.24	12.95	39.83	12.59	15.47	16.29	17.04	120.61	164.24	218.08	45.34	51.12	62.21	87.72
New Zealand	196	—	—	.05	.72	1.37	3.89	7.14	3.99	4.14	7.55	.93	2.14	3.90	3.58
Austria	122	12.15	11.41	22.32	28.34	27.88	39.37	73.20	47.57	61.36	101.50	139.71	157.94	213.77	281.86
Belgium	124	74.88	104.73	154.08	259.01	226.24	175.10	288.98	124.47	142.58	158.80	266.39	345.25	482.36	706.85
Cyprus	423	2.28	68.34	58.21	7.67	6.06	23.42	6.00	.60	68.82	52.91	74.49	12.63	6.35	5.56
Denmark	128	205.55	278.94	338.74	442.74	511.18	593.47	697.28	185.50	223.62	278.64	445.34	467.72	558.98	669.38
Finland	172	63.78	64.32	109.72	81.09	117.12	122.30	229.18	145.58	174.36	240.57	415.66	474.97	564.35	684.57
France	132	150.34	224.37	363.19	590.03	829.97	588.68	626.05	239.36	297.07	407.35	396.82	434.19	612.59	856.52
Germany	134	575.78	567.73	709.49	952.59	1,105.36	1,219.88	1,798.44	1,094.48	1,308.80	1,583.34	2,073.27	2,344.17	2,888.04	3,664.26
Greece	174	.95	23.00	61.34	29.53	10.40	21.48	16.30	6.71	15.09	66.60	29.97	14.76	17.97	20.52
Iceland	176	1.03	2.40	5.78	19.11	67.43	97.57	129.86	5.38	14.41	12.41	14.78	13.35	15.94	18.03
Ireland	178	9.22	13.64	35.03	37.98	60.84	53.55	72.07	24.95	31.33	33.09	24.84	32.87	44.98	66.12
Italy	136	92.33	153.22	155.61	193.93	227.53	299.78	390.34	268.26	375.10	424.29	398.92	457.49	657.40	976.46
Luxembourg	137	.42	.46	.91	.30	1.24	6.71	29.83	7.19	10.97	8.77	26.72	11.62	11.36	21.36
Malta	181	.10	.17	1.19	7.60	1.85	2.91	8.42	.97	4.54	4.94	.33	.53	3.91	3.57
Netherlands	138	134.66	174.46	245.15	446.86	364.07	684.00	511.49	149.56	172.46	248.76	499.13	575.92	725.88	1,045.37
Norway	142	59.76	131.72	165.02	197.03	188.86	264.09	394.50	61.26	113.75	118.48	108.67	80.00	95.14	117.66
Portugal	182	5.96	10.21	11.75	32.36	65.88	44.18	40.59	14.50	13.35	17.33	16.40	15.33	15.97	19.36
Slovenia	961	.63	.45	1.76	3.50	4.30	6.43	12.62	25.12	33.28	34.30	37.45	41.95	52.18	71.95
Spain	184	61.85	59.69	63.15	174.41	319.87	267.30	241.41	80.87	97.50	129.71	118.57	157.18	228.43	412.57
Sweden	144	167.82	229.40	286.89	471.12	586.67	635.92	652.39	192.86	251.37	342.64	414.77	531.36	647.44	916.25
Switzerland	146	27.31	96.05	833.34	424.06	70.53	98.48	47.58	53.52	66.19	76.86	64.84	85.40	81.09	114.65
United Kingdom	112	633.15	730.64	455.27	494.09	553.85	623.99	782.49	212.95	252.11	325.52	289.55	342.72	517.93	687.91
Developing Countries	**202**	**2,089.4**	**2,287.4**	**2,801.9**	**3,850.9**	**5,495.2**	**7,360.8**	**9,568.1**	**2,974.2**	**3,450.4**	**4,467.9**	**6,262.4**	**8,508.2**	**10,566.2**	**12,437.7**
Africa	**607**	**11.3**	**7.7**	**25.6**	**20.1**	**26.8**	**50.0**	**114.9**	**26.2**	**50.9**	**46.6**	**23.1**	**35.5**	**65.1**	**55.6**
Algeria	612	3.37	1.91	1.68	.99	.48	.21	14.78	—	—	1.75	—	—	—	—
Angola	614	.12	.19	.90	.78	.36	.36	.38	—	—	—	—	—	—	—
Benin	638	.07	.08	.35	.12	.15	.46	.95	—	.02	.05	.02	.19	.19	—
Burkina Faso	748	.01	.03	.06	.43	.44	.48	.07	.29	—	—	—	—	—	—
Burundi	618	—	—	—	—	—	—	—	.03	—	—	—	—	—	—
Cameroon	622	.02	.09	.25	.62	.26	8.40	4.32	.14	.40	.33	.06	.42	.57	.41
Central African Rep.	626	—	—	—	.02	.02	—	.04	—	—	—	—	—	—	—
Comoros	632	—	—	—	—	—	.03	3.28	.01	.01	—	—	—	.32	—
Congo, Dem. Rep. of	636	—	—	—	.07	.18	.10	—	—	.01	.03	.02	.47	1.11	.10
Congo, Republic of	634	—	—	6.89	.03	.06	.21	.33	—	.04	.46	.08	.16	.11	.08
Côte d'Ivoire	662	—	.05	.16	.10	2.37	3.75	3.52	3.94	8.10	17.26	3.61	2.33	1.13	.80
Djibouti	611	—	—	—	.01	—	.01	22.01	—	—	—	—	—	.01	—
Equatorial Guinea	642	—	—	—	—	.03	—	—	—	—	—	—	—	—	—
Eritrea	643	—	.04	—	.01	—	—	—	—	—	—	—	—	—	—
Ethiopia	644	.40	.19	1.34	—	—	12.56	6.15	.09	.18	.23	.05	.15	.10	.27
Gabon	646	—	—	—	—	.04	.10	.11	—	.02	—	.02	—	—	.03
Gambia, The	648	—	.04	.16	.18	.20	.29	.52	—	—	—	—	—	—	—
Ghana	652	.04	.06	.05	.36	.42	.25	.18	.15	.21	.65	.08	.42	.64	.39
Guinea	656	.04	.04	.09	.35	.24	.15	.23	—	—	.26	—	.07	.08	—
Guinea-Bissau	654	—	—	—	—	.01	.01	.02	—	—	—	—	—	—	—
Kenya	664	—	.01	—	.02	.06	.11	9.81	.03	.13	.16	.01	.01	—	—
Liberia	668	.44	1.11	.13	6.67	11.07	.07	6.48	.13	17.03	.02	5.39	2.37	1.52	—
Madagascar	674	.02	.01	—	.01	.01	—	—	.01	.01	.02	—	—	—	—
Malawi	676	.10	.26	.16	.14	.12	.01	.05	.98	.84	.74	.13	.53	.83	2.61
Mali	678	—	—	—	.36	.11	.47	.16	.50	.23	.39	—	—	—	—
Mauritania	682	1.68	.89	.28	.30	.89	.77	.22	6.32	1.78	1.66	.01	.17	.24	.28
Mauritius	684	.02	—	.09	.11	.01	.09	—	.12	.07	.05	.02	.06	1.21	.35
Morocco	686	.26	.28	.27	6.39	2.14	3.48	27.47	7.00	9.06	13.54	11.81	24.56	52.98	41.67
Mozambique	688	.01	.04	.08	.06	3.70	5.01	.85	.59	.71	.78	.07	.68	.54	1.48
Namibia	728	.02	—	9.00	.14	.22	.22	.14	.08	6.02	.62	.42	.81	.21	.27
Niger	692	.59	.27	—	.01	.06	.01	.05	—	—	—	—	—	—	—
Nigeria	694	.32	.26	.24	.06	.08	.04	.14	.06	.15	.18	.01	.11	.13	.02
Rwanda	714	.37	.05	—	—	.24	.02	—	—	—	—	—	—	—	—
Senegal	722	.02	.12	.53	.23	.21	2.25	.47	.05	—	.01	—	—	—	—
Seychelles	718	.33	—	1.11	—	.66	.86	.97	—	—	—	—	—	—	—
Sierra Leone	724	—	—	.33	.18	.07	—	—	—	—	—	—	—	—	—
Somalia	726	—	.02	—	—	—	—	—	—	—	—	—	—	—	—
South Africa	199	.51	.50	.94	.65	.75	.97	1.98	3.83	3.72	5.67	.97	1.14	2.08	5.26
Sudan	732	.65	.88	—	—	.12	.01	.48	.01	.10	.11	—	—	—	—
Swaziland	734	—	—	—	—	—	—	—	—	.01	.01	—	—	.05	.10
Tanzania	738	.06	.01	.02	.18	.06	7.27	—	—	.01	.04	.04	.46	.67	.83

	Exports 2001	2002	2003	2004	2005	2006	2007	Imports 2001	2002	2003	2004	2005	2006	2007
	Millions of U.S. Dollars							Millions of U.S. Dollars						
Togo 742	.06	.03	.29	.35	.52	.54	.87	.01	—	.02	—	.01	—	—
Tunisia 744	1.70	.14	.12	.10	.46	.41	7.78	.44	.53	.73	.12	.33	.27	.59
Uganda 746	—	.01	.01	.05	.04	—	.11	—	.25	.04	.07	.04	.07	—
Zambia 754	.01	.04	.02	.03	—	—	—	.01	—	.05	.08	—	—	—
Zimbabwe 698	.02	.08	.09	.03	—	—	—	1.34	1.29	.72	.03	—	—	.01
Asia 507	**27.3**	**96.3**	**71.3**	**98.4**	**429.4**	**439.1**	**224.3**	**310.4**	**463.9**	**645.0**	**544.2**	**637.1**	**765.3**	**1,036.7**
Afghanistan, I.S. of 512	—	.18	.08	.25	10.38	3.52	7.60	—	—	.09	.03	.01	—	—
American Samoa 859	—	—	—	—	—	—	—	—	.02	—	—	—	—	—
Bangladesh 513	.45	.68	2.45	.58	1.35	3.92	.48	.50	.80	1.59	.20	.09	.50	.23
Cambodia 522	.01	—	—	—	.01	.05	.01	.12	.27	.31	—	.04	.53	.23
China,P.R.: Mainland 924	1.89	2.81	8.51	11.66	13.72	18.82	21.04	125.07	182.36	300.22	294.75	360.74	465.07	685.35
China,P.R.:Hong Kong 532	1.35	38.18	23.01	3.52	4.84	8.35	9.11	8.04	32.84	17.31	7.56	9.15	10.15	10.42
China,P.R.:Macao 546	—	—	—	—	.01	—	.13	.24	.57	.69	—	.02	.10	.18
India 534	3.81	4.86	6.25	18.41	29.33	19.12	13.12	19.11	24.87	31.16	23.20	19.77	23.84	31.13
Indonesia 536	.26	4.10	.89	7.03	.12	.22	.41	9.75	8.40	11.70	6.53	7.79	27.91	26.15
Korea 542	4.06	29.05	11.65	19.45	10.68	10.62	8.42	44.02	80.49	109.70	84.38	88.51	65.36	57.56
Lao People's Dem.Rep 544	—	—	—	—	—	—	—	.01	.01	.01	—	.06	—	—
Malaysia 548	3.59	2.28	6.10	7.68	9.62	11.04	36.99	20.54	28.17	40.65	24.77	33.82	35.97	27.75
Maldives 556	—	—	—	—	—	—	.04	—	—	—	—	—	—	—
Mongolia 948	.05	.09	.25	.43	.43	.39	4.02	—	—	—	—	—	—	—
Myanmar 518	—	.01	—	—	.47	—	—	.43	.14	.15	—	.39	—	—
Nepal 558	.10	.17	.01	.04	.09	.15	—	.01	.02	.04	.01	.01	.02	.04
Pakistan 564	3.92	7.23	1.84	9.56	17.44	25.98	31.84	3.95	3.87	7.14	13.35	11.13	12.36	16.59
Papua New Guinea 853	—	—	.02	.04	.06	.04	.10	—	—	—	—	—	—	—
Philippines 566	2.94	3.07	.52	1.43	.49	.36	.84	2.77	4.70	5.96	2.48	1.69	2.51	6.61
Singapore 576	1.01	.41	1.04	13.75	322.05	326.38	77.09	7.64	19.24	17.71	12.98	6.05	8.42	7.18
Sri Lanka 524	.71	.34	1.23	.39	1.26	.29	.98	3.95	3.52	3.44	3.14	3.53	3.23	4.03
Taiwan Province of China 528	1.79	1.63	1.10	2.46	2.82	6.67	8.97	44.70	54.61	61.09	50.72	70.79	85.48	88.24
Thailand 578	.81	.47	5.63	.77	2.90	1.24	2.04	12.88	14.86	31.28	16.26	18.64	15.80	61.73
Tonga 866	—	—	—	—	.01	—	—	—	.87	—	—	—	—	—
Vietnam 582	.59	.77	.75	.97	1.28	1.90	1.03	6.63	3.26	4.78	3.86	4.88	8.02	13.30
Europe 170	**2,035.1**	**2,149.7**	**2,688.1**	**3,687.5**	**4,964.9**	**6,760.9**	**9,003.5**	**2,562.4**	**2,854.0**	**3,661.3**	**5,599.4**	**7,728.5**	**9,508.2**	**11,161.4**
Albania 914	.01	.03	1.02	—	—	.02	.02	.01	.01	.02	—	—	.01	.01
Armenia 911	4.61	2.79	.82	.71	1.76	1.34	1.36	2.26	.61	.12	.04	.18	.05	.14
Azerbaijan 912	.78	1.69	2.55	7.00	8.19	8.76	12.24	2.81	4.22	4.64	7.58	6.88	4.13	6.69
Belarus 913	178.62	173.40	226.87	296.82	380.63	537.39	689.87	120.85	114.45	146.27	241.20	271.24	345.26	483.91
Bosnia & Herzegovina 963	.31	.62	1.58	1.00	1.19	.86	1.05	.17	.23	.16	.17	.18	.23	.24
Bulgaria 918	3.04	4.84	14.43	14.75	14.09	30.95	26.53	13.08	14.77	18.71	19.17	17.27	19.68	25.05
Croatia 960	.60	2.06	3.00	8.25	8.36	10.53	14.41	3.93	6.04	5.56	5.92	5.12	4.90	9.49
Czech Republic 935	21.30	24.73	26.64	45.55	68.58	114.27	154.39	86.02	99.38	146.90	190.00	230.50	277.57	382.71
Estonia 939	148.81	207.88	308.12	465.85	695.55	914.57	998.08	68.74	81.53	135.31	399.05	438.43	598.59	875.83
Faroe Islands 816	—	.34	.13	10.12	.29	1.35	1.67	1.39	1.86	.22	8.80	3.24	2.99	1.72
Georgia 915	2.26	2.11	2.02	5.28	17.96	6.13	15.17	.74	.66	.57	1.74	3.06	5.08	5.70
Gibraltar 823	—	—	.10	.02	—	1.35	9.24	—	—	—	—	.49	7.48	.04
Hungary 944	15.36	28.05	44.80	51.08	49.67	55.88	76.73	53.53	56.29	84.91	99.85	130.69	166.23	231.50
Kazakhstan 916	21.39	33.19	53.95	84.52	108.98	217.38	331.82	9.24	113.11	5.20	9.63	31.18	49.93	83.46
Kosovo 967	—	—	—	—	.04	.06	.19	—	—	—	—	—	—	—
Kyrgyz Republic 917	3.57	6.78	5.98	8.13	11.12	17.02	36.03	.13	.23	.17	.17	.07	.04	.07
Latvia 941	579.09	530.47	692.13	947.37	1,203.73	1,570.90	2,211.47	98.10	122.85	155.47	474.67	611.31	928.03	1,340.81
Macedonia, FYR 962	2.54	.65	.01	.31	.51	.62	.86	.12	.22	.13	.46	.89	.64	.48
Moldova 921	10.52	6.22	12.31	15.10	18.16	15.41	22.03	2.82	4.97	6.87	4.49	3.52	6.64	6.10
Montenegro, Rep. of 943	—	—	—	—	—	.48	.05	—	—	—	—	—	.01	.11
Poland 964	287.07	193.78	241.14	449.01	649.26	860.94	1,075.25	308.27	369.23	505.77	947.22	1,284.41	1,848.56	2,599.52
Romania 968	1.44	2.60	6.62	11.79	19.26	25.62	55.28	2.89	5.29	7.58	7.23	10.77	17.29	27.05
Russia 922	504.93	663.83	725.87	863.56	1,227.34	1,810.33	2,581.09	1,607.00	1,635.92	2,160.42	2,853.87	4,315.24	4,709.07	4,403.29
Serbia, Rep. of 942	—	—	—	—	—	3.15	4.24	—	—	—	—	—	1.26	2.24
Serbia & Montenegro 965	—	—	—	—	3.24	—	—	—	—	—	.86	4.93	—	—
Slovak Republic 936	5.41	7.10	9.93	11.85	18.25	21.57	31.93	16.69	25.45	41.09	45.97	60.99	93.25	125.23
Tajikistan 923	1.46	2.94	3.78	11.46	20.50	19.02	34.91	1.74	.74	1.83	2.46	1.31	1.04	.45
Turkey 186	65.04	94.87	120.63	150.73	149.07	134.59	130.19	41.18	61.35	82.99	88.11	100.83	134.59	188.97
Turkmenistan 925	.90	1.67	4.44	1.42	1.18	.43	.50	.98	.27	—	.62	.02	.47	.16
Ukraine 926	154.72	143.30	171.74	213.16	265.49	366.83	469.61	103.56	126.67	141.42	186.44	182.98	263.68	337.85
Uzbekistan 927	19.81	10.95	5.54	12.65	22.57	13.17	17.50	15.12	6.81	7.55	3.71	12.77	21.50	22.62
Yugoslavia n.s. 966	1.49	2.77	1.97	—	—	—	—	1.05	.81	1.46	—	—	—	—
Middle East 407	**7.5**	**10.5**	**9.5**	**12.3**	**27.3**	**57.4**	**146.1**	**11.6**	**12.8**	**19.6**	**22.3**	**26.6**	**35.0**	**60.7**
Bahrain 419	.04	.08	.04	.10	.16	.27	.36	—	.03	—	—	.02	—	.12
Egypt 469	.29	.71	.53	.46	.67	1.19	1.73	.43	.49	1.26	3.10	2.48	4.39	5.36
Iran, I.R. of 429	.32	.15	.93	.90	.76	.85	.90	3.34	3.65	4.77	3.57	4.13	7.87	14.72
Iraq 433	.01	.01	.09	.01	.65	.73	24.74	—	—	—	—	—	—	—
Israel 436	4.34	7.77	4.50	6.49	7.30	17.20	19.88	5.01	7.14	11.48	8.57	13.19	14.35	23.41
Jordan 439	.26	.06	.06	.29	9.85	.30	.49	2.08	.21	.68	4.08	4.63	.38	.11
Kuwait 443	.08	.42	.41	.38	1.12	.63	2.02	—	—	—	—	—	—	—
Lebanon 446	.14	.24	.37	.46	.18	.28	.33	.02	.04	.07	.32	.48	.64	.57
Libya 672	—	.02	.06	.11	.03	.33	15.97	.16	.06	.02	—	—	—	—
Oman 449	.01	.02	.08	.28	.58	1.18	.92	—	—	—	.04	.08	—	—
Qatar 453	—	.04	.04	.06	.07	.33	3.88	—	—	—	—	—	.10	.48
Saudi Arabia 456	.34	.25	.50	.72	2.41	29.61	66.38	.29	.76	.73	.30	.36	.48	6.22

	Exports 2001	Exports 2002	Exports 2003	Exports 2004	Exports 2005	Exports 2006	Exports 2007	Imports 2001	Imports 2002	Imports 2003	Imports 2004	Imports 2005	Imports 2006	Imports 2007
	Millions of U.S. Dollars							Millions of U.S. Dollars						
Syrian Arab Republic.......... 463	.07	.11	.20	.29	.48	.31	.22	.04	.08	.12	.09	.04	.03	.04
United Arab Emirates.......... 466	1.48	.61	1.69	1.80	3.02	4.22	8.21	.25	.37	.47	2.25	1.22	6.79	9.64
Yemen, Republic of.......... 474	.08	.06	.01	.01	—	.01	.05	—	—	—	—	—	—	—
Western Hemisphere.......... 207	**8.3**	**23.2**	**7.4**	**32.5**	**46.7**	**53.5**	**79.3**	**63.7**	**68.7**	**95.4**	**73.3**	**80.5**	**192.6**	**123.3**
Antigua and Barbuda.......... 311	.34	.01	.60	8.44	7.17	4.04	4.29	—	.21	—	6.30	4.39	3.31	.77
Argentina.......... 213	.08	.02	—	.07	.12	.11	12.37	9.35	10.47	19.08	12.93	10.91	16.21	20.21
Aruba.......... 314	.04	—	—	—	.01	—	.01	.09	—	—	—	—	—	—
Bahamas, The.......... 313	.16	.02	.01	3.50	3.91	.45	.04	.15	2.06	.07	3.22	2.98	19.68	12.03
Barbados.......... 316	—	—	—	—	1.21	.01	.01	—	.01	—	—	.82	1.69	—
Belize.......... 339	.04	.49	.74	.08	4.81	3.42	7.21	—	.95	.01	1.84	2.93	.82	5.96
Bolivia.......... 218	.15	.01	.02	.02	—	.02	.06	.17	.14	.32	—	.19	.29	.33
Brazil.......... 223	.14	.27	.14	.24	.56	3.04	3.18	18.38	16.86	20.87	11.22	21.37	32.19	28.58
Chile.......... 228	.35	.20	.22	.15	.64	1.24	.93	2.46	3.41	5.29	3.15	6.67	8.58	10.26
Colombia.......... 233	1.29	2.50	2.82	.33	.55	.46	1.19	.66	2.08	3.98	.88	1.12	1.52	33.57
Costa Rica.......... 238	—	.03	.02	.07	.04	.12	.21	1.10	.98	1.77	1.23	.32	.17	.35
Dominica.......... 321	—	—	—	.01	.02	—	.13	—	—	.01	—	—	—	—
Dominican Republic.......... 243	.82	.20	.02	.05	.02	.07	3.17	.06	.09	.17	.12	.01	.02	.04
Ecuador.......... 248	.01	.02	.03	.02	.03	.05	.20	14.94	13.61	16.61	7.37	9.67	3.12	.63
El Salvador.......... 253	—	—	—	—	—	.03	.04	.02	.02	.15	1.35	—	—	—
Falkland Islands.......... 323	—	—	—	—	—	—	—	.01	.03	.04	—	.10	.07	.67
Greenland.......... 326	—	—	—	1.43	.31	.08	.17	.04	.04	.02	.97	—	—	.06
Grenada.......... 328	—	—	.07	.01	—	—	—	—	.01	—	—	—	—	—
Guatemala.......... 258	.07	—	—	.02	.07	.10	.14	2.02	2.15	1.82	.01	.07	4.67	.14
Guyana.......... 336	.04	—	—	—	—	—	—	—	.01	—	.07	.02	—	—
Haiti.......... 263	—	—	—	—	—	.08	—	—	—	—	—	—	—	—
Honduras.......... 268	.01	.44	—	.01	.01	.01	.01	.02	.11	1.59	—	.04	.02	.02
Jamaica.......... 343	.31	.03	.02	—	1.62	.09	.03	.07	.04	.01	—	—	—	—
Mexico.......... 273	2.02	12.84	1.61	4.24	5.20	18.60	7.36	2.88	5.00	5.81	4.05	2.91	6.04	6.16
Netherlands Antilles.......... 353	—	—	—	.01	1.95	.04	—	.44	—	—	—	1.70	3.50	—
Nicaragua.......... 278	—	—	.02	.04	.02	.10	.01	.17	—	.03	—	.04	—	—
Panama.......... 283	1.12	1.54	.65	6.07	12.89	6.61	16.97	.12	3.82	6.04	6.92	6.69	8.73	.36
Paraguay.......... 288	—	—	—	—	—	.01	.11	.01	.01	—	—	—	.01	.11
Peru.......... 293	.22	.14	.25	.05	.06	2.01	.49	7.65	3.45	6.86	1.88	1.61	.61	1.64
St. Kitts and Nevis.......... 361	—	—	—	.01	—	.29	.01	—	—	—	—	—	.12	—
St. Vincent & Grens.......... 364	.02	3.14	.11	4.70	2.66	2.73	.87	—	1.50	—	4.65	1.16	1.71	—
Suriname.......... 366	.01	—	—	.10	—	.04	—	—	.07	.06	.04	—	.02	—
Trinidad and Tobago.......... 369	.01	—	—	—	.09	.09	.04	—	—	—	—	—	—	—
Uruguay.......... 298	.01	.02	—	.02	.03	6.66	.67	1.66	.32	1.51	1.45	1.11	.52	.55
Venezuela, Rep. Bol.......... 299	.24	.02	—	2.84	2.57	.26	.14	1.23	1.32	3.27	3.68	3.69	65.91	.84
Western Hem. n.s.......... 399	.80	1.27	.01	.02	.19	2.63	19.26	—	—	—	.01	—	13.02	—
Other Countries n.i.e.......... 910	**1.6**	**.1**	**.2**	**.1**	**.2**	**1.3**	**.3**	**1.3**	**.5**	**.8**	**.1**	**.1**	**.1**	**.2**
Cuba.......... 928	1.58	.05	.04	.05	.22	1.32	.33	.07	.08	.35	.03	.07	.06	.07
North Korea.......... 954	—	.01	.15	—	—	—	—	1.26	.41	.44	.08	.03	.02	.10
Countries & Areas n.s.......... 898	**3.3**	**4.8**	**6.8**	**7.6**	—	—	—	**95.9**	**125.4**	**128.2**	—	—	—	—
Special Categories.......... 899	—	—	—	—	**6.2**	**9.3**	**7.0**	—	—	—	—	—	—	—
Memorandum Items														
European Union.......... 998	3,248.88	3,707.19	4,396.55	6,223.87	7,705.35	8,946.59	11,024.93	3,452.87	4,288.45	5,528.51	7,825.10	9,174.93	12,162.13	16,666.05
Oil Exporting Ctys.......... 999	6.44	7.80	6.61	15.17	11.91	38.59	138.49	15.08	14.73	22.88	16.39	17.38	109.19	58.07
Non-Oil Develop.Ctys.......... 201	2,083.01	2,279.60	2,795.31	3,835.75	5,483.30	7,322.24	9,429.64	2,959.16	3,435.64	4,445.03	6,246.06	8,490.81	10,456.97	12,379.60
PERCENT DISTRIBUTION														
Industrial Countries.......... 101	**54.3**	**58.1**	**60.8**	**58.5**	**53.2**	**47.9**	**44.2**	**51.7**	**53.6**	**53.1**	**49.4**	**45.1**	**45.5**	**49.1**
Developing Countries.......... 202	**45.6**	**41.8**	**39.1**	**41.4**	**46.7**	**52.0**	**55.7**	**46.8**	**44.8**	**45.6**	**50.6**	**54.9**	**54.4**	**50.9**
Africa.......... 607	**.2**	**.1**	**.4**	**.2**	**.2**	**.4**	**.7**	**.4**	**.7**	**.5**	**.2**	**.2**	**.3**	**.2**
Asia.......... 507	**.6**	**1.8**	**1.0**	**1.1**	**3.6**	**3.1**	**1.3**	**4.9**	**6.0**	**6.6**	**4.4**	**4.1**	**3.9**	**4.2**
Europe.......... 170	**44.4**	**39.2**	**37.5**	**39.7**	**42.2**	**47.8**	**52.4**	**40.3**	**37.0**	**37.3**	**45.2**	**49.9**	**49.0**	**45.6**
Middle East.......... 407	**.2**	**.2**	**.1**	**.1**	**.2**	**.4**	**.9**	**.2**	**.2**	**.2**	**.2**	**.2**	**.2**	**.2**
Western Hemisphere.......... 207	**.2**	**.4**	**.1**	**.3**	**.4**	**.4**	**.5**	**1.0**	**.9**	**1.0**	**.6**	**.5**	**1.0**	**.5**
ANNUAL PERCENT CHANGE														
World.......... 001	**20.3**	**19.5**	**30.8**	**29.8**	**26.5**	**20.3**	**21.3**	**16.4**	**21.3**	**27.2**	**26.3**	**25.1**	**25.3**	**26.0**
Industrial Countries.......... 101	**16.5**	**27.9**	**36.7**	**24.9**	**15.1**	**8.3**	**12.0**	**20.3**	**25.9**	**26.0**	**17.5**	**14.1**	**26.7**	**35.9**
Developing Countries.......... 202	**25.2**	**9.5**	**22.5**	**37.4**	**42.7**	**34.0**	**30.0**	**12.5**	**16.0**	**29.5**	**40.2**	**35.9**	**24.2**	**17.7**
Africa.......... 607	**190.2**	**−31.9**	**234.1**	**−21.5**	**33.4**	**86.3**	**129.9**	**41.0**	**94.7**	**−8.5**	**−50.4**	**53.5**	**83.4**	**−14.6**
Asia.......... 507	**−3.6**	**252.5**	**−25.9**	**38.0**	**336.2**	**2.3**	**−48.9**	**38.1**	**49.5**	**39.0**	**−15.6**	**17.1**	**20.1**	**35.5**
Europe.......... 170	**26.4**	**5.6**	**25.0**	**37.2**	**34.6**	**36.2**	**33.2**	**9.5**	**11.4**	**28.3**	**52.9**	**38.0**	**23.0**	**17.4**
Middle East.......... 407	**−4.3**	**41.4**	**−9.9**	**29.9**	**121.1**	**110.4**	**154.4**	**8.7**	**10.5**	**52.5**	**14.0**	**19.2**	**31.6**	**73.2**
Western Hemisphere.......... 207	**−56.9**	**179.7**	**−68.3**	**342.5**	**43.7**	**14.4**	**48.3**	**30.0**	**7.9**	**38.8**	**−23.1**	**9.8**	**139.2**	**−36.0**
Other Countries n.i.e.......... 910	**−1.3**	**−95.8**	**185.8**	**−73.3**	**325.2**	**505.8**	**−75.1**	**80.0**	**−62.7**	**58.4**	**−85.1**	**−14.8**	**−18.4**	**114.8**

	Exports 2001	Exports 2002	Exports 2003	Exports 2004	Exports 2005	Exports 2006	Exports 2007	Imports 2001	Imports 2002	Imports 2003	Imports 2004	Imports 2005	Imports 2006	Imports 2007
	Millions of U.S. Dollars							*Millions of U.S. Dollars*						
IFS World Total	**8,238**	**8,495**	**9,979**	**12,175**	**12,696**	**14,174**	**16,053**	**11,151**	**11,597**	**13,691**	**16,826**	**17,564**	**19,433**	**22,090**
DOTS World Total 001	**10,321**	**10,191**	**13,322**	**16,258**	**18,716**	**22,853**	**22,459**	**12,164**	**13,146**	**16,179**	**20,052**	**21,820**	**26,547**	**27,457**
Industrial Countries 101	**9,194**	**9,280**	**12,089**	**14,734**	**16,439**	**20,373**	**19,373**	**10,529**	**11,119**	**12,993**	**16,225**	**17,150**	**19,906**	**21,374**
United States 111	286	280	267	312	393	470	408	597	513	289	590	680	742	968
Canada 156	45	43	37	58	64	76	85	66	29	82	47	70	75	217
Australia 193	16	13	17	19	23	30	35	2	1	2	4	3	2	3
Japan 158	49	44	48	44	45	33	47	146	130	171	223	168	191	143
New Zealand 196	8	9	7	8	5	6	5	—	—	—	—	—	—	—
Austria 122	111	130	216	309	412	550	416	108	102	136	138	155	179	191
Belgium 124	1,431	1,072	1,388	1,629	1,698	2,009	2,262	3,771	3,903	4,722	5,972	6,190	7,013	7,514
Cyprus 423	1	1	1	6	15	236	60	—	—	—	21	33	11	11
Denmark 128	66	75	125	173	258	390	337	29	26	36	38	39	42	42
Finland 172	110	107	131	167	194	220	183	16	11	14	28	45	66	59
France 132	1,890	2,051	2,533	3,212	3,243	3,532	3,659	1,403	1,739	1,859	2,403	2,082	2,254	2,524
Germany 134	2,384	2,432	3,106	3,609	3,903	4,406	4,744	2,774	3,025	3,738	4,527	4,742	5,361	6,541
Greece 174	39	44	71	91	90	98	134	3	3	3	6	5	5	7
Iceland 176	4	5	4	13	10	11	12	—	—	—	1	1	1	2
Ireland 178	107	50	73	61	73	74	84	51	39	90	121	109	110	116
Italy 136	633	625	909	1,194	1,376	2,176	1,666	190	220	314	443	527	562	541
Malta 181	1	1	1	1	1	16	12	—	—	—	—	—	1	—
Netherlands 138	418	445	578	694	790	1,014	1,202	564	604	778	842	1,105	1,122	1,361
Norway 142	32	61	60	63	56	90	81	7	7	7	5	7	6	6
Portugal 182	88	79	121	134	168	724	221	21	21	26	36	38	42	46
Slovenia 961	23	18	23	44	57	59	65	2	9	9	10	15	19	28
Spain 184	334	454	620	968	1,375	1,200	1,128	105	128	119	152	157	166	225
Sweden 144	123	150	307	351	480	611	728	51	55	63	60	64	85	157
Switzerland 146	153	205	234	192	182	185	203	162	113	149	285	475	392	211
United Kingdom 112	843	886	1,211	1,383	1,528	2,155	1,597	461	442	385	274	440	1,462	461
Developing Countries 202	**634**	**740**	**1,043**	**1,292**	**1,675**	**2,324**	**2,855**	**1,332**	**1,489**	**3,082**	**3,611**	**4,420**	**6,311**	**5,954**
Africa 607	**85**	**76**	**88**	**110**	**101**	**93**	**101**	**21**	**24**	**28**	**33**	**38**	**25**	**11**
Algeria 612	5	4	9	26	26	12	17	—	—	1	—	2	2	—
Angola 614	—	1	1	2	—	—	1	—	—	—	—	—	—	—
Benin 638	—	—	—	—	—	—	1	—	—	—	—	—	—	—
Burkina Faso 748	—	—	—	—	—	—	1	—	—	—	—	—	—	—
Cameroon 622	1	1	1	1	1	1	1	—	—	—	—	—	—	—
Cape Verde 624	2	1	2	—	—	—	—	—	—	—	—	—	—	—
Congo, Dem. Rep. of 636	—	1	1	1	1	1	2	—	—	—	—	—	—	—
Congo, Republic of 634	—	—	1	1	1	1	2	—	—	—	—	—	—	—
Côte d'Ivoire 662	8	10	8	8	6	6	6	—	2	3	7	6	9	1
Equatorial Guinea 642	14	—	—	1	—	1	1	—	—	—	—	—	—	—
Ethiopia 644	—	—	—	—	1	2	2	—	—	—	—	—	—	—
Gabon 646	—	1	1	1	1	1	1	—	—	—	—	—	—	—
Ghana 652	1	2	5	4	5	2	3	2	2	4	4	3	3	2
Guinea 656	7	4	5	3	4	5	3	—	—	—	—	—	—	—
Kenya 664	1	—	1	1	1	1	1	—	—	2	3	4	4	—
Madagascar 674	—	—	1	2	—	—	—	—	—	—	—	—	—	—
Malawi 676	—	—	—	—	—	—	—	—	—	1	—	1	—	—
Mali 678	—	—	1	—	1	1	1	—	—	—	—	—	—	—
Mauritania 682	—	—	1	—	—	—	—	—	—	—	—	—	—	—
Mauritius 684	—	—	—	—	—	1	1	—	—	—	—	—	—	—
Morocco 686	12	9	9	14	8	8	9	2	1	1	1	2	—	1
Mozambique 688	—	—	—	—	—	—	1	4	—	—	—	—	—	—
Namibia 728	—	1	—	—	—	—	—	—	—	—	—	—	—	—
Niger 692	—	—	—	—	—	3	—	—	—	—	—	—	—	—
Nigeria 694	6	10	15	10	9	8	10	—	—	—	—	—	—	—
Rwanda 714	—	—	1	—	—	1	—	—	—	—	—	—	—	—
Senegal 722	1	3	2	2	2	2	2	—	—	—	—	—	—	—
South Africa 199	11	14	17	20	25	28	24	3	1	2	6	12	2	4
Tanzania 738	—	1	1	1	2	2	3	4	6	—	—	2	—	—
Tunisia 744	10	6	5	7	5	3	5	5	4	5	8	5	4	3
Uganda 746	1	—	—	—	—	—	—	1	6	7	4	—	—	—
Zambia 754	—	1	—	—	—	—	1	—	—	—	—	—	—	—
Asia 507	**149**	**160**	**330**	**277**	**367**	**502**	**524**	**939**	**1,152**	**2,766**	**3,225**	**3,631**	**5,349**	**5,112**
Afghanistan, I.S. of 512	—	—	—	—	1	—	1	—	—	—	—	—	—	—
Bangladesh 513	—	—	1	—	—	2	—	1	—	—	1	—	—	—
Brunei Darussalam 516	—	1	—	—	—	—	—	—	—	—	—	—	—	—
Cambodia 522	1	2	3	4	4	5	6	1	3	5	6	7	7	8
China,P.R.: Mainland 924	49	56	145	120	161	284	266	68	70	1,781	2,529	2,759	4,453	4,701
China,P.R.:Hong Kong 532	25	24	72	19	42	51	63	71	57	93	116	187	242	202
China,P.R.:Macao 546	—	—	—	—	1	—	—	—	—	—	—	—	2	—
French Polynesia 887	1	1	—	1	1	1	1	—	—	—	—	—	—	—
India 534	11	9	12	14	18	31	41	9	8	15	15	17	16	30

	Exports							Imports						
	2001	2002	2003	2004	2005	2006	2007	2001	2002	2003	2004	2005	2006	2007
	Millions of U.S. Dollars							Millions of U.S. Dollars						
Indonesia........ 536	4	3	4	3	13	5	3	27	29	37	51	44	69	10
Korea........ 542	11	18	28	49	55	58	50	14	4	156	66	37	15	7
Malaysia........ 548	6	7	9	10	8	15	19	21	2	17	22	386	338	31
Mongolia........ 948	—	—	1	—	—	—	—	—	—	—	—	—	—	—
Nepal........ 558	—	1	1	—	1	—	—	—	—	—	—	—	—	—
New Caledonia........ 839	1	3	1	1	—	—	1	—	—	—	—	—	—	—
Pakistan........ 564	1	2	2	2	9	3	6	—	—	—	1	1	1	—
Philippines........ 566	3	2	6	2	5	2	1	10	1	24	130	1	17	18
Singapore........ 576	14	12	18	15	11	16	32	16	7	10	12	12	20	17
Sri Lanka........ 524	—	—	—	—	—	—	—	1	—	—	—	—	—	—
Taiwan Province of China........ 528	15	12	16	27	29	20	23	692	960	604	246	153	148	63
Thailand........ 578	4	4	6	6	8	7	5	4	9	24	30	26	21	25
Vietnam........ 582	2	3	7	3	1	—	4	2	1	—	—	—	—	—
Europe........ 170	**276**	**352**	**435**	**660**	**885**	**1,369**	**1,894**	**284**	**250**	**248**	**272**	**296**	**436**	**643**
Albania........ 914	1	—	—	1	1	1	2	—	—	—	—	—	—	—
Armenia........ 911	—	—	—	—	1	1	1	—	—	1	—	—	—	—
Azerbaijan........ 912	2	1	1	5	5	4	2	1	1	1	—	—	—	—
Belarus........ 913	3	4	2	2	3	2	2	3	5	4	5	5	4	4
Bosnia & Herzegovina........ 963	1	1	1	1	2	2	1	—	—	—	—	—	—	—
Bulgaria........ 918	4	8	5	6	4	9	32	—	1	1	1	1	5	1
Croatia........ 960	5	4	5	5	6	6	6	1	—	1	1	2	2	5
Czech Republic........ 935	55	77	87	119	143	204	277	192	160	106	54	76	100	112
Estonia........ 939	2	2	4	8	11	14	16	—	2	2	3	—	—	1
Faroe Islands........ 816	1	—	1	—	—	—	1	—	—	—	—	—	—	—
Georgia........ 915	3	1	—	1	1	—	—	—	—	—	—	—	—	—
Hungary........ 944	27	35	56	64	79	86	130	17	21	27	17	18	24	32
Kazakhstan........ 916	2	10	3	6	9	5	10	—	—	—	—	—	1	—
Kyrgyz Republic........ 917	—	—	—	—	—	1	—	—	—	—	—	—	—	—
Latvia........ 941	4	5	5	6	8	14	16	1	1	—	—	—	2	1
Lithuania........ 946	6	12	11	34	20	25	100	—	1	2	1	1	1	24
Macedonia, FYR........ 962	—	—	—	1	—	1	1	—	—	—	—	—	—	—
Moldova........ 921	1	1	1	—	—	1	—	—	—	—	—	—	—	—
Montenegro, Rep. of........ 943	—	—	—	—	—	1	1	—	—	—	—	—	—	—
Poland........ 964	82	92	122	167	232	373	421	22	33	42	71	65	56	144
Romania........ 968	5	6	9	18	21	38	82	1	2	3	4	7	5	3
Russia........ 922	27	39	45	84	76	147	202	8	7	15	82	50	152	236
Serbia, Rep. of........ 942	—	—	—	—	—	4	8	—	—	—	—	—	—	—
Serbia & Montenegro........ 965	2	2	3	4	1	—	—	—	—	—	1	1	—	—
Slovak Republic........ 936	3	6	10	28	47	66	99	28	4	32	9	18	17	18
Tajikistan........ 923	—	—	—	—	—	1	—	—	—	—	—	—	—	—
Turkey........ 186	26	29	36	77	183	318	449	8	10	10	17	26	28	55
Turkmenistan........ 925	—	—	—	—	2	—	—	—	—	—	—	—	—	—
Ukraine........ 926	14	13	23	19	26	47	31	—	—	1	5	24	37	6
Uzbekistan........ 927	—	—	1	2	3	2	3	—	—	—	—	—	—	—
Europe n.s........ 884	1	1	1	1	1	1	1	—	—	—	—	—	—	—
Middle East........ 407	**61**	**90**	**117**	**120**	**149**	**176**	**170**	**37**	**56**	**22**	**49**	**392**	**428**	**58**
Bahrain........ 419	1	—	1	4	20	4	3	—	—	—	—	—	—	—
Egypt........ 469	6	5	8	5	10	10	11	—	—	—	—	—	—	—
Iran, I.R. of........ 429	3	6	12	23	11	10	8	5	10	5	6	8	5	3
Iraq........ 433	—	4	—	—	1	1	2	—	—	—	—	—	—	—
Israel........ 436	17	22	13	13	20	22	24	27	41	4	7	8	3	7
Jordan........ 439	1	1	—	1	2	1	1	—	—	—	—	—	—	—
Kuwait........ 443	1	3	5	5	10	4	3	—	—	—	1	6	—	—
Lebanon........ 446	1	1	2	2	1	—	2	—	—	—	—	—	—	—
Libya........ 672	1	1	—	1	3	—	1	—	—	—	—	—	—	—
Oman........ 449	—	—	—	1	1	2	3	—	—	—	—	—	—	—
Qatar........ 453	—	—	2	1	5	2	3	—	—	—	—	—	—	—
Saudi Arabia........ 456	16	28	29	28	28	33	39	1	1	1	5	6	9	25
Syrian Arab Republic........ 463	1	1	2	2	2	1	1	—	—	—	—	—	—	—
United Arab Emirates........ 466	11	18	40	32	35	83	66	2	3	12	31	364	411	22
Yemen, Republic of........ 474	—	—	1	1	1	3	3	—	—	—	—	—	—	—
Western Hemisphere........ 207	**64**	**63**	**73**	**125**	**173**	**184**	**166**	**52**	**8**	**19**	**31**	**64**	**73**	**130**
Argentina........ 213	5	3	3	8	7	14	7	1	2	1	1	1	1	2
Aruba........ 314	—	—	—	1	—	—	—	—	—	—	—	—	—	—
Bahamas, The........ 313	—	—	—	—	—	3	—	—	—	—	—	—	—	—
Barbados........ 316	—	1	1	2	3	1	—	—	—	—	—	—	—	—
Belize........ 339	—	—	—	—	1	—	—	—	—	—	—	—	—	—
Brazil........ 223	22	9	9	31	49	37	48	47	3	13	28	59	25	28
Chile........ 228	4	11	11	13	13	10	6	3	—	—	—	—	—	1
Colombia........ 233	2	1	1	1	2	1	1	—	—	—	—	—	—	2
Costa Rica........ 238	—	—	—	—	1	2	4	—	—	—	—	—	—	1
Dominican Republic........ 243	1	3	2	2	4	1	2	—	—	—	—	—	—	—
Ecuador........ 248	4	7	10	13	13	11	8	—	—	—	—	—	—	1
El Salvador........ 253	—	1	3	—	1	1	—	—	—	—	—	—	—	—
Greenland........ 326	—	—	—	—	—	1	—	—	—	—	—	—	—	—
Grenada........ 328	—	—	—	—	1	—	—	—	—	—	—	—	—	—
Guatemala........ 258	1	1	1	—	1	—	—	—	—	—	—	—	—	—

	Exports							Imports						
	2001	2002	2003	2004	2005	2006	2007	2001	2002	2003	2004	2005	2006	2007
	Millions of U.S. Dollars							Millions of U.S. Dollars						
Guyana......336	2	1	3	2	3	1	—	—	—	—	—	—	—	—
Honduras......268	—	—	1	—	6	—	—	—	—	—	—	—	—	—
Jamaica......343	1	2	3	5	1	4	1	—	—	—	—	—	—	—
Mexico......273	17	15	17	35	53	58	79	—	1	4	1	2	18	58
Netherlands Antilles......353	—	—	—	—	2	—	—	—	—	—	—	—	—	—
Nicaragua......278	1	—	—	—	—	—	1	—	—	—	—	—	—	—
Panama......283	2	1	1	2	1	—	—	—	—	—	—	—	—	—
Paraguay......288	—	—	—	1	—	—	—	—	—	—	—	—	—	—
Peru......293	—	1	2	—	2	2	3	—	—	—	—	—	—	—
St. Lucia......362	—	—	—	—	1	1	—	—	—	—	—	—	—	—
St. Pierre-Miquelon......363	—	—	—	—	—	—	—	—	—	—	—	—	19	—
Suriname......366	—	1	—	1	2	—	1	—	—	—	—	—	—	—
Trinidad and Tobago......369	1	2	5	5	3	2	2	—	—	—	—	—	—	—
Venezuela, Rep. Bol......299	2	2	2	2	2	1	2	—	—	—	—	—	8	39
Western Hem. n.s......399	—	—	—	—	—	29	—	—	—	—	—	—	—	—
Other Countries n.i.e......910	**—**	**3**	**—**	**—**	**—**	**—**	**1**	**—**	**—**	**2**	**—**	**—**	**—**	**—**
Cuba......928	—	3	—	—	—	—	1	—	—	—	—	—	—	—
North Korea......954	—	—	—	—	—	—	—	—	—	2	—	—	—	—
Countries & Areas n.s......898	**24**	**41**	**5**	**27**	**602**	**156**	**230**	**301**	**538**	**102**	**216**	**250**	**330**	**129**
Special Categories......899	**469**	**127**	**185**	**205**	**—**	**—**	**—**	**1**	**—**	**—**	**—**	**—**	**—**	**—**
Memorandum Items														
European Union......998	8,780	8,850	11,708	14,452	16,202	20,253	19,555	9,808	10,547	12,504	15,226	15,925	18,699	20,156
Oil Exporting Ctys......999	49	79	117	133	144	162	159	36	43	55	93	429	503	100
Non-Oil Develop.Ctys......201	585	662	925	1,159	1,531	2,162	2,696	1,297	1,446	3,027	3,517	3,991	5,808	5,854
PERCENT DISTRIBUTION														
Industrial Countries......101	**89.1**	**91.1**	**90.7**	**90.6**	**87.8**	**89.1**	**86.3**	**86.6**	**84.6**	**80.3**	**80.9**	**78.6**	**75.0**	**77.8**
Developing Countries......202	**6.1**	**7.3**	**7.8**	**7.9**	**8.9**	**10.2**	**12.7**	**11.0**	**11.3**	**19.1**	**18.0**	**20.3**	**23.8**	**21.7**
Africa......607	**.8**	**.7**	**.7**	**.7**	**.5**	**.4**	**.4**	**.2**	**.2**	**.2**	**.2**	**.2**	**.1**	**—**
Asia......507	**1.4**	**1.6**	**2.5**	**1.7**	**2.0**	**2.2**	**2.3**	**7.7**	**8.8**	**17.1**	**16.1**	**16.6**	**20.1**	**18.6**
Europe......170	**2.7**	**3.5**	**3.3**	**4.1**	**4.7**	**6.0**	**8.4**	**2.3**	**1.9**	**1.5**	**1.4**	**1.4**	**1.6**	**2.3**
Middle East......407	**.6**	**.9**	**.9**	**.7**	**.8**	**.8**	**.8**	**.3**	**.4**	**.1**	**.2**	**1.8**	**1.6**	**.2**
Western Hemisphere......207	**.6**	**.6**	**.6**	**.8**	**.9**	**.8**	**.7**	**.4**	**.1**	**.1**	**.2**	**.3**	**.3**	**.5**
ANNUAL PERCENT CHANGE														
World......001	**25.2**	**−1.3**	**30.7**	**22.0**	**15.1**	**22.1**	**−1.7**	**6.8**	**8.1**	**23.1**	**23.9**	**8.8**	**21.7**	**3.4**
Industrial Countries......101	**20.9**	**.9**	**30.3**	**21.9**	**11.6**	**23.9**	**−4.9**	**1.9**	**5.6**	**16.9**	**24.9**	**5.7**	**16.1**	**7.4**
Developing Countries......202	**.2**	**16.7**	**40.8**	**23.9**	**29.6**	**38.8**	**22.9**	**33.4**	**11.8**	**107.0**	**17.1**	**22.4**	**42.8**	**−5.7**
Africa......607	**34.0**	**−11.2**	**15.7**	**26.1**	**−8.7**	**−8.1**	**8.9**	**10.9**	**11.4**	**19.3**	**19.0**	**12.8**	**−33.0**	**−54.5**
Asia......507	**−6.9**	**7.8**	**105.9**	**−16.2**	**32.5**	**36.9**	**4.2**	**28.6**	**22.7**	**140.1**	**16.6**	**12.6**	**47.3**	**−4.4**
Europe......170	**−1.6**	**27.4**	**23.6**	**51.7**	**34.0**	**54.8**	**38.3**	**71.1**	**−11.9**	**−1.1**	**9.8**	**8.8**	**47.4**	**47.5**
Middle East......407	**−7.3**	**48.0**	**29.8**	**2.9**	**24.7**	**17.6**	**−3.0**	**109.0**	**50.9**	**−61.0**	**126.5**	**698.5**	**9.2**	**−86.5**
Western Hemisphere......207	**—**	**−1.5**	**16.7**	**70.7**	**38.1**	**6.4**	**−9.7**	**−21.9**	**−84.7**	**137.0**	**65.5**	**105.0**	**14.2**	**78.5**
Other Countries n.i.e......910	**—**	**—**	**−92.6**	**62.9**	**11.8**	**−27.5**	**224.7**	**−23.5**	**−77.8**	**—**	**−97.8**	**−49.0**	**886.9**	**−54.6**

		Exports							Imports						
		2001	2002	2003	2004	2005	2006	2007	2001	2002	2003	2004	2005	2006	2007
		Millions of U.S. Dollars							*Millions of U.S. Dollars*						
IFS World Total		**1,157.5**	**1,115.5**	**1,367.0**	**1,675.9**	**2,041.3**	**2,397.5**	**3,302.1**	**1,693.6**	**1,995.2**	**2,306.4**	**2,931.6**	**3,228.0**	**3,752.0**	**5,177.1**
DOTS World Total	**001**	**1,155.1**	**1,115.3**	**1,366.6**	**1,675.4**	**2,040.9**	**2,399.6**	**3,602.8Y**	**1,687.6**	**1,995.1**	**2,306.3**	**2,931.3**	**3,224.9**	**3,762.0**	**4,546.3Y**
Industrial Countries	**101**	**732.0**	**705.4**	**870.9**	**1,027.7**	**1,131.3**	**1,336.3**	**2,016.8Y**	**938.4**	**1,149.7**	**1,268.5**	**1,455.0**	**1,461.2**	**1,614.9**	**2,343.6Y**
United States	111	99.71	77.40	72.80	72.06	44.28	22.42	69.73V	51.54	58.78	56.79	48.31	45.23	41.10	36.85V
Canada	156	.56	.65	.49	1.12	1.09	.97	8.12V	2.58	2.50	3.96	8.65	22.27	36.04	16.27V
Australia	193	2.03	2.51	2.47	2.52	1.71	2.27	3.46V	3.72	5.86	6.72	2.73	4.29	1.78	2.37V
Japan	158	3.83	4.33	5.76	2.72	8.40	1.23	5.81V	16.70	22.64	19.35	24.37	22.76	26.96	6.04V
New Zealand	196	.04	.12	.08	.02	.01	.05	.13V	.15	.18	.20	.17	.18	.27	.20V
Austria	122	6.22	6.50	7.68	8.51	9.00	14.99	18.41V	43.88	53.31	56.20	68.86	69.18	80.56	128.86V
Belgium	124	7.39	10.36	9.70	15.16	34.62	83.15	181.89V	14.40	15.74	16.70	22.10	27.28	26.22	38.01V
Cyprus	423	1.63	.61	.50	4.80	5.54	4.48	2.16V	2.62	4.17	4.08	4.69	3.47	1.50	.54V
Denmark	128	2.13	1.90	3.28	2.31	2.78	1.47	7.85V	7.97	7.26	11.30	14.83	14.29	16.86	21.99V
Finland	172	.20	.17	.18	.14	.16	.07	.12V	2.70	3.16	4.80	3.40	5.04	5.65	13.43V
France	132	15.97	24.79	54.66	77.32	19.92	10.29	20.51V	30.28	53.06	51.52	67.59	61.01	66.27	66.71V
Germany	134	237.50	234.00	279.39	317.22	364.01	375.48	523.59V	213.37	284.73	304.77	368.19	334.88	369.27	600.63V
Greece	174	101.36	116.95	180.40	228.76	312.93	361.16	375.14V	184.39	237.88	300.58	282.64	296.83	319.88	588.62V
Iceland	176	—	—	—	.03	—	—	.47V	.06	.08	.33	.13	.07	.08	.04V
Ireland	178	.07	.07	.07	.04	.05	.29	.33V	9.33	5.35	5.19	12.46	14.05	20.08	19.59V
Italy	136	88.69	81.93	95.41	134.55	169.61	236.85	364.71V	107.66	118.59	123.13	168.81	193.67	226.92	284.98V
Luxembourg	137	2.57	.22	.62	—	—	.07	.01V	.50	.57	.72	.72	.98	2.06	.76V
Malta	181	.06	.11	.46	.34	.89	.54	3.33V	.10	.12	.05	.09	.06	.01	—V
Netherlands	138	45.28	44.71	47.33	47.31	44.58	55.39	63.47V	45.75	51.86	49.60	57.13	53.23	59.77	128.30V
Norway	142	.11	.10	.22	.06	.07	.29	3.32V	1.66	1.56	.76	.42	.84	2.55	2.61V
Portugal	182	4.47	1.59	6.66	7.50	6.76	7.10	19.79V	1.24	.25	.46	1.51	2.93	3.96	2.45V
Slovenia	961	20.93	21.66	21.34	27.19	31.81	41.18	71.95V	118.87	129.67	139.07	140.34	127.99	129.41	226.68V
Spain	184	21.45	14.58	21.29	23.03	14.01	50.40	180.78V	9.91	12.67	24.61	30.97	32.31	51.73	37.45V
Sweden	144	2.77	3.60	5.65	5.75	8.34	19.44	16.41V	18.82	17.71	20.18	25.10	20.06	29.51	39.25V
Switzerland	146	40.48	27.62	19.31	6.76	7.80	10.32	12.61V	24.01	29.21	27.94	46.06	64.27	59.30	42.18V
United Kingdom	112	26.57	28.91	35.18	42.46	42.93	36.46	62.69V	26.18	32.78	39.48	54.75	44.03	37.17	38.85V
Developing Countries	**202**	**422.6**	**409.9**	**495.7**	**647.7**	**909.0**	**1,062.8**	**1,585.3Y**	**749.1**	**845.3**	**1,037.6**	**1,476.0**	**1,762.9**	**2,145.6**	**2,200.9Y**
Africa	**607**	**3.5**	**1.9**	**1.9**	**3.0**	**2.6**	**2.0**	**1.2Y**	**3.1**	**4.8**	**5.4**	**9.8**	**5.9**	**9.7**	**10.4Y**
Algeria	612	.02	.01	—	—	—	.07	.10Y	—	—	—	4.50	—	—	—Y
Angola	614	—	—	—	—	—	—	—Y	.02	—	—	—	—	—	—Y
Burundi	618	—	—	.02	—	—	—	—Y	.05	.01	—	—	—	—	—Y
Cameroon	622	.02	—	—	—	—	—	—Y	—	—	—	.03	.02	.09	.11Y
Central African Rep.	626	—	—	—	—	—	—	—Y	—	.01	—	—	—	—	—Y
Chad	628	—	—	—	—	—	—	—Y	.01	—	.01	.02	.14	.07	.08Y
Congo, Dem. Rep. of	636	—	—	—	—	—	—	—Y	—	—	.01	—	—	—	—Y
Congo, Republic of	634	—	—	—	—	—	.04	.05Y	—	—	.02	.01	—	—	—Y
Côte d'Ivoire	662	—	—	—	.01	.01	—	—Y	.11	.05	.15	.04	.02	.02	.03Y
Equatorial Guinea	642	—	—	—	—	—	—	—Y	—	.01	—	—	.01	.02	.02Y
Ethiopia	644	—	—	—	—	—	—	—Y	—	—	—	.03	.08	.05	.06Y
Gabon	646	—	—	—	—	—	—	—Y	—	.02	—	—	—	5.04	6.25Y
Gambia, The	648	—	—	—	—	—	—	—Y	—	—	.04	.02	—	—	—Y
Ghana	652	.01	—	—	—	—	—	—Y	.79	1.09	.52	.80	2.83	.75	.93Y
Guinea	656	—	—	—	1.11	—	—	—Y	—	—	—	—	—	—	—Y
Kenya	664	—	.01	.04	.01	—	—	—Y	.06	.02	—	.01	.01	.01	.01Y
Lesotho	666	—	—	—	—	—	—	—Y	.10	—	—	.01	—	—	—Y
Liberia	668	—	—	—	—	.01	—	—Y	—	—	—	—	—	—	—Y
Madagascar	674	—	—	—	—	—	—	—Y	—	—	—	.01	.02	.01	.01Y
Malawi	676	—	—	—	—	—	—	—Y	.29	.42	.22	.12	.31	.20	.25Y
Mali	678	....	....	....	....	....	....	....	—	—	—	.01	—	.01	.01Y
Mauritius	684	—	—	—	—	—	—	—V	—	.02	.01	.02	.03	.07	.01V
Morocco	686	.05	.01	.15	.14	.04	.06	.07Y	.02	.14	.09	.17	.14	.50	.62Y
Mozambique	688	—	—	—	—	—	—	—Y	.02	—	.02	.01	.02	.02	.03Y
Namibia	728	—	—	—	—	—	—	—Y	—	—	.01	.09	.02	.01	.01Y
Niger	692	.04	—	—	—	—	—	—Y	.01	—	—	—	—	.01	.01Y
Nigeria	694	2.84	1.39	.74	.93	1.30	.53	.69Y	—	—	.05	—	—	.12	.14Y
Rwanda	714	—	—	—	—	.03	—	—Y	—	—	—	—	—	—	—Y
São Tomé & Príncipe	716	....	....	....	....	....	....	....	—	—	—	—	—	.01	.01Y
Senegal	722	.02	—	—	—	—	—	—Y	—	—	—	—	—	—	—Y
Seychelles	718	....	....	....	....	....	....	....	.02	—	.05	.05	.42	.19	.24Y
Sierra Leone	724	—	—	—	.05	.01	—	—Y	.01	.01	.01	—	—	.01	.01Y
South Africa	199	.51	.39	.65	.57	.78	1.05	—V	.76	.56	1.03	2.95	1.11	1.57	.42V
Sudan	732	—	—	—	—	.08	.03	.04Y	.51	.13	.25	.11	.03	.01	.01Y
Swaziland	734	—	.04	—	—	—	—	—Y	—	.17	—	—	—	—	—Y
Tanzania	738	—	—	—	—	.15	—	—Y	.12	.48	.59	.20	—	.08	.10Y
Togo	742	—	—	—	—	—	—	—Y	—	1.10	.75	—	—	—	—Y
Tunisia	744	—	—	.25	.15	.16	.19	.24Y	—	.01	.83	.10	.19	.31	.39Y
Uganda	746	.01	—	—	—	.01	—	—Y	.20	.31	.54	.34	.12	.12	.15Y
Zambia	754	—	.01	—	—	—	—	—Y	—	—	—	—	.10	.29	.36Y
Zimbabwe	698	—	—	.01	—	.01	—	—Y	.06	.23	.22	.11	.32	.06	.08Y

	Exports 2001	Exports 2002	Exports 2003	Exports 2004	Exports 2005	Exports 2006	Exports 2007	Imports 2001	Imports 2002	Imports 2003	Imports 2004	Imports 2005	Imports 2006	Imports 2007
	Millions of U.S. Dollars							*Millions of U.S. Dollars*						
Asia....... 507	**1.6**	**2.4**	**17.2**	**9.5**	**25.0**	**5.3**	**13.6Y**	**47.2**	**54.7**	**92.0**	**154.0**	**215.0**	**278.7**	**142.8Y**
Afghanistan, I.S. of....... 512	—	.07	—	.03	.03	.02	.03Y	—	—	.01	—	—	.01	.01Y
Bangladesh....... 513	—	—	—	—	—	—	—V	.20	.30	.28	.20	.53	.69	.39Y
Cambodia....... 522	—	—	—	—	—	—	—Y	—	—	—	—	—	.03	.03Y
China,P.R.: Mainland....... 924	.50	.11	14.59	1.36	9.93	1.47	8.93V	18.73	24.47	48.32	82.02	115.03	139.39	82.32V
China,P.R.:Hong Kong....... 532	.05	.10	.22	.14	.06	.18	.06V	1.49	1.42	2.43	2.96	2.58	1.74	4.18V
China,P.R.:Macao....... 546	—	—	—	—	—	—	—V	—	—	—	.01	.01	.04	—V
India....... 534	.01	.05	.20	.11	1.29	.22	.27Y	4.00	3.95	4.35	7.04	10.25	14.59	18.11Y
Indonesia....... 536	.67	1.53	1.28	1.22	.63	.03	.10V	.87	1.21	1.72	2.40	15.30	39.57	1.97V
Kiribati....... 826	—	—	—	—	—	—	—Y	—	.01	—	.02	—	—	—Y
Korea....... 542	—	.04	.12	1.96	1.37	1.65	2.17V	6.69	8.92	14.02	23.38	33.64	41.24	11.34V
Lao People's Dem.Rep....... 544	—	—	—	.01	—	—	—Y	—	—	—	—	—	.01	.01Y
Malaysia....... 548	—	—	.05	—	.10	.19	.04V	3.25	1.87	3.37	5.57	8.13	9.49	1.70V
Maldives....... 556	—	—	—	—	—	—	—Y	—	—	—	—	—	.01	.01Y
Myanmar....... 518	....	....	....	....	....	....	....	—	—	.01	—	—	.07	.08Y
Pakistan....... 564	—	.46	.52	.42	.11	1.18	1.46Y	.76	.33	1.39	5.50	5.02	4.56	5.66Y
Philippines....... 566	.01	.02	—	—	—	.34	—V	.19	.19	.41	.69	.61	.53	.54V
Samoa....... 862	—	—	—	—	—	—	—Y	—	.01	—	—	—	—	—Y
Singapore....... 576	.04	—	.15	2.20	.27	.05	.06Y	.39	1.32	1.78	4.78	2.21	2.36	2.93Y
Solomon Islands....... 813	—	—	—	—	.02	—	—Y	—	—	—	—	—	—	—Y
Sri Lanka....... 524	—	—	—	—	2.87	—	—Y	.80	1.13	1.14	1.26	1.26	1.07	1.32Y
Taiwan Province of China....... 528	.32	—	.01	2.08	.01	.01	.47V	6.79	6.22	8.49	12.49	13.80	13.59	2.78V
Thailand....... 578	—	—	—	—	8.23	—	—Y	1.45	2.07	3.22	4.52	5.07	7.49	9.30Y
Tuvalu....... 869	—	—	—	—	—	—	—Y	—	—	—	.02	—	.01	.02Y
Vanuatu....... 846	—	—	—	—	—	—	—Y	—	—	—	—	—	.07	.09Y
Vietnam....... 582	—	—	.08	—	.13	—	—V	1.59	1.25	1.01	1.09	1.54	2.13	—V
Europe....... 170	**406.1**	**391.6**	**466.8**	**629.8**	**787.4**	**1,043.2**	**1,555.0Y**	**646.8**	**719.2**	**885.7**	**1,236.1**	**1,469.0**	**1,767.1**	**1,954.8Y**
Albania....... 914	10.15	13.87	17.42	23.59	27.52	40.56	73.24V	1.30	1.13	3.96	6.35	9.07	11.72	26.74V
Armenia....... 911	.06	.20	.16	.30	.15	.14	.20V	—	.16	.42	—	—	.02	—V
Azerbaijan....... 912	.03	.17	.13	.28	1.27	.80	.42V	—	.25	—	—	—	—	—V
Belarus....... 913	.12	.11	.12	.16	.50	.94	3.06V	.46	1.35	.63	.22	.24	.25	.33V
Bosnia & Herzegovina....... 963	16.24	18.31	23.79	33.23	50.46	64.70	80.29Y	4.15	14.30	11.75	16.31	23.58	26.53	32.93Y
Bulgaria....... 918	20.70	21.78	25.83	51.54	76.10	130.14	354.07V	103.39	128.48	149.21	209.75	234.33	250.17	436.22V
Croatia....... 960	58.42	59.08	66.17	80.16	81.05	124.23	201.06V	46.39	55.23	63.55	65.78	75.23	78.96	128.45V
Czech Republic....... 935	3.18	1.98	3.07	5.36	6.05	10.55	11.38V	10.73	9.03	11.95	17.47	23.34	32.79	46.61V
Estonia....... 939	.05	.03	.02	.03	.02	.03	.13V	.11	.18	.15	.26	.17	.10	.08V
Georgia....... 915	.06	.05	.04	.27	.10	.06	.04Y	—	.01	7.48	.01	.17	.03	.03Y
Gibraltar....... 823	—	—	—	—	—	—	—Y	.02	.10	—	.02	.01	.04	.05Y
Hungary....... 944	2.56	2.68	2.83	2.19	2.70	6.39	8.20V	17.50	28.70	29.14	30.99	36.25	38.06	178.56V
Kazakhstan....... 916	.21	.14	.35	.27	.29	.45	.56Y	.70	.95	.20	2.28	19.28	21.49	26.67Y
Kyrgyz Republic....... 917	—	—	—	—	—	—	—V	—	—	.03	.48	.16	.58	.73V
Latvia....... 941	.02	.01	.03	.13	.30	.23	.82V	.01	—	.01	—	.03	.08	.05V
Lithuania....... 946	.15	.02	.07	.55	.98	.34	.43V	.95	.21	.01	1.26	.42	.65	.94V
Moldova....... 921	.36	.14	.19	.04	.06	.17	.21Y	—	.13	.61	.32	.27	.13	.17Y
Poland....... 964	.93	.90	.49	2.62	4.04	6.33	7.43V	15.16	21.78	26.42	78.31	94.64	117.69	142.10V
Romania....... 968	.96	.95	1.39	1.83	4.19	13.30	20.82V	13.19	9.75	14.38	113.06	64.91	91.87	87.63V
Russia....... 922	13.94	14.43	13.74	19.67	21.42	25.48	40.75V	139.35	125.37	178.97	271.01	424.49	569.58	39.65V
Serbia & Montenegro....... 965	266.78	246.38	274.99	347.60	459.54	557.85	692.29Y	157.20	185.19	212.80	243.72	264.21	282.85	351.01Y
Slovak Republic....... 936	1.87	1.35	.84	3.59	1.48	3.40	6.91V	3.73	4.87	5.86	8.45	11.75	13.90	25.76V
Tajikistan....... 923	—	.09	.01	—	.02	—	—V	—	.06	1.19	1.10	.49	.01	.01Y
Turkey....... 186	8.58	8.46	32.81	53.95	46.31	55.18	50.36V	46.41	59.26	78.82	94.88	113.61	123.92	298.94V
Turkmenistan....... 925	—	—	—	.02	.62	—	—Y	—	—	—	—	.04	—	—Y
Ukraine....... 926	.78	.48	1.78	2.16	2.04	1.80	2.23Y	85.96	72.75	88.03	74.10	72.03	105.65	131.11Y
Uzbekistan....... 927	—	—	.09	.13	.03	.01	.01Y	.05	—	.06	.01	.24	.07	.09Y
Europe n.s....... 884	.01	—	.38	.14	.17	.07	.09Y	.05	.02	.02	.01	.01	—	.01Y
Middle East....... 407	**5.9**	**8.1**	**8.6**	**4.4**	**5.4**	**12.2**	**14.9Y**	**12.6**	**15.9**	**12.0**	**12.3**	**15.4**	**20.9**	**18.8Y**
Bahrain....... 419	—	.03	.03	—	.01	.09	.11Y	—	.09	—	—	—	.07	.09Y
Egypt....... 469	1.23	4.69	3.82	.58	1.25	2.43	3.01Y	2.78	4.32	1.68	1.15	2.74	3.29	4.09Y
Iran, I.R. of....... 429	2.10	.79	1.51	.47	.38	1.10	1.42Y	2.52	3.75	1.65	1.34	1.60	2.05	2.47Y
Iraq....... 433	.45	—	.01	.01	1.13	.05	.07Y	.01	—	—	—	—	.02	.03Y
Israel....... 436	.30	.12	.15	.68	.55	.83	.36V	2.52	2.84	4.17	6.65	7.55	10.73	6.49V
Jordan....... 439	.17	.06	.18	.16	.15	.05	.09V	—	—	—	.75	.04	.08	—V
Kuwait....... 443	—	.01	.04	.02	—	—	—Y	—	—	.02	.01	.02	—	—Y
Lebanon....... 446	.22	.09	.31	.03	—	.05	.06Y	.01	—	—	.01	.01	.01	.02Y
Libya....... 672	.39	.70	.07	.47	.09	.12	.16Y	.04	—	—	—	.05	.24	.29Y
Oman....... 449	.01	—	—	—	—	—	—Y	—	—	—	—	.39	.05	.06Y
Qatar....... 453	—	—	—	—	—	6.75	8.75Y	—	—	—	—	—	—	—Y
Saudi Arabia....... 456	.04	.03	.03	.06	.25	—	—Y	.06	.20	.11	.13	.05	.81	.97Y
Syrian Arab Republic....... 463	.03	—	.03	.42	.24	.33	.41Y	2.90	2.61	1.39	.49	.13	.19	.24Y
United Arab Emirates....... 466	.95	1.52	2.34	1.48	1.26	.34	.44Y	1.80	2.05	2.96	1.82	2.77	3.37	4.06Y
Yemen, Republic of....... 474	—	.04	.06	—	.12	—	—Y	—	—	—	—	—	—	—Y
Western Hemisphere....... 207	**5.4**	**5.9**	**1.2**	**.9**	**88.5**	**.1**	**.7Y**	**39.3**	**50.7**	**42.6**	**63.8**	**57.6**	**69.2**	**74.1Y**
Antigua and Barbuda....... 311	—	—	—	—	—	—	—Y	—	—	—	.01	.01	.04	.05Y
Argentina....... 213	.01	1.19	.01	.31	1.59	.01	.38V	7.50	4.83	5.59	9.88	8.74	10.68	2.78V
Bahamas, The....... 313	—	—	—	—	—	—	—Y	.11	—	.02	.01	.01	.01	.01Y
Barbados....... 316	—	—	—	—	—	—	—Y	—	—	—	—	—	—	.01Y
Belize....... 339	—	—	—	—	—	—	—Y	—	—	.03	.02	.01	—	—Y

	Exports							Imports						
	2001	2002	2003	2004	2005	2006	2007	2001	2002	2003	2004	2005	2006	2007
	Millions of U.S. Dollars							Millions of U.S. Dollars						
Bolivia........ 218	.04	—	—	—	—	—	—Y	8.59	5.88	3.81	—	.01	—	—Y
Brazil........ 223	—	—	—	—	.94	—	—V	10.68	23.21	23.25	41.07	37.66	39.64	36.79V
Chile........ 228	—	—	—	.08	—	.04	.02V	.06	.04	.04	.11	.19	.20	.09V
Colombia........ 233	—	—	—	—	—	—	.17V	2.62	.09	1.15	2.17	1.24	.57	11.62V
Costa Rica........ 238	—	.01	—	—	—	—	—Y	.04	.15	1.51	.84	.55	.78	.96Y
Dominica........ 321	—	—	—	—	—	—	—Y	—	—	—	—	—	.07	.08Y
Dominican Republic........ 243	—	—	—	—	—	.06	.07Y	—	.01	.03	.02	.03	.02	.03Y
Ecuador........ 248	—	—	—	—	—	—	—Y	.56	1.01	2.97	7.22	6.19	6.98	8.66Y
El Salvador........ 253	—	.02	.02	—	.19	—	—Y	—	3.52	—	—	—	—	—Y
Guatemala........ 258	.04	.01	—	—	—	—	—Y	.02	.10	.11	.17	.31	.49	.61Y
Guyana........ 336	—	.04	—	—	—	—	—Y	—	—	—	—	—	—	—Y
Honduras........ 268	—	—	—	—	—	—	—Y	.02	.08	.06	.03	.08	—	—Y
Jamaica........ 343	—	—	—	—	—	—	—V	—	—	—	.01	—	.02	—V
Mexico........ 273	.01	—	.15	.29	2.22	—	—Y	1.58	.38	.33	.79	.92	1.95	2.42Y
Nicaragua........ 278	—	—	—	—	—	—	—Y	—	.05	—	—	—	.01	.01Y
Panama........ 283	5.14	4.63	.73	—	—	.01	.01Y	4.78	4.73	.87	.20	.57	.50	.62Y
Paraguay........ 288	—	—	—	—	—	—	—Y	—	—	—	—	—	.01	.01Y
Peru........ 293	—	—	—	.05	—	—	.02Y	.89	2.74	1.47	.07	.11	.23	.16Y
St. Kitts and Nevis........ 361	—	—	—	—	—	—	—Y	—	—	—	.01	—	—	—Y
Trinidad and Tobago........ 369	—	—	.22	—	—	—	—Y	.01	—	—	—	—	—	—Y
Uruguay........ 298	—	—	.06	.04	.01	—	—Y	.31	.35	.80	1.14	.94	.71	.88Y
Venezuela, Rep. Bol........ 299	—	—	—	—	—	—	—Y	.04	—	—	—	—	5.43	6.55Y
Western Hem. n.s........ 399	.17	.04	—	.16	83.58	—	—Y	1.45	3.47	.51	.03	.07	.88	1.70Y
Other Countries n.i.e........ 910	**—**	**—**	**—**	**—**	**.6**	**.2**	**.3Y**	**—**	**—**	**.1**	**.3**	**.8**	**1.4**	**1.7Y**
Cuba........ 928	—	—	—	—	—	—	—Y	—	—	.07	.02	.07	.06	.07Y
North Korea........ 954	—	—	—	—	.56	.24	.29Y	.01	.02	.06	.29	.68	1.32	1.63Y
Special Categories........ 899	**.5**	**—**	**—**	**—**	**—**	**.3**	**.3Y**	**—**	**—**	**—**	**—**	**—**	**—**	**—Y**
Memorandum Items														
European Union........ 998	594.00	599.63	777.15	956.87	1,083.51	1,326.09	1,948.43Y	886.16	1,093.63	1,225.98	1,460.90	1,467.87	1,650.07	2,631.18Y
Oil Exporting Ctys........ 999	7.47	5.99	6.01	4.68	5.04	9.01	11.73Y	5.34	7.20	6.51	10.19	20.18	51.65	16.55Y
Non-Oil Develop.Ctys........ 201	415.10	403.88	489.65	642.99	903.98	1,053.74	1,573.61Y	743.72	838.05	1,031.11	1,465.79	1,742.70	2,093.99	2,184.35Y
PERCENT DISTRIBUTION														
Industrial Countries........ 101	**63.4**	**63.2**	**63.7**	**61.3**	**55.4**	**55.7**	**56.0**	**55.6**	**57.6**	**55.0**	**49.6**	**45.3**	**42.9**	**51.6**
Developing Countries........ 202	**36.6**	**36.8**	**36.3**	**38.7**	**44.5**	**44.3**	**44.0**	**44.4**	**42.4**	**45.0**	**50.4**	**54.7**	**57.0**	**48.4**
Africa........ 607	**.3**	**.2**	**.1**	**.2**	**.1**	**.1**	**—**	**.2**	**.2**	**.2**	**.3**	**.2**	**.3**	**.2**
Asia........ 507	**.1**	**.2**	**1.3**	**.6**	**1.2**	**.2**	**.4**	**2.8**	**2.7**	**4.0**	**5.3**	**6.7**	**7.4**	**3.1**
Europe........ 170	**35.2**	**35.1**	**34.2**	**37.6**	**38.6**	**43.5**	**43.2**	**38.3**	**36.0**	**38.4**	**42.2**	**45.6**	**47.0**	**43.0**
Middle East........ 407	**.5**	**.7**	**.6**	**.3**	**.3**	**.5**	**.4**	**.7**	**.8**	**.5**	**.4**	**.5**	**.6**	**.4**
Western Hemisphere........ 207	**.5**	**.5**	**.1**	**.1**	**4.3**	**—**	**—**	**2.3**	**2.5**	**1.8**	**2.2**	**1.8**	**1.8**	**1.6**
ANNUAL PERCENT CHANGE														
World........ 001	**–12.4**	**–3.4**	**22.5**	**22.6**	**21.8**	**17.6**	**50.1**	**–19.0**	**18.2**	**15.6**	**27.1**	**10.0**	**16.7**	**20.8**
Industrial Countries........ 101	**–11.5**	**–3.6**	**23.5**	**18.0**	**10.1**	**18.1**	**50.9**	**–13.3**	**22.5**	**10.3**	**14.7**	**.4**	**10.5**	**45.1**
Developing Countries........ 202	**–13.7**	**–3.0**	**20.9**	**30.7**	**40.4**	**16.9**	**49.2**	**–25.2**	**12.8**	**22.8**	**42.2**	**19.4**	**21.7**	**2.6**
Africa........ 607	**44.3**	**–47.2**	**1.3**	**57.9**	**–12.7**	**–23.9**	**–40.1**	**–73.7**	**52.6**	**12.8**	**80.2**	**–39.2**	**62.8**	**7.5**
Asia........ 507	**–21.0**	**48.3**	**625.3**	**–44.7**	**162.5**	**–78.7**	**154.2**	**1.9**	**15.8**	**68.2**	**67.4**	**39.6**	**29.6**	**–48.8**
Europe........ 170	**–14.2**	**–3.6**	**19.2**	**34.9**	**25.0**	**32.5**	**49.1**	**–27.1**	**11.2**	**23.1**	**39.6**	**18.8**	**20.3**	**10.6**
Middle East........ 407	**–46.0**	**37.5**	**6.2**	**–49.0**	**24.0**	**123.4**	**22.5**	**–24.2**	**25.6**	**–24.4**	**2.8**	**24.5**	**36.1**	**–10.1**
Western Hemisphere........ 207	**454.0**	**9.1**	**–79.9**	**–20.8**	**—**	**–99.9**	**464.5**	**1.8**	**29.0**	**–15.9**	**49.9**	**–9.7**	**20.1**	**7.0**
Other Countries n.i.e........ 910	**—**	**—**	**....**	**....**	**....**	**–57.3**	**24.1**	**–96.6**	**84.9**	**524.7**	**144.6**	**147.2**	**81.9**	**24.1**

		Exports							Imports						
		2001	2002	2003	2004	2005	2006	2007	2001	2002	2003	2004	2005	2006	2007
		Millions of U.S. Dollars							*Millions of U.S. Dollars*						
IFS World Total		**928.0**	**486.0**	**856.1**	**991.6**	**856.7**	**974.5**	**1,190.0**	**1,117.9**	**626.7**	**1,304.4**	**1,680.0**	**1,706.3**	**1,790.0**	**2,590.0**
DOTS World Total	**001**	**673.9**	**494.7**	**848.1**	**1,253.3Y**	**1,006.8Y**	**1,075.2Y**	**1,222.9Y**	**749.3**	**508.1**	**1,240.4**	**1,738.7Y**	**1,889.1Y**	**2,035.2Y**	**2,808.9Y**
Industrial Countries	**101**	**497.3**	**414.4**	**701.0**	**1,119.1Y**	**882.0Y**	**931.4Y**	**1,048.6Y**	**269.4**	**161.1**	**388.6**	**578.1Y**	**557.1Y**	**562.4Y**	**797.0Y**
United States	111	114.03	98.17	247.79	449.09V	311.45V	271.00V	325.18V	24.47	14.00	30.66	39.16V	30.91V	49.17V	35.09V
Canada	156	5.30	13.36	10.44	21.33V	11.88V	14.23V	17.04V	2.29	.39	1.97	1.04V	.78V	2.70V	11.54V
Australia	193	.75	.17	.20	.28V	.81V	.38V	.44V	4.06	1.10	4.07	3.98V	3.52V	5.70V	9.62V
Japan	158	21.87	23.73	13.94	28.65V	26.09V	27.66V	21.45V	28.83	10.93	29.35	28.75V	19.65V	22.82V	57.03V
New Zealand	196	.02	.01	.01	.02V	.03V	.08V	.07V	.61	.05	.10	1.74V	2.26V	1.88V	.15V
Austria	122	.30	.09	.23	.72V	.62V	.41V	.64V	.91	1.02	.86	.56V	1.20V	1.32V	2.56V
Belgium	124	9.51	8.30	7.00	12.27V	14.98V	24.05V	16.95V	8.11	7.79	20.64	61.38V	47.65V	44.39V	54.91V
Cyprus	423	.37	—	.03	.02V	.02Y	.12V	.24V	.03	.03	.03	.02V	.08V	.13V	.17V
Denmark	128	2.88	1.80	1.21	2.34V	2.84V	2.48V	1.75V	1.95	2.16	3.91	5.14V	5.84V	4.84V	4.41V
Finland	172	.25	.44	.01	.02V	.76V	.50V	.39V	.42	.15	.21	1.16V	.32V	6.92V	33.64V
France	132	250.04	194.22	316.71	385.64V	317.08V	344.74V	388.80V	127.26	83.68	178.88	297.36V	317.35V	296.34V	382.21V
Germany	134	27.76	27.48	46.88	96.89V	88.47V	64.75V	74.16V	26.21	14.41	37.27	37.40V	36.66V	35.23V	47.38V
Greece	174	.32	.40	.46	.40V	.63V	1.17V	2.72V	.27	.62	5.09	4.80V	8.06V	3.16V	2.80V
Iceland	176	—	—	—	.04V	.04V	.06V	.07V	—	—	.18	.02V	.05V	—V	—V
Ireland	178	.29	—	.03	.12V	.05V	.07V	.62V	.46	.39	.98	.06V	1.17V	.32V	.02V
Italy	136	10.72	7.89	14.03	43.48V	32.81V	53.87V	53.99V	15.47	8.71	36.17	28.82V	28.08V	27.37V	37.31V
Luxembourg	137	.01	—	.11	—V	—V	—V	—V	.16	.07	.43	1.77V	—V	.13V	.44V
Malta	181	.04	.01	.01	—V	—V	.05V	—V	.10	.19	.23	—V	.13V	.08V	.02V
Netherlands	138	12.37	6.38	10.94	21.15V	18.34V	30.15V	23.45V	4.99	2.80	6.20	8.91V	8.00V	9.21V	66.92V
Norway	142	.28	.02	.05	.68V	.81V	.82V	.92V	.15	.21	.13	.47V	.78V	.43V	.89V
Portugal	182	1.65	.42	1.01	1.57V	.83V	4.42V	4.31V	1.40	.88	.42	2.96V	.32V	2.98V	.65V
Slovenia	961	—	—	—	.17Y	.02V	.03V	2.27V	—	—	—	.08Y	.08V	.10V	.10V
Spain	184	12.82	12.14	7.12	16.35V	16.66V	30.65V	30.41V	7.48	5.29	11.40	28.64V	20.23V	24.69V	23.84V
Sweden	144	5.01	3.73	1.72	10.11V	8.42V	10.54V	17.30V	.90	.80	4.69	2.39V	1.63V	11.39V	6.25V
Switzerland	146	.62	1.16	5.31	1.94V	2.88V	5.31V	5.78V	2.87	1.34	2.75	2.87V	9.18V	2.50V	3.26V
United Kingdom	112	20.07	14.46	15.81	25.79V	25.47V	43.85V	59.70V	9.94	4.13	11.93	18.66V	13.15V	8.59V	15.81V
Developing Countries	**202**	**166.6**	**69.7**	**130.6**	**112.5Y**	**100.1Y**	**113.2Y**	**136.3Y**	**393.4**	**299.8**	**751.8**	**1,029.2Y**	**1,181.9Y**	**1,287.3Y**	**1,781.7Y**
Africa	**607**	**33.6**	**22.1**	**67.2**	**40.7Y**	**25.5Y**	**28.0Y**	**37.2Y**	**75.3**	**70.9**	**159.7**	**252.0Y**	**278.0Y**	**266.8Y**	**405.2Y**
Algeria	612	.03	.10	.11	.15Y	.19Y	.23Y	.30Y	.03	.05	.04	.05Y	.07Y	.08Y	.10Y
Angola	614	—	—	—	—Y	—Y	—Y	—Y	.01	—	—	—Y	—Y	—Y	—Y
Benin	638	—	.04	—	.01V	.02V	.02Y	.03Y	.03	—	—	.43V	.14V	.18Y	.22Y
Botswana	616	—	—	—	—Y	—Y	—Y	—Y	—	.02	—	—Y	—Y	—Y	—Y
Burkina Faso	748	.03	.02	—	—Y	—Y	—Y	—Y	—	.02	.21	.27Y	.31Y	.39Y	.48Y
Burundi	618	—	—	.08	—V	—V	—V	—Y	—	—	—	—Y	—Y	—Y	—Y
Cameroon	622	.03	.06	—	—Y	—Y	—Y	—Y	.02	—	.11	.15Y	.17Y	.21Y	.26Y
Central African Rep.	626	.04	—	.04	.05Y	.06Y	.07Y	.09Y	.01	—	—	—Y	—Y	—Y	—Y
Chad	628	—	.01	.04	.05Y	.05Y	.07Y	.08Y	.01	—	.06	.07Y	.08Y	.10Y	.13Y
Comoros	632	2.24	1.64	2.09	2.74Y	3.13Y	3.87Y	4.81Y	.10	.03	.15	.20Y	.23Y	.29Y	.36Y
Congo, Dem. Rep. of	636	.01	—	.15	.20Y	.23Y	.28Y	.35Y	.02	—	.04	.06Y	.07Y	.08Y	.10Y
Congo, Republic of	634	.04	.04	.01	—V	—Y	—Y	—Y	—	.04	—	—V	—Y	—Y	—Y
Côte d'Ivoire	662	.08	.04	.64	.47V	.24V	.17V	.21Y	2.21	.14	.39	1.28V	2.50V	1.00V	1.24Y
Djibouti	611	.02	.01	—	—Y	—Y	—Y	—Y	.29	.01	.02	.03Y	.03Y	.04Y	.05Y
Equatorial Guinea	642	.14	—	—	—Y	—Y	—Y	—Y	—	—	.64	.84Y	.96Y	1.18Y	1.47Y
Ethiopia	644	—	.06	.02	—V	—V	—Y	—Y	—	—	.01	—V	—V	—Y	—Y
Gabon	646	.02	—	.02	.02Y	.02Y	.03Y	.04Y	.25	.04	—	—Y	—Y	—Y	—Y
Gambia, The	648	.06	—	—	—Y	—Y	—Y	—Y	—	—	—	.01Y	.01Y	.01Y	.01Y
Ghana	652	—	—	.03	.03Y	.04Y	.05Y	.06Y	.01	—	.02	.03Y	.03Y	.04Y	.04Y
Guinea	656	—	—	—	—V	—Y	—Y	.01Y	.06	—	—	—V	—Y	—Y	—Y
Guinea-Bissau	654	—	—	.02	.02Y	.02Y	.03Y	.04Y	—	—	.01	.01Y	.01Y	.02Y	.02Y
Kenya	664	1.22	1.87	.43	.01V	.01Y	.01Y	.01Y	5.07	6.73	8.33	3.90V	4.46Y	5.51Y	6.84Y
Lesotho	666	.63	—	.52	.68Y	.77Y	.96Y	1.19Y	—	—	—	—Y	—Y	—Y	—Y
Liberia	668	—	—	.13	.17Y	.20Y	.25Y	.31Y	.04	—	.36	.47Y	.54Y	.66Y	.82Y
Malawi	676	—	—	—	—Y	—Y	—Y	—Y	—	.29	2.43	3.20Y	3.65Y	4.51Y	5.60Y
Mali	678	.02	—	.03	.04Y	.05Y	.06Y	.07Y	.08	—	—	.01Y	.01Y	.01Y	.01Y
Mauritania	682	—	—	.01	.01Y	.01Y	.01Y	.01Y	—	—	.01	.01Y	.01Y	.01Y	.02Y
Mauritius	684	23.44	15.63	44.01	30.82V	13.44V	13.71V	16.06V	16.97	14.71	39.09	107.57V	125.78V	114.07V	135.80V
Morocco	686	1.07	.83	1.25	2.31V	3.24V	4.00Y	4.97Y	1.12	.83	2.62	1.24V	2.29V	2.83Y	3.51Y
Mozambique	688	.15	—	.07	.09Y	—V	—V	—Y	.10	—	.10	—V	—V	—V	—Y
Namibia	728	—	—	.07	.13Y	.20Y	.27Y	.34Y	—	—	.03	.07Y	.10Y	.14Y	.17Y
Niger	692	—	.05	.12	—V	—Y	—Y	—Y	—	—	—	—V	—Y	—Y	—Y
Nigeria	694	.06	—	—	—Y	—Y	—Y	—Y	.07	13.80	.17	.22Y	.31Y	.38Y	.46Y
Rwanda	714	—	.01	—	—Y	—Y	—Y	—Y	—	—	—	—Y	—Y	—Y	—Y
São Tomé & Príncipe	716	.01	—	—	—Y	—Y	—Y	—Y	—	—	—	—Y	—Y	—Y	—Y
Senegal	722	.03	.08	.29	.08V	.03V	.04V	.05Y	.22	.05	.31	.36V	.71V	.11V	.14Y
Seychelles	718	.84	.51	.58	.77Y	.88Y	1.08Y	1.34Y	.07	3.11	1.81	2.38Y	2.72Y	3.36Y	4.17Y
Sierra Leone	724	.01	—	—	—Y	—Y	—Y	—Y	—	—	—	—Y	—Y	—Y	—Y
South Africa	199	2.05	.93	16.17	1.22V	1.75V	1.93V	5.88V	38.89	26.37	85.56	97.67V	93.38V	79.88V	179.25V
Sacca exc. South Afr.	608	—	—	—	—Y	—Y	—Y	—Y	—	—	—	7.20V	8.23Y	10.17Y	12.62Y
Sudan	732	.30	.03	.07	.07V	.33V	.35V	.33V	.08	—	.09	.02V	.01V	—V	.03V

	Exports							Imports						
	2001	2002	2003	2004	2005	2006	2007	2001	2002	2003	2004	2005	2006	2007
	Millions of U.S. Dollars							Millions of U.S. Dollars						
Swaziland.......... 734	—	—	.08	.11Y	.13Y	.16Y	.19Y	1.47	1.18	4.96	6.52Y	7.45Y	9.20Y	11.42Y
Tanzania.......... 738	.51	—	.03	.04Y	.05Y	.06Y	.08Y	.32	.84	3.17	4.17Y	4.76Y	5.89Y	7.30Y
Togo.......... 742	—	—	—	.08V	—V	—Y	—Y	.02	—	.01	—V	—V	—Y	—Y
Tunisia.......... 744	.49	.14	.07	.18V	.22V	.19V	.24Y	1.07	.50	1.00	1.02V	1.20V	3.47V	4.30Y
Uganda.......... 746	—	—	—	—Y	—Y	—Y	—Y	—	.01	—	—Y	—Y	—Y	—Y
Zambia.......... 754	—	—	—	—V	.01V	—V	—V	—	.01	—	—V	—V	—V	.03V
Zimbabwe.......... 698	—	—	.03	.12V	.18V	.14V	.17Y	.11	.13	.71	.09V	.09V	.01V	.01Y
Africa n.s.......... 799	—	—	—	—Y	—Y	—Y	—Y	6.49	1.95	7.20	12.45Y	17.70Y	22.95Y	28.20Y
Asia.......... 507	**129.8**	**45.1**	**58.2**	**65.8Y**	**64.7Y**	**74.9Y**	**87.1Y**	**150.0**	**93.6**	**389.9**	**486.4Y**	**544.1Y**	**579.4Y**	**834.1Y**
Afghanistan, I.S. of.......... 512	—	—	.08	.10Y	.11Y	.14Y	.17Y	—	—	—	—Y	—Y	—Y	—Y
Bangladesh.......... 513	.04	.10	—	—V	—V	—V	—V	.02	.03	.06	.15V	.99V	1.38Y	1.47Y
Cambodia.......... 522	.02	—	—	—V	—V	—V	.01Y	—	—	.01	—V	—V	.01V	.01Y
China,P.R.: Mainland.......... 924	7.11	6.11	8.47	12.73V	12.71V	22.17V	27.29V	51.39	32.26	191.87	167.76V	201.69V	244.84V	366.10V
China,P.R.:Hong Kong.......... 532	9.52	7.00	8.23	7.31V	11.11V	7.08V	8.28V	1.49	.76	23.77	114.19V	95.12V	97.03V	136.72V
China,P.R.:Macao.......... 546	—	—	—	.01V	.01V	.04V	.03V	—	—	—	—V	—V	—V	—V
Fiji.......... 819	—	—	—	—Y	—Y	—Y	—Y	.01	—	—	—Y	—Y	—Y	—Y
French Polynesia.......... 887	.07	—	.10	.13Y	.14Y	.18Y	.22Y	—	—	.33	.43Y	.49Y	.60Y	.75Y
India.......... 534	1.47	1.83	4.12	6.27V	12.76V	15.77Y	19.57Y	18.38	20.98	51.02	38.60V	49.45V	61.12Y	75.85Y
Indonesia.......... 536	22.44	.53	.15	.49V	.56V	2.22V	1.94V	17.95	12.23	23.82	10.90V	23.34V	18.74V	36.01V
Korea.......... 542	.26	.09	1.25	1.00V	1.13V	1.50V	1.73V	9.35	6.37	.10	16.26V	15.83V	17.64V	30.15V
Malaysia.......... 548	.18	.19	.48	3.57V	1.90V	.42V	1.27V	10.76	8.35	17.02	10.48V	14.69V	12.44V	25.56V
Nauru.......... 836	—	—	.35	.46Y	.52Y	.65Y	.80Y	—	—	.02	.03Y	.03Y	.04Y	.05Y
New Caledonia.......... 839	.03	.12	.03	.09V	.11Y	.13Y	.16Y	.06	—	.06	—V	—Y	—Y	—Y
Pakistan.......... 564	.32	.40	.39	1.49V	.86V	1.06Y	1.31Y	22.67	3.46	24.70	18.06V	30.89V	38.18Y	47.38Y
Papua New Guinea.......... 853	.15	—	—	—Y	—Y	—Y	—Y	—	—	—	—Y	—Y	—Y	—Y
Philippines.......... 566	—	.01	.04	—V	—V	—V	.04V	.10	.07	.28	.10V	.29V	.18V	.12V
Singapore.......... 576	81.52	20.74	24.77	26.89V	16.93V	19.12V	20.75V	6.34	3.30	12.16	48.03V	44.68V	39.06V	52.71V
Sri Lanka.......... 524	.15	.56	.25	1.26V	.65V	.19V	.13V	.07	.02	4.21	3.13V	3.22V	1.17V	.43V
Taiwan Province of China.......... 528	.38	.71	.57	.89V	1.28V	.78V	.97V	4.89	2.86	26.29	29.11V	26.28V	24.60V	24.87V
Thailand.......... 578	6.08	6.73	8.92	3.05V	3.93V	3.40V	2.44V	4.77	2.77	13.36	29.15V	37.12V	22.39V	35.91V
Vanuatu.......... 846	—	—	.01	.01Y	.01Y	.02Y	.02Y	—	—	—	—Y	—Y	—Y	—Y
Vietnam.......... 582	.09	.01	.04	—V	—V	—V	—V	1.76	.15	.82	—V	—V	—V	—V
Europe.......... 170	**.9**	**.3**	**.6**	**3.6Y**	**4.1Y**	**3.0Y**	**4.1Y**	**6.5**	**4.4**	**16.5**	**17.7Y**	**14.5Y**	**17.4Y**	**19.5Y**
Albania.......... 914	—	—	—	—V	.02V	.01V	—V	—	—	.01	—V	—V	.14V	.02V
Belarus.......... 913	—	—	—	.09V	—V	—V	.03V	—	—	—	—V	.14V	.35V	.40V
Bulgaria.......... 918	.16	.04	.04	.16V	1.28V	.34V	.04V	.35	.01	.04	.06V	.06V	1.28V	.28V
Croatia.......... 960	—	—	—	—V	—V	—V	—V	—	—	—	—V	—V	.13V	—V
Czech Republic.......... 935	.05	.01	.01	.67V	1.05V	.33V	.57V	.64	.33	.83	.59V	.19V	.75V	.44V
Estonia.......... 939	—	—	—	.01V	.01V	—V	.01V	—	—	—	.30V	—V	—V	—V
Faroe Islands.......... 816	—	—	—	—Y	—Y	—Y	—Y	.06	—	—	—Y	—Y	—Y	—Y
Gibraltar.......... 823	.09	—	—	—Y	—Y	—Y	—Y	—	.01	—	—Y	—Y	—Y	—Y
Hungary.......... 944	.07	—	—	.07V	.05V	.02V	.01V	.41	.30	.86	.29V	.19V	.80V	2.13V
Kazakhstan.......... 916	—	—	—	.01V	.01Y	.02Y	.02Y	—	—	—	—Y	—Y	—Y	—Y
Latvia.......... 941	—	—	—	.01V	.03V	.04V	.05V	—	—	—	.04V	.41V	.04V	—V
Lithuania.......... 946	—	—	—	—V	—V	—V	—V	—	—	—	.02V	.01V	—V	—V
Macedonia, FYR.......... 962	—	—	—	.01V	.01V	.01V	.01Y	—	—	—	—V	—V	—V	—Y
Moldova.......... 921	—	—	—	—V	—V	—Y	.01Y	....	....	....	....	....	....	....
Poland.......... 964	.30	.03	.29	.73V	.80V	.08V	.19V	.39	.52	.80	1.35V	.96V	.98V	.71V
Romania.......... 968	—	—	—	.14V	.33V	.38V	.05V	.10	.16	.24	.57V	.23V	.57V	.63V
Russia.......... 922	.07	.10	.08	.12V	.19V	.50V	1.39V	1.54	.51	6.43	.08V	—V	.01V	.07V
Serbia & Montenegro.......... 965	.03	.01	.09	.12Y	.13Y	.16Y	.20Y	.08	.04	.15	.19Y	.22Y	.27Y	.34Y
Slovak Republic.......... 936	—	—	—	—Y	—V	—V	.27V	—	—	—	—Y	.37V	.47V	.68V
Turkey.......... 186	.04	.01	.10	1.31V	.10V	1.02V	1.16V	2.36	1.32	6.32	12.97V	10.29V	9.86V	11.67V
Ukraine.......... 926	—	—	—	.18V	.04V	.05Y	.06Y	—	—	—	.08V	.11V	.13Y	.17Y
Europe n.s.......... 884	.08	.09	.01	.02Y	.02Y	.02Y	.03Y	.58	1.18	.86	1.14Y	1.30Y	1.60Y	1.99Y
Middle East.......... 407	**1.6**	**1.6**	**2.4**	**1.9Y**	**2.7Y**	**3.3Y**	**4.6Y**	**151.6**	**123.2**	**146.0**	**190.6Y**	**252.6Y**	**314.3Y**	**381.5Y**
Bahrain.......... 419	—	.37	.04	.05Y	.05Y	.06Y	.08Y	51.85	56.66	18.51	24.31Y	27.77Y	34.33Y	42.60Y
Egypt.......... 469	.25	.30	.38	.50Y	.57Y	.71Y	.88Y	1.86	2.57	8.43	11.07Y	12.65Y	15.64Y	19.40Y
Iran, I.R. of.......... 429	.01	—	.02	.02Y	.03Y	.03Y	.04Y	1.98	3.71	83.79	110.87Y	150.81Y	189.60Y	228.73Y
Iraq.......... 433	—	—	—	—Y	—Y	—Y	.01Y	.01	—	.01	.01Y	.01Y	.01Y	.02Y
Israel.......... 436	.39	.36	.25	—V	—V	—V	—V	.34	1.19	1.71	—V	—V	—V	—V
Jordan.......... 439	—	.05	—	—V	—V	.02V	.45V	—	—	.18	—V	—V	.02V	.69V
Kuwait.......... 443	—	—	—	—Y	—Y	—Y	—Y	.03	2.15	.05	.07Y	.10Y	.12Y	.15Y
Lebanon.......... 446	—	.01	—	—Y	—Y	—Y	—Y	.03	.01	—	—Y	—Y	—Y	—Y
Libya.......... 672	—	—	.03	.04Y	.05Y	.06Y	.08Y	—	—	.03	.03Y	.05Y	.06Y	.07Y
Oman.......... 449	—	—	—	—Y	—Y	—Y	—Y	.02	.02	.09	.12Y	.17Y	.21Y	.25Y
Qatar.......... 453	—	—	—	.11V	.05V	.02V	.03Y	28.67	17.55	.49	.78V	2.14V	.22V	.27Y
Saudi Arabia.......... 456	.13	.29	.81	.07V	.47V	.58Y	.75Y	6.68	3.61	6.14	8.12Y	11.05Y	13.89Y	16.76Y
Syrian Arab Republic.......... 463	.01	.06	.02	—V	—Y	—Y	—Y	—	.01	—	—V	—Y	—Y	—Y
United Arab Emirates.......... 466	.77	.18	.88	1.14Y	1.45Y	1.79Y	2.32Y	59.49	34.71	26.57	35.16Y	47.83Y	60.14Y	72.55Y
Yemen, Republic of.......... 474	.01	—	—	—V	—V	—Y	—Y	.67	1.06	.02	.07V	.03V	.03Y	.04Y
Western Hemisphere.......... 207	**.8**	**.5**	**2.1**	**.5Y**	**3.1Y**	**4.0Y**	**3.2Y**	**10.0**	**7.7**	**39.6**	**82.5Y**	**92.7Y**	**109.4Y**	**141.3Y**
Antigua and Barbuda.......... 311	.01	.01	—	—Y	—Y	—Y	—Y	—	—	—	—Y	—Y	—Y	—Y
Argentina.......... 213	—	—	.01	.10V	.19V	.11V	.59V	4.42	1.25	9.40	25.36V	14.89V	15.86V	33.62V
Bahamas, The.......... 313	—	—	—	—Y	—Y	—Y	—Y	.19	—	.04	.05Y	.05Y	.07Y	.08Y
Belize.......... 339	—	—	.01	.01Y	.01Y	.01Y	.01Y	—	—	—	—Y	—Y	—Y	—Y
Bermuda.......... 319	—	—	—	.01Y	—V	—V	—Y	—	—	—	—Y	—Y	—Y	—Y

	Exports							Imports						
	2001	2002	2003	2004	2005	2006	2007	2001	2002	2003	2004	2005	2006	2007
	Millions of U.S. Dollars							*Millions of U.S. Dollars*						
Brazil 223	.02	.03	.05	.21V	.14V	.26V	—V	4.20	4.99	7.44	13.77V	13.83V	7.55V	—V
Chile 228	.06	—	—	.11V	.07V	.07V	.14V	.05	.04	.01	.01V	.05V	—V	.03V
Colombia 233	.04	—	.01	.01V	.16V	.02V	.02V	.04	.09	.03	.26V	.01V	.10V	.16V
Costa Rica 238	—	—	—	.02V	.04V	.05Y	.06Y	—	—	.03	—V	—V	—Y	—Y
Dominican Republic 243	.37	.02	—	—Y	—Y	—Y	—Y	—	—	.52	.68Y	.78Y	.97Y	1.20Y
Ecuador 248	—	—	.04	—V	—V	—V	—Y	.02	.02	.07	.17V	.14V	.13V	.16Y
El Salvador 253	—	—	.03	—V	.38V	.98V	—V	—	—	.01	—V	—V	.03V	—V
Falkland Islands 323	—	—	—	—Y	—Y	—Y	—Y	.01	—	—	—Y	—Y	.01Y	.01Y
Greenland 326	—	—	—	—Y	—Y	—Y	—Y	—	.01	—	—Y	—Y	.01Y	.01Y
Guatemala 258	—	—	—	—V	—V	—Y	—Y	.02	—	—	—V	—V	—Y	—Y
Guyana 336	.02	.01	—	—Y	—Y	.01Y	.01Y	—	—	.01	.01Y	.01Y	.01Y	.01Y
Haiti 263	—	.02	.01	—V	—Y	—Y	—Y	—	.02	—	—Y	—Y	—Y	—Y
Honduras 268	—	—	—	.03V	.03Y	.04Y	.04Y	—	—	.01	—V	—Y	.01Y	.01Y
Jamaica 343	.01	—	—	—V	—V	—V	—V	—	—	—	.19V	—V	—V	—V
Mexico 273	.14	.37	.28	—V	1.95V	2.40V	2.19V	.10	.81	.92	—V	—V	—V	.03V
Netherlands Antilles 353	—	.01	.02	.03Y	.04Y	.05Y	.06Y	—	—	—	—Y	—Y	—Y	—Y
Nicaragua 278	—	—	.02	—V	—V	—V	—V	—	—	—	—V	—V	—V	—V
Panama 283	.08	—	1.54	—V	—V	—V	—V	.04	—	—	—Y	.03V	—V	.01V
Paraguay 288	—	—	—	—V	—V	—V	—Y	.10	.05	.06	—V	—V	—V	—Y
Peru 293	.01	—	—	—V	.01V	.01V	.06Y	.66	.42	.36	.56V	.68V	1.80V	2.35Y
St. Kitts and Nevis 361	—	—	—	—Y	—Y	—Y	—Y	.02	—	—	—Y	—Y	—Y	—Y
St. Vincent & Grens 364	—	.06	.09	—V	—V	—Y	—Y	—	—	—	—V	—V	—Y	—Y
Suriname 366	—	—	—	—Y	—Y	—Y	—Y	.13	—	—	—Y	—Y	—Y	—Y
Trinidad and Tobago 369	—	—	—	—Y	—Y	—Y	—Y	.02	—	—	—Y	—Y	.01Y	.01Y
Uruguay 298	—	—	—	—V	.01V	.01Y	.01Y	—	—	—	—V	—V	—Y	—Y
Venezuela, Rep. Bol. 299	—	—	—	—V	.05V	—V	—V	—	—	.01	—V	—V	—V	—Y
Western Hem. n.s. 399	—	—	—	—Y	—Y	—Y	—Y	—	.01	20.73	41.45Y	62.17Y	82.89Y	103.61Y
Other Countries n.i.e. 910	**—**	**.1**	**—**	**—Y**	**—Y**	**—Y**	**—Y**	**.1**	**—**	**14.3**	**18.7Y**	**21.4Y**	**26.5Y**	**32.8Y**
Cuba 928	—	—	—	—Y	—Y	—Y	—Y	.03	.01	.01	.01Y	.01Y	.01Y	.01Y
North Korea 954	.03	.08	.02	.02Y	.03Y	.03Y	.04Y	.08	.04	14.26	18.73Y	21.41Y	26.46Y	32.83Y
Countries & Areas n.s. 898	**—**	**—**	**—**	**.1Y**	**.1Y**	**.1Y**	**.1Y**	**45.1**	**11.7**	**28.5**	**37.5Y**	**42.8Y**	**52.9Y**	**65.7Y**
Special Categories 899	**9.9**	**10.6**	**16.0**	**21.1Y**	**24.1Y**	**29.7Y**	**36.9Y**	**41.3**	**35.4**	**57.2**	**75.1Y**	**85.9Y**	**106.1Y**	**131.7Y**
Memorandum Items														
European Union 998	354.83	277.82	423.59	618.51Y	529.94Y	612.34Y	678.78Y	207.52	134.26	321.84	502.69Y	492.09Y	480.25Y	683.42Y
Oil Exporting Ctys 999	23.44	1.10	2.00	2.02Y	2.85Y	4.95Y	5.47Y	114.91	87.82	141.21	166.35Y	235.88Y	283.46Y	355.37Y
Non-Oil Develop.Ctys 201	143.20	68.56	128.61	110.51Y	97.22Y	108.24Y	130.83Y	278.52	211.97	610.56	862.85Y	946.02Y	1,003.84Y	1,426.28Y
PERCENT DISTRIBUTION														
Industrial Countries 101	**73.8**	**83.8**	**82.7**	**89.3**	**87.6**	**86.6**	**85.8**	**35.9**	**31.7**	**31.3**	**33.3**	**29.5**	**27.6**	**28.4**
Developing Countries 202	**24.7**	**14.1**	**15.4**	**9.0**	**9.9**	**10.5**	**11.1**	**52.5**	**59.0**	**60.6**	**59.2**	**62.6**	**63.3**	**63.4**
Africa 607	**5.0**	**4.5**	**7.9**	**3.2**	**2.5**	**2.6**	**3.0**	**10.0**	**13.9**	**12.9**	**14.5**	**14.7**	**13.1**	**14.4**
Asia 507	**19.3**	**9.1**	**6.9**	**5.2**	**6.4**	**7.0**	**7.1**	**20.0**	**18.4**	**31.4**	**28.0**	**28.8**	**28.5**	**29.7**
Europe 170	**.1**	**.1**	**.1**	**.3**	**.4**	**.3**	**.3**	**.9**	**.9**	**1.3**	**1.0**	**.8**	**.9**	**.7**
Middle East 407	**.2**	**.3**	**.3**	**.2**	**.3**	**.3**	**.4**	**20.2**	**24.3**	**11.8**	**11.0**	**13.4**	**15.4**	**13.6**
Western Hemisphere 207	**.1**	**.1**	**.3**	**—**	**.3**	**.4**	**.3**	**1.3**	**1.5**	**3.2**	**4.7**	**4.9**	**5.4**	**5.0**
Other Countries n.i.e. 910	**—**	**—**	**—**	**—**	**—**	**—**	**—**	**—**	**—**	**1.2**	**1.1**	**1.1**	**1.3**	**1.2**
ANNUAL PERCENT CHANGE														
World 001	**−16.4**	**−26.6**	**71.4**	**47.8**	**−19.7**	**6.8**	**13.7**	**2.1**	**−32.2**	**144.1**	**40.2**	**8.6**	**7.7**	**38.0**
Industrial Countries 101	**−25.1**	**−16.7**	**69.2**	**59.6**	**−21.2**	**5.6**	**12.6**	**8.0**	**−40.2**	**141.1**	**48.8**	**−3.6**	**1.0**	**41.7**
Developing Countries 202	**63.2**	**−58.2**	**87.5**	**−13.8**	**−11.1**	**13.1**	**20.4**	**−7.7**	**−23.8**	**150.8**	**36.9**	**14.8**	**8.9**	**38.4**
Africa 607	**29.5**	**−34.2**	**204.2**	**−39.5**	**−37.3**	**10.0**	**32.8**	**59.5**	**−5.8**	**125.3**	**57.8**	**10.3**	**−4.0**	**51.9**
Asia 507	**79.7**	**−65.2**	**29.1**	**12.9**	**−1.6**	**15.7**	**16.4**	**11.8**	**−37.6**	**316.5**	**24.8**	**11.9**	**6.5**	**44.0**
Europe 170	**−44.7**	**−66.7**	**109.3**	**488.1**	**12.9**	**−26.9**	**37.0**	**−3.3**	**−32.9**	**278.1**	**7.0**	**−18.2**	**20.4**	**12.2**
Middle East 407	**19.5**	**2.9**	**49.9**	**−20.2**	**38.6**	**22.8**	**41.1**	**−28.6**	**−18.7**	**18.5**	**30.5**	**32.5**	**24.4**	**21.4**
Western Hemisphere 207	**−24.2**	**−30.6**	**300.3**	**−74.5**	**467.5**	**29.7**	**−19.9**	**−61.4**	**−23.3**	**415.0**	**108.2**	**12.3**	**18.1**	**29.1**
Other Countries n.i.e. 910	**−11.2**	**144.4**	**−78.2**	**31.3**	**14.3**	**23.6**	**24.1**	**−21.2**	**−59.1**	**—**	**31.3**	**14.3**	**23.6**	**24.1**

		Exports							Imports						
		2001	2002	2003	2004	2005	2006	2007	2001	2002	2003	2004	2005	2006	2007
		Millions of U.S. Dollars							Millions of U.S. Dollars						
IFS World Total		**457.9**	**404.6**	**520.2**	**483.1**	**501.5**	**542.6**	**670.0**	**579.4**	**690.2**	**785.0**	**932.5**	**1,163.9**	**1,209.2**	**1,380.0**
DOTS World Total	**001**	**426.3Y**	**421.1Y**	**507.0Y**	**501.0Y**	**626.3Y**	**620.6Y**	**791.7Y**	**430.4Y**	**594.0Y**	**584.0Y**	**758.6Y**	**748.5Y**	**802.2Y**	**937.2Y**
Industrial Countries	**101**	**275.0Y**	**246.2Y**	**299.3Y**	**239.5Y**	**335.6Y**	**248.5Y**	**324.2Y**	**90.5Y**	**142.1Y**	**112.1Y**	**160.0Y**	**140.1Y**	**205.7Y**	**230.2Y**
United States	111	76.55V	69.45V	75.27V	59.00V	112.18V	58.18V	57.82V	16.28V	33.00V	18.37V	23.76V	30.69V	50.27V	56.76V
Canada	156	1.37V	1.01V	1.10V	1.21V	1.15V	1.31V	1.63V	4.82V	4.22V	2.12V	2.14V	2.89V	5.00V	5.29V
Australia	193	6.08V	4.34V	6.22V	.94V	7.91V	11.12V	6.93V	1.37V	12.27V	1.05V	.46V	1.07V	.51V	.90V
Japan	158	32.67V	23.86V	25.47V	12.12V	30.27V	18.77V	23.52V	12.96V	16.91V	21.22V	9.75V	6.04V	10.43V	8.91V
New Zealand	196	1.80V	1.94V	2.90V	1.57V	.66V	.49V	.03V	.04V	.02V	.11V	.06V	.52V	.12V	.03V
Austria	122	3.45V	1.48V	6.90V	3.11V	3.34V	2.42V	3.25V	.72V	.75V	.81V	.91V	.17V	.68V	.17V
Belgium	124	4.00V	7.73V	8.97V	14.51V	6.53V	5.26V	15.72V	3.82V	8.26V	6.97V	13.94V	9.52V	17.27V	12.88V
Cyprus	423	.03V	.04V	.01V	—V	—Y	—V	—V	.08V	.08V	.58V	.21V	.28V	.15V	1.63V
Denmark	128	2.86V	2.92V	2.87V	4.96V	5.97V	5.12V	5.47V	1.90V	2.05V	2.97V	2.94V	2.87V	3.25V	4.72V
Finland	172	.93V	.50V	.41V	.38V	.38V	6.70V	1.09V	1.97V	.72V	.71V	1.72V	4.67V	3.00V	8.92V
France	132	11.34V	8.88V	7.60V	7.57V	10.16V	6.67V	9.96V	6.13V	11.20V	9.80V	13.45V	13.43V	13.72V	18.35V
Germany	134	55.92V	56.56V	62.70V	57.10V	43.68V	59.12V	93.00V	17.32V	14.36V	11.01V	29.17V	12.10V	35.75V	28.48V
Greece	174	1.56V	3.39V	4.78V	6.16V	6.12V	4.25V	3.74V	.06V	.01V	1.43V	.39V	3.44V	—V	10.34V
Iceland	176	—V	.01V	—V	—V	—V	.01V	.04V	—V	—V	—V	—V	—V	—V	—V
Ireland	178	.18V	.02V	.18V	.06V	.02V	.06V	.10V	1.04V	1.80V	1.74V	5.62V	6.69V	15.50V	9.07V
Italy	136	4.45V	1.82V	8.07V	8.31V	2.26V	3.26V	5.16V	2.56V	3.76V	3.38V	7.71V	6.27V	6.99V	8.48V
Luxembourg	137	—V	—V	1.00V	—V	.79V	—V	—V	—V	.31V	.01V	.04V	.07V	—V	.08V
Malta	181	—Y	—V	.01V	—V	—V	—V	—V	—Y	—V	.52V	4.81V	2.13V	2.47V	—V
Netherlands	138	27.05V	22.06V	23.97V	18.43V	42.89V	26.83V	35.67V	3.81V	3.46V	3.18V	6.41V	6.73V	9.15V	9.42V
Norway	142	.25V	.18V	.23V	.21V	.15V	.14V	.16V	.19V	2.31V	1.70V	1.08V	.36V	.54V	.17V
Portugal	182	10.47V	9.61V	26.55V	2.53V	16.02V	10.45V	19.23V	1.27V	.46V	.39V	.38V	.40V	.88V	.80V
Slovenia	961	.69V	.83V	.84V	1.11Y	—V	—V	—V	—V	.04V	—V	—Y	.01V	—V	.02V
Spain	184	8.81V	6.16V	8.88V	4.00V	14.05V	6.00V	9.28V	.74V	1.00V	.70V	7.80V	1.09V	.69V	1.81V
Sweden	144	1.05V	.96V	.32V	.18V	.17V	.72V	1.26V	.24V	2.80V	4.46V	2.46V	2.81V	7.70V	7.90V
Switzerland	146	3.95V	5.08V	6.63V	3.42V	4.74V	2.40V	3.73V	.22V	.29V	.56V	.69V	2.32V	.41V	5.51V
United Kingdom	112	19.56V	17.34V	17.48V	32.60V	26.18V	19.19V	27.39V	12.98V	22.07V	18.28V	24.10V	23.50V	21.24V	29.60V
Developing Countries	**202**	**149.9Y**	**173.4Y**	**205.7Y**	**259.1Y**	**287.8Y**	**368.6Y**	**463.1Y**	**339.9Y**	**451.8Y**	**471.9Y**	**598.6Y**	**608.4Y**	**596.4Y**	**706.9Y**
Africa	**607**	**65.4Y**	**74.9Y**	**106.4Y**	**126.9Y**	**138.4Y**	**189.4Y**	**215.6Y**	**291.7Y**	**390.4Y**	**385.7Y**	**479.4Y**	**501.9Y**	**452.9Y**	**519.5Y**
Algeria	612	1.00V	2.84V	3.15V	4.10Y	5.22Y	6.44Y	8.35Y	—V	—V	—Y	—Y	—Y	—Y	—Y
Benin	638	.15V	—V	—V	.01V	—V	—Y	—Y	—Y	—Y	—V	—V	—V	—Y	—Y
Burkina Faso	748	.01Y	.01Y	.01Y	.01Y	.02Y	.02Y	.03Y	—Y	—Y	—Y	—Y	—Y	—Y	—Y
Cameroon	622	.03V	.05V	—V	—Y	—Y	—Y	—Y	—V	—V	—V	—Y	—Y	—Y	—Y
Congo, Dem. Rep. of	636	.97Y	1.05Y	1.33Y	1.75Y	2.00Y	2.47Y	3.07Y	.03Y	.03Y	.04Y	.05Y	.06Y	.07Y	.09Y
Côte d'Ivoire	662	—V	.02V	.05V	.03V	—V	—V	—Y	—V	.01V	.19V	.04V	.01V	—V	—Y
Djibouti	611	—Y	—Y	—Y	—Y	—Y	—Y	—Y	.03Y	.03Y	.04Y	.06Y	.07Y	.08Y	.10Y
Gabon	646	.36Y	.39Y	.49Y	.64Y	.74Y	.91Y	1.13Y	—Y	—Y	—Y	—Y	—Y	—Y	—Y
Gambia, The	648	.02Y	.02Y	.03Y	.03Y	.04Y	.05Y	.06Y	—Y	—Y	—Y	—Y	—Y	—Y	—Y
Ghana	652	—Y	—Y	—Y	—Y	—Y	—Y	—Y	.06Y	.06Y	.08Y	.11Y	.12Y	.15Y	.19Y
Guinea	656	—V	—Y	—V	.10V	.12Y	.14Y	.18Y	....	....	....	....	....	....	....
Guinea-Bissau	654	.13Y	.14Y	.18Y	.24Y	.27Y	.33Y	.41Y	—Y	—Y	—Y	—Y	—Y	—Y	—Y
Kenya	664	11.02V	10.68V	13.44V	7.43V	8.49Y	10.49Y	13.02Y	5.26V	10.59V	11.00V	15.75V	17.99Y	22.24Y	27.60Y
Madagascar	674	—V	.26V	2.21V	2.91Y	3.32Y	4.10Y	5.09Y	—V	—V	—V	—Y	—Y	—Y	—Y
Mauritania	682	—Y	—Y	—Y	—Y	—Y	—Y	—Y	.04Y	.04Y	.05Y	.07Y	.08Y	.10Y	.12Y
Mauritius	684	.96V	.04V	.17V	.36V	.08V	.07V	.13V	—V	1.73V	.37V	.51V	.14V	.02V	.69V
Morocco	686	.84V	2.42V	1.42V	1.51V	.72V	.89Y	1.11Y	—V	—V	.01V	—V	—V	—Y	—Y
Mozambique	688	2.91V	2.58V	17.45V	22.10V	26.76V	16.06V	19.93Y	12.88V	11.41V	36.12V	54.85V	53.69V	27.21V	33.77Y
Nigeria	694	.01V	.23V	.16V	.21Y	.26Y	.33Y	.42Y	—V	—V	—V	—Y	—Y	—Y	—Y
Rwanda	714	.02Y	.02Y	.02Y	.03Y	.04Y	.05Y	.06Y	—Y	—Y	—Y	—Y	—Y	—Y	—Y
Senegal	722	.10V	.11V	.17V	.41V	.57V	.74V	.92Y	—V	—V	—V	—V	—V	—V	—Y
Seychelles	718	—V	.03V	.02V	.02Y	.03Y	.03Y	.04Y	—V	—V	—V	—Y	—Y	—Y	—Y
Sierra Leone	724	.36Y	.39Y	.49Y	.64Y	.74Y	.91Y	1.13Y	—Y	—Y	—Y	—Y	—Y	—Y	—Y
Somalia	726	—Y	—Y	—Y	—Y	—Y	—Y	—Y	.02Y	.02Y	.03Y	.04Y	.04Y	.06Y	.07Y
South Africa	199	37.57V	45.22V	49.81V	66.49V	70.17V	77.20V	79.39V	240.82V	246.98V	245.06V	266.07V	280.50V	271.65V	338.35V
Sacca exc. South Afr	608	.13V	.06V	—V	—Y	—Y	—Y	—Y	3.79V	5.97V	6.12V	4.32V	4.93Y	6.10Y	7.57Y
Sudan	732	.05Y	.05Y	.07Y	.09Y	.01V	.03V	—V	—Y	—Y	—Y	—Y	—V	.03V	—V
Tanzania	738	1.88V	1.32V	1.66Y	2.19Y	2.50Y	3.09Y	3.83Y	6.46V	19.54V	24.73Y	32.48Y	37.12Y	45.87Y	56.93Y
Tunisia	744	.65V	.06V	.25V	.21V	.48V	.74V	.92Y	—V	.04V	—V	—V	—V	—V	—Y
Uganda	746	.17V	—V	.27V	.36Y	.41Y	.51Y	.63Y	.02V	.10V	.61V	.80Y	.91Y	1.12Y	1.40Y
Zambia	754	3.07V	3.35V	8.57V	7.09V	12.74V	11.73V	11.25V	10.55V	13.14V	22.26V	53.03V	77.83V	63.40V	34.28V
Zimbabwe	698	2.99V	3.61V	4.92V	7.93V	2.64V	52.00V	64.53Y	11.68V	80.68V	39.00V	51.19V	28.39V	14.82V	18.40Y
Asia	**507**	**10.6Y**	**15.5Y**	**10.9Y**	**16.5Y**	**21.4Y**	**30.0Y**	**46.5Y**	**46.1Y**	**58.7Y**	**77.3Y**	**106.5Y**	**95.2Y**	**132.6Y**	**168.6Y**
Bangladesh	513	—V	—V	—V	—V	—V	—V	—V	.08V	—V	.09V	—V	—V	—Y	—Y
Brunei Darussalam	516	.01Y	.02Y	—V	—Y	—Y	.01Y	.01Y	....	....	....	....	....	....	....
China,P.R.: Mainland	924	.37V	.55V	.01V	.04V	1.88V	.90V	.91Y	4.94V	7.17V	11.87V	22.38V	17.96V	33.82V	46.27V
China,P.R.:Hong Kong	532	.09V	.19V	.19V	.23V	.12V	.06V	.08V	3.05V	1.37V	3.27V	2.18V	.89V	2.13V	1.07V
China,P.R.:Macao	546	—V	—V	—V	.02V	—V	—V	—V	—V	—V	—V	—V	—V	—V	—V
Fiji	819	.27Y	.29Y	.37Y	.48Y	.55Y	.68Y	.84Y	—Y	—Y	—Y	—Y	—Y	—Y	—Y
India	534	.38Y	1.55V	3.78V	4.48V	2.38V	2.94V	3.65Y	23.07Y	31.05V	39.99V	57.45V	51.71V	63.91Y	79.32Y
Indonesia	536	.08V	.13V	.03V	.42V	1.54V	4.63V	5.23V	.63V	.76V	1.12V	2.42V	3.09V	4.73V	6.53V

	Exports 2001	2002	2003	2004	2005	2006	2007	Imports 2001	2002	2003	2004	2005	2006	2007
	Millions of U.S. Dollars							Millions of U.S. Dollars						
Korea.......... 542	—V	.06V	.61V	1.29V	1.35V	3.90V	18.28V	2.40V	2.49V	3.39V	6.89V	6.53V	7.85V	8.76V
Malaysia.......... 548	1.02V	2.70V	.68V	2.41V	3.38V	5.17V	3.90V	.73V	3.11V	7.89V	3.10V	2.22V	3.63V	4.17V
Pakistan.......... 564	1.13V	1.02V	1.17V	1.43V	1.64V	2.03Y	2.52Y	1.65V	1.53V	1.67V	1.05V	1.93V	2.39Y	2.97Y
Papua New Guinea.......... 853	.64Y	.69Y	.88Y	1.15Y	1.31Y	1.62Y	2.02Y	—Y	—Y	—Y	—Y	—Y	—Y	—Y
Philippines.......... 566	2.75V	6.27V	1.02V	.86V	1.06V	1.31V	1.46V	—V	.03V	—V	—V	—V	—V	.01V
Solomon Islands.......... 813	.57Y	.62Y	.79Y	1.04Y	1.18Y	1.46Y	1.81Y	—Y	—Y	—Y	—Y	—Y	—Y	—Y
Sri Lanka.......... 524	—V	—V	—Y	—Y	—Y	—Y	—Y	.04V	—V	—V	.04V	.02V	.02V	.24V
Taiwan Province of China.......... 528	3.08V	1.43V	1.33V	1.88V	4.51V	4.02V	5.27V	7.94V	8.62V	6.47V	8.24V	7.42V	7.34V	9.15V
Thailand.......... 578	.23V	.01V	.01V	.81V	.47V	1.31V	.55V	1.55V	2.30V	1.43V	2.70V	3.43V	6.78V	10.12V
Vietnam.......... 582	.02V	—V	.03V	—V	—V	—V	—V	.03V	.20V	.08V	—V	—V	—V	—V
Asia n.s.......... 598	—Y	—Y	—Y	—Y	—Y	—Y	—Y	.02Y	.02Y	.02Y	.02Y	.02Y	.02Y	.02Y
Europe.......... 170	**44.4Y**	**54.3Y**	**49.3Y**	**67.2Y**	**66.8Y**	**78.6Y**	**113.7Y**	**1.0Y**	**1.4Y**	**5.0Y**	**5.1Y**	**4.6Y**	**3.9Y**	**5.6Y**
Belarus.......... 913	.24V	.02V	—V	—V	.08V	.18V	.64V	—V	—V	.40V	—V	—V	.08V	—V
Bulgaria.......... 918	.21V	.14V	.06V	.06V	—V	.01V	—V	.06V	.05V	—V	—V	.05V	.12V	.17V
Czech Republic.......... 935	3.31V	2.44V	4.17V	6.45V	4.30V	4.19V	3.32V	—V	—V	.60V	.13V	.23V	.07V	.20V
Estonia.......... 939	—V	—V	—V	—V	—V	—V	—V	—V	.06V	.06V	.12V	—V	.02V	.01V
Hungary.......... 944	6.15V	4.19V	4.45V	1.18V	.70V	.55V	.59V	.13V	.04V	.32V	1.10V	.22V	.72V	.96V
Kyrgyz Republic.......... 917	.13V	.03V	.04V	—V	—V	—V	—V	....	....	....	....	....	....	....
Latvia.......... 941	.07V	.16V	.08V	—V	.37V	.19V	.12V	—V	—V	—V	—V	—V	.03V	.05V
Lithuania.......... 946	.89V	.77V	.68V	.12V	.48V	.75V	2.37V	.11V	.29V	.18V	.16V	.13V	.01V	.05V
Macedonia, FYR.......... 962	.26V	.38V	.20V	.11V	.28V	.19V	.23Y	—V	—V	—V	—V	—V	—V	—Y
Poland.......... 964	9.75V	18.16V	2.93V	11.20V	6.69V	11.57V	16.92V	.43V	.82V	1.32V	1.40V	1.17V	1.06V	1.63V
Romania.......... 968	2.71V	1.39V	1.83V	.94V	1.57V	3.45V	5.37V	—V	—V	—V	—V	—V	—V	.16V
Russia.......... 922	10.23V	19.33V	20.29V	17.04V	28.77V	33.07V	45.85V	—V	—V	—V	—V	—V	.02V	—V
Slovak Republic.......... 936	.35V	.46V	.58Y	.77Y	—V	—V	—V	.03V	.06V	.08Y	.10Y	.20V	.08V	.21V
Turkey.......... 186	3.19V	1.85V	7.38V	19.07V	14.95V	13.85V	25.09V	.21V	.06V	2.08V	2.09V	2.33V	1.38V	1.74V
Ukraine.......... 926	6.90V	5.00V	6.60V	10.31V	8.61V	10.64Y	13.20Y	—V	—V	—V	—V	.25V	.31Y	.38Y
Middle East.......... 407	**25.2Y**	**27.2Y**	**34.7Y**	**43.0Y**	**48.8Y**	**60.2Y**	**75.4Y**	**.1Y**	**—Y**	**—Y**	**.7Y**	**2.5Y**	**.2Y**	**3.5Y**
Egypt.......... 469	23.04V	25.00Y	31.65Y	41.56Y	47.49Y	58.69Y	72.83Y	.01V	.01Y	.01Y	.02Y	.02Y	.02Y	.03Y
Israel.......... 436	—V	—V	—V	—V	.09V	—V	.36V	.11V	—V	—V	.11V	.11V	.22V	.11V
Jordan.......... 439	1.70V	1.71V	2.30V	.61V	—V	—V	.25V	—V	—V	—V	.62V	2.35V	—V	3.35V
Kuwait.......... 443	—Y	—Y	—Y	—Y	—Y	—Y	.01Y	—Y	—Y	—Y	—Y	—Y	—Y	—Y
Lebanon.......... 446	.46Y	.50Y	.63Y	.83Y	.95Y	1.18Y	1.46Y	—Y	—Y	—Y	—Y	—Y	—Y	—Y
Oman.......... 449	.02V	—V	—V	—Y	—Y	—Y	—Y	—V	—V	—V	—Y	—Y	—Y	—Y
Saudi Arabia.......... 456	—V	—V	.17V	.03V	.29V	.35Y	.46Y	—Y	—Y	—Y	—Y	—Y	—Y	—Y
Western Hemisphere.......... 207	**4.3Y**	**1.4Y**	**4.4Y**	**5.3Y**	**12.4Y**	**10.4Y**	**11.9Y**	**1.0Y**	**1.4Y**	**3.8Y**	**6.9Y**	**4.2Y**	**6.7Y**	**9.7Y**
Argentina.......... 213	1.32V	.99V	1.19V	1.05V	2.17V	1.87V	1.61V	.54V	.05V	.14V	2.21V	3.14V	5.18V	9.55V
Barbados.......... 316	.02V	.02V	.02V	.02V	.03V	.03V	.04Y	—V	—V	—V	—V	—V	—V	—Y
Brazil.......... 223	1.81V	—V	2.59V	3.42V	4.48V	2.17V	4.66V	.44V	1.33V	3.65V	4.63V	1.10V	1.35V	—V
Chile.......... 228	.01V	—V	—V	—V	.35V	—V	.21V	—V	—V	—V	.09V	—V	—V	—V
Colombia.......... 233	—V	—V	—V	—V	—V	—V	.11V	—V	—V	—V	—V	—V	.20V	.16V
Costa Rica.......... 238	.24V	—V	.23V	.28V	.35V	.43Y	.54Y	....	....	....	....	....	....	....
Dominican Republic.......... 243	.27V	.29Y	.37Y	.48Y	.55Y	.68Y	.85Y	....	....	....	....	....	....	....
Guatemala.......... 258	.16V	—V	—V	—Y	—V	—Y	—Y	—Y	—Y	—Y	—Y	—Y	—Y	—Y
Jamaica.......... 343	—V	—V	—V	—V	.02V	—V	—V	—V	—V	—V	—V	—V	—V	—V
Mexico.......... 273	—V	—V	—V	—V	4.34V	5.08V	3.72V	—V	—V	—V	—V	—V	—V	—V
Peru.......... 293	.35V	—V	—V	—V	.05V	—V	—Y	—V	—V	—V	—V	—V	—V	—Y
St. Vincent & Grens.......... 364	.01V	.01V	—V	—V	—V	—Y	—Y	—V	—V	—V	—V	—V	—Y	—Y
Trinidad and Tobago.......... 369	.07V	.04V	.06Y	.07Y	.08Y	.10Y	.13Y	—V	—V	—Y	—Y	—Y	—Y	—Y
Venezuela, Rep. Bol.......... 299	—V	.07V	—V	—V	—V	—V	—V	—V	—V	—V	—V	—V	—V	—Y
Countries & Areas n.s.......... 898	**1.4Y**	**1.5Y**	**1.9Y**	**2.5Y**	**2.8Y**	**3.5Y**	**4.4Y**	**—Y**	**—Y**	**—Y**	**—Y**	**.1Y**	**.1Y**	**.1Y**
Memorandum Items														
European Union.......... 998	172.88Y	166.48Y	194.42Y	180.72Y	191.10Y	173.31Y	253.65Y	55.37Y	74.39Y	69.52Y	125.07Y	98.15Y	140.42Y	155.77Y
Oil Exporting Ctys.......... 999	1.11Y	3.26Y	3.51Y	4.77Y	7.32Y	11.76Y	14.46Y	.63Y	.76Y	1.12Y	2.42Y	3.09Y	4.73Y	6.53Y
Non-Oil Develop.Ctys.......... 201	148.76Y	170.18Y	202.22Y	254.29Y	280.48Y	356.88Y	448.67Y	339.23Y	451.04Y	470.75Y	596.18Y	605.30Y	591.68Y	700.38Y
PERCENT DISTRIBUTION														
Industrial Countries.......... 101	**64.5**	**58.5**	**59.0**	**47.8**	**53.6**	**40.0**	**40.9**	**21.0**	**23.9**	**19.2**	**21.1**	**18.7**	**25.6**	**24.6**
Developing Countries.......... 202	**35.2**	**41.2**	**40.6**	**51.7**	**46.0**	**59.4**	**58.5**	**79.0**	**76.1**	**80.8**	**78.9**	**81.3**	**74.3**	**75.4**
Africa.......... 607	**15.3**	**17.8**	**21.0**	**25.3**	**22.1**	**30.5**	**27.2**	**67.8**	**65.7**	**66.1**	**63.2**	**67.0**	**56.5**	**55.4**
Asia.......... 507	**2.5**	**3.7**	**2.1**	**3.3**	**3.4**	**4.8**	**5.9**	**10.7**	**9.9**	**13.2**	**14.0**	**12.7**	**16.5**	**18.0**
Europe.......... 170	**10.4**	**12.9**	**9.7**	**13.4**	**10.7**	**12.7**	**14.4**	**.2**	**.2**	**.9**	**.7**	**.6**	**.5**	**.6**
Middle East.......... 407	**5.9**	**6.5**	**6.9**	**8.6**	**7.8**	**9.7**	**9.5**	**—**	**—**	**—**	**.1**	**.3**	**—**	**.4**
Western Hemisphere.......... 207	**1.0**	**.3**	**.9**	**1.1**	**2.0**	**1.7**	**1.5**	**.2**	**.2**	**.6**	**.9**	**.6**	**.8**	**1.0**
ANNUAL PERCENT CHANGE														
World.......... 001	**11.7**	**–1.2**	**20.4**	**–1.2**	**25.0**	**–.9**	**27.6**	**–23.5**	**38.0**	**–1.7**	**29.9**	**–1.3**	**7.2**	**16.8**
Industrial Countries.......... 101	**12.6**	**–10.5**	**21.6**	**–20.0**	**40.1**	**–26.0**	**30.5**	**–1.9**	**57.0**	**–21.1**	**42.8**	**–12.4**	**46.8**	**11.9**
Developing Countries.......... 202	**10.2**	**15.7**	**18.6**	**25.9**	**11.1**	**28.1**	**25.6**	**–27.7**	**32.9**	**4.4**	**26.9**	**1.6**	**–2.0**	**18.5**
Africa.......... 607	**4.9**	**14.6**	**41.9**	**19.3**	**9.0**	**36.9**	**13.9**	**–29.0**	**33.9**	**–1.2**	**24.3**	**4.7**	**–9.8**	**14.7**
Asia.......... 507	**–41.4**	**46.2**	**–29.8**	**51.7**	**29.4**	**40.4**	**54.9**	**–9.4**	**27.1**	**31.8**	**37.7**	**–10.6**	**39.3**	**27.1**
Europe.......... 170	**5.1**	**22.4**	**–9.3**	**36.5**	**–.7**	**17.7**	**44.6**	**–31.7**	**41.4**	**265.9**	**1.1**	**–10.4**	**–15.0**	**42.8**
Middle East.......... 407	**143.6**	**7.9**	**27.7**	**23.9**	**13.4**	**23.4**	**25.2**	**–57.1**	**–90.3**	**12.9**	**—**	**233.6**	**–90.2**	**—**
Western Hemisphere.......... 207	**41.7**	**–66.5**	**212.2**	**19.8**	**133.3**	**–16.5**	**14.4**	**–85.0**	**40.8**	**174.6**	**83.2**	**–38.8**	**58.8**	**44.2**

	Exports 2001	Exports 2002	Exports 2003	Exports 2004	Exports 2005	Exports 2006	Exports 2007	Imports 2001	Imports 2002	Imports 2003	Imports 2004	Imports 2005	Imports 2006	Imports 2007
	Millions of U.S. Dollars							*Millions of U.S. Dollars*						
IFS World Total	**88,005**	**93,265**	**99,369**	**125,744**	**140,870**	**160,573**	**176,025**	**73,866**	**79,869**	**81,948**	**105,298**	**114,411**	**131,080**	**146,773**
DOTS World Total........ 001	**88,201**	**93,387**	**104,968**	**126,509**	**140,977**	**160,664**	**176,207**	**73,358**	**79,513**	**82,734**	**104,304**	**113,609**	**130,477**	**146,982**
Industrial Countries........ 101	**44,807**	**44,170**	**48,339**	**57,118**	**63,031**	**70,683**	**73,002**	**38,777**	**39,312**	**39,752**	**48,152**	**48,919**	**53,240**	**58,159**
United States........ 111	17,816	18,826	20,540	23,749	27,763	30,191	27,531	11,839	13,099	12,851	15,263	14,789	16,424	15,928
Canada........ 156	547	567	606	792	752	1,028	955	298	333	360	463	563	656	749
Australia........ 193	2,052	2,108	2,614	4,153	4,766	4,553	5,939	1,564	1,425	1,264	1,788	2,157	2,426	2,970
Japan........ 158	11,770	10,530	11,222	12,777	13,181	14,241	16,091	14,211	14,168	14,282	16,773	16,634	17,338	19,085
New Zealand........ 196	297	325	357	444	538	674	755	342	310	303	341	339	338	487
Austria........ 122	141	220	231	237	247	283	114	96	94	113	141	142	199	360
Belgium........ 124	667	537	512	557	539	615	773	324	324	359	405	376	396	515
Cyprus........ 423	11	9	13	14	15	21	36	5	6	6	5	4	4	3
Denmark........ 128	135	116	157	161	190	362	259	109	122	114	142	154	140	171
Finland........ 172	206	208	228	280	500	676	600	135	144	108	182	218	260	288
France........ 132	959	1,367	1,770	1,876	1,848	2,193	2,171	1,142	1,121	1,201	1,460	1,495	2,102	2,244
Germany........ 134	2,044	2,096	2,407	2,759	2,973	3,487	4,318	2,743	2,939	3,891	4,703	5,088	5,750	6,813
Greece........ 174	83	75	82	106	90	134	184	10	10	7	8	8	25	25
Iceland........ 176	2	1	2	2	3	3	4	1	—	—	—	—	3	—
Ireland........ 178	390	324	292	380	473	447	456	1,000	700	655	591	709	806	799
Italy........ 136	469	479	622	767	707	989	1,104	754	663	635	952	1,239	1,143	1,313
Luxembourg........ 137	5	7	8	9	72	21	16	3	3	4	8	9	10	18
Malta........ 181	93	31	35	22	24	30	35	29	34	25	34	49	41	76
Netherlands........ 138	4,060	3,459	3,431	4,147	4,609	5,849	6,878	649	645	566	904	885	921	955
Norway........ 142	44	66	49	51	52	67	72	52	53	56	63	71	100	163
Portugal........ 182	48	56	58	81	180	180	189	18	45	27	163	115	76	356
Slovenia........ 961	13	7	5	10	12	11	15	3	10	7	7	8	9	14
Spain........ 184	296	270	408	594	583	935	854	162	158	196	216	256	332	421
Sweden........ 144	169	155	172	196	216	343	382	541	508	342	783	649	609	643
Switzerland........ 146	180	135	186	174	197	425	392	938	825	805	1,014	1,239	1,274	1,645
United Kingdom........ 112	2,310	2,198	2,335	2,778	2,501	2,924	2,880	1,808	1,571	1,577	1,747	1,722	1,858	2,115
Developing Countries........ 202	**43,355**	**49,191**	**56,594**	**69,323**	**77,872**	**89,920**	**103,119**	**33,708**	**39,085**	**42,708**	**55,937**	**64,552**	**76,515**	**87,320**
Africa........ 607	**571**	**766**	**943**	**1,182**	**1,533**	**1,816**	**2,411**	**326**	**267**	**321**	**587**	**615**	**1,074**	**1,700**
Algeria........ 612	31	114	75	91	51	67	113	2	2	2	—	1	7	6
Angola........ 614	4	6	14	22	23	42	55	—	—	—	—	—	—	—
Benin........ 638	3	4	22	12	26	98	211	1	—	1	2	1	—	2
Botswana........ 616	1	1	1	2	3	1	3	—	—	—	—	—	—	—
Burkina Faso........ 748	—	1	—	—	—	—	1	3	1	—	—	—	—	1
Burundi........ 618	—	—	—	—	—	1	—	—	—	—	—	—	—	—
Cameroon........ 622	4	7	5	7	9	23	36	2	1	2	45	30	42	21
Cape Verde........ 624	—	—	—	—	—	—	1	—	—	—	—	—	—	—
Central African Rep........ 626	—	—	—	3	—	—	1	—	—	—	—	—	—	—
Comoros........ 632	—	—	—	—	1	1	2	—	—	—	—	—	—	—
Congo, Dem. Rep. of........ 636	1	3	3	5	9	10	14	2	1	1	13	2	4	6
Congo, Republic of........ 634	1	—	1	7	17	18	38	—	—	—	—	—	—	15
Côte d'Ivoire........ 662	6	6	8	6	6	12	16	9	3	12	41	49	129	79
Djibouti........ 611	5	5	13	13	22	33	79	—	—	—	—	—	—	2
Equatorial Guinea........ 642	—	—	—	—	1	54	1	—	—	—	—	—	—	—
Eritrea........ 643	—	1	—	1	—	—	1	3	2	9	3	—	—	—
Ethiopia........ 644	6	6	6	9	8	12	13	2	1	1	2	6	4	2
Gabon........ 646	1	1	—	1	5	7	7	1	1	—	—	1	86	414
Gambia, The........ 648	1	4	9	15	16	17	30	1	4	1	2	—	2	—
Ghana........ 652	20	27	47	56	67	86	120	4	9	18	24	50	112	117
Guinea........ 656	3	1	3	5	3	9	14	—	—	1	—	—	—	2
Guinea-Bissau........ 654	—	—	—	—	—	—	2	—	—	—	—	—	—	—
Kenya........ 664	20	13	18	43	52	78	102	8	7	7	6	7	12	13
Lesotho........ 666	5	3	2	1	1	1	—	—	—	—	—	—	—	—
Liberia........ 668	1	2	4	6	8	8	12	1	—	1	5	59	12	309
Madagascar........ 674	7	8	7	10	13	11	23	1	1	—	4	2	—	1
Malawi........ 676	1	3	7	3	2	3	4	1	3	1	3	4	6	4
Mali........ 678	1	3	—	1	1	1	—	4	1	—	—	—	—	2
Mauritania........ 682	6	3	14	22	13	24	42	—	—	2	3	1	—	—
Mauritius........ 684	27	44	50	55	60	79	84	1	2	3	2	1	5	7
Morocco........ 686	16	15	18	27	34	49	59	2	3	7	7	15	34	25
Mozambique........ 688	5	62	17	16	15	24	35	—	1	—	—	1	2	2
Namibia........ 728	14	12	15	11	6	7	5	1	—	2	3	4	22	12
Niger........ 692	1	1	4	7	3	1	4	1	1	—	—	—	—	—
Nigeria........ 694	49	79	91	55	185	63	99	4	3	2	4	14	21	26
Rwanda........ 714	—	—	—	—	—	—	—	2	1	—	7	5	—	6
São Tomé & Príncipe........ 716	—	—	—	—	4	1	1	—	—	—	—	—	—	—
Senegal........ 722	1	2	8	8	16	10	15	1	—	—	—	—	—	1
Seychelles........ 718	2	5	3	4	6	10	11	—	—	—	1	—	1	—
Sierra Leone........ 724	2	2	2	6	6	10	20	—	—	—	—	—	—	—
Somalia........ 726	3	3	3	4	7	6	15	—	—	—	—	3	—	—

	Exports 2001	2002	2003	2004	2005	2006	2007	Imports 2001	2002	2003	2004	2005	2006	2007
	Millions of U.S. Dollars							Millions of U.S. Dollars						
South Africa 199	256	251	334	478	572	668	810	232	194	224	336	287	466	491
Sudan 732	19	18	41	39	128	52	53	—	—	1	—	—	—	42
Swaziland 734	1	1	2	2	1	4	2	1	1	2	1	6	5	4
Tanzania 738	16	14	26	23	30	68	123	6	5	3	11	22	37	38
Togo 742	5	16	35	58	50	72	94	2	1	2	3	1	5	9
Tunisia 744	12	13	22	33	39	61	26	11	3	8	6	4	13	20
Uganda 746	2	2	3	6	4	6	8	1	1	1	—	—	—	2
Zambia 754	1	2	1	3	3	3	4	13	12	13	52	36	44	13
Zimbabwe 698	11	6	6	7	5	3	1	5	2	3	2	2	2	4
Asia 507	**38,663**	**44,328**	**50,398**	**60,875**	**68,699**	**78,828**	**88,630**	**30,419**	**36,158**	**39,180**	**50,779**	**57,557**	**67,105**	**77,009**
Afghanistan, I.S. of 512	2	2	2	3	5	4	4	1	—	—	—	—	—	—
American Samoa 859	—	—	—	1	1	—	2	—	—	—	—	—	—	—
Bangladesh 513	171	226	320	364	409	422	407	15	21	15	17	22	23	32
Bhutan 514	1	—	1	—	—	1	—	—	—	—	—	—	—	—
Brunei Darussalam 516	273	257	318	317	353	346	402	5	4	32	14	13	76	96
Cambodia 522	60	55	65	84	109	108	134	19	20	8	8	8	20	21
China,P.R.: Mainland 924	3,821	5,253	6,810	8,460	9,303	11,646	15,452	3,804	6,157	7,300	10,339	13,177	15,887	18,908
China,P.R.:Hong Kong 532	4,063	5,307	6,784	7,549	8,241	7,947	8,145	1,892	2,323	2,258	2,858	2,852	3,452	4,273
China,P.R.:Macao 546	4	4	3	6	6	11	20	1	2	2	11	13	21	24
Fiji 819	10	10	16	20	25	29	25	—	—	—	—	—	2	—
French Polynesia 887	1	4	2	6	3	3	3	—	—	—	—	—	—	—
Guam 829	2	1	2	3	2	3	6	—	—	—	—	—	—	—
India 534	1,577	1,761	2,534	3,003	3,955	5,129	5,884	772	643	672	1,289	1,100	1,333	2,060
Indonesia 536	1,563	1,801	2,129	3,073	3,322	4,074	5,171	2,241	2,551	2,939	4,194	4,375	4,952	6,233
Korea 542	2,963	3,140	3,039	4,431	4,737	5,806	6,703	2,958	4,231	4,555	5,228	5,706	7,068	7,250
Lao People's Dem.Rep. 544	2	3	3	3	6	6	9	—	—	—	—	13	49	36
Maldives 556	29	20	22	36	54	67	112	—	—	2	—	—	—	—
Mongolia 948	2	2	3	5	4	6	10	—	—	—	—	—	—	—
Myanmar 518	197	239	140	149	246	165	211	78	77	80	107	134	125	139
Nauru 836	—	2	—	—	—	—	—	—	—	—	—	—	—	—
Nepal 558	7	8	6	7	9	10	12	—	—	—	—	—	—	1
New Caledonia 839	1	1	2	3	3	24	7	—	—	—	—	—	—	—
Pakistan 564	399	524	671	701	741	843	1,257	44	55	45	54	57	59	83
Papua New Guinea 853	28	32	39	41	77	78	97	9	6	10	18	30	41	38
Philippines 566	1,288	1,335	1,437	1,937	1,974	2,173	2,548	1,839	2,596	3,115	2,819	3,219	2,901	2,850
Samoa 862	1	—	1	1	1	2	1	—	—	—	—	—	—	—
Singapore 576	14,913	15,958	16,523	18,994	22,010	24,744	25,772	9,293	9,541	9,811	11,704	13,425	15,329	16,870
Solomon Islands 813	1	1	2	2	4	5	8	1	2	3	2	3	3	10
Sri Lanka 524	187	233	304	345	438	534	371	5	6	6	7	11	22	32
Taiwan Province of China 528	3,263	3,509	3,777	4,148	3,913	4,379	4,792	4,193	4,437	4,131	5,698	6,331	7,157	8,350
Thailand 578	3,360	3,972	4,615	6,040	7,585	8,502	8,730	2,927	3,158	3,829	5,789	6,045	7,167	7,863
Tonga 866	—	—	—	—	1	1	1	—	—	—	—	—	—	—
Vanuatu 846	—	—	—	—	—	1	2	—	1	1	41	—	—	1
Vietnam 582	474	664	827	1,140	1,160	1,758	2,329	318	327	366	580	1,022	1,415	1,838
Europe 170	**939**	**783**	**1,286**	**2,039**	**2,082**	**2,409**	**3,359**	**333**	**466**	**444**	**797**	**860**	**643**	**815**
Albania 914	—	—	—	2	—	1	1	—	—	—	—	—	1	2
Armenia 911	1	1	—	1	1	1	1	—	—	—	—	—	—	1
Azerbaijan 912	1	2	79	104	2	6	2	—	—	—	—	—	—	—
Belarus 913	3	—	—	—	—	15	21	—	—	—	—	—	10	17
Bosnia & Herzegovina 963	—	1	1	—	—	—	1	—	2	1	—	1	2	3
Bulgaria 918	19	20	15	22	20	19	43	3	4	5	6	9	12	19
Croatia 960	5	3	9	10	9	13	22	2	1	1	1	2	2	10
Czech Republic 935	87	122	119	152	193	243	201	21	37	37	55	60	57	62
Estonia 939	19	6	12	18	30	42	65	2	7	2	2	4	5	7
Georgia 915	1	1	88	36	1	2	9	1	1	1	1	1	1	5
Hungary 944	157	108	182	599	376	402	505	25	26	34	35	47	54	73
Kazakhstan 916	2	3	30	10	48	21	18	2	11	5	6	10	—	—
Kyrgyz Republic 917	—	—	—	—	1	1	2	—	4	2	—	—	—	—
Latvia 941	8	8	10	11	12	17	23	9	5	1	—	5	1	1
Lithuania 946	5	6	6	11	16	17	26	1	5	5	8	10	17	21
Macedonia, FYR 962	1	—	—	—	2	1	2	—	—	—	—	—	—	—
Moldova 921	1	1	—	—	—	—	—	—	—	—	—	—	—	—
Montenegro, Rep. of 943	—	—	—	—	—	—	1	—	—	—	—	—	—	—
Poland 964	58	52	75	115	127	182	334	39	54	50	76	55	75	95
Romania 968	19	21	26	30	33	38	101	8	4	11	7	11	22	20
Russia 922	131	171	251	407	476	470	630	136	174	191	469	432	220	256
Serbia, Rep. of 942	—	—	—	—	—	—	15	—	—	—	—	—	—	2
Serbia & Montenegro 965	7	5	6	7	11	14	—	3	3	4	4	1	1	—
Slovak Republic 936	13	13	16	22	32	79	130	1	2	2	16	33	22	15
Tajikistan 923	—	—	—	—	—	—	1	—	—	—	1	—	—	—
Turkey 186	367	211	318	398	534	640	907	43	59	43	55	71	63	93
Turkmenistan 925	—	—	—	1	1	3	5	—	—	2	—	—	1	1
Ukraine 926	34	25	41	75	148	171	259	39	67	45	51	108	75	107
Uzbekistan 927	2	2	2	5	9	12	36	—	—	3	—	—	—	3
Europe n.s. 884	—	—	—	—	—	—	—	—	—	—	1	1	1	2
Middle East 407	**2,015**	**2,280**	**2,934**	**3,750**	**3,958**	**4,752**	**6,064**	**1,811**	**1,373**	**1,829**	**2,530**	**3,748**	**5,495**	**5,176**
Bahrain 419	27	32	33	35	42	55	61	56	39	44	78	108	141	123
Egypt 469	210	296	455	365	457	342	477	10	16	23	31	37	49	86
Iran, I.R. of 429	178	229	328	346	359	441	618	149	130	100	258	348	581	428

	Exports 2001	Exports 2002	Exports 2003	Exports 2004	Exports 2005	Exports 2006	Exports 2007	Imports 2001	Imports 2002	Imports 2003	Imports 2004	Imports 2005	Imports 2006	Imports 2007
	Millions of U.S. Dollars							Millions of U.S. Dollars						
Iraq.......433	33	74	13	60	24	28	20	—	—	—	155	30	38	47
Jordan.......439	66	63	79	344	114	150	87	25	28	30	44	26	58	67
Kuwait.......443	63	71	90	108	122	160	168	67	46	54	68	272	307	602
Lebanon.......446	31	32	41	44	44	39	62	—	—	1	3	2	4	7
Libya.......672	4	9	21	31	16	32	75	1	—	1	6	11	—	24
Oman.......449	97	50	52	71	81	100	152	359	284	466	397	510	885	468
Qatar.......453	29	39	39	50	96	186	292	48	17	14	20	54	80	24
Saudi Arabia.......456	341	383	409	482	473	530	716	636	398	583	985	1,548	2,330	1,977
Syrian Arab Republic.......463	51	67	154	149	164	156	166	1	1	—	—	1	2	2
United Arab Emirates.......466	833	858	1,116	1,553	1,847	2,270	2,948	164	141	300	452	750	969	1,293
Yemen, Republic of.......474	51	77	105	111	119	262	221	295	273	212	31	49	52	29
Western Hemisphere.......207	**1,167**	**1,033**	**1,034**	**1,476**	**1,600**	**2,116**	**2,654**	**819**	**821**	**935**	**1,244**	**1,772**	**2,199**	**2,620**
Antigua and Barbuda.......311	—	15	1	1	1	1	1	—	—	—	—	—	—	—
Argentina.......213	55	21	47	67	103	131	179	301	223	183	376	613	607	726
Aruba.......314	—	—	1	—	—	1	—	—	—	—	—	—	—	—
Bahamas, The.......313	1	—	—	1	1	2	3	—	—	—	—	—	1	—
Barbados.......316	1	1	1	2	2	1	1	—	—	—	—	—	—	—
Belize.......339	—	—	1	1	—	1	1	—	—	6	1	—	—	—
Bolivia.......218	—	1	—	1	1	1	2	4	5	5	6	3	1	1
Brazil.......223	162	217	194	319	373	500	659	193	223	230	341	522	692	921
Chile.......228	80	44	58	95	87	88	83	48	32	74	137	149	165	178
Colombia.......233	11	18	16	23	36	64	54	1	2	2	2	2	3	4
Costa Rica.......238	21	10	13	38	43	38	52	61	77	241	191	231	411	431
Dominica.......321	1	1	—	—	—	1	1	—	—	—	1	—	—	2
Dominican Republic.......243	3	5	8	11	12	14	10	—	1	2	3	9	14	10
Ecuador.......248	7	4	4	9	10	11	13	1	—	1	1	2	2	5
El Salvador.......253	5	6	10	11	11	16	19	—	2	—	—	1	8	1
Greenland.......326	—	—	—	—	—	—	—	—	—	13	2	2	—	—
Guatemala.......258	4	6	6	11	10	19	20	7	8	13	14	10	14	13
Guyana.......336	—	1	1	1	7	11	4	—	—	—	—	—	—	1
Haiti.......263	4	8	21	35	36	45	41	—	—	—	—	—	—	—
Honduras.......268	2	1	6	18	10	9	18	—	—	1	—	—	12	1
Jamaica.......343	2	4	3	5	13	8	16	2	—	—	—	—	—	—
Mexico.......273	647	567	524	656	673	917	1,173	159	136	135	134	135	216	258
Netherlands Antilles.......353	—	1	—	2	2	3	4	—	1	2	—	—	—	2
Nicaragua.......278	—	1	1	5	2	6	5	—	—	—	—	—	—	4
Panama.......283	118	63	63	72	73	94	140	2	78	13	1	35	18	3
Paraguay.......288	1	1	1	2	4	3	5	—	—	—	1	—	2	—
Peru.......293	13	17	22	54	47	54	57	18	10	6	9	7	8	7
St. Vincent & Grens.......364	—	—	—	1	—	—	—	—	—	—	—	—	—	—
Suriname.......366	—	—	1	1	1	3	3	—	—	—	—	—	—	—
Trinidad and Tobago.......369	2	3	3	6	8	15	17	—	—	—	—	—	—	—
Uruguay.......298	12	6	13	8	7	15	17	7	20	4	18	34	12	16
Venezuela, Rep. Bol.......299	11	11	14	17	25	45	54	12	3	4	3	15	10	28
Western Hem. n.s.......399	—	1	—	1	1	1	1	—	—	—	—	—	—	7
Other Countries n.i.e.......910	**9**	**5**	**8**	**22**	**21**	**9**	**12**	**1**	**5**	**—**	**—**	**1**	**1**	**4**
Cuba.......928	2	1	1	2	3	2	4	—	5	—	—	1	1	1
North Korea.......954	7	4	7	20	18	7	8	1	—	—	—	—	—	2
Countries & Areas n.s.......898	**28**	**19**	**25**	**44**	**51**	**49**	**69**	**601**	**279**	**265**	**206**	**127**	**140**	**62**
Special Categories.......899	**—**	**—**	**—**	**—**	**—**	**—**	**—**	**265**	**825**	**—**	**—**	**—**	**570**	**1,427**
Memorandum Items														
European Union.......998	12,446	11,928	13,183	15,904	16,564	20,482	22,548	9,630	9,236	9,963	12,641	13,339	14,912	17,405
Oil Exporting Ctys.......999	3,233	3,719	4,377	5,938	6,601	7,996	10,427	3,683	3,576	4,464	6,543	7,927	10,179	11,156
Non-Oil Develop.Ctys.......201	40,122	45,472	52,217	63,385	71,271	81,924	92,692	30,025	35,509	38,244	49,394	56,624	66,336	76,164
PERCENT DISTRIBUTION														
Industrial Countries.......101	**50.8**	**47.3**	**46.1**	**45.1**	**44.7**	**44.0**	**41.4**	**52.9**	**49.4**	**48.0**	**46.2**	**43.1**	**40.8**	**39.6**
Developing Countries.......202	**49.2**	**52.7**	**53.9**	**54.8**	**55.2**	**56.0**	**58.5**	**46.0**	**49.2**	**51.6**	**53.6**	**56.8**	**58.6**	**59.4**
Africa.......607	**.6**	**.8**	**.9**	**.9**	**1.1**	**1.1**	**1.4**	**.4**	**.3**	**.4**	**.6**	**.5**	**.8**	**1.2**
Asia.......507	**43.8**	**47.5**	**48.0**	**48.1**	**48.7**	**49.1**	**50.3**	**41.5**	**45.5**	**47.4**	**48.7**	**50.7**	**51.4**	**52.4**
Europe.......170	**1.1**	**.8**	**1.2**	**1.6**	**1.5**	**1.5**	**1.9**	**.5**	**.6**	**.5**	**.8**	**.8**	**.5**	**.6**
Middle East.......407	**2.3**	**2.4**	**2.8**	**3.0**	**2.8**	**3.0**	**3.4**	**2.5**	**1.7**	**2.2**	**2.4**	**3.3**	**4.2**	**3.5**
Western Hemisphere.......207	**1.3**	**1.1**	**1.0**	**1.2**	**1.1**	**1.3**	**1.5**	**1.1**	**1.0**	**1.1**	**1.2**	**1.6**	**1.7**	**1.8**
ANNUAL PERCENT CHANGE														
World.......001	**–10.1**	**5.9**	**12.4**	**20.5**	**11.4**	**14.0**	**9.7**	**–10.8**	**8.4**	**4.1**	**26.1**	**8.9**	**14.8**	**12.7**
Industrial Countries.......101	**–10.8**	**–1.4**	**9.4**	**18.2**	**10.4**	**12.1**	**3.3**	**–10.3**	**1.4**	**1.1**	**21.1**	**1.6**	**8.8**	**9.2**
Developing Countries.......202	**–9.5**	**13.5**	**15.0**	**22.5**	**12.3**	**15.5**	**14.7**	**–10.0**	**16.0**	**9.3**	**31.0**	**15.4**	**18.5**	**14.1**
Africa.......607	**2.0**	**34.3**	**23.0**	**25.3**	**29.7**	**18.4**	**32.8**	**–5.7**	**–18.2**	**20.2**	**82.9**	**4.7**	**74.8**	**58.3**
Asia.......507	**–10.8**	**14.7**	**13.7**	**20.8**	**12.9**	**14.7**	**12.4**	**–11.4**	**18.9**	**8.4**	**29.6**	**13.3**	**16.6**	**14.8**
Europe.......170	**59.4**	**–16.7**	**64.3**	**58.6**	**2.1**	**15.7**	**39.5**	**–21.8**	**39.9**	**–4.8**	**79.6**	**7.9**	**–25.3**	**26.8**
Middle East.......407	**3.6**	**13.2**	**28.7**	**27.8**	**5.5**	**20.1**	**27.6**	**9.3**	**–24.2**	**33.2**	**38.3**	**48.2**	**46.6**	**–5.8**
Western Hemisphere.......207	**–20.8**	**–11.4**	**—**	**42.8**	**8.4**	**32.3**	**25.4**	**22.8**	**.3**	**13.9**	**33.1**	**42.5**	**24.1**	**19.2**
Other Countries n.i.e.......910	**392.2**	**–37.8**	**52.4**	**171.1**	**–7.1**	**–54.2**	**27.7**	**–27.5**	**280.1**	**–91.4**	**–49.6**	**572.6**	**–29.5**	**263.3**

		Exports							Imports						
		2001	2002	2003	2004	2005	2006	2007	2001	2002	2003	2004	2005	2006	2007
		Millions of U.S. Dollars							*Millions of U.S. Dollars*						
IFS World Total		**76.2**	**90.4**	**112.5**	**122.4**	**103.5**	**135.1**	**107.8**	**393.5**	**391.7**	**470.8**	**641.8**	**744.9**	**926.5**	**1,096.3**
DOTS World Total	**001**	**76.6**	**90.7**	**112.7**	**122.8**	**98.7**	**169.8Y**	**162.8Y**	**393.0**	**390.7**	**470.7**	**645.0**	**744.9**	**909.4Y**	**1,738.8Y**
Industrial Countries	**101**	**45.7**	**57.7**	**66.0**	**70.9**	**47.6**	**70.9Y**	**75.5Y**	**92.6**	**90.1**	**97.7**	**124.7**	**161.6**	**179.7Y**	**815.4Y**
United States	111	29.32	34.55	36.47	32.55	.77	2.18V	3.36V	8.15	4.99	5.94	8.41	8.48	19.36V	21.23V
Canada	156	.65	.05	.10	.02	.10	.37V	.58V	5.56	6.10	6.76	8.81	5.44	6.12V	612.70V
Australia	193	—	—	—	—	—	.64V	.66V	8.67	11.18	15.30	17.33	15.82	18.96V	22.31V
Japan	158	4.40	10.42	11.69	14.38	22.50	17.20V	10.44V	8.80	7.13	10.35	12.04	13.38	24.36V	15.92V
New Zealand	196	—	—	—	—	—	.02V	.01V	5.55	2.43	3.07	8.32	6.06	14.53V	13.67V
Austria	122	—	—	—	—	.01	.21V	.14V	.44	.49	1.00	.77	.79	2.12V	3.85V
Belgium	124	—	—	—	—	—	.12V	.04V	—	—	—	.33	1.20	2.36V	1.81V
Cyprus	423	—	—	—	—	—	—V	—V	.04	—	.02	.04	.03	.01V	.12V
Denmark	128	—	—	—	—	—	.04V	.04V	11.57	6.31	2.51	2.12	7.86	4.34V	4.31V
Finland	172	—	—	—	—	—	.01V	.01V	.07	3.26	.15	2.21	.61	.53V	.28V
France	132	.01	.14	.57	2.84	4.20	11.59V	14.36V	4.74	23.24	12.39	12.35	16.26	16.51V	14.50V
Germany	134	3.83	3.04	4.31	6.03	4.75	3.36V	5.25V	11.16	4.76	6.44	10.75	15.01	23.26V	36.45V
Greece	174	.43	.62	.35	.12	—	.90V	.43V	.29	.35	.47	.44	.42	.69V	1.63V
Iceland	176	—	—	—	—	—	.01V	.01V	—	—	—	—	—	—V	—V
Ireland	178	—	—	—	—	—	.50V	.44V	.12	.27	1.09	2.37	.20	.24V	.25V
Italy	136	.05	.03	.90	2.11	1.74	3.61V	6.61V	4.32	4.35	6.24	12.01	10.67	14.87V	23.98V
Luxembourg	137	—	—	—	—	—	—V	.03V	—	—	—	—	—	.04V	—V
Malta	181	—	—	—	—	—	—V	—V	.33	.52	.30	.64	.27	.74V	.74V
Netherlands	138	.43	.26	.50	.56	1.07	4.65V	3.95V	7.90	4.16	10.66	4.87	13.08	10.02V	9.81V
Norway	142	—	—	—	—	—	—V	.05V	.45	.33	.74	.44	3.44	.77V	3.14V
Portugal	182	—	—	—	—	—	.04V	—V	.12	.08	.01	.02	.01	.28V	.02V
Slovenia	961	—	—	—	—	—	—V	.06V	—	—	—	—	—	—V	—V
Spain	184	.55	—	—	.03	—	1.48V	.37V	.26	.37	.73	.69	1.02	1.63V	1.82V
Sweden	144	—	—	—	—	—	.03V	.06V	1.11	1.17	2.51	3.35	4.75	3.50V	8.65V
Switzerland	146	—	—	.16	.21	.01	.02V	—V	2.36	2.16	2.69	2.76	3.31	1.98V	2.68V
United Kingdom	112	6.01	8.63	10.96	12.00	12.41	23.96V	28.62V	10.56	6.45	8.28	13.71	33.53	12.52V	15.56V
Developing Countries	**202**	**30.9**	**33.0**	**46.7**	**52.0**	**51.2**	**98.8Y**	**87.3Y**	**299.8**	**300.0**	**372.3**	**519.1**	**582.2**	**728.3Y**	**921.7Y**
Africa	**607**	**—**	**—**	**—**	**—**	**—**	**14.9Y**	**19.0Y**	**1.9**	**2.4**	**13.7**	**6.3**	**2.4**	**5.4Y**	**6.2Y**
Algeria	612	—	—	—	—	—	10.27Y	13.30Y	—	—	—	—	—	—Y	—Y
Burkina Faso	748	—	—	—	—	—	—Y	—Y	—	—	—	—	.37	.46Y	.57Y
Kenya	664	—	—	—	—	—	.27Y	.34Y	—	—	—	—	.01	.01Y	.01Y
Mauritius	684	—	—	—	—	—	—V	—V	.01	.04	.05	.65	.55	.05V	.52V
Seychelles	718	—	—	—	—	—	.03Y	.04Y	—	—	11.80	.01	.04	.05Y	.06Y
South Africa	199	—	—	—	.05	—	—V	—V	1.85	2.35	1.86	5.66	.81	3.46V	3.35V
Sudan	732	....	....	....	....	....	....	....	—	—	—	—	.63	.78Y	.97Y
Tanzania	738	—	—	—	—	—	3.30Y	4.10Y	—	—	—	—	—	.56Y	.70Y
Tunisia	744	—	—	—	—	—	1.02V	1.26Y	—	—	—	—	—	—V	—Y
Zambia	754	—	—	—	—	—	—V	—V	—	—	—	—	.02	—V	—V
Asia	**507**	**30.8**	**32.8**	**45.7**	**51.8**	**51.1**	**83.7Y**	**67.8Y**	**262.2**	**264.7**	**320.1**	**406.1**	**438.0**	**544.7Y**	**702.5Y**
Bangladesh	513	—	—	—	—	—	—V	—V	.01	—	—	.01	.01	—Y	—Y
China,P.R.: Mainland	924	.01	—	.02	.05	.04	.54V	.26Y	1.55	2.71	2.89	7.98	16.01	16.95V	27.30V
China,P.R.:Hong Kong	532	3.11	1.73	2.06	.75	.80	1.34V	1.01V	4.40	9.03	9.64	10.42	7.95	4.23V	5.10V
China,P.R.:Macao	546	—	—	—	—	—	—V	—Y	—	—	—	—	—	.01V	.01V
India	534	1.21	.12	.35	.46	1.00	1.24Y	1.54Y	41.04	41.91	47.75	65.88	83.86	103.65Y	128.62Y
Indonesia	536	—	—	4.80	.98	.09	.23V	1.97V	14.38	12.23	12.40	12.80	18.15	21.78V	25.92V
Korea	542	.02	.12	.25	.17	1.72	.01V	.28V	1.10	1.78	1.71	1.64	1.90	3.54V	5.26V
Malaysia	548	1.48	.77	1.04	.65	.51	.38V	.24V	34.40	20.32	36.17	48.87	53.43	73.88V	123.65V
Myanmar	518	—	—	—	—	—	—Y	—Y	—	—	—	.02	—	—Y	—Y
Nepal	558	—	—	—	—	—	—Y	—Y	—	.02	—	—	.01	.01Y	.01Y
Pakistan	564	—	—	—	—	—	—Y	—Y	1.49	1.52	1.74	2.21	2.88	3.55Y	4.41Y
Philippines	566	—	—	—	—	—	.31V	.20V	.63	.41	.59	1.07	.71	.92V	1.50V
Singapore	576	1.72	2.79	3.26	4.83	5.74	2.89V	2.12V	98.37	101.06	117.06	160.75	179.70	216.29V	260.58V
Sri Lanka	524	15.78	13.94	15.34	15.13	16.16	21.44V	14.06V	50.62	59.52	64.69	68.39	42.58	32.61V	55.98V
Taiwan Province of China	528	.36	.08	.04	—	2.60	.04V	.08V	2.06	1.13	1.55	1.29	2.00	2.67V	3.36V
Thailand	578	7.06	13.28	18.51	28.82	22.41	55.30V	46.07V	12.16	13.05	23.89	24.51	28.50	64.64V	60.80V
Vietnam	582	....	....	....	....	....	....	....	—	—	.01	.28	.34	—V	—V
Europe	**170**	**—**	**—**	**—**	**—**	**—**	**—Y**	**—Y**	**.1**	**.2**	**.4**	**.9**	**2.8**	**2.3Y**	**3.4Y**
Bulgaria	918	—	—	—	—	.02	—V	—V	—	—	—	—	—	—V	.06V
Czech Republic	935	—	—	—	—	—	—V	.01V	—	—	—	—	—	.19V	.95V
Czechoslovakia n.s.	937	....	....	....	....	....	....	....	—	—	—	.01	.02	.03Y	.03Y
Estonia	939	—	—	—	—	—	—V	—V	—	—	—	—	—	.01V	—V
Hungary	944	—	—	—	—	—	—V	—V	—	—	—	—	—	.01V	.13V
Macedonia, FYR	962	—	—	—	—	—	.01V	.01Y	—	—	—	—	—	—V	—Y
Poland	964	—	—	—	—	—	—V	—V	—	.02	.02	—	—	.06V	.05V
Russia	922	—	—	—	—	.01	—V	—V	.01	.06	.03	—	.01	.03V	.17V
Slovak Republic	936	—	—	—	—	—	—V	.01V	—	—	—	—	—	—V	.41V
Turkey	186	—	—	—	—	—	—V	—V	.06	.13	.29	.82	2.72	1.89V	1.54V
Europe n.s.	884	....	....	....	....	....	....	....	—	—	.03	.02	.05	.06Y	.08Y

		Exports							Imports						
		2001	2002	2003	2004	2005	2006	2007	2001	2002	2003	2004	2005	2006	2007
		Millions of U.S. Dollars							Millions of U.S. Dollars						
Middle East	**407**	**—**	**.1**	**—**	**.1**	**—**	**.2Y**	**.2Y**	**34.4**	**31.6**	**37.5**	**104.1**	**136.1**	**170.8Y**	**206.7Y**
Bahrain	419	—	—	—	—	—	—Y	—Y	.46	2.62	.80	34.73	15.00	18.54Y	23.01Y
Egypt	469	....	....	....	....	....	....	....	.04	.09	.14	.31	.39	.48Y	.60Y
Iran, I.R. of	429	....	....	....	....	....	....	....	.03	.01	—	.01	.01	.02Y	.02Y
Jordan	439	—	—	—	—	—	—Y	—Y	—	—	—	.04	.09	.09V	.11V
Kuwait	443	—	—	—	—	—	—Y	—Y	—	—	—	.26	1.98	2.49Y	3.00Y
Lebanon	446	—	—	—	—	—	.10Y	.13Y	—	—	.02	.31	.04	.05Y	.06Y
Oman	449	—	—	—	—	—	—Y	—Y	.67	.35	.49	.53	.31	.39Y	.47Y
Qatar	453	—	—	—	—	—	—V	—Y	.01	—	—	—	.01	—V	—Y
Saudi Arabia	456	—	.01	.01	.07	.04	.06Y	.07Y	.73	.51	.42	1.29	1.13	1.42Y	1.72Y
United Arab Emirates	466	.02	.12	—	.01	—	—Y	.01Y	32.47	28.00	35.59	66.61	117.16	147.29Y	177.69Y
Western Hemisphere	**207**	**.1**	**—**	**1.0**	**—**	**—**	**—Y**	**.2Y**	**1.2**	**1.2**	**.7**	**1.8**	**2.8**	**5.1Y**	**2.9Y**
Argentina	213	—	—	—	—	—	—V	—V	—	—	.01	.11	.04	.03V	.07V
Bahamas, The	313	....	....	....	....	....	....	....	.15	.22	.02	.02	.04	.05Y	.06Y
Brazil	223	—	—	—	—	—	—V	—V	.71	.68	.45	1.07	.79	2.76V	—V
Colombia	233	—	—	—	—	—	—V	—V	—	—	—	—	—	.01V	.01V
Mexico	273	.07	—	—	—	—	—V	.21V	.06	.03	.01	.18	.03	.06V	.10V
Panama	283	.04	.01	1.02	—	—	—V	—V	—	—	—	—	—	—Y	—Y
Paraguay	288	—	—	—	—	—	—V	—Y	—	—	—	—	—	.03V	.03Y
St. Lucia	362	....	....	....	....	....	....	....	—	—	—	—	1.56	1.92Y	2.39Y
Uruguay	298	—	—	—	—	—	—Y	—Y	—	—	—	—	—	.04Y	.04Y
Western Hem. n.s.	399	—	—	—	—	—	—Y	—Y	.29	.22	.19	.38	.31	.24Y	.18Y
Countries & Areas n.s.	**898**	....	....	....	....	....	....	....	**.6**	**.6**	**.7**	**1.1**	**1.1**	**1.4Y**	**1.7Y**
Memorandum Items															
European Union	998	11.30	12.72	17.58	23.69	24.18	50.50Y	60.43Y	53.04	55.79	52.83	66.65	105.70	93.92Y	125.33Y
Oil Exporting Ctys	999	.02	.13	4.81	1.07	.14	10.56Y	15.35Y	48.30	41.11	48.91	81.50	138.76	173.39Y	208.82Y
Non-Oil Develop.Ctys	201	30.88	32.83	41.90	50.91	51.02	88.27Y	71.98Y	251.48	258.93	323.39	437.64	443.41	554.90Y	712.84Y
PERCENT DISTRIBUTION															
Industrial Countries	**101**	**59.7**	**63.7**	**58.6**	**57.7**	**48.2**	**41.8**	**46.4**	**23.6**	**23.1**	**20.8**	**19.3**	**21.7**	**19.8**	**46.9**
Developing Countries	**202**	**40.3**	**36.3**	**41.4**	**42.3**	**51.8**	**58.2**	**53.6**	**76.3**	**76.8**	**79.1**	**80.5**	**78.2**	**80.1**	**53.0**
Africa	**607**	—	—	—	—	—	**8.8**	**11.7**	**.5**	**.6**	**2.9**	**1.0**	**.3**	**.6**	**.4**
Asia	**507**	**40.2**	**36.2**	**40.5**	**42.2**	**51.7**	**49.3**	**41.7**	**66.7**	**67.7**	**68.0**	**63.0**	**58.8**	**59.9**	**40.4**
Europe	**170**	—	—	—	—	—	—	—	—	**.1**	**.1**	**.1**	**.4**	**.3**	**.2**
Middle East	**407**	—	**.1**	—	**.1**	—	**.1**	**.1**	**8.8**	**8.1**	**8.0**	**16.1**	**18.3**	**18.8**	**11.9**
Western Hemisphere	**207**	**.2**	—	**.9**	—	—	—	**.1**	**.3**	**.3**	**.1**	**.3**	**.4**	**.6**	**.2**
ANNUAL PERCENT CHANGE															
World	**001**	**.5**	**18.5**	**24.3**	**9.0**	**–19.6**	**72.0**	**–4.1**	**1.0**	**–.6**	**20.5**	**37.0**	**15.5**	**22.1**	**91.2**
Industrial Countries	**101**	**–10.8**	**26.4**	**14.3**	**7.4**	**–32.9**	**49.2**	**6.5**	**16.2**	**–2.7**	**8.4**	**27.7**	**29.6**	**11.2**	**353.7**
Developing Countries	**202**	**23.7**	**6.7**	**41.7**	**11.3**	**–1.6**	**93.2**	**–11.6**	**–3.0**	**.1**	**24.1**	**39.4**	**12.1**	**25.1**	**26.6**
Africa	**607**	—	....	—	....	—	....	**27.9**	**23.4**	**28.8**	**473.3**	**–53.9**	**–61.6**	**121.3**	**15.0**
Asia	**507**	**23.2**	**6.7**	**39.2**	**13.5**	**–1.5**	**64.0**	**–19.0**	**–3.4**	**.9**	**20.9**	**26.9**	**7.9**	**24.4**	**29.0**
Europe	**170**	—	—	—	....	....	**–27.1**	**56.1**	**–86.9**	**224.6**	**70.6**	**129.9**	**227.4**	**–18.5**	**49.4**
Middle East	**407**	**267.5**	**524.3**	**–92.8**	**845.6**	**–46.5**	**236.1**	**26.1**	**1.6**	**–8.2**	**18.6**	**177.8**	**30.8**	**25.5**	**21.0**
Western Hemisphere	**207**	....	**–88.3**	—	**–97.5**	....	....	—	**–30.3**	**–4.5**	**–42.0**	**161.3**	**58.3**	**84.7**	**–43.7**

Mali 678

		Exports							Imports						
		2001	2002	2003	2004	2005	2006	2007	2001	2002	2003	2004	2005	2006	2007
		Millions of U.S. Dollars							Millions of U.S. Dollars						
IFS World Total		**725.2**	**872.4**	**925.1**	**976.4**	**1,100.9**	**1,544.2**	**1,620.0**	**990.0**	**926.6**	**1,269.6**	**1,364.0**	**1,622.0**	**1,844.0**	**2,000.0**
DOTS World Total	**001**	**156.2Y**	**162.4Y**	**214.6Y**	**327.6Y**	**258.0Y**	**394.3Y**	**242.9Y**	**1,390.9Y**	**1,380.6Y**	**1,525.4Y**	**1,886.6Y**	**2,067.5Y**	**2,351.8Y**	**2,815.0Y**
Industrial Countries	**101**	**49.0Y**	**66.0Y**	**64.6Y**	**70.3Y**	**59.9Y**	**152.1Y**	**58.2Y**	**459.5Y**	**419.0Y**	**489.6Y**	**580.1Y**	**570.5Y**	**666.0Y**	**787.8Y**
United States	111	5.91V	2.45V	2.45V	3.45V	3.55V	7.45V	9.09V	35.86V	12.21V	34.32V	47.41V	35.53V	47.63V	35.09V
Canada	156	4.20V	1.96V	.77V	.32V	.18V	.35V	.43V	2.97V	2.20V	3.77V	7.34V	6.32V	10.51V	8.05V
Australia	193	.48V	.64V	.87V	.41V	6.54V	14.67V	8.00V	1.25V	1.89V	8.93V	9.70V	9.37V	11.22V	23.93V
Japan	158	.25V	.48V	.27V	.18V	.13V	.28V	.10V	6.65V	6.16V	5.77V	5.34V	5.79V	5.77V	5.16V
New Zealand	196	—V	—V	—V	—V	—V	—V	.02V	—V	1.88V	.48V	.02V	.54V	.64V	.02V
Austria	122	.16V	.02V	.06V	.01V	.18V	.11V	.01V	4.56V	3.95V	7.43V	6.47V	7.96V	12.09V	17.15V
Belgium	124	2.64V	5.10V	4.25V	5.65V	3.25V	2.73V	5.31V	34.71V	32.41V	32.01V	49.15V	59.32V	90.99V	102.34V
Cyprus	423	—V	—V	.01V	.10V	.04Y	.01V	.01V	.03V	.04V	.19V	.07V	.07V	.11V	.08V
Denmark	128	2.51V	.31V	.40V	1.46V	1.04V	.02V	2.58V	3.12V	2.06V	2.96V	2.97V	1.55V	1.21V	2.24V
Finland	172	.01V	.01V	—V	—V	.01V	.17V	—V	1.76V	3.37V	1.93V	6.67V	.39V	.55V	1.71V
France	132	4.66V	6.49V	7.72V	7.37V	10.97V	8.12V	10.98V	198.36V	192.07V	234.10V	268.74V	268.43V	302.63V	363.25V
Germany	134	6.30V	8.46V	7.26V	16.54V	9.85V	96.32V	2.14V	64.81V	54.43V	54.87V	73.73V	63.80V	68.71V	86.98V
Greece	174	.08V	.40V	—V	.21V	.44V	.23V	.33V	.61V	.09V	.37V	.36V	.43V	7.01V	7.93V
Iceland	176	—V	.01V	—V	—V	—V	—V	.07V	—V	—V	—V	—V	—V	—V	—V
Ireland	178	.02V	.03V	—V	.01V	—V	—V	.17V	7.25V	12.55V	3.76V	8.55V	13.06V	12.96V	17.72V
Italy	136	10.19V	16.92V	16.12V	22.38V	12.98V	7.10V	7.41V	22.19V	21.63V	23.69V	21.45V	27.27V	28.64V	34.99V
Luxembourg	137	—V	.01V	—V	—V	—V	—V	—V	.15V	.53V	.70V	.35V	.55V	1.08V	.66V
Malta	181	—Y	—V	—V	—V	—V	—V	.01V	—Y	—V	.06V	.33V	1.41V	.74V	.84V
Netherlands	138	.31V	.49V	.26V	.99V	4.20V	3.55V	4.13V	13.42V	12.82V	23.44V	20.40V	24.04V	24.59V	30.22V
Norway	142	.25V	.21V	.35V	.37V	.06V	.02V	.03V	.61V	.49V	.22V	.23V	.85V	.69V	1.53V
Portugal	182	3.20V	7.41V	4.40V	1.73V	1.95V	5.00V	1.71V	1.31V	1.44V	1.16V	.33V	1.19V	.58V	1.24V
Slovenia	961	.06V	.52V	1.31V	1.72V	1.20V	.33V	1.55V	.30V	.24V	.22V	.29Y	.02V	—V	.10V
Spain	184	5.35V	8.42V	4.67V	3.13V	1.19V	2.68V	2.51V	28.14V	20.69V	18.39V	21.82V	27.65V	22.05V	29.32V
Sweden	144	.04V	.06V	.12V	.03V	.01V	.01V	.02V	1.16V	1.36V	2.57V	.61V	1.23V	4.65V	4.33V
Switzerland	146	.50V	.73V	.74V	.86V	.19V	2.43V	.54V	3.31V	2.33V	1.53V	4.12V	2.65V	2.28V	3.71V
United Kingdom	112	1.94V	4.84V	12.50V	3.33V	2.00V	.47V	1.04V	26.98V	32.18V	26.72V	23.65V	11.05V	8.66V	9.25V
Developing Countries	**202**	**101.2Y**	**90.0Y**	**141.9Y**	**246.6Y**	**185.9Y**	**227.1Y**	**165.9Y**	**842.3Y**	**864.8Y**	**913.4Y**	**1,145.7Y**	**1,313.3Y**	**1,458.7Y**	**1,745.4Y**
Africa	**607**	**16.9Y**	**16.9Y**	**16.0Y**	**17.8Y**	**16.4Y**	**20.1Y**	**25.2Y**	**724.0Y**	**729.5Y**	**740.1Y**	**945.9Y**	**1,074.4Y**	**1,187.3Y**	**1,403.6Y**
Algeria	612	—V	—V	—Y	—Y	—Y	—Y	—Y	.04V	—V	.01Y	.01Y	.01Y	.01Y	.02Y
Benin	638	.09V	—V	.13V	.01V	.10V	.13Y	.16Y	.14V	.07V	.44V	8.44V	8.09V	10.00Y	12.41Y
Burkina Faso	748	2.12Y	2.30Y	2.91Y	3.82Y	4.37Y	5.40Y	6.70Y	3.72Y	4.03Y	5.10Y	6.70Y	7.66Y	9.47Y	11.75Y
Cameroon	622	—V	—V	.02V	.02Y	.02Y	.03Y	.04Y	.02V	.13V	.20V	.27Y	.31Y	.38Y	.47Y
Central African Rep.	626	.02Y	.02Y	.02Y	.03Y	.03Y	.04Y	.05Y	—Y	—Y	—Y	—Y	—Y	—Y	.01Y
Congo, Republic of	634	.04V	—V	.02V	—V	—Y	—Y	—Y	—V	—V	—V	—V	—Y	—Y	—Y
Côte d'Ivoire	662	2.10V	1.75V	.06V	.12V	.46V	.36V	.45Y	223.80V	194.78V	107.93V	158.56V	173.78V	246.40V	305.78Y
Gabon	646	.04Y	.04Y	.05Y	.06Y	.07Y	.09Y	.11Y	.09Y	.10Y	.13Y	.17Y	.19Y	.23Y	.29Y
Gambia, The	648	—Y	.01Y	.01Y	.01Y	.01Y	.01Y	.02Y	.04Y	.04Y	.05Y	.07Y	.08Y	.09Y	.12Y
Ghana	652	.01Y	.01Y	.02Y	.02Y	.03Y	.03Y	.04Y	.01Y	.01Y	.02Y	.02Y	.02Y	.03Y	.04Y
Guinea	656	.01V	.02Y	.01V	.06V	.07Y	.09Y	.11Y	.80V	.86Y	1.11V	2.05V	2.34Y	2.89Y	3.59Y
Kenya	664	2.93V	.12V	.06V	.29V	.34Y	.42Y	.52Y	.52V	.49V	1.14V	2.46V	2.81Y	3.48Y	4.32Y
Madagascar	674	.07V	—V	—V	.01Y	.01Y	.01Y	.01Y	.02V	—V	.03V	.04Y	.05Y	.06Y	.08Y
Mauritania	682	—Y	—Y	—Y	—Y	—Y	—Y	—Y	.72Y	.78Y	.98Y	1.29Y	1.47Y	1.82Y	2.26Y
Mauritius	684	2.90V	6.56V	2.60V	1.67V	1.08V	2.48V	3.73V	.03V	.14V	.02V	.06V	.06V	.19V	.04V
Morocco	686	1.73V	1.30V	3.19V	4.92V	5.31V	6.56Y	8.15Y	14.43V	14.77V	14.74V	13.58V	15.81V	19.54Y	24.25Y
Niger	692	.86V	.51V	.43V	.44V	.50Y	.62Y	.77Y	.32V	.21V	.42V	1.41V	1.62Y	2.00Y	2.48Y
Nigeria	694	1.10V	.06V	.47V	.61Y	.78Y	.96Y	1.25Y	26.88V	.26V	3.75V	4.96Y	6.74Y	8.48Y	10.23Y
Senegal	722	—V	.01V	.02V	1.32V	.23V	.03V	.04Y	59.74V	92.45V	117.77V	184.15V	268.10V	288.13V	357.57Y
South Africa	199	1.54V	.83V	.84V	1.68V	.82V	.64V	.45V	21.11V	19.29V	25.63V	63.00V	75.40V	52.13V	89.13V
Sacca exc. South Afr.	608	—V	.04V	—V	—Y	—Y	—Y	—Y	—Y	—Y	—Y	—Y	—Y	—Y	—Y
Tanzania	738	—V	.06V	.07Y	.10Y	.11Y	.14Y	.17Y	.06V	.68V	.86Y	1.12Y	1.28Y	1.59Y	1.97Y
Togo	742	—V	.01V	.15V	.01V	.05V	.06Y	.07Y	1.86V	3.62V	35.43V	47.84V	29.22V	36.11Y	44.81Y
Tunisia	744	1.16V	3.22V	4.81V	2.30V	1.87V	1.83V	2.28Y	2.20V	3.53V	4.97V	5.01V	8.94V	8.11V	10.06Y
Uganda	746	.07V	.02V	.04V	.06Y	.08Y	.10Y	.12Y	.02V	.01V	.02V	.03Y	.03Y	.04Y	.05Y
Zambia	754	.07V	.02V	.05V	.02V	—V	—V	.01V	.07V	.03V	.41V	—V	.01V	—V	—V
Zimbabwe	698	.06V	—V	—V	.21V	.03V	.02V	.02Y	—V	.08V	.06V	.07V	—V	—V	—Y
Africa n.s.	799	—Y	—Y	—Y	—Y	—Y	—Y	—Y	367.37Y	393.12Y	418.88Y	444.63Y	470.39Y	496.15Y	521.90Y
Asia	**507**	**67.5Y**	**63.1Y**	**119.6Y**	**217.2Y**	**157.3Y**	**196.4Y**	**118.8Y**	**86.8Y**	**89.2Y**	**108.1Y**	**121.6Y**	**123.7Y**	**140.3Y**	**206.5Y**
Bangladesh	513	—V	1.83V	13.12V	14.44V	11.08V	5.75V	7.10V	—V	—V	—V	—V	—V	—Y	—Y
Cambodia	522	....	....	....	....	....	....	....	—V	—V	—V	—V	—V	.05V	.07Y
China,P.R.: Mainland	924	.93V	1.57V	25.81V	102.09V	72.42V	103.82V	47.51Y	25.23V	23.78V	38.72V	64.77V	72.68V	82.43V	137.80V
China,P.R.:Hong Kong	532	.22V	.12V	.03V	1.25V	.05V	1.70V	.05V	17.93V	16.73V	11.22V	14.16V	13.17V	13.45V	14.33V
Fiji	819	.01Y	.02Y	.02Y	.03Y	.03Y	.04Y	.04Y	.01Y	.01Y	.01Y	.02Y	.02Y	.03Y	.03Y
India	534	12.19Y	13.98V	25.79V	15.51V	4.71V	5.83Y	7.23Y	19.64Y	27.65V	42.38V	29.63V	27.46V	33.94Y	42.12Y
Indonesia	536	4.75V	3.80V	4.09V	7.30V	6.25V	8.43V	10.86V	9.56V	9.82V	5.95V	5.01V	3.62V	2.23V	3.66V
Korea	542	6.87V	3.63V	2.22V	1.18V	.71V	.22V	.59V	2.76V	1.36V	2.71V	2.26V	1.71V	1.92V	1.52V
Malaysia	548	3.58V	1.11V	.01V	.33V	.23V	.39V	1.45V	1.54V	3.39V	.17V	.80V	1.00V	.61V	.50V
Pakistan	564	—V	.21V	1.73V	32.30V	6.31V	7.80Y	9.68Y	.47V	.09V	1.17V	.11V	.08V	.09Y	.12Y
Philippines	566	.16V	1.21V	1.51V	.48V	.01V	.09V	—V	1.65V	.44V	.98V	1.43V	.15V	.96V	.44V
Taiwan Province of China	528	6.82V	8.27V	10.11V	13.01V	19.14V	19.02V	8.73V	.31V	.11V	.06V	.75V	.83V	.10V	.51V

		Exports							Imports						
		2001	2002	2003	2004	2005	2006	2007	2001	2002	2003	2004	2005	2006	2007
		Millions of U.S. Dollars							*Millions of U.S. Dollars*						
Thailand	578	28.83V	23.87V	30.02V	22.66V	24.90V	27.37V	25.54V	5.04V	4.03V	2.58V	2.47V	2.74V	4.21V	5.16V
Vietnam	582	3.11V	3.49V	5.12V	6.64V	11.45V	15.91V	—V	2.49V	1.62V	1.88V	—V	—V	—V	—V
Asia n.s.	598	—Y	—Y	—Y	—Y	—Y	—Y	—Y	.18Y	.20Y	.21Y	.22Y	.24Y	.25Y	.26Y
Europe	**170**	**6.4Y**	**8.0Y**	**5.3Y**	**10.1Y**	**9.4Y**	**1.8Y**	**3.7Y**	**26.5Y**	**28.3Y**	**52.6Y**	**65.9Y**	**91.4Y**	**103.6Y**	**123.1Y**
Albania	914	—V	.32V	—V	.06V	.12V	.03V	.02V	—V	—V	—V	—V	—V	—V	—V
Belarus	913	—V	—V	—V	—V	—V	—V	—V	.13V	.12V	.07V	—V	—V	—V	—V
Bulgaria	918	—V	—V	—V	—V	.01V	—V	—V	.02V	.02V	.02V	.01V	.15V	1.87V	1.43V
Czech Republic	935	4.65V	5.31V	3.77V	4.64V	3.78V	.52V	1.43V	1.50V	1.38V	1.23V	11.83V	20.65V	24.65V	24.59V
Estonia	939	.03V	.68V	.01V	—V	—V	—V	—V	—V	—V	—V	—V	.01V	—V	.04V
Hungary	944	.10V	.64V	.53V	.05V	—V	—V	.02V	.35V	.01V	.18V	.19V	.04V	.27V	.52V
Kyrgyz Republic	917	—V	.01V	.05V	.01V	—V	—V	—V	....	....	....	....	....	....	....
Latvia	941	—V	—V	—V	—V	—V	—V	—V	.01V	.02V	—V	—V	.02V	.29V	.03V
Lithuania	946	.45V	.21V	.36V	—V	—V	—V	—V	—V	—V	—V	.39V	.12V	.52V	.18V
Macedonia, FYR	962	—V	—V	—V	.01V	—V	.01V	.01Y	—Y	—Y	—Y	—Y	—Y	—Y	—Y
Poland	964	1.08V	.80V	.35V	.55V	—V	.04V	.21V	1.29V	1.38V	1.09V	1.04V	1.02V	2.11V	1.51V
Romania	968	.01V	.05V	.15V	.68V	—V	—V	—V	.42V	.48V	3.65V	.86V	6.86V	.13V	.78V
Russia	922	—V	.01V	—V	3.74V	2.82V	—V	—V	1.41V	.74V	3.24V	2.50V	3.44V	5.96V	6.49V
Slovak Republic	936	—V	—V	—Y	.01Y	—V	—V	—V	.03V	.12V	.15Y	.20Y	.06V	.04V	.49V
Turkey	186	—V	—V	.04V	.36V	2.62V	1.21V	1.98V	2.87V	3.73V	5.47V	7.01V	11.00V	8.43V	13.35V
Ukraine	926	.07V	—V	—V	—V	—V	—Y	—Y	3.04V	3.57V	16.28V	13.98V	16.22V	20.05Y	24.88Y
Europe n.s.	884	—Y	—Y	—Y	—Y	—Y	—Y	—Y	15.44Y	16.75Y	21.20Y	27.85Y	31.82Y	39.32Y	48.80Y
Middle East	**407**	**.6Y**	**.7Y**	**.9Y**	**1.3Y**	**1.5Y**	**1.8Y**	**2.4Y**	**1.6Y**	**1.8Y**	**2.4Y**	**3.7Y**	**5.8Y**	**5.6Y**	**7.0Y**
Egypt	469	.49V	.53Y	.67Y	.88Y	1.01Y	1.25Y	1.55Y	.74V	.80Y	1.02Y	1.33Y	1.52Y	1.88Y	2.34Y
Iran, I.R. of	429	—V	.16V	.17Y	.23Y	.29Y	.36Y	.46Y	—Y	—Y	—Y	—Y	—Y	—Y	—Y
Israel	436	—V	—V	—V	—V	—V	—V	.18V	—V	—V	—V	.44V	1.65V	.66V	.99V
Jordan	439	—V	—V	—V	—V	—V	—V	—V	—V	—V	—V	—V	.01V	—V	—V
Kuwait	443	.01Y	.01Y	.02Y	.02Y	.03Y	.03Y	.04Y	—Y	—Y	—Y	—Y	—Y	—Y	—Y
Lebanon	446	.04Y	.04Y	.06Y	.07Y	.08Y	.10Y	.13Y	.24Y	.26Y	.33Y	.44Y	.50Y	.62Y	.77Y
Oman	449	....	....	....	....	....	....	....	.03V	.11V	.32V	.43Y	.58Y	.73Y	.88Y
Qatar	453	—V	—V	—V	.10V	.05V	.03V	.05Y	—V	—V	.02V	.13V	.24V	.02V	.03Y
Saudi Arabia	456	.06V	—V	.01V	—V	.02V	.02Y	.03Y	.54Y	.58Y	.70Y	.92Y	1.26Y	1.58Y	1.90Y
Yemen, Republic of	474	—V	—V	—Y	—V	—V	—Y	—Y	—V	—V	—Y	.06V	.08V	.10Y	.12Y
Western Hemisphere	**207**	**9.8Y**	**1.2Y**	**.2Y**	**.2Y**	**1.4Y**	**7.1Y**	**15.8Y**	**3.4Y**	**16.0Y**	**10.2Y**	**8.5Y**	**17.9Y**	**21.9Y**	**5.2Y**
Argentina	213	—V	—V	—V	—V	—V	—V	—V	.11V	2.75V	.50V	1.28V	1.59V	5.23V	1.91V
Barbados	316	.01V	.03V	.08V	.04V	.06V	.04V	.05Y	.01V	—V	—V	—V	—V	—V	—Y
Bolivia	218	.01V	.09V	.01V	—V	—V	—Y	—Y	....	....	....	....	....	....	....
Brazil	223	8.74V	.96V	.01V	—V	.03V	5.01V	11.28V	1.71V	10.30V	8.21V	5.45V	14.92V	14.01V	—V
Chile	228	—V	—V	—V	.06V	—V	.01V	—V	—V	—V	—V	—V	—V	—V	—V
Colombia	233	—V	.08V	—V	.02V	.32V	.04V	.08V	—V	1.56V	.03V	.41V	.07V	—V	.34V
Mexico	273	—V	—V	—V	—V	.88V	1.73V	4.01V	—V	—V	—V	—V	.08V	.04V	.03V
Peru	293	1.00V	—V	—V	—V	.01V	.20V	.31Y	1.60V	1.40V	1.50V	1.32V	1.19V	2.52V	2.79Y
Suriname	366	.02Y	.03Y	.03Y	.04Y	.05Y	.06Y	.08Y	—Y	—Y	—Y	—Y	—Y	—Y	—Y
Uruguay	298	....	....	....	....	....	....	....	—V	—Y	—Y	.06V	.06V	.07Y	.09Y
Venezuela, Rep. Bol.	299	—V	—V	.02V	—V	—V	—V	—V	—V	—V	—V	—V	—V	—V	—Y
Countries & Areas n.s.	**898**	**5.9Y**	**6.4Y**	**8.1Y**	**10.7Y**	**12.2Y**	**15.1Y**	**18.7Y**	**88.9Y**	**96.5Y**	**122.1Y**	**160.4Y**	**183.3Y**	**226.5Y**	**281.1Y**
Memorandum Items															
European Union	998	43.79Y	67.15Y	64.12Y	69.94Y	53.08Y	127.42Y	41.59Y	412.02Y	394.77Y	437.22Y	519.59Y	531.34Y	615.11Y	737.70Y
Oil Exporting Ctys.	999	5.93Y	4.03Y	4.79Y	8.26Y	7.42Y	9.83Y	12.68Y	37.06Y	10.77Y	10.74Y	11.45Y	12.45Y	13.05Y	16.71Y
Non-Oil Develop.Ctys.	201	95.28Y	85.97Y	137.11Y	238.34Y	178.43Y	217.27Y	153.26Y	805.24Y	854.04Y	902.62Y	1,134.25Y	1,300.84Y	1,445.66Y	1,728.68Y
PERCENT DISTRIBUTION															
Industrial Countries	**101**	**31.4**	**40.6**	**30.1**	**21.5**	**23.2**	**38.6**	**24.0**	**33.0**	**30.4**	**32.1**	**30.7**	**27.6**	**28.3**	**28.0**
Developing Countries	**202**	**64.8**	**55.4**	**66.1**	**75.3**	**72.0**	**57.6**	**68.3**	**60.6**	**62.6**	**59.9**	**60.7**	**63.5**	**62.0**	**62.0**
Africa	**607**	**10.8**	**10.4**	**7.4**	**5.4**	**6.3**	**5.1**	**10.4**	**52.1**	**52.8**	**48.5**	**50.1**	**52.0**	**50.5**	**49.9**
Asia	**507**	**43.2**	**38.9**	**55.7**	**66.3**	**61.0**	**49.8**	**48.9**	**6.2**	**6.5**	**7.1**	**6.4**	**6.0**	**6.0**	**7.3**
Europe	**170**	**4.1**	**5.0**	**2.5**	**3.1**	**3.6**	**.5**	**1.5**	**1.9**	**2.1**	**3.4**	**3.5**	**4.4**	**4.4**	**4.4**
Middle East	**407**	**.4**	**.5**	**.4**	**.4**	**.6**	**.5**	**1.0**	**.1**	**.1**	**.2**	**.2**	**.3**	**.2**	**.2**
Western Hemisphere	**207**	**6.3**	**.7**	**.1**	**.1**	**.5**	**1.8**	**6.5**	**.2**	**1.2**	**.7**	**.5**	**.9**	**.9**	**.2**
ANNUAL PERCENT CHANGE															
World	**001**	**–33.4**	**4.0**	**32.1**	**52.6**	**–21.2**	**52.8**	**–38.4**	**8.2**	**–.7**	**10.5**	**23.7**	**9.6**	**13.8**	**19.7**
Industrial Countries	**101**	**–50.8**	**34.5**	**–2.1**	**8.9**	**–14.7**	**153.7**	**–61.7**	**17.9**	**–8.8**	**16.8**	**18.5**	**–1.7**	**16.7**	**18.3**
Developing Countries	**202**	**–21.8**	**–11.1**	**57.7**	**73.8**	**–24.6**	**22.2**	**–26.9**	**3.3**	**2.7**	**5.6**	**25.4**	**14.6**	**11.1**	**19.7**
Africa	**607**	**–24.9**	**–.1**	**–5.5**	**11.5**	**–8.1**	**22.5**	**25.9**	**5.6**	**.8**	**1.5**	**27.8**	**13.6**	**10.5**	**18.2**
Asia	**507**	**–10.1**	**–6.5**	**89.5**	**81.6**	**–27.6**	**24.8**	**–39.5**	**–14.0**	**2.8**	**21.1**	**12.6**	**1.7**	**13.4**	**47.2**
Europe	**170**	**–23.9**	**25.6**	**–34.7**	**92.0**	**–7.3**	**–80.7**	**102.6**	**22.0**	**6.9**	**85.7**	**25.2**	**38.8**	**13.4**	**18.8**
Middle East	**407**	**410.8**	**23.4**	**25.0**	**39.8**	**13.2**	**21.2**	**35.6**	**–14.5**	**12.8**	**35.9**	**57.1**	**56.1**	**–4.4**	**25.7**
Western Hemisphere	**207**	**–57.9**	**–87.9**	**–86.7**	**11.8**	**671.1**	**422.4**	**123.0**	**–31.6**	**368.1**	**–36.0**	**–16.8**	**110.1**	**22.1**	**–76.4**

	Exports 2001	2002	2003	2004	2005	2006	2007	Imports 2001	2002	2003	2004	2005	2006	2007
	Millions of U.S. Dollars							Millions of U.S. Dollars						
IFS World Total	**1,957.8**	**2,225.2**	**2,467.1**	**2,627.1**	**2,375.5**	**2,707.2**	**2,982.5**	**2,725.7**	**2,839.4**	**3,398.1**	**3,823.9**	**3,807.3**	**4,078.6**	**4,507.7**
DOTS World Total ... 001	**2,241.0Y**	**2,215.4**	**2,460.7**	**2,624.0**	**2,393.0**	**2,668.1**	**2,922.0**	**4,743.4Y**	**2,828.1**	**3,396.4**	**3,803.2**	**3,671.7**	**3,979.8**	**4,373.1**
Industrial Countries ... 101	**1,379.0Y**	**1,450.0**	**1,562.6**	**1,702.4**	**1,634.2**	**1,774.9**	**1,876.8**	**3,289.4Y**	**2,316.7**	**2,758.5**	**3,093.4**	**3,089.5**	**3,079.1**	**3,507.8**
United States ... 111	338.55V	367.60	355.81	411.55	328.47	345.72	330.87	284.90V	265.92	275.64	197.19	198.61	224.37	174.31
Canada ... 156	6.86V	3.68	5.42	10.58	18.41	12.76	15.36	9.27V	7.88	9.01	5.93	7.29	13.83	7.49
Australia ... 193	2.84V	1.13	1.11	2.42	3.52	4.89	7.38	8.36V	8.23	9.09	5.35	5.31	6.89	4.53
Japan ... 158	26.56V	95.91	98.16	74.76	95.83	131.61	142.05	346.97V	64.46	77.54	95.19	65.43	88.01	88.08
New Zealand ... 196	.27V	.07	.07	.07	.13	.48	.36	5.72V	6.22	9.15	4.07	5.49	8.06	7.31
Austria ... 122	2.89V	2.08	3.42	4.26	4.10	9.46	7.36	26.69V	20.11	24.56	23.70	27.13	29.09	39.92
Belgium ... 124	63.86V	70.68	67.87	34.11	54.26	27.46	19.15	67.21V	32.33	57.77	62.39	72.14	67.85	90.71
Cyprus ... 423	15.88V	.35	.81	1.80	3.32	3.91	4.25	2.12V	2.13	2.42	3.53	4.13	5.69	6.41
Denmark ... 128	3.13V	3.80	5.36	4.78	6.24	12.14	16.43	24.69V	20.88	27.50	42.63	30.26	31.13	34.87
Finland ... 172	20.60V	8.70	11.01	12.93	6.02	55.73	65.31	3.89V	4.49	4.36	4.16	3.71	2.84	4.45
France ... 132	199.23V	276.80	318.62	407.94	352.44	406.63	368.44	474.40V	473.13	580.28	497.26	361.43	346.23	413.98
Germany ... 134	298.44V	215.65	252.46	282.70	292.60	333.47	400.50	313.09V	227.25	267.71	337.68	310.57	303.10	383.21
Greece ... 174	8.97V	1.90	1.79	1.82	5.04	3.40	2.98	166.26V	17.53	16.44	26.08	20.62	26.50	37.96
Iceland ... 176	.26V	.78	.68	4.41	3.77	5.59	2.67	.36V	3.14	1.57	8.74	3.71	4.09	1.98
Ireland ... 178	1.90V	10.79	6.92	7.69	3.55	2.31	10.15	16.25V	16.77	20.47	23.19	24.72	19.30	28.46
Italy ... 136	136.43V	75.31	83.50	78.45	123.15	93.16	117.24	795.85V	627.60	783.05	967.68	1,183.63	1,113.55	1,138.98
Luxembourg ... 137	.14V	.02	.03	.08	.01	.01	.01	.56V	.69	.52	.54	.53	.94	3.92
Netherlands ... 138	12.10V	23.75	18.05	21.46	21.74	23.96	16.19	114.71V	65.87	78.72	133.18	127.25	145.86	132.79
Norway ... 142	2.89V	2.94	5.35	3.36	2.95	4.00	5.45	127.49V	2.20	2.95	7.01	4.06	3.12	3.15
Portugal ... 182	13.01V	5.44	3.95	5.34	5.19	8.17	11.38	10.43V	9.83	16.02	15.36	12.56	11.12	11.01
Slovenia ... 961	4.87V	1.12	1.48	1.96	.52	.45	1.00	1.75V	1.31	1.52	2.56	2.61	3.40	8.17
Spain ... 184	19.86V	13.70	17.30	19.76	15.41	19.31	18.87	90.48V	75.57	94.38	119.11	126.56	122.43	135.67
Sweden ... 144	3.20V	5.31	10.42	11.08	8.39	8.39	10.64	15.94V	16.39	15.55	14.92	20.16	13.45	11.20
Switzerland ... 146	2.46V	3.56	3.97	5.11	10.37	9.60	10.71	37.77V	52.14	67.77	39.32	55.23	69.18	83.34
United Kingdom ... 112	193.79V	258.90	289.00	293.89	268.74	252.25	292.06	344.28V	294.64	314.49	456.69	416.39	419.06	655.93
Developing Countries ... 202	**717.3Y**	**620.4**	**742.2**	**787.9**	**734.1**	**874.0**	**1,014.4**	**1,453.7Y**	**511.1**	**637.6**	**705.3**	**578.7**	**898.6**	**862.4**
Africa ... 607	**19.7Y**	**23.0**	**30.6**	**37.7**	**66.3**	**61.8**	**75.4**	**31.0Y**	**18.6**	**18.1**	**19.9**	**17.1**	**20.0**	**19.9**
Algeria ... 612	5.12V	.43	.90	1.61	.78	1.72	6.89	13.34V	2.80	1.92	—	—	1.98	.01
Angola ... 614	.04Y	.95	2.78	4.41	3.55	4.01	3.37	—Y	—	—	—	—	—	—
Benin ... 638	.02V	.05	.12	.20	—	.15	.12	.16V	.02	—	—	—	—	—
Botswana ... 616	—Y	.92	—	.84	.83	.75	.85	—Y	—	—	—	—	—	—
Burkina Faso ... 748	—Y	—	—	—	.05	.08	—	—Y	—	—	—	—	—	—
Burundi ... 618	—V	.03	—	.17	1.34	.93	2.01	—V	—	—	—	—	—	—
Cameroon ... 622	.01V	.23	.87	.64	1.06	1.36	.85	.05V	—	.01	.02	.08	.05	.23
Cape Verde ... 624	.08V	.20	.09	.75	1.88	2.26	1.84	—V	—	—	—	—	—	—
Central African Rep. ... 626	—Y	—	—	—	.04	.02	.05	—Y	—	—	—	—	—	—
Chad ... 628	—Y	—	—	—	—	.25	.50	—Y	—	—	—	—	—	—
Congo, Dem. Rep. of ... 636	—Y	—	—	—	—	.03	.46	—Y	—	—	—	—	—	—
Congo, Republic of ... 634	—V	.08	.03	.30	.17	.35	.40	—V	—	—	—	—	—	—
Côte d'Ivoire ... 662	—V	—	.14	.61	.18	—	—	3.14V	.75	.68	.62	.97	.59	.55
Djibouti ... 611	3.57Y	2.03	1.84	1.90	1.46	1.99	1.48	—Y	—	—	—	—	—	—
Equatorial Guinea ... 642	—Y	—	—	—	—	.09	.01	—Y	—	—	—	—	—	—
Eritrea ... 643	—Y	—	—	—	.03	.03	—	—Y	—	—	—	—	—	—
Ethiopia ... 644	—V	—	.11	.07	.02	.57	.44	—V	.07	.28	—	—	.03	—
Gabon ... 646	.02Y	—	—	.15	.30	.30	.22	—Y	—	—	—	—	—	—
Gambia, The ... 648	—Y	.38	.34	.45	.66	.31	.36	—Y	—	—	—	—	—	—
Ghana ... 652	.32Y	1.61	1.63	.51	.78	.32	10.49	.06Y	.09	.22	.26	.42	.72	.39
Guinea ... 656	.05V	—	.17	.15	2.82	1.24	4.17	—V	—	—	—	—	—	—
Guinea-Bissau ... 654	—Y	.11	.38	.41	.67	.97	1.35	—Y	—	—	—	—	—	—
Kenya ... 664	.05V	.28	.11	.39	.28	.21	.38	.24V	.17	.28	.04	.42	2.75	2.13
Liberia ... 668	.02Y	—	.03	.15	.29	.26	.51	—Y	—	—	—	—	.03	—
Madagascar ... 674	.09V	.44	.26	—	.12	.07	.02	.05V	.07	.01	—	—	.05	—
Malawi ... 676	—Y	—	.48	4.35	1.94	2.25	—	—Y	—	.01	—	—	—	—
Mali ... 678	—Y	—	.06	.31	1.28	.67	.76	—Y	—	—	—	—	—	.01
Mauritania ... 682	.08Y	.13	.80	.14	.03	.22	.44	.02Y	—	.02	—	.01	—	.01
Mauritius ... 684	.03V	.06	.01	.06	.11	.06	.13	4.96V	3.04	3.49	3.79	2.24	2.39	1.51
Morocco ... 686	.16V	1.51	2.13	3.27	3.10	3.38	3.63	1.35V	4.28	4.85	1.85	2.29	3.01	4.77
Mozambique ... 688	—V	—	—	—	—	—	—	—V	.01	—	—	—	—	—
Namibia ... 728	—Y	.02	—	.33	.05	.15	.10	—Y	.01	.01	—	—	—	—
Niger ... 692	.04V	.04	—	.19	.24	.32	.44	—V	—	—	—	—	—	—
Nigeria ... 694	1.04V	.74	.74	.49	14.93	17.37	15.11	—V	—	—	—	—	—	—
Rwanda ... 714	—Y	—	—	—	—	.02	.89	—Y	—	—	—	—	—	—
St. Helena ... 856	—Y	—	—	—	—	—	—	—Y	—	—	—	—	.07	—
São Tomé & Príncipe ... 716	—Y	—	—	—	—	—	.09	—Y	—	—	—	—	—	—
Senegal ... 722	.53V	.75	2.23	3.07	3.12	2.44	2.07	—V	.09	.08	.09	.05	.02	.23
Seychelles ... 718	—V	—	.08	—	.01	—	—	.32V	.44	.25	.47	.65	.52	.30
Sierra Leone ... 724	.04Y	.09	.36	.67	.30	.18	.27	.01Y	—	.01	—	—	.01	.03
Somalia ... 726	.62Y	—	—	—	.34	—	.63	.40Y	.15	.16	.03	—	—	—
South Africa ... 199	.94V	4.99	3.37	.97	3.60	5.65	.44	1.43V	3.37	3.77	4.87	2.33	3.53	2.15

		Exports							Imports						
		2001	2002	2003	2004	2005	2006	2007	2001	2002	2003	2004	2005	2006	2007
		Millions of U.S. Dollars							*Millions of U.S. Dollars*						
Sudan	732	1.72Y	.87	.70	.38	.11	—	.22	—Y	—	—	—	—	—	—
Swaziland	734	—Y	—	—	.11	.05	—	—	—Y	.01	—	—	.03	.02	.11
Tanzania	738	.42V	.05	.05	.20	.14	.23	1.75	.06V	.19	.14	.05	.09	.11	.55
Togo	742	.42V	—	.25	.57	.57	.17	.13	—V	—	—	—	—	—	—
Tunisia	744	4.23V	4.45	6.71	8.84	16.27	9.17	11.52	5.41V	3.07	1.81	7.78	7.45	3.78	6.51
Uganda	746	—V	—	.01	—	—	—	—	—V	—	.06	—	.05	.11	.11
Zambia	754	—V	1.53	2.86	—	2.80	1.26	—	—V	—	—	—	—	—	—
Zimbabwe	698	—V	.01	.01	—	—	—	—	—V	.02	.03	.02	—	.19	.28
Asia	**507**	**493.1Y**	**440.7**	**533.6**	**529.3**	**411.4**	**577.0**	**699.0**	**1,000.8Y**	**333.8**	**464.0**	**464.7**	**421.2**	**731.3**	**648.3**
Afghanistan, I.S. of	512	—Y	—	—	.01	.50	.02	—	—Y	—	—	—	.01	—	—
Bangladesh	513	.71V	.01	.01	.02	—	.01	—	—V	.47	.98	.62	1.19	1.80	1.77
Bhutan	514	.01Y	—	—	—	.09	—	—	—Y	—	—	—	—	—	—
Cambodia	522	—V	.01	—	.01	—	—	—	—V	.03	.03	.07	.08	.11	.09
China,P.R.: Mainland	924	64.99V	5.01	9.27	19.31	21.76	66.90	37.25	88.31V	63.22	98.13	77.39	71.33	134.51	126.75
China,P.R.:Hong Kong	532	47.99V	48.96	60.84	78.53	70.93	112.91	179.51	26.84V	17.76	16.24	15.23	18.03	54.40	16.88
China,P.R.:Macao	546	—V	.46	—	.31	.06	—	—	.01V	.19	.20	.03	.14	.30	.02
Fiji	819	.03Y	—	—	—	—	—	—	—Y	—	—	—	—	—	—
Guam	829	—Y	—	—	—	.75	—	—	—Y	—	—	—	—	—	—
India	534	.53Y	2.53	.11	.50	1.16	1.96	4.13	15.65Y	17.46	16.54	16.03	20.57	20.99	27.68
Indonesia	536	1.08V	—	.30	.21	.03	1.54	.22	2.37V	2.73	5.36	2.53	4.52	4.10	6.07
Korea	542	46.40V	28.36	27.10	24.78	11.09	15.61	22.66	343.17V	17.99	28.30	24.13	33.86	38.72	67.11
Lao People's Dem.Rep	544	—Y	—	—	—	—	—	—	.02Y	.06	.06	.01	—	—	—
Malaysia	548	26.27V	.73	16.57	6.08	14.66	19.68	17.01	102.38V	41.19	65.30	94.50	46.89	83.26	57.46
Maldives	556	.30V	.35	.49	.60	.25	.67	.67	—Y	—	—	—	—	—	—
Myanmar	518	—Y	—	—	—	—	—	.05	.03Y	.02	.01	.01	.07	.08	.08
Nauru	836	—Y	—	—	—	—	—	—	—Y	—	—	—	.04	.01	.01
Nepal	558	.07Y	.05	.17	.82	.03	.05	.04	—Y	—	—	—	—	.01	—
New Caledonia	839	.01V	—	.03	—	—	—	—	—V	—	—	—	—	—	—
Pakistan	564	.13V	.22	.09	.20	.51	.94	.36	4.39V	1.96	3.62	2.49	3.37	3.61	2.08
Papua New Guinea	853	.01Y	—	—	—	—	—	—	—Y	—	—	.28	.18	.08	.10
Philippines	566	1.18V	.31	.77	11.45	4.90	.52	.60	.55V	12.99	25.51	26.95	20.46	24.87	29.68
Singapore	576	257.59V	350.44	413.22	381.36	279.79	352.15	419.99	381.46V	119.29	158.04	154.97	148.66	270.24	226.69
Sri Lanka	524	.02V	.18	.64	.55	.37	.51	.28	.22V	.83	.74	.32	.21	.33	.48
Taiwan Province of China	528	22.01V	1.92	2.45	1.83	1.00	.51	2.16	22.47V	26.77	33.14	39.35	38.57	73.35	67.60
Thailand	578	17.61V	1.17	1.51	2.63	3.35	3.04	14.05	12.69V	10.02	10.60	8.88	11.75	13.37	16.31
Vietnam	582	6.19V	—	.04	.10	.11	—	—	.22V	.77	1.21	.87	1.21	7.18	1.40
Europe	**170**	**89.4Y**	**38.9**	**54.1**	**61.3**	**74.4**	**89.7**	**81.9**	**301.0Y**	**94.1**	**109.4**	**100.8**	**81.8**	**85.4**	**124.0**
Albania	914	.24V	.13	.23	.14	.24	—	.02	—V	.02	.16	.03	—	—	—
Armenia	911	—V	—	—	—	—	—	—	—V	—	—	.01	—	.01	—
Azerbaijan	912	.18V	—	—	.01	.61	.04	.12	9.54V	—	—	—	1.42	1.66	.01
Belarus	913	—V	—	—	—	—	—	—	—V	—	.01	.04	.04	.01	.06
Bosnia & Herzegovina	963	—Y	—	—	—	—	—	—	—Y	—	—	—	.01	.82	—
Bulgaria	918	.17V	.25	.32	.32	.51	2.06	1.90	12.33V	3.46	3.15	11.92	2.13	3.63	3.61
Croatia	960	1.21V	.46	.51	.57	1.49	1.29	2.62	61.18V	.26	.45	.45	1.97	.30	1.13
Czech Republic	935	8.33V	3.86	3.27	4.15	16.03	20.93	14.91	4.60V	6.76	7.47	8.38	5.35	9.70	14.00
Estonia	939	2.35V	2.71	5.71	7.07	1.10	.48	—	14.45V	.08	.33	.28	.10	.16	.05
Georgia	915	.03V	—	—	—	—	.28	—	—V	—	2.26	3.22	1.02	1.64	.63
Gibraltar	823	—Y	.38	—	—	—	.03	—	—Y	2.60	—	2.87	—	.02	.69
Hungary	944	28.29V	15.79	37.12	33.95	30.61	27.39	18.26	6.38V	4.60	6.81	5.36	8.38	6.53	12.92
Kazakhstan	916	.37V	—	—	.03	—	9.46	1.31	.30V	—	—	—	—	—	—
Kyrgyz Republic	917	—V	2.75	1.04	1.55	1.41	.57	2.63	—V	—	—	—	—	—	—
Latvia	941	.08V	.18	.02	.03	.13	.05	.10	.48V	.01	.09	.22	.26	.58	.44
Lithuania	946	.88V	.01	.05	.01	—	.18	.18	.11V	.20	.32	.43	1.52	1.44	1.67
Macedonia, FYR	962	.09V	—	—	—	—	.10	—	.07V	—	—	—	1.66	.69	3.66
Moldova	921	.01V	—	.01	—	—	—	—	—V	—	.08	—	—	—	—
Poland	964	21.90V	.36	.77	2.11	5.42	10.41	20.75	23.68V	3.58	5.19	4.79	6.66	9.04	17.06
Romania	968	13.99V	.05	.33	.20	1.88	3.60	3.16	46.41V	1.49	2.08	1.59	2.24	1.89	8.89
Russia	922	1.68V	.09	.04	.91	1.52	2.27	2.94	40.41V	25.36	18.51	8.20	.97	2.28	.95
Serbia, Rep. of	942	—Y	—	—	—	—	1.95	.48	—Y	—	—	—	—	.18	2.27
Serbia & Montenegro	965	—Y	.12	—	—	—	—	—	—Y	.32	.44	1.30	—	—	—
Slovak Republic	936	1.12V	1.72	.76	1.35	.56	1.18	1.86	7.47V	.90	1.47	1.24	1.12	.88	2.47
Turkey	186	8.29V	9.95	3.86	4.87	4.50	4.20	10.35	69.23V	41.00	46.19	47.46	45.27	40.15	49.35
Turkmenistan	925	—V	—	—	3.57	8.29	2.76	.01	—V	—	—	—	—	—	—
Ukraine	926	.14V	.11	.09	.23	.10	.28	.36	4.39V	3.44	14.45	3.04	1.69	3.77	4.10
Europe n.s.	884	—Y	—	—	.25	—	.21	—	—Y	—	—	—	—	—	.02
Middle East	**407**	**84.3Y**	**111.6**	**105.4**	**144.5**	**153.3**	**129.4**	**127.4**	**111.6Y**	**47.5**	**23.7**	**82.4**	**32.5**	**29.6**	**32.9**
Bahrain	419	.77Y	.71	.78	.55	1.41	1.46	1.34	8.18Y	—	.13	.21	.15	.12	.11
Egypt	469	10.48V	5.91	3.77	5.04	6.82	10.43	5.14	21.59V	2.48	7.27	44.64	11.18	7.49	5.03
Iran, I.R. of	429	.05V	.18	.13	.56	1.22	2.50	2.81	5.95Y	.29	.38	.26	3.61	.16	.56
Iraq	433	—Y	—	1.57	6.50	1.36	.47	.55	—Y	—	—	—	—	.02	—
Israel	436	3.91V	1.49	7.99	9.78	9.34	5.67	7.88	23.32V	18.70	5.37	20.09	4.68	6.56	4.73
Jordan	439	.30V	1.82	1.46	.56	.96	.93	1.08	.16V	.15	.15	.30	.13	.22	.23
Kuwait	443	1.99Y	1.55	4.25	2.33	2.44	2.90	3.03	6.56Y	.08	.13	1.05	.04	.08	.02
Lebanon	446	.93Y	1.22	1.30	2.37	.54	.61	.65	.81Y	.27	.36	.26	.36	.69	.31
Libya	672	35.41Y	74.12	58.63	92.53	94.94	70.61	74.71	40.24Y	18.80	3.24	10.12	2.82	3.29	5.48
Oman	449	1.47V	.69	1.75	2.25	2.48	2.14	2.22	.05V	.06	.13	.33	.48	.64	1.19
Qatar	453	—V	.60	.86	1.11	.92	1.51	2.99	.01V	—	—	—	—	.08	—

	Exports 2001	Exports 2002	Exports 2003	Exports 2004	Exports 2005	Exports 2006	Exports 2007	Imports 2001	Imports 2002	Imports 2003	Imports 2004	Imports 2005	Imports 2006	Imports 2007
	Millions of U.S. Dollars							Millions of U.S. Dollars						
Saudi Arabia....456	8.29V	9.86	8.62	7.96	10.36	10.05	10.61	.40Y	.76	.89	.51	.44	.78	2.55
Syrian Arab Republic....463	.08Y	—	.08	.09	.13	5.79	.32	.26Y	4.76	3.18	.16	.18	.24	.51
United Arab Emirates....466	19.82V	11.35	12.43	10.55	17.69	12.05	12.45	4.04Y	1.14	2.49	4.52	8.48	9.26	12.11
Yemen, Republic of....474	.82V	2.09	1.75	2.32	2.70	2.30	1.58	—V	—	—	—	—	—	.04
Western Hemisphere....207	**30.8Y**	**6.1**	**18.4**	**15.1**	**28.7**	**16.1**	**30.8**	**9.3Y**	**17.1**	**22.4**	**37.5**	**26.1**	**32.3**	**37.4**
Antigua and Barbuda....311	—Y	.02	—	.10	.05	—	—	—Y	—	—	—	.10	.02	.01
Argentina....213	.75V	.24	.40	.24	.09	.26	.11	2.15V	3.99	7.64	7.80	1.93	2.69	2.38
Aruba....314	—V	.10	—	—	—	.01	—	—Y	—	—	—	—	—	—
Bahamas, The....313	—Y	—	—	—	.16	.11	.12	.33Y	.15	.22	.16	.39	.71	.02
Barbados....316	.03V	.04	—	—	.66	.01	—	.01V	—	—	—	—	.32	—
Belize....339	—Y	—	—	—	—	—	—	—Y	—	—	1.44	—	—	—
Bermuda....319	.01Y	—	—	—	—	—	—	.12Y	.18	—	—	—	—	—
Bolivia....218	—V	—	—	.02	—	—	—	—V	.04	.07	.04	—	—	—
Brazil....223	24.79V	1.19	15.19	6.29	14.58	6.97	7.98	6.24V	7.41	7.55	21.97	13.11	15.06	23.81
Chile....228	.15V	.03	.03	.01	1.45	.63	.57	.22V	.89	1.08	1.10	1.49	7.14	3.33
Colombia....233	.07V	.17	.06	.13	1.26	.06	.18	.10V	.44	.61	.70	1.48	1.03	.79
Costa Rica....238	—V	.08	.02	.13	.29	.05	.02	.03V	.23	.27	.29	1.10	.24	.01
Dominica....321	—V	—	.03	.04	—	.09	—	—V	—	—	—	—	—	—
Dominican Republic....243	.04V	.25	.70	3.40	.88	1.67	2.13	.01V	.06	.08	.02	—	.01	.02
Ecuador....248	.04V	.05	.07	.77	.04	.01	.03	—V	2.21	1.98	1.08	2.18	.38	.11
El Salvador....253	—V	—	—	—	.03	—	—	—V	.01	.01	—	—	—	—
Falkland Islands....323	—Y	—	—	—	—	—	—	—Y	—	—	—	—	.05	—
Guatemala....258	3.52V	.03	.08	.01	.01	.01	.80	—V	.05	.02	.01	—	.02	—
Guyana....336	.09Y	.08	.13	.06	.05	—	—	—Y	.01	.01	—	—	—	—
Haiti....263	—V	—	—	.33	2.16	—	—	—Y	—	—	—	—	—	—
Honduras....268	.02V	.07	.03	.01	—	—	—	—V	.01	.01	—	—	—	.01
Jamaica....343	.52V	.50	.19	.02	.20	.09	.05	—V	.02	.05	.03	—	—	—
Mexico....273	—V	1.05	.94	1.76	3.55	4.80	7.23	—V	.97	1.87	1.65	2.25	1.14	1.80
Netherlands Antilles....353	.01V	—	—	—	—	.46	—	.01V	—	—	—	—	—	.05
Nicaragua....278	—V	—	.09	.04	.09	—	—	—V	—	.02	—	—	2.51	4.10
Panama....283	—V	.48	.04	.29	—	—	.04	—V	.23	.44	.03	.98	.02	—
Paraguay....288	—V	—	—	—	1.21	.01	—	—V	—	—	—	—	—	—
Peru....293	.01V	.02	—	.21	.19	.04	.06	.05V	.16	.15	.15	.05	.13	.15
St. Lucia....362	—Y	—	—	—	—	.34	—	—Y	—	—	—	—	—	—
St. Vincent & Grens....364	—V	—	.02	—	.03	—	—	—V	—	—	—	—	—	—
Suriname....366	.02Y	—	.01	.15	.10	.01	.01	—Y	—	—	—	—	—	—
Trinidad and Tobago....369	.36V	.27	.20	.78	.13	.17	.22	—V	—	.02	—	—	—	.06
Uruguay....298	.13V	.47	—	.07	.71	.09	—	.03V	.06	.30	1.00	.89	.19	.06
Venezuela, Rep. Bol....299	.23V	.97	.17	.20	.75	—	11.13	—V	—	—	—	—	.02	.61
Western Hem. n.s....399	—Y	—	—	—	.03	.17	.08	—Y	—	—	—	.12	.62	.04
Other Countries n.i.e....910	**—Y**	**.1**	**—**	**—**	**—**	**.3**	**—**	**.3Y**	**.2**	**.3**	**1.3**	**.1**	**.2**	**.1**
Cuba....928	.01Y	.07	.05	—	.01	.29	—	.25Y	.23	.27	.11	.13	.10	.13
North Korea....954	—Y	—	—	—	—	—	—	—Y	—	—	1.20	—	.05	—
Countries & Areas n.s....898	**—Y**	**—**	**—**	**—**	**4.2**	**1.8**	**8.0**	**—Y**	**—**	**—**	**.9**	**2.3**	**1.6**	**1.2**
Special Categories....899	**144.7Y**	**145.0**	**155.9**	**133.8**	**20.6**	**17.1**	**22.7**	**—Y**	**—**	**—**	**2.3**	**1.0**	**.4**	**1.6**
Memorandum Items														
European Union....998	1,061.25Y	998.92	1,139.68	1,238.76	1,224.57	1,320.82	1,418.00	2,525.78Y	1,922.66	2,327.44	2,751.36	2,767.78	2,689.88	3,186.24
Oil Exporting Ctys....999	74.49Y	100.49	90.34	126.31	147.90	122.86	142.71	72.96Y	26.67	14.53	19.33	20.40	20.42	28.61
Non-Oil Develop.Ctys....201	642.79Y	519.87	651.86	661.55	586.15	751.12	871.70	1,380.74Y	484.46	623.11	686.01	558.27	878.22	833.78
PERCENT DISTRIBUTION														
Industrial Countries....101	**61.5**	**65.5**	**63.5**	**64.9**	**68.3**	**66.5**	**64.2**	**69.3**	**81.9**	**81.2**	**81.3**	**84.1**	**77.4**	**80.2**
Developing Countries....202	**32.0**	**28.0**	**30.2**	**30.0**	**30.7**	**32.8**	**34.7**	**30.6**	**18.1**	**18.8**	**18.5**	**15.8**	**22.6**	**19.7**
Africa....607	**.9**	**1.0**	**1.2**	**1.4**	**2.8**	**2.3**	**2.6**	**.7**	**.7**	**.5**	**.5**	**.5**	**.5**	**.5**
Asia....507	**22.0**	**19.9**	**21.7**	**20.2**	**17.2**	**21.6**	**23.9**	**21.1**	**11.8**	**13.7**	**12.2**	**11.5**	**18.4**	**14.8**
Europe....170	**4.0**	**1.8**	**2.2**	**2.3**	**3.1**	**3.4**	**2.8**	**6.3**	**3.3**	**3.2**	**2.7**	**2.2**	**2.1**	**2.8**
Middle East....407	**3.8**	**5.0**	**4.3**	**5.5**	**6.4**	**4.9**	**4.4**	**2.4**	**1.7**	**.7**	**2.2**	**.9**	**.7**	**.8**
Western Hemisphere....207	**1.4**	**.3**	**.7**	**.6**	**1.2**	**.6**	**1.1**	**.2**	**.6**	**.7**	**1.0**	**.7**	**.8**	**.9**
ANNUAL PERCENT CHANGE														
World....001	**–8.2**	**–1.1**	**11.1**	**6.6**	**–8.8**	**11.5**	**9.5**	**39.5**	**–40.4**	**20.1**	**12.0**	**–3.5**	**8.4**	**9.9**
Industrial Countries....101	**–21.8**	**5.1**	**7.8**	**8.9**	**–4.0**	**8.6**	**5.7**	**28.8**	**–29.6**	**19.1**	**12.1**	**–.1**	**–.3**	**13.9**
Developing Countries....202	**31.2**	**–13.5**	**19.6**	**6.2**	**–6.8**	**19.1**	**16.1**	**72.0**	**–64.8**	**24.8**	**10.6**	**–18.0**	**55.3**	**–4.0**
Africa....607	**9.9**	**17.0**	**33.3**	**22.9**	**75.9**	**–6.8**	**22.0**	**95.3**	**–39.9**	**–2.9**	**10.0**	**–14.1**	**16.9**	**–.4**
Asia....507	**11.6**	**–10.6**	**21.1**	**–.8**	**–22.3**	**40.3**	**21.1**	**46.6**	**–66.7**	**39.0**	**.1**	**–9.4**	**73.7**	**–11.4**
Europe....170	**369.4**	**–56.5**	**39.1**	**13.2**	**21.3**	**20.6**	**–8.7**	**416.3**	**–68.7**	**16.3**	**–7.9**	**–18.9**	**4.4**	**45.2**
Middle East....407	**35.2**	**32.4**	**–5.6**	**37.1**	**6.1**	**–15.6**	**–1.6**	**56.8**	**–57.4**	**–50.1**	**247.6**	**–60.5**	**–8.9**	**10.9**
Western Hemisphere....207	**442.1**	**–80.1**	**200.9**	**–18.2**	**90.6**	**–44.1**	**91.6**	**–46.4**	**83.9**	**30.7**	**67.4**	**–30.4**	**23.9**	**15.7**
Other Countries n.i.e....910	**10.4**	**438.9**	**–29.2**	**31.3**	**....**	**—**	**....**	**10.4**	**–7.9**	**14.1**	**393.4**	**–90.1**	**17.6**	**–17.1**

		Exports							Imports						
		2001	2002	2003	2004	2005	2006	2007	2001	2002	2003	2004	2005	2006	2007
		Millions of U.S. Dollars							Millions of U.S. Dollars						
IFS World Total		**348.0**	**322.0**	**306.0**	**422.0**	**556.3**	**1,294.0**	**1,360.0**	**465.2**	**431.2**	**542.1**	**1,305.0**	**1,347.6**	**1,089.0**	**1,510.0**
DOTS World Total	**001**	**548.0Y**	**543.4Y**	**594.2Y**	**803.2Y**	**943.1Y**	**1,399.1Y**	**1,691.6Y**	**711.0Y**	**882.4Y**	**1,001.4Y**	**1,123.5Y**	**1,367.7Y**	**1,466.8Y**	**1,852.2Y**
Industrial Countries	**101**	**361.7Y**	**400.9Y**	**424.2Y**	**540.6Y**	**686.7Y**	**757.6Y**	**824.9Y**	**434.7Y**	**493.3Y**	**590.8Y**	**651.4Y**	**811.7Y**	**757.9Y**	**932.0Y**
United States	111	.27V	.91V	.82V	6.82V	.82V	48.82V	.55V	28.05V	25.08V	38.50V	85.25V	94.38V	99.33V	112.75V
Canada	156	.29V	.37V	.50V	.33V	.49V	.29V	.76V	1.20V	2.19V	1.25V	4.49V	3.17V	4.36V	9.01V
Australia	193	—V	.01V	.03V	.17V	2.97V	.24V	.03V	3.67V	1.89V	1.53V	1.59V	10.15V	4.03V	6.43V
Japan	158	39.29V	38.22V	72.04V	102.69V	114.57V	75.67V	93.40V	17.11V	30.52V	41.58V	31.36V	31.72V	17.68V	20.91V
New Zealand	196	—V	—V	—V	—V	—V	—V	.01V	—V	.53V	5.50V	.46V	.72V	.44V	.25V
Austria	122	.01V	—V	.01V	—V	—V	.04V	—V	1.48V	1.91V	2.76V	2.45V	2.82V	2.98V	5.46V
Belgium	124	41.94V	53.45V	45.05V	58.40V	79.62V	94.88V	84.95V	54.90V	64.01V	50.17V	47.49V	58.58V	100.36V	106.74V
Cyprus	423	.21V	.23V	.17V	.02V	.02Y	—V	—V	.11V	.09V	.24V	.02V	—V	.14V	—V
Denmark	128	—V	.03V	—V	.03V	—V	.01V	.05V	.53V	3.71V	5.98V	1.54V	1.43V	.89V	.43V
Finland	172	6.51V	2.28V	—V	1.98V	5.23V	3.03V	22.22V	.08V	.16V	.11V	.32V	3.48V	2.44V	3.96V
France	132	73.56V	75.13V	86.04V	87.38V	112.16V	146.70V	159.97V	155.97V	151.00V	165.62V	159.00V	249.50V	175.01V	306.43V
Germany	134	30.21V	57.62V	43.08V	76.20V	77.66V	40.61V	51.25V	37.31V	43.27V	47.92V	48.52V	51.97V	51.05V	68.42V
Greece	174	3.10V	3.49V	7.66V	3.05V	5.70V	4.93V	5.61V	4.67V	14.45V	28.71V	42.03V	39.08V	20.40V	27.42V
Iceland	176	.01V	.01V	.02V	.02V	.02V	.03V	.03V	—V	—V	—V	—V	.03V	—V	.74V
Ireland	178	.01V	—V	—V	—V	.01V	—V	.08V	2.03V	.56V	.36V	.70V	.15V	.34V	.85V
Italy	136	73.95V	76.95V	59.87V	75.13V	140.17V	163.85V	144.51V	38.69V	30.61V	36.61V	35.97V	29.46V	86.87V	34.56V
Luxembourg	137	—V	—V	—V	.01V	—V	—V	—V	.13V	.50V	.56V	.14V	.43V	.21V	.35V
Malta	181	.02Y	—V	.02V	—V	.01V	—V	.01V	.09Y	.15V	.88V	.15V	.03V	.24V	.48V
Netherlands	138	9.27V	10.91V	22.66V	23.77V	41.28V	42.65V	88.95V	18.64V	24.38V	39.58V	41.86V	34.66V	31.65V	57.49V
Norway	142	3.76V	3.58V	3.91V	6.95V	8.66V	9.08V	8.43V	1.32V	.20V	1.02V	21.41V	25.44V	8.29V	4.77V
Portugal	182	10.18V	12.28V	12.58V	9.89V	10.84V	7.73V	2.20V	1.39V	3.18V	3.23V	3.63V	2.19V	13.17V	8.62V
Slovenia	961	—V	.01V	—V	.01Y	—V	—V	—V	—V	—V	—V	—Y	.01V	.02V	.06V
Spain	184	61.21V	63.03V	65.94V	76.18V	67.10V	96.07V	144.01V	37.54V	48.57V	75.97V	66.61V	67.83V	84.02V	123.65V
Sweden	144	—V	.01V	.01V	.11V	.01V	.07V	.10V	8.49V	1.85V	1.01V	3.02V	5.86V	5.86V	8.92V
Switzerland	146	.09V	.04V	.06V	.18V	.28V	.04V	—V	8.66V	20.27V	1.55V	1.95V	.75V	1.68V	1.97V
United Kingdom	112	7.83V	2.31V	3.69V	11.27V	19.09V	22.85V	17.74V	12.67V	24.25V	40.11V	51.43V	97.82V	46.43V	21.35V
Developing Countries	**202**	**179.4Y**	**135.0Y**	**160.6Y**	**250.2Y**	**242.1Y**	**623.9Y**	**844.9Y**	**213.2Y**	**320.7Y**	**324.0Y**	**358.4Y**	**426.1Y**	**548.3Y**	**721.0Y**
Africa	**607**	**115.3Y**	**76.7Y**	**99.7Y**	**140.8Y**	**169.3Y**	**188.6Y**	**236.1Y**	**76.3Y**	**91.8Y**	**96.9Y**	**95.4Y**	**124.5Y**	**152.2Y**	**184.1Y**
Algeria	612	2.99V	4.99V	5.54Y	7.21Y	9.18Y	11.33Y	14.68Y	11.84V	11.07V	13.42Y	17.76Y	24.16Y	30.37Y	36.64Y
Benin	638	3.62V	2.56V	4.35V	6.77V	4.25V	5.26Y	6.53Y	.01V	—V	1.60V	.19V	.05V	.06Y	.07Y
Burkina Faso	748	.39Y	.43Y	.54Y	.71Y	.81Y	1.00Y	1.25Y	.01Y	.01Y	.02Y	.02Y	.02Y	.03Y	.04Y
Cameroon	622	14.19V	12.95V	17.16V	22.53Y	25.74Y	31.82Y	39.49Y	—V	—V	.05V	.07Y	.08Y	.09Y	.12Y
Cape Verde	624	—V	—Y	—Y	—Y	—Y	—Y	—Y	.06V	.07Y	.09Y	.11Y	.13Y	.16Y	.20Y
Chad	628	.01Y	.01Y	.01Y	.02Y	.02Y	.03Y	.03Y	....	....	....	....	....	....	....
Congo, Dem. Rep. of	636	.02Y	.02Y	.03Y	.04Y	.04Y	.06Y	.07Y	—Y	—Y	—Y	—Y	—Y	—Y	—Y
Congo, Republic of	634	.98V	1.51V	7.01V	3.72V	4.25Y	5.25Y	6.52Y	—V	—V	.02V	—V	—Y	—Y	—Y
Côte d'Ivoire	662	18.70V	10.84V	24.33V	50.08V	67.16V	64.59V	80.16Y	5.79V	10.23V	7.16V	4.45V	3.21V	20.89V	25.92Y
Equatorial Guinea	642	.51Y	.56Y	.70Y	.93Y	1.06Y	1.31Y	1.62Y	—Y	—Y	—Y	—Y	—Y	—Y	—Y
Gabon	646	.44Y	.48Y	.61Y	.80Y	.91Y	1.13Y	1.40Y	.01Y	.01Y	.01Y	.02Y	.02Y	.02Y	.03Y
Gambia, The	648	.14Y	.15Y	.20Y	.26Y	.29Y	.36Y	.45Y	.11Y	.12Y	.15Y	.19Y	.22Y	.28Y	.34Y
Ghana	652	1.88Y	2.04Y	2.59Y	3.40Y	3.88Y	4.80Y	5.95Y	—Y	—Y	—Y	—Y	—Y	—Y	—Y
Guinea	656	—V	—Y	.04V	.03V	.03Y	.04Y	.04Y	.02V	.02Y	.21V	.05V	.06Y	.07Y	.09Y
Guinea-Bissau	654	.01Y	.01Y	.01Y	.01Y	.01Y	.01Y	.02Y	—Y	—Y	—Y	—Y	—Y	—Y	—Y
Kenya	664	—V	.04V	2.13V	—V	—Y	—Y	—Y	.07V	.09V	.07V	.24V	.28Y	.34Y	.43Y
Liberia	668	12.00Y	13.03Y	16.49Y	21.65Y	24.74Y	30.58Y	37.95Y	—Y	—Y	—Y	—Y	—Y	—Y	—Y
Madagascar	674	—V	—V	.01V	.01Y	.01Y	.01Y	.02Y	—V	—V	.01V	.01Y	.01Y	.01Y	.02Y
Malawi	676	.03Y	.04Y	.05Y	.06Y	.07Y	.09Y	.11Y	—Y	—Y	—Y	—Y	—Y	—Y	—Y
Mali	678	.66Y	.71Y	.90Y	1.18Y	1.35Y	1.67Y	2.07Y	—Y	—Y	—Y	—Y	—Y	—Y	—Y
Mauritius	684	—V	.93V	—V	—V	—V	—V	—V	—V	—V	—V	—V	.08V	.05V	.02V
Morocco	686	.01V	.52V	.37V	1.97V	.85V	1.05Y	1.30Y	19.07V	25.85V	26.13V	24.51V	23.84V	29.46Y	36.56Y
Niger	692	.07V	.03V	.02V	.16V	.19Y	.23Y	.29Y	.12V	—V	.01V	—V	—Y	.01Y	.01Y
Nigeria	694	49.29V	20.18V	11.29V	14.68Y	18.69Y	23.08Y	29.89Y	.01V	—V	.39V	.52Y	.70Y	.88Y	1.07Y
Senegal	722	.04V	.01V	.03V	.45V	1.16V	.54V	.67Y	33.38V	32.05V	32.20V	30.68V	39.52V	38.27V	47.49Y
South Africa	199	.07V	.08V	.16V	.12V	.09V	—V	—V	4.00V	9.85V	11.75V	8.06V	23.17V	20.48V	21.76V
Swaziland	734	—Y	—Y	—Y	—Y	—Y	—Y	—Y	.03Y	.04Y	.04Y	.06Y	.07Y	.08Y	.10Y
Tanzania	738	.06V	—V	—Y	—Y	—Y	—Y	—Y	.01V	.03V	.04Y	.05Y	.06Y	.07Y	.09Y
Togo	742	6.99V	4.09V	3.79V	2.97V	3.15V	3.89Y	4.82Y	.09V	.06V	.01V	.60V	1.02V	1.26Y	1.57Y
Tunisia	744	2.15V	.46V	1.31V	.91V	1.32V	.44V	.54Y	1.68V	2.28V	3.51V	7.81V	7.83V	9.32V	11.57Y
Zambia	754	—V	.01V	—V	—V	—V	—V	.22V	.02V	—V	—V	—V	—V	.01V	—V
Zimbabwe	698	—V	—V	—V	.11V	—V	.02V	.03Y	.01V	.04V	.01V	.04V	—V	—V	—Y
Asia	**507**	**21.4Y**	**25.4Y**	**18.8Y**	**56.1Y**	**9.3Y**	**370.7Y**	**521.3Y**	**90.6Y**	**111.1Y**	**121.7Y**	**149.4Y**	**169.3Y**	**236.4Y**	**315.0Y**
China,P.R.: Mainland	924	3.97V	8.88V	7.01V	47.72V	3.69V	365.47V	515.74V	32.86V	57.19V	62.13V	72.22V	81.73V	120.13V	150.86V
China,P.R.:Hong Kong	532	.83V	.92V	1.16V	1.84V	1.75V	1.25V	1.41V	4.99V	3.46V	2.41V	1.99V	2.77V	2.59V	.85V
India	534	—Y	.02V	.03V	.88V	.99V	1.22Y	1.52Y	15.27Y	22.39V	20.52V	24.49V	43.90V	54.26Y	67.34Y
Indonesia	536	—V	—V	.07V	—V	—V	—V	.07V	19.26V	14.78V	10.01V	15.43V	15.56V	11.59V	13.49V
Korea	542	.25V	.58V	.56V	.32V	.45V	.97V	1.37V	2.02V	2.50V	3.89V	2.31V	3.76V	2.70V	12.76V
Malaysia	548	.20V	.43V	1.87V	2.53V	1.17V	.07V	.01V	7.01V	3.16V	15.58V	24.19V	14.11V	26.30V	46.56V
New Caledonia	839	.01V	—V	.01V	.01V	.01Y	.01Y	.01Y	—V	—V	—Y	—Y	—Y	—Y	—Y
Pakistan	564	7.59V	7.67V	4.99V	—V	.01V	.02Y	.02Y	4.22V	3.06V	3.46V	2.22V	4.05V	5.01Y	6.22Y

Mauritania 682

		Exports							Imports						
		2001	2002	2003	2004	2005	2006	2007	2001	2002	2003	2004	2005	2006	2007
		Millions of U.S. Dollars							*Millions of U.S. Dollars*						
Philippines	566	—V	3.95V	1.02V	.13V	—V	—V	—V	.01V	—V	.01V	.01V	—V	.77V	.15V
Sri Lanka	524	—V	—V	—Y	—Y	—Y	—Y	—Y	.11V	—V	—V	.29V	.28V	.26V	.32V
Taiwan Province of China	528	.02V	.01V	.05V	.23V	.40V	1.24V	.15V	.34V	.43V	.69V	.60V	.66V	.53V	.77V
Thailand	578	8.40V	2.96V	2.05V	2.42V	.78V	.41V	.95V	3.22V	2.76V	2.40V	5.63V	2.50V	12.23V	15.64V
Vietnam	582	.12V	.01V	—V	—V	—V	—V	—V	1.26V	1.35V	.58V	—V	—V	—V	—V
Europe	**170**	**37.8Y**	**28.3Y**	**35.9Y**	**45.2Y**	**54.0Y**	**52.8Y**	**72.7Y**	**30.4Y**	**75.6Y**	**61.8Y**	**37.3Y**	**49.5Y**	**39.4Y**	**58.1Y**
Belarus	913	2.38V	2.57V	1.99V	1.63V	1.10V	3.26V	.60V	—V	—V	.13V	—V	—V	—V	.42V
Bulgaria	918	.20V	.20V	.08V	.01V	.01V	.03V	—V	1.39V	2.56V	3.53V	2.30V	4.23V	.06V	.20V
Czech Republic	935	.03V	—V	—V	—V	—V	—V	—V	.40V	.30V	1.37V	1.02V	3.83V	2.32V	2.50V
Estonia	939	.11V	.06V	.01V	.12V	—V	.12V	.38V	.67V	1.16V	.40V	.28V	.15V	.16V	.05V
Georgia	915	.03V	.15V	—V	—V	—V	—V	.03Y	—V	—V	—V	—V	—V	—V	—Y
Hungary	944	—V	—V	.01V	—V	—V	.03V	—V	.91V	.53V	.09V	.39V	.11V	1.19V	1.65V
Kazakhstan	916	—V	—V	—V	.01V	.01Y	.01Y	.01Y	—V	.05V	—V	—V	—Y	—Y	—Y
Latvia	941	1.09V	.60V	.32V	.02V	—V	.06V	.06V	.01V	.01V	.15V	—V	—V	—V	—V
Lithuania	946	5.74V	1.62V	1.51V	.01V	.15V	.22V	.25V	1.85V	.98V	.31V	.33V	.97V	.85V	.24V
Moldova	921	—V	—V	.01V	—V	—V	—Y	—Y	—V	—V	—V	—V	—V	—Y	—Y
Poland	964	.05V	.17V	.05V	2.12V	.03V	.30V	.22V	2.86V	18.22V	19.13V	13.29V	6.13V	1.15V	4.17V
Romania	968	—V	—V	—V	.12V	.01V	.06V	—V	1.65V	1.25V	.56V	1.63V	.39V	.06V	.15V
Russia	922	26.19V	19.99V	28.93V	35.96V	46.62V	42.12V	56.22V	1.45V	10.08V	20.06V	2.64V	3.73V	1.22V	8.59V
Slovak Republic	936	—V	—V	—Y	—Y	—V	—V	—V	.05V	—V	—Y	—Y	.57V	.01V	—V
Turkey	186	.02V	.70V	1.72V	3.76V	.89V	.19V	6.89V	4.79V	12.80V	4.72V	6.08V	11.07V	9.80V	12.08V
Ukraine	926	1.92V	2.21V	1.24V	1.42V	5.22V	6.45Y	8.01Y	14.35V	27.61V	11.30V	9.36V	18.29V	22.60Y	28.05Y
Europe n.s.	884	—Y	—Y	—Y	—Y	—Y	—Y	—Y	—Y	—Y	—Y	—Y	—Y	.01Y	.01Y
Middle East	**407**	**4.9Y**	**4.7Y**	**6.1Y**	**8.0Y**	**8.9Y**	**11.0Y**	**13.7Y**	**9.7Y**	**11.1Y**	**15.1Y**	**23.8Y**	**29.1Y**	**36.2Y**	**44.0Y**
Bahrain	419	.02Y	.02Y	.02Y	.03Y	.04Y	.04Y	.05Y	—Y	—Y	—Y	—Y	—Y	—Y	—Y
Egypt	469	2.19V	2.38Y	3.01Y	3.96Y	4.52Y	5.59Y	6.93Y	1.61V	1.75Y	2.22Y	2.91Y	3.32Y	4.11Y	5.10Y
Jordan	439	—V	.06V	.10V	.39V	.14V	.19V	.18V	.03V	.17V	1.13V	.30V	.30V	.38V	.14V
Kuwait	443	.12Y	.12Y	.13Y	.17Y	.22Y	.27Y	.35Y	—Y	—Y	—Y	—Y	—Y	—Y	—Y
Lebanon	446	1.73Y	1.87Y	2.37Y	3.11Y	3.56Y	4.40Y	5.46Y	2.25Y	2.44Y	3.09Y	4.05Y	4.63Y	5.72Y	7.10Y
Oman	449	—V	.04V	—V	—Y	—Y	—Y	—Y	.81V	1.42V	2.27V	3.01Y	4.09Y	5.15Y	6.21Y
Qatar	453	—V	—V	.01V	.04V	.01V	—V	—Y	.08V	.05V	—V	.05V	—V	—V	—Y
Saudi Arabia	456	.81V	.13V	.39V	.11V	.21V	.26Y	.34Y	3.46Y	3.68Y	4.46Y	5.90Y	8.02Y	10.09Y	12.17Y
Syrian Arab Republic	463	—Y	—Y	—Y	.20V	.23Y	.28Y	.35Y	1.13Y	1.23Y	1.56Y	6.92V	7.90Y	9.77Y	12.12Y
United Arab Emirates	466	—V	—V	—V	—Y	—Y	—Y	—Y	.33Y	.35Y	.42Y	.56Y	.76Y	.96Y	1.15Y
Yemen, Republic of	474	.01V	.04V	.04Y	.01V	—V	—Y	—Y	—V	—V	—Y	.12V	.01V	.02Y	.02Y
Western Hemisphere	**207**	**.1Y**	**—Y**	**.2Y**	**.2Y**	**.6Y**	**.8Y**	**1.2Y**	**6.2Y**	**31.1Y**	**28.5Y**	**52.4Y**	**53.7Y**	**84.1Y**	**119.7Y**
Argentina	213	.05V	.01V	.01V	.04V	.04V	.06V	.09V	.68V	1.48V	.32V	4.05V	4.53V	2.02V	11.46V
Barbados	316	—V	—V	—V	—V	—V	—V	—Y	.01V	—V	—V	—V	—V	—V	—Y
Bermuda	319	.01Y	.01Y	.01Y	.01Y	—V	—V	—Y	—Y	—Y	—Y	—Y	—Y	—Y	—Y
Brazil	223	.01V	—V	.03V	.01V	.01V	.09V	—V	5.36V	26.66V	21.42V	43.56V	48.01V	80.79V	106.19V
Chile	228	—V	—V	.02V	.06V	.05V	.06V	.10V	.02V	—V	—V	—V	.07V	—V	—V
Colombia	233	.01V	—V	—V	.01V	.01V	.04V	.20V	—V	2.94V	5.77V	—V	—V	.03V	.04V
Costa Rica	238	—V	—V	—V	—V	.02V	.02Y	.02Y	—V	—V	—V	—V	—V	—Y	—Y
El Salvador	253	—V	—V	—V	—V	—V	—V	—V	—V	—V	.01V	—V	—V	—V	—V
Haiti	263	—V	—V	.09V	—V	—Y	—Y	—Y	....	....	....	....	....	....	....
Mexico	273	—V	—V	—V	—V	.51V	.50V	.72V	—V	—V	—V	—V	.15V	.02V	.09V
Panama	283	—V	—V	—V	—V	—V	—V	—V	.11V	—V	—V	—V	—V	—V	—V
Paraguay	288	—V	—V	—V	—V	—V	.01V	.02Y	—V	—V	—V	.27V	—V	—V	—Y
Peru	293	.01V	—V	—V	—V	.01V	.01V	.01Y	—V	.05V	.77V	3.98V	.18V	.29V	.78Y
Trinidad and Tobago	369	—V	—V	—Y	—Y	—Y	—Y	—Y	—V	.01V	.01Y	.02Y	.02Y	.02Y	.03Y
Uruguay	298	—V	—Y	—V	—V	—V	—Y	—Y	—V	—Y	.21V	.53V	.75V	.93Y	1.16Y
Other Countries n.i.e.	**910**	**—Y**	**—Y**	**—Y**	**—Y**	**—Y**	**—Y**	**—Y**	**—Y**	**—Y**	**—Y**	**—Y**	**—Y**	**.1Y**	**.1Y**
Cuba	928	—Y	—Y	—Y	—Y	—Y	—Y	—Y	.02Y	.02Y	.03Y	.04Y	.04Y	.05Y	.07Y
Countries & Areas n.s.	**898**	**6.9Y**	**7.5Y**	**9.5Y**	**12.5Y**	**14.2Y**	**17.6Y**	**21.8Y**	**63.0Y**	**68.4Y**	**86.5Y**	**113.7Y**	**129.9Y**	**160.5Y**	**199.2Y**
Memorandum Items															
European Union	998	325.03Y	360.20Y	348.66Y	425.69Y	559.09Y	624.15Y	722.56Y	381.47Y	433.84Y	521.28Y	520.20Y	657.07Y	627.76Y	783.82Y
Oil Exporting Ctys	999	53.21Y	25.45Y	17.43Y	22.21Y	28.32Y	34.94Y	45.34Y	35.78Y	31.34Y	30.97Y	43.22Y	53.30Y	59.03Y	70.73Y
Non-Oil Develop.Ctys	201	126.20Y	109.59Y	143.12Y	227.98Y	213.82Y	588.98Y	799.55Y	177.41Y	289.32Y	293.05Y	315.16Y	372.81Y	489.30Y	650.23Y
PERCENT DISTRIBUTION															
Industrial Countries	**101**	**66.0**	**73.8**	**71.4**	**67.3**	**72.8**	**54.1**	**48.8**	**61.1**	**55.9**	**59.0**	**58.0**	**59.3**	**51.7**	**50.3**
Developing Countries	**202**	**32.7**	**24.9**	**27.0**	**31.1**	**25.7**	**44.6**	**49.9**	**30.0**	**36.3**	**32.4**	**31.9**	**31.2**	**37.4**	**38.9**
Africa	**607**	**21.0**	**14.1**	**16.8**	**17.5**	**17.9**	**13.5**	**14.0**	**10.7**	**10.4**	**9.7**	**8.5**	**9.1**	**10.4**	**9.9**
Asia	**507**	**3.9**	**4.7**	**3.2**	**7.0**	**1.0**	**26.5**	**30.8**	**12.7**	**12.6**	**12.2**	**13.3**	**12.4**	**16.1**	**17.0**
Europe	**170**	**6.9**	**5.2**	**6.0**	**5.6**	**5.7**	**3.8**	**4.3**	**4.3**	**8.6**	**6.2**	**3.3**	**3.6**	**2.7**	**3.1**
Middle East	**407**	**.9**	**.9**	**1.0**	**1.0**	**.9**	**.8**	**.8**	**1.4**	**1.3**	**1.5**	**2.1**	**2.1**	**2.5**	**2.4**
Western Hemisphere	**207**	**—**	**—**	**—**	**—**	**.1**	**.1**	**.1**	**.9**	**3.5**	**2.8**	**4.7**	**3.9**	**5.7**	**6.5**
ANNUAL PERCENT CHANGE															
World	**001**	**3.5**	**–.8**	**9.3**	**35.2**	**17.4**	**48.4**	**20.9**	**9.2**	**24.1**	**13.5**	**12.2**	**21.7**	**7.2**	**26.3**
Industrial Countries	**101**	**–1.7**	**10.8**	**5.8**	**27.4**	**27.0**	**10.3**	**8.9**	**5.4**	**13.5**	**19.8**	**10.3**	**24.6**	**–6.6**	**23.0**
Developing Countries	**202**	**15.6**	**–24.7**	**18.9**	**55.8**	**–3.2**	**157.7**	**35.4**	**17.3**	**50.4**	**1.0**	**10.6**	**18.9**	**28.7**	**31.5**
Africa	**607**	**4.9**	**–33.5**	**30.0**	**41.3**	**20.2**	**11.4**	**25.2**	**31.0**	**20.3**	**5.6**	**–1.5**	**30.5**	**22.2**	**21.0**
Asia	**507**	**6.5**	**18.9**	**–26.0**	**198.0**	**–83.5**	**—**	**40.6**	**3.7**	**22.6**	**9.5**	**22.8**	**13.4**	**39.6**	**33.2**
Europe	**170**	**112.6**	**–25.1**	**26.8**	**25.9**	**19.7**	**–2.2**	**37.5**	**20.3**	**148.7**	**–18.3**	**–39.5**	**32.5**	**–20.3**	**47.4**
Middle East	**407**	**141.3**	**–4.5**	**30.6**	**32.0**	**11.3**	**23.6**	**23.9**	**36.1**	**14.2**	**36.7**	**57.3**	**22.0**	**24.6**	**21.6**
Western Hemisphere	**207**	**–98.5**	**–74.7**	**628.8**	**–3.3**	**326.2**	**25.0**	**45.1**	**67.3**	**403.9**	**–8.4**	**83.8**	**2.5**	**56.6**	**42.4**
Other Countries n.i.e.	**910**	**—**	**—**	**....**	**....**	**....**	**....**	**....**	**10.4**	**8.5**	**26.6**	**31.3**	**14.3**	**23.6**	**24.1**

	Exports 2001	Exports 2002	Exports 2003	Exports 2004	Exports 2005	Exports 2006	Exports 2007	Imports 2001	Imports 2002	Imports 2003	Imports 2004	Imports 2005	Imports 2006	Imports 2007
	Millions of U.S. Dollars							*Millions of U.S. Dollars*						
IFS World Total	**1,627.8**	**1,801.4**	**1,898.1**	**1,993.1**	**2,138.4**	**2,328.6**	**2,230.7**	**1,986.6**	**2,159.1**	**2,363.4**	**2,770.9**	**3,156.8**	**3,626.8**	**3,895.1**
DOTS World Total 001	**1,524.9**	**1,746.4**	**1,808.0**	**1,914.1**	**2,000.2**	**2,110.4**	**1,971.4**	**1,996.3**	**2,165.9**	**2,387.6**	**2,774.0**	**3,161.8**	**3,639.1**	**3,864.1**
Industrial Countries 101	**1,363.1**	**1,542.6**	**1,550.9**	**1,634.1**	**1,554.4**	**1,532.1**	**1,550.3**	**833.5**	**872.2**	**951.2**	**1,065.2**	**1,230.7**	**1,469.0**	**1,430.8**
United States 111	302.37	343.90	325.54	282.50	191.23	181.49	152.59	62.79	69.33	62.47	60.36	67.28	73.65	88.94
Canada 156	7.81	8.31	6.95	5.21	3.02	4.36	3.91	3.36	3.59	3.18	3.23	2.03	2.68	5.30
Australia 193	3.87	3.24	3.80	5.06	3.92	3.95	4.34	81.81	86.47	77.21	103.46	91.49	97.92	87.90
Japan 158	7.60	26.48	16.25	15.94	17.18	17.07	9.85	73.45	75.82	83.37	112.10	113.00	102.61	138.02
New Zealand 196	.23	.58	.42	.25	.13	.24	2.01	14.88	13.26	19.99	18.41	27.89	26.85	42.18
Austria 122	4.07	3.17	3.63	2.64	6.80	4.34	6.29	3.11	3.85	4.57	5.71	6.34	6.03	8.65
Belgium 124	25.32	29.27	34.15	49.55	52.86	58.38	66.71	27.41	31.09	33.92	49.74	50.44	55.44	51.31
Cyprus 423	.08	.05	.01	.01	.02	.07	.19	.21	.62	1.33	.32	1.83	1.61	1.49
Denmark 128	1.88	2.99	8.02	6.23	4.20	6.45	2.38	5.38	7.27	10.14	7.11	34.23	7.57	13.46
Finland 172	1.79	.92	.97	1.10	1.08	.25	.60	1.92	4.47	28.19	29.88	152.05	87.79	37.90
France 132	308.78	386.47	343.64	385.55	339.16	274.54	283.01	187.50	240.75	285.96	251.68	239.97	519.04	411.67
Germany 134	55.92	52.87	55.54	46.11	36.28	40.85	54.21	107.76	74.10	77.58	103.74	128.61	145.50	104.36
Greece 174	.37	.58	.79	1.96	1.47	2.27	2.93	1.31	1.24	1.03	1.74	1.13	1.12	1.23
Iceland 176	—	—	—	—	—	.01	—	.01	—	.01	.09	.02	.04	.45
Ireland 178	3.76	4.77	3.66	2.45	1.63	2.29	1.90	5.83	5.26	6.75	6.81	8.59	9.36	12.28
Italy 136	56.08	64.30	68.59	78.43	112.21	86.87	114.03	65.65	69.94	75.62	88.40	81.43	93.04	106.09
Luxembourg 137	.30	.23	.02	.05	9.23	4.63	.14	.23	.42	.33	.45	.37	.12	.94
Malta 181	4.51	3.94	2.92	3.16	1.87	2.34	2.39	.03	.02	.02	.06	.10	.08	.13
Netherlands 138	26.84	27.79	30.72	33.24	24.51	27.45	34.80	22.89	24.76	17.65	16.82	15.81	21.04	20.95
Norway 142	1.38	.84	.97	.50	.41	.93	.40	.84	.45	.38	.44	.71	.75	1.16
Portugal 182	25.52	18.35	23.81	26.63	18.90	5.89	22.93	3.27	2.66	5.04	5.23	2.97	4.68	6.61
Slovenia 961	.05	.21	.06	.14	.01	.03	.02	.12	.08	.09	.23	.23	.30	.34
Spain 184	25.05	22.20	23.65	31.27	53.88	77.19	65.44	42.64	39.72	39.76	53.62	70.90	73.31	100.28
Sweden 144	6.45	4.87	3.19	1.43	1.00	4.03	.51	5.23	4.60	5.41	6.65	7.46	6.29	9.46
Switzerland 146	15.83	16.49	18.94	23.48	21.99	20.90	26.57	43.52	33.26	33.17	52.50	38.01	40.88	64.24
United Kingdom 112	477.30	519.76	574.67	631.17	651.45	705.26	692.13	72.39	79.18	77.99	86.44	87.78	91.26	115.48
Developing Countries 202	**161.7**	**203.8**	**251.7**	**273.0**	**445.1**	**578.2**	**420.9**	**1,161.8**	**1,293.1**	**1,433.4**	**1,701.4**	**1,925.9**	**2,168.0**	**2,430.6**
Africa 607	**137.8**	**135.1**	**185.1**	**174.1**	**181.8**	**194.3**	**237.9**	**353.6**	**374.4**	**391.8**	**407.0**	**359.5**	**374.4**	**413.8**
Algeria 612	—	—	—	—	—	.02	—	.02	.02	.05	.20	.09	.17	.07
Angola 614	.01	.05	—	1.00	.05	2.86	2.30	—	—	—	—	—	—	—
Benin 638	.04	.06	.16	.31	.35	.44	.53	—	1.14	.73	1.16	1.71	.34	.81
Botswana 616	.57	.43	.57	.66	.37	.17	.12	.10	.53	.11	.29	.38	.09	.78
Burkina Faso 748	.15	.52	.04	.07	.01	.56	.24	4.16	.85	4.14	2.23	.38	.84	1.10
Burundi 618	.33	.39	1.09	.63	.38	.18	.23	—	—	—	—	—	—	—
Cameroon 622	.30	.27	.69	.08	.06	1.42	.87	3.96	2.30	2.60	3.20	1.55	1.12	5.42
Central African Rep. 626	.01	—	—	—	—	—	—	.06	.34	—	—	—	—	—
Chad 628	—	—	—	—	—	—	—	.01	.02	.14	—	1.18	3.16	2.55
Comoros 632	3.60	3.20	4.55	4.34	3.75	4.27	5.47	—	.07	.73	.07	.01	.01	.02
Congo, Dem. Rep. of 636	.03	—	—	—	—	—	—	—	—	—	—	.01	—	—
Congo, Republic of 634	—	.11	.09	.17	.39	.46	.63	.78	.70	.33	.78	1.01	1.37	2.30
Côte d'Ivoire 662	.50	.41	.18	.27	.23	.32	.66	2.27	.60	.08	.18	.29	.58	2.00
Djibouti 611	.02	—	—	.01	.20	—	—	—	—	—	—	.07	—	—
Equatorial Guinea 642	—	—	—	—	.21	—	—	—	—	—	—	—	—	—
Ethiopia 644	.02	—	.32	.04	.80	.53	.11	.02	.02	.03	.04	.06	.08	.59
Gabon 646	.08	2.63	.02	.09	.19	.03	—	—	—	.03	—	—	—	—
Gambia, The 648	—	—	.06	.07	.14	.12	—	.03	—	—	—	—	—	—
Ghana 652	.31	.13	.27	.30	.70	1.90	1.13	—	—	—	.03	1.49	—	.07
Guinea 656	—	.15	.14	.03	.48	.36	.44	—	—	.07	.01	.13	.14	.09
Kenya 664	5.77	7.01	8.04	9.04	7.02	4.36	7.64	3.06	2.53	3.69	5.52	9.60	13.26	12.83
Lesotho 666	—	.01	.06	.21	.59	1.01	1.65	—	—	—	.49	.78	2.09	.90
Liberia 668	—	.01	—	—	—	—	.02	—	—	.63	—	—	—	—
Madagascar 674	95.18	68.34	117.00	97.79	114.35	103.70	123.45	33.50	22.28	50.42	33.90	14.78	15.08	17.66
Malawi 676	—	1.57	.33	.46	.13	.02	.63	1.06	.05	.19	.40	.08	.08	.14
Mali 678	.03	.13	.02	.05	.05	.18	.04	3.19	7.21	2.86	1.83	1.19	2.73	4.10
Mauritania 682	—	—	—	—	.08	.04	.02	—	1.03	—	—	—	—	—
Morocco 686	.34	.94	.34	.04	.03	.03	.17	2.59	3.06	3.90	3.34	3.22	4.56	5.91
Mozambique 688	1.03	1.80	1.79	3.31	1.29	1.11	.52	.82	7.52	4.77	11.03	15.62	5.23	3.23
Namibia 728	.02	.02	.52	.17	.11	—	.11	.29	.53	.39	.77	.31	.12	1.44
Niger 692	—	.02	—	—	.06	—	—	—	.01	—	—	—	—	—
Nigeria 694	.02	.01	.03	.23	.71	.21	.45	.08	.05	.12	.06	.02	.03	—
Rwanda 714	.99	.89	.82	1.24	1.03	.39	1.62	—	—	—	—	—	—	—
Senegal 722	.05	.07	.53	.49	.79	1.21	.99	.01	—	1.71	.34	.01	.02	.03
Seychelles 718	5.14	13.19	9.70	11.86	14.21	14.96	18.50	4.84	33.09	7.81	6.79	9.55	32.90	36.87
Sierra Leone 724	.07	.04	.01	—	—	.03	—	—	.02	.01	.01	1.03	.07	.35
Somalia 726	—	—	—	—	—	—	—	—	—	—	—	—	—	.09
South Africa 199	12.33	19.11	28.20	28.17	26.71	46.92	64.16	275.73	272.10	288.67	311.35	273.45	265.97	284.27
Sudan 732	.09	—	—	—	—	—	.09	.01	—	—	—	—	—	—
Swaziland 734	.07	—	.02	.02	.11	.13	.02	7.69	7.77	7.83	8.04	6.61	7.86	9.76
Tanzania 738	2.76	3.48	2.32	5.88	2.68	1.23	.85	3.03	.65	.72	3.03	2.62	1.23	1.35

		Exports							Imports						
		2001	2002	2003	2004	2005	2006	2007	2001	2002	2003	2004	2005	2006	2007
		Millions of U.S. Dollars							Millions of U.S. Dollars						
Togo	742	.07	.11	.02	2.00	.64	.23	.55	—	—	.68	.63	.01	—	—
Tunisia	744	1.08	1.13	.88	.16	.03	1.95	.15	.14	.07	.19	.25	.27	.72	2.17
Uganda	746	.36	1.06	1.38	.20	.57	.42	.68	—	.09	.15	.22	.54	.05	.27
Zambia	754	.29	.66	1.27	1.16	.53	.97	1.53	2.19	7.31	5.66	8.26	8.62	11.65	12.48
Zimbabwe	698	6.15	7.10	3.66	3.53	1.78	1.61	1.35	3.91	2.48	2.36	2.51	2.85	2.82	4.17
Asia	**507**	**15.8**	**59.9**	**48.1**	**53.1**	**71.6**	**107.9**	**70.0**	**628.1**	**684.3**	**762.0**	**904.0**	**970.5**	**1,262.5**	**1,748.4**
Afghanistan, I.S. of	512	—	—	—	.03	—	—	.02	—	—	.02	.02	.01	.04	.04
American Samoa	859	—	5.03	—	.15	.66	—	.01	—	—	—	—	—	—	.01
Bangladesh	513	.26	.40	.02	1.25	2.52	3.36	1.94	.12	.08	.05	.11	.24	.27	.48
Bhutan	514	—	—	—	—	—	—	—	.08	—	—	—	—	—	—
Brunei Darussalam	516	.04	.05	—	—	.03	.12	.05	.13	—	—	.01	.15	—	.02
Cambodia	522	.01	—	.05	.01	—	.04	.01	—	.07	.01	—	.01	.02	.02
China,P.R.: Mainland	924	1.55	9.44	7.51	6.33	6.34	5.24	4.19	142.58	182.67	199.63	257.03	310.75	314.99	439.83
China,P.R.:Hong Kong	532	3.66	17.31	6.67	6.42	6.58	7.10	8.50	47.39	40.11	37.65	28.03	22.09	18.82	18.57
China,P.R.:Macao	546	.01	—	—	.24	—	—	—	.12	.22	.05	.08	.04	.01	.04
Fiji	819	—	—	—	.09	—	15.17	.61	—	.11	.18	.15	.12	.02	.04
French Polynesia	887	2.27	.01	.05	—	7.78	.02	.03	—	—	—	—	.19	.20	.34
Guam	829	—	—	—	—	—	—	—	—	—	—	—	.11	—	—
India	534	2.25	3.37	6.06	18.14	8.72	12.06	10.57	159.86	157.75	194.98	254.16	219.03	494.74	818.71
Indonesia	536	.49	1.11	.55	.94	.63	2.12	1.76	46.98	41.67	40.74	56.67	71.62	73.98	90.36
Korea	542	1.33	7.91	2.07	.75	2.74	1.59	2.74	24.89	35.65	24.88	28.99	30.71	34.08	53.15
Lao People's Dem.Rep	544	—	—	—	—	—	—	—	—	.01	—	—	—	—	—
Malaysia	548	.43	.96	7.38	2.61	3.52	7.18	7.18	58.73	61.37	72.61	83.09	90.50	93.92	100.38
Maldives	556	—	—	.01	.56	.38	.05	.47	—	—	—	—	—	—	.01
Mongolia	948	—	—	—	—	—	—	—	—	—	—	—	.07	—	.07
Myanmar	518	.05	—	—	—	—	.01	—	.34	.47	.38	.59	.95	1.18	2.26
Nauru	836	—	—	—	—	—	—	—	—	—	.02	—	—	—	—
Nepal	558	—	.01	—	—	.02	—	—	—	—	—	.02	.04	.01	.01
New Caledonia	839	—	—	.01	.01	—	.02	.02	—	—	—	—	—	.02	—
Pakistan	564	.12	.17	.69	.74	.60	.71	.26	31.75	27.16	36.64	42.98	34.28	39.09	38.59
Papua New Guinea	853	.03	—	—	—	—	—	—	.01	—	—	—	—	—	—
Philippines	566	.05	.42	.57	.94	1.32	1.10	3.52	2.16	5.40	10.13	14.81	19.66	24.40	4.80
Singapore	576	1.40	7.74	11.99	5.24	7.42	4.43	8.96	42.01	47.25	60.24	42.73	53.77	34.80	42.57
Sri Lanka	524	1.08	1.40	1.07	2.58	1.62	.66	.36	1.85	2.30	3.78	4.47	2.97	2.48	2.51
Taiwan Province of China	528	.45	3.44	2.10	2.72	16.33	37.74	8.33	35.72	47.63	41.98	45.32	58.25	73.10	61.21
Thailand	578	.32	1.00	1.21	3.11	3.45	5.17	7.26	32.55	32.57	34.71	42.48	51.93	52.88	68.56
Vanuatu	846	—	—	—	—	.02	.12	.75	—	.09	1.39	—	—	—	.39
Vietnam	582	—	.13	.13	.28	.90	3.91	2.45	.82	1.72	1.98	2.25	3.01	3.46	5.46
Europe	**170**	**1.2**	**3.0**	**7.8**	**10.2**	**18.4**	**15.3**	**25.1**	**12.0**	**14.1**	**24.0**	**20.9**	**89.6**	**145.7**	**64.1**
Albania	914	—	—	—	—	—	—	—	.01	.01	.01	.01	.01	.01	—
Azerbaijan	912	—	—	—	—	—	—	—	—	—	—	.01	—	—	—
Belarus	913	—	—	—	—	—	—	—	—	—	—	—	—	.06	—
Bosnia & Herzegovina	963	—	—	.02	.04	.08	.12	.18	—	—	—	—	—	—	—
Bulgaria	918	—	—	.02	.01	.07	.19	.88	.19	.18	.27	.30	.23	.33	.45
Croatia	960	—	—	.08	.15	.23	.24	.14	.03	.09	.02	.03	1.04	.02	3.24
Czech Republic	935	.11	.07	.13	.25	.21	4.13	11.73	.77	1.16	1.31	2.38	3.19	3.17	4.18
Estonia	939	—	—	—	—	1.69	.01	.01	—	.01	.02	.46	.09	.01	.06
Faroe Islands	816	—	—	—	.01	—	—	—	—	—	—	—	—	—	—
Georgia	915	—	—	—	—	.03	—	—	—	.01	.03	.01	.01	.02	.01
Gibraltar	823	—	—	—	.04	—	—	—	—	—	—	—	.04	.01	—
Hungary	944	.04	.14	.08	.07	1.97	1.66	.13	.98	4.74	9.28	8.21	72.59	126.38	30.49
Kyrgyz Republic	917	—	—	—	—	—	—	.06	—	—	—	—	—	—	—
Latvia	941	—	—	.01	.30	.07	.16	.02	.03	.32	.39	.32	.37	.27	.29
Lithuania	946	—	—	.01	.01	.04	1.02	.31	—	—	.01	.06	.08	.17	.08
Macedonia, FYR	962	—	—	.01	.02	.01	.04	.01	—	—	—	—	—	—	—
Moldova	921	.01	—	—	.08	.02	.01	.01	.05	.01	.04	.03	—	.01	.01
Poland	964	.53	.67	1.07	2.06	3.66	3.21	2.93	.45	.53	1.01	2.18	3.55	3.23	4.87
Romania	968	.01	.03	2.49	.24	.72	.35	2.29	.06	.05	.13	.12	.28	.29	.42
Russia	922	.37	.62	.62	.79	1.92	2.04	2.15	2.33	.18	4.11	.99	.53	1.13	.39
Serbia & Montenegro	965	—	—	—	—	—	—	—	—	.05	.06	.01	.37	.61	—
Slovak Republic	936	—	—	—	—	.01	.02	.36	—	—	.05	.23	.35	.40	1.30
Turkey	186	.15	1.39	3.24	6.02	7.14	1.73	3.21	2.18	2.68	2.61	5.20	6.50	8.88	18.12
Ukraine	926	—	—	.02	.09	.53	.25	.66	4.90	4.05	4.60	.32	.30	.67	.15
Yugoslavia n.s.	966	—	.05	—	—	—	—	—	—	—	—	—	—	—	—
Europe n.s.	884	—	—	—	—	—	.15	—	—	—	—	.01	.08	—	—
Middle East	**407**	**4.8**	**4.2**	**6.7**	**31.8**	**168.8**	**256.0**	**80.4**	**134.4**	**174.2**	**201.4**	**309.7**	**448.9**	**332.7**	**135.9**
Bahrain	419	1.11	—	—	.31	.01	.07	—	33.11	36.90	92.13	146.22	172.41	42.53	.18
Egypt	469	.49	.63	.62	.27	.09	.15	.32	10.03	10.08	13.89	18.94	21.36	27.94	27.53
Iran, I.R. of	429	—	—	.01	.04	—	.03	.04	6.88	5.77	.67	7.06	2.00	2.38	2.84
Israel	436	.91	.97	1.24	1.45	1.75	2.73	1.03	8.86	5.76	10.17	10.31	9.31	7.63	12.29
Jordan	439	—	.09	—	.09	.12	.07	—	.01	1.08	.88	1.53	3.24	2.97	.17
Kuwait	443	.02	.02	.05	.03	.07	.13	.06	.20	1.53	1.48	7.91	.84	.58	.63
Lebanon	446	—	.05	.03	.23	.03	.01	—	.05	2.04	1.94	.08	.15	.17	.28
Libya	672	—	—	.01	—	—	—	.01	—	—	—	—	.01	—	—
Oman	449	.08	.92	.14	.90	.29	4.22	.30	.93	1.32	.42	1.75	1.18	9.86	1.08
Qatar	453	—	.01	—	.01	.01	—	—	—	—	—	—	.12	7.91	.13
Saudi Arabia	456	.06	.09	.01	.05	.11	.07	.26	38.19	50.54	58.72	51.56	115.57	126.15	42.99

	Exports							Imports						
	2001	2002	2003	2004	2005	2006	2007	2001	2002	2003	2004	2005	2006	2007
	Millions of U.S. Dollars							*Millions of U.S. Dollars*						
Syrian Arab Republic.................. 463	.03	.08	.05	.16	.06	.02	.01	.05	.16	.11	.05	.03	.18	.16
United Arab Emirates.................. 466	2.05	1.39	4.10	28.29	166.24	248.57	78.34	36.11	57.80	17.39	63.18	121.63	104.36	47.32
Yemen, Republic of..................... 474	.01	—	.02	—	—	—	—	—	1.21	3.56	1.02	.99	.08	.35
Middle East n.s.......................... 489	.01	—	.44	—	—	—	—	—	—	.05	.05	.01	—	—
Western Hemisphere............... 207	**2.0**	**1.6**	**4.0**	**3.7**	**4.6**	**4.5**	**7.6**	**33.8**	**46.1**	**54.1**	**59.9**	**57.4**	**52.8**	**68.3**
Antigua and Barbuda.................. 311	—	—	—	—	—	—	1.26	—	—	.01	—	—	.01	3.88
Argentina.................................. 213	.10	.01	.02	.14	.03	.03	.06	24.64	30.00	26.25	33.09	38.56	31.35	44.66
Bahamas, The............................ 313	.01	—	—	—	.01	.02	—	.01	.01	.04	.02	.02	.18	.13
Barbados................................... 316	—	.01	—	.01	.56	—	.38	—	—	—	—	.03	—	—
Belize.. 339	.01	—	.75	.28	—	—	—	.15	—	.16	.06	—	.13	.45
Bermuda................................... 319	.01	—	—	—	—	—	—	—	—	—	—	—	—	—
Bolivia....................................... 218	—	—	—	—	—	—	—	—	—	—	—	—	—	.10
Brazil.. 223	.05	.26	.10	.10	.48	.18	.06	6.27	5.33	11.09	17.19	13.37	9.16	10.74
Chile... 228	.57	.06	.10	.22	.16	.12	.24	.67	1.30	1.12	1.52	1.87	1.79	2.74
Colombia................................... 233	—	—	.03	—	—	—	—	.15	.05	.35	.17	.08	.47	.41
Costa Rica................................. 238	—	—	.07	—	.01	.01	—	.02	.26	.10	.37	.24	.36	.31
Dominican Republic.................... 243	—	—	.03	—	—	—	—	.05	.06	.11	.11	.08	.18	.42
Ecuador.................................... 248	—	—	—	—	—	—	.69	.01	.06	.05	.01	.07	.11	.09
El Salvador................................ 253	—	—	—	—	—	—	—	—	.04	—	—	—	.01	.01
Greenland................................. 326	—	—	—	—	—	—	—	—	.02	—	—	—	—	—
Guatemala................................. 258	—	—	—	—	—	—	—	.01	.10	.08	.09	.03	.08	.13
Guyana...................................... 336	—	—	—	—	.28	.02	.04	—	—	—	—	—	—	.14
Haiti.. 263	—	—	—	.01	—	.01	—	.02	.04	.03	.05	.02	.03	.03
Honduras.................................. 268	—	—	.02	.01	—	—	.12	—	.01	.02	.01	.03	.01	.03
Jamaica..................................... 343	—	—	—	—	—	—	—	—	—	—	.04	.03	.02	.01
Mexico...................................... 273	.58	.53	.75	.84	.91	1.60	1.56	.26	.72	.51	.83	1.51	2.47	2.07
Netherlands Antilles.................... 353	—	—	—	—	.02	—	.01	.46	—	6.30	5.16	—	4.88	.01
Nicaragua.................................. 278	—	—	—	—	—	.03	—	—	.02	—	—	—	—	.02
Panama..................................... 283	.69	.47	.75	1.90	1.97	2.31	2.73	.21	.22	.86	.14	.56	.36	.90
Paraguay................................... 288	—	—	—	—	.03	—	—	—	—	—	—	.13	.13	—
Peru.. 293	—	—	—	—	—	—	—	.85	1.03	.88	.62	.58	.82	.74
St. Kitts and Nevis...................... 361	—	—	—	.01	—	—	—	—	—	—	—	—	—	—
Trinidad and Tobago................... 369	.01	—	—	—	.05	.01	.03	—	.57	.02	—	—	—	—
Uruguay.................................... 298	.01	.26	1.30	.08	.08	.19	.40	—	6.26	6.11	.43	.19	.21	.28
Venezuela, Rep. Bol.................... 299	.01	—	—	.09	.02	—	—	—	.02	.04	—	.01	—	.01
Western Hem. n.s....................... 399	—	—	—	.05	—	—	—	—	—	—	—	—	.01	—
Other Countries n.i.e............... 910	**—**	**—**	**.2**	**—**	**—**	**—**	**—**	**.9**	**.6**	**1.0**	**1.4**	**1.6**	**.8**	**2.2**
Cuba... 928	—	.04	—	—	—	—	—	.12	.07	.08	.11	.11	.16	.15
North Korea............................... 954	.04	—	.23	.03	.01	—	—	.76	.48	.94	1.34	1.54	.67	2.00
Memorandum Items														
European Union......................... 998	1,024.74	1,143.62	1,179.33	1,303.80	1,324.21	1,313.33	1,366.10	555.11	596.78	683.45	728.45	970.44	1,257.19	1,043.90
Oil Exporting Ctys...................... 999	2.72	3.55	4.92	30.59	168.08	255.37	81.21	129.39	158.72	119.64	188.40	313.09	325.42	185.41
Non-Oil Develop.Ctys.................. 201	158.95	200.25	246.81	242.37	277.03	322.80	339.73	1,032.45	1,134.40	1,313.74	1,513.03	1,612.86	1,842.60	2,245.15
PERCENT DISTRIBUTION														
Industrial Countries................ 101	**89.4**	**88.3**	**85.8**	**85.4**	**77.7**	**72.6**	**78.6**	**41.8**	**40.3**	**39.8**	**38.4**	**38.9**	**40.4**	**37.0**
Developing Countries............. 202	**10.6**	**11.7**	**13.9**	**14.3**	**22.3**	**27.4**	**21.4**	**58.2**	**59.7**	**60.0**	**61.3**	**60.9**	**59.6**	**62.9**
Africa.................................... 607	**9.0**	**7.7**	**10.2**	**9.1**	**9.1**	**9.2**	**12.1**	**17.7**	**17.3**	**16.4**	**14.7**	**11.4**	**10.3**	**10.7**
Asia...................................... 507	**1.0**	**3.4**	**2.7**	**2.8**	**3.6**	**5.1**	**3.5**	**31.5**	**31.6**	**31.9**	**32.6**	**30.7**	**34.7**	**45.2**
Europe.................................. 170	**.1**	**.2**	**.4**	**.5**	**.9**	**.7**	**1.3**	**.6**	**.6**	**1.0**	**.8**	**2.8**	**4.0**	**1.7**
Middle East........................... 407	**.3**	**.2**	**.4**	**1.7**	**8.4**	**12.1**	**4.1**	**6.7**	**8.0**	**8.4**	**11.2**	**14.2**	**9.1**	**3.5**
Western Hemisphere............. 207	**.1**	**.1**	**.2**	**.2**	**.2**	**.2**	**.4**	**1.7**	**2.1**	**2.3**	**2.2**	**1.8**	**1.5**	**1.8**
Other Countries n.i.e............... 910	**—**	**—**	**—**	**—**	**—**	**—**	**—**	**—**	**—**	**—**	**.1**	**.1**	**—**	**.1**
ANNUAL PERCENT CHANGE														
World.................................... 001	**2.5**	**14.5**	**3.5**	**5.9**	**4.5**	**5.5**	**−6.6**	**−4.4**	**8.5**	**10.2**	**16.2**	**14.0**	**15.1**	**6.2**
Industrial Countries................ 101	**1.4**	**13.2**	**.5**	**5.4**	**−4.9**	**−1.4**	**1.2**	**−.7**	**4.6**	**9.1**	**12.0**	**15.5**	**19.4**	**−2.6**
Developing Countries............. 202	**12.2**	**26.1**	**23.5**	**8.4**	**63.1**	**29.9**	**−27.2**	**−6.9**	**11.3**	**10.8**	**18.7**	**13.2**	**12.6**	**12.1**
Africa.................................... 607	**21.8**	**−2.0**	**37.1**	**−6.0**	**4.4**	**6.9**	**22.4**	**−8.0**	**5.9**	**4.6**	**3.9**	**−11.7**	**4.1**	**10.6**
Asia...................................... 507	**−31.3**	**278.7**	**−19.7**	**10.4**	**34.6**	**50.8**	**−35.2**	**−10.6**	**8.9**	**11.4**	**18.6**	**7.4**	**30.1**	**38.5**
Europe.................................. 170	**22.4**	**140.6**	**161.9**	**30.5**	**80.7**	**−16.6**	**63.6**	**20.6**	**17.5**	**70.2**	**−12.9**	**329.2**	**62.5**	**−56.0**
Middle East........................... 407	**72.0**	**−11.1**	**59.3**	**372.2**	**430.0**	**51.7**	**−68.6**	**9.2**	**29.6**	**15.6**	**53.8**	**44.9**	**−25.9**	**−59.1**
Western Hemisphere............. 207	**−50.9**	**−20.4**	**144.3**	**−5.5**	**23.1**	**−1.3**	**67.3**	**19.0**	**36.6**	**17.4**	**10.7**	**−4.2**	**−8.1**	**29.4**
Other Countries n.i.e............... 910	**22.5**	**6.9**	**418.2**	**−86.4**	**−59.7**	**23.6**	**....**	**31.6**	**−37.3**	**84.1**	**42.4**	**13.8**	**−49.8**	**160.6**

	Exports 2001	2002	2003	2004	2005	2006	2007	Imports, f.o.b 2001	2002	2003	2004	2005	2006	2007
	Millions of U.S. Dollars							*Millions of U.S. Dollars*						
IFS World Total	**158,547**	**160,682**	**165,396**	**189,084**	**213,891**	**250,441**	**272,055**	**168,276**	**168,679**	**170,490**	**197,347**	**221,415**	**256,130**	**283,264**
DOTS World Total 001	**158,899**	**161,235**	**164,892**	**187,812**	**214,230**	**249,924**	**271,874**	**172,229**	**173,854**	**173,839**	**201,156**	**221,820**	**256,058**	**281,949**
Industrial Countries 101	**150,173**	**151,976**	**154,948**	**175,756**	**199,105**	**230,269**	**246,832**	**143,762**	**138,293**	**136,496**	**148,834**	**165,703**	**184,066**	**199,848**
United States 111	140,564	141,898	144,293	164,522	183,862	212,094	223,426	113,767	106,557	105,361	110,827	118,974	130,782	139,953
Canada 156	3,083	2,991	3,042	3,292	4,234	5,176	6,491	4,235	4,480	4,120	5,327	6,169	7,376	7,957
Australia 193	88	169	199	275	341	439	561	348	351	429	404	802	897	785
Japan 158	621	1,194	1,173	1,191	1,470	1,594	1,913	8,086	9,349	7,595	10,583	13,078	15,295	16,343
New Zealand 196	19	19	10	15	21	28	33	261	246	278	280	385	340	511
Austria 122	20	61	16	34	53	51	60	220	187	255	363	439	528	638
Belgium 124	—	—	—	—	534	687	840	—	—	—	—	839	805	761
Belgium-Luxembourg n.s. 127	318	482	344	442	—	—	—	630	557	573	715	—	—	—
Cyprus 423	—	—	—	—	4	6	7	—	—	—	—	1	1	1
Denmark 128	44	37	44	48	71	100	126	169	177	199	202	220	271	321
Finland 172	9	12	17	25	69	139	107	249	151	277	242	306	324	537
France 132	373	310	337	335	373	556	696	1,577	1,807	2,015	2,395	2,569	2,667	3,108
Germany 134	1,504	1,159	1,715	1,689	2,289	2,973	4,104	6,080	6,066	6,218	7,144	8,670	9,437	10,688
Greece 174	7	14	18	20	22	26	34	23	29	23	26	32	43	105
Iceland 176	—	—	—	—	—	—	—	—	—	—	—	3	4	6
Ireland 178	186	213	184	162	129	109	148	551	614	795	700	774	893	954
Italy 136	240	196	276	235	195	267	481	2,100	2,171	2,474	2,817	3,498	4,109	5,542
Luxembourg 137	—	—	—	—	5	5	5	—	—	—	—	67	64	108
Malta 181	—	—	—	—	2	1	17	—	—	—	—	208	159	143
Netherlands 138	508	797	701	246	801	1,326	1,905	471	547	556	267	925	1,547	2,466
Norway 142	6	8	10	29	36	59	41	143	93	96	147	216	260	262
Portugal 182	149	141	187	154	270	282	276	101	94	126	250	305	345	325
Slovenia 961	4	10	5	7	11	3	9	13	14	23	42	41	54	62
Spain 184	1,271	1,394	1,512	2,027	2,954	3,270	3,690	1,827	2,224	2,288	2,853	3,325	3,638	3,830
Sweden 144	37	43	29	80	53	59	81	806	451	733	867	972	966	903
Switzerland 146	451	164	103	90	117	95	219	763	778	820	925	1,020	1,122	1,246
United Kingdom 112	673	664	733	840	1,188	925	1,563	1,344	1,350	1,242	1,458	1,866	2,140	2,294
Developing Countries 202	**8,541**	**9,098**	**9,770**	**11,794**	**14,829**	**19,384**	**24,642**	**28,433**	**35,528**	**37,301**	**52,272**	**55,848**	**71,832**	**81,984**
Africa 607	**104**	**117**	**178**	**170**	**294**	**370**	**342**	**599**	**398**	**376**	**494**	**426**	**742**	**951**
Algeria 612	16	39	87	65	97	87	95	163	96	73	46	41	81	55
Angola 614	—	—	—	—	31	22	14	—	—	—	—	—	—	53
Cameroon 622	—	—	—	—	1	—	—	—	—	—	—	—	1	32
Central African Rep. 626	—	—	—	—	—	—	—	—	—	—	—	—	—	1
Congo, Republic of 634	—	3	—	—	—	3	13	2	5	2	3	2	4	1
Côte d'Ivoire 662	43	—	26	—	17	4	—	1	2	3	5	3	14	18
Equatorial Guinea 642	—	—	—	—	—	2	—	—	—	—	—	—	—	5
Ethiopia 644	—	—	—	—	—	—	3	—	—	—	—	—	1	1
Gabon 646	—	—	—	—	—	1	—	—	—	—	—	4	2	5
Ghana 652	—	—	—	—	1	—	2	—	—	—	—	6	2	3
Guinea 656	—	—	—	—	—	—	4	—	—	—	—	—	—	—
Kenya 664	—	—	—	—	1	6	1	6	4	3	3	3	3	9
Liberia 668	1	2	2	2	2	1	3	—	—	—	—	—	2	1
Madagascar 674	—	—	—	—	—	—	—	—	—	—	—	2	2	2
Malawi 676	—	—	—	—	—	—	—	—	—	—	—	4	5	4
Mali 678	—	—	—	—	—	—	—	—	—	—	—	1	2	4
Mauritania 682	—	—	—	—	—	—	—	—	—	—	—	1	—	1
Mauritius 684	—	—	—	—	—	—	—	—	—	—	—	4	6	5
Morocco 686	2	9	1	3	3	4	7	79	87	79	126	129	147	173
Mozambique 688	—	—	—	—	6	15	3	—	—	—	—	—	—	4
Niger 692	—	—	—	—	—	1	—	—	—	—	—	1	1	—
Nigeria 694	3	9	4	14	23	42	28	22	4	29	6	12	128	254
St. Helena 856	—	—	—	—	—	—	—	—	—	—	—	1	—	—
São Tomé & Príncipe 716	—	—	—	—	—	—	—	—	—	—	—	—	2	—
Senegal 722	—	—	—	—	1	—	—	—	—	—	—	3	3	2
Seychelles 718	—	—	—	—	—	1	—	—	—	—	—	—	—	—
South Africa 199	—	—	—	—	96	165	153	—	—	—	—	177	273	269
Sudan 732	—	—	—	—	4	1	2	—	—	—	—	11	15	18
Tanzania 738	—	—	—	—	—	4	—	—	—	—	—	2	1	2
Tunisia 744	—	—	—	—	8	9	14	—	—	—	—	13	41	22
Uganda 746	—	—	—	—	—	—	—	—	—	—	—	—	—	1
Zimbabwe 698	—	—	—	—	—	—	—	—	—	—	—	1	2	3
Africa n.s. 799	39	55	57	86	—	—	—	326	200	186	305	—	—	—
Asia 507	**1,636**	**2,129**	**2,470**	**2,743**	**2,961**	**4,204**	**5,050**	**20,585**	**26,728**	**27,037**	**37,481**	**39,810**	**52,779**	**61,943**
Afghanistan, I.S. of 512	—	—	—	—	—	—	—	—	—	—	—	—	1	1
Bangladesh 513	—	—	—	—	2	5	1	—	—	—	—	41	62	89
Bhutan 514	—	—	—	—	—	—	—	—	—	—	—	6	—	—
Brunei Darussalam 516	—	—	—	—	1	—	—	—	—	—	—	—	—	—
Cambodia 522	—	—	—	—	—	—	1	—	—	—	—	11	17	23
China,P.R.: Mainland 924	282	654	974	986	1,136	1,688	1,895	4,027	6,274	9,401	14,374	17,696	24,438	29,744

	Exports							Imports, f.o.b						
	2001	2002	2003	2004	2005	2006	2007	2001	2002	2003	2004	2005	2006	2007
	Millions of U.S. Dollars							Millions of U.S. Dollars						
China,P.R.:Hong Kong.......... 532	120	151	144	173	192	282	328	442	509	517	408	552	614	561
China,P.R.:Macao.......... 546	8	5	—	—	8	6	1	13	12	10	15	15	25	28
Fiji.......... 819	—	—	—	—	—	—	—	—	—	—	—	2	2	2
Guam.......... 829	—	—	—	—	—	—	—	—	—	—	—	1	—	—
India.......... 534	160	328	487	446	561	680	1,046	392	459	564	868	959	1,126	1,207
Indonesia.......... 536	14	17	25	27	66	46	43	457	527	448	614	654	812	886
Kiribati.......... 826	—	—	—	—	—	—	—	—	—	—	—	—	—	1
Korea.......... 542	293	162	181	219	250	464	684	3,532	3,910	4,113	5,228	6,566	10,676	12,658
Lao People's Dem.Rep.......... 544	—	—	—	—	—	—	—	—	—	—	—	—	—	1
Malaysia.......... 548	67	86	68	57	54	100	123	2,006	1,993	2,761	3,374	3,658	4,474	4,771
Maldives.......... 556	—	—	—	—	—	—	—	818	925	784	867	—	—	—
Mongolia.......... 948	—	—	—	—	—	—	—	—	—	—	—	15	8	7
Myanmar.......... 518	—	—	—	—	—	—	—	—	—	—	—	4	4	6
Nepal.......... 558	—	—	—	—	—	—	—	—	—	—	—	2	2	2
New Caledonia.......... 839	—	—	—	—	1	—	—	—	—	—	—	—	—	—
Pakistan.......... 564	4	10	11	10	14	28	23	54	67	72	103	114	114	110
Papua New Guinea.......... 853	—	—	—	—	—	—	5	—	—	—	—	2	1	—
Philippines.......... 566	16	20	20	18	41	58	75	818	925	784	867	1,323	1,232	1,198
Singapore.......... 576	242	199	189	312	327	254	336	1,147	1,555	1,338	2,212	2,226	1,955	2,087
Solomon Islands.......... 813	—	—	—	—	—	—	7	—	—	—	—	—	2	1
Sri Lanka.......... 524	1	3	3	2	3	4	3	41	51	52	54	64	70	81
Taiwan Province of China.......... 528	172	208	148	206	200	441	272	3,015	4,250	2,509	3,479	4,066	4,974	5,897
Thailand.......... 578	63	54	54	51	98	118	167	615	839	987	1,260	1,558	1,784	2,106
Vanuatu.......... 846	—	—	—	—	—	—	—	—	—	—	—	—	6	2
Vietnam.......... 582	—	—	—	—	8	29	39	—	—	—	—	274	377	473
Asia n.s.......... 598	194	232	163	235	—	—	—	3,208	4,430	2,699	3,760	—	—	—
Europe.......... 170	**85**	**143**	**194**	**197**	**324**	**441**	**703**	**1,196**	**1,250**	**1,377**	**2,415**	**1,895**	**2,434**	**2,153**
Albania.......... 914	—	—	—	—	—	—	—	—	—	—	—	1	—	—
Bulgaria.......... 918	—	1	2	4	4	1	8	19	32	23	27	47	47	34
Czech Republic.......... 935	—	—	—	—	29	67	65	—	—	—	—	244	295	339
Czechoslovakia n.s.......... 937	12	7	13	34	2	4	6	90	87	121	226	59	81	79
Hungary.......... 944	41	62	57	58	40	54	87	108	150	107	177	254	315	295
Lithuania.......... 946	—	—	—	—	3	2	6	—	—	—	—	11	12	14
Poland.......... 964	5	18	15	15	41	90	52	160	87	79	94	127	211	252
Romania.......... 968	1	6	4	7	58	36	20	24	41	20	29	48	93	89
Russia.......... 922	18	19	47	26	29	44	160	243	236	248	437	563	535	449
Turkey.......... 186	7	28	50	52	43	36	44	83	122	98	168	241	361	318
Ukraine.......... 926	—	2	5	1	4	15	15	118	83	80	245	219	378	182
U.S.S.R. n.s.......... 930	—	—	—	—	65	88	58	—	—	—	—	44	61	58
Yugoslavia n.s.......... 966	—	—	—	—	2	3	4	—	—	—	—	11	12	14
Europe n.s.......... 884	—	—	—	—	3	2	179	350	411	603	1,012	28	32	31
Middle East.......... 407	**137**	**192**	**188**	**203**	**337**	**595**	**740**	**512**	**459**	**529**	**688**	**901**	**902**	**1,505**
Bahrain.......... 419	—	—	—	—	—	1	2	—	—	—	—	—	11	6
Egypt.......... 469	8	17	17	30	44	61	61	3	3	3	4	134	76	340
Iran, I.R. of.......... 429	27	31	22	37	26	23	19	9	5	4	4	4	6	43
Iraq.......... 433	—	—	—	—	1	—	—	—	—	—	—	1	—	—
Israel.......... 436	39	56	61	62	87	91	130	258	250	313	402	371	429	441
Jordan.......... 439	—	—	—	—	2	4	6	—	—	—	—	5	5	6
Kuwait.......... 443	9	3	3	13	16	20	124	18	—	—	1	1	—	—
Lebanon.......... 446	3	3	6	5	4	6	5	—	—	—	—	—	—	2
Libya.......... 672	—	—	—	3	4	29	61	7	—	13	7	—	1	—
Oman.......... 449	—	—	—	—	1	9	2	—	—	—	—	2	2	1
Qatar.......... 453	—	—	—	—	13	38	46	—	—	—	—	3	35	—
Saudi Arabia.......... 456	6	15	35	25	89	235	105	187	187	172	258	357	304	589
Syrian Arab Republic.......... 463	—	—	—	—	14	13	4	—	—	—	—	2	4	2
United Arab Emirates.......... 466	—	—	—	—	33	63	175	—	—	—	—	9	27	73
Yemen, Republic of.......... 474	—	—	—	—	1	1	1	—	—	—	—	14	—	—
Middle East n.s.......... 489	45	67	44	27	—	—	—	31	14	22	13	—	—	1
Western Hemisphere.......... 207	**6,578**	**6,517**	**6,740**	**8,482**	**10,914**	**13,772**	**17,807**	**5,541**	**6,694**	**7,984**	**11,193**	**12,817**	**14,976**	**15,432**
Antigua and Barbuda.......... 311	—	—	—	—	2	2	3	—	—	—	—	—	—	1
Argentina.......... 213	244	125	235	569	672	952	1,130	441	687	867	1,108	1,303	1,799	1,610
Aruba.......... 314	—	—	—	—	1,448	1,469	1,518	—	—	—	—	27	140	73
Bahamas, The.......... 313	44	9	14	9	14	12	19	10	48	51	36	24	—	25
Barbados.......... 316	—	—	—	—	7	8	8	—	—	—	—	1	1	2
Belize.......... 339	36	67	59	60	81	87	102	2	2	3	5	8	8	8
Bermuda.......... 319	170	3	7	5	7	4	3	1	2	—	—	—	—	—
Bolivia.......... 218	24	19	23	33	37	35	48	14	24	29	31	30	39	59
Brazil.......... 223	585	658	621	863	890	1,147	2,010	2,101	2,565	3,267	4,341	5,214	5,558	5,575
Chile.......... 228	374	322	381	443	668	905	1,170	975	1,010	1,082	1,464	1,754	2,470	2,594
Colombia.......... 233	506	658	662	789	1,548	2,132	2,943	344	352	406	635	675	744	764
Costa Rica.......... 238	321	373	352	387	421	522	687	184	416	584	852	883	789	740
Dominica.......... 321	2	1	1	1	1	1	2	—	—	—	—	—	2	1
Dominican Republic.......... 243	465	426	367	430	543	650	783	16	18	17	38	102	114	143
Ecuador.......... 248	128	179	175	215	309	386	448	110	33	54	54	106	70	123
El Salvador.......... 253	274	292	286	317	472	497	518	30	36	44	50	59	59	62
Grenada.......... 328	—	—	—	—	1	1	—	—	—	—	—	—	—	1
Guatemala.......... 258	560	548	590	672	864	935	1,152	95	117	151	230	222	356	457

	Exports							Imports, f.o.b						
	2001	2002	2003	2004	2005	2006	2007	2001	2002	2003	2004	2005	2006	2007
	Millions of U.S. Dollars							*Millions of U.S. Dollars*						
Guyana......336	1	3	2	2	3	2	5	1	—	1	2	5	1	3
Haiti......263	6	13	10	11	11	12	13	2	—	2	4	6	12	12
Honduras......268	180	156	161	182	240	285	382	17	25	47	66	105	123	183
Jamaica......343	91	81	82	102	85	112	118	6	8	5	6	6	5	6
Netherlands Antilles......353	838	674	480	22	13	33	56	1	26	40	78	279	404	518
Nicaragua......278	92	93	131	151	324	522	730	31	27	38	52	159	78	91
Panama......283	247	304	320	316	463	568	731	45	35	38	44	79	61	114
Paraguay......288	12	9	9	11	14	27	47	2	2	4	37	9	9	9
Peru......293	173	233	194	250	345	533	677	141	152	131	282	445	470	383
St. Kitts and Nevis......361	—	—	—	—	1	1	1	—	—	—	—	1	1	1
St. Lucia......362	—	—	—	—	2	1	2	—	—	—	—	1	1	2
St. Vincent & Grens......364	—	—	—	—	1	1	1	—	—	—	—	—	—	—
Suriname......366	—	—	—	—	6	7	8	—	—	—	—	—	—	—
Trinidad and Tobago......369	28	25	20	27	57	61	58	34	72	79	206	265	410	528
Uruguay......298	107	26	34	37	66	66	90	85	92	101	136	263	262	333
Venezuela, Rep. Bol......299	697	666	421	828	1,289	1,783	2,333	503	532	566	916	783	980	1,009
Western Hem. n.s......399	372	553	1,105	1,749	11	10	9	348	411	377	519	2	10	3
Other Countries n.i.e......910	**176**	**143**	**163**	**177**	**222**	**194**	**190**	**26**	**24**	**20**	**21**	**20**	**43**	**16**
Cuba......928	176	143	163	177	222	194	190	26	24	20	21	20	43	16
Countries & Areas n.s......898	**9**	**18**	**11**	**86**	**74**	**77**	**211**	**8**	**9**	**21**	**28**	**248**	**116**	**102**
Memorandum Items														
European Union......998	5,389	5,613	6,190	6,416	9,137	10,998	14,358	16,429	16,675	17,982	20,611	25,691	28,823	33,684
Oil Exporting Ctys......999	771	781	597	1,012	1,659	2,376	3,030	1,366	1,351	1,306	1,851	1,865	2,377	2,910
Non-Oil Develop.Ctys......201	7,770	8,318	9,172	10,782	13,170	17,008	21,612	27,067	34,177	35,995	50,422	53,983	69,455	79,073
PERCENT DISTRIBUTION														
Industrial Countries......101	**94.5**	**94.3**	**94.0**	**93.6**	**92.9**	**92.1**	**90.8**	**83.5**	**79.5**	**78.5**	**74.0**	**74.7**	**71.9**	**70.9**
Developing Countries......202	**5.4**	**5.6**	**5.9**	**6.3**	**6.9**	**7.8**	**9.1**	**16.5**	**20.4**	**21.5**	**26.0**	**25.2**	**28.1**	**29.1**
Africa......607	**.1**	**.1**	**.1**	**.1**	**.1**	**.1**	**.1**	**.3**	**.2**	**.2**	**.2**	**.2**	**.3**	**.3**
Asia......507	**1.0**	**1.3**	**1.5**	**1.5**	**1.4**	**1.7**	**1.9**	**12.0**	**15.4**	**15.6**	**18.6**	**17.9**	**20.6**	**22.0**
Europe......170	**.1**	**.1**	**.1**	**.1**	**.2**	**.2**	**.3**	**.7**	**.7**	**.8**	**1.2**	**.9**	**1.0**	**.8**
Middle East......407	**.1**	**.1**	**.1**	**.1**	**.2**	**.2**	**.3**	**.3**	**.3**	**.3**	**.3**	**.4**	**.4**	**.5**
Western Hemisphere......207	**4.1**	**4.0**	**4.1**	**4.5**	**5.1**	**5.5**	**6.5**	**3.2**	**3.9**	**4.6**	**5.6**	**5.8**	**5.8**	**5.5**
Other Countries n.i.e......910	**.1**	**.1**	**.1**	**.1**	**.1**	**.1**	**.1**	**—**	**—**	**—**	**—**	**—**	**—**	**—**
ANNUAL PERCENT CHANGE														
World......001	**–4.4**	**1.5**	**2.3**	**13.9**	**14.1**	**16.7**	**8.8**	**–2.7**	**.9**	**—**	**15.7**	**10.3**	**15.4**	**10.1**
Industrial Countries......101	**–4.9**	**1.2**	**2.0**	**13.4**	**13.3**	**15.7**	**7.2**	**–6.7**	**–3.8**	**–1.3**	**9.0**	**11.3**	**11.1**	**8.6**
Developing Countries......202	**6.3**	**6.5**	**7.4**	**20.7**	**25.7**	**30.7**	**27.1**	**24.2**	**25.0**	**5.0**	**40.1**	**6.8**	**28.6**	**14.1**
Africa......607	**149.2**	**12.9**	**52.0**	**–4.8**	**73.4**	**25.9**	**–7.7**	**22.9**	**–33.6**	**–5.6**	**31.6**	**–13.8**	**74.1**	**28.2**
Asia......507	**29.6**	**30.1**	**16.0**	**11.1**	**7.9**	**42.0**	**20.1**	**30.8**	**29.8**	**1.2**	**38.6**	**6.2**	**32.6**	**17.4**
Europe......170	**–51.7**	**68.2**	**35.3**	**1.5**	**64.4**	**36.4**	**59.3**	**3.2**	**4.5**	**10.2**	**75.4**	**–21.6**	**28.5**	**–11.5**
Middle East......407	**26.3**	**40.1**	**–2.3**	**7.9**	**66.2**	**76.9**	**24.3**	**–18.4**	**–10.3**	**15.2**	**30.2**	**30.8**	**.1**	**66.9**
Western Hemisphere......207	**2.0**	**–.9**	**3.4**	**25.8**	**28.7**	**26.2**	**29.3**	**13.4**	**20.8**	**19.3**	**40.2**	**14.5**	**16.8**	**3.0**
Other Countries n.i.e......910	**–16.1**	**–18.4**	**13.8**	**8.4**	**25.3**	**–12.3**	**–2.5**	**–8.3**	**–5.4**	**–16.4**	**4.2**	**–4.1**	**113.8**	**–63.9**

Moldova 921

		Exports							Imports						
		2001	2002	2003	2004	2005	2006	2007	2001	2002	2003	2004	2005	2006	2007
		Millions of U.S. Dollars							*Millions of U.S. Dollars*						
IFS World Total		**568.1**	**643.9**	**789.2**	**980.2**	**1,091.3**	**1,051.6**	**1,341.8**	**892.7**	**1,038.5**	**1,402.8**	**1,772.8**	**2,293.0**	**2,693.2**	**3,689.9**
DOTS World Total	**001**	**565.5**	**643.8**	**789.9**	**985.2**	**1,054.7**	**1,242.8Y**	**1,760.9Y**	**892.2**	**1,038.0**	**1,402.3**	**1,768.5**	**2,293.0**	**3,499.8Y**	**4,663.8Y**
Industrial Countries	**101**	**154.8**	**194.1**	**227.8**	**313.3**	**284.9**	**433.8Y**	**523.9Y**	**306.7**	**346.7**	**460.9**	**525.8**	**681.9**	**899.8Y**	**1,205.8Y**
United States	111	26.99	37.40	33.65	44.90	38.23	35.64V	22.55V	28.06	48.07	34.55	29.38	40.76	33.33V	57.97V
Canada	156	2.33	6.34	4.42	1.15	.96	21.04V	2.29V	.78	.73	.74	1.55	1.74	.93V	1.60V
Australia	193	.09	.04	.15	.11	.15	.29V	.43V	.05	.03	.02	.21	.36	.38V	.03V
Japan	158	.06	.02	.01	.07	.27	2.28V	3.27V	7.97	5.52	11.71	15.87	21.34	2.24V	4.06V
New Zealand	196	—	—	—	.01	—	.01V	.06V	.04	.31	.30	.47	1.74	2.17V	2.93V
Austria	122	8.50	7.22	11.32	10.03	11.68	15.69V	27.36V	9.12	9.35	14.61	14.06	21.84	40.20V	73.01V
Belgium	124	4.59	6.23	7.25	11.78	—	11.66V	8.80V	12.23	11.89	18.43	21.68	30.10	48.37V	49.35V
Cyprus	423	.53	.65	.92	.78	1.28	2.39V	13.70V	.48	.19	.03	.69	.20	.65V	.97V
Denmark	128	.08	.02	.15	.46	.02	.18V	2.25V	2.87	5.11	6.89	6.01	7.59	6.19V	8.41V
Finland	172	—	—	.31	.13	.05	.12V	.14V	3.50	3.78	9.41	6.02	9.85	11.97V	15.62V
France	132	8.37	11.35	9.35	11.40	16.49	26.31V	29.31V	25.60	23.32	35.17	52.67	64.43	56.20V	92.36V
Germany	134	40.01	46.14	56.18	71.28	47.43	106.45V	149.20V	84.04	85.70	135.59	150.21	191.06	305.25V	408.07V
Greece	174	2.72	3.11	3.73	3.42	4.83	14.15V	20.61V	5.24	13.27	11.47	10.40	10.31	19.84V	21.70V
Iceland	176	—	.05	.21	—	—	.04V	.04V	.10	.27	.39	.46	.28	—V	.10V
Ireland	178	.20	.75	—	.02	.05	.13V	.14V	1.90	1.36	1.04	2.70	3.19	1.53V	.48V
Italy	136	45.45	56.82	82.39	136.44	133.45	142.42V	175.97V	64.43	87.78	116.59	131.63	151.96	212.29V	265.93V
Luxembourg	137	—	—	—	—	—	—V	—V	.23	.53	.19	.22	.16	.58V	.43V
Malta	181	—	—	—	—	—	—V	—V	.01	.05	.04	.07	.01	—V	—V
Netherlands	138	3.99	3.05	2.89	5.52	6.52	12.86V	16.32V	12.83	10.50	13.22	17.50	31.04	52.92V	87.94V
Norway	142	.30	.55	—	—	—	.78V	1.45V	3.13	2.46	2.22	2.57	4.40	3.26V	5.05V
Portugal	182	.06	.08	.09	.50	.41	5.21V	3.69V	3.43	3.41	6.03	6.81	7.71	2.33V	3.95V
Slovenia	961	2.66	3.52	2.10	.81	—	1.38V	1.01V	7.65	9.47	8.54	9.84	10.89	17.82V	19.34V
Spain	184	1.27	3.18	5.09	2.98	4.07	6.80V	1.93V	5.81	5.59	8.48	11.74	18.07	15.32V	18.21V
Sweden	144	.09	.52	.04	.36	.44	4.89V	12.59V	3.20	2.67	7.50	12.60	20.53	9.99V	14.92V
Switzerland	146	.86	1.71	1.98	1.10	7.38	2.19V	2.75V	12.95	5.59	4.30	7.82	14.24	18.96V	25.27V
United Kingdom	112	5.62	5.31	5.61	10.02	11.14	20.86V	28.03V	11.08	9.76	13.50	12.65	18.16	37.12V	28.13V
Developing Countries	**202**	**410.7**	**449.7**	**562.1**	**670.6**	**767.4**	**806.0Y**	**1,233.2Y**	**585.5**	**685.0**	**941.3**	**1,242.6**	**1,607.4**	**2,595.5Y**	**3,452.4Y**
Africa	**607**	**.4**	**1.2**	**.7**	**1.2**	**3.5**	**4.6Y**	**5.6Y**	**.8**	**1.6**	**2.5**	**3.2**	**4.9**	**3.7Y**	**4.4Y**
Algeria	612	—	.05	.01	—	—	—Y	—Y	—	.05	—	—	—	—Y	—Y
Angola	614	.20	.10	.57	—	.49	.60Y	.75Y	—	—	—	—	—	—Y	—Y
Burkina Faso	748	—	.10	—	—	—	—Y	—Y	—	.01	—	—	—	—Y	—Y
Cameroon	622	....	....	....	....	....	....	....	—	—	.05	—	—	—Y	—Y
Congo, Republic of	634	—	—	.06	.07	.26	.32Y	.39Y	....	....	....	....	....	....	....
Côte d'Ivoire	662	....	....	....	....	....	....	....	.64	.82	.83	1.32	.98	1.21Y	1.50Y
Eritrea	643	—	.01	.01	—	.02	.02Y	.02Y	....	....	....	....	....	....	....
Ghana	652	—	—	—	—	—	—Y	—Y	—	—	—	.04	.01	.01Y	.01Y
Guinea	656	—	.01	—	—	—	—Y	—Y	—	—	—	—	—	—Y	—Y
Kenya	664	—	—	—	—	—	—Y	—Y	—	—	—	.01	.02	.02Y	.03Y
Liberia	668	.01	.08	—	.22	—	—Y	—Y	—	—	—	—	—	—Y	—Y
Madagascar	674	....	....	....	....	....	....	....	—	—	—	—	—	—Y	.01Y
Malawi	676	....	....	....	....	....	....	....	.02	.03	—	—	—	—Y	—Y
Mauritania	682	—	—	—	—	—	—Y	—Y	—	—	.01	—	—	—Y	—Y
Mauritius	684	—	—	—	—	—	.01V	.01V	.02	.01	—	—	.01	.01V	.01V
Morocco	686	—	—	—	—	.01	.01Y	.02Y	.01	.02	.04	.07	.49	.61Y	.76Y
Mozambique	688	....	....	....	....	....	....	....	—	—	—	—	—	—Y	.01Y
Namibia	728	....	....	....	....	....	....	....	—	—	—	—	.01	.01Y	.02Y
Nigeria	694	.10	—	.03	—	—	—Y	—Y	—	—	.01	.01	—	—Y	—Y
Rwanda	714	—	.03	—	—	—	—Y	—Y	—	—	—	—	—	—Y	—Y
São Tomé & Príncipe	716	.01	.86	—	.37	.32	.39Y	.49Y	....	....	....	....	....	....	....
Senegal	722	....	....	....	....	....	....	....	—	—	.01	—	—	—Y	—Y
Seychelles	718	—	—	—	.50	1.97	2.43Y	3.02Y	—	—	—	—	—	—Y	—Y
Sierra Leone	724	—	—	—	—	.02	.02Y	.03Y	—	—	—	—	—	—Y	—Y
South Africa	199	—	—	—	—	—	—Y	—Y	.09	.61	1.57	1.67	2.08	.34V	.18V
Sudan	732	—	—	—	—	.14	.17Y	.21Y	—	—	—	—	—	—Y	—Y
Swaziland	734	—	.02	—	—	.28	.35Y	.43Y	—	.02	—	.02	1.21	1.50Y	1.86Y
Tunisia	744	.04	—	—	—	—	.03V	.03Y	—	.06	.03	.04	.06	—V	—Y
Uganda	746	—	—	—	—	—	.22Y	.26Y	.01	—	—	—	—	—Y	—Y
Zambia	754	—	—	—	—	—	—V	—V	—	—	—	—	—	—V	.02V
Asia	**507**	**.6**	**2.4**	**1.5**	**6.3**	**1.3**	**2.6Y**	**4.9Y**	**25.7**	**33.0**	**49.9**	**73.2**	**122.1**	**76.4Y**	**102.0Y**
Bangladesh	513	—	—	—	—	—	—V	—V	.58	.53	.88	1.38	1.96	1.89Y	2.09Y
Cambodia	522	—	—	—	—	—	—V	—Y	—	.02	.01	.01	.01	.01Y	.01Y
China,P.R.: Mainland	924	.01	1.32	.07	.08	.63	.51V	1.28V	8.41	11.84	21.47	37.70	73.89	34.80V	54.92V
China,P.R.:Hong Kong	532	—	—	.50	.02	.01	.08V	.16V	.32	.37	.24	.31	.64	12.39V	3.98V
China,P.R.:Macao	546	—	—	—	—	—	.01V	.03V	—	—	—	—	.01	—V	—V
French Polynesia	887	....	....	....	....	....	....	....	.01	—	—	—	—	—Y	—Y
India	534	.39	.96	.81	.26	.24	.30Y	.37Y	4.22	5.91	5.97	8.04	12.74	15.75Y	19.54Y
Indonesia	536	—	—	.02	.23	.16	.48V	.53V	.26	.38	.54	1.29	1.93	.35V	.50V
Korea	542	.01	.01	—	.03	.02	.72V	1.59V	4.49	5.37	9.97	13.74	13.92	6.05V	12.28V
Malaysia	548	—	—	—	—	—	—V	.01V	.77	2.05	1.49	2.66	3.26	.14V	.31V

	Exports 2001	2002	2003	2004	2005	2006	2007	Imports 2001	2002	2003	2004	2005	2006	2007
	Millions of U.S. Dollars							Millions of U.S. Dollars						
Maldives....556	—	—	—	—	—	—Y	—Y	—	.01	—	—	—	—Y	—Y
Mongolia....948	—	.02	—	—	.01	.01Y	.01Y	—	—	—	—	—	.39Y	.48Y
Myanmar....518	....	....	....	....	....	....	....	—	.13	.02	.01	.03	.03Y	.04Y
Pakistan....564	—	—	—	.26	.09	.11Y	.13Y	.64	.19	.14	.16	.25	.31Y	.39Y
Philippines....566	—	—	—	.01	—	—V	—V	.05	.14	.14	.27	.32	—V	.09V
Singapore....576	.01	—	.01	.03	—	—Y	—Y	.11	.17	.36	.63	.56	.70Y	.86Y
Sri Lanka....524	—	—	—	2.50	.02	.02Y	.03Y	.53	.55	.76	.83	.92	1.14Y	1.42Y
Taiwan Province of China....528	—	—	—	2.59	—	.20V	.68V	3.77	2.73	3.35	3.57	7.09	2.29V	4.74V
Thailand....578	—	—	—	.07	.02	.14V	.10V	.46	.64	.64	1.10	1.20	.14V	.32V
Timor-Leste....537	....	....	....	....	....	....	....	—	—	—	—	.01	.01Y	.02Y
Vanuatu....846	....	....	....	....	....	....	....	.01	—	—	—	—	—Y	—Y
Vietnam....582	.15	.04	.06	.22	.10	—V	—V	1.08	1.96	3.92	1.48	3.32	—V	—V
Europe....170	**406.7**	**440.5**	**552.5**	**650.9**	**747.4**	**777.9Y**	**1,190.6Y**	**541.7**	**629.7**	**873.6**	**1,146.6**	**1,447.3**	**2,440.6Y**	**3,284.3Y**
Albania....914	.27	.22	.50	.62	.53	4.99V	3.30V	—	.01	—	—	.01	.01V	—V
Armenia....911	.42	.82	2.19	2.74	2.24	2.47V	1.54V	.05	.14	.19	.22	.19	.92V	2.71V
Azerbaijan....912	.33	1.10	.99	1.23	3.72	4.24V	8.91V	.03	.10	.05	.06	4.53	.37V	.12V
Belarus....913	30.02	39.01	41.08	58.65	71.16	73.70V	74.49V	38.84	40.90	50.64	64.32	84.29	105.25V	159.01V
Bosnia & Herzegovina....963	.13	.55	.41	.11	—	—Y	—Y	—	.05	.12	.18	.72	.89Y	1.10Y
Bulgaria....918	3.67	3.39	6.19	5.50	7.64	10.34V	21.05V	20.49	20.70	30.14	29.59	28.98	26.35V	60.60V
Croatia....960	.10	.28	.20	.01	—	—V	—V	2.79	1.98	3.08	2.22	2.08	—V	—V
Czech Republic....935	.56	.89	1.52	1.87	—	4.52V	6.05V	11.33	12.88	18.98	21.52	28.75	39.78V	48.96V
Estonia....939	1.36	.79	.68	1.11	1.85	.67V	1.20V	2.45	3.02	1.95	1.96	1.79	4.41V	7.54V
Faroe Islands....816	....	....	....	....	....	....	....	—	—	.01	.01	.05	.06Y	.07Y
Georgia....915	.66	.41	1.08	2.07	5.25	3.20V	3.76Y	.11	.10	.13	.11	.28	.24V	.77Y
Gibraltar....823	.87	.54	.13	.21	.21	.26Y	.33Y	.06	—	.04	.03	.55	.68Y	.85Y
Hungary....944	7.23	9.17	8.01	14.46	14.74	10.33V	17.00V	18.09	16.84	19.58	22.93	33.80	55.12V	79.74V
Kazakhstan....916	4.47	6.52	9.21	15.42	17.30	21.38Y	26.53Y	3.38	9.58	48.33	50.26	66.99	82.79Y	102.74Y
Kyrgyz Republic....917	.26	.76	1.26	1.25	1.72	.78V	2.56V	.89	.59	.76	.43	.29	.39V	1.02V
Latvia....941	2.26	2.55	2.55	2.23	3.08	4.10V	5.27V	1.68	2.05	3.25	2.92	2.94	11.29V	11.61V
Lithuania....946	3.23	6.02	5.25	2.41	6.32	6.03V	5.55V	6.32	4.72	6.72	8.06	8.13	16.96V	24.24V
Macedonia, FYR....962	.10	.14	.10	.08	—	.12V	.15Y	.02	.22	.13	.11	.03	.19V	.24Y
Poland....964	1.67	2.67	4.47	6.55	25.30	31.68V	110.03V	17.99	24.66	39.52	44.76	65.07	154.19V	193.40V
Romania....968	37.91	56.71	90.23	98.92	111.67	124.96V	228.52V	93.44	90.36	97.94	164.14	257.33	471.13V	700.61V
Russia....922	246.97	238.86	308.41	353.34	347.48	293.89V	445.18V	143.95	153.40	182.92	212.27	268.20	729.82V	957.31V
Serbia & Montenegro....965	.31	.79	.35	.42	—	—Y	—Y	1.16	1.71	1.92	2.89	3.21	3.97Y	4.93Y
Slovak Republic....936	.40	1.20	1.16	1.70	—	24.90V	23.17V	5.99	8.86	8.66	11.45	14.91	22.99V	28.58V
Tajikistan....923	—	—	—	—	.15	.36V	.82V	—	—	.01	.01	.08	.12V	.11V
Turkey....186	2.26	4.12	7.24	12.26	24.66	28.50V	48.25V	19.68	32.73	48.25	69.09	93.03	118.11V	160.22V
Turkmenistan....925	2.74	.91	1.46	.55	.54	.67Y	.83Y	.30	.25	.13	.04	—	—Y	—Y
Ukraine....926	57.17	61.37	56.14	64.75	99.91	123.48Y	153.24Y	152.57	203.64	309.25	436.33	479.82	593.02Y	735.93Y
Uzbekistan....927	1.34	.66	1.75	2.41	1.89	2.34Y	2.90Y	.09	.16	.93	.72	1.22	1.51Y	1.88Y
Middle East....407	**3.1**	**5.6**	**7.4**	**12.2**	**11.4**	**15.2Y**	**23.5Y**	**5.1**	**5.8**	**6.3**	**10.2**	**15.5**	**15.3Y**	**21.3Y**
Egypt....469	—	—	.01	.84	.83	1.03Y	1.28Y	.66	.71	.72	1.79	4.21	5.20Y	6.45Y
Iran, I.R. of....429	—	—	—	.09	—	—Y	—Y	.05	.09	.22	.22	.52	.66Y	.79Y
Israel....436	.52	.49	.76	1.39	.69	.73V	1.00V	4.15	4.38	4.33	7.68	9.12	6.71V	11.33V
Jordan....439	1.36	2.13	1.81	1.78	.98	2.47V	7.48V	—	.08	—	.03	.15	.85V	.42V
Lebanon....446	.15	1.43	1.99	2.36	1.54	1.91Y	2.37Y	.05	.08	.26	.02	.36	.45Y	.56Y
Libya....672	—	—	—	.22	.25	.31Y	.40Y	—	—	—	—	—	—Y	—Y
Qatar....453	....	....	....	....	....	....	....	—	—	.01	—	—	—Y	—Y
Saudi Arabia....456	—	—	—	.07	—	—Y	—Y	—	.01	.02	.10	.24	.30Y	.36Y
Syrian Arab Republic....463	1.03	1.55	2.78	3.62	4.84	5.98Y	7.42Y	.06	.25	.14	.18	.38	.47Y	.59Y
United Arab Emirates....466	—	—	.03	1.77	2.23	2.75Y	3.56Y	.19	.23	.57	.22	.55	.70Y	.84Y
Yemen, Republic of....474	.01	.01	—	—	—	—Y	—Y	—	—	—	—	—	—Y	—Y
Western Hemisphere....207	**—**	**.1**	**—**	**—**	**3.9**	**5.8Y**	**8.5Y**	**12.1**	**14.8**	**9.0**	**9.4**	**17.6**	**59.5Y**	**40.4Y**
Argentina....213	—	—	—	—	—	.01V	—V	.17	.18	.66	.77	1.26	.91V	.40V
Bahamas, The....313	—	—	—	—	—	—Y	—Y	—	—	—	.01	.01	.01Y	.01Y
Barbados....316	—	—	—	—	—	—V	—Y	—	—	.01	—	.01	.02V	.03Y
Belize....339	....	....	....	....	....	....	....	—	—	.20	—	.01	.01Y	.01Y
Brazil....223	—	—	.03	.05	.30	1.30V	2.89V	11.01	13.12	6.57	5.97	12.42	57.43V	38.11V
Chile....228	—	—	—	—	—	—V	.01V	—	.13	.06	.35	.66	—V	.33V
Colombia....233	—	—	—	—	—	.01V	.01V	.06	.09	.08	.17	.16	—V	.11V
Costa Rica....238	—	—	—	—	—	—Y	—Y	.07	.03	.08	.09	.12	.15Y	.19Y
Dominica....321	....	....	....	....	....	....	....	—	—	—	.03	—	—Y	—Y
Dominican Republic....243	....	....	....	....	....	....	....	—	—	.02	.01	—	—Y	.01Y
Ecuador....248	—	.03	—	—	—	—V	—Y	.49	.82	1.02	1.44	2.07	—V	—Y
Grenada....328	....	....	....	....	....	....	....	.01	—	—	—	—	—Y	—Y
Guatemala....258	—	—	—	—	—	—Y	—Y	—	—	.03	—	.01	.01Y	.01Y
Honduras....268	....	....	....	....	....	....	....	.06	.03	—	—	.02	.03Y	.04Y
Jamaica....343	—	—	—	—	—	—V	—V	.04	—	—	—	—	—V	—V
Mexico....273	—	—	—	—	—	—Y	—Y	.11	.32	.25	.30	.34	.42Y	.52Y
Netherlands Antilles....353	....	....	....	....	....	....	....	—	—	—	—	.05	.07Y	.08Y
Panama....283	—	—	—	—	3.60	4.45Y	5.53Y	.03	.02	—	—	.02	.03Y	.03Y
Peru....293	—	—	—	—	—	—V	.02Y	.01	.01	—	.09	.16	—V	.07Y
St. Kitts and Nevis....361	—	.01	—	—	—	—Y	—Y	—	—	—	—	—	—Y	—Y
Suriname....366	....	....	....	....	....	....	....	—	—	—	.01	—	—Y	—Y
Uruguay....298	—	—	—	—	—	.01Y	.01Y	.04	.06	.01	.10	.33	.41Y	.51Y
Venezuela, Rep. Bol....299	—	—	.01	—	.01	.02Y	.02Y	—	—	—	.02	—	—Y	—Y
Western Hem. n.s....399	—	.02	—	—	—	—Y	—Y	.01	.02	—	—	—	—Y	—Y

Moldova 921

	Exports							Imports						
	2001	2002	2003	2004	2005	2006	2007	2001	2002	2003	2004	2005	2006	2007
	Millions of U.S. Dollars							*Millions of U.S. Dollars*						
Other Countries n.i.e. 910	—	—	—	—	—	—Y	—Y	.1	6.4	.1	—	—	.1Y	.1Y
Cuba 928	—	—	—	—	—	—Y	—Y	—	6.31	.06	—	—	—Y	—Y
North Korea 954	—	—	—	—	—	—Y	—Y	.05	.06	.03	.03	.04	.05Y	.06Y
Countries & Areas n.s. 898	—	—	—	1.3	2.5	3.0Y	3.8Y	—	—	—	.1	3.6	4.4Y	5.5Y
Memorandum Items														
European Union 998	140.86	171.26	211.03	296.26	289.17	453.73Y	659.32Y	317.51	356.77	505.35	581.11	752.47	1,143.29Y	1,502.88Y
Oil Exporting Ctys 999	.11	.05	.09	2.38	2.65	3.55Y	4.51Y	.49	.76	1.38	1.86	3.25	2.00Y	2.49Y
Non-Oil Develop.Ctys 201	410.63	449.69	562.01	668.19	764.77	802.46Y	1,228.67Y	584.96	684.20	939.94	1,240.75	1,604.14	2,593.50Y	3,449.95Y
PERCENT DISTRIBUTION														
Industrial Countries 101	27.4	30.1	28.8	31.8	27.0	34.9	29.8	34.4	33.4	32.9	29.7	29.7	25.7	25.9
Developing Countries 202	72.6	69.9	71.2	68.1	72.8	64.9	70.0	65.6	66.0	67.1	70.3	70.1	74.2	74.0
Africa 607	.1	.2	.1	.1	.3	.4	.3	.1	.2	.2	.2	.2	.1	.1
Asia 507	.1	.4	.2	.6	.1	.2	.3	2.9	3.2	3.6	4.1	5.3	2.2	2.2
Europe 170	71.9	68.4	69.9	66.1	70.9	62.6	67.6	60.7	60.7	62.3	64.8	63.1	69.7	70.4
Middle East 407	.5	.9	.9	1.2	1.1	1.2	1.3	.6	.6	.4	.6	.7	.4	.5
Western Hemisphere 207	—	—	—	—	.4	.5	.5	1.4	1.4	.6	.5	.8	1.7	.9
Other Countries n.i.e. 910	—	—	—	—	—	—	—	—	.6	—	—	—	—	—
ANNUAL PERCENT CHANGE														
World 001	19.9	13.9	22.7	24.7	7.1	17.8	41.7	14.9	16.3	35.1	26.1	29.7	52.6	33.3
Industrial Countries 101	26.6	25.4	17.4	37.5	–9.1	52.3	20.8	6.2	13.0	32.9	14.1	29.7	32.0	34.0
Developing Countries 202	17.5	9.5	25.0	19.3	14.4	5.0	53.0	20.1	17.0	37.4	32.0	29.4	61.5	33.0
Africa 607	–34.3	238.7	–46.1	75.5	198.0	30.8	24.1	16.7	106.0	56.4	24.3	54.2	–23.7	18.3
Asia 507	–80.7	311.5	–37.7	328.1	–79.6	99.6	91.4	51.8	28.4	51.1	46.8	66.7	–37.4	33.5
Europe 170	19.4	8.3	25.4	17.8	14.8	4.1	53.1	16.6	16.2	38.7	31.3	26.2	68.6	34.6
Middle East 407	–35.8	81.8	31.5	64.7	–6.5	33.6	54.9	39.8	13.1	7.7	63.3	51.6	–1.3	39.2
Western Hemisphere 207	445.4	....	–25.1	13.0	—	48.0	46.4	718.1	22.3	–39.4	4.0	88.7	237.1	–32.0
Other Countries n.i.e. 910	—	—	....	....	71.4	23.6	24.1	46.2	—	–98.6	–64.8	26.6	23.6	24.1

		Exports							Imports						
		2001	2002	2003	2004	2005	2006	2007	2001	2002	2003	2004	2005	2006	2007
		Millions of U.S. Dollars							Millions of U.S. Dollars						
IFS World Total		**521.4**	**524.0**	**615.9**	**869.7**	**1,064.9**	**1,542.8**	**1,889.0**	**637.7**	**690.7**	**801.0**	**1,021.1**	**1,184.3**	**1,485.6**	**2,117.3**
DOTS World Total	**001**	**521.4**	**524.0**	**615.9**	**851.9**	**1,053.8**	**1,453.9Y**	**1,672.1Y**	**637.7**	**690.7**	**801.4**	**1,011.3**	**1,160.3**	**1,773.7Y**	**2,350.0Y**
Industrial Countries	**101**	**209.4**	**224.2**	**231.9**	**386.1**	**427.8**	**348.3Y**	**377.6Y**	**143.9**	**140.8**	**202.7**	**234.2**	**243.6**	**381.8Y**	**425.1Y**
United States	111	144.52	165.72	142.94	152.88	150.05	106.07T	79.73V	14.87	23.36	23.54	46.85	36.04	42.48T	28.71V
Canada	156	.99	.56	.71	14.70	122.05	170.22T	179.46V	1.05	2.52	3.75	6.17	16.78	4.18T	10.40V
Australia	193	10.02	17.72	34.47	.09	14.25	11.00T	.51V	1.38	11.28	19.64	15.52	13.12	14.15T	14.95V
Japan	158	15.72	6.32	8.51	33.46	5.78	7.54T	14.85V	55.99	42.76	63.42	74.48	82.19	210.37T	169.31V
New Zealand	196	—	.01	—	—	.03	.02T	.08V	.03	.86	.92	1.87	1.31	1.18T	1.42V
Austria	122	.02	.03	—	—	.12	.34T	.64V	.72	.80	5.48	4.74	.87	2.33T	8.37V
Belgium	124	1.34	.23	.53	.72	1.10	.97T	9.27V	6.40	4.25	5.92	3.33	4.47	3.65T	7.76V
Cyprus	423	—	.02	—	—	—	—T	—V	—	.03	.02	.03	.16	1.69T	.52V
Denmark	128	—	—	—	—	.01	.04T	.18V	7.75	2.99	3.93	5.01	3.04	1.62T	3.78V
Finland	172	—	—	.02	.83	—	—T	.01V	3.87	3.44	2.66	2.47	2.79	3.40T	8.32V
France	132	.36	.14	1.87	14.88	.65	3.93T	12.39V	6.17	4.83	10.77	14.49	29.17	16.76T	18.69V
Germany	134	1.95	2.69	4.65	11.50	12.45	9.11T	11.81V	30.31	30.40	38.03	33.48	33.36	51.41T	82.73V
Greece	174	—	—	—	—	—	.04T	—V	.08	.08	.25	.32	.08	.51T	1.10V
Iceland	176	—	—	—	—	—	.01T	.08V	—	—	—	—	.10	.01T	.01V
Ireland	178	.24	—	.01	.02	.08	.09T	.30V	—	.03	.12	1.04	.29	.36T	.26V
Italy	136	16.86	8.59	9.05	17.33	24.59	28.37T	47.41V	3.44	2.75	3.26	3.01	3.27	8.51T	25.19V
Luxembourg	137	—	—	.03	—	.48	.01T	.01V	—	.05	.47	—	.07	.02T	—V
Netherlands	138	3.51	3.19	2.24	3.32	4.64	1.41T	6.70V	2.95	2.24	2.15	1.36	3.09	5.02T	6.34V
Norway	142	—	.01	.01	.11	.29	.12T	.07V	.16	.57	.24	.37	.58	.31T	.05V
Portugal	182	—	—	—	—	—	—T	—V	—	—	.01	.01	.02	.02T	.08V
Slovenia	961	—	—	—	—	—	—T	.04V	—	.08	.29	.31	.52	.93T	1.40V
Spain	184	—	.71	.10	.13	.03	.03T	1.03V	.14	.11	8.22	4.32	.89	2.42T	8.85V
Sweden	144	.01	.01	.10	.02	.02	.12T	.25V	.23	.93	1.32	6.73	2.05	3.36T	17.21V
Switzerland	146	1.39	.75	.52	2.12	4.19	1.85T	1.76V	4.55	3.65	4.38	4.40	1.04	1.03T	1.91V
United Kingdom	112	12.44	17.53	26.10	133.99	87.02	7.00T	10.99V	3.81	2.81	3.85	3.91	8.30	6.09T	7.75V
Developing Countries	**202**	**312.1**	**299.7**	**383.9**	**465.6**	**626.0**	**1,105.6Y**	**1,294.6Y**	**493.8**	**549.9**	**598.7**	**777.1**	**916.7**	**1,362.3Y**	**1,888.2Y**
Africa	**607**	**.1**	**—**	**1.7**	**—**	**.1**	**—Y**	**.3Y**	**—**	**.1**	**.9**	**—**	**.2**	**.1Y**	**.1Y**
Mauritius	684	—	—	—	—	—	—T	.07V	—	—	—	—	—	—T	—V
Morocco	686	.10	—	—	—	—	—T	—Y	—	—	—	—	—	—T	—Y
South Africa	199	—	—	.96	—	—	—T	.16V	—	.12	.16	.02	.19	—T	—V
Tanzania	738	—	—	.72	—	.09	—T	—Y	—	—	.72	—	—	—T	—Y
Tunisia	744	—	—	—	—	—	.02T	.02Y	—	.01	.01	.01	.01	.11T	.14Y
Asia	**507**	**258.8**	**243.3**	**329.9**	**436.4**	**573.4**	**1,052.2Y**	**1,227.6Y**	**216.6**	**279.3**	**288.3**	**352.8**	**412.7**	**681.8Y**	**1,051.2Y**
Afghanistan, I.S. of	512	—	.05	—	.01	.01	—T	—Y	—	.03	—	—	.05	—T	—Y
Bangladesh	513	—	.01	—	.01	.01	—T	—V	—	—	.01	—	.43	—T	—Y
China,P.R.: Mainland	924	231.59	217.30	284.24	407.07	507.07	1,040.92T	1,202.96V	120.14	139.47	172.35	238.17	317.85	521.67T	752.69V
China,P.R.:Hong Kong	532	6.66	3.23	2.78	.72	—	.47T	2.48V	16.01	28.22	23.91	15.39	—	7.49T	10.36V
Fiji	819	—	—	—	—	—	—T	—Y	—	—	—	—	.06	—T	—Y
India	534	.05	.01	.09	.64	.06	1.10T	1.37Y	1.38	1.05	.85	.62	1.49	1.05T	1.30Y
Indonesia	536	.01	.06	.01	—	.03	.13T	.28V	2.61	2.74	2.79	2.99	3.12	5.31T	6.30V
Korea	542	20.13	22.46	7.47	7.75	65.10	7.84T	18.84V	58.29	86.32	67.65	60.94	61.20	73.88T	186.73V
Malaysia	548	.06	—	.01	.09	—	.07T	.38V	2.79	2.99	4.68	5.50	6.69	4.61T	11.52V
Nepal	558	.11	.10	.09	.17	.22	.34T	.42Y	—	—	—	—	—	—T	—Y
Pakistan	564	—	—	.12	.01	.01	.01T	.02Y	.02	—	—	.01	.03	.04T	.05Y
Philippines	566	—	.02	—	.02	—	—T	—V	.11	.17	.53	2.16	1.06	.98T	.48V
Singapore	576	.20	.05	35.04	19.88	.61	.86T	.26V	10.37	11.23	10.38	14.94	15.26	18.45T	42.68V
Sri Lanka	524	—	—	—	—	—	—T	—Y	.02	.04	.07	.23	.28	.31T	.39Y
Taiwan Province of China	528	.01	.01	.01	.02	.21	.25T	.31Y	1.96	4.40	1.92	4.97	2.14	27.86T	34.57Y
Thailand	578	—	—	—	—	.03	.24T	.27V	.39	.65	1.44	4.68	.85	7.05T	4.18V
Vietnam	582	—	.02	.02	—	.01	—T	—V	2.48	2.02	1.73	2.21	2.18	13.10T	—V
Europe	**170**	**49.2**	**52.5**	**49.4**	**26.0**	**49.7**	**46.4Y**	**57.2Y**	**276.3**	**269.0**	**306.5**	**415.1**	**489.4**	**646.9Y**	**828.3Y**
Armenia	911	—	—	—	—	—	—T	.01V	—	—	—	—	—	—T	.02V
Azerbaijan	912	—	—	—	—	.02	.09T	—V	.11	.10	—	—	—	12.88T	.03V
Belarus	913	—	—	.01	—	.01	.06T	—V	7.81	5.62	2.96	5.50	5.07	5.62T	4.21V
Bulgaria	918	—	—	—	.01	.12	.06T	.01V	1.73	.94	1.50	1.71	1.63	3.17T	2.23V
Croatia	960	.15	—	—	—	—	—T	—V	—	—	—	—	—	—T	—V
Czech Republic	935	.01	.07	.05	.04	.16	.49T	.34V	7.09	3.60	5.77	4.55	4.81	6.50T	11.43V
Estonia	939	—	—	—	—	—	—T	—V	—	.01	.19	.81	1.53	.20T	.15V
Georgia	915	—	—	—	—	.03	—T	—Y	.32	.39	.51	.57	.40	.30T	.64Y
Hungary	944	—	—	.01	.04	.01	.03T	.04V	1.42	1.51	3.82	7.01	3.29	3.84T	3.87V
Kazakhstan	916	1.09	.83	2.79	.22	.53	.20T	.25Y	21.33	7.19	4.92	26.64	38.84	30.55T	37.91Y
Kyrgyz Republic	917	—	—	.01	—	.11	.22T	1.36V	.99	.93	.97	1.30	1.05	11.75T	1.92V
Latvia	941	—	—	—	—	—	—T	.10V	.29	.34	1.42	4.80	1.59	.61T	1.05V
Lithuania	946	—	—	—	—	—	—T	—V	.14	.07	.19	.49	.45	.38T	4.42V
Moldova	921	—	.08	.12	.24	.48	.36T	.44Y	—	—	—	—	.01	.01T	.01Y
Poland	964	2.89	.11	.02	.08	.14	.02T	.12V	5.27	5.69	8.05	8.46	9.29	12.81T	26.41V
Romania	968	—	—	—	.02	.07	.46T	.38V	.01	.13	.25	.13	.07	.12T	.48V
Russia	922	44.94	47.99	41.22	18.10	26.00	35.59T	43.83V	225.96	237.63	265.39	336.55	400.02	526.88T	691.74V
Slovak Republic	936	.03	.03	.01	—	.01	—T	—V	.11	.10	.10	.19	.09	.64T	.97V

	Exports							Imports						
	2001	2002	2003	2004	2005	2006	2007	2001	2002	2003	2004	2005	2006	2007
	Millions of U.S. Dollars							Millions of U.S. Dollars						
Tajikistan 923	—	—	—	—	—	.05T	.09V	.01	—	—	—	—	—T	—V
Turkey 186	.08	.39	1.45	.56	.52	.70T	.29V	1.23	1.22	1.23	1.48	2.27	6.15T	10.47V
Ukraine 926	.03	3.00	3.60	3.02	6.75	5.05T	6.27Y	2.34	3.45	9.21	14.83	18.81	24.17T	30.00Y
Uzbekistan 927	—	.04	.06	3.65	14.78	2.98T	3.70Y	.02	.09	.06	.08	.22	.27T	.33Y
Yugoslavia n.s. 966	—	—	—	—	—	—T	—Y	.15	—	—	—	—	—T	—Y
Middle East 407	**2.8**	**2.3**	**2.7**	**2.8**	**2.0**	**2.3Y**	**2.9Y**	**.7**	**.4**	**1.8**	**4.7**	**8.6**	**5.7Y**	**7.1Y**
Egypt 469	—	—	—	.18	.05	—T	—Y	.04	—	.03	—	.05	.03T	.04Y
Iran, I.R. of 429	—	—	.08	.01	—	—T	—Y	....	....	....	....	....	....	....
Israel 436	—	—	.09	.01	—	—T	—Y	.68	.40	.77	4.29	8.13	4.79T	5.94Y
Jordan 439	—	.07	—	—	—	—T	—V	.01	—	.03	—	—	—T	—V
Kuwait 443	.44	.56	.79	.65	.91	1.11T	1.43Y	—	—	.01	.02	.05	.54T	.66Y
Lebanon 446	.78	.58	.52	.78	.15	.03T	.03Y	—	—	—	—	—	—T	—Y
Qatar 453	—	.09	.41	.23	.12	.14T	.18Y	—	—	.41	—	—	—T	—Y
Saudi Arabia 456	.03	.38	.31	.55	.59	.73T	.95Y	—	—	—	—	—	.07T	.08Y
Syrian Arab Republic 463	.05	.37	.32	.18	.13	.24T	.30Y	—	—	.32	—	—	—T	—Y
United Arab Emirates 466	1.45	.25	.19	.16	.05	—T	—Y	.01	.01	.25	.41	.37	.28T	.34Y
Western Hemisphere 207	**1.2**	**1.6**	**.2**	**.5**	**.8**	**4.7Y**	**6.6Y**	**.2**	**1.0**	**1.1**	**4.4**	**5.7**	**27.9Y**	**1.5Y**
Argentina 213	—	—	.20	.39	.24	.04T	—V	—	—	.83	2.10	3.70	21.36T	.99V
Aruba 314	.07	—	—	—	—	—T	—Y	—	—	—	.01	—	.01T	.01Y
Brazil 223	—	—	—	—	—	.04T	—V	.18	.79	.22	1.72	1.68	1.14T	—V
Chile 228	—	.57	—	.02	.09	.03T	.03V	—	.14	.02	.04	—	—T	—V
Colombia 233	—	.03	—	.04	.31	.01T	—V	—	—	—	—	—	4.96T	—V
Dominica 321	—	—	—	—	—	—T	—Y	—	—	—	.01	—	—T	—Y
Ecuador 248	....	....	....	....	....	....	....	—	—	—	.02	—	.08T	.10Y
Mexico 273	1.09	.98	.04	—	.13	4.59T	6.53V	—	.07	.04	.19	.10	.01T	.03V
Panama 283	—	—	—	—	—	—T	—Y	—	—	—	.01	.25	.29T	.36Y
Paraguay 288	....	....	....	....	....	....	....	—	—	.01	.35	—	.01T	.01Y
Peru 293	—	—	—	.03	—	—T	.05Y	—	—	—	—	—	—T	—Y
Other Countries n.i.e. 910	**—**	**—**	**.1**	**.2**	**—**	**—Y**	**—Y**	**—**	**—**	**.1**	**—**	**—**	**29.5Y**	**36.6Y**
North Korea 954	.02	.03	.11	.18	—	—T	—Y	.02	.02	.06	.02	.04	29.50T	36.61Y
Memorandum Items														
European Union 998	39.66	33.35	44.80	182.90	131.51	52.03Y	101.62Y	80.19	67.14	106.30	110.90	113.48	133.09Y	246.64Y
Oil Exporting Ctys 999	1.93	1.34	1.80	1.60	1.70	2.12Y	2.86Y	2.62	2.75	3.46	3.42	3.54	6.21Y	7.38Y
Non-Oil Develop.Ctys 201	310.12	298.40	382.09	464.01	624.29	1,103.47Y	1,291.73Y	491.20	547.13	595.22	773.66	913.12	1,356.14Y	1,880.84Y
PERCENT DISTRIBUTION														
Industrial Countries 101	**40.2**	**42.8**	**37.6**	**45.3**	**40.6**	**24.0**	**22.6**	**22.6**	**20.4**	**25.3**	**23.2**	**21.0**	**21.5**	**18.1**
Developing Countries 202	**59.8**	**57.2**	**62.3**	**54.7**	**59.4**	**76.0**	**77.4**	**77.4**	**79.6**	**74.7**	**76.8**	**79.0**	**76.8**	**80.4**
Africa 607	**—**	**—**	**.3**	**—**	**—**	**—**	**—**	**—**	**—**	**.1**	**—**	**—**	**—**	**—**
Asia 507	**49.6**	**46.4**	**53.6**	**51.2**	**54.4**	**72.4**	**73.4**	**34.0**	**40.4**	**36.0**	**34.9**	**35.6**	**38.4**	**44.7**
Europe 170	**9.4**	**10.0**	**8.0**	**3.1**	**4.7**	**3.2**	**3.4**	**43.3**	**38.9**	**38.3**	**41.0**	**42.2**	**36.5**	**35.2**
Middle East 407	**.5**	**.4**	**.4**	**.3**	**.2**	**.2**	**.2**	**.1**	**.1**	**.2**	**.5**	**.7**	**.3**	**.3**
Western Hemisphere 207	**.2**	**.3**	**—**	**.1**	**.1**	**.3**	**.4**	**—**	**.1**	**.1**	**.4**	**.5**	**1.6**	**.1**
Other Countries n.i.e. 910	**—**	**—**	**—**	**—**	**—**	**—**	**—**	**—**	**—**	**—**	**—**	**—**	**1.7**	**1.6**
ANNUAL PERCENT CHANGE														
World 001	**–2.7**	**.5**	**17.5**	**38.3**	**23.7**	**38.0**	**15.0**	**3.8**	**8.3**	**16.0**	**26.2**	**14.7**	**52.9**	**32.5**
Industrial Countries 101	**5.8**	**7.1**	**3.4**	**66.5**	**10.8**	**–18.6**	**8.4**	**–16.4**	**–2.1**	**43.9**	**15.6**	**4.0**	**56.7**	**11.3**
Developing Countries 202	**–7.7**	**–3.9**	**28.1**	**21.3**	**34.4**	**76.6**	**17.1**	**11.7**	**11.4**	**8.9**	**29.8**	**18.0**	**48.6**	**38.6**
Africa 607	**—**	**—**	**....**	**–99.8**	**—**	**–77.6**	**—**	**—**	**....**	**589.8**	**–96.9**	**617.6**	**–41.3**	**23.4**
Asia 507	**–10.0**	**–6.0**	**35.6**	**32.3**	**31.4**	**83.5**	**16.7**	**5.3**	**29.0**	**3.2**	**22.4**	**17.0**	**65.2**	**54.2**
Europe 170	**—**	**6.7**	**–6.0**	**–47.4**	**91.4**	**–6.8**	**23.4**	**17.6**	**–2.6**	**14.0**	**35.4**	**17.9**	**32.2**	**28.0**
Middle East 407	**511.1**	**–16.4**	**18.1**	**1.5**	**–27.3**	**12.5**	**28.9**	**–50.3**	**–44.6**	**345.7**	**158.6**	**82.1**	**–33.6**	**23.6**
Western Hemisphere 207	**73.1**	**36.2**	**–84.8**	**95.2**	**62.3**	**519.3**	**40.4**	**91.5**	**455.6**	**11.1**	**300.0**	**29.2**	**385.3**	**–94.6**
Other Countries n.i.e. 910	**....**	**50.0**	**257.3**	**63.5**	**–99.0**	**16.7**	**24.1**	**....**	**—**	**179.0**	**–69.9**	**108.9**	**—**	**24.1**

	Exports 2001	2002	2003	2004	2005	2006	2007	Imports 2001	2002	2003	2004	2005	2006	2007
	Millions of U.S. Dollars							Millions of U.S. Dollars						
IFS World Total	**7,144**	**7,849**	**8,778**	**9,917**	**11,185**	**12,744**	**14,665**	**11,038**	**11,864**	**14,250**	**17,849**	**20,805**	**23,977**	**31,715**
DOTS World Total 001	**7,233**	**7,838**	**8,764**	**9,911**	**10,643**	**13,270Y**	**15,922Y**	**11,471**	**11,833**	**14,197**	**17,807**	**20,336**	**25,088Y**	**32,618Y**
Industrial Countries 101	**5,919**	**6,438**	**7,259**	**8,024**	**8,232**	**9,196Y**	**10,900Y**	**7,240**	**7,763**	**9,615**	**11,334**	**11,891**	**15,810Y**	**20,372Y**
United States 111	277	241	246	386	281	508V	604V	408	509	577	735	685	963V	1,477V
Canada 156	30	31	31	46	71	150V	205V	225	160	138	158	210	164V	257V
Australia 193	16	19	14	19	35	37V	39V	27	50	8	30	33	28V	17V
Japan 158	212	279	167	73	112	178V	290V	167	207	296	358	358	273V	408V
New Zealand 196	60	44	51	55	59	97V	104V	13	16	12	13	23	32V	26V
Austria 122	24	30	46	47	45	37V	44V	15	23	49	63	69	111V	103V
Belgium 124	—	—	—	—	—	413V	468V	—	—	—	—	—	747V	800V
Belgium-Luxembourg n.s. 127	181	161	193	233	305	—Y	—Y	161	241	278	326	355	—Y	—Y
Cyprus 423	1	—	—	1	1	—V	—V	5	1	3	1	1	1V	1V
Denmark 128	11	6	5	3	4	7V	4V	30	50	54	55	46	34V	47V
Finland 172	7	7	7	7	13	15V	20V	53	77	87	134	121	106V	156V
France 132	2,408	2,642	3,032	3,333	3,230	2,715V	3,032V	2,763	2,428	2,920	3,287	3,704	4,408V	5,251V
Germany 134	336	327	344	339	320	470V	497V	568	628	738	1,052	964	1,498V	1,927V
Greece 174	30	37	32	33	40	44V	80V	16	22	37	45	39	62V	71V
Iceland 176	—	—	—	—	1	3V	3V	—	1	1	1	—	1V	3V
Ireland 178	18	26	27	21	21	14V	15V	29	56	142	171	162	121V	115V
Italy 136	409	424	451	462	553	618V	778V	571	687	1,012	1,163	1,245	1,587V	2,193V
Luxembourg 137	—	—	—	—	—	—V	1V	—	—	—	—	—	9V	10V
Malta 181	1	4	3	2	2	3V	4V	—	—	2	8	8	4V	4V
Netherlands 138	152	168	219	228	313	251V	328V	178	194	338	296	395	719V	1,323V
Norway 142	18	15	20	26	23	45V	59V	26	10	21	39	61	58V	24V
Portugal 182	47	62	96	102	107	83V	106V	65	101	162	209	194	227V	301V
Slovenia 961	1	1	2	2	1	9V	10V	2	4	6	7	7	11V	19V
Spain 184	1,045	1,227	1,553	1,732	1,915	2,730V	3,377V	1,054	1,376	1,763	2,170	2,236	3,498V	4,437V
Sweden 144	7	5	9	6	9	10V	27V	143	199	199	191	308	312V	468V
Switzerland 146	41	61	74	110	112	123V	66V	120	142	213	235	207	249V	247V
United Kingdom 112	588	620	638	757	661	636V	738V	601	582	559	588	461	586V	687V
Developing Countries 202	**1,262**	**1,336**	**1,422**	**1,777**	**2,160**	**3,763Y**	**4,637Y**	**4,230**	**4,050**	**4,565**	**6,413**	**8,365**	**9,180Y**	**12,123Y**
Africa 607	**215**	**275**	**296**	**355**	**417**	**517Y**	**646Y**	**486**	**473**	**504**	**564**	**868**	**912Y**	**1,159Y**
Algeria 612	9	21	24	41	50	62Y	81Y	193	160	175	161	347	436Y	526Y
Angola 614	7	8	7	15	14	17Y	21Y	—	—	—	—	—	—Y	—Y
Benin 638	3	4	8	8	14	17Y	21Y	7	9	4	3	3	4Y	5Y
Burkina Faso 748	4	5	7	8	14	17Y	21Y	4	3	3	6	6	7Y	9Y
Cameroon 622	5	7	7	6	6	7Y	9Y	11	12	13	17	13	16Y	19Y
Cape Verde 624	—	—	1	1	1	1Y	1Y	—	—	—	—	2	2Y	2Y
Central African Rep. 626	—	—	—	1	1	1Y	2Y	—	—	—	1	1	1Y	2Y
Chad 628	—	1	1	1	2	2Y	3Y	3	2	5	2	2	2Y	3Y
Comoros 632	1	1	1	1	1	2Y	2Y	—	—	—	—	—	—Y	—Y
Congo, Dem. Rep. of 636	3	5	7	9	11	13Y	17Y	—	—	—	2	3	3Y	4Y
Congo, Republic of 634	8	10	8	11	14	18Y	22Y	4	4	5	5	5	6Y	8Y
Côte d'Ivoire 662	15	16	22	22	23	30V	37Y	15	15	19	19	13	11V	14Y
Equatorial Guinea 642	4	6	10	12	9	11Y	13Y	3	2	2	2	3	4Y	5Y
Ethiopia 644	—	9	—	—	—	—Y	—Y	2	2	2	2	1	1Y	1Y
Gabon 646	8	10	10	9	11	14Y	17Y	21	20	27	38	27	33Y	42Y
Gambia, The 648	4	6	7	7	9	11Y	14Y	—	—	—	—	—	—Y	—Y
Ghana 652	4	9	9	13	13	16Y	20Y	1	1	1	2	2	2Y	3Y
Guinea 656	8	9	8	9	18	23Y	28Y	8	6	6	7	7	9Y	11Y
Guinea-Bissau 654	1	1	1	—	1	1Y	1Y	—	—	—	—	—	—Y	—Y
Kenya 664	1	2	1	2	9	11Y	14Y	—	—	1	1	1	1Y	2Y
Liberia 668	3	3	4	4	5	6Y	8Y	1	2	1	1	2	2Y	3Y
Madagascar 674	1	2	1	1	2	3Y	3Y	1	1	2	3	4	4Y	5Y
Malawi 676	—	—	—	—	—	—Y	—Y	1	3	2	2	1	1Y	1Y
Mali 678	13	13	13	12	14	18Y	22Y	2	1	4	5	6	7Y	9Y
Mauritania 682	17	24	24	22	22	27Y	33Y	—	1	—	2	1	1Y	1Y
Mauritius 684	3	2	3	3	3	4V	5V	—	1	1	—	—	—V	—V
Namibia 728	—	—	—	—	—	—Y	—Y	—	1	—	—	—	—Y	—Y
Niger 692	1	1	5	5	5	6Y	7Y	—	—	—	—	—	—Y	—Y
Nigeria 694	18	18	22	21	26	32Y	41Y	6	4	3	38	6	8Y	9Y
Rwanda 714	—	—	—	—	—	—Y	—Y	—	—	—	—	—	1Y	1Y
St. Helena 856	—	—	—	—	—	—Y	—Y	—	—	—	—	2	2Y	3Y
Senegal 722	16	21	25	30	47	53V	66Y	1	5	3	6	7	30V	37Y
Sierra Leone 724	2	1	2	2	3	4Y	5Y	1	—	1	—	—	—Y	—Y
South Africa 199	1	6	5	7	8	7V	9V	145	152	139	144	263	177V	261V
Sudan 732	—	—	1	—	1	1V	—V	—	—	—	—	—	—V	—V
Tanzania 738	—	—	—	—	—	—Y	—Y	—	1	1	1	2	2Y	2Y
Togo 742	2	5	10	9	14	17Y	21Y	5	3	5	5	10	13Y	16Y
Tunisia 744	53	49	43	60	46	64V	80Y	45	55	71	85	125	119V	148Y
Uganda 746	—	—	—	—	—	—Y	—Y	1	4	4	2	3	4Y	5Y
Zimbabwe 698	—	—	—	—	—	—V	—Y	2	3	1	1	—	—V	—Y

	Exports							Imports						
	2001	2002	2003	2004	2005	2006	2007	2001	2002	2003	2004	2005	2006	2007
	Millions of U.S. Dollars							*Millions of U.S. Dollars*						
Asia.......... 507	**409**	**405**	**439**	**574**	**715**	**1,701Y**	**1,941Y**	**666**	**749**	**1,120**	**1,408**	**1,783**	**2,772Y**	**3,739Y**
Bangladesh.......... 513	4	—	—	—	1	—V	7V	1	2	1	2	3	4Y	6Y
China,P.R.: Mainland.......... 924	35	26	66	50	71	327V	384V	278	341	486	744	1,059	1,727V	2,379V
China,P.R.:Hong Kong.......... 532	1	3	3	2	3	181V	201V	27	24	38	30	30	72V	106V
India.......... 534	244	259	273	338	434	536Y	665Y	67	87	164	123	151	186Y	231Y
Indonesia.......... 536	6	12	17	6	24	52V	25V	37	36	61	54	49	60V	52V
Korea.......... 542	12	29	27	40	35	79V	96V	128	122	161	225	266	245V	429V
Malaysia.......... 548	—	—	1	—	3	31V	23V	26	25	38	39	48	53V	65V
New Caledonia.......... 839	1	1	1	1	1	1Y	1Y	—	—	—	—	—	—Y	—Y
Pakistan.......... 564	43	27	19	79	103	127Y	158Y	7	7	12	13	14	18Y	22Y
Philippines.......... 566	—	—	—	—	—	4V	—V	2	5	8	7	4	2V	2V
Singapore.......... 576	35	8	2	17	1	270V	278V	8	6	23	21	14	269V	253V
Sri Lanka.......... 524	—	1	3	3	4	1V	2V	2	1	1	3	3	2V	2V
Taiwan Province of China.......... 528	1	6	5	15	4	31V	36V	58	64	91	90	75	81V	87V
Thailand.......... 578	27	34	22	23	31	60V	64V	23	26	31	45	50	53V	106V
Vietnam.......... 582	—	—	—	—	—	—V	—V	3	4	6	12	16	—V	—V
Europe.......... 170	**245**	**209**	**205**	**252**	**359**	**600Y**	**773Y**	**1,234**	**886**	**1,248**	**1,971**	**2,384**	**1,583Y**	**2,422Y**
Albania.......... 914	—	—	—	—	1	1V	1V	—	—	—	—	—	—V	—V
Azerbaijan.......... 912	—	—	—	—	2	1V	1V	—	—	—	—	—	—V	—V
Belarus.......... 913	—	—	—	—	2	11V	11V	8	16	21	—	—	4V	6V
Bosnia & Herzegovina.......... 963	—	—	—	—	—	—Y	1Y	2	1	1	1	1	2Y	2Y
Bulgaria.......... 918	14	11	8	13	19	38V	57V	8	3	15	25	10	10V	21V
Croatia.......... 960	14	23	9	12	12	26V	38V	11	8	2	3	7	3V	5V
Czech Republic.......... 935	1	3	2	4	9	3V	3V	17	17	29	44	58	45V	169V
Estonia.......... 939	—	—	—	—	—	—V	2V	3	3	2	2	1	3V	6V
Georgia.......... 915	—	—	—	—	1	—V	—Y	—	—	6	1	—	—V	—Y
Gibraltar.......... 823	—	13	10	—	—	—Y	—Y	—	—	—	—	—	—Y	—Y
Hungary.......... 944	1	1	2	2	1	2V	4V	13	36	35	36	63	67V	80V
Kazakhstan.......... 916	—	—	—	—	—	—Y	—Y	1	4	3	2	—	—Y	—Y
Latvia.......... 941	—	—	2	3	2	3V	4V	1	2	—	11	3	2V	26V
Lithuania.......... 946	9	10	12	19	27	48V	38V	1	1	1	9	4	4V	30V
Macedonia, FYR.......... 962	—	—	—	—	—	—V	1Y	—	—	—	—	—	—V	—Y
Moldova.......... 921	—	—	—	—	—	—Y	—Y	4	2	2	15	8	10Y	13Y
Poland.......... 964	14	20	25	33	35	51V	75V	54	72	72	121	142	151V	169V
Romania.......... 968	6	6	9	11	13	18V	19V	38	54	42	42	67	80V	134V
Russia.......... 922	54	62	73	87	138	209V	303V	371	356	693	1,045	1,375	289V	580V
Slovak Republic.......... 936	2	2	3	2	3	26V	33V	2	4	8	12	19	27V	39V
Tajikistan.......... 923	—	—	—	—	—	—V	—V	1	1	—	2	1	—V	—V
Turkey.......... 186	35	56	49	64	90	158V	180V	112	150	210	363	398	607V	794V
Ukraine.......... 926	—	1	2	1	3	3Y	4Y	147	153	105	238	225	278Y	345Y
Uzbekistan.......... 927	—	—	—	—	—	—Y	—Y	3	2	1	1	2	3Y	3Y
Europe n.s.......... 884	94	—	—	—	—	—Y	—Y	437	—	—	—	—	—Y	—Y
Middle East.......... 407	**238**	**223**	**234**	**239**	**294**	**364Y**	**468Y**	**1,384**	**1,457**	**1,086**	**1,595**	**2,452**	**3,091Y**	**3,744Y**
Bahrain.......... 419	—	1	1	1	1	1Y	1Y	4	5	10	16	31	38Y	47Y
Egypt.......... 469	28	20	24	24	23	28Y	35Y	47	55	123	97	160	198Y	246Y
Iran, I.R. of.......... 429	26	26	31	39	39	48Y	63Y	282	290	45	277	565	710Y	857Y
Iraq.......... 433	35	14	1	—	—	—Y	1Y	411	273	—	67	63	79Y	95Y
Israel.......... 436	—	—	—	—	—	2V	2V	—	—	—	—	—	12V	18V
Jordan.......... 439	10	7	15	14	16	17V	24V	2	2	2	2	5	4V	7V
Kuwait.......... 443	3	2	3	4	6	8Y	10Y	6	11	13	22	26	33Y	40Y
Lebanon.......... 446	6	9	13	15	18	22Y	28Y	7	7	7	9	14	17Y	21Y
Libya.......... 672	58	68	46	33	19	24Y	31Y	69	83	60	46	70	88Y	106Y
Oman.......... 449	1	2	1	1	4	5Y	6Y	—	—	1	2	3	3Y	4Y
Qatar.......... 453	—	—	1	1	2	5V	6Y	2	6	9	23	21	29V	35Y
Saudi Arabia.......... 456	48	47	60	59	85	104Y	135Y	521	693	717	955	1,376	1,730Y	2,087Y
Syrian Arab Republic.......... 463	14	16	23	29	43	53Y	65Y	13	10	17	9	16	20Y	25Y
United Arab Emirates.......... 466	6	7	9	14	29	36Y	46Y	21	21	81	54	98	123Y	149Y
Yemen, Republic of.......... 474	2	4	5	6	9	12Y	14Y	1	—	—	17	4	5Y	6Y
Western Hemisphere.......... 207	**155**	**224**	**247**	**357**	**376**	**582Y**	**809Y**	**460**	**484**	**608**	**875**	**878**	**821Y**	**1,059Y**
Antigua and Barbuda.......... 311	11	—	—	—	—	—Y	—Y	—	—	—	—	—	—Y	—Y
Argentina.......... 213	5	9	3	4	18	58V	51V	146	124	211	252	258	256V	388V
Bolivia.......... 218	—	—	—	—	—	—Y	—Y	—	1	—	—	—	—Y	—Y
Brazil.......... 223	80	142	182	261	259	331V	532V	271	303	268	447	453	431V	482V
Chile.......... 228	1	1	1	1	1	3V	1V	10	10	16	14	23	14V	3V
Colombia.......... 233	1	2	1	2	6	7V	12V	2	2	12	39	9	9V	39V
Costa Rica.......... 238	—	—	—	—	—	—Y	—Y	1	1	1	1	2	3Y	3Y
Dominican Republic.......... 243	—	1	1	1	1	1Y	1Y	2	1	1	1	1	1Y	1Y
Ecuador.......... 248	—	—	—	—	—	—V	—Y	1	—	—	—	2	1V	1Y
El Salvador.......... 253	1	3	—	1	13	—V	1V	—	—	—	—	—	—V	—V
Guatemala.......... 258	—	—	—	—	—	—Y	—Y	—	—	6	—	1	1Y	1Y
Haiti.......... 263	—	—	—	1	1	1Y	1Y	—	—	—	—	—	—Y	—Y
Honduras.......... 268	—	—	—	1	1	1Y	1Y	—	—	1	—	—	—Y	—Y
Mexico.......... 273	43	51	48	63	48	147V	173V	7	11	13	7	13	4V	7V
Netherlands Antilles.......... 353	—	—	—	7	—	—Y	—Y	—	—	1	—	21	26Y	32Y
Panama.......... 283	—	—	2	3	2	—V	—V	3	8	5	7	2	—V	—V
Paraguay.......... 288	—	—	—	—	—	—V	—Y	3	—	20	63	34	—V	—Y
Peru.......... 293	2	4	4	2	4	7V	7Y	2	1	1	2	2	5V	13Y

	Exports							Imports						
	2001	2002	2003	2004	2005	2006	2007	2001	2002	2003	2004	2005	2006	2007
	Millions of U.S. Dollars							*Millions of U.S. Dollars*						
Trinidad and Tobago.................... 369	—	—	—	1	3	3Y	4Y	—	—	3	—	—	—Y	—Y
Uruguay.................................... 298	4	3	—	3	10	13Y	16Y	2	10	15	24	42	52Y	64Y
Venezuela, Rep. Bol..................... 299	7	7	4	6	9	8V	7V	8	10	34	18	16	20V	24Y
Other Countries n.i.e................ 910	**—**	**—**	**—**	**—**	**1**	**1Y**	**2Y**	**—**	**—**	**1**	**2**	**3**	**4Y**	**4Y**
Cuba.. 928	—	—	—	—	1	1Y	2Y	—	—	1	2	3	4Y	4Y
Countries & Areas n.s............... 898	**—**	**—**	**—**	**—**	**83**	**103Y**	**127Y**	**—**	**—**	**—**	**—**	**5**	**6Y**	**7Y**
Special Categories.................. 899	**52**	**64**	**83**	**110**	**167**	**206Y**	**256Y**	**—**	**19**	**16**	**58**	**73**	**90Y**	**111Y**
Memorandum Items														
European Union........................... 998	5,294	5,785	6,703	7,372	7,614	8,188Y	9,688Y	6,345	6,802	8,495	9,999	10,604	14,340Y	18,431Y
Oil Exporting Ctys........................ 999	216	225	220	224	293	384Y	451Y	1,556	1,587	1,200	1,717	2,640	3,319Y	3,983Y
Non-Oil Develop.Ctys................... 201	1,046	1,111	1,203	1,554	1,867	3,380Y	4,186Y	2,675	2,463	3,366	4,696	5,726	5,860Y	8,139Y
PERCENT DISTRIBUTION														
Industrial Countries................. 101	**81.8**	**82.1**	**82.8**	**81.0**	**77.3**	**69.3**	**68.5**	**63.1**	**65.6**	**67.7**	**63.6**	**58.5**	**63.0**	**62.5**
Developing Countries............. 202	**17.4**	**17.0**	**16.2**	**17.9**	**20.3**	**28.4**	**29.1**	**36.9**	**34.2**	**32.2**	**36.0**	**41.1**	**36.6**	**37.2**
Africa..................................... 607	**3.0**	**3.5**	**3.4**	**3.6**	**3.9**	**3.9**	**4.1**	**4.2**	**4.0**	**3.6**	**3.2**	**4.3**	**3.6**	**3.6**
Asia....................................... 507	**5.7**	**5.2**	**5.0**	**5.8**	**6.7**	**12.8**	**12.2**	**5.8**	**6.3**	**7.9**	**7.9**	**8.8**	**11.0**	**11.5**
Europe.................................... 170	**3.4**	**2.7**	**2.3**	**2.5**	**3.4**	**4.5**	**4.9**	**10.8**	**7.5**	**8.8**	**11.1**	**11.7**	**6.3**	**7.4**
Middle East............................ 407	**3.3**	**2.8**	**2.7**	**2.4**	**2.8**	**2.7**	**2.9**	**12.1**	**12.3**	**7.6**	**9.0**	**12.1**	**12.3**	**11.5**
Western Hemisphere.............. 207	**2.1**	**2.9**	**2.8**	**3.6**	**3.5**	**4.4**	**5.1**	**4.0**	**4.1**	**4.3**	**4.9**	**4.3**	**3.3**	**3.2**
ANNUAL PERCENT CHANGE														
World...................................... 001	**–2.5**	**8.4**	**11.8**	**13.1**	**7.4**	**24.7**	**20.0**	**–.5**	**3.2**	**20.0**	**25.4**	**14.2**	**23.4**	**30.0**
Industrial Countries................. 101	**–4.8**	**8.8**	**12.7**	**10.5**	**2.6**	**11.7**	**18.5**	**–8.8**	**7.2**	**23.9**	**17.9**	**4.9**	**33.0**	**28.9**
Developing Countries............. 202	**7.2**	**5.9**	**6.5**	**25.0**	**21.5**	**74.2**	**23.2**	**17.8**	**–4.3**	**12.7**	**40.5**	**30.4**	**9.7**	**32.1**
Africa..................................... 607	**7.8**	**28.1**	**7.7**	**19.8**	**17.6**	**23.9**	**25.0**	**13.8**	**–2.7**	**6.6**	**11.8**	**53.9**	**5.1**	**27.1**
Asia....................................... 507	**–3.8**	**–.9**	**8.5**	**30.7**	**24.4**	**138.1**	**14.1**	**4.1**	**12.5**	**49.5**	**25.7**	**26.6**	**55.5**	**34.9**
Europe.................................... 170	**23.2**	**–14.7**	**–1.7**	**22.8**	**42.1**	**67.2**	**28.9**	**108.7**	**–28.1**	**40.8**	**57.9**	**21.0**	**–33.6**	**53.0**
Middle East............................ 407	**8.7**	**–6.2**	**5.0**	**2.0**	**22.8**	**23.9**	**28.6**	**–11.5**	**5.3**	**–25.5**	**47.0**	**53.7**	**26.1**	**21.1**
Western Hemisphere.............. 207	**15.1**	**44.2**	**10.4**	**44.4**	**5.3**	**54.7**	**39.2**	**25.3**	**5.2**	**25.6**	**43.9**	**.4**	**–6.5**	**28.9**
Other Countries n.i.e................ 910	**—**	**–88.4**	**–54.4**	**72.7**	**—**	**23.6**	**24.1**	**–80.6**	**511.1**	**31.7**	**152.9**	**79.0**	**23.6**	**24.1**

		Exports							Imports						
		2001	2002	2003	2004	2005	2006	2007	2001	2002	2003	2004	2005	2006	2007
		Millions of U.S. Dollars							*Millions of U.S. Dollars*						
IFS World Total		**703.0**	**810.0**	**1,045.0**	**1,504.0**	**1,783.0**	**2,381.1**	**2,650.0**	**1,063.0**	**1,543.0**	**1,753.0**	**2,034.7**	**2,408.2**	**2,869.3**	**3,210.0**
DOTS World Total	**001**	**703.7**	**682.0**	**1,043.9**	**1,503.9**	**1,745.3**	**2,381.1**	**2,737.0Y**	**1,063.4**	**1,269.7**	**1,740.4**	**2,034.8**	**2,466.6**	**2,913.7**	**3,797.9Y**
Industrial Countries	**101**	**487.1**	**431.4**	**681.8**	**1,035.9**	**1,172.4**	**1,634.5**	**1,742.4Y**	**309.7**	**333.3**	**594.7**	**572.8**	**659.1**	**848.1**	**922.5Y**
United States	111	6.68	10.75	15.73	8.92	38.32	6.52	5.00V	31.97	65.70	104.28	48.28	63.76	65.10	126.39V
Canada	156	1.05	—	—	—	—	—	.23V	10.18	5.28	8.55	5.74	4.98	12.35	18.27V
Australia	193	.59	—	—	—	—	—	1.40V	70.88	52.16	211.32	2.70	16.16	3.37	321.64V
Japan	158	29.19	4.85	9.20	12.81	8.79	7.04	8.78V	6.94	42.95	29.80	16.58	20.44	18.61	71.24V
New Zealand	196	—	—	—	—	—	—	.49V	—	—	—	—	—	4.37	3.87V
Austria	122	—	—	—	—	—	—	8.44V	.29	—	.82	3.27	.84	—	5.15V
Belgium	124	307.37	288.88	454.52	8.62	.90	3.27	504.94V	5.52	5.06	7.30	15.34	12.20	20.80	11.48V
Cyprus	423	—	—	—	—	—	—	—V	—	—	—	—	—	—	.90V
Denmark	128	.28	—	—	.13	—	1.38	4.40V	4.21	4.08	3.72	41.05	9.69	9.61	2.87V
Finland	172	—	.42	—	—	—	12.85	2.46V	.46	.57	3.05	.96	1.77	6.62	11.38V
France	132	.68	.60	1.95	2.54	13.42	10.03	14.23V	12.07	21.44	35.33	34.52	21.86	23.14	43.53V
Germany	134	.40	.22	.71	.80	.75	25.87	46.41V	5.86	10.40	36.63	18.87	28.82	53.71	34.77V
Greece	174	—	—	—	—	—	—	1.66V	—	—	—	—	—	—	.10V
Iceland	176	—	—	—	—	—	—	—V	—	—	—	—	—	—	.02V
Ireland	178	—	.51	—	—	—	—	—V	10.07	1.31	2.54	.84	2.89	—	1.59V
Italy	136	20.63	19.52	30.05	.80	1.62	3.16	530.97V	12.31	11.73	22.06	24.78	20.55	20.04	48.08V
Luxembourg	137	—	—	—	—	—	—	—V	—	—	—	—	—	—	.80V
Netherlands	138	26.26	19.94	29.57	916.56	1,042.79	1,422.15	31.48V	9.38	6.65	9.22	223.17	283.17	453.40	28.80V
Norway	142	.01	—	—	—	.29	—	.10V	2.36	8.30	.20	.28	12.13	2.14	3.63V
Portugal	182	28.21	29.82	38.91	42.04	21.45	29.74	32.47V	90.13	78.16	62.39	67.02	88.89	95.20	135.27V
Spain	184	46.13	37.11	69.98	37.98	32.82	43.50	341.15V	20.44	5.46	27.58	24.55	30.39	25.33	20.77V
Sweden	144	.27	—	—	.31	—	—	.02V	.94	1.13	6.22	15.41	10.33	4.28	8.44V
Switzerland	146	.01	—	.61	1.45	3.12	52.64	7.96V	3.59	.92	3.73	13.14	10.01	10.94	3.85V
United Kingdom	112	19.34	18.79	30.60	2.89	8.15	16.31	199.76V	12.10	12.04	19.92	16.31	20.29	19.13	19.66V
Developing Countries	**202**	**174.9**	**201.1**	**290.9**	**383.2**	**486.1**	**611.7**	**827.1Y**	**586.9**	**519.1**	**928.4**	**1,212.0**	**1,612.1**	**1,591.5**	**2,287.1Y**
Africa	**607**	**158.8**	**174.4**	**260.2**	**291.4**	**393.1**	**480.4**	**539.1Y**	**451.5**	**402.1**	**697.9**	**925.1**	**1,171.5**	**1,151.3**	**1,517.9Y**
Angola	614	.50	.14	.86	.64	.82	1.54	1.91Y	.07	—	.12	.09	—	—	—Y
Botswana	616	.01	.13	1.74	.75	—	—	—Y	.12	—	.21	.08	2.02	—	—Y
Cameroon	622	—	—	—	—	—	—	—Y	—	—	—	—	—	—	.12Y
Congo, Dem. Rep. of	636	—	.06	.30	.74	.33	—	—Y	—	—	—	—	—	—	—Y
Congo, Republic of	634	.10	2.84	1.39	—	—	—	—Y	—	—	—	—	—	—	—Y
Côte d'Ivoire	662	—	—	—	—	—	—	.03Y	—	—	—	—	—	—	.28Y
Gambia, The	648	—	—	—	.12	—	—	—Y	—	—	—	—	—	—	—Y
Guinea	656	—	—	—	—	—	—	.27Y	—	—	—	—	—	—	—Y
Kenya	664	.66	.22	3.23	2.64	2.11	1.40	1.74Y	.77	.77	1.13	3.01	3.54	3.10	3.85Y
Lesotho	666	—	—	—	.13	.13	—	—Y	—	—	—	—	—	—	—Y
Malawi	676	11.71	10.37	32.84	49.86	48.81	24.74	30.70Y	3.20	2.84	19.19	24.31	29.44	17.67	21.92Y
Mauritius	684	.08	.07	.61	.20	.58	—	2.94V	.79	—	.92	14.13	5.61	3.25	.58V
Morocco	686	—	.16	—	—	—	—	—Y	—	—	—	—	—	—	—Y
Namibia	728	—	—	—	.18	—	—	—Y	—	—	6.34	16.62	22.25	20.04	17.83Y
Nigeria	694	—	—	—	—	—	—	.20Y	—	—	—	—	—	—	—Y
Senegal	722	—	—	—	—	—	—	.04Y	—	—	—	—	—	—	.38Y
Seychelles	718	.01	—	—	—	—	—	—Y	—	—	—	—	—	—	—Y
South Africa	199	107.63	120.41	169.63	193.99	282.87	361.71	336.01V	436.30	385.71	654.38	841.95	1,059.32	1,056.25	1,394.48V
Sacca exc. South Afr.	608	—	—	—	—	—	—	—Y	—	—	—	—	—	—	10.52Y
Sudan	732	—	—	—	—	.10	—	—V	—	—	—	—	—	—	.23V
Swaziland	734	.69	.49	17.45	2.68	3.88	8.23	10.21Y	.36	2.27	4.18	11.40	15.57	16.86	20.92Y
Tanzania	738	.18	—	1.26	2.23	.45	4.52	5.61Y	.79	.56	1.60	3.45	4.36	8.37	10.39Y
Togo	742	—	—	—	.23	—	—	—Y	—	—	—	—	—	—	—Y
Tunisia	744	—	—	—	—	—	—	—Y	—	—	—	—	—	—	5.01Y
Uganda	746	—	—	—	—	—	—	.49Y	—	—	—	—	—	—	.16Y
Zambia	754	.11	.31	.81	1.04	1.34	2.12	54.45V	.06	—	—	.69	2.98	1.54	1.17V
Zimbabwe	698	37.15	39.23	29.47	35.03	51.20	76.13	94.47Y	9.04	9.94	9.80	9.35	16.96	24.21	30.05Y
Africa n.s.	799	—	—	.58	.93	.50	—	—Y	—	—	—	—	9.49	—	—Y
Asia	**507**	**14.1**	**26.2**	**24.6**	**81.5**	**83.0**	**102.2**	**206.9Y**	**106.4**	**100.3**	**181.2**	**212.7**	**323.9**	**331.6**	**552.4Y**
Bangladesh	513	—	—	.96	3.88	.13	—	—V	.12	—	.22	.49	1.87	—	1.97Y
China,P.R.: Mainland	924	1.28	6.96	5.41	23.46	33.28	32.94	112.62V	21.73	16.56	40.64	40.31	62.22	76.52	176.43V
China,P.R.:Hong Kong	532	5.19	2.84	6.25	3.65	2.03	1.63	7.29V	3.32	1.34	5.05	16.65	8.49	8.60	2.67V
China,P.R.:Macao	546	—	—	—	—	—	—	.28V	—	—	—	—	—	—	—V
India	534	3.53	14.59	3.61	33.05	25.31	30.20	37.47Y	25.18	53.12	72.94	62.75	88.28	92.15	114.36Y
Indonesia	536	.02	.42	2.98	5.00	3.06	13.08	13.82V	4.61	2.03	4.76	11.08	14.86	29.31	39.72V
Korea	542	—	—	—	—	—	—	1.66V	4.19	7.79	8.77	10.16	13.41	11.69	25.08V
Malaysia	548	1.29	.30	1.48	4.02	3.85	9.02	1.39V	3.75	4.44	18.64	10.02	7.77	15.61	38.95V
Pakistan	564	.16	—	.42	1.30	1.48	6.25	7.76Y	30.91	7.17	14.31	11.24	25.78	34.93	43.35Y
Philippines	566	—	—	—	—	—	—	.11V	—	—	—	—	—	—	.13V
Singapore	576	1.17	.91	.50	2.23	2.43	3.49	2.52V	5.11	2.22	5.69	6.14	25.24	11.61	34.37V
Sri Lanka	524	—	—	—	—	—	—	.60V	—	—	—	—	—	—	.02V
Taiwan Province of China	528	1.30	—	.60	1.79	.17	—	11.54V	3.52	2.19	2.47	3.22	2.16	3.03	5.81V
Thailand	578	.13	.20	2.03	2.45	10.99	3.65	9.84V	3.51	3.40	6.66	30.91	42.20	37.00	69.54V
Vietnam	582	.02	—	.33	.64	.14	1.91	—V	.41	—	1.03	9.72	30.80	11.12	—V
Asia n.s.	598	—	—	—	—	.14	—	—Y	—	—	—	—	.82	—	—Y

		Exports							Imports						
		2001	2002	2003	2004	2005	2006	2007	2001	2002	2003	2004	2005	2006	2007
		Millions of U.S. Dollars							*Millions of U.S. Dollars*						
Europe	**170**	**—**	**—**	**.8**	**8.4**	**8.0**	**25.6**	**70.4Y**	**.5**	**.6**	**2.3**	**4.2**	**13.7**	**14.0**	**70.2Y**
Belarus	913	—	—	—	—	—	—	.14V	—	—	—	—	—	—	.19V
Bulgaria	918	—	—	—	—	—	—	—V	—	—	—	—	—	—	.40V
Czech Republic	935	—	—	—	—	—	—	4.34V	—	—	—	—	—	—	.21V
Hungary	944	—	—	—	—	—	—	.52V	—	—	—	.20	1.35	—	3.80V
Kazakhstan	916	—	—	—	—	—	—	.22Y	—	—	—	—	—	—	—Y
Latvia	941	—	—	—	—	—	—	—V	—	—	—	—	—	—	.05V
Lithuania	946	—	—	—	—	—	—	1.35V	—	—	—	—	—	—	.94V
Macedonia, FYR	962	—	—	—	—	—	—	.02Y	—	—	—	—	—	—	—Y
Poland	964	—	—	—	—	—	5.23	9.24V	—	—	—	—	—	—	9.20V
Romania	968	—	—	—	—	—	—	.63V	—	—	—	—	—	—	.02V
Russia	922	—	—	—	6.32	.10	8.90	28.52V	—	—	—	—	.39	—	12.53V
Slovak Republic	936	—	—	—	—	—	—	—V	—	—	—	—	—	—	.63V
Turkey	186	—	—	.85	2.12	6.91	7.44	16.79V	.49	.65	1.44	3.61	2.28	4.66	16.49V
Ukraine	926	—	—	—	—	—	—	3.64Y	—	—	—	—	—	—	14.12Y
Europe n.s.	884	—	—	—	—	.98	4.02	4.99Y	—	—	.91	.36	9.73	9.37	11.63Y
Middle East	**407**	**2.0**	**.4**	**.5**	**.8**	**1.9**	**3.5**	**5.1Y**	**14.2**	**11.2**	**29.7**	**29.9**	**48.5**	**61.2**	**76.2Y**
Egypt	469	—	—	—	—	—	—	—Y	—	—	—	—	1.81	—	—Y
Iran, I.R. of	429	.81	.10	—	—	—	—	—Y	—	—	—	—	—	—	—Y
Israel	436	—	—	—	—	—	—	—V	—	—	—	—	1.13	—	—V
Jordan	439	—	—	—	—	—	—	.54V	—	—	—	—	—	—	2.27V
Lebanon	446	—	—	—	—	.17	—	—Y	—	—	—	—	.66	—	—Y
Oman	449	—	—	—	—	—	—	—Y	—	—	—	—	—	—	.14Y
Saudi Arabia	456	.04	—	.24	—	—	—	—Y	.87	4.34	18.40	5.76	2.55	1.85	2.24Y
United Arab Emirates	466	1.11	.33	.24	.76	1.75	3.52	4.56Y	13.34	6.81	11.35	24.14	41.68	59.32	71.56Y
Yemen, Republic of	474	—	—	—	—	—	—	.05Y	—	—	—	—	—	—	—Y
Middle East n.s.	489	—	—	—	—	—	—	—Y	—	—	—	—	.67	—	—Y
Western Hemisphere	**207**	**—**	**—**	**4.8**	**1.2**	**—**	**—**	**5.6Y**	**14.3**	**4.9**	**17.3**	**40.1**	**54.4**	**33.5**	**70.5Y**
Argentina	213	—	—	—	—	—	—	1.19V	9.91	3.23	8.85	24.92	26.13	11.36	65.50V
Bolivia	218	—	—	—	—	—	—	.01Y	—	—	—	—	—	—	—Y
Brazil	223	—	—	1.90	.11	—	—	—V	4.42	1.70	8.42	15.20	27.88	22.10	—V
Chile	228	—	—	—	—	—	—	.01V	—	—	—	—	.35	—	.89V
Colombia	233	—	—	2.49	.37	—	—	—V	—	—	—	—	—	—	.49V
Mexico	273	—	—	—	—	—	—	4.40V	—	—	—	—	—	—	2.97V
Panama	283	—	—	.38	.68	—	—	—Y	—	—	—	—	—	—	—Y
Paraguay	288	—	—	—	—	—	—	—Y	—	—	—	—	—	—	.18Y
Peru	293	—	—	—	—	—	—	—Y	—	—	—	—	—	—	.29Y
Uruguay	298	—	—	—	—	—	—	—Y	—	—	—	—	—	—	.13Y
Countries & Areas n.s.	**898**	**41.7**	**49.5**	**71.2**	**84.8**	**86.8**	**135.0**	**167.5Y**	**166.8**	**417.2**	**217.3**	**250.0**	**195.4**	**474.0**	**588.3Y**
Memorandum Items															
European Union	998	449.58	415.81	656.29	1,012.68	1,121.89	1,573.49	1,733.83Y	183.78	158.02	236.77	486.29	533.02	731.26	388.41Y
Oil Exporting Ctys	999	1.98	.84	3.47	5.76	4.80	16.61	18.58Y	18.82	13.19	34.50	40.98	59.10	90.48	113.65Y
Non-Oil Develop.Ctys	201	172.90	200.22	287.40	377.48	481.25	595.07	808.54Y	568.06	505.91	893.89	1,170.99	1,552.97	1,501.07	2,173.48Y
PERCENT DISTRIBUTION															
Industrial Countries	**101**	**69.2**	**63.3**	**65.3**	**68.9**	**67.2**	**68.6**	**63.7**	**29.1**	**26.3**	**34.2**	**28.2**	**26.7**	**29.1**	**24.3**
Developing Countries	**202**	**24.9**	**29.5**	**27.9**	**25.5**	**27.9**	**25.7**	**30.2**	**55.2**	**40.9**	**53.3**	**59.6**	**65.4**	**54.6**	**60.2**
Africa	**607**	**22.6**	**25.6**	**24.9**	**19.4**	**22.5**	**20.2**	**19.7**	**42.5**	**31.7**	**40.1**	**45.5**	**47.5**	**39.5**	**40.0**
Asia	**507**	**2.0**	**3.8**	**2.4**	**5.4**	**4.8**	**4.3**	**7.6**	**10.0**	**7.9**	**10.4**	**10.5**	**13.1**	**11.4**	**14.5**
Europe	**170**	**—**	**—**	**.1**	**.6**	**.5**	**1.1**	**2.6**	**—**	**.1**	**.1**	**.2**	**.6**	**.5**	**1.8**
Middle East	**407**	**.3**	**.1**	**—**	**.1**	**.1**	**.1**	**.2**	**1.3**	**.9**	**1.7**	**1.5**	**2.0**	**2.1**	**2.0**
Western Hemisphere	**207**	**—**	**—**	**.5**	**.1**	**—**	**—**	**.2**	**1.3**	**.4**	**1.0**	**2.0**	**2.2**	**1.1**	**1.9**
ANNUAL PERCENT CHANGE															
World	**001**	**93.2**	**–3.1**	**53.1**	**44.1**	**16.1**	**36.4**	**14.9**	**1.6**	**19.4**	**37.1**	**16.9**	**21.2**	**18.1**	**30.3**
Industrial Countries	**101**	**285.4**	**–11.4**	**58.0**	**51.9**	**13.2**	**39.4**	**6.6**	**11.7**	**7.6**	**78.4**	**–3.7**	**15.1**	**28.7**	**8.8**
Developing Countries	**202**	**6.6**	**15.0**	**44.7**	**31.8**	**26.8**	**25.8**	**35.2**	**–8.4**	**–11.6**	**78.8**	**30.5**	**33.0**	**–1.3**	**43.7**
Africa	**607**	**21.0**	**9.8**	**49.2**	**12.0**	**34.9**	**22.2**	**12.2**	**–16.7**	**–10.9**	**73.6**	**32.6**	**26.6**	**–1.7**	**31.8**
Asia	**507**	**–55.4**	**86.0**	**–6.2**	**231.6**	**1.9**	**23.1**	**102.5**	**23.8**	**–5.7**	**80.7**	**17.4**	**52.3**	**2.4**	**66.6**
Europe	**170**	**4.1**	**—**	**....**	**893.7**	**–5.3**	**220.0**	**175.1**	**–88.6**	**32.1**	**261.2**	**77.9**	**230.1**	**2.1**	**400.1**
Middle East	**407**	**86.8**	**–78.2**	**14.6**	**55.2**	**153.3**	**83.5**	**46.0**	**442.5**	**–21.5**	**166.7**	**.5**	**62.2**	**26.1**	**24.6**
Western Hemisphere	**207**	**—**	**—**	**....**	**–75.6**	**–8.3**	**....**	**....**	**127.5**	**–65.6**	**250.1**	**132.3**	**35.5**	**–38.5**	**110.6**
Other Countries n.i.e.	**910**	**219.5**	**—**	**....**	**....**	**....**	**....**	**....**	**—**	**—**	**....**	**....**	**....**	**....**	**....**

		Exports							Imports						
		2001	2002	2003	2004	2005	2006	2007	2001	2002	2003	2004	2005	2006	2007
		Millions of U.S. Dollars							*Millions of U.S. Dollars*						
IFS World Total		**2,381.0**	**3,046.3**	**2,483.4**	**2,380.0**	**3,778.3**	**4,585.4**	**6,317.0**	**2,877.0**	**2,348.4**	**2,090.8**	**2,196.5**	**1,909.8**	**2,564.1**	**3,279.9**
DOTS World Total	**001**	**2,625.4Y**	**2,752.7Y**	**2,767.4Y**	**3,158.1Y**	**3,705.8Y**	**4,382.2Y**	**4,753.4Y**	**2,662.8Y**	**2,969.1Y**	**3,226.0Y**	**3,451.5Y**	**3,569.0Y**	**3,848.1Y**	**5,520.2Y**
Industrial Countries	**101**	**1,008.3Y**	**851.0Y**	**819.2Y**	**690.4Y**	**516.9Y**	**570.9Y**	**620.9Y**	**330.4Y**	**257.7Y**	**227.1Y**	**266.2Y**	**259.7Y**	**269.3Y**	**490.6Y**
United States	111	456.18V	345.36V	268.64V	—V	—V	—V	—V	12.65V	11.55V	7.48V	12.65V	5.83V	8.36V	9.46V
Canada	156	40.61V	29.56V	29.54V	18.97V	9.13V	7.43V	7.46V	.22V	.41V	.39V	1.49V	.33V	.14V	1.46V
Australia	193	11.12V	9.89V	10.06V	12.07V	11.11V	15.92V	18.02V	21.53V	9.78V	8.77V	22.42V	33.80V	28.69V	32.70V
Japan	158	92.78V	100.30V	126.89V	163.47V	184.85V	225.61V	269.20V	205.29V	126.87V	136.96V	115.83V	100.97V	114.08V	193.98V
New Zealand	196	1.07V	.73V	.71V	.44V	.63V	.78V	1.10V	7.25V	8.84V	4.45V	4.20V	2.06V	3.13V	3.85V
Austria	122	3.57V	4.53V	5.06V	8.33V	7.75V	7.26V	7.93V	3.46V	3.48V	6.18V	7.24V	6.77V	7.41V	9.38V
Belgium	124	17.85V	20.49V	20.76V	22.91V	16.39V	9.80V	9.18V	8.86V	11.32V	4.02V	2.69V	5.55V	10.38V	6.06V
Cyprus	423	.30V	.29V	.20V	.02V	.08Y	.19V	.36V	.48V	.46V	.28V	.47V	.48V	.64V	.34V
Denmark	128	17.48V	15.42V	14.93V	12.46V	11.40V	7.69V	9.03V	1.27V	1.20V	1.22V	1.29V	2.10V	1.21V	.79V
Finland	172	.95V	.44V	.18V	.18V	.19V	.58V	1.39V	.90V	.90V	.25V	.78V	.67V	.31V	.12V
France	132	72.13V	79.49V	56.67V	71.19V	39.69V	33.51V	18.24V	11.82V	31.88V	12.52V	39.30V	15.68V	9.66V	42.29V
Germany	134	100.29V	73.15V	93.99V	118.26V	102.19V	114.90V	110.20V	18.35V	20.10V	15.94V	27.89V	35.81V	44.06V	58.51V
Greece	174	.19V	.01V	1.33V	1.59V	1.29V	1.30V	1.36V	.30V	.01V	.01V	—V	—V	—V	—V
Iceland	176	.09V	.12V	.39V	.38V	.17V	.29V	.19V	—V	—V	—V	—V	—V	—V	—V
Ireland	178	1.63V	.79V	1.35V	1.95V	.19V	.04V	—V	1.52V	1.40V	.46V	1.83V	4.54V	.13V	1.43V
Italy	136	31.05V	34.08V	39.67V	55.26V	32.34V	34.50V	45.11V	11.85V	3.72V	6.01V	12.20V	5.82V	18.73V	105.24V
Luxembourg	137	.07V	.01V	.01V	.04V	—V	—V	—V	.27V	.40V	.05V	.06V	.04V	.08V	.01V
Malta	181	.03Y	.01V	.01V	.01V	.06V	.07V	.07V	—Y	—V	—V	—V	—V	—V	.05V
Netherlands	138	39.83V	16.58V	21.06V	30.59V	14.58V	19.67V	17.28V	5.63V	4.60V	5.70V	5.55V	13.27V	7.57V	9.26V
Norway	142	1.34V	1.29V	1.51V	1.55V	2.16V	1.44V	1.09V	.10V	.15V	.04V	.03V	—V	.13V	.04V
Portugal	182	.36V	.67V	.95V	.65V	.57V	.94V	.22V	.10V	.10V	.06V	.03V	.02V	.08V	.47V
Slovenia	961	.30V	.44V	.70V	.91Y	.40V	.40V	.50V	—V	—V	—V	—Y	—V	.06V	—V
Spain	184	25.42V	19.76V	24.19V	42.04V	19.89V	40.18V	43.01V	.92V	1.43V	2.10V	1.69V	1.71V	2.31V	2.28V
Sweden	144	2.02V	3.37V	3.91V	3.39V	3.40V	3.14V	3.34V	.77V	.25V	2.69V	.38V	.48V	.96V	2.17V
Switzerland	146	4.18V	6.38V	3.84V	1.18V	.45V	.63V	.67V	1.89V	6.81V	2.55V	3.84V	4.32V	3.82V	2.68V
United Kingdom	112	87.44V	87.79V	92.64V	122.60V	57.97V	44.61V	55.90V	14.92V	12.09V	8.94V	4.37V	19.47V	7.37V	8.04V
Developing Countries	**202**	**1,589.1Y**	**1,871.3Y**	**1,909.7Y**	**2,417.1Y**	**3,131.2Y**	**3,740.0Y**	**4,043.9Y**	**2,313.0Y**	**2,690.3Y**	**2,972.3Y**	**3,150.3Y**	**3,269.3Y**	**3,529.4Y**	**4,968.3Y**
Africa	**607**	**182.6Y**	**201.9Y**	**215.2Y**	**225.3Y**	**239.3Y**	**255.6Y**	**283.1Y**	**3.4Y**	**4.0Y**	**3.3Y**	**4.6Y**	**6.2Y**	**3.9Y**	**4.1Y**
Algeria	612	—V	—V	—Y	.01Y	.01Y	.01Y	.01Y	—V	—V	—Y	—Y	—Y	—Y	—Y
Benin	638	.07V	.06V	—V	—V	—V	—Y	—Y	—V	—V	—V	—V	—V	—Y	—Y
Cameroon	622	—V	4.60V	1.17V	1.54Y	1.76Y	2.17Y	2.70Y	—V	—V	—V	—Y	—Y	—Y	—Y
Central African Rep.	626	.31Y	.34Y	.43Y	.56Y	.64Y	.80Y	.99Y	....	....	....	....	....	....	....
Ghana	652	2.57Y	2.79Y	3.53Y	4.64Y	5.30Y	6.55Y	8.13Y	—Y	—Y	—Y	—Y	—Y	—Y	—Y
Guinea	656	—V	—Y	.34V	—V	—Y	—Y	—Y	....	....	....	....	....	....	....
Kenya	664	—V	—V	—V	—V	—Y	—Y	—Y	1.26V	1.09V	—V	—V	—Y	—Y	—Y
Mauritius	684	.31V	.43V	.35V	.53V	.86V	1.07V	2.06V	.05V	—V	—V	—V	—V	.01V	—V
Morocco	686	—V	.01V	.09V	.15V	.01V	.01Y	.01Y	—V	—V	—V	—V	—V	—Y	—Y
Namibia	728	—Y	—Y	—Y	—Y	—Y	—Y	—Y	1.47Y	1.57Y	1.68Y	1.78Y	1.88Y	1.99Y	2.09Y
Niger	692	.45V	—V	.51V	—V	—Y	—Y	—Y	—V	—V	—V	—V	—Y	—Y	—Y
Nigeria	694	.04V	.49V	.26V	.34Y	.44Y	.54Y	.70Y	—V	—V	—V	—Y	—Y	—Y	—Y
Senegal	722	—V	1.64V	4.21V	.97V	—V	—V	—Y	—V	—V	—V	—V	—V	—V	—Y
South Africa	199	.11V	.11V	.32V	.21V	1.22V	2.91V	14.39V	.26V	.64V	.65V	1.37V	2.97V	—V	—V
Sudan	732	—Y	—Y	—Y	—V	—V	—V	—V	.01Y	.01Y	—V	—V	—V	—V	—V
Tanzania	738	—V	—V	—Y	—Y	—Y	—Y	—Y	.26V	.64V	.81Y	1.07Y	1.22Y	1.51Y	1.87Y
Togo	742	.05V	.06V	—V	.01V	—V	—Y	—Y	....	....	....	....	....	....	....
Tunisia	744	—V	.11V	.19V	.06V	.23V	.15V	.19Y	—V	—V	—V	.04V	—V	—V	—Y
Zambia	754	—V	—V	—V	—V	—V	—V	—V	—V	—V	—V	—V	—V	.29V	—V
Zimbabwe	698	—V	—V	—V	—V	—V	—V	—Y	—V	—V	.04V	.27V	—V	.02V	.02Y
Africa n.s.	799	178.73Y	191.27Y	203.80Y	216.33Y	228.86Y	241.39Y	253.92Y	.08Y	.08Y	.09Y	.09Y	.10Y	.10Y	.11Y
Asia	**507**	**1,368.8Y**	**1,614.1Y**	**1,641.5Y**	**2,122.9Y**	**2,808.7Y**	**3,383.6Y**	**3,645.2Y**	**2,285.5Y**	**2,542.7Y**	**2,899.6Y**	**3,087.6Y**	**3,227.7Y**	**3,480.1Y**	**4,897.6Y**
Bangladesh	513	17.92V	21.61V	30.21V	24.82V	29.35V	24.45V	26.97V	.74V	1.06V	2.68V	2.08V	1.66V	3.62Y	6.35Y
Brunei Darussalam	516	.27Y	.29Y	.12V	.16Y	.18Y	.22Y	.27Y	—Y	—Y	.03V	.03Y	.04Y	.05Y	.06Y
Cambodia	522	.06V	—V	—V	—V	.38V	.12V	.15Y	—V	—V	—V	—V	.08V	.04V	.04Y
China,P.R.: Mainland	924	121.99V	124.47V	154.10V	187.68V	249.49V	229.70V	336.87V	547.26V	797.34V	998.75V	1,029.24V	1,028.40V	1,327.95V	1,861.12V
China,P.R.:Hong Kong	532	25.16V	22.47V	25.97V	36.65V	43.89V	48.91V	72.83V	70.06V	69.93V	48.36V	48.73V	39.36V	44.23V	54.17V
China,P.R.:Macao	546	.13V	.18V	.09V	.06V	.03V	.13V	.18V	.42V	.12V	.02V	—V	—V	.01V	.03V
Fiji	819	.02Y	.02Y	.02Y	.03Y	.04Y	.05Y	.06Y	—Y	—Y	—Y	—Y	—Y	—Y	—Y
India	534	179.83Y	314.22V	355.24V	363.68V	449.13V	555.10Y	688.87Y	58.35Y	78.68V	94.60V	115.18V	121.82V	150.56Y	186.85Y
Indonesia	536	18.93V	28.62V	13.59V	15.84V	12.87V	17.88V	27.63V	75.88V	59.80V	50.22V	66.31V	85.79V	151.48V	288.63V
Korea	542	46.07V	51.11V	26.63V	27.36V	51.14V	87.67V	73.35V	255.26V	157.81V	202.41V	178.16V	132.01V	133.44V	321.18V
Malaysia	548	71.09V	69.78V	72.62V	97.15V	121.51V	113.53V	126.64V	216.71V	263.11V	154.25V	164.28V	270.27V	181.53V	231.55V
Maldives	556	—V	—V	—V	.02V	—V	—Y	—Y	—Y	—Y	—Y	—Y	—Y	—Y	—Y
New Caledonia	839	.06V	.06V	.05V	.03V	.03Y	.04Y	.05Y	....	....	....	....	....	....	....
Pakistan	564	15.88V	13.73V	8.36V	19.17V	35.78V	44.22Y	54.87Y	3.59V	8.62V	5.87V	2.70V	2.47V	3.06Y	3.79Y
Philippines	566	2.80V	1.61V	2.08V	2.26V	1.09V	1.43V	2.39V	6.83V	4.06V	4.33V	8.04V	10.00V	8.34V	8.81V
Singapore	576	102.14V	97.26V	76.22V	64.51V	98.53V	63.18V	55.61V	465.56V	576.62V	715.96V	717.06V	656.11V	619.60V	855.83V
Sri Lanka	524	1.14V	1.07V	2.08V	1.85V	3.70V	2.58V	4.99V	.65V	.30V	.26V	.23V	2.69V	.13V	.56V
Taiwan Province of China	528	26.33V	31.08V	30.41V	33.74V	46.89V	—V	—V	187.71V	161.59V	124.68V	74.77V	86.56V	—V	—V
Thailand	578	735.41V	831.19V	826.96V	1,230.34V	1,622.98V	2,135.72V	2,104.89V	390.54V	355.88V	483.34V	665.37V	777.30V	837.90V	1,054.64V
Vietnam	582	3.61V	5.33V	16.68V	17.55V	41.64V	58.73V	68.55V	5.90V	7.84V	13.78V	15.40V	13.20V	18.15V	23.98V

	Exports 2001	Exports 2002	Exports 2003	Exports 2004	Exports 2005	Exports 2006	Exports 2007	Imports 2001	Imports 2002	Imports 2003	Imports 2004	Imports 2005	Imports 2006	Imports 2007
	Millions of U.S. Dollars							Millions of U.S. Dollars						
Europe....170	**6.0Y**	**21.5Y**	**6.2Y**	**12.1Y**	**10.7Y**	**16.1Y**	**16.2Y**	**18.0Y**	**136.8Y**	**58.3Y**	**46.7Y**	**23.3Y**	**31.8Y**	**53.4Y**
Belarus....913	—V	.10V	—V	—V	—V	.05V	.01V	—Y	—Y	—Y	—Y	—Y	—Y	.38V
Bulgaria....918	—V	1.18V	.04V	.10V	.15V	.15V	.13V	—V	—V	.02V	—V	.08V	.01V	.21V
Czech Republic....935	.82V	.82V	.74V	3.29V	1.33V	1.19V	.54V	.84V	.60V	.43V	.70V	.33V	.31V	.15V
Estonia....939	.12V	.12V	.27V	—V	.05V	—V	—V	.01V	.02V	.09V	.01V	.01V	—V	—V
Hungary....944	.60V	.91V	.80V	.12V	.48V	.33V	.28V	.26V	3.53V	.12V	.19V	.36V	.33V	.04V
Latvia....941	.07V	.05V	.06V	.04V	—V	.03V	—V	—V	—V	.01V	—V	—V	—V	—V
Lithuania....946	.39V	.12V	.14V	—V	.36V	—V	—V	—V	.02V	—V	—V	.52V	—V	—V
Poland....964	3.08V	1.77V	1.66V	3.66V	2.73V	4.26V	1.58V	.13V	.01V	.01V	.03V	.18V	.05V	—V
Romania....968	.01V	.53V	.05V	.18V	.32V	.63V	.42V	—V	.01V	.08V	—V	—V	.02V	—V
Russia....922	.12V	11.74V	.29V	1.51V	2.05V	2.73V	2.30V	2.48V	96.70V	11.72V	25.51V	.76V	7.20V	23.24V
Slovak Republic....936	.23V	.33V	.42Y	.55Y	—V	.01V	—V	5.93V	.86V	1.09Y	1.43Y	—V	—V	—V
Turkey....186	.55V	1.34V	1.51V	2.63V	3.04V	6.51V	10.73V	.06V	.71V	.16V	.36V	2.31V	.69V	.66V
Ukraine....926	—V	2.52V	.24V	.02V	.14V	.18Y	.22Y	8.24V	34.35V	44.57V	18.45V	18.73V	23.15Y	28.73Y
Middle East....407	**6.0Y**	**6.9Y**	**18.7Y**	**23.9Y**	**30.4Y**	**38.5Y**	**50.3Y**	**3.0Y**	**5.8Y**	**5.5Y**	**6.4Y**	**8.3Y**	**8.6Y**	**11.0Y**
Bahrain....419	.41Y	.45Y	.57Y	.74Y	.85Y	1.05Y	1.30Y	—Y	—Y	—Y	—Y	—Y	—Y	—Y
Egypt....469	2.20V	2.39Y	3.02Y	3.97Y	4.53Y	5.60Y	6.95Y	.02V	.02Y	.03Y	.04Y	.05Y	.06Y	.07Y
Iran, I.R. of....429	—V	.18V	.20Y	.26Y	.33Y	.41Y	.53Y	—Y	—Y	—Y	—Y	—Y	—Y	—Y
Israel....436	—V	—V	—V	—V	—V	.18V	.73V	.33V	1.10V	1.98V	1.76V	1.98V	.66V	1.43V
Jordan....439	.02V	.01V	.01V	.08V	.26V	.31V	.79V	—V	.03V	—V	—V	—V	—V	—V
Kuwait....443	2.07Y	2.14Y	2.38Y	3.09Y	3.93Y	4.86Y	6.29Y	—Y	—Y	—Y	—Y	—Y	—Y	—Y
Lebanon....446	.35Y	.38Y	.48Y	.63Y	.72Y	.89Y	1.11Y	—Y	—Y	—Y	—Y	—Y	—Y	—Y
Oman....449	.14V	.33V	1.12V	1.45Y	1.85Y	2.28Y	2.95Y	—V	.23V	.08V	.10Y	.14Y	.17Y	.21Y
Qatar....453	—V	.32V	.34V	.17V	.83V	1.79V	2.32Y	.01V	1.57V	—V	—V	—V	—V	—Y
Saudi Arabia....456	.77V	.69V	.65V	.62V	.71V	.88Y	1.13Y	2.64Y	2.81Y	3.41Y	4.51Y	6.14Y	7.71Y	9.31Y
United Arab Emirates....466	—V	—V	9.91V	12.89Y	16.41Y	20.26Y	26.24Y	—Y	—Y	—Y	—Y	—Y	—Y	—Y
Yemen, Republic of....474	.05V	.04V	.06Y	—V	—V	—Y	—Y	—V	—V	—Y	—V	—V	—Y	—Y
Western Hemisphere....207	**25.6Y**	**26.9Y**	**28.1Y**	**32.9Y**	**42.1Y**	**46.2Y**	**49.1Y**	**3.2Y**	**1.0Y**	**5.7Y**	**5.0Y**	**3.8Y**	**5.0Y**	**2.1Y**
Argentina....213	1.73V	.85V	1.05V	4.12V	6.83V	9.12V	8.98V	.02V	—V	.07V	.12V	.04V	.13V	.41V
Brazil....223	.12V	.17V	.05V	.11V	.48V	1.26V	—V	1.10V	.92V	5.07V	3.41V	2.25V	3.45V	—V
Chile....228	.18V	.64V	.01V	.03V	.07V	.21V	.19V	1.95V	—V	—V	—V	—V	—V	—V
Colombia....233	.01V	.01V	—V	.02V	.02V	.03V	.06V	.13V	.03V	.15V	.10V	—V	—V	—V
Costa Rica....238	.01V	—V	—V	—V	—V	—Y	—Y	—V	—V	.29V	1.20V	1.10V	1.36Y	1.68Y
Greenland....326	—Y	.01Y	.01Y	.01Y	.01Y	.01Y	.02Y	—Y	—Y	—Y	—Y	—Y	—Y	—Y
Guatemala....258	.01V	—V	.03V	—V	—V	—Y	—Y	—V	—V	.09V	.17Y	—V	—Y	—Y
Mexico....273	—V	—V	—V	—V	4.40V	3.53V	6.12V	—V	—V	—V	—V	.35V	.05V	.03V
Paraguay....288	—V	—V	—V	—V	.01V	.03V	.03Y	—V	—V	—V	—V	—V	—V	—Y
Peru....293	.01V	—V	.03V	.03V	—V	—V	.03Y	—V	—V	—V	—V	.05V	—V	—Y
Trinidad and Tobago....369	—V	.01V	.01Y	.01Y	.01Y	.01Y	.01Y	—V	—V	—Y	—Y	—Y	—Y	—Y
Uruguay....298	.03V	.03Y	.11V	.09V	.13V	.17Y	.21Y	—Y	—Y	—Y	—Y	—Y	—Y	—Y
Western Hem. n.s....399	23.52Y	25.17Y	26.82Y	28.47Y	30.12Y	31.77Y	33.42Y	.02Y	.02Y	.02Y	.03Y	.03Y	.03Y	.03Y
Other Countries n.i.e....910	**14.1Y**	**15.3Y**	**19.3Y**	**25.4Y**	**29.0Y**	**35.8Y**	**44.5Y**	**16.6Y**	**18.0Y**	**22.8Y**	**30.0Y**	**34.2Y**	**42.3Y**	**52.5Y**
North Korea....954	14.07Y	15.27Y	19.33Y	25.39Y	29.00Y	35.85Y	44.49Y	16.61Y	18.02Y	22.81Y	29.96Y	34.23Y	42.31Y	52.50Y
Countries & Areas n.s....898	**12.5Y**	**13.6Y**	**17.2Y**	**22.6Y**	**25.8Y**	**31.9Y**	**39.6Y**	**2.8Y**	**3.0Y**	**3.8Y**	**5.0Y**	**5.7Y**	**7.1Y**	**8.8Y**
Special Categories....899	**1.4Y**	**1.5Y**	**1.9Y**	**2.6Y**	**2.9Y**	**3.6Y**	**4.5Y**	**—Y**	**—Y**	**—Y**	**—Y**	**—Y**	**—Y**	**—Y**
Memorandum Items														
European Union....998	406.22Y	361.45Y	381.70Y	500.04Y	313.33Y	324.63Y	325.54Y	88.61Y	98.39Y	68.16Y	108.12Y	113.79Y	111.66Y	246.63Y
Oil Exporting Ctys....999	21.95Y	32.77Y	28.46Y	34.66Y	37.37Y	48.89Y	67.80Y	78.53Y	64.41Y	53.71Y	70.92Y	92.06Y	159.36Y	298.14Y
Non-Oil Develop.Ctys....201	1,567.19Y	1,838.58Y	1,881.28Y	2,382.45Y	3,093.81Y	3,691.09Y	3,976.13Y	2,234.49Y	2,625.91Y	2,918.58Y	3,079.40Y	3,177.25Y	3,370.02Y	4,670.12Y
PERCENT DISTRIBUTION														
Industrial Countries....101	**38.4**	**30.9**	**29.6**	**21.9**	**13.9**	**13.0**	**13.1**	**12.4**	**8.7**	**7.0**	**7.7**	**7.3**	**7.0**	**8.9**
Developing Countries....202	**60.5**	**68.0**	**69.0**	**76.5**	**84.5**	**85.3**	**85.1**	**86.9**	**90.6**	**92.1**	**91.3**	**91.6**	**91.7**	**90.0**
Africa....607	**7.0**	**7.3**	**7.8**	**7.1**	**6.5**	**5.8**	**6.0**	**.1**	**.1**	**.1**	**.1**	**.2**	**.1**	**.1**
Asia....507	**52.1**	**58.6**	**59.3**	**67.2**	**75.8**	**77.2**	**76.7**	**85.8**	**85.6**	**89.9**	**89.5**	**90.4**	**90.4**	**88.7**
Europe....170	**.2**	**.8**	**.2**	**.4**	**.3**	**.4**	**.3**	**.7**	**4.6**	**1.8**	**1.4**	**.7**	**.8**	**1.0**
Middle East....407	**.2**	**.3**	**.7**	**.8**	**.8**	**.9**	**1.1**	**.1**	**.2**	**.2**	**.2**	**.2**	**.2**	**.2**
Western Hemisphere....207	**1.0**	**1.0**	**1.0**	**1.0**	**1.1**	**1.1**	**1.0**	**.1**	**—**	**.2**	**.1**	**.1**	**.1**	**—**
Other Countries n.i.e....910	**.5**	**.6**	**.7**	**.8**	**.8**	**.8**	**.9**	**.6**	**.6**	**.7**	**.9**	**1.0**	**1.1**	**1.0**
ANNUAL PERCENT CHANGE														
World....001	**32.6**	**4.8**	**.5**	**14.1**	**17.3**	**18.3**	**8.5**	**–12.4**	**11.5**	**8.7**	**7.0**	**3.4**	**7.8**	**43.5**
Industrial Countries....101	**8.3**	**–15.6**	**–3.7**	**–15.7**	**–25.1**	**10.5**	**8.8**	**–11.0**	**–22.0**	**–11.9**	**17.2**	**–2.4**	**3.7**	**82.2**
Developing Countries....202	**55.2**	**17.8**	**2.1**	**26.6**	**29.5**	**19.4**	**8.1**	**–12.7**	**16.3**	**10.5**	**6.0**	**3.8**	**8.0**	**40.8**
Africa....607	**7.6**	**10.5**	**6.6**	**4.7**	**6.2**	**6.8**	**10.8**	**117.8**	**19.3**	**–19.0**	**41.7**	**33.5**	**–36.6**	**4.5**
Asia....507	**67.0**	**17.9**	**1.7**	**29.3**	**32.3**	**20.5**	**7.7**	**–12.7**	**11.3**	**14.0**	**6.5**	**4.5**	**7.8**	**40.7**
Europe....170	**14.3**	**258.9**	**–71.1**	**94.4**	**–11.8**	**50.7**	**.9**	**–25.2**	**662.0**	**–57.4**	**–19.9**	**–50.1**	**36.4**	**68.2**
Middle East....407	**45.9**	**14.9**	**170.6**	**27.6**	**27.3**	**26.5**	**30.8**	**–53.8**	**91.6**	**–4.6**	**16.7**	**29.4**	**3.7**	**28.0**
Western Hemisphere....207	**2.4**	**4.9**	**4.6**	**17.0**	**27.9**	**9.6**	**6.3**	**173.0**	**–69.8**	**484.6**	**–11.6**	**–24.1**	**31.4**	**–57.2**
Other Countries n.i.e....910	**10.4**	**8.5**	**26.6**	**31.3**	**14.3**	**23.6**	**24.1**	**10.4**	**8.5**	**26.6**	**31.3**	**14.3**	**23.6**	**24.1**

		Exports							Imports						
		2001	2002	2003	2004	2005	2006	2007	2001	2002	2003	2004	2005	2006	2007
		Millions of U.S. Dollars							Millions of U.S. Dollars						
IFS World Total		**737.2**	**568.2**	**661.7**	**772.1**	**863.2**	**837.9**	**887.7**	**1,473.8**	**1,418.7**	**1,754.6**	**1,938.7**	**2,283.3**	**2,491.8**	**2,904.4**
DOTS World Total	**001**	**753.5**	**610.3**	**641.2**	**729.5**	**812.6**	**829.6**	**1,008.4Y**	**1,566.1**	**1,395.6**	**1,594.8**	**1,842.3**	**2,070.0**	**2,397.7**	**3,122.2Y**
Industrial Countries	**101**	**366.5**	**226.9**	**266.5**	**253.9**	**222.0**	**220.3**	**231.6Y**	**289.3**	**230.3**	**190.4**	**178.8**	**185.4**	**186.5**	**248.9Y**
United States	111	202.80	122.00	163.10	131.40	105.10	96.70	88.64V	17.40	32.90	22.00	19.40	24.50	23.20	31.79V
Canada	156	5.00	4.00	4.90	7.40	7.30	8.91	13.32V	3.00	3.40	5.20	9.30	3.80	9.89	12.00V
Australia	193	1.00	.80	1.10	1.30	1.40	2.13	2.90V	11.10	8.70	9.30	17.20	21.10	19.57	30.20V
Japan	158	18.20	6.40	6.10	7.10	7.40	7.91	7.60V	44.80	28.30	24.30	22.90	35.60	26.76	48.65V
New Zealand	196	.90	.20	.20	.20	.30	.38	.59V	21.40	12.10	18.30	17.40	17.10	14.09	7.54V
Austria	122	2.20	1.60	.80	1.20	1.40	1.38	2.01V	2.50	2.70	3.30	5.00	2.00	.81	1.36V
Belgium	124	5.30	3.80	2.10	3.50	4.40	4.27	4.52V	7.00	5.20	18.60	15.30	11.40	3.32	9.26V
Cyprus	423	—	—	—	—	—	—	.01V	—	—	—	—	—	—	.22V
Denmark	128	.70	.30	.30	1.70	1.20	1.13	2.14V	3.60	4.20	4.40	4.60	3.40	4.24	3.82V
Finland	172	.10	.10	.10	.10	.30	.31	.23V	1.60	.70	.60	.70	1.20	.96	1.18V
France	132	9.20	6.20	5.80	7.90	8.60	17.94	15.21V	14.70	9.20	20.40	9.20	9.30	12.58	12.92V
Germany	134	83.70	52.60	45.70	48.30	43.30	39.32	41.15V	22.80	21.70	29.30	26.80	21.80	38.19	43.89V
Greece	174	.20	.10	.20	.20	.30	.19	.27V	—	.60	.20	.30	.20	.27	.04V
Iceland	176	—	—	—	—	—	—	.08V	—	—	—	—	—	—	.01V
Ireland	178	.20	.10	.20	.10	.10	.10	.17V	.10	.20	.10	.20	.40	.07	.21V
Italy	136	9.10	7.40	6.80	8.00	8.10	9.85	9.01V	5.60	3.00	6.80	6.10	2.60	5.46	6.82V
Luxembourg	137	.10	.10	—	—	—	.02	.06V	.10	—	—	.30	.20	.07	—V
Malta	181	—	—	—	—	—	—	—V	—	—	—	—	—	—	.05V
Netherlands	138	2.90	2.40	3.10	3.90	3.40	3.17	4.59V	3.90	2.50	3.30	3.10	5.20	4.21	9.42V
Norway	142	.20	.20	.20	.20	.40	.42	.61V	.70	1.60	1.00	.40	.30	.40	.85V
Portugal	182	.50	.40	5.30	.40	6.10	.18	8.87V	—	—	—	—	.20	.04	—V
Slovenia	961	—	—	—	—	—	—	.28V	—	—	—	—	—	—	.38V
Spain	184	2.50	2.00	2.60	2.80	3.10	3.91	3.49V	1.70	1.40	1.90	2.10	1.30	1.10	3.95V
Sweden	144	.50	.70	.70	1.30	.80	1.35	.95V	2.00	.80	.60	1.20	.50	1.18	2.00V
Switzerland	146	7.90	5.00	3.40	4.20	4.40	4.39	5.80V	5.70	54.70	7.10	3.30	3.10	6.79	10.24V
United Kingdom	112	13.30	10.50	13.80	22.70	14.60	16.37	19.07V	119.60	36.40	13.70	14.00	20.20	13.29	12.13V
Developing Countries	**202**	**373.8**	**375.4**	**353.8**	**438.6**	**560.9**	**589.2**	**751.9Y**	**1,243.6**	**1,063.1**	**1,399.7**	**1,591.7**	**1,800.0**	**1,943.8**	**2,541.5Y**
Africa	**607**	**.1**	**.1**	**.1**	**.2**	**.6**	**1.3**	**.7Y**	**.5**	**1.7**	**1.5**	**4.5**	**2.3**	**.4**	**3.4Y**
Benin	638	—	—	—	—	—	—	.05Y	—	—	—	—	—	—	—Y
Mauritius	684	—	—	—	—	.30	1.10	—V	—	—	—	—	—	—	—V
Morocco	686	—	—	—	—	—	—	—Y	—	.50	—	.10	—	—	—Y
South Africa	199	.10	.10	.10	.20	.30	.22	.61V	.50	1.20	1.50	4.40	2.30	.35	3.40V
Tanzania	738	—	—	—	—	—	—	.02Y	—	—	—	—	—	—	—Y
Tunisia	744	—	—	—	—	—	—	.03Y	—	—	—	—	—	—	.01Y
Zimbabwe	698	—	—	—	—	—	—	—Y	—	—	—	—	—	—	.03Y
Asia	**507**	**370.4**	**372.6**	**351.2**	**433.1**	**553.3**	**578.9**	**736.8Y**	**1,106.6**	**961.3**	**1,328.4**	**1,507.3**	**1,683.5**	**1,823.0**	**2,444.0Y**
Bangladesh	513	7.10	3.10	5.30	5.70	4.00	3.24	14.25V	2.70	8.40	4.30	9.10	2.90	1.45	4.93Y
Brunei Darussalam	516	—	—	—	—	—	.10	.13Y	.40	.30	.50	1.10	.40	.08	.10Y
Cambodia	522	—	—	—	—	—	—	.09Y	—	—	—	—	—	—	—Y
China,P.R.: Mainland	924	—	.20	.40	1.60	.70	1.50	13.45V	85.00	56.10	61.20	73.60	114.60	91.75	424.14V
China,P.R.:Hong Kong	532	1.90	.80	1.10	1.00	1.80	1.55	1.25V	75.60	32.00	29.30	22.20	17.90	12.87	29.77V
India	534	352.60	363.60	339.80	417.10	540.10	562.98	698.65Y	612.40	573.80	911.70	1,067.10	1,230.60	1,481.51	1,838.55Y
Indonesia	536	—	—	—	—	—	.04	.15V	30.80	37.40	51.10	44.10	72.50	78.09	13.66V
Korea	542	3.00	.80	.70	.80	.50	.35	.55V	30.30	32.50	43.40	41.70	38.60	24.74	20.60V
Malaysia	548	—	.10	.10	.10	.20	.49	.53V	42.70	62.70	51.50	49.80	39.20	34.22	13.66V
Maldives	556	—	—	—	—	—	—	.01Y	—	—	—	—	—	—	—Y
New Caledonia	839	—	—	—	—	—	—	.03Y	....	....	....	....	....	....	....
Pakistan	564	.30	.80	1.00	3.80	3.20	2.58	3.20Y	1.40	1.70	2.00	2.60	2.30	2.65	3.28Y
Philippines	566	—	—	—	—	—	—	1.75V	—	—	—	—	—	—	1.46V
Singapore	576	4.60	1.90	1.10	.80	.60	4.46	1.30V	163.70	102.10	116.20	117.90	107.50	46.67	46.57V
Sri Lanka	524	—	—	—	—	.10	.03	.07V	4.00	2.10	1.30	1.90	.50	.72	.20V
Taiwan Province of China	528	.50	.60	.60	.70	.90	.97	.75V	12.40	9.30	16.30	15.90	11.50	7.85	5.17V
Thailand	578	.40	.70	1.10	1.40	1.10	.56	.66V	44.80	42.60	38.40	58.50	43.30	35.98	41.87V
Vietnam	582	—	—	—	.10	.10	.02	—V	.40	.30	1.20	1.80	1.70	4.41	—V
Europe	**170**	**.6**	**.5**	**1.4**	**4.0**	**3.8**	**5.6**	**8.4Y**	**6.3**	**9.4**	**6.6**	**10.4**	**25.9**	**28.5**	**16.9Y**
Azerbaijan	912	—	—	—	—	—	—	—V	—	—	—	—	—	—	.11V
Belarus	913	—	—	—	—	—	—	.04V	—	—	—	—	—	—	.40V
Bulgaria	918	—	—	—	—	—	—	.03V	—	—	—	—	—	—	.06V
Czech Republic	935	.20	.20	.20	.30	.40	.95	.79V	1.10	.90	.50	1.70	.80	.86	1.23V
Estonia	939	—	—	—	—	—	—	.02V	—	—	—	—	—	—	—V
Hungary	944	—	—	—	—	—	—	.17V	—	.10	.80	2.90	3.40	.13	.13V
Latvia	941	—	—	—	—	—	—	.03V	—	—	—	—	—	—	.02V
Lithuania	946	—	—	—	—	—	—	.04V	—	—	—	—	—	—	—V
Poland	964	—	—	—	—	—	—	.44V	—	—	—	—	—	—	.41V
Romania	968	—	—	—	—	—	—	.04V	—	—	—	.10	.60	—	—V
Russia	922	.10	.10	.10	.10	.20	.81	.66V	1.50	7.10	3.10	3.10	9.30	12.45	2.65V
Slovak Republic	936	—	—	—	—	—	—	.03V	—	—	—	.60	1.50	—	.01V
Turkey	186	.30	.20	1.10	3.60	3.20	3.85	5.98V	2.50	.50	1.40	1.20	.60	6.65	1.37V
Ukraine	926	—	—	—	—	—	—	.07Y	1.16	.80	.80	.80	9.70	8.44	10.48Y

	Exports							Imports						
	2001	2002	2003	2004	2005	2006	2007	2001	2002	2003	2004	2005	2006	2007
	Millions of U.S. Dollars							*Millions of U.S. Dollars*						
Middle East.............................. 407	**1.8**	**1.8**	**.8**	**1.1**	**2.5**	**2.7**	**3.7Y**	**122.1**	**81.9**	**50.2**	**50.4**	**62.0**	**60.2**	**76.0Y**
Bahrain.. 419	—	—	—	—	—	.03	.04Y	1.30	.70	.20	—	.10	.86	1.07Y
Egypt.. 469	—	—	—	—	—	—	.05Y	—	—	—	—	—	—	.17Y
Iran, I.R. of.................................... 429	—	—	—	—	.10	.06	.08Y	.40	.20	.80	.80	2.50	3.93	4.74Y
Israel.. 436	.10	.10	.10	—	.10	.06	—V	.50	1.10	5.70	6.60	.90	.89	4.18V
Kuwait.. 443	—	—	—	—	—	.02	.03Y	9.60	13.90	.10	.30	—	.27	.32Y
Lebanon.. 446	—	—	—	—	—	—	.16Y	—	—	—	—	—	—	—Y
Oman.. 449	—	—	—	—	—	.01	.01Y	.80	.40	.50	.50	.90	.25	.30Y
Qatar.. 453	—	—	—	—	.10	.17	.23Y	3.00	1.10	1.50	2.20	3.30	6.67	8.05Y
Saudi Arabia.................................. 456	.50	—	—	—	.10	.11	.14Y	67.20	59.50	30.40	34.50	43.60	32.21	38.86Y
United Arab Emirates.................... 466	1.20	1.70	.70	1.10	2.10	2.28	2.95Y	39.30	5.00	11.00	5.50	10.70	15.15	18.28Y
Western Hemisphere................ 207	**.9**	**.4**	**.3**	**.2**	**.7**	**.7**	**2.4Y**	**8.2**	**8.8**	**13.0**	**19.1**	**26.3**	**31.7**	**1.2Y**
Argentina.. 213	—	—	—	—	—	.01	.01V	6.70	5.80	11.80	15.10	13.20	13.89	.03V
Brazil.. 223	.70	.20	—	—	.20	.28	—V	.40	1.90	.20	4.00	11.60	16.12	—V
Chile... 228	—	—	—	—	—	—	.09V	—	—	—	—	—	—	.03V
Colombia.. 233	—	—	—	—	—	—	.02V	—	—	—	—	—	—	—V
Costa Rica...................................... 238	—	—	—	—	—	—	.02Y	—	—	—	—	—	—	—Y
Mexico.. 273	.20	.20	.30	.20	.50	.37	2.19V	—	—	—	—	—	.01	.12V
Peru.. 293	—	—	—	—	—	—	.01Y	1.06	1.10	1.00	—	1.50	1.70	1.06Y
Countries & Areas n.s.............. 898	**13.2**	**8.0**	**20.9**	**37.0**	**29.7**	**20.0**	**24.9Y**	**33.2**	**102.2**	**4.7**	**71.8**	**84.6**	**267.4**	**331.8Y**
Memorandum Items														
European Union............................ 998	130.70	88.50	87.70	102.40	96.10	100.43	113.57Y	186.30	89.60	104.50	94.10	85.60	86.79	109.46Y
Oil Exporting Ctys......................... 999	1.70	1.70	.70	1.10	2.40	2.70	3.59Y	151.10	117.50	95.40	87.90	133.50	136.57	84.21Y
Non-Oil Develop.Ctys.................... 201	372.10	373.70	353.10	437.50	558.50	586.51	748.33Y	1,092.52	945.60	1,304.30	1,503.80	1,666.50	1,807.26	2,457.28Y
PERCENT DISTRIBUTION														
Industrial Countries................. 101	**48.6**	**37.2**	**41.6**	**34.8**	**27.3**	**26.6**	**23.0**	**18.5**	**16.5**	**11.9**	**9.7**	**9.0**	**7.8**	**8.0**
Developing Countries.............. 202	**49.6**	**61.5**	**55.2**	**60.1**	**69.0**	**71.0**	**74.6**	**79.4**	**76.2**	**87.8**	**86.4**	**87.0**	**81.1**	**81.4**
Africa...................................... 607	**—**	**—**	**—**	**—**	**.1**	**.2**	**.1**	**—**	**.1**	**.1**	**.2**	**.1**	**—**	**.1**
Asia.. 507	**49.2**	**61.1**	**54.8**	**59.4**	**68.1**	**69.8**	**73.1**	**70.7**	**68.9**	**83.3**	**81.8**	**81.3**	**76.0**	**78.3**
Europe.................................... 170	**.1**	**.1**	**.2**	**.5**	**.5**	**.7**	**.8**	**.4**	**.7**	**.4**	**.6**	**1.3**	**1.2**	**.5**
Middle East............................ 407	**.2**	**.3**	**.1**	**.2**	**.3**	**.3**	**.4**	**7.8**	**5.9**	**3.1**	**2.7**	**3.0**	**2.5**	**2.4**
Western Hemisphere............. 207	**.1**	**.1**	**—**	**—**	**.1**	**.1**	**.2**	**.5**	**.6**	**.8**	**1.0**	**1.3**	**1.3**	**—**
ANNUAL PERCENT CHANGE														
World....................................... 001	**4.6**	**–19.0**	**5.1**	**13.8**	**11.4**	**2.1**	**21.6**	**–.3**	**–10.9**	**14.3**	**15.5**	**12.4**	**15.8**	**30.2**
Industrial Countries................. 101	**–5.2**	**–38.1**	**17.5**	**–4.7**	**–12.6**	**–.8**	**5.1**	**–2.9**	**–20.4**	**–17.3**	**–6.1**	**3.7**	**.6**	**33.5**
Developing Countries.............. 202	**15.9**	**.4**	**–5.8**	**24.0**	**27.9**	**5.0**	**27.6**	**7.0**	**–14.5**	**31.7**	**13.7**	**13.1**	**8.0**	**30.7**
Africa...................................... 607	**—**	**—**	**—**	**100.0**	**200.0**	**121.7**	**–46.6**	**–58.3**	**240.0**	**–11.8**	**200.0**	**–48.9**	**–84.7**	**875.9**
Asia.. 507	**15.5**	**.6**	**–5.7**	**23.3**	**27.8**	**4.6**	**27.3**	**5.2**	**–13.1**	**38.2**	**13.5**	**11.7**	**8.3**	**34.1**
Europe.................................... 170	**–40.0**	**–16.7**	**180.0**	**185.7**	**–5.0**	**47.6**	**49.0**	**–.6**	**50.1**	**–29.8**	**57.6**	**149.0**	**10.2**	**–40.9**
Middle East............................ 407	**350.0**	**—**	**–55.6**	**37.5**	**127.3**	**9.8**	**34.4**	**35.1**	**–32.9**	**–38.7**	**.4**	**23.0**	**–2.9**	**26.1**
Western Hemisphere............. 207	**200.0**	**–55.6**	**–25.0**	**–33.3**	**250.0**	**–6.3**	**259.9**	**–37.2**	**7.8**	**47.7**	**46.9**	**37.7**	**20.6**	**–96.1**

		Exports							Imports						
		2001	2002	2003	2004	2005	2006	2007	2001	2002	2003	2004	2005	2006	2007
		Millions of U.S. Dollars							Millions of U.S. Dollars						
IFS World Total		**216,141**	**219,758**	**264,798**	**317,966**	**349,812**	**399,569**	**476,820**	**195,533**	**194,044**	**233,969**	**283,929**	**310,571**	**358,495**	**421,381**
DOTS World Total	**001**	**230,882**	**243,192**	**295,950**	**357,474**	**406,007**	**463,829**	**551,694**	**208,687**	**218,783**	**264,714**	**319,782**	**363,222**	**417,098**	**493,295**
Industrial Countries	**101**	**201,282**	**209,055**	**253,946**	**301,650**	**338,438**	**381,413**	**444,889**	**141,723**	**149,044**	**181,977**	**212,266**	**224,734**	**259,327**	**305,398**
United States	111	9,659	11,119	13,205	15,153	17,259	20,715	23,986	20,666	19,812	21,093	25,315	27,537	32,513	36,016
Canada	156	890	897	1,078	1,233	1,370	1,544	2,099	1,134	1,375	1,554	1,845	2,109	2,751	3,700
Australia	193	611	727	894	1,190	1,297	1,414	1,674	979	783	846	1,007	1,202	1,474	1,805
Japan	158	2,307	2,268	2,537	2,797	2,826	2,865	3,612	9,338	8,804	9,929	11,720	11,667	12,686	15,282
New Zealand	196	169	125	218	191	233	210	254	255	277	387	325	366	435	468
Austria	122	3,728	3,542	4,571	5,331	5,549	6,512	7,945	1,381	1,411	1,720	2,016	2,059	2,222	2,621
Belgium	124	26,578	30,772	36,858	43,118	52,804	64,669	74,912	18,088	21,182	26,786	31,138	33,856	39,341	45,781
Cyprus	423	112	133	171	240	318	365	449	16	22	26	53	143	150	107
Denmark	128	3,249	3,421	3,964	4,815	6,205	5,899	7,015	1,674	1,877	2,581	3,617	3,884	4,760	4,575
Finland	172	2,366	2,530	3,093	3,626	4,415	4,957	5,613	1,803	1,957	2,421	3,402	3,425	4,097	4,976
France	132	24,632	24,854	30,341	35,268	38,118	39,754	46,694	11,341	12,074	13,311	15,931	16,941	18,938	21,586
Germany	134	61,743	61,140	74,675	89,759	101,078	118,091	134,704	35,987	39,053	47,786	57,345	60,422	71,219	87,353
Greece	174	1,887	2,082	2,553	2,961	3,159	3,367	4,041	298	345	388	458	420	431	536
Iceland	176	151	161	241	285	515	484	585	300	349	448	545	568	780	1,151
Ireland	178	2,275	2,382	3,364	3,547	3,674	4,193	5,126	3,422	3,333	4,675	4,637	4,925	4,736	5,404
Italy	136	14,340	14,661	18,018	21,667	23,131	23,772	27,865	5,570	6,082	6,781	7,601	8,362	9,232	10,704
Luxembourg	137	723	765	1,010	1,301	1,662	1,748	1,798	472	464	752	802	884	1,084	1,369
Malta	181	104	96	115	143	147	195	223	13	13	19	17	31	31	23
Norway	142	1,685	1,914	2,257	2,820	3,214	3,354	4,370	2,381	2,564	5,919	7,660	7,706	9,097	11,338
Portugal	182	2,064	2,069	2,641	3,035	3,589	3,427	3,946	1,032	1,107	1,343	1,463	1,518	1,605	1,678
Slovenia	961	311	355	417	517	629	823	945	129	133	174	163	164	202	339
Spain	184	8,132	8,706	11,343	14,197	16,536	16,781	19,984	4,335	4,403	5,456	6,566	6,526	7,236	8,705
Sweden	144	4,708	4,609	5,798	7,180	8,164	8,442	9,744	3,934	4,309	5,059	5,779	5,793	6,818	8,233
Switzerland	146	3,528	3,813	4,550	5,085	5,397	6,355	6,861	2,138	2,279	2,906	2,546	3,010	2,844	3,180
United Kingdom	112	25,329	25,912	30,034	36,191	37,148	41,477	50,443	15,034	15,035	19,619	20,315	21,215	24,645	28,467
Developing Countries	**202**	**28,092**	**32,237**	**39,879**	**52,539**	**64,455**	**77,902**	**102,046**	**60,130**	**62,197**	**81,329**	**106,087**	**137,130**	**156,652**	**186,591**
Africa	**607**	**3,003**	**3,274**	**4,520**	**5,160**	**6,099**	**7,301**	**10,634**	**5,125**	**4,965**	**5,976**	**6,184**	**8,775**	**9,307**	**13,021**
Algeria	612	199	251	258	314	291	345	510	1,528	1,271	895	1,291	1,828	2,017	3,144
Angola	614	110	107	477	165	187	246	356	100	43	21	4	106	92	1,212
Benin	638	49	49	54	42	47	71	84	1	—	—	—	2	27	17
Botswana	616	17	16	18	6	8	6	9	—	—	1	1	1	1	2
Burkina Faso	748	8	9	16	14	17	17	17	1	1	1	3	3	2	3
Burundi	618	5	2	2	8	8	5	4	2	2	4	2	8	1	3
Cameroon	622	44	68	65	74	61	70	77	159	181	311	165	315	370	339
Cape Verde	624	23	21	30	35	32	61	84	—	—	—	—	—	5	—
Central African Rep.	626	2	2	2	4	21	41	40	—	—	—	—	—	1	—
Chad	628	14	9	14	13	18	13	20	—	—	—	—	—	—	—
Comoros	632	2	2	2	2	2	2	2	2	2	1	1	1	13	1
Congo, Dem. Rep. of	636	30	44	39	35	59	68	84	7	2	4	2	8	26	32
Congo, Republic of	634	37	34	33	44	54	59	78	12	7	111	44	7	6	9
Côte d'Ivoire	662	67	65	89	79	115	102	128	410	676	816	676	636	551	770
Djibouti	611	18	25	19	18	20	34	37	3	—	—	—	—	1	1
Equatorial Guinea	642	12	18	21	23	25	40	49	34	20	54	54	357	157	336
Eritrea	643	10	7	8	7	5	16	4	—	—	—	—	—	—	—
Ethiopia	644	21	19	63	68	54	47	55	4	7	8	13	35	41	64
Gabon	646	32	38	45	58	59	98	118	15	14	12	11	46	19	33
Gambia, The	648	22	20	25	24	24	29	41	1	1	—	1	—	1	2
Ghana	652	101	116	135	200	216	244	320	236	272	247	307	325	353	393
Guinea	656	24	23	44	63	54	97	165	4	5	11	2	7	5	38
Guinea-Bissau	654	3	3	4	6	7	7	8	—	—	—	—	—	—	—
Kenya	664	68	68	95	115	157	157	183	168	190	241	290	316	360	436
Lesotho	666	—	—	—	1	—	3	1	—	—	—	—	—	—	1
Liberia	668	12	9	12	32	28	29	49	4	2	3	7	7	1	1
Madagascar	674	13	4	12	8	7	8	61	32	55	22	23	20	33	26
Malawi	676	3	3	3	6	6	8	9	30	24	26	20	47	30	39
Mali	678	12	12	21	19	22	22	27	—	1	—	1	5	4	5
Mauritania	682	17	22	36	38	32	29	52	10	12	25	26	45	47	98
Mauritius	684	15	15	22	19	23	25	69	25	21	26	27	37	26	31
Morocco	686	263	303	377	495	628	654	1,203	201	219	294	269	294	276	361
Mozambique	688	6	14	6	9	15	26	26	58	46	43	10	70	32	35
Namibia	728	5	4	7	8	5	13	29	16	14	20	25	26	36	33
Niger	692	11	14	15	20	16	33	25	2	3	2	1	—	—	—
Nigeria	694	555	581	851	1,076	1,345	1,649	2,822	416	236	773	427	1,169	1,445	1,480
Rwanda	714	7	5	7	9	10	14	13	7	3	3	4	5	7	5
St. Helena	856	—	—	—	—	—	11	5	—	3	2	1	—	1	—
São Tomé & Príncipe	716	1	2	2	3	2	2	2	3	3	6	4	12	5	2
Senegal	722	59	75	69	73	102	205	448	18	12	11	15	18	18	27
Seychelles	718	4	6	6	6	10	10	9	11	22	24	16	25	17	13
Sierra Leone	724	37	33	28	24	30	28	30	1	1	5	2	3	16	13

		Exports							Imports						
		2001	2002	2003	2004	2005	2006	2007	2001	2002	2003	2004	2005	2006	2007
		Millions of U.S. Dollars							*Millions of U.S. Dollars*						
Somalia	726	2	3	1	1	4	5	4	—	—	—	—	—	—	—
South Africa	199	746	778	1,010	1,339	1,546	1,867	2,325	1,125	1,133	1,400	1,836	2,372	2,619	3,067
Sudan	732	57	56	78	124	189	160	108	13	10	17	9	7	21	12
Swaziland	734	1	1	1	2	2	2	5	10	10	20	15	13	28	83
Tanzania	738	31	35	43	61	84	82	90	49	79	86	89	87	108	126
Togo	742	23	53	79	45	93	141	276	4	5	10	22	40	29	46
Tunisia	744	181	205	237	275	288	334	362	155	150	185	236	241	245	392
Uganda	746	14	15	16	21	34	30	37	51	51	68	81	83	71	96
Zambia	754	5	5	9	12	26	37	43	52	40	45	50	37	42	50
Zimbabwe	698	13	13	21	23	20	14	37	146	117	118	101	107	103	143
Asia	**507**	**8,058**	**8,881**	**10,128**	**14,145**	**15,058**	**18,122**	**22,559**	**32,607**	**33,297**	**44,213**	**57,573**	**67,861**	**76,660**	**89,937**
Afghanistan, I.S. of	512	4	18	16	15	80	30	33	—	—	—	—	—	—	—
American Samoa	859	—	—	—	—	1	1	1	—	—	—	—	—	—	—
Bangladesh	513	63	70	50	85	58	56	58	320	287	351	402	404	520	528
Bhutan	514	—	—	—	—	1	1	—	—	—	—	—	—	—	—
Brunei Darussalam	516	10	8	6	12	10	10	14	1	—	1	2	1	—	—
Cambodia	522	1	1	1	2	4	3	6	36	32	32	38	26	32	35
China,P.R.: Mainland	924	1,108	1,485	1,898	2,915	3,254	4,200	5,116	9,354	11,077	16,722	23,696	31,989	39,006	51,936
China,P.R.:Hong Kong	532	910	952	1,029	1,159	1,152	1,287	1,509	1,384	1,412	1,593	2,275	2,557	2,940	2,689
China,P.R.:Macao	546	1	1	2	4	6	10	12	75	72	80	95	36	49	39
Fiji	819	4	2	3	5	4	15	4	1	4	1	1	2	1	2
French Polynesia	887	8	10	13	13	9	17	17	1	1	1	—	—	3	1
Guam	829	—	—	—	—	1	—	—	—	—	—	—	—	—	—
India	534	491	508	632	978	1,126	1,420	2,195	892	953	1,325	1,499	1,945	2,372	2,863
Indonesia	536	324	386	482	500	439	567	981	1,542	1,502	1,770	2,117	2,259	2,627	2,914
Korea	542	996	1,214	1,502	1,901	2,658	3,162	3,724	2,160	2,188	2,629	3,131	3,652	4,239	4,359
Lao People's Dem.Rep.	544	2	5	2	1	1	—	1	11	12	11	12	15	15	12
Malaysia	548	456	451	446	603	573	685	769	4,271	3,871	5,352	5,678	6,417	6,645	7,908
Maldives	556	7	5	11	8	11	9	9	3	4	3	5	5	5	4
Mongolia	948	3	2	7	2	3	4	6	4	1	—	—	—	1	7
Myanmar	518	5	4	5	5	12	7	8	44	18	23	34	16	22	19
Nauru	836	—	—	—	—	—	—	—	—	1	—	—	—	—	—
Nepal	558	3	3	3	4	6	7	9	6	5	5	5	4	4	5
New Caledonia	839	4	4	8	10	14	16	16	—	—	1	—	—	—	2
Pakistan	564	160	143	212	261	285	340	407	210	198	250	282	253	295	351
Papua New Guinea	853	5	5	7	8	5	13	19	17	16	30	34	42	21	48
Philippines	566	285	202	293	440	399	412	451	2,315	2,190	2,325	2,723	2,746	2,266	2,075
Singapore	576	996	1,310	1,232	1,762	1,644	2,047	2,676	3,091	3,179	3,506	4,686	4,252	4,415	4,562
Solomon Islands	813	—	—	—	—	—	—	—	—	—	—	2	—	—	—
Sri Lanka	524	42	39	47	47	61	76	76	89	76	83	97	89	118	135
Taiwan Province of China	528	1,559	1,449	1,452	2,500	2,244	2,537	2,953	4,504	4,165	5,594	7,301	7,560	6,800	4,674
Thailand	578	542	523	649	739	813	897	1,041	1,886	1,614	1,981	2,788	2,924	3,425	3,711
Vanuatu	846	—	—	—	—	1	—	—	—	1	—	1	1	—	1
Vietnam	582	69	81	116	164	185	293	447	393	418	544	667	665	836	1,055
Wallis-Futuna	857	—	—	—	—	1	—	—	—	—	—	—	—	—	—
Europe	**170**	**10,160**	**12,641**	**16,508**	**22,369**	**30,055**	**36,518**	**49,037**	**9,865**	**10,795**	**14,778**	**20,636**	**29,259**	**36,518**	**45,095**
Albania	914	19	9	12	23	24	27	43	2	2	1	3	2	3	36
Armenia	911	7	9	9	9	12	18	29	3	4	13	43	148	111	135
Azerbaijan	912	17	32	64	191	240	159	136	1	1	1	5	6	126	318
Belarus	913	98	90	115	138	169	240	342	57	65	87	97	117	87	122
Bosnia & Herzegovina	963	43	53	56	77	99	90	117	12	14	14	10	26	17	30
Bulgaria	918	157	202	273	366	391	454	722	106	116	135	145	151	196	208
Croatia	960	235	283	369	429	513	580	705	44	38	46	65	76	77	95
Czech Republic	935	1,167	1,495	1,855	3,110	5,057	6,271	8,073	848	908	1,365	1,992	2,169	2,587	3,368
Estonia	939	117	146	214	288	470	678	621	156	161	133	241	345	360	316
Faroe Islands	816	2	2	9	9	6	22	15	29	29	35	21	26	39	55
Georgia	915	13	19	21	25	37	57	61	3	45	24	26	13	9	29
Gibraltar	823	33	61	111	42	235	361	566	1	4	6	4	1	1	18
Hungary	944	1,064	1,301	1,785	2,541	3,322	3,474	4,177	1,143	1,285	1,241	1,666	1,813	1,733	2,446
Kazakhstan	916	121	119	147	298	353	407	558	115	131	325	369	433	466	863
Kosovo	967	—	—	—	—	7	10	11	—	—	—	—	—	1	3
Kyrgyz Republic	917	5	29	43	7	10	21	31	1	—	1	1	—	1	1
Latvia	941	162	169	201	224	308	426	514	87	109	118	123	151	198	252
Lithuania	946	178	218	304	344	490	623	836	149	205	205	253	272	316	341
Macedonia, FYR	962	54	56	71	72	82	89	117	48	46	50	51	60	66	70
Moldova	921	29	31	37	39	48	48	80	9	6	4	8	12	14	18
Montenegro, Rep. of	943	—	—	—	—	—	33	33	—	—	—	—	—	2	2
Poland	964	2,324	2,672	3,133	4,224	5,505	6,994	9,826	1,400	1,530	1,909	2,455	2,648	3,471	4,926
Romania	968	398	529	673	859	1,079	1,461	2,069	332	330	522	582	565	612	704
Russia	922	1,949	2,458	3,325	4,202	5,640	6,897	9,543	3,844	4,021	6,242	9,048	16,151	21,467	25,107
Serbia, Rep. of	942	—	—	—	—	—	279	432	—	—	—	—	—	85	112
Serbia & Montenegro	965	96	152	206	282	127	—	—	45	52	65	57	35	—	—
Slovak Republic	936	286	361	467	579	735	993	1,878	220	269	326	683	864	1,099	1,777
Tajikistan	923	6	3	3	5	2	6	7	1	3	3	15	24	30	29
Turkey	186	1,276	1,733	2,430	3,233	3,927	4,354	5,430	1,011	1,238	1,665	2,344	2,764	2,905	3,028
Turkmenistan	925	6	11	13	17	21	20	25	1	1	—	—	—	1	1
Ukraine	926	273	371	507	682	1,096	1,387	1,983	179	168	227	318	382	418	670

	Code	Exports 2001	2002	2003	2004	2005	2006	2007	Imports 2001	2002	2003	2004	2005	2006	2007
		Millions of U.S. Dollars							*Millions of U.S. Dollars*						
Uzbekistan	927	15	13	38	36	35	31	50	20	13	12	10	8	21	18
Europe n.s.	884	9	14	17	18	24	18	19	—	—	—	—	—	1	1
Middle East	**407**	**4,110**	**4,590**	**5,507**	**6,945**	**8,405**	**9,717**	**11,782**	**5,448**	**6,002**	**7,528**	**9,826**	**16,642**	**17,547**	**17,269**
Bahrain	419	68	68	79	102	118	144	162	16	17	12	27	73	121	232
Egypt	469	362	388	402	539	803	902	1,083	162	240	264	410	465	392	508
Iran, I.R. of	429	250	315	423	647	910	836	674	227	682	1,289	1,826	2,777	3,574	2,538
Iraq	433	38	35	38	96	75	63	70	791	594	297	275	324	588	1,358
Israel	436	920	1,003	1,095	1,323	1,494	1,686	1,927	801	909	1,154	1,286	1,460	1,449	1,875
Jordan	439	103	110	152	172	219	237	244	13	27	38	64	72	72	72
Kuwait	443	148	184	243	307	310	341	513	1,049	771	767	1,113	1,826	2,446	2,478
Lebanon	446	133	151	173	203	204	224	258	13	13	9	17	19	27	39
Libya	672	143	161	153	164	172	176	318	57	90	78	87	407	949	940
Oman	449	92	81	132	158	150	205	307	6	40	6	5	17	9	90
Qatar	453	95	89	120	153	197	288	442	2	7	9	6	20	34	48
Saudi Arabia	456	738	871	1,017	1,250	1,481	1,919	2,154	2,091	2,244	3,261	3,832	5,777	6,902	5,338
Syrian Arab Republic	463	89	109	130	134	172	171	322	64	228	66	31	140	179	229
United Arab Emirates	466	879	970	1,281	1,630	2,031	2,435	3,187	152	134	277	843	3,263	802	1,479
West Bank/Gaza Strip	487	4	4	5	6	8	9	10	3	4	4	4	5	4	5
Yemen, Republic of	474	51	55	70	69	69	89	121	3	6	1	4	1	2	47
Western Hemisphere	**207**	**2,761**	**2,851**	**3,215**	**3,920**	**4,839**	**6,244**	**8,033**	**7,086**	**7,137**	**8,834**	**11,867**	**14,592**	**16,620**	**21,269**
Antigua and Barbuda	311	2	18	6	10	4	4	5	—	—	—	2	—	—	3
Argentina	213	182	98	151	269	298	322	494	669	940	1,068	1,144	1,353	1,333	1,713
Aruba	314	67	84	114	137	89	94	111	30	37	38	44	109	47	12
Bahamas, The	313	66	8	14	21	47	101	109	1	2	3	1	5	—	—
Barbados	316	9	16	12	11	13	10	37	1	1	1	1	1	1	2
Belize	339	5	9	5	6	8	5	7	10	6	9	6	7	14	15
Bermuda	319	4	42	56	32	78	82	95	17	19	11	10	4	1	1
Bolivia	218	6	6	10	8	13	12	17	10	17	20	22	25	42	50
Brazil	223	730	709	670	811	934	1,127	1,727	2,861	2,946	3,825	4,960	5,196	5,510	8,291
Chile	228	194	151	209	270	287	432	657	562	541	764	1,490	2,303	3,375	3,474
Colombia	233	94	85	159	180	387	332	392	278	245	306	526	689	795	1,179
Costa Rica	238	65	116	157	141	95	159	163	969	943	1,083	1,524	1,723	1,822	1,789
Dominica	321	3	3	2	2	2	2	3	—	—	—	—	—	—	—
Dominican Republic	243	54	58	59	53	69	81	76	102	66	68	100	142	134	152
Ecuador	248	45	55	81	123	156	149	114	94	99	125	153	228	238	326
El Salvador	253	12	16	15	16	17	33	25	4	3	5	5	8	8	6
Falkland Islands	323	—	—	—	—	5	—	11	—	—	—	—	—	—	—
Greenland	326	—	—	—	1	2	4	2	1	2	1	—	2	4	7
Grenada	328	3	3	5	4	4	4	6	6	5	5	4	4	1	1
Guatemala	258	18	25	29	41	51	70	82	55	64	78	97	115	115	119
Guyana	336	12	13	15	14	16	27	16	13	11	15	20	25	32	41
Haiti	263	20	15	16	17	15	23	19	2	1	2	1	1	1	1
Honduras	268	26	18	25	24	26	37	32	25	30	28	39	44	77	79
Jamaica	343	20	22	29	24	39	31	25	103	83	85	147	143	151	227
Mexico	273	491	604	619	727	872	1,591	2,042	664	550	622	699	874	987	1,447
Netherlands Antilles	353	161	166	191	202	246	337	406	30	22	32	63	46	22	38
Nicaragua	278	5	3	7	6	9	17	12	11	12	9	10	10	10	22
Panama	283	34	28	65	36	67	58	71	9	14	16	26	28	81	81
Paraguay	288	9	6	7	7	10	10	22	74	54	76	89	80	77	90
Peru	293	46	43	66	64	90	102	138	98	107	184	280	485	494	671
St. Kitts and Nevis	361	—	—	—	—	2	3	2	—	—	—	—	2	6	—
St. Lucia	362	1	1	3	3	81	42	52	—	—	—	—	—	—	—
St. Pierre-Miquelon	363	—	—	—	—	—	1	1	—	—	—	—	—	—	—
St. Vincent & Grens.	364	1	1	4	2	3	6	3	—	—	—	—	1	—	—
Suriname	366	77	88	114	132	145	166	196	49	31	26	19	27	34	33
Trinidad and Tobago	369	46	32	40	60	63	58	57	62	69	35	18	16	71	170
Uruguay	298	37	22	25	27	30	46	65	43	47	84	89	79	94	114
Venezuela, Rep. Bol.	299	141	114	108	139	208	336	415	229	171	208	277	809	1,032	1,114
Western Hem. n.s.	399	74	172	125	297	356	330	326	1	1	—	—	5	9	3
Other Countries n.i.e.	**910**	**78**	**99**	**157**	**185**	**166**	**139**	**166**	**290**	**312**	**370**	**562**	**621**	**660**	**495**
Cuba	928	66	58	63	64	131	117	150	279	305	364	551	614	616	448
North Korea	954	11	41	94	120	35	22	16	12	7	7	11	7	44	47
Countries & Areas n.s.	**898**	**1,361**	**1,738**	**828**	**1,394**	**1,069**	**1,950**	**1,200**	**3,104**	**3,753**	**574**	**305**	**735**	**458**	**809**
Special Categories	**899**	**70**	**63**	**1,140**	**1,706**	**1,874**	**2,422**	**3,387**	**3,440**	**3,477**	**464**	**562**	—	—	—
Memorandum Items															
European Union	998	187,580	194,392	236,923	284,204	322,212	363,932	427,371	108,534	117,270	144,193	168,717	178,830	206,511	245,883
Oil Exporting Ctys.	999	3,602	4,040	5,106	6,432	7,609	9,160	12,394	8,091	7,741	9,628	12,098	20,476	22,425	22,920
Non-Oil Develop.Ctys.	201	24,490	28,197	34,772	46,108	56,847	68,741	89,652	52,039	54,456	71,700	93,989	116,654	134,227	163,672
PERCENT DISTRIBUTION															
Industrial Countries	**101**	**87.2**	**86.0**	**85.8**	**84.4**	**83.4**	**82.2**	**80.6**	**67.9**	**68.1**	**68.7**	**66.4**	**61.9**	**62.2**	**61.9**
Developing Countries	**202**	**12.2**	**13.3**	**13.5**	**14.7**	**15.9**	**16.8**	**18.5**	**28.8**	**28.4**	**30.7**	**33.2**	**37.8**	**37.6**	**37.8**
Africa	**607**	**1.3**	**1.3**	**1.5**	**1.4**	**1.5**	**1.6**	**1.9**	**2.5**	**2.3**	**2.3**	**1.9**	**2.4**	**2.2**	**2.6**
Asia	**507**	**3.5**	**3.7**	**3.4**	**4.0**	**3.7**	**3.9**	**4.1**	**15.6**	**15.2**	**16.7**	**18.0**	**18.7**	**18.4**	**18.2**
Europe	**170**	**4.4**	**5.2**	**5.6**	**6.3**	**7.4**	**7.9**	**8.9**	**4.7**	**4.9**	**5.6**	**6.5**	**8.1**	**8.8**	**9.1**
Middle East	**407**	**1.8**	**1.9**	**1.9**	**1.9**	**2.1**	**2.1**	**2.1**	**2.6**	**2.7**	**2.8**	**3.1**	**4.6**	**4.2**	**3.5**
Western Hemisphere	**207**	**1.2**	**1.2**	**1.1**	**1.1**	**1.2**	**1.3**	**1.5**	**3.4**	**3.3**	**3.3**	**3.7**	**4.0**	**4.0**	**4.3**
Other Countries n.i.e.	**910**	—	—	**.1**	**.1**	—	—	—	**.1**	**.1**	**.1**	**.2**	**.2**	**.2**	**.1**

	Exports							Imports						
	2001	2002	2003	2004	2005	2006	2007	2001	2002	2003	2004	2005	2006	2007
ANNUAL PERCENT CHANGE														
World.. 001	.5	5.3	21.7	20.8	13.6	14.2	18.9	–3.3	4.8	21.0	20.8	13.6	14.8	18.3
Industrial Countries................. 101	.3	3.9	21.5	18.8	12.2	12.7	16.6	–5.3	5.2	22.1	16.6	5.9	15.4	17.8
Developing Countries.............. 202	1.7	14.8	23.7	31.7	22.7	20.9	31.0	–1.2	3.4	30.8	30.4	29.3	14.2	19.1
Africa..................................... 607	10.3	9.0	38.1	14.1	18.2	19.7	45.7	19.6	–3.1	20.3	3.5	41.9	6.1	39.9
Asia.. 507	–8.1	10.2	14.0	39.7	6.5	20.3	24.5	–.7	2.1	32.8	30.2	17.9	13.0	17.3
Europe.................................... 170	3.5	24.4	30.6	35.5	34.4	21.5	34.3	3.2	9.4	36.9	39.6	41.8	24.8	23.5
Middle East............................ 407	9.8	11.7	20.0	26.1	21.0	15.6	21.3	–28.1	10.2	25.4	30.5	69.4	5.4	–1.6
Western Hemisphere.............. 207	7.1	3.3	12.8	21.9	23.4	29.0	28.7	7.5	.7	23.8	34.3	23.0	13.9	28.0
Other Countries n.i.e............... 910	–9.8	28.2	57.6	17.9	–10.2	–16.0	19.1	–13.0	7.4	18.8	51.8	10.5	6.3	–25.0

		Exports							Imports						
		2001	2002	2003	2004	2005	2006	2007	2001	2002	2003	2004	2005	2006	2007
		Millions of U.S. Dollars							*Millions of U.S. Dollars*						
IFS World Total		**2,398.0**	**1,609.0**	**1,161.0**	**762.0**	**962.0**	**1,125.0**	**1,179.9**	**2,826.0**	**2,268.0**	**2,606.0**	**1,948.0**	**2,277.0**	**2,590.0**	**2,880.0**
DOTS World Total	**001**	**2,397.5**	**1,609.4**	**1,171.1**	**2,109.9Y**	**3,065.5Y**	**3,919.3Y**	**3,891.2Y**	**2,825.0**	**2,267.4**	**2,615.5**	**9,883.9Y**	**11,879.5Y**	**10,728.2Y**	**12,937.6Y**
Industrial Countries	**101**	**667.7**	**533.1**	**341.9**	**585.4Y**	**1,043.1Y**	**1,538.0Y**	**1,107.2Y**	**748.3**	**621.1**	**677.2**	**1,594.2Y**	**2,199.2Y**	**3,217.1Y**	**3,627.5Y**
United States	111	472.69	374.99	249.19	422.55V	882.27V	1,058.00V	736.45V	387.28	305.03	356.08	960.19V	1,248.39V	1,633.72V	2,290.42V
Canada	156	94.33	68.60	14.21	27.33V	1.19V	57.19V	18.30V	9.86	6.55	6.45	20.80V	18.53V	24.86V	59.89V
Australia	193	3.08	3.55	1.02	3.08V	5.79V	7.82V	7.97V	2.35	.94	1.34	1.71V	8.71V	6.44V	4.76V
Japan	158	1.30	1.67	.61	1.35V	4.61V	6.81V	47.15V	45.48	36.71	29.80	53.96V	53.51V	71.88V	73.58V
New Zealand	196	—	—	.03	.21V	5.40V	1.40V	.07V	.21	.26	.37	.57V	.90V	1.99V	1.82V
Austria	122	—	.01	.01	.31V	1.26V	.01V	.02V	.24	.51	.22	5.94V	7.12V	6.64V	9.19V
Belgium	124	8.06	8.08	7.48	20.08V	13.78V	28.52V	25.87V	28.09	6.94	3.44	15.67V	21.82V	27.56V	25.60V
Cyprus	423	—	—	—	—V	—Y	—V	—V	—	—	.25	.17V	.06V	.25V	.23V
Denmark	128	3.77	.01	16.10	.53V	.27V	1.17V	.27V	1.72	1.82	4.36	7.23V	7.86V	7.21V	17.31V
Finland	172	.05	—	.01	1.76V	.02V	.18V	9.98V	6.59	.53	.63	3.43V	6.90V	4.74V	5.94V
France	132	18.05	4.19	2.66	6.78V	38.77V	6.29V	8.64V	3.75	5.00	15.32	49.74V	52.58V	79.94V	55.84V
Germany	134	.67	1.28	.41	12.95V	24.77V	239.92V	26.56V	34.74	38.96	18.40	44.89V	30.26V	35.66V	70.73V
Greece	174	.01	.01	.01	.09V	—V	—V	.02V	.12	.27	.08	.44V	1.13V	.79V	32.28V
Iceland	176	—	.61	—	—V	—V	—V	—V	.04	.04	.02	—V	—V	—V	—V
Ireland	178	.59	.58	—	.01V	—V	—V	—V	.29	.27	.20	1.73V	.43V	.43V	.23V
Italy	136	2.93	.20	.11	14.52V	1.41V	42.62V	90.85V	73.06	6.31	16.69	85.22V	287.15V	585.13V	152.75V
Luxembourg	137	—	—	—	.01V	—V	—V	—V	.04	—	—	.14V	2.24V	.31V	.27V
Malta	181	.01	—	.01	—V	—V	—V	.05V	.01	—	—	—V	—V	.51V	—V
Netherlands	138	55.35	66.75	42.68	57.36V	41.75V	20.02V	34.21V	141.18	184.77	204.11	222.18V	270.25V	370.49V	446.12V
Norway	142	—	.20	—	.19V	.01V	.01V	.03V	.67	.36	.40	1.78V	15.04V	1.79V	2.91V
Portugal	182	.03	.02	.01	.31V	.40V	.02V	1.68V	.95	1.24	1.04	1.35V	5.79V	2.53V	64.31V
Slovenia	961	—	—	—	.03Y	—V	—V	—V	—	—	—	.13Y	.17V	.36V	.09V
Spain	184	1.79	.71	.15	11.10V	2.16V	5.57V	62.66V	3.87	4.23	5.25	35.52V	58.68V	106.99V	23.33V
Sweden	144	.07	.10	.12	.07V	1.30V	.02V	2.69V	1.78	2.11	2.54	11.83V	32.53V	7.04V	8.06V
Switzerland	146	.03	.03	.01	1.12V	.11V	.23V	.22V	1.43	2.28	3.71	20.57V	22.88V	24.34V	29.06V
United Kingdom	112	4.84	1.48	7.06	3.66V	17.86V	62.24V	33.53V	4.54	15.96	6.53	49.02V	46.23V	215.47V	252.82V
Developing Countries	**202**	**1,589.9**	**1,013.4**	**728.0**	**1,391.5Y**	**1,870.4Y**	**2,193.5Y**	**2,550.9Y**	**2,061.1**	**1,628.7**	**1,894.3**	**8,231.9Y**	**9,614.4Y**	**7,429.6Y**	**9,208.9Y**
Africa	**607**	**20.2**	**17.8**	**32.9**	**48.5Y**	**86.0Y**	**92.0Y**	**110.8Y**	**1.8**	**3.6**	**1.5**	**13.3Y**	**10.9Y**	**7.9Y**	**8.4Y**
Angola	614	—	—	.03	.04Y	.04Y	.05Y	.07Y	—	—	—	—Y	—Y	—Y	—Y
Benin	638	—	—	—	—V	.05V	.06Y	.07Y	—	—	—	—V	—V	—Y	—Y
Cameroon	622	—	—	—	.01Y	.01Y	.01Y	.01Y	—	—	—	—Y	—Y	—Y	—Y
Central African Rep.	626	—	—	—	—Y	—Y	—Y	—Y	.04	—	.03	.04Y	.05Y	.06Y	.08Y
Congo, Republic of	634	—	—	—	.17V	.20Y	.24Y	.30Y	—	—	—	—V	—Y	—Y	—Y
Côte d'Ivoire	662	—	—	—	1.06V	.01V	—V	—Y	—	—	—	.09V	.19V	.66V	.82Y
Gabon	646	—	.02	—	—Y	—Y	—Y	—Y	.07	.09	—	—Y	—Y	—Y	—Y
Ghana	652	8.05	—	—	—Y	—Y	—Y	—Y	—	—	—	—Y	—Y	—Y	—Y
Guinea	656	—	.03	—	.05V	.05Y	.07Y	.08Y	—	—	—	—V	—Y	—Y	—Y
Liberia	668	1.07	—	13.36	17.54Y	20.04Y	24.77Y	30.74Y	—	—	—	—Y	—Y	—Y	—Y
Madagascar	674	—	—	—	—Y	—Y	—Y	—Y	—	—	—	.04Y	.04Y	.05Y	.06Y
Mauritius	684	—	—	—	4.69V	—V	4.44V	.01V	—	—	—	—V	.02V	—V	.01V
Morocco	686	.03	.07	—	—V	18.77V	23.20Y	28.79Y	.29	.14	.03	7.64V	.04V	.05Y	.07Y
Niger	692	.03	.01	—	—V	—Y	—Y	—Y	.04	.06	.20	—V	—Y	—Y	—Y
Nigeria	694	10.29	16.38	18.99	24.69Y	31.44Y	38.81Y	50.28Y	—	—	—	—Y	—Y	—Y	—Y
St. Helena	856	.07	—	—	—Y	—Y	—Y	—Y	—	—	—	—Y	—Y	—Y	—Y
Senegal	722	—	—	.01	—V	—V	.31V	.38Y	.03	.01	.03	—V	—V	—V	—Y
Sierra Leone	724	.06	—	—	—Y	—Y	—Y	—Y	—	—	.01	.02Y	.02Y	.02Y	.03Y
South Africa	199	.35	1.23	.55	.12V	15.32V	—V	—V	1.35	3.03	.84	5.27V	4.30V	6.70V	6.77V
Sudan	732	.28	.01	—	—V	—V	—V	—V	—	.13	.03	—V	—V	—V	—V
Tanzania	738	—	—	—	.01Y	.01Y	.01Y	.01Y	—	—	—	—Y	—Y	—Y	—Y
Togo	742	—	—	—	—V	.01V	.02Y	.02Y	—	—	—	—V	—V	—Y	—Y
Tunisia	744	—	—	—	.03V	.01V	.02V	.02Y	—	—	.08	—V	5.99V	.01V	.02Y
Zambia	754	—	—	—	.11V	.08V	—V	—V	—	—	—	—V	—V	.01V	.08V
Zimbabwe	698	—	—	—	—V	—V	—V	—Y	.01	.14	.13	—V	—V	.02V	.02Y
Africa n.s.	799	—	—	—	—Y	—Y	—Y	—Y	—	—	.09	.17Y	.26Y	.35Y	.44Y
Asia	**507**	**102.9**	**13.7**	**76.1**	**81.5Y**	**71.7Y**	**202.4Y**	**280.1Y**	**37.1**	**14.6**	**50.0**	**128.8Y**	**268.4Y**	**222.6Y**	**180.5Y**
Bangladesh	513	—	—	—	—V	—V	—V	—V	—	—	.03	.39V	2.18V	1.16Y	1.58Y
Brunei Darussalam	516	—	—	—	—Y	—Y	—Y	—Y	—	—	.01	.01Y	.01Y	.01Y	.01Y
China,P.R.: Mainland	924	.55	6.43	.44	.83V	1.20V	.15V	—Y	3.00	3.06	3.54	78.37V	94.15V	132.99V	75.56V
China,P.R.:Hong Kong	532	.01	—	.01	—V	—V	—V	—V	2.52	2.40	2.11	—V	—V	—V	—V
China,P.R.:Macao	546	—	—	—	—V	—V	—V	—V	.04	—	—	—V	—V	—V	—V
Guam	829	.91	—	—	—Y	—Y	—Y	—Y	—	—	—	—Y	—Y	—Y	—Y
India	534	.01	.77	.01	.05V	.04V	.05Y	.06Y	6.90	.91	23.55	7.83V	9.88V	12.21Y	15.15Y
Indonesia	536	—	—	—	4.86V	3.51V	8.38V	.47V	.92	.33	.59	9.82V	12.18V	6.71V	8.59V
Korea	542	—	.02	—	.19V	.31V	.55V	.30V	7.39	5.63	7.96	7.86V	11.83V	15.43V	15.39V
Malaysia	548	—	—	14.41	.03V	.31V	.28V	1.44V	.10	.12	.21	2.18V	1.91V	2.78V	4.59V
Nauru	836	....	....	....	....	....	....	....	.02	—	.09	.12Y	.14Y	.17Y	.21Y
Pakistan	564	—	—	—	1.09V	1.12V	1.39Y	1.73Y	—	—	—	.11V	.56V	.69Y	.85Y
Papua New Guinea	853	.01	—	—	—Y	—Y	—Y	—Y	—	—	—	—Y	—Y	—Y	—Y
Philippines	566	—	—	—	.06V	.02V	—V	—V	.21	.12	.15	.48V	.49V	.47V	.34V

		Exports							Imports						
		2001	2002	2003	2004	2005	2006	2007	2001	2002	2003	2004	2005	2006	2007
		Millions of U.S. Dollars							Millions of U.S. Dollars						
Samoa	862	—	—	—	—Y	.12V	.14Y	.18Y	....	....	....	....	....	....	....
Singapore	576	100.94	6.50	60.96	72.39V	59.54V	187.65V	267.88V	14.35	.15	9.45	15.29V	15.52V	24.50V	24.29V
Sri Lanka	524	—	—	—	.24V	.08V	—V	—V	—	—	—	.05V	109.94V	—V	—V
Taiwan Province of China	528	.01	—	—	—V	—V	—V	—V	.69	.89	1.12	—V	—V	—V	—V
Thailand	578	—	—	—	1.80V	5.43V	3.82V	8.00V	.90	.97	1.13	6.33V	9.60V	25.47V	33.88V
Vietnam	582	.47	—	.22	—V	—V	—V	—V	.02	.05	.07	—V	—V	—V	—V
Europe	**170**	**—**	**.9**	**.1**	**26.0Y**	**4.8Y**	**3.4Y**	**3.8Y**	**18.6**	**.3**	**.5**	**30.5Y**	**24.7Y**	**110.6Y**	**51.5Y**
Albania	914	—	—	—	—V	—V	—V	—V	.11	—	—	—V	—V	—V	—V
Azerbaijan	912	—	—	—	—V	.01V	—V	—V	—	—	—	—V	—V	—V	—V
Bulgaria	918	—	—	—	—V	—V	—V	.01V	.04	—	—	.02V	.15V	.61V	.29V
Czech Republic	935	—	—	—	.35V	2.46V	—V	—V	.02	—	.02	.17V	.18V	.52V	.19V
Estonia	939	—	—	—	—V	—V	—V	—V	—	—	—	.01V	5.68V	41.01V	.05V
Gibraltar	823	—	—	—	—Y	—Y	—Y	—Y	9.61	—	—	—Y	—Y	—Y	—Y
Hungary	944	—	—	—	1.14V	—V	—V	—V	.11	—	.06	.53V	.98V	.63V	2.00V
Latvia	941	—	—	—	—V	—V	—V	—V	—	—	—	.04V	.51V	.24V	.38V
Lithuania	946	—	—	—	—V	1.55V	3.18V	—V	—	—	—	.01V	2.14V	.05V	—V
Moldova	921	—	—	—	—V	.05V	.06Y	.07Y	....	....	....	....	....	....	....
Poland	964	.01	—	—	23.73V	—V	—V	—V	.02	.02	.07	26.97V	.43V	1.10V	2.74V
Romania	968	—	—	—	.14V	—V	.01V	2.17V	—	—	—	.14V	.13V	.35V	.04V
Russia	922	—	.69	—	—V	—V	.03V	.06V	8.57	.06	.02	—V	.04V	63.06V	41.38V
Slovak Republic	936	—	—	—	—Y	—V	—V	—V	—	—	—	—Y	.08V	.19V	.38V
Turkey	186	—	.07	.06	.64V	.73V	.06V	1.53V	.12	.17	.28	1.79V	14.41V	2.81V	4.03V
Ukraine	926	—	.11	—	—V	—V	—Y	—Y	.01	.05	.10	.79V	—V	—Y	—Y
Middle East	**407**	**—**	**45.8**	**—**	**—Y**	**—Y**	**—Y**	**—Y**	**237.1**	**152.2**	**.9**	**.2Y**	**.3Y**	**.4Y**	**.4Y**
Bahrain	419	—	4.86	—	—Y	—Y	—Y	—Y	—	—	—	—Y	—Y	—Y	—Y
Egypt	469	.01	—	—	—Y	—Y	—Y	—Y	28.17	—	.04	.05Y	.06Y	.07Y	.09Y
Iran, I.R. of	429	—	—	—	—Y	—Y	—Y	—Y	.06	.01	—	—Y	—Y	—Y	—Y
Iraq	433	....	....	....	....	....	....	....	208.45	151.05	—	—Y	—Y	—Y	—Y
Israel	436	.02	.33	.03	—V	—V	—V	—V	.14	.40	.68	—V	—V	—V	—V
Jordan	439	—	—	—	—V	—V	—V	—V	—	.05	—	—Y	—Y	—Y	—Y
Lebanon	446	—	.07	—	—Y	—Y	—Y	—Y	.07	.22	.05	.06Y	.07Y	.09Y	.11Y
Saudi Arabia	456	—	—	—	—Y	—V	—Y	—Y	.19	.46	.03	.04Y	.05Y	.06Y	.08Y
Syrian Arab Republic	463	—	—	—	—V	—Y	—Y	—Y	.01	—	—	—V	—Y	—Y	—Y
United Arab Emirates	466	—	40.58	—	—Y	—Y	—Y	—Y	.01	.04	.06	.08Y	.11Y	.14Y	.17Y
Western Hemisphere	**207**	**1,466.7**	**935.2**	**618.9**	**1,235.5Y**	**1,707.9Y**	**1,895.7Y**	**2,156.2Y**	**1,766.5**	**1,457.9**	**1,841.4**	**8,059.1Y**	**9,310.0Y**	**7,088.2Y**	**8,968.1Y**
Antigua and Barbuda	311	24.58	22.00	16.66	21.88Y	25.00Y	30.90Y	38.35Y	.06	.78	.90	1.18Y	1.34Y	1.66Y	2.06Y
Argentina	213	1.93	.01	—	5.02V	2.02V	5.99V	4.74V	.70	1.60	2.03	51.71V	87.60V	129.59V	48.29V
Aruba	314	26.14	22.65	25.12	22.67V	25.36V	30.37V	28.50V	4.79	4.23	10.55	9.79V	10.46V	9.91V	14.24V
Bahamas, The	313	128.62	129.91	89.06	116.97Y	133.65Y	165.18Y	204.99Y	.01	.01	26.56	34.88Y	39.85Y	49.26Y	61.13Y
Barbados	316	2.80	2.39	.51	15.35V	11.86V	1.02V	1.27Y	1.37	.56	1.02	3.83V	2.20V	4.18V	5.19Y
Belize	339	39.66	26.08	6.19	8.13Y	9.28Y	11.47Y	14.24Y	.01	.03	1.01	1.33Y	1.51Y	1.87Y	2.32Y
Bermuda	319	10.56	7.33	—	—Y	.43V	.33V	.41Y	.57	.71	1.21	1.59Y	1.82Y	2.25Y	2.79Y
Bolivia	218	.02	—	.69	.11V	.01V	.01Y	.01Y	.62	.20	.16	—V	—Y	—Y	—Y
Brazil	223	18.28	4.99	2.77	8.35V	6.95V	3.17V	7.54V	7.83	9.58	12.64	84.73V	88.72V	326.26V	912.77V
Chile	228	16.95	8.84	19.91	21.78V	16.82V	13.17V	10.47V	.93	1.62	1.75	4.14V	3.29V	2.93V	3.04V
Colombia	233	19.96	18.17	8.93	7.04V	2.52V	6.75V	10.49V	13.95	30.33	15.69	66.66V	35.89V	42.08V	30.40V
Costa Rica	238	45.92	3.34	2.61	33.50V	30.47V	37.65Y	46.73Y	2.62	3.25	3.75	6.49V	7.09V	8.77Y	10.88Y
Dominica	321	.08	.01	.03	.04Y	.05Y	.06Y	.08Y	.15	.01	—	—Y	—Y	.01Y	.01Y
Dominican Republic	243	34.03	15.63	3.37	4.43Y	5.06Y	6.25Y	7.76Y	1.54	1.67	4.69	6.16Y	7.04Y	8.70Y	10.80Y
Ecuador	248	15.62	10.80	6.98	28.92V	55.18V	27.46V	34.08Y	11.29	.45	1.35	3.67V	2.71V	2.03V	2.51Y
El Salvador	253	98.35	79.99	16.71	56.96V	82.15V	56.40V	55.81V	.37	.24	.51	1.49V	.80V	.18V	.22V
Greenland	326	.02	—	—	—Y	—Y	—Y	—Y	—	—	—	—Y	—Y	—Y	—Y
Grenada	328	6.61	4.36	.20	.26Y	.30Y	.37Y	.46Y	—	.01	—	—Y	—Y	—Y	—Y
Guatemala	258	117.56	66.44	52.16	183.06V	87.59V	108.25Y	134.34Y	.79	1.02	1.07	1.55V	2.24V	2.76Y	3.43Y
Guyana	336	120.11	69.69	11.55	15.16Y	17.33Y	21.42Y	26.58Y	.96	.07	3.83	5.04Y	5.75Y	7.11Y	8.83Y
Haiti	263	80.42	34.16	29.09	146.79V	167.72Y	207.29Y	257.24Y	.02	.01	.01	.01Y	.01Y	.02Y	.02Y
Honduras	268	168.64	74.21	57.06	87.71V	100.22Y	123.86Y	153.71Y	.15	.10	2.54	.26V	.30Y	.37Y	.46Y
Jamaica	343	16.62	1.31	1.30	12.87V	16.50V	9.52V	6.05V	.31	.32	.62	2.95V	2.12V	1.64V	2.94V
Mexico	273	35.58	5.48	1.70	77.58V	278.72V	403.88V	517.59V	3.01	3.29	4.95	24.17V	14.81V	36.71V	61.55V
Nicaragua	278	33.49	36.33	2.34	—V	—V	—V	—V	—	—	—	—V	—V	—V	—V
Panama	283	52.82	67.99	41.52	232.49V	431.99V	443.86V	444.69V	20.36	15.15	16.82	.90V	1.01V	1.03V	1.07V
Paraguay	288	—	.03	—	.03V	.08V	.07V	.09Y	.26	—	.39	2.96V	3.30V	3.39V	4.21Y
Peru	293	3.87	2.75	3.33	10.00V	13.10V	2.12V	3.76Y	1.01	.95	1.22	1.82V	7.63V	11.45V	13.85Y
St. Kitts and Nevis	361	2.45	.08	.06	.08Y	.09Y	.11Y	.14Y	.01	—	—	—Y	—Y	—Y	—Y
St. Lucia	362	.23	.07	.11	.14Y	.16Y	.19Y	.24Y	.08	.08	.15	.19Y	.22Y	.27Y	.34Y
St. Vincent & Grens	364	.06	.14	.20	.37V	.14V	.18Y	.22Y	—	—	.03	—V	.14V	.17Y	.21Y
Suriname	366	24.14	24.14	3.35	4.40Y	5.02Y	6.21Y	7.71Y	.56	.34	.66	.87Y	1.00Y	1.23Y	1.53Y
Trinidad and Tobago	369	13.51	3.18	4.24	5.57Y	6.36Y	7.86Y	9.76Y	6.79	7.10	8.42	11.05Y	12.63Y	15.61Y	19.37Y
Uruguay	298	.24	.17	.04	1.55V	2.22V	2.74Y	3.40Y	.06	.43	1.37	1.27V	.46V	.57Y	.71Y
Venezuela, Rep. Bol	299	271.89	169.84	187.47	81.78V	148.19V	135.36V	97.68V	1,683.11	1,370.81	1,693.95	7,688.22V	8,909.32V	6,338.80V	7,647.01Y
Western Hem. n.s	399	34.89	22.73	23.61	24.50Y	25.38Y	26.26Y	27.15Y	2.19	2.99	21.58	40.16Y	58.75Y	77.34Y	95.92Y
Other Countries n.i.e	**910**	**120.2**	**61.5**	**32.1**	**42.2Y**	**48.2Y**	**59.6Y**	**73.9Y**	**.2**	**.2**	**.2**	**.2Y**	**.3Y**	**.3Y**	**.4Y**
Cuba	928	120.15	61.54	32.13	42.20Y	48.21Y	59.59Y	73.95Y	.16	.20	.18	.24Y	.28Y	.34Y	.42Y
Countries & Areas n.s	**898**	**19.7**	**1.3**	**69.1**	**90.8Y**	**103.7Y**	**128.2Y**	**159.1Y**	**15.5**	**17.3**	**43.7**	**57.4Y**	**65.5Y**	**81.0Y**	**100.5Y**
Memorandum Items															
European Union	998	96.25	83.42	76.83	154.80Y	147.78Y	409.77Y	297.05Y	301.12	268.95	279.21	562.38Y	841.21Y	1,495.81Y	1,170.83Y
Oil Exporting Ctys	999	282.18	226.80	206.46	111.33Y	183.15Y	182.55Y	148.43Y	1,892.73	1,522.70	1,694.64	7,698.16Y	8,921.66Y	6,345.70Y	7,655.84Y
Non-Oil Develop.Ctys	201	1,307.74	786.63	521.51	1,280.21Y	1,687.26Y	2,010.96Y	2,402.52Y	168.35	106.03	199.66	533.75Y	692.72Y	1,083.92Y	1,553.03Y

	Exports							Imports						
	2001	2002	2003	2004	2005	2006	2007	2001	2002	2003	2004	2005	2006	2007
PERCENT DISTRIBUTION														
Industrial Countries.................. 101	27.8	33.1	29.2	27.7	34.0	39.2	28.5	26.5	27.4	25.9	16.1	18.5	30.0	28.0
Developing Countries.............. 202	66.3	63.0	62.2	66.0	61.0	56.0	65.6	73.0	71.8	72.4	83.3	80.9	69.3	71.2
Africa...................................... 607	.8	1.1	2.8	2.3	2.8	2.3	2.8	.1	.2	.1	.1	.1	.1	.1
Asia... 507	4.3	.9	6.5	3.9	2.3	5.2	7.2	1.3	.6	1.9	1.3	2.3	2.1	1.4
Europe.................................... 170	—	.1	—	1.2	.2	.1	.1	.7	—	—	.3	.2	1.0	.4
Middle East............................ 407	—	2.8	—	—	—	—	—	8.4	6.7	—	—	—	—	—
Western Hemisphere.............. 207	61.2	58.1	52.8	58.6	55.7	48.4	55.4	62.5	64.3	70.4	81.5	78.4	66.1	69.3
Other Countries n.i.e................ 910	5.0	3.8	2.7	2.0	1.6	1.5	1.9	—	—	—	—	—	—	—
ANNUAL PERCENT CHANGE														
World.. 001	20.9	−32.9	−27.2	80.2	45.3	27.9	−.7	−1.0	−19.7	15.3	277.9	20.2	−9.7	20.6
Industrial Countries.................. 101	17.6	−20.2	−35.9	71.2	78.2	47.4	−28.0	10.3	−17.0	9.0	135.4	37.9	46.3	12.8
Developing Countries.............. 202	14.5	−36.3	−28.2	91.2	34.4	17.3	16.3	−4.6	−21.0	16.3	334.6	16.8	−22.7	23.9
Africa...................................... 607	−49.0	−12.3	85.5	47.3	77.4	6.9	20.4	−92.8	95.6	−59.2	801.0	−17.7	−27.2	5.7
Asia... 507	47.7	−86.7	454.3	7.2	−12.1	182.4	38.4	75.9	−60.5	241.4	157.7	108.3	−17.1	−18.9
Europe.................................... 170	−87.3	—	−93.1	—	−81.5	−30.2	14.8	—	−98.3	73.7	—	−18.8	346.9	−53.4
Middle East............................ 407	−90.4	—	−99.9	.1	....	....	....	140.0	−35.8	−99.4	−72.7	25.3	24.8	22.2
Western Hemisphere.............. 207	14.7	−36.2	−33.8	99.6	38.2	11.0	13.7	−12.4	−17.5	26.3	337.7	15.5	−23.9	26.5
Other Countries n.i.e................ 910	785.3	−48.8	−47.8	31.3	14.3	23.6	24.1	4.4	24.5	−7.6	31.3	14.3	23.6	24.1

	Exports							Imports						
	2001	2002	2003	2004	2005	2006	2007	2001	2002	2003	2004	2005	2006	2007
	Millions of U.S. Dollars							*Millions of U.S. Dollars*						
IFS World Total	**13,730**	**14,382**	**16,527**	**20,344**	**21,729**	**22,434**	**26,972**	**13,308**	**15,046**	**18,559**	**23,195**	**26,234**	**26,430**	**30,900**
DOTS World Total 001	**13,478**	**14,186**	**16,325**	**20,340**	**21,766**	**22,441**	**26,997**	**13,367**	**15,098**	**18,476**	**23,094**	**26,133**	**26,363**	**30,781**
Industrial Countries 101	**8,467**	**9,162**	**10,620**	**12,895**	**13,796**	**13,676**	**15,756**	**9,372**	**10,425**	**12,616**	**15,514**	**16,642**	**15,858**	**18,030**
United States 111	2,027	2,199	2,371	2,926	3,067	2,947	3,103	2,152	2,061	2,188	2,618	2,882	3,107	2,984
Canada 156	264	297	315	347	392	358	398	198	174	335	410	337	449	430
Australia 193	2,534	2,875	3,546	4,259	4,657	4,598	5,928	2,925	3,336	4,109	5,164	5,460	5,399	6,362
Japan 158	1,682	1,627	1,788	2,287	2,301	2,303	2,474	1,467	1,813	2,173	2,588	2,880	2,417	2,918
Austria 122	8	4	8	11	14	12	18	48	78	77	98	111	122	132
Belgium 124	228	297	363	345	366	411	398	135	168	198	223	224	192	212
Cyprus 423	5	6	7	10	12	10	14	—	—	—	—	1	—	1
Denmark 128	41	40	86	145	127	96	140	61	69	92	165	117	174	170
Finland 172	9	7	9	13	15	17	21	81	71	81	137	130	107	118
France 132	154	180	227	263	289	266	315	260	316	528	699	708	510	490
Germany 134	348	414	431	484	558	566	557	644	778	985	1,208	1,272	1,172	1,445
Greece 174	30	31	37	41	53	41	44	5	7	8	9	14	12	16
Iceland 176	—	1	1	1	1	2	2	1	1	2	2	4	2	3
Ireland 178	14	12	18	33	25	31	46	65	68	80	105	121	142	130
Italy 136	229	215	258	290	316	332	340	309	391	457	557	618	541	707
Luxembourg 137	—	—	—	—	—	—	1	7	6	8	8	7	6	7
Malta 181	5	4	7	6	4	8	7	—	—	—	—	1	1	1
Netherlands 138	89	125	146	193	237	283	298	125	152	172	192	272	194	386
Norway 142	7	7	21	10	50	11	70	36	23	51	22	28	27	31
Portugal 182	20	15	23	18	22	22	22	16	18	19	20	18	15	18
Slovenia 961	—	—	3	1	4	2	3	4	4	5	6	7	6	8
Spain 184	64	76	95	159	172	151	179	70	77	98	113	134	150	200
Sweden 144	22	20	28	36	39	46	53	147	160	200	238	258	224	250
Switzerland 146	34	35	49	56	65	61	71	97	102	135	151	196	163	210
United Kingdom 112	652	675	785	961	1,012	1,103	1,252	518	555	618	783	844	724	799
Developing Countries 202	**4,835**	**4,867**	**5,540**	**7,137**	**7,664**	**8,459**	**10,791**	**3,916**	**4,344**	**5,857**	**7,578**	**9,489**	**10,503**	**12,745**
Africa 607	**134**	**177**	**198**	**282**	**363**	**519**	**651**	**151**	**194**	**262**	**328**	**413**	**321**	**345**
Algeria 612	38	65	53	73	96	139	183	—	—	—	—	—	—	—
Angola 614	1	1	2	4	9	14	12	—	—	—	—	—	—	—
Benin 638	—	—	2	3	4	1	1	—	—	—	—	—	—	—
Botswana 616	—	—	—	—	—	15	—	—	—	—	—	—	—	—
Burundi 618	—	—	—	—	1	—	—	—	—	—	—	—	—	—
Cameroon 622	—	—	—	—	2	3	4	—	—	—	—	—	—	—
Congo, Dem. Rep. of 636	—	—	1	2	4	7	5	—	—	—	—	—	—	—
Congo, Republic of 634	—	—	1	1	1	1	2	—	—	—	—	—	—	—
Côte d'Ivoire 662	1	1	2	3	4	3	2	—	—	—	—	—	—	—
Djibouti 611	—	—	—	—	—	1	2	—	—	—	—	—	—	—
Equatorial Guinea 642	—	—	—	—	—	—	—	—	—	—	8	—	—	—
Eritrea 643	—	—	1	1	—	—	—	—	—	—	—	—	—	—
Ethiopia 644	—	—	—	—	3	1	—	—	—	—	—	1	1	1
Gabon 646	—	—	—	1	—	1	3	—	—	—	—	—	—	—
Gambia, The 648	—	—	1	1	—	1	—	—	—	—	—	—	—	—
Ghana 652	3	2	5	5	7	23	34	—	1	1	1	1	2	3
Guinea 656	—	—	1	1	—	—	—	—	—	—	—	—	—	—
Kenya 664	1	1	2	2	3	4	6	1	2	1	1	2	2	2
Liberia 668	—	—	—	—	1	1	—	—	—	—	—	—	—	—
Madagascar 674	2	—	1	2	2	2	—	—	—	—	—	—	—	—
Malawi 676	—	—	—	—	—	—	—	2	2	3	2	1	1	—
Mali 678	—	2	—	—	—	1	—	—	—	—	—	—	—	—
Mauritania 682	—	—	5	—	1	—	—	—	—	—	—	—	—	—
Mauritius 684	12	11	15	20	26	23	36	1	—	—	—	—	—	—
Morocco 686	11	11	9	10	19	29	24	81	62	65	97	88	107	115
Mozambique 688	1	—	—	1	1	3	4	—	—	—	—	1	1	1
Niger 692	—	1	2	—	—	—	—	—	—	—	—	—	—	—
Nigeria 694	5	13	22	45	41	70	127	—	28	63	43	98	—	55
Senegal 722	1	2	4	2	2	17	5	—	—	—	—	—	—	—
Seychelles 718	1	1	1	1	2	1	5	—	—	—	1	1	—	1
Sierra Leone 724	—	1	—	—	—	1	—	—	—	—	—	—	—	—
South Africa 199	49	56	63	97	118	134	154	49	64	77	104	149	99	113
Sudan 732	1	1	1	3	7	12	27	—	—	—	—	—	51	—
Swaziland 734	—	—	—	1	—	—	—	—	13	28	44	52	35	39
Tanzania 738	1	1	1	2	2	3	4	—	—	—	1	1	1	1
Togo 742	—	—	—	—	—	—	—	6	10	13	13	8	6	—
Tunisia 744	4	3	3	2	3	5	7	8	8	6	8	9	14	11
Uganda 746	1	—	—	—	—	—	—	—	—	—	—	—	—	—
Zambia 754	—	—	—	—	1	—	1	—	—	1	1	—	1	—
Zimbabwe 698	—	—	—	—	2	—	—	3	3	3	3	1	1	—
Asia 507	**3,542**	**3,588**	**4,084**	**5,255**	**5,506**	**6,002**	**7,550**	**2,927**	**3,402**	**4,494**	**6,034**	**7,483**	**8,526**	**10,720**
Afghanistan, I.S. of 512	—	—	1	1	—	—	—	—	—	—	—	1	—	—
American Samoa 859	13	23	24	27	25	24	27	1	—	1	1	1	1	2
Bangladesh 513	10	12	11	18	13	17	28	4	5	6	4	4	5	5

Exports (Millions of U.S. Dollars)

	2001	2002	2003	2004	2005	2006	2007
Brunei Darussalam........ 516	1	2	1	2	2	67	2
Cambodia........ 522	1	—	—	—	1	1	1
China,P.R.: Mainland........ 924	541	655	792	1,150	1,104	1,220	1,443
China,P.R.:Hong Kong........ 532	323	287	324	369	369	363	431
China,P.R.:Macao........ 546	3	5	3	2	3	3	4
Fiji........ 819	102	131	154	237	250	243	252
French Polynesia........ 887	71	82	92	116	115	114	149
Guam........ 829	5	5	4	6	6	6	7
India........ 534	65	89	90	128	166	218	270
Indonesia........ 536	229	208	221	271	328	399	576
Kiribati........ 826	1	3	4	4	5	4	5
Korea........ 542	593	621	572	779	769	881	981
Lao People's Dem.Rep........ 544	1	—	—	1	—	—	1
Malaysia........ 548	295	274	307	348	331	323	480
Maldives........ 556	3	3	2	9	4	13	12
Mongolia........ 948	—	—	—	1	1	1	1
Myanmar........ 518	7	8	4	4	2	3	4
Nauru........ 836	1	—	—	—	—	—	—
Nepal........ 558	12	12	15	6	8	10	7
New Caledonia........ 839	37	41	55	82	86	88	122
Pakistan........ 564	9	11	15	19	29	46	64
Palau........ 565	—	—	—	1	—	—	—
Papua New Guinea........ 853	41	48	94	61	72	73	88
Philippines........ 566	236	213	282	333	355	334	492
Samoa........ 862	42	39	46	65	69	63	69
Singapore........ 576	168	177	184	241	306	346	510
Solomon Islands........ 813	5	5	6	11	9	12	14
Sri Lanka........ 524	69	60	82	105	127	134	177
Taiwan Province of China........ 528	296	313	358	464	545	497	568
Thailand........ 578	172	164	194	244	238	284	419
Tonga........ 866	22	24	39	41	39	35	40
Tuvalu........ 869	1	1	1	2	1	2	2
Vanuatu........ 846	10	12	11	15	18	22	32
Vietnam........ 582	155	59	92	93	108	158	271
Wallis-Futuna........ 857	1	—	—	—	—	—	2
Europe........ 170	**202**	**210**	**244**	**385**	**366**	**388**	**403**
Albania........ 914	—	1	—	—	—	—	1
Armenia........ 911	—	—	—	3	6	7	9
Azerbaijan........ 912	—	—	3	9	34	20	37
Belarus........ 913	—	—	—	—	1	—	1
Bulgaria........ 918	—	—	—	1	4	5	3
Croatia........ 960	1	—	1	3	4	4	6
Czech Republic........ 935	1	3	7	2	1	6	8
Estonia........ 939	6	2	4	1	2	2	2
Faroe Islands........ 816	1	1	1	1	2	2	2
Georgia........ 915	1	1	4	11	3	8	11
Gibraltar........ 823	—	—	—	—	—	—	1
Hungary........ 944	1	1	2	3	1	1	2
Kazakhstan........ 916	—	3	—	1	2	3	—
Latvia........ 941	23	24	3	3	2	3	3
Lithuania........ 946	3	2	5	5	5	7	6
Macedonia, FYR........ 962	1	—	—	—	—	—	—
Moldova........ 921	—	—	—	—	1	2	3
Poland........ 964	4	6	13	10	11	9	14
Romania........ 968	—	—	—	12	2	3	3
Russia........ 922	14	32	64	68	91	105	115
Serbia & Montenegro........ 965	—	—	—	—	—	1	—
Slovak Republic........ 936	—	—	—	—	—	—	—
Tajikistan........ 923	—	—	—	—	—	1	2
Turkey........ 186	15	19	17	20	29	32	39
Ukraine........ 926	—	1	—	1	2	5	11
Uzbekistan........ 927	—	—	—	—	—	3	3
Europe n.s........ 884	129	113	116	227	163	157	119
Middle East........ 407	**369**	**407**	**482**	**627**	**708**	**822**	**1,105**
Bahrain........ 419	8	7	8	12	12	10	16
Egypt........ 469	69	68	66	62	84	104	129
Iran, I.R. of........ 429	27	47	63	65	55	84	106
Iraq........ 433	—	—	—	—	1	—	—
Israel........ 436	5	6	6	36	12	9	14
Jordan........ 439	11	30	39	17	49	45	20
Kuwait........ 443	19	19	29	23	39	46	71
Lebanon........ 446	3	3	5	7	7	6	5
Libya........ 672	1	—	2	3	2	5	5
Oman........ 449	9	18	30	61	24	38	67
Qatar........ 453	4	3	5	6	8	10	14
Saudi Arabia........ 456	129	127	158	215	269	267	389

Imports (Millions of U.S. Dollars)

	2001	2002	2003	2004	2005	2006	2007
Brunei Darussalam........ 516	12	79	113	146	74	219	142
Cambodia........ 522	1	—	—	—	1	1	1
China,P.R.: Mainland........ 924	930	1,209	1,669	2,249	2,843	3,238	4,130
China,P.R.:Hong Kong........ 532	66	66	90	125	135	128	156
China,P.R.:Macao........ 546	1	1	2	2	3	4	4
Fiji........ 819	24	25	30	33	36	38	50
French Polynesia........ 887	1	2	2	2	2	3	1
Guam........ 829	—	—	—	—	—	—	—
India........ 534	80	89	105	135	157	163	198
Indonesia........ 536	179	184	236	278	445	575	840
Kiribati........ 826	—	—	—	—	—	—	—
Korea........ 542	306	367	495	661	727	778	837
Lao People's Dem.Rep........ 544	—	—	—	—	—	—	—
Malaysia........ 548	411	372	429	576	675	805	930
Maldives........ 556	—	—	—	—	—	—	—
Mongolia........ 948	—	—	—	—	—	—	—
Myanmar........ 518	1	1	1	—	1	1	1
Nauru........ 836	3	2	—	—	—	—	—
Nepal........ 558	—	—	—	—	—	1	1
New Caledonia........ 839	—	—	—	—	1	—	1
Pakistan........ 564	32	35	37	43	43	39	42
Palau........ 565	—	—	—	—	—	—	—
Papua New Guinea........ 853	39	40	47	25	63	40	60
Philippines........ 566	37	43	74	77	85	95	157
Samoa........ 862	1	2	2	1	1	2	3
Singapore........ 576	263	267	357	619	842	1,151	1,523
Solomon Islands........ 813	—	—	1	1	1	2	1
Sri Lanka........ 524	9	10	15	16	19	21	22
Taiwan Province of China........ 528	278	306	404	523	588	473	677
Thailand........ 578	215	260	335	440	661	644	831
Tonga........ 866	1	1	1	3	1	2	2
Tuvalu........ 869	—	—	—	—	—	—	—
Vanuatu........ 846	1	1	—	1	—	—	1
Vietnam........ 582	32	34	41	72	72	96	100
Wallis-Futuna........ 857	—	—	—	—	—	—	—
Europe........ 170	**56**	**72**	**123**	**132**	**193**	**142**	**185**
Albania........ 914	—	—	—	—	—	—	—
Armenia........ 911	—	—	—	—	—	—	—
Azerbaijan........ 912	—	—	—	—	—	—	—
Belarus........ 913	—	—	—	—	—	—	—
Bulgaria........ 918	—	1	1	1	2	2	3
Croatia........ 960	1	1	1	1	1	2	1
Czech Republic........ 935	5	13	15	18	23	20	24
Estonia........ 939	—	—	—	—	1	2	1
Faroe Islands........ 816	—	—	—	—	—	—	—
Georgia........ 915	—	—	—	—	—	—	—
Gibraltar........ 823	—	1	1	—	—	—	—
Hungary........ 944	8	9	14	19	23	22	35
Kazakhstan........ 916	2	1	2	2	4	1	4
Latvia........ 941	—	—	—	1	1	1	1
Lithuania........ 946	—	—	—	—	—	—	1
Macedonia, FYR........ 962	3	—	—	—	—	—	—
Moldova........ 921	—	—	—	—	—	—	—
Poland........ 964	4	6	8	16	25	16	23
Romania........ 968	1	2	4	4	4	3	3
Russia........ 922	6	14	42	13	22	6	9
Serbia & Montenegro........ 965	—	—	—	—	1	—	—
Slovak Republic........ 936	3	2	3	4	5	5	5
Tajikistan........ 923	—	—	—	—	—	—	—
Turkey........ 186	16	22	28	50	75	56	72
Ukraine........ 926	5	2	2	3	5	4	4
Uzbekistan........ 927	—	—	—	—	—	—	—
Europe n.s........ 884	—	—	—	—	—	—	—
Middle East........ 407	**616**	**499**	**785**	**840**	**1,097**	**1,245**	**1,151**
Bahrain........ 419	4	3	6	8	7	9	9
Egypt........ 469	1	1	3	4	2	4	5
Iran, I.R. of........ 429	10	39	24	29	8	113	4
Iraq........ 433	—	—	—	—	—	—	—
Israel........ 436	31	28	34	79	45	49	67
Jordan........ 439	—	—	—	—	1	1	1
Kuwait........ 443	95	18	69	18	71	78	96
Lebanon........ 446	—	—	—	—	—	—	1
Libya........ 672	—	—	—	—	27	—	—
Oman........ 449	141	136	141	120	100	48	—
Qatar........ 453	50	49	74	92	136	173	243
Saudi Arabia........ 456	165	127	115	171	262	320	322

	Exports							Imports						
	2001	2002	2003	2004	2005	2006	2007	2001	2002	2003	2004	2005	2006	2007
	Millions of U.S. Dollars							*Millions of U.S. Dollars*						
Syrian Arab Republic.................... 463	3	5	5	11	18	36	62	—	—	—	—	—	—	—
United Arab Emirates.................. 466	73	62	56	90	116	143	177	119	98	318	228	347	424	402
Yemen, Republic of...................... 474	8	10	9	19	13	20	32	—	—	—	91	90	26	—
Western Hemisphere............... 207	**588**	**485**	**532**	**588**	**722**	**727**	**1,082**	**166**	**176**	**193**	**244**	**304**	**268**	**345**
Antigua and Barbuda.................. 311	—	1	—	1	1	1	1	—	—	—	—	—	—	—
Argentina.................................. 213	14	4	6	11	8	11	17	7	11	12	16	20	17	35
Aruba... 314	—	—	—	—	—	—	1	—	—	—	—	—	—	—
Bahamas, The............................. 313	1	1	1	2	1	15	1	—	—	—	—	—	—	—
Barbados.................................... 316	8	10	11	13	13	12	16	—	—	—	—	—	1	1
Bermuda..................................... 319	2	2	2	3	3	3	3	—	—	—	—	—	—	—
Bolivia.. 218	—	—	—	—	1	2	2	1	1	—	—	—	1	1
Brazil.. 223	31	37	19	23	63	57	32	33	45	65	79	109	81	114
Chile... 228	20	16	19	35	37	37	40	11	11	20	26	33	26	29
Colombia.................................... 233	14	4	3	4	3	5	7	2	3	3	4	5	5	7
Costa Rica.................................. 238	1	3	2	1	1	1	2	1	1	2	2	3	2	3
Dominican Republic..................... 243	18	14	13	14	10	14	24	—	1	1	1	1	1	2
Ecuador...................................... 248	2	1	3	2	1	2	2	30	33	19	19	23	22	22
El Salvador................................. 253	43	22	21	18	22	14	13	—	—	—	—	—	—	1
Grenada...................................... 328	2	2	1	2	2	2	2	—	—	—	—	—	—	—
Guatemala.................................. 258	11	16	17	19	22	23	25	1	1	1	1	2	2	2
Guyana....................................... 336	4	4	4	4	5	5	7	1	—	—	—	1	—	1
Haiti... 263	—	—	—	1	1	—	—	—	—	—	—	—	—	—
Honduras.................................... 268	1	1	1	1	—	2	1	—	—	—	—	1	1	1
Jamaica...................................... 343	18	13	11	17	22	21	32	4	4	5	6	5	5	4
Mexico.. 273	220	216	241	264	310	278	446	71	55	57	70	85	90	102
Netherlands Antilles..................... 353	1	1	1	1	1	2	2	—	—	—	—	6	2	—
Nicaragua................................... 278	1	3	2	1	1	18	25	—	—	—	—	—	—	1
Panama....................................... 283	14	14	19	16	23	24	32	—	—	—	1	—	—	—
Paraguay..................................... 288	—	—	6	—	—	1	—	—	—	—	—	—	—	—
Peru... 293	36	21	22	25	17	18	25	2	5	6	10	8	10	14
St. Lucia..................................... 362	1	1	1	2	2	2	3	—	—	—	—	—	—	—
St. Vincent & Grens..................... 364	1	—	—	—	1	1	1	—	—	—	—	—	—	—
Suriname.................................... 366	—	—	—	—	—	—	—	—	—	—	—	—	—	3
Trinidad and Tobago.................... 369	10	10	12	15	24	21	33	—	—	—	—	—	—	—
Uruguay...................................... 298	3	3	5	5	3	3	7	—	—	—	—	—	—	1
Venezuela, Rep. Bol..................... 299	111	44	78	78	98	116	266	—	5	—	6	—	1	—
Western Hem. n.s........................ 399	—	20	10	11	24	14	16	—	—	—	—	—	—	—
Other Countries n.i.e................ 910	**46**	**32**	**40**	**55**	**42**	**46**	**84**	**1**	**1**	**1**	**1**	**1**	**1**	**1**
Cuba... 928	46	32	40	55	42	46	84	1	1	1	1	1	1	1
Countries & Areas n.s.............. 898	**—**	**—**	**—**	**—**	**1**	**—**	**65**	**—**	**244**	**—**	**—**	**—**	**—**	**—**
Special Categories................... 899	**101**	**91**	**77**	**181**	**185**	**188**	**210**	**67**	**83**	**—**	**—**	**—**	**—**	**—**
Memorandum Items														
European Union........................... 998	1,957	2,160	2,564	3,034	3,286	3,426	3,746	2,516	2,947	3,666	4,619	4,933	4,359	5,180
Oil Exporting Ctys........................ 999	643	608	716	930	1,077	1,318	1,980	759	683	1,040	984	1,494	1,733	1,963
Non-Oil Develop.Ctys................... 201	4,192	4,259	4,824	6,207	6,587	7,141	8,811	3,157	3,661	4,817	6,593	7,996	8,770	10,782
PERCENT DISTRIBUTION														
Industrial Countries................. 101	**62.8**	**64.6**	**65.1**	**63.4**	**63.4**	**60.9**	**58.4**	**70.1**	**69.1**	**68.3**	**67.2**	**63.7**	**60.2**	**58.6**
Developing Countries.............. 202	**35.9**	**34.3**	**33.9**	**35.1**	**35.2**	**37.7**	**40.0**	**29.3**	**28.8**	**31.7**	**32.8**	**36.3**	**39.8**	**41.4**
Africa..................................... 607	**1.0**	**1.2**	**1.2**	**1.4**	**1.7**	**2.3**	**2.4**	**1.1**	**1.3**	**1.4**	**1.4**	**1.6**	**1.2**	**1.1**
Asia.. 507	**26.3**	**25.3**	**25.0**	**25.8**	**25.3**	**26.7**	**28.0**	**21.9**	**22.5**	**24.3**	**26.1**	**28.6**	**32.3**	**34.8**
Europe.................................... 170	**1.5**	**1.5**	**1.5**	**1.9**	**1.7**	**1.7**	**1.5**	**.4**	**.5**	**.7**	**.6**	**.7**	**.5**	**.6**
Middle East............................ 407	**2.7**	**2.9**	**3.0**	**3.1**	**3.3**	**3.7**	**4.1**	**4.6**	**3.3**	**4.2**	**3.6**	**4.2**	**4.7**	**3.7**
Western Hemisphere............. 207	**4.4**	**3.4**	**3.3**	**2.9**	**3.3**	**3.2**	**4.0**	**1.2**	**1.2**	**1.0**	**1.1**	**1.2**	**1.0**	**1.1**
Other Countries n.i.e................ 910	**.3**	**.2**	**.2**	**.3**	**.2**	**.2**	**.3**	**—**	**—**	**—**	**—**	**—**	**—**	**—**
ANNUAL PERCENT CHANGE														
World....................................... 001	**5.8**	**5.3**	**15.1**	**24.6**	**7.0**	**3.1**	**20.3**	**−4.2**	**12.9**	**22.4**	**25.0**	**13.2**	**.9**	**16.8**
Industrial Countries................. 101	**2.1**	**8.2**	**15.9**	**21.4**	**7.0**	**−.9**	**15.2**	**−5.0**	**11.2**	**21.0**	**23.0**	**7.3**	**−4.7**	**13.7**
Developing Countries.............. 202	**12.9**	**.7**	**13.8**	**28.8**	**7.4**	**10.4**	**27.6**	**−2.4**	**10.9**	**34.8**	**29.4**	**25.2**	**10.7**	**21.3**
Africa..................................... 607	**14.0**	**32.0**	**12.0**	**42.2**	**28.7**	**43.2**	**25.4**	**−9.9**	**28.7**	**34.9**	**24.9**	**26.0**	**−22.1**	**7.2**
Asia.. 507	**11.7**	**1.3**	**13.8**	**28.7**	**4.8**	**9.0**	**25.8**	**6.3**	**16.2**	**32.1**	**34.3**	**24.0**	**13.9**	**25.7**
Europe.................................... 170	**−8.8**	**4.1**	**16.2**	**57.7**	**−4.9**	**6.1**	**3.8**	**−3.5**	**29.4**	**69.6**	**7.4**	**46.1**	**−26.3**	**30.2**
Middle East............................ 407	**3.0**	**10.3**	**18.5**	**30.1**	**12.9**	**16.2**	**34.4**	**−21.3**	**−19.0**	**57.3**	**7.0**	**30.5**	**13.6**	**−7.6**
Western Hemisphere............. 207	**42.4**	**−17.5**	**9.7**	**10.6**	**22.8**	**.7**	**48.8**	**−33.9**	**5.9**	**9.7**	**26.3**	**24.8**	**−11.7**	**28.4**
Other Countries n.i.e................ 910	**510.5**	**−31.6**	**26.8**	**36.6**	**−23.0**	**9.3**	**83.3**	**45.2**	**8.0**	**−5.6**	**30.3**	**20.6**	**1.3**	**33.6**

		Exports							Imports						
		2001	2002	2003	2004	2005	2006	2007	2001	2002	2003	2004	2005	2006	2007
		Millions of U.S. Dollars							*Millions of U.S. Dollars*						
IFS World Total		**589.4**	**561.0**	**604.5**	**755.6**	**857.9**	**1,027.4**	**1,193.8**	**1,775.3**	**1,753.7**	**1,879.4**	**2,212.3**	**2,595.1**	**3,000.3**	**3,579.2**
DOTS World Total	**001**	**589.4**	**561.0**	**604.5**	**759.8**	**866.0**	**1,049.5**	**1,202.2**	**1,775.3**	**1,753.7**	**1,879.8**	**2,209.6**	**2,623.2**	**2,991.5**	**3,621.6**
Industrial Countries	**101**	**313.1**	**312.0**	**312.9**	**433.7**	**460.1**	**578.9**	**624.9**	**731.3**	**718.6**	**722.4**	**762.3**	**827.5**	**928.1**	**1,140.9**
United States	111	201.88	221.33	217.16	293.00	306.80	369.42	380.76	493.78	476.43	464.13	495.20	524.90	615.37	815.24
Canada	156	19.66	19.41	21.35	36.00	32.50	45.32	69.45	30.40	19.15	15.69	22.20	21.90	22.91	27.50
Japan	158	3.17	4.43	4.18	7.50	10.40	9.26	12.80	88.22	93.79	81.87	96.90	118.00	111.25	121.42
Belgium	124	8.02	3.52	3.78	11.70	8.80	32.53	25.22	8.23	8.76	10.86	17.60	12.50	14.32	7.87
Finland	172	2.57	3.59	2.92	5.90	8.20	7.45	11.91	.51	.55	2.08	2.80	2.00	2.26	2.51
France	132	6.66	9.21	5.98	7.70	4.10	7.48	9.56	12.68	9.58	10.62	11.50	13.10	16.61	15.40
Germany	134	30.21	13.01	9.49	14.10	15.50	30.47	24.04	36.76	27.64	42.08	42.40	37.30	43.67	41.41
Italy	136	4.26	15.27	19.00	6.20	5.00	22.14	17.60	11.03	9.68	9.70	9.80	12.80	12.60	13.23
Netherlands	138	6.33	4.89	5.05	3.80	5.90	9.65	11.37	2.53	5.04	7.19	9.60	4.70	10.58	12.51
Norway	142	.09	.27	.60	.60	.50	.73	.79	.60	.45	.31	.30	.40	14.15	.24
Spain	184	10.91	11.20	15.89	21.70	34.00	34.62	43.61	27.00	32.39	26.85	29.30	43.70	36.29	37.77
Sweden	144	1.09	.84	.99	3.50	3.20	4.12	3.56	4.35	21.24	32.75	6.50	18.00	10.64	20.96
Switzerland	146	1.86	2.39	3.37	4.50	3.40	.29	.21	9.25	7.55	9.55	8.30	9.20	8.71	8.64
United Kingdom	112	16.37	2.61	3.13	17.50	21.80	5.44	14.05	5.94	6.38	8.71	9.90	9.00	8.70	16.23
Developing Countries	**202**	**267.9**	**246.8**	**290.0**	**323.3**	**402.7**	**467.4**	**573.1**	**1,026.7**	**1,023.5**	**1,149.6**	**1,439.3**	**1,789.6**	**2,052.3**	**2,464.6**
Asia	**507**	**2.0**	**1.5**	**4.3**	**9.1**	**22.8**	**12.6**	**22.1**	**128.5**	**157.3**	**176.6**	**212.9**	**279.2**	**363.2**	**486.1**
Korea	542	—	—	—	.90	1.00	—	.31	—	—	—	21.90	36.60	43.76	84.09
Taiwan Province of China	528	.41	.19	.21	1.90	4.00	5.38	10.22	19.83	19.11	17.07	16.20	16.20	16.42	15.42
Asia n.s.	598	1.63	1.28	4.07	6.30	17.80	7.23	11.62	108.69	138.18	159.53	174.80	226.40	303.01	386.56
Europe	**170**	**44.7**	**15.0**	**16.0**	**4.1**	**16.6**	**10.6**	**16.0**	**39.3**	**29.4**	**33.6**	**52.6**	**59.1**	**50.9**	**47.5**
Russia	922	—	—	—	1.20	13.70	7.80	9.06	—	—	—	20.10	28.00	24.86	24.17
Europe n.s.	884	44.68	15.04	15.97	2.90	2.90	2.78	6.92	39.30	29.36	33.61	32.50	31.10	26.00	23.31
Western Hemisphere	**207**	**221.2**	**230.3**	**269.8**	**310.1**	**363.3**	**444.2**	**535.0**	**858.8**	**836.8**	**939.3**	**1,173.8**	**1,451.3**	**1,638.3**	**1,931.0**
Argentina	213	—	.01	—	—	.10	.01	.02	5.54	6.17	8.23	20.30	47.40	68.15	66.68
Chile	228	—	.05	—	.10	4.00	1.19	3.55	7.01	9.19	8.43	13.10	12.70	38.51	35.95
Colombia	233	1.13	.12	.26	.80	1.30	1.95	2.61	9.18	6.95	8.51	8.60	9.80	12.78	14.82
Costa Rica	238	36.36	48.42	49.22	50.90	53.60	59.93	86.95	158.59	151.30	167.63	190.20	237.20	260.20	304.60
Dominican Republic	243	2.55	3.49	5.79	6.40	7.00	8.63	4.83	1.74	1.65	1.47	3.40	3.40	5.42	4.45
Ecuador	248	.55	.09	.10	—	.10	.29	.51	15.63	18.34	26.01	51.50	110.00	75.55	140.53
El Salvador	253	75.78	86.72	104.36	109.50	122.80	149.29	168.51	104.76	102.69	91.90	109.60	135.70	157.39	172.72
Guatemala	258	22.88	23.20	25.88	32.30	44.40	48.19	65.81	130.03	136.83	137.52	158.00	182.80	197.82	223.63
Honduras	268	39.63	38.41	43.52	56.60	68.10	98.15	111.22	21.47	9.71	32.41	51.60	61.20	75.64	104.16
Mexico	273	27.05	21.38	27.90	39.90	44.00	48.47	58.02	130.64	112.17	158.84	178.90	216.90	404.08	487.64
Panama	283	8.58	3.95	4.76	3.90	6.00	8.47	9.56	32.21	22.43	18.93	16.30	17.10	10.58	13.73
Venezuela, Rep. Bol	299	1.84	3.44	.88	1.40	3.50	2.07	6.28	195.16	196.13	183.24	280.10	307.20	220.66	232.42
Western Hem. n.s.	399	4.81	1.05	7.11	8.30	8.40	17.52	17.07	46.90	63.26	96.21	92.20	109.90	111.50	129.69
Other Countries n.i.e.	**910**	**1.1**	**1.0**	**.4**	**.1**	**.5**	**.4**	**.7**	**.7**	**.3**	**.4**	**.6**	**.3**	**1.0**	**6.3**
Cuba	928	1.13	1.01	.39	.10	.50	.37	.66	.68	.29	.40	.60	.30	.97	6.27
Countries & Areas n.s.	**898**	**7.3**	**1.2**	**1.3**	**2.7**	**2.7**	**2.8**	**3.5**	**16.7**	**11.4**	**7.5**	**7.4**	**5.8**	**10.1**	**9.8**
Memorandum Items															
European Union	998	86.40	64.15	66.21	92.10	106.50	153.90	160.92	109.03	121.26	150.84	139.40	153.10	155.69	167.89
Oil Exporting Ctys	999	1.84	3.44	.88	1.40	3.50	2.07	6.28	195.16	196.13	183.24	280.10	307.20	220.66	232.42
Non-Oil Develop.Ctys	201	266.04	243.41	289.14	321.90	399.20	465.29	566.80	831.50	827.33	966.31	1,159.20	1,482.40	1,831.67	2,232.18
PERCENT DISTRIBUTION															
Industrial Countries	**101**	**53.1**	**55.6**	**51.8**	**57.1**	**53.1**	**55.2**	**52.0**	**41.2**	**41.0**	**38.4**	**34.5**	**31.5**	**31.0**	**31.5**
Developing Countries	**202**	**45.5**	**44.0**	**48.0**	**42.6**	**46.5**	**44.5**	**47.7**	**57.8**	**58.4**	**61.2**	**65.1**	**68.2**	**68.6**	**68.1**
Asia	**507**	**.3**	**.3**	**.7**	**1.2**	**2.6**	**1.2**	**1.8**	**7.2**	**9.0**	**9.4**	**9.6**	**10.6**	**12.1**	**13.4**
Europe	**170**	**7.6**	**2.7**	**2.6**	**.5**	**1.9**	**1.0**	**1.3**	**2.2**	**1.7**	**1.8**	**2.4**	**2.3**	**1.7**	**1.3**
Western Hemisphere	**207**	**37.5**	**41.1**	**44.6**	**40.8**	**42.0**	**42.3**	**44.5**	**48.4**	**47.7**	**50.0**	**53.1**	**55.3**	**54.8**	**53.3**
Other Countries n.i.e.	**910**	**.2**	**.2**	**.1**	—	**.1**	—	**.1**	—	—	—	—	—	—	**.2**
ANNUAL PERCENT CHANGE															
World	**001**	**–8.3**	**–4.8**	**7.8**	**25.7**	**14.0**	**21.2**	**14.5**	**–1.7**	**–1.2**	**7.2**	**17.5**	**18.7**	**14.0**	**21.1**
Industrial Countries	**101**	**–23.8**	**–.4**	**.3**	**38.6**	**6.1**	**25.8**	**7.9**	**–1.6**	**–1.7**	**.5**	**5.5**	**8.6**	**12.2**	**22.9**
Developing Countries	**202**	**17.4**	**–7.9**	**17.5**	**11.5**	**24.6**	**16.1**	**22.6**	**–1.7**	**–.3**	**12.3**	**25.2**	**24.3**	**14.7**	**20.1**
Africa	**607**	—	—	—	....	**164.9**	....	**222.4**	—	—	—	....	**13.2**	....	**–41.6**
Asia	**507**	**–34.4**	**–27.7**	**190.3**	**112.7**	**150.5**	**–44.7**	**75.6**	**–6.4**	**22.4**	**12.3**	**20.6**	**31.1**	**30.1**	**33.8**
Europe	**170**	**189.3**	**–66.3**	**6.2**	**–74.3**	**304.9**	**–36.2**	**50.9**	**47.7**	**–25.3**	**14.5**	**56.5**	**12.4**	**–13.9**	**–6.6**
Middle East	**407**	—	—	....	....	**28.3**	....	**14.4**	—	—	—	....	**–37.7**	....	**–28.9**
Western Hemisphere	**207**	**5.5**	**4.1**	**17.1**	**15.0**	**17.2**	**22.3**	**20.4**	**–2.4**	**–2.6**	**12.3**	**25.0**	**23.6**	**12.9**	**17.9**
Other Countries n.i.e.	**910**	**–60.3**	**–10.3**	**–61.4**	**–74.4**	**400.0**	**–25.9**	**77.3**	**–43.5**	**–57.9**	**40.9**	**48.6**	**–50.0**	**224.6**	**543.9**

		Exports							Imports						
		2001	2002	2003	2004	2005	2006	2007	2001	2002	2003	2004	2005	2006	2007
		Millions of U.S. Dollars							Millions of U.S. Dollars						
IFS World Total		**272.4**	**279.5**	**352.0**	**437.0**	**477.6**	**520.8**	**650.0**	**412.1**	**468.3**	**622.0**	**750.0**	**805.0**	**950.0**	**970.0**
DOTS World Total	**001**	**162.4**	**168.6**	**199.7**	**222.5**	**299.4Y**	**428.9Y**	**384.5Y**	**325.0**	**395.7**	**495.0**	**588.0**	**838.4Y**	**1,009.2Y**	**1,097.1Y**
Industrial Countries	**101**	**88.2**	**94.0**	**116.3**	**152.0**	**212.1Y**	**274.4Y**	**242.3Y**	**129.7**	**150.5**	**190.1**	**243.2**	**425.2Y**	**480.2Y**	**526.5Y**
United States	111	.53	.07	.40	.27	60.27V	113.64V	8.73V	18.82	20.56	27.12	60.42	89.10V	142.12V	76.23V
Canada	156	.03	—	—	.05	2.49V	2.05V	.95V	.71	.38	.24	1.82	5.03V	6.23V	6.69V
Australia	193	—	—	—	—	.88V	6.95V	6.84V	.20	.10	.51	1.42	2.16V	4.90V	2.87V
Japan	158	25.32	23.08	30.95	34.10	1.55V	.20V	.20V	15.57	18.32	24.00	30.56	4.23V	4.67V	8.51V
New Zealand	196	—	—	—	—	—V	.01V	.10V	—	.06	.93	3.94	.03V	.27V	.17V
Austria	122	—	—	—	—	—V	—V	—V	.10	.18	.85	.14	.19V	.62V	1.07V
Belgium	124	.02	—	.22	.18	.01V	.25V	1.94V	3.62	5.90	8.17	12.64	38.13V	39.72V	94.03V
Cyprus	423	—	—	—	—	.01Y	—V	—V	—	—	—	.33	—V	—V	—V
Denmark	128	—	—	.01	—	.01V	.05V	.02V	2.09	1.30	2.22	3.17	5.53V	1.98V	1.34V
Finland	172	—	—	—	—	—V	.03V	—V	.26	.29	.21	.33	2.09V	.65V	.48V
France	132	56.07	64.54	76.14	91.19	142.19V	148.97V	219.28V	62.26	66.54	80.88	84.73	120.78V	122.08V	174.81V
Germany	134	.06	.11	.18	3.62	.72V	.14V	.39V	4.34	5.73	10.17	8.62	37.54V	30.16V	31.16V
Greece	174	—	—	—	—	—V	—V	.03V	.12	.06	.07	.02	12.42V	5.85V	13.43V
Iceland	176	—	—	—	—	—V	—V	—V	—	.02	.09	—	.05V	.01V	—V
Ireland	178	—	—	—	—	.01V	.01V	.02V	.82	1.22	.54	.93	1.15V	1.89V	2.49V
Italy	136	.07	.05	—	—	.38V	.20V	1.03V	4.72	7.08	5.11	5.02	56.27V	28.18V	26.91V
Luxembourg	137	—	—	—	—	.45V	—V	.24V	—	—	.70	.33	.19V	3.59V	.09V
Malta	181	—	—	—	—	—V	—V	—V	.04	.05	.02	.06	.26V	.35V	.48V
Netherlands	138	.02	.03	.02	.01	.20V	.34V	.10V	5.39	7.51	6.79	11.15	17.56V	35.78V	27.24V
Norway	142	—	—	—	—	—V	—V	.07V	.11	.76	.12	.14	.23V	14.38V	18.33V
Portugal	182	—	—	—	—	.07V	—V	—V	.21	1.47	.48	.76	.41V	.71V	.50V
Slovenia	961	—	—	—	—	—V	.01V	—V	—	—	—	—	—V	.14V	.15V
Spain	184	5.80	6.02	8.37	9.20	1.89V	.84V	1.58V	2.60	4.55	7.67	3.83	3.36V	2.81V	3.95V
Sweden	144	—	—	—	—	.02V	.01V	.06V	.33	.66	.75	.96	.54V	2.64V	8.30V
Switzerland	146	.25	.06	—	13.40	.61V	.33V	.39V	.24	.33	.81	.70	15.33V	21.10V	18.62V
United Kingdom	112	.02	—	.02	.01	.33V	.42V	.37V	7.12	7.41	11.71	11.20	12.62V	9.44V	8.62V
Developing Countries	**202**	**74.1**	**74.7**	**83.4**	**70.4**	**87.3Y**	**154.5Y**	**142.1Y**	**192.0**	**245.2**	**304.6**	**344.7**	**413.2Y**	**528.9Y**	**570.5Y**
Africa	**607**	**73.9**	**74.0**	**82.2**	**69.6**	**81.1Y**	**98.9Y**	**126.9Y**	**120.0**	**139.1**	**185.2**	**175.4**	**196.1Y**	**233.9Y**	**286.3Y**
Algeria	612	.34	.39	.30	.27	.34Y	.42Y	.54Y	1.36	2.62	4.57	4.59	6.24Y	7.85Y	9.47Y
Angola	614	—	—	—	—	—Y	—Y	—Y	—	—	—	.09	.11Y	.13Y	.17Y
Benin	638	1.91	4.92	3.59	1.56	.20V	.25Y	.31Y	6.32	9.61	14.10	22.86	19.70V	24.35Y	30.21Y
Botswana	616	—	—	—	—	—Y	—Y	—Y	—	.02	—	—	—Y	—Y	—Y
Burkina Faso	748	1.26	1.03	2.05	1.13	1.29Y	1.60Y	1.98Y	7.74	4.82	10.71	14.37	16.42Y	20.29Y	25.18Y
Burundi	618	—	—	—	.01	—V	—V	—Y	—	—	—	—	—V	—V	—Y
Cameroon	622	.05	—	—	—	—Y	—Y	—Y	.12	—	.36	.48	.54Y	.67Y	.83Y
Central African Rep.	626	—	—	—	—	—Y	—Y	—Y	—	—	.11	—	—Y	—Y	—Y
Chad	628	.64	.13	.10	.38	.44Y	.54Y	.67Y	—	.01	—	.01	.01Y	.01Y	.01Y
Comoros	632	—	.01	—	.01	.01Y	.01Y	.01Y	—	—	—	—	—Y	—Y	—Y
Congo, Republic of	634	—	—	—	—	—Y	—Y	—Y	—	.01	.11	.18	.21Y	.26Y	.32Y
Côte d'Ivoire	662	4.32	3.59	5.20	4.40	1.60V	1.19V	1.47Y	47.38	58.86	68.11	44.08	42.68V	49.79V	61.79Y
Equatorial Guinea	642	—	—	—	.12	.14Y	.17Y	.22Y	—	—	—	.02	.03Y	.03Y	.04Y
Gabon	646	.02	—	—	—	—Y	—Y	—Y	—	—	.04	.01	.01Y	.01Y	.02Y
Gambia, The	648	—	—	.01	—	—Y	—Y	—Y	—	—	.03	—	—Y	—Y	—Y
Ghana	652	3.35	8.92	10.37	8.94	10.21Y	12.62Y	15.67Y	6.36	7.88	7.91	5.07	5.79Y	7.16Y	8.89Y
Guinea	656	—	—	.02	.31	.36Y	.44Y	.55Y	—	.01	—	.02	.03Y	.03Y	.04Y
Kenya	664	—	—	—	—	—Y	—Y	—Y	.03	.01	.02	—	—Y	—Y	—Y
Liberia	668	—	—	—	—	—Y	—Y	—Y	—	.02	.01	.05	.06Y	.07Y	.09Y
Madagascar	674	—	—	.24	—	—Y	—Y	—Y	—	.04	—	—	—Y	—Y	—Y
Mali	678	.29	.19	.38	1.29	1.47Y	1.82Y	2.25Y	.95	.56	.47	.48	.55Y	.68Y	.85Y
Mauritania	682	.11	—	.01	—	—Y	.01Y	.01Y	.08	.04	.02	.18	.21Y	.25Y	.32Y
Mauritius	684	—	—	—	—	—V	—V	—V	—	.01	—	—	.07V	—V	—V
Morocco	686	—	—	—	—	.04V	.05Y	.06Y	.77	1.17	3.17	3.49	5.36V	6.62Y	8.22Y
Mozambique	688	—	—	—	—	—V	—V	—Y	—	—	.04	—	—V	—V	—Y
Namibia	728	—	—	—	—	—Y	—Y	—Y	.02	.02	—	—	—Y	.01Y	.01Y
Nigeria	694	61.46	53.75	59.20	49.90	63.54Y	78.44Y	101.61Y	33.44	29.08	38.33	45.73	62.21Y	78.21Y	94.35Y
Rwanda	714	—	—	—	—	—Y	—Y	—Y	—	—	.01	.02	.02Y	.02Y	.03Y
Senegal	722	.02	.01	.02	.21	—V	—V	—Y	.61	.35	2.53	3.79	5.39V	4.08V	5.06Y
Sierra Leone	724	—	—	—	.60	.69Y	.85Y	1.06Y	—	—	.05	—	—Y	—Y	—Y
South Africa	199	—	—	—	.01	.29V	.32V	.23V	1.85	2.60	10.31	17.11	6.11V	8.38V	9.52V
Sudan	732	—	—	—	—	—V	—V	—V	.01	—	—	—	—V	—V	—V
Tanzania	738	—	—	—	—	—Y	—Y	—Y	.31	.11	—	—	—Y	—Y	—Y
Togo	742	.13	1.06	.74	.47	.12V	.15Y	.19Y	8.67	13.56	14.82	8.32	11.92V	14.73Y	18.28Y
Tunisia	744	—	—	—	—	—V	—V	—Y	3.97	7.73	9.38	4.47	10.91V	10.14V	12.58Y
Uganda	746	—	—	—	—	—Y	—Y	—Y	—	—	.04	—	—Y	—Y	—Y
Zambia	754	—	—	—	—	.32V	.03V	.06V	—	—	—	—	.04V	.11V	.04V
Zimbabwe	698	—	—	—	—	.03V	—V	—Y	—	—	—	—	1.53V	—V	—Y
Asia	**507**	**—**	**.1**	**.4**	**.4**	**2.7Y**	**4.9Y**	**6.3Y**	**49.8**	**71.8**	**76.6**	**127.8**	**169.3Y**	**240.5Y**	**223.3Y**
Afghanistan, I.S. of	512	—	—	—	—	—Y	—Y	—Y	—	—	—	—	—Y	.01Y	.01Y
Bangladesh	513	—	.03	.20	.38	—V	.39V	—V	—	.11	.01	.08	.04V	.04Y	.05Y
China,P.R.: Mainland	924	.01	.01	.01	—	—V	.84V	.33Y	20.82	38.87	51.86	30.09	37.31V	78.94V	33.81V

	Exports 2001	2002	2003	2004	2005	2006	2007	Imports 2001	2002	2003	2004	2005	2006	2007
	Millions of U.S. Dollars							Millions of U.S. Dollars						
China,P.R.:Hong Kong.......... 532	—	—	—	.02	.43V	.11V	.05V	.40	.34	.15	.08	1.81V	2.01V	1.40V
China,P.R.:Macao.......... 546	—	—	—	—	.01V	.09V	.01V	—	—	—	—	—V	—V	—V
French Polynesia.......... 887	—	—	—	—	—Y	—Y	—Y	—	—	—	55.00	62.84Y	77.67Y	96.39Y
India.......... 534	—	.04	.22	.03	.65V	.80Y	.99Y	1.71	17.47	17.74	10.11	23.20V	28.67Y	35.58Y
Indonesia.......... 536	—	—	—	—	.12V	.26V	.08V	.70	5.38	.55	.46	8.17V	8.43V	3.18V
Korea.......... 542	—	—	—	—	1.24V	1.31V	4.59V	.68	.73	.32	.90	3.26V	7.10V	3.35V
Lao People's Dem.Rep.......... 544	....	....	....	....	....	....	....	.04	—	—	—	—Y	—Y	—Y
Malaysia.......... 548	—	—	—	—	.08V	.02V	.14V	.37	.56	1.55	2.43	2.77V	1.59V	4.92V
Myanmar.......... 518	—	—	—	—	—Y	—Y	—Y	.49	—	.56	—	—Y	—Y	—Y
New Caledonia.......... 839	—	—	—	—	—Y	—Y	—Y	—	.06	—	—	—Y	—Y	—Y
Pakistan.......... 564	—	—	—	—	.02V	.02Y	.03Y	20.12	4.69	.40	.89	26.17V	32.34Y	40.13Y
Philippines.......... 566	—	—	—	—	—V	—V	—V	.05	.03	.11	.02	—V	.03V	.10V
Samoa.......... 862	....	....	....	....	....	....	....	—	—	.01	—	—Y	—Y	—Y
Singapore.......... 576	—	—	—	—	—V	—V	—V	.19	.16	.25	.46	—V	—V	—V
Sri Lanka.......... 524	—	—	—	—	—Y	—Y	—Y	.01	.01	.01	.06	.07Y	.09Y	.11Y
Taiwan Province of China.......... 528	—	—	—	—	.04V	.88V	.03V	.40	.37	.31	.27	.71V	.33V	.17V
Thailand.......... 578	—	—	—	—	.15V	.15V	.07V	1.41	1.81	2.09	24.12	2.93V	3.26V	4.13V
Vietnam.......... 582	—	—	—	—	—V	—V	—V	2.34	1.17	.74	2.80	—V	—V	—V
Europe.......... 170	**—**	**—**	**—**	**—**	**.2Y**	**49.1Y**	**7.3Y**	**4.4**	**6.1**	**8.9**	**3.6**	**8.5Y**	**9.4Y**	**17.6Y**
Albania.......... 914	—	—	—	—	.01V	—V	—V	—	—	—	—	—V	—V	—V
Belarus.......... 913	....	....	....	....	....	....	....	—	—	—	—	.06V	.02V	—V
Bulgaria.......... 918	—	—	—	—	.03V	.02V	—V	.01	.07	.71	.13	.83V	.81V	.11V
Czech Republic.......... 935	—	—	—	—	.08V	—V	—V	—	—	—	—	.47V	.64V	.63V
Czechoslovakia n.s.......... 937	—	—	—	—	—Y	—Y	—Y	.01	.26	.70	—	—Y	—Y	—Y
Estonia.......... 939	—	—	—	—	—V	—V	—V	—	—	—	—	.07V	.19V	—V
Gibraltar.......... 823	—	—	—	—	—Y	—Y	—Y	—	.01	.02	—	—Y	—Y	—Y
Hungary.......... 944	—	—	—	—	—V	.02V	.02V	.29	.11	.08	.09	.23V	.34V	.17V
Latvia.......... 941	—	—	—	—	—V	—V	—V	—	—	—	—	—V	.16V	—V
Lithuania.......... 946	—	—	—	—	—V	—V	—V	—	—	—	—	.07V	.02V	.06V
Poland.......... 964	—	—	—	—	.01V	.02V	.09V	.81	.40	.31	.24	1.16V	.67V	1.75V
Romania.......... 968	—	—	—	—	—V	.01V	.11V	2.25	1.96	2.00	.44	.05V	.52V	.46V
Russia.......... 922	—	—	—	—	—V	48.47V	6.12V	.33	2.58	1.15	1.75	.04V	—V	—V
Slovak Republic.......... 936	—	—	—	—	—V	—V	—V	—	—	—	—	.06V	.24V	.42V
Turkey.......... 186	—	—	—	—	.12V	.53V	.96V	.73	.65	1.07	.88	4.27V	4.36V	12.23V
Ukraine.......... 926	—	—	—	—	—V	—Y	—Y	—	—	—	—	1.07V	1.32Y	1.64Y
Yugoslavia n.s.......... 966	....	....	....	....	....	....	....	—	.02	2.81	.08	.09Y	.11Y	.14Y
Europe n.s.......... 884	—	—	—	—	—Y	—Y	—Y	—	—	.03	.01	.02Y	.02Y	.02Y
Middle East.......... 407	**.2**	**.5**	**.6**	**.4**	**.7Y**	**.8Y**	**1.0Y**	**13.5**	**16.8**	**13.1**	**17.5**	**29.2Y**	**28.4Y**	**34.8Y**
Bahrain.......... 419	—	—	—	—	—Y	—Y	—Y	2.94	11.04	8.06	4.26	4.87Y	6.02Y	7.47Y
Egypt.......... 469	—	—	—	.04	.05Y	.06Y	.07Y	.16	.12	.35	1.50	1.72Y	2.13Y	2.64Y
Iran, I.R. of.......... 429	—	—	—	—	—Y	—Y	—Y	.11	.93	1.02	2.76	3.75Y	4.72Y	5.69Y
Iraq.......... 433	—	—	—	—	—Y	—Y	—Y	.02	—	.03	.04	.05Y	.06Y	.08Y
Israel.......... 436	—	—	—	—	—V	—V	—V	5.15	.98	.42	.24	7.04V	.66V	.88V
Jordan.......... 439	—	—	—	—	—V	—V	—V	—	—	—	.02	.03V	.03V	.21V
Kuwait.......... 443	—	—	—	—	—Y	—Y	—Y	.02	.05	.02	1.69	2.30Y	2.89Y	3.49Y
Lebanon.......... 446	—	—	—	—	—Y	—Y	—Y	.02	.02	—	.03	.03Y	.04Y	.05Y
Libya.......... 672	.19	.54	.65	.34	.44Y	.54Y	.70Y	.95	.26	1.01	.15	.21Y	.26Y	.31Y
Qatar.......... 453	—	—	—	—	.14V	.11V	.14Y	—	—	—	—	—V	.01V	.01Y
Saudi Arabia.......... 456	—	—	—	—	.06V	.07Y	.09Y	1.04	.29	.95	4.51	6.14Y	7.72Y	9.31Y
Syrian Arab Republic.......... 463	—	—	—	—	—Y	—Y	—Y	.03	.07	—	.32	.37Y	.45Y	.56Y
United Arab Emirates.......... 466	—	—	—	—	—Y	—Y	—Y	3.04	3.03	1.19	1.98	2.70Y	3.39Y	4.09Y
Western Hemisphere.......... 207	**—**	**—**	**.1**	**—**	**2.5Y**	**.9Y**	**.6Y**	**4.3**	**11.5**	**20.8**	**20.3**	**10.1Y**	**16.7Y**	**8.5Y**
Argentina.......... 213	—	—	.02	—	—V	—V	.20V	1.27	.90	2.74	5.20	8.94V	12.18V	8.22V
Bahamas, The.......... 313	....	....	....	....	....	....	....	—	.64	.01	—	—Y	—Y	—Y
Bermuda.......... 319	—	—	—	—	1.17V	—V	—Y	—	—	—	—	—Y	—Y	—Y
Bolivia.......... 218	.01	—	—	—	—Y	—Y	—Y	—	—	—	—	—Y	—Y	—Y
Brazil.......... 223	—	.02	.02	—	—V	.02V	—V	2.68	8.22	16.94	14.04	.64V	2.65V	—V
Chile.......... 228	—	—	—	—	—V	—V	—V	—	—	—	.64	.04V	—V	—V
Colombia.......... 233	—	—	—	—	.12V	—V	—V	—	—	.35	.04	—V	.11V	—V
Ecuador.......... 248	—	—	—	—	—V	—V	—Y	—	—	.01	.01	—V	—V	—Y
El Salvador.......... 253	....	....	....	....	....	....	....	.02	—	—	—	—Y	—Y	—Y
Guatemala.......... 258	—	—	—	—	.01V	.03Y	.04Y	—	—	—	—	.05V	.07Y	.08Y
Haiti.......... 263	....	....	....	....	....	....	....	—	.02	—	—	—Y	—Y	—Y
Jamaica.......... 343	....	....	....	....	....	....	....	.03	—	—	—	—V	—V	—V
Mexico.......... 273	—	—	—	—	1.20V	.80V	.31V	.02	.04	.34	.19	—V	1.58V	.10V
Paraguay.......... 288	....	....	....	....	....	....	....	—	—	—	—	.27V	.03V	.04Y
Peru.......... 293	—	—	—	—	—V	.01V	.03Y	.02	—	—	.01	—V	—V	—Y
Uruguay.......... 298	—	—	—	—	—V	—Y	—Y	.10	—	—	—	—V	—Y	—Y
Venezuela, Rep. Bol.......... 299	—	—	—	—	—V	—V	—V	—	.65	.18	.02	—V	—V	—Y
Western Hem. n.s.......... 399	—	—	.09	—	—Y	—Y	—Y	.20	.99	.20	.15	.10Y	.06Y	.01Y
Other Countries n.i.e.......... 910	**—**	**—**	**—**	**—**	**—Y**	**—Y**	**—Y**	**.1**	**.1**	**.2**	**—**	**—Y**	**—Y**	**.1Y**
North Korea.......... 954	—	—	—	—	—Y	—Y	—Y	.13	.06	.20	.03	.04Y	.05Y	.06Y
Countries & Areas n.s.......... 898	**.1**	**—**	**—**	**—**	**—Y**	**—Y**	**—Y**	**3.2**	**—**	**—**	**—**	**—Y**	**—Y**	**—Y**
Memorandum Items														
European Union.......... 998	62.06	70.76	84.95	104.20	146.39Y	151.31Y	225.18Y	95.11	110.47	136.73	144.56	311.10Y	288.83Y	398.07Y
Oil Exporting Ctys.......... 999	61.99	54.67	60.14	50.51	64.63Y	79.84Y	103.17Y	40.68	42.28	47.85	61.94	91.77Y	113.54Y	129.99Y
Non-Oil Develop.Ctys.......... 201	12.12	19.98	23.27	19.93	22.63Y	74.64Y	38.97Y	151.34	202.89	256.77	282.73	321.39Y	415.36Y	440.53Y

	Exports							Imports						
	2001	2002	2003	2004	2005	2006	2007	2001	2002	2003	2004	2005	2006	2007
PERCENT DISTRIBUTION														
Industrial Countries................. 101	54.3	55.7	58.2	68.3	70.9	64.0	63.0	39.9	38.0	38.4	41.4	50.7	47.6	48.0
Developing Countries.............. 202	45.6	44.3	41.8	31.7	29.1	36.0	37.0	59.1	62.0	61.5	58.6	49.3	52.4	52.0
Africa..................................... 607	45.5	43.9	41.2	31.3	27.1	23.1	33.0	36.9	35.2	37.4	29.8	23.4	23.2	26.1
Asia... 507	—	.1	.2	.2	.9	1.1	1.6	15.3	18.1	15.5	21.7	20.2	23.8	20.4
Europe.................................... 170	—	—	—	—	.1	11.4	1.9	1.4	1.5	1.8	.6	1.0	.9	1.6
Middle East............................ 407	.1	.3	.3	.2	.2	.2	.3	4.1	4.2	2.6	3.0	3.5	2.8	3.2
Western Hemisphere.............. 207	—	—	.1	—	.8	.2	.2	1.3	2.9	4.2	3.5	1.2	1.7	.8
ANNUAL PERCENT CHANGE														
World....................................... 001	–17.0	3.8	18.4	11.4	34.6	43.3	–10.4	–58.0	21.7	25.1	18.8	42.6	20.4	8.7
Industrial Countries................. 101	–11.7	6.6	23.8	30.7	39.5	29.4	–11.7	6.7	16.0	26.4	27.9	74.8	12.9	9.6
Developing Countries.............. 202	–22.6	.7	11.7	–15.6	23.9	77.0	–8.0	–70.4	27.7	24.2	13.1	19.9	28.0	7.9
Africa..................................... 607	–22.4	.1	11.1	–15.3	16.5	22.0	28.3	13.7	15.9	33.2	–5.3	11.8	19.3	22.4
Asia... 507	–63.7	—	380.2	2.4	532.0	78.9	29.6	32.4	44.2	6.8	66.7	32.5	42.1	–7.1
Europe.................................... 170	....	—	....	....	....	—	–85.1	38.0	36.7	46.6	–59.1	133.5	11.1	86.9
Middle East............................ 407	–66.5	183.3	19.1	–40.4	78.3	13.8	29.2	–97.3	24.5	–22.1	34.1	66.7	–2.8	22.6
Western Hemisphere.............. 207	....	18.3	662.1	35.8	....	–65.7	–31.1	178.9	163.6	81.2	–2.3	–50.5	66.0	–49.4
Other Countries n.i.e................ 910	—	....	—	....	....	....	....	61.6	–51.5	212.7	–82.9	14.3	23.6	24.1

	Exports 2001	Exports 2002	Exports 2003	Exports 2004	Exports 2005	Exports 2006	Exports 2007	Imports 2001	Imports 2002	Imports 2003	Imports 2004	Imports 2005	Imports 2006	Imports 2007
	Millions of U.S. Dollars							*Millions of U.S. Dollars*						
IFS World Total	**17,261**	**15,107**	**19,887**	**31,148**	**55,144**	**57,444**	**65,133**	**11,586**	**7,547**	**10,853**	**14,164**	**21,314**	**26,760**	**37,576**
DOTS World Total 001	**18,045**	**18,340**	**24,062**	**33,307Y**	**43,531Y**	**52,940Y**	**59,391Y**	**7,928**	**8,733**	**14,852**	**20,472Y**	**24,497Y**	**29,474Y**	**39,418Y**
Industrial Countries 101	**12,196**	**11,037**	**16,276**	**23,331Y**	**33,834Y**	**41,000Y**	**43,762Y**	**4,907**	**5,119**	**7,852**	**9,585Y**	**10,624Y**	**13,031Y**	**17,020Y**
United States 111	7,320	5,819	9,205	15,557V	22,827V	26,327V	30,673V	816	1,121	2,315	1,708V	1,777V	2,454V	3,065V
Canada 156	357	229	753	74V	148V	648V	260V	39	34	36	67V	101V	219V	189V
Australia 193	—	—	27	—V	—V	—V	—V	15	29	23	23V	24V	37V	31V
Japan 158	173	549	965	1,298V	902V	874V	617V	360	432	364	423V	571V	618V	807V
New Zealand 196	—	26	29	39V	89V	—V	50V	4	6	10	49V	45V	78V	140V
Austria 122	—	—	—	188V	487V	588V	148V	14	12	11	137V	143V	134V	247V
Belgium 124	—	489	—	59V	84V	114V	102V	438	518	533	238V	296V	595V	925V
Cyprus 423	—	—	—	—V	—Y	—V	—V	1	3	—	2V	2V	2V	2V
Denmark 128	—	—	1	1V	1V	2V	2V	27	85	34	86V	106V	112V	103V
Finland 172	—	—	—	—V	—V	—V	—V	7	7	8	39V	67V	135V	158V
France 132	1,142	997	1,359	1,092V	1,339V	2,261V	1,599V	372	363	480	1,112V	1,455V	1,633V	1,691V
Germany 134	244	365	505	340V	804V	1,585V	1,126V	781	531	1,088	984V	1,032V	1,314V	1,630V
Greece 174	—	—	—	15V	22V	16V	56V	44	32	46	45V	90V	50V	57V
Iceland 176	—	—	—	—V	—V	—V	—V	4	10	12	54V	56V	60V	64V
Ireland 178	—	—	—	1V	1V	1V	1V	35	55	68	166V	150V	206V	281V
Italy 136	854	722	688	538V	682V	935V	1,100V	201	260	636	814V	775V	1,069V	1,262V
Luxembourg 137	—	—	—	—V	—V	—V	—V	1	1	3	11V	10V	9V	11V
Malta 181	—	—	—	—V	—V	—V	—V	1	1	3	1V	16V	19V	17V
Netherlands 138	365	288	535	388V	1,063V	1,313V	1,346V	392	278	320	1,183V	1,479V	1,814V	3,105V
Norway 142	—	33	14	—V	—V	1V	1V	19	30	90	41V	52V	62V	80V
Portugal 182	461	491	589	774V	1,094V	881V	1,257V	9	5	22	28V	53V	19V	40V
Slovenia 961	—	—	—	—Y	—V	—V	—V	—	—	—	—Y	3V	4V	5V
Spain 184	1,175	1,019	1,483	2,327V	3,548V	4,325V	4,563V	108	84	142	357V	295V	267V	285V
Sweden 144	59	—	—	27V	53V	3V	—V	53	33	64	317V	285V	255V	407V
Switzerland 146	1	—	27	421V	424V	759V	255V	97	93	125	127V	105V	168V	192V
United Kingdom 112	45	11	96	191V	266V	366V	605V	1,070	1,095	1,420	1,573V	1,633V	1,698V	2,228V
Developing Countries 202	**5,598**	**7,034**	**7,543**	**9,655Y**	**9,260Y**	**11,390Y**	**14,967Y**	**3,006**	**3,605**	**4,750**	**7,961Y**	**10,148Y**	**11,844Y**	**16,440Y**
Africa 607	**1,146**	**1,732**	**2,010**	**3,135Y**	**3,807Y**	**4,806Y**	**5,983Y**	**712**	**398**	**747**	**1,285Y**	**1,513Y**	**1,671Y**	**2,071Y**
Algeria 612	—	1	—	1Y	1Y	1Y	1Y	1	—	1	1Y	1Y	1Y	1Y
Angola 614	1	20	—	1Y	1Y	1Y	1Y	1	6	2	3Y	4Y	5Y	6Y
Benin 638	4	61	15	24V	33V	41Y	49Y	177	31	13	18V	15V	19Y	24Y
Botswana 616	—	—	—	—Y	—Y	—Y	—Y	—	1	1	1Y	1Y	2Y	2Y
Burkina Faso 748	—	—	—	—Y	—Y	—Y	—Y	—	1	2	2Y	3Y	3Y	4Y
Cameroon 622	125	113	313	414Y	563Y	708Y	854Y	3	32	1	1Y	1Y	2Y	2Y
Cape Verde 624	—	—	—	—Y	—Y	—Y	—Y	—	1	—	—Y	—Y	—Y	—Y
Central African Rep. 626	—	—	—	1Y	1Y	1Y	1Y	—	—	—	—Y	—Y	—Y	—Y
Chad 628	2	—	7	9Y	12Y	15Y	18Y	—	—	—	1Y	1Y	1Y	1Y
Congo, Dem. Rep. of 636	—	—	—	—Y	—Y	—Y	1Y	1	1	—	1Y	1Y	1Y	1Y
Congo, Republic of 634	3	—	—	1V	1Y	1Y	2Y	1	—	—	—V	1Y	1Y	1Y
Côte d'Ivoire 662	341	270	360	871V	1,301V	1,460V	1,761Y	57	5	11	545V	632V	647V	838Y
Ethiopia 644	—	—	—	—V	—V	—Y	—Y	—	—	2	—V	—V	—Y	—Y
Gabon 646	—	1	6	8Y	10Y	13Y	16Y	6	8	11	14Y	18Y	23Y	29Y
Ghana 652	271	379	454	601Y	818Y	1,028Y	1,241Y	12	18	22	29Y	37Y	46Y	59Y
Guinea 656	—	9	—	4V	5Y	6Y	8Y	11	6	25	—V	—Y	—Y	—Y
Guinea-Bissau 654	—	—	—	—Y	—Y	—Y	—Y	—	3	13	17Y	21Y	26Y	34Y
Kenya 664	—	—	—	2V	2Y	3Y	4Y	8	12	15	17V	22Y	27Y	34Y
Liberia 668	—	—	—	—Y	—Y	—Y	—Y	—	1	1	1Y	1Y	2Y	2Y
Madagascar 674	—	—	—	—Y	—Y	—Y	—Y	1	—	1	1Y	1Y	1Y	2Y
Mali 678	24	—	3	5Y	6Y	8Y	9Y	1	—	1	1Y	1Y	1Y	1Y
Mauritania 682	—	—	—	—Y	1Y	1Y	1Y	54	22	12	16Y	21Y	25Y	33Y
Mauritius 684	—	—	—	—V	—V	—V	—V	27	10	20	—V	1V	—V	—V
Morocco 686	—	—	—	35V	6V	7Y	8Y	3	4	4	23V	29V	35Y	46Y
Namibia 728	—	—	—	—Y	—Y	—Y	—Y	8	4	6	7Y	9Y	11Y	13Y
Niger 692	2	—	1	42V	57Y	71Y	86Y	—	1	1	55V	70Y	86Y	112Y
Rwanda 714	—	—	—	—Y	—Y	—Y	—Y	—	1	—	—Y	—Y	—Y	—Y
St. Helena 856	—	—	—	—Y	—Y	—Y	—Y	—	—	1	1Y	1Y	1Y	1Y
Senegal 722	175	119	254	308V	333V	109V	132Y	2	3	31	5V	2V	6V	8Y
Sierra Leone 724	—	—	—	—Y	—Y	—Y	—Y	—	—	—	1Y	1Y	1Y	1Y
Somalia 726	—	—	—	—Y	—Y	—Y	—Y	7	11	5	6Y	8Y	10Y	13Y
South Africa 199	198	388	589	804V	651V	1,323V	1,782V	231	189	291	486V	580V	651V	750V
Sacca exc. South Afr. 608	—	—	—	—Y	—Y	—Y	—Y	—	—	—	—V	1Y	1Y	1Y
Sudan 732	—	—	1	—V	—V	1V	1V	—	—	—	13V	—V	—V	—V
Swaziland 734	—	—	—	—Y	—Y	—Y	—Y	2	4	2	2Y	3Y	4Y	5Y
Tanzania 738	—	—	—	—Y	—Y	—Y	—Y	—	—	4	5Y	6Y	8Y	10Y
Togo 742	—	370	4	6V	4V	6Y	7Y	90	21	242	8V	16V	20Y	26Y
Tunisia 744	—	—	—	—V	—V	—V	—Y	3	—	1	2V	3V	4V	5Y
Uganda 746	—	—	—	—Y	—Y	1Y	1Y	—	—	—	—Y	—Y	—Y	—Y
Zambia 754	—	—	—	—V	—V	—V	—V	—	—	1	—V	—V	—V	—V
Zimbabwe 698	—	—	—	—V	—V	—V	—Y	—	1	4	—V	—V	—V	—Y

	Exports 2001	2002	2003	2004	2005	2006	2007	Imports 2001	2002	2003	2004	2005	2006	2007
	Millions of U.S. Dollars							*Millions of U.S. Dollars*						
Asia.......... 507	**3,067**	**3,525**	**3,634**	**2,288Y**	**1,891Y**	**1,097Y**	**1,990Y**	**1,647**	**2,522**	**2,680**	**4,791Y**	**5,692Y**	**6,385Y**	**9,819Y**
Bangladesh.......... 513	—	—	—	6V	11V	7V	10V	1	—	—	2V	5V	4Y	4Y
Brunei Darussalam.......... 516	—	—	—	—Y	—Y	—Y	—Y	3	1	11	15Y	19Y	23Y	30Y
China,P.R.: Mainland.......... 924	127	73	123	360V	479V	253V	489V	527	739	1,067	1,899V	2,536V	3,141V	4,180V
China,P.R.:Hong Kong.......... 532	—	—	2	17V	23V	48V	44V	96	108	153	134V	96V	137V	215V
India.......... 534	2,083	2,157	2,392	50V	60V	76Y	91Y	316	310	377	661V	926V	1,143Y	1,480Y
Indonesia.......... 536	537	961	770	979V	867V	4V	552V	108	108	122	195V	186V	174V	215V
Korea.......... 542	75	41	100	501V	332V	569V	403V	223	311	434	748V	914V	890V	2,612V
Lao People's Dem.Rep.......... 544	—	—	—	—Y	—Y	—Y	—Y	—	—	—	—Y	—Y	1Y	1Y
Malaysia.......... 548	—	—	—	4V	12V	19V	24V	10	14	12	60V	204V	69V	108V
Maldives.......... 556	—	—	—	—V	—V	—Y	—Y	—	—	1	—V	—V	—Y	—Y
Myanmar.......... 518	—	—	—	—Y	—Y	—Y	—Y	—	1	—	—Y	—Y	1Y	1Y
Pakistan.......... 564	—	—	—	13V	10V	13Y	16Y	2	1	3	336V	56V	70Y	90Y
Philippines.......... 566	—	—	—	—V	—V	—V	5V	4	3	6	7V	13V	7V	9V
Singapore.......... 576	—	24	2	36V	2V	4V	5V	104	498	79	187V	182V	201V	280V
Sri Lanka.......... 524	—	—	—	1V	1V	—V	—V	—	—	—	1V	5V	1V	3V
Taiwan Province of China.......... 528	226	159	245	264V	—V	57V	319V	128	247	267	179V	196V	189V	208V
Thailand.......... 578	19	110	—	45V	65V	30V	33V	116	174	139	353V	335V	298V	381V
Vietnam.......... 582	—	—	—	13V	28V	17V	—V	9	6	7	13V	19V	36V	—V
Europe.......... 170	**—**	**—**	**1**	**183Y**	**222Y**	**357Y**	**469Y**	**258**	**240**	**354**	**586Y**	**917Y**	**1,037Y**	**1,182Y**
Azerbaijan.......... 912	—	—	—	—V	—V	—V	—V	—	—	—	—V	1V	—V	—V
Belarus.......... 913	—	—	—	—V	—V	—V	—V	—	—	—	5V	4V	20V	5V
Bulgaria.......... 918	—	—	—	—V	—V	3V	8V	3	5	4	12V	8V	3V	10V
Croatia.......... 960	—	—	—	—V	—V	—V	—V	—	—	—	35V	67V	10V	1V
Czech Republic.......... 935	—	—	—	9V	1V	2V	3V	2	1	3	19V	19V	90V	39V
Estonia.......... 939	—	—	—	—V	—V	—V	—V	—	—	—	1V	19V	39V	10V
Faroe Islands.......... 816	—	—	—	—Y	—Y	—Y	—Y	6	22	32	42Y	53Y	66Y	85Y
Gibraltar.......... 823	—	—	—	—Y	—Y	—Y	—Y	3	—	2	3Y	4Y	5Y	6Y
Hungary.......... 944	—	—	1	—V	—V	—V	—V	4	4	10	7V	42V	167V	213V
Kazakhstan.......... 916	—	—	—	—V	—Y	—Y	—Y	—	—	—	2V	2Y	3Y	3Y
Latvia.......... 941	—	—	—	—V	—V	—V	—V	—	—	—	2V	8V	3V	2V
Macedonia, FYR.......... 962	—	—	—	—V	—V	—V	—Y	—	—	—	1V	1V	1V	1Y
Poland.......... 964	—	—	—	3V	3V	1V	2V	16	24	28	39V	49V	39V	90V
Romania.......... 968	—	—	—	2V	1V	—V	2V	37	22	16	46V	113V	38V	23V
Russia.......... 922	—	—	—	7V	2V	1V	2V	116	91	145	82V	172V	158V	163V
Slovak Republic.......... 936	—	—	—	—Y	—V	—V	—V	—	—	—	5Y	12V	16V	10V
Turkey.......... 186	—	—	—	161V	213V	346V	449V	21	28	24	88V	108V	91V	147V
Ukraine.......... 926	—	—	—	1V	2V	2Y	3Y	49	41	88	198V	234V	288Y	373Y
Middle East.......... 407	**—**	**19**	**1**	**44Y**	**56Y**	**70Y**	**84Y**	**146**	**177**	**448**	**542Y**	**718Y**	**882Y**	**1,170Y**
Bahrain.......... 419	—	—	—	—Y	—Y	—Y	—Y	1	1	1	1Y	2Y	2Y	3Y
Egypt.......... 469	—	—	—	—Y	—Y	—Y	—Y	7	14	7	9Y	12Y	14Y	19Y
Iran, I.R. of.......... 429	—	—	—	—Y	—Y	—Y	—Y	1	3	1	1Y	1Y	1Y	2Y
Israel.......... 436	—	—	—	2V	1V	—V	—V	15	12	15	36V	52V	85V	225V
Jordan.......... 439	—	—	—	—V	—V	—V	—V	7	6	3	1V	2V	1V	2V
Kuwait.......... 443	—	—	—	—Y	—Y	—Y	—Y	2	3	2	2Y	3Y	3Y	4Y
Lebanon.......... 446	—	—	1	1Y	1Y	1Y	2Y	9	31	8	11Y	13Y	17Y	22Y
Libya.......... 672	—	—	—	—Y	—Y	—Y	—Y	2	—	—	—Y	—Y	—Y	—Y
Oman.......... 449	—	—	—	—Y	—Y	—Y	—Y	—	1	3	3Y	4Y	5Y	6Y
Qatar.......... 453	—	—	—	—V	—V	—V	—Y	—	1	—	11V	10V	11V	13Y
Saudi Arabia.......... 456	—	—	—	2V	2V	2Y	3Y	50	20	22	26Y	34Y	41Y	48Y
Syrian Arab Republic.......... 463	—	—	—	38V	51Y	64Y	77Y	4	18	2	2V	2Y	3Y	3Y
United Arab Emirates.......... 466	—	19	1	1Y	1Y	1Y	1Y	43	66	382	439Y	583Y	698Y	823Y
Yemen, Republic of.......... 474	—	—	—	1V	—V	—Y	—Y	5	2	3	—V	—V	—Y	—Y
Western Hemisphere.......... 207	**1,385**	**1,759**	**1,896**	**4,004Y**	**3,285Y**	**5,061Y**	**6,441Y**	**243**	**269**	**521**	**756Y**	**1,308Y**	**1,869Y**	**2,198Y**
Antigua and Barbuda.......... 311	—	—	—	—Y	—Y	—Y	—Y	—	—	1	1Y	2Y	2Y	3Y
Argentina.......... 213	55	30	33	14V	—V	1V	1V	23	31	30	109V	119V	174V	333V
Bahamas, The.......... 313	—	—	—	—Y	—Y	—Y	—Y	—	1	1	1Y	1Y	1Y	1Y
Barbados.......... 316	—	—	—	—V	—V	—V	—Y	—	—	1	—V	—V	—V	—Y
Belize.......... 339	—	—	—	—Y	—Y	—Y	—Y	1	1	6	7Y	9Y	11Y	15Y
Bermuda.......... 319	—	—	—	—Y	—V	—V	—Y	4	1	2	2Y	3Y	4Y	5Y
Brazil.......... 223	1,051	1,538	1,636	3,499V	2,652V	3,943V	5,273V	175	180	183	556V	1,048V	1,511V	1,664V
Chile.......... 228	110	141	86	342V	236V	413V	253V	4	10	22	24V	29V	52V	59V
Colombia.......... 233	—	—	—	—V	19V	—V	37V	—	—	—	2V	2V	4V	2V
Costa Rica.......... 238	—	—	—	—V	—V	—Y	—Y	—	—	1	—V	—V	—Y	—Y
Dominican Republic.......... 243	—	—	—	—Y	—Y	—Y	—Y	1	11	2	3Y	3Y	4Y	5Y
Ecuador.......... 248	—	—	—	—V	24V	49V	59Y	1	—	—	—V	—V	—V	—Y
El Salvador.......... 253	—	—	—	—V	—V	5V	6V	—	—	—	—V	—V	—V	—V
Greenland.......... 326	—	—	—	—Y	—Y	—Y	—Y	3	—	1	1Y	1Y	1Y	2Y
Guatemala.......... 258	—	—	—	—V	—V	—Y	—Y	—	1	—	—V	—V	—Y	—Y
Guyana.......... 336	—	—	—	—Y	—Y	—Y	—Y	—	—	1	1Y	1Y	2Y	2Y
Honduras.......... 268	—	—	—	3V	4Y	5Y	6Y	—	—	—	—V	—Y	—Y	—Y
Jamaica.......... 343	—	—	—	—V	20V	3V	28V	2	—	2	—V	—V	—V	—V
Mexico.......... 273	—	22	—	6V	12V	128V	254V	3	9	19	15V	25V	46V	30V
Netherlands Antilles.......... 353	—	—	—	—Y	—Y	—Y	—Y	7	5	11	15Y	19Y	23Y	30Y
Nicaragua.......... 278	—	—	—	—V	—V	—V	—V	—	—	1	—V	—V	—V	—V
Panama.......... 283	—	—	—	—V	—V	—V	—V	8	2	224	—V	—V	—V	—V
Paraguay.......... 288	—	—	—	—V	—V	—V	—Y	—	1	1	—V	—V	—V	—Y

	Exports 2001	2002	2003	2004	2005	2006	2007	Imports 2001	2002	2003	2004	2005	2006	2007
	Millions of U.S. Dollars							Millions of U.S. Dollars						
Peru.......... 293	24	28	115	—V	109V	254V	209Y	—	1	1	2V	7V	12V	20Y
St. Vincent & Grens.......... 364	—	—	—	—V	—V	—Y	—Y	—	—	1	—V	—V	—Y	—Y
Suriname.......... 366	—	—	—	—Y	—Y	—Y	—Y	1	1	1	1Y	1Y	1Y	1Y
Trinidad and Tobago.......... 369	—	—	—	—Y	—Y	—Y	—Y	3	2	—	—Y	—Y	1Y	1Y
Uruguay.......... 298	32	—	26	139V	207V	260Y	314Y	1	4	3	10V	15V	18Y	24Y
Venezuela, Rep. Bol.......... 299	113	—	—	1V	—V	—V	—V	3	—	7	5V	19V	—V	1Y
Western Hem. n.s.......... 399	—	—	—	—Y	—Y	—Y	—Y	3	6	1	1Y	1Y	1Y	1Y
Countries & Areas n.s.......... 898	**250**	**268**	**243**	**321Y**	**437Y**	**549Y**	**662Y**	**13**	**4**	**2,247**	**2,923Y**	**3,722Y**	**4,594Y**	**5,952Y**
Memorandum Items														
European Union.......... 998	4,345	4,381	5,257	5,953Y	9,449Y	12,396Y	11,909Y	3,575	3,393	4,920	7,165Y	8,040Y	9,689Y	12,817Y
Oil Exporting Ctys.......... 999	650	981	771	982Y	870Y	9Y	557Y	210	201	539	683Y	842Y	936Y	1,114Y
Non-Oil Develop.Ctys.......... 201	4,948	6,053	6,772	8,673Y	8,390Y	11,382Y	14,410Y	2,795	3,404	4,210	7,278Y	9,306Y	10,908Y	15,326Y
PERCENT DISTRIBUTION														
Industrial Countries.......... 101	67.6	60.2	67.6	70.0	77.7	77.4	73.7	61.9	58.6	52.9	46.8	43.4	44.2	43.2
Developing Countries.......... 202	31.0	38.4	31.3	29.0	21.3	21.5	25.2	37.9	41.3	32.0	38.9	41.4	40.2	41.7
Africa.......... 607	6.4	9.4	8.4	9.4	8.7	9.1	10.1	9.0	4.6	5.0	6.3	6.2	5.7	5.3
Asia.......... 507	17.0	19.2	15.1	6.9	4.3	2.1	3.4	20.8	28.9	18.0	23.4	23.2	21.7	24.9
Europe.......... 170	—	—	—	.5	.5	.7	.8	3.2	2.7	2.4	2.9	3.7	3.5	3.0
Middle East.......... 407	—	.1	—	.1	.1	.1	.1	1.8	2.0	3.0	2.6	2.9	3.0	3.0
Western Hemisphere.......... 207	7.7	9.6	7.9	12.0	7.5	9.6	10.8	3.1	3.1	3.5	3.7	5.3	6.3	5.6
ANNUAL PERCENT CHANGE														
World.......... 001	-33.3	1.6	31.2	38.4	30.7	21.6	12.2	36.1	10.1	70.1	37.8	19.7	20.3	33.7
Industrial Countries.......... 101	-33.8	-9.5	47.5	43.3	45.0	21.2	6.7	25.7	4.3	53.4	22.1	10.8	22.7	30.6
Developing Countries.......... 202	-34.2	25.6	7.2	28.0	-4.1	23.0	31.4	58.2	19.9	31.8	67.6	27.5	16.7	38.8
Africa.......... 607	-39.7	51.1	16.1	56.0	21.4	26.2	24.5	191.4	-44.1	87.9	72.1	17.7	10.4	23.9
Asia.......... 507	-41.6	14.9	3.1	-37.0	-17.4	-42.0	81.4	64.2	53.1	6.3	78.8	18.8	12.2	53.8
Europe.......... 170	—	-85.7	—	—	21.5	60.7	31.4	-14.0	-6.9	47.8	65.4	56.5	13.1	14.0
Middle East.......... 407	-99.4	—	-93.5	—	26.5	24.3	20.3	57.4	20.9	153.3	20.9	32.5	22.8	32.7
Western Hemisphere.......... 207	2.9	27.0	7.8	111.2	-18.0	54.1	27.3	-6.8	10.6	93.4	45.3	72.9	42.9	17.7
Other Countries n.i.e.......... 910	-100.1	—	—	....	....	....	....	-91.7	-95.4	—	30.1	27.3	23.5	29.5

		Exports							Imports						
		2001	2002	2003	2004	2005	2006	2007	2001	2002	2003	2004	2005	2006	2007
		Millions of U.S. Dollars							Millions of U.S. Dollars						
DOTS World Total	**001**	**958.3Y**	**960.3Y**	**913.7Y**	**1,207.6Y**	**1,247.3Y**	**1,334.1Y**	**1,609.9Y**	**3,293.6Y**	**2,276.0Y**	**2,240.4Y**	**2,787.4Y**	**2,890.6Y**	**3,131.5Y**	**3,445.3Y**
Industrial Countries	**101**	**278.2Y**	**298.7Y**	**219.1Y**	**226.3Y**	**190.4Y**	**249.1Y**	**85.8Y**	**1,460.7Y**	**535.1Y**	**424.3Y**	**474.7Y**	**311.0Y**	**234.6Y**	**156.5Y**
United States	111	—V	—V	.09V	1.36V	—V	—V	—V	.55V	27.61V	8.69V	26.07V	6.27V	—V	1.87V
Canada	156	9.49V	.05V	.07V	.07V	.04V	.07V	.15V	12.74V	14.85V	23.83V	26.29V	19.50V	16.84V	20.67V
Australia	193	2.41V	9.96V	5.93V	14.98V	13.62V	14.46V	7.43V	3.60V	3.05V	2.40V	9.19V	.36V	—V	—V
Japan	158	199.12V	209.04V	158.04V	148.39V	120.27V	67.46V	—V	1,169.63V	145.76V	100.48V	98.09V	68.71V	48.27V	10.24V
Austria	122	.55V	.85V	1.19V	1.01V	.48V	.57V	.55V	20.09V	14.18V	2.24V	5.86V	2.14V	2.65V	2.28V
Belgium	124	6.04V	4.20V	3.25V	4.33V	.32V	.37V	.89V	7.87V	10.63V	12.89V	17.00V	11.75V	14.09V	2.87V
Cyprus	423	—V	—V	—V	.32V	.45V	.09V	.14V	.02V	—V	.01V	—V	—V	—V	—V
Denmark	128	3.42V	2.56V	1.89V	1.90V	1.55V	2.52V	1.34V	14.14V	14.11V	13.63V	12.34V	12.12V	5.48V	7.02V
Finland	172	.15V	.01V	.03V	—V	—V	.14V	—V	1.18V	.18V	1.45V	.08V	2.65V	.27V	.21V
France	132	2.89V	1.30V	.91V	.92V	1.36V	1.71V	1.30V	7.37V	8.12V	4.79V	7.23V	8.43V	4.28V	3.58V
Germany	134	20.56V	26.51V	22.04V	20.57V	30.83V	14.71V	13.15V	90.32V	155.38V	76.88V	75.42V	69.86V	65.37V	40.92V
Greece	174	.14V	.17V	.08V	2.37V	.79V	78.51V	.42V	1.59V	8.97V	.71V	.54V	1.38V	1.51V	.47V
Iceland	176	—V	—V	—V	—V	—V	—V	—V	—V	—V	.21V	—V	—V	—V	—V
Ireland	178	7.26V	1.07V	4.15V	5.04V	3.96V	.13V	.08V	14.87V	.12V	.01V	.07V	.31V	—V	—V
Italy	136	2.45V	27.28V	3.24V	3.49V	.62V	1.40V	.61V	10.60V	17.08V	30.75V	11.99V	13.09V	12.74V	10.45V
Luxembourg	137	.06V	—V	1.80V	.03V	.01V	.12V	.09V	.03V	.04V	—V	.15V	—V	.02V	.02V
Malta	181	—Y	—V	—V	1.09V	—V	.05V	—V	—Y	—V	—V	—V	—V	—V	—V
Netherlands	138	10.52V	6.36V	5.93V	10.20V	6.17V	39.92V	42.70V	12.61V	45.18V	103.14V	132.19V	38.81V	24.20V	17.45V
Norway	142	—V	—V	—V	—V	—V	—V	—V	.38V	—V	—V	.01V	.10V	—V	30.27V
Portugal	182	—V	.02V	.02V	.08V	.20V	.08V	.19V	.28V	.01V	.11V	.05V	1.01V	.04V	—V
Slovenia	961	2.26V	1.56V	3.23V	4.24Y	.21V	.07V	.01V	.07V	.24V	.99V	1.30Y	1.42V	.74V	.94V
Spain	184	6.70V	5.54V	5.88V	4.29V	6.77V	9.27V	2.95V	34.33V	23.11V	12.19V	9.52V	10.43V	7.60V	2.21V
Sweden	144	1.50V	.03V	.33V	.20V	.30V	.72V	.13V	4.52V	4.59V	6.73V	31.29V	38.15V	26.67V	1.30V
Switzerland	146	.79V	.82V	.80V	.92V	1.23V	.73V	.39V	9.10V	14.47V	6.49V	5.45V	3.97V	3.17V	3.13V
United Kingdom	112	1.87V	1.33V	.21V	.48V	1.22V	16.04V	13.28V	44.79V	27.42V	15.72V	4.58V	.57V	.68V	.63V
Developing Countries	**202**	**680.2Y**	**661.6Y**	**694.6Y**	**981.3Y**	**1,056.9Y**	**1,085.0Y**	**1,524.1Y**	**1,832.9Y**	**1,740.9Y**	**1,816.0Y**	**2,312.7Y**	**2,579.5Y**	**2,896.8Y**	**3,288.7Y**
Africa	**607**	**27.6Y**	**32.6Y**	**50.9Y**	**69.0Y**	**79.3Y**	**97.6Y**	**124.7Y**	**329.0Y**	**436.2Y**	**308.5Y**	**285.4Y**	**378.6Y**	**552.2Y**	**714.6Y**
Algeria	612	4.86V	9.62V	10.69Y	13.91Y	17.71Y	21.86Y	28.31Y	97.83V	126.80V	153.72Y	203.40Y	276.69Y	347.85Y	419.63Y
Benin	638	1.21V	.63V	.49V	2.94V	.42V	.52Y	.64Y	—V	1.49V	.02V	—V	.31V	.39Y	.48Y
Burkina Faso	748	.24Y	.26Y	.33Y	.43Y	.49Y	.60Y	.75Y	—Y	—Y	—Y	—Y	—Y	—Y	—Y
Burundi	618	.27V	—V	—V	.05V	.20V	.07V	.09Y	—V	—V	—V	—V	—V	—V	—Y
Cameroon	622	—V	.01V	.14V	.18Y	.21Y	.26Y	.32Y	—V	—V	—V	—Y	—Y	—Y	—Y
Cape Verde	624	.17V	.19Y	.24Y	.31Y	.36Y	.44Y	.55Y	—V	—Y	—Y	—Y	—Y	—Y	—Y
Central African Rep.	626	.62Y	.68Y	.86Y	1.12Y	1.28Y	1.59Y	1.97Y	....	....	....	....	....	....	....
Congo, Dem. Rep. of	636	.33Y	.36Y	.45Y	.60Y	.68Y	.84Y	1.04Y	—Y	—Y	—Y	—Y	—Y	—Y	—Y
Congo, Republic of	634	—V	—V	—V	—V	—Y	—Y	—Y	228.02V	296.95V	143.28V	77.23V	88.24Y	109.06Y	135.34Y
Côte d'Ivoire	662	.16V	.04V	.02V	.27V	.27V	.01V	.01Y	.14V	—V	1.39V	—V	—V	—V	—Y
Djibouti	611	1.39Y	1.51Y	1.91Y	2.51Y	2.87Y	3.54Y	4.40Y	....	....	....	....	....	....	....
Ethiopia	644	.83V	1.90V	1.43V	4.88V	5.23V	6.47Y	8.03Y	.02V	.39V	.04V	.11V	1.24V	1.53Y	1.90Y
Gabon	646	.20Y	.22Y	.27Y	.36Y	.41Y	.51Y	.63Y	1.47Y	1.60Y	2.02Y	2.66Y	3.03Y	3.75Y	4.65Y
Ghana	652	8.70Y	9.44Y	11.95Y	15.69Y	17.93Y	22.16Y	27.50Y	.05Y	.05Y	.07Y	.09Y	.10Y	.12Y	.16Y
Guinea	656	.30V	.32Y	1.25V	.27V	.31Y	.38Y	.47Y	.01V	.01Y	.06V	.01V	.01Y	.02Y	.02Y
Kenya	664	3.08V	3.04V	2.30V	3.03V	3.46Y	4.28Y	5.31Y	.08V	.11V	.07V	.04V	.04Y	.05Y	.07Y
Madagascar	674	.08V	.03V	12.97V	17.03Y	19.46Y	24.05Y	29.85Y	.04V	.09V	.02V	.03Y	.03Y	.04Y	.05Y
Mauritius	684	.69V	.44V	.85V	1.21V	1.40V	.61V	1.81V	.05V	—V	.25V	.03V	.01V	—V	—V
Niger	692	.12V	.06V	.18V	.03V	.04Y	.04Y	.05Y	—V	—V	—V	—V	—Y	—Y	—Y
Senegal	722	.20V	.15V	.26V	.25V	.26V	.25V	.31Y	—V	—V	—V	.19V	.26V	.87V	1.08Y
Somalia	726	.50Y	.54Y	.68Y	.90Y	1.03Y	1.27Y	1.57Y	....	....	....	....	....	....	....
South Africa	199	1.04V	1.24V	.43V	.74V	1.56V	1.33V	3.01V	1.22V	8.42V	7.40V	1.45V	8.04V	87.84V	150.38V
Tanzania	738	.44V	.29V	.36Y	.48Y	.54Y	.67Y	.83Y	—V	.07V	.09Y	.12Y	.13Y	.16Y	.20Y
Togo	742	.91V	.24V	1.84V	.22V	.97V	1.20Y	1.49Y	—V	—V	.01V	—V	—V	—Y	—Y
Tunisia	744	1.18V	.98V	.87V	.90V	1.72V	4.24V	5.26Y	.01V	—V	.07V	.01V	.03V	.01V	.01Y
Uganda	746	.02V	.18V	.09V	.12Y	.13Y	.16Y	.20Y	.04V	.03V	—V	—Y	—Y	—Y	—Y
Zambia	754	.04V	.01V	.01V	.06V	.29V	.10V	.11V	.04V	—V	—V	—V	—V	.01V	.02V
Zimbabwe	698	.05V	.26V	.04V	.53V	.06V	.14V	.17Y	—V	.21V	.01V	.07V	.45V	.49V	.61Y
Asia	**507**	**299.1Y**	**375.8Y**	**454.0Y**	**655.5Y**	**694.4Y**	**657.3Y**	**753.2Y**	**1,147.2Y**	**1,071.4Y**	**1,233.4Y**	**1,447.0Y**	**1,686.6Y**	**1,866.1Y**	**2,044.7Y**
Bangladesh	513	38.11V	26.25V	13.04V	10.39V	20.93V	17.20V	10.91V	5.07V	4.93V	7.31V	11.36V	11.89V	21.71Y	30.08Y
Brunei Darussalam	516	.22Y	.23Y	.07V	.10Y	.11Y	.14Y	.17Y	.01Y	.01Y	.05V	.06Y	.07Y	.09Y	.11Y
Cambodia	522	.67V	—V	—V	—V	2.98V	3.80V	4.71Y	—V	—V	—V	—V	.01V	.11V	.14Y
China,P.R.: Mainland	924	151.63V	246.24V	359.59V	503.28V	451.37V	425.20V	528.66V	627.73V	514.04V	690.79V	876.13V	1,193.19V	1,355.03V	1,531.70V
China,P.R.:Hong Kong	532	29.55V	12.32V	6.09V	5.27V	4.74V	2.61V	2.01V	47.10V	32.62V	13.59V	12.39V	10.81V	8.44V	17.08V
China,P.R.:Macao	546	.58V	.01V	—V	.01V	.10V	—V	—V	.02V	.28V	.03V	.22V	.04V	—V	—V
Fiji	819	.37Y	.40Y	.50Y	.66Y	.75Y	.93Y	1.16Y	.03Y	.03Y	.04Y	.05Y	.06Y	.07Y	.09Y
India	534	18.69Y	3.93V	1.80V	2.84V	40.60V	50.18Y	62.28Y	175.78Y	195.10V	181.33V	144.30V	77.50V	95.79Y	118.87Y
Indonesia	536	1.92V	2.60V	.37V	6.18V	7.91V	.50V	2.43V	3.86V	1.72V	2.20V	4.05V	7.27V	14.69V	.47V
Korea	542	11.29V	19.87V	—V	—V	—V	—V	—V	—V	—V	—V	—V	—V	—V	—V
Malaysia	548	1.00V	.20V	.23V	.10V	.34V	.42V	2.25V	7.79V	4.34V	7.89V	22.54V	19.84V	8.20V	8.86V
Mongolia	948	.02V	.02V	.05V	.02V	.03V	26.82Y	33.28Y	.02V	.03V	.12V	.19V	—V	—Y	—Y
Myanmar	518	15.23Y	16.52Y	20.91Y	27.47Y	31.38Y	38.79Y	48.14Y	15.35Y	16.66Y	21.08Y	27.69Y	31.63Y	39.10Y	48.52Y
New Caledonia	839	.02V	.15V	.28V	.07V	.07Y	.09Y	.11Y	....	....	....	....	....	....	....

		Exports							Imports						
		2001	2002	2003	2004	2005	2006	2007	2001	2002	2003	2004	2005	2006	2007
		Millions of U.S. Dollars							Millions of U.S. Dollars						
Pakistan	564	.46V	.35V	.02V	8.96V	11.59V	14.32Y	17.78Y	.70V	.82V	1.56V	6.96V	4.77V	5.89Y	7.31Y
Papua New Guinea	853	1.47Y	1.60Y	2.02Y	2.66Y	3.03Y	3.75Y	4.65Y	—Y	—Y	—Y	—Y	—Y	—Y	—Y
Philippines	566	—V	—V	—V	—V	—V	—V	—V	.04V	.47V	.40V	.10V	.13V	.13V	—V
Singapore	576	2.76V	.73V	1.05V	1.46V	6.12V	5.97V	.93V	123.63V	92.01V	65.98V	60.24V	80.60V	66.03V	60.13V
Sri Lanka	524	—V	—V	—V	.04V	.04V	—V	—V	—V	—V	—V	—V	—V	—V	—V
Taiwan Province of China	528	3.22V	3.86V	1.38V	4.75V	3.72V	2.52V	2.97V	18.13V	14.16V	16.27V	17.15V	22.58V	24.68V	23.84V
Thailand	578	21.90V	40.48V	46.55V	81.26V	108.56V	64.05V	30.69V	116.57V	189.91V	224.80V	263.54V	226.18V	226.14V	197.51V
Tonga	866	.01Y	.01Y	.01Y	.01Y	.01Y	.02Y	.02Y	—Y	—Y	—Y	—Y	—Y	—Y	—Y
Vietnam	582	—V	—V	—V	—V	—V	—V	—V	5.41V	4.24V	—V	—V	—V	—V	—V
Europe	**170**	**55.8Y**	**36.3Y**	**33.6Y**	**41.9Y**	**54.9Y**	**46.0Y**	**51.8Y**	**78.2Y**	**63.3Y**	**147.4Y**	**256.3Y**	**287.1Y**	**239.1Y**	**168.9Y**
Azerbaijan	912	.14V	.01V	.54V	.14V	.63V	.13V	—V	—V	—V	—V	.01V	—V	—V	—V
Belarus	913	.25V	.09V	.07V	1.70V	1.94V	1.85V	2.14V	3.18V	2.13V	2.62V	2.30V	6.26V	1.57V	1.82V
Bulgaria	918	2.26V	2.39V	2.31V	2.76V	4.12V	2.94V	.15V	.41V	.14V	1.39V	4.56V	3.30V	1.18V	.20V
Czech Republic	935	.53V	.89V	2.79V	9.66V	9.06V	.21V	.04V	.40V	.57V	.28V	2.60V	.41V	1.56V	.11V
Estonia	939	.14V	.06V	.21V	.01V	—V	—V	—V	1.03V	—V	.01V	.01V	—V	.05V	—V
Georgia	915	.10V	.34V	.05V	.04V	.09V	.32V	.38Y	—V	.05V	.02V	.26V	.05V	2.62V	2.53Y
Hungary	944	.29V	.92V	1.59V	.37V	.19V	.26V	.21V	.51V	.03V	.29V	.41V	.20V	.11V	2.88V
Kazakhstan	916	.26V	.31V	.03V	.60V	.69Y	.85Y	1.05Y	.18V	.28V	10.91V	10.89V	12.45Y	15.38Y	19.09Y
Kyrgyz Republic	917	—V	—V	.05V	—V	.92V	—V	.03V	—V	.02V	.30V	.55V	.75V	.45V	.10V
Latvia	941	—V	—V	.01V	—V	—V	—V	—V	—V	—V	—V	—V	—V	—V	—V
Lithuania	946	1.15V	.38V	.40V	.08V	.03V	.02V	.09V	—V	.01V	.17V	—V	—V	—V	—V
Macedonia, FYR	962	.01V	.02V	.05V	.26V	.62V	1.20V	1.48Y	—V	—V	—V	—V	.61V	.26V	.32Y
Moldova	921	.05V	.05V	.03V	.03V	.04V	.04Y	.05Y	—V	—V	—V	—V	—V	—Y	—Y
Poland	964	10.41V	10.05V	7.53V	6.38V	15.90V	5.52V	.80V	2.38V	.74V	2.00V	1.84V	4.46V	3.46V	.57V
Romania	968	.92V	1.52V	2.53V	1.29V	2.19V	1.18V	.04V	—V	.01V	5.14V	1.05V	.41V	.60V	.72V
Russia	922	14.84V	9.67V	2.64V	4.34V	6.24V	18.26V	30.65V	63.78V	53.90V	121.63V	225.31V	251.04V	209.28V	138.73V
Slovak Republic	936	.31V	.86V	1.08Y	1.42Y	.09V	.01V	.06V	.53V	.05V	.07Y	.09Y	5.38V	.65V	.01V
Tajikistan	923	5.49V	—V	—V	—V	—V	—V	—V	1.51V	—V	—V	—V	—V	—V	—V
Turkey	186	4.98V	2.20V	2.22V	4.80V	3.49V	2.55V	1.39V	1.37V	1.76V	1.65V	1.47V	1.27V	1.32V	1.07V
Turkmenistan	925	3.36V	1.18V	4.49V	5.90Y	6.74Y	8.33Y	10.33Y	—V	.02V	.15V	.20Y	.23Y	.29Y	.36Y
Ukraine	926	10.28V	5.41V	4.96V	2.11V	1.91V	2.36Y	2.93Y	2.95V	3.58V	.76V	4.77V	.25V	.31Y	.38Y
Middle East	**407**	**43.7Y**	**87.1Y**	**38.4Y**	**89.8Y**	**90.4Y**	**111.6Y**	**140.5Y**	**23.5Y**	**31.7Y**	**30.6Y**	**81.3Y**	**53.4Y**	**66.9Y**	**81.1Y**
Bahrain	419	.29Y	.32Y	.40Y	.52Y	.60Y	.74Y	.92Y	—Y	—Y	—Y	—Y	—Y	—Y	—Y
Egypt	469	1.18V	1.28Y	1.63Y	2.14Y	2.44Y	3.02Y	3.74Y	—V	—Y	—Y	—Y	—Y	—Y	.01Y
Jordan	439	—V	.10V	.48V	.15V	.19V	.24V	—V	—V	—V	—V	.26V	—V	—V	—V
Lebanon	446	25.44Y	27.61Y	34.95Y	45.90Y	52.44Y	64.81Y	80.43Y	4.36Y	4.73Y	5.99Y	7.86Y	8.99Y	11.11Y	13.78Y
Libya	672	.08Y	.09Y	.10Y	.13Y	.16Y	.20Y	.26Y	—Y	—Y	—Y	—Y	—Y	—Y	—Y
Oman	449	.01V	—V	—V	—Y	—Y	—Y	—Y	....	....	....	....	....	....	....
Qatar	453	—V	—V	—V	33.48V	—V	—V	—Y	—V	6.59V	—V	40.51V	—V	—V	—Y
Saudi Arabia	456	15.42V	57.01V	—V	—V	33.17V	40.94Y	53.04Y	19.12Y	20.33Y	24.65Y	32.61Y	44.36Y	55.77Y	67.28Y
Yemen, Republic of	474	1.25V	.68V	.86Y	7.50V	1.38V	1.70Y	2.11Y	.02V	—V	—Y	.01V	—V	—Y	—Y
Western Hemisphere	**207**	**254.0Y**	**129.8Y**	**117.7Y**	**125.1Y**	**138.0Y**	**172.4Y**	**453.9Y**	**254.9Y**	**138.4Y**	**96.1Y**	**242.7Y**	**173.9Y**	**172.6Y**	**279.4Y**
Bahamas, The	313	.13Y	.14Y	.18Y	.23Y	.27Y	.33Y	.41Y	—Y	—Y	—Y	—Y	—Y	—Y	—Y
Barbados	316	—V	—V	.04V	.01V	1.04V	1.47V	1.82Y	—V	—V	—V	—V	—V	—V	—Y
Bermuda	319	.29Y	.32Y	.40Y	.53Y	—V	—V	—Y	—Y	—Y	—Y	—Y	—Y	—Y	—Y
Bolivia	218	1.01V	1.35V	.62V	.64V	.29V	.36Y	.45Y	.09V	.02V	.39V	.37V	.42Y	.52Y	.65Y
Brazil	223	62.47V	73.38V	65.61V	69.80V	71.56V	91.98V	109.30V	229.08V	109.19V	80.91V	186.93V	72.70V	70.89V	135.12V
Chile	228	26.17V	10.73V	3.17V	.51V	.23V	.26V	1.00V	1.14V	.99V	4.44V	15.58V	58.96V	19.14V	42.74V
Colombia	233	5.25V	4.35V	16.43V	8.67V	—V	8.12V	7.67V	.03V	—V	.01V	.42V	2.21V	4.26V	1.47V
Costa Rica	238	120.09V	1.92V	1.55V	2.94V	2.40V	2.96Y	3.68Y	1.70V	.69V	.30V	.01V	.07V	.09Y	.11Y
Dominica	321	.03V	.03Y	.04Y	.06Y	.07Y	.08Y	.10Y	—V	—Y	—Y	—Y	—Y	—Y	—Y
Ecuador	248	.08V	.14V	—V	—V	—V	—V	—Y	1.76V	.85V	.28V	24.30V	.30V	—V	—Y
El Salvador	253	—V	—V	—V	—V	.02V	.57V	—V	—V	—V	—V	—V	—V	—V	.15V
Greenland	326	.01Y	.01Y	.01Y	.02Y	.02Y	.03Y	.03Y	—Y	—Y	—Y	—Y	—Y	—Y	—Y
Guatemala	258	10.99V	5.50V	4.70V	7.50V	4.60V	5.69Y	7.06Y	—V	.05V	—V	—V	26.12V	32.28Y	40.06Y
Guyana	336	4.99Y	5.42Y	6.86Y	9.01Y	10.29Y	12.72Y	15.78Y	.16Y	.17Y	.21Y	.28Y	.32Y	.40Y	.49Y
Honduras	268	7.09V	2.83V	5.20V	3.36V	3.84Y	4.74Y	5.89Y	3.27V	4.66V	7.65V	8.98V	10.26Y	12.68Y	15.73Y
Jamaica	343	.91V	.51V	.68V	.37V	1.63V	2.12V	2.87V	—V	.02V	.01V	.10V	.02V	.03V	.16V
Paraguay	288	4.43V	2.75V	3.39V	8.23V	21.76V	22.62V	28.07Y	.61V	—V	.01V	1.06V	.84V	.17V	.21Y
Peru	293	1.14V	11.99V	.69V	.81V	2.37V	1.27V	1.94Y	11.45V	4.04V	1.50V	3.21V	1.06V	25.36V	34.38Y
St. Kitts and Nevis	361	.21Y	.22Y	.28Y	.37Y	.43Y	.53Y	.65Y	....	....	....	....	....	....	....
St. Lucia	362	.49Y	.53Y	.67Y	.88Y	1.01Y	1.24Y	1.54Y	—Y	—Y	—Y	—Y	—Y	—Y	—Y
St. Vincent & Grens.	364	.03V	.02V	.03V	.01V	.08V	.10Y	.12Y	—V	—V	—V	—V	—V	—Y	—Y
Suriname	366	2.79Y	3.03Y	3.84Y	5.04Y	5.76Y	7.12Y	8.83Y	—Y	—Y	—Y	—Y	—Y	—Y	—Y
Trinidad and Tobago	369	1.52V	2.25V	2.85Y	3.75Y	4.28Y	5.29Y	6.57Y	.37V	.27V	.34Y	.45Y	.51Y	.63Y	.79Y
Uruguay	298	1.24V	1.35Y	.22V	.44V	.30V	.38Y	.47Y	.24V	.26Y	.02V	1.02V	.09V	.12Y	.14Y
Venezuela, Rep. Bol.	299	2.61V	1.03V	.22V	1.86V	5.70V	2.47V	249.68V	5.03V	17.15V	.01V	—V	—V	5.98V	7.22Y
Memorandum Items															
European Union	998	79.17Y	91.94Y	67.79Y	78.50Y	80.53Y	172.43Y	79.02Y	269.55Y	330.77Y	285.04Y	314.55Y	222.57Y	172.18Y	93.91Y
Oil Exporting Ctys.	999	24.90Y	70.34Y	11.38Y	55.55Y	64.64Y	65.96Y	333.73Y	125.84Y	172.59Y	180.56Y	280.58Y	328.32Y	424.28Y	494.60Y
Non-Oil Develop.Ctys.	201	655.28Y	591.25Y	683.18Y	925.73Y	992.26Y	1,019.05Y	1,190.38Y	1,707.09Y	1,568.28Y	1,635.45Y	2,032.13Y	2,251.21Y	2,472.56Y	2,794.13Y
PERCENT DISTRIBUTION															
Industrial Countries	**101**	**29.0**	**31.1**	**24.0**	**18.7**	**15.3**	**18.7**	**5.3**	**44.3**	**23.5**	**18.9**	**17.0**	**10.8**	**7.5**	**4.5**
Developing Countries	**202**	**71.0**	**68.9**	**76.0**	**81.3**	**84.7**	**81.3**	**94.7**	**55.7**	**76.5**	**81.1**	**83.0**	**89.2**	**92.5**	**95.5**
Africa	**607**	**2.9**	**3.4**	**5.6**	**5.7**	**6.4**	**7.3**	**7.7**	**10.0**	**19.2**	**13.8**	**10.2**	**13.1**	**17.6**	**20.7**
Asia	**507**	**31.2**	**39.1**	**49.7**	**54.3**	**55.7**	**49.3**	**46.8**	**34.8**	**47.1**	**55.1**	**51.9**	**58.3**	**59.6**	**59.3**
Europe	**170**	**5.8**	**3.8**	**3.7**	**3.5**	**4.4**	**3.5**	**3.2**	**2.4**	**2.8**	**6.6**	**9.2**	**9.9**	**7.6**	**4.9**

	Exports 2001	2002	2003	2004	2005	2006	2007	Imports 2001	2002	2003	2004	2005	2006	2007
Middle East............................ 407	4.6	9.1	4.2	7.4	7.2	8.4	8.7	.7	1.4	1.4	2.9	1.8	2.1	2.4
Western Hemisphere............. 207	26.5	13.5	12.9	10.4	11.1	12.9	28.2	7.7	6.1	4.3	8.7	6.0	5.5	8.1
ANNUAL PERCENT CHANGE														
World....................................... 001	−1.9	.2	−4.9	32.2	3.3	7.0	20.7	56.6	−30.9	−1.6	24.4	3.7	8.3	10.0
Industrial Countries................. 101	−18.3	7.4	−26.6	3.3	−15.9	30.8	−65.6	231.1	−63.4	−20.7	11.9	−34.5	−24.6	−33.3
Developing Countries.............. 202	7.0	−2.7	5.0	41.3	7.7	2.7	40.5	10.3	−5.0	4.3	27.4	11.5	12.3	13.5
Africa...................................... 607	11.2	18.0	56.2	35.6	14.8	23.1	27.8	9.2	32.6	−29.3	−7.5	32.7	45.8	29.4
Asia... 507	41.7	25.6	20.8	44.4	5.9	−5.3	14.6	10.7	−6.6	15.1	17.3	16.6	10.6	9.6
Europe.................................... 170	7.0	−34.8	−7.6	24.8	31.1	−16.1	12.6	22.1	−19.1	132.9	73.9	12.0	−16.7	−29.4
Middle East............................ 407	−43.0	99.4	−55.9	133.8	.6	23.5	25.8	−75.3	34.7	−3.2	165.2	−34.3	25.4	21.2
Western Hemisphere............. 207	−6.4	−48.9	−9.3	6.3	10.3	25.0	163.2	53.8	−45.7	−30.6	152.6	−28.4	−.8	61.9

	Exports 2001	Exports 2002	Exports 2003	Exports 2004	Exports 2005	Exports 2006	Exports 2007	Imports 2001	Imports 2002	Imports 2003	Imports 2004	Imports 2005	Imports 2006	Imports 2007
	Millions of U.S. Dollars							Millions of U.S. Dollars						
IFS World Total	**59,191**	**59,702**	**67,479**	**81,750**	**101,938**	**120,464**	**137,998**	**32,955**	**34,890**	**39,486**	**48,085**	**54,792**	**63,366**	**79,762**
DOTS World Total....001	**57,621**	**60,523**	**68,315**	**82,369**	**103,750**	**122,122**	**136,376**	**31,953**	**34,156**	**40,052**	**48,441**	**55,481**	**64,278**	**80,281**
Industrial Countries....101	**52,983**	**54,617**	**61,656**	**74,910**	**94,455**	**103,625**	**122,076**	**26,255**	**27,799**	**31,847**	**38,014**	**42,720**	**48,855**	**60,855**
United States....111	4,628	5,191	5,905	6,945	6,842	6,987	8,389	2,196	2,105	2,064	2,359	2,850	3,432	3,875
Canada....156	2,415	2,167	2,498	3,272	3,927	3,784	3,990	873	723	811	1,137	1,410	1,724	3,415
Australia....193	107	143	144	154	192	194	286	104	45	68	78	83	96	160
Japan....158	885	1,001	973	1,024	1,016	1,193	1,319	1,004	1,064	1,445	1,642	1,760	1,728	1,772
New Zealand....196	17	20	29	19	24	20	27	14	17	20	24	23	21	32
Austria....122	136	144	152	194	235	332	406	286	308	336	385	440	515	776
Belgium....124	1,993	1,745	1,840	2,072	2,552	3,058	3,394	625	707	819	1,161	1,420	1,482	1,655
Cyprus....423	24	8	15	15	99	73	23	5	4	17	6	22	30	10
Denmark....128	2,120	2,236	2,614	3,021	3,682	4,288	4,406	2,341	2,757	3,145	3,545	4,056	4,430	5,145
Finland....172	1,098	1,118	1,175	1,244	1,315	1,909	1,722	1,138	1,152	1,293	1,966	1,748	2,056	2,959
France....132	6,858	6,981	5,610	7,924	9,650	10,055	10,948	1,699	1,631	1,737	2,064	2,202	2,528	2,928
Germany....134	6,751	7,477	8,888	10,605	13,056	15,033	16,793	4,167	4,565	5,310	6,595	7,452	8,648	10,899
Greece....174	242	145	163	156	194	195	251	47	52	60	56	84	70	150
Iceland....176	142	127	155	289	320	360	301	110	98	104	92	83	126	178
Ireland....178	903	738	539	545	1,851	2,158	2,210	486	497	563	697	886	896	949
Italy....136	1,092	1,813	2,415	1,985	2,960	3,846	3,740	1,096	1,345	1,585	1,707	1,821	2,183	2,638
Luxembourg....137	39	24	29	62	36	41	49	20	23	25	38	51	65	71
Malta....181	115	22	15	16	72	147	60	3	5	6	6	15	6	8
Netherlands....138	5,809	5,637	6,562	8,164	10,297	12,545	13,971	1,417	1,630	1,793	2,121	2,193	2,619	2,974
Portugal....182	528	455	481	612	575	767	871	184	186	190	187	193	203	217
Slovenia....961	12	12	17	15	19	61	16	33	44	52	57	59	63	93
Spain....184	878	1,017	1,632	2,379	2,510	2,624	3,223	443	523	636	835	1,252	1,465	1,777
Sweden....144	4,574	4,432	5,041	5,545	6,751	894	8,918	5,022	5,351	6,433	7,597	8,001	9,645	11,778
Switzerland....146	218	260	252	248	282	336	921	427	455	465	505	582	715	864
United Kingdom....112	11,399	11,702	14,514	18,407	25,997	32,727	35,843	2,515	2,514	2,869	3,156	4,033	4,110	5,530
Developing Countries....202	**4,561**	**5,853**	**6,487**	**7,427**	**9,260**	**18,452**	**14,219**	**5,566**	**6,356**	**8,205**	**10,425**	**12,761**	**15,397**	**19,406**
Africa....607	**304**	**314**	**423**	**333**	**572**	**8,423**	**934**	**265**	**287**	**372**	**504**	**689**	**785**	**1,079**
Algeria....612	5	6	3	3	4	14	15	—	13	1	10	1	1	—
Angola....614	67	60	47	35	162	192	207	—	—	—	—	5	7	2
Benin....638	—	2	2	1	1	1	—	—	—	—	—	—	—	—
Botswana....616	2	—	—	—	—	1	—	76	78	162	182	330	391	529
Burkina Faso....748	—	—	—	—	—	1	—	—	—	—	—	—	—	—
Burundi....618	—	—	—	—	1	—	—	—	—	—	—	—	—	—
Cameroon....622	—	4	1	2	3	7	7	—	—	—	—	—	—	—
Cape Verde....624	1	—	—	—	—	—	—	—	—	—	—	—	—	—
Chad....628	—	—	—	1	—	1	—	—	—	—	—	—	—	—
Congo, Dem. Rep. of....636	2	4	4	6	9	15	25	—	—	—	—	—	—	—
Congo, Republic of....634	6	5	5	5	5	10	101	3	—	2	22	20	29	7
Côte d'Ivoire....662	4	4	4	37	11	8	7	1	1	1	1	1	1	8
Djibouti....611	—	—	1	—	—	—	1	—	—	—	—	—	—	—
Equatorial Guinea....642	2	41	65	8	9	4	3	—	—	—	1	29	57	93
Eritrea....643	—	1	1	1	1	—	—	—	—	—	—	—	—	—
Ethiopia....644	—	1	3	2	5	2	4	—	2	3	2	5	14	9
Gabon....646	4	4	3	3	11	3	7	9	14	17	32	41	25	35
Ghana....652	4	8	11	17	30	13	14	6	4	5	7	8	11	14
Guinea....656	2	—	—	4	1	2	2	—	—	—	—	—	—	—
Kenya....664	12	10	7	11	22	9	10	4	6	7	9	12	11	12
Liberia....668	92	61	110	28	67	4	187	42	28	7	26	—	19	61
Madagascar....674	—	—	—	—	1	—	1	2	1	1	1	1	1	1
Malawi....676	—	2	2	1	—	—	—	—	—	—	—	—	—	—
Mali....678	1	—	—	—	1	1	1	—	—	—	—	—	—	—
Mauritania....682	1	—	1	19	23	8	4	4	4	4	8	10	10	9
Mauritius....684	—	1	—	1	1	1	1	—	1	2	2	2	3	3
Morocco....686	23	7	17	23	55	53	21	30	27	37	50	53	50	65
Mozambique....688	1	—	—	1	6	5	3	—	—	—	—	—	—	—
Namibia....728	4	15	2	2	1	3	3	3	9	9	9	10	10	12
Niger....692	—	—	—	1	—	13	17	—	—	—	—	—	—	—
Nigeria....694	30	32	60	37	48	57	73	—	—	—	—	—	1	1
Senegal....722	1	1	1	2	2	—	4	—	—	—	—	—	1	2
Seychelles....718	—	1	1	1	1	12	1	—	—	—	—	—	—	—
Sierra Leone....724	—	—	1	—	—	—	—	—	—	—	—	—	—	—
Somalia....726	—	—	—	1	—	—	—	—	—	—	—	—	—	—
South Africa....199	26	27	60	65	64	116	165	59	69	87	111	121	104	164
Sudan....732	1	5	2	5	14	7,854	8	1	1	1	1	—	1	1
Tanzania....738	4	3	3	4	3	3	20	5	4	4	5	7	7	11
Togo....742	—	1	1	1	—	—	—	—	—	—	—	—	—	—
Tunisia....744	5	2	3	2	4	8	11	12	15	13	15	23	24	32
Uganda....746	1	2	1	3	1	1	3	2	2	1	2	2	2	2
Zambia....754	—	1	1	1	1	1	5	1	1	1	2	1	—	1
Zimbabwe....698	1	1	1	1	1	1	—	5	5	4	6	6	4	4

		Exports							Imports						
		2001	2002	2003	2004	2005	2006	2007	2001	2002	2003	2004	2005	2006	2007
		Millions of U.S. Dollars							*Millions of U.S. Dollars*						
Asia	**507**	**1,827**	**2,444**	**2,637**	**2,837**	**3,339**	**3,616**	**5,696**	**2,414**	**2,753**	**3,651**	**4,572**	**5,719**	**6,930**	**8,164**
Afghanistan, I.S. of	512	1	—	3	4	2	12	6	—	—	—	—	—	—	1
Bangladesh	513	4	4	7	2	11	5	26	33	39	46	63	64	72	82
Bhutan	514	—	—	—	1	2	2	—	—	—	—	—	—	—	—
Brunei Darussalam	516	—	1	1	1	2	2	3	—	—	—	—	—	—	—
Cambodia	522	2	—	—	2	1	1	—	5	6	7	8	9	9	10
China,P.R.: Mainland	924	667	931	870	908	905	1,707	1,610	989	1,268	1,751	2,411	3,109	3,659	4,857
China,P.R.:Hong Kong	532	176	113	138	260	228	260	271	109	124	167	228	250	246	255
China,P.R.:Macao	546	1	—	1	1	1	1	1	6	5	6	17	12	5	6
Fiji	819	—	—	—	2	—	—	—	—	—	—	—	—	—	—
French Polynesia	887	—	—	—	—	—	—	3	—	—	—	—	—	—	—
Guam	829	1	—	1	—	—	—	1	—	—	—	—	—	—	—
India	534	48	65	70	128	200	337	594	97	105	134	176	213	233	290
Indonesia	536	25	30	33	44	54	82	129	90	88	97	103	127	119	125
Korea	542	368	600	501	736	788	739	1,226	336	214	454	367	569	948	740
Lao People's Dem.Rep	544	2	1	—	—	1	1	1	3	3	2	2	1	1	1
Malaysia	548	—	47	49	59	52	109	143	—	164	181	185	220	299	277
Maldives	556	—	—	1	—	3	1	3	—	—	—	—	—	—	—
Mongolia	948	—	—	—	1	—	—	—	—	—	—	—	—	—	—
Myanmar	518	—	—	—	—	—	—	—	1	1	2	2	2	2	1
Nepal	558	—	1	1	—	—	1	1	—	1	—	1	—	1	1
New Caledonia	839	1	3	1	1	3	3	5	—	—	—	—	—	—	—
Pakistan	564	9	8	8	16	20	18	20	106	38	45	46	56	67	71
Papua New Guinea	853	1	2	1	6	5	1	1	—	—	—	—	—	—	—
Philippines	566	32	15	15	19	21	17	22	33	37	28	38	50	43	48
Singapore	576	303	376	737	371	793	15	1,127	121	129	98	144	191	225	162
Solomon Islands	813	—	—	—	—	—	1	—	—	—	—	—	—	—	—
Sri Lanka	524	4	3	4	4	7	5	6	9	9	10	11	13	15	23
Taiwan Province of China	528	93	143	102	158	128	131	215	326	348	393	493	527	594	730
Thailand	578	82	95	88	97	94	140	223	105	124	160	187	201	277	341
Vanuatu	846	—	—	—	—	—	—	24	—	—	—	—	—	—	—
Vietnam	582	6	7	8	13	17	26	36	45	49	70	89	104	116	142
Europe	**170**	**1,502**	**1,810**	**2,317**	**2,844**	**3,636**	**4,558**	**5,405**	**1,967**	**2,408**	**2,916**	**3,992**	**4,680**	**5,808**	**7,762**
Albania	914	4	—	—	1	1	2	2	—	—	—	—	—	—	1
Armenia	911	—	1	1	1	—	—	—	—	—	—	—	—	—	—
Azerbaijan	912	3	30	28	83	25	38	24	—	—	2	5	1	3	2
Belarus	913	15	15	21	21	33	40	49	4	2	8	20	36	46	42
Bosnia & Herzegovina	963	2	2	1	3	4	3	3	1	1	2	3	3	6	8
Bulgaria	918	—	6	6	6	9	12	18	—	14	18	22	27	28	35
Croatia	960	35	38	47	52	50	69	79	6	6	7	10	11	16	18
Czech Republic	935	166	277	372	519	629	951	981	171	252	261	364	404	491	751
Czechoslovakia n.s.	937	—	—	—	—	11	—	—	—	—	—	—	6	—	—
Estonia	939	53	60	63	72	91	130	121	116	190	181	223	263	316	436
Faroe Islands	816	99	89	118	106	131	142	195	33	30	31	49	37	72	108
Georgia	915	—	1	7	—	2	3	2	—	—	—	—	—	—	—
Gibraltar	823	10	3	30	1	2	1	29	—	—	—	—	—	—	—
Hungary	944	29	34	37	41	47	37	76	107	140	226	316	302	339	443
Kazakhstan	916	2	5	8	11	20	14	89	2	5	6	2	6	4	10
Kyrgyz Republic	917	4	—	1	—	—	—	1	12	—	—	—	—	—	—
Latvia	941	52	62	101	85	116	231	170	54	64	112	148	162	192	275
Lithuania	946	62	62	72	90	106	134	157	81	127	163	218	248	349	510
Macedonia, FYR	962	1	1	—	1	1	2	2	1	1	1	2	2	2	4
Moldova	921	1	1	1	2	3	3	5	—	—	—	1	1	1	2
Montenegro, Rep. of	943	—	—	—	—	—	—	2	—	—	—	—	—	—	—
Poland	964	336	331	437	591	841	1,083	1,611	351	466	534	778	958	1,270	1,675
Romania	968	26	33	34	52	93	92	122	86	138	157	123	187	303	342
Russia	922	263	322	389	516	818	849	936	762	687	829	1,141	1,290	1,559	1,968
Serbia, Rep. of	942	—	—	—	—	—	16	16	—	—	—	—	—	9	6
Serbia & Montenegro	965	7	6	8	—	—	—	—	3	3	3	—	—	—	—
Slovak Republic	936	15	16	24	35	51	—	96	25	36	48	77	109	131	261
Tajikistan	923	—	—	—	—	1	—	—	11	56	37	81	119	134	185
Turkey	186	206	304	400	429	349	491	383	116	164	258	353	441	427	584
Turkmenistan	925	—	—	—	2	—	25	1	—	—	—	—	—	—	—
Ukraine	926	107	112	110	124	198	187	230	24	27	31	55	64	107	93
Uzbekistan	927	1	—	1	1	4	2	4	—	—	—	—	—	—	—
Europe n.s.	884	—	—	—	—	—	—	—	1	1	—	—	2	2	3
Middle East	**407**	**267**	**283**	**360**	**437**	**424**	**595**	**666**	**106**	**98**	**115**	**140**	**191**	**234**	**415**
Bahrain	419	3	5	5	6	6	7	9	14	6	6	8	9	22	20
Egypt	469	27	40	28	28	55	42	62	11	9	9	20	24	23	55
Iran, I.R. of	429	19	13	24	63	34	43	28	7	8	8	10	9	12	11
Iraq	433	—	—	1	4	5	1	4	—	—	—	—	—	—	—
Israel	436	70	64	72	64	66	87	77	62	60	67	73	88	101	108
Jordan	439	3	12	5	4	3	7	10	—	—	—	—	—	3	1
Kuwait	443	6	8	6	7	25	42	13	1	—	—	—	2	2	1
Lebanon	446	11	5	4	7	6	5	5	2	2	4	1	1	1	2
Libya	672	3	2	2	5	5	13	4	—	—	—	—	—	—	12

	Exports 2001	2002	2003	2004	2005	2006	2007	Imports 2001	2002	2003	2004	2005	2006	2007
	Millions of U.S. Dollars							Millions of U.S. Dollars						
Oman.......... 449	4	5	5	10	13	6	12	—	—	—	—	1	1	—
Qatar.......... 453	4	4	8	6	18	52	22	—	—	—	—	—	1	—
Saudi Arabia.......... 456	47	44	67	82	49	107	122	6	6	4	11	45	51	53
Syrian Arab Republic.......... 463	4	4	6	5	4	—	44	—	4	6	7	2	1	1
United Arab Emirates.......... 466	65	76	124	146	134	179	251	3	4	9	10	9	18	152
West Bank/Gaza Strip.......... 487	—	—	—	—	1	—	—	—	—	—	—	—	—	—
Yemen, Republic of.......... 474	2	2	2	2	2	2	4	—	—	—	—	—	—	—
Western Hemisphere.......... 207	**661**	**1,002**	**749**	**976**	**1,289**	**1,258**	**1,518**	**814**	**810**	**1,151**	**1,216**	**1,481**	**1,639**	**1,986**
Antigua and Barbuda.......... 311	1	1	12	1	2	17	68	—	—	—	—	1	—	2
Argentina.......... 213	9	5	11	19	18	22	27	37	53	34	42	55	37	42
Bahamas, The.......... 313	79	483	41	76	248	237	185	8	—	1	9	2	3	7
Barbados.......... 316	2	3	18	4	1	1	1	—	—	—	—	—	—	—
Belize.......... 339	—	—	—	11	—	2	1	—	—	—	—	—	—	—
Bermuda.......... 319	—	—	—	—	58	100	6	60	—	203	—	—	—	—
Bolivia.......... 218	1	1	1	3	3	4	7	—	—	—	—	1	1	2
Brazil.......... 223	174	217	253	303	408	315	476	254	206	350	392	514	621	853
Chile.......... 228	30	20	27	69	59	74	122	49	54	61	59	77	98	108
Colombia.......... 233	12	8	8	11	15	16	16	44	43	46	50	51	41	64
Costa Rica.......... 238	2	2	4	4	8	7	5	14	26	37	45	54	50	54
Dominica.......... 321	—	1	—	1	2	—	1	—	—	—	—	—	—	—
Dominican Republic.......... 243	26	29	24	32	30	32	166	1	1	3	3	5	4	5
Ecuador.......... 248	6	4	3	13	3	5	6	4	5	6	11	13	22	24
El Salvador.......... 253	1	1	1	1	1	3	1	1	1	1	—	1	1	—
Greenland.......... 326	46	35	31	15	14	24	18	12	3	2	7	5	8	3
Grenada.......... 328	2	1	1	1	1	1	2	—	—	—	—	—	—	—
Guatemala.......... 258	3	5	21	55	93	108	76	8	6	7	8	11	14	16
Guyana.......... 336	—	2	1	1	—	—	—	—	—	—	—	—	—	—
Haiti.......... 263	4	3	3	2	2	6	2	—	—	—	—	—	—	—
Honduras.......... 268	—	1	1	1	1	1	10	3	1	2	3	6	3	2
Jamaica.......... 343	8	13	15	13	19	19	15	121	171	121	118	145	139	69
Mexico.......... 273	110	68	78	109	140	66	90	42	31	44	48	74	85	110
Netherlands Antilles.......... 353	2	2	1	2	14	2	3	—	—	—	—	—	—	—
Nicaragua.......... 278	1	6	—	2	1	—	—	—	—	1	1	1	1	1
Panama.......... 283	86	42	44	155	38	13	27	4	1	14	31	26	8	48
Paraguay.......... 288	1	—	—	1	3	1	1	—	—	—	—	—	—	1
Peru.......... 293	3	4	10	5	32	6	15	36	58	51	47	134	137	194
St. Kitts and Nevis.......... 361	—	1	—	1	—	—	2	—	—	—	—	—	—	—
St. Vincent & Grens.......... 364	1	4	1	1	—	1	9	—	—	—	—	—	1	—
Suriname.......... 366	1	1	1	1	1	1	6	90	110	116	285	239	312	311
Trinidad and Tobago.......... 369	2	2	3	6	3	6	7	—	7	—	—	7	—	1
Uruguay.......... 298	5	2	2	4	2	5	5	17	10	19	28	51	53	67
Venezuela, Rep. Bol.......... 299	32	31	14	21	20	40	19	8	17	31	12	6	—	1
Western Hem. n.s.......... 399	11	7	117	34	48	120	124	—	3	—	15	—	—	—
Other Countries n.i.e.......... 910	**2**	**1**	**1**	**1**	**2**	**1**	**28**	**—**	**—**	**—**	**1**	**1**	**1**	**17**
Cuba.......... 928	2	1	1	1	2	1	1	—	—	—	1	1	1	17
North Korea.......... 954	—	—	—	—	—	—	28	—	—	—	—	—	—	—
Special Categories.......... 899	**56**	—	—	—	—	—	—	**131**	—	—	—	—	—	—
Memorandum Items														
European Union.......... 998	45,285	46,549	52,806	64,393	83,731	93,318	110,057	22,431	24,565	28,394	34,304	38,374	44,101	54,907
Oil Exporting Ctys.......... 999	239	252	347	427	409	636	692	115	137	151	157	200	206	357
Non-Oil Develop.Ctys.......... 201	4,322	5,601	6,140	7,000	8,851	17,816	13,527	5,452	6,220	8,054	10,269	12,561	15,191	19,049
PERCENT DISTRIBUTION														
Industrial Countries.......... 101	**92.0**	**90.2**	**90.3**	**90.9**	**91.0**	**84.9**	**89.5**	**82.2**	**81.4**	**79.5**	**78.5**	**77.0**	**76.0**	**75.8**
Developing Countries.......... 202	**7.9**	**9.7**	**9.5**	**9.0**	**8.9**	**15.1**	**10.4**	**17.4**	**18.6**	**20.5**	**21.5**	**23.0**	**24.0**	**24.2**
Africa.......... 607	**.5**	**.5**	**.6**	**.4**	**.6**	**6.9**	**.7**	**.8**	**.8**	**.9**	**1.0**	**1.2**	**1.2**	**1.3**
Asia.......... 507	**3.2**	**4.0**	**3.9**	**3.4**	**3.2**	**3.0**	**4.2**	**7.6**	**8.1**	**9.1**	**9.4**	**10.3**	**10.8**	**10.2**
Europe.......... 170	**2.6**	**3.0**	**3.4**	**3.5**	**3.5**	**3.7**	**4.0**	**6.2**	**7.1**	**7.3**	**8.2**	**8.4**	**9.0**	**9.7**
Middle East.......... 407	**.5**	**.5**	**.5**	**.5**	**.4**	**.5**	**.5**	**.3**	**.3**	**.3**	**.3**	**.3**	**.4**	**.5**
Western Hemisphere.......... 207	**1.1**	**1.7**	**1.1**	**1.2**	**1.2**	**1.0**	**1.1**	**2.5**	**2.4**	**2.9**	**2.5**	**2.7**	**2.5**	**2.5**
ANNUAL PERCENT CHANGE														
World.......... 001	**—**	**5.0**	**12.9**	**20.6**	**26.0**	**17.7**	**11.7**	**1.0**	**6.9**	**17.3**	**20.9**	**14.5**	**15.9**	**24.9**
Industrial Countries.......... 101	**–1.5**	**3.1**	**12.9**	**21.5**	**26.1**	**9.7**	**17.8**	**.9**	**5.9**	**14.6**	**19.4**	**12.4**	**14.4**	**24.6**
Developing Countries.......... 202	**20.1**	**28.3**	**10.8**	**14.5**	**24.7**	**99.3**	**–22.9**	**–1.0**	**14.2**	**29.1**	**27.1**	**22.4**	**20.7**	**26.0**
Africa.......... 607	**33.9**	**3.3**	**35.0**	**–21.3**	**71.4**	**—**	**–88.9**	**–2.0**	**8.3**	**29.7**	**35.5**	**36.5**	**14.0**	**37.4**
Asia.......... 507	**24.0**	**33.8**	**7.9**	**7.6**	**17.7**	**8.3**	**57.5**	**–3.6**	**14.0**	**32.6**	**25.2**	**25.1**	**21.2**	**17.8**
Europe.......... 170	**10.1**	**20.6**	**28.0**	**22.7**	**27.8**	**25.4**	**18.6**	**3.6**	**22.4**	**21.1**	**36.9**	**17.2**	**24.1**	**33.6**
Middle East.......... 407	**9.9**	**5.8**	**27.3**	**21.4**	**–2.9**	**40.3**	**11.8**	**8.3**	**–8.1**	**17.6**	**22.1**	**36.4**	**22.5**	**77.3**
Western Hemisphere.......... 207	**35.1**	**51.5**	**–25.3**	**30.3**	**32.1**	**–2.4**	**20.7**	**–4.7**	**–.5**	**42.1**	**5.7**	**21.8**	**10.6**	**21.2**
Other Countries n.i.e.......... 910	**4.2**	**–21.0**	**–38.5**	**6.8**	**115.7**	**–45.8**	**—**	**71.5**	**–4.6**	**–18.7**	**145.9**	**–44.3**	**31.6**	**—**

		Exports							Imports						
		2001	2002	2003	2004	2005	2006	2007	2001	2002	2003	2004	2005	2006	2007
		Millions of U.S. Dollars							*Millions of U.S. Dollars*						
IFS World Total		**11,074.1**	**11,171.7**	**11,668.7**	**13,341.5**	**18,691.8**	**21,585.2**	**24,135.8**	**5,797.9**	**6,005.5**	**6,572.2**	**8,865.3**	**8,827.0**	**10,915.2**	**15,977.6**
DOTS World Total	**001**	**10,681.1**	**11,126.7**	**10,361.7**	**12,725.5Y**	**17,420.9Y**	**24,109.4Y**	**22,805.5Y**	**5,796.8**	**6,005.3**	**6,572.2**	**7,690.7Y**	**9,644.8Y**	**11,580.9Y**	**15,834.9Y**
Industrial Countries	**101**	**2,912.1**	**2,890.1**	**2,304.1**	**2,404.6Y**	**3,633.3Y**	**3,978.8Y**	**4,672.0Y**	**2,742.1**	**2,911.8**	**3,194.4**	**4,263.0Y**	**4,851.9Y**	**5,581.5Y**	**8,174.2Y**
United States	111	292.96	259.86	343.09	408.55V	541.09V	872.91V	988.64V	394.93	393.48	409.57	362.78V	652.52V	939.18V	1,165.23V
Canada	156	1.80	4.27	4.23	5.63V	3.83V	5.42V	3.02V	16.75	29.24	23.95	51.87V	20.65V	54.32V	120.43V
Australia	193	1.04	2.58	2.73	1.48V	1.63V	2.09V	2.85V	141.57	108.43	154.82	198.83V	193.92V	226.58V	336.66V
Japan	158	2,228.21	2,082.64	1,674.33	1,476.02V	2,474.91V	2,568.23V	3,257.26V	892.12	968.77	1,123.04	1,278.01V	1,523.14V	1,902.76V	2,783.66V
New Zealand	196	121.15	158.16	56.32	108.68V	91.27V	43.91V	.16V	11.26	16.03	37.06	67.14V	26.80V	41.80V	73.79V
Austria	122	.06	.08	1.88	.60V	.53V	.32V	.35V	15.02	12.41	21.75	59.91V	59.98V	68.65V	116.74V
Belgium	124	25.65	26.96	22.90	10.97V	19.89V	5.59V	4.34V	48.61	101.34	63.41	95.95V	82.78V	137.43V	139.56V
Cyprus	423	1.05	.49	.89	2.14V	2.01V	1.48V	2.47V	3.75	5.38	5.50	3.63V	2.96V	3.50V	3.36V
Denmark	128	3.38	.67	.34	.59V	.82V	.30V	.24V	30.15	37.61	42.24	45.48V	44.43V	36.02V	86.89V
Finland	172	.06	.13	.13	.12V	.02V	.04V	.02V	17.41	14.56	16.54	21.01V	23.27V	38.24V	81.04V
France	132	6.68	71.22	11.08	33.40V	36.54V	20.21V	14.29V	180.44	142.67	157.92	144.50V	264.16V	217.80V	533.41V
Germany	134	11.69	12.05	15.17	13.17V	15.70V	27.16V	24.01V	245.30	264.10	291.12	395.10V	556.83V	624.34V	824.22V
Greece	174	3.07	3.61	6.14	6.39V	6.66V	6.06V	5.46V	2.77	9.22	19.21	1.77V	10.16V	12.53V	29.44V
Iceland	176	—	—	—	—V	—V	—V	—V	.03	.05	—	.03V	.01V	.02V	—V
Ireland	178	.33	.66	.97	1.66V	2.17V	2.76V	2.70V	38.55	28.14	28.10	20.29V	25.85V	28.95V	32.75V
Italy	136	6.30	7.48	8.94	15.47V	20.10V	35.18V	27.42V	122.87	183.93	159.45	465.65V	189.91V	272.13V	455.92V
Luxembourg	137	—	—	.03	—V	—V	—V	—V	.02	.75	.14	1.47V	.97V	1.84V	3.39V
Malta	181	.05	.18	.07	.30V	.43V	.58V	1.08V	1.61	.73	1.90	2.45V	2.73V	2.36V	2.44V
Netherlands	138	11.19	5.70	9.64	4.74V	15.88V	7.73V	81.58V	108.39	98.27	103.67	173.61V	165.00V	225.86V	338.01V
Norway	142	.57	5.60	.55	.15V	1.21V	.88V	.07V	4.88	5.81	5.63	11.02V	13.76V	7.14V	13.09V
Portugal	182	.40	.83	.94	2.34V	9.79V	.82V	.57V	.47	.56	.70	.87V	.92V	16.94V	10.03V
Slovenia	961	—	.01	.02	.03Y	—V	14.65V	—V	2.00	1.69	2.01	2.61Y	1.81V	1.48V	2.14V
Spain	184	137.91	177.26	59.78	122.36V	268.20V	204.70V	103.78V	29.87	31.05	35.10	49.00V	56.97V	71.23V	99.04V
Sweden	144	.28	1.50	2.50	2.16V	5.36V	1.73V	.76V	42.26	37.63	56.80	92.30V	113.70V	124.27V	161.23V
Switzerland	146	2.48	2.98	3.00	1.56V	.86V	14.75V	1.28V	42.85	55.58	63.28	68.71V	71.90V	97.57V	170.85V
United Kingdom	112	55.79	65.20	78.41	186.08V	114.39V	141.23V	149.62V	348.24	364.40	371.49	648.96V	746.76V	428.56V	590.85V
Developing Countries	**202**	**7,769.0**	**8,236.6**	**8,057.6**	**10,320.9Y**	**13,787.6Y**	**20,130.7Y**	**18,133.5Y**	**3,054.7**	**3,093.4**	**3,377.8**	**3,427.7Y**	**4,792.9Y**	**5,999.4Y**	**7,660.7Y**
Africa	**607**	**309.6**	**232.7**	**105.3**	**95.4Y**	**247.9Y**	**2,000.9Y**	**604.1Y**	**24.2**	**34.4**	**43.1**	**47.0Y**	**56.6Y**	**90.1Y**	**83.0Y**
Algeria	612	13.98	.84	1.02	1.17Y	1.55Y	1.86Y	2.19Y	.01	—	—	—Y	—Y	—Y	—Y
Angola	614	2.34	1.12	.94	1.25Y	1.70Y	2.14Y	2.58Y	—	.01	—	—Y	—Y	—Y	—Y
Benin	638	.09	—	.17	—V	—V	—Y	—Y	—	—	—	—V	—V	—Y	—Y
Botswana	616	—	—	—	—Y	—Y	—Y	—Y	.12	—	—	—Y	—Y	—Y	—Y
Burundi	618	.75	.63	1.38	—V	—V	—V	—Y	.80	.21	.18	.01V	.98V	1.11V	1.44Y
Cameroon	622	.39	.02	.99	1.31Y	1.78Y	2.24Y	2.71Y	.03	.13	.15	.20Y	.25Y	.31Y	.40Y
Cape Verde	624	—	—	—	.03Y	.04Y	.05Y	.06Y	....	....	....	....	....	....	....
Central African Rep.	626	—	—	.28	.38Y	.51Y	.64Y	.77Y	—	—	—	—Y	—Y	—Y	—Y
Chad	628	.33	2.97	5.10	6.75Y	9.18Y	11.54Y	13.92Y	—	.06	—	—Y	—Y	—Y	—Y
Comoros	632	.05	.12	.23	.31Y	.42Y	.52Y	.63Y	—	—	—	—Y	—Y	—Y	—Y
Congo, Dem. Rep. of	636	—	—	.14	.18Y	.24Y	.31Y	.37Y	—	—	—	—Y	—Y	—Y	—Y
Congo, Republic of	634	.48	.49	.80	.04V	.05Y	.07Y	.08Y	.01	—	—	—V	—Y	—Y	—Y
Côte d'Ivoire	662	—	—	—	.31V	.28V	.83V	1.00Y	.05	—	—	.01V	.04V	.02V	.03Y
Djibouti	611	2.16	5.27	8.52	11.27Y	15.33Y	19.27Y	23.25Y	—	—	—	—Y	—Y	—Y	—Y
Eritrea	643	.67	1.29	1.58	2.09Y	2.85Y	3.58Y	4.32Y	....	....	....	....	....	....	....
Ethiopia	644	2.29	4.50	8.98	—V	—V	—Y	—Y	.02	.01	.05	—V	—V	—Y	—Y
Gabon	646	.04	.01	.11	.14Y	.19Y	.24Y	.29Y	—	—	—	—Y	—Y	—Y	—Y
Gambia, The	648	—	—	.53	.70Y	.96Y	1.20Y	1.45Y	—	—	—	—Y	—Y	—Y	—Y
Ghana	652	.39	.84	1.29	1.71Y	2.32Y	2.92Y	3.52Y	.01	.03	.08	.10Y	.13Y	.16Y	.20Y
Guinea	656	.02	.19	.82	.02V	.03Y	.03Y	.04Y	—	—	—	—Y	—Y	—Y	—Y
Kenya	664	29.00	64.47	2.52	1.18V	1.60Y	2.02Y	2.43Y	.44	.58	1.31	.85V	1.08Y	1.34Y	1.73Y
Liberia	668	.47	.17	.60	.80Y	1.09Y	1.37Y	1.65Y	—	—	.04	.05Y	.06Y	.08Y	.10Y
Madagascar	674	.02	—	.12	.16Y	.21Y	.27Y	.32Y	—	—	—	—Y	—Y	—Y	—Y
Malawi	676	—	—	—	—Y	—Y	—Y	—Y	.02	—	—	—Y	—Y	—Y	—Y
Mali	678	.03	.10	.29	.39Y	.53Y	.66Y	.80Y	....	....	....	....	....	....	....
Mauritania	682	.73	1.29	2.07	2.74Y	3.72Y	4.68Y	5.64Y	—	.04	—	—Y	—Y	—Y	—Y
Mauritius	684	.42	.15	.19	1.59V	1.08V	8.96V	.98V	.25	.34	1.12	.99V	.32V	4.64V	.33V
Morocco	686	.95	.97	1.07	1.62V	2.38V	2.99Y	3.60Y	.81	2.63	.54	1.02V	4.03V	4.97Y	6.44Y
Mozambique	688	.08	.03	.05	.06Y	.08Y	.10Y	.13Y	.09	.34	—	—Y	—Y	—Y	—Y
Namibia	728	—	.08	—	—Y	—Y	—Y	—Y	—	—	—	—Y	—Y	—Y	—Y
Niger	692	.07	.22	.87	—V	—Y	—Y	—Y	.04	.13	—	—Y	—Y	—Y	—Y
Nigeria	694	3.13	2.95	—	—Y	—Y	—Y	—Y	.14	.12	.11	.13Y	.17Y	.21Y	.25Y
Rwanda	714	.13	.19	1.19	1.58Y	2.15Y	2.70Y	3.26Y	—	.04	—	—Y	—Y	—Y	—Y
Senegal	722	.87	.37	.21	.48V	.47V	1.87V	2.26Y	—	—	—	.03V	—V	—V	—Y
Seychelles	718	—	.11	—	—Y	—Y	—Y	—Y	—	—	—	—Y	—Y	—Y	—Y
Sierra Leone	724	.97	.30	.68	.90Y	1.23Y	1.54Y	1.86Y	—	—	—	—Y	—Y	—Y	—Y
Somalia	726	10.64	16.25	17.59	23.27Y	31.65Y	39.79Y	48.01Y	4.11	10.14	9.60	12.48Y	15.89Y	19.62Y	25.41Y
South Africa	199	121.52	4.37	5.72	3.72V	123.70V	1,821.41V	417.68V	9.11	14.40	21.96	28.07V	31.97V	55.39V	43.80V
Sudan	732	16.89	11.65	17.67	4.22V	9.69V	27.55V	13.10V	.29	.14	.19	.02V	—V	—V	.03V
Swaziland	734	.02	—	—	—Y	—Y	—Y	—Y	.09	—	—	—Y	—Y	—Y	—Y
Tanzania	738	64.65	74.77	16.08	21.27Y	28.94Y	36.38Y	43.89Y	1.46	.71	.86	1.12Y	1.43Y	1.77Y	2.29Y

	Exports 2001	2002	2003	2004	2005	2006	2007	Imports 2001	2002	2003	2004	2005	2006	2007
	Millions of U.S. Dollars							*Millions of U.S. Dollars*						
Togo.......... 742	.11	—	—	.02V	—V	—Y	—Y	—	—	—	—V	—V	—Y	—Y
Tunisia.......... 744	5.45	5.26	5.92	5.42V	4.42V	4.14V	5.00Y	3.52	1.90	1.17	1.58V	.21V	.37V	.47Y
Uganda.......... 746	.27	.03	.06	.08Y	.11Y	.14Y	.17Y	.05	.06	.02	.03Y	.04Y	.04Y	.06Y
Zambia.......... 754	29.82	31.67	.92	.38V	.30V	.49V	.50V	.87	1.91	5.37	—V	—V	—V	.02V
Zimbabwe.......... 698	—	.30	.22	.02V	—V	—V	—Y	1.83	.44	.32	.27V	.01V	.03V	.04Y
Asia.......... 507	**5,629.9**	**6,003.2**	**6,152.6**	**8,340.3Y**	**11,003.6Y**	**15,060.2Y**	**13,880.2Y**	**848.0**	**794.9**	**1,022.8**	**950.1Y**	**1,449.5Y**	**1,911.7Y**	**2,744.8Y**
Afghanistan, I.S. of.......... 512	1.21	4.73	14.21	18.80Y	25.58Y	32.16Y	38.79Y	—	—	—	—Y	—Y	—Y	—Y
Bangladesh.......... 513	.41	.81	.77	—V	—V	.53V	11.99V	1.36	1.32	.95	.87V	.74V	.71Y	.80Y
Brunei Darussalam.......... 516	.10	.14	.16	.21Y	.29Y	.36Y	.43Y	2.14	.03	—	—Y	—Y	—Y	—Y
Cambodia.......... 522	—	.10	.21	—V	.05V	.06V	.07Y	—	—	—	—Y	—Y	—Y	—Y
China,P.R.: Mainland.......... 924	1,245.57	1,345.42	1,913.05	3,788.74V	3,765.72V	5,572.90V	6,107.99V	97.07	96.45	159.26	115.13V	210.09V	373.21V	602.93V
China,P.R.:Hong Kong.......... 532	15.55	29.65	58.82	32.85V	27.49V	48.28V	70.14V	13.64	11.14	11.07	18.92V	18.06V	25.60V	34.44V
China,P.R.:Macao.......... 546	—	.01	—	.01V	—V	.01V	.01V	.01	.07	—	—V	—V	—V	—V
Fiji.......... 819	.05	—	—	—Y	—Y	—Y	—Y	....	....	....	....	....	....	....
India.......... 534	143.15	121.58	67.98	25.16V	179.68V	225.89Y	272.51Y	226.57	271.34	287.75	282.96V	407.38V	502.92Y	651.49Y
Indonesia.......... 536	32.35	17.04	118.38	.64V	.31V	11.37V	4.54V	42.09	35.65	40.91	22.95V	32.14V	49.96V	108.05V
Korea.......... 542	1,959.48	1,860.23	1,938.88	2,249.98V	3,368.28V	4,662.46V	3,467.15V	186.75	116.59	215.40	172.78V	334.74V	378.76V	596.69V
Malaysia.......... 548	303.24	268.78	342.28	361.26V	463.63V	804.10V	425.90V	80.99	72.46	85.11	78.59V	89.11V	109.79V	166.76V
Maldives.......... 556	.12	.18	.33	.48V	.28V	.35Y	.42Y	—	—	—	—Y	—Y	—Y	—Y
Myanmar.......... 518	—	.21	.07	.09Y	.12Y	.15Y	.19Y	.16	.36	1.23	1.60Y	2.03Y	2.51Y	3.25Y
Nepal.......... 558	.03	.08	.12	.45V	.82V	.22V	.27Y	.04	—	.13	—V	—V	.01V	.01Y
Pakistan.......... 564	7.38	13.61	11.94	28.11V	32.89V	41.35Y	49.88Y	52.71	55.24	46.25	61.66V	56.67V	69.96Y	90.63Y
Philippines.......... 566	245.11	151.54	2.42	.32V	.61V	.15V	.12V	1.97	2.46	3.60	1.64V	1.72V	1.69V	2.27V
Singapore.......... 576	508.61	425.13	277.26	73.92V	225.24V	204.70V	235.85V	56.34	60.02	75.58	95.44V	98.68V	109.64V	137.63V
Sri Lanka.......... 524	5.33	3.46	—	2.72V	3.26V	6.08V	59.84V	5.95	5.09	5.51	2.80V	7.06V	4.62V	4.51V
Taiwan Province of China.......... 528	130.30	476.48	137.49	432.58V	711.82V	931.38V	752.21V	30.30	22.80	25.52	13.65V	17.62V	26.15V	36.32V
Thailand.......... 578	1,031.74	1,283.84	1,267.19	1,323.98V	2,197.56V	2,517.69V	2,381.90V	48.24	42.88	63.29	81.16V	173.46V	256.14V	308.96V
Vietnam.......... 582	.15	.16	1.02	—V	—V	—V	—V	1.66	1.03	1.29	—V	—V	—V	—V
Europe.......... 170	**11.6**	**9.8**	**61.3**	**14.4Y**	**19.4Y**	**20.5Y**	**45.1Y**	**97.4**	**113.4**	**292.7**	**89.0Y**	**193.7Y**	**264.6Y**	**422.4Y**
Albania.......... 914	—	—	.12	—V	—V	—V	—V	—	—	—	—V	—V	—V	—V
Armenia.......... 911	.12	.07	1.83	.45V	.05V	.07V	.04V	.97	2.82	4.14	—V	—V	—V	—V
Azerbaijan.......... 912	.99	2.36	8.63	.09V	.14V	.44V	.16V	—	.01	—	—V	—V	.41V	.01V
Belarus.......... 913	—	—	—	—V	—V	—V	.01V	—	—	—	.01V	—V	—V	—V
Bulgaria.......... 918	.06	.08	.21	.03V	.01V	—V	—V	1.80	3.19	.25	.56V	.72V	1.52V	3.31V
Croatia.......... 960	.01	.05	.34	—V	—V	—V	—V	2.71	.03	—	—V	—V	—V	—V
Czech Republic.......... 935	—	—	.11	.23V	—V	.04V	.05V	.64	.62	20.28	4.99V	10.10V	12.22V	38.93V
Estonia.......... 939	—	—	—	—V	—V	—V	.02V	.09	.19	.12	.30V	.26V	.39V	.48V
Georgia.......... 915	—	.40	2.45	.37V	.48V	.35V	.38Y	.17	.02	—	—V	.03V	—V	—Y
Hungary.......... 944	—	.02	.02	.03V	.07V	.07V	.04V	.89	3.04	24.13	6.65V	8.34V	7.69V	29.96V
Kazakhstan.......... 916	4.58	4.25	17.38	1.64V	2.23Y	2.81Y	3.39Y	.16	2.95	—	.01V	.01Y	.02Y	.02Y
Kyrgyz Republic.......... 917	.01	—	.02	—V	—V	—V	—V	—	—	—	—V	—V	—V	—V
Latvia.......... 941	—	—	—	—V	.06V	.43V	.42V	—	.02	.22	.21V	.22V	.39V	.53V
Lithuania.......... 946	—	—	—	.04V	.07V	—V	—V	—	—	.19	.31V	.64V	1.29V	1.01V
Macedonia, FYR.......... 962	—	—	—	—V	.36V	.05V	.05Y	—	—	—	—V	—V	—V	—Y
Moldova.......... 921	.02	—	—	—V	—V	—Y	—Y	....	....	....	....	....	....	....
Poland.......... 964	.08	.12	8.28	1.53V	1.44V	.65V	1.56V	5.42	8.14	3.43	4.67V	18.92V	51.16V	57.46V
Romania.......... 968	3.67	—	.01	.18V	.30V	.69V	2.09V	.58	.94	1.57	2.55V	6.77V	13.16V	10.14V
Russia.......... 922	.61	.11	3.35	.42V	1.41V	1.24V	.44V	8.29	11.90	18.51	18.63V	43.82V	21.23V	85.95V
Slovak Republic.......... 936	—	.08	.02	.03Y	—V	—V	.04V	.40	.61	1.17	1.52Y	7.16V	11.98V	9.32V
Tajikistan.......... 923	.12	.10	3.31	.09V	—V	.09V	.18V	—	.33	—	—Y	—Y	—Y	—V
Turkey.......... 186	.07	.34	4.20	1.26V	3.52V	1.92V	22.12V	31.58	28.71	51.37	32.00V	43.96V	78.10V	100.99V
Turkmenistan.......... 925	.87	.85	4.36	5.77Y	7.84Y	9.86Y	11.90Y	—	.01	—	—Y	—Y	—Y	—Y
Ukraine.......... 926	.07	.43	6.07	1.50V	.42V	.53Y	.63Y	43.47	49.79	167.32	16.54V	52.70V	65.05Y	84.27Y
Uzbekistan.......... 927	.35	.54	.57	.75Y	1.02Y	1.29Y	1.55Y	.19	.07	.01	.02Y	.02Y	.03Y	.04Y
Middle East.......... 407	**1,817.5**	**1,990.2**	**1,737.8**	**1,870.4Y**	**2,514.3Y**	**3,045.5Y**	**3,596.9Y**	**2,012.1**	**2,075.2**	**1,929.6**	**2,256.3Y**	**2,968.3Y**	**3,551.0Y**	**4,227.7Y**
Bahrain.......... 419	15.36	22.44	21.30	28.18Y	38.33Y	48.19Y	58.14Y	43.19	86.49	132.90	172.84Y	220.08Y	271.68Y	351.94Y
Egypt.......... 469	147.65	5.83	8.60	11.38Y	15.49Y	19.47Y	23.49Y	13.88	17.18	22.56	29.35Y	37.37Y	46.13Y	59.76Y
Iran, I.R. of.......... 429	454.84	520.02	429.52	494.51Y	656.41Y	785.85Y	927.01Y	46.16	22.48	45.71	52.63Y	69.86Y	83.64Y	98.66Y
Iraq.......... 433	20.73	69.88	23.59	27.16Y	36.06Y	43.17Y	50.92Y	—	—	—	—Y	—Y	—Y	—Y
Jordan.......... 439	44.30	24.55	58.78	8.46V	10.92V	13.11V	14.48V	7.69	9.85	10.41	17.07V	30.42V	23.89V	25.25V
Kuwait.......... 443	25.38	26.23	44.33	51.04Y	67.75Y	81.11Y	95.68Y	42.18	28.01	34.76	40.02Y	53.12Y	63.59Y	75.02Y
Lebanon.......... 446	4.72	2.55	3.89	5.15Y	7.00Y	8.80Y	10.62Y	4.38	16.68	5.35	6.95Y	8.85Y	10.93Y	14.16Y
Libya.......... 672	18.12	18.68	38.52	44.35Y	58.87Y	70.48Y	83.13Y	—	—	.12	.14Y	.18Y	.22Y	.26Y
Qatar.......... 453	20.79	34.21	29.83	40.27V	70.22V	109.95V	129.70Y	8.57	11.97	16.23	30.02V	12.82V	14.39V	16.98Y
Saudi Arabia.......... 456	188.74	180.95	197.57	146.46V	220.80V	264.34Y	311.82Y	185.04	220.47	224.43	258.38Y	342.98Y	410.61Y	484.37Y
Syrian Arab Republic.......... 463	7.79	8.04	12.49	28.66V	38.99Y	49.01Y	59.13Y	11.60	8.64	5.29	11.34V	14.43Y	17.82Y	23.08Y
United Arab Emirates.......... 466	822.39	1,026.73	807.57	929.75Y	1,234.15Y	1,477.51Y	1,742.91Y	1,645.60	1,646.02	1,417.89	1,632.42Y	2,166.87Y	2,594.15Y	3,060.13Y
Yemen, Republic of.......... 474	46.68	50.10	61.81	55.05V	59.27V	74.51Y	89.89Y	3.69	7.29	13.88	5.15V	11.28V	13.93Y	18.04Y
Middle East n.s.......... 489	—	—	—	—Y	—Y	—Y	—Y	.08	.08	.03	.03Y	.03Y	.03Y	.03Y
Western Hemisphere.......... 207	**.4**	**.8**	**.7**	**.3Y**	**2.4Y**	**3.5Y**	**7.2Y**	**73.1**	**75.6**	**89.6**	**85.3Y**	**124.8Y**	**182.0Y**	**182.8Y**
Argentina.......... 213	.03	—	.19	—V	—V	.21V	—V	13.48	20.71	20.44	28.35V	48.06V	54.10V	27.96V
Bahamas, The.......... 313	....	....	....	....	....	....	....	.04	—	—	—Y	—Y	—Y	—Y
Barbados.......... 316	—	—	—	.01V	.21V	.05V	.06Y	—	—	—	—V	—V	.01V	.02Y
Bolivia.......... 218	—	—	—	—V	—V	—Y	—Y	—	.06	—	—V	—Y	—Y	—Y
Brazil.......... 223	.02	—	.14	.01V	.33V	.99V	5.43V	40.45	32.79	57.85	46.12V	59.69V	65.65V	102.81V
Chile.......... 228	.24	.41	.31	.11V	.07V	.11V	.06V	8.81	17.24	8.25	10.45V	15.18V	27.97V	19.13V
Colombia.......... 233	.02	.02	—	.05V	.01V	.31V	.01V	.03	.01	.01	—V	.10V	.04V	.11V

	Exports							Imports						
	2001	2002	2003	2004	2005	2006	2007	2001	2002	2003	2004	2005	2006	2007
	Millions of U.S. Dollars							*Millions of U.S. Dollars*						
Costa Rica........238	—	—	—	—Y	—Y	—Y	—Y	.18	.32	.16	.04V	.01V	.01Y	.01Y
Dominican Republic........243	—	—	—	—Y	—Y	—Y	—Y	—	.01	—	—Y	—Y	—Y	—Y
Ecuador........248	—	—	—	.02V	—V	.01V	.02Y	.50	—	—	—V	.05V	.12V	.15Y
El Salvador........253	—	—	—	—V	—V	—V	.13V	—	—	—	—Y	—Y	—Y	—Y
Guatemala........258	—	—	—	—V	—V	—Y	—Y	—	.58	.12	.32V	.42V	.52Y	.68Y
Guyana........336	.03	—	—	—Y	—Y	—Y	—Y	.01	.17	—	—Y	—Y	—Y	—Y
Honduras........268	—	.06	.01	.01Y	.01Y	.01Y	.02Y	.03	.14	.02	.03Y	.04Y	.05Y	.06Y
Jamaica........343	—	—	—	—V	—V	—V	—V	—	—	.01	—V	—V	—V	—V
Mexico........273	.01	.01	—	—V	1.63V	1.77V	1.39V	2.63	3.23	2.68	—V	1.17V	10.26V	1.88V
Nicaragua........278	—	—	—	—Y	—Y	—Y	—Y	.01	—	—	—Y	—Y	—Y	—Y
Panama........283	—	—	—	—Y	—Y	—Y	—Y	.17	—	—	—V	—V	—V	—V
Peru........293	—	—	—	.05V	.07V	.05V	—Y	6.65	—	—	—V	—V	23.05V	29.74Y
Uruguay........298	—	—	—	—V	—V	—Y	—Y	—	.04	—	.01V	.10V	.12Y	.15Y
Venezuela, Rep. Bol........299	.07	.27	—	.02V	.03V	—V	.04V	.05	.25	.06	.02V	.01V	.09V	.11Y
Western Hem. n.s........399	—	—	—	—Y	—Y	—Y	—Y	—	.06	—	—Y	—Y	—Y	—Y
Other Countries n.i.e........910	**—**	**—**	**—**	**—Y**	**—Y**	**—Y**	**—Y**	**.1**	**—**	**—**	**—Y**	**—Y**	**—Y**	**—Y**
Cuba........928	.03	.01	—	—Y	—Y	—Y	—Y	.06	.01	—	—Y	—Y	—Y	—Y
North Korea........954	....	....	....	....	....	....	....	.01	—	—	—Y	—Y	—Y	—Y
Memorandum Items														
European Union........998	263.97	374.25	228.28	404.38Y	520.11Y	471.74Y	420.82Y	1,245.16	1,347.04	1,426.60	2,243.22Y	2,394.83Y	2,397.24Y	3,648.15Y
Oil Exporting Ctys........999	1,600.51	1,897.80	1,690.33	1,735.36Y	2,346.15Y	2,845.63Y	3,347.94Y	1,969.85	1,964.98	1,780.22	2,036.70Y	2,678.16Y	3,216.87Y	3,843.82Y
Non-Oil Develop.Ctys........201	6,168.47	6,338.81	6,367.29	8,585.52Y	1,441.43Y	7,285.02Y	4,785.55Y	1,084.81	1,128.46	1,597.57	1,391.04Y	2,114.73Y	2,782.51Y	3,816.87Y
PERCENT DISTRIBUTION														
Industrial Countries........101	**27.3**	**26.0**	**22.2**	**18.9**	**20.9**	**16.5**	**20.5**	**47.3**	**48.5**	**48.6**	**55.4**	**50.3**	**48.2**	**51.6**
Developing Countries........202	**72.7**	**74.0**	**77.8**	**81.1**	**79.1**	**83.5**	**79.5**	**52.7**	**51.5**	**51.4**	**44.6**	**49.7**	**51.8**	**48.4**
Africa........607	**2.9**	**2.1**	**1.0**	**.8**	**1.4**	**8.3**	**2.6**	**.4**	**.6**	**.7**	**.6**	**.6**	**.8**	**.5**
Asia........507	**52.7**	**54.0**	**59.4**	**65.5**	**63.2**	**62.5**	**60.9**	**14.6**	**13.2**	**15.6**	**12.4**	**15.0**	**16.5**	**17.3**
Europe........170	**.1**	**.1**	**.6**	**.1**	**.1**	**.1**	**.2**	**1.7**	**1.9**	**4.5**	**1.2**	**2.0**	**2.3**	**2.7**
Middle East........407	**17.0**	**17.9**	**16.8**	**14.7**	**14.4**	**12.6**	**15.8**	**34.7**	**34.6**	**29.4**	**29.3**	**30.8**	**30.7**	**26.7**
Western Hemisphere........207	**—**	**—**	**—**	**—**	**—**	**—**	**—**	**1.3**	**1.3**	**1.4**	**1.1**	**1.3**	**1.6**	**1.2**
ANNUAL PERCENT CHANGE														
World........001	**.1**	**4.2**	**–6.9**	**22.8**	**36.9**	**38.4**	**–5.4**	**15.0**	**3.6**	**9.4**	**17.0**	**25.4**	**20.1**	**36.7**
Industrial Countries........101	**25.0**	**–.8**	**–20.3**	**4.4**	**51.1**	**9.5**	**17.4**	**15.6**	**6.2**	**9.7**	**33.5**	**13.8**	**15.0**	**46.5**
Developing Countries........202	**–6.8**	**6.0**	**–2.2**	**28.1**	**33.6**	**46.0**	**–9.9**	**14.5**	**1.3**	**9.2**	**1.5**	**39.8**	**25.2**	**27.7**
Africa........607	**91.1**	**–24.8**	**–54.7**	**–9.4**	**159.8**	**707.1**	**–69.8**	**14.9**	**42.2**	**25.3**	**9.1**	**20.5**	**59.1**	**–7.8**
Asia........507	**–16.1**	**6.6**	**2.5**	**35.6**	**31.9**	**36.9**	**–7.8**	**15.2**	**–6.3**	**28.7**	**–7.1**	**52.6**	**31.9**	**43.6**
Europe........170	**7.0**	**–15.8**	**525.0**	**–76.5**	**34.6**	**5.7**	**119.8**	**35.1**	**16.4**	**158.2**	**–69.6**	**117.7**	**36.6**	**59.6**
Middle East........407	**25.3**	**9.5**	**–12.7**	**7.6**	**34.4**	**21.1**	**18.1**	**13.4**	**3.1**	**–7.0**	**16.9**	**31.6**	**19.6**	**19.1**
Western Hemisphere........207	**–17.5**	**87.8**	**–15.5**	**–56.7**	**731.8**	**48.8**	**103.5**	**13.2**	**3.5**	**18.5**	**–4.8**	**46.3**	**45.8**	**.4**
Other Countries n.i.e........910	**....**	**–57.4**	**74.2**	**....**	**....**	**....**	**....**	**....**	**–80.2**	**24.7**	**....**	**....**	**....**	**....**

	Exports 2001	2002	2003	2004	2005	2006	2007	Imports 2001	2002	2003	2004	2005	2006	2007
	Millions of U.S. Dollars							Millions of U.S. Dollars						
IFS World Total	**9,238**	**9,913**	**11,930**	**13,379**	**16,051**	**16,930**	**17,837**	**10,191**	**11,233**	**13,037**	**17,949**	**25,357**	**29,825**	**32,590**
DOTS World Total....001	**9,211**	**9,880**	**11,928**	**13,284**	**16,046**	**16,981Y**	**19,349Y**	**10,166**	**11,238**	**13,048**	**17,756**	**25,410**	**33,866Y**	**39,203Y**
Industrial Countries....101	**5,267**	**5,644**	**6,652**	**7,614**	**8,739**	**7,990Y**	**8,378Y**	**3,325**	**3,868**	**4,506**	**6,294**	**8,554**	**10,539Y**	**10,582Y**
United States....111	2,234	2,419	2,752	3,119	3,979	3,604V	3,482V	569	723	788	1,726	1,532	2,188V	2,239V
Canada....156	164	192	200	177	212	248V	227V	73	78	191	209	213	386V	453V
Australia....193	102	113	115	125	120	116V	127V	243	277	218	395	452	258V	396V
Japan....158	187	141	139	160	143	187V	227V	528	675	862	1,153	1,633	1,936V	1,716V
New Zealand....196	25	30	31	37	40	36V	38V	10	10	16	15	26	50V	70V
Austria....122	24	26	26	26	31	36V	44V	14	21	25	52	88	171V	151V
Belgium....124	177	216	255	273	342	282V	329V	236	276	279	184	305	318V	332V
Cyprus....423	7	8	9	7	8	6V	7V	1	1	2	1	1	4V	5V
Denmark....128	35	36	42	48	51	51V	62V	25	23	33	43	94	75V	76V
Finland....172	17	18	21	25	39	21V	26V	17	29	42	79	310	135V	178V
France....132	259	255	315	380	363	324V	371V	133	165	130	173	297	558V	527V
Germany....134	479	486	608	664	725	639V	729V	405	489	576	707	1,145	1,395V	1,365V
Greece....174	47	59	76	99	94	67V	81V	6	11	6	15	22	34V	36V
Iceland....176	1	1	1	1	1	3V	3V	—	6	—	—	2	—V	—V
Ireland....178	18	23	27	34	41	38V	36V	17	16	16	32	36	38V	43V
Italy....136	251	276	402	531	583	487V	569V	183	250	279	333	437	746V	783V
Luxembourg....137	3	—	1	1	1	1V	—V	—	3	3	3	3	3V	6V
Malta....181	4	2	3	3	2	3V	2V	—	3	8	20	—	1V	—V
Netherlands....138	241	265	317	368	378	268V	319V	204	169	212	169	215	374V	448V
Norway....142	26	27	27	29	62	61V	65V	4	7	8	10	15	20V	22V
Portugal....182	82	66	84	103	104	115V	135V	1	3	8	8	7	14V	10V
Slovenia....961	1	1	2	4	7	8V	8V	3	7	24	14	19	25V	31V
Spain....184	167	189	268	322	386	377V	440V	47	63	67	78	100	126V	145V
Sweden....144	62	59	63	79	85	89V	94V	40	33	50	78	386	404V	309V
Switzerland....146	24	20	26	30	35	48V	54V	204	162	261	355	493	287V	302V
United Kingdom....112	627	716	842	970	908	874V	903V	360	367	403	441	721	991V	939V
Developing Countries....202	**3,938**	**4,232**	**5,274**	**5,663**	**7,296**	**8,978Y**	**10,954Y**	**6,839**	**7,369**	**8,541**	**11,452**	**16,840**	**23,307Y**	**28,596Y**
Africa....607	**435**	**422**	**511**	**795**	**862**	**894Y**	**1,075Y**	**341**	**327**	**326**	**518**	**694**	**796Y**	**1,031Y**
Algeria....612	4	6	8	9	13	16Y	20Y	—	—	—	—	1	1Y	1Y
Angola....614	—	4	8	9	10	13Y	16Y	—	—	—	—	1	1Y	1Y
Benin....638	13	7	4	3	32	40Y	49Y	1	3	2	7	1	2Y	2Y
Botswana....616	—	—	—	1	1	2Y	2Y	—	—	—	—	—	1Y	1Y
Burkina Faso....748	—	—	—	—	—	—Y	—Y	—	—	1	5	3	4Y	4Y
Burundi....618	—	—	—	—	—	12V	15Y	1	1	—	4	3	5V	7Y
Cameroon....622	6	3	4	8	47	58Y	72Y	2	2	3	15	11	13Y	16Y
Central African Rep....626	6	—	—	—	—	—Y	1Y	15	—	—	—	—	—Y	1Y
Chad....628	—	—	—	3	1	1Y	1Y	—	1	—	—	1	1Y	1Y
Comoros....632	—	—	1	5	7	8Y	10Y	—	—	—	—	—	—Y	—Y
Congo, Dem. Rep. of....636	—	—	—	—	2	2Y	3Y	—	—	1	—	1	1Y	1Y
Congo, Republic of....634	9	3	4	10	11	13Y	17Y	—	—	—	—	—	—Y	—Y
Côte d'Ivoire....662	17	—	—	8	43	52V	64Y	—	4	—	5	3	1V	1Y
Djibouti....611	1	4	5	2	4	5Y	6Y	2	9	6	1	1	1Y	1Y
Equatorial Guinea....642	—	—	—	1	1	1Y	1Y	—	—	1	—	—	—Y	—Y
Eritrea....643	—	—	—	1	—	—Y	—Y	—	—	—	—	—	—Y	—Y
Ethiopia....644	2	5	2	4	3	4Y	5Y	2	10	1	3	4	5Y	6Y
Gabon....646	2	—	—	—	—	—Y	—Y	—	—	—	—	—	—Y	—Y
Gambia, The....648	1	2	3	5	8	10Y	13Y	—	—	—	—	—	—Y	—Y
Ghana....652	1	1	5	4	27	33Y	41Y	—	—	—	—	1	1Y	1Y
Guinea....656	2	—	—	9	12	14Y	18Y	—	—	—	—	1	1Y	2Y
Guinea-Bissau....654	—	—	—	3	7	8Y	10Y	—	—	—	1	1	1Y	1Y
Kenya....664	28	93	85	60	66	82Y	102Y	137	124	142	152	181	224Y	278Y
Lesotho....666	2	1	—	1	6	7Y	9Y	—	—	—	—	—	—Y	—Y
Liberia....668	—	1	1	5	2	2Y	3Y	—	5	—	—	1	2Y	2Y
Madagascar....674	8	10	19	16	28	35Y	43Y	—	—	1	2	1	1Y	1Y
Malawi....676	1	1	2	1	2	2Y	3Y	1	1	1	2	2	2Y	3Y
Mali....678	—	—	1	—	—	—Y	—Y	—	—	2	36	7	9Y	11Y
Mauritania....682	4	3	3	2	4	5Y	6Y	8	8	5	—	—	—Y	—Y
Mauritius....684	30	25	34	36	34	36V	35V	—	4	4	1	1	1V	—V
Morocco....686	12	10	16	15	14	17Y	21Y	55	41	18	87	154	191Y	236Y
Mozambique....688	—	4	13	19	43	32V	39Y	—	—	2	2	2	7V	9Y
Namibia....728	—	—	—	—	—	—Y	1Y	—	—	—	—	2	3Y	5Y
Niger....692	14	13	7	12	24	29Y	36Y	—	—	—	1	—	—Y	—Y
Nigeria....694	40	42	89	306	51	63Y	82Y	—	1	4	14	11	14Y	17Y
Rwanda....714	—	—	1	1	1	1Y	1Y	2	2	1	5	7	8Y	10Y
Senegal....722	1	4	7	8	5	2V	2Y	—	—	—	2	—	—V	—Y
Seychelles....718	—	—	1	—	—	—Y	1Y	—	—	—	—	—	—Y	—Y
Sierra Leone....724	—	—	—	2	9	11Y	14Y	—	—	—	—	—	—Y	—Y
Somalia....726	4	4	4	4	3	4Y	5Y	1	1	1	3	4	6Y	7Y
South Africa....199	72	83	115	152	222	132V	137V	76	60	84	94	172	177V	243V

	Exports							Imports						
	2001	2002	2003	2004	2005	2006	2007	2001	2002	2003	2004	2005	2006	2007
	Millions of U.S. Dollars							*Millions of U.S. Dollars*						
Sudan.......... 732	8	15	12	16	24	31V	36V	4	5	11	14	16	10V	47V
Swaziland.......... 734	2	—	1	1	1	1Y	1Y	1	—	—	6	11	14Y	17Y
Tanzania.......... 738	23	29	21	14	15	19Y	24Y	15	13	10	19	13	16Y	20Y
Togo.......... 742	12	8	6	12	58	72Y	90Y	—	—	—	3	7	9Y	11Y
Tunisia.......... 744	13	13	13	15	12	10V	12Y	6	18	15	18	38	—V	—Y
Uganda.......... 746	4	3	8	9	4	5Y	6Y	2	1	1	4	7	8Y	10Y
Zambia.......... 754	2	3	3	3	3	1V	1V	6	8	7	10	22	54V	53V
Zimbabwe.......... 698	3	3	2	4	3	1V	2Y	1	2	3	3	2	1V	1Y
Africa n.s.......... 799	86	15	—	—	—	—Y	—Y	—	—	—	—	—	—Y	—Y
Asia.......... 507	**1,809**	**1,803**	**2,231**	**2,442**	**3,435**	**4,364Y**	**5,131Y**	**2,520**	**2,904**	**3,683**	**4,735**	**6,714**	**10,968Y**	**13,948Y**
Afghanistan, I.S. of.......... 512	143	223	409	465	1,065	1,316Y	1,634Y	26	31	31	49	53	66Y	82Y
Bangladesh.......... 513	119	104	166	197	234	155V	179V	26	31	43	45	68	68Y	88Y
Bhutan.......... 514	—	—	—	—	—	—Y	—Y	—	1	—	—	1	1Y	1Y
Brunei Darussalam.......... 516	1	3	5	1	2	2Y	3Y	2	—	1	—	1	2Y	2Y
Cambodia.......... 522	4	7	6	12	13	12V	15Y	1	1	—	1	1	—V	—Y
China,P.R.: Mainland.......... 924	289	236	260	300	436	916V	1,005V	485	700	958	1,499	2,349	4,665V	6,363V
China,P.R.:Hong Kong.......... 532	470	478	547	590	599	594V	576V	64	77	193	102	154	173V	188V
China,P.R.:Macao.......... 546	1	—	1	—	—	1V	1V	1	—	1	1	—	—V	—V
Fiji.......... 819	2	1	1	1	1	1Y	1Y	—	—	—	—	—	—Y	—Y
India.......... 534	66	49	84	158	337	417Y	517Y	241	163	226	455	577	714Y	886Y
Indonesia.......... 536	95	81	47	57	68	32V	43V	187	288	266	471	684	808V	1,029V
Korea.......... 542	282	247	206	182	200	310V	446V	329	322	349	429	655	740V	746V
Malaysia.......... 548	53	64	94	65	67	54V	76V	435	509	601	634	732	927V	1,383V
Maldives.......... 556	2	3	3	2	3	4Y	4Y	—	—	—	—	3	4Y	5Y
Mongolia.......... 948	—	—	—	—	—	—Y	—Y	1	—	—	—	—	—Y	—Y
Myanmar.......... 518	3	8	5	2	2	3Y	3Y	17	15	9	21	39	49Y	60Y
Nauru.......... 836	—	—	—	—	—	—Y	1Y	—	—	—	—	—	—Y	—Y
Nepal.......... 558	2	2	5	3	4	2V	3Y	1	1	2	4	4	3V	4Y
New Caledonia.......... 839	—	—	—	—	—	—Y	—Y	—	—	—	—	5	6Y	8Y
Philippines.......... 566	24	26	23	29	37	39V	39V	7	8	8	12	25	32V	43V
Singapore.......... 576	47	53	138	80	32	42V	48V	327	346	526	357	449	849V	931V
Sri Lanka.......... 524	75	71	84	134	154	133V	162V	27	32	43	46	59	64V	61V
Taiwan Province of China.......... 528	—	—	—	68	—	103V	155V	—	—	—	240	—	416V	452V
Thailand.......... 578	53	67	69	61	91	92V	62V	175	209	232	345	538	717V	728V
Tonga.......... 866	—	—	1	1	1	2Y	2Y	—	—	—	—	—	—Y	—Y
Vietnam.......... 582	15	31	20	32	36	30V	—V	7	8	11	20	19	72V	—V
Asia n.s.......... 598	62	49	59	—	51	102Y	154Y	162	162	182	—	296	593Y	889Y
Europe.......... 170	**166**	**208**	**329**	**394**	**534**	**668Y**	**854Y**	**206**	**262**	**255**	**550**	**1,331**	**1,608Y**	**1,697Y**
Albania.......... 914	—	—	—	—	—	—V	1V	—	—	—	—	1	—V	—V
Armenia.......... 911	—	—	—	—	—	3V	5V	—	—	—	—	1	—V	—V
Azerbaijan.......... 912	1	2	1	2	2	1V	2V	1	—	—	—	1	1V	1V
Belarus.......... 913	1	—	1	—	1	7V	10V	—	3	—	9	47	81V	93V
Bosnia & Herzegovina.......... 963	1	—	—	1	1	1Y	1Y	—	—	—	—	—	—Y	—Y
Bulgaria.......... 918	3	1	2	2	7	3V	6V	5	3	5	4	6	49V	12V
Croatia.......... 960	1	1	3	3	7	13V	18V	1	1	2	1	1	4V	2V
Czech Republic.......... 935	8	8	9	10	11	23V	29V	2	2	3	8	11	35V	80V
Estonia.......... 939	7	9	9	10	15	10V	9V	1	—	1	2	2	8V	2V
Georgia.......... 915	—	—	—	1	1	—V	—Y	—	—	—	—	—	—V	—Y
Hungary.......... 944	11	13	18	18	18	21V	20V	5	14	21	18	65	220V	168V
Kazakhstan.......... 916	7	9	10	9	10	12Y	15Y	—	—	—	1	1	1Y	1Y
Kyrgyz Republic.......... 917	1	1	3	5	2	1V	3V	—	—	—	—	—	—V	—V
Latvia.......... 941	1	2	3	1	3	3V	4V	—	1	1	2	1	3V	3V
Lithuania.......... 946	2	3	6	19	18	11V	15V	1	20	8	19	28	29V	35V
Macedonia, FYR.......... 962	—	—	—	—	—	4V	5Y	....	....	....	....	....	....	....
Poland.......... 964	11	24	25	36	40	37V	48V	9	9	6	33	53	36V	27V
Romania.......... 968	3	4	4	6	10	20V	15V	19	10	12	16	63	54V	43V
Russia.......... 922	8	6	17	31	48	102V	95V	90	65	75	222	356	329V	286V
Serbia & Montenegro.......... 965	—	1	1	1	2	2Y	3Y	—	—	—	—	—	—Y	—Y
Slovak Republic.......... 936	2	2	1	1	1	7V	11V	5	2	1	2	6	4V	13V
Tajikistan.......... 923	2	1	—	—	2	—V	1V	1	—	—	8	7	—V	—V
Turkey.......... 186	87	110	200	219	300	344V	483V	38	107	66	90	187	143V	173V
Turkmenistan.......... 925	3	3	2	1	1	1Y	2Y	1	1	—	9	12	14Y	18Y
Ukraine.......... 926	1	3	7	14	31	38Y	48Y	22	19	50	98	261	322Y	400Y
Uzbekistan.......... 927	6	7	3	3	2	3Y	3Y	5	4	1	6	12	14Y	18Y
Europe n.s.......... 884	—	—	—	—	—	—Y	—Y	—	—	—	—	210	260Y	322Y
Middle East.......... 407	**1,350**	**1,617**	**2,021**	**1,805**	**2,185**	**2,685Y**	**3,458Y**	**3,610**	**3,790**	**4,194**	**5,507**	**7,667**	**9,594Y**	**11,610Y**
Bahrain.......... 419	45	43	39	44	42	52Y	64Y	43	45	79	63	44	54Y	68Y
Egypt.......... 469	45	53	41	48	52	64Y	80Y	31	40	36	55	125	154Y	191Y
Iran, I.R. of.......... 429	29	42	82	103	178	220Y	285Y	218	204	301	272	363	456Y	550Y
Iraq.......... 433	23	33	4	4	18	22Y	28Y	3	—	—	—	1	2Y	2Y
Jordan.......... 439	25	24	25	21	26	21V	19V	52	35	29	31	40	8V	37V
Kuwait.......... 443	53	60	77	75	77	96Y	124Y	793	758	832	1,000	1,264	1,589Y	1,917Y
Lebanon.......... 446	12	9	11	15	21	26Y	33Y	1	—	1	5	15	18Y	23Y
Libya.......... 672	4	2	3	2	3	4Y	5Y	—	—	—	—	1	1Y	2Y
Oman.......... 449	49	48	42	56	52	64Y	82Y	6	13	8	31	36	45Y	55Y
Qatar.......... 453	35	32	34	38	40	47V	61Y	17	39	30	177	326	411V	496Y
Saudi Arabia.......... 456	296	390	469	336	355	438Y	568Y	1,138	1,315	1,417	2,067	2,819	3,545Y	4,276Y

	Exports							Imports						
	2001	2002	2003	2004	2005	2006	2007	2001	2002	2003	2004	2005	2006	2007
	Millions of U.S. Dollars							*Millions of U.S. Dollars*						
Syrian Arab Republic.................... 463	7	11	21	24	6	8Y	10Y	4	16	3	23	10	12Y	15Y
United Arab Emirates.................. 466	697	835	1,121	982	1,256	1,551Y	2,009Y	1,302	1,318	1,455	1,773	2,620	3,294Y	3,974Y
Yemen, Republic of...................... 474	30	35	53	56	58	72Y	90Y	3	7	4	10	3	4Y	5Y
Western Hemisphere................ 207	**178**	**181**	**182**	**226**	**279**	**367Y**	**437Y**	**162**	**86**	**83**	**141**	**434**	**342Y**	**310Y**
Argentina.................................. 213	25	3	14	27	35	37V	41V	31	53	44	42	69	64V	88V
Bahamas, The............................. 313	2	2	2	2	1	2Y	2Y	—	—	—	—	—	—Y	—Y
Bermuda..................................... 319	—	—	—	—	—	—V	—Y	1	—	1	—	—	—Y	—Y
Brazil.. 223	6	6	5	6	12	30V	50V	103	17	25	76	322	213V	163V
Chile... 228	35	38	37	47	51	52V	57V	—	—	1	3	3	2V	2V
Colombia.................................... 233	9	7	6	11	19	31V	40V	—	—	—	—	1	9V	3V
Costa Rica.................................. 238	1	1	1	1	3	4Y	5Y	—	—	—	—	—	—Y	—Y
Dominican Republic..................... 243	4	4	2	4	6	7Y	9Y	—	—	—	—	—	—Y	—Y
Ecuador...................................... 248	2	1	1	2	4	2V	3Y	—	—	—	—	1	—V	—Y
El Salvador.................................. 253	5	6	3	5	9	18V	20V	—	—	—	—	—	—V	1V
Falkland Islands.......................... 323	—	—	1	—	—	—Y	—Y	—	—	—	—	1	1Y	1Y
Greenland................................... 326	1	—	—	—	—	—Y	—Y	—	—	—	—	2	2Y	3Y
Guatemala................................... 258	10	12	4	7	10	13Y	16Y	2	1	3	2	2	2Y	3Y
Guyana....................................... 336	—	—	1	1	1	1Y	1Y	—	—	—	—	—	—Y	—Y
Haiti.. 263	1	2	4	4	3	3Y	4Y	—	—	—	—	—	—Y	—Y
Honduras.................................... 268	7	9	8	11	10	12Y	15Y	—	—	—	—	1	1Y	1Y
Jamaica...................................... 343	—	—	1	1	1	4V	1V	—	—	—	—	—	—V	—V
Mexico.. 273	25	49	54	55	57	114V	110V	12	7	6	7	14	31V	26V
Netherlands Antilles..................... 353	—	—	—	—	1	1Y	1Y	—	—	—	1	1	2Y	2Y
Nicaragua.................................... 278	2	6	10	9	10	—V	—V	—	—	—	—	1	—V	—V
Panama....................................... 283	10	10	11	12	14	1V	1V	—	—	1	—	—	—V	—V
Paraguay..................................... 288	2	1	1	2	4	2V	2Y	—	—	—	1	—	—V	—Y
Peru.. 293	4	5	5	3	6	8V	10Y	1	1	1	3	7	3V	2Y
St. Vincent & Grens...................... 364	—	—	—	—	—	—Y	—Y	—	—	—	—	—	—Y	1Y
Suriname.................................... 366	—	—	—	1	—	—Y	—Y	—	—	—	—	—	—Y	—Y
Trinidad and Tobago.................... 369	—	—	—	1	1	1Y	2Y	—	—	—	—	—	—Y	—Y
Uruguay...................................... 298	2	1	2	2	3	3Y	4Y	—	2	1	—	1	2Y	2Y
Venezuela, Rep. Bol..................... 299	17	11	4	10	16	13V	31V	1	3	1	1	2	—V	—Y
Western Hem. n.s........................ 399	6	5	4	—	3	6Y	9Y	8	—	—	3	4	7Y	10Y
Other Countries n.i.e................ 910	**1**	**1**	**2**	**7**	**5**	**6Y**	**7Y**	**1**	**1**	**1**	**10**	**14**	**17Y**	**22Y**
Cuba... 928	—	—	1	1	—	1Y	1Y	—	—	1	—	1	2Y	2Y
North Korea................................ 954	1	1	1	6	4	5Y	7Y	1	—	—	10	13	16Y	20Y
Countries & Areas n.s.............. 898	**1**	**—**	**—**	**—**	**—**	**—Y**	**—Y**	**—**	**—**	**—**	**—**	**—**	**—Y**	**—Y**
Memorandum Items														
European Union........................... 998	2,544	2,761	3,434	4,031	4,254	3,797Y	4,291Y	1,715	1,979	2,204	2,515	4,354	5,748Y	5,712Y
Oil Exporting Ctys........................ 999	1,342	1,582	1,980	1,978	2,128	2,566Y	3,339Y	3,666	3,939	4,314	5,807	8,129	10,167Y	12,319Y
Non-Oil Develop.Ctys................... 201	2,596	2,650	3,295	3,685	5,168	6,412Y	7,615Y	3,174	3,430	4,227	5,645	8,712	13,141Y	16,277Y
PERCENT DISTRIBUTION														
Industrial Countries................. 101	**57.2**	**57.1**	**55.8**	**57.3**	**54.5**	**47.0**	**43.3**	**32.7**	**34.4**	**34.5**	**35.4**	**33.7**	**31.1**	**27.0**
Developing Countries.............. 202	**42.7**	**42.8**	**44.2**	**42.6**	**45.5**	**52.9**	**56.6**	**67.3**	**65.6**	**65.5**	**64.5**	**66.3**	**68.8**	**72.9**
Africa...................................... 607	**4.7**	**4.3**	**4.3**	**6.0**	**5.4**	**5.3**	**5.6**	**3.4**	**2.9**	**2.5**	**2.9**	**2.7**	**2.4**	**2.6**
Asia... 507	**19.6**	**18.3**	**18.7**	**18.4**	**21.4**	**25.7**	**26.5**	**24.8**	**25.8**	**28.2**	**26.7**	**26.4**	**32.4**	**35.6**
Europe.................................... 170	**1.8**	**2.1**	**2.8**	**3.0**	**3.3**	**3.9**	**4.4**	**2.0**	**2.3**	**2.0**	**3.1**	**5.2**	**4.7**	**4.3**
Middle East............................ 407	**14.7**	**16.4**	**16.9**	**13.6**	**13.6**	**15.8**	**17.9**	**35.5**	**33.7**	**32.1**	**31.0**	**30.2**	**28.3**	**29.6**
Western Hemisphere.............. 207	**1.9**	**1.8**	**1.5**	**1.7**	**1.7**	**2.2**	**2.3**	**1.6**	**.8**	**.6**	**.8**	**1.7**	**1.0**	**.8**
Other Countries n.i.e................ 910	**—**	**—**	**—**	**.1**	**—**	**—**	**—**	**—**	**—**	**—**	**.1**	**.1**	**.1**	**.1**
ANNUAL PERCENT CHANGE														
World.. 001	**3.8**	**7.3**	**20.7**	**11.4**	**20.8**	**5.8**	**13.9**	**–5.2**	**10.6**	**16.1**	**36.1**	**43.1**	**33.3**	**15.8**
Industrial Countries................. 101	**–.7**	**7.2**	**17.9**	**14.5**	**14.8**	**–8.6**	**4.9**	**–6.3**	**16.3**	**16.5**	**39.7**	**35.9**	**23.2**	**.4**
Developing Countries.............. 202	**10.4**	**7.5**	**24.6**	**7.4**	**28.8**	**23.1**	**22.0**	**–4.6**	**7.7**	**15.9**	**34.1**	**47.1**	**38.4**	**22.7**
Africa...................................... 607	**34.2**	**–2.9**	**21.0**	**55.7**	**8.4**	**3.7**	**20.2**	**19.0**	**–4.2**	**–.2**	**58.7**	**34.1**	**14.6**	**29.6**
Asia... 507	**.9**	**–.3**	**23.7**	**9.4**	**40.7**	**27.0**	**17.6**	**3.9**	**15.2**	**26.8**	**28.6**	**41.8**	**63.4**	**27.2**
Europe.................................... 170	**–4.1**	**25.2**	**57.8**	**19.9**	**35.5**	**25.1**	**27.7**	**–8.5**	**27.5**	**–2.7**	**115.4**	**142.0**	**20.8**	**5.5**
Middle East............................ 407	**23.6**	**19.8**	**25.0**	**–10.7**	**21.1**	**22.8**	**28.8**	**–12.1**	**5.0**	**10.7**	**31.3**	**39.2**	**25.1**	**21.0**
Western Hemisphere.............. 207	**–3.7**	**1.8**	**.6**	**24.1**	**23.5**	**31.4**	**19.1**	**26.4**	**–47.0**	**–3.4**	**70.5**	**207.5**	**–21.2**	**–9.3**
Other Countries n.i.e................ 910	**–51.8**	**39.2**	**119.5**	**276.1**	**–34.0**	**23.6**	**24.1**	**–36.6**	**55.6**	**–3.8**	**—**	**39.8**	**23.6**	**24.1**

	Exports 2001	2002	2003	2004	2005	2006	2007	Imports 2001	2002	2003	2004	2005	2006	2007
	Millions of U.S. Dollars							*Millions of U.S. Dollars*						
IFS World Total	**910.5**	**846.4**	**864.2**	**943.7**	**1,018.3**	**1,093.2**	**1,163.6**	**2,963.5**	**2,982.0**	**3,086.1**	**3,594.2**	**4,180.0**	**4,831.0**	**6,872.1**
DOTS World Total 001	**827.2**	**760.3**	**795.2**	**891.5**	**977.1**	**1,038.0**	**1,126.1**	**3,339.4**	**3,035.7**	**2,731.7**	**3,592.2**	**4,158.2**	**5,392.3**	**6,459.0**
Industrial Countries 101	**583.1**	**545.9**	**617.2**	**673.8**	**708.5**	**756.2**	**788.1**	**1,410.1**	**1,467.4**	**1,567.2**	**1,523.2**	**1,678.0**	**1,921.9**	**3,027.2**
United States 111	402.43	360.92	414.47	444.96	432.64	407.50	400.62	985.52	1,042.64	1,096.36	1,048.89	1,142.09	1,307.07	2,120.50
Canada 156	4.18	5.32	3.77	2.32	1.96	3.35	2.51	26.61	20.04	20.20	19.97	22.30	27.63	50.64
Australia 193	—	—	.15	.17	.18	.50	.41	1.63	1.65	2.61	.91	1.12	1.62	3.14
Japan 158	12.07	10.22	5.98	2.51	3.41	4.01	3.88	128.98	164.61	193.23	189.83	188.16	229.24	328.95
New Zealand 196	.24	.07	.03	.39	.02	—	—	14.43	14.28	15.11	13.84	25.51	22.25	27.12
Austria 122	—	—	—	—	—	—	—	2.56	4.11	5.00	4.26	4.79	2.83	6.94
Belgium-Luxembourg n.s. 127	36.52	33.31	28.81	29.68	24.91	38.65	42.35	6.15	10.34	—	27.55	26.64	29.06	15.95
Cyprus 423	—	—	—	—	—	—	—	.02	.02	.01	—	—	—	—
Denmark 128	—	.01	.03	.02	.05	2.12	3.10	7.16	7.73	6.53	6.46	6.33	7.94	17.45
Finland 172	—	—	—	—	—	—	—	2.62	1.25	.91	2.22	11.32	9.65	25.46
France 132	1.54	1.48	3.13	3.11	2.11	3.38	2.89	45.73	17.73	18.24	18.06	24.37	26.28	58.21
Germany 134	25.83	6.72	3.66	5.05	1.99	6.17	3.18	51.95	45.75	49.18	44.81	52.77	56.83	87.35
Greece 174	.03	.02	1.44	.19	1.58	4.59	2.40	.84	.62	.35	.40	.69	.57	.79
Iceland 176	—	—	—	—	.01	.06	.12	.20	.26	.11	.07	.03	—	—
Ireland 178	.22	—	.51	1.03	6.33	4.16	.57	5.99	6.24	6.88	6.81	7.54	8.95	9.41
Italy 136	22.14	8.30	9.86	12.81	15.15	26.38	18.31	19.23	18.83	20.71	21.54	20.12	22.86	41.60
Luxembourg 137	—	—	—	—	—	—	—	—	—	14.10	—	—	—	—
Netherlands 138	12.04	12.84	15.06	38.78	47.06	68.31	114.64	16.63	18.22	16.02	15.88	31.73	22.67	44.18
Norway 142	.53	.85	—	—	—	—	—	2.07	2.83	1.76	1.85	1.40	.44	1.35
Portugal 182	13.82	30.02	28.65	23.24	12.65	11.73	13.08	.83	.87	.87	1.17	1.86	2.11	2.69
Slovenia 961	—	—	—	—	—	—	—	.33	.34	.26	.11	.40	—	—
Spain 184	18.14	21.98	45.60	45.00	85.63	83.44	55.79	50.92	41.62	48.69	50.91	63.15	73.93	106.96
Sweden 144	30.31	46.12	49.87	57.99	54.33	56.86	62.15	11.67	21.16	17.12	21.96	24.59	22.18	28.98
Switzerland 146	.36	.20	—	.02	.10	.30	.81	7.31	7.65	7.67	9.70	8.76	11.98	16.98
United Kingdom 112	2.74	7.59	6.25	6.57	18.43	34.65	61.24	20.66	18.59	25.26	15.97	12.29	35.79	32.58
Developing Countries 202	**242.5**	**212.4**	**177.2**	**207.4**	**255.0**	**264.7**	**334.9**	**1,514.2**	**1,134.4**	**1,099.8**	**1,495.2**	**2,265.8**	**2,670.5**	**3,405.7**
Africa 607	**.2**	**.1**	**.1**	**—**	**.2**	**.1**	**2.7**	**1.6**	**1.5**	**1.1**	**.9**	**1.7**	**1.0**	**.3**
Algeria 612	.06	.06	—	—	—	—	.36	—	—	—	—	—	—	—
Angola 614	—	—	.12	.02	.02	.05	.04	—	—	—	—	—	—	—
Congo, Republic of 634	—	—	—	—	—	—	—	.71	—	—	—	—	—	—
Kenya 664	.04	—	—	—	—	—	—	—	—	—	—	—	—	—
Madagascar 674	—	—	—	—	.03	—	.01	—	—	—	—	—	—	—
Mauritania 682	.10	—	—	—	—	—	—	—	—	—	—	—	—	—
Morocco 686	—	—	—	—	—	—	—	.01	.01	.06	.03	—	.03	—
Nigeria 694	—	.02	—	—	—	—	—	—	—	—	—	—	—	—
Senegal 722	—	—	—	—	—	.03	.24	—	—	—	—	—	—	—
South Africa 199	—	—	—	—	—	—	2.03	.86	1.46	1.09	.84	1.72	1.00	.31
Tanzania 738	....	....	....	....	....	....	....	—	.01	—	—	—	—	—
Tunisia 744	.02	—	—	—	.12	—	—	—	—	—	—	—	—	—
Asia 507	**22.1**	**14.9**	**28.9**	**52.9**	**52.9**	**52.7**	**124.4**	**136.2**	**160.4**	**165.3**	**237.2**	**273.6**	**420.3**	**742.3**
Bangladesh 513	—	—	—	.36	5.45	.27	.42	—	—	—	—	—	—	—
China,P.R.: Mainland 924	3.20	2.01	12.07	10.82	10.21	13.45	68.03	24.73	40.80	48.41	72.11	99.05	166.84	358.73
China,P.R.:Hong Kong 532	6.36	5.23	5.43	7.66	6.60	6.29	5.34	20.31	19.94	17.49	19.40	20.80	27.44	32.10
Guam 829	—	.01	—	—	—	—	—	....	....	....	....	....	....	....
India 534	.42	2.54	4.24	18.12	6.55	6.12	7.79	3.29	2.18	3.93	6.88	7.21	10.72	12.31
Indonesia 536	—	—	—	.58	.73	—	.31	1.23	1.37	1.52	1.73	2.15	3.11	4.26
Korea 542	.36	.05	.14	1.98	2.26	1.84	1.90	54.76	63.54	63.80	101.55	102.88	165.67	267.67
Malaysia 548	—	—	—	—	.01	.12	.31	.91	1.40	1.80	3.78	3.30	4.90	3.80
Pakistan 564	—	—	—	.01	—	—	.05	.48	.53	.62	.82	.85	.82	.98
Philippines 566	—	—	—	—	—	—	—	.89	.86	.27	.45	.52	.82	—
Singapore 576	—	.26	.13	.52	.07	.08	.14	.88	5.14	1.30	1.64	1.78	2.01	3.31
Sri Lanka 524	—	—	—	—	—	—	—	.16	.25	.33	.29	.42	.25	.32
Taiwan Province of China 528	11.72	4.81	6.86	11.39	20.05	23.66	38.92	24.45	18.79	19.48	21.64	26.72	24.99	32.78
Thailand 578	—	—	—	1.50	.95	.41	.38	4.04	5.54	6.12	6.39	7.48	12.04	24.80
Vietnam 582	—	—	—	—	.05	.42	.86	.08	.07	.23	.52	.46	.68	1.24
Europe 170	**.2**	**1.0**	**7.2**	**1.2**	**1.9**	**.4**	**4.4**	**11.7**	**13.3**	**10.7**	**25.6**	**19.3**	**35.7**	**10.8**
Albania 914	—	—	—	—	—	—	—	.02	—	—	—	—	—	—
Armenia 911	—	—	—	—	—	—	—	.03	—	—	—	—	—	—
Bulgaria 918	—	—	—	—	.17	—	—	—	.01	.04	.04	.16	.10	.38
Croatia 960	—	—	—	—	.01	—	1.14	—	—	—	—	—	—	—
Czech Republic 935	.01	—	—	—	.09	—	.08	1.20	1.52	1.85	2.89	1.63	1.93	1.75
Estonia 939	—	—	—	—	—	—	—	—	—	.01	.02	.01	.22	.04
Faroe Islands 816	—	—	—	—	—	—	.56	—	—	—	—	—	—	—
Georgia 915	—	—	—	.06	—	—	.71	—	—	—	—	—	—	—
Gibraltar 823	—	—	—	—	—	.02	—	—	—	—	—	—	—	—
Hungary 944	—	—	—	—	—	—	.12	.51	.04	—	.31	.09	.12	.08
Kazakhstan 916	—	—	—	—	—	—	—	—	—	—	—	.02	—	—
Latvia 941	—	—	—	.14	—	—	—	—	—	—	—	—	—	—
Lithuania 946	—	—	.02	.14	—	—	—	—	—	—	—	—	—	—

	Exports 2001	Exports 2002	Exports 2003	Exports 2004	Exports 2005	Exports 2006	Exports 2007	Imports 2001	Imports 2002	Imports 2003	Imports 2004	Imports 2005	Imports 2006	Imports 2007
	Millions of U.S. Dollars							*Millions of U.S. Dollars*						
Poland 964	.16	—	6.18	.84	1.26	—	—	.78	.33	.63	.52	1.32	1.45	2.72
Romania 968	—	—	—	—	—	—	.56	.03	.01	—	.11	2.09	.09	.19
Russia 922	—	.51	.98	—	.17	.36	—	—	—	1.27	.69	2.94	.94	3.11
Slovak Republic 936	—	—	—	—	—	—	—	.24	.34	.21	.07	.72	—	—
Turkey 186	—	—	—	.01	—	—	1.28	6.42	2.87	1.65	9.23	2.07	2.88	2.53
Ukraine 926	—	—	—	—	—	—	—	.44	6.93	5.07	11.77	5.26	28.02	—
U.S.S.R. n.s. 930	—	.51	—	—	.17	—	—	1.99	1.22	—	—	2.94	—	—
Yugoslavia n.s. 966	....	....	....	....	....	....	....	.02	—	—	—	—	—	—
Middle East 407	**—**	**.1**	**.6**	**.2**	**1.7**	**.1**	**1.2**	**15.3**	**4.5**	**3.3**	**2.5**	**6.2**	**5.2**	**9.0**
Egypt 469	—	—	—	—	—	—	—	.01	.03	.07	.11	.04	.04	.32
Iran, I.R. of 429	—	—	—	—	1.36	—	—	.01	—	—	—	—	.02	.13
Israel 436	—	.02	.02	.03	.10	.13	.10	5.51	3.59	2.53	2.30	5.39	4.51	8.18
Jordan 439	—	.11	.15	.07	—	—	—	—	—	—	—	—	—	—
Kuwait 443	—	—	—	—	—	—	—	—	.16	.08	.08	.07	.12	.03
Lebanon 446	—	—	—	—	—	—	—	.02	.02	—	.01	.08	.01	.03
Libya 672	—	—	.07	—	—	—	—	—	—	—	—	—	—	—
Qatar 453	—	—	—	—	—	—	—	.26	.25	.55	—	.60	.44	—
Saudi Arabia 456	.03	—	—	—	.01	.02	.02	9.49	.49	.09	.01	.06	.10	—
Syrian Arab Republic 463	—	—	.34	—	—	—	1.06	—	—	—	—	—	—	—
United Arab Emirates 466	—	—	—	.08	.22	—	—	.03	—	—	—	—	—	.36
Middle East n.s. 489	—	—	—	.02	—	—	—	—	—	—	—	—	—	—
Western Hemisphere 207	**220.0**	**196.2**	**140.5**	**153.1**	**198.3**	**211.5**	**202.2**	**1,349.5**	**954.7**	**919.3**	**1,229.0**	**1,964.9**	**2,208.2**	**2,643.2**
Argentina 213	.88	.14	.09	.01	.02	.02	.03	11.70	11.09	19.78	36.16	41.48	61.12	73.52
Aruba 314	1.19	.85	.78	.76	.65	1.00	.91	.38	12.86	31.06	16.16	.01	—	31.29
Bahamas, The 313	.30	12.72	.24	.29	.45	1.12	.50	.01	—	.16	—	—	—	—
Barbados 316	.03	.04	.47	.23	.20	.04	.13	.79	—	1.41	3.19	5.02	6.13	8.03
Belize 339	.20	.36	.15	.13	.58	.50	.37	.72	.04	—	.10	.09	—	.11
Bermuda 319	—	.07	.07	.10	.06	.03	.02	.04	—	—	—	—	—	—
Bolivia 218	.85	.40	.20	.17	.32	.32	.61	.04	—	.04	2.80	.06	.09	.09
Brazil 223	—	—	.05	.07	2.14	1.05	1.62	33.54	48.14	95.16	117.18	127.24	150.05	140.70
Chile 228	.82	.11	.34	.21	.12	.41	1.63	19.98	19.90	25.47	30.71	30.80	30.94	40.81
Colombia 233	24.47	5.75	8.58	11.89	15.46	18.81	19.14	169.00	179.63	122.91	132.03	143.64	169.91	192.11
Costa Rica 238	38.77	36.13	33.47	36.77	38.75	45.61	57.10	108.83	127.82	149.84	177.08	194.62	246.24	326.23
Dominican Republic 243	7.76	15.79	8.24	9.74	16.44	16.03	13.44	3.89	3.55	6.48	15.50	9.94	9.69	15.08
Ecuador 248	4.81	3.90	3.64	5.70	5.30	1.37	1.75	236.72	99.12	6.99	8.09	12.43	13.46	14.64
El Salvador 253	6.03	7.68	9.40	10.59	9.33	9.31	8.03	26.39	35.68	46.45	50.96	55.94	59.08	72.34
Greenland 326	—	.01	—	—	—	—	—	—	—	—	—	—	—	—
Grenada 328	—	—	—	—	.01	.03	—	—	—	—	—	—	—	—
Guatemala 258	17.13	15.90	13.25	11.61	21.39	33.02	16.71	57.98	62.95	71.10	73.87	83.66	84.86	107.37
Guyana 336	.19	.20	.07	.15	.13	.17	.11	.06	.07	.01	.59	.54	.12	.08
Haiti 263	.62	.09	1.78	2.66	3.82	1.73	.35	—	—	—	.01	.01	—	.06
Honduras 268	20.08	33.56	13.36	15.40	15.62	17.91	20.92	8.49	8.16	8.08	8.92	9.97	15.08	22.30
Jamaica 343	3.75	3.77	3.28	7.79	7.40	6.59	5.98	1.18	1.14	2.00	1.89	1.89	3.04	4.50
Mexico 273	15.10	14.91	12.07	13.92	17.11	10.45	9.25	119.39	112.44	119.15	143.32	154.06	173.02	212.02
Netherlands Antilles 353	6.13	1.09	.87	.82	.92	.94	.97	22.19	52.01	89.61	255.74	475.19	488.25	489.16
Nicaragua 278	41.13	20.91	24.81	18.23	21.38	17.25	12.88	7.20	3.27	4.39	3.75	6.37	7.39	6.95
Paraguay 288	.03	—	—	.03	.02	.03	.03	.02	.03	.03	.03	.01	.03	.12
Peru 293	.59	.62	.33	1.48	1.36	.90	.86	11.52	9.41	14.62	12.96	15.20	19.38	69.03
Suriname 366	—	.10	.41	.06	.26	1.66	2.03	.01	.01	.02	.05	.01	.01	—
Trinidad and Tobago 369	1.79	2.36	2.14	1.61	3.54	4.58	2.54	1.89	38.55	19.55	21.39	43.82	32.32	41.69
Uruguay 298	.13	.09	—	—	—	—	.43	.38	1.13	1.69	4.32	1.80	13.00	4.99
Venezuela, Rep. Bol. 299	18.19	8.58	2.30	2.15	1.27	1.29	2.78	154.27	127.68	83.24	112.21	44.79	51.50	55.40
Western Hem. n.s. 399	9.02	10.08	.07	.50	14.29	19.32	21.10	352.86	—	—	.03	506.31	573.49	714.61
Other Countries n.i.e. 910	**1.7**	**2.0**	**.7**	**.7**	**.5**	**.8**	**3.1**	**.6**	**.1**	**.2**	**.4**	**15.8**	**21.7**	**26.1**
Cuba 928	1.65	1.98	.71	.73	.47	.77	3.07	.61	.14	.22	.45	15.77	21.75	26.08
Special Categories 899	**—**	**—**	**—**	**9.5**	**13.1**	**16.4**	**—**	**414.5**	**433.8**	**64.5**	**573.3**	**198.7**	**778.1**	**—**
Memorandum Items														
European Union 998	163.49	168.37	199.06	224.59	271.55	340.43	379.90	246.04	215.65	232.83	241.94	292.38	325.36	483.13
Oil Exporting Ctys 999	18.28	8.66	2.38	2.81	3.59	1.31	3.46	165.29	129.94	85.48	114.03	47.67	55.30	60.18
Non-Oil Develop.Ctys 201	224.18	203.71	174.83	204.62	251.39	263.42	331.48	1,348.93	1,004.45	1,014.27	1,381.22	2,218.10	2,615.21	3,345.49
PERCENT DISTRIBUTION														
Industrial Countries 101	**70.5**	**71.8**	**77.6**	**75.6**	**72.5**	**72.8**	**70.0**	**42.2**	**48.3**	**57.4**	**42.4**	**40.4**	**35.6**	**46.9**
Developing Countries 202	**29.3**	**27.9**	**22.3**	**23.3**	**26.1**	**25.5**	**29.7**	**45.3**	**37.4**	**40.3**	**41.6**	**54.5**	**49.5**	**52.7**
Africa 607	**—**	**—**	**—**	**—**	**—**	**—**	**.2**	**—**	**—**	**—**	**—**	**—**	**—**	**—**
Asia 507	**2.7**	**2.0**	**3.6**	**5.9**	**5.4**	**5.1**	**11.1**	**4.1**	**5.3**	**6.1**	**6.6**	**6.6**	**7.8**	**11.5**
Europe 170	**—**	**.1**	**.9**	**.1**	**.2**	**—**	**.4**	**.3**	**.4**	**.4**	**.7**	**.5**	**.7**	**.2**
Middle East 407	**—**	**—**	**.1**	**—**	**.2**	**—**	**.1**	**.5**	**.1**	**.1**	**.1**	**.2**	**.1**	**.1**
Western Hemisphere 207	**26.6**	**25.8**	**17.7**	**17.2**	**20.3**	**20.4**	**18.0**	**40.4**	**31.4**	**33.7**	**34.2**	**47.3**	**41.0**	**40.9**
Other Countries n.i.e. 910	**.2**	**.3**	**.1**	**.1**	**—**	**.1**	**.3**	**—**	**—**	**—**	**—**	**.4**	**.4**	**.4**
ANNUAL PERCENT CHANGE														
World 001	**6.2**	**−8.1**	**4.6**	**12.1**	**9.6**	**6.2**	**8.5**	**−1.9**	**−9.1**	**−10.0**	**31.5**	**15.8**	**29.7**	**19.8**
Industrial Countries 101	**6.5**	**−6.4**	**13.1**	**9.2**	**5.1**	**6.7**	**4.2**	**−15.7**	**4.1**	**6.8**	**−2.8**	**10.2**	**14.5**	**57.5**
Developing Countries 202	**5.7**	**−12.4**	**−16.6**	**17.1**	**22.9**	**3.8**	**26.5**	**−11.8**	**−25.1**	**−3.1**	**36.0**	**51.5**	**17.9**	**27.5**
Africa 607	**−39.5**	**−65.5**	**58.3**	**−79.3**	**578.1**	**−57.0**	**—**	**−45.5**	**−5.8**	**−22.7**	**−24.7**	**99.3**	**−40.2**	**−69.6**
Asia 507	**−15.6**	**−32.4**	**93.7**	**83.3**	**—**	**−.5**	**136.3**	**−21.0**	**17.8**	**3.1**	**43.5**	**15.4**	**53.6**	**76.6**
Europe 170	**−95.0**	**495.2**	**609.0**	**−83.4**	**56.1**	**−79.8**	**—**	**−23.3**	**13.7**	**−19.2**	**139.1**	**−24.9**	**85.5**	**−69.8**
Middle East 407	**−86.8**	**374.7**	**316.4**	**−66.9**	**790.6**	**−91.2**	**696.9**	**68.1**	**−70.4**	**−26.9**	**−24.1**	**147.9**	**−15.9**	**72.5**
Western Hemisphere 207	**10.4**	**−10.8**	**−28.4**	**9.0**	**29.6**	**6.6**	**−4.4**	**−11.0**	**−29.3**	**−3.7**	**33.7**	**59.9**	**12.4**	**19.7**
Other Countries n.i.e. 910	**−3.6**	**19.7**	**−64.0**	**2.2**	**−34.9**	**63.4**	**296.8**	**−46.6**	**−76.7**	**55.7**	**101.8**	**—**	**37.9**	**19.9**

	Exports 2001	2002	2003	2004	2005	2006	2007	Imports, f.o.b 2001	2002	2003	2004	2005	2006	2007
	Millions of U.S. Dollars							Millions of U.S. Dollars						
IFS World Total	**1,805.2**	**1,640.9**	**2,206.8**	**2,551.9**	**3,273.5**	**4,165.8**	**4,681.2**	**932.0**	**1,074.1**	**1,188.6**	**1,460.5**	**1,503.3**	....	....
DOTS World Total 001	**2,627.3Y**	**2,667.7Y**	**3,667.5Y**	**4,265.2Y**	**5,237.7Y**	**6,412.9Y**	**7,418.9Y**	**1,021.2Y**	**1,085.7Y**	**1,228.9Y**	**1,458.0Y**	**1,834.8Y**	**2,150.0Y**	**2,697.1Y**
Industrial Countries 101	**1,239.3Y**	**1,251.4Y**	**1,719.2Y**	**1,949.6Y**	**2,528.6Y**	**2,985.7Y**	**3,458.5Y**	**662.4Y**	**698.9V**	**753.3V**	**891.4Y**	**1,257.5V**	**1,392.5V**	**1,786.4V**
United States 111	39.45V	87.91V	64.00V	52.18V	56.64V	80.09V	104.36V	22.30V	23.30V	30.20V	42.60V	55.30V	43.80V	65.70V
Canada 156	5.09V	.63V	2.19V	1.24V	2.36V	2.87V	3.09V	1.53V	.97V	1.90V	2.80V	5.61V	6.27V	3.47V
Australia 193	646.49V	645.47V	980.08V	1,198.26V	1,506.59V	1,895.34V	2,022.22V	521.90V	535.55V	547.31V	677.42V	1,002.92V	1,116.41V	1,384.51V
Japan 158	279.17V	252.48V	266.21V	247.56V	449.88V	511.74V	703.92V	46.94V	45.92V	42.77V	63.26V	79.59V	93.21V	152.49V
New Zealand 196	35.34V	36.03V	42.52V	22.71V	56.92V	36.66V	54.67V	40.86V	47.77V	94.20V	61.11V	72.03V	72.78V	88.16V
Austria 122	.43V	.05V	.12V	.59V	.70V	.63V	.14V	.11V	.12V	.26V	.06V	.09V	.18V	6.49V
Belgium 124	7.32V	13.68V	13.44V	18.50V	26.68V	18.25V	39.52V	.54V	.66V	.76V	1.63V	1.46V	1.10V	2.67V
Cyprus 423	—V	.16V	.09V	—V	.15Y	.10V	.04V	—V	—V	.01V	—V	—V	—V	—V
Denmark 128	.46V	.50V	1.39V	.68V	2.97V	3.73V	2.72V	2.37V	2.05V	2.64V	2.47V	2.93V	3.11V	4.00V
Finland 172	.41V	.57V	.16V	.56V	.01V	.23V	.05V	2.20V	1.65V	.65V	.42V	.35V	.42V	1.31V
France 132	1.26V	1.90V	15.06V	8.50V	5.50V	4.43V	6.01V	1.21V	1.93V	1.77V	6.87V	2.36V	2.19V	2.32V
Germany 134	106.10V	76.95V	135.26V	201.42V	207.07V	242.39V	244.36V	7.00V	7.57V	6.21V	4.57V	5.24V	16.34V	11.12V
Greece 174	.90V	.65V	3.56V	5.48V	6.04V	6.82V	9.84V	—V	—V	—V	—V	.01V	—V	—V
Iceland 176	.01V	.01V	—V	.01V	.05V	—V	.07V	—V	—V	—V	—V	—V	—V	.01V
Ireland 178	.54V	.34V	.65V	.95V	1.54V	1.26V	.63V	.04V	1.38V	.11V	1.34V	7.81V	7.69V	7.95V
Italy 136	27.94V	45.96V	49.72V	37.65V	37.89V	59.06V	86.79V	1.15V	1.88V	1.35V	1.51V	1.64V	1.64V	2.71V
Luxembourg 137	—V	—V	—V	—V	—V	—V	—V	.10V	.35V	.16V	.12V	.01V	.15V	.38V
Malta 181	—Y	—V	—V	.26V	.17V	.07V	.09V	.01Y	—V	—V	—V	—V	—V	—V
Netherlands 138	15.17V	14.16V	27.10V	30.59V	37.82V	19.47V	43.78V	5.08V	4.77V	7.46V	7.96V	4.52V	13.40V	18.94V
Norway 142	.01V	—V	.01V	.15V	.01V	—V	.09V	.57V	1.57V	.64V	6.18V	4.99V	.62V	1.38V
Portugal 182	1.34V	.83V	.67V	.39V	.41V	.45V	.48V	.21V	.01V	.08V	—V	.12V	.13V	.04V
Slovenia 961	—V	—V	.02V	.03Y	—V	—V	—V	.06V	.06V	.06V	.08Y	.04V	—V	—V
Spain 184	3.11V	5.77V	19.58V	19.78V	26.13V	30.71V	63.75V	.92V	1.58V	.30V	.45V	.40V	2.14V	.74V
Sweden 144	14.42V	.05V	7.20V	.36V	4.49V	2.53V	1.15V	.74V	.71V	1.18V	.72V	1.08V	1.76V	11.95V
Switzerland 146	.04V	.02V	.25V	.01V	.35V	1.23V	.18V	.25V	.48V	.49V	.25V	.53V	.28V	4.40V
United Kingdom 112	54.29V	67.25V	89.94V	101.73V	98.24V	67.64V	70.57V	6.28V	18.64V	12.84V	9.61V	8.47V	8.96V	15.65V
Developing Countries 202	**1,386.3Y**	**1,414.4Y**	**1,945.9Y**	**2,312.4Y**	**2,705.4Y**	**3,422.6Y**	**3,954.7Y**	**343.1Y**	**369.8Y**	**454.0Y**	**538.3Y**	**544.9Y**	**717.4Y**	**861.1Y**
Africa 607	**.3Y**	**.2Y**	**.7Y**	**1.6Y**	**1.8Y**	**2.2Y**	**.9Y**	**10.8Y**	**11.9Y**	**1.7Y**	**4.7Y**	**5.8Y**	**5.3Y**	**8.6Y**
Burkina Faso 748	.01Y	.01Y	.01Y	.01Y	.01Y	.01Y	.02Y	....	....	....	....	....	....	....
Côte d'Ivoire 662	—V	—V	.09V	—V	—V	—V	—Y	—V	—V	—V	—V	—V	—V	—Y
Kenya 664	.08V	—V	.21V	.16V	.18Y	.23Y	.28Y	—V	—V	.07V	.19V	.21Y	.27Y	.33Y
Liberia 668	—Y	—Y	—Y	—Y	—Y	—Y	—Y	—Y	—Y	.01Y	.01Y	.01Y	.01Y	.01Y
Madagascar 674	....	....	....	....	....	....	....	.15V	—V	—Y	—Y	—Y	—Y	—Y
Malawi 676	—Y	—Y	—Y	—Y	—Y	—Y	—Y	.63Y	.69Y	.87Y	1.14Y	1.30Y	1.61Y	2.00Y
Mauritania 682	—Y	—Y	—Y	—Y	—Y	—Y	—Y	—Y	—Y	.01Y	.01Y	.01Y	.01Y	.01Y
Mauritius 684	.01V	—V	—V	—V	—V	—V	—V	.03V	—V	—V	—V	—V	—V	—V
Morocco 686	.09V	—V	—V	—V	—V	—Y	—Y	—V	—V	—V	—V	—V	—Y	—Y
Nigeria 694	.01V	—V	—V	—Y	—Y	—Y	—Y	—V	—V	—V	—Y	—Y	—Y	—Y
Senegal 722	—V	—V	—V	—V	—V	—V	—Y	—V	—V	—V	1.97V	2.46V	1.14V	1.42Y
South Africa 199	—V	.04V	.22V	1.23V	1.41V	1.74V	.36V	.54V	.96V	.42V	.93V	1.27V	1.51V	3.94V
Sudan 732	—Y	—Y	—Y	—V	—V	—V	—V	9.11Y	9.89Y	—V	—V	—V	—V	—V
Swaziland 734	....	....	....	....	....	....	....	.01Y	.01Y	.01Y	.02Y	.02Y	.02Y	.03Y
Tanzania 738	—V	—V	.01Y	.01Y	.01Y	.01Y	.01Y	.28V	.28V	.36Y	.47Y	.54Y	.67Y	.83Y
Tunisia 744	—V	—V	—V	.05V	—V	—V	—Y	—V	—V	—V	—V	—V	—V	—Y
Uganda 746	—V	—V	—V	—Y	.01Y	.01Y	.01Y	—V	—V	.01V	.01Y	.01Y	.01Y	.01Y
Zambia 754	—V	—V	—V	—V	—V	.02V	—V	—V	—V	—V	—V	—V	—V	—V
Zimbabwe 698	—V	—V	—V	—V	—V	—V	—Y	—V	.05V	—V	—V	—V	—V	—Y
Africa n.s. 799	.12Y	.13Y	.14Y	.15Y	.16Y	.17Y	.18Y	—Y	—Y	—Y	—Y	—Y	—Y	—Y
Asia 507	**481.0Y**	**433.6Y**	**705.1Y**	**683.6Y**	**843.5Y**	**1,121.9Y**	**1,104.3Y**	**326.5Y**	**352.5Y**	**447.1Y**	**521.5Y**	**534.4Y**	**690.0Y**	**843.5Y**
Bangladesh 513	.53V	—V	—V	—V	—V	—V	—V	.53V	1.13V	1.32V	.91V	1.40V	1.06Y	1.91Y
Brunei Darussalam 516	.01Y	.01Y	—V	—Y	—Y	—Y	—Y	.06Y	.06Y	—V	—Y	—Y	—Y	—Y
Cambodia 522	—V	—V	—V	—V	.01V	.05V	.06Y	—V	—V	—V	—V	.01V	.02V	.03Y
China,P.R.: Mainland 924	111.26V	145.15V	210.06V	194.68V	281.33V	356.06V	425.77V	19.17V	27.25V	60.93V	50.42V	66.49V	126.40V	212.90V
China,P.R.:Hong Kong 532	5.31V	5.21V	6.69V	7.12V	8.01V	7.20V	14.56V	8.87V	8.89V	6.62V	6.53V	6.99V	5.33V	9.68V
China,P.R.:Macao 546	—V	—V	—V	.01V	—V	—V	—V	—V	—V	.01V	—V	—V	—V	—V
Fiji 819	1.37Y	1.48Y	1.88Y	2.46Y	2.82Y	3.48Y	4.32Y	2.98Y	3.24Y	4.10Y	5.38Y	6.15Y	7.60Y	9.43Y
French Polynesia 887	—Y	—Y	—Y	—Y	—Y	—Y	—Y	.04Y	.04Y	.05Y	.07Y	.08Y	.10Y	.12Y
Guam 829	.01Y	.02Y	.02Y	.03Y	.03Y	.04Y	.05Y	.27Y	.29Y	.36Y	.48Y	.55Y	.68Y	.84Y
India 534	.60Y	.29V	.74V	63.57V	65.36V	80.78Y	100.24Y	5.22Y	6.37V	4.79V	11.46V	10.44V	12.90Y	16.01Y
Indonesia 536	11.10V	60.05V	107.24V	84.91V	45.42V	167.38V	12.91V	28.38V	30.21V	34.23V	36.24V	49.08V	65.64V	69.90V
Kiribati 826	—Y	—Y	—Y	.01Y	.01Y	.01Y	.01Y	—Y	—Y	—Y	—Y	—Y	—Y	—Y
Korea 542	78.40V	29.27V	47.80V	35.31V	65.40V	86.39V	124.79V	9.31V	9.01V	7.77V	13.98V	16.86V	16.50V	18.39V
Malaysia 548	8.24V	5.35V	9.07V	16.29V	27.52V	37.17V	34.75V	28.23V	32.45V	39.39V	41.06V	76.68V	78.13V	96.80V
New Caledonia 839	1.47V	1.27V	1.18V	1.20V	1.37Y	1.69Y	2.10Y	—V	.01V	.03V	—V	—Y	—Y	—Y
Pakistan 564	.07V	.03V	.14V	.08V	.10V	.12Y	.15Y	.12V	.05V	.21V	.14V	.13V	.16Y	.20Y
Philippines 566	59.36V	12.77V	67.58V	60.31V	104.48V	158.27V	105.75V	1.86V	1.52V	2.41V	6.01V	4.74V	5.16V	19.71V
Samoa 862	—Y	—Y	—Y	—Y	.87V	1.08Y	1.34Y	—Y	—Y	—Y	—Y	—V	—Y	—Y
Singapore 576	19.98V	18.56V	56.86V	37.17V	36.14V	17.98V	22.99V	193.52V	204.50V	252.63V	315.55V	246.38V	269.75V	313.42V
Solomon Islands 813	3.79Y	4.11Y	5.21Y	6.84Y	7.81Y	9.66Y	11.98Y	.49Y	.53Y	.67Y	.88Y	1.00Y	1.24Y	1.54Y

		Exports							Imports, f.o.b						
		2001	2002	2003	2004	2005	2006	2007	2001	2002	2003	2004	2005	2006	2007
		Millions of U.S. Dollars							*Millions of U.S. Dollars*						
Sri Lanka	524	.13V	—V	.09V	.02V	.01V	.12V	.09V	.60V	.31V	.21V	.20V	.38V	.50V	.83V
Taiwan Province of China	528	11.31V	11.46V	12.00V	15.28V	13.95V	12.27V	10.45V	7.44V	8.56V	7.07V	7.45V	10.34V	45.14V	9.16V
Thailand	578	64.08V	27.51V	49.45V	29.55V	45.44V	35.61V	76.13V	15.27V	16.91V	21.22V	23.38V	35.22V	51.78V	60.27V
Vanuatu	846	1.66Y	1.80Y	2.28Y	3.00Y	3.43Y	4.24Y	5.26Y	.72Y	.78Y	.99Y	1.30Y	1.49Y	1.84Y	2.28Y
Vietnam	582	1.27V	—V	9.27V	—V	—V	—V	—V	3.37V	.40V	2.09V	—V	—V	—V	—V
Asia n.s.	598	101.03Y	109.28Y	117.54Y	125.80Y	134.05Y	142.31Y	150.57Y	.02Y	.02Y	.02Y	.02Y	.02Y	.03Y	.03Y
Europe	**170**	**902.0Y**	**977.4Y**	**1,236.7Y**	**1,623.4Y**	**1,854.4Y**	**2,293.4Y**	**2,845.1Y**	**.6Y**	**3.6Y**	**3.9Y**	**8.1Y**	**2.2Y**	**1.7Y**	**1.7Y**
Belarus	913	—V	—V	—V	—V	—V	—V	.01V	—V	—V	—V	—V	—V	.02V	—V
Bulgaria	918	.30V	.01V	—V	.03V	.03V	.01V	—V	—V	—V	—V	.02V	—V	—V	—V
Czech Republic	935	.05V	.18V	.11V	.11V	.15V	2.12V	1.15V	.05V	—V	—V	.04V	—V	.01V	.03V
Estonia	939	—V	—V	.03V	—V	—V	—V	—V	—V	—V	—V	—V	—V	—V	—V
Gibraltar	823	—Y	—Y	—Y	—Y	—Y	—Y	—Y	.01Y	.01Y	.02Y	.02Y	.03Y	.03Y	.04Y
Hungary	944	.07V	.09V	.05V	—V	—V	—V	—V	—V	.02V	.07V	—V	—V	—V	.10V
Lithuania	946	—V	—V	—V	—V	—V	—V	—V	—V	—V	.02V	.04V	.06V	.04V	.10V
Poland	964	2.40V	1.56V	1.36V	1.27V	.47V	.03V	1.27V	.03V	.06V	.09V	—V	.17V	.03V	.03V
Romania	968	—V	.01V	—V	.01V	.11V	.25V	—V	—V	—V	.02V	—V	—V	.02V	.07V
Russia	922	.46V	.69V	1.34V	1.62V	2.51V	3.12V	3.40V	.25V	3.28V	3.21V	7.30V	1.17V	.68V	.02V
Serbia, Rep. of	942	—Y	—Y	—Y	—Y	—Y	.01V	.01Y	....	....	....	....	....	....	....
Slovak Republic	936	.03V	.15V	.20Y	.26Y	—V	—V	—V	—V	—V	—Y	—Y	—V	—V	—V
Turkey	186	.60V	—V	.01V	—V	.01V	—V	.04V	.25V	.24V	.45V	.62V	.76V	.87V	1.34V
Ukraine	926	.06V	.03V	.02V	.02V	—V	—Y	—Y	—V	—V	—V	—V	—V	—Y	—Y
Europe n.s.	884	898.07Y	974.65Y	1,233.59Y	1,620.11Y	1,851.11Y	2,287.83Y	2,839.18Y	....	....	....	....	....	....	....
Middle East	**407**	**—Y**	**—Y**	**—Y**	**—Y**	**—Y**	**—Y**	**—Y**	**.3Y**	**.3Y**	**.3Y**	**1.0Y**	**.4Y**	**1.6Y**	**2.1Y**
Bahrain	419	.01Y	.01Y	.01Y	.02Y	.02Y	.02Y	.03Y	.02Y	.02Y	.02Y	.03Y	.03Y	.04Y	.05Y
Israel	436	—V	—V	—V	—V	—V	—V	—V	.10V	—V	.10V	.70V	.10V	1.20V	1.60V
Lebanon	446	—Y	—Y	—Y	—Y	—Y	—Y	—Y	.02Y	.02Y	.03Y	.04Y	.05Y	.06Y	.07Y
Qatar	453	....	....	....	....	....	....	....	—V	.10V	—V	—V	—V	—V	—Y
United Arab Emirates	466	—V	—V	—V	—Y	—Y	—Y	—Y	.11Y	.12Y	.14Y	.19Y	.26Y	.33Y	.39Y
Western Hemisphere	**207**	**2.9Y**	**3.1Y**	**3.4Y**	**3.7Y**	**5.7Y**	**5.1Y**	**4.5Y**	**5.0Y**	**1.5Y**	**1.0Y**	**3.0Y**	**2.0Y**	**18.9Y**	**5.2Y**
Argentina	213	—V	—V	—V	.01V	.01V	.01V	.02V	.01V	.02V	.03V	.03V	—V	.05V	.04V
Brazil	223	—V	—V	—V	.02V	—V	—V	—V	.81V	1.37V	.78V	1.86V	1.88V	18.42V	—V
Chile	228	—V	—V	—V	—V	—V	.02V	.15V	—V	—V	.16V	1.10V	.04V	—V	—V
Colombia	233	—V	—V	—V	.06V	—V	—V	—V	.06V	—V	—V	—V	.01V	—V	—V
Costa Rica	238	—V	—V	—V	—V	—V	—Y	—Y	.01V	—V	—V	.01V	.03V	.03Y	.04Y
Ecuador	248	—V	—V	—V	—V	—V	.01V	.02Y	—V	—V	—V	—V	—V	—V	—Y
Guyana	336	—Y	—Y	—Y	—Y	—Y	—Y	—Y	—Y	—Y	.01Y	.01Y	.01Y	.01Y	.01Y
Mexico	273	—V	—V	—V	—V	1.88V	1.07V	.11V	—V	—V	—V	—V	—V	—V	4.62V
Netherlands Antilles	353	—V	—V	—Y	—Y	—Y	—Y	—Y	.01V	—V	—V	—Y	—Y	—Y	—Y
Peru	293	—V	—V	—V	—V	—V	—V	—Y	.11V	.08V	—V	.01V	—V	.33V	.45Y
Trinidad and Tobago	369	—V	.02V	.02Y	.03Y	.03Y	.04Y	.05Y	—V	—V	—Y	—Y	—Y	—Y	—Y
Venezuela, Rep. Bol	299	—V	—V	—V	.03V	—V	—V	—V	4.00V	—V	—V	—V	—V	—V	—Y
Western Hem. n.s.	399	2.91Y	3.12Y	3.33Y	3.54Y	3.75Y	3.96Y	4.17Y	.01Y	.01Y	.01Y	.01Y	.01Y	.02Y	.02Y
Other Countries n.i.e	**910**	**—Y**	**—Y**	**—Y**	**—Y**	**—Y**	**—Y**	**—Y**	**1.5Y**	**1.6Y**	**2.0Y**	**2.6Y**	**3.0Y**	**3.7Y**	**4.6Y**
North Korea	954	—Y	—Y	—Y	—Y	—Y	—Y	—Y	1.46Y	1.58Y	2.01Y	2.63Y	3.01Y	3.72Y	4.62Y
Countries & Areas n.s	**898**	**1.2Y**	**1.3Y**	**1.7Y**	**2.2Y**	**2.5Y**	**3.1Y**	**3.8Y**	**13.2Y**	**14.4Y**	**18.2Y**	**23.9Y**	**27.3Y**	**33.7Y**	**41.8Y**
Special Categories	**899**	**—Y**	**—Y**	**—Y**	**—Y**	**—Y**	**—Y**	**—Y**	**1.0Y**	**1.1Y**	**1.4Y**	**1.8Y**	**2.0Y**	**2.5Y**	**3.1Y**
Memorandum Items															
European Union	998	236.24Y	230.82Y	365.70Y	429.09Y	456.43Y	459.94Y	572.35Y	28.08Y	43.43Y	36.01Y	37.90Y	36.78V	59.28V	86.53V
Oil Exporting Ctys	999	11.12Y	60.05Y	107.24Y	84.94Y	45.42Y	167.38Y	12.91Y	32.49Y	30.44Y	34.37Y	36.43Y	49.34Y	65.97Y	70.30Y
Non-Oil Develop.Ctys	201	1,375.15Y	1,354.30Y	1,838.62Y	2,227.45Y	2,660.00Y	3,255.23Y	3,941.82Y	310.59Y	339.35Y	419.65Y	501.83Y	495.55Y	651.47Y	790.79Y
PERCENT DISTRIBUTION															
Industrial Countries	**101**	**47.2**	**46.9**	**46.9**	**45.7**	**48.3**	**46.6**	**46.6**	**64.9**	**64.4**	**61.3**	**61.1**	**68.5**	**64.8**	**66.2**
Developing Countries	**202**	**52.8**	**53.0**	**53.1**	**54.2**	**51.7**	**53.4**	**53.3**	**33.6**	**34.1**	**36.9**	**36.9**	**29.7**	**33.4**	**31.9**
Africa	**607**	**—**	**—**	**—**	**—**	**—**	**—**	**—**	**1.1**	**1.1**	**.1**	**.3**	**.3**	**.2**	**.3**
Asia	**507**	**18.3**	**16.3**	**19.2**	**16.0**	**16.1**	**17.5**	**14.9**	**32.0**	**32.5**	**36.4**	**35.8**	**29.1**	**32.1**	**31.3**
Europe	**170**	**34.3**	**36.6**	**33.7**	**38.1**	**35.4**	**35.8**	**38.3**	**.1**	**.3**	**.3**	**.6**	**.1**	**.1**	**.1**
Middle East	**407**	**—**	**—**	**—**	**—**	**—**	**—**	**—**	**—**	**—**	**—**	**.1**	**—**	**.1**	**.1**
Western Hemisphere	**207**	**.1**	**.1**	**.1**	**.1**	**.1**	**.1**	**.1**	**.5**	**.1**	**.1**	**.2**	**.1**	**.9**	**.2**
Other Countries n.i.e	**910**	**—**	**—**	**—**	**—**	**—**	**—**	**—**	**.1**	**.1**	**.2**	**.2**	**.2**	**.2**	**.2**
ANNUAL PERCENT CHANGE															
World	**001**	**–6.6**	**1.5**	**37.5**	**16.3**	**22.8**	**22.4**	**15.7**	**–8.6**	**6.3**	**13.2**	**18.6**	**25.8**	**17.2**	**25.4**
Industrial Countries	**101**	**–17.4**	**1.0**	**37.4**	**13.4**	**29.7**	**18.1**	**15.8**	**–5.3**	**5.5**	**7.8**	**18.3**	**41.1**	**10.7**	**28.3**
Developing Countries	**202**	**5.7**	**2.0**	**37.6**	**18.8**	**17.0**	**26.5**	**15.5**	**–14.8**	**7.8**	**22.8**	**18.6**	**1.2**	**31.7**	**20.0**
Africa	**607**	**–31.6**	**–43.2**	**269.5**	**138.8**	**9.7**	**22.9**	**–60.6**	**11.1**	**10.5**	**–85.3**	**171.3**	**22.8**	**–9.9**	**63.3**
Asia	**507**	**–2.0**	**–9.8**	**62.6**	**–3.0**	**23.4**	**33.0**	**–1.6**	**–15.9**	**8.0**	**26.8**	**16.6**	**2.5**	**29.1**	**22.2**
Europe	**170**	**10.2**	**8.4**	**26.5**	**31.3**	**14.2**	**23.7**	**24.1**	**–64.9**	**516.5**	**7.2**	**107.6**	**–72.7**	**–22.1**	**1.2**
Middle East	**407**	**7.3**	**8.5**	**26.6**	**31.3**	**14.3**	**23.6**	**24.1**	**–58.7**	**5.2**	**12.8**	**223.2**	**–54.3**	**270.0**	**30.2**
Western Hemisphere	**207**	**6.8**	**7.7**	**6.8**	**10.0**	**54.0**	**–10.0**	**–11.6**	**108.6**	**–70.5**	**–33.0**	**204.5**	**–34.6**	**852.8**	**–72.5**
Other Countries n.i.e	**910**	**—**	**—**	**....**	**....**	**....**	**....**	**....**	**10.4**	**8.5**	**26.6**	**31.3**	**14.3**	**23.6**	**24.1**

	Exports 2001	2002	2003	2004	2005	2006	2007	Imports, f.o.b 2001	2002	2003	2004	2005	2006	2007
	Millions of U.S. Dollars							*Millions of U.S. Dollars*						
IFS World Total	**990.0**	**951.0**	**1,241.5**	**1,626.6**	**1,687.7**	**1,906.4**	**2,784.5**	**1,988.8**	**1,510.3**	**1,865.3**	**2,657.7**	**3,251.4**	**5,250.2**	**6,286.9**
DOTS World Total 001	**990.2**	**950.6**	**1,241.5**	**1,626.6**	**1,687.8**	**1,906.4**	**3,420.5Y**	**1,988.8**	**1,510.2**	**1,865.3**	**2,657.7**	**3,251.4**	**5,250.2**	**5,420.5Y**
Industrial Countries 101	**187.2**	**166.2**	**238.5**	**246.9**	**195.6**	**243.8**	**646.9Y**	**428.5**	**330.6**	**348.2**	**455.9**	**623.1**	**1,259.2**	**1,636.0V**
United States 111	29.33	38.04	44.96	55.10	54.86	66.62	72.55V	118.39	77.65	71.67	108.54	172.82	338.20	1,236.80V
Canada 156	1.93	3.66	4.56	5.87	4.22	5.14	15.20V	3.58	3.06	1.64	5.20	13.80	6.21	8.14V
Australia 193	.02	.02	.09	.08	.07	.16	.27V	.32	.61	.27	.76	1.68	5.44	1.36V
Japan 158	11.77	8.13	5.40	18.14	18.48	24.70	31.34V	86.24	49.61	65.53	86.71	93.40	435.16	76.09V
New Zealand 196	.03	.05	.07	—	—	.01	.07V	.23	.16	.03	.13	.18	.74	.44V
Austria 122	.04	.01	.14	.16	.11	.28	.13V	1.63	3.12	2.09	2.38	3.44	9.13	6.41V
Belgium 124	1.35	1.85	2.90	3.77	1.85	2.56	9.97V	5.72	4.53	5.39	4.16	3.13	—	9.85V
Cyprus 423	—	—	—	.01	—	—	.04V	—	—	—	.03	.01	—	—V
Denmark 128	.06	.37	.34	.19	.44	.21	.89V	1.42	1.17	1.08	1.26	1.79	1.59	1.94V
Finland 172	.01	.01	.12	.36	.04	.14	—V	.77	.89	1.06	1.46	4.95	5.84	4.50V
France 132	4.84	8.04	10.45	10.52	8.28	9.37	13.90V	21.32	17.61	15.48	35.52	38.14	39.43	33.47V
Germany 134	13.06	8.78	7.23	14.20	13.86	19.44	168.76V	50.26	45.56	34.15	44.83	50.68	125.41	98.69V
Greece 174	.29	.14	.22	.01	.01	.06	22.64V	1.05	1.28	1.09	.98	1.28	.27	.12V
Iceland 176	.01	.07	.01	.10	.11	—	.05V	—	—	—	—	—	—	—V
Ireland 178	.01	—	.04	.16	.01	.07	.06V	1.05	.61	.65	.97	.42	1.15	1.63V
Italy 136	42.09	34.91	40.42	24.57	16.33	21.20	103.56V	25.30	13.63	13.69	19.63	24.74	20.56	47.94V
Luxembourg 137	—	—	—	—	—	—	—V	—	—	—	—	—	—	.02V
Malta 181	—	—	—	—	—	—	—V	—	.03	.01	—	1.52	—	—V
Netherlands 138	29.38	19.19	12.52	33.15	47.19	41.66	82.13V	8.78	6.65	3.15	4.36	5.58	10.74	22.04V
Norway 142	.08	.06	.95	.07	1.01	.30	.52V	.98	.02	.03	.08	.16	.90	1.05V
Portugal 182	5.11	.61	.70	3.45	1.95	1.18	17.00V	.71	.35	.30	.37	.51	.68	1.96V
Slovenia 961	—	—	.01	—	—	—	.13V	.11	.07	.04	.02	.03	.08	.25V
Spain 184	10.85	7.66	8.73	9.30	10.05	12.01	98.95V	20.99	16.23	33.48	18.20	24.50	18.90	28.85V
Sweden 144	.02	.10	.04	.09	.07	1.09	.58V	7.88	6.62	7.20	26.88	18.05	30.95	19.97V
Switzerland 146	34.37	33.44	97.11	66.66	14.56	34.13	2.23V	36.61	59.12	56.30	64.62	136.98	176.18	12.97V
United Kingdom 112	2.56	1.10	1.46	.98	2.08	3.45	5.92V	35.11	22.03	33.90	28.84	25.30	31.66	21.50V
Developing Countries 202	**802.3**	**784.2**	**1,002.8**	**1,377.6**	**1,490.7**	**1,661.6**	**2,772.4Y**	**1,555.2**	**1,176.4**	**1,495.3**	**2,174.2**	**2,580.1**	**3,958.0**	**3,743.6Y**
Africa 607	**2.1**	**3.0**	**7.3**	**11.5**	**14.8**	**33.3**	**47.5Y**	**7.9**	**4.5**	**5.7**	**8.4**	**9.2**	**1.9**	**3.0Y**
Algeria 612	—	—	.02	.12	—	—	—Y	—	—	—	—	—	—	—Y
Angola 614	.14	.41	4.05	6.78	6.55	20.64	25.62Y	—	—	—	—	—	—	—Y
Benin 638	—	.18	—	—	—	—	—Y	—	—	—	—	—	—	—Y
Botswana 616	—	—	.05	—	—	—	—Y	—	—	—	.01	—	—	—Y
Burundi 618	—	—	—	—	.10	—	—Y	—	—	—	—	—	—	—Y
Cameroon 622	—	—	.03	—	—	.04	.05Y	—	—	—	—	—	—	—Y
Central African Rep. 626	—	.06	.23	—	—	—	—Y	—	—	—	—	—	—	—Y
Comoros 632	—	—	.13	—	.07	.12	.15Y	....	....	....	....	....	....	....
Congo, Republic of 634	—	—	.03	—	.17	.07	.08Y	—	—	—	—	—	—	—Y
Djibouti 611	.05	.03	.14	—	—	—	—Y	....	....	....	....	....	....	....
Equatorial Guinea 642	—	—	—	.25	.65	.08	.11Y	—	—	—	—	—	—	—Y
Ethiopia 644	—	—	—	—	—	—	—Y	—	—	.04	—	—	—	—Y
Gabon 646	.13	—	.08	—	.09	.95	1.17Y	—	—	—	—	—	—	—Y
Gambia, The 648	....	....	....	....	....	....	....	—	—	.01	—	—	—	—Y
Ghana 652	.18	—	.16	.06	.25	.46	.57Y	—	—	—	—	—	—	—Y
Guinea-Bissau 654	—	—	—	—	—	.05	.06Y	—	—	—	—	—	—	—Y
Kenya 664	—	—	—	—	—	—	—Y	—	—	—	.09	—	—	—Y
Liberia 668	—	—	—	—	.35	.22	.28Y	—	—	—	—	—	—	—Y
Madagascar 674	.04	.05	.03	—	—	—	—Y	—	—	—	—	—	—	—Y
Mauritania 682	—	—	—	.24	—	—	—Y	—	—	—	—	—	.01	.02Y
Mauritius 684	—	.05	.30	—	—	.05	—V	—	—	.02	.01	—	—	—V
Morocco 686	.07	.30	.41	.09	—	—	—Y	—	—	.01	—	.01	—	—Y
Mozambique 688	—	—	—	.11	—	.13	.16Y	—	—	—	—	—	—	—Y
Namibia 728	—	—	.01	.01	.27	.04	.08Y	—	—	—	—	—	—	—Y
Niger 692	—	—	—	—	.24	.03	.04Y	....	....	....	....	....	....	....
Nigeria 694	.25	.06	.33	—	—	—	—Y	—	—	—	—	—	—	—Y
Rwanda 714	—	—	—	—	—	.02	.03Y	....	....	....	....	....	....	....
Senegal 722	.02	.01	.13	.03	.06	—	—Y	.01	—	—	—	—	—	—Y
Seychelles 718	—	—	—	—	—	.44	.55Y	....	....	....	....	....	....	....
South Africa 199	1.09	1.84	1.05	2.18	4.93	9.12	17.85V	3.45	2.15	2.57	1.87	1.92	1.87	2.39V
Tanzania 738	....	....	....	....	....	....	....	—	—	—	—	—	—	.51Y
Togo 742	—	.02	—	.01	—	.01	.02Y	—	—	—	—	—	—	—Y
Tunisia 744	.14	—	—	.19	.02	—	—Y	—	—	—	.01	—	—	—Y
Zimbabwe 698	—	—	—	—	.02	—	—Y	2.59	2.15	3.02	6.19	7.21	—	—Y
Africa n.s. 799	.01	.01	.09	1.39	.99	.82	.75Y	1.81	.20	—	.21	.03	.03	.04Y
Asia 507	**76.9**	**40.5**	**48.7**	**97.3**	**105.4**	**53.8**	**65.0Y**	**313.3**	**250.7**	**308.6**	**568.0**	**842.2**	**1,726.7**	**757.3Y**
Bangladesh 513	.57	.12	.44	.75	.02	—	—V	.01	.08	.04	.11	—	.02	—Y
Brunei Darussalam 516	—	—	—	—	—	—	—Y	—	.03	—	—	—	—	—Y
Cambodia 522	.07	.86	—	—	—	—	—Y	.04	—	.01	.01	—	.01	.01Y
China,P.R.: Mainland 924	10.71	7.68	16.67	44.46	69.64	19.62	17.87V	219.26	180.36	236.73	439.40	667.44	1,416.64	464.84V
China,P.R.:Hong Kong 532	12.05	11.82	9.16	10.21	6.62	8.96	7.56V	12.03	7.56	6.95	25.05	7.78	11.83	102.49V

	Exports 2001	2002	2003	2004	2005	2006	2007	Imports, f.o.b 2001	2002	2003	2004	2005	2006	2007
	Millions of U.S. Dollars							Millions of U.S. Dollars						
China,P.R.:Macao........ 546	—	—	—	—	—	—	—V	—	—	.02	—	—	—	—V
Fiji........ 819	.03	—	—	—	—	—	—Y	—	—	—	—	—	—	—Y
French Polynesia........ 887	—	.01	.01	—	.23	.62	.77Y	—	—	—	—	—	—	—Y
India........ 534	28.46	2.80	.14	3.46	4.26	3.11	3.86Y	7.34	5.62	12.55	15.71	19.58	22.79	28.28Y
Indonesia........ 536	2.29	.46	2.53	9.30	2.04	.15	.24V	3.96	3.53	1.97	3.07	2.89	5.94	6.69V
Korea........ 542	.26	.13	.12	4.35	3.40	.79	1.68V	24.17	14.61	17.70	26.92	35.45	86.57	64.65V
Malaysia........ 548	1.88	.80	.32	4.86	.64	.04	.14V	9.20	7.50	7.13	10.78	30.54	65.13	4.88V
Maldives........ 556	—	—	—	—	—	.02	.03Y	—	—	—	—	—	—	—Y
Mongolia........ 948	—	—	.01	.11	—	—	—Y	....	....	....	....	....	....	....
Myanmar........ 518	—	—	—	—	—	—	—Y	—	—	—	—	.01	.03	.03Y
Pakistan........ 564	.79	—	.10	.26	.34	—	—Y	1.08	.82	.74	1.87	2.08	1.89	2.34Y
Philippines........ 566	2.49	.20	.38	.13	.14	.27	.18V	1.03	.93	.23	.50	.43	2.66	4.39V
Singapore........ 576	.18	.15	1.46	.46	.23	.64	.33V	8.17	4.31	2.96	2.64	9.12	30.47	2.87V
Sri Lanka........ 524	—	—	—	—	—	.01	.01Y	.09	.13	.18	.13	.13	.27	.33Y
Taiwan Province of China........ 528	11.65	11.00	11.54	7.55	5.66	5.17	14.55V	18.45	16.77	16.14	33.90	53.71	64.61	63.02V
Thailand........ 578	4.69	4.20	5.75	9.05	11.53	12.79	17.81V	7.81	8.12	4.83	7.44	11.79	15.12	12.46V
Tonga........ 866	—	—	.01	—	—	—	—Y	....	....	....	....	....	....	....
Vietnam........ 582	.80	.22	.08	2.35	.70	1.57	—V	.64	.35	.42	.48	1.25	2.74	—V
Europe........ 170	**8.9**	**4.7**	**10.9**	**57.2**	**107.2**	**230.6**	**166.3Y**	**3.4**	**2.7**	**3.9**	**5.6**	**4.1**	**7.4**	**10.9Y**
Albania........ 914	.04	.08	2.34	2.72	2.65	1.03	1.82V	—	—	—	—	—	—	—V
Belarus........ 913	—	—	—	—	—	—	.07V	—	—	—	—	—	—	—V
Bulgaria........ 918	—	—	—	—	—	—	.24V	.01	.08	.81	.80	.59	.32	.25V
Croatia........ 960	—	—	—	—	—	—	—V	.03	.03	.47	—	.56	2.63	—V
Czech Republic........ 935	—	.01	.17	.07	.05	.16	.05V	.73	.68	.31	.47	.32	.87	.51V
Estonia........ 939	—	—	—	—	—	—	—V	—	.03	—	.04	—	.02	.09V
Gibraltar........ 823	—	—	—	—	—	—	—Y	—	—	—	—	—	.02	.03Y
Hungary........ 944	—	—	—	—	—	—	—V	.05	.02	.12	.84	.15	.46	.44V
Latvia........ 941	—	—	—	—	—	—	.07V	—	—	—	—	—	—	.07V
Lithuania........ 946	—	—	.02	.07	.07	.05	.10V	—	.01	.02	.02	.03	.05	.11V
Moldova........ 921	—	—	.03	.26	.35	—	—Y	—	—	—	—	.04	—	—Y
Poland........ 964	.32	.24	.17	.75	1.04	1.03	2.72V	.23	.25	.13	.20	.29	1.15	.79V
Romania........ 968	1.97	—	.06	.15	.13	.11	5.96V	.30	.54	.14	.01	.33	.08	.11V
Russia........ 922	3.67	4.22	2.21	41.22	101.08	227.80	152.25V	.20	.13	.18	.22	.52	.31	.32V
Slovak Republic........ 936	.08	—	—	—	—	—	.14V	.71	.45	.04	.02	.31	.16	6.42V
Turkey........ 186	2.49	.10	.71	1.76	1.48	.19	2.67V	.62	.45	1.60	2.66	.78	1.20	1.55V
Ukraine........ 926	—	—	—	.04	.11	.16	.20Y	.49	.01	.04	.08	.13	.04	.05Y
Europe n.s........ 884	.30	.10	5.22	10.14	.25	.01	.02Y	—	.01	—	.22	.10	.09	.12Y
Middle East........ 407	**3.1**	**.9**	**12.4**	**39.6**	**44.5**	**30.0**	**36.4Y**	**4.7**	**3.1**	**3.8**	**6.0**	**5.2**	**23.0**	**12.8Y**
Bahrain........ 419	—	—	—	.23	.39	.41	.51Y	—	—	—	—	—	—	—Y
Egypt........ 469	.63	.03	.11	.18	4.47	.56	.70Y	.18	.03	.01	.03	.07	.08	.09Y
Iran, I.R. of........ 429	—	—	—	—	—	—	—Y	.01	—	.01	—	—	—	—Y
Iraq........ 433	—	—	—	.20	—	.14	.18Y	—	—	—	—	—	.01	.01Y
Israel........ 436	1.49	.40	2.78	14.85	13.48	16.22	20.55V	3.49	2.26	1.92	3.76	4.32	21.39	10.80V
Jordan........ 439	—	—	.05	.08	.14	.14	.01V	—	—	—	—	—	—	.03V
Kuwait........ 443	—	—	—	.45	.65	.20	.25Y	—	—	—	—	—	—	—Y
Lebanon........ 446	.03	.10	2.87	9.85	12.68	6.28	7.80Y	.11	.13	.08	.02	.08	.05	.07Y
Libya........ 672	—	—	.04	—	—	—	—Y	—	—	—	—	—	—	—Y
Oman........ 449	.05	—	—	—	—	—	—Y	—	—	—	—	—	—	—Y
Qatar........ 453	—	—	—	.07	—	—	.01Y	—	—	—	—	—	—	—Y
Saudi Arabia........ 456	.74	.22	6.01	7.55	6.03	1.20	1.55Y	.62	.59	.44	.42	.01	.01	.01Y
Syrian Arab Republic........ 463	.12	.07	.25	.05	.03	—	—Y	—	.05	1.33	1.72	.68	1.24	1.54Y
United Arab Emirates........ 466	—	.08	.28	2.50	2.69	1.28	1.66Y	.26	—	—	.03	.02	.22	.26Y
Middle East n.s........ 489	—	—	.04	3.62	3.97	3.56	3.15Y	—	—	—	—	—	—	—Y
Western Hemisphere........ 207	**711.3**	**735.1**	**923.5**	**1,172.0**	**1,218.8**	**1,314.0**	**2,457.2Y**	**1,226.1**	**915.5**	**1,173.4**	**1,586.3**	**1,719.4**	**2,199.0**	**2,959.7Y**
Argentina........ 213	60.83	34.72	66.36	101.84	107.30	168.50	960.38V	478.56	309.40	402.69	619.34	639.19	715.76	778.66V
Aruba........ 314	—	—	—	—	—	—	2.05V	—	—	—	—	—	—	.07V
Bahamas, The........ 313	—	—	—	—	—	—	—Y	42.78	28.48	54.37	8.86	2.26	—	—Y
Belize........ 339	.87	.67	.04	.10	—	—	—Y	—	—	.01	—	—	—	—Y
Bermuda........ 319	—	—	—	—	—	—	—Y	—	—	.11	—	—	—	—Y
Bolivia........ 218	27.19	16.19	21.39	22.43	25.76	29.49	36.59Y	3.12	3.10	2.70	9.41	12.71	25.80	32.02Y
Brazil........ 223	277.89	352.97	424.87	312.50	325.53	327.98	434.04V	563.59	477.58	605.06	821.01	883.94	1,052.63	1,648.19V
Chile........ 228	61.46	49.13	12.62	29.57	64.79	130.84	200.50V	42.01	19.29	32.67	35.59	38.21	73.06	68.93V
Colombia........ 233	10.50	3.02	1.36	1.53	2.36	2.64	18.35V	2.47	1.36	1.77	2.64	1.61	3.03	3.53V
Costa Rica........ 238	.03	1.42	.57	.52	.09	.12	.15Y	.09	.28	.04	.18	.23	.30	.37Y
Dominica........ 321	....	....	....	....	....	....	....	—	—	.01	—	—	—	—Y
Dominican Republic........ 243	.16	.12	.35	.63	.57	.18	.23Y	—	—	—	.02	1.13	—	—Y
Ecuador........ 248	1.48	2.59	2.28	7.09	5.20	3.90	4.84Y	.64	.44	.27	.50	.38	.59	.73Y
El Salvador........ 253	.03	.06	.08	.09	.14	.46	1.48V	.06	.07	.09	.24	.04	.03	.12V
Grenada........ 328	—	—	—	—	—	—	—Y	—	—	—	—	—	.01	.01Y
Guatemala........ 258	.51	.54	1.07	1.01	.40	.27	.33Y	.03	.03	.06	.04	.06	.01	.01Y
Guyana........ 336	—	—	—	.44	.06	—	—Y	—	—	—	—	—	—	—Y
Haiti........ 263	—	.05	—	—	—	—	—Y	—	—	—	—	—	—	—Y
Honduras........ 268	.05	.09	.10	.08	.07	.10	.13Y	—	—	.03	—	.01	.03	.03Y
Jamaica........ 343	.01	.03	—	.01	.02	—	.02V	.01	—	—	—	—	—	—V
Mexico........ 273	.77	1.34	3.20	4.95	4.12	6.64	9.26V	17.59	11.51	9.90	16.02	18.97	36.75	46.74V
Netherlands Antilles........ 353	.55	.18	1.08	2.69	3.00	3.08	3.83Y	—	.01	.03	.03	.08	.07	.09Y
Nicaragua........ 278	.06	.16	.14	.26	.17	.27	—V	—	—	—	.01	—	.17	—V

	Exports							Imports, f.o.b						
	2001	2002	2003	2004	2005	2006	2007	2001	2002	2003	2004	2005	2006	2007
	Millions of U.S. Dollars							*Millions of U.S. Dollars*						
Panama........283	1.17	.54	.51	2.94	1.11	1.59	.11V	2.06	.36	.54	1.22	1.03	.76	.03V
Peru........293	15.62	17.93	17.91	19.81	22.59	27.84	64.18Y	.98	.33	1.00	1.07	1.22	1.03	1.19Y
Trinidad and Tobago........369	.13	.15	.17	.06	.03	—	—Y	.13	.06	.02	—	.10	—	—Y
Uruguay........298	180.02	165.05	243.11	451.21	479.09	420.24	521.52Y	69.32	58.40	59.15	61.27	52.99	59.10	73.34Y
Venezuela, Rep. Bol........299	7.35	9.69	6.48	9.21	6.99	9.60	8.10V	2.61	4.75	2.85	6.08	5.70	139.92	168.80Y
Western Hem. n.s........399	64.67	78.41	119.79	203.07	169.40	180.24	191.08Y	—	—	—	2.72	59.52	89.91	136.80Y
Other Countries n.i.e........910	**.6**	**—**	**.1**	**1.0**	**.8**	**.2**	**.2Y**	**4.8**	**3.0**	**3.5**	**8.4**	**21.9**	**22.6**	**28.1Y**
Cuba........928	—	.05	.04	.01	.01	.04	.05Y	.32	.21	.07	.13	.10	.03	.03Y
North Korea........954	.56	—	.01	.96	.76	.15	.19Y	4.43	2.75	3.39	8.23	21.76	22.62	28.07Y
Countries & Areas n.s........898	**.1**	**.1**	**.1**	**.9**	**.7**	**.8**	**1.0Y**	**.4**	**.2**	**18.3**	**19.2**	**26.4**	**10.3**	**12.8Y**
Memorandum Items														
European Union........998	110.05	83.01	85.68	101.80	103.44	113.97	527.74Y	183.83	141.83	153.38	191.49	205.17	299.09	307.56V
Oil Exporting Ctys........999	10.69	10.52	15.69	29.39	18.39	12.57	11.98Y	7.46	8.88	5.27	9.59	8.62	146.10	175.77Y
Non-Oil Develop.Ctys........201	791.63	773.68	987.15	1,348.17	1,472.35	1,649.05	2,760.44Y	1,547.76	1,167.55	1,490.02	2,164.65	2,571.49	3,811.90	3,567.81Y
PERCENT DISTRIBUTION														
Industrial Countries........101	**18.9**	**17.5**	**19.2**	**15.2**	**11.6**	**12.8**	**18.9**	**21.5**	**21.9**	**18.7**	**17.2**	**19.2**	**24.0**	**30.2**
Developing Countries........202	**81.0**	**82.5**	**80.8**	**84.7**	**88.3**	**87.2**	**81.1**	**78.2**	**77.9**	**80.2**	**81.8**	**79.4**	**75.4**	**69.1**
Africa........607	**.2**	**.3**	**.6**	**.7**	**.9**	**1.7**	**1.4**	**.4**	**.3**	**.3**	**.3**	**.3**	**—**	**.1**
Asia........507	**7.8**	**4.3**	**3.9**	**6.0**	**6.2**	**2.8**	**1.9**	**15.8**	**16.6**	**16.5**	**21.4**	**25.9**	**32.9**	**14.0**
Europe........170	**.9**	**.5**	**.9**	**3.5**	**6.4**	**12.1**	**4.9**	**.2**	**.2**	**.2**	**.2**	**.1**	**.1**	**.2**
Middle East........407	**.3**	**.1**	**1.0**	**2.4**	**2.6**	**1.6**	**1.1**	**.2**	**.2**	**.2**	**.2**	**.2**	**.4**	**.2**
Western Hemisphere........207	**71.8**	**77.3**	**74.4**	**72.1**	**72.2**	**68.9**	**71.8**	**61.6**	**60.6**	**62.9**	**59.7**	**52.9**	**41.9**	**54.6**
Other Countries n.i.e........910	**.1**	**—**	**—**	**.1**	**—**	**—**	**—**	**.2**	**.2**	**.2**	**.3**	**.7**	**.4**	**.5**
ANNUAL PERCENT CHANGE														
World........001	**13.9**	**-4.0**	**30.6**	**31.0**	**3.8**	**12.9**	**79.4**	**-3.0**	**-24.1**	**23.5**	**42.5**	**22.3**	**61.5**	**3.2**
Industrial Countries........101	**19.1**	**-11.2**	**43.5**	**3.5**	**-20.8**	**24.6**	**165.4**	**-16.2**	**-22.8**	**5.3**	**30.9**	**36.7**	**102.1**	**29.9**
Developing Countries........202	**12.7**	**-2.3**	**27.9**	**37.4**	**8.2**	**11.5**	**66.9**	**1.1**	**-24.4**	**27.1**	**45.4**	**18.7**	**53.4**	**-5.4**
Africa........607	**192.6**	**42.0**	**140.1**	**57.8**	**28.9**	**125.5**	**42.8**	**73.3**	**-42.7**	**25.6**	**48.5**	**9.2**	**-79.1**	**54.8**
Asia........507	**118.3**	**-47.4**	**20.4**	**99.7**	**8.4**	**-49.0**	**20.9**	**-6.6**	**-20.0**	**23.1**	**84.1**	**48.3**	**105.0**	**-56.1**
Europe........170	**355.8**	**-46.5**	**130.4**	**422.6**	**87.6**	**115.0**	**-27.9**	**6.5**	**-20.6**	**44.4**	**44.8**	**-25.9**	**79.2**	**46.3**
Middle East........407	**369.3**	**-70.4**	**—**	**218.7**	**12.3**	**-32.6**	**21.2**	**-26.6**	**-34.4**	**24.1**	**57.9**	**-13.4**	**343.8**	**-44.3**
Western Hemisphere........207	**5.6**	**3.3**	**25.6**	**26.9**	**4.0**	**7.8**	**87.0**	**3.2**	**-25.3**	**28.2**	**35.2**	**8.4**	**27.9**	**34.6**
Other Countries n.i.e........910	**—**	**-91.5**	**7.2**	**—**	**-21.6**	**-74.5**	**24.1**	**203.0**	**-37.8**	**17.3**	**141.4**	**161.4**	**3.6**	**24.1**

	Exports							Imports, f.o.b						
	2001	2002	2003	2004	2005	2006	2007	2001	2002	2003	2004	2005	2006	2007
	Millions of U.S. Dollars							Millions of U.S. Dollars						
IFS World Total	**7,025.7**	**7,713.9**	**9,090.7**	**12,616.9**	**16,587.3**	**23,748.7**	**27,679.5**	**7,273.4**	**7,439.9**	**8,244.4**	**9,812.4**	**12,084.0**	**14,896.8**	**19,580.2**
DOTS World Total 001	**6,944.0**	**7,648.2**	**8,859.5**	**12,468.8**	**17,291.2**	**23,743.7**	**26,369.3Y**	**7,199.3**	**7,412.4**	**8,224.5**	**9,757.3**	**12,005.4**	**14,776.6**	**18,786.6S**
Industrial Countries 101	**4,520.0**	**5,158.0**	**5,952.7**	**7,925.8**	**10,801.7**	**14,919.5**	**15,315.4Y**	**3,362.7**	**3,906.4**	**4,610.3**	**5,652.3**	**4,325.6**	**5,052.2**	**7,190.1S**
United States 111	1,772.92	2,005.18	2,396.95	3,682.43	5,393.09	5,721.70	5,153.08S	1,714.20	1,998.08	2,350.13	2,956.37	2,154.58	2,445.31	3,858.23S
Canada 156	143.76	140.64	136.75	313.85	1,038.71	1,608.87	1,991.67S	146.61	74.83	86.98	105.89	187.09	258.51	298.70S
Australia 193	35.91	34.71	53.38	49.61	60.66	38.41	102.37S	41.84	27.01	32.39	39.25	67.61	72.88	80.07S
Japan 158	375.31	371.05	392.99	548.33	602.07	1,227.20	1,973.20S	393.06	218.16	172.77	155.60	420.84	513.96	642.85S
New Zealand 196	1.99	3.20	3.74	6.27	5.66	7.62	11.67S	34.21	22.21	15.24	22.38	17.12	18.71	23.36S
Austria 122	4.50	.76	.49	.44	1.39	1.03	5.65S	16.46	30.41	21.74	29.00	26.73	44.22	58.50S
Belgium 124	—	—	—	—	—	—	308.28S	—	—	—	—	—	—	62.66S
Belgium-Luxembourg n.s. 127	107.95	103.54	96.32	169.58	227.96	513.03	253.62S	53.30	75.53	76.62	85.97	57.84	67.65	49.97S
Cyprus 423	.90	.16	.20	.87	.16	.23	.78S	.01	.16	.19	.48	.13	.07	—S
Denmark 128	6.90	9.04	6.37	18.74	36.40	77.80	113.61S	15.76	13.53	15.90	22.74	21.28	25.94	29.13S
Finland 172	18.49	35.84	29.40	84.66	121.53	229.44	224.19S	41.90	36.51	33.93	47.84	77.27	88.73	75.36S
France 132	68.56	74.40	88.98	106.23	136.05	189.74	212.27S	131.57	88.35	106.46	99.67	136.93	164.39	169.32S
Germany 134	208.81	252.19	256.04	383.42	525.93	815.13	848.97S	214.33	251.61	275.79	300.38	387.18	487.44	654.36S
Greece 174	6.21	6.14	11.23	6.75	9.95	13.45	24.10S	2.81	.38	1.29	1.64	1.10	1.45	6.49S
Iceland 176	.01	.08	.07	.12	.18	.18	.60S	.11	.04	.06	.22	.16	.02	.02S
Ireland 178	1.38	1.57	2.08	2.84	3.24	6.19	3.98S	12.78	14.31	17.46	29.78	22.49	23.54	26.58S
Italy 136	140.62	175.17	189.02	283.65	398.47	770.12	831.05S	134.12	132.72	157.74	135.81	192.63	222.76	352.77S
Luxembourg 137	—	—	—	—	.02	.03	.01S	—	—	—	—	1.52	1.33	1.63S
Malta 181	.05	.16	.07	.14	.14	.13	.10S	.01	.02	.01	.06	.10	.06	.12S
Netherlands 138	96.68	151.28	162.66	385.52	561.05	752.03	584.55S	34.22	61.79	70.64	86.39	63.92	69.50	102.58S
Norway 142	26.08	26.51	12.03	24.20	13.15	26.38	117.83S	3.88	2.71	7.49	21.42	36.26	10.56	10.11S
Portugal 182	26.03	34.76	9.14	6.02	7.67	31.49	35.63S	4.30	2.91	3.49	3.77	8.23	9.47	8.29S
Slovenia 961	.51	.13	.02	.17	.34	.86	1.90S	.78	.25	.32	.37	.98	1.27	2.00S
Spain 184	213.72	241.68	301.60	422.25	560.59	775.37	1,078.52S	165.46	605.88	823.61	1,119.87	187.48	242.36	285.43S
Sweden 144	10.76	18.75	26.22	26.18	65.41	81.56	84.81S	53.79	44.53	45.67	59.33	85.81	109.21	157.79S
Switzerland 146	310.54	565.26	675.17	283.17	789.34	1,693.53	1,104.24S	58.35	122.25	219.33	211.95	76.94	72.76	89.94S
United Kingdom 112	941.44	905.79	1,101.83	1,120.34	242.52	337.97	248.74S	88.90	82.23	75.03	116.07	93.36	100.08	143.80S
Developing Countries 202	**2,409.1**	**2,484.1**	**2,902.6**	**4,536.2**	**6,485.4**	**8,797.3**	**11,017.7Y**	**3,831.7**	**3,489.9**	**3,604.0**	**4,097.3**	**7,670.5**	**9,716.9**	**11,585.6S**
Africa 607	**26.9**	**31.8**	**30.0**	**50.6**	**62.4**	**112.4**	**218.6Y**	**141.3**	**24.0**	**49.7**	**30.3**	**400.9**	**346.8**	**569.2S**
Algeria 612	7.89	15.43	14.36	18.29	28.64	58.94	81.02S	1.37	—	—	—	.11	.04	—S
Angola 614	.02	8.56	.73	4.88	.24	.73	.65S	—	—	—	—	259.02	55.33	306.87S
Benin 638	—	.04	.01	.10	.36	.43	.71S	1.61	—	.02	—	.24	.42	1.34S
Botswana 616	—	—	—	—	.77	—	—S	—	—	.01	—	—	—	—S
Burkina Faso 748	.45	.31	.32	.47	.25	.48	—S	.10	.14	—	—	.90	1.70	3.99S
Burundi 618	—	—	.07	.03	—	—	—S	—	—	—	—	—	—	—S
Cameroon 622	.98	.89	.81	1.02	2.08	3.43	3.35S	—	—	.23	.02	.21	.12	.05S
Cape Verde 624	—	—	.04	.06	—	.17	.50S	—	—	—	—	—	—	—S
Central African Rep. 626	—	—	—	—	.08	.86	—S	—	—	—	—	—	—	—S
Congo, Dem. Rep. of 636	.04	—	.02	—	.27	1.05	.34S	—	.02	.03	—	—	—	—S
Congo, Republic of 634	.03	.02	—	1.22	.10	1.37	2.38S	—	—	—	—	—	—	—S
Côte d'Ivoire 662	—	—	—	—	—	.02	.03S	.61	—	—	.43	.25	.29	.59S
Djibouti 611	.09	—	—	—	1.37	—	.06S	—	—	—	—	—	—	—S
Equatorial Guinea 642	—	—	.01	—	.01	.09	.19S	—	—	.01	—	—	—	7.27S
Ethiopia 644	—	—	—	.03	—	.04	—S	—	—	—	—	—	—	—S
Gabon 646	.13	—	.04	.04	.12	.74	.86S	.04	—	—	—	.01	—	—S
Gambia, The 648	.01	—	.31	.67	1.68	1.89	2.59S	—	—	—	—	—	—	—S
Ghana 652	.82	.26	.60	.16	.70	2.16	2.99S	.15	.01	.01	.02	.09	—	—S
Guinea 656	.01	—	.88	.61	1.76	1.56	1.58S	—	—	—	—	—	—	—S
Guinea-Bissau 654	—	—	—	.02	.10	.07	.09S	—	—	—	—	—	—	—S
Kenya 664	.35	.93	1.47	2.04	.04	—	—S	.04	.02	.01	.01	—	—	—S
Liberia 668	.03	—	.08	.40	.48	.88	1.12S	.01	.18	—	—	—	—	—S
Madagascar 674	.54	.30	.36	.51	.62	1.64	2.14S	—	—	—	—	.01	.01	.06S
Malawi 676	—	—	—	—	—	—	—S	.35	—	—	—	.05	—	—S
Mali 678	1.45	1.28	1.37	1.20	1.08	2.29	2.53S	1.00	—	—	—	.01	.20	.31S
Mauritania 682	—	.04	.70	3.62	.16	.27	.71S	.01	—	—	—	.01	.01	.01S
Mauritius 684	1.00	.52	.30	.52	.35	.59	.45S	.07	.43	.15	.04	.09	.18	.16S
Morocco 686	.85	.36	.30	1.42	2.17	4.67	11.63S	2.37	3.89	3.34	4.37	5.62	7.37	7.20S
Mozambique 688	.06	—	.01	—	.08	.12	.27S	—	—	—	—	—	.02	—S
Namibia 728	—	—	—	—	—	—	—S	—	—	—	.01	—	—	—S
Niger 692	—	—	—	—	—	—	—S	—	.03	.01	—	—	.01	.03S
Nigeria 694	1.46	1.09	.98	2.20	6.59	10.57	18.39S	114.72	.02	30.17	—	108.94	253.93	208.88S
Rwanda 714	—	—	—	—	.12	—	—S	—	—	.01	—	—	—	—S
São Tomé & Príncipe 716	—	—	—	.08	—	—	—S	—	—	—	—	.18	—	—S
Senegal 722	—	.60	1.55	3.27	4.90	5.84	4.59S	—	—	.01	—	—	—	—S
Seychelles 718	—	—	.03	—	—	.04	.08S	.07	.03	.01	.01	.01	.01	—S
Sierra Leone 724	.01	—	.04	—	.07	.02	.04S	.04	—	—	—	.01	.01	.01S
Somalia 726	—	—	—	—	.01	—	—S	—	—	—	—	—	—	—S
South Africa 199	6.26	.71	3.22	5.81	5.37	9.87	73.13S	18.26	18.72	15.02	24.94	24.46	25.97	31.33S
Sudan 732	3.83	—	.73	.96	.23	.50	.40S	—	.01	.02	.03	—	—	.03S

	Exports 2001	Exports 2002	Exports 2003	Exports 2004	Exports 2005	Exports 2006	Exports 2007	Imports, f.o.b 2001	Imports, f.o.b 2002	Imports, f.o.b 2003	Imports, f.o.b 2004	Imports, f.o.b 2005	Imports, f.o.b 2006	Imports, f.o.b 2007
	Millions of U.S. Dollars							*Millions of U.S. Dollars*						
Swaziland.......734	.44	.13	—	.01	—	—	—S	.27	.03	.16	.37	.05	.26	.30S
Tanzania.......738	.03	—	.08	.30	.47	.57	.70S	—	—	—	—	—	—	—S
Togo.......742	.01	.01	.09	.22	.93	.29	.93S	—	.32	.43	.01	—	—	—S
Tunisia.......744	.13	.05	.09	.08	.13	.02	3.97S	.03	.10	.04	.04	.55	.62	.65S
Zambia.......754	—	.27	.43	.36	.08	.13	.15S	—	—	—	—	.01	.07	—S
Zimbabwe.......698	—	—	—	—	—	—	—S	.14	—	—	—	.09	.18	.12S
Asia.......507	**846.4**	**1,015.5**	**1,152.5**	**1,870.3**	**2,659.9**	**3,589.6**	**5,021.7Y**	**916.5**	**697.4**	**798.2**	**912.5**	**1,961.9**	**2,555.9**	**3,356.6S**
Afghanistan, I.S. of.......512	—	—	—	.09	.02	—	—S	.06	.01	—	.01	.07	.06	.05S
American Samoa.......859	—	—	.05	.03	.18	.43	.71S	—	—	—	.01	—	—	—S
Bangladesh.......513	.62	.45	.65	.80	.29	4.49	.80S	.14	.02	.05	.55	9.29	2.85	4.51S
Brunei Darussalam.......516	—	—	—	.01	—	—	—S	.02	—	—	.02	—	—	—S
Cambodia.......522	—	—	—	.03	.07	.01	.01S	—	—	.04	.27	.66	.21	.33S
China,P.R.: Mainland.......924	425.87	598.98	680.11	1,239.53	1,885.65	2,277.26	3,352.05S	371.47	236.81	286.77	325.77	1,035.53	1,525.43	2,030.33S
China,P.R.:Hong Kong.......532	21.38	31.47	30.13	29.06	46.14	42.13	45.55S	11.92	64.90	73.95	104.24	18.62	14.34	81.92S
China,P.R.:Macao.......546	—	.04	.43	.01	.02	—	.05S	.20	.08	.25	.22	.67	.76	.24S
Fiji.......819	.20	.05	.02	—	—	.57	1.16S	—	—	—	—	—	.03	—S
French Polynesia.......887	.03	.03	.01	.07	.05	.02	.03S	—	—	—	—	—	—	—S
Guam.......829	—	—	—	.01	.01	.02	.04S	—	—	—	—	—	—	.01S
India.......534	36.63	21.75	19.12	49.64	79.37	102.65	134.56S	41.23	42.63	38.38	53.04	116.37	138.10	182.53S
Indonesia.......536	39.40	25.09	22.76	21.91	35.73	30.20	22.11S	40.31	15.55	18.56	19.67	55.09	59.47	53.70S
Kiribati.......826	.16	.02	.02	—	—	—	.02S	—	—	—	—	—	—	—S
Korea.......542	108.75	165.61	177.16	202.25	227.83	549.97	953.98S	244.77	186.57	214.20	190.11	327.16	370.73	479.29S
Lao People's Dem.Rep.......544	.02	—	.03	—	.02	.01	—S	.08	—	—	—	.08	.01	.01S
Malaysia.......548	14.84	9.36	5.53	12.37	9.05	7.20	3.91S	34.78	10.10	10.95	21.28	93.27	122.50	98.67S
Mongolia.......948	—	—	—	—	—	—	—S	—	—	—	.13	.04	—	.05S
Myanmar.......518	—	—	—	—	.04	—	—S	.01	—	.03	.03	—	—	.03S
Nauru.......836	—	—	—	—	—	.01	—S	—	—	.07	—	—	—	—S
Nepal.......558	.08	—	.48	.24	.16	.17	—S	.03	—	.01	—	.01	.01	.01S
New Caledonia.......839	.56	.34	.17	1.02	.82	.34	.92S	.01	—	—	.01	—	—	—S
Pakistan.......564	1.30	.60	.82	2.44	2.12	2.82	2.01S	3.44	4.47	5.76	3.26	5.98	8.42	10.02S
Papua New Guinea.......853	.11	.08	—	.01	—	.33	.45S	—	—	—	—	—	—	—S
Philippines.......566	20.52	14.02	11.12	8.97	6.93	45.06	7.44S	12.31	4.24	1.46	1.86	7.46	9.48	18.30S
Samoa.......862	.83	.25	.48	.13	—	.22	.63S	—	—	—	—	—	—	—S
Singapore.......576	7.94	6.77	16.20	10.95	5.49	4.61	7.11S	17.86	12.88	23.34	37.42	26.43	26.70	26.15S
Solomon Islands.......813	—	—	—	—	—	.03	.03S	—	—	—	—	—	—	—S
Sri Lanka.......524	1.39	1.69	1.81	1.08	1.04	1.14	1.41S	3.60	3.03	3.26	2.95	4.45	5.39	4.92S
Taiwan Province of China.......528	86.38	108.11	147.98	240.04	304.70	418.45	411.33S	109.18	101.18	104.58	125.22	180.76	169.60	224.03S
Thailand.......578	70.63	26.10	26.82	30.61	24.89	65.64	52.75S	20.50	13.72	15.46	24.84	61.79	80.71	128.33S
Timor-Leste.......537	—	—	—	.02	—	—	.01S	....	....	....	....	....	....	....
Tonga.......866	.05	.01	.07	.01	—	.13	.16S	—	—	—	—	—	—	—S
Vanuatu.......846	—	—	—	—	.03	.02	.10S	—	—	—	—	—	—	—S
Vietnam.......582	8.71	4.69	10.53	18.96	29.28	35.65	22.39S	4.48	1.20	1.07	1.56	18.21	21.14	13.14S
Europe.......170	**97.3**	**94.7**	**99.2**	**168.5**	**204.6**	**275.2**	**295.3Y**	**107.4**	**38.8**	**65.8**	**45.5**	**218.2**	**206.2**	**294.4S**
Albania.......914	—	—	—	.03	.17	—	.05S	.04	.06	.30	.50	.07	.04	—S
Armenia.......911	—	—	.01	—	.03	—	.04S	—	—	.01	.01	—	.05	.05S
Azerbaijan.......912	—	—	—	.04	—	—	.01S	.01	—	—	—	—	—	—S
Belarus.......913	—	—	.11	.99	—	.03	.64S	.20	.02	—	.06	4.77	5.07	6.18S
Bosnia & Herzegovina.......963	—	—	—	.02	.41	1.89	2.34S	.02	.01	.01	.03	.02	.03	.10S
Bulgaria.......918	13.91	28.50	46.87	70.43	91.86	142.52	159.65S	8.89	7.78	4.31	6.45	23.21	39.35	34.19S
Croatia.......960	.31	.18	.05	.06	.31	.26	1.66S	.08	.02	.03	.01	2.19	.71	.72S
Czech Republic.......935	.79	.36	.62	.85	1.11	2.31	6.02S	6.97	3.91	2.38	2.42	15.16	11.54	12.32S
Czechoslovakia n.s.......937	—	—	—	—	—	—	—S	.02	.01	—	.01	—	.03	.01S
Estonia.......939	.27	.36	.16	.33	.59	.74	1.22S	2.31	.91	—	.26	1.60	1.67	.70S
Faroe Islands.......816	—	—	.02	—	—	—	—S	—	—	—	—	—	—	—S
Georgia.......915	—	.15	.11	.20	—	.31	.85S	—	.01	.01	.03	.10	.25	.67S
Gibraltar.......823	—	—	—	—	—	—	—S	.06	.04	.09	3.42	—	—	—S
Hungary.......944	1.06	.73	.94	1.26	1.20	1.98	1.98S	3.70	1.44	1.42	1.88	4.38	7.05	10.82S
Kazakhstan.......916	.01	—	.01	.01	—	.04	.07S	7.38	.58	—	—	.07	.05	.07S
Kyrgyz Republic.......917	—	—	—	2.51	1.02	.49	.20S	—	—	—	.03	.06	.16	.14S
Latvia.......941	.72	.17	3.40	.04	.36	.17	.16S	15.76	5.00	15.93	3.79	15.72	5.16	18.09S
Lithuania.......946	25.52	18.56	7.07	11.86	6.99	1.76	2.34S	.65	.07	.04	.19	.65	6.69	2.63S
Macedonia, FYR.......962	—	—	—	—	—	—	—S	—	—	—	—	.01	.01	.03S
Moldova.......921	.04	—	—	—	—	—	.06S	.01	.01	—	—	—	—	.02S
Poland.......964	6.79	3.33	1.50	3.77	15.36	8.20	18.97S	4.39	2.53	3.14	4.68	13.78	10.71	12.28S
Romania.......968	5.84	6.31	3.12	9.58	10.01	8.25	8.76S	11.40	1.43	3.38	.45	8.73	13.14	5.49S
Russia.......922	32.17	23.98	14.25	24.99	31.83	25.71	17.33S	22.88	3.26	20.77	10.54	51.13	67.59	131.11S
Serbia & Montenegro.......965	.13	.52	.75	.87	.12	.11	.13S	.01	.01	.02	.03	.01	.12	1.40S
Slovak Republic.......936	.04	.05	.06	—	.01	.13	.34S	2.02	.32	.36	.15	7.31	4.67	2.71S
Tajikistan.......923	—	.01	—	—	—	—	—S	—	—	—	—	.71	.10	—S
Turkey.......186	9.52	11.02	18.84	39.60	41.39	41.26	71.07S	8.55	6.26	6.72	5.71	13.30	9.85	15.04S
Turkmenistan.......925	—	—	—	—	—	—	—S	.01	.01	—	—	—	—	—S
Ukraine.......926	.08	.37	1.20	.74	1.23	39.03	1.42S	10.72	2.23	6.70	4.55	55.11	21.97	39.59S
U.S.S.R. n.s.......930	—	—	—	—	—	—	—S	—	2.47	—	—	—	—	.01S
Uzbekistan.......927	.02	—	—	—	.10	—	—S	.01	—	.09	.12	.01	.22	.01S
Europe n.s.......884	.08	.15	.13	.28	.49	—	—S	1.31	.43	.06	.17	.07	.01	.01S
Middle East.......407	**54.7**	**50.2**	**35.7**	**26.1**	**25.4**	**52.5**	**65.8Y**	**29.6**	**14.0**	**15.0**	**27.0**	**66.5**	**43.3**	**101.8S**
Bahrain.......419	—	.05	.16	.14	.08	.07	.18S	.01	—	.07	—	.17	.30	.16S
Egypt.......469	4.72	3.04	3.01	3.16	3.22	6.01	6.27S	.37	.20	.83	.40	.79	.96	1.32S
Iran, I.R. of.......429	15.73	24.85	13.84	8.10	4.46	1.62	3.71S	.33	.40	.34	.59	1.07	.76	46.50S

	Exports 2001	2002	2003	2004	2005	2006	2007	Imports, f.o.b 2001	2002	2003	2004	2005	2006	2007
	Millions of U.S. Dollars							*Millions of U.S. Dollars*						
Iraq 433	—	—	—	—	.01	—	—S	.01	.03	—	—	.01	—	—S
Israel 436	5.33	3.97	4.67	5.09	6.61	4.49	5.23S	15.99	10.04	11.30	15.99	29.10	31.41	42.48S
Jordan 439	.99	1.38	.69	.74	1.13	.95	.28S	.33	.45	.54	.86	.90	.56	.46S
Kuwait 443	.55	.31	.67	.90	.72	.93	1.22S	—	—	—	—	21.58	—	—S
Lebanon 446	1.17	1.07	1.40	1.12	.73	1.46	1.01S	—	—	.01	—	.06	—	—S
Libya 672	—	—	.02	.19	.36	.23	1.10S	—	—	—	—	—	—	—S
Oman 449	.15	—	—	—	—	20.96	27.03S	.01	—	—	.05	.07	.05	—S
Qatar 453	.02	—	.01	.03	—	.32	.42S	.97	.37	.22	1.69	2.72	4.20	4.07S
Saudi Arabia 456	1.99	3.16	6.55	4.14	4.31	11.13	13.14S	9.49	.88	.14	.77	8.18	4.21	5.66S
Syrian Arab Republic 463	.79	.81	1.05	1.22	1.73	1.43	2.65S	1.87	.62	.74	.46	.44	.63	.84S
United Arab Emirates 466	22.61	10.99	3.04	1.26	1.89	2.74	3.40S	.16	.90	.80	6.20	1.44	.26	.32S
Yemen, Republic of 474	.65	.55	.62	—	.16	.12	.16S	—	.10	—	—	—	—	—S
Western Hemisphere 207	**1,383.8**	**1,291.9**	**1,585.2**	**2,420.7**	**3,533.0**	**4,767.7**	**5,416.3Y**	**2,637.1**	**2,715.7**	**2,675.4**	**3,082.0**	**5,022.9**	**6,564.6**	**7,263.6S**
Antigua and Barbuda 311	.04	.13	.16	.30	.32	.25	.36S	.01	.01	—	—	—	.95	2.08S
Argentina 213	20.62	13.25	19.37	36.46	53.77	74.27	110.74S	403.99	284.74	266.95	303.19	616.31	712.28	1,044.30S
Aruba 314	.65	2.25	1.28	1.58	1.84	1.94	2.02S	.09	11.56	11.29	14.69	.44	56.65	57.09S
Bahamas, The 313	4.63	14.59	5.79	3.24	2.64	3.10	3.76S	.17	99.00	55.14	50.75	.03	—	—S
Barbados 316	.17	.12	.13	.42	.58	.88	1.15S	—	6.43	25.87	8.24	.03	.05	.09S
Belize 339	.03	—	.28	.72	.54	.96	1.06S	—	13.81	2.36	.71	—	—	—S
Bermuda 319	.77	—	.04	.04	.04	.02	.02S	.20	27.04	28.08	30.58	—	.16	.60S
Bolivia 218	98.81	88.59	88.29	131.71	155.61	190.98	232.04S	57.07	69.96	76.57	112.18	112.44	122.97	142.55S
Brazil 223	228.16	194.35	232.21	357.52	459.75	812.28	973.35S	313.30	340.62	416.49	530.89	957.64	1,516.40	1,690.21S
Chile 228	284.01	255.34	414.46	637.03	1,097.57	1,429.30	1,561.96S	470.10	577.56	613.26	700.31	613.94	859.30	946.78S
Colombia 233	151.63	158.01	189.58	262.27	350.28	506.00	581.05S	359.56	330.47	368.18	504.55	728.47	906.21	901.42S
Costa Rica 238	7.66	8.99	9.18	11.05	16.92	27.58	27.78S	4.14	6.55	8.16	7.45	10.21	12.99	20.84S
Dominica 321	.02	.02	.05	.26	.23	.16	.22S	.11	.26	.02	.03	.05	.01	.02S
Dominican Republic 243	13.77	17.26	16.70	19.87	21.33	28.56	34.97S	.68	.19	.22	1.92	2.09	2.41	3.25S
Ecuador 248	124.13	137.69	156.34	207.09	295.97	328.15	385.55S	336.51	151.86	160.74	173.39	887.65	1,062.05	1,150.69S
El Salvador 253	13.01	21.30	8.29	17.15	38.91	20.28	54.56S	.14	.30	.42	.20	.31	.30	3.62S
Greenland 326	—	—	—	.02	—	—	—S	—	—	—	—	—	—	—S
Grenada 328	—	—	.03	.03	.02	.04	.02S	.01	—	—	—	—	—	—S
Guatemala 258	19.19	28.15	26.36	64.77	58.11	69.24	75.49S	8.00	3.27	2.77	8.73	11.23	29.94	32.27S
Guyana 336	.94	1.02	1.36	1.76	1.49	1.94	2.61S	.21	.03	.03	.02	.22	.16	.05S
Haiti 263	9.80	12.68	14.52	17.25	22.36	39.57	44.66S	—	—	—	—	.01	.02	.13S
Honduras 268	7.81	9.73	7.05	10.99	11.63	13.87	19.22S	.09	.16	.24	.12	.29	.18	.25S
Jamaica 343	3.83	1.05	.90	2.62	3.58	3.25	3.04S	.75	.86	.66	.67	.67	1.08	.64S
Mexico 273	128.69	130.17	108.59	229.95	333.44	391.85	339.86S	263.11	200.41	189.32	218.33	418.94	596.01	738.77S
Netherlands Antilles 353	8.01	14.73	1.13	1.66	6.94	10.41	12.59S	.92	33.16	21.12	10.00	13.10	2.12	3.76S
Nicaragua 278	2.00	3.08	3.07	10.71	4.17	6.20	2.87S	.12	.17	.12	.35	.39	3.39	1.31S
Panama 283	79.49	45.62	146.20	173.91	266.22	338.79	195.70S	4.63	100.16	105.70	108.32	9.07	23.34	2.10S
Paraguay 288	.82	.45	.32	.59	.38	.65	.80S	39.52	5.27	24.48	23.19	69.40	109.72	131.16S
St. Kitts and Nevis 361	—	—	.06	.56	.27	1.14	1.18S	.01	.01	—	—	—	—	—S
St. Lucia 362	.08	.01	.28	.82	.49	.66	.74S	—	—	—	—	—	—	—S
St. Vincent & Grens 364	5.78	.03	.13	.13	.24	.12	.29S	.01	—	—	—	—	—	—S
Suriname 366	.07	.11	.31	.39	.72	.91	.94S	.01	.08	.02	.20	.01	—	.01S
Trinidad and Tobago 369	18.47	13.70	14.42	11.71	20.10	42.82	46.23S	5.59	3.36	2.91	1.43	32.94	4.52	13.09S
Uruguay 298	4.30	5.03	8.68	8.98	6.47	8.49	10.15S	20.30	64.40	58.99	58.39	39.95	27.52	36.62S
Venezuela, Rep. Bol 299	146.29	114.36	109.51	196.87	299.83	413.06	688.50S	347.71	240.54	190.86	178.44	497.08	513.82	339.62S
Western Hem. n.s. 399	.10	.05	.13	.29	.23	.01	.82S	—	143.49	44.42	34.71	—	—	.25S
Other Countries n.i.e. 910	**13.4**	**4.4**	**3.7**	**5.4**	**4.0**	**26.4**	**35.8Y**	**1.6**	**12.4**	**1.1**	**1.2**	**3.0**	**1.8**	**2.5S**
Cuba 928	2.96	.78	2.34	2.52	3.03	3.36	4.53S	.46	.37	.37	.41	.65	.54	.59S
North Korea 954	10.41	3.67	1.37	2.92	.96	23.06	31.25S	1.14	11.99	.69	.81	2.37	1.27	1.94S
Countries & Areas n.s. 898	**—**	**1.3**	**—**	**—**	**—**	**.4**	**—S**	**3.1**	**3.5**	**.6**	**.5**	**5.9**	**4.9**	**7.5S**
Special Categories 899	**1.4**	**.3**	**.1**	**1.0**	**—**	**—**	**—S**	**.2**	**.1**	**8.4**	**5.9**	**.3**	**.8**	**.9S**
Memorandum Items														
European Union 998	1,888.67	2,034.95	2,295.42	3,035.92	2,924.43	4,610.90	4,891.77Y	1,006.29	1,455.30	1,749.15	2,152.54	1,423.59	1,706.96	2,246.36S
Oil Exporting Ctys 999	236.09	195.29	171.73	253.90	382.56	550.71	860.04Y	515.08	258.68	241.09	207.40	696.27	836.74	658.75S
Non-Oil Develop.Ctys 201	2,173.02	2,288.85	2,730.92	4,282.26	6,102.82	8,246.56	0,157.67Y	3,316.63	3,231.26	3,362.93	3,889.87	6,974.27	8,880.11	10,926.84S
PERCENT DISTRIBUTION														
Industrial Countries 101	**65.1**	**67.4**	**67.2**	**63.6**	**62.5**	**62.8**	**58.1**	**46.7**	**52.7**	**56.1**	**57.9**	**36.0**	**34.2**	**38.3**
Developing Countries 202	**34.7**	**32.5**	**32.8**	**36.4**	**37.5**	**37.1**	**41.8**	**53.2**	**47.1**	**43.8**	**42.0**	**63.9**	**65.8**	**61.7**
Africa 607	**.4**	**.4**	**.3**	**.4**	**.4**	**.5**	**.8**	**2.0**	**.3**	**.6**	**.3**	**3.3**	**2.3**	**3.0**
Asia 507	**12.2**	**13.3**	**13.0**	**15.0**	**15.4**	**15.1**	**19.0**	**12.7**	**9.4**	**9.7**	**9.4**	**16.3**	**17.3**	**17.9**
Europe 170	**1.4**	**1.2**	**1.1**	**1.4**	**1.2**	**1.2**	**1.1**	**1.5**	**.5**	**.8**	**.5**	**1.8**	**1.4**	**1.6**
Middle East 407	**.8**	**.7**	**.4**	**.2**	**.1**	**.2**	**.2**	**.4**	**.2**	**.2**	**.3**	**.6**	**.3**	**.5**
Western Hemisphere 207	**19.9**	**16.9**	**17.9**	**19.4**	**20.4**	**20.1**	**20.5**	**36.6**	**36.6**	**32.5**	**31.6**	**41.8**	**44.4**	**38.7**
Other Countries n.i.e. 910	**.2**	**.1**	**—**	**—**	**—**	**.1**	**.1**	**—**	**.2**	**—**	**—**	**—**	**—**	**—**
ANNUAL PERCENT CHANGE														
World 001	**1.1**	**10.1**	**15.8**	**40.7**	**38.7**	**37.3**	**11.1**	**–1.5**	**3.0**	**11.0**	**18.6**	**23.0**	**23.1**	**27.1**
Industrial Countries 101	**.6**	**14.1**	**15.4**	**33.1**	**36.3**	**38.1**	**2.7**	**–5.5**	**16.2**	**18.0**	**22.6**	**–23.5**	**16.8**	**42.3**
Developing Countries 202	**1.6**	**3.1**	**16.8**	**56.3**	**43.0**	**35.6**	**25.2**	**2.4**	**–8.9**	**3.3**	**13.7**	**87.2**	**26.7**	**19.2**
Africa 607	**–21.1**	**18.1**	**–5.6**	**68.5**	**23.4**	**80.0**	**94.6**	**53.5**	**–83.0**	**107.3**	**–39.0**	**—**	**–13.5**	**64.2**
Asia 507	**–7.8**	**20.0**	**13.5**	**62.3**	**42.2**	**34.9**	**39.9**	**21.1**	**–23.9**	**14.5**	**14.3**	**115.0**	**30.3**	**31.3**
Europe 170	**31.2**	**–2.6**	**4.7**	**69.8**	**21.4**	**34.5**	**7.3**	**25.5**	**–63.8**	**69.4**	**–30.8**	**379.7**	**–5.5**	**42.7**

	Exports							Imports, f.o.b						
	2001	2002	2003	2004	2005	2006	2007	2001	2002	2003	2004	2005	2006	2007
Middle East.......................... 407	−20.9	−8.3	−28.8	−27.0	−2.6	106.4	25.4	66.0	−52.7	7.2	80.0	146.4	−34.8	134.9
Western Hemisphere............. 207	8.4	−6.6	22.7	52.7	45.9	34.9	13.6	−5.4	3.0	−1.5	15.2	63.0	30.7	10.6
Other Countries n.i.e............... 910	188.8	−66.7	−16.7	46.8	−26.7	562.5	35.4	−70.6	675.7	−91.4	15.8	146.6	−40.0	39.1

	Exports 2001	2002	2003	2004	2005	2006	2007	Imports 2001	2002	2003	2004	2005	2006	2007
	Millions of U.S. Dollars							Millions of U.S. Dollars						
IFS World Total	**32,664**	**36,502**	**36,229**	**39,680**	**39,879**	**47,416**	**50,270**	**34,921**	**37,180**	**39,502**	**42,345**	**46,964**	**54,081**	**57,708**
DOTS World Total.....001	**32,150**	**35,208**	**36,231**	**39,680**	**41,215**	**46,976**	**50,458**	**33,057**	**35,426**	**37,505**	**44,039**	**47,414**	**51,532**	**55,513**
Industrial Countries.....101	**20,832**	**21,164**	**19,752**	**22,586**	**22,226**	**25,764**	**25,266**	**17,360**	**18,513**	**19,262**	**21,067**	**22,156**	**21,117**	**21,421**
United States.....111	8,994	8,691	7,275	7,209	7,429	8,608	8,601	6,412	7,289	7,407	8,276	9,105	8,404	7,843
Canada.....156	282	378	319	281	265	285	258	272	261	229	254	235	241	264
Australia.....193	225	356	407	482	455	480	528	645	575	492	579	531	627	717
Japan.....158	5,057	5,293	5,768	7,983	7,203	7,741	7,304	6,633	7,233	7,640	7,674	8,071	7,004	6,842
New Zealand.....196	19	21	36	38	39	53	114	228	222	256	273	276	271	357
Austria.....122	38	43	24	21	21	53	69	65	57	48	73	46	55	28
Belgium.....124	196	268	277	265	270	732	666	135	137	181	197	214	264	305
Cyprus.....423	1	1	4	4	2	1	2	1	—	1	1	—	1	1
Denmark.....128	30	34	39	27	17	23	33	40	29	36	48	57	55	64
Finland.....172	30	24	29	45	40	47	80	351	99	182	136	83	126	156
France.....132	253	252	217	186	187	212	266	297	291	281	357	398	343	606
Germany.....134	1,323	1,386	1,219	1,436	1,346	1,775	2,149	792	708	927	1,196	1,131	1,374	1,244
Greece.....174	7	7	11	12	30	14	16	2	5	5	2	3	6	2
Iceland.....176	1	—	—	—	—	—	1	—	—	—	—	—	—	—
Ireland.....178	113	138	187	123	123	96	70	278	373	221	312	523	892	1,394
Italy.....136	135	107	125	125	166	198	203	146	163	157	154	179	165	206
Luxembourg.....137	—	6	2	2	—	2	3	—	1	1	2	1	1	2
Malta.....181	—	10	21	32	19	23	22	1	1	1	1	—	1	—
Netherlands.....138	2,976	3,055	2,922	3,583	4,032	4,753	4,150	246	234	310	390	407	414	464
Norway.....142	10	7	5	5	8	9	12	14	6	6	8	10	24	47
Portugal.....182	14	18	16	16	18	15	18	7	7	6	7	7	11	12
Slovenia.....961	3	3	2	2	3	3	3	—	1	—	1	2	2	1
Spain.....184	65	68	109	112	73	96	152	89	103	110	153	92	106	121
Sweden.....144	22	18	18	13	15	27	26	117	94	88	145	103	123	141
Switzerland.....146	41	33	28	29	30	36	41	126	162	211	379	288	255	253
United Kingdom.....112	997	946	695	555	436	482	479	462	464	466	449	393	354	351
Developing Countries.....202	**11,304**	**14,028**	**16,462**	**17,076**	**18,972**	**21,196**	**25,167**	**15,693**	**16,903**	**18,235**	**22,965**	**25,250**	**30,408**	**34,090**
Africa.....607	**53**	**60**	**93**	**90**	**74**	**109**	**173**	**66**	**69**	**49**	**54**	**68**	**61**	**67**
Algeria.....612	3	3	3	2	1	1	2	—	2	1	—	4	8	1
Angola.....614	1	—	—	—	1	—	1	—	—	—	—	—	—	—
Benin.....638	1	1	1	—	—	1	1	—	—	1	—	—	—	—
Burundi.....618	—	—	1	—	—	1	—	—	—	—	—	—	—	—
Cameroon.....622	—	—	—	—	—	—	—	—	1	—	—	—	—	—
Côte d'Ivoire.....662	1	—	1	—	1	3	8	3	2	1	—	—	—	—
Ethiopia.....644	—	—	—	1	—	15	—	—	—	—	1	1	1	1
Ghana.....652	—	—	1	3	1	3	10	—	—	—	—	—	—	—
Guinea.....656	—	—	2	2	—	—	5	—	—	—	—	—	—	—
Guinea-Bissau.....654	—	—	2	—	—	—	1	—	—	—	—	—	—	—
Kenya.....664	—	1	1	1	1	4	9	2	1	4	2	3	1	2
Lesotho.....666	—	—	2	3	2	—	1	—	—	—	—	—	—	—
Liberia.....668	—	—	—	—	—	—	4	—	—	—	—	—	—	—
Madagascar.....674	1	—	1	—	—	—	—	—	—	—	—	—	—	—
Malawi.....676	—	—	—	—	—	—	—	3	7	1	1	1	1	2
Mali.....678	2	—	1	1	—	1	—	—	1	2	1	—	—	—
Mauritania.....682	—	—	—	—	—	1	—	—	4	1	—	—	—	—
Mauritius.....684	1	3	6	13	11	11	1	—	—	1	—	1	—	—
Morocco.....686	5	9	13	9	5	2	1	—	2	1	1	3	5	—
Mozambique.....688	1	—	1	—	1	—	—	1	—	1	—	—	1	—
Namibia.....728	—	1	—	—	—	—	—	—	—	—	—	—	—	—
Niger.....692	—	—	1	—	—	—	—	—	—	1	—	—	—	—
Nigeria.....694	5	6	7	6	12	6	8	—	4	—	—	—	—	5
St. Helena.....856	—	—	—	—	—	—	—	—	1	—	—	—	—	—
São Tomé & Príncipe.....716	—	1	—	—	—	—	—	1	—	1	—	—	—	—
Senegal.....722	—	—	—	1	—	1	2	—	—	—	—	—	—	—
Seychelles.....718	—	—	1	—	—	1	—	—	—	—	1	1	—	1
South Africa.....199	28	31	47	42	35	51	106	43	35	30	44	52	38	52
Sudan.....732	—	—	—	1	—	1	4	—	—	—	—	—	—	—
Swaziland.....734	1	—	—	1	—	—	2	—	1	—	—	—	—	1
Tanzania.....738	—	1	1	—	—	—	1	1	1	—	—	—	—	1
Togo.....742	—	—	—	—	—	—	—	11	—	—	—	—	1	—
Tunisia.....744	1	—	—	—	1	2	2	—	—	—	—	—	1	—
Zambia.....754	—	—	—	—	—	—	—	—	—	—	2	1	—	—
Zimbabwe.....698	—	—	—	—	—	—	—	1	4	—	1	—	2	1
Asia.....507	**10,643**	**13,200**	**15,788**	**16,150**	**18,025**	**20,084**	**23,803**	**11,836**	**13,581**	**14,473**	**19,097**	**20,129**	**23,978**	**27,124**
American Samoa.....859	—	—	1	1	1	—	1	—	—	—	—	—	—	—
Bangladesh.....513	8	6	10	7	19	31	23	10	—	1	3	4	18	5
Bhutan.....514	—	1	2	1	—	—	—	1	—	2	—	—	—	—
Brunei Darussalam.....516	4	3	3	4	9	6	6	—	24	1	—	1	—	—
Cambodia.....522	4	8	6	5	8	9	9	3	2	1	1	2	1	1

	Exports							Imports						
	2001	2002	2003	2004	2005	2006	2007	2001	2002	2003	2004	2005	2006	2007
	Millions of U.S. Dollars							*Millions of U.S. Dollars*						
China,P.R.: Mainland.................. 924	793	1,356	2,145	2,653	4,077	4,617	5,750	975	1,252	1,797	2,659	2,973	3,672	4,001
China,P.R.:Hong Kong................ 532	1,580	2,359	3,094	3,146	3,339	3,676	5,804	1,335	1,583	1,601	1,739	1,929	2,065	2,219
China,P.R.:Macao....................... 546	1	2	1	3	5	5	8	—	—	—	—	1	5	5
Fiji.. 819	2	1	1	3	2	2	2	—	—	—	1	—	—	—
French Polynesia......................... 887	—	—	—	—	—	2	1	—	—	—	—	—	—	—
Guam... 829	13	13	17	27	19	15	16	1	2	1	2	1	—	1
India... 534	71	89	102	89	86	119	244	248	428	304	283	344	401	490
Indonesia.................................... 536	133	205	296	376	476	364	524	760	765	829	939	1,003	990	1,250
Kiribati.. 826	—	—	—	1	—	—	—	—	—	1	—	—	—	2
Korea.. 542	1,044	1,339	1,314	1,113	1,391	1,408	1,784	2,082	2,754	2,401	2,740	2,294	3,218	3,278
Lao People's Dem.Rep................ 544	—	—	—	—	1	—	—	—	—	—	—	—	—	—
Malaysia...................................... 548	1,112	1,653	2,463	2,070	2,457	2,616	2,507	1,080	1,293	1,359	1,981	1,779	2,100	2,283
Maldives...................................... 556	—	—	1	1	1	1	1	—	—	—	—	—	—	—
Mongolia...................................... 948	—	—	—	—	1	—	—	—	—	—	—	—	—	—
Myanmar...................................... 518	6	4	4	7	9	8	8	3	2	2	2	1	2	3
Nauru.. 836	—	—	—	—	—	—	—	—	—	—	—	—	—	1
Nepal... 558	—	1	2	1	—	1	1	—	—	—	—	—	1	2
New Caledonia............................ 839	—	—	—	2	1	20	93	—	—	—	—	—	—	—
Pakistan...................................... 564	8	8	13	20	32	29	39	15	17	12	14	25	43	43
Palau... 565	—	—	—	—	6	10	6	—	—	—	—	1	—	1
Papua New Guinea...................... 853	2	2	2	6	5	5	20	65	14	74	66	115	174	116
Samoa.. 862	—	—	—	1	1	3	2	—	—	—	—	—	—	—
Singapore.................................... 576	2,308	2,472	2,431	2,631	2,706	3,449	3,139	2,073	2,311	2,542	3,421	3,727	4,356	6,219
Solomon Islands.......................... 813	—	—	—	—	—	1	1	8	10	11	9	11	11	15
Sri Lanka..................................... 524	7	8	9	8	12	10	8	3	5	7	6	9	10	6
Taiwan Province of China............ 528	2,127	2,485	2,492	2,228	1,887	2,008	1,973	1,970	1,784	1,861	3,214	3,549	4,145	4,062
Thailand...................................... 578	1,358	1,083	1,234	1,064	1,169	1,325	1,403	925	1,052	1,361	1,572	1,583	2,089	2,277
Timor-Leste................................. 537	—	—	—	—	—	—	2	—	—	—	—	—	—	—
Vanuatu....................................... 846	—	—	—	—	—	—	—	—	—	—	—	—	2	4
Vietnam....................................... 582	62	103	145	681	312	354	436	280	282	304	441	778	673	843
Europe..................................... 170	**99**	**148**	**148**	**311**	**286**	**268**	**305**	**365**	**469**	**548**	**562**	**544**	**445**	**371**
Azerbaijan................................... 912	—	—	—	—	1	—	—	—	—	—	—	—	—	—
Bosnia & Herzegovina................. 963	1	1	1	—	—	—	1	—	—	1	—	—	—	—
Bulgaria....................................... 918	1	2	1	—	2	2	4	1	1	2	6	7	14	9
Croatia... 960	3	1	1	2	1	1	3	—	—	—	—	—	—	—
Czech Republic............................ 935	4	25	58	146	37	26	72	3	5	12	22	62	85	98
Estonia.. 939	—	1	1	—	1	4	2	—	—	—	—	—	—	—
Gibraltar...................................... 823	—	—	—	—	—	—	—	1	—	—	—	—	—	—
Hungary....................................... 944	55	79	42	100	145	102	78	25	20	26	13	8	11	10
Kazakhstan.................................. 916	—	—	—	—	—	—	—	—	—	—	1	2	—	1
Kyrgyz Republic........................... 917	—	—	—	—	—	—	1	—	—	—	—	—	—	—
Latvia.. 941	—	—	—	—	—	1	1	—	—	—	—	—	—	—
Lithuania..................................... 946	—	—	—	1	1	1	1	—	—	—	—	—	—	—
Macedonia, FYR.......................... 962	1	3	2	—	—	—	—	—	—	—	—	—	—	—
Poland... 964	7	10	9	13	17	13	18	1	—	7	2	4	2	4
Romania...................................... 968	1	2	3	4	6	5	6	6	9	2	—	1	1	1
Russia.. 922	—	—	14	19	36	23	26	—	—	345	378	354	206	107
Slovak Republic........................... 936	2	—	—	—	1	4	2	1	—	1	2	15	55	91
Turkey.. 186	7	11	13	23	36	79	73	11	11	23	22	22	21	33
Ukraine.. 926	2	—	—	1	2	3	4	89	115	126	114	70	48	19
U.S.S.R. n.s................................. 930	14	11	—	—	—	—	—	227	306	—	—	—	—	—
Uzbekistan................................... 927	—	1	2	—	—	1	1	1	—	—	—	—	—	—
Europe n.s.................................. 884	1	—	—	—	—	2	11	—	—	—	—	—	—	—
Middle East............................. 407	**199**	**190**	**219**	**249**	**279**	**378**	**507**	**3,085**	**2,397**	**2,685**	**2,611**	**3,886**	**5,302**	**5,618**
Bahrain.. 419	3	3	3	3	3	5	16	13	4	7	2	6	7	5
Egypt... 469	4	8	5	6	8	9	17	1	1	2	4	9	12	15
Iran, I.R. of................................. 429	2	2	13	34	40	69	94	758	433	593	847	1,004	1,689	193
Israel... 436	36	18	20	25	29	24	34	375	97	162	199	169	171	240
Jordan.. 439	1	1	3	3	2	2	3	13	8	15	6	7	5	2
Kuwait.. 443	12	11	15	15	20	30	29	15	49	10	13	18	45	59
Lebanon....................................... 446	3	3	5	5	3	4	4	—	—	—	—	—	1	—
Libya.. 672	—	—	—	—	1	2	1	1	—	—	—	—	—	—
Oman... 449	3	1	3	1	2	2	2	246	216	26	—	1	—	—
Qatar.. 453	2	2	5	8	12	14	33	148	151	127	165	273	35	309
Saudi Arabia................................. 456	33	42	41	39	39	50	67	887	1,000	1,198	1,274	2,182	2,981	3,526
Syrian Arab Republic.................... 463	2	1	1	1	1	1	1	—	—	—	—	—	—	—
United Arab Emirates................... 466	97	97	103	107	117	164	203	606	368	477	100	216	356	1,268
Yemen, Republic of...................... 474	1	1	2	—	1	1	3	21	68	69	—	—	—	—
Western Hemisphere............... 207	**309**	**429**	**215**	**277**	**307**	**356**	**379**	**340**	**386**	**481**	**641**	**623**	**622**	**910**
Antigua and Barbuda................... 311	1	—	—	—	—	—	—	—	—	—	—	—	—	—
Argentina..................................... 213	6	1	4	6	11	25	28	86	155	202	264	247	221	322
Aruba... 314	1	1	—	1	—	—	—	—	—	1	1	—	—	—
Bahamas, The.............................. 313	1	2	1	1	1	1	2	—	—	—	—	—	—	—
Barbados...................................... 316	5	5	5	1	1	—	—	—	—	—	—	—	—	—
Belize... 339	3	1	2	—	—	—	—	1	—	—	—	—	—	—
Bermuda....................................... 319	2	—	1	—	1	—	—	1	—	—	—	—	—	19
Bolivia.. 218	—	—	—	—	—	—	1	—	—	—	—	—	—	—

	Exports							Imports						
	2001	2002	2003	2004	2005	2006	2007	2001	2002	2003	2004	2005	2006	2007
	Millions of U.S. Dollars							Millions of U.S. Dollars						
Brazil.......223	37	35	24	23	76	76	76	93	127	146	231	222	207	291
Chile.......228	12	12	9	12	19	21	27	40	38	53	52	8	22	81
Colombia.......233	1	2	2	4	6	5	3	6	7	6	5	9	6	8
Costa Rica.......238	9	9	7	8	25	43	26	51	15	20	22	48	45	47
Dominican Republic.......243	2	2	1	1	3	2	3	—	—	—	—	—	—	—
Ecuador.......248	—	1	2	3	1	1	2	1	—	—	—	—	1	—
El Salvador.......253	—	—	—	3	1	1	1	—	—	—	—	—	—	—
Guatemala.......258	1	1	1	1	1	4	2	—	1	—	—	—	—	—
Haiti.......263	2	2	—	—	—	—	—	1	—	—	—	—	—	—
Honduras.......268	1	3	8	6	2	2	2	1	—	—	—	1	—	—
Jamaica.......343	2	6	1	2	1	1	2	—	—	—	—	—	—	—
Mexico.......273	163	302	111	134	125	141	161	27	24	18	21	32	44	63
Netherlands Antilles.......353	1	1	—	—	—	—	—	—	—	—	—	—	—	—
Nicaragua.......278	—	—	—	—	—	1	1	—	—	—	1	9	—	—
Panama.......283	40	36	26	18	17	12	17	3	3	5	2	3	14	6
Paraguay.......288	1	1	1	—	1	1	4	—	—	—	—	—	—	—
Peru.......293	10	4	4	5	2	7	9	26	12	10	8	8	25	9
Trinidad and Tobago.......369	—	—	—	—	—	—	1	—	—	—	—	—	—	—
Uruguay.......298	2	1	1	6	3	2	2	2	1	16	33	35	35	42
Venezuela, Rep. Bol.......299	5	2	2	38	7	7	7	2	1	1	1	1	—	—
Western Hem. n.s.......399	—	—	—	—	—	—	1	—	1	—	—	—	1	22
Other Countries n.i.e.......910	**—**	**1**	**—**	**—**	**—**	**1**	**1**	**—**	**—**	**—**	**—**	**1**	**1**	**1**
Cuba.......928	—	—	—	—	—	—	1	—	—	—	—	1	1	1
Countries & Areas n.s.......898	**9**	**4**	**10**	**9**	**9**	**—**	**—**	**2**	**2**	**2**	**3**	**1**	**—**	**—**
Memorandum Items														
European Union.......998	6,272	6,500	6,025	6,818	7,000	8,703	8,581	3,059	2,791	3,068	3,663	3,727	4,445	5,300
Oil Exporting Ctys.......999	294	371	487	627	726	709	972	3,424	2,990	3,262	3,341	4,701	6,105	6,612
Non-Oil Develop.Ctys.......201	11,010	13,657	15,975	16,448	18,245	20,487	24,196	12,269	13,913	14,974	19,624	20,548	24,303	27,478
PERCENT DISTRIBUTION														
Industrial Countries.......101	**64.8**	**60.1**	**54.5**	**56.9**	**53.9**	**54.8**	**50.1**	**52.5**	**52.3**	**51.4**	**47.8**	**46.7**	**41.0**	**38.6**
Developing Countries.......202	**35.2**	**39.8**	**45.4**	**43.0**	**46.0**	**45.1**	**49.9**	**47.5**	**47.7**	**48.6**	**52.1**	**53.3**	**59.0**	**61.4**
Africa.......607	**.2**	**.2**	**.3**	**.2**	**.2**	**.2**	**.3**	**.2**	**.2**	**.1**	**.1**	**.1**	**.1**	**.1**
Asia.......507	**33.1**	**37.5**	**43.6**	**40.7**	**43.7**	**42.8**	**47.2**	**35.8**	**38.3**	**38.6**	**43.4**	**42.5**	**46.5**	**48.9**
Europe.......170	**.3**	**.4**	**.4**	**.8**	**.7**	**.6**	**.6**	**1.1**	**1.3**	**1.5**	**1.3**	**1.1**	**.9**	**.7**
Middle East.......407	**.6**	**.5**	**.6**	**.6**	**.7**	**.8**	**1.0**	**9.3**	**6.8**	**7.2**	**5.9**	**8.2**	**10.3**	**10.1**
Western Hemisphere.......207	**1.0**	**1.2**	**.6**	**.7**	**.7**	**.8**	**.8**	**1.0**	**1.1**	**1.3**	**1.5**	**1.3**	**1.2**	**1.6**
ANNUAL PERCENT CHANGE														
World.......001	**–15.9**	**9.5**	**2.9**	**9.5**	**3.9**	**14.0**	**7.4**	**–4.2**	**7.2**	**5.9**	**17.4**	**7.7**	**8.7**	**7.7**
Industrial Countries.......101	**–15.3**	**1.6**	**–6.7**	**14.3**	**–1.6**	**15.9**	**–1.9**	**–.8**	**6.6**	**4.0**	**9.4**	**5.2**	**–4.7**	**1.4**
Developing Countries.......202	**–17.0**	**24.1**	**17.4**	**3.7**	**11.1**	**11.7**	**18.7**	**–7.6**	**7.7**	**7.9**	**25.9**	**9.9**	**20.4**	**12.1**
Africa.......607	**4.1**	**13.1**	**54.6**	**–3.6**	**–17.7**	**48.5**	**58.2**	**–16.8**	**4.6**	**–29.7**	**10.9**	**25.0**	**–9.4**	**9.0**
Asia.......507	**–16.2**	**24.0**	**19.6**	**2.3**	**11.6**	**11.4**	**18.5**	**–6.3**	**14.7**	**6.6**	**32.0**	**5.4**	**19.1**	**13.1**
Europe.......170	**–58.4**	**48.5**	**.1**	**110.0**	**–7.8**	**–6.5**	**14.0**	**3.0**	**28.4**	**16.8**	**2.6**	**–3.2**	**–18.2**	**–16.6**
Middle East.......407	**2.5**	**–4.5**	**14.8**	**14.0**	**12.1**	**35.2**	**34.3**	**–15.2**	**–22.3**	**12.0**	**–2.8**	**48.8**	**36.5**	**5.9**
Western Hemisphere.......207	**–27.9**	**39.0**	**–49.8**	**28.3**	**11.1**	**16.1**	**6.4**	**18.7**	**13.6**	**24.4**	**33.3**	**–2.9**	**–.2**	**46.4**
Other Countries n.i.e.......910	**–46.7**	**224.3**	**–42.9**	**–30.6**	**–45.4**	**287.1**	**–1.8**	**–34.6**	**–99.3**	**—**	**–92.4**	**—**	**–34.1**	**–22.0**

	Exports 2001	2002	2003	2004	2005	2006	2007	Imports 2001	2002	2003	2004	2005	2006	2007
	Millions of U.S. Dollars							*Millions of U.S. Dollars*						
IFS World Total	**36,092**	**41,010**	**53,537**	**73,792**	**89,347**	**109,584**	**136,360**	**50,275**	**55,113**	**68,004**	**87,909**	**100,904**	**124,647**	**159,541**
DOTS World Total......001	**36,091**	**41,008**	**53,576**	**73,781**	**89,256**	**110,890**	**140,409**	**50,275**	**55,112**	**68,003**	**88,155**	**101,413**	**127,209**	**166,143**
Industrial Countries......101	**27,204**	**30,925**	**40,238**	**54,291**	**63,788**	**76,965**	**95,615**	**35,309**	**38,933**	**47,368**	**59,557**	**71,611**	**86,484**	**112,626**
United States......111	854	1,101	1,200	1,776	1,847	2,120	2,079	1,716	1,818	1,786	2,119	1,223	1,665	2,129
Canada......156	168	180	231	264	488	435	520	169	160	196	246	167	219	224
Australia......193	21	35	34	174	179	141	203	39	27	40	74	30	75	123
Japan......158	65	71	94	171	180	192	298	987	1,039	1,269	1,711	950	1,181	1,558
New Zealand......196	2	2	3	12	17	11	17	11	11	19	20	17	13	16
Austria......122	732	752	911	1,456	1,860	2,035	2,641	983	1,056	1,320	1,575	2,558	3,014	3,620
Belgium......124	1,114	1,330	1,730	2,358	2,662	3,063	3,761	1,369	1,529	1,781	2,239	3,597	4,064	5,342
Cyprus......423	54	98	57	68	31	47	95	47	94	42	39	47	28	82
Denmark......128	933	1,134	1,268	1,649	1,878	2,182	2,691	881	955	1,006	1,333	1,631	1,913	2,452
Finland......172	299	284	356	585	692	751	1,007	849	857	1,025	1,232	1,320	1,541	2,090
France......132	1,955	2,473	3,277	4,454	5,548	6,906	8,548	3,425	3,845	4,809	5,924	5,792	6,893	8,494
Germany......134	12,414	13,248	17,281	22,134	25,185	30,094	36,317	12,046	13,402	16,584	21,481	30,039	36,899	48,221
Greece......174	124	150	160	215	283	390	578	131	149	157	200	242	226	335
Iceland......176	198	39	37	39	118	103	127	25	54	34	42	66	66	38
Ireland......178	104	125	149	218	291	365	523	292	323	365	461	307	462	688
Italy......136	1,955	2,264	3,084	4,514	5,482	7,256	9,294	4,150	4,615	5,791	6,939	6,676	8,159	10,909
Luxembourg......137	32	45	51	78	86	82	167	70	77	108	141	221	262	375
Malta......181	22	11	10	47	9	15	23	24	14	29	40	4	8	21
Netherlands......138	1,707	1,841	2,407	3,166	3,716	4,264	5,363	1,786	1,935	2,302	3,072	5,993	7,250	9,452
Norway......142	408	729	1,130	1,319	1,877	2,136	2,515	491	673	1,204	1,268	1,365	1,314	1,325
Portugal......182	260	364	419	468	431	531	467	161	203	253	285	187	291	380
Slovenia......961	128	139	181	244	292	359	471	265	308	377	459	604	637	884
Spain......184	581	724	1,135	1,805	2,217	2,754	4,055	1,284	1,459	1,772	2,352	2,008	2,342	3,370
Sweden......144	984	1,329	1,933	2,577	2,749	3,559	4,516	1,351	1,458	1,778	2,381	2,598	3,268	4,419
Switzerland......146	289	331	402	513	680	835	1,003	667	731	791	1,000	817	888	1,096
United Kingdom......112	1,800	2,126	2,699	3,986	4,990	6,338	8,339	2,093	2,142	2,532	2,922	3,153	3,806	4,985
Developing Countries......202	**8,767**	**9,984**	**13,231**	**19,373**	**25,225**	**33,777**	**44,409**	**14,901**	**16,127**	**20,484**	**28,524**	**29,658**	**40,045**	**51,646**
Africa......607	**415**	**326**	**341**	**487**	**631**	**775**	**1,095**	**423**	**464**	**525**	**609**	**406**	**712**	**875**
Algeria......612	107	74	86	84	118	118	205	5	14	6	3	—	—	1
Angola......614	3	1	2	1	1	3	6	—	—	—	—	—	1	1
Benin......638	—	1	1	2	1	1	2	1	—	—	—	—	—	—
Botswana......616	2	1	1	—	—	—	—	—	—	1	2	—	—	—
Burkina Faso......748	1	1	1	1	1	1	—	—	—	—	1	—	—	—
Burundi......618	—	—	—	—	—	—	—	2	—	1	1	—	—	—
Cameroon......622	1	2	3	4	7	4	8	3	3	5	4	3	6	7
Chad......628	1	—	1	1	—	1	1	4	3	3	3	—	—	—
Comoros......632	—	—	—	—	—	—	—	—	—	1	—	—	—	—
Congo, Dem. Rep. of......636	—	—	1	1	—	—	1	—	—	—	1	1	22	39
Congo, Republic of......634	2	—	—	1	3	1	5	1	1	1	1	—	1	1
Côte d'Ivoire......662	3	4	3	7	12	11	23	66	84	115	97	103	104	104
Djibouti......611	6	5	8	9	1	1	1	—	—	—	—	—	—	—
Equatorial Guinea......642	—	—	—	—	—	3	1	—	—	—	—	—	—	—
Eritrea......643	1	1	1	1	1	—	—	—	—	1	—	—	—	—
Ethiopia......644	3	2	3	4	4	5	4	1	1	3	3	2	2	4
Gabon......646	—	1	2	1	2	2	3	1	1	2	2	—	2	1
Gambia, The......648	—	—	—	—	—	1	1	—	—	—	—	—	—	—
Ghana......652	10	10	9	17	15	12	16	5	5	6	10	9	21	20
Guinea......656	1	1	1	1	1	1	1	1	2	5	2	1	3	2
Kenya......664	1	—	2	1	4	7	7	10	9	9	13	12	12	10
Liberia......668	159	64	60	67	70	107	212	94	80	113	143	49	199	209
Madagascar......674	—	—	—	1	1	1	1	1	1	1	1	1	—	—
Malawi......676	—	1	1	1	1	1	1	11	20	3	12	7	13	19
Mali......678	1	1	1	1	1	2	1	1	1	—	1	—	—	—
Mauritania......682	3	17	17	12	6	1	4	—	—	—	2	—	—	—
Mauritius......684	—	3	1	1	3	2	2	1	2	2	5	4	4	2
Morocco......686	44	45	40	84	112	137	154	41	41	56	73	48	56	83
Mozambique......688	—	2	3	—	7	8	8	—	3	2	2	1	5	10
Namibia......728	—	—	—	—	—	—	—	—	1	1	2	1	2	2
Niger......692	1	—	—	—	1	1	2	—	—	—	—	—	—	—
Nigeria......694	25	37	39	35	44	35	82	4	2	1	3	3	1	2
Rwanda......714	—	—	—	—	—	—	—	—	1	—	—	—	1	—
St. Helena......856	—	—	—	—	—	—	—	—	—	1	—	—	—	—
São Tomé & Príncipe......716	1	—	1	—	—	—	—	1	—	—	1	—	—	—
Senegal......722	3	2	2	3	6	6	12	—	—	—	—	—	1	1
Seychelles......718	—	—	—	1	—	2	4	—	—	—	—	—	—	—
Sierra Leone......724	1	1	1	1	1	1	1	1	1	—	3	—	—	—
South Africa......199	20	35	36	102	169	222	253	80	85	93	123	107	198	258
Sudan......732	6	7	4	7	11	16	10	3	3	3	5	2	2	1
Tanzania......738	2	—	1	1	1	7	3	5	3	3	3	2	6	10

	Exports 2001	2002	2003	2004	2005	2006	2007	Imports 2001	2002	2003	2004	2005	2006	2007
	Millions of U.S. Dollars							Millions of U.S. Dollars						
Togo.......742	2	1	1	1	2	7	8	9	8	3	2	4	8	9
Tunisia.......744	4	4	7	29	19	42	48	44	56	64	67	25	27	43
Uganda.......746	—	—	1	1	2	2	2	7	6	9	11	15	8	8
Zambia.......754	—	—	—	—	—	—	3	1	1	—	1	1	3	23
Zimbabwe.......698	—	—	—	—	—	—	—	16	25	9	8	5	3	5
Asia.......507	**598**	**564**	**754**	**1,229**	**1,554**	**1,974**	**2,284**	**3,881**	**4,604**	**5,844**	**8,146**	**5,865**	**8,438**	**12,388**
Afghanistan, I.S. of.......512	3	2	3	3	5	20	3	1	—	—	—	—	—	—
Bangladesh.......513	4	3	3	1	7	5	3	13	14	20	37	24	35	39
Brunei Darussalam.......516	—	—	—	—	—	1	1	—	—	—	—	—	—	—
Cambodia.......522	—	1	2	10	9	12	4	2	2	2	4	—	—	1
China,P.R.: Mainland.......924	180	207	253	556	592	769	996	1,620	2,077	2,890	4,065	3,229	4,497	6,945
China,P.R.:Hong Kong.......532	38	30	41	40	59	90	163	46	42	59	53	40	69	126
China,P.R.:Macao.......546	—	1	—	—	—	1	1	3	3	4	8	1	2	2
French Polynesia.......887	—	—	—	—	—	—	1	—	—	3	—	—	—	—
Guam.......829	—	—	1	—	—	—	—	—	—	—	—	—	—	—
India.......534	94	34	81	84	200	203	163	157	183	225	310	269	354	539
Indonesia.......536	7	16	18	59	41	41	92	188	224	267	336	195	256	294
Kiribati.......826	—	—	—	—	—	—	—	—	1	—	—	—	—	—
Korea.......542	28	37	58	72	118	225	290	521	578	644	1,020	1,030	1,726	2,786
Lao People's Dem.Rep.......544	—	—	—	1	—	—	3	1	2	5	8	6	7	8
Malaysia.......548	33	41	41	57	46	98	127	259	273	342	438	151	295	226
Maldives.......556	—	—	—	—	—	—	—	—	—	—	1	—	—	—
Mongolia.......948	6	6	7	8	9	13	24	—	—	—	—	—	—	—
Myanmar.......518	—	—	—	—	—	—	—	3	2	2	4	3	5	2
Nauru.......836	1	—	—	—	—	—	—	—	—	—	1	—	—	—
Nepal.......558	—	4	—	4	—	—	—	1	—	—	—	—	—	—
New Caledonia.......839	—	—	—	—	—	1	1	—	—	—	—	—	—	—
Pakistan.......564	10	12	11	34	65	33	25	25	36	44	65	34	41	53
Papua New Guinea.......853	—	—	—	—	—	—	—	3	2	1	1	1	—	1
Philippines.......566	5	3	6	21	9	6	13	65	87	72	107	26	33	39
Samoa.......862	—	—	—	—	—	—	—	1	—	—	—	—	—	—
Singapore.......576	53	55	95	56	96	189	92	182	224	291	377	104	119	119
Sri Lanka.......524	4	4	4	9	34	19	21	18	16	22	29	20	26	34
Taiwan Province of China.......528	65	65	52	70	76	110	119	477	510	566	782	470	608	662
Thailand.......578	46	22	29	98	114	68	72	190	203	244	329	150	189	269
Tuvalu.......869	—	—	2	—	—	—	—	—	—	—	—	—	—	—
Vanuatu.......846	—	—	—	2	21	—	—	—	—	4	2	20	—	—
Vietnam.......582	21	19	44	42	53	70	69	103	124	134	168	92	175	241
Wallis-Futuna.......857	—	—	—	—	—	—	—	—	—	—	1	—	—	—
Europe.......170	**6,954**	**8,306**	**11,253**	**16,493**	**21,351**	**29,100**	**38,496**	**9,525**	**10,033**	**12,838**	**17,616**	**21,964**	**28,824**	**36,031**
Albania.......914	1	1	4	5	6	7	16	—	—	—	1	—	1	1
Armenia.......911	3	4	5	7	7	8	10	—	—	1	1	4	7	6
Azerbaijan.......912	30	27	34	45	52	70	70	2	3	5	7	9	6	4
Belarus.......913	276	261	396	565	722	988	1,134	145	227	386	699	851	1,071	1,136
Bosnia & Herzegovina.......963	41	73	88	84	120	67	91	4	5	5	9	38	68	43
Bulgaria.......918	90	83	124	178	256	403	548	60	62	89	131	150	220	244
Croatia.......960	103	122	172	229	279	342	480	32	30	43	62	46	105	107
Czech Republic.......935	1,432	1,640	2,172	3,189	4,072	6,144	7,777	1,738	1,788	2,332	3,188	3,863	4,834	6,412
Estonia.......939	104	122	172	259	408	569	802	40	39	60	81	116	113	164
Faroe Islands.......816	2	—	—	13	—	2	4	4	3	2	14	5	2	3
Georgia.......915	6	4	4	10	13	24	62	1	—	1	3	2	3	5
Gibraltar.......823	—	—	1	4	26	7	20	—	—	—	4	—	—	18
Hungary.......944	755	927	1,294	1,894	2,537	3,374	4,081	796	927	1,217	1,664	1,877	2,798	3,584
Kazakhstan.......916	62	62	98	155	212	350	479	103	95	123	446	476	293	408
Kosovo.......967	—	—	—	—	2	6	7	—	—	—	—	—	—	—
Kyrgyz Republic.......917	3	3	5	10	10	16	28	2	2	2	2	1	1	2
Latvia.......941	229	283	354	441	570	797	1,090	34	38	44	178	449	186	267
Lithuania.......946	757	933	1,327	1,250	1,232	1,650	2,293	278	191	304	476	703	811	1,004
Macedonia, FYR.......962	11	18	23	67	84	99	129	3	—	2	5	4	6	8
Moldova.......921	45	50	80	93	111	140	176	5	4	4	23	28	35	121
Montenegro, Rep. of.......943	—	—	—	—	—	10	23	—	—	—	—	—	—	—
Romania.......968	226	280	462	731	1,018	1,306	2,182	129	143	222	406	395	550	669
Russia.......922	1,059	1,332	1,512	2,843	3,958	4,756	6,506	4,422	4,407	5,215	6,391	8,775	12,147	14,398
Serbia, Rep. of.......942	—	—	—	—	—	223	225	—	—	—	—	—	77	102
Serbia & Montenegro.......965	37	55	101	142	89	—	—	10	11	19	29	24	—	—
Slovak Republic.......936	517	573	873	1,318	1,707	2,323	3,065	756	812	1,044	1,453	1,849	2,267	3,238
Tajikistan.......923	1	4	6	7	9	18	17	20	27	21	31	2	6	10
Turkey.......186	138	255	358	901	1,196	1,315	1,528	399	629	873	1,111	1,064	1,269	1,710
Turkmenistan.......925	4	2	4	7	20	21	17	4	1	46	105	79	3	1
Ukraine.......926	1,003	1,181	1,561	2,023	2,589	4,006	5,579	449	492	745	1,038	997	1,312	1,684
Uzbekistan.......927	19	11	25	24	46	63	64	91	45	33	58	158	633	681
Europe n.s.......884	1	1	—	—	—	—	—	—	52	—	1	—	—	—
Middle East.......407	**366**	**387**	**415**	**548**	**852**	**1,082**	**1,302**	**190**	**201**	**261**	**338**	**248**	**433**	**480**
Bahrain.......419	1	2	2	8	3	8	15	—	—	—	—	—	—	—
Egypt.......469	94	89	70	57	126	166	151	9	11	12	19	18	24	34
Iran, I.R. of.......429	52	34	73	65	125	108	106	16	26	53	19	10	15	12
Iraq.......433	—	1	7	21	93	75	72	—	—	—	—	—	—	—

	Exports 2001	Exports 2002	Exports 2003	Exports 2004	Exports 2005	Exports 2006	Exports 2007	Imports 2001	Imports 2002	Imports 2003	Imports 2004	Imports 2005	Imports 2006	Imports 2007
	Millions of U.S. Dollars							*Millions of U.S. Dollars*						
Israel.......... 436	52	58	50	91	120	177	216	123	111	117	153	139	199	264
Jordan.......... 439	5	6	10	15	35	27	25	4	7	14	20	15	12	—
Kuwait.......... 443	7	10	10	12	20	23	33	—	—	—	—	—	119	—
Lebanon.......... 446	12	8	6	13	13	20	21	1	1	1	7	1	3	3
Libya.......... 672	7	6	10	9	12	25	38	4	2	2	1	4	3	16
Oman.......... 449	3	7	1	4	17	47	52	1	1	—	2	2	1	2
Qatar.......... 453	1	1	5	3	11	11	16	—	—	—	—	—	—	—
Saudi Arabia.......... 456	36	67	67	120	98	147	202	12	14	29	61	21	12	112
Syrian Arab Republic.......... 463	20	13	14	24	22	18	38	1	1	1	6	9	16	22
United Arab Emirates.......... 466	43	52	80	94	143	221	306	18	27	33	51	30	30	13
Yemen, Republic of.......... 474	33	34	10	12	13	10	10	—	—	—	—	—	—	—
Western Hemisphere.......... 207	**434**	**401**	**468**	**615**	**837**	**847**	**1,231**	**882**	**825**	**1,017**	**1,815**	**1,175**	**1,637**	**1,873**
Antigua and Barbuda.......... 311	55	29	33	57	15	6	85	3	1	1	112	7	—	—
Argentina.......... 213	17	10	25	34	78	64	68	70	89	193	307	312	394	558
Aruba.......... 314	—	—	—	—	1	—	1	—	—	—	—	—	—	—
Bahamas, The.......... 313	24	11	45	42	239	213	292	51	24	76	220	217	324	368
Barbados.......... 316	—	16	—	—	—	—	—	—	16	—	—	—	—	3
Belize.......... 339	—	1	1	1	7	2	3	—	—	1	3	5	—	—
Bermuda.......... 319	27	47	7	—	66	—	1	—	5	7	—	5	—	—
Bolivia.......... 218	—	—	1	1	—	—	1	—	1	31	—	—	1	1
Brazil.......... 223	89	101	99	113	134	177	278	386	236	239	533	279	341	356
Chile.......... 228	7	19	16	16	32	39	46	16	20	25	33	39	250	272
Colombia.......... 233	7	9	17	20	18	25	33	24	21	24	33	21	18	27
Costa Rica.......... 238	3	2	3	5	6	4	5	25	25	20	40	20	6	6
Dominica.......... 321	1	—	5	5	—	—	2	—	—	3	—	—	—	—
Dominican Republic.......... 243	4	6	10	17	24	6	24	3	3	4	3	1	12	9
Ecuador.......... 248	3	5	3	5	5	6	5	89	74	78	78	73	51	42
El Salvador.......... 253	1	1	1	1	—	2	2	1	1	1	2	—	—	—
Greenland.......... 326	—	—	—	—	—	—	—	1	1	2	2	—	—	—
Guatemala.......... 258	3	3	2	2	5	3	5	4	4	3	2	1	2	5
Guyana.......... 336	—	—	—	—	—	—	—	—	—	—	1	—	—	—
Haiti.......... 263	1	—	1	—	1	1	—	—	—	—	—	—	—	—
Honduras.......... 268	—	1	—	3	2	2	1	22	41	55	10	1	2	2
Jamaica.......... 343	1	1	1	1	2	9	2	—	—	2	7	—	—	—
Mexico.......... 273	104	53	77	89	81	121	150	84	97	125	120	104	103	141
Netherlands Antilles.......... 353	—	—	2	25	—	1	2	—	3	1	26	—	—	—
Nicaragua.......... 278	—	1	—	—	—	—	1	—	—	—	1	—	—	1
Panama.......... 283	27	54	86	74	28	66	70	45	114	66	146	31	68	20
Paraguay.......... 288	—	—	—	—	—	1	1	4	1	—	1	1	1	3
Peru.......... 293	3	4	5	9	10	7	13	20	13	6	14	35	48	42
St. Vincent & Grens.......... 364	1	—	3	44	1	—	7	4	1	6	50	1	—	6
Suriname.......... 366	1	1	2	1	2	1	1	1	1	2	9	1	—	—
Trinidad and Tobago.......... 369	5	2	4	5	5	4	2	—	—	—	—	—	—	—
Uruguay.......... 298	3	1	5	3	4	5	5	23	27	36	37	8	10	8
Venezuela, Rep. Bol.......... 299	44	18	12	39	53	61	83	1	2	11	21	10	5	2
Western Hem. n.s.......... 399	3	1	1	3	18	20	41	2	1	1	2	3	—	—
Other Countries n.i.e.......... 910	**5**	**10**	**19**	**9**	**18**	**15**	**19**	**13**	**12**	**10**	**11**	**18**	**7**	**1**
Cuba.......... 928	3	9	17	8	14	12	19	2	1	1	4	—	1	1
North Korea.......... 954	2	1	2	2	4	3	1	11	11	8	7	17	6	1
Countries & Areas n.s.......... 898	**9**	**9**	**8**	**76**	**133**	**41**	**61**	**39**	**—**	**68**	**45**	**85**	**619**	**1,713**
Special Categories.......... 899	**64**	**60**	**69**	**26**	**65**	**67**	**83**	**7**	**—**	**28**	**—**	**38**	**3**	**—**
Memorandum Items														
European Union.......... 998	28,992	32,914	43,299	58,373	68,927	85,847	107,963	34,845	38,215	47,031	60,115	75,834	92,073	120,786
Oil Exporting Ctys.......... 999	331	323	409	545	775	911	1,287	250	312	402	496	274	443	453
Non-Oil Develop.Ctys.......... 201	8,436	9,662	12,822	18,828	24,450	32,867	43,122	14,651	15,815	20,082	28,028	29,384	39,602	51,193
PERCENT DISTRIBUTION														
Industrial Countries.......... 101	**75.4**	**75.4**	**75.1**	**73.6**	**71.5**	**69.4**	**68.1**	**70.2**	**70.6**	**69.7**	**67.6**	**70.6**	**68.0**	**67.8**
Developing Countries.......... 202	**24.3**	**24.3**	**24.7**	**26.3**	**28.3**	**30.5**	**31.6**	**29.6**	**29.3**	**30.1**	**32.4**	**29.2**	**31.5**	**31.1**
Africa.......... 607	**1.2**	**.8**	**.6**	**.7**	**.7**	**.7**	**.8**	**.8**	**.8**	**.8**	**.7**	**.4**	**.6**	**.5**
Asia.......... 507	**1.7**	**1.4**	**1.4**	**1.7**	**1.7**	**1.8**	**1.6**	**7.7**	**8.4**	**8.6**	**9.2**	**5.8**	**6.6**	**7.5**
Europe.......... 170	**19.3**	**20.3**	**21.0**	**22.4**	**23.9**	**26.2**	**27.4**	**18.9**	**18.2**	**18.9**	**20.0**	**21.7**	**22.7**	**21.7**
Middle East.......... 407	**1.0**	**.9**	**.8**	**.7**	**1.0**	**1.0**	**.9**	**.4**	**.4**	**.4**	**.4**	**.2**	**.3**	**.3**
Western Hemisphere.......... 207	**1.2**	**1.0**	**.9**	**.8**	**.9**	**.8**	**.9**	**1.8**	**1.5**	**1.5**	**2.1**	**1.2**	**1.3**	**1.1**
ANNUAL PERCENT CHANGE														
World.......... 001	**14.0**	**13.6**	**30.6**	**37.7**	**21.0**	**24.2**	**26.6**	**2.7**	**9.6**	**23.4**	**29.6**	**15.0**	**25.4**	**30.6**
Industrial Countries.......... 101	**12.4**	**13.7**	**30.1**	**34.9**	**17.5**	**20.7**	**24.2**	**1.6**	**10.3**	**21.7**	**25.7**	**20.2**	**20.8**	**30.2**
Developing Countries.......... 202	**18.7**	**13.9**	**32.5**	**46.4**	**30.2**	**33.9**	**31.5**	**5.3**	**8.2**	**27.0**	**39.2**	**4.0**	**35.0**	**29.0**
Africa.......... 607	**56.7**	**−21.4**	**4.5**	**43.0**	**29.4**	**22.8**	**41.3**	**37.8**	**9.8**	**13.1**	**16.1**	**−33.3**	**75.2**	**22.9**
Asia.......... 507	**2.4**	**−5.8**	**33.7**	**63.0**	**26.5**	**27.0**	**15.7**	**3.4**	**18.7**	**26.9**	**39.4**	**−28.0**	**43.9**	**46.8**
Europe.......... 170	**20.4**	**19.4**	**35.5**	**46.6**	**29.5**	**36.3**	**32.3**	**3.2**	**5.3**	**28.0**	**37.2**	**24.7**	**31.2**	**25.0**
Middle East.......... 407	**−4.4**	**5.9**	**7.2**	**32.1**	**55.4**	**26.9**	**20.4**	**−9.9**	**5.9**	**29.7**	**29.6**	**−26.7**	**74.7**	**10.8**
Western Hemisphere.......... 207	**14.0**	**−7.6**	**16.7**	**31.4**	**36.0**	**1.2**	**45.4**	**36.7**	**−6.5**	**23.3**	**78.5**	**−35.3**	**39.4**	**14.4**
Other Countries n.i.e.......... 910	**83.8**	**90.7**	**84.3**	**−50.0**	**93.5**	**−15.2**	**25.4**	**22.6**	**−8.2**	**−21.4**	**11.1**	**67.0**	**−63.2**	**−77.3**

	Exports 2001	Exports 2002	Exports 2003	Exports 2004	Exports 2005	Exports 2006	Exports 2007	Imports 2001	Imports 2002	Imports 2003	Imports 2004	Imports 2005	Imports 2006	Imports 2007
	Millions of U.S. Dollars							Millions of U.S. Dollars						
IFS World Total	**24,445**	**25,523**	**30,591**	**33,014**	**32,156**	**42,881**	**50,243**	**39,415**	**38,308**	**40,835**	**49,210**	**53,380**	**65,592**	**76,372**
DOTS World Total 001	**23,892**	**25,543**	**31,732**	**35,726**	**38,141**	**43,350**	**51,519**	**37,925**	**38,342**	**47,222**	**54,865**	**61,170**	**66,684**	**78,321**
Industrial Countries 101	**21,311**	**22,682**	**28,086**	**31,205**	**31,596**	**35,144**	**40,863**	**31,694**	**32,046**	**39,738**	**44,793**	**47,372**	**50,369**	**59,542**
United States 111	1,375	1,484	1,802	2,162	2,052	2,651	2,447	1,424	834	875	1,315	1,335	978	1,310
Canada 156	131	132	186	218	175	193	199	90	77	211	134	129	116	159
Australia 193	88	118	133	132	102	82	86	32	52	48	33	29	35	53
Japan 158	97	89	106	113	109	138	408	727	683	756	809	725	690	783
New Zealand 196	13	14	15	13	12	11	12	19	16	32	23	23	24	26
Austria 122	191	203	192	201	208	222	259	225	265	376	410	396	415	685
Belgium 124	1,289	1,159	1,405	1,425	1,417	1,345	1,294	1,164	1,158	1,369	1,529	1,745	1,770	2,202
Cyprus 423	13	14	18	19	20	24	39	3	1	7	3	5	6	5
Denmark 128	255	254	281	292	300	295	372	226	251	262	346	411	387	386
Finland 172	116	103	145	246	275	291	288	172	212	280	276	364	262	353
France 132	3,013	3,211	4,181	4,986	4,998	5,195	6,313	3,904	3,927	4,624	5,120	5,211	5,410	6,571
Germany 134	4,593	4,698	4,686	4,802	4,556	5,598	6,630	5,278	5,749	6,914	7,839	8,223	8,751	10,082
Greece 174	91	95	137	145	166	155	186	84	85	93	95	98	107	140
Iceland 176	15	10	8	6	10	12	9	109	79	54	50	42	34	64
Ireland 178	124	146	169	212	202	214	244	232	255	352	433	577	594	630
Italy 136	1,096	1,236	1,520	1,534	1,626	1,709	2,084	2,550	2,505	3,028	3,342	3,189	3,713	4,102
Luxembourg 137	27	24	28	40	40	44	132	86	94	133	152	148	190	215
Malta 181	9	9	16	13	12	10	15	14	5	7	4	16	9	11
Netherlands 138	996	965	1,195	1,429	1,482	1,574	1,708	1,842	1,736	2,216	2,524	2,633	2,946	3,564
Norway 142	270	194	258	119	118	139	140	744	450	612	658	655	866	950
Slovenia 961	9	7	10	20	38	35	38	14	19	23	22	25	34	45
Spain 184	4,440	5,173	7,573	8,906	9,894	11,493	13,941	10,048	10,780	14,204	16,058	17,715	19,309	23,116
Sweden 144	360	376	421	410	415	479	615	430	451	554	705	680	617	848
Switzerland 146	247	279	334	341	314	343	365	364	350	400	380	409	455	546
United Kingdom 112	2,453	2,688	3,265	3,422	3,054	2,892	3,037	1,913	2,009	2,311	2,533	2,587	2,653	2,698
Developing Countries 202	**2,424**	**2,677**	**3,459**	**4,169**	**4,931**	**6,606**	**8,808**	**6,211**	**6,275**	**7,460**	**10,026**	**11,941**	**14,037**	**16,579**
Africa 607	**978**	**1,133**	**1,425**	**1,709**	**1,848**	**2,531**	**3,609**	**1,558**	**1,427**	**1,689**	**2,343**	**3,805**	**3,434**	**4,218**
Algeria 612	41	38	47	52	69	91	110	127	187	249	612	1,362	1,115	801
Angola 614	448	541	736	836	994	1,525	2,317	116	61	3	2	33	69	508
Benin 638	1	1	2	1	1	1	1	3	3	3	3	6	7	13
Botswana 616	14	16	14	6	2	2	16	17	20	19	9	7	4	2
Burkina Faso 748	1	1	2	2	2	1	2	7	3	6	7	7	5	2
Burundi 618	—	—	1	—	1	—	—	—	—	—	—	—	—	—
Cameroon 622	2	2	4	3	3	10	5	35	35	31	70	27	73	39
Cape Verde 624	122	140	155	173	185	239	313	9	9	10	13	9	9	10
Central African Rep. 626	—	—	—	—	—	—	—	5	5	5	3	3	4	5
Chad 628	1	11	4	39	20	—	1	25	22	15	53	54	15	16
Congo, Dem. Rep. of 636	1	4	2	4	5	9	10	16	11	12	23	26	28	26
Congo, Republic of 634	3	8	4	4	5	5	6	17	29	39	24	19	15	15
Côte d'Ivoire 662	4	6	6	6	6	7	8	14	19	17	27	13	16	23
Djibouti 611	—	—	—	—	—	—	1	—	—	—	—	—	—	—
Equatorial Guinea 642	—	1	1	3	2	13	16	2	57	4	4	371	498	580
Ethiopia 644	—	1	4	—	1	1	2	1	8	9	11	10	9	18
Gabon 646	2	4	20	46	2	3	2	58	23	68	92	19	12	16
Gambia, The 648	1	—	1	1	1	3	1	—	—	—	—	—	—	—
Ghana 652	4	4	4	3	4	12	9	3	6	3	10	7	9	6
Guinea 656	1	1	2	1	8	7	5	5	2	3	2	3	3	—
Guinea-Bissau 654	20	19	19	22	30	34	47	2	3	2	1	1	1	1
Kenya 664	3	2	2	2	3	4	7	5	2	4	11	4	8	9
Liberia 668	1	—	—	3	1	1	—	2	1	1	—	—	—	—
Madagascar 674	3	1	2	3	—	3	1	4	2	1	2	1	5	5
Malawi 676	1	—	—	—	—	1	1	12	11	29	3	18	11	21
Mali 678	1	1	1	—	1	1	1	4	8	5	2	2	5	2
Mauritania 682	1	3	3	3	2	12	8	11	14	14	11	12	9	2
Mauritius 684	3	3	4	4	2	2	3	16	26	28	32	17	2	16
Morocco 686	95	111	146	179	163	206	274	46	67	68	71	70	91	117
Mozambique 688	57	51	61	68	80	93	123	35	35	44	33	39	36	36
Namibia 728	1	2	3	3	2	3	5	3	4	5	4	4	6	12
Niger 692	2	1	—	1	—	1	—	3	1	1	—	—	—	—
Nigeria 694	18	27	19	25	48	17	36	723	530	745	851	1,203	969	1,382
Rwanda 714	—	—	—	—	1	—	2	—	—	—	—	—	—	—
São Tomé & Príncipe 716	19	28	29	30	28	36	46	2	—	—	—	—	1	—
Senegal 722	6	8	12	13	12	10	10	11	10	12	12	18	14	17
Seychelles 718	—	1	—	—	—	—	—	1	—	—	—	—	—	—
Sierra Leone 724	—	—	—	—	—	—	1	—	—	—	—	—	4	6
South Africa 199	53	57	54	87	87	98	120	107	117	137	255	321	253	373
Sudan 732	2	3	3	7	8	6	3	1	1	1	1	12	—	—
Swaziland 734	1	1	1	—	—	—	1	16	8	10	10	12	15	21
Tanzania 738	1	—	—	1	1	1	1	10	10	11	16	14	18	32

	Exports							Imports						
	2001	2002	2003	2004	2005	2006	2007	2001	2002	2003	2004	2005	2006	2007
	Millions of U.S. Dollars							*Millions of U.S. Dollars*						
Togo 742	1	1	1	1	1	2	1	4	7	11	5	2	3	4
Tunisia 744	38	31	51	68	65	69	90	30	23	26	30	30	35	37
Uganda 746	—	—	—	—	—	1	1	12	15	15	11	12	16	18
Zambia 754	1	1	—	—	—	—	1	8	10	1	1	14	15	17
Zimbabwe 698	5	3	3	4	1	—	1	30	22	21	15	22	23	8
Asia 507	**326**	**409**	**645**	**833**	**1,075**	**1,572**	**2,067**	**1,319**	**1,262**	**1,441**	**1,797**	**2,024**	**2,459**	**3,225**
Bangladesh 513	1	1	1	2	1	4	1	8	9	7	10	11	13	16
Brunei Darussalam 516	—	—	—	—	—	—	3	—	—	—	—	—	—	—
Cambodia 522	1	—	—	—	—	—	—	1	1	—	—	—	—	—
China,P.R.: Mainland 924	53	77	170	126	210	270	247	314	326	421	570	706	974	1,462
China,P.R.:Hong Kong 532	77	63	60	75	123	115	78	26	22	26	37	38	38	57
China,P.R.:Macao 546	11	11	12	15	13	17	18	7	4	2	2	1	1	1
Fiji 819	—	—	—	—	—	—	—	13	9	6	5	—	—	—
French Polynesia 887	—	—	—	1	1	2	2	—	—	—	—	—	—	—
India 534	14	16	21	23	32	36	44	160	184	179	218	260	299	479
Indonesia 536	3	5	5	10	8	8	5	87	96	94	108	125	137	96
Korea 542	17	21	26	36	29	48	67	263	228	258	308	383	383	391
Lao People's Dem.Rep. 544	—	—	—	—	—	—	—	—	—	—	1	1	1	1
Malaysia 548	18	50	32	163	102	108	545	62	59	79	90	79	125	129
Myanmar 518	—	—	—	—	—	—	—	—	1	1	1	1	1	—
Nepal 558	—	—	—	—	—	—	—	1	1	6	—	6	—	10
New Caledonia 839	2	—	1	1	1	2	1	—	—	—	—	—	—	—
Pakistan 564	2	3	9	12	10	12	9	85	61	75	99	91	126	148
Papua New Guinea 853	—	—	—	—	—	—	—	1	1	1	—	—	—	1
Philippines 566	10	8	9	9	8	12	14	23	27	19	16	14	15	23
Singapore 576	78	116	262	301	472	884	976	26	31	54	64	35	57	74
Solomon Islands 813	—	—	—	1	—	—	—	—	—	—	—	—	—	—
Sri Lanka 524	2	2	5	6	3	2	3	5	3	6	5	5	4	5
Taiwan Province of China 528	16	18	12	23	29	16	20	101	108	94	125	133	140	120
Thailand 578	16	14	16	22	24	24	19	124	83	102	122	114	116	164
Vietnam 582	3	2	4	7	7	11	12	11	8	13	16	21	27	47
Europe 170	**432**	**552**	**760**	**848**	**1,089**	**1,390**	**1,725**	**1,319**	**1,447**	**1,812**	**2,617**	**2,330**	**3,144**	**3,355**
Albania 914	1	1	2	1	3	2	2	—	—	—	1	—	—	—
Armenia 911	—	1	1	1	—	—	1	—	—	—	—	—	—	—
Azerbaijan 912	1	1	1	1	1	5	1	—	6	—	4	—	45	83
Belarus 913	2	1	1	3	2	2	4	7	7	9	13	18	8	52
Bosnia & Herzegovina 963	1	1	3	—	3	8	15	5	—	3	3	3	4	1
Bulgaria 918	16	18	21	26	21	19	28	18	26	16	15	30	60	19
Croatia 960	4	5	7	10	9	14	21	5	1	2	2	5	8	7
Czech Republic 935	53	56	82	87	108	159	199	131	156	145	202	274	347	422
Estonia 939	5	6	8	10	10	12	23	5	24	43	60	32	6	7
Faroe Islands 816	1	2	2	2	4	3	3	—	—	—	—	—	—	—
Georgia 915	2	4	1	8	7	1	11	—	—	—	12	1	80	3
Gibraltar 823	1	19	16	4	22	35	10	1	—	1	—	1	—	2
Hungary 944	87	85	107	104	132	176	188	57	68	77	78	88	76	255
Kazakhstan 916	—	1	1	1	1	1	3	8	7	34	314	316	415	433
Kyrgyz Republic 917	—	—	—	—	—	—	—	—	—	1	2	2	2	2
Latvia 941	5	8	7	8	19	33	38	19	22	27	47	88	6	6
Lithuania 946	10	12	12	13	16	13	18	57	48	37	43	53	30	32
Macedonia, FYR 962	1	—	—	2	1	2	2	3	3	7	12	10	16	22
Moldova 921	3	3	5	6	6	2	4	3	2	15	48	7	6	4
Montenegro, Rep. of 943	—	—	—	—	—	—	—	—	—	—	—	—	1	—
Poland 964	103	132	169	165	206	281	359	256	354	364	397	306	397	331
Romania 968	19	30	54	57	69	103	185	20	34	41	51	68	46	35
Russia 922	20	30	45	65	97	136	197	388	336	588	759	464	812	774
Serbia, Rep. of 942	—	—	—	—	—	2	4	—	—	—	—	—	55	10
Serbia & Montenegro 965	5	5	4	2	2	—	—	4	—	3	1	26	—	—
Slovak Republic 936	15	21	30	36	40	59	69	32	30	32	37	38	46	135
Tajikistan 923	—	—	—	—	—	—	—	2	3	4	3	3	2	1
Turkey 186	68	100	170	216	286	292	308	246	242	313	438	447	600	608
Turkmenistan 925	—	—	—	—	1	—	—	1	2	5	7	8	10	6
Ukraine 926	5	7	9	16	19	25	29	30	53	26	50	25	53	90
Uzbekistan 927	—	—	—	—	—	—	1	20	19	18	18	11	11	14
Europe n.s. 884	3	3	3	4	5	4	5	—	1	1	1	3	2	1
Middle East 407	**243**	**231**	**284**	**342**	**417**	**363**	**473**	**811**	**808**	**1,061**	**1,351**	**1,574**	**2,253**	**2,707**
Bahrain 419	2	6	5	5	3	4	7	3	11	12	7	19	9	4
Egypt 469	24	24	23	22	44	31	50	89	60	82	66	45	115	108
Iran, I.R. of 429	10	10	23	22	22	19	19	91	145	60	145	137	370	401
Iraq 433	1	—	—	2	11	1	—	52	69	—	121	322	341	301
Israel 436	76	73	76	67	75	88	129	58	45	48	82	70	99	79
Jordan 439	11	9	9	12	15	18	19	2	3	2	4	4	3	2
Kuwait 443	8	9	28	30	58	11	13	8	22	32	36	20	—	59
Lebanon 446	18	11	11	12	11	9	13	2	1	1	2	3	—	1
Libya 672	2	4	3	14	9	7	12	62	56	408	447	380	583	1,083
Oman 449	1	—	—	1	1	15	9	1	1	1	3	11	1	1
Qatar 453	2	2	2	5	4	9	14	—	—	8	20	2	1	6
Saudi Arabia 456	58	53	63	68	71	65	67	369	334	357	375	526	671	592

	Exports 2001	2002	2003	2004	2005	2006	2007	Imports 2001	2002	2003	2004	2005	2006	2007
	Millions of U.S. Dollars							Millions of U.S. Dollars						
Syrian Arab Republic.................... 463	9	4	10	34	9	16	22	41	55	32	35	7	38	10
United Arab Emirates.................. 466	19	24	29	47	83	67	76	32	6	16	7	28	22	59
Yemen, Republic of..................... 474	2	1	1	1	1	2	21	1	1	1	1	1	1	—
Western Hemisphere............... 207	**444**	**351**	**345**	**437**	**502**	**750**	**935**	**1,205**	**1,330**	**1,458**	**1,919**	**2,208**	**2,748**	**3,075**
Antigua and Barbuda.................. 311	2	—	2	1	3	30	104	—	—	—	—	1	—	11
Argentina.................................. 213	49	25	29	37	45	62	81	175	161	205	198	188	124	253
Bahamas, The............................. 313	1	—	—	1	—	6	—	—	—	—	—	9	—	—
Barbados.................................... 316	1	—	1	1	—	—	1	—	1	—	—	—	—	—
Belize.. 339	—	—	—	—	—	—	—	2	—	—	4	—	9	9
Bermuda..................................... 319	1	1	1	1	1	1	1	—	—	—	—	—	—	—
Bolivia....................................... 218	1	1	—	—	—	1	3	—	—	—	—	1	1	1
Brazil... 223	201	154	146	193	220	321	356	498	620	752	1,060	1,217	1,543	1,900
Chile.. 228	52	42	50	61	64	71	77	32	29	34	45	47	46	47
Colombia.................................... 233	7	6	6	5	5	8	9	75	77	97	155	189	211	222
Costa Rica.................................. 238	4	3	6	5	2	4	5	45	44	55	53	39	47	64
Dominica.................................... 321	—	—	—	—	—	—	1	—	—	—	—	—	—	—
Dominican Republic.................... 243	4	6	4	3	3	5	5	—	—	—	—	—	1	—
Ecuador...................................... 248	1	3	2	3	3	4	4	31	27	33	39	48	24	15
El Salvador................................. 253	4	3	2	2	4	10	10	1	1	1	1	1	1	4
Guatemala.................................. 258	4	3	2	2	4	3	3	2	1	2	3	3	4	5
Guyana....................................... 336	—	—	—	—	—	—	—	22	31	41	65	57	49	68
Haiti... 263	1	1	1	1	—	—	—	—	—	—	—	—	—	—
Honduras.................................... 268	1	1	1	1	3	2	1	3	3	5	5	7	9	15
Jamaica...................................... 343	1	1	1	1	—	—	1	7	8	—	—	—	3	—
Mexico.. 273	60	69	66	88	107	173	165	128	163	145	195	319	327	312
Netherlands Antilles.................... 353	5	1	1	1	5	2	58	—	1	—	—	—	—	2
Nicaragua................................... 278	1	1	1	1	1	1	—	2	1	—	1	2	1	2
Panama...................................... 283	4	6	4	4	7	7	6	14	15	14	13	17	4	8
Paraguay.................................... 288	2	2	—	—	—	1	2	5	2	6	16	5	11	19
Peru... 293	5	3	4	8	5	7	8	4	5	8	8	10	25	40
St. Kitts and Nevis....................... 361	—	—	—	—	—	—	2	—	5	—	6	2	—	—
St. Pierre-Miquelon..................... 363	—	—	—	—	—	—	—	1	—	—	—	—	—	1
St. Vincent & Grens..................... 364	—	1	—	—	—	—	—	—	—	—	—	—	—	—
Suriname.................................... 366	—	—	—	—	—	—	1	4	1	—	—	2	2	1
Trinidad and Tobago................... 369	1	1	2	1	1	1	2	1	6	10	6	2	14	14
Uruguay..................................... 298	6	3	2	3	1	4	3	6	12	16	24	27	21	45
Venezuela, Rep. Bol..................... 299	24	13	7	12	15	22	22	150	113	29	21	14	270	17
Western Hem. n.s........................ 399	—	—	—	1	1	3	2	—	—	—	1	—	—	—
Other Countries n.i.e............... 910	**6**	**4**	**3**	**4**	**6**	**7**	**12**	**18**	**19**	**22**	**44**	**10**	**23**	**30**
Cuba... 928	5	4	3	4	5	7	12	18	19	22	44	10	23	30
North Korea................................ 954	—	—	—	—	1	—	—	—	—	—	—	—	—	—
Countries & Areas n.s............. 898	**31**	**56**	**34**	**54**	**1,382**	**1,300**	**1,394**	**1**	**1**	**—**	**1**	**1,847**	**2,254**	**2,165**
Special Categories.................. 899	**120**	**120**	**150**	**264**	**225**	**292**	**437**	**—**	**2**	**1**	**—**	**—**	**—**	**3**
Memorandum Items														
European Union.......................... 998	19,354	20,684	25,656	28,524	29,235	32,308	38,089	28,742	30,207	37,475	42,254	44,903	48,079	56,840
Oil Exporting Ctys....................... 999	188	186	228	288	399	333	385	1,702	1,559	2,000	2,747	4,130	4,480	4,798
Non-Oil Develop.Ctys.................. 201	2,236	2,491	3,231	3,881	4,532	6,274	8,423	4,509	4,715	5,460	7,280	7,811	9,557	11,782
PERCENT DISTRIBUTION														
Industrial Countries................ 101	**89.2**	**88.8**	**88.5**	**87.3**	**82.8**	**81.1**	**79.3**	**83.6**	**83.6**	**84.2**	**81.6**	**77.4**	**75.5**	**76.0**
Developing Countries............. 202	**10.1**	**10.5**	**10.9**	**11.7**	**12.9**	**15.2**	**17.1**	**16.4**	**16.4**	**15.8**	**18.3**	**19.5**	**21.1**	**21.2**
Africa.................................... 607	**4.1**	**4.4**	**4.5**	**4.8**	**4.8**	**5.8**	**7.0**	**4.1**	**3.7**	**3.6**	**4.3**	**6.2**	**5.1**	**5.4**
Asia...................................... 507	**1.4**	**1.6**	**2.0**	**2.3**	**2.8**	**3.6**	**4.0**	**3.5**	**3.3**	**3.1**	**3.3**	**3.3**	**3.7**	**4.1**
Europe.................................. 170	**1.8**	**2.2**	**2.4**	**2.4**	**2.9**	**3.2**	**3.3**	**3.5**	**3.8**	**3.8**	**4.8**	**3.8**	**4.7**	**4.3**
Middle East.......................... 407	**1.0**	**.9**	**.9**	**1.0**	**1.1**	**.8**	**.9**	**2.1**	**2.1**	**2.2**	**2.5**	**2.6**	**3.4**	**3.5**
Western Hemisphere............. 207	**1.9**	**1.4**	**1.1**	**1.2**	**1.3**	**1.7**	**1.8**	**3.2**	**3.5**	**3.1**	**3.5**	**3.6**	**4.1**	**3.9**
Other Countries n.i.e............... 910	**—**	**—**	**—**	**—**	**—**	**—**	**—**	**—**	**—**	**—**	**.1**	**—**	**—**	**—**
ANNUAL PERCENT CHANGE														
World..................................... 001	**2.6**	**6.9**	**24.2**	**12.6**	**6.8**	**13.7**	**18.8**	**–.8**	**1.1**	**23.2**	**16.2**	**11.5**	**9.0**	**17.5**
Industrial Countries................ 101	**2.1**	**6.4**	**23.8**	**11.1**	**1.3**	**11.2**	**16.3**	**–.3**	**1.1**	**24.0**	**12.7**	**5.8**	**6.3**	**18.2**
Developing Countries............. 202	**7.3**	**10.4**	**29.2**	**20.5**	**18.3**	**34.0**	**33.3**	**–3.0**	**1.0**	**18.9**	**34.4**	**19.1**	**17.6**	**18.1**
Africa.................................... 607	**8.0**	**15.8**	**25.8**	**19.9**	**8.2**	**36.9**	**42.6**	**—**	**–8.4**	**18.3**	**38.7**	**62.4**	**–9.8**	**22.8**
Asia...................................... 507	**–2.0**	**25.6**	**57.5**	**29.2**	**29.1**	**46.3**	**31.5**	**–12.9**	**–4.3**	**14.2**	**24.7**	**12.6**	**21.5**	**31.2**
Europe.................................. 170	**4.5**	**27.9**	**37.5**	**11.7**	**28.4**	**27.7**	**24.1**	**31.2**	**9.7**	**25.2**	**44.4**	**–11.0**	**34.9**	**6.7**
Middle East.......................... 407	**10.4**	**–5.0**	**23.0**	**20.5**	**21.9**	**–13.1**	**30.3**	**–35.4**	**–.3**	**31.2**	**27.4**	**16.5**	**43.1**	**20.1**
Western Hemisphere............. 207	**15.1**	**–21.0**	**–1.6**	**26.6**	**14.8**	**49.4**	**24.6**	**12.8**	**10.4**	**9.6**	**31.6**	**15.1**	**24.5**	**11.9**
Other Countries n.i.e............... 910	**–17.8**	**–25.4**	**–28.7**	**25.3**	**51.9**	**23.3**	**70.8**	**.7**	**3.1**	**19.4**	**96.3**	**–76.2**	**125.7**	**29.1**

		Exports							Imports						
		2001	2002	2003	2004	2005	2006	2007	2001	2002	2003	2004	2005	2006	2007
		Millions of U.S. Dollars							*Millions of U.S. Dollars*						
IFS World Total		....	10,978	13,382	18,685	25,762	34,051	36,970	....	4,052	4,897	6,004	10,061	16,441	22,045
DOTS World Total	001	10,868	10,977	13,380	18,546	18,001	25,090	38,624Y	3,758	4,051	4,897	6,052	9,093	12,688	22,800Y
Industrial Countries	101	6,269	5,742	6,772	8,802	11,360	15,842	18,710Y	2,452	2,523	3,022	3,839	5,977	7,902	15,104Y
United States	111	384	284	225	240	311	135	471V	516	528	596	577	1,163	1,621	3,038V
Canada	156	8	1	1	35	—	—	—V	23	32	33	23	45	85	92V
Australia	193	171	55	41	160	133	201	199V	73	59	81	69	124	208	181V
Japan	158	5,543	5,126	6,158	7,779	10,303	14,116	15,422V	357	427	513	314	1,171	1,973	2,028V
New Zealand	196	45	45	66	69	121	185	221V	5	5	6	4	12	16	15V
Austria	122	—	—	10	1	—	—	1V	14	16	21	23	60	93	153V
Belgium	124	4	4	6	3	16	93	661V	37	47	53	60	120	242	399V
Cyprus	423	—	—	1	1	1	—	—V	—	3	4	1	3	5	5V
Denmark	128	—	—	—	—	—	—	4V	17	18	20	13	61	37	64V
Finland	172	—	—	—	—	—	—	1V	—	10	14	23	83	97	160V
France	132	14	10	13	12	45	17	42V	167	169	163	1,607	425	635	1,796V
Germany	134	3	6	3	6	4	1	41V	343	284	472	316	924	1,533	1,656V
Greece	174	—	1	4	18	5	6	9V	7	6	4	3	11	23	11V
Ireland	178	—	1	1	1	3	3	6V	17	17	20	21	40	—	32V
Italy	136	1	107	10	26	15	43	56V	366	366	364	203	650	56	2,457V
Luxembourg	137	—	—	—	—	—	—	—V	—	1	1	—	4	4	3V
Malta	181	—	—	—	10	—	—	—V	—	1	1	—	1	1	3V
Netherlands	138	14	54	46	15	156	199	43V	87	93	93	76	184	215	487V
Norway	142	—	—	—	—	—	—	—V	5	6	9	9	11	145	24V
Portugal	182	—	—	—	—	1	1	6V	—	3	4	3	6	1	16V
Slovenia	961	—	—	—	—	—	—	—V	—	1	1	1	3	1	18V
Spain	184	56	23	151	347	245	836	1,174V	40	51	61	50	115	43	602V
Sweden	144	1	—	—	—	1	—	1V	22	23	35	29	48	17	222V
Switzerland	146	4	11	1	12	—	1	82V	55	52	62	108	140	29	355V
United Kingdom	112	19	14	36	67	1	4	269V	301	309	393	308	576	820	1,289V
Developing Countries	202	4,591	4,710	5,733	8,334	6,641	9,248	19,914Y	1,273	1,527	1,875	2,176	3,117	4,785	7,694Y
Africa	607	104	73	98	179	266	264	278Y	13	16	23	32	46	65	78Y
Algeria	612	—	2	2	8	5	8	9Y	—	—	—	—	—	3	3Y
Cameroon	622	—	—	—	1	1	1	1Y	—	—	—	1	—	—	—Y
Côte d'Ivoire	662	—	2	2	2	—	—	—Y	—	—	—	—	—	—	—Y
Eritrea	643	2	—	—	—	—	—	—Y	—	—	—	—	—	—	—Y
Ethiopia	644	1	3	4	11	8	12	15Y	—	—	—	—	—	—	—Y
Ghana	652	—	—	—	—	—	—	1Y	—	—	—	—	—	—	1Y
Kenya	664	4	4	7	10	35	23	28Y	—	—	—	1	4	2	2Y
Madagascar	674	23	—	—	1	2	—	—Y	—	—	—	—	—	—	—Y
Mauritius	684	—	1	—	1	—	—	—V	—	—	—	—	—	—	—V
Morocco	686	1	6	8	22	15	26	32Y	—	1	2	2	3	5	7Y
Mozambique	688	—	1	19	9	—	—	—Y	—	—	—	9	—	—	—Y
Nigeria	694	2	—	2	10	9	10	12Y	—	—	—	—	—	—	—Y
Senegal	722	—	1	2	2	2	1	1Y	—	—	—	—	—	—	—Y
Sierra Leone	724	—	—	1	—	—	—	—Y	—	—	—	—	—	—	—Y
Somalia	726	—	—	—	—	—	—	—Y	—	—	1	1	2	2	3Y
South Africa	199	51	47	38	77	160	133	106V	—	11	17	14	25	36	41V
Sudan	732	4	1	2	9	13	11	28V	—	1	2	1	1	1	—V
Swaziland	734	—	—	—	—	—	—	—Y	—	—	—	1	10	10	14Y
Tanzania	738	14	1	5	1	7	23	28Y	—	—	—	—	—	2	3Y
Tunisia	744	2	3	1	8	5	9	11Y	—	1	1	1	1	3	4Y
Uganda	746	—	—	—	—	—	3	3Y	—	—	—	—	—	—	—Y
Zimbabwe	698	2	2	3	4	4	2	3Y	—	—	—	—	—	—	—Y
Africa n.s.	799	—	—	2	—	—	—	—Y	13	—	—	—	—	—	—Y
Asia	507	3,979	3,603	4,893	7,013	4,935	7,203	17,486Y	606	674	843	742	1,054	1,456	3,753Y
Afghanistan, I.S. of	512	—	—	1	—	—	—	—Y	—	—	—	—	1	—	—Y
Bangladesh	513	4	2	9	4	8	30	47V	—	2	2	2	4	4	5Y
China,P.R.: Mainland	924	327	117	258	209	—	—	534V	107	128	166	184	—	—	684V
China,P.R.:Hong Kong	532	11	6	—	1	1	26	18V	18	37	15	11	14	18	39V
India	534	157	102	148	1,006	880	1,647	1,987Y	87	121	154	141	388	451	584Y
Indonesia	536	20	12	3	24	4	24	38V	36	43	44	43	105	131	161V
Korea	542	2,144	1,737	2,478	2,933	182	142	7,685V	164	145	243	112	22	7	1,280V
Malaysia	548	41	4	5	14	27	54	22V	51	59	59	39	119	236	321V
Myanmar	518	—	1	—	—	—	—	—Y	—	—	—	—	1	2	3Y
Nepal	558	1	1	1	1	2	7	8Y	—	—	—	—	—	—	—Y
Pakistan	564	13	17	16	117	207	374	451Y	32	29	32	26	45	52	67Y
Philippines	566	192	127	159	215	300	164	281V	11	8	8	6	32	29	37V
Singapore	576	738	1,017	1,274	1,695	2,104	3,209	3,808V	27	31	43	111	113	160	277V
Sri Lanka	524	12	23	23	11	17	44	44V	—	2	4	3	5	7	4V
Taiwan Province of China	528	23	27	87	255	654	534	626V	31	31	30	24	57	72	52V
Thailand	578	257	375	399	512	520	930	1,875V	32	35	42	38	144	257	238V
Vietnam	582	38	35	31	17	29	18	61V	—	1	2	2	6	30	—V
Asia n.s.	598	—	—	—	—	—	—	—Y	10	—	—	—	—	—	—Y

	Exports 2001	2002	2003	2004	2005	2006	2007	Imports 2001	2002	2003	2004	2005	2006	2007
	Millions of U.S. Dollars							*Millions of U.S. Dollars*						
Europe....170	**6**	**6**	**6**	**7**	**28**	**35**	**39Y**	**46**	**45**	**75**	**79**	**199**	**510**	**653Y**
Azerbaijan....912	—	—	—	—	—	—	—V	—	—	—	1	—	—	—V
Bosnia & Herzegovina....963	—	—	—	—	—	—	—Y	—	—	—	—	—	—	1Y
Bulgaria....918	—	—	—	—	—	—	—V	—	—	1	1	1	1	2V
Croatia....960	—	—	—	—	—	—	—V	—	—	3	—	16	25	—V
Czech Republic....935	—	—	—	—	1	—	—V	—	3	8	9	24	29	44V
Czechoslovakia n.s....937	....	....	....	....	....	....	....	—	—	—	—	10	12	15Y
Hungary....944	—	—	—	—	—	—	—V	—	3	4	6	22	35	36V
Lithuania....946	—	—	—	—	—	—	—V	—	—	—	—	—	2	4V
Macedonia, FYR....962	—	—	—	—	—	—	—Y	—	—	—	—	—	—	10Y
Poland....964	—	—	—	—	—	—	—V	—	3	3	3	11	22	18V
Romania....968	—	—	—	—	—	—	—V	2	4	7	5	14	16	—V
Russia....922	—	—	—	—	—	—	9V	—	4	5	2	5	4	1V
Slovak Republic....936	—	—	—	—	—	—	—V	—	1	2	2	10	12	7V
Turkey....186	5	6	5	7	27	33	27V	19	25	29	32	70	334	495V
Ukraine....926	—	—	—	—	—	—	—Y	—	2	13	18	16	17	22Y
Europe n.s....884	—	—	—	—	—	—	—Y	25	—	—	—	—	—	—Y
Middle East....407	**493**	**1,027**	**730**	**1,133**	**1,404**	**1,726**	**1,994Y**	**538**	**727**	**833**	**1,214**	**1,613**	**2,465**	**2,965Y**
Bahrain....419	30	29	35	37	46	52	63Y	22	34	65	79	62	122	158Y
Egypt....469	12	263	24	18	38	21	25Y	8	16	29	20	47	90	116Y
Iran, I.R. of....429	5	24	11	61	—	—	—Y	25	19	18	14	52	53	63Y
Iraq....433	—	—	4	3	—	1	1Y	—	—	—	—	—	—	—Y
Jordan....439	15	13	8	28	31	44	7V	15	20	15	15	24	38	65V
Kuwait....443	17	33	33	78	17	20	24Y	15	29	21	28	47	86	102Y
Lebanon....446	8	12	4	19	3	5	7Y	9	10	13	24	41	79	102Y
Libya....672	—	1	1	22	8	1	1Y	—	3	—	5	—	8	10Y
Oman....449	6	10	14	27	12	13	15Y	19	25	28	44	77	121	143Y
Saudi Arabia....456	151	191	197	194	173	216	255Y	200	252	291	571	575	839	990Y
Syrian Arab Republic....463	8	4	27	18	21	31	37Y	22	33	25	34	40	36	47Y
United Arab Emirates....466	233	436	369	616	1,050	1,318	1,555Y	195	286	326	379	647	991	1,169Y
Yemen, Republic of....474	8	9	3	13	5	4	5Y	—	1	1	—	1	2	2Y
Middle East n.s....489	—	—	—	—	—	—	—Y	6	—	—	—	—	—	—Y
Western Hemisphere....207	**9**	**1**	**6**	**2**	**8**	**21**	**117Y**	**70**	**67**	**100**	**108**	**204**	**289**	**245Y**
Argentina....213	5	—	—	—	—	—	22V	10	10	13	10	28	46	17V
Brazil....223	—	—	4	—	—	7	64V	35	40	45	57	119	149	149V
Chile....228	2	1	1	—	2	1	20V	—	3	3	1	6	8	3V
Colombia....233	—	—	—	—	1	1	5V	—	—	—	—	—	—	—V
Costa Rica....238	—	—	—	—	—	—	—Y	—	—	—	—	2	1	1Y
Dominican Republic....243	—	—	—	—	—	—	—Y	—	—	—	1	—	—	—Y
Ecuador....248	—	—	—	—	—	—	—Y	—	—	—	—	1	1	2Y
Guatemala....258	....	....	....	....	....	....	....	—	1	1	1	1	1	1Y
Mexico....273	—	—	—	—	—	7	—V	18	12	13	6	28	63	51V
Panama....283	—	—	—	—	—	—	—V	—	—	—	—	2	1	—V
Peru....293	1	—	1	2	4	4	4Y	—	—	—	—	—	—	—Y
Trinidad and Tobago....369	—	—	—	—	—	—	—Y	—	—	5	25	—	—	—Y
Uruguay....298	—	—	—	—	—	—	—Y	—	—	—	—	—	1	1Y
Venezuela, Rep. Bol....299	—	—	—	—	—	—	—V	—	—	20	7	18	17	20Y
Western Hem. n.s....399	—	—	—	—	—	—	—Y	7	—	—	—	—	—	—Y
Other Countries n.i.e....910	**—**	**6**	**—**	**37**	**—**	**—**	**—Y**	**—**	**—**	**—**	**37**	**—**	**1**	**1Y**
Cuba....928	—	—	—	—	—	—	—Y	—	—	—	—	—	1	1Y
North Korea....954	—	6	—	37	—	—	—Y	—	—	—	37	—	—	—Y
Countries & Areas n.s....898	**9**	**519**	**875**	**1,373**	**—**	**—**	**—Y**	**33**	**—**	**—**	**1**	**—**	**—**	**—Y**
Memorandum Items														
European Union....998	113	220	280	508	493	1,204	2,315Y	1,418	1,424	1,740	2,755	3,378	3,925	9,480Y
Oil Exporting Ctys....999	435	709	635	1,044	1,279	1,611	1,910Y	491	656	748	1,092	1,522	2,249	2,660Y
Non-Oil Develop.Ctys....201	4,156	4,001	5,098	7,290	5,362	7,637	18,004Y	781	871	1,127	1,084	1,594	2,536	5,034Y
PERCENT DISTRIBUTION														
Industrial Countries....101	**57.7**	**52.3**	**50.6**	**47.5**	**63.1**	**63.1**	**48.4**	**65.2**	**62.3**	**61.7**	**63.4**	**65.7**	**62.3**	**66.2**
Developing Countries....202	**42.2**	**42.9**	**42.8**	**44.9**	**36.9**	**36.9**	**51.6**	**33.9**	**37.7**	**38.3**	**36.0**	**34.3**	**37.7**	**33.7**
Africa....607	**1.0**	**.7**	**.7**	**1.0**	**1.5**	**1.1**	**.7**	**.3**	**.4**	**.5**	**.5**	**.5**	**.5**	**.3**
Asia....507	**36.6**	**32.8**	**36.6**	**37.8**	**27.4**	**28.7**	**45.3**	**16.1**	**16.6**	**17.2**	**12.3**	**11.6**	**11.5**	**16.5**
Europe....170	**.1**	**.1**	**—**	**—**	**.2**	**.1**	**.1**	**1.2**	**1.1**	**1.5**	**1.3**	**2.2**	**4.0**	**2.9**
Middle East....407	**4.5**	**9.4**	**5.5**	**6.1**	**7.8**	**6.9**	**5.2**	**14.3**	**17.9**	**17.0**	**20.1**	**17.7**	**19.4**	**13.0**
Western Hemisphere....207	**.1**	**—**	**—**	**—**	**—**	**.1**	**.3**	**1.9**	**1.6**	**2.0**	**1.8**	**2.2**	**2.3**	**1.1**
Other Countries n.i.e....910	**—**	**.1**	**—**	**.2**	**—**	**—**	**—**	**—**	**—**	**—**	**.6**	**—**	**—**	**—**
ANNUAL PERCENT CHANGE														
World....001	**−6.2**	**1.0**	**21.9**	**38.6**	**−2.9**	**39.4**	**53.9**	**15.5**	**7.8**	**20.9**	**23.6**	**50.3**	**39.5**	**79.7**
Industrial Countries....101	**6.6**	**−8.4**	**17.9**	**30.0**	**29.1**	**39.5**	**18.1**	**22.5**	**2.9**	**19.8**	**27.0**	**55.7**	**32.2**	**91.1**
Developing Countries....202	**1.6**	**2.6**	**21.7**	**45.4**	**−20.3**	**39.3**	**115.3**	**1.8**	**20.0**	**22.7**	**16.1**	**43.2**	**53.5**	**60.8**
Africa....607	**8.8**	**−29.8**	**33.2**	**82.9**	**49.1**	**−1.1**	**5.4**	**53.2**	**22.9**	**49.1**	**38.0**	**44.4**	**40.8**	**19.3**
Asia....507	**8.3**	**−9.4**	**35.8**	**43.3**	**−29.6**	**46.0**	**142.8**	**3.1**	**11.1**	**25.2**	**−12.0**	**42.1**	**38.1**	**157.8**
Europe....170	**−56.6**	**2.8**	**1.0**	**20.0**	**297.2**	**25.6**	**13.1**	**22.4**	**−1.7**	**68.3**	**5.4**	**150.1**	**156.7**	**28.1**
Middle East....407	**−31.8**	**108.1**	**−28.8**	**55.1**	**23.9**	**22.9**	**15.6**	**−5.0**	**35.2**	**14.6**	**45.8**	**32.9**	**52.8**	**20.3**
Western Hemisphere....207	**−27.0**	**−87.6**	**448.2**	**−65.2**	**255.8**	**171.7**	**450.4**	**38.8**	**−5.2**	**50.6**	**7.9**	**88.8**	**41.5**	**−15.2**
Other Countries n.i.e....910	**—**	**—**	**—**	**....**	**36.0**	**25.7**	**20.6**	**—**	**....**	**14.8**	**—**	**−99.2**	**213.8**	**29.5**

	Exports 2001	2002	2003	2004	2005	2006	2007	Imports, f.o.b 2001	2002	2003	2004	2005	2006	2007
	Millions of U.S. Dollars							Millions of U.S. Dollars						
IFS World Total	**11,391**	**13,876**	**17,619**	**23,485**	**27,730**	**32,336**	**40,042**	**14,363**	**16,487**	**22,155**	**30,149**	**37,348**	**47,172**	**64,354**
DOTS World Total 001	**11,386**	**13,874**	**17,616**	**23,476**	**27,645**	**32,479**	**40,342**	**14,139**	**16,200**	**21,758**	**29,614**	**36,682**	**46,664**	**63,710**
Industrial Countries 101	**8,413**	**10,305**	**12,978**	**16,735**	**18,352**	**20,662**	**25,390**	**9,102**	**10,524**	**13,878**	**18,450**	**21,449**	**27,289**	**37,665**
United States 111	357	605	619	667	1,075	807	814	446	487	504	850	1,020	1,149	858
Canada 156	36	48	50	74	96	75	56	54	44	113	160	176	235	142
Australia 193	4	4	5	9	10	7	19	78	23	38	43	46	83	144
Japan 158	18	12	16	48	79	104	117	140	197	271	399	529	603	390
New Zealand 196	—	1	1	1	1	—	1	1	1	1	2	3	5	2
Austria 122	342	421	567	732	859	857	1,034	401	539	770	1,038	1,358	1,756	3,088
Belgium 124	193	219	280	465	477	527	643	233	259	322	444	522	712	1,251
Cyprus 423	27	14	9	66	110	63	56	7	6	6	12	11	17	102
Denmark 128	29	26	31	53	60	80	86	62	70	99	105	126	189	286
Finland 172	4	7	12	18	28	39	70	45	50	78	88	145	213	212
France 132	919	1,056	1,295	1,995	2,057	2,435	3,118	890	1,036	1,589	2,106	2,473	3,047	3,978
Germany 134	1,781	2,166	2,771	3,514	3,869	5,093	6,829	2,150	2,414	3,236	4,425	5,120	7,079	10,938
Greece 174	316	388	426	628	590	636	688	297	240	295	401	421	551	975
Iceland 176	—	—	—	1	3	3	6	1	1	2	2	2	2	2
Ireland 178	64	15	31	39	45	53	119	53	63	91	145	225	276	247
Italy 136	2,854	3,489	4,288	5,025	5,340	5,819	6,924	2,829	3,376	4,270	5,099	5,650	6,776	8,134
Luxembourg 137	1	7	6	4	10	7	44	6	6	11	18	21	34	92
Malta 181	42	17	27	83	68	97	75	14	1	2	13	3	4	32
Netherlands 138	386	436	628	749	743	803	832	293	355	425	551	628	848	2,306
Norway 142	73	116	114	99	171	335	414	28	41	48	75	101	127	121
Portugal 182	21	33	38	46	56	42	56	29	45	80	88	115	147	125
Slovenia 961	66	81	69	118	128	115	227	61	78	107	150	171	220	606
Spain 184	179	204	314	466	668	759	933	200	263	396	652	817	1,091	1,292
Sweden 144	62	66	91	132	134	179	259	142	164	205	316	352	482	661
Switzerland 146	55	71	106	142	172	196	307	154	144	197	297	363	486	451
United Kingdom 112	587	805	1,182	1,561	1,504	1,528	1,661	490	621	722	972	1,051	1,156	1,229
Developing Countries 202	**2,927**	**3,543**	**4,606**	**6,714**	**8,881**	**11,151**	**14,887**	**4,580**	**5,591**	**7,774**	**11,067**	**14,885**	**18,941**	**25,996**
Africa 607	**176**	**155**	**195**	**239**	**392**	**444**	**445**	**76**	**110**	**100**	**125**	**134**	**121**	**155**
Algeria 612	18	28	52	61	70	84	105	—	28	—	1	—	—	1
Angola 614	1	1	2	4	1	1	2	—	—	—	—	—	—	—
Benin 638	—	—	1	4	1	—	—	—	—	—	—	—	—	—
Burkina Faso 748	—	—	—	3	—	—	—	....	....	....	....	....	....	....
Burundi 618	—	—	—	—	—	—	—	1	—	—	—	2	—	—
Cameroon 622	3	5	7	7	10	14	10	—	—	—	1	1	—	3
Cape Verde 624	1	—	1	—	—	—	—	—	—	—	—	—	—	—
Chad 628	—	—	—	1	—	—	—	....	....	....	....	....	....	....
Congo, Dem. Rep. of 636	—	—	—	—	—	2	—	—	—	—	1	—	—	—
Congo, Republic of 634	—	1	—	1	1	1	1	—	—	—	—	—	—	1
Côte d'Ivoire 662	2	5	21	6	2	3	4	2	2	3	6	7	10	10
Equatorial Guinea 642	—	—	—	1	—	—	—	....	....	....	....	....	....	....
Ethiopia 644	1	2	2	—	2	1	—	2	2	2	2	2	2	2
Gabon 646	—	—	1	1	1	1	1	—	—	—	1	3	1	1
Gambia, The 648	—	1	1	6	—	—	—	—	—	—	—	—	—	—
Ghana 652	1	1	2	4	10	2	2	—	2	2	2	2	4	1
Guinea 656	1	1	1	2	—	—	—	8	21	21	33	37	24	1
Kenya 664	2	1	14	23	9	35	5	—	—	1	2	2	2	2
Liberia 668	1	—	—	3	26	53	95	—	—	—	—	—	—	—
Madagascar 674	—	—	—	1	—	1	1	—	—	—	—	—	—	—
Mali 678	—	—	3	1	6	—	1	—	—	—	1	—	—	—
Mauritania 682	2	1	—	1	—	—	—	—	—	—	—	—	—	—
Mauritius 684	—	—	—	—	—	—	—	—	—	2	—	3	1	2
Morocco 686	31	38	36	26	67	73	122	9	9	12	19	23	18	19
Mozambique 688	—	1	—	3	—	6	—	—	—	—	—	—	—	1
Niger 692	1	1	—	—	—	—	—	—	—	—	—	—	—	—
Nigeria 694	68	38	23	41	103	35	21	—	—	3	2	1	—	2
Rwanda 714	—	—	—	—	—	—	1	1	2	1	2	2	2	2
Senegal 722	1	1	—	—	1	2	2	—	—	—	—	—	—	—
Seychelles 718	—	—	—	—	1	—	—	....	....	....	....	....	....	....
Sierra Leone 724	2	—	—	—	—	—	1	—	—	—	—	—	—	—
South Africa 199	3	4	3	5	6	10	13	39	29	38	38	24	33	63
Sudan 732	7	4	3	2	11	29	9	—	—	—	—	—	—	—
Tanzania 738	1	1	—	—	9	—	1	1	1	1	2	3	3	5
Togo 742	—	—	2	—	—	16	1	1	1	1	1	—	—	—
Tunisia 744	27	19	17	29	47	71	45	2	5	5	5	15	12	10
Uganda 746	1	—	—	—	1	—	1	1	1	1	2	3	3	2
Zambia 754	—	—	—	—	—	—	—	—	—	—	—	—	—	21
Zimbabwe 698	—	—	—	—	—	—	—	4	3	2	2	2	1	1
Asia 507	**314**	**673**	**689**	**616**	**786**	**716**	**926**	**590**	**1,023**	**1,403**	**2,052**	**2,797**	**3,750**	**3,721**
Afghanistan, I.S. of 512	—	—	2	3	—	—	12	—	—	—	—	—	—	—
Bangladesh 513	1	—	7	6	20	25	2	1	2	1	3	6	8	5
Brunei Darussalam 516	—	—	—	—	—	1	—	—	—	—	—	—	—	—

	Exports							Imports, f.o.b						
	2001	2002	2003	2004	2005	2006	2007	2001	2002	2003	2004	2005	2006	2007
	Millions of U.S. Dollars							*Millions of U.S. Dollars*						
Cambodia....... 522	—	—	1	—	—	—	—	....	....	....	....	....	....	....
China,P.R.: Mainland....... 924	89	209	282	195	207	219	215	230	339	602	967	1,477	1,993	2,090
China,P.R.:Hong Kong....... 532	31	230	99	36	20	30	17	14	24	24	21	27	33	25
China,P.R.:Macao....... 546	—	—	—	—	—	—	—	—	—	—	—	—	1	—
French Polynesia....... 887	—	26	—	—	1	1	1	—	—	—	—	—	—	—
India....... 534	39	48	54	130	271	241	453	29	48	71	123	161	197	322
Indonesia....... 536	5	11	5	25	8	5	8	32	34	44	144	68	79	71
Korea....... 542	40	44	76	96	67	28	60	152	206	226	324	498	694	753
Malaysia....... 548	7	6	9	7	10	16	14	42	55	76	107	114	147	81
Mongolia....... 948	—	—	—	—	—	—	—	—	—	—	—	1	—	—
Myanmar....... 518	—	—	—	—	—	—	—	—	1	—	—	—	1	—
New Caledonia....... 839	—	—	—	—	3	1	4	....	....	....	....	....	....	....
Pakistan....... 564	20	14	21	18	50	49	39	6	5	8	12	17	20	15
Philippines....... 566	16	7	5	1	1	2	1	12	21	29	41	32	50	18
Singapore....... 576	16	16	33	44	65	60	52	17	33	49	52	52	59	16
Sri Lanka....... 524	5	1	1	2	3	5	6	1	1	1	2	2	3	3
Taiwan Province of China....... 528	—	34	48	39	30	10	28	—	197	185	236	205	272	164
Thailand....... 578	39	20	23	—	24	15	10	38	45	71	—	111	149	122
Vietnam....... 582	6	7	24	14	5	9	6	15	13	16	20	26	41	35
Europe....... 170	**1,767**	**1,848**	**2,901**	**4,786**	**6,392**	**8,253**	**11,500**	**3,334**	**3,994**	**5,767**	**8,149**	**10,920**	**13,691**	**20,301**
Albania....... 914	13	21	15	20	15	31	51	1	—	—	—	2	1	4
Armenia....... 911	2	—	—	2	6	7	8	2	—	—	—	—	1	1
Azerbaijan....... 912	5	6	6	8	5	5	9	—	—	1	148	104	87	110
Belarus....... 913	2	2	2	5	5	9	12	26	24	34	75	60	59	77
Bosnia & Herzegovina....... 963	12	15	17	40	127	180	73	8	1	1	18	41	69	44
Bulgaria....... 918	202	177	289	451	733	914	1,303	135	133	208	317	358	442	760
Croatia....... 960	17	36	124	189	233	148	164	4	5	19	40	70	67	80
Czech Republic....... 935	36	52	96	168	263	369	557	250	316	445	642	841	1,154	1,549
Estonia....... 939	2	1	2	5	5	8	17	3	2	1	4	4	8	12
Faroe Islands....... 816	—	—	—	—	—	—	—	—	—	—	1	—	—	—
Georgia....... 915	39	26	62	78	160	198	142	1	13	2	—	7	7	—
Gibraltar....... 823	44	11	72	93	13	—	118	—	—	—	5	—	—	—
Hungary....... 944	371	431	617	898	1,144	1,603	2,249	545	581	789	940	1,213	1,526	4,416
Kazakhstan....... 916	15	23	23	26	35	36	91	138	307	219	534	1,194	1,484	1,236
Kosovo....... 967	—	—	—	—	—	—	11	....	....	....	....	....	....	....
Kyrgyz Republic....... 917	—	—	—	—	—	—	—	2	2	5	4	2	1	1
Latvia....... 941	2	3	5	7	8	7	14	—	1	1	3	6	4	20
Lithuania....... 946	2	3	4	9	12	20	35	2	3	11	13	23	27	48
Macedonia, FYR....... 962	12	7	13	115	60	98	80	2	1	2	1	4	13	21
Moldova....... 921	112	110	137	205	325	428	637	35	46	76	70	77	125	229
Montenegro, Rep. of....... 943	—	—	—	—	—	—	15	....	....	....	....	....	....	....
Poland....... 964	100	107	169	310	403	589	870	250	318	505	748	1,063	1,294	2,165
Russia....... 922	83	40	52	121	230	376	587	1,076	1,170	1,801	2,027	3,030	3,659	4,041
Serbia, Rep. of....... 942	—	—	—	—	—	—	427	....	....	....	....	....	....	....
Serbia & Montenegro....... 965	155	126	153	227	108	—	—	31	23	27	52	36	—	—
Slovak Republic....... 936	32	35	47	78	115	227	366	127	148	220	305	400	528	814
Tajikistan....... 923	—	—	24	2	—	—	—	1	1	1	3	2	3	2
Turkey....... 186	451	574	902	1,643	2,189	2,509	2,838	342	510	840	1,241	1,772	2,305	3,450
Turkmenistan....... 925	11	3	3	4	4	9	14	48	68	47	137	129	41	121
Ukraine....... 926	45	38	65	78	167	427	746	291	313	499	807	475	646	718
Uzbekistan....... 927	4	1	1	3	25	53	78	12	11	12	14	7	139	81
Middle East....... 407	**546**	**758**	**740**	**984**	**1,160**	**1,535**	**1,609**	**271**	**201**	**150**	**231**	**367**	**639**	**1,031**
Bahrain....... 419	2	5	8	4	6	9	6	1	—	—	—	—	—	—
Egypt....... 469	113	118	119	207	188	219	236	36	19	26	41	67	138	110
Iran, I.R. of....... 429	43	64	84	59	93	62	138	7	4	7	9	90	274	561
Iraq....... 433	13	30	11	20	26	65	27	47	—	1	2	—	—	—
Israel....... 436	121	150	98	106	117	147	168	137	98	103	150	160	184	214
Jordan....... 439	18	24	13	37	32	33	44	1	2	1	2	2	3	6
Kuwait....... 443	7	26	18	15	26	48	62	—	—	—	—	—	—	—
Lebanon....... 446	32	77	71	98	158	143	125	1	1	1	3	2	4	5
Libya....... 672	11	9	19	12	22	20	12	—	—	—	—	—	6	67
Oman....... 449	—	—	11	2	6	12	9	2	1	—	—	—	1	2
Qatar....... 453	1	2	7	4	6	10	—	....	....	....	....	....	....	....
Saudi Arabia....... 456	62	90	77	100	119	166	165	4	5	3	9	28	9	24
Syrian Arab Republic....... 463	69	96	124	145	87	88	118	32	68	4	6	13	13	20
United Arab Emirates....... 466	54	65	76	163	254	486	458	2	2	2	7	5	6	20
Yemen, Republic of....... 474	1	3	3	13	19	28	41	—	—	—	—	—	—	—
Western Hemisphere....... 207	**124**	**109**	**82**	**89**	**152**	**203**	**407**	**309**	**263**	**355**	**510**	**667**	**740**	**788**
Antigua and Barbuda....... 311	—	—	—	—	—	—	52	....	....	....	....	....	....	....
Argentina....... 213	21	4	7	15	18	18	27	10	15	14	21	26	29	76
Aruba....... 314	—	—	—	—	—	—	—	—	—	—	—	2	2	7
Bahamas, The....... 313	—	13	11	—	—	—	2	—	—	—	—	—	—	—
Bermuda....... 319	—	—	—	—	—	—	1	....	....	....	....	....	....	....
Bolivia....... 218	—	—	—	—	—	—	—	—	2	—	—	—	—	—
Brazil....... 223	16	9	6	10	17	15	70	196	176	232	361	448	516	485

	Exports							Imports, f.o.b						
	2001	2002	2003	2004	2005	2006	2007	2001	2002	2003	2004	2005	2006	2007
	Millions of U.S. Dollars							*Millions of U.S. Dollars*						
Chile....228	11	8	3	2	18	7	7	1	1	2	3	3	10	3
Colombia....233	4	7	4	7	36	76	97	11	6	6	8	10	9	10
Costa Rica....238	1	1	—	—	—	—	—	2	1	7	9	12	13	4
Dominica....321	—	1	—	—	—	—	—	—	—	—	—	—	—	—
Dominican Republic....243	—	1	—	1	3	1	5	—	—	—	1	1	1	2
Ecuador....248	1	—	1	1	3	1	1	14	20	27	39	54	61	75
El Salvador....253	—	—	1	—	—	—	—	—	—	—	—	—	1	—
Guatemala....258	—	3	1	1	1	3	2	—	—	2	1	2	3	9
Guyana....336	—	—	—	—	—	—	—	5	—	—	—	—	—	—
Honduras....268	—	—	—	1	1	1	—	3	3	5	4	2	3	1
Jamaica....343	—	1	—	—	—	—	—	—	3	20	—	—	—	13
Mexico....273	19	24	9	11	18	60	30	7	18	23	30	79	72	56
Netherlands Antilles....353	—	—	12	—	—	—	—	....	....	....	....	....	....	....
Nicaragua....278	—	—	—	—	—	—	—	—	—	1	1	1	1	—
Panama....283	2	1	1	4	4	3	88	1	1	—	—	—	1	3
Paraguay....288	—	—	—	—	—	—	—	9	—	—	—	—	—	6
Peru....293	10	7	9	10	8	3	4	7	9	5	8	7	11	9
St. Vincent & Grens....364	1	—	—	2	—	—	—	....	....	....	....	....	....	....
Suriname....366	—	—	—	—	—	—	—	—	—	—	—	—	—	13
Trinidad and Tobago....369	3	12	2	3	1	2	4	—	—	—	—	—	—	—
Uruguay....298	—	2	1	—	—	—	—	—	2	2	3	7	6	2
Venezuela, Rep. Bol....299	34	14	13	19	23	11	16	26	5	8	20	12	1	11
Other Countries n.i.e....910	**1**	**2**	**5**	**1**	**3**	**1**	**2**	**17**	**15**	**16**	**9**	**8**	**2**	**1**
Cuba....928	1	2	—	—	3	—	1	17	14	13	8	6	1	1
North Korea....954	—	—	5	1	—	1	1	1	2	3	1	2	1	—
Countries & Areas n.s....898	**45**	**24**	**26**	**25**	**408**	**665**	**29**	**439**	**70**	**90**	**87**	**339**	**432**	**48**
Memorandum Items														
European Union....998	8,417	10,079	13,007	17,170	18,697	21,958	27,763	9,379	10,953	14,678	19,276	22,758	29,140	44,580
Oil Exporting Ctys....999	315	377	396	521	757	1,003	1,021	121	79	69	196	203	376	761
Non-Oil Develop.Ctys....201	2,612	3,166	4,210	6,193	8,124	10,148	13,866	4,459	5,512	7,705	10,871	14,682	18,565	25,235
PERCENT DISTRIBUTION														
Industrial Countries....101	**73.9**	**74.3**	**73.7**	**71.3**	**66.4**	**63.6**	**62.9**	**64.4**	**65.0**	**63.8**	**62.3**	**58.5**	**58.5**	**59.1**
Developing Countries....202	**25.7**	**25.5**	**26.1**	**28.6**	**32.1**	**34.3**	**36.9**	**32.4**	**34.5**	**35.7**	**37.4**	**40.6**	**40.6**	**40.8**
Africa....607	**1.5**	**1.1**	**1.1**	**1.0**	**1.4**	**1.4**	**1.1**	**.5**	**.7**	**.5**	**.4**	**.4**	**.3**	**.2**
Asia....507	**2.8**	**4.9**	**3.9**	**2.6**	**2.8**	**2.2**	**2.3**	**4.2**	**6.3**	**6.4**	**6.9**	**7.6**	**8.0**	**5.8**
Europe....170	**15.5**	**13.3**	**16.5**	**20.4**	**23.1**	**25.4**	**28.5**	**23.6**	**24.7**	**26.5**	**27.5**	**29.8**	**29.3**	**31.9**
Middle East....407	**4.8**	**5.5**	**4.2**	**4.2**	**4.2**	**4.7**	**4.0**	**1.9**	**1.2**	**.7**	**.8**	**1.0**	**1.4**	**1.6**
Western Hemisphere....207	**1.1**	**.8**	**.5**	**.4**	**.5**	**.6**	**1.0**	**2.2**	**1.6**	**1.6**	**1.7**	**1.8**	**1.6**	**1.2**
Other Countries n.i.e....910	—	—	—	—	—	—	—	**.1**	**.1**	**.1**	—	—	—	—
ANNUAL PERCENT CHANGE														
World....001	**9.8**	**21.8**	**27.0**	**33.3**	**17.8**	**17.5**	**24.2**	**19.1**	**14.6**	**34.3**	**36.1**	**23.9**	**27.2**	**36.5**
Industrial Countries....101	**15.6**	**22.5**	**25.9**	**28.9**	**9.7**	**12.6**	**22.9**	**19.8**	**15.6**	**31.9**	**32.9**	**16.3**	**27.2**	**38.0**
Developing Countries....202	**−3.5**	**21.1**	**30.0**	**45.8**	**32.3**	**25.6**	**33.5**	**20.2**	**22.1**	**39.0**	**42.4**	**34.5**	**27.3**	**37.2**
Africa....607	**−10.4**	**−11.9**	**25.8**	**22.5**	**63.9**	**13.3**	**.3**	**38.8**	**45.3**	**−9.0**	**24.8**	**7.1**	**−9.3**	**28.0**
Asia....507	**37.7**	**114.3**	**2.3**	**−10.5**	**27.6**	**−9.0**	**29.4**	**16.5**	**73.4**	**37.1**	**46.3**	**36.3**	**34.1**	**−.8**
Europe....170	**−12.4**	**4.6**	**57.0**	**65.0**	**33.5**	**29.1**	**39.3**	**15.9**	**19.8**	**44.4**	**41.3**	**34.0**	**25.4**	**48.3**
Middle East....407	**6.9**	**39.0**	**−2.4**	**33.0**	**17.8**	**32.4**	**4.8**	**125.1**	**−26.0**	**−25.4**	**54.2**	**58.8**	**74.2**	**61.2**
Western Hemisphere....207	**50.6**	**−12.5**	**−24.9**	**8.5**	**71.3**	**33.9**	**100.7**	**22.0**	**−14.8**	**35.0**	**43.6**	**30.9**	**11.0**	**6.4**
Other Countries n.i.e....910	**−54.7**	**27.1**	**180.9**	**−74.6**	**129.6**	**−78.8**	**161.7**	**−8.5**	**−14.0**	**4.4**	**−39.7**	**−12.2**	**−78.3**	**−51.3**

	Exports							Imports						
	2001	2002	2003	2004	2005	2006	2007	2001	2002	2003	2004	2005	2006	2007
	Millions of U.S. Dollars							*Millions of U.S. Dollars*						
IFS World Total	**101,884**	**107,301**	**135,929**	**183,207**	**243,798**	**303,926**	**355,175**	**59,140**	**67,063**	**83,677**	**107,120**	**137,977**	**181,161**	**245,364**
DOTS World Total 001	**82,538**	**107,224**	**131,469**	**166,370**	**239,277**	**291,881**	**352,368**	**36,889**	**45,507**	**56,677**	**69,055**	**97,405**	**132,517**	**199,444**
Industrial Countries 101	**43,712**	**53,285**	**65,635**	**89,554**	**128,482**	**162,191**	**182,652**	**20,164**	**23,392**	**28,103**	**37,660**	**49,836**	**69,645**	**100,110**
United States 111	5,944	6,517	6,082	8,354	7,475	8,909	8,305	3,199	2,923	2,931	3,205	4,571	6,417	9,502
Canada 156	57	86	265	500	200	362	335	242	222	299	334	514	901	1,222
Australia 193	10	9	19	22	36	29	48	141	99	91	151	244	495	650
Japan 158	2,438	1,789	2,407	3,471	3,768	4,688	7,564	813	974	1,816	3,937	5,841	7,785	12,717
New Zealand 196	7	5	8	22	12	4	5	35	58	63	56	64	88	92
Austria 122	596	729	1,029	1,115	2,339	3,353	2,737	536	605	780	917	1,208	1,840	2,457
Belgium 124	557	795	1,119	1,821	2,462	2,646	2,809	639	760	860	1,176	1,472	2,169	3,185
Cyprus 423	1,398	1,555	4,363	5,310	4,875	4,530	4,831	28	14	14	22	47	42	35
Denmark 128	327	414	205	518	725	932	1,083	494	511	603	716	920	1,345	1,596
Finland 172	3,032	2,915	4,283	5,764	7,672	9,198	10,750	1,275	1,497	1,820	2,331	3,078	3,995	5,027
France 132	1,722	2,645	3,464	4,130	6,123	7,526	8,724	1,516	1,880	2,312	3,061	3,671	5,863	7,769
Germany 134	8,178	8,033	10,285	13,295	19,747	24,491	26,347	5,716	6,508	7,956	10,571	13,226	18,428	26,552
Greece 174	810	953	927	1,159	1,899	2,759	2,625	144	171	141	167	189	235	312
Iceland 176	4	1	3	2	8	8	46	6	8	11	28	37	77	67
Ireland 178	116	260	870	647	707	630	525	153	197	232	239	289	460	656
Italy 136	6,844	7,409	8,340	10,271	18,959	25,106	27,532	1,341	2,205	2,369	3,197	4,436	5,724	8,536
Luxembourg 137	18	56	33	108	64	142	195	15	11	33	57	58	86	155
Malta 181	37	141	83	104	125	372	423	2	3	3	9	16	85	16
Netherlands 138	3,870	7,185	8,554	15,207	24,564	35,877	42,826	840	1,078	1,232	1,373	1,935	2,680	3,858
Norway 142	199	268	301	402	686	714	615	196	285	320	464	745	1,110	977
Portugal 182	211	136	118	501	1,990	1,661	1,817	20	34	43	67	89	145	219
Slovenia 961	119	135	167	140	142	269	266	241	257	306	379	456	614	792
Spain 184	892	1,099	1,279	1,679	2,824	3,345	4,320	486	572	749	878	1,224	1,950	3,197
Sweden 144	1,622	997	924	1,568	2,331	2,192	2,998	711	1,005	1,175	1,610	1,854	2,141	3,124
Switzerland 146	1,522	5,352	5,736	7,798	10,462	12,059	13,910	394	417	535	650	879	1,296	1,753
United Kingdom 112	3,182	3,802	4,772	5,645	8,288	10,388	11,015	980	1,099	1,410	2,064	2,773	3,673	5,645
Developing Countries 202	**38,501**	**52,242**	**65,659**	**76,447**	**110,399**	**129,275**	**168,759**	**16,229**	**21,802**	**28,392**	**31,066**	**47,357**	**62,635**	**99,079**
Africa 607	**506**	**872**	**879**	**1,222**	**1,338**	**1,844**	**3,095**	**392**	**483**	**558**	**689**	**883**	**1,010**	**1,399**
Algeria 612	130	169	291	183	206	643	1,401	—	—	1	1	2	—	11
Angola 614	20	51	24	35	27	81	36	—	—	—	—	—	—	1
Botswana 616	—	—	—	—	—	—	—	—	—	—	—	—	—	1
Burkina Faso 748	2	1	3	4	8	6	8	1	—	—	—	—	—	—
Burundi 618	—	—	—	—	—	—	—	—	—	—	—	1	1	2
Cameroon 622	1	1	—	1	1	1	5	2	—	1	2	2	2	4
Cape Verde 624	—	—	1	—	—	—	—	—	—	—	—	—	—	—
Chad 628	—	9	1	—	1	6	1	—	—	—	—	—	—	—
Congo, Dem. Rep. of 636	—	—	2	2	3	3	2	—	1	—	2	1	2	7
Congo, Republic of 634	1	6	3	1	—	2	1	1	—	1	—	—	1	1
Côte d'Ivoire 662	20	11	6	21	13	14	13	73	144	130	132	137	144	169
Djibouti 611	—	2	—	—	—	4	7	—	—	—	—	—	—	—
Equatorial Guinea 642	—	—	—	2	1	12	7	—	—	—	—	—	—	—
Eritrea 643	—	—	4	37	8	2	17	—	—	—	—	—	—	—
Ethiopia 644	8	17	56	94	22	11	23	—	—	—	1	3	5	8
Gabon 646	—	—	—	—	—	—	—	—	—	—	—	—	1	1
Ghana 652	4	5	6	19	16	16	35	13	17	19	24	28	30	44
Guinea 656	3	3	3	10	10	6	8	79	62	78	165	214	173	198
Kenya 664	10	12	20	19	42	55	80	3	10	16	19	26	30	45
Liberia 668	10	129	40	28	36	64	48	—	—	—	1	—	1	10
Madagascar 674	1	—	—	—	—	—	—	—	—	—	—	—	1	2
Malawi 676	—	—	—	—	—	—	—	11	21	22	19	32	36	50
Mali 678	1	1	3	2	3	5	6	—	—	—	4	3	—	—
Mauritania 682	1	9	18	2	3	1	8	29	22	32	40	51	46	62
Mauritius 684	—	—	—	—	—	1	—	—	—	—	—	1	2	5
Morocco 686	134	197	111	346	396	262	528	47	58	78	87	144	230	334
Mozambique 688	—	—	—	—	—	4	11	6	7	6	4	10	22	31
Namibia 728	—	—	1	1	2	2	2	—	—	6	—	16	1	5
Niger 692	—	—	—	—	—	—	—	—	—	—	—	—	53	7
Nigeria 694	63	65	74	74	156	144	148	7	2	6	7	2	2	3
Rwanda 714	—	7	2	—	6	1	1	—	—	—	—	1	2	1
Senegal 722	11	7	11	7	3	14	19	—	—	—	—	—	—	—
Seychelles 718	3	8	10	2	4	28	5	—	—	—	—	1	3	1
Sierra Leone 724	1	1	7	1	—	—	—	—	—	—	2	1	1	3
South Africa 199	6	40	7	9	25	20	14	60	92	112	130	147	159	270
Sudan 732	4	21	55	149	94	106	68	2	1	1	1	—	3	10
Swaziland 734	—	—	—	—	—	—	—	11	—	—	—	—	—	1
Tanzania 738	6	6	3	2	35	33	47	5	4	9	14	18	24	34
Togo 742	4	2	7	13	2	6	57	—	1	1	—	—	—	—
Tunisia 744	55	91	99	192	221	282	479	6	1	5	5	13	11	26
Uganda 746	2	2	12	1	1	7	20	2	3	6	7	8	4	9

	Exports							Imports						
	2001	2002	2003	2004	2005	2006	2007	2001	2002	2003	2004	2005	2006	2007
	Millions of U.S. Dollars							*Millions of U.S. Dollars*						
Zambia........ 754	—	—	—	—	—	—	—	—	—	2	1	2	6	11
Zimbabwe........ 698	—	—	—	—	—	3	6	33	35	24	19	20	17	33
Asia........ 507	**7,564**	**12,179**	**15,312**	**19,282**	**22,666**	**24,957**	**31,377**	**3,821**	**5,032**	**6,596**	**9,288**	**14,829**	**24,642**	**40,328**
Afghanistan, I.S. of........ 512	8	32	54	76	104	82	125	3	5	6	4	4	12	9
Bangladesh........ 513	24	31	32	60	187	235	193	4	1	5	11	16	41	88
Cambodia........ 522	5	—	1	2	2	3	11	—	—	1	2	6	8	18
China,P.R.: Mainland........ 924	4,021	6,790	8,161	10,020	13,049	15,734	15,893	1,611	2,382	3,270	4,733	7,239	12,888	24,412
China,P.R.:Hong Kong........ 532	126	184	321	318	349	353	343	15	10	7	10	19	86	105
China,P.R.:Macao........ 546	—	—	—	1	1	—	—	—	—	—	—	—	1	3
Fiji........ 819	—	—	—	—	—	—	5	—	—	—	—	—	—	—
India........ 534	695	1,622	2,732	2,461	2,314	2,907	4,011	541	515	579	643	784	967	1,317
Indonesia........ 536	30	31	236	145	203	187	252	95	161	182	221	348	420	665
Korea........ 542	842	1,225	1,317	1,963	2,365	1,930	6,157	782	916	1,312	2,025	3,997	6,777	8,837
Lao People's Dem.Rep........ 544	4	4	2	6	11	4	2	—	—	—	—	—	1	1
Malaysia........ 548	261	348	423	114	150	239	440	157	228	297	423	672	893	1,469
Mongolia........ 948	211	231	284	363	443	490	629	35	49	36	21	22	38	48
Myanmar........ 518	2	88	11	23	1	7	21	—	13	—	2	2	3	3
Nepal........ 558	7	2	6	7	4	3	2	1	—	—	—	—	—	1
Pakistan........ 564	57	82	71	227	231	299	260	26	18	19	25	48	112	104
Papua New Guinea........ 853	—	3	3	7	1	1	—	1	1	1	2	3	3	4
Philippines........ 566	45	98	184	217	198	79	117	22	31	38	50	73	88	124
Singapore........ 576	719	521	158	186	307	790	1,088	106	87	89	162	317	436	452
Sri Lanka........ 524	11	8	5	8	14	32	22	77	102	119	156	163	204	258
Taiwan Province of China........ 528	263	463	827	1,999	1,446	931	903	163	206	258	342	490	756	885
Thailand........ 578	69	96	130	372	547	347	330	105	226	298	355	450	559	1,006
Vietnam........ 582	164	321	354	706	739	304	570	79	80	76	100	174	349	521
Europe........ 170	**27,050**	**34,645**	**44,222**	**49,000**	**76,243**	**91,185**	**118,755**	**10,274**	**14,384**	**18,568**	**18,241**	**26,908**	**30,369**	**48,800**
Albania........ 914	9	20	36	38	50	48	136	1	—	7	2	2	4	4
Armenia........ 911	60	95	126	135	191	392	655	51	56	75	73	101	103	166
Azerbaijan........ 912	130	277	408	621	856	1,372	1,397	73	86	92	139	205	259	328
Belarus........ 913	—	5,843	7,540	—	8,095	3,321	17,489	—	4,069	4,900	—	4,614	1,927	8,872
Bosnia & Herzegovina........ 963	40	28	53	43	81	95	90	5	1	2	19	3	4	7
Bulgaria........ 918	445	528	614	1,019	1,900	2,966	3,794	136	134	158	203	241	331	415
Croatia........ 960	358	380	357	563	850	802	1,255	77	42	63	79	80	179	156
Czech Republic........ 935	1,469	1,508	1,939	2,223	3,818	4,665	4,655	460	558	699	835	988	1,529	2,450
Estonia........ 939	1,237	1,662	1,426	1,532	2,104	2,706	1,633	102	104	125	178	245	325	377
Faroe Islands........ 816	—	—	1	—	—	—	1	—	—	1	3	3	24	23
Georgia........ 915	58	91	152	230	353	570	589	83	68	83	107	157	68	63
Gibraltar........ 823	310	54	141	497	428	205	209	—	—	—	—	—	—	1
Hungary........ 944	2,099	2,167	2,827	3,205	4,975	6,244	6,121	441	508	590	740	1,098	1,863	2,602
Kazakhstan........ 916	2,544	2,412	3,270	4,648	6,529	8,970	11,934	1,834	1,943	2,662	3,457	3,210	3,824	4,622
Kyrgyz Republic........ 917	83	104	160	265	397	561	879	61	74	103	150	145	194	290
Latvia........ 941	889	694	1,060	1,353	1,186	1,692	2,644	117	150	180	212	339	387	507
Lithuania........ 946	1,610	1,693	2,144	2,921	4,005	4,210	4,057	207	310	393	461	568	702	849
Macedonia, FYR........ 962	30	20	14	12	20	24	36	17	16	19	26	35	41	45
Moldova........ 921	210	269	305	374	448	663	870	344	281	397	496	548	323	490
Montenegro, Rep. of........ 943	—	—	—	—	—	—	155	—	—	—	—	—	—	—
Poland........ 964	3,952	3,719	4,606	5,682	8,621	11,478	13,298	950	1,294	1,682	2,302	2,744	3,400	4,630
Romania........ 968	749	939	1,280	1,674	3,045	3,272	3,211	86	61	68	130	233	540	731
Serbia, Rep. of........ 942	—	—	—	—	—	580	790	—	—	—	—	—	—	385
Serbia & Montenegro........ 965	—	—	—	—	—	300	93	—	—	—	—	—	—	19
Slovak Republic........ 936	2,013	2,032	2,296	2,426	3,189	4,583	5,151	131	158	294	405	502	769	1,411
Tajikistan........ 923	69	68	128	183	240	377	607	129	65	68	76	95	125	162
Turkey........ 186	2,980	3,349	4,754	7,200	10,859	14,348	18,463	509	724	916	1,225	1,738	2,681	4,182
Turkmenistan........ 925	139	143	221	242	224	229	384	39	32	28	43	77	79	69
Ukraine........ 926	4,931	5,852	7,531	10,663	12,378	14,976	16,424	3,777	3,219	4,369	6,097	7,776	9,239	13,326
Uzbekistan........ 927	364	453	503	767	861	1,086	1,729	580	342	480	612	902	1,290	1,464
Yugoslavia n.s........ 966	273	244	333	483	539	449	—	65	89	113	169	259	159	—
Europe n.s........ 884	—	—	—	2	—	—	6	—	—	—	—	1	—	154
Middle East........ 407	**2,532**	**3,791**	**4,296**	**5,647**	**6,751**	**6,558**	**10,348**	**201**	**269**	**347**	**421**	**691**	**1,021**	**1,192**
Bahrain........ 419	1	—	1	1	—	10	5	—	—	—	—	1	—	11
Egypt........ 469	426	489	374	777	1,050	1,239	1,952	12	21	39	56	82	132	173
Iran, I.R. of........ 429	894	752	1,319	1,892	1,930	1,895	2,958	34	50	61	111	141	238	349
Iraq........ 433	187	367	167	206	107	113	52	—	—	—	—	—	—	—
Israel........ 436	372	1,077	1,421	1,301	1,539	1,560	2,040	128	158	205	208	332	408	531
Jordan........ 439	20	18	33	54	104	65	418	—	2	3	2	4	4	11
Kuwait........ 443	9	82	3	1	23	10	18	—	—	—	1	—	—	—
Lebanon........ 446	228	112	137	149	237	142	196	5	4	2	6	8	11	9
Libya........ 672	11	24	54	119	166	72	232	—	—	—	—	—	—	—
Oman........ 449	3	6	5	17	40	19	78	1	—	1	—	2	1	—
Qatar........ 453	—	—	2	18	2	—	1	—	—	—	—	1	2	10
Saudi Arabia........ 456	66	137	208	139	230	273	427	1	2	2	6	5	6	10
Syrian Arab Republic........ 463	89	138	209	290	441	604	1,023	17	16	14	17	26	30	38
United Arab Emirates........ 466	222	386	273	482	692	461	771	3	15	3	14	90	187	49
Yemen, Republic of........ 474	5	205	89	202	189	95	179	—	—	18	—	—	—	—
Western Hemisphere........ 207	**848**	**755**	**949**	**1,296**	**3,401**	**4,731**	**5,184**	**1,541**	**1,634**	**2,324**	**2,427**	**4,046**	**5,595**	**7,360**
Argentina........ 213	10	26	7	33	72	153	259	100	189	227	355	620	958	1,125
Aruba........ 314	—	—	—	59	25	—	—	—	—	—	—	—	—	—
Bahamas, The........ 313	14	12	1	135	234	355	—	—	1	—	1	1	1	1

	Exports							Imports						
	2001	2002	2003	2004	2005	2006	2007	2001	2002	2003	2004	2005	2006	2007
	Millions of U.S. Dollars							Millions of U.S. Dollars						
Barbados.......316	—	—	1	—	1	—	—	—	—	—	—	—	—	—
Belize.......339	1	—	2	20	62	24	35	3	—	—	—	1	1	1
Bermuda.......319	118	—	—	2	—	—	—	—	—	—	—	—	1	1
Bolivia.......218	—	—	—	—	—	—	1	—	—	2	2	4	2	4
Brazil.......223	190	229	255	369	606	726	1,130	918	949	1,473	1,370	2,342	2,985	4,108
Chile.......228	21	45	9	3	11	14	22	16	30	45	82	129	152	259
Colombia.......233	17	46	15	42	48	47	115	34	34	22	67	94	89	144
Costa Rica.......238	1	1	3	12	25	14	13	22	10	10	6	30	31	34
Dominica.......321	—	—	—	2	—	—	—	—	—	—	—	—	—	—
Dominican Republic.......243	10	14	5	27	26	64	15	—	—	1	1	1	3	13
Ecuador.......248	33	16	18	36	22	89	42	166	191	262	361	468	530	755
El Salvador.......253	22	11	15	16	31	62	33	31	14	26	12	17	27	33
Falkland Islands.......323	....	....	....	....	....	....	....	—	—	—	—	—	—	1
Greenland.......326	—	7	—	—	—	—	—	—	—	2	1	1	2	8
Guatemala.......258	29	17	25	37	38	55	49	44	23	56	2	6	6	9
Guyana.......336	—	1	—	2	1	—	—	—	2	—	—	—	—	—
Haiti.......263	1	1	—	1	1	2	1	—	—	—	—	—	—	—
Honduras.......268	15	17	18	36	12	30	37	5	9	8	1	14	2	3
Jamaica.......343	1	—	—	2	2	3	2	28	11	21	1	22	31	97
Mexico.......273	94	101	98	181	208	248	285	50	50	60	63	87	185	412
Netherlands Antilles.......353	37	—	119	—	—	57	38	—	—	—	—	—	—	—
Nicaragua.......278	4	7	4	12	13	15	2	39	20	18	1	16	14	5
Panama.......283	172	86	87	102	268	70	16	1	24	4	2	4	21	8
Paraguay.......288	—	1	2	—	—	—	—	3	4	2	25	71	225	167
Peru.......293	35	49	60	62	70	107	183	30	16	28	15	29	21	27
St. Kitts and Nevis.......361	1	1	—	—	—	2	1	—	—	—	—	—	—	—
St. Vincent & Grens.......364	1	3	1	3	17	2	18	—	—	—	—	—	15	—
Suriname.......366	—	—	—	—	—	—	—	—	—	3	—	—	9	19
Trinidad and Tobago.......369	3	5	5	12	8	5	2	—	—	—	—	—	—	—
Uruguay.......298	11	54	196	83	143	22	90	5	21	23	19	35	222	110
Venezuela, Rep. Bol.......299	6	6	1	6	25	456	1,117	45	36	33	38	52	60	13
Western Hem. n.s.......399	3	—	—	—	1,432	2,106	1,679	—	—	—	—	—	1	5
Other Countries n.i.e.......910	**122**	**83**	**149**	**258**	**353**	**375**	**343**	**451**	**299**	**182**	**185**	**68**	**67**	**102**
Cuba.......928	64	34	38	53	125	184	217	435	288	179	181	61	47	68
North Korea.......954	58	49	111	205	228	190	126	16	11	3	5	7	20	34
Countries & Areas n.s.......898	**200**	**1,613**	**12**	**111**	**29**	**40**	**65**	**44**	**15**	**—**	**144**	**144**	**170**	**153**
Memorandum Items														
European Union.......998	46,798	52,734	67,112	88,325	133,733	170,995	189,383	17,544	21,487	26,002	33,967	43,424	60,448	85,957
Oil Exporting Ctys.......999	1,622	2,024	2,634	3,282	3,781	4,274	7,454	185	267	289	400	642	918	1,110
Non-Oil Develop.Ctys.......201	36,879	50,218	63,025	73,165	106,617	125,001	161,306	16,044	21,535	28,103	30,666	46,714	61,717	97,969
PERCENT DISTRIBUTION														
Industrial Countries.......101	**53.0**	**49.7**	**49.9**	**53.8**	**53.7**	**55.6**	**51.8**	**54.7**	**51.4**	**49.6**	**54.5**	**51.2**	**52.6**	**50.2**
Developing Countries.......202	**46.6**	**48.7**	**49.9**	**46.0**	**46.1**	**44.3**	**47.9**	**44.0**	**47.9**	**50.1**	**45.0**	**48.6**	**47.3**	**49.7**
Africa.......607	**.6**	**.8**	**.7**	**.7**	**.6**	**.6**	**.9**	**1.1**	**1.1**	**1.0**	**1.0**	**.9**	**.8**	**.7**
Asia.......507	**9.2**	**11.4**	**11.6**	**11.6**	**9.5**	**8.6**	**8.9**	**10.4**	**11.1**	**11.6**	**13.4**	**15.2**	**18.6**	**20.2**
Europe.......170	**32.8**	**32.3**	**33.6**	**29.5**	**31.9**	**31.2**	**33.7**	**27.9**	**31.6**	**32.8**	**26.4**	**27.6**	**22.9**	**24.5**
Middle East.......407	**3.1**	**3.5**	**3.3**	**3.4**	**2.8**	**2.2**	**2.9**	**.5**	**.6**	**.6**	**.6**	**.7**	**.8**	**.6**
Western Hemisphere.......207	**1.0**	**.7**	**.7**	**.8**	**1.4**	**1.6**	**1.5**	**4.2**	**3.6**	**4.1**	**3.5**	**4.2**	**4.2**	**3.7**
Other Countries n.i.e.......910	**.1**	**.1**	**.1**	**.2**	**.1**	**.1**	**.1**	**1.2**	**.7**	**.3**	**.3**	**.1**	**.1**	**.1**
ANNUAL PERCENT CHANGE														
World.......001	**–19.9**	**29.9**	**22.6**	**26.5**	**43.8**	**22.0**	**20.7**	**9.0**	**23.4**	**24.5**	**21.8**	**41.1**	**36.0**	**50.5**
Industrial Countries.......101	**–18.7**	**21.9**	**23.2**	**36.4**	**43.5**	**26.2**	**12.6**	**31.0**	**16.0**	**20.1**	**34.0**	**32.3**	**39.7**	**43.7**
Developing Countries.......202	**–21.7**	**35.7**	**25.7**	**16.4**	**44.4**	**17.1**	**30.5**	**–10.5**	**34.3**	**30.2**	**9.4**	**52.4**	**32.3**	**58.2**
Africa.......607	**–17.6**	**72.1**	**.9**	**38.9**	**9.5**	**37.8**	**67.9**	**4.2**	**23.2**	**15.4**	**23.5**	**28.1**	**14.4**	**38.6**
Asia.......507	**–18.8**	**61.0**	**25.7**	**25.9**	**17.6**	**10.1**	**25.7**	**59.7**	**31.7**	**31.1**	**40.8**	**59.7**	**66.2**	**63.7**
Europe.......170	**–23.5**	**28.1**	**27.6**	**10.8**	**55.6**	**19.6**	**30.2**	**–28.0**	**40.0**	**29.1**	**–1.8**	**47.5**	**12.9**	**60.7**
Middle East.......407	**–10.7**	**49.7**	**13.3**	**31.4**	**19.6**	**–2.8**	**57.8**	**–3.3**	**33.7**	**29.1**	**21.3**	**64.1**	**47.7**	**16.8**
Western Hemisphere.......207	**–16.4**	**–10.9**	**25.7**	**36.6**	**162.3**	**39.1**	**9.6**	**72.2**	**6.1**	**42.2**	**4.4**	**66.7**	**38.3**	**31.5**
Other Countries n.i.e.......910	**2.7**	**–31.7**	**78.3**	**73.3**	**37.1**	**6.0**	**–8.5**	**44.5**	**–33.8**	**–39.2**	**2.2**	**–63.2**	**–2.3**	**52.5**

	Exports 2001	2002	2003	2004	2005	2006	2007	Imports 2001	2002	2003	2004	2005	2006	2007
	Millions of U.S. Dollars							Millions of U.S. Dollars						
IFS World Total	**84.9**	**55.9**	**57.7**	**97.8**	**124.9**	**135.0**	**176.7**	**249.7**	**203.1**	**245.2**	**283.4**	**430.2**	**485.1**	**737.2**
DOTS World Total 001	**129.7Y**	**146.0Y**	**150.8Y**	**385.1Y**	**162.2Y**	**197.7Y**	**240.9Y**	**264.0Y**	**303.2Y**	**369.7Y**	**446.1Y**	**519.5Y**	**631.4Y**	**768.8Y**
Industrial Countries 101	**50.3Y**	**22.4Y**	**19.9Y**	**30.4Y**	**45.3Y**	**53.9Y**	**53.6Y**	**91.7Y**	**98.8Y**	**111.3Y**	**140.7Y**	**137.2Y**	**171.4Y**	**200.6Y**
United States 111	6.91V	3.00V	2.64V	5.27V	6.09V	8.36V	11.91V	19.25V	11.22V	8.80V	12.43V	11.55V	12.87V	17.71V
Canada 156	.01V	.53V	.01V	.04V	.30V	.14V	.27V	1.09V	1.20V	1.16V	1.17V	2.16V	1.05V	1.80V
Australia 193	.08V	.07V	.03V	—V	.18V	.14V	.07V	.76V	.18V	.08V	.30V	.21V	.11V	.17V
Japan 158	2.13V	.01V	.31V	—V	.06V	.07V	.57V	6.58V	6.01V	8.06V	3.90V	14.34V	7.28V	15.20V
New Zealand 196	—V	—V	—V	—V	.01V	—V	—V	.04V	.01V	—V	.04V	.08V	.09V	—V
Austria 122	.37V	.66V	.39V	.32V	2.32V	4.43V	7.35V	.65V	.54V	.16V	.27V	.24V	1.47V	.46V
Belgium 124	2.41V	4.35V	2.17V	3.74V	7.23V	7.10V	4.33V	22.55V	25.24V	23.13V	31.37V	30.38V	31.88V	45.34V
Cyprus 423	—V	—V	—V	—V	—Y	—V	—V	—V	—V	—V	—V	.08V	—V	.02V
Denmark 128	.43V	.48V	.94V	1.03V	.50V	.81V	.64V	2.29V	3.92V	3.22V	3.95V	1.85V	1.77V	1.32V
Finland 172	—V	—V	—V	—V	.09V	—V	—V	.57V	.21V	.42V	.26V	.02V	.37V	2.77V
France 132	.65V	.71V	.73V	1.14V	2.54V	5.25V	2.35V	8.82V	11.10V	17.63V	24.31V	11.14V	11.99V	13.39V
Germany 134	28.08V	4.77V	7.16V	10.55V	17.81V	18.82V	16.39V	6.78V	19.73V	26.56V	35.31V	29.36V	48.40V	47.41V
Greece 174	.10V	.15V	.19V	.09V	.08V	—V	—V	.05V	.02V	.31V	.22V	.12V	.18V	.07V
Iceland 176	.03V	—V	—V	—V	—V	—V	—V	—V	—V	—V	—V	—V	—V	—V
Ireland 178	—V	.03V	.03V	.09V	.05V	.03V	—V	.55V	.42V	.48V	.56V	.58V	.36V	.60V
Italy 136	.60V	.98V	.62V	.30V	.40V	.62V	1.09V	3.86V	3.28V	3.27V	5.48V	4.05V	10.89V	6.33V
Luxembourg 137	.01V	.01V	—V	.01V	—V	—V	—V	.51V	.35V	.58V	.40V	.33V	.80V	.22V
Malta 181	—Y	—V	—V	—V	—V	—V	—V	—Y	—V	—V	—V	—V	.02V	.98V
Netherlands 138	6.31V	2.68V	3.04V	4.02V	4.33V	5.95V	4.56V	7.29V	5.84V	7.47V	9.65V	11.24V	15.67V	14.43V
Norway 142	—V	—V	—V	—V	—V	.07V	—V	.04V	.09V	.15V	.07V	.37V	.10V	.22V
Portugal 182	.19V	.01V	—V	—V	—V	.03V	—V	.23V	.29V	.12V	.11V	.64V	.17V	2.44V
Slovenia 961	.04V	.01V	.01V	.02Y	—V	—V	.10V	—V	.22V	—V	—Y	—V	—V	.02V
Spain 184	1.16V	1.63V	.88V	2.98V	1.07V	.44V	.02V	.82V	1.64V	1.00V	1.03V	2.40V	.93V	8.40V
Sweden 144	.08V	.66V	.33V	.28V	1.10V	.92V	1.13V	.61V	1.22V	1.01V	.49V	6.36V	12.01V	4.36V
Switzerland 146	.05V	.04V	.03V	.06V	.28V	.28V	.03V	.40V	.53V	1.94V	.53V	.61V	5.68V	2.53V
United Kingdom 112	.63V	1.61V	.37V	.46V	.81V	.46V	2.80V	7.97V	5.53V	5.76V	8.83V	9.13V	7.34V	14.39V
Developing Countries 202	**42.3Y**	**83.3Y**	**79.9Y**	**287.7Y**	**40.3Y**	**49.2Y**	**69.8Y**	**109.5Y**	**136.2Y**	**172.0Y**	**192.0Y**	**252.8Y**	**299.9Y**	**369.6Y**
Africa 607	**11.0Y**	**4.7Y**	**3.2Y**	**4.7Y**	**6.0Y**	**6.7Y**	**7.5Y**	**77.2Y**	**100.8Y**	**141.2Y**	**155.9Y**	**172.6Y**	**220.6Y**	**264.3Y**
Benin 638	—V	—V	—V	—V	—V	—Y	—Y	—V	—V	—V	—V	—V	—Y	.01Y
Burundi 618	.44V	.75V	.67V	.67V	.81V	.94V	1.16Y	2.42V	3.44V	2.35V	4.62V	2.97V	3.43V	4.26Y
Cameroon 622	—V	—V	—V	—Y	—Y	—Y	—Y	—V	.06V	.49V	.64Y	.73Y	.90Y	1.12Y
Congo, Dem. Rep. of 636	1.13Y	1.23Y	1.55Y	2.04Y	2.33Y	2.88Y	3.57Y	6.82Y	7.41Y	9.37Y	12.31Y	14.07Y	17.39Y	21.57Y
Congo, Republic of 634	—V	—V	—V	—V	—Y	—Y	—Y	—V	—V	.01V	—V	—Y	—Y	—Y
Côte d'Ivoire 662	.01V	.01V	.02V	.03V	.01V	.01V	.01Y	.04V	.19V	—V	.11V	.14V	.07V	.09Y
Ethiopia 644	.14V	.02V	.03V	.06V	.07V	.09Y	.11Y	—V	—V	—V	—V	—V	—Y	—Y
Gabon 646	—Y	—Y	—Y	—Y	—Y	—Y	—Y	.02Y	.03Y	.03Y	.04Y	.05Y	.06Y	.07Y
Ghana 652	.01Y	.01Y	.01Y	.01Y	.01Y	.02Y	.02Y	—Y	—Y	—Y	—Y	—Y	—Y	—Y
Guinea 656	—V	—Y	—V	.02V	.03Y	.03Y	.04Y	—Y	—Y	—V	—V	—Y	—Y	—Y
Kenya 664	.03V	.07V	.06V	.19V	.21Y	.26Y	.33Y	49.23V	60.25V	87.08V	86.00V	98.26Y	121.44Y	150.71Y
Madagascar 674	—V	—V	—V	—Y	—Y	—Y	—Y	—V	.01V	—V	—Y	—Y	—Y	—Y
Malawi 676	—Y	—Y	—Y	—Y	—Y	—Y	—Y	.02Y	.02Y	.03Y	.04Y	.04Y	.05Y	.06Y
Mauritius 684	—V	—V	—V	—V	—V	—V	—V	1.09V	.98V	.90V	1.36V	1.13V	.43V	1.78V
Morocco 686	—V	.02V	.03V	.09V	.40V	.49Y	.61Y	—V	.10V	.13V	.10V	.13V	.16Y	.20Y
Niger 692	—V	—V	—V	.02V	.02Y	.02Y	.03Y	—V	—V	—V	—V	—Y	—Y	—Y
Nigeria 694	—V	.84V	.08V	.11Y	.14Y	.17Y	.22Y	—V	—V	—V	—Y	—Y	—Y	—Y
Senegal 722	—V	—V	—V	—V	.02V	—V	—Y	.01V	—V	—V	—V	.09V	.02V	.03Y
South Africa 199	8.81V	.40V	.16V	.13V	1.00V	.63V	.07V	10.02V	8.68V	12.42V	12.65V	11.90V	12.48V	16.46V
Sudan 732	—Y	—Y	—Y	.56V	—V	.03V	.01V	—Y	—Y	—V	—V	—V	—V	—V
Tanzania 738	.07V	.04V	.05Y	.07Y	.08Y	.10Y	.12Y	3.14V	4.26V	5.39Y	7.08Y	8.09Y	10.00Y	12.41Y
Togo 742	—V	.02V	—V	.01V	—V	—Y	—Y	—V	—V	—V	—V	.04V	.04Y	.05Y
Tunisia 744	—V	.02V	.02V	.05V	.12V	.09V	.11Y	.01V	.01V	.03V	—V	.23V	.01V	.01Y
Uganda 746	.32V	1.24V	.49V	.64Y	.73Y	.90Y	1.12Y	—V	14.16V	22.88V	30.05Y	34.34Y	42.44Y	52.67Y
Zambia 754	.01V	.01V	.01V	.02V	—V	.02V	—V	4.35V	1.11V	—V	.41V	.03V	11.62V	2.75V
Zimbabwe 698	—V	—V	—V	—V	—V	—V	—Y	—V	.11V	.07V	.49V	.40V	.04V	.05Y
Asia 507	**23.7Y**	**71.6Y**	**73.7Y**	**278.6Y**	**28.5Y**	**32.5Y**	**55.3Y**	**9.8Y**	**14.0Y**	**12.7Y**	**15.2Y**	**30.0Y**	**34.4Y**	**60.5Y**
China,P.R.: Mainland 924	5.79V	4.72V	6.47V	14.00V	10.48V	19.98V	21.50V	3.18V	4.25V	4.01V	5.06V	13.54V	13.65V	38.27V
China,P.R.:Hong Kong 532	12.32V	9.52V	3.84V	3.28V	4.19V	.48V	11.55V	.36V	.51V	.72V	.44V	1.16V	.71V	.08V
India 534	—Y	.01V	—V	.49V	.19V	.24Y	.29Y	4.07Y	6.19V	5.86V	7.34V	11.05V	13.66Y	16.95Y
Indonesia 536	—V	53.60V	60.10V	247.04V	—V	.06V	—V	.26V	.71V	.35V	.28V	.45V	.56V	.68V
Korea 542	.03V	.02V	—V	.06V	—V	—V	.09V	.85V	.40V	.41V	.51V	2.01V	1.42V	1.50V
Malaysia 548	1.57V	.83V	.43V	6.43V	4.77V	.27V	5.58V	.05V	.19V	.03V	.14V	.01V	.24V	.21V
Pakistan 564	2.24V	1.84V	1.06V	4.81V	6.01V	7.43Y	9.22Y	.15V	.33V	.78V	.89V	1.07V	1.33Y	1.65Y
Philippines 566	—V	—V	.02V	—V	—V	—V	—V	.01V	.02V	—V	—V	—V	.01V	.54V
Taiwan Province of China 528	.07V	—V	—V	—V	.01V	—V	.01V	.18V	.43V	.11V	.05V	.24V	.03V	.12V
Thailand 578	1.73V	.49V	1.75V	2.50V	2.86V	4.10V	7.06V	.55V	.69V	.45V	.44V	.47V	2.83V	.48V
Vietnam 582	—V	.58V	.01V	—V	—V	—V	—V	.10V	.24V	—V	—V	—V	—V	—V
Europe 170	**7.6Y**	**7.0Y**	**2.8Y**	**3.7Y**	**4.7Y**	**5.3Y**	**4.5Y**	**2.8Y**	**9.4Y**	**4.5Y**	**4.5Y**	**9.6Y**	**6.7Y**	**10.7Y**
Belarus 913	—V	.04V	—V	—V	—V	—V	—V	.03V	—V	—V	.53V	—V	—V	.03V
Bulgaria 918	—V	—V	—V	—V	—V	—V	—V	.01V	.02V	.03V	—V	—V	.01V	.03V
Czech Republic 935	.05V	.03V	.11V	—V	.04V	—V	.10V	.06V	.03V	—V	.10V	.05V	.03V	.11V

	Exports 2001	Exports 2002	Exports 2003	Exports 2004	Exports 2005	Exports 2006	Exports 2007	Imports 2001	Imports 2002	Imports 2003	Imports 2004	Imports 2005	Imports 2006	Imports 2007
	Millions of U.S. Dollars							Millions of U.S. Dollars						
Estonia.......... 939	.01V	—V	—V	—V	—V	—V	—V	.06V	—V	—V	—V	—V	—V	—V
Hungary.......... 944	.24V	.13V	.33V	.42V	.54V	.45V	.82V	.01V	—V	.12V	—V	.13V	.39V	2.17V
Kazakhstan.......... 916	6.16V	4.39V	—V	.54V	.62Y	.76Y	.95Y	.10V	—V	—V	—V	—Y	—Y	—Y
Latvia.......... 941	—Y	—Y	—Y	—Y	—V	—V	—V	—V	—V	—Y	—V	—V	.84V	—V
Lithuania.......... 946	—V	—V	—V	—V	—V	—V	—V	.41V	.05V	—V	—V	.26V	.02V	—V
Macedonia, FYR.......... 962	—V	—V	—V	—V	—V	—V	—Y	—V	—V	—V	—V	.03V	—V	—Y
Moldova.......... 921	—V	—V	—V	—V	—V	—Y	—Y	—V	.03V	—V	—V	—V	—Y	—Y
Poland.......... 964	.02V	.60V	.35V	.08V	—V	.59V	—V	.10V	.05V	.05V	.10V	.08V	.08V	.50V
Romania.......... 968	1.03V	1.65V	1.39V	2.44V	2.05V	1.89V	1.61V	.01V	.03V	.51V	—V	.17V	—V	.75V
Russia.......... 922	.04V	.04V	—V	—V	1.33V	1.38V	1.05V	.48V	7.58V	2.04V	.44V	6.46V	1.48V	.66V
Slovak Republic.......... 936	—V	.08V	.10Y	.13Y	—V	.01V	—V	—V	—V	.01Y	.01Y	—V	.06V	.08V
Turkey.......... 186	.01V	.01V	.50V	.12V	.11V	.16V	—V	.58V	.37V	.35V	.89V	.27V	1.08V	3.09V
Ukraine.......... 926	.02V	—V	—V	—V	—V	—Y	—Y	.05V	.18V	.10V	.74V	.25V	.31Y	.39Y
U.S.S.R. n.s.......... 930	....	....	....	....	....	....	....	.93Y	1.00Y	1.27Y	1.67Y	1.91Y	2.36Y	2.93Y
Middle East.......... 407	**—Y**	**—Y**	**.3Y**	**.5Y**	**.6Y**	**.8Y**	**1.1Y**	**19.5Y**	**12.0Y**	**13.0Y**	**16.3Y**	**40.3Y**	**36.9Y**	**34.0Y**
Egypt.......... 469	—V	—Y	—Y	—Y	—Y	—Y	—Y	.07V	.07Y	.09Y	.12Y	.14Y	.17Y	.21Y
Israel.......... 436	—V	—V	—V	.09V	—V	.09V	.18V	12.54V	4.62V	2.97V	2.97V	22.11V	14.19V	6.49V
Jordan.......... 439	—V	—V	—V	—V	—V	—V	—V	—V	—V	.03V	.02V	.10V	.05V	.13V
Oman.......... 449	—V	.03V	—V	—Y	—Y	—Y	—Y	.15V	.20V	1.31V	1.74Y	2.36Y	2.97Y	3.58Y
Saudi Arabia.......... 456	—V	—V	—V	—V	.08V	.10Y	.13Y	.94Y	1.00Y	1.22Y	1.61Y	2.19Y	2.76Y	3.33Y
United Arab Emirates.......... 466	—V	—V	.27V	.35Y	.45Y	.56Y	.72Y	5.75Y	6.11Y	7.41Y	9.81Y	13.34Y	16.77Y	20.24Y
Yemen, Republic of.......... 474	—V	.01V	.01Y	.02Y	.02Y	.03Y	.03Y	—V	—V	—Y	—Y	—Y	—Y	—Y
Western Hemisphere.......... 207	**—Y**	**—Y**	**—Y**	**.1Y**	**.6Y**	**3.9Y**	**1.4Y**	**.3Y**	**.1Y**	**.6Y**	**.2Y**	**.3Y**	**1.3Y**	**.1Y**
Argentina.......... 213	—V	—V	—V	—V	—V	—V	—V	.07V	—V	—V	.13V	—V	.63V	.01V
Barbados.......... 316	—V	—V	—V	—V	—V	—V	—Y	.01V	—V	—V	—V	—V	—V	—Y
Brazil.......... 223	—V	.01V	—V	—V	—V	.14V	—V	.19V	.09V	.60V	.05V	.08V	.58V	—V
Colombia.......... 233	—V	—V	—V	—V	—V	.05V	1.35V	—V	.02V	.01V	.01V	.04V	.02V	.05V
Costa Rica.......... 238	—V	—V	—V	—V	—V	—Y	.01Y	—V	—V	—V	—V	—V	—Y	—Y
El Salvador.......... 253	—V	—V	—V	.01V	—V	2.92V	—V	....	....	....	....	....	....	....
Guatemala.......... 258	—V	—V	—V	—V	.03V	.04Y	.05Y	—V	—V	—V	—V	—V	—Y	—Y
Mexico.......... 273	—V	—V	—V	—V	—V	.01V	.01V	—V	—V	—V	—V	—V	—V	—V
Paraguay.......... 288	....	....	....	....	....	....	....	—V	—V	—V	—V	—V	.03V	.03Y
Peru.......... 293	—V	—V	.01V	—V	—V	—V	—Y	—V	—V	—V	—V	.14V	—V	—Y
Venezuela, Rep. Bol.......... 299	—V	—V	—V	.11V	.58V	.76V	—V	—V	—V	—V	—V	—V	—V	—Y
Countries & Areas n.s.......... 898	**37.1Y**	**40.3Y**	**51.0Y**	**67.0Y**	**76.6Y**	**94.6Y**	**117.4Y**	**62.8Y**	**68.2Y**	**86.3Y**	**113.4Y**	**129.5Y**	**160.1Y**	**198.7Y**
Memorandum Items														
European Union.......... 998	41.37Y	19.58Y	17.76Y	25.66Y	38.92Y	45.92Y	41.69Y	64.18Y	79.68Y	91.30Y	122.44Y	108.44Y	145.67Y	165.81Y
Oil Exporting Ctys.......... 999	.01Y	54.48Y	60.45Y	247.61Y	1.25Y	1.65Y	1.08Y	7.10Y	8.03Y	10.30Y	13.44Y	18.35Y	23.06Y	27.83Y
Non-Oil Develop.Ctys.......... 201	42.30Y	28.84Y	19.49Y	40.04Y	39.09Y	47.51Y	68.77Y	102.36Y	128.21Y	161.75Y	178.58Y	234.41Y	276.79Y	341.77Y
PERCENT DISTRIBUTION														
Industrial Countries.......... 101	**38.8**	**15.3**	**13.2**	**7.9**	**27.9**	**27.3**	**22.3**	**34.7**	**32.6**	**30.1**	**31.5**	**26.4**	**27.2**	**26.1**
Developing Countries.......... 202	**32.6**	**57.1**	**53.0**	**74.7**	**24.9**	**24.9**	**29.0**	**41.5**	**44.9**	**46.5**	**43.0**	**48.7**	**47.5**	**48.1**
Africa.......... 607	**8.5**	**3.2**	**2.1**	**1.2**	**3.7**	**3.4**	**3.1**	**29.2**	**33.2**	**38.2**	**35.0**	**33.2**	**34.9**	**34.4**
Asia.......... 507	**18.3**	**49.1**	**48.8**	**72.4**	**17.6**	**16.5**	**23.0**	**3.7**	**4.6**	**3.4**	**3.4**	**5.8**	**5.5**	**7.9**
Europe.......... 170	**5.8**	**4.8**	**1.8**	**1.0**	**2.9**	**2.7**	**1.9**	**1.1**	**3.1**	**1.2**	**1.0**	**1.9**	**1.1**	**1.4**
Middle East.......... 407	**—**	**—**	**.2**	**.1**	**.3**	**.4**	**.4**	**7.4**	**4.0**	**3.5**	**3.6**	**7.7**	**5.8**	**4.4**
Western Hemisphere.......... 207	**—**	**—**	**—**	**—**	**.4**	**2.0**	**.6**	**.1**	**—**	**.2**	**—**	**—**	**.2**	**—**
ANNUAL PERCENT CHANGE														
World.......... 001	**31.2**	**12.5**	**3.3**	**155.3**	**–57.9**	**21.9**	**21.8**	**5.3**	**14.8**	**21.9**	**20.7**	**16.5**	**21.5**	**21.8**
Industrial Countries.......... 101	**28.3**	**–55.5**	**–11.2**	**53.0**	**48.8**	**19.1**	**–.6**	**6.3**	**7.7**	**12.7**	**26.4**	**–2.4**	**24.9**	**17.0**
Developing Countries.......... 202	**62.3**	**96.9**	**–4.0**	**259.8**	**–86.0**	**21.9**	**42.1**	**1.9**	**24.5**	**26.3**	**11.6**	**31.6**	**18.6**	**23.3**
Africa.......... 607	**51.6**	**–57.4**	**–31.8**	**47.7**	**27.0**	**11.7**	**12.8**	**–9.2**	**30.6**	**40.1**	**10.4**	**10.7**	**27.8**	**19.8**
Asia.......... 507	**65.6**	**201.6**	**2.9**	**278.2**	**–89.8**	**14.1**	**69.9**	**–6.2**	**43.1**	**–8.8**	**19.1**	**97.9**	**14.7**	**75.7**
Europe.......... 170	**68.9**	**–8.0**	**–60.0**	**34.0**	**25.2**	**12.3**	**–13.7**	**–46.5**	**232.8**	**–52.2**	**.5**	**113.8**	**–30.7**	**61.1**
Middle East.......... 407	**117.2**	**—**	**555.7**	**61.8**	**19.9**	**39.8**	**37.6**	**191.4**	**–38.2**	**8.5**	**24.8**	**147.4**	**–8.3**	**–8.0**
Western Hemisphere.......... 207	**–82.5**	**—**	**–5.7**	**—**	**407.5**	**536.0**	**–63.8**	**141.1**	**–60.2**	**462.7**	**–69.2**	**35.6**	**392.8**	**–92.4**

	Exports							Imports, f.o.b						
	2001	2002	2003	2004	2005	2006	2007	2001	2002	2003	2004	2005	2006	2007
	Millions of U.S. Dollars							*Millions of U.S. Dollars*						
DOTS World Total.................... 001	**1,731.6**	**1,025.8**	**443.0**	**454.1**	**504.3Y**	**599.0Y**	**717.7Y**	**311.4**	**222.3**	**148.3**	**169.3Y**	**180.8Y**	**207.6Y**	**249.2Y**
Industrial Countries................. 101	**1,554.3**	**727.4**	**208.1**	**268.2**	**288.8Y**	**332.6Y**	**386.3Y**	**208.3**	**143.3**	**112.6**	**135.7Y**	**141.9Y**	**159.5Y**	**189.6Y**
United States.............................. 111	39.13	73.72	103.26	123.10	132.54Y	152.66Y	177.29Y	50.51	28.75	20.54	24.75Y	25.87Y	29.05Y	34.53Y
Canada.. 156	.10	.33	.77	.52	.56Y	.64Y	.74Y	8.92	1.49	.70	.85Y	.88Y	.99Y	1.18Y
Australia..................................... 193	2.19	20.40	21.90	29.57	31.84Y	36.67Y	42.58Y	3.27	1.68	2.44	2.94Y	3.07Y	3.45Y	4.10Y
Japan.. 158	4.64	1.93	3.84	10.51	11.31Y	13.03Y	15.13Y	17.57	.88	7.64	9.20Y	9.62Y	10.80Y	12.84Y
New Zealand................................ 196	.04	21.38	25.40	38.73	41.70Y	48.03Y	55.78Y	.16	.29	—	—Y	—Y	—Y	—Y
Austria.. 122	—	—	—	—	—Y	—Y	—Y	.90	1.55	.25	.30Y	.31Y	.35Y	.42Y
Belgium....................................... 124	2.15	2.00	3.44	1.54	1.65Y	1.91Y	2.21Y	4.04	2.51	3.93	4.74Y	4.95Y	5.56Y	6.61Y
Cyprus... 423	—	—	—	—	—Y	—Y	—Y	.65	.77	.62	.81Y	.93Y	1.15Y	1.42Y
Denmark...................................... 128	.02	.05	—	—	—Y	—Y	—Y	1.14	1.76	.78	.93Y	.98Y	1.10Y	1.30Y
Finland.. 172	.36	—	.53	.52	.56Y	.64Y	.74Y	.62	1.33	26.36	31.77Y	33.20Y	37.28Y	44.31Y
France... 132	3.02	2.82	2.41	3.66	3.94Y	4.54Y	5.27Y	14.63	14.23	7.74	9.33Y	9.75Y	10.95Y	13.01Y
Germany...................................... 134	8.41	3.06	4.60	5.85	6.30Y	7.26Y	8.43Y	9.16	10.67	8.26	9.95Y	10.40Y	11.68Y	13.88Y
Greece... 174	.64	.40	.94	1.95	2.10Y	2.42Y	2.81Y	.23	—	—	—Y	—Y	—Y	—Y
Ireland... 178	.20	.38	.61	.72	.78Y	.90Y	1.04Y	1.05	1.77	.27	.32Y	.34Y	.38Y	.45Y
Italy.. 136	6.99	4.94	5.06	5.97	6.43Y	7.41Y	8.60Y	30.58	8.15	5.70	6.86Y	7.17Y	8.05Y	9.57Y
Netherlands................................. 138	3.73	3.92	5.94	10.43	11.23Y	12.94Y	15.03Y	2.82	2.65	1.49	1.79Y	1.88Y	2.11Y	2.50Y
Norway.. 142	34.12	9.99	.61	—	—Y	—Y	—Y	1.85	.13	—	—Y	—Y	—Y	—Y
Portugal....................................... 182	7.70	7.46	.79	1.06	1.14Y	1.32Y	1.53Y	5.54	5.78	.29	.35Y	.36Y	.41Y	.48Y
Spain... 184	1.26	1.66	1.86	2.26	2.43Y	2.80Y	3.25Y	2.44	4.25	2.81	3.39Y	3.54Y	3.98Y	4.72Y
Sweden.. 144	—	.04	.08	—	—Y	—Y	—Y	19.02	22.84	3.55	4.28Y	4.47Y	5.02Y	5.97Y
Switzerland.................................. 146	.31	.90	.20	.05	.06Y	.07Y	.08Y	1.50	2.70	.55	.66Y	.69Y	.78Y	.93Y
United Kingdom........................... 112	1,439.30	572.01	25.89	31.78	34.22Y	39.42Y	45.77Y	31.72	29.12	18.67	22.49Y	23.51Y	26.40Y	31.37Y
Developing Countries............. 202	**177.3**	**298.4**	**234.9**	**185.9**	**205.2Y**	**253.6Y**	**315.7Y**	**103.0**	**79.0**	**35.7**	**33.6Y**	**38.9Y**	**48.1Y**	**59.6Y**
Africa.. 607	**114.8**	**235.9**	**147.3**	**113.2**	**129.4Y**	**160.0Y**	**198.6Y**	**47.2**	**18.4**	**.8**	**1.0Y**	**1.1Y**	**1.4Y**	**1.7Y**
Angola... 614	4.13	8.98	3.30	12.52	14.31Y	17.68Y	21.94Y	....	....	....	....	....	....	....
Congo, Dem. Rep. of.................. 636	4.62	1.94	.18	.32	.36Y	.45Y	.55Y	—	—	—	—Y	—Y	—Y	—Y
Ghana.. 652	.03	.25	—	.12	.14Y	.18Y	.22Y	....	....	....	....	....	....	....
Kenya.. 664	11.80	32.07	28.98	35.55	40.62Y	50.20Y	62.30Y	.15	.70	—	—Y	—Y	—Y	—Y
Madagascar................................. 674	3.12	1.67	4.49	6.55	7.48Y	9.24Y	11.47Y	....	....	....	....	....	....	....
Malawi... 676	3.44	5.43	5.57	3.92	4.48Y	5.54Y	6.88Y	.13	.06	—	—Y	—Y	—Y	—Y
Mali... 678	—	—	—	—	—Y	—Y	—Y	—	.04	—	—Y	—Y	—Y	—Y
Mauritius..................................... 684	8.11	7.65	7.85	6.75	7.71Y	9.53Y	11.83Y	.53	—	—	—Y	—Y	—Y	—Y
Mozambique............................... 688	6.22	5.91	6.46	5.46	6.24Y	7.71Y	9.57Y	—	.67	—	—Y	—Y	—Y	—Y
Nigeria.. 694	1.07	.94	.29	.39	.50Y	.62Y	.80Y	....	....	....	....	....	....	....
Seychelles................................... 718	.11	.44	.38	.24	.28Y	.34Y	.42Y	....	....	....	....	....	....	....
Sudan.. 732	.03	.32	—	—	—Y	—Y	—Y	....	....	....	....	....	....	....
Tanzania...................................... 738	15.34	16.54	14.22	14.77	16.88Y	20.86Y	25.89Y	.09	—	—	—Y	—Y	—Y	—Y
Tunisia... 744	—	.77	—	1.27	1.45Y	1.79Y	2.22Y	....	....	....	....	....	....	....
Uganda.. 746	5.55	7.26	7.43	14.03	16.03Y	19.82Y	24.59Y	....	....	....	....	....	....	....
Zambia... 754	5.99	11.44	5.41	4.37	4.99Y	6.17Y	7.66Y	.62	.70	—	—Y	—Y	—Y	—Y
Zimbabwe.................................... 698	45.30	134.27	62.75	6.97	7.96Y	9.84Y	12.21Y	45.72	16.25	.76	.99Y	1.13Y	1.40Y	1.74Y
Asia.. 507	**51.7**	**58.3**	**86.6**	**70.1**	**72.5Y**	**89.6Y**	**111.9Y**	**37.2**	**44.2**	**26.6**	**21.7Y**	**25.2Y**	**31.2Y**	**38.6Y**
China,P.R.: Mainland.................. 924	26.39	17.41	64.94	42.00	47.99Y	59.31Y	73.61Y	9.08	15.24	5.41	7.11Y	8.12Y	10.04Y	12.45Y
China,P.R.:Hong Kong................ 532	.62	1.61	.46	.27	.31Y	.38Y	.47Y	3.55	4.70	1.81	2.38Y	2.72Y	3.36Y	4.17Y
India.. 534	.18	.59	.20	.27	.30Y	.37Y	.47Y	12.34	3.01	1.36	1.79Y	2.04Y	2.52Y	3.13Y
Indonesia.................................... 536	10.52	6.58	6.14	7.95	10.12Y	12.49Y	16.18Y	1.68	1.76	1.55	2.05Y	2.79Y	3.50Y	4.22Y
Korea... 542	5.17	5.90	5.85	6.01	6.86Y	8.48Y	10.53Y	5.80	5.45	—	—Y	—Y	—Y	—Y
Malaysia...................................... 548	....	....	....	....	....	....	....	.99	1.26	1.69	2.22Y	2.54Y	3.14Y	3.90Y
Pakistan...................................... 564	—	—	—	—	—Y	—Y	—Y	.12	.23	.64	.84Y	.96Y	1.19Y	1.47Y
Philippines.................................. 566	1.16	.51	—	—	—Y	—Y	—Y	....	....	....	....	....	....	....
Singapore.................................... 576	.16	.11	.04	.42	.48Y	.60Y	.74Y	2.35	.94	2.47	3.25Y	3.71Y	4.59Y	5.69Y
Sri Lanka..................................... 524	—	—	—	—	—Y	—Y	—Y	.27	.27	—	—Y	—Y	—Y	—Y
Taiwan Province of China............ 528	—	12.35	8.71	7.50	—V	—V	—V	—	9.96	10.10	—V	—V	—V	—V
Thailand...................................... 578	7.54	13.24	.27	5.66	6.47Y	7.99Y	9.92Y	1.06	1.41	1.55	2.03Y	2.32Y	2.87Y	3.56Y
Europe..................................... 170	**—**	**—**	**—**	**.2**	**.2Y**	**.2Y**	**.3Y**	**.4**	**—**	**.2**	**.3Y**	**.4Y**	**.5Y**	**.6Y**
Hungary...................................... 944	—	—	—	—	—Y	—Y	—Y	.21	—	—	—Y	—Y	—Y	—Y
Romania...................................... 968	—	—	—	.15	.17Y	.21Y	.27Y	....	....	....	....	....	....	....
Turkey... 186	—	—	—	—	—Y	—Y	—Y	.12	—	—	—Y	—Y	—Y	—Y
Ukraine....................................... 926	—	—	—	—	—Y	—Y	—Y	.02	—	.25	.33Y	.37Y	.46Y	.57Y
Middle East............................. 407	**10.8**	**4.2**	**.9**	**2.4**	**3.1Y**	**3.8Y**	**4.9Y**	**5.7**	**10.7**	**5.9**	**7.7Y**	**8.9Y**	**10.9Y**	**13.6Y**
Egypt... 469	—	.04	—	—	—Y	—Y	—Y	1.04	.98	1.37	1.80Y	2.05Y	2.54Y	3.15Y
Iran, I.R. of................................. 429	—	—	—	—	—Y	—Y	—Y	.34	—	—	—Y	—Y	—Y	—Y
Israel... 436	10.27	3.22	.07	.19	.22Y	.27Y	.34Y	3.07	9.08	4.40	5.78Y	6.60Y	8.16Y	10.12Y
Saudi Arabia................................ 456	.27	.79	.59	1.14	1.45Y	1.79Y	2.32Y	—	—	—	—Y	—Y	—Y	—Y
United Arab Emirates.................. 466	.23	.17	.28	1.11	1.42Y	1.75Y	2.27Y	1.27	.66	.11	.15Y	.20Y	.26Y	.31Y
Western Hemisphere............... 207	**—**	**—**	**—**	**—**	**—Y**	**—Y**	**—Y**	**12.5**	**5.6**	**2.2**	**2.9Y**	**3.3Y**	**4.1Y**	**5.1Y**
Argentina.................................... 213	—	—	—	—	—Y	—Y	—Y	8.43	3.23	.15	.20Y	.23Y	.29Y	.35Y
Brazil... 223	—	—	—	—	—Y	—Y	—Y	2.35	1.91	1.14	1.50Y	1.71Y	2.12Y	2.63Y
Dominica..................................... 321	—	—	—	—	—Y	—Y	—Y	.08	—	—	—Y	—Y	—Y	—Y
Mexico.. 273	—	—	—	—	—Y	—Y	—Y	1.63	.43	.92	1.21Y	1.38Y	1.71Y	2.12Y

	Exports 2001	2002	2003	2004	2005	2006	2007	Imports, f.o.b 2001	2002	2003	2004	2005	2006	2007
	Millions of U.S. Dollars							Millions of U.S. Dollars						
Other Countries n.i.e.............. 910	—	—	—	—	—Y	—Y	—Y	—	—	—	—Y	—Y	—Y	—Y
Cuba.. 928	—	.02	—	—	—Y	—Y	—Y	....	....	....	....	....	....	....
Countries & Areas n.s.............. 898	—	—	—	—	2.3Y	2.8Y	3.5Y	—	—	—	—Y	—Y	—Y	—Y
Special Categories.................. 899	—	—	—	—	8.0Y	9.9Y	12.2Y	—	—	—	—Y	—Y	—Y	—Y
Memorandum Items														
European Union.......................... 998	1,473.79	598.75	52.15	65.75	70.80Y	81.54Y	94.69Y	124.74	107.38	80.70	97.31Y	101.78Y	114.41Y	136.02Y
Oil Exporting Ctys....................... 999	12.08	8.48	7.30	10.59	13.49Y	16.65Y	21.57Y	3.29	2.42	1.66	2.20Y	2.99Y	3.76Y	4.53Y
Non-Oil Develop.Ctys.................. 201	165.25	289.91	227.56	175.31	191.74Y	236.97Y	294.08Y	99.75	76.55	34.02	31.42Y	35.90Y	44.36Y	55.06Y
PERCENT DISTRIBUTION														
Industrial Countries................. 101	89.8	70.9	47.0	59.1	57.3	55.5	53.8	66.9	64.5	75.9	80.1	78.5	76.8	76.1
Developing Countries.............. 202	10.2	29.1	53.0	40.9	40.7	42.3	44.0	33.1	35.5	24.1	19.9	21.5	23.2	23.9
Africa..................................... 607	6.6	23.0	33.3	24.9	25.7	26.7	27.7	15.2	8.3	.5	.6	.6	.7	.7
Asia....................................... 507	3.0	5.7	19.6	15.4	14.4	15.0	15.6	12.0	19.9	17.9	12.8	13.9	15.0	15.5
Europe.................................. 170	—	—	—	—	—	—	—	.1	—	.2	.2	.2	.2	.2
Middle East........................... 407	.6	.4	.2	.5	.6	.6	.7	1.8	4.8	4.0	4.6	4.9	5.3	5.4
Western Hemisphere............. 207	....	....	....	....	....	....	....	4.0	2.5	1.5	1.7	1.8	2.0	2.0
ANNUAL PERCENT CHANGE														
World...................................... 001	–26.9	–40.8	–56.8	2.5	11.1	18.8	19.8	–22.9	–28.6	–33.3	14.2	6.8	14.8	20.0
Industrial Countries................. 101	–29.3	–53.2	–71.4	28.9	7.7	15.2	16.1	–23.4	–31.2	–21.4	20.6	4.6	12.4	18.9
Developing Countries.............. 202	4.8	68.3	–21.3	–20.8	10.4	23.6	24.5	–21.9	–23.4	–54.8	–5.8	15.7	23.8	23.8
Africa..................................... 607	–11.1	105.4	–37.5	–23.1	14.3	23.6	24.1	3.6	–61.0	–95.9	31.3	14.3	23.6	24.1
Asia....................................... 507	110.7	12.7	48.6	–19.1	3.5	23.6	24.9	–49.7	18.8	–39.9	–18.5	16.3	23.8	23.7
Europe.................................. 170	—	—	—	....	14.3	23.6	24.1	–4.6	–22.4	12.1	31.3	14.3	23.6	24.1
Middle East........................... 407	–30.2	–60.9	–77.8	162.0	26.3	23.5	29.2	–32.5	87.5	–45.2	31.4	14.7	23.6	24.0
Western Hemisphere............. 207	....	....	....	....	....	....	....	264.6	–55.3	–60.2	31.3	14.3	23.6	24.1
Other Countries n.i.e.............. 910	10.4	8.5	26.6	31.3	....	....	....	....	....	....	....	....	....	....

	Exports 2001	2002	2003	2004	2005	2006	2007	Imports 2001	2002	2003	2004	2005	2006	2007
	Millions of U.S. Dollars							Millions of U.S. Dollars						
IFS World Total	**31.0**	**27.0**	**48.0**	**42.0**	**34.0**	**39.7**	**40.5**	**189.0**	**201.0**	**205.0**	**182.4**	**210.2**	**249.5**	**275.0**
DOTS World Total 001	**62.5Y**	**68.4Y**	**69.4Y**	**70.0Y**	**83.6Y**	**84.2Y**	**83.6Y**	**168.4Y**	**187.3Y**	**241.5Y**	**404.7Y**	**298.7Y**	**383.4Y**	**468.3Y**
Industrial Countries 101	**55.9Y**	**63.2Y**	**64.1Y**	**60.9Y**	**71.7Y**	**69.0Y**	**64.4Y**	**113.9Y**	**140.8Y**	**185.0Y**	**154.6Y**	**214.5Y**	**277.4Y**	**327.3Y**
United States 111	40.09V	46.27V	43.27V	40.18V	50.73V	51.91V	55.45V	72.71V	76.45V	88.66V	89.65V	138.82V	187.33V	223.41V
Canada 156	3.96V	4.73V	6.26V	6.31V	6.64V	7.88V	4.13V	13.75V	18.05V	10.82V	4.57V	6.89V	9.05V	11.35V
Australia 193	—V	—V	.01V	.04V	—V	.40V	.04V	.19V	.09V	.11V	.22V	.38V	.18V	.18V
Japan 158	.35V	.02V	.05V	.68V	.07V	1.28V	.08V	4.19V	7.33V	7.30V	9.48V	12.49V	13.63V	15.01V
New Zealand 196	—V	—V	—V	.14V	.04V	.03V	.02V	.05V	.11V	.15V	.14V	.20V	.10V	.16V
Austria 122	—V	—V	.05V	—V	.14V	.01V	.08V	.43V	.02V	.01V	.07V	.38V	.68V	1.01V
Belgium 124	—V	—V	.01V	—V	1.26V	—V	.01V	1.09V	.28V	.38V	1.00V	3.67V	4.67V	.43V
Denmark 128	.50V	.37V	.28V	.06V	.44V	.26V	.32V	1.18V	12.05V	13.12V	5.43V	3.68V	2.78V	5.32V
Finland 172	—V	.01V	—V	—V	—V	.01V	—V	.02V	6.18V	.02V	.02V	2.89V	3.34V	.76V
France 132	.15V	.10V	.04V	.05V	.05V	.14V	.38V	2.64V	2.14V	3.51V	1.37V	13.27V	3.07V	9.28V
Germany 134	1.51V	2.07V	2.90V	1.93V	2.65V	.68V	1.24V	1.48V	2.44V	3.68V	7.68V	5.70V	5.81V	8.36V
Greece 174	—V	—V	.02V	.07V	.12V	.04V	1.67V	.01V	.03V	.01V	.04V	.37V	.33V	.28V
Ireland 178	—V	—V	—V	—V	—V	—V	.11V	.15V	.19V	.10V	.15V	.27V	.18V	.66V
Italy 136	.02V	.07V	.06V	.88V	.27V	.09V	.13V	.44V	.45V	39.74V	3.71V	1.40V	5.15V	6.48V
Luxembourg 137	—V	—V	—V	.01V	—V	—V	—V	—V	—V	—V	—V	—V	—V	—V
Netherlands 138	.02V	.01V	—V	—V	2.21V	5.50V	.01V	.36V	.37V	.42V	.41V	2.54V	2.91V	2.57V
Norway 142	—V	.01V	—V	—V	.03V	—V	—V	.31V	.64V	.35V	1.26V	.01V	.54V	2.44V
Portugal 182	—V	4.16V	—V	5.79V	2.08V	.01V	—V	.07V	—V	—V	—V	.18V	.50V	1.76V
Spain 184	—V	—V	.01V	.01V	.23V	.03V	.03V	.83V	1.17V	.13V	.10V	.60V	17.66V	6.97V
Sweden 144	.03V	.09V	.02V	—V	.07V	.06V	.05V	.07V	.03V	.05V	3.73V	3.99V	.82V	1.63V
Switzerland 146	.02V	.01V	.30V	.05V	.04V	.07V	.02V	.20V	.08V	.19V	.39V	.84V	1.58V	3.15V
United Kingdom 112	9.26V	5.28V	10.82V	4.65V	4.62V	.65V	.66V	13.70V	12.72V	16.20V	25.17V	15.93V	17.10V	26.07V
Developing Countries 202	**6.4Y**	**5.0Y**	**5.1Y**	**8.8Y**	**11.5Y**	**14.7Y**	**18.6Y**	**54.2Y**	**46.1Y**	**56.0Y**	**249.5Y**	**83.5Y**	**105.1Y**	**139.9Y**
Africa 607	**.1Y**	**.1Y**	**.1Y**	**.1Y**	**2.7Y**	**.1Y**	**.1Y**	**.4Y**	**.5Y**	**1.5Y**	**.1Y**	**.2Y**	**—Y**	**.2Y**
Benin 638	.01V	—V	—V	—V	—V	—Y	—Y	....	....	....	....	....	....	....
Djibouti 611	—Y	—Y	—Y	—Y	—Y	.01Y	.01Y	—Y	—Y	—Y	—Y	—Y	.01Y	.01Y
Kenya 664	—Y	—Y	—Y	—Y	—Y	—Y	—Y	—V	.10V	.01V	.02V	.02Y	.03Y	.04Y
Madagascar 674	.02V	—V	—V	—Y	—Y	—Y	—Y	—V	—V	—V	—Y	—Y	—Y	—Y
Mauritius 684	—V	—V	—V	—V	—V	—V	—V	—V	—V	—V	.01V	—V	—V	—V
South Africa 199	—V	.08V	.10V	.03V	2.66V	—V	—V	.11V	.36V	1.35V	.09V	.17V	—V	.16V
Swaziland 734	....	....	....	....	....	....	....	—Y	—Y	—Y	—Y	.01Y	.01Y	.01Y
Tanzania 738	.02V	.03V	.03Y	.04Y	.05Y	.06Y	.07Y	—V	—V	—Y	—Y	—Y	—Y	—Y
Zimbabwe 698	.02V	—V	—V	—V	—V	—V	—Y	.25V	—V	.08V	—V	—V	—V	—Y
Asia 507	**.4Y**	**.1Y**	**—Y**	**—Y**	**—Y**	**.2Y**	**.9Y**	**1.6Y**	**2.1Y**	**2.5Y**	**2.7Y**	**2.8Y**	**3.4Y**	**7.3Y**
Afghanistan, I.S. of 512	....	....	....	....	....	....	....	.02Y	.02Y	.03Y	.04Y	.04Y	.05Y	.06Y
China,P.R.: Mainland 924	.01V	—V	—V	—V	—V	—V	.01Y	.12V	.30V	.17V	.19V	.66V	.70V	2.83V
China,P.R.:Hong Kong 532	—Y	—Y	—Y	—Y	—Y	—Y	—Y	.10Y	.11Y	.14Y	.18Y	.21Y	.26Y	.32Y
India 534	.01Y	—V	—V	—V	.01V	.01Y	.01Y	.18Y	.07V	.28V	.49V	.45V	.55Y	.69Y
Indonesia 536	.21V	.04V	.01V	—V	—V	—V	—V	.62V	.99V	.53V	.24V	.19V	.24V	.46V
Korea 542	.14V	.03V	.02V	.02V	—V	.08V	.09V	.28V	.24V	.44V	.52V	.81V	.67V	1.95V
Malaysia 548	.01V	—V	—V	—V	—V	.02V	.03V	—V	.08V	.17V	.41V	.10V	.09V	.07V
Pakistan 564	....	....	....	....	....	....	....	.01Y	.01Y	—V	—V	—V	—Y	—Y
Singapore 576	....	....	....	....	....	....	....	.03Y	.04Y	.05Y	.06Y	.07Y	.09Y	.11Y
Taiwan Province of China 528	.05V	—V	—V	—V	.02V	.07V	.78V	.05V	—V	.28V	.37V	.05V	.56V	.49V
Thailand 578	....	....	....	....	....	....	....	.09Y	.09Y	.12Y	.16Y	.18Y	.22Y	.28Y
Vietnam 582	....	....	....	....	....	....	....	.08V	.13V	.32V	—V	—V	—V	—V
Europe 170	**2.3Y**	**1.1Y**	**.6Y**	**3.1Y**	**1.5Y**	**5.2Y**	**6.8Y**	**2.4Y**	**1.6Y**	**2.4Y**	**182.9Y**	**6.1Y**	**11.2Y**	**22.2Y**
Azerbaijan 912	.82V	.10V	.20V	.37V	.74V	3.28V	2.64V	—V	—V	.02V	—V	—V	.58V	—V
Belarus 913	—V	—V	—V	—V	—V	—V	—V	—V	—V	—V	—V	—V	.46V	—V
Bulgaria 918	—V	.01V	—V	—V	—V	—V	—V	—V	—V	—V	—V	—V	1.17V	12.39V
Czech Republic 935	—V	.21V	.29V	.68V	.38V	.83V	1.20V	—V	.24V	—V	—V	.13V	.14V	.10V
Estonia 939	—V	—V	—V	—V	—V	—V	—V	.02V	.03V	.03V	—V	—V	—V	—V
Georgia 915	.03V	—V	—V	.01V	—V	—V	—Y	—V	—V	—V	—V	—V	—V	—Y
Hungary 944	.14V	—V	.03V	1.55V	—V	.03V	.08V	—V	.01V	—V	.03V	.03V	—V	.19V
Kazakhstan 916	.39V	.20V	.04V	.01V	.02Y	.02Y	.02Y	....	....	....	....	....	....	....
Kyrgyz Republic 917	.07V	.01V	—V	—V	—V	—V	—V	....	....	....	....	....	....	....
Latvia 941	—V	—V	—V	—V	—V	—V	—V	—V	—V	.02V	1.23V	.63V	.01V	.20V
Lithuania 946	—V	—V	—V	—V	—V	.11V	—V	—V	—V	—V	.01V	—V	.32V	.01V
Macedonia, FYR 962	—V	—V	—V	.01V	—V	—V	—Y	—V	—V	—V	—V	—V	—V	—Y
Moldova 921	—V	—V	—V	—V	—V	—Y	—Y	—V	.01V	—V	—V	—V	—Y	—Y
Poland 964	.02V	.10V	.02V	.13V	—V	—V	—V	—V	.07V	.15V	.09V	.14V	.29V	.41V
Romania 968	—V	.01V	—V	—V	.08V	—V	—V	—V	—V	—V	—V	—V	—V	.02V
Russia 922	.04V	.09V	—V	.24V	.19V	.04V	.01V	1.60V	.63V	.44V	.12V	.47V	2.30V	1.29V
Turkey 186	—V	—V	.04V	—V	—V	.86V	2.73V	.07V	.21V	.82V	.36V	.53V	.70V	1.16V
Ukraine 926	.74V	.38V	—V	.12V	.05V	.06Y	.08Y	.74V	.41V	.97V	181.01V	4.21V	5.20Y	6.45Y
Middle East 407	**—Y**	**—Y**	**—Y**	**—Y**	**—Y**	**—Y**	**—Y**	**.1Y**	**.1Y**	**.1Y**	**.2Y**	**.2Y**	**.3Y**	**.3Y**
Iran, I.R. of 429	....	....	....	....	....	....	....	—Y	—Y	—Y	—Y	—Y	.01Y	.01Y
Israel 436	—V	—V	—V	—V	—V	—V	—V	.08Y	.09Y	.11Y	.14Y	.16Y	.20Y	.25Y
Qatar 453	....	....	....	....	....	....	....	.02Y	.02Y	.02Y	.03Y	.04Y	.05Y	.06Y

	Exports							Imports						
	2001	2002	2003	2004	2005	2006	2007	2001	2002	2003	2004	2005	2006	2007
	Millions of U.S. Dollars							Millions of U.S. Dollars						
Western Hemisphere................ 207	**3.7Y**	**3.7Y**	**4.3Y**	**5.6Y**	**7.3Y**	**9.2Y**	**10.9Y**	**49.7Y**	**41.8Y**	**49.5Y**	**63.7Y**	**74.1Y**	**90.2Y**	**109.8Y**
Antigua and Barbuda.................. 311	.17Y	.19Y	.24Y	.32Y	.36Y	.45Y	.55Y	1.06Y	1.15Y	1.45Y	1.91Y	2.18Y	2.70Y	3.35Y
Argentina.................................. 213	—V	—V	—V	—V	—V	—V	.48V	.19V	.21V	.08V	.19V	.27V	.29V	.20V
Aruba.. 314	.03V	—V	—V	.09V	—V	—V	.04V	.01V	—V	—V	.01V	—V	.02V	—V
Bahamas, The............................ 313	—Y	—Y	—Y	—Y	—Y	—Y	—Y	.01Y	.01Y	.01Y	.02Y	.02Y	.03Y	.03Y
Barbados................................... 316	.37V	.17V	.10V	.16V	.07V	.13V	.16Y	6.24V	7.17V	7.37V	8.59V	11.28V	11.88V	14.75Y
Belize.. 339	.01Y	.01Y	.01Y	.01Y	.01Y	.02Y	.02Y	—Y	—Y	—Y	—Y	—Y	—Y	—Y
Bermuda.................................... 319	—Y	—Y	—Y	—Y	—V	—V	—Y	—Y	—Y	—Y	—Y	—Y	—Y	.01Y
Bolivia....................................... 218	—V	—V	—V	—V	—V	—Y	—Y	.04V	—V	—V	—V	—Y	—Y	—Y
Brazil... 223	.17V	.08V	.01V	—V	.05V	.01V	—V	.32V	.32V	.44V	.70V	.94V	1.94V	—V
Colombia................................... 233	.02V	.01V	—V	.01V	.01V	.47V	.12V	.88V	.52V	.24V	.43V	.52V	.18V	1.37V
Costa Rica................................. 238	—V	—V	—V	—V	—V	—Y	—Y	.05V	.12V	.09V	.14V	.13V	.17Y	.21Y
Dominica................................... 321	.40V	.44Y	.55Y	.73Y	.83Y	1.03Y	1.28Y	1.60V	1.74Y	2.20Y	2.89Y	3.31Y	4.09Y	5.07Y
Dominican Republic................... 243	.01V	.02Y	.02Y	.03Y	.03Y	.04Y	.05Y	.54V	.59Y	.74Y	.98Y	1.12Y	1.38Y	1.71Y
Grenada.................................... 328	.01Y	.01Y	.02Y	.02Y	.03Y	.03Y	.04Y	1.50Y	1.63Y	2.06Y	2.71Y	3.10Y	3.83Y	4.75Y
Guatemala................................. 258	.02V	—V	—V	—Y	—Y	—Y	—Y	—V	—V	.08V	.01V	.01V	.01Y	.01Y
Guyana...................................... 336	.01Y	.01Y	.02Y	.02Y	.03Y	.03Y	.04Y	.16Y	.17Y	.21Y	.28Y	.32Y	.40Y	.49Y
Haiti.. 263	—V	—V	.01V	—V	—Y	—Y	—Y	.02Y	.02Y	.02Y	.03Y	.04Y	.05Y	.06Y
Honduras................................... 268	....	....	....	....	....	....	....	.02Y	.02Y	.03Y	.04Y	.04Y	.05Y	.07Y
Jamaica..................................... 343	.01V	.06V	—V	—V	.13V	.52V	.22V	1.79V	1.72V	1.90V	2.44V	2.35V	2.63V	2.60V
Mexico...................................... 273	—V	—V	—V	—V	.90V	.80V	1.20V	—V	—V	—V	—V	.60V	.76V	1.59V
Netherlands Antilles.................. 353	.01V	—V	—V	—Y	—Y	—Y	—Y	2.70V	.09V	.07V	.09Y	.10Y	.12Y	.15Y
Panama..................................... 283	....	....	....	....	....	....	....	1.05Y	1.13Y	1.44Y	1.89Y	2.16Y	2.66Y	3.31Y
Peru.. 293	.01V	.01V	—V	—V	—V	—V	—Y	—V	—V	.07V	.62V	.30V	1.26V	1.30Y
St. Lucia.................................... 362	.73Y	.79Y	1.00Y	1.32Y	1.50Y	1.86Y	2.31Y	.63Y	.68Y	.86Y	1.14Y	1.30Y	1.60Y	1.99Y
St. Vincent & Grens.................... 364	.02V	.03V	.06V	.16V	.24V	.29Y	.36Y	1.65V	1.59V	1.33V	1.17V	1.32V	1.63Y	2.03Y
Trinidad and Tobago.................. 369	.23V	.02V	.03Y	.04Y	.05Y	.06Y	.07Y	27.90V	21.41V	27.10Y	35.60Y	40.67Y	50.27Y	62.38Y
Uruguay..................................... 298	—V	—Y	—V	—V	—V	—Y	—Y	—V	—Y	—V	—V	.07V	.08Y	.10Y
Western Hem. n.s....................... 399	1.40Y	1.82Y	2.24Y	2.66Y	3.08Y	3.49Y	3.91Y	1.32Y	1.49Y	1.66Y	1.83Y	1.99Y	2.16Y	2.33Y
Other Countries n.i.e............... 910	....	....	....	....	....	....	....	**.2Y**	**.2Y**	**.3Y**	**.4Y**	**.5Y**	**.6Y**	**.7Y**
North Korea............................... 954	....	....	....	....	....	....	....	.23Y	.25Y	.31Y	.41Y	.47Y	.58Y	.72Y
Special Categories.................. 899	**.2Y**	**.2Y**	**.2Y**	**.3Y**	**.4Y**	**.5Y**	**.6Y**	**—Y**	**—Y**	**—Y**	**—Y**	**—Y**	**—Y**	**—Y**
Memorandum Items														
European Union......................... 998	11.67Y	12.48Y	14.55Y	15.80Y	14.53Y	8.44Y	5.98Y	22.49Y	38.42Y	77.59Y	50.25Y	55.79Y	65.75Y	72.50Y
Oil Exporting Ctys...................... 999	.21Y	.04Y	.01Y	—Y	—Y	—Y	—Y	.64Y	1.01Y	.55Y	.28Y	.23Y	.30Y	.53Y
Non-Oil Develop.Ctys.................. 201	6.20Y	4.93Y	5.10Y	8.80Y	11.53Y	14.72Y	18.61Y	53.53Y	45.04Y	55.49Y	249.22Y	83.22Y	104.79Y	139.34Y
PERCENT DISTRIBUTION														
Industrial Countries................ 101	**89.5**	**92.4**	**92.3**	**87.0**	**85.8**	**82.0**	**77.1**	**67.6**	**75.2**	**76.6**	**38.2**	**71.8**	**72.4**	**69.9**
Developing Countries............. 202	**10.3**	**7.3**	**7.4**	**12.6**	**13.8**	**17.5**	**22.3**	**32.2**	**24.6**	**23.2**	**61.6**	**27.9**	**27.4**	**29.9**
Africa..................................... 607	**.1**	**.2**	**.2**	**.1**	**3.3**	**.1**	**.1**	**.2**	**.3**	**.6**	**—**	**.1**	**—**	**—**
Asia....................................... 507	**.7**	**.1**	**.1**	**—**	**—**	**.2**	**1.1**	**.9**	**1.1**	**1.0**	**.7**	**.9**	**.9**	**1.5**
Europe.................................... 170	**3.6**	**1.6**	**.9**	**4.5**	**1.8**	**6.2**	**8.1**	**1.4**	**.9**	**1.0**	**45.2**	**2.1**	**2.9**	**4.7**
Middle East............................ 407	**—**	**—**	**—**	**—**	**—**	**—**	**—**	**.1**	**.1**	**.1**	**—**	**.1**	**.1**	**.1**
Western Hemisphere............. 207	**5.8**	**5.4**	**6.2**	**8.0**	**8.8**	**11.0**	**13.0**	**29.5**	**22.3**	**20.5**	**15.7**	**24.8**	**23.5**	**23.5**
Other Countries n.i.e............... 910	....	....	....	....	....	....	....	**.1**	**.1**	**.1**	**.1**	**.2**	**.2**	**.2**
ANNUAL PERCENT CHANGE														
World...................................... 001	**91.1**	**9.4**	**1.6**	**.8**	**19.5**	**.8**	**–.7**	**–14.1**	**11.2**	**29.0**	**67.6**	**–26.2**	**28.4**	**22.1**
Industrial Countries................ 101	**93.9**	**13.0**	**1.4**	**–5.0**	**17.8**	**–3.7**	**–6.7**	**–24.8**	**23.7**	**31.4**	**–16.4**	**38.7**	**29.3**	**18.0**
Developing Countries............. 202	**72.8**	**–22.3**	**2.7**	**72.2**	**31.1**	**27.7**	**26.4**	**22.6**	**–15.0**	**21.7**	**345.2**	**–66.5**	**25.9**	**33.1**
Africa..................................... 607	**—**	**76.3**	**17.7**	**–39.7**	**—**	**–97.6**	**23.2**	**224.9**	**28.9**	**207.0**	**–90.8**	**52.9**	**–78.0**	**383.2**
Asia....................................... 507	**157.8**	**–83.0**	**–43.4**	**–30.7**	**9.1**	**501.1**	**397.9**	**6.3**	**31.5**	**21.1**	**4.9**	**4.2**	**24.3**	**111.3**
Europe.................................... 170	....	**–50.8**	**–44.2**	**402.8**	**–53.2**	**258.4**	**28.9**	**—**	**–33.8**	**51.9**	**—**	**–96.6**	**81.5**	**99.2**
Middle East............................ 407	**—**	**—**	....	....	....	....	....	**9.9**	**8.1**	**25.5**	**31.5**	**18.3**	**24.0**	**23.3**
Western Hemisphere............. 207	**3.3**	**.5**	**17.4**	**28.9**	**31.6**	**26.1**	**17.6**	**17.4**	**–15.9**	**18.5**	**28.7**	**16.4**	**21.7**	**21.8**
Other Countries n.i.e............... 910	....	....	....	....	....	....	....	**10.4**	**8.5**	**26.6**	**31.3**	**14.3**	**23.6**	**24.1**

		Exports							Imports						
		2001	2002	2003	2004	2005	2006	2007	2001	2002	2003	2004	2005	2006	2007
		Millions of U.S. Dollars							Millions of U.S. Dollars						
IFS World Total		**51.2**	**49.1**	**85.3**	**62.6**	**64.0**	**65.0**	**77.0**	**355.0**	**309.0**	**403.0**	**437.0**	**479.0**	**592.0**	**635.0**
DOTS World Total	**001**	**84.0Y**	**68.2Y**	**52.2Y**	**82.4Y**	**165.1Y**	**289.6Y**	**132.9Y**	**526.8Y**	**567.3Y**	**346.8Y**	**378.1Y**	**670.1Y**	**708.9Y**	**1,789.0Y**
Industrial Countries	**101**	**68.4Y**	**51.7Y**	**37.1Y**	**49.6Y**	**106.3Y**	**256.3Y**	**90.4Y**	**164.7Y**	**182.0Y**	**209.9Y**	**225.9Y**	**400.6Y**	**492.3Y**	**383.6Y**
United States	111	27.82V	18.36V	12.45V	13.55V	30.55V	29.27V	32.55V	97.35V	107.69V	133.21V	113.74V	148.06V	166.76V	182.05V
Canada	156	.14V	.25V	.19V	.29V	.42V	.14V	.29V	7.05V	6.61V	6.50V	7.59V	9.14V	13.17V	17.37V
Australia	193	—V	—V	.02V	.01V	—V	.01V	.02V	1.11V	1.89V	2.03V	1.66V	1.14V	1.88V	1.03V
Japan	158	.08V	.15V	.06V	.02V	.01V	.03V	.02V	10.48V	7.07V	9.45V	13.40V	17.83V	25.22V	25.92V
New Zealand	196	—V	—V	—V	—V	—V	—V	—V	1.41V	1.20V	1.46V	2.06V	2.23V	2.58V	3.00V
Austria	122	.01V	.01V	—V	—V	—V	—V	—V	.56V	.02V	.22V	.25V	.09V	.62V	1.97V
Belgium	124	.01V	—V	—V	—V	.01V	—V	.08V	1.01V	.92V	1.98V	1.15V	14.53V	2.64V	3.22V
Denmark	128	.01V	.06V	.06V	.02V	.01V	.03V	.02V	.70V	.32V	.45V	.61V	.55V	.80V	1.32V
Finland	172	—V	—V	.02V	.01V	.04V	—V	.07V	.76V	.32V	.65V	28.82V	18.95V	.22V	.40V
France	132	18.41V	.59V	.31V	.30V	51.35V	200.72V	30.87V	7.01V	7.84V	6.37V	7.39V	29.26V	93.17V	20.97V
Germany	134	.20V	.08V	.06V	.08V	.48V	.18V	.49V	5.10V	5.64V	4.91V	4.56V	6.23V	6.86V	17.56V
Greece	174	—V	—V	—V	—V	—V	—V	.13V	.12V	.02V	.02V	—V	.25V	.01V	—V
Ireland	178	—V	—V	—V	—V	.11V	.01V	.01V	.38V	.81V	.19V	.14V	.21V	.25V	.40V
Italy	136	.08V	.07V	.24V	.96V	.02V	.23V	.02V	1.69V	1.94V	1.69V	1.84V	22.41V	71.31V	10.23V
Luxembourg	137	—V	—V	—V	—V	—V	—V	—V	.02V	.03V	.08V	—V	.63V	1.17V	—V
Malta	181	—Y	—V	—V	—V	—V	—V	—V	—Y	—V	—V	—V	—V	.37V	—V
Netherlands	138	.01V	.03V	.03V	.16V	.28V	.22V	.17V	1.49V	1.57V	3.18V	3.37V	89.07V	46.13V	56.93V
Norway	142	—V	—V	—V	—V	—V	—V	—V	.40V	.50V	.44V	.47V	.20V	.53V	.17V
Portugal	182	—V	—V	—V	—V	—V	.08V	—V	.04V	.02V	—V	.04V	.12V	.10V	.25V
Slovenia	961	—V	—V	—V	—Y	—V	—V	—V	—V	—V	—V	—Y	—V	.01V	.01V
Spain	184	—V	—V	—V	—V	—V	—V	—V	.37V	2.29V	.53V	1.11V	1.07V	1.07V	1.10V
Sweden	144	—V	—V	—V	.10V	.06V	.02V	.01V	.28V	14.66V	7.80V	1.67V	1.55V	1.30V	3.75V
Switzerland	146	—V	—V	.03V	.01V	.02V	.05V	.08V	.44V	1.30V	1.56V	3.33V	2.91V	1.84V	3.73V
United Kingdom	112	21.63V	32.12V	23.62V	34.08V	22.93V	25.30V	25.60V	26.96V	19.27V	27.18V	32.67V	34.16V	54.27V	32.22V
Developing Countries	**202**	**15.6Y**	**16.5Y**	**15.1Y**	**32.8Y**	**58.8Y**	**33.3Y**	**42.5Y**	**361.5Y**	**384.7Y**	**136.1Y**	**151.2Y**	**268.3Y**	**215.0Y**	**1,403.4Y**
Africa	**607**	**—Y**	**—Y**	**—Y**	**—Y**	**—Y**	**.1Y**	**.1Y**	**.3Y**	**.3Y**	**.4Y**	**.5Y**	**.5Y**	**.4Y**	**.5Y**
Gabon	646	—Y	—Y	—Y	—Y	—Y	—Y	—Y	.02Y	.02Y	.02Y	.03Y	.04Y	.05Y	.06Y
Gambia, The	648	.02Y	.02Y	.03Y	.04Y	.04Y	.05Y	.06Y	.03Y	.03Y	.04Y	.05Y	.06Y	.08Y	.10Y
Kenya	664	—V	—V	—V	—V	—Y	—Y	—Y	—V	.01V	—V	—V	—Y	—Y	—Y
Nigeria	694	.01V	—V	—V	—Y	—Y	—Y	—Y	—V	—V	—V	—Y	—Y	—Y	—Y
São Tomé & Príncipe	716	—Y	—Y	.01Y	.01Y	.01Y	.01Y	.01Y	—Y	—Y	—Y	—Y	—Y	—Y	—Y
South Africa	199	—Y	—Y	—Y	—Y	—Y	—Y	—Y	.13Y	.13Y	.15Y	.18Y	.19Y	—V	—V
Sudan	732	—Y	—Y	—Y	—Y	—Y	—Y	—Y	.04Y	.04Y	.02Y	.03Y	.04Y	.05Y	.06Y
Swaziland	734	—Y	—Y	—Y	—Y	—Y	—Y	—Y	.09Y	.10Y	.13Y	.17Y	.20Y	.24Y	.30Y
Asia	**507**	**.1Y**	**.1Y**	**.1Y**	**.2Y**	**31.6Y**	**2.0Y**	**2.5Y**	**8.3Y**	**8.4Y**	**6.9Y**	**9.7Y**	**11.5Y**	**15.1Y**	**22.0Y**
Bangladesh	513	.01Y	.01Y	.02Y	.02Y	.03Y	.03Y	.04Y	.05Y	.05Y	.06Y	.08Y	.09Y	.12Y	.14Y
China,P.R.: Mainland	924	—V	—V	.01V	.03V	29.73V	.02V	.10V	3.33V	2.96V	1.69V	2.77V	2.73V	4.53V	7.52V
China,P.R.:Hong Kong	532	.01Y	.02Y	.02Y	.03Y	.03Y	.04Y	.04Y	.95Y	1.03Y	1.31Y	1.72Y	1.96Y	2.43Y	3.01Y
Guam	829	—Y	—Y	—Y	—Y	—Y	—Y	—Y	—Y	—Y	—Y	—Y	.01Y	.01Y	.01Y
India	534	.02Y	—V	—V	—V	.01V	.01Y	.01Y	.62Y	.43V	.45V	.50V	.67V	.82Y	1.02Y
Indonesia	536	—V	—V	—V	—V	—V	—V	—V	.20V	.36V	.29V	.18V	.64V	.94V	.85V
Korea	542	—V	—V	.01V	.08V	.02V	—V	—V	.53V	.73V	.83V	1.36V	2.29V	2.42V	4.04V
Malaysia	548	—V	—V	—V	—V	—V	—V	—V	.13V	.19V	.10V	.10V	.14V	.28V	.28V
Maldives	556	—V	—V	—V	—V	1.42V	1.75Y	2.17Y	....	....	....	....	....	....	....
Pakistan	564	—Y	—Y	—Y	—Y	—Y	—Y	—Y	.78Y	.49Y	—V	—V	—V	—Y	—Y
Philippines	566	—V	—V	—V	—V	—V	—V	—V	—V	—V	—V	.18V	—V	.01V	—V
Taiwan Province of China	528	—V	—V	—V	.02V	.31V	.11V	.01V	.45V	.55V	.53V	.69V	.50V	.51V	1.37V
Thailand	578	.03Y	.03Y	.04Y	.05Y	.06Y	.07Y	.09Y	1.18Y	1.28Y	1.62Y	2.13Y	2.43Y	3.01Y	3.73Y
Vietnam	582	—V	.02V	—V	—V	—V	—V	—V	.11V	.32V	.03V	—V	—V	—V	—V
Europe	**170**	**—Y**	**—Y**	**—Y**	**—Y**	**—Y**	**—Y**	**—Y**	**.2Y**	**.2Y**	**.4Y**	**.7Y**	**.5Y**	**.5Y**	**.6Y**
Bulgaria	918	—V	.01V	—V	—V	.01V	—V	—V	—V	.02V	—V	—V	—V	—V	—V
Czech Republic	935	—V	—V	.04V	—V	—V	—V	—V	—V	—V	.04V	.05V	—V	.01V	.02V
Czechoslovakia n.s.	937	—Y	—Y	—Y	—Y	—Y	—Y	—Y	.08Y	.08Y	.11Y	.14Y	.16Y	.20Y	.25Y
Hungary	944	—Y	—V	—V	—V	—V	—V	.01V	—V	—V	—V	.30V	—V	.01V	—V
Poland	964	—V	—V	—V	—V	—V	—V	—V	.02V	.03V	.12V	.02V	.01V	.03V	.20V
Romania	968	—V	—V	—V	—V	.02V	.01V	—V	—V	—V	—V	—V	—V	—V	—V
Russia	922	—Y	—Y	—Y	—Y	—Y	—Y	—Y	—V	—V	—V	—V	.08V	—V	—V
Slovak Republic	936	—V	—V	—Y	—Y	—V	.01V	—V	.01V	—V	—Y	—Y	—V	—V	.01V
Turkey	186	—V	—V	—V	—V	.01V	—V	—V	.03V	.05V	.10V	.21V	.22V	.23V	.14V
Ukraine	926	—V	.04V	—V	—V	—V	—Y	—Y	—V	—V	—V	—V	—V	—Y	—Y
U.S.S.R. n.s.	930	—Y	—Y	—Y	—Y	—Y	—Y	—Y	.01Y	.01Y	.01Y	.01Y	.02Y	.02Y	.02Y
Middle East	**407**	**—Y**	**—Y**	**—Y**	**—Y**	**—Y**	**—Y**	**—Y**	**.5Y**	**.5Y**	**.6Y**	**.8Y**	**1.0Y**	**1.2Y**	**1.5Y**
Iran, I.R. of	429	—V	—V	—Y	—Y	—Y	—Y	—Y	.01Y	.01Y	.01Y	.02Y	.02Y	.03Y	.03Y
Israel	436	—V	—V	—V	—V	—V	—V	—V	.04Y	.05Y	.06Y	.08Y	.09Y	.11Y	.13Y
Jordan	439	—Y	—Y	—Y	—Y	—Y	—Y	—Y	.24Y	.26Y	.32Y	.42Y	.49Y	.60Y	.74Y
Saudi Arabia	456	—V	—V	—V	—V	—V	—Y	—Y	—Y	—Y	—Y	—Y	.01Y	.01Y	.01Y
United Arab Emirates	466	—V	—V	—Y	—Y	—Y	—Y	—Y	.16Y	.17Y	.21Y	.27Y	.37Y	.47Y	.57Y
Western Hemisphere	**207**	**15.5Y**	**16.4Y**	**14.9Y**	**32.5Y**	**27.1Y**	**31.2Y**	**39.9Y**	**352.3Y**	**375.3Y**	**127.8Y**	**139.5Y**	**254.9Y**	**197.8Y**	**1,378.8Y**
Antigua and Barbuda	311	2.12Y	2.30Y	2.91Y	3.82Y	4.37Y	5.40Y	6.70Y	.59Y	.64Y	.82Y	1.07Y	1.22Y	1.51Y	1.88Y
Argentina	213	—V	—V	—V	—V	—V	—V	—V	.03V	.36V	1.14V	1.24V	43.57V	.61V	1.06V
Aruba	314	—V	—V	—V	—V	—V	.08V	—V	.11V	.08V	.05V	.04V	.03V	—V	—V

	Exports 2001	2002	2003	2004	2005	2006	2007	Imports 2001	2002	2003	2004	2005	2006	2007
	Millions of U.S. Dollars							Millions of U.S. Dollars						
Bahamas, The.......... 313	—Y	—Y	—Y	—Y	—Y	.01Y	.01Y	.05Y	.06Y	.07Y	.09Y	.11Y	.13Y	.16Y
Barbados.......... 316	6.02V	5.04V	.48V	4.73V	5.27V	4.72V	5.85Y	15.18V	12.56V	12.88V	15.77V	24.03V	24.92V	30.93Y
Belize.......... 339	.16Y	.18Y	.23Y	.30Y	.34Y	.42Y	.52Y	.04Y	.04Y	.05Y	.06Y	.07Y	.09Y	.11Y
Brazil.......... 223	—V	—V	—V	9.52V	—V	.01V	—V	193.11V	267.96V	1.93V	2.67V	3.50V	4.44V	1,138.28V
Chile.......... 228	—V	—V	—V	—V	—V	—V	—V	.36V	.22V	.22V	.41V	.51V	.58V	.70V
Colombia.......... 233	.11V	—V	—V	.04V	—V	—V	—V	2.13V	1.26V	1.56V	1.85V	3.59V	3.95V	5.68V
Costa Rica.......... 238	—V	—V	—V	—V	—V	—Y	—Y	.29V	.39V	.75V	.62V	.77V	.95Y	1.18Y
Dominica.......... 321	2.06V	2.24Y	2.84Y	3.72Y	4.25Y	5.26Y	6.53Y	1.83V	1.98Y	2.51Y	3.30Y	3.77Y	4.65Y	5.78Y
Dominican Republic.......... 243	.03V	.04Y	.04Y	.06Y	.07Y	.08Y	.10Y	.91V	.99Y	1.25Y	1.64Y	1.88Y	2.32Y	2.88Y
Grenada.......... 328	1.40Y	1.52Y	1.93Y	2.53Y	2.89Y	3.58Y	4.44Y	2.69Y	2.92Y	3.70Y	4.86Y	5.55Y	6.86Y	8.52Y
Guatemala.......... 258	—V	—V	—V	—V	—V	—Y	—Y	.01V	.16V	.12V	.04V	.05V	.07Y	.08Y
Guyana.......... 336	.38Y	.41Y	.52Y	.69Y	.79Y	.97Y	1.20Y	4.29Y	4.65Y	5.89Y	7.73Y	8.84Y	10.92Y	13.56Y
Haiti.......... 263	—V	—V	—V	—V	—Y	—Y	—Y	.02Y	.02Y	.02Y	.03Y	.03Y	.04Y	.05Y
Honduras.......... 268	—V	.04V	—V	.03V	.03Y	.04Y	.05Y	—V	2.00V	2.00V	1.60V	1.83Y	2.26Y	2.81Y
Jamaica.......... 343	.05V	.24V	.12V	.22V	.53V	.64V	.86V	2.65V	4.03V	3.92V	3.62V	4.52V	4.15V	3.97V
Mexico.......... 273	—V	—V	—V	—V	1.40V	1.25V	2.04V	—V	—V	—V	—V	2.39V	1.40V	2.54V
Netherlands Antilles.......... 353	.07V	.07V	.13V	.18Y	.20Y	.25Y	.31Y	.25V	.08V	.12V	.15Y	.17Y	.21Y	.27Y
Panama.......... 283	—Y	—Y	—Y	—Y	—Y	—Y	—Y	.93Y	1.01Y	1.28Y	1.68Y	1.92Y	2.38Y	2.95Y
Peru.......... 293	—V	—V	—V	—V	—V	—V	—Y	.09V	.02V	.31V	.90V	.54V	.73V	.81Y
St. Kitts and Nevis.......... 361	.52Y	.56Y	.71Y	.93Y	1.06Y	1.32Y	1.63Y	.14Y	.16Y	.20Y	.26Y	.30Y	.37Y	.45Y
St. Vincent & Grens.......... 364	.80V	1.34V	2.00V	1.94V	1.47V	1.82Y	2.25Y	4.00V	3.82V	4.32V	4.63V	4.80V	5.93Y	7.36Y
Suriname.......... 366	.10Y	.11Y	.13Y	.18Y	.20Y	.25Y	.31Y	.03Y	.04Y	.05Y	.06Y	.07Y	.09Y	.11Y
Trinidad and Tobago.......... 369	1.28V	1.87V	2.37Y	3.11Y	3.55Y	4.39Y	5.45Y	65.15V	50.19V	63.53Y	83.43Y	95.33Y	117.82Y	146.21Y
Uruguay.......... 298	—V	—Y	—V	—V	—V	—Y	—Y	—V	—Y	.02V	—V	.13V	.16Y	.19Y
Venezuela, Rep. Bol.......... 299	.04V	.05V	.06V	.07V	.16V	.25V	1.10V	57.20V	19.54V	18.98V	1.52V	45.20V	.07V	.09Y
Western Hem. n.s.......... 399	.33Y	.36Y	.39Y	.43Y	.47Y	.50Y	.54Y	.15Y	.15Y	.16Y	.17Y	.17Y	.18Y	.19Y
Other Countries n.i.e.......... 910	**—Y**	**—Y**	**—Y**	**—Y**	**—Y**	**—Y**	**—Y**	**.6Y**	**.7Y**	**.8Y**	**1.1Y**	**1.2Y**	**1.5Y**	**1.9Y**
Cuba.......... 928	—Y	—Y	—Y	—Y	—Y	—Y	—Y	.07Y	.07Y	.09Y	.12Y	.14Y	.17Y	.21Y
North Korea.......... 954	—Y	—Y	—Y	—Y	—Y	—Y	—Y	.54Y	.58Y	.74Y	.97Y	1.11Y	1.37Y	1.70Y
Memorandum Items														
European Union.......... 998	40.37Y	32.96Y	24.38Y	35.72Y	75.29Y	226.80Y	57.48Y	46.52Y	55.72Y	55.42Y	83.99Y	219.08Y	280.37Y	150.57Y
Oil Exporting Ctys.......... 999	.05Y	.05Y	.07Y	.07Y	.16Y	.25Y	1.10Y	57.58Y	20.09Y	19.49Y	2.00Y	46.24Y	1.52Y	1.54Y
Non-Oil Develop.Ctys.......... 201	15.56Y	16.48Y	14.99Y	32.71Y	58.60Y	33.09Y	41.36Y	303.92Y	364.65Y	116.61Y	149.20Y	222.09Y	213.49Y	1,401.89Y
PERCENT DISTRIBUTION														
Industrial Countries.......... 101	**81.4**	**75.8**	**71.1**	**60.2**	**64.4**	**88.5**	**68.0**	**31.3**	**32.1**	**60.5**	**59.7**	**59.8**	**69.5**	**21.4**
Developing Countries.......... 202	**18.6**	**24.2**	**28.9**	**39.8**	**35.6**	**11.5**	**32.0**	**68.6**	**67.8**	**39.2**	**40.0**	**40.0**	**30.3**	**78.4**
Africa.......... 607	**—**	**—**	**.1**	**.1**	**—**	**—**	**.1**	**.1**	**.1**	**.1**	**.1**	**.1**	**.1**	**—**
Asia.......... 507	**.1**	**.1**	**.2**	**.3**	**19.1**	**.7**	**1.9**	**1.6**	**1.5**	**2.0**	**2.6**	**1.7**	**2.1**	**1.2**
Europe.......... 170	**—**	**.1**	**.1**	**—**	**—**	**—**	**—**	**—**	**—**	**.1**	**.2**	**.1**	**.1**	**—**
Middle East.......... 407	**—**	**—**	**—**	**—**	**—**	**—**	**—**	**.1**	**.1**	**.2**	**.2**	**.1**	**.2**	**.1**
Western Hemisphere.......... 207	**18.4**	**24.0**	**28.5**	**39.5**	**16.4**	**10.8**	**30.0**	**66.9**	**66.2**	**36.8**	**36.9**	**38.0**	**27.9**	**77.1**
Other Countries n.i.e.......... 910	**—**	**—**	**—**	**—**	**—**	**—**	**—**	**.1**	**.1**	**.2**	**.3**	**.2**	**.2**	**.1**
ANNUAL PERCENT CHANGE														
World.......... 001	**86.0**	**–18.8**	**–23.6**	**57.9**	**100.4**	**75.5**	**–54.1**	**50.5**	**7.7**	**–38.9**	**9.0**	**77.2**	**5.8**	**152.4**
Industrial Countries.......... 101	**106.6**	**–24.4**	**–28.3**	**33.7**	**114.4**	**141.1**	**–64.7**	**–31.2**	**10.5**	**15.4**	**7.6**	**77.3**	**22.9**	**–22.1**
Developing Countries.......... 202	**29.4**	**5.9**	**–8.9**	**117.7**	**79.2**	**–43.3**	**27.4**	**228.5**	**6.4**	**–64.6**	**11.1**	**77.5**	**–19.9**	**552.7**
Africa.......... 607	**63.8**	**–24.9**	**22.4**	**34.8**	**11.3**	**23.6**	**24.1**	**–29.2**	**7.6**	**13.4**	**26.9**	**10.6**	**–20.2**	**24.1**
Asia.......... 507	**–48.6**	**–3.1**	**25.6**	**128.1**	**—**	**–93.5**	**21.1**	**–50.1**	**.7**	**–17.5**	**40.1**	**18.0**	**31.6**	**45.8**
Europe.......... 170	**–23.0**	**—**	**–11.4**	**–87.5**	**452.2**	**–37.0**	**–28.8**	**–36.0**	**28.1**	**97.6**	**92.6**	**–34.5**	**3.0**	**28.3**
Middle East.......... 407	**–97.8**	**—**	**....**	**....**	**....**	**23.5**	**29.5**	**7.5**	**7.7**	**24.5**	**31.7**	**22.3**	**24.5**	**22.7**
Western Hemisphere.......... 207	**30.5**	**5.7**	**–9.1**	**118.5**	**–16.7**	**15.3**	**27.8**	**281.8**	**6.6**	**–65.9**	**9.1**	**82.8**	**–22.4**	**597.1**
Other Countries n.i.e.......... 910	**10.4**	**8.5**	**26.6**	**31.3**	**14.3**	**23.6**	**24.1**	**10.4**	**8.5**	**26.6**	**31.3**	**14.3**	**23.6**	**24.1**

St. Vincent and the Grenadines 364

		Exports							Imports						
		2001	2002	2003	2004	2005	2006	2007	2001	2002	2003	2004	2005	2006	2007
		Millions of U.S. Dollars							*Millions of U.S. Dollars*						
IFS World Total		**41.5**	**38.0**	**38.2**	**36.6**	**39.9**	**38.1**	**50.0**	**185.9**	**174.0**	**201.1**	**225.6**	**240.4**	**271.3**	**310.0**
DOTS World Total	**001**	**41.6**	**39.3**	**38.1**	**36.6**	**39.9**	**195.5Y**	**157.7Y**	**171.8**	**178.5**	**201.3**	**225.2**	**240.5**	**576.3Y**	**583.7Y**
Industrial Countries	**101**	**18.8**	**17.7**	**16.8**	**14.7**	**14.6**	**148.0Y**	**115.6Y**	**107.2**	**113.9**	**124.9**	**137.8**	**138.7**	**304.5Y**	**273.6Y**
United States	111	1.18	2.06	5.05	1.95	3.66	1.82V	1.09V	65.88	73.18	82.94	84.36	79.98	64.02V	75.90V
Canada	156	.15	.10	.23	.12	.13	.26V	.51V	4.92	4.14	5.97	6.05	9.21	10.31V	10.87V
Australia	193	—	—	—	—	—	.01V	.04V	1.74	1.10	2.29	1.14	1.84	.52V	1.39V
Japan	158	—	—	—	—	.01	.06V	.41V	6.53	6.33	6.59	8.33	10.04	14.26V	23.10V
New Zealand	196	—	—	—	—	—	—V	.02V	.64	.31	.45	.52	.72	.77V	.76V
Austria	122	—	—	—	—	—	—V	—V	.04	.04	.04	.18	.16	.10V	.49V
Belgium	124	—	—	—	—	.02	—V	—V	.39	.45	.28	.50	.73	.47V	6.85V
Cyprus	423	—	—	—	—	—	—V	—V	.01	.11	.01	.01	.01	.02V	—V
Denmark	128	—	—	—	—	—	—V	.03V	.59	.66	.84	1.13	1.18	1.25V	8.07V
Finland	172	—	—	—	—	—	.12V	—V	.05	.91	.10	.09	.19	.18V	.28V
France	132	.62	.27	.33	.14	.16	50.50V	18.86V	2.47	3.28	1.35	3.00	2.44	22.68V	10.62V
Germany	134	.01	.01	—	—	—	.01V	6.71V	1.46	1.84	1.23	1.29	2.54	25.25V	3.57V
Greece	174	—	—	—	—	—	40.97V	44.75V	.02	.01	.01	.01	.05	12.41V	3.69V
Iceland	176	—	—	—	—	—	—V	—V	—	.19	—	—	.03	—V	—V
Ireland	178	—	—	—	—	—	—V	—V	.79	.59	1.24	.87	1.16	.42V	.56V
Italy	136	.01	.06	—	—	—	36.38V	23.00V	1.27	1.32	.96	3.64	2.78	63.31V	77.42V
Luxembourg	137	—	—	—	—	—	—V	—V	—	—	—	—	.18	—V	.01V
Malta	181	—	—	—	—	—	—V	—V	—	.01	—	—	.03	—V	—V
Netherlands	138	.02	—	.03	.18	—	.13V	.02V	1.23	.93	1.58	1.41	1.29	6.83V	3.32V
Norway	142	—	—	—	—	—	.51V	—V	.41	.51	.41	.57	.53	.96V	9.51V
Portugal	182	—	—	—	—	—	—V	—V	.05	.02	.03	.03	.03	.10V	.39V
Slovenia	961	—	—	—	—	—	—V	—V	—	—	—	—	—	.10V	.01V
Spain	184	—	—	—	—	—	1.07V	7.19V	.18	.07	.13	.12	.21	54.85V	13.84V
Sweden	144	—	—	—	.07	—	.02V	—V	.17	2.35	3.50	.60	.40	.31V	4.23V
Switzerland	146	.01	—	—	—	—	2.96V	1.17V	.08	.57	.13	.32	.46	7.43V	.84V
United Kingdom	112	16.82	15.24	11.15	12.27	10.65	13.17V	11.82V	18.31	14.95	14.79	23.64	22.56	17.93V	17.83V
Developing Countries	**202**	**22.8**	**21.5**	**21.2**	**21.9**	**25.2**	**47.5Y**	**42.1Y**	**64.6**	**64.6**	**76.4**	**87.4**	**101.7**	**271.8Y**	**310.0Y**
Africa	**607**	**—**	**—**	**—**	**—**	**—**	**—Y**	**—Y**	**.1**	**.1**	**.2**	**.7**	**.1**	**4.0Y**	**2.6Y**
Congo, Dem. Rep. of	636	—	—	—	—	—	—Y	—Y	—	—	—	.03	—	—Y	—Y
Côte d'Ivoire	662	—	—	—	—	—	—V	—Y	—	—	—	—	—	.46V	.57Y
Gabon	646	—	—	—	—	—	—Y	—Y	—	.02	.01	—	—	—Y	—Y
Ghana	652	—	—	—	—	—	—Y	—Y	—	—	—	.01	—	—Y	—Y
Malawi	676	—	—	—	—	—	—Y	—Y	.01	.01	—	—	—	—Y	—Y
Mauritius	684	.01	—	—	—	—	—V	—V	—	—	—	—	—	—V	—V
Morocco	686	—	—	—	.02	—	—Y	—Y	.01	—	—	—	—	—Y	—Y
Nigeria	694	—	—	—	—	.01	.01Y	.01Y	—	—	—	—	—	—Y	—Y
Sierra Leone	724	—	—	—	—	—	—Y	—Y	.01	—	—	.07	—	—Y	—Y
South Africa	199	—	—	—	—	—	—V	—V	.10	.02	.19	.54	.12	3.50V	2.04V
Swaziland	734	—	—	—	—	—	—Y	—Y	—	—	—	.01	.01	.01Y	.01Y
Tunisia	744	—	—	—	—	—	—V	—Y	.01	—	—	—	—	—V	—Y
Asia	**507**	**—**	**—**	**—**	**—**	**.1**	**2.9Y**	**.2Y**	**3.5**	**3.7**	**5.6**	**9.8**	**14.7**	**122.6Y**	**128.4Y**
Afghanistan, I.S. of	512	—	—	—	—	—	—Y	—Y	.05	—	—	.01	—	—Y	—Y
Bangladesh	513	—	—	—	—	—	—Y	—Y	—	—	.01	.02	.04	.05Y	.06Y
Bhutan	514	....	....	....	....	....	....	....	—	.01	—	—	—	—Y	—Y
China,P.R.: Mainland	924	.03	—	—	.01	.04	—V	—Y	1.33	1.21	1.79	3.41	6.56	16.33V	29.19V
China,P.R.:Hong Kong	532	—	—	—	—	—	—V	—V	.22	.16	.27	.52	.62	—V	—V
India	534	—	—	—	—	—	—Y	—Y	.18	.15	.36	.56	2.45	3.02Y	3.75Y
Indonesia	536	—	—	.01	—	—	2.72V	.05V	.24	.21	1.00	.93	.61	.37V	.52V
Korea	542	—	—	—	—	—	—V	.04V	.24	.22	.12	.29	1.23	.64V	.68V
Malaysia	548	—	—	—	—	—	—V	.03V	.21	.13	.14	.16	.30	.18V	.29V
Nauru	836	....	....	....	....	....	....	....	—	.01	—	—	—	—Y	—Y
Pakistan	564	—	—	—	—	—	—Y	—Y	.01	.02	.03	.04	.05	.06Y	.07Y
Philippines	566	—	—	—	—	—	—V	—V	—	—	.01	.01	.01	—V	—V
Singapore	576	—	—	—	—	.01	.01V	—V	.11	.09	.14	.26	.22	100.22V	92.61V
Sri Lanka	524	—	—	—	—	—	—Y	—Y	.03	.03	.03	.03	.05	.06Y	.07Y
Taiwan Province of China	528	—	—	—	—	.01	.15V	.04V	.60	1.40	1.55	3.08	2.06	.41V	.64V
Thailand	578	—	—	—	—	—	—V	.01V	.20	.08	.20	.42	.49	1.25V	.51V
Vietnam	582	—	—	—	—	—	—V	—V	.05	.02	—	.03	.01	—V	—V
Europe	**170**	**—**	**—**	**—**	**—**	**—**	**16.3Y**	**6.6Y**	**.1**	**.1**	**.3**	**.4**	**.4**	**40.7Y**	**51.8Y**
Belarus	913	—	—	—	—	—	—V	—V	—	—	—	—	—	—V	.15V
Bulgaria	918	—	—	—	—	—	.01V	.01V	—	—	—	—	—	4.29V	3.97V
Czech Republic	935	—	—	—	—	—	—V	—V	—	—	—	.03	.01	.15V	.03V
Estonia	939	—	—	—	—	—	—V	—V	—	—	—	—	—	.08V	.17V
Hungary	944	—	—	—	—	—	—V	.02V	.05	.01	.01	—	.05	—V	.08V
Latvia	941	—	—	—	—	—	—V	—V	—	—	—	—	—	3.10V	.93V
Lithuania	946	—	—	—	—	—	1.55V	—V	—	—	—	—	—	3.00V	.96V
Poland	964	—	—	—	—	—	—V	5.63V	.02	.03	.02	.01	.01	.04V	7.51V
Romania	968	—	—	—	—	—	—V	—V	.02	.02	—	.03	—	.54V	.48V
Russia	922	—	—	—	—	—	13.89V	—V	.01	—	—	—	.01	2.67V	19.92V

St. Vincent and the Grenadines 364

	Exports							Imports						
	2001	2002	2003	2004	2005	2006	2007	2001	2002	2003	2004	2005	2006	2007
	Millions of U.S. Dollars							*Millions of U.S. Dollars*						
Slovak Republic.......... 936	—	—	—	—	—	—V	—V	—	—	—	—	.01	.12V	.02V
Turkey.......... 186	—	—	—	—	—	.81V	.96V	.03	.03	.07	.27	.09	26.40V	17.21V
Ukraine.......... 926	—	—	—	—	—	—Y	—Y	.01	.01	.01	.07	—	.01Y	.01Y
Europe n.s.......... 884	—	—	—	—	—	—Y	—Y	—	.01	.16	—	.25	.30Y	.38Y
Middle East.......... 407	**—**	**—**	**—**	**—**	**—**	**—Y**	**—Y**	**.1**	**—**	**.1**	**.1**	**.1**	**.1Y**	**.1Y**
Egypt.......... 469	—	—	—	—	—	—Y	—Y	.01	—	.04	—	—	—Y	—Y
Iran, I.R. of.......... 429	—	—	—	—	—	—Y	—Y	—	.03	.01	.04	—	—Y	—Y
Israel.......... 436	—	—	—	—	—	—Y	—Y	.03	—	—	.07	.01	—V	—V
Jordan.......... 439	—	—	—	—	—	—Y	—Y	.02	.02	.01	—	—	—Y	—Y
Lebanon.......... 446	—	—	—	—	—	—Y	—Y	.01	—	.01	.01	.02	.02Y	.03Y
Saudi Arabia.......... 456	—	—	.02	—	—	—Y	—Y	—	—	—	—	.03	.03Y	.04Y
Syrian Arab Republic.......... 463	....	....	....	....	....	....	....	—	—	—	—	.01	.01Y	.01Y
Western Hemisphere.......... 207	**22.7**	**21.5**	**21.2**	**21.8**	**25.2**	**28.3Y**	**35.3Y**	**60.7**	**60.7**	**70.2**	**76.4**	**86.4**	**104.4Y**	**127.0Y**
Antigua and Barbuda.......... 311	2.54	2.37	2.73	3.02	2.47	3.05Y	3.78Y	.18	.27	.18	.10	.06	.08Y	.10Y
Argentina.......... 213	—	—	—	—	—	—V	—V	.11	.20	.29	.44	.73	—V	.25V
Aruba.......... 314	—	—	—	—	.01	.01Y	.01Y	—	—	.01	—	—	—V	—V
Bahamas, The.......... 313	—	.01	—	—	.01	.01Y	.01Y	.14	.15	.14	.02	.04	.05Y	.06Y
Barbados.......... 316	4.47	4.48	4.27	4.78	5.08	4.46V	5.54Y	7.54	7.08	7.63	8.93	9.47	15.44V	19.16Y
Belize.......... 339	—	—	—	—	—	—Y	—Y	.07	.10	.04	.06	.09	.12Y	.14Y
Bermuda.......... 319	—	—	—	—	—	—V	—Y	—	—	.03	.07	—	—Y	—Y
Brazil.......... 223	—	—	—	—	.02	—V	—V	2.00	1.94	2.16	3.26	2.93	2.83V	—V
Chile.......... 228	—	—	—	—	—	—V	—V	.05	.06	.15	.23	.26	—V	.01V
Colombia.......... 233	—	.01	—	—	—	—V	—V	.54	.52	2.89	1.31	2.46	2.17V	2.63V
Costa Rica.......... 238	—	—	—	—	.03	.03Y	.04Y	.24	.37	.53	.72	.62	.76Y	.95Y
Dominica.......... 321	1.35	1.33	1.38	1.51	2.86	3.54Y	4.39Y	.58	.64	.49	.57	.58	.72Y	.89Y
Dominican Republic.......... 243	—	—	—	—	—	—Y	—Y	.75	1.00	.89	.77	1.18	1.46Y	1.82Y
Ecuador.......... 248	—	—	—	—	—	—V	—Y	.01	.01	—	.04	.09	.11Y	.14Y
El Salvador.......... 253	—	—	—	—	—	—V	—V	—	.02	.01	.01	.01	—V	—V
Grenada.......... 328	1.20	1.28	1.30	1.95	2.73	3.38Y	4.19Y	.56	.54	.74	.56	.54	.67Y	.83Y
Guatemala.......... 258	—	—	—	—	—	—Y	—Y	.45	.58	.57	.08	.06	.07Y	.09Y
Guyana.......... 336	.26	.17	.14	.12	.15	.19Y	.24Y	2.16	2.10	1.65	2.55	1.95	2.41Y	2.99Y
Haiti.......... 263	.02	—	—	—	—	—Y	—Y	.02	.03	.02	.02	.02	.02Y	.03Y
Honduras.......... 268	—	—	—	—	—	—Y	—Y	.56	.75	1.05	.81	1.81	2.24Y	2.78Y
Jamaica.......... 343	1.85	1.71	.97	.80	.73	.18V	.34V	1.76	1.30	1.85	1.45	1.63	1.44V	2.22V
Mexico.......... 273	—	—	—	—	—	.01V	.03V	.94	.70	1.01	.82	1.66	.65V	.99V
Netherlands Antilles.......... 353	—	.01	—	—	.13	.16Y	.20Y	.40	.59	.56	.41	.16	.19Y	.24Y
Panama.......... 283	—	—	—	—	—	—V	—V	1.54	1.62	1.15	1.48	.23	—V	—V
Paraguay.......... 288	—	—	—	—	—	—V	—Y	—	—	.01	—	—	—V	—Y
Peru.......... 293	—	—	—	—	—	—V	—Y	.07	.16	.19	.10	.43	.13V	.31Y
St. Kitts and Nevis.......... 361	1.50	1.45	1.21	1.07	1.20	1.49Y	1.84Y	.03	.04	.06	.17	.26	.32Y	.40Y
St. Lucia.......... 362	3.63	3.47	3.93	4.21	4.36	5.39Y	6.69Y	.88	1.47	2.20	2.13	1.62	2.00Y	2.48Y
Suriname.......... 366	—	—	—	—	.10	.13Y	.16Y	—	.01	—	.07	.04	.05Y	.06Y
Trinidad and Tobago.......... 369	4.80	3.92	4.22	3.62	4.90	6.06Y	7.52Y	37.19	36.97	41.61	48.04	56.82	70.22Y	87.15Y
Uruguay.......... 298	—	—	—	—	—	—Y	—Y	.57	.01	—	—	—	—Y	—Y
Venezuela, Rep. Bol.......... 299	.07	.03	.04	.03	.03	.01V	.10V	1.18	1.29	1.78	.98	.61	.26V	.32Y
Western Hem. n.s.......... 399	1.05	1.27	.99	.71	.36	.25Y	.23Y	.20	.13	.28	.24	.02	.02Y	.02Y
Other Countries n.i.e.......... 910	**—**	**—**	**.1**	**—**	**—**	**—Y**	**—Y**	**—**	**—**	**—**	**—**	**.1**	**.1Y**	**.1Y**
Cuba.......... 928	.01	.03	.09	—	—	—Y	—Y	—	—	—	—	.01	.01Y	.01Y
North Korea.......... 954	—	—	—	—	—	—Y	—Y	.03	.02	.03	.01	.09	.11Y	.14Y
Memorandum Items														
European Union.......... 998	17.48	15.58	11.52	12.67	10.83	143.91Y	118.04Y	27.10	27.58	26.10	36.56	36.02	212.71Y	160.88Y
Oil Exporting Ctys.......... 999	.07	.03	.07	.03	.04	2.74Y	.16Y	1.42	1.52	2.79	1.96	1.24	.67Y	.88Y
Non-Oil Develop.Ctys.......... 201	22.72	21.49	21.13	21.84	25.20	44.76Y	41.95Y	63.14	63.09	73.59	85.45	100.45	271.09Y	309.10Y
PERCENT DISTRIBUTION														
Industrial Countries.......... 101	**45.2**	**45.1**	**44.1**	**40.3**	**36.7**	**75.7**	**73.3**	**62.4**	**63.8**	**62.0**	**61.2**	**57.7**	**52.8**	**46.9**
Developing Countries.......... 202	**54.7**	**54.8**	**55.6**	**59.7**	**63.3**	**24.3**	**26.7**	**37.6**	**36.2**	**37.9**	**38.8**	**42.3**	**47.2**	**53.1**
Africa.......... 607	**—**	**—**	**—**	**.1**	**—**	**—**	**—**	**.1**	**—**	**.1**	**.3**	**.1**	**.7**	**.5**
Asia.......... 507	**.1**	**—**	**—**	**—**	**.2**	**1.5**	**.1**	**2.0**	**2.1**	**2.8**	**4.3**	**6.1**	**21.3**	**22.0**
Europe.......... 170	**—**	**—**	**—**	**—**	**—**	**8.3**	**4.2**	**.1**	**.1**	**.1**	**.2**	**.2**	**7.1**	**8.9**
Middle East.......... 407	**—**	**—**	**—**	**—**	**—**	**—**	**—**	**—**	**—**	**—**	**.1**	**—**	**—**	**—**
Western Hemisphere.......... 207	**54.6**	**54.7**	**55.6**	**59.6**	**63.1**	**14.5**	**22.4**	**35.3**	**34.0**	**34.9**	**33.9**	**35.9**	**18.1**	**21.8**
Other Countries n.i.e.......... 910	**—**	**.1**	**.2**	**—**	**—**	**—**	**—**	**—**	**—**	**—**	**—**	**—**	**—**	**—**
ANNUAL PERCENT CHANGE														
World.......... 001	**–17.7**	**–5.6**	**–3.1**	**–3.9**	**8.9**	**390.1**	**–19.3**	**6.3**	**3.9**	**12.8**	**11.9**	**6.8**	**139.6**	**1.3**
Industrial Countries.......... 101	**–24.7**	**–5.8**	**–5.3**	**–12.3**	**–.7**	**910.9**	**–21.8**	**7.0**	**6.2**	**9.7**	**10.4**	**.7**	**119.5**	**–10.2**
Developing Countries.......... 202	**–10.9**	**–5.5**	**–1.5**	**3.1**	**15.5**	**88.2**	**–11.3**	**5.1**	**.1**	**18.2**	**14.4**	**16.3**	**167.2**	**14.1**
Africa.......... 607	**—**	**–81.6**	**–75.4**	**—**	**–64.6**	**23.5**	**29.5**	**141.2**	**–63.3**	**302.0**	**198.9**	**–78.9**	**—**	**–33.6**
Asia.......... 507	**–20.3**	**–90.8**	**249.3**	**–37.7**	**996.0**	**—**	**–94.0**	**18.4**	**6.8**	**51.4**	**72.8**	**50.4**	**735.2**	**4.8**
Europe.......... 170	**–99.9**	**471.4**	**–98.8**	**—**	**84.7**	**—**	**–59.3**	**–47.9**	**–22.9**	**141.0**	**55.4**	**2.9**	**—**	**27.3**
Middle East.......... 407	**–104.2**	**–971.6**	**—**	**30.1**	**....**	**....**	**....**	**–36.1**	**–37.2**	**48.3**	**76.1**	**–48.1**	**9.7**	**22.6**
Western Hemisphere.......... 207	**–3.6**	**–5.4**	**–1.6**	**3.1**	**15.3**	**12.6**	**24.6**	**4.6**	**–.1**	**15.7**	**8.9**	**13.0**	**20.9**	**21.7**
Other Countries n.i.e.......... 910	**—**	**266.5**	**143.5**	**31.3**	**....**	**....**	**....**	**61.0**	**–40.4**	**48.6**	**–68.4**	**946.7**	**23.6**	**24.1**

	Exports 2001	2002	2003	2004	2005	2006	2007	Imports 2001	2002	2003	2004	2005	2006	2007
	Millions of U.S. Dollars							Millions of U.S. Dollars						
IFS World Total	**15.5**	**13.7**	**15.0**	**10.7**	**11.9**	**10.7**	**15.5**	**119.5**	**127.6**	**128.9**	**155.2**	**187.2**	**218.7**	**227.1**
DOTS World Total....001	**70.5Y**	**77.7Y**	**104.8Y**	**95.9Y**	**233.1**	**131.3Y**	**162.5Y**	**277.1Y**	**179.2Y**	**255.2Y**	**288.9Y**	**641.0**	**319.2Y**	**346.2Y**
Industrial Countries....101	**60.5Y**	**61.0Y**	**77.9Y**	**74.5Y**	**197.9**	**65.9Y**	**88.0Y**	**199.1Y**	**108.0Y**	**139.4Y**	**137.3Y**	**487.5**	**154.6Y**	**151.7Y**
United States....111	8.73V	7.09V	5.00V	5.36V	15.13	4.45V	5.55V	77.11V	7.70V	12.10V	13.31V	86.69	20.24V	18.37V
Canada....156	.17V	.09V	.01V	.02V	—	.04V	.28V	.17V	.12V	.33V	.39V	.21	.40V	.33V
Australia....193	47.83V	46.86V	67.27V	63.01V	176.81	57.83V	78.22V	35.34V	28.53V	39.13V	25.41V	144.91	27.98V	27.39V
Japan....158	1.09V	2.57V	1.30V	1.06V	.92	.94V	.42V	27.25V	23.81V	30.13V	21.49V	47.94	27.92V	23.50V
New Zealand....196	1.11V	1.78V	1.60V	1.06V	4.66	1.60V	2.92V	46.64V	42.42V	50.37V	71.52V	198.70	69.68V	76.35V
Austria....122	—V	.01V	—V	.03V	—	—V	.04V	.01V	.01V	.02V	—V	—	.34V	.01V
Belgium....124	—V	.03V	—V	.40V	.01	—V	—V	—V	.14V	.71V	.60V	.14	.11V	.26V
Cyprus....423	—V	—V	—V	—V	—	—V	—V	.01V	—V	—V	.04V	—	—V	—V
Denmark....128	—V	—V	.01V	—V	—	.04V	—V	.95V	.04V	—V	.06V	.03	.07V	.06V
Finland....172	—V	—V	—V	—V	—	—V	—V	.82V	—V	.01V	—V	.01	—V	—V
France....132	.04V	.10V	.80V	.10V	.02	—V	—V	.09V	.15V	.15V	2.67V	.31	.23V	.04V
Germany....134	1.46V	1.97V	.78V	1.41V	—	.03V	—V	1.18V	1.01V	1.53V	.63V	2.25	.95V	1.18V
Greece....174	—V	—V	—V	—V	—	—V	—V	—V	—V	—V	—V	—	.01V	—V
Iceland....176	—V	—V	—V	—V	—	—V	—V	—V	—V	—V	—V	.01	—V	—V
Ireland....178	—V	—V	—V	—V	—	—V	—V	.01V	.01V	.03V	—V	1.47	.69V	.49V
Italy....136	.01V	.23V	.59V	.64V	.22	—V	—V	1.36V	.85V	.18V	.19V	.64	.22V	1.40V
Netherlands....138	.01V	—V	—V	.43V	—	.02V	.01V	.07V	.27V	.01V	.02V	.12	.12V	.05V
Norway....142	—V	—V	—V	—V	—	—V	—V	—V	—V	.02V	—V	—	—V	.01V
Portugal....182	—V	—V	—V	—V	—	—V	—V	.53V	.18V	.10V	.18V	—	—V	—V
Spain....184	—V	.04V	—V	.01V	—	.09V	.03V	—V	.28V	.35V	.26V	.07	.03V	.02V
Sweden....144	.07V	.17V	.01V	.02V	—	—V	.08V	—V	—V	3.22V	.04V	.14	5.43V	.77V
Switzerland....146	—V	.01V	—V	—V	.01	.13V	.18V	.06V	.39V	.22V	.14V	.07	.03V	.04V
United Kingdom....112	.01V	.11V	.52V	.92V	.14	.74V	.31V	7.50V	2.14V	.78V	.35V	3.76	.13V	1.44V
Developing Countries....202	**8.8Y**	**15.5Y**	**25.3Y**	**19.3Y**	**34.7**	**64.8Y**	**73.8Y**	**76.6Y**	**69.6Y**	**113.9Y**	**149.1Y**	**153.5**	**162.0Y**	**191.3Y**
Africa....607	**—Y**	**—Y**	**—Y**	**.1Y**	**—**	**—Y**	**—Y**	**.4Y**	**1.9Y**	**.6Y**	**.9Y**	**.3**	**2.7Y**	**—Y**
Benin....638	—V	—V	.02V	—V	—	—Y	—Y	....	....	....	....	....	....	....
Côte d'Ivoire....662	.01V	—V	—V	—V	—	—V	—Y	—V	—V	—V	—V	—	—V	—Y
Namibia....728	....	....	....	....	....	....	....	—Y	—Y	—Y	—Y	.01	.01Y	.02Y
Niger....692	—V	—V	.01V	—V	—	—Y	—Y	....	....	....	....	....	....	....
South Africa....199	—V	—V	—V	.11V	—	—V	—V	—V	1.49V	.56V	.89V	.31	2.69V	—V
Tunisia....744	—V	—V	—V	—V	—	—V	—Y	—V	—V	—V	.04V	—	.02V	.03Y
Zimbabwe....698	.01V	—V	—V	—V	—	—V	—Y	.36V	.40V	.04V	.01V	—	—V	—Y
Asia....507	**8.2Y**	**15.1Y**	**25.0Y**	**18.8Y**	**34.7**	**64.2Y**	**73.2Y**	**66.2Y**	**65.5Y**	**107.1Y**	**141.4Y**	**147.3**	**152.7Y**	**184.7Y**
American Samoa....859	1.67Y	1.81Y	2.29Y	3.01Y	31.74	39.23Y	48.68Y	2.33Y	2.53Y	3.20Y	4.21Y	.59	.73Y	.90Y
Bangladesh....513	—V	—V	—V	—V	—	—V	—V	.15V	—V	—V	—V	—	—Y	—Y
China,P.R.: Mainland....924	—V	—V	.32V	.87V	.02	.01V	.27Y	2.39V	3.07V	3.12V	5.66V	29.56	14.25V	12.71V
China,P.R.:Hong Kong....532	.22V	8.40V	.66V	.01V	.03	.03V	.03V	.56V	1.43V	.91V	.63V	3.50	.75V	1.75V
China,P.R.:Macao....546	—V	—V	—V	—V	—	—V	—V	—V	—V	.02V	—V	—	—V	—V
Fiji....819	.28Y	.30Y	.38Y	.50Y	.64	.79Y	.98Y	34.07Y	36.98Y	46.80Y	61.46Y	38.71	47.84Y	59.37Y
French Polynesia....887	—Y	—Y	—Y	—Y	.01	.01Y	.01Y	—Y	—Y	—Y	—Y	—	—Y	—Y
India....534	.35Y	—V	—V	—V	—	.05Y	.06Y	1.18Y	.72V	.52V	.33V	1.22	1.51Y	1.88Y
Indonesia....536	.02V	.05V	15.44V	5.01V	.01	.02V	.05V	6.50V	6.01V	7.07V	6.77V	12.97	10.82V	18.67V
Kiribati....826	....	....	....	....	....	....	....	—Y	—Y	—Y	—Y	.45	.55Y	.68Y
Korea....542	.01V	.01V	—V	—V	—	.10V	.25V	3.93V	6.00V	4.52V	5.30V	7.43	7.74V	6.23V
Malaysia....548	.05V	—V	.03V	—V	—	—V	—V	.58V	.39V	.72V	1.38V	15.43	1.79V	1.38V
New Caledonia....839	.01V	—V	—V	—V	.01	.01Y	.02Y	.41V	.61V	.45V	1.58V	—	2.23Y	2.77Y
Pakistan....564	—V	—V	—V	.01V	—	.22Y	.27Y	.06V	—V	.01V	.08V	.07	.09Y	.11Y
Papua New Guinea....853	—Y	—Y	—Y	—Y	—	—Y	—Y	—Y	—Y	—Y	—Y	.96	1.19Y	1.47Y
Philippines....566	—V	.04V	.06V	—V	—	—V	.02V	.05V	.04V	.04V	.90V	3.89	3.24V	2.21V
Singapore....576	—V	—V	—V	.02V	.53	.03V	.11V	1.31V	.97V	11.34V	24.22V	18.51	42.81V	55.74V
Sri Lanka....524	—V	—V	—Y	—Y	—	—Y	—Y	—V	—V	—Y	—Y	.33	.40Y	.50Y
Taiwan Province of China....528	1.52V	.04V	.77V	3.06V	—	14.76V	13.00V	10.80V	4.87V	26.73V	26.05V	3.07	5.84V	7.58V
Thailand....578	.10V	.02V	.02V	.80V	—	.66V	.16V	1.28V	1.21V	.96V	2.07V	9.97	9.71V	9.33V
Tonga....866	.17Y	.18Y	.23Y	.31Y	1.71	2.11Y	2.62Y	.17Y	.18Y	.23Y	.30Y	.65	.80Y	.99Y
Asia n.s....598	3.81Y	4.28Y	4.76Y	5.24Y	—	6.19Y	6.66Y	.45Y	.45Y	.45Y	.45Y	—	.45Y	.45Y
Europe....170	**.5Y**	**.1Y**	**—Y**	**.1Y**	**—**	**.1Y**	**—Y**	**.3Y**	**.4Y**	**.5Y**	**.7Y**	**—**	**.5Y**	**.6Y**
Albania....914	—V	—V	—V	—V	—	.02V	—V	—V	—V	—V	—V	—	—V	—V
Czech Republic....935	—V	—V	—V	—V	—	.04V	—V	.06V	—V	—V	—V	—	.02V	.01V
Estonia....939	—V	—V	—V	—V	—	—V	—V	—V	—V	.12V	—V	—	—V	—V
Macedonia, FYR....962	—V	.01V	—V	—V	—	—V	—Y	—V	—V	—V	—V	.01	—V	—Y
Poland....964	.49V	.08V	.03V	.07V	—	—V	—V	.04V	.14V	.07V	.02V	.03	.03V	.01V
Turkey....186	—V	—V	—V	.03V	—	—V	—V	.01V	.03V	—V	.31V	—	—V	.01V
Europe n.s....884	—Y	—Y	—Y	—Y	—	—Y	—Y	.19Y	.21Y	.27Y	.35Y	—	.50Y	.61Y
Middle East....407	**—Y**	**—Y**	**—Y**	**—Y**	**—**	**.1Y**	**.2Y**	**.3Y**	**.3Y**	**.4Y**	**.5Y**	**.8**	**.8Y**	**1.0Y**
Egypt....469	—V	.01Y	.01Y	.01Y	—	.01Y	.02Y	.02V	.03Y	.03Y	.04Y	.11	.14Y	.17Y
Iran, I.R. of....429	—V	—V	—Y	—Y	—	—Y	—Y	—Y	—Y	—Y	—Y	.55	.69Y	.83Y
Israel....436	—V	—V	—V	—V	—	—V	—V	—V	—V	—V	—V	.13	—V	—V
Lebanon....446	.01Y	.01Y	.01Y	.02Y	—	.03Y	.03Y	—Y	—Y	—Y	—Y	—	—Y	—Y
Saudi Arabia....456	—V	—V	—V	—V	—	—Y	—Y	.26Y	.28Y	.34Y	.45Y	—	—Y	—Y
Yemen, Republic of....474	—V	—V	—Y	—V	—	.10Y	.13Y	—Y	—Y	—Y	—Y	—	—Y	—Y

	Exports 2001	2002	2003	2004	2005	2006	2007	Imports 2001	2002	2003	2004	2005	2006	2007
	Millions of U.S. Dollars							Millions of U.S. Dollars						
Western Hemisphere.......... 207	**—Y**	**.2Y**	**.3Y**	**.2Y**	**—**	**.4Y**	**.4Y**	**9.4Y**	**1.6Y**	**5.4Y**	**5.6Y**	**5.0**	**5.2Y**	**4.8Y**
Argentina.......... 213	—V	—V	—V	—V	—	—V	—V	—V	—V	—V	—V	.01	.10V	.03V
Bahamas, The.......... 313	.01Y	.01Y	.01Y	.01Y	—	.02Y	.02Y	—Y	—Y	—Y	—Y	.60	.74Y	.92Y
Brazil.......... 223	—V	.11V	.12V	.03V	—	.09V	—V	2.42V	1.32V	.78V	1.23V	1.22	.87V	—V
Chile.......... 228	—V	—V	.01V	—V	—	—V	—V	1.10V	—V	4.05V	3.34V	3.01	2.82V	2.12V
Colombia.......... 233	—V	.02V	—V	—V	—	—V	.03V	.01V	.01V	—V	—V	—	—V	.70V
Costa Rica.......... 238	—V	—V	.02V	.03V	—	—Y	—Y	....	....	....	....	....	....	....
Ecuador.......... 248	.02V	.04V	.08V	.05V	—	.07V	.09Y	5.01V	—V	—V	.86V	—	.02V	.03Y
Haiti.......... 263	—V	—V	—Y	.07V	—	.09Y	.12Y	....	....	....	....	....	....	....
Jamaica.......... 343	—V	—V	—Y	—Y	—	—Y	—Y	—V	—V	—Y	—Y	.02	.02Y	.03Y
Mexico.......... 273	—V	—V	—V	—V	—	.09V	.09V	—V	—V	—V	—V	.02	.20V	.12V
Netherlands Antilles.......... 353	....	....	....	....	....	....	....	—V	—V	—Y	—Y	.13	.16Y	.20Y
Peru.......... 293	—V	—V	—V	—V	—	—V	—Y	.91V	.27V	.53V	.14V	—	.24V	.69Y
Trinidad and Tobago.......... 369	—V	.02V	.02Y	.03Y	—	.04Y	.05Y	—V	—V	—Y	—Y	—	—Y	—Y
Venezuela, Rep. Bol.......... 299	—V	—V	—V	—V	—	—V	—V	—V	—V	—V	.01V	—	—V	—Y
Countries & Areas n.s.......... 898	**—Y**	**—Y**	**—Y**	**—Y**	**—**	**—Y**	**—Y**	**1.0Y**	**1.1Y**	**1.3Y**	**1.8Y**	**—**	**2.5Y**	**3.1Y**
Memorandum Items														
European Union.......... 998	2.09Y	2.73Y	2.75Y	4.04Y	.39	.96Y	.46Y	12.63Y	5.21Y	7.29Y	5.07Y	8.97	8.40Y	5.76Y
Oil Exporting Ctys.......... 999	.02Y	.05Y	15.44Y	5.01Y	.01	.03Y	.06Y	6.76Y	6.29Y	7.41Y	7.23Y	13.52	11.51Y	19.50Y
Non-Oil Develop.Ctys.......... 201	8.74Y	15.41Y	9.89Y	14.31Y	34.68	64.81Y	73.71Y	69.86Y	63.34Y	106.48Y	141.87Y	139.95	150.51Y	171.77Y
PERCENT DISTRIBUTION														
Industrial Countries.......... 101	**85.9**	**78.5**	**74.3**	**77.7**	**84.9**	**50.2**	**54.2**	**71.9**	**60.3**	**54.6**	**47.5**	**76.0**	**48.4**	**43.8**
Developing Countries.......... 202	**12.4**	**19.9**	**24.2**	**20.1**	**14.9**	**49.4**	**45.4**	**27.7**	**38.9**	**44.6**	**51.6**	**23.9**	**50.8**	**55.3**
Africa.......... 607	**—**	**—**	**—**	**.1**	**—**	**—**	**—**	**.1**	**1.1**	**.2**	**.3**	**.1**	**.9**	**—**
Asia.......... 507	**11.6**	**19.5**	**23.8**	**19.6**	**14.9**	**48.9**	**45.0**	**23.9**	**36.5**	**42.0**	**49.0**	**23.0**	**47.9**	**53.4**
Europe.......... 170	**.7**	**.1**	**—**	**.1**	**—**	**—**	**—**	**.1**	**.2**	**.2**	**.2**	**—**	**.2**	**.2**
Middle East.......... 407	**—**	**—**	**—**	**—**	**—**	**.1**	**.1**	**.1**	**.2**	**.1**	**.2**	**.1**	**.3**	**.3**
Western Hemisphere.......... 207	**—**	**.3**	**.2**	**.2**	**—**	**.3**	**.2**	**3.4**	**.9**	**2.1**	**1.9**	**.8**	**1.6**	**1.4**
ANNUAL PERCENT CHANGE														
World.......... 001	**2.5**	**10.4**	**34.8**	**–8.5**	**143.1**	**–43.7**	**23.7**	**1.1**	**–35.3**	**42.4**	**13.2**	**121.9**	**–50.2**	**8.5**
Industrial Countries.......... 101	**20.8**	**.8**	**27.6**	**–4.4**	**165.7**	**–66.7**	**33.5**	**–4.9**	**–45.7**	**29.0**	**–1.5**	**255.0**	**–68.3**	**–1.8**
Developing Countries.......... 202	**–50.1**	**76.4**	**63.9**	**–23.8**	**79.6**	**86.9**	**13.8**	**20.4**	**–9.1**	**63.6**	**30.9**	**2.9**	**5.6**	**18.0**
Africa.......... 607	**–56.9**	**–87.9**	**—**	**335.7**	**—**	**—**	**....**	**245.6**	**420.1**	**–68.2**	**55.7**	**–65.5**	**745.5**	**–98.3**
Asia.......... 507	**–52.8**	**84.7**	**65.0**	**–24.6**	**84.1**	**85.2**	**14.0**	**16.0**	**–1.1**	**63.6**	**32.0**	**4.2**	**3.7**	**21.0**
Europe.......... 170	**—**	**–81.5**	**–63.6**	**224.4**	**–62.2**	**....**	**....**	**–32.8**	**23.3**	**21.6**	**49.0**	**–94.3**	**—**	**17.3**
Middle East.......... 407	**64.1**	**8.5**	**26.6**	**31.6**	**–89.9**	**—**	**24.2**	**8.1**	**6.5**	**21.7**	**32.2**	**63.0**	**4.3**	**21.2**
Western Hemisphere.......... 207	**–68.2**	**475.0**	**32.2**	**–13.3**	**11.8**	**....**	**–1.9**	**66.3**	**–83.1**	**236.3**	**4.2**	**–10.4**	**3.4**	**–6.8**

		Exports 2001	Exports 2002	Exports 2003	Exports 2004	Exports 2005	Exports 2006	Exports 2007	Imports 2001	Imports 2002	Imports 2003	Imports 2004	Imports 2005	Imports 2006	Imports 2007
		Millions of U.S. Dollars							*Millions of U.S. Dollars*						
IFS World Total		**2.6**	**5.0**	**6.6**	**3.5**	**3.4**	**3.8**	**3.0**	**28.5**	**31.1**	**40.7**	**41.4**	**49.7**	**70.9**	**67.0**
DOTS World Total	**001**	**11.5Y**	**8.6Y**	**11.8Y**	**9.5Y**	**18.3Y**	**10.8Y**	**7.8Y**	**53.5Y**	**61.8Y**	**63.6Y**	**64.5Y**	**64.3Y**	**79.9Y**	**80.9Y**
Industrial Countries	**101**	**8.0Y**	**7.2Y**	**9.9Y**	**6.3Y**	**15.0Y**	**7.7Y**	**6.0Y**	**47.7Y**	**54.8Y**	**55.9Y**	**55.6Y**	**52.6Y**	**69.3Y**	**69.8Y**
United States	111	.27V	.27V	—V	—V	.18V	—V	.45V	11.77V	2.09V	1.65V	3.96V	11.11V	4.07V	9.35V
Canada	156	.82V	.87V	1.85V	.11V	.10V	.22V	.01V	.02V	.03V	.51V	.02V	.04V	.07V	.12V
Australia	193	—V	—V	—V	—V	—V	—V	.02V	—V	.07V	.01V	—V	.08V	1.34V	.08V
Japan	158	.29V	.22V	.01V	—V	.12V	.03V	.07V	.87V	.94V	.31V	2.34V	.74V	.13V	.03V
New Zealand	196	—V	—V	—V	—V	—V	.01V	.01V	—V	.02V	—V	—V	—V	—V	—V
Austria	122	.01V	.03V	—V	—V	—V	—V	.01V	.21V	.07V	.02V	.02V	—V	.19V	.06V
Belgium	124	.33V	.56V	.57V	.73V	1.66V	1.68V	1.84V	2.56V	3.68V	3.17V	2.67V	3.43V	4.10V	3.17V
Denmark	128	—V	—V	—V	—V	.24V	—V	.02V	.09V	.10V	.30V	.17V	.15V	.05V	.23V
Finland	172	—V	—V	—V	—V	—V	—V	—V	—V	.07V	.10V	.01V	—V	—V	.07V
France	132	.22V	.37V	.48V	.47V	.40V	.35V	1.00V	2.18V	1.73V	2.43V	2.29V	1.70V	15.81V	1.54V
Germany	134	.05V	.71V	.92V	.62V	.57V	.02V	.02V	.59V	6.20V	7.38V	6.21V	.50V	.71V	.86V
Greece	174	—V	.01V	.01V	—V	—V	—V	—V	.76V	.17V	.10V	—V	.01V	—V	—V
Iceland	176	—V	—V	—V	—V	—V	—V	.01V	—V	—V	—V	—V	—V	—V	—V
Ireland	178	—V	—V	—V	—V	—V	—V	—V	—V	—V	—V	.16V	.04V	—V	.14V
Italy	136	.02V	.03V	.06V	.21V	.02V	.08V	.24V	.20V	.45V	3.61V	.25V	.21V	.18V	.35V
Luxembourg	137	—V	—V	—V	—V	—V	—V	—V	—V	—V	—V	.01V	—V	—V	—V
Malta	181	—Y	—V	—V	—V	—V	—V	—V	—Y	—V	—V	—V	—V	—V	.10V
Netherlands	138	3.01V	2.77V	5.06V	3.53V	11.07V	4.23V	1.84V	1.28V	2.24V	2.69V	3.23V	2.14V	2.73V	2.50V
Norway	142	—V	.01V	—V	—V	—V	—V	—V	.02V	—V	—V	.01V	.04V	—V	.08V
Portugal	182	2.10V	.40V	.31V	.31V	.29V	.82V	.32V	20.89V	30.41V	31.58V	32.90V	30.59V	39.07V	50.36V
Slovenia	961	.01V	—V	—V	—Y	—V	—V	—V	—V	—V	—V	—Y	—V	—V	—V
Spain	184	.65V	.67V	.03V	—V	.17V	.01V	.13V	.68V	1.65V	.69V	.25V	.44V	.14V	.35V
Sweden	144	.01V	.02V	.03V	—V	.03V	—V	—V	.01V	.08V	.01V	—V	—V	—V	.04V
Switzerland	146	.02V	.17V	.08V	.10V	.04V	.01V	.01V	.29V	.28V	.52V	.28V	.01V	.03V	.02V
United Kingdom	112	.17V	.09V	.47V	.24V	.16V	.23V	.01V	5.30V	4.55V	.82V	.77V	1.42V	.65V	.32V
Developing Countries	**202**	**3.5Y**	**1.4Y**	**1.9Y**	**3.2Y**	**3.3Y**	**3.1Y**	**1.7Y**	**5.8Y**	**6.9Y**	**7.7Y**	**9.0Y**	**11.7Y**	**10.6Y**	**11.2Y**
Africa	**607**	**.2Y**	**.5Y**	**.2Y**	**.3Y**	**.5Y**	**.5Y**	**.7Y**	**1.7Y**	**3.7Y**	**2.6Y**	**5.5Y**	**3.6Y**	**4.4Y**	**5.7Y**
Benin	638	—V	.02V	—V	—V	—V	—Y	—Y	—V	—V	—V	—V	—V	—Y	—Y
Cameroon	622	—V	.04V	.05V	.07Y	.07Y	.09Y	.11Y	—V	1.06V	.47V	.62Y	.71Y	.87Y	1.08Y
Cape Verde	624	—V	—Y	—Y	—Y	—Y	—Y	—Y	.01V	.01Y	.01Y	.01Y	.02Y	.02Y	.03Y
Congo, Republic of	634	—V	—V	—V	—V	—Y	—Y	—Y	—V	—V	.02V	—V	—Y	—Y	—Y
Côte d'Ivoire	662	—V	—V	—V	—V	—V	—V	—Y	.32V	.05V	.02V	—V	.20V	.13V	.16Y
Gabon	646	.01Y	.01Y	.01Y	.01Y	.02Y	.02Y	.03Y	1.15Y	1.24Y	1.57Y	2.07Y	2.36Y	2.92Y	3.62Y
Ghana	652	—Y	—Y	—Y	—Y	—Y	—Y	—Y	.01Y	.01Y	.01Y	.01Y	.02Y	.02Y	.02Y
Guinea	656	—V	—Y	.01V	—V	—Y	—Y	—Y	....	....	....	....	....	....	....
Kenya	664	.10V	.04V	.01V	.10V	.12Y	.15Y	.18Y	—V	.04V	—V	—V	—Y	—Y	—Y
Madagascar	674	—V	—V	—Y	—Y	—Y	—Y	—Y	.01V	—V	—V	—Y	—Y	—Y	—Y
Nigeria	694	—V	.32V	.11V	.14Y	.18Y	.22Y	.29Y	—V	—V	—V	—Y	—Y	—Y	—Y
South Africa	199	—V	—V	.03V	—V	.10V	—V	—V	.22V	1.13V	.51V	2.80V	.33V	.49V	.77V
Tanzania	738	.03V	—V	—Y	—Y	—Y	.01Y	.01Y	—V	—V	—Y	—Y	—Y	—Y	—Y
Tunisia	744	—V	—V	—V	—V	—V	—V	—Y	.01V	.02V	—V	—V	—V	—V	—Y
Zambia	754	—V	.03V	—V	—V	—V	—V	.01V	—V	.12V	—V	—V	—V	—V	—V
Zimbabwe	698	.01V	—V	—V	—V	—V	.02V	.03Y	—V	—V	—V	—V	—V	—V	—Y
Asia	**507**	**.8Y**	**.6Y**	**1.3Y**	**1.4Y**	**.8Y**	**.3Y**	**.4Y**	**2.5Y**	**2.0Y**	**2.9Y**	**2.0Y**	**5.7Y**	**4.2Y**	**4.2Y**
China,P.R.: Mainland	924	—V	—V	.03V	1.22V	—V	—V	—Y	1.38V	.17V	.22V	.22V	.61V	1.34V	1.96V
India	534	—Y	.03V	.01V	—V	.01V	.01Y	.02Y	—Y	.29V	1.55V	.57V	.27V	.33Y	.41Y
Indonesia	536	.04V	—V	.01V	—V	—V	—V	—V	.77V	.76V	.58V	.68V	.59V	.65V	.75V
Korea	542	.01V	.04V	.17V	.01V	.73V	.06V	.21V	.01V	.02V	.05V	.05V	.10V	.15V	.03V
Malaysia	548	.04V	.08V	.06V	.04V	.01V	.01V	—V	.10V	.04V	.01V	.03V	3.98V	1.39V	.66V
Philippines	566	.67V	.36V	.81V	.12V	—V	—V	—V	.17V	.71V	.43V	.24V	.12V	.14V	—V
Taiwan Province of China	528	—V	—V	—V	—V	—V	—V	.01V	.02V	.03V	.06V	.03V	.02V	.12V	.08V
Thailand	578	.04V	.08V	.23V	.03V	.05V	.19V	.13V	.05V	.01V	.02V	.13V	.01V	.08V	.36V
Europe	**170**	**2.4Y**	**.2Y**	**.1Y**	**.9Y**	**1.0Y**	**—Y**	**.1Y**	**1.2Y**	**1.0Y**	**1.7Y**	**.7Y**	**1.2Y**	**1.1Y**	**1.1Y**
Bulgaria	918	—V	—V	—V	—V	—V	—V	—V	.34V	.06V	—V	—V	.01V	—V	—V
Czech Republic	935	.05V	—V	—V	.11V	.04V	—V	—V	—V	—V	—V	—V	.04V	—V	—V
Estonia	939	—V	—V	—V	—V	—V	—V	—V	.08V	—V	—V	—V	—V	—V	—V
Hungary	944	—V	—V	.02V	.02V	—V	—V	—V	—V	.06V	.03V	.06V	—V	—V	—V
Macedonia, FYR	962	—V	—V	—V	—V	—V	.01V	.01Y	....	....	....	....	....	....	....
Poland	964	1.03V	.08V	.04V	.50V	—V	—V	—V	.62V	.53V	1.20V	.37V	—V	—V	—V
Romania	968	—V	—V	—V	—V	—V	—V	—V	.09V	—V	—V	—V	—V	—V	.07V
Russia	922	—V	—V	—V	—V	—V	—V	—V	.02V	.34V	.29V	—V	.04V	.15V	—V
Slovak Republic	936	—V	—V	—Y	—Y	—V	—V	—V	—V	—V	—Y	—Y	—V	.02V	—V
Turkey	186	1.36V	.09V	—V	.24V	1.01V	—V	.12V	.05V	.03V	.19V	.30V	.60V	.27V	.27V
Ukraine	926	—V	—V	—V	—V	—V	—Y	—Y	.02V	—V	.03V	—V	.51V	.63Y	.78Y
Middle East	**407**	**—Y**	**—Y**	**—Y**	**—Y**	**.1Y**	**.1Y**	**.1Y**	**—Y**	**—Y**	**—Y**	**—Y**	**—Y**	**—Y**	**—Y**
Egypt	469	.01V	.01Y	.01Y	.02Y	.02Y	.03Y	.03Y	—V	—Y	—Y	—Y	—Y	—Y	—Y
Lebanon	446	.01Y	.01Y	.01Y	.02Y	.02Y	.03Y	.03Y	—Y	—Y	—Y	—Y	—Y	—Y	—Y
Yemen, Republic of	474	—V	—V	—Y	—V	.01V	.01Y	.01Y	—V	—V	—Y	—V	—V	—Y	—Y

São Tomé and Príncipe 716

	Exports 2001	2002	2003	2004	2005	2006	2007	Imports 2001	2002	2003	2004	2005	2006	2007
	Millions of U.S. Dollars							*Millions of U.S. Dollars*						
Western Hemisphere............... 207	**.1Y**	**.1Y**	**.3Y**	**.5Y**	**.9Y**	**2.2Y**	**.5Y**	**.4Y**	**.2Y**	**.4Y**	**.8Y**	**1.2Y**	**.9Y**	**.1Y**
Argentina.................................. 213	—V	—V	—V	—V	—V	—V	—V	—V	—V	—V	.22V	.22V	—V	.04V
Barbados.................................. 316	—V	.02V	.02V	—V	—V	—V	—Y	.09V	—V	.13V	—V	—V	—V	—Y
Bolivia....................................... 218	—V	—V	—V	—V	.05V	.06Y	.07Y	....	....	....	....	....	....	....
Brazil... 223	—V	—V	.13V	.39V	.11V	—V	—V	.18V	.11V	.29V	.33V	.79V	.86V	—V
Colombia.................................. 233	—V	—V	—V	—V	—V	—V	—V	.02V	.08V	—V	.09V	.09V	—V	—V
Costa Rica................................. 238	....	....	....	....	....	....	....	.04V	—V	—V	.01V	.02V	.02Y	.03Y
Dominican Republic.................... 243	.08V	.09Y	.11Y	.15Y	.17Y	.21Y	.26Y	.01V	.01Y	.02Y	.02Y	.02Y	.03Y	.04Y
Ecuador...................................... 248	—V	.03V	—V	—V	—V	—V	—Y	....	....	....	....	....	....	....
Mexico....................................... 273	—V	—V	—V	—V	.34V	1.96V	.18V	—V	—V	—V	—V	—V	—V	—V
Peru... 293	—V	—V	—V	—V	.18V	—V	—Y	—V	—V	—V	.08V	—V	—V	—Y
St. Lucia..................................... 362	—Y	—Y	—Y	—Y	—Y	—Y	—Y	—Y	—Y	.01Y	.01Y	.01Y	.01Y	.01Y
Memorandum Items														
European Union......................... 998	7.67Y	5.74Y	8.00Y	6.75Y	14.64Y	7.42Y	5.43Y	35.46Y	51.99Y	54.12Y	49.37Y	40.67Y	63.66Y	60.10Y
Oil Exporting Ctys...................... 999	.04Y	.32Y	.12Y	.14Y	.18Y	.22Y	.29Y	.77Y	.76Y	.58Y	.68Y	.59Y	.65Y	.75Y
Non-Oil Develop.Ctys.................. 201	3.46Y	1.06Y	1.76Y	3.06Y	3.08Y	2.87Y	1.46Y	5.01Y	6.16Y	7.13Y	8.29Y	11.09Y	9.98Y	10.42Y
PERCENT DISTRIBUTION														
Industrial Countries................ 101	**69.6**	**83.9**	**84.0**	**66.4**	**82.2**	**71.4**	**77.5**	**89.2**	**88.8**	**87.9**	**86.1**	**81.8**	**86.7**	**86.2**
Developing Countries............. 202	**30.4**	**16.1**	**16.0**	**33.6**	**17.8**	**28.6**	**22.5**	**10.8**	**11.2**	**12.1**	**13.9**	**18.2**	**13.3**	**13.8**
Africa..................................... 607	**1.3**	**5.4**	**1.9**	**3.4**	**2.7**	**4.8**	**8.5**	**3.2**	**6.0**	**4.1**	**8.5**	**5.6**	**5.6**	**7.0**
Asia....................................... 507	**6.9**	**6.8**	**11.2**	**14.8**	**4.5**	**2.5**	**4.8**	**4.7**	**3.3**	**4.6**	**3.0**	**8.9**	**5.3**	**5.2**
Europe................................... 170	**21.3**	**2.0**	**.5**	**9.2**	**5.7**	**.1**	**1.7**	**2.3**	**1.7**	**2.7**	**1.1**	**1.9**	**1.3**	**1.4**
Middle East........................... 407	**.2**	**.3**	**.2**	**.4**	**.3**	**.6**	**1.0**	**—**	**—**	**—**	**—**	**—**	**—**	**—**
Western Hemisphere............. 207	**.7**	**1.6**	**2.2**	**5.7**	**4.7**	**20.6**	**6.5**	**.7**	**.3**	**.7**	**1.2**	**1.8**	**1.2**	**.1**
ANNUAL PERCENT CHANGE														
World...................................... 001	**–34.8**	**–25.3**	**37.2**	**–19.0**	**92.0**	**–41.1**	**–28.0**	**34.6**	**15.4**	**3.0**	**1.4**	**–.3**	**24.2**	**1.3**
Industrial Countries................ 101	**–46.4**	**–9.9**	**37.4**	**–36.0**	**137.8**	**–48.8**	**–21.8**	**40.0**	**14.9**	**1.9**	**–.6**	**–5.2**	**31.6**	**.7**
Developing Countries............. 202	**29.3**	**–60.5**	**36.1**	**70.5**	**1.7**	**–5.2**	**–43.5**	**2.2**	**19.7**	**11.4**	**16.4**	**30.2**	**–9.0**	**5.0**
Africa..................................... 607	**157.9**	**208.0**	**–51.9**	**46.8**	**50.2**	**4.1**	**27.7**	**–33.6**	**113.9**	**–28.9**	**111.0**	**–34.2**	**22.6**	**27.8**
Asia....................................... 507	**–.6**	**–26.7**	**125.1**	**7.5**	**–42.1**	**–66.7**	**36.1**	**190.7**	**–19.4**	**44.7**	**–32.8**	**190.6**	**–26.3**	**1.0**
Europe................................... 170	**38.5**	**–93.0**	**–67.8**	**—**	**18.9**	**–98.7**	**866.8**	**–29.3**	**–16.0**	**71.0**	**–58.2**	**64.8**	**–11.5**	**5.2**
Middle East........................... 407	**125.1**	**8.5**	**26.6**	**47.3**	**24.5**	**23.6**	**24.1**	**—**	**—**	**....**	**....**	**....**	**....**	**....**
Western Hemisphere............. 207	**17.7**	**68.2**	**85.8**	**110.8**	**56.3**	**160.6**	**–77.2**	**–29.2**	**–39.7**	**105.9**	**75.6**	**50.0**	**–20.0**	**–87.1**

	Exports							Imports						
	2001	2002	2003	2004	2005	2006	2007	2001	2002	2003	2004	2005	2006	2007
	Millions of U.S. Dollars							*Millions of U.S. Dollars*						
IFS World Total	**67,973**	**72,453**	**93,245**	**125,997**	**180,711**	**211,306**	**228,550**	**31,181**	**32,293**	**36,915**	**44,744**	**59,459**	**69,800**	**90,215**
DOTS World Total............001	**68,832Y**	**66,140Y**	**86,547Y**	**112,687Y**	**156,967Y**	**191,048Y**	**197,954Y**	**31,181**	**32,290**	**36,916**	**44,745**	**59,509**	**70,616Y**	**91,136Y**
Industrial Countries............101	**36,274Y**	**35,161Y**	**45,969Y**	**57,424Y**	**80,444Y**	**93,811Y**	**91,995Y**	**21,629**	**21,304**	**23,842**	**27,741**	**36,008**	**41,105Y**	**52,550Y**
United States............111	13,104V	12,629V	17,750V	20,457V	26,333V	30,079V	33,786V	5,543	5,267	5,551	6,845	8,803	8,589V	11,439V
Canada............156	502V	477V	650V	790V	1,415V	1,505V	1,761V	376	352	370	499	518	526V	713V
Australia............193	579V	674V	585V	763V	1,023V	946V	841V	1,262	1,126	989	1,281	1,673	1,843V	1,806V
Japan............158	11,197V	10,580V	13,241V	16,803V	25,978V	33,624V	32,357V	3,478	3,575	3,818	4,366	5,362	5,103V	7,398V
New Zealand............196	150V	115V	104V	156V	239V	291V	293V	120	108	157	212	305	294V	428V
Austria............122	103V	137V	303V	339V	367V	337V	267V	130	171	349	308	455	625V	658V
Belgium............124	186V	222V	266V	364V	692V	1,072V	1,250V	504	557	616	595	870	1,303V	1,441V
Cyprus............423	15V	10V	18V	17V	13V	18V	57V	8	6	6	7	10	9V	12V
Denmark............128	4V	5V	3V	4V	11V	4V	7V	208	243	319	360	395	309V	431V
Finland............172	1V	1V	—V	1V	1V	1V	6V	232	341	353	298	1,033	1,148V	1,186V
France............132	2,144V	2,221V	2,404V	3,559V	4,242V	4,427V	3,371V	1,193	1,160	1,350	1,565	2,052	2,499V	2,925V
Germany............134	779V	727V	951V	1,198V	1,534V	1,530V	1,110V	2,507	2,725	3,301	3,612	4,867	6,020V	8,017V
Greece............174	949V	799V	1,120V	1,455V	2,024V	2,200V	1,155V	45	52	52	65	84	74V	80V
Iceland............176	—V	—V	1V	—V	—V	—V	1V	1	2	—	—	—	—V	—V
Ireland............178	1V	21V	4V	2V	2V	4V	6V	302	293	318	350	432	440V	538V
Italy............136	1,740V	1,638V	2,266V	3,319V	4,771V	4,837V	4,515V	1,212	1,388	1,469	1,524	2,260	3,373V	4,588V
Luxembourg............137	1V	1V	1V	4V	5V	8V	23V	11	19	25	31	33	36V	43V
Malta............181	—Y	1V	1V	—V	—V	1V	2V	9	4	11	12	12	11V	12V
Netherlands............138	1,901V	2,040V	2,965V	3,484V	5,252V	6,275V	4,853V	584	545	739	806	988	2,111V	2,369V
Norway............142	6V	5V	4V	10V	41V	46V	48V	63	36	50	197	56	117V	134V
Portugal............182	336V	303V	324V	341V	478V	610V	538V	46	41	52	50	69	71V	73V
Slovenia............961	1V	2V	3V	4Y	—V	—V	1V	15	16	19	31	23	35V	90V
Spain............184	1,106V	1,367V	1,649V	2,155V	2,774V	3,484V	3,915V	444	411	489	598	670	930V	1,384V
Sweden............144	135V	24V	32V	85V	53V	93V	77V	439	397	560	745	967	1,159V	1,269V
Switzerland............146	44V	175V	161V	81V	172V	259V	291V	755	537	713	845	1,284	1,075V	1,421V
United Kingdom............112	1,290V	988V	1,164V	2,034V	3,024V	2,160V	1,463V	2,143	1,931	2,167	2,541	2,787	3,402V	4,093V
Developing Countries............202	**32,516Y**	**30,935Y**	**40,524Y**	**55,192Y**	**76,425Y**	**97,115Y**	**105,812Y**	**9,481**	**10,653**	**12,553**	**16,355**	**22,888**	**28,754Y**	**37,605Y**
Africa............607	**3,187Y**	**2,801Y**	**4,093Y**	**5,333Y**	**3,778Y**	**8,195Y**	**8,946Y**	**517**	**611**	**588**	**943**	**1,017**	**872Y**	**1,125Y**
Algeria............612	34V	27V	30Y	35Y	46Y	55Y	65Y	1	—	—	1	2	3Y	3Y
Angola............614	—Y	—Y	—Y	—Y	—Y	1Y	1Y	—	—	—	—	—	—Y	—Y
Benin............638	5V	4V	2V	1V	9V	11Y	14Y	2	—	—	—	—	—Y	—Y
Burkina Faso............748	—Y	—Y	—Y	—Y	—Y	—Y	—Y	1	—	—	—	—	—Y	—Y
Burundi............618	14V	3V	1V	—V	9V	49V	60Y	—	—	—	—	—	—V	—Y
Cameroon............622	15V	11V	3V	4Y	5Y	6Y	7Y	2	3	3	3	2	3Y	3Y
Central African Rep............626	—Y	—Y	—Y	—Y	—Y	—Y	—Y	—	—	—	—	1	2Y	2Y
Chad............628	8Y	9Y	11Y	14Y	19Y	24Y	29Y	—	—	—	—	—	—Y	—Y
Comoros............632	—Y	—Y	—Y	—Y	—Y	—Y	—Y	—	—	—	—	1	1Y	1Y
Congo, Republic of............634	3V	8V	2V	1V	1Y	1Y	1Y	—	—	—	—	1	1Y	1Y
Côte d'Ivoire............662	22V	14V	17V	17V	23V	21V	25Y	—	1	1	3	4	8V	10Y
Djibouti............611	106Y	112Y	136Y	180Y	245Y	308Y	372Y	—	—	—	—	—	—Y	—Y
Eritrea............643	13Y	14Y	17Y	22Y	30Y	38Y	46Y	—	—	—	—	1	1Y	1Y
Ethiopia............644	183V	101V	231V	346V	546V	686Y	827Y	26	25	34	50	66	82Y	106Y
Gambia, The............648	2Y	3Y	3Y	4Y	6Y	7Y	8Y	—	—	—	—	—	—Y	—Y
Ghana............652	2Y	2Y	3Y	4Y	5Y	7Y	8Y	4	4	4	3	7	9Y	11Y
Guinea............656	1V	1Y	3V	1V	2Y	2Y	3Y	—	—	—	—	—	—Y	—Y
Kenya............664	183V	155V	291V	362V	492Y	619Y	747Y	6	5	5	11	8	10Y	13Y
Lesotho............666	—Y	—Y	—Y	—Y	—Y	—Y	—Y	—	—	—	2	—	—Y	—Y
Madagascar............674	6V	3V	6V	7Y	10Y	13Y	15Y	—	—	—	—	1	1Y	1Y
Malawi............676	—Y	—Y	—Y	—Y	—Y	—Y	—Y	—	—	—	—	—	—Y	1Y
Mali............678	1Y	1Y	1Y	1Y	1Y	1Y	2Y	—	—	—	—	—	—Y	—Y
Mauritania............682	3Y	3Y	4Y	5Y	7Y	9Y	11Y	1	—	—	—	—	—Y	—Y
Mauritius............684	35V	46V	53V	47V	105V	115V	39V	—	1	1	1	1	—V	—V
Morocco............686	474V	630V	651V	868V	1,251V	1,573Y	1,897Y	72	35	52	73	106	131Y	169Y
Mozambique............688	1V	4V	17V	5V	2V	2V	2Y	—	—	—	—	—	—V	—Y
Namibia............728	14Y	18Y	21Y	25Y	29Y	32Y	36Y	3	—	—	1	—	—Y	—Y
Niger............692	1V	—V	1V	4V	6Y	7Y	8Y	—	—	—	—	—	—Y	—Y
Nigeria............694	45V	18V	20V	23Y	31Y	37Y	44Y	1	1	1	2	2	2Y	3Y
Rwanda............714	1Y	1Y	1Y	1Y	2Y	3Y	3Y	—	—	—	—	—	—Y	—Y
St. Helena............856	—Y	1Y	1Y	1Y	1Y	1Y	2Y	—	—	—	—	—	—Y	—Y
Senegal............722	9V	8V	7V	8V	16V	7V	9Y	—	—	—	—	—	—V	—Y
Seychelles............718	37V	53V	59V	78Y	106Y	133Y	161Y	—	—	—	—	—	—Y	—Y
Sierra Leone............724	—Y	—Y	—Y	—Y	1Y	1Y	1Y	—	—	—	—	—	—Y	—Y
Somalia............726	4Y	5Y	6Y	7Y	10Y	13Y	15Y	7	6	8	7	9	11Y	14Y
South Africa............199	1,730V	1,294V	1,944V	2,644V	—V	3,599V	3,624V	238	216	184	414	431	324V	370V
Sacca exc. South Afr............608	—V	—V	—V	—Y	—Y	—Y	—Y	—	—	—	—	—	2Y	3Y
Sudan............732	141Y	150Y	400Y	429V	570V	590V	595V	29	164	139	194	143	139V	108V
Swaziland............734	—Y	—Y	—Y	—Y	—Y	—Y	—Y	—	—	—	1	1	1Y	1Y
Tanzania............738	53V	43V	52Y	69Y	94Y	118Y	142Y	2	2	2	2	4	5Y	6Y
Togo............742	2V	4V	9V	14V	4V	5Y	7Y	—	2	4	3	—	—Y	—Y

		Exports							Imports						
		2001	2002	2003	2004	2005	2006	2007	2001	2002	2003	2004	2005	2006	2007
		Millions of U.S. Dollars							*Millions of U.S. Dollars*						
Tunisia	744	40V	55V	94V	103V	98V	111V	134Y	25	7	11	27	66	45V	59Y
Uganda	746	7V	7V	11V	15Y	20Y	25Y	30Y	—	—	—	—	—	—Y	—Y
Zambia	754	3V	4V	1V	4V	—V	2V	—V	93	136	135	144	159	93V	238V
Zimbabwe	698	1V	2V	—V	3V	4V	1V	1Y	2	1	1	2	1	—V	—Y
Asia	**507**	**22,689Y**	**21,206Y**	**27,622Y**	**36,829Y**	**55,152Y**	**67,571Y**	**72,015Y**	**4,902**	**5,387**	**6,669**	**8,460**	**11,889**	**16,035Y**	**22,021Y**
Afghanistan, I.S. of	512	—Y	—Y	—Y	1Y	1Y	1Y	1Y	—	1	—	—	1	1Y	1Y
Bangladesh	513	216V	94V	182V	149V	266V	364V	312V	20	19	17	18	27	34Y	38Y
Brunei Darussalam	516	—Y	—Y	1V	2Y	2Y	3Y	3Y	—	—	—	—	—	—Y	—Y
Cambodia	522	—V	—V	—V	—V	—V	2V	2Y	—	1	3	1	1	—V	—Y
China,P.R.: Mainland	924	2,476V	3,124V	4,731V	6,838V	11,169V	13,715V	15,951V	1,441	1,718	2,186	2,968	4,409	5,560V	8,596V
China,P.R.:Hong Kong	532	167V	202V	238V	339V	397V	439V	428V	24	22	96	39	150	404V	449V
China,P.R.:Macao	546	9V	8V	9V	11V	12V	18V	25V	1	1	2	1	1	—V	—V
Fiji	819	—Y	—Y	—Y	—Y	—Y	—Y	—Y	—	—	—	1	1	2Y	2Y
India	534	1,197Y	450V	618V	1,027V	1,398V	1,758Y	2,121Y	750	882	1,091	1,417	1,837	2,268Y	2,938Y
Indonesia	536	1,195V	1,003V	1,362V	1,788V	2,466V	3,077V	3,066V	375	361	352	411	542	739V	1,039V
Korea	542	7,325V	6,864V	8,425V	10,727V	14,642V	18,684V	19,240V	1,022	1,064	1,360	1,702	2,172	3,276V	4,428V
Malaysia	548	579V	362V	530V	896V	1,407V	2,118V	1,797V	304	300	371	446	546	583V	788V
Maldives	556	1V	—V	—V	1V	1V	1Y	2Y	—	—	—	—	—	—Y	—Y
Myanmar	518	2Y	3Y	3Y	4Y	6Y	7Y	9Y	1	1	1	1	1	1Y	1Y
Nepal	558	61V	54V	28V	31V	40V	29V	35Y	—	—	—	—	—	—V	—Y
Pakistan	564	1,034V	1,196V	1,288V	1,879V	2,563V	3,222Y	3,887Y	127	127	152	170	199	246Y	318Y
Philippines	566	806V	909V	1,089V	1,159V	1,984V	2,710V	3,205V	44	51	60	67	88	55V	73V
Singapore	576	3,845V	3,467V	3,566V	4,590V	8,143V	8,449V	8,012V	135	160	179	198	292	818V	922V
Sri Lanka	524	32V	141V	68V	162V	134V	134V	138V	31	29	27	33	40	31V	57V
Taiwan Province of China	528	2,496V	2,188V	3,887V	5,053V	6,760V	8,873V	9,463V	314	309	349	407	519	583V	806V
Thailand	578	1,226V	1,113V	1,560V	2,113V	3,676V	3,873V	4,199V	296	326	399	552	1,019	1,379V	1,506V
Vietnam	582	21V	26V	35V	60V	83V	93V	119V	16	17	21	28	45	54V	57V
Europe	**170**	**696Y**	**761Y**	**954Y**	**1,242Y**	**1,838Y**	**2,156Y**	**2,441Y**	**873**	**1,094**	**1,425**	**1,846**	**2,690**	**2,948Y**	**4,206Y**
Albania	914	1V	1V	2V	—V	1V	1V	—V	—	—	—	—	—	—V	—V
Armenia	911	—Y	—Y	—Y	—Y	—Y	1V	2V	—	—	—	—	—	—V	—V
Azerbaijan	912	2V	2V	1V	1V	1V	1V	1V	1	—	—	—	—	—V	—V
Belarus	913	—V	—V	—V	—V	1V	4V	2V	—	—	5	—	—	4V	8V
Bosnia & Herzegovina	963	—Y	—Y	—Y	—Y	—Y	—Y	—Y	—	—	—	—	1	1Y	1Y
Bulgaria	918	—V	1V	—V	1V	2V	4V	1V	23	27	14	21	28	44V	72V
Croatia	960	1V	2V	3V	8V	12V	17V	7V	4	5	6	20	19	17V	75V
Czech Republic	935	1V	3V	4V	7V	8V	1V	1V	57	72	60	86	134	106V	157V
Estonia	939	—V	—V	—V	—V	—V	—V	1V	3	3	3	3	5	14V	58V
Georgia	915	—V	—V	—V	1V	—V	—V	—Y	—	—	1	—	—	—V	—Y
Hungary	944	2V	3V	4V	1V	—V	—V	1V	58	95	124	179	320	264V	305V
Kazakhstan	916	2V	2V	1V	—V	1Y	1Y	1Y	59	15	13	140	75	93Y	120Y
Kyrgyz Republic	917	—V	—V	—V	—V	—V	—V	—V	—	—	12	6	2	—V	—V
Latvia	941	—V	—V	—V	—V	—V	—V	—V	1	2	2	2	2	2V	8V
Lithuania	946	—V	1V	1V	—V	—V	—V	6V	1	1	2	3	12	33V	73V
Macedonia, FYR	962	—V	—V	—V	—V	—V	1V	1Y	—	—	—	1	1	—V	—Y
Moldova	921	....	....	....	....	....	....	....	1	—	—	—	2	3Y	4Y
Poland	964	11V	13V	26V	55V	19V	11V	102V	48	76	94	122	162	161V	222V
Romania	968	4V	5V	3V	9V	28V	9V	24V	70	85	71	115	154	183V	182V
Russia	922	1V	2V	2V	5V	4V	6V	10V	103	137	196	264	400	300V	469V
Serbia & Montenegro	965	....	....	....	....	....	....	....	—	—	—	—	2	2Y	3Y
Slovak Republic	936	—V	1V	1Y	2Y	—V	—V	—V	7	6	8	26	48	42V	41V
Tajikistan	923	—V	—V	—V	—V	—V	—V	—V	—	—	2	—	1	—V	—V
Turkey	186	663V	722V	881V	1,120V	1,717V	2,047V	2,218V	352	392	559	599	838	1,082V	1,635V
Turkmenistan	925	3V	2V	20V	26Y	35Y	44Y	54Y	—	—	—	—	—	—Y	—Y
Ukraine	926	3V	1V	1V	2V	3V	3Y	4Y	85	171	250	257	484	597Y	774Y
Uzbekistan	927	1Y	1Y	1Y	1Y	1Y	2Y	2Y	—	5	—	1	—	—Y	—Y
Europe n.s.	884	1Y	1Y	2Y	2Y	3Y	3Y	4Y	—	—	—	—	—	—Y	—Y
Middle East	**407**	**4,859Y**	**5,260Y**	**6,755Y**	**10,227Y**	**13,851Y**	**17,137Y**	**19,909Y**	**2,134**	**2,648**	**2,793**	**3,746**	**5,103**	**6,389Y**	**7,788Y**
Bahrain	419	1,554Y	1,653Y	2,004Y	2,651Y	3,606Y	4,534Y	5,470Y	199	275	204	450	573	707Y	916Y
Egypt	469	617V	656Y	795Y	1,052Y	1,432Y	1,800Y	2,171Y	186	217	303	424	798	985Y	1,276Y
Iran, I.R. of	429	201V	304V	339Y	390Y	518Y	620Y	731Y	119	90	115	274	487	583Y	688Y
Iraq	433	—Y	—Y	—Y	—Y	—Y	—Y	—Y	—	—	—	—	—	—Y	1Y
Jordan	439	142V	131V	589V	1,470V	2,255V	2,668V	2,589V	142	142	171	196	269	436V	456V
Kuwait	443	540Y	509Y	567Y	652Y	866Y	1,037Y	1,223Y	110	125	130	205	223	267Y	315Y
Lebanon	446	162Y	172Y	209Y	276Y	375Y	472Y	569Y	126	87	100	112	129	159Y	206Y
Libya	672	4Y	4Y	4Y	5Y	6Y	7Y	9Y	1	—	—	—	7	8Y	9Y
Oman	449	168V	200V	204V	235Y	312Y	373Y	440Y	136	119	152	161	243	291Y	343Y
Qatar	453	182V	229V	265V	519V	523V	763V	900Y	135	145	169	188	128	238V	281Y
Syrian Arab Republic	463	122Y	130Y	157Y	1,237V	1,683Y	2,116Y	2,552Y	272	539	403	407	519	641Y	830Y
United Arab Emirates	466	888V	951V	1,235V	1,422Y	1,887Y	2,260Y	2,665Y	633	818	958	1,187	1,564	1,873Y	2,209Y
Yemen, Republic of	474	278V	320V	388Y	318V	388V	488Y	589Y	75	88	86	140	161	199Y	258Y
Middle East n.s.	489	—Y	—Y	—Y	—Y	—Y	—Y	—Y	2	3	2	2	1	1Y	—Y
Western Hemisphere	**207**	**1,085Y**	**907Y**	**1,100Y**	**1,561Y**	**1,807Y**	**2,055Y**	**2,501Y**	**1,054**	**912**	**1,078**	**1,359**	**2,188**	**2,510Y**	**2,464Y**
Argentina	213	13V	11V	5V	10V	1V	—V	21V	62	83	140	142	276	378V	410V
Aruba	314	—V	—V	—V	—V	—V	—V	—V	—	—	—	—	16	—V	—V
Bahamas, The	313	20Y	21Y	26Y	34Y	47Y	59Y	71Y	—	—	—	—	—	—Y	—Y
Bermuda	319	—Y	—Y	—Y	—Y	—V	—V	—Y	1	—	—	—	—	—Y	—Y
Brazil	223	816V	677V	888V	1,232V	1,340V	1,617V	1,709V	648	553	626	781	1,313	1,634V	1,626V

	Exports							Imports						
	2001	2002	2003	2004	2005	2006	2007	2001	2002	2003	2004	2005	2006	2007
	Millions of U.S. Dollars							*Millions of U.S. Dollars*						
Chile........ 228	5V	4V	—V	1V	5V	2V	31V	64	48	92	101	92	81V	110V
Colombia........ 233	1V	1V	3V	1V	4V	3V	2V	6	3	5	4	6	5V	5V
Costa Rica........ 238	6V	—V	—V	—V	—V	—Y	1Y	1	1	4	7	16	20Y	25Y
Dominica........ 321	—V	—Y	—Y	—Y	—Y	—Y	—Y	—	—	1	—	1	2Y	2Y
Dominican Republic........ 243	1V	1Y	1Y	1Y	1Y	2Y	2Y	—	—	1	1	2	2Y	2Y
Ecuador........ 248	13V	—V	—V	16V	39V	53V	64Y	30	16	17	35	32	16V	20Y
El Salvador........ 253	—V	—V	—V	—V	—V	—V	—V	13	—	1	—	—	—V	—V
Guatemala........ 258	—V	—V	—V	2V	1V	1Y	1Y	58	58	47	45	44	54Y	70Y
Guyana........ 336	—Y	—Y	—Y	1Y	1Y	1Y	1Y	—	—	—	—	—	—Y	—Y
Honduras........ 268	—V	—V	—V	—V	—Y	—Y	—Y	2	1	—	—	1	1Y	2Y
Mexico........ 273	187V	187V	172V	258V	357V	304V	589V	158	138	124	183	343	258V	116V
Panama........ 283	9V	—V	—V	—V	—V	—V	—V	—	—	—	10	3	—V	—V
Paraguay........ 288	1V	1V	—V	—V	—V	—V	—Y	1	1	6	8	6	1V	2Y
Peru........ 293	9V	1V	—V	1V	8V	4V	6Y	2	2	8	6	4	12V	14Y
Trinidad and Tobago........ 369	—V	—V	—Y	—Y	—Y	—Y	1Y	—	—	—	—	—	—Y	—Y
Uruguay........ 298	1V	1Y	1V	2V	—V	—Y	—Y	5	6	3	33	22	28Y	36Y
Venezuela, Rep. Bol........ 299	2V	1V	—V	1V	1V	7V	1V	1	1	1	1	9	16V	18Y
Western Hem. n.s........ 399	1Y	1Y	1Y	1Y	1Y	1Y	1Y	—	—	—	—	1	3Y	4Y
Other Countries n.i.e........ 910	**18Y**	**19Y**	**23Y**	**31Y**	**42Y**	**53Y**	**63Y**	**18**	**63**	**—**	**—**	**37**	**45Y**	**59Y**
Cuba........ 928	—Y	—Y	—Y	1Y	1Y	1Y	1Y	1	—	—	—	—	—Y	1Y
North Korea........ 954	18Y	19Y	23Y	30Y	41Y	52Y	62Y	17	63	—	—	36	45Y	58Y
Countries & Areas n.s........ 898	**24Y**	**25Y**	**30Y**	**40Y**	**55Y**	**69Y**	**83Y**	**54**	**270**	**520**	**648**	**577**	**712Y**	**922Y**
Memorandum Items														
European Union........ 998	10,707Y	10,526Y	13,510Y	18,430Y	25,272Y	27,073Y	22,728Y	10,207	10,556	12,486	13,917	18,689	24,179Y	30,075Y
Oil Exporting Ctys........ 999	3,260Y	3,247Y	4,026Y	5,069Y	6,656Y	8,235Y	9,144Y	1,512	1,660	1,880	2,430	3,208	4,021Y	4,910Y
Non-Oil Develop.Ctys........ 201	29,257Y	27,688Y	36,498Y	50,123Y	69,770Y	88,879Y	96,668Y	7,969	8,992	10,673	13,925	19,680	24,733Y	32,696Y
PERCENT DISTRIBUTION														
Industrial Countries........ 101	**52.7**	**53.2**	**53.1**	**51.0**	**51.2**	**49.1**	**46.5**	**69.4**	**66.0**	**64.6**	**62.0**	**60.5**	**58.2**	**57.7**
Developing Countries........ 202	**47.2**	**46.8**	**46.8**	**49.0**	**48.7**	**50.8**	**53.5**	**30.4**	**33.0**	**34.0**	**36.6**	**38.5**	**40.7**	**41.3**
Africa........ 607	**4.6**	**4.2**	**4.7**	**4.7**	**2.4**	**4.3**	**4.5**	**1.7**	**1.9**	**1.6**	**2.1**	**1.7**	**1.2**	**1.2**
Asia........ 507	**33.0**	**32.1**	**31.9**	**32.7**	**35.1**	**35.4**	**36.4**	**15.7**	**16.7**	**18.1**	**18.9**	**20.0**	**22.7**	**24.2**
Europe........ 170	**1.0**	**1.1**	**1.1**	**1.1**	**1.2**	**1.1**	**1.2**	**2.8**	**3.4**	**3.9**	**4.1**	**4.5**	**4.2**	**4.6**
Middle East........ 407	**7.1**	**8.0**	**7.8**	**9.1**	**8.8**	**9.0**	**10.1**	**6.8**	**8.2**	**7.6**	**8.4**	**8.6**	**9.0**	**8.5**
Western Hemisphere........ 207	**1.6**	**1.4**	**1.3**	**1.4**	**1.2**	**1.1**	**1.3**	**3.4**	**2.8**	**2.9**	**3.0**	**3.7**	**3.6**	**2.7**
Other Countries n.i.e........ 910	**—**	**—**	**—**	**—**	**—**	**—**	**—**	**.1**	**.2**	**—**	**—**	**.1**	**.1**	**.1**
ANNUAL PERCENT CHANGE														
World........ 001	**–7.9**	**–3.9**	**30.9**	**30.2**	**39.3**	**21.7**	**3.6**	**1.9**	**3.6**	**14.3**	**21.2**	**33.0**	**18.7**	**29.1**
Industrial Countries........ 101	**–11.6**	**–3.1**	**30.7**	**24.9**	**40.1**	**16.6**	**–1.9**	**3.0**	**–1.5**	**11.9**	**16.4**	**29.8**	**14.2**	**27.8**
Developing Countries........ 202	**–3.5**	**–4.9**	**31.0**	**36.2**	**38.5**	**27.1**	**9.0**	**–.2**	**12.4**	**17.8**	**30.3**	**39.9**	**25.6**	**30.8**
Africa........ 607	**–4.4**	**–12.1**	**46.2**	**30.3**	**–29.2**	**116.9**	**9.2**	**–25.4**	**18.3**	**–3.8**	**60.3**	**7.9**	**–14.3**	**29.0**
Asia........ 507	**–4.2**	**–6.5**	**30.3**	**33.3**	**49.7**	**22.5**	**6.6**	**1.6**	**9.9**	**23.8**	**26.9**	**40.5**	**34.9**	**37.3**
Europe........ 170	**–22.0**	**9.3**	**25.4**	**30.2**	**48.0**	**17.3**	**13.2**	**35.6**	**25.3**	**30.2**	**29.6**	**45.7**	**9.6**	**42.7**
Middle East........ 407	**3.9**	**8.3**	**28.4**	**51.4**	**35.4**	**23.7**	**16.2**	**19.2**	**24.1**	**5.5**	**34.1**	**36.2**	**25.2**	**21.9**
Western Hemisphere........ 207	**–1.8**	**–16.4**	**21.3**	**41.9**	**15.8**	**13.7**	**21.7**	**–32.0**	**–13.5**	**18.3**	**26.1**	**61.0**	**14.7**	**–1.8**
Other Countries n.i.e........ 910	**7.9**	**6.3**	**21.2**	**32.3**	**36.0**	**25.7**	**20.6**	**–68.9**	**253.5**	**–99.6**	**86.4**	**—**	**23.5**	**29.5**

		Exports							Imports						
		2001	2002	2003	2004	2005	2006	2007	2001	2002	2003	2004	2005	2006	2007
		Millions of U.S. Dollars							*Millions of U.S. Dollars*						
IFS World Total		**1,003.1**	**1,066.6**	**1,257.1**	**1,509.0**	**1,578.1**	**1,556.0**	**1,650.0**	**1,730.1**	**2,031.0**	**2,390.9**	**2,848.8**	**3,197.0**	**3,434.0**	**4,250.0**
DOTS World Total	**001**	**783.6**	**948.7**	**1,158.9**	**1,275.7**	**1,443.5**	**1,363.6**	**1,722.9Y**	**1,727.1**	**1,957.6**	**2,358.5**	**2,854.1**	**3,215.3**	**3,423.0**	**4,953.4Y**
Industrial Countries	**101**	**341.2**	**334.7**	**368.2**	**394.8**	**415.1**	**397.5**	**506.2Y**	**1,042.5**	**1,184.5**	**1,266.3**	**1,487.4**	**1,674.1**	**2,025.2**	**2,951.1Y**
United States	111	2.49	2.49	8.06	3.69	16.40	6.66	19.36V	72.00	106.10	84.47	92.97	134.39	108.34	168.30V
Canada	156	.54	1.05	.99	.58	.99	.82	1.08V	17.08	11.17	17.02	24.00	25.52	15.06	35.87V
Australia	193	.01	.16	.01	—	.01	.12	2.12V	1.77	1.33	.44	.71	4.91	3.69	15.16V
Japan	158	.28	.60	7.25	12.27	11.20	13.35	12.76V	46.48	50.91	52.62	64.43	57.37	95.29	32.57V
New Zealand	196	—	—	—	—	—	—	.40V	.96	1.23	2.91	1.51	.63	12.47	5.41V
Austria	122	—	.15	2.44	.17	.12	.17	.15V	3.47	2.89	5.31	2.62	8.71	3.45	12.24V
Belgium	124	—	—	—	—	—	—	49.47V	—	—	—	—	—	—	221.15V
Belgium-Luxembourg n.s.	127	17.24	10.48	7.83	9.25	10.81	10.08	—Y	57.50	66.86	64.79	83.71	92.24	87.23	—Y
Cyprus	423	.04	.03	—	—	—	.02	.33V	.01	.02	.01	1.58	.08	.03	.17V
Denmark	128	.66	.67	.09	.33	.98	.21	.22V	3.58	17.02	5.26	5.85	7.32	15.32	15.01V
Finland	172	—	—	.01	.89	.06	3.42	.15V	1.89	15.07	3.01	5.21	8.86	62.96	16.16V
France	132	131.27	122.97	137.55	127.64	137.45	113.40	156.38V	479.71	500.34	587.32	706.36	734.13	858.43	1,100.13V
Germany	134	7.34	8.44	5.69	4.69	4.18	2.98	5.62V	82.67	104.84	81.06	76.39	80.57	84.73	94.93V
Greece	174	57.20	72.91	16.57	27.27	32.33	22.43	24.36V	.87	1.66	11.31	4.13	3.69	5.12	2.38V
Iceland	176	—	—	—	.05	.05	.06	.02V	—	.16	.01	—	.03	.03	.12V
Ireland	178	—	.01	—	.08	.02	.03	.23V	26.28	28.19	28.58	44.47	47.91	50.00	67.89V
Italy	136	46.73	41.86	95.64	92.44	78.73	66.81	102.50V	68.69	87.95	84.09	102.97	91.28	116.02	153.63V
Luxembourg	137	—	—	—	—	—	—	—V	—	—	—	—	—	—	2.10V
Malta	181	—	—	—	.01	.05	5.71	.21V	.58	.61	1.95	1.81	2.15	13.76	2.27V
Netherlands	138	21.31	15.45	9.80	8.80	11.87	15.89	24.14V	56.91	61.57	68.80	71.97	67.73	107.98	492.92V
Norway	142	.01	.05	.03	.03	.10	.08	1.53V	1.01	1.24	.60	1.33	1.02	.78	4.39V
Portugal	182	8.13	10.33	8.65	8.85	10.06	11.35	15.86V	9.70	6.57	12.43	14.15	13.53	23.69	11.46V
Slovenia	961	—	—	—	—	—	—	—V	—	—	—	—	—	—	.20V
Spain	184	31.30	30.56	56.33	84.27	87.69	70.20	55.98V	74.26	78.63	100.88	118.16	118.78	138.05	155.31V
Sweden	144	—	.01	.01	—	.05	.03	.90V	4.84	6.00	7.59	9.96	27.86	28.75	14.16V
Switzerland	146	6.80	5.31	8.59	6.71	4.13	46.31	6.13V	8.47	9.19	9.72	9.60	15.70	14.41	19.84V
United Kingdom	112	9.81	11.22	2.67	6.72	7.82	7.37	26.24V	23.78	24.99	36.09	43.47	129.69	179.65	307.33V
Developing Countries	**202**	**347.1**	**522.1**	**634.4**	**719.1**	**859.1**	**749.6**	**948.1Y**	**683.8**	**772.1**	**1,090.6**	**1,363.9**	**1,538.0**	**1,395.0**	**1,998.8Y**
Africa	**607**	**234.6**	**310.1**	**450.4**	**502.2**	**621.8**	**612.5**	**759.5Y**	**300.9**	**318.1**	**485.2**	**587.0**	**640.2**	**478.7**	**583.6Y**
Algeria	612	—	.09	.39	.55	.16	.02	.03Y	1.67	1.01	.94	6.98	2.43	.70	.85Y
Angola	614	.19	.32	1.20	2.28	1.52	2.43	3.01Y	—	10.22	.04	.02	—	—	—Y
Benin	638	6.77	21.74	32.34	23.92	14.19	13.26	16.46Y	1.42	.55	6.54	2.18	.56	3.78	4.69Y
Botswana	616	—	—	—	.04	.02	—	.01Y	.01	—	—	.01	—	—	—Y
Burkina Faso	748	2.99	6.39	29.40	22.47	14.99	17.23	21.38Y	.06	.10	.04	.06	.10	.07	.09Y
Burundi	618	—	—	—	—	—	.01	.01Y	—	—	—	—	—	.01	.01Y
Cameroon	622	9.14	7.21	10.08	10.30	8.35	10.01	12.42Y	6.40	6.94	8.28	12.68	13.23	11.74	14.56Y
Cape Verde	624	1.21	5.80	1.61	1.63	4.03	2.17	2.69Y	.09	.05	.01	.07	.08	.01	.01Y
Central African Rep.	626	.59	.66	.85	1.01	.86	.59	.73Y	.03	—	.07	.08	.09	.01	.02Y
Chad	628	2.15	.50	1.14	3.61	1.34	.85	1.05Y	—	—	—	—	—	—	—Y
Comoros	632	—	—	—	—	—	.04	.05Y	—	—	—	.01	.03	—	—Y
Congo, Dem. Rep. of	636	.11	.87	.43	.60	1.03	2.13	2.64Y	.14	.13	—	.50	.01	.02	.03Y
Congo, Republic of	634	9.81	9.38	6.59	6.68	10.81	12.65	15.70Y	10.19	7.32	11.59	13.29	13.68	7.57	9.39Y
Côte d'Ivoire	662	25.84	32.85	60.89	39.44	34.09	37.49	46.52Y	49.35	55.41	83.82	95.09	92.92	108.42	134.55Y
Djibouti	611	—	.02	—	—	.04	.02	.02Y	—	.01	—	.03	—	—	—Y
Equatorial Guinea	642	.33	.34	2.72	2.88	4.13	1.16	1.44Y	.08	—	—	.64	4.03	14.15	17.56Y
Ethiopia	644	—	—	.05	.07	.08	.08	.09Y	—	—	—	.03	—	.01	.01Y
Gabon	646	9.48	8.40	3.68	4.98	4.52	7.21	8.95Y	3.95	6.53	5.63	9.95	20.23	51.50	63.91Y
Gambia, The	648	26.87	33.54	41.65	64.76	66.29	72.68	90.20Y	—	.19	.01	1.53	1.43	.03	.03Y
Ghana	652	3.55	5.14	3.44	3.97	3.58	3.36	4.18Y	5.36	6.99	13.61	14.87	14.62	11.94	14.82Y
Guinea	656	16.17	16.52	28.64	36.97	39.91	37.05	45.97Y	.19	.64	.73	1.48	2.26	2.30	2.86Y
Guinea-Bissau	654	14.37	19.87	52.34	34.39	35.31	29.62	36.76Y	.01	—	.73	.18	—	—	—Y
Kenya	664	.01	.03	—	.56	.75	.82	1.02Y	.23	.50	.85	1.01	1.19	.79	.98Y
Liberia	668	2.17	2.53	7.80	4.22	7.18	3.92	4.86Y	3.03	3.06	3.51	—	—	.02	.02Y
Madagascar	674	.02	.20	.64	.32	.65	.10	.12Y	.07	.07	.15	.09	.03	.04	.05Y
Malawi	676	—	—	—	—	—	—	—Y	.11	.12	.18	.45	.62	.82	1.01Y
Mali	678	54.31	84.05	107.06	167.41	243.73	261.94	325.06Y	—	.01	.02	1.45	.25	.03	.04Y
Mauritania	682	30.35	29.13	29.28	27.89	35.93	34.79	43.17Y	.04	.01	.03	.50	1.27	.59	.74Y
Mauritius	684	—	—	.53	—	—	.01	.03V	.01	.05	.36	.60	1.15	.69	1.09V
Morocco	686	1.24	2.96	3.37	5.44	10.16	27.37	33.96Y	13.25	16.34	19.59	25.48	32.84	58.75	72.91Y
Mozambique	688	.08	.09	.06	—	—	.28	.35Y	—	—	—	.11	.02	.03	.04Y
Namibia	728	—	—	—	—	.53	—	—Y	.01	.01	—	—	.23	.18	.14Y
Niger	692	.56	.70	3.10	3.51	4.90	3.71	4.60Y	.02	—	.01	.02	—	—	—Y
Nigeria	694	5.45	4.33	1.76	4.48	1.95	5.59	7.24Y	169.19	170.18	287.16	338.43	366.03	120.12	144.91Y
Rwanda	714	.01	—	—	—	.08	.02	.02Y	—	—	—	—	.02	—	—Y
Seychelles	718	—	—	—	—	—	—	—Y	—	—	—	—	.01	.02	.03Y
Sierra Leone	724	1.25	3.49	3.25	5.05	6.34	4.23	5.25Y	.05	.08	.11	.04	—	.17	.21Y
Somalia	726	—	—	—	.02	—	—	—Y	—	—	—	—	—	—	—Y
South Africa	199	.25	.57	.30	1.36	.89	.39	.47V	22.67	21.65	25.16	39.95	44.47	55.03	63.02V
Sudan	732	—	—	—	.07	44.92	.51	—V	—	—	.05	—	.01	.96	—V

		Exports							Imports						
		2001	2002	2003	2004	2005	2006	2007	2001	2002	2003	2004	2005	2006	2007
		Millions of U.S. Dollars							*Millions of U.S. Dollars*						
Swaziland	734	—	—	—	—	—	—	—Y	—	.01	—	—	.08	—	—Y
Tanzania	738	.05	.19	.23	1.09	2.85	1.68	2.09Y	.38	.68	1.40	.49	.29	1.02	1.26Y
Togo	742	6.34	8.65	14.25	16.34	13.55	15.72	19.51Y	2.95	.72	1.78	2.97	2.88	1.98	2.46Y
Tunisia	744	2.71	3.09	.99	3.46	1.70	1.09	1.36Y	9.16	7.57	11.14	15.22	22.66	24.87	30.86Y
Uganda	746	—	.02	—	.01	—	.01	.01Y	.03	—	.03	.01	.33	.19	.24Y
Zambia	754	.28	.42	.36	.37	.49	.31	.04V	.03	.10	—	—	—	—	.09V
Zimbabwe	698	—	.02	—	.02	—	—	—Y	.70	.86	1.64	.53	.13	.11	.13Y
Asia	**507**	**108.2**	**209.3**	**179.5**	**207.5**	**223.1**	**106.3**	**145.3Y**	**252.8**	**284.6**	**337.7**	**403.9**	**448.4**	**501.8**	**836.9Y**
Afghanistan, I.S. of	512	—	—	—	.06	.05	.02	.02Y	.14	—	.01	.11	.09	—	—Y
Bangladesh	513	—	.54	.83	—	.95	.13	—V	.09	.09	.45	.61	.19	.35	.22Y
Brunei Darussalam	516	—	—	—	.91	.07	.01	.01Y	—	.01	—	—	—	—	—Y
Cambodia	522	—	—	—	—	—	—	—Y	—	—	—	.01	—	—	—Y
China,P.R.: Mainland	924	7.51	8.62	15.28	6.36	14.67	9.28	20.48V	42.22	44.86	62.99	97.79	122.37	153.41	366.64V
China,P.R.:Hong Kong	532	1.50	1.13	1.08	2.73	3.51	3.79	11.41V	4.81	4.96	5.06	7.00	5.76	6.21	21.96V
China,P.R.:Macao	546	—	—	—	.02	.26	.58	.01V	—	—	—	—	—	—	—V
India	534	97.31	196.79	147.35	182.78	189.48	79.08	98.14Y	20.13	40.63	50.83	42.57	85.80	88.56	109.90Y
Indonesia	536	—	.31	2.99	.58	1.37	.59	.95V	9.18	8.40	8.39	11.13	10.09	9.11	12.42V
Korea	542	—	—	5.82	.88	1.21	3.08	7.91V	10.43	10.16	11.16	12.10	13.73	22.37	36.16V
Lao People's Dem.Rep	544	.15	—	—	—	—	.12	.15Y	—	—	.03	.02	—	.01	.01Y
Malaysia	548	1.08	—	.26	.01	.21	—	.58V	2.55	3.60	6.80	7.94	20.80	10.55	16.48V
Myanmar	518	—	—	—	—	—	—	—Y	—	1.81	4.63	1.06	—	—	—Y
New Caledonia	839	—	—	.03	—	—	.03	.03Y	—	—	—	—	—	.01	.01Y
Pakistan	564	—	.72	—	2.68	.04	.04	.05Y	.36	1.50	.95	3.95	2.49	2.11	2.62Y
Papua New Guinea	853	—	—	—	1.97	2.46	1.14	1.42Y	—	—	—	—	—	—	—Y
Philippines	566	—	.17	.03	.01	.04	.03	—V	.19	.13	.09	.16	1.68	.79	2.07V
Singapore	576	—	.06	—	.12	.15	.64	—V	2.84	1.65	2.84	4.14	6.89	3.68	—V
Sri Lanka	524	—	—	—	—	—	.01	.01Y	.02	.03	.03	.04	.02	.06	.08Y
Taiwan Province of China	528	.16	.34	3.13	6.41	5.12	5.05	.87V	3.13	2.86	3.53	3.92	3.85	2.78	12.20V
Thailand	578	.37	.58	2.38	2.02	2.62	2.16	3.27V	132.25	140.41	159.13	173.16	137.52	163.27	256.15V
Vietnam	582	.08	—	.30	—	.92	.49	—V	24.45	23.55	20.84	38.17	37.08	38.49	—V
Europe	**170**	**.4**	**.5**	**.2**	**1.5**	**3.0**	**2.0**	**3.0Y**	**53.2**	**62.7**	**94.3**	**146.7**	**127.3**	**121.8**	**200.0Y**
Albania	914	—	—	—	.09	.42	.21	—V	—	—	—	—	.05	—	—V
Armenia	911	—	—	—	—	—	—	—V	—	.06	.01	.16	.22	.13	.16Y
Belarus	913	—	—	—	—	—	—	.01V	—	—	—	1.00	2.19	—	.40V
Bulgaria	918	.02	—	—	.25	.15	.07	—V	2.72	.25	1.64	.65	1.55	.46	1.20V
Czech Republic	935	—	—	—	—	—	.57	.05V	1.43	1.46	2.74	—	—	4.42	8.27V
Czechoslovakia n.s.	937	—	—	—	.01	.01	—	—Y	—	—	—	2.49	7.84	—	—Y
Estonia	939	—	—	—	—	—	—	—V	—	—	—	—	.15	5.15	.36V
Faroe Islands	816	—	—	—	—	—	—	—Y	.01	—	—	—	—	—	—Y
Gibraltar	823	—	—	—	—	—	—	—Y	.26	—	—	.84	—	—	—Y
Hungary	944	—	—	—	—	—	.05	.02V	.43	1.08	1.06	2.21	1.08	3.13	3.83V
Latvia	941	—	—	—	—	—	—	—V	—	—	—	—	.01	—	.03V
Lithuania	946	—	—	—	—	—	—	—V	—	1.34	.27	2.17	.08	1.96	.51V
Poland	964	.14	.10	—	.77	1.82	.32	1.26V	3.09	2.05	3.09	6.80	5.54	4.14	12.93V
Romania	968	—	—	.01	—	.04	.03	.05V	.15	.37	.48	1.06	1.21	1.66	2.44V
Russia	922	—	—	.04	—	—	.07	.07V	—	—	—	—	—	14.67	20.58V
Serbia & Montenegro	965	—	—	—	—	—	—	—Y	1.14	.30	1.44	—	—	.68	.84Y
Slovak Republic	936	—	—	—	—	—	—	—V	—	.01	.12	.17	.29	.15	3.47V
Turkey	186	.18	.13	.09	.43	.56	.67	1.48V	12.76	15.49	22.05	18.87	24.95	26.18	71.62V
Ukraine	926	—	—	—	—	.01	.02	.02Y	—	8.01	18.40	65.83	55.96	59.09	73.32Y
U.S.S.R. n.s.	930	.07	.25	.04	—	—	—	—Y	31.26	32.24	43.01	43.69	25.23	—	—Y
Yugoslavia n.s.	966	—	—	—	—	.03	—	—Y	—	—	—	.79	.94	—	—Y
Europe n.s.	884	—	—	—	—	—	—	—Y	—	—	—	.01	—	—	—Y
Middle East	**407**	**2.0**	**1.1**	**3.2**	**4.9**	**7.0**	**22.3**	**29.1Y**	**31.9**	**43.0**	**55.1**	**77.4**	**107.6**	**62.3**	**76.4Y**
Bahrain	419	—	—	—	.01	.37	.21	.26Y	.95	5.51	6.09	.72	.04	.27	.34Y
Egypt	469	.03	.03	.01	.03	.14	.35	.43Y	6.08	11.14	12.00	20.22	39.68	12.00	14.89Y
Iran, I.R. of	429	—	—	—	.04	.24	.10	.13Y	.90	.35	1.06	.93	.83	1.19	1.44Y
Iraq	433	—	—	—	—	—	—	—Y	—	.01	.01	—	.29	.10	.12Y
Israel	436	.10	.09	.18	.07	.14	.17	.55V	7.24	3.75	3.39	6.35	6.78	6.18	7.81V
Jordan	439	—	.01	.48	—	.09	.01	—V	.84	.16	.41	.66	.98	.07	.03V
Kuwait	443	—	—	—	.05	—	—	—Y	.23	.15	.10	.41	.26	.01	.02Y
Lebanon	446	1.73	.91	2.32	1.94	1.32	1.22	1.51Y	1.48	3.71	2.85	5.17	5.93	8.69	10.79Y
Libya	672	.05	.02	.13	.01	—	.02	.03Y	.01	.22	.32	.34	2.26	1.18	1.43Y
Oman	449	—	—	—	.03	—	—	—Y	.30	.51	.31	.53	.51	2.06	2.49Y
Qatar	453	—	—	—	—	—	—	—Y	.06	.77	2.10	1.86	3.48	1.74	2.10Y
Saudi Arabia	456	.06	.05	.06	1.36	.22	.04	.06Y	9.86	8.54	7.81	8.67	17.60	7.96	9.60Y
Syrian Arab Republic	463	—	—	—	—	—	.01	.02Y	.72	1.07	1.59	2.60	2.08	5.55	6.89Y
United Arab Emirates	466	—	—	.05	1.37	4.42	20.12	26.06Y	3.24	6.91	17.05	28.91	26.82	15.33	18.49Y
Yemen, Republic of	474	—	—	—	—	.01	.01	.01Y	—	.18	.01	—	.03	—	—Y
Western Hemisphere	**207**	**1.9**	**1.1**	**1.1**	**2.9**	**4.2**	**6.5**	**11.2Y**	**45.0**	**63.7**	**118.2**	**149.0**	**214.5**	**230.4**	**301.9Y**
Argentina	213	—	—	—	—	—	.01	—V	10.46	22.77	31.21	25.09	38.04	79.99	61.86V
Bahamas, The	313	—	—	—	—	—	—	—Y	—	—	—	.01	.01	.01	.01Y
Bermuda	319	—	—	—	—	—	—	—Y	—	—	—	1.64	.14	.13	.16Y
Bolivia	218	—	—	—	.01	—	—	—Y	—	—	—	—	—	—	—Y
Brazil	223	1.49	.75	—	.12	.05	.20	—V	27.68	34.33	70.81	104.72	145.15	82.80	174.51V
Chile	228	—	—	.01	—	—	—	.03V	.56	.17	.02	.24	1.25	.27	—V
Colombia	233	—	—	—	1.77	.07	4.85	8.15V	.61	.70	1.84	1.01	1.26	13.56	.52V

	Exports							Imports						
	2001	2002	2003	2004	2005	2006	2007	2001	2002	2003	2004	2005	2006	2007
	Millions of U.S. Dollars							Millions of U.S. Dollars						
Costa Rica.......... 238	—	—	—	.04	—	—	—Y	.01	.01	—	—	.01	.05	.06Y
Dominica.......... 321	—	—	—	—	—	.04	.04Y	—	—	—	—	—	—	—Y
Ecuador.......... 248	—	—	—	—	—	—	—Y	.05	.12	.11	—	.01	.01	.02Y
El Salvador.......... 253	—	—	—	—	—	—	—V	—	.01	.02	—	—	—	—V
Greenland.......... 326	—	—	—	—	.03	—	—Y	—	—	—	—	—	—	—Y
Guatemala.......... 258	—	—	—	—	—	—	—Y	.01	—	—	—	—	—	—Y
Haiti.......... 263	—	—	—	—	2.54	—	—Y	—	—	.04	—	—	—	—Y
Honduras.......... 268	—	—	—	—	.12	.01	.02Y	—	—	—	.41	—	—	—Y
Jamaica.......... 343	—	—	—	—	—	—	.06V	—	—	—	—	—	—	—V
Mexico.......... 273	.41	.33	1.07	.87	.62	.81	2.40V	.16	.13	.32	.13	.92	.48	.25V
Netherlands Antilles.......... 353	—	—	—	—	—	—	—Y	—	—	1.04	—	—	.34	.42Y
Panama.......... 283	—	—	—	.01	.63	.24	—V	—	—	.01	—	—	.05	.27V
Paraguay.......... 288	—	—	—	.01	—	—	—Y	.39	.04	.12	.05	.10	.23	.29Y
Peru.......... 293	—	.01	—	.01	—	—	—Y	—	.70	3.25	4.75	5.44	6.29	6.39Y
St. Pierre-Miquelon.......... 363	—	—	—	—	—	—	—Y	—	—	—	.12	—	.03	.04Y
Suriname.......... 366	—	—	—	—	.02	—	—Y	—	—	—	—	—	—	—Y
Trinidad and Tobago.......... 369	—	—	—	—	—	—	—Y	.96	1.87	5.71	5.61	9.68	19.81	24.58Y
Uruguay.......... 298	—	—	—	—	—	—	—Y	1.81	.41	2.44	4.61	11.03	21.73	26.97Y
Venezuela, Rep. Bol.......... 299	—	—	—	—	—	—	—V	2.30	2.36	1.16	.38	1.36	4.57	5.51Y
Western Hem. n.s.......... 399	—	—	—	.05	.09	.32	.54Y	.02	.06	.06	.20	.09	.03	.03Y
Other Countries n.i.e.......... 910	**—**	**—**	**—**	**.2**	**.2**	**.8**	**1.0Y**	**.3**	**.3**	**.7**	**.6**	**1.0**	**1.1**	**1.3Y**
Cuba.......... 928	—	—	—	—	—	—	—Y	.10	.15	.42	.32	.69	.78	.97Y
North Korea.......... 954	—	—	—	.17	.24	.79	.98Y	.22	.16	.29	.28	.28	.28	.35Y
Countries & Areas n.s.......... 898	**.8**	**2.1**	**1.5**	**—**	**.1**	**—**	**—Y**	**.4**	**.5**	**.8**	**—**	**—**	**—**	**—Y**
Special Categories.......... 899	**94.6**	**89.8**	**154.8**	**161.7**	**169.0**	**215.7**	**267.7Y**	**.1**	**.1**	**.1**	**.7**	**.8**	**1.8**	**2.2Y**
Memorandum Items														
European Union.......... 998	331.18	325.19	343.29	372.20	384.03	331.05	464.10Y	899.68	1,009.15	1,105.78	1,304.14	1,441.68	1,794.11	2,698.84Y
Oil Exporting Ctys.......... 999	5.56	4.80	5.38	8.49	8.36	26.49	34.50Y	196.94	199.42	326.42	398.57	431.96	164.07	199.36Y
Non-Oil Develop.Ctys.......... 201	341.54	517.26	629.03	710.61	850.74	723.07	913.58Y	486.91	572.70	764.17	965.38	1,106.00	1,230.92	1,799.45Y
PERCENT DISTRIBUTION														
Industrial Countries.......... 101	**43.5**	**35.3**	**31.8**	**30.9**	**28.8**	**29.2**	**29.4**	**60.4**	**60.5**	**53.7**	**52.1**	**52.1**	**59.2**	**59.6**
Developing Countries.......... 202	**44.3**	**55.0**	**54.7**	**56.4**	**59.5**	**55.0**	**55.0**	**39.6**	**39.4**	**46.2**	**47.8**	**47.8**	**40.8**	**40.4**
Africa.......... 607	**29.9**	**32.7**	**38.9**	**39.4**	**43.1**	**44.9**	**44.1**	**17.4**	**16.3**	**20.6**	**20.6**	**19.9**	**14.0**	**11.8**
Asia.......... 507	**13.8**	**22.1**	**15.5**	**16.3**	**15.5**	**7.8**	**8.4**	**14.6**	**14.5**	**14.3**	**14.2**	**13.9**	**14.7**	**16.9**
Europe.......... 170	**.1**	**.1**	**—**	**.1**	**.2**	**.1**	**.2**	**3.1**	**3.2**	**4.0**	**5.1**	**4.0**	**3.6**	**4.0**
Middle East.......... 407	**.3**	**.1**	**.3**	**.4**	**.5**	**1.6**	**1.7**	**1.8**	**2.2**	**2.3**	**2.7**	**3.3**	**1.8**	**1.5**
Western Hemisphere.......... 207	**.2**	**.1**	**.1**	**.2**	**.3**	**.5**	**.7**	**2.6**	**3.3**	**5.0**	**5.2**	**6.7**	**6.7**	**6.1**
Other Countries n.i.e.......... 910	**—**	**—**	**—**	**—**	**—**	**.1**	**.1**	**—**	**—**	**—**	**—**	**—**	**—**	**—**
ANNUAL PERCENT CHANGE														
World.......... 001	**13.1**	**21.1**	**22.2**	**10.1**	**13.1**	**−5.5**	**26.4**	**18.1**	**13.3**	**20.5**	**21.0**	**12.7**	**6.5**	**44.7**
Industrial Countries.......... 101	**−.1**	**−1.9**	**10.0**	**7.2**	**5.1**	**−4.2**	**27.3**	**19.2**	**13.6**	**6.9**	**17.5**	**12.6**	**21.0**	**45.7**
Developing Countries.......... 202	**14.3**	**50.4**	**21.5**	**13.3**	**19.5**	**−12.8**	**26.5**	**16.4**	**12.9**	**41.2**	**25.1**	**12.8**	**−9.3**	**43.3**
Africa.......... 607	**20.0**	**32.2**	**45.3**	**11.5**	**23.8**	**−1.5**	**24.0**	**−1.0**	**5.7**	**52.5**	**21.0**	**9.1**	**−25.2**	**21.9**
Asia.......... 507	**7.4**	**93.5**	**−14.2**	**15.6**	**7.5**	**−52.4**	**36.8**	**19.5**	**12.6**	**18.7**	**19.6**	**11.0**	**11.9**	**66.8**
Europe.......... 170	**−16.4**	**20.5**	**−61.3**	**713.3**	**96.6**	**−33.8**	**47.2**	**45.9**	**17.7**	**50.5**	**55.6**	**−13.3**	**−4.3**	**64.1**
Middle East.......... 407	**−39.6**	**−44.1**	**192.8**	**52.5**	**41.4**	**220.3**	**30.5**	**200.6**	**34.8**	**28.1**	**40.4**	**39.0**	**−42.1**	**22.6**
Western Hemisphere.......... 207	**−46.9**	**−42.7**	**−1.2**	**167.5**	**44.1**	**56.1**	**73.2**	**81.6**	**41.5**	**85.6**	**26.1**	**44.0**	**7.4**	**31.0**
Other Countries n.i.e.......... 910	**—**	**—**	**....**	**....**	**37.6**	**236.9**	**24.1**	**56.4**	**−4.3**	**128.8**	**−15.2**	**61.3**	**9.5**	**24.1**

		Exports							Imports						
		2001	2002	2003	2004	2005	2006	2007	2001	2002	2003	2004	2005	2006	2007
		Millions of U.S. Dollars							*Millions of U.S. Dollars*						
DOTS World Total	**001**	**1,142.3Y**	**1,436.8Y**	**1,721.7Y**	**2,249.8Y**	**1,725.8Y**	....	....	**3,865.4Y**	**4,849.3Y**	**6,093.3Y**	**7,718.5Y**	**5,330.8Y**	....	....
Industrial Countries	**101**	**943.1Y**	**1,215.6Y**	**1,439.1Y**	**1,876.8Y**	**1,262.3Y**	....	....	**2,732.4Y**	**3,657.2Y**	**4,382.1Y**	**5,900.2Y**	**3,445.9Y**	....	....
United States	111	5.55V	9.55V	14.36V	88.82V	54.36V	....	....	60.72V	85.91V	55.00V	157.19V	145.31V	....	....
Canada	156	—V	5.49V	5.39V	6.57V	10.98V	....	....	—V	5.68V	6.21V	7.64V	9.64V	....	....
Australia	193	—V	.94V	1.74V	1.81V	2.69V	....	....	—V	1.75V	.84V	1.76V	.84V	....	....
Japan	158	2.90V	1.72V	1.94V	1.86V	2.85V	....	....	4.41V	7.12V	21.39V	13.02V	11.28V	....	....
New Zealand	196	—V	.20V	.38V	.22V	.51V	....	....	—V	.08V	.11V	.26V	.21V	....	....
Austria	122	44.53V	83.70V	107.39V	156.76V	73.44V	....	....	273.98V	383.97V	505.60V	635.30V	217.13V	....	....
Belgium	124	18.56V	21.92V	27.04V	44.32V	19.47V	....	....	67.99V	98.19V	134.90V	177.79V	76.94V	....	....
Cyprus	423	1.53V	6.47V	2.49V	2.59V	4.39V	....	....	2.85V	3.90V	2.18V	4.81V	3.90V	....	....
Denmark	128	3.00V	5.09V	5.34V	6.62V	3.20V	....	....	45.04V	54.49V	66.42V	69.26V	23.38V	....	....
Finland	172	1.67V	2.14V	2.95V	3.28V	1.74V	....	....	5.60V	9.12V	20.33V	23.19V	8.02V	....	....
France	132	48.34V	63.91V	103.24V	110.53V	56.32V	....	....	147.81V	196.28V	273.25V	342.15V	150.92V	....	....
Germany	134	247.90V	279.44V	300.22V	371.24V	420.58V	....	....	651.22V	906.00V	1,104.07V	1,414.36V	1,460.93V	....	....
Greece	174	82.94V	96.74V	101.13V	159.36V	72.20V	....	....	171.59V	197.70V	265.18V	299.29V	91.55V	....	....
Iceland	176	—V	.22V	.07V	.17V	.46V	....	....	—V	.03V	.08V	.06V	.05V	....	....
Ireland	178	.06V	.02V	2.27V	1.57V	.61V	....	....	14.20V	10.12V	11.51V	20.09V	7.82V	....	....
Italy	136	344.33V	441.72V	542.22V	647.18V	307.43V	....	....	722.69V	816.70V	959.39V	1,259.80V	500.06V	....	....
Luxembourg	137	.29V	.37V	—V	.81V	.03V	....	....	2.26V	2.43V	2.93V	4.89V	—V	....	....
Malta	181	—Y	.29V	.40V	1.15V	—V	....	....	—Y	.13V	.01V	—V	—V	....	....
Netherlands	138	40.58V	46.92V	58.99V	51.43V	27.35V	....	....	105.71V	167.06V	226.10V	310.40V	121.10V	....	....
Norway	142	2.26V	2.65V	3.00V	—V	—V	....	....	7.33V	6.98V	8.72V	—V	—V	....	....
Portugal	182	3.60V	.44V	2.34V	.80V	8.86V	....	....	5.08V	5.73V	4.47V	2.31V	.35V	....	....
Slovenia	961	36.92V	53.00V	69.76V	91.61Y	86.30V	....	....	205.00V	362.51V	389.84V	511.99Y	287.07V	....	....
Spain	184	17.34V	39.16V	35.40V	25.05V	18.20V	....	....	57.63V	69.21V	89.17V	118.30V	44.82V	....	....
Sweden	144	9.41V	10.30V	—V	20.29V	—V	....	....	100.34V	164.09V	116.20V	200.06V	—V	....	....
Switzerland	146	—V	—V	—V	15.36V	18.82V	....	....	—V	—V	—V	192.69V	171.85V	....	....
United Kingdom	112	31.42V	43.20V	51.03V	67.40V	71.52V	....	....	80.94V	102.05V	118.23V	133.57V	112.74V	....	....
Developing Countries	**202**	**199.1Y**	**221.1Y**	**282.6Y**	**373.0Y**	**463.4Y**	....	....	**1,133.0Y**	**1,192.0Y**	**1,711.2Y**	**1,818.3Y**	**1,884.9Y**	....	....
Africa	**607**	**10.9Y**	**19.3Y**	**21.2Y**	**31.0Y**	**34.3Y**	....	....	**49.2Y**	**43.8Y**	**47.4Y**	**63.0Y**	**85.7Y**	....	....
Algeria	612	8.54V	17.18V	19.10Y	24.84Y	31.63Y	....	....	42.61V	38.15V	46.25Y	61.19Y	83.24Y	....	....
Burkina Faso	748	.01Y	.01Y	.01Y	.01Y	.02Y	....	....	....	....	....	....	....	....	....
Cameroon	622	.14V	.17V	.04V	.06Y	.07Y	....	....	2.59V	3.32V	—V	—Y	—Y	....	....
Cape Verde	624	.01V	.01Y	.01Y	.01Y	.01Y	....	....	....	....	....	....	....	....	....
Côte d'Ivoire	662	1.09V	.58V	.41V	2.22V	.26V	....	....	3.85V	.86V	1.18V	1.76V	2.27V	....	....
Kenya	664	.12V	.21V	.23V	—V	—Y	....	....	.13V	1.42V	—V	—V	—Y	....	....
South Africa	199	1.01Y	1.10Y	1.39Y	1.82Y	—V	....	....	—Y	—Y	—Y	—Y	—V	....	....
Tunisia	744	—V	—V	—V	2.00V	2.31V	....	....	—V	—V	—V	.06V	.24V	....	....
Asia	**507**	**14.7Y**	**7.4Y**	**22.8Y**	**19.2Y**	**35.2Y**	....	....	**130.2Y**	**116.4Y**	**237.1Y**	**263.5Y**	**296.1Y**	....	....
China,P.R.: Mainland	924	9.07V	2.39V	12.67V	11.07V	19.47V	....	....	96.26V	80.81V	149.18V	173.17V	221.30V	....	....
China,P.R.:Hong Kong	532	2.42V	.63V	.48V	.13V	.14V	....	....	5.95V	6.62V	8.82V	13.88V	13.63V	....	....
China,P.R.:Macao	546	—V	—V	—V	—V	.02V	....	....	.02V	—V	—V	.05V	.04V	....	....
India	534	—Y	1.31V	2.75V	3.65V	2.29V	....	....	—Y	5.32V	15.15V	12.07V	9.34V	....	....
Korea	542	—V	—V	2.86V	.37V	2.32V	....	....	—V	—V	42.76V	19.68V	20.03V	....	....
Malaysia	548	2.79V	2.74V	3.48V	3.40V	.84V	....	....	7.23V	5.80V	6.08V	7.79V	11.67V	....	....
New Caledonia	839	—V	—V	.01V	.08V	.09Y	....	....	....	....	....	....	....	....	....
Pakistan	564	.19V	.12V	.32V	.35V	.07V	....	....	.31V	1.04V	.93V	.66V	1.95V	....	....
Taiwan Province of China	528	.17V	.20V	.21V	.18V	9.97V	....	....	20.04V	15.93V	13.20V	36.20V	18.15V	....	....
Vietnam	582	.01V	—V	—V	—V	—V	....	....	.38V	.90V	.93V	—V	—V	....	....
Europe	**170**	**144.0Y**	**163.8Y**	**204.4Y**	**257.3Y**	**307.9Y**	....	....	**815.3Y**	**877.7Y**	**1,233.7Y**	**1,217.5Y**	**1,165.1Y**	....	....
Albania	914	5.45V	11.78V	7.71V	11.97V	14.87V	....	....	10.50V	8.23V	11.59V	33.07V	6.08V	....	....
Belarus	913	5.83V	6.95V	4.36V	7.01V	11.19V	....	....	17.17V	18.00V	18.93V	30.14V	38.66V	....	....
Bulgaria	918	18.63V	21.70V	30.78V	47.91V	78.62V	....	....	233.83V	190.44V	273.49V	380.79V	384.44V	....	....
Estonia	939	—V	—V	—V	.92V	.23V	....	....	—V	—V	—V	2.38V	.85V	....	....
Georgia	915	.39V	.88V	.80V	1.34V	1.06V	....	....	.14V	.02V	.05V	.35V	1.03V	....	....
Hungary	944	50.48V	60.75V	67.79V	—V	56.95V	....	....	210.76V	246.90V	343.78V	—V	260.63V	....	....
Kazakhstan	916	.93V	2.20V	.90V	1.41V	1.61Y	....	....	2.67V	.23V	1.54V	.12V	.13Y	....	....
Kyrgyz Republic	917	.06V	.17V	.24V	.24V	—V	....	....	—V	.03V	.07V	.13V	—V	....	....
Moldova	921	1.05V	1.56V	1.74V	2.63V	2.92V	....	....	.34V	.87V	.38V	.46V	—V	....	....
Poland	964	9.36V	9.92V	17.40V	26.25V	—V	....	....	41.02V	60.34V	111.53V	155.93V	—V	....	....
Romania	968	31.10V	23.23V	27.09V	51.91V	36.23V	....	....	170.05V	138.85V	168.44V	249.26V	119.28V	....	....
Russia	922	—V	—V	—V	—V	—V	....	....	—V	—V	—V	—V	—V	....	....
Slovak Republic	936	13.89V	14.51V	18.37Y	24.12Y	16.32V	....	....	39.36V	79.57V	100.71Y	132.26Y	70.33V	....	....
Tajikistan	923	—V	—V	—V	2.18V	—V	....	....	....	....	....	....	....	....	....
Turkey	186	6.80V	10.13V	27.26V	79.46V	87.93V	....	....	89.50V	134.26V	203.14V	232.63V	283.63V	....	....
Middle East	**407**	**28.4Y**	**30.3Y**	**33.3Y**	**64.4Y**	**84.4Y**	....	....	**130.3Y**	**141.1Y**	**176.1Y**	**240.9Y**	**309.0Y**	....	....
Bahrain	419	.03Y	.03Y	.04Y	.05Y	.06Y	....	....	....	....	....	....	....	....	....
Egypt	469	2.59V	2.81Y	3.56Y	4.68Y	5.35Y	....	....	.91V	.98Y	1.24Y	1.63Y	1.87Y	....	....
Israel	436	3.45V	4.45V	3.55V	10.82V	13.18V	....	....	4.84V	7.81V	14.41V	26.40V	17.71V	....	....
Jordan	439	.59V	.29V	.31V	.28V	5.28V	....	....	.12V	.06V	.02V	.03V	.24V	....	....
Libya	672	18.23Y	18.85Y	20.95Y	27.25Y	34.70Y	....	....	124.01Y	131.86Y	159.86Y	211.53Y	287.74Y	....	....

	Exports 2001	2002	2003	2004	2005	2006	2007	Imports 2001	2002	2003	2004	2005	2006	2007
	Millions of U.S. Dollars							Millions of U.S. Dollars						
Qatar.....453	—Y	.02V	.02V	.01V	—V	....	....	....	....	....	....	....	....	....
Saudi Arabia.....456	—V	—V	—V	—V	1.48V	....	....	....	....	....	....	....	....	....
Syrian Arab Republic.....463	3.55Y	3.85Y	4.88Y	21.17V	24.19Y	....	....	.38Y	.41Y	.52Y	1.30V	1.48Y	....	....
Yemen, Republic of.....474	—V	—V	—Y	.13V	.20V	....	....	—V	—V	—Y	—V	—V	....	....
Western Hemisphere.....207	**1.1Y**	**.4Y**	**.9Y**	**1.1Y**	**1.6Y**	....	....	**8.1Y**	**13.0Y**	**17.0Y**	**33.4Y**	**28.9Y**	....	....
Argentina.....213	.68V	.18V	.44V	.33V	.44V	....	....	3.22V	1.49V	2.32V	2.32V	3.12V	....	....
Bolivia.....218	—V	—V	.01V	—V	.01V	....	....	—V	—V	—V	—V	—Y	....	....
Brazil.....223	.31V	.05V	.33V	.52V	.62V	....	....	3.70V	9.46V	13.66V	29.81V	25.25V	....	....
Chile.....228	.03V	—V	.04V	—V	—V	....	....	.04V	.44V	—V	.20V	.26V	....	....
Colombia.....233	—V	—V	—V	—V	—V	....	....	—V	—V	—V	—V	—V	....	....
Peru.....293	.01V	.01V	.02V	.03V	.01V	....	....	.14V	.57V	.83V	.96V	.13V	....	....
Uruguay.....298	—V	—Y	.06V	.01V	.07V	....	....	.96V	1.04Y	.22V	.09V	.16V	....	....
Venezuela, Rep. Bol.....299	.11V	.14V	.03V	.19V	.39V	....	....	—V	—V	—V	—V	—V	....	....
Memorandum Items														
European Union.....998	1,006.15Y	1,280.02Y	1,515.76Y	1,813.27Y	1,245.15Y	....	....	2,951.08Y	3,936.48Y	4,845.80Y	5,818.15Y	3,438.55Y	....	....
Oil Exporting Ctys.....999	26.88Y	36.19Y	40.10Y	52.29Y	68.20Y	....	....	166.62Y	170.01Y	206.10Y	272.72Y	370.98Y	....	....
Non-Oil Develop.Ctys.....201	172.25Y	184.96Y	242.53Y	320.73Y	395.21Y	....	....	966.40Y	1,022.03Y	1,505.11Y	1,545.58Y	1,513.89Y	....	....
PERCENT DISTRIBUTION														
Industrial Countries.....101	**82.6**	**84.6**	**83.6**	**83.4**	**73.1**	....	....	**70.7**	**75.4**	**71.9**	**76.4**	**64.6**	....	....
Developing Countries.....202	**17.4**	**15.4**	**16.4**	**16.6**	**26.9**	....	....	**29.3**	**24.6**	**28.1**	**23.6**	**35.4**	....	....
Africa.....607	**1.0**	**1.3**	**1.2**	**1.4**	**2.0**	....	....	**1.3**	**.9**	**.8**	**.8**	**1.6**	....	....
Asia.....507	**1.3**	**.5**	**1.3**	**.9**	**2.0**	....	....	**3.4**	**2.4**	**3.9**	**3.4**	**5.6**	....	....
Europe.....170	**12.6**	**11.4**	**11.9**	**11.4**	**17.8**	....	....	**21.1**	**18.1**	**20.2**	**15.8**	**21.9**	....	....
Middle East.....407	**2.5**	**2.1**	**1.9**	**2.9**	**4.9**	....	....	**3.4**	**2.9**	**2.9**	**3.1**	**5.8**	....	....
Western Hemisphere.....207	**.1**	**—**	**.1**	**—**	**.1**	....	....	**.2**	**.3**	**.3**	**.4**	**.5**	....	....
ANNUAL PERCENT CHANGE														
World.....001	**11.1**	**25.8**	**19.8**	**30.7**	**–23.3**	....	....	**18.1**	**25.5**	**25.7**	**26.7**	**–30.9**	....	....
Industrial Countries.....101	**27.8**	**28.9**	**18.4**	**30.4**	**–32.7**	....	....	**32.0**	**33.8**	**19.8**	**34.6**	**–41.6**	....	....
Developing Countries.....202	**–31.3**	**11.1**	**27.8**	**32.0**	**24.2**	....	....	**–5.8**	**5.2**	**43.6**	**6.3**	**3.7**	....	....
Africa.....607	**–24.1**	**76.2**	**10.0**	**46.2**	**10.7**	....	....	**19.4**	**–11.0**	**8.4**	**32.9**	**36.1**	....	....
Asia.....507	**–27.7**	**–49.5**	**207.7**	**–15.5**	**83.0**	....	....	**50.7**	**–10.6**	**103.6**	**11.2**	**12.4**	....	....
Europe.....170	**–32.7**	**13.8**	**24.8**	**25.9**	**19.7**	....	....	**–14.6**	**7.7**	**40.6**	**–1.3**	**–4.3**	....	....
Middle East.....407	**–28.3**	**6.6**	**9.9**	**93.3**	**31.1**	....	....	**9.2**	**8.3**	**24.8**	**36.8**	**28.3**	....	....
Western Hemisphere.....207	**–36.0**	**–66.8**	**146.4**	**17.0**	**43.0**	....	....	**326.3**	**61.4**	**30.9**	**96.2**	**–13.4**	....	....

	Code	Exports 2001	2002	2003	2004	2005	2006	2007	Imports 2001	2002	2003	2004	2005	2006	2007
		Millions of U.S. Dollars							*Millions of U.S. Dollars*						
IFS World Total		**216.5**	**227.9**	**273.0**	**290.8**	**339.7**	**379.9**	**360.0**	**478.3**	**422.1**	**412.3**	**496.7**	**675.7**	**757.4**	**775.0**
DOTS World Total	**001**	**152.4**	**174.8**	**213.9**	**367.9Y**	**416.8Y**	**350.2Y**	**333.7Y**	**469.8**	**414.5**	**414.2**	**551.2Y**	**762.9Y**	**846.2Y**	**1,008.2Y**
Industrial Countries	**101**	**142.3**	**169.2**	**207.9**	**321.9Y**	**366.9Y**	**287.8Y**	**252.3Y**	**294.2**	**215.0**	**182.4**	**254.7Y**	**321.6Y**	**313.7Y**	**431.2Y**
United States	111	.02	—	1.74	5.45V	5.45V	9.27V	9.45V	123.45	5.75	3.57	11.77V	23.21V	10.34V	10.23V
Canada	156	.02	.02	.02	3.12V	2.55V	3.52V	3.58V	1.31	.42	1.13	.36V	.77V	1.62V	1.34V
Australia	193	.39	.46	.06	.71V	1.72V	2.54V	2.77V	4.42	6.00	4.98	3.00V	3.30V	4.96V	12.43V
Japan	158	.43	1.88	1.28	31.48V	41.24V	28.93V	27.85V	9.88	4.20	4.54	4.88V	6.39V	12.40V	17.68V
New Zealand	196	—	—	—	1.08V	.52V	.40V	.73V	2.07	1.28	1.83	.76V	2.02V	1.53V	5.07V
Austria	122	1.21	.75	—	.01V	.01V	.03V	.01V	.12	.05	.06	2.43V	1.29V	1.14V	1.10V
Belgium	124	.60	.02	—	6.43V	—V	1.25V	.87V	—	—	—	3.88V	4.27V	3.92V	7.03V
Cyprus	423	.09	—	.07	.30V	.32Y	.13V	.21V	.02	.35	.13	.18V	.09V	.10V	.08V
Denmark	128	1.11	.73	1.68	.68V	1.14V	.77V	.98V	1.88	3.21	3.28	3.53V	4.36V	1.78V	2.32V
Finland	172	4.92	1.66	1.67	2.15V	.36V	.15V	.31V	1.45	1.72	.57	1.09V	1.30V	6.14V	19.06V
France	132	38.46	52.21	67.64	58.30V	48.71V	61.38V	66.23V	46.32	49.40	40.24	57.21V	54.92V	64.38V	82.09V
Germany	134	9.47	14.82	15.94	20.43V	24.51V	2.41V	6.56V	5.43	33.78	3.44	12.87V	25.63V	29.54V	108.48V
Greece	174	.68	.64	.74	.52V	.38V	.20V	.15V	.02	.11	—	.15V	.39V	.21V	.22V
Iceland	176	—	—	—	—V	.07V	—V	—V	—	—	—	.44V	.01V	.01V	.02V
Ireland	178	—	—	.07	—V	1.20V	1.54V	2.80V	1.25	1.17	1.06	1.44V	1.98V	1.96V	2.34V
Italy	136	23.03	16.72	31.03	27.67V	31.60V	41.61V	19.10V	30.27	35.05	38.12	36.94V	43.52V	39.68V	32.61V
Luxembourg	137	—	—	—	—V	—V	—V	—V	—	—	—	—V	.08V	.04V	—V
Malta	181	.29	.71	.26	.42V	.59V	.47V	.27V	—	—	—	—V	.01V	—V	—V
Netherlands	138	3.21	3.85	2.39	14.68V	22.90V	15.12V	12.27V	3.29	4.16	5.31	6.83V	10.53V	10.89V	10.31V
Norway	142	—	—	—	.10V	.01V	—V	.14V	.05	.07	.04	1.01V	.96V	13.58V	.66V
Portugal	182	.82	.18	—	—V	—V	—V	—V	.03	.26	.11	.23V	.20V	.30V	.24V
Slovenia	961	—	—	—	—Y	.77V	—V	—V	—	—	—	.05Y	2.45V	.99V	1.56V
Spain	184	—	.29	.07	46.63V	84.33V	28.59V	17.17V	31.28	36.13	43.12	73.71V	104.58V	67.30V	76.96V
Sweden	144	.50	.36	.19	.02V	.03V	—V	.06V	.19	.49	.20	4.76V	1.02V	6.24V	2.22V
Switzerland	146	—	.04	.13	.06V	.48V	.31V	1.86V	2.63	3.89	3.00	1.43V	1.63V	1.08V	1.77V
United Kingdom	112	57.11	73.85	82.88	101.61V	97.97V	89.22V	78.93V	28.82	27.50	27.70	25.74V	26.65V	33.53V	35.41V
Developing Countries	**202**	**9.6**	**5.2**	**5.6**	**45.6Y**	**49.4Y**	**61.7Y**	**80.6Y**	**174.3**	**198.5**	**186.1**	**236.5Y**	**372.7Y**	**447.7Y**	**471.8Y**
Africa	**607**	**5.6**	**3.3**	**1.0**	**21.6Y**	**19.7Y**	**35.2Y**	**44.1Y**	**45.2**	**70.2**	**58.9**	**55.2Y**	**127.0Y**	**102.7Y**	**92.1Y**
Cameroon	622	—	—	—	—Y	—Y	—Y	—Y	.02	.11	.19	.24Y	.28Y	.34Y	.43Y
Côte d'Ivoire	662	—	—	—	—V	4.30V	—V	—Y	—	—	—	.03V	—V	—V	—Y
Ghana	652	—	—	.09	.12Y	.14Y	.17Y	.21Y	—	—	—	—Y	—Y	—Y	—Y
Kenya	664	—	—	—	.04V	.04Y	.05Y	.07Y	3.76	4.89	4.43	3.36V	3.84Y	4.75Y	5.89Y
Madagascar	674	3.57	2.65	.15	.19Y	.22Y	.27Y	.34Y	.32	1.24	.13	.17Y	.19Y	.24Y	.30Y
Malawi	676	—	—	—	—Y	—Y	—Y	—Y	—	.04	.02	.02Y	.03Y	.03Y	.04Y
Mauritius	684	.10	.11	.20	6.17V	8.68V	29.91V	33.52V	8.38	18.07	9.18	13.04V	15.63V	16.46V	20.35V
Morocco	686	—	—	—	.08V	.04V	.05Y	.06Y	—	—	—	—V	—V	—Y	—Y
Mozambique	688	—	.13	—	—Y	—V	—V	—Y	—	—	—	—V	—V	—V	—Y
Namibia	728	—	—	—	—Y	—Y	—Y	—Y	—	.02	.02	.02Y	.02Y	.02Y	.02Y
Senegal	722	—	—	—	—V	.01V	.02V	.02Y	—	—	—	—V	—V	—V	—Y
South Africa	199	1.91	.42	.57	4.27V	2.77V	2.22V	6.20V	32.30	45.16	44.68	37.65V	106.32V	80.12V	64.12V
Sacca exc. South Afr.	608	—	—	—	—Y	—Y	—Y	—Y	—	—	—	.26V	.30Y	.37Y	.46Y
Sudan	732	—	—	—	—Y	.72V	.83V	1.09V	—	—	—	—Y	—V	—V	—V
Swaziland	734	—	—	—	—Y	—Y	—Y	—Y	.20	.11	—	—Y	—Y	—Y	—Y
Tanzania	738	—	—	—	—Y	—Y	—Y	—Y	.09	.33	.19	.24Y	.28Y	.34Y	.43Y
Tunisia	744	—	—	—	3.66V	—V	—V	—Y	—	—	—	.06V	.02V	.01V	.01Y
Uganda	746	—	—	—	—Y	—Y	—Y	—Y	—	.04	—	—Y	—Y	—Y	—Y
Zambia	754	—	—	—	.01V	.06V	.13V	.71V	—	.07	.02	—V	—V	—V	—V
Zimbabwe	698	—	—	—	7.02V	2.67V	1.54V	1.91Y	.15	.11	.07	.14V	.06V	.04V	.05Y
Asia	**507**	**.5**	**.8**	**2.0**	**10.2Y**	**15.9Y**	**11.9Y**	**15.8Y**	**53.9**	**61.8**	**54.6**	**70.0Y**	**91.7Y**	**120.5Y**	**123.0Y**
China,P.R.: Mainland	924	—	—	—	.02V	.01V	1.02V	4.11Y	3.19	2.90	2.61	1.96V	3.74V	5.81V	8.16V
China,P.R.:Hong Kong	532	.36	.02	.24	.84V	2.06V	2.68V	2.02V	1.43	1.46	1.67	.96V	.88V	1.67V	1.72V
Fiji	819	.03	—	—	—Y	—Y	—Y	—Y	.03	—	—	—Y	—Y	—Y	—Y
India	534	.02	—	.02	.41V	.91V	1.13Y	1.40Y	6.49	8.27	7.67	11.11V	11.60V	14.33Y	17.79Y
Indonesia	536	—	.04	—	.05V	.17V	.13V	.15V	2.17	1.61	3.35	2.57V	3.77V	5.76V	3.42V
Korea	542	—	—	—	.02V	.11V	.56V	.23V	.50	.46	.26	4.15V	5.85V	6.94V	9.24V
Malaysia	548	.05	.02	—	.58V	.26V	.48V	.07V	4.80	7.79	2.96	4.83V	7.14V	10.80V	12.09V
Maldives	556	—	—	—	.01V	.04V	.05Y	.06Y	—	—	.02	.02Y	.03Y	.03Y	.04Y
New Caledonia	839	—	—	—	.02V	.03Y	.03Y	.04Y	—	—	—	—Y	—Y	—Y	—Y
Pakistan	564	.02	.02	—	—V	.07V	.08Y	.10Y	.31	.44	.24	.22V	.40V	.49Y	.61Y
Philippines	566	—	.31	.28	.79V	.59V	.24V	.57V	.10	.09	.02	.16V	.10V	1.59V	.45V
Singapore	576	.05	.05	.93	.70V	.71V	2.35V	1.78V	27.69	31.06	29.37	38.78V	52.87V	59.95V	58.12V
Sri Lanka	524	—	—	.56	1.30V	.71V	.39V	.21V	.89	.20	.24	.20V	1.05V	2.39V	3.30V
Taiwan Province of China	528	—	.35	—	—V	.02V	.10V	.03V	.77	2.90	1.24	1.15V	.59V	1.30V	1.46V
Thailand	578	—	—	—	5.43V	10.21V	2.69V	5.01V	5.55	4.60	4.89	3.86V	3.71V	9.41V	6.58V
Vietnam	582	—	—	—	—V	—V	—V	—V	—	.02	.06	—V	—V	—V	—V
Europe	**170**	**.2**	**.1**	**.1**	**8.7Y**	**6.4Y**	**4.7Y**	**2.6Y**	**1.8**	**.3**	**.1**	**15.6Y**	**24.5Y**	**60.4Y**	**59.8Y**
Belarus	913	—	—	—	—V	.05V	—V	—V	—	—	—	—V	.02V	.02V	1.04V
Bulgaria	918	—	—	—	.01V	.01V	—V	.12V	—	—	—	.10V	—V	.06V	11.54V
Czech Republic	935	—	—	—	.03V	.15V	.09V	.18V	.07	.04	.04	6.76V	.60V	6.39V	13.24V

	Exports 2001	2002	2003	2004	2005	2006	2007	Imports 2001	2002	2003	2004	2005	2006	2007
	Millions of U.S. Dollars							*Millions of U.S. Dollars*						
Estonia........ 939	—	—	—	.01V	.01V	—V	—V	—	—	—	.04V	1.54V	.17V	.04V
Hungary........ 944	.05	.11	.04	5.86V	2.62V	.80V	—V	.05	.11	.04	3.72V	4.47V	2.79V	7.12V
Lithuania........ 946	—	—	—	—V	—V	—V	—V	—	—	—	—V	.73V	.95V	1.07V
Macedonia, FYR........ 962	—	—	—	.05V	.38V	.18V	.22Y	—	—	—	—Y	—Y	—Y	—Y
Moldova........ 921	—	—	—	—V	—V	—Y	—Y	—	—	—	.55V	2.16V	2.68Y	3.32Y
Poland........ 964	—	—	—	.18V	.04V	.03V	—V	—	—	—	.59V	.44V	2.72V	4.12V
Romania........ 968	—	—	—	.05V	.05V	.05V	—V	—	—	—	.03V	1.03V	.01V	.04V
Russia........ 922	—	—	—	.43V	.59V	2.32V	.68V	—	—	—	2.51V	4.19V	31.26V	5.60V
Slovak Republic........ 936	—	—	—	—Y	—V	—V	—V	—	—	—	.01Y	.59V	.30V	.09V
Turkey........ 186	.12	—	—	2.04V	1.70V	.23V	.18V	1.69	.13	.02	.78V	4.43V	7.80V	6.08V
Turkmenistan........ 925	....	....	....	....	....	....	....	—	—	—	.29Y	.33Y	.41Y	.51Y
Ukraine........ 926	—	—	—	.02V	.75V	.92Y	1.14Y	—	—	—	.12V	3.87V	4.79Y	5.94Y
U.S.S.R. n.s........ 930	—	—	—	—Y	—Y	—Y	—Y	.02	.02	.04	.05Y	.06Y	.07Y	.09Y
Europe n.s........ 884	—	—	.02	.02Y	.03Y	.03Y	.04Y	—	—	—	—Y	—Y	—Y	—Y
Middle East........ 407	**3.3**	**.9**	**.1**	**.1Y**	**.1Y**	**.1Y**	**.1Y**	**73.0**	**65.5**	**71.7**	**95.6Y**	**129.1Y**	**162.3Y**	**195.8Y**
Bahrain........ 419	—	.16	—	—Y	—Y	—Y	—Y	7.61	.05	.07	.10Y	.11Y	.14Y	.17Y
Egypt........ 469	—	—	—	—Y	—Y	—Y	—Y	.07	.02	—	—Y	—Y	—Y	—Y
Iran, I.R. of........ 429	.03	.24	.02	.02Y	.03Y	.04Y	.05Y	.02	—	—	—Y	—Y	—Y	—Y
Israel........ 436	—	.07	.09	—V	—V	—V	—V	—	.07	.09	.12Y	.14Y	.17Y	.21Y
Jordan........ 439	—	—	—	—V	—V	—V	—V	—	—	—	—V	—V	.04V	—V
Kuwait........ 443	.07	.15	—	—Y	—Y	—Y	—Y	—	—	.02	.02Y	.03Y	.04Y	.05Y
Oman........ 449	.02	.07	—	—Y	—Y	—Y	—Y	—	.33	.02	.02Y	.03Y	.04Y	.05Y
Saudi Arabia........ 456	—	—	—	—V	—V	—Y	—Y	40.61	58.49	64.84	85.80Y	116.72Y	146.73Y	177.02Y
United Arab Emirates........ 466	.07	.07	.04	.05Y	.06Y	.08Y	.10Y	21.48	6.55	6.68	8.84Y	12.03Y	15.13Y	18.25Y
Yemen, Republic of........ 474	—	—	—	—V	—V	—Y	—Y	3.18	—	—	.64V	.04V	.05Y	.06Y
Middle East n.s........ 489	3.11	.18	—	—Y	—Y	—Y	—Y	—	—	—	—Y	—Y	—Y	—Y
Western Hemisphere........ 207	**—**	**—**	**2.4**	**5.1Y**	**7.4Y**	**9.8Y**	**18.0Y**	**.3**	**.8**	**.7**	**.1Y**	**.5Y**	**1.8Y**	**1.1Y**
Argentina........ 213	—	—	—	—V	.04V	.07V	.05V	—	—	.31	.12V	.30V	.25V	.21V
Barbados........ 316	—	—	—	—V	—V	—V	—Y	—	—	—	—V	.04V	—V	—Y
Brazil........ 223	—	—	—	—V	—V	—V	—V	.31	.57	.43	—V	—V	—V	—V
Chile........ 228	—	—	—	—V	—V	—V	5.73V	—	—	—	—V	—V	—V	—V
Colombia........ 233	—	—	—	.27V	—V	—V	—V	.02	.11	—	.01V	—V	—V	—V
Jamaica........ 343	—	—	—	—V	.04V	—V	—V	—	.09	—	—V	—V	—V	—V
Mexico........ 273	—	—	—	—V	.05V	.12V	.16V	—	—	—	—V	.03V	.87V	—V
Paraguay........ 288	....	....	....	....	....	....	....	—	—	—	—V	—V	.49V	.60Y
Peru........ 293	—	—	—	.01V	.01V	.01V	—Y	—	—	—	—V	—V	.04V	.09Y
Uruguay........ 298	—	—	—	—V	.01V	.01Y	.01Y	—	—	—	—V	.10V	.12Y	.15Y
Western Hem. n.s........ 399	—	—	2.41	4.81Y	7.22Y	9.63Y	12.04Y	—	—	—	—Y	—Y	—Y	—Y
Other Countries n.i.e........ 910	**—**	**—**	**—**	**—Y**	**—Y**	**—Y**	**—Y**	**—**	**—**	**—**	**—Y**	**—Y**	**—Y**	**—Y**
Cuba........ 928	—	—	—	—Y	—Y	—Y	—Y	—	.02	—	—Y	—Y	—Y	—Y
Countries & Areas n.s........ 898	**.5**	**.5**	**.4**	**.5Y**	**.5Y**	**.7Y**	**.8Y**	**1.3**	**1.0**	**45.7**	**60.0Y**	**68.6Y**	**84.8Y**	**105.2Y**
Memorandum Items														
European Union........ 998	141.54	166.90	204.68	285.92Y	317.65Y	243.77Y	206.09Y	150.47	193.52	163.42	242.16Y	291.63Y	281.48Y	407.71Y
Oil Exporting Ctys........ 999	.19	.57	.06	.13Y	.26Y	.24Y	.29Y	64.28	66.97	74.92	97.26Y	132.58Y	167.70Y	198.78Y
Non-Oil Develop.Ctys........ 201	9.39	4.60	5.59	45.49Y	49.13Y	61.48Y	80.33Y	109.98	131.57	111.19	139.22Y	240.16Y	280.05Y	272.99Y
PERCENT DISTRIBUTION														
Industrial Countries........ 101	**93.4**	**96.8**	**97.2**	**87.5**	**88.0**	**82.2**	**75.6**	**62.6**	**51.9**	**44.0**	**46.2**	**42.2**	**37.1**	**42.8**
Developing Countries........ 202	**6.3**	**3.0**	**2.6**	**12.4**	**11.9**	**17.6**	**24.2**	**37.1**	**47.9**	**44.9**	**42.9**	**48.9**	**52.9**	**46.8**
Africa........ 607	**3.7**	**1.9**	**.5**	**5.9**	**4.7**	**10.1**	**13.2**	**9.6**	**16.9**	**14.2**	**10.0**	**16.6**	**12.1**	**9.1**
Asia........ 507	**.3**	**.5**	**.9**	**2.8**	**3.8**	**3.4**	**4.7**	**11.5**	**14.9**	**13.2**	**12.7**	**12.0**	**14.2**	**12.2**
Europe........ 170	**.1**	**.1**	**—**	**2.4**	**1.5**	**1.3**	**.8**	**.4**	**.1**	**—**	**2.8**	**3.2**	**7.1**	**5.9**
Middle East........ 407	**2.2**	**.5**	**.1**	**—**	**—**	**—**	**—**	**15.5**	**15.8**	**17.3**	**17.3**	**16.9**	**19.2**	**19.4**
Western Hemisphere........ 207	**—**	**—**	**1.1**	**1.4**	**1.8**	**2.8**	**5.4**	**.1**	**.2**	**.2**	**—**	**.1**	**.2**	**.1**
ANNUAL PERCENT CHANGE														
World........ 001	**23.3**	**14.7**	**22.3**	**72.0**	**13.3**	**–16.0**	**–4.7**	**39.0**	**–11.8**	**–.1**	**33.1**	**38.4**	**10.9**	**19.1**
Industrial Countries........ 101	**24.0**	**18.8**	**22.9**	**54.8**	**14.0**	**–21.5**	**–12.3**	**98.1**	**–26.9**	**–15.1**	**39.6**	**26.3**	**–2.4**	**37.5**
Developing Countries........ 202	**15.7**	**–46.1**	**9.4**	**707.7**	**8.3**	**25.0**	**30.6**	**–7.6**	**13.9**	**–6.3**	**27.1**	**57.6**	**20.1**	**5.4**
Africa........ 607	**12.7**	**–40.8**	**–69.2**	**—**	**–8.8**	**79.0**	**25.4**	**–11.6**	**55.2**	**–16.0**	**–6.2**	**129.8**	**–19.1**	**–10.3**
Asia........ 507	**–13.6**	**51.7**	**151.4**	**404.0**	**56.2**	**–25.0**	**32.5**	**–8.8**	**14.6**	**–11.7**	**28.2**	**31.1**	**31.3**	**2.1**
Europe........ 170	**....**	**–35.9**	**–49.3**	**—**	**–26.7**	**–27.1**	**–44.8**	**286.6**	**–84.0**	**–55.6**	**—**	**57.0**	**147.0**	**–1.0**
Middle East........ 407	**21.5**	**–71.2**	**–84.4**	**–51.2**	**27.3**	**23.5**	**29.5**	**–5.9**	**–10.2**	**9.5**	**33.2**	**35.1**	**25.7**	**20.6**
Western Hemisphere........ 207	**—**	**—**	**....**	**111.8**	**44.5**	**33.5**	**82.9**	**–15.8**	**136.3**	**–3.4**	**–82.4**	**262.3**	**275.9**	**–40.7**

	Exports							Imports						
	2001	2002	2003	2004	2005	2006	2007	2001	2002	2003	2004	2005	2006	2007
	Millions of U.S. Dollars							*Millions of U.S. Dollars*						
IFS World Total	**29.0**	**48.7**	**92.3**	**138.6**	**158.5**	**216.0**	**244.5**	**182.0**	**264.3**	**303.4**	**286.5**	**344.7**	**389.4**	**444.7**
DOTS World Total 001	**55.9Y**	**105.8Y**	**140.6Y**	**184.0Y**	**196.0Y**	**208.9Y**	**267.7Y**	**420.3Y**	**495.9Y**	**602.0Y**	**523.0Y**	**609.3Y**	**564.6Y**	**642.6Y**
Industrial Countries 101	**43.9Y**	**91.4Y**	**124.6Y**	**157.9Y**	**172.4Y**	**186.3Y**	**235.4Y**	**297.0Y**	**360.9Y**	**398.2Y**	**295.0Y**	**316.3Y**	**216.5Y**	**249.3Y**
United States 111	4.27V	3.64V	6.18V	10.00V	9.00V	39.91V	54.82V	30.58V	27.83V	31.24V	44.66V	41.58V	43.23V	60.94V
Canada 156	1.87V	1.58V	2.41V	2.93V	2.01V	1.64V	10.94V	1.38V	3.55V	2.53V	2.63V	4.16V	4.93V	12.34V
Australia 193	.10V	.01V	.09V	.19V	.48V	2.94V	2.13V	.61V	.25V	.56V	.78V	2.64V	3.77V	4.94V
Japan 158	2.65V	.77V	.03V	.15V	.23V	.80V	3.08V	6.01V	5.78V	5.17V	4.03V	7.81V	1.68V	3.16V
New Zealand 196	—V	—V	.04V	—V	—V	.10V	.30V	.36V	.93V	.37V	.28V	.21V	.59V	.40V
Austria 122	.07V	.07V	.04V	.01V	—V	.05V	.03V	2.26V	7.84V	6.97V	1.17V	.40V	.43V	.59V
Belgium 124	21.22V	41.57V	81.89V	113.82V	128.87V	108.79V	131.83V	15.97V	13.63V	16.36V	16.09V	10.95V	17.91V	16.38V
Cyprus 423	—V	—V	.15V	.06V	.07Y	.43V	.02V	.01V	.16V	.05V	.01V	—V	—V	.01V
Denmark 128	.99V	1.26V	1.24V	.26V	.04V	.33V	.17V	17.66V	16.07V	19.82V	13.20V	6.82V	3.10V	4.41V
Finland 172	.03V	.03V	.03V	.03V	.05V	.02V	.01V	.11V	.74V	.52V	.70V	.50V	.95V	4.14V
France 132	1.22V	1.98V	.66V	.69V	.31V	1.01V	1.90V	16.73V	15.61V	42.71V	21.18V	14.10V	23.62V	17.20V
Germany 134	3.64V	31.87V	18.62V	21.89V	26.26V	3.15V	2.07V	24.33V	128.91V	137.75V	74.23V	114.34V	14.74V	20.10V
Greece 174	.99V	.17V	.19V	.03V	—V	—V	.01V	5.48V	5.20V	3.14V	3.36V	1.10V	.73V	.33V
Iceland 176	—V	—V	—V	—V	—V	—V	—V	—V	—V	—V	.01V	.02V	—V	—V
Ireland 178	1.31V	.61V	.40V	.07V	.07V	.07V	.05V	4.53V	4.07V	1.69V	.88V	1.04V	.56V	.98V
Italy 136	.41V	2.90V	1.44V	2.23V	.13V	1.07V	.33V	21.58V	21.15V	20.79V	18.66V	8.58V	17.64V	12.20V
Luxembourg 137	—V	.03V	.06V	.02V	—V	—V	—V	.41V	.42V	.20V	.16V	.03V	.01V	.01V
Malta 181	.01Y	—V	.01V	—V	—V	.01V	.02V	.05Y	.10V	.40V	.74V	.33V	.20V	.30V
Netherlands 138	.61V	.81V	4.39V	1.74V	2.44V	14.16V	12.13V	40.35V	36.83V	30.67V	26.69V	32.51V	30.89V	32.48V
Norway 142	—V	.02V	—V	—V	—V	—V	—V	.41V	.44V	.57V	.44V	.45V	.29V	.37V
Portugal 182	.05V	—V	.01V	.01V	.01V	3.41V	5.46V	.09V	.12V	.30V	.26V	.18V	.27V	.87V
Slovenia 961	—V	—V	—V	—Y	.01V	.18V	.06V	.54V	2.10V	2.16V	2.84Y	—V	.02V	—V
Spain 184	.09V	.06V	.19V	—V	.36V	.49V	2.75V	3.80V	9.94V	9.54V	6.50V	3.99V	3.95V	5.14V
Sweden 144	.35V	.32V	.33V	.33V	.02V	.04V	.11V	5.09V	4.71V	5.75V	6.21V	12.36V	9.04V	10.66V
Switzerland 146	.01V	.05V	.03V	.02V	.02V	.14V	1.46V	.63V	1.04V	.56V	.73V	.61V	.41V	1.61V
United Kingdom 112	3.99V	3.64V	6.22V	3.43V	2.03V	7.52V	5.67V	98.03V	53.45V	58.37V	48.52V	51.62V	37.56V	39.74V
Developing Countries 202	**11.6Y**	**13.9Y**	**15.3Y**	**25.3Y**	**22.6Y**	**21.5Y**	**30.9Y**	**111.2Y**	**121.9Y**	**187.2Y**	**206.3Y**	**268.1Y**	**317.3Y**	**355.1Y**
Africa 607	**7.1Y**	**7.4Y**	**7.0Y**	**7.7Y**	**11.9Y**	**11.1Y**	**14.0Y**	**36.5Y**	**49.0Y**	**71.2Y**	**91.4Y**	**118.3Y**	**106.0Y**	**123.4Y**
Benin 638	.04V	.30V	.30V	—V	1.08V	1.34Y	1.66Y	.08V	—V	.04V	.02V	—V	—Y	—Y
Cameroon 622	—V	.01V	—V	—Y	—Y	.01Y	.01Y	.02V	.03V	1.61V	2.11Y	2.41Y	2.98Y	3.70Y
Côte d'Ivoire 662	.15V	.34V	.01V	.53V	2.06V	.69V	.86Y	22.13V	30.50V	43.16V	46.78V	67.52V	51.86V	64.36Y
Gambia, The 648	—Y	—Y	—Y	—Y	—Y	—Y	—Y	.03Y	.04Y	.04Y	.06Y	.07Y	.08Y	.10Y
Ghana 652	—Y	—Y	—Y	—Y	—Y	—Y	—Y	.16Y	.17Y	.21Y	.28Y	.32Y	.40Y	.49Y
Guinea 656	.01V	.01Y	.17V	.53V	.61Y	.75Y	.94Y	1.20V	1.30Y	1.78V	2.21V	2.52Y	3.12Y	3.87Y
Kenya 664	.13V	.97V	.64V	.49V	.56Y	.69Y	.86Y	.51V	.02V	.24V	.41V	.47Y	.58Y	.71Y
Liberia 668	—Y	—Y	—Y	—Y	—Y	—Y	—Y	2.87Y	3.12Y	3.94Y	5.18Y	5.92Y	7.32Y	9.08Y
Madagascar 674	....	....	....	....	....	....	....	.01V	—V	—V	—Y	—Y	—Y	—Y
Malawi 676	—Y	—Y	—Y	—Y	—Y	—Y	—Y	.39Y	.43Y	.54Y	.71Y	.81Y	1.00Y	1.24Y
Mauritius 684	—V	.02V	.01V	.01V	.94V	.06V	.32V	.07V	.04V	.01V	—V	—V	.03V	—V
Morocco 686	.76V	.37V	.86V	.22V	.24V	.30Y	.37Y	1.79V	1.55V	2.17V	2.56V	3.35V	4.14Y	5.13Y
Niger 692	—V	—V	.05V	—V	—Y	—Y	—Y	—V	—V	—V	.66V	.76Y	.94Y	1.16Y
Nigeria 694	.10V	—V	.40V	.52Y	.67Y	.82Y	1.06Y	—V	—V	—V	—Y	—Y	—Y	—Y
Senegal 722	.04V	.07V	.10V	.03V	—V	.15V	.19Y	1.37V	3.84V	3.57V	5.56V	6.97V	4.65V	5.77Y
South Africa 199	2.45V	1.78V	.41V	.77V	.67V	.66V	1.49V	5.60V	5.79V	11.93V	21.87V	23.94V	25.26V	23.22V
Tanzania 738	.04V	.04V	.05Y	.06Y	.07Y	.09Y	.11Y	.17V	1.35V	1.70Y	2.24Y	2.56Y	3.16Y	3.92Y
Togo 742	—V	—V	—V	—V	—V	—Y	—Y	.03V	.12V	.01V	.07V	.03V	.04Y	.05Y
Tunisia 744	.13V	.01V	.06V	.02V	—V	.01V	.01Y	.03V	.06V	.18V	.59V	.67V	.42V	.52Y
Uganda 746	.18V	.13V	.02V	.02Y	.02Y	.02Y	.02Y	.02V	.04V	.02V	.03Y	.03Y	.04Y	.04Y
Zambia 754	.25V	—V	—V	.07V	.03V	—V	—V	.01V	.35V	.01V	—V	—V	.01V	.01V
Zimbabwe 698	—V	.02V	.03V	—V	.01V	—V	—Y	—V	.23V	.01V	.03V	—V	—V	—Y
Africa n.s. 799	2.77Y	3.32Y	3.86Y	4.40Y	4.95Y	5.51Y	6.07Y	—Y	—Y	—Y	—Y	—Y	—Y	—Y
Asia 507	**1.9Y**	**4.7Y**	**6.9Y**	**6.1Y**	**6.7Y**	**7.0Y**	**10.8Y**	**53.5Y**	**56.7Y**	**59.1Y**	**80.5Y**	**108.9Y**	**132.6Y**	**180.7Y**
Bangladesh 513	—Y	—Y	—Y	—Y	—V	—V	—V	.24V	.18V	.08V	1.13V	.12V	.15Y	.18Y
Cambodia 522	—V	—Y	—Y	—Y	—Y	—Y	—Y	—V	—V	—V	—V	.02V	—V	—Y
China,P.R.: Mainland 924	—V	.14V	—V	1.46V	1.35V	.89V	5.17V	13.19V	15.85V	18.27V	29.47V	33.84V	42.88V	64.32V
China,P.R.:Hong Kong 532	.01V	.11V	.16V	.83V	.73V	.07V	.20V	11.60V	10.78V	10.63V	10.21V	9.08V	9.36V	11.73V
China,P.R.:Macao 546	—V	—V	—V	—V	—V	—V	—V	—V	—V	—V	—V	—V	—V	.04V
India 534	.78Y	2.93V	5.35V	3.02V	2.95V	3.64Y	4.52Y	4.83Y	13.82V	13.56V	13.76V	19.69V	24.33Y	30.20Y
Indonesia 536	.01V	.04V	.15V	.07V	.06V	—V	.06V	5.29V	4.02V	4.73V	8.58V	6.94V	13.33V	20.18V
Korea 542	.46V	.49V	.05V	.05V	.45V	.46V	.67V	7.70V	4.04V	2.24V	1.87V	2.48V	3.12V	5.96V
Malaysia 548	.18V	.27V	.43V	.31V	.17V	.15V	.09V	1.68V	1.66V	2.32V	6.98V	6.24V	10.68V	22.03V
Myanmar 518	—Y	—Y	—Y	—Y	—Y	—Y	—Y	.66Y	.71Y	.90Y	1.19Y	1.36Y	1.68Y	2.08Y
New Caledonia 839	—V	—V	.01V	—V	—Y	—Y	—Y	....	....	....	....	....	....	....
Pakistan 564	.04V	.10V	—V	—V	.04V	.06Y	.07Y	—V	.16V	.28V	1.97V	9.83V	12.15Y	15.08Y
Philippines 566	—V	.05V	—V	.04V	.04V	.04V	.03V	—V	—V	—V	—V	.05V	.06V	—V
Taiwan Province of China 528	—V	—V	—V	.07V	.08V	1.24V	—V	1.88V	1.74V	1.39V	1.42V	2.93V	3.49V	4.25V
Thailand 578	.37V	.29V	.32V	.30V	.85V	.49V	.03V	4.84V	3.01V	4.14V	3.93V	16.35V	11.38V	4.69V
Vietnam 582	.07V	.26V	.40V	—V	—V	—V	—V	1.59V	.76V	.55V	—V	—V	—V	—V
Europe 170	**2.0Y**	**1.6Y**	**1.3Y**	**11.2Y**	**3.7Y**	**2.7Y**	**5.3Y**	**10.1Y**	**7.1Y**	**42.7Y**	**12.6Y**	**14.3Y**	**18.2Y**	**28.0Y**
Albania 914	—V	.02V	.05V	.03V	.03V	.02V	.01V	—V	—V	—V	—V	—V	—V	—V
Azerbaijan 912	—V	—V	—V	—V	—V	—V	.04V	—V	.02V	—V	—V	—V	—V	—V
Belarus 913	—V	—V	—V	—V	.45V	.03V	.10V	—V	.04V	.01V	.02V	.64V	.06V	.15V

	Exports							Imports						
	2001	2002	2003	2004	2005	2006	2007	2001	2002	2003	2004	2005	2006	2007
	Millions of U.S. Dollars							*Millions of U.S. Dollars*						
Bulgaria.......................... 918	.01V	.01V	—V	—V	—V	—V	.05V	.04V	.02V	.05V	—V	—V	.50V	.33V
Czech Republic.......................... 935	.63V	.76V	.47V	6.26V	1.62V	—V	.08V	.29V	.94V	.31V	.30V	2.43V	.33V	3.03V
Estonia.......................... 939	.25V	.07V	.21V	—V	—V	—V	.03V	—V	—V	—V	—V	.04V	—V	—V
Hungary.......................... 944	.22V	.05V	.11V	.22V	.03V	.10V	.04V	.96V	.42V	.34V	.28V	.92V	4.40V	5.81V
Kazakhstan.......................... 916	.25V	.06V	—V	—V	—Y	—Y	—Y	—V	—V	—V	—V	—Y	—Y	—Y
Latvia.......................... 941	—V	—V	—Y	—V	—V	—V	.12V	—V	—V	—V	—V	—V	—V	.02V
Lithuania.......................... 946	—V	—V	—V	—V	—V	—V	—V	—V	—V	.37V	.20V	.07V	—V	—V
Macedonia, FYR.......................... 962	.01V	.01V	.01V	—V	—V	.01V	.01Y	—V	—V	.01V	.05V	.01V	—V	—Y
Poland.......................... 964	.46V	.49V	.24V	3.13V	—V	—V	.02V	1.58V	1.10V	1.45V	1.57V	.94V	1.16V	1.06V
Romania.......................... 968	—V	—V	.01V	—V	.01V	.01V	.20V	2.62V	.08V	.23V	.50V	.02V	.40V	.76V
Russia.......................... 922	.09V	.01V	.08V	1.41V	1.00V	.53V	2.67V	1.53V	.93V	7.88V	.70V	.12V	.09V	.19V
Slovak Republic.......................... 936	.03V	.05V	.06Y	.08Y	—V	.01V	—V	.01V	.22V	.28Y	.37Y	—V	—V	.03V
Turkey.......................... 186	.01V	—V	—V	.01V	.04V	1.37V	1.14V	1.89V	1.43V	5.09V	7.35V	5.91V	7.28V	11.71V
Ukraine.......................... 926	.01V	—V	—V	—V	.42V	.52Y	.65Y	1.20V	1.85V	26.65V	1.22V	3.19V	3.95Y	4.90Y
Europe n.s.......................... 884	.05Y	.05Y	.07Y	.09Y	.10Y	.12Y	.15Y	....	....	....	....	....	....	....
Middle East.......................... 407	**.2Y**	**.1Y**	**.1Y**	**.1Y**	**.1Y**	**.1Y**	**.1Y**	**5.6Y**	**5.0Y**	**7.8Y**	**9.3Y**	**13.3Y**	**12.7Y**	**15.7Y**
Egypt.......................... 469	.02V	.03Y	.03Y	.04Y	.05Y	.06Y	.08Y	2.22V	2.41Y	3.05Y	4.01Y	4.58Y	5.66Y	7.03Y
Israel.......................... 436	—V	—V	—V	—V	—V	—V	—V	.22V	.11V	.11V	.77V	2.86V	.22V	.22V
Jordan.......................... 439	—V	—V	—V	—V	—V	—V	—V	.02V	.03V	.06V	.01V	.42V	—V	.05V
Lebanon.......................... 446	.01Y	.01Y	.01Y	.02Y	.02Y	.03Y	.03Y	1.71Y	1.86Y	2.35Y	3.09Y	3.53Y	4.36Y	5.41Y
Oman.......................... 449	—V	—V	—V	—Y	—Y	—Y	—Y	1.07V	.33V	.75V	.99Y	1.35Y	1.70Y	2.05Y
Qatar.......................... 453	—Y	—Y	—Y	—Y	—Y	—Y	—Y	.07V	.02V	1.16V	—V	—V	—V	—Y
Saudi Arabia.......................... 456	.17V	.02V	—V	.03V	.02V	.03Y	.04Y	.25Y	.27Y	.33Y	.43Y	.59Y	.74Y	.89Y
Yemen, Republic of.......................... 474	—V	—V	—Y	—V	—V	—Y	—Y	—V	—V	—Y	.03V	.02V	.02Y	.03Y
Western Hemisphere.......................... 207	**.4Y**	**.2Y**	**.1Y**	**.1Y**	**.2Y**	**.5Y**	**.7Y**	**5.6Y**	**4.1Y**	**6.5Y**	**12.5Y**	**13.2Y**	**47.8Y**	**7.3Y**
Argentina.......................... 213	.01V	—V	—V	—V	.05V	.22V	.15V	.42V	.55V	1.13V	4.21V	3.54V	8.97V	6.97V
Barbados.......................... 316	.07V	.11V	.10V	—V	.05V	.01V	.01Y	—V	—V	.01V	.01V	.05V	.14V	.17Y
Brazil.......................... 223	—V	—V	.01V	.02V	—V	.16V	—V	2.82V	3.51V	5.23V	8.23V	9.46V	38.51V	—V
Chile.......................... 228	—V	—V	—V	—V	—V	—V	.19V	—V	—V	—V	—V	—V	—V	—V
Colombia.......................... 233	—V	—V	—V	—V	—V	—V	.01V	.03V	—V	—V	—V	—V	—V	.05V
Costa Rica.......................... 238	—V	—V	—V	—V	—V	—Y	—Y	.02V	—V	—V	—V	—V	—Y	—Y
Ecuador.......................... 248	—Y	—Y	—Y	—Y	—Y	—Y	—Y	—V	—V	—V	.01V	—V	—V	—Y
Guatemala.......................... 258	—V	—V	—V	—V	—V	—Y	—Y	2.14V	—V	—V	—V	—V	—Y	—Y
Haiti.......................... 263	.24V	—V	—V	—V	—Y	—Y	—Y	....	....	....	....	....	....	....
Jamaica.......................... 343	.01V	—V	—V	—V	—V	—V	—V	.01V	—V	—V	—V	—V	.05V	—V
Mexico.......................... 273	—V	—V	—V	—V	.06V	.07V	.26V	—V	—V	—V	—V	.02V	.05V	.04V
Netherlands Antilles.......................... 353	—V	—V	.01V	.01Y	.02Y	.02Y	.03Y	.07V	—V	—V	—Y	—Y	—Y	—Y
Peru.......................... 293	.04V	—V	—V	—V	.01V	.01V	.01Y	.01V	—V	.05V	—V	.08V	.03V	.05Y
St. Vincent & Grens.......................... 364	.01V	—V	—V	.06V	—V	—Y	—Y	—V	—V	—V	—V	—V	—Y	—Y
Trinidad and Tobago.......................... 369	—V	—V	—Y	—Y	—Y	—Y	—Y	—V	.01V	.01Y	.01Y	.01Y	.01Y	.02Y
Uruguay.......................... 298	—V	—Y	—V	—V	—V	—Y	—Y	—V	—Y	.04V	—V	.01V	.01Y	.01Y
Venezuela, Rep. Bol.......................... 299	—V	.10V	—V	—V	—V	—V	—V	—V	—V	—V	—V	—V	—V	—Y
Western Hem. n.s.......................... 399	—Y	—Y	—Y	—Y	—Y	—Y	—Y	.02Y	.02Y	.03Y	.03Y	.03Y	.03Y	.03Y
Countries & Areas n.s.......................... 898	**.4Y**	**.5Y**	**.6Y**	**.8Y**	**.9Y**	**1.1Y**	**1.4Y**	**2.9Y**	**3.1Y**	**3.9Y**	**5.2Y**	**5.9Y**	**7.3Y**	**9.1Y**
Special Categories.......................... 899	**—Y**	**—Y**	**—Y**	**—Y**	**—Y**	**—Y**	**—Y**	**9.2Y**	**10.0Y**	**12.7Y**	**16.6Y**	**19.0Y**	**23.5Y**	**29.1Y**
Memorandum Items														
European Union.......................... 998	36.57Y	86.74Y	116.96Y	154.30Y	162.32Y	140.85Y	162.92Y	259.85Y	323.73Y	359.92Y	244.12Y	263.24Y	167.52Y	175.48Y
Oil Exporting Ctys.......................... 999	.28Y	.17Y	.55Y	.62Y	.74Y	.85Y	1.16Y	6.68Y	4.65Y	6.97Y	10.01Y	8.88Y	15.77Y	23.12Y
Non-Oil Develop.Ctys.......................... 201	11.30Y	13.76Y	14.75Y	24.66Y	21.88Y	20.63Y	29.76Y	104.56Y	117.24Y	180.27Y	196.28Y	259.24Y	301.51Y	332.01Y
PERCENT DISTRIBUTION														
Industrial Countries.......................... 101	**78.5**	**86.4**	**88.7**	**85.8**	**88.0**	**89.2**	**87.9**	**70.7**	**72.8**	**66.1**	**56.4**	**51.9**	**38.4**	**38.8**
Developing Countries.......................... 202	**20.7**	**13.2**	**10.9**	**13.7**	**11.5**	**10.3**	**11.6**	**26.5**	**24.6**	**31.1**	**39.4**	**44.0**	**56.2**	**55.3**
Africa.......................... 607	**12.6**	**7.0**	**4.9**	**4.2**	**6.1**	**5.3**	**5.2**	**8.7**	**9.9**	**11.8**	**17.5**	**19.4**	**18.8**	**19.2**
Asia.......................... 507	**3.5**	**4.4**	**4.9**	**3.3**	**3.4**	**3.4**	**4.1**	**12.7**	**11.4**	**9.8**	**15.4**	**17.9**	**23.5**	**28.1**
Europe.......................... 170	**3.6**	**1.5**	**.9**	**6.1**	**1.9**	**1.3**	**2.0**	**2.4**	**1.4**	**7.1**	**2.4**	**2.3**	**3.2**	**4.4**
Middle East.......................... 407	**.4**	**.1**	**—**	**—**	**—**	**.1**	**.1**	**1.3**	**1.0**	**1.3**	**1.8**	**2.2**	**2.3**	**2.4**
Western Hemisphere.......................... 207	**.7**	**.2**	**.1**	**.1**	**.1**	**.2**	**.2**	**1.3**	**.8**	**1.1**	**2.4**	**2.2**	**8.5**	**1.1**
ANNUAL PERCENT CHANGE														
World.......................... 001	**−55.7**	**89.2**	**32.9**	**30.9**	**6.5**	**6.6**	**28.2**	**32.9**	**18.0**	**21.4**	**−13.1**	**16.5**	**−7.3**	**13.8**
Industrial Countries.......................... 101	**−61.4**	**108.3**	**36.4**	**26.7**	**9.2**	**8.0**	**26.4**	**23.9**	**21.5**	**10.3**	**−25.9**	**7.2**	**−31.5**	**15.1**
Developing Countries.......................... 202	**−4.9**	**20.2**	**9.9**	**65.1**	**−10.5**	**−5.1**	**44.0**	**69.4**	**9.6**	**53.6**	**10.2**	**30.0**	**18.3**	**11.9**
Africa.......................... 607	**−7.4**	**4.9**	**−6.0**	**10.5**	**55.1**	**−6.9**	**25.8**	**73.8**	**34.1**	**45.4**	**28.4**	**29.5**	**−10.4**	**16.4**
Asia.......................... 507	**−25.7**	**142.6**	**46.9**	**−10.6**	**9.2**	**4.9**	**54.0**	**42.1**	**6.0**	**4.1**	**36.3**	**35.3**	**21.7**	**36.3**
Europe.......................... 170	**49.9**	**−21.8**	**−17.1**	**760.4**	**−67.1**	**−26.2**	**94.2**	**302.2**	**−30.2**	**504.4**	**−70.6**	**13.9**	**27.0**	**54.1**
Middle East.......................... 407	**25.9**	**−69.4**	**−18.9**	**82.4**	**2.4**	**23.6**	**25.4**	**125.5**	**−9.5**	**55.3**	**19.5**	**42.9**	**−4.8**	**23.4**
Western Hemisphere.......................... 207	**−18.0**	**−46.2**	**−43.3**	**−6.2**	**83.1**	**141.3**	**35.8**	**173.3**	**−26.3**	**58.8**	**92.2**	**5.6**	**262.0**	**−84.6**

	Exports 2001	Exports 2002	Exports 2003	Exports 2004	Exports 2005	Exports 2006	Exports 2007	Imports 2001	Imports 2002	Imports 2003	Imports 2004	Imports 2005	Imports 2006	Imports 2007
	Millions of U.S. Dollars							*Millions of U.S. Dollars*						
IFS World Total....................	**121,751**	**125,177**	**144,181**	**198,637**	**229,649**	**271,807**	**299,272**	**116,000**	**116,448**	**127,939**	**163,854**	**200,047**	**238,710**	**263,155**
DOTS World Total.................. 001	**121,826**	**125,219**	**160,073**	**198,694**	**229,447**	**272,057**	**299,173**	**116,020**	**116,483**	**136,327**	**172,697**	**200,197**	**238,797**	**263,325**
Industrial Countries............. 101	**49,646**	**48,837**	**56,426**	**68,955**	**74,199**	**85,691**	**87,898**	**54,488**	**50,515**	**55,181**	**67,185**	**72,143**	**84,137**	**94,141**
United States.......................... 111	18,755	19,106	20,570	23,282	23,880	27,622	26,643	19,159	16,605	18,003	20,744	23,482	30,353	32,867
Canada................................. 156	402	370	433	564	517	820	1,985	417	576	553	652	812	915	1,074
Australia............................... 193	3,171	3,373	4,681	6,612	8,429	10,186	11,191	2,406	2,159	2,185	2,300	2,910	3,739	3,166
Japan................................... 158	9,341	8,935	9,696	11,567	12,536	14,855	14,389	16,091	14,576	15,396	19,096	19,244	19,928	21,542
New Zealand.......................... 196	402	417	573	947	1,164	1,393	1,558	180	195	220	269	320	352	469
Austria................................. 122	112	105	121	156	117	115	116	302	212	325	503	568	758	1,046
Belgium................................ 124	674	694	626	691	827	1,326	1,592	629	529	521	723	764	737	862
Cyprus................................. 423	160	136	192	239	49	382	288	3	3	10	49	1	3	200
Denmark............................... 128	136	137	201	269	299	346	233	218	181	232	295	305	383	459
Finland................................. 172	349	349	417	654	653	428	341	276	208	337	425	350	359	420
France.................................. 132	1,606	1,481	2,081	2,510	3,628	3,526	4,849	2,079	2,117	2,481	4,158	3,854	5,374	6,187
Germany............................... 134	4,297	4,059	4,444	6,241	6,309	6,563	5,942	3,835	3,960	4,857	5,671	5,955	6,829	8,132
Greece................................. 174	145	146	183	181	205	274	364	37	30	45	49	25	95	123
Ireland................................. 178	1,113	871	1,099	1,069	1,212	1,774	1,360	432	642	667	902	1,043	849	779
Italy..................................... 136	425	397	413	486	595	584	713	1,313	1,301	1,593	2,091	2,177	2,623	3,130
Luxembourg........................... 137	17	16	29	37	189	211	47	20	11	10	14	27	20	24
Malta.................................... 181	347	242	304	318	295	544	511	283	476	564	511	375	449	522
Netherlands........................... 138	4,035	4,303	4,616	5,437	5,480	5,435	5,730	1,144	1,302	1,091	1,644	1,805	2,063	2,938
Norway................................. 142	162	171	157	186	227	260	283	303	272	267	276	406	541	1,009
Portugal............................... 182	38	41	66	62	53	61	144	66	109	241	235	290	204	361
Slovenia............................... 961	5	7	4	13	13	16	30	3	4	5	7	8	11	15
Spain.................................... 184	402	373	392	461	409	577	398	380	304	337	338	386	499	607
Sweden................................. 144	80	113	79	94	127	230	166	517	532	677	784	783	924	1,114
Switzerland........................... 146	623	407	474	583	668	899	900	1,955	1,858	2,017	2,312	2,309	1,839	2,288
United Kingdom..................... 112	2,851	2,589	4,576	6,296	6,315	7,266	8,124	2,440	2,353	2,546	3,141	3,944	4,290	4,808
Developing Countries............ 202	**71,793**	**75,950**	**103,115**	**129,051**	**154,418**	**185,337**	**210,445**	**61,259**	**65,713**	**80,960**	**104,775**	**126,290**	**153,613**	**169,096**
Africa.................................. 607	**1,201**	**1,249**	**1,547**	**1,865**	**2,219**	**3,107**	**3,869**	**569**	**610**	**635**	**815**	**916**	**1,091**	**1,103**
Algeria................................. 612	8	4	5	16	13	26	44	—	—	—	28	—	—	22
Angola.................................. 614	37	35	51	57	64	94	102	—	65	1	—	46	21	8
Benin.................................... 638	12	14	15	26	57	93	56	—	—	—	—	—	—	—
Cameroon.............................. 622	6	10	18	21	15	19	20	—	1	—	32	1	1	3
Cape Verde............................ 624	—	—	2	1	1	—	—	—	—	—	—	—	—	—
Comoros............................... 632	1	2	2	4	3	3	5	7	3	2	6	4	3	3
Congo, Dem. Rep. of.............. 636	5	10	—	—	—	—	—	1	—	—	—	—	—	—
Côte d'Ivoire......................... 662	18	20	13	12	23	11	17	2	3	17	18	4	4	7
Djibouti................................ 611	9	12	16	13	10	13	9	—	—	—	—	—	—	1
Ethiopia............................... 644	4	3	8	7	9	8	16	2	2	1	1	2	—	3
Gabon.................................. 646	5	4	5	6	9	14	18	8	77	31	8	43	128	95
Ghana.................................. 652	18	31	37	42	40	48	61	2	4	6	5	9	31	53
Guinea................................. 656	8	8	9	10	9	10	20	—	—	—	—	—	1	1
Guinea-Bissau....................... 654	—	—	—	—	—	1	2	—	—	—	—	—	—	—
Kenya................................... 664	17	26	22	22	41	49	48	20	11	6	7	10	11	10
Liberia.................................. 668	333	372	483	539	743	977	1,771	—	—	—	—	2	—	2
Madagascar........................... 674	37	28	40	44	41	36	48	78	21	30	30	19	21	23
Mauritius.............................. 684	83	76	86	99	120	97	115	7	8	8	16	6	8	11
Morocco................................ 686	20	48	108	193	174	245	230	174	182	205	225	283	297	306
Mozambique.......................... 688	4	5	14	11	10	14	31	1	—	—	1	1	1	3
Nigeria................................. 694	244	239	234	170	166	183	254	1	24	12	40	2	4	6
Seychelles............................ 718	22	24	27	35	48	55	53	—	—	1	1	1	3	2
South Africa......................... 199	260	240	307	475	550	1,047	733	217	179	282	327	425	487	434
Sudan.................................. 732	23	15	22	31	41	29	27	11	12	11	38	16	17	24
Swaziland............................. 734	2	2	2	2	2	2	4	1	3	3	3	6	2	5
Tanzania............................... 738	10	9	11	13	13	19	28	19	4	9	13	7	4	4
Tunisia................................. 744	9	7	8	11	9	10	13	1	1	2	2	13	23	3
Zambia................................. 754	1	2	2	1	2	3	3	4	2	1	7	8	7	3
Zimbabwe............................. 698	3	2	2	3	7	4	4	11	8	6	6	8	18	15
Africa n.s............................. 799	—	—	—	—	—	—	136	—	—	—	—	—	—	56
Asia.................................... 507	**65,098**	**68,744**	**95,067**	**118,981**	**140,237**	**168,688**	**190,120**	**49,057**	**53,195**	**66,917**	**86,521**	**101,655**	**124,577**	**136,955**
Afghanistan, I.S. of............... 512	3	1	2	1	4	6	8	—	—	—	—	3	5	6
Bangladesh........................... 513	847	749	682	742	696	932	936	68	67	103	132	95	113	85
Brunei Darussalam................ 516	410	456	462	488	496	574	697	181	214	174	155	149	220	140
Cambodia............................. 522	370	352	307	348	303	460	438	55	84	75	48	100	111	84
China,P.R.: Mainland............ 924	5,329	6,863	10,134	15,392	19,752	26,514	28,927	7,195	8,869	11,073	16,211	20,526	27,243	31,890
China,P.R.:Hong Kong........... 532	10,820	11,475	14,423	17,647	21,570	27,571	31,335	2,785	2,842	3,092	3,652	4,209	4,102	3,855
China,P.R.:Macao................. 546	24	18	21	16	22	24	35	8	5	5	13	15	19	18
Fiji....................................... 819	58	122	173	259	363	417	433	1	1	1	2	5	4	6
French Polynesia.................. 887	15	14	15	109	253	275	256	2	1	1	—	2	1	—
Guam................................... 829	181	164	180	252	439	517	485	1	1	4	4	5	4	5
India.................................... 534	2,744	2,649	3,092	4,174	5,897	7,673	10,000	1,118	1,158	1,444	2,787	4,079	4,884	5,869

	Exports							Imports						
	2001	2002	2003	2004	2005	2006	2007	2001	2002	2003	2004	2005	2006	2007
	Millions of U.S. Dollars							*Millions of U.S. Dollars*						
Indonesia.......536	—	—	15,777	19,020	22,109	24,901	29,467	—	—	8,330	9,729	10,452	14,757	14,657
Korea.......542	4,688	5,208	6,058	7,387	8,053	8,736	10,609	3,823	4,303	4,960	6,936	8,599	10,477	12,814
Lao People's Dem.Rep.......544	26	26	20	38	40	41	39	—	—	—	1	1	1	1
Malaysia.......548	21,122	21,807	22,793	27,280	30,405	35,537	38,626	20,094	21,218	21,549	24,956	27,347	31,157	34,419
Maldives.......556	105	93	113	186	197	197	237	3	7	6	4	3	3	2
Mongolia.......948	12	12	13	17	19	25	39	—	—	—	—	—	—	—
Myanmar.......518	423	524	651	652	596	563	778	112	107	84	71	108	69	61
Nepal.......558	74	69	65	57	35	34	42	9	4	4	3	2	3	1
New Caledonia.......839	92	104	139	190	285	277	348	—	—	7	1	—	—	—
Pakistan.......564	365	393	456	557	647	771	846	49	57	44	48	37	46	53
Papua New Guinea.......853	194	204	253	316	246	270	313	22	20	63	41	40	20	25
Philippines.......566	3,085	3,039	3,236	3,916	4,185	5,080	6,130	2,555	2,503	2,827	4,215	4,650	5,650	5,811
Samoa.......862	1	1	10	22	38	39	51	—	—	—	—	—	—	—
Solomon Islands.......813	19	18	26	33	49	55	86	1	4	7	5	4	3	2
Sri Lanka.......524	396	382	485	592	681	922	836	33	50	52	74	59	53	70
Taiwan Province of China.......528	6,264	6,196	6,897	8,336	8,970	9,478	9,147	4,932	5,329	6,470	9,369	11,835	15,250	15,490
Thailand.......578	5,304	5,710	6,156	7,757	9,431	11,313	12,390	5,159	5,409	5,514	6,710	7,518	8,731	8,497
Vanuatu.......846	22	10	15	18	36	30	34	—	2	2	2	1	1	2
Vietnam.......582	2,105	2,082	2,412	3,179	4,421	5,459	6,517	850	938	1,024	1,352	1,814	1,650	2,140
Asia n.s.......598	—	—	—	—	—	—	32	—	—	—	—	—	—	948
Europe.......170	**605**	**986**	**1,121**	**1,443**	**1,579**	**1,871**	**2,272**	**794**	**857**	**1,153**	**1,532**	**1,763**	**2,144**	**2,706**
Belarus.......913	—	—	—	—	—	—	7	3	2	2	2	3	29	7
Bulgaria.......918	31	5	8	8	8	20	5	3	4	41	103	150	171	233
Croatia.......960	7	7	9	12	19	16	18	1	1	1	11	4	7	9
Czech Republic.......935	35	71	94	87	80	88	329	49	66	116	169	100	99	116
Hungary.......944	214	492	415	487	629	679	665	166	116	82	210	222	177	192
Kazakhstan.......916	3	5	8	12	18	18	27	—	4	—	—	—	2	2
Latvia.......941	2	1	2	5	29	24	7	—	26	1	64	44	112	92
Lithuania.......946	3	5	8	9	21	5	10	—	—	77	1	5	12	62
Poland.......964	46	66	145	183	110	137	188	21	21	46	48	87	145	101
Romania.......968	2	4	3	11	22	29	25	21	20	47	52	76	67	61
Russia.......922	133	174	250	375	387	459	501	291	318	276	323	399	734	752
Slovak Republic.......936	—	—	—	—	—	—	10	—	—	—	—	—	—	11
Turkey.......186	119	122	160	223	222	305	330	110	115	116	119	108	194	361
Ukraine.......926	9	34	17	30	34	89	81	127	165	347	430	565	396	544
Europe n.s.......884	—	—	—	—	—	—	67	—	—	—	—	—	—	164
Middle East.......407	**2,340**	**2,451**	**2,828**	**3,550**	**5,789**	**5,685**	**6,523**	**9,827**	**9,973**	**11,132**	**14,302**	**20,001**	**23,371**	**25,276**
Bahrain.......419	21	30	31	38	170	56	54	199	74	61	75	146	353	251
Egypt.......469	126	128	110	129	152	292	331	46	85	125	253	287	84	66
Iran, I.R. of.......429	251	320	395	534	494	456	534	571	598	754	1,026	1,283	1,747	1,345
Israel.......436	192	144	169	226	345	357	464	353	300	337	428	434	521	542
Jordan.......439	14	23	19	36	34	43	55	1	3	20	16	3	6	43
Kuwait.......443	67	67	89	77	102	121	249	1,361	1,746	2,113	3,159	3,687	4,508	5,087
Lebanon.......446	39	22	18	20	22	24	27	—	1	1	1	1	1	1
Libya.......672	16	18	22	22	30	24	39	2	5	19	—	—	—	23
Oman.......449	73	48	83	87	90	100	125	554	445	201	81	248	225	259
Qatar.......453	39	44	63	91	116	182	252	703	1,070	1,373	1,945	2,373	2,436	4,189
Saudi Arabia.......456	313	356	336	323	424	744	838	4,229	3,814	3,923	5,049	8,958	9,293	8,813
Syrian Arab Republic.......463	20	16	17	32	80	43	19	75	109	143	58	3	1	—
United Arab Emirates.......466	1,147	1,216	1,452	1,903	3,693	3,194	3,486	1,365	1,572	1,887	1,857	2,538	4,180	4,592
Yemen, Republic of.......474	24	20	23	33	39	50	51	367	152	176	355	41	15	62
Western Hemisphere.......207	**2,550**	**2,520**	**2,553**	**3,212**	**4,593**	**5,986**	**7,661**	**1,013**	**1,077**	**1,122**	**1,604**	**1,955**	**2,430**	**3,056**
Antigua and Barbuda.......311	44	31	49	99	114	133	195	—	—	—	—	12	—	—
Argentina.......213	66	19	36	158	69	77	125	25	20	14	19	23	44	43
Bahamas, The.......313	164	145	154	162	250	296	477	—	36	45	26	25	59	398
Bermuda.......319	21	20	17	21	28	60	96	25	5	1	—	—	—	—
Brazil.......223	262	274	235	366	847	1,273	1,257	276	415	321	601	713	714	864
Chile.......228	35	29	19	26	38	34	88	29	40	70	81	105	159	154
Colombia.......233	24	27	28	24	26	49	56	13	9	11	27	49	127	42
Costa Rica.......238	8	7	6	13	19	22	18	20	18	75	162	176	214	230
Dominican Republic.......243	42	4	3	5	7	11	11	1	2	1	2	12	21	20
Ecuador.......248	5	5	4	4	8	9	15	17	4	4	5	5	10	6
El Salvador.......253	2	3	4	4	6	5	5	1	13	12	10	9	16	17
Guatemala.......258	7	6	14	21	31	4	6	13	24	10	6	4	4	8
Guyana.......336	1	1	1	1	2	4	5	—	—	—	—	1	—	—
Honduras.......268	45	63	7	7	8	10	6	—	—	—	—	—	1	—
Jamaica.......343	4	5	6	11	54	38	43	1	1	—	1	1	1	4
Mexico.......273	736	745	719	837	971	1,009	1,088	352	331	289	447	451	519	503
Netherlands Antilles.......353	11	8	6	14	14	22	22	120	80	187	80	65	206	295
Panama.......283	973	1,049	1,156	1,299	1,908	2,696	3,847	3	10	5	11	44	2	5
Paraguay.......288	6	7	9	15	8	4	3	—	—	1	—	—	1	—
Peru.......293	14	15	11	21	21	15	25	2	12	4	12	5	29	12
St. Vincent & Grens.......364	34	36	45	45	79	91	84	—	—	—	—	—	—	—
Trinidad and Tobago.......369	3	3	10	35	54	78	67	5	13	5	6	1	3	—
Uruguay.......298	10	5	5	10	8	7	7	8	11	5	12	15	18	15
Venezuela, Rep. Bol.......299	31	13	7	13	24	39	41	99	34	61	96	237	281	363
Western Hem. n.s.......399	—	—	—	—	—	—	75	—	—	—	—	—	—	74

	Exports							Imports						
	2001	2002	2003	2004	2005	2006	2007	2001	2002	2003	2004	2005	2006	2007
	Millions of U.S. Dollars							*Millions of U.S. Dollars*						
Other Countries n.i.e.................910	**114**	**85**	**61**	**57**	**75**	**71**	**62**	**5**	**8**	**3**	**4**	**9**	**10**	**5**
Cuba..928	1	2	1	2	2	11	8	2	8	1	2	2	3	4
North Korea................................954	112	84	60	55	73	60	55	3	1	1	2	7	7	1
Countries & Areas n.s...............898	**163**	**214**	**309**	**415**	**495**	**467**	**71**	**266**	**246**	**183**	**733**	**1,755**	**1,035**	**76**
Memorandum Items														
European Union...........................998	17,089	16,695	20,507	25,984	27,647	30,590	32,158	14,212	14,503	16,861	22,030	23,119	27,015	32,300
Oil Exporting Ctys.......................999	2,188	2,325	18,463	22,255	27,260	29,969	35,328	8,885	9,307	18,675	23,011	29,778	37,432	39,358
Non-Oil Develop.Ctys..................201	69,606	73,625	84,652	106,796	127,157	155,368	175,116	52,374	56,406	62,285	81,764	96,511	116,182	129,738
PERCENT DISTRIBUTION														
Industrial Countries.................. 101	**40.8**	**39.0**	**35.3**	**34.7**	**32.3**	**31.5**	**29.4**	**47.0**	**43.4**	**40.5**	**38.9**	**36.0**	**35.2**	**35.8**
Developing Countries.............. 202	**58.9**	**60.7**	**64.4**	**64.9**	**67.3**	**68.1**	**70.3**	**52.8**	**56.4**	**59.4**	**60.7**	**63.1**	**64.3**	**64.2**
Africa.......................................607	**1.0**	**1.0**	**1.0**	**.9**	**1.0**	**1.1**	**1.3**	**.5**	**.5**	**.5**	**.5**	**.5**	**.5**	**.4**
Asia.. 507	**53.4**	**54.9**	**59.4**	**59.9**	**61.1**	**62.0**	**63.5**	**42.3**	**45.7**	**49.1**	**50.1**	**50.8**	**52.2**	**52.0**
Europe...................................170	**.5**	**.8**	**.7**	**.7**	**.7**	**.7**	**.8**	**.7**	**.7**	**.8**	**.9**	**.9**	**.9**	**1.0**
Middle East............................ 407	**1.9**	**2.0**	**1.8**	**1.8**	**2.5**	**2.1**	**2.2**	**8.5**	**8.6**	**8.2**	**8.3**	**10.0**	**9.8**	**9.6**
Western Hemisphere.............207	**2.1**	**2.0**	**1.6**	**1.6**	**2.0**	**2.2**	**2.6**	**.9**	**.9**	**.8**	**.9**	**1.0**	**1.0**	**1.2**
Other Countries n.i.e...............910	**.1**	**.1**	**—**	**—**	**—**	**—**	**—**	**—**	**—**	**—**	**—**	**—**	**—**	**—**
ANNUAL PERCENT CHANGE														
World....................................... 001	**–11.7**	**2.8**	**27.8**	**24.1**	**15.5**	**18.6**	**10.0**	**–13.8**	**.4**	**17.0**	**26.7**	**15.9**	**19.3**	**10.3**
Industrial Countries.................. 101	**–14.6**	**–1.6**	**15.5**	**22.2**	**7.6**	**15.5**	**2.6**	**–15.7**	**–7.3**	**9.2**	**21.8**	**7.4**	**16.6**	**11.9**
Developing Countries.............. 202	**–9.8**	**5.8**	**35.8**	**25.2**	**19.7**	**20.0**	**13.5**	**–11.7**	**7.3**	**23.2**	**29.4**	**20.5**	**21.6**	**10.1**
Africa.......................................607	**–23.1**	**4.1**	**23.9**	**20.5**	**19.0**	**40.0**	**24.5**	**4.6**	**7.2**	**4.0**	**28.5**	**12.3**	**19.1**	**1.1**
Asia.. 507	**–10.3**	**5.6**	**38.3**	**25.2**	**17.9**	**20.3**	**12.7**	**–12.4**	**8.4**	**25.8**	**29.3**	**17.5**	**22.5**	**9.9**
Europe...................................170	**1.6**	**63.0**	**13.7**	**28.7**	**9.4**	**18.5**	**21.5**	**–9.4**	**8.0**	**34.6**	**32.9**	**15.1**	**21.6**	**26.3**
Middle East............................ 407	**5.7**	**4.8**	**15.4**	**25.5**	**63.1**	**–1.8**	**14.7**	**–10.6**	**1.5**	**11.6**	**28.5**	**39.9**	**16.8**	**8.1**
Western Hemisphere.............207	**–3.5**	**–1.2**	**1.3**	**25.8**	**43.0**	**30.3**	**28.0**	**5.2**	**6.3**	**4.2**	**43.0**	**21.8**	**24.3**	**25.7**
Other Countries n.i.e...............910	**123.1**	**–25.0**	**–28.0**	**–7.6**	**32.5**	**–6.2**	**–11.7**	**–14.4**	**82.3**	**–69.3**	**42.6**	**148.9**	**6.8**	**–50.4**

	Exports							Imports						
	2001	2002	2003	2004	2005	2006	2007	2001	2002	2003	2004	2005	2006	2007
	Millions of U.S. Dollars							*Millions of U.S. Dollars*						
IFS World Total	**12,641**	**14,478**	**21,966**	**27,605**	**31,997**	**41,939**	**57,770**	**15,501**	**17,460**	**23,760**	**30,469**	**36,168**	**47,309**	**62,139**
DOTS World Total 001	**12,645**	**14,366**	**20,427Y**	**24,908Y**	**31,794**	**41,957**	**58,320**	**16,258**	**18,146**	**23,397Y**	**29,469Y**	**34,531**	**44,938**	**60,408**
Industrial Countries 101	**8,149**	**9,470**	**14,279Y**	**16,853Y**	**20,080**	**26,572**	**36,935**	**9,040**	**10,329**	**13,324Y**	**15,697Y**	**17,585**	**21,600**	**28,593**
United States 111	162	207	944V	1,129V	993	1,336	1,447	314	387	127V	145V	270	282	538
Canada 156	16	23	100V	88V	63	111	119	21	22	12V	26V	17	30	79
Australia 193	10	11	12V	16V	33	78	95	16	15	6V	3V	6	14	13
Japan 158	11	145	67V	115V	88	111	129	261	337	71V	117V	365	556	655
New Zealand 196	1	1	3V	4V	7	14	15	3	3	—V	—V	—	1	1
Austria 122	1,027	1,104	1,974V	2,056V	2,268	2,532	3,376	674	764	1,544V	1,932V	2,158	2,492	3,089
Belgium 124	304	298	263V	352V	630	777	1,239	271	328	484V	722V	656	784	1,047
Cyprus 423	12	4	6V	6V	59	40	47	3	4	4V	7V	12	14	74
Denmark 128	60	105	103V	143V	224	364	567	75	86	113V	122V	148	230	280
Finland 172	49	69	53V	93V	226	457	377	98	121	112V	99V	125	149	171
France 132	499	600	501V	575V	1,228	1,809	3,925	627	800	812V	888V	1,096	1,410	2,375
Germany 134	3,424	3,732	7,499V	8,610V	8,216	9,811	12,461	4,009	4,105	6,418V	7,638V	8,351	10,314	13,324
Greece 174	81	48	68V	79V	118	230	364	27	30	28V	36V	42	77	108
Iceland 176	1	1	3V	4V	7	6	9	1	3	—V	—V	—	2	2
Ireland 178	15	18	17V	18V	56	96	140	57	62	51V	50V	76	119	133
Italy 136	1,125	1,548	1,090V	1,511V	2,116	2,735	3,712	1,037	1,250	1,314V	1,503V	1,555	1,960	2,367
Luxembourg 137	40	17	29V	8V	38	41	41	4	7	11V	30V	46	70	140
Malta 181	7	1	1V	1V	2	1	3	1	1	1V	1V	1	1	6
Netherlands 138	356	437	297V	621V	1,088	1,778	2,078	239	319	514V	636V	829	1,012	1,337
Norway 142	30	48	44V	70V	60	83	154	25	24	26V	38V	31	49	60
Portugal 182	28	28	29V	34V	54	78	196	32	57	33V	39V	44	69	96
Slovenia 961	123	146	168V	220Y	302	363	467	98	153	202V	266Y	229	246	382
Spain 184	155	233	280V	287V	645	1,197	1,817	391	570	591V	440V	478	540	768
Sweden 144	104	123	130V	180V	335	577	879	131	172	188V	264V	295	343	488
Switzerland 146	198	182	209V	221V	254	318	484	210	249	234V	262V	215	237	343
United Kingdom 112	311	341	389V	413V	970	1,628	2,796	413	460	427V	431V	540	599	719
Developing Countries 202	**4,476**	**4,883**	**6,130Y**	**8,031Y**	**11,679**	**15,346**	**21,312**	**7,076**	**7,668**	**9,884Y**	**13,523Y**	**16,936**	**23,326**	**31,790**
Africa 607	**32**	**35**	**50Y**	**92Y**	**154**	**201**	**218**	**41**	**40**	**36Y**	**42Y**	**44**	**67**	**60**
Algeria 612	2	4	4Y	5Y	15	36	20	—	—	—Y	—Y	—	—	—
Angola 614	4	1	1Y	1Y	5	8	9	—	—	—Y	—Y	—	—	—
Benin 638	—	1	1Y	—V	—	1	—	—	—	—Y	—V	—	—	—
Burundi 618	—	—	—V	—V	—	—	1	—	—	—Y	—Y	—	—	—
Cameroon 622	—	—	1V	1Y	—	—	—	1	—	—Y	1Y	—	—	—
Central African Rep. 626	—	—	—Y	—Y	2	1	1	—	—	—Y	—Y	—	—	—
Congo, Dem. Rep. of 636	—	—	—Y	—Y	—	1	—	—	—	—Y	—Y	—	—	—
Congo, Republic of 634	1	—	—V	—V	1	—	—	—	—	—Y	—Y	—	—	—
Côte d'Ivoire 662	—	—	—Y	—Y	1	2	2	12	20	25Y	33Y	17	7	—
Ethiopia 644	—	—	—Y	—Y	9	7	3	—	1	1Y	1Y	—	1	1
Gabon 646	—	—	—Y	—Y	1	1	1	—	—	—Y	—Y	—	—	—
Gambia, The 648	—	—	—Y	—Y	—	—	1	—	—	—Y	—Y	—	—	—
Ghana 652	1	1	2Y	2Y	3	3	7	—	—	—Y	—Y	—	—	—
Kenya 664	—	—	1V	1V	2	3	3	—	—	—V	—V	—	1	1
Madagascar 674	—	—	—Y	—Y	—	—	1	—	—	—Y	—Y	—	—	—
Malawi 676	—	—	—Y	—Y	—	—	—	—	1	1Y	1Y	—	—	—
Mauritania 682	—	—	—Y	—Y	1	—	—	—	—	—Y	—Y	—	—	—
Mauritius 684	—	—	—V	—V	—	—	1	—	—	—V	—V	—	—	—
Morocco 686	3	6	7V	11V	30	25	35	5	8	3V	2V	17	28	36
Mozambique 688	—	—	—Y	—Y	1	1	1	—	—	—Y	—Y	—	—	—
Nigeria 694	8	3	4Y	5Y	11	15	9	—	—	—Y	—Y	—	—	—
Senegal 722	—	—	—V	—V	3	1	3	—	—	—V	—V	—	—	—
Seychelles 718	—	—	—Y	—Y	1	—	—	—	—	—Y	—Y	—	—	—
South Africa 199	5	6	23V	58V	53	71	98	17	6	2V	1V	1	12	18
Sudan 732	1	1	1Y	2Y	1	3	4	—	—	—Y	—Y	—	—	—
Tanzania 738	—	—	1Y	1Y	1	—	—	—	—	—Y	—Y	3	14	1
Tunisia 744	4	5	2V	4V	9	19	14	2	2	—V	—V	4	4	2
Uganda 746	—	2	—V	—Y	2	1	2	—	—	—V	—Y	—	—	—
Zambia 754	—	3	—V	—V	—	—	—	—	—	—V	—V	—	—	—
Zimbabwe 698	—	—	—V	—V	1	—	—	1	1	2V	—V	—	—	—
Asia 507	**108**	**130**	**169Y**	**219Y**	**371**	**522**	**828**	**681**	**904**	**426Y**	**863Y**	**1,908**	**3,633**	**6,906**
Afghanistan, I.S. of 512	1	1	1Y	1Y	—	31	46	—	—	—Y	—Y	—	—	—
Bangladesh 513	2	2	—V	—V	1	2	3	1	3	—V	1V	2	12	35
Brunei Darussalam 516	—	—	—Y	—Y	2	1	2	—	—	—Y	—Y	6	—	—
Cambodia 522	—	—	—V	—V	1	—	—	—	—	—V	—V	—	—	2
China,P.R.: Mainland 924	13	40	111V	115V	127	221	444	256	378	151V	175V	502	937	2,169
China,P.R.:Hong Kong 532	7	7	9V	10V	37	50	32	18	22	27V	49V	23	28	37
China,P.R.:Macao 546	—	—	—V	—V	—	—	—	—	—	—V	—V	2	3	1
India 534	43	30	10V	18V	39	26	58	30	43	17V	23V	40	50	89
Indonesia 536	4	2	1V	2V	5	4	5	35	48	2V	29V	78	74	93
Korea 542	5	10	16V	21V	30	56	56	44	60	121V	392V	771	1,518	2,867

	Exports 2001	2002	2003	2004	2005	2006	2007	Imports 2001	2002	2003	2004	2005	2006	2007
	Millions of U.S. Dollars							Millions of U.S. Dollars						
Malaysia 548	3	7	2V	15V	34	18	29	79	90	17V	25V	82	138	182
Mongolia 948	—	—	—V	—V	1	1	1	—	—	—V	—V	—	—	—
Myanmar 518	5	1	1Y	1Y	—	—	—	—	—	—Y	1Y	—	—	—
Nepal 558	—	—	—V	1V	—	—	—	—	—	—Y	—Y	—	—	—
New Caledonia 839	—	—	—V	1V	2	2	2	—	—	—Y	—Y	—	—	—
Pakistan 564	1	1	1V	2V	13	4	12	6	10	2V	2V	2	8	13
Philippines 566	1	1	1V	2V	11	39	52	10	16	—V	—V	5	10	16
Singapore 576	11	14	—V	—V	21	22	28	27	28	—V	—V	23	42	53
Sri Lanka 524	1	6	—V	—V	3	1	2	2	2	—V	—V	1	2	10
Taiwan Province of China 528	3	3	14V	27V	30	28	35	129	145	27V	86V	321	736	1,121
Thailand 578	6	4	—Y	—Y	13	13	17	25	41	52Y	69Y	36	59	132
Vietnam 582	1	2	1V	3V	3	3	3	17	18	9V	9V	12	16	89
Europe 170	**4,220**	**4,623**	**5,783Y**	**7,512Y**	**10,816**	**14,172**	**19,721**	**6,237**	**6,591**	**9,340Y**	**12,496Y**	**14,885**	**19,526**	**24,715**
Albania 914	—	—	1V	3V	6	4	4	—	—	—V	—V	—	—	—
Armenia 911	1	3	4V	3V	5	4	7	—	—	—V	—V	—	—	—
Azerbaijan 912	1	—	—V	1V	5	14	14	—	—	1V	1V	—	—	—
Belarus 913	11	13	23V	39V	40	64	104	30	19	25V	52V	51	71	77
Bosnia & Herzegovina 963	15	27	34Y	45Y	52	50	76	1	2	3Y	4Y	5	7	8
Bulgaria 918	34	40	64V	96V	95	125	225	10	12	19V	42V	43	76	96
Croatia 960	65	90	128V	134V	129	198	224	20	22	25V	29V	61	98	66
Czech Republic 935	2,101	2,184	2,656V	3,419V	4,512	5,763	7,339	2,449	2,749	4,277V	6,261V	6,763	8,105	10,426
Estonia 939	5	6	21V	14V	28	22	44	3	3	6V	6V	11	8	11
Georgia 915	—	—	1V	1V	6	3	4	—	—	—V	3V	4	1	2
Gibraltar 823	—	—	—Y	—Y	1	—	—	—	—	—Y	—Y	—	—	—
Hungary 944	680	784	844V	1,072V	1,883	2,563	3,474	415	496	927V	1,150V	1,580	2,719	4,041
Kazakhstan 916	15	14	20V	22V	31	50	76	17	18	84V	116V	10	18	38
Kosovo 967	—	—	—Y	—Y	—	1	1	—	—	—Y	—Y	—	—	1
Kyrgyz Republic 917	—	—	—V	1V	1	2	6	—	1	1V	1V	—	—	—
Latvia 941	22	25	31V	46V	57	86	147	9	8	10V	11V	11	28	27
Lithuania 946	26	40	37V	42V	73	112	157	5	9	11V	13V	19	22	35
Macedonia, FYR 962	5	4	5V	8V	13	16	23	2	1	1V	4V	5	5	8
Moldova 921	13	13	8V	10V	19	21	26	1	2	1V	2V	21	27	25
Montenegro, Rep. of 943	—	—	—Y	—Y	—	3	5	—	—	—Y	—Y	—	—	—
Poland 964	736	767	949V	1,321V	2,000	2,611	3,627	527	584	960V	1,450V	1,632	2,209	2,980
Romania 968	124	146	220V	305V	501	640	1,047	35	48	52V	86V	127	237	274
Russia 922	130	143	267V	368V	491	688	1,322	2,399	2,277	2,525V	2,668V	3,694	5,037	5,535
Serbia, Rep. of 942	—	—	—Y	—Y	—	158	308	—	—	—Y	—Y	—	45	104
Serbia & Montenegro 965	36	72	92Y	120Y	133	—	—	15	16	20Y	27Y	39	—	—
Tajikistan 923	—	—	—V	—V	—	6	1	7	24	—V	5V	1	—	—
Turkey 186	47	87	187V	212V	307	407	660	72	87	66V	119V	147	191	301
Turkmenistan 925	—	1	—V	—Y	4	1	1	1	—	2V	2Y	148	53	—
Ukraine 926	146	156	182V	221V	411	547	791	214	206	318V	438V	515	563	653
Uzbekistan 927	6	4	6Y	7Y	11	12	11	5	4	6Y	7Y	—	5	7
Europe n.s. 884	—	1	1Y	1Y	—	—	—	—	—	—Y	—Y	—	—	—
Middle East 407	**80**	**71**	**91Y**	**152Y**	**236**	**298**	**317**	**24**	**27**	**23Y**	**27Y**	**34**	**33**	**40**
Bahrain 419	—	—	—Y	1Y	2	5	5	—	—	—Y	—Y	—	—	—
Egypt 469	31	14	18Y	23Y	30	34	56	2	2	3Y	4Y	5	4	6
Iran, I.R. of 429	4	3	3Y	4Y	8	6	10	3	5	6Y	8Y	12	4	5
Iraq 433	1	—	—Y	1Y	8	3	7	—	—	—Y	—Y	—	—	—
Israel 436	7	9	13V	10V	28	27	32	16	16	11V	12V	14	19	23
Jordan 439	2	1	2V	1V	8	12	3	1	1	—V	1V	1	2	3
Kuwait 443	1	1	1Y	1Y	15	27	20	—	—	—Y	—Y	—	—	—
Lebanon 446	7	11	14Y	19Y	11	10	10	—	—	—Y	—Y	—	—	—
Libya 672	3	5	5Y	7Y	1	2	3	—	—	—Y	—Y	—	—	1
Oman 449	1	1	1V	1Y	7	11	8	—	—	—V	—Y	—	—	—
Qatar 453	—	—	2V	2V	5	9	6	—	—	—V	—V	—	—	—
Saudi Arabia 456	2	5	8V	24V	31	38	37	—	1	2Y	2Y	—	—	—
Syrian Arab Republic 463	7	5	7Y	38V	7	10	9	—	—	1Y	—V	—	1	—
United Arab Emirates 466	11	13	15Y	19Y	74	102	110	1	1	1Y	1Y	2	2	2
Yemen, Republic of 474	3	2	3Y	2V	2	1	1	—	—	—Y	—V	—	—	—
Western Hemisphere 207	**37**	**23**	**37Y**	**56Y**	**102**	**153**	**229**	**93**	**106**	**59Y**	**95Y**	**65**	**67**	**69**
Argentina 213	9	1	7V	11V	6	14	16	5	9	1V	—V	3	3	5
Brazil 223	3	4	13V	22V	25	35	65	26	48	25V	42V	39	40	40
Chile 228	1	1	2V	4V	3	5	5	1	1	—V	—V	—	—	—
Colombia 233	3	2	4V	3V	3	5	7	5	9	1V	—V	3	2	2
Costa Rica 238	1	2	—V	1V	4	4	2	3	8	—V	—V	—	—	1
Dominican Republic 243	—	—	—Y	—Y	5	5	5	—	—	1Y	1Y	—	—	—
Ecuador 248	2	1	—V	—V	2	2	—	11	4	—V	—V	1	—	1
El Salvador 253	1	—	—V	—V	—	—	—	1	—	—V	—V	—	—	—
Guatemala 258	—	1	1V	2V	1	3	2	—	—	—V	1V	—	—	—
Guyana 336	—	—	—Y	—Y	1	—	1	—	—	—Y	—Y	—	—	—
Honduras 268	—	—	—V	—V	1	1	1	2	1	—V	—V	—	—	—
Jamaica 343	—	—	—V	—V	—	—	1	—	—	9V	22V	—	—	—
Mexico 273	7	6	7Y	10Y	37	61	84	21	11	13Y	18Y	14	19	17
Panama 283	2	1	—V	—V	1	1	1	7	6	8Y	11Y	—	—	—
Paraguay 288	1	—	—V	—V	—	—	6	—	—	—V	—V	—	—	—
Peru 293	1	1	—V	—V	4	3	1	10	6	—V	—V	—	—	1

	Exports 2001	2002	2003	2004	2005	2006	2007	Imports 2001	2002	2003	2004	2005	2006	2007
	Millions of U.S. Dollars							Millions of U.S. Dollars						
Trinidad and Tobago.................... 369	1	1	1Y	1Y	2	1	2	—	—	—Y	—Y	—	—	—
Uruguay...................................... 298	—	—	—V	—V	1	—	1	1	1	—V	—V	—	—	—
Venezuela, Rep. Bol...................... 299	3	1	—V	1V	5	8	25	1	1	—V	—V	3	—	—
Western Hem. n.s......................... 399	1	1	—Y	—Y	1	3	1	—	—	—Y	—Y	—	—	—
Other Countries n.i.e................ 910	**2**	**—**	**1Y**	**1Y**	**18**	**9**	**27**	**1**	**1**	**2Y**	**2Y**	**—**	**1**	**1**
Cuba.. 928	1	—	—Y	1Y	14	8	27	—	—	1Y	1Y	—	1	1
North Korea.................................. 954	—	—	—Y	—Y	5	1	—	—	1	1Y	2Y	—	—	—
Countries & Areas n.s.............. 898	**18**	**14**	**17Y**	**23Y**	**10**	**24**	**39**	**11**	**10**	**13Y**	**17Y**	**9**	**12**	**24**
Special Categories.................. 899	**—**	**—**	**—Y**	**—Y**	**4**	**6**	**5**	**131**	**137**	**174Y**	**228Y**	**—**	**—**	**—**
Memorandum Items														
European Union........................... 998	11,288	12,657	17,436Y	21,120Y	27,128	35,673	49,271	11,597	13,139	19,037Y	23,997Y	26,698	33,521	44,421
Oil Exporting Ctys........................ 999	39	38	43Y	72Y	183	262	262	40	56	11Y	41Y	95	81	102
Non-Oil Develop.Ctys.................... 201	4,437	4,845	6,087Y	7,959Y	11,496	15,085	21,051	7,036	7,612	9,873Y	13,482Y	16,841	23,245	31,688
PERCENT DISTRIBUTION														
Industrial Countries................. 101	**64.4**	**65.9**	**69.9**	**67.7**	**63.2**	**63.3**	**63.3**	**55.6**	**56.9**	**56.9**	**53.3**	**50.9**	**48.1**	**47.3**
Developing Countries.............. 202	**35.4**	**34.0**	**30.0**	**32.2**	**36.7**	**36.6**	**36.5**	**43.5**	**42.3**	**42.2**	**45.9**	**49.0**	**51.9**	**52.6**
Africa...................................... 607	**.3**	**.2**	**.2**	**.4**	**.5**	**.5**	**.4**	**.3**	**.2**	**.2**	**.1**	**.1**	**.1**	**.1**
Asia.. 507	**.9**	**.9**	**.8**	**.9**	**1.2**	**1.2**	**1.4**	**4.2**	**5.0**	**1.8**	**2.9**	**5.5**	**8.1**	**11.4**
Europe.................................... 170	**33.4**	**32.2**	**28.3**	**30.2**	**34.0**	**33.8**	**33.8**	**38.4**	**36.3**	**39.9**	**42.4**	**43.1**	**43.5**	**40.9**
Middle East........................... 407	**.6**	**.5**	**.4**	**.6**	**.7**	**.7**	**.5**	**.1**	**.1**	**.1**	**.1**	**.1**	**.1**	**.1**
Western Hemisphere............. 207	**.3**	**.2**	**.2**	**.2**	**.3**	**.4**	**.4**	**.6**	**.6**	**.3**	**.3**	**.2**	**.1**	**.1**
Other Countries n.i.e................ 910	**—**	**—**	**—**	**—**	**.1**	**—**	**—**	**—**	**—**	**—**	**—**	**—**	**—**	**—**
ANNUAL PERCENT CHANGE														
World....................................... 001	**6.5**	**13.6**	**42.2**	**21.9**	**27.6**	**32.0**	**39.0**	**15.7**	**11.6**	**28.9**	**26.0**	**17.2**	**30.1**	**34.4**
Industrial Countries................. 101	**7.3**	**16.2**	**50.8**	**18.0**	**19.1**	**32.3**	**39.0**	**17.0**	**14.3**	**29.0**	**17.8**	**12.0**	**22.8**	**32.4**
Developing Countries.............. 202	**5.2**	**9.1**	**25.5**	**31.0**	**45.4**	**31.4**	**38.9**	**13.8**	**8.4**	**28.9**	**36.8**	**25.2**	**37.7**	**36.3**
Africa...................................... 607	**–3.2**	**9.7**	**41.3**	**85.3**	**67.5**	**30.6**	**8.1**	**3.5**	**–1.2**	**–10.1**	**15.3**	**4.0**	**54.7**	**–11.3**
Asia.. 507	**–22.3**	**21.2**	**29.7**	**29.8**	**69.3**	**40.6**	**58.6**	**32.4**	**32.7**	**–52.9**	**102.7**	**121.1**	**90.4**	**90.1**
Europe.................................... 170	**6.7**	**9.5**	**25.1**	**29.9**	**44.0**	**31.0**	**39.2**	**12.1**	**5.7**	**41.7**	**33.8**	**19.1**	**31.2**	**26.6**
Middle East........................... 407	**–.4**	**–10.6**	**27.5**	**67.0**	**55.4**	**26.1**	**6.4**	**10.3**	**10.3**	**–11.9**	**17.3**	**25.1**	**–5.2**	**23.8**
Western Hemisphere............. 207	**–24.9**	**–37.6**	**62.6**	**48.0**	**82.9**	**50.6**	**49.5**	**24.1**	**14.2**	**–44.2**	**61.3**	**–31.5**	**2.1**	**4.4**
Other Countries n.i.e................ 910	**–66.6**	**–73.3**	**26.6**	**31.3**	**—**	**–51.0**	**203.0**	**–42.1**	**110.4**	**26.6**	**31.3**	**–80.1**	**18.0**	**32.6**

	Exports 2001	Exports 2002	Exports 2003	Exports 2004	Exports 2005	Exports 2006	Exports 2007	Imports 2001	Imports 2002	Imports 2003	Imports 2004	Imports 2005	Imports 2006	Imports 2007
	Millions of U.S. Dollars							*Millions of U.S. Dollars*						
IFS World Total	**9,252**	**10,357**	**12,767**	**15,879**	**17,896**	**20,985**	**26,553**	**10,148**	**10,932**	**13,853**	**17,571**	**19,626**	**23,014**	**29,481**
DOTS World Total........001	**9,190**	**10,357**	**12,728**	**14,606Y**	**19,159**	**23,151**	**30,017**	**10,125**	**10,932**	**13,851**	**18,532Y**	**20,286**	**24,174**	**31,619**
Industrial Countries........101	**6,174**	**6,695**	**8,201**	**9,228Y**	**11,779**	**13,955**	**17,202**	**7,531**	**8,127**	**10,182**	**14,591Y**	**14,780**	**17,195**	**21,156**
United States........111	246	285	465	484V	371	507	461	297	314	335	211V	185	249	385
Canada........156	19	26	24	42V	33	46	60	40	35	52	39V	54	41	87
Australia........193	20	24	31	39V	36	41	42	12	9	16	9V	12	12	14
Japan........158	12	15	18	35V	24	28	34	145	143	203	130V	155	91	128
New Zealand........196	2	2	3	5V	5	5	6	3	2	3	2V	3	3	4
Austria........122	693	731	935	1,675V	1,511	1,959	2,237	843	903	1,193	2,743V	2,424	2,824	3,695
Belgium........124	100	91	106	140V	216	257	262	157	161	192	409V	417	522	680
Cyprus........423	3	3	2	13V	7	5	13	1	1	1	1V	11	6	7
Denmark........128	87	91	115	132V	183	223	262	56	64	76	94V	88	103	112
Finland........172	27	25	30	46V	49	67	86	55	68	85	54V	59	91	114
France........132	626	690	722	1,085V	1,520	1,449	1,781	1,078	1,118	1,390	1,877V	1,439	1,416	1,582
Germany........134	2,426	2,561	2,948	2,663V	3,714	4,445	5,620	1,948	2,094	2,670	3,660V	3,927	4,712	5,734
Greece........174	29	34	45	51V	74	76	99	32	49	43	68V	53	264	233
Iceland........176	1	1	1	6V	3	9	8	—	—	—	—V	—	—	1
Ireland........178	13	13	19	14V	26	32	39	37	37	56	36V	44	50	58
Italy........136	1,154	1,251	1,674	1,839V	2,378	2,891	3,755	1,789	1,957	2,535	3,408V	3,743	4,302	5,400
Luxembourg........137	3	7	30	9V	60	70	65	22	27	37	48V	70	71	87
Malta........181	2	1	1	2V	1	4	6	5	2	2	2V	—	—	1
Netherlands........138	154	173	223	148V	261	305	461	197	226	291	568V	710	867	1,047
Norway........142	17	21	25	52V	35	44	67	18	14	22	16V	16	11	17
Portugal........182	15	21	22	20V	63	75	87	15	17	25	22V	50	46	51
Spain........184	90	110	187	159V	328	415	509	264	335	282	453V	611	625	725
Sweden........144	73	92	118	138V	192	210	250	103	110	154	164V	157	183	227
Switzerland........146	102	174	174	163V	240	199	266	153	177	228	263V	258	324	291
United Kingdom........112	259	254	284	267V	446	592	728	260	263	290	310V	293	380	477
Developing Countries........202	**3,013**	**3,661**	**4,526**	**5,377Y**	**7,366**	**9,187**	**12,803**	**2,590**	**2,802**	**3,665**	**3,935Y**	**5,503**	**6,973**	**10,374**
Africa........607	**36**	**38**	**41**	**68Y**	**161**	**208**	**216**	**104**	**89**	**116**	**117Y**	**165**	**175**	**186**
Algeria........612	10	7	9	12Y	62	107	125	72	51	55	73Y	105	115	116
Angola........614	—	—	—	—Y	—	—	1	—	—	—	—Y	—	—	—
Benin........638	—	—	—	—V	—	—	—	1	1	—	—V	—	1	—
Burkina Faso........748	—	—	—	—Y	—	—	—	—	—	1	1Y	—	1	1
Cameroon........622	—	—	1	1Y	—	—	—	3	4	5	7Y	8	14	4
Central African Rep........626	—	—	—	—Y	—	—	—	—	—	—	—Y	—	—	1
Chad........628	—	—	—	—Y	—	—	—	2	—	1	1Y	—	—	—
Côte d'Ivoire........662	1	1	1	1Y	—	—	—	3	1	1	1Y	1	—	5
Djibouti........611	1	1	—	—Y	1	1	1	—	—	—	—Y	—	—	—
Ethiopia........644	1	—	2	3Y	5	1	1	—	—	—	—Y	—	—	—
Gabon........646	—	—	—	—Y	—	1	—	—	—	—	—Y	—	—	—
Ghana........652	1	1	2	2Y	2	3	4	—	—	—	1Y	—	—	—
Guinea........656	2	3	4	6Y	—	—	—	4	—	—	—Y	—	—	—
Kenya........664	—	2	1	—V	—	2	1	—	—	—	—V	—	—	—
Liberia........668	—	—	—	—Y	—	—	—	—	1	2	3Y	1	4	6
Madagascar........674	—	—	—	—Y	—	—	—	—	—	—	—Y	—	—	2
Malawi........676	—	—	—	—Y	—	—	—	1	1	1	1Y	—	—	—
Mali........678	—	—	—	—Y	—	—	—	—	1	1	2Y	1	—	2
Mauritius........684	—	—	—	—V	1	1	1	—	1	1	—V	—	—	—
Morocco........686	2	2	2	6V	8	10	17	3	4	5	2V	13	10	11
Nigeria........694	2	4	3	4Y	3	4	4	—	—	—	—Y	—	—	—
Seychelles........718	—	—	—	—Y	2	1	1	—	—	—	—Y	1	—	—
Sierra Leone........724	—	2	2	3Y	—	—	—	—	—	—	—Y	—	—	—
South Africa........199	8	8	9	12Y	45	42	34	7	10	14	18Y	15	19	28
Sudan........732	—	—	1	1Y	6	4	2	—	—	—	—Y	—	—	—
Swaziland........734	—	—	—	—Y	—	1	1	—	—	—	—Y	—	—	—
Tanzania........738	—	—	—	—Y	—	—	—	1	1	1	1Y	14	2	—
Tunisia........744	4	4	3	14V	22	27	21	3	5	19	1V	4	6	6
Uganda........746	—	—	—	—Y	—	—	—	1	1	1	1Y	—	—	1
Zambia........754	—	—	—	—V	—	—	—	1	2	2	—V	—	—	—
Zimbabwe........698	—	—	—	—V	—	—	—	1	3	4	—V	1	1	2
Asia........507	**82**	**109**	**145**	**163Y**	**202**	**295**	**327**	**444**	**551**	**730**	**560Y**	**589**	**826**	**2,013**
Afghanistan, I.S. of........512	—	—	1	1Y	1	6	—	—	—	—	—Y	—	—	—
Bangladesh........513	1	1	—	—V	1	1	—	3	3	5	—V	3	7	4
Cambodia........522	—	—	—	—Y	1	1	3	—	1	1	—V	—	1	1
China,P.R.: Mainland........924	11	22	30	37V	54	71	95	158	225	330	221V	263	385	614
China,P.R.:Hong Kong........532	7	8	9	12V	23	39	34	13	13	15	43V	12	15	16
China,P.R.:Macao........546	—	—	—	1V	1	—	9	1	1	1	1V	—	—	—
French Polynesia........887	—	—	—	—Y	—	—	1	—	—	—	—Y	—	—	—
India........534	15	18	28	28V	26	43	58	31	32	44	61V	60	70	117
Indonesia........536	2	3	5	3V	5	5	7	39	42	50	34V	45	68	78
Korea........542	11	15	22	19V	20	21	28	63	68	93	83V	95	162	1,034

	Exports							Imports						
	2001	2002	2003	2004	2005	2006	2007	2001	2002	2003	2004	2005	2006	2007
	Millions of U.S. Dollars							*Millions of U.S. Dollars*						
Malaysia.......548	7	8	8	7V	8	10	14	29	32	38	11V	17	13	17
Mongolia.......948	—	—	—	—V	1	1	1	—	—	—	—Y	—	—	—
Myanmar.......518	—	—	—	—Y	—	—	—	—	1	1	1Y	—	—	1
New Caledonia.......839	—	—	—	—V	1	—	2	—	—	—	—Y	—	—	—
Pakistan.......564	8	9	14	13V	20	23	28	2	3	4	4V	6	9	9
Philippines.......566	—	1	1	1V	1	2	1	7	5	7	2V	2	2	4
Singapore.......576	3	3	3	6V	7	9	15	14	17	21	14V	15	11	11
Sri Lanka.......524	—	1	—	—V	3	4	2	2	2	2	—V	1	2	3
Taiwan Province of China.......528	12	14	18	27V	16	42	12	63	81	81	52V	47	52	67
Thailand.......578	5	6	6	7Y	11	12	11	13	17	23	30Y	12	17	24
Vietnam.......582	—	—	1	—V	1	3	3	6	8	11	—V	9	11	13
Europe.......170	**2,709**	**3,295**	**4,093**	**4,786Y**	**6,626**	**8,268**	**11,645**	**1,906**	**1,994**	**2,541**	**3,011Y**	**4,435**	**5,555**	**7,528**
Albania.......914	9	11	14	16V	26	42	46	—	—	1	—V	2	2	1
Armenia.......911	—	1	1	2V	3	3	7	—	—	—	—V	—	—	—
Azerbaijan.......912	2	2	2	1V	3	6	8	2	—	—	13V	12	—	1
Belarus.......913	18	19	27	31V	35	48	61	2	4	7	6V	6	7	3
Bosnia & Herzegovina.......963	397	466	533	700Y	688	720	910	62	65	89	117Y	361	508	570
Bulgaria.......918	32	40	59	84V	113	131	219	31	35	43	32V	60	131	257
Croatia.......960	797	902	1,142	1,068V	1,749	2,030	2,400	402	397	504	660V	849	1,111	1,466
Czech Republic.......935	167	190	232	347V	450	552	876	249	272	348	423V	471	503	695
Estonia.......939	5	5	7	9V	14	21	28	1	1	2	2V	1	2	6
Georgia.......915	3	3	3	4V	5	7	9	—	24	8	—V	—	5	—
Gibraltar.......823	—	—	—	—Y	1	2	2	—	—	—	—Y	—	—	3
Hungary.......944	156	185	252	396V	449	661	1,150	314	322	398	594V	749	843	1,042
Kazakhstan.......916	9	11	21	32V	46	75	72	8	9	12	—V	18	20	19
Kosovo.......967	—	—	—	—Y	56	101	120	—	—	—	—Y	1	6	6
Kyrgyz Republic.......917	—	1	1	1V	2	3	5	—	—	—	—V	—	—	—
Latvia.......941	9	12	17	12V	15	24	39	3	3	4	3V	3	3	3
Lithuania.......946	25	34	35	34V	39	55	96	2	2	3	4V	4	6	9
Macedonia, FYR.......962	132	151	162	128V	171	164	206	27	24	25	30V	37	49	79
Moldova.......921	6	9	8	9V	13	16	18	2	2	2	1V	1	2	1
Montenegro, Rep. of.......943	—	—	—	—Y	—	120	193	—	—	—	—Y	—	24	33
Poland.......964	242	288	352	417V	519	717	989	144	159	215	268V	297	381	488
Romania.......968	58	75	103	150V	197	283	606	85	92	80	130V	169	144	200
Russia.......922	281	303	395	344V	733	983	1,330	281	252	353	154V	424	467	672
Serbia, Rep. of.......942	—	—	—	—Y	—	824	1,171	—	—	—	—Y	—	327	526
Serbia & Montenegro.......965	186	330	354	465Y	693	—	—	41	58	77	101Y	243	—	—
Slovak Republic.......936	83	125	184	241Y	291	384	638	143	153	184	242Y	261	325	389
Tajikistan.......923	—	—	—	—V	—	1	3	—	2	4	—V	2	34	16
Turkey.......186	39	49	81	185V	195	184	211	85	93	146	207V	423	623	997
Turkmenistan.......925	—	—	—	—Y	—	1	1	—	—	—	—Y	—	1	—
Ukraine.......926	48	82	105	104V	168	196	331	15	19	31	16V	39	35	50
Uzbekistan.......927	3	1	4	5Y	7	11	20	7	4	6	7Y	2	1	1
Europe n.s.......884	—	—	—	—Y	—	1	—	—	—	—	—Y	—	—	—
Middle East.......407	**135**	**185**	**202**	**283Y**	**305**	**322**	**499**	**50**	**39**	**52**	**49Y**	**103**	**110**	**212**
Bahrain.......419	—	—	—	—Y	15	16	7	1	—	—	—Y	—	1	9
Egypt.......469	31	31	35	46Y	47	51	62	5	6	6	8Y	9	12	16
Iran, I.R. of.......429	29	57	69	90Y	66	54	86	1	2	2	2Y	2	3	6
Iraq.......433	—	3	10	14Y	11	2	1	—	—	—	—Y	—	—	—
Israel.......436	18	16	20	25V	23	23	33	38	28	37	26V	85	69	150
Jordan.......439	2	5	2	1V	8	9	11	—	—	—	—V	—	—	—
Kuwait.......443	1	3	2	3Y	13	16	18	1	1	2	2Y	—	—	—
Lebanon.......446	2	2	2	2Y	5	3	7	—	—	1	1Y	3	3	4
Libya.......672	6	5	4	5Y	11	22	33	2	—	1	1Y	—	—	25
Oman.......449	1	1	2	2Y	2	1	2	—	—	—	—Y	—	16	—
Qatar.......453	—	1	1	1V	3	4	16	—	—	—	—V	—	—	—
Saudi Arabia.......456	18	26	22	28V	29	32	82	1	2	3	4Y	—	—	1
Syrian Arab Republic.......463	9	11	9	33V	14	12	21	—	—	1	4V	3	5	—
United Arab Emirates.......466	16	22	22	29Y	42	59	103	—	—	—	—Y	—	1	1
Yemen, Republic of.......474	2	2	1	2V	15	16	17	—	—	—	—V	—	—	—
Western Hemisphere.......207	**50**	**34**	**44**	**77Y**	**71**	**94**	**117**	**86**	**128**	**226**	**199Y**	**211**	**307**	**435**
Argentina.......213	4	1	2	4V	3	5	6	9	46	110	14V	48	92	163
Belize.......339	—	—	—	—Y	—	1	2	—	—	—	—Y	—	—	—
Bolivia.......218	—	—	—	—V	—	—	1	—	—	—	—V	—	—	—
Brazil.......223	21	8	8	19V	15	24	30	41	41	72	146V	115	151	199
Chile.......228	2	2	2	4V	3	3	4	6	7	6	1V	9	14	17
Colombia.......233	4	5	3	3V	4	5	6	6	7	8	29V	15	11	13
Costa Rica.......238	—	—	—	—V	5	2	—	2	1	3	—V	—	—	1
Dominican Republic.......243	—	1	1	1Y	—	—	—	—	—	—	—Y	—	—	—
Ecuador.......248	2	1	1	—V	2	3	3	8	8	9	—V	12	6	6
Falkland Islands.......323	—	—	—	—Y	—	—	—	—	—	—	—Y	—	—	1
Grenada.......328	—	—	—	—Y	—	—	—	2	—	—	—Y	—	—	—
Guatemala.......258	1	—	—	—Y	—	—	—	—	—	1	1Y	—	—	—
Honduras.......268	—	—	—	—V	—	—	—	—	—	1	—V	—	—	—
Jamaica.......343	1	1	—	—V	—	—	—	—	—	—	—V	—	—	—
Mexico.......273	10	11	21	42V	29	38	46	9	12	14	7V	11	11	11
Panama.......283	1	1	1	—V	2	2	2	—	3	—	—Y	—	—	—

	Exports 2001	Exports 2002	Exports 2003	Exports 2004	Exports 2005	Exports 2006	Exports 2007	Imports 2001	Imports 2002	Imports 2003	Imports 2004	Imports 2005	Imports 2006	Imports 2007
	Millions of U.S. Dollars							Millions of U.S. Dollars						
Paraguay.......288	—	—	—	—V	—	—	—	1	—	—	—V	—	1	—
Peru.......293	—	—	—	—V	1	1	2	2	1	1	—V	—	1	2
Suriname.......366	—	—	—	—Y	—	—	1	—	—	—	—Y	—	—	—
Uruguay.......298	—	1	1	1V	—	—	2	—	1	1	—V	—	—	—
Venezuela, Rep. Bol.......299	3	2	2	2V	3	3	7	—	—	—	—V	—	18	20
Western Hem. n.s.......399	—	—	—	—Y	2	5	3	—	—	—	—Y	—	—	—
Other Countries n.i.e.......910	**—**	**—**	**1**	**1Y**	**1**	**1**	**1**	**3**	**3**	**4**	**5Y**	**—**	**—**	**—**
Cuba.......928	—	—	—	—Y	—	—	—	1	1	1	1Y	—	—	—
North Korea.......954	—	—	1	1Y	1	1	1	2	2	4	5Y	—	—	—
Countries & Areas n.s.......898	**3**	**—**	**—**	**—Y**	**12**	**8**	**11**	**—**	**—**	**—**	**—Y**	**3**	**6**	**88**
Memorandum Items														
European Union.......998	6,442	6,988	8,540	9,858Y	12,810	15,491	20,073	7,717	8,345	10,475	15,457Y	15,883	18,526	22,861
Oil Exporting Ctys.......999	88	134	151	192Y	251	310	485	117	98	114	117Y	152	222	246
Non-Oil Develop.Ctys.......201	2,924	3,527	4,375	5,185Y	7,115	8,877	12,319	2,472	2,704	3,551	3,818Y	5,351	6,751	10,128
PERCENT DISTRIBUTION														
Industrial Countries.......101	**67.2**	**64.6**	**64.4**	**63.2**	**61.5**	**60.3**	**57.3**	**74.4**	**74.3**	**73.5**	**78.7**	**72.9**	**71.1**	**66.9**
Developing Countries.......202	**32.8**	**35.4**	**35.6**	**36.8**	**38.4**	**39.7**	**42.7**	**25.6**	**25.6**	**26.5**	**21.2**	**27.1**	**28.8**	**32.8**
Africa.......607	**.4**	**.4**	**.3**	**.5**	**.8**	**.9**	**.7**	**1.0**	**.8**	**.8**	**.6**	**.8**	**.7**	**.6**
Asia.......507	**.9**	**1.0**	**1.1**	**1.1**	**1.1**	**1.3**	**1.1**	**4.4**	**5.0**	**5.3**	**3.0**	**2.9**	**3.4**	**6.4**
Europe.......170	**29.5**	**31.8**	**32.2**	**32.8**	**34.6**	**35.7**	**38.8**	**18.8**	**18.2**	**18.3**	**16.2**	**21.9**	**23.0**	**23.8**
Middle East.......407	**1.5**	**1.8**	**1.6**	**1.9**	**1.6**	**1.4**	**1.7**	**.5**	**.4**	**.4**	**.3**	**.5**	**.5**	**.7**
Western Hemisphere.......207	**.5**	**.3**	**.3**	**.5**	**.4**	**.4**	**.4**	**.9**	**1.2**	**1.6**	**1.1**	**1.0**	**1.3**	**1.4**
ANNUAL PERCENT CHANGE														
World.......001	**5.3**	**12.7**	**22.9**	**14.8**	**31.2**	**20.8**	**29.7**	**.3**	**8.0**	**26.7**	**33.8**	**9.5**	**19.2**	**30.8**
Industrial Countries.......101	**2.5**	**8.4**	**22.5**	**12.5**	**27.7**	**18.5**	**23.3**	**–.8**	**7.9**	**25.3**	**43.3**	**1.3**	**16.3**	**23.0**
Developing Countries.......202	**11.5**	**21.5**	**23.6**	**18.8**	**37.0**	**24.7**	**39.4**	**3.7**	**8.2**	**30.8**	**7.4**	**39.8**	**26.7**	**48.8**
Africa.......607	**16.9**	**5.5**	**9.3**	**63.1**	**138.2**	**29.0**	**4.1**	**6.3**	**–14.7**	**30.4**	**.7**	**40.9**	**6.0**	**6.4**
Asia.......507	**–10.2**	**32.3**	**33.8**	**12.1**	**24.2**	**45.9**	**10.6**	**7.1**	**24.2**	**32.4**	**–23.3**	**5.3**	**40.2**	**143.8**
Europe.......170	**12.4**	**21.6**	**24.2**	**16.9**	**38.4**	**24.8**	**40.8**	**4.1**	**4.7**	**27.4**	**18.5**	**47.3**	**25.3**	**35.5**
Middle East.......407	**11.0**	**36.9**	**9.4**	**39.8**	**7.7**	**5.7**	**54.9**	**–29.3**	**–21.8**	**35.0**	**–7.0**	**112.2**	**6.3**	**93.6**
Western Hemisphere.......207	**7.4**	**–31.9**	**28.1**	**75.3**	**–7.4**	**32.1**	**24.0**	**1.9**	**49.0**	**76.0**	**–12.0**	**6.3**	**45.4**	**41.5**
Other Countries n.i.e.......910	**–49.1**	**274.0**	**297.2**	**31.3**	**9.5**	**–32.3**	**13.5**	**210.6**	**–20.7**	**51.6**	**31.3**	**–95.4**	**–63.7**	**–52.0**

		Exports							Imports, f.o.b						
		2001	2002	2003	2004	2005	2006	2007	2001	2002	2003	2004	2005	2006	2007
		Millions of U.S. Dollars							Millions of U.S. Dollars						
IFS World Total		**46.9**	**57.6**	**74.0**	**97.0**	**105.0**	**120.0**	**165.5**	....	....	....	....	....	....	....
DOTS World Total	**001**	**86.6Y**	**97.9Y**	**126.2Y**	**179.4Y**	**209.8Y**	**242.3Y**	**326.3Y**	**104.0Y**	**91.4Y**	**124.8Y**	**144.3Y**	**188.7Y**	**232.9Y**	**303.8Y**
Industrial Countries	**101**	**25.5Y**	**22.2Y**	**24.2Y**	**36.6Y**	**36.4Y**	**41.9Y**	**50.8Y**	**48.9Y**	**39.1V**	**48.8V**	**59.3Y**	**74.6V**	**105.4V**	**118.5V**
United States	111	2.64V	.73V	1.36V	3.18V	1.91V	2.64V	1.55V	7.40V	1.80V	1.90V	2.60V	2.30V	5.70V	5.50V
Canada	156	.09V	.04V	.02V	.05V	.11V	.10V	.13V	—V	.09V	.06V	.15V	.04V	.11V	.23V
Australia	193	1.34V	.78V	3.28V	3.77V	2.76V	3.00V	5.59V	30.12V	28.68V	34.22V	35.59V	49.43V	59.33V	77.31V
Japan	158	17.09V	18.78V	16.25V	16.60V	13.45V	21.14V	18.63V	3.70V	2.11V	3.50V	5.48V	7.17V	18.24V	14.03V
New Zealand	196	.22V	.23V	.60V	.56V	.68V	1.70V	1.21V	5.15V	4.60V	5.79V	11.22V	8.91V	11.79V	13.56V
Austria	122	—V	—V	—V	—V	—V	.02V	—V	.02V	—V	—V	—V	.01V	.01V	.11V
Belgium	124	.03V	.02V	1.05V	2.40V	3.78V	1.47V	.73V	.09V	.02V	.19V	.13V	.24V	.32V	.16V
Cyprus	423	—V	—V	—V	—V	—Y	—V	—V	—V	—V	—V	—V	.01V	—V	—V
Denmark	128	.13V	—V	.03V	—V	—V	.12V	.08V	.04V	.01V	.12V	.05V	.13V	.71V	.33V
Finland	172	—V	—V	—V	—V	.01V	—V	—V	—V	.02V	—V	—V	.19V	.04V	.04V
France	132	.03V	.04V	.03V	.11V	.27V	.29V	.17V	.02V	.10V	.51V	.29V	1.10V	.48V	.28V
Germany	134	.42V	.84V	1.31V	3.88V	3.75V	.04V	.01V	1.54V	.59V	1.09V	.67V	1.61V	2.17V	2.89V
Greece	174	—V	—V	—V	—V	—V	—V	—V	.06V	—V	—V	—V	—V	—V	—V
Ireland	178	—V	—V	—V	—V	—V	—V	—V	—V	.09V	—V	.05V	.04V	.03V	.06V
Italy	136	—V	.02V	.14V	4.11V	8.87V	10.49V	11.98V	.02V	.06V	.95V	1.04V	.98V	2.58V	.21V
Luxembourg	137	—V	—V	—V	—V	—V	—V	.01V	—V	.05V	.02V	.05V	.14V	.12V	—V
Netherlands	138	.07V	—V	—V	1.82V	.02V	.08V	.01V	.16V	.09V	.17V	.26V	.33V	.21V	.30V
Norway	142	—V	—V	—V	.01V	—V	—V	—V	—V	—V	—V	—V	.01V	.68V	—V
Portugal	182	—V	—V	.05V	—V	—V	—V	—V	.02V	.08V	.04V	.70V	.01V	—V	—V
Slovenia	961	—V	—V	—V	—Y	—V	—V	.02V	—V	—V	—V	—Y	—V	—V	—V
Spain	184	2.79V	.73V	—V	.01V	—V	—V	3.87V	.04V	—V	.01V	.01V	.01V	.02V	.05V
Sweden	144	—V	—V	—V	—V	—V	—V	—V	.06V	.09V	.08V	—V	.14V	.18V	.23V
Switzerland	146	—V	—V	—V	—V	.01V	—V	.03V	.02V	.01V	.03V	.04V	.04V	.04V	.30V
United Kingdom	112	.63V	.03V	.06V	.12V	.72V	.76V	6.76V	.39V	.58V	.15V	.98V	1.76V	2.69V	2.92V
Developing Countries	**202**	**54.1Y**	**68.1Y**	**92.4Y**	**130.2Y**	**159.0Y**	**182.6Y**	**253.4Y**	**54.1Y**	**51.1Y**	**74.5Y**	**83.0Y**	**111.9Y**	**124.7Y**	**181.9Y**
Africa	**607**	**.1Y**	**—Y**	**.1Y**	**.1Y**	**.1Y**	**.2Y**	**.2Y**	**.6Y**	**.7Y**	**.8Y**	**1.1Y**	**1.2Y**	**1.4Y**	**1.8Y**
Malawi	676	—Y	—Y	—Y	—Y	—Y	—Y	—Y	.57Y	.62Y	.78Y	1.03Y	1.17Y	1.45Y	1.80Y
Nigeria	694	—V	—V	.09V	.12Y	.15Y	.18Y	.24Y	—V	—V	—V	—Y	—Y	—Y	—Y
South Africa	199	.07V	.03V	—V	—V	—V	—V	—V	—V	.03V	—V	.05V	—V	—V	—V
Asia	**507**	**53.6Y**	**67.8Y**	**92.0Y**	**129.7Y**	**158.6Y**	**179.9Y**	**252.0Y**	**50.1Y**	**46.7Y**	**68.9Y**	**76.0Y**	**104.0Y**	**114.7Y**	**163.1Y**
Bangladesh	513	1.32V	—V	—V	—V	—V	—V	—V	.04V	.04V	—V	—V	—V	—Y	—Y
China,P.R.: Mainland	924	5.40V	16.56V	29.67V	47.49V	87.39V	113.51V	165.75V	1.03V	1.07V	2.12V	3.02V	5.08V	5.01V	10.20V
China,P.R.:Hong Kong	532	3.74V	3.16V	1.37V	.75V	1.29V	.51V	1.38V	2.95V	1.49V	2.01V	1.46V	2.24V	1.57V	2.23V
Fiji	819	.11Y	.12Y	.16Y	.21Y	.24Y	.29Y	.36Y	3.88Y	4.21Y	5.33Y	7.00Y	7.99Y	9.88Y	12.26Y
India	534	2.51Y	1.81V	1.82V	.71V	1.96V	2.42Y	3.00Y	.55Y	.29V	4.65V	1.72V	.23V	.29Y	.36Y
Indonesia	536	—V	.07V	.57V	.06V	—V	.40V	1.05V	1.47V	1.67V	1.77V	1.72V	3.71V	4.09V	5.76V
Korea	542	15.41V	14.44V	21.43V	29.15V	28.29V	25.48V	22.93V	.52V	.77V	.86V	1.18V	2.44V	1.13V	1.49V
Malaysia	548	1.28V	2.18V	2.44V	1.87V	2.69V	3.00V	8.76V	1.19V	.94V	2.26V	2.12V	3.75V	5.39V	8.04V
New Caledonia	839	.14V	.11V	.22V	.22V	.25Y	.31Y	.39Y	.06V	.06V	—V	—V	—Y	—Y	—Y
Papua New Guinea	853	1.30Y	1.41Y	1.78Y	2.34Y	2.67Y	3.30Y	4.09Y	3.77Y	4.09Y	5.18Y	6.80Y	7.77Y	9.61Y	11.92Y
Philippines	566	7.32V	9.20V	9.91V	8.21V	9.67V	9.95V	13.92V	.30V	.04V	.11V	.15V	.27V	.68V	.67V
Singapore	576	.95V	3.63V	6.69V	4.97V	3.24V	3.04V	1.63V	19.13V	18.03V	25.84V	33.42V	48.51V	54.75V	85.60V
Taiwan Province of China	528	.04V	.02V	.02V	.93V	.05V	.06V	.29V	.33V	.51V	1.81V	.42V	1.32V	.31V	1.17V
Thailand	578	7.42V	6.71V	7.43V	27.02V	14.80V	11.05V	21.16V	2.83V	.58V	1.15V	2.28V	5.02V	5.43V	6.02V
Vanuatu	846	1.00Y	1.08Y	1.37Y	1.80Y	2.06Y	2.54Y	3.15Y	—Y	—Y	—Y	—Y	—Y	—Y	—Y
Vietnam	582	1.81V	3.35V	3.17V	—V	—V	—V	—V	.02V	.01V	2.06V	—V	—V	—V	—V
Asia n.s.	598	3.89Y	3.93Y	3.96Y	4.00Y	4.03Y	4.07Y	4.11Y	12.01Y	12.91Y	13.82Y	14.72Y	15.63Y	16.53Y	17.44Y
Europe	**170**	**.4Y**	**.3Y**	**.3Y**	**.3Y**	**.2Y**	**.2Y**	**.3Y**	**2.6Y**	**2.8Y**	**3.7Y**	**4.8Y**	**5.3Y**	**6.6Y**	**8.2Y**
Czech Republic	935	—V	—V	—V	.11V	—V	—V	—V	—V	—V	—V	—V	—V	—V	—V
Hungary	944	—V	.09V	—V	.02V	—V	—V	—V	—V	—V	—V	.01V	—V	.02V	.02V
Macedonia, FYR	962	—V	—V	—V	—V	—V	—V	—Y	—V	—V	—V	—V	.02V	—V	—Y
Poland	964	.14V	.05V	.14V	.01V	—V	—V	—V	.01V	.02V	.13V	—V	—V	—V	—V
Romania	968	—V	.04V	—V	—V	—V	—V	—V	—V	—V	—V	.10V	.01V	—V	—V
Russia	922	.14V	—V	—V	—V	—V	—V	—V	....	....	....	....	....	....	....
Slovak Republic	936	—V	—V	—Y	—Y	—V	—V	—V	—V	.01V	.01Y	.02Y	—V	—V	—V
Turkey	186	—V	—V	—V	—V	—V	—V	—V	—V	—V	—V	.05V	.03V	.07V	.06V
Europe n.s.	884	.08Y	.09Y	.11Y	.15Y	.17Y	.21Y	.26Y	2.57Y	2.79Y	3.53Y	4.64Y	5.30Y	6.55Y	8.12Y
Middle East	**407**	**—Y**	**—Y**	**—Y**	**—Y**	**—Y**	**—Y**	**.1Y**	**—Y**	**—Y**	**—Y**	**—Y**	**—Y**	**.1Y**	**.1Y**
Bahrain	419	.02Y	.02Y	.02Y	.03Y	.03Y	.04Y	.05Y	....	....	....	....	....	....	....
Yemen, Republic of	474	—V	—V	—Y	.02V	.01V	.01Y	.01Y	—V	—V	—Y	—V	.04V	.05Y	.07Y
Western Hemisphere	**207**	**—Y**	**—Y**	**—Y**	**—Y**	**.1Y**	**2.3Y**	**.9Y**	**.9Y**	**.9Y**	**1.1Y**	**1.1Y**	**1.3Y**	**1.9Y**	**8.6Y**
Brazil	223	—V	—V	—V	—V	—V	—V	—V	—V	—V	.02V	.05V	.17V	.63V	—V
Chile	228	—V	—V	—V	—V	—V	—V	—V	—V	—V	.06V	.02V	.04V	—V	—V
Dominican Republic	243	—V	—Y	—Y	.01Y	.01Y	.01Y	.01Y	—V	—Y	—Y	—Y	—Y	—Y	—Y
Haiti	263	—V	—V	—Y	.02V	.03Y	.03Y	.04Y	—Y	—Y	—Y	—Y	—Y	—Y	—Y
Mexico	273	—V	—V	—V	—V	.01V	2.22V	.86V	—V	—V	—V	—V	—V	—V	7.34V
Peru	293	—V	—V	—V	—V	—V	—V	—Y	—V	—V	—V	—V	—V	.03V	.03Y
Western Hem. n.s.	399	.01Y	.01Y	.01Y	.01Y	.01Y	.01Y	.01Y	.87Y	.93Y	1.00Y	1.07Y	1.13Y	1.20Y	1.26Y

	Exports							Imports, f.o.b						
	2001	2002	2003	2004	2005	2006	2007	2001	2002	2003	2004	2005	2006	2007
Memorandum Items														
European Union.......... 998	4.25Y	1.82Y	2.82Y	12.59Y	17.43Y	13.28Y	23.65Y	2.47Y	1.82Y	3.48Y	4.26Y	6.70V	9.57V	7.60V
Oil Exporting Ctys.......... 999	—Y	.07Y	.66Y	.18Y	.15Y	.58Y	1.29Y	1.47Y	1.67Y	1.77Y	1.72Y	3.71Y	4.09Y	5.76Y
Non-Oil Develop.Ctys.......... 201	54.10Y	68.07Y	91.73Y	130.03Y	158.88Y	182.06Y	252.16Y	52.62Y	49.46Y	72.70Y	81.32Y	108.16Y	120.58Y	176.10Y
PERCENT DISTRIBUTION														
Industrial Countries.......... 101	**29.4**	**22.7**	**19.2**	**20.4**	**17.3**	**17.3**	**15.6**	**47.0**	**42.8**	**39.1**	**41.1**	**39.5**	**45.3**	**39.0**
Developing Countries.......... 202	**62.5**	**69.6**	**73.2**	**72.6**	**75.8**	**75.4**	**77.7**	**52.0**	**55.9**	**59.7**	**57.5**	**59.3**	**53.5**	**59.9**
Africa.......... 607	**.1**	**—**	**.1**	**.1**	**.1**	**.1**	**.1**	**.5**	**.7**	**.6**	**.7**	**.6**	**.6**	**.6**
Asia.......... 507	**62.0**	**69.2**	**72.9**	**72.3**	**75.6**	**74.3**	**77.2**	**48.1**	**51.1**	**55.2**	**52.7**	**55.1**	**49.2**	**53.7**
Europe.......... 170	**.4**	**.3**	**.2**	**.2**	**.1**	**.1**	**.1**	**2.5**	**3.1**	**2.9**	**3.3**	**2.8**	**2.8**	**2.7**
Western Hemisphere.......... 207	**—**	**—**	**—**	**—**	**—**	**.9**	**.3**	**.8**	**1.0**	**.9**	**.8**	**.7**	**.8**	**2.8**
ANNUAL PERCENT CHANGE														
World.......... 001	**–14.4**	**13.1**	**28.8**	**42.2**	**16.9**	**15.5**	**34.7**	**–7.8**	**–12.2**	**36.6**	**15.6**	**30.8**	**23.4**	**30.5**
Industrial Countries.......... 101	**–28.7**	**–12.8**	**8.9**	**51.3**	**–.7**	**15.2**	**21.3**	**–5.6**	**–20.0**	**25.0**	**21.4**	**25.8**	**41.3**	**12.4**
Developing Countries.......... 202	**–8.4**	**25.9**	**35.6**	**40.9**	**22.1**	**14.8**	**38.8**	**–9.9**	**–5.5**	**45.6**	**11.5**	**34.7**	**11.4**	**45.9**
Africa.......... 607	**. . . .**	**–50.9**	**165.0**	**30.1**	**27.3**	**25.6**	**29.4**	**4.2**	**14.3**	**20.2**	**38.3**	**8.5**	**23.6**	**24.1**
Asia.......... 507	**–8.9**	**26.4**	**35.7**	**41.0**	**22.3**	**13.4**	**40.0**	**–10.9**	**–6.7**	**47.5**	**10.3**	**36.8**	**10.3**	**42.3**
Europe.......... 170	**191.4**	**–26.4**	**–5.1**	**10.7**	**–40.4**	**23.0**	**24.4**	**7.9**	**9.4**	**30.3**	**31.2**	**11.0**	**24.1**	**23.6**
Middle East.......... 407	**10.4**	**8.5**	**26.6**	**102.7**	**–9.2**	**23.6**	**24.1**	**. . . .**	**–7.6**	**26.6**	**13.9**	**—**	**23.6**	**24.1**
Western Hemisphere.......... 207	**–28.3**	**18.4**	**18.6**	**109.4**	**23.4**	**—**	**–59.6**	**–5.4**	**7.5**	**15.0**	**5.4**	**18.3**	**38.6**	**365.2**

	Exports							Imports						
	2001	2002	2003	2004	2005	2006	2007	2001	2002	2003	2004	2005	2006	2007
	Millions of U.S. Dollars							*Millions of U.S. Dollars*						
DOTS World Total 001	**77.2Y**	**112.9Y**	**150.5Y**	**190.1Y**	**250.6Y**	**301.2Y**	**380.5Y**	**337.8Y**	**388.0Y**	**421.8Y**	**547.3Y**	**626.3Y**	**792.7Y**	**886.6Y**
Industrial Countries 101	**4.2Y**	**3.1Y**	**2.3Y**	**3.6Y**	**2.3Y**	**3.0Y**	**6.0Y**	**37.0Y**	**41.6Y**	**26.6Y**	**37.5Y**	**27.6Y**	**42.1Y**	**45.1Y**
United States 111	.27V	.27V	—V	.64V	.27V	.36V	—V	7.26V	6.71V	7.81V	10.12V	9.79V	22.00V	22.88V
Canada 156	.03V	.20V	.09V	.06V	.09V	.03V	.04V	2.19V	.14V	.09V	.06V	1.14V	1.86V	1.71V
Australia 193	—V	—V	—V	.04V	.01V	.04V	.15V	.13V	.57V	.26V	.17V	.09V	.16V	.11V
Japan 158	.17V	.08V	.44V	1.18V	.50V	.50V	.29V	.22V	.36V	.13V	.20V	.28V	.26V	1.35V
New Zealand 196	—V	—V	.02V	.01V	—V	—V	.02V	—V	—V	.01V	.01V	.01V	.06V	.06V
Austria 122	—V	—V	—V	—V	—V	—V	—V	3.05V	.64V	.28V	.12V	.67V	.42V	.02V
Belgium 124	—V	—V	—V	—V	.12V	—V	.04V	1.12V	.12V	.16V	.09V	.42V	.81V	1.34V
Cyprus 423	—V	—V	—V	—V	—Y	—V	—V	.26V	.08V	.18V	.07V	.37V	.25V	.18V
Denmark 128	—V	—V	—V	—V	—V	—V	—V	.57V	.43V	.20V	.28V	.14V	.25V	.11V
Finland 172	—V	—V	—V	—V	—V	—V	—V	.04V	—V	.06V	.02V	.09V	—V	.15V
France 132	.47V	.28V	.21V	.27V	.31V	.40V	.24V	3.53V	.64V	.69V	1.26V	.95V	2.32V	4.02V
Germany 134	.75V	.31V	.28V	.75V	.43V	.72V	3.86V	.63V	1.63V	3.47V	1.98V	1.40V	1.41V	2.64V
Greece 174	.05V	.02V	.03V	—V	—V	—V	—V	.20V	.04V	—V	.06V	.05V	—V	—V
Iceland 176	—V	—V	—V	—V	—V	—V	—V	.01V	—V	—V	—V	—V	—V	—V
Ireland 178	—V	—V	—V	.03V	—V	—V	—V	.30V	.14V	.04V	.05V	.05V	.01V	.06V
Italy 136	1.72V	1.57V	.73V	.14V	.35V	.78V	.82V	4.30V	8.29V	5.19V	6.31V	2.61V	3.54V	3.01V
Luxembourg 137	—V	—V	—V	—V	—V	—V	—V	—V	.08V	—V	—V	—V	.27V	—V
Malta 181	.36Y	.14V	.14V	.03V	—V	—V	—V	.69Y	—V	—V	—V	.37V	—V	.69V
Netherlands 138	—V	.05V	.01V	.04V	.02V	.01V	.01V	2.56V	3.57V	1.15V	1.19V	3.85V	5.58V	4.04V
Norway 142	—V	—V	—V	—V	.01V	—V	—V	—V	.40V	.13V	.59V	.15V	.41V	.17V
Portugal 182	.02V	.04V	—V	.01V	—V	—V	—V	.20V	.48V	.13V	.14V	.37V	.08V	.25V
Slovenia 961	.01V	.05V	.07V	.09Y	—V	—V	—V	—V	—V	—V	—Y	—V	—V	—V
Spain 184	.05V	.06V	.05V	.01V	.02V	.02V	—V	.05V	.33V	.20V	.38V	.83V	.01V	.04V
Sweden 144	.02V	.01V	—V	—V	.02V	.03V	.20V	.04V	1.33V	.06V	.07V	.09V	.80V	.29V
Switzerland 146	—V	.02V	.12V	.21V	.01V	.02V	.06V	.25V	.02V	.10V	.16V	.01V	.09V	.07V
United Kingdom 112	.28V	.04V	.11V	.05V	.18V	.12V	.32V	9.45V	15.64V	6.29V	14.23V	3.82V	1.55V	1.89V
Developing Countries 202	**73.0Y**	**109.8Y**	**148.1Y**	**186.5Y**	**248.2Y**	**298.1Y**	**374.4Y**	**260.4Y**	**302.5Y**	**339.6Y**	**436.9Y**	**515.4Y**	**647.7Y**	**713.8Y**
Africa 607	**7.4Y**	**10.8Y**	**6.4Y**	**9.1Y**	**11.5Y**	**13.3Y**	**16.6Y**	**131.8Y**	**170.3Y**	**187.7Y**	**220.9Y**	**253.0Y**	**312.2Y**	**388.0Y**
Algeria 612	—V	.06V	.06Y	.08Y	.10Y	.13Y	.17Y	—V	—V	—Y	—Y	—Y	—Y	—Y
Benin 638	—V	—V	.03V	—V	—V	—Y	—Y	—V	—V	—V	—V	—V	—Y	—Y
Chad 628	.01Y	.01Y	.01Y	.01Y	.02Y	.02Y	.03Y	—Y	—Y	—Y	—Y	—Y	—Y	—Y
Côte d'Ivoire 662	—V	—V	.50V	.96V	.51V	.76V	.95Y	.02V	—V	—V	—V	—V	—V	—Y
Djibouti 611	.40Y	.44Y	.55Y	.72Y	.83Y	1.02Y	1.27Y	96.52Y	104.75Y	132.57Y	174.11Y	198.94Y	245.87Y	305.13Y
Ghana 652	.11Y	.12Y	.15Y	.20Y	.23Y	.29Y	.35Y	—Y	—Y	—Y	—Y	—Y	—Y	—Y
Guinea 656	.02V	.02Y	—V	.03V	.03Y	.04Y	.05Y	—V	—Y	—Y	—Y	—Y	—Y	—Y
Kenya 664	.11V	.03V	.11V	1.03V	1.18Y	1.46Y	1.81Y	33.97V	63.65V	54.23V	45.51V	51.99Y	64.26Y	79.75Y
Malawi 676	.02Y	.02Y	.03Y	.04Y	.04Y	.05Y	.06Y	—Y	—Y	—Y	—Y	—Y	—Y	—Y
Mauritius 684	—V	—V	—V	—V	—V	—V	.08V	—V	—V	—V	—V	—V	—V	—V
Morocco 686	.01V	—V	.05V	.06V	.01V	.01Y	.01Y	.03V	—V	—V	—V	.06V	.07Y	.09Y
Nigeria 694	6.48V	10.05V	4.40V	5.72Y	7.29Y	8.99Y	11.65Y	—V	—V	—V	—Y	—Y	—Y	—Y
Senegal 722	—V	—V	—V	—V	—V	—V	—Y	—V	—V	—V	.03V	—V	—V	—Y
South Africa 199	.24V	.04V	.12V	—V	.99V	—V	—V	.16V	.40V	.15V	.18V	.81V	.49V	1.23V
Sudan 732	.02Y	.02Y	.33Y	.19V	.29V	.54V	.17V	.85Y	.92Y	.01V	—V	—V	—V	—V
Swaziland 734	—Y	—Y	—Y	—Y	—Y	—Y	—Y	.12Y	.13Y	.17Y	.22Y	.25Y	.31Y	.38Y
Tanzania 738	.01V	.01V	.01Y	.01Y	.01Y	.01Y	.01Y	.16V	.37V	.47Y	.62Y	.71Y	.88Y	1.09Y
Tunisia 744	—V	.01V	.01V	—V	—V	.01V	.01Y	—V	—V	—V	—V	—V	.02V	.02Y
Uganda 746	—V	—V	—V	—Y	—Y	—Y	—Y	—V	.06V	.14V	.19Y	.21Y	.26Y	.32Y
Asia 507	**6.9Y**	**26.1Y**	**20.6Y**	**22.9Y**	**27.1Y**	**24.4Y**	**25.9Y**	**52.7Y**	**51.7Y**	**69.8Y**	**85.9Y**	**95.5Y**	**119.8Y**	**147.7Y**
Afghanistan, I.S. of 512	.01Y	.01Y	.01Y	.01Y	.01Y	.02Y	.02Y	—Y	—Y	—Y	—Y	—Y	—Y	—Y
Bangladesh 513	—V	—V	—V	—V	—V	—V	—V	—V	.09V	—V	—V	—V	—Y	—Y
China,P.R.: Mainland 924	.47V	1.42V	6.02V	6.71V	3.02V	2.82V	1.57V	1.23V	2.02V	4.29V	10.68V	18.28V	30.33V	29.29V
China,P.R.:Hong Kong 532	.44V	.11V	.34V	.75V	.69V	.44V	.20V	—V	—V	.08V	.10V	.05V	.14V	.22V
India 534	2.53Y	21.42V	12.65V	6.65V	9.58V	11.84Y	14.69Y	8.99Y	20.58V	38.57V	49.60V	52.68V	65.11Y	80.80Y
Indonesia 536	—V	.17V	.01V	—V	—V	—V	—V	13.77V	3.57V	1.39V	1.24V	9.79V	6.44V	8.60V
Korea 542	—V	—V	.43V	.27V	.12V	—V	—V	2.45V	1.17V	1.08V	1.45V	1.96V	.99V	.28V
Malaysia 548	.03V	.04V	.01V	.01V	2.43V	—V	—V	2.88V	3.77V	3.76V	4.63V	8.00V	6.85V	16.95V
Pakistan 564	.92V	.98V	.53V	2.92V	4.07V	5.03Y	6.24Y	3.89V	3.87V	4.82V	4.18V	3.28V	4.05Y	5.03Y
Philippines 566	—V	.33V	.14V	—V	—V	—V	—V	.07V	.01V	—V	.01V	.01V	.01V	.01V
Taiwan Province of China 528	—V	.01V	—V	.02V	.02V	.01V	.12V	—V	.01V	.15V	.26V	.16V	.11V	5.36V
Thailand 578	2.47V	1.58V	.46V	5.59V	7.15V	4.29V	3.07V	18.82V	16.58V	15.54V	13.75V	1.31V	5.71V	1.21V
Vietnam 582	—V	—V	.01V	—V	—V	—V	—V	.55V	.04V	.14V	—V	—V	—V	—V
Asia n.s. 598	—Y	—Y	—Y	—Y	—Y	—Y	—Y	.01Y	.01Y	.01Y	.01Y	.01Y	.01Y	.01Y
Europe 170	**.9Y**	**.2Y**	**1.9Y**	**.9Y**	**.8Y**	**2.4Y**	**1.7Y**	**.7Y**	**.6Y**	**.3Y**	**1.6Y**	**6.1Y**	**8.5Y**	**8.5Y**
Bulgaria 918	—V	.01V	—V	—V	—V	—V	—V	—V	—V	—V	—V	—V	—V	—V
Czech Republic 935	.34V	—V	—V	—V	—V	—V	—V	.38V	—V	—V	—V	—V	—V	—V
Hungary 944	—V	—V	—V	.03V	—V	—V	—V	—V	.03V	—V	—V	—V	1.95V	.54V
Lithuania 946	—V	—V	—V	—V	—V	—V	—V	—V	.02V	—V	—V	—V	—V	—V
Poland 964	—V	.11V	.24V	.01V	—V	—V	—V	.02V	.14V	.08V	.02V	.05V	—V	.01V
Romania 968	.01V	—V	—V	—V	—V	.04V	—V	—V	—V	—V	—V	.10V	—V	—V
Russia 922	.01V	—V	—V	—V	—V	—V	—V	—V	—V	—V	—V	—V	—V	—V

	Exports							Imports						
	2001	2002	2003	2004	2005	2006	2007	2001	2002	2003	2004	2005	2006	2007
	Millions of U.S. Dollars							*Millions of U.S. Dollars*						
Slovak Republic.......... 936	—V	—V	—Y	—Y	—V	—V	—V	—V	—V	—Y	—Y	.03V	—V	—V
Tajikistan.......... 923	.18V	—V	—V	—V	—V	—V	—V	—V	—V	—V	—V	—V	—V	—V
Turkey.......... 186	.29V	.11V	1.66V	.84V	.76V	2.32V	1.65V	.22V	.44V	.24V	.83V	2.43V	2.22V	2.55V
Ukraine.......... 926	.05V	—V	—V	—V	—V	.01Y	.01Y	.11V	.01V	—V	.75V	3.53V	4.36Y	5.42Y
Middle East.......... 407	**57.7Y**	**72.6Y**	**119.2Y**	**153.3Y**	**208.8Y**	**258.0Y**	**330.0Y**	**41.1Y**	**49.5Y**	**58.0Y**	**79.8Y**	**111.4Y**	**139.5Y**	**169.5Y**
Bahrain.......... 419	2.10Y	2.28Y	2.88Y	3.78Y	4.32Y	5.34Y	6.63Y	.01Y	.01Y	.01Y	.01Y	.01Y	.02Y	.02Y
Egypt.......... 469	.42V	.45Y	.57Y	.75Y	.86Y	1.07Y	1.32Y	.11V	.12Y	.15Y	.20Y	.23Y	.29Y	.35Y
Jordan.......... 439	.87V	.25V	.41V	.47V	.61V	.52V	.42V	.55V	1.02V	1.02V	1.05V	.42V	.64V	.56V
Kuwait.......... 443	3.07Y	3.18Y	3.53Y	4.60Y	5.85Y	7.22Y	9.36Y	—Y	—Y	—Y	—Y	—Y	—Y	—Y
Lebanon.......... 446	.39Y	.42Y	.54Y	.71Y	.81Y	1.00Y	1.24Y	—Y	—Y	—Y	—Y	—Y	—Y	—Y
Oman.......... 449	3.73V	9.22V	8.72V	11.35Y	14.45Y	17.83Y	23.10Y	11.71V	17.88V	19.34V	25.60Y	34.82Y	43.77Y	52.81Y
Qatar.......... 453	—V	.41V	.49V	.52V	1.47V	2.21V	2.86Y	.08V	.07V	.01V	—V	—V	.05V	.05Y
Saudi Arabia.......... 456	6.54V	5.38V	6.88V	6.37V	7.82V	9.66Y	12.51Y	4.71Y	5.01Y	6.07Y	8.03Y	10.93Y	13.74Y	16.58Y
Syrian Arab Republic.......... 463	—Y	—Y	—Y	—V	—Y	—Y	—Y	.26Y	.28Y	.36Y	.13V	.15Y	.18Y	.23Y
United Arab Emirates.......... 466	38.18V	33.36V	72.82V	94.70Y	120.59Y	148.86Y	192.84Y	14.13Y	15.02Y	18.21Y	24.09Y	32.78Y	41.20Y	49.71Y
Yemen, Republic of.......... 474	2.38V	17.62V	22.30Y	30.03V	51.98V	64.24Y	79.73Y	9.59V	10.10V	12.78Y	20.68V	32.07V	39.63Y	49.18Y
Western Hemisphere.......... 207	**.1Y**	**.1Y**	**.1Y**	**.3Y**	**.1Y**	**—Y**	**.2Y**	**34.1Y**	**30.4Y**	**23.8Y**	**48.8Y**	**49.4Y**	**67.7Y**	**—Y**
Argentina.......... 213	—V	—V	—V	.01V	.01V	—V	.08V	—V	—V	—V	—V	—V	—V	—V
Barbados.......... 316	—V	—V	.01V	.01V	—V	—V	—Y	—V	—V	—V	—V	—V	—V	—Y
Bermuda.......... 319	.03Y	.04Y	.05Y	.06Y	—V	—V	—Y	—Y	—Y	—Y	—Y	—Y	—Y	—Y
Brazil.......... 223	.06V	.01V	.05V	.20V	.06V	—V	—V	34.06V	30.42V	23.80V	48.78V	49.39V	67.68V	—V
Mexico.......... 273	—V	—V	—V	—V	—V	.02V	.09V	—V	—V	—V	—V	—V	.04V	—V
Peru.......... 293	—V	—V	—V	—V	—V	—V	—Y	—V	—V	—V	—V	.01V	—V	—Y
Other Countries n.i.e.......... 910	**—Y**	**—Y**	**—Y**	**—Y**	**—Y**	**—Y**	**—Y**	**.5Y**	**.6Y**	**.7Y**	**1.0Y**	**1.1Y**	**1.4Y**	**1.7Y**
North Korea.......... 954	....	....	....	....	....	....	....	.54Y	.59Y	.75Y	.98Y	1.12Y	1.38Y	1.72Y
Countries & Areas n.s.......... 898	**—Y**	**—Y**	**—Y**	**.1Y**	**.1Y**	**.1Y**	**.1Y**	**9.0Y**	**9.7Y**	**12.3Y**	**16.2Y**	**18.5Y**	**22.9Y**	**28.4Y**
Special Categories.......... 899	**—Y**	**—Y**	**—Y**	**—Y**	**—Y**	**—Y**	**—Y**	**30.9Y**	**33.5Y**	**42.4Y**	**55.7Y**	**63.6Y**	**78.6Y**	**97.6Y**
Memorandum Items														
European Union.......... 998	4.08Y	2.70Y	1.89Y	1.47Y	1.45Y	2.08Y	5.48Y	27.39Y	33.64Y	18.18Y	26.23Y	16.17Y	19.26Y	19.28Y
Oil Exporting Ctys.......... 999	58.01Y	61.84Y	96.92Y	123.34Y	157.57Y	194.91Y	252.49Y	44.40Y	41.55Y	45.02Y	58.96Y	88.31Y	105.20Y	127.74Y
Non-Oil Develop.Ctys.......... 201	14.95Y	47.93Y	51.21Y	63.13Y	90.66Y	103.20Y	121.89Y	216.01Y	260.99Y	294.62Y	377.98Y	427.14Y	542.50Y	586.03Y
PERCENT DISTRIBUTION														
Industrial Countries.......... 101	**5.4**	**2.8**	**1.5**	**1.9**	**.9**	**1.0**	**1.6**	**11.0**	**10.7**	**6.3**	**6.9**	**4.4**	**5.3**	**5.1**
Developing Countries.......... 202	**94.5**	**97.2**	**98.4**	**98.1**	**99.0**	**99.0**	**98.4**	**77.1**	**78.0**	**80.5**	**79.8**	**82.3**	**81.7**	**80.5**
Africa.......... 607	**9.6**	**9.6**	**4.2**	**4.8**	**4.6**	**4.4**	**4.4**	**39.0**	**43.9**	**44.5**	**40.3**	**40.4**	**39.4**	**43.8**
Asia.......... 507	**8.9**	**23.1**	**13.7**	**12.1**	**10.8**	**8.1**	**6.8**	**15.6**	**13.3**	**16.6**	**15.7**	**15.3**	**15.1**	**16.7**
Europe.......... 170	**1.1**	**.2**	**1.3**	**.5**	**.3**	**.8**	**.4**	**.2**	**.2**	**.1**	**.3**	**1.0**	**1.1**	**1.0**
Middle East.......... 407	**74.7**	**64.3**	**79.2**	**80.6**	**83.3**	**85.6**	**86.7**	**12.2**	**12.8**	**13.7**	**14.6**	**17.8**	**17.6**	**19.1**
Western Hemisphere.......... 207	**.1**	**—**	**.1**	**.2**	**—**	**—**	**—**	**10.1**	**7.8**	**5.6**	**8.9**	**7.9**	**8.5**	**—**
Other Countries n.i.e.......... 910	**—**	**—**	**—**	**—**	**—**	**—**	**—**	**.2**	**.2**	**.2**	**.2**	**.2**	**.2**	**.2**
ANNUAL PERCENT CHANGE														
World.......... 001	**-34.3**	**46.3**	**33.2**	**26.3**	**31.9**	**20.2**	**26.3**	**2.8**	**14.9**	**8.7**	**29.8**	**14.4**	**26.6**	**11.8**
Industrial Countries.......... 101	**106.2**	**-25.2**	**-26.5**	**54.0**	**-34.4**	**29.8**	**99.3**	**-23.0**	**12.4**	**-36.0**	**40.8**	**-26.6**	**53.0**	**6.9**
Developing Countries.......... 202	**-36.8**	**50.4**	**35.0**	**25.9**	**33.1**	**20.1**	**25.6**	**6.7**	**16.2**	**12.3**	**28.6**	**18.0**	**25.7**	**10.2**
Africa.......... 607	**21.7**	**45.7**	**-41.3**	**42.7**	**27.1**	**15.7**	**24.7**	**.2**	**29.2**	**10.3**	**17.6**	**14.5**	**23.4**	**24.3**
Asia.......... 507	**154.6**	**279.3**	**-20.9**	**11.3**	**18.1**	**-9.8**	**6.0**	**8.3**	**-1.8**	**35.0**	**23.1**	**11.2**	**25.4**	**23.4**
Europe.......... 170	**454.9**	**-72.6**	**695.1**	**-53.7**	**-13.1**	**207.5**	**-29.9**	**-49.1**	**-11.0**	**-49.8**	**399.0**	**283.2**	**39.0**	**-.2**
Middle East.......... 407	**-45.8**	**25.8**	**64.2**	**28.6**	**36.2**	**23.6**	**27.9**	**-1.2**	**20.3**	**17.1**	**37.7**	**39.6**	**25.2**	**21.5**
Western Hemisphere.......... 207	**11.3**	**-47.5**	**105.6**	**168.8**	**-70.4**	**-75.3**	**746.6**	**64.8**	**-10.7**	**-21.8**	**105.0**	**1.3**	**37.1**	**—**
Other Countries n.i.e.......... 910	**—**	**—**	**....**	**....**	**....**	**....**	**....**	**10.4**	**8.5**	**26.6**	**31.3**	**14.3**	**23.6**	**24.1**

	Exports 2001	2002	2003	2004	2005	2006	2007	Imports, f.o.b 2001	2002	2003	2004	2005	2006	2007
	Millions of U.S. Dollars							Millions of U.S. Dollars						
IFS World Total	**29,258**	**29,723**	**36,482**	**46,146**	**51,626**	**58,175**	**69,788**	**25,023**	**25,969**	**34,302**	**47,285**	**54,830**	**67,617**	**79,873**
DOTS World Total 001	**29,510**	**29,899**	**36,353**	**45,555**	**51,562**	**52,439**	**63,484**	**25,236**	**25,950**	**33,958**	**47,168**	**54,230**	**67,983**	**85,574**
Industrial Countries 101	**13,263**	**13,834**	**19,972**	**25,752**	**30,243**	**33,983**	**38,882**	**16,414**	**17,165**	**21,813**	**27,888**	**33,495**	**34,864**	**45,950**
United States 111	2,338	2,427	3,824	4,659	4,895	6,070	7,538	3,010	2,974	3,346	3,998	4,283	5,180	6,155
Canada 156	180	168	210	357	651	438	778	176	229	271	295	3,425	496	739
Australia 193	440	484	741	1,020	1,412	1,191	1,277	701	737	788	1,118	1,147	1,406	1,454
Japan 158	1,270	1,482	3,129	4,083	5,126	6,234	7,025	1,706	1,812	2,405	3,241	3,707	4,465	5,254
New Zealand 196	40	41	57	94	102	87	101	50	54	64	83	113	131	152
Austria 122	82	85	105	167	223	168	118	263	277	360	426	523	609	767
Belgium 124	801	861	980	1,119	1,423	1,492	1,745	366	370	500	594	745	840	986
Cyprus 423	4	4	5	16	8	16	9	1	2	1	3	3	3	2
Denmark 128	78	66	94	112	133	174	186	117	119	166	177	191	222	272
Finland 172	27	22	27	30	21	82	101	304	157	200	373	457	686	744
France 132	567	667	747	898	1,078	1,203	1,307	945	1,052	2,038	2,850	2,444	2,316	2,670
Germany 134	1,971	1,874	2,426	3,223	3,340	3,944	5,104	3,733	4,079	5,069	6,719	7,718	8,565	9,306
Greece 174	52	41	58	42	44	102	89	10	10	14	19	22	32	66
Iceland 176	1	2	7	9	9	23	43	3	2	4	4	6	5	5
Ireland 178	91	88	142	156	184	164	195	346	289	372	629	641	633	807
Italy 136	772	739	908	1,182	1,163	1,346	1,425	935	938	1,116	1,431	1,621	2,045	2,218
Luxembourg 137	4	8	2	5	6	3	13	17	19	28	28	37	32	26
Malta 181	1	6	2	5	2	10	5	1	4	5	4	5	19	12
Netherlands 138	1,120	1,182	1,500	1,829	2,349	2,745	2,882	474	476	573	702	852	1,103	1,277
Norway 142	25	35	42	41	46	70	188	29	32	48	54	71	88	152
Portugal 182	81	98	94	111	144	199	223	52	55	71	123	100	109	142
Slovenia 961	—	—	—	—	—	—	34	—	—	—	—	—	—	—
Spain 184	554	638	826	1,103	1,388	1,471	1,755	278	336	506	667	877	1,037	7,035
Sweden 144	73	70	109	184	238	426	429	300	315	439	635	765	858	1,154
Switzerland 146	205	239	758	1,121	1,245	1,696	1,411	472	452	461	479	708	601	710
United Kingdom 112	2,487	2,506	3,179	4,187	5,014	4,630	4,901	2,124	2,373	2,966	3,237	3,036	3,382	3,846
Developing Countries 202	**8,586**	**8,635**	**11,010**	**13,996**	**16,322**	**18,376**	**24,465**	**8,776**	**8,723**	**12,051**	**19,109**	**20,507**	**33,114**	**39,618**
Africa 607	**3,950**	**4,093**	**4,988**	**5,851**	**7,117**	**7,663**	**9,416**	**675**	**871**	**1,049**	**1,983**	**2,060**	**3,282**	**5,320**
Algeria 612	32	29	35	29	64	170	123	—	—	—	1	23	3	1
Angola 614	305	321	445	477	545	679	773	1	11	2	261	296	366	1,660
Benin 638	8	12	12	12	13	23	24	2	2	3	4	2	4	5
Burkina Faso 748	3	2	4	8	9	15	21	—	—	—	1	—	—	—
Burundi 618	3	4	4	5	6	7	7	—	—	1	—	1	—	3
Cameroon 622	28	34	66	33	35	40	47	3	1	18	29	3	1	3
Cape Verde 624	2	1	3	1	2	2	1	—	—	—	—	—	—	—
Central African Rep. 626	1	1	—	1	1	5	8	—	—	1	—	—	—	1
Chad 628	2	1	3	3	5	5	5	—	—	—	—	—	—	—
Comoros 632	9	13	16	12	7	8	12	—	—	—	—	—	—	—
Congo, Dem. Rep. of 636	107	153	163	206	265	364	622	2	2	4	7	4	7	8
Congo, Republic of 634	30	34	38	41	57	62	69	2	3	8	13	21	3	4
Côte d'Ivoire 662	36	44	46	47	47	47	63	13	15	17	16	17	18	26
Djibouti 611	7	6	4	6	6	16	10	....	....	....	....	....	....	....
Equatorial Guinea 642	1	3	5	10	13	12	13	....	....	....	....	....	....	....
Eritrea 643	2	2	3	3	4	4	6	....	....	....	....	....	....	....
Ethiopia 644	13	16	17	37	26	34	34	—	1	2	4	1	4	4
Gabon 646	15	19	15	23	29	45	44	66	67	7	25	105	175	25
Gambia, The 648	7	3	4	8	6	10	7	1	—	—	—	—	—	1
Ghana 652	87	93	147	188	241	254	308	3	7	7	10	11	12	14
Guinea 656	6	11	43	43	37	38	41	—	—	1	2	2	2	3
Guinea-Bissau 654	—	—	—	1	1	2	3	—	—	—	—	—	—	—
Kenya 664	218	221	286	447	459	477	643	10	10	14	50	31	24	28
Liberia 668	1	2	4	5	6	18	19	1	1	1	1	1	186	4
Madagascar 674	53	39	99	89	85	73	163	2	3	2	1	2	2	6
Malawi 676	219	225	223	242	255	247	308	38	45	50	66	70	77	79
Mali 678	19	18	23	57	69	47	81	2	1	1	2	1	1	—
Mauritania 682	4	9	11	7	21	19	20	—	—	—	—	—	—	—
Mauritius 684	244	254	270	268	338	289	270	18	9	16	16	26	38	62
Morocco 686	95	101	61	73	163	161	237	2	5	6	7	8	7	9
Mozambique 688	664	597	741	782	994	910	1,268	29	37	34	30	30	44	336
Niger 692	3	5	8	5	6	8	9	—	9	—	—	—	—	—
Nigeria 694	198	257	332	442	527	592	682	234	342	401	804	651	1,323	1,782
Rwanda 714	9	8	11	12	11	11	15	9	—	—	—	1	1	—
St. Helena 856	4	4	6	7	9	10	32	—	—	—	—	—	—	—
São Tomé & Príncipe 716	—	1	—	3	—	—	1	—	—	—	—	—	—	—
Senegal 722	20	20	29	31	41	48	57	—	—	—	1	—	1	—
Seychelles 718	26	34	39	34	97	73	58	4	1	3	4	3	2	6
Sierra Leone 724	5	5	11	20	22	23	21	2	2	—	1	1	1	1
Somalia 726	—	—	—	—	1	—	1	—	—	—	—	1	—	—
Sudan 732	20	29	41	47	66	63	93	—	—	—	1	—	—	1

	Exports 2001	Exports 2002	Exports 2003	Exports 2004	Exports 2005	Exports 2006	Exports 2007	Imports, f.o.b 2001	Imports, f.o.b 2002	Imports, f.o.b 2003	Imports, f.o.b 2004	Imports, f.o.b 2005	Imports, f.o.b 2006	Imports, f.o.b 2007
	Millions of U.S. Dollars							*Millions of U.S. Dollars*						
Tanzania......738	180	191	247	339	419	400	383	4	9	18	32	39	43	52
Togo......742	9	5	20	11	10	15	29	7	4	5	5	—	8	5
Tunisia......744	5	3	4	3	6	10	16	5	7	9	3	15	12	11
Uganda......746	57	55	62	86	87	104	153	2	2	5	6	6	6	12
Zambia......754	568	523	534	729	845	1,157	1,424	48	71	73	154	202	268	322
Zimbabwe......698	625	689	854	923	1,165	1,070	1,196	165	200	342	426	488	646	845
Asia......507	**2,820**	**2,847**	**4,007**	**5,543**	**6,332**	**6,834**	**10,049**	**3,496**	**3,940**	**5,613**	**8,723**	**11,448**	**15,561**	**18,409**
Afghanistan, I.S. of......512	1	—	6	1	8	—	—	—	—	—	1	—	—	—
American Samoa......859	—	—	1	1	—	—	1	—	—	—	—	—	—	—
Bangladesh......513	4	5	6	7	10	26	20	7	3	5	6	7	12	24
Brunei Darussalam......516	1	—	1	2	5	2	2	—	—	—	—	—	—	—
Cambodia......522	—	—	1	1	—	1	—	—	—	—	—	1	2	5
China,P.R.: Mainland......924	456	448	884	1,049	1,376	2,085	4,167	1,055	1,353	2,194	3,559	4,929	6,813	8,585
China,P.R.:Hong Kong......532	304	314	421	525	589	558	657	239	223	303	415	390	391	398
China,P.R.:Macao......546	4	7	10	2	4	3	18	1	—	1	1	2	2	3
Fiji......819	1	1	2	3	4	4	2	—	—	—	—	—	—	1
French Polynesia......887	—	1	—	—	—	—	—	....	....	....	....	....	....	....
Guam......829	—	—	1	1	—	—	—	—	—	—	—	—	—	—
India......534	362	350	378	563	1,182	782	1,351	245	279	413	703	1,100	1,586	1,776
Indonesia......536	99	104	163	161	238	211	223	153	184	251	307	354	438	635
Korea......542	441	475	577	694	834	901	1,166	447	426	552	1,005	1,449	1,736	1,789
Lao People's Dem.Rep......544	—	2	1	3	3	3	—	—	—	—	—	—	—	—
Malaysia......548	153	165	225	265	237	347	407	284	344	398	588	687	847	1,065
Maldives......556	2	1	2	5	2	3	3	—	—	—	—	—	—	—
Myanmar......518	—	1	1	1	3	—	—	—	—	—	—	1	3	14
Nauru......836	—	—	—	—	—	—	—	—	—	—	7	—	—	—
Nepal......558	1	1	2	4	2	1	3	—	—	—	—	—	2	1
New Caledonia......839	—	—	1	1	—	1	2	2	4	20	48	44	47	163
Pakistan......564	64	43	86	84	157	161	221	37	38	54	85	104	132	137
Papua New Guinea......853	1	1	—	1	1	2	4	—	—	—	1	1	2	—
Philippines......566	43	29	36	49	62	36	34	45	51	68	87	93	104	130
Samoa......862	—	1	1	1	2	2	—	—	—	—	—	—	—	—
Singapore......576	232	168	227	307	415	492	359	171	207	276	403	451	1,037	653
Sri Lanka......524	22	25	24	25	29	23	25	10	11	12	12	12	15	20
Taiwan Province of China......528	449	483	657	1,359	789	875	892	525	514	614	784	869	1,132	1,136
Thailand......578	169	188	215	351	270	266	431	256	282	422	660	877	1,168	1,737
Tonga......866	—	—	1	—	—	—	4	—	—	—	—	—	—	—
Tuvalu......869	—	—	1	—	—	—	—	—	—	—	—	—	—	—
Vanuatu......846	—	—	—	—	3	—	—	....	....	....	....	....	....	....
Vietnam......582	12	33	78	77	106	49	57	20	21	30	48	75	93	135
Europe......170	**226**	**258**	**359**	**476**	**577**	**899**	**1,129**	**243**	**406**	**545**	**925**	**1,411**	**1,846**	**2,803**
Albania......914	—	1	—	—	—	1	1	—	—	—	—	—	—	—
Armenia......911	—	2	1	1	1	2	1	—	—	—	—	—	—	—
Azerbaijan......912	—	1	—	4	8	1	2	—	—	—	—	—	—	—
Belarus......913	—	—	—	1	—	—	—	—	1	—	3	1	2	7
Bosnia & Herzegovina......963	1	—	—	1	1	1	3	—	1	1	1	1	2	1
Bulgaria......918	9	3	3	4	6	16	53	3	4	4	6	12	10	14
Croatia......960	3	5	7	6	15	8	7	4	3	1	3	11	45	53
Czech Republic......935	13	21	31	64	69	99	110	41	68	100	148	242	273	348
Estonia......939	—	1	2	9	9	9	5	1	2	2	7	18	7	3
Georgia......915	1	1	2	9	1	7	4	—	—	—	—	—	1	—
Gibraltar......823	1	—	—	9	8	—	—	—	—	—	—	—	—	—
Hungary......944	3	8	5	6	11	16	33	46	59	147	284	366	430	580
Kazakhstan......916	—	—	—	4	1	9	17	—	15	9	—	—	9	—
Kyrgyz Republic......917	—	—	—	1	3	1	—	—	—	—	—	—	—	1
Latvia......941	—	2	1	1	3	3	3	2	4	1	1	1	2	64
Lithuania......946	—	1	1	5	2	2	8	1	—	4	2	20	3	10
Macedonia, FYR......962	—	—	—	1	—	—	—	—	—	—	—	—	—	—
Moldova......921	1	1	1	2	1	—	—	—	—	—	—	—	—	—
Poland......964	22	21	31	44	94	186	253	23	40	60	117	201	208	293
Romania......968	18	9	21	28	5	13	66	7	8	8	12	17	21	27
Russia......922	29	42	75	97	70	104	166	40	93	36	40	98	267	561
Serbia & Montenegro......965	—	—	—	—	—	4	5	—	—	—	—	—	1	—
Slovak Republic......936	1	1	2	1	2	3	3	8	12	23	58	66	58	114
Turkey......186	116	127	151	158	225	369	316	59	76	129	196	313	476	695
Ukraine......926	1	3	16	17	37	24	53	6	18	16	46	39	11	17
Uzbekistan......927	—	2	4	3	3	—	—	—	—	—	—	—	—	—
Yugoslavia n.s......966	4	4	4	1	1	—	—	1	2	2	2	2	2	1
Europe n.s......884	—	1	—	1	1	22	18	—	—	—	—	—	20	13
Middle East......407	**934**	**914**	**1,119**	**1,406**	**1,543**	**1,968**	**2,449**	**3,233**	**2,625**	**3,648**	**5,667**	**3,405**	**9,512**	**8,643**
Bahrain......419	6	9	11	12	15	12	23	44	11	2	24	47	34	35
Egypt......469	31	18	35	25	39	32	67	8	10	47	17	27	95	29
Iran, I.R. of......429	57	35	40	53	129	212	213	1,027	917	1,238	2,357	2,257	2,710	2,957
Iraq......433	3	1	4	16	12	32	48	63	87	—	—	—	155	258
Israel......436	510	518	506	632	760	666	854	123	132	180	263	258	316	375
Jordan......439	13	14	10	14	25	23	13	—	8	5	5	5	8	8
Kuwait......443	15	9	19	22	29	23	40	94	18	83	53	47	22	1

	Exports 2001	2002	2003	2004	2005	2006	2007	Imports, f.o.b 2001	2002	2003	2004	2005	2006	2007
	Millions of U.S. Dollars							*Millions of U.S. Dollars*						
Lebanon....446	5	7	6	6	8	7	27	—	—	—	1	2	—	—
Libya....672	4	7	6	7	6	—	—	—	—	—	—	—	—	—
Oman....449	5	5	10	26	29	50	40	21	1	2	4	124	1,821	418
Qatar....453	9	4	7	10	12	21	37	22	41	45	106	142	183	106
Saudi Arabia....456	122	126	152	223	—	295	336	1,730	1,294	1,944	2,644	—	3,599	3,624
Syrian Arab Republic....463	4	6	15	3	6	8	11	1	1	1	1	1	1	1
United Arab Emirates....466	144	150	295	340	437	552	710	99	67	73	108	413	570	691
Yemen, Republic of....474	5	3	3	17	36	34	29	—	40	27	85	82	—	142
Western Hemisphere....207	**657**	**523**	**537**	**719**	**752**	**1,011**	**1,423**	**1,130**	**881**	**1,197**	**1,811**	**2,182**	**2,913**	**4,444**
Antigua and Barbuda....311	1	—	—	2	3	5	3	—	—	—	—	—	—	—
Argentina....213	77	33	43	60	87	100	90	221	228	287	542	436	954	1,789
Aruba....314	—	2	—	—	3	—	—	—	—	—	—	—	—	—
Bahamas, The....313	2	32	2	1	2	10	5	1	1	—	—	4	3	13
Barbados....316	—	1	1	1	1	1	13	—	—	—	—	—	—	—
Belize....339	—	—	1	—	1	2	1	—	1	2	3	4	—	—
Bermuda....319	—	—	—	—	—	—	90	1	—	—	—	—	—	4
Bolivia....218	—	—	—	—	—	1	2	—	—	—	1	—	2	17
Brazil....223	269	176	176	243	317	405	520	685	463	705	991	1,306	1,377	1,659
Chile....228	53	46	45	71	53	59	59	14	22	45	38	53	75	106
Colombia....233	16	20	18	19	17	17	36	7	4	14	32	31	44	229
Costa Rica....238	2	3	1	1	1	12	6	7	9	16	35	45	35	29
Dominica....321	—	—	2	1	—	—	—	—	—	—	—	1	—	—
Dominican Republic....243	3	3	2	1	2	2	2	1	1	1	2	4	6	7
Ecuador....248	6	11	4	3	3	4	3	2	3	4	3	3	8	73
El Salvador....253	—	1	1	1	1	1	1	—	—	—	—	1	1	1
Falkland Islands....323	—	—	—	—	—	—	—	—	—	1	1	2	—	—
Guatemala....258	1	1	3	1	2	7	2	2	1	2	4	3	2	2
Guyana....336	—	—	1	1	1	1	2	—	—	—	—	—	—	—
Haiti....263	—	—	—	1	1	—	1	—	—	—	—	—	—	—
Honduras....268	—	1	1	1	1	—	1	—	1	1	—	1	1	1
Jamaica....343	3	2	2	4	9	2	46	4	6	10	9	13	9	—
Mexico....273	92	79	82	127	147	216	180	63	74	80	109	169	283	302
Netherlands Antilles....353	1	11	5	5	4	6	6	—	—	—	—	15	—	—
Nicaragua....278	2	2	7	2	7	54	31	—	1	—	—	—	—	1
Panama....283	4	5	7	21	19	41	21	1	—	2	5	60	10	1
Paraguay....288	3	4	2	1	2	2	2	1	2	2	3	6	8	18
Peru....293	15	17	27	21	18	25	76	2	2	3	2	3	5	72
St. Kitts and Nevis....361	—	—	1	—	—	—	—	—	—	—	—	3	—	—
St. Vincent & Grens....364	—	—	—	—	—	3	2	—	—	—	—	—	—	—
Suriname....366	—	—	3	1	—	—	—	—	6	—	—	—	—	—
Trinidad and Tobago....369	4	3	2	4	3	3	4	—	3	—	—	—	3	9
Uruguay....298	10	5	7	5	7	9	181	13	10	10	14	12	36	26
Venezuela, Rep. Bol....299	16	15	4	14	17	21	39	—	1	2	4	3	51	84
Western Hem. n.s....399	77	46	87	104	22	1	—	105	39	7	9	3	—	—
Other Countries n.i.e....910	**1**	**8**	**7**	**2**	**8**	**80**	**137**	**2**	**2**	**2**	**3**	**4**	**5**	**5**
Cuba....928	—	—	—	—	1	—	—	1	1	1	2	3	3	2
North Korea....954	1	8	7	1	7	80	137	1	1	—	1	2	1	3
Countries & Areas n.s....898	**7,060**	**6,926**	**4,836**	**5,525**	**4,687**	—	—	**28**	**37**	**49**	**115**	**179**	—	—
Special Categories....899	**599**	**496**	**528**	**281**	**301**	—	—	**16**	**22**	**43**	**53**	**44**	—	—
Memorandum Items														
European Union....998	8,804	9,010	11,277	14,499	16,946	18,493	20,937	10,388	11,056	14,764	19,234	20,950	23,469	32,741
Oil Exporting Ctys....999	705	744	1,067	1,344	1,500	2,180	2,493	3,444	2,952	4,039	6,387	4,014	10,873	10,555
Non-Oil Develop.Ctys....201	7,881	7,891	9,943	12,652	14,821	16,195	21,972	5,332	5,771	8,012	12,722	16,493	22,241	29,063
PERCENT DISTRIBUTION														
Industrial Countries....101	**44.9**	**46.3**	**54.9**	**56.5**	**58.7**	**64.8**	**61.2**	**65.0**	**66.1**	**64.2**	**59.1**	**61.8**	**51.3**	**53.7**
Developing Countries....202	**29.1**	**28.9**	**30.3**	**30.7**	**31.7**	**35.0**	**38.5**	**34.8**	**33.6**	**35.5**	**40.5**	**37.8**	**48.7**	**46.3**
Africa....607	**13.4**	**13.7**	**13.7**	**12.8**	**13.8**	**14.6**	**14.8**	**2.7**	**3.4**	**3.1**	**4.2**	**3.8**	**4.8**	**6.2**
Asia....507	**9.6**	**9.5**	**11.0**	**12.2**	**12.3**	**13.0**	**15.8**	**13.9**	**15.2**	**16.5**	**18.5**	**21.1**	**22.9**	**21.5**
Europe....170	**.8**	**.9**	**1.0**	**1.0**	**1.1**	**1.7**	**1.8**	**1.0**	**1.6**	**1.6**	**2.0**	**2.6**	**2.7**	**3.3**
Middle East....407	**3.2**	**3.1**	**3.1**	**3.1**	**3.0**	**3.8**	**3.9**	**12.8**	**10.1**	**10.7**	**12.0**	**6.3**	**14.0**	**10.1**
Western Hemisphere....207	**2.2**	**1.8**	**1.5**	**1.6**	**1.5**	**1.9**	**2.2**	**4.5**	**3.4**	**3.5**	**3.8**	**4.0**	**4.3**	**5.2**
Other Countries n.i.e....910	—	—	—	—	—	**.2**	**.2**	—	—	—	—	—	—	—
ANNUAL PERCENT CHANGE														
World....001	**−3.0**	**1.3**	**21.6**	**25.3**	**13.2**	**1.7**	**21.1**	**−5.4**	**2.8**	**30.9**	**38.9**	**15.0**	**25.4**	**25.9**
Industrial Countries....101	**−1.9**	**4.3**	**44.4**	**28.9**	**17.4**	**12.4**	**14.4**	**−7.0**	**4.6**	**27.1**	**27.9**	**20.1**	**4.1**	**31.8**
Developing Countries....202	**−2.8**	**.6**	**27.5**	**27.1**	**16.6**	**12.6**	**33.1**	**−2.1**	**−.6**	**38.2**	**58.6**	**7.3**	**61.5**	**19.6**
Africa....607	**−1.1**	**3.6**	**21.9**	**17.3**	**21.6**	**7.7**	**22.9**	**21.1**	**29.1**	**20.5**	**89.0**	**3.9**	**59.3**	**62.1**
Asia....507	**−5.5**	**.9**	**40.8**	**38.3**	**14.2**	**7.9**	**47.0**	**−6.8**	**12.7**	**42.5**	**55.4**	**31.2**	**35.9**	**18.3**
Europe....170	**2.7**	**14.3**	**39.1**	**32.7**	**21.3**	**55.7**	**25.5**	**−18.5**	**67.1**	**34.1**	**69.9**	**52.5**	**30.8**	**51.8**
Middle East....407	**−2.7**	**−2.1**	**22.4**	**25.7**	**9.8**	**27.5**	**24.4**	**−12.5**	**−18.8**	**38.9**	**55.3**	**−39.9**	**179.4**	**−9.1**
Western Hemisphere....207	**−3.0**	**−20.3**	**2.6**	**33.9**	**4.6**	**34.4**	**40.7**	**70.8**	**−22.0**	**35.9**	**51.3**	**20.5**	**33.5**	**52.5**
Other Countries n.i.e....910	**−13.6**	**458.1**	**−11.5**	**−76.7**	**379.2**	**921.7**	**71.0**	**−2.2**	**9.5**	**−18.7**	**60.0**	**44.9**	**10.6**	**14.5**

		Exports							Imports						
		2001	2002	2003	2004	2005	2006	2007	2001	2002	2003	2004	2005	2006	2007
		Millions of U.S. Dollars							*Millions of U.S. Dollars*						
IFS World Total		**115,155**	**123,507**	**155,995**	**182,107**	**190,982**	**213,341**	**248,917**	**153,607**	**163,501**	**208,512**	**257,591**	**287,617**	**326,033**	**384,955**
DOTS World Total	**001**	**108,952**	**118,219**	**155,400**	**181,699**	**191,974**	**212,634**	**239,843**	**142,624**	**154,756**	**208,772**	**258,289**	**288,979**	**328,870**	**372,972**
Industrial Countries	**101**	**84,481**	**92,035**	**122,748**	**142,020**	**147,078**	**160,165**	**176,993**	**105,168**	**114,252**	**156,985**	**190,525**	**200,868**	**217,910**	**244,867**
United States	111	5,047	5,409	6,411	7,179	7,880	9,401	10,151	5,990	5,653	6,254	7,416	7,638	8,872	11,380
Canada	156	480	607	712	805	855	956	991	564	564	619	1,035	1,134	887	1,176
Australia	193	398	509	653	939	917	938	1,403	394	446	506	580	790	1,042	1,049
Japan	158	1,101	978	1,090	1,429	1,412	1,561	1,749	3,062	3,166	4,294	5,734	5,919	5,980	6,467
New Zealand	196	51	54	77	80	106	121	173	95	88	115	161	198	180	183
Austria	122	960	1,073	1,420	1,601	1,646	1,767	1,869	1,608	1,844	2,359	2,650	2,373	2,752	3,550
Belgium	124	3,093	3,083	4,662	5,518	5,459	6,246	6,831	4,813	5,245	7,558	9,472	10,703	11,638	12,945
Cyprus	423	133	129	188	206	199	244	278	19	23	17	19	25	24	38
Denmark	128	700	870	1,027	1,168	1,360	1,710	1,812	923	1,174	1,705	1,944	2,083	2,452	2,633
Finland	172	395	449	619	729	800	916	997	1,050	1,061	1,544	1,643	1,629	2,002	2,412
France	132	20,811	22,439	29,988	35,400	37,061	40,005	45,095	24,254	26,232	35,085	41,113	42,582	43,951	47,305
Germany	134	12,753	13,506	18,650	21,243	21,936	23,335	25,903	22,774	25,528	34,959	43,238	44,107	48,637	58,610
Greece	174	1,165	1,369	1,888	2,232	2,138	2,396	2,865	314	348	619	531	639	841	955
Iceland	176	83	28	36	41	50	54	159	45	55	81	101	105	114	70
Ireland	178	657	735	892	1,127	1,177	1,314	1,353	1,961	2,249	2,865	3,258	4,108	4,832	4,257
Italy	136	9,586	11,002	15,180	16,508	16,140	18,264	20,450	11,964	13,266	19,050	23,618	24,710	27,175	31,351
Luxembourg	137	131	129	192	237	203	226	321	261	292	530	740	884	998	1,018
Malta	181	82	193	118	143	109	114	421	22	32	49	23	25	22	479
Netherlands	138	3,775	3,800	5,318	6,098	6,018	7,074	7,831	6,634	7,376	10,314	12,860	14,326	16,136	17,228
Norway	142	506	463	517	885	1,414	1,570	1,390	668	648	1,408	1,852	2,377	2,361	2,680
Portugal	182	10,459	11,280	15,037	17,830	18,460	19,058	20,648	3,793	4,597	6,844	8,589	9,507	10,914	12,151
Slovenia	961	286	332	361	412	505	552	645	102	117	158	175	250	311	528
Sweden	144	1,065	1,085	1,492	1,837	1,862	2,058	2,281	1,683	1,858	3,108	3,350	3,606	4,260	4,476
Switzerland	146	1,124	1,215	1,639	1,895	3,165	3,264	3,268	2,177	2,454	3,167	3,979	4,321	4,484	4,192
United Kingdom	112	9,640	11,299	14,582	16,482	16,207	17,020	18,111	9,998	9,936	13,777	16,445	16,825	17,045	17,734
Developing Countries	**202**	**22,014**	**23,979**	**29,749**	**35,963**	**39,970**	**46,435**	**55,835**	**37,314**	**40,343**	**51,633**	**67,522**	**87,771**	**110,613**	**127,831**
Africa	**607**	**3,537**	**4,078**	**5,319**	**6,371**	**7,343**	**8,032**	**9,924**	**9,024**	**8,901**	**11,192**	**13,340**	**17,490**	**20,513**	**22,599**
Algeria	612	518	707	854	1,025	1,529	1,341	1,813	2,913	2,765	3,149	3,534	5,055	5,763	6,040
Angola	614	78	57	106	83	111	247	242	153	343	33	210	671	469	592
Benin	638	23	22	24	20	22	29	43	10	8	4	1	5	5	2
Botswana	616	1	1	1	1	1	3	14	—	—	1	2	1	1	1
Burkina Faso	748	11	20	20	22	22	18	37	5	3	3	7	3	1	1
Burundi	618	—	1	1	1	2	—	3	1	—	—	—	1	—	—
Cameroon	622	34	37	45	41	41	33	48	316	353	547	577	691	1,100	1,095
Cape Verde	624	11	11	12	22	25	37	43	—	—	—	—	11	18	12
Central African Rep.	626	6	4	1	2	1	5	1	17	13	13	12	11	13	9
Chad	628	1	1	1	2	1	5	5	5	4	4	2	—	—	1
Comoros	632	—	1	2	2	3	—	1	—	—	—	—	—	—	—
Congo, Dem. Rep. of	636	3	5	7	11	10	19	20	1	24	3	3	4	4	5
Congo, Republic of	634	10	10	12	20	17	19	36	19	69	30	33	32	26	27
Côte d'Ivoire	662	71	73	81	61	61	62	94	173	225	340	252	234	286	331
Djibouti	611	2	6	3	2	3	5	4	—	—	—	—	—	—	—
Equatorial Guinea	642	45	59	90	110	110	143	165	590	495	737	686	739	1,037	1,254
Eritrea	643	3	4	2	1	1	1	1	—	—	—	—	—	—	—
Ethiopia	644	12	11	16	13	22	65	50	4	4	3	3	6	5	7
Gabon	646	20	29	20	25	58	40	57	52	29	29	74	128	165	118
Gambia, The	648	6	8	10	9	9	9	12	1	1	—	—	—	—	1
Ghana	652	49	57	67	86	85	67	127	42	67	82	72	64	178	101
Guinea	656	16	16	17	22	27	21	85	102	92	92	130	148	135	163
Guinea-Bissau	654	2	2	6	4	3	3	6	—	—	—	—	—	—	1
Kenya	664	103	31	31	46	42	86	64	12	15	18	28	26	32	36
Lesotho	666	5	—	—	—	—	—	—	—	—	—	—	—	—	—
Liberia	668	9	3	158	18	125	163	30	10	9	21	—	165	140	92
Madagascar	674	12	14	23	26	18	22	22	29	23	15	18	18	34	33
Malawi	676	1	1	1	7	1	1	2	10	7	10	4	15	7	10
Mali	678	26	19	17	20	25	20	27	6	9	5	3	1	3	3
Mauritania	682	34	44	69	61	62	76	112	67	69	73	84	74	106	158
Mauritius	684	31	30	36	36	40	42	64	31	25	27	22	40	63	58
Morocco	686	1,316	1,550	2,039	2,632	2,700	3,180	4,034	1,067	1,271	1,755	2,265	2,553	3,003	3,715
Mozambique	688	25	15	19	13	27	17	19	46	48	110	190	248	254	375
Namibia	728	10	21	34	14	28	16	19	212	174	233	244	212	214	252
Niger	692	3	5	4	4	3	3	4	—	—	1	2	2	1	2
Nigeria	694	173	188	206	324	268	242	259	1,922	1,384	2,279	2,560	3,903	4,758	5,020
Rwanda	714	1	1	1	1	2	1	8	1	2	1	3	1	—	—
St. Helena	856	—	1	6	2	6	16	11	1	1	2	1	1	1	—
São Tomé & Príncipe	716	1	2	1	—	—	—	—	1	1	—	—	—	—	—
Senegal	722	69	87	128	115	110	122	141	36	33	51	64	58	57	62
Seychelles	718	23	33	50	67	95	61	70	14	22	20	51	93	31	19
Sierra Leone	724	3	9	9	6	4	4	5	—	—	—	—	—	1	3

	Exports 2001	2002	2003	2004	2005	2006	2007	Imports 2001	2002	2003	2004	2005	2006	2007
	Millions of U.S. Dollars							*Millions of U.S. Dollars*						
Somalia.......... 726	—	—	—	—	1	—	—	—	—	—	—	—	—	—
South Africa.......... 199	295	332	415	605	808	967	1,086	745	880	1,041	1,438	1,546	1,686	1,995
Sudan.......... 732	12	11	16	22	34	31	32	6	4	5	3	3	1	2
Swaziland.......... 734	—	2	—	—	3	2	1	2	2	2	2	2	2	3
Tanzania.......... 738	9	12	23	24	15	13	21	14	13	15	114	18	22	31
Togo.......... 742	13	19	16	23	19	21	42	10	11	9	9	14	10	9
Tunisia.......... 744	436	489	601	704	729	737	917	313	345	361	566	608	800	887
Uganda.......... 746	4	12	16	8	9	8	17	20	21	28	24	25	23	32
Zambia.......... 754	2	2	5	5	3	5	7	4	2	2	3	14	20	7
Zimbabwe.......... 698	5	6	3	4	3	3	5	39	35	36	41	43	39	33
Asia.......... 507	**2,988**	**3,378**	**3,956**	**4,703**	**5,668**	**6,240**	**7,797**	**10,645**	**11,435**	**15,133**	**19,504**	**24,114**	**30,505**	**39,149**
Afghanistan, I.S. of.......... 512	—	3	3	4	9	10	8	—	—	—	—	1	—	—
American Samoa.......... 859	—	—	—	—	1	—	2	—	—	—	—	—	—	—
Bangladesh.......... 513	27	37	46	72	58	64	75	114	150	234	354	384	503	515
Brunei Darussalam.......... 516	1	2	3	6	5	3	1	—	14	—	—	1	—	—
Cambodia.......... 522	1	1	2	2	2	2	3	13	17	20	35	41	95	127
China,P.R.: Mainland.......... 924	567	745	1,240	1,438	1,888	2,154	2,726	3,956	4,494	6,409	8,899	12,135	15,252	21,587
China,P.R.:Hong Kong.......... 532	454	451	440	503	625	624	686	222	233	258	281	434	567	526
China,P.R.:Macao.......... 546	13	8	4	7	5	5	6	24	21	30	27	13	24	30
Fiji.......... 819	1	1	1	1	1	1	1	—	—	1	—	—	—	2
French Polynesia.......... 887	9	9	11	10	11	14	21	1	—	—	2	2	2	1
Guam.......... 829	—	—	—	—	1	1	1	—	—	—	—	—	—	—
India.......... 534	200	255	275	474	698	683	1,000	770	885	1,142	1,505	1,801	2,155	2,781
Indonesia.......... 536	171	150	214	195	275	191	262	1,149	1,163	1,431	1,206	1,549	1,909	2,361
Kiribati.......... 826	—	—	—	1	—	—	—	—	—	—	—	—	—	—
Korea.......... 542	271	347	380	449	510	641	723	1,740	1,877	2,299	3,033	3,341	4,602	4,569
Lao People's Dem.Rep.......... 544	—	1	—	—	—	—	—	4	5	3	3	4	3	4
Malaysia.......... 548	153	157	187	198	225	284	479	371	334	458	635	646	786	898
Maldives.......... 556	—	1	1	1	1	1	2	1	1	1	1	—	2	—
Mongolia.......... 948	—	—	8	4	1	2	8	—	1	—	—	—	—	1
Myanmar.......... 518	1	1	2	2	2	2	2	28	22	27	46	22	44	47
Nepal.......... 558	2	2	2	2	2	2	4	3	3	3	3	4	4	4
New Caledonia.......... 839	13	14	18	18	18	23	25	43	41	64	88	97	142	224
Pakistan.......... 564	50	62	79	102	120	115	131	185	214	294	345	339	414	484
Papua New Guinea.......... 853	1	2	—	—	—	2	1	3	6	22	22	29	34	70
Philippines.......... 566	114	122	146	189	127	126	156	89	88	148	159	122	175	262
Singapore.......... 576	369	446	298	342	320	545	531	227	247	271	257	315	538	339
Solomon Islands.......... 813	—	—	—	—	—	—	—	3	1	—	—	—	—	4
Sri Lanka.......... 524	13	12	16	16	25	24	39	37	34	36	46	63	59	69
Taiwan Province of China.......... 528	283	269	266	303	367	342	419	790	754	887	1,059	1,153	1,306	1,890
Thailand.......... 578	219	198	219	259	281	279	350	666	598	815	1,079	1,112	1,223	1,489
Tuvalu.......... 869	—	—	—	—	5	—	—	—	—	—	—	—	—	—
Vanuatu.......... 846	—	—	—	2	—	—	1	—	—	—	—	—	—	—
Vietnam.......... 582	54	81	93	102	85	100	133	207	231	281	416	508	664	867
Wallis-Futuna.......... 857	—	—	1	—	—	—	—	—	—	—	—	—	—	—
Europe.......... 170	**5,969**	**7,209**	**9,570**	**12,011**	**13,260**	**15,596**	**19,641**	**5,997**	**7,660**	**10,249**	**14,820**	**18,705**	**24,864**	**29,921**
Albania.......... 914	17	21	30	37	37	37	45	—	—	—	1	1	2	4
Armenia.......... 911	7	4	7	7	9	12	21	—	1	1	4	1	2	10
Azerbaijan.......... 912	4	9	13	13	18	24	26	7	30	7	13	2	6	444
Belarus.......... 913	17	23	31	34	41	48	75	16	38	44	93	173	126	247
Bosnia & Herzegovina.......... 963	30	36	36	39	33	35	43	7	4	22	30	30	22	14
Bulgaria.......... 918	102	133	201	239	264	306	314	175	211	186	319	415	517	264
Croatia.......... 960	109	159	219	257	251	316	376	39	32	37	35	57	68	59
Czech Republic.......... 935	660	747	962	1,086	1,233	1,500	1,803	591	685	945	1,176	1,486	1,903	2,486
Estonia.......... 939	32	47	71	91	113	143	154	85	71	43	88	80	171	62
Faroe Islands.......... 816	2	8	1	1	50	1	9	1	1	1	2	1	2	3
Georgia.......... 915	5	8	16	10	22	22	28	112	35	49	130	54	117	64
Gibraltar.......... 823	332	347	454	542	824	1,040	1,222	30	8	16	42	40	53	24
Hungary.......... 944	536	598	828	962	973	1,059	1,309	491	615	940	1,391	1,714	2,063	2,342
Kazakhstan.......... 916	17	24	59	60	39	51	84	50	122	218	536	637	1,038	791
Kosovo.......... 967	—	—	—	—	4	7	8	—	—	—	—	—	1	2
Kyrgyz Republic.......... 917	1	1	1	2	2	2	3	1	7	1	11	3	—	—
Latvia.......... 941	49	54	72	69	85	105	153	25	20	47	107	141	257	326
Lithuania.......... 946	135	149	128	124	161	225	447	146	153	215	124	225	294	185
Macedonia, FYR.......... 962	12	16	27	30	24	40	34	23	11	17	28	26	52	199
Moldova.......... 921	5	6	9	12	14	14	17	25	33	24	21	4	7	2
Montenegro, Rep. of.......... 943	—	—	—	—	—	9	29	—	—	—	—	—	—	2
Poland.......... 964	1,031	1,201	1,525	1,833	1,931	2,315	3,141	616	681	1,239	1,931	1,662	2,303	3,735
Romania.......... 968	165	225	366	540	707	939	1,170	198	276	329	450	651	720	637
Russia.......... 922	668	743	918	1,112	1,338	1,876	2,821	1,764	2,486	3,210	4,436	6,369	9,138	10,547
Serbia, Rep. of.......... 942	—	—	—	—	—	98	141	—	—	—	—	—	94	75
Serbia & Montenegro.......... 965	52	63	81	108	107	—	—	19	43	39	28	67	—	—
Slovak Republic.......... 936	304	465	537	400	455	566	618	131	194	308	316	519	907	846
Tajikistan.......... 923	2	2	—	1	—	—	—	2	2	2	3	2	2	10
Turkey.......... 186	1,013	1,358	1,965	3,201	3,315	3,468	3,973	985	1,253	1,918	2,909	3,406	4,282	5,563
Turkmenistan.......... 925	2	2	2	4	2	1	3	15	8	19	37	27	34	10
Ukraine.......... 926	87	109	177	220	205	325	438	407	602	315	484	819	571	877
Uzbekistan.......... 927	13	10	6	5	9	5	9	11	8	9	11	5	3	8
Europe n.s.......... 884	560	643	829	974	998	1,014	1,135	26	31	47	64	91	109	83

	Exports 2001	2002	2003	2004	2005	2006	2007	Imports 2001	2002	2003	2004	2005	2006	2007
	Millions of U.S. Dollars							*Millions of U.S. Dollars*						
Middle East.......407	**3,102**	**3,081**	**3,770**	**4,682**	**4,108**	**4,640**	**6,173**	**5,518**	**5,604**	**6,813**	**9,887**	**13,066**	**16,727**	**16,681**
Bahrain.......419	29	34	35	42	51	64	76	21	31	18	16	68	42	126
Egypt.......469	359	312	407	823	511	521	615	227	243	347	559	1,311	1,966	1,998
Iran, I.R. of.......429	277	307	459	552	466	412	600	827	703	1,043	1,077	1,910	2,506	2,093
Iraq.......433	93	69	52	47	30	27	30	383	411	332	1,288	1,223	1,627	1,669
Israel.......436	759	633	636	616	630	727	850	552	433	576	684	719	924	1,218
Jordan.......439	104	76	123	124	85	98	135	12	8	16	25	33	31	27
Kuwait.......443	113	127	144	161	151	167	229	14	26	22	91	55	68	72
Lebanon.......446	156	177	204	169	154	160	193	18	21	23	18	17	13	14
Libya.......672	76	91	142	137	215	106	152	1,734	1,480	2,040	2,521	2,977	3,748	3,509
Oman.......449	30	32	43	45	52	65	90	104	144	64	135	295	225	114
Qatar.......453	28	47	49	489	84	232	547	84	205	279	710	975	1,409	1,292
Saudi Arabia.......456	624	582	648	696	752	845	1,258	1,217	1,504	1,813	2,371	3,051	3,833	4,307
Syrian Arab Republic.......463	96	97	140	163	148	185	213	249	250	121	271	262	191	97
United Arab Emirates.......466	336	474	664	595	755	1,003	1,156	67	140	99	111	138	107	127
West Bank/Gaza Strip.......487	1	1	3	1	7	2	2	—	—	—	—	—	—	—
Yemen, Republic of.......474	21	24	26	24	24	27	28	8	5	19	13	32	40	18
Western Hemisphere.......207	**6,419**	**6,233**	**7,132**	**8,195**	**9,591**	**11,926**	**12,301**	**6,130**	**6,744**	**8,246**	**9,972**	**14,396**	**18,003**	**19,482**
Antigua and Barbuda.......311	21	7	5	5	70	86	146	7	5	1	—	68	84	114
Argentina.......213	668	283	482	542	591	678	921	1,194	1,354	1,632	1,752	1,823	2,038	2,624
Aruba.......314	4	3	3	3	5	7	18	9	1	2	34	139	68	18
Bahamas, The.......313	94	108	152	132	614	573	397	110	132	151	203	768	536	372
Barbados.......316	4	4	6	12	6	4	8	—	2	5	20	46	8	—
Belize.......339	2	6	3	4	31	10	9	2	—	1	—	3	7	16
Bermuda.......319	28	19	15	54	19	496	2	47	15	23	38	229	297	87
Bolivia.......218	22	29	21	38	31	26	38	13	10	12	20	22	22	27
Brazil.......223	1,216	954	983	1,342	1,251	1,402	1,758	1,232	1,264	1,856	2,293	2,532	2,673	4,093
Chile.......228	435	385	515	518	605	685	854	418	446	599	912	1,125	1,546	1,445
Colombia.......233	255	265	271	280	351	409	480	169	262	247	288	425	642	678
Costa Rica.......238	97	122	123	121	98	106	126	57	53	53	46	41	41	83
Dominica.......321	—	—	—	1	—	—	—	—	—	—	—	—	—	—
Dominican Republic.......243	372	328	255	248	222	289	381	24	30	40	97	59	81	135
Ecuador.......248	117	162	146	172	204	221	220	93	91	167	157	245	354	406
El Salvador.......253	67	51	59	55	53	59	53	6	13	16	35	63	54	86
Falkland Islands.......323	14	9	22	25	—	13	24	60	66	125	107	131	110	140
Greenland.......326	27	—	—	—	—	—	—	—	—	—	20	26	9	—
Grenada.......328	1	1	—	—	—	1	—	2	—	—	—	—	—	—
Guatemala.......258	84	91	91	119	109	125	134	35	30	37	41	58	66	68
Guyana.......336	1	1	1	2	1	1	2	—	13	4	6	4	4	5
Haiti.......263	7	8	7	9	17	14	9	1	1	2	1	2	3	3
Honduras.......268	36	48	118	72	63	64	85	28	28	43	54	52	58	68
Jamaica.......343	15	15	21	19	37	47	44	20	23	23	20	3	1	4
Mexico.......273	1,780	2,185	2,445	2,793	3,230	3,738	4,192	1,406	1,495	1,612	2,162	3,284	3,351	3,784
Netherlands Antilles.......353	6	32	8	32	53	97	21	19	21	30	12	2	6	69
Nicaragua.......278	20	30	30	31	33	26	42	12	12	17	24	32	38	54
Panama.......283	96	93	137	148	316	646	401	29	39	47	45	299	575	170
Paraguay.......288	20	27	28	20	21	20	29	55	11	61	13	15	54	109
Peru.......293	164	147	159	197	190	229	284	230	263	352	452	606	830	1,162
St. Kitts and Nevis.......361	1	1	—	—	1	16	6	—	—	—	—	—	—	—
St. Lucia.......362	—	2	—	1	1	1	1	—	—	—	—	—	—	—
St. Pierre-Miquelon.......363	—	—	—	—	—	—	—	—	—	—	1	2	2	3
St. Vincent & Grens.......364	11	28	40	42	5	50	13	6	39	14	56	3	1	8
Suriname.......366	1	1	2	3	2	3	6	—	1	1	1	1	3	17
Trinidad and Tobago.......369	12	22	25	323	29	28	34	48	64	38	32	110	787	638
Uruguay.......298	128	87	83	71	68	92	107	93	96	108	129	173	156	190
Venezuela, Rep. Bol.......299	495	559	340	453	550	628	749	613	666	338	407	962	2,291	2,038
Western Hem. n.s.......399	98	120	535	307	710	1,036	706	88	200	591	491	1,043	1,206	770
Other Countries n.i.e.......910	**590**	**468**	**527**	**545**	**610**	**801**	**912**	**127**	**158**	**151**	**160**	**171**	**178**	**193**
Cuba.......928	559	447	516	536	600	794	910	119	152	145	156	163	168	190
North Korea.......954	31	21	11	9	9	7	2	7	6	6	5	7	10	3
Countries & Areas n.s.......898	**425**	**373**	**475**	**600**	**2,380**	**2,585**	**2,567**	**15**	**3**	**3**	**63**	**20**	**9**	**—**
Special Categories.......899	**1,440**	**1,364**	**1,901**	**2,521**	**1,781**	**2,534**	**3,481**	**—**	**—**	**—**	**—**	**—**	**—**	**—**
Memorandum Items														
European Union.......998	78,437	86,034	115,737	133,333	136,231	148,213	165,333	94,256	103,596	144,277	174,800	184,212	201,887	227,651
Oil Exporting Ctys.......999	2,934	3,334	3,813	4,718	5,128	5,260	7,145	11,028	10,590	12,889	16,010	22,093	28,243	28,641
Non-Oil Develop.Ctys.......201	19,080	20,645	25,936	31,244	34,842	41,175	48,691	26,286	29,753	38,744	51,512	65,678	82,370	99,190
PERCENT DISTRIBUTION														
Industrial Countries.......101	**77.5**	**77.9**	**79.0**	**78.2**	**76.6**	**75.3**	**73.8**	**73.7**	**73.8**	**75.2**	**73.8**	**69.5**	**66.3**	**65.7**
Developing Countries.......202	**20.2**	**20.3**	**19.1**	**19.8**	**20.8**	**21.8**	**23.3**	**26.2**	**26.1**	**24.7**	**26.1**	**30.4**	**33.6**	**34.3**
Africa.......607	**3.2**	**3.4**	**3.4**	**3.5**	**3.8**	**3.8**	**4.1**	**6.3**	**5.8**	**5.4**	**5.2**	**6.1**	**6.2**	**6.1**
Asia.......507	**2.7**	**2.9**	**2.5**	**2.6**	**3.0**	**2.9**	**3.3**	**7.5**	**7.4**	**7.2**	**7.6**	**8.3**	**9.3**	**10.5**
Europe.......170	**5.5**	**6.1**	**6.2**	**6.6**	**6.9**	**7.3**	**8.2**	**4.2**	**5.0**	**4.9**	**5.7**	**6.5**	**7.6**	**8.0**
Middle East.......407	**2.8**	**2.6**	**2.4**	**2.6**	**2.1**	**2.2**	**2.6**	**3.9**	**3.6**	**3.3**	**3.8**	**4.5**	**5.1**	**4.5**
Western Hemisphere.......207	**5.9**	**5.3**	**4.6**	**4.5**	**5.0**	**5.6**	**5.1**	**4.3**	**4.4**	**3.9**	**3.9**	**5.0**	**5.5**	**5.2**
Other Countries n.i.e.......910	**.5**	**.4**	**.3**	**.3**	**.3**	**.4**	**.4**	**.1**	**.1**	**.1**	**.1**	**.1**	**.1**	**.1**

	Exports 2001	2002	2003	2004	2005	2006	2007	Imports 2001	2002	2003	2004	2005	2006	2007
ANNUAL PERCENT CHANGE														
World....... 001	.7	8.5	31.5	16.9	5.7	10.8	12.8	–1.4	8.5	34.9	23.7	11.9	13.8	13.4
Industrial Countries....... 101	.3	8.9	33.4	15.7	3.6	8.9	10.5	–1.9	8.6	37.4	21.4	5.4	8.5	12.4
Developing Countries....... 202	2.8	8.9	24.1	20.9	11.1	16.2	20.2	.2	8.1	28.0	30.8	30.0	26.0	15.6
Africa....... 607	11.2	15.3	30.4	19.8	15.3	9.4	23.5	–.2	–1.4	25.7	19.2	31.1	17.3	10.2
Asia....... 507	3.4	13.1	17.1	18.9	20.5	10.1	24.9	2.1	7.4	32.3	28.9	23.6	26.5	28.3
Europe....... 170	–3.5	20.8	32.8	25.5	10.4	17.6	25.9	13.0	27.7	33.8	44.6	26.2	32.9	20.3
Middle East....... 407	4.0	–.7	22.4	24.2	–12.3	12.9	33.0	–15.0	1.6	21.6	45.1	32.2	28.0	–.3
Western Hemisphere....... 207	4.0	–2.9	14.4	14.9	17.0	24.4	3.1	2.6	10.0	22.3	20.9	44.4	25.1	8.2
Other Countries n.i.e....... 910	3.1	–20.8	12.6	3.5	11.9	31.3	13.9	–32.9	24.6	–4.3	6.0	6.5	4.2	8.7

	Exports							Imports						
	2001	2002	2003	2004	2005	2006	2007	2001	2002	2003	2004	2005	2006	2007
	Millions of U.S. Dollars							*Millions of U.S. Dollars*						
IFS World Total	**4,815.8**	**4,699.1**	**5,125.2**	**5,756.9**	**6,346.8**	**6,885.5**	**7,740.4**	**5,972.8**	**6,104.8**	**6,671.9**	**7,972.9**	**8,833.7**	**10,258.2**	**11,300.5**
DOTS World Total 001	**4,722.4**	**4,678.4**	**5,133.3**	**5,757.2**	**6,383.6**	**6,883.0**	**7,740.0**	**5,730.8**	**6,021.8**	**6,671.9**	**7,999.8**	**8,863.2**	**10,253.0**	**11,301.0**
Industrial Countries 101	**3,530.8**	**3,447.4**	**3,540.5**	**4,043.3**	**4,280.7**	**4,668.4**	**5,180.8**	**1,794.9**	**1,818.6**	**2,073.5**	**2,310.2**	**2,255.9**	**2,624.3**	**2,705.4**
United States 111	1,925.84	1,764.22	1,776.42	1,869.29	1,988.09	2,005.48	1,969.98	265.55	217.84	198.34	240.09	204.52	200.65	412.14
Canada 156	68.76	61.63	64.34	71.68	78.76	77.11	78.44	23.73	13.44	36.53	43.50	80.53	214.96	79.42
Australia 193	45.21	47.17	57.59	53.88	64.59	65.32	79.96	160.92	167.28	99.41	160.62	100.08	104.20	104.75
Japan 158	185.78	140.32	160.98	157.60	144.61	163.56	159.64	336.88	354.19	448.13	411.71	379.69	449.58	413.17
New Zealand 196	5.74	5.97	7.89	8.12	10.02	12.50	12.52	70.51	64.04	81.33	88.99	95.08	137.13	156.64
Austria 122	7.66	6.66	6.58	6.83	9.52	11.70	13.31	7.59	14.23	15.20	21.35	18.68	22.06	17.00
Belgium-Luxembourg n.s. 127	120.27	258.28	172.09	295.20	315.88	359.84	400.18	162.68	170.35	203.04	212.70	242.89	241.14	220.20
Cyprus 423	5.50	1.04	.93	1.11	1.80	2.05	2.33	8.42	10.12	19.25	9.50	28.51	12.85	1.91
Denmark 128	8.77	9.62	8.69	11.30	12.05	21.08	23.12	12.41	12.05	15.00	18.14	27.78	24.64	24.77
Finland 172	12.93	16.81	15.58	16.52	22.73	15.14	29.17	18.64	13.03	6.39	65.25	18.68	27.64	37.41
France 132	106.93	93.27	87.12	102.27	121.36	154.09	175.94	79.86	78.46	140.81	123.40	142.08	140.13	154.59
Germany 134	198.48	199.30	232.44	274.06	271.83	328.81	437.85	138.00	121.21	142.97	193.98	177.97	222.77	229.48
Greece 174	7.22	7.09	7.79	7.89	8.19	8.08	12.06	1.55	15.24	8.76	.85	8.19	1.29	1.20
Iceland 176	.32	—	—	.29	.15	.91	.44	.02	—	—	.05	.12	.11	.24
Ireland 178	15.12	14.45	14.62	17.24	18.99	21.35	25.94	5.86	7.72	7.38	6.83	8.27	9.07	8.57
Italy 136	61.06	71.94	117.48	152.86	199.62	258.02	394.88	66.02	83.29	122.36	135.94	150.57	157.63	204.68
Luxembourg 137	—	—	—	—	—	.19	.06	—	—	—	—	—	.02	.10
Malta 181	.20	.33	.26	.04	.20	.15	.48	.02	.23	.32	1.06	.43	.56	.32
Netherlands 138	86.47	77.53	88.55	107.06	99.95	121.51	151.10	78.17	50.46	50.78	51.39	67.66	76.84	74.96
Norway 142	7.05	6.46	6.62	7.14	8.65	12.02	16.45	5.19	5.92	4.16	7.79	6.56	6.17	7.81
Portugal 182	5.95	4.22	5.66	6.56	5.28	4.14	5.68	1.99	.95	1.30	1.41	2.19	1.03	2.27
Slovenia 961	.21	.24	.67	.27	.53	.84	.78	.26	.59	.68	.45	2.96	3.37	.84
Spain 184	34.80	27.25	29.73	39.36	56.63	54.46	62.77	11.29	12.08	17.65	16.57	22.57	29.04	34.69
Sweden 144	16.70	18.31	20.17	24.45	26.48	36.67	57.54	42.89	54.71	79.27	78.77	83.78	113.57	113.69
Switzerland 146	27.44	24.97	17.81	33.07	37.56	53.29	52.14	75.84	89.16	101.58	107.79	109.60	124.41	174.70
United Kingdom 112	576.33	590.30	640.45	779.17	777.26	880.10	1,018.04	220.61	262.06	272.85	312.10	276.49	303.37	229.82
Developing Countries 202	**1,148.9**	**1,163.0**	**1,376.0**	**1,660.9**	**1,954.2**	**1,902.7**	**2,180.5**	**3,917.8**	**4,189.0**	**4,433.3**	**5,680.5**	**6,595.5**	**7,568.0**	**8,518.3**
Africa 607	**34.2**	**38.9**	**44.5**	**47.2**	**45.7**	**49.9**	**52.9**	**26.5**	**34.3**	**30.0**	**64.6**	**68.2**	**31.3**	**30.5**
Congo, Dem. Rep. of 636	—	.01	.11	.16	.20	—	—	—	—	—	—	—	—	—
Ethiopia 644	.76	.20	.42	.42	.50	.35	.23	—	.32	.32	.01	.08	—	.42
Ghana 652	.14	.30	.97	1.70	2.40	2.48	3.00	—	—	—	.08	.09	.87	.77
Guinea 656	.78	1.41	1.80	.62	.69	.82	1.39	—	—	—	—	—	1.62	8.02
Kenya 664	1.56	2.59	3.32	5.40	4.40	4.33	4.40	2.28	1.63	3.47	34.88	6.90	6.97	.52
Madagascar 674	1.57	1.88	5.33	2.84	2.93	1.06	.39	.08	.42	.15	1.38	.71	.20	.14
Malawi 676	.03	—	—	.04	.02	.02	.22	—	—	—	—	—	—	—
Mauritania 682	.10	—	—	.27	.25	.24	.29	—	—	—	—	—	—	—
Mauritius 684	1.22	1.72	3.20	3.64	2.51	1.94	1.77	1.15	1.08	1.19	3.05	32.38	3.13	.02
Morocco 686	.97	.63	.94	1.44	1.82	1.75	2.18	.14	.46	.35	.59	1.00	.59	2.03
Mozambique 688	—	—	—	—	—	.08	.02	—	—	—	—	.03	.02	.66
Nigeria 694	1.55	1.86	.90	.79	4.12	1.24	3.07	.24	.33	.30	.56	.76	.17	.27
Seychelles 718	.39	—	—	.18	.95	2.17	3.00	—	—	—	1.43	.78	.42	.23
South Africa 199	10.14	10.59	12.97	12.00	11.56	15.71	18.11	21.99	29.63	22.45	21.95	25.18	16.61	16.45
Sudan 732	.03	.04	.16	.29	.50	.13	.23	—	—	.11	.07	.03	—	—
Tanzania 738	.19	—	—	1.66	1.71	2.39	4.11	.18	—	—	.08	.11	.68	.86
Tunisia 744	11.01	10.44	7.32	9.01	10.84	14.77	10.40	—	.03	.18	.18	.06	—	.05
Zambia 754	.10	.06	.84	.11	.20	.16	.06	—	.35	—	—	—	—	—
Zimbabwe 698	.07	.10	.09	.12	.13	.29	—	.21	.09	.07	—	.04	.01	—
Africa n.s. 799	3.58	7.02	6.15	6.57	—	—	—	.26	—	1.37	.37	—	—	—
Asia 507	**389.5**	**491.7**	**602.0**	**772.3**	**949.0**	**939.2**	**1,017.3**	**3,338.9**	**3,214.2**	**3,741.8**	**4,557.8**	**5,289.5**	**6,141.6**	**6,824.1**
Afghanistan, I.S. of 512	.06	.40	.48	1.28	2.04	.68	—	.02	.09	.27	.12	.12	.31	—
Bangladesh 513	10.08	10.18	11.17	13.92	15.77	18.68	22.75	2.05	3.89	5.64	7.70	8.87	7.99	10.92
China,P.R.: Mainland 924	4.94	12.22	16.25	20.86	29.41	25.40	34.20	220.40	257.72	329.02	454.04	630.56	779.74	923.81
China,P.R.:Hong Kong 532	52.66	56.77	77.02	68.81	64.17	71.92	65.80	500.31	489.66	559.45	619.40	648.19	659.05	724.81
Fiji 819	1.06	1.07	1.44	1.45	2.07	1.98	1.78	—	—	—	.37	.02	.09	.03
India 534	71.99	170.57	245.05	391.51	566.41	489.46	515.28	601.48	832.07	1,076.16	1,439.15	1,835.43	2,172.85	2,610.14
Indonesia 536	5.46	8.41	8.56	8.74	25.16	47.29	48.42	142.85	147.30	163.43	174.80	218.87	224.83	246.72
Korea 542	28.24	33.20	28.91	19.26	23.27	25.49	28.72	335.48	302.81	282.89	245.94	210.32	186.18	183.14
Malaysia 548	6.65	8.66	12.46	9.04	14.46	24.74	35.63	207.63	203.86	270.41	329.18	393.50	444.81	283.48
Maldives 556	50.45	45.91	55.46	61.43	27.27	29.65	50.89	35.11	31.12	22.65	19.84	21.09	23.59	15.46
Myanmar 518	.59	.27	.24	.21	2.45	.11	.51	1.25	1.18	2.29	2.03	4.07	2.84	5.49
Nepal 558	.33	.88	1.66	.29	.40	3.57	.18	.01	.19	—	.08	.11	.07	.07
Pakistan 564	24.87	28.84	36.73	39.45	43.56	58.36	55.44	73.82	65.69	70.98	107.92	115.64	146.58	178.05
Papua New Guinea 853	.60	.31	.21	.20	.38	.50	.83	.15	—	.10	.02	.01	.14	.09
Philippines 566	4.37	6.28	7.71	3.36	3.34	6.13	4.61	6.71	8.43	6.39	6.77	7.46	6.48	7.99
Singapore 576	57.12	72.25	65.86	86.48	79.39	74.70	80.19	410.43	431.96	522.20	698.45	736.86	992.75	1,118.54
Taiwan Province of China 528	12.37	11.98	12.17	12.56	12.37	17.17	14.74	322.77	287.09	276.15	290.84	278.66	274.83	263.60
Thailand 578	36.88	14.16	11.54	19.41	27.40	38.72	44.70	147.35	145.73	145.89	152.14	168.29	202.96	230.81
Vietnam 582	7.39	9.30	9.12	5.71	9.75	4.61	12.63	8.02	5.46	7.83	9.01	11.44	15.52	20.95
Asia n.s. 598	13.42	—	—	8.29	—	—	—	323.11	—	—	—	—	—	—

		Exports							Imports						
		2001	2002	2003	2004	2005	2006	2007	2001	2002	2003	2004	2005	2006	2007
		Millions of U.S. Dollars							Millions of U.S. Dollars						
Europe	**170**	**224.5**	**185.3**	**214.4**	**303.4**	**242.4**	**282.3**	**334.1**	**20.8**	**22.0**	**38.1**	**30.6**	**69.0**	**79.0**	**94.3**
Bulgaria	918	.31	.67	1.35	.57	1.11	.98	1.74	5.19	1.99	2.82	2.18	2.13	1.99	3.45
Czech Republic	935	—	—	2.23	3.70	4.71	5.97	7.62	—	—	1.32	1.23	1.55	3.28	3.38
Czechoslovakia n.s.	937	1.27	—	—	—	—	—	—	.67	—	—	—	—	—	—
Hungary	944	1.64	.76	1.12	1.56	2.25	2.35	2.33	1.03	1.04	.98	.95	1.39	1.18	.76
Poland	964	11.98	9.28	12.64	18.06	19.97	26.95	34.14	1.49	1.33	2.94	4.72	13.62	16.95	23.79
Romania	968	.15	.33	.45	.67	.03	3.57	3.92	.78	.77	1.04	.79	—	2.80	5.00
Russia	922	115.61	126.57	140.82	150.98	157.66	188.18	202.60	2.75	2.66	1.63	1.87	8.91	22.77	9.86
Slovak Republic	936	—	—	—	.27	.16	1.79	7.59	—	—	—	.34	.04	.42	1.51
Turkey	186	46.19	47.67	55.77	75.95	56.56	52.55	74.13	6.02	14.18	27.34	18.56	41.36	29.56	46.56
Europe n.s.	884	47.32	—	—	51.64	—	—	—	2.82	—	—	—	—	—	—
Middle East	**407**	**433.4**	**380.4**	**445.4**	**434.1**	**517.9**	**529.0**	**640.6**	**507.8**	**879.3**	**595.4**	**921.4**	**1,065.1**	**1,253.7**	**1,526.5**
Bahrain	419	1.81	2.65	3.30	5.05	4.84	4.11	3.98	19.32	104.65	4.04	36.30	3.65	6.34	5.44
Egypt	469	13.61	—	11.12	12.51	14.48	18.41	18.62	3.78	—	3.87	1.28	1.73	8.93	11.25
Iran, I.R. of	429	29.45	35.05	35.28	57.89	74.14	83.39	117.15	233.20	183.19	249.51	418.75	523.86	758.93	844.19
Iraq	433	19.06	22.72	8.72	10.84	20.25	24.33	26.45	—	.01	—	.12	—	.05	.01
Israel	436	55.31	39.42	45.00	28.96	50.95	47.13	47.19	43.42	49.57	41.30	41.68	42.41	46.40	55.17
Jordan	439	22.05	23.18	29.02	31.63	27.47	26.41	21.25	.64	3.02	6.52	8.99	15.32	4.14	.98
Kuwait	443	9.09	9.69	9.99	10.06	12.23	12.77	13.44	7.03	96.70	17.17	14.92	7.71	8.02	7.61
Lebanon	446	7.65	5.58	7.21	6.57	6.14	6.03	10.06	.93	.11	.31	.70	.20	.08	.59
Libya	672	36.91	10.16	34.23	2.86	21.38	11.32	22.98	—	—	—	—	—	.37	—
Oman	449	4.63	4.94	3.13	2.54	6.42	4.20	4.10	3.55	2.28	3.29	3.00	3.59	6.68	65.82
Qatar	453	.88	.99	1.08	1.90	2.95	4.40	3.95	9.13	15.54	13.70	14.77	21.21	45.73	48.34
Saudi Arabia	456	31.06	30.30	29.98	31.03	38.59	28.51	51.38	35.59	155.26	75.33	177.76	147.84	147.69	151.56
Syrian Arab Republic	463	55.67	65.04	62.54	65.88	67.24	82.60	90.09	.10	.05	.03	.05	.06	.08	.69
United Arab Emirates	466	145.38	130.04	163.51	137.78	170.29	174.77	209.17	150.98	268.91	179.96	202.69	296.31	219.58	333.22
Yemen, Republic of	474	.82	.63	1.26	1.00	.59	.63	.81	.11	—	.36	.42	1.23	.70	1.59
Middle East n.s.	489	—	—	—	27.56	—	—	—	—	—	—	—	—	—	—
Western Hemisphere	**207**	**67.3**	**66.8**	**69.7**	**103.9**	**199.1**	**102.2**	**135.6**	**23.8**	**39.2**	**28.2**	**106.1**	**103.7**	**62.5**	**43.0**
Argentina	213	3.18	1.79	3.06	4.77	5.10	6.24	4.74	.38	11.17	1.03	61.51	60.08	3.03	3.44
Barbados	316	.41	.08	.09	.02	.03	.06	.04	.01	—	.01	—	—	—	—
Bolivia	218	—	—	—	—	—	1.66	1.62	—	—	—	.13	.01	.01	—
Brazil	223	2.62	2.58	3.77	8.00	13.18	12.15	17.75	4.93	7.62	7.49	20.15	13.12	31.39	5.92
Chile	228	11.17	11.12	9.56	11.71	15.65	17.78	20.66	15.01	17.10	15.73	16.31	20.65	22.76	28.73
Colombia	233	2.55	2.87	2.98	3.22	3.44	4.48	4.08	.66	.69	.77	2.91	4.95	1.43	1.14
Dominica	321	.40	.07	.02	.04	.22	.23	.26	.06	.06	—	.02	.50	.03	.38
Ecuador	248	1.41	1.80	1.60	2.15	2.21	3.24	3.78	.13	.10	.07	.57	.10	.66	.11
El Salvador	253	.87	—	—	.68	.45	.57	.97	—	—	—	—	—	—	—
Guatemala	258	2.07	2.20	1.97	1.31	2.36	2.45	2.12	—	—	—	1.80	—	—	—
Guyana	336	—	—	1.80	.07	—	.02	.05	—	—	—	—	—	—	—
Honduras	268	.42	—	—	.89	.39	.84	.91	—	—	—	—	—	—	—
Mexico	273	30.60	38.27	37.65	38.08	46.21	46.86	62.76	.99	1.01	.80	1.01	2.27	2.19	1.94
Netherlands Antilles	353	.09	.05	—	.05	99.95	—	—	—	—	—	.27	.08	—	—
Panama	283	2.92	2.76	1.43	2.32	4.49	4.99	6.04	—	—	.08	.05	1.55	—	—
Peru	293	3.73	2.66	5.11	2.40	4.54	.53	4.82	1.38	1.21	2.07	1.01	.39	.85	.93
Uruguay	298	.83	.40	.56	.63	.51	.15	.58	—	.01	.01	.28	—	.13	.37
Venezuela, Rep. Bol.	299	.50	.18	.06	.27	.37	—	4.46	.14	.26	.10	.05	.02	—	.04
Western Hem. n.s.	399	3.58	—	—	27.31	—	—	—	.08	—	—	—	—	—	—
Other Countries n.i.e.	**910**	—	—	—	—	—	—	—	—	—	—	—	—	—	—
North Korea	954	—	—	—	—	—	—	—	—	—	—	.05	.04	—	—
Countries & Areas n.s.	**898**	**42.7**	**68.0**	**216.9**	**53.1**	**148.7**	**311.9**	**378.7**	**18.1**	**14.2**	**165.1**	**9.0**	**11.7**	**60.7**	**77.3**
Memorandum Items															
European Union	998	1,278.23	1,406.67	1,464.80	1,865.76	1,975.38	2,315.28	2,862.90	858.78	909.14	1,109.25	1,256.94	1,296.30	1,408.88	1,385.94
Oil Exporting Ctys	999	283.98	254.33	295.43	264.72	375.89	392.20	504.58	582.70	869.77	702.80	1,007.41	1,220.17	1,412.06	1,697.78
Non-Oil Develop.Ctys	201	864.95	908.69	1,080.55	1,396.18	1,578.36	1,510.45	1,675.94	3,335.10	3,319.27	3,730.54	4,673.10	5,375.35	6,155.98	6,820.55
PERCENT DISTRIBUTION															
Industrial Countries	**101**	74.8	73.7	69.0	70.2	67.1	67.8	66.9	31.3	30.2	31.1	28.9	25.5	25.6	23.9
Developing Countries	**202**	24.3	24.9	26.8	28.8	30.6	27.6	28.2	68.4	69.6	66.4	71.0	74.4	73.8	75.4
Africa	**607**	.7	.8	.9	.8	.7	.7	.7	.5	.6	.4	.8	.8	.3	.3
Asia	**507**	8.2	10.5	11.7	13.4	14.9	13.6	13.1	58.3	53.4	56.1	57.0	59.7	59.9	60.4
Europe	**170**	4.8	4.0	4.2	5.3	3.8	4.1	4.3	.4	.4	.6	.4	.8	.8	.8
Middle East	**407**	9.2	8.1	8.7	7.5	8.1	7.7	8.3	8.9	14.6	8.9	11.5	12.0	12.2	13.5
Western Hemisphere	**207**	1.4	1.4	1.4	1.8	3.1	1.5	1.8	.4	.7	.4	1.3	1.2	.6	.4
ANNUAL PERCENT CHANGE															
World	**001**	−13.5	−.9	9.7	12.2	10.9	7.8	12.5	−14.3	5.1	10.8	19.9	10.8	15.7	10.2
Industrial Countries	**101**	−14.3	−2.4	2.7	14.2	5.9	9.1	11.0	−20.5	1.3	14.0	11.4	−2.4	16.3	3.1
Developing Countries	**202**	−7.0	1.2	18.3	20.7	17.7	−2.6	14.6	−11.3	6.9	5.8	28.1	16.1	14.7	12.6
Africa	**607**	−9.3	13.6	14.6	6.1	−3.2	9.1	5.9	−24.8	29.3	−12.7	115.7	5.5	−54.1	−2.7
Asia	**507**	−22.1	26.2	22.4	28.3	22.9	−1.0	8.3	−10.3	−3.7	16.4	21.8	16.1	16.1	11.1
Europe	**170**	3.2	−17.5	15.7	41.5	−20.1	16.5	18.3	21.2	5.9	73.2	−19.5	125.2	14.4	19.4
Middle East	**407**	8.3	−12.2	17.1	−2.5	19.3	2.1	21.1	−15.8	73.2	−32.3	54.8	15.6	17.7	21.8
Western Hemisphere	**207**	−15.4	−.8	4.2	49.2	91.6	−48.6	32.7	−35.2	64.9	−28.2	276.6	−2.2	−39.8	−31.2
Other Countries n.i.e.	**910**	—	—	....	....	....	....	....	−104.8	—	....	....	−12.3	23.6	24.1

	Exports 2001	2002	2003	2004	2005	2006	2007	Imports 2001	2002	2003	2004	2005	2006	2007
	Millions of U.S. Dollars							*Millions of U.S. Dollars*						
IFS World Total	**1,698.7**	**1,949.1**	**2,542.2**	**3,777.8**	**4,824.3**	**5,656.6**	**8,866.3**	**2,300.9**	**2,446.4**	**2,881.9**	**4,075.2**	**6,756.8**	**8,073.5**	**8,450.0**
DOTS World Total 001	**1,699.9Y**	**1,941.6Y**	**2,609.4**	**3,773.7**	**4,821.8**	**5,654.6**	**8,866.4**	**1,864.3Y**	**2,168.2Y**	**2,713.9Y**	**4,085.9**	**6,689.2**	**8,072.2**	**8,739.2**
Industrial Countries 101	**479.4Y**	**446.7Y**	**428.4**	**583.8**	**781.8**	**686.1**	**996.7**	**804.4Y**	**787.0Y**	**889.7Y**	**1,236.4**	**1,961.0**	**2,355.8**	**2,159.5**
United States 111	3.27V	1.36V	6.75	2.85	12.35	4.90	9.40	19.14V	11.88V	17.42S	33.97	129.66	104.03	154.44
Canada 156	.50V	.15V	11.80	12.79	63.03	63.17	60.27	41.05V	36.19V	32.19S	62.46	81.03	77.71	163.30
Australia 193	.09V	.08V	28.22	.02	—	—	—	74.42V	87.18V	83.93S	168.92	221.84	223.10	178.05
Japan 158	266.77V	264.13V	39.09	402.23	577.53	522.58	744.45	37.97V	54.35V	84.15S	165.08	341.85	535.77	367.81
New Zealand 196	—V	.01V	2.49	—	—	—	—	1.52V	1.23V	2.05S	4.24	7.64	13.35	21.22
Austria 122	.01V	.02V	1.12	—	—	.01	—	8.16V	11.24V	12.75S	14.70	10.77	13.79	23.70
Belgium 124	3.31V	3.84V	—	—	5.16	2.71	2.69	27.29V	21.84V	12.52S	—	37.95	42.21	32.21
Belgium-Luxembourg n.s. 127	—Y	—Y	3.34	14.92	—	—	—	—Y	—Y	11.71S	36.60	—	—	—
Cyprus 423	.07V	.17V	2.54	.19	.01	—	.20	4.01V	4.22V	6.74S	12.00	7.24	11.46	8.63
Denmark 128	.15V	.41V	7.03	.32	.24	.66	.35	10.78V	9.54V	15.82S	12.05	42.07	49.64	23.68
Finland 172	.22V	7.95V	.42	.60	1.12	1.56	.86	18.13V	2.99V	2.95S	9.03	14.81	38.92	28.84
France 132	94.60V	41.24V	32.15	23.84	26.10	7.14	12.70	111.29V	82.24V	110.24S	72.78	220.71	372.96	257.56
Germany 134	29.40V	32.35V	85.34	34.33	27.28	13.23	11.47	143.67V	116.11V	133.23S	185.15	81.24	.02	—
Greece 174	11.51V	5.23V	4.10	8.49	1.69	5.93	1.29	5.65V	5.17V	8.09S	18.47	21.81	9.01	7.77
Iceland 176	.11V	.12V	—	—	—	—	—	—V	—V	—S	—	—	—	—
Ireland 178	.64V	1.00V	2.97	—	1.91	.24	.59	13.48V	14.47V	9.78S	11.30	18.39	19.55	19.21
Italy 136	34.56V	61.76V	34.40	14.27	19.13	9.85	22.36	49.63V	76.83V	67.42S	118.50	257.58	271.61	328.80
Luxembourg 137	—V	—V	—	—	—	—	—	.11V	.16V	.08S	—	—	—	—
Malta 181	—Y	—V	.52	—	—	—	—	1.90Y	.95V	1.41S	.45	.01	.10	.01
Netherlands 138	11.57V	8.83V	26.95	7.32	5.48	13.99	96.11	62.40V	61.06V	53.06S	60.12	93.43	109.14	108.35
Norway 142	1.13V	.81V	.04	—	—	—	—	1.18V	5.45V	.44S	3.40	4.39	5.56	5.04
Portugal 182	1.24V	.70V	.81	.90	11.72	.18	.26	2.19V	2.90V	1.93S	1.23	1.72	1.14	2.01
Slovenia 961	.09V	.10V	—	—	—	—	—	.30V	.34V	.16S	—	—	—	—
Spain 184	5.72V	3.18V	4.68	2.14	1.38	.48	.70	13.06V	12.61V	10.65S	7.07	15.00	21.39	24.37
Sweden 144	.96V	2.39V	6.99	2.48	5.82	4.00	3.51	12.36V	31.46V	43.74S	46.60	82.02	96.39	99.62
Switzerland 146	.31V	.31V	29.50	—	.02	16.52	.10	18.26V	19.08V	31.62S	41.01	48.00	31.07	54.27
United Kingdom 112	13.12V	10.51V	97.15	56.06	21.79	18.99	29.40	126.42V	117.47V	135.59S	151.28	221.87	307.84	250.62
Developing Countries 202	**1,219.3Y**	**1,493.6Y**	**2,159.6**	**3,180.9**	**4,025.0**	**4,933.2**	**7,861.0**	**1,059.8Y**	**1,381.1Y**	**1,727.3Y**	**2,378.5**	**4,644.1**	**5,515.2**	**6,281.9**
Africa 607	**20.7Y**	**11.3Y**	**52.2**	**24.7**	**64.2**	**57.9**	**36.9**	**69.8Y**	**85.4Y**	**120.7Y**	**115.4**	**160.2**	**174.3**	**214.1**
Algeria 612	.49V	.93V	.15	1.16	.73	.46	.39	.03V	.06V	.04S	.03	9.62	4.80	2.91
Angola 614	—Y	—Y	—	—	—	—	—	—Y	—Y	—S	—	.20	—	.10
Burundi 618	—V	—V	.02	—	—	—	—	—V	—V	.12S	.24	.52	.27	4.02
Cameroon 622	—V	—V	—	—	—	—	—	—V	—V	.07S	—	—	—	—
Central African Rep. 626	.01Y	.01Y	—	—	—	—	—	.44Y	.48Y	.30S	—	—	—	—
Chad 628	—Y	—Y	—	—	—	—	—	.46Y	.50Y	.30S	—	—	—	—
Comoros 632	—Y	—Y	—	—	—	—	—	—Y	—Y	—S	—	—	.26	.05
Congo, Dem. Rep. of 636	—Y	—Y	—	—	—	—	—	—Y	—Y	.01S	—	1.01	7.01	.66
Congo, Republic of 634	—V	—V	—	—	—	—	—	—V	—V	—S	—	2.07	.20	.80
Côte d'Ivoire 662	—V	—V	—	—	—	—	—	—V	.02V	—S	—	—	—	—
Djibouti 611	—Y	—Y	.04	—	—	—	—	—Y	—Y	.02S	—	.21	.02	.31
Eritrea 643	—Y	—Y	—	—	2.50	1.93	.89	—Y	—Y	—S	—	.77	1.53	2.36
Ethiopia 644	.80V	.74V	.54	1.57	55.13	50.31	28.51	—V	2.48V	4.29S	.26	2.15	13.45	15.96
Ghana 652	.04Y	.05Y	—	—	—	—	—	—Y	—Y	—S	—	—	—	—
Kenya 664	11.92V	2.93V	15.70	2.18	2.22	—	—	34.27V	39.37V	53.45S	37.14	40.67	39.85	57.23
Liberia 668	—Y	—Y	—	—	—	1.05	—	....	....	....	....	....	....	....
Madagascar 674	.07V	—V	.06	.02	.01	—	.03	.33V	.03V	.05S	.08	.36	.38	.36
Malawi 676	—Y	—Y	—	—	—	.02	—	.05Y	.06Y	.02S	—	.01	.03	—
Mauritius 684	.01V	—V	.02	—	—	—	—	.09V	—V	.14S	—	.30	.75	.29
Morocco 686	.20V	.13V	.39	—	.06	—	.32	.11V	.08V	.34S	1.51	4.59	1.05	.29
Mozambique 688	—V	—V	—	—	—	—	.21	—V	—V	—S	—	—	—	—
Namibia 728	—Y	—Y	—	—	—	—	—	—Y	—Y	—S	—	3.19	.09	.07
Nigeria 694	.31V	.01V	.09	12.07	.01	—	—	—V	—V	.49S	—	.40	.67	.75
Rwanda 714	—Y	—Y	—	—	—	—	—	—Y	—Y	—S	.62	—	.03	.01
Seychelles 718	—V	—V	—	—	—	—	—	—V	—V	—S	—	.79	.91	1.20
Somalia 726	.78Y	.84Y	.01	—	—	—	—	.02Y	.03Y	.36S	.21	.32	.59	.19
South Africa 199	.16V	.33V	11.99	—	—	—	—	22.31V	31.71V	31.55S	47.86	44.00	—	—
Sacca exc. South Afr. 608	—Y	—Y	—	—	—	—	—	.03V	.35V	—S	—	—	—	—
Swaziland 734	—Y	—Y	—	—	—	—	—	—Y	—Y	—S	—	15.48	59.89	86.97
Tanzania 738	.04V	.10V	—	—	—	—	—	.26V	.30V	.16S	—	—	—	—
Togo 742	—V	—V	—	—	—	—	—	—V	.01V	—S	—	—	—	—
Tunisia 744	5.72V	5.11V	2.01	7.60	6.02	6.04	7.47	.07V	.53V	.74S	.25	4.68	1.90	8.10
Uganda 746	.13V	.05V	6.40	—	—	—	—	10.07V	6.34V	16.82S	22.79	29.22	42.18	33.84
Zambia 754	.05V	.07V	—	—	—	—	—	.10V	—V	—S	.05	—	—	—
Zimbabwe 698	.01V	—V	6.67	—	—	—	—	1.16V	3.08V	6.55S	4.35	.39	—	—
Africa n.s. 799	—Y	—Y	8.09	.10	—	—	.01	—Y	—Y	4.88S	—	—	—	—
Asia 507	**1,047.1Y**	**1,199.3Y**	**1,283.3**	**2,709.5**	**3,558.3**	**4,317.0**	**7,401.6**	**601.4Y**	**840.0Y**	**751.4Y**	**990.1**	**2,158.2**	**2,930.4**	**3,641.7**
Bangladesh 513	5.05V	4.03V	15.81	14.41	19.69	13.67	13.07	2.72V	18.35V	36.98S	14.45	14.79	17.79	15.63
China,P.R.: Mainland 924	852.84V	1,052.15V	1,067.08	2,523.90	3,427.10	4,243.98	7,276.88	249.31V	431.53V	386.01S	529.59	1,382.99	1,679.43	2,436.21
China,P.R.:Hong Kong 532	4.46V	4.11V	.84	.92	1.42	.24	.15	3.02V	4.46V	2.70S	1.51	3.11	16.71	8.49

		Exports 2001	2002	2003	2004	2005	2006	2007	Imports 2001	2002	2003	2004	2005	2006	2007
		Millions of U.S. Dollars							*Millions of U.S. Dollars*						
India	534	7.68Y	19.75V	79.00	27.91	30.77	22.50	16.44	110.78Y	120.37V	114.82S	197.07	317.84	599.04	546.50
Indonesia	536	31.31V	.24V	36.18	50.64	40.08	2.39	1.59	68.35V	101.84V	41.47S	50.17	49.85	71.60	79.13
Korea	542	101.38V	72.56V	36.50	23.53	7.93	6.19	49.57	79.05V	77.63V	70.83S	99.34	149.78	335.37	305.58
Malaysia	548	.21V	.16V	12.59	.10	—	—	—	21.44V	19.72V	50.24S	40.93	143.38	92.19	83.85
Myanmar	518	.01Y	.01Y	—	—	—	—	—	—Y	—Y	—S	—	—	—	—
Pakistan	564	3.80V	4.63V	14.63	7.30	18.08	8.81	42.31	9.24V	16.86V	9.80S	15.23	23.93	34.05	39.81
Papua New Guinea	853	9.19Y	9.97Y	—	—	—	—	—	—Y	—Y	—S	—	—	—	—
Philippines	566	.39V	.32V	—	—	—	—	—	.44V	.27V	.40S	—	—	—	—
Singapore	576	9.80V	10.64V	5.57	49.69	5.83	15.96	.02	25.42V	16.79V	14.59S	9.94	28.11	16.76	23.54
Sri Lanka	524	—V	—V	—	—	—	—	—	.04V	.04V	.08S	—	—	—	—
Taiwan Province of China	528	13.63V	10.81V	.60	.98	1.75	1.36	1.22	10.21V	8.12V	6.23S	13.85	10.60	15.09	17.46
Thailand	578	6.36V	9.53V	14.14	10.13	5.67	1.92	.38	20.06V	23.35V	16.85S	17.98	33.79	52.39	85.47
Vietnam	582	.95V	.36V	—	—	—	—	—	1.27V	.64V	.43S	—	—	—	—
Asia n.s.	598	—Y	—Y	.38	—	—	—	—	—Y	—Y	—S	—	—	—	—
Europe	**170**	**10.3Y**	**18.7Y**	**34.3**	**14.6**	**11.5**	**6.7**	**5.3**	**105.6Y**	**153.8Y**	**106.6Y**	**122.7**	**336.2**	**319.1**	**324.2**
Albania	914	—V	1.83V	—	—	—	—	—	—V	—V	—S	—	—	—	—
Belarus	913	—V	—V	—	—	—	—	—	4.68V	10.17V	6.19S	—	—	—	—
Bulgaria	918	.82V	.57V	2.07	1.41	.07	.24	.11	3.64V	3.17V	4.67S	7.35	13.95	7.41	5.41
Croatia	960	.04V	.10V	—	—	—	—	—	.08V	8.56V	.14S	—	—	—	—
Czech Republic	935	1.60V	.64V	—	—	—	—	—	5.38V	2.92V	.98S	—	—	—	—
Czechoslovakia n.s.	937	—Y	—Y	—	—	—	.03	—	—Y	—Y	1.15S	3.72	—	—	—
Estonia	939	.01V	—V	—	—	—	—	—	.45V	.31V	1.32S	—	—	—	—
Hungary	944	.54V	.11V	.77	—	.01	—	.04	.40V	.65V	1.62S	.06	.48	1.67	7.24
Kazakhstan	916	.01V	—V	—	—	—	—	—	—V	9.94V	.56S	—	—	—	—
Latvia	941	—V	—V	—	—	—	—	—	.14V	.17V	.08S	—	—	—	—
Lithuania	946	.01V	.09V	—	—	—	—	—	.72V	.96V	—S	—	—	—	—
Macedonia, FYR	962	.46V	.12V	—	—	—	—	—	—V	—V	—S	—	—	—	—
Poland	964	2.89V	2.46V	4.80	1.83	2.08	—	.41	6.20V	7.91V	3.98S	5.32	12.29	15.90	9.24
Romania	968	.17V	.14V	1.58	.56	.64	1.10	.78	8.16V	4.11V	6.07S	3.56	2.17	—	—
Russia	922	2.17V	1.20V	—	—	.62	—	.68	4.52V	23.26V	12.40S	—	57.50	—	—
Slovak Republic	936	.02V	.03V	—	—	—	—	—	1.32V	1.21V	.69S	—	—	—	—
Turkey	186	1.27V	11.28V	24.84	10.55	8.05	.37	1.32	60.03V	65.23V	51.99S	102.65	154.65	206.27	205.84
Ukraine	926	.30V	.16V	—	—	—	4.94	1.85	9.86V	15.24V	14.74S	—	95.09	87.89	96.44
Yugoslavia n.s.	966	—Y	—Y	—	—	—	—	.11	—Y	—Y	—S	—	.07	—	—
Europe n.s.	884	—Y	—Y	.28	.20	—	—	—	—Y	—Y	—S	—	—	—	—
Middle East	**407**	**136.5Y**	**263.8Y**	**764.5**	**416.6**	**377.9**	**541.0**	**414.8**	**263.6Y**	**280.2Y**	**732.0Y**	**1,076.6**	**1,802.3**	**1,843.2**	**1,962.1**
Bahrain	419	2.11Y	2.29Y	37.93	—	—	—	—	—Y	—Y	13.82S	36.72	183.14	85.74	59.83
Egypt	469	58.24Y	63.21Y	62.27	108.50	78.69	96.82	54.44	36.69V	39.82Y	104.21S	208.75	369.45	428.22	492.97
Iran, I.R. of	429	—V	2.00V	5.42	—	—	—	—	—Y	—Y	15.07S	27.45	56.29	47.14	49.46
Iraq	433	—Y	—Y	.06	—	—	.01	—	—Y	—Y	.02S	—	.08	—	—
Jordan	439	14.89V	10.18V	21.19	9.56	3.12	3.40	3.39	26.69V	38.43V	32.26S	35.08	45.33	54.11	69.09
Kuwait	443	.62Y	.64Y	2.27	.74	1.56	1.83	1.00	—Y	—Y	3.17S	10.15	16.24	30.85	17.15
Lebanon	446	15.37Y	16.68Y	18.17	24.98	42.53	17.28	17.22	3.24Y	3.52Y	5.68S	9.24	13.23	17.21	26.81
Libya	672	—Y	—Y	4.49	3.19	1.62	5.38	2.92	2.24Y	2.38Y	1.56S	.01	12.41	.99	23.70
Oman	449	.27V	.13V	1.77	.02	—	—	.03	18.58V	12.82V	13.51S	4.64	10.66	30.31	14.41
Qatar	453	—V	1.36V	1.50	.60	.40	.26	.13	4.21V	1.21V	1.46S	.99	26.44	15.70	30.92
Saudi Arabia	456	26.08V	149.24V	447.27	164.19	136.43	126.38	98.07	152.07Y	161.70Y	438.01S	471.49	627.46	649.33	654.62
Syrian Arab Republic	463	13.93Y	15.11Y	16.98	15.84	12.69	18.01	10.66	10.33Y	11.21Y	14.36S	22.47	46.76	38.91	42.82
United Arab Emirates	466	—V	—V	140.30	85.53	90.04	227.43	224.95	6.77Y	7.20Y	86.89S	239.25	394.76	444.67	480.37
Yemen, Republic of	474	5.00V	3.01V	—	—	10.85	44.21	1.94	2.75V	1.93V	1.22S	—	.08	—	—
Middle East n.s.	489	—Y	—Y	4.88	3.45	—	—	—	—Y	—Y	.76S	10.33	—	—	—
Western Hemisphere	**207**	**4.7Y**	**.5Y**	**25.3**	**15.5**	**13.1**	**10.6**	**2.4**	**19.4Y**	**21.6Y**	**16.6Y**	**73.8**	**187.3**	**248.1**	**139.9**
Argentina	213	.07V	.01V	2.18	—	—	—	—	5.70V	4.76V	.60S	1.34	30.77	2.37	6.01
Aruba	314	4.26V	.03V	—	—	—	—	—	....	....	....	....	....	....	....
Barbados	316	—V	—V	—	—	—	—	—	.01V	.01V	—S	—	—	—	—
Brazil	223	.13V	.02V	1.84	—	—	—	—	8.97V	16.45V	6.76S	23.94	54.27	149.67	94.69
Colombia	233	.16V	.08V	—	—	—	—	—	.09V	.03V	—S	—	—	—	—
Ecuador	248	—V	—V	9.51	—	—	—	—	—V	—V	6.89S	44.71	96.44	92.11	35.26
Guatemala	258	.03V	—V	—	—	—	—	—	.15V	.37V	.05S	—	—	—	—
Guyana	336	—Y	.01Y	—	—	—	—	—	—Y	—Y	—S	—	—	—	—
Honduras	268	—V	.02V	—	—	—	—	—	—V	—V	—S	—	—	—	—
Jamaica	343	—V	—V	—	—	—	—	—	—V	—V	.05S	.12	.91	.40	1.05
Mexico	273	—V	—V	2.36	15.32	13.11	10.61	2.28	—V	—V	.50S	2.65	4.54	3.53	2.69
Netherlands Antilles	353	—V	.12V	—	—	—	—	—	.31V	.01V	—S	—	—	—	—
Panama	283	—V	—V	.17	—	—	—	—	—V	—V	.83S	.23	.34	.02	.15
Peru	293	—V	.01V	—	—	—	—	—	4.21V	—V	—S	—	—	—	—
St. Lucia	362	.03Y	.03Y	—	—	—	—	—	—Y	—Y	—S	—	—	—	—
Suriname	366	—Y	—Y	—	—	—	—	—	.01Y	.02Y	.01S	—	—	—	—
Venezuela, Rep. Bol	299	—V	.14V	—	—	—	—	—	—V	—V	.03S	—	—	—	—
Western Hem. n.s.	399	—Y	—Y	9.21	.22	—	—	.14	—Y	—Y	.86S	.82	—	—	—
Countries & Areas n.s.	**898**	**1.2Y**	**1.3Y**	**21.4**	**9.1**	**15.0**	**35.3**	**8.6**	**.2Y**	**.2Y**	**92.5S**	**310.0**	**84.1**	**201.3**	**297.7**
Special Categories	**899**	**—Y**	**—Y**	**—**	**—**	**—**	**—**	**—**	**—Y**	**—Y**	**4.5S**	**161.0**	**—**	**—**	**—**
Memorandum Items															
European Union	998	212.25Y	183.02Y	316.09	167.68	130.93	78.95	182.94	625.45Y	585.73Y	646.53Y	762.70	1,139.38	1,382.74	1,231.86
Oil Exporting Ctys	999	59.07Y	154.67Y	639.50	318.13	270.85	364.14	329.08	252.26Y	287.21Y	601.74Y	804.18	1,204.22	1,296.06	1,353.42
Non-Oil Develop.Ctys	201	1,160.24Y	1,338.94Y	1,520.10	2,862.76	3,754.13	4,569.05	7,531.96	807.54Y	1,093.86Y	1,125.56Y	1,574.32	3,439.91	4,219.11	4,928.53

	Exports 2001	2002	2003	2004	2005	2006	2007	Imports 2001	2002	2003	2004	2005	2006	2007
PERCENT DISTRIBUTION														
Industrial Countries.................. 101	28.2	23.0	16.4	15.5	16.2	12.1	11.2	43.1	36.3	32.8	30.3	29.3	29.2	24.7
Developing Countries.............. 202	71.7	76.9	82.8	84.3	83.5	87.2	88.7	56.8	63.7	63.6	58.2	69.4	68.3	71.9
Africa..................................... 607	1.2	.6	2.0	.7	1.3	1.0	.4	3.7	3.9	4.4	2.8	2.4	2.2	2.5
Asia.. 507	61.6	61.8	49.2	71.8	73.8	76.3	83.5	32.3	38.7	27.7	24.2	32.3	36.3	41.7
Europe.................................... 170	.6	1.0	1.3	.4	.2	.1	.1	5.7	7.1	3.9	3.0	5.0	4.0	3.7
Middle East............................ 407	8.0	13.6	29.3	11.0	7.8	9.6	4.7	14.1	12.9	27.0	26.3	26.9	22.8	22.5
Western Hemisphere.............. 207	.3	—	1.0	.4	.3	.2	—	1.0	1.0	.6	1.8	2.8	3.1	1.6
ANNUAL PERCENT CHANGE														
World.. 001	5.0	14.2	34.4	44.6	27.8	17.3	56.8	28.3	16.3	25.2	50.6	63.7	20.7	8.3
Industrial Countries.................. 101	7.7	−6.8	−4.1	36.3	33.9	−12.2	45.3	34.4	−2.2	13.1	39.0	58.6	20.1	−8.3
Developing Countries.............. 202	4.0	22.5	44.6	47.3	26.5	22.6	59.3	24.1	30.3	25.1	37.7	95.3	18.8	13.9
Africa..................................... 607	173.6	−45.5	361.7	−52.7	159.9	−9.8	−36.2	34.7	22.4	41.3	−4.4	38.8	8.9	22.8
Asia.. 507	9.7	14.5	7.0	111.1	31.3	21.3	71.5	33.1	39.7	−10.5	31.8	118.0	35.8	24.3
Europe.................................... 170	−25.0	81.7	83.3	−57.6	−21.2	−41.7	−20.8	38.1	45.7	−30.7	15.1	174.1	−5.1	1.6
Middle East............................ 407	−26.4	93.3	189.8	−45.5	−9.3	43.2	−23.3	4.5	6.3	161.2	47.1	67.4	2.3	6.5
Western Hemisphere.............. 207	−56.5	−89.9	—	−38.5	−15.6	−19.1	−77.1	−11.6	11.3	−23.4	345.5	153.7	32.5	−43.6

		Exports							Imports						
		2001	2002	2003	2004	2005	2006	2007	2001	2002	2003	2004	2005	2006	2007
		Millions of U.S. Dollars							Millions of U.S. Dollars						
IFS World Total		**403.0**	**469.0**	**638.0**	**895.0**	**949.6**	**1,200.0**	**1,310.0**	**461.0**	**492.0**	**704.0**	**742.5**	**769.7**	**820.0**	**940.0**
DOTS World Total	**001**	**498.1Y**	**475.2Y**	**584.2Y**	**880.4Y**	**923.8Y**	**1,188.1Y**	**1,398.8Y**	**665.8Y**	**593.9Y**	**680.1Y**	**750.9Y**	**922.6Y**	**968.6Y**	**1,246.0Y**
Industrial Countries	**101**	**434.5Y**	**404.9Y**	**462.9Y**	**744.0Y**	**767.0Y**	**956.9Y**	**1,107.3Y**	**335.7Y**	**373.9Y**	**467.6Y**	**489.1Y**	**593.1Y**	**610.2Y**	**783.3Y**
United States	111	134.82V	126.91V	134.27V	134.09V	155.64V	156.00V	123.91V	174.24V	137.28V	211.86V	196.24V	267.85V	283.91V	336.60V
Canada	156	35.08V	29.80V	.71V	110.35V	152.10V	190.81V	374.69V	4.29V	2.86V	5.00V	11.70V	10.30V	9.92V	10.35V
Australia	193	—V	—V	.07V	.01V	.10V	.26V	.32V	.56V	.59V	.82V	1.29V	1.11V	2.02V	2.23V
Japan	158	17.03V	16.87V	12.13V	11.81V	10.70V	7.65V	7.98V	23.68V	35.55V	43.11V	49.42V	47.46V	48.94V	63.60V
New Zealand	196	—V	—V	—V	—V	—V	—V	2.73V	.21V	.02V	.06V	.04V	.39V	.39V	.09V
Austria	122	—V	.01V	.03V	.01V	—V	.01V	2.89V	.26V	.43V	.65V	1.32V	1.64V	1.14V	6.72V
Belgium	124	3.93V	19.00V	72.14V	90.35V	91.22V	125.21V	129.10V	11.41V	11.17V	14.64V	17.90V	23.62V	14.44V	18.72V
Cyprus	423	—V	—V	—V	—V	.01Y	—V	.01V	.01V	—V	.07V	.02V	.05V	.15V	.18V
Denmark	128	.45V	.03V	.10V	—V	.02V	—V	.03V	.96V	1.53V	2.69V	2.46V	3.98V	1.03V	1.97V
Finland	172	—V	—V	—V	.04V	—V	—V	—V	1.20V	5.16V	.36V	.63V	1.35V	.61V	.76V
France	132	51.07V	41.09V	58.19V	74.75V	74.81V	105.03V	100.15V	6.65V	46.27V	6.32V	8.34V	12.49V	10.76V	11.59V
Germany	134	.16V	3.76V	1.68V	1.47V	3.08V	.33V	.52V	7.20V	12.23V	20.72V	17.53V	23.91V	16.00V	23.98V
Greece	174	.03V	.19V	.02V	—V	.02V	.01V	.08V	.44V	.13V	.12V	.12V	.12V	.13V	.14V
Iceland	176	32.27V	29.88V	26.52V	34.28V	26.93V	51.50V	19.95V	—V	.01V	—V	—V	—V	.02V	—V
Ireland	178	.01V	.05V	.01V	.01V	—V	—V	—V	.17V	.20V	.38V	.59V	.92V	1.01V	1.28V
Italy	136	.07V	1.33V	25.38V	8.33V	6.68V	.65V	15.26V	2.99V	3.93V	9.25V	4.64V	8.57V	8.29V	41.29V
Luxembourg	137	.01V	.02V	—V	.05V	—V	—V	—V	.27V	1.08V	.47V	.63V	1.73V	.33V	1.26V
Malta	181	—Y	—V	—V	—V	—V	—V	—V	.02Y	—V	.01V	.16V	.11V	.02V	.01V
Netherlands	138	44.27V	27.88V	23.92V	17.22V	24.18V	30.54V	29.56V	84.91V	96.58V	125.49V	145.20V	160.01V	182.27V	215.78V
Norway	142	82.20V	100.96V	105.56V	259.15V	217.33V	283.68V	282.59V	1.48V	.71V	.62V	.70V	.58V	.82V	6.31V
Portugal	182	3.32V	.88V	.28V	.22V	2.24V	1.49V	1.15V	.14V	.20V	.12V	.40V	.15V	.42V	.69V
Slovenia	961	.09V	—V	—V	—Y	—V	—V	—V	.09V	.27V	.19V	.25Y	.06V	.03V	1.17V
Spain	184	.32V	1.22V	1.10V	1.04V	.81V	2.63V	15.44V	.93V	1.58V	2.09V	3.42V	2.14V	2.89V	6.24V
Sweden	144	.15V	.06V	—V	.01V	.09V	.03V	.51V	.44V	.55V	2.20V	4.01V	4.69V	2.77V	13.20V
Switzerland	146	.03V	.03V	.29V	.10V	.17V	.14V	.04V	.44V	.47V	2.23V	2.27V	1.56V	2.32V	1.62V
United Kingdom	112	29.25V	4.92V	.49V	.71V	.86V	.92V	.38V	12.71V	15.05V	18.15V	19.86V	18.27V	19.62V	17.57V
Developing Countries	**202**	**63.4Y**	**70.1Y**	**121.1Y**	**136.1Y**	**156.4Y**	**230.8Y**	**291.0Y**	**326.9Y**	**216.6Y**	**208.2Y**	**256.2Y**	**323.1Y**	**350.4Y**	**452.8Y**
Africa	**607**	**11.4Y**	**15.3Y**	**11.3Y**	**14.8Y**	**16.8Y**	**20.8Y**	**25.6Y**	**.6Y**	**.5Y**	**3.4Y**	**1.6Y**	**.6Y**	**.5Y**	**.6Y**
Algeria	612	.04V	—V	—Y	—Y	—Y	—Y	—Y	—V	—V	—Y	—Y	—Y	—Y	—Y
Benin	638	.01V	—V	—V	—V	—V	—Y	—Y	—V	—V	—V	—V	—V	—Y	—Y
Cameroon	622	2.60V	—V	—V	—Y	—Y	—Y	—Y	—V	—V	—V	—Y	—Y	—Y	—Y
Ghana	652	.04Y	.04Y	.06Y	.07Y	.08Y	.10Y	.13Y	—Y	—Y	—Y	—Y	—Y	—Y	—Y
Liberia	668	7.58Y	8.23Y	10.41Y	13.68Y	15.63Y	19.31Y	23.97Y	.04Y	.04Y	.06Y	.07Y	.08Y	.10Y	.13Y
Madagascar	674	.12V	—V	—V	—Y	—Y	—Y	—Y	—V	—V	—V	—Y	—Y	—Y	—Y
Mali	678	—Y	—Y	—Y	—Y	—Y	—Y	—Y	.03Y	.03Y	.04Y	.05Y	.06Y	.07Y	.08Y
Morocco	686	.01V	.01V	.01V	—V	.02V	.03Y	.03Y	.14V	.07V	.04V	.09V	.10V	.13Y	.16Y
Nigeria	694	.53V	.97V	.46V	.60Y	.77Y	.95Y	1.23Y	—V	—V	.04V	.06Y	.08Y	.10Y	.12Y
Senegal	722	—V	—V	—V	—V	—V	—V	—Y	—V	—V	—V	—V	.02V	—V	—Y
South Africa	199	—V	5.95V	.18V	.31V	.11V	.22V	—V	.05V	.20V	3.18V	1.27V	.17V	—V	—V
Sudan	732	.01Y	.01Y	.01Y	—V	—V	—V	—V	—Y	—Y	—V	—V	—V	—V	—V
Tanzania	738	.49V	.09V	.12Y	.15Y	.17Y	.21Y	.26Y	.05V	.02V	.03Y	.04Y	.05Y	.06Y	.07Y
Tunisia	744	—V	—V	.01V	—V	—V	—V	—Y	.07V	.10V	.05V	.06V	—V	—V	—Y
Zambia	754	—V	—V	—V	—V	.02V	—V	—V	—V	—V	—V	.01V	—V	—V	—V
Zimbabwe	698	—V	—V	—V	—V	—V	—V	—Y	.25V	—V	—V	—V	—V	—V	—Y
Asia	**507**	**9.3Y**	**10.5Y**	**20.8Y**	**5.1Y**	**15.3Y**	**12.8Y**	**14.4Y**	**184.0Y**	**91.2Y**	**72.7Y**	**75.2Y**	**105.0Y**	**102.6Y**	**144.6Y**
China,P.R.: Mainland	924	7.62V	5.12V	16.32V	1.35V	6.47V	3.58V	2.78V	167.43V	73.73V	50.07V	34.19V	59.50V	47.58V	73.89V
China,P.R.:Hong Kong	532	.96V	1.08V	1.37V	2.13V	3.21V	2.62V	3.04V	2.73V	2.91V	2.01V	1.97V	2.18V	2.02V	5.03V
India	534	.15Y	2.28V	1.09V	.73V	4.64V	5.73Y	7.11Y	1.52Y	1.88V	3.58V	15.13V	17.63V	21.79Y	27.04Y
Indonesia	536	.08V	.08V	.01V	—V	.04V	.05V	—V	1.81V	1.91V	2.53V	3.58V	2.58V	2.88V	3.46V
Korea	542	—V	.03V	.02V	—V	.05V	.06V	.32V	2.93V	2.19V	3.15V	4.15V	5.83V	7.17V	9.57V
Malaysia	548	.25V	.28V	.05V	.04V	.01V	.01V	.03V	.42V	.43V	1.01V	1.42V	1.57V	2.77V	3.58V
Pakistan	564	.07V	.04V	.01V	.02V	.18V	.22Y	.28Y	.03V	.08V	.16V	.65V	.34V	.42Y	.52Y
Philippines	566	.02V	—V	.39V	.05V	—V	—V	—V	.04V	.14V	.30V	.33V	.12V	.01V	.09V
Taiwan Province of China	528	.06V	.28V	.27V	.09V	.12V	.07V	.71V	3.20V	3.09V	3.87V	4.74V	4.60V	5.08V	5.55V
Thailand	578	.11V	1.07V	1.27V	.72V	.58V	.42V	.10V	3.29V	4.52V	5.80V	9.06V	10.62V	12.91V	15.88V
Vietnam	582	—V	.19V	.05V	—V	—V	—V	—V	.56V	.29V	.20V	—V	—V	—V	—V
Europe	**170**	**1.2Y**	**1.5Y**	**4.2Y**	**8.7Y**	**1.7Y**	**8.3Y**	**31.4Y**	**2.1Y**	**3.4Y**	**4.4Y**	**4.5Y**	**6.2Y**	**4.8Y**	**5.7Y**
Albania	914	—V	.20V	.04V	—V	.02V	.02V	.05V	—V	—V	—V	—V	—V	—V	—V
Azerbaijan	912	.01V	—V	—V	—V	—V	—V	—V	—V	.04V	—V	—V	—V	—V	—V
Bulgaria	918	.08V	—V	.01V	—V	—V	—V	.02V	.01V	—V	—V	—V	.01V	.01V	.13V
Czech Republic	935	.03V	.12V	.08V	.59V	.41V	.01V	.02V	.09V	.17V	.19V	.35V	.14V	.54V	.43V
Estonia	939	.01V	—V	—V	—V	—V	—V	—V	.01V	—V	—V	—V	—V	—V	.02V
Hungary	944	.03V	—V	.05V	.08V	.01V	.01V	.02V	.01V	.01V	.07V	.04V	—V	.08V	.15V
Latvia	941	—V	—V	—Y	—V	—V	—V	—V	—V	—V	—Y	—V	.04V	.03V	.03V
Lithuania	946	—V	.06V	.05V	.04V	—V	.02V	—V	.01V	—V	—V	.11V	—V	.04V	—V
Poland	964	1.03V	1.08V	1.51V	8.03V	1.16V	.16V	.03V	.97V	1.16V	2.72V	1.63V	2.48V	.85V	1.30V
Romania	968	—V	—V	—V	—V	—V	.08V	13.48V	—V	—V	—V	.17V	—V	.05V	.01V
Russia	922	—V	—V	2.48V	.01V	.02V	7.93V	17.71V	.01V	—V	—V	.15V	—V	.01V	—V
Slovak Republic	936	—V	—V	—Y	—Y	—V	—V	—V	.05V	.12V	.15Y	.19Y	.15V	.06V	.22V
Turkey	186	—V	—V	.02V	—V	.01V	—V	.08V	.98V	1.91V	1.26V	1.88V	3.28V	3.05V	3.27V
Ukraine	926	—V	.01V	.01V	—V	.03V	.04Y	.05Y	—V	—V	.01V	—V	.10V	.12Y	.15Y

	Exports							Imports						
	2001	2002	2003	2004	2005	2006	2007	2001	2002	2003	2004	2005	2006	2007
	Millions of U.S. Dollars							*Millions of U.S. Dollars*						
Middle East.............................. 407	**.1Y**	**.2Y**	**42.0Y**	**54.7Y**	**69.5Y**	**85.8Y**	**111.2Y**	**—Y**	**—Y**	**—Y**	**—Y**	**—Y**	**—Y**	**—Y**
Iran, I.R. of.................................. 429	—V	.09V	.10Y	.12Y	.16Y	.19Y	.25Y	—Y	—Y	—Y	—Y	—Y	—Y	—Y
Lebanon..................................... 446	.01Y	.01Y	.01Y	.02Y	.02Y	.03Y	.03Y	—Y	—Y	—Y	—Y	—Y	—Y	—Y
Saudi Arabia............................... 456	.10V	.06V	.04V	.15V	.11V	.14Y	.18Y	—Y	—Y	—Y	—Y	—Y	—Y	—Y
United Arab Emirates.................. 466	—V	—V	41.82V	54.39Y	69.25Y	85.49Y	110.74Y	.01Y	.01Y	.02Y	.02Y	.03Y	.04Y	.05Y
Western Hemisphere................ 207	**41.3Y**	**42.7Y**	**42.8Y**	**52.7Y**	**53.1Y**	**103.1Y**	**108.3Y**	**140.2Y**	**121.6Y**	**127.7Y**	**174.8Y**	**211.3Y**	**242.5Y**	**301.8Y**
Antigua and Barbuda.................. 311	.20Y	.22Y	.28Y	.36Y	.41Y	.51Y	.64Y	.28Y	.31Y	.39Y	.51Y	.58Y	.72Y	.89Y
Argentina.................................... 213	4.26V	.02V	—V	—V	—V	—V	—V	.94V	1.15V	2.59V	3.75V	4.08V	4.76V	5.90V
Aruba.. 314	2.75V	2.88V	.59V	.62V	.30V	.47V	1.16V	.03V	.10V	.05V	.22V	.90V	1.08V	1.83V
Bahamas, The.............................. 313	—Y	—Y	—Y	—Y	—Y	—Y	—Y	.08Y	.09Y	.11Y	.15Y	.17Y	.21Y	.25Y
Barbados..................................... 316	7.43V	12.80V	11.14V	11.66V	6.55V	15.30V	18.99Y	5.14V	5.84V	3.56V	4.06V	3.67V	2.55V	3.16Y
Belize.. 339	—Y	—Y	—Y	—Y	—Y	—Y	—Y	.01Y	.01Y	.01Y	.01Y	.01Y	.02Y	.02Y
Bolivia... 218	.01V	—V	—V	—V	—V	—Y	—Y	.11V	—V	—V	—V	—Y	—Y	—Y
Brazil... 223	.11V	—V	—V	.74V	.01V	29.81V	19.17V	10.25V	11.73V	18.01V	31.12V	39.34V	34.39V	40.26V
Chile.. 228	—V	—V	—V	—V	—V	—V	—V	.22V	—V	.52V	1.10V	1.11V	1.22V	1.05V
Colombia..................................... 233	.01V	—V	.03V	—V	—V	.72V	.06V	3.31V	4.15V	5.74V	6.24V	10.05V	10.08V	17.42V
Costa Rica................................... 238	.04V	.28V	.01V	.04V	.01V	.01Y	.01Y	.98V	.25V	2.02V	2.55V	3.19V	3.94Y	4.89Y
Dominica..................................... 321	.02V	.02Y	.03Y	.04Y	.04Y	.05Y	.07Y	.58V	.63Y	.79Y	1.04Y	1.19Y	1.47Y	1.83Y
Dominican Republic.................... 243	.02V	.03Y	.03Y	.04Y	.05Y	.06Y	.08Y	2.56V	2.78Y	3.52Y	4.62Y	5.28Y	6.52Y	8.09Y
Ecuador....................................... 248	—V	—V	.02V	.02V	.05V	—V	—Y	.05V	—V	.10V	.04V	.19V	.22V	.28Y
El Salvador.................................. 253	—V	—V	—V	—V	—V	—V	—V	.07V	.02V	—V	—V	—V	.13V	.24V
Grenada....................................... 328	.06Y	.07Y	.08Y	.11Y	.13Y	.15Y	.19Y	.04Y	.04Y	.05Y	.07Y	.08Y	.09Y	.12Y
Guatemala.................................... 258	—V	—V	.02V	—V	—V	—Y	—Y	.89V	.88V	.38V	.50V	.63V	.78Y	.96Y
Guyana.. 336	6.28Y	6.82Y	8.63Y	11.33Y	12.94Y	16.00Y	19.85Y	3.15Y	3.42Y	4.33Y	5.69Y	6.50Y	8.03Y	9.97Y
Haiti... 263	.13V	.05V	—V	.02V	.02Y	.02Y	.03Y	—Y	—Y	—Y	—Y	—Y	—Y	—Y
Honduras..................................... 268	—V	.04V	—V	—V	—Y	—Y	—Y	—V	.02V	.39V	.90V	1.03Y	1.27Y	1.58Y
Jamaica.. 343	6.47V	7.74V	7.26V	7.82V	10.68V	12.64V	14.50V	.95V	.80V	1.07V	1.75V	1.18V	1.95V	2.52V
Mexico... 273	—V	—V	—V	—V	.10V	.37V	.01V	—V	—V	—V	—V	6.47V	7.95V	8.38V
Netherlands Antilles.................... 353	.51V	.31V	.60V	.79Y	.91Y	1.12Y	1.39Y	26.56V	26.56V	3.68V	4.84Y	5.53Y	6.83Y	8.48Y
Panama.. 283	.01V	.01V	.02V	.04V	.01V	.01V	—V	—V	.12V	.46V	.07V	.29V	1.83V	2.23V
Peru... 293	.01V	.08V	.02V	.20V	.01V	—V	.01Y	.07V	.12V	.34V	.43V	.80V	1.00V	1.03Y
St. Lucia...................................... 362	.03Y	.03Y	.04Y	.06Y	.07Y	.08Y	.10Y	.11Y	.12Y	.15Y	.19Y	.22Y	.27Y	.34Y
St. Vincent & Grens..................... 364	—V	.01V	—V	.06V	.03V	.04Y	.05Y	—V	—V	—V	—V	.11V	.14Y	.18Y
Trinidad and Tobago.................... 369	12.22V	10.92V	13.82Y	18.14Y	20.73Y	25.62Y	31.80Y	82.72V	61.09V	77.32Y	101.54Y	116.02Y	143.39Y	177.95Y
Uruguay....................................... 298	—V	—Y	—V	—V	.05V	.06Y	.08Y	.01V	.01Y	.88V	1.38V	.22V	.28Y	.34Y
Venezuela, Rep. Bol.................... 299	.68V	.38V	.19V	.64V	—V	—V	.15V	1.10V	1.36V	1.25V	2.02V	2.50V	1.35V	1.63Y
Other Countries n.i.e................ 910	**.2Y**	**.2Y**	**.2Y**	**.3Y**	**.4Y**	**.4Y**	**.6Y**	**3.1Y**	**3.4Y**	**4.3Y**	**5.6Y**	**6.4Y**	**7.9Y**	**9.8Y**
Cuba.. 928	.17Y	.19Y	.24Y	.31Y	.36Y	.44Y	.55Y	.04Y	.04Y	.06Y	.07Y	.08Y	.10Y	.13Y
North Korea................................. 954	—Y	—Y	—Y	—Y	—Y	—Y	—Y	3.07Y	3.34Y	4.22Y	5.54Y	6.33Y	7.83Y	9.72Y
Memorandum Items														
European Union........................... 998	134.22Y	101.70Y	185.03Y	202.94Y	205.60Y	267.04Y	295.14Y	131.95Y	197.82Y	207.03Y	229.79Y	266.62Y	263.51Y	364.70Y
Oil Exporting Ctys........................ 999	1.43Y	1.57Y	42.61Y	55.90Y	70.33Y	86.83Y	112.56Y	2.92Y	3.28Y	3.84Y	5.67Y	5.19Y	4.37Y	5.25Y
Non-Oil Develop.Ctys................... 201	61.92Y	68.52Y	78.48Y	80.23Y	86.07Y	143.96Y	178.44Y	324.01Y	213.34Y	204.40Y	250.49Y	317.91Y	346.05Y	447.50Y
PERCENT DISTRIBUTION														
Industrial Countries................. 101	**87.2**	**85.2**	**79.2**	**84.5**	**83.0**	**80.5**	**79.2**	**50.4**	**63.0**	**68.8**	**65.1**	**64.3**	**63.0**	**62.9**
Developing Countries.............. 202	**12.7**	**14.8**	**20.7**	**15.5**	**16.9**	**19.4**	**20.8**	**49.1**	**36.5**	**30.6**	**34.1**	**35.0**	**36.2**	**36.3**
Africa...................................... 607	**2.3**	**3.2**	**1.9**	**1.7**	**1.8**	**1.8**	**1.8**	**.1**	**.1**	**.5**	**.2**	**.1**	**—**	**—**
Asia... 507	**1.9**	**2.2**	**3.6**	**.6**	**1.7**	**1.1**	**1.0**	**27.6**	**15.4**	**10.7**	**10.0**	**11.4**	**10.6**	**11.6**
Europe.................................... 170	**.2**	**.3**	**.7**	**1.0**	**.2**	**.7**	**2.2**	**.3**	**.6**	**.6**	**.6**	**.7**	**.5**	**.5**
Middle East............................ 407	**—**	**—**	**7.2**	**6.2**	**7.5**	**7.2**	**8.0**	**—**	**—**	**—**	**—**	**—**	**—**	**—**
Western Hemisphere............. 207	**8.3**	**9.0**	**7.3**	**6.0**	**5.7**	**8.7**	**7.7**	**21.1**	**20.5**	**18.8**	**23.3**	**22.9**	**25.0**	**24.2**
Other Countries n.i.e............... 910	**—**	**—**	**—**	**—**	**—**	**—**	**—**	**.5**	**.6**	**.6**	**.7**	**.7**	**.8**	**.8**
ANNUAL PERCENT CHANGE														
World....................................... 001	**–.1**	**–4.6**	**23.0**	**50.7**	**4.9**	**28.6**	**17.7**	**38.8**	**–10.8**	**14.5**	**10.4**	**22.9**	**5.0**	**28.6**
Industrial Countries................. 101	**–.8**	**–6.8**	**14.3**	**60.7**	**3.1**	**24.8**	**15.7**	**7.5**	**11.4**	**25.1**	**4.6**	**21.2**	**2.9**	**28.4**
Developing Countries.............. 202	**5.2**	**10.6**	**72.8**	**12.4**	**14.9**	**47.6**	**26.1**	**98.7**	**–33.7**	**–3.9**	**23.0**	**26.1**	**8.5**	**29.2**
Africa...................................... 607	**32.2**	**33.7**	**–26.5**	**31.7**	**13.4**	**23.9**	**23.0**	**–96.8**	**–26.9**	**643.4**	**–52.3**	**–66.2**	**–18.5**	**23.4**
Asia... 507	**188.0**	**11.9**	**99.5**	**–75.3**	**197.0**	**–16.5**	**12.5**	**491.3**	**–50.4**	**–20.3**	**3.5**	**39.6**	**–2.2**	**40.9**
Europe.................................... 170	**60.0**	**24.1**	**187.4**	**106.1**	**–81.0**	**398.2**	**280.9**	**–15.6**	**59.2**	**29.1**	**2.8**	**37.0**	**–21.8**	**18.1**
Middle East............................ 407	**–86.1**	**42.7**	**—**	**30.3**	**27.2**	**23.5**	**29.5**	**7.9**	**6.3**	**21.2**	**32.3**	**36.0**	**25.7**	**20.6**
Western Hemisphere............. 207	**–11.8**	**3.5**	**.2**	**23.3**	**.7**	**94.1**	**5.1**	**26.4**	**–13.3**	**5.1**	**36.9**	**20.9**	**14.7**	**24.5**
Other Countries n.i.e............... 910	**10.4**	**8.5**	**26.6**	**31.3**	**14.3**	**23.6**	**24.1**	**10.4**	**8.5**	**26.6**	**31.3**	**14.3**	**23.6**	**24.1**

		Exports							Imports						
		2001	2002	2003	2004	2005	2006	2007	2001	2002	2003	2004	2005	2006	2007
		Millions of U.S. Dollars							Millions of U.S. Dollars						
IFS World Total		**78,208**	**82,919**	**102,407**	**123,295**	**130,885**	**147,904**	**169,153**	**64,326**	**67,644**	**84,199**	**100,782**	**111,581**	**127,652**	**151,351**
DOTS World Total	**001**	**78,178**	**82,890**	**102,230**	**122,990**	**130,913**	**147,864**	**169,251**	**63,542**	**67,451**	**83,259**	**100,220**	**111,593**	**127,692**	**151,533**
Industrial Countries	**101**	**62,429**	**66,407**	**81,301**	**97,223**	**101,831**	**115,005**	**129,491**	**54,071**	**56,760**	**69,188**	**81,916**	**88,950**	**100,359**	**119,420**
United States	111	8,641	9,433	11,732	13,145	13,796	13,662	12,797	3,450	3,275	3,253	3,494	4,010	4,431	4,719
Canada	156	836	983	1,282	1,393	1,411	1,547	1,632	255	261	293	339	394	461	523
Australia	193	724	881	1,168	1,321	1,497	1,939	1,935	140	221	193	292	343	395	408
Japan	158	2,432	1,963	1,992	2,270	1,986	2,291	2,061	1,427	1,502	1,838	2,117	2,550	2,808	3,002
New Zealand	196	101	107	134	177	179	157	194	27	29	35	38	50	47	55
Austria	122	751	832	1,062	1,271	1,223	1,414	1,725	720	808	1,093	1,095	1,186	1,333	1,629
Belgium	124	3,465	3,795	4,583	5,549	5,606	6,778	7,767	2,401	2,621	3,494	4,035	4,386	5,296	6,246
Cyprus	423	61	69	65	119	58	72	89	6	7	8	11	15	38	20
Denmark	128	4,640	5,042	6,525	8,200	8,968	10,645	12,584	5,423	6,064	7,508	9,202	10,581	12,273	13,892
Finland	172	4,249	4,692	5,825	7,020	7,845	9,240	10,758	3,429	3,539	4,661	6,429	6,667	7,480	9,210
France	132	3,884	4,169	4,942	5,886	6,292	7,278	8,511	4,112	3,731	4,597	5,468	5,730	6,028	7,502
Germany	134	8,146	8,296	10,167	12,500	13,511	14,671	17,644	11,240	12,346	15,579	18,787	20,234	22,852	27,854
Greece	174	415	395	566	725	721	793	790	115	128	154	153	171	188	279
Iceland	176	149	163	235	340	455	504	709	25	28	26	28	31	28	37
Ireland	178	435	418	530	737	731	843	904	1,160	1,173	1,344	1,408	1,543	1,669	1,839
Italy	136	2,727	3,059	3,635	4,544	4,395	4,989	5,339	2,138	2,367	2,873	3,436	3,682	4,317	5,377
Luxembourg	137	23	34	58	69	99	98	115	110	121	306	389	514	680	775
Malta	181	14	13	19	28	19	24	35	4	4	5	11	19	12	11
Netherlands	138	3,835	4,317	5,005	5,874	5,932	7,100	8,566	4,505	4,682	5,663	6,766	7,021	7,575	8,736
Norway	142	6,546	7,166	8,801	10,622	11,193	13,517	15,881	5,368	5,350	6,634	7,637	8,732	10,417	12,535
Portugal	182	427	439	552	705	660	734	882	348	345	368	375	382	450	657
Slovenia	961	106	87	134	149	122	185	228	73	84	113	152	169	223	250
Spain	184	1,990	2,177	3,233	3,617	3,729	4,560	4,765	1,005	1,095	1,385	1,603	1,815	1,969	2,210
Switzerland	146	991	1,101	1,136	1,356	1,242	1,315	1,527	924	1,084	1,071	1,182	1,110	1,221	1,298
United Kingdom	112	6,839	6,777	7,919	9,605	10,160	10,649	12,053	5,668	5,895	6,696	7,468	7,616	8,169	10,355
Developing Countries	**202**	**15,722**	**16,462**	**20,584**	**25,290**	**28,297**	**31,890**	**38,634**	**9,467**	**10,690**	**14,068**	**18,301**	**22,617**	**27,295**	**32,062**
Africa	**607**	**943**	**1,034**	**1,492**	**1,829**	**2,475**	**2,455**	**3,359**	**232**	**207**	**231**	**344**	**520**	**535**	**810**
Algeria	612	49	71	147	199	356	186	297	6	14	15	4	32	19	48
Angola	614	17	12	25	28	30	41	75	1	—	—	—	5	—	—
Benin	638	2	2	3	2	2	13	17	—	—	5	2	5	—	—
Botswana	616	27	37	59	76	77	8	17	—	—	—	—	—	—	—
Burkina Faso	748	—	—	1	2	9	8	14	—	—	—	—	—	1	—
Burundi	618	—	1	—	—	1	—	—	—	—	1	2	3	3	4
Cameroon	622	14	7	13	11	12	28	27	—	—	—	19	—	—	—
Cape Verde	624	1	—	—	—	—	3	3	—	—	—	—	—	—	—
Central African Rep.	626	—	—	—	—	1	2	1	—	—	—	—	—	—	—
Chad	628	1	—	1	4	11	8	11	—	—	—	3	5	3	1
Congo, Dem. Rep. of	636	3	1	2	13	16	28	44	—	—	—	—	—	—	—
Congo, Republic of	634	10	11	6	8	13	9	18	—	—	1	—	—	1	—
Côte d'Ivoire	662	11	9	9	13	14	24	27	—	1	1	1	1	1	2
Djibouti	611	2	1	3	4	4	3	9	—	—	—	—	—	—	—
Equatorial Guinea	642	—	2	—	—	—	—	1	—	—	—	—	—	—	—
Eritrea	643	3	4	3	2	1	6	3	—	—	—	—	—	—	—
Ethiopia	644	16	14	26	29	72	24	42	1	2	4	7	14	16	16
Gabon	646	3	3	5	11	8	18	25	—	—	—	—	—	—	—
Gambia, The	648	1	1	2	2	2	4	4	—	—	—	—	—	—	—
Ghana	652	34	37	55	60	109	103	148	2	8	4	1	2	8	—
Guinea	656	2	1	3	3	5	8	35	11	1	—	—	—	—	—
Guinea-Bissau	654	—	—	—	2	—	1	4	—	—	—	—	—	—	—
Kenya	664	23	15	19	27	40	47	59	7	9	14	15	28	28	37
Lesotho	666	1	2	—	—	—	—	—	—	—	—	—	—	—	—
Liberia	668	1	—	1	4	11	10	19	—	—	—	—	—	—	—
Madagascar	674	2	1	5	2	1	10	6	8	6	4	11	9	12	19
Malawi	676	—	3	4	2	3	7	7	1	1	—	—	—	1	1
Mali	678	1	1	2	1	1	4	4	—	—	—	—	—	—	—
Mauritania	682	8	2	1	3	5	5	8	—	—	—	—	—	—	—
Mauritius	684	4	4	5	6	5	6	6	7	6	4	2	1	1	1
Morocco	686	122	157	162	157	285	284	425	15	7	10	10	9	11	30
Mozambique	688	2	2	4	15	19	6	8	—	—	—	—	1	—	—
Namibia	728	1	1	2	2	4	5	9	—	—	—	—	—	1	1
Niger	692	—	—	1	2	—	2	8	—	—	—	—	—	—	—
Nigeria	694	127	170	257	288	259	232	370	53	31	1	30	59	3	—
Rwanda	714	1	1	1	—	6	11	4	—	1	—	—	1	1	1
St. Helena	856	—	—	—	1	—	1	—	—	—	—	—	—	—	—
Senegal	722	4	4	6	7	23	9	13	—	—	—	—	—	—	1
Seychelles	718	—	—	1	4	1	6	2	—	—	—	—	—	—	—
Sierra Leone	724	5	4	5	6	11	8	10	—	—	—	—	—	—	—
Somalia	726	—	1	—	—	—	1	—	—	—	—	—	—	—	—
South Africa	199	272	282	444	607	734	849	1,084	89	89	136	200	303	387	600

	Exports							Imports						
	2001	2002	2003	2004	2005	2006	2007	2001	2002	2003	2004	2005	2006	2007
	Millions of U.S. Dollars							*Millions of U.S. Dollars*						
Sudan....732	11	29	43	47	91	132	116	1	3	1	4	7	4	3
Swaziland....734	—	—	4	2	3	2	3	—	—	—	—	—	—	—
Tanzania....738	12	15	36	26	74	44	90	—	—	2	2	5	3	1
Togo....742	—	1	1	2	6	8	10	—	—	—	—	—	—	—
Tunisia....744	126	111	108	108	85	141	139	15	18	21	25	27	25	34
Uganda....746	10	5	7	20	24	23	59	1	1	3	1	1	2	2
Zambia....754	12	7	8	19	26	61	71	—	—	1	—	1	—	—
Zimbabwe....698	5	4	4	5	16	24	10	10	5	1	—	1	2	2
Asia....507	**5,518**	**5,551**	**6,733**	**7,889**	**7,825**	**9,125**	**10,503**	**3,854**	**4,030**	**5,177**	**6,309**	**7,896**	**9,687**	**11,792**
Afghanistan, I.S. of....512	—	—	1	5	2	7	18	—	—	—	—	—	—	—
Bangladesh....513	45	30	39	139	174	213	304	83	87	124	163	148	185	203
Bhutan....514	—	—	2	—	1	2	6	—	—	—	—	—	—	—
Brunei Darussalam....516	2	2	1	1	1	5	2	—	—	—	—	—	—	—
Cambodia....522	1	2	1	2	2	5	9	9	13	11	10	13	14	19
China,P.R.: Mainland....924	1,925	1,591	2,242	2,588	2,518	2,807	3,293	1,088	1,158	1,891	2,391	3,970	4,917	6,453
China,P.R.:Hong Kong....532	399	399	485	586	541	496	577	769	783	879	943	312	464	457
China,P.R.:Macao....546	3	2	2	13	7	8	10	3	5	6	8	12	18	14
Fiji....819	—	1	—	1	4	2	5	—	—	—	—	—	—	—
French Polynesia....887	1	1	1	2	2	2	3	—	—	—	—	—	—	—
Guam....829	—	—	—	—	1	—	—	—	—	—	—	—	—	—
India....534	359	642	879	1,129	934	1,346	1,580	202	205	267	309	395	443	619
Indonesia....536	293	351	260	365	440	656	633	133	131	134	134	190	205	184
Kiribati....826	—	—	—	—	—	—	—	—	—	—	—	—	—	1
Korea....542	412	507	600	638	797	826	1,030	396	425	630	916	1,048	1,258	1,222
Lao People's Dem.Rep....544	1	9	7	4	2	2	4	1	1	4	3	2	2	3
Malaysia....548	442	382	300	390	408	454	555	183	211	165	197	285	456	534
Maldives....556	1	1	2	2	2	3	8	—	—	—	—	—	—	—
Mongolia....948	2	1	3	3	3	6	16	—	—	—	—	—	—	—
Myanmar....518	1	—	2	—	—	1	2	2	4	4	4	4	3	4
Nepal....558	2	1	1	2	1	—	2	1	1	1	2	1	1	1
New Caledonia....839	1	1	11	2	4	3	13	—	—	—	—	1	5	—
Pakistan....564	50	43	64	120	253	367	281	53	61	65	79	85	98	103
Palau....565	1	—	—	—	—	—	—	—	—	—	—	—	—	—
Papua New Guinea....853	1	1	1	1	1	2	12	16	—	8	—	5	3	1
Philippines....566	120	103	112	146	118	126	134	29	30	32	35	45	52	61
Samoa....862	—	—	3	—	—	5	1	—	—	—	—	—	—	—
Singapore....576	472	507	671	649	590	695	953	112	126	75	108	174	136	127
Sri Lanka....524	25	39	67	57	64	90	72	16	20	23	29	32	38	56
Taiwan Province of China....528	547	495	563	608	497	477	456	450	461	482	546	665	703	814
Thailand....578	354	367	310	303	335	379	347	238	227	264	306	351	475	659
Vanuatu....846	—	—	—	—	—	—	1	—	—	—	—	—	—	—
Vietnam....582	59	74	101	133	123	140	175	70	80	111	128	158	211	256
Europe....170	**4,978**	**5,885**	**7,649**	**9,664**	**11,315**	**13,485**	**16,811**	**3,735**	**4,994**	**6,897**	**9,468**	**11,761**	**14,755**	**16,772**
Albania....914	19	8	13	11	16	11	9	—	1	1	6	7	9	24
Armenia....911	10	1	3	3	2	4	31	—	—	—	—	—	—	—
Azerbaijan....912	9	10	35	77	65	67	43	—	—	—	—	—	—	—
Belarus....913	23	32	43	46	61	92	139	11	17	14	34	54	130	65
Bosnia & Herzegovina....963	13	13	18	29	29	23	31	3	4	6	8	13	19	28
Bulgaria....918	52	49	78	100	150	168	197	27	31	40	47	57	73	96
Croatia....960	83	94	160	183	178	176	195	24	23	46	129	86	93	73
Czech Republic....935	433	436	550	662	1,489	906	1,167	324	406	517	605	1,051	1,370	1,811
Czechoslovakia n.s....937	91	149	106	—	—	—	—	10	11	18	—	—	—	—
Estonia....939	445	522	688	708	757	1,234	1,428	616	637	817	921	846	992	1,117
Faroe Islands....816	15	15	18	24	26	30	45	2	2	2	2	3	4	5
Georgia....915	1	3	10	6	9	20	25	—	—	—	—	—	—	—
Gibraltar....823	2	14	43	126	95	32	41	—	—	2	2	—	—	—
Hungary....944	301	419	537	607	664	1,240	1,262	272	298	495	830	861	859	1,076
Kazakhstan....916	35	37	64	128	165	221	267	27	5	29	24	115	144	207
Kosovo....967	—	—	—	—	—	—	—	—	—	—	—	—	—	10
Kyrgyz Republic....917	1	3	1	4	4	12	8	2	1	—	—	—	—	1
Latvia....941	227	255	348	402	397	498	668	374	451	468	501	412	438	661
Lithuania....946	186	272	351	377	443	571	780	235	273	493	550	637	647	541
Macedonia, FYR....962	19	12	14	19	13	19	36	3	3	5	6	8	24	18
Moldova....921	1	1	3	5	13	9	14	—	2	3	4	4	5	14
Montenegro, Rep. of....943	—	—	—	—	—	2	37	—	—	—	—	—	—	1
Poland....964	1,239	1,304	1,688	2,165	2,339	3,071	4,155	956	1,291	1,898	2,527	2,606	3,417	4,395
Romania....968	126	132	191	322	319	408	404	68	72	97	153	157	194	208
Russia....922	867	1,136	1,405	1,852	2,133	2,432	3,373	376	1,007	1,278	2,192	3,732	4,830	4,642
Serbia & Montenegro....965	91	149	106	182	—	—	—	10	11	—	22	—	—	—
Slovak Republic....936	102	134	171	240	228	278	315	76	97	143	198	223	416	608
Tajikistan....923	—	2	2	3	4	10	2	—	—	—	—	5	—	—
Turkey....186	397	474	759	984	1,156	1,294	1,416	300	335	507	681	819	1,008	1,089
Turkmenistan....925	1	1	2	1	—	3	3	—	—	—	—	—	8	9
Ukraine....926	181	189	229	389	534	622	709	15	14	17	26	64	74	83
Uzbekistan....927	9	19	10	9	27	28	10	—	—	—	—	—	—	—
Europe n.s....884	—	1	1	1	1	1	1	—	—	—	—	—	—	—
Middle East....407	**2,156**	**2,428**	**2,725**	**3,373**	**3,835**	**3,768**	**4,226**	**919**	**540**	**804**	**723**	**769**	**476**	**483**
Bahrain....419	32	26	32	30	26	32	32	—	1	1	1	1	3	—
Egypt....469	231	175	244	305	431	523	651	51	6	8	11	23	16	28
Iran, I.R. of....429	216	331	635	950	1,056	490	345	561	330	640	456	175	148	139

		Exports							Imports						
		2001	2002	2003	2004	2005	2006	2007	2001	2002	2003	2004	2005	2006	2007
		Millions of U.S. Dollars							Millions of U.S. Dollars						
Iraq	433	73	57	20	91	58	50	51	—	—	—	—	—	—	1
Israel	436	314	288	269	325	362	350	365	138	122	83	106	129	120	147
Jordan	439	48	56	59	70	65	70	100	1	1	1	1	1	2	4
Kuwait	443	42	59	87	111	102	128	168	4	1	—	16	1	1	12
Lebanon	446	35	33	51	47	42	44	47	3	6	6	9	10	10	13
Libya	672	56	54	111	87	96	106	144	—	26	8	—	24	36	33
Oman	449	40	37	40	84	103	113	147	—	5	1	2	6	2	1
Qatar	453	17	21	37	38	63	106	202	—	2	3	1	2	1	1
Saudi Arabia	456	734	883	783	691	873	1,054	1,154	149	27	35	93	58	103	85
Syrian Arab Republic	463	45	70	72	129	95	71	96	1	1	2	2	2	5	5
United Arab Emirates	466	255	315	259	389	436	598	683	9	12	16	21	337	30	14
West Bank/Gaza Strip	487	—	—	1	1	—	—	—	—	—	—	1	—	—	—
Yemen, Republic of	474	20	23	24	26	26	34	42	1	—	—	3	—	—	—
Western Hemisphere	**207**	**2,128**	**1,564**	**1,985**	**2,536**	**2,847**	**3,056**	**3,736**	**726**	**919**	**959**	**1,458**	**1,671**	**1,843**	**2,205**
Antigua and Barbuda	311	1	8	2	1	2	2	3	—	1	—	—	—	—	—
Argentina	213	138	39	72	193	203	172	212	33	56	90	69	38	50	82
Aruba	314	1	6	3	1	—	—	1	—	—	—	—	17	2	1
Bahamas, The	313	2	6	28	2	3	3	45	—	—	—	1	51	1	—
Barbados	316	12	12	29	5	6	19	16	1	—	1	—	—	—	—
Belize	339	1	2	1	1	1	—	1	—	—	1	1	—	—	—
Bermuda	319	—	3	12	2	1	58	1	—	40	38	25	75	63	—
Bolivia	218	16	8	10	17	28	22	33	1	1	—	—	1	—	1
Brazil	223	661	523	540	704	756	917	1,176	197	245	268	554	506	544	712
Chile	228	139	129	169	213	330	259	299	116	139	139	302	353	419	521
Colombia	233	92	47	59	66	95	111	126	33	33	29	35	62	59	62
Costa Rica	238	20	20	18	72	51	28	38	39	35	50	88	81	72	71
Dominica	321	—	—	2	—	2	—	2	—	—	—	—	—	—	—
Dominican Republic	243	15	19	16	19	30	32	63	4	8	11	3	2	3	3
Ecuador	248	28	14	19	21	31	28	24	3	3	3	3	7	13	17
El Salvador	253	18	8	8	30	25	36	67	—	—	—	1	3	3	3
Greenland	326	2	2	14	65	126	106	144	—	2	1	—	—	2	16
Grenada	328	—	1	4	1	1	1	2	—	—	—	—	—	—	—
Guatemala	258	16	13	20	51	38	86	94	11	9	8	6	8	9	13
Guyana	336	1	1	2	2	1	9	4	—	—	—	—	—	2	2
Haiti	263	1	—	2	1	16	50	27	—	—	—	—	—	—	—
Honduras	268	4	5	13	21	36	40	71	10	6	6	6	9	12	10
Jamaica	343	92	125	27	29	22	29	17	32	31	25	38	11	1	11
Mexico	273	688	366	717	778	704	693	734	26	43	36	65	78	97	122
Netherlands Antilles	353	6	10	9	11	30	6	7	—	—	—	—	1	—	3
Nicaragua	278	5	21	17	17	19	9	25	2	1	2	3	4	4	3
Panama	283	23	39	34	42	36	52	79	53	57	54	29	11	24	22
Paraguay	288	6	6	2	23	10	10	20	—	—	—	—	—	1	1
Peru	293	30	27	36	49	70	86	149	9	26	26	54	57	74	90
St. Kitts and Nevis	361	—	—	—	3	4	1	1	—	—	—	—	—	—	—
St. Lucia	362	—	13	7	2	1	1	3	—	—	—	—	—	—	—
St. Vincent & Grens.	364	—	—	5	1	—	—	4	—	—	—	—	—	—	—
Suriname	366	—	—	2	4	4	3	12	—	—	—	—	—	—	1
Trinidad and Tobago	369	4	6	6	7	29	29	16	—	—	2	—	3	—	—
Uruguay	298	15	6	8	17	12	27	34	6	8	11	16	26	21	40
Venezuela, Rep. Bol.	299	81	70	58	62	112	123	184	147	172	140	156	264	365	399
Western Hem. n.s.	399	9	9	12	5	13	8	4	—	—	16	2	—	—	1
Other Countries n.i.e.	**910**	**26**	**14**	**26**	**55**	**53**	**45**	**44**	**3**	**1**	**2**	**3**	**3**	**3**	**1**
Cuba	928	22	10	19	27	18	20	43	1	1	2	3	2	3	1
North Korea	954	4	4	6	28	35	24	1	2	—	—	—	—	1	—
Countries & Areas n.s.	**898**	—	**2**	—	**1**	**135**	**145**	**246**	—	—	—	—	**24**	**33**	**49**
Special Categories	**899**	—	**2**	**318**	**417**	**596**	**767**	**834**	—	—	—	—	—	—	—
Memorandum Items															
European Union	998	44,941	47,952	59,155	71,759	76,389	87,873	102,531	45,310	48,465	60,677	72,920	78,366	88,690	107,052
Oil Exporting Ctys.	999	1,983	2,420	2,694	3,353	3,954	3,843	4,378	1,063	752	993	914	1,147	912	916
Non-Oil Develop.Ctys.	201	13,740	14,043	17,891	21,937	24,343	28,046	34,257	8,404	9,938	13,075	17,387	21,470	26,383	31,146
PERCENT DISTRIBUTION															
Industrial Countries	**101**	**79.9**	**80.1**	**79.5**	**79.0**	**77.8**	**77.8**	**76.5**	**85.1**	**84.2**	**83.1**	**81.7**	**79.7**	**78.6**	**78.8**
Developing Countries	**202**	**20.1**	**19.9**	**20.1**	**20.6**	**21.6**	**21.6**	**22.8**	**14.9**	**15.8**	**16.9**	**18.3**	**20.3**	**21.4**	**21.2**
Africa	**607**	**1.2**	**1.2**	**1.5**	**1.5**	**1.9**	**1.7**	**2.0**	**.4**	**.3**	**.3**	**.3**	**.5**	**.4**	**.5**
Asia	**507**	**7.1**	**6.7**	**6.6**	**6.4**	**6.0**	**6.2**	**6.2**	**6.1**	**6.0**	**6.2**	**6.3**	**7.1**	**7.6**	**7.8**
Europe	**170**	**6.4**	**7.1**	**7.5**	**7.9**	**8.6**	**9.1**	**9.9**	**5.9**	**7.4**	**8.3**	**9.4**	**10.5**	**11.6**	**11.1**
Middle East	**407**	**2.8**	**2.9**	**2.7**	**2.7**	**2.9**	**2.5**	**2.5**	**1.4**	**.8**	**1.0**	**.7**	**.7**	**.4**	**.3**
Western Hemisphere	**207**	**2.7**	**1.9**	**1.9**	**2.1**	**2.2**	**2.1**	**2.2**	**1.1**	**1.4**	**1.2**	**1.5**	**1.5**	**1.4**	**1.5**
ANNUAL PERCENT CHANGE															
World	**001**	**−11.0**	**6.0**	**23.3**	**20.3**	**6.4**	**12.9**	**14.5**	**−12.9**	**6.2**	**23.4**	**20.4**	**11.3**	**14.4**	**18.7**
Industrial Countries	**101**	**−11.1**	**6.4**	**22.4**	**19.6**	**4.7**	**12.9**	**12.6**	**−13.5**	**5.0**	**21.9**	**18.4**	**8.6**	**12.8**	**19.0**
Developing Countries	**202**	**−10.9**	**4.7**	**25.0**	**22.9**	**11.9**	**12.7**	**21.2**	**−9.6**	**12.9**	**31.6**	**30.1**	**23.6**	**20.7**	**17.5**
Africa	**607**	**−6.8**	**9.7**	**44.3**	**22.6**	**35.3**	**−.8**	**36.8**	**−12.9**	**−10.7**	**11.3**	**48.7**	**51.5**	**2.7**	**51.6**
Asia	**507**	**−7.7**	**.6**	**21.3**	**17.2**	**−.8**	**16.6**	**15.1**	**−13.0**	**4.6**	**28.5**	**21.8**	**25.2**	**22.7**	**21.7**
Europe	**170**	**−11.8**	**18.2**	**30.0**	**26.4**	**17.1**	**19.2**	**24.7**	**−10.9**	**33.7**	**38.1**	**37.3**	**24.2**	**25.5**	**13.7**
Middle East	**407**	**−6.0**	**12.6**	**12.2**	**23.8**	**13.7**	**−1.7**	**12.1**	**28.8**	**−41.2**	**48.8**	**−10.1**	**6.3**	**−38.1**	**1.4**
Western Hemisphere	**207**	**−21.9**	**−26.5**	**27.0**	**27.7**	**12.3**	**7.3**	**22.2**	**−16.2**	**26.5**	**4.4**	**52.0**	**14.6**	**10.2**	**19.7**
Other Countries n.i.e.	**910**	**39.9**	**−45.2**	**81.4**	**114.9**	**−3.4**	**−15.8**	**−1.9**	**−38.6**	**−74.5**	**161.6**	**44.6**	**−7.6**	**28.4**	**−69.6**

	Exports							Imports						
	2001	2002	2003	2004	2005	2006	2007	2001	2002	2003	2004	2005	2006	2007
	Millions of U.S. Dollars							*Millions of U.S. Dollars*						
IFS World Total	**78,066**	**87,359**	**100,724**	**117,816**	**126,083**	**141,669**	**164,797**	**77,070**	**82,377**	**95,581**	**110,321**	**119,770**	**132,021**	**153,171**
DOTS World Total....001	**82,062**	**91,695**	**104,814**	**122,833**	**130,884**	**147,695**	**171,797**	**84,077**	**87,188**	**100,238**	**115,799**	**126,523**	**141,283**	**160,963**
Industrial Countries....101	**64,196**	**71,190**	**81,186**	**94,204**	**100,821**	**112,101**	**127,791**	**72,529**	**76,095**	**87,927**	**100,967**	**109,222**	**120,503**	**137,640**
United States....111	9,547	10,989	11,730	12,871	14,248	16,364	16,748	5,646	6,137	5,856	6,294	7,086	8,726	9,345
Canada....156	816	1,001	1,068	1,604	1,822	2,196	2,413	301	300	396	539	660	806	951
Australia....193	653	677	780	1,035	1,150	1,313	1,652	102	103	115	123	133	142	159
Japan....158	3,190	3,325	4,017	4,602	4,732	5,365	5,606	2,009	1,757	2,113	2,450	2,344	2,476	2,919
New Zealand....196	80	84	111	131	164	141	187	58	62	73	83	74	74	81
Austria....122	2,650	3,041	3,461	3,941	4,151	4,664	5,262	3,010	3,501	4,205	4,894	5,798	6,071	6,741
Belgium....124	1,608	1,936	2,048	2,297	2,355	2,582	3,267	2,511	2,531	2,993	3,417	3,850	4,489	4,925
Cyprus....423	57	97	60	81	54	60	69	3	4	2	4	3	8	9
Denmark....128	653	670	762	833	906	1,091	1,110	674	732	799	902	855	868	946
Finland....172	472	467	555	616	678	802	857	628	638	618	696	681	954	974
France....132	7,373	8,414	9,241	10,894	11,384	12,689	14,380	8,625	9,353	11,361	12,149	12,694	14,122	15,270
Germany....134	17,785	18,634	21,701	24,867	25,452	29,028	34,923	25,328	26,846	31,737	37,267	39,940	44,807	52,414
Greece....174	539	622	818	954	929	1,041	1,343	91	98	115	126	201	252	188
Iceland....176	17	21	26	31	49	39	34	41	30	42	47	30	85	56
Ireland....178	401	577	645	764	728	723	835	3,157	3,295	3,562	3,774	4,539	3,721	5,028
Italy....136	6,546	8,196	9,498	11,032	11,907	13,039	14,984	7,891	8,706	10,453	12,745	13,276	14,919	17,367
Luxembourg....137	147	106	147	312	464	287	266	128	135	161	214	228	299	349
Malta....181	34	39	58	69	59	72	63	3	3	4	4	8	8	24
Netherlands....138	2,502	2,676	3,330	3,589	4,456	4,846	5,187	4,533	4,307	4,868	5,621	6,065	6,638	7,357
Norway....142	360	347	378	428	480	567	697	175	192	182	228	242	274	339
Portugal....182	520	546	647	698	743	793	906	310	327	359	395	379	410	423
Slovenia....961	155	171	221	239	248	281	332	97	121	130	180	166	165	206
Spain....184	2,586	2,923	3,650	4,815	5,303	5,566	6,316	1,479	1,709	2,374	2,768	3,198	3,242	3,452
Sweden....144	955	955	1,209	1,328	1,290	1,410	1,584	881	972	1,244	1,348	1,192	1,412	1,413
United Kingdom....112	4,549	4,676	5,026	6,174	7,070	7,141	8,772	4,847	4,236	4,165	4,698	5,582	5,537	6,704
Developing Countries....202	**17,831**	**20,434**	**23,595**	**28,595**	**30,022**	**35,566**	**43,980**	**11,528**	**11,055**	**12,287**	**14,793**	**17,275**	**20,757**	**23,298**
Africa....607	**878**	**1,058**	**1,093**	**1,336**	**1,325**	**1,679**	**1,990**	**936**	**999**	**1,246**	**1,693**	**1,800**	**2,392**	**1,669**
Algeria....612	85	91	105	155	119	198	328	100	127	97	136	163	104	5
Angola....614	15	8	6	10	12	22	34	—	—	—	—	—	60	204
Benin....638	21	16	16	9	9	13	20	—	—	—	—	—	—	—
Botswana....616	1	2	25	53	2	2	3	—	—	—	—	—	—	—
Burkina Faso....748	1	1	1	1	1	2	2	1	1	1	1	—	—	—
Burundi....618	1	1	—	1	8	3	1	2	1	2	1	6	4	1
Cameroon....622	9	8	9	12	11	18	12	2	3	4	4	3	9	3
Cape Verde....624	—	1	—	—	1	1	1	—	—	—	—	—	1	—
Central African Rep....626	—	—	—	—	1	1	—	—	—	—	—	—	—	—
Chad....628	1	—	1	1	2	12	3	—	—	—	—	—	5	—
Congo, Dem. Rep. of....636	3	3	4	4	5	3	3	—	1	3	—	—	—	1
Congo, Republic of....634	3	3	10	3	2	3	7	1	—	—	1	1	1	1
Côte d'Ivoire....662	18	17	22	34	17	21	47	11	14	17	13	16	12	21
Djibouti....611	—	—	—	2	—	—	1	—	—	—	—	—	—	—
Equatorial Guinea....642	—	—	—	—	3	—	1	—	—	—	—	2	—	—
Eritrea....643	1	1	1	2	2	—	—	—	—	—	—	—	—	1
Ethiopia....644	7	103	6	13	21	22	24	4	3	3	6	7	5	9
Gabon....646	5	5	6	10	9	6	3	1	—	—	8	1	—	1
Gambia, The....648	1	3	1	1	1	1	4	—	—	—	—	—	—	—
Ghana....652	11	11	12	21	19	18	20	18	21	33	27	36	41	50
Guinea....656	10	13	19	13	8	6	4	—	—	1	2	2	—	—
Guinea-Bissau....654	1	—	—	—	1	1	1	—	—	—	—	—	—	—
Kenya....664	17	20	21	24	26	43	57	11	13	17	19	26	26	30
Lesotho....666	—	—	1	—	—	—	—	—	—	—	—	—	—	—
Liberia....668	10	10	8	11	12	14	11	—	—	—	1	—	1	1
Madagascar....674	3	1	2	3	8	2	3	2	3	4	2	3	6	6
Malawi....676	—	—	1	1	2	—	5	4	6	7	4	5	3	4
Mali....678	3	2	1	4	2	2	3	1	1	1	1	—	3	1
Mauritania....682	8	18	1	2	1	2	2	—	—	—	—	—	—	—
Mauritius....684	27	27	30	37	30	34	57	19	20	24	23	21	21	30
Morocco....686	91	97	118	150	174	226	225	38	59	65	111	108	135	72
Mozambique....688	1	4	1	3	3	2	4	—	—	2	1	5	6	9
Namibia....728	2	2	2	17	1	2	1	1	2	1	1	3	1	1
Niger....692	3	13	10	11	14	19	17	—	—	1	1	1	—	—
Nigeria....694	87	102	111	116	95	152	174	297	275	268	464	466	835	281
Rwanda....714	—	—	2	—	1	5	2	—	—	—	—	—	—	—
Senegal....722	12	10	13	13	14	10	18	5	3	2	2	4	9	7
Seychelles....718	2	1	1	1	1	1	2	—	—	—	—	1	—	2
Sierra Leone....724	1	1	1	1	1	—	1	—	—	—	—	—	—	2
South Africa....199	303	333	390	446	536	582	672	377	408	642	815	875	1,006	873
Sudan....732	17	17	22	27	34	49	44	—	—	1	—	—	1	1
Swaziland....734	—	1	1	1	1	1	1	—	—	—	—	—	—	—

		Exports							Imports						
		2001	2002	2003	2004	2005	2006	2007	2001	2002	2003	2004	2005	2006	2007
		Millions of U.S. Dollars							Millions of U.S. Dollars						
Tanzania	738	4	9	6	8	13	22	25	1	2	4	8	7	60	12
Togo	742	9	12	13	13	13	17	17	2	1	1	1	1	2	3
Tunisia	744	71	79	69	86	76	95	100	14	15	19	20	24	23	29
Uganda	746	3	3	4	4	3	31	19	5	9	10	10	3	3	3
Zambia	754	2	1	3	9	7	7	4	1	1	1	1	—	1	—
Zimbabwe	698	8	6	18	6	7	4	8	18	8	13	8	6	5	4
Asia	**507**	**7,531**	**8,750**	**10,033**	**12,346**	**12,746**	**14,752**	**18,152**	**3,987**	**4,353**	**4,928**	**6,040**	**7,205**	**7,757**	**9,205**
Afghanistan, I.S. of	512	—	1	1	2	3	1	1	1	—	1	—	—	—	—
American Samoa	859	—	—	—	—	—	—	—	—	—	—	—	—	1	—
Bangladesh	513	53	44	46	72	75	78	80	39	42	48	62	66	86	97
Bhutan	514	—	—	—	1	—	1	1	—	—	—	—	—	—	—
Brunei Darussalam	516	3	3	6	3	2	13	16	—	4	—	—	6	14	12
Cambodia	522	5	3	6	5	5	8	8	5	8	11	16	18	17	21
China,P.R.: Mainland	924	988	1,328	1,845	2,499	2,784	3,274	4,515	1,338	1,422	1,799	2,285	2,713	3,135	3,984
China,P.R.:Hong Kong	532	2,393	3,058	3,078	3,407	3,222	3,743	4,413	403	694	681	884	1,345	1,162	988
China,P.R.:Macao	546	3	3	6	5	9	16	40	4	4	5	6	3	2	5
Fiji	819	—	—	1	2	2	1	2	—	—	—	—	—	—	—
French Polynesia	887	1	1	2	1	2	1	5	1	—	1	1	1	1	2
Guam	829	—	—	—	—	—	16	11	—	—	—	—	—	—	—
India	534	389	423	563	832	1,114	1,505	1,919	347	337	379	447	531	587	791
Indonesia	536	161	189	217	234	263	260	324	127	109	134	127	126	120	142
Korea	542	627	707	821	1,056	1,035	1,341	1,579	338	355	387	493	602	615	665
Lao People's Dem.Rep	544	—	1	1	1	2	2	2	2	2	3	3	4	2	3
Malaysia	548	328	286	334	505	466	411	535	143	132	134	156	169	196	246
Maldives	556	1	1	2	2	1	2	2	—	—	—	—	—	—	—
Mongolia	948	4	3	5	2	1	1	2	—	—	1	3	3	1	2
Myanmar	518	2	6	2	3	4	3	2	5	7	4	1	—	1	1
Nauru	836	—	—	—	—	—	1	—	—	—	—	—	—	—	—
Nepal	558	3	3	2	4	4	4	9	6	4	4	8	5	5	6
New Caledonia	839	1	1	1	2	2	2	6	—	—	—	—	—	—	—
Pakistan	564	141	132	186	274	288	261	275	23	29	27	34	37	53	60
Papua New Guinea	853	—	—	—	—	1	—	4	—	—	—	—	—	1	—
Philippines	566	142	152	155	175	169	173	215	66	76	67	75	67	67	75
Singapore	576	936	982	1,014	1,207	1,312	1,473	1,757	188	190	234	262	289	332	398
Sri Lanka	524	37	37	43	62	56	61	56	23	20	28	45	49	50	57
Taiwan Province of China	528	775	762	989	1,199	1,081	1,162	1,303	479	430	401	467	435	492	590
Thailand	578	477	547	609	682	750	824	871	356	393	464	529	581	639	843
Vietnam	582	59	75	98	111	93	112	199	93	95	113	138	157	179	216
Europe	**170**	**3,845**	**4,590**	**5,779**	**7,256**	**7,946**	**9,777**	**12,227**	**4,518**	**3,098**	**3,414**	**3,995**	**4,475**	**5,907**	**7,187**
Albania	914	6	14	13	26	21	24	26	—	—	1	—	1	1	1
Armenia	911	5	9	6	6	9	12	19	3	1	1	1	1	2	14
Azerbaijan	912	10	16	17	43	33	81	70	1	3	5	6	10	35	31
Belarus	913	18	17	21	35	57	55	80	5	2	3	3	4	4	6
Bosnia & Herzegovina	963	17	23	27	32	36	41	63	2	3	5	10	7	14	17
Bulgaria	918	84	101	135	231	187	254	247	36	44	46	53	71	101	94
Croatia	960	110	131	160	182	180	216	265	25	30	34	51	68	53	77
Czech Republic	935	550	613	773	927	1,025	1,156	1,519	398	544	663	793	878	1,113	1,422
Estonia	939	20	24	32	41	56	69	81	23	23	25	27	29	46	60
Faroe Islands	816	—	—	—	—	9	1	8	1	2	1	2	1	2	2
Georgia	915	2	3	6	7	8	12	19	—	—	—	—	—	—	1
Gibraltar	823	11	21	19	25	20	38	43	17	43	22	35	33	48	75
Hungary	944	411	461	631	712	777	803	1,008	376	417	533	621	618	618	915
Kazakhstan	916	27	49	58	84	68	173	153	5	48	41	88	158	386	664
Kyrgyz Republic	917	1	2	1	2	3	5	6	—	—	—	—	—	—	—
Latvia	941	49	65	77	100	105	131	192	8	7	6	10	32	17	19
Lithuania	946	45	49	70	77	87	102	149	12	16	21	37	40	34	44
Macedonia, FYR	962	17	26	26	37	36	33	38	10	9	7	6	9	10	14
Moldova	921	13	5	14	17	12	17	23	—	1	2	2	1	2	3
Montenegro, Rep. of	943	—	—	—	—	—	149	18	—	—	—	—	—	29	1
Poland	964	717	742	849	1,083	1,140	1,388	1,804	239	308	382	534	657	750	885
Romania	968	172	159	242	376	477	655	610	58	69	106	144	197	166	209
Russia	922	494	568	801	975	1,249	1,791	2,438	2,826	1,001	893	838	822	1,494	1,292
Serbia, Rep. of	942	—	—	—	—	—	4	193	—	—	—	—	—	—	35
Serbia & Montenegro	965	—	—	—	175	156	—	—	—	—	—	17	21	—	—
Slovak Republic	936	152	169	213	238	273	323	453	184	181	230	243	271	349	488
Tajikistan	923	2	1	—	3	2	2	5	1	—	—	1	9	5	1
Turkey	186	713	1,076	1,257	1,606	1,650	1,851	2,198	260	298	328	425	495	539	716
Turkmenistan	925	6	2	5	5	4	8	9	1	—	—	—	—	—	—
Ukraine	926	94	116	150	187	233	340	446	10	32	41	44	38	80	99
Uzbekistan	927	17	24	20	20	26	36	38	6	4	2	1	5	5	3
Yugoslavia n.s.	966	74	98	145	—	—	—	—	10	11	14	—	—	—	—
Europe n.s.	884	7	7	8	5	7	5	5	—	1	—	1	1	—	1
Middle East	**407**	**3,121**	**3,582**	**3,921**	**4,499**	**4,854**	**5,541**	**6,836**	**1,095**	**1,456**	**1,647**	**1,929**	**2,518**	**3,059**	**3,009**
Bahrain	419	59	126	86	142	111	140	204	11	26	28	40	22	40	61
Egypt	469	316	302	308	315	313	334	390	11	15	21	28	30	27	23
Iran, I.R. of	429	263	310	402	470	599	599	640	105	102	127	149	47	29	32
Iraq	433	44	79	29	81	39	61	70	—	—	—	—	—	—	—

	Exports							Imports						
	2001	2002	2003	2004	2005	2006	2007	2001	2002	2003	2004	2005	2006	2007
	Millions of U.S. Dollars							*Millions of U.S. Dollars*						
Israel 436	756	475	527	600	624	731	887	265	306	280	335	334	348	462
Jordan 439	66	64	92	115	121	146	161	—	—	7	7	4	9	5
Kuwait 443	104	148	182	191	226	270	317	15	38	40	39	47	65	57
Lebanon 446	114	187	187	238	240	236	323	102	99	150	154	193	168	303
Libya 672	66	88	91	153	150	191	232	463	423	562	638	1,084	1,338	1,382
Oman 449	81	51	73	62	65	89	155	2	7	17	2	1	16	1
Qatar 453	89	75	87	191	191	230	322	1	4	4	79	48	228	91
Saudi Arabia 456	589	855	998	895	895	978	1,292	49	193	177	89	189	285	320
Syrian Arab Republic 463	66	100	81	106	117	102	152	1	1	3	4	4	1	2
United Arab Emirates 466	489	695	746	911	1,126	1,399	1,642	70	240	234	364	514	506	270
West Bank/Gaza Strip 487	1	2	4	9	12	9	15	—	—	—	—	—	—	—
Yemen, Republic of 474	20	27	31	27	36	35	49	—	—	—	—	1	1	—
Western Hemisphere 207	**2,456**	**2,453**	**2,768**	**3,158**	**3,151**	**3,817**	**4,774**	**991**	**1,149**	**1,053**	**1,136**	**1,277**	**1,643**	**2,229**
Antigua and Barbuda 311	3	2	3	4	5	5	4	—	—	1	1	—	—	—
Argentina 213	202	113	185	207	253	289	309	37	37	44	40	51	46	54
Aruba 314	4	6	8	12	10	6	89	—	—	—	8	—	—	—
Bahamas, The 313	46	66	96	50	55	80	114	51	44	69	40	44	69	134
Barbados 316	2	2	3	7	8	11	14	2	2	1	—	—	1	—
Belize 339	—	1	—	1	2	2	5	—	—	—	—	—	—	1
Bermuda 319	10	11	42	22	18	26	12	23	—	7	18	—	3	55
Bolivia 218	6	5	6	6	9	7	13	1	1	1	1	1	2	1
Brazil 223	733	709	865	1,006	915	1,164	1,555	449	457	335	408	516	622	831
Chile 228	97	91	99	109	132	157	161	43	38	41	48	43	50	71
Colombia 233	114	122	141	171	189	183	256	74	192	40	58	119	312	378
Costa Rica 238	39	41	24	37	38	45	50	40	56	63	52	54	55	67
Dominica 321	—	1	1	1	1	1	1	—	—	—	1	—	—	—
Dominican Republic 243	13	16	16	11	14	18	16	8	12	15	11	9	11	10
Ecuador 248	35	34	34	39	45	55	60	21	27	33	40	48	60	81
El Salvador 253	16	11	8	8	9	15	11	2	5	2	2	5	1	1
Greenland 326	—	—	—	—	—	—	2	—	—	—	—	—	—	—
Grenada 328	—	—	—	—	—	—	1	—	—	1	2	—	—	—
Guatemala 258	23	18	18	22	19	22	24	15	10	12	9	15	15	21
Guyana 336	1	1	1	1	1	1	1	—	—	—	1	1	—	—
Haiti 263	1	1	1	2	1	1	1	1	1	2	2	2	3	3
Honduras 268	14	19	14	15	11	16	21	9	8	8	7	14	13	14
Jamaica 343	8	12	12	13	13	14	15	3	1	2	3	1	1	1
Mexico 273	657	635	679	840	796	1,020	1,139	100	122	166	148	110	94	141
Netherlands Antilles 353	12	19	21	19	21	22	26	1	1	1	1	—	—	—
Nicaragua 278	5	5	2	3	1	2	18	6	2	2	3	2	2	2
Panama 283	174	191	164	168	185	199	290	24	29	31	29	63	65	83
Paraguay 288	12	8	8	8	9	10	13	2	2	2	2	3	3	2
Peru 293	39	44	46	53	78	69	85	10	10	15	18	19	26	30
St. Kitts and Nevis 361	—	—	—	—	1	1	3	—	—	—	—	—	—	—
St. Lucia 362	—	1	1	3	3	2	3	—	—	—	—	—	—	—
St. Vincent & Grens. 364	—	1	1	2	1	7	1	1	3	—	—	1	3	1
Suriname 366	—	—	2	2	1	2	1	—	—	—	—	—	—	—
Trinidad and Tobago 369	6	18	4	8	10	8	7	—	1	6	1	1	1	6
Uruguay 298	41	51	59	60	67	83	83	7	8	7	18	12	5	20
Venezuela, Rep. Bol. 299	120	129	70	99	133	186	248	5	4	15	5	9	14	88
Western Hem. n.s. 399	22	65	133	149	98	88	123	56	78	129	161	133	165	132
Other Countries n.i.e. 910	**22**	**17**	**13**	**16**	**19**	**23**	**23**	**19**	**20**	**23**	**24**	**26**	**23**	**24**
Cuba 928	13	4	7	11	15	20	20	19	19	22	23	24	23	23
North Korea 954	8	13	6	5	4	3	3	1	1	1	1	1	1	—
Countries & Areas n.s. 898	**—**	**41**	**4**	**—**	**—**	**—**	**—**	**—**	**17**	**1**	**—**	**—**	**—**	**—**
Memorandum Items														
European Union 998	51,478	56,870	65,723	76,680	81,638	90,090	105,660	65,437	69,010	81,010	93,468	101,178	110,849	127,623
Oil Exporting Ctys 999	2,179	2,812	3,110	3,558	3,903	4,613	5,746	1,234	1,522	1,673	2,092	2,694	3,538	2,670
Non-Oil Develop.Ctys 201	15,652	17,621	20,484	25,037	26,118	30,954	38,234	10,294	9,533	10,614	12,701	14,581	17,218	20,629
PERCENT DISTRIBUTION														
Industrial Countries 101	**78.2**	**77.6**	**77.5**	**76.7**	**77.0**	**75.9**	**74.4**	**86.3**	**87.3**	**87.7**	**87.2**	**86.3**	**85.3**	**85.5**
Developing Countries 202	**21.7**	**22.3**	**22.5**	**23.3**	**22.9**	**24.1**	**25.6**	**13.7**	**12.7**	**12.3**	**12.8**	**13.7**	**14.7**	**14.5**
Africa 607	**1.1**	**1.2**	**1.0**	**1.1**	**1.0**	**1.1**	**1.2**	**1.1**	**1.1**	**1.2**	**1.5**	**1.4**	**1.7**	**1.0**
Asia 507	**9.2**	**9.5**	**9.6**	**10.1**	**9.7**	**10.0**	**10.6**	**4.7**	**5.0**	**4.9**	**5.2**	**5.7**	**5.5**	**5.7**
Europe 170	**4.7**	**5.0**	**5.5**	**5.9**	**6.1**	**6.6**	**7.1**	**5.4**	**3.6**	**3.4**	**3.4**	**3.5**	**4.2**	**4.5**
Middle East 407	**3.8**	**3.9**	**3.7**	**3.7**	**3.7**	**3.8**	**4.0**	**1.3**	**1.7**	**1.6**	**1.7**	**2.0**	**2.2**	**1.9**
Western Hemisphere 207	**3.0**	**2.7**	**2.6**	**2.6**	**2.4**	**2.6**	**2.8**	**1.2**	**1.3**	**1.1**	**1.0**	**1.0**	**1.2**	**1.4**
ANNUAL PERCENT CHANGE														
World 001	**1.9**	**11.7**	**14.3**	**17.2**	**6.6**	**12.8**	**16.3**	**1.9**	**3.7**	**15.0**	**15.5**	**9.3**	**11.7**	**13.9**
Industrial Countries 101	**1.2**	**10.9**	**14.0**	**16.0**	**7.0**	**11.2**	**14.0**	**2.0**	**4.9**	**15.5**	**14.8**	**8.2**	**10.3**	**14.2**
Developing Countries 202	**4.3**	**14.6**	**15.5**	**21.2**	**5.0**	**18.5**	**23.7**	**.9**	**–4.1**	**11.2**	**20.4**	**16.8**	**20.2**	**12.2**
Africa 607	**4.8**	**20.5**	**3.3**	**22.2**	**–.8**	**26.7**	**18.6**	**–5.9**	**6.7**	**24.7**	**35.9**	**6.3**	**32.9**	**–30.2**
Asia 507	**2.7**	**16.2**	**14.7**	**23.1**	**3.2**	**15.7**	**23.0**	**–7.8**	**9.2**	**13.2**	**22.6**	**19.3**	**7.7**	**18.7**
Europe 170	**9.2**	**19.4**	**25.9**	**25.6**	**9.5**	**23.0**	**25.1**	**15.6**	**–31.4**	**10.2**	**17.0**	**12.0**	**32.0**	**21.7**
Middle East 407	**2.9**	**14.8**	**9.4**	**14.8**	**7.9**	**14.2**	**23.4**	**–2.2**	**32.9**	**13.1**	**17.1**	**30.6**	**21.5**	**–1.6**
Western Hemisphere 207	**3.9**	**–.1**	**12.9**	**14.1**	**–.2**	**21.1**	**25.1**	**–7.8**	**15.9**	**–8.3**	**7.9**	**12.4**	**28.6**	**35.7**
Other Countries n.i.e. 910	**121.8**	**–21.4**	**–24.2**	**22.1**	**19.3**	**21.5**	**.7**	**.5**	**4.9**	**10.7**	**7.8**	**5.9**	**–8.6**	**1.5**

Syrian Arab Republic 463

	Exports 2001	Exports 2002	Exports 2003	Exports 2004	Exports 2005	Exports 2006	Exports 2007	Imports 2001	Imports 2002	Imports 2003	Imports 2004	Imports 2005	Imports 2006	Imports 2007
	Millions of U.S. Dollars							Millions of U.S. Dollars						
IFS World Total	**21,661.4**	**26,864.4**	**23,611.4**	**30,838.8**	**37,799.6**	**....**	**....**	**19,665.4**	**21,002.6**	**21,092.9**	**34,655.3**	**44,754.5**	**....**	**....**
DOTS World Total 001	**6,205.3Y**	**6,796.5Y**	**6,052.7Y**	**23,585.9**	**10,226.0Y**	**12,091.2Y**	**14,458.5Y**	**6,413.9Y**	**7,153.5Y**	**8,598.2Y**	**26,331.4**	**15,759.0Y**	**18,881.3Y**	**23,491.4Y**
Industrial Countries 101	**3,702.1Y**	**3,825.3Y**	**3,373.7Y**	**12,782.2**	**3,632.8Y**	**4,170.2Y**	**4,304.6Y**	**2,676.8Y**	**2,868.2Y**	**3,250.3Y**	**6,755.6**	**4,320.0Y**	**4,704.1Y**	**5,703.5Y**
United States 111	151.09V	145.18V	256.00V	747.57	319.55V	208.64V	108.45V	249.04V	301.51V	235.51V	1,235.32	172.70V	246.73V	397.65V
Canada 156	39.60V	31.84V	68.44V	6.91	18.30V	22.04V	77.24V	11.52V	12.11V	15.69V	91.43	60.60V	46.93V	66.04V
Australia 193	.52V	.54V	1.02V	4.98	1.41V	1.74V	1.80V	12.01V	13.21V	12.81V	54.12	11.79V	4.46V	5.27V
Japan 158	14.93V	19.87V	43.82V	82.70	15.31V	8.75V	20.88V	201.59V	199.34V	202.44V	678.20	277.51V	374.89V	528.33V
New Zealand 196	.03V	.02V	.21V	1.12	.20V	.14V	.16V	3.79V	5.46V	5.89V	39.98	20.05V	39.26V	68.43V
Austria 122	168.91V	161.08V	119.47V	43.97	56.87V	254.53V	299.98V	33.36V	35.91V	40.29V	73.32	95.29V	62.96V	70.83V
Belgium 124	26.98V	57.77V	28.78V	73.05	23.67V	22.82V	63.86V	174.92V	192.85V	227.87V	229.54	266.79V	291.90V	230.40V
Cyprus 423	137.57V	132.46V	107.62V	98.43	12.24V	14.86V	10.71V	63.83V	28.52V	18.48V	5.22	3.23V	3.64V	3.75V
Denmark 128	3.15V	3.96V	1.90V	5.01	2.70V	1.27V	2.15V	19.24V	19.69V	25.50V	53.96	36.82V	29.05V	36.69V
Finland 172	.14V	.35V	.12V	1.71	.05V	.29V	.64V	27.61V	31.53V	41.10V	77.35	52.44V	49.14V	66.59V
France 132	535.49V	440.44V	334.56V	4,253.29	506.85V	476.18V	712.14V	389.16V	313.76V	490.56V	577.73	625.86V	708.52V	468.68V
Germany 134	1,163.74V	1,133.71V	1,308.48V	116.52	1,017.52V	1,482.46V	1,397.04V	441.27V	525.77V	598.11V	862.91	719.26V	901.12V	1,100.03V
Greece 174	15.70V	12.04V	20.10V	140.13	22.09V	21.62V	31.95V	46.26V	36.05V	94.95V	144.80	213.16V	222.38V	98.23V
Iceland 176	.01V	.01V	.02V	—	.02V	.01V	.01V	—V	—V	—V	—	1.17V	.01V	.02V
Ireland 178	.57V	1.67V	.24V	1.80	1.25V	.92V	.55V	9.69V	6.30V	9.32V	30.85	12.36V	18.28V	26.44V
Italy 136	1,004.77V	1,028.11V	785.34V	5,352.06	1,035.58V	810.01V	1,162.57V	535.54V	571.57V	588.73V	1,139.31	924.07V	918.82V	1,418.57V
Luxembourg 137	.02V	.01V	.01V	.08	—V	—V	—V	1.58V	.82V	2.12V	.18	2.48V	1.15V	.74V
Malta 181	.23Y	4.33V	2.89V	.76	.16V	.22V	.46V	.08Y	—V	.09V	.07	.15V	6.37V	.36V
Netherlands 138	58.09V	207.66V	60.20V	522.82	126.97V	163.02V	208.42V	98.41V	120.23V	142.69V	277.16	188.86V	187.89V	354.62V
Norway 142	.29V	3.96V	5.47V	.46	2.11V	.64V	.62V	4.81V	4.13V	7.06V	21.53	3.90V	—V	48.63V
Portugal 182	37.54V	50.19V	29.02V	50.55	6.82V	34.27V	8.88V	10.40V	4.63V	10.49V	35.40	10.36V	17.73V	24.00V
Slovenia 961	.02V	.08V	.76V	3.36	2.84V	4.33V	.31V	9.99V	11.82V	10.40V	36.78	15.49V	13.46V	23.09V
Spain 184	226.10V	227.37V	109.97V	845.92	237.95V	173.49V	88.35V	105.68V	106.39V	153.60V	260.11	162.36V	203.38V	234.28V
Sweden 144	.83V	1.11V	1.57V	5.44	1.91V	4.62V	4.31V	49.07V	77.51V	79.63V	248.79	104.94V	77.84V	105.19V
Switzerland 146	.72V	1.07V	2.33V	29.41	3.95V	1.06V	1.72V	72.20V	109.90V	89.28V	202.23	129.01V	112.59V	167.04V
United Kingdom 112	115.05V	160.47V	85.41V	394.19	216.52V	462.25V	101.41V	105.73V	139.20V	147.73V	379.30	209.40V	165.57V	159.64V
Developing Countries 202	**2,348.2Y**	**2,802.9Y**	**2,466.1Y**	**10,803.4**	**6,592.8Y**	**7,920.7Y**	**10,153.5Y**	**2,636.7Y**	**3,091.1Y**	**3,836.4Y**	**19,575.8**	**11,439.0Y**	**14,177.2Y**	**17,787.8Y**
Africa 607	**64.2Y**	**166.8Y**	**167.9Y**	**358.5**	**332.8Y**	**380.2Y**	**482.3Y**	**54.1Y**	**56.3Y**	**76.7Y**	**268.8**	**158.2Y**	**195.0Y**	**227.4Y**
Algeria 612	22.30V	114.78V	127.58Y	178.18	226.88Y	280.09Y	362.83Y	10.09V	8.11V	9.83Y	9.18	12.49Y	15.70Y	18.94Y
Benin 638	.16V	.27V	.17V	—	.04V	.05Y	.06Y	—V	—V	—V	—	—V	—Y	—Y
Cameroon 622	.01V	.03V	.09V	—	—Y	—Y	—Y	1.13V	.35V	.87V	—	—Y	—Y	—Y
Congo, Republic of 634	....	....	....	....	....	....	....	—V	.01V	.16V	.69	.79Y	.98Y	1.22Y
Côte d'Ivoire 662	.30V	.55V	.44V	5.52	.62V	.86V	1.07Y	.32V	.55V	1.33V	4.74	3.56V	2.00V	2.48Y
Ghana 652	—Y	—Y	—Y	2.30	2.63Y	3.25Y	4.04Y	—Y	—Y	—Y	5.14	5.88Y	7.26Y	9.01Y
Kenya 664	—V	.01V	.01V	.86	.98Y	1.21Y	1.51Y	.49V	.39V	.51V	1.96	2.24Y	2.76Y	3.43Y
Madagascar 674	—V	—V	—V	—	—Y	—Y	—Y	.01V	.07V	.02V	—	—Y	—Y	—Y
Mauritania 682	1.03Y	1.12Y	1.42Y	6.29	7.18Y	8.88Y	11.02Y	—Y	—Y	—Y	.22	.25Y	.31Y	.38Y
Mauritius 684	.05V	.15V	.10V	—	.02V	.16V	.15V	.03V	.09V	.06V	—	.06V	.02V	.01V
Morocco 686	11.43V	9.29V	15.18V	36.43	14.74V	18.22Y	22.61Y	15.90V	18.07V	25.44V	101.81	46.91V	57.98Y	71.95Y
Niger 692	.03V	.06V	—V	—	—Y	—Y	—Y	—V	—V	—V	—	—Y	—Y	—Y
Nigeria 694	4.03V	16.19V	1.82V	1.54	1.97Y	2.43Y	3.14Y	—V	—V	—V	41.30	56.18Y	70.63Y	85.20Y
Senegal 722	.66V	.98V	1.45V	14.71	1.89V	5.05V	6.26Y	—V	—V	—V	—	—V	.02V	.02Y
Somalia 726	.24Y	.26Y	.33Y	.12	.13Y	.17Y	.21Y	—Y	—Y	—Y	—	—Y	—Y	—Y
South Africa 199	.60V	.61V	.73V	2.72	.67V	.60V	.75V	4.91V	6.31V	15.99V	22.31	6.77V	8.87V	12.28V
Sudan 732	9.39Y	10.19Y	13.05Y	78.67	42.51V	35.37V	38.93V	15.32Y	16.62Y	18.68V	66.43	13.96V	19.81V	11.73V
Tanzania 738	.08V	.02V	.03Y	—	—Y	—Y	—Y	—V	.04V	.05Y	—	—Y	—Y	—Y
Togo 742	.02V	.03V	.02V	—	.03V	.04Y	.05Y	....	....	....	....	....	....	....
Tunisia 744	13.78V	11.93V	5.28V	30.88	32.39V	23.64V	29.34Y	5.12V	5.70V	3.76V	15.04	9.10V	8.69V	10.79Y
Uganda 746	.06V	.05V	.09V	—	—Y	—Y	—Y	—Y	—Y	—Y	—	—Y	—Y	—Y
Zambia 754	.02V	.06V	.04V	.24	.05V	.11V	.27V	—V	—V	.02V	—	—V	—V	—V
Zimbabwe 698	.01V	.25V	.01V	—	.01V	.04V	.05Y	.77V	—V	—V	—	—V	—V	—Y
Asia 507	**136.6Y**	**190.0Y**	**189.9Y**	**562.4**	**63.6Y**	**131.0Y**	**44.9Y**	**1,124.7Y**	**1,356.5Y**	**1,613.3Y**	**5,534.4**	**2,405.7Y**	**3,058.5Y**	**3,930.7Y**
Bangladesh 513	17.88V	1.67V	—V	—	—V	5.92V	4.63V	23.69V	33.73V	18.67V	—	10.05V	15.14Y	12.96Y
Brunei Darussalam 516	—Y	—Y	.03V	—	—Y	—Y	—Y	—Y	—Y	.10V	—	—Y	—Y	—Y
Cambodia 522	—V	—V	—V	—	.01V	—V	—Y	—V	—V	—V	—	—V	.12V	.15Y
China,P.R.: Mainland 924	.01V	12.85V	23.96V	88.53	16.19V	46.09V	7.52V	245.82V	392.59V	528.86V	2,040.89	977.07V	1,492.46V	2,055.47V
China,P.R.:Hong Kong 532	3.88V	1.80V	.28V	2.12	.45V	1.92V	1.74V	26.16V	24.60V	24.49V	1.64	45.44V	19.27V	27.38V
India 534	7.93Y	7.71V	5.18V	13.60	4.27V	5.27Y	6.54Y	87.07Y	127.07V	199.54V	588.25	295.36V	365.04Y	453.01Y
Indonesia 536	13.52V	14.08V	6.64V	42.65	10.95V	6.08V	.44V	65.75V	65.13V	43.75V	197.19	53.29V	61.29V	87.43V
Korea 542	2.61V	12.00V	2.01V	70.60	10.57V	27.51V	5.93V	361.75V	328.28V	301.25V	1,220.35	440.10V	532.48V	668.52V
Malaysia 548	.78V	.87V	.37V	193.33	1.36V	1.53V	1.54V	55.71V	73.16V	169.70V	539.27	180.68V	171.77V	183.00V
Mongolia 948	—V	.34V	.29V	—	—V	—Y	—Y	.06V	.41V	.35V	—	.14V	.26Y	.33Y
New Caledonia 839	—V	.01V	.01V	—	.01Y	.01Y	.01Y	....	....	....	....	....	....	....
Pakistan 564	3.79V	14.42V	2.41V	138.87	8.88V	10.98Y	13.63Y	7.48V	11.74V	23.30V	103.12	7.06V	8.73Y	10.83Y
Philippines 566	.09V	.28V	.13V	—	—V	—V	—V	2.22V	1.41V	.98V	—	1.51V	.72V	1.17V
Singapore 576	68.38V	99.02V	129.80V	—	2.47V	.98V	.22V	22.53V	17.34V	18.75V	—	87.68V	47.70V	20.75V
Sri Lanka 524	.09V	.05V	.03V	.03	.06V	.07V	.63V	61.24V	71.54V	68.79V	240.85	73.96V	90.86V	99.10V
Taiwan Province of China 528	6.28V	1.36V	11.26V	2.50	.47V	23.73V	1.39V	114.56V	116.37V	107.31V	359.57	127.03V	144.53V	178.03V
Thailand 578	10.36V	23.08V	7.06V	5.69	7.88V	.91V	.63V	48.94V	91.66V	103.50V	231.32	106.37V	108.13V	132.55V
Vietnam 582	1.00V	.41V	.46V	4.49	—V	—V	—V	1.67V	1.43V	3.97V	11.94	—V	—V	—V

	Exports 2001	Exports 2002	Exports 2003	Exports 2004	Exports 2005	Exports 2006	Exports 2007	Imports 2001	Imports 2002	Imports 2003	Imports 2004	Imports 2005	Imports 2006	Imports 2007
	Millions of U.S. Dollars							Millions of U.S. Dollars						
Europe....170	**631.5Y**	**887.3Y**	**874.7Y**	**3,514.2**	**415.0Y**	**294.2Y**	**572.9Y**	**829.0Y**	**951.4Y**	**1,266.4Y**	**7,262.4**	**2,194.3Y**	**2,635.5Y**	**3,706.4Y**
Albania....914	.96V	.20V	.30V	—	1.34V	.99V	1.22V	—V	—V	—V	—	—V	—V	—V
Armenia....911	5.09V	1.09V	1.09V	—	1.90V	3.95V	1.78V	.08V	.22V	.54V	—	.52V	.25V	.17V
Azerbaijan....912	.75V	.77V	.47V	—	.54V	.72V	1.15V	—V	.06V	1.01V	—	.32V	.01V	19.86V
Belarus....913	.03V	.11V	.13V	.06	.30V	1.13V	3.59V	16.92V	16.11V	16.97V	179.40	34.31V	48.51V	47.12V
Bulgaria....918	3.85V	26.45V	23.93V	43.02	15.23V	16.89V	18.15V	22.02V	19.61V	13.55V	83.71	22.71V	39.05V	113.93V
Croatia....960	130.35V	202.29V	300.06V	288.78	52.36V	3.07V	2.32V	2.43V	1.50V	5.38V	12.77	25.99V	6.05V	6.47V
Czech Republic....935	14.09V	103.70V	141.46V	8.57	16.07V	2.89V	.89V	43.03V	48.35V	32.24V	101.59	43.20V	57.49V	68.12V
Estonia....939	.01V	1.91V	.05V	.67	.03V	—V	—V	1.34V	.80V	1.21V	5.15	.08V	.92V	1.07V
Georgia....915	.39V	.34V	.38V	—	2.31V	2.30V	2.86Y	.59V	.65V	—V	—	.08V	—V	.01Y
Hungary....944	.90V	.69V	1.00V	3.85	5.15V	2.60V	81.30V	20.91V	22.05V	26.62V	74.78	63.95V	52.11V	64.55V
Kazakhstan....916	.06V	.06V	.19V	—	.31Y	.38Y	.47Y	9.20V	9.23V	9.36V	—	11.46Y	14.16Y	17.57Y
Kyrgyz Republic....917	.18V	.12V	.13V	—	.08V	—V	.01V	.33V	.22V	—V	—	.22V	.22V	.14V
Latvia....941	—V	—V	—V	.78	.10V	—V	.01V	—V	—V	.15V	—	—V	.01V	.06V
Lithuania....946	.04V	.07V	.11V	.70	.04V	.02V	.03V	.07V	.13V	.22V	.85	.52V	.34V	.25V
Macedonia, FYR....962	2.63V	2.37V	1.27V	—	.12V	.17V	.21Y	.03V	—V	.04V	—	.27V	.36V	.45Y
Moldova....921	.05V	.23V	.12V	—	.35V	.43Y	.53Y	1.13V	1.71V	3.06V	—	5.32V	6.58Y	8.17Y
Poland....964	.56V	.58V	.70V	19.86	7.78V	14.47V	20.28V	21.97V	13.78V	15.28V	89.72	24.26V	20.18V	41.91V
Romania....968	32.29V	68.13V	4.28V	18.96	13.23V	13.38V	19.75V	75.39V	105.82V	136.81V	458.62	95.35V	96.58V	129.91V
Russia....922	15.33V	14.91V	12.30V	35.94	23.60V	27.24V	34.54V	97.36V	151.55V	229.40V	1,415.03	485.46V	664.17V	1,125.24V
Serbia & Montenegro....965	.34Y	.37Y	.47Y	1.18	1.35Y	1.67Y	2.07Y	3.91Y	4.24Y	5.37Y	23.29	26.61Y	32.89Y	40.81Y
Slovak Republic....936	.06V	.40V	.50Y	.20	.02V	.49V	.31V	7.67V	5.81V	7.35Y	42.02	7.53V	11.45V	9.59V
Tajikistan....923	—V	.09V	.09V	—	.18V	.09V	.09V	—V	—V	—V	—	—V	—V	—V
Turkey....186	421.34V	460.22V	375.77V	3,037.56	247.44V	170.23V	342.69V	309.26V	293.45V	451.83V	2,480.49	606.79V	670.36V	877.04V
Ukraine....926	2.21V	2.24V	9.90V	54.04	25.18V	31.12Y	38.62Y	195.34V	256.15V	309.99V	2,295.04	739.35V	913.78Y	1,134.00Y
Middle East....407	**1,495.2Y**	**1,549.4Y**	**1,217.3Y**	**6,336.7**	**5,716.9Y**	**7,030.6Y**	**9,029.2Y**	**434.8Y**	**490.2Y**	**641.4Y**	**5,115.1**	**6,276.8Y**	**7,879.2Y**	**9,509.9Y**
Bahrain....419	11.35Y	12.32Y	15.59Y	15.52	17.73Y	21.92Y	27.20Y	4.35Y	4.72Y	5.98Y	7.54	8.61Y	10.64Y	13.21Y
Egypt....469	44.11V	47.87Y	60.59Y	457.44	522.66Y	645.97Y	801.65Y	61.52V	66.77Y	84.50Y	827.13	945.07Y	1,168.03Y	1,449.52Y
Iran, I.R. of....429	1.55V	31.56V	35.08Y	25.03	31.87Y	39.34Y	50.96Y	48.59Y	51.67Y	62.64Y	493.39	671.16Y	843.77Y	1,017.90Y
Iraq....433	—Y	—Y	—Y	2,132.95	2,715.89Y	3,352.77Y	4,343.24Y	—Y	—Y	—Y	404.32	549.99Y	691.44Y	834.14Y
Jordan....439	60.42V	88.12V	139.31V	627.99	207.20V	238.22V	330.93V	43.84V	76.72V	106.81V	346.04	222.92V	296.45V	295.34V
Kuwait....443	64.46Y	66.67Y	74.10Y	232.53	296.08Y	365.52Y	473.50Y	20.93Y	22.25Y	26.98Y	160.60	218.47Y	274.66Y	331.34Y
Lebanon....446	284.29Y	308.53Y	390.50Y	821.31	938.41Y	1,159.81Y	1,439.31Y	31.30Y	33.96Y	42.99Y	528.61	603.98Y	746.47Y	926.37Y
Libya....672	31.22Y	32.29Y	35.89Y	151.39	192.77Y	237.97Y	308.27Y	26.36Y	28.03Y	33.98Y	164.67	223.99Y	281.60Y	339.72Y
Oman....449	10.54V	7.86V	4.81V	10.30	13.12Y	16.20Y	20.98Y	8.57V	8.84V	13.74V	31.53	42.89Y	53.92Y	65.04Y
Qatar....453	19.73V	30.03V	23.17V	100.07	35.98V	32.88V	42.60Y	8.55V	4.35V	29.88V	109.77	23.10V	34.12V	41.17Y
Saudi Arabia....456	246.89V	489.67V	366.12V	1,469.31	471.87V	582.53Y	754.61Y	133.97Y	142.45Y	172.70Y	1,360.92	1,851.24Y	2,327.36Y	2,807.68Y
United Arab Emirates....466	715.45V	426.00V	61.36V	200.67	255.51Y	315.43Y	408.62Y	46.53Y	49.48Y	59.99Y	668.81	909.77Y	1,143.75Y	1,379.80Y
Yemen, Republic of....474	5.14V	8.49V	10.75Y	92.18	17.84V	22.05Y	27.36Y	.26V	.98V	1.24Y	11.80	5.63V	6.95Y	8.63Y
Western Hemisphere....207	**20.8Y**	**9.4Y**	**16.3Y**	**31.7**	**64.5Y**	**84.7Y**	**24.2Y**	**194.1Y**	**236.6Y**	**238.5Y**	**1,395.1**	**403.9Y**	**409.1Y**	**413.4Y**
Argentina....213	.34V	.24V	.25V	.70	.32V	.34V	.53V	111.54V	123.78V	145.91V	598.81	179.79V	142.73V	158.52V
Barbados....316	.01V	.01V	.01V	—	—V	—V	—Y	—V	—V	—V	—	—V	—V	—Y
Bermuda....319	—Y	—Y	—Y	—	.01V	—V	—Y	—Y	—Y	—Y	—	—Y	—Y	—Y
Bolivia....218	.12V	.16V	.13V	—	.14V	.18Y	.22Y	—V	.04V	—V	—	—Y	—Y	—Y
Brazil....223	11.83V	3.68V	11.21V	14.73	55.03V	40.91V	9.50V	71.98V	96.30V	73.26V	609.78	182.62V	224.37V	215.24V
Chile....228	.43V	.27V	—V	.77	.74V	.52V	.85V	1.29V	—V	.01V	4.49	.21V	.09V	5.56V
Colombia....233	2.93V	1.63V	.77V	1.88	1.40V	1.12V	1.31V	2.57V	6.76V	7.31V	33.20	2.01V	14.10V	11.31V
Costa Rica....238	.11V	.07V	.03V	—	.02V	.03Y	.04Y	.13V	.18V	.15V	—	.05V	.06Y	.08Y
Dominican Republic....243	.03V	.03Y	.04Y	—	.05Y	.07Y	.08Y	—V	—Y	—Y	—	—Y	—Y	—Y
Ecuador....248	1.08V	1.16V	.84V	4.25	1.74V	1.98V	2.46Y	.26V	1.62V	1.16V	86.25	15.60V	4.01V	4.97Y
Guatemala....258	.13V	.12V	.05V	.18	.06V	.08Y	.10Y	5.33V	5.27V	5.02V	32.82	5.74V	7.09Y	8.80Y
Honduras....268	.21V	.17V	.19V	—	—Y	—Y	—Y	.03V	.01V	.02V	—	—Y	—Y	—Y
Jamaica....343	.05V	.02V	.01V	—	.04V	—V	—V	—V	—V	—V	—	—V	—V	—V
Mexico....273	—V	—V	—V	3.93	1.63V	3.74V	2.30V	—V	—V	—V	29.46	15.77V	14.73V	4.51V
Netherlands Antilles....353	.01V	—V	—V	—	—Y	—Y	—Y	—V	—V	—V	—	—Y	—Y	—Y
Panama....283	—V	—V	—V	—	—V	—V	—V	—V	—V	.37V	—	—V	—V	1.16V
Paraguay....288	—V	.05V	1.33V	—	.68V	1.24V	1.54Y	.13V	.08V	.27V	—	.03V	—V	—Y
Peru....293	1.87V	.62V	.74V	—	.44V	.63V	.84Y	.87V	.89V	1.16V	—	1.91V	1.58V	2.91Y
St. Vincent & Grens....364	—V	—V	—V	—	—V	.01Y	.01Y	—Y	—Y	—Y	—	—Y	—Y	—Y
Trinidad and Tobago....369	.33V	.17V	.21Y	—	—Y	—Y	—Y	—V	—V	—Y	—	—Y	—Y	—Y
Uruguay....298	—V	—Y	—V	—	.07V	.09Y	.11Y	—V	—Y	3.86V	—	.17V	.21Y	.27Y
Venezuela, Rep. Bol....299	1.26V	1.01V	.53V	5.23	2.14V	33.74V	4.33V	.01V	1.68V	.04V	.26	.02V	.08V	.10Y
Other Countries n.i.e....910	**.2Y**	**.2Y**	**.3Y**	**.3**	**.3Y**	**.4Y**	**.5Y**	**7.2Y**	**7.8Y**	**9.8Y**	**—**	**—Y**	**—Y**	**—Y**
Cuba....928	.19Y	.20Y	.26Y	.27	.31Y	.38Y	.48Y	7.16Y	7.77Y	9.83Y	—	—Y	—Y	—Y
Countries & Areas n.s....898	**154.8Y**	**168.0Y**	**212.6Y**	**—**	**—Y**	**—Y**	**—Y**	**1,093.2Y**	**1,186.5Y**	**1,501.7Y**	**—**	**—Y**	**—Y**	**—Y**
Memorandum Items														
European Union....998	3,510.55Y	3,730.17Y	3,140.24Y	11,943.72	3,301.18Y	3,947.62Y	4,196.53Y	2,216.84Y	2,313.46Y	2,764.72Y	4,746.89	3,782.86Y	4,021.70Y	4,607.69Y
Oil Exporting Ctys....999	1,130.97Y	1,230.13Y	737.11Y	4,549.87	4,255.04Y	5,264.97Y	6,773.53Y	369.36Y	381.99Y	453.52Y	3,641.93	4,612.58Y	5,798.31Y	7,008.47Y
Non-Oil Develop.Ctys....201	1,217.26Y	1,572.81Y	1,729.00Y	6,253.54	2,337.79Y	2,655.71Y	3,379.92Y	2,267.32Y	2,709.08Y	3,382.83Y	15,933.91	6,826.38Y	8,378.93Y	0,779.38Y
PERCENT DISTRIBUTION														
Industrial Countries....101	**59.7**	**56.3**	**55.7**	**54.2**	**35.5**	**34.5**	**29.8**	**41.7**	**40.1**	**37.8**	**25.7**	**27.4**	**24.9**	**24.3**
Developing Countries....202	**37.8**	**41.2**	**40.7**	**45.8**	**64.5**	**65.5**	**70.2**	**41.1**	**43.2**	**44.6**	**74.3**	**72.6**	**75.1**	**75.7**
Africa....607	**1.0**	**2.5**	**2.8**	**1.5**	**3.3**	**3.1**	**3.3**	**.8**	**.8**	**.9**	**1.0**	**1.0**	**1.0**	**1.0**
Asia....507	**2.2**	**2.8**	**3.1**	**2.4**	**.6**	**1.1**	**.3**	**17.5**	**19.0**	**18.8**	**21.0**	**15.3**	**16.2**	**16.7**
Europe....170	**10.2**	**13.1**	**14.5**	**14.9**	**4.1**	**2.4**	**4.0**	**12.9**	**13.3**	**14.7**	**27.6**	**13.9**	**14.0**	**15.8**

	Exports							Imports						
	2001	2002	2003	2004	2005	2006	2007	2001	2002	2003	2004	2005	2006	2007
Middle East.......... 407	24.1	22.8	20.1	26.9	55.9	58.1	62.4	6.8	6.9	7.5	19.4	39.8	41.7	40.5
Western Hemisphere.......... 207	.3	.1	.3	.1	.6	.7	.2	3.0	3.3	2.8	5.3	2.6	2.2	1.8
Other Countries n.i.e.......... 910	—	—	—	—	—	—	—	.1	.1	.1	—	—	—	—
ANNUAL PERCENT CHANGE														
World.......... 001	30.4	9.5	–10.9	289.7	–56.6	18.2	19.6	18.7	11.5	20.2	206.2	–40.2	19.8	24.4
Industrial Countries.......... 101	16.8	3.3	–11.8	278.9	–71.6	14.8	3.2	16.4	7.2	13.3	107.8	–36.1	8.9	21.2
Developing Countries.......... 202	61.9	19.4	–12.0	338.1	–39.0	20.1	28.2	25.1	17.2	24.1	410.3	–41.6	23.9	25.5
Africa.......... 607	8.9	159.8	.6	113.6	–7.2	14.2	26.9	33.7	4.1	36.2	250.5	–41.2	23.3	16.6
Asia.......... 507	75.4	39.0	—	196.1	–88.7	106.0	–65.8	25.7	20.6	18.9	243.0	–56.5	27.1	28.5
Europe.......... 170	8.7	40.5	–1.4	301.8	–88.2	–29.1	94.7	22.0	14.8	33.1	473.5	–69.8	20.1	40.6
Middle East.......... 407	106.0	3.6	–21.4	420.6	–9.8	23.0	28.4	15.4	12.8	30.8	697.5	22.7	25.5	20.7
Western Hemisphere.......... 207	195.6	–54.7	73.7	93.8	103.7	31.2	–71.4	67.4	21.9	.8	484.8	–71.0	1.3	1.1
Other Countries n.i.e.......... 910	10.4	8.5	26.6	6.4	14.3	23.6	24.1	10.4	8.5	26.6	31.3	....	....	....

	Exports							Imports						
	2001	2002	2003	2004	2005	2006	2007	2001	2002	2003	2004	2005	2006	2007
	Millions of U.S. Dollars							Millions of U.S. Dollars						
DOTS World Total....................001	**652.9**	**736.9**	**797.1**	**914.9**	**908.7**	**1,398.9**	**1,468.1**	**693.5**	**720.5**	**880.8**	**1,191.1**	**1,330.0**	**1,725.3**	**2,537.7**
Industrial Countries................101	**266.9**	**308.8**	**303.3**	**467.9**	**476.7**	**619.7**	**616.6**	**48.6**	**68.0**	**61.9**	**147.3**	**129.5**	**154.4**	**192.7**
United States..........................111	1.20	.70	.60	.50	.20	.38	.40	2.80	6.10	5.30	79.20	11.70	12.00	38.40
Canada..................................156	—	—	—	—	—	.01	.10	.10	1.00	.60	.20	.30	.20	.40
Australia...............................193	—	—	—	—	—	.01	—	.60	.90	.40	.30	.50	.30	.70
Japan.....................................158	—	—	.70	—	.10	.03	.10	1.20	.80	.60	1.10	5.90	1.80	3.60
New Zealand...........................196	—	—	—	—	—	—	—	—	—	—	.20	—	—	—
Austria...................................122	.80	—	1.10	.20	—	—	—	.80	.50	2.50	1.20	2.00	.70	1.60
Belgium..................................124	6.00	9.50	7.60	7.20	4.90	4.21	1.40	2.50	1.50	2.30	1.30	2.30	1.60	5.30
Cyprus....................................423	—	.10	.10	—	—	—	—	—	.80	—	—	.90	—	—
Denmark.................................128	—	—	—	—	—	—	—	.30	1.00	.40	2.00	.80	.80	2.00
Finland...................................172	.10	—	—	—	—	.23	.10	.30	.30	.80	.90	.50	2.80	5.50
France....................................132	.10	.20	—	—	—	.18	.10	.30	.20	1.10	1.40	3.90	6.30	4.00
Germany.................................134	.20	.10	.20	.20	.50	.44	1.10	4.10	3.90	12.10	29.30	17.40	22.80	21.90
Greece....................................174	—	.10	—	—	—	—	—	7.40	17.40	—	6.00	12.50	17.10	5.80
Iceland....................................176	—	—	—	—	—	—	—	—	—	—	—	.10	.20	.10
Ireland....................................178	—	—	—	—	—	—	—	—	.10	—	—	—	—	.20
Italy..136	5.70	6.90	8.40	11.40	15.60	16.52	16.30	20.00	25.80	22.80	13.80	51.70	61.60	80.40
Luxembourg............................137	—	—	—	—	—	—	—	—	—	—	.10	—	1.10	—
Netherlands............................138	194.40	216.90	200.80	379.20	423.40	569.42	570.50	.30	.50	1.10	.50	2.00	2.10	2.60
Norway...................................142	—	—	—	—	—	—	—	.40	—	—	.10	.60	.50	—
Portugal..................................182	1.60	.70	2.80	2.80	2.80	1.26	1.30	—	—	—	—	—	—	—
Slovenia..................................961	—	—	—	—	—	—	—	—	—	.10	—	.20	.50	.90
Spain.......................................184	2.00	.90	1.50	2.10	.90	1.54	.30	2.90	2.30	4.30	.20	.30	.10	—
Sweden...................................144	.10	.10	—	—	—	—	—	—	.70	.70	.90	.90	2.30	2.30
Switzerland.............................146	52.20	68.70	77.00	63.40	27.00	24.48	24.40	2.10	1.00	3.10	2.70	8.40	5.40	6.30
United Kingdom......................112	2.50	3.90	2.50	.90	1.30	.97	.50	2.50	3.20	3.70	5.90	6.60	14.20	10.70
Developing Countries............. 202	**384.6**	**428.1**	**493.8**	**447.0**	**432.0**	**779.2**	**851.5**	**638.9**	**652.5**	**818.9**	**1,043.8**	**1,200.5**	**1,570.9**	**2,345.0**
Africa.....................................607	**.4**	**.1**	**.2**	**.2**	**.2**	**—**	**.1**	**.5**	**6.2**	**8.3**	**—**	**.1**	**23.3**	**.1**
Benin.......................................638	—	—	—	—	—	—	.10	—	—	—	—	—	—	—
Congo, Republic of..................634	.20	—	.10	—	—	—	—	.10	.20	.20	—	—	—	—
Côte d'Ivoire...........................662	—	.10	—	—	—	—	—	—	.10	—	—	—	—	—
Djibouti...................................611	.20	—	—	—	—	—	—	.20	—	—	—	—	—	—
Guinea.....................................656	....	....	....	....	....	....	....	—	5.90	8.00	—	—	23.30	—
Morocco..................................686	—	—	—	.10	.10	—	—	—	—	—	—	—	—	—
Somalia...................................726	—	—	—	—	—	—	—	.20	—	—	—	—	—	—
South Africa............................199	—	—	—	—	—	.01	—	—	—	.10	—	.10	—	.10
Tunisia....................................744	—	—	.10	.10	.10	—	—	—	—	—	—	—	—	—
Asia.......................................507	**13.8**	**14.8**	**16.7**	**20.0**	**22.9**	**31.5**	**23.9**	**45.2**	**43.2**	**34.7**	**70.3**	**108.9**	**181.8**	**339.9**
Afghanistan, I.S. of..................512	3.10	6.30	5.80	7.70	12.10	18.64	12.10	.10	.30	1.60	4.00	3.40	6.50	27.10
Bangladesh..............................513	—	—	—	.40	—	—	—	—	—	—	—	—	—	—
China,P.R.: Mainland...............924	1.40	2.10	5.70	6.10	5.70	9.94	8.30	6.00	7.60	26.70	57.00	92.50	148.90	275.30
China,P.R.:Hong Kong.............532	—	.10	—	—	—	—	—	—	—	—	—	.30	—	.70
India..534	—	—	—	.20	.10	.01	.10	34.40	31.50	3.20	3.30	1.40	9.60	8.50
Indonesia.................................536	—	—	—	—	.20	—	—	—	—	.30	—	.10	.20	.20
Korea.......................................542	7.00	4.10	3.20	3.20	2.10	.91	1.50	4.20	3.30	2.60	4.20	9.00	14.70	24.30
Malaysia..................................548	—	—	—	—	—	—	—	.10	.10	.10	.60	.50	1.20	1.70
Mongolia..................................948	—	—	—	—	—	—	—	—	—	—	.10	—	.10	.10
Pakistan...................................564	.20	—	.10	.20	.30	.14	.40	.10	.10	—	.30	1.70	.30	.80
Philippines...............................566	—	—	—	—	—	—	—	—	—	—	.10	—	—	.10
Singapore.................................576	—	—	—	—	—	.14	—	.10	.20	.10	.70	—	.30	.70
Taiwan Province of China.........528	—	.10	—	—	—	—	—	—	—	.10	—	—	—	—
Thailand...................................578	—	—	.10	.10	—	—	—	—	—	—	—	—	—	.30
Vietnam...................................582	2.10	2.10	1.80	2.10	2.40	1.75	1.50	.20	.10	—	—	—	—	.10
Europe...................................170	**340.1**	**383.4**	**424.5**	**396.9**	**371.5**	**670.0**	**748.5**	**569.9**	**580.3**	**698.7**	**930.4**	**1,004.9**	**1,245.5**	**1,806.1**
Albania....................................914	....	....	....	....	....	....	....	—	—	—	—	—	.10	—
Armenia...................................911	—	—	—	—	—	—	.20	.10	1.40	—	—	—	—	.20
Azerbaijan................................912	.50	.50	.70	—	.60	2.65	.80	33.50	41.10	62.30	86.00	114.90	138.20	74.10
Belarus....................................913	1.40	1.50	1.60	1.60	1.10	1.98	3.30	2.60	2.90	7.50	18.90	13.70	19.00	22.90
Bosnia & Herzegovina..............963	—	—	—	—	—	—	—	—	.10	—	29.30	15.60	—	23.60
Bulgaria...................................918	.10	.10	—	2.90	1.80	1.71	3.50	.30	.30	.30	.20	.30	.20	.10
Croatia.....................................960	—	—	—	—	—	—	—	—	—	.10	—	—	.20	.50
Czech Republic........................935	—	2.40	.10	2.20	.10	.02	.30	.50	.80	1.00	.80	2.30	4.70	2.00
Estonia.....................................939	—	.60	.60	—	—	—	—	.10	.10	.60	1.00	2.50	6.30	13.50
Georgia....................................915	—	2.50	—	2.10	—	3.33	—	.80	1.10	.90	1.60	1.50	3.10	3.20
Gibraltar..................................823	—	1.10	—	—	—	—	—	—	—	.20	.10	.10	.10	—
Hungary...................................944	38.80	39.90	12.00	22.10	—	.05	.60	.70	12.20	3.40	2.40	.70	3.20	4.90
Kazakhstan..............................916	3.10	3.50	4.60	3.50	19.70	27.85	24.00	89.10	72.20	95.80	152.60	168.30	186.70	332.80
Kyrgyz Republic.......................917	2.00	3.70	3.70	4.40	3.20	11.21	3.30	5.70	5.20	27.50	17.60	20.60	28.20	58.60
Latvia.......................................941	11.70	30.90	78.00	64.80	44.20	35.10	31.00	2.70	2.80	12.10	12.30	8.60	9.70	8.30
Lithuania.................................946	—	—	.30	—	—	—	.10	2.60	2.40	8.70	15.70	21.90	24.60	60.70
Macedonia, FYR......................962	....	....	....	....	....	....	....	—	.10	—	—	—	—	—

		Exports 2001	Exports 2002	Exports 2003	Exports 2004	Exports 2005	Exports 2006	Exports 2007	Imports 2001	Imports 2002	Imports 2003	Imports 2004	Imports 2005	Imports 2006	Imports 2007
		Millions of U.S. Dollars							Millions of U.S. Dollars						
Moldova	921	—	.30	.20	—	.10	.11	.10	—	—	.10	.10	.10	.40	.90
Poland	964	.20	.10	.60	.10	.30	2.83	5.10	4.90	3.20	2.80	3.60	4.50	9.40	7.90
Romania	968	.20	—	.80	1.60	.90	.32	.80	10.80	—	38.90	13.10	61.70	46.40	—
Russia	922	104.70	87.50	52.20	60.50	82.80	65.44	97.30	129.40	163.50	178.10	240.80	256.50	423.70	813.70
Serbia & Montenegro	965	....	....	....	....	....	....	....	—	—	—	2.40	—	.02	—
Slovak Republic	936	2.60	1.50	.40	4.30	2.90	1.01	.60	.10	—	—	.40	.50	3.70	.60
Turkey	186	75.10	118.50	193.20	139.70	143.40	442.78	477.60	9.30	10.50	29.50	37.90	21.90	36.60	72.90
Turkmenistan	925	9.70	10.00	2.20	7.60	—	.06	4.30	62.30	47.10	31.60	33.70	53.80	60.30	38.20
Ukraine	926	2.80	5.90	6.20	13.60	3.90	6.09	8.60	63.60	80.50	62.40	53.80	82.00	64.30	52.60
Uzbekistan	927	87.20	72.90	67.10	65.90	66.50	67.43	87.00	150.70	132.40	132.70	168.80	152.90	176.40	213.90
Yugoslavia n.s.	966	—	—	—	—	—	—	—	.10	.40	2.20	37.30	—	—	—
Middle East	**407**	**30.3**	**29.8**	**52.4**	**29.9**	**37.4**	**77.6**	**79.0**	**15.0**	**22.8**	**38.1**	**43.1**	**56.6**	**68.9**	**130.3**
Egypt	469	.10	—	—	—	.20	—	.10	—	—	—	—	—	—	.40
Iran, I.R. of	429	29.90	28.40	51.40	29.60	36.70	76.11	75.50	10.00	15.60	23.70	26.30	30.90	34.20	60.90
Iraq	433	—	—	—	—	.10	1.21	—	—	—	—	—	—	—	—
Israel	436	—	.20	—	—	.10	.06	—	.10	.10	.40	.30	.70	1.50	3.50
Jordan	439	—	—	.30	—	—	—	—	—	—	—	—	—	—	—
Kuwait	443	—	—	—	—	—	—	—	—	—	—	—	.50	—	—
Lebanon	446	—	—	—	—	—	—	—	—	—	—	—	—	—	.10
Oman	449	—	—	—	—	—	—	—	—	.10	.10	.10	—	.10	.20
Saudi Arabia	456	—	—	—	—	—	—	—	—	—	—	—	—	—	.10
Syrian Arab Republic	463	—	—	—	—	—	—	—	—	.10	.10	.20	.20	.10	.10
United Arab Emirates	466	.30	1.20	.70	.30	.30	.21	3.40	4.90	6.90	13.80	16.20	24.30	33.00	65.00
Western Hemisphere	**207**	—	—	—	—	—	**.1**	—	**8.3**	—	**39.1**	—	**30.0**	**51.4**	**68.6**
Argentina	213	—	—	—	—	—	.07	—	—	—	—	—	.10	—	—
Bahamas, The	313	....	....	....	....	....	....	....	—	—	—	—	.40	.10	—
Brazil	223	—	—	—	—	—	—	—	—	—	26.00	—	.20	.40	15.60
Jamaica	343	—	—	—	—	—	—	—	—	—	13.10	—	16.20	39.90	53.00
Panama	283	—	—	—	—	—	—	—	—	—	—	—	.20	—	—
Venezuela, Rep. Bol	299	—	—	—	—	—	—	—	8.30	—	—	—	12.90	11.00	—
Other Countries n.i.e	**910**	**1.4**	—	—	—	—	—	—	**6.0**	—	—	—	—	—	—
North Korea	954	1.37	—	—	—	—	—	—	6.04	—	—	—	—	—	—
Memorandum Items															
European Union	998	266.80	314.80	317.00	497.50	496.90	633.78	629.30	53.00	79.70	80.50	99.70	143.00	195.60	241.10
Oil Exporting Ctys	999	30.20	29.60	52.10	29.90	37.30	77.52	78.90	23.20	22.60	37.90	42.60	68.70	78.50	126.40
Non-Oil Develop.Ctys	201	354.40	398.50	441.70	417.10	394.70	701.66	772.60	615.70	629.90	781.00	1,001.20	1,131.80	1,492.42	2,218.60
PERCENT DISTRIBUTION															
Industrial Countries	**101**	**40.9**	**41.9**	**38.1**	**51.1**	**52.5**	**44.3**	**42.0**	**7.0**	**9.4**	**7.0**	**12.4**	**9.7**	**8.9**	**7.6**
Developing Countries	**202**	**58.9**	**58.1**	**61.9**	**48.9**	**47.5**	**55.7**	**58.0**	**92.1**	**90.6**	**93.0**	**87.6**	**90.3**	**91.1**	**92.4**
Africa	**607**	**.1**	—	—	—	—	—	—	**.1**	**.9**	**.9**	—	—	**1.4**	—
Asia	**507**	**2.1**	**2.0**	**2.1**	**2.2**	**2.5**	**2.3**	**1.6**	**6.5**	**6.0**	**3.9**	**5.9**	**8.2**	**10.5**	**13.4**
Europe	**170**	**52.1**	**52.0**	**53.3**	**43.4**	**40.9**	**47.9**	**51.0**	**82.2**	**80.5**	**79.3**	**78.1**	**75.6**	**72.2**	**71.2**
Middle East	**407**	**4.6**	**4.0**	**6.6**	**3.3**	**4.1**	**5.5**	**5.4**	**2.2**	**3.2**	**4.3**	**3.6**	**4.3**	**4.0**	**5.1**
Western Hemisphere	**207**	—	—	—	—	—	—	—	**1.2**	—	**4.4**	—	**2.3**	**3.0**	**2.7**
Other Countries n.i.e	**910**	**.2**	—	—	—	—	—	—	**.9**	—	—	—	—	—	—
ANNUAL PERCENT CHANGE															
World	**001**	**–15.2**	**12.9**	**8.2**	**14.8**	**–.7**	**53.9**	**4.9**	**3.4**	**3.9**	**22.2**	**35.2**	**11.7**	**29.7**	**47.1**
Industrial Countries	**101**	**–8.9**	**15.7**	**–1.8**	**54.3**	**1.9**	**30.0**	**–.5**	**74.2**	**39.9**	**–9.0**	**138.0**	**–12.1**	**19.2**	**24.8**
Developing Countries	**202**	**–19.4**	**11.3**	**15.3**	**–9.5**	**–3.4**	**80.4**	**9.3**	**–.6**	**2.1**	**25.5**	**27.5**	**15.0**	**30.9**	**49.3**
Africa	**607**	**–60.0**	**–75.0**	**100.0**	—	—	**–93.6**	**675.2**	**25.0**	—	**33.9**	**–99.4**	**14.3**	—	**–99.6**
Asia	**507**	**–26.2**	**7.2**	**12.8**	**19.8**	**14.5**	**37.7**	**–24.2**	**211.7**	**–4.4**	**–19.7**	**102.6**	**54.9**	**66.9**	**87.0**
Europe	**170**	**–23.4**	**12.7**	**10.7**	**–6.5**	**–6.4**	**80.3**	**11.7**	**–7.6**	**1.8**	**20.4**	**33.2**	**8.0**	**23.9**	**45.0**
Middle East	**407**	**131.3**	**–1.7**	**75.8**	**–42.9**	**25.1**	**107.4**	**1.8**	**37.6**	**52.0**	**67.1**	**13.1**	**31.3**	**21.7**	**89.1**
Western Hemisphere	**207**	—	—	—	....	....	....	**–95.8**	....	**–99.9**	—	**–99.9**	**49.8**	**71.3**	**33.5**

		Exports 2001	2002	2003	2004	2005	2006	2007	Imports 2001	2002	2003	2004	2005	2006	2007
		Millions of U.S. Dollars							Millions of U.S. Dollars						
IFS World Total		**776.2**	**902.4**	**1,129.5**	**1,473.6**	**1,675.4**	**1,735.8**	**2,022.4**	**1,714.4**	**1,660.3**	**2,125.2**	**2,726.3**	**3,287.1**	**4,246.2**	**5,337.1**
DOTS World Total	**001**	**774.4**	**948.6**	**934.1Y**	**1,220.7Y**	**1,476.0Y**	**1,572.1Y**	**1,766.1Y**	**1,780.2**	**1,749.5**	**2,496.0Y**	**3,073.7Y**	**3,554.5Y**	**4,286.5Y**	**5,470.6Y**
Industrial Countries	**101**	**526.6**	**597.2**	**418.7Y**	**540.2Y**	**590.5Y**	**576.3Y**	**594.5Y**	**780.4**	**718.7**	**731.3Y**	**935.8Y**	**1,008.5Y**	**1,237.4Y**	**1,612.5Y**
United States	111	15.20	13.52	23.73V	23.55V	32.18V	32.91V	43.55V	65.31	91.38	72.71V	140.47V	106.15V	176.88V	191.18V
Canada	156	.54	1.40	2.13V	11.02V	131.74V	37.57V	1.98V	23.08	17.69	21.02V	25.66V	29.66V	36.69V	48.67V
Australia	193	2.48	3.00	3.20V	2.46V	3.77V	8.16V	4.47V	141.19	72.49	37.96V	59.97V	33.90V	26.99V	25.76V
Japan	158	68.54	96.29	89.80V	71.64V	68.00V	83.72V	69.33V	150.70	138.72	85.17V	86.65V	104.47V	126.61V	183.07V
New Zealand	196	.06	.06	.08V	.56V	.48V	.58V	.75V	.96	1.38	1.41V	2.74V	2.03V	3.38V	4.57V
Austria	122	.05	.09	20.24V	31.93V	6.70V	.79V	4.13V	5.82	2.68	4.10V	7.08V	4.83V	11.86V	8.30V
Belgium	124	10.57	21.23	37.45V	35.67V	26.14V	32.91V	32.05V	22.04	23.18	31.45V	42.13V	47.98V	76.65V	81.17V
Cyprus	423	.19	.16	.11V	.21V	.36Y	.40V	.48V	.81	.54	.81V	8.65V	1.08V	1.82V	2.18V
Denmark	128	2.24	1.63	1.96V	1.75V	1.35V	1.03V	1.45V	17.50	15.67	13.81V	12.91V	8.68V	9.19V	12.57V
Finland	172	.87	.33	1.15V	1.04V	1.04V	1.58V	5.47V	4.79	16.32	16.29V	20.25V	16.38V	20.81V	116.77V
France	132	138.39	154.45	6.35V	14.18V	13.91V	14.23V	17.63V	41.56	38.94	63.79V	79.61V	86.08V	54.73V	154.67V
Germany	134	38.28	27.59	50.06V	48.58V	65.50V	65.80V	111.98V	68.12	60.01	91.45V	103.17V	122.49V	170.54V	181.34V
Greece	174	1.89	5.30	8.37V	6.86V	9.83V	11.38V	9.93V	1.44	1.73	2.00V	1.81V	1.87V	6.18V	1.03V
Iceland	176	2.18	1.05	.13V	.09V	.21V	.07V	.02V	.11	.13	.05V	.07V	.10V	.06V	—V
Ireland	178	27.92	14.06	.11V	.04V	.15V	.18V	.23V	5.24	8.25	7.99V	10.03V	9.60V	15.75V	13.42V
Italy	136	7.82	24.44	11.58V	15.76V	29.23V	35.59V	44.67V	50.97	44.96	55.54V	60.22V	78.67V	141.54V	122.91V
Luxembourg	137	—	—	.13V	.14V	1.50V	.08V	—V	.70	.82	1.25V	1.05V	2.17V	1.86V	3.60V
Malta	181	.06	.02	.13V	.05V	.08V	.10V	.50V	.46	.03	.05V	.22V	.15V	.26V	1.92V
Netherlands	138	51.71	53.95	77.98V	80.65V	78.83V	98.07V	114.14V	30.89	27.38	47.36V	67.53V	92.31V	90.58V	98.91V
Norway	142	.15	.24	3.74V	4.39V	6.40V	6.36V	9.71V	4.10	6.05	3.26V	4.87V	3.66V	3.56V	22.05V
Portugal	182	4.99	3.99	10.30V	14.10V	12.42V	16.46V	28.93V	.67	.34	.37V	.71V	1.26V	.97V	.80V
Slovenia	961	—	—	.62V	.81Y	12.35V	1.79V	.38V	—	—	.07V	.10Y	.12V	.05V	.09V
Spain	184	7.68	6.69	13.52V	103.55V	16.42V	20.02V	28.19V	10.27	10.26	25.00V	26.45V	16.28V	14.33V	22.93V
Sweden	144	.14	.18	1.70V	1.44V	4.56V	3.14V	1.04V	12.51	21.97	39.79V	29.07V	81.31V	47.91V	98.52V
Switzerland	146	4.25	5.71	3.67V	7.64V	6.68V	54.65V	10.71V	10.57	22.84	6.98V	8.83V	14.65V	23.80V	27.50V
United Kingdom	112	140.44	161.80	50.45V	62.15V	60.63V	48.68V	52.78V	110.62	94.91	101.63V	135.56V	142.58V	174.39V	188.61V
Developing Countries	**202**	**247.5**	**343.8**	**505.8Y**	**667.7Y**	**871.0Y**	**977.9Y**	**1,149.3Y**	**999.1**	**1,030.4**	**1,764.2Y**	**2,137.1Y**	**2,545.2Y**	**3,048.1Y**	**3,856.8Y**
Africa	**607**	**90.4**	**133.6**	**155.1Y**	**200.0Y**	**263.8Y**	**283.3Y**	**310.8Y**	**344.3**	**320.5**	**688.1Y**	**850.1Y**	**844.4Y**	**912.5Y**	**1,092.7Y**
Algeria	612	.02	.41	.45Y	.59Y	.75Y	.93Y	1.20Y	—	—	—Y	—Y	—Y	—Y	—Y
Angola	614	.51	1.40	1.77Y	2.33Y	2.66Y	3.28Y	4.08Y	—	—	—Y	—Y	—Y	—Y	—Y
Benin	638	—	—	—V	—V	.29V	.35Y	.44Y	—	—	—V	.01V	—V	—Y	—Y
Botswana	616	.23	.04	.05Y	.06Y	.07Y	.09Y	.11Y	.16	.26	.33Y	.43Y	.50Y	.61Y	.76Y
Burkina Faso	748	—	—	—Y	—Y	—Y	—Y	—Y	.01	—	—Y	—Y	—Y	—Y	—Y
Burundi	618	6.75	7.01	16.71V	13.54V	11.71V	6.90V	8.56Y	.16	.01	.04V	.17V	—V	.01V	.01Y
Cameroon	622	—	.06	.06V	.08Y	.10Y	.12Y	.15Y	.02	.01	.08V	.10Y	.12Y	.14Y	.18Y
Cape Verde	624	—	—	—Y	—Y	—Y	—Y	—Y	.01	—	—Y	—Y	—Y	—Y	—Y
Comoros	632	.02	.36	.45Y	.60Y	.68Y	.84Y	1.05Y	—	—	—Y	—Y	—Y	—Y	—Y
Congo, Dem. Rep. of	636	8.66	15.84	20.04Y	26.32Y	30.08Y	37.17Y	46.13Y	.10	.37	.47Y	.62Y	.70Y	.87Y	1.08Y
Congo, Republic of	634	.02	.06	.05V	—V	—Y	—Y	—Y	.24	.23	—V	—V	—Y	—Y	—Y
Côte d'Ivoire	662	—	—	.08V	.12V	—V	.01V	.01Y	3.90	.45	1.19V	14.92V	2.66V	1.53V	1.90Y
Djibouti	611	.03	.05	.06Y	.08Y	.10Y	.12Y	.15Y	—	—	—Y	—Y	—Y	.01Y	.01Y
Eritrea	643	.34	.23	.30Y	.39Y	.45Y	.55Y	.68Y	.05	.01	.01Y	.01Y	.01Y	.02Y	.02Y
Ethiopia	644	.73	.37	—V	—V	—V	—Y	—Y	.53	.69	—V	1.09V	1.39V	1.71Y	2.13Y
Gabon	646	—	.05	.06Y	.08Y	.09Y	.11Y	.14Y	.22	.10	.13Y	.17Y	.19Y	.23Y	.29Y
Gambia, The	648	.09	.09	.12Y	.16Y	.18Y	.22Y	.27Y	.17	.05	.06Y	.08Y	.09Y	.11Y	.14Y
Ghana	652	.10	—	.01Y	.01Y	.01Y	.01Y	.01Y	.42	.38	.48Y	.64Y	.73Y	.90Y	1.11Y
Guinea	656	—	.11	.11V	—V	—Y	—Y	—Y	.03	.04	.06V	.04V	.05Y	.06Y	.07Y
Kenya	664	38.41	35.34	16.37V	23.08V	26.37Y	32.59Y	40.44Y	96.08	95.21	211.32V	248.98V	284.48Y	351.60Y	436.34Y
Madagascar	674	.67	.69	2.88V	3.79Y	4.33Y	5.35Y	6.64Y	1.35	—	.04V	.05Y	.05Y	.07Y	.08Y
Malawi	676	5.87	17.77	22.49V	29.53Y	33.74Y	41.70Y	51.75Y	2.06	1.45	1.83Y	2.40Y	2.75Y	3.40Y	4.21Y
Mali	678	.06	.61	.78Y	1.02Y	1.17Y	1.44Y	1.79Y	.01	.06	.08Y	.11Y	.12Y	.15Y	.19Y
Mauritania	682	.01	.03	.04Y	.05Y	.05Y	.07Y	.08Y	.07	—	—Y	—Y	—Y	—Y	—Y
Mauritius	684	.33	.29	.65V	2.76V	2.38V	1.12V	1.23V	4.17	1.73	2.55V	6.47V	2.95V	1.35V	.94V
Morocco	686	.41	.44	1.29V	.51V	1.43V	1.77Y	2.19Y	.01	.01	.37V	.39V	.27V	.34Y	.42Y
Mozambique	688	1.50	1.63	1.46V	3.14V	3.97V	7.61V	9.45Y	.43	.03	1.39V	2.45V	.50V	4.97V	6.17Y
Namibia	728	.04	.03	.03Y	.02Y	.02Y	.02Y	.02Y	.19	.63	1.06Y	1.49Y	1.93Y	2.36Y	2.79Y
Niger	692	.02	.30	—V	—V	—Y	—Y	—Y	.24	.74	—V	—V	—Y	—Y	—Y
Nigeria	694	.02	.66	3.54V	4.60Y	5.86Y	7.23Y	9.37Y	.45	.63	.02V	.02Y	.03Y	.04Y	.05Y
Rwanda	714	2.85	3.87	4.90Y	6.44Y	7.35Y	9.09Y	11.28Y	.08	.04	.06Y	.07Y	.08Y	.10Y	.13Y
St. Helena	856	1.31	2.52	3.19Y	4.19Y	4.79Y	5.92Y	7.35Y	.65	3.76	4.76Y	6.26Y	7.15Y	8.83Y	10.96Y
São Tomé & Príncipe	716	—	—	—Y	—Y	—Y	—Y	—Y	.03	—	—Y	—Y	.01Y	.01Y	.01Y
Senegal	722	.01	.18	1.28V	.44V	.27V	.93V	1.15Y	.08	.06	.26V	1.20V	3.14V	1.85V	2.30Y
Seychelles	718	.03	.28	.17V	.22Y	.25Y	.31Y	.39Y	.01	—	—V	—Y	—Y	—Y	—Y
Sierra Leone	724	.15	1.22	1.55Y	2.03Y	2.32Y	2.87Y	3.56Y	.05	.04	.05Y	.07Y	.08Y	.10Y	.12Y
Somalia	726	.15	.34	.43Y	.56Y	.64Y	.80Y	.99Y	.01	.01	.01Y	.01Y	.01Y	.01Y	.02Y
South Africa	199	8.95	16.53	17.66V	31.85V	38.68V	42.97V	51.95V	203.43	188.78	272.18V	373.14V	460.56V	440.40V	420.86V
Sacca exc. South Afr.	608	—	—	—V	—Y	—Y	—Y	—Y	—	—	15.64V	16.25V	18.57Y	22.95Y	28.48Y
Sudan	732	.24	.27	.15Y	—V	—V	—V	—V	.05	.12	—V	—V	—V	—V	—V
Swaziland	734	—	.37	.47Y	.62Y	.71Y	.88Y	1.09Y	12.65	15.62	19.77Y	25.96Y	29.66Y	36.66Y	45.50Y

		Exports							Imports						
		2001	2002	2003	2004	2005	2006	2007	2001	2002	2003	2004	2005	2006	2007
		Millions of U.S. Dollars							*Millions of U.S. Dollars*						
Togo	742	—	—	.01V	.01V	.46V	.57Y	.71Y	—	.01	—V	—V	—V	—Y	—Y
Tunisia	744	.01	.04	.03V	.08V	.07V	.02V	.02Y	.04	.01	.19V	.06V	.30V	2.48V	3.08Y
Uganda	746	5.64	5.49	9.81V	12.88Y	14.72Y	18.19Y	22.57Y	11.37	2.66	6.42V	8.43Y	9.63Y	11.90Y	14.77Y
Zambia	754	6.09	17.45	21.39V	27.39V	62.29V	49.24V	21.42V	1.80	4.32	145.06V	132.63V	12.65V	15.20V	105.78V
Zimbabwe	698	.44	1.40	4.56V	.79V	5.24V	2.44V	3.03Y	3.01	1.98	2.18V	5.40V	3.05V	1.51V	1.87Y
Asia	**507**	**119.3**	**102.9**	**204.8Y**	**275.0Y**	**363.6Y**	**396.2Y**	**478.2Y**	**319.0**	**363.1**	**647.4Y**	**690.8Y**	**876.0Y**	**1,107.0Y**	**1,523.9Y**
Afghanistan, I.S. of	512	—	.28	.36Y	.47Y	.54Y	.66Y	.82Y	.02	.02	.03Y	.03Y	.04Y	.05Y	.06Y
American Samoa	859	—	.02	.02Y	.03Y	.03Y	.04Y	.05Y	.02	.01	.01Y	.02Y	.02Y	.03Y	.03Y
Bangladesh	513	.90	1.16	—V	—V	—V	1.21V	1.15V	1.03	.21	2.70V	.40V	.37V	.27Y	.46Y
Brunei Darussalam	516	—	—	.07V	.09Y	.10Y	.12Y	.15Y	.13	—	—V	—Y	—Y	—Y	—Y
Cambodia	522	....	....	....	....	....	....	....	—	—	—V	—V	.05V	—V	—Y
China,P.R.: Mainland	924	.71	.71	25.07V	59.82V	155.39V	137.98V	181.33V	70.55	78.97	211.00V	229.46V	334.19V	421.28V	655.44V
China,P.R.:Hong Kong	532	8.66	11.16	16.92V	18.76V	17.50V	16.85V	24.55V	7.07	7.82	13.29V	18.56V	23.01V	31.88V	36.36V
China,P.R.:Macao	546	.03	.04	.01V	.01V	.01V	—V	—V	—	—	—V	—V	—V	—V	—V
India	534	82.20	64.24	95.25V	112.32V	111.32V	137.58Y	170.73Y	87.47	106.84	176.77V	187.23V	245.77V	303.75Y	376.95Y
Indonesia	536	3.30	4.10	11.27V	11.38V	8.30V	8.18V	14.78V	48.24	62.00	77.78V	88.47V	92.93V	88.47V	69.43V
Korea	542	.75	.37	16.08V	1.20V	1.57V	7.29V	2.61V	15.75	18.36	34.04V	28.86V	33.67V	46.37V	74.70V
Lao People's Dem.Rep	544	—	—	—Y	—Y	—Y	—Y	—Y	.01	—	—Y	—Y	—Y	—Y	—Y
Malaysia	548	2.96	2.93	2.92V	9.95V	19.66V	33.66V	34.10V	18.21	12.55	29.09V	25.43V	33.10V	74.92V	135.62V
Maldives	556	.26	.22	.27Y	.36Y	.41Y	.51Y	.63Y	3.07	1.55	1.96Y	2.57Y	2.94Y	3.63Y	4.51Y
Mongolia	948	—	—	.66V	—V	—V	—Y	—Y	—	.01	.80V	—V	.10V	—Y	—Y
Myanmar	518	.23	.58	.74Y	.97Y	1.11Y	1.37Y	1.70Y	—	—	—Y	—Y	—Y	—Y	—Y
Nauru	836	.04	.01	.01Y	.01Y	.01Y	.02Y	.02Y	.05	.06	.08Y	.11Y	.12Y	.15Y	.19Y
Nepal	558	—	—	—Y	—Y	—Y	—Y	—Y	—	.01	.01Y	.01Y	.01Y	.01Y	.02Y
New Caledonia	839	—	—	—V	—V	—Y	—Y	—Y	—	.01	—Y	—Y	—Y	—Y	—Y
Pakistan	564	7.01	8.80	8.79V	17.37V	12.08V	14.93Y	18.52Y	9.84	21.34	23.34V	15.19V	16.96V	20.96Y	26.02Y
Papua New Guinea	853	.28	.28	.36Y	.47Y	.54Y	.67Y	.83Y	—	—	.01Y	.01Y	.01Y	.01Y	.01Y
Philippines	566	.28	.13	.01V	.01V	.32V	.35V	.49V	.99	2.25	1.06V	.47V	.31V	.20V	1.23V
Singapore	576	5.95	3.95	7.81V	12.04V	6.20V	3.34V	3.80V	8.99	5.77	12.44V	13.92V	14.06V	20.97V	30.57V
Sri Lanka	524	.14	.08	—V	.07V	.10V	.62V	.79V	.19	.40	—V	1.83V	1.89V	2.63V	4.52V
Taiwan Province of China	528	1.00	1.68	3.91V	5.21V	7.34V	15.32V	10.47V	5.05	7.92	7.30V	7.79V	10.79V	12.61V	14.55V
Thailand	578	4.28	1.73	13.07V	24.49V	21.08V	15.54V	10.70V	37.37	35.95	32.93V	42.89V	40.93V	53.93V	93.20V
Tuvalu	869	....	....	....	....	....	....	....	.01	—	—Y	—Y	—Y	—Y	—Y
Vietnam	582	.33	.45	1.16V	—V	—V	—V	—V	4.99	1.00	22.73V	27.50V	24.75V	24.86V	—V
Europe	**170**	**17.6**	**69.8**	**103.6Y**	**138.8Y**	**172.9Y**	**211.3Y**	**249.5Y**	**75.0**	**98.0**	**112.0Y**	**151.4Y**	**252.5Y**	**296.0Y**	**363.2Y**
Albania	914	—	—	—V	—V	—V	—V	—V	.10	.42	—V	—V	—V	—V	—V
Armenia	911	.18	.33	—V	—V	—V	.03V	.11V	—	—	—Y	—Y	—Y	—Y	—Y
Azerbaijan	912	—	—	.01V	—V	—V	—V	—V	—	—	—V	—V	—V	—V	—V
Belarus	913	—	—	.04V	—V	.03V	.06V	.20V	—	—	.17V	.13V	.91V	.13V	.45V
Bosnia & Herzegovina	963	.01	—	—Y	—Y	.01Y	.01Y	.01Y	—	—	—Y	—Y	—Y	—Y	—Y
Bulgaria	918	1.43	.64	.10V	.13V	.20V	.09V	.13V	1.79	1.69	.10V	.47V	.29V	.58V	.13V
Croatia	960	.09	—	—V	—V	—V	—V	—V	—	—	—V	—V	—V	—V	—V
Czech Republic	935	.05	.02	2.93V	4.53V	3.75V	2.28V	2.87V	.41	.54	1.09V	4.45V	9.88V	4.78V	2.68V
Estonia	939	—	—	—V	—V	—V	—V	.13V	—	—	—V	.07V	—V	3.36V	.57V
Gibraltar	823	11.12	14.22	18.00Y	23.64Y	27.01Y	33.38Y	41.43Y	.70	.01	.01Y	.01Y	.01Y	.02Y	.02Y
Hungary	944	2.06	1.49	4.58V	2.33V	15.32V	1.58V	2.36V	.41	.41	.16V	.11V	.90V	2.18V	20.41V
Latvia	941	—	—	.13V	.13V	—V	.01V	—V	—	—	.31V	.07V	.80V	.59V	.07V
Lithuania	946	—	—	.04V	.03V	.42V	.61V	.76V	—	—	.02V	.19V	.07V	8.00V	—V
Macedonia, FYR	962	—	—	.53V	.18V	—V	.07V	.09Y	—	—	—V	—V	.17V	—V	—Y
Poland	964	1.45	1.56	2.31V	3.03V	1.61V	5.86V	8.87V	1.90	.70	.85V	.78V	1.59V	7.37V	2.99V
Romania	968	.02	.01	.57V	1.68V	2.64V	2.68V	5.40V	.96	1.24	.13V	.04V	10.44V	.37V	.61V
Russia	922	.68	2.58	8.61V	12.49V	16.21V	21.58V	31.33V	12.51	10.14	3.82V	2.52V	37.97V	36.66V	51.93V
Slovak Republic	936	—	—	—Y	—Y	2.65V	12.37V	.90V	—	.01	.01Y	.01Y	1.25V	.50V	.13V
Turkey	186	.25	1.85	4.38V	9.89V	9.12V	14.58V	10.87V	2.24	3.20	6.59V	8.25V	25.32V	30.10V	33.24V
Ukraine	926	.01	.03	1.80V	2.56V	4.63V	5.72Y	7.10Y	4.63	3.04	1.84V	7.00V	17.49V	21.61Y	26.82Y
Yugoslavia n.s.	966	.24	.01	.01Y	.01Y	.02Y	.02Y	.02Y	.06	.02	.03Y	.04Y	.04Y	.05Y	.07Y
Europe n.s.	884	—	47.02	59.51Y	78.16Y	89.31Y	110.38Y	136.98Y	49.26	76.57	96.91Y	127.28Y	145.42Y	179.73Y	223.05Y
Middle East	**407**	**19.4**	**36.1**	**41.6Y**	**53.2Y**	**67.9Y**	**84.6Y**	**107.7Y**	**248.3**	**235.9**	**308.0Y**	**405.9Y**	**522.3Y**	**677.1Y**	**816.1Y**
Bahrain	419	.04	—	—Y	—Y	—Y	—Y	—Y	56.77	70.37	89.07Y	116.97Y	133.65Y	165.18Y	204.99Y
Egypt	469	1.83	1.66	2.11Y	2.77Y	3.16Y	3.91Y	4.85Y	6.81	5.24	6.63Y	8.70Y	9.94Y	12.29Y	15.25Y
Iran, I.R. of	429	.05	.16	.18Y	.24Y	.30Y	.37Y	.48Y	5.33	3.87	4.69Y	6.21Y	8.44Y	10.61Y	12.80Y
Israel	436	1.90	4.34	4.18V	4.64V	5.73V	6.27V	6.45V	3.54	4.15	5.06V	9.68V	9.35V	20.57V	16.61V
Jordan	439	.09	—	.04V	.06V	.10V	.08V	.09V	.39	.30	1.21V	5.20V	2.04V	1.68V	3.38V
Kuwait	443	.04	—	—Y	—Y	—Y	—Y	—Y	2.24	1.40	1.70Y	2.25Y	3.06Y	3.84Y	4.64Y
Lebanon	446	.33	—	—Y	—Y	—Y	—Y	—Y	.16	.32	.40Y	.53Y	.60Y	.74Y	.92Y
Libya	672	—	—	—Y	—Y	—Y	—Y	—Y	—	—	—Y	.01Y	.01Y	.01Y	.01Y
Oman	449	.54	.07	.79V	1.02Y	1.30Y	1.61Y	2.08Y	4.22	4.36	17.69V	23.40Y	31.83Y	40.02Y	48.28Y
Qatar	453	—	—	.07V	.09V	.13V	1.79V	2.32Y	.53	.55	5.32V	1.26V	7.94V	25.57V	30.85Y
Saudi Arabia	456	4.89	15.44	1.73V	1.99V	3.34V	4.13Y	5.35Y	58.23	47.28	57.31Y	75.84Y	103.16Y	129.69Y	156.46Y
Syrian Arab Republic	463	—	.03	.04Y	—V	—Y	—Y	—Y	.08	.03	.03Y	—V	—Y	—Y	—Y
United Arab Emirates	466	9.55	14.40	32.45V	42.21Y	53.74Y	66.35Y	85.95Y	108.97	97.08	117.69Y	155.73Y	211.84Y	266.33Y	321.29Y
Yemen, Republic of	474	.10	.03	.04Y	.15V	.08V	.10Y	.13Y	.98	.93	1.18Y	.09V	.41V	.50Y	.63Y
Western Hemisphere	**207**	**.9**	**1.3**	**.7Y**	**.7Y**	**2.8Y**	**2.4Y**	**3.0Y**	**12.6**	**12.9**	**8.7Y**	**39.0Y**	**50.0Y**	**55.5Y**	**60.9Y**
Antigua and Barbuda	311	.03	.05	.06Y	.08Y	.09Y	.11Y	.13Y	—	.01	.01Y	.01Y	.01Y	.02Y	.02Y
Argentina	213	—	.06	—V	—V	—V	.02V	.04V	3.03	4.04	2.38V	28.09V	26.67V	22.30V	49.74V
Bahamas, The	313	—	—	—Y	—Y	—Y	—Y	—Y	.01	—	—Y	—Y	—Y	—Y	—Y
Barbados	316	—	—	.01V	—V	—V	—V	—Y	—	—	—V	—V	.03V	—V	—Y

		Exports							Imports						
		2001	2002	2003	2004	2005	2006	2007	2001	2002	2003	2004	2005	2006	2007
		Millions of U.S. Dollars							Millions of U.S. Dollars						
Belize	339	—	—	—Y	—Y	—Y	—Y	—Y	.19	.04	.06Y	.07Y	.09Y	.11Y	.13Y
Bermuda	319	—	—	—Y	—Y	—V	—V	—Y	—	.39	.49Y	.64Y	.73Y	.91Y	1.12Y
Brazil	223	.23	.49	.01V	.01V	.26V	.30V	—V	4.64	3.04	5.19V	9.02V	15.48V	20.66V	—V
Chile	228	—	—	.11V	.11V	.02V	—V	—V	1.10	.24	.05V	.17V	.96V	.02V	1.30V
Colombia	233	—	.09	.04V	—V	.04V	.04V	.12V	.02	.03	.01V	.09V	.45V	.37V	.47V
Costa Rica	238	—	—	—V	—V	—V	—Y	—Y	.01	.32	—V	—V	—V	—Y	—Y
Dominica	321	.05	.02	.02Y	.03Y	.04Y	.04Y	.05Y	.06	.03	.04Y	.05Y	.06Y	.07Y	.09Y
Ecuador	248	—	—	—V	—V	—V	—V	—Y	2.50	1.57	—V	—V	.12V	.04V	.05Y
Grenada	328	.03	—	—Y	—Y	—Y	—Y	—Y	—	.04	.05Y	.07Y	.08Y	.10Y	.13Y
Guatemala	258	—	.01	.06V	—V	—V	—Y	—Y	.01	—	—V	—V	4.08V	5.05Y	6.26Y
Guyana	336	.09	.04	.05Y	.07Y	.08Y	.10Y	.13Y	.01	.10	.13Y	.17Y	.19Y	.23Y	.29Y
Haiti	263	—	—	.02V	—V	—Y	—Y	—Y	—	—	—Y	—Y	—Y	—Y	—Y
Honduras	268	—	.07	.01V	—V	—Y	—Y	—Y	.01	.01	—V	—V	—Y	—Y	—Y
Jamaica	343	.01	—	—V	—V	.01V	—V	—V	.02	.03	—V	—V	—V	—V	—V
Mexico	273	.27	.28	—V	—V	1.62V	1.19V	1.80V	.20	.95	—V	—V	.16V	4.66V	.05V
Netherlands Antilles	353	.08	—	—V	—Y	—Y	—Y	—Y	—	.02	—V	.01Y	.01Y	.01Y	.01Y
Nicaragua	278	—	—	—V	—V	—V	—V	—V	.06	—	—V	—V	—V	—V	—V
Panama	283	—	—	—V	—V	—V	—V	—V	.04	.01	.01Y	.01Y	.01Y	.02Y	.02Y
Paraguay	288	—	.18	.22Y	.29Y	.33Y	.41Y	.51Y	....	....	....	....	....	....	....
Peru	293	—	—	—V	—V	—V	—V	—Y	.02	—	.08V	.33V	.52V	.63V	.77Y
St. Kitts and Nevis	361	—	—	—Y	—Y	—Y	—Y	—Y	.02	.03	.03Y	.05Y	.05Y	.06Y	.08Y
St. Pierre-Miquelon	363	—	—	—Y	—Y	—Y	—Y	—Y	—	—	—Y	.01Y	.01Y	.01Y	.01Y
Suriname	366	.04	.02	.03Y	.04Y	.04Y	.05Y	.06Y	.54	.10	.13Y	.17Y	.19Y	.23Y	.29Y
Uruguay	298	—	—	—V	—V	—V	—Y	—Y	—	—	—V	—V	.03V	.03Y	.04Y
Venezuela, Rep. Bol	299	—	.03	—V	.10V	.25V	.16V	.20V	.06	1.93	.03V	—V	.07V	—V	—Y
Western Hem. n.s.	399	.04	—	—Y	—Y	—Y	—Y	—Y	—	—	—Y	—Y	—Y	—Y	—Y
Other Countries n.i.e.	**910**	**.1**	**.1**	**.1Y**	**.1Y**	**.1Y**	**.1Y**	**.2Y**	**.5**	**.3**	**.4Y**	**.5Y**	**.6Y**	**.7Y**	**.9Y**
Cuba	928	.11	—	—Y	—Y	—Y	—Y	—Y	—	—	—Y	—Y	—Y	—Y	—Y
North Korea	954	—	.06	.08Y	.11Y	.12Y	.15Y	.18Y	.49	.32	.40Y	.52Y	.60Y	.74Y	.92Y
Countries & Areas n.s.	**898**	**.2**	**7.6**	**9.6Y**	**12.6Y**	**14.4Y**	**17.8Y**	**22.2Y**	**.2**	**.1**	**.1Y**	**.2Y**	**.2Y**	**.2Y**	**.3Y**
Memorandum Items															
European Union	998	436.79	478.98	302.20Y	428.95Y	364.75Y	374.95Y	469.86Y	387.12	369.63	505.19Y	612.23Y	728.33Y	866.19Y	1,136.59Y
Oil Exporting Ctys	999	18.43	35.27	50.48Y	62.21Y	73.98Y	90.75Y	121.72Y	228.27	219.09	282.24Y	353.19Y	459.33Y	564.60Y	643.82Y
Non-Oil Develop.Ctys	201	229.09	308.52	455.27Y	605.50Y	797.04Y	887.12Y	1,027.55Y	770.83	811.27	1,481.92Y	1,783.93Y	2,085.91Y	2,483.48Y	3,212.95Y
PERCENT DISTRIBUTION															
Industrial Countries	**101**	**68.0**	**63.0**	**44.8**	**44.3**	**40.0**	**36.7**	**33.7**	**43.8**	**41.1**	**29.3**	**30.4**	**28.4**	**28.9**	**29.5**
Developing Countries	**202**	**32.0**	**36.2**	**54.1**	**54.7**	**59.0**	**62.2**	**65.1**	**56.1**	**58.9**	**70.7**	**69.5**	**71.6**	**71.1**	**70.5**
Africa	**607**	**11.7**	**14.1**	**16.6**	**16.4**	**17.9**	**18.0**	**17.6**	**19.3**	**18.3**	**27.6**	**27.7**	**23.8**	**21.3**	**20.0**
Asia	**507**	**15.4**	**10.8**	**21.9**	**22.5**	**24.6**	**25.2**	**27.1**	**17.9**	**20.8**	**25.9**	**22.5**	**24.6**	**25.8**	**27.9**
Europe	**170**	**2.3**	**7.4**	**11.1**	**11.4**	**11.7**	**13.4**	**14.1**	**4.2**	**5.6**	**4.5**	**4.9**	**7.1**	**6.9**	**6.6**
Middle East	**407**	**2.5**	**3.8**	**4.5**	**4.4**	**4.6**	**5.4**	**6.1**	**13.9**	**13.5**	**12.3**	**13.2**	**14.7**	**15.8**	**14.9**
Western Hemisphere	**207**	**.1**	**.1**	**.1**	**.1**	**.2**	**.2**	**.2**	**.7**	**.7**	**.3**	**1.3**	**1.4**	**1.3**	**1.1**
ANNUAL PERCENT CHANGE															
World	**001**	**5.3**	**22.5**	**–1.5**	**30.7**	**20.9**	**6.5**	**12.3**	**17.1**	**–1.7**	**42.7**	**23.1**	**15.6**	**20.6**	**27.6**
Industrial Countries	**101**	**22.8**	**13.4**	**–29.9**	**29.0**	**9.3**	**–2.4**	**3.2**	**14.1**	**–7.9**	**1.8**	**28.0**	**7.8**	**22.7**	**30.3**
Developing Countries	**202**	**–19.1**	**38.9**	**47.1**	**32.0**	**30.4**	**12.3**	**17.5**	**19.5**	**3.1**	**71.2**	**21.1**	**19.1**	**19.8**	**26.5**
Africa	**607**	**–35.1**	**47.9**	**16.1**	**28.9**	**31.9**	**7.4**	**9.7**	**11.6**	**–6.9**	**114.7**	**23.5**	**–.7**	**8.1**	**19.8**
Asia	**507**	**–14.5**	**–13.7**	**98.9**	**34.3**	**32.2**	**9.0**	**20.7**	**4.2**	**13.8**	**78.3**	**6.7**	**26.8**	**26.4**	**37.7**
Europe	**170**	**68.6**	**296.8**	**48.5**	**34.0**	**24.6**	**22.2**	**18.1**	**334.3**	**30.7**	**14.3**	**35.1**	**66.8**	**17.2**	**22.7**
Middle East	**407**	**32.8**	**86.4**	**15.2**	**27.7**	**27.7**	**24.6**	**27.3**	**42.5**	**–5.0**	**30.6**	**31.8**	**28.7**	**29.6**	**20.5**
Western Hemisphere	**207**	**–59.2**	**51.6**	**–51.4**	**13.5**	**277.2**	**–12.5**	**24.9**	**–57.9**	**2.9**	**–32.6**	**347.5**	**28.3**	**11.1**	**9.6**
Other Countries n.i.e	**910**	**39.7**	**–44.7**	**26.6**	**31.3**	**14.3**	**23.6**	**24.1**	**120.0**	**–35.0**	**26.6**	**31.3**	**14.3**	**23.6**	**24.1**

		Exports							Imports						
		2001	2002	2003	2004	2005	2006	2007	2001	2002	2003	2004	2005	2006	2007
		Millions of U.S. Dollars							Millions of U.S. Dollars						
IFS World Total		**64,919**	**68,108**	**80,324**	**96,248**	**110,178**	**130,803**	**153,100**	**61,960**	**64,645**	**75,824**	**94,410**	**118,158**	**128,723**	**140,795**
DOTS World Total	**001**	**65,113**	**68,850**	**80,318**	**96,214**	**110,158**	**130,555**	**152,459**	**62,057**	**64,721**	**75,824**	**94,407**	**118,143**	**130,605**	**141,346**
Industrial Countries	**101**	**36,820**	**37,059**	**41,241**	**47,425**	**51,642**	**60,438**	**66,239**	**31,581**	**31,144**	**36,099**	**42,750**	**50,727**	**52,565**	**56,737**
United States	111	13,246	13,522	13,669	15,492	16,950	19,626	19,250	7,198	6,197	7,185	7,270	8,724	9,782	9,653
Canada	156	787	807	941	1,057	1,028	1,245	1,365	345	414	392	500	523	514	634
Australia	193	1,358	1,640	2,167	2,460	3,151	4,379	5,726	1,380	1,506	1,585	2,210	3,255	3,453	3,838
Japan	158	9,964	10,000	11,395	13,452	14,979	16,492	18,122	13,881	14,902	18,267	22,379	26,026	26,034	28,674
New Zealand	196	182	205	267	329	518	529	616	210	189	212	238	253	326	417
Austria	122	99	101	130	183	232	298	338	93	86	135	213	155	188	258
Belgium	124	1,417	1,358	1,131	1,189	1,276	1,445	1,662	456	486	468	708	616	698	723
Cyprus	423	38	32	30	42	39	35	55	2	3	2	2	4	3	3
Denmark	128	171	160	190	242	253	351	421	203	120	149	197	195	235	208
Finland	172	117	137	185	291	317	426	487	404	307	195	290	275	312	320
France	132	833	821	951	1,203	1,289	1,435	1,651	930	849	1,010	1,046	1,868	1,468	1,313
Germany	134	1,568	1,533	1,799	1,798	1,994	2,343	2,874	2,562	2,482	2,533	2,841	3,203	3,323	3,957
Greece	174	143	115	141	195	219	255	316	17	12	12	19	28	20	35
Iceland	176	9	3	5	7	10	9	9	9	10	9	6	7	5	6
Ireland	178	242	233	338	384	440	583	557	165	125	141	186	180	182	196
Italy	136	675	701	955	1,335	1,245	1,502	1,843	668	724	821	1,010	1,133	1,507	1,372
Luxembourg	137	8	15	20	27	21	18	23	5	3	5	6	5	7	8
Malta	181	12	12	11	13	10	12	16	19	27	53	70	35	42	40
Netherlands	138	2,028	1,890	2,373	2,589	2,755	3,260	3,801	523	495	617	652	716	748	886
Norway	142	49	54	65	79	91	197	159	100	105	101	115	108	178	263
Portugal	182	111	84	100	115	101	141	155	22	18	18	20	33	51	33
Spain	184	526	440	619	878	919	1,088	1,297	218	215	231	272	337	359	414
Sweden	144	241	228	269	321	344	421	527	346	332	317	383	444	461	446
Switzerland	146	670	576	902	725	675	926	1,418	838	681	712	845	1,324	1,331	1,511
United Kingdom	112	2,328	2,391	2,587	3,021	2,784	3,421	3,552	985	853	931	1,273	1,281	1,336	1,531
Developing Countries	**202**	**28,151**	**30,907**	**38,787**	**48,448**	**58,143**	**69,787**	**85,699**	**28,868**	**32,003**	**38,256**	**50,100**	**65,514**	**76,058**	**82,044**
Africa	**607**	**1,345**	**1,311**	**1,384**	**2,174**	**2,476**	**2,870**	**3,866**	**740**	**888**	**907**	**1,228**	**1,537**	**1,953**	**1,949**
Algeria	612	33	59	59	87	93	86	137	8	10	67	126	213	309	338
Angola	614	17	21	25	73	36	50	124	42	127	2	4	112	142	90
Benin	638	39	30	74	124	174	186	281	13	16	22	14	12	12	8
Botswana	616	—	—	1	1	5	17	18	—	—	78	86	113	96	111
Burkina Faso	748	1	1	2	4	3	5	5	5	8	22	15	24	22	38
Burundi	618	1	1	1	1	6	1	1	—	—	—	—	—	—	—
Cameroon	622	13	15	17	37	104	55	51	21	11	13	11	11	13	20
Cape Verde	624	—	3	1	—	—	1	4	—	—	—	—	—	—	—
Central African Rep.	626	—	—	—	—	—	—	1	—	1	1	—	—	—	—
Chad	628	—	—	—	—	1	1	1	1	1	1	3	4	32	14
Comoros	632	3	4	4	3	3	2	4	—	—	—	—	—	—	—
Congo, Republic of	634	23	20	27	28	25	36	41	31	49	3	8	25	19	74
Côte d'Ivoire	662	77	73	66	85	61	142	164	14	14	16	12	11	21	8
Djibouti	611	4	2	5	6	7	14	15	—	—	—	—	—	—	—
Ethiopia	644	8	15	10	12	22	30	41	2	2	1	1	2	2	1
Gabon	646	16	9	13	15	16	29	25	1	2	3	42	106	221	109
Gambia, The	648	8	5	4	5	14	8	20	1	—	1	2	1	1	—
Ghana	652	33	43	67	117	83	96	166	6	6	10	16	6	9	18
Guinea	656	8	2	5	10	13	10	12	—	—	—	4	—	2	—
Guinea-Bissau	654	4	4	2	2	2	1	1	43	25	—	—	—	—	—
Kenya	664	29	28	36	59	66	72	105	10	7	11	9	17	15	14
Liberia	668	2	1	1	2	3	5	5	1	—	51	51	49	52	—
Madagascar	674	5	4	12	27	34	20	33	5	2	5	3	4	4	3
Malawi	676	1	2	1	2	3	6	9	—	—	—	1	1	1	1
Mali	678	5	4	2	2	2	4	5	32	26	33	25	27	30	28
Mauritania	682	3	3	2	5	2	11	14	9	3	2	3	1	—	1
Mauritius	684	27	26	28	33	42	48	65	3	1	1	3	5	4	6
Morocco	686	17	17	25	32	40	48	96	50	63	38	46	52	66	70
Mozambique	688	11	9	11	41	43	34	63	1	2	4	5	7	8	11
Namibia	728	1	1	2	2	2	4	4	—	1	—	2	1	3	1
Niger	692	—	1	1	1	3	3	4	—	—	1	1	—	—	—
Nigeria	694	349	291	223	321	304	271	346	31	82	62	49	71	33	36
Rwanda	714	—	1	—	—	—	3	—	2	1	2	3	3	5	8
Senegal	722	137	137	105	144	147	125	233	2	1	4	3	5	3	4
Seychelles	718	2	3	5	4	3	9	6	13	21	42	6	11	3	6
Sierra Leone	724	4	3	4	4	15	10	4	—	—	—	—	1	1	—
Somalia	726	17	15	14	12	1	5	1	3	2	1	6	8	5	3
South Africa	199	315	332	379	656	840	1,101	1,322	243	234	276	421	371	346	560
Sudan	732	18	21	18	26	46	90	87	7	10	19	13	8	3	26
Swaziland	734	3	2	2	7	6	10	6	7	17	15	31	74	162	25
Tanzania	738	34	33	30	39	37	49	85	8	9	14	27	23	17	12
Togo	742	25	16	21	47	56	41	100	5	7	5	9	9	8	9

	Exports 2001	2002	2003	2004	2005	2006	2007	Imports 2001	2002	2003	2004	2005	2006	2007
	Millions of U.S. Dollars							*Millions of U.S. Dollars*						
Tunisia 744	15	16	28	36	44	59	63	—	1	—	1	1	3	4
Uganda 746	11	10	9	11	10	13	14	—	1	1	2	3	3	7
Zambia 754	1	2	2	5	7	5	8	68	67	53	116	96	249	252
Zimbabwe 698	4	8	11	10	10	10	19	50	31	25	48	47	27	32
Africa n.s. 799	19	16	26	33	40	45	53	—	26	—	—	—	2	—
Asia 507	**23,048**	**25,333**	**32,353**	**39,753**	**47,405**	**55,893**	**66,926**	**20,307**	**23,259**	**27,145**	**34,493**	**44,381**	**51,789**	**56,879**
Afghanistan, I.S. of 512	2	3	11	8	58	63	150	—	—	—	1	—	—	1
Bangladesh 513	231	229	273	373	393	470	511	29	25	30	13	29	36	14
Brunei Darussalam 516	37	40	42	56	68	83	91	387	454	325	390	203	129	112
Cambodia 522	467	515	688	723	913	1,243	1,356	12	11	12	28	31	35	49
China,P.R.: Mainland 924	2,863	3,553	5,707	7,098	9,105	11,810	14,834	3,711	4,928	6,067	8,182	11,153	13,801	16,382
China,P.R.:Hong Kong 532	3,298	3,699	4,331	4,924	6,123	7,214	8,686	825	910	1,075	1,331	1,505	1,561	1,454
China,P.R.:Macao 546	7	5	5	5	6	8	16	1	2	2	5	4	3	4
Fiji 819	15	16	20	30	59	49	51	1	—	1	—	2	1	—
French Polynesia 887	7	8	14	19	26	28	26	2	2	19	17	11	3	3
Guam 829	4	4	12	5	8	5	7	2	—	—	—	—	—	—
India 534	482	413	641	910	1,520	1,822	2,664	673	776	879	1,140	1,276	1,640	2,085
Indonesia 536	1,366	1,678	2,274	3,207	3,953	3,336	4,768	1,364	1,559	1,771	2,323	3,130	3,484	4,025
Kiribati 826	—	—	1	1	2	1	1	10	6	1	1	—	1	—
Korea 542	1,229	1,398	1,588	1,854	2,244	2,688	2,967	2,121	2,527	2,919	3,590	3,888	5,198	5,338
Lao People's Dem.Rep 544	411	404	456	581	769	1,023	1,312	89	94	104	115	225	523	475
Malaysia 548	2,722	2,835	3,887	5,295	5,781	6,656	7,792	3,078	3,640	4,540	5,549	8,092	8,599	8,703
Maldives 556	13	14	21	29	38	59	55	6	22	26	32	45	61	51
Mongolia 948	—	—	1	1	1	2	4	—	—	—	—	—	—	—
Myanmar 518	355	324	439	605	707	762	959	809	914	910	1,353	1,785	2,349	2,315
Nauru 836	—	—	—	—	—	—	—	2	—	—	—	—	—	—
Nepal 558	30	22	28	37	25	25	38	1	—	1	2	1	—	1
New Caledonia 839	5	6	14	17	21	29	35	—	—	—	—	—	—	—
Pakistan 564	178	228	338	435	588	652	662	54	86	94	61	84	101	69
Papua New Guinea 853	15	17	21	23	35	52	60	70	30	54	33	50	39	84
Philippines 566	1,156	1,274	1,622	1,828	2,042	2,588	2,899	1,129	1,081	1,352	1,547	1,881	2,143	2,163
Samoa 862	1	1	1	2	7	9	8	—	—	—	1	—	1	—
Singapore 576	5,287	5,554	5,873	7,009	7,641	8,411	9,535	2,854	2,904	3,270	4,153	5,375	5,760	6,343
Solomon Islands 813	3	1	1	2	5	5	6	8	7	8	30	16	12	23
Sri Lanka 524	141	152	161	182	193	297	274	39	7	8	10	13	27	37
Taiwan Province of China 528	1,916	1,968	2,591	2,598	2,703	3,386	3,321	2,599	2,905	3,229	3,977	4,501	5,175	5,789
Tonga 866	5	1	1	1	3	2	4	—	—	—	—	—	—	—
Vanuatu 846	1	1	1	2	5	4	5	6	20	28	106	119	159	175
Vietnam 582	797	947	1,267	1,873	2,348	3,094	3,803	327	240	337	439	890	909	1,122
Asia n.s. 598	5	23	24	18	15	18	27	96	109	80	66	71	36	61
Europe 170	**533**	**686**	**968**	**1,315**	**1,760**	**2,385**	**3,563**	**808**	**1,132**	**1,151**	**1,823**	**2,276**	**2,055**	**2,204**
Albania 914	2	—	—	—	1	1	2	—	—	—	—	—	—	—
Armenia 911	—	—	—	1	2	1	2	—	—	1	—	—	1	2
Azerbaijan 912	—	2	—	2	2	2	3	1	—	—	10	—	40	52
Belarus 913	—	—	1	1	1	3	10	3	7	2	2	2	—	3
Bulgaria 918	8	6	5	9	14	22	29	7	13	8	12	18	127	30
Czech Republic 935	46	68	96	147	251	355	522	87	55	43	52	63	100	111
Estonia 939	4	14	18	22	28	50	57	6	4	9	12	3	17	2
Faroe Islands 816	—	—	1	—	—	—	—	1	2	4	4	2	2	2
Gibraltar 823	11	1	—	1	—	—	—	—	—	—	—	—	—	—
Hungary 944	138	118	145	174	185	270	384	22	25	36	33	35	72	68
Kazakhstan 916	2	4	6	10	15	27	40	7	25	27	71	52	18	20
Kyrgyz Republic 917	1	—	—	—	2	—	1	—	—	—	—	—	—	—
Latvia 941	4	4	7	12	16	22	29	—	—	1	2	1	1	1
Lithuania 946	3	5	14	19	20	15	62	1	1	1	1	1	2	3
Moldova 921	—	—	—	—	—	—	—	—	5	3	—	7	—	—
Poland 964	73	82	85	106	141	233	413	62	47	66	112	122	96	70
Romania 968	23	18	29	44	61	66	104	26	29	20	24	29	17	14
Russia 922	81	150	274	300	323	387	573	315	503	584	1,021	1,605	1,291	1,552
Tajikistan 923	—	—	—	—	—	—	—	1	—	—	1	—	—	1
Turkey 186	97	159	208	332	559	739	967	44	55	94	106	80	168	116
Turkmenistan 925	—	—	1	1	3	2	2	—	—	—	—	—	1	—
Ukraine 926	15	17	29	51	70	92	151	195	336	230	333	200	49	115
Uzbekistan 927	2	2	1	2	2	1	2	7	5	—	2	3	7	7
Yugoslavia n.s. 966	2	4	—	—	—	—	—	1	1	—	—	—	—	—
Europe n.s. 884	18	29	47	79	66	95	210	20	19	22	25	50	46	34
Middle East 407	**2,141**	**2,449**	**2,891**	**3,686**	**4,442**	**5,756**	**7,435**	**5,977**	**5,704**	**7,535**	**10,856**	**15,247**	**18,401**	**18,639**
Bahrain 419	33	35	41	51	66	79	96	57	57	94	87	118	214	130
Egypt 469	142	126	173	217	266	380	479	9	10	53	83	64	16	7
Iran, I.R. of 429	132	177	298	452	315	566	775	76	62	72	40	41	57	88
Iraq 433	58	76	111	169	143	199	203	77	41	27	115	229	330	62
Israel 436	456	500	530	564	579	587	701	324	445	475	501	527	499	525
Jordan 439	39	53	76	94	110	148	174	9	6	5	8	13	12	10
Kuwait 443	65	67	82	94	152	193	225	338	129	168	310	311	285	163
Lebanon 446	53	50	49	66	70	76	113	1	1	3	5	1	2	2
Libya 672	17	31	60	113	113	139	267	4	2	15	—	—	1	12
Oman 449	40	43	52	74	158	233	281	1,264	1,201	1,401	1,456	2,417	2,769	2,620

	Exports 2001	2002	2003	2004	2005	2006	2007	Imports 2001	2002	2003	2004	2005	2006	2007
	Millions of U.S. Dollars							*Millions of U.S. Dollars*						
Qatar.......... 453	19	22	28	49	112	194	216	255	424	473	701	839	1,552	2,062
Saudi Arabia.......... 456	348	394	435	617	1,003	1,253	1,369	1,349	1,225	1,716	2,324	4,044	4,261	4,618
Syrian Arab Republic.......... 463	44	83	94	70	97	98	120	11	25	8	2	9	1	1
United Arab Emirates.......... 466	636	717	759	965	1,168	1,486	2,207	1,529	1,428	2,039	3,711	5,699	7,219	6,898
Yemen, Republic of.......... 474	58	76	104	92	93	125	208	674	648	987	1,511	934	1,184	1,439
Western Hemisphere.......... 207	**1,083**	**1,128**	**1,190**	**1,520**	**2,061**	**2,884**	**3,910**	**1,037**	**1,019**	**1,517**	**1,701**	**2,073**	**1,860**	**2,374**
Argentina.......... 213	78	15	41	97	268	353	382	381	350	501	360	385	265	478
Bahamas, The.......... 313	1	1	1	1	3	3	3	—	—	2	—	—	—	1
Barbados.......... 316	2	1	2	4	7	9	10	—	—	—	—	—	—	1
Belize.......... 339	4	4	3	1	3	2	3	6	1	2	10	3	2	23
Bermuda.......... 319	—	1	1	1	2	1	1	—	—	—	—	—	—	—
Bolivia.......... 218	2	3	3	3	3	4	7	1	1	3	1	2	2	1
Brazil.......... 223	161	162	300	385	454	632	937	267	366	563	806	1,079	879	1,046
Chile.......... 228	64	96	109	104	122	264	319	65	60	80	173	160	234	272
Colombia.......... 233	38	39	47	71	86	130	222	6	5	6	8	9	14	12
Costa Rica.......... 238	13	14	12	20	23	28	59	2	4	12	23	29	25	29
Dominica.......... 321	1	1	1	1	1	2	4	—	—	—	—	1	1	1
Dominican Republic.......... 243	40	43	19	29	44	50	73	1	—	—	2	5	3	11
Ecuador.......... 248	20	25	23	47	133	168	224	27	1	3	5	2	8	3
El Salvador.......... 253	14	18	20	16	20	22	37	—	2	—	1	1	1	1
Greenland.......... 326	—	—	—	—	—	—	—	25	20	16	14	16	11	5
Grenada.......... 328	—	—	—	—	1	1	1	—	—	—	—	—	—	—
Guatemala.......... 258	16	20	26	31	35	52	80	—	—	—	—	2	1	2
Guyana.......... 336	2	2	1	2	3	4	3	—	—	—	—	2	1	1
Haiti.......... 263	3	3	3	11	4	7	8	—	—	—	—	2	2	11
Honduras.......... 268	11	14	17	20	25	37	61	—	—	—	—	1	—	1
Jamaica.......... 343	11	10	12	12	21	26	32	—	—	1	1	2	5	8
Mexico.......... 273	427	500	413	460	464	641	852	127	145	173	161	201	232	292
Netherlands Antilles.......... 353	7	6	5	6	9	23	31	1	2	2	2	6	4	9
Nicaragua.......... 278	5	7	7	7	9	13	26	—	—	—	—	—	—	—
Panama.......... 283	73	59	47	58	102	119	161	2	2	62	26	52	14	3
Paraguay.......... 288	6	6	2	8	6	5	12	6	6	5	9	12	13	20
Peru.......... 293	14	22	20	32	44	58	116	91	32	37	42	45	93	87
St. Vincent & Grens.......... 364	—	—	—	—	—	1	—	—	—	—	—	—	—	—
Suriname.......... 366	3	4	5	8	10	12	14	—	1	1	1	1	—	—
Trinidad and Tobago.......... 369	13	12	14	22	31	64	72	—	—	—	6	2	2	1
Uruguay.......... 298	18	3	4	8	8	10	12	13	14	38	38	50	42	44
Venezuela, Rep. Bol.......... 299	26	19	11	29	51	83	118	12	4	6	8	3	2	11
Western Hem. n.s.......... 399	10	15	20	26	70	61	32	3	1	4	1	1	3	1
Other Countries n.i.e.......... 910	**111**	**177**	**212**	**250**	**216**	**237**	**185**	**25**	**45**	**52**	**90**	**120**	**71**	**36**
Cuba.......... 928	5	4	8	11	10	31	5	1	1	1	1	1	1	2
North Korea.......... 954	106	173	204	240	206	206	180	24	45	51	89	119	70	34
Countries & Areas n.s.......... 898	**30**	**706**	**77**	**88**	**155**	**93**	**335**	**1,583**	**1,528**	**1,417**	**1,467**	**1,782**	**1,911**	**2,530**
Memorandum Items														
European Union.......... 998	10,823	10,543	12,195	14,306	14,880	17,980	21,042	7,796	7,271	7,794	9,399	10,734	11,229	11,997
Oil Exporting Ctys.......... 999	3,090	3,574	4,391	6,177	7,564	8,038	10,911	6,308	6,167	7,816	11,163	16,997	20,301	20,934
Non-Oil Develop.Ctys.......... 201	25,061	27,333	34,395	42,271	50,579	61,749	74,788	22,560	25,837	30,440	38,937	48,517	55,756	61,109
PERCENT DISTRIBUTION														
Industrial Countries.......... 101	**56.5**	**53.8**	**51.3**	**49.3**	**46.9**	**46.3**	**43.4**	**50.9**	**48.1**	**47.6**	**45.3**	**42.9**	**40.2**	**40.1**
Developing Countries.......... 202	**43.2**	**44.9**	**48.3**	**50.4**	**52.8**	**53.5**	**56.2**	**46.5**	**49.4**	**50.5**	**53.1**	**55.5**	**58.2**	**58.0**
Africa.......... 607	**2.1**	**1.9**	**1.7**	**2.3**	**2.2**	**2.2**	**2.5**	**1.2**	**1.4**	**1.2**	**1.3**	**1.3**	**1.5**	**1.4**
Asia.......... 507	**35.4**	**36.8**	**40.3**	**41.3**	**43.0**	**42.8**	**43.9**	**32.7**	**35.9**	**35.8**	**36.5**	**37.6**	**39.7**	**40.2**
Europe.......... 170	**.8**	**1.0**	**1.2**	**1.4**	**1.6**	**1.8**	**2.3**	**1.3**	**1.7**	**1.5**	**1.9**	**1.9**	**1.6**	**1.6**
Middle East.......... 407	**3.3**	**3.6**	**3.6**	**3.8**	**4.0**	**4.4**	**4.9**	**9.6**	**8.8**	**9.9**	**11.5**	**12.9**	**14.1**	**13.2**
Western Hemisphere.......... 207	**1.7**	**1.6**	**1.5**	**1.6**	**1.9**	**2.2**	**2.6**	**1.7**	**1.6**	**2.0**	**1.8**	**1.8**	**1.4**	**1.7**
Other Countries n.i.e.......... 910	**.2**	**.3**	**.3**	**.3**	**.2**	**.2**	**.1**	**—**	**.1**	**.1**	**.1**	**.1**	**.1**	**—**
ANNUAL PERCENT CHANGE														
World.......... 001	**–5.6**	**5.7**	**16.7**	**19.8**	**14.5**	**18.5**	**16.8**	**.2**	**4.3**	**17.2**	**24.5**	**25.1**	**10.5**	**8.2**
Industrial Countries.......... 101	**–5.6**	**.6**	**11.3**	**15.0**	**8.9**	**17.0**	**9.6**	**.5**	**–1.4**	**15.9**	**18.4**	**18.7**	**3.6**	**7.9**
Developing Countries.......... 202	**–4.4**	**9.8**	**25.5**	**24.9**	**20.0**	**20.0**	**22.8**	**–1.3**	**10.9**	**19.5**	**31.0**	**30.8**	**16.1**	**7.9**
Africa.......... 607	**18.2**	**–2.6**	**5.6**	**57.0**	**13.9**	**15.9**	**34.7**	**–6.1**	**20.1**	**2.1**	**35.4**	**25.2**	**27.1**	**–.2**
Asia.......... 507	**–6.2**	**9.9**	**27.7**	**22.9**	**19.2**	**17.9**	**19.7**	**–1.2**	**14.5**	**16.7**	**27.1**	**28.7**	**16.7**	**9.8**
Europe.......... 170	**–11.6**	**28.7**	**41.1**	**35.8**	**33.8**	**35.5**	**49.4**	**2.5**	**40.2**	**1.7**	**58.3**	**24.9**	**–9.7**	**7.2**
Middle East.......... 407	**2.6**	**14.4**	**18.1**	**27.5**	**20.5**	**29.6**	**29.2**	**–5.4**	**–4.6**	**32.1**	**44.1**	**40.4**	**20.7**	**1.3**
Western Hemisphere.......... 207	**2.7**	**4.1**	**5.5**	**27.8**	**35.5**	**39.9**	**35.6**	**25.8**	**–1.7**	**48.9**	**12.1**	**21.9**	**–10.3**	**27.6**
Other Countries n.i.e.......... 910	**–41.4**	**59.4**	**20.2**	**17.9**	**–13.9**	**9.8**	**–22.0**	**21.4**	**82.0**	**14.7**	**73.5**	**33.8**	**–40.7**	**–49.7**

	Exports 2001	Exports 2002	Exports 2003	Exports 2004	Exports 2005	Exports 2006	Exports 2007	Imports 2001	Imports 2002	Imports 2003	Imports 2004	Imports 2005	Imports 2006	Imports 2007
	Millions of U.S. Dollars							*Millions of U.S. Dollars*						
IFS World Total	**356.6**	**429.4**	**599.4**	**601.3**	**658.8**	**612.0**	**690.0**	**553.1**	**594.2**	**775.3**	**882.5**	**1,193.4**	**1,330.0**	**1,450.0**
DOTS World Total 001	**220.4**	**249.0**	**415.6**	**407.8**	**364.1**	**567.4Y**	**699.7Y**	**354.8**	**396.6**	**563.3**	**556.6**	**589.5**	**2,630.7Y**	**4,157.7Y**
Industrial Countries 101	**34.4**	**41.2**	**91.0**	**67.5**	**40.9**	**142.0Y**	**174.8Y**	**197.0**	**226.3**	**315.2**	**262.1**	**281.1**	**1,152.8Y**	**1,407.0Y**
United States 111	5.22	.93	5.33	1.49	4.07	3.55V	5.18V	10.13	18.50	6.50	13.45	6.93	119.24V	316.36V
Canada 156	.05	.04	.21	.02	.03	1.57V	2.17V	23.24	23.44	9.85	7.42	9.63	7.90V	15.52V
Australia 193	4.36	9.16	4.49	6.49	3.45	2.20V	.05V	.01	.03	.33	.53	.10	3.05V	2.54V
Japan 158	.52	.04	.55	.39	.03	.13V	.05V	8.14	7.72	8.24	9.05	10.88	14.68V	24.72V
New Zealand 196	2.89	8.44	5.45	7.45	3.11	5.53V	.01V	—	.01	.01	.03	.01	.45V	.42V
Austria 122	—	—	—	.05	—	.05V	.02V	.56	.14	.10	.28	.17	5.45V	2.94V
Belgium 124	2.60	1.24	1.39	10.52	3.23	34.74V	26.73V	11.95	20.42	21.88	26.86	23.28	150.53V	87.30V
Cyprus 423	—	—	—	—	.95	—V	—V	.17	.07	—	.01	—	—V	.04V
Denmark 128	.59	.70	.54	.76	.60	.11V	.26V	1.55	2.94	4.54	3.16	4.95	2.96V	25.35V
Finland 172	—	—	.01	—	2.97	—V	.39V	.15	.05	—	.01	—	.31V	.51V
France 132	4.36	2.32	3.47	15.53	5.02	14.21V	9.89V	67.75	82.05	118.71	108.54	104.89	231.71V	291.45V
Germany 134	1.84	1.16	1.76	2.03	7.53	30.86V	64.52V	15.79	20.33	25.71	18.26	17.36	56.53V	54.21V
Greece 174	1.91	4.22	2.74	.29	.02	.01V	.20V	.04	.13	.11	5.54	.82	1.13V	23.31V
Iceland 176	.02	—	—	.23	.07	—V	—V	.03	—	.03	.03	.01	—V	—V
Ireland 178	—	—	—	—	.15	1.69V	.05V	.46	.51	.55	.68	.83	7.85V	14.83V
Italy 136	4.69	4.43	4.33	3.34	3.10	7.18V	8.31V	21.48	14.54	25.11	20.77	26.58	59.25V	91.99V
Luxembourg 137	—	—	—	—	—	—V	—V	.05	.02	.07	.33	.21	.50V	.24V
Malta 181	—	—	—	—	—	—V	—V	.46	.01	.14	.03	—	.18V	.14V
Netherlands 138	1.82	4.91	53.95	15.39	3.92	26.21V	41.41V	7.34	12.95	68.25	18.64	23.48	154.91V	303.26V
Norway 142	.03	—	1.27	.27	—	.01V	—V	1.03	.73	.74	.37	2.11	.43V	.42V
Portugal 182	.37	.71	1.78	1.03	.28	2.78V	3.27V	.33	.20	.12	.19	3.57	1.80V	1.62V
Slovenia 961	—	—	—	—	—	—V	—V	—	—	—	—	—	.15V	.04V
Spain 184	2.12	1.52	1.65	.93	1.93	8.72V	8.59V	11.83	10.63	17.18	15.94	25.14	23.23V	46.14V
Sweden 144	.01	.10	.02	—	—	.01V	.10V	5.02	3.63	.03	.08	6.96	9.11V	11.08V
Switzerland 146	.76	1.00	2.01	1.34	.47	1.61V	2.56V	1.23	.55	1.79	.54	.87	18.55V	18.37V
United Kingdom 112	.25	.23	.11	—	—	.81V	1.06V	8.22	6.73	5.24	11.34	12.30	282.94V	74.24V
Developing Countries 202	**184.2**	**205.4**	**321.8**	**333.8**	**317.0**	**417.8Y**	**515.4Y**	**143.9**	**167.3**	**233.2**	**281.6**	**287.8**	**1,452.4Y**	**2,719.0Y**
Africa 607	**140.8**	**153.2**	**243.0**	**259.3**	**261.7**	**320.9Y**	**394.9Y**	**63.1**	**68.9**	**111.2**	**102.7**	**104.1**	**198.9Y**	**258.4Y**
Algeria 612	—	.24	.32	.04	.17	.21Y	.27Y	—	—	—	—	—	—Y	—Y
Angola 614	—	.19	.21	—	.01	.01Y	.01Y	—	.01	—	—	—	—Y	—Y
Benin 638	37.19	32.94	39.61	47.45	41.69	51.53Y	63.95Y	3.28	2.97	9.65	14.71	12.08	14.93Y	18.53Y
Burkina Faso 748	22.86	32.37	69.07	50.81	66.37	82.03Y	101.80Y	.84	3.41	5.40	18.05	2.79	3.44Y	4.27Y
Burundi 618	—	—	—	—	—	—V	—Y	—	—	—	—	.01	.02Y	.02Y
Cameroon 622	.50	.18	.53	.17	.08	.10Y	.12Y	.53	.53	.91	1.05	11.55	14.28Y	17.72Y
Cape Verde 624	.02	.13	—	—	—	—Y	—Y	—	—	—	—	—	—Y	—Y
Central African Rep. 626	.04	.05	.02	.07	.03	.04Y	.04Y	—	.02	—	.01	—	—Y	—Y
Chad 628	1.34	1.30	1.11	1.24	2.16	2.67Y	3.31Y	—	—	—	—	—	—Y	—Y
Comoros 632	—	—	—	—	—	—Y	—Y	—	—	—	.01	—	—Y	—Y
Congo, Dem. Rep. of 636	.07	.15	.07	.42	.18	.23Y	.28Y	.01	.01	.01	.02	.02	.02Y	.03Y
Congo, Republic of 634	1.12	.40	.82	1.14	.93	1.15Y	1.42Y	.02	3.87	.17	.11	.09	.11Y	.13Y
Côte d'Ivoire 662	.51	1.52	2.72	2.57	6.23	2.77V	3.44Y	20.35	25.32	32.96	33.71	38.54	102.37V	127.04Y
Djibouti 611	—	—	—	—	—	—Y	—Y	—	.06	—	—	—	—Y	—Y
Equatorial Guinea 642	.02	—	.01	—	.06	.07Y	.09Y	—	—	—	.04	—	—Y	—Y
Ethiopia 644	.03	.02	—	.08	.38	.47Y	.58Y	—	.01	.02	—	.01	.01Y	.02Y
Gabon 646	.67	.44	.52	.64	.62	.76Y	.94Y	.59	.04	3.68	.06	2.07	2.56Y	3.18Y
Gambia, The 648	.02	.02	.09	.06	—	—Y	—Y	.01	—	.01	.12	.02	.03Y	.04Y
Ghana 652	49.45	53.47	63.63	64.78	76.76	94.87Y	117.73Y	7.19	8.09	13.54	9.74	8.04	9.93Y	12.33Y
Guinea 656	1.45	.51	.07	.08	.06	.08Y	.10Y	—	—	.02	.01	.04	.05Y	.06Y
Guinea-Bissau 654	—	—	.02	—	—	—Y	—Y	—	—	.11	—	.21	.26Y	.32Y
Kenya 664	—	—	.02	—	—	—Y	—Y	—	.01	—	.01	.01	.02Y	.02Y
Lesotho 666	—	—	.06	—	—	—Y	—Y	—	—	.01	—	—	—Y	—Y
Liberia 668	.34	.06	.13	.64	.37	.46Y	.57Y	.17	.17	.09	.11	.10	.13Y	.16Y
Madagascar 674	.02	.02	—	—	—	—Y	—Y	.01	—	—	.09	—	—Y	—Y
Mali 678	1.69	3.29	32.21	43.49	26.56	32.83Y	40.74Y	—	.01	.17	.02	.05	.07Y	.08Y
Mauritania 682	.08	.05	.01	.54	.93	1.15Y	1.42Y	7.69	4.49	4.17	3.27	3.46	4.28Y	5.31Y
Mauritius 684	—	—	.73	—	—	—V	—V	.01	.29	.08	.01	.08	.25V	.61V
Morocco 686	2.00	2.64	4.13	2.97	6.51	8.04Y	9.98Y	.74	.69	.73	.77	1.39	1.72Y	2.13Y
Namibia 728	—	—	—	—	—	—Y	—Y	—	—	.01	—	—	—Y	—Y
Niger 692	9.77	11.51	15.08	13.05	10.84	13.39Y	16.62Y	.09	.07	1.19	.08	.13	.16Y	.20Y
Nigeria 694	4.28	5.00	5.92	7.34	14.70	18.14Y	23.51Y	5.06	4.53	5.95	6.28	4.95	6.22Y	7.51Y
Rwanda 714	—	—	—	—	.03	.04Y	.05Y	—	.02	—	.01	—	—Y	—Y
São Tomé & Príncipe 716	.03	.03	.08	.01	.06	.08Y	.10Y	—	.09	—	—	.01	.01Y	.01Y
Senegal 722	.71	.66	1.63	14.72	3.19	1.80V	2.23Y	6.37	5.48	8.08	4.90	4.66	17.29V	21.46Y
Sierra Leone 724	.03	.11	.01	.06	.03	.03Y	.04Y	—	—	—	—	—	—Y	—Y
Somalia 726	—	—	—	—	—	—Y	—Y	—	—	.01	—	.01	.01Y	.01Y
South Africa 199	6.45	5.86	3.76	5.29	.95	7.57V	5.11V	7.31	8.00	23.59	7.98	11.31	16.79V	32.28V
Sudan 732	—	.01	—	—	—	—V	—V	—	—	—	—	—	—V	—V
Swaziland 734	—	.02	—	—	—	—Y	—Y	.01	—	—	.02	—	—Y	.01Y
Tanzania 738	.01	—	—	—	—	—Y	—Y	—	.01	.01	.01	.51	.63Y	.78Y

	Exports 2001	2002	2003	2004	2005	2006	2007	Imports 2001	2002	2003	2004	2005	2006	2007
	Millions of U.S. Dollars							*Millions of U.S. Dollars*						
Tunisia........ 744	—	—	.30	1.62	1.77	.38V	.47Y	2.75	.63	.61	.87	1.91	3.30V	4.10Y
Uganda........ 746	.04	.01	.11	—	—	—Y	—Y	.01	.02	—	—	.02	.02Y	.02Y
Zimbabwe........ 698	.06	—	—	—	—	—V	—Y	—	—	—	—	—	—V	—Y
Africa n.s........ 799	—	—	—	—	—	—Y	—Y	—	—	—	.63	—	—Y	—Y
Asia........ 507	**31.1**	**40.6**	**67.0**	**66.3**	**41.9**	**78.3Y**	**95.9Y**	**46.5**	**42.2**	**67.4**	**102.2**	**129.2**	**1,016.9Y**	**1,863.5Y**
Bangladesh........ 513	.07	2.34	2.38	5.82	.26	—V	—V	.07	.02	.04	.15	.22	.27Y	.33Y
Cambodia........ 522	—	—	—	—	—	—Y	—Y	—	—	.02	—	—	—V	—Y
China,P.R.: Mainland........ 924	.25	2.53	10.55	17.30	7.94	19.64V	23.73V	10.08	11.68	23.44	46.36	78.44	774.45V	1,511.15V
China,P.R.:Hong Kong........ 532	.21	.02	1.45	.03	.06	4.31V	4.36V	6.38	7.22	10.13	14.22	12.19	29.44V	22.42V
China,P.R.:Macao........ 546	—	.01	—	.01	—	—V	—V	—	—	.01	—	—	—V	—V
French Polynesia........ 887	—	—	—	—	—	—Y	—Y	.09	—	.01	.02	.01	.02Y	.02Y
India........ 534	4.23	4.97	10.25	15.60	21.25	26.26Y	32.59Y	5.39	4.76	8.20	9.74	14.06	17.38Y	21.57Y
Indonesia........ 536	2.99	2.88	8.19	8.01	1.32	3.75V	4.82V	4.81	7.87	10.50	11.43	5.87	37.60V	51.33V
Korea........ 542	—	.52	.06	.01	.81	3.17V	1.82V	8.08	1.11	.90	2.45	.82	21.07V	24.79V
Malaysia........ 548	.98	5.00	5.42	2.45	1.70	4.61V	8.56V	3.11	2.17	7.23	7.76	4.77	79.13V	103.31V
Maldives........ 556	—	.03	.02	.04	—	—Y	.01Y	.06	—	—	—	—	—Y	—Y
Myanmar........ 518	—	—	—	—	.01	.01Y	.01Y	.06	.06	—	.01	—	—Y	—Y
Nauru........ 836	—	—	—	—	—	—Y	—Y	.02	—	.02	.20	—	—Y	—Y
Nepal........ 558	—	—	—	—	—	—Y	—Y	.05	.02	—	—	—	—Y	—Y
New Caledonia........ 839	—	—	—	—	—	—Y	.01Y	—	—	—	—	—	—Y	—Y
Pakistan........ 564	—	.83	5.97	3.47	4.79	5.91Y	7.34Y	1.24	1.13	.51	.21	.99	1.23Y	1.52Y
Papua New Guinea........ 853	—	—	—	—	—	—Y	—Y	—	—	—	.01	.01	.01Y	.01Y
Philippines........ 566	13.81	—	—	—	.01	1.29V	.02V	—	.02	—	—	—	.04V	—V
Samoa........ 862	....	....	....	....	....	....	....	—	—	—	.01	—	—Y	—Y
Singapore........ 576	.35	.65	.09	.09	.48	.60Y	.74Y	1.46	1.82	2.08	5.24	2.99	3.69Y	4.58Y
Sri Lanka........ 524	—	.11	—	—	—	—Y	—Y	.02	.04	.02	.02	.01	.01Y	.01Y
Taiwan Province of China........ 528	5.99	15.69	17.99	8.83	1.20	1.29V	3.70V	.85	.54	.85	.37	3.97	7.81V	11.99V
Thailand........ 578	1.19	4.25	2.56	3.66	1.45	7.43V	8.19V	4.47	3.41	3.07	3.47	4.07	44.77V	110.48V
Tonga........ 866	—	—	—	—	—	—Y	—Y	—	—	—	.03	—	—Y	—Y
Vanuatu........ 846	....	....	....	....	....	....	....	—	.06	—	—	—	—Y	—Y
Vietnam........ 582	.99	.76	2.09	.97	.63	—V	—V	.24	.21	.35	.49	.83	—V	—V
Europe........ 170	**6.3**	**7.4**	**4.8**	**1.7**	**5.9**	**12.3Y**	**11.4Y**	**18.4**	**28.0**	**24.2**	**26.4**	**18.7**	**164.8Y**	**511.6Y**
Belarus........ 913	—	—	—	—	—	—Y	—V	—	.50	—	—	.01	—V	—V
Bulgaria........ 918	—	—	—	—	—	—V	—V	.04	.02	.02	.02	.04	3.98V	8.75V
Czech Republic........ 935	.02	—	—	—	—	—V	—V	.54	—	—	—	—	1.04V	3.68V
Estonia........ 939	—	—	—	—	—	—V	—V	—	—	—	—	—	108.36V	398.47V
Faroe Islands........ 816	....	....	....	....	....	....	....	—	—	—	—	.03	.04Y	.05Y
Gibraltar........ 823	—	—	—	—	—	—Y	—Y	—	—	.01	—	—	—Y	—Y
Hungary........ 944	.01	—	—	—	—	.03V	.10V	.01	—	—	.01	—	.87V	2.08V
Latvia........ 941	—	—	—	—	—	—V	—V	—	—	—	—	—	.01V	.56V
Poland........ 964	5.59	5.83	.76	1.31	3.66	7.64V	7.96V	2.54	.66	.38	.47	.41	7.74V	9.32V
Romania........ 968	.49	.53	1.20	—	.58	.01V	—V	.32	.19	1.39	6.47	.01	17.82V	.61V
Russia........ 922	—	—	—	—	—	—V	—V	7.00	—	—	6.05	8.41	6.46V	62.17V
Slovak Republic........ 936	—	—	—	—	—	—V	—V	—	—	—	—	—	.06V	.08V
Turkey........ 186	.21	1.04	2.81	—	—	2.56V	.76V	1.14	10.68	5.14	1.05	2.17	8.97V	14.10V
Ukraine........ 926	—	—	.02	.39	1.69	2.09Y	2.59Y	3.96	12.87	17.20	12.35	7.65	9.45Y	11.73Y
Yugoslavia n.s........ 966	.01	—	—	—	—	—Y	—Y	2.85	3.07	.06	.02	.02	.02Y	.03Y
Middle East........ 407	**.9**	**.5**	**.3**	**1.3**	**.5**	**.6Y**	**.8Y**	**12.0**	**19.2**	**19.4**	**30.3**	**18.5**	**26.5Y**	**33.8Y**
Bahrain........ 419	.01	.02	—	—	—	—Y	—Y	.75	3.76	2.40	2.80	.74	.91Y	1.13Y
Egypt........ 469	—	—	—	—	—	—Y	—Y	.40	6.34	3.68	6.31	.49	.60Y	.75Y
Iran, I.R. of........ 429	—	.01	—	—	—	—Y	—Y	1.02	.43	.07	.02	.01	.01Y	.02Y
Iraq........ 433	—	—	—	—	—	—Y	—Y	.01	—	—	—	—	—Y	—Y
Israel........ 436	.42	.19	.27	—	—	—V	—V	2.27	.03	1.44	.03	.13	3.41V	5.83V
Jordan........ 439	—	.02	.05	—	.04	—V	—V	—	.01	.01	—	—	—V	—V
Kuwait........ 443	—	—	—	—	—	—Y	—Y	.03	1.72	.02	4.17	10.40	13.07Y	15.77Y
Lebanon........ 446	—	—	—	.01	.01	.01Y	.02Y	.10	.12	.42	.28	.34	.42Y	.52Y
Libya........ 672	—	—	—	—	—	—Y	—Y	—	2.07	.60	.01	.01	.01Y	.02Y
Oman........ 449	—	.04	—	—	—	—Y	—Y	.07	.04	.01	.02	—	—Y	—Y
Saudi Arabia........ 456	.27	—	.01	1.13	.01	.02Y	.02Y	2.11	4.02	9.60	14.92	4.72	5.94Y	7.16Y
Syrian Arab Republic........ 463	—	—	—	—	—	—Y	—Y	.02	.03	.03	.04	.04	.05Y	.06Y
United Arab Emirates........ 466	.19	.19	—	.17	.48	.59Y	.77Y	5.21	.57	.98	1.58	1.62	2.04Y	2.46Y
Yemen, Republic of........ 474	—	—	—	—	—	—Y	—Y	.03	.05	.08	.11	.04	.04Y	.05Y
Middle East n.s........ 489	—	—	—	—	—	—Y	—Y	—	—	.01	—	—	—Y	—Y
Western Hemisphere........ 207	**5.1**	**3.7**	**6.6**	**5.3**	**7.0**	**5.7Y**	**12.3Y**	**3.9**	**9.1**	**11.1**	**19.9**	**17.3**	**45.3Y**	**51.7Y**
Antigua and Barbuda........ 311	—	—	—	.02	—	—Y	—Y	—	—	—	—	—	.01Y	.01Y
Argentina........ 213	—	—	—	—	—	—V	—V	.51	.01	1.01	.17	.52	10.34V	8.36V
Bahamas, The........ 313	—	—	—	—	—	—Y	—Y	.31	.09	.04	.01	—	—Y	—Y
Barbados........ 316	—	—	.11	—	—	—Y	—Y	—	—	—	—	—	—V	—Y
Belize........ 339	—	—	—	—	—	—Y	—Y	—	.01	—	—	—	—Y	—Y
Bermuda........ 319	.35	.50	.28	.03	—	—V	—Y	....	....	....	....	....	....	....
Bolivia........ 218	—	—	—	—	—	—Y	—Y	—	.01	—	—	.08	.10Y	.12Y
Brazil........ 223	1.49	.62	3.32	4.28	6.32	4.73V	11.12V	2.67	2.93	8.00	13.96	16.23	33.84V	41.39V
Chile........ 228	—	.01	.01	—	—	—V	—V	.02	.24	.73	.10	—	.12V	—V
Colombia........ 233	.96	.09	—	—	—	—V	—V	.02	—	.01	.11	.08	.03V	.25V
Costa Rica........ 238	—	—	—	—	.02	.03Y	.03Y	—	.02	—	—	—	—Y	—Y
Dominica........ 321	....	....	....	....	....	....	....	—	.01	—	.02	—	—Y	—Y
Dominican Republic........ 243	—	—	—	—	—	—Y	—Y	—	—	.03	—	—	—Y	—Y

	Exports							Imports						
	2001	2002	2003	2004	2005	2006	2007	2001	2002	2003	2004	2005	2006	2007
	Millions of U.S. Dollars							*Millions of U.S. Dollars*						
Ecuador.......... 248	—	—	—	—	—	.12V	.15Y	—	—	—	.01	—	—V	—Y
Falkland Islands.......... 323	—	—	—	—	—	—Y	—Y	.01	.01	.01	.88	—	—Y	—Y
Greenland.......... 326	—	.01	—	—	—	—Y	—Y	—	—	.02	—	—	—Y	—Y
Grenada.......... 328	—	—	—	—	—	—Y	—Y	.04	—	—	—	—	—Y	—Y
Guatemala.......... 258	.50	.01	—	—	—	—Y	—Y	.02	.02	.02	—	—	—Y	—Y
Guyana.......... 336	—	—	.14	—	—	—Y	—Y	.18	.02	.04	—	.04	.05Y	.06Y
Honduras.......... 268	—	.60	—	.46	.02	.02Y	.02Y	.01	—	.02	—	.01	.01Y	.01Y
Jamaica.......... 343	—	.01	—	—	—	—V	—V	.05	.04	.04	.06	.08	—V	—V
Mexico.......... 273	—	.70	.94	—	—	.05V	.05V	—	.31	.27	.09	.01	.17V	.04V
Netherlands Antilles.......... 353	.01	—	—	—	—	—Y	—Y	—	4.56	.17	.01	.01	.02Y	.02Y
Panama.......... 283	—	.16	—	—	—	—V	—V	.01	.05	.42	—	.01	—V	—V
Paraguay.......... 288	—	—	—	.02	—	—V	—Y	—	.02	—	—	—	.01V	.02Y
Peru.......... 293	—	.12	.28	—	—	—V	—Y	—	—	—	—	—	.32V	1.02Y
St. Kitts and Nevis.......... 361	....	....	....	....	....	....	....	—	—	—	.01	—	—Y	—Y
St. Vincent & Grens.......... 364	—	—	—	—	—	—Y	—Y	—	—	.01	—	—	—Y	—Y
Suriname.......... 366	—	—	—	—	—	—Y	—Y	.01	.03	—	—	.01	.01Y	.01Y
Trinidad and Tobago.......... 369	—	—	.01	—	—	—Y	—Y	.02	.01	.01	.01	.01	.02Y	.02Y
Uruguay.......... 298	1.48	.87	1.52	.43	.58	.72Y	.90Y	—	—	—	4.26	.07	.08Y	.10Y
Venezuela, Rep. Bol.......... 299	.30	—	—	—	.03	—V	—V	—	.01	.19	.20	—	—V	—Y
Western Hem. n.s.......... 399	.01	.01	—	—	.01	.01Y	.02Y	.02	.69	.03	—	.08	.16Y	.24Y
Other Countries n.i.e.......... 910	**—**	**—**	**—**	**—**	**—**	**—Y**	**—Y**	**1.0**	**.3**	**2.0**	**.2**	**1.1**	**1.3Y**	**1.7Y**
Cuba.......... 928	—	—	—	—	—	—Y	—Y	.05	.01	.01	—	.02	.02Y	.03Y
North Korea.......... 954	—	—	.01	—	—	—Y	—Y	1.00	.27	2.02	.24	1.07	1.32Y	1.64Y
Countries & Areas n.s.......... 898	**1.0**	**1.8**	**1.6**	**5.3**	**4.6**	**5.7Y**	**7.1Y**	**.2**	**—**	**1.5**	**1.0**	**.7**	**.9Y**	**1.1Y**
Special Categories.......... 899	**.8**	**.6**	**1.2**	**1.1**	**1.6**	**1.9Y**	**2.4Y**	**12.5**	**2.6**	**11.3**	**11.7**	**18.7**	**23.1Y**	**28.6Y**
Memorandum Items														
European Union.......... 998	26.16	27.39	72.49	51.17	33.35	135.05Y	172.89Y	156.25	176.02	288.12	231.14	250.95	1,106.60Y	1,442.87Y
Oil Exporting Ctys.......... 999	8.02	8.36	14.44	16.69	16.71	22.72Y	29.39Y	18.32	21.27	27.93	38.63	27.58	64.90Y	84.26Y
Non-Oil Develop.Ctys.......... 201	176.17	197.04	307.32	317.13	300.31	395.09Y	485.96Y	125.53	146.05	205.28	242.95	260.26	1,387.52Y	2,634.72Y
PERCENT DISTRIBUTION														
Industrial Countries.......... 101	**15.6**	**16.5**	**21.9**	**16.6**	**11.2**	**25.0**	**25.0**	**55.5**	**57.1**	**56.0**	**47.1**	**47.7**	**43.8**	**33.8**
Developing Countries.......... 202	**83.6**	**82.5**	**77.4**	**81.9**	**87.1**	**73.6**	**73.7**	**40.5**	**42.2**	**41.4**	**50.6**	**48.8**	**55.2**	**65.4**
Africa.......... 607	**63.9**	**61.5**	**58.5**	**63.6**	**71.9**	**56.6**	**56.4**	**17.8**	**17.4**	**19.7**	**18.5**	**17.7**	**7.6**	**6.2**
Asia.......... 507	**14.1**	**16.3**	**16.1**	**16.3**	**11.5**	**13.8**	**13.7**	**13.1**	**10.6**	**12.0**	**18.4**	**21.9**	**38.7**	**44.8**
Europe.......... 170	**2.9**	**3.0**	**1.2**	**.4**	**1.6**	**2.2**	**1.6**	**5.2**	**7.1**	**4.3**	**4.7**	**3.2**	**6.3**	**12.3**
Middle East.......... 407	**.4**	**.2**	**.1**	**.3**	**.1**	**.1**	**.1**	**3.4**	**4.8**	**3.4**	**5.4**	**3.1**	**1.0**	**.8**
Western Hemisphere.......... 207	**2.3**	**1.5**	**1.6**	**1.3**	**1.9**	**1.0**	**1.8**	**1.1**	**2.3**	**2.0**	**3.6**	**2.9**	**1.7**	**1.2**
Other Countries n.i.e.......... 910	**—**	**—**	**—**	**—**	**—**	**—**	**—**	**.3**	**.1**	**.4**	**—**	**.2**	**.1**	**—**
ANNUAL PERCENT CHANGE														
World.......... 001	**14.6**	**13.0**	**66.9**	**–1.9**	**–10.7**	**55.8**	**23.3**	**9.6**	**11.8**	**42.0**	**–1.2**	**5.9**	**346.2**	**58.0**
Industrial Countries.......... 101	**–4.2**	**19.7**	**121.1**	**–25.8**	**–39.4**	**247.0**	**23.2**	**5.7**	**14.9**	**39.3**	**–16.9**	**7.2**	**310.1**	**22.1**
Developing Countries.......... 202	**22.0**	**11.5**	**56.6**	**3.8**	**–5.0**	**31.8**	**23.3**	**11.6**	**16.3**	**39.4**	**20.7**	**2.2**	**404.6**	**87.2**
Africa.......... 607	**74.6**	**8.8**	**58.6**	**6.7**	**.9**	**22.6**	**23.1**	**–14.0**	**9.2**	**61.5**	**–7.6**	**1.3**	**91.1**	**29.9**
Asia.......... 507	**–19.5**	**30.6**	**65.1**	**–1.1**	**–36.8**	**86.7**	**22.5**	**45.7**	**–9.3**	**59.8**	**51.7**	**26.5**	**686.8**	**83.3**
Europe.......... 170	**–26.2**	**17.1**	**–35.2**	**–64.5**	**248.0**	**107.9**	**–7.4**	**20.2**	**52.3**	**–13.6**	**9.2**	**–29.1**	**779.3**	**210.4**
Middle East.......... 407	**–91.4**	**–46.7**	**–28.9**	**288.5**	**–58.8**	**15.0**	**29.4**	**82.9**	**59.7**	**.8**	**56.6**	**–38.8**	**43.0**	**27.4**
Western Hemisphere.......... 207	**–60.1**	**–27.3**	**78.2**	**–20.6**	**32.9**	**–18.4**	**115.9**	**116.5**	**132.6**	**22.1**	**79.6**	**–13.4**	**162.5**	**14.1**
Other Countries n.i.e.......... 910	**....**	**—**	**....**	**31.3**	**14.3**	**....**	**....**	**795.2**	**–73.8**	**641.1**	**–88.1**	**348.8**	**23.6**	**24.1**

Tonga 866

		Exports							Imports						
		2001	2002	2003	2004	2005	2006	2007	2001	2002	2003	2004	2005	2006	2007
		Millions of U.S. Dollars							*Millions of U.S. Dollars*						
IFS World Total		**6.6**	**14.4**	**17.7**	**15.0**	**10.0**	**11.0**	**8.0**	**72.3**	**89.1**	**93.7**	**104.8**	**120.1**	**130.0**	**142.8**
DOTS World Total	**001**	**23.8Y**	**27.8Y**	**31.0Y**	**33.9Y**	**19.3Y**	**22.1Y**	**18.4Y**	**73.9Y**	**86.6Y**	**101.3Y**	**121.7Y**	**127.8Y**	**139.2Y**	**160.8Y**
Industrial Countries	**101**	**22.5Y**	**24.6Y**	**28.0Y**	**22.2Y**	**16.9Y**	**17.3Y**	**14.2Y**	**46.7Y**	**57.5Y**	**68.6Y**	**72.0Y**	**76.9Y**	**79.5Y**	**78.4Y**
United States	111	8.18V	10.27V	13.73V	6.00V	6.45V	8.64V	6.73V	5.28V	12.32V	6.27V	7.70V	10.78V	11.44V	14.52V
Canada	156	.02V	.02V	.14V	.12V	.05V	.06V	.09V	.49V	.67V	.43V	.08V	.12V	.15V	.59V
Australia	193	.37V	.36V	.38V	.38V	.48V	.44V	.41V	8.30V	11.39V	11.13V	11.16V	13.38V	10.46V	11.88V
Japan	158	12.20V	10.83V	9.61V	12.54V	8.09V	6.04V	3.97V	3.06V	1.91V	1.99V	2.75V	3.04V	1.97V	3.37V
New Zealand	196	1.05V	.89V	.88V	2.50V	1.22V	1.79V	1.86V	24.53V	26.59V	42.69V	45.25V	42.69V	38.44V	44.21V
Austria	122	—V	.02V	—V	.01V	—V	.01V	—V	—V	.11V	—V	.03V	—V	.22V	—V
Belgium	124	—V	—V	.01V	—V	—V	—V	.02V	—V	—V	.60V	.03V	.03V	.01V	.21V
Denmark	128	.07V	.05V	.01V	.02V	.01V	—V	.02V	.08V	.15V	.18V	.07V	.08V	—V	.20V
Finland	172	.01V	—V	—V	—V	—V	—V	—V	—V	—V	—V	—V	—V	—V	—V
France	132	.08V	.03V	.02V	.07V	.03V	.01V	.09V	2.01V	.82V	.64V	.40V	.92V	7.90V	.58V
Germany	134	.16V	.82V	.01V	.32V	.20V	.02V	.13V	.07V	.34V	2.12V	3.18V	.95V	1.79V	.68V
Greece	174	—V	.96V	2.56V	—V	—V	—V	.06V	.09V	.85V	.05V	.03V	—V	.01V	.08V
Iceland	176	—V	.03V	—V	—V	—V	—V	—V	—Y	—Y	—Y	—Y	—Y	—V	—V
Ireland	178	—V	—V	—V	—V	—V	—V	.01V	.10V	.01V	.02V	—V	—V	—V	—V
Italy	136	.02V	.28V	.61V	.18V	.16V	.21V	.19V	.07V	.57V	.25V	.18V	.23V	.43V	.09V
Netherlands	138	.04V	—V	—V	—V	.04V	.02V	.01V	.17V	.07V	.06V	.04V	.05V	.11V	.03V
Norway	142	—V	—V	—V	—V	—V	—V	—V	.35V	.03V	—V	—V	—V	—V	—V
Portugal	182	—V	—V	—V	—V	—V	—V	—V	.01V	.21V	.06V	.07V	.01V	.04V	—V
Spain	184	—V	—V	.02V	—V	—V	—V	—V	.01V	.05V	.06V	—V	—V	.01V	—V
Sweden	144	—V	—V	—V	—V	—V	.01V	.04V	.01V	.03V	.02V	.01V	.05V	.03V	.05V
Switzerland	146	—V	—V	—V	—V	—V	.02V	—V	.01V	.01V	.10V	.01V	—V	.03V	—V
United Kingdom	112	.33V	.04V	.08V	.03V	.15V	.01V	.57V	2.01V	1.35V	1.90V	.94V	4.58V	6.47V	1.89V
Developing Countries	**202**	**1.2Y**	**3.1Y**	**3.0Y**	**11.6Y**	**2.4Y**	**4.8Y**	**4.1Y**	**27.2Y**	**29.1Y**	**32.7Y**	**49.7Y**	**50.8Y**	**59.6Y**	**82.4Y**
Africa	**607**	**—Y**	**—Y**	**—Y**	**—Y**	**—Y**	**—Y**	**—Y**	**.1Y**	**.2Y**	**.9Y**	**.1Y**	**.1Y**	**.1Y**	**4.2Y**
South Africa	199	—V	—V	—V	—V	—V	—V	—V	.09V	.15V	.88V	.08V	.06V	.14V	4.18V
Tunisia	744	—V	—V	—V	—V	—V	—V	—Y	—V	.03V	.02V	—V	—V	—V	—Y
Asia	**507**	**1.2Y**	**2.2Y**	**2.6Y**	**11.1Y**	**2.3Y**	**4.8Y**	**4.0Y**	**26.5Y**	**28.3Y**	**30.7Y**	**48.9Y**	**49.5Y**	**58.4Y**	**76.5Y**
American Samoa	859	.18Y	.20Y	.25Y	.32Y	.37Y	.46Y	.57Y	.11Y	.12Y	.15Y	.20Y	.23Y	.29Y	.35Y
China,P.R.: Mainland	924	.01V	.01V	.05V	6.34V	—V	.01V	.04V	1.29V	5.31V	2.25V	10.90V	3.23V	4.12V	8.05V
China,P.R.:Hong Kong	532	.11V	.04V	.06V	.26V	.09V	.46V	.21V	.30V	.54V	.21V	.39V	.39V	.23V	.28V
Fiji	819	.34Y	.37Y	.47Y	.61Y	.70Y	.86Y	1.07Y	16.51Y	17.92Y	22.68Y	29.78Y	34.03Y	42.06Y	52.19Y
French Polynesia	887	.03Y	.03Y	.04Y	.05Y	.05Y	.07Y	.08Y	—Y	—Y	—Y	.01Y	.01Y	.01Y	.01Y
India	534	—Y	.75V	.81V	.18V	.08V	.09Y	.12Y	.33Y	.32V	.87V	.83V	.56V	.69Y	.86Y
Indonesia	536	—V	—V	—V	—V	—V	—V	—V	.53V	1.04V	1.04V	2.65V	1.96V	2.63V	2.64V
Korea	542	—V	.02V	.04V	.13V	.11V	2.01V	.64V	.34V	.41V	.53V	.39V	1.16V	.36V	.23V
Malaysia	548	—V	—V	.01V	.02V	—V	.02V	—V	.16V	.08V	.44V	.36V	.70V	.78V	.82V
New Caledonia	839	—V	.01V	—V	—V	—Y	—Y	.01Y	—V	.01V	—V	.01V	.01Y	.02Y	.02Y
Pakistan	564	—V	—V	—V	—V	—V	—Y	—Y	—V	—V	.68V	1.14V	1.47V	1.82Y	2.26Y
Philippines	566	—V	—V	—V	—V	—V	—V	—V	.02V	—V	.01V	.03V	.16V	.07V	.10V
Samoa	862	.15Y	.16Y	.21Y	.27Y	.59Y	.73Y	.90Y	.19Y	.20Y	.26Y	.34Y	1.88V	2.32Y	2.88Y
Taiwan Province of China	528	.21V	.62V	.61V	2.95V	.31V	.05V	.38V	.63V	1.34V	.86V	.93V	.79V	.84V	1.19V
Thailand	578	.13V	—V	.09V	—V	—V	—V	—V	6.03V	.97V	.74V	.92V	2.91V	2.11V	4.58V
Vanuatu	846	—Y	—Y	—Y	—Y	—Y	—Y	—Y	.02Y	.03Y	.03Y	.05Y	.05Y	.06Y	.08Y
Europe	**170**	**—Y**	**.8Y**	**.2Y**	**.3Y**	**—Y**	**—Y**	**—Y**	**.3Y**	**.6Y**	**.5Y**	**.1Y**	**—Y**	**.1Y**	**—Y**
Bulgaria	918	—V	—V	—V	—V	—V	—V	—V	.07V	.37V	.38V	.05V	.03V	—V	—V
Georgia	915	.01V	—V	—V	—V	—V	—V	—Y	—Y	—Y	—Y	—Y	—Y	—Y	—Y
Hungary	944	—V	—V	—V	—V	—V	—V	—V	—V	—V	—V	.01V	—V	.01V	—V
Latvia	941	—V	—V	—Y	—Y	—V	—V	—V	—V	.01V	.01Y	.01Y	—V	—V	—V
Lithuania	946	—V	.79V	—V	—V	—V	—V	—V	—V	—V	—Y	—Y	.01V	—V	—V
Poland	964	.03V	.03V	.01V	—V	—V	—V	—V	.15V	.05V	.07V	.01V	—V	—V	.03V
Romania	968	—V	—V	—V	—V	—V	—V	—V	.02V	.07V	.02V	—V	—V	—V	—V
Russia	922	—V	—V	—V	—V	—V	—V	—V	—V	—V	—Y	—Y	—Y	.04Y	—V
Slovak Republic	936	—V	—V	—Y	—Y	—V	—V	—V	.01V	.01V	.01Y	.01Y	—V	—V	—V
Turkey	186	—V	—V	.15V	.31V	—V	—V	—V	.07V	.04V	.01V	.01V	—V	—V	—V
Middle East	**407**	**—Y**	**.1Y**	**.1Y**	**—Y**	**—Y**	**—Y**	**—Y**	**—Y**	**—Y**	**—Y**	**—Y**	**—Y**	**—Y**	**—Y**
Lebanon	446	.01Y	.01Y	.01Y	.02Y	.02Y	.03Y	.03Y	—Y	—Y	—Y	—Y	—Y	—Y	—Y
Qatar	453	—V	.10V	.05V	—V	—V	—V	—Y	—V	—V	—V	—V	—V	—V	—Y
Western Hemisphere	**207**	**—Y**	**—Y**	**.1Y**	**.2Y**	**.1Y**	**—Y**	**—Y**	**.3Y**	**.1Y**	**.6Y**	**.6Y**	**1.2Y**	**1.0Y**	**1.6Y**
Argentina	213	—V	—V	—V	—V	—V	—V	.01V	—V	—V	—V	—V	—V	.01V	—V
Brazil	223	—V	—V	.11V	.18V	.06V	—V	—V	.01V	.11V	.05V	.03V	.25V	.26V	—V
Chile	228	—V	—V	—V	—V	—V	—V	—V	.22V	—V	.45V	.56V	.92V	.36V	.97V
Mexico	273	—V	—V	—V	—V	—V	—V	—V	—V	—V	—V	—V	—V	.26V	.50V
Paraguay	288	....	....	....	....	....	....	....	—V	—V	.01V	—V	—V	—V	—Y
Peru	293	—V	—V	—V	—V	—V	—V	—Y	.05V	.02V	.08V	.01V	—V	.15V	.18Y
Other Countries n.i.e.	**910**	**—Y**	**—Y**	**—Y**	**—Y**	**—Y**	**—Y**	**—Y**	**—Y**	**—Y**	**—Y**	**—Y**	**—Y**	**—Y**	**—Y**
North Korea	954	—Y	—Y	—Y	—Y	—Y	—Y	—Y	.01Y	.01Y	.01Y	.01Y	.01Y	.02Y	.02Y
Memorandum Items															
European Union	998	.74Y	3.01Y	3.32Y	.63Y	.58Y	.28Y	1.14Y	4.81Y	4.62Y	6.04Y	5.03Y	6.92Y	17.02Y	3.84Y
Oil Exporting Ctys	999	—Y	.10Y	.05Y	—Y	—Y	—Y	—Y	.53Y	1.04Y	1.04Y	2.65Y	1.96Y	2.63Y	2.64Y
Non-Oil Develop.Ctys	201	1.21Y	3.03Y	2.91Y	11.65Y	2.38Y	4.79Y	4.06Y	26.63Y	28.10Y	31.70Y	47.06Y	48.86Y	57.00Y	79.76Y

	Exports 2001	2002	2003	2004	2005	2006	2007	Imports 2001	2002	2003	2004	2005	2006	2007
PERCENT DISTRIBUTION														
Industrial Countries......... 101	94.8	88.6	90.3	65.5	87.3	78.0	77.3	63.2	66.3	67.7	59.1	60.2	57.1	48.7
Developing Countries......... 202	5.1	11.3	9.5	34.4	12.3	21.7	22.2	36.8	33.6	32.3	40.9	39.8	42.8	51.2
Africa......... 607	—	—	—	—	—	—	—	.1	.2	.9	.1	—	.1	2.6
Asia......... 507	4.9	7.9	8.4	32.9	11.9	21.5	21.9	35.8	32.6	30.3	40.2	38.8	42.0	47.6
Europe......... 170	.2	2.9	.5	.9	—	—	—	.4	.6	.5	.1	—	—	—
Middle East......... 407	—	.4	.2	.1	.1	.1	.2	—	—	—	—	—	—	—
Western Hemisphere......... 207	—	—	.3	.5	.3	—	.1	.4	.1	.6	.5	.9	.7	1.0
ANNUAL PERCENT CHANGE														
World......... 001	34.8	16.7	11.9	9.1	–42.9	14.5	–17.0	–10.7	17.3	17.0	20.1	5.0	8.9	15.6
Industrial Countries......... 101	39.2	9.1	14.0	–20.9	–23.9	2.2	–17.8	–12.3	23.1	19.3	4.9	6.9	3.4	–1.4
Developing Countries......... 202	–15.1	158.1	–5.5	294.0	–79.5	101.0	–15.1	–7.8	7.3	12.3	51.8	2.2	17.3	38.2
Africa......... 607	–92.8	–76.8	219.6	31.3	....	–40.6	....	—	106.5	382.0	–91.1	–20.4	116.7	—
Asia......... 507	–10.4	90.8	18.8	325.1	–79.3	106.7	–15.5	–9.7	6.8	8.7	59.1	1.2	17.9	31.1
Europe......... 170	–63.2	—	–79.7	87.8	14.2	....	....	—	73.3	–9.1	–80.3	–52.6	13.8	–41.2
Middle East......... 407	10.4	984.5	–42.3	–71.2	14.3	23.6	24.1	—	—	—	....	....	....	....
Western Hemisphere......... 207	....	—	—	68.2	–67.0	–89.5	79.4	95.0	–55.6	364.3	1.2	94.7	–11.2	58.4
Other Countries n.i.e......... 910	—	—	....	....	....	....	....	10.4	8.5	26.6	31.3	14.3	23.6	24.1

		Exports							Imports						
		2001	2002	2003	2004	2005	2006	2007	2001	2002	2003	2004	2005	2006	2007
		Millions of U.S. Dollars							Millions of U.S. Dollars						
IFS World Total		**4,274.8**	**3,882.2**	**5,177.6**	**6,374.0**	**9,611.2**	**14,154.7**	**14,700.0**	**3,576.3**	**3,643.7**	**3,891.8**	**4,858.0**	**5,724.6**	**6,484.1**	**7,457.2**
DOTS World Total	**001**	**4,284.9**	**3,850.8**	**6,565.1Y**	**8,461.4Y**	**11,013.8Y**	**13,167.7Y**	**14,769.1Y**	**3,561.5**	**3,660.4**	**3,648.6Y**	**5,069.7Y**	**5,305.5Y**	**5,855.8Y**	**6,933.4Y**
Industrial Countries	**101**	**2,568.2**	**2,480.2**	**4,939.4Y**	**6,369.0Y**	**8,362.3Y**	**9,987.4Y**	**10,422.8Y**	**2,263.2**	**2,165.3**	**2,193.1Y**	**3,352.3Y**	**2,822.2Y**	**2,945.5Y**	**3,375.7Y**
United States	111	1,920.43	1,940.57	4,280.82V	5,696.36V	7,583.82V	8,020.36V	8,492.45V	1,323.49	1,242.42	1,170.62V	1,327.81V	1,583.01V	1,776.28V	1,957.34V
Canada	156	98.06	91.87	165.82V	114.85V	197.60V	271.30V	393.06V	91.21	103.55	98.91V	131.97V	145.13V	194.87V	232.42V
Australia	193	1.04	1.34	2.60V	2.25V	2.83V	4.05V	4.81V	26.32	17.27	26.55V	19.37V	11.10V	18.92V	19.18V
Japan	158	155.88	1.38	13.84V	15.75V	3.26V	179.47V	223.69V	133.64	160.28	158.64V	191.54V	316.42V	223.30V	247.40V
New Zealand	196	.13	—	.07V	.12V	.18V	.15V	.33V	11.38	10.46	13.34V	16.38V	26.65V	23.36V	35.85V
Austria	122	.01	.01	.01V	.04V	.20V	.10V	.22V	8.29	9.11	9.95V	7.28V	12.70V	10.03V	16.72V
Belgium	124	18.30	11.10	20.07V	13.63V	58.13V	37.88V	23.10V	14.56	9.89	22.60V	30.60V	21.07V	20.02V	30.68V
Cyprus	423	.02	7.01	.06V	—V	.01Y	—V	—V	.03	7.73	.14V	.15V	.22V	.16V	.08V
Denmark	128	.07	.14	.22V	.55V	.73V	.11V	.31V	6.04	3.04	8.35V	8.17V	9.71V	17.47V	13.27V
Finland	172	2.20	—	.02V	—V	—V	—V	—V	9.27	1.38	3.32V	1.25V	1.60V	3.64V	10.12V
France	132	192.70	175.79	228.23V	307.70V	244.03V	334.24V	255.26V	29.34	38.06	42.60V	47.86V	96.16V	49.60V	58.24V
Germany	134	14.54	2.02	11.56V	32.64V	13.11V	17.17V	21.78V	130.41	252.23	243.77V	624.17V	135.02V	145.17V	183.91V
Greece	174	.44	7.03	.42V	.65V	.84V	1.39V	1.03V	.60	.40	.42V	.69V	.78V	2.24V	2.39V
Iceland	176	—	—	—V	—V	—V	—V	—V	.13	.01	—V	.01V	—V	—V	.01V
Ireland	178	.04	.08	.23V	.19V	.35V	.51V	.52V	21.11	23.26	21.21V	16.93V	13.48V	16.28V	21.87V
Italy	136	6.24	25.74	22.16V	13.66V	14.01V	18.63V	29.67V	178.66	56.57	91.62V	282.50V	89.64V	92.03V	147.81V
Luxembourg	137	—	—	—V	—V	—V	—V	—V	1.14	.62	5.05V	5.36V	3.74V	1.75V	1.93V
Malta	181	—	.08	.02V	—V	—V	—V	.06V	.40	.16	.22V	.84V	.14V	.18V	.25V
Netherlands	138	52.01	58.47	31.53V	16.22V	14.98V	64.88V	154.22V	32.58	45.22	44.22V	66.42V	69.27V	63.36V	62.69V
Norway	142	.05	4.93	.09V	.19V	6.55V	.22V	.53V	2.39	2.59	3.14V	6.61V	3.61V	6.90V	7.97V
Portugal	182	.41	3.73	8.70V	5.03V	1.92V	12.95V	13.10V	.73	1.75	2.58V	.93V	.80V	.87V	2.20V
Slovenia	961	—	—	—V	—Y	.06V	—V	.03V	—	—	.10V	.13Y	.18V	.54V	.29V
Spain	184	35.91	92.07	34.93V	29.32V	100.39V	715.39V	579.96V	66.62	21.46	27.50V	355.12V	32.42V	30.25V	36.99V
Sweden	144	5.84	.04	1.48V	.10V	2.77V	.09V	.11V	5.53	14.82	6.54V	7.17V	32.09V	32.03V	17.48V
Switzerland	146	.43	.07	5.33V	.58V	1.02V	1.08V	5.32V	10.47	12.29	4.36V	8.30V	10.57V	8.92V	7.78V
United Kingdom	112	63.48	56.70	111.17V	119.14V	115.54V	307.42V	223.28V	158.82	130.77	187.37V	194.80V	206.64V	207.35V	260.86V
Developing Countries	**202**	**1,645.6**	**1,315.7**	**1,556.3Y**	**2,001.3Y**	**2,547.3Y**	**3,051.6Y**	**4,186.5Y**	**1,295.3**	**1,491.3**	**1,450.8Y**	**1,711.1Y**	**2,476.2Y**	**2,901.4Y**	**3,546.7Y**
Africa	**607**	**12.6**	**6.5**	**12.1Y**	**10.0Y**	**14.3Y**	**27.2Y**	**39.6Y**	**77.6**	**399.7**	**240.2Y**	**317.8Y**	**386.6Y**	**448.2Y**	**555.9Y**
Angola	614	—	.39	.50Y	.66Y	.75Y	.93Y	1.15Y	—	43.26	54.75Y	71.91Y	82.16Y	101.55Y	126.02Y
Benin	638	—	—	.01V	—V	—V	—Y	.01Y	—	—	—V	—V	—V	—Y	—Y
Burkina Faso	748	—	.01	.02Y	.02Y	.02Y	.03Y	.03Y	.06	—	—Y	—Y	—Y	—Y	—Y
Cameroon	622	—	—	—V	—Y	—Y	—Y	—Y	—	—	33.11V	43.49Y	49.69Y	61.41Y	76.21Y
Cape Verde	624	.15	1.75	2.22Y	2.91Y	3.33Y	4.12Y	5.11Y	—	—	—Y	—Y	—Y	—Y	—Y
Central African Rep.	626	—	—	—Y	—Y	—Y	—Y	—Y	—	.01	.02Y	.02Y	.02Y	.03Y	.04Y
Comoros	632	.01	.02	.02Y	.03Y	.04Y	.05Y	.06Y	—	—	—Y	—Y	—Y	—Y	—Y
Congo, Republic of	634	—	.02	—V	—V	—Y	—Y	—Y	—	144.76	—V	—V	—Y	—Y	—Y
Côte d'Ivoire	662	—	—	.78V	—V	—V	—V	—Y	.31	.31	.09V	.20V	23.81V	—V	—Y
Ethiopia	644	—	—	—V	—V	—Y	—Y	—Y	—	.02	—V	—V	—V	—Y	—Y
Gabon	646	—	.01	.01Y	.01Y	.01Y	.01Y	.02Y	70.25	117.59	148.83Y	195.46Y	223.33Y	276.01Y	342.53Y
Gambia, The	648	.03	.10	.13Y	.17Y	.19Y	.24Y	.29Y	—	—	—Y	—Y	—Y	—Y	—Y
Ghana	652	.27	.14	.18Y	.23Y	.27Y	.33Y	.41Y	.03	—	—Y	—Y	—Y	—Y	—Y
Kenya	664	.01	.01	.01V	.02V	.02Y	.03Y	.04Y	—	.08	—V	.02V	.02Y	.03Y	.04Y
Liberia	668	2.57	—	—Y	—Y	—Y	—Y	—Y	.03	—	—Y	—Y	—Y	—Y	—Y
Madagascar	674	—	—	—V	—Y	—Y	—Y	.01Y	.02	.01	—V	—Y	—Y	—Y	—Y
Malawi	676	—	—	—Y	—Y	—Y	—Y	—Y	.07	.05	.06Y	.08Y	.09Y	.11Y	.14Y
Mauritania	682	—	.01	.01Y	.01Y	.02Y	.02Y	.02Y	—	—	—Y	—Y	—Y	—Y	—Y
Mauritius	684	—	—	.01V	—V	—V	—V	—V	—	—	—V	—V	.06V	.01V	.03V
Morocco	686	.33	.70	2.54V	—V	—V	—Y	—Y	—	.07	.09V	1.08V	2.88V	3.56Y	4.42Y
Mozambique	688	—	—	—Y	—Y	—Y	—Y	—Y	—	.01	.01Y	.02Y	.02Y	.02Y	.03Y
Namibia	728	.10	.01	.01Y	.01Y	.01Y	.01Y	.01Y	.11	.02	.02Y	.02Y	.02Y	.02Y	.02Y
Niger	692	—	—	—V	—V	—Y	—Y	—Y	.04	—	—V	—V	—Y	—Y	—Y
Nigeria	694	6.30	—	.22V	.29Y	.37Y	.46Y	.59Y	.11	87.70	—V	—Y	—Y	—Y	—Y
Senegal	722	2.57	—	5.19V	5.10V	8.80V	18.01V	22.35Y	—	—	—V	—V	—V	—V	—Y
Sierra Leone	724	—	—	.01Y	.01Y	.01Y	.01Y	.01Y	—	—	—Y	—Y	—Y	—Y	—Y
South Africa	199	.24	3.18	.23V	.41V	.42V	2.94V	9.44V	6.43	4.98	2.16V	4.14V	2.94V	3.46V	4.04V
Swaziland	734	—	—	—Y	—Y	—Y	—Y	—Y	.01	.65	.82Y	1.08Y	1.23Y	1.52Y	1.89Y
Tanzania	738	—	.02	.02Y	.03Y	.04Y	.04Y	.05Y	.03	.17	.22Y	.29Y	.33Y	.41Y	.50Y
Togo	742	—	—	.01V	.01V	.01V	.02Y	.02Y	—	—	.01V	—V	—V	—Y	—Y
Tunisia	744	—	.11	—V	.01V	—V	—V	—Y	.04	.03	—V	—V	—V	.02V	.02Y
Zimbabwe	698	—	.01	—V	—V	—V	—V	—Y	.03	—	—Y	—V	—V	—V	—Y
Asia	**507**	**8.3**	**13.6**	**27.4Y**	**47.9Y**	**35.4Y**	**110.4Y**	**269.3Y**	**174.8**	**183.1**	**184.0Y**	**263.7Y**	**362.7Y**	**546.5Y**	**702.7Y**
Afghanistan, I.S. of	512	—	—	—Y	—Y	—Y	—Y	—Y	.02	.05	.07Y	.09Y	.10Y	.12Y	.15Y
Bangladesh	513	.08	.02	—V	—V	—V	1.79V	—V	.08	.11	—V	—V	—V	—Y	—Y
Cambodia	522	.01	—	—Y	—Y	—Y	—Y	—Y	—	.10	.12Y	.16Y	.19Y	.23Y	.28Y
China,P.R.: Mainland	924	.20	1.90	9.31V	3.39V	16.57V	9.28V	18.67V	65.92	72.19	64.38V	82.66V	104.26V	181.18V	289.66V
China,P.R.:Hong Kong	532	.04	.05	.29V	.10V	.37V	.44V	.40V	4.95	3.05	10.45V	9.48V	9.27V	9.09V	8.10V
China,P.R.:Macao	546	—	—	—V	.05V	.01V	.02V	—V	.02	.01	—V	—V	—V	—V	—V
Fiji	819	—	—	—Y	—Y	—Y	—Y	—Y	—	.04	.05Y	.06Y	.07Y	.09Y	.11Y
India	534	.24	1.34	5.04V	8.98V	4.41V	5.46Y	6.77Y	16.76	20.07	22.34V	28.11V	62.46V	77.20Y	95.80Y

		Exports							Imports						
		2001	2002	2003	2004	2005	2006	2007	2001	2002	2003	2004	2005	2006	2007
		Millions of U.S. Dollars							*Millions of U.S. Dollars*						
Indonesia	536	1.99	4.62	6.65V	16.58V	9.57V	6.70V	39.00V	4.87	4.75	2.55V	6.77V	3.90V	8.83V	6.29V
Korea	542	.40	.40	.31V	6.26V	.27V	23.98V	164.12V	23.85	32.31	21.36V	25.22V	39.60V	52.06V	69.91V
Malaysia	548	.02	.04	.23V	—V	.01V	.04V	—V	4.42	5.83	2.99V	6.88V	8.45V	16.18V	18.91V
Myanmar	518	—	—	—Y	—Y	—Y	—Y	—Y	—	.01	.01Y	.01Y	.01Y	.01Y	.02Y
New Caledonia	839	—	.02	—V	—V	—Y	—Y	—Y	—	.01	—Y	—Y	—Y	—Y	—Y
Pakistan	564	—	.02	—V	.08V	.09V	.12Y	.15Y	5.45	4.01	.45V	1.47V	1.12V	1.38Y	1.72Y
Papua New Guinea	853	—	—	—Y	—Y	—Y	—Y	—Y	—	.02	.02Y	.03Y	.04Y	.04Y	.05Y
Philippines	566	—	—	.03V	—V	.01V	.02V	—V	.91	.83	.24V	.38V	.17V	.32V	1.33V
Samoa	862	—	—	—Y	—Y	—Y	—Y	—Y	—	.02	.02Y	.03Y	.04Y	.04Y	.05Y
Singapore	576	4.85	4.53	4.86V	5.16V	.81V	3.05V	.32V	4.97	2.63	10.63V	38.47V	59.76V	85.34V	74.11V
Sri Lanka	524	—	.03	.03Y	.04Y	.05Y	.06Y	.07Y	1.04	.72	.91Y	1.20Y	1.37Y	1.69Y	2.10Y
Taiwan Province of China	528	.48	.62	.65V	2.01V	1.64V	57.88V	39.00V	22.48	19.48	32.04V	38.37V	37.84V	42.46V	54.98V
Thailand	578	.01	—	—V	5.25V	1.56V	1.56V	.82V	17.83	16.33	15.00V	24.27V	34.03V	70.24V	79.13V
Vietnam	582	—	.02	.02V	—V	—V	—V	—V	1.27	.56	.33V	—V	—V	—V	—V
Europe	**170**	**.1**	**.4**	**3.6Y**	**3.3Y**	**7.5Y**	**9.5Y**	**.6Y**	**22.9**	**23.2**	**25.9Y**	**43.9Y**	**40.9Y**	**63.4Y**	**74.5Y**
Albania	914	.04	.30	—V	.02V	.02V	.01V	—V	—	.01	—V	—V	—V	—V	—V
Azerbaijan	912	.01	—	.03V	.05V	—V	—V	.04V	....	....	....	....	....	....	....
Bulgaria	918	—	—	—V	—V	.02V	—V	—V	.06	.10	.03V	.04V	.09V	19.74V	25.22V
Czech Republic	935	—	—	1.60V	3.15V	7.38V	9.30V	.02V	.03	—	1.49V	7.31V	1.47V	1.97V	2.31V
Czechoslovakia n.s.	937	—	—	—Y	—Y	—Y	—Y	—Y	2.44	2.34	2.96Y	3.89Y	4.45Y	5.50Y	6.82Y
Estonia	939	—	—	—V	—V	—V	.01V	—V	.01	.21	.10V	.08V	.91V	.02V	—V
Georgia	915	—	—	—V	—V	—V	—V	—Y	.03	.02	2.17V	—V	—V	—V	—Y
Hungary	944	—	—	.01V	.04V	—V	.01V	—V	.72	.90	1.04V	.61V	1.07V	1.34V	2.99V
Kazakhstan	916	....	....	....	....	....	....	....	.56	.11	.05V	.73V	.83Y	1.03Y	1.27Y
Latvia	941	—	—	—Y	—Y	—V	—V	—V	.06	.03	.01V	.11V	.16V	.04V	.02V
Lithuania	946	—	—	—V	—V	—V	—V	—V	.03	.02	—V	—V	.09V	.09V	.05V
Macedonia, FYR	962	—	—	—V	—V	—V	—V	—Y	—	—	.24V	—V	—V	—V	—Y
Poland	964	—	—	.11V	.01V	.01V	.01V	—V	3.30	4.39	3.87V	5.23V	5.06V	3.86V	2.27V
Romania	968	—	—	—V	—V	.02V	.01V	.15V	3.05	2.24	1.78V	2.87V	1.22V	1.67V	3.89V
Russia	922	.01	—	.13V	—V	—V	—V	.06V	5.13	5.34	5.54V	12.90V	8.88V	4.97V	2.12V
Slovak Republic	936	—	—	—Y	—Y	—V	—V	—V	—	—	—Y	—Y	1.77V	1.34V	2.10V
Turkey	186	—	.07	1.68V	.03V	.01V	.11V	.34V	3.09	4.79	3.62V	4.64V	4.46V	8.94V	9.44V
Ukraine	926	—	—	.01V	—V	.01V	.01Y	.02Y	4.21	2.69	2.93V	5.44V	10.34V	12.78Y	15.86Y
Uzbekistan	927	....	....	....	....	....	....	....	.02	.01	.02Y	.02Y	.02Y	.03Y	.04Y
Yugoslavia n.s.	966	—	—	—Y	—Y	—Y	—Y	—Y	.13	.03	.03Y	.04Y	.05Y	.06Y	.08Y
Middle East	**407**	**.1**	**2.0**	**4.9Y**	**23.4Y**	**.8Y**	**1.0Y**	**1.2Y**	**9.4**	**19.8**	**14.7Y**	**18.7Y**	**27.5Y**	**29.4Y**	**31.9Y**
Egypt	469	.03	.36	.46Y	.60Y	.69Y	.85Y	1.06Y	.82	8.68	10.99Y	14.43Y	16.49Y	20.38Y	25.29Y
Iran, I.R. of	429	—	.03	.04Y	.05Y	.06Y	.08Y	.10Y	.04	.26	.32Y	.42Y	.58Y	.72Y	.87Y
Israel	436	—	.01	—V	—V	—V	—V	—V	7.89	10.06	2.64V	3.08V	9.46V	7.04V	4.18V
Jordan	439	—	.01	—V	—V	—V	—V	—V	.09	.09	—V	—V	—V	—V	—V
Kuwait	443	—	—	—Y	—Y	—Y	—Y	—Y	.05	—	—Y	—Y	—Y	—Y	—Y
Lebanon	446	.01	—	—Y	.01Y	.01Y	.01Y	.01Y	—	—	—Y	.01Y	.01Y	.01Y	.01Y
Libya	672	—	—	—Y	—Y	—Y	—Y	—Y	—	.01	.01Y	.01Y	.02Y	.02Y	.03Y
Oman	449	.02	.01	—V	—Y	—Y	—Y	—Y	—	.02	—V	—Y	—Y	—Y	—Y
Qatar	453	—	.01	4.33V	22.74V	—V	—V	—Y	.03	—	—Y	—Y	—Y	—Y	—Y
Saudi Arabia	456	.01	.01	.11V	.04V	.03V	.04Y	.05Y	.08	.20	.24Y	.31Y	.43Y	.54Y	.65Y
Syrian Arab Republic	463	—	—	—Y	—V	—Y	—Y	—Y	.36	.18	.23Y	—V	—Y	—Y	—Y
United Arab Emirates	466	.03	1.50	—V	—Y	—Y	—Y	—Y	.04	.25	.30Y	.40Y	.55Y	.69Y	.83Y
Yemen, Republic of	474	.01	—	—Y	—V	—V	—Y	—Y	.04	—	—Y	—V	—V	—Y	—Y
Western Hemisphere	**207**	**1,624.5**	**1,293.3**	**1,508.2Y**	**1,916.7Y**	**2,489.3Y**	**2,903.5Y**	**3,875.7Y**	**1,010.6**	**865.5**	**986.0Y**	**1,067.0Y**	**1,658.5Y**	**1,813.9Y**	**2,181.7Y**
Antigua and Barbuda	311	17.60	18.74	23.72Y	31.15Y	35.59Y	43.99Y	54.59Y	.12	.12	.15Y	.19Y	.22Y	.27Y	.34Y
Argentina	213	.51	2.48	.08V	3.32V	—V	.01V	14.90V	5.51	6.00	17.61V	26.28V	29.78V	31.75V	30.20V
Aruba	314	4.84	7.32	5.26V	4.66V	5.28V	4.68V	3.38V	.03	.01	.15V	.04V	.59V	.74V	.22V
Bahamas, The	313	19.55	23.79	30.11Y	39.55Y	45.19Y	55.85Y	69.30Y	22.07	2.29	2.89Y	3.80Y	4.34Y	5.37Y	6.66Y
Barbados	316	273.60	178.44	214.95V	268.72V	320.94V	332.82V	413.02Y	23.24	30.57	31.20V	32.06V	42.75V	53.57V	66.48Y
Belize	339	7.76	9.84	12.46Y	16.36Y	18.69Y	23.10Y	28.67Y	15.99	3.51	4.44Y	5.84Y	6.67Y	8.24Y	10.23Y
Bermuda	319	19.10	13.38	16.94Y	22.25Y	1.50V	2.79V	3.46Y	.01	.01	.01Y	.01Y	.01Y	.01Y	.02Y
Bolivia	218	.24	.22	.19V	.11V	.05V	.06Y	.07Y	.14	.02	.40V	.06V	.06Y	.08Y	.10Y
Brazil	223	13.61	18.42	44.62V	48.65V	95.47V	108.50V	113.22V	199.16	208.97	245.40V	591.99V	759.63V	696.97V	759.50V
Chile	228	.09	.06	.02V	5.92V	6.55V	.05V	17.06V	3.91	4.33	6.53V	5.91V	6.48V	12.58V	16.33V
Colombia	233	28.89	53.00	30.33V	35.41V	161.11V	84.93V	281.61V	150.13	62.17	108.41V	77.92V	217.52V	227.22V	376.49V
Costa Rica	238	11.48	3.27	13.67V	17.04V	9.28V	11.47Y	14.24Y	3.10	3.41	16.02V	18.11V	22.40V	27.68Y	34.35Y
Dominica	321	20.34	15.77	19.96Y	26.21Y	29.95Y	37.01Y	45.93Y	2.20	2.36	2.99Y	3.92Y	4.48Y	5.54Y	6.88Y
Dominican Republic	243	180.40	78.31	99.11Y	130.17Y	148.72Y	183.81Y	228.11Y	4.34	4.42	5.60Y	7.35Y	8.40Y	10.38Y	12.89Y
Ecuador	248	1.49	3.74	20.22V	6.74V	11.09V	44.36V	55.05Y	1.27	3.62	3.12V	1.43V	33.51V	1.55V	1.92Y
El Salvador	253	35.42	22.51	41.12V	13.01V	13.15V	12.30V	17.45V	.49	.43	1.00V	1.08V	1.22V	1.12V	1.14V
Grenada	328	45.65	44.74	56.62Y	74.36Y	84.97Y	105.01Y	130.32Y	.25	.14	.18Y	.23Y	.27Y	.33Y	.41Y
Guatemala	258	57.78	46.11	2.54V	15.32V	1.25V	1.55Y	1.92Y	11.77	12.77	2.20V	5.80V	12.27V	15.17Y	18.82Y
Guyana	336	92.64	82.49	104.40Y	137.11Y	156.66Y	193.62Y	240.28Y	16.25	15.74	19.93Y	26.17Y	29.90Y	36.96Y	45.86Y
Haiti	263	4.20	4.52	5.55V	7.01V	8.01Y	9.90Y	12.29Y	.16	.15	.19Y	.26Y	.29Y	.36Y	.45Y
Honduras	268	44.92	33.92	58.07V	57.87V	66.12Y	81.72Y	101.42Y	8.40	6.78	6.79V	4.79V	5.48Y	6.77Y	8.40Y
Jamaica	343	355.52	292.44	371.48V	438.77V	600.46V	697.40V	963.14V	20.02	17.39	19.61V	19.34V	19.36V	19.90V	22.09V
Mexico	273	32.32	54.46	78.57V	206.20V	264.66V	410.23V	528.33V	44.15	42.07	21.93V	29.34V	63.02V	67.07V	64.32V
Netherlands Antilles	353	61.22	55.22	7.65V	10.05Y	11.48Y	14.19Y	17.61Y	10.19	6.20	4.66V	6.12Y	7.00Y	8.65Y	10.73Y
Nicaragua	278	11.38	8.29	—V	—V	—V	—V	—V	3.40	.05	—V	—V	—V	—V	—V
Panama	283	21.51	29.08	17.77V	19.45V	39.84V	29.38V	37.90V	2.64	4.06	2.35V	1.77V	3.89V	5.04V	2.79V
Paraguay	288	.12	.02	.02V	—V	.10V	—V	—Y	—	.07	.18V	.07V	.04V	—V	—Y

	Exports 2001	2002	2003	2004	2005	2006	2007	Imports 2001	2002	2003	2004	2005	2006	2007
	Millions of U.S. Dollars							*Millions of U.S. Dollars*						
Peru.......... 293	5.77	5.74	2.91V	1.43V	32.94V	4.52V	13.09Y	3.65	11.10	15.86V	12.88V	22.11V	47.10V	50.85Y
St. Kitts and Nevis.......... 361	25.37	19.47	24.64Y	32.36Y	36.97Y	45.70Y	56.71Y	.26	.03	.03Y	.04Y	.05Y	.06Y	.08Y
St. Lucia.......... 362	59.23	45.63	57.75Y	75.85Y	86.66Y	107.11Y	132.92Y	1.41	2.06	2.61Y	3.42Y	3.91Y	4.83Y	6.00Y
St. Pierre-Miquelon.......... 363	.06	.01	.01Y	.01Y	.01Y	.01Y	.01Y	—	—	—Y	—Y	—Y	—Y	—Y
St. Vincent & Grens.......... 364	37.93	34.13	37.83V	43.67V	51.65V	63.84Y	79.22Y	5.22	5.51	4.64V	3.98V	5.39V	6.66Y	8.27Y
Suriname.......... 366	75.20	55.53	70.29Y	92.31Y	105.47Y	130.36Y	161.77Y	13.44	12.01	15.20Y	19.96Y	22.80Y	28.18Y	34.98Y
Uruguay.......... 298	.06	—	.02V	1.02V	.05V	.06Y	.08Y	1.86	.30	.96V	10.03V	8.52V	10.53Y	13.07Y
Venezuela, Rep. Bol.......... 299	50.85	23.91	30.59V	25.08V	29.06V	51.80V	26.24V	435.72	396.82	422.72V	146.80V	316.15V	473.19V	570.85Y
Western Hem. n.s.......... 399	7.87	8.31	8.74Y	9.56Y	10.38Y	11.37Y	12.36Y	.05	.01	.01Y	.01Y	.01Y	.01Y	.01Y
Other Countries n.i.e.......... 910	**13.5**	**12.9**	**16.3Y**	**21.4Y**	**24.5Y**	**30.2Y**	**37.5Y**	**1.8**	**2.7**	**3.4Y**	**4.5Y**	**5.1Y**	**6.3Y**	**7.9Y**
Cuba.......... 928	13.13	12.64	16.00Y	21.01Y	24.01Y	29.67Y	36.82Y	.08	.22	.28Y	.37Y	.42Y	.52Y	.65Y
North Korea.......... 954	.34	.25	.31Y	.41Y	.47Y	.58Y	.72Y	1.67	2.48	3.14Y	4.12Y	4.71Y	5.82Y	7.22Y
Countries & Areas n.s.......... 898	**—**	**.6**	**.8Y**	**1.0Y**	**1.2Y**	**1.4Y**	**1.8Y**	**—**	**.1**	**.2Y**	**.2Y**	**.2Y**	**.3Y**	**.4Y**
Special Categories.......... 899	**57.6**	**41.3**	**52.2Y**	**68.6Y**	**78.4Y**	**96.8Y**	**120.2Y**	**1.2**	**.9**	**1.2Y**	**1.6Y**	**1.8Y**	**2.2Y**	**2.8Y**
Memorandum Items														
European Union.......... 998	392.22	440.03	472.52Y	542.07Y	574.48Y	1,520.09Y	1,302.68Y	668.30	622.01	724.04Y	1,663.69Y	736.20Y	701.66Y	877.50Y
Oil Exporting Ctys.......... 999	59.20	30.10	41.94Y	64.78Y	39.10Y	59.07Y	65.99Y	440.93	490.01	426.14Y	154.72Y	321.62Y	484.00Y	579.52Y
Non-Oil Develop.Ctys.......... 201	1,586.40	1,285.65	1,514.37Y	1,936.52Y	2,508.21Y	2,992.50Y	4,120.52Y	854.35	1,001.32	1,024.61Y	1,556.35Y	2,154.58Y	2,417.38Y	2,967.18Y
PERCENT DISTRIBUTION														
Industrial Countries.......... 101	**59.9**	**64.4**	**75.2**	**75.3**	**75.9**	**75.8**	**70.6**	**63.5**	**59.2**	**60.1**	**66.1**	**53.2**	**50.3**	**48.7**
Developing Countries.......... 202	**38.4**	**34.2**	**23.7**	**23.7**	**23.1**	**23.2**	**28.3**	**36.4**	**40.7**	**39.8**	**33.8**	**46.7**	**49.5**	**51.2**
Africa.......... 607	**.3**	**.2**	**.2**	**.1**	**.1**	**.2**	**.3**	**2.2**	**10.9**	**6.6**	**6.3**	**7.3**	**7.7**	**8.0**
Asia.......... 507	**.2**	**.4**	**.4**	**.6**	**.3**	**.8**	**1.8**	**4.9**	**5.0**	**5.0**	**5.2**	**6.8**	**9.3**	**10.1**
Europe.......... 170	**—**	**—**	**.1**	**—**	**.1**	**.1**	**—**	**.6**	**.6**	**.7**	**.9**	**.8**	**1.1**	**1.1**
Middle East.......... 407	**—**	**.1**	**.1**	**.3**	**—**	**—**	**—**	**.3**	**.5**	**.4**	**.4**	**.5**	**.5**	**.5**
Western Hemisphere.......... 207	**37.9**	**33.6**	**23.0**	**22.7**	**22.6**	**22.1**	**26.2**	**28.4**	**23.6**	**27.0**	**21.0**	**31.3**	**31.0**	**31.5**
Other Countries n.i.e.......... 910	**.3**	**.3**	**.2**	**.3**	**.2**	**.2**	**.3**	**—**	**.1**	**.1**	**.1**	**.1**	**.1**	**.1**
ANNUAL PERCENT CHANGE														
World.......... 001	**40.9**	**–10.1**	**70.5**	**28.9**	**30.2**	**19.6**	**12.2**	**51.4**	**2.8**	**–.3**	**38.9**	**4.7**	**10.4**	**18.4**
Industrial Countries.......... 101	**37.6**	**–3.4**	**99.2**	**28.9**	**31.3**	**19.4**	**4.4**	**81.0**	**–4.3**	**1.3**	**52.9**	**–15.8**	**4.4**	**14.6**
Developing Countries.......... 202	**48.1**	**–20.0**	**18.3**	**28.6**	**27.3**	**19.8**	**37.2**	**17.9**	**15.1**	**–2.7**	**17.9**	**44.7**	**17.2**	**22.2**
Africa.......... 607	**–28.3**	**–48.2**	**86.6**	**–18.0**	**43.9**	**90.1**	**45.5**	**–15.7**	**415.3**	**–39.9**	**32.3**	**21.6**	**15.9**	**24.0**
Asia.......... 507	**–32.5**	**63.5**	**101.6**	**74.6**	**–26.1**	**211.9**	**144.0**	**55.9**	**4.7**	**.5**	**43.3**	**37.5**	**50.7**	**28.6**
Europe.......... 170	**55.3**	**459.5**	**874.7**	**–7.7**	**126.2**	**26.7**	**–93.3**	**60.7**	**1.5**	**11.4**	**69.6**	**–6.9**	**55.1**	**17.5**
Middle East.......... 407	**–63.9**	**—**	**152.4**	**374.1**	**–96.6**	**23.6**	**24.7**	**179.9**	**109.3**	**–25.4**	**26.7**	**47.4**	**6.8**	**8.4**
Western Hemisphere.......... 207	**50.3**	**–20.4**	**16.6**	**27.1**	**29.9**	**16.6**	**33.5**	**15.3**	**–14.4**	**13.9**	**8.2**	**55.4**	**9.4**	**20.3**
Other Countries n.i.e.......... 910	**–53.0**	**–4.3**	**26.6**	**31.3**	**14.3**	**23.6**	**24.1**	**–41.5**	**53.6**	**26.6**	**31.3**	**14.3**	**23.6**	**24.1**

		Exports							Imports						
		2001	2002	2003	2004	2005	2006	2007	2001	2002	2003	2004	2005	2006	2007
		Millions of U.S. Dollars							*Millions of U.S. Dollars*						
IFS World Total		**6,621.1**	**6,871.3**	**8,026.9**	**9,684.9**	**10,493.6**	**11,513.0**	**15,028.8**	**9,528.8**	**9,525.9**	**10,909.9**	**12,817.7**	**13,177.0**	**14,865.0**	**18,980.1**
DOTS World Total	**001**	**6,605.6**	**6,856.2**	**8,027.1**	**9,679.0**	**10,631.2**	**11,687.9**	**14,593.2Y**	**9,520.5**	**9,503.1**	**10,895.6**	**12,814.7**	**13,327.2**	**15,028.5**	**20,053.9Y**
Industrial Countries	**101**	**5,405.3**	**5,559.4**	**6,733.4**	**8,234.3**	**8,686.0**	**9,565.3**	**11,762.7Y**	**7,453.6**	**7,392.3**	**8,499.8**	**9,590.9**	**9,823.2**	**10,514.0**	**14,857.3Y**
United States	111	63.46	53.48	48.51	115.21	102.50	262.55	434.45V	384.18	301.15	269.89	360.34	331.14	430.99	443.30V
Canada	156	4.15	3.98	6.29	8.35	9.94	11.54	46.53V	45.46	90.14	91.03	42.00	28.91	85.82	111.72V
Australia	193	1.20	1.59	1.30	2.08	1.84	3.56	9.36V	5.19	9.64	5.36	5.91	5.32	8.43	12.74V
Japan	158	10.94	8.11	13.77	22.48	22.27	26.75	94.35V	170.71	158.31	198.59	255.04	213.02	249.81	84.42V
New Zealand	196	4.07	3.98	3.75	2.20	3.29	7.09	10.35V	4.71	4.83	3.01	1.61	4.09	5.90	8.20V
Austria	122	6.02	8.56	10.28	10.66	11.81	11.88	115.91V	35.78	36.79	47.27	49.76	58.79	66.67	116.75V
Belgium	124	322.65	292.02	315.05	288.16	288.09	276.17	485.18V	332.63	295.19	321.16	357.27	348.07	341.67	609.94V
Cyprus	423	.25	.44	.31	.73	.78	1.75	2.89V	1.36	1.32	1.26	1.48	1.04	1.12	.78V
Denmark	128	4.38	7.14	8.02	5.49	4.46	3.71	6.42V	23.25	26.71	29.89	29.91	31.37	30.67	73.73V
Finland	172	.98	5.07	1.22	1.95	2.85	1.40	.81V	58.59	55.98	71.33	94.91	73.58	82.85	97.89V
France	132	1,913.68	2,129.39	2,613.32	3,203.28	3,490.81	3,775.29	4,563.83V	2,454.95	2,429.91	2,839.31	3,189.14	3,100.75	3,400.32	4,773.10V
Germany	134	774.30	780.65	858.06	887.36	891.34	916.80	1,247.30V	908.25	847.94	981.33	1,075.39	1,092.89	1,182.29	1,942.37V
Greece	174	35.62	11.01	16.69	21.05	22.97	23.29	32.69V	45.56	52.68	38.07	61.41	66.32	59.84	54.13V
Iceland	176	1.19	.57	.40	.72	.94	.45	6.17V	.03	.01	.06	.23	.23	.17	.01V
Ireland	178	10.33	7.82	8.85	10.44	9.79	11.97	15.79V	22.07	20.18	25.45	41.22	42.09	40.97	67.16V
Italy	136	1,534.04	1,463.83	1,770.61	2,449.99	2,549.80	2,582.20	3,058.19V	1,821.28	1,851.61	2,176.79	2,417.65	2,858.65	2,898.39	4,401.28V
Luxembourg	137	3.23	3.64	4.88	7.91	4.87	4.09	2.81V	8.91	12.50	7.17	6.51	4.35	5.40	5.96V
Malta	181	4.91	4.65	7.90	13.83	18.26	4.88	5.92V	4.65	6.56	24.16	10.86	9.73	10.37	12.67V
Netherlands	138	162.55	148.90	185.57	213.32	235.03	233.23	355.95V	174.59	172.24	221.40	228.27	252.75	232.14	398.15V
Norway	142	4.19	3.67	3.52	3.77	4.78	3.76	29.42V	2.73	7.14	4.18	5.08	4.95	7.56	12.14V
Portugal	182	16.45	20.44	25.71	33.01	32.15	32.76	33.53V	30.72	33.20	56.59	66.99	65.92	70.23	99.07V
Slovenia	961	1.23	.75	1.54	1.31	1.75	2.42	5.87V	4.45	3.61	4.50	15.63	16.16	19.93	22.75V
Spain	184	319.75	324.20	373.91	585.76	587.60	747.87	806.24V	433.76	469.27	581.14	673.76	679.04	698.44	1,009.03V
Sweden	144	13.16	18.41	22.81	27.57	36.11	21.79	31.24V	146.62	148.64	128.95	181.90	100.77	151.68	153.42V
Switzerland	146	35.32	87.12	169.34	39.38	48.23	258.28	26.25V	104.50	132.02	128.12	141.23	142.89	170.91	110.23V
United Kingdom	112	157.28	169.98	261.80	278.30	303.69	339.87	335.23V	228.66	224.78	243.75	277.45	290.32	261.38	236.38V
Developing Countries	**202**	**910.5**	**1,035.9**	**1,015.8**	**1,150.2**	**1,559.6**	**1,813.2**	**2,446.6Y**	**1,904.5**	**1,948.0**	**2,200.0**	**3,152.4**	**3,387.2**	**4,376.4**	**5,025.1Y**
Africa	**607**	**184.1**	**215.6**	**238.6**	**279.1**	**427.7**	**469.1**	**605.4Y**	**209.3**	**205.7**	**237.8**	**283.1**	**262.9**	**328.4**	**410.8Y**
Algeria	612	75.79	89.02	103.54	108.85	182.84	187.96	243.49Y	82.80	90.10	130.02	156.11	135.41	194.64	234.81Y
Angola	614	.10	.40	.49	1.04	1.04	2.26	2.80Y	—	—	—	—	—	.02	.03Y
Benin	638	2.08	2.77	3.06	3.03	2.82	2.32	2.87Y	1.06	—	.39	.01	.21	1.09	1.35Y
Botswana	616	—	—	—	—	—	.09	.11Y	.06	.01	—	.01	.09	.01	.01Y
Burkina Faso	748	2.63	6.12	7.44	6.07	11.89	12.78	15.85Y	.31	.67	.98	.31	1.16	2.28	2.83Y
Burundi	618	—	—	—	—	—	.06	.08Y	—	—	.05	.09	.14	—	—Y
Cameroon	622	2.74	2.02	3.34	4.43	2.92	4.08	5.06Y	9.79	7.34	6.41	6.10	10.15	8.30	10.30Y
Cape Verde	624	—	—	—	.05	.04	—	—Y	—	—	—	—	—	—	—Y
Central African Rep.	626	—	—	—	—	.08	.37	.46Y	.31	.58	.44	.49	.12	.03	.03Y
Chad	628	.38	.60	.38	.61	1.64	2.41	2.99Y	1.58	—	.01	.03	—	—	—Y
Comoros	632	.30	.08	.01	—	.58	.03	.04Y	.01	.01	.03	—	.02	.02	.02Y
Congo, Dem. Rep. of	636	—	—	—	—	—	.01	.01Y	—	—	—	—	.02	—	—Y
Congo, Republic of	634	3.86	4.10	4.62	5.24	6.03	6.97	8.65Y	.79	.96	1.11	1.86	1.59	1.66	2.06Y
Côte d'Ivoire	662	7.69	11.60	6.49	6.56	10.26	16.68	20.70Y	17.80	18.61	18.29	15.94	20.65	24.41	30.29Y
Djibouti	611	7.27	1.52	1.02	.33	.55	.70	.87Y	—	—	.04	.07	.04	.03	.03Y
Equatorial Guinea	642	.88	.41	.74	2.69	.80	2.13	2.64Y	—	—	—	—	—	—	—Y
Eritrea	643	.09	.66	.02	—	.16	—	—Y	.02	.02	—	—	.01	.07	.08Y
Ethiopia	644	.36	.03	—	.13	2.87	18.10	22.47Y	.05	.13	.12	.27	.39	.27	.34Y
Gabon	646	1.88	2.93	2.92	4.05	5.45	7.78	9.65Y	1.67	5.99	1.79	2.35	4.70	2.75	3.41Y
Gambia, The	648	.52	.92	.52	.46	.43	.73	.91Y	—	.03	.06	.01	—	—	—Y
Ghana	652	2.44	2.73	3.10	4.09	4.86	5.48	6.80Y	.98	.28	1.51	2.71	.17	.54	.66Y
Guinea	656	1.04	1.52	1.92	1.08	.95	1.77	2.20Y	.34	—	.02	—	.03	.02	.02Y
Guinea-Bissau	654	.02	.02	.03	.03	.05	.08	.10Y	—	—	.02	.07	.03	.01	.01Y
Kenya	664	.32	1.07	.19	2.04	.10	8.40	10.43Y	2.67	.08	.11	.12	.09	.14	.17Y
Lesotho	666	—	—	—	—	—	—	—Y	—	—	—	—	.03	.03	.04Y
Liberia	668	.03	.06	1.41	1.40	.33	.26	.33Y	.52	.36	.88	—	—	—	—Y
Madagascar	674	1.68	.80	.91	.92	1.09	3.15	3.91Y	2.06	.04	.25	.19	.24	.21	.26Y
Malawi	676	—	.04	—	—	—	—	—Y	.73	.07	.27	.23	.52	.82	1.02Y
Mali	678	2.00	3.28	4.51	4.56	8.13	7.37	9.15Y	1.28	3.57	5.33	2.53	2.06	2.02	2.50Y
Mauritania	682	1.52	2.03	3.17	7.10	7.12	8.47	10.52Y	2.39	.50	1.44	1.00	1.45	.48	.60Y
Mauritius	684	.07	.03	.10	.05	.25	.09	1.98V	.03	.35	.64	.46	.66	1.34	.17V
Morocco	686	40.83	50.81	54.07	74.22	109.34	108.61	134.79Y	64.68	57.43	46.74	62.68	60.08	70.87	87.95Y
Mozambique	688	—	.06	.06	6.51	2.04	3.67	4.55Y	—	—	.40	.04	—	—	—Y
Namibia	728	—	—	—	—	.07	—	—Y	—	—	—	—	—	.09	.18Y
Niger	692	5.56	10.36	12.63	6.61	9.92	9.22	11.44Y	—	.02	.01	.02	—	—	—Y
Nigeria	694	2.07	1.51	.75	1.59	2.78	3.22	4.17Y	—	.17	.01	.02	.02	.11	.13Y
Rwanda	714	.01	.01	.02	—	.21	.01	.01Y	—	.02	.02	.05	.13	.10	.12Y
São Tomé & Príncipe	716	.01	.01	—	—	—	—	—Y	—	—	—	—	—	—	—Y
Senegal	722	11.34	11.62	12.31	18.19	40.20	32.46	40.29Y	3.01	2.55	1.06	2.95	1.53	1.67	2.07Y
Seychelles	718	—	—	—	.06	.02	.01	.01Y	.09	.04	1.24	4.02	—	—	—Y
Sierra Leone	724	.03	.05	.16	.54	.61	.38	.47Y	.14	.01	.07	.02	—	.01	.01Y

	Exports							Imports						
	2001	2002	2003	2004	2005	2006	2007	2001	2002	2003	2004	2005	2006	2007
	Millions of U.S. Dollars							*Millions of U.S. Dollars*						
Somalia....726	—	—	—	—	—	.02	.02Y	—	.01	.01	—	—	.01	.01Y
South Africa....199	6.69	4.57	6.55	1.44	1.79	1.89	10.54V	5.11	6.18	6.79	6.35	8.29	5.65	17.40V
Sacca exc. South Afr....608	—	—	—	—	—	—	—Y	—	—	—	—	—	—	2.44Y
Sudan....732	.06	.47	.66	2.89	1.36	3.69	7.36V	6.29	5.63	8.10	10.03	7.74	7.73	8.22V
Swaziland....734	—	—	—	—	—	—	—Y	.11	.99	.07	—	.01	.60	.74Y
Tanzania....738	.10	—	.17	.05	.27	2.26	2.80Y	.01	—	.03	.09	.08	.02	.02Y
Togo....742	1.86	2.01	1.27	2.13	5.90	3.00	3.72Y	.19	1.73	.90	3.29	2.47	.42	.52Y
Uganda....746	—	.01	—	.05	.02	.09	.12Y	.36	1.10	.89	1.29	.01	.02	.03Y
Zambia....754	—	—	—	—	—	.05	.05V	—	—	—	.01	—	—	—V
Zimbabwe....698	—	—	—	—	—	—	—Y	2.12	.16	1.28	1.30	2.56	—	—Y
Asia....507	**136.2**	**155.9**	**107.9**	**155.3**	**223.0**	**234.7**	**270.8Y**	**464.0**	**439.8**	**514.8**	**746.8**	**840.4**	**1,059.9**	**1,045.1Y**
Afghanistan, I.S. of....512	.10	.05	.03	.70	.27	.67	.83Y	1.58	1.12	1.52	.78	1.22	1.41	1.75Y
Bangladesh....513	10.29	11.18	8.44	10.82	40.43	13.17	—V	1.59	.57	2.65	1.70	1.81	3.08	2.50Y
Bhutan....514	—	—	—	—	—	—	—Y	.01	—	—	—	—	—	—Y
Brunei Darussalam....516	.04	—	—	—	—	—	—Y	.08	—	—	.02	—	—	—Y
Cambodia....522	.02	.02	.03	.02	—	—	—Y	—	.01	.13	.03	.04	.12	.15Y
China,P.R.: Mainland....924	15.69	15.29	17.27	25.50	17.84	42.48	27.51V	130.53	139.29	185.25	291.09	382.27	491.83	530.04V
China,P.R.:Hong Kong....532	2.58	2.23	2.91	4.37	6.96	4.86	9.88V	12.82	11.85	12.16	21.97	16.32	21.63	36.73V
China,P.R.:Macao....546	—	—	.10	.02	.03	—	.60V	.03	.03	.03	.05	.01	.03	—V
Fiji....819	—	—	—	—	.03	—	—Y	—	—	—	—	—	—	—Y
French Polynesia....887	.14	.24	.58	.82	.52	.47	.58Y	.08	.01	.07	.08	.06	.01	.01Y
India....534	82.25	80.79	46.36	85.87	97.66	131.04	162.62Y	44.46	68.27	76.53	109.37	110.88	110.68	137.35Y
Indonesia....536	6.76	6.10	3.30	2.01	11.76	11.82	10.00V	22.58	13.48	17.59	14.61	20.34	43.40	44.61V
Korea....542	2.32	1.04	1.61	1.62	1.46	1.48	22.86V	97.93	74.26	65.38	97.17	97.03	118.06	111.58V
Lao People's Dem.Rep....544	—	—	—	—	—	—	—Y	—	.01	—	.15	.02	.01	.01Y
Malaysia....548	5.39	4.67	6.15	4.99	3.65	6.10	18.21V	24.06	19.99	28.74	46.26	43.76	36.83	28.07V
Maldives....556	—	—	—	—	—	—	—Y	—	—	.72	5.00	—	1.12	1.39Y
Mongolia....948	—	—	—	—	—	—	—Y	—	—	—	—	—	.04	.04Y
Myanmar....518	—	—	—	.04	—	—	—Y	—	.13	.21	.06	.26	.17	.21Y
Nauru....836	—	—	—	—	.03	.13	.16Y	.02	.24	—	.04	—	—	—Y
Nepal....558	—	—	—	.02	.04	—	—Y	—	.03	.01	.02	.01	.02	.03Y
New Caledonia....839	.01	.06	.01	.01	.02	.36	.45Y	—	—	.05	.01	.09	—	—Y
Pakistan....564	5.30	17.55	16.41	10.92	36.98	.20	.25Y	20.33	20.11	19.00	20.25	16.52	11.00	13.65Y
Papua New Guinea....853	—	—	—	—	—	—	—Y	—	—	—	.06	—	—	—Y
Philippines....566	.01	.01	—	.39	.16	2.35	.02V	1.91	1.12	1.92	2.24	6.68	22.67	1.85V
Samoa....862	—	—	—	.04	—	.02	.02Y	—	—	—	—	—	—	—Y
Singapore....576	.86	2.09	2.07	.39	.55	1.68	2.68V	12.14	10.07	12.59	15.58	13.40	24.60	14.82V
Sri Lanka....524	.08	—	—	.23	.01	—	.04V	12.50	11.01	8.90	8.61	12.61	15.03	11.44V
Taiwan Province of China....528	.10	.10	.29	.34	.38	1.69	10.30V	56.40	42.58	43.56	54.20	51.31	67.67	39.22V
Thailand....578	.37	.42	.21	.12	.24	.27	3.76V	21.24	24.14	35.19	54.97	61.70	86.43	69.68V
Tonga....866	—	.03	.01	—	—	—	—Y	—	—	—	—	—	—	—Y
Tuvalu....869	—	—	—	.02	—	—	—Y	—	—	—	—	—	—	—Y
Vietnam....582	3.93	14.01	2.15	6.04	3.95	15.86	—V	3.67	1.50	2.61	2.49	4.10	4.08	—V
Europe....170	**94.3**	**84.7**	**107.9**	**129.1**	**162.7**	**171.0**	**318.9Y**	**537.9**	**615.6**	**650.7**	**1,079.5**	**1,134.6**	**1,516.8**	**1,817.9Y**
Albania....914	1.88	2.39	2.42	3.05	4.71	5.83	1.56V	.01	.50	—	.01	.02	.07	.02V
Armenia....911	—	—	—	.02	—	—	.14V	—	—	—	—	—	—	—V
Azerbaijan....912	.04	.08	.01	.06	.07	—	—V	.07	.11	.26	.42	.05	.12	.18V
Belarus....913	—	—	—	—	.02	.07	.85V	.01	.02	.07	.37	.61	5.12	5.98V
Bosnia & Herzegovina....963	—	—	.02	.08	.36	.15	.19Y	.77	.89	1.25	1.28	.59	1.03	1.28Y
Bulgaria....918	.84	.34	2.15	4.39	2.06	.47	4.88V	27.52	25.98	13.49	32.08	39.52	66.39	73.95V
Croatia....960	.20	.88	1.63	2.29	1.62	1.55	17.24V	6.64	.97	7.42	.81	1.08	10.01	.86V
Czech Republic....935	1.36	4.18	2.31	8.71	11.40	7.75	4.63V	10.45	12.93	21.88	21.85	28.41	49.83	43.47V
Estonia....939	—	.02	—	—	.01	.42	.09V	.11	.06	.13	.39	.95	3.38	.29V
Faroe Islands....816	—	.01	—	.06	.04	—	—Y	.01	—	—	—	—	—	—Y
Georgia....915	—	.02	.01	.01	—	—	—Y	—	—	.01	—	.01	—	—Y
Gibraltar....823	—	—	.02	—	.31	.13	.16Y	—	—	.14	—	—	—	—Y
Hungary....944	.99	1.06	1.00	2.00	3.44	3.79	5.19V	39.25	33.56	39.86	36.38	57.89	67.26	58.63V
Kazakhstan....916	.03	.09	.01	.12	.03	.06	.07Y	1.55	12.51	2.32	7.98	8.29	23.23	28.82Y
Kyrgyz Republic....917	—	—	—	—	—	.02	—V	—	—	—	.04	.01	—	—Y
Latvia....941	—	.10	.13	.09	.10	—	.03V	.03	.11	.32	.71	3.65	11.74	12.47V
Lithuania....946	—	.05	.10	.09	.17	.21	.54V	4.95	2.22	.41	.77	.83	2.00	8.56V
Macedonia, FYR....962	—	—	—	—	—	—	—Y	—	—	—	—	—	.06	.08Y
Moldova....921	—	—	—	—	—	—	—Y	.02	.01	.31	2.62	1.38	.03	.04Y
Poland....964	12.12	12.12	12.60	12.78	13.54	19.11	39.14V	14.32	17.28	15.33	41.48	32.87	47.39	52.52V
Romania....968	2.75	2.80	2.94	2.78	6.70	2.78	9.59V	36.04	20.60	27.68	30.81	50.90	48.89	49.40V
Russia....922	3.23	1.33	1.71	5.24	9.94	5.34	23.40V	173.11	185.58	223.17	390.31	375.47	567.59	526.46V
Serbia & Montenegro....965	.67	.79	.70	.05	.21	.64	.79Y	1.16	1.34	.77	2.20	2.54	.38	.47Y
Slovak Republic....936	.07	.14	.10	.31	.73	1.12	1.87V	2.52	2.02	2.58	4.12	8.81	7.72	15.20V
Tajikistan....923	—	—	—	—	.03	—	—V	.04	.07	.18	.05	.07	.38	—V
Turkey....186	65.35	56.02	79.65	86.21	106.64	121.26	208.21V	143.41	147.35	198.68	321.93	297.80	317.33	583.29V
Turkmenistan....925	.12	—	—	—	—	—	—Y	.30	.12	.02	.01	.01	.01	.01Y
Ukraine....926	4.58	2.24	.27	.57	.44	.29	.36Y	63.97	149.03	92.70	181.86	221.23	285.91	354.81Y
Uzbekistan....927	—	—	.01	—	—	—	—Y	2.75	2.26	.92	.95	1.58	.85	1.06Y
Europe n.s....884	.09	.06	.04	.14	.14	—	—Y	8.93	.09	.75	.03	.03	.05	.06Y
Middle East....407	**470.7**	**528.4**	**497.4**	**504.5**	**676.0**	**838.6**	**1,079.2Y**	**507.3**	**457.2**	**591.4**	**684.4**	**824.1**	**1,105.6**	**1,341.3Y**
Bahrain....419	7.96	8.51	5.96	8.51	10.84	13.35	16.57Y	8.15	6.42	8.11	6.14	7.73	11.46	14.22Y
Egypt....469	32.46	25.94	27.95	31.15	48.00	49.83	61.84Y	53.98	47.21	48.72	62.58	68.63	106.28	131.89Y
Iran, I.R. of....429	47.32	35.46	41.29	43.32	37.30	61.02	79.04Y	5.38	2.65	9.04	1.14	2.15	2.64	3.18Y

	Exports							Imports						
	2001	2002	2003	2004	2005	2006	2007	2001	2002	2003	2004	2005	2006	2007
	Millions of U.S. Dollars							*Millions of U.S. Dollars*						
Iraq........ 433	77.66	87.80	23.17	27.50	6.06	1.78	2.31Y	12.94	1.82	6.07	2.69	.09	—	—Y
Jordan........ 439	4.36	3.88	8.16	4.69	10.46	5.75	4.67V	6.54	6.58	6.19	7.10	9.63	8.73	12.82V
Kuwait........ 443	1.62	1.13	.47	.55	1.14	7.81	10.12Y	8.83	7.64	11.66	19.01	15.79	39.31	47.42Y
Lebanon........ 446	6.22	5.95	3.55	3.88	4.64	7.22	8.96Y	8.28	4.08	5.30	6.63	10.60	9.31	11.55Y
Libya........ 672	248.46	327.03	352.17	347.36	479.85	620.41	803.69Y	323.93	287.06	357.36	423.06	510.18	725.69	875.46Y
Oman........ 449	1.70	1.68	.22	1.43	.19	.33	.43Y	1.79	.87	1.64	5.96	4.86	4.56	5.50Y
Qatar........ 453	.69	.65	.24	.63	1.55	3.04	3.93Y	2.05	3.11	4.39	6.76	7.78	8.40	10.13Y
Saudi Arabia........ 456	23.67	17.86	25.34	23.90	50.87	41.36	53.58Y	44.25	60.33	103.79	113.18	107.99	121.94	147.11Y
Syrian Arab Republic........ 463	4.71	5.34	3.41	5.12	8.28	7.90	9.81Y	15.23	12.90	5.77	13.04	35.63	26.01	32.27Y
United Arab Emirates........ 466	11.69	5.22	5.02	5.70	15.82	16.73	21.68Y	15.49	15.42	22.47	15.25	41.75	40.27	48.59Y
Yemen, Republic of........ 474	2.18	1.94	.42	.74	1.05	2.04	2.54Y	.46	1.11	.91	1.92	1.31	.97	1.21Y
Western Hemisphere........ 207	**25.1**	**51.4**	**64.1**	**82.3**	**70.1**	**99.9**	**172.4Y**	**185.9**	**229.7**	**205.2**	**358.6**	**325.2**	**365.7**	**409.9Y**
Antigua and Barbuda........ 311	.52	.06	.01	.37	.17	—	—Y	.08	.01	.01	.01	.04	.02	.02Y
Argentina........ 213	3.59	11.66	15.11	10.93	3.53	12.84	12.27V	97.06	132.23	112.41	162.57	138.04	121.09	183.16V
Bahamas, The........ 313	.03	.04	.02	.04	—	.02	.02Y	—	.02	.01	.01	—	.02	.02Y
Barbados........ 316	.03	.03	—	—	—	.01	.01Y	.01	—	—	—	—	.01	.01Y
Belize........ 339	—	—	—	—	.77	—	—Y	—	—	.01	—	.04	.01	.01Y
Bermuda........ 319	.02	.33	.05	—	.16	.02	.02Y	.16	—	.03	.04	.02	—	—Y
Bolivia........ 218	.05	.13	.02	.15	.02	.02	.03Y	—	—	—	—	—	.03	.03Y
Brazil........ 223	18.50	32.21	44.28	65.02	47.76	70.76	121.04V	71.69	76.45	68.19	156.61	154.01	210.60	186.15V
Chile........ 228	.62	2.42	.05	.10	.04	.02	.95V	1.32	1.17	2.11	1.86	1.89	1.18	.03V
Colombia........ 233	.01	.02	.26	.11	.06	.18	—V	1.68	5.03	7.30	1.62	1.36	1.06	.06V
Costa Rica........ 238	—	.04	—	—	—	—	—Y	.36	.18	.19	.66	.62	.55	.69Y
Dominica........ 321	.03	—	.03	—	.04	.14	.18Y	—	—	—	—	—	—	—Y
Dominican Republic........ 243	—	—	—	—	—	—	—Y	1.22	.18	.09	.10	.15	.18	.23Y
Ecuador........ 248	—	.08	.02	.01	.02	.01	.01Y	3.19	4.17	4.23	13.52	4.61	4.54	5.63Y
El Salvador........ 253	—	.01	—	—	—	—	—V	—	—	—	—	—	.08	—V
Falkland Islands........ 323	—	.04	.01	.02	.04	.76	.94Y	.05	.06	—	.01	—	—	—Y
Greenland........ 326	—	—	—	—	—	.15	.19Y	—	—	—	—	—	—	—Y
Grenada........ 328	—	—	—	—	—	—	—Y	.02	—	.10	—	.02	—	—Y
Guatemala........ 258	.06	.16	.03	—	—	—	—Y	1.02	3.46	2.64	—	.01	.03	.04Y
Guyana........ 336	—	—	3.70	.41	.05	.13	.17Y	.11	—	—	.06	.09	—	—Y
Haiti........ 263	—	—	.01	—	—	—	—Y	—	—	—	—	—	—	—Y
Honduras........ 268	—	.01	—	.08	—	.45	.56Y	.01	.03	.01	.01	—	.02	.02Y
Jamaica........ 343	.01	—	—	—	.37	—	—V	.02	.22	.12	—	.01	—	—V
Mexico........ 273	.04	.10	.24	.89	1.44	2.76	22.21V	5.63	4.63	6.79	5.92	11.55	13.53	15.12V
Netherlands Antilles........ 353	.02	.01	—	—	5.44	.01	.02Y	.96	.20	.11	.03	.01	.02	.02Y
Panama........ 283	.21	.18	.07	1.71	.37	.85	—V	.98	.38	—	.20	.41	.97	—V
Paraguay........ 288	.02	.03	—	—	.01	—	—Y	.18	.23	.06	6.16	3.36	2.11	2.62Y
Peru........ 293	—	.09	.07	.08	.08	.05	.39Y	.13	.06	.11	.16	.25	.20	4.47Y
St. Vincent & Grens........ 364	.08	.04	.02	—	—	—	—Y	.01	—	—	—	—	—	—Y
Suriname........ 366	.06	.09	.05	.06	—	—	—Y	—	—	.01	—	—	—	—Y
Trinidad and Tobago........ 369	—	—	—	—	—	.01	.02Y	—	.01	—	.02	—	—	—Y
Uruguay........ 298	.27	3.15	—	2.20	9.46	10.12	12.56Y	.04	.07	.70	7.66	2.82	4.56	5.66Y
Venezuela, Rep. Bol........ 299	.89	.41	.04	.16	.31	.59	.80V	—	.72	—	1.32	5.72	4.74	5.72Y
Western Hem. n.s........ 399	—	—	—	—	—	—	—Y	—	.16	—	—	.17	.18	.20Y
Other Countries n.i.e........ 910	**15.2**	**3.5**	**3.7**	**—**	**—**	**—**	**—Y**	**14.8**	**15.1**	**9.8**	**6.8**	**2.0**	**4.9**	**6.1Y**
Cuba........ 928	15.15	3.52	3.61	—	—	.02	.02Y	13.48	13.98	8.85	5.80	.12	.28	.35Y
North Korea........ 954	.01	—	.07	.01	.02	—	.01Y	1.29	1.07	.95	1.00	1.89	4.66	5.79Y
Countries & Areas n.s........ 898	**221.1**	**226.9**	**229.5**	**266.2**	**298.1**	**279.0**	**346.3Y**	**144.2**	**140.4**	**172.8**	**53.2**	**69.5**	**69.5**	**86.3Y**
Special Categories........ 899	**53.6**	**30.5**	**44.7**	**28.2**	**87.5**	**30.1**	**37.3Y**	**3.4**	**7.3**	**13.2**	**11.4**	**45.2**	**63.7**	**79.1Y**
Memorandum Items														
European Union........ 998	5,295.35	5,414.55	6,502.76	8,064.11	8,521.57	9,023.77	1,157.29Y	6,807.71	6,757.27	7,880.04	8,885.21	9,226.03	9,743.68	4,265.68Y
Oil Exporting Ctys........ 999	498.31	573.87	555.55	562.99	790.47	956.08	1,233.23Y	520.04	483.37	664.07	759.10	852.10	1,185.68	1,422.64Y
Non-Oil Develop.Ctys........ 201	412.14	462.06	460.26	587.25	769.08	857.16	1,213.42Y	1,384.44	1,464.64	1,535.92	2,393.32	2,535.14	3,190.69	3,602.47Y
PERCENT DISTRIBUTION														
Industrial Countries........ 101	81.8	81.1	83.9	85.1	81.7	81.8	80.6	78.3	77.8	78.0	74.8	73.7	70.0	74.1
Developing Countries........ 202	13.8	15.1	12.7	11.9	14.7	15.5	16.8	20.0	20.5	20.2	24.6	25.4	29.1	25.1
Africa........ 607	2.8	3.1	3.0	2.9	4.0	4.0	4.1	2.2	2.2	2.2	2.2	2.0	2.2	2.0
Asia........ 507	2.1	2.3	1.3	1.6	2.1	2.0	1.9	4.9	4.6	4.7	5.8	6.3	7.1	5.2
Europe........ 170	1.4	1.2	1.3	1.3	1.5	1.5	2.2	5.7	6.5	6.0	8.4	8.5	10.1	9.1
Middle East........ 407	7.1	7.7	6.2	5.2	6.4	7.2	7.4	5.3	4.8	5.4	5.3	6.2	7.4	6.7
Western Hemisphere........ 207	.4	.7	.8	.9	.7	.9	1.2	2.0	2.4	1.9	2.8	2.4	2.4	2.0
Other Countries n.i.e........ 910	.2	.1	—	—	—	—	—	.2	.2	.1	.1	—	—	—
ANNUAL PERCENT CHANGE														
World........ 001	13.1	3.8	17.1	20.6	9.8	9.9	24.9	11.2	–.2	14.7	17.6	4.0	12.8	33.4
Industrial Countries........ 101	12.8	2.9	21.1	22.3	5.5	10.1	23.0	10.6	–.8	15.0	12.8	2.4	7.0	41.3
Developing Countries........ 202	10.7	13.8	–1.9	13.2	35.6	16.3	34.9	13.3	2.3	12.9	43.3	7.4	29.2	14.8
Africa........ 607	37.7	17.1	10.7	17.0	53.2	9.7	29.1	2.2	–1.7	15.6	19.0	–7.2	24.9	25.1
Asia........ 507	–9.5	14.4	–30.8	43.8	43.6	5.2	15.4	16.9	–5.2	17.1	45.1	12.5	26.1	–1.4
Europe........ 170	9.2	–10.2	27.3	19.7	26.1	5.1	86.5	23.5	14.4	5.7	65.9	5.1	33.7	19.9
Middle East........ 407	18.7	12.3	–5.9	1.4	34.0	24.0	28.7	–1.3	–9.9	29.4	15.7	20.4	34.1	21.3
Western Hemisphere........ 207	–54.3	104.9	24.8	28.5	–14.8	42.5	72.5	43.3	23.5	–10.6	74.7	–9.3	12.5	12.1
Other Countries n.i.e........ 910	21.1	–76.8	4.5	–99.7	140.3	–8.6	24.1	45.7	1.9	–34.9	–30.7	–70.4	146.0	24.1

	Exports							Imports						
	2001	2002	2003	2004	2005	2006	2007	2001	2002	2003	2004	2005	2006	2007
	Millions of U.S. Dollars							*Millions of U.S. Dollars*						
IFS World Total	**31,334**	**34,561**	**46,576**	**61,682**	**71,928**	**81,912**	**106,851**	**41,399**	**49,663**	**65,637**	**96,368**	**98,998**	**133,584**	**168,527**
DOTS World Total....001	**31,323**	**36,045**	**47,233**	**62,989**	**73,451**	**85,492**	**107,113**	**41,399**	**51,554**	**69,339**	**97,340**	**116,562**	**139,480**	**169,986**
Industrial Countries....101	**20,085**	**22,925**	**29,574**	**39,112**	**43,118**	**48,851**	**57,692**	**24,746**	**31,109**	**41,172**	**54,562**	**59,351**	**65,978**	**77,474**
United States....111	3,132	3,362	3,758	4,840	4,942	5,100	4,217	3,264	3,100	3,499	4,699	5,375	6,258	8,145
Canada....156	172	240	221	342	365	379	370	129	321	245	369	444	675	866
Australia....193	84	100	136	227	228	289	292	211	286	229	283	294	366	635
Japan....158	124	130	156	190	234	263	247	1,307	1,466	1,927	2,683	3,107	3,215	3,703
New Zealand....196	12	16	21	35	43	38	51	16	18	17	18	27	33	37
Austria....122	341	367	473	561	659	710	844	418	588	824	1,071	939	1,073	1,351
Belgium....124	688	693	886	1,183	1,292	1,381	1,736	985	1,150	1,524	1,992	2,231	2,476	2,869
Cyprus....423	—	—	—	—	6	12	8	—	—	—	—	—	—	—
Denmark....128	272	365	454	637	733	827	1,008	196	293	345	343	435	446	656
Finland....172	71	136	214	256	297	359	412	302	372	480	708	957	1,139	1,208
France....132	1,895	2,135	2,826	3,669	3,806	4,604	5,975	2,284	3,053	4,164	6,201	5,884	7,236	7,832
Germany....134	5,367	5,869	7,485	8,743	9,455	9,684	11,994	5,335	7,042	9,453	12,513	13,620	14,743	17,547
Greece....174	476	590	920	1,167	1,127	1,602	2,262	266	312	428	593	727	1,044	950
Iceland....176	3	3	10	10	18	22	11	2	3	2	9	8	5	6
Ireland....178	147	183	262	433	405	575	637	378	477	501	700	724	800	862
Italy....136	2,342	2,376	3,193	4,625	5,617	6,752	7,479	3,484	4,097	5,472	6,864	7,561	8,653	9,967
Luxembourg....137	—	16	13	20	28	24	74	—	133	368	533	122	94	151
Malta....181	63	142	157	98	279	227	621	9	28	73	73	46	21	99
Netherlands....138	892	1,056	1,526	2,134	2,470	2,539	3,018	1,042	1,311	1,657	1,908	2,142	2,158	2,655
Norway....142	70	115	171	206	245	261	375	251	366	423	474	373	496	496
Portugal....182	286	227	315	395	396	563	551	68	101	155	237	398	382	408
Slovenia....961	63	69	103	188	332	418	487	49	57	93	203	217	201	232
Spain....184	950	1,127	1,793	2,617	3,011	3,721	4,580	1,066	1,419	2,004	3,249	3,550	3,831	4,342
Sweden....144	214	296	458	561	662	787	883	544	535	822	1,118	1,426	1,487	1,716
Switzerland....146	243	289	353	436	553	901	935	1,227	2,143	2,968	3,404	4,054	4,013	5,269
United Kingdom....112	2,175	3,025	3,670	5,540	5,917	6,813	8,626	1,914	2,438	3,500	4,317	4,690	5,134	5,471
Developing Countries....202	**9,438**	**11,036**	**15,529**	**21,228**	**27,152**	**33,474**	**45,595**	**15,597**	**18,845**	**26,912**	**41,894**	**56,308**	**72,448**	**91,222**
Africa....607	**1,027**	**1,194**	**1,513**	**2,132**	**2,547**	**3,351**	**4,409**	**1,879**	**1,824**	**2,076**	**3,012**	**3,786**	**4,714**	**5,703**
Algeria....612	422	514	573	806	807	1,021	1,232	1,064	1,126	1,082	1,256	1,693	1,865	2,108
Angola....614	8	11	14	22	27	45	48	—	—	—	—	9	27	1
Benin....638	4	5	5	5	5	6	37	11	5	—	—	2	3	2
Botswana....616	—	—	—	—	—	—	1	—	—	—	—	—	—	1
Burkina Faso....748	1	2	3	3	4	4	5	1	1	1	2	—	3	7
Burundi....618	—	—	—	—	2	1	1	—	—	—	—	—	—	—
Cameroon....622	9	15	20	21	17	15	24	6	12	21	35	35	26	52
Cape Verde....624	3	7	6	5	3	5	8	—	—	—	—	—	—	—
Central African Rep....626	1	1	—	—	1	—	1	—	1	2	4	6	6	6
Chad....628	1	3	2	1	1	1	3	—	1	—	—	—	—	—
Comoros....632	—	—	—	2	2	2	2	—	—	—	2	1	2	13
Congo, Dem. Rep. of....636	1	1	1	2	2	4	4	—	—	—	—	—	1	1
Congo, Republic of....634	4	6	5	9	16	15	19	1	3	7	12	14	15	15
Côte d'Ivoire....662	9	15	14	14	27	30	32	17	32	44	43	31	44	86
Djibouti....611	7	4	5	9	7	11	45	—	—	—	—	—	—	—
Equatorial Guinea....642	—	—	—	2	5	11	10	—	1	2	2	6	34	46
Eritrea....643	5	10	15	19	12	15	20	....	....	....	....	....	....	....
Ethiopia....644	32	32	51	78	109	92	146	—	8	20	18	30	24	43
Gabon....646	2	4	3	3	5	6	23	7	7	8	18	23	15	24
Gambia, The....648	3	6	10	14	10	11	18	—	—	—	—	—	—	—
Ghana....652	18	23	37	32	32	33	84	36	39	95	81	73	57	41
Guinea....656	5	6	8	8	12	17	18	—	—	—	—	—	—	1
Guinea-Bissau....654	—	—	—	—	—	—	1	—	—	—	—	—	—	—
Kenya....664	10	8	13	18	51	85	98	3	2	2	2	2	4	12
Lesotho....666	—	—	—	—	1	1	1	—	—	—	—	—	—	—
Liberia....668	9	2	20	47	48	10	100	7	19	6	24	11	2	1
Madagascar....674	3	4	5	12	9	9	11	—	—	—	1	—	1	1
Malawi....676	—	—	2	2	2	1	2	4	2	8	21	16	15	28
Mali....678	3	3	5	6	10	8	12	—	—	—	—	3	1	2
Mauritania....682	4	12	4	6	10	9	11	—	1	2	4	1	—	8
Mauritius....684	1	1	2	4	6	8	23	1	1	2	9	10	6	9
Morocco....686	98	138	181	330	370	551	722	38	68	77	106	143	174	198
Mozambique....688	1	1	5	4	6	9	15	—	1	—	7	12	14	18
Namibia....728	1	1	—	1	—	1	1	—	—	—	3	1	3	6
Niger....692	1	1	2	3	4	4	11	—	—	—	—	—	1	1
Nigeria....694	69	63	66	80	99	83	133	228	182	223	177	234	380	494
Rwanda....714	1	—	—	1	—	1	3	—	—	1	—	—	—	—
São Tomé & Príncipe....716	—	—	—	—	1	—	—	1	—	—	—	1	—	—
Senegal....722	13	19	27	26	35	40	65	—	—	—	—	—	1	2
Seychelles....718	2	1	2	1	4	7	6	1	1	—	2	2	—	—
Sierra Leone....724	2	1	5	7	5	7	11	—	—	—	—	—	2	1

		Exports							Imports						
		2001	2002	2003	2004	2005	2006	2007	2001	2002	2003	2004	2005	2006	2007
		Millions of U.S. Dollars							*Millions of U.S. Dollars*						
Somalia	726	—	—	—	1	2	2	2	—	—	2	1	1	3	2
South Africa	199	78	88	122	190	316	598	654	345	211	336	1,004	1,260	1,793	2,172
Sudan	732	55	59	64	84	145	217	180	1	12	7	12	8	8	8
Swaziland	734	—	—	—	—	—	—	1	—	—	1	3	2	1	—
Tanzania	738	3	4	6	7	23	27	30	1	4	5	11	10	16	12
Togo	742	2	8	2	6	5	8	13	3	3	4	5	2	3	1
Tunisia	744	141	121	220	256	295	325	530	73	72	98	100	117	150	229
Uganda	746	1	—	1	3	4	7	9	1	1	1	3	12	6	6
Zambia	754	—	—	—	1	2	2	3	1	—	—	2	1	5	21
Zimbabwe	698	2	1	—	—	1	1	2	24	5	17	41	11	6	22
Asia	**507**	**862**	**1,260**	**1,579**	**1,523**	**1,868**	**2,322**	**3,037**	**3,354**	**4,618**	**7,157**	**11,924**	**16,410**	**20,670**	**27,458**
Afghanistan, I.S. of	512	7	20	36	71	113	91	109	—	1	3	7	8	10	13
Bangladesh	513	15	15	40	33	91	92	63	22	32	42	84	100	168	246
Brunei Darussalam	516	—	—	—	1	1	1	1	—	—	—	—	—	—	—
Cambodia	522	2	1	2	2	2	5	5	—	—	1	3	9	7	12
China,P.R.: Mainland	924	199	268	505	392	550	693	1,039	926	1,368	2,610	4,464	6,868	9,657	13,224
China,P.R.:Hong Kong	532	146	150	95	144	115	148	180	102	114	114	129	120	142	164
China,P.R.:Macao	546	2	2	1	1	—	1	1	2	3	5	6	3	5	7
French Polynesia	887	—	—	1	—	—	—	—	—	—	—	—	—	—	—
India	534	74	73	71	136	220	222	347	355	564	723	1,046	1,279	1,578	2,300
Indonesia	536	32	29	47	54	81	85	174	202	327	450	623	748	1,031	1,360
Korea	542	62	55	58	80	100	156	152	759	900	1,312	2,572	3,479	3,552	4,369
Lao People's Dem.Rep.	544	1	1	1	1	—	—	—	—	—	—	—	1	1	1
Malaysia	548	35	152	227	52	57	60	83	239	245	391	646	784	934	1,253
Maldives	556	—	—	—	1	2	2	1	—	—	—	—	—	—	—
Mongolia	948	1	2	1	3	4	6	10	—	—	2	1	—	1	—
Myanmar	518	—	1	—	—	2	1	1	1	1	2	3	3	7	12
Nepal	558	—	1	1	1	5	3	1	1	2	4	5	4	7	7
New Caledonia	839	3	—	1	1	1	1	2	—	—	—	—	—	—	—
Pakistan	564	31	57	70	86	188	130	157	101	118	192	240	315	379	532
Papua New Guinea	853	—	—	—	1	1	1	1	1	—	—	—	—	—	—
Philippines	566	13	15	27	36	31	43	40	36	44	60	112	117	130	196
Singapore	576	105	99	100	76	79	357	390	111	132	130	175	216	254	284
Sri Lanka	524	13	16	29	30	53	37	45	5	10	17	22	23	35	53
Taiwan Province of China	528	67	230	130	163	78	80	95	316	522	753	1,206	1,526	1,648	1,884
Thailand	578	37	45	108	124	51	61	63	152	195	292	500	676	936	1,229
Vanuatu	846	—	—	—	—	—	—	—	—	—	—	—	20	—	—
Vietnam	582	13	26	25	34	44	45	77	21	38	55	80	110	189	313
Europe	**170**	**3,798**	**4,679**	**6,562**	**8,962**	**11,642**	**15,571**	**22,367**	**6,165**	**7,904**	**11,181**	**18,574**	**24,479**	**32,029**	**41,853**
Albania	914	73	80	114	161	191	214	294	4	4	5	16	16	13	24
Azerbaijan	912	225	231	315	404	528	695	1,046	78	65	123	136	272	340	330
Belarus	913	20	20	20	25	50	65	96	11	21	29	42	47	45	80
Bosnia & Herzegovina	963	28	43	63	100	128	151	445	5	6	8	11	15	9	21
Bulgaria	918	299	380	622	893	1,179	1,568	2,061	394	508	689	955	1,190	1,662	1,950
Croatia	960	30	43	86	118	168	214	356	17	9	17	35	86	61	77
Czech Republic	935	109	130	189	222	290	378	578	127	317	444	655	698	680	1,169
Estonia	939	13	18	23	36	57	75	82	1	1	14	44	59	98	167
Faroe Islands	816	—	—	—	1	—	—	1	—	—	—	—	—	—	—
Georgia	915	144	103	155	200	272	408	646	127	138	274	303	303	345	289
Gibraltar	823	14	41	52	102	41	240	149	—	—	1	—	—	—	5
Hungary	944	170	201	285	350	379	486	776	187	326	417	705	945	1,285	1,423
Kazakhstan	916	120	160	234	356	460	697	1,080	90	204	267	441	558	994	1,284
Kyrgyz Republic	917	17	24	41	75	90	132	181	6	18	11	13	14	27	45
Latvia	941	16	20	27	38	81	77	105	—	—	1	1	3	8	36
Lithuania	946	33	54	86	123	149	167	236	78	110	136	171	159	145	122
Macedonia, FYR	962	90	101	123	149	162	173	272	9	15	27	52	52	56	55
Moldova	921	28	40	47	66	81	107	146	3	5	11	27	31	31	53
Poland	964	241	343	486	697	830	1,060	1,437	168	245	415	996	1,244	1,436	1,645
Romania	968	392	566	873	1,231	1,785	2,350	3,651	481	662	956	1,694	2,285	2,669	3,113
Russia	922	924	1,172	1,368	1,859	2,377	3,238	4,727	3,436	3,892	5,451	9,027	12,870	17,806	23,506
Serbia & Montenegro	965	81	122	185	211	258	363	615	7	11	30	87	97	52	74
Slovak Republic	936	28	33	60	109	123	170	285	49	112	206	233	377	437	648
Tajikistan	923	16	11	29	42	47	72	118	14	41	57	63	47	118	143
Turkmenistan	925	105	110	170	215	181	281	339	72	106	124	176	161	190	397
Ukraine	926	289	313	445	572	821	1,121	1,481	758	991	1,332	2,480	2,641	3,058	4,518
Uzbekistan	927	90	94	138	145	151	176	225	36	75	99	179	260	416	614
Europe n.s.	884	201	225	326	465	761	892	940	7	21	37	33	49	46	65
Middle East	**407**	**3,375**	**3,592**	**5,588**	**8,097**	**10,444**	**11,390**	**14,824**	**3,751**	**3,855**	**5,320**	**6,908**	**9,639**	**12,572**	**13,098**
Bahrain	419	11	17	29	54	42	35	77	15	19	15	18	19	45	119
Egypt	469	421	326	346	473	687	709	903	92	118	189	255	267	393	679
Iran, I.R. of	429	361	334	534	810	913	1,066	1,387	840	921	1,861	1,961	3,470	5,626	6,614
Iraq	433	—	—	829	1,815	2,749	2,589	2,812	—	—	113	468	459	376	645
Israel	436	805	861	1,083	1,309	1,467	1,529	1,658	529	544	459	714	803	782	1,081
Jordan	439	119	117	150	229	288	322	389	14	18	17	14	28	9	12
Kuwait	443	105	139	166	266	210	219	221	123	27	16	26	41	56	90
Lebanon	446	184	187	148	234	196	241	393	26	42	72	146	144	127	116
Libya	672	67	165	255	337	384	489	644	848	754	1,073	1,514	1,984	2,297	400

	Exports 2001	2002	2003	2004	2005	2006	2007	Imports 2001	2002	2003	2004	2005	2006	2007
	Millions of U.S. Dollars							*Millions of U.S. Dollars*						
Oman.......... 449	31	31	22	29	40	71	92	—	—	1	1	4	2	24
Qatar.......... 453	8	16	16	35	82	342	450	6	11	8	18	51	66	30
Saudi Arabia.......... 456	501	555	741	768	962	983	1,486	730	794	969	1,232	1,889	2,252	2,440
Syrian Arab Republic.......... 463	281	267	411	393	552	609	797	463	506	413	358	272	187	377
United Arab Emirates.......... 466	380	457	703	1,139	1,675	1,986	3,241	65	101	114	182	205	352	470
West Bank/Gaza Strip.......... 487	6	5	6	9	9	21	21	—	—	—	1	—	1	1
Yemen, Republic of.......... 474	100	119	156	204	197	198	274	—	—	—	1	3	—	—
Western Hemisphere.......... 207	**377**	**310**	**287**	**515**	**651**	**841**	**958**	**448**	**643**	**1,178**	**1,476**	**1,993**	**2,463**	**3,111**
Antigua and Barbuda.......... 311	—	4	18	1	23	1	4	—	—	1	—	—	—	—
Argentina.......... 213	23	2	11	20	38	44	64	70	112	265	265	261	301	418
Aruba.......... 314	—	—	—	—	1	—	—	1	—	—	—	—	—	11
Bahamas, The.......... 313	18	23	29	56	33	45	29	—	—	4	1	4	1	1
Barbados.......... 316	—	1	1	1	2	3	3	—	—	—	1	1	1	1
Belize.......... 339	—	—	—	1	1	1	2	1	—	1	1	1	1	2
Bermuda.......... 319	—	—	—	—	—	49	—	—	—	—	—	—	—	—
Bolivia.......... 218	—	1	1	1	—	1	2	—	—	—	1	—	—	2
Brazil.......... 223	90	49	50	69	103	122	230	212	236	402	566	797	934	1,173
Chile.......... 228	20	20	16	25	25	35	42	73	79	160	176	293	442	528
Colombia.......... 233	11	8	17	26	45	52	79	1	4	76	96	175	205	207
Costa Rica.......... 238	14	6	3	8	3	10	10	3	21	32	46	53	48	41
Dominica.......... 321	2	1	—	—	—	—	—	—	—	—	—	—	—	—
Dominican Republic.......... 243	19	15	4	17	6	8	7	—	1	1	3	3	3	4
Ecuador.......... 248	8	5	2	26	7	26	25	14	23	28	39	46	71	97
El Salvador.......... 253	5	1	1	1	2	2	1	—	1	—	—	3	—	—
Guatemala.......... 258	9	3	6	5	6	12	10	—	1	2	—	2	3	4
Guyana.......... 336	3	2	2	2	2	2	2	—	—	—	—	—	—	—
Haiti.......... 263	10	11	8	7	5	6	7	—	—	—	—	—	—	—
Honduras.......... 268	3	2	2	3	4	6	3	—	1	2	2	5	2	1
Jamaica.......... 343	11	12	16	19	13	22	15	—	—	—	—	—	—	—
Mexico.......... 273	52	77	40	151	164	141	197	31	52	100	117	196	262	352
Netherlands Antilles.......... 353	11	1	1	2	13	3	4	—	—	—	1	1	—	2
Nicaragua.......... 278	2	1	—	2	2	1	1	—	—	—	—	1	—	—
Panama.......... 283	29	23	20	34	84	78	117	2	17	20	31	10	10	23
Paraguay.......... 288	1	1	1	1	1	1	2	5	44	4	23	22	12	3
Peru.......... 293	9	14	7	7	7	9	15	17	12	22	49	37	61	70
St. Kitts and Nevis.......... 361	—	—	1	—	—	1	1	—	—	—	—	—	1	3
St. Vincent & Grens.......... 364	3	5	1	7	10	24	16	—	6	1	1	2	1	1
Suriname.......... 366	1	2	1	2	3	3	3	—	—	—	—	—	—	—
Trinidad and Tobago.......... 369	2	3	3	4	4	8	9	—	—	2	—	—	—	—
Uruguay.......... 298	5	2	2	2	3	4	8	16	18	36	12	20	16	36
Venezuela, Rep. Bol.......... 299	16	16	22	13	39	42	42	2	13	20	43	59	88	132
Western Hem. n.s.......... 399	—	—	—	2	1	79	7	—	1	—	—	—	—	—
Other Countries n.i.e.......... 910	**5**	**3**	**5**	**4**	**3**	**10**	**33**	**6**	**3**	**3**	**5**	**6**	**4**	**3**
Cuba.......... 928	4	2	3	2	2	9	32	—	—	—	—	2	1	1
North Korea.......... 954	1	2	1	1	1	1	1	5	2	2	5	4	3	2
Countries & Areas n.s.......... 898	**858**	**631**	**185**	**18**	**86**	**88**	**633**	**741**	**1,012**	**652**	**64**	**122**	**99**	**62**
Special Categories.......... 899	**934**	**1,438**	**1,928**	**2,562**	**2,973**	**2,967**	**2,940**	**303**	**575**	**589**	**811**	**758**	**944**	**1,221**
Memorandum Items														
European Union.......... 998	16,854	19,470	25,903	34,401	38,400	44,012	54,695	18,949	24,519	33,495	45,428	49,155	55,008	63,527
Oil Exporting Ctys.......... 999	1,992	2,318	3,974	6,153	8,040	8,977	11,913	4,108	4,254	5,929	7,500	10,837	14,392	14,807
Non-Oil Develop.Ctys.......... 201	7,446	8,718	11,555	15,075	19,112	24,498	33,682	11,489	14,591	20,983	34,394	45,471	58,057	76,415
PERCENT DISTRIBUTION														
Industrial Countries.......... 101	**64.1**	**63.6**	**62.6**	**62.1**	**58.7**	**57.1**	**53.9**	**59.8**	**60.3**	**59.4**	**56.1**	**50.9**	**47.3**	**45.6**
Developing Countries.......... 202	**30.1**	**30.6**	**32.9**	**33.7**	**37.0**	**39.2**	**42.6**	**37.7**	**36.6**	**38.8**	**43.0**	**48.3**	**51.9**	**53.7**
Africa.......... 607	**3.3**	**3.3**	**3.2**	**3.4**	**3.5**	**3.9**	**4.1**	**4.5**	**3.5**	**3.0**	**3.1**	**3.2**	**3.4**	**3.4**
Asia.......... 507	**2.8**	**3.5**	**3.3**	**2.4**	**2.5**	**2.7**	**2.8**	**8.1**	**9.0**	**10.3**	**12.2**	**14.1**	**14.8**	**16.2**
Europe.......... 170	**12.1**	**13.0**	**13.9**	**14.2**	**15.8**	**18.2**	**20.9**	**14.9**	**15.3**	**16.1**	**19.1**	**21.0**	**23.0**	**24.6**
Middle East.......... 407	**10.8**	**10.0**	**11.8**	**12.9**	**14.2**	**13.3**	**13.8**	**9.1**	**7.5**	**7.7**	**7.1**	**8.3**	**9.0**	**7.7**
Western Hemisphere.......... 207	**1.2**	**.9**	**.6**	**.8**	**.9**	**1.0**	**.9**	**1.1**	**1.2**	**1.7**	**1.5**	**1.7**	**1.8**	**1.8**
ANNUAL PERCENT CHANGE														
World.......... 001	**12.8**	**15.1**	**31.0**	**33.4**	**16.6**	**16.4**	**25.3**	**−24.0**	**24.5**	**34.5**	**40.4**	**19.7**	**19.7**	**21.9**
Industrial Countries.......... 101	**8.3**	**14.1**	**29.0**	**32.2**	**10.2**	**13.3**	**18.1**	**−27.1**	**25.7**	**32.3**	**32.5**	**8.8**	**11.2**	**17.4**
Developing Countries.......... 202	**19.0**	**16.9**	**40.7**	**36.7**	**27.9**	**23.3**	**36.2**	**−17.2**	**20.8**	**42.8**	**55.7**	**34.4**	**28.7**	**25.9**
Africa.......... 607	**14.0**	**16.2**	**26.7**	**40.9**	**19.5**	**31.6**	**31.6**	**5.1**	**−2.9**	**13.8**	**45.1**	**25.7**	**24.5**	**21.0**
Asia.......... 507	**7.7**	**46.3**	**25.3**	**−3.6**	**22.7**	**24.3**	**30.8**	**−29.4**	**37.7**	**55.0**	**66.6**	**37.6**	**26.0**	**32.8**
Europe.......... 170	**16.0**	**23.2**	**40.2**	**36.6**	**29.9**	**33.8**	**43.6**	**−19.0**	**28.2**	**41.5**	**66.1**	**31.8**	**30.8**	**30.7**
Middle East.......... 407	**26.1**	**6.4**	**55.6**	**44.9**	**29.0**	**9.1**	**30.2**	**−7.4**	**2.8**	**38.0**	**29.8**	**39.5**	**30.4**	**4.2**
Western Hemisphere.......... 207	**33.4**	**−17.7**	**−7.6**	**79.5**	**26.5**	**29.1**	**13.9**	**−28.8**	**43.6**	**83.2**	**25.2**	**35.0**	**23.6**	**26.3**
Other Countries n.i.e.......... 910	**53.5**	**−33.9**	**38.5**	**−26.5**	**−16.9**	**243.0**	**232.4**	**−42.2**	**−53.7**	**−2.8**	**113.2**	**4.9**	**−31.1**	**−22.5**

	Exports 2001	2002	2003	2004	2005	2006	2007	Imports 2001	2002	2003	2004	2005	2006	2007
	Millions of U.S. Dollars							Millions of U.S. Dollars						
DOTS World Total.................... 001	**2,555.0**	**2,815.7**	**3,449.1**	**4,062.6Y**	**5,698.7Y**	**6,229.9Y**	**7,283.4Y**	**2,210.0**	**2,127.9**	**2,510.9**	**2,729.3Y**	**2,703.2Y**	**2,780.8Y**	**3,637.1Y**
Industrial Countries................ 101	**612.4**	**668.1**	**755.9**	**387.1Y**	**499.3Y**	**492.1Y**	**531.9Y**	**701.9**	**371.2**	**379.9**	**939.4Y**	**721.0Y**	**675.6Y**	**799.9Y**
United States.............................. 111	31.70	48.97	56.51	78.73V	132.55V	73.64V	213.00V	208.80	137.33	47.13	323.84V	260.92V	124.08V	203.17V
Canada.. 156	.10	2.53	1.99	3.48V	3.21V	5.18V	.95V	2.90	7.61	.26	14.42V	30.19V	19.02V	7.88V
Australia..................................... 193	—	—	—	.17V	.13V	.88V	.05V	.80	.04	.31	.40V	.29V	.60V	.73V
Japan.. 158	—	.10	.19	.18V	.01V	.09V	.07V	161.20	8.29	3.37	56.21V	16.08V	57.48V	101.56V
New Zealand............................... 196	—	—	—	—V	.01V	—V	—V	—	—	.21	—V	—V	—V	—V
Austria.. 122	1.90	—	.10	12.35V	.28V	.24V	35.57V	15.80	4.88	16.51	19.05V	44.76V	8.75V	52.33V
Belgium...................................... 124	—	.29	.44	6.34V	2.85V	4.35V	1.20V	7.30	8.12	8.09	21.42V	16.21V	12.80V	18.46V
Cyprus.. 423	26.40	90.70	4.94	.01V	.01Y	—V	.01V	1.10	1.01	.25	—V	—V	.09V	—V
Denmark..................................... 128	—	—	—	—V	.01V	—V	—V	.10	.58	4.23	2.64V	6.47V	3.25V	7.41V
Finland.. 172	1.90	—	.42	.08V	.09V	.15V	.23V	6.80	5.00	8.98	3.67V	4.40V	6.87V	8.55V
France.. 132	3.60	3.52	1.10	5.70V	22.93V	38.87V	1.49V	10.90	32.60	82.63	136.44V	97.00V	95.47V	55.90V
Germany...................................... 134	5.10	4.01	11.62	41.66V	46.79V	41.31V	4.09V	197.90	103.75	106.28	219.53V	146.35V	215.36V	238.17V
Greece.. 174	.90	—	5.61	30.93V	49.13V	10.41V	25.10V	—	.05	.02	.15V	.13V	.38V	.57V
Iceland.. 176	—	—	—	.01V	.04V	.02V	.01V	.80	.62	.59	—V	—V	—V	—V
Ireland.. 178	—	.82	—	—V	—V	.04V	—V	.60	2.59	1.47	.08V	—V	.18V	.61V
Italy.. 136	473.00	486.85	624.78	158.17V	201.06V	220.98V	197.40V	2.30	7.23	3.81	81.77V	27.82V	34.90V	22.39V
Luxembourg................................ 137	—	20.03	20.89	—V	—V	.01V	—V	—	6.76	13.24	.18V	1.74V	.01V	.08V
Malta... 181	—	.02	—	—V	—V	—V	—V	—	—	2.95	3.93V	9.12V	3.03V	.01V
Netherlands................................ 138	1.10	1.65	.39	.02V	.27V	1.11V	.65V	39.30	8.48	8.04	19.05V	23.44V	21.48V	27.47V
Norway.. 142	—	—	—	.16V	.37V	.43V	.19V	.50	.35	.34	2.00V	.23V	26.99V	.65V
Portugal...................................... 182	—	—	—	6.23V	7.44V	9.17V	5.18V	—	—	.49	.08V	.72V	.18V	.01V
Slovenia...................................... 961	—	—	—	—Y	—V	1.35V	.06V	.10	.26	.32	.42Y	.52V	.77V	1.13V
Spain.. 184	—	2.05	.77	33.43V	24.83V	31.05V	8.70V	.80	.60	—	4.88V	2.15V	.63V	3.69V
Sweden....................................... 144	—	.05	.55	—V	.40V	7.00V	7.93V	1.20	.55	4.01	.95V	.45V	3.01V	2.88V
Switzerland................................. 146	47.30	3.81	18.28	.13V	.22V	.07V	.07V	20.10	13.41	49.04	5.52V	4.66V	8.45V	9.41V
United Kingdom.......................... 112	19.40	2.72	7.30	9.27V	6.68V	45.79V	30.01V	22.60	21.06	17.31	22.73V	27.30V	31.82V	36.79V
Developing Countries.............. 202	**1,942.6**	**2,068.0**	**2,421.3**	**3,604.4Y**	**5,118.1Y**	**5,637.4Y**	**6,626.8Y**	**1,504.4**	**1,454.2**	**1,977.9**	**1,783.0Y**	**1,974.4Y**	**2,095.4Y**	**2,825.2Y**
Africa.. 607	**.9**	**.3**	**.2**	**.3Y**	**.3Y**	**.4Y**	**.5Y**	**—**	**—**	**—**	**—Y**	**—Y**	**—Y**	**—Y**
Morocco...................................... 686	—	—	—	.02V	—V	.01Y	.01Y	—	—	—	—V	—V	—Y	—Y
Seychelles.................................. 718	.90	.28	.20	.26Y	.30Y	.37Y	.46Y	....	....	....	....	....	....	....
Tunisia.. 744	—	—	—	.01V	.01V	.01V	.01Y	—	—	—	—V	—V	—V	—Y
Asia... 507	**32.1**	**34.8**	**83.6**	**139.0Y**	**161.7Y**	**194.9Y**	**295.5Y**	**74.2**	**132.4**	**133.7**	**132.2Y**	**134.0Y**	**218.0Y**	**382.0Y**
Afghanistan, I.S. of..................... 512	21.90	28.56	73.76	96.87Y	110.68Y	136.80Y	169.76Y	1.20	.01	.25	.32Y	.37Y	.46Y	.57Y
Bangladesh................................. 513	—	—	—	11.00V	10.61V	13.39V	46.60V	—	—	—	—V	—V	—Y	—Y
China,P.R.: Mainland.................. 924	4.50	3.71	3.17	12.84V	17.26V	14.56V	44.68V	59.80	109.68	104.92	93.90V	99.49V	178.70V	332.49V
China,P.R.:Hong Kong................ 532	.10	.48	—	—V	.01V	.01V	.01V	.10	.68	.23	.75V	.81V	.86V	.53V
India.. 534	1.90	1.27	.57	9.23V	10.89V	13.46Y	16.71Y	7.20	15.27	18.59	17.33V	19.51V	24.12Y	29.93Y
Indonesia.................................... 536	—	—	—	.02V	.01V	.75V	.07V	.30	.26	2.15	.89V	1.02V	.13V	.66V
Korea.. 542	.10	—	—	.15V	1.21V	1.63V	.63V	1.80	.98	1.33	15.54V	7.09V	6.57V	7.57V
Malaysia..................................... 548	—	—	.30	.34V	.35V	.56V	.46V	.10	.49	.34	.70V	1.32V	2.77V	6.00V
New Caledonia........................... 839	—	—	—	—V	—Y	—Y	.01Y	....	....	....	....	....	....	....
Pakistan...................................... 564	—	.70	—	8.48V	10.49V	12.97Y	16.09Y	1.90	2.54	3.39	1.04V	1.08V	1.34Y	1.66Y
Singapore................................... 576	3.60	.02	5.85	—Y	—Y	—Y	—Y	1.60	2.14	1.77	—Y	—Y	—Y	—Y
Sri Lanka.................................... 524	—	—	—	—Y	—Y	—Y	—Y	.10	.07	.22	.29Y	.33Y	.40Y	.50Y
Taiwan Province of China............ 528	—	—	—	.09V	.14V	.27V	.44V	—	—	.09	.06V	.11V	.22V	.02V
Thailand...................................... 578	—	—	—	—V	—V	.47V	—V	.10	.22	.38	1.35V	2.86V	2.49V	2.03V
Europe...................................... 170	**1,580.3**	**1,608.5**	**1,683.4**	**2,612.6Y**	**3,879.7Y**	**4,119.7Y**	**4,625.0Y**	**1,088.9**	**1,039.4**	**1,524.3**	**1,221.1Y**	**1,276.8Y**	**1,168.6Y**	**1,597.3Y**
Armenia...................................... 911	2.30	2.12	1.16	93.70V	103.21V	10.78V	8.67V	18.10	4.51	17.22	.67V	1.14V	1.98V	2.77V
Azerbaijan.................................. 912	7.10	8.14	8.68	104.04V	220.86V	335.46V	36.63V	61.70	28.16	46.91	157.76V	300.94V	10.48V	14.96V
Belarus....................................... 913	1.10	.09	.06	.40V	.99V	.99V	.83V	12.20	26.57	45.65	18.64V	48.25V	15.98V	95.64V
Bulgaria...................................... 918	—	.04	1.12	1.30V	.03V	.07V	—V	5.40	4.65	4.46	1.11V	.84V	3.28V	1.16V
Croatia.. 960	—	—	—	.07V	.02V	.02V	.01V	—	—	—	.02V	.01V	2.24V	.15V
Czech Republic.......................... 935	.20	.59	—	1.41V	26.59V	.17V	.15V	5.00	7.25	10.37	11.43V	4.62V	8.61V	9.05V
Estonia....................................... 939	—	.08	.02	.02V	.23V	.80V	.65V	1.40	1.78	1.01	.10V	.28V	3.11V	1.80V
Georgia...................................... 915	3.00	10.61	15.12	29.70V	86.42V	91.87V	115.11Y	3.90	28.55	53.52	124.79V	83.41V	78.99V	76.35Y
Gibraltar..................................... 823	—	—	—	—Y	—Y	—Y	—Y	—	6.19	27.56	36.20Y	41.36Y	51.12Y	63.44Y
Hungary...................................... 944	—	—	.24	56.65V	300.30V	159.34V	.35V	8.10	1.84	1.85	2.21V	3.66V	12.32V	18.97V
Kazakhstan................................. 916	13.10	1.88	3.10	68.69V	78.48Y	97.00Y	120.37Y	15.10	26.55	76.73	28.70V	32.79Y	40.53Y	50.30Y
Kyrgyz Republic.......................... 917	6.90	1.13	.69	1.25V	11.85V	1.61V	1.03V	4.00	4.90	7.07	4.44V	3.11V	2.35V	1.85V
Latvia... 941	2.90	.02	5.81	.22V	.32V	.95V	.76V	3.90	2.11	4.61	.38V	1.25V	.84V	1.20V
Lithuania.................................... 946	—	—	.01	.57V	.02V	.43V	.15V	8.80	3.14	2.75	1.57V	1.30V	.47V	.55V
Macedonia, FYR......................... 962	—	—	—	—V	.03V	—V	—Y	—	—	.31	.02V	.69V	—V	—Y
Moldova...................................... 921	.50	.11	.76	.03V	—V	—Y	—Y	11.00	7.86	9.88	.60V	.59V	.73Y	.91Y
Poland.. 964	.20	.77	3.56	95.22V	71.39V	2.54V	1.21V	10.10	4.97	4.74	8.06V	22.53V	23.08V	18.42V
Romania..................................... 968	—	.02	.08	137.32V	129.01V	41.16V	121.28V	23.10	20.03	.83	4.15V	4.53V	9.78V	15.92V
Russia... 922	153.50	22.95	27.02	39.31V	69.91V	71.74V	62.83V	396.70	360.86	538.91	266.57V	246.45V	251.67V	422.60V
Slovak Republic.......................... 936	.50	.59	1.48	1.95Y	134.20V	47.89V	.31V	.20	.40	.36	.48Y	4.74V	.93V	.93V
Tajikistan.................................... 923	50.40	33.62	25.94	30.64V	48.91V	54.82V	34.73V	19.10	14.70	3.84	8.36V	—V	.07V	4.73V
Turkey... 186	126.80	168.14	224.71	159.71V	145.95V	172.94V	360.79V	163.60	233.49	236.56	236.32V	198.70V	309.46V	372.87V
Ukraine....................................... 926	1,198.00	1,346.08	1,352.96	1,776.10V	2,434.61V	3,009.00Y	3,734.14Y	264.90	213.26	382.68	247.57V	205.87V	254.44Y	315.75Y

	Exports							Imports						
	2001	2002	2003	2004	2005	2006	2007	2001	2002	2003	2004	2005	2006	2007
	Millions of U.S. Dollars							Millions of U.S. Dollars						
Uzbekistan........ 927	13.80	11.52	10.79	14.17Y	16.19Y	20.01Y	24.84Y	52.60	37.55	45.90	60.28Y	68.88Y	85.13Y	105.65Y
Yugoslavia n.s........ 966	—	.01	.08	.11Y	.12Y	.15Y	.18Y	—	.08	.56	.73Y	.84Y	1.03Y	1.28Y
Middle East........ 407	**311.7**	**391.6**	**603.2**	**785.9Y**	**1,000.4Y**	**1,234.1Y**	**1,598.2Y**	**330.9**	**267.3**	**311.9**	**414.5Y**	**553.4Y**	**692.0Y**	**837.4Y**
Bahrain........ 419	—	—	.01	.01Y	.01Y	.01Y	.01Y	....	....	....	....	....	....	....
Egypt........ 469	—	.01	.06	.07Y	.09Y	.11Y	.13Y	1.20	—	—	—Y	—Y	—Y	—Y
Iran, I.R. of........ 429	301.60	355.61	507.92	660.57Y	841.10Y	1,038.34Y	1,345.09Y	121.40	80.93	93.25	123.39Y	167.85Y	211.02Y	254.57Y
Israel........ 436	—	2.10	—	1.45V	1.45V	.91V	.73V	67.20	2.45	6.18	9.90V	2.86V	.11V	2.42V
Jordan........ 439	—	—	—	—V	.04V	.06V	—V	—	—	—	—V	.22V	.04V	.38V
Kuwait........ 443	—	.07	—	—Y	—Y	—Y	—Y	.10	.26	.19	.25Y	.34Y	.43Y	.52Y
Lebanon........ 446	—	.01	—	—Y	—Y	—Y	—Y	—	—	—	—Y	—Y	—Y	—Y
Qatar........ 453	....	....	....	....	....	....	....	—	—	—	.03V	—V	—V	—Y
Saudi Arabia........ 456	—	—	—	.02V	.06V	.07Y	.09Y	2.90	1.74	21.58	28.56Y	38.85Y	48.84Y	58.92Y
United Arab Emirates........ 466	10.10	33.85	95.20	123.81Y	157.65Y	194.62Y	252.11Y	138.10	181.92	190.70	252.35Y	343.27Y	431.55Y	520.61Y
Western Hemisphere........ 207	**17.6**	**32.8**	**50.9**	**66.6Y**	**76.1Y**	**88.2Y**	**107.7Y**	**10.4**	**15.2**	**8.1**	**15.2Y**	**10.2Y**	**16.8Y**	**8.5Y**
Argentina........ 213	—	—	—	—V	—V	—V	—V	—	—	—	—V	.01V	—V	2.18V
Bahamas, The........ 313	—	—	1.51	1.98Y	2.27Y	2.80Y	3.48Y	.10	.16	.01	.01Y	.02Y	.02Y	.02Y
Bermuda........ 319	15.30	17.36	42.11	55.30Y	63.19Y	78.10Y	96.92Y	—	—	—	—Y	—Y	—Y	—Y
Brazil........ 223	.40	.32	—	1.94V	3.37V	.06V	—V	.10	.40	1.73	8.82V	3.88V	10.43V	—V
Chile........ 228	—	—	—	.04V	—V	—V	.01V	—	—	—	—V	—V	—V	—V
Panama........ 283	—	—	—	—Y	—Y	—Y	—Y	.10	—	—	—Y	—Y	—Y	—Y
St. Kitts and Nevis........ 361	—	—	—	—Y	—Y	—Y	—Y	.20	.40	—	—Y	—Y	—Y	—Y
Western Hem. n.s........ 399	1.90	15.17	7.29	7.29Y	7.29Y	7.29Y	7.29Y	9.90	14.22	6.31	6.31Y	6.31Y	6.31Y	6.31Y
Other Countries n.i.e........ 910	**—**	**—**	**.1**	**.2Y**	**.2Y**	**.3Y**	**.3Y**	**3.7**	**1.3**	**4.9**	**6.5Y**	**7.4Y**	**9.2Y**	**11.4Y**
North Korea........ 954	—	.02	.14	.18Y	.21Y	.26Y	.32Y	3.70	1.30	4.94	6.48Y	7.41Y	9.16Y	11.36Y
Countries & Areas n.s........ 898	**—**	**8.5**	**54.0**	**70.9Y**	**81.1Y**	**100.2Y**	**124.3Y**	**—**	**.7**	**.1**	**.1Y**	**.1Y**	**.2Y**	**.2Y**
Special Categories........ 899	**—**	**71.1**	**217.7**	**—Y**	**—Y**	**—Y**	**—Y**	**—**	**300.5**	**147.9**	**—Y**	**—Y**	**—Y**	**—Y**
Memorandum Items														
European Union........ 998	537.10	614.77	690.05	460.22Y	895.84Y	623.93Y	321.18Y	344.30	225.03	304.31	561.20Y	446.96Y	488.37Y	527.38Y
Oil Exporting Ctys........ 999	311.70	389.53	603.12	784.43Y	998.81Y	1,233.78Y	1,597.36Y	262.80	265.11	307.88	405.47Y	551.33Y	691.97Y	835.28Y
Non-Oil Develop.Ctys........ 201	1,630.90	1,678.50	1,818.22	2,819.97Y	4,119.32Y	4,403.57Y	5,029.47Y	1,241.60	1,189.11	1,670.00	1,377.49Y	1,423.04Y	1,403.46Y	1,989.87Y
PERCENT DISTRIBUTION														
Industrial Countries........ 101	**24.0**	**23.7**	**21.9**	**9.5**	**8.8**	**7.9**	**7.3**	**31.8**	**17.4**	**15.1**	**34.4**	**26.7**	**24.3**	**22.0**
Developing Countries........ 202	**76.0**	**73.4**	**70.2**	**88.7**	**89.8**	**90.5**	**91.0**	**68.1**	**68.3**	**78.8**	**65.3**	**73.0**	**75.4**	**77.7**
Asia........ 507	**1.3**	**1.2**	**2.4**	**3.4**	**2.8**	**3.1**	**4.1**	**3.4**	**6.2**	**5.3**	**4.8**	**5.0**	**7.8**	**10.5**
Europe........ 170	**61.9**	**57.1**	**48.8**	**64.3**	**68.1**	**66.1**	**63.5**	**49.3**	**48.8**	**60.7**	**44.7**	**47.2**	**42.0**	**43.9**
Middle East........ 407	**12.2**	**13.9**	**17.5**	**19.3**	**17.6**	**19.8**	**21.9**	**15.0**	**12.6**	**12.4**	**15.2**	**20.5**	**24.9**	**23.0**
Western Hemisphere........ 207	**.7**	**1.2**	**1.5**	**1.6**	**1.3**	**1.4**	**1.5**	**.5**	**.7**	**.3**	**.6**	**.4**	**.6**	**.2**
Other Countries n.i.e........ 910	**—**	**—**	**—**	**—**	**—**	**—**	**—**	**.2**	**.1**	**.2**	**.2**	**.3**	**.3**	**.3**
ANNUAL PERCENT CHANGE														
World........ 001	**2.0**	**10.2**	**22.5**	**17.8**	**40.3**	**9.3**	**16.9**	**23.6**	**–3.7**	**18.0**	**8.7**	**–1.0**	**2.9**	**30.8**
Industrial Countries........ 101	**–2.0**	**9.1**	**13.1**	**–48.8**	**29.0**	**–1.4**	**8.1**	**81.7**	**–47.1**	**2.3**	**147.3**	**–23.3**	**–6.3**	**18.4**
Developing Countries........ 202	**5.4**	**6.5**	**17.1**	**48.9**	**42.0**	**10.1**	**17.6**	**16.3**	**–3.3**	**36.0**	**–9.9**	**10.7**	**6.1**	**34.8**
Africa........ 607	**–79.5**	**–69.2**	**–27.3**	**44.3**	**9.1**	**22.7**	**24.1**	**—**	**—**	**....**	**....**	**....**	**235.4**	**....**
Asia........ 507	**–34.5**	**8.3**	**140.7**	**66.2**	**16.3**	**20.5**	**51.6**	**107.3**	**78.4**	**1.0**	**–1.1**	**1.4**	**62.7**	**75.2**
Europe........ 170	**4.0**	**1.8**	**4.7**	**55.2**	**48.5**	**6.2**	**12.3**	**7.9**	**–4.5**	**46.7**	**–19.9**	**4.6**	**–8.5**	**36.7**
Middle East........ 407	**24.8**	**25.6**	**54.0**	**30.3**	**27.3**	**23.4**	**29.5**	**37.6**	**–19.2**	**16.7**	**32.9**	**33.5**	**25.0**	**21.0**
Western Hemisphere........ 207	**–10.2**	**86.6**	**55.0**	**30.8**	**14.3**	**15.9**	**22.0**	**30.0**	**46.0**	**–47.0**	**88.2**	**–32.6**	**64.0**	**–49.2**
Other Countries n.i.e........ 910	**....**	**....**	**....**	**....**	**....**	**....**	**....**	**23.3**	**–64.8**	**279.2**	**31.3**	**14.3**	**23.6**	**24.1**

		Exports							Imports						
		2001	2002	2003	2004	2005	2006	2007	2001	2002	2003	2004	2005	2006	2007
		Millions of U.S. Dollars							*Millions of U.S. Dollars*						
IFS World Total		**456.6**	**442.9**	**561.8**	**884.0**	**821.4**	**970.0**	**1,555.4**	**1,593.8**	**1,111.5**	**1,249.7**	**2,022.7**	**1,895.5**	**2,504.6**	**3,465.8**
DOTS World Total	**001**	**451.6**	**465.6**	**532.6**	**574.1Y**	**671.4Y**	**688.4Y**	**852.6Y**	**1,006.2**	**1,073.5**	**1,374.9**	**1,494.4Y**	**1,702.3Y**	**2,134.1Y**	**2,841.9Y**
Industrial Countries	**101**	**223.5**	**255.0**	**249.3**	**332.1Y**	**369.7Y**	**357.8Y**	**453.8Y**	**364.1**	**364.5**	**474.2**	**455.1Y**	**513.8Y**	**590.3Y**	**862.4Y**
United States	111	6.74	9.19	12.69	26.73V	26.27V	21.64V	25.64V	28.13	35.84	78.13	70.29V	68.75V	58.74V	88.44V
Canada	156	.94	.83	1.76	3.83V	2.57V	2.71V	2.38V	8.85	6.70	8.28	4.48V	9.15V	7.46V	13.39V
Australia	193	5.40	4.64	9.21	4.65V	4.13V	3.80V	6.72V	20.55	26.45	31.98	3.51V	2.43V	4.43V	4.88V
Japan	158	8.03	13.35	10.01	8.48V	6.83V	6.16V	9.56V	75.02	87.31	90.36	69.06V	67.09V	90.04V	137.44V
New Zealand	196	.02	.01	.12	.42V	.24V	.01V	.01V	.04	.23	.26	.19V	.08V	.17V	.18V
Austria	122	.55	.11	.34	.53V	.84V	.77V	.31V	1.88	.65	1.65	1.33V	1.46V	4.66V	9.73V
Belgium	124	16.09	21.90	12.90	62.09V	76.93V	68.26V	83.29V	15.74	16.59	23.09	47.83V	56.69V	39.25V	52.79V
Cyprus	423	—	.13	.56	.14V	.10Y	.19V	.28V	—	.03	.08	.51V	.62V	1.05V	1.08V
Denmark	128	.18	.86	.50	3.90V	2.98V	2.22V	3.27V	7.02	7.41	10.99	8.04V	5.24V	8.78V	9.77V
Finland	172	—	—	.02	.02V	.64V	—V	.22V	.97	1.93	1.91	6.08V	11.86V	24.79V	64.83V
France	132	4.07	6.87	5.13	30.23V	55.48V	54.32V	61.47V	25.88	12.86	15.67	38.34V	43.24V	56.46V	63.32V
Germany	134	13.92	13.40	12.02	30.01V	40.02V	52.84V	67.66V	38.21	30.31	39.15	43.50V	57.91V	73.39V	97.15V
Greece	174	.68	1.07	2.76	2.25V	3.05V	2.33V	4.55V	2.21	.24	.45	2.02V	7.82V	2.14V	2.03V
Iceland	176	.01	—	.13	—V	.05V	.10V	.08V	.08	.46	.71	—V	.70V	.02V	—V
Ireland	178	.06	—	.04	.03V	.04V	.20V	.35V	2.10	1.67	3.63	4.57V	4.40V	6.81V	11.94V
Italy	136	5.04	5.59	5.17	15.64V	15.04V	14.26V	31.36V	17.75	25.03	23.33	20.13V	23.89V	30.02V	53.04V
Luxembourg	137	—	1.09	2.15	3.47V	.28V	.22V	.25V	.02	.02	—	.28V	.12V	.03V	.19V
Malta	181	—	.06	—	—V	.04V	.10V	.10V	—	—	.05	—V	—V	—V	—V
Netherlands	138	52.80	56.00	48.96	73.80V	75.30V	64.39V	86.97V	14.84	18.84	25.02	22.59V	37.12V	32.90V	40.96V
Norway	142	.59	1.08	.20	1.48V	2.01V	1.75V	1.63V	4.48	2.04	1.04	2.87V	1.16V	.60V	2.93V
Portugal	182	.61	1.88	2.50	10.45V	10.93V	14.09V	16.61V	.21	.08	.19	.34V	.31V	.89V	.68V
Slovenia	961	—	—	.11	.15Y	.23V	.22V	.73V	—	.02	.06	.07Y	.05V	.03V	—V
Spain	184	7.96	17.73	14.53	21.57V	22.94V	20.97V	28.69V	3.17	3.96	15.89	9.13V	10.03V	9.06V	19.00V
Sweden	144	.37	.13	.65	.99V	.73V	1.67V	2.26V	18.11	9.15	8.81	22.17V	26.35V	25.10V	65.16V
Switzerland	146	70.67	69.01	73.00	9.18V	2.82V	2.94V	2.61V	6.63	8.92	7.06	4.43V	3.12V	34.37V	20.66V
United Kingdom	112	28.81	30.01	33.88	22.08V	19.16V	21.64V	16.79V	72.25	67.74	86.41	73.36V	74.23V	79.14V	102.81V
Developing Countries	**202**	**207.9**	**199.8**	**247.9**	**195.6Y**	**248.8Y**	**265.1Y**	**317.6Y**	**642.0**	**708.9**	**900.6**	**1,039.1Y**	**1,188.3Y**	**1,543.5Y**	**1,979.3Y**
Africa	**607**	**133.6**	**158.7**	**189.6**	**106.1Y**	**122.7Y**	**156.8Y**	**182.6Y**	**372.0**	**462.1**	**484.2**	**659.2Y**	**742.5Y**	**912.8Y**	**1,159.4Y**
Algeria	612	—	.01	—	—Y	—Y	—Y	—Y	—	—	.15	.20Y	.27Y	.34Y	.41Y
Angola	614	—	.19	.03	.03Y	.04Y	.05Y	.06Y	—	—	—	—Y	—Y	—Y	—Y
Benin	638	—	—	.12	—V	.27V	.33Y	.41Y	—	—	—	—V	—V	—Y	—Y
Botswana	616	.02	.01	.11	.15Y	.17Y	.21Y	.25Y	.09	.06	.13	.17Y	.19Y	.24Y	.29Y
Burkina Faso	748	—	—	.01	.01Y	.01Y	.02Y	.02Y	—	—	—	—Y	—Y	—Y	—Y
Burundi	618	4.78	6.27	10.08	10.04V	10.34V	15.38V	19.09Y	—	.06	.03	.76V	1.01V	1.29V	1.60Y
Cameroon	622	.02	.45	.14	.19Y	.21Y	.26Y	.33Y	.03	—	.04	.05Y	.05Y	.07Y	.08Y
Central African Rep.	626	—	—	.27	.35Y	.41Y	.50Y	.62Y	—	44.03	—	—Y	—Y	—Y	—Y
Chad	628	—	.02	—	—Y	—Y	—Y	—Y	.02	—	—	—Y	—Y	—Y	—Y
Congo, Dem. Rep. of	636	8.83	7.55	12.89	16.93Y	19.34Y	23.91Y	29.67Y	.04	.18	.30	.40Y	.45Y	.56Y	.69Y
Congo, Republic of	634	8.22	10.15	14.26	—V	—Y	—Y	—Y	.08	.10	.45	—V	—Y	—Y	—Y
Côte d'Ivoire	662	.22	.19	—	—V	.09V	.01V	.01Y	.07	.21	.15	1.13V	1.61V	2.43V	3.02Y
Djibouti	611	—	.02	—	.01Y	.01Y	.01Y	.01Y	.01	—	—	—Y	—Y	—Y	—Y
Eritrea	643	—	1.96	1.44	1.89Y	2.16Y	2.67Y	3.31Y	.15	.04	.08	.11Y	.13Y	.16Y	.19Y
Ethiopia	644	2.40	.22	.16	—V	—V	—Y	—Y	.04	.09	.06	.19V	.01V	.01Y	.02Y
Gambia, The	648	.05	—	—	—Y	—Y	—Y	—Y	—	.05	.05	.07Y	.08Y	.10Y	.12Y
Ghana	652	—	.02	.17	.22Y	.25Y	.31Y	.39Y	.01	.05	.06	.07Y	.08Y	.10Y	.13Y
Guinea	656	—	—	.04	—V	—Y	—Y	.01Y	.08	.01	.03	—V	—Y	—Y	—Y
Guinea-Bissau	654	.01	—	—	—Y	—Y	—Y	—Y	....	....	....	....	....	....	....
Kenya	664	59.06	61.50	78.43	11.60V	13.26Y	16.39Y	20.34Y	281.49	312.87	357.33	514.90V	588.31Y	727.11Y	902.34Y
Lesotho	666	.02	.01	—	—Y	—Y	—Y	—Y	—	—	.01	.01Y	.02Y	.02Y	.03Y
Liberia	668	.21	.74	—	—Y	—Y	—Y	—Y	.01	—	—	—Y	—Y	—Y	—Y
Malawi	676	.02	.09	.55	.72Y	.83Y	1.02Y	1.27Y	.19	—	.30	.40Y	.45Y	.56Y	.70Y
Mali	678	.02	.01	.02	.03Y	.03Y	.04Y	.04Y	.07	.02	.04	.05Y	.06Y	.08Y	.09Y
Mauritania	682	—	—	.21	.27Y	.31Y	.38Y	.47Y	—	—	—	—Y	—Y	—Y	—Y
Mauritius	684	.09	—	.79	.20V	.50V	.04V	.25V	.56	1.32	2.48	.22V	.63V	.46V	.74V
Morocco	686	—	.12	.59	1.83V	2.79V	3.45Y	4.28Y	—	.02	.06	—V	.04V	.04Y	.05Y
Mozambique	688	.07	.12	.06	.08Y	.09Y	.12Y	.15Y	—	.02	.24	.31Y	.35Y	.44Y	.54Y
Namibia	728	.01	.01	—	—Y	—Y	—Y	—Y	.02	.11	.20	.30Y	.40Y	.49Y	.59Y
Niger	692	—	.01	—	—V	—Y	—Y	—Y	—	.15	.06	—V	—Y	—Y	—Y
Nigeria	694	.50	.14	.11	.15Y	.19Y	.23Y	.30Y	.74	.24	.49	.65Y	.89Y	1.12Y	1.35Y
Rwanda	714	—	12.87	20.80	27.32Y	31.22Y	38.58Y	47.88Y	.35	1.37	.54	.70Y	.80Y	.99Y	1.23Y
St. Helena	856	—	—	—	—Y	—Y	—Y	—Y	.01	—	.01	.01Y	.01Y	.01Y	.02Y
São Tomé & Príncipe	716	.02	.04	—	—Y	—Y	—Y	—Y	.06	.02	—	—Y	—Y	—Y	—Y
Senegal	722	.04	.01	.04	.01V	.30V	.18V	.22Y	.03	.05	.07	.01V	—V	.01V	.01Y
Seychelles	718	—	1.06	—	—Y	—Y	—Y	—Y	.02	.10	—	—Y	—Y	—Y	—Y
Sierra Leone	724	.02	.04	.02	.02Y	.03Y	.03Y	.04Y	.20	.14	.02	.02Y	.03Y	.04Y	.04Y
Somalia	726	—	.05	.13	.17Y	.19Y	.24Y	.29Y	—	—	—	—Y	—Y	—Y	—Y
South Africa	199	24.08	43.00	29.63	5.96V	5.62V	5.72V	11.81V	72.85	83.66	98.98	94.32V	96.19V	114.75V	168.29V
Sacca exc. South Afr.	608	—	—	—	—Y	—Y	—Y	—Y	—	—	—	15.44V	17.64Y	21.80Y	27.05Y
Sudan	732	9.15	5.76	13.76	20.72V	26.56V	38.35V	30.76V	.14	.06	.01	—V	—V	—V	—V

		Exports							Imports						
		2001	2002	2003	2004	2005	2006	2007	2001	2002	2003	2004	2005	2006	2007
		Millions of U.S. Dollars							*Millions of U.S. Dollars*						
Swaziland	734	.27	.05	.04	.05Y	.05Y	.07Y	.08Y	5.23	8.21	10.00	13.14Y	15.01Y	18.55Y	23.02Y
Tanzania	738	6.69	5.77	5.83	7.66Y	8.75Y	10.82Y	13.42Y	6.65	7.51	10.79	14.17Y	16.19Y	20.01Y	24.83Y
Togo	742	—	—	.01	—V	.01V	.02Y	.02Y	.03	—	—	—V	—V	—Y	—Y
Tunisia	744	.05	—	—	1.17V	—V	.02V	.03Y	—	.15	.01	.05V	.03V	.10V	.13Y
Zambia	754	8.61	2.15	.25	.23V	.43V	.13V	.05V	1.60	.58	.21	.59V	1.05V	.89V	1.83V
Zimbabwe	698	.12	.05	.06	.01V	.39V	.04V	.05Y	1.30	.69	.85	.90V	.63V	.14V	.17Y
Asia	**507**	**38.9**	**24.2**	**30.6**	**42.4Y**	**58.2Y**	**49.3Y**	**61.5Y**	**184.7**	**161.0**	**291.6**	**210.1Y**	**224.8Y**	**324.4Y**	**434.2Y**
Afghanistan, I.S. of	512	—	.01	—	—Y	—Y	—Y	—Y	.02	.01	.09	.12Y	.14Y	.17Y	.22Y
American Samoa	859	....	....	....	....	....	....	....	—	.01	—	—Y	—Y	—Y	—Y
Bangladesh	513	—	—	.02	—V	—V	—V	—V	1.18	.93	.80	.51V	1.58V	1.70Y	2.11Y
Brunei Darussalam	516	—	.02	.01	.01Y	.01Y	.01Y	.01Y	—	.07	—	—Y	—Y	—Y	—Y
Cambodia	522	—	.01	.03	.04Y	.05Y	.06Y	.07Y	.04	—	—	—V	—V	—V	—Y
China,P.R.: Mainland	924	.24	.76	.82	11.32V	18.18V	16.09V	18.05V	36.23	—	70.25	81.00V	87.43V	151.64V	222.69V
China,P.R.:Hong Kong	532	26.51	13.36	12.30	11.19V	11.30V	11.00V	12.54V	19.65	17.45	16.80	4.94V	7.03V	9.87V	12.19V
China,P.R.:Macao	546	—	—	—	—V	—V	.01V	—V	—	—	—	.01V	—V	—V	—V
India	534	.33	.16	1.13	4.82V	3.42V	4.23Y	5.24Y	66.55	71.91	102.16	84.50V	95.90V	118.53Y	147.10Y
Indonesia	536	.13	—	—	4.68V	7.42V	4.25V	4.56V	4.02	3.79	4.69	3.03V	2.69V	3.24V	4.72V
Kiribati	826	.01	—	—	—Y	—Y	—Y	—Y	....	....	....	....	....	....	....
Korea	542	.27	.02	.84	1.85V	2.53V	1.54V	2.79V	4.91	4.76	6.97	5.68V	7.12V	9.50V	11.76V
Lao People's Dem.Rep	544	—	—	—	.01Y	.01Y	.01Y	.01Y	—	—	—	—Y	—Y	—Y	—Y
Malaysia	548	1.53	.46	.67	.43V	.16V	.32V	1.80V	23.16	32.06	42.06	6.31V	4.95V	7.07V	9.19V
Mongolia	948	—	—	.05	.06Y	.07Y	.09Y	.11Y	....	....	....	....	....	....	....
Pakistan	564	2.33	.46	.22	3.60V	6.01V	7.43Y	9.22Y	5.70	9.98	18.29	10.33V	4.02V	4.97Y	6.17Y
Papua New Guinea	853	—	—	.01	.01Y	.01Y	.01Y	.01Y	—	—	—	.01Y	.01Y	.01Y	.01Y
Philippines	566	—	—	—	—V	.32V	.26V	.02V	.05	.18	.12	.23V	.26V	.29V	.08V
Singapore	576	7.28	8.72	13.86	—V	—V	—V	—V	5.13	6.25	11.37	—V	—V	—V	—V
Solomon Islands	813	.11	—	—	—Y	—Y	—Y	—Y	....	....	....	....	....	....	....
Sri Lanka	524	—	.01	—	—Y	.01Y	.01Y	.01Y	.06	.35	.23	.31Y	.35Y	.43Y	.54Y
Taiwan Province of China	528	.15	.10	.50	2.79V	5.98V	1.28V	.56V	1.98	2.78	2.52	1.22V	1.99V	2.99V	2.31V
Thailand	578	.02	.05	.03	1.62V	2.74V	2.70V	6.53V	8.65	5.29	8.77	11.87V	11.33V	14.01V	15.11V
Vietnam	582	.03	.04	.09	—V	—V	—V	—V	7.33	5.20	6.48	—V	—V	—V	—V
Europe	**170**	**18.8**	**4.2**	**6.2**	**25.9Y**	**41.2Y**	**25.7Y**	**30.7Y**	**2.5**	**4.6**	**9.6**	**23.7Y**	**27.4Y**	**62.1Y**	**90.8Y**
Albania	914	—	.11	—	—V	—V	—V	—V	—	—	—	—V	—V	—V	—V
Armenia	911	—	—	—	—Y	—Y	—V	.03V	—	.01	—	—Y	—Y	—V	—V
Azerbaijan	912	....	....	....	....	....	....	....	—	—	.01	.02Y	.02Y	.03Y	.03Y
Belarus	913	.02	—	—	—V	—V	.01V	.01V	—	—	.01	.02V	—V	—V	.01V
Bulgaria	918	.67	.06	.01	.14V	.44V	.48V	.84V	.04	.08	.03	—V	.23V	2.25V	.39V
Czech Republic	935	—	.62	—	.62V	.91V	.16V	1.21V	.13	1.13	.70	2.45V	1.60V	1.98V	2.72V
Estonia	939	—	—	—	—V	—V	—V	—V	—	—	.05	—V	.04V	.02V	—V
Georgia	915	—	—	.03	—V	—V	—V	—Y	—	.05	.10	—V	—V	—V	—Y
Hungary	944	.70	.60	.96	3.24V	3.52V	2.96V	2.74V	.43	.51	.89	2.02V	5.42V	25.32V	33.77V
Kazakhstan	916	—	—	.08	.10Y	.12Y	.15Y	.18Y	—	—	1.26	1.65Y	1.89Y	2.34Y	2.90Y
Kyrgyz Republic	917	—	—	—	—V	—V	—V	—V	—	.02	—	—Y	—Y	—Y	—Y
Latvia	941	—	—	—	—V	.16V	.04V	—V	—	—	—	—V	—V	.08V	.34V
Lithuania	946	—	—	—	.07V	.04V	.06V	—V	—	—	—	.06V	.05V	—V	.12V
Macedonia, FYR	962	—	—	—	.31V	.11V	.11V	.14Y	—	—	—	—V	.01V	—V	—Y
Moldova	921	—	—	—	—V	—V	—Y	—Y	—	.04	.09	.12Y	.13Y	.16Y	.20Y
Poland	964	.29	.65	3.07	9.59V	13.23V	7.24V	7.46V	.12	.15	.19	1.35V	2.36V	2.49V	2.44V
Romania	968	16.62	.06	.03	1.75V	2.89V	3.28V	1.82V	.41	.23	.07	.25V	.60V	.55V	.61V
Russia	922	—	1.31	1.97	6.11V	6.83V	3.36V	8.05V	—	.49	3.11	.58V	.67V	7.72V	22.54V
Slovak Republic	936	—	.16	—	—Y	.14V	.44V	.02V	—	.03	.15	.19Y	1.74V	.76V	2.04V
Turkey	186	—	.03	—	3.00V	10.94V	5.13V	5.49V	—	.24	1.83	3.10V	4.25V	7.99V	9.78V
Turkmenistan	925	....	....	....	....	....	....	....	—	.10	—	—Y	—Y	—Y	—Y
Ukraine	926	.49	.60	.02	.92V	1.80V	2.23Y	2.77Y	1.41	1.47	1.10	11.86V	8.42V	10.41Y	12.92Y
Middle East	**407**	**15.2**	**11.1**	**21.2**	**20.6Y**	**25.7Y**	**31.9Y**	**41.0Y**	**73.9**	**78.4**	**108.1**	**137.7Y**	**185.5Y**	**235.7Y**	**284.6Y**
Bahrain	419	.01	—	—	—Y	—Y	—Y	—Y	.05	.01	.18	.23Y	.27Y	.33Y	.41Y
Egypt	469	5.28	1.95	2.67	3.51Y	4.01Y	4.96Y	6.15Y	4.58	4.53	6.43	8.45Y	9.65Y	11.93Y	14.80Y
Iran, I.R. of	429	—	.01	—	—Y	—Y	.01Y	.01Y	1.36	1.21	1.88	2.49Y	3.39Y	4.26Y	5.14Y
Iraq	433	—	—	—	—Y	—Y	—Y	—Y	.01	—	—	—Y	—Y	—Y	—Y
Israel	436	3.08	2.04	5.26	—V	—V	—V	—V	1.79	1.71	4.04	—V	—V	—V	—V
Jordan	439	—	—	—	—V	.25V	.45V	.64V	.09	.10	.13	.18V	.35V	.66V	.61V
Kuwait	443	—	—	.08	.10Y	.13Y	.16Y	.20Y	.87	1.31	2.14	2.83Y	3.84Y	4.83Y	5.83Y
Lebanon	446	.05	.05	.17	.22Y	.26Y	.32Y	.39Y	.15	.03	.07	.09Y	.11Y	.13Y	.16Y
Libya	672	—	—	.03	.03Y	.04Y	.05Y	.07Y	—	—	.01	.01Y	.01Y	.01Y	.02Y
Oman	449	.48	.08	.10	.13Y	.16Y	.20Y	.26Y	.41	.09	.29	.38Y	.52Y	.65Y	.78Y
Qatar	453	—	—	—	.25V	—V	.02V	.03Y	.17	.14	.16	.44V	.54V	3.12V	3.76Y
Saudi Arabia	456	.14	.04	.35	.03V	.07V	.09Y	.11Y	8.09	7.33	12.27	16.24Y	22.09Y	27.77Y	33.50Y
Syrian Arab Republic	463	—	—	—	—V	—Y	—Y	—Y	.06	.06	.10	—V	—Y	—Y	—Y
United Arab Emirates	466	6.12	6.91	12.53	16.29Y	20.74Y	25.61Y	33.17Y	56.26	61.92	80.42	106.41Y	144.75Y	181.98Y	219.53Y
Yemen, Republic of	474	—	—	.01	—V	—V	—Y	—Y	—	—	.04	—V	.02V	.02Y	.02Y
Western Hemisphere	**207**	**1.4**	**1.6**	**.4**	**.6Y**	**1.1Y**	**1.5Y**	**1.6Y**	**8.9**	**2.7**	**7.1**	**8.4Y**	**8.0Y**	**8.6Y**	**10.2Y**
Antigua and Barbuda	311	.02	—	—	—Y	—Y	—Y	—Y	—	—	1.07	1.41Y	1.61Y	1.99Y	2.47Y
Argentina	213	—	—	.01	—V	.28V	—V	—V	.86	.23	2.19	1.90V	.82V	2.56V	6.47V
Aruba	314	....	....	....	....	....	....	....	—	—	—	.01Y	.01Y	.01Y	.01Y
Barbados	316	—	—	—	—V	.01V	—V	—Y	—	—	—	—V	—V	—V	—Y
Belize	339	—	—	.01	.02Y	.02Y	.02Y	.03Y	—	—	.05	.06Y	.07Y	.09Y	.11Y
Brazil	223	.03	.05	.02	—V	—V	.84V	—V	3.83	1.51	3.12	3.95V	4.78V	2.68V	—V

	Exports 2001	2002	2003	2004	2005	2006	2007	Imports 2001	2002	2003	2004	2005	2006	2007
	Millions of U.S. Dollars							*Millions of U.S. Dollars*						
Chile 228	—	—	.08	—V	—V	—V	—V	—	—	.02	.11V	.01V	—V	—V
Colombia 233	.20	.29	.17	.15V	.14V	.16V	.03V	2.56	.03	.01	—V	.01V	.13V	.08V
Costa Rica 238	—	—	—	.01V	—V	—Y	—Y	.05	—	—	—Y	—Y	—Y	—Y
Dominica 321	.10	—	.02	.02Y	.03Y	.04Y	.04Y	.30	.09	.10	.13Y	.15Y	.19Y	.23Y
Dominican Republic 243	.10	.23	—	—Y	—Y	—Y	—Y	....	....	....	....	....	....	....
Ecuador 248	.03	—	—	.08V	—V	—V	—Y	.04	.28	—	.01V	—V	—V	—Y
El Salvador 253	....	....	....	....	....	....	....	.03	—	—	—Y	—Y	—Y	—Y
Grenada 328	—	—	.02	.02Y	.03Y	.03Y	.04Y	.04	—	.02	.03Y	.03Y	.04Y	.05Y
Guatemala 258	—	—	—	.10Y	.01V	.01Y	.01Y	.01	—	—	.47V	.01V	.02Y	.02Y
Guyana 336	—	—	—	—Y	—Y	—Y	—Y	.01	—	.03	.03Y	.04Y	.05Y	.06Y
Haiti 263	—	.01	—	—Y	—Y	—Y	—Y	—	—	—	—Y	—Y	—Y	—Y
Honduras 268	—	.01	.06	.19V	.22Y	.27Y	.34Y	—	—	.02	.02Y	.03Y	.03Y	.04Y
Jamaica 343	—	.02	—	—V	.07V	—V	—V	.06	.02	.10	.04V	.04V	—V	—V
Mexico 273	—	—	—	—V	.29V	.09V	1.13V	.18	.03	.17	—V	.20V	.51V	.34V
Netherlands Antilles 353	—	—	—	—Y	—Y	—Y	—Y	.01	—	.10	.13Y	.15Y	.18Y	.23Y
Nicaragua 278	—	.06	—	—V	—V	—V	—V	.03	.02	—	—Y	—Y	—Y	.01Y
Panama 283	—	—	—	—V	—V	—V	—V	.04	—	.03	.04Y	.05Y	.06Y	.07Y
St. Vincent & Grens 364	—	—	—	—Y	—Y	—Y	—Y	.04	—	—	—Y	—Y	—Y	—Y
Suriname 366	—	—	—	—Y	—Y	—Y	—Y	—	.10	—	—Y	—Y	—Y	—Y
Trinidad and Tobago 369	.03	.02	—	—Y	—Y	—Y	—Y	.66	.38	—	—Y	—Y	—Y	—Y
Venezuela, Rep. Bol 299	.88	.87	—	—Y	—Y	—Y	—Y	—	.02	.06	—V	—V	—V	—Y
Western Hem. n.s. 399	—	.05	—	—Y	—Y	—Y	—Y	.14	.02	.03	.03Y	.04Y	.04Y	.05Y
Other Countries n.i.e. 910	**.3**	**.2**	**.1**	**.1Y**	**.1Y**	**.2Y**	**.2Y**	**—**	**.2**	**.1**	**.1Y**	**.1Y**	**.2Y**	**.2Y**
Cuba 928	.23	.20	.10	.13Y	.14Y	.18Y	.22Y	.01	.02	—	—Y	—Y	—Y	.01Y
North Korea 954	.04	.03	—	—Y	—Y	—Y	—Y	.02	.19	.10	.13Y	.15Y	.18Y	.22Y
Countries & Areas n.s. 898	**19.9**	**10.6**	**35.2**	**46.2Y**	**52.8Y**	**65.3Y**	**81.0Y**	**—**	**—**	**—**	**—Y**	**—Y**	**—Y**	**—Y**
Memorandum Items														
European Union 998	132.13	158.87	146.25	290.86Y	342.74Y	329.60Y	416.61Y	221.04	198.34	258.33	306.37Y	372.54Y	425.14Y	635.91Y
Oil Exporting Ctys 999	8.26	8.08	13.19	21.66Y	28.76Y	30.62Y	38.71Y	71.93	76.05	102.55	132.67Y	178.98Y	227.31Y	275.04Y
Non-Oil Develop.Ctys 201	199.62	191.72	234.73	173.93Y	220.06Y	234.48Y	278.85Y	570.10	632.81	798.07	906.43Y	1,009.31Y	1,316.23Y	1,704.21Y
PERCENT DISTRIBUTION														
Industrial Countries 101	49.5	54.8	46.8	57.9	55.1	52.0	53.2	36.2	34.0	34.5	30.5	30.2	27.7	30.3
Developing Countries 202	46.0	42.9	46.6	34.1	37.1	38.5	37.2	63.8	66.0	65.5	69.5	69.8	72.3	69.6
Africa 607	29.6	34.1	35.6	18.5	18.3	22.8	21.4	37.0	43.0	35.2	44.1	43.6	42.8	40.8
Asia 507	8.6	5.2	5.7	7.4	8.7	7.2	7.2	18.4	15.0	21.2	14.1	13.2	15.2	15.3
Europe 170	4.2	.9	1.2	4.5	6.1	3.7	3.6	.3	.4	.7	1.6	1.6	2.9	3.2
Middle East 407	3.4	2.4	4.0	3.6	3.8	4.6	4.8	7.3	7.3	7.9	9.2	10.9	11.0	10.0
Western Hemisphere 207	.3	.3	.1	.1	.2	.2	.2	.9	.3	.5	.6	.5	.4	.4
Other Countries n.i.e. 910	.1	.1	—	—	—	—	—	—	—	—	—	—	—	—
ANNUAL PERCENT CHANGE														
World 001	12.4	3.1	14.4	7.8	17.0	2.5	23.9	5.0	6.7	28.1	8.7	13.9	25.4	33.2
Industrial Countries 101	.1	14.1	−2.2	33.2	11.3	−3.2	26.8	8.8	.1	30.1	−4.0	12.9	14.9	46.1
Developing Countries 202	25.1	−3.9	24.1	−21.1	27.2	6.5	19.8	3.0	10.4	27.1	15.4	14.4	29.9	28.2
Africa 607	7.3	18.8	19.5	−44.0	15.6	27.8	16.4	−2.8	24.2	4.8	36.2	12.6	22.9	27.0
Asia 507	25.0	−37.9	26.4	38.8	37.2	−15.3	24.8	18.0	−12.8	81.1	−28.0	7.0	44.3	33.8
Europe 170	873.7	−77.7	47.1	319.0	59.2	−37.7	19.8	−35.5	78.9	110.6	147.0	15.9	126.3	46.2
Middle East 407	98.3	−27.0	91.1	−2.9	24.7	24.1	28.8	11.6	6.1	37.9	27.4	34.7	27.0	20.7
Western Hemisphere 207	49.2	15.8	−76.3	60.0	79.1	34.0	11.5	−35.9	−69.4	161.5	18.0	−4.1	6.6	19.4
Other Countries n.i.e. 910	....	−11.3	−59.1	31.3	14.3	23.6	24.1	−74.3	601.4	−52.6	31.3	14.3	23.6	24.1

	Exports 2001	2002	2003	2004	2005	2006	2007	Imports 2001	2002	2003	2004	2005	2006	2007
	Millions of U.S. Dollars							Millions of U.S. Dollars						
IFS World Total	**16,265**	**17,957**	**23,067**	**32,666**	**34,228**	**38,368**	**49,296**	**15,775**	**16,977**	**23,020**	**28,997**	**36,136**	**45,039**	**60,618**
DOTS World Total....001	**16,263**	**17,943**	**24,267**	**32,629**	**33,959**	**39,413Y**	**51,964Y**	**15,777**	**16,977**	**24,091**	**28,995**	**36,153**	**58,537Y**	**75,649Y**
Industrial Countries....101	**3,918**	**4,578**	**6,199**	**8,387**	**7,563**	**8,609Y**	**9,964Y**	**4,378**	**5,076**	**7,176**	**8,286**	**10,399**	**18,829Y**	**25,157Y**
United States....111	569	519	719	1,507	956	1,604V	1,199V	458	473	499	571	710	832V	1,476V
Canada....156	28	41	36	83	90	172V	110V	23	23	74	44	87	103V	133V
Australia....193	3	2	2	7	10	21V	22V	46	50	52	56	104	67V	74V
Japan....158	67	83	88	100	82	153V	143V	165	185	378	423	548	743V	1,193V
New Zealand....196	4	2	2	4	4	4V	3V	1	1	1	1	2	6V	12V
Austria....122	174	237	258	249	317	361V	474V	202	224	324	353	458	994V	1,220V
Belgium....124	85	121	138	278	198	215V	209V	157	187	228	260	314	683V	865V
Cyprus....423	99	201	273	168	217	68V	46V	8	17	17	4	5	5V	11V
Denmark....128	30	37	58	115	107	131V	196V	93	102	151	163	176	283V	337V
Finland....172	38	30	27	31	29	35V	58V	127	168	295	274	351	641V	785V
France....132	103	113	158	204	200	314V	483V	296	349	530	655	799	1,096V	1,350V
Germany....134	711	755	1,423	1,891	1,285	1,334V	1,674V	1,380	1,658	2,273	2,773	3,384	6,803V	8,932V
Greece....174	138	103	152	118	137	242V	354V	39	39	47	55	68	96V	149V
Iceland....176	1	—	—	2	1	1V	2V	3	3	4	8	13	8V	13V
Ireland....178	3	2	4	8	7	9V	13V	29	25	27	29	45	33V	57V
Italy....136	840	839	1,285	1,638	1,898	2,475V	2,988V	412	463	646	880	1,031	2,310V	2,984V
Luxembourg....137	1	4	7	6	27	34V	6V	12	12	18	15	22	52V	34V
Malta....181	4	5	27	19	15	3V	4V	—	—	1	—	—	—V	—V
Netherlands....138	207	285	480	525	515	380V	609V	177	214	281	340	464	1,526V	2,182V
Norway....142	20	17	9	23	47	98V	84V	56	61	66	71	128	205V	253V
Portugal....182	23	82	45	27	20	48V	82V	8	10	16	22	28	27V	32V
Slovenia....961	11	13	24	15	32	32V	46V	46	69	93	114	125	215V	364V
Spain....184	245	373	211	522	574	519V	798V	88	102	154	174	234	357V	482V
Sweden....144	19	19	20	28	42	67V	76V	171	223	247	405	547	685V	780V
Switzerland....146	126	155	443	473	396	73V	90V	150	156	190	204	253	374V	491V
United Kingdom....112	368	537	310	347	358	215V	195V	229	263	565	392	503	684V	950V
Developing Countries....202	**12,336**	**13,354**	**18,058**	**24,230**	**26,374**	**30,776Y**	**41,965Y**	**11,379**	**11,890**	**16,895**	**20,694**	**25,750**	**39,704Y**	**50,486Y**
Africa....607	**568**	**691**	**937**	**1,352**	**1,523**	**1,908Y**	**2,415Y**	**188**	**170**	**240**	**259**	**388**	**446Y**	**574Y**
Algeria....612	173	217	351	594	617	762Y	987Y	4	3	4	4	5	6Y	7Y
Angola....614	8	4	3	2	5	6Y	8Y	—	—	—	—	—	—Y	—Y
Benin....638	1	8	1	2	6	8Y	10Y	—	—	—	—	—	—Y	—Y
Burkina Faso....748	1	1	7	9	12	15Y	18Y	—	—	—	—	—	—Y	—Y
Burundi....618	—	1	1	—	1	1Y	1Y	—	—	—	—	—	—Y	—Y
Cameroon....622	9	7	9	12	16	20Y	25Y	—	—	—	—	1	1Y	2Y
Cape Verde....624	—	—	—	—	1	1Y	1Y	—	—	—	—	—	—Y	—Y
Chad....628	4	6	7	6	4	6Y	7Y	1	—	—	—	—	—Y	—Y
Congo, Dem. Rep. of....636	1	2	—	—	—	—Y	—Y	—	—	—	—	—	—Y	—Y
Congo, Republic of....634	—	—	2	2	2	3Y	4Y	—	—	—	—	—	—Y	—Y
Côte d'Ivoire....662	9	13	11	10	12	15Y	19Y	20	36	57	42	41	51Y	63Y
Djibouti....611	—	—	1	—	11	13Y	16Y	—	—	—	—	—	—Y	—Y
Equatorial Guinea....642	1	1	—	2	—	—Y	1Y	—	—	—	—	—	—Y	—Y
Eritrea....643	1	14	4	5	8	10Y	12Y	—	—	—	—	—	—Y	—Y
Ethiopia....644	6	17	38	23	40	49Y	61Y	—	—	—	—	—	—Y	—Y
Gabon....646	—	—	1	1	1	1Y	1Y	—	3	14	61	75	93Y	116Y
Gambia, The....648	—	1	—	6	3	4Y	5Y	—	—	—	—	—	—Y	—Y
Ghana....652	18	10	12	21	24	30Y	37Y	40	31	68	55	55	69Y	85Y
Guinea....656	10	4	7	9	10	12Y	15Y	78	61	46	45	116	143Y	178Y
Kenya....664	2	7	6	15	27	33Y	41Y	—	1	—	—	1	1Y	1Y
Liberia....668	4	3	2	1	1	2Y	2Y	1	1	—	—	1	2Y	2Y
Madagascar....674	—	2	—	—	—	—Y	—Y	1	1	1	—	—	—Y	—Y
Malawi....676	—	—	—	—	—	—Y	—Y	8	6	7	11	9	12Y	15Y
Mali....678	3	3	15	13	15	18Y	23Y	—	—	—	—	—	—Y	—Y
Mauritania....682	13	25	10	9	17	21Y	25Y	2	2	1	2	6	7Y	9Y
Mauritius....684	2	—	1	—	—	1V	—V	1	—	—	—	—	—V	1V
Morocco....686	92	106	78	163	128	159Y	197Y	1	1	3	3	5	6Y	8Y
Mozambique....688	—	1	—	1	8	10Y	13Y	1	1	1	1	3	3Y	4Y
Namibia....728	—	1	9	5	—	—Y	—Y	—	—	—	1	1	2Y	3Y
Niger....692	—	—	—	1	1	1Y	1Y	—	—	—	—	—	—Y	—Y
Nigeria....694	134	90	194	180	212	262Y	340Y	2	1	1	1	2	2Y	3Y
Rwanda....714	—	—	—	1	—	—Y	—Y	—	—	—	—	—	—Y	—Y
São Tomé & Príncipe....716	—	—	—	—	—	1Y	1Y	—	—	—	—	—	—Y	—Y
Senegal....722	5	10	13	39	47	54V	67Y	—	—	—	—	—	—V	—Y
Seychelles....718	1	—	—	—	4	4Y	5Y	—	—	—	—	1	1Y	1Y
Sierra Leone....724	1	2	24	1	3	4Y	4Y	—	—	—	—	—	1Y	1Y
Somalia....726	—	—	—	1	3	4Y	5Y	—	—	—	—	—	—Y	—Y
South Africa....199	1	14	15	7	25	11V	17V	5	9	28	21	52	26V	58V
Sacca exc. South Afr....608	—	—	—	—	—	—Y	1Y	—	—	—	—	—	—Y	—Y
Sudan....732	9	14	30	48	51	80V	88V	—	—	—	—	—	5V	2V
Tanzania....738	3	3	2	6	16	20Y	24Y	2	3	2	3	5	6Y	8Y

		Exports 2001	Exports 2002	Exports 2003	Exports 2004	Exports 2005	Exports 2006	Exports 2007	Imports 2001	Imports 2002	Imports 2003	Imports 2004	Imports 2005	Imports 2006	Imports 2007
		Millions of U.S. Dollars							*Millions of U.S. Dollars*						
Togo	742	5	10	8	10	6	7Y	9Y	—	—	—	—	—	—Y	—Y
Tunisia	744	49	102	78	142	184	260V	323Y	10	4	—	2	1	—V	—Y
Uganda	746	1	1	1	11	8	9Y	12Y	—	—	1	1	2	2Y	3Y
Zambia	754	—	1	—	—	—	—V	—V	—	1	—	—	2	—V	—V
Zimbabwe	698	—	—	—	—	—	—V	—Y	10	5	5	5	3	4V	5Y
Asia	**507**	**1,630**	**2,399**	**2,763**	**3,371**	**3,307**	**3,118Y**	**3,936Y**	**581**	**703**	**1,166**	**1,671**	**3,361**	**6,547Y**	**10,261Y**
Afghanistan, I.S. of	512	4	6	8	11	7	9Y	11Y	—	—	—	—	—	—Y	—Y
Bangladesh	513	9	11	12	21	18	69V	27V	—	—	—	—	2	3Y	5Y
Cambodia	522	—	—	—	—	1	—V	—Y	—	—	—	—	1	2V	2Y
China,P.R.: Mainland	924	542	700	1,003	829	711	398V	605V	196	260	519	741	1,810	4,095V	6,453V
China,P.R.:Hong Kong	532	11	35	87	114	5	9V	14V	5	4	5	6	10	148V	224V
China,P.R.:Macao	546	—	—	—	—	—	1V	1V	—	—	—	—	—	—V	—V
India	534	130	158	203	482	737	911Y	1,130Y	96	111	154	234	321	397Y	493Y
Indonesia	536	119	148	207	283	216	314V	489V	38	68	58	79	124	228V	386V
Korea	542	131	185	182	358	202	199V	268V	102	126	229	327	649	973V	1,701V
Lao People's Dem.Rep	544	1	—	—	—	—	—Y	—Y	—	—	—	—	—	—Y	1Y
Malaysia	548	20	65	49	29	26	68V	97V	45	30	42	85	162	188V	285V
Mongolia	948	2	6	10	15	20	24Y	30Y	5	5	8	7	12	8Y	10Y
Myanmar	518	7	31	41	17	17	21Y	26Y	—	3	—	—	—	—Y	—Y
Nepal	558	2	2	1	5	2	8V	10Y	—	—	—	—	—	—Y	—Y
New Caledonia	839	—	—	—	—	—	—Y	—Y	4	1	—	24	16	20Y	25Y
Pakistan	564	33	25	93	168	274	339Y	420Y	3	3	4	9	10	12Y	15Y
Philippines	566	136	184	195	105	133	44V	17V	3	4	3	3	6	3V	4V
Singapore	576	93	126	132	286	490	360V	494V	9	8	16	11	18	98V	89V
Sri Lanka	524	13	3	10	14	26	32Y	40Y	18	17	19	18	23	29Y	36Y
Taiwan Province of China	528	132	245	151	213	135	164V	118V	25	28	48	67	97	169V	239V
Thailand	578	169	251	153	244	142	44V	105V	13	13	33	30	58	101V	166V
Vietnam	582	77	218	228	177	145	107V	35V	20	23	25	28	41	71V	128V
Europe	**170**	**8,259**	**8,399**	**11,015**	**15,673**	**17,435**	**20,608Y**	**29,277Y**	**10,274**	**10,587**	**13,832**	**18,282**	**21,360**	**32,033Y**	**38,846Y**
Albania	914	12	16	35	52	54	106V	99V	—	1	1	1	1	—V	—V
Armenia	911	22	33	50	71	97	148V	229V	11	7	6	8	13	25V	51V
Azerbaijan	912	46	105	143	216	290	289V	423V	8	5	8	9	28	42V	32V
Belarus	913	244	261	340	551	891	1,112V	1,395V	407	263	344	545	940	1,357V	1,619V
Bosnia & Herzegovina	963	11	22	12	7	15	19Y	23Y	—	—	1	1	3	4Y	5Y
Bulgaria	918	299	274	318	499	543	663V	1,960V	65	58	60	83	109	124V	251V
Croatia	960	30	8	20	52	60	73V	89V	7	11	19	17	19	30V	76V
Czech Republic	935	194	173	216	299	377	542V	567V	203	223	314	431	594	1,058V	1,309V
Estonia	939	56	87	364	278	125	95V	140V	67	52	68	80	103	163V	179V
Faroe Islands	816	—	—	—	—	—	—Y	—Y	—	—	—	1	5	6Y	7Y
Georgia	915	36	57	102	148	200	291V	412Y	11	16	40	19	41	63V	84Y
Gibraltar	823	4	17	2	7	—	—Y	—Y	—	—	—	—	—	—Y	—Y
Hungary	944	469	525	850	808	689	806V	1,209V	172	189	270	471	648	1,476V	2,118V
Kazakhstan	916	117	200	307	623	667	825Y	1,023Y	666	383	493	395	186	230Y	286Y
Kyrgyz Republic	917	5	6	12	21	32	38V	70V	3	4	4	5	6	5V	7V
Latvia	941	251	235	267	377	311	111V	155V	36	35	56	60	65	120V	137V
Lithuania	946	141	198	238	469	209	240V	307V	110	121	136	174	200	404V	517V
Macedonia, FYR	962	42	20	43	50	36	96V	119Y	1	1	2	2	3	2V	2Y
Moldova	921	274	302	486	660	679	839Y	1,041Y	64	56	57	67	84	104Y	129Y
Poland	964	497	506	763	980	1,010	1,192V	1,531V	451	537	802	1,008	1,406	4,407V	6,137V
Romania	968	266	338	497	732	489	646V	718V	28	29	46	91	212	469V	821V
Russia	922	3,680	3,189	4,311	5,886	7,490	8,399V	12,115V	5,813	6,317	8,646	12,128	12,843	16,473V	18,067V
Slovak Republic	936	243	292	289	398	508	512V	594V	140	136	201	243	304	601V	870V
Tajikistan	923	35	43	32	29	47	58V	48V	2	3	4	8	5	7V	9V
Turkey	186	1,009	1,235	902	1,869	2,027	2,780V	4,107V	138	196	312	374	608	1,234V	1,629V
Turkmenistan	925	107	113	177	225	187	231Y	287Y	1,654	1,886	1,746	1,954	2,678	3,310Y	4,108Y
Uzbekistan	927	109	68	84	129	151	186Y	231Y	193	28	160	70	205	254Y	315Y
Yugoslavia n.s.	966	61	75	153	240	251	310Y	385Y	23	28	35	37	53	66Y	81Y
Middle East	**407**	**1,470**	**1,497**	**1,684**	**2,919**	**3,607**	**4,281Y**	**5,346Y**	**82**	**74**	**101**	**145**	**175**	**273Y**	**340Y**
Bahrain	419	—	1	1	—	6	7Y	9Y	—	—	—	—	—	—Y	—Y
Egypt	469	204	318	292	368	799	987Y	1,225Y	10	7	9	20	37	46Y	57Y
Iran, I.R. of	429	161	165	296	435	577	712Y	923Y	3	7	9	9	18	23Y	28Y
Iraq	433	293	123	13	88	78	96Y	124Y	—	—	—	—	—	—Y	—Y
Israel	436	133	155	188	288	291	155V	141V	57	51	58	84	63	141V	178V
Jordan	439	45	55	78	289	182	255V	298V	2	1	6	7	11	7V	8V
Kuwait	443	1	10	16	16	16	20Y	26Y	—	—	—	—	1	1Y	1Y
Lebanon	446	99	60	87	76	102	127Y	157Y	1	1	1	2	2	2Y	3Y
Libya	672	104	32	18	33	64	79Y	102Y	—	—	—	—	1	1Y	2Y
Oman	449	3	1	2	15	48	59Y	77Y	—	—	—	2	—	1Y	1Y
Qatar	453	—	—	11	11	13	15V	20Y	—	—	—	—	—	—V	—Y
Saudi Arabia	456	124	183	237	242	386	477Y	618Y	3	1	2	2	3	4Y	5Y
Syrian Arab Republic	463	178	233	282	604	672	831Y	1,031Y	2	2	11	13	28	34Y	42Y
United Arab Emirates	466	118	148	137	426	345	426Y	552Y	2	3	5	5	10	13Y	16Y
Yemen, Republic of	474	6	13	27	29	28	35Y	43Y	—	—	—	—	—	—Y	—Y
Western Hemisphere	**207**	**409**	**368**	**1,659**	**915**	**502**	**861Y**	**992Y**	**253**	**357**	**1,556**	**337**	**466**	**405Y**	**465Y**
Antigua and Barbuda	311	—	—	6	—	—	—Y	—Y	—	—	3	—	—	—Y	—Y
Argentina	213	8	3	—	22	16	26V	108V	6	8	—	17	39	54V	88V
Aruba	314	—	—	7	—	—	—V	—V	—	—	14	—	—	—V	—V

		Exports							Imports						
		2001	2002	2003	2004	2005	2006	2007	2001	2002	2003	2004	2005	2006	2007
		Millions of U.S. Dollars							Millions of U.S. Dollars						
Bahamas, The	313	7	2	—	—	1	1Y	1Y	2	1	—	—	1	1Y	1Y
Barbados	316	—	—	—	1	12	—V	—Y	—	—	—	—	—	—V	—Y
Belize	339	—	2	—	—	15	19Y	23Y	—	1	1	—	—	—Y	—Y
Bermuda	319	—	—	1	—	—	—V	—Y	—	—	—	—	—	—Y	—Y
Bolivia	218	—	—	—	—	2	2Y	3Y	—	—	—	—	—	—Y	—Y
Brazil	223	36	48	178	189	110	151V	378V	112	134	361	270	312	243V	301V
Chile	228	13	16	20	47	38	65V	28V	1	2	2	3	10	17V	20V
Colombia	233	10	9	22	56	31	45V	50V	1	3	15	3	8	7V	5V
Costa Rica	238	5	12	10	30	10	12Y	15Y	2	—	1	1	5	6Y	7Y
Dominica	321	—	—	—	—	—	—Y	—Y	2	—	—	—	—	—Y	—Y
Dominican Republic	243	21	33	12	24	7	8Y	11Y	—	—	—	1	—	—Y	1Y
Ecuador	248	26	19	18	31	34	37V	46Y	15	17	22	19	66	6V	8Y
El Salvador	253	12	19	10	10	2	—V	—V	6	—	2	3	3	—V	—V
Guatemala	258	13	14	17	20	16	20Y	25Y	1	4	8	7	1	2Y	2Y
Guyana	336	—	—	—	—	—	—Y	—Y	15	2	2	—	—	—Y	—Y
Honduras	268	10	12	16	21	8	9Y	12Y	1	1	1	1	1	1Y	2Y
Jamaica	343	—	1	1	—	—	—V	—V	—	—	—	—	—	—V	—V
Mexico	273	67	49	44	188	117	378V	182V	2	4	5	5	8	16V	17V
Netherlands Antilles	353	—	—	—	1	—	—Y	—Y	—	—	—	—	—	—Y	—Y
Nicaragua	278	3	5	9	8	5	—V	—V	—	—	3	—	—	—Y	—Y
Panama	283	10	13	9	49	16	25V	—V	3	—	1	2	4	5Y	6Y
Peru	293	6	25	15	31	37	22V	40Y	2	1	6	3	3	43V	2Y
St. Kitts and Nevis	361	1	—	1	165	4	5Y	6Y	1	—	—	—	—	—Y	—Y
St. Vincent & Grens	364	5	1	—	—	5	6Y	7Y	—	—	2	—	—	—Y	—Y
Trinidad and Tobago	369	2	4	3	5	9	12Y	14Y	—	—	—	—	—	—Y	—Y
Uruguay	298	4	—	—	1	—	—Y	—Y	—	—	6	1	3	4Y	4Y
Venezuela, Rep. Bol.	299	14	9	15	18	8	16V	43V	—	1	—	—	—	—V	—Y
Western Hem. n.s.	399	135	71	1,248	—	—	—Y	—Y	83	176	1,102	—	—	—Y	—Y
Other Countries n.i.e.	**910**	**8**	**12**	**10**	**12**	**22**	**27Y**	**33Y**	**20**	**10**	**20**	**15**	**4**	**4Y**	**5Y**
Cuba	928	5	8	9	8	22	27Y	33Y	9	4	14	12	1	2Y	2Y
North Korea	954	3	3	1	4	—	—Y	—Y	11	6	5	2	2	3Y	3Y
Memorandum Items															
European Union	998	4,950	5,774	7,887	9,796	9,207	9,981Y	12,813Y	4,655	5,419	7,759	9,374	11,872	24,721Y	32,780Y
Oil Exporting Ctys	999	1,246	1,126	1,496	2,341	2,581	3,238Y	4,300Y	53	84	79	102	165	280Y	448Y
Non-Oil Develop.Ctys	201	11,091	12,228	16,561	21,889	23,793	27,538Y	37,665Y	11,325	11,806	16,817	20,592	25,585	39,424Y	50,039Y
PERCENT DISTRIBUTION															
Industrial Countries	**101**	**24.1**	**25.5**	**25.5**	**25.7**	**22.3**	**21.8**	**19.2**	**27.7**	**29.9**	**29.8**	**28.6**	**28.8**	**32.2**	**33.3**
Developing Countries	**202**	**75.9**	**74.4**	**74.4**	**74.3**	**77.7**	**78.1**	**80.8**	**72.1**	**70.0**	**70.1**	**71.4**	**71.2**	**67.8**	**66.7**
Africa	**607**	**3.5**	**3.9**	**3.9**	**4.1**	**4.5**	**4.8**	**4.6**	**1.2**	**1.0**	**1.0**	**.9**	**1.1**	**.8**	**.8**
Asia	**507**	**10.0**	**13.4**	**11.4**	**10.3**	**9.7**	**7.9**	**7.6**	**3.7**	**4.1**	**4.8**	**5.8**	**9.3**	**11.2**	**13.6**
Europe	**170**	**50.8**	**46.8**	**45.4**	**48.0**	**51.3**	**52.3**	**56.3**	**65.1**	**62.4**	**57.4**	**63.1**	**59.1**	**54.7**	**51.3**
Middle East	**407**	**9.0**	**8.3**	**6.9**	**8.9**	**10.6**	**10.9**	**10.3**	**.5**	**.4**	**.4**	**.5**	**.5**	**.5**	**.4**
Western Hemisphere	**207**	**2.5**	**2.1**	**6.8**	**2.8**	**1.5**	**2.2**	**1.9**	**1.6**	**2.1**	**6.5**	**1.2**	**1.3**	**.7**	**.6**
Other Countries n.i.e.	**910**	**—**	**.1**	**—**	**—**	**.1**	**.1**	**.1**	**.1**	**.1**	**.1**	**.1**	**—**	**—**	**—**
ANNUAL PERCENT CHANGE															
World	**001**	**11.6**	**10.3**	**35.2**	**34.5**	**4.1**	**16.1**	**31.8**	**13.1**	**7.6**	**41.9**	**20.4**	**24.7**	**61.9**	**29.2**
Industrial Countries	**101**	**9.2**	**16.8**	**35.4**	**35.3**	**–9.8**	**13.8**	**15.7**	**16.8**	**15.9**	**41.4**	**15.5**	**25.5**	**81.1**	**33.6**
Developing Countries	**202**	**12.4**	**8.3**	**35.2**	**34.2**	**8.9**	**16.7**	**36.4**	**11.6**	**4.5**	**42.1**	**22.5**	**24.4**	**54.2**	**27.2**
Africa	**607**	**11.6**	**21.7**	**35.6**	**44.3**	**12.7**	**25.3**	**26.5**	**42.1**	**–9.9**	**41.4**	**8.1**	**49.6**	**14.8**	**28.9**
Asia	**507**	**–2.5**	**47.2**	**15.2**	**22.0**	**–1.9**	**–5.7**	**26.3**	**26.5**	**21.0**	**65.8**	**43.3**	**101.2**	**94.8**	**56.7**
Europe	**170**	**10.1**	**1.7**	**31.1**	**42.3**	**11.2**	**18.2**	**42.1**	**10.1**	**3.0**	**30.7**	**32.2**	**16.8**	**50.0**	**21.3**
Middle East	**407**	**69.1**	**1.8**	**12.5**	**73.3**	**23.6**	**18.7**	**24.9**	**2.2**	**–10.3**	**37.3**	**42.8**	**20.7**	**56.4**	**24.7**
Western Hemisphere	**207**	**–2.7**	**–10.0**	**350.8**	**–44.8**	**–45.2**	**71.5**	**15.2**	**32.4**	**41.3**	**336.2**	**–78.3**	**38.1**	**–13.0**	**14.8**
Other Countries n.i.e.	**910**	**–55.9**	**49.9**	**–13.7**	**18.7**	**83.0**	**23.6**	**24.1**	**75.9**	**–49.2**	**92.5**	**–26.6**	**–75.5**	**23.6**	**24.1**

		Exports							Imports						
		2001	2002	2003	2004	2005	2006	2007	2001	2002	2003	2004	2005	2006	2007
		Millions of U.S. Dollars							Millions of U.S. Dollars						
IFS World Total		**48,414**	**52,163**	**67,135**	**90,997**	**117,287**	**142,505**	**154,000**	**37,293**	**42,652**	**52,074**	**72,082**	**84,654**	**97,864**	**121,100**
DOTS World Total	**001**	**39,879Y**	**39,136Y**	**50,096Y**	**66,788Y**	**93,182Y**	**112,758Y**	**125,238Y**	**29,608**	**30,353**	**38,827**	**74,752Y**	**99,709Y**	**115,160Y**	**146,038Y**
Industrial Countries	**101**	**15,806Y**	**14,447Y**	**18,960Y**	**24,627Y**	**35,762Y**	**38,487Y**	**41,040Y**	**16,876**	**17,596**	**20,222**	**35,738Y**	**49,842Y**	**56,019Y**	**68,140Y**
United States	111	1,167V	907V	1,103V	1,104V	1,401V	1,315V	1,267V	2,263	2,352	2,622	4,470V	9,324V	13,113V	12,770V
Canada	156	47V	19V	21V	71V	54V	84V	28V	163	225	219	347V	534V	765V	1,178V
Australia	193	438V	208V	633V	691V	296V	947V	1,821V	636	649	686	1,039V	1,039V	1,583V	2,822V
Japan	158	11,682V	10,552V	13,024V	16,658V	22,887V	28,836V	29,591V	2,345	2,635	3,406	5,071V	5,327V	6,646V	8,869V
New Zealand	196	108V	89V	289V	207V	315V	386V	366V	51	56	53	99V	127V	157V	195V
Austria	122	4V	5V	9V	8V	57V	53V	50V	82	93	154	305V	398V	576V	771V
Belgium	124	399V	387V	784V	1,370V	1,450V	1,443V	1,752V	506	499	—	1,291V	1,643V	1,985V	2,561V
Cyprus	423	11V	14V	24V	38V	83V	89V	66V	13	14	15	61V	37V	61V	21V
Denmark	128	47V	19V	57V	301V	683V	414V	177V	122	136	169	261V	264V	300V	348V
Finland	172	7V	3V	2V	5V	6V	7V	11V	201	219	371	1,375V	1,546V	1,146V	1,268V
France	132	440V	485V	495V	747V	1,530V	637V	721V	1,763	2,000	2,597	4,524V	4,678V	4,675V	5,463V
Germany	134	155V	156V	238V	364V	421V	616V	454V	2,241	2,161	3,124	4,860V	5,886V	7,064V	8,688V
Greece	174	12V	8V	34V	40V	37V	50V	55V	50	50	46	143V	283V	264V	305V
Iceland	176	—V	—V	1V	—V	—V	—V	1V	—	—	—	—V	—V	45V	82V
Ireland	178	26V	21V	27V	46V	32V	40V	37V	113	127	123	197V	208V	297V	433V
Italy	136	136V	103V	189V	286V	296V	304V	405V	1,386	1,544	1,681	2,921V	3,512V	4,587V	6,719V
Luxembourg	137	2V	2V	11V	28V	331V	373V	20V	9	14	—	35V	38V	91V	73V
Malta	181	4Y	1V	2V	4V	8V	8V	11V	22	16	13	12V	19V	13V	14V
Netherlands	138	138V	122V	252V	766V	2,966V	729V	1,344V	635	746	576	1,793V	2,234V	2,678V	3,506V
Norway	142	3V	4V	8V	9V	8V	16V	138V	47	55	64	160V	148V	197V	276V
Portugal	182	29V	6V	14V	6V	25V	20V	54V	23	26	41	51V	91V	73V	84V
Slovenia	961	—V	—V	—V	—Y	—V	1V	1V	14	14	21	27Y	46V	65V	113V
Spain	184	61V	127V	90V	101V	125V	97V	115V	302	354	443	655V	831V	1,103V	1,272V
Sweden	144	8V	11V	14V	19V	307V	27V	13V	237	274	277	428V	479V	658V	751V
Switzerland	146	63V	219V	212V	331V	468V	460V	246V	1,653	1,105	1,327	1,002V	1,239V	1,539V	1,806V
United Kingdom	112	817V	978V	1,425V	1,426V	1,974V	1,534V	2,296V	2,001	2,236	2,198	4,609V	9,909V	6,338V	7,753V
Developing Countries	**202**	**18,184Y**	**18,427Y**	**23,545Y**	**32,116Y**	**43,757Y**	**57,093Y**	**63,475Y**	**12,732**	**12,756**	**18,299**	**38,616Y**	**49,360Y**	**58,516Y**	**77,088Y**
Africa	**607**	**1,038Y**	**902Y**	**1,421Y**	**2,017Y**	**3,008Y**	**3,850Y**	**4,390Y**	**424**	**402**	**556**	**1,028Y**	**1,458Y**	**2,090Y**	**2,251Y**
Algeria	612	21V	47V	52Y	60Y	79Y	95Y	112Y	—	—	1	1Y	1Y	1Y	2Y
Benin	638	—V	1V	1V	7V	2V	2Y	3Y	—	—	—	1V	3V	4Y	5Y
Burkina Faso	748	—Y	—Y	—Y	—Y	—Y	1Y	1Y	—	—	—	—Y	—Y	—Y	—Y
Cameroon	622	—V	7V	5V	7Y	10Y	12Y	15Y	—	—	1	1Y	1Y	2Y	2Y
Comoros	632	4Y	5Y	6Y	7Y	10Y	13Y	15Y	—	—	—	—Y	—Y	—Y	—Y
Congo, Dem. Rep. of	636	—Y	—Y	—Y	—Y	—Y	—Y	—Y	—	—	—	—Y	—Y	1Y	1Y
Congo, Republic of	634	....	....	....	....	....	....	....	—	—	—	4V	6Y	7Y	9Y
Côte d'Ivoire	662	2V	2V	3V	4V	6V	11V	13Y	3	4	4	9V	7V	13V	17Y
Djibouti	611	10Y	11Y	13Y	18Y	24Y	30Y	36Y	—	—	5	7Y	9Y	11Y	14Y
Ethiopia	644	—V	—V	—V	—V	—V	—Y	—Y	—	—	34	—V	—V	—Y	—Y
Gabon	646	—Y	—Y	1Y	1Y	1Y	1Y	1Y	....	....	....	....	....	....	....
Gambia, The	648	3Y	3Y	3Y	5Y	6Y	8Y	9Y	—	—	—	—Y	—Y	—Y	—Y
Ghana	652	2Y	2Y	2Y	3Y	4Y	5Y	6Y	—	—	12	15Y	19Y	24Y	31Y
Guinea	656	5V	5Y	7V	8V	11Y	14Y	17Y	—	—	—	—V	—Y	—Y	—Y
Kenya	664	480V	335V	382V	517V	703Y	884Y	1,066Y	40	33	26	33V	42Y	52Y	68Y
Madagascar	674	54V	32V	24V	32Y	43Y	55Y	66Y	—	—	2	3Y	4Y	4Y	6Y
Mauritania	682	—Y	—Y	—Y	1Y	1Y	1Y	1Y	—	—	—	—Y	—Y	—Y	—Y
Mauritius	684	33V	53V	16V	57V	111V	95V	43V	—	—	1	31V	183V	273V	86V
Morocco	686	19V	19V	74V	49V	89V	112Y	135Y	8	10	17	15V	32V	39Y	51Y
Mozambique	688	12V	6V	10V	22V	38V	54V	65Y	1	1	1	1V	2V	4V	5Y
Niger	692	3V	3V	1V	2V	2Y	3Y	4Y	....	....	....	....	....	....	....
Nigeria	694	39V	60V	347V	399Y	530Y	635Y	749Y	2	2	13	15Y	20Y	23Y	28Y
Rwanda	714	5Y	6Y	7Y	9Y	12Y	15Y	18Y	—	—	—	—Y	—Y	1Y	1Y
Senegal	722	3V	6V	16V	26V	24V	14V	17Y	—	—	1	2V	5V	22V	29Y
Seychelles	718	20V	6V	6V	8Y	11Y	14Y	17Y	—	—	—	—Y	—Y	—Y	—Y
Somalia	726	13Y	14Y	17Y	22Y	30Y	37Y	45Y	42	37	80	104Y	133Y	164Y	212Y
South Africa	199	99V	67V	73V	108V	413V	570V	691V	280	205	267	374V	481V	608V	782V
Sacca exc. South Afr.	608	1V	1V	—V	—Y	—Y	—Y	—Y	—	—	—	1V	2Y	2Y	2Y
Sudan	732	14Y	15Y	78Y	217V	359V	404V	437V	—	—	33	94V	99V	250V	247V
Swaziland	734	—Y	—Y	—Y	—Y	—Y	—Y	—Y	—	—	—	—Y	—Y	1Y	1Y
Tanzania	738	99V	88V	107Y	142Y	193Y	242Y	292Y	13	11	36	46Y	59Y	73Y	95Y
Togo	742	5V	1V	1V	1V	1V	2Y	2Y	....	....	....	....	....	....	....
Tunisia	744	14V	14V	21V	14V	38V	37V	44Y	—	—	6	6V	17V	18V	24Y
Uganda	746	51V	56V	73V	97Y	132Y	165Y	200Y	—	—	13	16Y	21Y	26Y	33Y
Zambia	754	11V	15V	61V	133V	87V	285V	231V	—	—	—	1V	—V	89V	54V
Zimbabwe	698	5V	12V	4V	30V	25V	22V	26Y	—	—	4	13V	11V	11V	14Y
Africa n.s.	799	10Y	10Y	11Y	11Y	12Y	12Y	13Y	35	101	—	233Y	300Y	366Y	432Y
Asia	**507**	**11,995Y**	**11,435Y**	**15,623Y**	**21,782Y**	**29,555Y**	**39,066Y**	**42,302Y**	**8,521**	**9,162**	**12,407**	**27,984Y**	**35,229Y**	**41,604Y**	**55,824Y**
Afghanistan, I.S. of	512	2Y	2Y	3Y	4Y	5Y	6Y	8Y	—	—	3	4Y	5Y	7Y	9Y
Bangladesh	513	102V	138V	172V	198V	321V	356V	313V	13	14	12	22V	23V	23Y	31Y
Brunei Darussalam	516	2Y	2Y	3V	4Y	5Y	6Y	7Y	—	—	—	—Y	—Y	1Y	1Y

		Exports							Imports						
		2001	2002	2003	2004	2005	2006	2007	2001	2002	2003	2004	2005	2006	2007
		Millions of U.S. Dollars							Millions of U.S. Dollars						
Cambodia	522	—V	—V	—V	—V	1V	1V	1Y	—	—	—	2V	2V	2V	3Y
China,P.R.: Mainland	924	407V	405V	704V	1,176V	1,860V	2,542V	2,733V	2,229	2,477	3,805	7,396V	9,606V	12,553V	18,740V
China,P.R.:Hong Kong	532	620V	855V	1,085V	1,185V	1,205V	1,278V	1,366V	407	352	458	2,119V	2,113V	2,272V	2,851V
China,P.R.:Macao	546	—V	—V	—V	—V	—V	—V	—V	1	1	—	2V	—V	1V	2V
India	534	1,057Y	860V	1,622V	3,592V	3,995V	5,022Y	6,059Y	1,847	2,030	3,219	7,265V	9,110V	11,246Y	14,568Y
Indonesia	536	158V	105V	103V	309V	312V	314V	173V	533	586	567	819V	997V	1,175V	1,457V
Korea	542	4,212V	3,827V	5,233V	6,627V	9,108V	11,755V	11,506V	1,552	1,611	1,280	2,846V	3,006V	3,186V	4,075V
Malaysia	548	149V	128V	273V	411V	682V	881V	1,176V	334	384	702	1,709V	2,032V	2,497V	3,242V
Maldives	556	30V	25V	32V	61V	107V	134Y	162Y	—	—	—	—V	—V	—Y	—Y
Myanmar	518	—Y	—Y	—Y	—Y	—Y	—Y	—Y	—	—	11	14Y	18Y	22Y	29Y
Nepal	558	36V	5V	10V	5V	10V	14V	17Y	—	—	1	1V	2V	3V	3Y
New Caledonia	839	—V	—V	—V	—V	—Y	—Y	1Y	....	....	....	....	....	....	....
Pakistan	564	1,184V	1,198V	1,323V	1,611V	2,382V	2,994Y	3,612Y	303	332	405	1,080V	1,382V	1,706Y	2,210Y
Philippines	566	551V	335V	434V	91V	197V	324V	1,153V	62	60	69	117V	129V	181V	223V
Singapore	576	1,241V	1,429V	1,715V	1,688V	2,307V	3,800V	4,175V	758	795	665	2,093V	4,063V	3,513V	3,835V
Sri Lanka	524	137V	244V	164V	184V	269V	200V	303V	—	—	97	152V	187V	192V	230V
Taiwan Province of China	528	704V	545V	839V	1,205V	1,540V	2,829V	3,160V	—	—	531	1,178V	1,134V	1,236V	1,630V
Thailand	578	1,390V	1,298V	1,854V	3,374V	5,181V	6,562V	6,271V	482	521	543	1,061V	1,285V	1,635V	2,427V
Vietnam	582	9V	26V	49V	49V	63V	40V	100V	—	—	39	103V	134V	155V	258V
Asia n.s.	598	5Y	6Y	6Y	6Y	6Y	7Y	7Y	—	—	—	—Y	—Y	—Y	—Y
Europe	**170**	**337Y**	**449Y**	**510Y**	**661Y**	**845Y**	**1,208Y**	**1,419Y**	**632**	**266**	**1,482**	**4,223Y**	**5,430Y**	**5,909Y**	**8,056Y**
Albania	914	—V	2V	1V	1V	1V	1V	2V	—	—	—	—V	—V	—V	—V
Armenia	911	43V	39V	14V	12V	19V	17V	17V	2	3	3	10V	11V	6V	7V
Azerbaijan	912	17V	17V	24V	28V	30V	34V	46V	1	1	1	9V	17V	13V	5V
Belarus	913	1V	1V	1V	2V	2V	2V	3V	—	—	—	23V	5V	27V	18V
Bulgaria	918	1V	3V	24V	29V	9V	7V	21V	5	5	14	11V	24V	86V	20V
Croatia	960	1V	1V	1V	5V	2V	2V	12V	4	4	5	61V	128V	159V	95V
Czech Republic	935	11V	25V	58V	21V	20V	14V	22V	79	79	—	408V	536V	534V	598V
Czechoslovakia n.s.	937	....	....	....	....	....	....	....	—	—	103	134Y	170Y	210Y	272Y
Estonia	939	1V	1V	—V	1V	—V	—V	2V	—	—	1	2V	4V	7V	48V
Georgia	915	8V	6V	18V	42V	66V	99V	148Y	—	—	—	3V	4V	25V	32Y
Hungary	944	1V	1V	4V	4V	11V	16V	26V	19	19	191	649V	611V	501V	586V
Kazakhstan	916	31V	36V	23V	18V	25Y	31Y	38Y	11	7	7	35V	45Y	55Y	71Y
Kyrgyz Republic	917	6V	7V	7V	7V	5V	10V	12V	—	—	—	195V	190V	10V	15V
Latvia	941	2V	2V	2V	5V	4V	4V	2V	—	—	—	2V	2V	3V	9V
Lithuania	946	—V	—V	—V	2V	1V	6V	9V	1	1	1	2V	3V	5V	9V
Macedonia, FYR	962	2V	2V	3V	2V	3V	3V	4Y	—	—	1	2V	1V	—V	—Y
Moldova	921	—V	—V	1V	—V	1V	1Y	1Y	—	—	—	2V	2V	3Y	4Y
Poland	964	17V	25V	30V	46V	27V	27V	12V	35	34	57	103V	157V	243V	337V
Romania	968	2V	2V	2V	7V	5V	6V	20V	49	59	50	179V	279V	534V	503V
Russia	922	3V	13V	2V	12V	82V	170V	45V	49	49	259	530V	762V	507V	849V
Slovak Republic	936	1V	1V	1Y	1Y	2V	2V	2V	3	3	—	5Y	81V	112V	121V
Tajikistan	923	4V	6V	13V	15V	22V	30V	59V	5	3	—	—V	—V	—V	4V
Turkey	186	59V	92V	103V	166V	186V	320V	427V	320	—	713	1,253V	1,843V	2,184V	3,565V
Turkmenistan	925	126V	165V	173V	229Y	312Y	392Y	473Y	1	—	—	136Y	173Y	214Y	277Y
Ukraine	926	2V	2V	4V	4V	9V	12Y	14Y	47	—	76	469V	380V	469Y	607Y
Yugoslavia n.s.	966	....	....	....	....	....	....	....	—	—	1	1Y	2Y	2Y	3Y
Middle East	**407**	**4,671Y**	**5,537Y**	**5,959Y**	**7,566Y**	**10,238Y**	**12,554Y**	**14,915Y**	**2,874**	**2,651**	**3,167**	**4,247Y**	**5,937Y**	**7,325Y**	**8,946Y**
Bahrain	419	112Y	119Y	144Y	191Y	260Y	327Y	394Y	152	162	247	321Y	409Y	504Y	653Y
Egypt	469	101V	107Y	130Y	172Y	234Y	295Y	355Y	86	102	167	217Y	277Y	342Y	443Y
Iran, I.R. of	429	1,485V	1,957V	2,177Y	2,506Y	3,327Y	3,983Y	4,698Y	348	365	381	438Y	582Y	697Y	822Y
Iraq	433	—Y	—Y	—Y	—Y	—Y	—Y	—Y	—	—	2	3Y	3Y	4Y	5Y
Jordan	439	53V	71V	131V	132V	193V	195V	261V	115	118	191	126V	188V	321V	473V
Kuwait	443	275Y	260Y	289Y	332Y	441Y	528Y	623Y	104	105	178	204Y	271Y	325Y	383Y
Lebanon	446	47Y	50Y	60Y	80Y	109Y	137Y	165Y	114	117	164	213Y	271Y	335Y	434Y
Libya	672	27Y	25Y	28Y	33Y	43Y	52Y	61Y	8	5	99	114Y	151Y	180Y	213Y
Oman	449	1,496V	1,496V	1,289V	1,484Y	1,970Y	2,358Y	2,782Y	27	17	25	29Y	38Y	46Y	54Y
Qatar	453	178V	260V	297V	345V	588V	901V	1,063Y	139	129	181	678V	1,155V	1,450V	1,710Y
Saudi Arabia	456	576V	744V	871V	1,079V	1,422V	1,703Y	2,008Y	977	1,047	1,359	1,564Y	2,076Y	2,485Y	2,932Y
Syrian Arab Republic	463	42Y	45Y	55Y	608V	827Y	1,040Y	1,254Y	787	469	68	221V	281Y	347Y	449Y
Yemen, Republic of	474	280V	403V	488Y	604V	824V	1,036Y	1,250Y	18	16	107	120V	234V	289Y	374Y
Western Hemisphere	**207**	**142Y**	**104Y**	**32Y**	**89Y**	**111Y**	**416Y**	**449Y**	**282**	**276**	**688**	**1,133Y**	**1,306Y**	**1,588Y**	**2,012Y**
Argentina	213	29V	2V	2V	3V	1V	—V	16V	49	29	58	209V	238V	175V	210V
Bahamas, The	313	—Y	—Y	—Y	—Y	—Y	—Y	—Y	—	—	—	—Y	—Y	—Y	1Y
Barbados	316	—V	—V	—V	—V	—V	—V	—Y	—	—	—	—V	—V	—V	1Y
Bolivia	218	—V	—V	—V	—V	—V	—Y	—Y	—	—	—	2V	3Y	4Y	5Y
Brazil	223	104V	91V	19V	64V	77V	347V	320V	181	193	404	778V	801V	1,149V	1,316V
Chile	228	1V	1V	1V	1V	2V	13V	2V	32	34	52	61V	88V	67V	127V
Colombia	233	—V	—V	1V	1V	1V	1V	2V	2	2	1	5V	15V	6V	9V
Costa Rica	238	—V	—V	—V	1V	1V	1Y	1Y	—	—	2	1V	1V	2Y	2Y
Dominican Republic	243	1V	1Y	1Y	1Y	1Y	2Y	2Y	—	—	—	—Y	—Y	—Y	—Y
Ecuador	248	—V	—V	—V	—V	—V	—V	—Y	1	1	1	—V	—V	—V	—Y
El Salvador	253	—V	—V	1V	—V	—V	—V	—V	—	—	—	—V	—V	—V	—V
Guatemala	258	—V	2V	1V	1V	3V	4Y	5Y	—	—	14	8V	10V	13Y	17Y
Haiti	263	—V	—V	—V	—V	—Y	1Y	1Y	—	—	—	—Y	—Y	—Y	—Y
Honduras	268	1V	—V	1V	2V	3Y	4Y	5Y	—	—	—	—V	—Y	—Y	—Y
Jamaica	343	—V	—V	1V	1V	—V	—V	1V	—	1	—	—V	29V	—V	—V

	Exports 2001	2002	2003	2004	2005	2006	2007	Imports 2001	2002	2003	2004	2005	2006	2007
	Millions of U.S. Dollars							*Millions of U.S. Dollars*						
Mexico.......................... 273	—V	—V	—V	—V	9V	27V	73V	—	—	106	—V	36V	69V	192V
Panama.......................... 283	—V	—V	—V	—V	—V	—V	—V	1	1	—	—V	—V	—V	—V
Paraguay.......................... 288	—V	—V	—V	—V	—V	—V	—Y	—	—	1	3V	3V	1V	2Y
Peru.......................... 293	—V	1V	1V	6V	1V	—V	—Y	16	15	1	1V	2V	3V	4Y
St. Lucia.......................... 362	—Y	—Y	—Y	—Y	—Y	—Y	1Y	—	—	—	—Y	—Y	—Y	—Y
Suriname.......................... 366	—Y	—Y	—Y	—Y	—Y	—Y	—Y	—	—	46	60Y	76Y	94Y	122Y
Trinidad and Tobago.......................... 369	—V	—V	—Y	—Y	—Y	1Y	1Y	—	1	—	—Y	—Y	—Y	—Y
Uruguay.......................... 298	4V	4Y	—V	—V	—V	—Y	—Y	—	—	1	2V	1V	2Y	2Y
Venezuela, Rep. Bol.......................... 299	1V	1V	3V	7V	9V	12V	20V	—	—	2	4V	1V	2V	2Y
Other Countries n.i.e.......................... 910	**—Y**	**—Y**	**—Y**	**—Y**	**—Y**	**—Y**	**—Y**	**—**	**—**	**1**	**1Y**	**1Y**	**2Y**	**2Y**
Cuba.......................... 928	—Y	—Y	—Y	—Y	—Y	—Y	—Y	—	—	1	1Y	1Y	2Y	2Y
Countries & Areas n.s.......................... 898	**5,889Y**	**6,262Y**	**7,591Y**	**10,045Y**	**13,664Y**	**17,178Y**	**20,723Y**	**—**	**—**	**305**	**397Y**	**505Y**	**624Y**	**808Y**
Memorandum Items														
European Union.......................... 998	2,330Y	2,504Y	3,764Y	5,638Y	10,397Y	6,513Y	7,658Y	9,857	10,657	12,096	24,720Y	33,498Y	33,378Y	41,849Y
Oil Exporting Ctys.......................... 999	4,255Y	4,953Y	5,455Y	6,555Y	8,722Y	10,580Y	12,289Y	2,138	2,255	2,807	3,868Y	5,296Y	6,389Y	7,608Y
Non-Oil Develop.Ctys.......................... 201	13,929Y	13,473Y	18,090Y	25,561Y	35,034Y	46,513Y	51,186Y	10,594	10,501	15,493	34,748Y	44,064Y	52,127Y	69,481Y
PERCENT DISTRIBUTION														
Industrial Countries.......................... 101	**39.6**	**36.9**	**37.8**	**36.9**	**38.4**	**34.1**	**32.8**	**57.0**	**58.0**	**52.1**	**47.8**	**50.0**	**48.6**	**46.7**
Developing Countries.......................... 202	**45.6**	**47.1**	**47.0**	**48.1**	**47.0**	**50.6**	**50.7**	**43.0**	**42.0**	**47.1**	**51.7**	**49.5**	**50.8**	**52.8**
Africa.......................... 607	**2.6**	**2.3**	**2.8**	**3.0**	**3.2**	**3.4**	**3.5**	**1.4**	**1.3**	**1.4**	**1.4**	**1.5**	**1.8**	**1.5**
Asia.......................... 507	**30.1**	**29.2**	**31.2**	**32.6**	**31.7**	**34.6**	**33.8**	**28.8**	**30.2**	**32.0**	**37.4**	**35.3**	**36.1**	**38.2**
Europe.......................... 170	**.8**	**1.1**	**1.0**	**1.0**	**.9**	**1.1**	**1.1**	**2.1**	**.9**	**3.8**	**5.6**	**5.4**	**5.1**	**5.5**
Middle East.......................... 407	**11.7**	**14.1**	**11.9**	**11.3**	**11.0**	**11.1**	**11.9**	**9.7**	**8.7**	**8.2**	**5.7**	**6.0**	**6.4**	**6.1**
Western Hemisphere.......................... 207	**.4**	**.3**	**.1**	**.1**	**.1**	**.4**	**.4**	**1.0**	**.9**	**1.8**	**1.5**	**1.3**	**1.4**	**1.4**
ANNUAL PERCENT CHANGE														
World.......................... 001	**–2.3**	**–1.9**	**28.0**	**33.3**	**39.5**	**21.0**	**11.1**	**16.3**	**2.5**	**27.9**	**92.5**	**33.4**	**15.5**	**26.8**
Industrial Countries.......................... 101	**–8.4**	**–8.6**	**31.2**	**29.9**	**45.2**	**7.6**	**6.6**	**12.2**	**4.3**	**14.9**	**76.7**	**39.5**	**12.4**	**21.6**
Developing Countries.......................... 202	**.5**	**1.3**	**27.8**	**36.4**	**36.2**	**30.5**	**11.2**	**22.1**	**.2**	**43.5**	**111.0**	**27.8**	**18.5**	**31.7**
Africa.......................... 607	**–28.4**	**–13.1**	**57.6**	**41.9**	**49.1**	**28.0**	**14.0**	**51.5**	**–5.2**	**38.4**	**85.0**	**41.8**	**43.4**	**7.7**
Asia.......................... 507	**–2.3**	**–4.7**	**36.6**	**39.4**	**35.7**	**32.2**	**8.3**	**12.8**	**7.5**	**35.4**	**125.6**	**25.9**	**18.1**	**34.2**
Europe.......................... 170	**1.7**	**33.1**	**13.5**	**29.8**	**27.7**	**43.0**	**17.4**	**24.4**	**–57.9**	**457.4**	**184.9**	**28.6**	**8.8**	**36.3**
Middle East.......................... 407	**18.0**	**18.5**	**7.6**	**27.0**	**35.3**	**22.6**	**18.8**	**50.6**	**–7.8**	**19.5**	**34.1**	**39.8**	**23.4**	**22.1**
Western Hemisphere.......................... 207	**87.8**	**–26.6**	**–69.1**	**176.0**	**24.6**	**275.5**	**8.1**	**56.1**	**–2.0**	**149.1**	**64.8**	**15.3**	**21.6**	**26.7**
Other Countries n.i.e.......................... 910	**—**	**—**	**....**	**....**	**....**	**....**	**....**	**—**	**—**	**300.0**	**30.1**	**27.3**	**23.5**	**29.5**

		Exports							Imports						
		2001	2002	2003	2004	2005	2006	2007	2001	2002	2003	2004	2005	2006	2007
		Millions of U.S. Dollars							Millions of U.S. Dollars						
IFS World Total		**267,349**	**276,299**	**304,185**	**341,596**	**371,370**	**428,359**	**434,904**	**320,973**	**335,438**	**380,712**	**451,680**	**483,017**	**547,476**	**620,709**
DOTS World Total	**001**	**268,571**	**275,795**	**305,943**	**341,970**	**370,275**	**422,689**	**441,185**	**322,844**	**335,342**	**383,634**	**453,191**	**482,615**	**546,797**	**624,132**
Industrial Countries	**101**	**211,895**	**219,656**	**237,838**	**260,434**	**279,182**	**324,735**	**336,823**	**236,187**	**245,702**	**279,458**	**316,843**	**332,400**	**374,037**	**433,532**
United States	111	42,794	42,854	48,167	52,197	55,852	58,604	62,646	45,056	39,899	39,234	42,137	41,868	48,562	53,916
Canada	156	4,647	4,705	5,339	6,109	5,952	7,102	6,564	5,455	5,544	6,205	7,827	7,697	9,270	11,170
Australia	193	3,345	3,194	3,755	4,407	4,573	4,467	5,023	2,646	2,665	2,985	3,473	3,843	3,935	4,342
Japan	158	5,342	5,408	6,115	6,966	6,955	7,391	7,563	13,502	12,734	13,483	15,064	15,918	14,679	15,404
New Zealand	196	448	470	577	751	740	671	693	807	820	923	1,080	1,087	1,123	1,324
Austria	122	1,619	1,784	1,961	1,835	2,172	2,838	2,723	2,470	3,212	4,164	3,927	3,493	4,240	4,934
Belgium	124	13,016	14,244	17,052	17,506	18,563	22,078	23,501	15,418	16,647	18,955	22,027	22,389	24,720	29,577
Cyprus	423	419	410	515	561	550	1,261	825	360	378	417	338	329	1,263	361
Denmark	128	3,007	3,827	3,350	3,312	3,766	5,691	4,323	3,400	3,826	4,617	4,916	6,200	7,196	6,786
Finland	172	2,147	2,069	2,287	2,296	2,541	3,230	3,882	4,030	3,980	4,251	4,047	3,998	5,073	5,213
France	132	25,716	25,965	29,152	31,381	32,799	44,087	35,921	24,939	26,253	31,146	33,387	34,391	37,869	43,348
Germany	134	31,163	30,935	32,235	36,796	39,028	46,148	49,057	37,918	43,373	51,983	59,088	61,932	69,856	88,462
Greece	174	1,509	1,718	1,959	2,392	2,297	2,567	2,684	600	760	967	1,078	1,143	1,159	1,250
Iceland	176	227	212	239	315	334	350	399	431	467	508	675	652	771	768
Ireland	178	18,492	21,964	19,932	23,318	27,104	29,876	35,321	12,413	12,664	15,152	17,069	17,232	18,311	22,532
Italy	136	11,364	12,062	13,352	14,206	14,640	15,798	18,241	13,008	14,783	17,927	19,411	19,526	21,295	26,379
Luxembourg	137	349	492	435	436	355	2,042	540	390	659	970	1,342	1,439	2,391	1,367
Malta	181	313	341	422	446	391	543	721	213	258	306	323	257	254	351
Netherlands	138	19,609	19,748	21,008	20,433	20,385	26,498	29,988	19,962	21,215	24,363	30,123	31,765	35,894	45,559
Norway	142	2,732	2,726	3,140	3,584	4,036	3,871	5,480	8,460	8,332	10,773	15,828	22,529	26,937	29,059
Portugal	182	2,132	2,148	2,271	2,705	2,788	3,650	2,935	2,103	2,307	3,008	3,223	2,964	3,625	2,910
Slovenia	961	228	272	260	282	279	340	405	221	263	280	293	323	490	634
Spain	184	10,715	11,749	13,565	15,336	16,221	19,160	19,853	9,186	11,030	13,177	14,804	15,519	17,089	20,232
Sweden	144	5,300	5,397	6,004	7,448	7,647	8,741	9,737	6,217	6,198	7,219	8,789	8,607	9,725	10,488
Switzerland	146	5,262	4,963	4,745	5,416	9,214	7,731	7,798	6,985	7,433	6,447	6,574	7,300	8,312	7,167
Developing Countries	**202**	**49,407**	**50,343**	**62,283**	**72,486**	**83,241**	**86,673**	**101,940**	**76,943**	**81,208**	**95,852**	**122,733**	**137,681**	**158,840**	**181,619**
Africa	**607**	**6,004**	**6,201**	**7,523**	**8,595**	**9,103**	**9,957**	**10,959**	**9,331**	**9,479**	**10,548**	**13,323**	**14,530**	**15,719**	**16,601**
Algeria	612	171	198	310	307	264	310	335	336	510	427	686	831	1,761	1,703
Angola	614	133	100	169	218	286	380	547	104	40	16	18	27	30	315
Benin	638	48	65	76	66	60	70	86	1	11	5	10	—	1	—
Botswana	616	35	25	22	29	29	26	41	1,552	1,548	1,815	2,118	2,065	2,252	1,051
Burkina Faso	748	11	4	6	6	8	5	8	5	—	—	—	1	1	3
Burundi	618	3	3	3	3	3	2	2	1	1	1	—	1	1	—
Cameroon	622	52	54	54	49	48	42	48	58	98	160	387	322	130	124
Cape Verde	624	6	9	10	6	8	8	6	4	6	5	3	1	1	1
Central African Rep.	626	3	3	1	1	1	1	1	—	—	2	1	—	—	—
Chad	628	5	7	6	9	9	6	12	—	—	2	—	1	—	2
Comoros	632	1	1	1	2	1	—	1	5	—	—	—	—	—	—
Congo, Dem. Rep. of	636	14	8	13	12	21	31	23	1	1	2	9	11	1	2
Congo, Republic of	634	24	25	21	32	37	50	92	5	9	12	8	14	18	30
Côte d'Ivoire	662	88	60	72	126	102	73	82	122	140	178	158	137	146	206
Djibouti	611	17	19	36	19	10	9	12	—	—	1	3	2	4	—
Equatorial Guinea	642	36	55	176	63	71	84	78	8	10	13	21	30	32	21
Eritrea	643	7	5	13	8	10	4	5	—	—	—	—	—	—	—
Ethiopia	644	42	62	74	65	57	71	110	22	105	25	34	38	40	36
Gabon	646	50	37	55	87	53	52	63	6	9	39	12	18	12	12
Gambia, The	648	27	25	31	29	30	26	28	11	6	4	6	6	6	4
Ghana	652	208	211	249	314	281	351	426	192	181	234	250	216	271	322
Guinea	656	31	40	43	25	40	60	48	—	4	2	5	8	3	3
Guinea-Bissau	654	2	2	1	1	1	1	—	—	—	—	—	—	—	—
Kenya	664	249	238	281	343	349	396	431	305	324	354	404	407	471	497
Lesotho	666	3	2	—	—	1	2	1	3	2	1	—	1	1	2
Liberia	668	15	9	8	16	21	22	28	17	5	24	1	5	18	18
Madagascar	674	10	5	10	17	12	8	14	36	26	27	28	28	48	66
Malawi	676	12	20	17	22	21	19	27	22	19	19	36	29	21	30
Mali	678	25	29	24	22	10	8	8	2	5	14	4	2	1	1
Mauritania	682	12	22	36	47	89	42	19	9	3	4	12	21	25	20
Mauritius	684	75	85	77	80	86	83	104	487	508	532	629	644	680	689
Morocco	686	533	502	584	626	479	533	624	657	706	746	954	778	700	812
Mozambique	688	18	21	26	19	20	21	18	11	6	14	5	16	11	220
Namibia	728	18	13	17	32	32	25	24	455	270	172	406	508	652	376
Niger	692	8	9	10	11	11	9	8	15	1	5	1	—	—	—
Nigeria	694	984	1,078	1,228	1,430	1,485	1,544	2,025	99	144	145	211	292	403	666
Rwanda	714	7	5	5	8	8	7	13	1	2	—	1	1	1	3
St. Helena	856	14	19	10	14	30	17	20	1	1	2	1	2	2	1
São Tomé & Príncipe	716	5	4	1	1	1	1	—	—	—	1	—	—	—	—
Senegal	722	59	56	86	124	186	349	279	16	16	13	13	14	14	29
Seychelles	718	19	20	22	23	24	30	32	69	93	88	112	108	98	87
Sierra Leone	724	89	49	53	44	47	34	36	4	4	7	4	2	8	6

Country	Code	Exports 2001	2002	2003	2004	2005	2006	2007
		Millions of U.S. Dollars						
Somalia	726	9	14	6	13	3	1	2
South Africa	199	2,228	2,416	2,909	3,452	3,789	4,025	4,292
Sudan	732	115	107	145	168	253	286	229
Swaziland	734	6	4	3	7	12	11	10
Tanzania	738	95	92	92	123	130	159	171
Togo	742	49	39	62	50	178	257	67
Tunisia	744	204	203	239	278	243	237	215
Uganda	746	50	51	60	67	67	72	93
Zambia	754	34	29	35	43	54	65	71
Zimbabwe	698	52	51	48	48	40	36	45
Asia	**507**	**18,683**	**18,520**	**22,753**	**26,684**	**30,305**	**30,862**	**36,532**
Afghanistan, I.S. of	512	5	4	16	26	26	42	83
American Samoa	859	—	1	4	1	8	1	1
Bangladesh	513	98	99	92	125	145	139	121
Bhutan	514	2	2	3	7	1	1	2
Brunei Darussalam	516	86	91	210	124	80	147	1,660
Cambodia	522	5	6	6	8	6	5	5
China,P.R.: Mainland	924	2,474	2,251	3,157	4,355	5,119	6,054	7,553
China,P.R.:Hong Kong	532	3,889	3,783	4,087	4,847	5,641	5,247	5,127
China,P.R.:Macao	546	28	19	24	28	31	39	34
Fiji	819	5	5	8	12	9	10	10
French Polynesia	887	9	12	18	15	16	11	13
Guam	829	5	5	7	5	7	13	7
India	534	2,568	2,648	3,741	4,121	5,118	4,993	5,908
Indonesia	536	453	495	736	722	678	585	574
Korea	542	1,833	2,226	2,389	2,662	2,981	3,143	3,614
Lao People's Dem.Rep.	544	3	2	5	2	3	2	7
Malaysia	548	1,492	1,326	1,698	1,827	1,976	1,626	1,908
Maldives	556	7	5	10	14	16	11	14
Mongolia	948	3	4	4	3	9	7	7
Myanmar	518	14	11	8	4	18	7	7
Nauru	836	1	1	1	1	—	—	—
Nepal	558	9	10	11	12	10	8	11
New Caledonia	839	13	13	14	20	18	18	30
Pakistan	564	330	366	481	635	839	900	854
Palau	565	—	—	—	—	1	—	—
Papua New Guinea	853	6	19	13	10	8	9	16
Philippines	566	566	533	629	579	509	448	496
Samoa	862	7	2	1	—	1	—	1
Singapore	576	2,307	2,185	2,598	3,148	3,784	4,283	4,924
Solomon Islands	813	—	1	—	1	2	3	3
Sri Lanka	524	205	191	200	254	205	193	190
Taiwan Province of China	528	1,270	1,285	1,480	1,746	1,719	1,686	1,875
Thailand	578	857	799	937	1,174	1,166	1,048	1,205
Timor-Leste	537	—	—	—	—	—	—	2
Tonga	866	2	1	2	1	4	6	2
Tuvalu	869	—	—	—	—	—	—	—
Vanuatu	846	1	1	—	—	3	1	2
Vietnam	582	130	120	164	193	148	176	269
Europe	**170**	**9,894**	**11,013**	**14,318**	**16,667**	**18,047**	**22,250**	**26,766**
Albania	914	31	28	16	21	27	31	37
Armenia	911	11	8	9	10	9	21	24
Azerbaijan	912	53	85	229	481	386	882	481
Belarus	913	47	51	65	98	103	116	133
Bosnia & Herzegovina	963	21	24	21	28	44	35	37
Bulgaria	918	174	201	252	285	399	415	404
Croatia	960	127	142	228	231	214	270	317
Czech Republic	935	1,553	1,549	1,635	1,661	1,711	2,154	2,762
Estonia	939	118	148	151	185	195	545	455
Faroe Islands	816	40	10	21	13	12	21	41
Georgia	915	28	26	42	86	48	70	66
Gibraltar	823	184	192	254	290	314	472	424
Hungary	944	884	1,125	1,403	1,639	1,450	1,474	1,709
Kazakhstan	916	132	138	169	253	280	388	591
Kosovo	967	—	—	—	—	—	—	1
Kyrgyz Republic	917	4	3	3	6	5	6	7
Latvia	941	124	116	186	162	167	217	290
Lithuania	946	197	226	309	250	277	413	616
Macedonia, FYR	962	35	31	30	36	37	33	35
Moldova	921	14	8	10	9	18	34	26
Montenegro, Rep. of	943	—	—	—	—	—	3	17
Poland	964	1,870	1,978	2,379	2,485	2,619	3,823	4,706
Romania	968	492	648	831	1,118	1,164	1,121	1,322
Russia	922	1,293	1,488	2,319	2,698	3,400	3,807	5,623
Serbia, Rep. of	942	—	—	—	—	—	133	189
Serbia & Montenegro	965	74	93	107	121	102	6	—
Slovak Republic	936	294	302	388	392	433	462	756
Tajikistan	923	1	1	4	6	9	9	3

Country	Code	Imports 2001	2002	2003	2004	2005	2006	2007
		Millions of U.S. Dollars						
Somalia	726	—	—	—	—	—	—	—
South Africa	199	4,241	4,208	4,918	6,119	7,335	7,313	8,555
Sudan	732	14	12	10	26	33	19	40
Swaziland	734	48	53	52	61	60	65	63
Tanzania	738	51	58	56	68	67	54	58
Togo	742	2	2	2	1	1	1	1
Tunisia	744	173	172	231	353	324	297	369
Uganda	746	12	16	15	24	21	24	18
Zambia	754	17	16	57	30	23	33	74
Zimbabwe	698	131	128	95	88	79	49	61
Asia	**507**	**43,015**	**44,645**	**52,010**	**66,259**	**72,240**	**81,568**	**93,354**
Afghanistan, I.S. of	512	1	—	1	4	1	20	1
American Samoa	859	—	—	—	—	—	1	5
Bangladesh	513	655	726	935	1,163	1,083	1,374	1,541
Bhutan	514	3	1	1	6	—	—	—
Brunei Darussalam	516	50	54	93	123	51	140	89
Cambodia	522	123	134	165	197	133	170	233
China,P.R.: Mainland	924	8,592	10,514	14,020	19,469	23,916	28,766	45,665
China,P.R.:Hong Kong	532	8,611	8,686	9,235	10,787	12,165	13,847	4,765
China,P.R.:Macao	546	57	47	71	72	42	44	188
Fiji	819	74	72	107	120	117	139	125
French Polynesia	887	1	1	—	1	1	2	2
Guam	829	—	—	—	1	2	1	1
India	534	2,714	2,809	3,509	4,284	5,148	5,857	7,321
Indonesia	536	1,716	1,620	1,567	1,761	1,656	1,879	2,087
Korea	542	4,099	4,307	4,284	5,730	5,605	5,747	5,621
Lao People's Dem.Rep.	544	10	15	15	30	9	1	47
Malaysia	548	2,898	2,702	3,134	3,783	3,363	3,568	3,675
Maldives	556	9	11	11	19	21	26	31
Mongolia	948	13	5	3	4	3	9	12
Myanmar	518	96	97	102	135	64	49	61
Nauru	836	—	—	—	—	—	—	1
Nepal	558	14	13	17	19	18	19	21
New Caledonia	839	—	—	—	2	1	2	—
Pakistan	564	630	735	870	1,034	904	962	993
Palau	565	—	—	—	—	—	—	—
Papua New Guinea	853	60	74	99	112	108	74	78
Philippines	566	1,729	1,465	1,197	1,229	1,317	1,388	1,427
Samoa	862	—	—	1	1	2	1	—
Singapore	576	3,094	3,054	4,460	6,333	7,064	7,025	7,189
Solomon Islands	813	1	—	—	—	1	1	7
Sri Lanka	524	577	633	670	855	833	935	1,037
Taiwan Province of China	528	4,167	3,716	3,686	4,381	4,118	4,410	5,277
Thailand	578	2,404	2,420	2,761	3,297	3,181	3,618	4,166
Timor-Leste	537	—	—	—	—	—	—	—
Tonga	866	—	—	—	—	—	—	1
Tuvalu	869	—	1	1	—	—	—	—
Vanuatu	846	—	—	—	1	2	2	1
Vietnam	582	616	733	993	1,308	1,310	1,492	1,688
Europe	**170**	**13,012**	**15,306**	**19,707**	**26,241**	**31,128**	**39,386**	**48,129**
Albania	914	2	4	6	3	3	3	7
Armenia	911	1	1	103	1	1	5	1
Azerbaijan	912	14	17	27	28	75	428	623
Belarus	913	26	51	37	138	497	1,342	1,181
Bosnia & Herzegovina	963	4	6	7	7	10	15	17
Bulgaria	918	145	179	206	275	299	366	473
Croatia	960	76	105	82	100	100	127	149
Czech Republic	935	1,620	1,911	2,344	2,217	2,678	3,634	5,946
Estonia	939	416	510	438	687	612	784	452
Faroe Islands	816	157	152	184	174	177	191	198
Georgia	915	8	4	9	16	35	434	94
Gibraltar	823	21	34	42	27	122	56	67
Hungary	944	1,044	1,302	1,863	2,739	3,049	3,529	4,741
Kazakhstan	916	101	52	84	67	81	151	476
Kosovo	967	—	—	—	—	—	—	—
Kyrgyz Republic	917	—	—	—	1	—	11	—
Latvia	941	611	707	831	1,171	1,171	1,465	1,188
Lithuania	946	347	409	474	464	430	493	598
Macedonia, FYR	962	26	26	40	52	45	47	69
Moldova	921	7	4	5	5	11	23	31
Montenegro, Rep. of	943	—	—	—	—	—	1	3
Poland	964	1,717	1,939	2,566	3,159	3,418	4,989	7,371
Romania	968	660	801	1,131	1,446	1,409	1,528	1,864
Russia	922	3,012	2,972	4,061	6,499	9,475	10,691	10,415
Serbia, Rep. of	942	—	—	—	—	—	110	141
Serbia & Montenegro	965	35	48	56	74	79	8	—
Slovak Republic	936	260	324	428	454	550	1,175	2,542
Tajikistan	923	2	2	2	—	1	1	23

		Exports							Imports						
		2001	2002	2003	2004	2005	2006	2007	2001	2002	2003	2004	2005	2006	2007
		Millions of U.S. Dollars							*Millions of U.S. Dollars*						
Turkey	186	1,736	2,075	2,798	3,619	4,035	4,572	4,705	2,556	3,487	4,471	6,174	6,568	7,458	9,159
Turkmenistan	925	10	10	12	21	25	29	33	3	7	3	10	7	50	33
Ukraine	926	295	274	402	409	506	622	864	104	220	157	203	170	237	215
Uzbekistan	927	29	22	30	38	39	52	73	39	33	48	49	53	34	52
Europe n.s.	884	24	11	15	17	19	14	20	—	—	1	1	1	—	1
Middle East	**407**	**10,224**	**9,959**	**12,951**	**15,362**	**20,322**	**17,176**	**20,132**	**5,569**	**5,514**	**6,477**	**8,354**	**10,419**	**11,213**	**10,715**
Bahrain	419	225	200	253	289	325	490	427	147	117	130	130	294	304	266
Egypt	469	655	697	756	1,184	993	1,080	1,413	607	648	724	933	683	1,250	1,108
Iran, I.R. of	429	620	602	774	816	841	793	796	42	54	50	79	70	131	128
Iraq	433	87	71	216	159	233	143	266	1	—	—	1	2	3	6
Israel	436	1,965	2,152	2,248	2,555	2,468	2,384	2,345	1,405	1,361	1,439	1,725	1,861	1,812	1,866
Jordan	439	243	270	287	294	339	295	325	24	48	29	37	40	36	41
Kuwait	443	514	468	621	654	791	825	902	449	433	558	764	718	1,419	1,341
Lebanon	446	261	239	344	386	385	384	446	23	30	27	31	37	38	77
Libya	672	266	322	393	396	384	376	453	275	252	329	362	639	1,098	1,158
Oman	449	435	383	433	590	679	390	537	99	130	144	205	126	155	165
Qatar	453	251	305	516	614	660	896	1,171	46	43	89	157	176	363	296
Saudi Arabia	456	2,182	2,094	3,010	2,945	2,907	3,093	3,721	1,419	1,086	1,281	2,237	3,327	2,376	1,610
Syrian Arab Republic	463	96	127	134	163	190	151	145	127	177	94	96	238	508	112
United Arab Emirates	466	2,317	1,916	2,832	4,190	9,009	5,762	7,048	899	1,076	1,567	1,569	2,172	1,688	2,526
West Bank/Gaza Strip	487	—	—	—	—	—	—	2	—	—	—	—	—	—	3
Yemen, Republic of	474	106	112	132	123	113	114	135	7	59	15	27	36	29	15
Middle East n.s.	489	—	—	1	3	4	2	1	—	—	1	1	1	2	1
Western Hemisphere	**207**	**4,603**	**4,650**	**4,739**	**5,177**	**5,465**	**6,429**	**7,551**	**6,015**	**6,264**	**7,109**	**8,556**	**9,364**	**10,953**	**12,819**
Antigua and Barbuda	311	25	27	29	21	22	56	45	5	3	16	58	10	10	11
Argentina	213	383	192	222	328	307	399	453	310	369	422	500	527	664	819
Aruba	314	47	42	23	20	41	57	49	20	6	22	27	55	10	67
Bahamas, The	313	22	54	45	71	67	110	37	10	31	8	9	80	137	10
Barbados	316	80	59	86	77	100	87	98	58	37	34	36	42	36	40
Belize	339	20	21	28	17	17	15	23	50	48	68	82	85	154	64
Bermuda	319	49	46	69	60	37	36	90	65	27	110	100	30	132	38
Bolivia	218	15	16	10	9	20	11	15	18	17	17	20	26	19	35
Brazil	223	1,171	1,331	1,356	1,452	1,523	1,703	2,153	1,911	2,126	2,477	2,893	3,216	3,567	4,300
Chile	228	189	175	200	249	276	346	364	693	712	692	885	885	973	1,008
Colombia	233	151	126	174	214	215	246	279	461	327	372	519	553	565	713
Costa Rica	238	62	76	66	71	73	62	92	197	479	714	1,074	1,021	920	1,025
Dominica	321	14	14	10	15	11	11	11	17	24	14	18	25	26	10
Dominican Republic	243	65	77	66	56	94	95	109	46	80	80	77	96	207	170
Ecuador	248	49	67	52	57	56	76	71	48	55	52	78	76	81	135
El Salvador	253	25	20	28	37	62	48	20	11	11	80	13	10	8	11
Falkland Islands	323	29	26	45	52	44	50	51	10	8	15	13	7	15	8
Greenland	326	4	1	1	2	1	2	3	5	2	—	—	—	1	10
Grenada	328	10	8	12	12	18	13	12	1	2	3	1	4	—	—
Guatemala	258	51	50	42	61	47	53	49	19	21	25	28	26	34	32
Guyana	336	33	28	38	30	33	38	49	88	78	85	78	83	65	81
Haiti	263	15	18	26	13	8	13	9	1	2	1	1	1	1	8
Honduras	268	16	15	24	20	17	14	19	45	29	39	47	43	33	48
Jamaica	343	101	123	100	98	107	132	125	169	157	194	172	187	240	245
Mexico	273	988	1,065	1,135	1,149	1,155	1,374	1,529	1,011	785	831	771	827	834	2,071
Netherlands Antilles	353	51	28	33	45	42	196	230	10	21	9	4	20	68	37
Nicaragua	278	4	7	6	7	4	6	5	14	9	9	7	12	21	13
Panama	283	93	111	141	132	143	201	340	14	16	10	15	36	32	27
Paraguay	288	34	20	24	29	23	25	22	3	3	2	2	1	3	7
Peru	293	59	66	74	77	85	97	135	239	236	208	248	230	369	281
St. Kitts and Nevis	361	12	12	15	23	14	16	24	10	6	12	5	5	1	1
St. Lucia	362	25	18	25	30	31	49	29	24	35	26	37	25	28	28
St. Pierre-Miquelon	363	4	1	—	—	—	—	1	—	—	—	—	—	3	—
St. Vincent & Grens.	364	13	10	15	16	13	16	16	20	22	16	22	14	14	13
Suriname	366	12	14	16	18	17	18	16	32	5	1	1	1	1	—
Trinidad and Tobago	369	132	122	170	177	188	188	237	77	85	122	131	127	338	246
Uruguay	298	71	46	52	56	68	74	70	51	69	72	80	107	120	116
Venezuela, Rep. Bol.	299	453	462	237	344	428	437	502	239	283	191	390	709	1,118	1,013
Western Hem. n.s.	399	27	55	44	34	58	60	169	15	35	61	114	161	103	78
Other Countries n.i.e.	**910**	**59**	**42**	**42**	**25**	**29**	**39**	**34**	**19**	**14**	**15**	**23**	**18**	**32**	**25**
Cuba	928	19	17	28	21	28	38	33	17	12	15	22	16	15	10
North Korea	954	41	25	14	4	1	1	1	2	1	—	1	1	18	15
Countries & Areas n.s.	**898**	**7,188**	**5,724**	**5,732**	**9,017**	**7,808**	**11,225**	**2,375**	**9,690**	**8,414**	**8,302**	**13,587**	**12,508**	**13,870**	**8,950**
Memorandum Items															
European Union	998	152,139	160,568	172,212	187,465	198,379	243,635	251,952	158,862	174,907	207,845	235,076	243,414	276,518	333,221
Oil Exporting Ctys.	999	8,733	8,394	11,307	13,167	18,359	15,152	18,332	5,620	5,631	6,349	8,423	10,718	12,394	12,698
Non-Oil Develop.Ctys.	201	40,674	41,949	50,976	59,318	64,882	71,521	83,608	71,323	75,577	89,504	114,310	126,963	146,446	168,920
PERCENT DISTRIBUTION															
Industrial Countries	**101**	**78.9**	**79.6**	**77.7**	**76.2**	**75.4**	**76.8**	**76.3**	**73.2**	**73.3**	**72.8**	**69.9**	**68.9**	**68.4**	**69.5**
Developing Countries	**202**	**18.4**	**18.3**	**20.4**	**21.2**	**22.5**	**20.5**	**23.1**	**23.8**	**24.2**	**25.0**	**27.1**	**28.5**	**29.0**	**29.1**
Africa	**607**	**2.2**	**2.2**	**2.5**	**2.5**	**2.5**	**2.4**	**2.5**	**2.9**	**2.8**	**2.7**	**2.9**	**3.0**	**2.9**	**2.7**
Asia	**507**	**7.0**	**6.7**	**7.4**	**7.8**	**8.2**	**7.3**	**8.3**	**13.3**	**13.3**	**13.6**	**14.6**	**15.0**	**14.9**	**15.0**

	Exports 2001	2002	2003	2004	2005	2006	2007	Imports 2001	2002	2003	2004	2005	2006	2007
Europe.................................170	3.7	4.0	4.7	4.9	4.9	5.3	6.1	4.0	4.6	5.1	5.8	6.4	7.2	7.7
Middle East.......................... 407	3.8	3.6	4.2	4.5	5.5	4.1	4.6	1.7	1.6	1.7	1.8	2.2	2.1	1.7
Western Hemisphere............. 207	1.7	1.7	1.5	1.5	1.5	1.5	1.7	1.9	1.9	1.9	1.9	1.9	2.0	2.1
ANNUAL PERCENT CHANGE														
World.................................... 001	–5.0	2.7	10.9	11.8	8.3	14.2	4.4	–3.6	3.9	14.4	18.1	6.5	13.3	14.1
Industrial Countries................ 101	–7.9	3.7	8.3	9.5	7.2	16.3	3.7	–7.6	4.0	13.7	13.4	4.9	12.5	15.9
Developing Countries.............. 202	–4.7	1.9	23.7	16.4	14.8	4.1	17.6	–1.8	5.5	18.0	28.0	12.2	15.4	14.3
Africa.................................. 607	3.0	3.3	21.3	14.2	5.9	9.4	10.1	19.1	1.6	11.3	26.3	9.1	8.2	5.6
Asia..................................... 507	–5.9	–.9	22.9	17.3	13.6	1.8	18.4	–7.8	3.8	16.5	27.4	9.0	12.9	14.4
Europe.................................170	–5.6	11.3	30.0	16.4	8.3	23.3	20.3	15.3	17.6	28.8	33.2	18.6	26.5	22.2
Middle East.......................... 407	–4.4	–2.6	30.0	18.6	32.3	–15.5	17.2	–7.5	–1.0	17.5	29.0	24.7	7.6	–4.4
Western Hemisphere............. 207	–8.3	1.0	1.9	9.3	5.5	17.7	17.5	–7.5	4.1	13.5	20.3	9.5	17.0	17.0
Other Countries n.i.e................910	1.6	–29.0	.2	–40.3	14.9	33.1	–12.8	–2.4	–28.1	11.5	52.3	–23.6	85.2	–24.4

	Exports 2001	2002	2003	2004	2005	2006	2007	Imports 2001	2002	2003	2004	2005	2006	2007
	Millions of U.S. Dollars							Millions of U.S. Dollars						
IFS World Total (Billions).........	**729**	**693**	**725**	**819**	**907**	**1,038**	**1,163**	**1,179**	**1,200**	**1,303**	**1,526**	**1,732**	**1,919**	**2,017**
DOTS World Total (Billions)...... 001	**731**	**693**	**724**	**816**	**904**	**1,037**	**1,163**	**1,180**	**1,202**	**1,305**	**1,525**	**1,733**	**1,919**	**2,017**
Industrial Countries................. 101	**406,407**	**381,179**	**398,438**	**438,958**	**480,761**	**536,107**	**592,962**	**601,581**	**596,898**	**627,600**	**705,394**	**774,084**	**823,825**	**854,407**
Canada.. 156	163,725	160,799	169,481	187,713	211,420	230,257	248,437	220,138	213,954	227,652	259,807	291,944	307,823	317,604
Australia..................................... 193	10,945	13,084	13,104	14,271	15,771	17,782	19,207	6,811	6,824	6,744	7,916	7,677	8,563	8,971
Japan.. 158	57,639	51,440	52,064	54,400	55,410	59,649	62,665	129,708	124,633	121,233	133,339	141,950	152,244	149,423
New Zealand................................ 196	2,134	1,814	1,849	2,076	2,648	2,929	2,813	2,384	2,471	2,601	3,178	3,368	3,326	3,316
Austria.. 122	2,626	2,424	1,793	1,958	2,598	2,987	3,172	4,113	3,939	4,631	5,979	6,312	8,527	10,893
Belgium....................................... 124	13,524	13,343	15,218	16,877	18,605	21,347	25,292	10,384	10,067	10,401	12,812	13,399	14,790	15,677
Cyprus... 423	268	193	327	96	84	240	169	36	27	26	27	32	55	18
Denmark...................................... 128	1,611	1,496	1,548	2,147	1,913	2,268	2,927	3,524	3,346	3,854	4,020	5,303	5,707	6,233
Finland.. 172	1,554	1,537	1,714	2,067	2,248	2,648	3,133	3,530	3,607	3,778	4,092	4,531	5,176	5,501
France... 132	20,125	19,347	17,394	21,557	22,538	24,386	27,820	30,984	29,031	29,902	32,619	34,774	38,089	42,498
Germany...................................... 134	30,114	26,629	28,848	31,381	34,149	41,320	49,652	60,492	63,884	69,618	79,117	86,938	91,222	96,640
Greece... 174	1,296	1,153	1,191	2,063	1,190	1,554	2,111	555	602	672	811	1,005	1,070	1,297
Iceland.. 176	226	219	242	308	510	366	630	246	310	297	290	282	262	217
Ireland.. 178	7,150	6,749	7,699	8,166	9,335	8,515	9,011	18,626	22,485	25,959	27,569	28,770	28,778	30,491
Italy.. 136	9,923	10,098	10,579	10,719	11,541	12,588	14,174	24,954	25,419	26,665	29,408	32,419	34,107	36,471
Luxembourg................................ 137	550	480	279	706	782	580	1,003	324	317	280	311	410	559	553
Malta... 181	259	210	202	182	194	163	207	372	314	379	390	289	380	336
Netherlands................................ 138	19,525	18,334	20,703	24,286	26,496	31,102	32,986	9,954	10,308	11,438	13,175	15,503	18,081	19,140
Norway.. 142	1,839	1,408	1,471	1,605	1,935	2,401	3,054	5,472	6,075	5,470	6,857	7,112	7,380	7,590
Portugal...................................... 182	1,258	863	863	1,046	1,129	1,471	2,478	1,620	1,740	2,045	2,333	2,415	3,145	3,175
Slovenia...................................... 961	120	131	140	192	234	239	297	301	322	498	533	430	506	507
Spain... 184	5,811	5,226	5,935	6,640	6,934	7,405	9,879	5,582	6,063	7,141	7,931	9,128	10,402	11,075
Sweden.. 144	3,548	3,154	3,226	3,265	3,709	4,126	4,494	9,128	9,552	11,451	13,097	14,228	14,230	13,401
Switzerland................................. 146	9,842	7,796	8,676	9,279	10,760	14,392	17,056	9,975	9,785	11,101	12,107	13,483	14,774	15,285
United Kingdom.......................... 112	40,798	33,253	33,896	35,960	38,629	45,393	50,296	42,367	41,825	43,764	47,677	52,380	54,630	58,096
Developing Countries............. 202	**324,230**	**311,510**	**324,717**	**376,770**	**422,776**	**500,424**	**568,693**	**578,526**	**605,459**	**677,649**	**820,038**	**958,403**	**1,095,415**	**1,162,940**
Africa....................................... 607	**8,557**	**7,740**	**7,931**	**10,273**	**12,236**	**14,450**	**17,795**	**25,843**	**21,876**	**32,675**	**46,555**	**63,992**	**78,638**	**89,141**
Algeria... 612	1,047	985	487	972	1,161	1,102	1,653	2,906	2,560	5,126	7,927	10,835	16,089	18,432
Angola... 614	276	373	492	594	928	1,550	1,280	3,277	3,275	4,506	4,797	8,846	12,174	12,926
Benin... 638	32	35	30	45	71	116	289	1	1	1	1	1	1	5
Botswana.................................... 616	43	32	26	54	67	27	54	21	30	14	74	180	254	189
Burkina Faso............................... 748	4	19	11	22	25	18	33	5	3	1	—	2	1	2
Burundi....................................... 618	5	2	3	17	8	7	7	3	1	7	3	5	2	1
Cameroon.................................... 622	184	156	91	100	117	120	133	112	184	226	335	171	292	315
Cape Verde.................................. 624	8	10	9	51	10	14	6	2	2	6	4	3	1	2
Central African Rep...................... 626	4	7	7	30	15	25	20	2	2	2	9	6	4	3
Chad.. 628	137	127	64	40	54	60	71	6	6	24	828	1,580	2,021	2,240
Comoros...................................... 632	1	—	1	1	—	—	—	11	5	4	17	2	2	1
Congo, Dem. Rep. of................... 636	19	28	31	67	64	71	113	167	209	183	132	269	86	209
Congo, Republic of...................... 634	90	52	79	65	104	138	140	527	211	457	898	1,697	3,185	3,182
Côte d'Ivoire............................... 662	97	76	103	118	124	147	162	358	399	514	762	1,282	756	639
Djibouti....................................... 611	19	56	34	43	48	48	59	1	2	1	1	1	3	5
Equatorial Guinea........................ 642	80	109	336	215	249	552	236	477	554	963	1,259	1,675	1,825	1,862
Eritrea... 643	22	29	87	54	31	9	6	—	—	—	—	1	1	—
Ethiopia....................................... 644	61	60	409	459	515	137	168	32	28	34	45	67	85	93
Gabon.. 646	75	65	63	93	98	135	478	1,735	1,665	2,074	2,620	2,955	1,416	2,243
Gambia, The................................ 648	9	10	27	23	31	21	20	1	—	—	1	—	—	—
Ghana.. 652	200	193	209	306	338	290	416	205	129	93	160	173	210	212
Guinea... 656	78	63	36	59	125	65	74	106	85	87	80	90	115	139
Guinea-Bissau............................. 654	1	2	1	1	2	6	7	—	—	2	28	—	1	—
Kenya.. 664	577	271	197	394	632	526	584	137	202	266	374	368	375	342
Lesotho....................................... 666	1	2	5	6	4	4	7	224	343	420	493	421	428	462
Liberia.. 668	37	28	33	61	75	68	76	45	48	62	89	97	144	118
Madagascar................................. 674	21	15	46	36	28	45	32	285	226	401	494	343	298	358
Malawi.. 676	15	30	17	22	28	46	52	84	76	83	65	123	64	64
Mali... 678	33	11	31	43	32	43	32	7	3	3	4	4	8	10
Mauritania.................................. 682	26	23	35	78	86	90	103	—	1	1	8	1	54	1
Mauritius.................................... 684	29	27	32	29	31	36	50	296	301	316	285	233	230	197
Morocco...................................... 686	286	566	465	523	528	876	1,343	467	425	415	553	474	559	664
Mozambique............................... 688	29	98	63	76	62	65	115	8	9	9	11	13	18	6
Namibia....................................... 728	256	58	28	73	114	127	128	39	59	128	251	133	119	223
Niger... 692	64	41	34	35	81	129	69	5	1	4	28	66	125	10
Nigeria.. 694	957	1,057	1,029	1,552	1,615	2,231	2,787	9,180	6,219	10,949	17,112	25,109	28,959	33,741
Rwanda....................................... 714	18	10	8	11	11	12	16	8	3	3	6	7	9	13
St. Helena.................................... 856	4	2	2	7	3	2	3	3	4	6	5	3	2	5
São Tomé & Príncipe.................... 716	11	2	2	4	10	4	9	—	—	—	—	—	—	1
Senegal....................................... 722	85	75	102	89	158	97	153	104	4	5	3	4	22	21
Seychelles................................... 718	176	8	7	11	21	9	9	24	27	14	6	6	10	10
Sierra Leone............................... 724	28	25	28	41	38	39	55	5	4	7	11	10	44	60

	Exports 2001	2002	2003	2004	2005	2006	2007	Imports 2001	2002	2003	2004	2005	2006	2007
	Millions of U.S. Dollars							*Millions of U.S. Dollars*						
Somalia 726	7	6	7	9	9	20	21	—	—	—	1	—	—	—
South Africa 199	2,962	2,525	2,821	3,172	3,882	4,462	5,518	4,588	4,183	4,831	6,168	6,071	7,751	9,291
Sudan 732	17	11	26	68	103	77	67	4	2	3	4	14	7	8
Swaziland 734	12	12	8	12	12	12	29	69	123	174	209	207	165	154
Tanzania 738	64	62	66	128	97	161	174	29	27	26	26	35	36	48
Togo 742	17	14	15	24	28	108	288	14	3	6	2	7	4	6
Tunisia 744	278	195	171	258	261	363	403	130	98	107	225	243	524	478
Uganda 746	33	23	43	64	63	53	80	21	17	38	29	29	24	28
Zambia 754	16	36	19	26	29	52	70	16	8	13	33	32	29	49
Zimbabwe 698	32	49	42	47	45	48	105	96	109	61	81	98	107	75
Asia 507	**122,649**	**123,271**	**135,401**	**155,392**	**167,890**	**199,404**	**228,431**	**289,803**	**316,702**	**352,392**	**423,196**	**484,957**	**552,133**	**588,920**
Afghanistan, I.S. of 512	6	80	61	158	261	418	489	1	5	63	25	68	46	77
Bangladesh 513	308	269	227	289	319	332	456	2,504	2,286	2,213	2,465	2,881	3,497	3,635
Bhutan 514	1	1	1	2	3	3	4	1	1	1	—	1	1	1
Brunei Darussalam 516	104	47	36	49	50	48	140	424	306	446	429	590	575	421
Cambodia 522	30	29	58	59	70	75	139	1,017	1,146	1,336	1,592	1,875	2,328	2,599
China,P.R.: Mainland 924	19,235	22,053	28,419	34,721	41,837	55,224	65,238	109,392	133,490	163,255	210,526	259,838	305,788	340,118
China,P.R.:Hong Kong 532	14,072	12,612	13,542	15,809	16,323	17,779	20,121	10,074	9,775	9,287	9,782	9,302	8,285	7,321
China,P.R.:Macao 546	71	79	55	86	102	200	226	1,281	1,308	1,430	1,574	1,320	1,290	1,144
Fiji 819	19	17	20	25	28	33	30	199	170	186	227	188	173	190
French Polynesia 887	83	79	92	93	112	108	124	49	46	49	68	61	59	63
India 534	3,764	4,098	4,986	6,095	7,958	10,091	17,592	10,291	12,450	13,752	16,437	19,875	22,993	25,114
Indonesia 536	2,500	2,581	2,520	2,669	3,045	3,078	4,235	10,907	10,385	10,271	11,680	12,947	14,342	15,208
Kiribati 826	6	4	1	1	2	1	1	1	1	2	2	1	2	2
Korea 542	22,197	22,596	24,099	26,333	27,670	32,455	34,703	36,491	36,910	38,346	47,814	45,523	47,636	49,319
Lao People's Dem.Rep 544	4	4	5	6	10	7	13	4	3	4	4	5	9	21
Malaysia 548	9,380	10,348	10,920	10,897	10,451	12,550	11,680	23,072	24,734	26,190	29,051	34,676	37,521	33,701
Maldives 556	7	4	7	10	9	18	19	103	122	98	87	6	2	4
Mongolia 948	12	66	21	28	22	23	26	153	172	195	253	153	121	88
Myanmar 518	12	11	7	12	5	8	9	502	380	296	—	—	—	—
Nauru 836	4	3	2	1	2	4	8	—	1	—	—	—	—	1
Nepal 558	14	20	16	25	25	17	29	218	166	186	156	120	108	98
New Caledonia 839	25	37	43	45	38	44	58	15	10	13	20	28	52	80
Pakistan 564	543	694	840	1,811	1,247	1,990	2,035	2,420	2,482	2,734	3,090	3,493	3,964	3,831
Papua New Guinea 853	22	23	30	43	55	44	66	43	97	70	57	62	88	115
Philippines 566	7,665	7,270	7,992	7,072	6,893	7,617	7,713	11,775	11,431	10,496	9,581	9,694	10,137	9,813
Samoa 862	70	7	11	12	15	18	17	10	8	6	6	9	5	6
Singapore 576	17,692	16,221	16,576	19,601	20,647	24,683	26,285	15,262	15,093	15,490	15,595	15,388	18,069	18,692
Solomon Islands 813	7	2	2	3	2	6	6	3	1	2	4	2	3	2
Sri Lanka 524	183	172	155	164	198	237	227	2,100	1,924	1,926	2,080	2,215	2,282	2,179
Taiwan Province of China 528	18,152	18,394	17,488	21,731	22,050	23,023	26,359	34,779	33,520	33,018	36,211	36,387	39,797	39,853
Thailand 578	5,995	4,860	5,842	6,363	7,233	8,152	8,445	15,566	15,683	16,106	18,646	21,035	23,685	23,793
Timor-Leste 537	—	—	1	10	9	12	11	—	—	—	—	1	—	—
Tonga 866	5	11	6	7	10	10	13	9	11	15	7	7	10	7
Vanuatu 846	1	1	1	9	9	9	24	1	3	1	2	3	2	1
Vietnam 582	461	580	1,324	1,163	1,192	1,100	1,903	1,139	2,585	4,910	5,727	7,206	9,265	11,425
Wallis-Futuna 857	—	—	1	—	—	—	—	—	—	—	—	—	—	—
Europe 170	**10,242**	**9,955**	**10,348**	**12,942**	**15,776**	**20,180**	**27,015**	**18,608**	**19,652**	**23,671**	**31,202**	**37,391**	**43,680**	**44,054**
Albania 914	15	15	10	20	19	28	34	8	6	5	12	39	25	10
Armenia 911	50	112	103	91	65	81	111	34	32	39	48	47	48	34
Azerbaijan 912	65	70	121	159	132	231	178	25	37	13	47	50	742	1,942
Belarus 913	35	19	84	33	35	74	102	118	137	237	375	381	585	1,101
Bosnia & Herzegovina 963	43	32	21	28	18	51	20	13	17	13	12	73	27	27
Bulgaria 918	110	101	156	172	268	293	306	367	366	478	546	493	495	453
Croatia 960	110	78	197	130	159	147	247	148	150	186	300	373	361	342
Czech Republic 935	707	654	672	822	1,052	1,123	1,262	1,173	1,293	1,459	1,843	2,305	2,456	2,525
Estonia 939	58	82	121	133	146	221	242	259	174	195	433	547	560	311
Faroe Islands 816	20	5	14	9	2	4	3	14	17	19	8	5	5	9
Georgia 915	107	99	132	226	212	266	364	35	19	60	84	206	118	200
Gibraltar 823	10	26	14	138	163	301	594	3	1	3	2	5	1	3
Hungary 944	687	688	934	1,142	1,022	1,188	1,292	3,013	2,693	2,760	2,644	2,633	2,645	2,869
Kazakhstan 916	163	605	168	320	538	646	753	364	348	409	568	1,165	998	1,290
Kyrgyz Republic 917	28	31	39	30	31	71	49	4	6	12	11	5	5	2
Latvia 941	111	91	124	121	177	245	381	160	210	402	394	386	317	355
Lithuania 946	100	103	163	295	389	567	720	182	320	378	526	684	611	496
Macedonia, FYR 962	33	19	26	21	32	23	34	117	79	65	83	51	45	77
Moldova 921	36	31	25	39	40	30	53	74	42	46	53	53	39	25
Montenegro, Rep. of 943	—	—	—	—	—	—	45	—	—	—	—	—	—	6
Poland 964	788	687	759	928	1,267	1,961	3,123	1,023	1,172	1,420	1,952	2,074	2,377	2,350
Romania 968	375	249	367	502	632	550	680	555	745	785	919	1,310	1,194	1,125
Russia 922	2,724	2,399	2,450	2,959	3,942	4,717	7,365	6,532	7,146	9,085	12,560	16,150	20,731	20,221
Serbia, Rep. of 942	—	—	—	—	—	—	110	—	—	—	—	—	—	61
Serbia & Montenegro 965	55	78	50	143	132	147	—	6	11	16	98	60	72	—
Slovak Republic 936	70	93	115	132	150	511	680	250	271	1,039	1,242	994	1,386	1,603
Tajikistan 923	29	33	50	56	29	43	53	5	1	8	8	249	62	—
Turkey 186	3,107	3,107	2,904	3,361	4,274	5,730	6,585	3,255	3,760	4,062	5,322	5,584	5,774	4,897
Turkmenistan 925	249	47	34	294	237	113	185	50	63	82	87	146	81	234
Ukraine 926	205	255	231	398	532	756	1,342	765	458	310	935	1,226	1,765	1,319

		Exports							Imports						
		2001	2002	2003	2004	2005	2006	2007	2001	2002	2003	2004	2005	2006	2007
		Millions of U.S. Dollars							Millions of U.S. Dollars						
Uzbekistan	927	148	138	257	230	74	54	89	57	81	88	90	98	153	166
Europe n.s.	884	8	11	8	12	10	9	14	—	1	—	1	1	3	—
Middle East	**407**	**23,088**	**21,827**	**22,024**	**26,655**	**35,145**	**43,685**	**52,190**	**39,672**	**37,262**	**45,202**	**56,021**	**69,562**	**79,900**	**86,298**
Bahrain	419	433	419	509	301	351	491	591	451	419	401	432	455	654	655
Egypt	469	3,778	2,866	2,660	3,105	3,169	4,104	5,347	939	1,417	1,219	1,439	2,221	2,574	2,545
Iran, I.R. of	429	8	27	99	85	96	85	146	149	163	167	156	180	162	178
Iraq	433	46	32	316	856	1,372	1,494	1,575	6,298	3,798	4,913	9,204	9,647	12,231	11,894
Israel	436	7,482	7,039	6,878	9,198	9,732	10,965	13,019	12,158	12,644	13,010	14,790	17,129	19,399	21,078
Jordan	439	343	404	492	552	643	650	857	242	438	705	1,145	1,320	1,489	1,388
Kuwait	443	906	1,015	1,509	1,519	1,974	2,135	2,485	2,211	2,052	2,478	3,473	4,614	4,182	4,313
Lebanon	446	418	318	314	463	464	934	826	93	66	96	78	91	93	110
Libya	672	9	18	—	39	84	435	510	—	—	—	346	1,657	2,629	3,540
Oman	449	306	357	323	330	593	854	1,059	455	423	748	449	595	960	1,088
Qatar	453	336	314	408	455	986	1,331	2,762	580	535	373	430	490	284	518
Saudi Arabia	456	5,970	4,779	4,596	5,245	6,830	7,808	10,399	14,414	13,892	19,525	22,502	28,966	33,087	37,165
Syrian Arab Republic	463	226	274	214	211	157	224	362	166	160	282	297	352	230	119
United Arab Emirates	466	2,640	3,598	3,510	4,064	8,477	11,921	11,609	1,284	998	1,213	1,214	1,542	1,447	1,394
West Bank/Gaza Strip	487	2	—	—	—	4	2	18	7	9	2	1	4	4	4
Yemen, Republic of	474	185	366	195	232	217	255	642	233	258	72	67	303	479	313
Western Hemisphere	**207**	**159,694**	**148,717**	**149,013**	**171,508**	**191,730**	**222,705**	**243,263**	**204,601**	**209,968**	**223,710**	**263,065**	**302,501**	**341,065**	**354,528**
Antigua and Barbuda	311	96	82	127	125	190	194	240	4	4	14	5	5	6	9
Argentina	213	3,928	1,591	2,435	3,386	4,100	4,773	5,854	3,257	3,432	3,435	4,067	4,945	4,277	4,820
Aruba	314	279	465	355	374	547	511	529	1,104	803	1,011	1,862	3,026	2,922	3,070
Bahamas, The	313	1,022	975	1,084	1,182	1,769	2,288	2,473	328	478	500	667	726	475	523
Barbados	316	286	269	302	348	393	443	457	41	36	45	38	33	35	40
Belize	339	173	137	200	152	217	239	234	103	84	106	113	104	156	113
Bermuda	319	371	415	401	472	489	638	660	67	23	16	25	88	17	24
Bolivia	218	217	192	182	194	218	215	278	173	167	192	273	308	378	377
Brazil	223	15,928	12,409	11,218	13,863	15,346	19,227	24,628	15,259	16,722	18,965	22,734	26,221	28,031	27,193
Chile	228	3,131	2,612	2,719	3,625	5,198	6,790	8,311	4,083	4,350	4,323	5,422	7,446	10,291	9,784
Colombia	233	3,606	3,589	3,755	4,504	5,415	6,708	8,560	6,068	5,936	6,790	7,766	9,424	9,826	10,034
Costa Rica	238	2,496	3,132	3,414	3,304	3,596	4,132	4,581	3,091	3,339	3,582	3,504	3,602	4,084	4,209
Dominica	321	31	45	34	36	61	68	84	6	5	6	4	4	3	2
Dominican Republic	243	4,436	4,262	4,214	4,343	4,708	5,348	6,091	4,286	4,271	4,558	4,638	4,721	4,649	4,328
Ecuador	248	1,420	1,607	1,448	1,666	1,980	2,728	2,937	2,316	2,391	3,030	4,691	6,215	7,572	6,540
El Salvador	253	1,771	1,665	1,824	1,868	1,846	2,157	2,313	1,935	2,038	2,077	2,112	2,053	1,919	2,118
Falkland Islands	323	—	—	1	—	9	2	1	7	6	5	7	9	13	5
Greenland	326	5	4	3	4	5	3	5	30	24	14	15	18	12	10
Grenada	328	60	57	68	70	82	76	83	25	7	8	5	6	5	9
Guatemala	258	1,877	2,042	2,274	2,548	2,813	3,518	4,076	2,747	2,976	3,151	3,360	3,342	3,326	3,269
Guyana	336	141	128	117	136	175	179	188	161	134	136	138	133	141	147
Haiti	263	550	582	640	663	688	809	711	272	264	341	381	459	509	500
Honduras	268	2,437	2,565	2,845	3,077	3,244	3,693	4,462	3,249	3,396	3,454	3,804	3,920	3,893	4,101
Jamaica	343	1,407	1,420	1,469	1,431	1,687	2,035	2,318	496	421	524	343	411	562	789
Mexico	273	101,509	97,531	97,457	110,775	120,049	134,167	136,541	132,778	136,144	139,702	157,821	172,485	200,516	212,889
Netherlands Antilles	353	818	742	747	873	1,135	1,485	2,082	518	382	646	465	971	1,164	810
Nicaragua	278	443	438	503	592	620	755	890	631	707	801	1,030	1,227	1,580	1,663
Panama	283	1,333	1,408	1,848	1,820	2,169	2,707	3,740	312	321	319	336	349	405	391
Paraguay	288	396	433	489	622	896	911	1,237	37	48	60	69	62	68	80
Peru	293	1,567	1,557	1,707	2,095	2,289	2,927	4,119	1,970	2,077	2,572	3,912	5,395	6,155	5,489
St. Kitts and Nevis	361	66	70	81	82	126	170	203	44	51	48	44	56	57	61
St. Lucia	362	89	98	121	103	135	152	166	31	20	14	15	34	32	36
St. Pierre-Miquelon	363	1	1	—	1	1	—	—	4	4	3	2	1	1	2
St. Vincent & Grens	364	40	40	47	45	45	58	69	23	17	4	4	16	2	1
Suriname	366	158	125	193	178	244	258	306	148	140	148	148	171	172	136
Trinidad and Tobago	369	1,090	1,018	1,064	1,207	1,439	1,615	1,779	2,590	2,664	4,709	6,266	8,342	8,822	9,342
Uruguay	298	414	210	327	324	355	482	641	241	203	271	622	784	547	524
Venezuela, Rep. Bol	299	5,684	4,447	2,840	4,782	6,408	9,012	10,200	16,141	15,828	18,074	26,316	35,292	38,386	41,011
Western Hem. n.s	399	418	360	460	640	1,043	1,231	1,217	28	57	56	41	99	56	80
Other Countries n.i.e	**910**	**7**	**170**	**269**	**424**	**367**	**348**	**449**	—	—	—	**2**	—	—	—
Cuba	928	7	145	261	400	362	348	447	—	—	—	—	—	—	—
North Korea	954	1	25	8	24	6	—	2	—	—	—	2	—	—	—
Countries & Areas n.s	**898**	**262**	**264**	**186**	**223**	**222**	**124**	**428**	—	—	—	—	—	—	—
Memorandum Items															
European Union	998	162,577	147,017	154,440	172,880	186,508	214,147	246,801	232,906	238,979	260,154	290,934	317,892	339,805	362,510
Oil Exporting Ctys	999	20,410	19,209	17,638	22,568	32,641	41,485	49,419	64,524	56,853	73,838	100,810	131,874	152,759	168,482
Non-Oil Develop.Ctys	201	303,820	292,301	307,080	354,202	390,135	458,939	519,274	514,003	548,605	603,811	719,228	826,529	942,656	994,459
PERCENT DISTRIBUTION															
Industrial Countries	**101**	**55.6**	**55.0**	**55.1**	**53.8**	**53.2**	**51.7**	**51.0**	**51.0**	**49.6**	**48.1**	**46.2**	**44.7**	**42.9**	**42.4**
Developing Countries	**202**	**44.4**	**44.9**	**44.9**	**46.1**	**46.8**	**48.3**	**48.9**	**49.0**	**50.4**	**51.9**	**53.8**	**55.3**	**57.1**	**57.6**
Africa	**607**	**1.2**	**1.1**	**1.1**	**1.3**	**1.4**	**1.4**	**1.5**	**2.2**	**1.8**	**2.5**	**3.1**	**3.7**	**4.1**	**4.4**
Asia	**507**	**16.8**	**17.8**	**18.7**	**19.0**	**18.6**	**19.2**	**19.6**	**24.6**	**26.3**	**27.0**	**27.7**	**28.0**	**28.8**	**29.2**
Europe	**170**	**1.4**	**1.4**	**1.4**	**1.6**	**1.7**	**1.9**	**2.3**	**1.6**	**1.6**	**1.8**	**2.0**	**2.2**	**2.3**	**2.2**
Middle East	**407**	**3.2**	**3.1**	**3.0**	**3.3**	**3.9**	**4.2**	**4.5**	**3.4**	**3.1**	**3.5**	**3.7**	**4.0**	**4.2**	**4.3**
Western Hemisphere	**207**	**21.8**	**21.5**	**20.6**	**21.0**	**21.2**	**21.5**	**20.9**	**17.3**	**17.5**	**17.1**	**17.2**	**17.5**	**17.8**	**17.6**
Other Countries n.i.e	**910**	—	—	—	.1	—	—	—	—	—	—	—	—	—	—

	Exports							Imports						
	2001	2002	2003	2004	2005	2006	2007	2001	2002	2003	2004	2005	2006	2007
ANNUAL PERCENT CHANGE														
World........ 001	–5.3	–5.2	4.4	12.8	10.8	14.7	12.1	–4.7	1.9	8.6	16.9	13.6	10.8	5.1
Industrial Countries........ 101	–5.5	–6.2	4.5	10.2	9.5	11.5	10.6	–4.3	–.8	5.1	12.4	9.7	6.4	3.7
Developing Countries........ 202	–5.1	–3.9	4.2	16.0	12.2	18.4	13.6	–5.1	4.7	11.9	21.0	16.9	14.3	6.2
Africa........ 607	13.1	–9.5	2.5	29.5	19.1	18.1	23.1	–4.2	–15.4	49.4	42.5	37.5	22.9	13.4
Asia........ 507	–8.0	.5	9.8	14.8	8.0	18.8	14.6	–7.0	9.3	11.3	20.1	14.6	13.9	6.7
Europe........ 170	–.8	–2.8	3.9	25.1	21.9	27.9	33.9	–6.4	5.6	20.5	31.8	19.8	16.8	.9
Middle East........ 407	.3	–5.5	.9	21.0	31.8	24.3	19.5	–1.7	–6.1	21.3	23.9	24.2	14.9	8.0
Western Hemisphere........ 207	–4.7	–6.9	.2	15.1	11.8	16.2	9.2	–2.9	2.6	6.5	17.6	15.0	12.7	3.9
Other Countries n.i.e........ 910	28.1	—	58.5	57.7	–13.4	–5.4	29.0	....	....	....	....	....	....	....

	Exports 2001	2002	2003	2004	2005	2006	2007	Imports 2001	2002	2003	2004	2005	2006	2007
	Millions of U.S. Dollars							*Millions of U.S. Dollars*						
IFS World Total	**2,060.4**	**1,861.0**	**2,206.0**	**2,930.8**	**3,404.5**	**3,953.2**	**4,485.2**	**3,060.8**	**1,964.3**	**2,190.4**	**3,113.6**	**3,878.9**	**4,757.4**	**5,726.1**
DOTS World Total 001	**2,057.6**	**2,183.0Y**	**2,197.2**	**2,929.9**	**3,402.6**	**4,291.1Y**	**5,082.2Y**	**3,048.1**	**2,629.4Y**	**2,190.4**	**3,118.6**	**3,878.7**	**6,168.1Y**	**7,408.0Y**
Industrial Countries 101	**658.7**	**762.3Y**	**871.3**	**1,321.5**	**1,547.9**	**1,533.1Y**	**1,743.5Y**	**941.5**	**811.7Y**	**535.2**	**675.4**	**761.6**	**1,859.8Y**	**1,987.6Y**
United States 111	176.89	184.55V	250.72	600.69	788.95	497.64V	475.91V	273.70	230.45V	167.49	223.90	260.85	530.53V	704.55V
Canada 156	64.87	30.58V	86.84	105.14	87.11	48.15V	87.50V	19.01	6.97V	10.47	12.02	21.59	23.52V	25.97V
Australia 193	2.77	4.86V	2.16	1.99	1.20	11.90V	21.98V	8.61	13.98V	7.29	9.32	5.26	15.13V	18.50V
Japan 158	12.10	47.64V	12.44	15.12	32.15	105.24V	84.56V	49.70	33.53V	28.09	42.82	42.89	75.02V	86.42V
New Zealand 196	.23	.36V	.42	.38	.33	.29V	.48V	3.42	3.20V	5.27	3.96	3.65	3.63V	7.80V
Austria 122	1.01	1.73V	1.43	.38	.32	.51V	1.76V	6.52	6.90V	2.64	4.86	6.68	82.83V	28.16V
Belgium 124	23.18	18.31V	—	—	—	23.71V	53.94V	14.77	13.63V	—	—	—	23.22V	62.69V
Belgium-Luxembourg n.s. 127	—	—Y	18.15	19.56	14.64	16.86Y	19.58Y	—	—Y	12.38	12.82	12.35	13.86Y	16.48Y
Cyprus 423	2.81	.94V	1.32	.39	.93	.76V	.93V	.25	.09V	.02	.02	.04	.06V	.04V
Denmark 128	1.86	2.18V	2.45	2.80	3.42	5.62V	5.90V	8.69	12.01V	9.57	7.67	8.26	16.09V	24.25V
Finland 172	1.23	5.84V	5.66	8.23	8.46	18.96V	46.07V	8.57	4.71V	3.13	6.06	10.89	222.21V	102.07V
France 132	16.78	23.50V	19.47	32.73	31.07	42.04V	41.07V	128.58	64.89V	50.54	52.44	67.82	144.86V	155.54V
Germany 134	96.45	118.83V	145.05	151.54	143.29	203.68V	245.70V	93.31	81.56V	61.70	82.65	87.76	200.34V	198.39V
Greece 174	2.13	3.90V	2.07	2.34	1.05	2.48V	2.03V	6.10	3.43V	4.06	2.87	2.50	2.25V	2.57V
Iceland 176	—	.03V	.01	—	.06	.11V	.26V	.09	.16V	—	.01	.03	.69V	.50V
Ireland 178	.47	1.07V	.12	.54	.39	5.47V	2.21V	4.64	5.54V	5.35	6.16	8.85	7.47V	14.49V
Italy 136	70.91	90.63V	88.92	89.29	92.57	121.87V	115.06V	100.34	89.63V	50.21	66.25	75.76	133.14V	133.57V
Luxembourg 137	—	.02V	—	—	—	.05V	.08V	.90	.19V	.01	.03	.05	.51V	.28V
Malta 181	.03	.06V	.53	1.67	.91	.17V	.05V	.14	.52V	.01	—	—	.10V	—V
Netherlands 138	32.22	43.09V	37.15	53.68	46.90	85.31V	103.56V	25.19	24.71V	13.08	13.68	18.88	50.25V	71.45V
Norway 142	12.27	8.97V	9.62	21.95	23.80	47.76V	61.03V	1.31	1.67V	1.72	3.45	2.64	5.87V	5.72V
Portugal 182	3.71	10.63V	19.61	10.77	10.20	19.32V	41.14V	3.47	3.69V	2.21	2.31	2.77	3.87V	3.60V
Slovenia 961	—	.54V	.18	.03	—	.37V	.17V	.43	.99V	.62	.92	.68	.20V	1.77V
Spain 184	64.21	87.01V	75.52	95.24	130.79	142.27V	172.53V	100.81	96.05V	42.83	55.67	48.08	101.09V	117.55V
Sweden 144	5.52	7.09V	9.71	11.71	19.69	18.96V	35.99V	16.11	6.52V	10.37	18.21	22.51	30.07V	36.87V
Switzerland 146	1.45	6.98V	3.40	3.88	25.02	4.14V	18.18V	28.54	55.70V	21.22	18.55	16.75	91.32V	91.49V
United Kingdom 112	65.61	62.95V	78.37	91.45	84.67	109.43V	105.80V	38.28	50.94V	24.97	28.77	34.11	81.71V	76.90V
Developing Countries 202	**1,376.2**	**1,396.1Y**	**1,290.7**	**1,508.6**	**1,718.1**	**2,589.2Y**	**3,129.3Y**	**2,104.9**	**1,815.9Y**	**1,654.4**	**2,439.2**	**3,113.0**	**4,303.2Y**	**5,414.0Y**
Africa 607	**37.8**	**49.2Y**	**63.3**	**61.8**	**101.7**	**135.9Y**	**152.3Y**	**85.4**	**50.4Y**	**72.5**	**169.5**	**334.3**	**422.4Y**	**701.9Y**
Algeria 612	1.28	18.08V	24.69	9.76	15.05	18.58Y	24.06Y	—	—V	—	.02	—	—Y	—Y
Angola 614	.38	.41Y	.33	.43	.80	.99Y	1.23Y	—	—Y	32.46	—	42.59	52.64Y	65.33Y
Benin 638	—	.01V	.05	.05	.15	.18Y	.23Y	—	—Y	—	—	—	—Y	—Y
Botswana 616	.09	.10Y	.21	.07	—	—Y	—Y	—	—Y	—	—	—	—Y	—Y
Burkina Faso 748	—	—Y	—	—	.01	.01Y	.01Y	—	—Y	—	—	—	—Y	—Y
Cameroon 622	—	—V	1.22	1.29	5.15	6.37Y	7.90Y	—	—V	—	—	14.90	18.42Y	22.85Y
Cape Verde 624	—	—Y	.03	.01	—	—Y	—Y	—	—Y	.01	—	—	—Y	—Y
Congo, Dem. Rep. of 636	.16	.17Y	—	.36	.78	.96Y	1.19Y	—	—Y	—	.01	—	—Y	—Y
Congo, Republic of 634	—	.35V	.77	—	—	—Y	—Y	—	—V	—	—	—	—Y	—Y
Côte d'Ivoire 662	—	.11V	.32	.47	.41	1.61V	2.00Y	—	—V	—	—	.06	—V	—Y
Equatorial Guinea 642	....	....	....	....	....	....	....	10.96	11.90Y	—	—	20.63	25.50Y	31.65Y
Gabon 646	—	—Y	.55	.82	1.66	2.05Y	2.54Y	—	—Y	—	—	—	—Y	—Y
Gambia, The 648	—	—Y	.03	—	—	—Y	—Y	—	—Y	—	—	—	—Y	—Y
Ghana 652	.72	.78Y	.29	.64	3.48	4.30Y	5.33Y	—	—Y	—	—	.10	.12Y	.15Y
Guinea 656	—	—Y	.04	.02	.12	.15Y	.19Y	—	—Y	—	—	—	—Y	—Y
Guinea-Bissau 654	—	—Y	—	—	—	—Y	—Y	23.09	25.06Y	—	—	—	—Y	—Y
Kenya 664	.07	.06V	.14	.04	.12	.15Y	.18Y	—	—V	—	—	.01	.01Y	.01Y
Liberia 668	—	—Y	.20	.72	.30	.38Y	.47Y	—	—Y	—	—	—	—Y	—Y
Madagascar 674	—	—V	—	—	—	—Y	—Y	.02	—V	—	—	.01	.01Y	.01Y
Mali 678	—	—Y	—	.05	.05	.07Y	.08Y	....	....	....	....	....	....	....
Mauritania 682	—	—Y	.19	.48	.69	.85Y	1.05Y	—	—Y	—	—	—	—Y	—Y
Mauritius 684	.70	5.69V	.09	.04	.17	.20V	.25V	—	.29V	.01	.01	.01	.20V	.44V
Morocco 686	2.10	8.97V	8.44	11.58	17.65	21.82Y	27.07Y	4.38	2.80V	.09	2.29	13.22	16.34Y	20.28Y
Mozambique 688	—	—V	.02	.13	.08	.09Y	.12Y	—	—V	—	—	—	—Y	—Y
Namibia 728	—	—Y	—	.03	.01	.02Y	.02Y	....	....	....	....	....	....	....
Niger 692	—	—V	—	.02	—	—Y	—Y	36.84	—V	—	—	—	—Y	—Y
Nigeria 694	3.17	3.82V	10.54	9.52	13.62	16.82Y	21.79Y	—	—V	27.27	152.88	227.92	286.53Y	345.67Y
Senegal 722	.77	.37V	2.98	6.92	15.05	19.76V	24.52Y	—	—V	—	—	—	—V	—Y
Seychelles 718	—	—V	—	—	.09	.11Y	.13Y	—	—V	—	—	.01	.01Y	.01Y
Sierra Leone 724	—	—Y	.04	—	.01	.01Y	.01Y	—	—Y	—	—	—	—Y	—Y
South Africa 199	27.33	10.15V	11.72	13.50	24.15	36.08V	26.47V	7.90	5.81V	7.58	5.77	5.57	9.68V	199.42V
Tanzania 738	—	—V	—	—	.03	.03Y	.04Y	—	—V	—	—	—	—Y	—Y
Togo 742	—	—V	—	.14	.15	.19Y	.23Y	1.81	.96V	3.13	1.94	1.47	1.82Y	2.25Y
Tunisia 744	.97	.06V	.33	4.62	1.81	4.15V	5.14Y	.39	3.49V	1.96	6.59	7.82	11.13V	13.82Y
Uganda 746	—	—Y	.07	—	—	—Y	—Y	—	—Y	—	—	—	—Y	—Y
Zambia 754	—	.04V	.01	.02	.07	.02V	.02V	—	—V	—	—	—	—V	—V
Zimbabwe 698	.12	.04V	.04	.02	.08	—V	—Y	—	.04V	—	—	—	—V	—Y
Asia 507	**195.1**	**164.2Y**	**197.6**	**217.7**	**244.3**	**416.9Y**	**515.6Y**	**262.7**	**250.3Y**	**178.9**	**287.8**	**427.6**	**720.2Y**	**1,007.1Y**
Afghanistan, I.S. of 512	—	—Y	.03	—	.02	.03Y	.04Y	.03	.03Y	—	.01	—	—Y	—Y
Bangladesh 513	.39	—V	.38	.69	1.54	.33V	1.60V	.41	.17V	.25	.48	.73	.42Y	.52Y
Cambodia 522	—	—Y	.09	.24	.82	1.01Y	1.25Y	—	—V	.01	.02	.02	.12V	.15Y

	Exports 2001	Exports 2002	Exports 2003	Exports 2004	Exports 2005	Exports 2006	Exports 2007	Imports 2001	Imports 2002	Imports 2003	Imports 2004	Imports 2005	Imports 2006	Imports 2007
	Millions of U.S. Dollars							*Millions of U.S. Dollars*						
China,P.R.: Mainland.................. 924	102.86	71.00V	95.24	112.95	119.59	245.43V	310.59V	121.51	104.42V	86.02	172.72	242.29	447.58V	677.02V
China,P.R.:Hong Kong................ 532	24.44	30.58V	14.01	15.65	17.32	25.40V	33.17V	24.10	28.53V	6.88	9.89	11.68	37.63V	40.27V
China,P.R.:Macao........................ 546	.15	.23V	.51	.51	.38	.47V	.31V	.02	.04V	.04	.02	.03	.06V	.02V
French Polynesia........................ 887	—	—Y	—	.82	3.52	4.36Y	5.41Y	—	—Y	—	—	—	—Y	—Y
India.. 534	1.77	3.97V	10.19	4.29	3.71	4.58Y	5.69Y	23.07	21.07V	13.05	22.19	37.31	46.11Y	57.22Y
Indonesia.................................. 536	1.64	3.46V	1.58	1.03	1.31	1.34V	1.03V	5.70	4.38V	2.86	3.49	3.72	5.21V	7.98V
Korea.. 542	5.50	5.13V	6.09	11.93	22.67	27.30V	36.98V	45.21	38.12V	36.74	33.33	48.93	59.66V	78.80V
Lao People's Dem.Rep................ 544	....	....	....	....	....	....	....	—	—Y	—	.02	—	—Y	—Y
Malaysia.................................... 548	32.68	18.60V	2.21	.82	1.87	10.71V	14.69V	5.77	6.18V	2.53	3.96	7.88	15.97V	18.33V
Maldives.................................... 556	—	—Y	—	—	.03	.03Y	.04Y	—	—Y	—	—	—	—Y	—Y
Mongolia.................................... 948	....	....	....	....	....	....	....	—	—Y	—	.01	.01	.01Y	.01Y
Myanmar.................................... 518	....	....	....	....	....	....	....	.03	.04Y	.13	.10	.15	.18Y	.23Y
Nepal... 558	—	—Y	.03	—	—	—Y	—Y	—	—Y	—	—	—	—Y	—Y
Pakistan.................................... 564	.05	1.95V	1.71	.09	2.83	3.50Y	4.35Y	2.82	1.15V	1.09	2.80	3.09	3.82Y	4.74Y
Philippines................................. 566	5.65	1.29V	5.86	5.64	7.85	31.63V	37.97V	1.09	1.51V	.87	1.16	2.07	2.44V	2.71V
Singapore.................................. 576	2.52	10.36V	2.31	3.93	4.14	16.58V	13.97V	2.62	5.86V	2.78	5.18	6.03	8.06V	7.58V
Sri Lanka.................................... 524	—	.01V	—	.57	—	.12V	.34V	1.02	.44V	.68	.64	.63	.16V	.64V
Taiwan Province of China............ 528	2.34	3.54V	4.59	5.67	3.23	6.32V	8.49V	22.37	34.49V	20.39	26.28	54.80	82.07V	98.21V
Thailand..................................... 578	12.92	12.30V	50.13	47.78	44.74	37.81V	39.71V	6.26	2.86V	4.14	4.76	6.95	10.69V	12.66V
Vietnam...................................... 582	2.21	1.82V	2.63	5.13	8.75	—V	—V	.69	1.02V	.43	.73	1.24	—V	—V
Europe...................................... 170	**13.3**	**70.1Y**	**54.7**	**49.5**	**62.4**	**241.4Y**	**159.1Y**	**56.7**	**76.9Y**	**272.4**	**358.6**	**326.0**	**59.8Y**	**125.6Y**
Albania...................................... 914	.08	.10V	.02	—	.27	.78V	.31V	—	—V	—	—	—	—V	.07V
Armenia...................................... 911	....	....	....	....	....	....	....	—	—Y	—	—	—	—V	.01V
Azerbaijan.................................. 912	—	.59V	—	—	—	.02V	.09V	—	—V	—	—	—	—V	—V
Belarus....................................... 913	—	.07V	.09	.10	.03	.84V	1.11V	.02	—V	.37	.68	3.33	.03V	—V
Bosnia & Herzegovina.................. 963	—	—Y	—	.05	1.09	1.35Y	1.68Y	—	—Y	—	—	.01	.01Y	.01Y
Bulgaria..................................... 918	—	1.39V	1.12	.57	1.10	3.00V	6.60V	.68	1.70V	2.15	1.28	.91	1.52V	.12V
Croatia...................................... 960	.09	—V	—	.56	2.04	—V	—V	.07	—V	.03	.05	.05	—V	—V
Czech Republic........................... 935	—	1.89V	.33	.90	1.15	.58V	1.27V	1.62	9.74V	—	1.31	3.20	10.08V	6.43V
Czechoslovakia n.s...................... 937	—	—Y	—	—	—	—Y	—Y	—	—Y	.92	—	—	—Y	—Y
Estonia....................................... 939	.13	.23V	.85	.19	.27	.05V	—V	.54	.01V	.01	1.55	.13	4.40V	.32V
Faroe Islands.............................. 816	—	—Y	—	.03	—	—Y	—Y	—	—Y	—	—	—	—Y	—Y
Georgia...................................... 915	.06	.01V	.47	.20	.12	.35V	.48Y	4.80	—V	—	—	—	.17V	.12Y
Gibraltar..................................... 823	—	—Y	—	1.07	.04	.05Y	.06Y	—	—Y	—	—	—	—Y	—Y
Hungary...................................... 944	.12	.80V	.40	.59	.27	.13V	.15V	2.38	.82V	.70	1.05	1.28	1.71V	2.17V
Kazakhstan................................. 916	—	.21V	—	—	.03	.04Y	.05Y	—	—V	—	—	—	—Y	—Y
Latvia... 941	—	.41V	.29	.11	.07	.02V	.05V	1.30	.02V	.01	2.25	.02	.05V	.36V
Lithuania.................................... 946	.53	.29V	4.26	6.98	1.82	.47V	.50V	—	.02V	.01	.33	.03	7.33V	.74V
Macedonia, FYR.......................... 962	—	.32V	.55	.50	.35	.65V	.80Y	—	—V	—	—	—	—V	—Y
Moldova...................................... 921	—	.06V	—	—	.18	.22Y	.28Y	—	—V	—	—	—	—Y	.01Y
Poland.. 964	2.10	24.81V	1.85	5.07	4.69	8.67V	7.53V	3.32	1.19V	8.34	2.69	3.32	4.96V	5.48V
Romania..................................... 968	.02	1.54V	.12	.37	1.08	6.02V	2.19V	6.73	1.95V	.45	.36	.26	.33V	.26V
Russia.. 922	6.51	19.38V	20.07	17.11	37.78	201.51V	99.93V	25.95	58.96V	257.05	342.32	308.65	24.57V	98.73V
Serbia & Montenegro.................. 965	.87	.95Y	.20	.09	.14	.18Y	.22Y	—	—Y	.06	.01	.08	.10Y	.13Y
Slovak Republic.......................... 936	.04	.57V	.08	.06	.08	.12V	.23V	.18	.02V	—	.15	.08	.19V	1.28V
Turkey.. 186	2.70	16.41V	23.32	13.83	8.03	14.15V	32.81V	5.76	2.32V	2.13	3.28	4.45	4.15V	9.17V
Ukraine....................................... 926	.07	.06V	.49	.96	1.70	2.10Y	2.60Y	3.16	.02V	.03	1.25	.12	.15Y	.18Y
Uzbekistan.................................. 927	—	—Y	—	—	—	—Y	—Y	.01	.01Y	.05	.04	.04	.05Y	.06Y
Europe n.s.................................. 884	—	—Y	.20	.19	.11	.13Y	.16Y	.12	.13Y	.06	.01	—	—Y	—Y
Middle East............................. 407	**79.9**	**106.3Y**	**77.1**	**123.1**	**161.8**	**235.2Y**	**275.9Y**	**45.9**	**47.1Y**	**6.9**	**128.9**	**12.6**	**13.8Y**	**16.5Y**
Bahrain....................................... 419	—	—Y	—	—	—	—Y	—Y	.99	1.08Y	—	—	—	—Y	—Y
Egypt.. 469	1.83	1.98Y	3.44	9.35	28.30	34.98Y	43.41Y	25.98	28.19Y	.86	6.02	3.17	3.92Y	4.86Y
Iran, I.R. of................................. 429	24.34	38.80V	15.84	43.37	80.73	99.66Y	129.10Y	—	—Y	—	114.92	.72	.91Y	1.09Y
Iraq... 433	—	—Y	—	3.11	—	—Y	—Y	—	—Y	—	—	—	—Y	—Y
Israel... 436	45.55	58.91V	40.06	26.10	25.89	64.36V	61.91V	10.10	8.36V	4.63	5.35	8.16	7.92V	9.13V
Jordan... 439	.38	.66V	4.72	8.33	9.43	13.71V	12.38V	—	—V	—	.03	.03	.08V	.23V
Kuwait... 443	.07	.08Y	.24	.61	1.40	1.73Y	2.24Y	2.63	2.80Y	—	—	—	—Y	—Y
Lebanon...................................... 446	.01	.01Y	.29	.61	.88	1.09Y	1.35Y	.72	.79Y	.01	.26	.01	.02Y	.02Y
Libya... 672	—	—Y	—	.07	.23	.29Y	.38Y	—	—Y	—	—	—	—Y	—Y
Oman.. 449	—	.03V	—	.01	.09	.11Y	.14Y	—	—V	.01	—	—	—Y	—Y
Qatar... 453	—	.19V	.21	.03	.01	1.04V	1.35Y	—	—V	—	—	.07	.41V	.50Y
Saudi Arabia................................ 456	6.96	5.66V	7.90	29.96	13.52	16.69Y	21.62Y	1.49	1.59Y	1.26	2.16	.09	.11Y	.13Y
Syrian Arab Republic................... 463	—	—Y	3.50	.11	.16	.19Y	.24Y	—	—Y	—	.01	.08	.10Y	.12Y
United Arab Emirates.................. 466	.74	—V	.85	1.40	1.12	1.39Y	1.80Y	4.01	4.27Y	.15	.15	.29	.37Y	.44Y
Yemen, Republic of..................... 474	—	—V	.04	—	—	—Y	—Y	—	—V	—	—	—	—Y	—Y
Western Hemisphere............... 207	**1,050.1**	**1,006.3Y**	**897.9**	**1,056.5**	**1,147.9**	**1,559.7Y**	**2,026.4Y**	**1,654.2**	**1,391.2Y**	**1,123.7**	**1,494.4**	**2,012.5**	**3,086.9Y**	**3,562.9Y**
Antigua and Barbuda.................. 311	.01	.01Y	—	.01	.48	.59Y	.73Y	....	....	....	....	....	....	....
Argentina.................................... 213	316.37	111.32V	154.91	223.30	266.93	281.31V	425.27V	705.79	595.77V	571.68	691.46	785.72	1,315.93V	1,325.36V
Aruba.. 314	.07	.08V	1.00	1.26	.38	1.00V	.59V	—	—V	—	.42	.04	—V	—V
Bahamas, The............................. 313	.59	.64Y	.31	.65	1.58	1.96Y	2.43Y	—	—Y	.01	.05	.03	.03Y	.04Y
Barbados..................................... 316	—	.09V	—	.95	2.61	3.21V	3.98Y	.01	—V	—	—	—	—V	—Y
Belize.. 339	.16	.18Y	.04	.03	.20	.25Y	.31Y	.02	.02Y	.04	.03	.02	.02Y	.03Y
Bermuda...................................... 319	—	—Y	—	.02	—	.01V	.01Y	.12	.13Y	.12	—	—	—Y	—Y
Bolivia... 218	2.63	3.52V	2.44	3.17	4.61	5.70Y	7.07Y	1.13	1.24V	.74	1.08	1.20	1.48Y	1.83Y
Brazil... 223	440.69	484.86V	470.82	483.64	458.25	618.22V	786.20V	625.88	451.54V	459.77	676.52	824.68	1,106.71V	1,417.28V
Chile.. 228	44.42	58.27V	71.46	61.09	83.15	—V	—V	67.13	45.10V	41.46	58.43	69.60	99.63V	109.14V

	Exports							Imports						
	2001	2002	2003	2004	2005	2006	2007	2001	2002	2003	2004	2005	2006	2007
	Millions of U.S. Dollars							*Millions of U.S. Dollars*						
Colombia........ 233	21.66	20.54V	12.97	13.27	13.51	28.53V	36.00V	4.73	5.89V	2.22	2.67	1.95	6.12V	9.99V
Costa Rica........ 238	.77	4.61V	.77	.68	.99	1.22Y	1.51Y	1.14	.67V	.67	.89	1.26	1.56Y	1.93Y
Dominica........ 321	—	—Y	—	—	.02	.02Y	.03Y	—	—Y	—	—	—	—Y	—Y
Dominican Republic........ 243	8.66	9.40Y	2.50	2.94	3.65	4.50Y	5.59Y	.51	.55Y	.13	.12	.07	.09Y	.11Y
Ecuador........ 248	1.56	21.26V	2.12	1.39	10.44	53.43V	66.30Y	10.08	1.32V	1.18	1.50	2.89	3.30V	4.09Y
El Salvador........ 253	.23	1.00V	3.98	1.58	1.04	23.66V	27.88V	.06	.02V	.01	.03	.01	.01V	.15V
Grenada........ 328	—	—Y	.03	—	—	—Y	—Y	.06	.06Y	.06	.05	.01	.01Y	.01Y
Guatemala........ 258	2.02	9.00V	3.97	2.92	3.33	4.12Y	5.11Y	.02	.45V	.04	.04	.08	.10Y	.12Y
Guyana........ 336	—	—Y	—	—	—	—Y	—Y	—	—Y	—	—	.05	.06Y	.07Y
Haiti........ 263	7.17	5.23V	.05	3.27	2.64	3.26Y	4.05Y	—	—Y	—	—	—	—Y	—Y
Honduras........ 268	.15	.70V	1.29	1.08	.47	.58Y	.72Y	.02	.25V	—	—	.09	.11Y	.13Y
Jamaica........ 343	.22	.72V	.18	.58	.66	1.50V	7.28V	—	—V	—	.02	.10	—V	—V
Mexico........ 273	76.20	91.57V	90.80	117.72	139.43	262.28V	333.25V	37.12	28.49V	20.47	29.60	50.87	73.13V	98.65V
Netherlands Antilles........ 353	.50	.39V	.67	1.16	.42	.52Y	.65Y	.23	.19V	—	1.70	2.44	3.01Y	3.74Y
Nicaragua........ 278	1.36	—V	.10	.07	.23	—V	—V	—	—V	.01	—	.02	—V	—V
Panama........ 283	1.02	1.03V	15.19	9.62	17.20	11.82V	4.54V	3.06	.09V	.76	1.54	.80	—V	.47V
Paraguay........ 288	82.80	58.40V	47.80	58.53	55.81	59.10V	73.34Y	18.33	181.56V	10.66	16.14	20.15	462.27V	573.67Y
Peru........ 293	16.89	64.40V	8.77	24.47	37.05	27.52V	36.62Y	4.22	5.53V	10.14	8.99	5.53	9.34V	11.17Y
St. Kitts and Nevis........ 361	—	—Y	—	—	.06	.08Y	.09Y	—	—Y	—	—	—	—Y	—Y
St. Lucia........ 362	—	—Y	.02	—	.11	.14Y	.18Y	—	—Y	—	—	—	—Y	—Y
St. Vincent & Grens........ 364	—	.01V	.09	—	.51	.63Y	.78Y	—	—V	—	—	—	—Y	—Y
Suriname........ 366	.01	.01Y	.80	1.26	.20	.25Y	.31Y	—	—Y	—	—	.06	.07Y	.09Y
Trinidad and Tobago........ 369	1.46	.28V	.87	9.12	7.75	9.57Y	11.88Y	.05	—V	.02	1.12	.05	.07Y	.08Y
Venezuela, Rep. Bol........ 299	22.42	58.76V	3.93	32.69	33.49	153.37V	181.62V	174.50	72.37V	1.10	1.82	244.75	3.78V	4.56Y
Western Hem. n.s........ 399	.01	.01Y	.05	.08	.68	1.36Y	2.03Y	—	—Y	2.35	.16	.06	.10Y	.14Y
Other Countries n.i.e........ 910	**.8**	**.9Y**	**.8**	**9.7**	**33.8**	**41.7Y**	**51.8Y**	**1.6**	**1.7Y**	**.6**	**.7**	**.7**	**.8Y**	**1.1Y**
Cuba........ 928	.59	.64Y	.74	8.78	33.68	41.62Y	51.65Y	.20	.21Y	.34	.24	.35	.43Y	.54Y
North Korea........ 954	.21	.23Y	.02	.93	.08	.10Y	.13Y	1.37	1.49Y	.24	.48	.33	.41Y	.51Y
Countries & Areas n.s........ 898	**1.7**	**1.8Y**	**—**	**—**	**—**	**—Y**	**—Y**	**.1**	**.1Y**	**—**	**—**	**—**	**—Y**	**—Y**
Special Categories........ 899	**20.2**	**21.9Y**	**34.3**	**89.8**	**102.7**	**127.0Y**	**157.6Y**	**—**	**—Y**	**—**	**3.3**	**3.4**	**4.3Y**	**5.3Y**
Memorandum Items														
European Union........ 998	391.05	507.32Y	513.77	586.25	597.64	827.92Y	1,003.30Y	566.46	477.83Y	302.77	370.71	416.05	1,142.85Y	1,063.42Y
Oil Exporting Ctys........ 999	60.61	128.88Y	65.80	131.55	160.57	311.00Y	385.12Y	188.34	85.41Y	32.66	275.43	477.55	297.30Y	360.36Y
Non-Oil Develop.Ctys........ 201	1,315.59	1,267.25Y	1,224.90	1,377.08	1,557.57	2,278.24Y	2,744.19Y	1,916.59	1,730.48Y	1,621.71	2,163.76	2,635.40	4,005.86Y	5,053.64Y
PERCENT DISTRIBUTION														
Industrial Countries........ 101	**32.0**	**34.9**	**39.7**	**45.1**	**45.5**	**35.7**	**34.3**	**30.9**	**30.9**	**24.4**	**21.7**	**19.6**	**30.2**	**26.8**
Developing Countries........ 202	**66.9**	**64.0**	**58.7**	**51.5**	**50.5**	**60.3**	**61.6**	**69.1**	**69.1**	**75.5**	**78.2**	**80.3**	**69.8**	**73.1**
Africa........ 607	**1.8**	**2.3**	**2.9**	**2.1**	**3.0**	**3.2**	**3.0**	**2.8**	**1.9**	**3.3**	**5.4**	**8.6**	**6.8**	**9.5**
Asia........ 507	**9.5**	**7.5**	**9.0**	**7.4**	**7.2**	**9.7**	**10.1**	**8.6**	**9.5**	**8.2**	**9.2**	**11.0**	**11.7**	**13.6**
Europe........ 170	**.6**	**3.2**	**2.5**	**1.7**	**1.8**	**5.6**	**3.1**	**1.9**	**2.9**	**12.4**	**11.5**	**8.4**	**1.0**	**1.7**
Middle East........ 407	**3.9**	**4.9**	**3.5**	**4.2**	**4.8**	**5.5**	**5.4**	**1.5**	**1.8**	**.3**	**4.1**	**.3**	**.2**	**.2**
Western Hemisphere........ 207	**51.0**	**46.1**	**40.9**	**36.1**	**33.7**	**36.3**	**39.9**	**54.3**	**52.9**	**51.3**	**47.9**	**51.9**	**50.0**	**48.1**
Other Countries n.i.e........ 910	**—**	**—**	**—**	**.3**	**1.0**	**1.0**	**1.0**	**.1**	**.1**	**—**	**—**	**—**	**—**	**—**
ANNUAL PERCENT CHANGE														
World........ 001	**−10.3**	**6.1**	**.7**	**33.3**	**16.1**	**26.1**	**18.4**	**−12.1**	**−13.7**	**−16.7**	**42.4**	**24.4**	**59.0**	**20.1**
Industrial Countries........ 101	**−3.3**	**15.7**	**14.3**	**51.7**	**17.1**	**−1.0**	**13.7**	**−14.5**	**−13.8**	**−34.1**	**26.2**	**12.8**	**144.2**	**6.9**
Developing Countries........ 202	**−13.4**	**1.4**	**−7.6**	**16.9**	**13.9**	**50.7**	**20.9**	**−10.4**	**−13.7**	**−8.9**	**47.4**	**27.6**	**38.2**	**25.8**
Africa........ 607	**−8.8**	**30.0**	**28.7**	**−2.5**	**64.7**	**33.6**	**12.1**	**−35.6**	**−41.0**	**44.0**	**133.8**	**97.2**	**26.4**	**66.2**
Asia........ 507	**7.2**	**−15.8**	**20.3**	**10.2**	**12.2**	**70.6**	**23.7**	**2.8**	**−4.7**	**−28.5**	**60.8**	**48.6**	**68.4**	**39.8**
Europe........ 170	**2.1**	**425.9**	**−21.9**	**−9.5**	**26.0**	**286.6**	**−34.1**	**−58.5**	**35.8**	**254.1**	**31.7**	**−9.1**	**−81.6**	**110.0**
Middle East........ 407	**−27.4**	**33.1**	**−27.5**	**59.6**	**31.5**	**45.4**	**17.3**	**46.2**	**2.5**	**−85.3**	**—**	**−90.2**	**9.6**	**19.5**
Western Hemisphere........ 207	**−15.5**	**−4.2**	**−10.8**	**17.7**	**8.6**	**35.9**	**29.9**	**−7.7**	**−15.9**	**−19.2**	**33.0**	**34.7**	**53.4**	**15.4**
Other Countries n.i.e........ 910	**−79.5**	**8.5**	**−12.7**	**—**	**247.7**	**23.6**	**24.1**	**38.2**	**8.5**	**−66.1**	**25.6**	**−5.3**	**23.6**	**24.1**

	Exports 2001	Exports 2002	Exports 2003	Exports 2004	Exports 2005	Exports 2006	Exports 2007	Imports 2001	Imports 2002	Imports 2003	Imports 2004	Imports 2005	Imports 2006	Imports 2007
	Millions of U.S. Dollars							*Millions of U.S. Dollars*						
DOTS World Total.................... 001	**2,078.9Y**	**1,567.9Y**	**1,975.0Y**	**2,697.4Y**	**3,467.5Y**	**4,952.4Y**	**5,942.6Y**	**2,292.8Y**	**2,075.7Y**	**2,484.6Y**	**3,156.1Y**	**3,551.5Y**	**4,354.5Y**	**6,317.5Y**
Industrial Countries................. 101	**566.5Y**	**476.6Y**	**453.4Y**	**545.3Y**	**649.9Y**	**650.9Y**	**899.8Y**	**739.9Y**	**655.7Y**	**846.0Y**	**877.3Y**	**804.9Y**	**773.6Y**	**1,115.1Y**
United States............................. 111	51.55V	74.00V	79.55V	81.82V	88.64V	139.27V	150.55V	162.47V	151.91V	282.48V	252.89V	80.85V	59.29V	97.57V
Canada.. 156	26.72V	5.26V	7.54V	27.87V	46.48V	.36V	33.05V	9.83V	2.72V	1.26V	3.58V	7.78V	4.62V	8.14V
Australia..................................... 193	.01V	.01V	.05V	.01V	.07V	.03V	.02V	1.94V	.63V	1.50V	1.61V	1.14V	.67V	1.05V
Japan... 158	47.98V	66.67V	84.34V	78.36V	113.04V	161.71V	147.57V	19.46V	18.74V	47.70V	56.80V	38.82V	18.07V	71.51V
New Zealand................................ 196	—V	—V	.01V	.01V	.06V	.01V	.01V	.12V	.19V	.38V	.01V	.01V	2.84V	3.59V
Austria.. 122	15.20V	6.94V	22.77V	59.01V	114.96V	4.06V	1.45V	13.36V	9.85V	19.34V	33.99V	32.24V	45.78V	75.91V
Belgium....................................... 124	44.70V	33.66V	35.47V	38.07V	24.88V	29.82V	27.02V	11.89V	14.01V	13.86V	14.41V	15.36V	19.56V	37.28V
Cyprus... 423	.06V	—V	—V	—V	—Y	—V	—V	.12V	.01V	—V	—V	.10V	—V	.12V
Denmark...................................... 128	.08V	.01V	.06V	.08V	.02V	.72V	.08V	10.01V	7.13V	6.70V	5.93V	2.42V	4.10V	6.82V
Finland.. 172	.10V	.07V	.06V	.14V	.17V	.50V	8.03V	20.74V	15.85V	13.06V	13.35V	21.34V	20.14V	30.77V
France... 132	44.20V	29.24V	22.78V	34.20V	39.57V	57.46V	189.82V	118.78V	38.69V	48.52V	43.17V	54.53V	59.99V	77.53V
Germany...................................... 134	56.35V	43.21V	34.53V	60.43V	52.91V	48.91V	79.19V	227.22V	224.54V	235.69V	242.91V	313.42V	306.51V	395.92V
Greece... 174	30.05V	10.44V	24.62V	28.38V	31.62V	24.18V	74.36V	1.08V	3.87V	3.98V	3.35V	2.25V	1.22V	2.46V
Ireland... 178	1.34V	.24V	.27V	—V	—V	—V	—V	1.23V	.64V	2.12V	2.50V	1.18V	1.76V	2.15V
Italy... 136	155.20V	133.77V	54.31V	48.73V	61.78V	115.15V	100.76V	45.53V	69.17V	48.90V	76.32V	68.22V	44.79V	74.05V
Luxembourg................................ 137	—V	.09V	.41V	.37V	—V	.03V	—V	.05V	.43V	1.45V	2.18V	3.60V	2.68V	2.79V
Netherlands................................ 138	17.80V	11.50V	11.28V	9.26V	7.36V	19.18V	16.38V	16.19V	14.10V	41.70V	39.65V	38.42V	34.10V	55.45V
Norway.. 142	—V	.02V	—V	—V	—V	—V	.11V	1.61V	.38V	.58V	.80V	4.74V	1.67V	4.42V
Portugal...................................... 182	18.39V	17.50V	16.17V	16.68V	9.67V	10.08V	12.35V	.01V	.04V	.08V	.23V	.13V	.09V	1.11V
Slovenia...................................... 961	6.28V	4.02V	5.00V	6.57Y	1.87V	1.07V	1.36V	3.68V	1.41V	3.86V	5.06Y	7.78V	12.41V	22.49V
Spain... 184	9.58V	6.96V	8.47V	9.71V	4.36V	3.02V	7.67V	14.37V	10.52V	6.26V	5.38V	9.64V	5.45V	10.37V
Sweden.. 144	.27V	.04V	.04V	.02V	—V	.10V	.04V	9.57V	20.93V	11.05V	10.35V	29.36V	30.55V	11.48V
Switzerland................................. 146	5.53V	3.26V	2.11V	1.19V	4.13V	4.10V	2.32V	18.65V	25.99V	22.36V	21.47V	28.77V	39.57V	41.26V
United Kingdom.......................... 112	35.14V	29.69V	43.53V	44.40V	48.30V	31.15V	47.60V	32.03V	23.98V	33.18V	41.32V	42.76V	57.70V	80.83V
Developing Countries.............. 202	**1,512.4Y**	**1,091.3Y**	**1,521.7Y**	**2,152.1Y**	**2,817.6Y**	**4,301.5Y**	**5,042.8Y**	**1,552.9Y**	**1,420.0Y**	**1,638.6Y**	**2,278.9Y**	**2,746.7Y**	**3,581.0Y**	**5,202.5Y**
Africa.. 607	**5.2Y**	**3.7Y**	**1.9Y**	**1.7Y**	**3.4Y**	**3.1Y**	**3.9Y**	**.3Y**	**2.5Y**	**4.4Y**	**3.2Y**	**3.0Y**	**—Y**	**—Y**
Morocco...................................... 686	2.67V	1.70V	1.00V	.82V	1.92V	2.37Y	2.94Y	.04V	.04V	.05V	—V	—V	—Y	—Y
South Africa................................ 199	....	....	....	....	....	....	....	.30V	2.42V	4.32V	3.22V	2.84V	—V	—V
Tunisia.. 744	2.49V	2.05V	.85V	.87V	1.44V	.78V	.96Y	—V	—V	.02V	—V	—V	—V	—Y
Zimbabwe................................... 698	—V	—V	—V	—V	—V	—V	—Y	—V	—V	—V	—V	.14V	—V	—Y
Asia.. 507	**203.0Y**	**205.9Y**	**391.5Y**	**599.1Y**	**659.6Y**	**847.4Y**	**773.5Y**	**464.3Y**	**347.6Y**	**466.6Y**	**625.8Y**	**862.7Y**	**1,230.1Y**	**1,770.4Y**
Bangladesh.................................. 513	22.30V	41.89V	92.25V	101.42V	163.14V	231.17V	257.92V	.13V	.13V	.27V	1.14V	1.44V	2.99Y	1.60Y
China,P.R.: Mainland.................. 924	6.92V	24.91V	182.07V	371.32V	410.01V	514.41V	330.33V	55.85V	114.63V	160.86V	182.90V	253.24V	446.71V	842.56V
China,P.R.:Hong Kong................ 532	.25V	.17V	.64V	1.42V	.96V	.07V	.65V	1.68V	1.43V	2.84V	6.83V	3.18V	4.15V	5.16V
India... 534	11.24Y	17.93V	23.55V	26.36V	24.86V	30.72Y	38.13Y	11.57V	5.98V	13.89V	20.38V	25.47V	31.48Y	39.06Y
Indonesia.................................... 536	2.69V	2.41V	2.81V	2.47V	9.32V	8.51V	24.23V	.50V	.72V	1.19V	.69V	1.50V	1.30V	1.78V
Korea.. 542	124.30V	88.01V	71.78V	69.95V	26.21V	36.44V	94.45V	380.26V	207.33V	271.85V	394.95V	542.40V	714.23V	823.13V
Malaysia..................................... 548	.11V	.17V	2.29V	.21V	.03V	.04V	2.95V	2.22V	1.90V	2.43V	5.53V	10.00V	13.53V	40.13V
Mongolia..................................... 948	.02V	.08V	.06V	.07V	.20V	.24Y	.30Y	—V	.04V	.07V	4.01V	16.26V	3.28Y	4.07Y
Pakistan...................................... 564	4.95V	3.82V	1.18V	5.76V	10.52V	13.00Y	16.14Y	6.29V	7.63V	3.62V	3.37V	2.49V	3.08Y	3.82Y
Philippines.................................. 566	.78V	.33V	.25V	—V	.03V	—V	—V	.11V	.58V	1.83V	.33V	.23V	.67V	1.07V
Taiwan Province of China........... 528	11.31V	13.10V	12.45V	12.73V	4.75V	3.00V	2.10V	2.05V	4.96V	6.73V	3.52V	4.36V	7.35V	6.16V
Thailand...................................... 578	6.23V	4.74V	.22V	1.75V	3.00V	6.35V	6.28V	2.50V	1.90V	.94V	2.17V	2.06V	1.31V	1.89V
Vietnam...................................... 582	11.95V	8.36V	1.98V	5.64V	6.55V	3.45V	—V	1.13V	.32V	.07V	—V	—V	—V	—V
Europe...................................... 170	**1,257.4Y**	**821.1Y**	**1,062.9Y**	**1,473.2Y**	**2,054.3Y**	**3,328.3Y**	**4,107.5Y**	**1,067.5Y**	**1,024.8Y**	**1,154.1Y**	**1,624.0Y**	**1,862.6Y**	**2,328.3Y**	**3,394.1Y**
Armenia...................................... 911	1.10V	1.08V	1.40V	7.76V	2.83V	1.69V	9.49V	.07V	.28V	.56V	.93V	.48V	1.29V	1.67V
Azerbaijan................................... 912	5.54V	1.28V	1.87V	72.42V	90.73V	24.99V	17.39V	3.42V	4.21V	1.62V	3.09V	3.13V	7.54V	4.90V
Belarus....................................... 913	15.98V	10.87V	9.70V	10.24V	12.61V	14.76V	19.66V	18.28V	20.85V	23.91V	43.05V	46.30V	59.66V	102.38V
Bulgaria...................................... 918	5.96V	1.84V	.47V	.94V	2.01V	8.81V	1.70V	3.30V	3.13V	2.15V	2.96V	2.79V	4.51V	5.89V
Czech Republic........................... 935	28.97V	29.57V	19.76V	18.53V	11.33V	4.51V	3.79V	21.72V	38.91V	9.54V	15.69V	23.06V	23.23V	40.16V
Estonia....................................... 939	21.86V	15.24V	10.24V	.73V	2.78V	8.43V	4.89V	3.53V	3.50V	3.37V	4.30V	4.79V	4.77V	9.65V
Georgia....................................... 915	1.36V	.34V	.93V	13.62V	3.02V	5.72V	9.75Y	1.26V	2.82V	1.25V	2.44V	2.36V	2.80V	2.83Y
Hungary...................................... 944	6.99V	4.18V	6.41V	20.31V	16.99V	140.56V	358.61V	6.24V	4.51V	9.75V	16.83V	11.35V	20.84V	24.99V
Kazakhstan.................................. 916	73.72V	78.66V	81.56V	206.92V	236.42Y	292.20Y	362.61Y	165.26V	111.13V	151.68V	221.86V	253.49Y	313.30Y	388.80Y
Kyrgyz Republic.......................... 917	60.68V	54.68V	35.65V	47.11V	54.65V	59.09V	115.58V	52.73V	30.62V	17.88V	16.16V	18.80V	30.64V	80.28V
Latvia.. 941	2.07V	2.03V	4.56V	6.74V	13.48V	8.74V	9.99V	6.55V	4.51V	5.39V	9.65V	9.89V	12.44V	15.33V
Lithuania..................................... 946	13.74V	6.19V	6.86V	3.38V	11.61V	19.55V	20.56V	21.79V	12.04V	6.10V	13.91V	24.83V	14.49V	19.26V
Macedonia, FYR......................... 962	.04V	—V	.05V	.01V	.22V	.07V	.08Y	—V	—V	.10V	.15V	.03V	.01V	.01Y
Moldova...................................... 921	.08V	.14V	.85V	.66V	1.11V	1.37Y	1.71Y	1.48V	.73V	1.93V	2.65V	2.08V	2.57Y	3.19Y
Poland... 964	82.32V	41.35V	29.90V	53.12V	143.29V	575.59V	619.02V	20.96V	11.91V	27.98V	25.97V	50.26V	69.23V	70.41V
Romania...................................... 968	12.05V	10.76V	12.22V	13.89V	6.88V	139.23V	80.99V	3.94V	1.18V	1.21V	3.29V	27.60V	58.68V	85.44V
Russia... 922	527.15V	310.56V	436.73V	556.23V	820.00V	1,172.44V	1,330.75V	400.23V	498.69V	553.56V	843.62V	946.58V	1,194.89V	1,901.93V
Slovak Republic........................... 936	4.69V	4.03V	5.10Y	6.70Y	.15V	4.22V	6.10V	6.73V	4.93V	6.23Y	8.19Y	11.96V	12.78V	12.20V
Tajikistan..................................... 923	137.00V	120.36V	120.64V	153.45V	139.00V	160.36V	194.45V	95.92V	80.19V	73.81V	72.49V	73.15V	74.17V	95.70V
Turkey... 186	32.77V	68.49V	90.42V	162.39V	235.95V	377.90V	558.01V	98.70V	103.11V	152.26V	159.75V	166.18V	193.60V	247.59V
Turkmenistan.............................. 925	47.82V	34.14V	41.73V	54.80Y	62.62Y	77.39Y	96.04Y	15.18V	12.67V	11.87V	15.59Y	17.81Y	22.01Y	27.32Y
Ukraine.. 926	175.48V	25.29V	145.85V	63.25V	186.65V	230.69V	286.29Y	120.21V	74.94V	91.95V	141.39V	165.70V	204.80Y	254.15Y
Middle East............................. 407	**43.3Y**	**60.6Y**	**60.8Y**	**78.0Y**	**98.9Y**	**121.6Y**	**157.7Y**	**20.7Y**	**43.4Y**	**8.5Y**	**12.8Y**	**9.6Y**	**16.7Y**	**32.1Y**
Bahrain.. 419	.33Y	.36Y	.45Y	.59Y	.68Y	.83Y	1.04Y	....	....	....	....	....	....	....
Egypt... 469	.04V	.05V	.06Y	.08Y	.09Y	.11Y	.14Y	.06V	.07Y	.09Y	.11Y	.13Y	.16Y	.20Y
Iran, I.R. of................................ 429	40.06V	52.03V	57.83Y	75.22Y	95.77Y	118.23Y	153.16Y	—Y	—Y	—Y	—Y	—Y	—Y	—Y

	Exports							Imports						
	2001	2002	2003	2004	2005	2006	2007	2001	2002	2003	2004	2005	2006	2007
	Millions of U.S. Dollars							Millions of U.S. Dollars						
Israel........ 436	2.09V	2.73V	1.64V	1.09V	1.18V	1.18V	1.82V	19.58V	41.91V	6.93V	10.67V	6.82V	13.20V	27.83V
Jordan........ 439	.11V	.36V	.33V	.01V	.60V	.59V	.71V	—V	.07V	—V	—V	—V	.01V	—V
Lebanon........ 446	.24Y	.26Y	.33Y	.43Y	.50Y	.61Y	.76Y	.04Y	.04Y	.05Y	.07Y	.08Y	.09Y	.12Y
Oman........ 449	.17V	.07V	.01V	.02Y	.02Y	.03Y	.03Y	.39V	.59V	.62V	.83Y	1.12Y	1.41Y	1.71Y
Saudi Arabia........ 456	.20V	4.73V	.11V	.51V	.04V	.05Y	.07Y	.64Y	.68Y	.82Y	1.08Y	1.48Y	1.85Y	2.24Y
Western Hemisphere........ 207	**3.6Y**	**—Y**	**4.6Y**	**.2Y**	**1.5Y**	**1.0Y**	**.2Y**	**—Y**	**1.8Y**	**5.0Y**	**13.1Y**	**8.8Y**	**5.9Y**	**5.9Y**
Argentina........ 213	.05V	—V	4.45V	.01V	—V	—V	.03V	—V	1.71V	2.01V	1.93V	.01V	—V	5.78V
Barbados........ 316	—V	—V	—V	.01V	—V	—V	—Y	....	....	....	....	....	....	....
Brazil........ 223	3.50V	—V	—V	—V	1.36V	.61V	—V	.02V	—V	2.98V	11.18V	8.60V	5.81V	—V
Chile........ 228	—V	—V	—V	.01V	—V	.02V	—V	—V	—V	—V	—V	—V	—V	—V
Colombia........ 233	—V	.01V	.01V	—V	.10V	.08V	.10V	—V	.01V	—V	—V	—V	—V	—V
Ecuador........ 248	....	....	....	....	....	....	....	—V	.05V	—V	—V	.05V	.08V	.10Y
Greenland........ 326	—Y	—Y	—Y	—Y	—Y	.01Y	.01Y	—Y	—Y	—Y	—Y	—Y	—Y	—Y
Peru........ 293	.01V	—V	.09V	.12V	.01V	.22V	.01Y	.02V	—V	—V	—V	.11V	—V	—Y
Trinidad and Tobago........ 369	.01V	.01V	.01Y	.02Y	.02Y	.03Y	.03Y	....	....	....	....	....	....	....
Uruguay........ 298	.01V	.01Y	.05V	.04V	.03V	.04Y	.05Y	—V	—Y	—V	—V	—V	—Y	—Y
Memorandum Items														
European Union........ 998	595.37Y	429.96Y	362.60Y	465.55Y	597.08Y	1,107.00Y	1,589.08Y	613.38Y	535.47Y	558.11Y	634.67Y	778.91Y	804.64Y	1,079.54Y
Oil Exporting Ctys........ 999	43.13Y	59.24Y	60.76Y	78.22Y	105.16Y	126.82Y	177.50Y	1.52Y	1.98Y	2.64Y	2.60Y	4.10Y	4.57Y	5.72Y
Non-Oil Develop.Ctys........ 201	1,469.28Y	1,032.11Y	1,460.91Y	2,073.92Y	2,712.48Y	4,174.69Y	4,865.31Y	1,551.34Y	1,418.01Y	1,635.97Y	2,276.28Y	2,742.56Y	3,576.40Y	5,196.74Y
PERCENT DISTRIBUTION														
Industrial Countries........ 101	**27.2**	**30.4**	**23.0**	**20.2**	**18.7**	**13.1**	**15.1**	**32.3**	**31.6**	**34.0**	**27.8**	**22.7**	**17.8**	**17.7**
Developing Countries........ 202	**72.8**	**69.6**	**77.0**	**79.8**	**81.3**	**86.9**	**84.9**	**67.7**	**68.4**	**66.0**	**72.2**	**77.3**	**82.2**	**82.3**
Africa........ 607	**.2**	**.2**	**.1**	**.1**	**.1**	**.1**	**.1**	**—**	**.1**	**.2**	**.1**	**.1**	**—**	**—**
Asia........ 507	**9.8**	**13.1**	**19.8**	**22.2**	**19.0**	**17.1**	**13.0**	**20.2**	**16.7**	**18.8**	**19.8**	**24.3**	**28.2**	**28.0**
Europe........ 170	**60.5**	**52.4**	**53.8**	**54.6**	**59.2**	**67.2**	**69.1**	**46.6**	**49.4**	**46.5**	**51.5**	**52.4**	**53.5**	**53.7**
Middle East........ 407	**2.1**	**3.9**	**3.1**	**2.9**	**2.9**	**2.5**	**2.7**	**.9**	**2.1**	**.3**	**.4**	**.3**	**.4**	**.5**
Western Hemisphere........ 207	**.2**	**—**	**.2**	**—**	**—**	**—**	**—**	**—**	**.1**	**.2**	**.4**	**.2**	**.1**	**.1**
ANNUAL PERCENT CHANGE														
World........ 001	**–4.7**	**–24.6**	**26.0**	**36.6**	**28.5**	**42.8**	**20.0**	**10.7**	**–9.5**	**19.7**	**27.0**	**12.5**	**22.6**	**45.1**
Industrial Countries........ 101	**4.2**	**–15.9**	**–4.9**	**20.3**	**19.2**	**.2**	**38.2**	**2.7**	**–11.4**	**29.0**	**3.7**	**–8.3**	**–3.9**	**44.1**
Developing Countries........ 202	**–7.6**	**–27.8**	**39.4**	**41.4**	**30.9**	**52.7**	**17.2**	**14.9**	**–8.6**	**15.4**	**39.1**	**20.5**	**30.4**	**45.3**
Africa........ 607	**74.4**	**–27.4**	**–50.4**	**–9.4**	**99.1**	**–6.2**	**24.1**	**—**	**616.1**	**78.0**	**–26.4**	**–7.6**	**—**	**24.1**
Asia........ 507	**7.1**	**1.4**	**90.1**	**53.0**	**10.1**	**28.5**	**–8.7**	**41.8**	**–25.1**	**34.2**	**34.1**	**37.8**	**42.6**	**43.9**
Europe........ 170	**–8.3**	**–34.7**	**29.5**	**38.6**	**39.4**	**62.0**	**23.4**	**5.6**	**–4.0**	**12.6**	**40.7**	**14.7**	**25.0**	**45.8**
Middle East........ 407	**–10.7**	**40.1**	**.3**	**28.3**	**26.8**	**23.0**	**29.7**	**69.9**	**109.4**	**–80.4**	**49.9**	**–24.6**	**73.9**	**91.7**
Western Hemisphere........ 207	**–85.7**	**–99.2**	**—**	**–95.4**	**618.1**	**–35.0**	**–76.2**	**–97.0**	**—**	**182.9**	**162.4**	**–33.2**	**–32.8**	**–.1**

	Exports							Imports						
	2001	2002	2003	2004	2005	2006	2007	2001	2002	2003	2004	2005	2006	2007
	Millions of U.S. Dollars							*Millions of U.S. Dollars*						
IFS World Total	**20.0**	**20.2**	**27.3**	**38.0**	**37.8**	**36.9**	**29.9**	**89.9**	**90.1**	**105.8**	**128.0**	**149.2**	**160.8**	**201.8**
DOTS World Total 001	**57.3Y**	**57.8Y**	**77.0Y**	**202.6Y**	**228.4Y**	**248.4Y**	**272.6Y**	**174.0Y**	**132.7Y**	**211.6Y**	**229.7Y**	**267.9Y**	**271.5Y**	**318.0Y**
Industrial Countries 101	**19.9Y**	**13.2Y**	**16.4Y**	**42.6Y**	**38.6Y**	**41.3Y**	**39.3Y**	**111.9Y**	**74.7Y**	**75.1Y**	**100.2Y**	**134.1Y**	**153.8Y**	**173.5Y**
United States 111	.55V	2.55V	1.09V	1.91V	2.55V	2.09V	1.00V	.88V	.66V	1.54V	10.23V	10.01V	10.01V	26.29V
Canada 156	.05V	.03V	.07V	.53V	3.80V	.34V	.05V	—V	.37V	.06V	.20V	.99V	.52V	.28V
Australia 193	1.73V	2.57V	3.93V	2.41V	3.38V	2.49V	1.76V	27.26V	29.33V	32.74V	38.30V	49.31V	55.82V	65.89V
Japan 158	6.50V	3.89V	7.53V	15.30V	16.04V	27.74V	30.67V	43.72V	25.54V	22.89V	26.41V	44.60V	53.57V	6.05V
New Zealand 196	.63V	.51V	.34V	.76V	.37V	.41V	1.18V	11.32V	13.36V	12.62V	16.69V	19.35V	23.96V	35.59V
Austria 122	.01V	—V	—V	—V	—V	.02V	.03V	—V	—V	—V	—V	—V	—V	—V
Belgium 124	—V	.83V	.65V	11.03V	6.10V	5.66V	1.68V	—V	.06V	.03V	.08V	.01V	.10V	.21V
Denmark 128	.05V	—V	—V	.02V	.01V	.03V	.01V	.01V	.04V	.02V	.07V	.02V	.03V	.08V
Finland 172	—V	—V	—V	—V	—V	—V	—V	.04V	—V	.02V	.06V	—V	.06V	.05V
France 132	.28V	1.14V	1.22V	1.44V	.66V	.65V	.90V	7.87V	2.85V	3.22V	4.10V	3.56V	5.51V	5.46V
Germany 134	1.39V	.84V	1.28V	5.36V	3.66V	.06V	.08V	17.98V	.56V	.41V	.32V	.51V	.51V	1.34V
Greece 174	8.27V	—V	—V	2.70V	—V	—V	—V	.37V	—V	.01V	.02V	.77V	.57V	.03V
Ireland 178	—V	—V	—V	—V	—V	—V	—V	—V	.01V	.02V	—V	—V	.01V	—V
Italy 136	.21V	.10V	—V	.01V	—V	.04V	.01V	.43V	.53V	.93V	.53V	1.01V	.95V	.57V
Luxembourg 137	—V	—V	—V	—V	—V	—V	—V	—V	—V	.01V	.11V	—V	—V	—V
Netherlands 138	—V	.47V	—V	.55V	.50V	.11V	.77V	.51V	.19V	.14V	.14V	.55V	.37V	.12V
Norway 142	—V	—V	—V	—V	—V	—V	—V	.37V	.09V	—V	—V	—V	—V	26.94V
Portugal 182	—V	.04V	—V	—V	—V	—V	—V	—V	.08V	—V	—V	—V	—V	—V
Slovenia 961	—V	—V	—V	—Y	—V	—V	—V	.02V	—V	—V	—Y	—V	—V	—V
Spain 184	.01V	.01V	—V	.03V	.05V	.15V	.01V	.03V	.10V	.10V	2.39V	.16V	.12V	1.44V
Sweden 144	—V	—V	—V	—V	—V	—V	—V	.06V	.05V	.06V	.09V	.21V	.08V	1.38V
Switzerland 146	.13V	—V	—V	—V	—V	—V	—V	.27V	.16V	.08V	.03V	.03V	.02V	.06V
United Kingdom 112	.08V	.25V	.33V	.57V	1.51V	1.45V	1.12V	.74V	.66V	.22V	.43V	3.03V	1.63V	1.72V
Developing Countries 202	**37.2Y**	**44.3Y**	**60.2Y**	**159.5Y**	**189.3Y**	**206.5Y**	**232.5Y**	**59.6Y**	**55.3Y**	**133.1Y**	**125.0Y**	**128.7Y**	**111.3Y**	**136.6Y**
Africa 607	**.2Y**	**.3Y**	**1.6Y**	**.4Y**	**.5Y**	**.6Y**	**1.1Y**	**.5Y**	**.6Y**	**.4Y**	**.6Y**	**3.4Y**	**1.3Y**	**2.3Y**
Côte d'Ivoire 662	—V	—V	—V	—V	—V	—V	—Y	.52V	.64V	.30V	.35V	.19V	1.16V	1.44Y
Gabon 646	.14Y	.15Y	.19Y	.25Y	.28Y	.35Y	.43Y	—Y	—Y	—Y	—Y	—Y	—Y	—Y
Madagascar 674	—V	—V	—V	—Y	—Y	—Y	—Y	—V	—V	.01V	.01Y	.02Y	.02Y	.02Y
Mauritius 684	—V	.08V	1.26V	—V	—V	—V	.35V	—V	—V	—V	—V	.02V	.14V	.82V
Morocco 686	—V	—V	—V	—V	—V	—Y	—Y	—V	—V	.01V	—V	—V	—Y	—Y
Nigeria 694	.04V	.04V	.11V	.14Y	.18Y	.22Y	.28Y	—V	—V	—V	—Y	—Y	—Y	—Y
South Africa 199	—Y	—Y	—Y	—Y	—Y	—Y	—Y	—V	—V	.08V	.26V	3.22V	—V	—V
Zimbabwe 698	—V	.01V	—V	—V	—V	—V	—Y	—V	—V	—V	—V	—V	—V	—Y
Asia 507	**36.4Y**	**43.2Y**	**53.9Y**	**155.2Y**	**150.9Y**	**197.7Y**	**226.9Y**	**58.4Y**	**53.9Y**	**132.0Y**	**122.2Y**	**101.4Y**	**108.8Y**	**133.2Y**
Bangladesh 513	.68V	—V	—V	—V	—V	—V	—V	—V	—V	—V	—V	—V	—Y	—Y
China,P.R.: Mainland 924	.29V	.24V	.18V	10.02V	.43V	.96V	.37Y	1.26V	1.55V	3.17V	7.82V	8.58V	20.16V	23.03V
China,P.R.:Hong Kong 532	.84V	1.15V	.98V	.86V	.86V	1.17V	1.33V	1.52V	1.59V	1.85V	1.67V	1.65V	1.69V	2.31V
Fiji 819	.06Y	.07Y	.08Y	.11Y	.13Y	.16Y	.19Y	8.17Y	8.87Y	11.23Y	14.74Y	16.84Y	20.82Y	25.84Y
French Polynesia 887	.84Y	.91Y	1.15Y	1.51Y	1.72Y	2.13Y	2.64Y	.45Y	.49Y	.62Y	.82Y	.93Y	1.15Y	1.43Y
Guam 829	....	....	....	....	....	....	....	.05Y	.05Y	.07Y	.09Y	.10Y	.13Y	.16Y
India 534	23.81Y	3.05V	10.31V	3.24V	32.84V	40.59V	50.37Y	6.07Y	.14V	.47V	1.47V	1.97V	2.44Y	3.02Y
Indonesia 536	.11V	5.02V	9.59V	—V	—V	.01V	—V	.52V	.40V	.50V	2.10V	1.92V	2.39V	4.26V
Korea 542	.58V	8.28V	.06V	.09V	.85V	.20V	.14V	1.36V	1.09V	1.07V	2.11V	3.75V	2.13V	3.75V
Malaysia 548	.03V	.55V	.47V	37.63V	.07V	.20V	.80V	.22V	.21V	.40V	.46V	.46V	1.16V	2.13V
New Caledonia 839	1.04V	1.06V	1.42V	1.61V	1.84Y	2.28Y	2.83Y	4.50V	4.05V	7.77V	8.21V	9.38Y	11.60Y	14.39Y
Pakistan 564	—Y	—Y	—V	—V	—V	—Y	—Y	—V	—V	—V	—V	.07V	.09Y	.11Y
Papua New Guinea 853	.73Y	.79Y	1.00Y	1.31Y	1.50Y	1.85Y	2.30Y	1.83Y	1.98Y	2.51Y	3.30Y	3.77Y	4.66Y	5.78Y
Philippines 566	—V	—V	—V	—V	—V	1.42V	3.21V	.01V	.02V	.14V	.06V	.27V	.20V	.23V
Singapore 576	.31V	1.67V	2.17V	1.47V	1.06V	1.21V	2.16V	24.41V	10.70V	16.45V	19.66V	39.31V	32.79V	37.66V
Solomon Islands 813	.40Y	.43Y	.54Y	.71Y	.81Y	1.01Y	1.25Y	1.09Y	1.18Y	1.49Y	1.96Y	2.24Y	2.77Y	3.44Y
Taiwan Province of China 528	.76V	.16V	.35V	.52V	.15V	.20V	.18V	6.12V	20.98V	80.51V	55.78V	4.59V	.21V	.44V
Thailand 578	5.89V	18.13V	25.43V	96.11V	108.59V	144.25V	159.04V	.76V	.56V	1.45V	1.96V	5.58V	4.42V	5.18V
Tonga 866	.02Y	.02Y	.03Y	.04Y	.05Y	.06Y	.07Y	—Y	—Y	—Y	—Y	—Y	—Y	—Y
Vietnam 582	—V	1.71V	.09V	—V	—V	—V	—V	.01V	.04V	2.25V	—V	—V	—V	—V
Europe 170	**—Y**	**—Y**	**3.7Y**	**1.5Y**	**36.5Y**	**.2Y**	**.2Y**	**.3Y**	**.6Y**	**.4Y**	**2.1Y**	**23.2Y**	**.4Y**	**.5Y**
Bulgaria 918	—V	—V	—V	.02V	—V	.07V	—V	.01V	—V	—V	—V	—V	—V	—V
Estonia 939	—V	—V	—V	—V	—V	—V	.02V	.02V	.24V	.10V	.01V	.05V	—V	—V
Hungary 944	—V	—V	—V	—V	—V	—V	—V	—Y	—Y	—Y	—Y	—V	.01V	—V
Latvia 941	—V	—V	—Y	—V	—V	—V	—V	—V	—V	—V	—V	—V	.21V	—V
Macedonia, FYR 962	—V	—V	—V	—V	—V	.06V	.08Y	—V	—V	—V	—V	—V	—V	—Y
Poland 964	.01V	.04V	3.70V	1.44V	18.46V	.07V	.03V	.11V	.38V	.32V	1.93V	22.90V	.02V	—V
Romania 968	—V	—V	—V	—V	—V	—V	—V	—V	—V	—V	—V	—V	.01V	—V
Russia 922	—V	—V	—V	.01V	.01V	—V	.01V	—V	—V	—V	—V	.01V	—V	—V
Slovak Republic 936	—V	—V	—Y	—Y	—V	—V	—V	.10V	—V	—Y	—Y	—V	—V	—V
Turkey 186	—V	—V	—V	—V	17.99V	—V	—V	.02V	.01V	—V	.11V	.26V	.19V	.53V
Ukraine 926	—V	—V	—V	—V	.03V	.03Y	.04Y	.03V	—V	—V	—V	—V	—Y	—Y
Middle East 407	**.6Y**	**.6Y**	**.8Y**	**1.0Y**	**1.2Y**	**1.5Y**	**1.8Y**	**—Y**	**—Y**	**—Y**	**—Y**	**—Y**	**—Y**	**—Y**
Egypt 469	.57V	.62Y	.79Y	1.03Y	1.18Y	1.46Y	1.81Y	—V	—Y	—Y	—Y	—Y	—Y	—Y
Yemen, Republic of 474	—Y	—Y	—Y	—Y	—Y	—Y	—Y	—V	—V	—Y	.01V	—V	—Y	—Y

	Exports							Imports						
	2001	2002	2003	2004	2005	2006	2007	2001	2002	2003	2004	2005	2006	2007
	Millions of U.S. Dollars							Millions of U.S. Dollars						
Western Hemisphere............... 207	**—Y**	**.1Y**	**.3Y**	**1.4Y**	**.3Y**	**6.6Y**	**2.6Y**	**.5Y**	**.1Y**	**.3Y**	**.1Y**	**.6Y**	**.8Y**	**.6Y**
Argentina.................................. 213	—V	—V	—V	—V	—V	—V	—V	—V	.01V	—V	—V	.21V	.28V	.15V
Brazil.. 223	.02V	.02V	—V	—V	—V	—V	—V	—V	—V	—V	—V	—V	.01V	—V
Chile... 228	—V	—V	.07V	1.19V	.05V	.24V	.01V	.35V	—V	.28V	.08V	.27V	.31V	.32V
Colombia.................................... 233	.01V	—V	—V	—V	—V	.05V	.02V	—V	—V	—V	.01V	—V	.11V	—V
Costa Rica.................................. 238	....	....	....	....	....	....	....	.03V	.02V	—V	—V	—V	—Y	—Y
Ecuador...................................... 248	—V	.04V	.21V	.22V	.11V	.02V	.03Y	.09V	.09V	—V	—V	—V	—V	—Y
Mexico.. 273	—V	—V	—V	—V	.10V	6.27V	2.50V	—V	—V	—V	—V	.05V	.05V	.02V
Peru.. 293	—V	—V	—V	—V	—V	—V	—Y	—V	—V	—V	—V	.03V	.02V	.11Y
Countries & Areas n.s............. 898	**.3Y**	**.3Y**	**.4Y**	**.5Y**	**.5Y**	**.7Y**	**.8Y**	**2.5Y**	**2.7Y**	**3.4Y**	**4.5Y**	**5.1Y**	**6.3Y**	**7.9Y**
Memorandum Items														
European Union......................... 998	10.32Y	3.72Y	7.18Y	23.14Y	30.94Y	8.24Y	4.66Y	28.30Y	5.77Y	5.60Y	10.29Y	32.78Y	10.17Y	12.40Y
Oil Exporting Ctys....................... 999	.15Y	5.06Y	9.70Y	.14Y	.18Y	.22Y	.28Y	.52Y	.40Y	.50Y	2.10Y	1.92Y	2.39Y	4.26Y
Non-Oil Develop.Ctys.................. 201	37.01Y	39.19Y	50.48Y	159.38Y	189.11Y	206.31Y	232.21Y	59.12Y	54.89Y	132.57Y	122.88Y	126.73Y	108.93Y	132.34Y
PERCENT DISTRIBUTION														
Industrial Countries................ 101	**34.7**	**22.9**	**21.4**	**21.0**	**16.9**	**16.6**	**14.4**	**64.3**	**56.3**	**35.5**	**43.6**	**50.1**	**56.7**	**54.6**
Developing Countries............. 202	**64.8**	**76.6**	**78.2**	**78.7**	**82.9**	**83.1**	**85.3**	**34.3**	**41.7**	**62.9**	**54.4**	**48.0**	**41.0**	**43.0**
Africa..................................... 607	**.3**	**.5**	**2.0**	**.2**	**.2**	**.2**	**.4**	**.3**	**.5**	**.2**	**.3**	**1.3**	**.5**	**.7**
Asia.. 507	**63.5**	**74.9**	**70.0**	**76.6**	**66.1**	**79.6**	**83.2**	**33.5**	**40.6**	**62.4**	**53.2**	**37.9**	**40.1**	**41.9**
Europe.................................... 170	**—**	**.1**	**4.8**	**.7**	**16.0**	**.1**	**.1**	**.2**	**.5**	**.2**	**.9**	**8.7**	**.2**	**.2**
Middle East........................... 407	**1.0**	**1.1**	**1.0**	**.5**	**.5**	**.6**	**.7**	**—**	**—**	**—**	**—**	**—**	**—**	**—**
Western Hemisphere............. 207	**—**	**.1**	**.4**	**.7**	**.1**	**2.6**	**.9**	**.3**	**.1**	**.1**	**—**	**.2**	**.3**	**.2**
ANNUAL PERCENT CHANGE														
World...................................... 001	**–33.6**	**.8**	**33.3**	**163.2**	**12.7**	**8.8**	**9.7**	**40.4**	**–23.8**	**59.5**	**8.5**	**16.6**	**1.3**	**17.1**
Industrial Countries................ 101	**–34.9**	**–33.5**	**24.3**	**159.3**	**–9.4**	**6.8**	**–4.8**	**53.3**	**–33.3**	**.6**	**33.4**	**33.9**	**14.7**	**12.8**
Developing Countries............. 202	**–33.1**	**19.1**	**36.0**	**165.1**	**18.7**	**9.1**	**12.6**	**22.6**	**–7.3**	**140.7**	**–6.1**	**2.9**	**–13.5**	**22.7**
Africa..................................... 607	**44.8**	**55.5**	**450.9**	**–75.2**	**19.1**	**23.4**	**88.0**	**114.6**	**21.7**	**–36.9**	**53.6**	**457.5**	**–61.6**	**73.2**
Asia.. 507	**–34.1**	**18.9**	**24.5**	**188.2**	**–2.8**	**31.0**	**14.8**	**22.2**	**–7.6**	**144.8**	**–7.4**	**–17.0**	**7.2**	**22.4**
Europe.................................... 170	**–93.6**	**254.3**	**—**	**–60.5**	**—**	**–99.3**	**–23.5**	**33.4**	**115.5**	**–34.1**	**391.8**	**—**	**–98.2**	**24.8**
Middle East........................... 407	**....**	**8.5**	**26.6**	**31.3**	**14.3**	**23.6**	**24.1**	**—**	**—**	**....**	**....**	**....**	**....**	**....**
Western Hemisphere............. 207	**–56.9**	**137.5**	**372.1**	**391.1**	**–81.4**	**—**	**–61.2**	**3.9**	**–74.8**	**145.3**	**–70.0**	**543.2**	**39.8**	**–24.1**

	Exports							Imports						
	2001	2002	2003	2004	2005	2006	2007	2001	2002	2003	2004	2005	2006	2007
	Millions of U.S. Dollars							Millions of U.S. Dollars						
IFS World Total	**25,353**	**25,890**	**23,990**	**33,994**	**51,859**	**59,208**	**69,165**	**18,323**	**12,963**	**9,256**	**16,679**	**24,027**	**33,616**	**46,097**
DOTS World Total 001	**26,936**	**26,641**	**27,170**	**39,668**	**55,472**	**65,214**	**87,253Y**	**21,695**	**15,004**	**9,174**	**16,680**	**24,034**	**33,760**	**46,101**
Industrial Countries 101	**15,264**	**14,353**	**15,268**	**19,581**	**32,407**	**32,054**	**45,946Y**	**10,796**	**7,859**	**5,624**	**9,290**	**12,304**	**16,438**	**19,841**
United States 111	12,849	12,024	11,635	16,946	26,975	25,503	37,282V	6,258	4,299	3,044	5,485	7,584	10,286	12,243
Canada 156	567	280	295	400	984	353	1,400V	409	298	214	380	399	492	521
Australia 193	1	3	2	1	1	1	2V	9	52	6	9	14	16	20
Japan 158	148	54	135	204	232	252	447V	782	455	196	546	783	1,139	1,262
New Zealand 196	—	3	1	—	—	—	—V	57	34	60	38	40	58	106
Austria 122	—	—	—	—	—	1	81V	24	22	79	24	62	44	70
Belgium 124	137	101	107	183	264	318	593V	181	161	127	217	280	339	386
Belgium-Luxembourg n.s. 127	—	—	—	—	—	—	—Y	—	1	2	—	—	—	1
Cyprus 423	1	—	—	—	—	—	—V	—	6	—	4	—	44	—
Denmark 128	1	2	2	1	2	1	12V	34	40	34	20	25	101	63
Finland 172	—	—	—	—	—	3	—V	80	33	40	20	32	69	111
France 132	53	145	59	55	256	731	227V	303	221	228	211	298	451	521
Germany 134	289	114	137	183	362	270	1,127V	618	620	359	583	672	849	1,034
Greece 174	11	17	4	2	5	1	43V	5	2	3	3	8	3	4
Iceland 176	5	—	—	—	12	7	2V	—	—	—	—	1	—	1
Ireland 178	5	1	2	—	—	—	1V	39	27	27	32	47	68	84
Italy 136	169	161	128	139	314	348	429V	609	546	282	473	546	735	1,029
Luxembourg 137	—	—	—	—	—	—	36V	—	—	2	—	—	—	—
Malta 181	—	—	—	—	—	—	1V	—	—	—	3	—	—	—
Netherlands 138	289	338	2,076	566	1,510	854	1,013V	229	166	128	176	280	291	361
Norway 142	18	13	15	14	1	—	1V	26	19	33	14	85	31	25
Portugal 182	10	102	8	13	5	10	15V	25	12	7	11	15	22	32
Slovenia 961	3	—	—	—	—	—	18V	2	1	1	2	2	2	4
Spain 184	555	533	213	292	719	1,901	1,853V	525	358	366	419	555	658	966
Sweden 144	13	182	11	1	3	1	363V	73	67	44	53	108	111	162
Switzerland 146	36	48	41	63	109	76	80V	137	114	90	141	186	280	397
United Kingdom 112	103	232	397	517	651	1,426	921V	370	305	253	425	282	347	441
Developing Countries 202	**8,442**	**8,554**	**7,932**	**13,033**	**14,757**	**13,780**	**17,928Y**	**7,910**	**5,000**	**3,436**	**7,272**	**11,623**	**17,098**	**25,827**
Africa 607	**27**	**24**	**12**	**7**	**148**	**34**	**108Y**	**251**	**26**	**20**	**40**	**39**	**27**	**32**
Algeria 612	—	1	—	—	23	1	1Y	2	—	—	—	—	—	—
Benin 638	—	—	—	—	—	1	2Y	1	—	1	—	—	—	—
Cameroon 622	—	2	5	—	—	—	—Y	3	—	—	1	—	2	—
Ghana 652	16	10	—	—	—	—	—Y	2	—	—	—	3	—	—
Kenya 664	—	—	—	—	—	—	—Y	1	1	—	—	—	—	—
Liberia 668	—	—	—	—	—	—	—Y	—	—	7	11	—	—	—
Morocco 686	4	3	3	1	6	18	22Y	4	1	2	4	4	9	8
Nigeria 694	6	5	3	4	18	—	—Y	213	6	—	1	—	—	—
Rwanda 714	—	—	—	—	—	—	—Y	—	—	—	—	1	1	—
South Africa 199	—	—	—	1	98	13	84V	22	17	8	15	25	14	22
Sudan 732	—	—	—	—	—	—	—V	—	—	1	1	2	—	—
Tanzania 738	—	2	—	—	—	—	—Y	1	1	—	—	—	—	—
Togo 742	—	—	—	—	—	—	—Y	1	—	—	—	—	—	—
Tunisia 744	—	—	—	—	2	—	—Y	1	—	—	—	—	—	1
Africa n.s. 799	—	—	—	—	—	—	—Y	—	—	—	6	4	—	—
Asia 507	**84**	**289**	**423**	**870**	**835**	**1,173**	**3,379Y**	**1,230**	**762**	**445**	**1,014**	**1,935**	**3,247**	**5,235**
Afghanistan, I.S. of 512	—	—	—	—	—	—	—Y	—	—	—	—	1	—	—
Bangladesh 513	—	2	—	—	—	—	—V	—	—	—	—	—	—	1
China,P.R.: Mainland 924	42	91	165	277	293	145	2,731V	348	227	173	431	889	1,634	3,081
China,P.R.:Hong Kong 532	6	9	11	2	3	1	100V	176	95	39	79	161	290	382
China,P.R.:Macao 546	1	8	37	32	3	2	—V	135	81	55	113	169	184	270
India 534	4	3	4	10	21	41	49Y	53	36	27	55	94	149	190
Indonesia 536	4	3	1	4	11	3	4V	29	21	25	51	74	71	84
Korea 542	6	23	—	—	—	—	91V	—	—	—	—	—	—	—
Malaysia 548	1	1	2	1	7	7	26V	16	10	9	34	32	39	61
Pakistan 564	1	4	1	—	—	—	—Y	8	5	1	10	15	14	34
Papua New Guinea 853	4	—	—	—	—	—	—Y	—	—	—	—	—	—	—
Philippines 566	1	1	—	—	1	1	—V	4	1	2	2	4	6	7
Singapore 576	1	124	201	500	434	933	330V	21	15	12	24	31	72	57
Taiwan Province of China 528	—	—	—	—	—	—	11V	—	—	—	—	—	—	—
Thailand 578	4	2	1	2	1	7	10V	21	17	10	25	49	68	65
Vietnam 582	—	—	—	—	—	—	—V	5	2	6	4	7	12	—
Asia n.s. 598	9	19	—	40	62	32	26Y	414	251	86	185	409	707	1,004
Europe 170	**75**	**34**	**25**	**48**	**129**	**48**	**177Y**	**83**	**84**	**74**	**130**	**168**	**236**	**690**
Albania 914	—	—	—	—	—	—	—V	—	—	—	—	1	1	—
Belarus 913	—	—	—	—	—	—	1V	—	—	—	—	—	—	—
Bulgaria 918	—	6	—	—	4	—	14V	2	1	2	3	1	2	3
Croatia 960	—	—	—	—	4	—	6V	—	—	—	—	—	1	—
Czech Republic 935	—	—	—	—	—	—	1V	5	4	2	1	3	29	10
Czechoslovakia n.s. 937	3	—	—	—	—	—	—Y	—	—	—	—	—	—	—

Venezuela, República Bolivariana de 299

	Exports 2001	2002	2003	2004	2005	2006	2007	Imports 2001	2002	2003	2004	2005	2006	2007
	Millions of U.S. Dollars							*Millions of U.S. Dollars*						
Estonia........ 939	—	—	—	—	—	—	—V	1	1	—	10	4	5	3
Hungary........ 944	—	—	—	—	—	—	3V	2	3	2	3	3	4	7
Latvia........ 941	—	—	—	—	—	—	—V	—	—	—	3	6	—	—
Lithuania........ 946	—	—	—	—	—	—	1V	—	—	—	5	2	8	37
Macedonia, FYR........ 962	—	—	—	—	—	—	6Y	—	—	—	—	—	—	—
Poland........ 964	—	—	—	8	31	12	2V	11	15	7	25	51	41	74
Romania........ 968	—	—	1	10	22	11	11V	17	18	2	14	28	13	18
Russia........ 922	23	22	23	28	50	24	11V	17	19	21	30	13	63	435
Slovak Republic........ 936	—	—	—	—	—	—	—V	1	—	—	1	—	3	7
Turkey........ 186	—	2	1	1	19	—	120V	14	10	19	14	36	43	49
Ukraine........ 926	4	1	—	—	—	—	—Y	11	11	18	18	14	18	47
Yugoslavia n.s........ 966	2	—	—	—	—	—	—Y	—	—	—	—	—	—	—
Europe n.s........ 884	42	3	—	—	—	—	—Y	2	1	—	1	3	5	—
Middle East........ 407	**51**	**35**	**67**	**28**	**48**	**68**	**85Y**	**43**	**23**	**23**	**29**	**83**	**134**	**127**
Egypt........ 469	1	1	1	22	23	38	46Y	1	1	1	1	2	3	2
Iran, I.R. of........ 429	—	—	—	1	—	14	16Y	—	—	1	—	17	40	43
Iraq........ 433	42	—	—	—	—	—	—Y	—	—	—	—	—	2	—
Israel........ 436	1	5	1	1	1	—	4V	33	16	17	17	49	28	50
Jordan........ 439	—	—	—	—	—	—	—V	—	—	—	1	—	1	—
Kuwait........ 443	—	—	—	—	—	—	—Y	—	—	—	—	1	—	—
Lebanon........ 446	—	—	—	—	—	—	—Y	—	—	—	—	—	1	2
Libya........ 672	1	—	—	—	—	—	—Y	2	2	—	—	—	—	—
Qatar........ 453	4	5	20	—	7	—	—Y	—	—	—	—	—	—	—
Saudi Arabia........ 456	1	1	1	1	15	14	17Y	3	1	—	1	1	8	1
Syrian Arab Republic........ 463	—	2	—	—	—	—	—Y	1	1	1	1	2	37	5
United Arab Emirates........ 466	1	21	2	3	1	2	2Y	1	1	4	8	10	13	22
Middle East n.s........ 489	—	—	43	—	—	—	—Y	—	—	—	—	—	—	—
Western Hemisphere........ 207	**8,205**	**8,172**	**7,405**	**12,081**	**13,596**	**12,457**	**14,178Y**	**6,304**	**4,105**	**2,874**	**6,059**	**9,399**	**13,453**	**19,744**
Antigua and Barbuda........ 311	5	5	1	2	2	2	2Y	—	—	—	—	1	24	—
Argentina........ 213	22	9	12	207	70	361	21V	299	206	254	488	570	931	1,429
Aruba........ 314	—	—	—	—	—	—	22V	—	—	—	—	—	—	—
Bahamas, The........ 313	8	218	64	57	133	348	420Y	—	—	2	44	—	15	1
Barbados........ 316	2	1	—	1	1	1	1Y	1	1	—	—	5	2	9
Belize........ 339	—	1	1	1	1	1	1Y	—	1	—	—	3	—	1
Bermuda........ 319	1	—	1	—	—	—	—Y	—	—	1	1	1	—	—
Bolivia........ 218	2	4	4	4	5	8	10Y	109	102	73	63	14	31	33
Brazil........ 223	374	548	260	165	237	532	346V	1,077	830	608	1,341	2,188	3,388	4,402
Chile........ 228	125	112	71	104	118	129	194V	319	222	151	274	373	565	928
Colombia........ 233	718	741	651	1,043	1,087	1,165	1,242V	1,593	1,068	799	1,878	2,650	3,438	6,241
Costa Rica........ 238	91	278	211	304	399	530	639Y	29	23	21	30	36	67	28
Dominica........ 321	3	2	1	1	1	1	2Y	—	—	—	1	—	—	1
Dominican Republic........ 243	193	758	188	525	765	885	1,067Y	8	5	4	4	5	10	12
Ecuador........ 248	189	342	199	381	299	257	309Y	174	65	58	126	173	292	484
El Salvador........ 253	7	57	89	170	120	102	102V	7	4	3	2	4	6	5
Grenada........ 328	2	3	1	2	1	1	1Y	—	—	—	—	2	—	—
Guatemala........ 258	187	188	75	93	71	27	32Y	11	19	6	64	37	22	21
Guyana........ 336	8	6	5	10	9	23	28Y	3	2	1	1	1	—	2
Haiti........ 263	14	16	8	6	6	14	16Y	—	—	—	—	—	—	—
Honduras........ 268	14	73	41	54	18	22	26Y	1	—	4	1	1	1	3
Jamaica........ 343	126	101	70	85	249	507	551V	7	7	8	26	20	48	46
Mexico........ 273	257	335	377	616	471	681	1,009V	835	586	431	785	1,666	1,998	2,386
Netherlands Antilles........ 353	4,381	3,408	2,531	6,989	8,099	5,763	6,952Y	208	198	25	90	163	149	107
Nicaragua........ 278	184	131	123	384	108	120	211V	1	2	1	1	1	2	13
Panama........ 283	190	163	112	34	235	60	50V	452	264	185	469	931	1,620	2,282
Paraguay........ 288	3	4	5	2	4	1	1Y	9	17	12	7	8	13	9
Peru........ 293	279	201	238	562	164	483	397Y	151	126	120	189	314	495	832
St. Lucia........ 362	52	18	17	1	41	—	—Y	—	—	—	—	—	—	1
St. Vincent & Grens........ 364	1	1	1	1	30	—	—Y	1	—	—	—	—	—	—
Suriname........ 366	1	1	1	2	2	1	1Y	1	—	—	1	—	—	—
Trinidad and Tobago........ 369	600	361	384	133	287	430	519Y	48	160	34	28	32	57	29
Uruguay........ 298	1	66	1	2	1	3	4Y	108	65	42	95	136	169	200
Western Hem. n.s........ 399	165	21	1,662	140	561	—	—Y	851	133	31	48	62	112	236
Other Countries n.i.e........ 910	**478**	**321**	**10**	**1,081**	**1,712**	**2,151**	**2,595Y**	**18**	**6**	**114**	**118**	**100**	**37**	**329**
Cuba........ 928	473	305	10	1,081	1,712	2,145	2,588Y	15	5	114	116	94	34	54
North Korea........ 954	5	16	—	—	—	5	7Y	3	1	—	2	6	3	275
Countries & Areas n.s........ 898	**2,752**	**3,413**	**3,961**	**5,973**	**6,596**	**17,229**	**20,785Y**	—	—	—	—	**5**	**150**	**102**
Special Categories........ 899	—	—	—	—	—	—	—Y	**2,970**	**2,138**	—	—	—	—	—
Memorandum Items														
European Union........ 998	1,640	1,927	3,145	1,961	4,123	5,876	6,737Y	3,138	2,611	1,993	2,727	3,281	4,226	5,404
Oil Exporting Ctys........ 999	59	37	27	13	75	34	40Y	250	32	29	61	103	136	150
Non-Oil Develop.Ctys........ 201	8,383	8,518	7,905	13,020	14,681	13,746	17,888Y	7,660	4,968	3,407	7,212	11,520	16,962	25,677
PERCENT DISTRIBUTION														
Industrial Countries........ 101	**56.7**	**53.9**	**56.2**	**49.4**	**58.4**	**49.2**	**52.7**	**49.8**	**52.4**	**61.3**	**55.7**	**51.2**	**48.7**	**43.0**
Developing Countries........ 202	**31.3**	**32.1**	**29.2**	**32.9**	**26.6**	**21.1**	**20.5**	**36.5**	**33.3**	**37.5**	**43.6**	**48.4**	**50.6**	**56.0**
Africa........ 607	**.1**	**.1**	—	—	**.3**	**.1**	**.1**	**1.2**	**.2**	**.2**	**.2**	**.2**	**.1**	**.1**
Asia........ 507	**.3**	**1.1**	**1.6**	**2.2**	**1.5**	**1.8**	**3.9**	**5.7**	**5.1**	**4.8**	**6.1**	**8.1**	**9.6**	**11.4**

	Exports							Imports						
	2001	2002	2003	2004	2005	2006	2007	2001	2002	2003	2004	2005	2006	2007
Europe.......170	.3	.1	.1	.1	.2	.1	.2	.4	.6	.8	.8	.7	.7	1.5
Middle East.......407	.2	.1	.2	.1	.1	.1	.1	.2	.2	.3	.2	.3	.4	.3
Western Hemisphere.......207	30.5	30.7	27.3	30.5	24.5	19.1	16.2	29.1	27.4	31.3	36.3	39.1	39.9	42.8
Other Countries n.i.e.......910	1.8	1.2	—	2.7	3.1	3.3	3.0	.1	—	1.2	.7	.4	.1	.7
ANNUAL PERCENT CHANGE														
World.......001	–19.3	–1.1	2.0	46.0	39.8	17.6	33.8	14.4	–30.8	–38.9	81.8	44.1	40.5	36.6
Industrial Countries.......101	–22.3	–6.0	6.4	28.3	65.5	–1.1	43.3	4.5	–27.2	–28.4	65.2	32.4	33.6	20.7
Developing Countries.......202	–23.8	1.3	–7.3	64.3	13.2	–6.6	30.1	28.9	–36.8	–31.3	111.6	59.8	47.1	51.1
Africa.......607	124.0	–8.8	–52.4	–40.8	—	–77.3	222.2	136.6	–89.4	–23.1	98.6	–2.5	–30.9	16.8
Asia.......507	–58.8	242.9	46.6	105.5	–3.9	40.4	188.0	13.8	–38.1	–41.6	127.8	90.9	67.8	61.2
Europe.......170	–22.7	–55.3	–25.6	90.4	171.6	–62.8	268.2	–3.7	1.1	–11.5	76.1	28.5	40.7	192.5
Middle East.......407	–6.2	–30.5	90.7	–58.2	69.8	42.3	25.4	47.8	–46.5	.9	27.1	180.6	62.1	–5.0
Western Hemisphere.......207	–23.4	–.4	–9.4	63.2	12.5	–8.4	13.8	30.3	–34.9	–30.0	110.8	55.1	43.1	46.8
Other Countries n.i.e.......910	–49.4	–32.8	–97.0	—	58.4	25.6	20.6	109.7	–64.9	—	3.1	–14.9	–63.5	798.8

		Exports							Imports						
		2001	2002	2003	2004	2005	2006	2007	2001	2002	2003	2004	2005	2006	2007
		Millions of U.S. Dollars							Millions of U.S. Dollars						
IFS World Total		**15,029**	**16,706**	**20,149**	**26,485**	**32,442**	**39,605**	**48,302**	**16,218**	**19,746**	**25,256**	**31,969**	**36,978**	**44,410**	**60,869**
DOTS World Total	**001**	**15,020**	**16,705**	**20,144**	**26,485**	**32,447**	**39,826**	**48,561**	**16,217**	**19,745**	**25,255**	**31,969**	**36,761**	**44,891**	**62,682**
Industrial Countries	**101**	**7,867**	**9,631**	**12,421**	**15,709**	**18,843**	**24,288**	**29,132**	**4,711**	**5,364**	**7,368**	**8,663**	**9,132**	**11,525**	**15,454**
United States	111	1,066	2,453	3,940	5,025	5,924	7,845	10,089	411	459	1,144	1,134	863	987	1,700
Canada	156	107	138	171	270	356	441	539	57	64	77	97	174	179	287
Australia	193	1,042	1,328	1,421	1,885	2,723	3,745	3,557	266	286	278	459	499	1,100	1,059
Japan	158	2,510	2,437	2,909	3,542	4,340	5,240	6,070	2,183	2,505	2,982	3,553	4,074	4,702	6,178
New Zealand	196	18	21	25	47	48	54	67	142	60	90	109	119	160	246
Austria	122	29	30	38	60	89	98	112	35	72	44	57	51	56	64
Belgium	124	341	337	391	516	544	688	849	72	95	168	138	171	225	312
Cyprus	423	2	1	2	3	5	6	7	11	3	4	9	11	7	8
Denmark	128	50	63	71	80	88	110	138	65	75	72	77	70	111	171
Finland	172	20	24	29	42	57	69	93	19	35	33	54	43	82	79
France	132	469	439	497	555	653	797	884	301	299	411	617	448	421	1,155
Germany	134	722	729	855	1,065	1,086	1,445	1,855	397	558	615	694	662	915	1,309
Greece	174	21	34	42	45	55	65	82	1	3	1	2	5	2	7
Iceland	176	5	2	1	4	2	4	5	8	1	3	3	2	6	6
Ireland	178	21	19	17	28	25	38	55	5	12	16	15	22	22	41
Italy	136	238	265	331	370	470	653	817	197	277	374	310	288	335	686
Luxembourg	137	—	—	—	—	—	—	—	1	—	3	—	—	—	—
Malta	181	—	—	1	—	—	—	—	7	—	9	—	—	—	—
Netherlands	138	365	404	493	582	659	857	1,182	115	114	325	179	312	361	510
Norway	142	15	17	21	24	33	38	49	5	6	7	18	16	24	25
Portugal	182	6	6	10	16	23	33	52	7	4	3	4	12	11	10
Slovenia	961	2	2	2	—	—	—	—	—	1	1	—	—	—	—
Spain	184	159	179	234	312	411	558	760	47	67	79	94	77	97	139
Sweden	144	53	62	90	109	134	171	202	74	63	114	125	139	164	209
Switzerland	146	95	67	75	120	104	156	237	114	139	296	687	894	1,357	1,016
United Kingdom	112	512	572	755	1,010	1,016	1,180	1,431	172	167	220	228	182	202	237
Developing Countries	**202**	**6,784**	**6,913**	**7,581**	**10,356**	**12,753**	**14,630**	**16,195**	**11,376**	**14,248**	**17,777**	**23,140**	**27,438**	**32,995**	**45,799**
Africa	**607**	**146**	**108**	**194**	**244**	**332**	**313**	**116**	**43**	**59**	**130**	**135**	**171**	**120**	**73**
Algeria	612	12	3	18	14	31	34	—	—	—	—	—	—	—	—
Angola	614	28	21	28	35	76	60	—	—	—	—	—	—	—	—
Benin	638	—	1	1	—	—	—	—	1	—	1	—	—	—	—
Burkina Faso	748	1	—	—	—	—	—	—	1	2	5	—	—	—	—
Cameroon	622	—	—	—	—	—	—	—	1	—	—	—	—	—	—
Congo, Dem. Rep. of	636	1	1	3	—	—	—	—	—	—	—	—	—	—	—
Congo, Republic of	634	1	—	—	—	—	—	—	—	—	—	—	—	—	—
Côte d'Ivoire	662	1	2	4	—	—	—	—	6	3	5	8	13	14	—
Gabon	646	3	—	6	—	—	—	—	—	—	—	—	—	—	—
Gambia, The	648	1	2	1	—	—	—	—	—	—	—	—	—	—	—
Ghana	652	5	9	15	32	23	38	—	—	—	1	—	—	—	—
Guinea	656	1	1	1	9	7	15	—	1	—	—	—	—	—	—
Kenya	664	4	3	6	—	—	—	—	1	2	1	—	—	—	—
Liberia	668	1	1	—	—	—	—	—	—	—	—	6	—	4	—
Madagascar	674	3	—	1	—	—	—	—	—	—	—	—	—	—	—
Mali	678	2	1	2	—	—	—	—	3	4	6	7	13	18	—
Mauritania	682	1	1	1	—	—	—	—	—	—	—	—	—	—	—
Mauritius	684	—	1	1	—	—	—	—	—	—	1	—	—	—	—
Morocco	686	2	3	3	—	—	—	—	—	—	—	—	—	—	—
Mozambique	688	—	—	6	—	—	—	—	3	3	1	—	—	—	—
Niger	692	—	1	1	—	—	—	—	—	—	—	—	—	—	—
Nigeria	694	8	9	11	11	17	33	—	11	6	10	14	31	19	—
Rwanda	714	—	—	—	—	—	—	—	—	1	—	—	—	—	—
São Tomé & Príncipe	716	—	—	—	—	—	—	—	—	—	1	—	—	—	—
Senegal	722	21	14	34	57	42	10	—	—	—	1	—	—	—	—
Sierra Leone	724	1	1	—	—	—	—	—	—	—	—	—	—	—	—
Somalia	726	1	—	—	—	—	—	—	—	—	—	—	—	—	—
South Africa	199	29	16	23	57	112	101	116	5	25	79	91	108	54	73
Sudan	732	1	1	1	—	—	—	—	1	—	—	—	—	—	—
Swaziland	734	3	7	—	4	2	—	—	—	—	—	—	—	—	—
Tanzania	738	8	6	21	25	23	23	—	2	1	1	—	—	—	—
Togo	742	3	1	1	—	—	—	—	—	1	3	—	—	—	—
Tunisia	744	1	1	2	—	—	—	—	4	6	6	6	5	10	—
Uganda	746	1	—	—	—	—	—	—	—	—	—	—	—	—	—
Zambia	754	—	—	1	—	—	—	—	—	4	5	3	1	2	—
Asia	**507**	**5,582**	**5,692**	**6,524**	**8,980**	**11,105**	**12,382**	**14,324**	**10,478**	**12,913**	**16,130**	**21,147**	**25,036**	**31,070**	**43,940**
Bangladesh	513	7	10	6	20	22	22	—	13	7	11	21	32	27	—
Brunei Darussalam	516	1	1	1	—	—	—	—	—	—	—	—	—	—	—
Cambodia	522	146	178	267	384	556	781	991	23	65	95	131	160	170	202
China,P.R.: Mainland	924	1,417	1,518	1,883	2,899	3,228	3,243	3,357	1,606	2,159	3,139	4,595	5,900	7,391	12,502
China,P.R.:Hong Kong	532	317	340	369	380	353	453	583	538	805	991	1,074	1,235	1,441	1,941

	Exports 2001	2002	2003	2004	2005	2006	2007	Imports 2001	2002	2003	2004	2005	2006	2007
	Millions of U.S. Dollars							Millions of U.S. Dollars						
China,P.R.:Macao........ 546	1	—	1	—	—	—	—	—	—	—	—	—	—	—
Fiji........ 819	1	1	1	—	—	—	—	—	—	—	—	—	—	—
Guam........ 829	1	—	1	—	—	—	—	—	1	—	—	—	—	—
India........ 534	45	52	32	79	98	138	180	228	325	457	594	596	880	1,357
Indonesia........ 536	266	334	467	453	469	958	1,105	289	363	551	663	700	1,013	1,354
Korea........ 542	406	469	492	608	664	843	1,253	1,887	2,280	2,625	3,359	3,594	3,908	5,334
Lao People's Dem.Rep........ 544	64	65	52	68	69	95	104	68	63	61	74	98	167	208
Malaysia........ 548	337	348	454	624	1,028	1,254	1,390	464	683	925	1,215	1,257	1,482	2,290
Mongolia........ 948	1	1	1	—	—	—	—	—	1	—	—	—	—	—
Myanmar........ 518	5	7	13	14	12	17	22	4	6	18	19	46	65	75
Nepal........ 558	—	1	1	—	—	—	—	—	—	—	—	—	—	—
Pakistan........ 564	9	22	23	40	42	66	—	14	28	17	30	38	33	—
Palau........ 565	—	—	1	—	—	—	—	—	—	—	—	—	—	—
Papua New Guinea........ 853	3	—	2	—	—	—	—	1	—	10	—	—	—	—
Philippines........ 566	368	315	340	499	829	783	965	54	101	141	188	210	343	414
Samoa........ 862	—	15	—	—	—	—	—	—	—	—	—	—	—	—
Singapore........ 576	1,044	961	1,025	1,485	1,917	1,812	2,202	2,478	2,533	2,876	3,618	4,482	6,274	7,609
Solomon Islands........ 813	—	—	2	—	—	—	—	2	4	3	—	—	—	—
Sri Lanka........ 524	10	7	6	22	20	21	—	7	8	11	7	10	19	—
Taiwan Province of China........ 528	806	818	749	891	935	969	1,139	2,009	2,525	2,916	3,698	4,304	4,825	6,917
Thailand........ 578	323	227	335	515	863	930	1,034	792	955	1,282	1,859	2,374	3,034	3,737
Timor-Leste........ 537	—	—	—	—	—	—	—	—	—	5	—	—	—	—
Vanuatu........ 846	—	—	2	—	—	—	—	—	2	—	—	—	—	—
Europe........ 170	**409**	**417**	**408**	**483**	**552**	**955**	**1,302**	**559**	**838**	**893**	**1,049**	**1,128**	**752**	**816**
Albania........ 914	—	1	—	—	—	—	—	—	—	—	—	—	—	—
Armenia........ 911	—	1	2	—	—	—	—	—	—	—	—	—	—	—
Azerbaijan........ 912	—	—	—	—	—	—	—	1	1	1	—	—	—	—
Belarus........ 913	3	1	2	—	—	—	—	6	11	6	11	23	23	—
Bosnia & Herzegovina........ 963	—	—	—	—	—	—	—	1	—	—	—	—	—	—
Bulgaria........ 918	14	8	6	8	11	22	36	3	2	7	3	6	7	10
Croatia........ 960	1	1	3	—	—	—	—	—	—	1	—	—	—	—
Czech Republic........ 935	39	40	39	43	49	70	102	8	9	14	14	16	22	23
Estonia........ 939	1	2	2	—	—	—	—	1	1	—	—	—	—	—
Georgia........ 915	4	4	3	9	4	7	—	1	—	1	1	1	—	—
Gibraltar........ 823	—	—	—	—	—	—	—	—	—	1	—	—	—	—
Hungary........ 944	17	21	18	22	27	33	63	15	14	19	16	19	26	29
Kazakhstan........ 916	—	—	1	—	—	—	—	5	15	33	—	—	—	—
Latvia........ 941	2	1	3	—	—	—	—	—	—	—	—	—	—	—
Lithuania........ 946	1	5	4	—	—	—	—	—	—	—	—	—	—	—
Macedonia, FYR........ 962	—	1	1	—	—	—	—	—	—	—	—	—	—	—
Moldova........ 921	—	1	1	—	—	—	—	—	—	—	—	—	—	—
Poland........ 964	79	68	84	82	82	160	221	18	14	38	39	43	58	110
Romania........ 968	7	11	12	14	16	21	32	3	2	23	12	10	7	9
Russia........ 922	194	187	160	216	252	413	459	376	501	492	672	767	456	552
Serbia & Montenegro........ 965	—	1	1	—	—	—	—	—	—	—	—	—	—	—
Slovak Republic........ 936	5	7	8	9	12	23	72	2	2	1	3	2	3	2
Tajikistan........ 923	—	—	—	—	—	—	—	1	2	1	—	—	—	—
Turkey........ 186	12	24	31	47	60	142	202	8	16	25	31	43	28	42
Turkmenistan........ 925	—	—	—	—	—	—	—	2	—	—	—	—	—	—
Ukraine........ 926	26	30	26	33	39	65	116	95	239	224	241	192	118	39
Uzbekistan........ 927	1	—	—	—	—	—	—	13	9	2	6	7	4	—
Middle East........ 407	**531**	**561**	**305**	**407**	**431**	**443**	**301**	**166**	**288**	**365**	**493**	**640**	**449**	**330**
Bahrain........ 419	—	—	—	—	—	—	—	10	6	6	9	8	13	—
Egypt........ 469	29	22	15	40	45	49	—	—	1	7	3	19	8	—
Iran, I.R. of........ 429	10	10	14	20	83	16	—	14	20	24	41	22	55	—
Iraq........ 433	405	440	151	185	101	118	15	3	—	1	—	—	—	—
Israel........ 436	18	19	20	32	32	44	—	14	17	22	35	36	41	—
Jordan........ 439	4	1	4	—	—	—	—	4	3	13	5	6	20	—
Kuwait........ 443	3	3	7	4	12	11	—	46	151	173	257	359	145	22
Lebanon........ 446	3	4	4	—	—	—	—	—	—	—	—	—	—	—
Libya........ 672	—	—	1	—	—	—	—	—	—	—	—	—	—	—
Oman........ 449	1	1	1	—	—	—	—	—	—	—	—	—	—	—
Qatar........ 453	—	—	—	—	—	—	—	—	31	26	26	29	20	67
Saudi Arabia........ 456	14	18	17	22	31	49	52	23	29	38	66	91	102	131
Syrian Arab Republic........ 463	2	1	4	—	—	—	—	1	—	1	—	—	—	—
United Arab Emirates........ 466	33	41	66	94	122	141	235	10	28	54	54	69	44	110
Yemen, Republic of........ 474	9	—	1	11	7	15	—	—	—	—	—	—	—	—
Middle East n.s........ 489	—	—	—	—	—	—	—	40	—	—	—	—	—	—
Western Hemisphere........ 207	**117**	**135**	**150**	**243**	**333**	**538**	**152**	**131**	**150**	**259**	**315**	**464**	**604**	**640**
Antigua and Barbuda........ 311	1	—	—	—	—	—	—	—	—	—	—	—	—	—
Argentina........ 213	5	1	6	9	17	31	50	59	90	165	172	271	241	409
Aruba........ 314	1	—	—	—	—	—	—	—	—	—	—	—	—	—
Bahamas, The........ 313	—	—	—	—	—	—	—	8	—	1	—	—	—	—
Belize........ 339	—	—	—	—	—	—	—	23	—	2	—	—	—	—
Brazil........ 223	15	12	23	25	32	62	103	13	29	33	47	76	147	231
Chile........ 228	9	10	10	22	31	46	—	3	9	20	44	78	105	—
Colombia........ 233	3	7	3	8	11	23	—	—	—	—	—	—	—	—

	Exports 2001	Exports 2002	Exports 2003	Exports 2004	Exports 2005	Exports 2006	Exports 2007	Imports 2001	Imports 2002	Imports 2003	Imports 2004	Imports 2005	Imports 2006	Imports 2007
	Millions of U.S. Dollars							*Millions of U.S. Dollars*						
Costa Rica.......... 238	1	—	1	—	—	—	—	—	—	1	—	—	—	—
Dominica.......... 321	—	1	1	—	—	—	—	—	—	2	—	—	—	—
Dominican Republic.......... 243	2	—	—	—	—	—	—	—	1	—	—	—	—	—
Ecuador.......... 248	2	3	5	—	—	—	—	—	—	—	—	—	—	—
El Salvador.......... 253	1	1	—	—	—	—	—	—	—	—	—	—	—	—
Guatemala.......... 258	3	4	1	—	—	—	—	—	—	—	—	—	—	—
Haiti.......... 263	1	—	—	—	—	—	—	—	—	1	—	—	—	—
Honduras.......... 268	—	2	1	—	—	—	—	—	—	1	—	—	—	—
Mexico.......... 273	44	60	78	128	192	286	—	6	6	11	13	8	19	—
Netherlands Antilles.......... 353	—	3	—	—	—	—	—	—	—	1	—	—	—	—
Panama.......... 283	15	13	14	45	43	78	—	7	6	5	23	—	54	—
Paraguay.......... 288	1	—	—	—	—	—	—	—	—	—	—	—	—	—
Peru.......... 293	2	1	2	6	8	13	—	10	4	11	17	32	39	—
Suriname.......... 366	1	—	—	—	—	—	—	—	—	—	—	—	—	—
Trinidad and Tobago.......... 369	1	—	—	—	—	—	—	1	—	—	—	—	—	—
Uruguay.......... 298	2	1	—	—	—	—	—	1	2	3	—	—	—	—
Venezuela, Rep. Bol.......... 299	6	4	1	—	—	—	—	—	—	—	—	—	—	—
Western Hem. n.s.......... 399	—	5	—	—	—	—	—	—	—	—	—	—	—	—
Other Countries n.i.e.......... 910	**49**	**51**	**65**	**105**	**207**	**153**	**—**	**1**	**—**	**—**	**—**	**—**	**—**	**—**
Cuba.......... 928	44	47	65	105	207	153	—	1	—	—	—	—	—	—
North Korea.......... 954	5	4	—	—	—	—	—	—	—	—	—	—	—	—
Countries & Areas n.s.......... 898	**314**	**107**	**76**	**314**	**644**	**755**	**3,235**	**129**	**132**	**110**	**166**	**190**	**371**	**1,429**
Memorandum Items														
European Union.......... 998	3,153	3,312	4,018	4,948	5,483	7,053	8,976	1,567	1,885	2,565	2,676	2,572	3,120	5,100
Oil Exporting Ctys.......... 999	758	865	754	802	864	1,360	1,406	397	629	878	1,120	1,301	1,398	1,684
Non-Oil Develop.Ctys.......... 201	6,027	6,049	6,827	9,555	11,888	13,270	14,789	10,979	13,619	16,899	22,020	26,138	31,597	44,115
PERCENT DISTRIBUTION														
Industrial Countries.......... 101	**52.4**	**57.7**	**61.7**	**59.3**	**58.1**	**61.0**	**60.0**	**29.1**	**27.2**	**29.2**	**27.1**	**24.8**	**25.7**	**24.7**
Developing Countries.......... 202	**45.2**	**41.4**	**37.6**	**39.1**	**39.3**	**36.7**	**33.3**	**70.1**	**72.2**	**70.4**	**72.4**	**74.6**	**73.5**	**73.1**
Africa.......... 607	**1.0**	**.6**	**1.0**	**.9**	**1.0**	**.8**	**.2**	**.3**	**.3**	**.5**	**.4**	**.5**	**.3**	**.1**
Asia.......... 507	**37.2**	**34.1**	**32.4**	**33.9**	**34.2**	**31.1**	**29.5**	**64.6**	**65.4**	**63.9**	**66.1**	**68.1**	**69.2**	**70.1**
Europe.......... 170	**2.7**	**2.5**	**2.0**	**1.8**	**1.7**	**2.4**	**2.7**	**3.4**	**4.2**	**3.5**	**3.3**	**3.1**	**1.7**	**1.3**
Middle East.......... 407	**3.5**	**3.4**	**1.5**	**1.5**	**1.3**	**1.1**	**.6**	**1.0**	**1.5**	**1.4**	**1.5**	**1.7**	**1.0**	**.5**
Western Hemisphere.......... 207	**.8**	**.8**	**.7**	**.9**	**1.0**	**1.4**	**.3**	**.8**	**.8**	**1.0**	**1.0**	**1.3**	**1.3**	**1.0**
Other Countries n.i.e.......... 910	**.3**	**.3**	**.3**	**.4**	**.6**	**.4**	**—**	**—**	**—**	**—**	**—**	**—**	**—**	**—**
ANNUAL PERCENT CHANGE														
World.......... 001	**3.7**	**11.2**	**20.6**	**31.5**	**22.5**	**22.7**	**21.9**	**3.7**	**21.8**	**27.9**	**26.6**	**15.0**	**22.1**	**39.6**
Industrial Countries.......... 101	**1.7**	**22.4**	**29.0**	**26.5**	**19.9**	**28.9**	**19.9**	**4.5**	**13.9**	**37.4**	**17.6**	**5.4**	**26.2**	**34.1**
Developing Countries.......... 202	**2.5**	**1.9**	**9.7**	**36.6**	**23.1**	**14.7**	**10.7**	**3.3**	**25.2**	**24.8**	**30.2**	**18.6**	**20.3**	**38.8**
Africa.......... 607	**18.9**	**–25.9**	**79.9**	**25.7**	**36.2**	**–5.8**	**–63.1**	**–4.4**	**38.5**	**120.0**	**3.8**	**26.6**	**–29.7**	**–39.1**
Asia.......... 507	**–1.6**	**2.0**	**14.6**	**37.6**	**23.7**	**11.5**	**15.7**	**1.8**	**23.2**	**24.9**	**31.1**	**18.4**	**24.1**	**41.4**
Europe.......... 170	**34.6**	**2.0**	**–2.2**	**18.4**	**14.3**	**73.1**	**36.4**	**34.5**	**50.0**	**6.5**	**17.5**	**7.5**	**–33.3**	**8.5**
Middle East.......... 407	**25.1**	**5.6**	**–45.7**	**33.5**	**5.9**	**2.8**	**–32.0**	**–13.2**	**73.7**	**26.8**	**35.3**	**29.7**	**–29.8**	**–26.4**
Western Hemisphere.......... 207	**23.8**	**15.4**	**11.3**	**61.2**	**37.2**	**61.6**	**–71.7**	**91.6**	**14.3**	**72.7**	**21.6**	**47.4**	**30.1**	**6.0**
Other Countries n.i.e.......... 910	**37.3**	**3.6**	**28.3**	**61.3**	**96.7**	**–26.2**	**24.1**	**....**	**–77.8**	**–6.5**	**31.3**	**14.3**	**....**	**....**

	Exports 2001	Exports 2002	Exports 2003	Exports 2004	Exports 2005	Exports 2006	Exports 2007	Imports 2001	Imports 2002	Imports 2003	Imports 2004	Imports 2005	Imports 2006	Imports 2007
	Millions of U.S. Dollars							*Millions of U.S. Dollars*						
IFS World Total	**3,374.0**	**3,684.0**	**3,924.0**	**4,676.0**	**6,380.0**	**7,316.4**	**7,160.0**	**2,466.0**	**2,921.0**	**3,675.0**	**3,986.1**	**4,864.5**	**5,293.7**	**5,890.0**
DOTS World Total 001	**3,370.2**	**3,271.0**	**3,724.0Y**	**4,076.4**	**5,606.3**	**6,439.3Y**	**6,833.6Y**	**2,465.6**	**2,776.9**	**4,403.7Y**	**3,984.5**	**4,799.8**	**7,073.6Y**	**9,112.8Y**
Industrial Countries 101	**303.9**	**283.7**	**267.1Y**	**326.2**	**995.8**	**918.2Y**	**1,052.1Y**	**736.8**	**741.8**	**1,292.5Y**	**1,341.9**	**1,479.8**	**1,714.6Y**	**2,730.5Y**
United States 111	138.98	176.99	65.45V	47.45	182.46	435.73V	284.73V	121.89	131.17	214.61V	186.04	216.17	280.83V	706.42V
Canada 156	1.13	.03	.15V	.15	.16	.20V	.17V	12.13	17.34	26.18V	20.62	14.48	26.81V	27.83V
Australia 193	—	—	19.89V	28.79	35.68	75.56V	.01V	44.31	32.85	64.81V	65.31	33.50	123.67V	97.23V
Japan 158	17.79	47.25	107.22V	110.54	354.88	227.12V	493.63V	67.18	61.85	127.60V	154.41	96.15	223.89V	231.21V
New Zealand 196	—	—	—V	68.82	64.28	23.32V	—V	5.78	7.40	10.11V	15.92	14.59	21.46V	34.92V
Austria 122	—	—	—V	.23	.03	1.36V	.43V	9.86	7.48	9.09V	18.43	20.98	17.94V	30.53V
Belgium 124	.79	1.98	3.91V	3.20	7.97	3.43V	7.26V	18.10	16.55	24.86V	28.31	39.36	56.74V	103.97V
Cyprus 423	—	.02	.35V	—	—	13.28V	.01V	.94	1.07	.77V	2.33	1.92	2.78V	2.94V
Denmark 128	.05	.03	—V	—	.72	.03V	2.59V	21.48	21.58	43.10V	36.94	33.01	28.68V	43.67V
Finland 172	.01	.02	.08V	—	.02	.10V	.01V	.59	1.93	7.74V	6.67	60.06	24.96V	15.90V
France 132	28.80	4.75	20.67V	4.44	3.67	21.22V	61.86V	115.06	104.18	179.67V	129.85	105.73	162.34V	255.02V
Germany 134	1.62	1.85	5.00V	3.66	2.95	6.21V	109.54V	52.70	47.19	143.06V	143.82	137.40	247.05V	438.82V
Greece 174	1.02	3.06	.07V	16.90	15.42	29.50V	.64V	4.29	5.01	10.36V	2.80	1.23	4.28V	26.49V
Iceland 176	—	—	—V	—	—	—V	.03V	—	—	.16V	.01	.12	—V	.01V
Ireland 178	—	.01	—V	—	—	—V	—V	3.85	3.42	3.74V	3.44	4.72	4.09V	6.57V
Italy 136	72.22	10.84	11.59V	7.09	6.08	15.47V	17.91V	35.68	47.09	108.34V	75.63	68.23	132.36V	243.31V
Luxembourg 137	—	—	.01V	—	—	.02V	—V	—	—	.82V	—	.04	3.75V	3.07V
Malta 181	—	—	—V	—	—	—V	.04V	.91	1.69	1.93V	1.41	2.05	2.53V	1.74V
Netherlands 138	.70	.29	.66V	.78	.26	1.64V	42.62V	49.46	35.11	77.13V	67.33	48.17	97.45V	133.56V
Norway 142	.01	.02	.03V	—	—	.02V	.02V	.21	.12	1.87V	1.08	1.38	2.64V	4.24V
Portugal 182	.12	.80	1.21V	.29	.42	.61V	.32V	.13	.25	.73V	.61	.51	1.85V	23.44V
Slovenia 961	—	—	.01V	—	—	—V	—V	.39	1.47	1.45V	2.45	.67	17.78V	19.06V
Spain 184	5.32	3.06	16.83V	6.18	7.58	35.99V	16.60V	16.44	19.85	28.68V	17.64	14.25	30.05V	31.32V
Sweden 144	.05	.02	.37V	.03	.09	.19V	.04V	14.26	10.95	26.66V	23.24	20.67	36.94V	46.32V
Switzerland 146	16.78	26.95	.24V	23.51	307.17	.93V	.39V	48.26	81.32	34.13V	154.57	410.52	38.40V	54.11V
United Kingdom 112	18.46	5.74	13.40V	4.11	5.97	26.29V	13.27V	92.84	84.89	144.93V	183.05	133.90	125.32V	148.80V
Developing Countries 202	**2,909.6**	**2,980.5**	**3,448.3Y**	**3,723.4**	**4,577.8**	**5,480.7Y**	**5,731.3Y**	**1,623.4**	**2,017.5**	**3,088.7Y**	**2,631.9**	**3,286.6**	**5,317.6Y**	**6,331.0Y**
Africa 607	**133.9**	**82.5**	**76.8Y**	**153.6**	**65.3**	**59.6Y**	**216.2Y**	**78.5**	**85.0**	**137.8Y**	**93.9**	**148.7**	**233.9Y**	**217.4Y**
Algeria 612	.10	.77	.86Y	.37	.30	.37Y	.48Y	.10	.04	.05Y	.04	.08	.10Y	.12Y
Angola 614	—	—	—Y	.02	.07	.09Y	.11Y	—	—	—Y	—	—	—Y	—Y
Cameroon 622	—	—	—V	—	—	—Y	—Y	.02	.99	—V	—	.02	.03Y	.04Y
Central African Rep. 626	—	.01	.01Y	—	—	—Y	—Y	—	—	—Y	.02	—	—Y	—Y
Congo, Dem. Rep. of 636	—	—	—Y	.02	—	—Y	—Y	—	.02	.03Y	—	—	—Y	—Y
Côte d'Ivoire 662	—	—	—V	.01	—	.08V	.10Y	—	—	—V	.35	—	—V	—Y
Djibouti 611	6.89	9.08	11.49Y	10.24	9.44	11.67Y	14.48Y	50.74	37.38	47.31Y	14.92	10.27	12.69Y	15.75Y
Equatorial Guinea 642	—	—	—Y	—	—	—Y	—Y	—	—	—Y	.01	—	—Y	—Y
Eritrea 643	3.03	3.59	4.54Y	1.91	4.62	5.71Y	7.09Y	.05	.16	.21Y	.09	.22	.27Y	.34Y
Ethiopia 644	3.35	2.51	9.16V	4.31	6.41	7.92Y	9.83Y	4.85	5.42	17.79V	6.56	9.84	12.17Y	15.10Y
Gabon 646	....	....	....	....	....	....	....	—	—	—Y	.04	—	—Y	—Y
Gambia, The 648	—	—	—Y	.01	.22	.27Y	.34Y	—	—	—Y	.02	—	—Y	—Y
Ghana 652	.03	.09	.11Y	.52	.39	.48Y	.59Y	.18	—	—Y	—	—	—Y	—Y
Guinea 656	.01	.01	.01V	.02	.18	.22Y	.27Y	.05	—	—V	.06	.01	.01Y	.01Y
Kenya 664	.06	.13	7.45V	.45	.28	.35Y	.43Y	6.94	9.23	34.63V	12.61	13.60	16.80Y	20.85Y
Liberia 668	—	—	—Y	.08	.04	.04Y	.06Y	.10	—	—Y	—	—	—Y	—Y
Madagascar 674	—	.10	.02V	.07	.02	.03Y	.04Y	—	—	—V	—	—	—Y	—Y
Mali 678	—	—	—Y	.05	.07	.09Y	.11Y	—	—	—Y	—	—	—Y	—Y
Mauritania 682	—	—	—Y	.11	.01	.02Y	.02Y	.01	.04	.05Y	.01	—	—Y	—Y
Mauritius 684	—	—	3.24V	.02	—	.07V	.32V	—	—	.03V	.03	—	—V	—V
Morocco 686	.27	.31	.14V	.14	.06	.08Y	.09Y	.51	2.66	5.82V	2.91	7.61	9.40Y	11.67Y
Mozambique 688	—	—	—Y	—	—	—Y	—Y	—	—	—Y	.09	.03	.04Y	.05Y
Niger 692	—	—	—V	—	—	—Y	—Y	.01	—	—Y	—	—	—Y	—Y
Nigeria 694	.04	—	2.73V	—	.16	.20Y	.26Y	.61	1.39	—V	1.37	.34	.42Y	.51Y
Rwanda 714	—	—	—Y	—	—	—Y	—Y	—	.01	.02Y	—	—	.03Y	.04Y
São Tomé & Príncipe 716	—	—	—Y	—	—	—Y	—Y	—	—	—Y	—	.01	.01Y	.02Y
Senegal 722	—	—	.01V	.02	.07	—V	—Y	—	—	—V	—	.20	.01V	.02Y
Seychelles 718	—	.24	—V	.58	.04	.05Y	.06Y	—	—	—V	—	—	—Y	—Y
Sierra Leone 724	—	—	—Y	.03	.02	.02Y	.02Y	—	—	—Y	—	—	—Y	—Y
Somalia 726	8.72	9.18	11.62Y	18.80	29.15	36.03Y	44.71Y	2.62	19.38	24.53Y	33.04	57.18	70.67Y	87.70Y
South Africa 199	111.51	57.92	26.82V	113.46	2.95	—V	141.89V	3.52	2.38	3.51V	12.46	24.69	37.24V	31.52V
Sudan 732	2.50	1.76	2.22Y	3.08	13.73	—V	—V	5.50	3.31	2.10Y	3.51	4.12	48.63V	2.14V
Swaziland 734	—	—	—Y	—	.14	.17Y	.21Y	—	—	—Y	3.30	18.58	22.97Y	28.50Y
Tanzania 738	.02	—	—Y	.09	.37	.46Y	.57Y	.03	.04	.05Y	.17	.09	.11Y	.14Y
Togo 742	—	—	.07V	—	—	.04Y	.05Y	—	—	—V	—	—	—Y	—Y
Tunisia 744	.43	.42	.83V	1.12	1.22	.88V	1.10Y	1.04	1.14	.46V	1.32	.96	2.25V	2.79Y
Uganda 746	—	—	.04V	—	.01	.02Y	.02Y	—	.12	.01V	—	—	—Y	—Y
Zambia 754	—	—	.01V	—	—	—V	—V	—	—	—V	—	.02	—V	—V
Zimbabwe 698	—	—	—V	—	—	—V	—Y	1.67	1.45	1.38V	1.12	1.08	.32V	.39Y
Asia 507	**2,590.6**	**2,561.9**	**3,001.0Y**	**3,262.2**	**3,984.5**	**4,771.0Y**	**4,631.2Y**	**451.3**	**537.8**	**1,081.7Y**	**725.8**	**740.0**	**1,812.6Y**	**2,276.5Y**
Afghanistan, I.S. of 512	—	—	—Y	—	—	—Y	—Y	.01	—	—Y	.08	—	—Y	—Y
Bangladesh 513	.30	.05	—V	.65	.03	—V	—V	.94	.96	1.98V	.84	1.16	1.73Y	2.25Y
Bhutan 514	—	—	—Y	—	—	—Y	—Y	.02	.70	.89Y	—	—	—Y	—Y

		Exports							Imports						
		2001	2002	2003	2004	2005	2006	2007	2001	2002	2003	2004	2005	2006	2007
		Millions of U.S. Dollars							*Millions of U.S. Dollars*						
Brunei Darussalam	516	—	—	—Y	—	.01	.02Y	.02Y	....	....	....	....	....	....	....
Cambodia	522	—	—	—Y	—	—	—Y	—Y	.02	.01	.01Y	—	—	—Y	—Y
China,P.R.: Mainland	924	322.31	502.15	1,405.74V	1,169.06	1,978.89	2,028.55V	1,589.39V	98.02	173.08	389.67V	255.33	295.11	886.81V	1,060.60V
China,P.R.:Hong Kong	532	.58	.97	5.05V	9.57	5.77	12.36V	11.79V	1.89	2.21	4.80V	2.81	2.71	6.75V	8.76V
China,P.R.:Macao	546	—	—	.01V	—	—	—V	—V	—	—	.05V	—	—	—V	—V
Fiji	819	—	—	—Y	—	—	—Y	—Y	—	.01	.01Y	—	—	—Y	—Y
India	534	618.52	545.96	29.89V	540.26	910.63	1,125.48Y	1,396.71Y	135.17	106.72	224.51V	161.18	136.29	168.45Y	209.04Y
Indonesia	536	.90	50.96	26.57V	.35	.23	.17V	.58V	25.57	32.51	57.66V	37.09	32.44	99.22V	267.57V
Korea	542	445.37	407.22	216.70V	130.60	352.64	453.72V	232.14V	24.11	42.86	65.94V	39.15	59.68	103.00V	135.34V
Lao People's Dem.Rep.	544	....	....	....	....	....	....	....	—	—	—Y	—	.01	.02Y	.02Y
Malaysia	548	218.27	199.45	192.86V	29.97	26.30	47.34V	26.13V	65.79	64.63	115.05V	78.55	97.09	288.63V	242.78V
Mongolia	948	—	—	—Y	—	—	—Y	—Y	—	.05	.07Y	.05	—	—Y	—Y
Myanmar	518	—	—	—Y	—	—	—Y	—Y	.06	.05	.06Y	—	—	—Y	—Y
Nepal	558	—	—	—Y	—	—	—Y	—Y	.14	.02	.02Y	—	—	—Y	—Y
Pakistan	564	1.29	1.76	3.51V	6.04	2.07	2.56Y	3.17Y	14.02	19.48	57.92V	21.25	21.31	26.34Y	32.68Y
Philippines	566	19.34	54.84	62.35V	—	—	—V	—V	.04	.06	1.84V	.20	.32	.79V	2.81V
Samoa	862	....	....	....	....	....	....	....	—	—	—Y	—	.09	.11Y	.14Y
Singapore	576	316.80	123.72	159.56V	192.70	39.99	13.43V	56.81V	34.10	27.72	25.59V	53.09	46.18	54.88V	56.13V
Solomon Islands	813	—	—	—Y	—	.04	.05Y	.07Y	—	—	—Y	.02	.01	.01Y	.01Y
Sri Lanka	524	.22	.09	.33V	.33	.54	.64V	1.44V	.52	2.15	1.39V	.38	.10	.70V	.89V
Taiwan Province of China	528	40.98	54.95	.75V	1.32	.59	10.77V	4.80V	6.69	5.75	18.80V	9.56	7.16	21.84V	28.25V
Thailand	578	605.68	619.81	897.55V	1,180.85	666.30	1,075.92V	1,308.15V	41.10	58.81	113.93V	61.59	37.68	137.23V	229.23V
Vanuatu	846	—	—	—Y	.01	—	—Y	—Y	....	....	....	....	....	....	....
Vietnam	582	—	—	.09V	.51	.50	—V	—V	—	—	1.52V	4.61	2.62	16.06V	—V
Asia n.s.	598	—	—	—Y	—	—	—Y	—Y	3.11	—	—Y	—	—	—Y	—Y
Europe	**170**	**.2**	**.9**	**16.5Y**	**1.1**	**3.7**	**3.5Y**	**4.6Y**	**61.1**	**95.8**	**345.4Y**	**160.1**	**250.1**	**477.7Y**	**640.0Y**
Albania	914	—	—	—V	—	—	—V	.15V	—	.04	—V	.17	.01	—V	.11V
Armenia	911	—	—	—Y	.02	—	—Y	—Y	—	—	—Y	.69	.03	—V	—V
Azerbaijan	912	—	—	.03V	—	—	.01V	—V	—	—	5.15V	—	—	2.46V	—V
Belarus	913	—	—	—V	—	—	.03V	—V	.14	—	.23V	—	—	.01V	1.74V
Bosnia & Herzegovina	963	.03	—	—Y	—	—	—Y	—Y	—	—	—Y	.06	.56	.69Y	.86Y
Bulgaria	918	.02	.06	—V	—	—	—V	.02V	.10	1.88	1.44V	.74	6.42	36.51V	9.15V
Croatia	960	—	.36	—V	—	—	.05V	—V	.13	.05	—V	.12	.25	—V	—V
Czech Republic	935	—	.11	—V	—	—	—V	.02V	.14	3.02	2.51V	3.23	2.13	9.22V	10.80V
Estonia	939	—	—	—V	—	—	—V	—V	.02	—	—V	.03	.01	.64V	2.19V
Georgia	915	—	—	—V	.01	—	—V	—Y	—	—	—V	—	.19	6.12V	6.38Y
Gibraltar	823	—	—	—Y	.01	—	—Y	—Y	—	—	—Y	—	—	—Y	—Y
Hungary	944	—	—	—V	—	—	—V	.01V	.56	1.35	7.43V	1.94	9.68	17.68V	5.27V
Kazakhstan	916	—	—	—V	—	—	—Y	—Y	.46	—	—V	—	5.27	6.52Y	8.09Y
Kyrgyz Republic	917	—	—	—Y	—	—	—Y	—Y	—	.07	—V	—	—	—V	—V
Latvia	941	—	—	—V	.09	—	—V	—V	.22	.39	1.04V	.11	.48	1.32V	1.20V
Lithuania	946	—	.03	—V	—	—	—V	—V	—	.05	.01V	1.30	—	.01V	.05V
Macedonia, FYR	962	—	—	—V	—	—	—V	—Y	—	—	.07V	—	—	—V	—Y
Poland	964	—	.07	.13V	.24	.21	.09V	.41V	2.90	7.69	11.31V	6.83	5.55	11.07V	10.89V
Romania	968	—	.04	.01V	.02	.03	.08V	—V	.99	1.31	2.81V	2.63	5.69	31.00V	45.57V
Russia	922	—	—	16.13V	—	—	.09V	.17V	1.45	2.68	98.35V	17.59	39.64	104.24V	196.54V
Serbia & Montenegro	965	—	—	—Y	—	—	—Y	—Y	—	—	—Y	.14	.22	.28Y	.34Y
Slovak Republic	936	—	—	—Y	—	—	—V	—V	.10	.12	.15Y	1.73	.35	1.52V	1.01V
Tajikistan	923	—	—	—V	.01	—	—V	—V	—	—	—V	.11	.02	—V	—V
Turkey	186	.08	.10	.12V	.56	1.28	.40V	.42V	51.03	64.12	171.68V	98.29	148.75	217.66V	301.65V
Ukraine	926	—	—	—V	.04	2.20	2.71Y	3.37Y	.94	2.19	29.60V	24.06	11.82	14.61Y	18.13Y
Europe n.s.	884	.06	.09	.12Y	.08	.01	.02Y	.02Y	1.94	10.80	13.67Y	.27	13.03	16.11Y	19.99Y
Middle East	**407**	**184.9**	**335.2**	**346.7Y**	**306.1**	**523.9**	**646.2Y**	**879.0Y**	**895.2**	**1,138.7**	**1,362.7Y**	**1,476.0**	**1,900.2**	**2,394.9Y**	**2,895.1Y**
Bahrain	419	10.40	13.48	17.06Y	.36	.53	.66Y	.82Y	11.65	30.43	38.51Y	1.64	6.78	8.38Y	10.40Y
Egypt	469	10.96	14.30	18.10Y	12.85	22.38	27.66Y	34.32Y	27.23	43.88	55.54Y	88.76	111.00	137.19Y	170.25Y
Iran, I.R. of	429	.05	.27	.30Y	3.00	.10	.12Y	.16Y	4.79	4.98	6.04Y	8.31	4.65	5.85Y	7.06Y
Iraq	433	4.89	3.47	3.86Y	10.73	21.16	26.13Y	33.84Y	.09	—	—Y	.61	.82	1.03Y	1.25Y
Jordan	439	1.40	1.25	1.97V	1.36	1.63	3.82V	48.78V	14.46	17.70	24.91V	23.64	23.37	39.78V	47.08V
Kuwait	443	64.18	103.31	114.83Y	59.42	117.13	144.60Y	187.31Y	128.19	152.87	185.33Y	246.71	319.33	401.45Y	484.31Y
Lebanon	446	.35	.38	.48Y	.18	.74	.91Y	1.13Y	6.16	3.75	4.75Y	6.32	9.82	12.13Y	15.06Y
Libya	672	.07	.03	.03Y	3.54	.51	.63Y	.82Y	—	.02	.02Y	.85	—	—Y	—Y
Oman	449	2.93	17.51	12.62V	4.68	10.26	12.66Y	16.40Y	80.38	78.43	67.99V	60.55	65.20	81.97Y	98.88Y
Qatar	453	1.72	.38	.86V	.72	3.08	1.39V	1.80Y	2.92	1.88	3.53V	3.07	4.93	4.26V	5.14Y
Saudi Arabia	456	67.88	93.41	78.22V	96.39	128.39	158.50Y	205.32Y	305.99	352.21	426.99Y	349.78	427.35	537.26Y	648.14Y
Syrian Arab Republic	463	.24	.89	1.13Y	4.13	5.11	6.32Y	7.84Y	5.66	9.34	11.82Y	20.99	19.62	24.25Y	30.10Y
United Arab Emirates	466	19.83	86.54	97.27V	108.79	212.88	262.80Y	340.44Y	307.68	443.21	537.30Y	664.67	906.28	1,139.36Y	1,374.51Y
Middle East n.s.	489	—	—	—Y	—	—	—Y	—Y	—	—	—Y	.15	1.09	2.02Y	2.96Y
Western Hemisphere	**207**	**—**	**—**	**7.3Y**	**.4**	**.3**	**.4Y**	**.4Y**	**137.2**	**160.2**	**161.1Y**	**176.1**	**247.5**	**398.6Y**	**302.1Y**
Argentina	213	.01	—	—V	.07	—	—V	.01V	39.72	52.53	42.31V	44.49	83.43	75.73V	111.90V
Aruba	314	—	—	—V	.01	.01	—V	—V	....	....	....	....	....	....	....
Bahamas, The	313	—	—	—Y	—	.06	.08Y	.09Y	—	—	—Y	.21	—	—Y	—Y
Belize	339	—	—	—Y	—	—	—Y	—Y	—	—	—Y	.01	—	—Y	—Y
Bolivia	218	—	—	—V	—	—	—Y	—Y	.01	—	—Y	—	—	—Y	—Y
Brazil	223	.01	—	—V	—	—	.01V	—V	94.68	103.34	115.95V	125.99	150.02	312.67V	178.30V
Chile	228	—	—	—V	—	—	—V	—V	.11	.06	1.79V	2.03	1.66	—V	—V

	Exports							Imports						
	2001	2002	2003	2004	2005	2006	2007	2001	2002	2003	2004	2005	2006	2007
	Millions of U.S. Dollars							Millions of U.S. Dollars						
Colombia.......233	—	.02	—V	—	.03	.01V	—V	—	.05	.01V	2.67	6.15	1.22V	.35V
Costa Rica.......238	—	—	—V	—	—	—Y	—Y	—	.01	.01Y	.03	—	—Y	—Y
Dominica.......321	—	—	—Y	.21	.07	.09Y	.11Y	—	—	—Y	—	—	—Y	—Y
Dominican Republic.......243	—	—	—Y	—	.04	.05Y	.06Y	....	....	....	....	....	....	....
Ecuador.......248	—	—	7.29V	—	—	—V	—Y	—	—	.02V	.02	.02	—V	—Y
El Salvador.......253	—	—	—V	—	—	—V	—V	—	—	—V	—	.91	—V	—V
Grenada.......328	—	—	—Y	—	—	—Y	—Y	—	—	—Y	.39	—	—Y	—Y
Guatemala.......258	—	—	—V	—	—	—Y	—Y	—	—	.07V	.10	.06	.07Y	.09Y
Haiti.......263	....	....	....	....	....	....	....	—	—	—Y	.01	—	—Y	—Y
Honduras.......268	—	—	—V	—	—	.01Y	.01Y	—	1.66	.02V	—	.60	.74Y	.91Y
Jamaica.......343	—	—	—Y	—	—	—Y	—Y	—	—	—Y	—	.01	.02Y	.02Y
Mexico.......273	—	—	—V	.08	—	.14V	.12V	2.72	2.41	—V	.15	.33	1.60V	.82V
Nicaragua.......278	....	....	....	....	....	....	....	—	—	—Y	—	.16	.19Y	.24Y
Panama.......283	.03	—	—V	—	.03	—V	—V	—	—	—Y	—	.02	.02Y	.03Y
Peru.......293	—	—	—V	—	—	—V	—Y	—	—	.69V	.01	.09	.14V	.18Y
Uruguay.......298	—	—	—V	—	—	—Y	—Y	—	—	.05V	—	1.00	—Y	—Y
Venezuela, Rep. Bol.......299	—	—	—V	—	.03	—V	—V	—	.14	.17Y	—	.02	.02Y	.03Y
Western Hem. n.s.......399	—	—	—Y	—	—	—Y	—Y	—	—	—Y	—	3.07	6.15Y	9.22Y
Other Countries n.i.e.......910	**—**	**—**	**—Y**	**—**	**—**	**—Y**	**—Y**	**1.4**	**.8**	**1.0Y**	**8.3**	**1.5**	**1.9Y**	**2.3Y**
Cuba.......928	—	—	—Y	—	.01	.01Y	.02Y	.02	—	—Y	.08	.01	.01Y	.01Y
North Korea.......954	.02	—	—Y	.01	—	—Y	—Y	1.37	.75	.95Y	8.25	1.51	1.87Y	2.32Y
Countries & Areas n.s.......898	**156.6**	**6.6**	**8.3Y**	**—**	**6.6**	**8.1Y**	**10.1Y**	**104.1**	**17.0**	**21.5Y**	**2.3**	**31.9**	**39.4Y**	**49.0Y**
Special Categories.......899	**—**	**.1**	**.2Y**	**26.8**	**26.1**	**32.3Y**	**40.0Y**	**—**	**—**	**—Y**	**—**	**—**	**—Y**	**—Y**
Memorandum Items														
European Union.......998	129.17	32.69	74.30Y	47.25	51.40	155.42Y	273.59Y	440.93	422.34	835.51Y	759.09	711.10	1,038.36Y	1,605.95Y
Oil Exporting Ctys.......999	162.58	356.65	338.16Y	287.99	494.23	607.57Y	787.41Y	856.31	1,067.67	1,285.09Y	1,373.05	1,761.44	2,270.95Y	2,887.49Y
Non-Oil Develop.Ctys.......201	2,747.07	2,623.89	3,110.18Y	3,435.44	4,083.56	4,873.12Y	4,943.92Y	767.07	949.79	1,803.64Y	1,258.89	1,525.14	3,046.69Y	3,443.53Y
PERCENT DISTRIBUTION														
Industrial Countries.......101	**9.0**	**8.7**	**7.2**	**8.0**	**17.8**	**14.3**	**15.4**	**29.9**	**26.7**	**29.4**	**33.7**	**30.8**	**24.2**	**30.0**
Developing Countries.......202	**86.3**	**91.1**	**92.6**	**91.3**	**81.7**	**85.1**	**83.9**	**65.8**	**72.7**	**70.1**	**66.1**	**68.5**	**75.2**	**69.5**
Africa.......607	**4.0**	**2.5**	**2.1**	**3.8**	**1.2**	**.9**	**3.2**	**3.2**	**3.1**	**3.1**	**2.4**	**3.1**	**3.3**	**2.4**
Asia.......507	**76.9**	**78.3**	**80.6**	**80.0**	**71.1**	**74.1**	**67.8**	**18.3**	**19.4**	**24.6**	**18.2**	**15.4**	**25.6**	**25.0**
Europe.......170	**—**	**—**	**.4**	**—**	**.1**	**.1**	**.1**	**2.5**	**3.4**	**7.8**	**4.0**	**5.2**	**6.8**	**7.0**
Middle East.......407	**5.5**	**10.2**	**9.3**	**7.5**	**9.3**	**10.0**	**12.9**	**36.3**	**41.0**	**30.9**	**37.0**	**39.6**	**33.9**	**31.8**
Western Hemisphere.......207	**—**	**—**	**.2**	**—**	**—**	**—**	**—**	**5.6**	**5.8**	**3.7**	**4.4**	**5.2**	**5.6**	**3.3**
Other Countries n.i.e.......910	**—**	**—**	**—**	**—**	**—**	**—**	**—**	**.1**	**—**	**—**	**.2**	**—**	**—**	**—**
ANNUAL PERCENT CHANGE														
World.......001	**–17.3**	**–2.9**	**13.8**	**9.5**	**37.5**	**14.9**	**6.1**	**6.1**	**12.6**	**58.6**	**–9.5**	**20.5**	**47.4**	**28.8**
Industrial Countries.......101	**–39.2**	**–6.6**	**–5.8**	**22.1**	**205.3**	**–7.8**	**14.6**	**–4.8**	**.7**	**74.2**	**3.8**	**10.3**	**15.9**	**59.3**
Developing Countries.......202	**–16.0**	**2.4**	**15.7**	**8.0**	**22.9**	**19.7**	**4.6**	**7.9**	**24.3**	**53.1**	**–14.8**	**24.9**	**61.8**	**19.1**
Africa.......607	**74.5**	**–38.4**	**–6.9**	**99.9**	**–57.5**	**–8.7**	**262.4**	**–15.4**	**8.3**	**62.1**	**–31.8**	**58.3**	**57.3**	**–7.1**
Asia.......507	**–16.6**	**–1.1**	**17.1**	**8.7**	**22.1**	**19.7**	**–2.9**	**2.6**	**19.2**	**101.1**	**–32.9**	**2.0**	**145.0**	**25.6**
Europe.......170	**–99.6**	**344.4**	**—**	**–93.5**	**246.7**	**–7.0**	**32.1**	**–27.9**	**56.7**	**260.7**	**–53.7**	**56.3**	**91.0**	**34.0**
Middle East.......407	**7.7**	**81.3**	**3.4**	**–11.7**	**71.1**	**23.3**	**36.0**	**11.4**	**27.2**	**19.7**	**8.3**	**28.7**	**26.0**	**20.9**
Western Hemisphere.......207	**–99.9**	**–59.1**	**—**	**–94.8**	**–28.5**	**36.8**	**4.7**	**64.7**	**16.7**	**.5**	**9.3**	**40.5**	**61.0**	**–24.2**
Other Countries n.i.e.......910	**....**	**—**	**—**	**....**	**21.2**	**23.6**	**24.1**	**234.9**	**–46.0**	**26.6**	**775.8**	**–81.7**	**23.6**	**24.1**

	Exports							Imports						
	2001	2002	2003	2004	2005	2006	2007	2001	2002	2003	2004	2005	2006	2007
	Millions of U.S. Dollars							*Millions of U.S. Dollars*						
IFS World Total	**985.0**	**929.5**	**980.7**	**1,575.6**	**1,809.8**	**3,770.4**	**4,876.0**	**1,307.0**	**1,252.7**	**1,573.6**	**2,017.1**	**2,575.0**	**2,920.0**	**4,013.6**
DOTS World Total 001	**979.6**	**875.3**	**947.6**	**1,574.9**	**1,839.6**	**3,706.7**	**4,615.5**	**1,080.1**	**1,071.9**	**1,547.1**	**2,151.0**	**2,566.3**	**3,080.9**	**4,005.5**
Industrial Countries 101	**616.4**	**505.6**	**435.2**	**690.1**	**1,017.7**	**1,930.6**	**2,243.6**	**227.2**	**227.3**	**305.9**	**609.0**	**720.2**	**670.4**	**861.6**
United States 111	7.84	5.11	6.12	17.84	14.29	19.26	27.91	16.23	15.52	32.57	35.05	41.34	58.09	65.16
Canada 156	.37	.07	1.05	1.72	.36	.16	.15	9.56	7.72	10.23	9.50	17.49	14.71	17.54
Australia 193	1.16	.57	.02	.51	1.47	.55	.71	1.94	3.57	5.38	18.91	27.17	28.11	32.36
Japan 158	1.53	7.74	15.49	6.99	30.25	23.42	37.33	31.03	34.32	23.39	28.90	41.72	47.17	51.91
New Zealand 196	.01	.61	—	.50	.13	.14	.10	1.45	.46	.15	.66	.51	.69	.47
Austria 122	2.33	.25	.27	.72	.02	.09	.03	1.16	1.24	.51	1.21	1.94	4.58	8.96
Belgium 124	7.61	17.02	27.40	36.68	31.90	20.94	46.55	5.30	7.38	6.58	7.97	7.59	14.43	16.90
Cyprus 423	.92	.70	.01	—	—	.02	—	.08	.26	.59	.34	.56	.36	.40
Denmark 128	.13	.02	.05	1.81	.37	2.46	1.11	3.09	7.42	12.32	6.93	17.81	12.73	21.48
Finland 172	.23	5.59	12.21	11.26	.04	7.99	.27	3.29	6.39	26.34	22.68	12.33	13.19	55.20
France 132	.51	2.39	5.10	16.64	46.11	78.21	53.31	5.13	12.03	28.80	71.79	90.11	23.73	117.47
Germany 134	14.97	8.96	7.35	10.81	12.71	11.00	9.69	16.04	13.18	22.82	22.09	36.20	43.74	81.35
Greece 174	.01	.02	—	.12	.04	.40	.03	—	.25	.07	.71	.50	.19	.07
Iceland 176	.48	.56	1.14	.01	—	—	.01	.05	—	.01	.17	.02	.10	—
Ireland 178	.23	.29	.40	1.18	—	.97	.68	2.95	2.70	5.62	8.86	5.57	12.06	17.34
Italy 136	3.53	2.47	1.55	3.12	6.45	3.44	2.72	3.52	7.16	5.36	4.77	9.55	17.15	11.25
Luxembourg 137	—	—	.01	—	—	.09	.02	1.02	.05	.04	—	—	.03	—
Malta 181	—	—	—	—	—	—	—	—	.01	—	—	—	—	—
Netherlands 138	21.82	15.88	26.46	47.69	46.55	45.13	50.11	7.04	5.90	10.44	11.24	30.03	45.43	77.01
Norway 142	1.03	.52	.26	.13	.18	.33	.15	.15	1.67	.80	.93	1.54	123.28	2.41
Portugal 182	7.83	.75	.12	.17	28.15	12.20	25.49	.09	.14	.06	.01	.40	11.96	8.65
Slovenia 961	—	—	.20	—	—	—	—	.01	.06	.08	.04	.02	.06	.10
Spain 184	1.58	.42	.47	1.48	4.91	1.68	2.44	1.37	.45	.61	1.84	2.20	4.41	4.70
Sweden 144	1.64	.11	.04	.28	.30	.42	1.43	5.08	4.95	9.19	18.65	36.55	57.39	89.36
Switzerland 146	60.76	56.10	76.92	255.40	527.91	1,420.06	1,927.91	3.94	6.45	11.71	18.15	16.42	23.91	20.78
United Kingdom 112	479.82	379.48	252.51	274.99	265.62	281.63	55.45	107.66	88.00	92.23	317.58	322.68	112.88	160.73
Developing Countries 202	**363.2**	**369.6**	**512.4**	**884.8**	**821.8**	**1,775.8**	**2,371.9**	**852.8**	**844.5**	**1,241.1**	**1,541.9**	**1,845.7**	**2,410.4**	**3,143.8**
Africa 607	**306.5**	**318.2**	**431.4**	**777.3**	**746.7**	**1,340.2**	**1,111.1**	**737.2**	**726.0**	**1,047.7**	**1,230.9**	**1,507.8**	**1,840.0**	**2,366.5**
Algeria 612	—	—	—	.01	.01	.02	.05	—	—	—	—	—	—	—
Angola 614	.03	.32	1.12	.40	.57	.39	.57	—	.01	—	.11	.01	.02	.07
Benin 638	—	—	—	—	—	—	—	.09	—	—	—	—	—	—
Botswana 616	3.84	2.62	3.59	2.94	42.12	5.77	19.96	4.57	3.99	6.54	9.43	11.53	18.92	23.31
Burkina Faso 748	—	—	—	—	—	—	.01	—	—	—	—	—	—	—
Burundi 618	1.88	1.96	2.32	2.29	.02	.06	1.82	—	—	—	.01	—	—	.05
Cameroon 622	—	—	—	—	—	—	.01	—	—	—	—	—	.01	.02
Chad 628	—	—	—	—	—	—	.01	—	—	—	—	—	—	—
Congo, Dem. Rep. of 636	32.27	29.96	36.79	105.81	99.03	140.96	245.63	.64	1.55	11.99	14.11	21.86	31.39	127.89
Congo, Republic of 634	.21	.07	.21	.01	—	—	—	—	—	—	—	—	—	.10
Côte d'Ivoire 662	—	—	—	—	—	.23	—	.05	.09	.08	.09	.39	.14	.18
Djibouti 611	—	—	—	—	—	—	—	.05	—	—	—	—	—	—
Eritrea 643	—	—	—	.02	—	—	—	.01	—	.01	—	—	—	.02
Ethiopia 644	—	.23	.01	.02	.08	.17	.03	.02	.07	.13	.05	.03	.15	.12
Gabon 646	—	—	—	—	—	—	—	—	—	.11	—	—	—	.18
Gambia, The 648	—	—	—	—	.08	.01	—	.04	.03	—	—	.08	—	—
Ghana 652	—	.05	—	.01	.01	.45	.09	.07	.04	.04	.10	1.84	.26	.12
Guinea 656	—	—	—	—	—	—	—	—	—	—	—	—	—	.02
Guinea-Bissau 654	—	—	—	—	—	—	—	.01	—	—	—	—	—	—
Kenya 664	12.60	4.25	5.60	9.08	13.82	29.54	29.50	5.27	10.94	23.29	34.15	37.58	56.21	78.38
Lesotho 666	.02	.06	.16	2.55	.65	4.87	.99	.17	.16	—	.01	—	.01	.01
Liberia 668	—	—	—	—	.01	—	—	—	—	—	—	—	—	.01
Madagascar 674	—	—	—	—	—	—	.03	—	—	—	—	.02	—	—
Malawi 676	9.60	11.95	20.24	48.21	63.36	55.42	31.16	3.38	3.68	9.43	7.80	14.39	13.53	12.38
Mali 678	.07	.03	.37	—	.01	—	—	.07	.02	.06	.02	—	—	.01
Mauritania 682	.02	—	—	—	—	.01	—	—	.01	—	—	—	—	.24
Mauritius 684	2.87	5.80	3.72	3.82	1.50	.67	.04	4.07	5.31	2.10	2.77	1.99	2.38	8.13
Morocco 686	—	.05	—	.01	—	.03	—	.04	—	.02	—	.01	—	—
Mozambique 688	.02	.08	.60	1.51	.82	.85	1.06	4.87	2.76	9.47	2.27	10.32	15.85	59.90
Namibia 728	.84	1.15	1.24	4.32	8.83	11.74	39.40	2.18	2.82	3.55	5.73	6.34	8.45	12.31
Niger 692	.03	.05	—	.06	.04	.10	.04	.29	.25	.13	.09	.36	.03	.07
Nigeria 694	.03	—	—	.02	.02	.01	.11	.13	.19	.18	.27	.23	.24	.28
Rwanda 714	3.95	1.01	—	.37	.02	—	2.50	.01	.01	.01	.02	—	.02	—
St. Helena 856	—	—	—	.12	.92	—	—	.01	—	.06	—	—	—	—
São Tomé & Príncipe 716	—	.11	—	—	—	—	—	—	.04	—	—	—	—	.01
Senegal 722	—	—	—	—	.05	.06	.08	.04	.04	.04	.12	.05	.04	.05
Seychelles 718	—	.01	.01	—	—	—	—	—	—	—	.01	.05	.15	.78
Sierra Leone 724	.01	.32	.01	—	—	.01	—	.27	—	—	.07	.03	—	—
South Africa 199	216.97	194.28	204.65	384.93	342.44	796.80	555.18	603.32	585.04	748.90	993.44	1,220.36	1,458.28	1,898.20
Sudan 732	.09	—	—	—	—	.17	.07	.06	.07	—	.08	—	.08	.03
Swaziland 734	.23	.55	.24	.48	.93	3.06	3.42	2.94	2.12	4.37	5.37	3.76	5.46	8.34

		Exports Millions of U.S. Dollars							Imports Millions of U.S. Dollars						
		2001	2002	2003	2004	2005	2006	2007	2001	2002	2003	2004	2005	2006	2007
Tanzania	738	3.77	51.69	131.87	120.57	94.29	234.73	96.16	7.29	10.56	23.53	30.13	65.71	53.08	23.56
Togo	742	—	—	—	—	—	—	—	.01	—	—	—	—	—	—
Tunisia	744	—	—	—	—	—	—	—	—	.03	—	.02	—	—	.06
Uganda	746	1.30	.31	.25	.53	.94	.80	1.66	.01	2.92	5.31	.25	.47	.14	.05
Zimbabwe	698	15.88	11.32	18.35	89.18	76.17	53.20	81.52	97.22	93.21	198.40	124.41	110.42	175.10	111.66
Asia	**507**	**50.9**	**42.5**	**66.2**	**102.7**	**72.1**	**417.7**	**759.5**	**85.9**	**89.9**	**113.8**	**142.5**	**218.8**	**223.9**	**485.7**
American Samoa	859	—	—	—	—	—	—	—	—	—	—	—	.01	—	—
Bangladesh	513	—	—	—	—	.08	.04	.07	.18	.01	.06	.11	.01	.01	—
Bhutan	514	—	.03	.19	.12	.02	—	.06	.01	—	.01	.04	—	—	—
Cambodia	522	—	.03	—	—	—	—	—	—	—	—	—	—	—	—
China,P.R.: Mainland	924	.37	3.46	15.96	33.89	39.06	380.78	188.88	38.13	28.17	42.54	46.10	85.73	83.69	239.66
China,P.R.:Hong Kong	532	9.79	7.59	9.56	2.56	2.27	6.22	5.11	2.53	2.95	8.76	7.41	10.19	12.30	15.31
China,P.R.:Macao	546	—	—	—	—	.01	.07	.10	—	—	—	—	—	—	—
India	534	31.89	29.09	34.09	16.82	25.84	18.06	52.06	19.23	40.90	34.38	50.73	80.10	85.96	164.88
Indonesia	536	.01	.02	—	.02	.11	—	.01	1.66	.40	.77	1.02	.68	1.04	10.38
Korea	542	.35	.31	.08	—	.02	.12	94.25	4.27	2.74	8.02	12.41	15.39	8.80	14.61
Malaysia	548	—	.01	—	—	—	—	54.17	8.35	2.24	2.65	1.90	1.84	3.27	4.61
Myanmar	518	—	—	—	—	—	.28	—	—	—	—	—	—	—	—
Nauru	836	—	.01	—	—	—	—	—	—	—	—	—	.02	—	—
Nepal	558	—	—	—	.07	—	—	—	—	—	—	—	—	—	—
Pakistan	564	.01	—	.05	—	—	.08	48.38	2.04	1.84	2.39	2.48	2.06	1.35	1.60
Papua New Guinea	853	—	—	—	—	—	—	—	—	—	—	—	—	.02	—
Philippines	566	—	—	—	2.84	.03	.25	.17	.06	.09	.19	.28	.47	.29	.04
Samoa	862	—	—	—	—	—	—	—	—	—	—	—	.01	—	—
Singapore	576	.06	.03	.39	.52	1.26	3.58	3.30	1.83	2.08	5.26	6.41	6.52	9.77	10.51
Sri Lanka	524	.06	—	—	—	—	—	—	.01	.05	.06	.12	.02	.23	.07
Taiwan Province of China	528	.38	.01	1.89	44.69	2.72	8.11	39.19	4.87	5.61	6.77	10.14	10.18	11.13	10.96
Thailand	578	7.96	1.84	4.00	1.11	.12	.10	273.73	2.38	2.75	1.51	3.04	5.29	5.40	10.59
Vietnam	582	—	—	—	—	.56	—	—	.29	.12	.42	.34	.26	.63	2.44
Europe	**170**	**.5**	**2.6**	**.5**	**1.3**	**.6**	**4.0**	**2.9**	**1.9**	**1.8**	**1.4**	**2.2**	**2.4**	**3.9**	**3.9**
Albania	914	—	—	—	—	—	—	—	—	—	—	—	—	—	.02
Azerbaijan	912	—	—	—	—	—	—	—	.01	—	.04	.01	.12	.08	.16
Belarus	913	—	—	—	—	—	—	—	.02	—	.19	.01	—	—	.94
Bulgaria	918	.03	.51	—	.23	.08	1.23	.37	.28	.20	.31	.01	.23	.28	.02
Croatia	960	—	—	.08	—	—	—	—	—	—	—	—	—	—	—
Czech Republic	935	—	.01	.01	.16	.01	—	.01	.90	.16	.24	.92	1.04	.20	.34
Faroe Islands	816	—	—	—	—	—	—	—	—	—	—	.01	—	—	—
Georgia	915	.01	.03	—	.03	—	.03	—	.21	.03	.04	—	.01	.06	—
Gibraltar	823	—	—	—	—	—	—	—	—	.01	.09	.04	.01	.04	.10
Hungary	944	.01	—	—	—	—	.01	—	.02	.06	—	.11	.01	.76	.35
Kyrgyz Republic	917	—	—	—	—	—	.06	—	—	—	—	—	—	—	—
Latvia	941	—	—	—	—	—	—	.12	—	—	—	.01	.01	.01	.07
Moldova	921	—	—	—	—	—	—	.02	—	—	—	—	—	—	—
Poland	964	.22	.24	.14	.69	.50	1.45	1.95	.01	.02	.01	—	.03	.06	.23
Romania	968	—	—	—	.19	—	.30	—	—	—	—	.01	.02	.01	.03
Russia	922	.13	1.82	.05	—	—	.66	.23	.03	.01	.02	.04	.05	.04	.02
Slovak Republic	936	—	.01	—	—	—	—	—	—	.03	.03	—	.01	.08	.06
Turkey	186	.05	—	—	—	—	.20	.03	.16	.05	.20	.95	.83	1.94	1.52
Ukraine	926	—	.01	.21	—	—	.02	.01	.18	1.16	.08	.01	.02	—	—
Yugoslavia n.s.	966	.03	—	—	—	—	—	—	.04	—	.06	—	.01	—	—
Europe n.s.	884	—	—	—	—	—	.03	.14	—	.10	.11	.02	.03	.29	.07
Middle East	**407**	**4.2**	**5.8**	**10.2**	**3.3**	**2.2**	**2.5**	**498.3**	**18.0**	**22.7**	**72.5**	**158.5**	**107.2**	**334.8**	**271.0**
Bahrain	419	—	—	—	—	—	—	—	.09	.07	.02	.01	.29	1.72	.01
Egypt	469	.07	.27	.88	.74	.10	.55	231.91	.67	.50	1.85	3.81	6.25	6.65	9.30
Iran, I.R. of	429	.01	—	1.09	—	.30	—	.09	.75	.32	.36	.59	.31	1.51	1.75
Iraq	433	—	—	—	—	—	—	—	—	—	—	—	—	—	.03
Israel	436	.19	.45	1.17	1.43	1.45	1.31	.46	.80	.24	1.03	2.23	2.01	2.16	.97
Jordan	439	—	—	—	—	—	—	—	.06	.03	.04	.13	.13	.01	—
Kuwait	443	—	.01	.08	.01	—	—	.23	.07	.02	—	.01	.01	—	.09
Lebanon	446	.02	—	—	.10	—	—	.01	.07	.15	.24	.51	2.25	1.21	3.38
Libya	672	—	—	—	.01	—	—	—	—	—	.03	—	—	—	.11
Oman	449	—	.01	—	—	—	—	.02	.02	—	.13	.42	.33	.52	.55
Qatar	453	—	—	—	—	—	—	—	.01	—	—	—	.87	.05	—
Saudi Arabia	456	—	.12	.02	.01	.01	.01	216.36	2.96	4.47	1.57	4.87	.25	1.65	.16
Syrian Arab Republic	463	—	—	.02	—	—	—	—	.02	.07	.04	.05	.05	.13	.29
United Arab Emirates	466	3.94	4.95	6.97	1.06	.33	.57	49.24	12.53	16.83	67.15	145.83	94.42	319.24	254.30
Yemen, Republic of	474	—	—	—	—	.03	—	—	—	—	.01	—	—	—	—
Western Hemisphere	**207**	**1.0**	**.5**	**4.1**	**.3**	**.2**	**11.5**	**.1**	**9.9**	**4.1**	**5.7**	**7.9**	**9.5**	**7.9**	**16.7**
Antigua and Barbuda	311	—	—	—	—	—	—	.03	.21	.05	—	.02	—	—	.05
Argentina	213	—	—	—	—	.09	—	—	7.85	2.42	.41	.31	.98	.91	3.50
Aruba	314	—	—	—	—	—	—	—	—	—	—	—	—	—	.01
Bahamas, The	313	—	—	—	.05	—	—	—	—	.01	—	—	—	—	—
Barbados	316	—	—	—	—	—	—	—	—	—	—	—	—	.05	—
Belize	339	—	—	—	—	—	—	—	.05	.20	—	—	—	.09	—
Bermuda	319	—	—	—	—	—	—	—	—	.01	—	—	—	—	—
Bolivia	218	—	—	—	—	.03	—	—	—	—	—	—	—	—	—
Brazil	223	.01	—	—	.21	—	—	.01	.95	1.03	3.01	6.13	6.34	5.65	8.32

	Exports 2001	Exports 2002	Exports 2003	Exports 2004	Exports 2005	Exports 2006	Exports 2007	Imports 2001	Imports 2002	Imports 2003	Imports 2004	Imports 2005	Imports 2006	Imports 2007
	Millions of U.S. Dollars							*Millions of U.S. Dollars*						
Chile.......228	—	—	—	—	—	—	—	.22	—	—	.21	.07	.10	.71
Colombia.......233	—	—	—	—	—	—	—	—	—	—	—	.05	.02	.11
Costa Rica.......238	—	.47	3.88	—	—	—	—	—	—	—	.02	.02	—	—
Dominica.......321	—	—	—	—	—	—	—	.02	—	—	.03	—	—	—
Ecuador.......248	—	—	—	—	—	—	—	—	—	—	—	.01	—	—
El Salvador.......253	—	—	—	—	—	—	—	—	—	—	—	.07	—	—
Falkland Islands.......323	—	—	—	—	—	—	—	—	—	—	—	—	.01	—
Grenada.......328	—	—	—	—	—	—	—	—	.01	—	—	—	—	—
Guatemala.......258	.01	—	—	—	—	—	—	.01	.01	—	—	—	—	—
Jamaica.......343	—	—	.02	—	.03	—	—	—	.03	.03	.01	.01	.02	—
Mexico.......273	.15	—	—	—	—	—	—	.06	.02	1.67	.01	—	.67	.03
Netherlands Antilles.......353	.03	—	.02	—	—	.01	.08	.13	.01	.15	.12	.09	—	—
Nicaragua.......278	.26	—	—	.02	—	—	—	.33	.18	.08	.32	1.68	.03	.06
Panama.......283	—	—	—	—	—	—	—	—	—	—	—	—	.01	—
Peru.......293	.01	—	.21	—	.01	.06	—	—	.01	.26	.29	.04	.19	.10
St. Kitts and Nevis.......361	—	—	—	—	—	11.45	—	—	—	—	—	—	—	—
Suriname.......366	—	—	—	.01	—	—	—	—	—	—	—	.02	—	—
Uruguay.......298	.01	—	—	—	—	—	—	.01	.04	.04	.26	.08	.02	.02
Venezuela, Rep. Bol.......299	—	—	—	—	—	—	—	—	.01	.04	.13	.09	.04	.06
Western Hem. n.s.......399	.57	—	—	—	—	—	—	—	—	—	—	.01	.03	3.71
Other Countries n.i.e.......910	**.1**	**—**	**—**	**—**	**—**	**—**	**—**	**—**	**—**	**—**	**.1**	**.3**	**.1**	**.1**
Cuba.......928	.02	—	—	—	—	—	—	—	—	—	—	—	—	—
North Korea.......954	.04	—	—	—	—	.01	.02	.05	.01	.01	.07	.33	.10	.12
Memorandum Items														
European Union.......998	543.40	434.62	334.31	407.79	443.68	468.13	251.40	163.78	157.85	221.95	497.75	575.15	375.42	672.01
Oil Exporting Ctys.......999	4.00	5.12	8.16	1.14	.78	.63	266.11	18.12	22.23	70.23	153.15	97.18	324.29	267.72
Non-Oil Develop.Ctys.......201	359.17	364.49	504.26	883.70	821.04	1,775.21	2,105.82	834.73	822.29	1,170.92	1,388.78	1,748.55	2,086.10	2,876.07
PERCENT DISTRIBUTION														
Industrial Countries.......101	**62.9**	**57.8**	**45.9**	**43.8**	**55.3**	**52.1**	**48.6**	**21.0**	**21.2**	**19.8**	**28.3**	**28.1**	**21.8**	**21.5**
Developing Countries.......202	**37.1**	**42.2**	**54.1**	**56.2**	**44.7**	**47.9**	**51.4**	**79.0**	**78.8**	**80.2**	**71.7**	**71.9**	**78.2**	**78.5**
Africa.......607	**31.3**	**36.4**	**45.5**	**49.4**	**40.6**	**36.2**	**24.1**	**68.3**	**67.7**	**67.7**	**57.2**	**58.8**	**59.7**	**59.1**
Asia.......507	**5.2**	**4.9**	**7.0**	**6.5**	**3.9**	**11.3**	**16.5**	**7.9**	**8.4**	**7.4**	**6.6**	**8.5**	**7.3**	**12.1**
Europe.......170	**.1**	**.3**	**.1**	**.1**	**—**	**.1**	**.1**	**.2**	**.2**	**.1**	**.1**	**.1**	**.1**	**.1**
Middle East.......407	**.4**	**.7**	**1.1**	**.2**	**.1**	**.1**	**10.8**	**1.7**	**2.1**	**4.7**	**7.4**	**4.2**	**10.9**	**6.8**
Western Hemisphere.......207	**.1**	**.1**	**.4**	**—**	**—**	**.3**	**—**	**.9**	**.4**	**.4**	**.4**	**.4**	**.3**	**.4**
ANNUAL PERCENT CHANGE														
World.......001	**29.3**	**–10.6**	**8.3**	**66.2**	**16.8**	**101.5**	**24.5**	**–1.9**	**–.8**	**44.3**	**39.0**	**19.3**	**20.1**	**30.0**
Industrial Countries.......101	**70.6**	**–18.0**	**–13.9**	**58.6**	**47.5**	**89.7**	**16.2**	**–11.8**	**—**	**34.6**	**99.1**	**18.3**	**–6.9**	**28.5**
Developing Countries.......202	**–8.3**	**1.8**	**38.6**	**72.7**	**–7.1**	**116.1**	**33.6**	**2.1**	**–1.0**	**47.0**	**24.2**	**19.7**	**30.6**	**30.4**
Africa.......607	**–3.1**	**3.8**	**35.6**	**80.2**	**–3.9**	**79.5**	**–17.1**	**–2.9**	**–1.5**	**44.3**	**17.5**	**22.5**	**22.0**	**28.6**
Asia.......507	**85.8**	**–16.6**	**56.0**	**55.0**	**–29.7**	**479.2**	**81.8**	**72.1**	**4.8**	**26.5**	**25.2**	**53.5**	**2.3**	**116.9**
Europe.......170	**–3.7**	**430.7**	**–81.4**	**165.8**	**–53.5**	**562.1**	**–27.8**	**136.9**	**–2.0**	**–22.6**	**51.7**	**13.1**	**58.2**	**2.1**
Middle East.......407	**367.5**	**37.6**	**75.6**	**–67.2**	**–34.2**	**11.2**	**—**	**–5.5**	**25.8**	**219.2**	**118.7**	**–32.4**	**212.5**	**–19.1**
Western Hemisphere.......207	**–98.0**	**–53.9**	**765.5**	**–93.1**	**–47.3**	**—**	**–98.9**	**62.0**	**–58.8**	**40.6**	**37.9**	**21.4**	**–17.7**	**112.6**
Other Countries n.i.e.......910	**–64.3**	**–98.6**	**138.5**	**31.3**	**....**	**....**	**102.3**	**94.7**	**–84.6**	**86.6**	**396.2**	**384.5**	**–70.8**	**22.1**

Zimbabwe 698

	Exports							Imports, f.o.b						
	2001	2002	2003	2004	2005	2006	2007	2001	2002	2003	2004	2005	2006	2007
	Millions of U.S. Dollars							*Millions of U.S. Dollars*						
IFS World Total	**1,207.0**	**2,012.0**	**1,670.0**	**1,887.0**	**1,840.0**	**2,020.0**	**2,050.0**	**1,491.3**	**1,522.6**	**1,487.0**	**1,916.3**	**2,026.1**	**1,956.5**	**2,104.4**
DOTS World Total........001	**2,221.8**	**2,009.5**	**3,344.8**	**1,768.5**	**1,394.8**	**940.6**	**2,496.5Y**	**1,561.4**	**2,114.3**	**624.8**	**1,957.0**	**1,883.3**	**2,556.8**	**2,357.4Y**
Industrial Countries........101	**729.6**	**1,115.6**	**885.0**	**635.3**	**431.0**	**209.2**	**722.5Y**	**272.4**	**338.1**	**90.7**	**257.1**	**208.5**	**300.0**	**344.7V**
United States........111	61.46	83.39	34.66	40.06	96.77	98.28	68.36V	44.03	60.78	8.98	36.76	27.01	125.74	105.20V
Canada........156	.52	1.58	1.21	1.74	1.37	.54	2.89V	2.69	3.04	1.05	4.27	1.78	2.48	6.44V
Australia........193	4.05	7.17	5.35	4.13	1.32	.37	9.17V	6.90	4.42	1.30	5.73	9.48	9.70	1.19V
Japan........158	117.06	189.65	220.26	54.26	6.18	2.27	203.29V	26.81	48.93	12.90	21.30	24.99	19.89	22.03V
New Zealand........196	2.70	1.93	2.43	.90	.28	.32	.45V	2.21	.82	.06	.21	.74	.05	.23V
Austria........122	9.31	3.42	2.18	5.37	.55	.37	.56V	9.03	2.84	.23	.97	.69	1.46	.97V
Belgium........124	12.71	16.18	10.13	7.73	33.93	15.96	14.87V	8.89	7.68	.96	10.05	6.21	3.95	12.65V
Cyprus........423	—	.23	.01	.01	.09	—	.01V	.31	.47	.06	.50	1.25	.16	.18V
Denmark........128	15.11	6.61	8.44	5.59	11.04	.27	4.15V	2.56	4.46	.94	2.96	3.75	1.60	2.27V
Finland........172	9.27	.43	.81	.01	—	.02	.30V	2.71	5.66	.51	2.23	.99	7.60	8.46V
France........132	27.93	52.80	17.36	9.68	7.97	21.90	13.44V	25.17	16.09	7.31	18.18	4.16	8.92	15.98V
Germany........134	155.75	151.05	181.26	75.39	28.71	8.34	64.20V	43.32	67.84	12.12	33.31	42.44	26.14	51.42V
Greece........174	11.77	6.08	3.73	9.59	3.11	1.08	3.55V	.03	.27	.07	.13	.29	.09	.67V
Iceland........176	.01	.08	.04	—	—	—	.10V	.90	.13	.08	.02	.03	.01	—V
Ireland........178	14.38	.83	11.25	19.06	.51	2.35	.15V	3.21	2.88	.67	4.13	6.16	2.71	.94V
Italy........136	40.64	48.56	36.47	61.47	17.65	6.81	102.38V	7.82	12.23	20.41	8.00	10.16	4.06	10.20V
Luxembourg........137	.08	.96	1.13	.73	.79	.11	—V	.04	.03	—	.03	.02	.01	—V
Malta........181	—	.02	—	.06	—	—	.26V	—	.01	.03	.52	.14	—	—V
Netherlands........138	25.76	53.07	51.99	26.39	41.24	8.04	130.37V	11.59	10.01	1.69	10.24	14.15	8.24	37.38V
Norway........142	8.50	42.72	7.25	12.55	2.82	.60	3.68V	.92	2.08	.06	.68	.50	.54	.27V
Portugal........182	31.74	21.75	23.12	12.84	4.70	6.45	7.51V	4.31	3.14	.29	2.88	.47	.31	.64V
Slovenia........961	.01	.02	—	—	—	.03	1.43V	—	—	.01	.13	.09	.06	—V
Spain........184	32.51	102.02	26.04	28.50	9.25	1.45	30.35V	4.51	4.60	.30	2.58	1.06	1.08	5.17V
Sweden........144	5.57	2.82	.25	.37	.19	.13	2.17V	5.01	8.53	.50	4.00	9.99	5.84	9.85V
Switzerland........146	12.49	164.40	114.72	130.60	89.12	21.88	3.40V	9.37	9.83	6.17	13.30	10.94	15.68	7.97V
United Kingdom........112	130.25	157.83	124.96	128.23	73.38	11.67	55.39V	50.01	61.38	13.96	74.02	31.08	53.71	44.62V
Developing Countries........202	**485.3**	**893.7**	**2,459.7**	**1,133.2**	**963.4**	**731.0**	**1,773.5Y**	**1,100.5**	**1,526.4**	**446.7**	**1,513.4**	**1,492.4**	**2,171.0**	**1,906.3Y**
Africa........607	**192.2**	**676.7**	**952.8**	**790.2**	**818.0**	**628.9**	**1,390.8Y**	**972.3**	**1,208.5**	**393.7**	**1,258.6**	**1,256.0**	**1,994.8**	**1,528.4Y**
Algeria........612	.51	4.08	.71	.01	—	—	.01Y	—	—	—	—	—	—	—Y
Angola........614	.95	3.58	2.44	3.69	.77	.06	.07Y	.01	—	.13	.03	.04	—	—Y
Benin........638	.01	—	—	—	—	—	—Y	....	....	....	....	....	....	....
Botswana........616	13.11	40.03	66.96	47.18	29.58	148.13	183.83Y	30.58	47.47	11.39	79.00	95.13	81.19	100.76Y
Burkina Faso........748	.04	.10	—	.02	—	—	—Y	—	—	—	—	—	—	—Y
Burundi........618	.20	.24	.20	.28	.10	.06	.08Y	—	—	—	—	.02	.17	.22Y
Cameroon........622	.36	.61	.23	.37	.12	—	—Y	—	—	—	—	.02	—	—Y
Cape Verde........624	—	—	—	—	.03	—	—Y	—	—	—	—	—	—	—Y
Central African Rep........626	—	—	.05	—	—	.01	.01Y	—	—	—	—	—	—	—Y
Congo, Dem. Rep. of........636	2.67	15.87	7.67	12.37	7.14	166.00	206.01Y	87.34	4.13	3.45	6.27	70.62	29.67	36.81Y
Congo, Republic of........634	.33	2.45	.96	.63	34.34	.78	.97Y	.26	.08	.05	.40	10.23	12.90	16.01Y
Côte d'Ivoire........662	—	.26	.06	.01	.01	—	—Y	.01	—	—	—	.95	.01	.02Y
Djibouti........611	—	—	—	.38	.09	—	.01Y	—	—	—	—	—	—	—Y
Equatorial Guinea........642	—	—	.01	—	—	—	—Y	....	....	....	....	....	....	....
Ethiopia........644	.12	.13	.07	.45	1.67	.22	.28Y	—	.13	—	.16	.07	.01	.01Y
Gabon........646	—	—	.11	.50	.07	.24	.29Y	.32	.01	—	—	.01	—	—Y
Gambia, The........648	—	.01	—	—	—	—	—Y	.01	.42	.06	.31	.08	—	—Y
Ghana........652	.88	.56	.33	.28	.04	.01	.01Y	.18	.10	.01	.06	—	—	—Y
Guinea........656	—	.08	.15	—	.01	—	—Y	—	—	—	—	—	—	—Y
Guinea-Bissau........654	—	.01	—	—	—	—	—Y	....	....	....	....	....	....	....
Kenya........664	3.88	7.08	6.11	3.32	1.96	.63	.78Y	1.87	31.15	.63	1.76	4.93	1.92	2.38Y
Lesotho........666	.97	.41	.31	3.23	.20	.08	.10Y	.01	—	.04	—	—	.01	.01Y
Liberia........668	—	.01	—	—	—	.02	.03Y	—	—	—	—	—	—	—Y
Madagascar........674	.01	.34	.04	.08	.08	.01	.01Y	—	.01	—	.12	.18	.14	.17Y
Malawi........676	10.62	73.35	35.46	46.53	25.81	13.48	16.72Y	2.99	3.61	4.92	7.93	2.64	52.00	64.53Y
Mali........678	—	.07	.06	.06	—	—	—Y	.06	—	—	.21	.03	.02	.02Y
Mauritania........682	.01	.03	.01	.03	—	—	—Y	—	—	—	.11	—	.02	.03Y
Mauritius........684	.16	3.70	1.93	1.61	1.46	.77	3.79V	9.69	9.47	.96	4.74	4.15	3.87	1.35V
Morocco........686	.11	1.86	.03	.82	.42	—	—Y	.09	.06	—	.01	.28	.01	.01Y
Mozambique........688	3.70	37.66	39.37	19.12	39.09	22.20	27.55Y	81.71	157.83	36.22	44.13	4.15	3.87	4.81Y
Namibia........728	11.44	17.86	31.12	13.89	11.75	5.94	.13Y	4.46	2.13	.61	1.23	.75	1.50	2.25Y
Niger........692	—	.10	.01	—	1.39	—	—Y	.08	.02	—	.28	.03	—	—Y
Nigeria........694	1.89	1.71	.82	.28	.37	.01	.02Y	.17	.29	.20	.27	.34	.09	.10Y
Rwanda........714	—	.10	.06	.44	.36	.04	.05Y	—	—	—	—	—	—	—Y
São Tomé & Príncipe........716	—	—	—	—	—	—	—Y	.01	—	—	—	—	.02	.03Y
Senegal........722	—	.22	.06	.14	.10	.01	.01Y	.02	—	—	—	.19	—	—Y
Seychelles........718	.01	.19	.02	.13	.05	.03	.04Y	.01	.02	—	7.02	2.67	1.54	1.91Y
Sierra Leone........724	—	.21	.01	.03	—	—	—Y	—	.02	.03	—	.01	—	—Y
South Africa........199	124.69	329.75	700.16	557.67	579.53	233.53	844.88V	729.81	902.34	314.93	1,029.83	281.81	1,042.70	1,196.10V
Sacca exc. South Afr........608	—	—	—	—	—	—	1.74Y	—	—	—	—	—	—	12.21Y
Sudan........732	1.06	2.80	2.18	.57	.27	.16	—V	.01	—	—	—	—	—	—V

		Exports							Imports, f.o.b						
		2001	2002	2003	2004	2005	2006	2007	2001	2002	2003	2004	2005	2006	2007
		Millions of U.S. Dollars							*Millions of U.S. Dollars*						
Swaziland	734	.03	.56	.08	.18	.46	.05	.07Y	9.67	35.57	1.62	7.91	1.08	3.18	3.95Y
Tanzania	738	2.08	5.82	1.99	4.91	2.77	1.37	1.70Y	.05	1.89	4.56	.79	5.24	2.44	3.03Y
Togo	742	—	.02	.01	—	—	—	—Y	—	—	—	—	—	—	—Y
Tunisia	744	.24	.03	.03	.13	.01	—	—Y	—	.20	—	—	.01	—	—Y
Uganda	746	.44	.82	.41	.82	.57	.13	.16Y	.02	.01	.11	.01	.39	.04	.05Y
Zambia	754	11.65	123.96	52.53	70.00	77.38	34.90	101.51V	12.80	11.58	13.77	66.06	769.91	757.30	81.52V
Asia	**507**	**199.6**	**131.3**	**1,413.8**	**266.7**	**104.8**	**41.7**	**258.8Y**	**85.2**	**102.0**	**33.6**	**119.8**	**120.8**	**88.9**	**269.9Y**
Afghanistan, I.S. of	512	—	—	—	.04	—	—	—Y	—	—	—	—	—	—	—Y
American Samoa	859	—	—	—	—	—	—	—Y	.01	—	—	—	—	—	—Y
Bangladesh	513	2.41	.27	.79	.26	.17	.37	5.81V	1.53	.99	—	.10	.08	—	—Y
Bhutan	514	.04	—	.08	—	—	—	—Y	—	—	—	—	—	—	—Y
Cambodia	522	—	—	—	.07	—	—	—Y	—	—	—	—	—	—	—Y
China,P.R.: Mainland	924	104.79	29.43	1,301.99	107.88	70.67	25.82	129.39V	18.67	22.25	5.84	51.55	46.04	41.73	197.50V
China,P.R.:Hong Kong	532	7.34	7.15	20.62	4.85	2.47	.44	4.37V	5.53	9.10	1.61	7.54	9.54	6.20	1.19V
China,P.R.:Macao	546	—	—	—	—	—	—	.05V	—	—	—	—	—	—	—V
Fiji	819	—	—	—	.03	—	—	—Y	—	—	—	—	—	—	—Y
French Polynesia	887	.01	—	—	—	—	—	—Y	.70	1.78	.17	—	—	—	—Y
India	534	12.05	14.73	20.46	4.15	.37	1.55	1.92Y	10.94	15.25	8.59	12.71	31.94	18.75	23.27Y
Indonesia	536	18.94	23.00	12.17	43.96	8.40	1.59	12.78V	4.72	7.37	1.05	7.34	2.48	1.62	5.29V
Korea	542	.19	2.56	3.61	23.22	.98	1.19	45.72V	8.96	12.84	1.03	7.80	9.30	4.72	14.49V
Malaysia	548	1.98	1.68	8.18	1.17	.53	.02	3.64V	17.04	6.06	.96	7.65	2.04	1.14	1.35V
Mongolia	948	—	—	—	—	—	—	—Y	—	—	.07	—	—	—	—Y
Myanmar	518	—	—	.04	.25	—	.02	.02Y	—	—	—	—	—	—	—Y
Nauru	836	—	—	—	—	.01	—	—Y	.08	—	—	—	.01	—	—Y
Nepal	558	—	—	—	—	—	.02	.03Y	—	—	—	—	—	—	—Y
New Caledonia	839	—	—	.01	—	—	—	—Y	—	—	—	—	—	—	—Y
Pakistan	564	.69	1.21	2.87	3.06	.28	.48	.59Y	.74	2.43	.25	1.59	.81	1.34	1.67Y
Papua New Guinea	853	—	.05	—	—	—	—	—Y	—	—	—	—	—	—	—Y
Philippines	566	4.85	2.21	.21	3.21	.02	.02	1.24V	.18	.06	.01	.03	.06	.04	—V
Samoa	862	.33	.36	.03	.01	—	—	—Y	.01	—	—	—	—	—	—Y
Singapore	576	3.88	8.88	4.18	7.82	7.53	5.63	13.52V	3.15	3.73	1.43	5.54	2.96	3.41	3.82V
Sri Lanka	524	.01	.03	.71	.03	.01	.01	—V	.11	.15	—	.02	—	—	—V
Taiwan Province of China	528	17.96	15.07	10.03	20.71	6.42	.35	10.97V	7.92	13.76	1.00	10.61	7.79	5.30	2.28V
Thailand	578	20.72	23.32	25.12	41.82	5.96	4.12	28.69V	3.70	6.15	11.61	7.26	7.17	4.26	19.04V
Vanuatu	846	—	—	—	—	—	—	—Y	—	.01	—	—	—	—	—Y
Vietnam	582	3.44	1.34	2.73	4.15	.95	.08	—V	1.21	.09	—	—	.56	.43	—V
Europe	**170**	**45.0**	**39.6**	**41.1**	**39.8**	**21.5**	**44.8**	**70.9Y**	**7.3**	**2.4**	**.4**	**2.4**	**1.3**	**2.4**	**11.2Y**
Albania	914	—	.09	—	—	—	—	.02V	—	—	—	—	—	—	—V
Armenia	911	.07	.08	—	.12	—	—	—V	—	—	—	—	—	—	—V
Azerbaijan	912	2.00	—	—	—	—	.04	.32V	—	—	—	.02	—	—	—V
Belarus	913	—	.16	—	.01	.02	—	.83V	—	—	—	.01	.35	.02	.07V
Bosnia & Herzegovina	963	—	.04	.42	.03	—	.22	.28Y	—	—	—	—	—	—	—Y
Bulgaria	918	6.79	4.54	3.18	9.41	1.45	36.08	3.51V	.02	.11	.05	1.42	.15	.05	.18V
Croatia	960	3.91	1.96	1.19	.85	.09	—	.51V	.08	.01	—	—	—	—	—V
Czech Republic	935	—	.04	.59	.03	.01	.04	.01V	.13	.94	.03	.19	.09	.06	.32V
Estonia	939	—	.01	—	—	—	—	—V	—	—	—	—	—	—	—V
Faroe Islands	816	—	.06	—	—	—	—	—Y	—	—	—	—	—	—	—Y
Georgia	915	.36	.02	—	.02	—	—	—Y	.03	.02	—	.01	—	—	—Y
Gibraltar	823	—	.02	—	.01	—	.01	.01Y	—	—	.12	.01	—	.02	.03Y
Hungary	944	.09	1.21	.01	.35	.14	.02	5.08V	.02	.03	.01	.04	.04	—	.84V
Kazakhstan	916	—	—	2.92	3.37	.37	.23	.29Y	—	.04	—	—	—	—	—Y
Latvia	941	1.33	.74	.70	.15	.02	.08	.05V	—	—	—	—	—	—	.03V
Lithuania	946	1.00	1.30	.37	.11	—	—	.01V	—	—	.01	—	—	—	—V
Poland	964	1.60	6.76	2.94	2.65	1.50	.80	4.35V	.10	.02	—	.02	.02	—	.32V
Romania	968	2.34	.19	.94	.38	.01	.01	.58V	2.21	.08	.05	—	—	—	.01V
Russia	922	12.27	17.67	4.23	9.53	16.47	2.79	29.69V	1.30	.02	—	—	.10	.02	6.14V
Slovak Republic	936	1.23	3.14	2.20	.17	—	.01	.04V	.06	.05	—	.01	.09	.04	.27V
Turkey	186	7.65	1.48	20.98	11.85	1.12	.52	20.43V	1.60	.87	.05	.11	.04	.99	1.55V
Ukraine	926	3.99	.04	.39	.76	.11	3.72	4.62Y	1.58	.17	.04	.14	.10	.12	.15Y
Uzbekistan	927	—	—	—	—	.13	—	—Y	—	—	—	—	—	—	—Y
Yugoslavia n.s.	966	.40	—	—	—	.11	.22	.27Y	.11	.01	.02	—	—	.80	.99Y
Europe n.s.	884	—	—	—	.01	—	.01	.01Y	.08	.04	.02	.43	.33	.24	.30Y
Middle East	**407**	**33.1**	**37.2**	**45.2**	**35.3**	**18.7**	**14.6**	**40.2Y**	**21.3**	**200.0**	**15.2**	**99.7**	**110.6**	**80.1**	**95.1Y**
Bahrain	419	—	—	—	—	—	.01	.01Y	—	—	—	—	—	—	—Y
Egypt	469	14.36	3.07	2.40	5.77	1.84	.88	1.09Y	2.67	2.67	1.06	1.55	.94	.82	1.01Y
Iran, I.R. of	429	6.81	8.97	17.34	1.54	—	.39	.51Y	.54	.84	.06	18.96	1.75	.32	.39Y
Iraq	433	—	—	.02	—	.22	.01	.01Y	—	—	—	—	—	—	—Y
Israel	436	6.33	6.78	3.23	3.69	1.75	.74	.45V	3.97	4.59	1.59	4.23	2.57	3.40	2.50V
Jordan	439	.40	6.97	9.53	10.11	4.56	1.85	24.25V	.01	1.11	.02	.03	.07	—	.01V
Kuwait	443	.01	.13	.01	.01	.03	—	.01Y	7.08	174.54	8.03	39.34	75.67	52.50	63.33Y
Lebanon	446	—	.56	.01	—	.01	—	—Y	.04	.18	.05	.37	.19	.17	.21Y
Libya	672	—	1.02	.23	.02	.05	.14	.18Y	—	—	—	—	—	—	—Y
Oman	449	—	.30	2.05	.25	.01	.03	.04Y	—	—	.02	.02	—	—	—Y
Qatar	453	—	—	.04	—	.03	.02	.02Y	1.24	1.65	.18	2.19	.51	.24	.28Y
Saudi Arabia	456	.04	1.15	.84	.63	.01	.09	.12Y	.79	1.72	.31	2.78	3.83	.72	.87Y
Syrian Arab Republic	463	.70	—	—	—	—	—	—Y	.01	.25	.01	.15	.01	.04	.05Y
United Arab Emirates	466	3.38	6.08	8.24	11.70	9.77	10.14	13.14Y	4.96	12.42	3.92	30.12	25.04	21.93	26.46Y
Yemen, Republic of	474	1.11	2.12	1.26	1.56	.42	.29	.36Y	.01	—	—	—	—	—	—Y

	Exports 2001	Exports 2002	Exports 2003	Exports 2004	Exports 2005	Exports 2006	Exports 2007	Imports, f.o.b 2001	Imports, f.o.b 2002	Imports, f.o.b 2003	Imports, f.o.b 2004	Imports, f.o.b 2005	Imports, f.o.b 2006	Imports, f.o.b 2007
	Millions of U.S. Dollars							*Millions of U.S. Dollars*						
Western Hemisphere................ 207	**15.3**	**9.0**	**6.8**	**1.3**	**.4**	**.9**	**12.8Y**	**14.4**	**13.5**	**3.8**	**32.9**	**3.8**	**4.8**	**1.6Y**
Antigua and Barbuda.................. 311	.03	.04	—	.01	.01	—	—Y	.10	.01	.01	.02	.01	—	—Y
Argentina.................................. 213	1.01	.19	.01	.22	.01	.02	.04V	10.52	5.15	1.54	28.68	1.76	2.42	.07V
Bahamas, The............................. 313	—	—	—	.01	—	—	—Y	—	—	—	.12	—	—	—Y
Barbados.................................... 316	—	—	—	.06	—	.02	.02Y	—	—	—	—	—	—	—Y
Belize.. 339	—	—	—	—	—	—	—Y	—	—	—	—	.02	—	—Y
Bermuda.................................... 319	—	.01	—	—	—	—	—Y	—	—	—	.99	.42	1.20	1.49Y
Bolivia....................................... 218	—	—	.01	—	—	—	—Y	—	—	—	—	—	—	—Y
Brazil... 223	10.59	7.06	5.96	.66	.02	—	6.00V	1.92	5.82	.95	2.44	1.34	1.11	—V
Chile.. 228	—	.10	—	.03	—	.05	—V	1.31	—	—	.19	.05	—	—V
Colombia.................................... 233	.13	—	.43	—	.17	.57	3.67V	—	—	—	—	—	—	.01V
Costa Rica.................................. 238	1.72	—	—	—	—	—	—Y	—	—	—	—	—	—	—Y
Dominica.................................... 321	.01	—	—	—	—	—	—Y	.22	—	.01	—	.02	—	—Y
Dominican Republic.................... 243	—	—	—	—	.02	.01	.02Y	—	—	—	—	—	—	—Y
Ecuador...................................... 248	—	—	—	—	—	—	—Y	.01	—	—	—	—	—	—Y
El Salvador................................. 253	—	—	—	—	—	—	.04V	—	—	—	—	—	—	—V
Grenada..................................... 328	—	—	—	—	—	—	—Y	—	—	—	—	—	.01	.02Y
Guatemala.................................. 258	—	.27	.02	—	—	—	—Y	—	—	—	—	—	—	—Y
Haiti... 263	.82	—	—	—	.01	—	—Y	—	—	—	—	—	—	—Y
Jamaica...................................... 343	—	.01	—	—	—	.05	.02V	—	—	.01	.01	—	—	—V
Mexico....................................... 273	.12	.31	.08	.19	.03	.20	2.95V	.04	.04	.03	—	—	.04	—V
Netherlands Antilles.................... 353	—	.06	.12	—	—	.02	.02Y	.03	—	—	—	—	—	—Y
Nicaragua................................... 278	—	—	—	—	.03	—	—V	—	—	—	—	—	.02	—V
Panama...................................... 283	.02	—	—	—	—	—	—V	.06	—	—	.08	.02	—	—V
Paraguay.................................... 288	.08	—	—	—	—	—	—Y	—	—	—	—	—	.02	.02Y
Peru... 293	.33	.29	.10	.01	—	—	.04Y	—	—	—	—	—	—	—Y
St. Kitts and Nevis...................... 361	.22	—	.08	—	—	—	—Y	.02	—	—	—	—	—	—Y
Suriname.................................... 366	.23	—	—	—	—	—	—Y	—	—	—	—	—	—	—Y
Trinidad and Tobago................... 369	—	.06	—	—	—	—	—Y	.01	2.42	—	—	—	—	—Y
Uruguay...................................... 298	—	.04	—	—	.02	—	—Y	.13	.04	1.21	.08	.08	—	—Y
Venezuela, Rep. Bol.................... 299	.01	—	—	—	—	—	—V	—	—	—	—	—	—	—Y
Western Hem. n.s........................ 399	—	.57	.01	.08	.04	—	—Y	—	—	—	.24	.02	—	—Y
Other Countries n.i.e................ 910	—	**.2**	—	**.1**	**.4**	**.4**	**.6Y**	**.1**	**.3**	—	**.5**	**.1**	**.1**	**.2Y**
North Korea................................ 954	—	.19	.01	.06	.41	.45	.55Y	.05	.26	.04	.53	.06	.14	.17Y
Countries & Areas n.s.............. 898	—	—	**.1**	—	—	—	**—Y**	**187.8**	**249.5**	**87.3**	**185.9**	**182.3**	**85.6**	**106.2Y**
Special Categories.................. 899	**1,006.9**	—	—	—	—	—	**—Y**	**.8**	—	—	—	—	—	**—Y**
Memorandum Items														
European Union.......................... 998	528.05	637.88	505.93	394.47	234.81	85.92	440.65Y	178.84	209.14	60.10	175.13	133.32	126.05	203.17V
Oil Exporting Ctys....................... 999	31.58	46.44	42.48	58.40	18.90	12.43	26.82Y	19.51	198.84	13.77	101.02	109.61	77.42	96.73Y
Non-Oil Develop.Ctys.................. 201	453.71	847.27	2,417.24	1,074.79	944.52	718.52	1,746.70Y	1,080.94	1,327.61	432.97	1,412.41	1,382.77	2,093.59	1,809.53Y
PERCENT DISTRIBUTION														
Industrial Countries................. 101	**32.8**	**55.5**	**26.5**	**35.9**	**30.9**	**22.2**	**28.9**	**17.4**	**16.0**	**14.5**	**13.1**	**11.1**	**11.7**	**14.6**
Developing Countries.............. 202	**21.8**	**44.5**	**73.5**	**64.1**	**69.1**	**77.7**	**71.0**	**70.5**	**72.2**	**71.5**	**77.3**	**79.2**	**84.9**	**80.9**
Africa...................................... 607	**8.6**	**33.7**	**28.5**	**44.7**	**58.6**	**66.9**	**55.7**	**62.3**	**57.2**	**63.0**	**64.3**	**66.7**	**78.0**	**64.8**
Asia.. 507	**9.0**	**6.5**	**42.3**	**15.1**	**7.5**	**4.4**	**10.4**	**5.5**	**4.8**	**5.4**	**6.1**	**6.4**	**3.5**	**11.4**
Europe.................................... 170	**2.0**	**2.0**	**1.2**	**2.2**	**1.5**	**4.8**	**2.8**	**.5**	**.1**	**.1**	**.1**	**.1**	**.1**	**.5**
Middle East............................ 407	**1.5**	**1.8**	**1.4**	**2.0**	**1.3**	**1.6**	**1.6**	**1.4**	**9.5**	**2.4**	**5.1**	**5.9**	**3.1**	**4.0**
Western Hemisphere.............. 207	**.7**	**.4**	**.2**	**.1**	—	**.1**	**.5**	**.9**	**.6**	**.6**	**1.7**	**.2**	**.2**	**.1**
ANNUAL PERCENT CHANGE														
World.. 001	**–32.3**	**–9.6**	**66.5**	**–47.1**	**–21.1**	**–32.6**	**165.4**	**–6.8**	**35.4**	**–70.5**	**213.2**	**–3.8**	**35.8**	**–7.8**
Industrial Countries................. 101	**–17.5**	**52.9**	**–20.7**	**–28.2**	**–32.2**	**–51.5**	**245.3**	**–42.6**	**24.1**	**–73.2**	**183.7**	**–18.9**	**43.9**	**14.9**
Developing Countries.............. 202	**–48.6**	**84.2**	**175.2**	**–53.9**	**–15.0**	**–24.1**	**142.6**	**8.5**	**38.7**	**–70.7**	**238.8**	**–1.4**	**45.5**	**–12.2**
Africa...................................... 607	**–66.5**	**252.1**	**40.8**	**–17.1**	**3.5**	**–23.1**	**121.2**	**17.0**	**24.3**	**–67.4**	**219.7**	**–.2**	**58.8**	**–23.4**
Asia.. 507	**–19.1**	**–34.2**	**976.8**	**–81.1**	**–60.7**	**–60.2**	**520.2**	**–35.9**	**19.8**	**–67.0**	**256.2**	**.9**	**–26.4**	**203.5**
Europe.................................... 170	**–11.8**	**–12.2**	**3.9**	**–3.2**	**–45.8**	**107.9**	**58.3**	**4.6**	**–67.0**	**–83.5**	**514.3**	**–46.3**	**79.4**	**375.5**
Middle East............................ 407	**–25.7**	**12.2**	**21.7**	**–21.9**	**–47.0**	**–22.0**	**175.3**	**–17.1**	**837.3**	**–92.4**	**554.2**	**10.9**	**–27.5**	**18.7**
Western Hemisphere.............. 207	**–45.3**	**–41.2**	**–24.2**	**–81.4**	**–71.7**	**163.1**	—	**–18.4**	**–6.0**	**–72.1**	**771.5**	**–88.6**	**28.5**	**–66.6**
Other Countries n.i.e............... 910	**–95.1**	—	**–95.1**	**561.9**	**555.8**	**8.8**	**24.1**	**–70.9**	**394.0**	**–85.3**	—	**–88.7**	**129.2**	**24.1**

NOTES

Aruba 314

As of January 2000, reported *DOTS* data include trade in the Aruba free trade zone.

Bahamas 313

Reported *DOTS* data in 1999 and *IFS* data beginning in 1990 exclude certain oil and chemical products.

Bahrain 419

Reported exports in *DOTS* and *IFS* include partial oil exports only. Beginning in 1998, reported imports from Saudi Arabia include oil imports as compiled by the Bahrain Ministry of Oil & industry and published in the Monthly Bulletin of the Bahrain Monetary Agency.

Belgium 124

Prior to 1997, trade data for Belgium are recorded as trade of the Belgium-Luxembourg Economic Union (BLEU). Belgium and BLEU trade data are not comparable due to the employment of different compilation methodologies.

China, P.R.:Mainland 924

Discrepancies in bilateral trade statistics as reported by China and its trading partners exist, particularly with industrial countries. Trade with these countries is classified by China as trade with Hong Kong Special Administrative Region (HKSAR) if it passes through HKSAR ports.

China, P.R.:Hong Kong 532

Reported exports and imports data with Belgium include trade with Luxembourg.

Czeschoslovakia 934

Czeschoslovakia (The Czech and Slovak Federal Republic) ceased to be a member of the Fund on January 1, 1993.

Dominican Republic 243

IFS data exclude trade in free trade processing zone. Beginning in 1994, *DOTS* data include trade in free trade processing zone.

El Salvador 253

IFS data exclude trade in free trade processing zone. Beginning in 2000, *DOTS* data include trade in free trade processing zone.

Estonia 939

IFS data are compiled according to the general trade system of recording trade transactions and *DOTS* data are compiled according to the special trade system.

European Union 998

The data for the European Union (EU) for all periods cover Austria, Belgium, Cyprus, Czech Republic, Denmark, Estonia, Finland, France, Germany, Greece, Hungary, Ireland, Italy, Latvia, Lithuania, Luxembourg, Malta, Netherlands, Poland, Portugal, Slovak Republic, Slovenia, Spain, Sweden, and the United Kingdom.

France 132

Beginning in 1997, reported exports and imports data include trade of French Guiana, Guadeloupe, Martinique, and Réunion with the rest of the world.

French Guiana 333

Beginning in January 1997, exports and imports data of French Guiana are combined with exports and imports data for France.

Guadeloupe 329

Beginning in January 1997, exports and imports data of Guadeloupe are combined with exports and imports data for France.

Guatemala 258

IFS data exclude trade in free trade processing zone. Beginning in 2004, *DOTS* data include trade in free trade processing zone.

India 534

Data from 1997 to 2000, and for 2003 were adjusted to calendar year from reported data based on fiscal year beginning April.

Israel 436

IFS imports data include military goods.

Lithuania 946

Data from 2004 are compiled according to the special trade system.

Luxembourg 137

Prior to 1997, trade data for Luxembourg are recorded as trade of the Belgium-Luxembourg Economic Union (BLEU).

Martinique 349

Beginning in January 1997, exports and imports data of Martinique are combined with exports and imports data for France.

Mexico 273

DOTS and *IFS* reported exports and imports data include trade in maquiladoras.

Netherlands 138

From 1993 through 1998, *DOTS* reported exports and imports exclude estimation of underreporting as a result of the establishment of the internal European market. Trade revisions are made in the monthly data and may not necessarily be reflected in the quarterly and annual data.

Nigeria 694

Beginning in 1995, *IFS* data are valued at an average (unitary) exchange rate of 70.36 naira to the U.S. dollar. This exchange rate is the weighted average of the official rate and the market rate that went into effect in February, 1995.

Oil Exporting Countries 999

The oil Exporting Countries comprise Algeria, Indonesia, the Islamic Republic of Iran, Iraq, Kuwait, Libya, Nigeria, Oman, Qatar, Saudi Arabia, the United Arab Emirates, and República Bolivariana de Venezuela.

Panama 283

Reported *IFS* and *DOTS* world totals exclude exports and imports of the COLON free trade processing zone. Beginning in Q1 2001 imports from Japan reflect reported exports of Japan to Panama which may represent flags of convenience.

Réunion 696

Beginning in January 1997, exports and imports data of Reunion are combined with exports and imports data for France.

Russia 922

DOTS data exclude adjustments for unrecorded trade (including shuttle trade) and, prior to 1994 exclude trade with the countries of the former U.S.S.R.

SACCA 198

Data are presented through 1997 and refer to the South African Common Customs Area (SACCA), which includes Botswana, Lesotho, Namibia, South Africa, and Swaziland. Beginning in 1998, SACCA trade are reported separately as South Africa and SACCA excluding South Africa.

SACCA excluding South Africa 608

The South African Common Customs Area (SACCA) excluding South Africa is composed of Botswana, Lesotho, Namibia, and Swaziland.

Singapore 576

Trade data published in the Singapore Trade Statistics by the Singapore Trade Development Board exclude trade with Indonesia. Starting January 2003, Singapore reports its trade with Indonesia.

South Africa 199

Prior to 1998, trade data for South Africa are included in the trade of the South African Common Customs Area (country code 198).

Switzerland 146

Beginning in 1992, *IFS* data exclude diamonds, nonmonetary gold, works of art, collectors' pieces, antiques, and precious metals.

Syrian Arab Republic 463

Beginning in 2000, *IFS* exports and imports totals are calculated using a flexible exchange rate determined by the Ministry of Economy and Foreign Trade.

Turkmenistan 925

Special category exports for 1996 and 1997 consist of natural gas sales unclassified by partner country.

Yugoslavia, SFR 188

Yugoslavia: The Socialist Federal Republic of Yugoslavia ceased to be a member of the Fund on December 14, 1992.

Non Specified Countries as Partners

For the years that a country reports trade with Czech Republic, Slovak Republic and Czechoslovakia n.s., it is assumed that the reported trade with Czechoslovakia n.s. refers to the combined trade with Czech Republic and Slovak Republic.

For the years that a country reports trade separately with the former republics of U.S.S.R. and U.S.S.R. n.s., it is assumed that the reported trade with U.S.S.R. n.s. refers to the combined trade with the former U.S.S.R. republics.

For the years that a country reports trade separately with the former republics of Yugoslavia and Yugoslavia n.s., it is assumed that the reported trade with Yugoslavia n.s. refers to the combined trade with the former Yugoslavia republics.

Notes

Notes

Notes